# Sports Illustrated 2010 Almanac

## By the Editors of Sports Illustrated

YEAR IN SPORTS
CALENDAR

BASEBALL

PRO
FOOTBALL

COLLEGE
FOOTBALL

PRO
BASKETBALL

COLLEGE
BASKETBALL

HOCKEY

TENNIS

GOLF

BOXING/
MIXED MARTIAL ARTS

HORSE
RACING

MOTOR
SPORTS

Time Inc.
1271 Avenue of the Americas
New York, New York 10020

First Edition
ISBN10: 1-60320-826-7
ISBN 13: 978-1-60320-826-0

SPORTS ILLUSTRATED 2010 Almanac was prepared by
Touchpoint Sports Publishing, of White Plains, N.Y.

Editorial Director: Morin Bishop          Managing Editor: Reed Richardson
Art Director: Barbara Chilenskas          Associate Editor: Max Berry
Photo Editor: John Blackmar

Cover photography credits:
BEN ROETHLISBERGER: Al Tielemans
TIGER WOODS: Robert Beck
USAIN BOLT: MICHAEL KAPPELER/AFP/Getty Images
ALBERT PUJOLS: Porter Binks

Back cover photography credits:
TYLER HANSBROUGH: John Biever
TIM TEBOW: Kim Klement-US PRESSWIRE
SERENA WILLIAMS: Bob Martin

Spine photography credit:
LEBRON JAMES: REUTERS/Jeff Haynes (United States Sport Basketball)

## TIME INC. HOME ENTERTAINMENT

Publisher ............................................................. Richard Fraiman
General Manager ...................................................... Steven Sandonato
Executive Director, Marketing Services ............................... Carol Pittard
Director, Retail & Special Sales ..................................... Tom Mifsud
Director, New Product Development .................................... Peter Harper
Assistant Director, Bookazine Marketing .............................. Laura Adam
Assistant Director, Brand Marketing .................................. Joy Butts
Associate Counsel .................................................... Helen Wan
Brand & Licensing Manager ............................................ Alexandra Bliss
Design & Prepress Manager ............................................ Anne-Michelle Gallero
Book Production Manager .............................................. Susan Chodakiewicz
Associate Brand Manager .............................................. Allison Parker

Special thanks: Christine Austin, Glenn Buonocore, Jim Childs, Rose Cirrincione, Jacqueline
Fitzgerald, Lauren Hall, Jennifer Jacobs, Suzanne Janso, Brynn Joyce, Mona Li, Robert Marasco,
Amy Migliaccio, Brooke Reger, Dave Rozzelle, Ilene Schreider, Adriana Tierno, Alex Voznesenskiy,
Sydney Webber and Robert Yalen

We welcome your comments and suggestions about Sports Illustrated Books. Please write to us
at: Sports Illustrated Books, Attention: Book Editors, P.O. Box 11016, Des Moines, IA 50336-1016
If you would like to order any of our hardcover Collector's Edition books, please call us at
1-800-327-6388. (Monday through Friday, 7:00 a.m.- 8:00 p.m. or Saturday, 7:00 a.m.- 6:00 p.m.
Central Time)

# CONTENTS

In compiling the Sports Illustrated 2010 Almanac, the editors would like to extend their gratitude to the media relations offices of the following organizations for their help in providing information and materials relating to their sports: Major League Baseball; Elias Sports Bureau, the Canadian Football League; the National Football League, Arena Football League; the National Collegiate Athletic Association; the National Basketball Association; the National Hockey League; the Association of Tennis Professionals; the Women's Tennis Association; the U.S. Tennis Association; the U.S. Golf Association; the Ladies Professional Golf Association; the Professional Golfers Association; National Thoroughbred Racing Association; the Breeders' Cup; Churchill Downs; the New York Racing Association, Inc.; the Jockey's Guild, Inc.; the International Motor Sports Association; the National Association for Stock Car Auto Racing; the Professional Bowlers Association; the United Soccer Leagues; Major League Soccer; the Fédération Internationale de Futbol Association; the U.S. Soccer Federation; the U.S. Olympic Committee; USA Track & Field; U.S. Swimming; U.S. Diving; U.S. Skiing; U.S. Figure Skating Association; U.S. Curling; the Iditarod Trail Committee; USA Gymnastics; U.S. Handball Association; the Lacrosse Foundation; the American Power Boat Association; the Unlimited Hydroplane Racing Association; the Professional Rodeo Cowboys Association; U.S. Rowing; the Amateur Softball Association of America; U.S. Speed Skating; U.S. Rugby Football Union; USA Triathlon; the National Archery Association; USA Wrestling; the U.S. Squash Racquets Association; the U.S. Polo Association; NBC Sports; and the U.S. Volleyball Association.

The following outside sources were consulted in gathering information:

**Baseball** mlb.com, worldseries.com, baseballhalloffame.org, baseball-almanac.com, *Associated Press* (LCS, WS game recaps)

**Pro Football** nfl.com, superbowl.com, nfleurope.com arenafootball.com, arenabowl.com, profootballhof.com

**College Football** ncaasports.com, heisman.com, *Official 2009 NCAA Division I-A and I-AA Football Records Book, Official 2009 Division II and III Football Records Book*

**Pro Basketball** nba.com, hoophall.com

**College Basketball** ncaasports.com, *Official 2010 NCAA Division I Men's Basketball Records Book, Official 2010 NCAA Division I Women's Basketball Records Book, Official 2010 NCAA Division II and III Men's Basketball Records Book*

**Hockey** nhl.com, hhof.com, ushockeyhall.com

**Tennis** atptennis.com, sonyericssonwtatour.com, usopen.org, australianopen.com, wimbledon.org, rolandgarros.com, masters-cup.com, daviscup.com, fedcup.com, tennisfame.com

**Golf** pgatour.com, masters.org, usopen.org, usga.org, opengolf.com, pga.com, randa.org, lpga.com, knc.com, ussenioropen.com, usamateur.org, rydercup.com, walkercup.org, curtiscup.org, pinggolf.com

# SOURCES *(Cont.)*

**Boxing** wbaonline.com, wbcboxing.com, ibf-usba-boxing.com, ibhof.com, thering-online.com, usaboxing.org, olympic.org

**Horse Racing** ntra.com, equibase.com, kentuckyderby.com, preakness.com, belmontstakes.nyra.com

**Motor Sports** nascar.com, formula1.com, indycar.com, americanlemans.com, lemans.org, indy500.com, daytona24hr.com

**Soccer** fifa.com, mlsnet.com, ussoccer.com, uslsoccer.com, soccernet.com

**NCAA Sports** ncaasports.com

**Olympics** olympic.org, usoc.org

**Track and Field** iaaf.org, usatf.org, usoc.org, *Track and Field News*

**Swimming** fina.org, usaswimming.org, ishof.org, usoc.org

**Miscellaneous Sports** letour.fr, usarchery.org, pba.com, fide.com, worldcurling.org, usacurl.org, usacycling.org, uci.ch, iditarod.com, usfigureskating.org, isu.org, usoc.org, fig-gymnastics.com, usa-gymnastics.org, ushandball.org, uscla.com, nll.com, littleleague.org, abrahydroplanes.com, us-polo.org, prorodeo.org, usrowing.org, usarugby.org, rugbyworldcup.com, amnrl.com, ussailing.org, fis-ski.com, asasoftball.com, us-squash.org, ironmanlive.com, usatriathlon.org, fivb.org, usavolleyball.org, themat.com

**Obituaries** *Associated Press*

Woods (l.) and Federer had resurgent years in 2009 and ruled the past decade, winning a combined total of 27 major titles

# The Year In Sports

# Aughts End Hot

The year offered a wealth of dramatic champions and near-champions, including a pair of storied franchises adding yet another title to their lengthy resumes

## BY HANK HERSCH

IT HAPPENED SO FAST. ONE MINUTE we were counting down the seconds to the new millennium, hoping to usher in a glitch-free Y2K, the next we were closing out the first decade of the '00s, wondering at life's wildly accelerating pace. In sports, the two-thousand-aughts were fraught with the major achievements of a Swiss tennis player, with the unbridled quest of an NBA superstar for a ring to call his own, and with the sustained excellence of the greatest golfer in history, who stacked up victories as casually as firewood. Yet if anyone represented the decade whizzing past, it was a former Jamaican cricketer with the mind-bending ability to turn back time.

At the decade's last IAAF World Track and Field Championships, in Berlin, 22-year-old Usain Bolt eradicated his own sprint records in the 100 and 200 meters by margins that not only unsettled the foundations of the sport but also stretched ideas of human possibility. He won the 100 in 9.58, which surpassed his 9.69 at the 2008 Olympics, which had demolished the previous record of 9.77. The progression in the 200: to 19.19, down from Bolt's own 19.30, down from Michael Johnson's 12-year-old standard of 19.32. These weren't the usual incremental drops; they were seismic movements. As Ato Boldon, a four-time Olympic sprint medalist, watched the 6'5" Bolt streak to the 200 record, he expressed the feelings shared by perhaps the entire planet: "Oh...my...God!"

Time got twisted in other ways during 2009. At 59, Tom Watson turned it back at the British Open in Turnberry; he needed only to par the 72nd hole to become, by 11 years, the oldest winner of a major title. But he made a poor putt from a fluffy lie behind the green, missed the ensuing 10-footer and lost in a playoff to Stewart Cink. "One of the things I want out of life is for my peers to say, 'That Watson, he was a hell of a golfer,'" the runner-up said. During a year in which Tiger Woods, returning from knee surgery, won six tournaments and $10.5 million, Watson's turn-back-the-clock run turned out to be the highlight.

The Tiger of tennis, Roger Federer, did what Woods could not: He added to his major victories. In fact, by taking the French Open for the first time and Wimbledon for the sixth—only after beating Andy Roddick 16–14 in the fifth set of the final—he upped his total to 15, eclipsing Pete Sampras's career men's record. Although Juan Martin Del Potro would upset him in a five-set final at the U.S. Open, Federer closed out the decade as the undisputed king of his sport. "He gets a lot of credit for a lot of things," said Roddick. "But not a lot of the time is [it for] how many matches he kind of digs deep and toughs out."

In partnership with Shaquille O'Neal, Lakers star Kobe Bryant began the Aughts with a bang: NBA championships in 2000, 2001 and 2002. But in each victory Shaq was the Finals MVP, and since his exit from Los

Angeles in '04, Bryant had been driven to prove he could earn a ring on his own. While 24-year-old LeBron James would succeed him as MVP and challenge Bryant's unofficial title as the best player on the planet, Bryant took his team where James couldn't, reaching the Finals against the Magic. He dedicated himself to winning it all, becoming so ornery that his two daughters began calling him Grumpy, from Snow White. But in the end he was Happy, averaging 32.4 points to carry the Lakers to a five-game victory that gave Phil Jackson his record-breaking 10th championship as a coach.

Some athletic brand names that had experienced titleless droughts doubled down in the Aughts, including the Penguins, who brought the Stanley Cup back to Pittsburgh for the first time since 1992. The Steelers, who dominated the 1970s, hadn't won another Super Bowl until 2006. In Super Bowl XLIII at Tampa, they reestablished themselves as an NFL force, defeating the Cardinals 27–23 in a thriller for the franchise's record sixth victory. Quarterback Ben Roethlisberger, who had struggled in Super Bowl XL, claimed his second ring at age 26 by leading Pittsburgh on a 78-yard march in the final 2:30. His missile to wide-out Santonio Holmes in the corner of the end zone with 35 seconds left thwarted a fourth-quarter Arizona comeback from 13 points down. "Do or die," said Roethlisberger, recounting his thoughts in the huddle before the winning drive. "I've said it all along: I want the ball in my hands."

In 2005, under coach Roy Williams, North Carolina won its first NCAA basketball championship in 12 seasons. Four years later Williams took a team loaded with talent and laden with expectations to the finals in Detroit against local favorite Michigan State. But the four Tar Heels who chose to return to Chapel Hill rather than turn pro—seniors Tyler Hansbrough and Danny Green, and juniors Wayne Ellington and Ty Lawson—weren't to be denied, combining for 64 points in an 89–72 victory. "It was the best decision I ever made," said Naismith Player of the Year Hansbrough when it was over, standing on the court with one of the nets hanging from his neck. "All the hard work I put in, all the tough practices, all the weight room [sessions], that was what this was about."

After taking the NCAA finals in 2002, '03 and '04, the UConn women's basketball team closed out the decade with an unprecedented

**Connecticut women's head coach Geno Auriemma ended the Aughts just like he started them—with an NCAA championship. He also led the Huskies to three consecutive titles between 2002–04.**

DAVID E. KLUTHO

ularly stalwart. For the Yankees *arrivistes* like pitchers C.C. Sabathia, the iron man of the staff throughout the postseason, and the mercurial A.J. Burnett, the victory offered sweet justification for the massive sums expended by the team to acquire them in the offseason. For the regulars who came after the title in 2000 and suffered through the Yankees drought since then, the Series provided the single pedigree every Yankee must possess before he can truly enter the team pantheon: a world title. Alex Rodriguez, who delivered key hit after key hit throughout the Yankees' October run may have forever put to rest the widespread perception that he wilts in the clutch. And Hideki Matsui, who struggled in the Yankees previous playoff victories over the Twins and Angels, and who had become the forgotten man of the Yankees lineup, offered a vivid reminder of what a fearsome hitter he still can be. With eight hits in 13 at bats, including three homers and eight RBIs (six of them in the deciding Game 6), Matsui was a deserving if somewhat sentimental MVP selection. The Philadelphia Phillies, champions in '08, were scrappy in defeat but ultimately were unable to overcome a bullpen without a closer or a reliable setup man. Even a Series record-tying five home runs from Chase Utley and a pair of fine pitching performances from Cliff Lee were not enough to stop the Yankees juggernaut.

And so as the Aughts give way to a new decade, New York's win in a brand-new Yankee Stadium restores order and a sense of stability to the sporting universe. Federer, Woods, the Steelers, the Yankees—constants all amidst our changing times.

bang, not only going undefeated but also winning all 39 of its games by double digits. And while Florida quarterback Tim Tebow came up short in his bid to win a second straight Heisman Trophy—that honor went to Oklahoma QB Sam Bradford—the junior did guide the Gators to their second national championship in three years, throwing for 232 yards and two TDs to beat Bradford's Sooners 24–14 in the BCS title game.

Finally, as the Aughts wound closer yet to their conclusion, there were the mighty Yankees, whose triumph in the World Series proved that some verities in sports transcend even the ravages of time. The Yankees have won titles in eight of the nine decades since 1920—the benighted '80s being the only exception—and the results in '09 hardly suggest a decline in that tradition. Their titles in 2000 and '09 bookended the decade, with each of the four holdovers from the Yankees' earlier Series win—Jorge Posada, Derek Jeter, Andy Pettitte and Mariano Rivera—all contributing mightily to the title in '09. Pettite, with two gutty wins and the ageless Rivera with a pair of saves and a pair of closeouts in the four victories were partic-

# THE YEAR IN SPORTS CALENDAR

## NOVEMBER 2008

**11/2:** Paula Radcliffe and Marilson Gomes des Santos win the women's and men's New York Marathon, respectively. Two runners die after completing the race.

**11/7:** Eventual champions North Carolina and Connecticut are ranked No. 1 in the *Associated Press* preseason men's and women's Division I basketball poll.

**11/8:** Boxer Joe Calzaghe remains undefeated after 46 career fights when he beats Roy Jones Jr. in a 12-round unanimous decision at New York's Madison Square Garden.

**11/16:** Jimmie Johnson wins the Sprint Cup Championship for the third consecutive season, a feat equaled only by Cale Yarborough (1976-78).

**11/17:** Albert Pujols wins his second career NL MVP award.

**11/19:** Don Wakamatsu is named the new manager of the Seattle Mariners, making him the first Asian-American manager in major league history.

**11/22:** In one of the biggest upsets in rugby history, New Zealand defeats Australia 34–20 to win its first Rugby League World Cup.

## DECEMBER 2008

**12/6:** Manny Pacquiao defeats Oscar De La Hoya by an eighth-round TKO at Las Vegas' MGM Grand.

**12/7:** Michelle Wie earns her Tour card by finishing tied for seventh at the LPGA's Final Qualifying Tournament in Daytona Beach, Florida.

**12/8:** Pitcher Greg Maddux, who has 355 career wins and 18 Gold Gloves, retires after 23 seasons.

**12/12:** At MLB's winter meetings in Las Vegas, the New York Yankees sign free agent pitcher C.C. Sabathia to a seven-year, $161-million contract.

**12/14:** Oklahoma QB Sam Bradford wins the 2008 Heisman Trophy, beating out Texas' Colt McCoy and Florida's Tim Tebow.

**12/14:** LPGA Hall-of-Fame golfer Annika Sorenstam ends her career with a birdie on 18 at the Dubai Ladies Masters tournament, six shots off the pace.

**12/20:** Division III football dynasty Mount Union avenges its 2007 championship defeat at the hands of the UW-Whitewater Warhawks by beating that team 31–26 in the 2008 Amos Alonzo Stagg Bowl, giving the school its third NCAA football title in the past four years and 10th championship since 1993.

**12/28:** Completing an amazing turnaround from their 1–15 season the year before, the Miami Dolphins defeat the New York Jets 24–17 to finish the 2008 regular season with an 11–5 record.

## JANUARY 2009

**1/1:** MLB's TV network begins broadcasting.

**1/1:** NHL's Winter Classic is played at Wrigley Field, where the hometown Chicago Blackhawks are defeated 6–4 by the Detroit Red Wings.

**1/4:** Phil Taylor defeats Raymond van Barneveld 7–1 to win the PDC World Championship of Darts.

**1/7:** Boston College football coach Jeff Jagodzinski is fired after interviewing for a coaching job with the New York Jets that he does not get.

**1/8:** The Florida Gators defeat the Oklahoma Sooners 24–14 to win their second BCS Championship in three years.

**1/12:** After a 27-year coaching career, Indianapolis Colts head coach Tony Dungy announces his retirement from the NFL.

**1/18:** Police arrest two men in Chandler, Arizona, for burning the words "Go Cards" into the front yard of Philadelphia Eagles quarterback Donovan McNabb's off-season home.

**1/19:** After failing to make the playoffs despite an 8–3 start, the New York Jets hire former Ravens defensive coordinator Rex Ryan as their new head coach, three weeks after having fired Eric Mangini.

**1/20:** Seven time Tour de France champion Lance Armstrong begins his first cycling race in three years in Adelaide, Australia.

**1/21:** The New Jersey Institute of Technology's basketball team, the Highlanders, defeats Bryant College 61–51 to end a 51-game, nearly two-year-long losing streak.

**1/22:** Jay McGwire, estranged brother of former major league slugger Mark McGwire, claims in a book proposal that the former single-season home run king used steroids and HGH during his career.

**1/23:** After starting the year 11–30, the Memphis Grizzlies fire head coach Marc Iavaroni, becoming the seventh NBA team to make a coaching change thus far in the 2008-09 season.

**1/23:** At the Australian Open, rival Serbian and Bosnian fans brawl following a Novak Djokovic win and a half-naked man streaks across the court at a doubles match featuring the Williams sisters.

**1/24:** Shane Mosley, 37, upsets 30-year-old Antonio Margarito in a ninth round TKO to claim the World Boxing Association welterweight title.

**1/25:** The East earns a 12–11 shootout victory over the West in the NHL All-Star game. The Montreal Canadiens' Alex Kovalev is named MVP.

**1/26:** The Atlanta Hawks set an ignominious franchise record by going over 13 minutes without a field goal in a 95–79 loss to the Miami Heat.

**1/27:** For the fourth time in his career, Novak Djokovic retires from a Grand Slam match, this time quitting when he was down two sets to one in his Australian Open quarterfinal match against Andy Roddick.

**1/28:** With her victory over Elena Dementieva in the Australian Open semifinals, Serena Williams sets a record for career earnings by a female athlete.

## FEBRUARY

**2/1:** Rafael Nadal halts Roger Federer's bid for a 14th Grand Slam title when he defeats him in five sets in the Australian Open men's final.

**2/1:** The Pittsburgh Steelers defeat the Arizona Cardinals 27–23 in Super Bowl XLIII for an NFL-record sixth Super Bowl title.

**2/2:** Kobe Bryant sets a Madison Square Garden scoring record with 61 points in the Los Angeles Lakers' 126–117 defeat of the New York Knicks.

**2/3:** In a Cleveland Cavaliers victory over the Toronto Raptors, LeBron James, aged 24 years, 35 days, becomes the youngest player in NBA history to score 12,000 career points.

**2/5:** Coach Pat Summitt becomes the first Division I basketball coach—male or female—to reach 1,000 career victories as the Lady Vols defeat the Georgia Bulldogs 73–43.

**2/5:** Michael Phelps is suspended for 3 months from USA Swimming and loses an endorsement deal with Kellogg's in the wake of a photo in a London tabloid of the star swimmer holding a marijuana pipe.

**2/5:** Alexander Ovechkin scores his 200th career goal in the Capitals' 5–4 loss to the L.A. Kings.

**2/7:** *Sports Illustrated* reports that Alex Rodriguez tested positive for anabolic steroids in 2003.

**2/10:** In a 105–98 victory over Oklahoma, Kobe Bryant becomes the youngest NBA player in history to score 23,000 points.

**2/15:** The West beats the East in the NBA All-Star Game 146–119 as Shaquille O'Neal and Kobe Bryant, playing on the same team for the first time since 2004, share MVP honors.

**2/15:** With 48 laps remaining, Matt Kenseth wins the Daytona 500 after the race is ended due to heavy rain.

**2/19:** After its decision to deny Israeli women's tennis player Shahar Peer a visa to compete in a tournament in Dubai sparked controversy, the United Arab Emirates decides to issue Peer's countryman Andy Ram a visa to compete in the men's event.

**2/22:** Matt Kenseth, after going winless in 2008, wins his second race in as many tries at the Auto Club 500, marking the first time since 1997 that the same driver has won the first two Sprint Cup races of the season.

**2/22:** The Trinity College men's squash team wins its 11th-straight College Squash Association national title—and 202nd straight match—in a 5–4 victory over Princeton.

**2/23:** The Indianapolis Colts agree to release 13-year veteran Marvin Harrison after the franchise's all-time leading receiver refuses a pay cut.

**2/23:** Former NBA star Charles Barkley pleads guilty to drunk driving charges stemming from a December 31 traffic stop and agrees to spend five days in jail and pay more than $2,000 in fines.

**2/25:** After sitting out eight months recovering from knee surgery, Tiger Woods returns to the PGA Tour at the World Match Play Championships in Marana, Arizona.

**2/25:** With the league reeling from the faltering U.S. economy, NFL commissioner Roger Goddell agrees to take a 20-percent pay cut and trims league staff by 15 percent.

**2/27:** In the first hours of NFL free agency, the Washington Redskins sign All-Pro defensive tackle Albert Haynesworth to a seven-year, $100-million contract.

## MARCH

**3/3:** Gunmen in Pakistan attack the visiting Sri Lankan cricket team, killing six policemen and a driver and wounding seven players, an umpire and a coach.

**3/3:** The Coast Guard ends its three-day search for NFL players Corey Smith and Marquis Cooper, whose fishing boat capsized off the Florida Gulf Coast on March 1.

**3/5:** After undergoing surgery to repair a detached retina, Phoenix forward Amare Stoudemire is forced to miss the remainder of the Suns' season.

**3/7:** Just days after being cut by the Dallas Cowboys, Terrell Owens signs a one-year, $6.5-million deal with the Buffalo Bills.

**3/8:** Alex Rodriguez changes his mind and opts to undergo hip surgery that will force him to miss the first five weeks of the MLB regular season.

**3/10:** The Netherlands stuns a Dominican Republic team stacked with MLB players to advance to the second round of the World Baseball Classic.

**3/11:** Lindsey Vonn becomes the first two-time women's skiing World Cup champion when she wins the last downhill race of the season at the Cup finals in Sweden.

**3/11:** A month after opting not to renew Michael Phelps' endorsement contract, Kellogg's donates thousands of boxes of cereal with the Olympic swimmer's picture on them to a San Francisco food bank.

**3/15:** After winning the CA Championship at Doral, Phil Mickelson moves up to No. 2 in the world golf rankings.

**3/15:** For the first time in NCAA men's tournament history, three of the four No. 1 seeds are from the same conference as the Big East's Connecticut, Pittsburgh and Louisville receive top honors.

**3/17:** New Jersey Devils goalie Martin Brodeur becomes the winningest goaltender in NHL history with his 552nd career victory.

**3/18:** Houston Astros' infielder Aaron Boone announces he may retire following non-emergency heart surgery to replace an aortic valve.

**3/19:** Twelfth-seeded Western Kentucky notches the first major upset of the NCAA tournament as the Hilltoppers beat No. 5 seed Illinois 76–72.

**3/23:** Red Sox pitcher—and three-time World Series champion with Boston and Arizona—Curt Schilling announces his retirement from baseball.

**3/23:** Japan defeats South Korea 5–3 to win the World Baseball Classic.

**3/26:** Two years after retiring from professional tennis, Kim Clijsters announces she will return to the WTA Tour in 2009.

**3/29:** Tiger Woods comes back from five strokes down to win his first Tour title since returning from knee surgery at the Arnold Palmer Invitational.

### APRIL

**4/1:** Cleveland Browns wide receiver Dante Stallworth is charged with manslaughter after killing a pedestrian while driving drunk in Miami the month before.

**4/1:** John Calipari announces that he will take over as head coach at the University of Kentucky. His eight-year, $31.65-million salary makes him the nations' highest paid college basketball coach.

**4/3:** The New York Giants release Plaxico Burress.

**4/5:** In the opening game of the 2009 MLB season the Atlanta Braves defeat the defending World Series champion Philadelphia Phillies 4–1.

**4/6:** Michael Jordan is named to the Basketball Hall of Fame along with John Stockton, David Robinson, Utah coach Jerry Sloan, and Rutgers women's coach C. Vivian Stringer.

**4/6:** North Carolina defeats Michigan State 89–72 to win the NCAA men's basketball tournament.

**4/7:** UConn's women's basketball team caps an undefeated season with a 76–54 victory over Louisville in the NCAA women's championship game.

**4/9:** Rookie Los Angeles Angels pitcher Nick Adenhart, just 22, is killed in a hit-and-run car crash.

**4/12:** Golfer Angel Cabrera wins The Masters in a three-hole playoff against Kenny Perry and Chad Campbell.

**4/13:** Jermaine Dye and Paul Konerko of the Chicago White Sox hit back-to-back home runs in a game against the Detroit Tigers, marking the 300th career home run for each.

**4/14:** Boxer Oscar De La Hoya officially retires.

**4/15:** In Texas' 19–6 win over Baltimore, Ian Kinsler scores six runs and becomes the sixth Ranger in franchise history to hit for the cycle.

**4/16:** Pro Football Hall of Fame coach and longtime TV analyst John Madden announces his retirement from broadcasting after more than 30 years of calling games for four different networks.

**4/16:** Just as the New York Mets did the previous week, the New York Yankees lose the inaugural game in their new stadium.

**4/19:** At a polo match in Florida, 21 horses suddenly die, a tragedy that is later attributed to a pharmacy error involving toxic equine supplements.

**4/20:** After leading the Cavaliers to a franchise-record 66–16 record, Mike Brown is named NBA Coach of the Year.

**4/21:** Mackenzie Brown, a 12-year-old Little League player in Bayonne, New Jersey, becomes the first girl in the town's history to pitch a perfect game, striking out all 18 boys she faced.

**4/22:** The Milwaukee Brewers give away minor league outfielder Jason Tyner to the Detroit Tigers in what cannot technically be deemed a trade, as the Brewers apparently get nothing in return.

**4/25:** The Detroit Lions, 0–16 in the 2008 season, select Georgia quarterback Matthew Stafford with the first overall pick in the 2009 NFL draft.

**4/26:** Seven NASCAR fans are hurt when Carl Edwards' car flies into a fence and showers fans with debris after a crash with eventual winner Brad Keselowski at Talladega.

**4/26:** Jacoby Ellsbury becomes the first Red Sox player since 1999 to steal home and helps Boston sweep a series against the New York Yankees.

**4/27:** The Denver Nuggets, playing on the road, beat the New Orleans Hornets 121–63, the widest margin of victory in an NBA playoff game since the Minneapolis Lakers defeated the St. Louis Hawks 133–75 in 1956.

**4/29:** Six Beijing Olympians, including Bahrain's first track and field gold medalist, test positive for blood doping in retests of their Beijing samples.

**4/30:** The Alabama High School Athletic Association cancels all sports events due to concerns over the potential spread of swine flu.

### MAY

**5/2:** Ridden by jockey Calvin Borel, 50-1 long shot Mine That Bird wins the 135th Kentucky Derby.

**5/2:** The Dallas Cowboys' tent-like practice facility collapses under high winds, injuring 12 people.

**5/3:** Carl Crawford goes 4-for-4 at the plate and steals six bases—tying a modern major league record—in the Tampa Bay Rays' 5–3 win over the Boston Red Sox.

**5/4:** LeBron James is named NBA MVP for the 2008–09 regular season.

**5/5:** News reports note that Brett Favre is in talks with the Minnesota Vikings to return to the NFL.

**5/6:** The Los Angeles Dodgers win their 13th-straight game at home, defeating the Washington Nationals 10–3, and set a major league record for most home games won to begin a season.

**5/7:** MLB suspends Manny Ramirez for 50 games after the Dodgers outfielder tests positive for a women's fertility drug commonly used to mitigate the side effects of steroids.

**5/II:** French tennis player Richard Gasquet is suspended indefinitely after testing positive for cocaine, an offense that could see him banned from the sport for two years.

**5/12:** Cowboys quarterback Tony Romo tries—and fails—to qualify for golf's U.S. Open on a local course in Dallas.

**5/13:** Southern Indiana's Screaming Eagles forfeit their entire 2008–09 basketball season after two players are declared ineligible and an NCAA investigation finds five other violations.

**5/13:** Adam LaRoche and Ross Gload become the first major league baseball players to have home runs revoked under the league's video-review policy.

**5/15:** The North Dakota State Board of Higher Education votes unanimously that the University of North Dakota must retire its Fighting Sioux nickname and logo by October 1, 2009 unless the Spirit Lake and Standing Rock Sioux tribes vote to approve the nickname.

**5/16:** Rachel Alexandra, with Calvin Borel aboard, becomes the first filly in 85 years—and just the fifth overall—to win the Preakness Stakes.

**5/18:** ESPN announces that former Tampa Bay head coach Jon Gruden will replace Tony Kornheiser on Monday Night Football's announcing crew.

**5/19:** FINA approves 202 high-tech swimsuits for use in 2009 competition, but rejects 10 others.

**5/20:** Former NFL QB Michael Vick, suspended from the league and jailed for two years for financing an illegal dogfighting ring, is released from prison to begin home confinement in Virginia.

**5/25:** NASCAR driver David Reutimann wins a rain-shortened Coca-Cola 600.

**5/31:** Four-time defending champion Rafael Nadal loses at the French Open for the first time in his career, going down 2–6, 7–6, 4–6, 6–7 to Sweden's Robin Soderling.

### JUNE

**6/I:** Phil Mickelson, on sabbatical from the PGA Tour while his wife receives treatment for breast cancer, announces he will return to play the St. Jude Championship and the U.S. Open.

**6/3:** The Atlanta Braves release 300-game winning pitcher Tom Glavine.

**6/4:** In guiding the San Francisco Giants to a 5–1 victory over the Washington Nationals, 45-year-old Randy Johnson becomes only the 24th pitcher in major league history to earn 300 wins.

**6/6:** Summer Bird ends jockey Calvin Borel's personal Triple Crown bid by beating Borel and his horse Mine That Bird at the Belmont Stakes.

**6/7:** Tiger Woods wins his second tournament since returning to the PGA Tour, hitting every fairway en route to winning the Memorial tournament.

**6/7:** Roger Federer completes a career Grand Slam and ties Pete Sampras's record of 14 Grand Slam singles titles with a straight-sets win over Robin Soderling in the French Open final.

**6/II:** Don Briggs, a high school baseball umpire in West Burlington, Iowa, ejects a crowd of over 100 fans from a game between West Burlington and Winfield-Mt. Union, citing unruly crowd behavior.

**6/II:** The Cleveland Indians beat the Kansas City Royals when Shin-Soo Choo's line drive ricochets off a low-flying seagull and rolls past Kansas City centerfielder Mark DeRosa.

**6/12:** The Pittsburgh Penguins take the Stanley Cup with a 2–1 win over the Detroit Red Wings in Game 7.

**6/14:** The Los Angeles Lakers win their 15th NBA title with a 99–86 Game 5 win; Finals MVP Kobe Bryant earns his fourth career title and head coach Phil Jackson walks away with his tenth ring.

**6/18:** For the second straight year, the Washington Capitals' Alexander Ovechkin is awarded the Hart Memorial Trophy as the NHL's most valuable player.

**6/22:** U.S. golfer Lucas Glover wins his first major title at the U.S. Open at Bethpage Black.

**6/23:** For one game, the minor league Brooklyn Cyclones rename themselves the Barack-lyn Cyclones in honor of President Barack Obama.

**6/24:** Dubbed the "Miracle on Grass," the U.S. soccer team defeats world No. 1-ranked Spain 2–0 in the semifinals of the Confederations Cup.

**6/25:** The Cleveland Cavaliers trade Ben Wallace and Sasha Pavlovic to Phoenix in exchange for Shaquille O'Neal, who will begin the 2009–10 season playing for his third team in two years.

**6/25:** The Astana cycling team chooses 2007 Tour de France champion Alberto Contador—not Lance Armstrong—as its leader for the 2009 race.

**6/28:** Mariano Rivera becomes only the second pitcher in major league history to earn 500 saves as the Yankees beat the Mets 4–2.

**6/29:** A match is played indoors at Wimbledon for the first time ever, as the new retractable roof over Centre Court is closed for the match between Dinara Safina and Amelie Mauresmo.

## JULY

**7/4:** Serena Williams avenges her loss to sister Venus in last year's Wimbledon final with a 7–6, 6–2 win in the 2009 championship match.

**7/5:** In a match concluding with the longest set in Wimbledon history, Roger Federer defeats Andy Roddick to win his 15th Grand Slam title, breaking Pete Sampras' all-time career Grand Slam record.

**7/8:** Nashville police rule former Tennessee Titans QB Steve McNair's death a homicide, allegedly committed by distraught girlfriend Sahel Kazemi before she killed herself.

**7/14:** The American League wins the MLB All-Star Game for the seventh straight year, beating the National League 4–3.

**7/19:** Stewart Cink beats 59-year-old Tom Watson —who was bidding to become golf's oldest major champion—in a four-hole playoff to win the British Open at Turnberry.

**7/20:** Manny Ramirez hits his 537th career home run off Cincinnati Reds pitcher Micah Owings to pass Mickey Mantle and move into 15th on MLB's all-time home run list.

**7/24:** FINA votes to ban—as of 2010—the high-tech swimsuits that have helped swimmers set nearly 150 world records over the past two years.

**7/28:** Pitching five days after his perfect game, Chicago White Sox lefthander Mark Buehrle retires the first seventeen Minnesota Twins to set a new major league record of 45 consecutive outs.

**7/29:** One day after Germany's Paul Biedermann beat his 200-meter freestyle world record, Michael Phelps breaks his own 200-meter butterfly world record at the FINA World Championships in Rome.

## AUGUST

**8/3:** NASCAR driver Denny Hamlin wins the Pennsylvania 500, ending a 50-race winless skid.

**8/5:** New York Giants QB Eli Manning signs the most lucrative contract in NFL history, agreeing to a six-year extension worth $97.5 million.

**8/6:** San Jose Sharks forward Jeremy Roenick, who has scored the third-most points of any U.S.-born player in NHL history, announces his retirement after 20 seasons.

**8/6:** Orlando Magic forward Rashard Lewis is suspended for 10 games after testing positive for an elevated testosterone level, which Lewis attributes to over-the-counter supplements.

**8/14:** The Philadelphia Eagles sign newly reinstated QB Michael Vick to a one-year, $1.6-million contract with a team option for a second year at $5.2 million.

**8/16:** Korean golfer Y.E. Yang overcomes a two-shot, final-round deficit at the PGA Championship to upset Tiger Woods and become the first Asian-born golfer to win a major title.

**8/17:** Pitching phenom and No. 1 overall MLB draft pick Stephen Strasburg signs a record four-year, $15.1-million deal with the Washington Nationals.

**8/20:** Jamaican sprinter Usain Bolt breaks his second world record in four days, running the 200-meter dash in 19.19 seconds at the IAAF World Track and Field Championships in Berlin.

**8/21:** During a preseason game at the new Cowboys Stadium, play is abruptly halted after a punt from Tennessee Titan A.J. Trapasso caroms off the huge video screen that hangs 90 feet above the field.

**8/22:** In the inaugural championship match of the Women's Professional Soccer league, Sky Blue FC defeats the Los Angeles Sol 1–0.

**8/23:** The U.S. women's golf team wins its third-straight Solheim Cup with a 16–12 victory over Europe.

**8/23:** Philadelphia Phillies shortstop Eric Bruntlett turns the first-ever game-ending unassisted triple play in National League history against the New York Mets, cementing a 9–7 victory.

**8/24:** A federal appeals court rules against Delaware Governor Jack Markell's plan to allow betting on individual sports games in his state.

**8/25:** The NHL files a bid in U.S. Bankruptcy Court to buy the Phoenix Coyotes franchise and keep the financially struggling team in Arizona.

**8/30:** A team from Chula Vista, California rallies from a three-run deficit to defeat Chinese Taipei and win the Little League World Series 6–3.

## SEPTEMBER

**9/1:** Five months after open-heart surgery, Houston Astros third baseman Aaron Boone returns to play.

**9/7:** American John Isner loses his fourth-round U.S. Open match, marking the first time since 1881 that no U.S. men's player will make it into that tournament's quarterfinals.

**9/9:** The Chicago Cubs smack eight straight hits to start a game against the Philadelphia Phillies, setting a major league record.

**9/10:** The NFL regular season kicks off with the Super Bowl–champion Pittsburgh Steelers defeating the Tennessee Titans 13–10 in overtime.

**9/19:** Floyd Mayweather Jr. dominates the smaller Juan Manual Marquez throughout their highly touted fight, winning by unanimous decision.

**9/21:** The LPGA Tour announces it will lose the Kingsmill tournament in 2010, making it the seventh event the Tour has lost since 2007.

**9/22:** Former New York Giants wide receiver Plaxico Burress is sentenced to two years in prison for possession of an unlicensed gun in 2008.

**9/24:** Two-time World Cup champion skier Bode Miller rejoins the U.S. ski team after a nearly 18-month-long absence.

**9/27:** Phil Mickelson shoots a bogey-free final-round 65 to win The Tour Championship, but second-place finisher Tiger Woods takes home the FedEx Cup and the $10-million playoff bonus.

**9/27:** For the first time since December 27, 2007—a 19-game drought—the Detroit Lions claim victory, beating the Washington Redskins at home 19–14.

**9/29:** Diana Taurasi, who led the league in scoring and who will lead the Phoenix Mercury to a WNBA title in October, is named the league MVP.

**9/30:** Golfing legend Arnold Palmer receives the Congressional Gold Medal from President Barack Obama at the White House.

## OCTOBER

**10/2:** President Barack Obama travels to Copenhagen to make a personal pitch for Chicago, his former hometown, to host the 2016 Games. The International Olympic Committee instead chooses Brazil's Rio de Janeiro as host city.

**10/5:** Fans tune in to watch new Minnesota Vikings QB Brett Favre face his old Green Bay Packers teammates on *Monday Night Football*, making it the most-watched show in cable TV history.

**10/6:** In a one-game playoff to determine the AL Central champion, the Minnesota Twins defeat the Detroit Tigers at the Metrodome in 12 innings, 6–5.

**10/10:** The U.S. national soccer team clinches a berth in the 2010 FIFA World Cup in South Africa with a thrilling 3–2 victory over Honduras.

**10/11:** Tiger Woods finishes a perfect 5–0 in tourney play and helps to lead the U.S. team to a 19½–14½ Presidents Cup victory over the International team.

**10/12:** In a move designed to smooth the team's eventual sale for $845 million, the Chicago Cubs file for Chapter 11 bankruptcy.

**10/13:** An half-ton chainsaw-carved wooden statue of former Buffalo Bills RB Thurman Thomas, which had gone missing from a parking lot across from Ralph Wilson Stadium, is rescued after being found by a man in Ontario, Canada.

**10/14:** In its inaugural Hall of Fame class, NASCAR selects two members of the league's founding family—Bill France and Bill France Jr.—as well as three legendary drivers—Dale Earnhardt, Richard Petty and Junior Johnson.

**10/17:** The Super Six Boxing Classic, a round-robin middleweight tournament, kicks off with a 12th-round knockout victory by Arthur Abraham over Jermain Taylor.

**10/18:** New England Patriots QB Tom Brady sets a new NFL record by tossing five TD passes in the second quarter of a 59–0 shellacking of the Tennessee Titans.

**10/18:** Racecar driver Jenson Button wins his first Formula One season championship after finishing fifth in the Brazilian Grand Prix.

**10/18:** Only hours after helping the Connecticut Huskies football team earn a homecoming victory, UConn cornerback Jasper Howard is stabbed to death in an on-campus altercation.

**10/19:** A team official tells the *Associated Press* that a group of prospective investors in the WNBA's Detroit Shock would relocate the team to Tulsa.

**10/22:** The flame that will eventually make its way to the 2010 Winter Olympics in Vancouver, Canada, is lit in ancient Olympia, Greece.

**10/23:** 2009 No. 1 overall NBA draft pick Blake Griffin breaks his left kneecap in the Los Angeles Clippers' final exhibition game, forcing him to miss the first quarter of the regular season.

**10/23:** After numerous cracks appear in the pedestrian ramps at the new $1.5-billion Yankee Stadium, team officials hire an outside contractor to study the problem.

**10/23:** Just days before the start of the regular season, NBA referees end their lockout and agree to a new two-year contract with the league.

**10/25:** Stirring controversy, New York Jets QB Mark Sanchez is caught by TV cameras munching on a hot dog on the sidelines in the closing minutes of the Jets' 38–0 blowout of the Oakland Raiders.

**10/26:** Former slugger and suspected steroids user Mark McGwire is named by St. Louis Cardinals manager Tony LaRussa as the team's new hitting coach.

**10/28:** Oklahoma QB and 2008 Heisman Trophy winner Sam Bradford undergoes shoulder surgery that will sideline him for the remainder of the 2009 college football season.

**10/31:** In just the second-ever World Series game held on Halloween, the New York Yankees rally to beat the Philadelphia Phillies 8–5, thanks in part to Alex Rodriguez's two-run, fourth-inning home run, a play that marked the first-ever use of instant replay in the Fall Classic.

## NOVEMBER

**11/1:** In a rare, same-city, two-sport doubleheader, the NFL's Philadelphia Eagles defeat the New York Giants at home 40–17 on the same day that the Philadelphia Phillies lose at home to the New York Yankees 7–4 in Game 4 of the World Series.

**11/1:** For the first time since Alberto Salazar did it in 1982, an American man—Meb Keflezighi—wins the New York City Marathon.

**11/1:** Ted Ginn Jr. of the Miami Dolphins becomes the first player in NFL history to score two kickoff return TDs of 100 yards or more in one game, helping Miami defeat the New York Jets 30–25.

**11/2:** World Series MVP Hideki Matsui drives in six runs for the Yankees in Game 6, tying a single-game World Series record, and New York powers past the Phillies 7–3 to win its 27th championship.

# Baseball

New York Yankees captain Derek Jeter (c.) celebrates the team's 27th World Series victory

DAMIAN STROHMEYER

# A New Empire Strikes Back

After winning the Hot Stove bidding wars and rolling through the regular season, the New York Yankees fought past the Phillies to a 27th World Series title

## BY MERRELL NODEN

THE LAST TIME THE NEW YORK Yankees won the World Series was in 2000. That was the team's 26th championship overall and its third in a row. Given the Yankees' apparent willingness to spend whatever it took to keep on winning, it seemed as if the string might go on forever. But it didn't. In 2008 the mighty Yankees didn't even make the playoffs.

So when, in Game 6 of the 2009 World Series, Yankee manager Joe Girardi handed the ball to reliever Mariano Rivera with one out in the eighth and the Yankees leading the defending champion Philadelphia Phillies 7–3, it seemed as if a cruel order was being restored in the baseball world. Rivera was one of a remarkable Yankees quartet—shortstop and captain Derek Jeter, catcher Jorge Posada, starting pitcher Andy Pettitte, and the seemingly unflappable Rivera—all of whom had played on the last three Yankees championship teams. (Posada was not on the '96 postseason roster.) Oh, they had help this season and in the World Series, most notably in the latter from Hideki Matsui and Johnny Damon. But make no mistake: Nine years later those four veterans were the steady, beating heart of this team. When Rivera got Shane Victorino to ground out to end the game, they had calmly led the team to their 27th title.

The regular season had begun with the Yankees in their new $1.5-billion home, right across the street from the House that Ruth Built. In the off-season the team had spent $243.5 million on pitching alone, acquiring C.C. Sabathia and A.J. Burnett. When they added slugger Mark Teixeira for $180 million, the Yankees looked invincible.

But if the Yankees front office expected their glittering lineup to guarantee dominance and ticket sales, they were wrong on both counts—at least for a time. At the end of April New York was 12–10, the same record boasted by Kansas City, whose pitcher Zack Greinke started the season with 24 straight scoreless innings on his way to a 16–8 record and a major league-leading 2.16 ERA.

Besides starting the season flat, the Yankees were having trouble selling the most expensive seats in their new stadium (some priced at $2,625!) and had to reduce prices dramatically. It would be a tough year at the turnstiles everywhere. Overall major league attendance dropped 6.8%, and the average crowd fell from 32,543 to 30,338.

By May 9 the Yankees had slipped to 13–15, but there was good news too: Alex Rodriguez was coming back after off-season hip surgery. Rodriguez was returning with a Pandora's Box of controversies, ranging from his admission to using steroids for two

years earlier in his career to other rumors that he'd used them more than that. But Rodriguez hit a home run in his return at bat, and with him in the lineup the Yankees finally caught fire, going 90–44 the rest of the year to finish the season with 103 wins, best in the majors.

Just as A-Rod was coming back, the Dodgers' Manny Ramirez was exiting, suspended for 50 games for violating the league's drug policy. But if the Dodgers missed Ramirez, they didn't show it. At the All-Star break they had the best record in baseball (56–32) and the biggest divisional lead (seven games).

The defending champion Phillies were powered in the early going by Raul Ibanez, whom they'd acquired in the offseason. At the end of May Ibanez, 37, led the league in RBIs, and by the end of the season he was one of four Phillies with 30-plus homers, a quartet paced by Ryan Howard, who had 45 along with a major league-leading 141 RBIs (tying him with the Brewers' Prince Fielder).

The totally unexpected problem for Philadelphia was Brad Lidge. A perfect 48-for-48 in saves last year, Lidge was a baffling liability in 2009, blowing 11 saves, going 0–8, and recording an ERA of 7.21. The good news was the acquisition of Cliff Lee from Cleveland. The 2008 Cy Young Award winner won his first five starts for the Phillies and would prove especially valuable in the postseason.

In the NL Central the Cardinals pulled away over the second half of the season, led by Albert Pujols, who for a long time looked

**In 2009, three of the major league's most prodigious sluggers—(l. to r.) Ramirez, Rodriguez, and David Ortiz—were embroiled in controversy, thanks to steroids scandals.**

like a Triple Crown threat. Despite trailing off in September, Pujols won his first home run crown with 47, finished third in RBIs (135), and batted .327. The Cardinals' other great assets were pitchers Adam Wainwright and Chris Carpenter, who led the league with a 2.24 ERA. In a season with no 20-game winners this pair stood tall, going 17–4 and 19–8, respectively.

Out west, the Dodgers got Ramirez back on July 2. But the Manny who returned, on July 3, was not the same slugger who'd left. He hit .218 in September, forcing the Dodgers to rely on more Ramirez's young outfield mates, Andre Ethier and Matt Kemp, both of whom topped 100 RBIs. In the meantime, the last-place Rockies had fired manager Clint Hurdle in May 29, replacing him with bench coach Jim Tracy. Under Tracy, Colorado went 74–42 and almost caught the Dodgers in September.

No such worries for either the Yankees or the Angels, who sailed through September with comfortable leads. Led by veteran Bobby Abreu and slugging first baseman Kendry Morales, who defected from Cuba, the Angels enjoyed the biggest cushion of any division winner, 10 games. The Red Sox had led the Yankees by two games at the All-Star break but were slowed by multiple injuries yet still won the AL wild card slot.

The really interesting race in the American

After flirting with .400 through June, Joe Mauer's batting average faded down the stretch, but he still finished at .365 and led the Twins to an AL Central title.

League was in the Central, where the Tigers had started September with a seven-game lead on the Twins, only to see it disappear. The final game of the season was a one-game playoff pitting the struggling Tigers—the first team ever to lose a three-game lead with just four games to play—against the surging Twins, who had won 16 of their final 20. Their one-game playoff was a classic. The Twins overcame one-run deficits in the seventh and tenth innings and got out of a bases loaded, one out jam in the 12th to win 6–5.

It was a great ending to a season full of notable achievements. Among them: Randy Johnson got his 300th win, Rivera passed 500 saves and Arizona third baseman Mark Reynolds topped his own single-season strikeout record, set last year, with 223. Mark Buerle pitched the 18th perfect game in major league history, while Phillies infielder Eric Bruntlett did something even rarer when he turned history's 15th unassisted triple play. Minnesota's Joe Mauer became the first catcher to win back-to-back batting titles, hitting .365, a record for his position, and easily good enough to claim his third batting title in four years. And then there was Jeter who, on September 11, passed Lou Gehrig as the all-time Yankees hit leader, finishing the season with 2,747 hits.

The Yankees captain had his share of hits in the World Series as well, which looked to be one of the most intriguing World Series match-ups in years. The Phillies won the first game on the road, behind the awesome pitching of Lee, who went nine innings in the rain, with 10 strikeouts and no walks, to beat the Yankees, 6–1. Chase Utley was likewise impressive, hitting two solo home runs, the first of a record-tying five for the World Series.

Virtually absent were some of the two teams' biggest hitters. Kept off balance by a steady barrage of breaking balls, Howard needed only six games to set a World Series record with 13 strikeouts, Yankees slugger Mark Teixeira was just as bad, hitting a mere .136. Even A-Rod was a shadow of his new clutch self, hitting .250.

In the end, the Phillies' starting pitching let them down as much as their anemic hitting. Cole Hamels, the MVP of last years's Series, pitched poorly in his one start. In Game 2 Pedro Martinez pitched well but lost and he was hardly the pitcher you'd want to start the potentially deciding Game 6. In that game, he gave up four earned runs in four innings, all of them to Hideki Matsui. The 35-year-old Japanese veteran had a home run, a double, and a single to drive in a World Series single-game-tying record of six RBIs. After hitting .615 for the Series with 8 RBIs, he was voted the Series MVP, the first Japanese player to be so honored. In the last year of his contract, Matsui has expressed a fervent desire to stay and keep playing alongside his four veteran teammates.

Who wouldn't want to? In the Series Posada batted .263 and Jeter .407; Pettitte won the clinching game, just as he did in the Yankees' two previous playoff series; and Rivera was merely perfect with an ERA of 0.00. It was quite a comeback for the four old friends.

"The funny thing about those four guys is the team in the 1990s couldn't have won without them, and the team now couldn't have won without them," said their former teammate Paul O'Neill, who's now a Yankees broadcaster. "I don't think you'll ever see that again, four constants like that."

# FOR THE RECORD•2009

## 2009 Final Regular Season Standings

### National League

#### EASTERN DIVISION

| Team | Won | Lost | Pct | GB | Home | Away |
|---|---|---|---|---|---|---|
| Philadelphia | 93 | 69 | .574 | -- | 45–36 | 48–33 |
| Florida | 87 | 75 | .537 | 6.0 | 43–38 | 44–37 |
| Atlanta | 86 | 76 | .531 | 7.0 | 40–41 | 46–35 |
| NY Mets | 70 | 92 | .432 | 23.0 | 41–40 | 29–52 |
| Washington | 59 | 103 | .364 | 34.0 | 33–48 | 26–55 |

#### CENTRAL DIVISION

| Team | Won | Lost | Pct | GB | Home | Away |
|---|---|---|---|---|---|---|
| St. Louis | 91 | 71 | .562 | -- | 46–35 | 45–36 |
| Chicago | 83 | 78 | .516 | 7.5 | 46–34 | 37–44 |
| Milwaukee | 80 | 82 | .494 | 11.0 | 40–41 | 40–41 |
| Cincinnati | 78 | 84 | .481 | 13.0 | 40–41 | 38–43 |
| Houston | 74 | 88 | .457 | 17.0 | 44–37 | 30–51 |
| Pittsburgh | 62 | 99 | .385 | 28.5 | 40–41 | 22–58 |

#### WESTERN DIVISION

| Team | Won | Lost | Pct | GB | Home | Away |
|---|---|---|---|---|---|---|
| LA Dodgers | 95 | 67 | .586 | -- | 50–31 | 45–36 |
| †Colorado | 92 | 70 | .568 | 3.0 | 51–30 | 41–40 |
| San Francisco | 88 | 74 | .543 | 7.0 | 52–29 | 36–45 |
| San Diego | 75 | 87 | .463 | 20.0 | 42–48 | 33–48 |
| Arizona | 70 | 82 | .432 | 25.0 | 34–47 | 34–47 |

†Wild-card teams.

### American League

#### EASTERN DIVISION

| Team | Won | Lost | Pct | GB | Home | Away |
|---|---|---|---|---|---|---|
| NY Yankees | 103 | 59 | .636 | -- | 57–24 | 46–35 |
| †Boston | 95 | 67 | .586 | 8.0 | 56–25 | 39–42 |
| Tampa Bay | 84 | 78 | .519 | 19.0 | 52–29 | 32–49 |
| Toronto | 75 | 87 | .463 | 28.0 | 44–37 | 31–50 |
| Baltimore | 64 | 98 | .395 | 39.0 | 39–42 | 25–56 |

#### CENTRAL DIVISION

| Team | Won | Lost | Pct | GB | Home | Away |
|---|---|---|---|---|---|---|
| *Minnesota | 86 | 76 | .531 | -- | 48–33 | 38–43 |
| Detroit | 86 | 76 | .531 | - | 51–30 | 35–46 |
| Chicago | 79 | 83 | .488 | 7.0 | 43–38 | 36–45 |
| Kansas City | 65 | 97 | .401 | 21.0 | 33–48 | 32–49 |
| Cleveland | 65 | 97 | .401 | 21.0 | 35–46 | 30–51 |

#### WESTERN DIVISION

| Team | Won | Lost | Pct | GB | Home | Away |
|---|---|---|---|---|---|---|
| LA Angels | 97 | 69 | .599 | -- | 49–32 | 48–33 |
| Texas | 87 | 75 | .537 | 10.0 | 48–33 | 39–42 |
| Seattle | 85 | 77 | .525 | 12.0 | 48–33 | 37–44 |
| Oakland | 75 | 87 | .463 | 22.0 | 40–41 | 25–46 |

*won division in one-game tiebreaker at home vs. Detroit.

## 2009 Playoffs

### National League Division Playoffs

Oct 7 ..............Colorado 1 at Philadelphia 5
Oct 8 ..............Colorado 5 at Philadelphia 4

Oct 11 ............. Philadelphia 6 at Colorado 5
Oct 12 ............. Philadelphia 5 at Colorado 4

(Philadelphia won series 3–1)

Oct 7 ..............St. Louis 3 at Los Angeles 5
Oct 8 ..............St. Louis 2 at Los Angeles 3

Oct 10 .............Los Angeles 5 at St. Louis 1

(LA Dodgers won series 3–0)

### National League Championship Series

Oct 15 .............Philadelphia 8 at Los Angeles 6
Oct 16 .............Philadelphia 1 at Los Angeles 2
Oct 18 .............Los Angeles 0 at Philadelphia 11

Oct 19 .............Los Angeles 4 at Philadelphia 5
Oct 21 .............Los Angeles 4 at Philadelphia 10

(Philadelphia won series 4–1)

#### GAME I

| | | | | | | | | | | | |
|---|---|---|---|---|---|---|---|---|---|---|---|
| Philadelphia | 0 | 0 | 0 | 0 | 5 | 0 | 0 | 3 | 0 | **8** | **8** | **I** |
| Los Angeles | 0 | 1 | 0 | 0 | 3 | 0 | 0 | 2 | 0 | **6** | **I4** | **0** |

W—Phi: Hamels. L—LA: Kershaw. SV—Phi: Lidge.
LOB—Phi: 5; LA: 10. 2B—Phi: Howard; LA: Ethier,
Martin. HR—Phi: Ruiz, Ibanez; LA: Loney, Ramirez.
RBI—Phi: Ruiz (3), Howard (2), Ibanez (3); LA: Loney,
Furcal, Ethier, Ramirez (2), Martin. GIDP—LA: Blake.
SAC—Phi: Hamels. SF—LA: Furcal. E—Phi: Utley.
T—4:02. A—56,000.
Recap: Carlos Ruiz and Raul Ibanez hit three-run
homers, reliever Ryan Madson got a key out and
closer Brad Lidge finished off the Phillies' 8–6 victory
over the Los Angeles Dodgers in Game 1 of the NLCS.
Manny Ramirez homered, but grounded out weakly
with two runners on against a struggling Madson to
end the Dodgers' two-run rally in the eighth. L.A.'s 14
hits set an LCS single-game club record, but they
stranded 10 runners. Lidge, aided by a double play,
worked around a single and a walk in the ninth.

#### GAME 2

| | | | | | | | | | | | |
|---|---|---|---|---|---|---|---|---|---|---|---|
| Philadelphia | 0 | 0 | 0 | 1 | 0 | 0 | 0 | 0 | 0 | **I** | **4** | **I** |
| Los Angeles | 0 | 0 | 0 | 0 | 0 | 0 | 0 | 2 | x | **2** | **5** | **0** |

W—LA: Kuo. L—Phi: Park. SV—LA: Broxton. LOB—
Phi: 2; LA: 5. HR—Phi: Howard. RBI—Phi: Howard;
LA: Ethier. GIDP—Phi: Werth, Francisco. SB—Phi:
Ruiz. CS—LA: Kemp. SAC—LA: Padilla. HBP—LA:
Martin. E—Phi: Utley.
T—3:05. A—56,000.
Recap: In a matchup of castoff starting pitchers,
Vincente Padilla and Pedro Martinez dueled for
seven innings. Martinez allowed no runs and just two
hits, but after he left the game, the Phillies' bullpen
collapsed. A throwing error by Chase Utley, a pinch-
hit single by Jim Thome and two walks were part of a
crazy eighth inning that plated two runs and gave the
Dodgers a victory over the Phillies. The Dodgers took
the lead after Andre Ethier drew a bases-loaded, two-
out walk from Phillies' rookie J.A. Happ, capping the
Dodgers' third comeback win of this postseason.

## National League Championship Series *(Cont.)*

### GAME 3

| | | | | | | | | | | | | | |
|---|---|---|---|---|---|---|---|---|---|---|---|---|---|
| Los Angeles | 0 | 0 | 0 | 0 | 0 | 0 | 0 | 0 | 0 | **0** | **3** | **0** |
| Philadelphia | 4 | 2 | 0 | 0 | 2 | 0 | 0 | 3 | x | **11** | **11** | **0** |

**W**—Phi: Lee. **L**—LA: Kuroda. **LOB**—Phi 6; LA: 2. **2B**—Phi: Ruiz, Rollins. **3B**—Phi: Howard, Feliz. **HR**—Phi: Howard, Werth, Victorino. **RBI**—Phi: Howard (3), Werth (2), Rollins, Feliz, Ruiz, Victorino (3). **SB**—Phi: Victorino. **SAC**—Phi: Lee. **PB**—LA: Martin. **GIDP**—Phi: Feliz; LA: Loney. **WP**—LA: Elbert. **T**—3:12. **A**—45,721.

**Recap:** Cliff Lee provided another brilliant playoff start, becoming the only pitcher in postseason history to have 10-plus strikeouts with no walks while not allowing a run in a game. On offense, Ryan Howard had three RBIs and ran hard for a triple, while Jayson Werth homered and the Phillies led 6–0 by the second inning. Victorino's three-run home run to deep right field in the eighth put an emphatic exclamation point on the rout.

### GAME 4

| | | | | | | | | | | | | | |
|---|---|---|---|---|---|---|---|---|---|---|---|---|---|
| Los Angeles | 0 | 0 | 0 | 2 | 1 | 1 | 0 | 0 | 0 | **4** | **8** | **0** |
| Philadelphia | 2 | 0 | 0 | 0 | 0 | 1 | 0 | 0 | 2 | **5** | **5** | **1** |

**W**—Phi: Lidge. **L**—LA: Broxton. **LOB**—LA: 8; Phi: 6. **2B**—Phi: Rollins. **3B**—Phi: Victorino. **HR**—LA: Kemp; Phi: Howard. **RBI**—LA: Loney, Martin, Kemp, Blake; Phi: Howard (2), Utley, Rollins (2). **SB**—LA: Blake, Belliard, Furcal. **CS**—LA: Ethier. **HBP**—Phi: Victorino, Ruiz. **WP**—LA: Sherrill; Phi: Lidge. **E**—Phi: Feliz. **T**—3:44. **A**—46,157.

**Recap:** Jimmy Rollins didn't just finish off Game 4, he wrote a chapter of postseason history, lining a two-run walkoff double with two outs in the ninth inning off Dodgers' closer Jonathan Broxton, to rally the Phillies past the Dodgers 5–4. Trailing 4–3, the Phillies started their comeback with one out in the ninth when pinch-hitter Matt Stairs walked on four pitches and Carlos Ruiz was hit by a pitch. Rollins later ripped a 99 mph fastball to the wall in right-center and Andre Ethier's throw home was too late.

### GAME 5

| | | | | | | | | | | | | | |
|---|---|---|---|---|---|---|---|---|---|---|---|---|---|
| Los Angeles | 1 | 1 | 0 | 0 | 1 | 0 | 0 | 1 | 0 | **4** | **8** | **0** |
| Philadelphia | 3 | 1 | 0 | 2 | 0 | 2 | 1 | 1 | x | **10** | **8** | **0** |

**W**—Phi: Durbin. **L**—LA: Padilla. **LOB**—LA: 7; Phi: 5. **2B**—Phi: Ibanez, Victorino; LA: Furcal. **HR**—Phi: Werth (2), Feliz, Victorino; LA: Ethier, Loney, Hudson. **RBI**—LA: Ethier, Loney, Hudson, Kemp; Phi: Werth (4), Feliz, Ibanez, Victorino (3). **SAC**—Phi: Hamels. **HBP**—Phi: Rollins (2), Victorino. **WP**—LA: Belisario. **T**—3:40. **A**—46,214.

**Recap:** Jayson Werth homered twice, Shane Victorino and Pedro Feliz also connected and the Phillies beat the Dodgers 10–4 to win their second straight NL pennant. With two homers in Wednesday's win, the Phillies' Jayson Werth became the sixth player from a winning team to record a multi-homer game in an LCS clincher. Meanwhile, slugger Manny Ramirez, manager Joe Torre and the rest of the Dodgers go home after leading the NL with 95 wins in the regular season and sweeping the St. Louis Cardinals in the division series. With their latest big night at the plate, the Phillies overcame another shaky outing by 2008 NLCS and World Series MVP Cole Hamels. Los Angeles closed to 9-4 in the eighth, but Ryan Madson escaped a bases-loaded jam by striking out Russell Martin and retiring Casey Blake on a grounder. Brad Lidge closed it out, Ryan Howard was selected NLCS MVP and the Phillies became the first team to reach consecutive World Series since the New York Yankees in 2000–01.

## American League Division Playoffs

Oct 8 ...............Boston 0 at Los Angeles 5
Oct 9 ...............Boston 1 at Los Angeles 4
Oct 11 .............Los Angeles 7 at Boston 6

(Los Angeles won series 3–0)

Oct 7 ...............Minnesota 2 at New York 7
Oct 9 ...............Minnesota 3 at New York 4
Oct 11 .............New York 4 at Minnesota 1

(New York won series 3–0)

## American League Championship Series

Oct 16 .............Los Angeles 1 at New York 4
Oct 18 .............Los Angeles 3 at New York 4 (13 inn.)
Oct 19 .............New York 4 at Los Angeles 5 (11 inn.)
Oct 20 .............New York 10 at Los Angeles 1
Oct 22 .............New York 6 at Los Angeles 7
Oct 24 .............Los Angeles 2 at New York 5

(New York won series 4–2)

### GAME 1

| | | | | | | | | | | | | | |
|---|---|---|---|---|---|---|---|---|---|---|---|---|---|
| Los Angeles | 0 | 0 | 0 | 1 | 0 | 0 | 0 | 0 | 0 | **1** | **4** | **3** |
| New York | 2 | 0 | 0 | 1 | 1 | 0 | 0 | 0 | x | **4** | **10** | **0** |

**W**—NY: Sabathia. **L**—LA: Lackey. **SV**—NY: Rivera. **LOB**—LA: 5; NY: 11. **2B**—LA: Guerrero; NY: Damon, Matsui. **RBI**—LA: Morales; NY: Rodriguez, Matsui (2), Jeter. **SF**—NY: Rodriguez. **WP**—LA: Bulger. **HBP**—NY: Cano. **E**—LA: Rivera, Lackey, Hunter. **T**—3:18. **A**—49,688.

### GAME 1 *(CONT.)*

**Recap:** On a blustery night more suited to bobsleds than baseballs, C.C. Sabathia pitched eight superb innings of four-hit ball to win his second straight postseason start and post a 1.23 ERA in his two playoff starts as a Yankee. The Angels looked like chilled Californians withering in the unseasonable wintry weather, making three errors that led to two unearned runs and allowing an infield popup to drop untouched for an RBI single.

## American League Championship Series *(Cont.)*

### GAME 2

| | | | | | | | | | | | | | | | | |
|---|---|---|---|---|---|---|---|---|---|---|---|---|---|---|---|---|
| Los Angeles | 0 0 0 | 0 2 0 | 0 0 0 | 0 1 0 | 0 | **3** | **8** | **2** |
| New York | 0 1 1 | 0 0 0 | 0 0 0 | 0 1 0 | 1 | **4** | **13** | **3** |

**W**—NY: Robertson. **L**—LA: Santana. **LOB**—LA: 16; NY: 12. **2B**—LA: Hunter, Izturis, Mathis. **3B**—NY: Cano. **HR**—NY: Jeter, Rodriguez. **RBI**—LA: Aybar, Figgins; NY: Cano, Jeter, Rodriguez. **SB**—LA: Aybar. **SAC**—LA: Aybar, Figgins; NY: Gardner. **GIDP**—LA: Hunter; NY: Jeter Matsui, Cano. **IBB**—LA: Abreu (2), Izturis; NY: Jeter, Cano. **E**—LA: Figgins, Izturis; NY: Cano (2), Jeter. **HBP**—LA: Morales, Figgins. **WP**—NY: Burnett. **T**—5:10. **A**—49,922.

**Recap:** Coming through under pressure once again, Alex Rodriguez hit a tying homer in the 11th inning and the New York Yankees edged Los Angeles 4–3 on Maicer Izturis' error in the 13th. After the rain came and went on another chilly night, New York pulled out its latest late-inning thriller when pinch-hitter Jerry Hairston Jr. opened the 13th with a single off losing pitcher Ervin Santana in his first postseason at-bat. Brett Gardner sacrificed and Robinson Cano was intentionally walked. Melky Cabrera then hit a bouncer in the hole between first and second, and Izturis made an ill-advised attempt to throw back across his body for a force at second. The low toss skipped past shortstop Erick Aybar and rolled behind third, where Chone Figgins tried to pick it up. Figgins fumbled the ball and Hairston, who had slowed up, sped home and slid in with the winning run.

### GAME 3

| | | | | | | | | | | | | |
|---|---|---|---|---|---|---|---|---|---|---|---|---|
| New York | 1 0 0 | 1 1 0 | 0 1 0 | 0 0 | **4** | **8** | **0** |
| Los Angeles | 0 0 0 | 0 1 2 | 1 0 0 | 0 1 | **5** | **13** | **0** |

**W**—LA: Santana. **L**—NY: Aceves. **LOB**—NY: 10; LA:7. **2B**—LA: Aybar, Abreu, Mathis (2). **3B**—LA: Kendrick. **HR**—NY: Jeter, Rodriguez, Damon, Posada; LA: Kendrick, Guerrero. **RBI**—NY: Jeter, Rodriguez, Damon, Posada; LA: Kendrick, Guerrero (2), Izturis, Mathis. **SB**—LA: Aybar. **CS**—NY: Gardner; LA: Hunter. **SAC**—LA: Aybar. **SF**—LA: Izturis. **GIDP**—LA: Hunter, Morales. **IBB**—NY: Rodriguez; LA: Abreu. **T**—4:21. **A**—44,911.

**Recap:** After more than 280 minutes, 14 pitchers, six homers and several big blunders, a winning hit by a backup catcher left only one thing certain in this series: The Los Angeles Angels won't be trampled by the mighty Yankees. Jeff Mathis drove home Howie Kendrick with a two-out double in the 11th inning, and the Angels survived a second straight ALCS thriller, beating New York 5-4. Kendrick, himself a part-time infielder, homered and tripled before singling with two outs in the 11th off rookie Alfredo Aceves. Mathis, a .211 hitter in the regular season, followed with his drive up against the left-field wall, and Kendrick slid home well ahead of a desperate throw, setting off an on-field celebration of the backups' bonanza.

### GAME 4

| | | | | | | | | |
|---|---|---|---|---|---|---|---|---|
| New York | 0 0 0 | 3 2 0 | 0 2 3 | **10** | **13** | **0** |
| Los Angeles | 0 0 0 | 0 1 0 | 0 0 0 | **1** | **5** | **1** |

**W**—NY: Sabathia. **L**—LA: Kazmir. **LOB**—LA: 5; NY: 9. **2B**—NY: Posada, Cano, Rodriguez, Cabrera. **HR**—NY: Rodriguez, Damon; LA: Morales. **RBI**—LA: Morales; NY: Damon (2), Cabrera (4), Rodriguez (2), Cano. **SB**—NY: Rodriguez, Posada. **CS**—NY: Jeter, Gardner. **GIDP**—LA: Rivera. **E**—LA: Abreu. **HBP**—NY: Swisher. **WP**—LA: Kazmir. **T**—3:38. **A**—45,160.

**Recap:** Alex Rodriguez limited the celebration of his latest playoff homer to a brisk trot and a few high-fives. C.C. Sabathia barely even pumped a fist while mowing down the Angels for eight innings. Although none of the Yankees' 26 World Series championships included these two stars, their no-nonsense excellence resulted in a 10–1 victory and put New York one win from routing the Los Angeles Angels and playing for another title. Rodriguez homered in the third straight game of his outstanding postseason, while Sabathia pitched five-hit ball on three days' rest.

### GAME 5

| | | | | | | | | |
|---|---|---|---|---|---|---|---|---|
| New York | 0 0 0 | 0 0 0 | 6 0 0 | **6** | **9** | **0** |
| Los Angeles | 4 0 0 | 0 0 0 | 3 0 0 | **7** | **12** | **0** |

**W**—LA: Jepsen. **L**—NY: Hughes. **SV**—LA: Fuentes. **LOB**—NY: 10; LA: 7. **2B**—NY: Rodriguez, Cabrera, Teixeira; LA: Abreu, Guerrero, Mathis, Rivera. **3B**—NY: Cano. **RBI**—NY: Teixeira (3), Matsui, Cano (2); LA: Hunter (2), Guerrero (2), Morales (2), Abreu. **SAC**—LA: Figgins. **SB**—LA: Hunter, Aybar. **GIDP**—LA: Rivera, Aybar. **IBB**—NY: Rodriguez (2). **HBP**—NY: Cano. **WP**—NY: Burnett. **T**—3:34. **A**—45,113.

**Recap:** Kendry Morales drove in the go-ahead run with a two-out single in the seventh inning as the Angels responded to the Yankees' six-run comeback moments earlier with a three-run rally of their own, each hit more improbable than the last. When closer Brian Fuentes retired Nick Swisher on a bases-loaded, full-count popup for the final, perilous out, the Angels and their rally monkey had held on——and evoked the faintest echoes of the Yankees' last trip to this stage of the postseason, which ended in their unprecedented four-game flameout in 2004.

### GAME 6

| | | | | | | | | |
|---|---|---|---|---|---|---|---|---|
| Los Angeles | 0 0 1 | 0 0 0 | 0 1 0 | **2** | **9** | **2** |
| New York | 0 0 0 | 3 0 0 | 0 2 x | **5** | **9** | **0** |

**W**—NY: Pettitte. **L**—LA: Saunders. **SV**—NY: Rivera. **LOB**—LA: 6; NY: 12. **2B**—LA: Mathis, Guerrero. **RBI**—LA: Abreu, Guerrero; NY: Damon (2), Rodriguez, Teixeira. **SAC**—NY: Cabrera (2), Swisher. **SF**—NY: Teixeira. **GIDP**—LA: Aybar; NY: Posada (2), Teixeira. **E**—LA: Kendrick, Kazmir. **T**—3:40. **A**—50,173.

**Recap:** The Yankees, baseball's biggest spenders, finally cashed in with their first pennant in six years, beating the Angels 5-2 in Game 6 of the AL Championship Series behind the savvy pitching of that old October pro, Andy Pettitte. Ridiculed in the past for his October flops, three-time MVP Alex Rodriguez played a huge role in helping his team advance through the playoffs, batting .438 with five home runs and 12 RBIs overall and 2-for-2 with one RBI in the ALCS-clinching game. Thriving under late-inning pressure this time around, the slugger earned his first trip to the Fall Classic during a 16-year career in which he's accomplished almost everything else. For his part, Pettitte allowed only one earned run in 6⅓ innings to earn his 16th career postseason win and his fifth career win in a postseason series-clinching game. Both marks are the best in baseball history.

Oct 28 .............Philadelphia 6 at New York 1
Oct 29 .............Philadelphia 1 at New York 3
Oct 31 .............New York 8 at Philadelphia 5

Nov 1...............New York 7 at Philadelphia 4
Nov 2...............New York 6 at Philadelphia 8
Nov 4...............Philadelphia 3 at New York 7

(New York won series 4–2)

## GAME 1

| | | | | | | | | | | | | |
|---|---|---|---|---|---|---|---|---|---|---|---|---|
| Philadelphia | 0 | 0 | 1 | 0 | 0 | 1 | 0 | 2 | 2 | **6** | **9** | **1** |
| New York | 0 | 0 | 0 | 0 | 0 | 0 | 0 | 0 | 1 | **1** | **6** | **0** |

**W**—Phi: Lee. **L**—NY: Sabathia. **LOB**—Phi: 7; NY: 4.
**2B**—Phi: Howard (2), Ruiz; NY: Jeter. **HR**—Phi: Utley (2).
**RBI**—Phi: Utley (2), Ibanez (2), Victorino, Howard.
**SB**—Phi: Rollins. **GIDP**—Phi: Feliz. **E**—Phi: Rollins.
**T**—3:27. **A**—50,207.

**Recap:** Cliff Lee outdueled C.C. Sabathia, Chase Utley homered twice and the Phillies kept rolling through October, beating New York 6–1 on a misty night in Game 1. Lee bamboozled the Yankees with a spiked curveball, deceptive changeup and his usual pinpoint fastball, pitching a six-hitter while striking out 10 without a walk. The lefty blanked the Yankees until a run scored on shortstop Jimmy Rollins' throwing error in the ninth inning. A pair of nonchalant fielding plays, including a behind-the-back stop on Robinson Cano's one-hopper to the mound left observers wondering just how easy the game was for Lee. In addition to Utley's two solo shots, Howard reprised his NL championship series MVP performance, doubling twice and driving in the final run.

## GAME 2

| | | | | | | | | | | | | |
|---|---|---|---|---|---|---|---|---|---|---|---|---|
| Philadelphia | 0 | 1 | 0 | 0 | 0 | 0 | 0 | 0 | 0 | **1** | **6** | **0** |
| New York | 0 | 0 | 0 | 1 | 0 | 1 | 0 | 1 | 0 | X | **3** | **8** | **0** |

**W**—NY: Burnett. **L**—Phi: Martinez. **SV**—NY: Rivera.
**LOB**—Phi: 6, NY: 7. **2B**—Phi: Ibanez, Ruiz; NY: Jeter.
**HR**—NY: Teixeira, Matsui. **RBI**—Phi: Stairs; NY:
Teixeira, Matsui, Posada. **GIDP**—Phi: Utley. **IBB**—Phi:
Utley, Matsui. **HBP**—NY: Teixeira.
**T**—3:25. **A**—50,181.

**Recap:** Mark Teixeira and Hideki Matsui hit solo homers off familiar foe Pedro Martinez, backing a sharp performance by A.J. Burnett and giving the Yankees a 3–1 victory over the Phillies in Game 2. Burnett became the third Yankee pitcher to throw seven-plus innings in the World Series with nine or more strikeouts while allowing four or fewer hits and one or fewer earned runs. A night after getting shut down by Cliff Lee in the opener, the Yanks' spirits recovered despite facing an early deficit, sparked by a pickoff throw from backup catcher Jose Molina. They won in the Series for the first time since taking a 2–1 lead against the Florida Marlins in 2003. Light-hitting Matt Stairs put the Phillies on top with an RBI single in the second, but Burnett used a biting curveball to keep Philadelphia from advancing another runner past second base against him after that. Teixeira, in an 8-for-44 (.182) postseason slump, tied the score when he led off the fourth by driving a high changeup into the Yankees bullpen in right field. Matsui put New York ahead with two outs in the sixth, reaching down for a low curveball and sending it several rows into the seats in right.

## GAME 3

| | | | | | | | | | | | | |
|---|---|---|---|---|---|---|---|---|---|---|---|---|
| New York | 0 | 0 | 0 | 2 | 3 | 1 | 1 | 1 | 0 | **8** | **8** | **1** |
| Philadelphia | 0 | 0 | 3 | 0 | 0 | 1 | 0 | 0 | 1 | **5** | **6** | **0** |

**W**—NY: Pettitte. **L**—Phi: Hamels. **LOB**—NY: 6; Phi: 5.
**2B**—NY: Swisher, Damon; Phi: Feliz. **HR**—NY:
Rodriguez, Swisher, Matsui; Phi: Werth (2), Ruiz.
**RBI**—NY: Rodriguez (2), Pettitte, Damon (2), Swisher,
Posada, Matsui; Phi: Werth (2), Rollins, Victorino, Ruiz.
**SAC**—Phi: Hamels. **SF**—Phi: Victorino. **SB**—NY: Damon;
Phi: Rollins. **HBP**—NY: Rodriguez (2).**E**—NY: Rodriguez.
**T**—3:25 (1:20 delayed start). **A**—46,061.

**Recap:** Alex Rodriguez, whose double clanked off a television camera in the right-field corner and was ruled a home run in the first instant replay call in World Series history, woke up the Yankees offense en route to a Game 3 comeback win. Yankees starter Andy Pettitte struck out seven Phillies and helped out with his bat as well as with a game-tying single in the fifth to earn his 17th career postseason victory. After pitching dominated the first two games in the Bronx, the Yankees and defending champion Phillies flexed their hitting muscles, combining for six home runs at cozy Citizens Bank Park. Jayson Werth connected twice for Philadelphia. Rain affected the Series schedule in Philly for the second straight year, delaying the start by 80 minutes. Once they hit the field in front of their boisterous fans, the Phillies built a 3–0 lead—but it was squandered by a struggling Cole Hamels, last year's World Series MVP. Mariano Rivera got the last two outs to tie Whitey Ford for the most World Series games pitched with 22.

## GAME 4

| | | | | | | | | | | | | |
|---|---|---|---|---|---|---|---|---|---|---|---|---|
| New York | 2 | 0 | 0 | 0 | 2 | 0 | 0 | 0 | 3 | **7** | **9** | **1** |
| Philadelphia | 1 | 0 | 0 | 1 | 0 | 0 | 1 | 1 | 0 | **4** | **8** | **1** |

**W**—Phi: Chamberlain. **L**—Phi: Lidge. **SV**—NY: Rivera.
**LOB**—NY: Phi: 7. **2B**—NY: Damon, Rodriguez; Phi:
Victorino, Utley. **HR**—Phi: Utley, Feliz. **RBI**—NY:
Teixeira, Posada (3), Jeter, Damon, Rodriguez; Phi:
Utley (2), Feliz (2). **SF**—NY: Posada. **SB**—NY: Damon (2);
Phi: Howard. **IBB**—Phi: Werth, Ruiz. **HBP**—NY: Teixeira,
Rodriguez. **E**—NY: Posada; Phi: Ibanez.
**T**—3:25. **A**—46,125.

**Recap:** Thanks to Johnny Damon's patience at the plate and hustle in the ninth inning and to Alex Rodriguez's go-ahead, two-out double off Brad Lidge, the Yankees beat the Phillies 7–4. "There's no question—I've never had a bigger hit," Rodriguez said. Derek Jeter came through again with a leadoff single in a two-run first inning and Mariano Rivera recorded his second save of the Series as the Yankees moved within one win of that elusive 27th championship and their first since 2000. Chase Utley and Pedro Feliz had hit late home runs for the Phillies but Lidge, the Phillies closer, who has struggled in 2009 after a sterling 2008 postseason, blew the save in the ninth. With two outs, Damon capped a nine-pitch at-bat with a single, beat a one-hop throw to steal second, and then advanced to third when he noticed no one was covering. Rodriguez then lined a solid double for a 5-4 lead and the Philadelphia crowd was still silent when Jorge Posada followed with a two-run single.

## GAME 5

| | | | | | | | | | | |
|---|---|---|---|---|---|---|---|---|---|---|
| New York | 1 0 0 | 0 1 0 | 0 3 1 | **6 10 0** |
| Philadelphia | 3 0 3 | 0 0 0 | 2 0 x | **8 9 0** |

**W**—Phi: Lee. **L**—NY: Burnett. **SV**—Phi: Madson.
**LOB**—NY: 6. Phi: 5. **2B**—NY: Rodriguez, Teixeira, Posada. **HR**—Phi: Utley (2), Ibanez. **RBI**—NY: Damon, Rodriguez (3), Cano; Phi: Utley (4), Werth, Ibanez (2), Ruiz. **SF**—NY: Cano. **SB**—Phi: Utley. **WP**—NY: Aceves. **GIDP**—NY: Jeter; Phi: Stairs. **HBP**—Phi: Victorino. **T**—3:26. **A**—46,178.

**Recap:** Desperate to hang on somehow, Chase Utley and the Phillies did just that in the ninth inning as Derek Jeter grounded into a double play, Mark Teixeira struck out, and Philadelphia staved off the Yankees and elimination with an 8–6 win in Game 5. Philadelphia replicated its winning formula from the opener, when Utley hit two solo homers and Lee pitched a six-hitter. Raul Ibanez set off fireworks from the Liberty Bell one last time, adding a second solo shot in the seventh off Phil Coke that made it 8–2. Utley's two home runs raised his Series total to a record-tying five, while Cliff Lee won again. But by the end, Phillies fans were preparing for the worst as the Yankees were at it again. Ahead 8–2, the Phillies watched New York score three times in the eighth inning and put its first two batters on in the ninth. Jeter's grounder drove in a run, but the fans on their feet couldn't exhale until Teixeira struck out as the tying run.

## GAME 6

| | | | | | | | | | | |
|---|---|---|---|---|---|---|---|---|---|---|
| Philadelphia | 0 0 1 | 0 0 2 | 0 0 0 | **3 6 0** |
| New York | 0 2 2 | 0 3 0 | 0 0 x | **7 8 0** |

**W**—NY: Pettitte **L**—Phi: Martinez. **LOB**—Phi: 8; NY: 7. **2B**—Phi: Ibanez (2); NY: Jeter, Matsui. **HR**—Phi: Howard; NY: Matsui. **RBI**—Phi: Rollins, Howard (2); NY: Matsui (6), Teixeira. **SAC**—NY: Hairston Jr. **SF**—Phi: Rollins. **SB**—Phi: Rollins; NY: Rodriguez. **WP**—NY: Pettitte. **GIDP**—Phi: Utley, Rollins. **HBP**—NY: Teixeira. **IBB**—NY: Posada.
**T**—3:52. **A**—50,315.

**Recap:** Hideki Matsui drove in six runs, Andy Pettitte won on short rest and the Yankees beat the Phillies 7–3 in Game 6, finally seizing that elusive 27th title—the most in all of sports. Matsui, the Series MVP, who tied Bobby Richardson's record for most RBIs in a World Series game, powered a quick rout of old foe Pedro Martinez. And when Mariano Rivera got the final out, it was ecstasy in the Bronx for George Steinbrenner's go-for-broke bunch. With the championship, the Yankees season certainly ended a lot better than it started—with a steroids scandal involving Alex Rodriguez, who followed that up with hip surgery that kept him out until May. In the end, second-year manager Joe Girardi, A-Rod and the rest of the Yankees christened the team's new $1.5 billion ballpark with a title: One season, one World Series crown—the team's first since winning three straight from 1998–2000. "It feels better than I remember it, man," captain Derek Jeter said. "It's been a long time."

## 2009 World Series Composite Box Score

### NEW YORK

| BATTING | AB | R | H | HR | RBI | Avg |
|---|---|---|---|---|---|---|
| Jeter | 27 | 5 | 11 | 0 | 1 | .407 |
| Damon | 22 | 6 | 8 | 0 | 4 | .364 |
| Teixeira | 22 | 5 | 3 | 1 | 3 | .136 |
| Cano | 22 | 0 | 3 | 0 | 1 | .136 |
| Rodriguez | 20 | 5 | 5 | 1 | 6 | .250 |
| Posada | 19 | 1 | 5 | 0 | 5 | .263 |
| Swisher | 15 | 3 | 2 | 1 | 1 | .133 |
| Matsui | 13 | 3 | 8 | 3 | 8 | .615 |
| Cabrera | 13 | 1 | 2 | 0 | 0 | .154 |
| Gardner | 10 | 1 | 0 | 0 | 0 | .000 |
| Hairston Jr. | 6 | 0 | 1 | 0 | 0 | .167 |
| Molina | 2 | 0 | 0 | 0 | 0 | .000 |
| Hinske | 0 | 1 | 0 | 0 | 0 | — |
| Pitchers | 7 | 1 | 1 | 0 | 1 | .143 |
| **Totals** | **198** | **32** | **49** | **6** | **30** | **.247** |

| PITCHING | G | IP | H | BB | SO | ERA |
|---|---|---|---|---|---|---|
| Sabathia | 2 | 13.2 | 11 | 6 | 12 | 3.29 |
| Pettitte | 2 | 11.2 | 9 | 8 | 10 | 5.40 |
| Burnett | 2 | 9.0 | 8 | 6 | 11 | 7.00 |
| Rivera | 4 | 5.1 | 3 | 2 | 3 | 0.00 |
| Chamberlain | 3 | 3.0 | 2 | 1 | 4 | 3.00 |
| Marte | 4 | 2.2 | 0 | 0 | 5 | 0.00 |
| Robertson | 2 | 2.1 | 2 | 1 | 2 | 0.00 |
| Aceves | 1 | 2.0 | 1 | 0 | 1 | 0.00 |
| Hughes | 3 | 1.2 | 2 | 2 | 1 | 16.20 |
| Coke | 2 | 1.1 | 3 | 0 | 1 | 13.50 |
| Bruney | 1 | 0.1 | 3 | 0 | 0 | 54.00 |
| **Totals** | **6** | **53.0** | **44** | **26** | **50** | **4.58** |

### PHILADELPHIA

| BATTING | AB | R | H | HR | RBI | Avg |
|---|---|---|---|---|---|---|
| Howard | 23 | 3 | 4 | 1 | 3 | .174 |
| Ibanez | 23 | 2 | 7 | 1 | 4 | .304 |
| Feliz | 23 | 2 | 4 | 1 | 2 | .174 |
| Rollins | 23 | 3 | 5 | 0 | 2 | .217 |
| Victorino | 22 | 3 | 4 | 0 | 2 | .182 |
| Utley | 21 | 7 | 6 | 5 | 8 | .286 |
| Werth | 19 | 3 | 5 | 2 | 3 | .263 |
| Ruiz | 18 | 4 | 6 | 1 | 2 | .333 |
| Stairs | 8 | 0 | 1 | 0 | 1 | .125 |
| Francisco | 7 | 0 | 0 | 0 | 0 | .000 |
| Bruntlett | 1 | 1 | 0 | 0 | 0 | .000 |
| Pitchers | 6 | 0 | 2 | 0 | 0 | .333 |
| **Totals** | **194** | **28** | **44** | **11** | **27** | **.227** |

| PITCHING | G | IP | H | BB | SO | ERA |
|---|---|---|---|---|---|---|
| Lee | 2 | 16.0 | 13 | 3 | 13 | 2.81 |
| Martinez | 2 | 10.0 | 9 | 4 | 13 | 6.30 |
| Blanton | 1 | 6.0 | 5 | 2 | 7 | 6.00 |
| Madson | 5 | 4.1 | 6 | 2 | 6 | 2.08 |
| Hamels | 1 | 4.1 | 5 | 2 | 3 | 10.38 |
| Park | 4 | 3.1 | 2 | 1 | 3 | 0.00 |
| Happ | 2 | 2.2 | 2 | 1 | 4 | 3.38 |
| Eyre | 2 | 2.0 | 0 | 1 | 2 | 0.00 |
| Durbin | 2 | 1.1 | 3 | 2 | 2 | 27.00 |
| Myers | 1 | 1.0 | 1 | 0 | 2 | 9.00 |
| Lidge | 1 | 1.0 | 3 | 0 | 1 | 27.00 |
| **Totals** | **6** | **52.0** | **49** | **18** | **56** | **5.36** |

## National League Batting

### BATTING AVERAGE

| | |
|---|---|
| Hanley Ramirez, Fla | 342 |
| Pablo Sandoval, SF | 330 |
| Albert Pujols, StL | 327 |
| Todd Helton, Col | 325 |
| Joey Votto, Cin | 322 |
| Chris Coghlan, Fla | 321 |
| Ryan Braun, Mil | 320 |
| Miguel Tejada, Hou | 313 |
| Felipe Lopez, Mil/Ari | 310 |
| Nyjer Morgan, Was/Pit | 307 |
| David Wright, NYM | 307 |
| Martin Prado, Atl | 307 |

### HITS

| | |
|---|---|
| Ryan Braun, Mil | 203 |
| Miguel Tejada, Hou | 199 |
| Hanley Ramirez, Fla | 197 |
| Pablo Sandoval, SF | 189 |
| Felipe Lopez, Ari | 187 |
| Albert Pujols, StL | 186 |
| Carlos Lee, Hou | 183 |
| Shane Victorino, Phi | 181 |
| Matt Kemp, LA | 180 |

### DOUBLES

| | |
|---|---|
| Miguel Tejada, Hou | 46 |
| Albert Pujols, StL | 45 |
| Pablo Sandoval, SF | 44 |
| Jimmy Rollins, Phi | 43 |
| Brad Hawpe, Col | 42 |
| Jorge Cantu, Fla | 42 |
| Andre Ethier, LA | 42 |
| Hanley Ramirez, Fla | 42 |

### TRIPLES

| | |
|---|---|
| Shane Victorino, Phi | 13 |
| Stephen Drew, Ari | 12 |
| Michael Bourn, Hou | 12 |
| Angel Pagan, NYM | 11 |
| Dexter Fowler, SF | 10 |

### STOLEN BASES

| | |
|---|---|
| Michael Bourn, Hou | 61 |
| Nyjer Morgan, Was/Pit | 42 |
| Matt Kemp, LAD | 34 |
| Jimmy Rollins, Phi | 31 |
| Juan Pierre, LAD | 30 |
| David Wright, NYM | 27 |
| Hanley Ramirez, Fla | 27 |
| Dexter Fowler, Col | 27 |

### HOME RUNS

| | |
|---|---|
| Albert Pujols, StL | 47 |
| Prince Fielder, Mil | 46 |
| Ryan Howard, Phi | 45 |
| Mark Reynolds, Ari | 44 |
| Adrian Gonzalez, SD | 40 |
| Adam Dunn, Ari | 38 |
| Jayson Werth, Phi | 36 |
| Derrek Lee, CHC | 35 |
| Raul Ibanez, Phi | 34 |
| Ryan Zimmerman, Was | 33 |
| Troy Tulowitzki, Col | 32 |
| Ryan Braun, Mil | 32 |
| Chase Utley, Phi | 31 |
| Dan Uggla, Fla | 31 |
| Andre Ethier, LAD | 31 |

### RUNS SCORED

| | |
|---|---|
| Albert Pujols, StL | 124 |
| Ryan Braun, Mil | 113 |
| Chase Utley, Phi | 112 |
| Ryan Zimmerman, Was | 110 |
| Ryan Howard, Phi | 105 |
| Prince Fielder, Mil | 103 |
| Shane Victorino, Phi | 102 |
| Hanley Ramirez, Fla | 101 |
| Troy Tulowitzki, Col | 101 |
| Jimmy Rollins, Phi | 100 |
| Jayson Werth, Phi | 98 |
| Mark Reynolds, Ari | 98 |

### RUNS BATTED IN

| | |
|---|---|
| Ryan Howard, Phi | 141 |
| Prince Fielder, Mil | 141 |
| Albert Pujols, StL | 135 |
| Ryan Braun, Mil | 114 |
| Derrek Lee, CHC | 111 |
| Hanley Ramirez, Fla | 106 |
| Ryan Zimmerman, Was | 106 |
| Andre Ethier, LAD | 106 |
| Adam Dunn, Was | 105 |
| Mark Reynolds, Ari | 102 |
| Carlos Lee, Hou | 102 |
| Matt Kemp, LAD | 101 |
| Jorge Cantu, Fla | 100 |
| Jayson Werth, Phi | 99 |
| Adrian Gonzalez, SD | 99 |
| Brandon Phillips, Cin | 98 |

### SLUGGING PERCENTAGE

| | |
|---|---|
| Albert Pujols, StL | 658 |
| Prince Fielder, Mil | 602 |
| Derrek Lee, CHC | 579 |
| Ryan Howard, Phi | 571 |
| Joey Votto, Cin | 567 |
| Pablo Sandoval, SF | 556 |

### ON-BASE PERCENTAGE

| | |
|---|---|
| Albert Pujols, StL | 443 |
| Nick Johnson, Was/Fla | 426 |
| Todd Helton, Col | 416 |
| Joey Votto, Cin | 414 |
| Prince Fielder, Mil | 412 |
| Hanley Ramirez, Fla | 410 |

### BASES ON BALLS

| | |
|---|---|
| Adrian Gonzalez, SD | 119 |
| Adam Dunn, Ari | 116 |
| Albert Pujols, StL | 115 |
| Prince Fielder, Mil | 110 |
| Chipper Jones, Atl | 101 |
| Nick Johnson, Was/Fla | 99 |

## National League Pitching

### EARNED RUN AVERAGE

| | |
|---|---|
| Chris Carpenter, StL | 2.24 |
| Tim Lincecum, SF | 2.48 |
| Jair Jurrjens, Atl | 2.60 |
| Adam Wainwright, StL | 2.63 |
| Clayton Kershaw, LAD | 2.79 |
| Javier Vazquez, Atl | 2.87 |
| Matt Cain, SF | 2.89 |
| J.A. Happ, Phi | 2.93 |
| Wandy Rodriguez, Hou | 3.02 |
| Randy Wells, CHC | 3.05 |

### SAVES

| | |
|---|---|
| Heath Bell, SD | 42 |
| Francisco Cordero, Cin | 39 |
| Ryan Franklin, StL | 38 |
| Brian Wilson, SF | 38 |
| Trevor Hoffman, Mil | 37 |
| Jonathan Broxton, LAD | 36 |
| Francisco Rodriguez, NYM | 35 |
| Huston Street, Col | 35 |
| Brad Lidge, Phi | 31 |
| Rafael Soriano, Atl | 27 |
| Matt Capps, Pit | 27 |

### WINS

| | |
|---|---|
| Adam Wainwright, StL | 19 |
| Chris Carpenter, StL | 17 |
| Jorge De La Rosa, Col | 16 |

Eight tied with 15.

### GAMES PITCHED

| | |
|---|---|
| Pedro Feliciano, NYM | 88 |
| Peter Moylan, Atl | 87 |
| Mike Gonzalez, Atl | 80 |
| Ryan Madson, Phi | 79 |
| Sean Green, NYM | 79 |
| Carlos Marmol, CHC | 79 |
| Todd Coffey, Mil | 78 |

### INNINGS PITCHED

| | |
|---|---|
| Adam Wainwright, StL | 233.0 |
| Dan Haren, Ari | 229.1 |
| Tim Lincecum, SF | 225.1 |
| Bronson Arroyo, Cin | 220.1 |
| Javier Vazquez, Atl | 219.1 |
| Ubaldo Jimenez, Col | 218.0 |
| Matt Cain, SF | 217.2 |

### STRIKEOUTS

| | |
|---|---|
| Tim Lincecum, SF | 261 |
| Javier Vazquez, Atl | 238 |
| Dan Haren, Ari | 223 |
| Adam Wainwright, StL | 212 |
| Yovani Gallardo, Mil | 204 |
| Ubaldo Jimenez, Col | 198 |
| Ricky Nolasco, Fla | 195 |
| Jorge De La Rosa, Col | 193 |
| Wandy Rodriguez, Hou | 193 |
| Josh Johnson, Fla | 191 |

### COMPLETE GAMES

| | |
|---|---|
| Matt Cain, SF | 4 |
| Tim Lincecum, SF | 4 |

Nine tied with 3.

### SHUTOUTS

| | |
|---|---|
| Joel Pineiro, StL | 2 |
| J.A. Happ, Phi | 2 |
| Bronson Arroyo, Cin | 2 |
| Cole Hamels, Phi | 2 |
| Tim Lincecum, SF | 2 |

## American League Batting

### BATTING AVERAGE

Joe Mauer, Min ..................... .364
Ichiro Suzuki, Sea ................ .352
Derek Jeter, NYY .................. .334
Miguel Cabrera, Det ............. .323
Michael Young, Tex .............. .322
Robinson Cano, NYY ............ .320
Jason Bartlett, TB ................ .320
Denard Span, Min ................ .312
Erick Aybar, LAA .................. .312
Magglio Ordonez, Det .......... .309
Asdrubal Cabrera, Cle ......... .308
Kendry Morales, LAA ........... .306
Kevin Youkilis, Bos .............. .305

### HITS

Ichiro Suzuki, Sea ...............225
Derek Jeter, NYY .................212
Robinson Cano, NYY ............204
Miguel Cabrera, Det .............196
Aaron Hill, Tor .....................195
Joe Mauer, Min ....................189
Nick Markakis, Bal ...............188
Jacoby Ellsbury, Bos ............188
Carl Crawford, TB ................185
Dustin Pedroia, Bos .............185
Orlando Cabrera, Min/Oak .....185

### DOUBLES

Brian Roberts, Bal ................56
Billy Butler, KC ....................51
Robinson Cano, NYY ............48
Dustin Pedroia, Bos .............48
Adam Lind, Tor ....................46
Nick Markakis, Bal ...............45

### TRIPLES

Jacoby Ellsbury, Bos .............10
Denard Span, Min ................10
David DeJesus, KC ................9
Erick Aybar, LAA ...................9

Five tied with 8.

### EARNED RUN AVERAGE

Zack Greinke, KC .................2.16
Felix Hernandez, Sea ...........2.49
Roy Halladay, Tor .................2.79
Cliff Lee, Cle .......................2.54
C.C. Sabathia, NYY ..............3.37
Jon Lester, Bos ...................3.41
Justin Verlander, Det ............3.45
Edwin Jackson, Det ..............3.62
Kevin Millwood, Tex .............3.67
Jered Weaver, LAA ...............3.75
John Danks, CHW .................3.77

### SAVES

Brian Fuentes, LAA ...............48
Joe Nathan, Min ...................47
Mariano Rivera, NYY .............44
Jonathan Papelbon, Bos ........38
David Aardsma, Sea ..............38
Fernando Rodney, Det ...........37
Joakim Soria, KC ..................30
Bobby Jenks, CWS ................29
Andrew Bailey, Oak ...............26
Frank Francisco, Tex .............25

### STOLEN BASES

Jacoby Ellsbury, Bos .............70
Carl Crawford, TB .................60
Chone Figgins, LAA ..............42
B.J Upton, TB ......................42
Rajai Davis, Oak ..................41
Elvis Andrus, Tex .................33
Ian Kinsler, Tex ...................31

Five tied with 30.

### HOME RUNS

Carlos Pena, TB ...................39
Mark Teixeira, NYY ...............39
Jason Bay, Bos ....................36
Aaron Hill, Tor .....................36
Adam Lind, Tor ....................35
Kendry Morales, LAA .............34
Miguel Cabrera, Det ..............33
Nelson Cruz, Tex ..................33
Evan Longoria, TB .................33
Michael Cuddyer, Min ............32
Ian Kinsler, Tex ...................31
Russell Branyan, Sea ............31
Justin Morneau, Min ..............30
Curtis Granderson, Det ..........30
Alex Rodriguez, NYY ..............30

### RUNS SCORED

Dustin Pedroia, Bos ..............115
Chone Figgins, LAA ..............114
Brian Roberts, Bal ................110
Derek Jeter, NYY ..................107
Johnny Damon, NYY ..............107
Mark Teixeira, NYY ...............103
Jason Bay, Bos ....................103
Aaron Hill, Tor .....................103
Robinson Cano, NYY .............103
Ian Kinsler, Tex ...................101
Michael Young, Tex ...............102
Marco Scutaro, Tor ...............100
Evan Longoria, TB .................100

## American League Pitching

### WINS

C.C. Sabathia, NYY ...............19
Felix Hernandez, Sea ............19
Justin Verlander, Det .............19
Roy Halladay, Tor .................17
Josh Beckett, Bos .................17
Scott Feldman, Tex ...............17

### GAMES PITCHED

Matt Guerrier, Min .................78
Craig Breslow, Min/Oak ..........77
Mark Lowe, Sea ....................75
Russ Springer, Oak/TB ...........74
Michael Wuertz, Oak .............74
C.J. Wilson, Tex ...................74

### INNINGS PITCHED

Justin Verlander, Det ............240.0
Roy Halladay, Tor .................239.0
Felix Hernandez, Sea ...........238.2
C.C. Sabathia, NYY ..............230.0
Zack Greinke, KC .................229.1
James Shields, TB ................219.2
Edwin Jackson, Det ..............214.0

### RUNS BATTED IN

Mark Teixeira, NYY ...............122
Jason Bay, Bos ....................119
Adam Lind, Tor ....................114
Evan Longoria, TB .................113
Victor Martinez, Cle/Bos ........108
Kendry Morales, LAA .............108
Aaron Hill, Tor .....................108
Bobby Abreu, LAA .................103
Jason Kubel, Min ..................102
Miguel Cabrera, Det ..............101
Nick Markakis, Bal ................101
Carlos Pena, TB ...................100
Justin Morneau, Min ..............100
Alex Rodriguez, NYY ..............100
David Ortiz, Bos ...................99
Joe Mauer, Min ....................96
Jose Lopez, Sea ...................96

### SLUGGING PERCENTAGE

Joe Mauer, Min .................... .586
Kendry Morales, LAA ............ .569
Mark Teixeira, NYY ............... .565
Adam Lind, Tor .................... .562
Kevin Youkillis, Bos .............. .548
Ben Zobrist, TB .................... .543
Miguel Cabrera, Det .............. .541

### ON-BASE PERCENTAGE

Joe Mauer, Min .................... .442
Kevin Youkilis, Bos ............... .413
Derek Jeter, NYY .................. .406
Ben Zobrist, TB .................... .405
Alex Rodriguez, NYY ............. .402

### BASES ON BALLS

Chone Figgins, LAA ..............101
Nick Swisher, NYY ................97
Jason Bay, Bos ....................94
Bobby Abreu, LAA .................94
Jack Cust, Oak .....................93
Ben Zobrist, TB ....................91

### COMPLETE GAMES

Roy Halladay, Tor .................9
Zack Greinke, KC .................6
Josh Beckett, Bos .................4
Jered Weaver, LAA ................4

Four tied with 3.

### SHUTOUTS

Roy Halladay, Tor .................4
Zack Greinke, KC .................3

Four tied with 2.

### STRIKEOUTS

Justin Verlander, Det .............269
Zack Greinke, KC .................242
Jon Lester, Bos ...................225
Felix Hernandez, Sea ............217
Roy Halladay, Tor .................208
Josh Beckett, Bos .................199
C.C. Sabathia, NYY ..............197
A.J. Burnett, NYY .................195
Matt Garza, TB ....................189
Jered Weaver, LAA ...............174

## National League

| TEAM BATTING | G | AB | R | H | 2B | 3B | HR | TB | RBI | OBP | SLG | OPS | BAVG |
|---|---|---|---|---|---|---|---|---|---|---|---|---|---|
| Los Angeles Dodgers..162 | | 5592 | 780 | 1511 | 278 | 39 | 145 | 2302 | 739 | .346 | .412 | .758 | .270 |
| New York Mets ..........162 | | 5453 | 671 | 1472 | 295 | 49 | 95 | 2150 | 631 | .335 | .394 | .729 | .270 |
| Florida Marlins...........162 | | 5572 | 772 | 1493 | 296 | 25 | 159 | 2316 | 727 | .340 | .416 | .756 | .268 |
| St. Louis Cardinals ....162 | | 5465 | 730 | 1436 | 294 | 29 | 160 | 2268 | 694 | .332 | .415 | .747 | .263 |
| Atlanta Braves....:......162 | | 5539 | 735 | 1459 | 300 | 20 | 149 | 2246 | 700 | .339 | .405 | .744 | .263 |
| Milwaukee Brewers ...162 | | 5510 | 785 | 1447 | 281 | 37 | 182 | 2348 | 757 | .341 | .426 | .767 | .263 |
| Colorado Rockies......162 | | 5398 | 804 | 1408 | 300 | 50 | 190 | 2378 | 760 | .343 | .441 | .784 | .261 |
| Houston Astros..........162 | | 5436 | 643 | 1415 | 270 | 32 | 142 | 2175 | 616 | .319 | .400 | .719 | .260 |
| Washington Nationals..162 | | 5493 | 710 | 1416 | 271 | 38 | 156 | 2231 | 685 | .337 | .406 | .743 | .258 |
| Philadelphia Phillies ..162 | | 5578 | 820 | 1439 | 312 | 35 | 224 | 2493 | 788 | .334 | .447 | .781 | .258 |
| San Francisco Giants.162 | | 5493 | 657 | 1411 | 275 | 43 | 122 | 2138 | 612 | .309 | .389 | .699 | .257 |
| Chicago Cubs ...........161 | | 5486 | 707 | 1398 | 293 | 29 | 161 | 2232 | 678 | .332 | .407 | .738 | .255 |
| Arizona Diamondbacks.162 | | 5565 | 720 | 1408 | 307 | 45 | 173 | 2324 | 686 | .324 | .418 | .742 | .253 |
| Pittsburgh Pirates......161 | | 5417 | 636 | 1364 | 289 | 34 | 125 | 2096 | 612 | .318 | .387 | .705 | .252 |
| Cincinnati Reds.........162 | | 5462 | 673 | 1349 | 280 | 25 | 158 | 2153 | 637 | .318 | .394 | .712 | .247 |
| San Diego Padres .....162 | | 5425 | 638 | 1315 | 265 | 31 | 141 | 2065 | 605 | .321 | .381 | .701 | .242 |

| TEAM PITCHING | GP | W | L | SV | SVO | CG | SHO | R | IP | Ks | BB | ERA |
|---|---|---|---|---|---|---|---|---|---|---|---|---|
| Los Angeles Dodgers..162 | | 95 | 67 | 44 | 70 | 1 | 9 | 611 | 1473.1 | 1272 | 584 | 3.41 |
| San Francisco Giants..162 | | 88 | 74 | 41 | 58 | 11 | 18 | 611 | 1446.0 | 1302 | 584 | 3.55 |
| Atlanta Braves...........162 | | 86 | 76 | 38 | 60 | 3 | 10 | 641 | 1462.2 | 1232 | 530 | 3.57 |
| St. Louis Cardinals ....162 | | 91 | 71 | 43 | 58 | 8 | 11 | 640 | 1440.2 | 1049 | 460 | 3.66 |
| Chicago Cubs ...........161 | | 83 | 78 | 40 | 58 | 3 | 8 | 672 | 1445.1 | 1272 | 586 | 3.84 |
| Philadelphia Phillies ..162 | | 93 | 69 | 44 | 66 | 8 | 9 | 709 | 1455.2 | 1153 | 489 | 4.16 |
| Cincinnati Reds.........162 | | 78 | 84 | 41 | 53 | 6 | 12 | 723 | 1458.1 | 1069 | 577 | 4.18 |
| Colorado Rockies......162 | | 92 | 70 | 45 | 61 | 5 | 7 | 715 | 1438.1 | 1154 | 528 | 4.22 |
| Florida Marlins...........162 | | 87 | 75 | 45 | 69 | 5 | 5 | 766 | 1446.1 | 1248 | 601 | 4.29 |
| San Diego Padres .....162 | | 75 | 87 | 45 | 68 | 2 | 9 | 769 | 1450.2 | 1187 | 603 | 4.37 |
| Arizona Diamondbacks..162 | | 70 | 92 | 36 | 55 | 4 | 12 | 782 | 1447.2 | 1158 | 525 | 4.42 |
| New York Mets ..........162 | | 70 | 92 | 39 | 60 | 3 | 12 | 757 | 1426.0 | 1031 | 616 | 4.45 |
| Houston Astros..........162 | | 74 | 88 | 39 | 65 | 5 | 10 | 770 | 1430.0 | 1144 | 546 | 4.54 |
| Pittsburgh Pirates......161 | | 62 | 99 | 28 | 45 | 5 | 7 | 768 | 1418.1 | 919 | 563 | 4.59 |
| Milwaukee Brewers ...162 | | 80 | 82 | 44 | 66 | 1 | 8 | 818 | 1435.0 | 1104 | 607 | 4.83 |
| Washington Nationals..162 | | 59 | 103 | 33 | 58 | 6 | 3 | 874 | 1424.1 | 911 | 629 | 5.00 |

## American League

| TEAM BATTING | G | AB | R | H | 2B | 3B | HR | TB | RBI | OBP | SLG | OPS | BAVG |
|---|---|---|---|---|---|---|---|---|---|---|---|---|---|
| Los Angeles Angels | 162 | 5622 | 883 | 1604 | 293 | 33 | 173 | 2482 | 841 | .350 | .441 | .792 | .285 |
| New York Yankees | 162 | 5660 | 915 | 1604 | 325 | 21 | 244 | 2703 | 881 | .362 | .478 | .839 | .283 |
| Minnesota Twins | 163 | 5608 | 817 | 1539 | 271 | 40 | 172 | 2406 | 770 | .345 | .429 | .774 | .274 |
| Boston Red Sox | 162 | 5543 | 872 | 1495 | 335 | 25 | 212 | 2516 | 822 | .352 | .454 | .806 | .270 |
| Baltimore Orioles | 162 | 5618 | 741 | 1508 | 307 | 19 | 160 | 2333 | 708 | .332 | .415 | .747 | .268 |
| Toronto Blue Jays | 162 | 5696 | 798 | 1516 | 339 | 13 | 209 | 2508 | 766 | .333 | .440 | .773 | .266 |
| Cleveland Indians | 162 | 5568 | 773 | 1468 | 314 | 28 | 161 | 2321 | 730 | .339 | .417 | .756 | .264 |
| Tampa Bay Rays | 162 | 5462 | 803 | 1434 | 297 | 36 | 199 | 2400 | 765 | .343 | .439 | .782 | .263 |
| Oakland Athletics | 162 | 5584 | 759 | 1464 | 307 | 21 | 135 | 2218 | 723 | .328 | .397 | .726 | .262 |
| Detroit Tigers | 163 | 5540 | 743 | 1443 | 245 | 35 | 183 | 2307 | 718 | .331 | .416 | .747 | .260 |
| Texas Rangers | 162 | 5526 | 784 | 1436 | 296 | 27 | 224 | 2458 | 748 | .320 | .445 | .764 | .260 |
| Kansas City Royals | 162 | 5532 | 686 | 1432 | 276 | 51 | 144 | 2242 | 657 | .318 | .405 | .724 | .259 |
| Seattle Mariners | 162 | 5543 | 640 | 1430 | 280 | 19 | 160 | 2228 | 613 | .314 | .402 | .716 | .258 |
| Chicago White Sox | 163 | 5463 | 724 | 1410 | 246 | 20 | 184 | 2248 | 695 | .329 | .411 | .740 | .258 |

| TEAM PITCHING | GP | W | L | SV | SVO | CG | SHO | R | IP | Ks | BB | ERA |
|---|---|---|---|---|---|---|---|---|---|---|---|---|
| Seattle Mariners | 162 | 85 | 77 | 49 | 77 | 4 | 10 | 692 | 1452.2 | 1043 | 534 | 3.87 |
| Chicago White Sox | 162 | 79 | 83 | 36 | 54 | 4 | 11 | 732 | 1439.2 | 1119 | 507 | 4.14 |
| Oakland Athletics | 162 | 75 | 87 | 38 | 50 | 2 | 10 | 761 | 1447.1 | 1124 | 523 | 4.26 |
| New York Yankees | 162 | 103 | 59 | 51 | 66 | 3 | 8 | 753 | 1450.0 | 1260 | 574 | 4.26 |
| Detroit Tigers | 163 | 86 | 77 | 42 | 66 | 4 | 9 | 745 | 1447.0 | 1102 | 594 | 4.29 |
| Tampa Bay Rays | 162 | 84 | 78 | 41 | 63 | 3 | 5 | 754 | 1427.1 | 1125 | 515 | 4.33 |
| Boston Red Sox | 162 | 95 | 67 | 41 | 59 | 8 | 11 | 736 | 1436.2 | 1230 | 530 | 4.35 |
| Texas Rangers | 162 | 87 | 75 | 45 | 58 | 8 | 11 | 740 | 1434.2 | 1016 | 531 | 4.38 |
| Los Angeles Angels | 162 | 97 | 65 | 51 | 70 | 9 | 13 | 761 | 1445.0 | 1062 | 523 | 4.45 |
| Toronto Blue Jays | 162 | 75 | 87 | 25 | 41 | 10 | 10 | 771 | 1451.0 | 1181 | 551 | 4.47 |
| Minnesota Twins | 163 | 87 | 76 | 48 | 64 | 4 | 7 | 765 | 1453.0 | 1052 | 466 | 4.50 |
| Kansas City Royals | 162 | 65 | 97 | 34 | 56 | 10 | 9 | 842 | 1426.0 | 1153 | 600 | 4.83 |
| Cleveland Indians | 162 | 65 | 97 | 25 | 43 | 5 | 6 | 865 | 1434.0 | 986 | 598 | 5.06 |
| Baltimore Orioles | 162 | 64 | 98 | 31 | 53 | 2 | 3 | 876 | 1429.0 | 933 | 546 | 5.15 |

### Arizona Diamondbacks

| BATTING | G | AB | R | H | 2B | 3B | HR | RBI | TB | BB | SO | SB | OBP | SLG | BAVG |
|---|---|---|---|---|---|---|---|---|---|---|---|---|---|---|---|
| Mark Reynolds | 155 | 578 | 98 | 150 | 30 | 1 | 44 | 102 | 314 | 76 | 223 | 24 | .349 | .543 | .260 |
| Stephen Drew | 135 | 533 | 71 | 139 | 29 | 12 | 12 | 65 | 228 | 49 | 87 | 5 | .320 | .428 | .261 |
| Justin Upton | 138 | 526 | 84 | 158 | 30 | 7 | 26 | 86 | 280 | 55 | 137 | 20 | .366 | .532 | .300 |
| Gerardo Parra | 120* | 455 | 59 | 132 | 21 | 8 | 5 | 60 | 184 | 25 | 89 | 5 | .324 | .404 | .290 |
| Chris B. Young | 134 | 433 | 54 | 92 | 28 | 4 | 15 | 42 | 173 | 59 | 133 | 11 | .311 | .400 | .212 |
| Miguel Montero | 128 | 425 | 61 | 125 | 30 | 0 | 16 | 59 | 203 | 38 | 78 | 1 | .355 | .478 | .294 |
| *Felipe Lopez | 85 | 345 | 44 | 104 | 18 | 1 | 6 | 25 | 142 | 34 | 59 | 6 | .364 | .412 | .301 |
| Ryan Roberts | 110 | 305 | 41 | 85 | 17 | 2 | 7 | 25 | 127 | 40 | 55 | 7 | .367 | .416 | .279 |
| Augie Ojeda | 103 | 264 | 38 | 65 | 17 | 3 | 1 | 16 | 91 | 32 | 28 | 3 | .340 | .345 | .246 |
| Chad Tracy | 98 | 257 | 29 | 61 | 15 | 0 | 8 | 39 | 100 | 26 | 38 | 1 | .306 | .389 | .237 |
| Eric Byrnes | 84 | 239 | 26 | 54 | 14 | 1 | 8 | 31 | 94 | 12 | 30 | 9 | .270 | .393 | .226 |
| Chris Snyder | 61 | 165 | 20 | 33 | 7 | 0 | 6 | 22 | 58 | 32 | 47 | 0 | .333 | .352 | .200 |
| Alex Romero | 66 | 145 | 14 | 36 | 6 | 2 | 1 | 18 | 49 | 11 | 23 | 2 | .306 | .338 | .248 |
| Josh Whitesell | 46 | 108 | 7 | 21 | 7 | 0 | 1 | 14 | 31 | 24 | 29 | 0 | .346 | .287 | .194 |
| Brandon Allen | 32 | 104 | 13 | 21 | 7 | 0 | 4 | 14 | 40 | 12 | 40 | 0 | .284 | .385 | .202 |
| Conor Jackson | 30 | 99 | 8 | 18 | 4 | 0 | 1 | 14 | 25 | 11 | 16 | 5 | .264 | .253 | .182 |

| PITCHING | GP | GS | W–L | SV | SHO | R | ERA | IP | Ks | BB |
|---|---|---|---|---|---|---|---|---|---|---|
| Dan Haren | 33 | 33 | 14–10 | 0 | 1 | 83 | 3.14 | 229.1 | 223 | 38 |
| Doug Davis | 34 | 34 | 9–14 | 0 | 0 | 101 | 4.12 | 203.1 | 146 | 103 |
| Max Scherzer | 30 | 30 | 9–11 | 0 | 0 | 94 | 4.12 | 170.1 | 174 | 63 |
| *Jon Garland | 27 | 27 | 8–11 | 0 | 0 | 90 | 2.73 | 167.2 | 83 | 52 |
| Yusmeiro Petit | 23 | 17 | 3–10 | 0 | 0 | 62 | 5.82 | 89.2 | 74 | 34 |
| Billy Buckner | 16 | 13 | 4–6 | 0 | 0 | 57 | 6.40 | 77.1 | 64 | 29 |
| Juan Guiterrez | 65 | 0 | 4–3 | 9 | 0 | 33 | 4.06 | 71.0 | 66 | 30 |
| *Jon Rauch | 58 | 0 | 2–2 | 2 | 0 | 27 | 4.14 | 54.1 | 35 | 17 |
| Esmerling Vasquez | 53 | 0 | 3–3 | 0 | 0 | 27 | 4.42 | 53.0 | 45 | 29 |
| Chad Qualls | 51 | 0 | 2–2 | 24 | 0 | 23 | 3.63 | 52.0 | 45 | 7 |
| Clay Zavada | 49 | 0 | 3–3 | 0 | 0 | 22 | 3.35 | 51.0 | 52 | 24 |
| Leo Rosales | 33 | 0 | 2–1 | 0 | 0 | 24 | 4.76 | 45.1 | 31 | 12 |

### Atlanta Braves

| BATTING | G | AB | R | H | 2B | 3B | HR | RBI | TB | BB | SO | SB | OBP | SLG | BAVG |
|---|---|---|---|---|---|---|---|---|---|---|---|---|---|---|---|
| Yunel Escobar | 141 | 528 | 89 | 158 | 26 | 2 | 14 | 76 | 230 | 57 | 62 | 5 | .377 | .436 | .299 |
| Garret Anderson | 135 | 496 | 52 | 133 | 27 | 0 | 13 | 61 | 199 | 27 | 73 | 1 | .303 | .401 | .268 |
| Chipper Jones | 143 | 488 | 80 | 129 | 23 | 2 | 18 | 71 | 210 | 101 | 89 | 4 | .388 | .430 | .264 |
| Brian McCann | 138 | 488 | 63 | 137 | 35 | 1 | 21 | 94 | 237 | 49 | 83 | 4 | .349 | .486 | .281 |
| Martin Prado | 128 | 450 | 64 | 138 | 38 | 0 | 11 | 49 | 209 | 36 | 59 | 1 | .358 | .464 | .307 |
| Matt Diaz | 125 | 371 | 56 | 116 | 18 | 4 | 13 | 58 | 181 | 35 | 90 | 12 | .390 | .488 | .313 |
| *Nate McLouth | 84 | 339 | 59 | 87 | 20 | 1 | 11 | 36 | 142 | 47 | 70 | 12 | .354 | .419 | .257 |
| Kelly Johnson | 106 | 303 | 47 | 68 | 20 | 3 | 8 | 29 | 118 | 32 | 54 | 7 | .303 | .389 | .224 |
| Casey Kotchman | 87 | 298 | 28 | 84 | 20 | 0 | 6 | 41 | 122 | 32 | 28 | 0 | .354 | .409 | .282 |
| *Adam LaRoche | 57 | 212 | 30 | 69 | 11 | 1 | 12 | 40 | 118 | 28 | 59 | 0 | .401 | .557 | .325 |
| Omar Infante | 70 | 203 | 24 | 62 | 9 | 1 | 2 | 27 | 79 | 19 | 28 | 2 | .361 | .389 | .305 |
| Jordan Schaefer | 50 | 167 | 18 | 34 | 8 | 0 | 2 | 8 | 48 | 27 | 63 | 2 | .313 | .287 | .204 |
| David Ross | 54 | 128 | 18 | 35 | 9 | 0 | 7 | 20 | 65 | 21 | 39 | 0 | .380 | .508 | .273 |
| *Ryan Church | 44 | 127 | 20 | 33 | 12 | 0 | 2 | 18 | 51 | 16 | 22 | 0 | .347 | .402 | .260 |
| Diory Hernandez | 33 | 85 | 6 | 12 | 3 | 0 | 1 | 6 | 18 | 6 | 22 | 0 | .198 | .212 | .141 |
| Greg Norton | 95 | 76 | 3 | 11 | 2 | 0 | 0 | 7 | 13 | 20 | 20 | 0 | .330 | .171 | .145 |

| PITCHING | GP | GS | W–L | SV | SHO | R | ERA | IP | Ks | BB |
|---|---|---|---|---|---|---|---|---|---|---|
| Javier Vazquez | 32 | 32 | 15–10 | 0 | 0 | 75 | 2.87 | 219.1 | 238 | 44 |
| Jair Jurrjens | 34 | 34 | 14–10 | 0 | 0 | 71 | 2.60 | 215.0 | 152 | 75 |
| Derek Lowe | 34 | 34 | 15–10 | 0 | 0 | 109 | 4.67 | 194.2 | 111 | 63 |
| Kenshin Kawakami | 32 | 25 | 7–12 | 1 | 0 | 73 | 3.86 | 156.1 | 105 | 57 |
| Tommy Hanson | 21 | 21 | 11–4 | 0 | 0 | 42 | 2.89 | 127.2 | 116 | 46 |
| Rafael Soriano | 77 | 0 | 1–6 | 27 | 0 | 25 | 2.97 | 75.2 | 102 | 27 |
| Mike Gonzalez | 80 | 0 | 5–4 | 10 | 0 | 28 | 2.42 | 74.1 | 90 | 33 |
| Peter Moylan | 87 | 0 | 6–2 | 0 | 0 | 29 | 2.84 | 73.0 | 61 | 35 |
| Kris Medlen | 37 | 4 | 3–5 | 0 | 0 | 34 | 4.26 | 67.2 | 72 | 30 |
| Eric O'Flaherty | 78 | 0 | 2–1 | 0 | 0 | 23 | 3.04 | 56.1 | 39 | 18 |
| Tim Hudson | 7 | 7 | 2–1 | 0 | 0 | 17 | 3.61 | 42.1 | 30 | 13 |
| Manny Acosta | 36 | 0 | 1–1 | 0 | 0 | 19 | 4.34 | 37.1 | 32 | 19 |
| *Jeff Bennett | 33 | 0 | 2–4 | 0 | 0 | 13 | 3.18 | 34.0 | 23 | 21 |
| Jo-Jo Reyes | 6 | 5 | 0–2 | 0 | 0 | 25 | 7.00 | 27.0 | 21 | 13 |
| Buddy Carlyle | 16 | 0 | 0–1 | 0 | 0 | 23 | 8.86 | 21.1 | 12 | 12 |

*Mid-season trade.

## Chicago Cubs

| BATTING | G | AB | R | H | 2B | 3B | HR | RBI | TB | BB | SO | SB | OBP | SLG | BAVG |
|---|---|---|---|---|---|---|---|---|---|---|---|---|---|---|---|
| Ryan Theriot | 154 | 602 | 81 | 171 | 20 | 5 | 7 | 54 | 222 | 51 | 93 | 21 | .343 | .369 | .284 |
| Derek Lee | 141 | 532 | 91 | 163 | 36 | 2 | 35 | 111 | 308 | 76 | 109 | 1 | .393 | .579 | .306 |
| Kosuke Fukudome | 146 | 499 | 79 | 129 | 38 | 5 | 11 | 54 | 210 | 93 | 112 | 6 | .375 | .421 | .259 |
| Alfonso Soriano | 117 | 477 | 64 | 115 | 25 | 1 | 20 | 55 | 202 | 40 | 118 | 9 | .303 | .423 | .241 |
| Milton Bradley | 124 | 393 | 61 | 101 | 17 | 1 | 12 | 40 | 156 | 66 | 95 | 2 | .378 | .397 | .257 |
| Mike Fontenot | 135 | 377 | 38 | 89 | 22 | 2 | 9 | 43 | 142 | 35 | 83 | 4 | .301 | .377 | .236 |
| Geovany Soto | 102 | 331 | 27 | 72 | 19 | 1 | 11 | 47 | 126 | 50 | 77 | 1 | .321 | .381 | .218 |
| Aramis Ramirez | 82 | 306 | 46 | 97 | 14 | 1 | 15 | 65 | 158 | 28 | 43 | 2 | .389 | .516 | .317 |
| Koyle Hill | 83 | 253 | 26 | 60 | 12 | 2 | 2 | 24 | 82 | 27 | 78 | 0 | .312 | .324 | .237 |
| Micah Hoffpauir | 105 | 234 | 28 | 56 | 12 | 1 | 10 | 35 | 100 | 20 | 46 | 1 | .300 | .427 | .239 |
| Jeff Baker | 81 | 226 | 27 | 65 | 15 | 2 | 4 | 24 | 96 | 18 | 53 | 1 | .343 | .425 | .288 |
| Jake Fox | 82 | 216 | 23 | 56 | 12 | 0 | 11 | 44 | 101 | 14 | 47 | 0 | .311 | .468 | .259 |
| Reed Johnson | 65 | 165 | 23 | 42 | 10 | 2 | 4 | 22 | 68 | 13 | 27 | 2 | .330 | .412 | .255 |
| Aaron Miles | 74 | 157 | 17 | 29 | 7 | 1 | 0 | 5 | 38 | 8 | 21 | 3 | .224 | .242 | .185 |

| PITCHING | GP | GS | W-L | SV | SHO | R | ERA | IP | Ks | BB |
|---|---|---|---|---|---|---|---|---|---|---|
| Ryan Dempster | 31 | 31 | 11–9 | 0 | 1 | 94 | 3.65 | 200.0 | 172 | 65 |
| Ted Lilly | 27 | 27 | 12–9 | 0 | 0 | 66 | 3.10 | 177.0 | 151 | 36 |
| Carlos Zambrano | 28 | 28 | 9–7 | 0 | 1 | 78 | 3.77 | 169.1 | 152 | 78 |
| Randy Wells | 27 | 27 | 12–10 | 0 | 0 | 67 | 3.05 | 165.1 | 104 | 46 |
| Rich Harden | 26 | 26 | 9–9 | 0 | 0 | 74 | 4.09 | 141.0 | 171 | 67 |
| Sean Marshall | 55 | 9 | 3–7 | 0 | 0 | 43 | 4.32 | 85.1 | 68 | 32 |
| Carlos Marmol | 79 | 0 | 2–4 | 15 | 0 | 29 | 3.41 | 74.0 | 93 | 65 |
| Aaron Heilman | 70 | 0 | 4–4 | 1 | 0 | 34 | 4.11 | 72.1 | 65 | 34 |
| Kevin Gregg | 72 | 0 | 5–6 | 23 | 0 | 38 | 4.72 | 68.2 | 71 | 30 |
| Angel Guzman | 55 | 0 | 3–3 | 1 | 0 | 20 | 2.95 | 61.0 | 47 | 23 |
| Jeff Samardzija | 20 | 2 | 1–3 | 0 | 0 | 29 | 7.53 | 34.2 | 21 | 15 |
| *Tom Gorzelanny | 13 | 7 | 4–2 | 0 | 0 | 25 | 5.63 | 38.1 | 40 | 7 |
| David Patton | 20 | 0 | 3–1 | 0 | 0 | 22 | 6.83 | 27.2 | 23 | 19 |
| *John Grabow | 30 | 0 | 0–0 | 0 | 0 | 9 | 3.24 | 25.0 | 16 | 12 |

## Cincinnati Reds

| BATTING | G | AB | R | H | 2B | 3B | HR | RBI | TB | BB | SO | SB | OBP | SLG | BAVG |
|---|---|---|---|---|---|---|---|---|---|---|---|---|---|---|---|
| Brandon Phillips | 153 | 584 | 78 | 161 | 30 | 5 | 20 | 98 | 261 | 44 | 75 | 25 | .329 | .447 | .276 |
| Joey Votto | 131 | 469 | 82 | 151 | 38 | 1 | 25 | 84 | 266 | 70 | 106 | 4 | .414 | .567 | .322 |
| Willy Taveras | 102 | 404 | 56 | 97 | 11 | 2 | 1 | 15 | 115 | 18 | 58 | 25 | .275 | .285 | .240 |
| Jay Bruce | 101 | 345 | 47 | 77 | 15 | 2 | 22 | 58 | 162 | 38 | 75 | 3 | .303 | .470 | .223 |
| Laynce Nix | 116 | 309 | 42 | 74 | 26 | 1 | 15 | 46 | 147 | 22 | 81 | 0 | .291 | .476 | .239 |
| *Jerry Hairston Jr. | 86 | 307 | 47 | 78 | 18 | 1 | 8 | 27 | 122 | 21 | 46 | 7 | .305 | .397 | .254 |
| Ramon Hernandez | 81 | 287 | 25 | 74 | 13 | 1 | 5 | 37 | 104 | 33 | 34 | 1 | .336 | .362 | .258 |
| Jonny Gomes | 98 | 281 | 39 | 75 | 17 | 0 | 20 | 51 | 152 | 26 | 85 | 3 | .338 | .541 | .267 |
| Paul Janish | 90 | 256 | 36 | 54 | 21 | 0 | 1 | 16 | 78 | 26 | 40 | 2 | .296 | .305 | .211 |
| Chris Dickerson | 97 | 255 | 31 | 70 | 13 | 3 | 2 | 15 | 95 | 39 | 66 | 11 | .370 | .373 | .275 |
| Ryan Hanigan | 90 | 251 | 22 | 66 | 6 | 1 | 3 | 11 | 83 | 37 | 31 | 0 | .361 | .331 | .263 |
| *Alex Gonzalez | 68 | 243 | 16 | 51 | 12 | 0 | 3 | 26 | 72 | 15 | 36 | 0 | .258 | .296 | .210 |
| Adam Rosales | 87 | 230 | 23 | 49 | 10 | 1 | 4 | 19 | 73 | 26 | 46 | 1 | .303 | .317 | .213 |
| Drew Stubbs | 42 | 180 | 27 | 48 | 5 | 1 | 8 | 17 | 79 | 15 | 49 | 10 | .323 | .439 | .267 |
| *Edwin Encarnacion | 43 | 139 | 10 | 29 | 6 | 1 | 5 | 16 | 52 | 24 | 38 | 1 | .333 | .374 | .209 |
| *Scott Rolen | 40 | 137 | 24 | 37 | 7 | 1 | 3 | 24 | 55 | 19 | 20 | 1 | .364 | .401 | .270 |

| PITCHING | GP | GS | W-L | SV | SHO | R | ERA | IP | Ks | BB |
|---|---|---|---|---|---|---|---|---|---|---|
| Bronson Arroyo | 33 | 33 | 15–13 | 0 | 2 | 101 | 3.84 | 220.1 | 127 | 65 |
| Johnny Cueto | 30 | 30 | 11–11 | 0 | 0 | 90 | 4.41 | 171.1 | 132 | 61 |
| Aaron Harang | 26 | 26 | 6–14 | 0 | 0 | 82 | 4.21 | 162.1 | 142 | 43 |
| Micah Owings | 26 | 19 | 7–12 | 1 | 0 | 75 | 5.34 | 119.2 | 68 | 64 |
| Homer Bailey | 20 | 20 | 8–5 | 0 | 0 | 61 | 4.53 | 113.1 | 86 | 52 |
| Nick Masset | 74 | 0 | 5–1 | 0 | 0 | 22 | 2.37 | 76.0 | 70 | 24 |
| *Kip Wells | 10 | 7 | 2–3 | 2 | 0 | 24 | 4.66 | 46.1 | 25 | 22 |
| Francisco Cordero | 68 | 0 | 2–6 | 39 | 0 | 21 | 2.16 | 66.2 | 58 | 30 |
| Justin Lehr | 11 | 11 | 5–3 | 0 | 1 | 39 | 5.37 | 65.1 | 33 | 28 |
| Daniel Herrera | 70 | 0 | 4–4 | 0 | 0 | 30 | 3.06 | 61.2 | 44 | 24 |
| Jared Burton | 53 | 0 | 1–0 | 0 | 0 | 30 | 4.40 | 59.1 | 45 | 23 |
| Arthur Rhodes | 66 | 0 | 1–1 | 0 | 0 | 16 | 2.53 | 53.1 | 48 | 20 |
| Carlos Fisher | 39 | 0 | 1–1 | 0 | 0 | 26 | 4.47 | 52.1 | 48 | 31 |
| Edinson Volquez | 9 | 9 | 4–2 | 0 | 0 | 25 | 4.35 | 49.2 | 47 | 32 |
| Matt Maloney | 7 | 7 | 2–4 | 0 | 0 | 22 | 4.87 | 40.2 | 28 | 8 |
| Mike Lincoln | 19 | 0 | 1–1 | 0 | 0 | 21 | 8.22 | 23.0 | 9 | 19 |

*Mid-season trade.

### Colorado Rockies

| BATTING | G | AB | R | H | 2B | 3B | HR | RBI | TB | BB | SO | SB | OBP | SLG | BAVG |
|---|---|---|---|---|---|---|---|---|---|---|---|---|---|---|---|
| Clint Barmes | 154 | 550 | 69 | 135 | 32 | 3 | 23 | 76 | 242 | 31 | 121 | 12 | .294 | .440 | .245 |
| Todd Helton | 151 | 544 | 79 | 177 | 38 | 3 | 15 | 86 | 266 | 89 | 73 | 0 | .416 | .489 | .325 |
| Troy Tulowitzki | 151 | 543 | 101 | 161 | 25 | 9 | 32 | 92 | 300 | 73 | 112 | 20 | .377 | .552 | .297 |
| Brad Hawpe | 145 | 501 | 82 | 143 | 42 | 3 | 23 | 86 | 260 | 79 | 145 | 1 | .384 | .519 | .285 |
| Dexter Fowler | 135 | 433 | 73 | 115 | 29 | 10 | 4 | 34 | 176 | 67 | 116 | 27 | .363 | .406 | .266 |
| Ian Stewart | 147 | 425 | 74 | 97 | 19 | 3 | 25 | 70 | 197 | 56 | 138 | 7 | .322 | .464 | .228 |
| Garrett Atkins | 126 | 354 | 37 | 80 | 12 | 1 | 9 | 48 | 121 | 41 | 58 | 0 | .308 | .342 | .226 |
| Ryan Spilborghs | 133 | 352 | 55 | 85 | 24 | 3 | 8 | 48 | 139 | 34 | 79 | 9 | .310 | .395 | .241 |
| Seth Smith | 133 | 335 | 61 | 98 | 20 | 4 | 15 | 55 | 171 | 46 | 67 | 4 | .378 | .510 | .293 |
| Chris Iannetta | 93 | 289 | 41 | 66 | 15 | 2 | 16 | 52 | 133 | 43 | 75 | 0 | .344 | .460 | .228 |
| Carlos Gonzalez | 89 | 278 | 53 | 79 | 14 | 7 | 13 | 29 | 146 | 28 | 70 | 16 | .353 | .525 | .284 |
| Yorvit Torrealba | 64 | 213 | 27 | 62 | 11 | 1 | 2 | 31 | 81 | 21 | 42 | 1 | .351 | .380 | .291 |

| PITCHING | GP | GS | W-L | SV | SHO | R | ERA | IP | Ks | BB |
|---|---|---|---|---|---|---|---|---|---|---|
| Ubaldo Jimenez | 33 | 33 | 15-12 | 0 | 0 | 87 | 3.47 | 218.0 | 198 | 85 |
| Jason Marquis | 33 | 33 | 15-13 | 0 | 1 | 104 | 4.04 | 216.0 | 115 | 80 |
| Jorge De La Rosa | 33 | 32 | 16-9 | 0 | 0 | 95 | 4.38 | 185.0 | 193 | 83 |
| Jason Hammel | 34 | 30 | 10-8 | 0 | 0 | 94 | 4.33 | 176.2 | 133 | 42 |
| Aaron Cook | 27 | 27 | 11-6 | 0 | 1 | 76 | 4.16 | 158.0 | 78 | 47 |
| Huston Street | 64 | 0 | 4-1 | 35 | 0 | 22 | 3.06 | 61.2 | 70 | 13 |
| Matt Daley | 57 | 0 | 1-1 | 0 | 0 | 24 | 4.24 | 51.0 | 55 | 18 |
| Josh Fogg | 24 | 1 | 0-2 | 0 | 0 | 20 | 3.74 | 45.2 | 27 | 20 |
| Franklin Morales | 40 | 2 | 3-2 | 7 | 0 | 22 | 4.50 | 40.0 | 41 | 23 |
| Manny Corpas | 35 | 0 | 1-3 | 1 | 0 | 22 | 5.88 | 33.2 | 24 | 7 |
| Matt Belisle | 24 | 0 | 3-1 | 0 | 0 | 21 | 5.52 | 31.0 | 22 | 5 |
| *Juan Rincon | 26 | 0 | 3-2 | 0 | 0 | 23 | 7.52 | 26.1 | 25 | 20 |
| *Rafael Betancourt | 32 | 0 | 3-1 | 1 | 0 | 5 | 1.78 | 25.1 | 29 | 5 |
| Alan Embree | 36 | 0 | 2-2 | 0 | 0 | 18 | 5.84 | 24.2 | 12 | 12 |
| Joel Peralta | 27 | 0 | 0-3 | 0 | 0 | 17 | 6.20 | 24.2 | 22 | 12 |
| Jason Grilli | 22 | 0 | 0-1 | 0 | 0 | 13 | 6.05 | 19.1 | 22 | 13 |
| Glendon Rusch | 11 | 0 | 2-0 | 0 | 0 | 15 | 6.75 | 18.2 | 13 | 3 |

### Florida Marlins

| BATTING | G | AB | R | H | 2B | 3B | HR | RBI | TB | BB | SO | SB | OBP | SLG | BAVG |
|---|---|---|---|---|---|---|---|---|---|---|---|---|---|---|---|
| Jorge Cantu | 149 | 585 | 67 | 169 | 42 | 0 | 16 | 100 | 259 | 47 | 81 | 3 | .345 | .443 | .289 |
| Hanley Ramirez | 151 | 576 | 101 | 197 | 42 | 1 | 24 | 106 | 313 | 61 | 101 | 27 | .410 | .543 | .342 |
| Dan Uggla | 158 | 564 | 84 | 137 | 27 | 1 | 31 | 90 | 259 | 92 | 150 | 2 | .354 | .459 | .243 |
| Cody Ross | 151 | 559 | 73 | 151 | 37 | 1 | 24 | 90 | 262 | 34 | 122 | 5 | .321 | .469 | .270 |
| Chris Coghlan | 128 | 504 | 84 | 162 | 31 | 6 | 9 | 47 | 232 | 53 | 77 | 8 | .390 | .460 | .321 |
| Emilio Bonifacio | 127 | 461 | 72 | 116 | 11 | 6 | 1 | 27 | 142 | 34 | 95 | 21 | .303 | .308 | .252 |
| Jeremy Hermida | 129 | 429 | 48 | 111 | 14 | 2 | 13 | 47 | 168 | 56 | 101 | 5 | .348 | .392 | .259 |
| John Baker | 112 | 373 | 59 | 101 | 25 | 0 | 9 | 50 | 153 | 41 | 89 | 0 | .349 | .410 | .271 |
| Ronnie Paulino | 80 | 239 | 24 | 65 | 10 | 1 | 8 | 27 | 101 | 25 | 48 | 1 | .340 | .423 | .272 |
| Ross Gload | 125 | 230 | 33 | 60 | 10 | 2 | 6 | 30 | 92 | 23 | 30 | 0 | .329 | .400 | .261 |
| Wes Helms | 113 | 214 | 18 | 58 | 11 | 0 | 3 | 33 | 78 | 13 | 54 | 1 | .318 | .364 | .271 |
| Cameron Maybin | 54 | 176 | 30 | 44 | 12 | 2 | 4 | 13 | 72 | 17 | 51 | 1 | .318 | .409 | .250 |
| Brett Carroll | 92 | 141 | 18 | 33 | 8 | 2 | 3 | 18 | 54 | 11 | 33 | 0 | .306 | .383 | .234 |
| *Nick Johnson | 35 | 104 | 24 | 29 | 8 | 0 | 2 | 18 | 43 | 36 | 18 | 0 | .477 | .413 | .295 |
| Alfredo Amezaga | 27 | 69 | 6 | 15 | 3 | 0 | 0 | 5 | 18 | 5 | 16 | 1 | .267 | .261 | .217 |

| PITCHING | GP | GS | W-L | SV | SHO | R | ERA | IP | Ks | BB |
|---|---|---|---|---|---|---|---|---|---|---|
| Josh Johnson | 33 | 33 | 15-5 | 0 | 0 | 77 | 3.23 | 209.0 | 191 | 58 |
| Ricky Nolasco | 31 | 31 | 13-9 | 0 | 0 | 111 | 5.06 | 185.0 | 195 | 44 |
| Chris Volstad | 29 | 29 | 9-13 | 0 | 1 | 100 | 5.21 | 159.0 | 107 | 59 |
| Sean West | 20 | 20 | 8-6 | 0 | 0 | 62 | 4.79 | 103.1 | 70 | 44 |
| Anibal Sanchez | 16 | 16 | 4-8 | 0 | 0 | 39 | 3.87 | 86.0 | 71 | 46 |
| Andrew Miller | 20 | 14 | 3-5 | 0 | 0 | 52 | 4.84 | 80.0 | 59 | 43 |
| Burke Badenhop | 35 | 2 | 7-4 | 0 | 0 | 32 | 3.75 | 72.0 | 57 | 24 |
| Leo Nunez | 75 | 0 | 4-6 | 26 | 0 | 33 | 4.06 | 68.2 | 60 | 27 |
| Renyel Pinto | 73 | 0 | 4-1 | 0 | 0 | 25 | 3.23 | 61.1 | 58 | 45 |
| Kiko Calero | 67 | 0 | 2-2 | 0 | 0 | 13 | 1.95 | 60.0 | 69 | 30 |
| Rick VandenHurk | 11 | 11 | 3-2 | 0 | 0 | 29 | 4.30 | 58.2 | 49 | 21 |
| Dan Meyer | 71 | 0 | 3-2 | 2 | 0 | 24 | 3.09 | 58.1 | 56 | 21 |
| Brian Sanches | 47 | 0 | 4-2 | 0 | 0 | 18 | 2.56 | 56.1 | 51 | 26 |
| Matt Lindstrom | 54 | 0 | 2-1 | 15 | 0 | 35 | 5.89 | 47.1 | 39 | 24 |
| Christhian Martinez | 15 | 0 | 1-1 | 0 | 0 | 16 | 5.13 | 26.1 | 18 | 8 |
| Brendan Donnelly | 30 | 0 | 3-0 | 2 | 0 | 8 | 1.78 | 25.1 | 25 | 9 |

*Mid-season trade.

## Houston Astros

| BATTING | G | AB | R | H | 2B | 3B | HR | RBI | TB | BB | SO | SB | OBP | SLG | BAVG |
|---|---|---|---|---|---|---|---|---|---|---|---|---|---|---|---|
| Miguel Tejada | 158 | 635 | 83 | 199 | 46 | 1 | 14 | 86 | 289 | 19 | 48 | 5 | .340 | .455 | .313 |
| Carlos Lee | 160 | 610 | 65 | 183 | 35 | 1 | 26 | 102 | 298 | 41 | 51 | 5 | .343 | .489 | .300 |
| Michael Bourn | 157 | 606 | 97 | 173 | 27 | 12 | 3 | 35 | 233 | 63 | 140 | 61 | .354 | .384 | .285 |
| Hunter Pence | 159 | 585 | 76 | 165 | 26 | 5 | 25 | 72 | 276 | 58 | 109 | 14 | .346 | .472 | .282 |
| Kazuo Matsui | 132 | 476 | 56 | 119 | 20 | 2 | 9 | 46 | 170 | 34 | 85 | 19 | .302 | .357 | .250 |
| Lance Berkman | 136 | 460 | 73 | 126 | 31 | 1 | 25 | 80 | 234 | 97 | 98 | 7 | .399 | .509 | .274 |
| Geoff Blum | 120 | 381 | 34 | 94 | 14 | 1 | 10 | 49 | 140 | 33 | 61 | 0 | .314 | .367 | .247 |
| Ivan Rodriguez | 93 | 327 | 41 | 82 | 15 | 2 | 8 | 34 | 125 | 13 | 74 | 0 | .280 | .382 | .251 |
| Jeff Keppinger | 107 | 305 | 35 | 78 | 13 | 3 | 7 | 29 | 118 | 27 | 33 | 0 | .320 | .387 | .256 |
| Humberto Quintero | 60 | 157 | 11 | 37 | 8 | 1 | 4 | 14 | 59 | 7 | 41 | 0 | .286 | .376 | .236 |
| Jason Michaels | 102 | 135 | 17 | 32 | 12 | 1 | 4 | 16 | 58 | 16 | 38 | 1 | .322 | .430 | .237 |
| Darren Erstad | 107 | 134 | 13 | 26 | 8 | 2 | 2 | 11 | 44 | 14 | 31 | 0 | .268 | .328 | .194 |
| *Chris Coste | 43 | 103 | 3 | 21 | 5 | 0 | 0 | 10 | 26 | 8 | 28 | 0 | .259 | .252 | .204 |
| Edwin Maysonet | 39 | 69 | 9 | 20 | 2 | 0 | 1 | 7 | 25 | 5 | 19 | 0 | .333 | .362 | .290 |

| PITCHING | GP | GS | W–L | SV | SHO | R | ERA | IP | Ks | BB |
|---|---|---|---|---|---|---|---|---|---|---|
| Wandy Rodriguez | 33 | 33 | 14–12 | 0 | 1 | 77 | 3.02 | 205.2 | 193 | 63 |
| Roy Oswalt | 30 | 30 | 8–6 | 0 | 0 | 83 | 4.12 | 181.1 | 138 | 42 |
| Brian Moehler | 29 | 29 | 8–12 | 0 | 0 | 101 | 5.47 | 154.2 | 91 | 51 |
| Mike Hampton | 21 | 21 | 7–10 | 0 | 0 | 71 | 5.30 | 112.0 | 74 | 46 |
| Felipe Paulino | 23 | 17 | 3–11 | 0 | 0 | 73 | 6.27 | 97.2 | 93 | 37 |
| Russ Ortiz | 23 | 13 | 3–6 | 0 | 0 | 56 | 5.57 | 85.2 | 65 | 48 |
| Jeff Fulchino | 61 | 0 | 6–4 | 0 | 0 | 33 | 3.40 | 82.0 | 71 | 27 |
| LaTroy Hawkins | 65 | 0 | 1–4 | 11 | 0 | 16 | 2.13 | 63.1 | 45 | 16 |
| Tim Byrdak | 76 | 0 | 1–2 | 0 | 0 | 23 | 3.23 | 61.1 | 58 | 36 |
| Bud Norris | 11 | 10 | 6–3 | 0 | 0 | 29 | 4.53 | 55.2 | 54 | 25 |
| Chris Sampson | 49 | 0 | 4–2 | 3 | 0 | 34 | 5.04 | 55.1 | 33 | 21 |
| Jose Valverde | 52 | 0 | 4–2 | 25 | 0 | 15 | 2.33 | 54.0 | 56 | 21 |
| Alberto Arias | 42 | 0 | 2–1 | 0 | 0 | 21 | 3.35 | 45.2 | 39 | 19 |
| Wesley Wright | 49 | 0 | 3–4 | 0 | 0 | 27 | 5.44 | 44.2 | 47 | 25 |
| Yorman Bazardo | 10 | 6 | 1–3 | 0 | 0 | 31 | 7.88 | 32.0 | 17 | 22 |

## Los Angeles Dodgers

| BATTING | G | AB | R | H | 2B | 3B | HR | RBI | TB | BB | SO | SB | OBP | SLG | BAVG |
|---|---|---|---|---|---|---|---|---|---|---|---|---|---|---|---|
| Rafael Furcal | 150 | 613 | 92 | 165 | 28 | 5 | 9 | 47 | 230 | 61 | 89 | 12 | .335 | .375 | .269 |
| Matt Kemp | 159 | 606 | 97 | 180 | 25 | 7 | 26 | 101 | 297 | 52 | 139 | 34 | .352 | .490 | .297 |
| Andre Ethier | 160 | 596 | 92 | 162 | 42 | 3 | 31 | 106 | 303 | 72 | 116 | 6 | .361 | .508 | .272 |
| James Loney | 158 | 576 | 73 | 162 | 25 | 2 | 13 | 90 | 230 | 70 | 68 | 7 | .357 | .399 | .281 |
| Orlando Hudson | 149 | 551 | 74 | 156 | 35 | 6 | 9 | 62 | 230 | 62 | 99 | 8 | .357 | .417 | .283 |
| Russell Martin | 143 | 505 | 63 | 126 | 19 | 0 | 7 | 53 | 166 | 69 | 80 | 11 | .352 | .329 | .250 |
| Casey Blake | 139 | 485 | 84 | 136 | 25 | 6 | 18 | 79 | 227 | 63 | 116 | 3 | .363 | .468 | .280 |
| Juan Pierre | 145 | 380 | 57 | 117 | 16 | 8 | 0 | 31 | 149 | 27 | 27 | 30 | .365 | .392 | .308 |
| Manny Ramirez | 104 | 352 | 62 | 102 | 24 | 2 | 19 | 63 | 187 | 71 | 81 | 0 | .418 | .531 | .290 |
| Ronnie Belliard | 110 | 264 | 39 | 73 | 14 | 1 | 10 | 39 | 119 | 20 | 56 | 3 | .325 | .451 | .277 |
| Mark Loretta | 107 | 181 | 19 | 42 | 8 | 0 | 0 | 25 | 50 | 20 | 21 | 1 | .309 | .276 | .232 |
| Juan Castro | 57 | 112 | 18 | 31 | 4 | 0 | 1 | 9 | 38 | 6 | 25 | 0 | .311 | .339 | .277 |
| Brad Ausmus | 36 | 95 | 9 | 28 | 4 | 0 | 1 | 9 | 35 | 5 | 21 | 1 | .343 | .368 | .295 |
| Blake DeWitt | 31 | 49 | 4 | 10 | 3 | 0 | 2 | 4 | 19 | 3 | 7 | 0 | .245 | .388 | .204 |

| PITCHING | GP | GS | W–L | SV | SHO | R | ERA | IP | Ks | BB |
|---|---|---|---|---|---|---|---|---|---|---|
| Randy Wolf | 34 | 34 | 11–7 | 0 | 0 | 81 | 3.23 | 214.1 | 160 | 58 |
| Jon Garland | 33 | 33 | 11–13 | 0 | 0 | 106 | 4.01 | 204.0 | 109 | 61 |
| Chad Billingsley | 33 | 32 | 12–11 | 0 | 0 | 94 | 4.03 | 196.1 | 179 | 86 |
| Clayton Kershaw | 31 | 30 | 8–8 | 0 | 0 | 55 | 2.79 | 171.0 | 185 | 91 |
| Hiroki Kuroda | 21 | 20 | 8–7 | 0 | 0 | 59 | 3.76 | 117.1 | 87 | 24 |
| Ramon Troncoso | 73 | 0 | 5–4 | 6 | 0 | 30 | 2.72 | 82.2 | 55 | 34 |
| Jeff Weaver | 28 | 7 | 6–4 | 0 | 0 | 34 | 3.65 | 79.0 | 64 | 33 |
| Jonathan Broxton | 73 | 0 | 7–2 | 36 | 0 | 24 | 2.61 | 76.0 | 114 | 29 |
| Ronald Belisario | 69 | 0 | 4–3 | 0 | 0 | 21 | 2.04 | 70.2 | 64 | 29 |
| Guillermo Mota | 61 | 0 | 3–4 | 0 | 0 | 25 | 3.44 | 65.1 | 39 | 24 |
| James McDonald | 45 | 4 | 5–5 | 0 | 0 | 34 | 4.00 | 63.0 | 54 | 34 |
| Eric Stults | 10 | 10 | 4–3 | 0 | 1 | 27 | 4.86 | 50.0 | 33 | 26 |
| Vincente Padilla | 8 | 7 | 4–0 | 0 | 0 | 15 | 3.20 | 39.1 | 38 | 12 |
| Hong-Chih Kuo | 35 | 0 | 2–0 | 0 | 0 | 10 | 3.00 | 30.0 | 32 | 13 |
| George Sherrill | 30 | 0 | 1–0 | 1 | 0 | 2 | 0.65 | 27.2 | 22 | 11 |
| Cory Wade | 27 | 0 | 2–3 | 0 | 0 | 17 | 5.53 | 27.2 | 18 | 10 |
| Eric Milton | 5 | 5 | 2–1 | 0 | 0 | 12 | 3.80 | 23.2 | 20 | 6 |

*Mid-season trade.

## Milwaukee Brewers

| BATTING | G | AB | R | H | 2B | 3B | HR | RBI | TB | BB | SO | SB | OBP | SLG | BAVG |
|---|---|---|---|---|---|---|---|---|---|---|---|---|---|---|---|
| Ryan Braun | 158 | 635 | 113 | 203 | 39 | 6 | 32 | 114 | 350 | 57 | 121 | 20 | .386 | .551 | .320 |
| Prince Fielder | 162 | 591 | 103 | 177 | 35 | 3 | 46 | 141 | 356 | 110 | 138 | 2 | .412 | .602 | .299 |
| Mike Cameron | 149 | 544 | 78 | 136 | 32 | 3 | 24 | 70 | 246 | 75 | 156 | 7 | .342 | .452 | .250 |
| Jason Kendall | 134 | 452 | 48 | 109 | 19 | 2 | 2 | 43 | 138 | 46 | 58 | 7 | .331 | .305 | .241 |
| Corey Hart | 115 | 419 | 64 | 109 | 24 | 3 | 12 | 48 | 175 | 43 | 92 | 11 | .335 | .418 | .260 |
| J.J. Hardy | 115 | 414 | 53 | 95 | 16 | 2 | 11 | 47 | 148 | 43 | 85 | 0 | .302 | .357 | .229 |
| Craig Counsell | 130 | 404 | 61 | 115 | 22 | 8 | 4 | 39 | 165 | 42 | 54 | 3 | .357 | .408 | .285 |
| Casey McGehee | 116 | 355 | 58 | 107 | 20 | 1 | 16 | 66 | 177 | 34 | 67 | 0 | .360 | .499 | .301 |
| *Felipe Lopez | 66 | 259 | 44 | 83 | 20 | 2 | 3 | 32 | 116 | 37 | 41 | 0 | .407 | .448 | .320 |
| *Bill Hall | 76 | 214 | 22 | 43 | 12 | 0 | 6 | 24 | 73 | 19 | 72 | 1 | .265 | .341 | .201 |
| *Jody Gerut | 85 | 161 | 23 | 38 | 7 | 0 | 5 | 21 | 60 | 14 | 21 | 4 | .299 | .373 | .236 |
| Rickie Weeks | 37 | 147 | 28 | 40 | 5 | 2 | 9 | 24 | 76 | 12 | 39 | 2 | .340 | .517 | .272 |
| Frank Catalanotto | 77 | 144 | 18 | 40 | 6 | 3 | 1 | 9 | 55 | 14 | 23 | 2 | .346 | .382 | .278 |
| Mat Gamel | 61 | 128 | 11 | 31 | 6 | 1 | 5 | 20 | 54 | 18 | 54 | 1 | .338 | .422 | .242 |

| PITCHING | GP | GS | W-L | SV | SHO | R | ERA | IP | Ks | BB |
|---|---|---|---|---|---|---|---|---|---|---|
| Braden Looper | 34 | 34 | 14–7 | 0 | 0 | 123 | 5.22 | 194.2 | 100 | 64 |
| Yovani Gallardo | 30 | 30 | 13–12 | 0 | 0 | 78 | 3.73 | 185.2 | 204 | 94 |
| Jeff Suppan | 30 | 30 | 7–12 | 0 | 0 | 106 | 5.29 | 161.2 | 80 | 74 |
| Manny Parra | 27 | 27 | 11–11 | 0 | 0 | 108 | 6.36 | 140.0 | 116 | 77 |
| Dave Bush | 22 | 21 | 5–9 | 0 | 0 | 84 | 6.38 | 114.1 | 89 | 37 |
| Carlos Villanueva | 64 | 6 | 4–10 | 3 | 0 | 58 | 5.34 | 96.0 | 83 | 35 |
| Todd Coffey | 78 | 0 | 4–4 | 2 | 0 | 28 | 2.90 | 83.2 | 65 | 21 |
| Seth McClung | 41 | 2 | 3–3 | 0 | 0 | 34 | 4.94 | 62.0 | 40 | 39 |
| Trevor Hoffman | 55 | 0 | 3–2 | 37 | 0 | 11 | 1.83 | 54.0 | 48 | 14 |
| Mark DiFelice | 59 | 0 | 4–1 | 0 | 0 | 36 | 3.66 | 51.2 | 48 | 15 |
| Mike Burns | 15 | 8 | 3–5 | 0 | 0 | 21 | 5.75 | 51.2 | 39 | 17 |
| Chris Narveson | 21 | 4 | 2–0 | 0 | 0 | 22 | 3.83 | 47.0 | 46 | 16 |
| Chris Smith | 35 | 0 | 0–0 | 0 | 0 | 21 | 4.11 | 46.0 | 35 | 19 |
| Mitch Stetter | 71 | 0 | 4–1 | 1 | 0 | 19 | 3.60 | 45.0 | 44 | 27 |

## New York Mets

| BATTING | G | AB | R | H | 2B | 3B | HR | RBI | TB | BB | SO | SB | OBP | SLG | BAVG |
|---|---|---|---|---|---|---|---|---|---|---|---|---|---|---|---|
| David Wright | 144 | 535 | 88 | 164 | 39 | 3 | 10 | 72 | 239 | 74 | 140 | 27 | .390 | .447 | .307 |
| Daniel Murphy | 155 | 508 | 60 | 135 | 38 | 4 | 12 | 63 | 217 | 38 | 69 | 4 | .313 | .427 | .266 |
| Luis Castillo | 142 | 486 | 77 | 147 | 12 | 3 | 1 | 40 | 168 | 69 | 58 | 20 | .387 | .346 | .302 |
| Angel Pagan | 88 | 343 | 54 | 105 | 22 | 11 | 6 | 32 | 167 | 25 | 56 | 14 | .350 | .487 | .306 |
| Fernando Tatis | 125 | 340 | 42 | 96 | 21 | 4 | 8 | 48 | 149 | 22 | 54 | 4 | .339 | .438 | .282 |
| Carlos Beltran | 81 | 308 | 50 | 100 | 22 | 1 | 10 | 48 | 154 | 47 | 43 | 11 | .415 | .500 | .325 |
| *Jeff Francoeur | 75 | 289 | 40 | 90 | 20 | 2 | 10 | 41 | 144 | 11 | 46 | 1 | .338 | .498 | .311 |
| Omir Santos | 96 | 281 | 28 | 73 | 14 | 1 | 7 | 40 | 110 | 15 | 44 | 0 | .296 | .391 | .260 |
| Alex Cora | 82 | 271 | 31 | 68 | 11 | 1 | 1 | 18 | 84 | 25 | 28 | 8 | .320 | .310 | .251 |
| Gary Sheffield | 100 | 268 | 44 | 74 | 13 | 2 | 10 | 43 | 121 | 40 | 46 | 2 | .372 | .451 | .276 |
| *Ryan Church | 67 | 232 | 26 | 65 | 16 | 0 | 2 | 22 | 87 | 17 | 36 | 6 | .332 | .375 | .280 |
| Brian Schneider | 59 | 170 | 11 | 37 | 11 | 0 | 3 | 24 | 57 | 18 | 21 | 0 | .292 | .335 | .218 |
| Jeremy Reed | 126 | 161 | 9 | 39 | 6 | 2 | 0 | 9 | 49 | 14 | 36 | 0 | .301 | .304 | .242 |
| Jose Reyes | 36 | 147 | 18 | 41 | 7 | 2 | 2 | 15 | 58 | 18 | 19 | 11 | .355 | .395 | .279 |
| Cory Sullivan | 64 | 136 | 17 | 34 | 2 | 5 | 2 | 15 | 52 | 19 | 22 | 7 | .338 | .382 | .250 |
| *Anderson Hernandez | 46 | 135 | 14 | 34 | 6 | 2 | 2 | 14 | 50 | 13 | 22 | 2 | .315 | .370 | .252 |
| Carlos Delgado | 26 | 94 | 15 | 28 | 7 | 1 | 4 | 23 | 49 | 12 | 20 | 0 | .393 | .521 | .298 |

| PITCHING | GP | GS | W-L | SV | SHO | R | ERA | IP | Ks | BB |
|---|---|---|---|---|---|---|---|---|---|---|
| Mike Pelfrey | 31 | 31 | 10–12 | 0 | 0 | 112 | 5.03 | 184.1 | 107 | 66 |
| Johan Santana | 25 | 25 | 13–9 | 0 | 0 | 67 | 3.13 | 166.2 | 146 | 46 |
| *Livan Hernandez | 23 | 23 | 7–8 | 0 | 0 | 83 | 5.47 | 135.0 | 75 | 51 |
| Tim Redding | 30 | 17 | 3–6 | 0 | 0 | 72 | 5.10 | 120.0 | 76 | 50 |
| Bobby Parnell | 68 | 8 | 4–8 | 1 | 0 | 56 | 5.30 | 88.1 | 74 | 46 |
| John Maine | 15 | 15 | 7–3 | 0 | 0 | 42 | 4.43 | 81.1 | 55 | 38 |
| Nelson Figueroa | 16 | 10 | 3–8 | 0 | 1 | 33 | 4.09 | 70.1 | 59 | 24 |
| Brian Stokes | 69 | 0 | 2–4 | 0 | 0 | 33 | 3.97 | 70.1 | 45 | 38 |
| Sean Green | 79 | 0 | 1–4 | 1 | 0 | 37 | 4.52 | 69.2 | 54 | 36 |
| Francisco Rodriguez | 70 | 0 | 3–6 | 35 | 0 | 34 | 3.71 | 68.0 | 73 | 38 |
| Oliver Perez | 14 | 14 | 3–4 | 0 | 0 | 51 | 6.82 | 66.0 | 62 | 58 |
| Pedro Feliciano | 88 | 0 | 6–4 | 0 | 0 | 31 | 3.03 | 59.1 | 59 | 18 |
| *Pat Misch | 22 | 7 | 3–4 | 0 | 1 | 25 | 4.12 | 59.0 | 23 | 19 |
| Fernando Nieve | 8 | 7 | 3–3 | 0 | 0 | 13 | 2.95 | 36.2 | 23 | 19 |
| Elmer Dessens | 28 | 0 | 0–0 | 0 | 0 | 12 | 3.31 | 32.2 | 14 | 10 |
| J. J. Putz | 29 | 0 | 1–4 | 2 | 0 | 18 | 5.22 | 29.1 | 19 | 10 |

*Mid-season trade.

## Philadelphia Phillies

| BATTING | G | AB | R | H | 2B | 3B | HR | RBI | TB | BB | SO | SB | OBP | SLG | BAVG |
|---|---|---|---|---|---|---|---|---|---|---|---|---|---|---|---|
| Jimmy Rollins | 155 | 672 | 100 | 168 | 43 | 5 | 21 | 77 | 284 | 44 | 70 | 31 | .296 | .423 | .250 |
| Shane Victorino | 156 | 620 | 102 | 181 | 39 | 13 | 10 | 62 | 276 | 60 | 71 | 25 | .358 | .445 | .292 |
| Ryan Howard | 160 | 616 | 105 | 172 | 37 | 4 | 45 | 141 | 352 | 75 | 186 | 8 | .360 | .571 | .279 |
| Pedro Feliz | 158 | 580 | 62 | 154 | 30 | 2 | 12 | 82 | 224 | 35 | 68 | 0 | .308 | .386 | .266 |
| Chase Utley | 156 | 571 | 112 | 161 | 28 | 4 | 31 | 93 | 290 | 88 | 110 | 23 | .397 | .508 | .282 |
| Jayson Werth | 159 | 571 | 98 | 153 | 26 | 1 | 36 | 99 | 289 | 91 | 156 | 20 | .373 | .506 | .268 |
| Raul Ibanez | 134 | 500 | 93 | 136 | 32 | 3 | 34 | 93 | 276 | 56 | 119 | 4 | .347 | .552 | .272 |
| Carlos Ruiz | 107 | 322 | 32 | 82 | 26 | 1 | 9 | 43 | 137 | 47 | 39 | 3 | .355 | .425 | .255 |
| Greg Dobbs | 97 | 154 | 15 | 38 | 6 | 0 | 5 | 20 | 59 | 11 | 29 | 1 | .296 | .383 | .247 |
| Paul Bako | 44 | 116 | 12 | 26 | 4 | 0 | 3 | 9 | 39 | 13 | 32 | 0 | .308 | .336 | .224 |
| Eric Bruntlett | 72 | 105 | 15 | 18 | 7 | 0 | 0 | 7 | 25 | 5 | 26 | 2 | .224 | .238 | .171 |
| Matt Stairs | 99 | 103 | 15 | 20 | 4 | 0 | 5 | 17 | 39 | 23 | 30 | 0 | .357 | .379 | .194 |
| *Chris Coste | 45 | 102 | 12 | 25 | 8 | 0 | 2 | 8 | 39 | 14 | 27 | 0 | .342 | .382 | .245 |
| *Ben Francisco | 37 | 97 | 10 | 27 | 9 | 0 | 5 | 13 | 51 | 5 | 24 | 1 | .317 | .526 | .278 |

| PITCHING | GP | GS | W–L | SV | SHO | R | ERA | IP | Ks | BB |
|---|---|---|---|---|---|---|---|---|---|---|
| Joe Blanton | 31 | 31 | 12–8 | 0 | 0 | 89 | 4.05 | 195.1 | 163 | 59 |
| Cole Hamels | 32 | 32 | 10–11 | 0 | 2 | 95 | 4.32 | 193.2 | 168 | 43 |
| J.A. Happ | 35 | 23 | 12–4 | 0 | 2 | 55 | 2.93 | 166.0 | 119 | 56 |
| Jamie Moyer | 30 | 25 | 12–10 | 0 | 0 | 91 | 4.94 | 162.0 | 94 | 33 |
| Chan Ho Park | 45 | 7 | 3–3 | 0 | 0 | 43 | 4.43 | 83.1 | 73 | 10 |
| *Cliff Lee | 12 | 12 | 7–4 | 0 | 1 | 35 | 3.39 | 79.2 | 74 | 22 |
| Ryan Madson | 79 | 0 | 5–5 | 10 | 0 | 29 | 3.26 | 77.1 | 78 | 23 |
| Brett Myers | 18 | 10 | 4–3 | 0 | 0 | 38 | 4.84 | 70.2 | 50 | 47 |
| Chad Durbin | 59 | 0 | 2–2 | 2 | 0 | 38 | 4.39 | 69.2 | 62 | 34 |
| Brad Lidge | 67 | 0 | 0–8 | 31 | 0 | 51 | 7.21 | 58.2 | 61 | 8 |
| Pedro Martinez | 9 | 9 | 5–1 | 0 | 0 | 18 | 3.63 | 44.2 | 37 | 14 |
| Clay Condrey | 45 | 0 | 6–2 | 1 | 0 | 17 | 3.00 | 42.0 | 25 | 9 |
| Tyler Walker | 32 | 0 | 2–1 | 0 | 0 | 12 | 3.06 | 35.1 | 27 | 6 |
| Scott Eyre | 42 | 0 | 2–1 | 0 | 0 | 6 | 1.50 | 30.0 | 22 | 16 |
| Rodrigo Lopez | 7 | 5 | 3–1 | 0 | 0 | 24 | 5.70 | 30.0 | 19 | 11 |
| Jack Taschner | 24 | 0 | 1–1 | 0 | 0 | 18 | 4.91 | 29.1 | 19 | 20 |
| Kyle Kendrick | 9 | 2 | 3–1 | 0 | 0 | 11 | 3.42 | 26.1 | 15 | 9 |

## Pittsburgh Pirates

| BATTING | G | AB | R | H | 2B | 3B | HR | RBI | TB | BB | SO | SB | OBP | SLG | BAVG |
|---|---|---|---|---|---|---|---|---|---|---|---|---|---|---|---|
| Andy LaRoche | 150 | 524 | 64 | 135 | 29 | 5 | 12 | 64 | 210 | 50 | 84 | 3 | .330 | .401 | .258 |
| Andrew McCutchen | 108 | 433 | 74 | 124 | 26 | 9 | 12 | 54 | 204 | 54 | 83 | 22 | .365 | .471 | .286 |
| Brandon Moss | 133 | 385 | 47 | 91 | 20 | 4 | 7 | 41 | 140 | 34 | 84 | 1 | .304 | .364 | .236 |
| *Freddy Sanchez | 86 | 355 | 45 | 105 | 28 | 3 | 6 | 34 | 157 | 20 | 60 | 5 | .334 | .442 | .296 |
| Delwyn Young | 124 | 354 | 40 | 94 | 16 | 2 | 7 | 43 | 135 | 29 | 90 | 2 | .326 | .381 | .266 |
| *Adam LaRoche | 87 | 324 | 46 | 80 | 25 | 1 | 12 | 40 | 143 | 41 | 81 | 2 | .329 | .441 | .247 |
| Garrett Jones | 82 | 314 | 45 | 92 | 21 | 1 | 21 | 44 | 178 | 40 | 76 | 10 | .372 | .567 | .293 |
| Ryan Doumit | 75 | 280 | 31 | 70 | 16 | 0 | 10 | 38 | 116 | 20 | 49 | 4 | .299 | .414 | .250 |
| *Nyjer Morgan | 71 | 278 | 39 | 77 | 6 | 5 | 2 | 27 | 99 | 29 | 49 | 18 | .351 | .356 | .277 |
| *Jack Wilson | 75 | 266 | 26 | 71 | 18 | 1 | 4 | 31 | 103 | 15 | 31 | 2 | .304 | .387 | .267 |
| *Lastings Milledge | 58 | 220 | 20 | 64 | 11 | 0 | 4 | 20 | 87 | 12 | 37 | 6 | .333 | .395 | .291 |
| Jason Jaramillo | 63 | 206 | 20 | 52 | 14 | 0 | 3 | 26 | 75 | 17 | 33 | 1 | .309 | .364 | .252 |
| Ramon Vazquez | 101 | 204 | 17 | 47 | 7 | 0 | 1 | 16 | 57 | 31 | 47 | 1 | .335 | .279 | .230 |
| *Nate McLouth | 45 | 168 | 27 | 43 | 7 | 1 | 9 | 34 | 79 | 21 | 29 | 7 | .349 | .470 | .256 |
| Steve Pearce | 60 | 165 | 19 | 34 | 13 | 1 | 4 | 16 | 61 | 21 | 43 | 1 | .296 | .370 | .206 |
| *Ronny Cedeno | 46 | 155 | 17 | 40 | 4 | 1 | 5 | 21 | 61 | 9 | 29 | 2 | .307 | .394 | .258 |

| PITCHING | GP | GS | W–L | SV | SHO | R | ERA | IP | Ks | BB |
|---|---|---|---|---|---|---|---|---|---|---|
| Zach Duke | 32 | 32 | 11–16 | 0 | 1 | 101 | 4.06 | 213.0 | 106 | 49 |
| Paul Maholm | 31 | 31 | 8–9 | 0 | 0 | 102 | 4.44 | 194.2 | 119 | 60 |
| Ross Ohlendorf | 29 | 29 | 11–10 | 0 | 0 | 80 | 3.92 | 176.2 | 109 | 53 |
| Jeff Karstens | 39 | 13 | 4–6 | 0 | 0 | 66 | 5.42 | 108.0 | 52 | 45 |
| Charlie Morton | 18 | 18 | 5–9 | 0 | 1 | 49 | 4.55 | 97.0 | 62 | 40 |
| *Ian Snell | 15 | 15 | 2–8 | 0 | 0 | 50 | 5.36 | 80.2 | 52 | 44 |
| Jesse Chavez | 73 | 0 | 1–4 | 0 | 0 | 33 | 4.01 | 67.1 | 47 | 22 |
| Matt Capps | 57 | 0 | 4–8 | 27 | 0 | 36 | 5.80 | 54.1 | 46 | 17 |
| *Kevin Hart | 10 | 10 | 1–8 | 0 | 0 | 55 | 6.92 | 53.1 | 39 | 26 |
| *John Grabow | 45 | 0 | 3–0 | 0 | 0 | 19 | 3.42 | 47.1 | 41 | 28 |
| Evan Meek | 41 | 0 | 1–1 | 0 | 0 | 18 | 3.45 | 47.0 | 42 | 29 |
| Virgil Vasquez | 14 | 7 | 2–5 | 0 | 0 | 30 | 5.84 | 44.2 | 29 | 18 |
| Steven Jackson | 40 | 0 | 2–3 | 0 | 0 | 20 | 3.14 | 43.0 | 21 | 22 |
| Daniel McCutchen | 6 | 6 | 1–2 | 0 | 0 | 17 | 4.21 | 36.1 | 19 | 11 |

*Mid-season trade.

## St. Louis Cardinals

| BATTING | G | AB | R | H | 2B | 3B | HR | RBI | TB | BB | SO | SB | OBP | SLG | BAVG |
|---|---|---|---|---|---|---|---|---|---|---|---|---|---|---|---|
| Albert Pujols | 160 | 568 | 124 | 186 | 45 | 1 | 47 | 135 | 374 | 115 | 64 | 16 | .443 | .658 | .327 |
| Skip Schumaker | 153 | 532 | 85 | 161 | 34 | 1 | 4 | 35 | 209 | 52 | 69 | 2 | .364 | .393 | .303 |
| Ryan Ludwick | 139 | 486 | 63 | 129 | 20 | 1 | 22 | 97 | 217 | 41 | 106 | 4 | .329 | .447 | .265 |
| Yadier Molina | 140 | 481 | 45 | 141 | 23 | 1 | 6 | 54 | 184 | 50 | 39 | 9 | .366 | .383 | .293 |
| Colby Rasmus | 147 | 474 | 72 | 119 | 22 | 2 | 16 | 52 | 193 | 36 | 95 | 3 | .307 | .407 | .251 |
| Brendan Ryan | 129 | 390 | 55 | 114 | 19 | 7 | 3 | 37 | 156 | 24 | 56 | 14 | .340 | .400 | .292 |
| Rick Ankiel | 122 | 372 | 50 | 86 | 21 | 2 | 11 | 38 | 144 | 26 | 99 | 4 | .285 | .387 | .231 |
| Joe Thurston | 124 | 267 | 27 | 60 | 17 | 4 | 1 | 25 | 88 | 33 | 56 | 4 | .316 | .330 | .225 |
| Chris Duncan | 87 | 260 | 25 | 59 | 15 | 2 | 5 | 32 | 93 | 41 | 67 | 0 | .329 | .358 | .227 |
| *Mark DeRosa | 68 | 237 | 31 | 54 | 10 | 1 | 10 | 28 | 96 | 18 | 58 | 2 | .291 | .405 | .228 |
| *Matt Holliday | 63 | 235 | 42 | 83 | 16 | 2 | 13 | 55 | 142 | 26 | 43 | 2 | .419 | .604 | .353 |
| Khalil Greene | 77 | 170 | 21 | 34 | 7 | 0 | 6 | 24 | 59 | 15 | 35 | 2 | .272 | .347 | .200 |
| *Julio Lugo | 51 | 148 | 24 | 41 | 9 | 4 | 2 | 13 | 64 | 17 | 27 | 6 | .351 | .432 | .277 |
| Tyler Greene | 48 | 108 | 9 | 24 | 5 | 0 | 2 | 7 | 35 | 4 | 32 | 3 | .270 | .324 | .222 |
| Jason LaRue | 51 | 104 | 10 | 25 | 3 | 0 | 2 | 6 | 34 | 3 | 22 | 1 | .288 | .327 | .240 |
| Brian Barden | 52 | 103 | 13 | 24 | 3 | 0 | 4 | 10 | 39 | 6 | 21 | 0 | .286 | .379 | .233 |

| PITCHING | GP | GS | W–L | SV | SHO | R | ERA | IP | Ks | BB |
|---|---|---|---|---|---|---|---|---|---|---|
| Adam Wainwright | 34 | 34 | 19–8 | 0 | 0 | 75 | 2.63 | 233.0 | 212 | 66 |
| Joel Pineiro | 32 | 32 | 15–12 | 0 | 2 | 94 | 3.49 | 214.0 | 105 | 27 |
| Chris Carpenter | 28 | 28 | 17–4 | 0 | 1 | 49 | 2.24 | 192.2 | 144 | 38 |
| Todd Wellemeyer | 28 | 21 | 7–10 | 0 | 0 | 88 | 5.89 | 122.1 | 78 | 57 |
| Kyle Lohse | 23 | 22 | 6–10 | 0 | 1 | 69 | 4.74 | 117.2 | 77 | 36 |
| Brad Thompson | 32 | 8 | 2–6 | 0 | 0 | 45 | 4.84 | 80.0 | 34 | 23 |
| Kyle McClellan | 66 | 0 | 4–4 | 3 | 0 | 27 | 3.38 | 66.2 | 51 | 34 |
| Ryan Franklin | 62 | 0 | 4–3 | 38 | 0 | 13 | 1.92 | 61.0 | 44 | 24 |
| Mitchell Boggs | 16 | 9 | 2–3 | 0 | 0 | 28 | 4.19 | 58.0 | 46 | 33 |
| Jason Motte | 69 | 0 | 4–4 | 0 | 0 | 32 | 4.76 | 56.2 | 54 | 23 |
| Trever Miller | 70 | 0 | 4–1 | 0 | 0 | 11 | 2.06 | 43.2 | 46 | 11 |
| Dennys Reyes | 75 | 0 | 0–2 | 1 | 0 | 17 | 3.29 | 41.0 | 33 | 21 |
| Blake Hawksworth | 30 | 0 | 4–0 | 0 | 0 | 10 | 2.03 | 40.0 | 20 | 15 |
| *John Smoltz | 7 | 7 | 1–3 | 0 | 0 | 18 | 4.26 | 38.0 | 40 | 9 |
| *Chris Perez | 29 | 0 | 1–1 | 1 | 0 | 12 | 4.18 | 23.2 | 30 | 15 |

## San Diego Padres

| BATTING | G | AB | R | H | 2B | 3B | HR | RBI | TB | BB | SO | SB | OBP | SLG | BAVG |
|---|---|---|---|---|---|---|---|---|---|---|---|---|---|---|---|
| Adrian Gonzalez | 160 | 552 | 90 | 153 | 27 | 2 | 40 | 99 | 304 | 119 | 109 | 1 | .407 | .551 | .277 |
| Chase Headley | 156 | 543 | 62 | 142 | 31 | 2 | 12 | 64 | 213 | 62 | 133 | 10 | .342 | .392 | .262 |
| Kevin Kouzmanoff | 141 | 529 | 50 | 135 | 31 | 1 | 18 | 88 | 222 | 27 | 106 | 1 | .302 | .420 | .255 |
| David Eckstein | 136 | 503 | 64 | 131 | 27 | 2 | 3 | 51 | 168 | 39 | 46 | 3 | .323 | .334 | .260 |
| Tony Gwynn Jr. | 119 | 393 | 59 | 106 | 11 | 6 | 2 | 21 | 135 | 48 | 65 | 11 | .350 | .344 | .270 |
| Everth Cabrera | 103 | 377 | 59 | 96 | 18 | 8 | 2 | 31 | 136 | 46 | 88 | 25 | .342 | .361 | .255 |
| Will Venable | 95 | 293 | 38 | 75 | 14 | 2 | 12 | 38 | 129 | 25 | 89 | 6 | .323 | .440 | .256 |
| Nick Hundley | 78 | 256 | 23 | 61 | 15 | 2 | 8 | 30 | 104 | 28 | 76 | 5 | .313 | .406 | .238 |
| Brian Giles | 61 | 225 | 18 | 43 | 10 | 1 | 2 | 23 | 61 | 26 | 31 | 1 | .277 | .271 | .191 |
| Luis Rodriguez. | 93 | 208 | 18 | 42 | 6 | 0 | 2 | 16 | 54 | 37 | 23 | 1 | .319 | .260 | .202 |
| Henry Blanco | 67 | 204 | 21 | 48 | 12 | 0 | 6 | 16 | 78 | 26 | 50 | 0 | .320 | .382 | .235 |
| *Scott Hairston | 56 | 197 | 26 | 59 | 14 | 1 | 10 | 29 | 105 | 17 | 45 | 8 | .358 | .533 | .299 |
| Edgar Gonzalez | 82 | 153 | 16 | 33 | 8 | 2 | 4 | 18 | 57 | 11 | 36 | 1 | .278 | .373 | .216 |
| Kyle Blanks | 54 | 148 | 24 | 37 | 9 | 0 | 10 | 22 | 76 | 18 | 55 | 1 | .355 | .514 | .250 |
| Eliezer Alfonso | 37 | 114 | 6 | 20 | 3 | 0 | 2 | 8 | 29 | 3 | 34 | 0 | .197 | .254 | .175 |

| PITCHING | GP | GS | W–L | SV | SHO | R | ERA | IP | Ks | BB |
|---|---|---|---|---|---|---|---|---|---|---|
| Kevin Correia | 33 | 33 | 12–11 | 0 | 1 | 92 | 3.91 | 198.0 | 142 | 64 |
| *Chad Gaudin | 20 | 19 | 4–10 | 0 | 0 | 66 | 5.13 | 105.1 | 105 | 56 |
| Josh Geer | 19 | 17 | 1–7 | 0 | 0 | 73 | 5.96 | 102.2 | 54 | 23 |
| Edward Mujica | 67 | 4 | 3–5 | 2 | 0 | 47 | 3.94 | 93.2 | 76 | 19 |
| *Jake Peavy | 13 | 13 | 6–6 | 0 | 0 | 38 | 3.97 | 81.2 | 92 | 28 |
| Chris R. Young | 14 | 14 | 4–6 | 0 | 0 | 47 | 5.21 | 76.0 | 50 | 40 |
| Luke Gregerson | 72 | 0 | 2–4 | 1 | 0 | 29 | 3.24 | 75.0 | 93 | 31 |
| Tim Stauffer | 14 | 14 | 4–7 | 0 | 0 | 31 | 3.58 | 73.0 | 53 | 31 |
| Heath Bell | 68 | 0 | 6–4 | 42 | 0 | 21 | 2.71 | 69.2 | 79 | 24 |
| *Clayton Richard | 12 | 12 | 5–2 | 0 | 0 | 31 | 4.08 | 64.0 | 48 | 34 |
| Luis Perdomo | 35 | 0 | 1–0 | 0 | 0 | 36 | 4.80 | 60.0 | 55 | 34 |
| Mat Lantos | 10 | 10 | 4–5 | 0 | 0 | 29 | 4.62 | 50.2 | 39 | 23 |
| Wade LeBlanc | 9 | 9 | 3–1 | 0 | 0 | 19 | 3.69 | 46.1 | 30 | 19 |

*Mid-season trade.

## San Francisco Giants

| BATTING | G | AB | R | H | 2B | 3B | HR | RBI | TB | BB | SO | SB | OBP | SLG | BAVG |
|---|---|---|---|---|---|---|---|---|---|---|---|---|---|---|---|
| Pablo Sandoval | 153 | 572 | 79 | 189 | 44 | 5 | 25 | 90 | 318 | 52 | 83 | 5 | .387 | .556 | .330 |
| Randy Winn | 149 | 538 | 65 | 141 | 33 | 5 | 2 | 51 | 190 | 47 | 93 | 16 | .318 | .353 | .262 |
| Aaron Rowand | 144 | 499 | 61 | 130 | 30 | 2 | 15 | 64 | 209 | 30 | 125 | 4 | .319 | .419 | .261 |
| Bengie Molina | 132 | 491 | 52 | 130 | 25 | 1 | 20 | 80 | 217 | 13 | 68 | 0 | .285 | .442 | .265 |
| Edgar Renteria | 124 | 460 | 20 | 115 | 19 | 1 | 5 | 48 | 151 | 39 | 69 | 7 | .307 | .328 | .250 |
| Juan Uribe | 122 | 398 | 50 | 115 | 26 | 4 | 16 | 55 | 197 | 25 | 82 | 3 | .329 | .495 | .289 |
| Travis Ishikawa | 120 | 326 | 49 | 85 | 10 | 2 | 9 | 39 | 126 | 30 | 89 | 2 | .329 | .387 | .261 |
| Fred Lewis | 122 | 295 | 49 | 76 | 21 | 3 | 4 | 20 | 115 | 36 | 84 | 8 | .348 | .390 | .258 |
| Eugenio Velez | 84 | 285 | 40 | 76 | 13 | 5 | 5 | 31 | 114 | 16 | 55 | 11 | .308 | .400 | .267 |
| Nate Schierholtz | 116 | 285 | 33 | 76 | 19 | 2 | 5 | 29 | 114 | 16 | 58 | 3 | .302 | .400 | .267 |
| Emmanuel Burriss | 61 | 202 | 18 | 48 | 6 | 0 | 0 | 13 | 54 | 14 | 34 | 11 | .292 | .267 | .238 |
| Andres Torres | 75 | 152 | 30 | 41 | 6 | 8 | 6 | 23 | 81 | 16 | 45 | 6 | .343 | .533 | .270 |
| Eli Whiteside | 49 | 127 | 15 | 29 | 6 | 1 | 2 | 13 | 43 | 4 | 30 | 0 | .269 | .339 | .228 |
| Rich Aurilia | 60 | 122 | 10 | 26 | 2 | 0 | 2 | 16 | 34 | 8 | 24 | 0 | .256 | .279 | .213 |
| *Ryan Garko | 40 | 115 | 10 | 27 | 3 | 1 | 2 | 12 | 38 | 9 | 10 | 0 | .307 | .330 | .235 |
| *Freddy Sanchez | 25 | 102 | 11 | 29 | 1 | 0 | 1 | 7 | 33 | 2 | 16 | 0 | .295 | .324 | .284 |

| PITCHING | GP | GS | W–L | SV | SHO | R | ERA | IP | Ks | BB |
|---|---|---|---|---|---|---|---|---|---|---|
| Tim Lincecum | 32 | 32 | 15–7 | 0 | 2 | 69 | 2.48 | 225.1 | 261 | 68 |
| Matt Cain | 33 | 33 | 14–8 | 0 | 0 | 73 | 2.89 | 217.2 | 171 | 73 |
| Barry Zito | 33 | 33 | 10–13 | 0 | 0 | 89 | 4.03 | 192.0 | 154 | 81 |
| Jonathan Sanchez | 32 | 29 | 8–12 | 0 | 1 | 82 | 4.24 | 163.1 | 177 | 88 |
| Randy Johnson | 22 | 17 | 8–6 | 0 | 0 | 55 | 4.88 | 96.0 | 86 | 31 |
| Brian Wilson | 68 | 0 | 5–6 | 38 | 0 | 27 | 2.74 | 72.1 | 83 | 27 |
| Brandon Medders | 61 | 0 | 5–1 | 1 | 0 | 26 | 3.01 | 68.2 | 58 | 32 |
| Bob Howry | 63 | 0 | 2–6 | 0 | 0 | 26 | 3.39 | 63.2 | 46 | 23 |
| Jeremy Affeldt | 74 | 0 | 2–2 | 0 | 0 | 14 | 1.73 | 62.1 | 55 | 31 |
| Justin Miller | 44 | 0 | 3–3 | 0 | 0 | 20 | 3.18 | 56.2 | 36 | 27 |
| Merkin Valdez | 48 | 0 | 2–1 | 0 | 0 | 33 | 5.66 | 49.1 | 38 | 28 |
| *Brad Penny | 6 | 6 | 4–1 | 0 | 0 | 13 | 2.59 | 41.2 | 20 | 9 |
| Sergio Romo | 45 | 0 | 5–2 | 2 | 0 | 15 | 3.97 | 34.0 | 41 | 11 |

## Washington Nationals

| BATTING | G | AB | R | H | 2B | 3B | HR | RBI | TB | BB | SO | SB | OBP | SLG | BAVG |
|---|---|---|---|---|---|---|---|---|---|---|---|---|---|---|---|
| Ryan Zimmerman | 157 | 610 | 110 | 178 | 37 | 3 | 33 | 106 | 320 | 72 | 119 | 2 | .364 | .525 | .292 |
| Adam Dunn | 159 | 546 | 81 | 146 | 29 | 0 | 38 | 105 | 289 | 116 | 177 | 0 | .398 | .529 | .267 |
| Cristian Guzman | 135 | 531 | 74 | 151 | 24 | 7 | 6 | 52 | 207 | 16 | 75 | 4 | .306 | .390 | .284 |
| Josh Willingham | 133 | 427 | 70 | 111 | 29 | 0 | 24 | 61 | 212 | 61 | 104 | 4 | .367 | .496 | .260 |
| Elijah Dukes | 107 | 364 | 38 | 91 | 20 | 4 | 8 | 58 | 143 | 46 | 74 | 3 | .337 | .393 | .250 |
| *Nick Johnson | 98 | 353 | 47 | 104 | 16 | 2 | 6 | 44 | 142 | 63 | 66 | 2 | .408 | .402 | .295 |
| Willie Harris | 137 | 323 | 47 | 76 | 18 | 6 | 7 | 27 | 127 | 57 | 62 | 11 | .364 | .393 | .235 |
| Alberto Gonzalez | 105 | 291 | 31 | 77 | 16 | 3 | 1 | 33 | 102 | 14 | 27 | 1 | .299 | .351 | .265 |
| Josh Bard | 90 | 274 | 20 | 63 | 18 | 0 | 6 | 31 | 99 | 24 | 50 | 0 | .293 | .361 | .230 |
| *Anderson Hernandez | 77 | 231 | 25 | 58 | 9 | 2 | 1 | 23 | 74 | 20 | 41 | 5 | .310 | .320 | .251 |
| Wil Nieves | 72 | 224 | 20 | 58 | 6 | 0 | 1 | 26 | 67 | 17 | 45 | 1 | .313 | .299 | .259 |
| *Nyjer Morgan | 49 | 191 | 35 | 67 | 9 | 2 | 1 | 12 | 83 | 11 | 25 | 24 | .396 | .435 | .351 |
| *Ronnie Belliard | 86 | 187 | 26 | 46 | 7 | 1 | 5 | 22 | 70 | 14 | 40 | 2 | .296 | .374 | .246 |
| Austin Kearns | 80 | 174 | 20 | 34 | 6 | 2 | 3 | 17 | 53 | 32 | 51 | 1 | .336 | .305 | .195 |
| Jesus Flores | 29 | 93 | 13 | 28 | 3 | 2 | 4 | 15 | 47 | 11 | 26 | 0 | .371 | .505 | .301 |

| PITCHING | GP | GS | W–L | SV | SHO | R | ERA | IP | Ks | BB |
|---|---|---|---|---|---|---|---|---|---|---|
| John Lannan | 33 | 33 | 9–13 | 0 | 1 | 100 | 3.88 | 201.0 | 89 | 68 |
| Craig Stammen | 19 | 19 | 4–7 | 0 | 0 | 67 | 5.11 | 105.2 | 48 | 24 |
| Jordan Zimmerman | 16 | 16 | 3–5 | 0 | 0 | 51 | 4.63 | 91.1 | 92 | 29 |
| Garrett Mock | 28 | 15 | 3–10 | 0 | 0 | 65 | 5.62 | 91.1 | 72 | 44 |
| Shairon Mathis | 15 | 15 | 5–3 | 9 | 0 | 40 | 5.25 | 85.2 | 34 | 39 |
| J.D. Martin | 15 | 15 | 5–4 | 0 | 0 | 40 | 4.44 | 77.0 | 37 | 24 |
| Ross Detwiler | 15 | 14 | 1–6 | 0 | 0 | 43 | 5.00 | 75.2 | 43 | 33 |
| Scott Olsen | 11 | 11 | 2–4 | 0 | 0 | 45 | 6.03 | 62.2 | 42 | 25 |
| Tyler Clippard | 41 | 0 | 4–2 | 0 | 0 | 20 | 2.69 | 60.1 | 67 | 32 |
| *Mike MacDougal | 52 | 0 | 1–1 | 20 | 0 | 25 | 3.60 | 50.0 | 31 | 31 |
| Ron Villone | 63 | 0 | 5–6 | 1 | 0 | 25 | 4.25 | 48.2 | 33 | 29 |
| *Livan Hernandez | 8 | 8 | 2–4 | 0 | 0 | 29 | 5.36 | 48.2 | 27 | 16 |
| Jason Bergmann | 56 | 0 | 2–4 | 0 | 0 | 28 | 4.50 | 48.0 | 40 | 25 |
| *Daniel Cabrera | 9 | 8 | 0–5 | 0 | 0 | 39 | 5.85 | 40.0 | 16 | 35 |
| *Joe Beimel | 45 | 0 | 1–5 | 1 | 0 | 17 | 3.40 | 39.2 | 24 | 15 |

*Mid-season trade.

## Baltimore Orioles

| BATTING | G | AB | R | H | 2B | 3B | HR | RBI | TB | BB | SO | SB | OBP | SLG | BAVG |
|---|---|---|---|---|---|---|---|---|---|---|---|---|---|---|---|
| Nick Markakis | 161 | 642 | 94 | 188 | 45 | 2 | 18 | 101 | 291 | 56 | 98 | 6 | .347 | .453 | .293 |
| Brian Roberts | 159 | 632 | 110 | 179 | 56 | 1 | 16 | 79 | 285 | 74 | 112 | 30 | .356 | .451 | .283 |
| Adam Jones | 119 | 473 | 83 | 131 | 22 | 3 | 19 | 70 | 216 | 36 | 93 | 10 | .335 | .457 | .277 |
| Melvin Mora | 125 | 450 | 44 | 117 | 20 | 0 | 8 | 48 | 161 | 34 | 60 | 3 | .321 | .358 | .260 |
| Luke Scott | 128 | 449 | 61 | 116 | 26 | 1 | 25 | 77 | 219 | 55 | 104 | 0 | .340 | .488 | .258 |
| *Aubrey Huff | 110 | 430 | 51 | 109 | 24 | 1 | 13 | 72 | 174 | 41 | 74 | 0 | .321 | .405 | .253 |
| Ty Wigginton | 122 | 410 | 44 | 112 | 19 | 0 | 11 | 41 | 164 | 23 | 57 | 1 | .314 | .400 | .273 |
| Cesar Izturis | 114 | 387 | 34 | 99 | 14 | 4 | 2 | 30 | 127 | 18 | 38 | 12 | .294 | .328 | .256 |
| Nolan Reimold | 104 | 358 | 49 | 100 | 18 | 2 | 15 | 45 | 167 | 47 | 77 | 8 | .365 | .466 | .279 |
| Matt Wieters | 96 | 354 | 35 | 102 | 15 | 1 | 9 | 43 | 146 | 28 | 86 | 0 | .340 | .412 | .288 |
| Felix Pie | 101 | 252 | 38 | 67 | 10 | 3 | 9 | 29 | 110 | 24 | 58 | 1 | .326 | .437 | .266 |
| Robert Andino | 78 | 198 | 31 | 44 | 7 | 0 | 2 | 10 | 57 | 15 | 47 | 3 | .274 | .288 | .222 |
| *Gregg Zaun | 56 | 168 | 23 | 41 | 10 | 0 | 4 | 13 | 63 | 27 | 30 | 0 | .355 | .375 | .244 |
| Michael Aubrey | 31 | 90 | 12 | 26 | 7 | 0 | 4 | 14 | 45 | 5 | 10 | 0 | .326 | .500 | .289 |

| PITCHING | GP | GS | W–L | SV | SHO | R | ERA | IP | Ks | BB |
|---|---|---|---|---|---|---|---|---|---|---|
| Jeremy Guthrie | 33 | 33 | 10–17 | 0 | 0 | 120 | 5.04 | 200.0 | 110 | 60 |
| Brad Bergesen | 19 | 19 | 7–5 | 0 | 0 | 52 | 3.43 | 123.1 | 65 | 32 |
| Jason Berken | 24 | 24 | 6–12 | 0 | 0 | 92 | 6.54 | 119.2 | 66 | 44 |
| Mark Hendrickson | 53 | 11 | 6–5 | 1 | 0 | 59 | 4.37 | 105.0 | 61 | 33 |
| Daniel Hernandez | 20 | 19 | 4–10 | 0 | 0 | 62 | 5.42 | 101.1 | 68 | 46 |
| Brian Bass | 48 | 0 | 5–3 | 0 | 0 | 52 | 4.90 | 86.1 | 54 | 44 |
| Danys Baez | 59 | 0 | 4–6 | 0 | 0 | 36 | 4.02 | 71.2 | 40 | 22 |
| Jim Johnson | 64 | 0 | 4–6 | 10 | 0 | 32 | 4.11 | 70.0 | 49 | 23 |
| Matt Albers | 56 | 0 | 3–6 | 0 | 0 | 43 | 5.51 | 67.0 | 49 | 36 |
| Koji Uehara | 12 | 12 | 2–4 | 0 | 0 | 33 | 4.05 | 66.2 | 48 | 12 |
| Chris Tillman | 12 | 12 | 2–5 | 0 | 0 | 40 | 5.40 | 65.0 | 39 | 24 |
| Rich Hill | 14 | 13 | 3–3 | 0 | 0 | 53 | 7.80 | 57.2 | 46 | 40 |
| Brian Matusz | 8 | 8 | 5–2 | 0 | 0 | 24 | 4.63 | 44.2 | 38 | 14 |
| Chris Ray | 46 | 0 | 0–4 | 0 | 0 | 36 | 7.27 | 43.1 | 39 | 23 |
| *George Sherrill | 42 | 0 | 0–1 | 20 | 0 | 11 | 2.40 | 41.1 | 39 | 13 |
| *Adam Eaton | 8 | 8 | 2–5 | 0 | 0 | 39 | 8.56 | 41.0 | 28 | 19 |

## Boston Red Sox

| BATTING | G | AB | R | H | 2B | 3B | HR | RBI | TB | BB | SO | SB | OBP | SLG | BAVG |
|---|---|---|---|---|---|---|---|---|---|---|---|---|---|---|---|
| Dustin Pedroia | 154 | 626 | 115 | 185 | 48 | 1 | 15 | 72 | 280 | 74 | 45 | 20 | .371 | .447 | .296 |
| Jacoby Ellsbury | 153 | 624 | 94 | 188 | 27 | 10 | 8 | 60 | 259 | 49 | 74 | 70 | .355 | .415 | .301 |
| David Ortiz | 150 | 541 | 77 | 129 | 35 | 1 | 28 | 99 | 250 | 74 | 134 | 0 | .332 | .462 | 238 |
| Jason Bay | 151 | 531 | 103 | 142 | 29 | 3 | 36 | 119 | 285 | 94 | 162 | 13 | .384 | .537 | .267 |
| Kevin Youkilis | 136 | 491 | 99 | 150 | 36 | 1 | 27 | 94 | 269 | 77 | 125 | 7 | .413 | .548 | .305 |
| J.D. Drew | 137 | 452 | 84 | 126 | 30 | 4 | 24 | 68 | 236 | 82 | 109 | 2 | .392 | .522 | .279 |
| Mike Lowell | 119 | 445 | 54 | 129 | 29 | 1 | 17 | 75 | 211 | 33 | 61 | 2 | .337 | .474 | .290 |
| Jason Varitek | 109 | 364 | 41 | 76 | 24 | 0 | 14 | 51 | 142 | 54 | 90 | 0 | .313 | .390 | .209 |
| Nick Green | 104 | 276 | 35 | 65 | 18 | 0 | 6 | 35 | 101 | 20 | 69 | 1 | .303 | .366 | .236 |
| *Victor Martinez | 56 | 211 | 32 | 71 | 12 | 0 | 8 | 41 | 107 | 24 | 23 | 1 | .405 | .507 | .336 |
| Rocco Baldelli | 62 | 150 | 23 | 38 | 4 | 1 | 7 | 23 | 65 | 11 | 37 | 1 | .311 | .433 | .253 |
| *Alex Gonzalez | 44 | 148 | 26 | 42 | 10 | 0 | 5 | 15 | 67 | 5 | 29 | 2 | .316 | .453 | .284 |
| *Julio Lugo | 37 | 109 | 16 | 31 | 4 | 1 | 1 | 8 | 40 | 12 | 18 | 3 | .352 | .367 | .284 |
| George Kottaras | 45 | 93 | 15 | 22 | 11 | 0 | 1 | 10 | 36 | 11 | 25 | 0 | .308 | .387 | .237 |
| *Casey Kotchman | 39 | 87 | 9 | 19 | 13 | 0 | 1 | 7 | 25 | 7 | 14 | 1 | .284 | .287 | 218 |

| PITCHING | GP | GS | W–L | SV | SHO | R | ERA | IP | Ks | BB |
|---|---|---|---|---|---|---|---|---|---|---|
| Josh Beckett | 32 | 32 | 17–6 | 0 | 2 | 99 | 3.86 | 212.1 | 199 | 55 |
| Jon Lester | 32 | 32 | 15–8 | 0 | 0 | 80 | 3.41 | 203.1 | 225 | 64 |
| *Brad Penny | 24 | 24 | 7–8 | 0 | 0 | 89 | 5.61 | 131.2 | 89 | 42 |
| Tim Wakefield | 21 | 21 | 11–5 | 0 | 0 | 67 | 4.58 | 129.2 | 72 | 50 |
| Clay Buchholz | 16 | 16 | 7–4 | 0 | 0 | 44 | 4.21 | 92.0 | 68 | 36 |
| *Justin Masterson | 31 | 6 | 3–3 | 0 | 0 | 38 | 4.50 | 72.0 | 67 | 25 |
| Ramon Rodriguez | 70 | 0 | 7–4 | 0 | 0 | 26 | 2.84 | 69.2 | 52 | 32 |
| Jonathan Papelbon | 66 | 0 | 1–1 | 38 | 0 | 15 | 1.85 | 68.0 | 76 | 24 |
| Hideki Okajima | 68 | 0 | 6–0 | 0 | 0 | 23 | 3.39 | 61.0 | 53 | 21 |
| Manny Delcarmen | 64 | 0 | 5–2 | 0 | 0 | 34 | 4.53 | 59.2 | 44 | 34 |
| Daisuke Matsuzaka | 12 | 12 | 4–6 | 0 | 0 | 38 | 5.76 | 59.1 | 54 | 30 |
| Takashi Saito | 56 | 0 | 3–3 | 2 | 0 | 16 | 2.43 | 55.2 | 52 | 25 |
| Daniel Bard | 49 | 0 | 2–2 | 1 | 0 | 24 | 3.65 | 49.1 | 63 | 22 |
| *John Smoltz | 8 | 8 | 2–5 | 0 | 0 | 37 | 8.33 | 40.0 | 33 | 9 |
| Paul Byrd | 7 | 6 | 1–3 | 0 | 0 | 22 | 5.82 | 34.0 | 11 | 11 |

*Mid-season trade.

## Chicago White Sox

| BATTING | G | AB | R | H | 2B | 3B | HR | RBI | TB | BB | SO | SB | OBP | SLG | BAVG |
|---|---|---|---|---|---|---|---|---|---|---|---|---|---|---|---|
| Paul Konerko | 152 | 546 | 75 | 151 | 30 | 1 | 28 | 88 | 267 | 58 | 89 | 1 | .353 | .489 | .277 |
| Alexei Ramirez | 148 | 542 | 71 | 150 | 14 | 1 | 15 | 68 | 211 | 49 | 66 | 14 | .333 | .389 | .277 |
| Scott Podsednik | 132 | 537 | 75 | 163 | 25 | 6 | 7 | 48 | 221 | 39 | 74 | 30 | .353 | .412 | .304 |
| A.J. Pierzynski | 138 | 504 | 57 | 151 | 22 | 1 | 13 | 49 | 214 | 24 | 52 | 1 | .331 | .425 | .300 |
| Jermaine Dye | 141 | 503 | 78 | 126 | 19 | 1 | 27 | 81 | 228 | 64 | 108 | 0 | .340 | .453 | .250 |
| Gordon Beckham | 103 | 378 | 58 | 102 | 28 | 1 | 14 | 63 | 174 | 41 | 65 | 7 | .347 | .460 | .270 |
| Chris Getz | 107 | 375 | 49 | 98 | 18 | 4 | 2 | 31 | 130 | 30 | 54 | 25 | .324 | .347 | .261 |
| Carlos Quentin | 99 | 351 | 47 | 83 | 14 | 0 | 21 | 56 | 160 | 31 | 52 | 3 | .323 | .456 | .236 |
| *Jim Thome | 107 | 345 | 55 | 86 | 15 | 0 | 23 | 74 | 170 | 69 | 116 | 0 | .372 | .493 | .249 |
| Jayson Nix | 94 | 255 | 36 | 57 | 11 | 0 | 12 | 32 | 104 | 28 | 64 | 10 | .308 | .408 | .224 |
| Josh Fields | 79 | 239 | 29 | 53 | 5 | 2 | 7 | 30 | 83 | 25 | 76 | 2 | .301 | .347 | .222 |
| *Brian Anderson | 65 | 185 | 25 | 44 | 9 | 0 | 2 | 13 | 59 | 20 | 49 | 3 | .322 | .319 | .238 |
| *Alex Rios | 41 | 146 | 11 | 29 | 6 | 0 | 3 | 9 | 44 | 6 | 29 | 5 | .229 | .301 | .199 |
| Dewayne Wise | 84 | 142 | 17 | 32 | 8 | 3 | 2 | 11 | 52 | 3 | 27 | 4 | .262 | .366 | .225 |
| *Mark Kotsay | 40 | 113 | 12 | 33 | 7 | 0 | 3 | 18 | 49 | 11 | 9 | 1 | .349 | .434 | .292 |

| PITCHING | GP | GS | W–L | SV | SHO | R | ERA | IP | Ks | BB |
|---|---|---|---|---|---|---|---|---|---|---|
| Mark Buehrle | 33 | 33 | 13–10 | 0 | 1 | 97 | 3.84 | 213.1 | 105 | 45 |
| John Danks | 32 | 32 | 13–11 | 0 | 0 | 89 | 3.77 | 200.1 | 149 | 73 |
| Gavin Floyd | 30 | 30 | 11–11 | 0 | 0 | 93 | 4.06 | 193.0 | 163 | 59 |
| *Jose Contreras | 21 | 21 | 5–13 | 0 | 0 | 83 | 5.42 | 114.2 | 89 | 45 |
| D.J. Carrasco | 49 | 1 | 5–1 | 0 | 0 | 42 | 3.76 | 93.1 | 62 | 29 |
| *Clayton Richard | 26 | 14 | 4–3 | 0 | 0 | 50 | 4.65 | 89.0 | 66 | 37 |
| Matt Thornton | 70 | 0 | 6–3 | 4 | 0 | 22 | 2.74 | 72.1 | 87 | 20 |
| Octavio Dotel | 62 | 0 | 3–3 | 0 | 0 | 26 | 3.32 | 62.1 | 75 | 36 |
| Bartolo Colon | 12 | 12 | 3–6 | 0 | 0 | 42 | 4.19 | 62.1 | 38 | 21 |
| Scott Linebrink | 57 | 0 | 3–7 | 2 | 0 | 34 | 4.66 | 56.0 | 55 | 23 |
| Freddy Garcia | 9 | 9 | 3–4 | 0 | 0 | 27 | 4.34 | 56.0 | 37 | 12 |
| Bobby Jenks | 52 | 0 | 3–4 | 29 | 0 | 24 | 3.71 | 53.1 | 49 | 16 |
| *Tony Pena | 35 | 0 | 1–2 | 1 | 0 | 17 | 3.75 | 36.0 | 29 | 9 |
| Carlos Torres | 8 | 5 | 1–2 | 0 | 0 | 20 | 6.04 | 28.1 | 22 | 17 |
| *Jake Peavy | 3 | 3 | 3–0 | 0 | 0 | 3 | 1.35 | 20.0 | 18 | 6 |

## Cleveland Indians

| BATTING | G | AB | R | H | 2B | 3B | HR | RBI | TB | BB | SO | SB | OBP | SLG | BAVG |
|---|---|---|---|---|---|---|---|---|---|---|---|---|---|---|---|
| Shin-Soo Choo | 156 | 583 | 87 | 175 | 38 | 6 | 20 | 86 | 285 | 78 | 151 | 21 | .394 | .489 | .300 |
| Jhonny Peralta | 151 | 582 | 57 | 148 | 35 | 1 | 11 | 83 | 218 | 51 | 134 | 0 | .316 | .375 | .254 |
| Asdrubal Cabrera | 131 | 523 | 81 | 161 | 42 | 4 | 6 | 68 | 229 | 44 | 89 | 17 | .361 | .438 | .308 |
| Grady Sizemore | 106 | 436 | 73 | 108 | 20 | 6 | 18 | 64 | 194 | 60 | 92 | 13 | .343 | .445 | .248 |
| *Victor Martinez | 99 | 377 | 56 | 107 | 21 | 1 | 15 | 67 | 175 | 51 | 51 | 0 | .368 | .464 | .284 |
| Luis Valbuena | 103 | 368 | 52 | 92 | 25 | 3 | 10 | 31 | 153 | 26 | 83 | 2 | .298 | .416 | .250 |
| Travis Hafner | 94 | 338 | 46 | 92 | 19 | 0 | 16 | 49 | 159 | 41 | 67 | 0 | .355 | .470 | .272 |
| Jamey Carroll | 93 | 315 | 53 | 87 | 10 | 2 | 2 | 26 | 107 | 36 | 63 | 4 | .355 | .340 | .276 |
| *Ben Francisco | 89 | 308 | 48 | 77 | 21 | 1 | 10 | 33 | 130 | 33 | 59 | 13 | .336 | .422 | .250 |
| Mark DeRosa | 71 | 278 | 47 | 75 | 13 | 0 | 13 | 50 | 127 | 29 | 63 | 1 | .342 | .457 | .270 |
| Kelly Shoppach | 89 | 271 | 33 | 58 | 14 | 0 | 12 | 40 | 108 | 33 | 98 | 0 | .335 | .399 | .214 |
| *Ryan Garko | 78 | 239 | 29 | 68 | 10 | 0 | 11 | 39 | 111 | 20 | 40 | 0 | .362 | .464 | .285 |
| Trevor Crowe | 68 | 183 | 22 | 43 | 9 | 3 | 1 | 17 | 61 | 11 | 39 | 6 | .278 | .333 | .235 |
| Matt LaPorta | 52 | 181 | 29 | 46 | 13 | 0 | 7 | 21 | 80 | 12 | 37 | 2 | .308 | .442 | .254 |
| Andy Marte | 47 | 155 | 20 | 36 | 6 | 1 | 6 | 25 | 62 | 14 | 30 | 0 | .293 | .400 | .232 |

| PITCHING | GP | GS | W–L | SV | SHO | R | ERA | IP | Ks | BB |
|---|---|---|---|---|---|---|---|---|---|---|
| *Cliff Lee | 22 | 22 | 7–9 | 0 | 1 | 53 | 3.14 | 152.0 | 107 | 33 |
| David Huff | 23 | 23 | 11–8 | 0 | 0 | 82 | 5.61 | 128.1 | 65 | 41 |
| *Carl Pavano | 21 | 21 | 9–8 | 0 | 0 | 80 | 5.37 | 125.2 | 88 | 23 |
| Fausto Carmona | 24 | 24 | 5–12 | 0 | 0 | 97 | 6.32 | 125.1 | 79 | 70 |
| Jeremy Sowers | 23 | 22 | 6–11 | 0 | 0 | 73 | 5.25 | 123.1 | 51 | 52 |
| Aaron Laffey | 25 | 19 | 7–9 | 1 | 0 | 69 | 4.44 | 121.2 | 59 | 57 |
| Tomo Ohka | 18 | 6 | 1–5 | 0 | 0 | 47 | 5.96 | 71.0 | 31 | 19 |
| Jensen Lewis | 47 | 0 | 2–4 | 1 | 0 | 37 | 4.61 | 66.1 | 62 | 29 |
| *Justin Masterson | 11 | 10 | 1–7 | 0 | 0 | 73 | 4.55 | 57.1 | 52 | 35 |
| Kerry Wood | 58 | 0 | 3–3 | 20 | 0 | 26 | 4.25 | 55.0 | 63 | 28 |
| Rafael Perez | 54 | 0 | 4–3 | 0 | 0 | 41 | 7.31 | 48.0 | 32 | 25 |
| Tony Sipp | 46 | 0 | 2–0 | 0 | 0 | 16 | 2.93 | 40.0 | 48 | 25 |
| Anthony Reyes | 8 | 8 | 1–1 | 0 | 0 | 30 | 6.57 | 38.1 | 22 | 23 |
| Joe Smith | 37 | 0 | 0–0 | 0 | 0 | 16 | 3.44 | 34.0 | 30 | 13 |
| *Chris Perez | 32 | 0 | 0–1 | 1 | 0 | 16 | 4.32 | 33.1 | 38 | 12 |
| *Rafael Betancourt | 29 | 0 | 1–2 | 1 | 0 | 15 | 3.52 | 30.2 | 32 | 15 |

*Mid-season trade.

## Detroit Tigers

| BATTING | G | AB | R | H | 2B | 3B | HR | RBI | TB | BB | SO | SB | OBP | SLG | BAVG |
|---|---|---|---|---|---|---|---|---|---|---|---|---|---|---|---|
| Curtis Granderson | 160 | 631 | 91 | 157 | 23 | 8 | 30 | 71 | 286 | 72 | 141 | 20 | .327 | .453 | .249 |
| Placido Polanco | 153 | 618 | 82 | 176 | 31 | 4 | 10 | 72 | 245 | 36 | 46 | 7 | .331 | .396 | .285 |
| Miguel Cabrera | 160 | 611 | 96 | 198 | 34 | 0 | 34 | 103 | 334 | 68 | 107 | 6 | .396 | .547 | .324 |
| Brandon Inge | 161 | 562 | 71 | 129 | 16 | 1 | 27 | 84 | 228 | 54 | 170 | 2 | .314 | .406 | .230 |
| Magglio Ordonez | 131 | 465 | 64 | 144 | 24 | 2 | 9 | 50 | 199 | 51 | 65 | 3 | .376 | .428 | .310 |
| Gerald Laird | 135 | 413 | 49 | 93 | 23 | 2 | 4 | 33 | 132 | 40 | 68 | 5 | .306 | .320 | .225 |
| Adam Everett | 118 | 345 | 43 | 82 | 21 | 0 | 3 | 44 | 112 | 22 | 61 | 5 | .288 | .325 | .238 |
| Carlos Guillen | 81 | 277 | 36 | 67 | 10 | 3 | 11 | 41 | 116 | 39 | 56 | 1 | .339 | .419 | .242 |
| Clete Thomas | 102 | 275 | 46 | 66 | 13 | 3 | 7 | 39 | 106 | 33 | 77 | 3 | .324 | .385 | .240 |
| Ramon Santiago | 93 | 262 | 29 | 70 | 6 | 2 | 7 | 35 | 101 | 17 | 57 | 1 | .318 | .385 | .267 |
| Ryan Raburn | 113 | 261 | 44 | 76 | 11 | 2 | 16 | 45 | 139 | 26 | 60 | 5 | .259 | .533 | .291 |
| Marcus Thames | 87 | 258 | 33 | 65 | 11 | 1 | 13 | 36 | 117 | 29 | 72 | 0 | .323 | .453 | .252 |
| *Josh Anderson | 74 | 165 | 22 | 40 | 4 | 4 | 0 | 16 | 52 | 8 | 22 | 13 | .282 | .315 | .242 |
| *Aubrey Huff | 40 | 106 | 8 | 20 | 6 | 0 | 2 | 13 | 32 | 10 | 13 | 0 | .265 | .302 | .189 |

| PITCHING | GP | GS | W-L | SV | SHO | R | ERA | IP | Ks | BB |
|---|---|---|---|---|---|---|---|---|---|---|
| Justin Verlander | 35 | 35 | 19-9 | 0 | 1 | 99 | 3.45 | 240.0 | 269 | 63 |
| Edwin Jackson | 33 | 33 | 13-9 | 0 | 0 | 93 | 3.62 | 214.0 | 161 | 70 |
| Rick Porcello | 31 | 31 | 14-9 | 0 | 1 | 81 | 3.96 | 170.2 | 89 | 52 |
| Armando Galarraga | 29 | 25 | 6-10 | 0 | 0 | 93 | 5.64 | 143.2 | 95 | 67 |
| Zach Miner | 51 | 5 | 7-5 | 1 | 0 | 49 | 4.29 | 92.1 | 62 | 45 |
| Brandon Lyon | 65 | 0 | 6-5 | 3 | 0 | 25 | 2.86 | 78.2 | 57 | 31 |
| Fernando Rodney | 73 | 0 | 2-5 | 37 | 0 | 38 | 4.40 | 75.2 | 61 | 41 |
| Ryan Perry | 53 | 0 | 0-1 | 0 | 0 | 30 | 3.79 | 61.2 | 60 | 38 |
| Nate Robertson | 28 | 6 | 2-3 | 0 | 0 | 33 | 5.44 | 49.2 | 35 | 28 |
| Bobby Seay | 67 | 0 | 6-3 | 0 | 0 | 23 | 4.25 | 48.2 | 37 | 17 |
| *Jarrod Washburn | 8 | 8 | 1-3 | 0 | 0 | 35 | 7.33 | 43.0 | 21 | 16 |
| Eddie Bonine | 10 | 4 | 1-1 | 0 | 0 | 19 | 4.46 | 34.1 | 19 | 12 |
| Dontrelle Willis | 7 | 7 | 1-4 | 0 | 0 | 28 | 7.49 | 33.2 | 17 | 28 |
| Joel Zumaya | 29 | 0 | 3-3 | 1 | 0 | 18 | 4.94 | 31.0 | 30 | 22 |

## Kansas City Royals

| BATTING | G | AB | R | H | 2B | 3B | HR | RBI | TB | BB | SO | SB | OBP | SLG | BAVG |
|---|---|---|---|---|---|---|---|---|---|---|---|---|---|---|---|
| Billy Butler | 159 | 608 | 78 | 183 | 51 | 1 | 21 | 93 | 299 | 58 | 103 | 1 | .362 | .492 | .301 |
| Alberto Callaspo | 155 | 576 | 79 | 173 | 41 | 8 | 11 | 73 | 263 | 52 | 51 | 2 | .356 | .457 | .300 |
| David DeJesus | 144 | 558 | 74 | 157 | 28 | 9 | 13 | 71 | 242 | 51 | 87 | 4 | .347 | .434 | .281 |
| Mark Teahen | 144 | 524 | 69 | 145 | 34 | 1 | 12 | 50 | 214 | 37 | 123 | 8 | .325 | .408 | .271 |
| Willie Bloomquist | 125 | 434 | 52 | 115 | 11 | 8 | 4 | 29 | 154 | 27 | 73 | 25 | .308 | .355 | .265 |
| Mike Jacobs | 128 | 434 | 46 | 99 | 16 | 1 | 19 | 61 | 174 | 41 | 132 | 0 | .297 | .401 | .228 |
| Miguel Olivo | 114 | 390 | 51 | 97 | 15 | 5 | 23 | 65 | 191 | 19 | 126 | 5 | .292 | .490 | .249 |
| Mitch Maier | 127 | 341 | 42 | 83 | 15 | 3 | 3 | 31 | 113 | 43 | 76 | 9 | .333 | .331 | .243 |
| Jose Guillen | 81 | 281 | 30 | 68 | 8 | 0 | 9 | 40 | 103 | 22 | 50 | 1 | .314 | .367 | .242 |
| *Yuniesky Betancourt | 71 | 246 | 25 | 59 | 10 | 5 | 4 | 27 | 91 | 11 | 26 | 0 | .269 | .370 | .240 |
| John Buck | 59 | 186 | 16 | 46 | 12 | 4 | 8 | 36 | 90 | 13 | 55 | 1 | .299 | .484 | .247 |
| Coco Crisp | 49 | 180 | 30 | 41 | 8 | 5 | 3 | 14 | 68 | 29 | 23 | 13 | .336 | .378 | .228 |
| Brayan Pena | 64 | 165 | 17 | 45 | 10 | 0 | 6 | 18 | 73 | 12 | 18 | 0 | .318 | .442 | .273 |
| Alex Gordon | 49 | 164 | 28 | 38 | 6 | 0 | 6 | 22 | 62 | 21 | 43 | 5 | .324 | .378 | .232 |
| Mike Aviles | 36 | 120 | 10 | 22 | 3 | 1 | 1 | 8 | 30 | 4 | 26 | 1 | .208 | .250 | .183 |
| *Josh Anderson | 44 | 118 | 20 | 28 | 3 | 0 | 1 | 8 | 34 | 5 | 21 | 12 | .268 | .288 | .237 |

| PITCHING | GP | GS | W-L | SV | SHO | R | ERA | IP | Ks | BB |
|---|---|---|---|---|---|---|---|---|---|---|
| Zack Greinke | 33 | 33 | 16-8 | 0 | 3 | 64 | 2.16 | 229.1 | 242 | 51 |
| Brian Bannister | 26 | 26 | 7-12 | 0 | 0 | 94 | 4.73 | 154.0 | 98 | 50 |
| Luke Hochevar | 25 | 25 | 7-13 | 0 | 1 | 109 | 6.55 | 143.0 | 106 | 46 |
| Gil Meche | 23 | 23 | 6-10 | 0 | 1 | 81 | 5.09 | 129.0 | 95 | 58 |
| Kyle Davies | 22 | 22 | 8-9 | 0 | 0 | 76 | 5.27 | 123.0 | 86 | 66 |
| Jamey Wright | 65 | 0 | 3-5 | 0 | 0 | 51 | 4.33 | 79.0 | 60 | 44 |
| Robinson Tejeda | 35 | 6 | 4-2 | 0 | 0 | 30 | 3.54 | 73.2 | 87 | 50 |
| Bruce Chen | 17 | 9 | 1-6 | 0 | 0 | 42 | 5.78 | 62.1 | 45 | 25 |
| Sidney Ponson | 14 | 9 | 1-7 | 0 | 0 | 50 | 7.36 | 58.2 | 32 | 25 |
| Joakim Soria | 47 | 0 | 3-2 | 30 | 0 | 14 | 2.21 | 53.0 | 69 | 16 |
| Juan Cruz | 46 | 0 | 3-4 | 2 | 0 | 34 | 5.72 | 50.1 | 38 | 29 |
| Roman Colon | 43 | 0 | 2-3 | 0 | 0 | 27 | 4.83 | 50.1 | 29 | 22 |
| *Ron Mahay | 41 | 0 | 1-1 | 0 | 0 | 26 | 4.79 | 41.1 | 34 | 19 |
| Kyle Farnsworth | 41 | 0 | 1-5 | 0 | 0 | 22 | 4.58 | 37.1 | 42 | 14 |

*Mid-season trade.

## Los Angeles Angels of Anaheim

| BATTING | G | AB | R | H | 2B | 3B | HR | RBI | TB | BB | SO | SB | OBP | SLG | BAVG |
|---|---|---|---|---|---|---|---|---|---|---|---|---|---|---|---|
| Chone Figgins | 158 | 615 | 114 | 183 | 30 | 7 | 5 | 54 | 242 | 101 | 114 | 42 | .395 | .393 | .298 |
| Kendry Morales | 152 | 566 | 86 | 173 | 43 | 2 | 34 | 108 | 322 | 46 | 117 | 3 | .355 | .569 | .306 |
| Bobby Abreu | 152 | 563 | 96 | 165 | 29 | 3 | 15 | 103 | 245 | 94 | 113 | 30 | .390 | .435 | .293 |
| Juan Rivera | 138 | 529 | 72 | 152 | 24 | 1 | 25 | 88 | 253 | 36 | 57 | 0 | .332 | .478 | .287 |
| Erick Aybar | 137 | 504 | 70 | 157 | 23 | 9 | 5 | 58 | 213 | 30 | 54 | 14 | .353 | .423 | .312 |
| Torii Hunter | 119 | 451 | 74 | 135 | 26 | 1 | 22 | 90 | 229 | 47 | 92 | 18 | .366 | .508 | .299 |
| Maicer Izturis | 114 | 387 | 74 | 116 | 22 | 3 | 8 | 65 | 168 | 35 | 41 | 13 | .359 | .434 | .300 |
| Vladimir Guerrero | 100 | 383 | 59 | 113 | 16 | 1 | 15 | 50 | 176 | 19 | 56 | 2 | .334 | .460 | .295 |
| Mike Napoli | 114 | 382 | 60 | 104 | 22 | 1 | 20 | 56 | 188 | 40 | 103 | 3 | .350 | .492 | .272 |
| Howie Kendrick | 105 | 374 | 61 | 109 | 21 | 3 | 10 | 61 | 166 | 20 | 71 | 11 | .334 | .444 | .291 |
| Gary Matthews Jr. | 103 | 316 | 44 | 79 | 19 | 2 | 4 | 50 | 114 | 40 | 74 | 4 | .336 | .361 | .250 |
| Jeff Mathis | 84 | 237 | 26 | 50 | 8 | 0 | 5 | 28 | 73 | 22 | 73 | 2 | .288 | .308 | .211 |
| Robb Quinlan | 54 | 115 | 13 | 28 | 5 | 0 | 2 | 14 | 39 | 5 | 30 | 1 | .275 | .339 | .243 |
| Reggie Willits | 49 | 80 | 16 | 17 | 2 | 0 | 0 | 6 | 19 | 5 | 17 | 5 | .256 | .238 | .213 |

| PITCHING | GP | GS | W–L | SV | SHO | R | ERA | IP | Ks | BB |
|---|---|---|---|---|---|---|---|---|---|---|
| Jered Weaver | 33 | 33 | 16–8 | 0 | 2 | 91 | 3.75 | 211.0 | 174 | 66 |
| Joe Saunders | 31 | 31 | 16–7 | 0 | 1 | 102 | 4.60 | 186.0 | 101 | 64 |
| John Lackey | 27 | 27 | 11–8 | 0 | 1 | 84 | 3.83 | 176.1 | 139 | 47 |
| Ervin Santana | 24 | 23 | 8–8 | 0 | 2 | 83 | 5.03 | 139.2 | 107 | 47 |
| Matt Palmer | 40 | 13 | 11–2 | 0 | 0 | 55 | 3.93 | 121.0 | 69 | 55 |
| Darren Oliver | 63 | 1 | 5–1 | 0 | 0 | 22 | 2.71 | 73.0 | 65 | 22 |
| Jason Bulger | 64 | 0 | 6–1 | 1 | 0 | 26 | 3.56 | 65.2 | 68 | 30 |
| Shane Loux | 18 | 6 | 2–3 | 0 | 0 | 42 | 5.86 | 58.1 | 19 | 19 |
| Brian Fuentes | 65 | 0 | 1–5 | 48 | 0 | 24 | 3.93 | 55.0 | 46 | 24 |
| Kevin Jepsen | 54 | 0 | 6–4 | 1 | 0 | 33 | 4.94 | 54.2 | 48 | 19 |
| Sean O'Sullivan | 12 | 10 | 4–2 | 0 | 0 | 34 | 5.92 | 51.2 | 29 | 16 |
| Jose Arredondo | 43 | 0 | 2–3 | 0 | 0 | 30 | 6.00 | 45.0 | 47 | 23 |
| Justin Speier | 41 | 0 | 4–2 | 0 | 0 | 33 | 5.18 | 40.0 | 39 | 15 |
| *Scott Kazmir | 6 | 6 | 2–2 | 0 | 0 | 8 | 1.73 | 36.1 | 26 | 10 |

## Minnesota Twins

| BATTING | G | AB | R | H | 2B | 3B | HR | RBI | TB | BB | SO | SB | OBP | SLG | BAVG |
|---|---|---|---|---|---|---|---|---|---|---|---|---|---|---|---|
| Michael Cuddyer | 153 | 588 | 93 | 162 | 34 | 7 | 32 | 94 | 306 | 54 | 118 | 6 | .342 | .520 | .276 |
| Denard Span | 145 | 578 | 97 | 180 | 16 | 10 | 8 | 68 | 240 | 70 | 89 | 23 | .392 | .415 | .311 |
| Joe Mauer | 138 | 523 | 94 | 191 | 30 | 1 | 28 | 96 | 307 | 76 | 63 | 4 | .444 | .587 | .365 |
| Jason Kubel | 146 | 514 | 73 | 154 | 35 | 2 | 28 | 103 | 277 | 56 | 106 | 1 | .369 | .539 | .300 |
| Justin Morneau | 135 | 508 | 85 | 139 | 31 | 1 | 30 | 100 | 262 | 72 | 86 | 0 | .363 | .516 | .274 |
| Brendan Harris | 123 | 414 | 44 | 108 | 22 | 1 | 6 | 37 | 150 | 29 | 78 | 0 | .310 | .362 | .261 |
| Delmon Young | 180 | 395 | 50 | 112 | 16 | 2 | 12 | 60 | 168 | 12 | 92 | 2 | .308 | .425 | .284 |
| Nick Punto | 125 | 359 | 56 | 82 | 15 | 1 | 1 | 38 | 102 | 61 | 70 | 16 | .337 | .284 | .228 |
| Joe Crede | 90 | 333 | 42 | 75 | 16 | 1 | 15 | 48 | 138 | 29 | 56 | 0 | .289 | .414 | .225 |
| Carlos Gomez | 137 | 315 | 51 | 72 | 15 | 5 | 3 | 28 | 106 | 22 | 72 | 14 | .287 | .337 | .229 |
| *Orlando Cabrera | 59 | 242 | 42 | 70 | 13 | 3 | 5 | 36 | 104 | 11 | 32 | 2 | .313 | .430 | .289 |
| Alexi Casilla | 80 | 228 | 25 | 46 | 7 | 3 | 0 | 17 | 59 | 22 | 36 | 11 | .280 | .259 | .202 |
| Matt Tolbert | 71 | 198 | 28 | 46 | 7 | 1 | 2 | 19 | 61 | 21 | 37 | 6 | .303 | .308 | .232 |
| Brian Buscher | 61 | 136 | 14 | 32 | 3 | 1 | 2 | 12 | 43 | 24 | 35 | 0 | .360 | .316 | .235 |
| Mike Redmond | 45 | 135 | 9 | 32 | 5 | 1 | 0 | 7 | 39 | 11 | 19 | 0 | .299 | .289 | .237 |
| Jose Morales | 54 | 119 | 14 | 37 | 6 | 0 | 0 | 7 | 43 | 14 | 22 | 0 | .381 | .361 | .311 |

| PITCHING | GP | GS | W–L | SV | SHO | R | ERA | IP | Ks | BB |
|---|---|---|---|---|---|---|---|---|---|---|
| Nick Blackburn | 33 | 33 | 11–11 | 0 | 0 | 103 | 4.03 | 205.2 | 98 | 41 |
| Scott Baker | 33 | 33 | 15–9 | 0 | 1 | 99 | 4.37 | 200.0 | 162 | 48 |
| Francisco Liriano | 29 | 24 | 5–13 | 0 | 0 | 93 | 5.80 | 136.2 | 122 | 65 |
| Glen Perkins | 18 | 17 | 6–7 | 0 | 0 | 64 | 5.89 | 96.1 | 45 | 23 |
| Kevin Slowey | 16 | 16 | 10–3 | 0 | 0 | 50 | 4.86 | 90.2 | 75 | 15 |
| *Brian Duensing | 24 | 9 | 5–2 | 0 | 0 | 37 | 3.64 | 84.0 | 53 | 31 |
| Matt Guerrier | 79 | 0 | 5–1 | 1 | 0 | 23 | 2.36 | 76.1 | 47 | 16 |
| *Carl Pavano | 12 | 12 | 5–4 | 0 | 1 | 39 | 4.64 | 73.2 | 59 | 16 |
| Joe Nathan | 70 | 0 | 2–2 | 47 | 0 | 16 | 2.10 | 68.2 | 89 | 22 |
| R.A. Dickey | 35 | 1 | 1–1 | 0 | 0 | 34 | 4.62 | 64.1 | 42 | 30 |
| Jose Mijares | 71 | 0 | 2–2 | 0 | 0 | 17 | 2.34 | 61.2 | 55 | 23 |
| Anthony Swarzak | 12 | 12 | 3–7 | 0 | 0 | 43 | 6.25 | 59.0 | 34 | 20 |
| Bobby Keppel | 37 | 0 | 1–1 | 0 | 0 | 30 | 4.83 | 54.0 | 32 | 21 |
| Jesse Crain | 56 | 0 | 7–4 | 0 | 0 | 28 | 4.70 | 51.2 | 43 | 27 |
| *Luis Ayala | 28 | 0 | 1–2 | 0 | 0 | 18 | 4.18 | 32.1 | 21 | 8 |
| Jeff Manship | 11 | 5 | 1–1 | 0 | 0 | 21 | 5.68 | 31.0 | 21 | 15 |

*Mid-season trade.

### New York Yankees

| BATTING | G | AB | R | H | 2B | 3B | HR | RBI | TB | BB | SO | SB | OBP | SLG | BAVG |
|---|---|---|---|---|---|---|---|---|---|---|---|---|---|---|---|
| Robinson Cano | 161 | 637 | 103 | 204 | 48 | 2 | 25 | 85 | 331 | 30 | 63 | 5 | .352 | .520 | .320 |
| Derek Jeter | 153 | 634 | 107 | 212 | 27 | 1 | 18 | 66 | 295 | 72 | 90 | 30 | .406 | .465 | .334 |
| Mark Teixeira | 156 | 609 | 103 | 178 | 43 | 3 | 39 | 122 | 344 | 81 | 114 | 2 | .383 | .565 | .292 |
| Johnny Damon | 143 | 550 | 107 | 155 | 36 | 3 | 24 | 82 | 269 | 71 | 98 | 12 | .365 | .489 | .282 |
| Nick Swisher | 150 | 498 | 84 | 124 | 35 | 1 | 29 | 82 | 248 | 97 | 126 | 0 | .371 | .498 | .249 |
| Melky Cabrera | 154 | 485 | 66 | 133 | 28 | 1 | 13 | 68 | 202 | 43 | 59 | 10 | .336 | .416 | .274 |
| Hideki Matsui | 142 | 456 | 62 | 125 | 21 | 1 | 28 | 90 | 232 | 64 | 75 | 0 | .367 | .509 | .274 |
| Alex Rodriguez | 124 | 444 | 78 | 127 | 17 | 1 | 30 | 100 | 236 | 80 | 97 | 14 | .402 | .532 | .286 |
| Jorge Posada | 111 | 383 | 55 | 109 | 25 | 0 | 22 | 81 | 200 | 48 | 101 | 1 | .363 | .522 | .285 |
| Brett Gardner | 108 | 248 | 48 | 67 | 6 | 6 | 3 | 23 | 94 | 26 | 40 | 26 | .345 | .379 | .270 |
| Jose Molina | 52 | 138 | 15 | 30 | 4 | 0 | 1 | 11 | 37 | 14 | 28 | 0 | .292 | .268 | .217 |
| Ramiro Pena | 69 | 115 | 17 | 33 | 6 | 1 | 1 | 10 | 44 | 5 | 20 | 4 | .317 | .383 | .287 |
| Francisco Cervelli | 42 | 94 | 13 | 28 | 4 | 0 | 1 | 11 | 35 | 2 | 11 | 0 | .309 | .372 | .298 |
| *Eric Hinske | 39 | 84 | 13 | 19 | 3 | 0 | 7 | 14 | 43 | 10 | 25 | 1 | .316 | .512 | .226 |
| Cody Ransom | 31 | 79 | 11 | 15 | 9 | 1 | 0 | 10 | 26 | 7 | 25 | 2 | .256 | .329 | .190 |
| *Jerry Hairston Jr. | 45 | 76 | 15 | 18 | 5 | 0 | 2 | 12 | 29 | 11 | 8 | 0 | .352 | .382 | .237 |

| PITCHING | GP | GS | W–L | SV | SHO | R | ERA | IP | Ks | BB |
|---|---|---|---|---|---|---|---|---|---|---|
| C.C. Sabathia | 34 | 34 | 19–8 | 0 | 1 | 96 | 3.37 | 230.0 | 197 | 67 |
| A.J. Burnett | 33 | 33 | 13–9 | 0 | 0 | 99 | 4.04 | 207.0 | 195 | 97 |
| Andy Pettitte | 32 | 32 | 14–8 | 0 | 0 | 90 | 4.16 | 194.2 | 148 | 76 |
| Joba Chamberlain | 32 | 31 | 9–6 | 0 | 0 | 94 | 4.75 | 157.1 | 133 | 76 |
| Phil Hughes | 51 | 7 | 8–3 | 3 | 0 | 31 | 3.03 | 86.0 | 96 | 28 |
| Alfredo Aceves | 43 | 1 | 10–1 | 1 | 0 | 36 | 3.54 | 84.0 | 69 | 16 |
| Mariano Rivera | 66 | 0 | 3–3 | 44 | 0 | 14 | 1.76 | 66.1 | 72 | 12 |
| Phil Coke | 72 | 0 | 4–3 | 2 | 0 | 34 | 4.50 | 60.0 | 49 | 20 |
| Sergio Mitre | 12 | 9 | 3–3 | 0 | 0 | 45 | 6.79 | 51.2 | 32 | 13 |
| David Robertson | 45 | 0 | 2–1 | 1 | 0 | 19 | 3.30 | 43.2 | 63 | 23 |
| *Chad Gaudin | 11 | 6 | 2–0 | 0 | 0 | 16 | 3.43 | 42.0 | 34 | 20 |
| Chien-Ming Wang | 12 | 9 | 1–6 | 0 | 0 | 46 | 9.64 | 42.0 | 29 | 19 |
| Brian Bruney | 44 | 0 | 5–0 | 0 | 0 | 17 | 3.92 | 39.0 | 36 | 23 |
| Jonathan Albaladejo | 32 | 0 | 5–1 | 0 | 0 | 23 | 5.24 | 34.1 | 21 | 16 |
| *Jose Veras | 25 | 0 | 3–1 | 0 | 0 | 17 | 5.96 | 25.2 | 18 | 14 |
| Edwar Ramirez | 20 | 0 | 0–0 | 0 | 0 | 15 | 5.73 | 22.0 | 22 | 18 |
| *Brett Tomko | 15 | 0 | 1–2 | 0 | 0 | 12 | 5.23 | 20.2 | 11 | 7 |

### Oakland Athletics

| BATTING | G | AB | R | H | 2B | 3B | HR | RBI | TB | BB | SO | SB | OBP | SLG | BAVG |
|---|---|---|---|---|---|---|---|---|---|---|---|---|---|---|---|
| Kurt Suzuki | 147 | 570 | 74 | 156 | 37 | 1 | 15 | 88 | 240 | 28 | 59 | 8 | .313 | .421 | .274 |
| Adam Kennedy | 129 | 529 | 65 | 153 | 29 | 1 | 11 | 63 | 217 | 45 | 86 | 20 | .348 | .410 | .289 |
| Jack Cust | 149 | 513 | 88 | 123 | 16 | 0 | 25 | 70 | 214 | 93 | 185 | 4 | .356 | .417 | .240 |
| Ryan Sweeney | 134 | 484 | 68 | 142 | 31 | 3 | 6 | 53 | 197 | 40 | 67 | 6 | .348 | .407 | .293 |
| *Orlando Cabrera | 101 | 414 | 41 | 116 | 23 | 0 | 4 | 41 | 151 | 25 | 39 | 11 | .318 | .365 | .280 |
| Rajai Davis | 125 | 390 | 65 | 119 | 27 | 5 | 3 | 48 | 165 | 29 | 70 | 41 | .360 | .423 | .305 |
| Mark Ellis | 105 | 377 | 52 | 99 | 23 | 0 | 10 | 61 | 152 | 23 | 54 | 10 | .305 | .403 | .263 |
| *Matt Holliday | 93 | 346 | 52 | 99 | 23 | 1 | 11 | 54 | 157 | 46 | 58 | 12 | .378 | .454 | .286 |
| *Jason Giambi | 83 | 269 | 39 | 65 | 13 | 0 | 11 | 40 | 98 | 50 | 72 | 0 | .332 | .364 | .193 |
| Bobby Crosby | 97 | 238 | 35 | 53 | 10 | 2 | 6 | 29 | 85 | 24 | 44 | 2 | .295 | .357 | .223 |
| *Scott Hairston | 60 | 233 | 24 | 55 | 13 | 1 | 7 | 35 | 91 | 8 | 38 | 3 | .262 | .391 | .236 |
| Cliff Pennington | 60 | 208 | 27 | 58 | 11 | 3 | 4 | 21 | 87 | 19 | 46 | 7 | .342 | .418 | .279 |
| Daric Barton | 54 | 160 | 31 | 43 | 12 | 1 | 3 | 24 | 66 | 26 | 25 | 0 | .372 | .413 | .269 |
| Nomar Garciaparra | 65 | 160 | 17 | 45 | 8 | 0 | 3 | 16 | 62 | 8 | 28 | 2 | .314 | .388 | .281 |

| PITCHING | GP | GS | W–L | SV | SHO | R | ERA | IP | Ks | BB |
|---|---|---|---|---|---|---|---|---|---|---|
| Trevor Cahill | 32 | 32 | 10–13 | 0 | 0 | 99 | 4.63 | 178.2 | 90 | 72 |
| Brett Anderson | 30 | 30 | 11–11 | 0 | 1 | 94 | 4.06 | 175.1 | 150 | 45 |
| Dallas Braden | 22 | 22 | 8–9 | 0 | 0 | 63 | 3.89 | 136.2 | 81 | 42 |
| Gio Gonzalez | 20 | 17 | 6–7 | 0 | 0 | 68 | 5.75 | 98.2 | 109 | 56 |
| Vin Mazzaro | 17 | 17 | 4–9 | 0 | 0 | 61 | 5.32 | 91.1 | 59 | 39 |
| Andrew Bailey | 68 | 0 | 6–3 | 26 | 0 | 17 | 1.84 | 83.1 | 91 | 24 |
| Michael Wuertz | 74 | 0 | 6–1 | 4 | 0 | 25 | 2.63 | 78.2 | 102 | 23 |
| Brad Ziegler | 69 | 0 | 2–4 | 7 | 0 | 27 | 3.07 | 73.1 | 54 | 28 |
| Josh Outman | 14 | 12 | 4–1 | 0 | 0 | 30 | 3.48 | 67.1 | 53 | 25 |
| Edgar Gonzalez | 26 | 6 | 0–4 | 0 | 0 | 41 | 5.51 | 65.1 | 39 | 28 |
| *Craig Breslow | 60 | 0 | 7–5 | 0 | 0 | 20 | 2.60 | 55.1 | 44 | 18 |
| Santiago Casilla | 46 | 0 | 1–2 | 0 | 0 | 36 | 5.96 | 48.1 | 35 | 25 |
| Dana Eveland | 13 | 9 | 2–4 | 0 | 0 | 39 | 7.16 | 44.0 | 22 | 26 |
| *Russ Springer | 48 | 0 | 0–1 | 0 | 0 | 20 | 4.10 | 41.2 | 47 | 14 |

*Mid-season trade.

## Seattle Mariners

| BATTING | G | AB | R | H | 2B | 3B | HR | RBI | TB | BB | SO | SB | OBP | SLG | BAVG |
|---|---|---|---|---|---|---|---|---|---|---|---|---|---|---|---|
| Ichiro Suzuki | 146 | 639 | 88 | 225 | 31 | 4 | 11 | 46 | 297 | 32 | 71 | 26 | .386 | .465 | .352 |
| Jose Lopez | 153 | 613 | 69 | 167 | 42 | 0 | 25 | 96 | 284 | 24 | 69 | 3 | .303 | .463 | .272 |
| Franklin Guiterrez | 153 | 565 | 85 | 160 | 24 | 1 | 18 | 70 | 240 | 46 | 122 | 16 | .339 | .425 | .283 |
| Adrian Beltre | 111 | 449 | 54 | 119 | 27 | 0 | 8 | 44 | 170 | 19 | 74 | 13 | .304 | .379 | .265 |
| Russell Branyan | 116 | 431 | 64 | 108 | 21 | 1 | 31 | 76 | 224 | 58 | 149 | 2 | .347 | .520 | .251 |
| Ken Griffey Jr. | 117 | 387 | 44 | 83 | 19 | 0 | 19 | 57 | 159 | 63 | 80 | 0 | .324 | .411 | .214 |
| Rob Johnson | 80 | 258 | 21 | 55 | 19 | 2 | 2 | 27 | 84 | 26 | 60 | 1 | .289 | .326 | .213 |
| Mike Sweeney | 74 | 242 | 25 | 68 | 15 | 0 | 8 | 34 | 107 | 17 | 31 | 0 | .335 | .442 | .281 |
| Kenji Johjima | 71 | 239 | 24 | 59 | 11 | 0 | 9 | 22 | 97 | 12 | 28 | 2 | .296 | .406 | .247 |
| *Yuniesky Betancourt | 63 | 224 | 15 | 56 | 10 | 1 | 2 | 22 | 74 | 10 | 18 | 3 | .278 | .330 | .250 |
| *Ronny Cedeno | 59 | 186 | 15 | 31 | 4 | 2 | 5 | 17 | 54 | 10 | 50 | 3 | .213 | .290 | .167 |
| Endy Chavez | 54 | 161 | 17 | 44 | 3 | 1 | 2 | 13 | 55 | 14 | 22 | 9 | .328 | .342 | .273 |
| *Wladimir Balentien | 56 | 155 | 18 | 33 | 10 | 0 | 4 | 13 | 55 | 13 | 43 | 1 | .271 | .355 | .213 |
| *Jack Hannahan | 51 | 148 | 15 | 34 | 8 | 0 | 3 | 11 | 51 | 17 | 35 | 1 | .311 | .345 | .230 |
| *Josh Wilson | 45 | 128 | 16 | 32 | 8 | 1 | 3 | 10 | 51 | 6 | 32 | 1 | .294 | .398 | .250 |

| PITCHING | GP | GS | W–L | SV | SHO | R | ERA | IP | Ks | BB |
|---|---|---|---|---|---|---|---|---|---|---|
| Felix Hernandez | 34 | 34 | 19–5 | 0 | 1 | 81 | 2.49 | 238.2 | 217 | 71 |
| *Jarrod Washburn | 20 | 20 | 8–6 | 0 | 0 | 42 | 2.64 | 133.0 | 79 | 33 |
| Ryan Rowland-Smith | 15 | 15 | 5–4 | 0 | 0 | 43 | 3.74 | 96.1 | 52 | 27 |
| Chris Jakubauskas | 35 | 8 | 6–7 | 0 | 0 | 60 | 5.32 | 93.0 | 47 | 27 |
| Jason Vargas | 23 | 14 | 3–6 | 0 | 0 | 53 | 4.91 | 91.2 | 54 | 24 |
| Erik Bedard | 15 | 15 | 5–3 | 0 | 0 | 29 | 2.82 | 83.0 | 90 | 34 |
| Garrett Olson | 31 | 11 | 3–5 | 0 | 0 | 52 | 5.60 | 80.1 | 47 | 34 |
| Mark Lowe | 75 | 0 | 2–7 | 3 | 0 | 39 | 3.26 | 80.0 | 69 | 29 |
| David Aardsma | 73 | 0 | 3–6 | 38 | 0 | 23 | 2.52 | 71.1 | 80 | 34 |
| Miguel Batista | 56 | 0 | 7–4 | 1 | 0 | 37 | 4.04 | 71.1 | 52 | 39 |
| Brandon Morrow | 26 | 10 | 2–4 | 6 | 0 | 38 | 4.39 | 69.2 | 63 | 44 |
| Sean White | 52 | 0 | 3–2 | 1 | 0 | 23 | 2.80 | 64.1 | 28 | 20 |
| *Ian Snell | 12 | 12 | 5–2 | 0 | 0 | 32 | 4.20 | 64.1 | 37 | 39 |
| Doug Fister | 11 | 10 | 3–4 | 0 | 0 | 29 | 4.13 | 61.0 | 36 | 15 |
| Shawn Kelley | 41 | 0 | 5–4 | 0 | 0 | 23 | 4.50 | 46.0 | 41 | 9 |

## Tampa Bay Rays

| BATTING | G | AB | R | H | 2B | 3B | HR | RBI | TB | BB | SO | SB | OBP | SLG | BAVG |
|---|---|---|---|---|---|---|---|---|---|---|---|---|---|---|---|
| Carl Crawford | 156 | 606 | 96 | 185 | 28 | 8 | 15 | 68 | 274 | 51 | 99 | 60 | .364 | .452 | .305 |
| Evan Longoria | 157 | 584 | 100 | 164 | 44 | 0 | 33 | 113 | 307 | 72 | 140 | 9 | .364 | .526 | .281 |
| B.J. Upton | 144 | 560 | 79 | 135 | 33 | 4 | 11 | 55 | 209 | 57 | 152 | 42 | .313 | .373 | .241 |
| Ben Zobrist | 152 | 501 | 91 | 149 | 28 | 7 | 27 | 91 | 272 | 91 | 104 | 17 | .405 | .543 | .297 |
| Jason Bartlett | 137 | 500 | 90 | 160 | 29 | 7 | 14 | 66 | 245 | 54 | 89 | 30 | .389 | .490 | 320 |
| Carlos Pena | 135 | 471 | 91 | 107 | 25 | 2 | 39 | 100 | 253 | 87 | 163 | 3 | .356 | .537 | .227 |
| Pat Burrell | 122 | 412 | 45 | 91 | 16 | 1 | 14 | 64 | 151 | 57 | 119 | 2 | .315 | .367 | .221 |
| Dioner Navarro | 115 | 376 | 38 | 82 | 15 | 0 | 8 | 32 | 121 | 18 | 51 | 5 | .261 | .322 | .218 |
| Willy Aybar | 105 | 296 | 38 | 75 | 12 | 0 | 12 | 41 | 123 | 34 | 54 | 1 | .331 | .416 | .253 |
| Gabe Gross | 115 | 282 | 31 | 64 | 16 | 1 | 6 | 36 | 100 | 42 | 79 | 6 | .326 | .355 | .227 |
| Akinori Iwamura | 69 | 231 | 28 | 67 | 16 | 2 | 1 | 22 | 90 | 24 | 44 | 9 | .355 | .390 | .290 |
| Gabe Kapler | 99 | 205 | 26 | 49 | 15 | 1 | 8 | 32 | 90 | 29 | 39 | 5 | .329 | .439 | .239 |
| Michel Hernandez | 35 | 99 | 12 | 24 | 3 | 1 | 1 | 12 | 32 | 7 | 12 | 2 | .292 | .323 | .242 |
| *Gregg Zaun | 34 | 94 | 11 | 27 | 7 | 0 | 4 | 14 | 46 | 4 | 18 | 0 | .323 | .489 | .287 |
| Reid Brignac | 31 | 90 | 10 | 25 | 8 | 2 | 1 | 6 | 40 | 3 | 20 | 2 | .301 | .444 | .278 |

| PITCHING | GP | GS | W–L | SV | SHO | R | ERA | IP | Ks | BB |
|---|---|---|---|---|---|---|---|---|---|---|
| James Shields | 33 | 33 | 11–12 | 0 | 0 | 113 | 4.14 | 219.2 | 167 | 52 |
| Matt Garza | 32 | 32 | 8–12 | 0 | 0 | 93 | 3.95 | 203.0 | 189 | 79 |
| Jeff Niemann | 31 | 30 | 13–6 | 0 | 2 | 84 | 3.94 | 180.2 | 125 | 59 |
| David Price | 23 | 23 | 10–7 | 0 | 0 | 72 | 4.42 | 128.1 | 102 | 54 |
| *Scott Kazmir | 20 | 20 | 8–7 | 0 | 0 | 77 | 5.92 | 111.0 | 91 | 50 |
| Andy Sonnanstine | 22 | 18 | 6–9 | 0 | 0 | 85 | 6.77 | 99.2 | 60 | 34 |
| Lance Cormier | 53 | 0 | 3–3 | 2 | 0 | 31 | 3.26 | 77.1 | 36 | 25 |
| Grant Balfour | 73 | 0 | 5–4 | 4 | 0 | 38 | 4.81 | 67.1 | 69 | 33 |
| J.P. Howell | 69 | 0 | 7–5 | 17 | 0 | 22 | 2.84 | 66.2 | 79 | 33 |
| Dan Wheeler | 69 | 0 | 4–5 | 2 | 0 | 22 | 3.28 | 57.2 | 45 | 9 |
| Joe Nelson | 42 | 0 | 3–0 | 3 | 0 | 22 | 4.02 | 40.1 | 36 | 27 |
| Randy Choate | 61 | 0 | 1–0 | 5 | 0 | 15 | 3.47 | 36.1 | 28 | 11 |
| Wade Davis | 6 | 6 | 2–2 | 0 | 1 | 19 | 3.72 | 36.1 | 36 | 13 |
| Brian Shouse | 45 | 0 | 1–1 | 0 | 0 | 15 | 4.50 | 28.0 | 17 | 7 |
| *Russ Springer | 26 | 0 | 1–3 | 1 | 0 | 7 | 4.11 | 15.1 | 11 | 3 |

*Mid-season trade.

## Texas Rangers

### BATTING

| | G | AB | R | H | 2B | 3B | HR | RBI | TB | BB | SO | SB | OBP | SLG | BAVG |
|---|---|---|---|---|---|---|---|---|---|---|---|---|---|---|---|
| Ian Kinsler | 144 | 566 | 101 | 143 | 32 | 4 | 31 | 86 | 276 | 59 | 77 | 31 | .327 | .488 | .253 |
| Marlon Byrd | 146 | 547 | 66 | 155 | 43 | 2 | 20 | 89 | 262 | 32 | 98 | 8 | .329 | .479 | .283 |
| Michael Young | 135 | 541 | 76 | 174 | 36 | 2 | 22 | 68 | 280 | 47 | 90 | 8 | .374 | .518 | .322 |
| Elvis Andrus | 145 | 480 | 72 | 128 | 17 | 8 | 6 | 40 | 179 | 40 | 77 | 33 | .329 | .373 | .267 |
| Nelson Cruz | 128 | 462 | 75 | 120 | 21 | 1 | 33 | 76 | 242 | 49 | 118 | 20 | .332 | .524 | .260 |
| Hank Blalock | 123 | 462 | 62 | 108 | 21 | 4 | 25 | 66 | 212 | 26 | 108 | 2 | .277 | .459 | .234 |
| David Murphy | 128 | 432 | 61 | 116 | 24 | 1 | 17 | 57 | 193 | 49 | 106 | 9 | .338 | .447 | .269 |
| Chris Davis | 113 | 391 | 48 | 93 | 15 | 1 | 21 | 59 | 173 | 24 | 150 | 0 | .284 | .442 | .238 |
| Josh Hamilton | 89 | 336 | 43 | 90 | 19 | 2 | 10 | 54 | 143 | 24 | 79 | 8 | .315 | .426 | .268 |
| Jarrod Saltalamacchia | 84 | 283 | 34 | 66 | 12 | 0 | 9 | 34 | 105 | 22 | 97 | 0 | .290 | .371 | .233 |
| Andruw Jones | 82 | 281 | 43 | 60 | 18 | 0 | 17 | 43 | 129 | 45 | 72 | 5 | .323 | .459 | .214 |
| Taylor Teagarden | 60 | 198 | 26 | 43 | 13 | 0 | 6 | 24 | 74 | 14 | 76 | 0 | .270 | .374 | .217 |
| Omar Vizquel | 62 | 177 | 17 | 47 | 7 | 2 | 1 | 14 | 61 | 13 | 27 | 4 | .316 | .345 | .266 |
| Julio Borbon | 46 | 157 | 30 | 49 | 4 | 0 | 4 | 20 | 65 | 15 | 28 | 19 | .376 | .414 | .312 |
| *Ivan Rodriguez | 28 | 98 | 14 | 24 | 8 | 0 | 2 | 13 | 38 | 5 | 18 | 1 | .279 | .388 | .245 |

### PITCHING

| | GP | GS | W–L | SV | SHO | R | ERA | IP | Ks | BB |
|---|---|---|---|---|---|---|---|---|---|---|
| Kevin Millwood | 31 | 31 | 13–10 | 0 | 0 | 88 | 3.67 | 198.2 | 123 | 71 |
| Scott Feldman | 34 | 31 | 17–8 | 0 | 0 | 87 | 4.08 | 189.2 | 113 | 65 |
| Derek Holland | 33 | 21 | 8–13 | 0 | 1 | 98 | 6.12 | 138.1 | 107 | 47 |
| Tommy Hunter | 19 | 19 | 9–6 | 0 | 0 | 55 | 4.10 | 112.0 | 64 | 33 |
| *Vincente Padilla | 18 | 18 | 8–6 | 0 | 0 | 61 | 4.92 | 108.0 | 59 | 42 |
| Brandon McCarthy | 17 | 17 | 7–4 | 0 | 1 | 55 | 4.62 | 97.1 | 65 | 36 |
| C.J. Wilson | 74 | 0 | 5–6 | 14 | 0 | 29 | 2.81 | 73.2 | 84 | 32 |
| Dustin Nippert | 20 | 10 | 5–3 | 0 | 0 | 31 | 3.88 | 69.2 | 54 | 29 |
| Matt Harrison | 11 | 11 | 4–5 | 0 | 1 | 43 | 6.11 | 63.1 | 34 | 23 |
| Jason Jennings | 44 | 0 | 2–4 | 1 | 0 | 31 | 4.13 | 61.0 | 44 | 28 |
| *Darren O'Day | 64 | 0 | 2–1 | 2 | 0 | 12 | 1.94 | 55.2 | 54 | 17 |
| Frank Francisco | 51 | 0 | 2–3 | 25 | 0 | 21 | 3.83 | 49.1 | 57 | 15 |
| Doug Mathis | 24 | 2 | 0–1 | 1 | 0 | 17 | 3.16 | 42.2 | 25 | 10 |
| Eddie Guardado | 48 | 0 | 1–2 | 0 | 0 | 21 | 4.46 | 38.1 | 20 | 15 |
| Neftali Feliz | 20 | 0 | 1–0 | 2 | 0 | 13 | 1.74 | 31.0 | 39 | 8 |
| *Jason Grilli | 30 | 0 | 2–2 | 0 | 0 | 14 | 4.78 | 26.1 | 27 | 14 |
| Kris Benson | 8 | 2 | 1–1 | 0 | 0 | 23 | 8.46 | 22.1 | 11 | 12 |

## Toronto Blue Jays

### BATTING

| | G | AB | R | H | 2B | 3B | HR | RBI | TB | BB | SO | SB | OBP | SLG | BAVG |
|---|---|---|---|---|---|---|---|---|---|---|---|---|---|---|---|
| Aaron Hill | 158 | 682 | 103 | 195 | 37 | 0 | 36 | 108 | 340 | 42 | 98 | 6 | .330 | .499 | .286 |
| Vernon Wells | 158 | 630 | 84 | 164 | 37 | 3 | 15 | 66 | 252 | 48 | 86 | 17 | .311 | .400 | .260 |
| Adam Lind | 151 | 587 | 93 | 179 | 46 | 0 | 35 | 114 | 330 | 58 | 110 | 1 | .370 | .562 | .305 |
| Marco Scutaro | 144 | 574 | 100 | 162 | 35 | 1 | 12 | 60 | 235 | 90 | 75 | 14 | .379 | .409 | .282 |
| *Alex Rios | 108 | 436 | 52 | 115 | 25 | 2 | 14 | 62 | 186 | 31 | 78 | 19 | .317 | .427 | .264 |
| Rod Barajas | 125 | 429 | 43 | 97 | 19 | 0 | 19 | 71 | 173 | 20 | 76 | 1 | .258 | .403 | .226 |
| Lyle Overbay | 132 | 423 | 57 | 112 | 35 | 1 | 16 | 64 | 197 | 74 | 95 | 0 | .372 | .466 | .265 |
| *Scott Rolen | 88 | 338 | 52 | 108 | 29 | 0 | 8 | 43 | 161 | 26 | 42 | 4 | .370 | .476 | .320 |
| Jose Bautista | 113 | 336 | 54 | 79 | 13 | 3 | 13 | 40 | 137 | 56 | 85 | 4 | .349 | .408 | .235 |
| Kevin Millar | 78 | 251 | 29 | 56 | 14 | 0 | 7 | 29 | 91 | 31 | 49 | 0 | .311 | .363 | .223 |
| Travis Snider | 77 | 241 | 34 | 58 | 14 | 1 | 9 | 29 | 101 | 29 | 78 | 1 | .328 | .419 | .241 |
| Raul Chavez | 51 | 159 | 10 | 41 | 8 | 0 | 2 | 15 | 55 | 6 | 23 | 1 | .285 | .346 | .258 |
| *Edwin Encarnacion | 42 | 154 | 25 | 37 | 5 | 1 | 8 | 23 | 68 | 13 | 29 | 1 | .306 | .442 | .240 |
| John McDonald | 73 | 151 | 18 | 39 | 7 | 0 | 4 | 13 | 58 | 1 | 18 | 0 | .271 | .384 | .258 |
| Randy Ruiz | 33 | 115 | 25 | 36 | 7 | 0 | 10 | 17 | 73 | 10 | 35 | 1 | .385 | .635 | .313 |
| Joe Inglett | 36 | 89 | 11 | 25 | 4 | 1 | 0 | 6 | 31 | 8 | 21 | 3 | .347 | .348 | .281 |

### PITCHING

| | GP | GS | W–L | SV | SHO | R | ERA | IP | Ks | BB |
|---|---|---|---|---|---|---|---|---|---|---|
| Roy Halladay | 32 | 32 | 17–10 | 0 | 4 | 82 | 2.79 | 239.0 | 208 | 35 |
| Ricky Romero | 29 | 29 | 13–9 | 0 | 0 | 88 | 4.30 | 178.0 | 141 | 79 |
| Brian Tallet | 37 | 25 | 7–9 | 0 | 0 | 99 | 5.32 | 160.2 | 120 | 72 |
| Scott Richmond | 27 | 24 | 8–11 | 0 | 0 | 90 | 5.52 | 138.2 | 117 | 59 |
| Brett Cecil | 18 | 17 | 7–4 | 0 | 0 | 59 | 5.30 | 93.1 | 69 | 38 |
| Shawn Camp | 59 | 0 | 2–6 | 1 | 0 | 73 | 3.50 | 79.2 | 58 | 29 |
| Brandon League | 67 | 0 | 3–6 | 0 | 0 | 40 | 4.58 | 74.2 | 76 | 21 |
| Jesse Carlson | 73 | 0 | 1–6 | 0 | 0 | 37 | 4.66 | 67.2 | 51 | 21 |
| Marc Rzepczynski | 11 | 11 | 2–4 | 0 | 0 | 27 | 3.67 | 61.1 | 60 | 30 |
| Jason Frasor | 61 | 0 | 7–3 | 11 | 0 | 17 | 2.50 | 57.2 | 56 | 16 |
| David Purcey | 9 | 9 | 1–3 | 0 | 0 | 35 | 6.19 | 48.0 | 39 | 30 |
| Scott Downs | 48 | 0 | 1–3 | 9 | 0 | 28 | 3.09 | 46.2 | 43 | 13 |
| Casey Janssen | 21 | 5 | 2–4 | 1 | 0 | 29 | 5.85 | 40.0 | 24 | 14 |

*Mid-season trade.

## The World Series

### Results

| | |
|---|---|
| 1903...............Boston (A) 5, Pittsburgh (N) 3 | 1957...............Milwaukee (N) 4, New York (A) 3 |
| 1904...............No series | 1958...............New York (A) 4, Milwaukee (N) 3 |
| 1905...............New York (N) 4, Philadelphia (A) 1 | 1959...............Los Angeles (N) 4, Chicago (A) 2 |
| 1906...............Chicago (A) 4, Chicago (N) 2 | 1960...............Pittsburgh (N) 4, New York (A) 3 |
| 1907...............Chicago (N) 4, Detroit (A) 0; 1 tie | 1961...............New York (A) 4, Cincinnati (N) 1 |
| 1908...............Chicago (N) 4, Detroit (A) 1 | 1962...............New York (A) 4, San Francisco (N) 3 |
| 1909...............Pittsburgh (N) 4, Detroit (A) 3 | 1963...............Los Angeles (N) 4, New York (A) 0 |
| 1910...............Philadelphia (A) 4, Chicago (N) 1 | 1964...............St. Louis (N) 4, New York (A) 3 |
| 1911...............Philadelphia (A) 4, New York (N) 2 | 1965...............Los Angeles (N) 4, Minnesota (A) 3 |
| 1912...............Boston (A) 4, New York (N) 3; 1 tie | 1966...............Baltimore (A) 4, Los Angeles (N) 0 |
| 1913...............Philadelphia (A) 4, New York (N) 1 | 1967...............St. Louis (N) 4, Boston (A) 3 |
| 1914...............Boston (N) 4, Philadelphia (A) 0 | 1968...............Detroit (A) 4, St. Louis (N) 3 |
| 1915...............Boston (A) 4, Philadelphia (N) 1 | 1969...............New York (N) 4, Baltimore (A) 1 |
| 1916...............Boston (A) 4, Brooklyn (N) 1 | 1970...............Baltimore (A) 4, Cincinnati (N) 1 |
| 1917...............Chicago (A) 4, New York (N) 2 | 1971...............Pittsburgh (N) 4, Baltimore (A) 3 |
| 1918...............Boston (A) 4, Chicago (N) 2 | 1972...............Oakland (A) 4, Cincinnati (N) 3 |
| 1919...............Cincinnati (N) 5, Chicago (A) 3 | 1973...............Oakland (A) 4, New York (N) 3 |
| 1920...............Cleveland (A) 5, Brooklyn (N) 2 | 1974...............Oakland (A) 4, Los Angeles (N) 1 |
| 1921...............New York (N) 5, New York (A) 3 | 1975...............Cincinnati (N) 4, Boston (A) 3 |
| 1922...............New York (N) 4, New York (A) 0; 1 tie | 1976...............Cincinnati (N) 4, New York (A) 0 |
| 1923...............New York (A) 4, New York (N) 2 | 1977...............New York (A) 4, Los Angeles (N) 2 |
| 1924...............Washington (A) 4, New York (N) 3 | 1978...............New York (A) 4, Los Angeles (N) 2 |
| 1925...............Pittsburgh (N) 4, Washington (A) 3 | 1979...............Pittsburgh (N) 4, Baltimore (A) 3 |
| 1926...............St. Louis (N) 4, New York (A) 3 | 1980...............Philadelphia (N) 4, Kansas City (A) 2 |
| 1927...............New York (A) 4, Pittsburgh (N) 0 | 1981...............Los Angeles (N) 4, New York (A) 2 |
| 1928...............New York (A) 4, St. Louis (N) 0 | 1982...............St. Louis (N) 4, Milwaukee (A) 3 |
| 1929...............Philadelphia (A) 4, Chicago (N) 1 | 1983...............Baltimore (A) 4, Philadelphia (N) 1 |
| 1930...............Philadelphia (A) 4, St. Louis (N) 2 | 1984...............Detroit (A) 4, San Diego (N) 1 |
| 1931...............St. Louis (N) 4, Philadelphia (A) 3 | 1985...............Kansas City (A) 4, St. Louis (N) 3 |
| 1932...............New York (A) 4, Chicago (N) 0 | 1986...............New York (N) 4, Boston (A) 3 |
| 1933...............New York (N) 4, Washington (A) 1 | 1987...............Minnesota (A) 4, St. Louis (N) 3 |
| 1934...............St. Louis (N) 4, Detroit (A) 3 | 1988...............Los Angeles (N) 4, Oakland (A) 1 |
| 1935...............Detroit (A) 4, Chicago (N) 2 | 1989...............Oakland (A) 4, San Francisco (N) 0 |
| 1936...............New York (A) 4, New York (N) 2 | 1990...............Cincinnati (N) 4, Oakland (A) 0 |
| 1937...............New York (A) 4, New York (N) 1 | 1991...............Minnesota (A) 4, Atlanta (N) 3 |
| 1938...............New York (A) 4, Chicago (N) 0 | 1992...............Toronto (A) 4, Atlanta (N) 2 |
| 1939...............New York (A) 4, Cincinnati (N) 0 | 1993...............Toronto (A) 4, Philadelphia (N) 2 |
| 1940...............Cincinnati (N) 4, Detroit (A) 3 | 1994...............Series canceled due to players' strike. |
| 1941...............New York (A) 4, Brooklyn (N) 1 | 1995...............Atlanta (N) 4, Cleveland (A) 2 |
| 1942...............St. Louis (N) 4, New York (A) 1 | 1996...............New York (A) 4, Atlanta (N) 2 |
| 1943...............New York (A) 4, St. Louis (N) 1 | 1997...............Florida (N) 4, Cleveland (A) 3 |
| 1944...............St. Louis (N) 4, St. Louis (A) 2 | 1998...............New York (A) 4, San Diego (N) 0 |
| 1945...............Detroit (A) 4, Chicago (N) 3 | 1999...............New York (A) 4, Atlanta (N) 0 |
| 1946...............St. Louis (N) 4, Boston (A) 3 | 2000...............New York (A) 4 , New York (N) 1 |
| 1947...............New York (A) 4, Brooklyn (N) 3 | 2001...............Arizona (N) 4, New York (A) 3 |
| 1948...............Cleveland (A) 4, Boston (N) 2 | 2002...............Anaheim (A) 4, San Francisco (N) 3 |
| 1949...............New York (A) 4, Brooklyn (N) 1 | 2003...............Florida (N) 4, New York (A) 2 |
| 1950...............New York (A) 4, Philadelphia (N) 0 | 2004...............Boston (A) 4, St. Louis (N) 0 |
| 1951...............New York (A) 4, New York (N) 2 | 2005...............Chicago (A) 4, Houston (N) 0 |
| 1952...............New York (A) 4, Brooklyn (N) 3 | 2006...............St. Louis (N) 4, Detroit (A) 1 |
| 1953...............New York (A) 4, Brooklyn (N) 2 | 2007...............Boston (A) 4, Colorado (N) 0 |
| 1954...............New York (N) 4, Cleveland (A) 0 | 2008...............Philadelphia (N) 4, Tampa Bay (A) 1 |
| 1955...............Brooklyn (N) 4, New York (A) 3 | 2009...............New York (A) 4, Philadelphia (N) 2 |
| 1956...............New York (A) 4, Brooklyn (N) 3 | |

## Most Valuable Players

| | |
|---|---|
| 1955 .............................Johnny Podres, Bklyn | 1983 ............................Rick Dempsey, Balt |
| 1956 ..............................Don Larsen, NY (A) | 1984 .............................Alan Trammell, Det |
| 1957 ..............................Lew Burdette, Mil | 1985 ............................Bret Saberhagen, KC |
| 1958 ..............................Bob Turley, NY (A) | 1986 ............................Ray Knight, NY (N) |
| 1959 ..............................Larry Sherry, LA | 1987 ............................Frank Viola, Minn |
| 1960 ..............................Bobby Richardson, NY (A) | 1988 ............................Orel Hershiser, LA |
| 1961 ..............................Whitey Ford, NY (A) | 1989 ............................Dave Stewart, Oak |
| 1962 ..............................Ralph Terry, NY (A) | 1990 ............................Jose Rijo, Cin |
| 1963 ..............................Sandy Koufax, LA | 1991 ............................Jack Morris, Minn |
| 1964 ..............................Bob Gibson, StL | 1992 ............................Pat Borders, Tor |
| 1965 ..............................Sandy Koufax, LA | 1993 ............................Paul Molitor, Tor |
| 1966 ..............................Frank Robinson, Balt | 1994 ............................Series canceled due to strike. |
| 1967 ..............................Bob Gibson, StL | 1995 ............................Tom Glavine, Atl |
| 1968 ..............................Mickey Lolich, Det | 1996 ............................John Wetteland, NY (A) |
| 1969 ..............................Donn Clendenon, NY (N) | 1997 ............................Livan Hernandez, Fla |
| 1970 ..............................Brooks Robinson, Balt | 1998 ............................Scott Brosius, NY (A) |
| 1971 ..............................Roberto Clemente, Pitt | 1999 ............................Mariano Rivera, NY (A) |
| 1972 ..............................Gene Tenace, Oak | 2000 ............................Derek Jeter, NY (A) |
| 1973 ..............................Reggie Jackson, Oak | 2001 ............................Randy Johnson, Ariz |
| 1974 ..............................Rollie Fingers, Oak | Curt Schilling, Ariz |
| 1975 ..............................Pete Rose, Cin | 2002 ............................Troy Glaus, Ana |
| 1976 ..............................Johnny Bench, Cin | 2003 ............................Josh Beckett, Fla |
| 1977 ..............................Reggie Jackson, NY (A) | 2004 ............................Manny Ramirez, Bos |
| 1978 ..............................Bucky Dent, NY (A) | 2005 ............................Jermaine Dye, Chi (A) |
| 1979 ..............................Willie Stargell, Pitt | 2006 ............................David Eckstein, StL |
| 1980 ..............................Mike Schmidt, Phil | 2007 ............................Mike Lowell, Bos |
| 1981 ..............................Ron Cey, LA; Steve Yeager, LA; | 2008 ............................Cole Hamels, Phi |
| Pedro Guerrero, LA | 2009 ............................Hideki Matsui, NY (A) |
| 1982 ..............................Darrell Porter, StL | |

## Career Batting Leaders (Minimum 40 at bats)

### GAMES

| | |
|---|---|
| Yogi Berra | 75 |
| Mickey Mantle | 65 |
| Elston Howard | 54 |
| Hank Bauer | 53 |
| Gil McDougald | 53 |
| Phil Rizzuto | 52 |
| Joe DiMaggio | 51 |
| Frankie Frisch | 50 |
| Pee Wee Reese | 44 |
| Roger Maris | 41 |
| Babe Ruth | 41 |

### AT BATS

| | |
|---|---|
| Yogi Berra | 259 |
| Mickey Mantle | 230 |
| Joe DiMaggio | 199 |
| Frankie Frisch | 197 |
| Gil McDougald | 190 |
| Hank Bauer | 188 |
| Phil Rizzuto | 183 |
| Elston Howard | 171 |
| Pee Wee Reese | 169 |
| Derek Jeter | 156 |
| Roger Maris | 152 |

### BATTING AVERAGE

| | |
|---|---|
| Bobby Brown | .439 |
| Paul Molitor | .418 |
| Pepper Martin | .418 |
| Hal McRae | .400 |
| Lou Brock | .391 |
| Marquis Grissom | .390 |
| Thurman Munson | .373 |
| George Brett | .373 |
| Pat Borders | .372 |
| Hank Aaron | .364 |

### RUNS

| | |
|---|---|
| Mickey Mantle | 42 |
| Yogi Berra | 41 |
| Babe Ruth | 37 |
| Derek Jeter | 32 |
| Lou Gehrig | 30 |
| Joe DiMaggio | 27 |
| Derek Jeter | 27 |
| Roger Maris | 26 |
| Elston Howard | 25 |
| Gil McDougald | 23 |
| Jackie Robinson | 22 |

### RUNS BATTED IN

| | |
|---|---|
| Mickey Mantle | 40 |
| Yogi Berra | 39 |
| Lou Gehrig | 35 |
| Babe Ruth | 33 |
| Joe DiMaggio | 30 |
| Bill Skowron | 29 |
| Duke Snider | 26 |
| Reggie Jackson | 24 |
| Bill Dickey | 24 |
| Hank Bauer | 24 |
| Gil McDougald | 24 |

### TOTAL BASES

| | |
|---|---|
| Mickey Mantle | 123 |
| Yogi Berra | 117 |
| Babe Ruth | 96 |
| Lou Gehrig | 87 |
| Joe DiMaggio | 84 |
| Duke Snider | 79 |
| Hank Bauer | 75 |
| Reggie Jackson | 74 |
| Frankie Frisch | 74 |
| Gil McDougald | 72 |
| Derek Jeter | 70 |

### HOME RUNS

| | |
|---|---|
| Mickey Mantle | 18 |
| Babe Ruth | 15 |
| Yogi Berra | 12 |
| Duke Snider | 11 |
| Reggie Jackson | 10 |
| Lou Gehrig | 10 |
| Frank Robinson | 8 |
| Bill Skowron | 8 |
| Joe DiMaggio | 8 |
| Goose Goslin | 7 |
| Hank Bauer | 7 |
| Gil McDougald | 7 |
| Chase Utley | 7 |

### HITS

| | |
|---|---|
| Yogi Berra | 71 |
| Mickey Mantle | 59 |
| Frankie Frisch | 58 |
| Joe DiMaggio | 54 |
| Derek Jeter | 50 |
| Pee Wee Reese | 46 |
| Hank Bauer | 46 |
| Phil Rizzuto | 45 |
| Gil McDougald | 45 |
| Lou Gehrig | 43 |
| Eddie Collins | 42 |
| Babe Ruth | 42 |
| Elston Howard | 42 |

### STOLEN BASES

| | |
|---|---|
| Lou Brock | 14 |
| Eddie Collins | 14 |
| Frank Chance | 10 |
| Davey Lopes | 10 |
| Phil Rizzuto | 10 |
| Honus Wagner | 9 |
| Frankie Frisch | 9 |
| Kenny Lofton | 9 |

## Career Batting Leaders *(Cont.)*

### STOLEN BASES (CONT.)

| | |
|---|---|
| Johnny Evers | 8 |
| Roberto Alomar | 7 |
| Joe Tinker | 7 |
| Pepper Martin | 7 |
| Joe Morgan | 7 |
| Rickey Henderson | 7 |

### SLUGGING AVERAGE

| | |
|---|---|
| Reggie Jackson | .755 |
| Babe Ruth | .744 |
| Lou Gehrig | .731 |
| Bobby Brown | .707 |
| Lenny Dykstra | .700 |
| Al Simmons | .658 |
| Lou Brock | .655 |
| Pepper Martin | .636 |
| Paul Molitor | .636 |
| Joe Harris | .625 |

### STRIKEOUTS

| | |
|---|---|
| Mickey Mantle | 54 |
| Derek Jeter | 39 |
| Elston Howard | 37 |
| Duke Snider | 33 |
| Jorge Posada | 31 |
| Babe Ruth | 30 |
| David Justice | 30 |
| Gil McDougald | 29 |
| Bill Skowron | 26 |
| Bernie Williams | 26 |
| Hank Bauer | 25 |

## Career Pitching Leaders

### GAMES

| | |
|---|---|
| Mariano Rivera | 24 |
| Whitey Ford | 22 |
| Mike Stanton | 19 |
| Jeff Nelson | 16 |
| Rollie Fingers | 16 |
| Allie Reynolds | 15 |
| Bob Turley | 15 |
| Clay Carroll | 14 |
| Clem Labine | 13 |
| Mark Wohlers | 13 |
| Andy Pettitte | 13 |

### INNINGS PITCHED

| | |
|---|---|
| Whitey Ford | 146 |
| Christy Mathewson | 101.2 |
| Red Ruffing | 85.2 |
| Chief Bender | 85 |
| Waite Hoyt | 83.2 |
| Bob Gibson | 81 |
| Art Nehf | 79 |
| Andy Pettitte | 77.2 |
| Allie Reynolds | 77 |

### WINS

| | |
|---|---|
| Whitey Ford | 10 |
| Bob Gibson | 7 |
| Red Ruffing | 7 |
| Allie Reynolds | 7 |
| Lefty Gomez | 6 |
| Chief Bender | 6 |
| Waite Hoyt | 6 |
| Jack Coombs | 5 |
| Three Finger Brown | 5 |
| Herb Pennock | 5 |
| Christy Mathewson | 5 |
| Vic Raschi | 5 |
| Catfish Hunter | 5 |
| Andy Pettitte | 5 |

### LOSSES

| | |
|---|---|
| Whitey Ford | 8 |
| Eddie Plank | 5 |
| Schoolboy Rowe | 5 |
| Joe Bush | 5 |
| Rube Marquard | 5 |
| Christy Mathewson | 5 |

### SAVES

| | |
|---|---|
| Mariano Rivera | 11 |
| Rollie Fingers | 6 |
| Allie Reynolds | 4 |
| Johnny Murphy | 4 |
| John Wetteland | 4 |
| Robb Nen | 4 |

### *EARNED RUN AVERAGE

| | |
|---|---|
| Jack Billingham | 0.36 |
| Harry Brecheen | 0.83 |
| Babe Ruth | 0.87 |
| Sherry Smith | 0.89 |
| Sandy Koufax | 0.95 |
| Mariano Rivera | 0.99 |
| Hippo Vaughn | 1.00 |
| Monte Pearson | 1.01 |
| Christy Mathewson | 1.06 |
| Babe Adams | 1.29 |

### SHUTOUTS

| | |
|---|---|
| Christy Mathewson | 4 |
| Three Finger Brown | 3 |
| Whitey Ford | 3 |
| Bill Hallahan | 2 |
| Lew Burdette | 2 |
| Bill Dinneen | 2 |
| Sandy Koufax | 2 |
| Allie Reynolds | 2 |
| Art Nehf | 2 |
| Bob Gibson | 2 |

*Minimum 25 innings pitched.

### COMPLETE GAMES

| | |
|---|---|
| Christy Mathewson | 10 |
| Chief Bender | 9 |
| Bob Gibson | 8 |
| Red Ruffing | 7 |
| Whitey Ford | 7 |
| George Mullin | 6 |
| Eddie Plank | 6 |
| Art Nehf | 6 |
| Waite Hoyt | 6 |

### STRIKEOUTS

| | |
|---|---|
| Whitey Ford | 94 |
| Bob Gibson | 92 |
| Allie Reynolds | 62 |
| Sandy Koufax | 61 |
| Red Ruffing | 61 |
| Chief Bender | 59 |
| Andy Pettitte | 56 |
| George Earnshaw | 56 |
| John Smoltz | 52 |
| Waite Hoyt | 49 |
| Roger Clemens | 49 |
| Christy Mathewson | 48 |

### BASES ON BALLS

| | |
|---|---|
| Whitey Ford | 34 |
| Allie Reynolds | 32 |
| Art Nehf | 32 |
| Jim Palmer | 31 |
| Bob Turley | 29 |
| Paul Derringer | 27 |
| Red Ruffing | 27 |
| Don Gullett | 26 |
| Burleigh Grimes | 26 |
| Andy Pettitte | 26 |
| Vic Raschi | 25 |

## Alltime Team Rankings, by Championships

| Team | W | L | Appearances | Pct. | Most Recent App. | Last Championship |
|---|---|---|---|---|---|---|
| New York Yankees | 27 | 13 | 40 | .675 | 2009 | 2009 |
| St. Louis Cardinals | 10 | 7 | 17 | .588 | 2006 | 2006 |
| Phila./K.C./Oakland Athletics | 9 | 5 | 14 | .643 | 1990 | 1989 |
| Boston Red Sox | 7 | 5 | 12 | .583 | 2007 | 2007 |
| Brooklyn/Los Angeles Dodgers | 6 | 12 | 18 | .333 | 1988 | 1988 |
| Pittsburgh Pirates | 5 | 2 | 7 | .714 | 1979 | 1979 |
| Cincinnati Reds | 5 | 4 | 9 | .556 | 1990 | 1990 |
| New York/San Francisco Giants | 5 | 12 | 17 | .294 | 2002 | 1954 |
| Detroit Tigers | 4 | 6 | 10 | .400 | 2006 | 1984 |
| Chicago White Sox | 3 | 2 | 5 | .600 | 2005 | 2005 |
| Wash. Senators/Minnesota Twins | 3 | 3 | 6 | .500 | 1991 | 1991 |
| St. Louis Browns/Baltimore Orioles | 3 | 4 | 7 | .429 | 1983 | 1983 |
| Boston/Milwaukee/Atlanta Braves | 3 | 6 | 9 | .333 | 1999 | 1995 |

# The World Series (Cont.)

## Alltime Team Rankings, by Championships (Cont.)

| Team | W | L | Appearances | Pct. | Most Recent App. | Last Championship |
|---|---|---|---|---|---|---|
| Florida Marlins | 2 | 0 | 2 | 1.000 | 2003 | 2003 |
| Toronto Blue Jays | 2 | 0 | 2 | 1.000 | 1993 | 1993 |
| New York Mets | 2 | 2 | 4 | .500 | 2000 | 1986 |
| Cleveland Indians | 2 | 3 | 5 | .400 | 1997 | 1948 |
| Philadelphia Phillies | 2 | 5 | 7 | .286 | 2009 | 2008 |
| Chicago Cubs | 2 | 8 | 10 | .200 | 1945 | 1908 |
| California/Anaheim/L.A. Angels | 1 | 0 | 1 | 1.000 | 2002 | 2002 |
| Arizona Diamondbacks | 1 | 0 | 1 | 1.000 | 2001 | 2001 |
| Kansas City Royals | 1 | 1 | 2 | .500 | 1985 | 1985 |
| Tampa Bay Rays | 0 | 1 | 1 | .000 | 2008 | — |
| Colorado Rockies | 0 | 1 | 1 | .000 | 2007 | — |
| Houston Astros | 0 | 1 | 1 | .000 | 2005 | — |
| Seattle Pilots/Milwaukee Brewers | 0 | 1 | 1 | .000 | 1982 | — |
| San Diego Padres | 0 | 2 | 2 | .000 | 1998 | — |

# League Pennant Winners

## National League

| Year | Team | Manager | W | L | Pct | GA |
|---|---|---|---|---|---|---|
| 1900 | Brooklyn | Ned Hanlon | 82 | 54 | .603 | 4½ |
| 1901 | Pittsburgh | Fred Clarke | 90 | 49 | .647 | 7½ |
| 1902 | Pittsburgh | Fred Clarke | 103 | 36 | .741 | 27½ |
| 1903 | Pittsburgh | Fred Clarke | 91 | 49 | .650 | 6½ |
| 1904 | New York | John McGraw | 106 | 47 | .693 | 13 |
| 1905 | New York | John McGraw | 105 | 48 | .686 | 9 |
| 1906 | Chicago | Frank Chance | 116 | 36 | .763 | 20 |
| 1907 | Chicago | Frank Chance | 107 | 45 | .704 | 17 |
| 1908 | Chicago | Frank Chance | 99 | 55 | .643 | 1 |
| 1909 | Pittsburgh | Fred Clarke | 110 | 42 | .724 | 6½ |
| 1910 | Chicago | Frank Chance | 104 | 50 | .675 | 13 |
| 1911 | New York | John McGraw | 99 | 54 | .647 | 7½ |
| 1912 | New York | John McGraw | 103 | 48 | .682 | 10 |
| 1913 | New York | John McGraw | 101 | 51 | .664 | 12½ |
| 1914 | Boston | George Stallings | 94 | 59 | .614 | 10½ |
| 1915 | Philadelphia | Pat Moran | 90 | 62 | .592 | 7 |
| 1916 | Brooklyn | Wilbert Robinson | 94 | 60 | .610 | 2½ |
| 1917 | New York | John McGraw | 98 | 56 | .636 | 10 |
| 1918 | Chicago | Fred Mitchell | 84 | 45 | .651 | 10½ |
| 1919 | Cincinnati | Pat Moran | 96 | 44 | .686 | 9 |
| 1920 | Brooklyn | Wilbert Robinson | 93 | 61 | .604 | 7 |
| 1921 | New York | John McGraw | 94 | 59 | .614 | 4 |
| 1922 | New York | John McGraw | 93 | 61 | .604 | 7 |
| 1923 | New York | John McGraw | 95 | 58 | .621 | 4½ |
| 1924 | New York | John McGraw | 93 | 60 | .608 | 1½ |
| 1925 | Pittsburgh | Bill McKechnie | 95 | 58 | .621 | 8½ |
| 1926 | St. Louis | Rogers Hornsby | 89 | 65 | .578 | 2 |
| 1927 | Pittsburgh | Donie Bush | 94 | 60 | .610 | 1½ |
| 1928 | St. Louis | Bill McKechnie | 95 | 59 | .617 | 2 |
| 1929 | Chicago | Joe McCarthy | 98 | 54 | .645 | 10½ |
| 1930 | St. Louis | Gabby Street | 92 | 62 | .597 | 2 |
| 1931 | St. Louis | Gabby Street | 101 | 53 | .656 | 13 |
| 1932 | Chicago | Charlie Grimm | 90 | 64 | .584 | 4 |
| 1933 | New York | Bill Terry | 91 | 61 | .599 | 5 |
| 1934 | St. Louis | Frankie Frisch | 95 | 58 | .621 | 2 |
| 1935 | Chicago | Charlie Grimm | 100 | 54 | .649 | 4 |
| 1936 | New York | Bill Terry | 92 | 62 | .597 | 5 |
| 1937 | New York | Bill Terry | 95 | 57 | .625 | 3 |
| 1938 | Chicago | Gabby Hartnett | 89 | 63 | .586 | 2 |
| 1939 | Cincinnati | Bill McKechnie | 97 | 57 | .630 | 4½ |
| 1940 | Cincinnati | Bill McKechnie | 100 | 53 | .654 | 12 |
| 1941 | Brooklyn | Leo Durocher | 100 | 54 | .649 | 2½ |
| 1942 | St. Louis | Billy Southworth | 106 | 48 | .688 | 2 |
| 1943 | St. Louis | Billy Southworth | 105 | 49 | .682 | 18 |
| 1944 | St. Louis | Billy Southworth | 105 | 49 | .682 | 14½ |
| 1945 | Chicago | Charlie Grimm | 98 | 56 | .636 | 3 |
| 1946 | St. Louis* | Eddie Dyer | 98 | 58 | .628 | 2 |

## National League (Cont.)

| Year | Team | Manager | W | L | Pct | GA |
|------|------|---------|---|---|-----|-----|
| 1947 ................Brooklyn | | Burt Shotton | 94 | 60 | .610 | 5 |
| 1948 ................Boston | | Billy Southworth | 91 | 62 | .595 | 6½ |
| 1949 ................Brooklyn | | Burt Shotton | 97 | 57 | .630 | 1 |
| 1950 ................Philadelphia | | Eddie Sawyer | 91 | 63 | .591 | 2 |
| 1951 ................New York† | | Leo Durocher | 98 | 59 | .624 | 1 |
| 1952 ................Brooklyn | | Chuck Dressen | 96 | 57 | .627 | 4½ |
| 1953 ................Brooklyn | | Chuck Dressen | 105 | 49 | .682 | 13 |
| 1954 ................New York | | Leo Durocher | 97 | 57 | .630 | 5 |
| 1955 ................Brooklyn | | Walter Alston | 98 | 55 | .641 | 13½ |
| 1956 ................Brooklyn | | Walter Alston | 93 | 61 | .604 | 1 |
| 1957 ................Milwaukee | | Fred Haney | 95 | 59 | .617 | 8 |
| 1958 ................Milwaukee | | Fred Haney | 92 | 62 | .597 | 8 |
| 1959 ................Los Angeles‡ | | Walter Alston | 88 | 68 | .564 | 2 |
| 1960 ................Pittsburgh | | Danny Murtaugh | 95 | 59 | .617 | 7 |
| 1961 ................Cincinnati | | Fred Hutchinson | 93 | 61 | .604 | 4 |
| 1962 ................San Francisco# | | Al Dark | 103 | 62 | .624 | 1 |
| 1963 ................Los Angeles | | Walter Alston | 99 | 63 | .611 | 6 |
| 1964 ................St. Louis | | Johnny Keane | 93 | 69 | .574 | 1 |
| 1965 ................Los Angeles | | Walter Alston | 97 | 65 | .599 | 2 |
| 1966 ................Los Angeles | | Walter Alston | 95 | 67 | .586 | 1½ |
| 1967 ................St. Louis | | Red Schoendienst | 101 | 60 | .627 | 10½ |
| 1968 ................St. Louis | | Red Schoendienst | 97 | 65 | .599 | 9 |
| 1969 ................New York (E)†† | | Gil Hodges | 100 | 62 | .617 | 8 |
| 1970 ................Cincinnati (W)†† | | Sparky Anderson | 102 | 60 | .630 | 14½ |
| 1971 ................Pittsburgh (E)†† | | Danny Murtaugh | 97 | 65 | .599 | 7 |
| 1972 ................Cincinnati (W)†† | | Sparky Anderson | 95 | 59 | .617 | 10½ |
| 1973 ................New York (E)†† | | Yogi Berra | 82 | 79 | .509 | 1½ |
| 1974 ................Los Angeles (W)†† | | Walter Alston | 102 | 60 | .630 | 4 |
| 1975 ................Cincinnati (W)†† | | Sparky Anderson | 108 | 54 | .667 | 20 |
| 1976 ................Cincinnati (W)†† | | Sparky Anderson | 102 | 60 | .630 | 10 |
| 1977 ................Los Angeles (W)†† | | Tommy Lasorda | 98 | 64 | .605 | 10 |
| 1978 ................Los Angeles (W)†† | | Tommy Lasorda | 95 | 67 | .586 | 2½ |
| 1979 ................Pittsburgh (E)†† | | Chuck Tanner | 98 | 64 | .605 | 2 |
| 1980 ................Philadelphia (E)†† | | Dallas Green | 91 | 71 | .562 | 1 |
| 1981 ................Los Angeles (W)†† | | Tommy Lasorda | 63 | 47 | .573 | ** |
| 1982 ................St. Louis (E)†† | | Whitey Herzog | 92 | 70 | .568 | 3 |
| 1983 ................Philadelphia (E)†† | | Pat Corrales/ Paul Owens | 90 | 72 | .556 | 6 |
| 1984 ................San Diego (W)†† | | Dick Williams | 92 | 70 | .568 | 12 |
| 1985 ................St. Louis (E)†† | | Whitey Herzog | 101 | 61 | .623 | 3 |
| 1986 ................New York (E)†† | | Davey Johnson | 108 | 54 | .667 | 21½ |
| 1987 ................St. Louis (E)†† | | Whitey Herzog | 95 | 67 | .586 | 3 |
| 1988 ................Los Angeles (W)†† | | Tommy Lasorda | 94 | 67 | .584 | 7 |
| 1989 ................San Francisco (W)†† | | Roger Craig | 92 | 70 | .568 | 3 |
| 1990 ................Cincinnati (W)†† | | Lou Piniella | 91 | 71 | .562 | 5 |
| 1991 ................Atlanta (W)†† | | Bobby Cox | 94 | 68 | .580 | 1 |
| 1992 ................Atlanta (W)†† | | Bobby Cox | 98 | 64 | .605 | 8 |
| 1993 ................Philadelphia (E)†† | | Jim Fregosi | 97 | 65 | .599 | 3 |
| 1994 ................Season ended Aug. 11 due to players' strike. | | | | | | |
| 1995 ................Atlanta (E)†† | | Bobby Cox | 90 | 54 | .625 | 21 |
| 1996 ................Atlanta (E)†† | | Bobby Cox | 96 | 66 | .593 | 8 |
| 1997 ................Florida (wc)†† | | Jim Leyland | 92 | 70 | .568 | -9 |
| 1998 ................San Diego (W)†† | | Bruce Bochy | 98 | 64 | .605 | 9½ |
| 1999 ................Atlanta (E)†† | | Bobby Cox | 103 | 59 | .636 | 6½ |
| 2000 ................New York (wc)†† | | Bobby Valentine | 94 | 68 | .580 | -6½ |
| 2001 ................Arizona (W)†† | | Bob Brenly | 92 | 70 | .568 | 2 |
| 2002 ................San Francisco (wc)†† | | Dusty Baker | 95 | 66 | .590 | -2½ |
| 2003 ................Florida (wc)†† | | Jack McKeon | 91 | 71 | .562 | -10 |
| 2004 ................St. Louis (C)†† | | Tony LaRussa | 105 | 57 | .648 | 13 |
| 2005 ................Houston (wc)†† | | Phil Garner | 89 | 73 | .549 | -11 |
| 2006 ................St. Louis (C)†† | | Tony LaRussa | 83 | 78 | .516 | 1½ |
| 2007 ................Colorado (wc)††§ | | Clint Hurdle | 89 | 73 | .549 | -1 |
| 2008 ................Philadelphia (E)†† | | Charlie Manuel | 92 | 70 | .568 | 3 |
| 2009 ................Philadelphia (E)†† | | Charlie Manuel | 93 | 69 | .574 | 6 |

*Defeated Brooklyn, two games to none, in playoff for pennant. †Defeated Brooklyn, two games to one, in playoff for pennant. ‡Defeated Milwaukee, two games to none, in playoff for pennant. #Defeated Los Angeles, two games to one, in playoff for pennant. § Defeated San Diego in one-game playoff for wild card. ††Won Championship Series. **First half 36–21; second half 27–26, in season split by strike; defeated Houston in playoff for Western Division title.

## American League

| Year | Team | Manager | W | L | Pct | GA |
|------|------|---------|---|---|-----|----|
| 1901 | Chicago | Clark Griffith | 83 | 53 | .610 | 4 |
| 1902 | Philadelphia | Connie Mack | 83 | 53 | .610 | 5 |
| 1903 | Boston | Jimmy Collins | 91 | 47 | .659 | 14½ |
| 1904 | Boston | Jimmy Collins | 95 | 59 | .617 | 1½ |
| 1905 | Philadelphia | Connie Mack | 92 | 56 | .622 | 2 |
| 1906 | Chicago | Fielder Jones | 93 | 58 | .616 | 3 |
| 1907 | Detroit | Hughie Jennings | 92 | 58 | .613 | 1½ |
| 1908 | Detroit | Hughie Jennings | 90 | 63 | .588 | ½ |
| 1909 | Detroit | Hughie Jennings | 98 | 54 | .645 | 3½ |
| 1910 | Philadelphia | Connie Mack | 102 | 48 | .680 | 14½ |
| 1911 | Philadelphia | Connie Mack | 101 | 50 | .669 | 13½ |
| 1912 | Boston | Jake Stahl | 105 | 47 | .691 | 14 |
| 1913 | Philadelphia | Connie Mack | 96 | 57 | .627 | 6½ |
| 1914 | Philadelphia | Connie Mack | 99 | 53 | .651 | 8½ |
| 1915 | Boston | Bill Carrigan | 101 | 50 | .669 | 2½ |
| 1916 | Boston | Bill Carrigan | 91 | 63 | .591 | 2 |
| 1917 | Chicago | Pants Rowland | 100 | 54 | .649 | 9 |
| 1918 | Boston | Ed Barrow | 75 | 51 | .595 | 2½ |
| 1919 | Chicago | Kid Gleason | 88 | 52 | .629 | 3½ |
| 1920 | Cleveland | Tris Speaker | 98 | 56 | .636 | 2 |
| 1921 | New York | Miller Huggins | 98 | 55 | .641 | 4½ |
| 1922 | New York | Miller Huggins | 94 | 60 | .610 | 1 |
| 1923 | New York | Miller Huggins | 98 | 54 | .645 | 16 |
| 1924 | Washington | Bucky Harris | 92 | 62 | .597 | 2 |
| 1925 | Washington | Bucky Harris | 96 | 55 | .636 | 8½ |
| 1926 | New York | Miller Huggins | 91 | 63 | .591 | 3 |
| 1927 | New York | Miller Huggins | 110 | 44 | .714 | 19 |
| 1928 | New York | Miller Huggins | 101 | 53 | .656 | 2½ |
| 1929 | Philadelphia | Connie Mack | 104 | 46 | .693 | 18 |
| 1930 | Philadelphia | Connie Mack | 102 | 52 | .662 | 8 |
| 1931 | Philadelphia | Connie Mack | 107 | 45 | .704 | 13½ |
| 1932 | New York | Joe McCarthy | 107 | 47 | .695 | 13 |
| 1933 | Washington | Joe Cronin | 99 | 53 | .651 | 7 |
| 1934 | Detroit | Mickey Cochrane | 101 | 53 | .656 | 7 |
| 1935 | Detroit | Mickey Cochrane | 93 | 58 | .616 | 3 |
| 1936 | New York | Joe McCarthy | 102 | 51 | .667 | 19½ |
| 1937 | New York | Joe McCarthy | 102 | 52 | .662 | 13 |
| 1938 | New York | Joe McCarthy | 99 | 53 | .651 | 9½ |
| 1939 | New York | Joe McCarthy | 106 | 45 | .702 | 17 |
| 1940 | Detroit | Del Baker | 90 | 64 | .584 | 1 |
| 1941 | New York | Joe McCarthy | 101 | 53 | .656 | 17 |
| 1942 | New York | Joe McCarthy | 103 | 51 | .669 | 9 |
| 1943 | New York | Joe McCarthy | 98 | 56 | .636 | 13½ |
| 1944 | St. Louis | Luke Sewell | 89 | 65 | .578 | 1 |
| 1945 | Detroit | Steve O'Neill | 88 | 65 | .575 | 1½ |
| 1946 | Boston | Joe Cronin | 104 | 50 | .675 | 12 |
| 1947 | New York | Bucky Harris | 97 | 57 | .630 | 12 |
| 1948 | Cleveland† | Lou Boudreau | 97 | 58 | .626 | 1 |
| 1949 | New York | Casey Stengel | 97 | 57 | .630 | 1 |
| 1950 | New York | Casey Stengel | 98 | 56 | .636 | 3 |
| 1951 | New York | Casey Stengel | 98 | 56 | .636 | 5 |
| 1952 | New York | Casey Stengel | 95 | 59 | .617 | 2 |
| 1953 | New York | Casey Stengel | 99 | 52 | .656 | 8½ |
| 1954 | Cleveland | Al Lopez | 111 | 43 | .721 | 8 |
| 1955 | New York | Casey Stengel | 96 | 58 | .623 | 3 |
| 1956 | New York | Casey Stengel | 97 | 57 | .630 | 9 |
| 1957 | New York | Casey Stengel | 98 | 56 | .636 | 8 |
| 1958 | New York | Casey Stengel | 92 | 62 | .597 | 10 |
| 1959 | Chicago | Al Lopez | 94 | 60 | .610 | 5 |
| 1960 | New York | Casey Stengel | 97 | 57 | .630 | 8 |
| 1961 | New York | Ralph Houk | 109 | 53 | .673 | 8 |
| 1962 | New York | Ralph Houk | 96 | 66 | .593 | 5 |
| 1963 | New York | Ralph Houk | 104 | 57 | .646 | 10½ |
| 1964 | New York | Yogi Berra | 99 | 63 | .611 | 1 |
| 1965 | Minnesota | Sam Mele | 102 | 60 | .630 | 7 |
| 1966 | Baltimore | Hank Bauer | 97 | 63 | .606 | 9 |
| 1967 | Boston | Dick Williams | 92 | 70 | .568 | 1 |
| 1968 | Detroit | Mayo Smith | 103 | 59 | .636 | 12 |

## American League *(Cont.)*

| Year | Team | Manager | W | L | Pct | GA |
|---|---|---|---|---|---|---|
| 1969 | Baltimore (E)‡ | Earl Weaver | 109 | 53 | .673 | 19 |
| 1970 | Baltimore (E)‡ | Earl Weaver | 108 | 54 | .667 | 15 |
| 1971 | Baltimore (E)‡ | Earl Weaver | 101 | 57 | .639 | 12 |
| 1972 | Oakland (W)‡ | Dick Williams | 93 | 62 | .600 | 5½ |
| 1973 | Oakland (W)‡ | Dick Williams | 94 | 68 | .580 | 6 |
| 1974 | Oakland (W)‡ | Al Dark | 90 | 72 | .556 | 5 |
| 1975 | Boston (E)‡ | Darrell Johnson | 95 | 65 | .594 | 4½ |
| 1976 | New York (E)‡ | Billy Martin | 97 | 62 | .610 | 10½ |
| 1977 | New York (E)‡ | Billy Martin | 100 | 62 | .617 | 2½ |
| 1978 | New York (E)†‡ | Billy Martin, Bob Lemon | 100 | 63 | .613 | 1 |
| 1979 | Baltimore (E)‡ | Earl Weaver | 102 | 57 | .642 | 8 |
| 1980 | Kansas City (W)‡ | Jim Frey | 97 | 65 | .599 | 14 |
| 1981 | New York (E)‡ | Gene Michael/Bob Lemon | 59 | 48 | .551 | # |
| 1982 | Milwaukee (E)‡ | Buck Rodgers, Harvey Kuenn | 95 | 67 | .586 | 1 |
| 1983 | Baltimore (E)‡ | Joe Altobelli | 98 | 64 | .605 | 6 |
| 1984 | Detroit (E)‡ | Sparky Anderson | 104 | 58 | .642 | 15 |
| 1985 | Kansas City (W)‡ | Dick Howser | 91 | 71 | .562 | 1 |
| 1986 | Boston (E)‡ | John McNamara | 95 | 66 | .590 | 5½ |
| 1987 | Minnesota (W)‡ | Tom Kelly | 85 | 77 | .525 | 2 |
| 1988 | Oakland (W)‡ | Tony LaRussa | 104 | 58 | .642 | 13 |
| 1989 | Oakland (W)‡ | Tony LaRussa | 99 | 63 | .611 | 7 |
| 1990 | Oakland (W)‡ | Tony LaRussa | 103 | 59 | .636 | 9 |
| 1991 | Minnesota (W)‡ | Tom Kelly | 95 | 67 | .586 | 8 |
| 1992 | Toronto‡ | Cito Gaston | 96 | 66 | .593 | 4 |
| 1993 | Toronto‡ | Cito Gaston | 95 | 67 | .586 | 7 |
| 1994 | Season ended Aug. 11 due to players' strike. | | | | | |
| 1995 | Cleveland (C)‡ | Mike Hargrove | 100 | 44 | .694 | 30 |
| 1996 | New York (E)‡ | Joe Torre | 92 | 70 | .568 | 4 |
| 1997 | Cleveland (C)‡ | Mike Hargrove | 86 | 75 | .534 | 6 |
| 1998 | New York (E)‡ | Joe Torre | 114 | 48 | .704 | 22 |
| 1999 | New York (E)‡ | Joe Torre | 98 | 64 | .605 | 4 |
| 2000 | New York (E)‡ | Joe Torre | 87 | 74 | .540 | 2½ |
| 2001 | New York (E)‡ | Joe Torre | 95 | 65 | .594 | 13½ |
| 2002 | Anaheim (wc)‡ | Mike Scioscia | 99 | 63 | .611 | -4 |
| 2003 | New York (E)‡ | Joe Torre | 101 | 61 | .623 | 6 |
| 2004 | Boston (wc)‡ | Terry Francona | 98 | 64 | .605 | -3 |
| 2005 | Chicago (C)‡ | Ozzie Guillen | 99 | 63 | .611 | 6 |
| 2006 | Detroit (wc)‡ | Jim Leyland | 95 | 67 | .586 | -1 |
| 2007 | Boston (E)‡ | Terry Francona | 96 | 66 | .593 | 2 |
| 2008 | Tampa Bay (E)‡ | Joe Maddon | 97 | 65 | .599 | 2 |
| 2009 | New York (E)‡ | Joe Girardi | 103 | 59 | .636 | 8 |

†Defeated Boston in one-game playoff. ‡Won championship series.
#First half 34–22; second half 25–26, in season split by strike; defeated Milwaukee in playoff for Eastern Divison title.

# League Championship Series

## National League

|  |  |
|------|--------|
| 1969 | New York (E) 3, Atlanta (W) 0 |
| 1970 | Cincinnati (W) 3, Pittsburgh (E) 0 |
| 1971 | Pittsburgh (E) 3, San Francisco (W) 1 |
| 1972 | Cincinnati (W) 3, Pittsburgh (E) 2 |
| 1973 | New York (E) 3, Cincinnati (W) 2 |
| 1974 | Los Angeles (W) 3, Pittsburgh (E) 1 |
| 1975 | Cincinnati (W) 3, Pittsburgh (E) 0 |
| 1976 | Cincinnati (W) 3, Philadelphia (E) 0 |
| 1977 | Los Angeles (W) 3, Philadelphia (E) 1 |
| 1978 | Los Angeles (W) 3, Philadelphia (E) 1 |
| 1979 | Pittsburgh (E) 3, Cincinnati (W) 0 |
| 1980 | Philadelphia (E) 3, Houston (W) 2 |
| 1981 | Los Angeles (W) 3, Montreal (E) 2 |
| 1982 | St. Louis (E) 3, Atlanta (W) 0 |
| 1983 | Philadelphia (E) 3, Los Angeles (W) 1 |
| 1984 | San Diego (W) 3, Chicago (E) 2 |
| 1985 | St. Louis (E) 4, Los Angeles (W) 2 |
| 1986 | New York (E) 4, Houston (W) 2 |
| 1987 | St. Louis (E) 4, San Francisco (W) 3 |
| 1988 | Los Angeles (W) 4, New York (E) 3 |
| 1989 | San Francisco (W) 4, Chicago (E) 1 |
| 1990 | Cincinnati (W) 4, Pittsburgh (E) 2 |
| 1991 | Atlanta (W) 4, Pittsburgh (E) 3 |
| 1992 | Atlanta (W) 4, Pittsburgh (E) 3 |
| 1993 | Philadelphia (E) 4, Atlanta (W) 2 |
| 1994 | Playoffs canceled due to players' strike. |
| 1995 | Atlanta (E) 4, Cincinnati (C) 0 |
| 1996 | Atlanta (E) 4, St. Louis (C) 3 |
| 1997 | Florida (wc) 4, Atlanta (E) 2 |
| 1998 | San Diego (W) 4, Atlanta (E) 2 |
| 1999 | Atlanta (E) 4, New York (wc) 2 |
| 2000 | New York (wc) 4, St. Louis (C) 1 |
| 2001 | Arizona (W) 4, Atlanta (E) 1 |
| 2002 | San Francisco (wc) 4, St. Louis (C) 1 |
| 2003 | Florida (wc) 4, Chicago (C) 3 |
| 2004 | St. Louis (C) 4, Houston (wc) 3 |
| 2005 | Houston (wc) 4, St. Louis (C) 2 |
| 2006 | St. Louis (C) 4, New York (E) 3 |
| 2007 | Colorado (wc) 4, Arizona (W) 0 |
| 2008 | Philadelphia (E) 4, Los Angeles (W) 1 |
| 2009 | Philadelphia (E) 4, Los Angeles (W) 1 |

## American League

|  |  |
|------|--------|
| 1969 | Baltimore (E) 3, Minnesota (W) 0 |
| 1970 | Baltimore (E) 3, Minnesota (W) 0 |
| 1971 | Baltimore (E) 3, Oakland (W) 0 |
| 1972 | Oakland (W) 3, Detroit (E) 2 |
| 1973 | Oakland (W) 3, Baltimore (E) 2 |
| 1974 | Oakland (W) 3, Baltimore (E) 1 |
| 1975 | Boston (E) 3, Oakland (W) 0 |
| 1976 | New York (E) 3, Kansas City (W) 2 |
| 1977 | New York (E) 3, Kansas City (W) 2 |
| 1978 | New York (E) 3, Kansas City (W) 1 |
| 1979 | Baltimore (E) 3, California (W) 1 |
| 1980 | Kansas City (W) 3, New York (E) 0 |
| 1981 | New York (E) 3, Oakland (W) 0 |
| 1982 | Milwaukee (E) 3, California (W) 2 |
| 1983 | Baltimore (E) 3, Chicago (W) 1 |
| 1984 | Detroit (E) 3, Kansas City (W) 0 |
| 1985 | Kansas City (W) 4, Toronto (E) 3 |
| 1986 | Boston (E) 4, California (W) 3 |
| 1987 | Minnesota (W) 4, Detroit (E) 1 |
| 1988 | Oakland (W) 4, Boston (E) 0 |
| 1989 | Oakland (W) 4, Toronto (E) 1 |
| 1990 | Oakland (W) 4, Boston (E) 0 |
| 1991 | Minnesota (W) 4, Toronto (E) 1 |
| 1992 | Toronto (E) 4, Oakland (W) 2 |
| 1993 | Toronto (E) 4, Chicago (W) 2 |
| 1994 | Playoffs canceled due to players' strike. |
| 1995 | Cleveland (C) 4, Seattle (W) 2 |
| 1996 | New York (E) 4, Baltimore (wc) 1 |
| 1997 | Cleveland (C) 4, Baltimore (E) 2 |
| 1998 | New York (E) 4, Cleveland (C) 2 |
| 1999 | New York (E) 4, Boston (wc) 1 |
| 2000 | New York (E) 4, Seattle (wc) 2 |
| 2001 | New York (E) 4, Seattle (W) 1 |
| 2002 | Anaheim (wc) 4, Minnesota (C) 1 |
| 2003 | New York (E) 4, Boston (wc) 3 |
| 2004 | Boston (wc) 4, New York (E) 3 |
| 2005 | Chicago (C) 4, Los Angeles (W) 1 |
| 2006 | Detroit (wc) 4, Oakland (W) 0 |
| 2007 | Boston (E) 4, Cleveland (C) 3 |
| 2008 | Tampa Bay (E) 4, Boston (wc) 3 |
| 2009 | New York (E) 4, Los Angeles (W) 2 |

## NLCS Most Valuable Player

|  |  |
|------|--------|
| 1977 | Dusty Baker, LA |
| 1978 | Steve Garvey, LA |
| 1979 | Willie Stargell, Pitt |
| 1980 | Manny Trillo, Phi |
| 1981 | Burt Hooton, LA |
| 1982 | Darrell Porter, StL |
| 1983 | Gary Matthews, Phi |
| 1984 | Steve Garvey, SD |
| 1985 | Ozzie Smith, StL |
| 1986 | Mike Scott, Hou |
| 1987 | Jeffrey Leonard, SF |
| 1988 | Orel Hershiser, LA |
| 1989 | Will Clark, SF |
| 1990 | R. Myers/R. Dibble, Cin |
| 1991 | Steve Avery, Atl |
| 1992 | John Smoltz, Atl |
| 1993 | Curt Schilling, Phi |
| 1994 | Playoffs canceled |
| 1995 | Mike Devereaux, Atl |
| 1996 | Javier Lopez, Atl |
| 1997 | Livan Hernandez, Fla |
| 1998 | Sterling Hitchcock, SD |
| 1999 | Eddie Perez, Atl |
| 2000 | Mike Hampton, NY |
| 2001 | Craig Counsell, Ariz |
| 2002 | Benito Santiago, SF |
| 2003 | Ivan Rodriguez, Fla |
| 2004 | Albert Pujols, StL |
| 2005 | Roy Oswalt, Hou |
| 2006 | Jeff Suppan, StL |
| 2007 | Matt Holliday, Col |
| 2008 | Cole Hamels, Phi |
| 2009 | Ryan Howard, Phi |

## ALCS Most Valuable Player

|  |  |
|------|--------|
| 1980 | Frank White, KC |
| 1981 | Graig Nettles, NY |
| 1982 | Fred Lynn, Calif |
| 1983 | Mike Boddicker, Balt |
| 1984 | Kirk Gibson, Det |
| 1985 | George Brett, KC |
| 1986 | Marty Barrett, Bos |
| 1987 | Gary Gaetti, Minn |
| 1988 | Dennis Eckersley, Oak |
| 1989 | Rickey Henderson, Oak |
| 1990 | Dave Stewart, Oak |
| 1991 | Kirby Puckett, Minn |
| 1992 | Roberto Alomar, Tor |
| 1993 | Dave Stewart, Tor |
| 1994 | Playoffs canceled |
| 1995 | Orel Hershiser, Clev |
| 1996 | Bernie Williams, NY |
| 1997 | Marquis Grissom, Clev |
| 1998 | David Wells, NY |
| 1999 | Orlando Hernandez, NY |
| 2000 | David Justice, NY |
| 2001 | Andy Pettitte, NY |
| 2002 | Adam Kennedy, Ana |
| 2003 | Mariano Rivera, NY |
| 2004 | David Ortiz, Bos |
| 2005 | Paul Konerko, Chi |
| 2006 | Placido Polanco, Det |
| 2007 | Josh Beckett, Bos |
| 2008 | Matt Garza, TB |
| 2009 | C.C. Sabathia, NY |

# Divisional Playoffs

## National League

1995 ................Atlanta (E) 3, Colorado (wc) 1
Cincinnati (C) 3, Los Angeles (W) 0
1996 ................St. Louis (C) 3, San Diego (W) 0
Atlanta (E) 3, Los Angeles (wc) 0
1997 ................Atlanta (E) 3, Houston (C) 0
Florida (wc) 3, San Francisco (W) 0
1998 ................San Diego (W) 3, Houston (C) 1
Atlanta (E) 3, Chicago (wc) 0
1999 ................Atlanta (E) 3, Houston (C) 1
New York (wc) 3, Arizona (W) 1
2000 ................St. Louis (C) 3, Atlanta (E) 0
New York (wc) 3, San Francisco (W) 1
2001 ................Atlanta (E) 3, Houston (C) 0
Arizona (W) 3, St. Louis (wc) 2
2002 ................St. Louis (C) 3, Arizona (W) 0
San Francisco (wc) 3, Atlanta (E) 2
2003 ................Chicago (C) 3, Atlanta (E) 2
Florida (wc) 3, San Francisco (W) 1
2004 ................St. Louis (C) 3, Los Angeles (W) 1
Houston (wc) 3, Atlanta (E) 2
2005 ................Houston (wc) 3, Atlanta (E) 1
St. Louis (C) 3, San Diego (W) 1
2006 ................St. Louis (C) 3, San Diego (W) 1
New York (E) 3, Los Angeles (wc) 0
2007 ................Colorado (wc) 3, Philadelphia (E) 0
Arizona (W) 3, Chicago (C) 0
2008 ................Los Angeles (W) 3, Chicago (C) 0
Philadelphia (E) 3, Milwaukee (wc) 1
2009 ................Los Angeles (W) 3, St. Louis (C) 0
Philadelphia (E) 3, Colorado (wc) 1

## American League

1995 ................Cleveland (C) 3, Boston (E) 0
Seattle (W) 3, New York (wc) 2
1996 ................Baltimore (wc) 3, Cleveland (C) 1
New York (E) 3, Texas (W) 1
1997 ................Baltimore (E) 3, Seattle (W) 1
Cleveland (C) 3, New York (wc) 2
1998 ................New York (E) 3, Texas (W) 0
Cleveland (C) 3, Boston (wc) 1
1999 ................New York (E) 3, Texas (W) 1
Boston (wc) 3, Cleveland (C) 2
2000 ................New York (E) 3, Oakland (W) 2
Seattle (W) 3, Chicago (C) 0
2001 ................Seattle (W) 3, Cleveland (wc) 2
New York (E) 3, Oakland (wc) 2
2002 ................Minnesota (C) 3, Oakland (W) 2
Anaheim (wc) 3, New York (E) 1
2003 ................New York (E) 3, Minnesota (C) 1
Boston (wc) 3, Oakland (W) 2
2004 ................New York (E) 3, Minnesota (C) 1
Boston (wc) 3 Anaheim (W) 0
2005 ................Los Angeles (W) 3, New York (E) 2
Chicago (C) 3, Boston (wc) 0
2006 ................Oakland (W) 3, Minnesota (C) 0
Detroit (wc) 3, New York (E) 1
2007 ................Boston (E) 3, Los Angeles (W) 0
Cleveland (C) 3, New York (wc) 1
2008 ................Boston (wc) 3, Los Angeles (W) 1
Tampa Bay (E) 3, Chicago (C) 1
2009 ................Los Angeles (W) 3, Boston (wc) 0
New York (E) 3, Minnesota (C) 0

# The All-Star Game

## Results

| Date | Winner | Score | Site |
|------|--------|-------|------|
| 7-6-33 | American | 4–2 | Comiskey Park, Chi |
| 7-10-34 | American | 9–7 | Polo Grounds, NY |
| 7-8-35 | American | 4–1 | Municipal Stadium, Clev |
| 7-7-36 | National | 4–3 | Braves Field, Bos |
| 7-7-37 | American | 8–3 | Griffith Stadium, Wash |
| 7-6-38 | National | 4–1 | Crosley Field, Cin |
| 7-11-39 | American | 3–1 | Yankee Stadium, NY |
| 7-10-40 | National | 4–0 | Sportsman's Park, StL |
| 7-8-41 | American | 7–5 | Briggs Stadium, Det |
| 7-6-42 | American | 3–1 | Polo Grounds, NY |
| 7-13-43 | American | 5–3 | Shibe Park, Phi |
| 7-11-44 | National | 7–1 | Forbes Field, Pitt |
| 1945 | No game due to wartime travel restrictions. | | |
| 7-9-46 | American | 12–0 | Fenway Park, Bos |
| 7-8-47 | American | 2–1 | Wrigley Field, Chi |
| 7-13-48 | American | 5–2 | Sportsman's Park, StL |
| 7-12-49 | American | 11–7 | Ebbets Field, Bklyn |
| 7-11-50 | National | 4–3 | Comiskey Park, Chi |
| 7-10-51 | National | 8–3 | Briggs Stadium, Det |
| 7-8-52 | National | 3–2 | Shibe Park, Phi |
| 7-14-53 | National | 5–1 | Crosley Field, Cin |
| 7-13-54 | American | 11–9 | Municipal Stadium, Clev |
| 7-12-55 | National | 6–5 | County Stadium, Mil |
| 7-10-56 | National | 7–3 | Griffith Stadium, Wash |
| 7-9-57 | American | 6–5 | Busch Stadium, StL |
| 7-8-58 | American | 4–3 | Memorial Stadium, Balt |
| 7-7-59 | National | 5–4 | Forbes Field, Pitt |
| 8-3-59 | American | 5–3 | Memorial Coliseum, LA |
| 7-11-60 | National | 5–3 | Municipal Stadium, KC |
| 7-13-60 | National | 6–0 | Yankee Stadium, NY |
| 7-11-61 | National | 5–4 | Candlestick Park, SF |
| 7-31-61 | Tie* | 1–1 | Fenway Park, Bos |
| 7-10-62 | National | 3–1 | D.C. Stadium, Wash |
| 7-30-62 | American | 9–4 | Wrigley Field, Chi |
| 7-9-63 | National | 5–3 | Municipal Stadium, Clev |
| 7-7-64 | National | 7–4 | Shea Stadium, NY |
| 7-13-65 | National | 6–5 | Metro. Stadium, Minn |
| 7-12-66 | National | 2–1 | Busch Stadium, StL |
| 7-11-67 | National | 2–1 | Anaheim Stadium, Cal |
| 7-9-68 | National | 1–0 | Astrodome, Hou |
| 7-23-69 | National | 9–3 | R.F.K. Stadium, Wash. |
| 7-14-70 | National | 5–4 | Riverfront Stadium, Cin |
| 7-13-71 | American | 6–4 | Tiger Stadium, Det |
| 7-25-72 | National | 4–3 | Atlanta Stadium, Atl |
| 7-24-73 | National | 7–1 | Royals Stadium, KC |
| 7-23-74 | National | 7–2 | Three Rivers Stadium, Pitt |
| 7-15-75 | National | 6–3 | County Stadium, Mil |
| 7-13-76 | National | 7–1 | Veterans Stadium, Phi |
| 7-19-77 | National | 7–5 | Yankee Stadium, NY |
| 7-11-78 | National | 7–3 | Jack Murphy Stadium, SD |
| 7-17-79 | National | 7–6 | Kingdome, Sea |
| 7-8-80 | National | 4–2 | Dodger Stadium, LA |
| 8-9-81 | National | 5–4 | Municipal Stadium, Clev |
| 7-13-82 | National | 4–1 | Olympic Stadium, Mtl |
| 7-6-83 | American | 13–3 | Comiskey Park, Chi |
| 7-10-84 | National | 3–1 | Candlestick Park, SF |
| 7-16-85 | National | 6–1 | Metrodome, Minn |
| 7-15-86 | American | 3–2 | Astrodome, Hou |
| 7-14-87 | National | 2–0 | Oakland Coliseum, Oak |
| 7-12-88 | American | 2–1 | Riverfront Stadium, Cin |
| 7-11-89 | American | 5–3 | Anaheim Stadium, Cal |
| 7-10-90 | American | 2–0 | Wrigley Field, Chi |
| 7-9-91 | American | 4–2 | SkyDome, Tor |
| 7-14-92 | American | 13–6 | Jack Murphy Stadium, SD |
| 7-13-93 | American | 9–3 | Camden Yards, Balt |
| 7-12-94 | National | 8–7 | Three Rivers Stadium, Pitt |
| 7-11-95 | National | 3–2 | Ballpark in Arlington, Tex |
| 7-9-96 | National | 6–0 | Veterans Stadium, Phi |

*Game called because of rain after nine innings.

## Results *(Cont.)*

| Date | Winner | Score | Site | Date | Winner | Score | Site |
|------|--------|-------|------|------|--------|-------|------|
| 7-8-97 | American | 3–1 | Jacobs Field, Cle | 7-13-04 | American | 9–4 | Minute Maid Park, Hou |
| 7-7-98 | American | 13–8 | Coors Field, Col | 7-12-05 | American | 7–5 | Comerica Park, Det |
| 7-13-99 | American | 4–1 | Fenway Park, Bos | 7-11-06 | American | 3–2 | PNC Park, Pitt |
| 7-11-00 | American | 6–3 | Turner Field, Atl | 7-10-07 | American | 5–4 | AT&T Park, SF |
| 7-10-01 | American | 4–1 | Safeco Field, Sea | 7-15-08 | American | 4–3 | Yankee Stadium, NY |
| 7-9-02 | Tie (11 inn) | 7–7 | Miller Park, Mil | 7-14-09 | American | 4–3 | Busch Stadium, StL |
| 7-15-03 | American | 7–6 | Comiskey Park, Chi | | | | |

### Most Valuable Players

| Year | Player | Lg | Year | Player | Lg | Year | Player | Lg |
|------|--------|----|------|--------|----|------|--------|----|
| 1962 | Maury Wills, LA | NL | 1977 | Don Sutton, LA | NL | 1994 | Fred McGriff, Atl | NL |
| | Leon Wagner, LA | AL | 1978 | Steve Garvey, LA | NL | 1995 | Jeff Conine, Fla | NL |
| 1963 | Willie Mays, SF | NL | 1979 | Dave Parker, Pitt | NL | 1996 | Mike Piazza, LA | NL |
| 1964 | Johnny Callison, Phi | NL | 1980 | Ken Griffey, Cin | NL | 1997 | Sandy Alomar, Clev | AL |
| 1965 | Juan Marichal, SF | NL | 1981 | Gary Carter, Mtl | NL | 1998 | Roberto Alomar, Balt | AL |
| 1966 | Brooks Robinson, Balt | AL | 1982 | Dave Concepcion, Cin | NL | 1999 | Pedro Martinez, Bos | AL |
| 1967 | Tony Perez, Cin | NL | 1983 | Fred Lynn, Calif | AL | 2000 | Derek Jeter, NY | AL |
| 1968 | Willie Mays, SF | NL | 1984 | Gary Carter, Mtl | NL | 2001 | Cal Ripken Jr., Balt | AL |
| 1969 | Willie McCovey, SF | NL | 1985 | LaMarr Hoyt, SD | NL | 2002 | None selected | |
| 1970 | Carl Yastrzemski, Bos | AL | 1986 | Roger Clemens, Bos | AL | 2003 | Garret Anderson, Ana | AL |
| 1971 | Frank Robinson, Balt | AL | 1987 | Tim Raines, Mtl | NL | 2004 | Alfonso Soriano, Tex | AL |
| 1972 | Joe Morgan, Cin | NL | 1988 | Terry Steinbach, Oak | AL | 2005 | Miguel Tejada, Balt | AL |
| 1973 | Bobby Bonds, SF | NL | 1989 | Bo Jackson, KC | AL | 2006 | Michael Young, Tex | AL |
| 1974 | Steve Garvey, LA | NL | 1990 | Julio Franco, Tex | AL | 2007 | Ichiro Suzuki, Sea | AL |
| 1975 | Bill Madlock, Chi | NL | 1991 | Cal Ripken Jr., Balt | AL | 2008 | J.D. Drew, Bos | AL |
| | Jon Matlack, NY | NL | 1992 | Ken Griffey Jr., Sea | AL | 2009 | Carl Crawford, TB | AL |
| 1976 | George Foster, Cin | NL | 1993 | Kirby Puckett, Minn | AL | | | |

# The Regular Season

## Most Valuable Players
### NATIONAL LEAGUE

| Year | Name and Team | Position | Noteworthy |
|------|---------------|----------|------------|
| 1911 | Wildfire Schulte, Chi | Outfield | 21 HR†, 121 RBI†, .300 |
| 1912 | *Larry Doyle, NY | Second base | 10 HR, 90 RBI, .330 |
| 1913 | Jake Daubert, Bklyn | First base | 52 RBI, .350† |
| 1914 | *Johnny Evers, Bos | Second base | FA .976†, .279 |
| 1915–23 | No selection | | |
| 1924 | Dazzy Vance, Bklyn | Pitcher | 28†–6, 2.16 ERA†, 262 K† |
| 1925 | Rogers Hornsby, StL | Second base, Manager | 39 HR†, 143 RBI†, .403† |
| 1926 | *Bob O'Farrell, StL | Catcher | 7 HR, 68 RBI, .293 |
| 1927 | *Paul Waner, Pitt | Outfield | 237 hits†, 131 RBI†, .380† |
| 1928 | *Jim Bottomley, StL | First base | 31 HR†, 136 RBI†, .325 |
| 1929 | *Rogers Hornsby, Chi | Second base | 39 HR, 149 RBI, 156 runs†, .380 |
| 1930 | No selection | | |
| 1931 | *Frankie Frisch, StL | Second base | 4 HR, 82 RBI, 28 SB†, .311 |
| 1932 | Chuck Klein, Phi | Outfield | 38 HR†, 137 RBI, 226 hits†, .348 |
| 1933 | *Carl Hubbell, NY | Pitcher | 23†–12, 1.66 ERA†, 10 SO† |
| 1934 | *Dizzy Dean, StL | Pitcher | 30†–7, 2.66 ERA, 195 K† |
| 1935 | *Gabby Hartnett, Chi | Catcher | 13 HR, 91 RBI, .344 |
| 1936 | *Carl Hubbell, NY | Pitcher | 26†–6, 2.31 ERA† |
| 1937 | Joe Medwick, StL | Outfield | 31 HR‡, 154 RBI†, 111 runs†, .374† |
| 1938 | Ernie Lombardi, Cin | Catcher | 19 HR, 95 RBI, .342† |
| 1939 | *Bucky Walters, Cin | Pitcher | 27†–11, 2.29 ERA†, 137 K‡ |
| 1940 | *Frank McCormick, Cin | First base | 19 HR, 127 RBI, 191 hits†, .309 |
| 1941 | *Dolph Camilli, Bklyn | First base | 34 HR†, 120 RBI†, .285 |
| 1942 | *Mort Cooper, StL | Pitcher | 22†–7, 1.78 ERA†, 10 SO† |
| 1943 | Stan Musial, StL | Outfield | 13 HR, 81 RBI, 220 hits†, .357† |
| 1944 | *Marty Marion, StL | Shortstop | FA .972†, 63 RBI |
| 1945 | *Phil Cavarretta, Chi | First base | 6 HR, 97 RBI, .355† |
| 1946 | *Stan Musial, StL | First base, Outfield | 103 RBI, 124 runs†, 228 hits†, .365† |
| 1947 | Bob Elliott, Bos | Third base | 22 HR, 113 RBI, .317 |
| 1948 | Stan Musial, StL | Outfield | 39 HR, 131 RBI†, .376† |
| 1949 | *Jackie Robinson, Bklyn | Second base | 16 HR, 124 RBI, 37 SB†, .342† |
| 1950 | *Jim Konstanty, Phi | Pitcher | 16–7, 22 saves†, 2.66 ERA |
| 1951 | Roy Campanella, Bklyn | Catcher | 33 HR, 108 RBI, .325 |
| 1952 | Hank Sauer, Chi | Outfield | 37 HR‡, 121 RBI†, .270 |

*Played for pennant or, after 1968, division winner. †Led league. ‡Tied for league lead.

## Most Valuable Players (Cont.)
### NATIONAL LEAGUE (Cont.)

| Year | Name and Team | Position | Noteworthy |
|---|---|---|---|
| 1953 | *Roy Campanella, Bklyn | Catcher | 41 HR, 142 RBI†, .312 |
| 1954 | *Willie Mays, NY | Outfield | 41 HR, 110 RBI, 13 3B†, .345† |
| 1955 | *Roy Campanella, Bklyn | Catcher | 32 HR, 107 RBI, .318 |
| 1956 | *Don Newcombe, Bklyn | Pitcher | 27†–7, 3.06 ERA |
| 1957 | *Hank Aaron, Mil | Outfield | 44 HR†, 132 RBI†, .322 |
| 1958 | Ernie Banks, Chi | Shortstop | 47 HR†, 129 RBI†, .313 |
| 1959 | Ernie Banks, Chi | Shortstop | 45 HR, 143 RBI†, .304 |
| 1960 | *Dick Groat, Pitt | Shortstop | 2 HR, 50 RBI, .325† |
| 1961 | *Frank Robinson, Cin | Outfield | 37 HR, 124 RBI, .323 |
| 1962 | Maury Wills, LA | Shortstop | 104 SB†, 208 hits, .299, GG |
| 1963 | *Sandy Koufax, LA | Pitcher | 25‡–5, 1.88 ERA†, 306 K† |
| 1964 | *Ken Boyer, StL | Third Base | 24 HR, 119 RBI†, .295 |
| 1965 | Willie Mays, SF | Outfield | 52 HR†, 112 RBI, .317, GG |
| 1966 | Roberto Clemente, Pitt | Outfield | 29 HR, 119 RBI, 202 hits, .317, GG |
| 1967 | *Orlando Cepeda, StL | First base | 25 HR, 111 RBI†, .325 |
| 1968 | *Bob Gibson, StL | Pitcher | 22–9, 1.12 ERA†, 268 K†, 13 SO†, GG |
| 1969 | Willie McCovey, SF | First base | 45 HR†, 126 RBI†, .320 |
| 1970 | *Johnny Bench, Cin | Catcher | 45 HR†, 148 RBI†, .293, GG |
| 1971 | Joe Torre, StL | Third base | 24 HR, 137 RBI†, .363† |
| 1972 | *Johnny Bench, Cin | Catcher | 40 HR†, 125 RBI†, .270, GG |
| 1973 | *Pete Rose, Cin | Outfield | 5 HR, 64 RBI, .338†, 230 hits† |
| 1974 | *Steve Garvey, LA | First base | 21 HR, 111 RBI, 200 hits, .312, GG |
| 1975 | *Joe Morgan, Cin | Second base | 17 HR, 94 RBI, 67 SB, .327, GG |
| 1976 | *Joe Morgan, Cin | Second base | 27 HR, 111 RBI, 60 SB, .320, GG |
| 1977 | George Foster, Cin | Outfield | 52 HR†, 149 RBI†, .320 |
| 1978 | Dave Parker, Pitt | Outfield | 30 HR, 117 RBI, .334†, GG |
| 1979 | Keith Hernandez, StL | First base | 11 HR, 105 RBI, 210 hits, .344†, GG |
|  | *Willie Stargell, Pitt | First base | 32 HR, 82 RBI, .281 |
| 1980 | *Mike Schmidt, Phi | Third base | 48 HR†, 121 RBI†, .286, GG |
| 1981 | Mike Schmidt, Phi | Third base | 31 HR†, 91 RBI†, 78 runs†, .316, GG |
| 1982 | *Dale Murphy, Atl | Outfield | 36 HR, 109 RBI‡, .281, GG |
| 1983 | Dale Murphy, Atl | Outfield | 36 HR, 121 RBI†, .302, GG |
| 1984 | *Ryne Sandberg, Chi | Second base | 19 HR, 84 RBI, 114 runs†, .314, GG |
| 1985 | *Willie McGee, StL | Outfield | 10 HR, 82 RBI, 18 3B†, .353†, GG |
| 1986 | Mike Schmidt, Phi | Third base | 37 HR†, 119 RBI†, .290, GG |
| 1987 | Andre Dawson, Chi | Outfield | 49 HR†, 137 RBI†, .287, GG |
| 1988 | *Kirk Gibson, LA | Outfield | 25 HR, 76 RBI, 106 runs, .290 |
| 1989 | *Kevin Mitchell, SF | Outfield | 47 HR†, 125 RBI†, .291 |
| 1990 | *Barry Bonds, Pitt | Outfield | 33 HR, 114 RBI, .301 |
| 1991 | *Terry Pendleton, Atl | Third base | 23 HR, 86 RBI, .319† |
| 1992 | Barry Bonds, Pitt | Outfield | 34 HR, 103 RBI, .311 |
| 1993 | Barry Bonds, SF | Outfield | 46 HR†, 123 RBI†, .336 |
| 1994 | Jeff Bagwell, Hou | First base | 39 HR, 116 RBI†, .368 |
| 1995 | *Barry Larkin, Cin | Shortstop | 15 HR, 66 RBI, 51 SB, .319 |
| 1996 | *Ken Caminiti, SD | Third base | 40 HR, 130 RBI, .326 |
| 1997 | Larry Walker, Col | Outfield | 49 HR†, 130 RBI, .452 OBA†, .366, GG |
| 1998 | Sammy Sosa, Chi | Outfield | 66 HR†, 158 RBI†, 134 runs†, 416 TB†, .308 |
| 1999 | *Chipper Jones, Atl | Third Base | 45 HR, 110 RBI, 116 runs, .319 |
| 2000 | *Jeff Kent, SF | Second Base | 33 HR, 125 RBI, 114 runs, .334 |
| 2001 | Barry Bonds, SF | Outfield | 73 HR†, 137 RBI, 177 BB†, .328, .863 SLG† |
| 2002 | Barry Bonds, SF | Outfield | 46 HR, 110 RBI, .582 OBP, 198 BB†, .370 |
| 2003 | Barry Bonds, SF | Outfield | 45 HR, .341, .529 OBP†, .749 SLG† |
| 2004 | Barry Bonds, SF | Outfield | 45HR, 101 RBI, .609 OBP, .812 SLG |
| 2005 | Albert Pujols, StL | First Base | 41 HR, 117 RBI, .330, .430 OBP‡, .609 SLG† |
| 2006 | Ryan Howard, Phi | First Base | 58 HR†, 149 RBI†, .313, .425 OBP, .659 SLG |
| 2007 | Jimmy Rollins, Phi | Shortstop | 30 HR, 94 RBI, .296, 139 runs, 41 SB |
| 2008 | Albert Pujols, StL | First Base | 37HR, 116RBI, 100 runs, .357, .653 SLG |

*Played for pennant or, after 1968, division winner. †Led league. ‡Tied for league lead.

## Most Valuable Players *(Cont.)*
### AMERICAN LEAGUE

| Year | Name and Team | Position | Noteworthy |
|------|---------------|----------|------------|
| 1911 | Ty Cobb, Det | Outfield | 8 HR, 144 RBI†, 24 3B†, .420† |
| 1912 | *Tris Speaker, Bos | Outfield | 10 HR‡, 98 RBI, 53 2B†, .383 |
| 1913 | *Walter Johnson, Wash | Pitcher | 36†–7, 1.09 ERA†, 11 SO†, 243 K† |
| 1914 | *Eddie Collins, Phi | Second base | 2 HR, 85 RBI, 122 runs†, .344 |
| 1915–21 | No selection | | |
| 1922 | George Sisler, StL | First base | 8 HR, 105 RBI, 246 hits†, .420† |
| 1923 | *Babe Ruth, NY | Outfield | 41 HR†, 131 RBI†, .393 |
| 1924 | *Walter Johnson, Wash | Pitcher | 23†–7, 2.72 ERA†, 158 K† |
| 1925 | *Roger Peckinpaugh, Wash | Shortstop | 4 HR, 64 RBI, .294 |
| 1926 | George Burns, Clev | First base | 114 RBI, 216 hits‡, 64 2B†, .358 |
| 1927 | *Lou Gehrig, NY | First base | 47 HR, 175 RBI†, 52 2B†, .373 |
| 1928 | Mickey Cochrane, Phi | Catcher | 10 HR, 57 RBI, .293 |
| 1929 | No selection | | |
| 1930 | No selection | | |
| 1931 | *Lefty Grove, Phi | Pitcher | 31†–4, 2.06 ERA†, 175 K† |
| 1932 | Jimmie Foxx, Phi | First base | 58 HR†, 169 RBI†, 151 runs†, .364 |
| 1933 | Jimmie Foxx, Phi | First base | 48 HR†, 163 RBI†, .356† |
| 1934 | *Mickey Cochrane, Det | Catcher | 2 HR, 76 RBI, .320 |
| 1935 | *Hank Greenberg, Det | First base | 36 HR‡, 170 RBI†, 203 hits, .328 |
| 1936 | *Lou Gehrig, NY | First base | 49 HR†, 152 RBI, 167 runs†, .354 |
| 1937 | Charlie Gehringer, Det | Second base | 14 HR, 96 RBI, 133 runs, .371† |
| 1938 | Jimmie Foxx, Bos | First base | 50 HR, 175 RBI†, .349† |
| 1939 | *Joe DiMaggio, NY | Outfield | 30 HR, 126 RBI, .381† |
| 1940 | *Hank Greenberg, Det | Outfield | 41 HR†, 150 RBI†, 50 2B†, .340 |
| 1941 | *Joe DiMaggio, NY | Outfield | 30 HR, 125 RBI†, .357 |
| 1942 | *Joe Gordon, NY | Second base | 18 HR, 103 RBI, .322 |
| 1943 | *Spud Chandler, NY | Pitcher | 20†–4, 1.64 ERA†, 5 SO‡ |
| 1944 | Hal Newhouser, Det | Pitcher | 29†–9, 2.22 ERA†, 187 K† |
| 1945 | *Hal Newhouser, Det | Pitcher | 25†–9, 1.81 ERA†, 8 SO†, 212 K† |
| 1946 | *Ted Williams, Bos | Outfield | 38 HR, 123 RBI, 142 runs†, .342 |
| 1947 | *Joe DiMaggio, NY | Outfield | 20 HR, 97 RBI, .315 |
| 1948 | *Lou Boudreau, Clev | Shortstop | 18 HR, 106 RBI, .355 |
| 1949 | Ted Williams, Bos | Outfield | 43 HR†, 159 RBI‡, 150 runs†, .343 |
| 1950 | *Phil Rizzuto, NY | Shortstop | 125 runs, 200 hits, .324 |
| 1951 | *Yogi Berra, NY | Catcher | 27 HR, 88 RBI, .294 |
| 1952 | Bobby Shantz, Phi | Pitcher | 24†–7, 2.48 ERA |
| 1953 | Al Rosen, Clev | Third base | 43 HR†, 145 RBI†, 115 runs†, .336 |
| 1954 | Yogi Berra, NY | Catcher | 22 HR, 125 RBI, .307 |
| 1955 | *Yogi Berra, NY | Catcher | 27 HR, 108 RBI, .272 |
| 1956 | *Mickey Mantle, NY | Outfield | 52 HR†, 130 RBI†, 132 runs†, .353† |
| 1957 | *Mickey Mantle, NY | Outfield | 34 HR, 94 RBI, 121 runs†, .365 |
| 1958 | Jackie Jensen, Bos | Outfield | 35 HR, 122 RBI†, .286 |
| 1959 | *Nellie Fox, Chi | Second base | 2 HR, 70 RBI, .306, GG |
| 1960 | *Roger Maris, NY | Outfield | 39 HR, 112 RBI†, .283, GG |
| 1961 | *Roger Maris, NY | Outfield | 61 HR†, 142 RBI†, .269 |
| 1962 | *Mickey Mantle, NY | Outfield | 30 HR, 89 RBI, .321, GG |
| 1963 | *Elston Howard, NY | Catcher | 28 HR, 85 RBI, .287, GG |
| 1964 | Brooks Robinson, Balt | Third base | 28 HR, 118 RBI†, .317, GG |
| 1965 | *Zoilo Versalles, Minn | Shortstop | 126 runs†, 45 2B†, 12 3B‡, GG |
| 1966 | *Frank Robinson, Balt | Outfield | 49 HR†, 122 RBI†, 122 runs†, .316† |
| 1967 | *Carl Yastrzemski, Bos | Outfield | 44 HR‡, 121 RBI†, 112 runs†, .326†, GG |
| 1968 | *Denny McLain, Det | Pitcher | 31†–6, 1.96 ERA, 280 K |
| 1969 | *Harmon Killebrew, Minn | Third base, First base | 49 HR†, 140 RBI†, .276 |
| 1970 | *Boog Powell, Balt | First base | 35 HR, 114 RBI, .297 |
| 1971 | *Vida Blue, Oak | Pitcher | 24–8, 1.82 ERA†, 8 SO†, 301 K |
| 1972 | Dick Allen, Chi | First base | 37 HR†, 113 RBI†, .308 |
| 1973 | *Reggie Jackson, Oak | Outfield | 32 HR†, 117 RBI†, 99 runs†, .293 |
| 1974 | Jeff Burroughs, Tex | Outfield | 25 HR, 118 RBI†, .301 |
| 1975 | *Fred Lynn, Bos | Outfield | 21 HR, 105 RBI, 103 runs†, .331, GG |
| 1976 | *Thurman Munson, NY | Catcher | 17 HR, 105 RBI, .302 |
| 1977 | Rod Carew, Minn | First base | 100 RBI, 128 runs†, 239 hits†, .388† |
| 1978 | Jim Rice, Bos | Outfield, DH | 46 HR†, 139 RBI†, 213 hits†, .315 |
| 1979 | *Don Baylor, Calif | Outfield, DH | 36 HR, 139 RBI†, 120 runs†, .296 |
| 1980 | *George Brett, KC | Third base | 24 HR, 118 RBI, .390† |
| 1981 | *Rollie Fingers, Mil | Pitcher | 6–3, 28 saves†, 1.04 ERA |
| 1982 | *Robin Yount, Mil | Shortstop | 29 HR, 114 RBI, 210 hits†, .331, GG |

## Most Valuable Players *(Cont.)*
### AMERICAN LEAGUE *(Cont.)*

| Year | Name and Team | Position | Noteworthy |
|---|---|---|---|
| 1983 | *Cal Ripken Jr., Balt | Shortstop | 27 HR, 102 RBI, 121 runs†, 211 hits†, .318 |
| 1984 | *Willie Hernandez, Det | Pitcher | 9–3, 32 saves, 1.92 ERA |
| 1985 | Don Mattingly, NY | First base | 35 HR, 145 RBI†, 48 2B†, .324, GG |
| 1986 | *Roger Clemens, Bos | Pitcher | 24†–4, 2.48 ERA†, 238 K |
| 1987 | George Bell, Tor | Outfield | 47 HR, 134 RBI†, .308 |
| 1988 | *Jose Canseco, Oak | Outfield | 42 HR†, 124 RBI†, 40 SB, .307 |
| 1989 | Robin Yount, Mil | Outfield | 21 HR, 103 RBI, 101 runs, .318 |
| 1990 | *Rickey Henderson, Oak | Outfield | 28 HR, 119 runs†, 65 SB†, .325 |
| 1991 | Cal Ripken Jr., Balt | Shortstop | 34 HR, 114 RBI, .323 |
| 1992 | Dennis Eckersley, Oak | Pitcher | 7–1, 1.91 ERA, 51 saves |
| 1993 | Frank Thomas, Chi | First base | 41 HR, 128 RBI, .317 |
| 1994 | Frank Thomas, Chi | First base | 38 HR, 101 RBI, .353 |
| 1995 | *Mo Vaughn, Bos | First base | 39 HR, 126 RBI, .300 |
| 1996 | *Juan Gonzalez, Tex | Outfield | 47 HR, 144 RBI, .314 |
| 1997 | *Ken Griffey Jr., Sea | Outfield | 56 HR†, 125 runs†, 393 TB†, 147 RBI†, .304 |
| 1998 | *Juan Gonzalez, Tex | Outfield | 45 HR, 157 RBI†, 50 2B†, .318 |
| 1999 | *Ivan Rodriguez, Tex | Catcher | 35 HR, 113 RBI, 116 runs, .332, GG |
| 2000 | *Jason Giambi, Oak | First Base | 43 HR, 137 RBI, .333 |
| 2001 | *Ichiro Suzuki, Sea | Outfield | .350†, 242 H†, 127 runs, 56 SB† |
| 2002 | *Miguel Tejada, Oak | Shortstop | 34 HR, 131 RBI, .308 |
| 2003 | Alex Rodriguez, Tex | Shortstop | 47 HR†, 118 RBI, .600 SLG† |
| 2004 | *Vladimir Guerrero, Ana | Outfield | 39 HR, 126 RBI, .598 SLG |
| 2005 | *Alex Rodriguez, NYY | Third Base | 48 HR†, 130 RBI, .610 SLG† |
| 2006 | Justin Morneau, Min | First Base | 30HR, 130 RBI, .321, 190 hits |
| 2007 | Alex Rodriguez, NYY | Third Base | 54 HR, 156 RBI, .314, 183 hits, 24 SB |
| 2008 | Dustin Pedroia, Bos | Second Base | 17 HR, 118 runs, 213 hits, .326, 20 SB |

*Played for pennant or, after 1968, division winner. †Led league. ‡Tied for league lead.
Notes: 2B=doubles; 3B=triples; FA=fielding average; GG=won Gold Glove, award begun in 1957;
K=strikeouts; O=shutouts; SB=stolen bases; TB=total bases.

## Rookies of the Year

| NATIONAL LEAGUE | AMERICAN LEAGUE |
|---|---|
| 1947* Jackie Robinson, Bklyn (1B) | 1949 Roy Sievers, StL (OF) |
| 1948* Alvin Dark, Bos (SS) | 1950 Walt Dropo, Bos (1B) |
| 1949 Don Newcombe, Bklyn (P) | 1951 Gil McDougald, NY (3B) |
| 1950 Sam Jethroe, Bos (OF) | 1952 Harry Byrd, Phi (P) |
| 1951 Willie Mays, NY (OF) | 1953 Harvey Kuenn, Det (SS) |
| 1952 Joe Black, Bklyn (P) | 1954 Bob Grim, NY (P) |
| 1953 Junior Gilliam, Bklyn (2B) | 1955 Herb Score, Clev (P) |
| 1954 Wally Moon, StL (OF) | 1956 Luis Aparicio, Chi (SS) |
| 1955 Bill Virdon, StL (OF) | 1957 Tony Kubek, NY (OF, SS) |
| 1956 Frank Robinson, Cin (OF) | 1958 Albie Pearson, Wash (OF) |
| 1957 Jack Sanford, Phi (P) | 1959 Bob Allison, Wash (OF) |
| 1958 Orlando Cepeda, SF (1B) | 1960 Ron Hansen, Balt (SS) |
| 1959 Willie McCovey, SF (1B) | 1961 Don Schwall, Bos (P) |
| 1960 Frank Howard, LA (OF) | 1962 Tom Tresh, NY (SS) |
| 1961 Billy Williams, Chi (OF) | 1963 Gary Peters, Chi (P) |
| 1962 Ken Hubbs, Chi (2B) | 1964 Tony Oliva, Minn (OF) |
| 1963 Pete Rose, Cin (2B) | 1965 Curt Blefary, Balt (OF) |
| 1964 Dick Allen, Phi (3B) | 1966 Tommie Agee, Chi (OF) |
| 1965 Jim Lefebvre, LA (2B) | 1967 Rod Carew, Minn (2B) |
| 1966 Tommy Helms, Cin (2B) | 1968 Stan Bahnsen, NY (P) |
| 1967 Tom Seaver, NY (P) | 1969 Lou Piniella, KC (OF) |
| 1968 Johnny Bench, Cin (C) | 1970 Thurman Munson, NY (C) |
| 1969 Ted Sizemore, LA (2B) | 1971 Chris Chambliss, Clev (1B) |
| 1970 Carl Morton, Mtl(P) | 1972 Carlton Fisk, Bos (C) |
| 1971 Earl Williams, Atl (C) | 1973 Al Bumbry, Balt (OF) |
| 1972 Jon Matlack, NY (P) | 1974 Mike Hargrove, Tex (1B) |
| 1973 Gary Matthews, SF (OF) | 1975 Fred Lynn, Bos (OF) |
| 1974 Bake McBride, StL (OF) | 1976 Mark Fidrych, Det (P) |
| 1975 John Montefusco, SF (P) | 1977 Eddie Murray, Balt (DH) |
| 1976 Pat Zachry, Cin (P) | 1978 Lou Whitaker, Det (2B) |
| Butch Metzger, SD (P) | 1979 Alfredo Griffin, Tor (SS) |
| 1977 Andre Dawson, Mtl (OF) | John Castino, Minn (3B) |
| 1978 Bob Horner, Atl (3B) | 1980 Joe Charboneau, Clev (OF) |
| 1979 Rick Sutcliffe, LA (P) | 1981 Dave Righetti, NY (P) |
| 1980 Steve Howe, LA (P) | 1982 Cal Ripken Jr., Balt (SS) |

*Just one selection for both leagues.

## Rookies of the Year *(Cont.)*

### NATIONAL LEAGUE *(Cont.)*

|  |  |
|---|---|
| 1981 | Fernando Valenzuela, LA (P) |
| 1982 | Steve Sax, LA (2B) |
| 1983 | Darryl Strawberry, NY (OF) |
| 1984 | Dwight Gooden, NY (P) |
| 1985 | Vince Coleman, StL (OF) |
| 1986 | Todd Worrell, StL (P) |
| 1987 | Benito Santiago, SD (C) |
| 1988 | Chris Sabo, Cin (3B) |
| 1989 | Jerome Walton, Chi (OF) |
| 1990 | Dave Justice, Atl (OF) |
| 1991 | Jeff Bagwell, Hou (3B) |
| 1992 | Eric Karros, LA (1B) |
| 1993 | Mike Piazza, LA (C) |
| 1994 | Raul Mondesi, LA (OF) |
| 1995 | Hideo Nomo, LA (P) |
| 1996 | Todd Hollandsworth, LA (OF) |
| 1997 | Scott Rolen, Phi (3B) |
| 1998 | Kerry Wood, Chi (P) |
| 1999 | Scott Williamson, Cin (P) |
| 2000 | Rafael Furcal, Atl (SS) |
| 2001 | Albert Pujols, StL (OF) |
| 2002 | Jason Jennings, Col (P) |
| 2003 | Dontrelle Willis, Fla (P) |
| 2004 | Jason Bay, Pit (OF) |
| 2005 | Ryan Howard, Phi (1B) |
| 2006 | Hanley Ramirez, Fla (SS) |
| 2007 | Ryan Braun, Mil (OF) |
| 2008 | Geovany Soto, Chi (C) |

### AMERICAN LEAGUE *(Cont.)*

|  |  |
|---|---|
| 1983 | Ron Kittle, Chi (OF) |
| 1984 | Alvin Davis, Sea (1B) |
| 1985 | Ozzie Guillen, Chi (SS) |
| 1986 | Jose Canseco, Oak (OF) |
| 1987 | Mark McGwire, Oak (1B) |
| 1988 | Walt Weiss, Oak (SS) |
| 1989 | Gregg Olson, Balt (P) |
| 1990 | Sandy Alomar Jr, Clev (C) |
| 1991 | Chuck Knoblauch, Minn (2B) |
| 1992 | Pat Listach, Mil (SS) |
| 1993 | Tim Salmon, Calif (OF) |
| 1994 | Bob Hamelin, KC (DH) |
| 1995 | Marty Cordova, Minn (OF) |
| 1996 | Derek Jeter, NY (SS) |
| 1997 | Nomar Garciaparra, Bos (SS) |
| 1998 | Ben Grieve, Oak (OF) |
| 1999 | Carlos Beltran, KC (OF) |
| 2000 | Kazuhiro Sasaki, Sea (P) |
| 2001 | Ichiro Suzuki, Sea (OF) |
| 2002 | Eric Hinske, Tor (3B) |
| 2003 | Angel Berroa, KC (SS) |
| 2004 | Bobby Crosby, Oak (SS) |
| 2005 | Huston Street, Oak (P) |
| 2006 | Justin Verlander, Det (P) |
| 2007 | Dustin Pedroia, Bos (2B) |
| 2008 | Evan Longoria, TB (3B) |

## Cy Young Award

| Year | | W–L | Sv | ERA | Year | | W–L | Sv | ERA |
|---|---|---|---|---|---|---|---|---|---|
| 1956 | *Don Newcombe, Bklyn (NL) | 27–7 | 0 | 3.06 | 1962 | Don Drysdale, LA (NL) | 25–9 | 1 | 2.83 |
| 1957 | Warren Spahn, Mil (NL) | 21–11 | 3 | 2.69 | 1963 | *Sandy Koufax, LA (NL) | 25–5 | 0 | 1.88 |
| 1958 | Bob Turley, NY (AL) | 21–7 | 1 | 2.97 | 1964 | Dean Chance, LA (AL) | 20–9 | 4 | 1.65 |
| 1959 | Early Wynn, Chi (AL) | 22–10 | 0 | 3.17 | 1965 | Sandy Koufax, LA (NL) | 26–8 | 2 | 2.04 |
| 1960 | Vernon Law, Pitt (NL) | 20–9 | 0 | 3.08 | 1966 | Sandy Koufax, LA (NL) | 27–9 | 0 | 1.73 |
| 1961 | Whitey Ford, NY (AL) | 25–4 | 0 | 3.21 | | | | | |

### NATIONAL LEAGUE

| Year | | W–L | Sv | ERA |
|---|---|---|---|---|
| 1967 | Mike McCormick, SF | 22–10 | 0 | 2.85 |
| 1968 | *Bob Gibson, StL | 22–9 | 0 | 1.12 |
| 1969 | Tom Seaver, NY | 25–7 | 0 | 2.21 |
| 1970 | Bob Gibson, StL | 23–7 | 0 | 3.12 |
| 1971 | Ferguson Jenkins, Chi | 24–13 | 0 | 2.77 |
| 1972 | Steve Carlton, Phi | 27–10 | 0 | 1.97 |
| 1973 | Tom Seaver, NY | 19–10 | 0 | 2.08 |
| 1974 | Mike Marshall, LA | 15–12 | 21 | 2.42 |
| 1975 | Tom Seaver, NY | 22–9 | 0 | 2.38 |
| 1976 | Randy Jones, SD | 22–14 | 0 | 2.74 |
| 1977 | Steve Carlton, Phi | 23–10 | 0 | 2.64 |
| 1978 | Gaylord Perry, SD | 21–6 | 0 | 2.72 |
| 1979 | Bruce Sutter, Chi | 6–6 | 37 | 2.23 |
| 1980 | Steve Carlton, Phi | 24–9 | 0 | 2.34 |
| 1981 | Fernando Valenzuela, LA | 13–7 | 0 | 2.48 |
| 1982 | Steve Carlton, Phi | 23–11 | 0 | 3.10 |
| 1983 | John Denny, Phi | 19–6 | 0 | 2.37 |
| 1984 | †Rick Sutcliffe, Chi | 16–1 | 0 | 2.69 |
| 1985 | Dwight Gooden, NY | 24–4 | 0 | 1.53 |
| 1986 | Mike Scott, Hou | 18–10 | 0 | 2.22 |
| 1987 | Steve Bedrosian, Phi | 5–3 | 40 | 2.83 |
| 1988 | Orel Hershiser, LA | 23–8 | 1 | 2.26 |
| 1989 | Mark Davis, SD | 4–3 | 44 | 1.85 |
| 1990 | Doug Drabek, Pitt | 22–6 | 0 | 2.76 |
| 1991 | Tom Glavine, Atl | 20–11 | 0 | 2.55 |
| 1992 | Greg Maddux, Chi | 20–11 | 0 | 2.18 |
| 1993 | Greg Maddux, Atl | 20–10 | 0 | 2.36 |
| 1994 | Greg Maddux, Atl | 16–6 | 0 | 1.56 |

### AMERICAN LEAGUE

| Year | | W–L | Sv | ERA |
|---|---|---|---|---|
| 1967 | Jim Lonborg, Bos | 22–9 | 0 | 3.16 |
| 1968 | *Denny McLain, Det | 31–6 | 0 | 1.96 |
| 1969 | Denny McLain, Det | 24–9 | 0 | 2.80 |
| | Mike Cuellar, Balt | 23–11 | 0 | 2.38 |
| 1970 | Jim Perry, Minn | 24–12 | 0 | 3.03 |
| 1971 | *Vida Blue, Oak | 24–8 | 0 | 1.82 |
| 1972 | Gaylord Perry, Clev | 24–16 | 1 | 1.92 |
| 1973 | Jim Palmer, Balt | 22–9 | 1 | 2.40 |
| 1974 | Catfish Hunter, Oak | 25–12 | 0 | 2.49 |
| 1975 | Jim Palmer, Balt | 23–11 | 1 | 2.09 |
| 1976 | Jim Palmer, Balt | 22–13 | 0 | 2.51 |
| 1977 | Sparky Lyle, NY | 13–5 | 26 | 2.17 |
| 1978 | Ron Guidry, NY | 25–3 | 0 | 1.74 |
| 1979 | Mike Flanagan, Balt | 23–9 | 0 | 3.08 |
| 1980 | Steve Stone, Balt | 25–7 | 0 | 3.23 |
| 1981 | *Rollie Fingers, Mil | 6–3 | 28 | 1.04 |
| 1982 | Pete Vuckovich, Mil | 18–6 | 0 | 3.34 |
| 1983 | LaMarr Hoyt, Chi | 24–10 | 0 | 3.66 |
| 1984 | *Willie Hernandez, Det | 9–3 | 32 | 1.92 |
| 1985 | Bret Saberhagen, KC | 20–6 | 0 | 2.87 |
| 1986 | *Roger Clemens, Bos | 24–4 | 0 | 2.48 |
| 1987 | Roger Clemens, Bos | 20–9 | 0 | 2.97 |
| 1988 | Frank Viola, Minn | 24–7 | 0 | 2.64 |
| 1989 | Bret Saberhagen, KC | 23–6 | 0 | 2.16 |
| 1990 | Bob Welch, Oak | 27–6 | 0 | 2.95 |
| 1991 | Roger Clemens, Bos | 18–10 | 0 | 2.62 |
| 1992 | *Dennis Eckersley, Oak | 7–1 | 51 | 1.91 |
| 1993 | Jack McDowell, Chi | 22–10 | 0 | 3.37 |

## Cy Young Award

| NATIONAL LEAGUE | | | | AMERICAN LEAGUE | | | |
|---|---|---|---|---|---|---|---|
| Year | W–L | Sv | ERA | Year | W–L | Sv | ERA |
| 1995.....Greg Maddux, Atl | 19–2 | 0 | 1.63 | 1994.....David Cone, KC | 16–4 | 0 | 2.94 |
| 1996.....John Smoltz, Atl | 24–8 | 0 | 2.94 | 1995.....Randy Johnson, Sea | 18–2 | 0 | 2.48 |
| 1997.....Pedro Martinez, Mtl | 17–8 | 0 | 1.90 | 1996.....Pat Hentgen, Tor | 20–10 | 0 | 3.22 |
| 1998.....Tom Glavine, Atl | 20–6 | 0 | 2.47 | 1997.....Roger Clemens, Tor | 21–7 | 0 | 2.05 |
| 1999.....Randy Johnson, Ariz | 17–9 | 0 | 2.48 | 1998.....Roger Clemens, Tor | 20–6 | 0 | 2.65 |
| 2000.....Randy Johnson, Ariz | 19–7 | 0 | 2.64 | 1999.....Pedro Martinez, Bos | 23–4 | 0 | 1.55 |
| 2001.....Randy Johnson, Ariz | 21–6 | 0 | 2.49 | 2000.....Pedro Martinez, Bos | 18–6 | 0 | 1.74 |
| 2002.....Randy Johnson, Ariz | 24–5 | 0 | 2.32 | 2001.....Roger Clemens, NY | 20–3 | 0 | 3.51 |
| 2003.....Eric Gagne, LA | 2–3 | 55 | 1.20 | 2002.....Barry Zito, Oak | 23–5 | 0 | 2.75 |
| 2004.....Roger Clemens, Hou | 18-4 | 0 | 2.98 | 2003.....Roy Halladay, Tor | 22–7 | 0 | 3.25 |
| 2005.....Chris Carpenter, StL | 21-5 | 0 | 2.83 | 2004.....Johan Santana, Min | 20-6 | 0 | 2.61 |
| 2006.....Brandon Webb, Ariz | 16–8 | 0 | 3.10 | 2005.....Bartolo Colon, LAA | 21-8 | 0 | 3.48 |
| 2007.....Jake Peavy, SD | 19–6 | 0 | 2.54 | 2006.....Johan Santana, Min | 19–6 | 0 | 2.77 |
| 2008.....Tim Lincecum, SF | 18–5 | 0 | 2.62 | 2007.....C.C. Sabathia, Cle | 19–7 | 0 | 3.21 |
| | | | | 2008.....Cliff Lee, Cle | 22–3 | 0 | 2.54 |

*Won the MVP and Cy Young awards in the same season.
†NL games only. Sutcliffe pitched 15 games with Cleveland before being traded to the Cubs.

## Career Individual Batting

### GAMES

| | |
|---|---|
| Pete Rose | 3562 |
| Carl Yastrzemski | 3308 |
| Hank Aaron | 3298 |
| Rickey Henderson | 3081 |
| Ty Cobb | 3034 |
| Eddie Murray | 3026 |
| Stan Musial | 3026 |
| Cal Ripken Jr. | 3001 |
| Willie Mays | 2992 |
| Barry Bonds | 2986 |
| Dave Winfield | 2973 |
| Rusty Staub | 2951 |
| Brooks Robinson | 2896 |
| Robin Yount | 2856 |
| Craig Biggio | 2850 |
| Al Kaline | 2834 |
| Rafael Palmeiro | 2831 |
| Harold Baines | 2830 |
| Eddie Collins | 2826 |
| Reggie Jackson | 2820 |
| Frank Robinson | 2808 |
| Honus Wagner | 2792 |
| Tris Speaker | 2789 |

### RUNS

| | |
|---|---|
| Rickey Henderson | 2295 |
| Ty Cobb | 2246 |
| Barry Bonds | 2227 |
| Hank Aaron | 2174 |
| Babe Ruth | 2174 |
| Pete Rose | 2165 |
| Willie Mays | 2062 |
| Cap Anson | 1996 |
| Stan Musial | 1949 |
| Lou Gehrig | 1888 |
| Tris Speaker | 1882 |
| Mel Ott | 1859 |
| Craig Biggio | 1834 |
| Frank Robinson | 1829 |
| Eddie Collins | 1821 |
| Carl Yastrzemski | 1816 |
| Ted Williams | 1798 |
| Paul Molitor | 1782 |
| Charlie Gehringer | 1774 |
| Jimmie Foxx | 1751 |
| Honus Wagner | 1736 |

### HOME RUNS

| | |
|---|---|
| Barry Bonds | 762 |
| Hank Aaron | 755 |
| Babe Ruth | 714 |
| Willie Mays | 660 |
| *Ken Griffey Jr. | 630 |
| Sammy Sosa | 609 |
| Frank Robinson | 586 |
| Mark McGwire | 583 |
| *Alex Rodriguez | 583 |
| Harmon Killebrew | 573 |
| Rafael Palmeiro | 569 |
| *Jim Thome | 564 |
| Reggie Jackson | 563 |
| Mike Schmidt | 548 |
| *Manny Ramirez | 546 |
| Mickey Mantle | 536 |
| Jimmie Foxx | 534 |
| Willie McCovey | 521 |
| Ted Williams | 521 |
| Frank Thomas | 521 |
| Ernie Banks | 512 |
| Eddie Mathews | 512 |
| Mel Ott | 511 |

### BATTING AVERAGE (5,000 AB)

| | |
|---|---|
| Ty Cobb | .367 |
| Rogers Hornsby | .358 |
| Ed Delahanty | .346 |
| Tris Speaker | .345 |
| Billy Hamilton | .344 |
| Ted Williams | .344 |
| Dan Brouthers | .342 |
| Harry Heilmann | .342 |
| Babe Ruth | .342 |
| Willie Keeler | .341 |
| Bill Terry | .341 |
| Lou Gehrig | .340 |
| George Sisler | .340 |
| Jesse Burkett | .338 |
| Tony Gwynn | .338 |
| Nap Lajoie | .338 |
| Al Simmons | .334 |
| *Albert Pujols | .334 |
| *Ichiro Suzuki | .333 |
| Cap Anson | .333 |
| Eddie Collins | .333 |
| Paul Waner | .333 |

### HITS

| | |
|---|---|
| Pete Rose | 4256 |
| Ty Cobb | 4191 |
| Hank Aaron | 3771 |
| Stan Musial | 3630 |
| Tris Speaker | 3515 |
| Carl Yastrzemski | 3419 |
| Cap Anson | 3418 |
| Honus Wagner | 3415 |
| Paul Molitor | 3319 |
| Eddie Collins | 3313 |
| Willie Mays | 3283 |
| Eddie Murray | 3255 |
| Nap Lajoie | 3251 |
| Cal Ripken Jr. | 3184 |
| George Brett | 3154 |
| Paul Waner | 3152 |
| Robin Yount | 3142 |
| Tony Gwynn | 3141 |
| Dave Winfield | 3110 |
| Craig Biggio | 3060 |
| Rickey Henderson | 3055 |
| Rod Carew | 3053 |
| Lou Brock | 3023 |
| Rafael Palmeiro | 3020 |
| Wade Boggs | 3010 |
| Al Kaline | 3007 |
| Roberto Clemente | 3000 |

### AT BATS

| | |
|---|---|
| Pete Rose | 14053 |
| Hank Aaron | 12364 |
| Carl Yastrzemski | 11988 |
| Cal Ripken Jr. | 11551 |
| Ty Cobb | 11434 |
| Eddie Murray | 11336 |
| Robin Yount | 11008 |
| Dave Winfield | 11003 |
| Stan Musial | 10972 |
| Rickey Henderson | 10961 |
| Willie Mays | 10881 |
| Craig Biggio | 10876 |
| Paul Molitor | 10835 |
| Brooks Robinson | 10654 |
| Rafael Palmeiro | 10472 |
| Honus Wagner | 10430 |
| George Brett | 10349 |
| Lou Brock | 10332 |

* Active in 2009.

## Career Individual Batting *(Cont.)*

### DOUBLES

| | |
|---|---|
| Tris Speaker | 792 |
| Pete Rose | 746 |
| Stan Musial | 725 |
| Ty Cobb | 724 |
| Craig Biggio | 668 |
| George Brett | 665 |
| Nap Lajoie | 657 |
| Carl Yastrzemski | 646 |
| Honus Wagner | 640 |
| Hank Aaron | 624 |
| Paul Molitor | 605 |
| Paul Waner | 605 |
| Cal Ripken Jr. | 603 |
| Barry Bonds | 601 |
| *Luis Gonzalez | 596 |
| Rafael Palmeiro | 585 |
| Robin Yount | 583 |
| Cap Anson | 581 |
| Wade Boggs | 578 |
| Charlie Gehringer | 574 |

### TRIPLES

| | |
|---|---|
| Sam Crawford | 309 |
| Ty Cobb | 295 |
| Honus Wagner | 252 |
| Jake Beckley | 243 |
| Roger Connor | 233 |
| Tris Speaker | 222 |
| Fred Clarke | 220 |
| Dan Brouthers | 205 |
| Joe Kelley | 194 |
| Paul Waner | 191 |
| Bid McPhee | 188 |
| Eddie Collins | 187 |
| Ed Delahanty | 185 |
| Sam Rice | 184 |
| Jesse Burkett | 182 |
| Ed Konetchy | 182 |
| Edd Roush | 182 |
| Buck Ewing | 178 |
| Rabbit Maranville | 177 |
| Stan Musial | 177 |

### BASES ON BALLS

| | |
|---|---|
| Barry Bonds | 2558 |
| Rickey Henderson | 2190 |
| Babe Ruth | 2062 |
| Ted Williams | 2021 |
| Joe Morgan | 1865 |
| Carl Yastrzemski | 1845 |
| Mickey Mantle | 1733 |
| Mel Ott | 1708 |
| *Frank Thomas | 1667 |
| Eddie Yost | 1614 |
| Darrell Evans | 1605 |
| Stan Musial | 1599 |
| Pete Rose | 1566 |
| Harmon Killebrew | 1559 |
| *Jim Thome | 1550 |
| Lou Gehrig | 1508 |
| Mike Schmidt | 1507 |
| Eddie Collins | 1499 |
| Willie Mays | 1464 |
| Jimmie Foxx | 1452 |
| Eddie Mathews | 1444 |
| *Gary Sheffield | 1435 |

*Active in 2009.

### RUNS BATTED IN

| | |
|---|---|
| Hank Aaron | 2297 |
| Babe Ruth | 2213 |
| Cap Anson | 2076 |
| Barry Bonds | 1996 |
| Lou Gehrig | 1995 |
| Stan Musial | 1951 |
| Ty Cobb | 1937 |
| Jimmie Foxx | 1922 |
| Eddie Murray | 1917 |
| Willie Mays | 1903 |
| Mel Ott | 1860 |
| Carl Yastrzemski | 1844 |
| Ted Williams | 1839 |
| Rafael Palmeiro | 1835 |
| Dave Winfield | 1833 |
| *Ken Griffey Jr. | 1829 |
| Al Simmons | 1827 |
| Frank Robinson | 1812 |
| *Manny Ramirez | 1788 |
| Honus Wagner | 1732 |
| *Alex Rodriguez | 1706 |

### SLUGGING AVERAGE (5,000 AB)

| | |
|---|---|
| Babe Ruth | .690 |
| Ted Williams | .634 |
| Lou Gehrig | .632 |
| *Albert Pujols | .628 |
| Jimmie Foxx | .609 |
| Barry Bonds | .607 |
| Hank Greenberg | .605 |
| *Manny Ramirez | .591 |
| Mark McGwire | .588 |
| Joe Dimaggio | .579 |
| Rogers Hornsby | .577 |
| *Alex Rodriguez | .576 |
| *Vladimir Guerrero | .568 |
| *Todd Helton | .567 |
| Larry Walker | .565 |
| Albert Belle | .564 |
| Johnny Mize | .562 |
| *Juan Gonzalez | .561 |
| Stan Musial | .559 |
| Mickey Mantle | .557 |
| Willie Mays | .557 |
| *Jim Thome | .557 |

### STOLEN BASES

| | |
|---|---|
| Rickey Henderson | 1406 |
| Lou Brock | 938 |
| Billy Hamilton | 912 |
| Ty Cobb | 892 |
| Tim Raines | 808 |
| Vince Coleman | 752 |
| Eddie Collins | 745 |
| Max Carey | 738 |
| Honus Wagner | 722 |
| Joe Morgan | 689 |
| Willie Wilson | 668 |
| Bert Campaneris | 649 |
| *Kenny Lofton | 622 |
| Otis Nixon | 620 |
| George Davis | 616 |
| Tom Brown | 615 |
| Dummy Hoy | 594 |
| Maury Wills | 586 |
| George Van Haltren | 583 |
| Ozzie Smith | 580 |

### ON-BASE PERCENTAGE (5,000 AB)

| | |
|---|---|
| Ted Williams | .482 |
| Babe Ruth | .469 |
| Barry Bonds | .444 |
| Lou Gehrig | .442 |
| *Todd Helton | .427 |
| *Albert Pujols | .427 |
| Jimmie Foxx | .425 |
| Ty Cobb | .424 |
| Rogers Hornsby | .424 |
| Mickey Mantle | .422 |
| Frank Thomas | .419 |
| Edgar Martinez | .418 |
| Stan Musial | .417 |
| Tris Speaker | .417 |
| Wade Boggs | .415 |
| *Lance Berkman | .412 |
| *Manny Ramirez | .411 |
| Mel Ott | .410 |
| Mickey Cochrane | .409 |
| Hank Greenberg | .409 |
| Jeff Bagwell | .408 |
| Eddie Collins | .406 |
| *Chipper Jones | .406 |

### TOTAL BASES

| | |
|---|---|
| Hank Aaron | 6856 |
| Stan Musial | 6134 |
| Willie Mays | 6066 |
| Barry Bonds | 5976 |
| Ty Cobb | 5859 |
| Babe Ruth | 5793 |
| Pete Rose | 5752 |
| Carl Yastrzemski | 5539 |
| Eddie Murray | 5397 |
| Rafael Palmeiro | 5388 |
| Frank Robinson | 5373 |
| *Ken Griffey Jr. | 5251 |
| Dave Winfield | 5221 |
| Cal Ripken Jr. | 5168 |
| Tris Speaker | 5101 |
| Lou Gehrig | 5060 |
| George Brett | 5044 |
| Mel Ott | 5041 |
| Jimmie Foxx | 4956 |
| Ted Williams | 4884 |

### STRIKEOUTS

| | |
|---|---|
| Reggie Jackson | 2597 |
| *Jim Thome | 2313 |
| Sammy Sosa | 2306 |
| Andres Galarraga | 2003 |
| Jose Canseco | 1942 |
| Willie Stargell | 1936 |
| Mike Schmidt | 1883 |
| Fred McGriff | 1882 |
| Tony Perez | 1867 |
| Dave Kingman | 1816 |
| *Mike Cameron | 1798 |
| *Ken Griffey Jr. | 1762 |
| Bobby Bonds | 1757 |
| Craig Biggio | 1753 |
| Dale Murphy | 1748 |
| *Manny Ramirez | 1748 |
| *Carlos Delgado | 1745 |
| *Alex Rodriguez | 1738 |
| Lou Brock | 1730 |
| Mickey Mantle | 1710 |

## The 30–30 Club (30 HR, 30 SB in single season)

| Year | | HR | SB | Year | | HR | SB |
|---|---|---|---|---|---|---|---|
| 1922 | Kenny Williams, StL | 39 | 37 | 1996 | Dante Bichette, Col | 31 | 31 |
| 1956 | Willie Mays, NYG | 36 | 40 | 1997 | Larry Walker, Col | 49 | 33 |
| 1957 | Willie Mays, NYG | 35 | 38 | 1997 | Jeff Bagwell, Hou | 43 | 31 |
| 1963 | Hank Aaron, Mil | 44 | 31 | 1997 | Raul Mondesi, LA | 30 | 32 |
| 1969 | Bobby Bonds, SF | 32 | 45 | 1997 | Barry Bonds, SF | 40 | 37 |
| 1970 | Tommy Harper, Mil | 31 | 38 | 1998 | Alex Rodriguez, Sea | 42 | 46 |
| 1973 | Bobby Bonds, SF | 39 | 43 | 1998 | Shawn Green, Tor | 35 | 35 |
| 1975 | Bobby Bonds, NYY | 32 | 30 | 1999 | Jeff Bagwell, Hou | 42 | 30 |
| 1977 | Bobby Bonds, Cal | 37 | 41 | 1999 | Raul Mondesi, LA | 33 | 36 |
| 1978 | Bobby Bonds, Chi/Tex | 31 | 43 | 2000 | Preston Wilson, Fla | 31 | 36 |
| 1983 | Dale Murphy, Atl | 36 | 30 | 2001 | Vladimir Guerrero, Mtl | 34 | 37 |
| 1987 | Joe Carter, Clev | 32 | 31 | 2001 | Jose Cruz Jr., Tor | 34 | 32 |
| 1987 | Eric Davis, Cin | 37 | 50 | 2001 | Bobby Abreu, Phi | 31 | 36 |
| 1987 | Darryl Strawberry, NYM | 39 | 36 | 2002 | Alfonso Soriano, NYY | 39 | 41 |
| 1987 | Howard Johnson, NYM | 36 | 32 | 2002 | Vladimir Guerrero, Mtl | 39 | 40 |
| 1988 | Jose Canseco, Oak | 42 | 40 | 2003 | Alfonso Soriano, NYY | 38 | 35 |
| 1989 | Howard Johnson, NYM | 36 | 41 | 2004 | Carlos Beltran, KC/Hou | 38 | 42 |
| 1990 | Ron Gant, Atl | 32 | 33 | 2004 | Bobby Abreu, Phi | 30 | 40 |
| 1990 | Barry Bonds, Pitt | 33 | 52 | 2005 | Alfonso Soriano, Tex | 36 | 30 |
| 1991 | Ron Gant, Atl | 32 | 34 | 2006 | Alfonso Soriano, Wash | 46 | 41 |
| 1991 | Howard Johnson, NYM | 38 | 30 | 2007 | Brandon Phillips, Cin | 30 | 32 |
| 1992 | Barry Bonds, Pitt | 34 | 39 | 2007 | Jimmy Rollins, Phi | 30 | 41 |
| 1993 | Sammy Sosa, ChiC | 33 | 36 | 2007 | David Wright, NYM | 30 | 34 |
| 1995 | Barry Bonds, SF | 33 | 31 | 2008 | Grady Sizemore, Cle | 33 | 38 |
| 1995 | Sammy Sosa, ChiC | 36 | 34 | 2008 | Hanley Ramirez, Fla | 33 | 35 |
| 1996 | Barry Bonds, SF | 42 | 40 | 2009 | Ian Kinsler, Tex | 31 | 31 |
| 1996 | Ellis Burks, Col | 40 | 32 | | | | |
| 1996 | Barry Larkin, Cin | 33 | 36 | | | | |

## Career Individual Pitching

### GAMES

| | |
|---|---|
| Jesse Orosco | 1251 |
| *Mike Stanton | 1178 |
| John Franco | 1119 |
| Dennis Eckersley | 1071 |
| Hoyt Wilhelm | 1070 |
| Dan Plesac | 1064 |
| *Mike Timlin | 1058 |
| Kent Tekulve | 1050 |
| Jose Mesa | 1022 |
| Lee Smith | 1022 |
| Roberto Hernandez | 1010 |
| Mike Jackson | 1005 |
| Goose Gossage | 1002 |
| Lindy McDaniel | 987 |
| *Trevor Hoffman | 984 |
| *Todd Jones | 982 |
| *David Weathers | 964 |
| Rollie Fingers | 944 |
| Gene Garber | 931 |
| *Mariano Rivera | 917 |
| *Eddie Guardado | 908 |
| Cy Young | 906 |
| Sparky Lyle | 899 |
| Jim Kaat | 898 |
| *Tom Gordon | 890 |

### INNINGS PITCHED

| | |
|---|---|
| Cy Young | 7356.0 |
| Pud Galvin | 6003.1 |
| Walter Johnson | 5914.1 |
| Phil Niekro | 5404.1 |
| Nolan Ryan | 5386.0 |
| Gaylord Perry | 5350.1 |
| Don Sutton | 5282.1 |
| Warren Spahn | 5243.1 |
| Steve Carlton | 5217.1 |
| Grover Alexander | 5190.0 |
| Kid Nichols | 5056.1 |
| Tim Keefe | 5049.2 |
| *Greg Maddux | 5008.1 |
| Bert Blyleven | 4970.0 |
| Bobby Mathews | 4956.0 |
| Roger Clemens | 4916.2 |
| Mickey Welch | 4802.0 |
| Tom Seaver | 4782.2 |
| Christy Mathewson | 4780.2 |
| Tommy John | 4710.1 |
| Robin Roberts | 4688.2 |
| Early Wynn | 4564.0 |
| John Clarkson | 4536.1 |
| Charley Radbourn | 4535.1 |
| Tony Mullane | 4531.1 |

### WINS

| | |
|---|---|
| Cy Young | 511 |
| Walter Johnson | 417 |
| Grover Alexander | 373 |
| Christy Mathewson | 373 |
| Pud Galvin | 365 |
| Warren Spahn | 363 |
| Kid Nichols | 361 |
| Greg Maddux | 355 |
| Roger Clemens | 354 |
| Tim Keefe | 342 |
| Steve Carlton | 329 |
| John Clarkson | 328 |
| Eddie Plank | 326 |
| Nolan Ryan | 324 |
| Don Sutton | 324 |
| Phil Niekro | 318 |
| Gaylord Perry | 314 |
| Tom Seaver | 311 |
| Charley Radbourn | 309 |
| Mickey Welch | 307 |
| *Tom Glavine | 305 |
| *Randy Johnson | 303 |
| Lefty Grove | 300 |
| Early Wynn | 300 |
| Bobby Matthews | 297 |

* Active in 2009.

## Career Individual Pitching *(Cont.)*

### LOSSES

| | |
|---|---|
| Cy Young | 316 |
| Pud Galvin | 310 |
| Nolan Ryan | 292 |
| Walter Johnson | 279 |
| Phil Niekro | 274 |
| Gaylord Perry | 265 |
| Don Sutton | 256 |
| Jack Powell | 254 |
| Eppa Rixey | 251 |
| Bert Blyleven | 250 |
| Bobby Mathews | 248 |
| Robin Roberts | 245 |
| Warren Spahn | 245 |
| Steve Carlton | 244 |
| Early Wynn | 244 |
| Jim Kaat | 237 |
| Frank Tanana | 236 |
| Gus Weyhing | 232 |
| Tommy John | 231 |
| Bob Friend | 230 |
| Ted Lyons | 230 |

### WINNING PERCENTAGE**

| | |
|---|---|
| Al Spalding | .795 |
| Spud Chandler | .717 |
| Whitey Ford | .690 |
| Dave Foutz | .690 |
| Bob Caruthers | .688 |
| *Pedro Martinez | .687 |
| Don Gullett | .686 |
| Lefty Grove | .680 |
| Joe Wood | .672 |
| *Johan Santana | .670 |
| Vic Raschi | .667 |
| Roger Clemens | .667 |
| Larry Corcoran | .665 |
| Christy Mathewson | .665 |
| *Roy Oswalt | .662 |
| *Roy Halladay | .661 |
| Sam Leever | .660 |
| Sal Maglie | .657 |
| Dick McBride | .656 |
| Sandy Koufax | .655 |
| *Tim Hudson | .655 |

### SAVES

| | |
|---|---|
| *Trevor Hoffman | 591 |
| *Mariano Rivera | 526 |
| Lee Smith | 478 |
| John Franco | 424 |
| Dennis Eckersley | 390 |
| *Billy Wagner | 385 |
| Jeff Reardon | 367 |
| *Troy Percival | 358 |
| Randy Myers | 347 |
| Rollie Fingers | 341 |
| John Wetteland | 330 |
| Roberto Hernandez | 326 |
| Jose Mesa | 321 |
| *Todd Jones | 319 |
| Rick Aguilera | 318 |
| Robb Nen | 314 |
| Tom Henke | 311 |
| Goose Gossage | 310 |
| Jeff Montgomery | 304 |
| Doug Jones | 303 |
| Bruce Sutter | 300 |

### EARNED RUN AVERAGE (2,000 IP)

| | |
|---|---|
| Ed Walsh | 1.82 |
| Addie Joss | 1.89 |
| Al Spalding | 2.04 |
| Three Finger Brown | 2.06 |
| John Ward | 2.10 |
| Christy Mathewson | 2.13 |
| Tommy Bond | 2.14 |
| Rube Waddell | 2.16 |
| Walter Johnson | 2.17 |
| Ed Reulbach | 2.28 |
| Will White | 2.28 |
| Eddie Plank | 2.35 |
| Larry Corcoran | 2.36 |
| Eddie Cicotte | 2.38 |
| Candy Cummings | 2.39 |
| Doc White | 2.39 |
| Nap Rucker | 2.42 |
| George Bradley | 2.43 |
| Jim McCormick | 2.43 |
| Chief Bender | 2.46 |

### SHUTOUTS

| | |
|---|---|
| Walter Johnson | 110 |
| Grover Alexander | 90 |
| Christy Mathewson | 79 |
| Cy Young | 76 |
| Eddie Plank | 69 |
| Warren Spahn | 63 |
| Nolan Ryan | 61 |
| Tom Seaver | 61 |
| Bert Blyleven | 60 |
| Don Sutton | 58 |
| Pud Galvin | 57 |
| Ed Walsh | 57 |
| Bob Gibson | 56 |
| Three Finger Brown | 55 |
| Steve Carlton | 55 |
| Jim Palmer | 53 |
| Gaylord Perry | 53 |
| Juan Marichal | 52 |
| Rube Waddell | 50 |
| Vic Willis | 50 |

### COMPLETE GAMES

| | |
|---|---|
| Cy Young | 749 |
| Pud Galvin | 639 |
| Tim Keefe | 554 |
| Walter Johnson | 531 |
| Kid Nichols | 531 |
| Mickey Welch | 525 |
| Bobby Mathews | 525 |
| Charley Radbourn | 489 |
| John Clarkson | 485 |
| Tony Mullane | 468 |
| Jim McCormick | 466 |
| Gus Weyhing | 448 |
| Grover Alexander | 437 |
| Christy Mathewson | 434 |
| Jack Powell | 422 |
| Eddie Plank | 410 |
| Will White | 394 |
| Amos Rusie | 392 |
| Vic Willis | 388 |
| Tommy Bond | 386 |

### STRIKEOUTS

| | |
|---|---|
| Nolan Ryan | 5714 |
| *Randy Johnson | 4875 |
| Roger Clemens | 4672 |
| Steve Carlton | 4136 |
| Bert Blyleven | 3701 |
| Tom Seaver | 3640 |
| Don Sutton | 3574 |
| Gaylord Perry | 3534 |
| Walter Johnson | 3509 |
| Greg Maddux | 3371 |
| Phil Niekro | 3342 |
| Ferguson Jenkins | 3192 |
| *Pedro Martinez | 3154 |
| Bob Gibson | 3117 |
| Curt Schilling | 3116 |
| *John Smoltz | 3084 |
| Jim Bunning | 2855 |
| Mickey Lolich | 2832 |
| Mike Mussina | 2813 |
| Cy Young | 2803 |

### BASES ON BALLS

| | |
|---|---|
| Nolan Ryan | 2795 |
| Steve Carlton | 1833 |
| Phil Niekro | 1809 |
| Early Wynn | 1775 |
| Bob Feller | 1764 |
| Bobo Newsom | 1732 |
| Amos Rusie | 1707 |
| Charlie Hough | 1665 |
| Roger Clemens | 1580 |
| Gus Weyhing | 1566 |
| Red Ruffing | 1541 |
| *Tom Glavine | 1500 |
| *Randy Johnson | 1497 |
| Bump Hadley | 1442 |
| Warren Spahn | 1434 |
| Earl Whitehill | 1431 |
| Tony Mullane | 1408 |
| Sad Sam Jones | 1396 |
| Jack Morris | 1390 |
| Tom Seaver | 1390 |

* Active in 2009.   ** Minumum 100 victories.

## Alltime Winningest Managers

### CAREER

| | W | L | Pct | Yrs | | W | L | Pct | Yrs |
|---|---|---|---|---|---|---|---|---|---|
| Connie Mack | 3755 | 3967 | .486 | 53 | Casey Stengel | 1942 | 1868 | .510 | 25 |
| John McGraw | 2810 | 1987 | .586 | 33 | Gene Mauch | 1907 | 2044 | .483 | 26 |
| *Tony LaRussa | 2609 | 2264 | .535 | 31 | Bill McKechnie | 1904 | 1737 | .523 | 25 |
| *Bobby Cox | 2479 | 1994 | .554 | 28 | *Lou Piniella | 1807 | 1663 | .521 | 22 |
| Sparky Anderson | 2238 | 1855 | .547 | 26 | Ralph Houk | 1627 | 1539 | .514 | 20 |
| *Joe Torre | 2326 | 1969 | .542 | 28 | Fred Clarke | 1609 | 1189 | .575 | 19 |
| Bucky Harris | 2168 | 2228 | .493 | 29 | Dick Williams | 1592 | 1474 | .519 | 21 |
| Joe McCarthy | 2155 | 1346 | .616 | 24 | Tommy Lasorda | 1589 | 1434 | .526 | 20 |
| Walter Alston | 2063 | 1634 | .558 | 23 | Earl Weaver | 1506 | 1080 | .582 | 17 |
| Leo Durocher | 2015 | 1717 | .540 | 24 | Clark Griffith | 1491 | 1367 | .522 | 20 |

### REGULAR SEASON

| | W | L | Pct | Yrs | | W | L | Pct | Yrs |
|---|---|---|---|---|---|---|---|---|---|
| Connie Mack | 3731 | 3948 | .486 | 53 | Casey Stengel | 1905 | 1842 | .508 | 25 |
| John McGraw | 2784 | 1959 | .587 | 33 | Gene Mauch | 1902 | 2037 | .483 | 26 |
| *Tony LaRussa | 2552 | 2217 | .535 | 31 | Bill McKechnie | 1896 | 1723 | .524 | 25 |
| *Bobby Cox | 2413 | 1930 | .556 | 28 | *Lou Piniella | 1784 | 1639 | .521 | 22 |
| Sparky Anderson | 2194 | 1834 | .545 | 26 | Ralph Houk | 1619 | 1531 | .514 | 20 |
| Bucky Harris | 2157 | 2218 | .493 | 29 | Fred Clarke | 1602 | 1181 | .576 | 19 |
| *Joe Torre | 2246 | 1915 | .540 | 28 | Dick Williams | 1571 | 1451 | .520 | 21 |
| Joe McCarthy | 2125 | 1333 | .615 | 24 | Tommy Lasorda | 1558 | 1404 | .526 | 20 |
| Walter Alston | 2040 | 1613 | .558 | 23 | Lou Piniella | 1519 | 1420 | .523 | 19 |
| Leo Durocher | 2008 | 1709 | .540 | 24 | Clark Griffith | 1491 | 1367 | .522 | 20 |

### WORLD SERIES

| | W | L | T | Pct | App | WS | | W | L | T | Pct | App | WS |
|---|---|---|---|---|---|---|---|---|---|---|---|---|---|
| Casey Stengel | 37 | 26 | 0 | .587 | 10 | 7 | Billy Southworth | 11 | 11 | 0 | .500 | 4 | 2 |
| Joe McCarthy | 30 | 13 | 0 | .698 | 9 | 7 | Earl Weaver | 11 | 13 | 0 | .458 | 4 | 1 |
| John McGraw | 26 | 28 | 2 | .482 | 9 | 2 | *Bobby Cox | 11 | 18 | 0 | .379 | 5 | 1 |
| Connie Mack | 24 | 19 | 0 | .558 | 8 | 5 | Whitey Herzog | 10 | 11 | 0 | .476 | 3 | 1 |
| *Joe Torre | 21 | 11 | 0 | .657 | 6 | 4 | *Tony LaRussa | 9 | 13 | 0 | .409 | 5 | 2 |
| Walter Alston | 20 | 20 | 0 | .500 | 7 | 4 | *Terry Francona | 8 | 0 | 0 | 1.000 | 2 | 2 |
| Miller Huggins | 18 | 15 | 1 | .544 | 6 | 3 | Bill Carrigan | 8 | 2 | 0 | .800 | 2 | 2 |
| Sparky Anderson | 16 | 12 | 0 | .571 | 5 | 3 | Cito Gaston | 8 | 4 | 0 | .667 | 2 | 2 |
| Tommy Lasorda | 12 | 11 | 0 | .522 | 4 | 2 | Danny Murtaugh | 8 | 6 | 0 | .571 | 2 | 2 |
| Dick Williams | 12 | 14 | 0 | .462 | 4 | 2 | Tom Kelly | 8 | 6 | 0 | .571 | 2 | 2 |
| Frank Chance | 11 | 9 | 1 | .548 | 4 | 2 | Ralph Houk | 8 | 8 | 0 | .500 | 3 | 2 |
| Bucky Harris | 11 | 10 | 0 | .524 | 3 | 2 | Bill McKechnie | 8 | 14 | 0 | .364 | 4 | 2 |

* Active in 2009.

## Individual Batting Records (Single Season)

### HITS

| | |
|---|---|
| Ichiro Suzuki, 2004 | 262 |
| George Sisler, 1920 | 257 |
| Lefty O'Doul, 1929 | 254 |
| Bill Terry, 1930 | 254 |
| Al Simmons, 1925 | 253 |
| Rogers Hornsby, 1922 | 250 |
| Chuck Klein, 1930 | 250 |
| Ty Cobb, 1911 | 248 |
| George Sisler, 1922 | 246 |
| Ichiro Suzuki, 2001 | 242 |

### BATTING AVERAGE

| | |
|---|---|
| Levi Meyerle, 1871 | .492 |
| Hugh Duffy, 1894 | .440 |
| Tip O'Neill, 1887 | .435 |
| Ross Barnes, 1872 | .432 |
| Cal McVey, 1871 | .431 |
| Ross Barnes, 1876 | .429 |
| Nap Lajoie, 1901 | .426 |
| Ross Barnes, 1873 | .425 |
| Willie Keeler, 1897 | .424 |
| Rogers Hornsby, 1924 | .424 |

### DOUBLES

| | |
|---|---|
| Earl Webb, 1931 | 67 |
| George Burns, 1926 | 64 |
| Joe Medwick, 1936 | 64 |
| Hank Greenberg, 1934 | 63 |
| Paul Waner, 1932 | 62 |
| Charlie Gehringer, 1936 | 60 |
| Tris Speaker, 1923 | 59 |
| Chuck Klein, 1930 | 59 |
| Todd Helton, 2000 | 59 |
| Billy Herman, 1936 | 57 |
| Billy Herman, 1935 | 57 |
| Carlos Delgado, 2000 | 57 |

### TOTAL BASES

| | |
|---|---|
| Babe Ruth, 1921 | 457 |
| Rogers Hornsby, 1922 | 450 |
| Lou Gehrig, 1927 | 447 |
| Chuck Klein, 1930 | 445 |
| Jimmie Foxx, 1932 | 438 |
| Stan Musial, 1948 | 429 |
| Sammy Sosa, 2001 | 425 |
| Hack Wilson, 1930 | 423 |
| Chuck Klein, 1932 | 420 |
| Luis Gonzalez, 2001 | 419 |
| Lou Gehrig, 1930 | 419 |

### TRIPLES

| | |
|---|---|
| Chief Wilson, 1912 | 36 |
| Dave Orr, 1886 | 31 |
| Heinie Reitz, 1894 | 31 |
| Perry Werden, 1893 | 29 |
| Harry Davis, 1897 | 28 |
| George Davis, 1893 | 27 |
| Sam Thompson, 1894 | 27 |
| Jimmy Williams, 1899 | 27 |
| Sam Crawford, 1914 | 26 |
| Kiki Cuyler, 1925 | 26 |
| Joe Jackson, 1912 | 26 |
| John Reilly,1890 | 26 |
| George Treadway | 26 |

### HOME RUNS

| | |
|---|---|
| Barry Bonds, 2001 | 73 |
| Mark McGwire, 1998 | 70 |
| Sammy Sosa, 1998 | 66 |
| Mark McGwire, 1999 | 65 |
| Sammy Sosa, 2001 | 64 |
| Sammy Sosa, 1999 | 63 |
| Roger Maris, 1961 | 61 |
| Babe Ruth, 1927 | 60 |
| Babe Ruth, 1921 | 59 |
| Jimmie Foxx, 1932 | 58 |
| Hank Greenberg, 1938 | 58 |
| Mark McGwire, 1997 | 58 |
| Ryan Howard, 2006 | 58 |

### RUNS BATTED IN

| | |
|---|---|
| Hack Wilson, 1930 | 191 |
| Lou Gehrig, 1931 | 184 |
| Hank Greenberg, 1937 | 183 |
| Lou Gehrig, 1927 | 175 |
| Jimmie Foxx, 1938 | 175 |
| Lou Gehrig, 1930 | 174 |
| Babe Ruth, 1921 | 171 |
| Chuck Klein, 1930 | 170 |
| Hank Greenberg, 1935 | 170 |
| Jimmie Foxx, 1932 | 169 |

### STRIKEOUTS

| | |
|---|---|
| Mark Reynolds, 2009 | 223 |
| Mark Reynolds, 2008 | 204 |
| Ryan Howard, 2008 | 199 |
| Ryan Howard, 2007 | 199 |
| Jack Cust, 2008 | 197 |
| Adam Dunn, 2004 | 195 |
| Bobby Bonds, 1970 | 189 |
| Jose Hernandez, 2002 | 188 |
| Bobby Bonds, 1969 | 187 |
| Preston Wilson, 2000 | 187 |
| Ryan Howard, 2009 | 186 |
| Rob Deer, 1987 | 186 |
| Jack Cust, Oakland | 185 |
| Jose Hernandez, 2001 | 185 |
| Pete Incaviglia, 1986 | 185 |
| Jim Thome, 2001 | 185 |

### RUNS

| | |
|---|---|
| Billy Hamilton, 1894 | 192 |
| Tom Brown, 1891 | 177 |
| Babe Ruth, 1921 | 177 |
| Lou Gehrig, 1936 | 167 |
| Tip O'Neill, 1887 | 167 |
| Billy Hamilton, 1895 | 166 |
| Willie Keeler, 1894 | 165 |
| Joe Kelley, 1894 | 165 |
| Lou Gehrig, 1931 | 163 |
| Arlie Latham, 1887 | 163 |
| Babe Ruth, 1928 | 163 |

### STOLEN BASES

| | |
|---|---|
| Hugh Nicol, 1887 | 138 |
| Rickey Henderson, 1982 | 130 |
| Arlie Latham, 1887 | 129 |
| Lou Brock, 1974 | 118 |
| Charlie Comiskey, 1887 | 117 |
| Billy Hamilton, 1891 | 111 |
| Billy Hamilton, 1889 | 111 |
| John Ward, 1887 | 111 |
| Vince Coleman, 1985 | 110 |
| Vince Coleman, 1987 | 109 |
| Arlie Latham, 1888 | 109 |

### BASES ON BALLS

| | |
|---|---|
| Barry Bonds, 2004 | 232 |
| Barry Bonds, 2002 | 198 |
| Barry Bonds, 2001 | 177 |
| Babe Ruth, 1923 | 170 |
| Ted Williams, 1947 | 162 |
| Ted Williams, 1949 | 162 |
| Mark McGwire, 1998 | 162 |
| Ted Williams, 1946 | 156 |
| Barry Bonds,1996 | 151 |
| Eddie Yost, 1956 | 151 |
| Babe Ruth, 1920 | 150 |

### SLUGGING AVERAGE

| | |
|---|---|
| Barry Bonds, 2001 | .863 |
| Babe Ruth, 1920 | .847 |
| Babe Ruth, 1921 | .846 |
| Barry Bonds, 2004 | .812 |
| Barry Bonds, 2002 | .799 |
| Babe Ruth, 1927 | .772 |
| Lou Gehrig, 1927 | .765 |
| Babe Ruth, 1923 | .764 |
| Rogers Hornsby, 1925 | .756 |
| Mark McGwire, 1998 | .752 |

## Individual Pitching Records (Single Season)

### GAME APPEARANCES

Mike Marshall, 1974 ...........106
Kent Tekulve, 1979 ...............94
Salomon Torres, 2006...........94
Mike Marshall, 1973 ..............92
Kent Tekulve, 1978 ...............91
Wayne Granger, 1969...........90
Mike Marshall, 1979 ..............90
Kent Tekulve, 1987 ...............90
Steve Kline, 2001...................89
Jim Brower, 2004...................89
Mark Eichhorn, 1987 .............89
Steve Kline, 2001...................89

### GAMES STARTED

Will White, 1879 .....................75
Pud Galvin, 1883 ...................75
Jim McCormick, 1880 ...........74
Charley Radbourn, 1884 .......73
Guy Hecker, 1884...................73
Jim Galvin, 1884.....................72
John Clarkson, 1889...............72
Bill Hutchison, 1892...............71
John Clarkson, 1885...............70
Bobby Mathews, 1875...........70

### INNINGS PITCHED

Will White, 1878 ...............680.0
Charley Radbourn, 1884 ...678.2
Guy Hecker, 1884............670.2
Jim McCormick, 1880 .......657.2
Jim Galvin, 1883................656.1
Jim Galvin, 1884.................636.1
Charley Radbourn, 1883 ...632.1
Bill Hutchison, 1892...........627.0
Bobby Mathews, 1875........626.2
John Clarkson, 1885........623.0

### WINS

Charley Radbourn, 1884 .......59
Al Spalding, 1875 ..................55
John Clarkson, 1885..............53
Guy Hecker, 1884..................52
Al Spalding, 1874 ..................52
John Clarkson, 1889..............49
Charlie Buffinton, 1884 ..........48
Charley Radbourn, 1883 .......48
Al Spalding, 1876 ..................47
John Ward, 1879 ...................47
Matt Kilroy, 1887 ...................46

### LOSSES

John Coleman, 1883 .............48
Will White, 1880.....................42
Larry McKeon, 1884..............41
George Bradley, 1879 ...........40
Jim McCormick, 1879 ...........40
Bobby Mathews, 1875...........38
Kid Carsey, 1891 ..................37
George Cobb, 1892 ..............37
Henry Porter, 1888.................37

### WINNING PERCENTAGE

Roy Face, 1959 .................. .947
Johnny Allen, 1937............... .938
Greg Maddux, 1995 .......... .905
Randy Johnson, 1995 ........ .900
Ron Guidry, 1978 .............. .893
Freddie Fitzsimmons, 1940... .889
Lefty Grove, 1931............... .886
Bob Stanley, 1978 .............. .882
Preacher Roe, 1951 .......... .880
Cliff Lee, 2008 .................... .880
Fred Goldsmith, 1880.......... .875
Tom Seaver, 1981 .............. .875

### SAVES

Francisco Rodriguez, 2008 ...62
Bobby Thigpen, 1990...........57
Eric Gagne, 2003 .................55
John Smoltz, 2002................55
Mariano Rivera, 2004 ..........53
Randy Myers, 1993 ..............53
Trevor Hoffman, 1998 ...........53
Eric Gagne, 2002 .................52
Rod Beck, 1998....................51
Dennis Eckersley, 1992 ........51
Mariano Rivera, 2001 ...........50

### EARNED RUN AVERAGE

Tim Keefe, 1880 .................0.86
Dutch Leonard, 1914...........0.96
Three Finger Brown, 1906 ...1.04
Bob Gibson, 1968 ...............1.12
Christy Mathewson, 1909...1.14
Walter Johnson, 1913.........1.15
Jack Pfiester, 1907 .............1.15
Addie Joss, 1908.................1.16
Carl Lundgren, 1907 ...........1.17
Denny Driscoll, 1882 ..........1.21

### SHUTOUTS

Grover Alexander, 1916.........16
George Bradley, 1876 ..........16
Jack Coombs, 1910 .............13
Bob Gibson, 1968 ................13
Grover Alexander, 1915.........12
Jim Galvin, 1884....................12
Ed Morris, 1886 ....................12
Tommy Bond, 1879................11
Dean Chance, 1964 .............11
Dave Foutz, 1886 .................11
Walter Johnson, 1913............11
Sandy Koufax, 1963 .............11
Christy Mathewson, 1908......11
Charles Radbourn, 1884 .......11
Ed Walsh, 1908 ....................11

### COMPLETE GAMES

Will White, 1879 .....................75
Charley Radbourn, 1884 .......73
Pud Galvin, 1883 ...................72
Guy Hecker, 1884..................72
Jim McCormick,1880.............72
Pud Galvin, 1884 ..................71
Bobby Mathews, 1875...........69
John Clarkson, 1885..............68
John Clarkson, 1889..............68

### STRIKEOUTS

Matt Kilroy, 1886 .................513
Toad Ramsey, 1886 .............499
Hugh Daily, 1884 .................483
Dupee Shaw, 1884 ..............451
Charley Radbourn, 1884 .....441
Charlie Buffinton, 1884 ........417
Guy Hecker, 1884.................385
Nolan Ryan, 1973.................383
Sandy Koufax, 1965 .............382

### BASES ON BALLS

Amos Rusie, 1890 ................289
Mark Baldwin, 1889...............274
Amos Rusie, 1892 ................267
Amos Rusie, 1891 ................262
Mark Baldwin, 1890...............249
Jack Stivetts, 1891 ...............232
Mark Baldwin, 1891...............227
Phil Knell, 1891.....................226
Bob Barr, 1890 ....................219

## Manager of the Year

| NATIONAL LEAGUE | AMERICAN LEAGUE |
|---|---|
| 1983 .................Tommy Lasorda, LA | 1983 ..................Tony LaRussa, Chi |
| 1984 .................Jim Frey, Chi | 1984 ..................Sparky Anderson, Det |
| 1985 .................Whitey Herzog, StL | 1985 ..................Bobby Cox, Tor |
| 1986 .................Hal Lanier, Hou | 1986 ..................John McNamara, Bos |
| 1987 .................Buck Rodgers, Mtl | 1987 ..................Sparky Anderson, Det |
| 1988 .................Tommy Lasorda, LA | 1988 ..................Tony LaRussa, Oak |
| 1989 .................Don Zimmer, Chi | 1989 ..................Frank Robinson, Balt |
| 1990 .................Jim Leyland, Pitt | 1990 ..................Jeff Torborg, Chi |
| 1991 .................Bobby Cox, Atl | 1991 ..................Tom Kelly, Minn |
| 1992 .................Jim Leyland, Pitt | 1992 ..................Tony LaRussa, Oak |
| 1993 .................Dusty Baker, SF | 1993 ..................Gene Lamont, Chi |
| 1994 .................Felipe Alou, Mtl | 1994 ..................Buck Showalter, NY |
| 1995 .................Don Baylor, Col | 1995 ..................Lou Piniella, Sea |
| 1996 .................Bruce Bochy, SD | 1996 ..................Joe Torre, NY/Johnny Oates, Tex |
| 1997 .................Dusty Baker, SF | 1997 ..................Davey Johnson, Balt |
| 1998 .................Larry Dierker, Hou | 1998 ..................Joe Torre, NY |

### Manager of the Year (*Cont.*)

| NATIONAL LEAGUE | | AMERICAN LEAGUE | |
|---|---|---|---|
| 1999 | Jack McKeon, Cin | 1999 | Jimy Williams, Bos |
| 2000 | Dusty Baker, SF | 2000 | Jerry Manuel, Chi |
| 2001 | Larry Bowa, Phi | 2001 | Lou Piniella, Sea |
| 2002 | Tony LaRussa, StL | 2002 | Mike Scioscia, Ana |
| 2003 | Jack McKeon, Fla | 2003 | Tony Pena, KC |
| 2004 | Bobby Cox, Atl | 2004 | Buck Showalter, Tex |
| 2005 | Bobby Cox, Atl | 2005 | Ozzie Guillen, Chi |
| 2006 | Joe Girardi, Fla | 2006 | Jim Leyland, Det |
| 2007 | Bob Melvin, Ari | 2007 | Eric Wedge, Cle |

## Individual Batting Records (Single Game)

### MOST RUNS

7 .......Guy Hecker, Lou        Aug 15, 1886

### MOST HITS

7 ......Wilbert Robinson, Balt        June 10, 1892
Rennie Stennett, Pitt        Sept 16, 1975

### MOST HOME RUNS

4 .......Bobby Lowe, Bos (N)        May 30, 1894
Ed Delahanty, Phi        July 13, 1896
Lou Gehrig, NY (A)        June 3, 1932
Gil Hodges, Bklyn        Aug 31, 1950
Joe Adcock, Mil (N)        July 31, 1954
Rocky Colavito, Clev        June 10, 1959
Willie Mays, SF        April 30, 1961
Mike Schmidt, Phi        April 17, 1976
Bob Horner, Atl        July 6, 1986
Mark Whiten, StL        Sept 7, 1993
Mike Cameron, Sea        May 2, 2002
Shawn Green, LA        May 23, 2002
Carlos Delgado, Tor        Sept 25, 2003

Note: All single-game hitting records for a nine-inning game.

### MOST GRAND SLAMS

2 .......Tony Lazzeri, NY (A)        May 24, 1936
Jim Tabor, Bos (A)        July 4, 1939
Rudy York, Bos (A)        July 27, 1946
Jim Gentile, Balt        May 9, 1961
Tony Cloninger, Atl        July 3, 1966
Jim Northrup, Det        June 24, 1968
Frank Robinson, Balt        June 26, 1970
Robin Ventura, Chi (A)        Sept 4, 1995
Chris Hoiles, Balt        Aug 14, 1998
Fernando Tatis, StL        Apr 23, 1999
N. Garciaparra, Bos        May 10, 1999
Bill Mueller, Bos        July 29, 2003

### MOST RBIs

12 .....Jim Bottomley, StL        Sept 16, 1924
Mark Whiten, StL        Sept 7, 1993

## Individual Batting Records (Single Inning)

### MOST RUNS

3 .......Tommy Burns, Chi (N) Sept 6, 1883, 7th inning
Ned Williamson, Chi (N) Sept 6, 1883, 7th inning
Sammy White, Bos (A)  June 18, 1953, 7th inning

### MOST HITS

3 .......Tommy Burns, Chi (N) Sept 6, 1883, 7th inning
Fred Pfeiffer, Chi (N)  Sept 6, 1883, 7th inning
Ned Williamson, Chi (N) Sept 6, 1883, 7th inning
Gene Stephens, Bos (A) June 18, 1953, 7th inning
Johnny Damon, Bos (A), June 27, 2003, 1st inning

### MOST RBIs

8.......Fernando Tatis, StL    Apr 23, 1999, 3rd inning

## Individual Pitching Records (Single Game)

### MOST INNINGS PITCHED

26 .....Leon Cadore, Bklyn        May 1, 1920, tie 1–1
Joe Oeschger, Bos (N)        May 1, 1920, tie 1–1

### MOST RUNS ALLOWED

24 .....Al Travers, Det        May 18, 1912

### MOST HITS ALLOWED

36 .....Jack Wadsworth, Lou        Aug 17, 1894

### MOST STRIKEOUTS

20 .....Roger Clemens, Bos        April 29, 1986
20 .....Roger Clemens, Bos        Sept 18, 1996
20 .....Kerry Wood, Chi (N)        May 6, 1998
20 .....Randy Johnson, Ariz        May 8, 2001

### MOST WALKS ALLOWED

16 .....Bill George, NY (N)        May 30, 1887
George Van Haltren,        June 27, 1887
Chi (N)
Henry Gruber, Clev        Apr 19, 1890
Bruno Haas, Phi (A)        June 2, 1915

### MOST WILD PITCHES

6 .......J.R. Richard, Hou        April 10, 1979
Phil Niekro, Atl        Aug 14, 1979
Bill Gullickson, Mtl        April 10, 1982

### Individual Pitching Records (Single Inning)

| MOST RUNS ALLOWED | | | MOST WILD PITCHES | | |
|---|---|---|---|---|---|
| 13 | Lefty O'Doul, Bos (A) | July 7, 1923 | 4 | Walter Johnson, Wash | Sept 21, 1914 |
| | | | | Phil Niekro, Atl | Aug 14, 1979 |
| **MOST WALKS ALLOWED** | | | | Kevin Gregg, Ana | July 25, 2004 |
| 8 | Dolly Gray, Wash | Aug 28, 1909 | | Ryan Madson, Phi | July 25, 2006 |

### Miscellaneous Records

| LONGEST GAME, BY INNINGS | | | LONGEST NINE-INNING GAME, BY TIME | | |
|---|---|---|---|---|---|
| 26 | Brooklyn 1, Boston 1 | May 1, 1920 | 4:45 | New York (A) 14, Boston 11 | Aug 18, 2006 |

## Baseball Hall of Fame

### Players

| | Position | Career | Selected | | Position | Career | Selected |
|---|---|---|---|---|---|---|---|
| Hank Aaron | OF | 1954–76 | 1982 | Candy Cummings | P | 1872–77 | 1939 |
| Grover Alexander | P | 1911–30 | 1938 | Kiki Cuyler | OF | 1921–38 | 1968 |
| Cap Anson | 1B | 1876–97 | 1939 | Ray Dandridge* | 3B | | 1987 |
| Luis Aparicio | SS | 1956–73 | 1984 | George Davis | SS | 1890–1909 | 1998 |
| Luke Appling | SS | 1930–50 | 1964 | Leon Day* | P | | 1995 |
| Richie Ashburn | OF | 1948–62 | 1995 | Dizzy Dean | P | 1930–47 | 1953 |
| Earl Averill | OF | 1929–41 | 1975 | Ed Delahanty | OF | 1888–1903 | 1945 |
| Jose Mendez Baez* | P | 1908–26 | 2006 | Bill Dickey | C | 1928–46 | 1954 |
| Frank Baker | 3B | 1908–22 | 1955 | Martin Dihigo* | P-OF | | 1977 |
| Dave Bancroft | SS | 1915–30 | 1971 | Joe DiMaggio | OF | 1936–51 | 1955 |
| Ernie Banks | SS-1B | 1953–71 | 1977 | Larry Doby | OF | 1947–59 | 1998 |
| Jake Beckley | 1B | 1888–1907 | 1971 | Bobby Doerr | 2B | 1937–51 | 1986 |
| Cool Papa Bell* | OF | | 1974 | Don Drysdale | P | 1956–69 | 1984 |
| Johnny Bench | C | 1967–83 | 1989 | Hugh Duffy | OF | 1888–1906 | 1945 |
| Chief Bender | P | 1903–25 | 1953 | Dennis Eckersley | P | 1975–98 | 2004 |
| Yogi Berra | C | 1946–65 | 1972 | Johnny Evers | 2B | 1902–29 | 1939 |
| Wade Boggs | 3B | 1982-99 | 2005 | Buck Ewing | C | 1880–97 | 1946 |
| Jim Bottomley | 1B | 1922–37 | 1974 | Red Faber | P | 1914–33 | 1964 |
| Lou Boudreau | SS | 1938–52 | 1970 | Bob Feller | P | 1936–56 | 1962 |
| Roger Bresnahan | C | 1897–1915 | 1945 | Rick Ferrell | C | 1929–47 | 1984 |
| George Brett | 3B | 1973–93 | 1999 | Rollie Fingers | P | 1968–85 | 1992 |
| Lou Brock | OF | 1961–79 | 1985 | Carlton Fisk | C | 1969–93 | 2000 |
| Dan Brouthers | 1B | 1879–1904 | 1945 | Elmer Flick | OF | 1898–1910 | 1963 |
| Ray Brown* | P | 1930–48 | 2006 | Whitey Ford | P | 1950–67 | 1974 |
| Three Finger Brown | P | 1903–16 | 1949 | Bill Foster* | P | | 1996 |
| Willard Jesse Brown* | OF | 1935–58 | 2006 | Nellie Fox | 2B | 1947–65 | 1997 |
| Jim Bunning | P | 1955–71 | 1996 | Jimmie Foxx | 1B | 1925–45 | 1951 |
| Jesse Burkett | OF | 1890–1905 | 1946 | Frankie Frisch | 2B | 1919–37 | 1947 |
| Roy Campanella | C | 1948–57 | 1969 | Pud Galvin | P | 1879–92 | 1965 |
| Rod Carew | 1B-2B | 1967–85 | 1991 | Lou Gehrig | 1B | 1923–39 | 1939 |
| Max Carey | OF | 1910–29 | 1961 | Charlie Gehringer | 2B | 1924–42 | 1949 |
| Steve Carlton | P | 1965–88 | 1994 | Bob Gibson | P | 1959–75 | 1981 |
| Gary Carter | C | 1974–92 | 2003 | Josh Gibson* | C | | 1972 |
| Orlando Cepeda | 1B | 1958–74 | 1999 | Lefty Gomez | P | 1930–43 | 1972 |
| Frank Chance | 1B | 1898–1914 | 1946 | Joe Gordon | 2B | 1938-43/46-50 | 2009 |
| Oscar Charleston* | OF | | 1976 | Goose Goslin | OF | 1921–38 | 1968 |
| Jack Chesbro | P | 1899–1909 | 1946 | Rich "Goose" Gossage | P | 1972-94 | 2008 |
| Fred Clarke | OF | 1894–1915 | 1945 | Ulysses F. Grant* | 2B | 1886–1903 | 2006 |
| John Clarkson | P | 1882–94 | 1963 | Hank Greenberg | 1B | 1930–47 | 1956 |
| Roberto Clemente | OF | 1955–72 | 1973 | Burleigh Grimes | P | 1916–34 | 1964 |
| Ty Cobb | OF | 1905–28 | 1936 | Lefty Grove | P | 1925–41 | 1947 |
| Mickey Cochrane | C | 1925–37 | 1947 | Tony Gwynn | OF | 1982–2001 | 2007 |
| Eddie Collins | 2B | 1906–30 | 1939 | Chick Hafey | OF | 1924–37 | 1971 |
| Jimmy Collins | 3B | 1895–1908 | 1945 | Jesse Haines | P | 1918–37 | 1970 |
| Earle Combs | OF | 1924–35 | 1970 | Billy Hamilton | OF | 1888–1901 | 1961 |
| Roger Connor | 1B | 1880–97 | 1976 | Gabby Hartnett | C | 1922–41 | 1955 |
| Andrew Cooper* | P | 1920–41 | 2006 | Harry Heilmann | OF | 1914–32 | 1952 |
| Stan Coveleski | P | 1912–28 | 1969 | Rickey Henderson | OF | 1979–2003 | 2009 |
| Sam Crawford | OF | 1899–1917 | 1957 | Billy Herman | 2B | 1931–47 | 1975 |
| Joe Cronin | SS | 1926–45 | 1956 | Joseph Hill* | OF | 1899–1925 | 2006 |

Note: Career dates indicate first and last appearances in the majors.
*Elected on the basis of their career in the Negro leagues.

## Players *(Cont.)*

| | Position | Career | Selected | | Position | Career | Selected |
|---|---|---|---|---|---|---|---|
| Harry Hooper | OF | 1909–25 | 1971 | Cal Ripken Jr. | SS | 1981–2001 | 2007 |
| Rogers Hornsby | 2B | 1915–37 | 1942 | Eppa Rixey | P | 1912–33 | 1963 |
| Waite Hoyt | P | 1918–38 | 1969 | Phil Rizzuto | SS | 1941–56 | 1994 |
| Carl Hubbell | P | 1928–43 | 1947 | Robin Roberts | P | 1948–66 | 1976 |
| Catfish Hunter | P | 1965–79 | 1987 | Brooks Robinson | 3B | 1955–77 | 1983 |
| Monte Irvin* | OF | 1949–56 | 1973 | Frank Robinson | OF | 1956–76 | 1982 |
| Reggie Jackson | OF | 1967–87 | 1993 | Jackie Robinson | 2B | 1947–56 | 1962 |
| Travis Jackson | SS | 1922–36 | 1982 | Joe (Bullet) Rogan* | P | | 1998 |
| Ferguson Jenkins | P | 1965–83 | 1991 | Edd Roush | OF | 1913–31 | 1962 |
| Hugh Jennings | SS | 1891–1918 | 1945 | Red Ruffing | P | 1924–47 | 1967 |
| Judy Johnson* | 3B | | 1975 | Amos Rusie | P | 1889–1901 | 1977 |
| Walter Johnson | P | 1907–27 | 1936 | Babe Ruth | OF | 1914–35 | 1936 |
| Addie Joss | P | 1902–10 | 1978 | Nolan Ryan | P | 1966–93 | 1999 |
| Al Kaline | OF | 1953–74 | 1980 | Ryne Sandberg | 2B | 1981-97 | 2005 |
| Tim Keefe | P | 1880–93 | 1964 | Louis Santop* | C | 1909–26 | 2006 |
| Willie Keeler | OF | 1892–1910 | 1939 | Ray Schalk | C | 1912–29 | 1955 |
| George Kell | 3B | 1943–57 | 1983 | Mike Schmidt | 3B | 1972–89 | 1995 |
| Joe Kelley | OF | 1891–1908 | 1971 | Red Schoendienst | 2B | 1945–63 | 1989 |
| George Kelly | 1B | 1915–32 | 1973 | Tom Seaver | P | 1967–86 | 1992 |
| King Kelly | C | 1878–93 | 1945 | Joe Sewell | SS | 1920–33 | 1977 |
| Harmon Killebrew | 1B-3B | 1954–75 | 1984 | Al Simmons | OF | 1924–44 | 1953 |
| Ralph Kiner | OF | 1946–55 | 1975 | George Sisler | 1B | 1915–30 | 1939 |
| Chuck Klein | OF | 1928–44 | 1980 | Enos Slaughter | OF | 1938–59 | 1985 |
| Sandy Koufax | P | 1955–66 | 1972 | Hilton Smith* | P | | 2001 |
| Nap Lajoie | 2B | 1896–1916 | 1937 | Ozzie Smith | SS | 1978–96 | 2002 |
| Tony Lazzeri | 2B | 1926–39 | 1991 | Duke Snider | OF | 1947–64 | 1980 |
| Bob Lemon | P | 1941–58 | 1976 | Warren Spahn | P | 1942–65 | 1973 |
| Buck Leonard* | 1B | | 1977 | Al Spalding | P | 1871–78 | 1939 |
| Fred Lindstrom | 3B | 1924–36 | 1976 | Tris Speaker | OF | 1907–28 | 1937 |
| Pop Lloyd* | SS-1B | | 1977 | Willie Stargell | OF-1B | 1962–82 | 1988 |
| Ernie Lombardi | C | 1931–47 | 1986 | Turkey Stearns* | CF | | 2000 |
| Ted Lyons | P | 1923–46 | 1955 | Don Sutton | P | 1966–88 | 1998 |
| James Mackey* | C | 1920–47 | 2006 | Bruce Sutter | P | 1976–88 | 2006 |
| Mickey Mantle | OF | 1951–68 | 1974 | George Suttles* | C | 1923–44 | 2006 |
| Heinie Manush | OF | 1923–39 | 1964 | Benjamin Harrison Taylor* | P-1B | 1908–29 | 2006 |
| Rabbit Maranville | SS-2B | 1912–35 | 1954 | Bill Terry | 1B | 1923–36 | 1954 |
| Juan Marichal | P | 1960–75 | 1983 | Sam Thompson | OF | 1885–1906 | 1974 |
| Rube Marquard | P | 1908–25 | 1971 | Joe Tinker | SS | 1902–16 | 1946 |
| Eddie Mathews | 3B | 1952–68 | 1978 | Cristóbal Torriente* | OF | 1913–32 | 2006 |
| Christy Mathewson | P | 1900–16 | 1936 | Pie Traynor | 3B | 1920–37 | 1948 |
| Willie Mays | OF | 1951–73 | 1979 | Dazzy Vance | P | 1915–35 | 1955 |
| Bill Mazeroski | 2B | 1956–72 | 2001 | Arky Vaughan | SS | 1932–48 | 1985 |
| Tommy McCarthy | OF | 1884–96 | 1946 | Rube Waddell | P | 1897–1910 | 1946 |
| Willie McCovey | 1B | 1959–80 | 1986 | Honus Wagner | SS | 1897–1917 | 1936 |
| Joe McGinnity | P | 1899–1908 | 1946 | Bobby Wallace | SS | 1894–1918 | 1953 |
| Bid McPhee | 2B | 1882–99 | 2000 | Ed Walsh | P | 1904–17 | 1946 |
| Joe Medwick | OF | 1932–48 | 1968 | Lloyd Waner | OF | 1927–45 | 1967 |
| Johnny Mize | 1B | 1936–53 | 1981 | Paul Waner | OF | 1926–45 | 1952 |
| Paul Molitor | 3B | 1978–98 | 2004 | John Ward | 2B-P | 1878–94 | 1964 |
| Joe Morgan | 2B | 1963–84 | 1990 | Mickey Welch | P | 1880–92 | 1973 |
| Eddie Murray | 1B | 1977–97 | 2003 | Willie Wells* | SS | 1924–49 | 1997 |
| Stan Musial | OF-1B | 1941–63 | 1969 | Zach Wheat | OF | 1909–27 | 1959 |
| Hal Newhouser | P | 1939–55 | 1992 | Hoyt Wilhelm | P | 1952–72 | 1985 |
| Kid Nichols | P | 1890–1906 | 1949 | Billy Williams | OF | 1959–76 | 1987 |
| Phil Niekro | P | 1964–87 | 1997 | Ted Williams | OF | 1939–60 | 1966 |
| Jim O'Rourke | OF | 1876–1904 | 1945 | Vic Willis | P | 1898–1910 | 1995 |
| Mel Ott | OF | 1926–47 | 1951 | Ernest Judson Wilson*- | 3B | 1922–45 | 2006 |
| Satchel Paige* | P | 1948–65 | 1971 | Hack Wilson | OF | 1923–34 | 1979 |
| Jim Palmer | P | 1965–84 | 1990 | Dave Winfield | OF | 1973–95 | 2001 |
| Herb Pennock | P | 1912–34 | 1948 | Early Wynn | P | 1939–63 | 1972 |
| Tony Perez | 1B | 1964–86 | 2000 | Carl Yastrzemski | OF | 1961–83 | 1989 |
| Gaylord Perry | P | 1962–83 | 1991 | Cy Young | P | 1890–1911 | 1937 |
| Eddie Plank | P | 1901–17 | 1946 | Ross Youngs | OF | 1917–26 | 1972 |
| Kirby Puckett | OF | 1984–95 | 2001 | Robin Yount | SS | 1974–93 | 1999 |
| Charley Radbourn | P | 1880–91 | 1939 | | | | |
| Pee Wee Reese | SS | 1940–58 | 1984 | | | | |
| Jim Rice | OF | 1974–89 | 2009 | | | | |
| Sam Rice | OF | 1915–35 | 1963 | *Elected on the basis of their career in the Negro leagues. | | | |

## Pioneers/Executives

| | Selected |
|---|---|
| Ed Barrow (manager-executive) | 1953 |
| Morgan Bulkeley (executive) | 1937 |
| Alexander Cartwright (executive) | 1938 |
| Henry Chadwick (writer-executive) | 1938 |
| Happy Chandler (commissioner) | 1982 |
| Charles Comiskey (manager-executive) | 1939 |
| Barney Dreyfuss (executive) | 2008 |
| Ford Frick (commissioner-executive) | 1970 |
| Warren Giles (executive) | 1979 |
| Clark Griffith (executive) | 1946 |
| Will Harridge (executive) | 1972 |
| William Hulbert (executive) | 1995 |
| Ban Johnson (executive) | 1937 |
| Kenesaw M. Landis (commissioner) | 1944 |
| Bowie Kuhn (commissioner) | 2008 |
| Larry MacPhail Sr. (executive) | 1978 |
| Lee MacPhail Jr. (executive) | 1998 |
| Effa Manley (executive) | 2006 |
| Walter O'Malley (executive) | 2008 |
| Alex Pompez (executive) | 2006 |
| Cum Posey (player-manager-owner) | 2006 |
| Branch Rickey (manager-executive) | 1967 |
| Al Spalding (player-manager) | 1939 |
| Bill Veeck Jr. (owner) | 1991 |
| George Weiss (executive) | 1971 |
| Sol White (player-manager) | 2006 |
| J.L. Wilkinson (executive) | 2006 |
| George Wright (player-manager) | 1937 |
| Harry Wright (player-manager-executive) | 1953 |
| Tom Yawkey (executive) | 1980 |

## Managers

| | Managed | Selected |
|---|---|---|
| Walter Alston | 1954–76 | 1983 |
| Sparky Anderson | 1970–94 | 2000 |
| Leo Durocher | 1939–73 | 1994 |
| Rube Foster | 1907–26 | 1981 |
| Bucky Harris | 1924–56 | 1975 |
| Ned Hanlon | 1899–1907 | 1996 |
| Miller Huggins | 1913–29 | 1964 |
| Tommy Lasorda | 1977–96 | 1997 |
| Al Lopez | 1951–69 | 1977 |
| Connie Mack | 1894–1950 | 1937 |
| Joe McCarthy | 1926–50 | 1957 |
| John McGraw | 1899–1932 | 1937 |
| Bill McKechnie | 1915–46 | 1962 |
| Wilbert Robinson | 1902–31 | 1945 |
| Frank Selee | 1890–1905 | 1999 |
| Billy Southworth | 1929, 1940–51 | 2008 |
| Casey Stengel | 1934–65 | 1966 |
| Earl Weaver | 1968–82, 85–86 | 1996 |
| Dick Williams | 1967–69, 1971–88 | 2008 |

## Umpires

| | Selected |
|---|---|
| Al Barlick | 1989 |
| Nestor Chylak | 1999 |
| Jocko Conlan | 1974 |
| Tom Connolly | 1953 |
| Billy Evans | 1973 |
| Cal Hubbard | 1976 |
| Bill Klem | 1953 |
| Bill McGowan | 1992 |

# Notable Achievements

## No-Hit Games, Nine Innings or More

### NATIONAL LEAGUE

| Date | Pitcher and Game |
|---|---|
| 1876......July 15 | George Bradley, StL vs Hart 2–0 |
| 1880......June 12 | John Richmond, Wor vs Clev 1–0 (perfect game) |
| June 17 | Monte Ward, Prov vs Buff 5–0 (perfect game) |
| Aug 19 | Larry Corcoran, Chi vs Bos 6–0 |
| Aug 20 | Pud Galvin, Buff vs Wor 1–0 |
| 1882......Sept 20 | Larry Corcoran, Chi vs Wor 5–0 |
| Sept 22 | Tim Keefe, Bklyn vs NY 4–0 |
| 1883......July 25 | Hoss Radbourn, Prov vs Clev 8–0 |
| Sept 13 | Hugh Daily, Clev vs Phi 1–0 |
| 1884......June 27 | Larry Corcoran, Chi vs Prov 6–0 |
| Aug 4 | Pud Galvin, Buff vs Det 18–0 |
| 1885......July 27 | John Clarkson, Chi vs Prov 4–0 |
| Aug 29 | Charles Ferguson, Phi vs Prov 1–0 |
| 1891......July 31 | Amos Rusie, NY vs Bklyn 6–0 |
| June 22 | Tom Lovett, Bklyn vs NY 4–0 |
| 1892......Aug 6 | Jack Stivetts, Bos vs Bklyn 11–0 |
| Aug 22 | Alex Sanders, Lou vs Balt 6–2 |
| 1892......Oct 15 | Bumpus Jones, Cin vs Pitt 7–1 (first major league game) |
| 1893......Aug 16 | Bill Hawke, Balt vs Wash 5–0 |
| 1897......Sept 18 | Cy Young, Clev vs Cin 6–0 |
| 1898......Apr 22 | Ted Breitenstein, Cin vs Pitt 11–0 |
| Apr 22 | Jim Hughes, Balt vs Bos 8–0 |
| July 8 | Frank Donahue, Phi vs Bos 5–0 |
| Aug 21 | Walter Thornton, Chi vs Bklyn 2–0 |

| Date | Pitcher and Game |
|---|---|
| 1899......May 25 | Deacon Phillippe, Lou vs NY 7–0 |
| Aug 7 | Vic Willis, Bos vs Wash 7–1 |
| 1900......July 12 | Noodles Hahn, Cin vs Phi 4–0 |
| 1901......July 15 | Christy Mathewson, NY vs StL 5–0 |
| 1903......Sept 18 | Chick Fraser, Phi vs Chi 10–0 |
| 1904......June 11 | Bob Wicker, Chi at NY 1–0 (hit in 10th; won in 12th) |
| 1905......June 13 | Christy Mathewson, NY vs Chi 1–0 |
| 1906......May 1 | John Lush, Phi vs Bklyn 6–0 |
| July 20 | Mal Eason, Bklyn vs StL 2–0 |
| 1906......Aug 1 | Harry McIntire, Bklyn vs Pitt 0–1 (hit in 11th; lost in 13th) |
| 1907......May 8 | Frank Pfeffer, Bos vs Cin 6–0 |
| Sept 20 | Nick Maddox, Pitt vs Bklyn 2–1 |
| 1908......July 4 | George Wiltse, NY vs Phi 1–0 (10 innings) |
| Sept 5 | Nap Rucker, Bklyn vs Bos 6–0 |
| 1909......Apr 15 | Leon Ames, NY vs Bklyn 0–3 (hit in 10th; lost in 13th) |
| 1912......Sept 6 | Jeff Tesreau, NY vs Phi 3–0 |
| 1914......Sept 9 | George Davis, Bos vs Phi 7–0 |
| 1915......Apr 15 | Rube Marquard, NY vs Bklyn 2–0 |
| Aug 31 | Jimmy Lavender, Chi vs NY 2–0 |
| 1916......June 16 | Tom Hughes, Bos vs Pitt 2–0 |
| 1917......May 2 | Jim Vaughn, Cin vs Chi 0–1 (hit in 10th; lost in 10th) |
| May 2 | Fred Toney, Cin vs Chi 1–0 (10 innings) |

## No-Hit Games, Nine Innings or More *(Cont.)*
### NATIONAL LEAGUE *(Cont.)*

| Date | Pitcher and Game | Date | Pitcher and Game |
|---|---|---|---|
| 1919......May 11 | Hod Eller, Cin vs StL 6–0 | 1971......June 3 | Ken Holtzman, Chi vs Cin 1–0 |
| 1922......May 7 | Jesse Barnes, NY vs Phi 6–0 | June 23 | Rick Wise, Phi vs Cin 4–0 |
| 1924......July 17 | Jesse Haines, StL vs Bos 5–0 | Aug 14 | Bob Gibson, StL vs Pitt 11–0 |
| 1925......Sept 13 | Dazzy Vance, Bklyn vs Phi 10–1 | 1972......Apr 16 | Burt Hooton, Chi vs Phi 4–0 |
| 1929......May 8 | Carl Hubbell, NY vs Pitt 11–0 | Sept 2 | Milt Pappas, Chi vs SD 8–0 |
| 1934......Sept 21 | Paul Dean, StL vs Bklyn 3–0 | Oct 2 | Bill Stoneman, Mtl vs NY 7–0 |
| 1938......June 11 | Johnny Vander Meer, Cin vs Bos 3–0 | 1973......Aug 5 | Phil Niekro, Atl vs SD 9–0 |
| June 15 | Johnny Vander Meer, Cin vs Bklyn 6–0 | 1975......Aug 24 | Ed Halicki, SF vs NY 6–0 |
| 1940......Apr 30 | Tex Carleton, Bklyn vs Cin, 3–0 | 1976......July 9 | Larry Dierker, Hou vs Mtl 6–0 |
| 1941......Aug 30 | Lon Warneke, StL vs Cin 2–0 | Aug 9 | John Candelaria, Pitt vs LA 2–0 |
| 1944......Apr 27 | Jim Tobin, Bos vs Bklyn 2–0 | Sept 29 | John Montefusco, SF vs Atl 9–0 |
| May 15 | Clyde Shoun, Cin vs Bos 1–0 | 1978......Apr 16 | Bob Forsch, StL vs Phi 5–0 |
| 1946......Apr 23 | Ed Head, Bklyn vs Bos 5–0 | June 16 | Tom Seaver, Cin vs StL 4–0 |
| 1947......June 18 | Ewell Blackwell, Cin vs Bos 6–0 | 1979......Apr 7 | Ken Forsch, Hou vs Atl 6–0 |
| 1948......Sept 9 | Rex Barney, Bklyn vs NY 2–0 | 1980......June 27 | Jerry Reuss, LA vs SF 8–0 |
| 1950......Aug 11 | Vern Bickford, Bos vs Bklyn 7–0 | 1981......May 10 | Charlie Lea, Mtl vs SF 4–0 |
| 1951......May 6 | Cliff Chambers, Pitt vs Bos 3–0 | Sept 26 | Nolan Ryan, Hou vs LA 5–0 |
| 1952......June 19 | Carl Erskine, Bklyn vs Chi 5–0 | 1983......Sept 26 | Bob Forsch, StL vs Mtl 3–0 |
| 1954......June 12 | Jim Wilson, Mil vs Phi 2–0 | 1986......Sept 25 | Mike Scott, Hou vs SF 2–0 |
| 1955......May 12 | Sam Jones, Chi vs Pitt 4–0 | 1988......Sept 16 | Tom Browning, Cin vs LA 1–0 |
| 1956......May 12 | Carl Erskine, Bklyn vs NY 3–0 | | (perfect game) |
| Sept 25 | Sal Maglie, Bklyn vs Phi 5–0 | 1990......June 29 | Fernando Valenzuela, LA vs StL 6–0 |
| 1959......May 26 | Harvey Haddix, Pitt vs Mil 0–1 | 1990......Aug 15 | Terry Mulholland, Phi vs SF 6–0 |
| | (hit in 13th; lost in 13th) | 1991......May 23 | Tommy Greene, Phi vs Mtl 2–0 |
| 1960......May 15 | Don Cardwell, Chi vs StL 4–0 | July 26 | Mark Gardner, Mtl vs LA 0–1 |
| Aug 18 | Lew Burdette, Mil vs Phi 1–0 | | (hit in 10th, lost in 10th) |
| Sept 16 | Warren Spahn, Mil vs Phi 4–0 | July 28 | Dennis Martinez, Mtl vs LA 2–0 |
| 1961......Apr 28 | Warren Spahn, Mil vs SF 1–0 | | (perfect game) |
| 1962......June 30 | Sandy Koufax, LA vs NY 5–0 | Sept 11 | Kent Mercker (6), Mark Wohlers (2), |
| 1963......May 11 | Sandy Koufax, LA vs SF 8–0 | | and Alejandro Pena (1), Atl vs SD 1–0 |
| May 17 | Don Nottebart, Hou vs Phi 4–1 | 1992......Aug 17 | Kevin Gross, LA vs SF 2–0 |
| June 15 | Juan Marichal, SF vs Hou 1–0 | 1993......Sept 8 | Darryl Kile, Hou vs NY 7–1 |
| 1964......Apr 23 | Ken Johnson, Hou vs Cin 0–1 | 1994......Apr 8 | Kent Mercker, Atl vs LA 6–0 |
| June 4 | Sandy Koufax, LA vs Phi 3–0 | 1995......June 3 | Pedro Martinez, Mtl vs SD 1–0 |
| June 21 | Jim Bunning, Phi vs NY 6–0 | | (perfect through nine, hit in 10th) |
| | (perfect game) | July 14 | Ramon Martinez, LA vs Fla 7–0 |
| 1965......June 14 | Jim Maloney, Cin vs NY 0–1 | 1996......May 11 | Al Leiter, Fla vs Col 11–0 |
| | (hit in 11th; lost in 11th) | Sept 17 | Hideo Nomo, LA vs Col 9–0 |
| Aug 19 | Jim Maloney, Cin vs Chi 1–0 | 1997......June 10 | Kevin Brown, Fla vs SF 9–0 |
| | (10 innings) | July 12 | Francisco Cordova (9) and |
| Sept 9 | Sandy Koufax, LA vs Chi 1–0 | | Ricardo Rincon (1), Pitt vs Col 3–0 |
| | (perfect game) | 1999......June 25 | Jose Jimenez, StL vs Ariz 1–0 |
| 1967......June 18 | Don Wilson, Hou vs Atl 2–0 | 2001......May 12 | A.J. Burnett, Fla vs SD 3–0 |
| 1968......July 29 | George Culver, Cin vs Phi 6–1 | Sept 3 | Bud Smith, StL vs SD 4–0 |
| Sept 17 | Gaylord Perry, SF vs StL 1–0 | 2003......June 11 | R. Oswalt (1), P. Munro (2.2), K. |
| Sept 18 | Ray Washburn, StL vs SF 2–0 | | Saarloos (1.1), B. Lidge (2), O. Dotel |
| 1969......Apr 17 | Bill Stoneman, Mtl vs Phi 7–0 | | (1), B. Wagner (1), Hou vs NYY 8–0 |
| Apr 30 | Jim Maloney, Cin vs Hou 10–0 | April 27 | Kevin Millwood, Phi vs SF 1–0 |
| May 1 | Don Wilson, Hou vs Cin 4–0 | 2004......May 18 | Randy Johnson, Ariz vs Atl 2–0 |
| Aug 19 | Ken Holtzman, Chi vs Atl 3–0 | | (perfect game) |
| Sept 20 | Bob Moose, Pitt vs NY 4–0 | 2006......Sept 6 | Anibal Sanchez, Fla vs Ariz 2–0 |
| 1970......June 12 | Dock Ellis, Pitt vs SD 2–0 | 2008......Sept 14 | †Carlos Zambrano, Chi vs Hou 5–0 |
| July 20 | Bill Singer, LA vs Phi 5–0 | 2009......July 10 | Jonathan Sanchez, SF vs SD 8–0 |

Note: Includes the games struck from the official record book on Sept. 4, 1991, when baseball's committee on statistical accuracy voted to define no-hitters as games of nine innings or more that end with a team getting no hits.

†Game played in Milwaukee due to weather-related closure of Houston's home field.

## No-Hit Games, Nine Innings or More *(Cont.)*

### AMERICAN LEAGUE

| Date | | Pitcher and Game | Date | | Pitcher and Game |
|---|---|---|---|---|---|
| 1901 | May 9 | Earl Moore, Clev vs Chi 2–4 (hit in 10th; lost in 10th) | 1966 | Oct 8 | Don Larsen, NY (A) vs Bklyn (N) 2–0 (World Series) (perfect game) |
| 1902 | Sept 20 | Jimmy Callahan, Chi vs Det 3–0 | 1957 | Aug 20 | Bob Keegan, Chi vs Wash 6–0 |
| 1904 | May 5 | Cy Young, Bos vs Phi 3–0 (perfect game) | 1958 | July 20 | Jim Bunning, Det vs Bos 3–0 |
| | Aug 17 | Jesse Tannehill, Bos vs Chi 6–0 | | Sept 20 | Hoyt Wilhelm, Balt vs NY 1–0 |
| 1905 | July 22 | Weldon Henley, Phi vs StL 6–0 | 1962 | May 5 | Bo Belinsky, LA vs Balt 2–0 |
| | Sept 6 | Frank Smith, Chi vs Det 15–0 | | June 26 | Earl Wilson, Bos vs LA 2–0 |
| | Sept 27 | Bill Dinneen, Bos vs Chi 2–0 | | Aug 1 | Bill Monbouquette, Bos vs Chi 1–0 |
| 1908 | June 30 | Cy Young, Bos vs NY 8–0 | | Aug 26 | Jack Kralick, Minn vs KC 1–0 |
| | Sept 18 | Bob Rhoades, Clev vs Bos 2–1 | 1965 | Sept 16 | Dave Morehead, Bos vs Clev 2–0 |
| | Sept 20 | Frank Smith, Chi vs Phi 1–0 | 1966 | June 10 | Sonny Siebert, Clev vs Wash 2–0 |
| 1908 | Oct 2 | Addie Joss, Clev vs Chi 1–0 (perfect game) | 1967 | Apr 30 | Steve Barber (8⅔) and Stu Miller (⅓), Balt vs Det 1–2 |
| 1910 | Apr 20 | Addie Joss, Clev vs Chi 1–0 | | Aug 25 | Dean Chance, Minn vs Clev 2–1 |
| | May 12 | Chief Bender, Phi vs Clev 4–0 | | Sept 10 | Joel Horlen, Chi vs Det 6–0 |
| | Aug 30 | Tom Hughes, NY vs Clev 0–5 (hit in 10th; lost in 11th) | 1968 | Apr 27 | Tom Phoebus, Balt vs Bos 6–0 |
| 1911 | July 29 | Joe Wood, Bos vs StL 5–0 | | May 8 | Catfish Hunter, Oak vs Minn 4–0 (perfect game) |
| | Aug 27 | Ed Walsh, Chi vs Bos 5–0 | 1969 | Aug 13 | Jim Palmer, Balt vs Oak 8–0 |
| 1912 | July 4 | George Mullin, Det vs StL 7–0 | 1970 | July 3 | Clyde Wright, Cal vs Oak 4–0 |
| | Aug 30 | Earl Hamilton, StL vs Det 5–1 | | Sept 21 | Vida Blue, Oak vs Minn 6–0 |
| 1914 | May 14 | Jim Scott, Chi vs Wash 0–1 (hit in 10th; lost in 10th) | 1973 | Apr 27 | Steve Busby, KC vs Det 3–0 |
| | May 31 | Joe Benz, Chi vs Clev 6–1 | | May 15 | Nolan Ryan, Cal vs KC 3–0 |
| 1916 | June 21 | George Foster, Bos vs NY 2–0 | | July 15 | Nolan Ryan, Cal vs Det 6–0 |
| | Aug 26 | Joe Bush, Phi vs Clev 5–0 | | July 30 | Jim Bibby, Tex vs Oak 6–0 |
| | Aug 30 | Dutch Leonard, Bos vs StL 4–0 | 1974 | June 19 | Steve Busby, KC vs Mil 2–0 |
| 1917 | Apr 14 | Ed Cicotte, Chi vs StL 11–0 | | July 19 | Dick Bosman, Clev vs Oak 4–0 |
| | Apr 24 | George Mogridge, NY vs Bos 2–1 | | Sept 28 | Nolan Ryan, Cal vs Minn 4–0 |
| | May 5 | Ernie Koob, StL vs Chi 1–0 | 1975 | June 1 | Nolan Ryan, Cal vs Balt 1–0 |
| | May 6 | Bob Groom, StL vs Chi 3–0 | | Sept 28 | Vida Blue (5), Glenn Abbott and Paul Lindblad (1), Rollie Fingers (2), Oak vs Cal 5–0 |
| | June 23 | Ernie Shore, Bos vs Wash 4–0 (perfect game) | 1976 | July 28 | John Odom (5) and Francisco Barrios (4), Chi vs Oak 2–1 |
| 1918 | June 3 | Dutch Leonard, Bos vs Det 5–0 | 1977 | May 14 | Jim Colborn, KC vs Tex 6–0 |
| 1919 | Sept 10 | Ray Caldwell, Clev vs NY 3–0 | | May 30 | Dennis Eckersley, Clev vs Cal 1–0 |
| 1920 | July 1 | Walter Johnson, Wash vs Bos 1–0 | | Sept 22 | Bert Blyleven, Tex vs Cal 6–0 |
| 1922 | Apr 30 | Charlie Robertson, Chi vs Det 2–0 (perfect game) | 1981 | May 15 | Len Barker, Clev vs Tor 3–0 (perfect game) |
| 1923 | Sept 4 | Sam Jones, NY vs Phi 2–0 | 1983 | July 4 | Dave Righetti, NY vs Bos 4–0 |
| | Sept 7 | Howard Ehmke, Bos vs Phi 4–0 | | Sept 29 | Mike Warren, Oak vs Chi 3–0 |
| 1926 | Aug 21 | Ted Lyons, Chi vs Bos 6–0 | 1984 | Apr 7 | Jack Morris, Det vs Chi 4–0 |
| 1931 | Apr 29 | Wes Ferrell, Clev vs StL 9–0 | | Sept 30 | Mike Witt, Cal vs Tex 1–0 (perfect game) |
| | Aug 8 | Bob Burke, Wash vs Bos 5–0 | 1986 | Sept 19 | Joe Cowley, Chi vs Cal 7–1 |
| 1934 | Sept 18 | Bobo Newsom, StL vs Bos 1–2 (hit in 10th; lost in 10th) | 1987 | Apr 15 | Juan Nieves, Mil vs Balt 7–0 |
| 1935 | Aug 31 | Vern Kennedy, Chi vs Clev 5–0 | 1990 | Apr 11 | Mark Langston (7), Mike Witt (2), Cal vs Sea 1–0 |
| 1937 | June 1 | Bill Dietrich, Chi vs StL 8–0 | | June 2 | Randy Johnson, Sea vs Det 2–0 |
| 1938 | Aug 27 | Mtle Pearson, NY vs Clev 13–0 | | June 11 | Nolan Ryan, Tex vs Oak 5–0 |
| 1940 | Apr 16 | Bob Feller, Clev vs Chi 1–0 (opening day) | | June 29 | Dave Stewart, Oak vs Tor 5–0 |
| 1945 | Sept 9 | Dick Fowler, Phi vs StL 1–0 | 1990 | July 1 | Andy Hawkins, NY vs Chi 0–4 (pitched eight of nine–inning game) |
| 1946 | Apr 30 | Bob Feller, Clev vs NY 1–0 | | Sept 2 | Dave Stieb, Tor vs Clev 3–0 |
| 1947 | July 10 | Don Black, Clev vs Phi 3–0 | 1991 | May 1 | Nolan Ryan, Tex vs Tor 3–0 |
| | Sep 3 | Bill McCahan, Phi vs Wash 3–0 | | July 13 | Bob Milacki (6), Mike Flanagan (1), Mark Williamson (1), and Gregg Olson (1), Balt vs Oak 2–0 |
| 1948 | June 30 | Bob Lemon, Clev vs Det 2–0 | | Aug 11 | Wilson Alvarez, Chi vs Balt 7–0 |
| 1951 | July 1 | Bob Feller, Clev vs Det 2–1 | | Aug 26 | Bret Saberhagen, KC vs Chi 7–0 |
| | July 12 | Allie Reynolds, NY vs Clev 1–0 | 1993 | Apr 22 | Chris Bosio, Sea vs Bos 7–0 |
| | Sept 28 | Allie Reynolds, NY vs Bos 8–0 | | Sept 4 | Jim Abbott, NY vs Clev 4–0 |
| 1952 | May 15 | Virgil Trucks, Det vs Wash 1–0 | | | |
| | Aug 25 | Virgil Trucks, Det vs NY 1–0 | | | |
| 1953 | May 6 | Bobo Holloman, StL vs Phi 6–0 (first major league start) | | | |
| 1956 | July 14 | Mel Parnell, Bos vs Chi 4–0 | | | |

### No-Hit Games, Nine Innings or More *(Cont.)*

**AMERICAN LEAGUE** *(Cont.)*

| Date | Pitcher and Game | Date | Pitcher and Game |
|---|---|---|---|
| 1994......Apr 27 | Scott Erickson, Minn vs Mil 6–0 | 2001......Apr 4 | Hideo Nomo, Bos vs Balt 3–0 |
| July 28 | Kenny Rogers, Texas vs Cal 4–0 (perfect game) | 2002......Apr 27 | Derek Lowe, Bos vs TB 10–0 |
| 1996......May 14 | Dwight Gooden, NY vs Sea 2–0 | 2007......Apr 19 | Mark Buehrle, Chi vs Tex, 6–0 |
| 1998......May 17 | David Wells, NY vs Minn 4–0 (perfect game) | June 12 | Justin Verlander, Det vs Mil 4–0 |
| | | Sep 1 | Clay Buchholz, Bos vs Balt 10–0 |
| 1999......July 18 | David Cone, NY vs Mtl 6–0 (perfect game) | 2008......May 19 | Jon Lester, Bos vs KC 7–0 |
| Sept 11 | Eric Milton, Minn vs Ana 7–0 | 2009......July 23 | Mark Buehrle, Chi vs TB 5–0 (perfect game) |

### Longest Hitting Streaks

**NATIONAL LEAGUE**

| Player and Team | Year | G |
|---|---|---|
| Willie Keeler, Balt | 1897 | 44 |
| Pete Rose, Cin | 1978 | 44 |
| Bill Dahlen, Chi | 1894 | 42 |
| Tommy Holmes, Bos | 1945 | 37 |
| Billy Hamilton, Phi | 1894 | 36 |
| Jimmy Rollins, Phi | 2005–06 | 36 |
| Luis Castillo, Fla | 2002 | 35 |
| Fred Clarke, Lou | 1895 | 35 |
| Chase Utley, Phi | 2006 | 35 |
| Benito Santiago, SD | 1987 | 34 |
| George Davis, NY | 1893 | 33 |
| Rogers Hornsby, StL | 1922 | 33 |

**AMERICAN LEAGUE**

| Player and Team | Year | G |
|---|---|---|
| Joe DiMaggio, NY | 1941 | 56 |
| George Sisler, StL | 1922 | 41 |
| Ty Cobb, Det | 1911 | 40 |
| Paul Molitor, Mil | 1987 | 39 |
| Ty Cobb, Det | 1917 | 35 |
| George Sisler, StL | 1925 | 34 |
| George McQuinn, StL | 1938 | 34 |
| Dom DiMaggio, Bos | 1949 | 34 |
| Hal Chase, NY | 1907 | 33 |
| Heinie Manush, Wash | 1933 | 33 |

### Triple Crown Hitters

**NATIONAL LEAGUE**

| Player and Team | Year | HR | RBI | BA |
|---|---|---|---|---|
| Paul Hines, Prov | 1878 | 4 | 50 | .358 |
| Hugh Duffy, Bos | 1894 | 18 | 145 | .438 |
| Heinie Zimmerman*, Chi | 1912 | 14 | 103 | .372 |
| Rogers Hornsby, StL | 1922 | 42 | 152 | .401 |
| | 1925 | 39 | 143 | .403 |
| Chuck Klein, Phi | 1933 | 28 | 120 | .368 |
| Joe Medwick, StL | 1937 | 31 | 154 | .374 |

**AMERICAN LEAGUE**

| Player and Team | Year | HR | RBI | BA |
|---|---|---|---|---|
| Nap Lajoie, Phi | 1901 | 14 | 125 | .422 |
| Ty Cobb, Det | 1909 | 9 | 115 | .377 |
| Jimmie Foxx, Phi | 1933 | 48 | 163 | .356 |
| Lou Gehrig, NY | 1934 | 49 | 165 | .363 |
| Ted Williams, Bos | 1942 | 36 | 137 | .356 |
| | 1947 | 32 | 114 | .343 |
| Mickey Mantle, NY | 1956 | 52 | 130 | .353 |
| Frank Robinson, Balt | 1966 | 49 | 122 | .316 |
| Carl Yastrzemski, Bos | 1967 | 44 | 121 | .326 |

*Zimmerman ranked first in RBIs as calculated by Ernie Lanigan, but only third as calculated by Information Concepts Inc.

## Triple Crown Pitchers

### NATIONAL LEAGUE

| Player and Team | Year | W | L | SO | ERA |
|---|---|---|---|---|---|
| Tommy Bond, Bos | 1877 | 40 | 17 | 170 | 2.11 |
| Hoss Radbourn, Prov | 1884 | 60 | 12 | 441 | 1.38 |
| Tim Keefe, NY | 1888 | 35 | 12 | 333 | 1.74 |
| John Clarkson, Bos | 1889 | 49 | 19 | 284 | 2.73 |
| Amos Rusie, NY | 1894 | 36 | 13 | 195 | 2.78 |
| Christy Mathewson, NY | 1905 | 31 | 8 | 206 | 1.27 |
| | 1908 | 37 | 11 | 259 | 1.43 |
| Grover Alexander, Phi | 1915 | 31 | 10 | 241 | 1.22 |
| | 1916 | 33 | 12 | 167 | 1.55 |
| | 1917 | 30 | 13 | 201 | 1.86 |
| Hippo Vaughn, Chi | 1918 | 22 | 10 | 148 | 1.74 |
| Dazzy Vance, Bklyn | 1924 | 28 | 6 | 262 | 2.16 |
| Bucky Walters, Cin | 1939 | 27 | 11 | 137 | 2.29 |
| Sandy Koufax, LA | 1963 | 25 | 5 | 306 | 1.88 |
| | 1965 | 26 | 8 | 382 | 2.04 |
| | 1966 | 27 | 9 | 317 | 1.73 |
| Steve Carlton, Phi | 1972 | 27 | 10 | 310 | 1.97 |
| Dwight Gooden, NY | 1985 | 24 | 4 | 268 | 1.53 |
| Randy Johnson, Ariz | 2002 | 24 | 5 | 334 | 2.32 |

### AMERICAN LEAGUE

| Player and Team | Year | W | L | SO | ERA |
|---|---|---|---|---|---|
| Cy Young, Bos | 1901 | 33 | 10 | 158 | 1.62 |
| Rube Waddell, Phi | 1905 | 26 | 11 | 287 | 1.48 |
| Walter Johnson, Wash | 1913 | 36 | 7 | 303 | 1.09 |
| | 1918 | 23 | 13 | 162 | 1.27 |
| | 1924 | 23 | 7 | 158 | 2.72 |
| Lefty Grove, Phi | 1930 | 28 | 5 | 209 | 2.54 |
| | 1931 | 31 | 4 | 175 | 2.06 |
| Lefty Gomez, NY | 1934 | 26 | 5 | 158 | 2.33 |
| | 1937 | 21 | 11 | 194 | 2.33 |
| Hal Newhouser, Det | 1945 | 25 | 9 | 212 | 1.81 |
| Roger Clemens, Tor | 1997 | 21 | 7 | 292 | 2.05 |
| | 1998 | 20 | 6 | 271 | 2.64 |
| Pedro Martinez, Bos | 1999 | 23 | 4 | 313 | 2.07 |
| *Johan Santana, Minn | 2006 | 19 | 6 | 245 | 2.77 |

*Tied with another pitcher for most wins

## Consecutive Games Played, 500 or More Games

| | | | |
|---|---|---|---|
| Cal Ripken Jr. | 2,632 | Frank McCormick | 652 |
| Lou Gehrig | 2,130 | Sandy Alomar Sr. | 648 |
| Everett Scott | 1,307 | Eddie Brown | 618 |
| Steve Garvey | 1,207 | Roy McMillan | 585 |
| Miguel Tejada | 1,152 | George Pinckney | 577 |
| Billy Williams | 1,117 | Steve Brodie | 574 |
| Joe Sewell | 1,103 | Aaron Ward | 565 |
| Stan Musial | 895 | Alex Rodriguez | 546 |
| Eddie Yost | 829 | Candy LaChance | 540 |
| Gus Suhr | 822 | Buck Freeman | 535 |
| Nellie Fox | 798 | Fred Luderus | 533 |
| Pete Rose | 745 | Hideki Matsui | 518 |
| Dale Murphy | 740 | Clyde Milan | 511 |
| Richie Ashburn | 730 | Charlie Gehringer | 511 |
| Ernie Banks | 717 | Vada Pinson | 508 |
| Pete Rose | 678 | Tony Cuccinello | 504 |
| Earl Averill | 673 | Charlie Gehringer | 504 |

## Unassisted Triple Plays

| Player and Team | Date | Pos | Opp | Opp Batter |
|---|---|---|---|---|
| Neal Ball, Clev | 7-19-09 | SS | Bos | Amby McConnell |
| Bill Wambsganss, Clev | 10-10-20 | 2B | Bklyn | Clarence Mitchell |
| George Burns, Bos | 9-14-23 | 1B | Clev | Frank Brower |
| Ernie Padgett, Bos | 10-6-23 | SS | Phi | Walter Holke |
| Glenn Wright, Pitt | 5-7-25 | SS | StL | Jim Bottomley |
| Jimmy Cooney, Chi | 5-30-27 | SS | Pitt | Paul Waner |
| Johnny Neun, Det | 5-31-27 | 1B | Clev | Homer Summa |
| Ron Hansen, Wash | 7-30-68 | SS | Clev | Joe Azcue |
| Mickey Morandini, Phi | 9-20-92 | 2B | Pitt | Jeff King |
| John Valentin, Bos | 7-15-94 | SS | Minn | Marc Newfield |
| Randy Velarde, Oak | 5-29-00 | 2B | NYY | Shane Spencer |
| Rafael Furcal, Atl | 8-10-03 | SS | StL | Woody Williams |
| Troy Tulowitzki, Col | 4-29-07 | SS | Atl | Chipper Jones |
| Asdrubal Cabrera, Cle | 5-12-08 | 2B | Tor | Lyle Overbay |
| Eric Bruntlett, Phi | 8-23-09 | 2B | NYM | Jeff Francoeur |

## Leading Batsmen

| Year | Player and Team | BA | Year | Player and Team | BA |
|---|---|---|---|---|---|
| 1900 | Honus Wagner, Pitt | .381 | 1955 | Richie Ashburn, Phi | .338 |
| 1901 | Jesse Burkett, StL | .382 | 1956 | Hank Aaron, Mil | .328 |
| 1902 | Ginger Beaumtl, Pitt | .357 | 1957 | Stan Musial, StL | .351 |
| 1903 | Honus Wagner, Pitt | .355 | 1958 | Richie Ashburn, Phi | .350 |
| 1904 | Honus Wagner, Pitt | .349 | 1959 | Hank Aaron, Mil | .355 |
| 1905 | Cy Seymour, Cin | .377 | 1960 | Dick Groat, Pitt | .325 |
| 1906 | Honus Wagner, Pitt | .339 | 1961 | Roberto Clemente, Pitt | .351 |
| 1907 | Honus Wagner, Pitt | .350 | 1962 | Tommy Davis, LA | .346 |
| 1908 | Honus Wagner, Pitt | .354 | 1963 | Tommy Davis, LA | .326 |
| 1909 | Honus Wagner, Pitt | .339 | 1964 | Roberto Clemente, Pitt | .339 |
| 1910 | Sherry Magee, Phi | .331 | 1965 | Roberto Clemente, Pitt | .329 |
| 1911 | Honus Wagner, Pitt | .334 | 1966 | Matty Alou, Pitt | .342 |
| 1912 | Heinie Zimmerman, Chi | .372 | 1967 | Roberto Clemente, Pitt | .357 |
| 1913 | Jake Daubert, Bklyn | .350 | 1968 | Pete Rose, Cin | .335 |
| 1914 | Jake Daubert, Bklyn | .329 | 1969 | Pete Rose, Cin | .348 |
| 1915 | Larry Doyle, NY | .320 | 1970 | Rico Carty, Atl | .366 |
| 1916 | Hal Chase, Cin | .339 | 1971 | Joe Torre, StL | .363 |
| 1917 | Edd Roush, Cin | .341 | 1972 | Billy Williams, Chi | .333 |
| 1918 | Zach Wheat, Bklyn | .335 | 1973 | Pete Rose, Cin | .338 |
| 1919 | Edd Roush, Cin | .321 | 1974 | Ralph Garr, Atl | .353 |
| 1920 | Rogers Hornsby, StL | .370 | 1975 | Bill Madlock, Chi | .354 |
| 1921 | Rogers Hornsby, StL | .397 | 1976 | Bill Madlock, Chi | .339 |
| 1922 | Rogers Hornsby, StL | .401 | 1977 | Dave Parker, Pitt | .338 |
| 1923 | Rogers Hornsby, StL | .384 | 1978 | Dave Parker, Pitt | .334 |
| 1924 | Rogers Hornsby, StL | .424 | 1979 | Keith Hernandez, StL | .344 |
| 1925 | Rogers Hornsby, StL | .403 | 1980 | Bill Buckner, Chi | .324 |
| 1926 | Bubbles Hargrave, Cin | .353 | 1981 | Bill Madlock, Pitt | .341 |
| 1927 | Paul Waner, Pitt | .380 | 1982 | Al Oliver, Mtl | .331 |
| 1928 | Rogers Hornsby, Bos | .387 | 1983 | Bill Madlock, Pitt | .323 |
| 1929 | Lefty O'Doul, Phi | .398 | 1984 | Tony Gwynn, SD | .351 |
| 1930 | Bill Terry, NY | .401 | 1985 | Willie McGee, StL | .353 |
| 1931 | Chick Hafey, StL | .349 | 1986 | Tim Raines, Mtl | .334 |
| 1932 | Lefty O'Doul, Bklyn | .368 | 1987 | Tony Gwynn, SD | .370 |
| 1933 | Chuck Klein, Phi | .368 | 1988 | Tony Gwynn, SD | .313 |
| 1934 | Paul Waner, Pitt | .362 | 1989 | Tony Gwynn, SD | .336 |
| 1935 | Arky Vaughan, Pitt | .385 | 1990 | Willie McGee, StL | .335 |
| 1936 | Paul Waner, Pitt | .373 | 1991 | Terry Pendleton, Atl | .319 |
| 1937 | Joe Medwick, StL | .374 | 1992 | Gary Sheffield, SD | .330 |
| 1938 | Ernie Lombardi, Cin | .342 | 1993 | Andres Galarraga, Col | .370 |
| 1939 | Johnny Mize, StL | .349 | 1994 | Tony Gwynn, SD | .394 |
| 1940 | Debs Garms, Pitt | .355 | 1995 | Tony Gwynn, SD | .368 |
| 1941 | Pete Reiser, Bklyn | .343 | 1996 | Tony Gwynn, SD | .353 |
| 1942 | Ernie Lombardi, Bos | .330 | 1997 | Tony Gwynn, SD | .372 |
| 1943 | Stan Musial, StL | .357 | 1998 | Larry Walker, Col | .363 |
| 1944 | Dixie Walker, Bklyn | .357 | 1999 | Larry Walker, Col | .379 |
| 1945 | Phil Cavarretta, Chi | .355 | 2000 | Todd Helton, Col | .372 |
| 1946 | Stan Musial, StL | .365 | 2001 | Larry Walker, Col | .350 |
| 1947 | Harry Walker, StL-Phi | .363 | 2002 | Barry Bonds, SF | .370 |
| 1948 | Stan Musial, StL | .376 | 2003 | Albert Pujols, StL | .359 |
| 1949 | Jackie Robinson, Bklyn | .342 | 2004 | Barry Bonds, SF | .362 |
| 1950 | Stan Musial, StL | .346 | 2005 | Derrek Lee, Chi | .335 |
| 1951 | Stan Musial, StL | .355 | 2006 | Freddy Sanchez, Pitt | .334 |
| 1952 | Stan Musial, StL | .336 | 2007 | Matt Holliday, Col | .340* |
| 1953 | Carl Furillo, Bklyn | .344 | 2008 | Chipper Jones, Atl | .364 |
| 1954 | Willie Mays, NY | .345 | 2009 | Hanley Ramirez, Fla | .342 |

*Includes one-game NL playoff tiebreaker.

## Leaders in Runs Scored

| Year | Player and Team | Runs | Year | Player and Team | Runs |
|---|---|---|---|---|---|
| 1900 | Roy Thomas, Phi | 131 | 1955 | Duke Snider, Bklyn | 126 |
| 1901 | Jesse Burkett, StL | 139 | 1956 | Frank Robinson, Cin | 122 |
| 1902 | Honus Wagner, Pitt | 105 | 1957 | Hank Aaron, Mil | 118 |
| 1903 | Ginger Beaumont, Pitt | 137 | 1958 | Willie Mays, SF | 121 |
| 1904 | George Browne, NY | 99 | 1959 | Vada Pinson, Cin | 131 |
| 1905 | Mike Donlin, NY | 124 | 1960 | Bill Bruton, Mil | 112 |
| 1906 | Honus Wagner, Pitt | 103 | 1961 | Willie Mays, SF | 129 |
| | Frank Chance, Chi | 103 | 1962 | Frank Robinson, Cin | 134 |
| 1907 | Spike Shannon, NY | 104 | 1963 | Hank Aaron, Mil | 121 |
| 1908 | Fred Tenney, NY | 101 | 1964 | Dick Allen, Phi | 125 |
| 1909 | Tommy Leach, Pitt | 126 | 1965 | Tommy Harper, Cin | 126 |
| 1910 | Sherry Magee, Phi | 110 | 1966 | Felipe Alou, Atl | 122 |
| 1911 | Jimmy Sheckard, Chi | 121 | 1967 | Hank Aaron, Atl | 113 |
| 1912 | Bob Bescher, Cin | 120 | | Lou Brock, StL | 113 |
| 1913 | Tommy Leach, Chi | 99 | 1968 | Glenn Beckert, Chi | 98 |
| | Max Carey, Pitt | 99 | 1969 | Bobby Bonds, SF | 120 |
| 1914 | George Burns, NY | 100 | | Pete Rose, Cin | 120 |
| 1915 | Gavvy Cravath, Phi | 89 | 1970 | Billy Williams, Chi | 137 |
| 1916 | George Burns, NY | 105 | 1971 | Lou Brock, StL | 126 |
| 1917 | George Burns, NY | 103 | 1972 | Joe Morgan, Cin | 122 |
| 1918 | Heinie Groh, Cin | 88 | 1973 | Bobby Bonds, SF | 131 |
| 1919 | George Burns, NY | 86 | 1974 | Pete Rose, Cin | 110 |
| 1920 | George Burns, NY | 115 | 1975 | Pete Rose, Cin | 112 |
| 1921 | Rogers Hornsby, StL | 131 | 1976 | Pete Rose, Cin | 130 |
| 1922 | Rogers Hornsby, StL | 141 | 1977 | George Foster, Cin | 124 |
| 1923 | Ross Youngs, NY | 121 | 1978 | Ivan DeJesus, Chi | 104 |
| 1924 | Frankie Frisch, NY | 121 | 1979 | Keith Hernandez, StL | 116 |
| | Rogers Hornsby, StL | 121 | 1980 | Keith Hernandez, StL | 111 |
| 1925 | Kiki Cuyler, Pitt | 144 | 1981 | Mike Schmidt, Phi | 78 |
| 1926 | Kiki Cuyler, Pitt | 113 | 1982 | Lonnie Smith, StL | 120 |
| 1927 | Lloyd Waner, Pitt | 133 | 1983 | Tim Raines, Mtl | 133 |
| | Rogers Hornsby, NY | 133 | 1984 | Ryne Sandberg, Chi | 114 |
| 1928 | Paul Waner, Pitt | 142 | 1985 | Dale Murphy, Atl | 118 |
| 1929 | Rogers Hornsby, Chi | 156 | 1986 | Von Hayes, Phi | 107 |
| 1930 | Chuck Klein, Phi | 158 | | Tony Gwynn, SD | 107 |
| 1931 | Bill Terry, NY | 121 | 1987 | Tim Raines, Mtl | 123 |
| | Chuck Klein, Phi | 121 | 1988 | Brett Butler, SF | 109 |
| 1932 | Chuck Klein, Phi | 152 | 1989 | Howard Johnson, NY | 104 |
| 1933 | Pepper Martin, StL | 122 | | Will Clark, SF | 104 |
| 1934 | Paul Waner, Pitt | 122 | | Ryne Sandberg, Chi | 104 |
| 1935 | Augie Galan, Chi | 133 | 1990 | Ryne Sandberg, Chi | 116 |
| 1936 | Arky Vaughan, Pitt | 122 | 1991 | Brett Butler, LA | 112 |
| 1937 | Joe Medwick, StL | 111 | 1992 | Barry Bonds, Pitt | 109 |
| 1938 | Mel Ott, NY | 116 | 1993 | Lenny Dykstra, Phi | 143 |
| 1939 | Billy Werber, Cin | 115 | 1994 | Jeff Bagwell, Hou | 104 |
| 1940 | Arky Vaughan, Pitt | 113 | 1995 | Craig Biggio, Hou | 123 |
| 1941 | Pete Reiser, Bklyn | 117 | 1996 | Ellis Burks, Col | 142 |
| 1942 | Mel Ott, NY | 118 | 1997 | Craig Biggio, Hou | 146 |
| 1943 | Arky Vaughan, Bklyn | 112 | 1998 | Sammy Sosa, Chi | 134 |
| 1944 | Bill Nicholson, Chi | 116 | 1999 | Jeff Bagwell, Hou | 143 |
| 1945 | Eddie Stanky, Bklyn | 128 | 2000 | Jeff Bagwell, Hou | 152 |
| 1946 | Stan Musial, StL | 124 | 2001 | Sammy Sosa, Chi | 146 |
| 1947 | Johnny Mize, NY | 137 | 2002 | Sammy Sosa, Chi | 122 |
| 1948 | Stan Musial, StL | 135 | 2003 | Albert Pujols, StL | 137 |
| 1949 | Pee Wee Reese, Bklyn | 132 | 2004 | Albert Pujols, StL | 133 |
| 1950 | Earl Torgeson, Bos | 120 | 2005 | Albert Pujols, StL | 129 |
| 1951 | Stan Musial, StL | 124 | 2006 | Chase Utley, Phi | 131 |
| | Ralph Kiner, Pitt | 124 | 2007 | Jimmy Rollins, Phi | 139 |
| 1952 | Stan Musial, StL | 105 | 2008 | Hanley Ramirez, Fla | 125 |
| | Solly Hemus, StL | 105 | 2009 | Albert Pujols, StL | 124 |
| 1953 | Duke Snider, Bklyn | 132 | | | |
| 1954 | Stan Musial, StL | 120 | | | |
| | Duke Snider, Bklyn | 120 | | | |

## Leaders in Hits

| Year | Player and Team | Hits | Year | Player and Team | Hits |
|---|---|---|---|---|---|
| 1900 | Willie Keeler, Bklyn | 208 | 1957 | Red Schoendienst, NY-Mil | 200 |
| 1901 | Jesse Burkett, StL | 228 | 1958 | Richie Ashburn, Phi | 215 |
| 1902 | Ginger Beaumont, Pitt | 194 | 1959 | Hank Aaron, Mil | 223 |
| 1903 | Ginger Beaumont, Pitt | 209 | 1960 | Willie Mays, SF | 190 |
| 1904 | Ginger Beaumont, Pitt | 185 | 1961 | Vada Pinson, Cin | 208 |
| 1905 | Cy Seymour, Cin | 219 | 1962 | Tommy Davis, LA | 230 |
| 1906 | Harry Steinfeldt, Chi | 176 | 1963 | Vada Pinson, Cin | 204 |
| 1907 | Ginger Beaumont, Bos | 187 | 1964 | Roberto Clemente, Pitt | 211 |
| 1908 | Honus Wagner, Pitt | 201 | | Curt Flood, StL | 211 |
| 1909 | Larry Doyle, NY | 172 | 1965 | Pete Rose, Cin | 209 |
| 1910 | Honus Wagner, Pitt | 178 | 1966 | Felipe Alou, Atl | 218 |
| | Bobby Byrne, Pitt | 178 | 1967 | Roberto Clemente, Pitt | 209 |
| 1911 | Doc Miller, Bos | 192 | 1968 | Felipe Alou, Atl | 210 |
| 1912 | Heinie Zimmerman, Chi | 207 | | Pete Rose, Cin | 210 |
| 1913 | Gavvy Cravath, Phi | 179 | 1969 | Matty Alou, Pitt | 231 |
| 1914 | Sherry Magee, Phi | 171 | 1970 | Pete Rose, Cin | 205 |
| 1915 | Larry Doyle, NY | 189 | | Billy Williams, Chi | 205 |
| 1916 | Hal Chase, Cin | 184 | 1971 | Joe Torre, StL | 230 |
| 1917 | Heinie Groh, Cin | 182 | 1972 | Pete Rose, Cin | 198 |
| 1918 | Charlie Hollocher, Chi | 161 | 1973 | Pete Rose, Cin | 230 |
| 1919 | Ivy Olson, Bklyn | 164 | 1974 | Ralph Garr, Atl | 214 |
| 1920 | Rogers Hornsby, StL | 218 | 1975 | Dave Cash, Phi | 213 |
| 1921 | Rogers Hornsby, StL | 235 | 1976 | Pete Rose, Cin | 215 |
| 1922 | Rogers Hornsby, StL | 250 | 1977 | Dave Parker, Pitt | 215 |
| 1923 | Frankie Frisch, NY | 223 | 1978 | Steve Garvey, LA | 202 |
| 1924 | Rogers Hornsby, StL | 227 | 1979 | Garry Templeton, StL | 211 |
| 1925 | Jim Bottomley, StL | 227 | 1980 | Steve Garvey, LA | 200 |
| 1926 | Eddie Brown, Bos | 201 | 1981 | Pete Rose, Phi | 140 |
| 1927 | Paul Waner, Pitt | 237 | 1982 | Al Oliver, Mtl | 204 |
| 1928 | Freddy Lindstrom, NY | 231 | 1983 | Jose Cruz, Hou | 189 |
| 1929 | Lefty O'Doul, Phi | 254 | | Andre Dawson, Mtl | 189 |
| 1930 | Bill Terry, NY | 254 | 1984 | Tony Gwynn, SD | 213 |
| 1931 | Lloyd Waner, Pitt | 214 | 1985 | Willie McGee, StL | 216 |
| 1932 | Chuck Klein, Phi | 226 | 1986 | Tony Gwynn, SD | 211 |
| 1933 | Chuck Klein, Phi | 223 | 1987 | Tony Gwynn, SD | 218 |
| 1934 | Paul Waner, Pitt | 217 | 1988 | Andres Galarraga, Mtl | 184 |
| 1935 | Billy Herman, Chi | 227 | 1989 | Tony Gwynn, SD | 203 |
| 1936 | Joe Medwick, StL | 223 | 1990 | Brett Butler, SF | 192 |
| 1937 | Joe Medwick, StL | 237 | | Lenny Dykstra, Phi | 192 |
| 1938 | Frank McCormick, Cin | 209 | 1991 | Terry Pendleton, Atl | 187 |
| 1939 | Frank McCormick, Cin | 209 | 1992 | Terry Pendleton, Atl | 199 |
| 1940 | Stan Hack, Chi | 191 | | Andy Van Slyke, Pitt | 199 |
| | Frank McCormick, Cin | 191 | 1993 | Lenny Dykstra, Phi | 194 |
| 1941 | Stan Hack, Chi | 186 | 1994 | Tony Gwynn, SD | 165 |
| 1942 | Enos Slaughter, StL | 188 | 1995 | Dante Bichette, Col | 197 |
| 1943 | Stan Musial, StL | 220 | | Tony Gwynn, SD | 197 |
| 1944 | Stan Musial, StL | 197 | 1996 | Lance Johnson, NY | 227 |
| | Phil Cavarretta, Chi | 197 | 1997 | Tony Gwynn, SD | 220 |
| 1945 | Tommy Holmes, Bos | 224 | 1998 | Dante Bichette, Col | 219 |
| 1946 | Stan Musial, StL | 228 | 1999 | Luis Gonzalez, Ariz | 206 |
| 1947 | Tommy Holmes, Bos | 191 | 2000 | Todd Helton, Col | 216 |
| 1948 | Stan Musial, StL | 230 | 2001 | Rich Aurilia, SF | 206 |
| 1949 | Stan Musial, StL | 207 | 2002 | Vladimir Guerrero | 206 |
| 1950 | Duke Snider, Bklyn | 199 | 2003 | Albert Pujols, StL | 212 |
| 1951 | Richie Ashburn, Phi | 221 | 2004 | Juan Pierre, Fla | 221 |
| 1952 | Stan Musial, StL | 194 | 2005 | Derrek Lee, Chi | 199 |
| 1953 | Richie Ashburn, Phi | 205 | 2006 | Juan Pierre, Chi | 204 |
| 1954 | Don Mueller, NY | 212 | 2007 | Matt Holliday, Col | 216* |
| 1955 | Ted Kluszewski, Cin | 192 | 2008 | Jose Reyes, NYM | 204 |
| 1956 | Hank Aaron, Mil | 200 | 2009 | Ryan Braun, Mil | 203 |

*includes NL Wild Card tiebreaker

## Home Run Leaders

| Year | Player and Team | HR | Year | Player and Team | HR |
|------|-----------------|----|----|------|-----------------|----|
| 1900 | Herman Long, Bos | 12 | 1952 | Ralph Kiner, Pitt | 37 |
| 1901 | Sam Crawford, Cin | 16 | | Hank Sauer, Chi | 37 |
| 1902 | Tommy Leach, Pitt | 6 | 1953 | Eddie Mathews, Mil | 47 |
| 1903 | Jimmy Sheckard, Bklyn | 9 | 1954 | Ted Kluszewski, Cin | 49 |
| 1904 | Harry Lumley, Bklyn | 9 | 1955 | Willie Mays, NY | 51 |
| 1905 | Fred Odwell, Cin | 9 | 1956 | Duke Snider, Bklyn | 43 |
| 1906 | Tim Jordan, Bklyn | 12 | 1957 | Hank Aaron, Mil | 44 |
| 1907 | Dave Brain, Bos | 10 | 1958 | Ernie Banks, Chi | 47 |
| 1908 | Tim Jordan, Bklyn | 12 | 1959 | Eddie Mathews, Mil | 46 |
| 1909 | Red Murray, NY | 7 | 1960 | Ernie Banks, Chi | 41 |
| 1910 | Fred Beck, Bos | 10 | 1961 | Orlando Cepeda, SF | 46 |
| | Wildfire Schulte, Chi | 10 | 1962 | Willie Mays, SF | 49 |
| 1911 | Wildfire Schulte, Chi | 21 | 1963 | Hank Aaron, Mil | 44 |
| 1912 | Heinie Zimmerman, Chi | 14 | | Willie McCovey, SF | 44 |
| 1913 | Gavvy Cravath, Phi | 19 | 1964 | Willie Mays, SF | 47 |
| 1914 | Gavvy Cravath, Phi | 19 | 1965 | Willie Mays, SF | 52 |
| 1915 | Gavvy Cravath, Phi | 24 | 1966 | Hank Aaron, Atl | 44 |
| 1916 | Dave Robertson, NY | 12 | 1967 | Hank Aaron, Atl | 39 |
| | Cy Williams, Chi | 12 | 1968 | Willie McCovey, SF | 36 |
| 1917 | Dave Robertson, NY | 12 | 1969 | Willie McCovey, SF | 45 |
| | Gavvy Cravath, Phi | 12 | 1970 | Johnny Bench, Cin | 45 |
| 1918 | Gavvy Cravath, Phi | 8 | 1971 | Willie Stargell, Pitt | 48 |
| 1919 | Gavvy Cravath, Phi | 12 | 1972 | Johnny Bench, Cin | 40 |
| 1920 | Cy Williams, Phi | 15 | 1973 | Willie Stargell, Pitt | 44 |
| 1921 | George Kelly, NY | 23 | 1974 | Mike Schmidt, Phi | 36 |
| 1922 | Rogers Hornsby, StL | 42 | 1975 | Mike Schmidt, Phi | 38 |
| 1923 | Cy Williams, Phi | 41 | 1976 | Mike Schmidt, Phi | 38 |
| 1924 | Jack Fournier, Bklyn | 27 | 1977 | George Foster, Cin | 52 |
| 1925 | Rogers Hornsby, StL | 39 | 1978 | George Foster, Cin | 40 |
| 1926 | Hack Wilson, Chi | 21 | 1979 | Dave Kingman, Chi | 48 |
| 1927 | Hack Wilson, Chi | 30 | 1980 | Mike Schmidt, Phi | 48 |
| | Cy Williams, Phi | 30 | 1981 | Mike Schmidt, Phi | 31 |
| 1928 | Hack Wilson, Chi | 31 | 1982 | Dave Kingman, NY | 37 |
| | Jim Bottomley, StL | 31 | 1983 | Mike Schmidt, Phi | 40 |
| 1929 | Chuck Klein, Phi | 43 | 1984 | Dale Murphy, Atl | 36 |
| 1930 | Hack Wilson, Chi | 56 | | Mike Schmidt, Phi | 36 |
| 1931 | Chuck Klein, Phi | 31 | 1985 | Dale Murphy, Atl | 37 |
| 1932 | Chuck Klein, Phi | 38 | 1986 | Mike Schmidt, Phi | 37 |
| | Mel Ott, NY | 38 | 1987 | Andre Dawson, Chi | 49 |
| 1933 | Chuck Klein, Phi | 28 | 1988 | Darryl Strawberry, NY | 39 |
| 1934 | Ripper Collins, StL | 35 | 1989 | Kevin Mitchell, SF | 47 |
| | Mel Ott, NY | 35 | 1990 | Ryne Sandberg, Chi | 40 |
| 1935 | Wally Berger, Bos | 34 | 1991 | Howard Johnson, NY | 38 |
| 1936 | Mel Ott, NY | 33 | 1992 | Fred McGriff, SD | 35 |
| 1937 | Mel Ott, NY | 31 | 1993 | Barry Bonds, SF | 46 |
| | Joe Medwick, StL | 31 | 1994 | Matt Williams, SF | 43 |
| 1938 | Mel Ott, NY | 36 | 1995 | Dante Bichette, Col | 40 |
| 1939 | Johnny Mize, StL | 28 | 1996 | Andres Galarraga, Col | 47 |
| 1940 | Johnny Mize, StL | 43 | 1997 | Larry Walker, Col | 49 |
| 1941 | Dolph Camilli, Bklyn | 34 | 1998 | Mark McGwire, StL | 70 |
| 1942 | Mel Ott, NY | 30 | 1999 | Mark McGwire, StL | 65 |
| 1943 | Bill Nicholson, Chi | 29 | 2000 | Sammy Sosa, Chi | 50 |
| 1944 | Bill Nicholson, Chi | 33 | 2001 | Barry Bonds, SF | 73 |
| 1945 | Tommy Holmes, Bos | 28 | 2002 | Sammy Sosa, Chi | 49 |
| 1946 | Ralph Kiner, Pitt | 23 | 2003 | Jim Thome, Phi | 47 |
| 1947 | Ralph Kiner, Pitt | 51 | 2004 | Adrian Beltre, LA | 48 |
| | Johnny Mize, NY | 51 | 2005 | Andruw Jones, Atl | 51 |
| 1948 | Ralph Kiner, Pitt | 40 | 2006 | Ryan Howard, Phi | 58 |
| | Johnny Mize, NY | 40 | 2007 | Prince Fielder, Mil | 50 |
| 1949 | Ralph Kiner, Pitt | 54 | 2008 | Ryan Howard, Phi | 48 |
| 1950 | Ralph Kiner, Pitt | 47 | 2009 | Albert Pujols, StL | 47 |
| 1951 | Ralph Kiner, Pitt | 42 | | | |

## Runs Batted In Leaders

| Year | Player and Team | RBI | Year | Player and Team | RBI |
|---|---|---|---|---|---|
| 1900 | Elmer Flick, Phi | 110 | 1955 | Duke Snider, Bklyn | 136 |
| 1901 | Honus Wagner, Pitt | 126 | 1956 | Stan Musial, StL | 109 |
| 1902 | Honus Wagner, Pitt | 91 | 1957 | Hank Aaron, Mil | 132 |
| 1903 | Sam Mertes, NY | 104 | 1958 | Ernie Banks, Chi | 129 |
| 1904 | Bill Dahlen, NY | 80 | 1959 | Ernie Banks, Chi | 143 |
| 1905 | Cy Seymour, Cin | 121 | 1960 | Hank Aaron, Mil | 126 |
| 1906 | Jim Nealon, Pitt | 83 | 1961 | Orlando Cepeda, SF | 142 |
|  | Harry Steinfeldt, Chi | 83 | 1962 | Tommy Davis, LA | 153 |
| 1907 | Sherry Magee, Phi | 85 | 1963 | Hank Aaron, Mil | 130 |
| 1908 | Honus Wagner, Pitt | 109 | 1964 | Ken Boyer, StL | 119 |
| 1909 | Honus Wagner, Pitt | 100 | 1965 | Deron Johnson, Cin | 130 |
| 1910 | Sherry Magee, Phi | 123 | 1966 | Hank Aaron, Atl | 127 |
| 1911 | Wildfire Schulte, Chi | 121 | 1967 | Orlando Cepeda, StL | 111 |
| 1912 | Heinie Zimmerman, Chi | 103 | 1968 | Willie McCovey, SF | 105 |
| 1913 | Gavvy Cravath, Phi | 128 | 1969 | Willie McCovey, SF | 126 |
| 1914 | Sherry Magee, Phi | 103 | 1970 | Johnny Bench, Cin | 148 |
| 1915 | Gavvy Cravath, Phi | 115 | 1971 | Joe Torre, StL | 137 |
| 1916 | Heinie Zimmerman, Chi-NY | 83 | 1972 | Johnny Bench, Cin | 125 |
| 1917 | Heinie Zimmerman, NY | 102 | 1973 | Willie Stargell, Pitt | 119 |
| 1918 | Sherry Magee, Phi | 76 | 1974 | Johnny Bench, Cin | 129 |
| 1919 | Hi Myers, Bklyn | 73 | 1975 | Greg Luzinski, Phi | 120 |
| 1920 | George Kelly, NY | 94 | 1976 | George Foster, Cin | 121 |
|  | Rogers Hornsby, StL | 94 | 1977 | George Foster, Cin | 149 |
| 1921 | Rogers Hornsby, StL | 126 | 1978 | George Foster, Cin | 120 |
| 1922 | Rogers Hornsby, StL | 152 | 1979 | Dave Winfield, SD | 118 |
| 1923 | Irish Meusel, NY | 125 | 1980 | Mike Schmidt, Phi | 121 |
| 1924 | George Kelly, NY | 136 | 1981 | Mike Schmidt, Phi | 91 |
| 1925 | Rogers Hornsby, StL | 143 | 1982 | Dale Murphy, Atl | 109 |
| 1926 | Jim Bottomley, StL | 120 |  | Al Oliver, Mtl | 109 |
| 1927 | Paul Waner, Pitt | 131 | 1983 | Dale Murphy, Atl | 121 |
| 1928 | Jim Bottomley, StL | 136 | 1984 | Gary Carter, Mtl | 106 |
| 1929 | Hack Wilson, Chi | 159 |  | Mike Schmidt, Phi | 106 |
| 1930 | Hack Wilson, Chi | 190 | 1985 | Dave Parker, Cin | 125 |
| 1931 | Chuck Klein, Phi | 121 | 1986 | Mike Schmidt, Phi | 119 |
| 1932 | Don Hurst, Phi | 143 | 1987 | Andre Dawson, Chi | 137 |
| 1933 | Chuck Klein, Phi | 120 | 1988 | Will Clark, SF | 109 |
| 1934 | Mel Ott, NY | 135 | 1989 | Kevin Mitchell, SF | 125 |
| 1935 | Wally Berger, Bos | 130 | 1990 | Matt Williams, SF | 122 |
| 1936 | Joe Medwick, StL | 138 | 1991 | Howard Johnson, NY | 117 |
| 1937 | Joe Medwick, StL | 154 | 1992 | Darren Daulton, Phi | 109 |
| 1938 | Joe Medwick, StL | 122 | 1993 | Barry Bonds, SF | 123 |
| 1939 | Frank McCormick, Cin | 128 | 1994 | Jeff Bagwell, Hou | 116 |
| 1940 | Johnny Mize, StL | 137 | 1995 | Dante Bichette, Col | 128 |
| 1941 | Dolph Camilli, Bklyn | 120 | 1996 | Andres Galarraga, Col | 150 |
| 1942 | Johnny Mize, NY | 110 | 1997 | Andres Galarraga, Col | 140 |
| 1943 | Bill Nicholson, Chi | 128 | 1998 | Sammy Sosa, Chi | 158 |
| 1944 | Bill Nicholson, Chi | 122 | 1999 | Mark McGwire, StL | 147 |
| 1945 | Dixie Walker, Bklyn | 124 | 2000 | Todd Helton, Col | 147 |
| 1946 | Enos Slaughter, StL | 130 | 2001 | Sammy Sosa, Chi | 160 |
| 1947 | Johnny Mize, NY | 138 | 2002 | Lance Berkman, Hou | 128 |
| 1948 | Stan Musial, StL | 131 | 2003 | Preston Wilson, Col | 141 |
| 1949 | Ralph Kiner, Pitt | 127 | 2004 | Vinny Castilla, Col | 131 |
| 1950 | Del Ennis, Phi | 126 | 2005 | Andruw Jones, Atl | 128 |
| 1951 | Monte Irvin, NY | 121 | 2006 | Ryan Howard, Phi | 149 |
| 1952 | Hank Sauer, Chi | 121 | 2007 | Matt Holliday, Col | 137* |
| 1953 | Roy Campanella, Bklyn | 142 | 2008 | Ryan Howard, Phi | 146 |
| 1954 | Ted Kluszewski, Cin | 141 | 2009 | Ryan Howard, Phi | 141 |
|  |  |  |  | Prince Fielder, Mil | 141 |

*Includes one-game NL playoff tiebreaker.

## Leading Base Stealers

| Year | Player and Team | SB | Year | Player and Team | SB |
|------|-----------------|-----|------|-----------------|-----|
| 1900 | George Van Haltren, NY | 45 | 1953 | Bill Bruton, Mil | 26 |
|      | Patsy Donovan, StL | 45 | 1954 | Bill Bruton, Mil | 34 |
| 1901 | Honus Wagner, Pitt | 48 | 1955 | Bill Bruton, Mil | 35 |
| 1902 | Honus Wagner, Pitt | 43 | 1956 | Willie Mays, NY | 40 |
| 1903 | Jimmy Sheckard, Bklyn | 67 | 1957 | Willie Mays, NY | 38 |
|      | Frank Chance, Chi | 67 | 1958 | Willie Mays, SF | 31 |
| 1904 | Honus Wagner, Pitt | 53 | 1959 | Willie Mays, SF | 27 |
| 1905 | Billy Maloney, Chi | 59 | 1960 | Maury Wills, LA | 50 |
|      | Art Devlin, NY | 59 | 1961 | Maury Wills, LA | 35 |
| 1906 | Frank Chance, Chi | 57 | 1962 | Maury Wills, LA | 104 |
| 1907 | Honus Wagner, Pitt | 61 | 1963 | Maury Wills, LA | 40 |
| 1908 | Honus Wagner, Pitt | 53 | 1964 | Maury Wills, LA | 53 |
| 1909 | Bob Bescher, Cin | 54 | 1965 | Maury Wills, LA | 94 |
| 1910 | Bob Bescher, Cin | 70 | 1966 | Lou Brock, StL | 74 |
| 1911 | Bob Bescher, Cin | 80 | 1967 | Lou Brock, StL | 52 |
| 1912 | Bob Bescher, Cin | 67 | 1968 | Lou Brock, StL | 62 |
| 1913 | Max Carey, Pitt | 61 | 1969 | Lou Brock, StL | 53 |
| 1914 | George Burns, NY | 62 | 1970 | Bobby Tolan, Cin | 57 |
| 1915 | Max Carey, Pitt | 36 | 1971 | Lou Brock, StL | 64 |
| 1916 | Max Carey, Pitt | 63 | 1972 | Lou Brock, StL | 63 |
| 1917 | Max Carey, Pitt | 46 | 1973 | Lou Brock, StL | 70 |
| 1918 | Max Carey, Pitt | 58 | 1974 | Lou Brock, StL | 118 |
| 1919 | George Burns, NY | 40 | 1975 | Davey Lopes, LA | 77 |
| 1920 | Max Carey, Pitt | 52 | 1976 | Davey Lopes, LA | 63 |
| 1921 | Frankie Frisch, NY | 49 | 1977 | Frank Taveras, Pitt | 70 |
| 1922 | Max Carey, Pitt | 51 | 1978 | Omar Moreno, Pitt | 71 |
| 1923 | Max Carey, Pitt | 51 | 1979 | Omar Moreno, Pitt | 77 |
| 1924 | Max Carey, Pitt | 49 | 1980 | Ron LeFlore, Mtl | 97 |
| 1925 | Max Carey, Pitt | 46 | 1981 | Tim Raines, Mtl | 71 |
| 1926 | Kiki Cuyler, Pitt | 35 | 1982 | Tim Raines, Mtl | 78 |
| 1927 | Frankie Frisch, StL | 48 | 1983 | Tim Raines, Mtl | 90 |
| 1928 | Kiki Cuyler, Chi | 37 | 1984 | Tim Raines, Mtl | 75 |
| 1929 | Kiki Cuyler, Chi | 43 | 1985 | Vince Coleman, StL | 110 |
| 1930 | Kiki Cuyler, Chi | 37 | 1986 | Vince Coleman, StL | 107 |
| 1931 | Frankie Frisch, StL | 28 | 1987 | Vince Coleman, StL | 109 |
| 1932 | Chuck Klein, Phi | 20 | 1988 | Vince Coleman, StL | 81 |
| 1933 | Pepper Martin, StL | 26 | 1989 | Vince Coleman, StL | 65 |
| 1934 | Pepper Martin, StL | 23 | 1990 | Vince Coleman, StL | 77 |
| 1935 | Augie Galan, Chi | 22 | 1991 | Marquis Grissom, Mtl | 76 |
| 1936 | Pepper Martin, StL | 23 | 1992 | Marquis Grissom, Mtl | 78 |
| 1937 | Augie Galan, Chi | 23 | 1993 | Chuck Carr, Fla | 58 |
| 1938 | Stan Hack, Chi | 16 | 1994 | Craig Biggio, Hou | 39 |
| 1939 | Stan Hack, Chi | 17 | 1995 | Quilvio Veras, Fla | 56 |
|      | Lee Handley, Pitt | 17 | 1996 | Eric Young, Col | 53 |
| 1940 | Lonny Frey, Cin | 22 | 1997 | Tony Womack, Pitt | 60 |
| 1941 | Danny Murtaugh, Phi | 18 | 1998 | Tony Womack, Pitt | 58 |
| 1942 | Pete Reiser, Bklyn | 20 | 1999 | Tony Womack, Ariz | 72 |
| 1943 | Arky Vaughan, Bklyn | 20 | 2000 | Luis Castillo, Fla | 62 |
| 1944 | Johnny Barrett, Pitt | 28 | 2001 | Juan Pierre, Col | 46 |
| 1945 | Red Schoendienst, StL | 26 | 2002 | Luis Castillo, Fla | 48 |
| 1946 | Pete Reiser, Bklyn | 34 | 2003 | Juan Pierre, Fla | 65 |
| 1947 | Jackie Robinson, Bklyn | 29 | 2004 | Scott Podsednik, Mil | 70 |
| 1948 | Richie Ashburn, Phi | 32 | 2005 | Jose Reyes, NY | 60 |
| 1949 | Jackie Robinson, Bklyn | 37 | 2006 | Jose Reyes, NY | 64 |
| 1950 | Sam Jethroe, Bos | 35 | 2007 | Jose Reyes, NY | 78 |
| 1951 | Sam Jethroe, Bos | 35 | 2008 | Willy Taveras, Hou | 68 |
| 1952 | Pee Wee Reese, Bklyn | 30 | 2009 | Michael Bourn, Hou | 61 |

## Leading Pitchers—Winning Percentage

| Year | Pitcher and Team | W | L | Pct | Year | Pitcher and Team | W | L | Pct |
|------|------------------|---|---|-----|------|------------------|---|---|-----|
| 1900 | Jesse Tannehill, Pitt | 20 | 6 | .769 | 1956 | Don Newcombe, Bklyn | 27 | 7 | .794 |
| 1901 | Jack Chesbro, Pitt | 21 | 10 | .677 | 1957 | Bob Buhl, Mil | 18 | 7 | .720 |
| 1902 | Jack Chesbro, Pitt | 28 | 6 | .824 | 1958 | Warren Spahn, Mil | 22 | 11 | .667 |
| 1903 | Sam Leever, Pitt | 25 | 7 | .781 | | Lew Burdette, Mil | 20 | 10 | .667 |
| 1904 | Joe McGinnity, NY | 35 | 8 | .814 | 1959 | Roy Face, Pitt | 18 | 1 | .947 |
| 1905 | Sam Leever, Pitt | 20 | 5 | .800 | 1960 | Ernie Broglio, StL | 21 | 9 | .700 |
| 1906 | Ed Reulbach, Chi | 19 | 4 | .826 | 1961 | Johnny Podres, LA | 18 | 5 | .783 |
| 1907 | Ed Reulbach, Chi | 17 | 4 | .810 | 1962 | Bob Purkey, Cin | 23 | 5 | .821 |
| 1908 | Ed Reulbach, Chi | 24 | 7 | .774 | 1963 | Ron Perranoski, Cin | 16 | 3 | .842 |
| 1909 | Christy Mathewson, NY | 25 | 6 | .806 | 1964 | Sandy Koufax, LA | 19 | 5 | .792 |
| | Howie Camnitz, Pitt | 25 | 6 | .806 | 1965 | Sandy Koufax, LA | 26 | 8 | .765 |
| 1910 | King Cole, Chi | 20 | 4 | .833 | 1966 | Juan Marichal, SF | 25 | 6 | .806 |
| 1911 | Rube Marquard, NY | 24 | 7 | .774 | 1967 | Dick Hughes, StL | 16 | 6 | .727 |
| 1912 | Claude Hendrix, Pitt | 24 | 9 | .727 | 1968 | Steve Blass, Pitt | 18 | 6 | .750 |
| 1913 | Bert Humphries, Chi | 16 | 4 | .800 | 1969 | Tom Seaver, NY | 25 | 7 | .781 |
| 1914 | Bill James, Bos | 26 | 7 | .788 | 1970 | Bob Gibson, StL | 23 | 7 | .767 |
| 1915 | Grover Alexander, Phi | 31 | 10 | .756 | 1971 | Don Gullett, Cin | 16 | 6 | .727 |
| 1916 | Tom Hughes, Bos | 16 | 3 | .842 | 1972 | Gary Nolan, Cin | 15 | 5 | .750 |
| 1917 | Ferdie Schupp, NY | 21 | 7 | .750 | 1973 | Tommy John, LA | 16 | 7 | .696 |
| 1918 | Claude Hendrix, Chi | 19 | 7 | .731 | 1974 | Andy Messersmith, LA | 20 | 6 | .769 |
| 1919 | Dutch Ruether, Cin | 19 | 6 | .760 | 1975 | Don Gullett, Cin | 15 | 4 | .789 |
| 1920 | Burleigh Grimes, Bklyn | 23 | 11 | .676 | 1976 | Steve Carlton, Phi | 20 | 7 | .741 |
| 1921 | Bill Doak, StL | 15 | 6 | .714 | 1977 | John Candelaria, Pitt | 20 | 5 | .800 |
| 1922 | Pete Donohue, Cin | 18 | 9 | .667 | 1978 | Gaylord Perry, SD | 21 | 6 | .778 |
| 1923 | Dolf Luque, Cin | 27 | 8 | .771 | 1979 | Tom Seaver, Cin | 16 | 6 | .727 |
| 1924 | Emil Yde, Pitt | 16 | 3 | .842 | 1980 | Jim Bibby, Pitt | 19 | 6 | .760 |
| 1925 | Bill Sherdel, StL | 15 | 6 | .714 | 1981* | Tom Seaver, Cin | 14 | 2 | .875 |
| 1926 | Ray Kremer, Pitt | 20 | 6 | .769 | 1982 | Phil Niekro, Atl | 17 | 4 | .810 |
| 1927 | Larry Benton, Bos-NY | 17 | 7 | .708 | 1983 | John Denny, Phi | 19 | 6 | .760 |
| 1928 | Larry Benton, NY | 25 | 9 | .735 | 1984 | Rick Sutcliffe, Chi | 16 | 1 | .941 |
| 1929 | Charlie Root, Chi | 19 | 6 | .760 | 1985 | Orel Hershiser, LA | 19 | 3 | .864 |
| 1930 | Freddie Fitzsimmons, NY | 19 | 7 | .731 | 1986 | Bob Ojeda, NY | 18 | 5 | .783 |
| 1931 | Paul Derringer, StL | 18 | 8 | .692 | 1987 | Dwight Gooden, NY | 15 | 7 | .682 |
| 1932 | Lon Warneke, Chi | 22 | 6 | .786 | 1988 | David Cone, NY | 20 | 3 | .870 |
| 1933 | Ben Cantwell, Bos | 20 | 10 | .667 | 1989 | Mike Bielecki, Chi | 18 | 7 | .720 |
| 1934 | Dizzy Dean, StL | 30 | 7 | .811 | 1990 | Doug Drabeck, Pitt | 22 | 6 | .786 |
| 1935 | Bill Lee, Chi | 20 | 6 | .769 | 1991 | John Smiley, Pitt | 20 | 8 | .714 |
| 1936 | Carl Hubbell, NY | 26 | 6 | .813 | | Jose Rijo, Cin | 15 | 6 | .714 |
| 1937 | Carl Hubbell, NY | 22 | 8 | .733 | 1992 | Bob Tewksbury, StL | 16 | 5 | .762 |
| 1938 | Bill Lee, Chi | 22 | 9 | .710 | 1993 | Tom Glavine, Atl | 22 | 6 | .786 |
| 1939 | Paul Derringer, Cin | 25 | 7 | .781 | 1994 | Ken Hill, Mtl | 16 | 5 | .762 |
| 1940 | Freddie Fitzsimmons, Bklyn | 16 | 2 | .889 | 1995 | Greg Maddux, Atl | 19 | 2 | .905 |
| 1941 | Elmer Riddle, Cin | 19 | 4 | .826 | 1996 | John Smoltz, Atl | 24 | 8 | .750 |
| 1942 | Larry French, Bklyn | 15 | 4 | .789 | 1997 | Denny Neagle, Atl | 20 | 5 | .800 |
| 1943 | Mort Cooper, StL | 21 | 8 | .724 | 1998 | John Smoltz, Atl | 17 | 3 | .850 |
| 1944 | Ted Wilks, StL | 17 | 4 | .810 | 1999 | Mike Hampton, Hou | 22 | 4 | .846 |
| 1945 | Harry Brecheen, StL | 15 | 4 | .789 | 2000 | Randy Johnson, Ariz | 19 | 7 | .730 |
| 1946 | Murray Dickson, StL | 15 | 6 | .714 | 2001 | Curt Schilling, Ariz | 22 | 6 | .786 |
| 1947 | Larry Jansen, NY | 21 | 5 | .808 | 2002 | Randy Johnson, Ariz | 24 | 5 | .828 |
| 1948 | Harry Brecheen, StL | 20 | 7 | .741 | 2003 | Jason Schmidt, SF | 17 | 5 | .773 |
| 1949 | Preacher Roe, Bklyn | 15 | 6 | .714 | 2004 | Roger Clemens, Hou | 18 | 4 | .818 |
| 1950 | Sal Maglie, NY | 18 | 4 | .818 | 2005 | Chris Carpenter, StL | 21 | 5 | .808 |
| 1951 | Preacher Roe, Bklyn | 22 | 3 | .880 | 2006 | Carlos Zambrano, Chi | 16 | 7 | .695 |
| 1952 | Hoyt Wilhelm, NY | 15 | 3 | .833 | 2007 | Brad Penny, LA | 16 | 4 | .800 |
| 1953 | Carl Erskine, Bklyn | 20 | 6 | .769 | 2008 | Tim Lincecum, SF | 18 | 5 | .783 |
| 1954 | Johnny Antonelli, NY | 21 | 7 | .750 | 2009 | Chris Carpenter, StL | 17 | 4 | .810 |
| 1955 | Don Newcombe, Bklyn | 20 | 5 | .800 | | | | | |

*1981 percentages based on 10 or more victories. Note: Percentages based on 15 or more victories in all other years.

### Leading Pitchers—Earned Run Average

| Year | Player and Team | ERA | Year | Player and Team | ERA |
|------|-----------------|-----|------|-----------------|-----|
| 1900 | Rube Waddell, Pitt | 2.37 | 1955 | Bob Friend, Pitt | 2.84 |
| 1901 | Jesse Tannehill, Pitt | 2.18 | 1956 | Lew Burdette, Mil | 2.71 |
| 1902 | Jack Taylor, Chi | 1.33 | 1957 | Johnny Podres, Bklyn | 2.66 |
| 1903 | Sam Leever, Pitt | 2.06 | 1958 | Stu Miller, SF | 2.47 |
| 1904 | Joe McGinnity, NY | 1.61 | 1959 | Sam Jones, SF | 2.82 |
| 1905 | Christy Mathewson, NY | 1.27 | 1960 | Mike McCormick, SF | 2.70 |
| 1906 | Three Finger Brown, Chi | 1.04 | 1961 | Warren Spahn, Mil | 3.01 |
| 1907 | Jack Pfiester, Chi | 1.15 | 1962 | Sandy Koufax, LA | 2.54 |
| 1908 | Christy Mathewson, NY | 1.43 | 1963 | Sandy Koufax, LA | 1.88 |
| 1909 | Christy Mathewson, NY | 1.14 | 1964 | Sandy Koufax, LA | 1.74 |
| 1910 | George McQuillan, Phi | 1.60 | 1965 | Sandy Koufax, LA | 2.04 |
| 1911 | Christy Mathewson, NY | 1.99 | 1966 | Sandy Koufax, LA | 1.73 |
| 1912 | Jeff Tesreau, NY | 1.96 | 1967 | Phil Niekro, Atl | 1.87 |
| 1913 | Christy Mathewson, NY | 2.06 | 1968 | Bob Gibson, StL | 1.12 |
| 1914 | Bill Doak, StL | 1.72 | 1969 | Juan Marichal, SF | 2.10 |
| 1915 | Grover Alexander, Phi | 1.22 | 1970 | Tom Seaver, NY | 2.81 |
| 1916 | Grover Alexander, Phi | 1.55 | 1971 | Tom Seaver, NY | 1.76 |
| 1917 | Grover Alexander, Phi | 1.83 | 1972 | Steve Carlton, Phi | 1.98 |
| 1918 | Hippo Vaughn, Chi | 1.74 | 1973 | Tom Seaver, NY | 2.08 |
| 1919 | Grover Alexander, Chi | 1.72 | 1974 | Buzz Capra, Atl | 2.28 |
| 1920 | Grover Alexander, Chi | 1.91 | 1975 | Randy Jones, SD | 2.24 |
| 1921 | Bill Doak, StL | 2.58 | 1976 | John Denny, StL | 2.52 |
| 1922 | Rosy Ryan, NY | 3.00 | 1977 | John Candelaria, Pitt | 2.34 |
| 1923 | Dolf Luque, Cin | 1.93 | 1978 | Craig Swan, NY | 2.43 |
| 1924 | Dazzy Vance, Bklyn | 2.16 | 1979 | J.R. Richard, Hou | 2.71 |
| 1925 | Dolf Luque, Cin | 2.63 | 1980 | Don Sutton, LA | 2.21 |
| 1926 | Ray Kremer, Pitt | 2.61 | 1981 | Nolan Ryan, Hou | 1.69 |
| 1927 | Ray Kremer, Pitt | 2.47 | 1982 | Steve Rogers, Mtl | 2.40 |
| 1928 | Dazzy Vance, Bklyn | 2.09 | 1983 | Atlee Hammaker, SF | 2.25 |
| 1929 | Bill Walker, NY | 3.08 | 1984 | Alejandro Pena, LA | 2.48 |
| 1930 | Dazzy Vance, Bklyn | 2.61 | 1985 | Dwight Gooden, NY | 1.53 |
| 1931 | Bill Walker, NY | 2.26 | 1986 | Mike Scott, Hou | 2.22 |
| 1932 | Lon Warneke, Chi | 2.37 | 1987 | Nolan Ryan, Hou | 2.76 |
| 1933 | Carl Hubbell, NY | 1.66 | 1988 | Joe Magrane, StL | 2.18 |
| 1934 | Carl Hubbell, NY | 2.30 | 1989 | Scott Garrelts, SF | 2.28 |
| 1935 | Cy Blanton, Pitt | 2.59 | 1990 | Danny Darwin, Hou | 2.21 |
| 1936 | Carl Hubbell, NY | 2.31 | 1991 | Dennis Martinez, Mtl | 2.39 |
| 1937 | Jim Turner, Bos | 2.38 | 1992 | Bill Swift, SF | 2.08 |
| 1938 | Bill Lee, Chi | 2.66 | 1993 | Greg Maddux, Atl | 2.36 |
| 1939 | Bucky Walters, Cin | 2.29 | 1994 | Greg Maddux, Atl | 1.56 |
| 1940 | Bucky Walters, Cin | 2.48 | 1995 | Greg Maddux, Atl | 1.63 |
| 1941 | Elmer Riddle, Cin | 2.24 | 1996 | Kevin Brown, Fla | 1.89 |
| 1942 | Mort Cooper, StL | 1.77 | 1997 | Pedro Martinez, Mtl | 1.90 |
| 1943 | Howie Pollet, StL | 1.75 | 1998 | Greg Maddux, Atl | 1.98 |
| 1944 | Ed Heusser, Cin | 2.38 | 1999 | Randy Johnson, Ariz | 2.48 |
| 1945 | Hank Borowy, Chi | 2.14 | 2000 | Kevin Brown, LA | 2.58 |
| 1946 | Howie Pollet, StL | 2.10 | 2001 | Randy Johnson, Ariz | 2.49 |
| 1947 | Warren Spahn, Bos | 2.33 | 2002 | Randy Johnson, Ariz | 2.32 |
| 1948 | Harry Brecheen, StL | 2.24 | 2003 | Jason Schmidt, SF | 2.34 |
| 1949 | Dave Koslo, NY | 2.50 | 2004 | Jake Peavy, SD | 2.27 |
| 1950 | Jim Hearn, StL-NY | 2.49 | 2005 | Roger Clemens, Hou | 1.87 |
| 1951 | Chet Nichols, Bos | 2.88 | 2006 | Roy Oswalt, Hou | 2.98 |
| 1952 | Hoyt Wilhelm, NY | 2.43 | 2007 | Jake Peavy, SD | 2.54* |
| 1953 | Warren Spahn, Mil | 2.10 | 2008 | Johan Santana, NYM | 2.53 |
| 1954 | Johnny Antonelli, NY | 2.29 | 2009 | Chris Carpenter, StL | 2.24 |

*includes NL play-in tiebreaker

Note: Based on 10 complete games through 1950, then 154 innings until National League expanded in 1962, when it became 162 innings. In strike-shortened 1981, one inning per game required.

## Leading Pitchers—Strikeouts

| Year | Player and Team | SO | Year | Player and Team | SO |
|------|-----------------|-----|------|-----------------|-----|
| 1900 | Rube Waddell, Pitt | 133 | 1954 | Robin Roberts, Phi | 185 |
| 1901 | Noodles Hahn, Cin | 233 | 1955 | Sam Jones, Chi | 198 |
| 1902 | Vic Willis, Bos | 226 | 1956 | Sam Jones, Chi | 176 |
| 1903 | Christy Mathewson, NY | 267 | 1957 | Jack Sanford, Phi | 188 |
| 1904 | Christy Mathewson, NY | 212 | 1958 | Sam Jones, StL | 225 |
| 1905 | Christy Mathewson, NY | 206 | 1959 | Don Drysdale, LA | 242 |
| 1906 | Fred Beebe, Chi-StL | 171 | 1960 | Don Drysdale, LA | 246 |
| 1907 | Christy Mathewson, NY | 178 | 1961 | Sandy Koufax, LA | 269 |
| 1908 | Christy Mathewson, NY | 259 | 1962 | Don Drysdale, LA | 232 |
| 1909 | Orval Overall, Chi | 205 | 1963 | Sandy Koufax, LA | 306 |
| 1910 | Christy Mathewson, NY | 190 | 1964 | Bob Veale, Pitt | 250 |
| 1911 | Rube Marquard, NY | 237 | 1965 | Sandy Koufax, LA | 382 |
| 1912 | Grover Alexander, Phi | 195 | 1966 | Sandy Koufax, LA | 317 |
| 1913 | Tom Seaton, Phi | 168 | 1967 | Jim Bunning, Phi | 253 |
| 1914 | Grover Alexander, Phi | 214 | 1968 | Bob Gibson, StL | 268 |
| 1915 | Grover Alexander, Phi | 241 | 1969 | Ferguson Jenkins, Chi | 273 |
| 1916 | Grover Alexander, Phi | 167 | 1970 | Tom Seaver, NY | 283 |
| 1917 | Grover Alexander, Phi | 200 | 1971 | Tom Seaver, NY | 289 |
| 1918 | Hippo Vaughn, Chi | 148 | 1972 | Steve Carlton, Phi | 310 |
| 1919 | Hippo Vaughn, Chi | 141 | 1973 | Tom Seaver, NY | 251 |
| 1920 | Grover Alexander, Chi | 173 | 1974 | Steve Carlton, Phi | 240 |
| 1921 | Burleigh Grimes, Bklyn | 136 | 1975 | Tom Seaver, NY | 243 |
| 1922 | Dazzy Vance, Bklyn | 134 | 1976 | Tom Seaver, NY | 235 |
| 1923 | Dazzy Vance, Bklyn | 197 | 1977 | Phil Niekro, Atl | 262 |
| 1924 | Dazzy Vance, Bklyn | 262 | 1978 | J.R. Richard, Hou | 303 |
| 1925 | Dazzy Vance, Bklyn | 221 | 1979 | J.R. Richard, Hou | 313 |
| 1926 | Dazzy Vance, Bklyn | 140 | 1980 | Steve Carlton, Phi | 286 |
| 1927 | Dazzy Vance, Bklyn | 184 | 1981 | Fernando Valenzuela, LA | 180 |
| 1928 | Dazzy Vance, Bklyn | 200 | 1982 | Steve Carlton, Phi | 286 |
| 1929 | Pat Malone, Chi | 166 | 1983 | Steve Carlton, Phi | 275 |
| 1930 | Bill Hallahan, StL | 177 | 1984 | Dwight Gooden, NY | 276 |
| 1931 | Bill Hallahan, StL | 159 | 1985 | Dwight Gooden, NY | 268 |
| 1932 | Dizzy Dean, StL | 191 | 1986 | Mike Scott, Hou | 306 |
| 1933 | Dizzy Dean, StL | 199 | 1987 | Nolan Ryan, Hou | 270 |
| 1934 | Dizzy Dean, StL | 195 | 1988 | Nolan Ryan, Hou | 228 |
| 1935 | Dizzy Dean, StL | 182 | 1989 | Jose DeLeon, StL | 201 |
| 1936 | Van Lingle Mungo, Bklyn | 238 | 1990 | David Cone, NY | 233 |
| 1937 | Carl Hubbell, NY | 159 | 1991 | David Cone, NY | 241 |
| 1938 | Clay Bryant, Chi | 135 | 1992 | John Smoltz, Atl | 215 |
| 1939 | Claude Passeau, Phi-Chi | 137 | 1993 | Jose Rijo, Cin | 227 |
| | Bucky Walters, Cin | 137 | 1994 | Andy Benes, SD | 189 |
| 1940 | Kirby Higbe, Phi | 137 | 1995 | Hideo Nomo, LA | 236 |
| 1941 | Johnny Vander Meer, Cin | 202 | 1996 | John Smoltz, Atl | 276 |
| 1942 | Johnny Vander Meer, Cin | 186 | 1997 | Curt Schilling, Phi | 319 |
| 1943 | Johnny Vander Meer, Cin | 174 | 1998 | Curt Schilling, Phi | 300 |
| 1944 | Bill Voiselle, NY | 161 | 1999 | Randy Johnson, Ariz | 364 |
| 1945 | Preacher Roe, Pitt | 148 | 2000 | Randy Johnson, Ariz | 347 |
| 1946 | Johnny Schmitz, Chi | 135 | 2001 | Randy Johnson, Ariz | 372 |
| 1947 | Ewell Blackwell, Cin | 193 | 2002 | Randy Johnson, Ariz | 334 |
| 1948 | Harry Brecheen, StL | 149 | 2003 | Kerry Wood, Chi | 266 |
| 1949 | Warren Spahn, Bos | 151 | 2004 | Randy Johnson, Ariz | 290 |
| 1950 | Warren Spahn, Bos | 191 | 2005 | Jake Peavy, SD | 216 |
| 1951 | Warren Spahn, Bos | 164 | 2006 | Aaron Harang, Cin | 216 |
| | Don Newcombe, Bklyn | 164 | 2007 | Jake Peavy, SD | 240* |
| 1952 | Warren Spahn, Bos | 183 | 2008 | Tim Lincecum, SF | 265 |
| 1953 | Robin Roberts, Phi | 198 | 2009 | Tim Lincecum, SF | 261 |

*includes NL play-in tiebreaker

## Leading Pitchers—Saves

| Year | Player and Team | SV | Year | Player and Team | SV |
|------|-----------------|----|------|-----------------|----|
| 1947 | Hugh Casey, Bklyn | 18 | 1978 | Rollie Fingers, SD | 37 |
| 1948 | Harry Gumpert, Cin | 17 | 1979 | Bruce Sutter, Chi | 37 |
| 1949 | Ted Wilks, StL | 9 | 1980 | Bruce Sutter, Chi | 28 |
| 1950 | Jim Konstanty, Phi | 22 | 1981 | Bruce Sutter, StL | 25 |
| 1951 | Ted Wilks, StL, Pitt | 13 | 1982 | Bruce Sutter, StL | 36 |
| 1952 | Al Brazle, StL | 16 | 1983 | Lee Smith, Chi | 29 |
| 1953 | Al Brazle, StL | 18 | 1984 | Bruce Sutter, StL | 45 |
| 1954 | Jim Hughes, Bklyn | 24 | 1985 | Jeff Reardon, Mtl | 41 |
| 1955 | Jack Meyer, Phi | 16 | 1986 | Todd Worrell, StL | 36 |
| 1956 | Clem Labine, Bklyn | 19 | 1987 | Steve Bedrosian, Phi | 40 |
| 1957 | Clem Labine, Bklyn | 17 | 1988 | John Franco, Cin | 39 |
| 1958 | Roy Face, Pitt | 20 | 1989 | Mark Davis, SD | 44 |
| 1959 | Lindy McDaniel, StL | 15 | 1990 | John Franco, NY | 33 |
|  | Don McMahon, Mil | 15 | 1991 | Lee Smith, StL | 47 |
| 1960 | Lindy McDaniel, StL | 26 | 1992 | Lee Smith, StL | 42 |
| 1961 | Stu Miller, SF | 17 | 1993 | Randy Myers, Chi | 53 |
|  | Roy Face, Pitt | 17 | 1994 | John Franco, NY | 30 |
| 1962 | Roy Face, Pitt | 28 | 1995 | Randy Myers, Chi | 38 |
| 1963 | Lindy McDaniel, Chi | 22 | 1996 | Jeff Brantley, Cin | 44 |
| 1964 | Hal Woodeshick, Hou | 23 |  | Todd Worrell, LA | 44 |
| 1965 | Ted Abernathy, Chi | 31 | 1997 | Jeff Shaw, Cin | 42 |
| 1966 | Phil Regan, LA | 21 | 1998 | Trevor Hoffman, SD | 53 |
| 1967 | Ted Abernathy, Cin | 28 | 1999 | Ugueth Urbina, Mtl | 41 |
| 1968 | Phil Regan, Chi, LA | 25 | 2000 | Antonio Alfonseca, Fla | 45 |
| 1969 | Fred Gladding, Hou | 29 | 2001 | Robb Nen, SF | 45 |
| 1970 | Wayne Granger, Cin | 35 | 2002 | John Smoltz, Atl | 55 |
| 1971 | Dave Giusti, Pitt | 30 | 2003 | Eric Gagne, LA | 55 |
| 1972 | Clay Carroll, Cin | 37 | 2004 | Armando Benitez, Fla | 47 |
| 1973 | Mike Marshall, Mtl | 13 |  | Jason Isringhausen, StL | 47 |
| 1974 | Mike Marshall, LA | 21 | 2005 | Chad Cordero, Wash | 47 |
| 1975 | Al Hrabosky, StL | 22 | 2006 | Trevor Hoffman, SD | 46 |
|  | Rawly Eastwick, Cin | 22 | 2007 | Jose Valverde, Ariz | 47 |
| 1976 | Rawly Eastwick, Cin | 26 | 2008 | Jose Valverde, Hou | 44 |
| 1977 | Rollie Fingers, SD | 35 | 2009 | Heath Bell, SD | 42 |

## Leading Batsmen

| Year | Player and Team | BA | Year | Player and Team | BA |
|------|-----------------|-----|------|-----------------|-----|
| 1901 | Nap Lajoie, Phi | .422 | 1956 | Mickey Mantle, NY | .353 |
| 1902 | Ed Delahanty, Wash | .376 | 1957 | Ted Williams, Bos | .388 |
| 1903 | Nap Lajoie, Clev | .355 | 1958 | Ted Williams, Bos | .328 |
| 1904 | Nap Lajoie, Clev | .381 | 1959 | Harvey Kuenn, Det | .353 |
| 1905 | Elmer Flick, Clev | .306 | 1960 | Pete Runnels, Bos | .320 |
| 1906 | George Stone, StL | .358 | 1961 | Norm Cash, Det | .361 |
| 1907 | Ty Cobb, Det | .350 | 1962 | Pete Runnels, Bos | .326 |
| 1908 | Ty Cobb, Det | .324 | 1963 | Carl Yastrzemski, Bos | .321 |
| 1909 | Ty Cobb, Det | .377 | 1964 | Tony Oliva, Minn | .323 |
| 1910 | Nap Lajoie, Clev† | .383 | 1965 | Tony Oliva, Minn | .321 |
| 1911 | Ty Cobb, Det | .420 | 1966 | Frank Robinson, Balt | .316 |
| 1912 | Ty Cobb, Det | .410 | 1967 | Carl Yastrzemski, Bos | .326 |
| 1913 | Ty Cobb, Det | .390 | 1968 | Carl Yastrzemski, Bos | .301 |
| 1914 | Ty Cobb, Det | .368 | 1969 | Rod Carew, Minn | .332 |
| 1915 | Ty Cobb, Det | .369 | 1970 | Alex Johnson, Cal | .329 |
| 1916 | Tris Speaker, Clev | .386 | 1971 | Tony Oliva, Minn | .337 |
| 1917 | Ty Cobb, Det | .383 | 1972 | Rod Carew, Minn | .318 |
| 1918 | Ty Cobb, Det | .382 | 1973 | Rod Carew, Minn | .350 |
| 1919 | Ty Cobb, Det | .384 | 1974 | Rod Carew, Minn | .364 |
| 1920 | George Sisler, StL | .407 | 1975 | Rod Carew, Minn | .359 |
| 1921 | Harry Heilmann, Det | .394 | 1976 | George Brett, KC | .333 |
| 1922 | George Sisler, StL | .420 | 1977 | Rod Carew, Minn | .388 |
| 1923 | Harry Heilmann, Det | .403 | 1978 | Rod Carew, Minn | .333 |
| 1924 | Babe Ruth, NY | .378 | 1979 | Fred Lynn, Bos | .333 |
| 1925 | Harry Heilmann, Det | .393 | 1980 | George Brett, KC | .390 |
| 1926 | Heinie Manush, Det | .378 | 1981 | Carney Lansford, Bos | .336 |
| 1927 | Harry Heilmann, Det | .398 | 1982 | Willie Wilson, KC | .332 |
| 1928 | Goose Goslin, Wash | .379 | 1983 | Wade Boggs, Bos | .361 |
| 1929 | Lew Fonseca, Clev | .369 | 1984 | Don Mattingly, NY | .343 |
| 1930 | Al Simmons, Phi | .381 | 1985 | Wade Boggs, Bos | .368 |
| 1931 | Al Simmons, Phi | .390 | 1986 | Wade Boggs, Bos | .357 |
| 1932 | Dale Alexander, Det-Bos | .367 | 1987 | Wade Boggs, Bos | .363 |
| 1933 | Jimmie Foxx, Phi | .356 | 1988 | Wade Boggs, Bos | .366 |
| 1934 | Lou Gehrig, NY | .363 | 1989 | Kirby Puckett, Minn | .339 |
| 1935 | Buddy Myer, Wash | .349 | 1990 | George Brett, KC | .329 |
| 1936 | Luke Appling, Chi | .388 | 1991 | Julio Franco, Tex | .341 |
| 1937 | Charlie Gehringer, Det | .371 | 1992 | Edgar Martinez, Sea | .343 |
| 1938 | Jimmie Foxx, Bos | .349 | 1993 | John Olerud, Tor | .363 |
| 1939 | Joe DiMaggio, NY | .381 | 1994 | Paul O'Neill, NY | .359 |
| 1940 | Joe DiMaggio, NY | .352 | 1995 | Edgar Martinez, Sea | .356 |
| 1941 | Ted Williams, Bos | .406 | 1996 | Alex Rodriguez, Sea | .358 |
| 1942 | Ted Williams, Bos | .356 | 1997 | Frank Thomas, Chi | .347 |
| 1943 | Luke Appling, Chi | .328 | 1998 | Bernie Williams, NY | .339 |
| 1944 | Lou Boudreau, Clev | .327 | 1999 | Nomar Garciaparra, Bos | .357 |
| 1945 | Snuffy Stirnweiss, NY | .309 | 2000 | Nomar Garciaparra, Bos | .372 |
| 1946 | Mickey Vernon, Wash | .353 | 2001 | Ichiro Suzuki, Sea | .350 |
| 1947 | Ted Williams, Bos | .343 | 2002 | Manny Ramirez, Bos | .349 |
| 1948 | Ted Williams, Bos | .369 | 2003 | Bill Mueller, Bos | .326 |
| 1949 | George Kell, Det | .343 | 2004 | Ichiro Suzuki, Sea | .372 |
| 1950 | Billy Goodman, Bos | .354 | 2005 | Michael Young, Tex | .331 |
| 1951 | Ferris Fain, Phi | .344 | 2006 | Joe Mauer, Minn | .347 |
| 1952 | Ferris Fain, Phi | .327 | 2007 | Magglio Ordonez, Det | .363 |
| 1953 | Mickey Vernon, Wash | .337 | 2008 | Joe Mauer, Minn | .330 |
| 1954 | Bobby Avila, Clev | .341 | 2009 | Joe Mauer, Minn* | .365 |
| 1955 | Al Kaline, Det | .340 | | | |

†League president Ban Johnson declared Ty Cobb batting champion with a .385 average, beating Lajoie's .384. However, subsequent research has led to the revision of Lajoie's average to .383 and Cobb's to .382.
*Includes one-game AL Central playoff tiebreaker.

## Leaders in Runs Scored

| Year | Player and Team | Runs | Year | Player and Team | Runs |
|---|---|---|---|---|---|
| 1901 | Nap Lajoie, Phi | 145 | 1957 | Mickey Mantle, NY | 121 |
| 1902 | Dave Fultz, Phi | 110 | 1958 | Mickey Mantle, NY | 127 |
| 1903 | Patsy Dougherty, Bos | 108 | 1959 | Eddie Yost, Det | 115 |
| 1904 | Patsy Dougherty, Bos-NY | 113 | 1960 | Mickey Mantle, NY | 119 |
| 1905 | Harry Davis, Phi | 92 | 1961 | Mickey Mantle, NY | 132 |
| 1906 | Elmer Flick, Clev | 98 | | Roger Maris, NY | 132 |
| 1907 | Sam Crawford, Det | 102 | 1962 | Albie Pearson, LA | 115 |
| 1908 | Matty McIntyre, Det | 105 | 1963 | Bob Allison, Minn | 99 |
| 1909 | Ty Cobb, Det | 116 | 1964 | Tony Oliva, Minn | 109 |
| 1910 | Ty Cobb, Det | 106 | 1965 | Zoilo Versalles, Minn | 126 |
| 1911 | Ty Cobb, Det | 147 | 1966 | Frank Robinson, Balt | 122 |
| 1912 | Eddie Collins, Phi | 137 | 1967 | Carl Yastrzemski, Bos | 112 |
| 1913 | Eddie Collins, Phi | 125 | 1968 | Dick McAuliffe, Det | 95 |
| 1914 | Eddie Collins, Phi | 122 | 1969 | Reggie Jackson, Oak | 123 |
| 1915 | Ty Cobb, Det | 144 | 1970 | Carl Yastrzemski, Bos | 125 |
| 1916 | Ty Cobb, Det | 113 | 1971 | Don Buford, Balt | 99 |
| 1917 | Donie Bush, Det | 112 | 1972 | Bobby Murcer, NY | 102 |
| 1918 | Ray Chapman, Clev | 84 | 1973 | Reggie Jackson, Oak | 99 |
| 1919 | Babe Ruth, Bos | 103 | 1974 | Carl Yastrzemski, Bos | 93 |
| 1920 | Babe Ruth, NY | 158 | 1975 | Fred Lynn, Bos | 103 |
| 1921 | Babe Ruth, NY | 177 | 1976 | Roy White, NY | 104 |
| 1922 | George Sisler, StL | 134 | 1977 | Rod Carew, Minn | 128 |
| 1923 | Babe Ruth, NY | 151 | 1978 | Ron LeFlore, Det | 126 |
| 1924 | Babe Ruth, NY | 143 | 1979 | Don Baylor, Cal | 120 |
| 1925 | Johnny Mostil, Chi | 135 | 1980 | Willie Wilson, KC | 133 |
| 1926 | Babe Ruth, NY | 139 | 1981 | Rickey Henderson, Oak | 89 |
| 1927 | Babe Ruth, NY | 158 | 1982 | Paul Molitor, Mil | 136 |
| 1928 | Babe Ruth, NY | 163 | 1983 | Cal Ripken, Balt | 121 |
| 1929 | Charlie Gehringer, Det | 131 | 1984 | Dwight Evans, Bos | 121 |
| 1930 | Al Simmons, Phi | 152 | 1985 | Rickey Henderson, NY | 146 |
| 1931 | Lou Gehrig, NY | 163 | 1986 | Rickey Henderson, NY | 130 |
| 1932 | Jimmie Foxx, Phi | 151 | 1987 | Paul Molitor, Mil | 114 |
| 1933 | Lou Gehrig, NY | 138 | 1988 | Wade Boggs, Bos | 128 |
| 1934 | Charlie Gehringer, Det | 134 | 1989 | Rickey Henderson, NY-Oak | 113 |
| 1935 | Lou Gehrig, NY | 125 | | Wade Boggs, Bos | 113 |
| 1936 | Lou Gehrig, NY | 167 | 1990 | Rickey Henderson, Oak | 119 |
| 1937 | Joe DiMaggio, NY | 151 | 1991 | Paul Molitor, Mil | 133 |
| 1938 | Hank Greenberg, Det | 144 | 1992 | Tony Philips, Det | 114 |
| 1939 | Red Rolfe, NY | 139 | 1993 | Rafael Palmeiro, Tex | 124 |
| 1940 | Ted Williams, Bos | 134 | 1994 | Frank Thomas, Chi | 106 |
| 1941 | Ted Williams, Bos | 135 | 1995 | Albert Belle, Clev | 121 |
| 1942 | Ted Williams, Bos | 141 | | Edgar Martinez, Sea | 121 |
| 1943 | George Case, Wash | 102 | 1996 | Alex Rodriguez, Sea | 141 |
| 1944 | Snuffy Stirnweiss, NY | 125 | 1997 | Ken Griffey Jr., Sea | 125 |
| 1945 | Snuffy Stirnweiss, NY | 107 | 1998 | Derek Jeter, NY | 127 |
| 1946 | Ted Williams, Bos | 142 | 1999 | Roberto Alomar, Clev | 138 |
| 1947 | Ted Williams, Bos | 125 | 2000 | Johnny Damon, KC | 136 |
| 1948 | Tommy Henrich, NY | 138 | 2001 | Alex Rodriguez, Tex | 133 |
| 1949 | Ted Williams, Bos | 150 | 2002 | Alfonso Soriano, NY | 128 |
| 1950 | Dom DiMaggio, Bos | 131 | 2003 | Alex Rodriguez, Tex | 124 |
| 1951 | Dom DiMaggio, Bos | 113 | 2004 | Vladimir Guerrero, Ana | 124 |
| 1952 | Larry Doby, Clev | 104 | 2005 | Alex Rodriguez, NY | 124 |
| 1953 | Al Rosen, Clev | 115 | 2006 | Grady Sizemore, Clev | 134 |
| 1954 | Mickey Mantle, NY | 129 | 2007 | Alex Rodriguez, NY | 143 |
| 1955 | Al Smith, Clev | 123 | 2008 | Dustin Pedroia, Bos | 118 |
| 1956 | Mickey Mantle, NY | 132 | 2009 | Dustin Pedroia, Bos | 115 |

## Leaders in Hits

| Year | Player and Team | Hits | Year | Player and Team | Hits |
|------|-----------------|------|------|-----------------|------|
| 1901 | Nap Lajoie, Phi | 229 | 1955 | Al Kaline, Det | 200 |
| 1902 | Piano Legs Hickman, Bos-Clev | 194 | 1956 | Harvey Kuenn, Det | 196 |
| 1903 | Patsy Dougherty, Bos | 195 | 1957 | Nellie Fox, Chi | 196 |
| 1904 | Nap Lajoie, Clev | 211 | 1958 | Nellie Fox, Chi | 187 |
| 1905 | George Stone, StL | 187 | 1959 | Harvey Kuenn, Det | 198 |
| 1906 | Nap Lajoie, Clev | 214 | 1960 | Minnie Minoso, Chi | 184 |
| 1907 | Ty Cobb, Det | 212 | 1961 | Norm Cash, Det | 193 |
| 1908 | Ty Cobb, Det | 188 | 1962 | Bobby Richardson, NY | 209 |
| 1909 | Ty Cobb, Det | 216 | 1963 | Carl Yastrzemski, Bos | 183 |
| 1910 | Nap Lajoie, Clev | 227 | 1964 | Tony Oliva, Minn | 217 |
| 1911 | Ty Cobb, Det | 248 | 1965 | Tony Oliva, Minn | 185 |
| 1912 | Ty Cobb, Det | 227 | 1966 | Tony Oliva, Minn | 191 |
| 1913 | Joe Jackson, Clev | 197 | 1967 | Carl Yastrzemski, Bos | 189 |
| 1914 | Tris Speaker, Bos | 193 | 1968 | Bert Campaneris, Oak | 177 |
| 1915 | Ty Cobb, Det | 208 | 1969 | Tony Oliva, Minn | 197 |
| 1916 | Tris Speaker, Clev | 211 | 1970 | Tony Oliva, Minn | 204 |
| 1917 | Ty Cobb, Det | 225 | 1971 | Cesar Tovar, Minn | 204 |
| 1918 | George Burns, Phi | 178 | 1972 | Joe Rudi, Oak | 181 |
| 1919 | Ty Cobb, Det | 191 | 1973 | Rod Carew, Minn | 203 |
|      | Bobby Veach, Det | 191 | 1974 | Rod Carew, Minn | 218 |
| 1920 | George Sisler, StL | 257 | 1975 | George Brett, KC | 195 |
| 1921 | Harry Heilmann, Det | 237 | 1976 | George Brett, KC | 215 |
| 1922 | George Sisler, StL | 246 | 1977 | Rod Carew, Minn | 239 |
| 1923 | Charlie Jamieson, Clev | 222 | 1978 | Jim Rice, Bos | 213 |
| 1924 | Sam Rice, Wash | 216 | 1979 | George Brett, KC | 212 |
| 1925 | Al Simmons, Phi | 253 | 1980 | Willie Wilson, KC | 230 |
| 1926 | George Burns, Clev | 216 | 1981 | Rickey Henderson, Oak | 135 |
|      | Sam Rice, Wash | 216 | 1982 | Robin Yount, Mil | 210 |
| 1927 | Earle Combs, NY | 231 | 1983 | Cal Ripken Jr., Balt | 211 |
| 1928 | Heinie Manush, StL | 241 | 1984 | Don Mattingly, NY | 207 |
| 1929 | Dale Alexander, Det | 215 | 1985 | Wade Boggs, Bos | 240 |
|      | Charlie Gehringer, Det | 215 | 1986 | Don Mattingly, NY | 238 |
| 1930 | Johnny Hodapp, Clev | 225 | 1987 | Kirby Puckett, Minn | 207 |
| 1931 | Lou Gehrig, NY | 211 |      | Kevin Seitzer, KC | 207 |
| 1932 | Al Simmons, Phi | 216 | 1988 | Kirby Puckett, Minn | 234 |
| 1933 | Heinie Manush, Wash | 221 | 1989 | Kirby Puckett, Minn | 215 |
| 1934 | Charlie Gehringer, Det | 214 | 1990 | Rafael Palmeiro, Tex | 191 |
| 1935 | Joe Vosmik, Clev | 216 | 1991 | Paul Molitor, Mil | 216 |
| 1936 | Earl Averill, Clev | 232 | 1992 | Kirby Puckett, Minn | 210 |
| 1937 | Beau Bell, StL | 218 | 1993 | Paul Molitor, Tor | 211 |
| 1938 | Joe Vosmik, Bos | 201 | 1994 | Kenny Lofton, Clev | 160 |
| 1939 | Red Rolfe, NY | 213 | 1995 | Lance Johnson, Chi | 186 |
| 1940 | Rip Radcliff, StL | 200 | 1996 | Paul Molitor, Minn | 225 |
|      | Barney McCosky, Det | 200 | 1997 | Nomar Garciaparra, Bos | 209 |
|      | Doc Cramer, Bos | 200 | 1998 | Alex Rodriguez, Sea | 213 |
| 1941 | Cecil Travis, Wash | 218 | 1999 | Derek Jeter, NY | 219 |
| 1942 | Johnny Pesky, Bos | 205 | 2000 | Darin Erstad, Ana | 240 |
| 1943 | Dick Wakefield, Det | 200 | 2001 | Ichiro Suzuki, Sea | 242 |
| 1944 | Snuffy Stirnweiss, NY | 205 | 2002 | Alfonso Soriano, NY | 209 |
| 1945 | Snuffy Stirnweiss, NY | 195 | 2003 | Vernon Wells, Tor | 215 |
| 1946 | Johnny Pesky, Bos | 208 | 2004 | Ichiro Suzuki, Sea | 262 |
| 1947 | Johnny Pesky, Bos | 207 | 2005 | Michael Young, Tex | 221 |
| 1948 | Bob Dillinger, StL | 207 | 2006 | Ichiro Suzuki, Sea | 224 |
| 1949 | Dale Mitchell, Clev | 203 | 2007 | Ichiro Suzuki, Sea | 238 |
| 1950 | George Kell, Det | 218 | 2008 | Dustin Pedroia, Bos | 213 |
| 1951 | George Kell, Det | 191 |      | Ichiro Suzuki, Sea | 213 |
| 1952 | Nellie Fox, Chi | 192 | 2009 | Ichiro Suzuki, Sea | 225 |
| 1953 | Harvey Kuenn, Det | 209 |      |                 |      |
| 1954 | Nellie Fox, Chi | 201 |      |                 |      |
|      | Harvey Kuenn, Det | 201 |      |                 |      |

## Home Run Leaders

| Year | Player and Team | HR | Year | Player and Team | HR |
|------|-----------------|----|------|-----------------|----|
| 1901 | Nap Lajoie, Phi | 13 | 1959 | Rocky Colavito, Clev | 42 |
| 1902 | Socks Seybold, Phi | 16 | | Harmon Killebrew, Wash | 42 |
| 1903 | Buck Freeman, Bos | 13 | 1960 | Mickey Mantle, NY | 40 |
| 1904 | Harry Davis, Phi | 10 | 1961 | Roger Maris, NY | 61 |
| 1905 | Harry Davis, Phi | 8 | 1962 | Harmon Killebrew, Minn | 48 |
| 1906 | Harry Davis, Phi | 12 | 1963 | Harmon Killebrew, Minn | 45 |
| 1907 | Harry Davis, Phi | 8 | 1964 | Harmon Killebrew, Minn | 49 |
| 1908 | Sam Crawford, Det | 7 | 1965 | Tony Conigliaro, Bos | 32 |
| 1909 | Ty Cobb, Det | 9 | 1966 | Frank Robinson, Balt | 49 |
| 1910 | Jake Stahl, Bos | 10 | 1967 | Harmon Killebrew, Minn | 44 |
| 1911 | Frank Baker, Phi | 9 | | Carl Yastrzemski, Bos | 44 |
| 1912 | Frank Baker, Phi | 10 | 1968 | Frank Howard, Wash | 44 |
| | Tris Speaker, Bos | 10 | 1969 | Harmon Killebrew, Minn | 49 |
| 1913 | Frank Baker, Phi | 13 | 1970 | Frank Howard, Wash | 44 |
| 1914 | Frank Baker, Phi | 9 | 1971 | Bill Melton, Chi | 33 |
| 1915 | Braggo Roth, Chi-Clev | 7 | 1972 | Dick Allen, Chi | 37 |
| 1916 | Wally Pipp, NY | 12 | 1973 | Reggie Jackson, Oak | 32 |
| 1917 | Wally Pipp, NY | 9 | 1974 | Dick Allen, Chi | 32 |
| 1918 | Babe Ruth, Bos | 11 | 1975 | Reggie Jackson, Oak | 36 |
| | Tilly Walker, Phi | 11 | | George Scott, Mil | 36 |
| 1919 | Babe Ruth, Bos | 29 | 1976 | Graig Nettles, NY | 32 |
| 1920 | Babe Ruth, NY | 54 | 1977 | Jim Rice, Bos | 39 |
| 1921 | Babe Ruth, NY | 59 | 1978 | Jim Rice, Bos | 46 |
| 1922 | Ken Williams, StL | 39 | 1979 | Gorman Thomas, Mil | 45 |
| 1923 | Babe Ruth, NY | 41 | 1980 | Reggie Jackson, NY | 41 |
| 1924 | Babe Ruth, NY | 46 | | Ben Oglivie, Mil | 41 |
| 1925 | Bob Meusel, NY | 33 | 1981 | Tony Armas, Oak | 22 |
| 1926 | Babe Ruth, NY | 47 | 1981 | Dwight Evans, Bos | 22 |
| 1927 | Babe Ruth, NY | 60 | | Bobby Grich, Cal | 22 |
| 1928 | Babe Ruth, NY | 54 | | Eddie Murray, Balt | 22 |
| 1929 | Babe Ruth, NY | 46 | 1982 | Reggie Jackson, Cal | 39 |
| 1930 | Babe Ruth, NY | 49 | | Gorman Thomas, Mil | 39 |
| 1931 | Babe Ruth/ Lou Gehrig NY | 46 | 1983 | Jim Rice, Bos | 39 |
| 1932 | Jimmie Foxx, Phi | 58 | 1984 | Tony Armas, Bos | 43 |
| 1933 | Jimmie Foxx, Phi | 48 | 1985 | Darrell Evans, Det | 40 |
| 1934 | Lou Gehrig, NY | 49 | 1986 | Jesse Barfield, Tor | 40 |
| 1935 | Jimmie Foxx, Phi | 36 | 1987 | Mark McGwire, Oak | 49 |
| | Hank Greenberg, Det | 36 | 1988 | Jose Canseco, Oak | 42 |
| 1936 | Lou Gehrig, NY | 49 | 1989 | Fred McGriff, Tor | 36 |
| 1937 | Joe DiMaggio, NY | 46 | 1990 | Cecil Fielder, Det | 51 |
| 1938 | Hank Greenberg, Det | 58 | 1991 | Jose Canseco, Oak | 44 |
| 1939 | Jimmie Foxx, Bos | 35 | | Cecil Fielder, Det | 44 |
| 1940 | Hank Greenberg, Det | 41 | 1992 | Juan Gonzalez, Tex | 43 |
| 1941 | Ted Williams, Bos | 37 | 1993 | Juan Gonzalez, Tex | 46 |
| 1942 | Ted Williams, Bos | 36 | 1994 | Ken Griffey Jr., Sea | 40 |
| 1943 | Rudy York, Det | 34 | 1995 | Albert Belle, Clev | 50 |
| 1944 | Nick Etten, NY | 22 | 1996 | Mark McGwire, Oak | 52 |
| 1945 | Vern Stephens, StL | 24 | 1997 | Ken Griffey Jr., Sea | 56 |
| 1946 | Hank Greenberg, Det | 44 | 1998 | Ken Griffey Jr., Sea | 56 |
| 1947 | Ted Williams, Bos | 32 | 1999 | Ken Griffey Jr., Sea | 48 |
| 1948 | Joe DiMaggio, NY | 39 | 2000 | Troy Glaus, Ana | 47 |
| 1949 | Ted Williams, Bos | 43 | 2001 | Alex Rodriguez, Tex | 52 |
| 1950 | Al Rosen, Clev | 37 | 2002 | Alex Rodriguez, Tex | 57 |
| 1951 | Gus Zernial, Chi-Phi | 33 | 2003 | Alex Rodriguez, Tex | 47 |
| 1952 | Larry Doby, Clev | 32 | 2004 | Manny Ramirez, Bos | 43 |
| 1953 | Al Rosen, Clev | 43 | 2005 | Alex Rodriguez, NY | 48 |
| 1954 | Larry Doby, Clev | 32 | 2006 | David Ortiz, Bos | 54 |
| 1955 | Mickey Mantle, NY | 37 | 2007 | Alex Rodriguez, NY | 54 |
| 1956 | Mickey Mantle, NY | 52 | 2008 | Miguel Cabrera, Det | 37 |
| 1957 | Roy Sievers, Wash | 42 | 2009 | Carlos Pena, TB | 39 |
| 1958 | Mickey Mantle, NY | 42 | | Mark Teixeira, NY | 39 |

## Runs Batted In Leaders

| Year | Player and Team | RBI | Year | Player and Team | RBI |
|---|---|---|---|---|---|
| 1907 | Ty Cobb, Det | 116 | 1958 | Jackie Jensen, Bos | 122 |
| 1908 | Ty Cobb, Det | 108 | 1959 | Jackie Jensen, Bos | 112 |
| 1909 | Ty Cobb, Det | 107 | 1960 | Roger Maris, NY | 112 |
| 1910 | Sam Crawford, Det | 120 | 1961 | Roger Maris, NY | 142 |
| 1911 | Ty Cobb, Det | 144 | 1962 | Harmon Killebrew, Minn | 126 |
| 1912 | Frank Baker, Phi | 133 | 1963 | Dick Stuart, Bos | 118 |
| 1913 | Frank Baker, Phi | 126 | 1964 | Brooks Robinson, Balt | 118 |
| 1914 | Sam Crawford, Det | 104 | 1965 | Rocky Colavito, Clev | 108 |
| 1915 | Sam Crawford, Det | 112 | 1966 | Frank Robinson, Balt | 122 |
| | Bobby Veach, Det | 112 | 1967 | Carl Yastrzemski, Bos | 121 |
| 1916 | Del Pratt, StL | 103 | 1968 | Ken Harrelson, Bos | 109 |
| 1917 | Bobby Veach, Det | 103 | 1969 | Harmon Killebrew, Minn | 140 |
| 1918 | Bobby Veach, Det | 78 | 1970 | Frank Howard, Wash | 126 |
| 1919 | Babe Ruth, Bos | 114 | 1971 | Harmon Killebrew, Minn | 119 |
| 1920 | Babe Ruth, NY | 137 | 1972 | Dick Allen, Chi | 113 |
| 1921 | Babe Ruth, NY | 171 | 1973 | Reggie Jackson, Oak | 117 |
| 1922 | Ken Williams, StL | 155 | 1974 | Jeff Burroughs, Tex | 118 |
| 1923 | Babe Ruth, NY | 131 | 1975 | George Scott, Mil | 109 |
| 1924 | Goose Goslin, Wash | 129 | 1976 | Lee May, Balt | 109 |
| 1925 | Bob Meusel, NY | 138 | 1977 | Larry Hisle, Minn | 119 |
| 1926 | Babe Ruth, NY | 145 | 1978 | Jim Rice, Bos | 139 |
| 1927 | Lou Gehrig, NY | 175 | 1979 | Don Baylor, Cal | 139 |
| 1928 | Babe Ruth/ Lou Gehrig, NY | 142 | 1980 | Cecil Cooper, Mil | 122 |
| 1929 | Al Simmons, Phi | 157 | 1981 | Eddie Murray, Balt | 78 |
| 1930 | Lou Gehrig, NY | 174 | 1982 | Hal McRae, KC | 133 |
| 1931 | Lou Gehrig, NY | 184 | 1983 | Cecil Cooper, Mil | 126 |
| 1932 | Jimmie Foxx, Phi | 169 | | Jim Rice, Bos | 126 |
| 1933 | Jimmie Foxx, Phi | 163 | 1984 | Tony Armas, Bos | 123 |
| 1934 | Lou Gehrig, NY | 165 | 1985 | Don Mattingly, NY | 145 |
| 1935 | Hank Greenberg, Det | 170 | 1986 | Joe Carter, Clev | 121 |
| 1936 | Hal Trosky, Clev | 162 | 1987 | George Bell, Tor | 134 |
| 1937 | Hank Greenberg, Det | 183 | 1988 | Jose Canseco, Oak | 124 |
| 1938 | Jimmie Foxx, Bos | 175 | 1989 | Ruben Sierra, Tex | 119 |
| 1939 | Ted Williams, Bos | 145 | 1990 | Cecil Fielder, Det | 132 |
| 1940 | Hank Greenberg, Det | 150 | 1991 | Cecil Fielder, Det | 133 |
| 1941 | Joe DiMaggio, NY | 125 | 1992 | Cecil Fielder, Det | 124 |
| 1942 | Ted Williams, Bos | 137 | 1993 | Albert Belle, Clev | 129 |
| 1943 | Rudy York, Det | 118 | 1994 | Kirby Puckett, Minn | 112 |
| 1944 | Vern Stephens, StL | 109 | 1995 | Albert Belle, Clev | 126 |
| 1945 | Nick Etten, NY | 111 | | Mo Vaughn, Bos | 126 |
| 1946 | Hank Greenberg, Det | 127 | 1996 | Albert Belle, Clev | 148 |
| 1947 | Ted Williams, Bos | 114 | 1997 | Ken Griffey Jr., Sea | 147 |
| 1948 | Joe DiMaggio, NY | 155 | 1998 | Juan Gonzales, Tex | 157 |
| 1949 | Ted Williams, Bos | 159 | 1999 | Manny Ramirez, Clev | 165 |
| | Vern Stephens, Bos | 159 | 2000 | Edgar Martinez, Sea | 145 |
| 1950 | Walt Dropo, Bos | 144 | 2001 | Bret Boone, Sea | 141 |
| | Vern Stephens, Bos | 144 | 2002 | Alex Rodriguez, Tex | 142 |
| 1951 | Gus Zernial, Chi-Phi | 129 | 2003 | Carlos Delgado, Tor | 145 |
| 1952 | Al Rosen, Clev | 105 | 2004 | Miguel Tejada, Balt | 150 |
| 1953 | Al Rosen, Clev | 145 | 2005 | David Ortiz, Bos | 148 |
| 1954 | Larry Doby, Clev | 126 | 2006 | David Ortiz, Bos | 137 |
| 1955 | Ray Boone, Det | 116 | 2007 | Alex Rodriguez, NY | 156 |
| | Jackie Jensen, Bos | 116 | 2008 | Josh Hamilton, Tex | 130 |
| 1956 | Mickey Mantle, NY | 130 | 2009 | Mark Teixeira, NY | 122 |
| 1957 | Roy Sievers, Wash | 114 | | | |

## Leading Base Stealers

| Year | Player and Team | SB | Year | Player and Team | SB |
|---|---|---|---|---|---|
| 1901 | Frank Isbell, Chi | 48 | 1910 | Eddie Collins, Phi | 81 |
| 1902 | Topsy Hartsel, Phi | 54 | 1911 | Ty Cobb, Det | 83 |
| 1903 | Harry Bay, Clev | 46 | 1912 | Clyde Milan, Wash | 88 |
| 1904 | Elmer Flick, Clev | 42 | 1913 | Clyde Milan, Wash | 75 |
| | Harry Bay, Clev | 42 | 1914 | Fritz Maisel, NY | 74 |
| 1905 | Danny Hoffman, Phi | 46 | 1915 | Ty Cobb, Det | 96 |
| 1906 | Elmer Flick, Clev | 39 | 1916 | Ty Cobb, Det | 68 |
| | John Anderson, Wash | 39 | 1917 | Ty Cobb, Det | 55 |
| 1907 | Ty Cobb, Det | 49 | 1918 | George Sisler, StL | 45 |
| 1908 | Patsy Dougherty, Chi | 47 | 1919 | Eddie Collins, Chi | 33 |
| 1909 | Ty Cobb, Det | 76 | 1920 | Sam Rice, Wash | 63 |

Note: Runs Batted In not compiled before 1907; officially adopted in 1920.

## Leading Base Stealers *(Cont.)*

| Year | Player and Team | SB | Year | Player and Team | SB |
|---|---|---|---|---|---|
| 1921 | George Sisler, StL | 35 | 1966 | Bert Campaneris, KC | 52 |
| 1922 | George Sisler, StL | 51 | 1967 | Bert Campaneris, KC | 55 |
| 1923 | Eddie Collins, Chi | 49 | 1968 | Bert Campaneris, Oak | 62 |
| 1924 | Eddie Collins, Chi | 42 | 1969 | Tommy Harper, Sea | 73 |
| 1925 | John Mostil, Chi | 43 | 1970 | Bert Campaneris, Oak | 42 |
| 1926 | John Mostil, Chi | 35 | 1971 | Amos Otis, KC | 52 |
| 1927 | George Sisler, StL | 27 | 1972 | Bert Campaneris, Oak | 52 |
| 1928 | Buddy Myer, Bos | 30 | 1973 | Tommy Harper, Bos | 54 |
| 1929 | Charlie Gehringer, Det | 27 | 1974 | Bill North, Oak | 54 |
| 1930 | Marty McManus, Det | 23 | 1975 | Mickey Rivers, Cal | 70 |
| 1931 | Ben Chapman, NY | 61 | 1976 | Bill North, Oak | 75 |
| 1932 | Ben Chapman, NY | 38 | 1977 | Freddie Patek, KC | 53 |
| 1933 | Ben Chapman, NY | 27 | 1978 | Ron LeFlore, Det | 68 |
| 1934 | Bill Werber, Bos | 40 | 1979 | Willie Wilson, KC | 83 |
| 1935 | Bill Werber, Bos | 29 | 1980 | Rickey Henderson, Oak | 100 |
| 1936 | Lyn Lary, StL | 37 | 1981 | Rickey Henderson, Oak | 56 |
| 1937 | Bill Werber, Phi | 35 | 1982 | Rickey Henderson, Oak | 130 |
|  | Ben Chapman, Wash-Bos | 35 | 1983 | Rickey Henderson, Oak | 108 |
| 1938 | Frank Crosetti, NY | 27 | 1984 | Rickey Henderson, Oak | 66 |
| 1939 | George Case, Wash | 51 | 1985 | Rickey Henderson, NY | 80 |
| 1940 | George Case, Wash | 35 | 1986 | Rickey Henderson, NY | 87 |
| 1941 | George Case, Wash | 33 | 1987 | Harold Reynolds, Sea | 60 |
| 1942 | George Case, Wash | 44 | 1988 | Rickey Henderson, NY | 93 |
| 1943 | George Case, Wash | 61 | 1989 | Rickey Henderson, NY-Oak | 77 |
| 1944 | Snuffy Stirnweiss, NY | 55 | 1990 | Rickey Henderson, Oak | 65 |
| 1945 | Snuffy Stirnweiss, NY | 33 | 1991 | Rickey Henderson, Oak | 58 |
| 1946 | George Case, Clev | 28 | 1992 | Kenny Lofton, Clev | 66 |
| 1947 | Bob Dillinger, StL | 34 | 1993 | Kenny Lofton, Clev | 70 |
| 1948 | Bob Dillinger, StL | 28 | 1994 | Kenny Lofton, Clev | 60 |
| 1949 | Bob Dillinger, StL | 20 | 1995 | Kenny Lofton, Clev | 54 |
| 1950 | Dom DiMaggio, Bos | 15 | 1996 | Kenny Lofton, Clev | 75 |
| 1951 | Minnie Minoso, Clev-Chi | 31 | 1997 | Brian Hunter, Det | 74 |
| 1952 | Minnie Minoso, Chi | 22 | 1998 | Rickey Henderson, Oak | 66 |
| 1953 | Minnie Minoso, Chi | 25 | 1999 | Brian Hunter, Sea | 44 |
| 1954 | Jackie Jensen, Bos | 22 | 2000 | Johnny Damon, KC | 46 |
| 1955 | Jim Rivera, Chi | 25 | 2001 | Ichiro Suzuki, Sea | 56 |
| 1956 | Luis Aparicio, Chi | 21 | 2002 | Alfonso Soriano, NY | 41 |
| 1957 | Luis Aparicio, Chi | 28 | 2003 | Carl Crawford, TB | 55 |
| 1958 | Luis Aparicio, Chi | 29 | 2004 | Carl Crawford, TB | 59 |
| 1959 | Luis Aparicio, Chi | 56 | 2005 | Chone Figgins, LA | 62 |
| 1960 | Luis Aparicio, Chi | 51 | 2006 | Carl Crawford, TB | 58 |
| 1961 | Luis Aparicio, Chi | 53 | 2007 | Carl Crawford, TB | 50 |
| 1962 | Luis Aparicio, Chi | 31 |  | Brian Roberts, Balt | 50 |
| 1963 | Luis Aparicio, Balt | 40 | 2008 | Jacoby Ellsbury, Bos | 50 |
| 1964 | Luis Aparicio, Balt | 57 | 2009 | Jacoby Ellsbury, Bos | 70 |
| 1965 | Bert Campaneris, KC | 51 |  |  |  |

## Leading Pitchers—Winning Percentage

| Year | Pitcher and Team | W | L | Pct | Year | Pitcher and Team | W | L | Pct |
|---|---|---|---|---|---|---|---|---|---|
| 1901 | Clark Griffith, Chi | 24 | 7 | .774 | 1920 | Jim Bagby, Clev | 31 | 12 | .721 |
| 1902 | Bill Bernhard, Phi-Clev | 18 | 5 | .783 | 1921 | Carl Mays, NY | 27 | 9 | .750 |
| 1903 | Earl Moore, Clev | 22 | 7 | .759 | 1922 | Joe Bush, NY | 26 | 7 | .788 |
| 1904 | Jack Chesbro, NY | 41 | 12 | .774 | 1923 | Herb Pennock, NY | 19 | 6 | .760 |
| 1905 | Jess Tannehill, Bos | 22 | 9 | .710 | 1924 | Walter Johnson, Wash | 23 | 7 | .767 |
| 1906 | Eddie Plank, Phi | 19 | 6 | .760 | 1925 | Stan Coveleski, Wash | 20 | 5 | .800 |
| 1907 | Wild Bill Donovan, Det | 25 | 4 | .862 | 1926 | George Uhle, Clev | 27 | 11 | .711 |
| 1908 | Ed Walsh, Chi | 40 | 15 | .727 | 1927 | Waite Hoyt, NY | 22 | 7 | .759 |
| 1909 | George Mullin, Det | 29 | 8 | .784 | 1928 | General Crowder, StL | 21 | 5 | .808 |
| 1910 | Chief Bender, Phi | 23 | 5 | .821 | 1929 | Lefty Grove, Phi | 20 | 6 | .769 |
| 1911 | Chief Bender, Phi | 17 | 5 | .773 | 1930 | Lefty Grove, Phi | 28 | 5 | .848 |
| 1912 | Smoky Joe Wood, Bos | 34 | 5 | .872 | 1931 | Lefty Grove, Phi | 31 | 4 | .886 |
| 1913 | Walter Johnson, Wash | 36 | 7 | .837 | 1932 | Johnny Allen, NY | 17 | 4 | .810 |
| 1914 | Chief Bender, Phi | 17 | 3 | .850 | 1933 | Lefty Grove, Phi | 24 | 8 | .750 |
| 1915 | Smoky Joe Wood, Bos | 15 | 5 | .750 | 1934 | Lefty Gomez, NY | 26 | 5 | .839 |
| 1916 | Eddie Cicotte, Chi | 15 | 7 | .682 | 1935 | Eldon Auker, Det | 18 | 7 | .720 |
| 1917 | Reb Russell, Chi | 15 | 5 | .750 | 1936 | Monte Pearson, NY | 19 | 7 | .731 |
| 1918 | Sad Sam Jones, Bos | 16 | 5 | .762 | 1937 | Johnny Allen, Clev | 15 | 1 | .938 |
| 1919 | Eddie Cicotte, Chi | 29 | 7 | .806 | 1938 | Red Ruffing, NY | 21 | 7 | .750 |

## Leading Pitchers—Winning Percentage *(Cont.)*

| Year | Pitcher and Team | W | L | Pct | Year | Pitcher and Team | W | L | Pct |
|---|---|---|---|---|---|---|---|---|---|
| 1939 | Lefty Grove, Bos | 15 | 4 | .789 | 1975 | Mike Torrez, Balt | 20 | 9 | .690 |
| 1940 | Schoolboy Rowe, Det | 16 | 3 | .842 | 1976 | Bill Campbell, Minn | 17 | 5 | .773 |
| 1941 | Lefty Gomez, NY | 15 | 5 | .750 | 1977 | Paul Splittorff, KC | 16 | 6 | .727 |
| 1942 | Ernie Bonham, NY | 21 | 5 | .808 | 1978 | Ron Guidry, NY | 25 | 3 | .893 |
| 1943 | Spud Chandler, NY | 20 | 4 | .833 | 1979 | Mike Caldwell, Mil | 16 | 6 | .727 |
| 1944 | Tex Hughson, Bos | 18 | 5 | .783 | 1980 | Steve Stone, Balt | 25 | 7 | .781 |
| 1945 | Hal Newhouser, Det | 25 | 9 | .735 | 1981* | Pete Vuckovich, Mil | 14 | 4 | .778 |
| 1946 | Boo Ferriss, Bos | 25 | 6 | .806 | 1982 | Pete Vuckovich, Mil | 18 | 6 | .750 |
| 1947 | Allie Reynolds, NY | 19 | 8 | .704 | | Jim Palmer, Balt | 15 | 5 | .750 |
| 1948 | Jack Kramer, Bos | 18 | 5 | .783 | 1983 | Richard Dotson, Chi | 22 | 7 | .759 |
| 1949 | Ellis Kinder, Bos | 23 | 6 | .793 | 1984 | Doyle Alexander, Tor | 17 | 6 | .739 |
| 1950 | Vic Raschi, NY | 21 | 8 | .724 | 1985 | Ron Guidry, NY | 22 | 6 | .786 |
| 1951 | Bob Feller, Clev | 22 | 8 | .733 | 1986 | Roger Clemens, Bos | 24 | 4 | .857 |
| 1952 | Bobby Shantz, Phi | 24 | 7 | .774 | 1987 | Roger Clemens, Bos | 20 | 9 | .690 |
| 1953 | Ed Lopat, NY | 16 | 4 | .800 | 1988 | Frank Viola, Minn | 24 | 7 | .774 |
| 1954 | Sandy Consuegra, Chi | 16 | 3 | .842 | 1989 | Bret Saberhagen, KC | 23 | 6 | .793 |
| 1955 | Tommy Byrne, NY | 16 | 5 | .762 | 1990 | Bob Welch, Oak | 27 | 6 | .818 |
| 1956 | Whitey Ford, NY | 19 | 6 | .760 | 1991 | Scott Erickson, Minn | 20 | 8 | .714 |
| 1957 | Dick Donovan, Chi | 16 | 6 | .727 | 1992 | Mike Mussina, Balt | 18 | 5 | .783 |
| | Tom Sturdivant, NY | 16 | 6 | .727 | 1993 | Jimmy Key, NY | 18 | 6 | .750 |
| 1958 | Bob Turley, NY | 21 | 7 | .750 | 1994 | Jimmy Key, NY | 17 | 4 | .810 |
| 1959 | Bob Shaw, Chi | 18 | 6 | .750 | 1995 | Randy Johnson, Sea | 18 | 2 | .900 |
| 1960 | Jim Perry, Clev | 18 | 10 | .643 | 1996 | Charles Nagy, Clev | 17 | 5 | .773 |
| 1961 | Whitey Ford, NY | 25 | 4 | .862 | 1997 | Randy Johnson, Sea | 20 | 4 | .833 |
| 1962 | Ray Herbert, Chi | 20 | 9 | .690 | 1998 | David Wells, NY | 18 | 4 | .818 |
| 1963 | Whitey Ford, NY | 24 | 7 | .774 | 1999 | Pedro Martinez, Bos | 23 | 4 | .852 |
| 1964 | Wally Bunker, Balt | 19 | 5 | .792 | 2000 | Tim Hudson, Oak | 20 | 6 | .769 |
| 1965 | Mudcat Grant, Minn | 21 | 7 | .750 | 2001 | Roger Clemens, NY | 20 | 3 | .870 |
| 1966 | Sonny Siebert, Clev | 16 | 8 | .667 | 2002 | Pedro Martinez, Bos | 20 | 4 | .833 |
| 1967 | Joel Horlen, Chi | 19 | 7 | .731 | 2003 | Roy Halladay, Tor | 22 | 7 | .759 |
| 1968 | Denny McLain, Det | 31 | 6 | .838 | 2004 | Curt Schilling, Bos | 21 | 6 | .778 |
| 1969 | Jim Palmer, Balt | 16 | 4 | .800 | 2005 | Cliff Lee, Cle | 18 | 5 | .783 |
| 1970 | Mike Cuellar, Balt | 24 | 8 | .750 | 2006 | Roy Halladay, Tor | 16 | 5 | .762 |
| 1971 | Dave McNally, Balt | 21 | 5 | .808 | 2007 | Justin Verlander, Det | 18 | 6 | .750 |
| 1972 | Catfish Hunter, Oak | 21 | 7 | .750 | 2008 | Cliff Lee, Cle | 22 | 3 | .880 |
| 1973 | Catfish Hunter, Oak | 21 | 5 | .808 | 2009 | Felix Hernandez, Sea | 19 | 5 | .792 |
| 1974 | Mike Cuellar, Balt | 22 | 10 | .688 | | | | | |

*1981 percentages based on 10 or more victories. Note: Percentages based on 15 or more victories in all other years.

## Leading Pitchers—Earned Run Average

| Year | Player and Team | ERA | Year | Player and Team | ERA |
|---|---|---|---|---|---|
| 1913 | Walter Johnson, Wash | 1.14 | 1940 | Bob Feller, Clev† | 2.62 |
| 1914 | Dutch Leonard, Bos | 1.01 | 1941 | Thornton Lee, Chi | 2.37 |
| 1915 | Smoky Joe Wood, Bos | 1.49 | 1942 | Ted Lyons, Chi | 2.10 |
| 1916 | Babe Ruth, Bos | 1.75 | 1943 | Spud Chandler, NY | 1.64 |
| 1917 | Eddie Cicotte, Chi | 1.53 | 1944 | Dizzy Trout, Det | 2.12 |
| 1918 | Walter Johnson, Wash | 1.27 | 1945 | Hal Newhouser, Det | 1.81 |
| 1919 | Walter Johnson, Wash | 1.49 | 1946 | Hal Newhouser, Det | 1.94 |
| 1920 | Bob Shawkey, NY | 2.46 | 1947 | Spud Chandler, NY | 2.46 |
| 1921 | Red Faber, Chi | 2.47 | 1948 | Gene Bearden, Clev | 2.43 |
| 1922 | Red Faber, Chi | 2.80 | 1949 | Mel Parnell, Bos | 2.78 |
| 1923 | Stan Coveleski, Clev | 2.76 | 1950 | Early Wynn, Clev | 3.20 |
| 1924 | Walter Johnson, Wash | 2.72 | 1951 | Saul Rogovin, Det-Chi | 2.78 |
| 1925 | Stan Coveleski, Wash | 2.84 | 1952 | Allie Reynolds, NY | 2.07 |
| 1926 | Lefty Grove, Phi | 2.51 | 1953 | Ed Lopat, NY | 2.43 |
| 1927 | Wilcy Moore, NY# | 2.28 | 1954 | Mike Garcia, Clev | 2.64 |
| 1928 | Garland Braxton, Wash | 2.52 | 1955 | Billy Pierce, Chi | 1.97 |
| 1929 | Lefty Grove, Phi | 2.81 | 1956 | Whitey Ford, NY | 2.47 |
| 1930 | Lefty Grove, Phi | 2.54 | 1957 | Bobby Shantz, NY | 2.45 |
| 1931 | Lefty Grove, Phi | 2.06 | 1958 | Whitey Ford, NY | 2.01 |
| 1932 | Lefty Grove, Phi | 2.84 | 1959 | Hoyt Wilhelm, Balt | 2.19 |
| 1933 | Monte Pearson, Clev | 2.33 | 1960 | Frank Baumann, Chi | 2.68 |
| 1934 | Lefty Gomez, NY | 2.33 | 1961 | Dick Donovan, Wash | 2.40 |
| 1935 | Lefty Grove, Bos | 2.70 | 1962 | Hank Aguirre, Det | 2.21 |
| 1936 | Lefty Grove, Bos | 2.81 | 1963 | Gary Peters, Chi | 2.33 |
| 1937 | Lefty Gomez, NY | 2.33 | 1964 | Dean Chance, LA | 1.65 |
| 1938 | Lefty Grove, Bos | 3.07 | 1965 | Sam McDowell, Clev | 2.18 |
| 1939 | Lefty Grove, Bos | 2.54 | 1966 | Gary Peters, Chi | 1.98 |

## Leading Pitchers—Earned Run Average *(Cont.)*

| Year | Player and Team | ERA | Year | Player and Team | ERA |
|------|-----------------|-----|------|-----------------|-----|
| 1967 | Joe Horlen, Chi | 2.06 | 1989 | Bret Saberhagen, KC | 2.16 |
| 1968 | Luis Tiant, Clev | 1.60 | 1990 | Roger Clemens, Bos | 1.93 |
| 1969 | Dick Bosman, Wash | 2.19 | 1991 | Roger Clemens, Bos | 2.62 |
| 1970 | Diego Segui, Oak | 2.56 | 1992 | Roger Clemens, Bos | 2.41 |
| 1971 | Vida Blue, Oak | 1.82 | 1993 | Kevin Appier, KC | 2.56 |
| 1972 | Luis Tiant, Bos | 1.91 | 1994 | Steve Ontiveros, Oak | 2.65 |
| 1973 | Jim Palmer, Balt | 2.40 | 1995 | Randy Johnson, Sea | 2.48 |
| 1974 | Catfish Hunter, Oak | 2.49 | 1996 | Juan Guzman, Tor | 2.93 |
| 1975 | Jim Palmer, Balt | 2.09 | 1997 | Roger Clemens, Tor | 2.05 |
| 1976 | Mark Fidrych, Det | 2.34 | 1998 | Roger Clemens, Tor | 2.64 |
| 1977 | Frank Tanana, Cal | 2.54 | 1999 | Pedro Martinez, Bos | 2.07 |
| 1978 | Ron Guidry, NY | 1.74 | 2000 | Pedro Martinez, Bos | 1.74 |
| 1979 | Ron Guidry, NY | 2.78 | 2001 | Freddy Garcia, Sea | 3.05 |
| 1980 | Rudy May, NY | 2.47 | 2002 | Pedro Martinez, Bos | 2.26 |
| 1981 | Steve McCatty, Oak | 2.32 | 2003 | Pedro Martinez, Bos | 2.22 |
| 1982 | Rick Sutcliffe, Clev | 2.96 | 2004 | Johan Santana, Minn | 2.61 |
| 1983 | Rick Honeycutt, Tex | 2.42 | 2005 | Kevin Millwood, Cle | 2.86 |
| 1984 | Mike Boddicker, Balt | 2.79 | 2006 | Johan Santana, Minn | 2.77 |
| 1985 | Dave Stieb, Tor | 2.48 | 2007 | John Lackey, LA | 3.01 |
| 1986 | Roger Clemens, Bos | 2.48 | 2008 | Cliff Lee, Cle | 2.54 |
| 1987 | Jimmy Key, Tor | 2.76 | 2009 | Zack Greinke, KC | 2.16 |
| 1988 | Allan Anderson, Minn | 2.45 | | | |

Note: Based on 10 complete games through 1950, then 154 innings until the American League expanded in 1961, when it became 162 innings. In strike-shortened 1981, one inning per game required. Earned runs not tabulated in American League prior to 1913. #Wilcy Moore pitched only six complete games—he started 12—in 1927 but was recognized as leader because of 213 innings pitched. †Ernie Bonham, New York, had 1.91 ERA and 10 complete games in 1940 but appeared in only 12 games and 99 innings, and Bob Feller was recognized as the leader.

## Leading Pitchers—Strikeouts

| Year | Player and Team | SO | Year | Player and Team | SO |
|------|-----------------|-----|------|-----------------|-----|
| 1901 | Cy Young, Bos | 159 | 1940 | Bob Feller, Clev | 261 |
| 1902 | Rube Waddell, Phi | 210 | 1941 | Bob Feller, Clev | 260 |
| 1903 | Rube Waddell, Phi | 301 | 1942 | Bobo Newsom, Wash | |
| 1904 | Rube Waddell, Phi | 349 | | Tex Hughson, Bos | 113 |
| 1905 | Rube Waddell, Phi | 286 | 1943 | Allie Reynolds, Clev | 151 |
| 1906 | Rube Waddell, Phi | 203 | 1944 | Hal Newhouser, Det | 187 |
| 1907 | Rube Waddell, Phi | 226 | 1945 | Hal Newhouser, Det | 212 |
| 1908 | Ed Walsh, Chi | 269 | 1946 | Bob Feller, Clev | 348 |
| 1909 | Frank Smith, Chi | 177 | 1947 | Bob Feller, Clev | 196 |
| 1910 | Walter Johnson, Wash | 313 | 1948 | Bob Feller, Clev | 164 |
| 1911 | Ed Walsh, Chi | 255 | 1949 | Virgil Trucks, Det | 153 |
| 1912 | Walter Johnson, Wash | 303 | 1950 | Bob Lemon, Clev | 170 |
| 1913 | Walter Johnson, Wash | 243 | 1951 | Vic Raschi, NY | 164 |
| 1914 | Walter Johnson, Wash | 225 | 1952 | Allie Reynolds, NY | 160 |
| 1915 | Walter Johnson, Wash | 203 | 1953 | Billy Pierce, Chi | 186 |
| 1916 | Walter Johnson, Wash | 228 | 1954 | Bob Turley, Balt | 185 |
| 1917 | Walter Johnson, Wash | 188 | 1955 | Herb Score, Clev | 245 |
| 1918 | Walter Johnson, Wash | 162 | 1956 | Herb Score, Clev | 263 |
| 1919 | Walter Johnson, Wash | 147 | 1957 | Early Wynn, Clev | 184 |
| 1920 | Stan Coveleski, Clev | 133 | 1958 | Early Wynn, Chi | 179 |
| 1921 | Walter Johnson, Wash | 143 | 1959 | Jim Bunning, Det | 201 |
| 1922 | Urban Shocker, StL | 149 | 1960 | Jim Bunning, Det | 201 |
| 1923 | Walter Johnson, Wash | 130 | 1961 | Camilo Pascual, Minn | 221 |
| 1924 | Walter Johnson, Wash | 158 | 1962 | Camilo Pascual, Minn | 206 |
| 1925 | Lefty Grove, Phi | 116 | 1963 | Camilo Pascual, Minn | 202 |
| 1926 | Lefty Grove, Phi | 194 | 1964 | Al Downing, NY | 217 |
| 1927 | Lefty Grove, Phi | 174 | 1965 | Sam McDowell, Clev | 325 |
| 1928 | Lefty Grove, Phi | 183 | 1966 | Sam McDowell, Clev | 225 |
| 1929 | Lefty Grove, Phi | 170 | 1967 | Jim Lonborg, Bos | 246 |
| 1930 | Lefty Grove, Phi | 209 | 1968 | Sam McDowell, Clev | 283 |
| 1931 | Lefty Grove, Phi | 175 | 1969 | Sam McDowell, Clev | 279 |
| 1932 | Red Ruffing, NY | 190 | 1970 | Sam McDowell, Clev | 304 |
| 1933 | Lefty Gomez, NY | 163 | 1971 | Mickey Lolich, Det | 308 |
| 1934 | Lefty Gomez, NY | 158 | 1972 | Nolan Ryan, Cal | 329 |
| 1935 | Tommy Bridges, Det | 163 | 1973 | Nolan Ryan, Cal | 383 |
| 1936 | Tommy Bridges, Det | 175 | 1974 | Nolan Ryan, Cal | 367 |
| 1937 | Lefty Gomez, NY | 194 | 1975 | Frank Tanana, Cal | 269 |
| 1938 | Bob Feller, Clev | 240 | 1976 | Nolan Ryan, Cal | 327 |
| 1939 | Bob Feller, Clev | 246 | 1977 | Nolan Ryan, Cal | 341 |

# American League (Cont.)

## Leading Pitchers—Strikeouts (Cont.)

| Year | Player and Team | SO | Year | Player and Team | SO |
|---|---|---|---|---|---|
| 1978 | Nolan Ryan, Cal | 260 | 1995 | Randy Johnson, Sea | 294 |
| 1979 | Nolan Ryan, Cal | 223 | 1996 | Roger Clemens, Bos | 257 |
| 1980 | Len Barker, Clev | 187 | 1997 | Roger Clemens, Tor | 292 |
| 1981 | Len Barker, Clev | 127 | 1998 | Roger Clemens, Tor | 271 |
| 1982 | Floyd Bannister, Sea | 209 | 1999 | Pedro Martinez, Bos | 313 |
| 1983 | Jack Morris, Det | 232 | 2000 | Pedro Martinez, Bos | 284 |
| 1984 | Mark Langston, Sea | 204 | 2001 | Hideo Nomo, Bos | 220 |
| 1985 | Bert Blyleven, Clev-Minn | 206 | 2002 | Pedro Martinez, Bos | 239 |
| 1986 | Mark Langston, Sea | 245 | 2003 | Esteban Loaiza, Chi | 207 |
| 1987 | Mark Langston, Sea | 262 | 2004 | Johan Santana, Minn | 265 |
| 1988 | Roger Clemens, Bos | 291 | 2005 | Johan Santana, Minn | 238 |
| 1989 | Nolan Ryan, Tex | 301 | 2006 | Johan Santana, Minn | 245 |
| 1990 | Nolan Ryan, Tex | 232 | 2007 | Scott Kazmir, TB | 239 |
| 1991 | Roger Clemens, Bos | 241 | 2008 | A.J. Burnett, Tor | 231 |
| 1992 | Randy Johnson, Sea | 241 | 2009 | Justin Verlander, Det | 269 |
| 1993 | Randy Johnson, Sea | 308 | | | |
| 1994 | Randy Johnson, Sea | 204 | | | |

## Leading Pitchers—Saves

| FYear | Player and Team | SV | Year | Player and Team | SV |
|---|---|---|---|---|---|
| 1947 | Joe Page, NY | 17 | 1979 | Mike Marshall, Minn | 32 |
| 1948 | Russ Christopher, Clev | 17 | 1980 | Dan Quisenberry, KC | 33 |
| 1949 | Joe Page, NY | 29 | 1981 | Rollie Fingers, Mil | 28 |
| 1950 | Mickey Harris, Wash | 15 | 1982 | Dan Quisenberry, KC | 35 |
| 1951 | Ellis Kinder, Bos | 14 | 1983 | Dan Quisenberry, KC | 35 |
| 1952 | Harry Dorish, Chi | 11 | 1984 | Dan Quisenberry, KC | 44 |
| 1953 | Ellis Kinder, Bos | 27 | 1985 | Dan Quisenberry, KC | 37 |
| 1954 | Johnny Sain, NY | 22 | 1986 | Dave Righetti, NY | 46 |
| 1955 | Ray Narleski, Clev | 19 | 1987 | Tom Henke, Tor | 34 |
| 1956 | George Zuverink, Bal | 16 | 1988 | Dennis Eckersley, Oak | 45 |
| 1957 | Bob Grim, NY | 19 | 1989 | Jeff Russell, Tex | 38 |
| 1958 | Ryne Duren, NY | 20 | 1990 | Bobby Thigpen, Chi | 57 |
| 1959 | Turk Lown, Chi | 15 | 1991 | Bryan Harvey, Cal | 46 |
| 1960 | Mike Fornieles, Bos | 14 | 1992 | Dennis Eckersley, Oak | 51 |
| | Johnny Klippstein, Clev | 14 | 1993 | Jeff Montgomery, KC | 45 |
| 1961 | Luis Arroyo, NY | 29 | | Duane Ward, Tor | 45 |
| 1962 | Dick Radatz, Bos | 24 | 1994 | Lee Smith, Bal | 33 |
| 1963 | Stu Miller, Bal | 27 | 1995 | Jose Mesa, Clev | 46 |
| 1964 | Dick Radatz, Bos | 29 | 1996 | John Wetteland, NY | 43 |
| 1965 | Ron Kline, Wash | 29 | 1997 | Randy Myers, Balt | 45 |
| 1966 | Jack Aker, KC | 32 | 1998 | Tom Gordon, Bos | 46 |
| 1967 | Minnie Rojas, Cal | 27 | 1999 | Mariano Rivera, NY | 45 |
| 1968 | Al Worthington, Minn | 18 | 2000 | Todd Jones, Det | 42 |
| 1969 | Ron Perranoski, Minn | 31 | 2001 | Mariano Rivera, NY | 50 |
| 1970 | Ron Perranoski, Minn | 34 | 2002 | Eddie Guardado, Minn | 45 |
| 1971 | Ken Sanders, Mil | 31 | 2003 | Keith Foulke, Oak | 43 |
| 1972 | Sparky Lyle, NY | 35 | 2004 | Mariano Rivera, NY | 53 |
| 1973 | John Hiller, Det | 38 | 2005 | Francisco Rodríguez, LA | 45 |
| 1974 | Terry Forster, Chi | 24 | | Bob Wickman, Cle | 45 |
| 1975 | Goose Gossage, Chi | 26 | 2006 | Francisco Rodriguez, LA | 47 |
| 1976 | Sparky Lyle, NY | 23 | 2007 | Joe Borowski, Cle | 45 |
| 1977 | Bill Campbell, Bos | 31 | 2008 | Francisco Rodriguez, LA | 62 |
| 1978 | Goose Gossage, NY | 27 | 2009 | Brian Fuentes, LA | 48 |

# The Commissioners of Baseball

Kenesaw Mountain Landis.....Elected Nov. 12, 1920. Served until his death on Nov. 25, 1944.
Happy Chandler....................Elected April 24, 1945. Served until July 15, 1951.
Ford Frick ..............................Elected Sept. 20, 1951. Served until Nov. 16, 1965.
William Eckert........................Elected Nov. 17, 1965. Served until Dec. 20, 1968.
Bowie Kuhn ...........................Elected Feb. 8, 1969. Served until Sept. 30, 1984.
Peter Ueberroth.....................Elected March 3, 1984. Took office Oct. 1, 1984. Served through March 31, 1989.
A. Bartlett Giamatti ................Elected Sept. 8, 1988. Took office April 1, 1989. Served until his death on Sept. 1, 1989.
Francis Vincent Jr. ................Appointed Acting Commissioner Sept. 2, 1989. Elected Commissioner Sept. 13, 1989. Served through Sept. 7, 1992.
Allan H. (Bud) Selig...............Elected chairman of the executive council and given the powers of interim commissioner on Sept. 9, 1992. Unanimously elected Commissioner July 9, 1998.

# Pro
# Football

Santonio Holmes caught the
Super Bowl XLIII-winning pass
for the Pittsburgh Steelers
with just 42 seconds remaining

AL TIELEMANS

# Steel Rings

In 2008, a topsy-turvy season culminated with a see-saw Super Bowl thriller, where a storied Pittsburgh franchise edged an upstart Arizona team for a record sixth title

## BY HANK HERSCH

DIRECTIONS FOR WINNING Super Bowl XLIII: Start by steering clear of the obvious choice for coach; turn to your top playmakers on offense and defense to pick up momentum; then leave the late-night driving to a quarterback who's intimately familiar with the route. Once you've arrived in Tampa, find a worthy opponent and put on a second half that will go down as one of the most exciting in the history of the game.

Thanks to quarterback Ben Roethlisberger's pinpoint six-yard touchdown pass to wideout Santonio Holmes with 42 seconds remaining, the Pittsburgh Steelers defeated the Arizona Cardinals 27–23 to win their record sixth Super Bowl ring (one for the *other* thumb, as it were). But it wasn't merely Pittsburgh's winning play that put an exemplary coda on the 2008 NFL season: It was the tension that built as Roethlisberger and his counterpart, 37-year-old Kurt Warner, traded clutch throws; as Arizona receiver Larry Fitzgerald answered Pittsburgh outside linebacker James Harrison's 100-yard interception return with a pair of TDs of his own; and as the league's most pitiful franchise of the last six decades—coached by an also-ran for the Steelers' job—rallied to take the lead from its most successful.

"Do or die," said Roethlisberger, recalling his thoughts when he took over on his own 12-yard line, trailing by three with 2:30 remaining. "I've said it all along, I want the ball in my hands."

At 26, Big Ben earned the second title of his five-year career, though in Super Bowl XL, his performance was hardly distinguished. Warner was vying for his second, too. Even though he began the season as Matt Leinart's backup, it was Warner's steady leadership and big-play gunslinging that turned around the losingest team in NFL history. "When you go somewhere and no one expects anything, you're able to be part of change" he said. "When you do something like this, you're a part of it forever."

Still, Arizona dropped four of its last five games and limped into the playoffs with a 9–7 record. No wonder that, as the team reached its first championship game since 1947 by beating the Atlanta Falcons, Carolina Panthers and Philadelphia Eagles—with Fitzgerald reaching triple figures in receiving yards each time—one sign stood out from the 32–25 NFC title win over Philly in Glendale, Arizona: FINALLY A COLD DAY IN HELL.

That must have been what it felt like in New England just 7:33 into the season, when Kansas City Chiefs safety Bernard Pollard hit Patriots quarterback Tom Brady in the backfield, sidelining him for the season with a left knee injury. Seven months

after their Super Bowl loss to the New York Giants ended their bid for a 19–0 season, the Pats had to start over with Brady's understudy for three years, Matt Cassel, who had attempted all of 39 career passes. But the seventh-round pick from USC more than held up his end of the bargain, completing 63.4% of his throws for 3,693 yards and leading New England to an 11–5 record. That wasn't enough to win the AFC East, though: The Miami Dolphins, after going 1–15 in 2007, roared to the divisional title, thanks in part to their Wildcat offense, a direct snap to the tailback that drew more and more imitators throughout the league as the season wore on.

Two first-year QBs burst on the scene in '08, lifting their teams into the postseason. Showing poise and a sure right arm, rookie Matt Ryan, the No. 3 pick out of Boston College, guided the Atlanta Falcons, picked by some to finish last in the league, to an 11–5 mark. "I hate to compare," said Atlanta safety Lawyer Milloy, a former Patriot, "but I see a lot in Matt that I saw in Tom Brady—how to manage a game, poise under pressure, presence in the pocket." Still, that was not enough to win the Rookie of the Year award, which

**After having won only one playoff game since their 1947 NFL title, the Cardinals franchise made a magical and highly unexpected and run to Super Bowl XLIII.**

went instead to former Delaware star Joe Flacco, whose precociously steady hand guided the Baltimore Ravens to nine wins in their last 11 regular-season dates. It also guided them to the AFC title game.

In the divisional round, Flacco & Co. eliminated what appeared to be the league's most balanced and formidable team: the Tennessee Titans, who rode the running punch of LenDale White and rookie Chris Johnson and the runner-punishing of defensive tackle Albert Haynesworth to wins in their first 10 games. Their first loss came against the New York Jets, who prevailed 34–19 in what was to be a high point of '08 for quarterback Brett Favre. When four losses in five games followed, Favre, who had been lured out of retirement before the season, re-retired, albeit only temporarily, as by August he was suited up with the Packers' archenemy, the Minnesota Vikings.

Dallas went in like a lion—"I'll give anybody a loan who bet against the Cowboys,"

JOHN IACONO

burned through 37 coaches in 87 seasons, with Whisenhunt taking the job of head coach. Said Tomlin just days before the Super Bowl, "I'm committed to winning. I'm committed to a brand of football that I believe in. It's a physical game. You win by attrition. You impose your will on your opponent."

So it would seem the Steelers did, at the most unlikely time. Trailing 10–7 with 18 seconds remaining before halftime, Arizona had driven to the Pittsburgh one. Warner tried to hit wideout Anquan Boldin, but Harrison, dropped back in coverage, stepped into the path of the throw and took off. When Fitzgerald tried to bring him down 100 yards later at the goal line, Harrison did a somersault, landing on his head in the end zone. A potential 14–10 deficit at the break was suddenly a 17–7 Pittsburgh lead.

But Warner and Fitzgerald remained undaunted. Over the game's final 11 minutes they hooked up six times for 115 yards—64 of them on a slant pattern that put the Cards up 23–20 late in the fourth quarter. "The challenge," said Fitzgerald, "is when people know things are going to be run through you, but you still deliver."

The final delivery belonged to Roethlisberger. On the last drive he connected with Holmes—the game's MVP—on four throws, including a 40-yard gain that carried to the Arizona six. Then, after failing to haul in a Roethlisberger rocket, Holmes snatched the game-winner with his fingertips in the right corner of the end zone, dragging his outstretched toes.

Deep into the night, the Steelers passed around Lombardi Trophy number 6. "I ain't even touched it!" complained Tomlin before heading to the team bus. Even so, his fingerprints were all over it.

boasted Jerry Jones after his team went 3–0 to start the year—then, in a storm of injuries and internal dissension, went out like a lamb, failing to reach the postseason. The Detroit Lions played like lambs throughout, becoming the first team in NFL history to go 0–16.

Pittsburgh always had something it could rely on: a top-ranked 3–4 D, which finished first against the pass and second against the rush. Its architect was 71-year-old coordinator Dick Lebeau; its linchpin was Harrison, the NFL Defensive Player of the Year, who had a career-high 16 sacks while forcing a league-best seven fumbles; and its overseer was coach Mike Tomlin, the former Minnesota Vikings defensive coordinator. After having just two coaches in four decades, the Rooney family hired Tomlin in 2006, sensing that he was, like Chuck Noll and Bill Cowher, a once-in-a-generation leader.

In choosing Tomlin, the Rooneys passed over their lead top assistants, Ken Whisenhunt and Russ Grimm. They would leave and join forces with the Cardinals, who had

# FOR THE RECORD•2008–2009

## 2008 NFL Final Standings

### American Football Conference

#### EAST DIVISION

|  | W | L | T | Pct | Pts | OP |
|---|---|---|---|---|---|---|
| Miami | 11 | 5 | 0 | .688 | 345 | 317 |
| New England | 11 | 5 | 0 | .688 | 410 | 309 |
| NY Jets | 9 | 7 | 0 | .563 | 405 | 356 |
| Buffalo | 7 | 9 | 0 | .438 | 336 | 342 |

#### NORTH DIVISION

|  | W | L | T | Pct | Pts | OP |
|---|---|---|---|---|---|---|
| Pittsburgh | 12 | 4 | 0 | .750 | 347 | 223 |
| *Baltimore | 11 | 5 | 0 | .688 | 385 | 244 |
| Cincinnati | 4 | 11 | 1 | .281 | 204 | 364 |
| Cleveland | 4 | 12 | 0 | .250 | 232 | 350 |

#### SOUTH DIVISION

|  | W | L | T | Pct | Pts | OP |
|---|---|---|---|---|---|---|
| Tennessee | 13 | 3 | 0 | .813 | 375 | 234 |
| *Indianapolis | 12 | 4 | 0 | .750 | 377 | 298 |
| Houston | 8 | 8 | 0 | .500 | 366 | 394 |
| Jacksonville | 5 | 11 | 0 | .313 | 302 | 367 |

#### WEST DIVISION

|  | W | L | T | Pct | Pts | OP |
|---|---|---|---|---|---|---|
| San Diego | 8 | 8 | 0 | .500 | 439 | 347 |
| Denver | 8 | 8 | 0 | .500 | 370 | 448 |
| Oakland | 5 | 11 | 0 | .313 | 263 | 388 |
| Kansas City | 2 | 14 | 0 | .125 | 291 | 440 |

### National Football Conference

#### EAST DIVISION

|  | W | L | T | Pct | Pts | OP |
|---|---|---|---|---|---|---|
| NY Giants | 12 | 4 | 0 | .750 | 427 | 294 |
| *Philadelphia | 9 | 6 | 1 | .594 | 416 | 289 |
| Dallas | 9 | 7 | 0 | .563 | 362 | 365 |
| Washington | 8 | 8 | 0 | .500 | 265 | 296 |

#### NORTH DIVISION

|  | W | L | T | Pct | Pts | OP |
|---|---|---|---|---|---|---|
| Minnesota | 10 | 6 | 0 | .625 | 379 | 333 |
| Chicago | 9 | 7 | 0 | .563 | 375 | 350 |
| Green Bay | 6 | 10 | 0 | .375 | 419 | 380 |
| Detroit | 0 | 16 | 0 | .000 | 268 | 517 |

#### SOUTH DIVISION

|  | W | L | T | Pct | Pts | OP |
|---|---|---|---|---|---|---|
| Carolina | 12 | 4 | 0 | .750 | 414 | 329 |
| *Atlanta | 11 | 5 | 0 | .688 | 391 | 325 |
| Tampa Bay | 9 | 7 | 0 | .563 | 361 | 323 |
| New Orleans | 8 | 8 | 0 | .500 | 463 | 393 |

#### WEST DIVISION

|  | W | L | T | Pct | Pts | OP |
|---|---|---|---|---|---|---|
| Arizona | 9 | 7 | 0 | .563 | 427 | 426 |
| San Francisco | 7 | 9 | 0 | .438 | 339 | 381 |
| Seattle | 4 | 12 | 0 | .250 | 294 | 392 |
| St. Louis | 2 | 14 | 0 | .125 | 232 | 465 |

* Wild-card team.

## 2008–09 NFL Playoffs

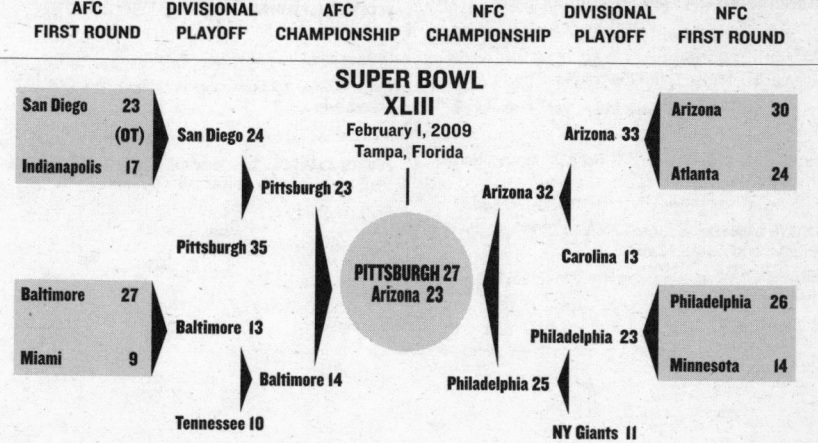

|  | AFC FIRST ROUND | AFC DIVISIONAL PLAYOFF | AFC CHAMPIONSHIP | NFC CHAMPIONSHIP | NFC DIVISIONAL PLAYOFF | NFC FIRST ROUND |
|---|---|---|---|---|---|---|

SUPER BOWL XLIII

February 1, 2009
Tampa, Florida

San Diego 23 (OT)
Indianapolis 17
San Diego 24
Pittsburgh 23
Pittsburgh 35
Baltimore 27
Miami 9
Baltimore 13
Baltimore 14
Tennessee 10

PITTSBURGH 27
Arizona 23

Arizona 30
Atlanta 24
Arizona 33
Arizona 32
Carolina 13
Philadelphia 26
Minnesota 14
Philadelphia 23
Philadelphia 25
NY Giants 11

# NFL Playoff Recaps

## AFC Wild-card Games

| Indianapolis | 7 | 3 | 7 | 0 | 0—17 |
|---|---|---|---|---|---|
| San Diego | 0 | 14 | 0 | 3 | 6—23 |

**FIRST QUARTER:** Indianapolis: TD Addai 1 run (Vinatieri kick), 2:59.

**SECOND QUARTER:** San Diego: TD Tomlinson 3 run (Kaeding kick), 10:15.

Indianapolis: FG Vinatieri 43, 6:46.

San Diego: TD Sproles 3 run (Kaeding kick), 0:42.

**THIRD QUARTER:** Indianapolis: TD Wayne 72 pass from Manning (Vinatieri kick), 8:10.

**FOURTH QUARTER:** San Diego: FG Kaeding 26, 0:31.

**OVERTIME:** San Diego: TD Sproles 22 run, 8:40.

A: 68.082.

| Baltimore | 3 | 10 | 7 | 7—27 |
|---|---|---|---|---|
| Miami | 3 | 0 | 0 | 6—9 |

**FIRST QUARTER:** Miami: FG Carpenter 19, 8:17.

Baltimore: FG Stover 23, 2:47.

**SECOND QUARTER:** Baltimore: TD Reed interception return 64 (Stover kick), 2:30.

Baltimore: FG Stover 31, 0:16.

**THIRD QUARTER:** Baltimore: TD McClain 8 run (Stover kick), 7:33.

**FOURTH QUARTER:** Miami: TD Brown 2 pass from Pennington (extra point blocked), 13:09.

Baltimore: TD Flacco 5 run (Stover kick), 3:53.

A: 72,240.

## NFC Wild-card Games

| Atlanta | 0 | 17 | 0 | 7—24 |
|---|---|---|---|---|
| Arizona | 7 | 7 | 14 | 2—30 |

**FIRST QUARTER:** Arizona: TD Fitzgerald 42 pass from Warner (Rackers kick), 10:28.

**SECOND QUARTER:** Atlanta: FG Elam 30, 10:00.

Arizona: TD Boldin 71 pass from Warner (Rackers Kick), 8:58.

Atlanta: TD Turner 7 run (Elam kick), 2:55.

Atlanta: TD Peelle 71 pass from Ryan (Elam kick), 0:23.

**THIRD QUARTER:** Arizona: TD Rolle 27 fumble return, (Rackers kick), 14:08.

Arizona: TD Hightower 4 run, (Rackers kick), 2:48.

**FOURTH QUARTER:** Arizona: Safety (A. Smith sacked Ryan in end zone), 12:37.

Atlanta: TD White 5 from Ryan (Elam kick), 4:15.

A: 62,848.

| Philadelphia | 6 | 10 | 0 | 10—26 |
|---|---|---|---|---|
| Minnesota | 0 | 14 | 0 | 0—14 |

**FIRST QUARTER:** Philadelphia: FG Akers 43, 6:44.

Philadelphia: FG Akers 51, 0:00.

**SECOND QUARTER:** Minnesota: TD Peterson 40 run (Longwell kick), 11:05.

Philadelphia: FG Akers 31, 7:29.

Philadelphia: TD Samuel interception return 44 (Akers kick), 6:34.

Minnesota: TD Peterson 3 run (Longwell kick), 1:51.

**FOURTH QUARTER:** Philadelphia: TD Westbrook 71 pass from McNabb (Akers kick), 6:37.

Philadelphia: FG Akers 45, 1:55.

A: 61,746.

### AFC Divisional Games

| | | | | |
|---|---|---|---|---|
| Baltimore | 7 | 0 | 0 | 6—13 |
| Tennessee | 7 | 0 | 0 | 3—10 |

**FIRST QUARTER:** Tennessee: TD Johnson 8 run (Bironas kick), 4:38.

Baltimore: TD Mason 48 pass from Flacco (Stover kick), 1:20.

**FOURTH QUARTER:** Baltimore: FG Stover 21, 14:10.

Tennessee: FG Bironas 27, 4:23.

Baltimore: FG Stover 43, 0:53.

A: 69,143.

| | | | | |
|---|---|---|---|---|
| San Diego | 7 | 3 | 0 | 14—24 |
| Pittsburgh | 7 | 7 | 7 | 14—35 |

**FIRST QUARTER:** San Diego: TD Jackson 41 pass from Rivers (Kaeding kick), 12:59.

Pittsburgh: TD Holmes 67 punt return (Reed kick), 7:41.

**SECOND QUARTER:** San Diego: FG Kaeding 42, 1:56.

Pittsburgh: TD Parker 3 run (Reed kick), 0:40.

**THIRD QUARTER:** Pittsburgh: TD Miller 8 pass from Roethlisberger (Reed kick), 7:04.

**FOURTH QUARTER:** Pittsburgh: TD Russell 1 run (Reed kick), 12:52.

San Diego: TD Naanee 4 pass from Rivers (Kaeding kick), 9:09.

Pittsburgh: TD Parker 16 run (Reed kick), 4:11.

San Diego: TD Sproles 62 pass from Rivers (Kaeding kick), 1:53.

A: 63,899.

### NFC Divisional Games

| | | | | |
|---|---|---|---|---|
| Arizona | 14 | 13 | 3 | 3—33 |
| Carolina | 7 | 0 | 0 | 6—13 |

**FIRST QUARTER:** Carolina: TD Stewart 9 run (Kasay kick), 11:56.

Arizona: TD Hightower 3 pass from Warner (Rackers kick), 2:43.

Arizona: TD James 4 run (Rackers kick), 1:47.

**SECOND QUARTER:** Arizona: FG Rackers 49, 10:16.

Arizona: FG Rackers 30, 5:28.

Arizona: TD Fitzgerald 29 pass from Warner (Rackers kick), 3:32.

**THIRD QUARTER:** Arizona: FG Rackers 33, 4:40.

**FOURTH QUARTER:** Arizona: FG Rackers 20, 3:10.

Carolina: TD Smith 8 pass from Delhomme (2-pt. conversion failed, 0:50.

A: 73,695.

| | | | | |
|---|---|---|---|---|
| Philadelphia | 7 | 3 | 3 | 10—23 |
| NY Giants | 3 | 5 | 3 | 0—11 |

**FIRST QUARTER:** NY Giants: FG Carney 22, 9:59.

Philadelphia: TD McNabb 1 run (Akers kick), 5:58.

**SECOND QUARTER:** NY Giants: Safety (McNabb intentional grounding in end zone), 12:34.

NY Giants: FG Carney 34, 1:33.

Philadelphia: FG Akers 25, 0:00.

**THIRD QUARTER:** NY Giants: FG Carney 36, 12:33.

Philadelphia: FG Akers 35, 7:45.

**FOURTH QUARTER:** Philadelphia: TD Celek 1 pass from McNabb (Akers kick), 14:56.

Philadelphia: FG Akers 20, 3:58.

A: 79,193.

# NFL Playoff Recaps (Cont.)

## AFC Championship

| | | | | |
|---|---|---|---|---|
| Baltimore | 0 | 7 | 0 | 7—14 |
| Pittsburgh | 6 | 7 | 3 | 7—23 |

**FIRST QUARTER:** Pittsburgh: FG Reed 34, 11:22.
Pittsburgh: FG Reed 42, 6:11.

**SECOND QUARTER:** Pittsburgh: TD Holmes 65 pass from Roethlisberger (Reed kick), 13:58.
Baltimore: TD McGahee 3 run (Stover kick), 2:40.

**THIRD QUARTER:** Pittsburgh: FG Reed 46, 3:38.

**FOURTH QUARTER:** Baltimore: TD McGahee 1 run (Stover kick), 9:29.
Pittsburgh: TD Polamalu interception return 40 (Reed kick), 4:24.

A: 65,350.

## NFC Championship

| | | | | |
|---|---|---|---|---|
| Philadelphia | 3 | 3 | 13 | 6—25 |
| Arizona | 7 | 17 | 0 | 8—32 |

**FIRST QUARTER:** Arizona: TD Fitzgerald 62 pass from Warner (Rackers kick), 9:20.
Philadelphia: FG Akers 45, 4:43.

**SECOND QUARTER:** Arizona: TD Fitzgerald 9 pass from Warner (Rackers kick), 13:19.
Philadelphia: FG Akers 33, 9:02.
Arizona: TD Fitzgerald 1 pass from Warner (Rackers kick), 3:06.
Arizona: FG Rackers 49, 0:00.

**THIRD QUARTER:** Philadelphia: TD Celek 6 pass from McNabb (Akers kick), 4:08.
Philadelphia: TD Celek 31 pass from McNabb (PAT failed), 0:49.

**FOURTH QUARTER:** Philadelphia: TD Jackson 62 pass from McNabb (2-pt. conversion failed), 10:45.
Arizona: TD Hightower 8 pass from Warner (2-pt. conversion Patrick pass from Warner), 2:53.

A: 70,650.

# Super Bowl XLIII Recap

| | | | | |
|---|---|---|---|---|
| Pittsburgh | 3 | 14 | 3 | 7—27 |
| Arizona | 0 | 7 | 0 | 16—23 |

**FIRST QUARTER:** Pittsburgh: FG Reed 18, 9:45.
**Pittsburgh 3-0.**

**SECOND QUARTER:** Pittsburgh: TD Russell 1 run (Reed kick), 14:01.
**Pittsburgh 10-0.**
Arizona: TD Patrick 1 pass from Warner (Rackers kick), 8:34.
**Pittsburgh 10-7.**
Pittsburgh: TD Harrison 100 INT run (Reed kick), 0:00.
**Pittsburgh 17-7.**

**THIRD QUARTER:** Pittsburgh: FG Reed 21, 2:11.
**Pittsburgh 20-7.**

**FOURTH QUARTER:** Arizona: TD Fitzgerald 1 pass from Warner (Rackers kick), 7:33.
**Pittsburgh 20-14.**
Arizona: Safety (Hartwig, offensive holding penalty in end zone), 2:58.
**Pittsburgh 20-16.**
Arizona: TD Fitzgerald 64 pass from Warner (Rackers kick), 2:37.
**Arizona 23-20.**
Pittsburgh: TD Holmes 6 pass from Roethlisberger (Reed kick), 0:35.
**Pittsburgh 27-23.**

A: 70,774.

# Super Bowl XLIII Box Score

## Team Statistics

| | Pittsburgh | Arizona |
|---|---|---|
| FIRST DOWNS | 20 | 23 |
| Rushing | 58 | 33 |
| Passing | 21–30 | 31–43 |
| Penalty | 7–56 | 11–106 |
| THIRD DOWN EFF | 4–10 | 3–8 |
| FOURTH DOWN EFF | 0–0 | 0–0 |
| TOTAL NET YARDS | 292 | 407 |
| Total plays | 58 | 57 |
| Avg gain | 5.0 | 7.1 |
| NET YARDS RUSHING | 58 | 33 |
| Rushes | 25 | 12 |
| Avg per rush | 2.3 | 2.8 |
| NET YARDS PASSING | 234 | 374 |
| Completed–Att–Int | 21–30–1 | 31–43–1 |
| Yards per pass | 7.8 | 8.7 |
| Sacked–yards lost | 2–22 | 2–3 |
| Had intercepted | 1 | 0 |
| PUNTS–Avg | 3–46.3 | 5–36.0 |
| PENALTIES–Yds | 7–56 | 11–106 |
| FUMBLES–Lost | 0–0 | 1–1 |

## Passing

### PITTSBURGH

| | Comp | Att | Yds | Int | TD |
|---|---|---|---|---|---|
| Roethlisberger | 21 | 30 | 256 | 1 | 1 |

### ARIZONA

| | Comp | Att | Yds | Int | TD |
|---|---|---|---|---|---|
| Warner | 31 | 43 | 377 | 1 | 3 |

## Rushing

### PITTSBURGH

| | No. | Yds | Lg | TD |
|---|---|---|---|---|
| Parker | 19 | 53 | 15 | 0 |
| Moore | 1 | 6 | 6 | 0 |
| Roethlisberger | 4 | 2 | 4 | 0 |
| Russell | 2 | -3 | 1 | 1 |

### ARIZONA

| | No. | Yds | Lg | TD |
|---|---|---|---|---|
| James | 9 | 33 | 9 | 0 |
| Warner | 1 | 0 | 0 | 0 |
| Hightower | 1 | 0 | 0 | 0 |
| Arrington | 1 | 0 | 0 | 0 |

## Receiving

### PITTSBURGH

| | No. | Yds | Lg | TD |
|---|---|---|---|---|
| Holmes | 9 | 131 | 40 | 1 |
| Miller | 5 | 57 | 21 | 0 |
| Ward | 2 | 43 | 38 | 0 |
| Washington | 1 | 11 | 11 | 0 |
| Davis | 1 | 6 | 6 | 0 |
| Spaeth | 1 | 6 | 6 | 0 |
| Moore | 1 | 4 | 4 | 0 |
| Parker | 1 | -2 | 0 | 0 |

### ARIZONA

| | No. | Yds | Lg | TD |
|---|---|---|---|---|
| Fitzgerald | 7 | 127 | 64 | 2 |
| Boldin | 8 | 84 | 45 | 0 |
| Breaston | 6 | 71 | 23 | 0 |
| Arrington | 2 | 35 | 22 | 0 |
| James | 4 | 28 | 11 | 0 |
| Urban | 1 | 18 | 18 | 0 |
| Hightower | 2 | 13 | 10 | 0 |
| Patrick | 1 | 1 | 1 | 1 |

## Defense

### PITTSBURGH

| | Tck | Ast | Int | Sack |
|---|---|---|---|---|
| Taylor | 8 | 3 | 0 | 0 |
| Farrior | 7 | 1 | 0 | 0 |
| Timmons | 5 | 0 | 0 | 0 |
| Keisel | 5 | 1 | 0 | 0 |
| Clark | 5 | 3 | 0 | 0 |
| Woodley | 4 | 1 | 0 | 2 |
| Harrison | 4 | 1 | 1 | 0 |
| McFadden | 3 | 0 | 0 | 0 |
| Townsend | 3 | 1 | 0 | 0 |
| Madison | 2 | 0 | 0 | 0 |
| Carter | 2 | 0 | 0 | 0 |
| Gay | 2 | 0 | 0 | 0 |
| Foote | 2 | 0 | 0 | 0 |
| Hampton | 2 | 1 | 0 | 0 |
| Polamalu | 2 | 2 | 0 | 0 |
| Davis | 1 | 0 | 0 | 0 |
| Moore | 1 | 0 | 0 | 0 |
| Russell | 1 | 0 | 0 | 0 |
| Bailey | 1 | 0 | 0 | 0 |
| Kirschke | 1 | 0 | 0 | 0 |
| Holmes | 1 | 1 | 0 | 0 |
| Smith | 1 | 1 | 0 | 0 |

### ARIZONA

| | Tck | Ast | Int | Sack |
|---|---|---|---|---|
| Dansby | 8 | 3 | 1 | 0 |
| Wilson | 7 | 0 | 0 | 0 |
| Hayes | 7 | 3 | 0 | 0 |
| Okeafor | 6 | 0 | 0 | 0 |
| Dockett | 6 | 1 | 0 | 2 |
| Hood | 6 | 1 | 0 | 0 |
| Rodgers-Cromartie | 5 | 0 | 0 | 0 |
| Beisel | 5 | 3 | 0 | 0 |
| Rolle | 3 | 2 | 0 | 0 |
| Campbell | 2 | 0 | 0 | 0 |
| Brown | 2 | 0 | 0 | 0 |
| Smith | 2 | 1 | 0 | 0 |
| LaBoy | 1 | 0 | 0 | 0 |
| Hightower | 1 | 0 | 0 | 0 |
| Francisco | 1 | 0 | 0 | 0 |
| Iwebema | 1 | 0 | 0 | 0 |
| Brown | 1 | 0 | 0 | 0 |
| Adams | 1 | 0 | 0 | 0 |
| Watson | 1 | 0 | 0 | 0 |
| Morey | 1 | 0 | 0 | 0 |

# 2008 Associated Press All-Pro Team

## First Team

### OFFENSE

| | |
|---|---|
| Peyton Manning, Indianapolis | Quarterback |
| Adrian Peterson, Minnesota | Running Back |
| Michael Turner, Atlanta | Running Back |
| Le'Ron McClain, Baltimore | Fullback |
| Tony Gonzalez, Kansas City | Tight End |
| Andre Johnson, Houston | Wide Receiver |
| Larry Fitzgerald, Arizona | Wide Receiver |
| Jordan Gross, Carolina | Tackle |
| Michael Roos, Tennessee | Tackle |
| Chris Snee, NY Giants | Guard |
| Steve Hutchinson, Minnesota | Guard |
| Kevin Mawae, Tennessee | Center |

### DEFENSE

| | |
|---|---|
| Jared Allen, Minnesota | Defensive End |
| Justin Tuck, NY Giants | Defensive End |
| Kevin Williams, Minnesota | Defensive Tackle |
| Albert Haynesworth, Tennessee | Defensive Tackle |
| DeMarcus Ware, Dallas | Linebacker |
| James Harrison, Pittsburgh | Linebacker |
| Ray Lewis, Baltimore | Linebacker |
| Jon Beason, Carolina | Linebacker |
| Nnamdi Asomugha, Oakland | Cornerback |
| Cortland Finnegan, Tennessee | Cornerback |
| Ed Reed, Baltimore | Safety |
| Troy Polamalu, Pittsburgh | Safety |

### SPECIALISTS

| | |
|---|---|
| Stephen Gostkowski, New England | Kicker |
| Leon Washington, NY Jets | Kick Returner |
| Shane Lechler, Oakland | Punter |

## Second Team

### OFFENSE

| | |
|---|---|
| Drew Brees, New Orleans | Quarterback |
| DeAngelo Williams, Carolina | Running Back |
| Clinton Portis, Washington | Running Back |
| Madison Hedgecock, NY Giants | Fullback |
| Jason Witten, Dallas | Tight End |
| Steve Smith, Carolina | Wide Receiver |
| Wes Welker, New England | Wide Receiver |
| Ryan Clady, Denver | Tackle |
| David Stewart, Tennessee (tie) | Tackle |
| Walter Jones, Seattle (tie) | Tackle |
| Jason Peters, Buffalo (tie) | Tackle |
| David Diehl, NY Giants (tie) | Tackle |
| Joe Thomas, Cleveland (tie) | Tackle |
| Kris Dielman, San Diego | Guard |
| Alan Faneca, NY Jets | Guard |
| Shaun O'Hara, NY Giants | Center |

### DEFENSE

| | |
|---|---|
| Julius Peppers, Carolina | Defensive End |
| John Abraham, Atlanta | Defensive End |
| Kris Jenkins, NY Jets | Defensive Tackle |
| Haloti Ngata, Baltimore | Defensive Tackle |
| Joey Porter, Miami | Linebacker |
| Terrell Suggs, Baltimore | Linebacker |
| Patrick Willis, San Francisco | Linebacker |
| James Farrior, Pittsburgh | Linebacker |
| Charles Woodson, Green Bay | Cornerback |
| Antoine Winfield, Minnesota | Cornerback |
| Adrian Wilson, Arizona | Safety |
| Quintin Mikell, Philadelphia (tie) | Safety |
| Nick Collins, Green Bay (tie) | Safety |

### SPECIALISTS

| | |
|---|---|
| John Carney, NY Giants | Kicker |
| Clifton Smith, Tampa Bay | Kick Returner |
| Donnie Jones, Miami | Punter |

## BALTIMORE RAVENS (11-5)

| | | |
|---|---|---|
| 17 | CINCINNATI | 10 |
| 28 | CLEVELAND | 10 |
| *20 | at Pittsburgh | 23 |
| 10 | TENNESSEE | 13 |
| 3 | at Indianapolis | 31 |
| 27 | at Miami | 13 |
| 29 | OAKLAND | 10 |
| 37 | at Cleveland | 27 |
| 41 | at Houston | 13 |
| 10 | at NY Giants | 30 |
| 36 | PHILADELPHIA | 7 |
| 34 | at Cincinnati | 3 |
| 24 | WASHINGTON | 10 |
| 9 | PITTSBURGH | 13 |
| 33 | at Dallas | 24 |
| 27 | JACKSONVILLE | 7 |
| 385 | | 244 |

## BUFFALO BILLS (7-9)

| | | |
|---|---|---|
| 34 | SEATTLE | 10 |
| 20 | at Jacksonville | 16 |
| 24 | OAKLAND | 23 |
| 31 | at St. Louis | 14 |
| 17 | at Arizona | 41 |
| 23 | SAN DIEGO | 14 |
| 16 | at Miami | 25 |
| 17 | NY JETS | 26 |
| 10 | at New England | 20 |
| 27 | CLEVELAND | 29 |
| 54 | at Kansas City | 31 |
| 3 | SAN FRANCISCO | 10 |
| 3 | MIAMI | 16 |
| 27 | at NY Jets | 31 |
| 30 | at Denver | 23 |
| 0 | NEW ENGLAND | 13 |
| 336 | | 342 |

## CINCINNATI BENGALS (4-11-1)

| | | |
|---|---|---|
| 10 | at Baltimore | 17 |
| 7 | TENNESSEE | 24 |
| *23 | at NY Giants | 26 |
| 12 | CLEVELAND | 20 |
| 22 | at Dallas | 31 |
| 14 | at NY Jets | 26 |
| 10 | PITTSBURGH | 38 |
| 6 | at Houston | 35 |
| 21 | JACKSONVILLE | 19 |
| *13 | PHILADELPHIA | 13 |
| 10 | at Pittsburgh | 27 |
| 3 | BALTIMORE | 34 |
| 3 | at Indianapolis | 35 |
| 20 | WASHINGTON | 13 |
| 14 | at Cleveland | 0 |
| 16 | KANSAS CITY | 6 |
| 204 | | 364 |

## CLEVELAND BROWNS (4-12)

| | | |
|---|---|---|
| 10 | DALLAS | 28 |
| 6 | PITTSBURGH | 10 |
| 10 | at Baltimore | 28 |
| 20 | at Cincinnati | 12 |
| 35 | NY GIANTS | 14 |
| 11 | at Washington | 14 |
| 23 | at Jacksonville | 17 |
| 27 | BALTIMORE | 37 |
| 30 | DENVER | 34 |
| 29 | at Buffalo | 27 |
| 6 | HOUSTON | 16 |
| 6 | INDIANAPOLIS | 10 |
| 9 | at Tennessee | 28 |
| 10 | at Philadelphia | 30 |
| 0 | CINCINNATI | 14 |
| 0 | at Pittsburgh | 31 |
| 232 | | 350 |

## DENVER BRONCOS (8-8)

| | | |
|---|---|---|
| 41 | at Oakland | 14 |
| 39 | SAN DIEGO | 38 |
| 34 | NEW ORLEANS | 32 |
| 19 | at Kansas City | 33 |
| 16 | TAMPA BAY | 13 |
| 17 | JACKSONVILLE | 24 |
| 7 | at New England | 41 |
| 17 | MIAMI | 26 |
| 34 | at Cleveland | 30 |
| 24 | at Atlanta | 20 |
| 10 | OAKLAND | 31 |
| 34 | at NY Jets | 17 |
| 24 | KANSAS CITY | 17 |
| 10 | at Carolina | 30 |
| 23 | BUFFALO | 30 |
| 21 | at San Diego | 52 |
| 370 | | 448 |

## HOUSTON TEXANS (8-8)

| | | |
|---|---|---|
| 17 | at Pittsburgh | 38 |
| 12 | at Tennessee | 31 |
| *27 | at Jacksonville | 30 |
| 27 | INDIANAPOLIS | 31 |
| 29 | MIAMI | 28 |
| 28 | DETROIT | 21 |
| 35 | CINCINNATI | 6 |
| 21 | at Minnesota | 28 |
| 13 | BALTIMORE | 41 |
| 27 | at Indianapolis | 33 |
| 16 | at Cleveland | 6 |
| 30 | JACKSONVILLE | 17 |
| 24 | at Green Bay | 21 |
| 13 | TENNESSEE | 12 |
| 16 | at Oakland | 27 |
| 31 | CHICAGO | 24 |
| 366 | | 394 |

## INDIANAPOLIS COLTS (12-4)

| | | |
|---|---|---|
| 13 | CHICAGO | 29 |
| 18 | at Minnesota | 15 |
| 21 | JACKSONVILLE | 23 |
| 31 | at Houston | 27 |
| 31 | BALTIMORE | 3 |
| 14 | at Green Bay | 34 |
| 21 | at Tennessee | 31 |
| 18 | NEW ENGLAND | 15 |
| 24 | at Pittsburgh | 20 |
| 33 | HOUSTON | 27 |
| 23 | at San Diego | 20 |
| 10 | at Cleveland | 6 |
| 35 | CINCINNATI | 3 |
| 31 | DETROIT | 21 |
| 31 | at Jacksonville | 24 |
| 23 | TENNESSEE | 0 |
| 377 | | 298 |

## JACKSONVILLE JAGUARS (5-11)

| | | |
|---|---|---|
| 10 | at Tennessee | 17 |
| 16 | BUFFALO | 20 |
| 23 | at Indianapolis | 21 |
| *30 | HOUSTON | 27 |
| 21 | PITTSBURGH | 26 |
| 24 | at Denver | 17 |
| 17 | CLEVELAND | 23 |
| 19 | at Cincinnati | 21 |
| 38 | at Detroit | 14 |
| 14 | TENNESSEE | 24 |
| 12 | MINNESOTA | 30 |
| 17 | at Houston | 30 |
| 10 | at Chicago | 23 |
| 20 | GREEN BAY | 16 |
| 24 | INDIANAPOLIS | 31 |
| 7 | at Baltimore | 27 |
| 302 | | 367 |

## KANSAS CITY CHIEFS (2-14)

| | | |
|---|---|---|
| 10 | at New England | 17 |
| 8 | OAKLAND | 23 |
| 14 | at Atlanta | 38 |
| 33 | DENVER | 19 |
| 0 | at Carolina | 34 |
| 10 | TENNESSEE | 34 |
| 24 | at NY Jets | 28 |
| *27 | TAMPA BAY | 30 |
| 19 | at San Diego | 20 |
| 20 | NEW ORLEANS | 30 |
| 31 | BUFFALO | 54 |
| 20 | at Oakland | 13 |
| 17 | at Dennver | 24 |
| 21 | SAN DIEGO | 22 |
| 31 | MIAMI | 38 |
| 6 | at Cincinnati | 16 |
| 291 | | 440 |

## MIAMI DOLPHINS (11-5)

| | | | | | |
|---|---|---|---|---|---|
| 14 | NY JETS | 20 | 21 | SEATTLE | 19 |
| 10 | at Arizona | 31 | 17 | OAKLAND | 15 |
| 38 | at New England | 13 | 28 | NEW ENGLAND | 48 |
| 17 | SAN DIEGO | 10 | 16 | at St. Louis | 12 |
| 28 | at Houston | 29 | 16 | at Buffalo | 3 |
| 13 | BALTIMORE | 27 | 14 | SAN FRANCISCO | 9 |
| 25 | BUFFALO | 16 | 38 | at Kansas City | 31 |
| 26 | at Denver | 17 | 24 | at NY Jets | 17 |
| | | | 345 | | 317 |

* overtime

### NEW ENGLAND PATRIOTS (11–5)

| | | |
|---|---|---|
| 17 | KANSAS CITY | 10 |
| 19 | at NY Jets | 10 |
| 13 | MIAMI | 38 |
| 30 | at San Francisco | 21 |
| 10 | at San Diego | 30 |
| 41 | DENVER | 7 |
| 23 | ST. LOUIS | 16 |
| 15 | at Indianapolis | 18 |
| 20 | BUFFALO | 10 |
| *31 | NY JETS | 34 |
| 48 | at Miami | 28 |
| 10 | PITTSBURGH | 33 |
| 24 | at Seattle | 21 |
| 49 | at Oakland | 26 |
| 47 | ARIZONA | 7 |
| 13 | at Buffalo | 0 |
| 410 | | 309 |

### NEW YORK JETS (9–7)

| | | |
|---|---|---|
| 20 | at Miami | 14 |
| 10 | NEW ENGLAND | 19 |
| 29 | at San Diego | 48 |
| 56 | ARIZONA | 35 |
| 26 | CINCINNATI | 14 |
| *13 | at Oakland | 16 |
| 28 | KANSAS CITY | 24 |
| 26 | at Buffalo | 17 |
| 47 | ST. LOUIS | 3 |
| *34 | at New England | 31 |
| 34 | at Tennessee | 13 |
| 17 | DENVER | 34 |
| 14 | at San Francisco | 24 |
| 31 | BUFFALO | 27 |
| 3 | at Seattle | 13 |
| 17 | MIAMI | 24 |
| 405 | | 356 |

### OAKLAND RAIDERS (5–11)

| | | |
|---|---|---|
| 14 | DENVER | 41 |
| 23 | at Kansas City | 8 |
| 23 | at Buffalo | 24 |
| 18 | SAN DIEGO | 28 |
| 3 | at New Orleans | 34 |
| *16 | NY JETS | 13 |
| 10 | at Baltimore | 29 |
| 0 | ATLANTA | 24 |
| 6 | CAROLINA | 17 |
| 15 | at Miami | 17 |
| 31 | at Denver | 10 |
| 13 | KANSAS CITY | 20 |
| 7 | at San Diego | 34 |
| 26 | NEW ENGLAND | 49 |
| 27 | HOUSTON | 16 |
| 31 | at Tampa Bay | 24 |
| 263 | | 388 |

### PITTSBURGH STEELERS (12–4)

| | | |
|---|---|---|
| 38 | HOUSTON | 17 |
| 10 | at Cleveland | 6 |
| 6 | at Philadelphia | 15 |
| *23 | BALTIMORE | 20 |
| 26 | at Jacksonville | 21 |
| 38 | at Cincinnati | 10 |
| 14 | NY GIANTS | 21 |
| 23 | at Washington | 6 |
| 20 | INDIANAPOLIS | 24 |
| 11 | SAN DIEGO | 10 |
| 27 | CINCINNATI | 10 |
| 33 | at New England | 10 |
| 20 | DALLAS | 13 |
| 13 | at Baltimore | 9 |
| 14 | at Tennessee | 31 |
| 31 | CLEVELAND | 0 |
| 347 | | 223 |

### SAN DIEGO CHARGERS (8–8)

| | | |
|---|---|---|
| 24 | CAROLINA | 26 |
| 38 | at Denver | 39 |
| 48 | NY JETS | 29 |
| 28 | at Oakland | 18 |
| 10 | at Miami | 17 |
| 30 | NEW ENGLAND | 10 |
| 14 | at Buffalo | 23 |
| 32 | at New Orleans | 37 |
| 20 | KANSAS CITY | 19 |
| 10 | at Pittsburgh | 11 |
| 23 | INDIANAPOLIS | 23 |
| 16 | ATLANTA | 22 |
| 34 | OAKLAND | 7 |
| 22 | at Kansas City | 21 |
| 41 | at Tampa Bay | 24 |
| 52 | DENVER | 21 |
| 439 | | 347 |

### TENNESSEE TITANS (13–3)

| | | |
|---|---|---|
| 17 | JACKSONVILLE | 10 |
| 24 | at Cincinnati | 7 |
| 31 | HOUSTON | 12 |
| 30 | MINNESOTA | 17 |
| 13 | at Baltimore | 10 |
| 34 | at Kansas City | 10 |
| 31 | INDIANAPOLIS | 21 |
| *19 | GREEN BAY | 16 |
| 21 | at Chicago | 14 |
| 24 | at Jacksonville | 14 |
| 13 | NY JETS | 34 |
| 47 | at Detroit | 10 |
| 28 | CLEVELAND | 9 |
| 12 | at Houston | 13 |
| 31 | PITTSBURGH | 14 |
| 0 | at Indianapolis | 23 |
| 375 | | 234 |

## 2008 NFC Team-by-Team Results

### ARIZONA CARDINALS (9–7)

| | | |
|---|---|---|
| 23 | at San Francisco | 13 |
| 31 | MIAMI | 10 |
| 17 | at Washington | 24 |
| 35 | at NY Jets | 56 |
| 41 | BUFFALO | 17 |
| *30 | DALLAS | 24 |
| 23 | at Carolina | 27 |
| 34 | at St. Louis | 13 |
| 29 | SAN FRANCISCO | 24 |
| 26 | at Seattle | 20 |
| 29 | NY GIANTS | 37 |
| 20 | at Philadelphia | 48 |
| 34 | ST. LOUIS | 10 |
| 14 | MINNESOTA | 35 |
| 7 | at New England | 47 |
| 34 | SEATTLE | 21 |
| 427 | | 426 |

### ATLANTA FALCONS (11–5)

| | | |
|---|---|---|
| 34 | DETROIT | 21 |
| 9 | at Tampa Bay | 24 |
| 38 | KANSAS CITY | 14 |
| 9 | at Carolina | 24 |
| 27 | at Green Bay | 24 |
| 22 | CHICAGO | 20 |
| 14 | at Philadelphia | 27 |
| 24 | at Oakland | 0 |
| 34 | NEW ORLEANS | 20 |
| 20 | DENVER | 24 |
| 45 | CAROLINA | 28 |
| 22 | at San Diego | 16 |
| 25 | at New Orleans | 29 |
| *13 | TAMPA BAY | 10 |
| 24 | at Minnesota | 17 |
| 31 | ST. LOUIS | 27 |
| 391 | | 325 |

### CAROLINA PANTHERS (12–4)

| | | |
|---|---|---|
| 26 | at San Diego | 24 |
| 20 | CHICAGO | 17 |
| 10 | at Minnesota | 20 |
| 24 | ATLANTA | 9 |
| 34 | KANSAS CITY | 0 |
| 3 | at Tampa Bay | 27 |
| 30 | NEW ORLEANS | 7 |
| 27 | ARIZONA | 23 |
| 17 | at Oakland | 6 |
| 31 | DETROIT | 22 |
| 28 | at Atlanta | 45 |
| 35 | at Green Bay | 31 |
| 38 | TAMPA BAY | 23 |
| 30 | DENVER | 10 |
| *28 | at NY Giants | 34 |
| 33 | at New Orleans | 31 |
| 414 | | 329 |

* overtime

## CHICAGO BEARS (9-7)

| | | |
|---|---|---|
| 29 | at Indianapolis | 13 |
| 17 | at Carolina | 20 |
| *24 | TAMPA BAY | 27 |
| 24 | PHILADELPHIA | 20 |
| 34 | at Detroit | 7 |
| 20 | at Atlanta | 22 |
| 48 | MINNESOTA | 41 |
| 27 | DETROIT | 23 |
| 14 | TENNESSEE | 21 |
| 3 | at Green Bay | 37 |
| 27 | at St. Louis | 3 |
| 14 | at Minnesota | 34 |
| 23 | JACKSONVILLE | 10 |
| *27 | NEW ORLEANS | 24 |
| *20 | GREEN BAY | 17 |
| 24 | at Houston | 31 |
| 375 | | 350 |

## DALLAS COWBOYS (9-7)

| | | |
|---|---|---|
| 28 | at Cleveland | 10 |
| 41 | PHILADELPHIA | 37 |
| 27 | at Green Bay | 16 |
| 24 | WASHINGTON | 26 |
| 31 | CINCINNATI | 22 |
| *24 | at Arizona | 30 |
| 14 | at St. Louis | 34 |
| 13 | TAMPA BAY | 9 |
| 14 | at NY Giants | 35 |
| 14 | at Washington | 10 |
| 35 | SAN FRANCISCO | 22 |
| 34 | SEATTLE | 9 |
| 13 | at Pittsburgh | 20 |
| 20 | NY GIANTS | 8 |
| 24 | BALTIMORE | 33 |
| 6 | at Philadelphia | 44 |
| 362 | | 365 |

## DETROIT LIONS (0-16)

| | | |
|---|---|---|
| 21 | at Atlanta | 34 |
| 25 | GREEN BAY | 48 |
| 13 | at San Francisco | 31 |
| 7 | CHICAGO | 34 |
| 10 | at Minnesota | 12 |
| 21 | at Houston | 28 |
| 17 | WASHINGTON | 25 |
| 23 | at Chicago | 27 |
| 14 | JACKSONVILLE | 38 |
| 22 | at Carolina | 31 |
| 20 | TAMPA BAY | 38 |
| 10 | TENNESSEE | 47 |
| 16 | MINNESOTA | 20 |
| 21 | at Indianapolis | 31 |
| 7 | NEW ORLEANS | 42 |
| 21 | at Green Bay | 31 |
| 268 | | 517 |

## GREEN BAY PACKERS (6-10)

| | | |
|---|---|---|
| 24 | MINNESOTA | 19 |
| 48 | at Detroit | 25 |
| 16 | DALLAS | 27 |
| 21 | at Tampa Bay | 30 |
| 24 | ATLANTA | 27 |
| 27 | at Seattle | 17 |
| 34 | INDIANAPOLIS | 14 |
| *16 | at Tennessee | 19 |
| 27 | at Minnesota | 28 |
| 37 | CHICAGO | 3 |
| 29 | at New Orleans | 51 |
| 31 | CAROLINA | 35 |
| 21 | HOUSTON | 24 |
| 16 | at Jacksonville | 20 |
| *17 | at Chicago | 20 |
| 31 | DETROIT | 21 |
| 419 | | 380 |

## MINNESOTA VIKINGS (10-6)

| | | |
|---|---|---|
| 19 | at Green Bay | 24 |
| 15 | INDIANAPOLIS | 18 |
| 20 | CAROLINA | 10 |
| 17 | at Tennessee | 30 |
| 30 | at New Orleans | 27 |
| 12 | DETROIT | 10 |
| 41 | at Chicago | 48 |
| 28 | HOUSTON | 21 |
| 28 | GREEN BAY | 27 |
| 13 | at Tampa Bay | 19 |
| 30 | at Jacksonville | 12 |
| 34 | CHICAGO | 14 |
| 20 | at Detroit | 16 |
| 35 | at Arizona | 14 |
| 17 | ATLANTA | 24 |
| 20 | NY GIANTS | 19 |
| 379 | | 333 |

## NEW ORLEANS SAINTS (8-8)

| | | |
|---|---|---|
| 24 | TAMPA BAY | 20 |
| 24 | at Washington | 29 |
| 32 | at Denver | 34 |
| 31 | SAN FRANCISCO | 17 |
| 27 | MINNESOTA | 30 |
| 34 | OAKLAND | 3 |
| 7 | at Carolina | 30 |
| 37 | SAN DIEGO | 32 |
| 20 | at Atlanta | 34 |
| 30 | at Kansas City | 20 |
| 51 | GREEN BAY | 29 |
| 20 | at Tampa Bay | 23 |
| 29 | ATLANTA | 25 |
| *24 | at Chicago | 27 |
| 42 | at Detroit | 7 |
| 31 | CAROLINA | 33 |
| 463 | | 393 |

## NEW YORK GIANTS (12-4)

| | | |
|---|---|---|
| 16 | WASHINGTON | 7 |
| 41 | at St. Louis | 13 |
| *26 | CINCINNATI | 23 |
| 44 | SEATTLE | 6 |
| 14 | at Cleveland | 35 |
| 29 | SAN FRANCISCO | 17 |
| 21 | at Pittsburgh | 14 |
| 35 | DALLAS | 14 |
| 36 | at Philadelphia | 31 |
| 30 | BALTIMORE | 10 |
| 37 | at Arizona | 29 |
| 23 | at Washington | 7 |
| 14 | PHILADELPHIA | 20 |
| 8 | at Dallas | 20 |
| *34 | CAROLINA | 28 |
| 19 | at Minnesota | 20 |
| 427 | | 294 |

## PHILADELPHIA EAGLES (9-6-1)

| | | |
|---|---|---|
| 38 | ST. LOUIS | 3 |
| 37 | at Dallas | 41 |
| 15 | PITTSBURGH | 6 |
| 20 | at Chicago | 24 |
| 17 | WASHINGTON | 23 |
| 40 | at San Francisco | 26 |
| 27 | ATLANTA | 14 |
| 26 | at Seattle | 7 |
| 31 | NY GIANTS | 36 |
| *13 | at Cincinnati | 13 |
| 7 | at Baltimore | 36 |
| 48 | ARIZONA | 20 |
| 20 | at NY Giants | 14 |
| 30 | CLEVELAND | 10 |
| 3 | at Washington | 10 |
| 44 | DALLAS | 6 |
| 416 | | 289 |

## SAN FRANCISCO 49ERS (7-9)

| | | |
|---|---|---|
| 13 | ARIZONA | 23 |
| *33 | at Seattle | 30 |
| 31 | DETROIT | 13 |
| 17 | at New Orleans | 31 |
| 21 | NEW ENGLAND | 30 |
| 26 | PHILADELPHIA | 40 |
| 17 | at NY Giants | 29 |
| 13 | SEATTLE | 34 |
| 24 | at Arizona | 29 |
| 35 | ST. LOUIS | 16 |
| 22 | at Dallas | 35 |
| 10 | at Buffalo | 3 |
| 24 | NY JETS | 14 |
| 9 | at Miami | 14 |
| 17 | at St. Louis | 16 |
| 27 | WASHINGTON | 24 |
| 339 | | 381 |

* overtime

## SEATTLE SEAHAWKS (4-12)

| | | |
|---|---|---|
| 10 | at Buffalo | 34 |
| *30 | SAN FRANCISCO | 33 |
| 37 | ST. LOUIS | 13 |
| 6 | at NY Giants | 44 |
| 17 | GREEN BAY | 27 |
| 10 | at Tampa Bay | 20 |
| 34 | at San Francisco | 13 |
| 7 | PHILADELPHIA | 26 |
| 19 | at Miami | 21 |
| 20 | ARIZONA | 26 |
| 17 | WASHINGTON | 20 |
| 9 | at Dallas | 34 |
| 21 | NEW ENGLAND | 24 |
| 23 | at St. Louis | 20 |
| 13 | NY JETS | 3 |
| 21 | at Arizona | 34 |
| **294** | | **392** |

## ST. LOUIS RAMS (2-14)

| | | |
|---|---|---|
| 3 | at Philadelphia | 38 |
| 13 | NY GIANTS | 41 |
| 13 | at Seattle | 37 |
| 14 | BUFFALO | 31 |
| 19 | at Washington | 17 |
| 34 | DALLAS | 14 |
| 16 | at New England | 23 |
| 13 | ARIZONA | 34 |
| 3 | at NY Jets | 47 |
| 16 | at San Francisco | 35 |
| 3 | CHICAGO | 27 |
| 12 | MIAMI | 16 |
| 10 | at Arizona | 34 |
| 20 | SEATTLE | 23 |
| 16 | SAN FRANCISCO | 17 |
| 27 | at Atlanta | 31 |
| **232** | | **465** |

## TAMPA BAY BUCCANEERS (9-7)

| | | |
|---|---|---|
| 20 | at New Orleans | 24 |
| 24 | ATLANTA | 9 |
| *27 | at Chicago | 24 |
| 30 | GREEN BAY | 21 |
| 13 | at Denver | 16 |
| 27 | CAROLINA | 3 |
| 20 | SEATTLE | 10 |
| 9 | at Dallas | 13 |
| *30 | at Kansas City | 27 |
| 19 | MINNESOTA | 13 |
| 38 | at Detroit | 20 |
| 23 | NEW ORLEANS | 20 |
| 23 | at Carolina | 38 |
| *10 | at Atlanta | 13 |
| 24 | SAN DIEGO | 41 |
| 24 | OAKLAND | 31 |
| **361** | | **323** |

## WASHINGTON REDSKINS (8-8)

| | | | | | | |
|---|---|---|---|---|---|---|
| 7 | at NY Giants | 16 | | 6 | PITTSBURGH | 23 |
| 29 | NEW ORLEANS | 24 | | 10 | DALLAS | 14 |
| 24 | ARIZONA | 17 | | 20 | at Seattle | 17 |
| 26 | at Dallas | 24 | | 7 | NY GIANTS | 23 |
| 23 | at Philadelphia | 17 | | 10 | at Baltimore | 24 |
| 17 | ST. LOUIS | 19 | | 13 | at Cincinnati | 20 |
| 14 | CLEVELAND | 11 | | 10 | PHILADELPHIA | 3 |
| 25 | at Detroit | 17 | | 24 | at San Francisco | 27 |
| | | | | **265** | | **296** |

\* overtime

# 2008 NFL Individual Leaders

## American Football Conference

### Scoring

| TOUCHDOWNS | TD | Rush | Rec | Ret | 2PT | Pts |
|---|---|---|---|---|---|---|
| T. Jones, NYJ | 15 | 13 | 2 | 0 | 0 | 90 |
| L. White, Ten | 15 | 15 | 0 | 0 | 0 | 90 |
| Jones-Drew, Jax | 14 | 12 | 2 | 0 | 0 | 84 |
| Tomlinson, SD | 12 | 11 | 1 | 0 | 0 | 72 |
| Moss, NE | 11 | 0 | 11 | 0 | 0 | 66 |
| McClain, Balt | 11 | 10 | 1 | 0 | 0 | 66 |
| Gonzalez, KC | 10 | 0 | 10 | 0 | 0 | 60 |
| R. Brown, Mia | 10 | 10 | 0 | 0 | 0 | 60 |
| C. Johnson, Ten | 10 | 9 | 1 | 0 | 0 | 60 |
| Slaton, Hou | 10 | 9 | 1 | 0 | 0 | 60 |

| KICKING | PAT | FG | Pts |
|---|---|---|---|
| Gostkowski, NE | 40 | 36 | 148 |
| Bironas, Ten | 40 | 29 | 127 |
| Kaeding, SD | 46 | 27 | 127 |
| Lindell, Buf | 34 | 30 | 124 |
| Brown, Hou | 37 | 29 | 124 |
| Stover, Bal | 41 | 27 | 122 |
| Reed, Pit | 36 | 27 | 117 |
| Prater, Den | 39 | 25 | 114 |
| Feely, NYJ | 39 | 24 | 111 |
| Dawson, Clev | 18 | 30 | 108 |

### Passing

| | Att | Comp | Yds | TD | Int | Lg | Rating Pts |
|---|---|---|---|---|---|---|---|
| Rivers, SD | 478 | 312 | 4009 | 34 | 11 | 67 | 105.5 |
| Pennington, Mia | 476 | 321 | 3653 | 19 | 7 | 80 | 97.4 |
| P. Manning, Ind | 555 | 371 | 4002 | 27 | 12 | 75 | 95.0 |
| Schaub, Hou | 380 | 251 | 3043 | 15 | 10 | 65 | 92.7 |
| Cassel, NE | 516 | 327 | 3693 | 21 | 11 | 76 | 89.4 |
| Cutler, Den | 616 | 384 | 4526 | 25 | 18 | 93 | 86.0 |
| Edwards, Buf | 374 | 245 | 2699 | 11 | 10 | 65 | 85.4 |
| Garrard, Jax | 535 | 335 | 3620 | 15 | 13 | 41 | 81.7 |
| Favre, NYJ | 522 | 343 | 3472 | 22 | 22 | 56 | 81.0 |
| Flacco, Balt | 428 | 257 | 2971 | 14 | 12 | 70 | 80.3 |

## American Football Conference *(Cont.)*

### Pass Receiving

| RECEPTIONS | No. | Yds | Avg | Lg | TD | YARDS | Yds | No. | Avg | Lg | TD |
|---|---|---|---|---|---|---|---|---|---|---|---|
| A. Johnson, Hou | 115 | 1575 | 13.7 | 65 | 8 | A. Johnson, Hou | 1575 | 115 | 13.7 | 65 | 8 |
| Welker, NE | 111 | 1165 | 10.5 | 64 | 3 | Marshall, Den | 1265 | 104 | 12.2 | 47 | 6 |
| Marshall, Den | 104 | 1265 | 12.2 | 47 | 6 | Welker, NE | 1165 | 111 | 10.5 | 64 | 3 |
| Gonzalez, KC | 96 | 1058 | 11.0 | 35 | 10 | Wayne, Ind | 1145 | 82 | 14.0 | 65 | 6 |
| Houshmandzadeh, Cin | 92 | 904 | 9.9 | 46 | 4 | V. Jackson, SD | 1098 | 59 | 18.6 | 60 | 7 |
| Royal, Den | 91 | 980 | 10.8 | 93 | 5 | Gonzalez, KC | 1058 | 96 | 11.0 | 35 | 10 |
| Bowe, KC | 86 | 1022 | 11.9 | 36 | 7 | Ward, Pit | 1043 | 81 | 12.9 | 49 | 7 |
| Wayne, Ind | 82 | 1145 | 14.0 | 65 | 6 | Mason, Balt | 1037 | 80 | 13.0 | 54 | 5 |
| Ward, Pit | 81 | 1043 | 12.9 | 49 | 7 | Bowe, KC | 1022 | 86 | 11.9 | 36 | 7 |
| Mason, Balt | 80 | 1037 | 13.0 | 54 | 5 | Evans, Buf | 1017 | 63 | 16.1 | 87 | 3 |

### Rushing

| | Att | Yds | Avg | Lg | TD |
|---|---|---|---|---|---|
| T. Jones, NYJ | 290 | 1312 | 4.5 | 59 | 13 |
| Slaton, Hou | 268 | 1282 | 4.8 | 71 | 9 |
| C. Johnson, Ten | 251 | 1228 | 4.9 | 66 | 9 |
| Tomlinson, SD | 292 | 1110 | 3.8 | 45 | 11 |
| Lynch, Buff | 250 | 1036 | 4.1 | 50 | 8 |
| Lewis, Clev | 279 | 1002 | 3.6 | 29 | 4 |
| R. Brown, Mia | 214 | 916 | 4.3 | 62 | 10 |
| McClain, Balt | 232 | 902 | 3.9 | 82 | 10 |
| L. Johnson, KC | 193 | 874 | 4.5 | 65 | 5 |
| Fargas, Oak | 218 | 853 | 3.9 | 42 | 1 |
| Jones-Drew, Jax | 197 | 824 | 4.2 | 46 | 12 |
| Parker, Pit | 210 | 791 | 3.8 | 34 | 5 |
| L. White, Ten | 200 | 773 | 3.9 | 80 | 15 |
| Benson, Cin | 214 | 747 | 3.5 | 46 | 2 |
| Morris, NE | 156 | 727 | 4.7 | 35 | 7 |

### Interceptions

| | No. | Yds | Lg | TD |
|---|---|---|---|---|
| Reed, Balt | 9 | 264 | 107 | 2 |
| Griffin, Ten | 7 | 172 | 83 | 1 |
| Polamalu, Pit | 7 | 59 | 23 | 0 |
| McDonald, Clev | 5 | 146 | 98 | 1 |
| Finnegan, Ten | 5 | 100 | 99 | 1 |
| Goodman, Mia | 5 | 53 | 55 | 0 |
| Revis, NYJ | 5 | 38 | 32 | 1 |
| Nine tied at 4. | | | | |

### Sacks

| | |
|---|---|
| Porter, Mia | 17.5 |
| J. Harrison, Pit | 16.0 |
| Williams, Hou | 12.0 |
| Woodley, Pit | 11.5 |
| Mathis, Ind | 11.5 |
| Freeney, Ind | 10.5 |
| Haynesworth, Ten | 8.5 |

### Punting

| | No. | Yds | Avg | Net Avg | TB | In 20 | Lg | Blk | Ret | Ret Avg |
|---|---|---|---|---|---|---|---|---|---|---|
| Lechler, Oak | 90 | 4391 | 48.8 | 41.2 | 13 | 33 | 70 | 0 | 43 | 9.9 |
| Kern, Den | 46 | 2150 | 46.7 | 37.8 | 4 | 13 | 64 | 0 | 28 | 11.8 |
| Scifres, SD | 51 | 2332 | 45.7 | 40.9 | 5 | 19 | 67 | 0 | 23 | 6.3 |
| Zastudil, Clev | 75 | 3410 | 45.5 | 39.4 | 11 | 23 | 65 | 0 | 32 | 7.3 |
| H. Smith, Ind | 53 | 2345 | 44.2 | 38.8 | 2 | 23 | 64 | 0 | 27 | 9.2 |

### Punt Returns

| | No. | Yds | Avg | Lg | TD |
|---|---|---|---|---|---|
| Parrish, Buf | 21 | 322 | 15.3 | 63 | 1 |
| Higgins, Oak | 44 | 570 | 13.0 | 93 | 3 |
| J. Jones, Hou | 32 | 386 | 12.1 | 73 | 2 |
| Leonhard, Balt | 20 | 232 | 11.6 | 46 | 0 |
| Sproles, SD | 22 | 249 | 11.3 | 43 | 0 |

### Kickoff Returns

| | No. | Yds | Avg | Lg | TD |
|---|---|---|---|---|---|
| Hobbs, NE | 45 | 1281 | 28.5 | 95 | 1 |
| McKelvin, Buf | 52 | 1468 | 28.2 | 98 | 1 |
| Carr, Ten | 35 | 984 | 28.1 | 52 | 0 |
| Royal, Den | 23 | 600 | 26.1 | 95 | 0 |
| Sproles, SD | 53 | 1376 | 26.0 | 103 | 1 |

## National Football Conference

### Scoring

| TOUCHDOWNS | TD | Rush | Rec | Ret | 2PT | Pts | KICKING | PAT | FG | Pts |
|---|---|---|---|---|---|---|---|---|---|---|
| D. Williams, Car | 20 | 18 | 2 | 0 | 1 | 122 | Akers, Phi | 45 | 33 | 144 |
| Turner, Atl | 17 | 17 | 0 | 0 | 0 | 102 | Carney, NYG | 38 | 35 | 143 |
| Jacobs, NYG | 15 | 15 | 0 | 0 | 0 | 90 | Bryant, TB | 35 | 32 | 131 |
| Westbrook, Phi | 14 | 9 | 5 | 0 | 0 | 84 | Kasay, Car | 46 | 28 | 130 |
| C. Johnson, Det | 12 | 0 | 12 | 0 | 1 | 74 | Elam, Atl | 42 | 49 | 129 |
| Fitzgerald, Ari | 12 | 0 | 12 | 0 | 0 | 72 | Longwell, Min | 40 | 29 | 127 |
| P. Thomas, NO | 12 | 9 | 3 | 0 | 0 | 72 | Crosby, GB | 46 | 27 | 127 |
| Forte, Chi | 12 | 8 | 4 | 0 | 0 | 72 | Nedney, SF | 34 | 29 | 121 |
| Boldin, Ari | 11 | 0 | 11 | 0 | 0 | 66 | Rackers, Ari | 44 | 25 | 119 |
| Owens, Dal | 10 | 0 | 10 | 0 | 0 | 60 | Gould, Chi | 41 | 26 | 119 |
| L. Moore, NO | 10 | 0 | 10 | 0 | 0 | 60 | Brown, Sea | 19 | 31 | 112 |
| Peterson, Min | 10 | 10 | 0 | 0 | 0 | 60 | Suisham, Wash | 25 | 26 | 103 |
| J. Stewart, Car | 10 | 10 | 0 | 0 | 0 | 60 | Mare, Sea | 30 | 24 | 102 |
| Hightower, Ari | 10 | 10 | 0 | 0 | 0 | 60 | Folk, Dal | 42 | 20 | 102 |

### National Football Conference *(Cont.)*

#### Passing

| | Att | Comp | Yds | TD | Int | Lg | Rating Pts |
|---|---|---|---|---|---|---|---|
| Warner, Ari | 598 | 401 | 4583 | 30 | 14 | 79 | 96.9 |
| Brees, NO | 635 | 413 | 5069 | 34 | 17 | 84 | 96.2 |
| Rodgers, GB | 533 | 341 | 4038 | 28 | 13 | 71 | 93.8 |
| Romo, Dal | 450 | 276 | 3448 | 26 | 14 | 75 | 91.4 |
| Garcia, TB | 376 | 244 | 2712 | 12 | 6 | 71 | 90.2 |
| Ryan, Atl | 434 | 265 | 3440 | 16 | 11 | 70 | 87.7 |
| Hill, SF | 288 | 181 | 2046 | 13 | 8 | 48 | 87.5 |
| Wallace, Sea | 242 | 141 | 1532 | 11 | 3 | 90 | 87.0 |
| McNabb, Phi | 571 | 345 | 3916 | 23 | 11 | 90 | 86.4 |
| E. Manning, NYG | 479 | 289 | 3238 | 21 | 10 | 48 | 86.4 |

#### Pass Receiving

| RECEPTIONS | No. | Yds | Avg | Lg | TD | YARDS | Yds | No. | Avg | Lg | TD |
|---|---|---|---|---|---|---|---|---|---|---|---|
| Fitzgerald, Ari | 96 | 1431 | 14.9 | 78 | 12 | Fitzgerald, Ari | 1431 | 96 | 14.9 | 78 | 12 |
| Boldin, Ari | 89 | 1038 | 11.7 | 79 | 11 | S. Smith, Car | 1421 | 78 | 18.2 | 65 | 6 |
| White, Atl | 88 | 1382 | 15.7 | 70 | 7 | White, Atl | 1382 | 88 | 15.7 | 70 | 7 |
| Bryant, TB | 83 | 1248 | 15.0 | 71 | 7 | C. Johnson, Det | 1331 | 78 | 17.1 | 96 | 12 |
| Cooley, Wash | 83 | 849 | 10.2 | 28 | 1 | Jennings, GB | 1292 | 80 | 16.2 | 63 | 9 |
| Witten, Dal | 81 | 952 | 11.8 | 42 | 4 | Bryant, TB | 1248 | 83 | 15.0 | 71 | 7 |
| Jennings, GB | 80 | 1292 | 16.2 | 63 | 9 | Owens, Dal | 1052 | 69 | 15.2 | 75 | 10 |
| Moss, Wash | 79 | 1044 | 13.2 | 67 | 6 | Moss, Wash | 1044 | 79 | 13.2 | 67 | 6 |
| L. Moore, NO | 79 | 928 | 11.7 | 70 | 10 | Boldin, Ari | 1038 | 89 | 11.7 | 79 | 11 |
| S. Smith, Car | 78 | 1421 | 18.2 | 65 | 6 | Driver, GB | 1012 | 74 | 13.7 | 71 | 5 |
| C. Johnson, Det | 78 | 1331 | 17.1 | 96 | 12 | Breaston, Ari | 1006 | 77 | 13.1 | 58 | 3 |

#### Rushing

| | Att | Yds | Avg | Lg | TD |
|---|---|---|---|---|---|
| Peterson, Min | 363 | 1760 | 4.8 | 67 | 10 |
| Turner, Atl | 376 | 1699 | 4.5 | 70 | 17 |
| D. Williams, Car | 273 | 1515 | 5.5 | 69 | 18 |
| Portis, Wash | 342 | 1487 | 4.3 | 31 | 9 |
| Forte, Chi | 316 | 1238 | 3.9 | 50 | 8 |
| Grant, GB | 312 | 1203 | 3.9 | 57 | 4 |
| Jacobs, NYG | 219 | 1089 | 5.0 | 44 | 15 |
| Jackson, StL | 253 | 1042 | 4.1 | 56 | 7 |
| Gore, SF | 240 | 1036 | 4.3 | 41 | 6 |
| Ward, NYG | 182 | 1025 | 5.6 | 51 | 2 |
| K. Smith, Det | 238 | 976 | 4.1 | 50 | 8 |
| Westbrook, Phi | 233 | 936 | 4.0 | 39 | 9 |
| Barber, Dal | 238 | 885 | 3.7 | 35 | 7 |
| Stewart, Car | 184 | 836 | 4.5 | 41 | 10 |
| Dunn, TB | 186 | 786 | 4.2 | 40 | 2 |

#### Interceptions

| | No. | Yds | Lg | TD |
|---|---|---|---|---|
| Collins, GB | 7 | 295 | 62 | 3 |
| Woodson, GB | 7 | 169 | 62 | 2 |
| Atogwe, StL | 5 | 91 | 43 | 0 |
| David, NO | 5 | 83 | 42 | 0 |
| T. Williams, GB | 5 | 78 | 39 | 0 |
| Seven tied with 4. | | | | |

#### Sacks

| | |
|---|---|
| Ware, Dal | 20.0 |
| Abraham, Atl | 16.5 |
| J. Allen, Min | 14.5 |
| Peppers, Car | 14.5 |
| Tuck, NYG | 12.0 |
| D. Howard, Phi | 10.0 |
| Kampman, GB | 9.5 |
| Cole, Phi | 9.0 |
| K. Williams, Min | 8.5 |
| Four tied with 8.0. | |

#### Punting

| | No. | Yds | Avg | Net Avg | TB | In 20 | Lg | Blk | Ret | Ret Avg |
|---|---|---|---|---|---|---|---|---|---|---|
| D. Jones, StL | 82 | 4100 | 50.0 | 41.1 | 7 | 20 | 68 | 0 | 57 | 10.4 |
| A. Lee, SF | 66 | 3155 | 47.8 | 39.6 | 9 | 13 | 82 | 1 | 39 | 9.3 |
| Kluwe, Min | 73 | 3473 | 47.6 | 35.5 | 13 | 23 | 62 | 1 | 42 | 14.9 |
| J. Ryan, Sea | 78 | 3557 | 45.6 | 38.4 | 12 | 22 | 63 | 1 | 38 | 8.5 |
| Bidwell, TB | 77 | 3426 | 44.5 | 37.6 | 7 | 27 | 64 | 0 | 39 | 10.1 |

#### Punt Returns

| | No. | Yds | Avg | Lg | TD |
|---|---|---|---|---|---|
| C. Smith, TB | 23 | 324 | 14.1 | 70 | 1 |
| Bush, NO | 20 | 270 | 13.5 | 71 | 3 |
| M. Jones, Car | 39 | 443 | 11.4 | 55 | 0 |
| Blackmon, GB | 36 | 398 | 11.1 | 76 | 2 |
| Hixon, NYG | 24 | 242 | 10.1 | 50 | 0 |
| Forsett, Sea | 23 | 227 | 9.9 | 29 | 0 |
| D. Jackson, Phi | 50 | 440 | 8.8 | 68 | 1 |

#### Kickoff Returns

| | No. | Yds | Avg | Lg | TD |
|---|---|---|---|---|---|
| D. Manning, Chi | 36 | 1070 | 29.7 | 83 | 1 |
| C. Smith, TB | 36 | 992 | 27.6 | 97 | 1 |
| Rossum, SF | 47 | 1259 | 26.8 | 104 | 1 |
| Norwood, Atl | 51 | 1311 | 25.7 | 92 | 0 |
| J. Arrington, Ari | 36 | 923 | 25.6 | 93 | 1 |
| Cartwright, Wash | 51 | 1307 | 25.6 | 87 | 0 |
| P. Thomas, NO | 31 | 793 | 25.6 | 88 | 0 |

# 2008 NFL Team Statistics

## AFC Total Offense

| | Total Plays | Yds/Game | Pts/Game | 1st Dwns/Game | Time of Poss |
|---|---|---|---|---|---|
| Denver | 1019 | 395.8 | 23.1 | 22.1 | 28:44 |
| Houston | 1019 | 382.1 | 22.9 | 21.2 | 32:05 |
| New England | 1095 | 365.4 | 25.6 | 22.2 | 32:25 |
| San Diego | 924 | 349.0 | 27.4 | 18.8 | 28:53 |
| Miami | 965 | 345.6 | 21.6 | 19.2 | 31:03 |
| Indianapolis | 969 | 335.5 | 23.6 | 20.1 | 28:39 |
| NY Jets | 981 | 331.7 | 25.3 | 19.2 | 31:06 |
| Baltimore | 1058 | 324.0 | 24.1 | 18.8 | 33:22 |
| Jacksonville | 1005 | 319.1 | 18.9 | 19.5 | 31:29 |
| Tennessee | 973 | 313.6 | 23.4 | 16.8 | 29:19 |
| Pittsburgh | 1015 | 311.9 | 21.7 | 18.1 | 31:41 |
| Kansas City | 957 | 308.7 | 18.2 | 17.1 | 28:04 |
| Buffalo | 956 | 305.1 | 21.0 | 17.9 | 30:04 |
| Oakland | 919 | 272.2 | 16.4 | 14.1 | 28:31 |
| Cleveland | 921 | 249.1 | 14.5 | 14.6 | 27:33 |
| Cincinnati | 984 | 245.4 | 12.8 | 15.3 | 29:18 |

## AFC Total Defense

| | Opp Total Plays | Opp Yds/Game | Opp Yds/Play | Opp Pts/Game |
|---|---|---|---|---|
| Pittsburgh | 974 | 237.2 | 3.9 | 13.9 |
| Baltimore | 928 | 261.1 | 4.5 | 15.3 |
| Tennessee | 1022 | 293.6 | 4.6 | 14.6 |
| New England | 920 | 309.0 | 5.4 | 19.3 |
| Indianapolis | 983 | 310.9 | 5.1 | 18.6 |
| Cincinnati | 1013 | 325.5 | 5.1 | 22.8 |
| Buffalo | 971 | 326.1 | 5.4 | 21.4 |
| Miami | 979 | 329.0 | 5.4 | 19.8 |
| NY Jets | 1020 | 329.4 | 5.2 | 22.3 |
| Jacksonville | 922 | 330.9 | 5.7 | 22.9 |
| Houston | 935 | 336.6 | 5.8 | 24.6 |
| San Diego | 1041 | 349.9 | 5.4 | 21.7 |
| Cleveland | 1004 | 356.5 | 5.7 | 21.9 |
| Oakland | 1045 | 360.9 | 5.5 | 24.3 |
| Denver | 990 | 374.6 | 6.1 | 28.0 |
| Kansas City | 1041 | 393.2 | 6.0 | 27.5 |

## NFC Total Offense

| | Total Plays | Yds/Game | Pts/Game | 1st Dwns/Game | Time of Poss |
|---|---|---|---|---|---|
| New Orleans | 1047 | 410.7 | 28.9 | 22.1 | 30:28 |
| Arizona | 998 | 365.8 | 26.7 | 20.5 | 30:11 |
| Atlanta | 1011 | 361.2 | 24.4 | 19.6 | 31:10 |
| NY Giants | 1021 | 355.9 | 26.7 | 21.1 | 33:19 |
| Green Bay | 1012 | 351.1 | 26.2 | 18.7 | 31:37 |
| Philadelphia | 1056 | 350.5 | 26.0 | 19.9 | 31:24 |
| Carolina | 938 | 349.7 | 25.9 | 17.9 | 29:28 |
| Dallas | 979 | 344.5 | 22.6 | 18.2 | 30:02 |
| Tampa Bay | 1045 | 341.0 | 22.6 | 18.6 | 32:14 |
| Minnesota | 1014 | 330.9 | 23.7 | 18.2 | 31:19 |
| Washington | 1026 | 320.0 | 16.6 | 18.4 | 31:31 |
| San Francisco | 961 | 311.1 | 21.2 | 17.9 | 29:31 |
| Chicago | 991 | 295.9 | 23.4 | 16.5 | 28:36 |
| St. Louis | 982 | 287.2 | 14.5 | 15.6 | 29:32 |
| Seattle | 927 | 274.1 | 18.4 | 16.6 | 26:38 |
| Detroit | 913 | 268.2 | 16.8 | 14.6 | 26:59 |

## NFC Total Defense

| | Opp Total Plays | Opp Yds/Game | Opp Yds/Play | Opp Pts/Game |
|---|---|---|---|---|
| Philadelphia | 994 | 274.3 | 4.4 | 18.1 |
| Washington | 933 | 288.8 | 5.0 | 18.5 |
| NY Giants | 931 | 292.0 | 5.0 | 18.4 |
| Minnesota | 946 | 292.4 | 4.9 | 20.8 |
| Dallas | 969 | 294.3 | 4.9 | 22.8 |
| Tampa Bay | 945 | 306.1 | 5.2 | 20.2 |
| San Francisco | 1027 | 326.0 | 5.1 | 23.8 |
| Carolina | 1026 | 331.2 | 5.2 | 20.6 |
| Arizona | 993 | 331.5 | 5.3 | 26.6 |
| Green Bay | 1003 | 334.3 | 5.3 | 23.8 |
| Chicago | 1087 | 334.7 | 4.9 | 21.9 |
| New Orleans | 999 | 339.5 | 5.4 | 24.6 |
| Atlanta | 998 | 348.2 | 5.6 | 20.3 |
| St. Louis | 975 | 371.9 | 6.1 | 29.1 |
| Seattle | 1058 | 378.0 | 5.7 | 24.5 |
| Detroit | 1009 | 404.4 | 6.4 | 32.3 |

## Takeaways/Giveaways

### American Football Conference

| | Takeaways Int | Fum | Total | Giveaways Int | Fum | Total | Net Diff |
|---|---|---|---|---|---|---|---|
| Miami | 18 | 12 | 30 | 7 | 6 | 13 | 17 |
| Tennessee | 20 | 11 | 31 | 9 | 8 | 17 | 14 |
| Baltimore | 26 | 8 | 34 | 12 | 9 | 21 | 13 |
| Indianapolis | 15 | 11 | 26 | 12 | 5 | 17 | 9 |
| Kansas City | 13 | 16 | 29 | 16 | 8 | 24 | 5 |
| Cleveland | 23 | 8 | 31 | 20 | 6 | 26 | 5 |
| Pittsburgh | 20 | 9 | 29 | 15 | 10 | 25 | 4 |
| San Diego | 15 | 9 | 24 | 11 | 9 | 20 | 4 |
| New England | 14 | 8 | 22 | 11 | 10 | 21 | 1 |
| Oakland | 16 | 8 | 24 | 11 | 12 | 23 | 1 |
| NY Jets | 14 | 16 | 30 | 23 | 8 | 31 | -1 |
| Cincinnati | 12 | 12 | 24 | 15 | 11 | 26 | -2 |
| Jacksonville | 13 | 4 | 17 | 13 | 11 | 24 | -7 |
| Buffalo | 10 | 12 | 22 | 15 | 15 | 30 | -8 |
| Houston | 12 | 10 | 22 | 20 | 12 | 32 | -10 |
| Denver | 6 | 7 | 13 | 18 | 12 | 30 | -17 |

### National Football Conference

| | Takeaways Int | Fum | Total | Giveaways Int | Fum | Total | Net Diff |
|---|---|---|---|---|---|---|---|
| NY Giants | 17 | 5 | 22 | 10 | 3 | 13 | 9 |
| Green Bay | 22 | 6 | 28 | 13 | 8 | 21 | 7 |
| Carolina | 12 | 13 | 25 | 12 | 7 | 19 | 6 |
| Chicago | 22 | 10 | 32 | 14 | 13 | 27 | 5 |
| Tampa Bay | 22 | 8 | 30 | 13 | 13 | 26 | 4 |
| Philadelphia | 15 | 14 | 29 | 16 | 10 | 26 | 3 |
| Arizona | 13 | 17 | 30 | 15 | 15 | 30 | 0 |
| Washington | 13 | 5 | 18 | 6 | 12 | 18 | 0 |
| Atlanta | 10 | 8 | 18 | 11 | 10 | 21 | -3 |
| New Orleans | 15 | 7 | 22 | 18 | 8 | 26 | -4 |
| St. Louis | 12 | 14 | 26 | 19 | 12 | 31 | -5 |
| Minnesota | 12 | 13 | 25 | 17 | 14 | 31 | -6 |
| Seattle | 9 | 11 | 20 | 15 | 12 | 27 | -7 |
| Detroit | 4 | 16 | 20 | 19 | 10 | 29 | -9 |
| Dallas | 8 | 14 | 22 | 20 | 13 | 33 | -11 |
| San Francisco | 12 | 6 | 18 | 19 | 16 | 35 | -17 |

## Baltimore Ravens

### SCORING

| | Rush | Rec | Ret | PAT | FG | S | Pts |
|---|---|---|---|---|---|---|---|
| Stover | 0 | 0 | 0 | 41 | 27 | 0 | 122 |
| McClain | 10 | 1 | 0 | 0 | 0 | 0 | 66 |
| McGahee | 7 | 0 | 0 | 0 | 0 | 0 | 42 |
| Mason | 0 | 5 | 0 | 0 | 0 | 0 | 30 |
| Clayton | 1 | 3 | 0 | 0 | 0 | 0 | 24 |
| Heap | 0 | 3 | 0 | 0 | 0 | 0 | 18 |
| Flacco | 2 | 0 | 0 | 0 | 0 | 0 | 12 |
| Wilcox | 0 | 2 | 0 | 0 | 0 | 0 | 12 |

### RUSHING

| | No. | Yds | Avg | Lg | TD |
|---|---|---|---|---|---|
| McClain | 232 | 902 | 3.9 | 82 | 10 |
| McGahee | 170 | 671 | 3.9 | 77 | 7 |

### PASSING

| | Att | Comp | Pct Comp | Yds | Avg Gain | TD | Int | Rating Pts |
|---|---|---|---|---|---|---|---|---|
| Flacco | 428 | 257 | 60.0 | 2971 | 6.9 | 12 | 12 | 80.3 |
| T. Smith | 4 | 3 | 75.0 | 82 | 20.5 | 1 | 0 | 156.2 |

### RECEIVING

| | No. | Yds | Avg | Lg | TD |
|---|---|---|---|---|---|
| Mason | 80 | 1037 | 13.0 | 54 | 5 |
| Clayton | 41 | 695 | 17.0 | 70 | 3 |
| Heap | 35 | 403 | 11.5 | 30 | 3 |
| Rice | 33 | 273 | 8.3 | 40 | 0 |
| McGahee | 24 | 173 | 7.2 | 35 | 0 |
| McClain | 19 | 123 | 6.5 | 25 | 1 |

**INTERCEPTIONS:** Reed, 9

### PUNTING

| | No. | Yds | Avg | Net Avg | TB | In 20 | Lg | Blk |
|---|---|---|---|---|---|---|---|---|
| Koch | 84 | 3777 | 45.0 | 39.9 | 9 | 34 | 74 | 1 |

**SACKS:** Suggs, 8

## Buffalo Bills

### SCORING

| | Rush | Rec | Ret | PAT | FG | S | Pts |
|---|---|---|---|---|---|---|---|
| Lindell | 0 | 0 | 0 | 34 | 30 | 0 | 124 |
| Lynch | 8 | 1 | 0 | 0 | 0 | 0 | 54 |
| Edwards | 3 | 0 | 0 | 0 | 0 | 0 | 18 |
| Evans | 0 | 3 | 0 | 0 | 0 | 0 | 18 |
| Jackson | 3 | 0 | 0 | 0 | 0 | 0 | 18 |

### RUSHING

| | No. | Yds | Avg | Lg | TD |
|---|---|---|---|---|---|
| Lynch | 250 | 1036 | 4.1 | 50 | 8 |
| Jackson | 130 | 571 | 4.4 | 32 | 3 |

### PASSING

| | Att | Comp | Pct Comp | Yds | Avg Gain | TD | Int | Rating Pts |
|---|---|---|---|---|---|---|---|---|
| Edwards | 374 | 245 | 65.5 | 2699 | 7.2 | 11 | 10 | 85.4 |
| Losman | 104 | 63 | 60.6 | 584 | 5.6 | 2 | 5 | 62.3 |

### RECEIVING

| | No. | Yds | Avg | Lg | TD |
|---|---|---|---|---|---|
| Evans | 63 | 1017 | 16.1 | 87 | 3 |
| Reed | 56 | 597 | 10.7 | 24 | 1 |
| Lynch | 47 | 300 | 6.4 | 42 | 1 |
| Jackson | 37 | 317 | 8.6 | 65 | 0 |
| Royal | 33 | 351 | 10.6 | 30 | 1 |
| Parrish | 24 | 232 | 9.7 | 22 | 1 |

**INTERCEPTIONS:** McGee, 3

### PUNTING

| | No. | Yds | Avg | Net Avg | TB | In 20 | Lg | Blk |
|---|---|---|---|---|---|---|---|---|
| Moorman | 58 | 2557 | 44.1 | 39.1 | 5 | 23 | 63 | 0 |

**SACKS:** Mitchell, Denney, 4

## Cincinnati Bengals

### SCORING

| | Rush | Rec | Ret | PAT | FG | S | Pts |
|---|---|---|---|---|---|---|---|
| Graham | 0 | 0 | 0 | 15 | 21 | 0 | 78 |
| Houshmandzadeh | 0 | 4 | 0 | 0 | 0 | 0 | 24 |
| C. Johnson | 0 | 4 | 0 | 0 | 0 | 0 | 24 |

### RUSHING

| | No. | Yds | Avg | Lg | TD |
|---|---|---|---|---|---|
| Benson | 214 | 747 | 3.5 | 46 | 2 |
| Perry | 104 | 269 | 2.6 | 25 | 2 |

### PASSING

| | Att | Comp | Pct Comp | Yds | Avg Gain | TD | Int | Rating Pts |
|---|---|---|---|---|---|---|---|---|
| Fitzpatrick | 372 | 221 | 59.4 | 1905 | 5.1 | 8 | 9 | 70.0 |
| Palmer | 129 | 75 | 58.1 | 731 | 5.7 | 3 | 4 | 69.0 |

### RECEIVING

| | No. | Yds | Avg | Lg | TD |
|---|---|---|---|---|---|
| Houshmandzadeh | 92 | 904 | 9.8 | 46 | 4 |
| C. Johnson | 53 | 540 | 10.2 | 26 | 4 |
| Henry | 19 | 220 | 11.6 | 22 | 2 |
| Kelly | 31 | 207 | 6.7 | 31 | 0 |
| Chatman | 21 | 194 | 9.2 | 25 | 0 |
| Benson | 20 | 185 | 9.3 | 79 | 0 |

**INTERCEPTIONS:** Hall, 3

### PUNTING

| | No. | Yds | Avg | Net Avg | TB | In 20 | Lg | Blk |
|---|---|---|---|---|---|---|---|---|
| Larson | 100 | 3449 | 39.5 | 34.1 | 3 | 28 | 57 | 1 |

**SACKS:** Ndukwe, Odom, Thornton, 3

## Cleveland Browns

### SCORING

| | Rush | Rec | Ret | PAT | FG | S | Pts |
|---|---|---|---|---|---|---|---|
| Dawson | 0 | 0 | 0 | 18 | 30 | 0 | 108 |
| Lewis | 4 | 0 | 0 | 0 | 0 | 0 | 24 |
| Cribbs | 1 | 1 | 1 | 0 | 0 | 0 | 18 |
| Edwards | 0 | 3 | 0 | 0 | 0 | 0 | 18 |
| Winslow | 0 | 3 | 0 | 0 | 0 | 0 | 18 |
| Harrison | 1 | 1 | 0 | 0 | 0 | 0 | 12 |

### RUSHING

| | No. | Yds | Avg | Lg | TD |
|---|---|---|---|---|---|
| Lewis | 279 | 1002 | 3.6 | 29 | 4 |
| Harrison | 34 | 246 | 7.2 | 72 | 1 |

### PASSING

| | Att | Comp | Pct Comp | Yds | Avg Gain | TD | Int | Rating Pts |
|---|---|---|---|---|---|---|---|---|
| Anderson | 283 | 142 | 50.2 | 1615 | 5.7 | 9 | 8 | 66.5 |
| Dorsey | 91 | 43 | 47.3 | 370 | 4.1 | 0 | 7 | 26.4 |
| Quinn | 89 | 45 | 50.6 | 518 | 5.8 | 2 | 2 | 66.6 |

### RECEIVING

| | No. | Yds | Avg | Lg | TD |
|---|---|---|---|---|---|
| Edwards | 55 | 873 | 15.9 | 70 | 3 |
| Winslow | 43 | 428 | 10.0 | 30 | 3 |
| Heiden | 23 | 248 | 10.8 | 51 | 0 |
| Steptoe | 19 | 182 | 9.6 | 53 | 0 |
| Lewis | 23 | 178 | 7.7 | 18 | 0 |
| Stallworth | 17 | 170 | 10.0 | 19 | 1 |

**INTERCEPTIONS:** McDonald, 5

### PUNTING

| | No. | Yds | Avg | Net Avg | TB | In 20 | Lg | Blk |
|---|---|---|---|---|---|---|---|---|
| Zastudil | 49 | 2046 | 41.8 | 34.6 | 4 | 14 | 64 | 0 |

**SACKS:** Rogers, Wimbley, 4

## Denver Broncos

| SCORING | Rush | TD Rec | Ret | PAT | FG | S | Pts |
|---|---|---|---|---|---|---|---|
| Prater | 0 | 0 | 0 | 39 | 25 | 0 | 114 |
| Hillis | 1 | 5 | 0 | 0 | 0 | 0 | 36 |
| Marshall | 0 | 6 | 0 | 0 | 0 | 0 | 36 |
| Royal | 0 | 5 | 0 | 0 | 0 | 0 | 30 |
| Graham | 0 | 4 | 0 | 0 | 0 | 0 | 24 |
| Pittman | 4 | 0 | 0 | 0 | 0 | 0 | 24 |

| RUSHING | No. | Yds | Avg | Lg | TD |
|---|---|---|---|---|---|
| Pittman | 76 | 320 | 4.2 | 20 | 4 |
| Hillis | 68 | 343 | 5.0 | 19 | 5 |
| S. Young | 61 | 303 | 5.0 | 49 | 1 |

| PASSING | Att | Comp | Pct Comp | Yds | Avg Gain | TD | Int | Rating Pts |
|---|---|---|---|---|---|---|---|---|
| Cutler | 616 | 384 | 62.3 | 4526 | 7.3 | 25 | 18 | 86.0 |

| RECEIVING | No. | Yds | Avg | Lg | TD |
|---|---|---|---|---|---|
| Marshall | 104 | 1265 | 12.2 | 47 | 6 |
| Royal | 91 | 980 | 10.8 | 93 | 5 |
| Scheffler | 40 | 645 | 16.1 | 72 | 3 |
| Stokley | 49 | 528 | 10.8 | 36 | 3 |
| Graham | 32 | 389 | 12.2 | 28 | 4 |

**INTERCEPTIONS:** Bly, 2

| PUNTING | No. | Yds | Avg | Net Avg | TB | In 20 | Lg | Blk |
|---|---|---|---|---|---|---|---|---|
| Kern | 46 | 2150 | 46.7 | 37.8 | 4 | 13 | 64 | 0 |

**SACKS:** Dumervil, Ekuban, 5

## Indianapolis Colts

| SCORING | Rush | TD Rec | Ret | PAT | FG | S | Pts |
|---|---|---|---|---|---|---|---|
| Vinatieri | 0 | 0 | 0 | 43 | 20 | 0 | 103 |
| Rhodes | 6 | 3 | 0 | 0 | 0 | 0 | 54 |
| Addai | 5 | 2 | 0 | 0 | 0 | 0 | 42 |
| Clark | 0 | 6 | 0 | 0 | 0 | 0 | 36 |
| Wayne | 0 | 6 | 0 | 0 | 0 | 0 | 36 |
| Harrison | 0 | 5 | 0 | 0 | 0 | 0 | 30 |
| A. Gonzalez | 0 | 4 | 0 | 0 | 0 | 0 | 24 |

| RUSHING | No. | Yds | Avg | Lg | TD |
|---|---|---|---|---|---|
| Addai | 155 | 544 | 3.5 | 23 | 5 |
| Rhodes | 152 | 538 | 3.5 | 38 | 6 |

| PASSING | Att | Comp | Pct Comp | Yds | Avg Gain | TD | Int | Rating Pts |
|---|---|---|---|---|---|---|---|---|
| Manning | 555 | 371 | 66.8 | 4002 | 7.2 | 27 | 12 | 95.0 |

| RECEIVING | No. | Yds | Avg | Lg | TD |
|---|---|---|---|---|---|
| Wayne | 82 | 1145 | 14.0 | 65 | 6 |
| Clark | 77 | 848 | 11.0 | 33 | 6 |
| A. Gonzalez | 57 | 664 | 11.6 | 58 | 4 |
| Harrison | 60 | 636 | 10.6 | 67 | 5 |
| Rhodes | 45 | 302 | 6.7 | 29 | 3 |
| Addai | 25 | 206 | 8.2 | 55 | 2 |

**INTERCEPTIONS:** Bullitt, 4

| PUNTING | No. | Yds | Avg | Net Avg | TB | In 20 | Lg | Blk |
|---|---|---|---|---|---|---|---|---|
| Smith | 53 | 2343 | 44.2 | 38.8 | 2 | 23 | 64 | 0 |

**SACKS:** Mathis, 11.5

## Houston Texans

| SCORING | Rush | TD Rec | Ret | PAT | FG | S | Pts |
|---|---|---|---|---|---|---|---|
| Brown | 0 | 0 | 0 | 37 | 29 | 0 | 124 |
| Slaton | 9 | 1 | 0 | 0 | 0 | 0 | 60 |
| A. Johnson | 0 | 8 | 0 | 0 | 0 | 0 | 48 |
| Walter | 0 | 8 | 0 | 0 | 0 | 0 | 48 |
| Green | 3 | 0 | 0 | 0 | 0 | 0 | 18 |

| RUSHING | No. | Yds | Avg | Lg | TD |
|---|---|---|---|---|---|
| Slaton | 268 | 1282 | 4.8 | 71 | 9 |
| Green | 74 | 294 | 4.0 | 14 | 3 |

| PASSING | Att | Comp | Pct Comp | Yds | Avg Gain | TD | Int | Rating Pts |
|---|---|---|---|---|---|---|---|---|
| Schaub | 380 | 251 | 66.1 | 3043 | 8.0 | 15 | 10 | 92.7 |
| Rosenfels | 174 | 116 | 66.7 | 1431 | 8.2 | 6 | 10 | 79.5 |

| RECEIVING | No. | Yds | Avg | Lg | TD |
|---|---|---|---|---|---|
| A. Johnson | 115 | 1575 | 13.7 | 65 | 8 |
| Walter | 60 | 899 | 15.0 | 61 | 8 |
| Daniels | 70 | 862 | 12.3 | 35 | 2 |
| Slaton | 50 | 377 | 7.5 | 46 | 1 |
| Anderson | 19 | 241 | 12.7 | 65 | 2 |
| Davis | 13 | 213 | 16.4 | 49 | 0 |

**INTERCEPTIONS:** Reeves, 4

| PUNTING | No. | Yds | Avg | Net Avg | TB | In 20 | Lg | Blk |
|---|---|---|---|---|---|---|---|---|
| Turk | 53 | 2240 | 42.3 | 35.2 | 7 | 17 | 59 | 0 |

**SACKS:** Williams, 12

## Jacksonville Jaguars

| SCORING | Rush | TD Rec | Ret | PAT | FG | S | Pts |
|---|---|---|---|---|---|---|---|
| Scobee | 0 | 0 | 0 | 33 | 19 | 0 | 90 |
| Jones-Drew | 12 | 2 | 0 | 0 | 0 | 0 | 84 |
| R. Williams | 0 | 3 | 0 | 0 | 0 | 0 | 18 |
| Garrard | 2 | 0 | 0 | 0 | 0 | 0 | 12 |
| M. Jones | 0 | 2 | 0 | 0 | 0 | 0 | 12 |
| M. Lewis | 0 | 2 | 0 | 0 | 0 | 0 | 12 |
| Northcutt | 0 | 2 | 0 | 0 | 0 | 0 | 12 |
| Owens | 2 | 0 | 0 | 0 | 0 | 0 | 12 |

| RUSHING | No. | Yds | Avg | Lg | TD |
|---|---|---|---|---|---|
| Jones-Drew | 197 | 824 | 4.2 | 46 | 12 |
| Taylor | 143 | 556 | 3.9 | 34 | 1 |

| PASSING | Att | Comp | Pct Comp | Yds | Avg Gain | TD | Int | Rating Pts |
|---|---|---|---|---|---|---|---|---|
| Garrard | 535 | 335 | 62.6 | 3620 | 6.8 | 15 | 13 | 81.7 |

| RECEIVING | No. | Yds | Avg | Lg | TD |
|---|---|---|---|---|---|
| M. Jones | 65 | 761 | 11.7 | 35 | 2 |
| Jones-Drew | 62 | 565 | 9.1 | 26 | 2 |
| Northcutt | 44 | 545 | 12.4 | 41 | 2 |
| M. Lewis | 41 | 489 | 11.9 | 30 | 2 |
| R. Williams | 37 | 364 | 9.8 | 32 | 3 |

**INTERCEPTIONS:** Mathis, Sensabaugh, 4

| PUNTING | No. | Yds | Avg | Ne Avg | TB | In 20 | Lg | Blk |
|---|---|---|---|---|---|---|---|---|
| Podlesh | 46 | 1989 | 43.2 | 36.6 | 5 | 12 | 60 | 0 |
| Weatherford | 21 | 915 | 43.6 | 37.7 | 3 | 2 | 57 | 0 |

**SACKS:** Spicer, Harvey, Hayward, 4

## Kansas City Chiefs

| SCORING | Rush | TD Rec | Ret | PAT | FG | S | Pts |
|---|---|---|---|---|---|---|---|
| T. Gonzalez | 0 | 10 | 0 | 0 | 0 | 0 | 60 |
| Barth | 0 | 0 | 0 | 24 | 10 | 0 | 54 |
| Bowe | 0 | 7 | 0 | 0 | 0 | 0 | 42 |
| L. Johnson | 5 | 0 | 0 | 0 | 0 | 0 | 30 |
| Novak | 0 | 0 | 0 | 7 | 6 | 0 | 25 |
| Thigpen | 3 | 1 | 0 | 0 | 0 | 0 | 24 |

| RUSHING | No. | Yds | Avg | Lg | TD |
|---|---|---|---|---|---|
| L. Johnson | 193 | 874 | 4.5 | 65 | 5 |
| Thigpen | 62 | 386 | 6.2 | 32 | 3 |
| Charles | 67 | 357 | 5.3 | 30 | 0 |

| PASSING | Att | Comp | Pct Comp | Yds | Avg Gain | TD | Int | Rating Pts |
|---|---|---|---|---|---|---|---|---|
| Thigpen | 420 | 230 | 54.8 | 2608 | 6.2 | 18 | 12 | 76.0 |
| Huard | 81 | 50 | 61.7 | 477 | 5.9 | 2 | 4 | 65.7 |

| RECEIVING | No. | Yds | Avg | Lg | TD |
|---|---|---|---|---|---|
| T. Gonzalez | 96 | 1058 | 11.0 | 35 | 10 |
| Bowe | 86 | 1022 | 11.9 | 36 | 7 |
| Bradley | 30 | 380 | 12.7 | 56 | 3 |
| Charles | 27 | 272 | 10.1 | 75 | 1 |
| Darling | 17 | 247 | 14.5 | 68 | 1 |

**INTERCEPTIONS:** Page, 4

| PUNTING | No. | Yds | Avg | Net Avg | TB | In 20 | Lg | Blk |
|---|---|---|---|---|---|---|---|---|
| Colquitt | 70 | 3110 | 44.4 | 39.2 | 8 | 27 | 73 | 0 |

**SACKS:** Hali, 3

## Miami Dolphins

| SCORING | Rush | TD Rec | Ret | PAT | FG | S | Pts |
|---|---|---|---|---|---|---|---|
| Carpenter | 0 | 0 | 0 | 40 | 21 | 0 | 103 |
| Brown | 10 | 0 | 0 | 0 | 0 | 0 | 60 |
| Fasano | 0 | 7 | 0 | 0 | 0 | 0 | 42 |
| R. Williams | 4 | 1 | 0 | 0 | 0 | 0 | 30 |
| Ginn | 2 | 2 | 0 | 0 | 0 | 0 | 24 |
| Cobbs | 1 | 2 | 0 | 0 | 0 | 0 | 18 |
| Martin | 0 | 3 | 0 | 0 | 0 | 0 | 18 |

| RUSHING | No. | Yds | Avg | Lg | TD |
|---|---|---|---|---|---|
| Brown | 214 | 916 | 4.3 | 62 | 10 |
| R. Williams | 160 | 659 | 4.1 | 51 | 4 |

| PASSING | Att | Comp | Pct Comp | Yds | Avg Gain | TD | Int | Rating Pts |
|---|---|---|---|---|---|---|---|---|
| Pennington | 476 | 321 | 67.4 | 3653 | 7.7 | 19 | 7 | 97.4 |

| RECEIVING | No. | Yds | Avg | Lg | TD |
|---|---|---|---|---|---|
| Ginn | 56 | 790 | 14.1 | 64 | 2 |
| Camarillo | 55 | 613 | 11.1 | 33 | 2 |
| Bess | 54 | 554 | 10.3 | 37 | 1 |
| Fasano | 34 | 454 | 13.4 | 24 | 7 |
| Martin | 31 | 450 | 14.5 | 61 | 3 |
| Cobbs | 19 | 275 | 14.5 | 80 | 2 |
| Brown | 33 | 254 | 7.7 | 39 | 0 |

**INTERCEPTIONS:** Goodman, 5

| PUNTING | No. | Yds | Avg | Net Avg | TB | In 20 | Lg | Blk |
|---|---|---|---|---|---|---|---|---|
| Fields | 74 | 3249 | 43.9 | 35.5 | 7 | 24 | 71 | 0 |

**SACKS:** Porter, 17.5

## New England Patriots

| SCORING | Rush | TD Rec | Ret | PAT | FG | S | Pts |
|---|---|---|---|---|---|---|---|
| Gostkowski | 0 | 0 | 0 | 40 | 36 | 0 | 148 |
| Moss | 0 | 11 | 0 | 0 | 0 | 0 | 66 |
| Morris | 7 | 0 | 0 | 0 | 0 | 0 | 42 |
| Faulk | 3 | 3 | 0 | 0 | 0 | 0 | 36 |
| Green-Ellis | 5 | 0 | 0 | 0 | 0 | 0 | 30 |
| Jordan | 4 | 0 | 0 | 0 | 0 | 0 | 24 |
| Welker | 0 | 3 | 0 | 0 | 0 | 0 | 18 |

| RUSHING | No. | Yds | Avg | Lg | TD |
|---|---|---|---|---|---|
| Morris | 85 | 384 | 4.5 | 49 | 3 |
| Faulk | 83 | 507 | 6.1 | 41 | 3 |
| Jordan | 80 | 363 | 4.5 | 49 | 4 |
| Green-Ellis | 74 | 275 | 3.7 | 15 | 5 |

| PASSING | Att | Comp | Pct Comp | Yds | Avg Gain | TD | Int | Rating Pts |
|---|---|---|---|---|---|---|---|---|
| Cassell | 516 | 327 | 63.4 | 3693 | 7.2 | 21 | 11 | 89.4 |
| Brady | 11 | 7 | 63.6 | 76 | 6.9 | 0 | 0 | 83.9 |

| RECEIVING | No. | Yds | Avg | Lg | TD |
|---|---|---|---|---|---|
| Welker | 111 | 1165 | 10.5 | 64 | 3 |
| Moss | 69 | 1008 | 14.6 | 76 | 11 |
| Faulk | 58 | 486 | 8.4 | 22 | 3 |
| Gaffney | 38 | 468 | 12.3 | 37 | 2 |
| Watson | 22 | 209 | 9.5 | 29 | 2 |

**INTERCEPTIONS:** Meriweather, 4

| PUNTING | No. | Yds | Avg | Net Avg | TB | In 20 | Lg | Blk |
|---|---|---|---|---|---|---|---|---|
| Hanson | 49 | 2143 | 43.7 | 36.4 | 10 | 19 | 70 | 0 |

**SACKS:** Seymour, 8

## New York Jets

| SCORING | Rush | TD Rec | Ret | PAT | FG | S | Pts |
|---|---|---|---|---|---|---|---|
| Feely | 0 | 0 | 0 | 39 | 24 | 0 | 111 |
| Jones | 13 | 2 | 0 | 0 | 0 | 0 | 90 |
| Washington | 6 | 2 | 1 | 0 | 0 | 0 | 54 |
| Coles | 0 | 7 | 0 | 0 | 0 | 0 | 42 |
| Cotchery | 0 | 5 | 0 | 0 | 0 | 0 | 30 |
| Keller | 0 | 3 | 0 | 0 | 0 | 0 | 18 |
| Stuckey | 0 | 3 | 0 | 0 | 0 | 0 | 18 |

| RUSHING | No. | Yds | Avg | Lg | TD |
|---|---|---|---|---|---|
| Jones | 290 | 1312 | 4.5 | 59 | 13 |
| Washington | 76 | 448 | 5.9 | 61 | 6 |

| PASSING | Att | Comp | Pct Comp | Yds | Avg Gain | TD | Int | Rating Pts |
|---|---|---|---|---|---|---|---|---|
| Favre | 522 | 343 | 65.7 | 3472 | 6.7 | 22 | 22 | 81.0 |

| RECEIVING | No. | Yds | Avg | Lg | TD |
|---|---|---|---|---|---|
| Cotchery | 71 | 858 | 12.1 | 56 | 5 |
| Coles | 70 | 850 | 12.1 | 54 | 7 |
| Keller | 48 | 535 | 11.1 | 54 | 3 |
| Stuckey | 32 | 359 | 11.2 | 31 | 3 |
| Washington | 47 | 355 | 7.6 | 40 | 2 |
| Jones | 36 | 207 | 5.8 | 19 | 2 |

**INTERCEPTIONS:** Revis, 5

| PUNTING | No. | Yds | Avg | Net Avg | TB | In 20 | Lg | Blk |
|---|---|---|---|---|---|---|---|---|
| Hodges | 44 | 1884 | 42.8 | 35.5 | 5 | 14 | 61 | 1 |

**SACKS:** Ellis, 8

### Oakland Raiders

| SCORING | Rush | Rec | Ret | PAT | FG | S | Pts |
|---|---|---|---|---|---|---|---|
| | | TD | | | | | |
| Janikowski | 0 | 0 | 0 | 25 | 24 | 0 | 97 |
| Higgins | 0 | 4 | 3 | 0 | 0 | 0 | 42 |
| McFadden | 4 | 0 | 0 | 0 | 0 | 0 | 24 |
| Bush | 3 | 0 | 0 | 0 | 0 | 0 | 18 |

| RUSHING | No. | Yds | Avg | Lg | TD |
|---|---|---|---|---|---|
| Fargas | 218 | 853 | 3.9 | 42 | 1 |
| McFadden | 113 | 499 | 4.4 | 50 | 4 |
| Bush | 95 | 421 | 4.4 | 67 | 3 |

| PASSING | Att | Comp | Pct Comp | Yds | Avg Gain | TD | Int | Rating Pts |
|---|---|---|---|---|---|---|---|---|
| Russell | 368 | 198 | 53.8 | 2423 | 6.6 | 13 | 8 | 77.1 |
| Walter | 49 | 22 | 204 | 44.9 | 4.2 | 0 | 3 | 31.3 |

| RECEIVING | No. | Yds | Avg | Lg | TD |
|---|---|---|---|---|---|
| Z. Miller | 56 | 778 | 13.9 | 63 | 1 |
| Higgins | 22 | 366 | 16.6 | 84 | 4 |
| McFadden | 29 | 285 | 9.8 | 27 | 0 |
| Schilens | 15 | 226 | 15.1 | 60 | 2 |
| Lelie | 11 | 197 | 17.9 | 51 | 2 |
| Walker | 15 | 196 | 13.1 | 29 | 1 |
| Curry | 19 | 181 | 9.5 | 16 | 2 |

**INTERCEPTIONS:** Johnson, Baker, 3

| PUNTING | No. | Yds | Avg | Net Avg | TB | In 20 | Lg | Blk |
|---|---|---|---|---|---|---|---|---|
| Lechler | 90 | 4391 | 48.8 | 41. | 13 | 33 | 70 | 0 |

**SACKS:** Edwards, Scott, 5

### San Diego Chargers

| SCORING | Rush | Rec | Ret | PAT | FG | S | Pts |
|---|---|---|---|---|---|---|---|
| | | TD | | | | | |
| Kaeding | 0 | 0 | 0 | 46 | 27 | 0 | 127 |
| Tomlinson | 11 | 1 | 0 | 0 | 0 | 0 | 72 |
| Gates | 0 | 8 | 0 | 0 | 0 | 0 | 48 |
| V. Jackson | 0 | 7 | 0 | 0 | 0 | 0 | 42 |
| Sproles | 1 | 5 | 1 | 0 | 0 | 0 | 42 |
| Chambers | 0 | 5 | 0 | 0 | 0 | 0 | 30 |
| Floyd | 0 | 4 | 0 | 0 | 0 | 0 | 24 |

| RUSHING | No. | Yds | Avg | Lg | TD |
|---|---|---|---|---|---|
| Tomlinson | 292 | 1110 | 3.8 | 45 | 11 |
| Sproles | 61 | 330 | 5.4 | 37 | 1 |

| PASSING | Att | Comp | Pct Comp | Yds | Avg Gain | TD | Int | Rating Pts |
|---|---|---|---|---|---|---|---|---|
| Rivers | 478 | 312 | 65.3 | 4009 | 8.4 | 34 | 11 | 105.5 |

| RECEIVING | No. | Yds | Avg | Lg | TD |
|---|---|---|---|---|---|
| V. Jackson | 59 | 1098 | 18.6 | 60 | 7 |
| Gates | 60 | 704 | 11.7 | 34 | 8 |
| Floyd | 27 | 465 | 17.2 | 49 | 4 |
| Chambers | 33 | 462 | 14.0 | 48 | 5 |
| Tomlinson | 52 | 426 | 8.2 | 32 | 1 |
| Sproles | 29 | 342 | 11.8 | 66 | 5 |
| Tolbert | 13 | 171 | 13.2 | 67 | 1 |
| Manumaleuna | 15 | 127 | 8.5 | 17 | 2 |

**INTERCEPTIONS:** Cooper, 4

| PUNTING | No. | Yds | Avg | Net Avg | TB | In 20 | Lg | Blk |
|---|---|---|---|---|---|---|---|---|
| Scifres | 51 | 2332 | 45.7 | 40.9 | 5 | 19 | 67 | 0 |

**SACKS:** Phillips, 7.5

### Pittsburgh Steelers

| SCORING | Rush | Rec | Ret | PAT | FG | S | Pts |
|---|---|---|---|---|---|---|---|
| | | TD | | | | | |
| Reed | 0 | 0 | 0 | 36 | 27 | 0 | 117 |
| Ward | 0 | 7 | 0 | 0 | 0 | 0 | 42 |
| Moore | 5 | 1 | 0 | 0 | 0 | 0 | 36 |
| Holmes | 0 | 5 | 0 | 0 | 0 | 0 | 30 |
| Parker | 5 | 0 | 0 | 0 | 0 | 0 | 30 |

| RUSHING | No. | Yds | Avg | Lg | TD |
|---|---|---|---|---|---|
| Parker | 210 | 791 | 3.8 | 34 | 5 |
| Moore | 140 | 588 | 4.2 | 32 | 5 |

| PASSING | Att | Comp | Pct Comp | Yds | Avg Gain | TD | Int | Rating Pts |
|---|---|---|---|---|---|---|---|---|
| Roethlisberger | 469 | 281 | 59.9 | 3301 | 7.0 | 17 | 15 | 80.1 |
| Leftwich | 36 | 21 | 58.3 | 303 | 8.4 | 2 | 0 | 104.3 |

| RECEIVING | No. | Yds | Avg | Lg | TD |
|---|---|---|---|---|---|
| Ward | 81 | 1043 | 12.9 | 49 | 7 |
| Holmes | 55 | 821 | 14.9 | 48 | 5 |
| N. Washington | 40 | 631 | 15.8 | 65 | 3 |
| Miller | 48 | 514 | 10.7 | 22 | 3 |
| Moore | 40 | 320 | 8.0 | 25 | 1 |
| Spaeth | 17 | 136 | 8.0 | 13 | 0 |

**INTERCEPTIONS:** Polamalu, 7

| PUNTING | No. | Yds | Avg | Net Avg | TB | In 20 | Lg | Blk |
|---|---|---|---|---|---|---|---|---|
| Berger | 66 | 2728 | 41.3 | 36.4 | 4 | 19 | 61 | 0 |

**SACKS:** Harrison, 16

### Tennessee Titans

| SCORING | Rush | Rec | Ret | PAT | FG | S | Pts |
|---|---|---|---|---|---|---|---|
| | | TD | | | | | |
| Bironas | 0 | 0 | 0 | 40 | 29 | 0 | 127 |
| White | 15 | 0 | 0 | 0 | 0 | 0 | 90 |
| C. Johnson | 9 | 1 | 0 | 0 | 0 | 0 | 60 |
| Gage | 0 | 6 | 0 | 0 | 0 | 0 | 36 |
| Scaife | 0 | 2 | 0 | 0 | 0 | 0 | 12 |
| A. Hall | 0 | 2 | 0 | 0 | 0 | 0 | 12 |

| RUSHING | No. | Yds | Avg | Lg | TD |
|---|---|---|---|---|---|
| C. Johnson | 251 | 1228 | 4.9 | 66 | 9 |
| White | 200 | 773 | 3.9 | 80 | 15 |

| PASSING | Att | Comp | Pct Comp | Yds | Avg Gain | TD | Int | Rating Pts |
|---|---|---|---|---|---|---|---|---|
| Collins | 415 | 242 | 58.3 | 2676 | 6.4 | 12 | 7 | 80.2 |
| Young | 36 | 22 | 61.1 | 219 | 6.1 | 1 | 2 | 64.5 |

| RECEIVING | No. | Yds | Avg | Lg | TD |
|---|---|---|---|---|---|
| Gage | 34 | 651 | 19.1 | 56 | 6 |
| Scaife | 58 | 561 | 9.7 | 44 | 2 |
| B. Jones | 41 | 449 | 11.0 | 40 | 1 |
| McCareins | 30 | 412 | 13.7 | 37 | 0 |
| C. Johnson | 43 | 260 | 6.0 | 25 | 1 |
| Crumpler | 24 | 257 | 10.7 | 28 | 1 |
| A. Hall | 13 | 138 | 10.6 | 54 | 2 |

**INTERCEPTIONS:** Griffin, 7

| PUNTING | No. | Yds | Avg | Net Avg | TB | In 20 | Lg | Blk |
|---|---|---|---|---|---|---|---|---|
| Hentrich | 87 | 3725 | 42.8 | 36.5 | 13 | 27 | 75 | 0 |

**SACKS:** Haynesworth, 8.5

### Arizona Cardinals

| SCORING | TD Rush | Rec | Ret | PAT | FG | S | Pts |
|---|---|---|---|---|---|---|---|
| Rackers | 0 | 0 | 0 | 44 | 25 | 0 | 119 |
| Fitzgerald | 0 | 12 | 0 | 0 | 0 | 0 | 72 |
| Boldin | 0 | 11 | 0 | 0 | 0 | 0 | 66 |
| Hightower | 10 | 0 | 0 | 0 | 0 | 0 | 60 |
| Urban | 0 | 4 | 0 | 0 | 0 | 0 | 24 |

| RUSHING | No. | Yds | Avg | Lg | TD |
|---|---|---|---|---|---|
| James | 133 | 514 | 3.9 | 35 | 3 |
| Hightower | 143 | 399 | 2.8 | 30 | 10 |
| Arrington | 31 | 187 | 6.0 | 30 | 1 |

| PASSING | Att | Comp | Pct Comp | Yds | Avg Gain | TD | Int | Rating Pts |
|---|---|---|---|---|---|---|---|---|
| Warner | 598 | 401 | 67.1 | 4583 | 7.7 | 30 | 14 | 96.9 |
| Leinart | 29 | 15 | 51.7 | 264 | 9.1 | 1 | 1 | 80.2 |

| RECEIVING | No. | Yds | Avg | Lg | TD |
|---|---|---|---|---|---|
| Fitzgerald | 96 | 1431 | 14.9 | 78 | 12 |
| Boldin | 89 | 1038 | 11.7 | 79 | 11 |
| Breaston | 77 | 1006 | 13.1 | 58 | 3 |
| Urban | 34 | 448 | 13.2 | 56 | 4 |
| Arrington | 29 | 255 | 8.8 | 35 | 1 |
| Hightower | 34 | 237 | 7.0 | 26 | 0 |

**INTERCEPTIONS:** Rodgers-Cromartie, 4

| PUNTING | No. | Yds | Avg | Net Avg | TB | In 20 | Lg | Blk |
|---|---|---|---|---|---|---|---|---|
| Johnson | 40 | 1670 | 41.8 | 35.2 | 4 | 13 | 59 | 0 |
| Graham | 20 | 839 | 42.0 | 32.0 | 0 | 7 | 59 | 0 |

**SACKS:** Berry, 5

### Carolina Panthers

| SCORING | TD Rush | Rec | Ret | PAT | FG | S | Pts |
|---|---|---|---|---|---|---|---|
| Kasay | 0 | 0 | 0 | 46 | 28 | 0 | 132 |
| D. Williams | 18 | 2 | 0 | 0 | 0 | 0 | 120 |
| Stewart | 10 | 0 | 0 | 0 | 0 | 0 | 60 |
| S. Smith | 0 | 6 | 0 | 0 | 0 | 0 | 36 |
| Muhammad | 0 | 5 | 0 | 0 | 0 | 0 | 30 |

| RUSHING | No. | Yds | Avg | Lg | TD |
|---|---|---|---|---|---|
| D. Williams | 273 | 1515 | 5.5 | 69 | 18 |
| Stewart | 184 | 836 | 4.5 | 41 | 10 |

| PASSING | Att | Comp | Pct Comp | Yds | Avg Gain | TD | Int | Rating Pts |
|---|---|---|---|---|---|---|---|---|
| Delhomme | 414 | 246 | 59.4 | 3288 | 7.9 | 15 | 12 | 84.7 |

| RECEIVING | No. | Yds | Avg | Lg | TD |
|---|---|---|---|---|---|
| S. Smith | 78 | 1421 | 18.2 | 65 | 6 |
| Muhammad | 65 | 923 | 14.2 | 60 | 5 |
| Rosario | 18 | 209 | 11.6 | 24 | 1 |
| King | 21 | 195 | 9.3 | 31 | 1 |
| Hackett | 13 | 181 | 13.9 | 37 | 0 |
| D. Williams | 22 | 121 | 5.5 | 25 | 2 |
| Jarrett | 10 | 119 | 11.9 | 25 | 0 |

**INTERCEPTIONS:** Beason, Gamble, 3

| PUNTING | No. | Yds | Avg | Net Avg | TB | In 20 | Lg | Blk |
|---|---|---|---|---|---|---|---|---|
| Baker | 73 | 3217 | 44.1 | 37.4 | 5 | 30 | 63 | 3 |

**SACKS:** Peppers, 14.5

### Atlanta Falcons

| SCORING | TD Rush | Rec | Ret | PAT | FG | S | Pts |
|---|---|---|---|---|---|---|---|
| Elam | 0 | 0 | 0 | 42 | 29 | 0 | 129 |
| Turner | 17 | 0 | 0 | 0 | 0 | 0 | 102 |
| White | 0 | 7 | 0 | 0 | 0 | 0 | 42 |
| Norwood | 4 | 2 | 0 | 0 | 0 | 0 | 36 |
| Jenkins | 0 | 3 | 0 | 0 | 0 | 0 | 18 |
| Douglas | 1 | 1 | 1 | 0 | 0 | 0 | 18 |

| RUSHING | No. | Yds | Avg | Lg | TD |
|---|---|---|---|---|---|
| Turner | 376 | 1699 | 4.5 | 70 | 17 |
| Norwood | 95 | 489 | 5.1 | 45 | 4 |

| PASSING | Att | Comp | Pct Comp | Yds | Avg Gain | TD | Int | Rating Pts |
|---|---|---|---|---|---|---|---|---|
| Ryan | 434 | 265 | 61.1 | 3440 | 67.9 | 16 | 11 | 87.7 |

| RECEIVING | No. | Yds | Avg | Lg | TD |
|---|---|---|---|---|---|
| White | 88 | 1382 | 15.7 | 70 | 7 |
| Jenkins | 50 | 777 | 15.5 | 62 | 3 |
| Norwood | 36 | 338 | 9.4 | 67 | 2 |
| Douglas | 23 | 320 | 13.9 | 69 | 1 |
| Finneran | 21 | 169 | 8.0 | 14 | 1 |
| Peelle | 15 | 159 | 10.6 | 18 | 2 |

**INTERCEPTIONS:** Coleman, 3

| PUNTING | No. | Yds | Avg | Net Avg | TB | In 20 | Lg | Blk |
|---|---|---|---|---|---|---|---|---|
| Koenen | 63 | 2566 | 40.7 | 40.7 | 4 | 25 | 60 | 2 |

**SACKS:** Abraham, 16.5

### Chicago Bears

| SCORING | TD Rush | Rec | Ret | PAT | FG | S | Pts |
|---|---|---|---|---|---|---|---|
| Gould | 0 | 0 | 0 | 41 | 26 | 0 | 119 |
| Forte | 8 | 4 | 0 | 0 | 0 | 0 | 72 |
| Olsen | 0 | 5 | 0 | 0 | 0 | 0 | 30 |
| Hester | 0 | 3 | 0 | 0 | 0 | 0 | 18 |
| McKie | 2 | 1 | 0 | 0 | 0 | 0 | 18 |
| Orton | 3 | 0 | 0 | 0 | 0 | 0 | 18 |

| RUSHING | No. | Yds | Avg | Lg | TD |
|---|---|---|---|---|---|
| Forte | 316 | 1238 | 3.9 | 50 | 8 |
| K. Jones | 34 | 109 | 3.2 | 16 | 0 |

| PASSING | Att | Comp | Pct Comp | Yds | Avg Gain | TD | Int | Rating Pts |
|---|---|---|---|---|---|---|---|---|
| Orton | 465 | 272 | 58.5 | 2972 | 6.4 | 18 | 12 | 79.6 |
| Grossman | 62 | 32 | 51.6 | 257 | 4.1 | 2 | 2 | 59.7 |

| RECEIVING | No. | Yds | Avg | Lg | TD |
|---|---|---|---|---|---|
| Hester | 51 | 665 | 13.0 | 65 | 3 |
| Olsen | 54 | 574 | 10.6 | 52 | 5 |
| Forte | 63 | 477 | 7.6 | 19 | 4 |
| R. Davis | 35 | 445 | 12.7 | 36 | 2 |
| Clark | 41 | 367 | 9.0 | 35 | 1 |
| Lloyd | 26 | 364 | 14.0 | 32 | 2 |
| Booker | 14 | 211 | 15.1 | 51 | 2 |

**INTERCEPTIONS:** Payne, 4

| PUNTING | No. | Yds | Avg | Net Avg | TB | In 20 | Lg | Blk |
|---|---|---|---|---|---|---|---|---|
| Maynard | 96 | 3957 | 41.2 | 38.1 | 5 | 40 | 67 | 0 |

**SACKS:** Brown, 6

## Dallas Cowboys

### SCORING

| | TD Rush | Rec | Ret | PAT | FG | S | Pts |
|---|---|---|---|---|---|---|---|
| Folk | 0 | 0 | 0 | 42 | 20 | 0 | 100 |
| Owens | 0 | 10 | 0 | 0 | 0 | 0 | 60 |
| Barber | 7 | 2 | 0 | 0 | 0 | 0 | 54 |

### RUSHING

| | No. | Yds | Avg | Lg | TD |
|---|---|---|---|---|---|
| Barber | 238 | 885 | 3.7 | 35 | 7 |
| Choice | 92 | 472 | 5.1 | 38 | 2 |
| F. Jones | 30 | 266 | 8.9 | 60 | 3 |

### PASSING

| | Att | Comp | Pct Comp | Yds | Avg Gain | TD | Int | Rating Pts |
|---|---|---|---|---|---|---|---|---|
| Romo | 450 | 276 | 61.3 | 3448 | 7.7 | 26 | 14 | 91.4 |
| B. Johnson | 78 | 41 | 52.6 | 427 | 5.5 | 2 | 5 | 50.5 |

### RECEIVING

| | No. | Yds | Avg | Lg | TD |
|---|---|---|---|---|---|
| Owens | 69 | 1052 | 15.2 | 75 | 10 |
| Witten | 81 | 952 | 11.8 | 42 | 4 |
| Crayton | 39 | 550 | 14.1 | 55 | 4 |
| Barber | 52 | 417 | 8.0 | 70 | 2 |
| Austin | 13 | 278 | 21.4 | 63 | 3 |
| Bennett | 20 | 283 | 14.2 | 37 | 4 |

**INTERCEPTIONS:** Newman, 4

### PUNTING

| | No. | Yds | Avg | Net Avg | TB | In 20 | Lg | Blk |
|---|---|---|---|---|---|---|---|---|
| Paulescu | 53 | 2213 | 41.8 | 35.2 | 5 | 14 | 70 | 0 |
| McBriar | 24 | 1175 | 49.0 | 38.8 | 3 | 5 | 66 | 1 |

**SACKS:** Ware, 20

## Green Bay Packers

### SCORING

| | TD Rush | Rec | Ret | PAT | FG | S | Pts |
|---|---|---|---|---|---|---|---|
| Crosby | 0 | 0 | 0 | 46 | 27 | 0 | 127 |
| Jennings | 0 | 9 | 0 | 0 | 0 | 0 | 54 |
| Driver | 0 | 5 | 0 | 0 | 0 | 0 | 30 |
| Grant | 4 | 1 | 0 | 0 | 0 | 0 | 30 |
| Lee | 0 | 5 | 0 | 0 | 0 | 0 | 30 |
| Rodgers | 4 | 0 | 0 | 0 | 0 | 0 | 24 |

### RUSHING

| | No. | Yds | Avg | Lg | TD |
|---|---|---|---|---|---|
| Grant | 312 | 1203 | 3.9 | 57 | 4 |
| B. Jackson | 45 | 248 | 5.5 | 32 | 1 |

### PASSING

| | Att | Comp | Pct Comp | Yds | Avg Gain | TD | Int | Rating Pts |
|---|---|---|---|---|---|---|---|---|
| Rodgers | 536 | 341 | 63.6 | 4038 | 7.5 | 28 | 13 | 93.8 |

### RECEIVING

| | No. | Yds | Avg | Lg | TD |
|---|---|---|---|---|---|
| Jennings | 80 | 1292 | 16.2 | 63 | 9 |
| Driver | 74 | 1012 | 13.7 | 71 | 5 |
| Nelson | 33 | 366 | 11.1 | 29 | 2 |
| Lee | 39 | 303 | 7.8 | 26 | 5 |
| J. Jones | 20 | 274 | 13.7 | 46 | 1 |
| B. Jackson | 30 | 185 | 6.2 | 18 | 0 |

**INTERCEPTIONS:** Collins, Woodson, 7

### PUNTING

| | No. | Yds | Avg | Net Avg | TB | In 20 | Lg | Blk |
|---|---|---|---|---|---|---|---|---|
| Frost | 48 | 2021 | 42.1 | 36.1 | 5 | 8 | 65 | 0 |
| Kapinos | 17 | 667 | 39.2 | 34.5 | 1 | 7 | 55 | 0 |

**SACKS:** Kampman, 9.5

## Detroit Lions

### SCORING

| | TD Rush | Rec | Ret | PAT | FG | S | Pts |
|---|---|---|---|---|---|---|---|
| Hanson | 0 | 0 | 0 | 25 | 21 | 0 | 88 |
| C. Johnson | 0 | 12 | 0 | 0 | 0 | 0 | 72 |
| K. Smith | 8 | 0 | 0 | 0 | 0 | 0 | 48 |
| R. Johnson | 1 | 1 | 0 | 0 | 0 | 0 | 12 |

### RUSHING

| | No. | Yds | Avg | Lg | TD |
|---|---|---|---|---|---|
| K. Smith | 238 | 976 | 4.1 | 50 | 8 |
| R. Johnson | 76 | 237 | 3.1 | 27 | 1 |

### PASSING

| | Att | Comp | Pct Comp | Yds | Avg Gain | TD | Int | Rating Pts |
|---|---|---|---|---|---|---|---|---|
| Orlovsky | 255 | 143 | 56.1 | 1616 | 6.3 | 8 | 8 | 72.6 |
| Kitna | 120 | 68 | 56.7 | 758 | 6.3 | 5 | 5 | 72.2 |
| Culpepper | 115 | 60 | 52.2 | 786 | 6.8 | 4 | 6 | 63.9 |

### RECEIVING

| | No. | Yds | Avg | Lg | TD |
|---|---|---|---|---|---|
| C. Johnson | 72 | 1331 | 17.1 | 96 | 12 |
| McDonald | 35 | 332 | 9.5 | 26 | 1 |
| K. Smith | 39 | 286 | 7.3 | 27 | 0 |
| Gaines | 23 | 260 | 11.3 | 33 | 1 |
| Standeford | 15 | 244 | 16.3 | 36 | 0 |
| Furrey | 18 | 181 | 10.1 | 25 | 0 |

**INTERCEPTIONS:** Bodden, Nece, Smith, D. White, 1

### PUNTING

| | No. | Yds | Avg | Net Avg | TB | In 20 | Lg | Blk |
|---|---|---|---|---|---|---|---|---|
| Harris | 90 | 3952 | 43.9 | 38.0 | 6 | 24 | 66 | 0 |

**SACKS:** D. White, 6.5

## Minnesota Vikings

### SCORING

| | TD Rush | Rec | Ret | PAT | FG | S | Pts |
|---|---|---|---|---|---|---|---|
| Longwell | 0 | 0 | 0 | 40 | 29 | 0 | 127 |
| Peterson | 10 | 0 | 0 | 0 | 0 | 0 | 60 |
| Berrian | 0 | 7 | 1 | 0 | 0 | 0 | 48 |
| Shiancoe | 0 | 7 | 0 | 0 | 0 | 0 | 42 |
| Rice | 0 | 4 | 0 | 0 | 0 | 0 | 24 |

### RUSHING

| | No. | Yds | Avg | Lg | TD |
|---|---|---|---|---|---|
| Peterson | 363 | 1760 | 4.8 | 67 | 10 |
| Taylor | 101 | 399 | 4.0 | 21 | 4 |
| Jackson | 26 | 145 | 5.6 | 29 | 0 |

### PASSING

| | Att | Comp | Pct Comp | Yds | Avg Gain | TD | Int | Rating Pts |
|---|---|---|---|---|---|---|---|---|
| Frerotte | 301 | 178 | 59.1 | 2157 | 7.2 | 12 | 15 | 73.7 |
| Jackson | 149 | 88 | 59.1 | 1056 | 7.1 | 9 | 2 | 95.4 |

### RECEIVING

| | No. | Yds | Avg | Lg | TD |
|---|---|---|---|---|---|
| Berrian | 48 | 964 | 20.1 | 99 | 7 |
| Wade | 53 | 645 | 12.2 | 59 | 2 |
| Shiancoe | 42 | 596 | 14.2 | 60 | 7 |
| Taylor | 45 | 399 | 8.9 | 47 | 2 |
| Rice | 15 | 141 | 9.4 | 23 | 4 |
| Peterson | 21 | 125 | 6.0 | 16 | 0 |

**INTERCEPTIONS:** Leber, Sapp, Winfield, M. Williams, 2

### PUNTING

| | No. | Yds | Avg | Net Avg | TB | In 20 | Lg | Blk |
|---|---|---|---|---|---|---|---|---|
| Kluwe | 73 | 3473 | 47.6 | 35.0 | 13 | 23 | 62 | 1 |

**SACKS:** J. Allen, 14.5

## New Orleans Saints

| SCORING | Rush | Rec | Ret | PAT | FG | S | Pts |
|---|---|---|---|---|---|---|---|
| Thomas | 9 | 3 | 0 | 0 | 0 | 0 | 72 |
| Hartley | 0 | 0 | 0 | 28 | 13 | 0 | 67 |
| Moore | 0 | 10 | 0 | 0 | 0 | 0 | 60 |
| Bush | 2 | 4 | 3 | 0 | 0 | 0 | 54 |
| McAllister | 5 | 1 | 0 | 0 | 0 | 0 | 36 |
| Colston | 0 | 5 | 0 | 0 | 0 | 0 | 30 |

| RUSHING | No. | Yds | Avg | Lg | TD |
|---|---|---|---|---|---|
| Thomas | 129 | 625 | 4.8 | 52 | 9 |
| McAllister | 107 | 418 | 3.9 | 19 | 5 |
| Bush | 106 | 404 | 3.8 | 43 | 2 |

| PASSING | Att | Comp | Pct Comp | Yds | Avg Gain | TD | Int | Rating Pts |
|---|---|---|---|---|---|---|---|---|
| Brees | 635 | 413 | 65.0 | 5069 | 8.0 | 34 | 17 | 96.2 |

| RECEIVING | No. | Yds | Avg | Lg | TD |
|---|---|---|---|---|---|
| Moore | 79 | 928 | 11.7 | 70 | 10 |
| Henderson | 32 | 793 | 24.8 | 84 | 3 |
| Colston | 47 | 760 | 16.2 | 70 | 5 |
| Miller | 45 | 579 | 12.9 | 41 | 1 |
| Shockey | 50 | 483 | 9.7 | 26 | 0 |
| Bush | 52 | 440 | 8.5 | 42 | 4 |
| Meachem | 12 | 289 | 24.1 | 74 | 3 |
| Thomas | 31 | 284 | 9.2 | 24 | 3 |

**INTERCEPTIONS:** David, 5

| PUNTING | No. | Yds | Avg | Net Avg | TB | In 20 | Lg | Blk |
|---|---|---|---|---|---|---|---|---|
| Pakulak | 24 | 1144 | 47.7 | 37.8 | 2 | 3 | 70 | 0 |
| Weatherford | 26 | 1094 | 42.1 | 34.2 | 3 | 5 | 61 | 0 |

**SACKS:** McCray, 6

## Philadelphia Eagles

| SCORING | Rush | Rec | Ret | PAT | FG | S | Pts |
|---|---|---|---|---|---|---|---|
| Akers | 0 | 0 | 0 | 45 | 33 | 0 | 144 |
| Westbrook | 9 | 5 | 0 | 0 | 0 | 0 | 84 |
| Curtis | 0 | 6 | 2 | 0 | 0 | 1 | 48 |
| D. Jackson | 1 | 2 | 1 | 0 | 0 | 0 | 24 |
| Buckhalter | 2 | 2 | 0 | 0 | 0 | 0 | 24 |

| RUSHING | No. | Yds | Avg | Lg | TD |
|---|---|---|---|---|---|
| Westbrook | 233 | 936 | 4.0 | 39 | 9 |
| Buckhalter | 76 | 369 | 4.9 | 33 | 2 |

| PASSING | Att | Comp | Pct Comp | Yds | Avg Gain | TD | Int | Rating Pts |
|---|---|---|---|---|---|---|---|---|
| McNabb | 571 | 345 | 60.4 | 3916 | 6.9 | 23 | 11 | 86.4 |

| RECEIVING | No. | Yds | Avg | Lg | TD |
|---|---|---|---|---|---|
| D. Jackson | 62 | 912 | 14.7 | 60 | 2 |
| Westbrook | 54 | 402 | 7.4 | 47 | 5 |
| Baskett | 33 | 440 | 13.3 | 90 | 3 |
| Curtis | 33 | 390 | 11.8 | 32 | 2 |
| Avant | 32 | 377 | 11.8 | 31 | 2 |
| Buckhalter | 26 | 324 | 12.5 | 59 | 2 |
| Celek | 27 | 318 | 11.8 | 44 | 1 |
| Smith | 37 | 298 | 8.1 | 25 | 3 |

**INTERCEPTIONS:** Samuel, 4

| PUNTING | No. | Yds | Avg | Net Avg | TB | In 20 | Lg | Blk |
|---|---|---|---|---|---|---|---|---|
| Rocca | 77 | 3334 | 43.3 | 37.9 | 4 | 24 | 65 | 1 |

**SACKS:** Howard, 10

## New York Giants

| SCORING | Rush | Rec | Ret | PAT | FG | S | Pts |
|---|---|---|---|---|---|---|---|
| Carney | 0 | 0 | 0 | 38 | 35 | 0 | 143 |
| Jacobs | 15 | 0 | 0 | 0 | 0 | 0 | 90 |
| Boss | 0 | 6 | 0 | 0 | 0 | 0 | 36 |
| Burress | 0 | 4 | 0 | 0 | 0 | 0 | 24 |
| Toomer | 0 | 4 | 0 | 0 | 0 | 0 | 24 |

| RUSHING | No. | Yds | Avg | Lg | TD |
|---|---|---|---|---|---|
| Jacobs | 219 | 1089 | 5.0 | 44 | 15 |
| Ward | 182 | 1025 | 5.6 | 51 | 2 |
| Bradshaw | 67 | 355 | 5.3 | 77 | 1 |

| PASSING | Att | Comp | Pct Comp | Yds | Avg Gain | TD | Int | Rating Pts |
|---|---|---|---|---|---|---|---|---|
| Manning | 479 | 289 | 60.3 | 3238 | 6.8 | 21 | 10 | 86.4 |

| RECEIVING | No. | Yds | Avg | Lg | TD |
|---|---|---|---|---|---|
| Hixon | 43 | 596 | 13.9 | 41 | 2 |
| Toomer | 48 | 580 | 12.1 | 40 | 4 |
| Smith | 57 | 574 | 10.1 | 30 | 1 |
| Burress | 35 | 454 | 13.0 | 33 | 4 |
| Ward | 41 | 384 | 9.4 | 48 | 0 |
| Boss | 33 | 384 | 11.6 | 28 | 6 |
| Si. Moss | 12 | 153 | 12.8 | 27 | 2 |
| Hedgecock | 8 | 52 | 6.5 | 13 | 1 |
| Bradshaw | 5 | 42 | 8.4 | 18 | 1 |

**INTERCEPTIONS:** Butler, Ross, Webster, 3

| PUNTING | No. | Yds | Avg | Net Avg | TB | In 20 | Lg | Blk |
|---|---|---|---|---|---|---|---|---|
| Feagles | 64 | 2814 | 404.0 | 40.2 | 5 | 23 | 61 | 0 |

**SACKS:** Tuck, 12

## St. Louis Rams

| SCORING | Rush | Rec | Ret | PAT | FG | S | Pts |
|---|---|---|---|---|---|---|---|
| Brown | 0 | 0 | 0 | 19 | 31 | 0 | 112 |
| S. Jackson | 7 | 1 | 0 | 0 | 0 | 0 | 48 |
| Avery | 1 | 3 | 0 | 0 | 0 | 0 | 24 |
| Holt | 0 | 3 | 0 | 0 | 0 | 0 | 18 |

| RUSHING | No. | Yds | Avg | Lg | TD |
|---|---|---|---|---|---|
| S. Jackson | 253 | 1042 | 4.1 | 56 | 7 |
| Pittman | 79 | 296 | 3.7 | 24 | 0 |

| PASSING | Att | Comp | Pct Comp | Yds | Avg Gain | TD | Int | Rating Pts |
|---|---|---|---|---|---|---|---|---|
| Bulger | 440 | 251 | 57.0 | 2720 | 6.2 | 11 | 13 | 71.4 |
| Green | 72 | 38 | 52.8 | 525 | 7.3 | 0 | 6 | 41.7 |

| RECEIVING | No. | Yds | Avg | Lg | TD |
|---|---|---|---|---|---|
| Holt | 64 | 796 | 12.4 | 45 | 3 |
| Avery | 53 | 674 | 12.7 | 69 | 3 |
| S. Jackson | 40 | 379 | 9.5 | 53 | 1 |
| Looker | 23 | 271 | 11.8 | 30 | 2 |
| Darby | 19 | 183 | 9.6 | 30 | 0 |
| Burton | 13 | 172 | 13.2 | 30 | 1 |
| McMichael | 11 | 139 | 12.6 | 31 | 0 |
| Pittman | 18 | 132 | 7.3 | 27 | 0 |

**INTERCEPTIONS:** Atogwe, 5

| PUNTING | No. | Yds | Avg | Net Avg | TB | In 20 | Lg | Blk |
|---|---|---|---|---|---|---|---|---|
| Jones | 82 | 4100 | 50.0 | 41.1 | 7 | 20 | 68 | 0 |

**SACKS:** Hall 6.5

## San Francisco 49ers

### SCORING
| | | TD | | | | | |
|---|---|---|---|---|---|---|---|
| SCORING | Rush | Rec | Ret | PAT | FG | S | Pts |
| Nedney | 0 | 0 | 0 | 34 | 29 | 0 | 121 |
| Gore | 6 | 2 | 0 | 0 | 0 | 0 | 48 |
| Bruce | 0 | 7 | 0 | 0 | 0 | 0 | 42 |
| B. Johnson | 0 | 3 | 0 | 0 | 0 | 0 | 18 |
| Morgan | 0 | 3 | 0 | 0 | 0 | 0 | 18 |

### RUSHING
| RUSHING | No. | Yds | Avg | Lg | TD |
|---|---|---|---|---|---|
| Gore | 240 | 1036 | 4.3 | 41 | 6 |
| Foster | 76 | 234 | 3.1 | 18 | 1 |

### PASSING
| PASSING | Att | Comp | Pct Comp | Yds | Avg Gain | TD | Int | Rating Pts |
|---|---|---|---|---|---|---|---|---|
| S. Hill | 288 | 181 | 62.8 | 2046 | 7.1 | 13 | 8 | 87.5 |
| O'Sullivan | 220 | 128 | 58.2 | 1678 | 7.6 | 8 | 11 | 73.6 |

### RECEIVING
| RECEIVING | No. | Yds | Avg | Lg | TD |
|---|---|---|---|---|---|
| Bruce | 61 | 835 | 13.7 | 63 | 7 |
| B. Johnson | 45 | 546 | 12.1 | 42 | 3 |
| Gore | 43 | 373 | 8.7 | 26 | 2 |
| V. Davis | 31 | 358 | 11.5 | 57 | 2 |
| Morgan | 20 | 319 | 16.0 | 48 | 3 |
| Battle | 24 | 318 | 13.3 | 36 | 0 |
| J. Hill | 30 | 317 | 10.6 | 33 | 2 |

**INTERCEPTIONS:** Harris, Spikes, 3

### PUNTING
| PUNTING | No. | Yds | Avg | Net Avg | TB | In 20 | Lg | Blk |
|---|---|---|---|---|---|---|---|---|
| Lee | 66 | 3155 | 47.8 | 39.0 | 9 | 13 | 82 | 1 |

**SACKS:** Haralson, 8

## Tampa Bay Buccaneers

### SCORING
| | | TD | | | | | |
|---|---|---|---|---|---|---|---|
| SCORING | Rush | Rec | Ret | PAT | FG | S | Pts |
| M. Bryant | 0 | 0 | 0 | 35 | 32 | 0 | 131 |
| A. Bryant | 0 | 7 | 0 | 0 | 0 | 0 | 42 |
| Graham | 4 | 0 | 0 | 0 | 0 | 0 | 24 |
| Hilliard | 0 | 4 | 0 | 0 | 0 | 0 | 24 |
| Williams | 4 | 0 | 0 | 0 | 0 | 0 | 24 |
| A. Smith | 0 | 3 | 0 | 0 | 0 | 0 | 18 |

### RUSHING
| RUSHING | No. | Yds | Avg | Lg | TD |
|---|---|---|---|---|---|
| Dunn | 186 | 786 | 4.2 | 40 | 2 |
| Graham | 132 | 563 | 4.3 | 68 | 4 |
| Williams | 63 | 233 | 3.7 | 28 | 4 |

### PASSING
| PASSING | Att | Comp | Pct Comp | Yds | Avg Gain | TD | Int | Rating Pts |
|---|---|---|---|---|---|---|---|---|
| Garcia | 376 | 244 | 64.9 | 2712 | 7.2 | 12 | 6 | 90.2 |
| Griese | 184 | 110 | 59.8 | 1073 | 5.8 | 5 | 7 | 69.4 |

### RECEIVING
| RECEIVING | No. | Yds | Avg | Lg | TD |
|---|---|---|---|---|---|
| A. Bryant | 83 | 1248 | 15.0 | 71 | 7 |
| Clayton | 38 | 484 | 12.7 | 58 | 1 |
| Hilliard | 47 | 424 | 9.0 | 36 | 4 |
| Stevens | 36 | 397 | 11.0 | 31 | 2 |
| Dunn | 47 | 330 | 7.0 | 36 | 0 |
| A. Smith | 21 | 250 | 11.9 | 34 | 3 |

**INTERCEPTIONS:** Barber, Talib, 4

### PUNTING
| PUNTING | No. | Yds | Avg | Net Avg | TB | In 20 | Lg | Blk |
|---|---|---|---|---|---|---|---|---|
| Bidwell | 77 | 3426 | 44.5 | 37.6 | 7 | 27 | 64 | 0 |

**SACKS:** Adams, 6.5

## Seattle Seahawks

### SCORING
| | | TD | | | | | |
|---|---|---|---|---|---|---|---|
| SCORING | Rush | Rec | Ret | PAT | FG | S | Pts |
| Mare | 0 | 0 | 0 | 30 | 27 | 0 | 111 |
| Duckett | 8 | 0 | 0 | 0 | 0 | 0 | 48 |
| Carlson | 0 | 5 | 0 | 0 | 0 | 0 | 30 |
| Branch | 0 | 4 | 0 | 0 | 0 | 0 | 24 |

### RUSHING
| RUSHING | No. | Yds | Avg | Lg | TD |
|---|---|---|---|---|---|
| J. Jones | 158 | 698 | 4.4 | 33 | 2 |
| Morris | 132 | 574 | 4.3 | 45 | 0 |
| Duckett | 62 | 172 | 2.8 | 29 | 8 |

### PASSING
| PASSING | Att | Comp | Pct Comp | Yds | Avg Gain | TD | Int | Rating Pts |
|---|---|---|---|---|---|---|---|---|
| Wallace | 242 | 141 | 58.3 | 1532 | 6.3 | 11 | 3 | 87.0 |
| Hasselbeck | 209 | 109 | 52.2 | 1216 | 5.8 | 5 | 10 | 57.8 |

### RECEIVING
| RECEIVING | No. | Yds | Avg | Lg | TD |
|---|---|---|---|---|---|
| Carlson | 55 | 627 | 11.4 | 33 | 5 |
| Engram | 47 | 489 | 10.4 | 37 | 0 |
| Branch | 30 | 412 | 13.7 | 63 | 4 |
| Robinson | 31 | 400 | 12.9 | 90 | 2 |
| Weaver | 20 | 222 | 11.1 | 62 | 2 |
| Morris | 19 | 136 | 7.2 | 13 | 2 |

**INTERCEPTIONS:** Wilson, 4

### PUNTING
| PUNTING | No. | Yds | Avg | Net Avg | TB | In 20 | Lg | Blk |
|---|---|---|---|---|---|---|---|---|
| Ryan | 78 | 3557 | 45.6 | 37.9 | 12 | 22 | 63 | 1 |

**SACKS:** Tapp, Mebane, 5.5

## Washington Redskins

### SCORING
| | | TD | | | | | |
|---|---|---|---|---|---|---|---|
| SCORING | Rush | Rec | Ret | PAT | FG | S | Pts |
| Suisham | 0 | 0 | 0 | 25 | 26 | 0 | 103 |
| Portis | 9 | 0 | 0 | 0 | 0 | 0 | 54 |
| Moss | 0 | 6 | 1 | 0 | 0 | 0 | 42 |
| Randle El | 0 | 4 | 0 | 0 | 0 | 0 | 24 |

### RUSHING
| RUSHING | No. | Yds | Avg | Lg | TD |
|---|---|---|---|---|---|
| Portis | 342 | 1487 | 4.3 | 31 | 9 |
| Campbell | 47 | 258 | 5.5 | 23 | 1 |
| Betts | 61 | 206 | 3.4 | 14 | 1 |

### PASSING
| PASSING | Att | Comp | Pct Comp | Yds | Avg Gain | TD | Int | Rating Pts |
|---|---|---|---|---|---|---|---|---|
| Campbell | 506 | 315 | 62.3 | 3245 | 6.4 | 13 | 6 | 84.3 |

### RECEIVING
| RECEIVING | No. | Yds | Avg | Lg | TD |
|---|---|---|---|---|---|
| Moss | 79 | 1044 | 13.2 | 67 | 6 |
| Cooley | 83 | 849 | 10.2 | 28 | 1 |
| Randle El | 53 | 593 | 11.2 | 31 | 4 |
| Portis | 28 | 218 | 7.8 | 29 | 0 |
| Betts | 22 | 200 | 9.1 | 27 | 0 |
| Thomas | 15 | 120 | 9.0 | 18 | 0 |
| Sellers | 12 | 98 | 8.2 | 20 | 1 |
| Thrash | 9 | 81 | 9.0 | 29 | 1 |

**INTERCEPTIONS:** Horton, 3

### PUNTING
| PUNTING | No. | Yds | Avg | Net Avg | TB | In 20 | Lg | Blk |
|---|---|---|---|---|---|---|---|---|
| Plackemeier | 55 | 2291 | 41.7 | 33.9 | 10 | 15 | 62 | 1 |
| Brooks | 26 | 1030 | 39.6 | 32.1 | 0 | 9 | 60 | 0 |

**SACKS:** Carter, Evans, Taylor, 4

First two rounds of the 73rd annual NFL Draft, held April 25–26, 2009 in New York City.

## First Round

| Team | Selection | Position |
|------|-----------|----------|
| 1. ...............Detroit | Matthew Stafford, Georgia | QB |
| 2. ...............St. Louis | Jason Smith, Baylor | OT |
| 3. ...............Kansas City | Tyson Jackson, LSU | DE |
| 4. ...............Seattle | Aaron Curry, Wake Forest | OLB |
| 5. ...............NY Jets (from Cleveland) | Mark Sanchez, USC | QB |
| 6. ...............Cincinnati | Andre Smith, Alabama | OT |
| 7. ...............Oakland | Darrius Heyward-Bey, Maryland | WR |
| 8. ...............Jacksonville | Eugene Monroe, Virginia | OT |
| 9. ...............Green Bay | B.J. Raji, Boston College | DT |
| 10. .............San Francisco | Michael Crabtree, Texas Tech | WR |
| 11. .............Buffalo | Aaron Maybin, Penn St | DE |
| 12. .............Denver | Knowshon Moreno, Georgia | RB |
| 13. .............Washington | Brian Orakpo, Texas | DE |
| 14. .............New Orleans | Malcolm Jenkins, Ohio St | CB |
| 15. .............Houston | Brian Cushing, USC | OLB |
| 16. .............San Diego | Larry English, Northern Illinois | DE |
| 17. .............Tampa Bay (from NY Jets through Cleveland) | Josh Freeman, Kansas St | QB |
| 18. .............Denver (from Chicago) | Robert Ayers, Tennessee | LB |
| 19. .............Philadelphia (from Tampa Bay through Cleveland) | Jeremy Maclin, Missouri | WR |
| 20. .............Detroit (from Dallas) | Brandon Pettigrew, Oklahoma St | TE |
| 21. .............Cleveland (from Philadelphia) | Alex Mack, California | C |
| 22. .............Minnesota | Percy Harvin, Florida | WR |
| 23. .............Baltimore (from New England) | Michael Oher, Mississippi | OT |
| 24. .............Atlanta | Peria Jerry, Mississippi | DT |
| 25. .............Miami | Vontae Davis, Illinois | CB |
| 26. .............Green Bay (from Baltimore through New England) | Clay Matthews, USC | OLB |
| 27. .............Indianapolis | Donald Brown, Connecticut | RB |
| 28. .............Buffalo (from Carolina through Philadelphia) | Eric Wood, Louisville | C |
| 29. .............NY Giants | Hakeem Nicks, North Carolina | WR |
| 30. .............Tennessee | Kenny Britt, Rutgers | WR |
| 31. .............Arizona | Chris Wells, Ohio St | RB |
| 32. .............Pittsburgh | Evander Hood, Missouri | DT |

## Second Round

| Team | Selection | Position |
|---|---|---|
| 33. ..............Detroit | Louis Delmas, Western Michigan | CB |
| 34. ..............New England (from Kansas City) | Patrick Chung, Oregon | SS |
| 35. ..............St. Louis | James Laurinaitis, Ohio St | LB |
| 36. ..............Cleveland | Brian Robiskie, Ohio St | WR |
| 37. ..............Denver (from Seattle) | Alphonso Smith, Wake Forest | CB |
| 38. ..............Cincinnati | Rey Maualaga, USC | LB |
| 39. ..............Jacksonville | Eben Britton, Arizona | OT |
| 40. ..............New England (from Oakland) | Ron Brace, Boston College | DT |
| 41. ..............New England (from Green Bay) | Darius Butler, Connecticut | CB |
| 42. ..............Buffalo | Jairus Byrd, Oregon | CB |
| 43. ..............Carolina (from San Francisco) | Everette Brown, Florida St | DE |
| 44. ..............Miami (from Washington) | Pat White, West Virginia | QB |
| 45. ..............NY Giants (from New Orleans) | Clint Sintim, Virginia | OLB |
| 46. ..............Houston | Connor Barwin, Cincinnati | DE |
| 47. ..............Oakland (from San Diego through New England) | Mike Mitchell, Ohio | SS |
| 48. ..............Denver | Darcel McBath, Texas Tech | CB |
| 49. ..............Seattle (from Chicago) | Max Unger, Oregon | OT |
| 50. ..............Cleveland (from Tampa Bay) | Mohamed Massaquoi, Georgia | WR |
| 51. ..............Buffalo (from Dallas) | Andy Levitre, Oregon St | OG |
| 52. ..............Cleveland (from NY Jets) | David Veikune, Hawaii | DE |
| 53. ..............Philadelphia | LeSean McCoy, Pittsburgh | RB |
| 54. ..............Minnesota | Phil Loadholt, Oklahoma | OG |
| 55. ..............Atlanta | William Moore, Missouri | S |
| 56. ..............Indianapolis (from Miami) | Fili Moala, USC | DT |
| 57. ..............Baltimore | Paul Kruger, Utah | DE |
| 58. ..............New England | Sebastian Vollmer, Houston | OG |
| 59. ..............Carolina | Sherrod Martin, Troy | S |
| 60. ..............NY Giants | William Beatty, Connecticut | OT |
| 61. ..............Miami (from Indianapolis) | Sean Smith, Utah | CB |
| 62. ..............Tennessee | Sen'Derrick Marks, Auburn | DT |
| 63. ..............Arizona | Cody Brown, Connecticut | DE |
| 64. ..............Denver (from Pittsburgh) | Richard Quinn, North Carolina | TE |

### Regular Season Results

| WESTERN DIVISION | W | L | T | Pts | PF | PA |
|---|---|---|---|---|---|---|
| †Calgary | 13 | 5 | 0 | 26 | 595 | 420 |
| *Saskatchewan | 12 | 6 | 0 | 24 | 500 | 471 |
| *British Columbia | 11 | 7 | 0 | 22 | 559 | 479 |
| *Edmonton | 10 | 8 | 0 | 20 | 512 | 526 |

| EASTERN DIVISION | W | L | T | Pts | PF | PA |
|---|---|---|---|---|---|---|
| †Montreal | 11 | 7 | 0 | 22 | 610 | 443 |
| *Winnipeg | 8 | 10 | 0 | 16 | 435 | 490 |
| Toronto | 4 | 14 | 0 | 8 | 397 | 627 |
| Hamilton | 3 | 15 | 0 | 6 | 441 | 593 |

†Clinched division title.

*Clinched playoff berth.

### Playoff Results

#### DIVISION SEMI-FINALS

Nov. 8, 2008

Edmonton 29, WINNIPEG 21

British Columbia 33, SASKATCHEWAN 12

#### DIVISION FINALS

Nov. 15, 2008

MONTREAL 36, Edmonton 26

CALGARY 22, British Columbia 18

Home team in caps.

### 2008 Grey Cup Championship

**Nov. 23, 2008, Olympic Stadium, Montreal, Quebec**

| | | | | |
|---|---|---|---|---|
| **Calgary Stampeders** | 0 | 10 | 6 | 6—22 |
| **Montreal Alouettes** | 3 | 10 | 1 | 0—14 |

**FIRST QUARTER:** Montreal: FG Duval 14, 10:45.
**Montreal 3–0.**

**SECOND QUARTER:** Calgary: FG DeAngelis 43, 14:08.
**3–3.**

Montreal: TD Cobourne 16 run (Duval kick), 8:05.
**Montreal 10–3.**

Montreal: FG Duval 19, 3:11.
**Montreal 13–3.**

Calgary: TD Ralph 20 pass from Burris
(DeAngelis kick), 0:44.
**Montreal 13–10.**

**THIRD QUARTER:** Calgary: FG DeAngelis 12, 5:53.
**13–13.**

Montreal: Punt single Duval 63 (9 deep), 3:12.
**Montreal 14–13.**

Calgary: FG DeAngelis 21, 0:10.
**Calgary 16–14.**

**FOURTH QUARTER:** Calgary: FG DeAngelis 30, 12:34.
**Calgary 19–14.**

Calgary: FG DeAngelis 50, 4:34.
**Calgary 22–14.**

A: 66,308.

## Season-by-Season NFL Final Standings

### 1920*

| | W | L | T | Pct | Pts | OP |
|---|---|---|---|---|---|---|
| Akron Pros | 8 | 0 | 3 | 1.000 | 95 | 7 |
| Decatur Staleys | 10 | 1 | 2 | .909 | 67 | 14 |
| Buffalo All-Americans | 9 | 1 | 1 | .900 | 74 | 19 |
| Chicago Cardinals | 6 | 2 | 2 | .750 | 34 | 26 |
| Rock Island Independents | 6 | 2 | 2 | .750 | 98 | 35 |
| Dayton Triangles | 5 | 2 | 2 | .714 | 127 | 47 |
| Rochester Jeffersons | 6 | 3 | 2 | .667 | 6 | 17 |
| Canton Bulldogs | 7 | 4 | 2 | .636 | 72 | 44 |
| Detroit Heralds | 2 | 3 | 3 | .400 | 6 | 61 |
| Cleveland Tigers | 2 | 4 | 2 | .333 | 22 | 63 |
| Chicago Tigers | 2 | 5 | 1 | .286 | 22 | 63 |
| Hammond Pros | 2 | 5 | 0 | .286 | 7 | 98 |
| Columbus Panhandles | 2 | 6 | 2 | .250 | 7 | 107 |
| Muncie Flyers | 0 | 1 | 0 | .000 | 0 | 45 |

*no official standings kept

### 1921

| | W | L | T | Pct | Pts | OP |
|---|---|---|---|---|---|---|
| Chicago Staleys | 9 | 1 | 1 | .900 | 128 | 53 |
| Buffalo All-Americans | 9 | 1 | 2 | .900 | 211 | 29 |
| Akron Pros | 8 | 3 | 1 | .727 | 148 | 31 |
| Canton Bulldogs | 5 | 2 | 3 | .714 | 106 | 55 |
| Rock Island Independents | 4 | 2 | 1 | .667 | 65 | 30 |
| Evansville Crimson Giants | 3 | 2 | 0 | .600 | 89 | 46 |
| Green Bay Packers | 3 | 2 | 1 | .600 | 70 | 55 |
| Dayton Triangles | 4 | 4 | 1 | .500 | 96 | 67 |
| Chicago Cardinals | 3 | 3 | 2 | .500 | 54 | 53 |
| Rochester Jeffersons | 2 | 3 | 0 | .400 | 85 | 76 |
| Cleveland Tigers | 3 | 5 | 0 | .375 | 95 | 58 |
| Washington Senators | 1 | 2 | 0 | .333 | 21 | 43 |
| Cincinnati Celts | 1 | 3 | 0 | .250 | 14 | 117 |
| Hammond Pros | 1 | 3 | 1 | .250 | 17 | 45 |
| Minneapolis Marines | 1 | 3 | 0 | .250 | 37 | 41 |
| Detroit Tigers | 1 | 5 | 1 | .167 | 19 | 109 |
| Columbus Panhandles | 1 | 8 | 0 | .111 | 47 | 222 |
| Tonawanda Kardex | 0 | 1 | 0 | .000 | 0 | 45 |
| Muncie Flyers | 0 | 2 | 0 | .000 | 0 | 28 |
| Louisville Brecks | 0 | 2 | 0 | .000 | 0 | 27 |
| New York Giants | 0 | 2 | 0 | .000 | 0 | 72 |

### 1922

| | W | L | T | Pct | Pts | OP |
|---|---|---|---|---|---|---|
| Canton Bulldogs | 10 | 0 | 2 | 1.000 | 184 | 15 |
| Chicago Bears | 9 | 3 | 0 | .750 | 123 | 44 |
| Chicago Cardinals | 8 | 3 | 0 | .727 | 96 | 50 |
| Toledo Maroons | 5 | 2 | 2 | .714 | 94 | 59 |
| Rock Island Independents | 4 | 2 | 1 | .667 | 154 | 27 |
| Racine Legion | 6 | 4 | 1 | .600 | 122 | 56 |
| Dayton Triangles | 4 | 3 | 1 | .571 | 80 | 62 |
| Green Bay Packers | 4 | 3 | 3 | .571 | 70 | 54 |
| Buffalo All-Americans | 5 | 4 | 1 | .556 | 87 | 41 |
| Akron Pros | 3 | 5 | 2 | .375 | 146 | 95 |
| Milwaukee Badgers | 2 | 4 | 3 | .333 | 51 | 71 |
| Oorang Indians | 3 | 6 | 0 | .333 | 69 | 190 |
| Minneapolis Marines | 1 | 3 | 0 | .250 | 19 | 40 |
| Louisville Brecks | 1 | 3 | 0 | .250 | 13 | 140 |
| Evansville Crimson Giants | 0 | 3 | 0 | .000 | 6 | 88 |
| Rochester Jeffersons | 0 | 4 | 1 | .000 | 13 | 76 |
| Hammond Pros | 0 | 5 | 1 | .000 | 0 | 69 |
| Columbus Panhandles | 0 | 8 | 0 | .000 | 24 | 174 |

### 1923

| | W | L | T | Pct | Pts | OP |
|---|---|---|---|---|---|---|
| Canton Bulldogs | 11 | 0 | 1 | 1.000 | 246 | 19 |
| Chicago Bears | 9 | 2 | 1 | .818 | 123 | 35 |
| Green Bay Packers | 7 | 2 | 1 | .778 | 85 | 34 |
| Milwaukee Badgers | 7 | 2 | 3 | .778 | 100 | 49 |
| Cleveland Indians | 3 | 1 | 3 | .750 | 52 | 49 |
| Chicago Cardinals | 8 | 4 | 0 | .667 | 139 | 37 |
| Duluth Kelleys | 4 | 3 | 0 | .571 | 35 | 33 |
| Buffalo All-Americans | 5 | 4 | 3 | .556 | 94 | 43 |
| Columbus Tigers | 5 | 4 | 1 | .556 | 119 | 35 |
| Racine Legion | 4 | 4 | 2 | .500 | 86 | 76 |
| Toledo Maroons | 3 | 3 | 2 | .500 | 35 | 66 |
| Rock Island Independents | 2 | 3 | 2 | .400 | 83 | 62 |
| Minneapolis Marines | 2 | 5 | 1 | .286 | 48 | 80 |
| St. Louis All-Stars | 1 | 4 | 2 | .200 | 14 | 32 |
| Hammond Pros | 1 | 5 | 1 | .167 | 14 | 59 |
| Dayton Triangles | 1 | 6 | 1 | .143 | 16 | 95 |
| Akron Pros | 1 | 6 | 0 | .143 | 25 | 74 |
| Oorang Indians | 1 | 10 | 0 | .091 | 24 | 235 |
| Louisville Brecks | 0 | 3 | 0 | .000 | 0 | 90 |
| Rochester Jeffersons | 0 | 4 | 0 | .000 | 6 | 141 |

### 1924

| | W | L | T | Pct | Pts | OP |
|---|---|---|---|---|---|---|
| Cleveland Bulldogs | 7 | 1 | 1 | .875 | 229 | 60 |
| Chicago Bears | 6 | 1 | 4 | .857 | 136 | 55 |
| Frankfort Yellow Jackets | 11 | 2 | 1 | .846 | 326 | 109 |
| Duluth Kelleys | 5 | 1 | 0 | .833 | 56 | 16 |
| Rock Island Independents | 5 | 2 | 2 | .714 | 81 | 15 |
| Green Bay Packers | 7 | 4 | 0 | .636 | 108 | 38 |
| Racine Legion | 4 | 3 | 3 | .571 | 69 | 47 |
| Chicago Cardinals | 5 | 4 | 1 | .556 | 90 | 67 |
| Buffalo Bisons | 6 | 5 | 0 | .545 | 120 | 140 |
| Columbus Tigers | 4 | 4 | 0 | .500 | 91 | 68 |
| Hammond Pros | 2 | 2 | 1 | .500 | 18 | 45 |
| Milwaukee Badgers | 5 | 8 | 0 | .385 | 142 | 188 |
| Akron Pros | 2 | 6 | 0 | .250 | 59 | 132 |
| Dayton Triangles | 2 | 6 | 0 | .250 | 45 | 148 |
| Kansas City Blues | 2 | 7 | 0 | .222 | 46 | 124 |
| Kenosha Maroons | 0 | 4 | 1 | .000 | 12 | 117 |
| Minneapolis Marines | 0 | 6 | 0 | .000 | 14 | 108 |
| Rochester Jeffersons | 0 | 7 | 0 | .000 | 14 | 179 |

### 1925

| | W | L | T | Pct | Pts | OP |
|---|---|---|---|---|---|---|
| Chicago Cardinals | 11 | 2 | 1 | .846 | 230 | 65 |
| Pottsville Maroons | 10 | 2 | 0 | .833 | 280 | 45 |
| Detroit Panthers | 8 | 2 | 2 | .800 | 118 | 42 |
| New York Giants | 8 | 4 | 0 | .667 | 122 | 67 |
| Akron Pros | 4 | 2 | 2 | .650 | 65 | 51 |
| Frankfort Yellow Jackets | 13 | 7 | 0 | .643 | 196 | 189 |
| Chicago Bears | 9 | 5 | 3 | .625 | 158 | 96 |
| Rock Island Independents | 5 | 3 | 3 | .615 | 99 | 58 |
| Green Bay Packers | 8 | 5 | 0 | .545 | 151 | 120 |
| Providence Steam Roller | 6 | 5 | 1 | .500 | 131 | 108 |
| Canton Bulldogs | 4 | 4 | 0 | .385 | 50 | 73 |
| Cleveland Bulldogs | 5 | 8 | 1 | .286 | 75 | 134 |
| Kansas City Cowboys | 2 | 5 | 1 | .200 | 68 | 106 |
| Hammond Pros | 1 | 4 | 0 | .143 | 23 | 87 |

## 1925 (Cont.)

| | W | L | T | Pct | Pts | OP |
|---|---|---|---|---|---|---|
| Buffalo Bisons .................1 | 6 | 2 | .143 | 33 | 113 |
| Duluth Kelleys .................0 | 3 | 0 | .000 | 6 | 25 |
| Rochester Jeffersons .......0 | 6 | 1 | .000 | 26 | 91 |
| Milwaukee Badgers .........0 | 6 | 0 | .000 | 7 | 191 |
| Dayton Triangles .............0 | 7 | 1 | .000 | 3 | 84 |
| Columbus Tigers .............0 | 9 | 0 | .000 | 28 | 124 |

## 1926

| | W | L | T | Pct | Pts | OP |
|---|---|---|---|---|---|---|
| Frankfort Yellow Jackets 14 | 1 | 2 | .765 | 223 | 43 |
| Chicago Bears .............12 | 1 | 3 | .844 | 216 | 63 |
| Pottsville Maroons .........10 | 2 | 2 | .714 | 155 | 29 |
| Kansas City Cowboys .....8 | 3 | 0 | .727 | 76 | 54 |
| Green Bay Packers .......7 | 3 | 3 | .462 | 144 | 68 |
| Los Angeles Buccaneers.6 | 3 | 1 | .600 | 67 | 57 |
| NY Giants .......................8 | 4 | 1 | .583 | 140 | 45 |
| Duluth Eskimos ..............6 | 5 | 3 | .429 | 114 | 81 |
| Buffalo Rangers .............4 | 4 | 2 | .400 | 53 | 62 |
| Chicago Cardinals ..........5 | 6 | 1 | .417 | 67 | 86 |
| Providence Steam Roller .5 | 7 | 1 | .417 | 94 | 96 |
| Detroit Panthers .............4 | 6 | 2 | .500 | 115 | 52 |
| Hartford Blues ...............3 | 7 | 0 | .300 | 57 | 99 |
| Brooklyn Lions ................3 | 8 | 0 | .273 | 60 | 150 |
| Milwaukee Badgers ........2 | 7 | 0 | .222 | 41 | 66 |
| Akron Indians .................1 | 4 | 3 | .125 | 23 | 89 |
| Dayton Triangles ............1 | 4 | 1 | .167 | 15 | 82 |
| Racine Tornadoes ...........1 | 4 | 0 | .200 | 8 | 92 |
| Columbus Tigers .............1 | 6 | 0 | .143 | 26 | 93 |
| Canton Bulldogs ..............1 | 9 | 3 | .077 | 46 | 172 |
| Hammond Pros ................0 | 4 | 0 | .000 | 3 | 56 |
| Louisville Colonels ..........0 | 4 | 0 | .000 | 0 | 108 |

## 1927

| | W | L | T | Pct | Pts | OP |
|---|---|---|---|---|---|---|
| NY Giants ......................11 | 1 | 1 | .917 | 197 | 20 |
| Green Bay Packers .........7 | 2 | 1 | .778 | 113 | 43 |
| Chicago Bears .............9 | 3 | 2 | .750 | 149 | 98 |
| Cleveland Bulldogs ........8 | 4 | 1 | .667 | 209 | 107 |
| Providence Steam Roller .8 | 5 | 1 | .615 | 105 | 88 |
| New York Yankees...........7 | 8 | 1 | .467 | 142 | 174 |
| Frankfort Yellow Jackets ..6 | 9 | 3 | .400 | 152 | 166 |
| Pottsville Maroons .........5 | 8 | 0 | .385 | 80 | 163 |
| Chicago Cardinals ..........3 | 7 | 1 | .300 | 69 | 134 |
| Dayton Triangles .............1 | 6 | 1 | .143 | 15 | 57 |
| Duluth Eskimos ..............1 | 8 | 0 | .111 | 68 | 134 |
| Buffalo Bisons .................0 | 5 | 0 | .000 | 8 | 123 |

## 1928

| | W | L | T | Pct | Pts | OP |
|---|---|---|---|---|---|---|
| Providence Steam Roller..8 | 1 | 1 | .889 | 128 | 36 |
| Frankfort Yellow Jackets 11 | 3 | 1 | .786 | 169 | 84 |
| Detroit Wolverines ...........7 | 2 | 1 | .778 | 189 | 76 |
| Green Bay Packers.........6 | 4 | 3 | .600 | 120 | 92 |
| Chicago Bears ................7 | 5 | 1 | .583 | 182 | 85 |
| NY Giants .......................4 | 7 | 2 | .364 | 79 | 137 |
| NY Yankees.....................4 | 8 | 1 | .333 | 104 | 179 |
| Pottsville Maroons ..........2 | 8 | 0 | .200 | 74 | 134 |
| Chicago Cardinals ...........1 | 5 | 0 | .167 | 7 | 107 |
| Dayton Triangles .............0 | 7 | 0 | .000 | 9 | 131 |

## 1929

| | W | L | T | Pct | Pts | OP |
|---|---|---|---|---|---|---|
| Green Bay Packers........12 | 0 | 1 | 1.000 | 198 | 22 |
| NY Giants.......................13 | 1 | 1 | .929 | 312 | 86 |
| Frankfort Yellow Jackets..10 | 4 | 5 | .714 | 139 | 128 |
| Chicago Cardinals ...........6 | 6 | 1 | .500 | 154 | 83 |
| Boston Bulldogs ..............4 | 4 | 0 | .500 | 98 | 73 |
| Staten Island Stapletons ..3 | 6 | 3 | .429 | 89 | 62 |
| Providence Steam Roller..4 | 5 | 2 | .400 | 107 | 117 |
| Orange Tornadoes ...........3 | 6 | 4 | .375 | 32 | 90 |
| Chicago Bears .................4 | 9 | 2 | .308 | 119 | 227 |
| Buffalo Bisons .................1 | 7 | 1 | .125 | 48 | 142 |
| Minneapolis Red Jackets..1 | 9 | 0 | .100 | 48 | 185 |
| Dayton Triangles ..............0 | 6 | 0 | .000 | 7 | 136 |

## 1930

| | W | L | T | Pct | Pts | OP |
|---|---|---|---|---|---|---|
| Green Bay Packers........10 | 3 | 1 | .769 | 234 | 111 |
| NY Giants.......................13 | 4 | 0 | .765 | 308 | 98 |
| Chicago Bears .................9 | 4 | 1 | .692 | 169 | 71 |
| Brooklyn Dodgers ............7 | 4 | 1 | .636 | 154 | 59 |
| Providence Steam Roller..6 | 4 | 1 | .600 | 90 | 125 |
| Staten Island Stapletons .5 | 5 | 2 | .500 | 95 | 112 |
| Chicago Cardinals ...........5 | 6 | 2 | .455 | 128 | 132 |
| Portsmouth Spartans .......5 | 6 | 3 | .455 | 176 | 161 |
| Frankfort Yellow Jackets ..4 | 13 | 1 | .222 | 113 | 321 |
| Minneapolis Red Jackets.1 | 7 | 1 | .125 | 27 | 165 |
| Newark Tornadoes ...........1 | 10 | 1 | .091 | 51 | 190 |

## 1931

| | W | L | T | Pct | Pts | OP |
|---|---|---|---|---|---|---|
| Green Bay Packers........12 | 2 | 0 | .857 | 318 | 94 |
| Portsmouth Spartans .....11 | 3 | 0 | .786 | 161 | 77 |
| Chicago Bears .............8 | 5 | 0 | .615 | 145 | 92 |
| Chicago Cardinals ........... 5 | 4 | 0 | .556 | 120 | 128 |
| NY Giants .......................7 | 6 | 1 | .538 | 161 | 127 |
| Providence Steam Roller..4 | 4 | 3 | .500 | 78 | 127 |
| Staten Island Stapletons..4 | 6 | 1 | .400 | 79 | 118 |
| Cleveland Indians ...........2 | 8 | 0 | .200 | 45 | 137 |
| Brooklyn Dodgers ...........2 | 12 | 0 | .143 | 64 | 199 |
| Frankfort Yellow Jackets ..1 | 6 | 1 | .143 | 13 | 85 |

## 1932

| | W | L | T | Pct | Pts | OP |
|---|---|---|---|---|---|---|
| Chicago Bears .................7 | 1 | 6 | .875 | 160 | 44 |
| Green Bay Packers........10 | 3 | 1 | .769 | 152 | 63 |
| Portsmouth Spartans .......6 | 2 | 4 | .750 | 116 | 71 |
| Boston Braves..................4 | 4 | 2 | .500 | 55 | 79 |
| NY Giants .......................4 | 6 | 2 | .400 | 93 | 113 |
| Brooklyn Dodgers ............3 | 9 | 0 | .250 | 63 | 131 |
| Chiago Cardinals .............2 | 6 | 2 | .250 | 72 | 114 |
| Staten Island Stapletons ..2 | 7 | 3 | .222 | 77 | 173 |

## 1933

| EAST | W | L | T | Pct | Pts | OP |
|---|---|---|---|---|---|---|
| NY Giants.......................11 | 3 | 0 | .786 | 244 | 101 |
| Brooklyn Dodgers ............5 | 4 | 1 | .556 | 93 | 54 |
| Boston Redskins ..............5 | 5 | 2 | .500 | 103 | 97 |
| Philadelphia Eagles .........3 | 5 | 1 | .375 | 77 | 158 |
| Pittsburgh Pirates............3 | 6 | 2 | .333 | 67 | 208 |

## 1933 (Cont.)

| WEST | W | L | T | Pct | Pts | OP |
|---|---|---|---|---|---|---|
| Chicago Bears | 10 | 2 | 1 | .833 | 133 | 82 |
| Portsmouth Spartans | 6 | 5 | 0 | .545 | 128 | 87 |
| Green Bay Packers | 5 | 7 | 1 | .417 | 170 | 107 |
| Cincinnati Reds | 3 | 6 | 1 | .333 | 38 | 110 |
| Chicago Cardinals | 1 | 9 | 1 | .100 | 52 | 101 |

## 1934

| EAST | W | L | T | Pct | Pts | OP |
|---|---|---|---|---|---|---|
| NY Giants | 8 | 5 | 0 | .615 | 147 | 107 |
| Boston Redskins | 6 | 6 | 0 | .500 | 107 | 93 |
| Brooklyn Dodgers | 4 | 7 | 0 | .364 | 60 | 153 |
| Philadelphia Eagles | 4 | 7 | 0 | .364 | 127 | 85 |
| Pittsburgh Pirates | 2 | 10 | 0 | .167 | 51 | 206 |

| WEST | W | L | T | Pct | Pts | OP |
|---|---|---|---|---|---|---|
| Chicago Bears | 13 | 0 | 0 | 1.000 | 286 | 86 |
| Detroit Lions | 10 | 3 | 0 | .769 | 238 | 59 |
| Green Bay Packers | 7 | 6 | 0 | .538 | 156 | 112 |
| Chicago Cardinals | 5 | 6 | 0 | .455 | 80 | 84 |
| St. Louis Gunners | 1 | 2 | 0 | .333 | 27 | 61 |
| Cincinnati Reds | 0 | 8 | 0 | .000 | 10 | 243 |

## 1935

| EAST | W | L | T | Pct | Pts | OP |
|---|---|---|---|---|---|---|
| NY Giants | 9 | 3 | 0 | .750 | 180 | 96 |
| Brooklyn Dodgers | 5 | 6 | 1 | .455 | 90 | 141 |
| Pittsburgh Pirates | 4 | 8 | 0 | .333 | 99 | 209 |
| Boston Redskins | 2 | 8 | 1 | .200 | 65 | 122 |
| Philadelphia Eagles | 2 | 9 | 0 | .182 | 60 | 179 |

| WEST | W | L | T | Pct | Pts | OP |
|---|---|---|---|---|---|---|
| Detroit Lions | 7 | 3 | 2 | .700 | 191 | 111 |
| Green Bay Packers | 8 | 4 | 0 | .667 | 181 | 96 |
| Chicago Bears | 6 | 4 | 2 | .600 | 192 | 106 |
| Chicago Cardinals | 6 | 4 | 2 | .600 | 99 | 97 |

## 1936

| EAST | W | L | T | Pct | Pts | OP |
|---|---|---|---|---|---|---|
| Boston Redskins | 7 | 5 | 0 | .583 | 149 | 110 |
| Pittsburgh Pirates | 6 | 6 | 0 | .500 | 98 | 187 |
| NY Giants | 5 | 6 | 1 | .455 | 115 | 163 |
| Brooklyn Dodgers | 3 | 8 | 1 | .273 | 92 | 161 |
| Philadelphia Eagles | 1 | 11 | 0 | .083 | 51 | 206 |

| WEST | W | L | T | Pct | Pts | OP |
|---|---|---|---|---|---|---|
| Green Bay | 10 | 1 | 1 | .909 | 248 | 118 |
| Chicago Bears | 9 | 3 | 0 | .750 | 222 | 94 |
| Detroit Lions | 8 | 4 | 0 | .667 | 235 | 102 |
| Chicago Cardinals | 3 | 8 | 1 | .273 | 74 | 143 |

## 1937

| EAST | W | L | T | Pct | Pts | OP |
|---|---|---|---|---|---|---|
| Washington Redskins | 8 | 3 | 0 | .727 | 195 | 120 |
| NY Giants | 6 | 3 | 2 | .667 | 128 | 109 |
| Pittsburgh Pirates | 4 | 7 | 0 | .364 | 122 | 145 |
| Brooklyn Dodgers | 3 | 7 | 1 | .300 | 82 | 174 |
| Philadelphia Eagles | 2 | 8 | 1 | .200 | 86 | 177 |

| WEST | W | L | T | Pct | Pts | OP |
|---|---|---|---|---|---|---|
| Chicago Bears | 9 | 1 | 1 | .900 | 201 | 100 |
| Green Bay Packers | 7 | 4 | 0 | .636 | 220 | 122 |
| Detroit Lions | 7 | 4 | 0 | .636 | 180 | 105 |
| Chicago Cardinals | 5 | 5 | 1 | .500 | 135 | 165 |
| Cleveland Rams | 1 | 10 | 0 | .091 | 75 | 207 |

## 1938

| EAST | W | L | T | Pct | Pts | OP |
|---|---|---|---|---|---|---|
| NY Giants | 8 | 2 | 1 | .800 | 194 | 79 |
| Washington Redskins | 6 | 3 | 2 | .667 | 148 | 154 |
| Brooklyn Dodgers | 4 | 4 | 3 | .500 | 131 | 161 |
| Philadelphia Eagles | 5 | 6 | 0 | .455 | 154 | 164 |
| Pittsburgh Pirates | 2 | 9 | 0 | .182 | 79 | 169 |

| WEST | W | L | T | Pct | Pts | OP |
|---|---|---|---|---|---|---|
| Green Bay Packers | 8 | 3 | 0 | .727 | 223 | 118 |
| Detroit Lions | 7 | 4 | 0 | .636 | 119 | 108 |
| Chicago Bears | 6 | 5 | 0 | .545 | 194 | 148 |
| Cleveland Rams | 4 | 7 | 0 | .364 | 131 | 215 |
| Chicago Cardinals | 2 | 9 | 0 | .182 | 111 | 168 |

## 1939

| EAST | W | L | T | Pct | Pts | OP |
|---|---|---|---|---|---|---|
| NY Giants | 9 | 1 | 1 | .168 | 168 | 85 |
| Washington Redskins | 8 | 2 | 1 | .242 | 242 | 94 |
| Brooklyn Dodgers | 4 | 6 | 1 | .108 | 108 | 219 |
| Philadelphia Eagles | 1 | 9 | 1 | .105 | 105 | 200 |
| Pittsburgh Pirates | 1 | 9 | 1 | .114 | 114 | 216 |

| WEST | W | L | T | Pct | Pts | OP |
|---|---|---|---|---|---|---|
| Green Bay Packers | 9 | 2 | 0 | .818 | 233 | 153 |
| Chicago Bears | 8 | 3 | 0 | .727 | 298 | 157 |
| Detroit Lions | 6 | 5 | 0 | .545 | 145 | 150 |
| Cleveland Rams | 5 | 5 | 1 | .195 | 195 | 164 |
| Chicago Cardinals | 1 | 10 | 0 | .091 | 84 | 254 |

## 1940

| EAST | W | L | T | Pct | Pts | OP |
|---|---|---|---|---|---|---|
| Washington Redskins | 9 | 2 | 0 | .818 | 245 | 142 |
| Brooklyn Dodgers | 8 | 2 | 0 | .800 | 179 | 110 |
| NY Giants | 6 | 4 | 1 | .545 | 131 | 133 |
| Pittsburgh Pirates | 2 | 7 | 2 | .182 | 67 | 174 |
| Philadelphia Eagles | 1 | 10 | 0 | .091 | 121 | 200 |

| WEST | W | L | T | Pct | Pts | OP |
|---|---|---|---|---|---|---|
| Chicago Bears | 8 | 3 | 0 | .727 | 238 | 152 |
| Green Bay Packers | 6 | 4 | 1 | .600 | 238 | 155 |
| Detroit Lions | 5 | 5 | 1 | .500 | 120 | 177 |
| Cleveland Rams | 4 | 6 | 1 | .400 | 181 | 191 |
| Chicago Cardinals | 2 | 7 | 2 | .222 | 139 | 222 |

## 1941

**EAST**

| | W | L | T | Pct | Pts | OP |
|---|---|---|---|---|---|---|
| NY Giants | 8 | 3 | 0 | .727 | 238 | 114 |
| Brooklyn Dodgers | 7 | 4 | 0 | .636 | 158 | 127 |
| Washington | 6 | 5 | 0 | .545 | 176 | 174 |
| Philadelphia | 2 | 8 | 1 | .200 | 119 | 218 |
| Pittsburgh Steelers | 1 | 9 | 1 | .100 | 103 | 276 |

**WEST**

| | W | L | T | Pct | Pts | OP |
|---|---|---|---|---|---|---|
| Green Bay | 10 | 1 | 0 | .909 | 258 | 120 |
| Chicago Bears | 10 | 1 | 0 | .909 | 396 | 147 |
| Detroit | 4 | 6 | 1 | .400 | 121 | 195 |
| Chicago Cardinals | 3 | 7 | 1 | .300 | 127 | 197 |
| Cleveland Rams | 2 | 9 | 0 | .182 | 116 | 244 |

## 1942

**EAST**

| | W | L | T | Pct | Pts | OP |
|---|---|---|---|---|---|---|
| Washington | 10 | 1 | 0 | .909 | 227 | 102 |
| Pittsburgh Steelers | 7 | 4 | 0 | .636 | 167 | 119 |
| NY Giants | 5 | 5 | 1 | .500 | 155 | 139 |
| Brooklyn Dodgers | 3 | 8 | 0 | .273 | 100 | 168 |
| Philadelphia | 2 | 9 | 0 | .182 | 134 | 239 |

**WEST**

| | W | L | T | Pct | Pts | OP |
|---|---|---|---|---|---|---|
| Chicago Bears | 11 | 0 | 0 | 1.000 | 376 | 84 |
| Green Bay | 8 | 2 | 1 | .800 | 300 | 215 |
| Cleveland Rams | 5 | 6 | 0 | .455 | 150 | 207 |
| Chicago Cardinals | 3 | 8 | 0 | .273 | 98 | 209 |
| Detroit | 0 | 11 | 0 | .000 | 38 | 263 |

## 1943

**EAST**

| | W | L | T | Pct | Pts | OP |
|---|---|---|---|---|---|---|
| Washington | 6 | 3 | 1 | .667 | 229 | 137 |
| NY Giants | 6 | 3 | 1 | .667 | 197 | 170 |
| Phi/Pitt Eagles/Steelers | 5 | 4 | 1 | .556 | 225 | 230 |
| Brooklyn Dodgers | 2 | 8 | 0 | .200 | 65 | 234 |

**WEST**

| | W | L | T | Pct | Pts | OP |
|---|---|---|---|---|---|---|
| Chicago Bears | 8 | 1 | 1 | .889 | 303 | 157 |
| Green Bay | 7 | 2 | 1 | .778 | 264 | 172 |
| Detroit | 3 | 6 | 1 | .333 | 178 | 218 |
| Chicago Cardinals | 0 | 10 | 0 | .000 | 95 | 238 |

## 1944

**EAST**

| | W | L | T | Pct | Pts | OP |
|---|---|---|---|---|---|---|
| NY Giants | 8 | 1 | 1 | .889 | 206 | 75 |
| Philadelphia | 7 | 1 | 2 | .875 | 267 | 131 |
| Washington | 6 | 3 | 1 | .667 | 169 | 180 |
| Boston Yanks | 2 | 8 | 0 | .200 | 82 | 233 |
| Brooklyn Tigers | 0 | 10 | 0 | .000 | 69 | 166 |

**WEST**

| | W | L | T | Pct | Pts | OP |
|---|---|---|---|---|---|---|
| Green Bay | 8 | 2 | 0 | .800 | 238 | 141 |
| Chicago Bears | 6 | 3 | 1 | .667 | 258 | 172 |
| Detroit | 6 | 3 | 1 | .667 | 216 | 151 |
| Cleveland Rams | 4 | 6 | 0 | .400 | 188 | 224 |
| Chi/Pitt Cards/Steelers | 0 | 10 | 0 | .000 | 116 | 336 |

## 1945

**EAST**

| | W | L | T | Pct | Pts | OP |
|---|---|---|---|---|---|---|
| Washington | 8 | 2 | 0 | .800 | 209 | 121 |
| Philadelphia | 7 | 3 | 0 | .700 | 272 | 133 |
| NY Giants | 3 | 6 | 1 | .333 | 179 | 198 |
| Bos/Bkn Yanks/Tigers | 3 | 6 | 1 | .333 | 123 | 211 |
| Pittsburgh | 2 | 8 | 0 | .200 | 79 | 220 |

**WEST**

| | W | L | T | Pct | Pts | OP |
|---|---|---|---|---|---|---|
| Cleveland Rams | 9 | 1 | 0 | .900 | 244 | 136 |
| Detroit | 7 | 3 | 0 | .700 | 195 | 194 |
| Green Bay | 6 | 4 | 0 | .600 | 258 | 173 |
| Chicago Bears | 3 | 7 | 0 | .300 | 192 | 235 |
| Chicago Cardinals | 1 | 9 | 0 | .100 | 98 | 228 |

## 1946

**EAST**

| | W | L | T | Pct | Pts | OP |
|---|---|---|---|---|---|---|
| NY Giants | 7 | 3 | 1 | .700 | 236 | 162 |
| Philadelphia | 6 | 5 | 0 | .545 | 231 | 220 |
| Washington | 5 | 5 | 1 | .500 | 171 | 191 |
| Pittsburgh | 5 | 5 | 1 | .500 | 136 | 117 |
| Boston Yanks | 2 | 8 | 1 | .200 | 189 | 273 |

**WEST**

| | W | L | T | Pct | Pts | OP |
|---|---|---|---|---|---|---|
| Chicago Bears | 8 | 2 | 1 | .800 | 289 | 193 |
| Los Angeles Rams | 6 | 4 | 1 | .600 | 277 | 257 |
| Chicago Cardinals | 6 | 5 | 0 | .545 | 260 | 198 |
| Green Bay | 6 | 5 | 0 | .545 | 148 | 158 |
| Detroit | 1 | 10 | 0 | .091 | 142 | 310 |

## 1947

**EAST**

| | W | L | T | Pct | Pts | OP |
|---|---|---|---|---|---|---|
| Pittsburgh | 8 | 4 | 0 | .667 | 240 | 259 |
| Philadelphia | 8 | 4 | 0 | .667 | 308 | 242 |
| Boston Yanks | 4 | 7 | 1 | .364 | 168 | 256 |
| Washington | 4 | 8 | 0 | .333 | 295 | 367 |
| NY Giants | 2 | 8 | 2 | .200 | 190 | 309 |

**WEST**

| | W | L | T | Pct | Pts | OP |
|---|---|---|---|---|---|---|
| Chicago Cardinals | 9 | 3 | 0 | .750 | 306 | 231 |
| Chicago Bears | 8 | 4 | 0 | .667 | 363 | 241 |
| Green Bay | 6 | 5 | 1 | .542 | 274 | 210 |
| LA Rams | 6 | 6 | 0 | .500 | 259 | 214 |
| Detroit Lions | 3 | 9 | 0 | .250 | 231 | 305 |

## 1948

**EAST**

| | W | L | T | Pct | Pts | OP |
|---|---|---|---|---|---|---|
| Philadelphia | 9 | 2 | 1 | .818 | 376 | 156 |
| Washington | 7 | 5 | 0 | .583 | 291 | 287 |
| Pittsburgh | 4 | 8 | 0 | .333 | 200 | 243 |
| NY Giants | 4 | 8 | 0 | .333 | 297 | 388 |
| Boston Yanks | 3 | 9 | 0 | .250 | 174 | 372 |

**WEST**

| | W | L | T | Pct | Pts | OP |
|---|---|---|---|---|---|---|
| Chicago Cardinals | 11 | 1 | 0 | .917 | 395 | 226 |
| Chicago Bears | 10 | 2 | 0 | .833 | 375 | 151 |
| LA Rams | 6 | 5 | 1 | .545 | 327 | 269 |
| Green Bay | 3 | 9 | 0 | .250 | 154 | 290 |
| Detroit Lions | 2 | 10 | 0 | .167 | 200 | 407 |

## 1949

### EAST

| | W | L | T | Pct | Pts | OP |
|---|---|---|---|---|---|---|
| Philadelphia | 11 | 1 | 0 | .917 | 364 | 134 |
| Pittsburgh | 6 | 5 | 1 | .545 | 224 | 214 |
| NY Giants | 6 | 6 | 0 | .500 | 287 | 298 |
| Washington | 4 | 7 | 1 | .364 | 268 | 339 |
| New York Bulldogs | 1 | 10 | 1 | .091 | 153 | 368 |

### WEST

| | W | L | T | Pct | Pts | OP |
|---|---|---|---|---|---|---|
| LA Rams | 8 | 2 | 2 | .800 | 360 | 239 |
| Chicago Bears | 9 | 3 | 0 | .750 | 332 | 218 |
| Chicago Cardinals | 6 | 5 | 1 | .545 | 360 | 301 |
| Detroit Lions | 4 | 8 | 0 | .333 | 237 | 259 |
| Green Bay | 2 | 10 | 0 | .167 | 114 | 329 |

## 1950

### EAST

| | W | L | T | Pct | Pts | OP |
|---|---|---|---|---|---|---|
| Cleveland Browns | 10 | 2 | 0 | .833 | 310 | 144 |
| NY Giants | 10 | 2 | 0 | .833 | 268 | 150 |
| Philadelphia | 6 | 6 | 0 | .500 | 254 | 141 |
| Pittsburgh | 6 | 6 | 0 | .500 | 180 | 195 |
| Chicago Cardinals | 5 | 7 | 0 | .417 | 233 | 287 |
| Washington | 3 | 9 | 0 | .250 | 232 | 326 |

### WEST

| | W | L | T | Pct | Pts | OP |
|---|---|---|---|---|---|---|
| Chicago Bears | 9 | 3 | 0 | .750 | 279 | 207 |
| LA Rams | 9 | 3 | 0 | .750 | 466 | 309 |
| New York Yanks | 7 | 5 | 0 | .583 | 366 | 367 |
| Detroit | 6 | 6 | 0 | .500 | 321 | 285 |
| San Francisco 49ers | 3 | 9 | 0 | .250 | 213 | 300 |
| Green Bay | 3 | 9 | 0 | .250 | 244 | 406 |
| Baltimore Colts | 1 | 11 | 0 | .067 | 213 | 462 |

## 1951

### AMERICAN

| | W | L | T | Pct | Pts | OP |
|---|---|---|---|---|---|---|
| Cleveland | 11 | 1 | 0 | .917 | 331 | 152 |
| NY Giants | 9 | 2 | 1 | .818 | 254 | 161 |
| Washington | 5 | 7 | 0 | .417 | 183 | 296 |
| Pittsburgh | 4 | 7 | 1 | .364 | 183 | 235 |
| Philadelphia | 4 | 8 | 0 | .333 | 234 | 264 |
| Chicago Cardinals | 3 | 9 | 0 | .250 | 210 | 287 |

### NATIONAL

| | W | L | T | Pct | Pts | OP |
|---|---|---|---|---|---|---|
| LA Rams | 8 | 4 | 0 | .667 | 392 | 261 |
| Detroit Lions | 7 | 4 | 1 | .636 | 336 | 259 |
| San Francisco 49ers | 7 | 4 | 1 | .636 | 255 | 205 |
| Chicago Bears | 7 | 5 | 0 | .583 | 286 | 282 |
| Green Bay | 3 | 9 | 0 | .250 | 254 | 375 |
| New York Yanks | 1 | 9 | 2 | .100 | 241 | 382 |

## 1952

### AMERICAN

| | W | L | T | Pct | Pts | OP |
|---|---|---|---|---|---|---|
| Cleveland | 8 | 4 | 0 | .667 | 310 | 213 |
| Philadelphia | 7 | 5 | 0 | .583 | 252 | 271 |
| NY Giants | 7 | 5 | 0 | .583 | 234 | 231 |
| Pittsburgh | 5 | 7 | 0 | .417 | 300 | 273 |
| Washington | 4 | 8 | 0 | .333 | 240 | 287 |
| Chicago Cardinals | 4 | 8 | 0 | .333 | 172 | 221 |

### NATIONAL

| | W | L | T | Pct | Pts | OP |
|---|---|---|---|---|---|---|
| Detroit | 9 | 3 | 0 | .750 | 344 | 192 |
| LA Rams | 9 | 3 | 0 | .750 | 349 | 234 |
| San Francisco | 7 | 5 | 0 | .583 | 285 | 221 |
| Green Bay | 6 | 6 | 0 | .500 | 295 | 312 |
| Chicago Bears | 5 | 7 | 0 | .417 | 245 | 326 |
| Dallas Texans | 1 | 11 | 0 | .083 | 182 | 427 |

## 1953

### EAST

| | W | L | T | Pct | Pts | OP |
|---|---|---|---|---|---|---|
| Cleveland | 11 | 1 | 0 | .917 | 348 | 162 |
| Philadelphia | 7 | 4 | 1 | .636 | 352 | 215 |
| Washington | 6 | 5 | 1 | .545 | 208 | 215 |
| Pittsburgh | 5 | 7 | 0 | .417 | 211 | 272 |
| NY Giants | 4 | 8 | 0 | .333 | 188 | 277 |
| Chicago Cardinals | 1 | 10 | 1 | .091 | 190 | 337 |

### WEST

| | W | L | T | Pct | Pts | OP |
|---|---|---|---|---|---|---|
| Detroit | 10 | 2 | 0 | .833 | 271 | 205 |
| San Francisco | 9 | 3 | 0 | .750 | 372 | 237 |
| LA Rams | 8 | 3 | 1 | .727 | 366 | 236 |
| Chicago Bears | 3 | 8 | 1 | .273 | 218 | 262 |
| Baltimore Colts | 3 | 9 | 0 | .250 | 182 | 350 |
| Green Bay | 2 | 9 | 1 | .182 | 200 | 338 |

## 1954

### EAST

| | W | L | T | Pct | Pts | OP |
|---|---|---|---|---|---|---|
| Cleveland | 9 | 3 | 0 | .750 | 336 | 162 |
| Philadelphia | 7 | 4 | 1 | .636 | 284 | 230 |
| NY Giants | 7 | 5 | 0 | .583 | 293 | 184 |
| Pittsburgh | 5 | 7 | 0 | .417 | 219 | 263 |
| Washington | 3 | 9 | 0 | .250 | 207 | 432 |
| Chicago Cardinals | 2 | 10 | 0 | .167 | 183 | 347 |

### WEST

| | W | L | T | Pct | Pts | OP |
|---|---|---|---|---|---|---|
| Detroit | 9 | 2 | 1 | .818 | 337 | 189 |
| Chicago Bears | 8 | 4 | 0 | .667 | 301 | 279 |
| San Francisco | 7 | 4 | 1 | .636 | 313 | 251 |
| LA Rams | 6 | 5 | 1 | .545 | 314 | 285 |
| Green Bay | 4 | 8 | 0 | .333 | 234 | 251 |
| Baltimore | 3 | 9 | 0 | .250 | 131 | 279 |

## 1955

### EAST

| | W | L | T | Pct | Pts | OP |
|---|---|---|---|---|---|---|
| Cleveland | 9 | 2 | 1 | .818 | 349 | 218 |
| Washington | 8 | 4 | 0 | .667 | 246 | 222 |
| NY Giants | 6 | 5 | 1 | .545 | 267 | 223 |
| Philadelphia | 4 | 7 | 1 | .364 | 248 | 231 |
| Chicago Cardinals | 4 | 7 | 1 | .364 | 224 | 252 |
| Pittsburgh | 4 | 8 | 0 | .333 | 195 | 285 |

### WEST

| | W | L | T | Pct | Pts | OP |
|---|---|---|---|---|---|---|
| LA Rams | 8 | 3 | 1 | .727 | 260 | 231 |
| Chicago Bears | 8 | 4 | 0 | .667 | 294 | 251 |
| Green Bay | 6 | 6 | 0 | .500 | 258 | 276 |
| Baltimore | 5 | 6 | 1 | .455 | 214 | 239 |
| San Francisco | 4 | 8 | 0 | .333 | 216 | 298 |
| Detroit | 3 | 9 | 0 | .250 | 230 | 275 |

## 1956

### EAST

| | W | L | T | Pct | Pts | OP |
|---|---|---|---|---|---|---|
| NY Giants | 8 | 3 | 1 | .727 | 264 | 197 |
| Chicago Cardinals | 7 | 5 | 0 | .583 | 240 | 182 |
| Washington | 6 | 6 | 0 | .500 | 183 | 225 |
| Pittsburgh | 5 | 7 | 0 | .417 | 217 | 250 |
| Cleveland | 5 | 7 | 0 | .417 | 167 | 177 |
| Philadelphia | 3 | 8 | 1 | .273 | 143 | 215 |

### WEST

| | W | L | T | Pct | Pts | OP |
|---|---|---|---|---|---|---|
| Chicago Bears | 9 | 2 | 1 | .818 | 269 | 169 |
| Detroit | 9 | 3 | 0 | .750 | 300 | 188 |
| San Francisco | 5 | 6 | 1 | .455 | 233 | 284 |
| Baltimore | 5 | 7 | 0 | .417 | 270 | 322 |
| Green Bay | 4 | 8 | 0 | .333 | 264 | 342 |
| LA Rams | 4 | 8 | 0 | .333 | 291 | 307 |

### 1957

**EAST**

| | W | L | T | Pct | Pts | OP |
|---|---|---|---|---|---|---|
| Cleveland | 9 | 2 | 1 | .818 | 269 | 169 |
| NY Giants | 7 | 5 | 0 | .583 | 251 | 211 |
| Pittsburgh | 6 | 6 | 0 | .500 | 155 | 178 |
| Washington | 5 | 6 | 1 | .455 | 251 | 230 |
| Philadelphia | 4 | 8 | 0 | .333 | 173 | 224 |
| Chicago Cardinals | 3 | 9 | 0 | .250 | 200 | 299 |

**WEST**

| | W | L | T | Pct | Pts | OP |
|---|---|---|---|---|---|---|
| San Francisco | 8 | 4 | 0 | .667 | 260 | 264 |
| Detroit | 8 | 4 | 0 | .667 | 251 | 231 |
| Baltimore | 7 | 5 | 0 | .583 | 303 | 235 |
| LA Rams | 6 | 6 | 0 | .500 | 307 | 278 |
| Chicago Bears | 5 | 7 | 0 | .417 | 203 | 211 |
| Green Bay | 3 | 9 | 0 | .250 | 218 | 311 |

### 1958

**EAST**

| | W | L | T | Pct | Pts | OP |
|---|---|---|---|---|---|---|
| Cleveland | 9 | 3 | 0 | .750 | 302 | 217 |
| NY Giants | 9 | 3 | 0 | .750 | 246 | 183 |
| Pittsburgh | 7 | 4 | 1 | .636 | 261 | 230 |
| Washington | 4 | 7 | 1 | .364 | 214 | 268 |
| Chicago Cardinals | 2 | 9 | 1 | .182 | 261 | 356 |
| Philadelphia | 2 | 9 | 1 | .182 | 235 | 306 |

**WEST**

| | W | L | T | Pct | Pts | OP |
|---|---|---|---|---|---|---|
| Baltimore | 9 | 3 | 0 | .750 | 381 | 203 |
| LA Rams | 8 | 4 | 0 | .667 | 344 | 278 |
| Chicago Bears | 8 | 4 | 0 | .667 | 298 | 230 |
| San Francisco | 6 | 6 | 0 | .500 | 257 | 324 |
| Detroit | 4 | 7 | 1 | .364 | 261 | 276 |
| Green Bay | 1 | 10 | 1 | .091 | 193 | 382 |

### 1959

**EAST**

| | W | L | T | Pct | Pts | OP |
|---|---|---|---|---|---|---|
| NY Giants | 10 | 2 | 0 | .833 | 284 | 167 |
| Philadelphia | 7 | 5 | 0 | .583 | 268 | 278 |
| Cleveland | 7 | 5 | 0 | .583 | 270 | 214 |
| Pittsburgh | 6 | 5 | 1 | .545 | 257 | 216 |
| Washington | 3 | 9 | 0 | .250 | 185 | 350 |
| Chicago Cardinals | 2 | 10 | 0 | .167 | 231 | 324 |

**WEST**

| | W | L | T | Pct | Pts | OP |
|---|---|---|---|---|---|---|
| Baltimore | 9 | 3 | 0 | .750 | 374 | 251 |
| Chicago Bears | 8 | 4 | 0 | .667 | 246 | 196 |
| Green Bay | 7 | 5 | 0 | .583 | 248 | 240 |
| San Francisco | 7 | 5 | 0 | .583 | 255 | 237 |
| Detroit | 3 | 8 | 1 | .273 | 203 | 275 |
| LA Rams | 2 | 10 | 0 | .167 | 242 | 315 |

### 1960

**NFL EAST**

| | W | L | T | Pct | Pts | OP |
|---|---|---|---|---|---|---|
| Philadelphia | 10 | 2 | 0 | .833 | 321 | 246 |
| Cleveland | 8 | 3 | 1 | .727 | 362 | 217 |
| NY Giants | 6 | 4 | 2 | .600 | 271 | 261 |
| St. Louis Cardinals | 6 | 5 | 1 | .545 | 288 | 230 |
| Pittsburgh | 5 | 6 | 1 | .455 | 240 | 275 |
| Washington | 1 | 9 | 2 | .100 | 178 | 309 |

**NFL WEST**

| | W | L | T | Pct | Pts | OP |
|---|---|---|---|---|---|---|
| Green Bay | 8 | 4 | 0 | .667 | 332 | 209 |
| Detroit | 7 | 5 | 0 | .583 | 239 | 212 |
| San Francisco | 7 | 5 | 0 | .583 | 208 | 205 |
| Baltimore | 6 | 6 | 0 | .500 | 288 | 234 |
| Chicago Bears | 5 | 6 | 1 | .455 | 194 | 299 |
| LA Rams | 4 | 7 | 1 | .364 | 265 | 297 |
| Dallas Cowboys | 0 | 11 | 1 | .000 | 177 | 369 |

**AFL EAST**

| | W | L | T | Pct | Pts | OP |
|---|---|---|---|---|---|---|
| Houston Oilers | 10 | 4 | 0 | .714 | 379 | 285 |
| NY Titans | 7 | 7 | 0 | .500 | 382 | 399 |
| Buffalo Bills | 5 | 8 | 1 | .385 | 296 | 303 |
| Boston Patriots | 5 | 9 | 0 | .357 | 286 | 349 |

**AFL WEST**

| | W | L | T | Pct | Pts | OP |
|---|---|---|---|---|---|---|
| Los Angeles Chargers | 10 | 4 | 0 | .714 | 373 | 336 |
| Dallas Texans | 8 | 6 | 0 | .571 | 361 | 253 |
| Oakland Raiders | 6 | 8 | 0 | .429 | 319 | 388 |
| Denver Broncos | 4 | 9 | 1 | .308 | 309 | 393 |

### 1961

**NFL EAST**

| | W | L | T | Pct | Pts | OP |
|---|---|---|---|---|---|---|
| NY Giants | 10 | 3 | 1 | .769 | 368 | 220 |
| Philadelphia | 10 | 4 | 0 | .714 | 361 | 297 |
| Cleveland | 8 | 5 | 1 | .615 | 319 | 270 |
| St. Louis Cardinals | 7 | 7 | 0 | .500 | 279 | 267 |
| Pittsburgh | 6 | 8 | 0 | .429 | 295 | 287 |
| Dallas Cowboys | 4 | 9 | 1 | .308 | 236 | 380 |
| Washington | 1 | 12 | 1 | .077 | 174 | 392 |

**NFL WEST**

| | W | L | T | Pct | Pts | OP |
|---|---|---|---|---|---|---|
| Green Bay | 11 | 3 | 0 | .786 | 391 | 223 |
| Detroit | 8 | 5 | 1 | .615 | 270 | 258 |
| Baltimore | 8 | 6 | 0 | .571 | 302 | 307 |
| Chicago | 8 | 6 | 0 | .571 | 326 | 302 |
| San Francisco | 7 | 6 | 1 | .538 | 346 | 272 |
| LA Rams | 4 | 10 | 0 | .286 | 263 | 407 |
| Minnesota Vikings | 3 | 11 | 0 | .214 | 285 | 407 |

**AFL EAST**

| | W | L | T | Pct | Pts | OP |
|---|---|---|---|---|---|---|
| Houston Oilers | 10 | 3 | 1 | .769 | 513 | 242 |
| Boston Patriots | 9 | 4 | 1 | .692 | 413 | 313 |
| New York Titans | 7 | 7 | 0 | .500 | 301 | 390 |
| Buffalo Bills | 6 | 8 | 0 | .429 | 294 | 342 |

**AFL WEST**

| | W | L | T | Pct | Pts | OP |
|---|---|---|---|---|---|---|
| San Diego Chargers | 12 | 2 | 0 | .857 | 396 | 219 |
| Dallas Texans | 6 | 8 | 0 | .429 | 334 | 343 |
| Denver | 3 | 11 | 0 | .214 | 251 | 432 |
| Oakland | 2 | 12 | 0 | .143 | 237 | 458 |

## 1962

### NFL EAST

| | W | L | T | Pct | Pts | OP |
|---|---|---|---|---|---|---|
| NY Giants | 12 | 2 | 0 | .857 | 398 | 283 |
| Pittsburgh | 9 | 5 | 0 | .642 | 312 | 363 |
| Cleveland | 7 | 6 | 1 | .538 | 291 | 257 |
| Washington | 5 | 7 | 2 | .417 | 305 | 376 |
| Dallas Cowboys | 5 | 8 | 1 | .385 | 398 | 402 |
| St. Louis Cardinals | 4 | 9 | 1 | .308 | 287 | 361 |
| Philadelphia | 3 | 10 | 1 | .231 | 282 | 356 |

### NFL WEST

| | W | L | T | Pct | Pts | OP |
|---|---|---|---|---|---|---|
| Green Bay | 13 | 1 | 0 | .929 | 415 | 148 |
| Detroit | 11 | 3 | 0 | .786 | 315 | 177 |
| Chicago | 9 | 5 | 0 | .643 | 321 | 287 |
| Baltimore | 7 | 7 | 0 | .500 | 293 | 288 |
| San Francisco | 6 | 8 | 0 | .429 | 282 | 331 |
| Minnesota | 2 | 11 | 1 | .154 | 254 | 410 |
| LA Rams | 1 | 12 | 1 | .077 | 220 | 334 |

### AFL EAST

| | W | L | T | Pct | Pts | OP |
|---|---|---|---|---|---|---|
| Houston | 11 | 3 | 0 | .786 | 387 | 270 |
| Boston | 9 | 4 | 1 | .692 | 346 | 295 |
| Buffalo | 7 | 6 | 1 | .538 | 309 | 272 |
| NY Titans | 5 | 9 | 0 | .357 | 278 | 423 |

### AFL WEST

| | W | L | T | Pct | Pts | OP |
|---|---|---|---|---|---|---|
| Dallas Texans | 11 | 3 | 0 | .786 | 389 | 233 |
| Denver | 6 | 7 | 0 | .462 | 323 | 313 |
| San Diego | 4 | 9 | 0 | .308 | 293 | 362 |
| Oakland | 1 | 13 | 0 | .071 | 213 | 370 |

## 1963

### NFL EAST

| | W | L | T | Pct | Pts | OP |
|---|---|---|---|---|---|---|
| NY Giants | 11 | 3 | 0 | .786 | 448 | 280 |
| Cleveland | 10 | 4 | 0 | .714 | 343 | 262 |
| St. Louis | 9 | 5 | 0 | .643 | 341 | 283 |
| Pittsburgh | 7 | 4 | 3 | .636 | 321 | 295 |
| Dallas Cowboys | 4 | 10 | 0 | .286 | 305 | 378 |
| Washington | 3 | 11 | 0 | .214 | 279 | 398 |
| Philadelphia | 2 | 10 | 2 | .214 | 242 | 381 |

### NFL WEST

| | W | L | T | Pct | Pts | OP |
|---|---|---|---|---|---|---|
| Chicago | 11 | 1 | 2 | .917 | 301 | 144 |
| Green Bay | 11 | 2 | 1 | .846 | 369 | 206 |
| Baltimore | 8 | 6 | 0 | .571 | 316 | 285 |
| Minnesota | 5 | 8 | 1 | .385 | 309 | 390 |
| Detroit | 5 | 8 | 1 | .385 | 32 | 265 |
| LA Rams | 5 | 9 | 0 | .357 | 210 | 350 |
| San Francisco | 2 | 12 | 0 | .143 | 198 | 391 |

### AFL EAST

| | W | L | T | Pct | Pts | OP |
|---|---|---|---|---|---|---|
| Boston | 7 | 6 | 1 | .538 | 327 | 257 |
| Buffalo | 7 | 6 | 1 | .538 | 304 | 291 |
| Houston | 6 | 8 | 0 | .429 | 302 | 372 |
| NY Jets | 5 | 8 | 1 | .385 | 249 | 399 |

### AFL WEST

| | W | L | T | Pct | Pts | OP |
|---|---|---|---|---|---|---|
| San Diego | 11 | 3 | 0 | .786 | 399 | 255 |
| Oakland | 10 | 4 | 0 | .714 | 363 | 282 |
| Kansas City Chiefs | 5 | 7 | 2 | .417 | 347 | 263 |
| Denver | 2 | 11 | 1 | .154 | 301 | 473 |

## 1964

### NFL EAST

| | W | L | T | Pct | Pts | OP |
|---|---|---|---|---|---|---|
| Cleveland | 10 | 3 | 1 | .769 | 415 | 293 |
| St. Louis | 9 | 3 | 2 | .750 | 357 | 331 |
| Philadelphia | 6 | 8 | 0 | .429 | 312 | 313 |
| Washington | 6 | 8 | 0 | .429 | 307 | 305 |
| Dallas | 5 | 8 | 1 | .385 | 250 | 289 |
| Pittsburgh | 5 | 9 | 0 | .357 | 253 | 315 |
| NY Giants | 2 | 10 | 2 | .167 | 241 | 399 |

### NFL WEST

| | W | L | T | Pct | Pts | OP |
|---|---|---|---|---|---|---|
| Baltimore | 12 | 2 | 0 | .857 | 428 | 225 |
| Green Bay | 8 | 5 | 1 | .615 | 342 | 245 |
| Minnesota | 8 | 5 | 1 | .615 | 355 | 296 |
| Detroit | 7 | 5 | 2 | .583 | 280 | 260 |
| LA Rams | 5 | 7 | 2 | .417 | 283 | 339 |
| Chicago | 5 | 9 | 0 | .357 | 260 | 379 |
| San Francisco | 4 | 10 | 0 | .286 | 236 | 330 |

### AFL EAST

| | W | L | T | Pct | Pts | OP |
|---|---|---|---|---|---|---|
| Buffalo | 12 | 2 | 0 | .857 | 400 | 242 |
| Boston | 10 | 3 | 1 | .769 | 365 | 297 |
| NY Jets | 5 | 8 | 1 | .385 | 278 | 315 |
| Houston | 4 | 10 | 0 | .286 | 310 | 355 |

### AFL WEST

| | W | L | T | Pct | Pts | OP |
|---|---|---|---|---|---|---|
| San Diego | 8 | 5 | 1 | .615 | 341 | 300 |
| Kansas City Chiefs | 7 | 7 | 0 | .500 | 366 | 306 |
| Oakland | 5 | 7 | 2 | .417 | 303 | 350 |
| Denver | 2 | 11 | 1 | .154 | 240 | 438 |

## 1965

### NFL EAST

| | W | L | T | Pct | Pts | OP |
|---|---|---|---|---|---|---|
| Cleveland | 11 | 3 | 0 | .786 | 363 | 325 |
| NY Giants | 7 | 7 | 0 | .500 | 270 | 338 |
| Dallas | 7 | 7 | 0 | .500 | 325 | 280 |
| Washington | 6 | 8 | 0 | .429 | 257 | 301 |
| St. Louis | 5 | 9 | 0 | .357 | 296 | 309 |
| Philadelphia | 5 | 9 | 0 | .357 | 363 | 359 |
| Pittsburgh | 2 | 12 | 0 | .143 | 202 | 397 |

### NFL WEST

| | W | L | T | Pct | Pts | OP |
|---|---|---|---|---|---|---|
| Green Bay | 10 | 3 | 1 | .769 | 316 | 224 |
| Baltimore | 9 | 3 | 1 | .769 | 389 | 263 |
| Chicago | 9 | 5 | 0 | .643 | 409 | 275 |
| San Francisco | 7 | 6 | 1 | .538 | 421 | 402 |
| Minnesota | 7 | 7 | 0 | .500 | 383 | 362 |
| Detroit | 6 | 7 | 1 | .462 | 257 | 295 |
| LA Rams | 4 | 10 | 0 | .286 | 269 | 328 |

### AFL EAST

| | W | L | T | Pct | Pts | OP |
|---|---|---|---|---|---|---|
| Buffalo | 10 | 3 | 1 | .769 | 313 | 226 |
| NY Jets | 5 | 8 | 1 | .385 | 285 | 303 |
| Boston | 4 | 8 | 2 | .333 | 244 | 302 |
| Houston | 4 | 10 | 0 | .286 | 298 | 429 |

### AFL WEST

| | W | L | T | Pct | Pts | OP |
|---|---|---|---|---|---|---|
| San Diego | 9 | 2 | 3 | .818 | 340 | 227 |
| Oakland | 8 | 5 | 1 | .615 | 298 | 239 |
| Kansas City | 7 | 5 | 2 | .583 | 322 | 285 |
| Denver | 4 | 10 | 0 | .286 | 303 | 392 |

## 1966

### NFL EAST
| | W | L | T | Pct | Pts | OP |
|---|---|---|---|---|---|---|
| Dallas | 10 | 3 | 1 | .769 | 445 | 239 |
| Cleveland | 9 | 5 | 0 | .643 | 403 | 259 |
| Philadelphia | 9 | 5 | 0 | .643 | 326 | 340 |
| St. Louis | 8 | 5 | 1 | .625 | 264 | 265 |
| Washington | 7 | 7 | 0 | .500 | 351 | 355 |
| Pittsburgh | 5 | 8 | 1 | .385 | 316 | 347 |
| Atlanta Falcons | 3 | 11 | 0 | .214 | 204 | 437 |
| NY Giants | 1 | 12 | 1 | .077 | 263 | 501 |

### NFL WEST
| | W | L | T | Pct | Pts | OP |
|---|---|---|---|---|---|---|
| Green Bay | 12 | 2 | 0 | .857 | 335 | 163 |
| Baltimore | 9 | 5 | 0 | .643 | 314 | 226 |
| LA Rams | 8 | 6 | 0 | .571 | 289 | 212 |
| San Francisco | 6 | 6 | 2 | .500 | 320 | 325 |
| Chicago | 5 | 7 | 2 | .417 | 234 | 272 |
| Detroit | 4 | 9 | 1 | .308 | 206 | 317 |
| Minnesota | 4 | 9 | 1 | .308 | 292 | 304 |

### AFL EAST
| | W | L | T | Pct | Pts | OP |
|---|---|---|---|---|---|---|
| Buffalo | 9 | 4 | 1 | .692 | 358 | 255 |
| Boston | 8 | 4 | 2 | .677 | 315 | 283 |
| NY Jets | 6 | 6 | 2 | .500 | 322 | 312 |
| Houston | 3 | 11 | 0 | .214 | 335 | 396 |
| Miami Dolphins | 3 | 11 | 0 | .214 | 213 | 362 |

### AFL WEST
| | W | L | T | Pct | Pts | OP |
|---|---|---|---|---|---|---|
| Kansas City | 11 | 2 | 1 | .846 | 448 | 276 |
| Oakland | 8 | 5 | 1 | .615 | 315 | 288 |
| San Diego | 7 | 6 | 1 | .538 | 335 | 284 |
| Denver | 4 | 10 | 0 | .286 | 196 | 381 |

## 1967

### NFL CAPITOL
| | W | L | T | Pct | Pts | OP |
|---|---|---|---|---|---|---|
| Dallas | 9 | 5 | 0 | .643 | 342 | 268 |
| Philadelphia | 6 | 7 | 1 | .462 | 351 | 409 |
| Washington | 5 | 6 | 3 | .455 | 347 | 353 |
| New Orleans Saints | 3 | 11 | 0 | .214 | 233 | 379 |

### NFL CENTURY
| | W | L | T | Pct | Pts | OP |
|---|---|---|---|---|---|---|
| Cleveland | 9 | 5 | 0 | .643 | 334 | 297 |
| NY Giants | 7 | 7 | 0 | .500 | 369 | 379 |
| St. Louis | 6 | 7 | 1 | .462 | 333 | 356 |
| Pittsburgh | 4 | 9 | 1 | .308 | 281 | 320 |

### NFL COASTAL
| | W | L | T | Pct | Pts | OP |
|---|---|---|---|---|---|---|
| LA Rams | 11 | 1 | 2 | .917 | 398 | 196 |
| Baltimore | 11 | 1 | 2 | .917 | 394 | 198 |
| San Francisco | 7 | 7 | 0 | .500 | 273 | 337 |
| Atlanta | 1 | 12 | 1 | .077 | 175 | 422 |

### NFL CENTRAL
| | W | L | T | Pct | Pts | OP |
|---|---|---|---|---|---|---|
| Green Bay | 9 | 4 | 1 | .692 | 332 | 209 |
| Chicago | 7 | 6 | 1 | .538 | 239 | 218 |
| Detroit | 5 | 7 | 2 | .417 | 260 | 259 |
| Minnesota | 3 | 8 | 3 | .273 | 233 | 294 |

### AFL EAST
| | W | L | T | Pct | Pts | OP |
|---|---|---|---|---|---|---|
| Houston | 9 | 4 | 1 | .692 | 258 | 199 |
| NY Jets | 8 | 5 | 1 | .615 | 371 | 329 |
| Buffalo | 4 | 10 | 0 | .286 | 237 | 285 |
| Miami | 4 | 10 | 0 | .286 | 219 | 407 |
| Boston | 3 | 10 | 1 | .231 | 280 | 389 |

## 1967 (Cont.)

### AFL WEST
| | W | L | T | Pct | Pts | OP |
|---|---|---|---|---|---|---|
| Oakland | 13 | 1 | 0 | .929 | 468 | 233 |
| Kansas City | 9 | 5 | 0 | .643 | 408 | 254 |
| San Diego | 8 | 5 | 1 | .615 | 360 | 352 |
| Denver | 3 | 11 | 0 | .214 | 256 | 409 |

## 1968

### NFL CAPITOL
| | W | L | T | Pct | Pts | OP |
|---|---|---|---|---|---|---|
| Dallas | 12 | 2 | 0 | .857 | 431 | 186 |
| NY Giants | 7 | 7 | 0 | .500 | 294 | 325 |
| Washington | 5 | 9 | 0 | .357 | 249 | 358 |
| Philadelphia | 2 | 12 | 0 | .143 | 202 | 351 |

### NFL CENTURY
| | W | L | T | Pct | Pts | OP |
|---|---|---|---|---|---|---|
| Cleveland | 10 | 4 | 0 | .714 | 394 | 273 |
| St. Louis | 9 | 4 | 1 | .692 | 325 | 289 |
| New Orleans | 4 | 9 | 1 | .308 | 246 | 327 |
| Pittsburgh | 2 | 11 | 1 | .154 | 244 | 397 |

### NFL COASTAL
| | W | L | T | Pct | Pts | OP |
|---|---|---|---|---|---|---|
| Baltimore | 13 | 1 | 0 | .929 | 402 | 144 |
| LA Rams | 10 | 3 | 1 | .769 | 312 | 200 |
| San Francisco | 7 | 6 | 1 | .538 | 303 | 310 |
| Atlanta | 2 | 12 | 0 | .143 | 202 | 351 |

### NFL CENTRAL
| | W | L | T | Pct | Pts | OP |
|---|---|---|---|---|---|---|
| Minnesota | 8 | 6 | 0 | .571 | 282 | 242 |
| Chicago | 7 | 7 | 0 | .500 | 250 | 333 |
| Green Bay | 6 | 7 | 1 | .462 | 281 | 227 |
| Detroit | 4 | 8 | 2 | .333 | 207 | 241 |

### AFL EAST
| | W | L | T | Pct | Pts | OP |
|---|---|---|---|---|---|---|
| NY Jets | 11 | 3 | 0 | .786 | 419 | 280 |
| Houston | 7 | 7 | 0 | .500 | 303 | 248 |
| Miami | 5 | 8 | 1 | .385 | 276 | 355 |
| Boston | 4 | 10 | 0 | .286 | 229 | 406 |
| Buffalo | 1 | 12 | 1 | .077 | 199 | 367 |

### AFL WEST
| | W | L | T | Pct | Pts | OP |
|---|---|---|---|---|---|---|
| Oakland | 12 | 2 | 0 | .857 | 453 | 233 |
| Kansas City | 12 | 2 | 0 | .857 | 371 | 170 |
| San Diego | 9 | 5 | 0 | .643 | 382 | 310 |
| Denver | 5 | 9 | 0 | .357 | 255 | 404 |
| Cincinnati Bengals | 3 | 11 | 0 | .214 | 215 | 329 |

## 1969

### NFL CAPITOL
| | W | L | T | Pct | Pts | OP |
|---|---|---|---|---|---|---|
| Dallas | 11 | 2 | 1 | .846 | 369 | 223 |
| Washington | 7 | 5 | 2 | .583 | 307 | 319 |
| New Orleans | 5 | 9 | 0 | .357 | 311 | 393 |
| Philadelphia | 4 | 9 | 1 | .308 | 279 | 377 |

### NFL CENTURY
| | W | L | T | Pct | Pts | OP |
|---|---|---|---|---|---|---|
| Cleveland | 10 | 3 | 1 | .769 | 351 | 300 |
| NY Giants | 6 | 8 | 0 | .429 | 264 | 298 |
| St. Louis | 4 | 9 | 1 | .308 | 314 | 389 |
| Pittsburgh | 1 | 13 | 0 | .071 | 218 | 404 |

### NFL COASTAL
| | W | L | T | Pct | Pts | OP |
|---|---|---|---|---|---|---|
| LA Rams | 11 | 3 | 0 | .786 | 320 | 243 |
| Baltimore | 7 | 5 | 2 | .615 | 307 | 319 |
| Atlanta | 6 | 8 | 0 | .429 | 276 | 268 |
| San Francisco | 4 | 8 | 2 | .333 | 277 | 319 |

## 1969 (Cont.)

### NFL CENTRAL

| | W | L | T | Pct | Pts | OP |
|---|---|---|---|---|---|---|
| Minnesota | 12 | 2 | 0 | .857 | 379 | 133 |
| Detroit | 9 | 4 | 1 | .692 | 259 | 188 |
| Green Bay | 8 | 6 | 0 | .571 | 269 | 221 |
| Chicago | 1 | 13 | 0 | .071 | 210 | 339 |

### AFL EAST

| | W | L | T | Pct | Pts | OP |
|---|---|---|---|---|---|---|
| NY Jets | 10 | 4 | 0 | .714 | 353 | 269 |
| Houston | 6 | 6 | 2 | .500 | 278 | 279 |
| Buffalo | 4 | 10 | 0 | .286 | 230 | 359 |
| Boston | 4 | 10 | 0 | .286 | 266 | 316 |
| Miami | 3 | 10 | 1 | .231 | 233 | 332 |

### AFL WEST

| | W | L | T | Pct | Pts | OP |
|---|---|---|---|---|---|---|
| Oakland | 12 | 1 | 1 | .923 | 377 | 242 |
| Kansas City | 11 | 3 | 0 | .786 | 359 | 177 |
| San Diego | 8 | 6 | 0 | .571 | 288 | 276 |
| Denver | 5 | 8 | 1 | .385 | 297 | 344 |
| Cincinnati | 4 | 9 | 1 | .308 | 280 | 367 |

## 1970

### AFC EAST

| | W | L | T | Pct | Pts | OP |
|---|---|---|---|---|---|---|
| Baltimore | 11 | 2 | 1 | .846 | 321 | 234 |
| Miami | 10 | 4 | 0 | .714 | 297 | 228 |
| NY Jets | 4 | 10 | 0 | .286 | 255 | 286 |
| Buffalo | 3 | 10 | 1 | .231 | 204 | 337 |
| Boston | 2 | 12 | 0 | .143 | 149 | 361 |

### AFC CENTRAL

| | W | L | T | Pct | Pts | OP |
|---|---|---|---|---|---|---|
| Cincinnati | 8 | 6 | 0 | .571 | 312 | 255 |
| Cleveland | 7 | 7 | 0 | .500 | 286 | 265 |
| Pittsburgh | 5 | 9 | 0 | .357 | 210 | 272 |
| Houston | 3 | 10 | 1 | .231 | 217 | 352 |

### AFC WEST

| | W | L | T | Pct | Pts | OP |
|---|---|---|---|---|---|---|
| Oakland | 8 | 4 | 2 | .667 | 300 | 293 |
| Kansas City | 7 | 5 | 2 | .583 | 272 | 244 |
| San Diego | 5 | 6 | 3 | .455 | 282 | 278 |
| Denver | 5 | 8 | 1 | .385 | 253 | 264 |

### NFC EAST

| | W | L | T | Pct | Pts | OP |
|---|---|---|---|---|---|---|
| Dallas | 10 | 4 | 0 | .714 | 299 | 221 |
| NY Giants | 9 | 5 | 0 | .643 | 301 | 270 |
| St. Louis | 8 | 5 | 1 | .615 | 325 | 228 |
| Washington | 6 | 8 | 0 | .429 | 297 | 314 |
| Philadelphia | 3 | 10 | 1 | .231 | 241 | 332 |

### NFC CENTRAL

| | W | L | T | Pct | Pts | OP |
|---|---|---|---|---|---|---|
| Minnesota | 12 | 2 | 0 | .857 | 335 | 143 |
| Detroit | 10 | 4 | 0 | .714 | 347 | 202 |
| Green Bay | 6 | 8 | 0 | .429 | 196 | 293 |
| Chicago | 6 | 8 | 0 | .429 | 256 | 261 |

### NFC WEST

| | W | L | T | Pct | Pts | OP |
|---|---|---|---|---|---|---|
| San Francisco | 10 | 3 | 1 | .769 | 352 | 267 |
| LA Rams | 9 | 4 | 1 | .692 | 325 | 202 |
| Atlanta | 4 | 8 | 2 | .333 | 206 | 261 |
| New Orleans | 2 | 11 | 1 | .154 | 172 | 347 |

## 1971

### AFC EAST

| | W | L | T | Pct | Pts | OP |
|---|---|---|---|---|---|---|
| Miami | 10 | 3 | 1 | .769 | 315 | 174 |
| Baltimore | 10 | 4 | 0 | .714 | 313 | 140 |
| New England Patriots | 6 | 8 | 0 | .429 | 238 | 325 |
| NY Jets | 6 | 8 | 0 | .429 | 212 | 299 |
| Buffalo | 1 | 13 | 0 | .071 | 184 | 394 |

### AFC CENTRAL

| | W | L | T | Pct | Pts | OP |
|---|---|---|---|---|---|---|
| Cleveland | 9 | 5 | 0 | .643 | 285 | 273 |
| Pittsburgh | 6 | 8 | 0 | .429 | 246 | 292 |
| Houston | 4 | 9 | 1 | .308 | 251 | 330 |
| Cincinnati | 4 | 10 | 0 | .286 | 284 | 265 |

### AFC WEST

| | W | L | T | Pct | Pts | OP |
|---|---|---|---|---|---|---|
| Kansas City | 10 | 3 | 1 | .769 | 302 | 208 |
| Oakland | 8 | 4 | 2 | .667 | 344 | 278 |
| San Diego | 6 | 8 | 0 | .429 | 311 | 341 |
| Denver | 4 | 9 | 1 | .308 | 203 | 275 |

### NFC EAST

| | W | L | T | Pct | Pts | OP |
|---|---|---|---|---|---|---|
| Dallas | 11 | 3 | 0 | .786 | 406 | 222 |
| Washington | 9 | 4 | 1 | .692 | 276 | 190 |
| Philadelphia | 6 | 7 | 1 | .462 | 221 | 302 |
| St. Louis | 4 | 9 | 1 | .308 | 231 | 279 |
| NY Giants | 4 | 10 | 0 | .286 | 228 | 362 |

### NFC CENTRAL

| | W | L | T | Pct | Pts | OP |
|---|---|---|---|---|---|---|
| Minnesota | 11 | 3 | 0 | .786 | 245 | 139 |
| Detroit | 7 | 6 | 1 | .538 | 341 | 286 |
| Chicago | 6 | 8 | 0 | .429 | 185 | 276 |
| Green Bay | 4 | 8 | 2 | .333 | 274 | 298 |

### NFC WEST

| | W | L | T | Pct | Pts | OP |
|---|---|---|---|---|---|---|
| San Francisco | 9 | 5 | 0 | .643 | 300 | 216 |
| LA Rams | 8 | 5 | 1 | .615 | 313 | 260 |
| Atlanta | 7 | 6 | 1 | .538 | 274 | 277 |
| New Orleans | 4 | 8 | 2 | .333 | 266 | 347 |

## 1972

### AFC EAST

| | W | L | T | Pct | Pts | OP |
|---|---|---|---|---|---|---|
| Miami | 14 | 0 | 0 | 1.000 | 385 | 171 |
| NY Jets | 7 | 7 | 0 | .500 | 367 | 324 |
| Baltimore | 5 | 9 | 0 | .357 | 235 | 252 |
| Buffalo | 4 | 9 | 1 | .321 | 257 | 377 |
| New England | 3 | 11 | 0 | .214 | 192 | 446 |

### AFC CENTRAL

| | W | L | T | Pct | Pts | OP |
|---|---|---|---|---|---|---|
| Pittsburgh | 11 | 3 | 0 | .786 | 343 | 175 |
| Cleveland | 10 | 4 | 0 | .714 | 268 | 249 |
| Cincinnati | 8 | 6 | 0 | .571 | 299 | 229 |
| Houston | 1 | 13 | 0 | .071 | 164 | 380 |

### AFC WEST

| | W | L | T | Pct | Pts | OP |
|---|---|---|---|---|---|---|
| Oakland | 10 | 3 | 1 | .750 | 365 | 248 |
| Kansas City | 8 | 6 | 0 | .571 | 287 | 254 |
| Denver | 5 | 9 | 0 | .357 | 325 | 350 |
| San Diego | 4 | 9 | 1 | .321 | 264 | 344 |

### NFC EAST

| | W | L | T | Pct | Pts | OP |
|---|---|---|---|---|---|---|
| Washington | 11 | 3 | 0 | .786 | 336 | 218 |
| Dallas | 10 | 4 | 0 | .286 | 319 | 240 |
| NY Giants | 8 | 6 | 0 | .571 | 331 | 247 |
| St. Louis | 4 | 9 | 1 | .321 | 193 | 303 |
| Philadelphia | 2 | 11 | 1 | .179 | 145 | 352 |

### 1972 (Cont.)

**NFC CENTRAL**

| | W | L | T | Pct | Pts | OP |
|---|---|---|---|---|---|---|
| Green Bay | 10 | 4 | 0 | .714 | 304 | 226 |
| Detroit | 8 | 5 | 1 | .607 | 339 | 290 |
| Minnesota | 7 | 7 | 0 | .500 | 301 | 252 |
| Chicago | 4 | 9 | 1 | .321 | 225 | 275 |

**NFC WEST**

| | W | L | T | Pct | Pts | OP |
|---|---|---|---|---|---|---|
| San Francisco | 8 | 5 | 1 | .607 | 353 | 249 |
| Atlanta | 7 | 7 | 0 | .500 | 269 | 274 |
| LA Rams | 6 | 7 | 1 | .464 | 291 | 286 |
| New Orleans | 2 | 11 | 1 | .179 | 215 | 361 |

### 1973

**AFC EAST**

| | W | L | T | Pct | Pts | OP |
|---|---|---|---|---|---|---|
| Miami | 12 | 2 | 0 | .857 | 343 | 150 |
| Buffalo | 9 | 5 | 0 | .643 | 259 | 230 |
| New England | 5 | 9 | 0 | .357 | 258 | 300 |
| Baltimore | 4 | 10 | 0 | .286 | 226 | 341 |
| NY Jets | 4 | 10 | 0 | .286 | 240 | 306 |

**AFC CENTRAL**

| | W | L | T | Pct | Pts | OP |
|---|---|---|---|---|---|---|
| Pittsburgh | 10 | 4 | 0 | .714 | 347 | 210 |
| Cincinnati | 10 | 4 | 0 | .714 | 286 | 231 |
| Cleveland | 7 | 5 | 2 | .571 | 234 | 255 |
| Houston | 1 | 13 | 0 | .071 | 199 | 447 |

**AFC WEST**

| | W | L | T | Pct | Pts | OP |
|---|---|---|---|---|---|---|
| Oakland | 9 | 4 | 1 | .679 | 292 | 175 |
| Kansas City | 7 | 5 | 2 | .571 | 231 | 192 |
| Denver | 7 | 5 | 2 | .571 | 354 | 296 |
| San Diego | 2 | 11 | 1 | .179 | 188 | 386 |

**NFC EAST**

| | W | L | T | Pct | Pts | OP |
|---|---|---|---|---|---|---|
| Washington | 10 | 4 | 0 | .714 | 325 | 198 |
| Dallas | 10 | 4 | 0 | .714 | 325 | 198 |
| Philadelphia | 5 | 8 | 1 | .393 | 310 | 393 |
| St. Louis | 4 | 9 | 1 | .321 | 286 | 365 |
| NY Giants | 2 | 11 | 1 | .179 | 226 | 362 |

**NFC CENTRAL**

| | W | L | T | Pct | Pts | OP |
|---|---|---|---|---|---|---|
| Minnesota | 12 | 2 | 0 | .857 | 296 | 168 |
| Detroit | 6 | 7 | 1 | .464 | 271 | 247 |
| Green Bay | 5 | 7 | 2 | .429 | 202 | 259 |
| Chicago | 3 | 11 | 0 | .214 | 195 | 334 |

**NFC WEST**

| | W | L | T | Pct | Pts | OP |
|---|---|---|---|---|---|---|
| LA Rams | 12 | 2 | 0 | .857 | 388 | 178 |
| Atlanta | 9 | 5 | 0 | .643 | 318 | 224 |
| New Orleans | 5 | 9 | 0 | .357 | 163 | 312 |
| San Francisco | 5 | 9 | 0 | .357 | 262 | 319 |

### 1974

**AFC EAST**

| | W | L | T | Pct | Pts | OP |
|---|---|---|---|---|---|---|
| Miami | 11 | 3 | 0 | .786 | 327 | 216 |
| Buffalo | 9 | 5 | 0 | .643 | 264 | 244 |
| NY Jets | 7 | 7 | 0 | .500 | 279 | 300 |
| New England | 7 | 7 | 0 | .500 | 348 | 289 |
| Baltimore | 2 | 12 | 0 | .143 | 190 | 329 |

**AFC CENTRAL**

| | W | L | T | Pct | Pts | OP |
|---|---|---|---|---|---|---|
| Pittsburgh | 10 | 3 | 1 | .750 | 305 | 189 |
| Houston | 7 | 7 | 0 | .500 | 236 | 282 |
| Cincinnati | 7 | 7 | 0 | .500 | 283 | 259 |
| Cleveland | 4 | 10 | 0 | .283 | 251 | 344 |

### 1974 (Cont.)

**AFC WEST**

| | W | L | T | Pct | Pts | OP |
|---|---|---|---|---|---|---|
| Oakland | 12 | 2 | 0 | .857 | 355 | 228 |
| Denver | 7 | 6 | 1 | .536 | 302 | 294 |
| Kansas City | 5 | 9 | 0 | .357 | 233 | 293 |
| San Diego | 5 | 9 | 0 | .357 | 212 | 285 |

**NFC EAST**

| | W | L | T | Pct | Pts | OP |
|---|---|---|---|---|---|---|
| Washington | 10 | 4 | 0 | .714 | 320 | 196 |
| St. Louis | 10 | 4 | 0 | .714 | 285 | 218 |
| Dallas | 8 | 6 | 0 | .571 | 297 | 235 |
| Philadelphia | 7 | 7 | 0 | .500 | 242 | 217 |
| NY Giants | 2 | 12 | 0 | .143 | 195 | 299 |

**NFC CENTRAL**

| | W | L | T | Pct | Pts | OP |
|---|---|---|---|---|---|---|
| Minnesota | 10 | 4 | 0 | .714 | 310 | 195 |
| Detroit | 7 | 7 | 0 | .500 | 256 | 270 |
| Green Bay | 6 | 8 | 0 | .429 | 210 | 206 |
| Chicago | 4 | 10 | 0 | .286 | 152 | 279 |

**NFC WEST**

| | W | L | T | Pct | Pts | OP |
|---|---|---|---|---|---|---|
| LA Rams | 10 | 4 | 0 | .714 | 263 | 181 |
| San Francisco | 6 | 8 | 0 | .429 | 226 | 236 |
| New Orleans | 5 | 9 | 0 | .357 | 166 | 263 |
| Atlanta | 3 | 11 | 0 | .214 | 111 | 271 |

### 1975

**AFC EAST**

| | W | L | T | Pct | Pts | OP |
|---|---|---|---|---|---|---|
| Miami | 10 | 4 | 0 | .714 | 357 | 222 |
| Baltimore | 10 | 4 | 0 | .714 | 395 | 269 |
| Buffalo | 8 | 6 | 0 | .571 | 420 | 355 |
| NY Jets | 3 | 11 | 0 | .214 | 258 | 433 |
| New England | 3 | 11 | 0 | .214 | 258 | 358 |

**AFC CENTRAL**

| | W | L | T | Pct | Pts | OP |
|---|---|---|---|---|---|---|
| Pittsburgh | 12 | 2 | 0 | .857 | 373 | 162 |
| Cincinnati | 11 | 3 | 0 | .786 | 340 | 246 |
| Houston | 10 | 4 | 0 | .714 | 293 | 226 |
| Cleveland | 3 | 11 | 0 | .214 | 218 | 372 |

**AFC WEST**

| | W | L | T | Pct | Pts | OP |
|---|---|---|---|---|---|---|
| Oakland | 11 | 3 | 0 | .786 | 375 | 255 |
| Denver | 6 | 8 | 0 | .429 | 254 | 307 |
| Kansas City | 5 | 9 | 0 | .357 | 282 | 341 |
| San Diego | 2 | 12 | 0 | .143 | 189 | 345 |

**NFC EAST**

| | W | L | T | Pct | Pts | OP |
|---|---|---|---|---|---|---|
| St. Louis | 11 | 3 | 0 | .786 | 356 | 276 |
| Dallas | 10 | 4 | 0 | .714 | 350 | 268 |
| Washington | 8 | 6 | 0 | .571 | 325 | 276 |
| NY Giants | 5 | 9 | 0 | .357 | 216 | 306 |
| Philadelphia | 4 | 10 | 0 | .286 | 225 | 302 |

**NFC CENTRAL**

| | W | L | T | Pct | Pts | OP |
|---|---|---|---|---|---|---|
| Minnesota | 12 | 2 | 0 | .857 | 377 | 180 |
| Detroit | 7 | 7 | 0 | .500 | 245 | 262 |
| Green Bay | 4 | 10 | 0 | .286 | 226 | 285 |
| Chicago | 4 | 10 | 0 | .286 | 191 | 379 |

**NFC WEST**

| | W | L | T | Pct | Pts | OP |
|---|---|---|---|---|---|---|
| LA Rams | 12 | 2 | 0 | .857 | 312 | 135 |
| San Francisco | 5 | 9 | 0 | .357 | 255 | 286 |
| Atlanta | 4 | 10 | 0 | .286 | 240 | 289 |
| New Orleans | 2 | 12 | 0 | .143 | 165 | 360 |

## 1976

### AFC EAST

| | W | L | T | Pct | Pts | OP |
|---|---|---|---|---|---|---|
| Baltimore | 11 | 3 | 0 | .786 | 417 | 246 |
| New England | 11 | 3 | 0 | .786 | 376 | 236 |
| Miami | 6 | 8 | 0 | .429 | 263 | 264 |
| NY Jets | 3 | 11 | 0 | .214 | 169 | 383 |
| Buffalo | 2 | 12 | 0 | .143 | 246 | 363 |

### AFC CENTRAL

| | W | L | T | Pct | Pts | OP |
|---|---|---|---|---|---|---|
| Cincinnati | 10 | 4 | 0 | .714 | 335 | 210 |
| Pittsburgh | 10 | 4 | 0 | .714 | 342 | 138 |
| Cleveland | 9 | 5 | 0 | .643 | 267 | 287 |
| Houston | 5 | 9 | 0 | .357 | 222 | 273 |

### AFC WEST

| | W | L | T | Pct | Pts | OP |
|---|---|---|---|---|---|---|
| Oakland | 13 | 1 | 0 | .929 | 350 | 237 |
| Denver | 9 | 5 | 0 | .643 | 315 | 206 |
| San Diego | 6 | 8 | 0 | .429 | 248 | 285 |
| Kansas City | 5 | 9 | 0 | .357 | 290 | 376 |
| Tampa Bay Buccaneers | 0 | 14 | 0 | .000 | 125 | 412 |

### NFC EAST

| | W | L | T | Pct | Pts | OP |
|---|---|---|---|---|---|---|
| Dallas | 11 | 3 | 0 | .786 | 296 | 194 |
| Washington | 10 | 4 | 0 | .714 | 291 | 217 |
| St. Louis | 10 | 4 | 0 | .714 | 309 | 267 |
| Philadelphia | 4 | 10 | 0 | .286 | 165 | 286 |
| NY Giants | 3 | 11 | 0 | .214 | 170 | 250 |

### NFC CENTRAL

| | W | L | T | Pct | Pts | OP |
|---|---|---|---|---|---|---|
| Minnesota | 11 | 2 | 1 | .821 | 305 | 176 |
| Chicago | 7 | 7 | 0 | .500 | 253 | 216 |
| Detroit | 6 | 8 | 0 | .429 | 218 | 299 |
| Green Bay | 5 | 9 | 0 | .357 | 218 | 299 |

### NFC WEST

| | W | L | T | Pct | Pts | OP |
|---|---|---|---|---|---|---|
| LA Rams | 10 | 3 | 1 | .750 | 351 | 190 |
| San Francisco | 8 | 6 | 0 | .571 | 270 | 190 |
| Atlanta | 4 | 10 | 0 | .286 | 172 | 312 |
| New Orleans | 4 | 10 | 0 | .286 | 253 | 346 |
| Seattle Seahawks | 2 | 12 | 0 | .143 | 229 | 429 |

## 1977

### AFC EAST

| | W | L | T | Pct | Pts | OP |
|---|---|---|---|---|---|---|
| Miami | 10 | 4 | 0 | .714 | 313 | 197 |
| Baltimore | 10 | 4 | 0 | .714 | 295 | 221 |
| New England | 9 | 5 | 0 | .643 | 279 | 217 |
| Buffalo | 3 | 11 | 0 | .214 | 160 | 313 |
| NY Jets | 3 | 11 | 0 | .214 | 191 | 313 |

### AFC CENTRAL

| | W | L | T | Pct | Pts | OP |
|---|---|---|---|---|---|---|
| Pittsburgh | 9 | 5 | 0 | .643 | 283 | 243 |
| Houston | 8 | 6 | 0 | .571 | 299 | 230 |
| Cincinnati | 8 | 6 | 0 | .571 | 238 | 235 |
| Cleveland | 6 | 8 | 0 | .429 | 269 | 267 |

### AFC WEST

| | W | L | T | Pct | Pts | OP |
|---|---|---|---|---|---|---|
| Denver | 12 | 2 | 0 | .857 | 274 | 148 |
| Oakland | 11 | 3 | 0 | .786 | 351 | 230 |
| San Diego | 7 | 7 | 0 | .500 | 222 | 205 |
| Seattle | 5 | 9 | 0 | .357 | 282 | 373 |
| Kansas City | 2 | 12 | 0 | .143 | 225 | 349 |

## 1977 (Cont.)

### NFC EAST

| | W | L | T | Pct | Pts | OP |
|---|---|---|---|---|---|---|
| Dallas | 12 | 2 | 0 | .857 | 345 | 212 |
| Washington | 9 | 5 | 0 | .643 | 196 | 189 |
| St. Louis | 7 | 7 | 0 | .500 | 272 | 287 |
| NY Giants | 5 | 9 | 0 | .357 | 181 | 265 |
| Philadelphia | 5 | 9 | 0 | .357 | 220 | 207 |

### NFC CENTRAL

| | W | L | T | Pct | Pts | OP |
|---|---|---|---|---|---|---|
| Chicago | 9 | 5 | 0 | .643 | 255 | 253 |
| Minnesota | 9 | 5 | 0 | .643 | 231 | 227 |
| Detroit | 6 | 8 | 0 | .429 | 183 | 252 |
| Green Bay | 4 | 10 | 0 | .286 | 134 | 219 |
| Tampa Bay | 2 | 12 | 0 | .143 | 103 | 223 |

### NFC WEST

| | W | L | T | Pct | Pts | OP |
|---|---|---|---|---|---|---|
| LA Rams | 10 | 4 | 0 | .714 | 302 | 146 |
| Atlanta | 7 | 7 | 0 | .500 | 179 | 129 |
| San Francisco | 5 | 9 | 0 | .357 | 220 | 260 |
| New Orleans | 3 | 11 | 0 | .214 | 232 | 336 |

## 1978

### AFC EAST

| | W | L | T | Pct | Pts | OP |
|---|---|---|---|---|---|---|
| New England | 11 | 5 | 0 | .688 | 358 | 286 |
| Miami | 11 | 5 | 0 | .688 | 372 | 254 |
| NY Jets | 8 | 8 | 0 | .500 | 359 | 364 |
| Buffalo | 5 | 11 | 0 | .313 | 302 | 354 |
| Baltimore | 5 | 11 | 0 | .313 | 239 | 421 |

### AFC CENTRAL

| | W | L | T | Pct | Pts | OP |
|---|---|---|---|---|---|---|
| Pittsburgh | 14 | 2 | 0 | .875 | 356 | 195 |
| Houston | 10 | 6 | 0 | .625 | 283 | 298 |
| Cleveland | 8 | 8 | 0 | .500 | 334 | 356 |
| Cincinnati | 4 | 12 | 0 | .250 | 252 | 284 |

### AFC WEST

| | W | L | T | Pct | Pts | OP |
|---|---|---|---|---|---|---|
| Denver | 10 | 6 | 0 | .625 | 282 | 198 |
| Seattle | 9 | 7 | 0 | .563 | 345 | 358 |
| Oakland | 9 | 7 | 0 | .563 | 311 | 283 |
| San Diego | 9 | 7 | 0 | .563 | 355 | 309 |
| Kansas City | 4 | 12 | 0 | .250 | 243 | 327 |

### NFC EAST

| | W | L | T | Pct | Pts | OP |
|---|---|---|---|---|---|---|
| Dallas | 12 | 4 | 0 | .750 | 384 | 208 |
| Philadelphia | 9 | 7 | 0 | .563 | 270 | 250 |
| Washington | 8 | 8 | 0 | .500 | 273 | 283 |
| St. Louis | 6 | 10 | 0 | .375 | 248 | 296 |
| NY Giants | 6 | 10 | 0 | .375 | 264 | 298 |

### NFC CENTRAL

| | W | L | T | Pct | Pts | OP |
|---|---|---|---|---|---|---|
| Green Bay | 8 | 7 | 1 | .531 | 249 | 269 |
| Minnesota | 8 | 7 | 1 | .531 | 294 | 306 |
| Detroit | 7 | 9 | 0 | .438 | 290 | 300 |
| Chicago | 7 | 9 | 0 | .438 | 253 | 274 |
| Tampa Bay | 5 | 11 | 0 | .313 | 241 | 259 |

### NFC WEST

| | W | L | T | Pct | Pts | OP |
|---|---|---|---|---|---|---|
| LA Rams | 12 | 4 | 0 | .750 | 316 | 245 |
| Atlanta | 9 | 7 | 0 | .563 | 240 | 290 |
| New Orleans | 7 | 9 | 0 | .438 | 281 | 298 |
| San Francisco | 2 | 14 | 0 | .125 | 219 | 350 |

## 1979

| AFC EAST | W | L | T | Pct | Pts | OP |
|---|---|---|---|---|---|---|
| Miami | 10 | 6 | 0 | .625 | 341 | 257 |
| New England | 9 | 7 | 0 | .563 | 411 | 326 |
| NY Jets | 8 | 8 | 0 | .500 | 337 | 383 |
| Buffalo | 7 | 9 | 0 | .438 | 268 | 279 |
| Baltimore | 5 | 11 | 0 | .313 | 271 | 351 |

| AFC CENTRAL | W | L | T | Pct | Pts | OP |
|---|---|---|---|---|---|---|
| Pittsburgh | 12 | 4 | 0 | .750 | 416 | 262 |
| Houston | 11 | 5 | 0 | .688 | 362 | 331 |
| Cleveland | 9 | 7 | 0 | .563 | 359 | 352 |
| Cincinnati | 4 | 12 | 0 | .250 | 337 | 421 |

| AFC WEST | W | L | T | Pct | Pts | OP |
|---|---|---|---|---|---|---|
| San Diego | 12 | 4 | 0 | .750 | 411 | 246 |
| Denver | 10 | 6 | 0 | .625 | 289 | 262 |
| Seattle | 9 | 7 | 0 | .563 | 378 | 372 |
| Oakland | 9 | 7 | 0 | .563 | 365 | 337 |
| Kansas City | 7 | 9 | 0 | .438 | 238 | 262 |

| NFC EAST | W | L | T | Pct | Pts | OP |
|---|---|---|---|---|---|---|
| Dallas | 11 | 5 | 0 | .688 | 371 | 313 |
| Philadelphia | 11 | 5 | 0 | .688 | 339 | 282 |
| Washington | 10 | 6 | 0 | .625 | 348 | 295 |
| NY Giants | 6 | 10 | 0 | .375 | 237 | 323 |
| St. Louis | 5 | 11 | 0 | .313 | 307 | 358 |

| NFC CENTRAL | W | L | T | Pct | Pts | OP |
|---|---|---|---|---|---|---|
| Chicago | 10 | 6 | 0 | .625 | 306 | 249 |
| Tampa Bay | 10 | 6 | 0 | .625 | 273 | 237 |
| Minnesota | 7 | 9 | 0 | .438 | 259 | 337 |
| Green Bay | 5 | 11 | 0 | .313 | 246 | 316 |
| Detroit | 2 | 14 | 0 | .125 | 219 | 365 |

| NFC WEST | W | L | T | Pct | Pts | OP |
|---|---|---|---|---|---|---|
| LA Rams | 9 | 7 | 0 | .563 | 323 | 309 |
| New Orleans | 8 | 8 | 0 | .500 | 370 | 360 |
| Atlanta | 6 | 10 | 0 | .375 | 300 | 388 |
| San Francisco | 2 | 14 | 0 | .125 | 308 | 416 |

## 1980

| AFC EAST | W | L | T | Pct | Pts | OP |
|---|---|---|---|---|---|---|
| Buffalo | 11 | 5 | 0 | .688 | 320 | 260 |
| New England | 10 | 6 | 0 | .625 | 441 | 325 |
| Miami | 8 | 8 | 0 | .500 | 266 | 305 |
| Baltimore | 7 | 9 | 0 | .438 | 355 | 387 |
| NY Jets | 4 | 12 | 0 | .250 | 302 | 395 |

| AFC CENTRAL | W | L | T | Pct | Pts | OP |
|---|---|---|---|---|---|---|
| Cleveland | 11 | 5 | 0 | .688 | 357 | 310 |
| Houston | 11 | 5 | 0 | .688 | 295 | 251 |
| Pittsburgh | 9 | 7 | 0 | .563 | 352 | 313 |
| Cincinnati | 6 | 10 | 0 | .375 | 244 | 312 |

| AFC WEST | W | L | T | Pct | Pts | OP |
|---|---|---|---|---|---|---|
| San Diego | 11 | 5 | 0 | .688 | 418 | 327 |
| Oakland | 11 | 5 | 0 | .688 | 364 | 306 |
| Denver | 8 | 8 | 0 | .500 | 310 | 323 |
| Kansas City | 8 | 8 | 0 | .500 | 319 | 336 |
| Seattle | 4 | 12 | 0 | .250 | 291 | 408 |

| NFC EAST | W | L | T | Pct | Pts | OP |
|---|---|---|---|---|---|---|
| Dallas | 12 | 4 | 0 | .750 | 454 | 311 |
| Philadelphia | 12 | 4 | 0 | .750 | 384 | 222 |
| Washington | 6 | 10 | 0 | .375 | 261 | 293 |
| St. Louis | 5 | 11 | 0 | .313 | 299 | 350 |
| NY Giants | 4 | 12 | 0 | .250 | 249 | 425 |

## 1980 (Cont.)

| NFC CENTRAL | W | L | T | Pct | Pts | OP |
|---|---|---|---|---|---|---|
| Detroit | 9 | 7 | 0 | .563 | 334 | 272 |
| Minnesota | 9 | 7 | 0 | .563 | 317 | 308 |
| Chicago | 7 | 9 | 0 | .438 | 304 | 264 |
| Tampa Bay | 5 | 10 | 1 | .344 | 271 | 341 |
| Green Bay | 5 | 10 | 1 | .344 | 231 | 371 |

| NFC WEST | W | L | T | Pct | Pts | OP |
|---|---|---|---|---|---|---|
| Atlanta | 12 | 4 | 0 | .750 | 405 | 272 |
| LA Rams | 11 | 5 | 0 | .688 | 424 | 289 |
| San Francisco | 6 | 10 | 0 | .375 | 320 | 415 |
| New Orleans | 1 | 15 | 0 | .063 | 291 | 487 |

## 1981

| AFC EAST | W | L | T | Pct | Pts | OP |
|---|---|---|---|---|---|---|
| Miami | 11 | 4 | 1 | .719 | 345 | 275 |
| NY Jets | 10 | 5 | 1 | .656 | 355 | 287 |
| Buffalo | 10 | 6 | 0 | .625 | 311 | 276 |
| Baltimore | 2 | 14 | 0 | .125 | 259 | 533 |
| New England | 2 | 14 | 0 | .125 | 322 | 370 |

| AFC CENTRAL | W | L | T | Pct | Pts | OP |
|---|---|---|---|---|---|---|
| Cincinnati | 12 | 4 | 0 | .750 | 421 | 304 |
| Pittsburgh | 8 | 8 | 0 | .500 | 356 | 297 |
| Houston | 7 | 9 | 0 | .438 | 281 | 355 |
| Cleveland | 5 | 11 | 0 | .313 | 276 | 375 |

| AFC WEST | W | L | T | Pct | Pts | OP |
|---|---|---|---|---|---|---|
| Denver | 10 | 6 | 0 | .625 | 321 | 289 |
| San Diego | 10 | 6 | 0 | .625 | 478 | 390 |
| Kansas City | 9 | 7 | 0 | .563 | 343 | 290 |
| Oakland | 7 | 9 | 0 | .438 | 273 | 343 |
| Seattle | 6 | 10 | 0 | .375 | 322 | 388 |

| NFC EAST | W | L | T | Pct | Pts | OP |
|---|---|---|---|---|---|---|
| Dallas | 12 | 4 | 0 | .750 | 367 | 277 |
| Philadelphia | 10 | 6 | 0 | .625 | 368 | 221 |
| NY Giants | 9 | 7 | 0 | .563 | 295 | 257 |
| Washington | 8 | 8 | 0 | .500 | 347 | 349 |
| St. Louis | 7 | 9 | 0 | .438 | 315 | 407 |

| NFC CENTRAL | W | L | T | Pct | Pts | OP |
|---|---|---|---|---|---|---|
| Tampa Bay | 9 | 7 | 0 | .563 | 315 | 268 |
| Detroit | 8 | 8 | 0 | .500 | 397 | 322 |
| Green Bay | 8 | 8 | 0 | .500 | 324 | 361 |
| Minnesota | 7 | 9 | 0 | .438 | 325 | 369 |
| Chicago | 6 | 10 | 0 | .375 | 253 | 324 |

| NFC WEST | W | L | T | Pct | Pts | OP |
|---|---|---|---|---|---|---|
| San Francisco | 13 | 3 | 0 | .813 | 357 | 250 |
| Atlanta | 7 | 9 | 0 | .438 | 426 | 355 |
| LA Rams | 6 | 10 | 0 | .375 | 303 | 351 |
| New Orleans | 4 | 12 | 0 | .250 | 207 | 378 |

## 1982

| AFC EAST | W | L | T | Pct | Pts | OP |
|---|---|---|---|---|---|---|
| Miami | 7 | 2 | 0 | .778 | 198 | 131 |
| NY Jets | 6 | 3 | 0 | .667 | 245 | 166 |
| New England | 5 | 4 | 0 | .556 | 143 | 157 |
| Buffalo | 4 | 5 | 0 | .444 | 150 | 154 |
| Baltimore | 0 | 8 | 1 | .056 | 113 | 236 |

## 1982 (Cont.)

### AFC CENTRAL

| | W | L | T | Pct | Pts | OP |
|---|---|---|---|---|---|---|
| Cincinnati | 7 | 2 | 0 | .778 | 232 | 177 |
| Pittsburgh | 6 | 3 | 0 | .667 | 204 | 146 |
| Cleveland | 4 | 5 | 0 | .444 | 140 | 182 |
| Houston | 1 | 8 | 0 | .111 | 136 | 245 |

### AFC WEST

| | W | L | T | Pct | Pts | OP |
|---|---|---|---|---|---|---|
| Los Angeles Raiders | 8 | 1 | 0 | .889 | 260 | 200 |
| San Diego | 6 | 3 | 0 | .667 | 288 | 221 |
| Seattle | 4 | 5 | 0 | .444 | 127 | 147 |
| Kansas City | 3 | 6 | 0 | .333 | 176 | 184 |
| Denver | 2 | 7 | 0 | .222 | 148 | 226 |

### NFC EAST

| | W | L | T | Pct | Pts | OP |
|---|---|---|---|---|---|---|
| Washington | 8 | 1 | 0 | .889 | 190 | 128 |
| Dallas | 6 | 3 | 0 | .667 | 226 | 145 |
| St. Louis | 5 | 4 | 0 | .556 | 135 | 170 |
| NY Giants | 4 | 5 | 0 | .444 | 164 | 160 |
| Philadelphia | 3 | 6 | 0 | .333 | 191 | 195 |

### NFC CENTRAL

| | W | L | T | Pct | Pts | OP |
|---|---|---|---|---|---|---|
| Green Bay | 5 | 3 | 1 | .611 | 226 | 169 |
| Tampa Bay | 5 | 4 | 0 | .556 | 158 | 178 |
| Minnesota | 5 | 4 | 0 | .556 | 187 | 198 |
| Detroit | 4 | 5 | 0 | .444 | 181 | 176 |
| Chicago | 3 | 6 | 0 | .333 | 141 | 174 |

### NFC WEST

| | W | L | T | Pct | Pts | OP |
|---|---|---|---|---|---|---|
| Atlanta | 5 | 4 | 0 | .556 | 183 | 199 |
| New Orleans | 4 | 5 | 0 | .444 | 129 | 160 |
| San Francisco | 3 | 6 | 0 | .333 | 209 | 206 |
| Los Angeles Rams | 2 | 7 | 0 | .222 | 200 | 250 |

## 1983

### AFC EAST

| | W | L | T | Pct | Pts | OP |
|---|---|---|---|---|---|---|
| Miami | 12 | 4 | 0 | .750 | 389 | 250 |
| Buffalo | 8 | 8 | 0 | .500 | 283 | 351 |
| New England | 8 | 8 | 0 | .500 | 274 | 289 |
| Baltimore | 7 | 9 | 0 | .438 | 264 | 354 |
| NY Jets | 7 | 9 | 0 | .438 | 313 | 331 |

### AFC CENTRAL

| | W | L | T | Pct | Pts | OP |
|---|---|---|---|---|---|---|
| Pittsburgh | 10 | 6 | 0 | .625 | 355 | 303 |
| Cleveland | 9 | 7 | 0 | .563 | 356 | 342 |
| Cincinnati | 7 | 9 | 0 | .438 | 346 | 302 |
| Houston | 2 | 14 | 0 | .125 | 288 | 460 |

### AFC WEST

| | W | L | T | Pct | Pts | OP |
|---|---|---|---|---|---|---|
| LA Raiders | 12 | 4 | 0 | .750 | 442 | 338 |
| Seattle | 9 | 7 | 0 | .563 | 403 | 397 |
| Denver | 9 | 7 | 0 | .563 | 302 | 327 |
| San Diego | 6 | 10 | 0 | .375 | 358 | 462 |
| Kansas City | 6 | 10 | 0 | .375 | 386 | 367 |

### NFC EAST

| | W | L | T | Pct | Pts | OP |
|---|---|---|---|---|---|---|
| Washington | 14 | 2 | 0 | .875 | 541 | 332 |
| Dallas | 12 | 4 | 0 | .750 | 479 | 360 |
| St. Louis | 8 | 7 | 1 | .531 | 374 | 428 |
| Philadelphia | 5 | 11 | 0 | .313 | 233 | 322 |
| NY Giants | 3 | 12 | 1 | .219 | 267 | 347 |

### NFC CENTRAL

| | W | L | T | Pct | Pts | OP |
|---|---|---|---|---|---|---|
| Detroit | 9 | 7 | 0 | .563 | 47 | 286 |
| Minnesota | 8 | 8 | 0 | .500 | 316 | 348 |
| Chicago | 8 | 8 | 0 | .500 | 311 | 301 |
| Green Bay | 8 | 8 | 0 | .500 | 429 | 439 |
| Tampa Bay | 2 | 14 | 0 | .125 | 241 | 380 |

## 1983 (Cont.)

### NFC WEST

| | W | L | T | Pct | Pts | OP |
|---|---|---|---|---|---|---|
| San Francisco | 10 | 6 | 0 | .625 | 432 | 293 |
| LA Rams | 9 | 7 | 0 | .563 | 361 | 344 |
| New Orleans | 8 | 8 | 0 | .500 | 319 | 337 |
| Atlanta | 7 | 9 | 0 | .438 | 370 | 389 |

## 1984

### AFC EAST

| | W | L | T | Pct | Pts | OP |
|---|---|---|---|---|---|---|
| Miami | 14 | 2 | 0 | .875 | 513 | 298 |
| New England | 9 | 7 | 0 | .563 | 362 | 352 |
| NY Jets | 7 | 9 | 0 | .438 | 332 | 364 |
| Indianapolis Colts | 4 | 12 | 0 | .250 | 239 | 414 |
| Buffalo | 2 | 14 | 0 | .125 | 250 | 454 |

### AFC CENTRAL

| | W | L | T | Pct | Pts | OP |
|---|---|---|---|---|---|---|
| Pittsburgh | 9 | 7 | 0 | .563 | 387 | 310 |
| Cincinnati | 8 | 8 | 0 | .500 | 339 | 339 |
| Cleveland | 5 | 11 | 0 | .313 | 250 | 297 |
| Houston | 3 | 13 | 0 | .188 | 240 | 437 |

### AFC WEST

| | W | L | T | Pct | Pts | OP |
|---|---|---|---|---|---|---|
| Denver | 13 | 3 | 0 | .813 | 353 | 241 |
| Seattle | 12 | 4 | 0 | .750 | 418 | 282 |
| LA Raiders | 11 | 5 | 0 | .313 | 368 | 278 |
| Kansas City | 8 | 8 | 0 | .500 | 314 | 324 |
| San Diego | 7 | 9 | 0 | .438 | 394 | 413 |

### NFC EAST

| | W | L | T | Pct | Pts | OP |
|---|---|---|---|---|---|---|
| Washington | 11 | 5 | 0 | .688 | 426 | 310 |
| NY Giants | 9 | 7 | 0 | .563 | 299 | 301 |
| Dallas | 9 | 7 | 0 | .563 | 308 | 308 |
| St. Louis | 9 | 7 | 0 | .563 | 423 | 345 |
| Philadelphia | 6 | 9 | 1 | .406 | 278 | 320 |

### NFC CENTRAL

| | W | L | T | Pct | Pts | OP |
|---|---|---|---|---|---|---|
| Chicago | 10 | 6 | 0 | .625 | 325 | 248 |
| Green Bay | 8 | 8 | 0 | .500 | 390 | 309 |
| Tampa Bay | 6 | 10 | 0 | .375 | 335 | 380 |
| Detroit | 4 | 11 | 1 | .281 | 283 | 408 |
| Minnesota | 3 | 13 | 0 | .188 | 276 | 484 |

| | W | L | T | Pct | Pts | OP |
|---|---|---|---|---|---|---|
| San Francisco | 15 | 1 | 0 | .938 | 475 | 227 |
| LA Rams | 10 | 6 | 0 | .625 | 346 | 316 |
| New Orleans | 7 | 9 | 0 | .438 | 298 | 361 |
| Atlanta | 4 | 12 | 0 | .20 | 281 | 382 |

## 1985

| AFC EAST | W | L | T | Pct | Pts | OP |
|---|---|---|---|---|---|---|
| Miami | 12 | 4 | 0 | .750 | 428 | 320 |
| New England | 11 | 5 | 0 | .688 | 362 | 290 |
| NY Jets | 11 | 5 | 0 | .688 | 393 | 264 |
| Indianapolis | 5 | 11 | 0 | .313 | 320 | 386 |
| Buffalo | 2 | 14 | 0 | .125 | 200 | 381 |

| AFC CENTRAL | W | L | T | Pct | Pts | OP |
|---|---|---|---|---|---|---|
| Cleveland | 8 | 8 | 0 | .500 | 287 | 294 |
| Cincinnati | 7 | 9 | 0 | .438 | 441 | 437 |
| Pittsburgh | 7 | 9 | 0 | .438 | 379 | 355 |
| Houston | 5 | 11 | 0 | .313 | 284 | 412 |

| AFC WEST | W | L | T | Pct | Pts | OP |
|---|---|---|---|---|---|---|
| LA Raiders | 12 | 4 | 0 | .750 | 354 | 308 |
| Denver | 11 | 5 | 0 | .688 | 380 | 329 |
| Seattle | 8 | 8 | 0 | .500 | 349 | 303 |
| San Diego | 8 | 8 | 0 | .500 | 467 | 435 |
| Kansas City | 6 | 10 | 0 | .375 | 317 | 360 |

| NFC EAST | W | L | T | Pct | Pts | OP |
|---|---|---|---|---|---|---|
| Washington | 10 | 6 | 0 | .625 | 297 | 312 |
| NY Giants | 10 | 6 | 0 | .625 | 399 | 283 |
| Dallas | 10 | 6 | 0 | .625 | 357 | 333 |
| Philadelphia | 7 | 9 | 0 | .438 | 286 | 310 |
| St. Louis | 5 | 11 | 0 | .313 | 278 | 414 |

| NFC CENTRAL | W | L | T | Pct | Pts | OP |
|---|---|---|---|---|---|---|
| Chicago | 15 | 1 | 0 | .938 | 456 | 198 |
| Green Bay | 8 | 8 | 0 | .500 | 337 | 355 |
| Detroit | 7 | 9 | 0 | .438 | 307 | 366 |
| Minnesota | 7 | 9 | 0 | .438 | 346 | 359 |
| Tampa Bay | 2 | 14 | 0 | .125 | 294 | 448 |

| NFC WEST | W | L | T | Pct | Pts | OP |
|---|---|---|---|---|---|---|
| LA Rams | 11 | 5 | 0 | .688 | 340 | 277 |
| San Francisco | 10 | 6 | 0 | .625 | 411 | 263 |
| New Orleans | 5 | 11 | 0 | .313 | 294 | 401 |
| Atlanta | 4 | 12 | 0 | .250 | 282 | 452 |

## 1986

| AFC EAST | W | L | T | Pct | Pts | OP |
|---|---|---|---|---|---|---|
| New England | 11 | 5 | 0 | .688 | 412 | 307 |
| NY Jets | 10 | 6 | 0 | .625 | 364 | 386 |
| Miami | 8 | 8 | 0 | .500 | 430 | 405 |
| Buffalo | 4 | 12 | 0 | .250 | 287 | 348 |
| Indianapolis | 3 | 13 | 0 | .188 | 299 | 400 |

| AFC CENTRAL | W | L | T | Pct | Pts | OP |
|---|---|---|---|---|---|---|
| Cleveland | 12 | 4 | 0 | .750 | 391 | 310 |
| Cincinnati | 10 | 6 | 0 | .625 | 409 | 394 |
| Pittsburgh | 6 | 10 | 0 | .375 | 307 | 336 |
| Houston | 5 | 11 | 0 | .313 | 274 | 329 |

| AFC WEST | W | L | T | Pct | Pts | OP |
|---|---|---|---|---|---|---|
| Denver | 11 | 5 | 0 | .688 | 378 | 327 |
| Kansas City | 10 | 6 | 0 | .625 | 358 | 326 |
| Seattle | 10 | 6 | 0 | .625 | 366 | 293 |
| LA Raiders | 8 | 8 | 0 | .500 | 323 | 346 |
| San Diego | 4 | 12 | 0 | .250 | 335 | 396 |

| NFC EAST | W | L | T | Pct | Pts | OP |
|---|---|---|---|---|---|---|
| NY Giants | 14 | 2 | 0 | .875 | 371 | 236 |
| Washington | 12 | 4 | 0 | .750 | 368 | 296 |
| Dallas | 7 | 9 | 0 | .438 | 346 | 337 |
| Philadelphia | 5 | 10 | 1 | .344 | 256 | 312 |
| St. Louis | 4 | 11 | 1 | .281 | 518 | 351 |

## 1986 (Cont.)

| NFC CENTRAL | W | L | T | Pct | Pts | OP |
|---|---|---|---|---|---|---|
| Chicago | 14 | 2 | 0 | .875 | 352 | 187 |
| Minnesota | 9 | 7 | 0 | .563 | 398 | 271 |
| Detroit | 5 | 11 | 0 | .313 | 277 | 326 |
| Green Bay | 4 | 12 | 0 | .250 | 254 | 418 |
| Tampa Bay | 2 | 14 | 0 | .125 | 239 | 473 |

| NFC WEST | W | L | T | Pct | Pts | OP |
|---|---|---|---|---|---|---|
| San Francisco | 10 | 5 | 1 | .656 | 374 | 247 |
| LA Rams | 10 | 6 | 0 | .625 | 309 | 267 |
| Atlanta | 7 | 8 | 1 | .469 | 280 | 280 |
| New Orleans | 7 | 9 | 0 | .438 | 288 | 287 |

## 1987

| AFC EAST | W | L | T | Pct | Pts | OP |
|---|---|---|---|---|---|---|
| Indianapolis | 9 | 6 | 0 | .643 | 300 | 238 |
| Miami | 8 | 7 | 0 | .533 | 362 | 335 |
| New England | 8 | 7 | 0 | .533 | 320 | 293 |
| Buffalo | 7 | 8 | 0 | .467 | 320 | 293 |
| NY Jets | 6 | 9 | 0 | .400 | 334 | 360 |

| AFC CENTRAL | W | L | T | Pct | Pts | OP |
|---|---|---|---|---|---|---|
| Cleveland | 10 | 5 | 0 | .700 | 390 | 239 |
| Houston | 9 | 6 | 0 | .600 | 345 | 349 |
| Pittsburgh | 8 | 7 | 0 | .533 | 285 | 299 |
| Cincinnati | 4 | 11 | 0 | .267 | 285 | 370 |

| AFC WEST | W | L | T | Pct | Pts | OP |
|---|---|---|---|---|---|---|
| Denver | 10 | 4 | 1 | .667 | 379 | 288 |
| Seattle | 9 | 6 | 0 | .600 | 371 | 314 |
| San Diego | 8 | 7 | 0 | .533 | 253 | 317 |
| LA Raiders | 5 | 10 | 0 | .333 | 301 | 289 |
| Kansas City | 4 | 11 | 0 | .267 | 276 | 388 |

| NFC EAST | W | L | T | Pct | Pts | OP |
|---|---|---|---|---|---|---|
| Washington | 11 | 4 | 0 | .733 | 379 | 285 |
| Dallas | 7 | 8 | 0 | .467 | 340 | 348 |
| St. Louis | 7 | 8 | 0 | .467 | 362 | 368 |
| Philadelphia | 7 | 8 | 0 | .467 | 337 | 380 |
| NY Giants | 6 | 9 | 0 | .400 | 280 | 312 |

| NFC CENTRAL | W | L | T | Pct | Pts | OP |
|---|---|---|---|---|---|---|
| Chicago | 11 | 4 | 0 | .733 | 356 | 282 |
| Minnesota | 8 | 7 | 0 | .533 | 336 | 335 |
| Green Bay | 5 | 9 | 1 | .367 | 255 | 300 |
| Tampa Bay | 4 | 11 | 0 | .267 | 286 | 360 |
| Detroit | 4 | 11 | 0 | .267 | 269 | 384 |

| NFC WEST | W | L | T | Pct | Pts | OP |
|---|---|---|---|---|---|---|
| San Francisco | 13 | 2 | 0 | .867 | 459 | 253 |
| New Orleans | 12 | 3 | 0 | .800 | 422 | 283 |
| LA Rams | 6 | 9 | 0 | .400 | 317 | 361 |
| Atlanta | 3 | 12 | 0 | .200 | 205 | 436 |

## 1988

### AFC EAST
| | W | L | T | Pct | Pts | OP |
|---|---|---|---|---|---|---|
| Buffalo | 12 | 4 | 0 | .750 | 329 | 237 |
| New England | 9 | 7 | 0 | .563 | 250 | 284 |
| Indianapolis | 9 | 7 | 0 | .563 | 354 | 315 |
| NY Jets | 8 | 7 | 1 | .531 | 372 | 354 |
| Miami | 6 | 10 | 0 | .375 | 319 | 380 |

### AFC CENTRAL
| | W | L | T | Pct | Pts | OP |
|---|---|---|---|---|---|---|
| Cincinnati | 12 | 4 | 0 | .750 | 448 | 329 |
| Cleveland | 10 | 6 | 0 | .625 | 304 | 288 |
| Houston | 10 | 6 | 0 | .625 | 424 | 365 |
| Pittsburgh | 5 | 1 | 0 | .313 | 336 | 421 |

### AFC WEST
| | W | L | T | Pct | Pts | OP |
|---|---|---|---|---|---|---|
| Seattle | 9 | 7 | 0 | .563 | 339 | 329 |
| Denver | 8 | 8 | 0 | .500 | 327 | 352 |
| LA Raiders | 7 | 9 | 0 | .438 | 325 | 369 |
| San Diego | 6 | 10 | 0 | .375 | 231 | 332 |
| Kansas City | 4 | 11 | 1 | .281 | 254 | 320 |

### NFC EAST
| | W | L | T | Pct | Pts | OP |
|---|---|---|---|---|---|---|
| NY Giants | 10 | 6 | 0 | .625 | 359 | 304 |
| Philadelphia | 10 | 6 | 0 | .625 | 379 | 319 |
| Phoenix Cardinals | 7 | 9 | 0 | .438 | 344 | 398 |
| Washington | 7 | 9 | 0 | .438 | 345 | 387 |
| Dallas | 3 | 13 | 0 | .188 | 265 | 381 |

### NFC CENTRAL
| | W | L | T | Pct | Pts | OP |
|---|---|---|---|---|---|---|
| Chicago | 12 | 4 | 0 | .750 | 312 | 215 |
| Minnesota | 11 | 5 | 0 | .688 | 406 | 233 |
| Tampa Bay | 5 | 11 | 0 | .313 | 261 | 350 |
| Detroit | 4 | 12 | 0 | .250 | 220 | 313 |
| Green Bay | 4 | 12 | 0 | .250 | 240 | 315 |

### NFC WEST
| | W | L | T | Pct | Pts | OP |
|---|---|---|---|---|---|---|
| New Orleans | 10 | 6 | 0 | .625 | 312 | 283 |
| San Francisco | 10 | 6 | 0 | .625 | 369 | 294 |
| LA Rams | 10 | 6 | 0 | .625 | 407 | 293 |
| Atlanta | 5 | 11 | 0 | .313 | 244 | 315 |

## 1989

### AFC EAST
| | W | L | T | Pct | Pts | OP |
|---|---|---|---|---|---|---|
| Buffalo | 9 | 7 | 0 | .563 | 407 | 317 |
| Miami | 8 | 8 | 0 | .500 | 331 | 379 |
| Indianapolis | 8 | 8 | 0 | .500 | 298 | 301 |
| New England | 5 | 11 | 0 | .313 | 297 | 391 |
| NY Jets | 4 | 12 | 0 | .250 | 253 | 411 |

### AFC CENTRAL
| | W | L | T | Pct | Pts | OP |
|---|---|---|---|---|---|---|
| Cleveland | 9 | 6 | 1 | .594 | 334 | 254 |
| Houston | 9 | 7 | 0 | .563 | 365 | 412 |
| Pittsburgh | 9 | 7 | 0 | .563 | 265 | 326 |
| Cincinnati | 8 | 8 | 0 | .500 | 404 | 285 |

### AFC WEST
| | W | L | T | Pct | Pts | OP |
|---|---|---|---|---|---|---|
| Denver | 11 | 5 | 0 | .688 | 362 | 226 |
| Kansas City | 8 | 7 | 1 | .531 | 318 | 286 |
| LA Raiders | 8 | 8 | 0 | .500 | 315 | 297 |
| Seattle | 7 | 9 | 0 | .438 | 241 | 327 |
| San Diego | 6 | 10 | 0 | .375 | 266 | 290 |

## 1989 (Cont.)

### NFC EAST
| | W | L | T | Pct | Pts | OP |
|---|---|---|---|---|---|---|
| NY Giants | 12 | 4 | 0 | .750 | 348 | 252 |
| Philadelphia | 11 | 5 | 0 | .688 | 342 | 274 |
| Washington | 10 | 6 | 0 | .625 | 386 | 308 |
| Phoenix | 5 | 11 | 0 | .313 | 258 | 377 |
| Dallas | 1 | 15 | 0 | .063 | 204 | 393 |

### NFC CENTRAL
| | W | L | T | Pct | Pts | OP |
|---|---|---|---|---|---|---|
| Green Bay | 10 | 6 | 0 | .625 | 362 | 356 |
| Minnesota | 10 | 6 | 0 | .625 | 351 | 275 |
| Detroit | 7 | 9 | 0 | .438 | 312 | 364 |
| Chicago | 6 | 10 | 0 | .375 | 358 | 377 |
| Tampa Bay | 5 | 11 | 0 | .313 | 320 | 419 |

### NFC WEST
| | W | L | T | Pct | Pts | OP |
|---|---|---|---|---|---|---|
| San Francisco | 14 | 2 | 0 | .875 | 442 | 253 |
| LA Rams | 11 | 5 | 0 | .688 | 426 | 344 |
| New Orleans | 9 | 7 | 0 | .563 | 386 | 301 |
| Atlanta | 3 | 13 | 0 | .188 | 279 | 437 |

## 1990

### AFC EAST
| | W | L | T | Pct | Pts | OP |
|---|---|---|---|---|---|---|
| Buffalo | 13 | 3 | 0 | .813 | 428 | 263 |
| Miami | 12 | 4 | 0 | .750 | 336 | 242 |
| Indianapolis | 7 | 9 | 0 | .438 | 281 | 353 |
| NY Jets | 6 | 10 | 0 | .375 | 295 | 345 |
| New England | 1 | 15 | 0 | .063 | 181 | 446 |

### AFC CENTRAL
| | W | L | T | Pct | Pts | OP |
|---|---|---|---|---|---|---|
| Pittsburgh | 9 | 7 | 0 | .563 | 292 | 240 |
| Cincinnati | 9 | 7 | 0 | .563 | 360 | 352 |
| Houston | 9 | 7 | 0 | .563 | 405 | 307 |
| Cleveland | 3 | 13 | 0 | .188 | 228 | 462 |

### AFC WEST
| | W | L | T | Pct | Pts | OP |
|---|---|---|---|---|---|---|
| LA Raiders | 12 | 4 | 0 | .750 | 337 | 268 |
| Kansas City | 11 | 5 | 0 | .688 | 369 | 257 |
| Seattle | 9 | 7 | 0 | .563 | 306 | 286 |
| San Diego | 6 | 10 | 0 | .375 | 315 | 281 |
| Denver | 5 | 11 | 0 | .313 | 331 | 374 |

### NFC EAST
| | W | L | T | Pct | Pts | OP |
|---|---|---|---|---|---|---|
| NY Giants | 13 | 3 | 0 | .813 | 335 | 211 |
| Washington | 10 | 6 | 0 | .625 | 381 | 301 |
| Philadelphia | 10 | 6 | 0 | .625 | 396 | 299 |
| Dallas | 7 | 9 | 0 | .438 | 244 | 308 |
| Phoenix | 5 | 11 | 0 | .313 | 268 | 396 |

### NFC CENTRAL
| | W | L | T | Pct | Pts | OP |
|---|---|---|---|---|---|---|
| Chicago | 11 | 5 | 0 | .688 | 348 | 280 |
| Green Bay | 6 | 10 | 0 | .375 | 271 | 347 |
| Minnesota | 6 | 10 | 0 | .375 | 351 | 326 |
| Detroit | 6 | 10 | 0 | .375 | 373 | 413 |
| Tampa Bay | 6 | 10 | 0 | .375 | 264 | 367 |

### NFC WEST
| | W | L | T | Pct | Pts | OP |
|---|---|---|---|---|---|---|
| San Francisco | 14 | 2 | 0 | .875 | 353 | 239 |
| New Orleans | 8 | 8 | 0 | .500 | 274 | 275 |
| LA Rams | 5 | 11 | 0 | .313 | 345 | 412 |
| Atlanta | 5 | 11 | 0 | .313 | 348 | 365 |

### 1991

**AFC EAST**

| | W | L | T | Pct | Pts | OP |
|---|---|---|---|---|---|---|
| Buffalo | 13 | 3 | 0 | .813 | 458 | 318 |
| Miami | 8 | 8 | 0 | .500 | 343 | 349 |
| NY Jets | 8 | 8 | 0 | .500 | 314 | 293 |
| New England | 6 | 10 | 0 | .375 | 211 | 305 |
| Indianapolis | 1 | 15 | 0 | .063 | 143 | 381 |

**AFC CENTRAL**

| | W | L | T | Pct | Pts | OP |
|---|---|---|---|---|---|---|
| Houston | 11 | 5 | 0 | .688 | 386 | 251 |
| Pittsburgh | 7 | 9 | 0 | .438 | 292 | 344 |
| Cleveland | 6 | 10 | 0 | .375 | 293 | 298 |
| Cincinnati | 3 | 13 | 0 | .188 | 263 | 435 |

**AFC WEST**

| | W | L | T | Pct | Pts | OP |
|---|---|---|---|---|---|---|
| Denver | 12 | 4 | 0 | .750 | 304 | 235 |
| Kansas City | 10 | 6 | 0 | .625 | 322 | 252 |
| LA Raiders | 9 | 7 | 0 | .563 | 298 | 297 |
| Seattle | 7 | 9 | 0 | .438 | 276 | 261 |
| San Diego | 4 | 12 | 0 | .250 | 274 | 342 |

**NFC EAST**

| | W | L | T | Pct | Pts | OP |
|---|---|---|---|---|---|---|
| Washington | 14 | 2 | 0 | .875 | 485 | 224 |
| Dallas | 11 | 5 | 0 | .688 | 342 | 310 |
| Philadelphia | 10 | 6 | 0 | .625 | 285 | 244 |
| NY Giants | 8 | 8 | 0 | .500 | 281 | 297 |
| Phoenix | 4 | 12 | 0 | .250 | 196 | 344 |

**NFC CENTRAL**

| | W | L | T | Pct | Pts | OP |
|---|---|---|---|---|---|---|
| Detroit | 12 | 4 | 0 | .750 | 339 | 295 |
| Chicago | 11 | 5 | 0 | .688 | 299 | 269 |
| Minnesota | 8 | 8 | 0 | .500 | 301 | 306 |
| Green Bay | 4 | 12 | 0 | .250 | 273 | 313 |
| Tampa Bay | 3 | 13 | 0 | .188 | 199 | 365 |

**NFC WEST**

| | W | L | T | Pct | Pts | OP |
|---|---|---|---|---|---|---|
| New Orleans | 11 | 5 | 0 | .688 | 341 | 211 |
| Atlanta | 10 | 6 | 0 | .625 | 361 | 338 |
| San Francisco | 10 | 6 | 0 | .625 | 393 | 239 |
| LA Rams | 3 | 13 | 0 | .188 | 234 | 390 |

### 1992

**AFC EAST**

| | W | L | T | Pct | Pts | OP |
|---|---|---|---|---|---|---|
| Buffalo | 11 | 5 | 0 | .688 | 381 | 283 |
| Miami | 11 | 5 | 0 | .688 | 340 | 281 |
| Indianapolis | 9 | 7 | 0 | .563 | 216 | 302 |
| NY Jets | 4 | 12 | 0 | .250 | 220 | 315 |
| New England | 2 | 14 | 0 | .125 | 205 | 363 |

**AFC CENTRAL**

| | W | L | T | Pct | Pts | OP |
|---|---|---|---|---|---|---|
| Pittsburgh | 11 | 5 | 0 | .688 | 299 | 225 |
| Houston | 10 | 6 | 0 | .625 | 352 | 258 |
| Cleveland | 7 | 9 | 0 | .438 | 272 | 275 |
| Cincinnati | 5 | 11 | 0 | .313 | 274 | 364 |

**AFC WEST**

| | W | L | T | Pct | Pts | OP |
|---|---|---|---|---|---|---|
| San Diego | 11 | 5 | 0 | .688 | 335 | 241 |
| Kansas City | 10 | 6 | 0 | .625 | 348 | 282 |
| Denver | 8 | 8 | 0 | .500 | 262 | 329 |
| LA Raiders | 7 | 9 | 0 | .438 | 249 | 281 |
| Seattle | 2 | 14 | 0 | .125 | 140 | 312 |

### 1992 (Cont.)

**NFC EAST**

| | W | L | T | Pct | Pts | OP |
|---|---|---|---|---|---|---|
| Dallas | 13 | 3 | 0 | .813 | 409 | 243 |
| Philadelphia | 11 | 5 | 0 | .688 | 354 | 245 |
| Washington | 9 | 7 | 0 | .563 | 300 | 255 |
| NY Giants | 6 | 10 | 0 | .375 | 306 | 367 |
| Phoenix | 4 | 12 | 0 | .250 | 243 | 332 |

**NFC CENTRAL**

| | W | L | T | Pct | Pts | OP |
|---|---|---|---|---|---|---|
| Minnesota | 11 | 5 | 0 | .688 | 374 | 249 |
| Green Bay | 9 | 7 | 0 | .563 | 276 | 296 |
| Tampa Bay | 5 | 11 | 0 | .313 | 267 | 365 |
| Detroit | 5 | 11 | 0 | .313 | 273 | 332 |
| Chicago | 5 | 11 | 0 | .313 | 295 | 361 |

**NFC WEST**

| | W | L | T | Pct | Pts | OP |
|---|---|---|---|---|---|---|
| San Francisco | 14 | 2 | 0 | .875 | 431 | 236 |
| New Orleans | 12 | 4 | 0 | .750 | 330 | 202 |
| Atlanta | 6 | 10 | 0 | .375 | 327 | 414 |
| LA Rams | 6 | 10 | 0 | .375 | 313 | 383 |

### 1993

**AFC EAST**

| | W | L | T | Pct | Pts | OP |
|---|---|---|---|---|---|---|
| Buffalo | 12 | 4 | 0 | .750 | 329 | 242 |
| Miami | 9 | 7 | 0 | .563 | 349 | 351 |
| NY Jets | 8 | 8 | 0 | .500 | 270 | 247 |
| New England | 5 | 11 | 0 | .313 | 238 | 286 |
| Indianapolis | 4 | 12 | 0 | .250 | 189 | 378 |

**AFC CENTRAL**

| | W | L | T | Pct | Pts | OP |
|---|---|---|---|---|---|---|
| Houston | 12 | 4 | 0 | .750 | 368 | 238 |
| Pittsburgh | 9 | 7 | 0 | .563 | 308 | 281 |
| Cleveland | 7 | 9 | 0 | .438 | 304 | 307 |
| Cincinnati | 3 | 13 | 0 | .188 | 187 | 319 |

**AFC WEST**

| | W | L | T | Pct | Pts | OP |
|---|---|---|---|---|---|---|
| Kansas City | 11 | 5 | 0 | .688 | 328 | 291 |
| LA Raiders | 10 | 6 | 0 | .625 | 306 | 326 |
| Denver | 9 | 7 | 0 | .563 | 373 | 284 |
| San Diego | 8 | 8 | 0 | .500 | 322 | 290 |
| Seattle | 6 | 10 | 0 | .375 | 280 | 314 |

**NFC EAST**

| | W | L | T | Pct | Pts | OP |
|---|---|---|---|---|---|---|
| Dallas | 12 | 4 | 0 | .750 | 376 | 229 |
| NY Giants | 11 | 5 | 0 | .688 | 288 | 205 |
| Philadelphia | 8 | 8 | 0 | .500 | 293 | 315 |
| Phoenix | 7 | 9 | 0 | .438 | 326 | 269 |
| Washington | 4 | 12 | 0 | .250 | 230 | 345 |

**NFC CENTRAL**

| | W | L | T | Pct | Pts | OP |
|---|---|---|---|---|---|---|
| Detroit | 10 | 6 | 0 | .625 | 298 | 292 |
| Green Bay | 9 | 7 | 0 | .563 | 340 | 282 |
| Minnesota | 9 | 7 | 0 | .563 | 277 | 290 |
| Chicago | 7 | 9 | 0 | .438 | 234 | 230 |
| Tampa Bay | 5 | 11 | 0 | .313 | 237 | 375 |

**NFC WEST**

| | W | L | T | Pct | Pts | OP |
|---|---|---|---|---|---|---|
| San Francisco | 10 | 6 | 0 | .625 | 473 | 295 |
| New Orleans | 8 | 8 | 0 | .500 | 317 | 343 |
| Atlanta | 6 | 10 | 0 | .375 | 316 | 385 |
| LA Rams | 5 | 11 | 0 | .313 | 221 | 367 |

### 1994

| AFC EAST | W | L | T | Pct | Pts | OP |
|---|---|---|---|---|---|---|
| Miami | 10 | 6 | 0 | .625 | 389 | 327 |
| New England | 10 | 6 | 0 | .625 | 351 | 312 |
| Indianapolis | 8 | 8 | 0 | .500 | 307 | 320 |
| Buffalo | 7 | 9 | 0 | .438 | 340 | 356 |
| NY Jets | 6 | 10 | 0 | .375 | 264 | 320 |

| AFC CENTRAL | W | L | T | Pct | Pts | OP |
|---|---|---|---|---|---|---|
| Pittsburgh | 12 | 4 | 0 | .750 | 316 | 234 |
| Cleveland | 11 | 5 | 0 | .688 | 340 | 204 |
| Cincinnati | 3 | 13 | 0 | .188 | 276 | 406 |
| Houston | 2 | 14 | 0 | .125 | 226 | 352 |

| AFC WEST | W | L | T | Pct | Pts | OP |
|---|---|---|---|---|---|---|
| San Diego | 11 | 5 | 0 | .688 | 384 | 306 |
| LA Raiders | 9 | 7 | 0 | .563 | 303 | 327 |
| Kansas City | 9 | 7 | 0 | .563 | 319 | 298 |
| Denver | 7 | 9 | 0 | .438 | 347 | 396 |
| Seattle | 6 | 10 | 0 | .375 | 287 | 323 |

| NFC EAST | W | L | T | Pct | Pts | OP |
|---|---|---|---|---|---|---|
| Dallas | 12 | 4 | 0 | .750 | 414 | 248 |
| NY Giants | 9 | 7 | 0 | .563 | 279 | 305 |
| Arizona Cardinals | 8 | 8 | 0 | .500 | 235 | 267 |
| Philadelphia | 7 | 9 | 0 | .438 | 308 | 308 |
| Washington | 3 | 13 | 0 | .188 | 320 | 412 |

| NFC CENTRAL | W | L | T | Pct | Pts | OP |
|---|---|---|---|---|---|---|
| Minnesota | 10 | 6 | 0 | .625 | 356 | 314 |
| Green Bay | 9 | 7 | 0 | .563 | 382 | 287 |
| Detroit | 9 | 7 | 0 | .563 | 357 | 342 |
| Chicago | 9 | 7 | 0 | .563 | 271 | 307 |
| Tampa Bay | 6 | 10 | 0 | .375 | 251 | 351 |

| NFC WEST | W | L | T | Pct | Pts | OP |
|---|---|---|---|---|---|---|
| San Francisco | 13 | 3 | 0 | .813 | 505 | 296 |
| New Orleans | 7 | 9 | 0 | .438 | 348 | 407 |
| Atlanta | 7 | 9 | 0 | .438 | 317 | 385 |
| LA Rams | 4 | 12 | 0 | .250 | 286 | 365 |

### 1995

| AFC EAST | W | L | T | Pct | Pts | OP |
|---|---|---|---|---|---|---|
| Buffalo | 10 | 6 | 0 | .625 | 350 | 335 |
| Miami | 9 | 7 | 0 | .563 | 398 | 332 |
| Indianapolis | 9 | 7 | 0 | .563 | 331 | 316 |
| New England | 6 | 10 | 0 | .375 | 294 | 377 |
| NY Jets | 3 | 13 | 0 | .188 | 233 | 384 |

| AFC CENTRAL | W | L | T | Pct | Pts | OP |
|---|---|---|---|---|---|---|
| Pittsburgh | 11 | 5 | 0 | .688 | 407 | 327 |
| Houston | 7 | 9 | 0 | .438 | 348 | 324 |
| Cincinnati | 7 | 9 | 0 | .438 | 349 | 374 |
| Cleveland | 5 | 11 | 0 | .313 | 289 | 356 |
| Jacksonville Jaguars | 4 | 12 | 0 | .250 | 275 | 404 |

| AFC WEST | W | L | T | Pct | Pts | OP |
|---|---|---|---|---|---|---|
| Kansas City | 13 | 3 | 0 | .813 | 358 | 241 |
| San Diego | 9 | 7 | 0 | .563 | 321 | 323 |
| Oakland Raiders | 8 | 8 | 0 | .500 | 348 | 332 |
| Denver | 8 | 8 | 0 | .500 | 388 | 345 |
| Seattle | 8 | 8 | 0 | .500 | 363 | 366 |

### 1995 (Cont.)

| NFC EAST | W | L | T | Pct | Pts | OP |
|---|---|---|---|---|---|---|
| Dallas | 12 | 4 | 0 | .750 | 435 | 291 |
| Philadelphia | 10 | 6 | 0 | .625 | 318 | 338 |
| Washington | 6 | 10 | 0 | .375 | 326 | 359 |
| NY Giants | 5 | 11 | 0 | .313 | 290 | 340 |
| Arizona | 4 | 12 | 0 | .250 | 275 | 422 |

| NFC CENTRAL | W | L | T | Pct | Pts | OP |
|---|---|---|---|---|---|---|
| Green Bay | 11 | 5 | 0 | .688 | 404 | 314 |
| Detroit | 10 | 6 | 0 | .625 | 436 | 336 |
| Chicago | 9 | 7 | 0 | .563 | 392 | 360 |
| Minnesota | 8 | 8 | 0 | .500 | 412 | 385 |
| Tampa Bay | 7 | 9 | 0 | .438 | 238 | 335 |

| NFC WEST | W | L | T | Pct | Pts | OP |
|---|---|---|---|---|---|---|
| San Francisco | 11 | 5 | 0 | .688 | 457 | 258 |
| Atlanta | 9 | 7 | 0 | .563 | 362 | 349 |
| St. Louis Rams | 7 | 9 | 0 | .438 | 309 | 418 |
| Carolina Panthers | 7 | 9 | 0 | .438 | 289 | 325 |
| New Orleans | 7 | 9 | 0 | .438 | 319 | 348 |

### 1996

| AFC EAST | W | L | T | Pct | Pts | OP |
|---|---|---|---|---|---|---|
| New England | 11 | 5 | 0 | .688 | 418 | 313 |
| Buffalo | 10 | 6 | 0 | .625 | 319 | 266 |
| Indianapolis | 9 | 7 | 0 | .563 | 317 | 334 |
| Miami | 8 | 8 | 0 | .500 | 339 | 325 |
| NY Jets | 1 | 15 | 0 | .063 | 279 | 454 |

| AFC CENTRAL | W | L | T | Pct | Pts | OP |
|---|---|---|---|---|---|---|
| Pittsburgh | 10 | 6 | 0 | .625 | 344 | 257 |
| Jacksonville | 9 | 7 | 0 | .563 | 325 | 334 |
| Houston | 8 | 8 | 0 | .500 | 345 | 319 |
| Cincinnati | 8 | 8 | 0 | .500 | 372 | 369 |
| Baltimore Ravens | 4 | 12 | 0 | .250 | 371 | 441 |

| AFC WEST | W | L | T | Pct | Pts | OP |
|---|---|---|---|---|---|---|
| Denver | 13 | 3 | 0 | .813 | 391 | 275 |
| Kansas City | 9 | 7 | 0 | .563 | 297 | 300 |
| San Diego | 8 | 8 | 0 | .500 | 310 | 376 |
| Seattle | 7 | 9 | 0 | .438 | 317 | 375 |
| Oakland | 7 | 9 | 0 | .438 | 340 | 293 |

| NFC EAST | W | L | T | Pct | Pts | OP |
|---|---|---|---|---|---|---|
| Dallas | 10 | 6 | 0 | .625 | 286 | 250 |
| Philadelphia | 10 | 6 | 0 | .625 | 363 | 341 |
| Washington | 9 | 7 | 0 | .563 | 364 | 312 |
| Arizona | 7 | 9 | 0 | .438 | 300 | 397 |
| NY Giants | 6 | 10 | 0 | .375 | 242 | 297 |

| NFC CENTRAL | W | L | T | Pct | Pts | OP |
|---|---|---|---|---|---|---|
| Green Bay | 13 | 3 | 0 | .813 | 456 | 210 |
| Minnesota | 9 | 7 | 0 | .563 | 298 | 315 |
| Chicago | 7 | 9 | 0 | .438 | 283 | 305 |
| Tampa Bay | 6 | 10 | 0 | .375 | 221 | 293 |
| Detroit | 5 | 11 | 0 | .313 | 302 | 368 |

| NFC WEST | W | L | T | Pct | Pts | OP |
|---|---|---|---|---|---|---|
| San Francisco | 12 | 4 | 0 | .750 | 398 | 257 |
| Carolina | 12 | 4 | 0 | .750 | 367 | 218 |
| St. Louis | 6 | 10 | 0 | .375 | 303 | 409 |
| New Orleans | 3 | 13 | 0 | .188 | 229 | 339 |
| Atlanta | 3 | 13 | 0 | .188 | 309 | 461 |

## 1997

### AFC EAST

| | W | L | T | Pct | Pts | OP |
|---|---|---|---|---|---|---|
| New England | 10 | 6 | 0 | .625 | 369 | 289 |
| Miami | 9 | 7 | 0 | .563 | 339 | 327 |
| NY Jets | 9 | 7 | 0 | .563 | 348 | 287 |
| Buffalo | 6 | 10 | 0 | .375 | 255 | 367 |
| Indianapolis | 3 | 13 | 0 | .188 | 313 | 401 |

### AFC CENTRAL

| | W | L | T | Pct | Pts | OP |
|---|---|---|---|---|---|---|
| Jacksonville | 11 | 5 | 0 | .688 | 394 | 318 |
| Pittsburgh | 11 | 5 | 0 | .688 | 372 | 307 |
| Tennessee Oilers | 8 | 8 | 0 | .500 | 333 | 310 |
| Cincinnati | 7 | 9 | 0 | .438 | 355 | 405 |
| Baltimore | 6 | 9 | 1 | .375 | 326 | 345 |

### AFC WEST

| | W | L | T | Pct | Pts | OP |
|---|---|---|---|---|---|---|
| Kansas City | 13 | 3 | 0 | .813 | 375 | 232 |
| Denver | 12 | 4 | 0 | .750 | 472 | 287 |
| Seattle | 8 | 8 | 0 | .500 | 365 | 362 |
| Oakland | 4 | 12 | 0 | .250 | 324 | 419 |
| San Diego | 4 | 12 | 0 | .250 | 266 | 425 |

### NFC EAST

| | W | L | T | Pct | Pts | OP |
|---|---|---|---|---|---|---|
| NY Giants | 10 | 5 | 1 | .656 | 307 | 265 |
| Washington | 8 | 7 | 1 | .531 | 327 | 289 |
| Philadelphia | 6 | 9 | 1 | .406 | 317 | 372 |
| Dallas | 6 | 10 | 0 | .375 | 304 | 314 |
| Arizona | 4 | 12 | 0 | .250 | 283 | 379 |

### NFC CENTRAL

| | W | L | T | Pct | Pts | OP |
|---|---|---|---|---|---|---|
| Green Bay | 13 | 3 | 0 | .813 | 422 | 282 |
| Tampa Bay | 10 | 6 | 0 | .625 | 299 | 263 |
| Detroit | 9 | 7 | 0 | .563 | 379 | 306 |
| Minnesota | 9 | 7 | 0 | .563 | 354 | 359 |
| Chicago | 4 | 12 | 0 | .250 | 263 | 421 |

### NFC WEST

| | W | L | T | Pct | Pts | OP |
|---|---|---|---|---|---|---|
| San Francisco | 13 | 3 | 0 | .813 | 375 | 265 |
| Carolina | 7 | 9 | 0 | .438 | 265 | 314 |
| Atlanta | 7 | 9 | 0 | .438 | 320 | 361 |
| New Orleans | 6 | 10 | 0 | .375 | 237 | 327 |
| St. Louis | 5 | 11 | 0 | .313 | 299 | 359 |

## 1998

### AFC EAST

| | W | L | T | Pct | Pts | OP |
|---|---|---|---|---|---|---|
| NY Jets | 12 | 4 | 0 | .750 | 416 | 266 |
| Miami | 10 | 6 | 0 | .625 | 321 | 265 |
| Buffalo | 10 | 6 | 0 | .625 | 400 | 333 |
| New England | 9 | 7 | 0 | .563 | 337 | 329 |
| Indianapolis | 3 | 13 | 0 | .188 | 310 | 444 |

### AFC CENTRAL

| | W | L | T | Pct | Pts | OP |
|---|---|---|---|---|---|---|
| Jacksonville | 11 | 5 | 0 | .688 | 392 | 338 |
| Tennessee | 8 | 8 | 0 | .500 | 330 | 320 |
| Pittsburgh | 7 | 9 | 0 | .438 | 263 | 303 |
| Baltimore | 6 | 10 | 0 | .375 | 269 | 335 |
| Cincinnati | 3 | 13 | 0 | .188 | 268 | 452 |

### AFC WEST

| | W | L | T | Pct | Pts | OP |
|---|---|---|---|---|---|---|
| Denver | 14 | 2 | 0 | .875 | 501 | 309 |
| Oakland | 8 | 8 | 0 | .500 | 288 | 356 |
| Seattle | 8 | 8 | 0 | .500 | 372 | 310 |
| Kansas City | 7 | 9 | 0 | .438 | 327 | 363 |
| San Diego | 5 | 11 | 0 | .313 | 241 | 342 |

## 1998 (Cont.)

### NFC EAST

| | W | L | T | Pct | Pts | OP |
|---|---|---|---|---|---|---|
| Dallas | 10 | 6 | 0 | .625 | 381 | 275 |
| Arizona | 9 | 7 | 0 | .563 | 325 | 378 |
| NY Giants | 8 | 8 | 0 | .500 | 287 | 309 |
| Washington | 6 | 10 | 0 | .375 | 319 | 421 |
| Philadelphia | 3 | 13 | 0 | .188 | 161 | 344 |

### NFC CENTRAL

| | W | L | T | Pct | Pts | OP |
|---|---|---|---|---|---|---|
| Minnesota | 15 | 1 | 0 | .938 | 556 | 296 |
| Green Bay | 11 | 5 | 0 | .688 | 408 | 319 |
| Tampa Bay | 8 | 8 | 0 | .500 | 314 | 295 |
| Detroit | 5 | 11 | 0 | .313 | 306 | 378 |
| Chicago | 4 | 12 | 0 | .250 | 276 | 368 |

### NFC WEST

| | W | L | T | Pct | Pts | OP |
|---|---|---|---|---|---|---|
| Atlanta | 14 | 2 | 0 | .875 | 442 | 289 |
| San Francisco | 12 | 4 | 0 | .750 | 479 | 328 |
| New Orleans | 6 | 10 | 0 | .375 | 305 | 359 |
| Carolina | 4 | 12 | 0 | .250 | 336 | 413 |
| St. Louis | 4 | 12 | 0 | .250 | 285 | 378 |

## 1999

### AFC EAST

| | W | L | T | Pct | Pts | OP |
|---|---|---|---|---|---|---|
| Indianapolis | 13 | 3 | 0 | .813 | 423 | 333 |
| Buffalo | 11 | 5 | 0 | .688 | 320 | 229 |
| Miami | 9 | 7 | 0 | .563 | 326 | 336 |
| NY Jets | 8 | 8 | 0 | .500 | 309 | 309 |
| New England | 8 | 8 | 0 | .500 | 299 | 284 |

### AFC CENTRAL

| | W | L | T | Pct | Pts | OP |
|---|---|---|---|---|---|---|
| Jacksonville | 14 | 2 | 0 | .875 | 396 | 217 |
| Tennessee Titans | 13 | 3 | 0 | .813 | 392 | 324 |
| Baltimore | 8 | 8 | 0 | .500 | 324 | 277 |
| Pittsburgh | 6 | 10 | 0 | .375 | 317 | 320 |
| Cincinnati | 4 | 12 | 0 | .250 | 283 | 460 |
| Cleveland Browns | 2 | 14 | 0 | .125 | 217 | 437 |

### AFC WEST

| | W | L | T | Pct | Pts | OP |
|---|---|---|---|---|---|---|
| Seattle | 9 | 7 | 0 | .563 | 338 | 298 |
| Kansas City | 9 | 7 | 0 | .563 | 390 | 322 |
| Oakland | 8 | 8 | 0 | .500 | 390 | 329 |
| San Diego | 8 | 8 | 0 | .500 | 269 | 316 |
| Denver | 6 | 10 | 0 | .375 | 314 | 318 |

### NFC EAST

| | W | L | T | Pct | Pts | OP |
|---|---|---|---|---|---|---|
| Washington | 10 | 6 | 0 | .625 | 443 | 377 |
| Dallas | 8 | 8 | 0 | .500 | 352 | 276 |
| NY Giants | 7 | 9 | 0 | .438 | 299 | 358 |
| Arizona | 6 | 10 | 0 | .375 | 245 | 382 |
| Philadelphia | 5 | 11 | 0 | .313 | 272 | 357 |

### NFC CENTRAL

| | W | L | T | Pct | Pts | OP |
|---|---|---|---|---|---|---|
| Tampa Bay | 11 | 5 | 0 | .688 | 270 | 235 |
| Minnesota | 10 | 6 | 0 | .625 | 399 | 335 |
| Green Bay | 8 | 8 | 0 | .500 | 357 | 341 |
| Detroit | 8 | 8 | 0 | .500 | 322 | 323 |
| Chicago | 6 | 10 | 0 | .375 | 272 | 341 |

### NFC WEST

| | W | L | T | Pct | Pts | OP |
|---|---|---|---|---|---|---|
| St. Louis | 13 | 3 | 0 | .813 | 526 | 242 |
| Carolina | 8 | 8 | 0 | .500 | 421 | 381 |
| Atlanta | 5 | 11 | 0 | .313 | 285 | 380 |
| San Francisco | 4 | 12 | 0 | .250 | 295 | 453 |
| New Orleans | 3 | 13 | 0 | .188 | 260 | 434 |

## 2000

### AFC EAST

| | W | L | T | Pct | Pts | OP |
|---|---|---|---|---|---|---|
| Miami | 11 | 5 | 0 | .688 | 323 | 226 |
| Indianapolis | 10 | 6 | 0 | .625 | 429 | 326 |
| NY Jets | 9 | 7 | 0 | .563 | 321 | 321 |
| Buffalo | 8 | 8 | 0 | .500 | 315 | 350 |
| New England | 5 | 11 | 0 | .313 | 276 | 338 |

### AFC CENTRAL

| | W | L | T | Pct | Pts | OP |
|---|---|---|---|---|---|---|
| Tennessee | 13 | 3 | 0 | .813 | 346 | 191 |
| Baltimore | 12 | 4 | 0 | .750 | 333 | 165 |
| Pittsburgh | 9 | 7 | 0 | .563 | 321 | 255 |
| Jacksonville | 7 | 9 | 0 | .438 | 367 | 327 |
| Cincinnati | 4 | 12 | 0 | .250 | 185 | 359 |
| Cleveland | 3 | 13 | 0 | .188 | 161 | 419 |

### AFC WEST

| | W | L | T | Pct | Pts | OP |
|---|---|---|---|---|---|---|
| Oakland | 12 | 4 | 0 | .750 | 479 | 299 |
| Denver | 11 | 5 | 0 | .688 | 485 | 369 |
| Kansas City | 7 | 9 | 0 | .438 | 355 | 354 |
| Seattle | 6 | 10 | 0 | .375 | 320 | 405 |
| San Diego | 1 | 15 | 0 | .063 | 269 | 440 |

### NFC EAST

| | W | L | T | Pct | Pts | OP |
|---|---|---|---|---|---|---|
| NY Giants | 12 | 4 | 0 | .750 | 328 | 246 |
| Philadelphia | 11 | 5 | 0 | .688 | 351 | 245 |
| Washington | 8 | 8 | 0 | .500 | 281 | 269 |
| Dallas | 5 | 11 | 0 | .313 | 294 | 361 |
| Arizona | 3 | 13 | 0 | .188 | 210 | 443 |

### NFC CENTRAL

| | W | L | T | Pct | Pts | OP |
|---|---|---|---|---|---|---|
| Minnesota | 11 | 5 | 0 | .688 | 397 | 371 |
| Tampa Bay | 10 | 6 | 0 | .625 | 388 | 269 |
| Green Bay | 9 | 7 | 0 | .563 | 353 | 323 |
| Detroit | 9 | 7 | 0 | .563 | 307 | 307 |
| Chicago | 5 | 11 | 0 | .313 | 216 | 355 |

### NFC WEST

| | W | L | T | Pct | Pts | OP |
|---|---|---|---|---|---|---|
| New Orleans | 10 | 6 | 0 | .625 | 354 | 306 |
| St. Louis | 10 | 6 | 0 | .625 | 540 | 471 |
| Carolina | 7 | 9 | 0 | .438 | 310 | 310 |
| San Francisco | 6 | 10 | 0 | .375 | 388 | 422 |
| Atlanta | 4 | 12 | 0 | .250 | 252 | 413 |

## 2001

### AFC EAST

| | W | L | T | Pct | Pts | OP |
|---|---|---|---|---|---|---|
| New England | 11 | 5 | 0 | .688 | 371 | 272 |
| Miami | 11 | 5 | 0 | .688 | 344 | 290 |
| NY Jets | 10 | 6 | 0 | .625 | 413 | 486 |
| Indianapolis | 6 | 10 | 0 | .375 | 413 | 486 |
| Buffalo | 3 | 13 | 0 | .188 | 265 | 420 |

### AFC CENTRAL

| | W | L | T | Pct | Pts | OP |
|---|---|---|---|---|---|---|
| Pittsburgh | 13 | 3 | 0 | .813 | 352 | 212 |
| Baltimore | 10 | 6 | 0 | .625 | 303 | 265 |
| Cleveland | 7 | 9 | 0 | .438 | 285 | 319 |
| Tennessee | 7 | 9 | 0 | .438 | 336 | 388 |
| Jacksonville | 6 | 10 | 0 | .375 | 294 | 286 |
| Cincinnati | 6 | 10 | 0 | .375 | 226 | 309 |

### AFC WEST

| | W | L | T | Pct | Pts | OP |
|---|---|---|---|---|---|---|
| Oakland | 10 | 6 | 0 | .625 | 399 | 327 |
| Seattle | 9 | 7 | 0 | .563 | 301 | 324 |
| Denver | 8 | 8 | 0 | .500 | 340 | 339 |
| Kansas City | 6 | 10 | 0 | .375 | 320 | 344 |
| San Diego | 5 | 11 | 0 | .313 | 332 | 321 |

## 2001 (Cont.)

### NFC EAST

| | W | L | T | Pct | Pts | OP |
|---|---|---|---|---|---|---|
| Philadelphia | 11 | 5 | 0 | .688 | 343 | 208 |
| Washington | 8 | 8 | 0 | .500 | 256 | 303 |
| NY Giants | 7 | 9 | 0 | .438 | 294 | 321 |
| Arizona | 7 | 9 | 0 | .438 | 295 | 343 |
| Dallas | 5 | 11 | 0 | .313 | 246 | 338 |

### NFC CENTRAL

| | W | L | T | Pct | Pts | OP |
|---|---|---|---|---|---|---|
| Chicago | 13 | 3 | 0 | .813 | 338 | 203 |
| Green Bay | 12 | 4 | 0 | .750 | 390 | 266 |
| Tampa Bay | 9 | 7 | 0 | .563 | 324 | 280 |
| Minnesota | 5 | 11 | 0 | .313 | 290 | 390 |
| Detroit | 2 | 14 | 0 | .125 | 270 | 424 |

### NFC WEST

| | W | L | T | Pct | Pts | OP |
|---|---|---|---|---|---|---|
| St. Louis | 14 | 2 | 0 | .875 | 503 | 273 |
| San Francisco | 12 | 4 | 0 | .750 | 409 | 282 |
| Atlanta | 7 | 9 | 0 | .438 | 291 | 377 |
| New Orleans | 7 | 9 | 0 | .438 | 333 | 409 |
| Carolina | 1 | 15 | 0 | .938 | 253 | 410 |

## 2002

### AFC EAST

| | W | L | T | Pct | Pts | OP |
|---|---|---|---|---|---|---|
| New England | 9 | 7 | 0 | .563 | 384 | 346 |
| Miami | 9 | 7 | 0 | .563 | 378 | 301 |
| NY Jets | 9 | 7 | 0 | .563 | 359 | 336 |
| Buffalo | 8 | 8 | 0 | .500 | 379 | 397 |

### AFC NORTH

| | W | L | T | Pct | Pts | OP |
|---|---|---|---|---|---|---|
| Pittsburgh | 10 | 5 | 1 | .656 | 390 | 345 |
| Cleveland | 9 | 7 | 0 | .563 | 344 | 320 |
| Baltimore | 7 | 9 | 0 | .438 | 316 | 354 |
| Cincinnati | 2 | 14 | 0 | .125 | 279 | 456 |

### AFC SOUTH

| | W | L | T | Pct | Pts | OP |
|---|---|---|---|---|---|---|
| Tennessee | 11 | 5 | 0 | .688 | 367 | 324 |
| Indianapolis | 10 | 6 | 0 | .625 | 349 | 313 |
| Jacksonville | 6 | 10 | 0 | .375 | 328 | 315 |
| Houston Texans | 4 | 12 | 0 | .250 | 213 | 356 |

### AFC WEST

| | W | L | T | Pct | Pts | OP |
|---|---|---|---|---|---|---|
| Oakland | 11 | 5 | 0 | .688 | 450 | 304 |
| Denver | 9 | 7 | 0 | .563 | 392 | 344 |
| Kansas City | 8 | 8 | 0 | .500 | 467 | 399 |
| San Diego | 8 | 8 | 0 | .500 | 333 | 367 |

### NFC EAST

| | W | L | T | Pct | Pts | OP |
|---|---|---|---|---|---|---|
| Philadelphia | 12 | 4 | 0 | .750 | 415 | 241 |
| NY Giants | 10 | 6 | 0 | .625 | 320 | 279 |
| Washington | 7 | 9 | 0 | .438 | 307 | 365 |
| Dallas | 5 | 11 | 0 | .313 | 217 | 329 |

### NFC NORTH

| | W | L | T | Pct | Pts | OP |
|---|---|---|---|---|---|---|
| Green Bay | 12 | 4 | 0 | .750 | 398 | 328 |
| Minnesota | 6 | 10 | 0 | .375 | 390 | 442 |
| Chicago | 4 | 12 | 0 | .250 | 281 | 379 |
| Detroit | 3 | 13 | 0 | .188 | 306 | 451 |

### 2002 (Cont.)

| NFC SOUTH | W | L | T | Pct | Pts | OP |
|---|---|---|---|---|---|---|
| Tampa Bay | 12 | 4 | 0 | .750 | 346 | 196 |
| Atlanta | 9 | 6 | 1 | .594 | 402 | 314 |
| New Orleans | 9 | 7 | 0 | .563 | 432 | 388 |
| Carolina | 7 | 9 | 0 | .438 | 258 | 302 |

| NFC WEST | W | L | T | Pct | Pts | OP |
|---|---|---|---|---|---|---|
| San Francisco | 10 | 6 | 0 | .625 | 367 | 351 |
| St. Louis | 7 | 9 | 0 | .438 | 316 | 367 |
| Seattle | 7 | 9 | 0 | .438 | 355 | 369 |
| Arizona | 5 | 11 | 0 | .313 | 262 | 417 |

### 2003

| AFC EAST | W | L | T | Pct | Pts | OP |
|---|---|---|---|---|---|---|
| New England | 14 | 2 | 0 | .875 | 348 | 238 |
| Miami | 10 | 6 | 0 | .625 | 311 | 261 |
| Buffalo | 6 | 10 | 0 | .375 | 243 | 279 |
| NY Jets | 6 | 10 | 0 | .375 | 283 | 299 |

| AFC NORTH | W | L | T | Pct | Pts | OP |
|---|---|---|---|---|---|---|
| Baltimore | 10 | 6 | 0 | .625 | 391 | 281 |
| Cincinnati | 8 | 8 | 0 | .500 | 346 | 384 |
| Pittsburgh | 6 | 10 | 0 | .375 | 300 | 327 |
| Cleveland | 5 | 11 | 0 | .313 | 254 | 322 |

| AFC SOUTH | W | L | T | Pct | Pts | OP |
|---|---|---|---|---|---|---|
| Indianapolis | 12 | 4 | 0 | .750 | 447 | 336 |
| Tennessee | 12 | 4 | 0 | .750 | 435 | 324 |
| Houston | 5 | 11 | 0 | .313 | 255 | 380 |
| Jacksonville | 5 | 11 | 0 | .313 | 276 | 331 |

| AFC WEST | W | L | T | Pct | Pts | OP |
|---|---|---|---|---|---|---|
| Kansas City | 13 | 3 | 0 | .813 | 484 | 332 |
| Denver | 10 | 6 | 0 | .625 | 381 | 301 |
| Oakland | 4 | 12 | 0 | .250 | 270 | 379 |
| San Diego | 4 | 12 | 0 | .250 | 313 | 441 |

| NFC EAST | W | L | T | Pct | Pts | OP |
|---|---|---|---|---|---|---|
| Philadelphia | 12 | 4 | 0 | .750 | 374 | 287 |
| Dallas | 10 | 6 | 0 | .625 | 289 | 260 |
| Washington | 5 | 11 | 0 | .313 | 287 | 372 |
| NY Giants | 4 | 12 | 0 | .250 | 243 | 387 |

| NFC NORTH | W | L | T | Pct | Pts | OP |
|---|---|---|---|---|---|---|
| Green Bay | 10 | 6 | 0 | .625 | 442 | 307 |
| Minnesota | 9 | 7 | 0 | .563 | 416 | 353 |
| Chicago | 7 | 9 | 0 | .438 | 283 | 346 |
| Detroit | 5 | 11 | 0 | .313 | 270 | 379 |

| NFC SOUTH | W | L | T | Pct | Pts | OP |
|---|---|---|---|---|---|---|
| Carolina | 11 | 5 | 0 | .688 | 325 | 304 |
| New Orleans | 8 | 8 | 0 | .500 | 340 | 326 |
| Tampa Bay | 7 | 9 | 0 | .438 | 301 | 264 |
| Atlanta | 5 | 11 | 0 | .313 | 299 | 422 |

| NFC WEST | W | L | T | Pct | Pts | OP |
|---|---|---|---|---|---|---|
| St. Louis | 12 | 4 | 0 | .750 | 447 | 328 |
| Seattle | 10 | 6 | 0 | .625 | 404 | 327 |
| San Francisco | 7 | 9 | 0 | .438 | 384 | 337 |
| Arizona | 4 | 12 | 0 | .250 | 225 | 452 |

### 2004

| AFC EAST | W | L | T | Pct | Pts | OP |
|---|---|---|---|---|---|---|
| New England | 14 | 2 | 0 | .875 | 437 | 260 |
| NY Jets | 10 | 6 | 0 | .625 | 333 | 261 |
| Buffalo | 9 | 7 | 0 | .562 | 395 | 284 |
| Miami | 4 | 12 | 0 | .250 | 275 | 354 |

| AFC NORTH | W | L | T | Pct | Pts | OP |
|---|---|---|---|---|---|---|
| Pittsburgh | 15 | 1 | 0 | .938 | 372 | 251 |
| Baltimore | 9 | 7 | 0 | .562 | 317 | 268 |
| Cincinnati | 8 | 8 | 0 | .500 | 374 | 372 |
| Cleveland | 4 | 12 | 0 | .250 | 275 | 354 |

| AFC SOUTH | W | L | T | Pct | Pts | OP |
|---|---|---|---|---|---|---|
| Indianapolis | 12 | 4 | 0 | .750 | 522 | 351 |
| Jacksonville | 9 | 7 | 0 | .562 | 261 | 280 |
| Houston | 7 | 9 | 0 | .438 | 309 | 339 |
| Tennessee | 5 | 11 | 0 | .312 | 344 | 439 |

| AFC WEST | W | L | T | Pct | Pts | OP |
|---|---|---|---|---|---|---|
| San Diego | 12 | 4 | 0 | .750 | 446 | 313 |
| Denver | 10 | 6 | 0 | .625 | 381 | 304 |
| Kansas City | 7 | 9 | 0 | .438 | 483 | 435 |
| Oakland | 5 | 11 | 0 | .312 | 320 | 442 |

| NFC EAST | W | L | T | Pct | Pts | OP |
|---|---|---|---|---|---|---|
| Philadelphia | 13 | 3 | 0 | .812 | 386 | 260 |
| NY Giants | 6 | 10 | 0 | .375 | 303 | 347 |
| Dallas | 6 | 10 | 0 | .375 | 293 | 405 |
| Washington | 6 | 10 | 0 | .375 | 240 | 265 |

| NFC NORTH | W | L | T | Pct | Pts | OP |
|---|---|---|---|---|---|---|
| Green Bay | 10 | 6 | 0 | .625 | 424 | 380 |
| Minnesota | 8 | 8 | 0 | .500 | 405 | 395 |
| Detroit | 6 | 10 | 0 | .375 | 296 | 350 |
| Chicago | 5 | 11 | 0 | .312 | 231 | 331 |

| NFC SOUTH | W | L | T | Pct | Pts | OP |
|---|---|---|---|---|---|---|
| Atlanta | 11 | 5 | 0 | .688 | 340 | 337 |
| New Orleans | 8 | 8 | 0 | .500 | 348 | 405 |
| Carolina | 7 | 9 | 0 | .438 | 355 | 339 |
| Tampa Bay | 5 | 11 | 0 | .312 | 301 | 304 |

| NFC WEST | W | L | T | Pct | Pts | OP |
|---|---|---|---|---|---|---|
| Seattle | 9 | 7 | 0 | .562 | 371 | 373 |
| St. Louis | 8 | 8 | 0 | .500 | 319 | 392 |
| Arizona | 6 | 10 | 0 | .375 | 284 | 322 |
| San Francisco | 2 | 14 | 0 | .125 | 259 | 452 |

### 2005

| AFC EAST | W | L | T | Pct | Pts | OP |
|---|---|---|---|---|---|---|
| New England | 10 | 6 | 0 | .625 | 379 | 338 |
| Miami | 9 | 7 | 0 | .562 | 318 | 317 |
| Buffalo | 5 | 11 | 0 | .312 | 271 | 367 |
| NY Jets | 4 | 12 | 0 | .250 | 240 | 355 |

| AFC NORTH | W | L | T | Pct | Pts | OP |
|---|---|---|---|---|---|---|
| Cincinnati | 11 | 5 | 0 | .688 | 421 | 350 |
| Pittsburgh | 11 | 5 | 0 | .688 | 389 | 258 |
| Cleveland | 6 | 10 | 0 | .375 | 232 | 301 |
| Baltimore | 6 | 10 | 0 | .375 | 265 | 299 |

| AFC SOUTH | W | L | T | Pct | Pts | OP |
|---|---|---|---|---|---|---|
| Indianapolis | 14 | 2 | 0 | .875 | 439 | 247 |
| Jacksonville | 12 | 4 | 0 | .750 | 361 | 269 |
| Tennessee | 4 | 12 | 0 | .250 | 299 | 421 |
| Houston | 2 | 14 | 0 | .125 | 260 | 431 |

## 2005 (Cont.)

### AFC WEST

| | W | L | T | Pct | Pts | OP |
|---|---|---|---|---|---|---|
| Denver | 13 | 3 | 0 | .812 | 395 | 258 |
| Kansas City | 10 | 6 | 0 | .625 | 403 | 325 |
| San Diego | 9 | 7 | 0 | .562 | 418 | 312 |
| Oakland | 4 | 12 | 0 | .250 | 290 | 383 |

### NFC EAST

| | W | L | T | Pct | Pts | OP |
|---|---|---|---|---|---|---|
| NY Giants | 11 | 5 | 0 | .688 | 422 | 314 |
| Washington | 10 | 6 | 0 | .625 | 359 | 293 |
| Dallas | 9 | 7 | 0 | .562 | 325 | 308 |
| Philadelphia | 6 | 10 | 0 | .375 | 310 | 388 |

### NFC NORTH

| | W | L | T | Pct | Pts | OP |
|---|---|---|---|---|---|---|
| Chicago | 11 | 5 | 0 | .688 | 260 | 202 |
| Minnesota | 9 | 7 | 0 | .562 | 306 | 344 |
| Detroit | 5 | 11 | 0 | .312 | 254 | 345 |
| Green Bay | 4 | 12 | 0 | .250 | 298 | 344 |

### NFC SOUTH

| | W | L | T | Pct | Pts | OP |
|---|---|---|---|---|---|---|
| Carolina | 11 | 5 | 0 | .688 | 391 | 259 |
| Tampa Bay | 11 | 5 | 0 | .688 | 300 | 274 |
| Atlanta | 8 | 8 | 0 | .500 | 351 | 341 |
| New Orleans | 3 | 13 | 0 | .188 | 235 | 398 |

### NFC WEST

| | W | L | T | Pct | Pts | OP |
|---|---|---|---|---|---|---|
| Seattle | 13 | 3 | 0 | .812 | 452 | 271 |
| St. Louis | 6 | 10 | 0 | .375 | 363 | 429 |
| Arizona | 5 | 11 | 0 | .312 | 311 | 387 |
| San Francisco | 4 | 12 | 0 | .250 | 239 | 428 |

## 2006

### AFC EAST

| | W | L | T | Pct | Pts | OP |
|---|---|---|---|---|---|---|
| New England | 12 | 4 | 0 | .750 | 385 | 237 |
| NY Jets | 10 | 6 | 0 | .625 | 316 | 295 |
| Buffalo | 7 | 9 | 0 | .438 | 300 | 311 |
| Miami | 6 | 10 | 0 | .375 | 260 | 283 |

### AFC NORTH

| | W | L | T | Pct | Pts | OP |
|---|---|---|---|---|---|---|
| Baltimore | 13 | 3 | 0 | .812 | 353 | 201 |
| Cincinnati | 8 | 8 | 0 | .500 | 373 | 331 |
| Pittsburgh | 8 | 8 | 0 | .500 | 353 | 315 |
| Cleveland | 4 | 12 | 0 | .250 | 238 | 356 |

### AFC SOUTH

| | W | L | T | Pct | Pts | OP |
|---|---|---|---|---|---|---|
| Indianapolis | 12 | 4 | 0 | .750 | 427 | 360 |
| Tennessee | 8 | 8 | 0 | .500 | 324 | 400 |
| Jacksonville | 8 | 8 | 0 | .500 | 371 | 274 |
| Houston | 6 | 10 | 0 | .375 | 267 | 366 |

### AFC WEST

| | W | L | T | Pct | Pts | OP |
|---|---|---|---|---|---|---|
| San Diego | 14 | 2 | 0 | .875 | 492 | 303 |
| Kansas City | 9 | 7 | 0 | .562 | 331 | 315 |
| Denver | 9 | 7 | 0 | .562 | 319 | 305 |
| Oakland | 2 | 14 | 0 | .125 | 168 | 332 |

### NFC EAST

| | W | L | T | Pct | Pts | OP |
|---|---|---|---|---|---|---|
| Philadelphia | 10 | 6 | 0 | .625 | 398 | 328 |
| Dallas | 9 | 7 | 0 | .562 | 425 | 350 |
| NY Giants | 8 | 8 | 0 | .500 | 355 | 362 |
| Washington | 5 | 11 | 0 | .312 | 307 | 376 |

### NFC NORTH

| | W | L | T | Pct | Pts | OP |
|---|---|---|---|---|---|---|
| Chicago | 13 | 3 | 0 | .812 | 427 | 255 |
| Green Bay | 8 | 8 | 0 | .500 | 301 | 366 |
| Minnesota | 6 | 10 | 0 | .375 | 282 | 327 |
| Detroit | 3 | 13 | 0 | .188 | 305 | 398 |

## 2006 (Cont.)

### NFC SOUTH

| | W | L | T | Pct | Pts | OP |
|---|---|---|---|---|---|---|
| New Orleans | 10 | 6 | 0 | .625 | 413 | 322 |
| Carolina | 8 | 8 | 0 | .500 | 270 | 305 |
| Atlanta | 7 | 9 | 0 | .438 | 292 | 328 |
| Tampa Bay | 4 | 12 | 0 | .250 | 211 | 353 |

### NFC WEST

| | W | L | T | Pct | Pts | OP |
|---|---|---|---|---|---|---|
| Seattle | 9 | 7 | 0 | .562 | 335 | 341 |
| St. Louis | 8 | 8 | 0 | .500 | 367 | 381 |
| San Francisco | 7 | 9 | 0 | .438 | 298 | 412 |
| Arizona | 5 | 11 | 0 | .312 | 314 | 389 |

## 2007

### AFC EAST

| | W | L | T | Pct | Pts | OP |
|---|---|---|---|---|---|---|
| New England | 16 | 0 | 0 | 1.000 | 589 | 274 |
| Buffalo | 7 | 9 | 0 | .438 | 252 | 354 |
| NY Jets | 4 | 12 | 0 | .250 | 268 | 355 |
| Miami | 1 | 15 | 0 | .063 | 267 | 437 |

### AFC NORTH

| | W | L | T | Pct | Pts | OP |
|---|---|---|---|---|---|---|
| Pittsburgh | 10 | 6 | 0 | .625 | 393 | 269 |
| Cleveland | 10 | 6 | 0 | .625 | 402 | 382 |
| Cincinnati | 7 | 9 | 0 | .438 | 380 | 385 |
| Baltimore | 5 | 11 | 0 | .313 | 275 | 384 |

### AFC SOUTH

| | W | L | T | Pct | Pts | OP |
|---|---|---|---|---|---|---|
| Indianapolis | 13 | 3 | 0 | .813 | 450 | 262 |
| Jacksonville | 11 | 5 | 0 | .688 | 411 | 304 |
| Tennessee | 10 | 6 | 0 | .625 | 301 | 297 |
| Houston | 8 | 8 | 0 | .500 | 379 | 384 |

### AFC WEST

| | W | L | T | Pct | Pts | OP |
|---|---|---|---|---|---|---|
| San Diego | 11 | 5 | 0 | .688 | 412 | 284 |
| Denver | 7 | 9 | 0 | .438 | 320 | 409 |
| Kansas City | 4 | 12 | 0 | .250 | 226 | 335 |
| Oakland | 4 | 12 | 0 | .250 | 286 | 398 |

### NFC EAST

| | W | L | T | Pct | Pts | OP |
|---|---|---|---|---|---|---|
| Dallas | 13 | 3 | 0 | .813 | 455 | 325 |
| NY Giants | 10 | 6 | 0 | .625 | 373 | 351 |
| Washington | 9 | 7 | 0 | .563 | 334 | 310 |
| Philadelphia | 8 | 8 | 0 | .500 | 336 | 300 |

### NFC NORTH

| | W | L | T | Pct | Pts | OP |
|---|---|---|---|---|---|---|
| Green Bay | 13 | 3 | 0 | .813 | 435 | 291 |
| Minnesota | 8 | 8 | 0 | .500 | 365 | 311 |
| Detroit | 7 | 9 | 0 | .438 | 346 | 444 |
| Chicago | 7 | 9 | 0 | .438 | 334 | 348 |

### NFC SOUTH

| | W | L | T | Pct | Pts | OP |
|---|---|---|---|---|---|---|
| Tampa Bay | 9 | 7 | 0 | .563 | 334 | 270 |
| Carolina | 7 | 9 | 0 | .438 | 267 | 347 |
| New Orleans | 7 | 9 | 0 | .438 | 379 | 388 |
| Atlanta | 4 | 12 | 0 | .250 | 259 | 414 |

### NFC WEST

| | W | L | T | Pct | Pts | OP |
|---|---|---|---|---|---|---|
| Seattle | 10 | 6 | 0 | .625 | 393 | 291 |
| Arizona | 8 | 8 | 0 | .500 | 404 | 399 |
| San Francisco | 5 | 11 | 0 | .313 | 219 | 364 |
| St. Louis | 3 | 13 | 0 | .188 | 263 | 438 |

# The Super Bowl

## Results

| | Date | Winner (Share) | Loser (Share) | Score | Site (Attendance) |
|---|---|---|---|---|---|
| I | 1-15-67 | Green Bay ($15,000) | Kansas City ($7,500) | 35–10 | Los Angeles (61,946) |
| II | 1-14-68 | Green Bay ($15,000) | Oakland ($7,500) | 33–14 | Miami (75,546) |
| III | 1-12-69 | NY Jets ($15,000) | Baltimore ($7,500) | 16–7 | Miami (75,389) |
| IV | 1-11-70 | Kansas City ($15,000) | Minnesota ($7,500) | 23–7 | New Orleans (80,562) |
| V | 1-17-71 | Baltimore ($15,000) | Dallas ($7,500) | 16–13 | Miami (79,204) |
| VI | 1-16-72 | Dallas ($15,000) | Miami ($7,500) | 24–3 | New Orleans (81,023) |
| VII | 1-14-73 | Miami ($15,000) | Washington ($7,500) | 14–7 | Los Angeles (90,182) |
| VIII | 1-13-74 | Miami ($15,000) | Minnesota ($7,500) | 24–7 | Houston (71,882) |
| IX | 1-12-75 | Pittsburgh ($15,000) | Minnesota ($7,500) | 16–6 | New Orleans (80,997) |
| X | 1-18-76 | Pittsburgh ($15,000) | Dallas ($7,500) | 21–17 | Miami (80,187) |
| XI | 1-9-77 | Oakland ($15,000) | Minnesota ($7,500) | 32–14 | Pasadena (103,438) |
| XII | 1-15-78 | Dallas ($18,000) | Denver ($9,000) | 27–10 | New Orleans (76,400) |
| XIII | 1-21-79 | Pittsburgh ($18,000) | Dallas ($9,000) | 35–31 | Miami (79,484) |
| XIV | 1-20-80 | Pittsburgh ($18,000) | Los Angeles ($9,000) | 31–19 | Pasadena (103,985) |
| XV | 1-25-81 | Oakland ($18,000) | Philadelphia ($9,000) | 27–10 | New Orleans (76,135) |
| XVI | 1-24-82 | San Francisco ($18,000) | Cincinnati ($9,000) | 26–21 | Pontiac, Mich. (81,270) |
| XVII | 1-30-83 | Washington ($18,000) | Miami ($18,000) | 27–17 | Pasadena (103,667) |
| XVIII | 1-22-84 | LA Raiders ($36,000) | Washington ($18,000) | 38–9 | Tampa (72,920) |
| XIX | 1-20-85 | San Francisco ($36,000) | Miami ($18,000) | 38–16 | Stanford, Calif. (84,059) |
| XX | 1-26-86 | Chicago ($36,000) | New England ($18,000) | 46–10 | New Orleans (73,818) |
| XXI | 1-25-87 | NY Giants ($36,000) | Denver ($18,000) | 39–20 | Pasadena (101,063) |
| XXII | 1-31-88 | Washington ($36,000) | Denver ($18,000) | 42–10 | San Diego (73,302) |
| XXIII | 1-22-89 | San Francisco ($36,000) | Cincinnati ($18,000) | 20–16 | Miami (75,129) |
| XXIV | 1-28-90 | San Francisco ($36,000) | Denver ($18,000) | 55–10 | New Orleans (72,919) |
| XXV | 1-27-91 | NY Giants ($36,000) | Buffalo ($18,000) | 20–19 | Tampa (73,813) |
| XXVI | 1-26-92 | Washington ($36,000) | Buffalo ($18,000) | 37–24 | Minneapolis (63,130) |
| XXVII | 1-31-93 | Dallas ($36,000) | Buffalo ($18,000) | 52–17 | Pasadena (98,374) |
| XXVIII | 1-30-94 | Dallas ($38,000) | Buffalo ($23,500) | 30–13 | Atlanta (72,817) |
| XXIX | 1-29-95 | San Francisco ($42,000) | San Diego ($26,000) | 49–26 | Miami (74,107) |
| XXX | 1-28-96 | Dallas ($42,000) | Pittsburgh ($27,000) | 27–17 | Tempe, Ariz. (76,347) |
| XXXI | 1-26-97 | Green Bay ($48,000) | New England ($29,000) | 35–21 | New Orleans (72,301) |
| XXXII | 1-25-98 | Denver ($48,000) | Green Bay ($27,500) | 31–24 | San Diego (68,912) |
| XXXIII | 1-31-99 | Denver ($53,000) | Atlanta ($32,500) | 34–19 | Miami (74,803) |
| XXXIV | 1-30-00 | St. Louis ($58,000) | Tennessee ($33,000) | 23–16 | Atlanta (72,625) |
| XXXV | 1-28-01 | Baltimore ($58,000) | NY Giants ($34,500) | 34–7 | Tampa (71,921) |
| XXXVI | 2-3-02 | New England ($63,000) | St. Louis ($34,500) | 20–17 | New Orleans (72,922) |
| XXXVII | 1-26-03 | Tampa Bay ($64,000) | Oakland ($35,000) | 48–21 | San Diego (67,603) |
| XXXVIII | 2-1-04 | New England ($64,000) | Carolina ($35,000) | 32–29 | Houston (71,525) |
| XXXIX | 2-6-05 | New England ($68,000) | Philadelphia ($36,500) | 24–21 | Jacksonville (78,125) |
| XL | 2-5-06 | Pittsburgh ($73,000) | Seattle ($38,000) | 21–10 | Detroit (68,206) |
| XLI | 2-4-07 | Indianapolis ($78,000) | Chicago ($40,000) | 29–17 | Miami (74,512) |
| XLII | 2-3-08 | NY Giants ($78,000) | New England ($40,000) | 17–14 | Glendale, Ariz. (71,101) |
| XLIII | 2-1-09 | Pittsburgh ($78,000) | Arizona ($40,000) | 27–23 | Tampa (70,774) |

## Most Valuable Players

| Super Bowl | Player/ Team | Position | Super Bowl | Player/ Team | Position |
|---|---|---|---|---|---|
| I | Bart Starr, GB | QB | XXII | Doug Williams, Wash | QB |
| II | Bart Starr, GB | QB | XXIII | Jerry Rice, SF | WR |
| III | Joe Namath, NYJ | QB | XXIV | Joe Montana, SF | QB |
| IV | Len Dawson, KC | QB | XXV | Ottis Anderson, NYG | RB |
| V | Chuck Howley, Dal | LB | XXVI | Mark Rypien, Wash | QB |
| VI | Roger Staubach, Dal | QB | XXVII | Troy Aikman, Dal | QB |
| VII | Jake Scott, Mia | S | XXVIII | Emmitt Smith, Dal | RB |
| VIII | Larry Csonka, Mia | RB | XXIX | Steve Young, SF | QB |
| IX | Franco Harris, Pit | RB | XXX | Larry Brown, Dal | CB |
| X | Lynn Swann, Pit | WR | XXXI | Desmond Howard, GB | KR |
| XI | Fred Biletnikoff, Oak | WR | XXXII | Terrell Davis, Den | RB |
| XII | Randy White, Dal | DT | XXXIII | John Elway, Den | QB |
| | Harvey Martin, Dal | DE | XXXIV | Kurt Warner, StL | QB |
| XIII | Terry Bradshaw, Pit | QB | XXXV | Ray Lewis, Balt | LB |
| XIV | Terry Bradshaw, Pit | QB | XXXVI | Tom Brady, NE | QB |
| XV | Jim Plunkett, Oak | QB | XXXVII | Dexter Jackson, TB | S |
| XVI | Joe Montana, SF | QB | XXXVIII | Tom Brady, NE | QB |
| XVII | John Riggins, Wash | RB | XXXIX | Deion Branch, NE | WR |
| XVIII | Marcus Allen, LA Rai | RB | XL | Hines Ward, Pit | WR |
| XIX | Joe Montana, SF | QB | XLI | Peyton Manning, Ind | QB |
| XX | Richard Dent, Chi | DE | XLII | Eli Manning, NYG | QB |
| XXI | Phil Simms, NYG | QB | XLIII | Santonio Holmes, Pit | WR |

## Composite Standings, by Win Percentage

|  | W | L | Pct | Pts | Opp Pts |
|---|---|---|---|---|---|
| San Francisco 49ers | 5 | 0 | 1.000 | 188 | 89 |
| Tampa Bay Buccaneers | 1 | 0 | 1.000 | 48 | 21 |
| Baltimore Ravens | 1 | 0 | 1.000 | 34 | 7 |
| New York Jets | 1 | 0 | 1.000 | 16 | 7 |
| Pittsburgh Steelers | 6 | 1 | .857 | 168 | 133 |
| Green Bay Packers | 3 | 1 | .750 | 127 | 76 |
| New York Giants | 3 | 1 | .750 | 83 | 87 |
| Baltimore/Indianapolis Colts | 2 | 1 | .667 | 52 | 46 |
| Dallas Cowboys | 5 | 3 | .625 | 221 | 132 |
| Oakland/LA Raiders | 3 | 2 | .600 | 132 | 114 |
| Washington Redskins | 3 | 2 | .600 | 122 | 103 |
| New England Patriots | 3 | 3 | .500 | 121 | 165 |
| Chicago Bears | 1 | 1 | .500 | 63 | 39 |
| Kansas City Chiefs | 1 | 1 | .500 | 33 | 42 |
| Miami Dolphins | 2 | 3 | .400 | 74 | 103 |
| Denver Broncos | 2 | 4 | .333 | 115 | 206 |
| Los Angeles/St. Louis Rams | 1 | 2 | .333 | 59 | 67 |
| Carolina Panthers | 0 | 1 | .000 | 29 | 32 |
| San Diego Chargers | 0 | 1 | .000 | 26 | 49 |
| Arizona Cardinals | 0 | 1 | .000 | 23 | 27 |
| Atlanta Falcons | 0 | 1 | .000 | 19 | 34 |
| Tennessee Titans | 0 | 1 | .000 | 16 | 23 |
| Seattle Seahawks | 0 | 1 | .000 | 10 | 21 |
| Cincinnati Bengals | 0 | 2 | .000 | 37 | 46 |
| Philadelphia Eagles | 0 | 2 | .000 | 31 | 51 |
| Buffalo Bills | 0 | 4 | .000 | 73 | 139 |
| Minnesota Vikings | 0 | 4 | .000 | 34 | 95 |

## Career Leaders

### Passing

|  | GP | Att | Comp | Pct Comp | Yds | Avg Gain | TD | Pct TD | Int | Pct Int | Lg | Rating Pts |
|---|---|---|---|---|---|---|---|---|---|---|---|---|
| Joe Montana, SF | 4 | 122 | 83 | 68.0 | 1142 | 9.36 | 11 | 9.0 | 0 | 0.0 | 44 | 127.8 |
| Jim Plunkett, Oak/LA Rai | 2 | 46 | 29 | 63.0 | 433 | 9.41 | 4 | 8.7 | 0 | 0.0 | t80 | 122.8 |
| Terry Bradshaw, Pit | 4 | 84 | 49 | 58.3 | 932 | 11.10 | 9 | 10.7 | 4 | 4.8 | t75 | 112.8 |
| Troy Aikman, Dal | 3 | 80 | 56 | 70.0 | 689 | 8.61 | 5 | 6.3 | 1 | 1.3 | t56 | 111.9 |
| Bart Starr, GB | 2 | 47 | 29 | 61.7 | 452 | 9.62 | 3 | 6.4 | 1 | 2.1 | t62 | 106.0 |
| Brett Favre, GB | 2 | 69 | 39 | 56.5 | 502 | 7.28 | 5 | 7.2 | 1 | 1.4 | t81 | 97.7 |
| Kurt Warner, StL, Ari | 3 | 132 | 83 | 62.9 | 1156 | 8.76 | 6 | 4.5 | 3 | 2.3 | t73 | 96.7 |
| Roger Staubach, Dal | 4 | 98 | 61 | 62.2 | 734 | 7.49 | 8 | 8.2 | 4 | 4.1 | t45 | 95.4 |
| Tom Brady, NE | 4 | 156 | 100 | 64.1 | 1001 | 6.42 | 7 | 4.5 | 1 | 0.1 | 52 | 94.5 |
| Len Dawson, KC | 2 | 44 | 28 | 63.6 | 353 | 8.02 | 2 | 4.5 | 2 | 4.5 | t46 | 84.8 |

Note: Minimum 40 attempts.

### Rushing Yards

|  | GP | Yds | Att | Avg | Lg | TD |
|---|---|---|---|---|---|---|
| Franco Harris, Pit | 4 | 354 | 101 | 3.5 | 25 | 4 |
| Larry Csonka, Mia | 3 | 297 | 57 | 5.2 | 49 | 2 |
| Emmitt Smith, Dal | 3 | 289 | 70 | 4.1 | 38 | 5 |
| Terrell Davis, Den | 2 | 259 | 55 | 4.7 | 27 | 3 |
| John Riggins, Wash | 2 | 230 | 64 | 3.6 | 43 | 2 |
| Timmy Smith, Wash | 1 | 204 | 22 | 9.3 | 58 | 2 |
| Thurman Thomas, Buf | 4 | 204 | 52 | 3.9 | 31 | 4 |
| Roger Craig, SF | 3 | 217 | 44 | 4.9 | 20 | 3 |
| Marcus Allen, LA Rai | 1 | 191 | 20 | 9.6 | t74 | 2 |
| Antowain Smith, NE | 2 | 175 | 44 | 4.0 | 17 | 1 |

### Receptions

|  | GP | No. | Yds | Avg | Lg | TD |
|---|---|---|---|---|---|---|
| Jerry Rice, SF | 4 | 33 | 589 | 17.9 | t48 | 8 |
| Andre Reed, Buf | 4 | 27 | 323 | 12.0 | 40 | 0 |
| Deion Branch, NE | 2 | 21 | 276 | 13.1 | 52 | 1 |
| Roger Craig, SF | 3 | 20 | 212 | 10.6 | 40 | 2 |
| Thurman Thomas, Buf | 4 | 20 | 144 | 7.2 | 24 | 0 |
| Jay Novacek, Dal | 3 | 17 | 148 | 8.7 | 23 | 2 |
| Lynn Swann, Pit | 4 | 16 | 364 | 22.8 | t74 | 3 |
| Michael Irvin, Dal | 3 | 16 | 256 | 16.0 | 25 | 2 |
| Troy Brown, NE | 3 | 16 | 182 | 11.4 | 23 | 0 |
| Chuck Foreman, Min | 3 | 15 | 139 | 9.3 | 26 | 0 |

t-scored touchdown

### Single-Game Leaders

#### Scoring

|  | Pts |
| --- | --- |
| Roger Craig: XIX, San Francisco vs Miami (1 rush, 2 rec) | 18 |
| Jerry Rice: XXIV, San Francisco vs Denver (3 rec); XXIX, SF vs San Diego (3 rec) | 18 |
| Ricky Watters: XXIX, San Francisco vs San Diego (1 rush, 2 rec) | 18 |
| Terrell Davis: XXXII, Denver vs Green Bay (3 rec) | 18 |

#### Rushing Yards

|  | Yds |
| --- | --- |
| Timmy Smith: XXII, Washington vs Denver | 204 |
| Marcus Allen: XVIII, LA Raiders vs Washington | 191 |
| John Riggins: XVII, Washington vs Miami | 166 |
| Franco Harris: IX, Pittsburgh vs Minnesota | 158 |
| Terrell Davis: XXXII, Denver vs Green Bay | 157 |
| Larry Csonka: VIII, Miami vs Minnesota | 145 |
| Clarence Davis: XI, Oakland vs Minnesota | 137 |
| Thurman Thomas: XXV, Buffalo vs NY Giants | 135 |
| Emmitt Smith: XXVIII, Dallas vs Buffalo | 132 |
| Michael Pittman: XXXVII, Tampa Bay vs Oakland | 124 |

#### Receptions

|  | No. |
| --- | --- |
| Deion Branch: XXXIX, New England vs Phila. | 11 |
| Jerry Rice: XXIII, San Francisco vs Cincinnati | 11 |
| Dan Ross: XVI, Cincinnati vs San Francisco | 11 |
| Wes Welker: XLII, New England vs NY Giants | 11 |
| Joseph Addai: XLI, Indianapolis vs Chicago | 10 |
| Deion Branch: XXXVIII, New England vs Carolina | 10 |
| Andre Hastings: XXX, Pittsburgh vs Dallas | 10 |
| Tony Nathan: XIX, Miami vs San Francisco | 10 |
| Jerry Rice: XXIX, San Francisco vs San Diego | 10 |
| Antonio Freeman: XXXII, Green Bay vs Denver | 9 |
| Santonio Holmes: XLIII, Pittsburgh vs Arizona | 9 |
| Terrell Owens: XXXIX, Philadelphia vs New England | 9 |
| Ricky Sanders: XXII, Washington vs Denver | 9 |
| Eight tied with eight. | |

#### Touchdown Passes

|  | No. |
| --- | --- |
| Steve Young: XXIX, San Francisco vs San Diego | 6 |
| Joe Montana: XXIV, San Francisco vs Denver | 5 |
| Terry Bradshaw: XIII, Pittsburgh vs Dallas | 4 |
| Doug Williams: XXII, Washington vs Denver | 4 |
| Troy Aikman: XXVII, Dallas vs Buffalo | 4 |
| Eight tied with three. | |

#### Passing Yards

|  | Yds |
| --- | --- |
| Kurt Warner: XXXIV, St. Louis vs Tennessee | 414 |
| Kurt Warner: XLIII, Arizona vs Pittsburgh | 377 |
| Kurt Warner: XXXVI, St. Louis vs New England | 365 |
| Donovan McNabb, XXXIX, Phila. vs New England | 357 |
| Joe Montana: XXIII, San Francisco vs Cincinnati | 357 |
| Tom Brady: XXXVIII, New England vs Carolina | 354 |
| Doug Williams: XXII, Washington vs Denver | 340 |
| John Elway: XXXIII, Denver vs Atlanta | 336 |
| Joe Montana: XIX, San Francisco vs Miami | 331 |
| Steve Young: XXIX, San Francisco vs San Diego | 325 |
| Jake Delhomme: XXXVIII Carolina vs New England | 323 |
| Terry Bradshaw: XIII, Pittsburgh vs Dallas | 318 |
| Dan Marino: XIX, Miami vs San Francisco | 318 |

#### Receiving Yards

|  | Yds |
| --- | --- |
| Jerry Rice: XXIII, San Francisco vs Cincinnati | 215 |
| Ricky Sanders: XXII, Washington vs Denver | 193 |
| Isaac Bruce: XXXIV, St. Louis vs Tennessee | 162 |
| Lynn Swann: X, Pittsburgh vs Dallas | 161 |
| Andre Reed: XXVII, Buffalo vs Dallas | 152 |
| Rod Smith: XXXIII, Denver vs Atlanta | 152 |
| Jerry Rice: XXIX, San Francisco vs San Diego | 149 |
| Jerry Rice: XXIV, San Francisco vs Denver | 148 |
| Deion Branch: XXXVIII, New England vs Carolina | 143 |

## I - 1967

| | | | | |
|---|---|---|---|---|
| Green Bay | 7 | 7 | 14 | 7—35 |
| Kansas City | 0 | 10 | 0 | 0—10 |

**FIRST QUARTER:** GB: McGee 37 pass from Starr (Chandler kick), 8:56. **Green Bay 7-0.**

**SECOND QUARTER:** KC: McClinton 7 pass from Dawson (Mercer kick), 4:20. **7-7.**
GB: Taylor 14 run (Chandler kick), 10:23. **Green Bay 14-7.**
KC: FG Mercer 31, 14:06. **Green Bay 14-10.**

**THIRD QUARTER:** GB: Pitts 5 run (Chandler kick), 2:27. **Green Bay 21-10.**
GB: McGee 13 pass from Starr (Chandler kick), 14:09. **Green Bay 28-10.**

**FOURTH QUARTER:** GB: Pitts 1 run (Chandler kick), 8:25. **Green Bay 35-10.**

A: 61,946

## II - 1968

| | | | | |
|---|---|---|---|---|
| Green Bay | 3 | 13 | 10 | 7—33 |
| Oakland | 0 | 7 | 0 | 7—14 |

**FIRST QUARTER:** GB: FG Chandler 39 5:07. **Green Bay 3-0.**

**SECOND QUARTER:** GB: FG Chandler, 20, 3:08. **Green Bay 6-0.**
GB: Dowler 62 pass from Starr (Chandler kick), 4:10. **Green Bay 13-0.**
Oak: Miller 23 pass from Lamonica (Blanda kick), 8:45. **Green Bay 13-7.**
GB: FG Chandler 43, 14:59. **Green Bay 16-7.**

**THIRD QUARTER:** GB: Anderson 2 run (Chandler kick), 9:06. **Green Bay 23-7.**
GB: FG Chandler 31, 14:58. **Green Bay 26-7.**

**FOURTH QUARTER:**
GB: Adderley 60 int return (Chandler kick), 3:57. **Green Bay 33-7.**
Oak: Miller 23 pass from Lamonica (Blanda kick), 5:47. **Green Bay 33-14.**

A: 75,546

## III - 1969

| | | | | |
|---|---|---|---|---|
| NY Jets | 0 | 7 | 6 | 3—16 |
| Baltimore | 0 | 0 | 0 | 7—7 |

**SECOND QUARTER:** Jets: Snell 4 run (Turner kick), 5:57. **Jets: 7-0.**

**THIRD QUARTER:** Jets: FG Turner 32, 4:52. **Jets: 10-0.**
Jets: FG Turner 30, 11:02. **Jets: 13-0.**

**FOURTH QUARTER:** Jets: FG Turner 9, 1:34. **Jets: 16-0.**
Balt: Hill 1 run (Michaels kick), 11:41. **Jets: 16-7.**

A: 75,389

## IV - 1970

| | | | | |
|---|---|---|---|---|
| Kansas City | 3 | 13 | 7 | 0—23 |
| Minnesota | 0 | 0 | 7 | 0—7 |

**FIRST QUARTER:** KC: FG Stenerud 48, 8:08. **Kansas City 3-0.**

**SECOND QUARTER:** KC: FG Stenerud 32, 1:40. **Kansas City 6-0.**
KC: FG Stenerud 25, 7:08. **Kansas City 9-0.**
KC: Garrett 5 run (Stenerud kick), 9:26. **Kansas City 16-0.**

**THIRD QUARTER:** Minn: Osborn 4 run (Cox kick), 10:28. **Kansas City 16-7.**
KC: Taylor 46 pass from Dawson (Stenerud kick), 13:38. **Kansas City 23-7.**

A: 80,562

## V - 1971

| | | | | |
|---|---|---|---|---|
| Baltimore | 0 | 6 | 0 | 10—16 |
| Dallas | 3 | 10 | 0 | 0—13 |

**FIRST QUARTER:** Dal (9:28): FG Clark 14, 9:28. **Dallas 3-0.**

**SECOND QUARTER:** Dal: FG Clark 30, 0:08. **Dallas 6-0.**
Balt: Mackey 75 pass from Unitas (kick blocked). 0:50. **6-6.**
Dal: Thomas 7 pass from Morton (Clark kick), 7:07. **Dallas 13-6.**

**FOURTH QUARTER:** Balt: Nowatzke 2 run (O'Brien kick), 7:25. **13-13.**
Balt: FG O'Brien 32, 14:55. **Baltimore 16-13.**

A: 79,204

## VI - 1972

| | | | | |
|---|---|---|---|---|
| Dallas | 3 | 7 | 7 | 7—24 |
| Miami | 0 | 3 | 0 | 0—3 |

**FIRST QUARTER:** Dal: FG Clark 9, 13:37. **Dallas 3-0.**

**SECOND QUARTER:** Dal: Alworth 7 pass from Staubach (Clark kick), 13:45. **Dallas 10-0.**
Mia: FG Yepremian, 31, 14:56. **Dallas 10-3.**

**THIRD QUARTER:** Dal: D. Thomas 3 run (Clark kick), 5:17. **Dallas 17-3.**

**FOURTH QUARTER:** Dal: Ditka 7 pass from Staubach (Clark kick), 3:18. **Dallas 24-3.**

A: 81,023

## VII - 1973

| | | | | |
|---|---|---|---|---|
| Miami | 7 | 7 | 0 | 0—14 |
| Washington | 0 | 0 | 0 | 7—7 |

**FIRST QUARTER:** Mia: Twilley 28 pass from Griese (Yepremian kick), 14:59. **Miami 7-0.**

**SECOND QUARTER:** Mia: Kiick 1 run (Yepremian kick), 14:42. **Miami 14-0.**

**FOURTH QUARTER:** Wash: Bass 49 fumble recovery return (Knight kick), 12:53. **Miami 14-7.**

A: 90,182

*From 1967 to 1999, Super Bowl scoring times indicate the time elapsed in each quarter. Starting in 2000, times listed give the time remaining in each quarter.

### VIII - 1974

| | | | |
|---|---|---|---|
| Miami | 14 | 3 | 7 | 0—24 |
| Minnesota | 0 | 0 | 0 | 7—7 |

**FIRST QUARTER:** Mia: Csonka 5 run (Yepremian kick), 5:27. **Miami 7-0.**
Mia: Kiick 1 run (Yepremian kick), 13:38. **Miami 14-0.**

**SECOND QUARTER:** Mia: FG Yepremian 28, 8:58. **Miami 17-0.**

**THIRD QUARTER:** Mia: Csonka 2 run (Yepremian kick), 6:16. **Miami 24-0.**

**FOURTH QUARTER:** Minn: Tarkenton 4 run (Cox kick), 1:35. **Miami 24-7.**

A: 71,882

### IX - 1975

| | | | |
|---|---|---|---|
| Pittsburgh | 0 | 2 | 7 | 7—16 |
| Minnesota | 0 | 0 | 0 | 6—6 |

**SECOND QUARTER:** Pit: White tackled Tarkenton for safety, 7:49. **Pittsburgh 2-0.**

**THIRD QUARTER:** Pit: Harris 9 run (Gerela kick), 1:35. **Pittsburgh 9-0.**

**FOURTH QUARTER:** Minn: T. Brown recovered blocked punt in end zone (kick failed), 4:27. **Pittsburgh 9-6.**
Pit: L. Brown 4 pass from Bradshaw (Gerela kick), 11:29. **Pittsburgh 16-6.**

A: 80,997

### X - 1976

| | | | |
|---|---|---|---|
| Pittsburgh | 7 | 0 | 0 | 14—21 |
| Dallas | 7 | 3 | 0 | 7—17 |

**FIRST QUARTER:** Dal: D. Pearson 29 pass from Staubach (Fritsch kick), 4:36. **Dallas 7-0.**
Pit: Grossman 7 pass from Bradshaw (Gerela kick), 9:03. **7-7.**

**SECOND QUARTER:** Dal: FG Fritsch 36, 0:15. **Dallas 10-7.**

**FOURTH QUARTER:** Pit: Harrison blocked Hoopes's punt for safety, 3:32. **Dallas 10-9.**
Pit: FG Gerela 36, 6:19. **Pittsburgh 12-10.**
Pit: FG Gerela 18, 8:32. **Pittsburgh 15-10.**
Pit: Swann 64 pass from Bradshaw (kick failed), 11:58. **Pittsburgh 21-10.**
Dal: P. Howard 34 pass from Staubach (Fritsch kick), 13:12. **Pittsburgh 21-17.**

A: 80,187

### XI - 1977

| | | | |
|---|---|---|---|
| Oakland | 0 | 16 | 3 | 13—32 |
| Minnesota | 0 | 0 | 7 | 7—14 |

**SECOND QUARTER:** Oak: FG Mann, 24, 0:48. **Oakland 3-0.**
Oak: Casper 1 pass from Stabler (Mann kick), 7:50. **Oakland 10-0.**
Oak: Banaszak 1 run (kick failed), 11:27. **Oakland 16-0.**

**THIRD QUARTER:** Oak: FG Mann, 40, 9:44. **Oakland 19-0.**
Min: S. White 8 pass from Tarkenton (Cox kick), 14:13. **Oakland 19-7.**

**FOURTH QUARTER:** Oak: Banaszak 2 run (Mann kick), 7:21. **Oakland 26-7.**
Oak: Brown 75 int return (kick failed), 9:17. **Oakland 32-7.**
Min: Voigt 13 pass from Lee (Cox kick), 14:35. **Oakland 32-14.**

A: 103,438

### XII - 1978

| | | | |
|---|---|---|---|
| Dallas | 10 | 3 | 7 | 7—27 |
| Denver | 0 | 0 | 10 | 0—10 |

**FIRST QUARTER: FIRST QUARTER:** Dal: Dorsett 3 run (Herrera kick), 10:31. **Dallas 7-0.**
Dal: FG Herrera 35, 13:29. **Dallas 10-0.**

**SECOND QUARTER:** Dal: FG Herrera 43, 3:44. **Dallas 13-0.**

**THIRD QUARTER:** Den: FG Turner 47, 2:28. **Dallas 13-3.**
Dal: Johnson 45 pass from Staubach (Herrera kick), 8:01. **Dallas 20-3.**
Den: Lytle 1 run (Turner kick), 9:21. **Dallas 20-10.**

**FOURTH QUARTER:** Dal: Richards 29 pass from Newhouse (Herrera kick), 7:56. **Dallas 27-10.**

A: 76,400

### XIII - 1979

| | | | |
|---|---|---|---|
| Pittsburgh | 7 | 14 | 0 | 14—35 |
| Dallas | 7 | 7 | 3 | 14—31 |

**FIRST QUARTER:** Pit: Stallworth 28 pass from Bradshaw (Gerela kick), 5:13. **Pittsburgh 7-0.**
Dal: Hill 39 pass from Staubach (Septien kick), 15:00. **7-7.**

**SECOND QUARTER:** Dal: Hegman 37 fumble recovery return (Septien kick), 2:52. **Dallas 14-7.**
Pit: Stallworth 75 pass from Bradshaw (Gerela kick), 4:35. **14-14.**
Pit: Bleier 7 pass from Bradshaw (Gerela kick), 14:34. **Pittsburgh 21-14.**

**THIRD QUARTER:** Dal: FG Septien 27, 12:24. **Pittsburgh 21-17.**

**FOURTH QUARTER:** Pit: Harris 22 run (Gerela kick), 7:50. **Pittsburgh 28-17.**
Pit: Swann 18 pass from Bradshaw (Gerela kick), 8:09. **Pittsburgh 35-17.**
Dal: DuPree 7 pass from Staubach (Septien kick), 12:33. **Pittsburgh 35-24.**
Dal: B. Johnson 4 pass from Staubach (Septien kick), 14:38. **Pittsburgh 35-31.**

A: 79,484

## XIV - 1980

| | | | | |
|---|---|---|---|---|
| Pittsburgh | 3 | 7 | 7 | 14—31 |
| LA Rams | 7 | 6 | 6 | 0—19 |

**FIRST QUARTER:** Pit: FG Bahr, 41, 7:29. **Pittsburgh 3–0.** LA: Bryant 1 run (Corral kick), 12:16. **LA Rams 7–3.**

**SECOND QUARTER:** Pit: Harris 1 run (Bahr kick), 2:08. **Pittsburgh 10–7.** LA: FG Corral 31, 7:39. **10–10.** LA: FG Corral 45, 14:46. **LA Rams 13–10.**

**THIRD QUARTER:** Pit: Swann 47 pass from Bradshaw (Bahr kick), 2:48. **Pittsburgh 17–13.** LA: Smith 24 pass from McCutcheon (kick failed), 4:45. **LA Rams 19–17.**

**FOURTH QUARTER:** Pit: Stallworth 73 pass from Bradshaw (Bahr kick), 2:56. **Pittsburgh 24–19.** Pit: Harris 1 run (Bahr kick), 13:11. **Pittsburgh 31–19.**

A: 103,985

## XV - 1981

| | | | | |
|---|---|---|---|---|
| Oakland | 14 | 0 | 10 | 3—27 |
| Philadelphia | 0 | 3 | 0 | 7—10 |

**FIRST QUARTER:** Oak: Branch 2 pass from Plunkett (Bahr kick), 6:04. **Oakland 7–0.** Oak: King 80 pass from Plunkett (Bahr kick), 14:51. **Oakland 14–0.**

**SECOND QUARTER:** Phi: FG Franklin 30, 4:32. **Oakland 14–3.**

**THIRD QUARTER:** Oak: Branch 29 pass from Plunkett (Bahr kick), 2:36. **Oakland 21–3.** Oak: FG Bahr 46, 10:25. **Oakland 24–3.**

**FOURTH QUARTER:** Phi: Krepfle 8 pass from Jaworski (Franklin kick), 1:01. **Oakland 24–10.** Oak: FG Bahr, 35, 6:31. **Oakland 27–10.**

A: 76,135

## XVI - 1982

| | | | | |
|---|---|---|---|---|
| San Francisco | 7 | 13 | 0 | 6—26 |
| Cincinnati | 0 | 0 | 7 | 14—21 |

**FIRST QUARTER:** SF: Montana 1 run (Wersching kick), 9:08. **San Francisco 7–0.**

**SECOND QUARTER:** SF: E. Cooper 11 pass from Montana (Wersching kick), 8:07. **San Francisco 14–0.** SF: FG Wersching 22, 14:45. **San Francisco 17–0.** SF: FG Wersching 26, 14:58. **San Francisco 20–0.**

**THIRD QUARTER:** Cin: Anderson 5 run (Breech kick), 3:35. **San Francisco 20–7.**

**FOURTH QUARTER:** Cin: Ross 4 pass from Anderson (Breech kick), 4:54. **San Francisco 20–14.** SF: FG Wersching 40, 9:35. **San Francisco 23–14.** SF: FG Wersching 23, 13:03. **San Francisco 26–14.** Cin: Ross 3 pass from Anderson (Breech kick), 14:44. **San Francisco 26–21.**

A: 81,270

## XVII - 1983

| | | | | |
|---|---|---|---|---|
| Washington | 0 | 10 | 3 | 14—27 |
| Miami | 7 | 10 | 0 | 0—17 |

**FIRST QUARTER:** Mia: Cefalo 76 pass from Woodley (Von Schamann kick), 6:49. **Miami 7–0.**

**SECOND QUARTER:** Wash: FG Moseley 31, 0:21. **Miami 7–3.** Mia: FG Von Schamann 20, 9:00. **Miami 10–3.** Wash: Garrett 4 pass from Theismann (Moseley kick), 13:09. **10–10.** Mia: Walker 98 kick return (Von Schamann kick), 13:22. **Miami 17–10.**

**THIRD QUARTER:** Wash: FG Moseley 20, 6:51. **Miami 17–13.**

**FOURTH QUARTER:** Wash: Riggins 43 run (Moseley kick), 4:59. **Washington 20–17.** Wash: Brown 6 pass from Theismann (Moseley kick), 13:05. **Washington 27–17.**

A: 103,667

## XVIII - 1984

| | | | | |
|---|---|---|---|---|
| LA Raiders | 7 | 14 | 14 | 3—38 |
| Washington | 0 | 3 | 6 | 0—9 |

**FIRST QUARTER:** LA: Jensen 0 blocked punt return (Bahr kick), 4:52. **LA Raiders 7–0.**

**SECOND QUARTER:** LA: Branch 12 pass from Plunkett (Bahr kick), 5:46. **LA Raiders 14–0.** Wash: FG Moseley 24, 11:55. **LA Raiders 14–3.** LA: Squirek 5 int return (Bahr kick), 14:53. **LA Raiders 21–3.**

**THIRD QUARTER:** Wash: Riggins 1 run (kick blocked), 4:08. **LA Raiders 21–9.** LA: Allen 5 run (Bahr kick), 7:54. **LA Raiders 28–9.** LA: Allen 74 run (Bahr kick), 15:00. **LA Raiders 35–9.**

**FOURTH QUARTER:** LA: FG Bahr 21, 12:36. **LA Raiders 38–9.**

A: 72,920

## XIX - 1985

| | | | | |
|---|---|---|---|---|
| San Francisco | 7 | 21 | 10 | 0—38 |
| Miami | 10 | 6 | 0 | 0—16 |

**FIRST QUARTER:** Mia: FG Von Schamann 37, 7:36. **Miami 3-0.**
SF: Monroe 33 pass from Montana (Wersching kick), 11:48. **San Francisco 7-3.**
Mia: D. Johnson 2 pass from Marino (Von Schamann kick), 14:15. **Miami 10-7.**

**SECOND QUARTER:** SF: Craig 8 pass from Montana (Wersching kick), 3:26. **San Francisco 14-10.**
SF: Montana 6 run (Wersching kick), 8:02. **San Francisco 21-10.**
SF: Craig 2 run (Wersching kick), 12:55. **San Francisco 28-10.**
Mia: FG Von Schamann 31, 14:48. **San Francisco 28-13.**
Mia: FG Von Schamann 30, 15:00. **San Francisco 28-16.**

**THIRD QUARTER:** SF: FG Wersching 27, 4:48. **San Francisco 31-16.**
SF: Craig 16 pass from Montana (Wershing kick), 8:42. **San Francisco 38-16.**

A: 84,059

## XX - 1986

| | | | | |
|---|---|---|---|---|
| Chicago | 13 | 10 | 21 | 2—46 |
| New England | 3 | 0 | 0 | 7—10 |

**FIRST QUARTER:** NE: FG Franklin 36, 1:19. **New England 3-0.**
Chi: FG Butler 28, 5:40. **3-3.**
Chi: FG Butler 24, 13:34. **Chicago 6-3.**
Chi: Suhey 11 run (Butler kick), 14:37. **Chicago 13-3.**

**SECOND QUARTER:** Chi: McMahon 2 run (Butler kick), 7:36. **Chicago 20-3.**
Chi: FG Butler 24, 15:00. **Chicago 23-3.**

**THIRD QUARTER:** Chi: McMahon 1 run (Butler kick), 7:38. **Chicago 30-3.**
Chi: Phillips 28 int return (Butler kick), 8:44. **Chicago 37-3.**
Chi: Perry 1 run (Butler kick), 11:38. **Chicago 44-3.**

**FOURTH QUARTER:** NE: Fryar 8 pass from Grogan (Franklin kick), 1:46. **Chicago 44-10.**
Chi: Waechter safety, 9:24. **Chicago 46-10.**

A: 73,818

## XXI - 1987

| | | | | |
|---|---|---|---|---|
| NY Giants | 7 | 2 | 17 | 13—39 |
| Denver | 10 | 0 | 0 | 10—20 |

**FIRST QUARTER:** Den: FG Karlis 48, 4:09. **Denver 3-0.**
NYG: Mowatt 6 pass from Simms (Allegre kick), 9:33. **NY Giants 7-3.**
Den: Elway 4 run (Karlis kick), 12:54. **Denver 10-7.**

**SECOND QUARTER:** NYG: Martin safety, 12:14. **Denver 10-9.**

**THIRD QUARTER:** NYG: Bavaro 13 pass from Simms (Allegre kick), 4:52. **NY Giants 16-10.**
NYG: FG Allegre 21, 11:06. **NY Giants 19-10.**
NYG: Morris 1 run (Allegre kick), 14:36. **NY Giants 26-10.**

**FOURTH QUARTER:** NYG: McConkey 6 pass from Simms (Allegre kick), 4:04. **NY Giants 33-10.**
Den: FG Karlis 28, 8:59. **NY Giants 33-13.**
NYG: Anderson 2 run (kick failed), 11:42. **NY Giants 39-13.**
Den: Johnson 47 pass from Elway (Karlis kick), 12:54. **NY Giants 39-20.**

A: 101,063

## XXII - 1988

| | | | | |
|---|---|---|---|---|
| Washington | 0 | 35 | 0 | 7—42 |
| Denver | 10 | 0 | 0 | 0—10 |

**FIRST QUARTER:** Den: Nattiel 56 pass from Elway (Karlis kick), 1:57. **Denver 7-0.**
Den: FG Karlis 24, 5:51. **Denver 10-0.**

**SECOND QUARTER:** Wash: Sanders 80 pass from D. Williams (Haji-Sheikh kick), 0:53. **Denver 10-7.**
Wash: Clark 27 pass from D. Williams (Haji-Sheikh kick), 4:45. **Washington 14-10.**
Wash: Smith 58 run (Haji-Sheikh kick), 8:33. **Washington 21-10.**
Wash: Sanders 50 pass from D. Williams (Haji-Sheikh kick), 11:18. **Washington 28-10.**
Wash: Didier 8 pass from D. Williams (Haji-Sheikh kick), 13:56. **Washington 35-10.**

**FOURTH QUARTER:** Wash: Smith 4 run (Haji-Sheikh kick), 1:51. **Washington 42-10.**

A: 73,302

## XXIII - 1989

| | | | | |
|---|---|---|---|---|
| San Francisco | 3 | 0 | 3 | 14—20 |
| Cincinnati | 0 | 3 | 10 | 3—16 |

**FIRST QUARTER:** SF: FG Cofer 41, 11:46. **San Francisco 3-0.**

**SECOND QUARTER:** Cin: FG Breech 34, 13:41. **3-3.**

**THIRD QUARTER:** Cin: FG Breech 43, 9:15. **Cincinnati 6-3.**
SF: FG Cofer 32, 14:10. **6-6.**
Cin: Jennings 93 kick return (Breech kick), 14:26. **Cincinnati 13-6.**

**FOURTH QUARTER:** SF: Rice 14 pass from Montana (Cofer kick), 0:57. **13-13.**
Cin: FG Breech 40, 11:40. **Cincinnati 16-13.**
SF: Taylor 10 pass from Montana (Cofer kick), 14:26. **San Francisco 20-16.**

A: 75,129

## XXIV - 1990

| | | | | |
|---|---|---|---|---|
| San Francisco | 13 | 14 | 14 | 14—55 |
| Denver | 3 | 0 | 7 | 0—10 |

**FIRST QUARTER:** SF: Rice 20 pass from Montana (Cofer kick), 4:54. **San Francisco 7-0.**
Den: FG Treadwell 42, 8:13. **San Francisco 7-3.**
SF: Jones 7 pass from Montana (kick failed), 14:57. **San Francisco 13-3.**

**SECOND QUARTER:** SF: Rathman 1 run (Cofer kick), 7:45. **San Francisco 20-3.**
SF: Rice 38 pass from Montana (Cofer kick), 14:26. **San Francisco 27-3.**

**THIRD QUARTER:** SF: Rice 28 pass from Montana (Cofer kick), 2:12. **San Francisco 34-3.**
SF: Taylor 35 pass from Montana (Cofer kick), 5:16. **San Francisco 41-3.**
Den: Elway 3 run (Treadwell kick), 8:07. **San Francisco 41-10.**

**FOURTH QUARTER:** SF: Rathman 3 run (Cofer kick), 0:03. **San Francisco 48-10.**
SF: Craig 1 run (Cofer kick), 1:13. **San Francisco 55-10.**

A: 72,919

## XXV - 1991

| | | | | |
|---|---|---|---|---|
| NY Giants | 3 | 7 | 7 | 3—20 |
| Buffalo | 3 | 9 | 0 | 7—19 |

**FIRST QUARTER:** NYG: FG Bahr 28, 7:46. **NY Giants 3-0.**
Buff: FG Norwood 23, 9:09. **3-3.**

**SECOND QUARTER:** Buff: D. Smith 1 run (Norwood kick), 2:30. **Buffalo 10-3.**
Buff: B. Smith safety 0, 6:33. **Buffalo 12-3.**
NYG: Baker 14 pass from Hostetler (Bahr kick), 14:35. **Buffalo 12-10.**

**THIRD QUARTER:** NYG: Anderson 1 run (Bahr kick), 9:29. **NY Giants 17-12.**

**FOURTH QUARTER:** Buff: Thomas 31 run (Norwood kick), 0:08. **Buffalo 19-17.**
NYG: FG Bahr 21, 7:40. **NY Giants 20-19.**

A: 73,813

## XXVI - 1992

| | | | | |
|---|---|---|---|---|
| Washington | 0 | 17 | 14 | 6—37 |
| Buffalo | 0 | 0 | 10 | 14—24 |

**SECOND QUARTER:** Wash: FG Lohmiller 34, 1:58. **Washington 3-0.**
Wash: Byner 10 pass from Rypien (Lohmiller kick), 5:06. **Washington 10-0.**
Wash: Riggs 1 run (Lohmiller kick), 7:43. **Washington 17-0.**

**THIRD QUARTER:** Wash: Riggs 2 run (Lohmiller kick), 0:16. **Washington 24-0.**
Buff: FG Norwood 21, 3:01. **Washington 24-3.**
Buff: Thomas 1 run (Norwood kick), 9:02. **Washington 24-10.**
Wash: Clark 30 pass from Rypien (Lohmiller kick), 13:36. **Washington 31-10.**

**FOURTH QUARTER:** Wash: FG Lohmiller 25, 0:06. **Washington 34-10.**
Wash: FG Lohmiller 39, 3:24. **Washington 37-10.**
Buff: Metzelaars 2 pass from Kelly (Norwood kick), 9:01. **Washington 37-17.**
Buff: Beebe 4 pass from Kelly (Norwood kick), 11:05. **Washington 37-24.**

A: 63,130.

## XXVII - 1993

| | | | | |
|---|---|---|---|---|
| Dallas | 14 | 14 | 3 | 21—52 |
| Buffalo | 7 | 3 | 7 | 0—17 |

**FIRST QUARTER:** Buff: Thomas 2 run (Christie kick), 5:00. **Buffalo 7-0.**
Dal: Novacek 23 pass from Aikman (Elliott kick), 13:24. **7-7.**
Dal: J.Jones 2 fumble return (Elliott kick), 13:39. **Dallas 14-7.**

**SECOND QUARTER:** Buff: FG Christie 21, 11:36. **Dallas 14-10.**
Dal: Irvin 19 pass from Aikman (Elliott kick)13:06. **Dallas 21-10.**
Dal: Irvin 18 pass from Aikman (Elliott kick), 13:24. **Dallas 28-10.**

**THIRD QUARTER:** Dal: FG Elliott 20, 6:39. **Dallas 31-10.**
Buff: Beebe 40 pass from Reich (Christie kick), 15:00. **Dallas 31-17.**

**FOURTH QUARTER:** Dal: Harper 45 pass from Aikman (Elliott kick), 4:56. **Dallas 38-17.**
Dal: E. Smith 10 run (Elliott kick), 6:48. **Dallas 45-17.**
Dal: Norton 9 fumble return (Elliott kick), 7:29. **Dallas 52-17.**

A: 98,374

## XXVIII - 1994

| | | | | |
|---|---|---|---|---|
| Dallas | 6 | 0 | 14 | 10—30 |
| Buffalo | 3 | 10 | 0 | 0—13 |

**FIRST QUARTER:** Dal: FG Murray 41, 2:19. **Dallas 3-0.**
Buff: FG Christie 54: 4:41. **3-3.**
Dal: FG Murray 24, 11:05. **Dallas 6-3.**

**SECOND QUARTER:** Buff: Thomas 4 run (Christie kick), 2:34. **Buffalo 10-6.**
Buff: FG Christie 28, 15:00. **Buffalo 13-6.**

**THIRD QUARTER:** Dal: Washington fumble return (Murray kick), 0:55. **13-13.**
Dal: Smith15 run (Murray kick), 0:55. **Dallas 20-13.**

**FOURTH QUARTER:** Dal: Smith1 run (Murray kick), 5:10. **Dallas 27-13.**
Dal: FG Murray 20, 12:10. **Dallas 30-13.**

A: 72,817

## XXIX - 1995

| | | | | |
|---|---|---|---|---|
| San Francisco | 14 | 14 | 14 | 7—49 |
| San Diego | 7 | 3 | 8 | 8—26 |

**FIRST QUARTER:** SF: Rice 44 pass from Young (Brien kick), 1:24. **San Francisco 7-0.**
SF: Watters 51 pass from Young (Brien kick, 4:55. **San Francisco 14-0.**
SD: Means 1 run (Carney kick), 12:16. **San Francisco 14-7.**

**SECOND QUARTER:** SF: Floyd 5 pass from Young (Brien kick), 1:58. **San Francisco 21-7.**
SF: Watters 8 pass from Young (Brien kick), 10:16. **San Francisco 28-7.**
SD: FG Carney 31, 13:16. **San Francisco 28-10.**

**THIRD QUARTER:** SF: Watters 9 run (Brien kick), 5:25. **San Francisco 35-10.**
SF: Rice 15 pass from Young (Brien kick), 11:42. **San Francisco 42-10.**
SD: Coleman 98 kickoff return (Humphries 2-pt conv pass to Seay), 11:59. **San Francisco 42-18.**

**FOURTH QUARTER:** SF: Rice 7 pass from Young (Brien kick), 1:11. **San Francisco 49-18.**
SD: Martin 30 pass from Humphries (Humphries 2 pt-conv pass to Pupunu), 12:35. **San Francisco 49-26.**

A: 74,107.

## XXX - 1996

| | | | | |
|---|---|---|---|---|
| Dallas | 10 | 3 | 7 | 7—27 |
| Pittsburgh | 0 | 7 | 0 | 10—17 |

**FIRST QUARTER:** Dal: FG Boniol 42, 2:55. **Dallas 3-0.**
Dal: Novacek 3 pass from Aikman (Boniol kick), 9:37. **Dallas 10-0.**

**SECOND QUARTER:** Dal: FG Boniol 35, 8:57. **Dallas 13-0.**
Pitt: Thigpen 6 pass from O'Donnell (N. Johnson kick), 14:47. **Dallas 13-7.**

**THIRD QUARTER:** Dal: E. Smith 1 run (Boniol kick), 8:18. **Dallas 20-7.**

**FOURTH QUARTER:** Pitt: FG N. Johnson 46, 3:40. **Dallas 20-10.**
Pitt: Morris 1 run (N. Johnson kick), 8:24. **Dallas 20-17.**
Dal: E. Smith 4 run (Boniol kick), 11:17. **Dallas 27-17.**

A: 76,347.

## XXXI - 1997

| | | | | |
|---|---|---|---|---|
| Green Bay | 10 | 17 | 8 | 0—35 |
| New England | 14 | 0 | 7 | 0—21 |

**FIRST QUARTER:** GB: Rison 54 pass from Favre (Jacke kick), 3:32. **Green Bay 7-0.**
GB: FG Jacke 37, 6:18. **Green Bay 10-0.**
NE: Byars 1 pass from Bledsoe (Vinatieri kick), 8:25. **Green Bay 10-7.**
NE: Coates 4 pass from Bledsoe (Vinatieri kick), 12:27. **New England 14-10.**

**SECOND QUARTER:** GB: Freeman 81 pass from Favre (Jacke kick), 0:56. **Green Bay 17-14.**
GB: FG Jacke 31, 6:45. **Green Bay 20-14.**
GB: Favre 2 run (Jacke kick), 13:49. **Green Bay 27-14.**

**THIRD QUARTER:** NE: Martin 18 run (Vinatieri kick), 11:33. **Green Bay 27-21.**
GB: Howard 99 kickoff return (Favre 2 pt conv pass to Chmura), 11:50. **Green Bay 35-21.**

A: 72,301.

## XXXII - 1998

| | | | | |
|---|---|---|---|---|
| Denver | 7 | 10 | 7 | 7—31 |
| Green Bay | 7 | 7 | 3 | 7—24 |

**FIRST QUARTER:** GB: Freeman 22 pass from Favre (Longwell kick), 4:02. **Green Bay 7-0.**
Den: Davis 1 run (Elam kick), 9:21. **7-7.**

**SECOND QUARTER:** Den: Elway 1 run (Elam kick), 0:05. **Denver 14-7.**
Den: FG Elam 51, 2:39. **Denver 17-7.**
GB: Chmura 6 pass from Favre (Longwell kick), 14:48. **Denver 17-14.**

**THIRD QUARTER:** GB: FG Longwell 27, 3:01. **17-17.**
Den: Davis 1 run (Elam kick), 14:26. **Denver 24-17.**

**FOURTH QUARTER:** GB: Freeman 13 pass from Favre (Longwell kick), 1:28. **24-24.**
Den: Davis 1 run (Elam kick), 13:15. **Denver 31-24.**

A: 68,912.

### XXXIII - 1999

| | | | | |
|---|---|---|---|---|
| Denver | 7 | 10 | 0 | 17—34 |
| Atlanta | 3 | 3 | 0 | 13—19 |

**FIRST QUARTER:** Atl: FG Andersen 32, 5:25.
**Atlanta 3-0.**
Den: Griffith 1 run (Elam kick), 11:05. **Denver 7-3.**

**SECOND QUARTER:** Den: FG Elam 26, 5:43.
**Denver 10-3.**
Den: Smith 80 pass from Elway (Elam kick), 10:06.
**Denver 17-3.**
Atl: FG Andersen 28, 12:35. **Denver 17-6.**

**FOURTH QUARTER:** Den: Griffith 1 run (Elam kick), 0:04.
**Denver 24-6.**
Den: Elway 3 run (Elam kick), 3:40. **Denver 31-6.**
Atl: Dwight 94 kickoff return (Andersen kick), 3:59.
**Denver 31-13.**
Den: FG Elam 37, 7:52. **Denver 34-13.**
Atl: Mathis 3 pass from Chandler (2-pt conv failed),
12:56. **Denver 34-19.**

A: 74,803

### XXXIV - 2000

| | | | | |
|---|---|---|---|---|
| St. Louis | 3 | 6 | 7 | 7—23 |
| Tennessee | 0 | 0 | 6 | 10—16 |

**FIRST QUARTER:** StL: FG Wilkins 27, 3:00.
**St. Louis 3-0.**

**SECOND QUARTER:** StL: FG Wilkins 29, 4:16.
**St. Louis 6-0.**
StL: FG Wilkins 28, 0:15. **St. Louis 9-0.**

**THIRD QUARTER:** StL: Holt 9 pass from Warner (Wilkins
kick), 7:20. **St. Louis 16-0.**
Tenn: George 1 run (2-pt conv failed), 0:14.
**St. Louis 16-6.**

**FOURTH QUARTER:** Tenn: George 2 run (Del Greco kick),
7:21. **St. Louis 16-13.**
Tenn: FG Del Greco 43, 2:15. **16-16.**
StL: : Bruce 73 pass from Warner, 1:54. **St. Louis 23-16.**

A: 72,265

### XXXV - 2001

| | | | | |
|---|---|---|---|---|
| Baltimore | 7 | 3 | 14 | 10—34 |
| NY Giants | 0 | 0 | 7 | 0—7 |

**FIRST QUARTER:** Balt: Stokely 38 pass from Dilfer
(Stover kick), 6:50. **Baltimore 7-0.**

**SECOND QUARTER:** Balt: FG Stover 47, 1:41.
**Baltimore 10-0.**

**THIRD QUARTER:** Balt: Starks 49 int return (Stover kick),
3:49. **Baltimore 17-0.**
NYG: Dixon 97 kickoff return (Daluiso kick), 3:31.
**Baltimore 17-7.**
Balt: Je. Lewis 84 kickoff return (Stover kick), 3:13.
**Baltimore 24-7.**

**FOURTH QUARTER:** Balt: Ja. Lewis 3 run (Stover kick),
8:45. **Baltimore 31-7.**
Balt: FG Stover 34, 5:28. **Baltimore 34-7.**

A: 71,921

### XXXVI - 2002

| | | | | |
|---|---|---|---|---|
| New England | 0 | 14 | 3 | 3—20 |
| St. Louis | 3 | 0 | 0 | 14—17 |

**FIRST QUARTER:** StL: FG Wilkins 50, 3:50.
**St. Louis 3-0.**

**SECOND QUARTER:** NE: Law 47 int return (Vinatieri kick),
8:49. **New England 7-3.**
NE: Patten 8 pass from Brady (Vinatieri kick), 0:31.
**New England 14-3.**

**THIRD QUARTER:** NE: FG Vinatieri 37, 1:18.
**New England 17-3.**

**FOURTH QUARTER:** StL: Warner 2 run (Wilkins kick), 9:31.
**New England 17-10.**
StL: Proehl 26 pass from Warner (Wilkins kick),
1:30. **17-17.**
NE: FG Vinatieri 48, 0:00. **New England 20-17.**

A: 72,922

### XXXVII - 2003

| | | | | |
|---|---|---|---|---|
| Tampa Bay | 3 | 17 | 14 | 14—48 |
| Oakland | 3 | 0 | 6 | 12—21 |

**FIRST QUARTER:** Oak: FG Janikowski 40, 10:20.
**Oakland 3-0.**
TB: FG Gramatica 31, 7:51. **3-3.**

**SECOND QUARTER:** TB: FG Gramatica 43, 11:16.
**Tampa Bay 6-3.**
TB: Alstott 2 run (Gramatica kick), 6:24.
**Tampa Bay 13-3.**
TB: McCardell 5 pass from B. Johnson (Gramatica
kick), 0:30. **Tampa Bay 20-3.**

**THIRD QUARTER:** TB: McCardell 8 pass from B. Johnson
(Gramatica kick), 5:30. **Tampa Bay 27-3.**
TB: Smith 44 int. return (Gramatica kick), 4:47.
**Tampa Bay 34-3.**
Oak: Porter 39 pass from Gannon (2-pt conv failed),
2:14. **Tampa Bay 34-9.**

**FOURTH QUARTER:** Oak: Johnson 13 return of blocked
punt (two-pt. conversion failed), 14:14.
**Tampa Bay 34-15.**
Oak: Rice 48 pass from Gannon (2-pt conv failed),
6:06. **Tampa Bay 34-21.**
TB: Brooks 44 int. return (Gramatica kick), 1:18.
**Tampa Bay 41-21.**
TB: Smith 50 int. return (Gramatica kick), 0:02.
**Tampa Bay 48-21.**

A: 67,603

## XXXVIII - 2004

| | | | | | |
|---|---|---|---|---|---|
| New England | 0 | 14 | 0 | 18 | 32 |
| Carolina | 0 | 10 | 0 | 19 | 29 |

**SECOND QUARTER:** NE: Branch 5 pass from Brady (Vinatieri kick), 3:11. **New England 7–0.**

Car: Smith 39 pass from Delhomme (Kasay kick), 1:17. **7–7.**

NE: Givens 5 pass from Brady (Vinatieri kick), 0:28. **New England 14–7.**

Car: FG Kasay 50, 0:00. **New England 14–10.**

**FOURTH QUARTER:** NE: Smith 2 run (Vinatieri kick), 14:49. **New England 21–10.**

Car: Foster 33 run (2-pt conv failed), 12:49. **New England 21–16.**

Car: Muhammad 85 pass from Delhomme (2-pt conv failed), 7:13. **Carolina 22–21.**

NE: Vrabel 1 pass from Brady (Faulk ran for 2-pt conv), 2:51. **New England 29–22.**

Car: Proehl 12 pass from Delhomme (Kasay kick), 1:18. **29–29.**

NE: FG Vinatieri 41, 0:04. **New England 32–29.**

A: 71,525

## XXXIX - 2005

| | | | | | |
|---|---|---|---|---|---|
| New England | 0 | 7 | 7 | 10 | 24 |
| Philadelphia | 0 | 7 | 7 | 7 | 21 |

**SECOND QUARTER:** Phil: Smith 6 pass from McNabb (Akers kick), 10:05. **Philadelphia 7–0.**
NE: Givens 4 pass from Brady (Vinatieri kick), 1:10. **7–7.**
**THIRD QUARTER:** NE: Vrabel 2 pass from Brady (Vinatieri kick), 11:04. **New England 14–7.**
Phil: Westbrook 10 pass from McNabb (Akers kick), 3:45. **14–14.**
**FOURTH QUARTER:** NE: Dillon 2 run (Vinatieri kick), 13:44. **New England 21–14.**
NE: FG Vinatieri 22, 9:40. **New England 24–14.**
Phil: Lewis 30 pass from McNabb (Akers kick), 13:12. **New England 24–21.**

A: 78,125

## XL - 2006

| | | | | | |
|---|---|---|---|---|---|
| Pittsburgh | 0 | 7 | 7 | 7 | 21 |
| Seattle | 3 | 0 | 7 | 0 | 10 |

**FIRST QUARTER:** Sea: FG Brown 47, 0:22. **Seattle 3–0.**
**SECOND QUARTER:** Pit: Roethlisberger 1 run (Reed kick), 1:55. **Pittsburgh 7–3.**
**THIRD QUARTER:** Pit: Parker 75 run (Reed kick), 14:38. **Pittsburgh 14–3.**
Sea: Stevens 16 pass from Hasselbeck (Brown kick), 6:45. **Pittsburgh 14–10.**
**FOURTH QUARTER:** Pit: Ward 43 pass from Randle El (Reed kick), 8:56. **Pittsburgh 21–10.**

A: 68,206

## XLI - 2007

| | | | | | |
|---|---|---|---|---|---|
| Indianapolis | 6 | 10 | 6 | 7 | 29 |
| Chicago | 14 | 0 | 3 | 0 | 17 |

**FIRST QUARTER:** Chicago: TD Hester 92 kick return (Gould kick) 14:46. **Chicago 7–0.**
Indianapolis: TD Wayne 53 pass from Manning, 6:50 (Vinatieri kick failed). **Chicago 7–6.**
Chicago: TD Muhammad 4 pass from Grossman (Gould kick), 4:34. **Chicago 14–6.**
**SECOND QUARTER:** Indianapolis: FG Vinatieri 29, 11:17. **Chicago 14–9.**
Indianapolis: TD Rhodes 1 run (Vinatieri kick), 6:09. **Indianapolis 16–14.**
**THIRD QUARTER:** Indianapolis: FG Vinatieri 24, 7:26. **Indianapolis 19–14.**
Indianapolis: FG Vinatieri 20, 3:16. **Indianapolis 22–14.**
Chicago: FG Gould 44, 1:14. **Indianapolis 22-17. FOURTH QUARTER:** Indianapolis: TD Hayden 56 interception return (Vinatieri kick) 11:44. **Indianapolis 29–17.**

A: 74,512

## XLII - 2008

| | | | | | |
|---|---|---|---|---|---|
| NY Giants | 3 | 0 | 0 | 14 | 17 |
| New England | 0 | 7 | 0 | 7 | 14 |

**FIRST QUARTER:** NY Giants: FG Tynes 32, 5:01. **NY Giants 3-0.**
**SECOND QUARTER:** New England: TD Maroney 1 run (Gostkowski kick), 14:57. **New England 7-3.**
**FOURTH QUARTER:** NY Giants: TD Tyree 5 pass from Manning (Tynes kick), 11:05. **NY Giants 10-7.**
New England: TD Moss 6 pass from Brady (Gostkowski kick), 02:42. **New England 14-10.**
NY Giants: TD Burress 13 pass from Manning (Tynes kick), 00:35. **NY Giants 17-14.**

A: 71,101

## XLIII - 2009

| | | | | | |
|---|---|---|---|---|---|
| Pittsburgh | 3 | 14 | 3 | 7 | 27 |
| Arizona | 0 | 7 | 0 | 16 | 23 |

**FIRST QUARTER:** Pit: FG Reed 18, 9:45. **Pittsburgh 3-0.**
**SECOND QUARTER:** Pit: Russell 1 run (Reed kick), 14:01. **Pittsburgh 10-0.**
Ari: Patrick 1 pass from Warner (Rackers kick), 8:34. **Pittsburgh 10-7.**
Pit: Harrison 100 Int return (Rackers kick), 0:00. **Pittsburgh 17-7.**
**THIRD QUARTER:** Pit: FG Reed 21, 2:11. **Pittsburgh 20-7.**
**FOURTH QUARTER:** Ari: Fitzgerald 1 pass from Warner (Rackers kick), 7:33. **Pittsburgh 20-14.**
Ari: Safety (Hartwig offensive holding penalty in end zone), 2:58. **Pittsburgh 20-16.**
Ari: Fitzgerald 64 pass from Warner (Rackers kick), 2:37. **Arizona 23-20.**
Pit: Holmes 6 pass from Roethlisberger (Reed kick), 0:35. **Pittsburgh 27-23.**

A: 70,774

**1933**
NFL championship  Chicago Bears 23, NY Giants 21

**1934**
NFL championship  NY Giants 30, Chicago Bears 13

**1935**
NFL championship  Detroit 26, NY Giants 7

**1936**
NFL championship  Green Bay 21, Boston 6

**1937**
NFL championship  Washington 28, Chicago Bears 21

**1938**
NFL championship  NY Giants 23, Green Bay 17

**1939**
NFL championship  Green Bay 27, NY Giants 0

**1940**
NFL championship  Chicago Bears 73, Washington 0

**1941**
W. div. playoff  Chicago Bears 33, Green Bay 14
NFL championship  Chicago Bears 37, NY Giants 9

**1942**
NFL championship  Washington 14, Chicago Bears 6

**1943**
E. div. playoff  Washington 28, NY Giants 0
NFL championship  Chicago Bears 41, Washington 21

**1944**
NFL championship  Green Bay 14, NY Giants 7

**1945**
NFL championship  Cleveland 15, Washington 14

**1946**
NFL championship  Chicago Bears 24, NY Giants 14

**1947**
E. div. playoff  Philadelphia 21, Pittsburgh 0
NFL championship  Chi Cardinals 28, Philadelphia 21

**1948**
NFL championship  Philadelphia 7, Chi Cardinals 0

**1949**
NFL championship  Philadelphia 14, Los Angeles 0

**1950**
Am. Conf. playoff  Cleveland 8, NY Giants 3
Nat. Conf. playoff  Los Angeles 24, Chicago Bears 14
NFL championship  Cleveland 30, Los Angeles 28

**1951**
NFL championship  Los Angeles 24, Cleveland 17

**1952**
Nat. Conf. playoff  Detroit 31, Los Angeles 21
NFL championship  Detroit 17, Cleveland 7

**1953**
NFL championship  Detroit 17, Cleveland 16

**1954**
NFL championship  Cleveland 56, Detroit 10

**1955**
NFL championship  Cleveland 38, Los Angeles 14

**1956**
NFL championship  NY Giants 47, Chicago Bears 7

**1957**
W. Conf. playoff  Detroit 31, San Francisco 27
NFL championship  Detroit 59, Cleveland 14

**1958**
E. Conf. playoff  NY Giants 10, Cleveland 0
NFL championship  Baltimore 23, NY Giants 17

**1959**
NFL championship  Baltimore 31, NY Giants 16

**1960**
NFL championship  Philadelphia 17, Green Bay 13
AFL championship  Houston 24, LA Chargers 16

**1961**
NFL championship  Green Bay 37, NY Giants 0
AFL championship  Houston 10, San Diego 3

**1962**
NFL championship  Green Bay 16, NY Giants 7
AFL championship  Dallas Texans 20, Houston 17

**1963**
NFL championship  Chicago 14, NY Giants 10
AFL E. div. playoff  Boston 26, Buffalo 8
AFL championship  San Diego 51, Boston 10

**1964**
NFL championship  Cleveland 27, Baltimore 0
AFL championship  Buffalo 20, San Diego 7

**1965**
NFL W. Conf.  Green Bay 13, Baltimore 10
playoff
NFL championship  Green Bay 23, Cleveland 12
AFL championship  Buffalo 23, San Diego 0

**1966**
NFL championship  Green Bay 34, Dallas 27
AFL championship  Kansas City 31, Buffalo 7

**1967**
NFL E. Conf.  Dallas 52, Cleveland 14
championship
NFL W. Conf.  Green Bay 28, Los Angeles 7
championship
NFL championship  Green Bay 21, Dallas 17
AFL championship  Oakland 40, Houston 7

**1968**
NFL E. Conf.  Cleveland 31, Dallas 20
championship
NFL W. Conf.  Baltimore 24, Minnesota 14
championship
NFL championship  Baltimore 34, Cleveland 0
AFL W. div. playoff  Oakland 41, Kansas City 6
AFL championship  NY Jets 27, Oakland 23

**1969**
NFL E. Conf.  Cleveland 38, Dallas 14
championship
NFL W. Conf.  Minnesota 23, Los Angeles 20
championship
NFL championship  Minnesota 27, Cleveland 7
AFL div. playoffs  Kansas City 13, NY Jets 6
Oakland 56, Houston 7
AFL championship  Kansas City 17, Oakland 7

**1970**

| | |
|---|---|
| AFC div. playoffs | Baltimore 17, Cincinnati 0 |
| | Oakland 21, Miami 14 |
| AFC championship | Baltimore 27, Oakland 17 |
| NFC div. playoffs | Dallas 5, Detroit 0 |
| | San Francisco 17, Minnesota 14 |
| NFC championship | Dallas 17, San Francisco 10 |

**1971**

| | |
|---|---|
| AFC div. playoffs | Miami 27, Kansas City 24 |
| | Baltimore 20, Cleveland 3 |
| AFC championship | Miami 21, Baltimore 0 |
| NFC div. playoffs | Dallas 20, Minnesota 12 |
| | San Francisco 24, Washington 20 |
| NFC championship | Dallas 14, San Francisco 3 |

**1972**

| | |
|---|---|
| AFC div. playoffs | Pittsburgh 13, Oakland 7 |
| | Miami 20, Cleveland 14 |
| AFC championship | Miami 21, Pittsburgh 17 |
| NFC div. playoffs | Dallas 30, San Francisco 28 |
| | Washington 16, Green Bay 3 |
| NFC championship | Washington 26, Dallas 3 |

**1973**

| | |
|---|---|
| AFC div. playoffs | Oakland 33, Pittsburgh 14 |
| | Miami 34, Cincinnati 16 |
| AFC championship | Miami 27, Oakland 10 |
| NFC div. playoffs | Minnesota 27, Washington 20 |
| | Dallas 27, Los Angeles 16 |
| NFC championship | Minnesota 27, Dallas 10 |

**1974**

| | |
|---|---|
| AFC div. playoffs | Oakland 28, Miami 26 |
| | Pittsburgh 32, Buffalo 14 |
| AFC championship | Pittsburgh 24, Oakland 13 |
| NFC div. playoffs | Minnesota 30, St Louis 14 |
| | Los Angeles 19, Washington 10 |
| NFC championship | Minnesota 14, Los Angeles 10 |

**1975**

| | |
|---|---|
| AFC div. playoffs | Pittsburgh 28, Baltimore 10 |
| | Oakland 31, Cincinnati 28 |
| AFC championship | Pittsburgh 16, Oakland 10 |
| NFC div. playoffs | Los Angeles 35, St Louis 23 |
| | Dallas 17, Minnesota 14 |
| NFC championship | Dallas 37, Los Angeles 7 |

**1976**

| | |
|---|---|
| AFC div. playoffs | Oakland 24, New England 21 |
| | Pittsburgh 40, Baltimore 14 |
| AFC championship | Oakland 24, Pittsburgh 7 |
| NFC div. playoffs | Minnesota 35, Washington 20 |
| | Los Angeles 14, Dallas 12 |
| NFC championship | Minnesota 24, Los Angeles 13 |

**1977**

| | |
|---|---|
| AFC div. playoffs | Denver 34, Pittsburgh 21 |
| | Oakland 37, Baltimore 31 |
| AFC championship | Denver 20, Oakland 17 |
| NFC div. playoffs | Dallas 37, Chicago 7 |
| | Minnesota 14, Los Angeles 7 |
| NFC championship | Dallas 23, Minnesota 6 |

**1978**

| | |
|---|---|
| AFC 1st-rd. playoff | Houston 17, Miami 9 |
| AFC div. playoffs | Houston 31, New England 14 |
| | Pittsburgh 33, Denver 10 |
| AFC championship | Pittsburgh 34, Houston 5 |
| NFC 1st-rd. playoff | Atlanta 14, Philadelphia 13 |
| NFC div. playoffs | Dallas 27, Atlanta 20 |
| | Los Angeles 34, Minnesota 10 |
| NFC championship | Dallas 28, Los Angeles 0 |

**1979**

| | |
|---|---|
| AFC 1st-rd. playoff | Houston 13, Denver 7 |
| AFC div. playoffs | Houston 17, San Diego 14 |
| | Pittsburgh 34, Miami 14 |
| AFC championship | Pittsburgh 27, Houston 13 |
| NFC 1st-rd. playoff | Philadelphia 27, Chicago 17 |
| NFC div. playoffs | Tampa Bay 24, Philadelphia 17 |
| | Los Angeles 21, Dallas 19 |
| NFC championship | Los Angeles 9, Tampa Bay 0 |

**1980**

| | |
|---|---|
| AFC 1st-rd. playoff | Oakland 27, Houston 7 |
| AFC div. playoffs | San Diego 20, Buffalo 14 |
| | Oakland 14, Cleveland 12 |
| AFC championship | Oakland 34, San Diego 27 |
| NFC 1st-rd. playoff | Dallas 34, Los Angeles 13 |
| NFC div. playoffs | Philadelphia 31, Minnesota 16 |
| | Dallas 30, Atlanta 27 |
| NFC championship | Philadelphia 20, Dallas 7 |

**1981**

| | |
|---|---|
| AFC 1st-rd. playoff | Buffalo 31, NY Jets 27 |
| AFC div. playoffs | San Diego 41, Miami 38 |
| | Cincinnati 28, Buffalo 21 |
| AFC championship | Cincinnati 27, San Diego 7 |
| NFC 1st-rd. playoff | NY Giants 27, Philadelphia 21 |
| NFC div. playoffs | Dallas 38, Tampa Bay 0 |
| | San Francisco 38, NY Giants 24 |
| NFC championship | San Francisco 28, Dallas 27 |

**1982**

| | |
|---|---|
| AFC 1st-rd. playoffs | Miami 28, New England 13 |
| | LA Raiders 27, Cleveland 10 |
| | NY Jets 44, Cincinnati 17 |
| | San Diego 31, Pittsburgh 28 |
| AFC div. playoffs | NY Jets 17, LA Raiders 14 |
| | Miami 34, San Diego 13 |
| AFC championship | Miami 14, NY Jets 0 |
| NFC 1st-rd. playoffs | Washington 31, Detroit 7 |
| | Green Bay 41, St Louis 16 |
| | Minnesota 30, Atlanta 24 |
| | Dallas 30, Tampa Bay 17 |
| NFC div. playoffs | Washington 21, Minnesota 7 |
| | Dallas 37, Green Bay 26 |
| NFC championship | Washington 31, Dallas 17 |

**1983**

| | |
|---|---|
| AFC 1st-rd. playoff | Seattle 31, Denver 7 |
| AFC div. playoffs | Seattle 27, Miami 20 |
| | LA Raiders 38, Pittsburgh 10 |
| AFC championship | LA Raiders 30, Seattle 14 |
| NFC 1st-rd. playoff | LA Rams 24, Dallas 17 |
| NFC div. playoffs | San Francisco 24, Detroit 23 |
| | Washington 51, LA Rams 7 |
| NFC championship | Washington 24, San Francisco 21 |

**1984**

| | |
|---|---|
| AFC 1st-rd. playoff | Seattle 13, LA Raiders 7 |
| AFC div. playoffs | Miami 31, Seattle 10 |
| | Pittsburgh 24, Denver 17 |
| AFC championship | Miami 45, Pittsburgh 28 |
| NFC 1st-rd. playoff | NY Giants 16, LA Rams 13 |
| NFC div. playoffs | San Francisco 21, NY Giants 10 |
| | Chicago 23, Washington 19 |
| NFC championship | San Francisco 23, Chicago 0 |

**1985**

| | |
|---|---|
| AFC 1st-rd. playoff | New England 26, NY Jets 14 |
| AFC div. playoffs | Miami 24, Cleveland 21 |
| | New England 27, LA Raiders 20 |
| AFC championship | New England 31, Miami 14 |
| NFC 1st-rd. playoff | NY Giants 17, San Francisco 3 |
| NFC div. playoffs | LA Rams 20, Dallas 0 |
| | Chicago 21, NY Giants 0 |
| NFC championship | Chicago 24, LA Rams 0 |

## 1986

| | |
|---|---|
| AFC 1st-rd. playoff | NY Jets 35, Kansas City 15 |
| AFC div. playoffs | Cleveland 23, NY Jets 20 |
| | Denver 22, New England 17 |
| AFC championship | Denver 23, Cleveland 20 |
| NFC 1st-rd. playoff | Washington 19, LA Rams 7 |
| NFC div playoffs | Washington 27, Chicago 13 |
| | NY Giants 49, San Francisco 3 |
| NFC championship | NY Giants 17, Washington 0 |

## 1987

| | |
|---|---|
| AFC 1st-rd. playoff | Houston 23, Seattle 20 |
| AFC div. playoffs | Cleveland 38, Indianapolis 21 |
| | Denver 34, Houston 10 |
| AFC championship | Denver 38, Cleveland 33 |
| NFC 1st-rd. playoff | Minnesota 44, New Orleans 10 |
| NFC div playoffs | Minnesota 36, San Francisco 24 |
| | Washington 21, Chicago 17 |
| NFC championship | Washington 17, Minnesota 10 |

## 1988

| | |
|---|---|
| AFC 1st-rd. playoff | Houston 24, Cleveland 23 |
| AFC div. playoffs | Cincinnati 21, Seattle 13 |
| | Buffalo 17, Houston 10 |
| AFC championship | Cincinnati 21, Buffalo 10 |
| NFC 1st-rd. playoff | Minnesota 28, LA Rams 17 |
| NFC div. playoffs | Chicago 20, Philadelphia 12 |
| | San Francisco 34, Minnesota 9 |
| NFC championship | San Francisco 28, Chicago 3 |

## 1989

| | |
|---|---|
| AFC 1st-rd. playoff | Pittsburgh 26, Houston 23 |
| AFC div. playoffs | Cleveland 34, Buffalo 30 |
| | Denver 24, Pittsburgh 23 |
| AFC championship | Denver 37, Cleveland 21 |
| NFC 1st-rd. playoff | LA Rams 21, Philadelphia 7 |
| NFC div. playoffs | LA Rams 19, NY Giants 13 |
| | San Francisco 41, Minnesota 13 |
| NFC championship | San Francisco 30, LA Rams 3 |

## 1990

| | |
|---|---|
| AFC 1st-rd. playoffs | Miami 17, Kansas City 16 |
| | Cincinnati 41, Houston 14 |
| AFC div. playoffs | Buffalo 44, Miami 34 |
| | LA Raiders 20, Cincinnati 10 |
| AFC championship | Buffalo 51, LA Raiders 3 |
| NFC 1st-rd. playoffs | Chicago 16, New Orleans 6 |
| NFC 1st-rd playoffs | Washington 20, Philadelphia 6 |
| NFC div. playoffs | NY Giants 31, Chicago 3 |
| | San Francisco 28, Washington 10 |
| NFC championship | NY Giants 15, San Francisco 13 |

## 1991

| | |
|---|---|
| AFC 1st-rd. playoffs | Houston 17, NY Jets 10 |
| | Kansas City 10, LA Raiders 6 |
| AFC div. playoffs | Denver 26, Houston 24 |
| | Buffalo 37, Kansas City 14 |
| AFC championship | Buffalo 10, Denver 7 |
| NFC 1st-rd. playoffs | Atlanta 27, New Orleans 20 |
| | Dallas 17, Chicago 13 |
| NFC div. playoffs | Washington 24, Atlanta 7 |
| | Detroit 38, Dallas 6 |
| NFC championship | Washington 41, Detroit 10 |

## 1992

| | |
|---|---|
| AFC 1st-rd. playoffs | San Diego 17, Kansas City 0 |
| | Buffalo 41, Houston 38 (OT) |
| AFC div. playoffs | Buffalo 24, Pittsburgh 3 |
| | Miami 31, San Diego 0 |
| AFC championship | Buffalo 29, Miami 10 |
| NFC 1st-rd. playoffs | Washington 24, Minnesota 7 |
| | Philadelphia 36, New Orleans 20 |
| NFC div. playoffs | San Francisco 20, Washington 13 |
| | Dallas 34, Philadelphia 10 |
| NFC championship | Dallas 30, San Francisco 20 |

## 1993

| | |
|---|---|
| AFC 1st-rd. playoffs | LA Raiders 42, Denver 24 |
| | Kansas City 27, Pittsburgh 24 (OT) |
| AFC div. playoffs | Buffalo 29, LA Raiders 23 |
| | Kansas City 28, Houston 20 |
| AFC championship | Buffalo 30, Kansas City 13 |
| NFC 1st-rd. playoffs | NY Giants 17, Minnesota 10 |
| | Green Bay 28, Detroit 24 |
| NFC div. playoffs | San Francisco 44, NY Giants 3 |
| | Dallas 27, Green Bay 17 |
| NFC championship | Dallas 38, San Francisco 21 |

## 1994

| | |
|---|---|
| AFC 1st-rd. playoffs | Miami 27, Kansas City 17 |
| | Cleveland 20, New England 13 |
| AFC div. playoffs | San Diego 22, Miami 21 |
| | Pittsburgh 29, Cleveland 9 |
| AFC championship | San Diego 17, Pittsburgh 13 |
| NFC 1st-rd. playoffs | Green Bay 16, Detroit 12 |
| | Chicago 35, Minnesota 18 |
| NFC div. playoffs | Dallas 35, Green Bay 9 |
| | San Francisco 44, Chicago 15 |
| NFC championship | San Francisco 38, Dallas 28 |

## 1995

| | |
|---|---|
| AFC 1st-rd. playoffs | Buffalo 37, Miami 22 |
| | Indianapolis 35, San Diego 20 |
| AFC div. playoffs | Pittsburgh 40, Buffalo 21 |
| | Indianapolis 10, Kansas City 7 |
| AFC championship | Pittsburgh 20, Indianapolis 16 |
| NFC 1st-rd. playoffs | Philadelphia 58, Detroit 37 |
| | Green Bay 37, Atlanta 20 |
| NFC div. playoffs | Dallas 30, Philadelphia 11 |
| | Green Bay 27, San Francisco 17 |
| NFC championship | Dallas 38, Green Bay 27 |

## 1996

| | |
|---|---|
| AFC 1st-rd. playoffs | Jacksonville 30, Buffalo 27 |
| | Pittsburgh 42, Indianapolis 14 |
| AFC div. playoffs | Jacksonville 30, Denver 27 |
| | New England 28, Pittsburgh 3 |
| AFC championship | New England 20, Jacksonville 6 |
| NFC 1st-rd. playoffs | Dallas 40, Minnesota 15 |
| | San Francisco 14, Philadelphia 0 |
| NFC div. playoffs | Green Bay 35, San Francisco 14 |
| | Carolina 26, Dallas 17 |
| NFC championship | Green Bay 30, Carolina 13 |

## 1997

| | |
|---|---|
| AFC 1st-rd. playoffs | Denver 42, Jacksonville 17 |
| | New England 17, Miami 3 |
| AFC div. playoffs | Denver 14, Kansas City 0 |
| | Pittsburgh 7, New England 6 |
| AFC championship | Denver 24, Pittsburgh 21 |
| NFC 1st-rd. playoffs | Minnesota 23, NY Giants 22 |
| | Tampa Bay 20, Detroit 10 |
| NFC div. playoffs | Green Bay 21, Tampa Bay 7 |
| | San Francisco 38, Minnesota 22 |
| NFC championship | Green Bay 23, San Francisco 10 |

## 1998

| | |
|---|---|
| AFC 1st-rd. playoffs | Miami 24, Buffalo 17 |
| | Jacksonville 25, New England 10 |
| AFC div. playoffs | Denver 38, Miami 3 |
| | NY Jets 34, Jacksonville 24 |
| AFC championship | Denver 23, NY Jets 10 |
| NFC 1st-rd. playoffs | Arizona 20, Dallas 7 |
| | San Francisco 30, Green Bay 27 |
| NFC div. playoffs | Atlanta 20, San Francisco 18 |
| | Minnesota 41, Arizona 21 |
| NFC championship | Atlanta 30, Minnesota 27 (OT) |

### 1999

AFC 1st-rd. playoffs  Tennessee 22, Buffalo 16
 Miami 20, Seattle 17
AFC div. playoffs  Jacksonville 62, Miami 7
 Tennessee 19, Indianapolis 16
AFC championship  Tennessee 33, Jacksonville 14
NFC 1st-rd. playoffs  Washington 27, Detroit 13
 Minnesota 27, Dallas 10
NFC div. playoffs  Tampa Bay 14, Washington 13
 St Louis 49, Minnesota 37
NFC championship  St Louis 11, Tampa Bay 6

### 2000

AFC 1st-rd. playoffs  Baltimore 21, Denver 3
 Miami 23, Indianapolis 17 (OT)
AFC div. playoffs  Baltimore 24, Tennessee 10
 Oakland 27, Miami 0
AFC championship  Baltimore 16, Oakland 3
NFC 1st-rd. playoffs  New Orleans 31, St. Louis 28
 Philadelphia 21, Tampa Bay 3
NFC div. playoffs  NY Giants 20, Philadelphia 10
 Minnesota 34, New Orleans 16
NFC championship  NY Giants 41, Minnesota 0

### 2001

AFC 1st-rd. playoffs  Oakland 38, NY Jets 24
 Baltimore 20, Miami 3
AFC div. playoffs  New England 16, Oakland 13(OT)
 Pittsburgh 27, Baltimore 10
AFC championship  New England 24, Pittsburgh 17
NFC 1st-rd. playoffs  Philadelphia 31, Tampa Bay 9
 Green Bay 25, San Francisco 15
NFC div. playoffs  Philadelphia 33, Chicago 19
 St. Louis 45, Green Bay 17
NFC championship  St. Louis 29, Philadelphia 24

### 2002

AFC 1st-rd. playoffs  NY Jets 41, Indianapolis 0
 Pittsburgh 36, Cleveland 33
AFC div. playoffs  Tennessee 34, Pittsburgh 31 (OT)
 Oakland 30, NY Jets 10
AFC championship  Oakland 41, Tennessee 24
NFC 1st-rd. playoffs  Atlanta 27, Green Bay 7
 San Francisco 39, NY Giants 38
NFC div. playoffs  Philadelphia 20, Atlanta 6
 Tampa Bay 31, San Francisco 6
NFC championship  Tampa Bay 27, Philadelphia 10

### 2003

AFC 1st-rd. playoffs  Tennessee 20, Baltimore 17
 Indianapolis 41, Denver 10
AFC div. playoffs  New England 17, Tennessee 14
 Indianapolis 38, Kansas City 31
AFC championship  New England 24, Indianapolis 14
NFC 1st-rd. playoffs  Carolina 29, Dallas 10
 Green Bay 37, Seattle 31 (OT)
NFC div. playoffs  Carolina 29, St. Louis 23
 Philadelphia 20, Green Bay 17 (OT)
NFC championship  Carolina 14, Philadelphia 3

### 2004

AFC 1st-rd. playoffs  Indianapolis 49, Denver 24
 NY Jets 20, San Diego 17
AFC div. playoffs  New England 20, Indianapolis 3
 Pittsburgh 20, NY Jets 17
AFC championship  New England 41, Pittsburgh 27
NFC 1st-rd. playoffs  Minnesota 31, Green Bay 17
 St. Louis 27, Seattle 20
NFC div. playoffs  Atlanta 47, St. Louis 17
 Philadelphia 27, Minnesota 14
NFC championship  Philadelphia 27, Atlanta 10

### 2005

AFC 1st-rd. playoffs  Pittsburgh 31, Cincinnati 17
 New England 28, Jacksonville 3
AFC div. playoffs  Pittsburgh 21, Indianapolis 18
 Denver 27, New England 13
AFC championship  Pittsburgh 34, Denver 17
NFC 1st-rd. playoffs  Washington 17, Tampa Bay 10
 Carolina 23, NY Giants 0
NFC div. playoffs  Seattle 20, Washington 10
 Carolina 29, Chicago 21
NFC championship  Seattle 34, Carolina 14

### 2006

AFC 1st-rd. playoffs  Indianapolis 23, Kansas City 8
 New England 37, NY Jets 16
AFC div. playoffs  Indianapolis 15, Baltimore 6
 New England 24, San Diego 21
AFC championship  Indianapolis 38, New England 34
NFC 1st-rd. playoffs  Seattle 21, Dallas 20
 Philadelphia 23, NY Giants 20
NFC div. playoffs  Chicago 27, Seattle 24
 New Orleans 27, Philadelphia 24
NFC championship  Chicago 39, New Orleans 14

### 2007

AFC 1st-rd. playoffs  Jacksonville 31, Pittsburgh 29
 San Diego 17, Tennessee 6
AFC Div. Playoffs  New England 31, Jacksonville 20
 San Diego 28, Indianapolis 24
AFC Championship  New England 21, San Diego 12
NFC 1st-rd. playoffs  Seattle 35, Washington 14
 NY Giants 24, Tampa Bay 14
NFC Div. Playoffs  NY Giants 21, Dallas 17
 Green Bay 42, Seattle 20
NFC Championship  NY Giants 23, Green Bay 20 (OT)

### 2008

AFC 1st-rd. playoffs  Baltimore 27, Miami 9
 San Diego 23, Indianapolis 17 (OT)
AFC Div. Playoffs  Baltimore 13, Tennessee 10
 Pittsburgh 35, San Diego 24
AFC Championship  Pittsburgh 23, Baltimore 14
NFC 1st-rd. playoffs  Philadelphia 26, Minnesota 14
 Arizona 30, Atlanta 24
NFC Div. Playoffs  Philadelphia 23, NY Giants 11
 Arizona 33, Carolina 13
NFC Championship  Arizona 32, Philadelphia 25

## Career Leaders

### Scoring

| | Yrs | TD | FG | PAT | Pts |
|---|---|---|---|---|---|
| Morten Andersen | 25 | 0 | 565 | 849 | 2,544 |
| Gary Anderson | 23 | 0 | 538 | 820 | 2,434 |
| George Blanda | 26 | 9 | 335 | 943 | 2,002 |
| †John Carney | 20 | 0 | 460 | 575 | 1,955 |
| †Matt Stover | 19 | 0 | 462 | 558 | 1,944 |
| †Jason Elam | 16 | 0 | 424 | 643 | 1,915 |
| †Jason Hanson | 17 | 0 | 406 | 529 | 1,747 |
| Norm Johnson | 18 | 0 | 366 | 638 | 1,736 |
| Nick Lowery | 18 | 0 | 383 | 562 | 1,711 |
| Jan Stenerud | 19 | 0 | 373 | 580 | 1,699 |
| †John Kasay | 16 | 0 | 386 | 476 | 1,634 |
| Lou Groza | 21 | 1 | 264 | 810 | 1,608 |
| Eddie Murray | 19 | 0 | 352 | 538 | 1,594 |
| Al Del Greco | 17 | 0 | 347 | 543 | 1,584 |
| †Adam Vinatieri | 13 | 0 | 331 | 497 | 1,492 |
| Steve Christie | 15 | 0 | 336 | 468 | 1,476 |

### Rushing

| | Yrs | Att | Yds | Avg | Lg | TD |
|---|---|---|---|---|---|---|
| Emmitt Smith | 15 | 4,409 | 18,355 | 4.2 | 75 | 164 |
| Walter Payton | 13 | 3,838 | 16,726 | 4.4 | 76 | 110 |
| Barry Sanders | 10 | 3,062 | 15,269 | 5.0 | 85 | 99 |
| Curtis Martin | 11 | 3,518 | 14,101 | 4.0 | 70 | 90 |
| Jerome Bettis | 13 | 3,479 | 13,662 | 3.9 | 71 | 91 |
| Eric Dickerson | 11 | 2,996 | 13,259 | 4.4 | 85 | 90 |
| Tony Dorsett | 12 | 2,936 | 12,739 | 4.3 | 99 | 77 |
| Jim Brown | 9 | 2,359 | 12,312 | 5.2 | 80 | 106 |
| Marshall Faulk | 12 | 2,836 | 12,279 | 4.3 | 71 | 100 |
| Marcus Allen | 16 | 3,022 | 12,243 | 4.1 | 61 | 123 |
| †Edgerrin James | 10 | 2,982 | 12,121 | 4.1 | 72 | 80 |
| Franco Harris | 13 | 2,949 | 12,120 | 4.1 | 75 | 91 |
| Thurman Thomas | 13 | 2,877 | 12,074 | 4.2 | 80 | 66 |
| †LaD. Tomlinson | 8 | 2,657 | 11,760 | 4.4 | 85 | 126 |
| John Riggins | 14 | 2,916 | 11,352 | 3.9 | 66 | 104 |
| †Fred Taylor | 11 | 2,428 | 11,271 | 4.6 | 80 | 62 |

### Touchdowns

| | Yrs | Rush | Rec | Ret | Total TD |
|---|---|---|---|---|---|
| Jerry Rice | 20 | 10 | 197 | 0 | 207 |
| Emmitt Smith | 15 | 164 | 11 | 0 | 175 |
| Marcus Allen | 16 | 123 | 21 | 0 | 144 |
| †Terrell Owens | 13 | 2 | 139 | 0 | 141 |
| †LaDainian Tomlinson | 8 | 126 | 15 | 0 | 141 |
| Marshall Faulk | 12 | 100 | 36 | 0 | 136 |
| †Randy Moss | 11 | 0 | 135 | 1 | 136 |
| Cris Carter | 16 | 0 | 130 | 0 | 130 |
| Jim Brown | 9 | 106 | 20 | 0 | 126 |
| Walter Payton | 13 | 110 | 15 | 0 | 125 |

| | Yrs | Rush | Rec | Ret | Total TD |
|---|---|---|---|---|---|
| †Marvin Harrison | 13 | 0 | 128 | 0 | 128 |
| John Riggins | 14 | 104 | 12 | 0 | 116 |
| Lenny Moore | 12 | 63 | 48 | 1 | 112 |
| †Shaun Alexander | 9 | 100 | 12 | 0 | 112 |
| Barry Sanders | 10 | 99 | 10 | 0 | 109 |
| Tim Brown | 17 | 1 | 100 | 4 | 105 |
| Don Hutson | 11 | 3 | 99 | 0 | 102 |
| Steve Largent | 14 | 1 | 100 | 0 | 101 |
| Curtis Martin | 12 | 90 | 10 | 0 | 100 |
| Franco Harris | 13 | 91 | 9 | 0 | 100 |

### Combined Yards Gained

| | Yrs | Total | Rush | Rec | Int Ret | Punt Ret | Kickoff Ret | Fum Ret |
|---|---|---|---|---|---|---|---|---|
| Jerry Rice | 20 | 23,546 | 645 | 22,895 | 0 | 0 | 6 | 0 |
| Brian Mitchell | 14 | 23,330 | 1,967 | 2,336 | 0 | 4,999 | 14,014 | 14 |
| Walter Payton | 13 | 21,803 | 16,726 | 4,538 | 0 | 0 | 539 | 0 |
| Emmitt Smith | 15 | 21,583 | 18,355 | 3,224 | 0 | 0 | 0 | 4 |
| Tim Brown | 17 | 19,682 | 190 | 14,934 | 0 | 3,320 | 1,235 | 3 |
| Marshall Faulk | 12 | 19,154 | 12,279 | 6,875 | 0 | 0 | 18 | 18 |
| Barry Sanders | 10 | 18,308 | 15,269 | 2,921 | 0 | 0 | 118 | 0 |
| Herschel Walker | 12 | 18,168 | 8,225 | 4,859 | 0 | 0 | 5,084 | 0 |
| Marcus Allen | 16 | 17,654 | 12,243 | 5,411 | 0 | 0 | 0 | 0 |
| Curtis Martin | 11 | 17,430 | 14,101 | 3,329 | 0 | 0 | 0 | 0 |
| Tiki Barber | 10 | 17,359 | 10,449 | 5,183 | 0 | 1,181 | 544 | 2 |
| Eric Metcalf | 13 | 17,230 | 2,392 | 5,572 | 0 | 3,453 | 5,813 | 0 |
| Thurman Thomas | 13 | 16,532 | 12,074 | 4,458 | 0 | 0 | 0 | 0 |
| Tony Dorsett | 12 | 16,293 | 12,739 | 3,554 | 0 | 0 | 0 | 0 |
| Henry Ellard | 16 | 15,718 | 50 | 13,777 | 0 | 1,527 | 364 | 0 |

†-Active in 2008.

## Career Leaders (Cont.)

### Passing

#### PASSER RATING*

| | Yrs | Att | Comp | Pct Comp | Yds | Avg Gain | TD | Pct TD | Int | Pct Int | Rating Pts |
|---|---|---|---|---|---|---|---|---|---|---|---|
| Steve Young | 15 | 4,149 | 2,667 | 64.3 | 33,124 | 8.0 | 232 | 5.6 | 107 | 2.6 | 96.8 |
| †Peyton Manning | 11 | 5,960 | 3,839 | 64.4 | 45,628 | 7.7 | 333 | 5.6 | 165 | 2.8 | 94.7 |
| †Kurt Warner | 11 | 3,557 | 2,327 | 65.4 | 28,891 | 8.0 | 182 | 5.1 | 114 | 3.2 | 93.8 |
| †Tom Brady | 9 | 3,653 | 2,301 | 63.0 | 26,446 | 7.2 | 197 | 5.4 | 86 | 2.4 | 92.9 |
| Joe Montana | 15 | 5,391 | 3,409 | 63.2 | 40,551 | 7.5 | 273 | 5.2 | 139 | 2.6 | 92.3 |
| †Chad Pennington | 9 | 2,395 | 1,580 | 66.0 | 17,391 | 7.3 | 101 | 4.2 | 62 | 2.6 | 90.6 |
| †Drew Brees | 8 | 3,650 | 2,334 | 63.9 | 26,258 | 7.2 | 168 | 4.6 | 99 | 2.7 | 89.4 |
| †Ben Roethlisberger | 5 | 1,905 | 1,189 | 62.4 | 14,974 | 7.9 | 101 | 5.3 | 69 | 3.6 | 89.4 |
| †Daunte Culpepper | 10 | 3,042 | 1,927 | 63.3 | 23,208 | 7.6 | 146 | 4.8 | 100 | 3.3 | 89.0 |
| †Carson Palmer | 6 | 2,165 | 1,380 | 63.7 | 15,630 | 7.2 | 107 | 4.9 | 67 | 3.1 | 88.9 |
| †Jeff Garcia | 10 | 3,676 | 2,264 | 61.6 | 25,537 | 6.9 | 161 | 4.4 | 83 | 2.3 | 87.5 |
| Dan Marino | 17 | 8,358 | 4,967 | 59.4 | 61,361 | 7.3 | 420 | 5.0 | 252 | 3.0 | 86.4 |
| †Trent Green | 15 | 3,740 | 2,266 | 60.6 | 28,475 | 7.6 | 162 | 4.3 | 114 | 3.0 | 86.0 |
| †Donovan McNabb | 10 | 4,303 | 2,534 | 58.9 | 29,320 | 6.8 | 194 | 4.5 | 90 | 2.1 | 85.9 |
| †Marc Bulger | 8 | 2,924 | 1,829 | 62.6 | 21,345 | 7.3 | 117 | 4.0 | 80 | 3.0 | 85.6 |
| †Brett Favre | 18 | 9,280 | 5,720 | 61.6 | 65,127 | 7.0 | 464 | 5.0 | 310 | 3.3 | 85.4 |
| †Jake Delhomme | 10 | 2,434 | 1,452 | 59.7 | 17,877 | 7.3 | 115 | 4.7 | 76 | 3.1 | 85.1 |
| Rich Gannon | 18 | 4,206 | 2,533 | 60.2 | 28,743 | 6.8 | 180 | 4.3 | 104 | 2.3 | 84.7 |
| †Matt Hasselbeck | 10 | 3,347 | 2,013 | 60.1 | 23,549 | 7.0 | 147 | 4.4 | 94 | 2.8 | 84.5 |
| Jim Kelly | 11 | 4,779 | 2,874 | 60.1 | 35,467 | 7.4 | 237 | 5.0 | 175 | 3.7 | 84.4 |
| †Mark Brunell | 16 | 4,594 | 2,738 | 59.6 | 31,826 | 6.9 | 182 | 4.0 | 106 | 2.3 | 84.2 |
| Roger Staubach | 11 | 2,958 | 1,685 | 57.0 | 22,700 | 7.7 | 153 | 5.2 | 109 | 3.7 | 83.4 |
| Steve McNair | 13 | 4,544 | 2,733 | 60.1 | 31,304 | 6.9 | 174 | 3.8 | 119 | 2.6 | 82.8 |

*1,500 or more attempts. The passer ratings are based on performance standards established for completion percentage, interception percentage, touchdown percentage and average gain. Passers are allocated points according to how their marks compare with those standards.

### YARDS

| | Yrs | Att | Comp | Pct Comp | Yds | | Yrs | Att | Comp | Pct Comp | Yds |
|---|---|---|---|---|---|---|---|---|---|---|---|
| †Brett Favre | 18 | 9,280 | 5,720 | 61.6 | 65,127 | Boomer Esiason | 14 | 5,205 | 2,969 | 57.0 | 37,920 |
| Dan Marino | 17 | 8,358 | 4,967 | 59.4 | 61,361 | †Kerry Collins | 14 | 5,669 | 3,160 | 55.7 | 37,393 |
| John Elway | 16 | 7,250 | 4,123 | 56.9 | 51,475 | Jim Kelly | 11 | 4,779 | 2,874 | 60.1 | 35,467 |
| Warren Moon | 17 | 6,823 | 3,988 | 58.5 | 49,325 | Jim Everett | 12 | 4,923 | 2,841 | 57.7 | 34,837 |
| Fran Tarkenton | 18 | 6,467 | 3,686 | 57.0 | 47,003 | Jim Hart | 19 | 5,076 | 2,593 | 51.1 | 34,665 |
| Vinny Testaverde | 21 | 6,701 | 3,787 | 56.5 | 46,233 | Steve DeBerg | 17 | 4,746 | 2,924 | 61.6 | 34,241 |
| †Peyton Manning | 11 | 5,960 | 3,839 | 64.4 | 45,628 | John Hadl | 16 | 4,687 | 2,363 | 50.4 | 33,503 |
| Drew Bledsoe | 14 | 6,717 | 3,839 | 57.2 | 44,611 | Phil Simms | 14 | 4,647 | 2,576 | 55.4 | 33,462 |
| Dan Fouts | 15 | 5,604 | 3,297 | 58.8 | 43,040 | Steve Young | 15 | 4,149 | 2,667 | 64.3 | 33,124 |
| Joe Montana | 15 | 5,391 | 3,409 | 63.2 | 40,551 | *Y.A. Tittle | 17 | 4,395 | 2,427 | 55.2 | 33,070 |
| Johnny Unitas | 18 | 5,186 | 2,830 | 54.6 | 40,239 | Troy Aikman | 12 | 4,715 | 2,898 | 61.5 | 32,942 |
| Dave Krieg | 19 | 5,311 | 3,105 | 58.5 | 38,147 | Ken Anderson | 16 | 4,475 | 2,654 | 59.3 | 32,838 |

### TOUCHDOWNS

| | No. | | No. | | No. |
|---|---|---|---|---|---|
| †Brett Favre | 464 | Dan Fouts | 254 | Jim Hart | 209 |
| Dan Marino | 420 | Drew Bledsoe | 251 | Randall Cunningham | 207 |
| Fran Tarkenton | 342 | Boomer Esiason | 247 | Jim Everett | 203 |
| †Peyton Manning | 333 | John Hadl | 244 | Roman Gabriel | 201 |
| John Elway | 300 | *Y.A. Tittle | 242 | Phil Simms | 199 |
| Warren Moon | 291 | Len Dawson | 239 | Ken Anderson | 197 |
| Johnny Unitas | 290 | Jim Kelly | 237 | †Tom Brady | 197 |
| Vinny Testaverde | 275 | George Blanda | 236 | Joe Ferguson | 196 |
| Joe Montana | 273 | Steve Young | 232 | Bobby Layne | 196 |
| Dave Krieg | 261 | John Brodie | 214 | Norm Snead | 196 |
| Sonny Jurgensen | 255 | Terry Bradshaw | 212 | Steve DeBerg | 196 |

* Includes 4,731 passing yards and 30 TDs with Baltimore Colts (1948–49) in All-American Football Conference.
† Active in 2008.

## Career Leaders *(Cont.)*

### Receiving

#### RECEPTIONS

| | Yrs | No. | Yds | Avg | Lg | TD | | Yrs | No. | Yds | Avg | Lg | TD |
|---|---|---|---|---|---|---|---|---|---|---|---|---|---|
| Jerry Rice | 20 | 1,549 | 22,895 | 14.8 | 96 | 197 | †Randy Moss | 11 | 843 | 13,201 | 15.7 | 82 | 135 |
| †Marvin Harrison | 12 | 1,102 | 14,580 | 13.2 | 80 | 128 | Larry Centers | 14 | 827 | 6,797 | 8.2 | 54 | 28 |
| Cris Carter | 16 | 1,101 | 13,899 | 12.6 | 80 | 130 | Steve Largent | 14 | 819 | 13,089 | 16.0 | 74 | 100 |
| Tim Brown | 17 | 1,094 | 14,934 | 13.7 | 80 | 100 | Shannon Sharpe | 15 | 815 | 10,060 | 12.3 | 82 | 62 |
| †Isaac Bruce | 15 | 1,003 | 14,944 | 14.9 | 80 | 91 | Henry Ellard | 16 | 814 | 13,777 | 16.9 | 81 | 65 |
| †Terrell Owens | 13 | 951 | 14,122 | 14.8 | 91 | 139 | Keyshawn Johnson | 11 | 814 | 10,571 | 13.0 | 76 | 64 |
| Andre Reed | 16 | 951 | 13,198 | 13.9 | 83 | 87 | †Muhsin Muhammad | 13 | 807 | 10,857 | 13.5 | 72 | 61 |
| Art Monk | 16 | 940 | 12,721 | 13.5 | 79 | 68 | †Hines Ward | 11 | 800 | 9,780 | 12.2 | 85 | 72 |
| †Tony Gonzalez | 12 | 916 | 10,940 | 11.9 | 73 | 76 | †Derrick Mason | 12 | 790 | 10,061 | 12.7 | 79 | 52 |
| Keenan McCardell | 17 | 883 | 11,373 | 12.9 | 76 | 63 | Marshall Faulk | 11 | 767 | 6,875 | 9.0 | 85 | 36 |
| †Torry Holt | 10 | 869 | 12,660 | 14.6 | 85 | 74 | James Lofton | 16 | 764 | 14,004 | 18.3 | 80 | 75 |
| Jimmy Smith | 13 | 862 | 12,287 | 14.3 | 75 | 67 | Eric Moulds | 12 | 764 | 9,995 | 13.1 | 84 | 49 |
| Irving Fryar | 17 | 851 | 12,785 | 15.0 | 80 | 84 | Michael Irvin | 12 | 750 | 11,904 | 15.9 | 87 | 65 |
| Rod Smith | 12 | 849 | 11,389 | 13.4 | 85 | 68 | Charlie Joiner | 18 | 750 | 12,146 | 16.2 | 87 | 65 |

#### YARDS

| | | | | | |
|---|---|---|---|---|---|
| Jerry Rice | 22,895 | †Randy Moss | 13,201 | Michael Irvin | 11,904 |
| †Isaac Bruce | 14,944 | Andre Reed | 13,198 | Don Maynard | 11,834 |
| Tim Brown | 14,934 | Steve Largent | 13,089 | Rod Smith | 11,389 |
| †Marvin Harrison | 14,580 | Irving Fryar | 12,785 | Keenan McCardell | 11,373 |
| †Terrell Owens | 14,122 | Art Monk | 12,721 | †Tony Gonzalez | 10,940 |
| James Lofton | 14,004 | †Torry Holt | 12,660 | †Muhsin Muhammad | 10,857 |
| Cris Carter | 13,899 | Jimmy Smith | 12,287 | Gary Clark | 10,856 |
| Henry Ellard | 13,777 | Charlie Joiner | 12,146 | Stanley Morgan | 10,716 |

#### SACKS

| | | | |
|---|---|---|---|
| Bruce Smith | 200.0 | Michael Strahan | 141.5 |
| Reggie White | 198.0 | John Randle | 137.5 |
| Kevin Greene | 160.0 | Richard Dent | 137.5 |
| Chris Doleman | 150.5 | Note: Stat officially compiled since 1982. | |

### Interceptions

| | Yrs | No. | Yds | Avg | Lg | TD |
|---|---|---|---|---|---|---|
| Paul Krause | 16 | 81 | 1,185 | 14.6 | 81 | 3 |
| Emlen Tunnell | 14 | 79 | 1,282 | 16.2 | 55 | 4 |
| Rod Woodson | 17 | 71 | 1,483 | 20.9 | 98 | 17 |
| Dick (Night Train) Lane | 14 | 68 | 1,207 | 17.8 | 80 | 5 |
| Ken Riley | 15 | 65 | 596 | 9.2 | 66 | 5 |

### Punting

| | Yrs | No. | Yds | Avg | Lg | Blk |
|---|---|---|---|---|---|---|
| †Shane Lechler | 9 | 682 | 31,902 | 46.8 | 73 | 3 |
| †Donnie Jones | 5 | 359 | 16,239 | 45.2 | 80 | 2 |
| Sammy Baugh | 16 | 338 | 15,245 | 45.1 | 85 | 9 |
| †Mat McBriar | 5 | 299 | 13,463 | 45.0 | 75 | 0 |
| Tommy Davis | 11 | 511 | 22,833 | 44.7 | 82 | 2 |
| †Chris Kluwe | 4 | 318 | 14,158 | 44.5 | 70 | 0 |
| †Andy Lee | 5 | 455 | 20,185 | 44.4 | 82 | 1 |

Note: 250 or more punts.

### Punt Returns

| | Yrs | No. | Yds | Avg | Lg | TD |
|---|---|---|---|---|---|---|
| †Roscoe Parrish | 4 | 94 | 1,312 | 14.0 | 82 | 3 |
| George McAfee | 8 | 112 | 1,431 | 12.8 | 74 | 2 |
| Jack Christiansen | 8 | 85 | 1,084 | 12.8 | 89 | 8 |
| Claude Gibson | 5 | 110 | 1,381 | 12.6 | 85 | 3 |
| Bill Dudley | 9 | 124 | 1,515 | 12.2 | 96 | 3 |
| †Devin Hester | 3 | 121 | 1,449 | 12.0 | 89 | 7 |
| †Santana Moss | 7 | 101 | 1,216 | 12.0 | 80 | 3 |

Note: 75 or more returns.

### Kickoff Returns

| | Yrs | No. | Yds | Avg | Lg | TD |
|---|---|---|---|---|---|---|
| Gale Sayers | 7 | 91 | 2,781 | 30.6 | 103 | 6 |
| Lynn Chandnois | 7 | 92 | 2,720 | 29.6 | 93 | 3 |
| Abe Woodson | 9 | 193 | 5,538 | 28.7 | 105 | 5 |
| Claude (Buddy) Young | 6 | 90 | 2,514 | 27.9 | 104 | 2 |
| †Ellis Hobbs | 4 | 105 | 2,913 | 27.7 | 108 | 3 |
| Travis Williams | 5 | 102 | 2,801 | 27.5 | 105 | 6 |

Note: 75 or more returns.

† Active in 2008.

## Single-Season Leaders
### Scoring

#### POINTS

| | Year | TD | PAT | FG | Pts |
|---|---|---|---|---|---|
| †LaDainian Tomlinson,SD | 2006 | 31 | 0 | 0 | 186 |
| Paul Hornung, GB | 1960 | 15 | 41 | 15 | 176 |
| †Shaun Alexander, Sea | 2005 | 28 | 0 | 0 | 168 |
| Gary Anderson, Min | 1998 | 0 | 59 | 35 | 164 |
| Jeff Wilkins, StL | 2003 | 0 | 46 | 39 | 163 |
| Priest Holmes, KC | 2003 | 27 | 0 | 0 | 162 |
| Mark Moseley, Wash | 1983 | 0 | 62 | 33 | 161 |
| Marshall Faulk, StL | 2000 | 26 | 2 | 0 | 160 |
| †Mike Vanderjagt, Ind | 2003 | 0 | 46 | 37 | 157 |
| Gino Cappelletti, Bos | 1964 | 7 | 37 | 25 | 155 |
| Emmitt Smith, Dal | 1995 | 25 | 0 | 0 | 150 |
| Chip Lohmiller, Wash | 1991 | 0 | 56 | 31 | 149 |
| †Jay Feely, NYG | 2005 | 0 | 43 | 35 | 148 |
| †Stephen Gostkowski | 2008 | 0 | 40 | 36 | 148 |
| Gino Cappelletti, Bos | 1961 | 8 | 48 | 17 | 147 |

Note: Faulk's (2) and Cappelletti's (1) totals include two-point conversions.

#### TOUCHDOWNS

| | Year | Rush | Rec | Ret | Total |
|---|---|---|---|---|---|
| †LaDainian Tomlinson, SD | 2006 | 28 | 3 | 0 | 31 |
| †Shaun Alexander, Sea | 2005 | 27 | 1 | 0 | 28 |
| Priest Holmes, KC | 2003 | 27 | 0 | 0 | 27 |
| Marshall Faulk, StL | 2000 | 18 | 8 | 0 | 26 |
| Emmitt Smith, Dal | 1995 | 25 | 0 | 0 | 25 |
| John Riggins, Wash | 1983 | 24 | 0 | 0 | 24 |
| Priest Holmes, KC | 2002 | 21 | 3 | 0 | 24 |
| O.J. Simpson, Buf | 1975 | 16 | 7 | 0 | 23 |
| Jerry Rice, SF | 1987 | 1 | 22 | 0 | 23 |
| Terrell Davis, Den | 1998 | 21 | 2 | 0 | 23 |
| †Randy Moss, NE | 2007 | 0 | 0 | 23 | 23 |

#### FIELD GOALS

| | Year | FGA | FGM |
|---|---|---|---|
| †Neil Rackers, Ari | 2005 | 42 | 40 |
| Jeff Wilkins, StL | 2003 | 42 | 39 |
| †Olindo Mare, Mia | 1999 | 46 | 39 |
| †Mike Vanderjagt, Ind | 2003 | 37 | 37 |
| †John Kasay, Car | 1996 | 45 | 37 |
| Al Del Greco, Ten | 1998 | 39 | 36 |
| Cary Blanchard, Ind | 1996 | 40 | 36 |
| †Stephen Gostkowski, NE | 2008 | 40 | 36 |

### Rushing

#### YARDS GAINED

| | Year | Att | Yds | Avg |
|---|---|---|---|---|
| Eric Dickerson, LA Rams | 1984 | 379 | 2,105 | 5.6 |
| †Jamal Lewis, Balt | 2003 | 387 | 2,066 | 5.3 |
| Barry Sanders, Det | 1997 | 335 | 2,053 | 6.1 |
| Terrell Davis, Den | 1998 | 392 | 2,008 | 5.1 |
| O.J. Simpson, Buf | 1973 | 332 | 2,003 | 6.0 |
| Earl Campbell, Hou | 1980 | 373 | 1,934 | 5.2 |
| †Ahman Green, GB | 2003 | 355 | 1,883 | 5.3 |
| Barry Sanders, Det | 1994 | 331 | 1,883 | 5.7 |
| †Shaun Alexander, Sea | 2005 | 370 | 1,880 | 5.1 |
| Jim Brown, Cle | 1963 | 291 | 1,863 | 6.4 |
| Tiki Barber, NYG | 2005 | 357 | 1,860 | 5.2 |
| †Ricky Williams, Mia | 2002 | 383 | 1,853 | 4.8 |

#### AVERAGE GAIN

| | Year | Avg |
|---|---|---|
| Beattie Feathers, Chi | 1934 | 8.44 |
| Randall Cunningham, Phil | 1990 | 7.98 |
| Michael Vick, Atl | 2004 | 7.50 |
| Michael Vick, Atl | 2002 | 6.88 |
| Bobby Douglass, Chi | 1972 | 6.87 |

Minimum 100 attempts.

#### TOUCHDOWNS

| | Year | No. |
|---|---|---|
| †LaDainian Tomlinson, SD | 2006 | 28 |
| †Shaun Alexander, Sea | 2005 | 27 |
| Priest Holmes, KC | 2003 | 27 |
| Emmitt Smith, Dal | 1995 | 25 |
| John Riggins, Wash | 1983 | 24 |
| Priest Holmes, KC | 2002 | 21 |
| Emmitt Smith, Dal | 1994 | 21 |
| Joe Morris, NYG | 1985 | 21 |
| Terry Allen, Wash | 1996 | 21 |
| Terrell Davis, Den | 1998 | 21 |

### Passing

#### YARDS GAINED

| | Year | Att | Comp | Pct | Yds |
|---|---|---|---|---|---|
| Dan Marino, Mia | 1984 | 564 | 362 | 64.2 | 5,084 |
| †Drew Brees, NO | 2008 | 635 | 413 | 65.0 | 5,069 |
| †Kurt Warner, StL Rams | 2001 | 546 | 375 | 68.7 | 4,830 |
| †Tom Brady, NE | 2007 | 578 | 398 | 68.9 | 4,806 |
| Dan Fouts, SD | 1981 | 609 | 360 | 59.1 | 4,802 |
| Dan Marino, Mia | 1986 | 623 | 378 | 60.7 | 4,746 |
| †Daunte Culpepper | 2004 | 548 | 379 | 69.2 | 4,717 |
| Dan Fouts, SD | 1980 | 589 | 348 | 59.1 | 4,715 |
| Warren Moon, Hou | 1991 | 655 | 404 | 61.7 | 4,690 |
| Warren Moon, Hou | 1990 | 584 | 362 | 62.0 | 4,689 |
| Rich Gannon, Oak | 2002 | 618 | 418 | 67.6 | 4,689 |
| Neil Lomax, StL Cards | 1984 | 560 | 345 | 61.6 | 4,614 |
| †Trent Green, StL Rams | 2004 | 556 | 369 | 66.4 | 4,591 |
| †Kurt Warner, Ari | 2008 | 598 | 401 | 67.1 | 4,583 |
| †Peyton Manning, Ind | 2004 | 497 | 336 | 67.6 | 4,557 |
| Drew Bledsoe, NE | 1994 | 691 | 400 | 57.9 | 4,555 |

#### PASSER RATING

| | Year | Rat. |
|---|---|---|
| †Peyton Manning, Ind | 2004 | 121.1 |
| †Tom Brady, NE | 2007 | 117.2 |
| Steve Young, SF | 1994 | 112.8 |
| Joe Montana, SF | 1989 | 112.4 |
| †Daunte Culpepper, Min | 2004 | 110.9 |
| Milt Plum, Clev | 1960 | 110.4 |

#### TOUCHDOWNS

| | Year | No. |
|---|---|---|
| †Tom Brady, NE | 2007 | 50 |
| †Peyton Manning, Ind | 2004 | 49 |
| Dan Marino, Mia | 1984 | 48 |
| Dan Marino, Mia | 1986 | 44 |
| †Kurt Warner, StL Rams | 1999 | 41 |
| †Daunte Culpepper, Min | 2004 | 39 |
| †Brett Favre, GB | 1996 | 39 |
| †Brett Favre, GB | 1995 | 38 |

Six tied with 36.

† Active in 2008.

## Single-Season Leaders (Cont.)

### Receiving

#### RECEPTIONS

| | Year | No. | Yds |
|---|---|---|---|
| †Marvin Harrison, Ind | 2002 | 143 | 1,722 |
| Herman Moore, Det | 1995 | 123 | 1,686 |
| Cris Carter, Min | 1994 | 122 | 1,256 |
| Jerry Rice, SF | 1995 | 122 | 1,848 |
| Cris Carter, Min | 1995 | 122 | 1,371 |
| †Isaac Bruce, StL Rams | 1995 | 119 | 1,781 |
| †Torry Holt, StL Rams | 2003 | 117 | 1,696 |
| Jimmy Smith, Jac | 1999 | 116 | 1,636 |
| †Marvin Harrison, Ind | 1999 | 115 | 1,663 |
| †Andre Johnson, Hous | 2008 | 115 | 1,575 |
| Rod Smith, Den | 2001 | 113 | 1,343 |
| Six tied at 112. | | | |

#### YARDS GAINED

| | Year | Yds |
|---|---|---|
| Jerry Rice, SF | 1995 | 1,848 |
| †Isaac Bruce, StL Rams | 1995 | 1,781 |
| Charley Hennigan, Hou | 1961 | 1,746 |
| †Marvin Harrison, Ind | 2002 | 1,722 |
| †Torry Holt, StL | 2003 | 1,696 |

#### TOUCHDOWNS

| | Year | No. |
|---|---|---|
| †Randy Moss, NE | 2007 | 23 |
| Jerry Rice, SF | 1987 | 22 |
| Mark Clayton, Mia | 1984 | 18 |
| Sterling Sharpe, GB | 1994 | 18 |
| Seven tied with 17. | | |

### All-Purpose Yards

| | Year | Run | Rec | Ret | Total |
|---|---|---|---|---|---|
| †Derrick Mason, Ten | 2000 | 1 | 895 | 1794 | 2690 |
| Michael Lewis, NO | 2002 | 15 | 200 | 2432 | 2647 |
| Lionel James, SD | 1985 | 516 | 1027 | 992 | 2535 |
| Brian Mitchell, Wash | 1994 | 311 | 236 | 1930 | 2477 |
| †Dante Hall, KC | 2003 | 73 | 423 | 1950 | 2446 |
| Mack Herron, NE | 1974 | 824 | 474 | 1146 | 2444 |
| Gale Sayers, Chi | 1966 | 1231 | 447 | 762 | 2440 |
| Terry Metcalf, StL Cards | 1975 | 816 | 378 | 1245 | 2439 |
| Marshall Faulk, StL Rams | 1999 | 1381 | 1048 | 0 | 2429 |
| Timmy Brown, Phi | 1963 | 841 | 487 | 1097 | 2425 |
| MarTay Jenkins, Ari | 2000 | -4 | 219 | 2187 | 2402 |
| Tiki Barber, NYG | 2005 | 1860 | 530 | 0 | 2390 |
| †LaD. Tomlinson, SD | 2003 | 1645 | 725 | 0 | 2370 |
| Barry Sanders, Det | 1997 | 2053 | 305 | 0 | 2358 |
| Brian Mitchell, Wash | 1998 | 208 | 306 | 1843 | 2357 |

#### Punting

| | Year | No. | Yds | Avg |
|---|---|---|---|---|
| Sammy Baugh, Wash | 1940 | 35 | 1,799 | 51.4 |
| †Donnie Jones, StL | 2008 | 82 | 4,100 | 50.0 |
| †Shane Lechler, Oak | 2007 | 73 | 3,585 | 49.1 |
| †Mat McBriar, Dal | 2008 | 24 | 1,175 | 49.0 |
| Yale Lary, Det | 1963 | 35 | 1,713 | 48.9 |
| †Shane Lechler, Oak | 2008 | 90 | 4,391 | 48.8 |
| Sammy Baugh, Wash | 1941 | 30 | 1,462 | 48.7 |
| Yale Lary, Det | 1961 | 52 | 2,519 | 48.4 |

#### Sacks

| | Year | No. |
|---|---|---|
| Michael Strahan, NYG | 2001 | 22.5 |
| Mark Gastineau, NYJ | 1984 | 22 |
| Reggie White, Phil | 1987 | 21 |
| Chris Doleman, Min | 1989 | 21 |
| Lawrence Taylor, NYG | 1986 | 20.5 |
| Derrick Thomas, KC | 1990 | 20 |
| †DeMarcus Ware, Dal | 2008 | 20 |
| Three tied with 19.0. | | |

### Interceptions

| | Year | No. |
|---|---|---|
| Dick (Night Train) Lane, LA Rams | 1952 | 14 |
| Dan Sandifer, Wash | 1948 | 13 |
| Spec Sanders, NY Yanks | 1950 | 13 |
| Lester Hayes, Oak | 1980 | 13 |
| Nine tied with 12. | | |

#### Kickoff Returns

| | Year | Avg |
|---|---|---|
| Travis Williams, GB | 1967 | 41.1 |
| Gale Sayers, Chi | 1967 | 37.7 |
| Ollie Matson, Chi Cards | 1958 | 35.5 |
| Jim Duncan, Balt Colts | 1970 | 35.4 |
| Lynn Chandnois, Pit | 1952 | 35.2 |

### Punt Returns

| | Year | Avg |
|---|---|---|
| Jack Christiansen, Det | 1952 | 21.5 |
| Dick Christy, NY Titans | 1961 | 21.3 |
| Bob Hayes, Dal | 1968 | 20.8 |
| Two tied at 19.1. | | |

## Single-Game Leaders

### Scoring

#### POINTS

| | Date | Pts |
|---|---|---|
| Ernie Nevers, Chi Cards vs Chi | 11-28-29 | 40 |
| Dub Jones, Clev vs Chi | 11-25-51 | 36 |
| Gale Sayers, Chi vs SF | 12-12-65 | 36 |
| Paul Hornung, GB vs Balt Colts | 10-8-61 | 33 |

On Thanksgiving Day, 1929, Nevers scored all the Cardinals' points on six rushing TDs and four PATs. The Cards defeated Red Grange and the Bears, 40–6. Jones and Sayers each rushed for four touchdowns and scored two more on returns in their teams' victories. Hornung scored four touchdowns and kicked 6 PATs and a field goal in a 45-7 win over the Colts.

#### FIELD GOALS

| | Date | No. |
|---|---|---|
| †Rob Bironas, Ten vs Hou | 10-21-07 | 8 |
| Jim Bakken, StL Cards vs Pit | 9-24-67 | 7 |
| Rich Karlis, Min vs LA Rams | 11-5-89 | 7 |
| Chris Boniol, Dal vs GB | 11-18-96 | 7 |
| Billy Cundiff, Dal vs NYG | 9-15-03 | 7 |

Bironas was 8 for 8.

Bakken was 7 for 9; Cundiff was 7 for 8; and Karlis and Boniol went 7 for 7.

† Active in 2008.

## Single-Game Leaders *(Cont.)*

### Scoring *(Cont.)*

#### TOUCHDOWNS

| | Date | No. |
|---|---|---|
| Ernie Nevers, Chi Cards vs Chi | 11-28-29 | 6 |
| Dub Jones, Clev vs Chi | 11-25-51 | 6 |
| Gale Sayers, Chi vs SF | 12-12-65 | 6 |
| Bob Shaw, Chi Cards vs Balt Colts | 10-2-50 | 5 |
| Jim Brown, Clev vs Balt Colts | 11-1-59 | 5 |
| Abner Haynes, Dal Texans vs Oak | 11-26-61 | 5 |
| Billy Cannon, Hou vs NY Titans | 12-10-61 | 5 |
| Cookie Gilchrist, Buf vs NYJ | 12-8-63 | 5 |
| Paul Hornung, GB vs Balt Colts | 12-12-65 | 5 |
| Kellen Winslow, SD vs Oak | 11-22-81 | 5 |
| Jerry Rice, SF vs Atl | 10-14-90 | 5 |
| James Stewart, Jac vs Phil | 10-12-97 | 5 |
| †Shaun Alexander, Sea vs Min | 9-29-02 | 5 |
| †Clinton Portis, Den vs KC | 12-07-03 | 5 |

### Rushing

#### YARDS GAINED

| | Date | Yds |
|---|---|---|
| †Adrian Peterson, Min vs SD | 11-4-07 | 296 |
| †Jamal Lewis, Balt vs Clev | 9-14-03 | 295 |
| Corey Dillon, Cin vs Den | 10-22-00 | 278 |
| Walter Payton, Chi vs Min | 11-20-77 | 275 |
| O.J. Simpson, Buf vs Det | 11-25-76 | 273 |

#### CARRIES

| | Date | No. |
|---|---|---|
| Jamie Morris, Wash vs Cin | 12-17-88 | 45 |
| Butch Woolfolk, NYG vs Phil | 11-20-83 | 43 |
| James Wilder, TB vs GB | 9-30-84 | 43 |
| †Rudi Johnson, Cin vs Hou | 11-9-03 | 43 |
| James Wilder, TB vs Pit | 10-30-83 | 42 |
| Terrell Davis, Den vs Buf (OT) | 10-26-97 | 42 |
| †Ricky Williams, Mia vs Buf | 9-21-03 | 42 |

#### TOUCHDOWNS

| | Date | No. |
|---|---|---|
| Ernie Nevers, Chi Cards vs Chi | 11-28-29 | 6 |
| Jim Brown, Clev vs Balt Colts | 11-1-59 | 5 |
| Cookie Gilchrist, Buf vs NYJ | 12-8-63 | 5 |
| James Stewart, Jac vs Phil | 10-12-97 | 5 |
| †Clinton Portis, Den vs KC | 12-7-03 | 5 |

### Passing

#### YARDS GAINED

| | Date | Yds |
|---|---|---|
| N. Van Brocklin, Rams vs NY Yanks | 9-28-51 | 554 |
| Warren Moon, Hou vs KC | 12-16-90 | 527 |
| Boomer Esiason, Ariz vs Wash | 11-10-96 | 522 |
| Dan Marino, Mia vs NYJ | 10-23-88 | 521 |
| Phil Simms, NYG vs Cin | 10-13-85 | 513 |

#### COMPLETIONS

| | Date | No. |
|---|---|---|
| Drew Bledsoe, NE vs Min | 11-13-94 | 45 |
| Rich Gannon, Oak vs Pit | 9-15-02 | 43 |
| Richard Todd, NYJ vs SF | 9-21-80 | 42 |
| Vinny Testaverde, NYJ vs Sea | 12-6-98 | 42 |
| Warren Moon, Hou vs Dal | 11-10-91 | 41 |
| Ken Anderson, Cin vs SD | 12-20-82 | 40 |
| Phil Simms, NYG vs Cin | 10-13-85 | 40 |
| †Brad Johnson, TB vs Chi | 11-18-01 | 40 |
| †Marc Bulger, StL Rams vs NYG | 10-02-05 | 40 |
| †Kurt Warner, Ari vs NYJ | 9-28-08 | 40 |

#### TOUCHDOWNS

| | Date | No. |
|---|---|---|
| Sid Luckman, Chi vs NYG | 11-14-43 | 7 |
| Adrian Burk, Phil vs Wash | 10-17-54 | 7 |
| George Blanda, Hou vs NY Titans | 11-19-61 | 7 |
| Y. A. Tittle, NYG vs Wash | 10-28-62 | 7 |
| Joe Kapp, Min vs Balt Colts | 9-28-69 | 7 |

### Receiving

#### YARDS GAINED

| | Date | Yds |
|---|---|---|
| Flipper Anderson, LA Rams vs NO | 11-26-89 | 336 |
| Stephone Paige, KC vs SD | 12-22-85 | 309 |
| Jim Benton, Clev vs Det | 11-22-45 | 303 |
| Cloyce Box, Det vs Balt Colts | 12-3-50 | 302 |
| Jimmy Smith, Jax vs Balt Ravens | 9-10-00 | 291 |

#### RECEPTIONS

| | Date | No. |
|---|---|---|
| †Terrell Owens, SF vs Chi | 12-17-00 | 20 |
| Tom Fears, Rams vs GB | 12-3-50 | 18 |
| †Brandon Marshall, Den vs SD | 9-14-08 | 18 |
| Clark Gaines, NYJ vs SF | 9-21-80 | 17 |
| Sonny Randle, StL Cards vs NYG | 11-4-62 | 16 |
| Jerry Rice, SF vs Rams | 11-20-94 | 16 |
| Keenan McCardell, Jax vs Rams | 10-20-96 | 16 |
| Troy Brown, NE vs KC | 9-22-02 | 16 |

† Active in 2008.

Six tied with 15.

## Single-Game Leaders *(Cont.)*

### Receiving *(Cont.)*
#### TOUCHDOWNS

| | Date | No. |
|---|---|---|
| Bob Shaw, Chi Cards vs Balt Colts | 10-2-50 | 5 |
| Kellen Winslow, SD vs Oak | 11-22-81 | 5 |
| Jerry Rice, SF vs Atl | 10-14-90 | 5 |

#### All-Purpose Yards

| | Date | Yds |
|---|---|---|
| Glyn Milburn, Den vs Sea | 12-10-95 | 404 |
| Billy Cannon, Hou vs NY Titans | 12-10-61 | 373 |
| Tyrone Hughes, NO vs LA Rams | 10-23-94 | 347 |
| Lionel James, SD vs LA Rai | 11-10-85 | 345 |
| Timmy Brown, Phi vs StL Cards | 12-16-62 | 341 |

## Longest Plays

| RUSHING | Opponent | Year | Yds |
|---|---|---|---|
| Tony Dorsett, Dal | Min | 1983 | 99 |
| †Ahman Green, GB | Den | 2003 | 98 |
| Andy Uram, GB | Chi Cards | 1939 | 97 |
| Bob Gage, Pit | Chi | 1949 | 97 |
| Jim Spavital, Balt Colts | GB | 1950 | 96 |
| Bob Hoernschemeyer, Det | NY Yanks | 1950 | 96 |
| Garrison Hearst, SF | NYJ | 1998 | 96 |
| Corey Dillon, Cin | Det | 2001 | 96 |

| PASSING | Opponent | Year | Yds |
|---|---|---|---|
| Frank Filchock to Andy Farkas, Wash | Pit | 1939 | 99 |
| George Izo to Bobby Mitchell, Wash | Clev | 1963 | 99 |
| Karl Sweetan to Pat Studstill, Det | Balt Colts | 1966 | 99 |
| Sonny Jurgensen to Gerry Allen, Wash | Chi | 1968 | 99 |
| Jim Plunkett to Cliff Branch, LA Rai | Wash | 1983 | 99 |
| Ron Jaworski to Mike Quick, Phil | Atl | 1985 | 99 |
| Stan Humphries to Tony Martin, SD | Sea | 1994 | 99 |
| †Brett Favre to Robert Brooks, GB | Chi | 1995 | 99 |
| Trent Green to Marc Boerigter, KC | SD | 2002 | 99 |
| †Jeff Garcia to Andre Davis, Clev | Cin | 2004 | 99 |
| Gus Frerotte to Bernard Berrian, Min | Chi | 2008 | 99 |

| FIELD GOALS | Opponent | Year | Yds |
|---|---|---|---|
| Tom Dempsey, NO | Det | 1970 | 63 |
| †Jason Elam, Den | Jac | 1998 | 63 |
| †Matt Bryant, TB | Phi | 2006 | 62 |
| †Rob Bironas, Ten | Ind | 2006 | 62 |

| PUNTS | Opponent | Year | Yds |
|---|---|---|---|
| Steve O'Neal, NYJ | Den | 1969 | 98 |
| Joe Lintzenich, Chi | NYG | 1931 | 94 |
| Shawn McCarthy, NE | Buf | 1991 | 93 |
| Randall Cunningham, Phil | NYG | 1989 | 91 |

| INTERCEPTION RETURNS | Opponent | Year | Yds |
|---|---|---|---|
| †Ed Reed, Balt | Phi | 2008 | 107 |
| †Ed Reed, Balt | Clev | 2004 | 106 |
| Vencie Glenn, SD | Den | 1987 | 103 |
| Louis Oliver, Mia | Buf | 1992 | 103 |
| Nine players tied at 102. | | | |

| KICKOFF RETURNS | Opponent | Year | Yds |
|---|---|---|---|
| †Ellis Hobbs, NE | NYJ | 2007 | 108 |
| Al Carmichael, GB | Chi | 1956 | 106 |
| Noland Smith, KC | Den | 1967 | 106 |
| Roy Green, StL Cards | Dal | 1979 | 106 |

| PUNT RETURNS | Opponent | Year | Yds |
|---|---|---|---|
| Robert Bailey, LA Rams | NO | 1994 | 103 |
| Gil LeFebvre, Cin | Brooklyn | 1933 | 98 |
| Charlie West, Min | Wash | 1968 | 98 |
| Dennis Morgan, Dal | StL Cards | 1974 | 98 |
| Terance Mathis, NYJ | Dal | 1990 | 98 |

| MISSED FIELD GOAL RETURNS | Opponent | Year | Yds |
|---|---|---|---|
| †Antonio Cromartie, SD | Min | 2007 | 109 |
| †Devin Hester, Chi | NYG | 2006 | 108 |
| †Nathan Vasher, Chi | SF | 2005 | 108 |
| †Chris McAllister, Balt | Den | 2002 | 107 |
| †Aaron Glenn, NYJ | Ind | 1998 | 104 |

† Active in 2008.

## Rushing

| Year | Player, Team | Att | Yards | Avg | TD | Year | Player, Team | Att | Yards | Avg | TD |
|------|--------------|-----|-------|-----|----|------|--------------|-----|-------|-----|----|
| 1932 | Cliff Battles, Bos | 148 | 576 | 3.9 | 3 | 1972 | O.J. Simpson, Buf, AFC | 292 | 1,251 | 4.3 | 6 |
| 1933 | Jim Musick, Bos | 173 | 809 | 4.7 | 5 | | Larry Brown, Wash, NFC | 285 | 1,216 | 4.3 | 8 |
| 1934 | Beattie Feathers, Chi | 119 | 1,004 | 8.4 | 8 | 1973 | O.J. Simpson, Buf, AFC | 332 | 2,003 | 6.0 | 12 |
| 1935 | Doug Russell, Chi Cards | 140 | 499 | 3.6 | 0 | | John Brockington, GB, NFC | 265 | 1,144 | 4.3 | 3 |
| 1936 | Alphonse Leemans, NY | 206 | 830 | 4.0 | 2 | 1974 | Otis Armstrong, Den, AFC | 263 | 1,407 | 5.3 | 9 |
| 1937 | Cliff Battles, Wash | 216 | 874 | 4.0 | 5 | | Lawrence McCutcheon, LA, NFC | 236 | 1,109 | 4.7 | 3 |
| 1938 | Byron White, Pit | 152 | 567 | 3.7 | 4 | 1975 | O.J. Simpson, Buf, AFC | 329 | 1,817 | 5.5 | 16 |
| 1939 | Bill Osmanski, Chi | 121 | 699 | 5.8 | 7 | | Jim Otis, StL, NFC | 269 | 1,076 | 4.0 | 5 |
| 1940 | Byron White, Det | 146 | 514 | 3.5 | 5 | 1976 | O.J. Simpson, Buf, AFC | 290 | 1,503 | 5.2 | 8 |
| 1941 | Clarence Manders, Bklyn | 111 | 486 | 4.4 | 5 | | Walter Payton, Chi, NFC | 311 | 1,390 | 4.5 | 13 |
| 1942 | Bill Dudley, Pit | 162 | 696 | 4.3 | 5 | 1977 | Walter Payton, Chi, NFC | 339 | 1,852 | 5.5 | 14 |
| 1943 | Bill Paschal, NY | 147 | 572 | 3.9 | 10 | | Mark van Eeghen, Oak, AFC | 324 | 1,273 | 3.9 | 7 |
| 1944 | Bill Paschal, NY | 196 | 737 | 3.8 | 9 | 1978 | Earl Campbell, Hou, AFC | 302 | 1,450 | 4.8 | 13 |
| 1945 | Steve Van Buren, Phil | 143 | 832 | 5.8 | 15 | | Walter Payton, Chi, NFC | 333 | 1,395 | 4.2 | 11 |
| 1946 | Bill Dudley, Pit | 146 | 604 | 4.1 | 3 | 1979 | Earl Campbell, Hou, AFC | 368 | 1,697 | 4.6 | 19 |
| 1947 | Steve Van Buren, Phil | 217 | 1,008 | 4.6 | 13 | | Walter Payton, Chi, NFC | 369 | 1,610 | 4.4 | 14 |
| 1948 | Steve Van Buren, Phil | 201 | 945 | 4.7 | 10 | 1980 | Earl Campbell, Hou, AFC | 373 | 1,934 | 5.2 | 13 |
| 1949 | Steve Van Buren, Phil | 263 | 1,146 | 4.4 | 11 | | Walter Payton, Chi, NFC | 317 | 1,460 | 4.6 | 6 |
| 1950 | Marion Motley, Clev | 140 | 810 | 5.8 | 3 | 1981 | George Rogers, NO, NFC | 378 | 1,674 | 4.4 | 13 |
| 1951 | Eddie Price, NY | 271 | 971 | 3.6 | 7 | | Earl Campbell, Hou, AFC | 361 | 1,376 | 3.8 | 10 |
| 1952 | Dan Towler, LA | 156 | 894 | 5.7 | 10 | 1982 | Freeman McNeil, NYJ, AFC | 151 | 786 | 5.2 | 6 |
| 1953 | Joe Perry, SF | 192 | 1,018 | 5.3 | 10 | | Tony Dorsett, Dal, NFC | 177 | 745 | 4.2 | 5 |
| 1954 | Joe Perry, SF | 173 | 1,049 | 6.1 | 8 | 1983 | Eric Dickerson, LA, NFC | 390 | 1,808 | 4.6 | 18 |
| 1955 | Alan Ameche, Balt | 213 | 961 | 4.5 | 9 | | Curt Warner, Sea, AFC | 335 | 1,449 | 4.3 | 13 |
| 1956 | Rick Casares, Chi | 234 | 1,126 | 4.8 | 12 | 1984 | Eric Dickerson, LA, NFC | 379 | 2,105 | 5.6 | 14 |
| 1957 | Jim Brown, Clev | 202 | 942 | 4.7 | 9 | | Earnest Jackson, SD, AFC | 296 | 1,179 | 4.0 | 8 |
| 1958 | Jim Brown, Clev | 257 | 1,527 | 5.9 | 17 | 1985 | Marcus Allen, LA, AFC | 380 | 1,759 | 4.6 | 11 |
| 1959 | Jim Brown, Clev | 290 | 1,329 | 4.6 | 14 | | Gerald Riggs, Atl, NFC | 397 | 1,719 | 4.3 | 10 |
| 1960 | Jim Brown, Clev, NFL | 215 | 1,257 | 5.8 | 9 | 1986 | Eric Dickerson, LA, NFC | 404 | 1,821 | 4.5 | 11 |
| | Abner Haynes, Dallas Texans, AFL | 156 | 875 | 5.6 | 9 | | Curt Warner, Sea, AFC | 319 | 1,481 | 4.6 | 13 |
| 1961 | Jim Brown, Clev, NFL | 305 | 1,408 | 4.6 | 8 | 1987 | Charles White, LA, NFC | 324 | 1,374 | 4.2 | 11 |
| | Billy Cannon, Hou, AFL | 200 | 948 | 4.7 | 6 | | Eric Dickerson, Ind, AFC | 223 | 1,011 | 4.5 | 5 |
| 1962 | Jim Taylor, GB, NFL | 272 | 1,474 | 5.4 | 19 | 1988 | Eric Dickerson, Ind, AFC | 388 | 1,659 | 4.3 | 14 |
| | Cookie Gilchrist, Buf, AFL | 214 | 1,096 | 5.1 | 13 | | Herschel Walker, Dal, NFC | 361 | 1,514 | 4.2 | 5 |
| 1963 | Jim Brown, Clev, NFL | 291 | 1,863 | 6.4 | 12 | 1989 | Christian Okoye, KC, AFC | 370 | 1,480 | 4.0 | 12 |
| | Clem Daniels, Oak, AFL | 215 | 1,099 | 5.1 | 3 | | Barry Sanders, Det, NFC | 280 | 1,470 | 5.3 | 14 |
| 1964 | Jim Brown, Clev, NFL | 280 | 1,446 | 5.2 | 7 | 1990 | Barry Sanders, Det, NFC | 255 | 1,304 | 5.1 | 13 |
| | Cookie Gilchrist, Buf, AFL | 230 | 981 | 4.3 | 6 | | Thurman Thomas, Buf, AFC | 271 | 1,297 | 4.8 | 11 |
| 1965 | Jim Brown, Clev, NFL | 289 | 1,544 | 5.3 | 17 | 1991 | Emmitt Smith, Dal, NFC | 365 | 1,563 | 4.3 | 12 |
| | Paul Lowe, SD, AFL | 222 | 1,121 | 5.0 | 7 | | Thurman Thomas, Buf, AFC | 288 | 1,407 | 4.9 | 7 |
| 1966 | Jim Nance, Bos, AFL | 299 | 1,458 | 4.9 | 11 | 1992 | Emmitt Smith, Dal, NFC | 373 | 1,713 | 4.6 | 18 |
| | Gale Sayers, Chi, NFL | 229 | 1,231 | 5.4 | 8 | | Barry Foster, Pit, AFC | 390 | 1,690 | 4.3 | 11 |
| 1967 | Jim Nance, Bos, AFL | 269 | 1,216 | 4.5 | 7 | 1993 | Emmitt Smith, Dal, NFC | 283 | 1,486 | 5.3 | 9 |
| | Leroy Kelly, Clev, NFL | 235 | 1,205 | 5.1 | 11 | | Thurman Thomas, Buf, AFC | 355 | 1,315 | 3.7 | 6 |
| 1968 | Leroy Kelly, Clev, NFL | 248 | 1,239 | 5.0 | 16 | | | | | | |
| | Paul Robinson, Cin, AFL | 238 | 1,023 | 4.3 | 8 | | | | | | |
| 1969 | Gale Sayers, Chi, NFL | 236 | 1,032 | 4.4 | 8 | | | | | | |
| | Dickie Post, SD, AFL | 182 | 873 | 4.8 | 6 | | | | | | |
| 1970 | Larry Brown, Wash, NFC | 237 | 1,125 | 4.7 | 5 | | | | | | |
| | Floyd Little, Den, AFC | 209 | 901 | 4.3 | 3 | | | | | | |
| 1971 | Floyd Little, Den, AFC | 284 | 1,133 | 4.0 | 6 | | | | | | |
| | John Brockington, GB, NFC | 216 | 1,105 | 5.1 | 4 | | | | | | |

## Rushing *(Cont.)*

| Year | Player, Team | Att | Yards | Avg | TD |
|------|--------------|-----|-------|-----|-----|
| 1994 | Barry Sanders, Det, NFC | 331 | 1,883 | 5.7 | 7 |
|  | Chris Warren, Sea, AFC | 333 | 1,545 | 4.6 | 9 |
| 1995 | Emmitt Smith, Dal, NFC | 377 | 1,773 | 4.7 | 25 |
|  | Curtis Martin, NE, AFC | 368 | 1,487 | 4.0 | 14 |
| 1996 | Barry Sanders, Det, NFC | 307 | 1,553 | 5.1 | 11 |
|  | Terrell Davis, Den, AFC | 345 | 1,538 | 4.5 | 13 |
| 1997 | Barry Sanders, Det, NFC | 335 | 2,053 | 6.1 | 11 |
|  | Terrell Davis, Den, AFC | 369 | 1,750 | 4.7 | 15 |
| 1998 | Terrell Davis, Den, AFC | 392 | 2,008 | 5.1 | 21 |
|  | Jamal Anderson, Atl, NFC | 410 | 1,846 | 4.5 | 14 |
| 1999 | Edgerrin James, Ind, AFC | 369 | 1,553 | 4.2 | 13 |
|  | Stephen Davis, Wash, NFC | 290 | 1,405 | 4.8 | 17 |
| 2000 | Edgerrin James, Ind, AFC | 387 | 1,709 | 4.4 | 13 |
|  | Robert Smith, Min, NFC | 295 | 1,521 | 5.2 | 7 |
| 2001 | Priest Holmes, Kan, AFC | 327 | 1,555 | 4.8 | 8 |
|  | Stephen Davis, Wash, NFC | 356 | 1,432 | 4.0 | 5 |
| 2002 | Ricky Williams, Mia, AFC | 383 | 1,853 | 4.8 | 16 |
|  | Deuce McAllister, NO, NFC | 325 | 1,388 | 4.3 | 13 |
| 2003 | Jamal Lewis, Balt, AFC | 387 | 2,066 | 5.3 | 14 |
|  | Ahman Green, GB, NFC | 355 | 1,883 | 5.3 | 15 |
| 2004 | Curtis Martin, NY Jets, AFC | 371 | 1,697 | 4.6 | 12 |
|  | Shaun Alexander, Sea, NFC | 353 | 1,696 | 4.8 | 16 |
| 2005 | Shaun Alexander, Sea, NFC | 370 | 1,880 | 5.1 | 27 |
|  | Larry Johnson, KC, AFC | 336 | 1,750 | 5.2 | 20 |
| 2006 | LaDainian Tomlinson, SD, AFC | 348 | 1,815 | 5.2 | 28 |
|  | Frank Gore, SF, NFC | 312 | 1,695 | 5.4 | 8 |
| 2007 | LaDainian Tomlinson, SD, AFC | 315 | 1,474 | 4.7 | 15 |
|  | Adrian Peterson, Min, NFC | 238 | 1,341 | 5.6 | 12 |
| 2008 | Adrian Peterson, Min, NFC | 363 | 1,760 | 4.8 | 10 |
|  | Thomas Jones, NYJ, AFC | 290 | 1,312 | 4.5 | 13 |

## Passing

| Year | Player, Team | Att | Comp | Yards | TD | Int |
|------|--------------|-----|------|-------|----|-----|
| 1932 | Arnie Herber, GB | 101 | 37 | 639 | 9 | 9 |
| 1933 | Harry Newman, NYG | 136 | 53 | 973 | 11 | 17 |
| 1934 | Arnie Herber, GB | 115 | 42 | 799 | 8 | 12 |
| 1935 | Ed Danowski, NYG | 113 | 57 | 794 | 10 | 9 |
| 1936 | Arnie Herber, GB | 173 | 77 | 1,239 | 11 | 13 |
| 1937 | Sammy Baugh, Wash | 171 | 81 | 1,127 | 8 | 14 |
| 1938 | Ed Danowski, NYG | 129 | 70 | 848 | 7 | 8 |
| 1939 | Parker Hall, Clev | 208 | 106 | 1,227 | 9 | 13 |
| 1940 | Sammy Baugh, Wash | 177 | 111 | 1,367 | 12 | 10 |
| 1941 | Cecil Isbell, GB | 206 | 117 | 1,479 | 15 | 11 |
| 1942 | Cecil Isbell, GB | 268 | 146 | 2,021 | 24 | 14 |
| 1943 | Sammy Baugh, Wash | 239 | 133 | 1,754 | 23 | 19 |
| 1944 | Frank Filchock, Wash | 147 | 84 | 1,139 | 13 | 9 |
| 1945 | Sammy Baugh, Wash | 182 | 128 | 1,669 | 11 | 4 |
|  | Sid Luckman, Chi | 217 | 117 | 1,725 | 14 | 10 |
| 1946 | Bob Waterfield, LA | 251 | 127 | 1,747 | 18 | 17 |
| 1947 | Sammy Baugh, Wash | 354 | 210 | 2,938 | 25 | 15 |
| 1948 | Tommy Thompson, Phil | 246 | 141 | 1,965 | 25 | 11 |
| 1949 | Sammy Baugh, Wash | 255 | 145 | 1,903 | 18 | 14 |
| 1950 | Norm Van Brocklin, LA | 233 | 127 | 2,061 | 18 | 14 |
| 1951 | Bob Waterfield, LA | 176 | 88 | 1,566 | 13 | 10 |
| 1952 | Norm Van Brocklin, LA | 205 | 113 | 1,736 | 14 | 17 |
| 1953 | Otto Graham, Clev | 258 | 167 | 2,722 | 11 | 9 |
| 1954 | Norm Van Brocklin, LA | 260 | 139 | 2,637 | 13 | 21 |
| 1955 | Otto Graham, Clev | 185 | 98 | 1,721 | 15 | 8 |
| 1956 | Ed Brown, Chi | 168 | 96 | 1,667 | 11 | 12 |
| 1957 | Tommy O'Connell, Clev | 110 | 63 | 1,229 | 9 | 8 |
| 1958 | Eddie LeBaron, Wash | 145 | 79 | 1,365 | 11 | 10 |
| 1959 | Charlie Conerly, NYG | 194 | 113 | 1,706 | 14 | 4 |
| 1960 | Milt Plum, Clev, NFL | 250 | 151 | 2,297 | 21 | 5 |
|  | Jack Kemp, LA, AFL | 406 | 211 | 3,018 | 20 | 25 |
| 1961 | George Blanda, Hou, AFL | 362 | 187 | 3,330 | 36 | 22 |
|  | Milt Plum, Clev, NFL | 302 | 177 | 2,416 | 18 | 10 |
| 1962 | Len Dawson, Dal, AFL | 310 | 189 | 2,759 | 29 | 17 |
|  | Bart Starr, GB, NFL | 285 | 178 | 2,438 | 12 | 9 |
| 1963 | Y.A. Tittle, NY, NFL | 367 | 221 | 3,145 | 36 | 14 |
|  | Tobin Rote, SD, AFL | 286 | 170 | 2,510 | 20 | 17 |
| 1964 | Len Dawson, KC, AFL | 354 | 199 | 2,879 | 30 | 18 |
|  | Bart Starr, GB, NFL | 272 | 163 | 2,144 | 15 | 4 |
| 1965 | Rudy Bukich, Chi, NFL | 312 | 176 | 2,641 | 20 | 9 |
|  | John Hadl, SD, AFL | 348 | 174 | 2,798 | 20 | 21 |
| 1966 | Bart Starr, GB, NFL | 251 | 156 | 2,257 | 14 | 3 |
|  | Len Dawson, KC, AFL | 284 | 159 | 2,527 | 26 | 10 |
| 1967 | Sonny Jurgensen, Wash, NFL | 508 | 288 | 3,747 | 31 | 16 |
|  | Daryle Lamonica, Oak, AFL | 425 | 220 | 3,228 | 30 | 20 |
| 1968 | Len Dawson, KC, AFL | 224 | 131 | 2,109 | 17 | 9 |
|  | Earl Morrall, Balt, NFL | 317 | 182 | 2,909 | 26 | 17 |
| 1969 | S. Jurgensen, Wash, NFL | 442 | 274 | 3,102 | 22 | 15 |
|  | Greg Cook, Cin, AFL | 197 | 106 | 1,854 | 15 | 11 |
| 1970 | John Brodie, SF, NFC | 378 | 223 | 2,941 | 24 | 10 |
|  | Daryle Lamonica, Oak, AFC | 356 | 179 | 2,516 | 22 | 15 |
| 1971 | Roger Staubach, Dal, NFC | 211 | 126 | 1,882 | 15 | 4 |
|  | Bob Griese, Mia, AFC | 263 | 145 | 2,089 | 19 | 9 |
| 1972 | Norm Snead, NY, NFC | 325 | 196 | 2,307 | 17 | 12 |
|  | Earl Morrall, Mia, AFC | 150 | 83 | 1,360 | 11 | 7 |

## Passing* *(Cont.)*

*Since 1973, the annual passing NFL leaders have been determined by a passer rating system that compares individual performances to a fixed performance standard. Before 1973, total passing yards gained was used.

| Year | Player, Team | Comp% | Yds | TD | Int | Rating |
|------|-------------|-------|-----|----|----|--------|
| 1973 | Roger Staubach, Dal, NFC | 62.6 | 2,428 | 23 | 15 | 94.6 |
| | Ken Stabler, Oak, AFC | 62.7 | 1,997 | 14 | 10 | 88.3 |
| 1974 | Ken Anderson, Cin, AFC | 64.9 | 2,667 | 18 | 10 | 95.7 |
| | Sonny Jurgensen, Wash, NFC | 64.1 | 1,185 | 11 | 5 | 94.5 |
| 1975 | Ken Anderson, Cin, AFC | 60.5 | 3,169 | 21 | 11 | 93.9 |
| | Fran Tarkenton, Min, NFC | 64.2 | 2,994 | 25 | 13 | 91.8 |
| 1976 | Ken Stabler, Oak, AFC | 66.7 | 2,737 | 27 | 17 | 103.4 |
| | James Harris, LA, NFC | 57.6 | 1,460 | 8 | 6 | 89.6 |
| 1977 | Bob Griese, Mia, AFC | 58.6 | 2,252 | 22 | 13 | 87.8 |
| | Roger Staubach, Dal, NFC | 58.2 | 2,620 | 18 | 9 | 87.0 |
| 1978 | Roger Staubach, Dal, NFC | 55.9 | 3,190 | 25 | 16 | 84.9 |
| | Terry Bradshaw, Pit, AFC | 56.3 | 2,915 | 28 | 20 | 84.7 |
| 1979 | Roger Staubach, Dal, NFC | 57.9 | 3,586 | 27 | 11 | 92.3 |
| | Dan Fouts, SD, AFC | 62.6 | 4,082 | 24 | 24 | 82.6 |
| 1980 | Brian Sipe, Clev, AFC | 60.8 | 4,132 | 30 | 14 | 91.4 |
| | Ron Jaworski, Phi, NFC | 57.0 | 3,529 | 27 | 12 | 91.0 |
| 1981 | Ken Anderson, Cin, AFC | 62.6 | 3,754 | 29 | 10 | 98.4 |
| | Joe Montana, SF, NFC | 63.7 | 3,565 | 19 | 12 | 88.4 |
| 1982 | Ken Anderson, Cin, AFC | 70.6 | 2,495 | 12 | 9 | 95.3 |
| | Joe Theismann, Wash, NFC | 63.9 | 2,033 | 13 | 9 | 91.3 |
| 1983 | Steve Bartkowski, Atl, NFC | 63.4 | 3,167 | 22 | 5 | 97.6 |
| | Dan Marino, Mia AFC | 58.4 | 2,210 | 20 | 6 | 96.0 |
| 1984 | Dan Marino, Mia, AFC | 64.2 | 5,084 | 48 | 17 | 108.9 |
| | Joe Montana, SF, NFC | 64.6 | 3,630 | 28 | 10 | 102.9 |
| 1985 | Ken O'Brien, NY, AFC | 60.9 | 3,888 | 25 | 8 | 96.2 |
| | Joe Montana, SF, NFC | 61.3 | 3,653 | 27 | 13 | 91.3 |
| 1986 | Tommy Kramer, Min, NFC | 55.9 | 3,000 | 24 | 10 | 92.6 |
| | Dan Marino, Mia, AFC | 60.7 | 4,746 | 44 | 23 | 92.5 |
| 1987 | Joe Montana, SF, NFC | 66.8 | 3,054 | 31 | 13 | 102.1 |
| | Bernie Kosar, Clev, AFC | 61.9 | 3,033 | 22 | 9 | 95.4 |
| 1988 | Boomer Esiason, Cin, AFC | 57.5 | 3,572 | 28 | 14 | 97.4 |
| | Wade Wilson, Min, NFC | 61.4 | 2,746 | 15 | 9 | 91.5 |
| 1989 | Joe Montana, SF, NFC | 70.2 | 3,521 | 26 | 8 | 112.4 |
| | Boomer Esiason, Cin, AFC | 56.7 | 3,525 | 28 | 11 | 92.1 |
| 1990 | Jim Kelly, Buf, AFC | 63.3 | 2,829 | 24 | 9 | 101.2 |
| | Phil Simms, NY, NFC | 59.2 | 2,284 | 15 | 4 | 92.7 |
| 1991 | Steve Young, SF, NFC | 64.5 | 2,517 | 17 | 8 | 101.8 |
| | Jim Kelly, Buf, AFC | 64.1 | 3,844 | 33 | 17 | 97.6 |
| 1992 | Steve Young, SF, NFC | 66.7 | 3,465 | 25 | 7 | 107.0 |
| | Warren Moon, Hou, AFC | 64.7 | 2,521 | 18 | 12 | 89.3 |
| 1993 | Steve Young, SF, NFC | 68.0 | 4,023 | 29 | 16 | 101.5 |
| | John Elway, Den, AFC | 63.2 | 4,030 | 25 | 10 | 92.8 |
| 1994 | Steve Young, SF, NFC | 70.3 | 3,969 | 35 | 10 | 112.8 |
| | Dan Marino, Mia, AFC | 62.0 | 4,453 | 30 | 17 | 89.2 |
| 1995 | Brett Favre, GB, NFC | 62.9 | 4,413 | 38 | 13 | 99.5 |
| | Jim Harbaugh, Ind, AFC | 61.2 | 2,575 | 17 | 5 | 100.7 |
| 1996 | John Elway, Den, AFC | 61.6 | 3,328 | 26 | 14 | 89.2 |
| | Steve Young, SF, NFC | 67.7 | 2,410 | 14 | 6 | 97.2 |
| 1997 | Steve Young, SF, NFC | 67.7 | 3,029 | 19 | 6 | 104.7 |
| | Mark Brunell, Jax, AFC | 60.7 | 3,281 | 18 | 7 | 91.2 |
| 1998 | Randall Cunningham, Min, NFC | 60.9 | 3,704 | 34 | 10 | 106.0 |
| | Vinny Testaverde, NYJ, AFC | 61.5 | 3,256 | 29 | 7 | 101.6 |
| 1999 | Kurt Warner, StL, NFC | 65.1 | 4,353 | 41 | 13 | 109.2 |
| | Peyton Manning, Ind, AFC | 62.1 | 4,135 | 26 | 15 | 90.7 |
| 2000 | Trent Green, StL, NFC | 60.4 | 2,063 | 16 | 5 | 101.8 |
| | Brian Griese, Den, AFC | 64.3 | 2,688 | 19 | 4 | 102.9 |
| 2001 | Kurt Warner, StL, NFC | 68.7 | 4,830 | 36 | 22 | 101.4 |
| | Rich Gannon, Oak, AFC | 65.8 | 3,828 | 27 | 9 | 95.5 |
| 2002 | Brad Johnson, TB, NFC | 62.3 | 3,049 | 22 | 6 | 92.9 |
| | Chad Pennington, NY, AFC | 68.9 | 3,120 | 22 | 6 | 104.2 |

## Passing *(Cont.)*

| Year | Player, Team | Comp% | Yds | TD | Int | Rating |
|------|--------------|-------|-----|-----|-----|--------|
| 2003 | Steve McNair, Ten, AFC | 62.5 | 3,215 | 24 | 7 | 100.4 |
|  | Daunte Culpepper, Min, NFC | 65.0 | 3,479 | 25 | 11 | 96.4 |
| 2004 | Peyton Manning, Ind, AFC | 67.6 | 4,557 | 49 | 10 | 121.1 |
|  | Daunte Culpepper, Min, NFC | 69.2 | 4,717 | 39 | 11 | 110.9 |
| 2005 | Peyton Manning, Ind, AFC | 67.3 | 3,747 | 28 | 10 | 104.1 |
|  | Matt Hasselbeck, GB, NFC | 65.5 | 3,459 | 24 | 9 | 98.2 |
| 2006 | Peyton Manning, Ind, AFC | 65.0 | 4,397 | 31 | 9 | 101.0 |
|  | Drew Brees, NO, NFC | 64.3 | 4,418 | 26 | 11 | 96.2 |
| 2007 | Tom Brady, NE, AFC | 68.9 | 4,806 | 50 | 8 | 117.2 |
|  | Tony Romo, Dal, NFC | 64.4 | 4,211 | 36 | 19 | 97.4 |
| 2008 | Philip Rivers, SD, AFC | 65.3 | 4,009 | 34 | 11 | 105.5 |
|  | Kurt Warner, Ari, NFC | 67.1 | 4,583 | 30 | 14 | 96.9 |

## Pass Receiving†

| Year | Player, Team | No. | Yds | Avg | TD |
|------|--------------|-----|-----|-----|-----|
| 1932 | Ray Flaherty, NY | 21 | 350 | 16.7 | 3 |
| 1933 | John Kelly, Brooklyn | 22 | 246 | 11.2 | 3 |
| 1934 | Joe Carter, Phil | 16 | 238 | 14.9 | 4 |
|  | Morris Badgro, NY | 16 | 206 | 12.9 | 1 |
| 1935 | Tod Goodwin, NY | 26 | 432 | 16.6 | 4 |
| 1936 | Don Hutson, GB | 34 | 536 | 15.8 | 8 |
| 1937 | Don Hutson, GB | 41 | 552 | 13.5 | 7 |
| 1938 | Gaynell Tinsley, Chi Cards | 41 | 516 | 12.6 | 1 |
| 1939 | Don Hutson, GB | 34 | 846 | 24.9 | 6 |
| 1940 | Don Looney, Phil | 58 | 707 | 12.2 | 4 |
| 1941 | Don Hutson, GB | 58 | 738 | 12.7 | 10 |
| 1942 | Don Hutson, GB | 74 | 1,211 | 16.4 | 17 |
| 1943 | Don Hutson, GB | 47 | 776 | 16.5 | 11 |
| 1944 | Don Hutson, GB | 58 | 866 | 14.9 | 9 |
| 1945 | Don Hutson, GB | 47 | 834 | 17.7 | 9 |
| 1946 | Jim Benton, LA | 63 | 981 | 15.6 | 6 |
| 1947 | Jim Keane, Chi | 64 | 910 | 14.2 | 10 |
| 1948 | Tom Fears, LA | 51 | 698 | 13.7 | 4 |
| 1949 | Tom Fears, LA | 77 | 1,013 | 13.2 | 9 |
| 1950 | Tom Fears, LA | 84 | 1,116 | 13.3 | 7 |
| 1951 | Elroy Hirsch, LA | 66 | 1,495 | 22.7 | 17 |
| 1952 | Mac Speedie, Clev | 62 | 911 | 14.7 | 5 |
| 1953 | Pete Pihos, Phil | 63 | 1,049 | 16.7 | 10 |
| 1954 | Pete Pihos, Phil | 60 | 872 | 14.5 | 10 |
|  | Billy Wilson, SF | 60 | 830 | 13.8 | 5 |
| 1955 | Pete Pihos, Phil | 62 | 864 | 13.9 | 7 |
| 1956 | Billy Wilson, SF | 60 | 889 | 14.8 | 5 |
| 1957 | Billy Wilson, SF | 52 | 757 | 14.6 | 6 |
| 1958 | Raymond Berry, Balt | 56 | 794 | 14.2 | 9 |
|  | Pete Retzlaff, Phil | 56 | 766 | 13.7 | 2 |
| 1959 | Raymond Berry, Balt | 66 | 959 | 14.5 | 14 |
| 1960 | Lionel Taylor, Den, AFL | 92 | 1,235 | 13.4 | 12 |
|  | Raymond Berry, Balt, NFL | 74 | 1,298 | 17.5 | 10 |
| 1961 | Lionel Taylor, Den, AFL | 100 | 1,176 | 11.8 | 4 |
|  | Jim Phillips, LA, NFL | 78 | 1,092 | 14.0 | 5 |
| 1962 | Lionel Taylor, Den, AFL | 77 | 908 | 11.8 | 4 |
|  | Bobby Mitchell, Wash, NFL | 72 | 1,384 | 19.2 | 11 |
| 1963 | Lionel Taylor, Den, AFL | 78 | 1,101 | 14.1 | 10 |
|  | Bobby Joe Conrad, St. Louis, NFL | 73 | 967 | 13.2 | 10 |
| 1964 | Charley Hennigan, Houston, AFL | 101 | 1,546 | 15.3 | 8 |
|  | Johnny Morris, Chi, NFL | 93 | 1,200 | 12.9 | 10 |
| 1965 | Lionel Taylor, Den, AFL | 85 | 1,131 | 13.3 | 6 |
|  | Dave Parks, SF, NFL | 80 | 1,344 | 16.8 | 12 |
| 1966 | Lance Alworth, SD, AFL | 73 | 1,383 | 18.9 | 13 |
|  | Charley Taylor, Wash, NFL | 72 | 1,119 | 15.5 | 12 |
| 1967 | George Sauer, NY, AFL | 75 | 1,189 | 15.9 | 6 |
|  | Charley Taylor, Wash, NFL | 70 | 990 | 14.1 | 9 |
| 1968 | Clifton McNeil, SF, NFL | 71 | 994 | 14.0 | 7 |
|  | Lance Alworth, SD, AFL | 68 | 1,312 | 19.3 | 10 |
| 1969 | Dan Abramowicz, NO, NFL | 73 | 1,015 | 13.9 | 7 |
|  | Lance Alworth, SD, AFL | 64 | 1,003 | 15.7 | 4 |
| 1970 | Dick Gordon, Chi, NFC | 71 | 1,026 | 14.5 | 13 |
|  | Marlin Briscoe, Buf, AFC | 57 | 1,036 | 18.2 | 8 |
| 1971 | Fred Biletnikoff, Oak, AFC | 61 | 929 | 15.2 | 9 |
|  | Bob Tucker, NY, NFC | 59 | 791 | 13.4 | 4 |
| 1972 | Harold Jackson, Phil, NFC | 62 | 1,048 | 16.9 | 4 |
|  | Fred Biletnikoff, Oak, AFC | 58 | 802 | 13.8 | 7 |
| 1973 | Harold Carmichael, Phil, NFC | 67 | 1,116 | 16.7 | 9 |
|  | Fred Willis, Hou, AFC | 57 | 371 | 6.5 | 1 |
| 1974 | Lydell Mitchell, Balt, AFC | 72 | 544 | 7.6 | 2 |
|  | Charles Young, Phil, NFC | 63 | 696 | 11.0 | 3 |
| 1975 | Chuck Foreman, Min, NFC | 73 | 691 | 9.5 | 9 |
|  | Reggie Rucker, Clev, AFC | 60 | 770 | 12.8 | 3 |
|  | Lydell Mitchell, Balt, AFC | 60 | 544 | 9.1 | 4 |
| 1976 | MacArthur Lane, KC, AFC | 66 | 686 | 10.4 | 1 |
|  | Drew Pearson, Dal, NFC | 58 | 806 | 13.9 | 6 |
| 1977 | Lydell Mitchell, Balt, AFC | 71 | 620 | 8.7 | 4 |
|  | Ahmad Rashad, Min, NFC | 51 | 681 | 13.4 | 2 |
| 1978 | Rickey Young, Min, NFC | 88 | 704 | 8.0 | 5 |
|  | Steve Largent, Sea, AFC | 71 | 1,168 | 16.5 | 8 |

†Most catches.

## Pass Receiving† *(Cont.)*

| Year | Player, Team | No. | Yds | Avg | TD | | Year | Player, Team | No. | Yds | Avg | TD |
|------|--------------|-----|-----|-----|----|---|------|--------------|-----|-----|-----|----|
| 1979 | Joe Washington, Balt, AFC | 82 | 750 | 9.1 | 3 | | 1994 | Cris Carter, Min, NFC | 122 | 1,256 | 10.3 | 7 |
| | Ahmad Rashad, Min, NFC | 80 | 1,156 | 14.5 | 9 | | | Ben Coates, NE, AFC | 96 | 1,174 | 12.2 | 7 |
| 1980 | Kellen Winslow, SD, AFC | 89 | 1,290 | 14.5 | 9 | | 1995 | Herman Moore, Det, NFC | 123 | 1,686 | 13.7 | 14 |
| | Earl Cooper, SF, NFC | 83 | 567 | 6.8 | 4 | | | Carl Pickens, Cin, AFC | 99 | 1,234 | 12.5 | 17 |
| 1981 | Kellen Winslow, SD, AFC | 88 | 1,075 | 12.2 | 10 | | 1996 | Jerry Rice, SF, NFC | 108 | 1,254 | 11.6 | 8 |
| | Dwight Clark, SF, NFC | 85 | 1,105 | 13.0 | 4 | | | Carl Pickens, Cin, AFC | 100 | 1,180 | 11.8 | 12 |
| 1982 | Dwight Clark, SF, NFC | 60 | 913 | 15.2 | 5 | | 1997 | Herman Moore, Det, NFC | 104 | 1,293 | 12.4 | 8 |
| | Kellen Winslow, SD, AFC | 54 | 721 | 13.4 | 6 | | | Tim Brown, Oak, AFC | 104 | 1,408 | 13.5 | 5 |
| 1983 | Todd Christensen, LA, AFC | 92 | 1,247 | 13.6 | 12 | | 1998 | Frank Sanders, Ariz, NFC | 89 | 1,145 | 12.9 | 3 |
| | Roy Green, StL, NFC | 78 | 1,227 | 15.7 | 14 | | | O.J. McDuffie, Mia, AFC | 90 | 1,050 | 11.7 | 7 |
| | Charlie Brown, Wash, NFC | 78 | 1,225 | 15.7 | 8 | | 1999 | Muhsin Muhammad, Car, NFC | 96 | 1,253 | 13.1 | 8 |
| | Earnest Gray, NY, NFC | 78 | 1,139 | 14.6 | 5 | | | Jimmy Smith, Jax, AFC | 116 | 1,636 | 14.1 | 6 |
| 1984 | Art Monk, Wash, NFC | 106 | 1,372 | 12.9 | 7 | | 2000 | Mushin Muhammad, Car, NFC | 102 | 1,183 | 11.6 | 6 |
| | Ozzie Newsome, Clev, AFC | 89 | 1,001 | 11.2 | 5 | | | Marvin Harrison, Ind, AFC | 102 | 1,413 | 13.9 | 14 |
| 1985 | Roger Craig, SF, NFC | 92 | 1,016 | 11.0 | 6 | | 2001 | Rod Smith, Den, NFC | 113 | 1,343 | 11.9 | 11 |
| | Lionel James, SD, AFC | 86 | 1,027 | 11.9 | 6 | | | Keyshawn Johnson, TB, NFC | 106 | 1,266 | 11.9 | 1 |
| 1986 | Todd Christensen, LA, AFC | 95 | 1,153 | 12.1 | 8 | | 2002 | Marvin Harrison, Ind, AFC | 143 | 1,722 | 12.0 | 11 |
| | Jerry Rice, SF, NFC | 86 | 1,570 | 18.3 | 15 | | | Randy Moss, Min, NFC | 106 | 1,347 | 12.7 | 7 |
| 1987 | J.T. Smith, StL Card, NFC | 91 | 1,117 | 12.3 | 8 | | 2003 | LaDainian Tomlinson, SD, AFC | 100 | 725 | 7.3 | 4 |
| | Al Toon, NY, AFC | 68 | 976 | 14.4 | 5 | | | Torry Holt, StL, NFC | 117 | 1,696 | 14.5 | 12 |
| 1988 | Al Toon, NY, AFC | 93 | 1,067 | 11.5 | 5 | | 2004 | Tony Gonzalez, KC, AFC | 102 | 1,258 | 12.3 | 7 |
| | Henry Ellard, LA, NFC | 86 | 1,414 | 16.4 | 10 | | | Joe Horn, NO, NFC | 94 | 1,399 | 14.9 | 11 |
| 1989 | Sterling Sharpe, GB, NFC | 90 | 1,423 | 15.8 | 12 | | 2005 | Chad Johnson, Cin, AFC | 97 | 1,432 | 14.8 | 9 |
| | Andre Reed, Buf, AFC | 88 | 1,312 | 14.9 | 9 | | | Steve Smith, Car, NFC | 103 | 1,563 | 15.2 | 12 |
| 1990 | Jerry Rice, SF, NFC | 100 | 1,502 | 15.0 | 13 | | 2006 | Chad Johnson, Cin, AFC | 87 | 1,369 | 15.7 | 7 |
| | Haywood Jeffires, Hou, AFC | 74 | 1,048 | 14.2 | 8 | | | Roy Williams, Det, NFC | 82 | 1,310 | 16.0 | 7 |
| | Drew Hill, Hou, AFC | 74 | 1,019 | 13.8 | 5 | | 2007 | Reggie Wayne, Ind, AFC | 104 | 1,510 | 14.5 | 10 |
| 1991 | Haywood Jeffires, Hou, AFC | 100 | 1,181 | 11.8 | 7 | | | Larry Fitzgerald, Ari, NFC | 100 | 1,409 | 14.1 | 10 |
| | Michael Irvin, Dal, NFC | 93 | 1,523 | 16.4 | 8 | | 2008 | Andre Johnson, Hou, AFC | 115 | 1,575 | 13.7 | 8 |
| 1992 | Sterling Sharpe, GB, NFC | 108 | 1,461 | 13.5 | 13 | | | Larry Fitzgerald, Ari, NFC | 96 | 1,431 | 14.9 | 12 |
| | Haywood Jeffires, Hou, AFC | 90 | 913 | 10.1 | 9 | | | | | | | |
| 1993 | Sterling Sharpe, GB, NFC | 112 | 1,274 | 11.4 | 11 | | | | | | | |
| | Reggie Langhorne, Ind, AFC | 85 | 1,038 | 12.2 | 3 | | | | | | | |

†Most catches.

## Scoring

| Year | Player, Team | TD | FG | PAT | TP | | Year | Player, Team | TD | FG | PAT | TP |
|------|--------------|----|----|-----|----|---|------|--------------|----|----|-----|----|
| 1932 | Earl Clark, Portsmouth | 6 | 3 | 10 | 55 | | 1942 | Don Hutson, GB | 17 | 1 | 33 | 138 |
| 1933 | Ken Strong, NY | 6 | 5 | 13 | 64 | | 1943 | Don Hutson, GB | 12 | 3 | 36 | 117 |
| | Glenn Presnell, Ports | 6 | 6 | 10 | 64 | | 1944 | Don Hutson, GB | 9 | 0 | 31 | 85 |
| 1934 | Jack Manders, Chi | 3 | 10 | 31 | 79 | | 1945 | Steve Van Buren, Phil | 18 | 0 | 2 | 110 |
| 1935 | Earl Clark, Det | 6 | 1 | 16 | 55 | | 1946 | Ted Fritsch, GB | 10 | 9 | 13 | 100 |
| 1936 | Earl Clark, Det | 7 | 4 | 19 | 73 | | 1947 | Pat Harder, Chicago Cards | 7 | 7 | 39 | 102 |
| 1937 | Jack Manders, Chi | 5 | 18 | 15 | 69 | | 1948 | Pat Harder, Chicago Cards | 6 | 7 | 53 | 110 |
| 1938 | Clarke Hinkle, GB | 7 | 3 | 7 | 58 | | 1949 | Pat Harder, Chicago Cards | 8 | 3 | 45 | 102 |
| 1939 | Andy Farkas, Wash | 11 | 0 | 2 | 68 | | | Gene Roberts, NY | 17 | 0 | 0 | 102 |
| 1940 | Don Hutson, GB | 7 | 0 | 15 | 57 | | 1950 | Doak Walker, Det | 11 | 8 | 38 | 128 |
| 1941 | Don Hutson, GB | 12 | 1 | 20 | 95 | | 1951 | Elroy Hirsch, LA | 17 | 0 | 0 | 102 |

## Scoring *(Cont.)*

| Year | Player, Team | TD | FG | PAT | TP | Year | Player, Team | TD | FG | PAT | TP |
|---|---|---|---|---|---|---|---|---|---|---|---|
| 1952 | Gordy Soltau, SF | 7 | 6 | 34 | 94 | 1983 | Mark Moseley, Wash, NFC | 0 | 33 | 62 | 161 |
| 1953 | Gordy Soltau, SF | 6 | 10 | 48 | 114 | | Gary Anderson, Pit, AFC | 0 | 27 | 38 | 119 |
| 1954 | Bobby Walston, Phil | 11 | 4 | 36 | 114 | 1984 | Ray Wersching, SF, NFC | 0 | 25 | 56 | 131 |
| 1955 | Doak Walker, Det | 7 | 9 | 27 | 96 | | Gary Anderson, Pit, AFC | 0 | 24 | 45 | 117 |
| 1956 | Bobby Layne, Det | 5 | 12 | 33 | 99 | 1985 | Kevin Butler, Chi, NFC | 0 | 31 | 51 | 144 |
| 1957 | Sam Baker, Wash | 1 | 14 | 29 | 77 | | Gary Anderson, Pit, AFC | 0 | 33 | 40 | 139 |
| | Lou Groza, Clev | 0 | 15 | 32 | 77 | 1986 | Tony Franklin, NE, AFC | 0 | 32 | 44 | 140 |
| 1958 | Jim Brown, Clev | 18 | 0 | 0 | 108 | | Kevin Butler, Chi, NFC | 0 | 28 | 36 | 120 |
| 1959 | Paul Hornung, GB | 7 | 7 | 31 | 94 | 1987 | Jerry Rice, SF, NFC | 23 | 0 | 0 | 138 |
| 1960 | Paul Hornung, GB, NFL | 15 | 15 | 41 | 176 | | Jim Breech, Cin, AFC | 0 | 24 | 25 | 97 |
| | Gene Mingo, Den, AFL | 6 | 18 | 33 | 123 | 1988 | Scott Norwood, Buf, AFC | 0 | 32 | 33 | 129 |
| 1961 | Gino Cappelletti, Bos, AFL | 8 | 17 | 48 | 147 | | Mike Cofer, SF, NFC | 0 | 27 | 40 | 121 |
| | Paul Hornung, GB, NFL | 10 | 15 | 41 | 146 | 1989 | Mike Cofer, SF, NFC | 0 | 29 | 49 | 136 |
| 1962 | Gene Mingo, Den, AFL | 4 | 27 | 32 | 137 | | David Treadwell, Den, AFC | 0 | 27 | 39 | 120 |
| | Jim Taylor, GB, NFL | 19 | 0 | 0 | 114 | 1990 | Nick Lowery, KC, AFC | 0 | 34 | 37 | 139 |
| 1963 | Gino Cappelletti, Bos, AFL | 2 | 22 | 35 | 113 | | Chip Lohmiller, Wash, NFC | 0 | 30 | 41 | 131 |
| | Don Chandler, NY, NFL | 0 | 18 | 52 | 106 | 1991 | Chip Lohmiller, Wash, NFC | 0 | 31 | 56 | 149 |
| 1964 | Gino Cappelletti, Bos, AFL | 7 | 25 | 36 | 155 | | Pete Stoyanovich, Mia, AFC | 0 | 31 | 28 | 121 |
| | Lenny Moore, Balt, NFL | 20 | 0 | 0 | 120 | 1992 | Pete Stoyanovich, Mia, AFC | 0 | 30 | 34 | 124 |
| 1965 | Gale Sayers, Chi, NFL | 22 | 0 | 0 | 132 | | Morten Anderson, NO, NFC | 0 | 29 | 33 | 120 |
| | Gino Cappelletti, Bos, AFL | 9 | 17 | 27 | 132 | | Chip Lohmiller, Wash, NFC | 0 | 30 | 30 | 120 |
| 1966 | Gino Cappelletti, Bos, AFL | 6 | 16 | 35 | 119 | 1993 | Jeff Jaeger, Rai, AFC | 0 | 35 | 27 | 132 |
| | Bruce Gossett, LA, NFL | 0 | 28 | 29 | 113 | | Jason Hanson, Det, NFC | 0 | 34 | 28 | 130 |
| 1967 | Jim Bakken, StL, NFL | 0 | 27 | 36 | 117 | 1994 | John Carney, SD, AFC | 0 | 34 | 33 | 135 |
| | George Blanda, Oak, AFL | 0 | 20 | 56 | 116 | | Fuad Reveiz, Min, NFC | 0 | 34 | 30 | 132 |
| 1968 | Jim Turner, NY, AFL | 0 | 34 | 43 | 145 | | Emmitt Smith, Dal, NFC | 22 | 0 | 0 | 132 |
| | Leroy Kelly, Clev, NFL | 20 | 0 | 0 | 120 | 1995 | Emmitt Smith, Dal, NFC | 25 | 0 | 0 | 150 |
| 1969 | Jim Turner, NY, AFL | 0 | 32 | 33 | 129 | | Norm Johnson, Pit, AFC | 0 | 34 | 39 | 141 |
| | Fred Cox, Min, NFL | 0 | 26 | 43 | 121 | 1996 | John Kasay, Car, NFC | 0 | 37 | 34 | 145 |
| 1970 | Fred Cox, Min, NFC | 0 | 30 | 35 | 125 | | Cary Blanchard, Ind, AFC | 0 | 36 | 27 | 135 |
| | Jan Stenerud, KC, AFC | 0 | 30 | 26 | 116 | 1997 | Richie Cunningham, Dal, NFC | 0 | 34 | 24 | 126 |
| 1971 | Garo Yepremian, Mia, AFC | 0 | 28 | 33 | 117 | | Mike Hollis, Jax, AFC | 0 | 41 | 31 | 134 |
| | Curt Knight, Wash, NFC | 0 | 29 | 27 | 114 | 1998 | Gary Anderson, Min, NFC | 0 | 35 | 59 | 164 |
| 1972 | Chester Marcol, GB, NFC | 0 | 33 | 29 | 128 | | Steve Christie, Buf, AFC | 0 | 33 | 41 | 140 |
| | Bobby Howfield, NY AFC | 0 | 27 | 40 | 121 | 1999 | Jeff Wilkins, StL, NFC | 0 | 20 | 64 | 124 |
| 1973 | David Ray, LA, NFC | 0 | 30 | 40 | 130 | | Mike Vanderjagt, Ind, AFC | 0 | 34 | 43 | 145 |
| | Roy Gerela, Pit, AFC | 0 | 29 | 36 | 123 | 2000 | Marshall Faulk, StL, NFC | 26 | 0 | 0 | 160 |
| 1974 | Chester Marcol, GB, NFC | 0 | 25 | 19 | 94 | | Matt Stover, Balt, AFC | 0 | 35 | 30 | 135 |
| | Roy Gerela, Pit, AFC | 0 | 20 | 33 | 93 | 2001 | Marshall Faulk, StL, NFC | 21 | 0 | 0 | 128 |
| 1975 | O.J. Simpson, Buf, AFC | 23 | 0 | 0 | 138 | | Mike Vanderjagt, Ind, AFC | 0 | 28 | 41 | 125 |
| | Chuck Foreman, Min, NFC | 22 | 0 | 0 | 132 | 2002 | Jay Feely, Atl, NFC | 0 | 32 | 42 | 138 |
| 1976 | Toni Linhart, Balt, AFC | 0 | 20 | 49 | 109 | | Priest Holmes, KC, AFC | 24 | 0 | 0 | 144 |
| | Mark Moseley, Wash, NFC | 0 | 22 | 31 | 97 | 2003 | Jeff Wilkins StL, NFC | 0 | 39 | 46 | 163 |
| 1977 | Errol Mann, Oak, AFC | 0 | 20 | 39 | 99 | | Priest Holmes, KC, AFC | 27 | 0 | 0 | 162 |
| | Walter Payton, Chi, NFC | 16 | 0 | 0 | 96 | 2004 | Adam Vinatieri, NE, AFC | 0 | 31 | 48 | 141 |
| 1978 | Frank Corral, LA, NFC | 0 | 29 | 31 | 118 | | David Akers, Phil, NFC | 0 | 27 | 41 | 122 |
| | Pat Leahy, NY, AFC | 0 | 22 | 41 | 107 | 2005 | Shayne Graham, Cin, AFC | 0 | 28 | 47 | 131 |
| 1979 | John Smith, NE, AFC | 0 | 23 | 46 | 115 | | Shaun Alexander, Sea, NFC | 28 | 0 | 0 | 168 |
| | Mark Moseley, Wash, NFC | 0 | 25 | 39 | 114 | 2006 | LaDainian Tomlinson, SD, AFC | 31 | 0 | 0 | 186 |
| 1980 | John Smith, NE, AFC | 0 | 26 | 51 | 129 | | Robbie Gould, Chi, NFC | 0 | 32 | 47 | 143 |
| | Ed Murray, Det, NFC | 0 | 27 | 35 | 116 | 2007 | Randy Moss, NE, AFC | 23 | 0 | 0 | 138 |
| 1981 | Ed Murray, Det, NFC | 0 | 25 | 46 | 121 | | Mason Crosby, GB, NFC | 0 | 31 | 48 | 141 |
| | Rafael Septien, Dal, NFC | 0 | 27 | 40 | 121 | 2008 | Stephen Gostkowski, NE, AFC | 0 | 36 | 40 | 148 |
| | Jim Breech, Cin, AFC | 0 | 22 | 49 | 115 | | David Akers, Phil, NFC | 0 | 33 | 45 | 144 |
| | Nick Lowery, KC, AFC | 0 | 26 | 37 | 115 | | | | | | |
| 1982 | Marcus Allen, LA, AFC | 14 | 0 | 0 | 84 | | | | | | |
| | Wendell Tyler, LA, NFC | 13 | 0 | 0 | 78 | | | | | | |

## Interceptions

| Year | Player, Team | Int | Yds |
|------|--------------|-----|-----|
| 1940 | Clarence Parker, Brooklyn | 6 | 146 |
| | Kent Ryan, Det | 6 | 65 |
| | Don Hutson, GB | 6 | 24 |
| 1941 | Marshall Goldberg, Chicago Card | 7 | 54 |
| | Art Jones, Pit | 7 | 35 |
| 1942 | Clyde Turner, Chicago Bears | 8 | 96 |
| 1943 | Sammy Baugh, Wash | 11 | 112 |
| 1944 | Howard Livingston, NYG | 9 | 172 |
| 1945 | Ray Zimmerman, Phil | 7 | 90 |
| 1946 | Bill Dudley, Pittsburgh | 10 | 242 |
| 1947 | Frank Reagan, NYG | 10 | 203 |
| | Frank Seno, Bos | 10 | 100 |
| 1948 | Dan Sandifier, Wash | 13 | 258 |
| 1949 | Bob Nussbaumer, Chicago Car | 12 | 157 |
| 1950 | Orban Sanders, NY Yanks | 13 | 199 |
| 1951 | Otto Schnellbacher, NYG | 11 | 194 |
| 1952 | Dick Lane, LA | 14 | 298 |
| 1953 | Jack Christiansen, Det | 12 | 238 |
| 1954 | Dick Lane, Chicago Card | 10 | 181 |
| 1955 | Will Sherman, LA | 11 | 101 |
| 1956 | Lindon Crow, Chicago Card | 11 | 170 |
| 1957 | Milt Davis, Balt | 10 | 219 |
| | Jack Christiansen, Det | 10 | 137 |
| | Jack Butler, Pit | 10 | 85 |
| 1958 | Jim Patton, NYG | 11 | 183 |
| 1959 | Dean Derby, Pit | 7 | 127 |
| | Milt Davis, Balt | 7 | 119 |
| | Don Shinnick, Balt | 7 | 70 |
| 1960 | Goose Gonsoulin, Den, AFL | 11 | 98 |
| | Dave Baker, SF, NFL | 10 | 96 |
| | Jerry Norton, StL, NFL | 10 | 96 |
| 1961 | Billy Atkins, Buf, AFL | 10 | 158 |
| | Dick Lynch, NYG, NFL | 9 | 60 |
| 1962 | Lee Riley, NY Titans, AFL | 11 | 122 |
| | Willie Wood, GB, NFL | 9 | 132 |
| 1963 | Fred Glick, Hous, AFL | 12 | 180 |
| | Dick Lynch, NYG, NFL | 9 | 251 |
| | Roosevelt Taylor, Chi, NFL | 9 | 172 |
| 1964 | Dainard Paulson, NYJ, AFL | 12 | 157 |
| | Paul Krause, Wash, NFL | 12 | 140 |
| 1965 | W. K. Hicks, Hous, AFL | 9 | 156 |
| | Bobby Boyd, Balt, NFL | 9 | 78 |
| 1966 | Larry Wilson, StL, NFL | 10 | 180 |
| | Johnny Robinson, KC, AFL | 10 | 136 |
| | Bobby Hunt, KC, AFL | 10 | 113 |
| 1967 | Lem Barney, Det, NFL | 10 | 232 |
| | Dave Whitsell, NO, NFL | 10 | 178 |
| | Miller Farr, Hous, AFL | 10 | 264 |
| | Tom Janik, Buf, AFL | 10 | 222 |
| | Dick Westmoreland, Mia, AFL | 10 | 127 |
| 1968 | Dave Grayson, Oak, AFL | 10 | 195 |
| | Willie Williams, NYG, NFL | 10 | 103 |
| 1969 | Mel Renfro, Dal, NFL | 10 | 118 |
| | Emmitt Thomas, KC, AFL | 9 | 146 |
| 1970 | Johnny Robinson, KC, AFC | 10 | 155 |
| | Dick LeBeau, Det, NFC | 9 | 96 |
| 1971 | Bill Bradley, Phil, NFC | 11 | 248 |
| | Ken Houston, Hou, AFC | 9 | 220 |
| 1972 | Bill Bradley, Phil, NFC | 9 | 73 |
| | Mike Sensibaugh, KC, AFC | 8 | 65 |
| 1973 | Dick Anderson, Mia, AFC | 8 | 163 |
| | Mike Wagner, Pit, AFC | 8 | 134 |
| | Bobby Bryant, Min, NFC | 7 | 105 |
| 1974 | Emmitt Thomas, KC, AFC | 12 | 214 |
| | Ray Brown, Atl, NFC | 8 | 164 |
| 1975 | Mel Blount, Pit, AFC | 11 | 121 |
| | Paul Krause, Min, NFC | 10 | 201 |
| 1976 | Monte Jackson, LA, NFC | 10 | 173 |
| | Ken Riley, Cin, AFC | 9 | 141 |
| 1977 | Lyle Blackwood, Balt, AFC | 10 | 163 |
| | Rolland Lawrence, Atl, NFC | 7 | 138 |
| 1978 | Thom Darden, Clev, AFC | 10 | 200 |
| | Ken Stone, StL, NFC | 9 | 139 |
| | Willie Buchanon, GB, NFC | 9 | 93 |
| 1979 | Mike Reinfeldt, Hou, AFC | 12 | 205 |
| | Lemar Parrish, Wash, NFC | 9 | 65 |
| 1980 | Lester Hayes, Oak, AFC | 13 | 273 |
| | Nolan Cromwell, LA, NFC | 8 | 140 |
| 1981 | Everson Walls, Dal, NFC | 11 | 133 |
| | John Harris, Sea, AFC | 10 | 155 |
| 1982 | Everson Walls, Dal, NFC | 7 | 61 |
| | Ken Riley, Cin, AFC | 5 | 88 |
| | Bobby Jackson, NYJ, AFC | 5 | 84 |
| | Dwayne Woodruff, Pit, AFC | 5 | 53 |
| | Donnie Shell, Pit, AFC | 5 | 27 |
| 1983 | Mark Murphy, Wash, NFC | 9 | 127 |
| | Ken Riley, Cin, AFC | 8 | 89 |
| | Vann McElroy, LA, AFC | 8 | 68 |
| 1984 | Ken Easley, Sea, AFC | 10 | 126 |
| | Tom Flynn, GB, NFC | 9 | 106 |
| 1985 | Everson Walls, Dal, NFC | 9 | 31 |
| | Albert Lewis, KC, AFC | 8 | 59 |
| | Eugene Daniel, Ind, AFC | 8 | 53 |
| 1986 | Ronnie Lott, SF, NFC | 10 | 134 |
| | Deron Cherry, KC, AFC | 9 | 150 |
| 1987 | Barry Wilburn, Wash, NFC | 9 | 135 |
| | Mike Prior, Ind, AFC | 6 | 57 |
| | Mark Kelso, Buf, AFC | 6 | 25 |
| | Keith Bostic, Hou, AFC | 6 | -14 |
| 1988 | Scott Case, Atl, NFC | 10 | 47 |
| | Erik McMillan, NYJ, AFC | 8 | 168 |
| 1989 | Felix Wright, Clev, AFC | 9 | 91 |
| | Eric Allen, Phil, NFC | 8 | 38 |
| 1990 | Mark Carrier, Chi, NFC | 10 | 39 |
| | Richard Johnson, Hou, AFC | 8 | 100 |
| 1991 | Ronnie Lott, LA, AFC | 8 | 52 |
| | Ray Crockett, Det, NFC | 6 | 141 |
| | Deion Sanders, Atl, NFC | 6 | 119 |
| | Aeneas Williams, Phoenix, NFC | 6 | 60 |
| | Tim McKyer, Atl, NFC | 6 | 24 |
| 1992 | Henry Jones, Buf, AFC | 8 | 263 |
| | Audray McMillian, Min, NFC | 8 | 157 |
| 1993 | Eugene Robinson, Sea, AFC | 9 | 80 |
| | Nate Odomes, Buf, AFC | 9 | 65 |
| | Deion Sanders, Atl, NFC | 7 | 91 |
| 1994 | Eric Turner, Clev, AFC | 9 | 199 |
| | Aeneas Williams, Ariz, NFC | 9 | 89 |

## Interceptions *(Cont.)*

| Year | Player, Team | Int | Yds | Year | Player, Team | Int | Yds |
|---|---|---|---|---|---|---|---|
| 1995 | Orlando Thomas, Min, NFC | 9 | 108 | 2003 | Brian Russell, Min, NFC | 9 | 185 |
| | Willie Williams, Pit, AFC | 7 | 122 | | Tony Parrish, SFo, NFC | 9 | 202 |
| 1996 | Tyrone Braxton, Den, AFC | 9 | 128 | | Patrick Surtain, Mia, AFC | 7 | 59 |
| | Keith Lyle, StL, NFC | 9 | 152 | | Ed Reed, Balt, AFC | 7 | 132 |
| 1997 | Ryan McNeil, StL, NFC | 9 | 127 | | Marcus Coleman, Hou, AFC | 7 | 95 |
| | Mark McMillian, KC, AFC | 8 | 274 | 2004 | Ed Reed, Balt, AFC | 9 | 358 |
| | Darryl Williams, Sea, AFC | 8 | 172 | | Chris Gamble, Car, NFC | 6 | 15 |
| 1998 | Ty Law, NE, AFC | 9 | 133 | | Ken Lucas, Sea, NFC | 6 | 46 |
| | Kwamie Lassiter, Ariz, NFC | 8 | 80 | 2005 | Ty Law, NYJ, AFC | 10 | 195 |
| 1999 | Rod Woodson, Balt, AFC | 7 | 195 | | Deltha O'Neal, Cin, AFC | 10 | 103 |
| | Sam Madison, Mia, AFC | 7 | 164 | | Darren Sharper, Min, NFC | 9 | 276 |
| | James Hasty, KC, AFC | 7 | 98 | 2006 | Champ Bailey, Den, AFC | 10 | 162 |
| | Donnie Abraham, TB, NFC | 7 | 115 | | Asante Samuel, NE, AFC | 10 | 120 |
| | Troy Vincent, Phil, NFC | 7 | 91 | | Walt Harris, SF, NFC | 8 | 84 |
| 2000 | Darren Sharper, GB, NFC | 9 | 109 | | Charles Woodson, GB, NFC | 8 | 61 |
| | Samari Rolle, Ten, AFC | 7 | 140 | 2007 | Antonio Cromartie, SD, AFC | 10 | 144 |
| | Brian Walker, Mia, AFC | 7 | 80 | | O. J. Atogwe, StL, NFC | 8 | 125 |
| 2001 | Ronde Barber, TB, NFC | 10 | 86 | 2008 | Ed Reed, Balt, AFC | 9 | 264 |
| | Anthony Henry, Clev, AFC | 10 | 177 | | Nick Collins, GB, NFC | 7 | 295 |
| 2002 | Rod Woodson, Oak, AFC | 8 | 225 | | Charles Woodson, GB, NFC | 7 | 169 |
| | Brian Kelly, TB, NFC | 8 | 68 | | | | |

## Sacks*

| Year | Player, Team | Sacks | Year | Player, Team | Int | Yds |
|---|---|---|---|---|---|---|
| 1982 | Doug Martin, Min, NFC | 11.5 | 1996 | Kevin Greene, Car, NFC | | 14.5 |
| | Jesse Baker, Hou, AFC | 7.5 | | Michael McCrary, Sea, AFC | | 13.5 |
| 1983 | Mark Gastineau, NYJ, AFC | 19.0 | | Bruce Smith, Buf, AFC | | 13.5 |
| | Fred Dean, SF, NFC | 17.5 | 1997 | John Randle, Min, NFC | | 15.5 |
| 1984 | Mark Gastineau, NYJ, AFC | 22.0 | | Bruce Smith, Buf, AFC | | 14.0 |
| | Richard Dent, Chi, NFC | 17.5 | 1998 | Michael Sinclair, Sea, AFC | | 16.5 |
| 1985 | Richard Dent, Chi, NFC | 17.0 | | Reggie White, GB, NFC | | 16.0 |
| | Andre Tippett, NE, AFC | 16.5 | 1999 | Kevin Carter, StL, NFC | | 17.0 |
| 1986 | Lawrence Taylor, NYG, NFC | 20.5 | | Jevon Kearse, Ten, AFC | | 14.5 |
| | Sean Jones, LA, AFC | 15.5 | 2000 | La'Roi Glover, NO, NFC | | 17.0 |
| 1987 | Reggie White, Phil, NFC | 21.0 | | Trace Armstrong, Mia, AFC | | 16.5 |
| | Andre Tippett, NE, AFC | 12.5 | 2001 | Michael Strahan, NYG, NFC | | 22.5 |
| 1988 | Reggie White, Phil, NFC | 18.0 | | Peter Boulware, Balt, AFC | | 15.0 |
| | G. Townsend, LA, AFC | 11.5 | 2002 | Jason Taylor, Mia, AFC | | 18.5 |
| 1989 | Chris Doleman, Min, NFC | 21.0 | | Simeon Rice, TB, NFC | | 15.5 |
| | Lee Williams, SD, AFC | 14.0 | 2003 | Michael Strahan, NYG, NFC | | 18.5 |
| 1990 | Derrick Thomas, KC, AFC | 20.0 | | Adewale Ogunleye, Mia, AFC | | 15.0 |
| | Charles Haley, SF, NFC | 16.0 | 2004 | Dwight Freeney, Ind, AFC | | 16.0 |
| 1991 | Pat Swilling, NO, NFC | 17.0 | | Bertrand Berry, Ariz, NFC | | 14.5 |
| | William Fuller, Hou, AFC | 15.0 | 2005 | Derrick Burgess, Oak, AFC | | 16.0 |
| 1992 | Clyde Simmons, Phil, NFC | 19.0 | | Osi Umenyiora, NYG, NFC | | 14.5 |
| | Leslie O'Neal, SD, AFC | 17.0 | 2006 | Shawne Merriman, SD, AFC | | 17.0 |
| 1993 | Neil Smith, KC, AFC | 15.0 | | Aaron Kampman, GB, NFC | | 15.5 |
| | Renaldo Turnbull, NO, NFC | 13.0 | 2007 | Jared Allen, KC, AFC | | 15.5 |
| | Reggie White, GB, NFC | 13.0 | | Patrick Kerney, Sea, NFC | | 14.5 |
| 1994 | Kevin Greene, Pit, AFC | 14.0 | 2008 | DeMarcus Ware, Dal, NFC | | 20.0 |
| | Ken Harvey, Wash, NFC | 13.5 | | Joey Porter, Mia, AFC | | 17.5 |
| | John Randle, Min, NFC | 13.5 | | | | |
| 1995 | Bryce Paup, Buf, AFC | 17.5 | | | | |
| | William Fuller, Phil, NFC | 13.0 | | | | |
| | Wayne Martin, NO, NFC | 13.0 | | | | |

*Sacks were not kept as an official NFL statistic until 1982.

# Pro Bowl Alltime Results

| Date | Result |
|------|--------|
| 1-15-39 | NY Giants 13, Pro All-Stars 10 |
| 1-14-40 | Green Bay 16, NFL All-Stars 7 |
| 12-29-40 | Chi Bears 28, NFL All-Stars 14 |
| 1-4-42 | Chi Bears 35, NFL All-Stars 24 |
| 12-27-42 | NFL All-Stars 17, Washington 14 |
| 1-14-51 | A. Conf. 28, N. Conf. 27 |
| 1-12-52 | N. Conf. 30, A. Conf. 13 |
| 1-10-53 | N. Conf. 27, A. Conf. 7 |
| 1-17-54 | East 20, West 9 |
| 1-16-55 | West 26, East 19 |
| 1-15-56 | East 31, West 30 |
| 1-13-57 | West 19, East 10 |
| 1-12-58 | West 26, East 7 |
| 1-11-59 | East 28, West 21 |
| 1-17-60 | West 38, East 21 |
| 1-15-61 | West 35, East 31 |
| 1-7-62 | AFL West 47, East 27 |
| 1-14-62 | NFL West 31, East 30 |
| 1-13-63 | AFL West 21, East 14 |
| 1-13-63 | NFL East 30, West 20 |
| 1-12-64 | NFL West 31, East 17 |
| 1-19-64 | AFL West 27, East 24 |

| Date | Result |
|------|--------|
| 1-10-65 | NFL West 34, East 14 |
| 1-16-65 | AFL West 38, East 14 |
| 1-15-66 | AFL All-Stars 30, Buffalo 19 |
| 1-15-66 | NFL East 36, West 7 |
| 1-21-67 | AFL East 30, West 23 |
| 1-22-67 | NFL East 20, West 10 |
| 1-21-68 | AFL East 25, West 24 |
| 1-21-68 | NFL West 38, East 20 |
| 1-19-69 | AFL West 38, East 25 |
| 1-19-69 | NFL West 10, East 7 |
| 1-17-70 | AFL West 26, East 3 |
| 1-18-70 | NFL West 16, East 13 |
| 1-24-71 | NFC 27, AFC 6 |
| 1-23-72 | AFC 26, NFC 13 |
| 1-21-73 | AFC 33, NFC 28 |
| 1-20-74 | AFC 15, NFC 13 |
| 1-20-75 | NFC 17, AFC 10 |
| 1-26-76 | NFC 23, AFC 20 |
| 1-17-77 | AFC 24, NFC 14 |
| 1-23-78 | NFC 14, AFC 13 |
| 1-29-79 | NFC 13, AFC 7 |
| 1-27-80 | NFC 37, AFC 27 |
| 2-1-81 | NFC 21, AFC 7 |
| 1-31-82 | AFC 16, NFC 13 |
| 2-6-83 | NFC 20, AFC 19 |
| 1-29-84 | NFC 45, AFC 3 |

| Date | Result |
|------|--------|
| 1-27-85 | AFC 22, NFC 14 |
| 2-2-86 | NFC 28, AFC 24 |
| 2-1-87 | AFC 10, NFC 6 |
| 2-7-88 | AFC 15, NFC 6 |
| 1-29-89 | NFC 34, AFC 3 |
| 2-4-90 | NFC 27, AFC 21 |
| 2-3-91 | AFC 23, NFC 21 |
| 2-2-92 | NFC 21, AFC 15 |
| 2-7-93 | AFC 23, NFC 20 |
| 2-6-94 | NFC 17, AFC 3 |
| 2-5-95 | AFC 41, NFC 13 |
| 2-4-96 | NFC 20, AFC 13 |
| 2-2-97 | AFC 26, NFC 23 |
| 2-1-98 | AFC 29, NFC 24 |
| 2-7-99 | AFC 23, NFC 10 |
| 2-6-00 | NFC 51, AFC 31 |
| 2-4-01 | AFC 38, NFC 17 |
| 2-10-02 | AFC 38, NFC 30 |
| 2-2-03 | AFC 45, NFC 20 |
| 2-8-04 | NFC 55, AFC 52 |
| 2-13-05 | AFC 38, NFC 27 |
| 2-12-06 | NFC 23, AFC 17 |
| 2-10-07 | AFC 31, NFC 28 |
| 2-10-08 | NFC 42, AFC 30 |
| 2-8-09 | NFC 30, AFC 21 |

# Chicago All-Star Game* Results

| Date | Result (Attendance) |
|------|---------------------|
| 8-31-34 | Chi Bears 0, All-Stars 0 (79,432) |
| 8-29-35 | Chi Bears 5, All-Stars 0 (77,450) |
| 9-2-36 | All-Stars 7, Detroit 7 (76,000) |
| 9-1-37 | All-Stars 6, Green Bay 0 (84,560) |
| 8-31-38 | All-Stars 28, Washington 16 (74,250) |
| 8-30-39 | NY Giants 9, All-Stars 0 (81,456) |
| 8-29-40 | Green Bay 45, All-Stars 28 (84,567) |
| 8-28-41 | Chi Bears 37, All-Stars 13 (98,203) |
| 8-28-42 | Chi Bears 21, All-Stars 0 (101,100) |
| 8-25-43 | All-Stars 27, Washington 7 (48,471) |
| 8-30-44 | Chi Bears 24, All-Stars 21 (48,769) |
| 8-30-45 | Green Bay 19, All-Stars 7 (92,753) |
| 8-23-46 | All-Stars 16, Los Angeles 0 (97,380) |
| 8-22-47 | All-Stars 16, Chi Bears 0 (105,840) |
| 8-20-48 | Chi Cardinals 28, All-Stars 0 (101,220) |
| 8-12-49 | Philadelphia 38, All-Stars 0 (93,780) |
| 8-11-50 | All-Stars 17, Philadelphia 7 (88,885) |
| 8-17-51 | Cleveland 33, All-Stars 0 (92,180) |
| 8-15-52 | Los Angeles 10, All-Stars 7 (88,316) |
| 8-14-53 | Detroit 24, All-Stars 10 (93,818) |
| 8-13-54 | Detroit 31, All-Stars 6 (93,470) |
| 8-12-55 | All-Stars 30, Cleveland 27 (75,000) |

| Date | Result (Attendance) |
|------|---------------------|
| 8-10-56 | Cleveland 26, All-Stars 0 (75,000) |
| 8-9-57 | NY Giants 22, All-Stars 12 (75,000) |
| 8-15-58 | All-Stars 35, Detroit 19 (70,000) |
| 8-14-59 | Baltimore 29, All-Stars 0 (70,000) |
| 8-12-60 | Baltimore 32, All-Stars 7 (70,000) |
| 8-4-61 | Philadelphia 28, All-Stars 14 (66,000) |
| 8-3-62 | Green Bay 42, All-Stars 20 (65,000) |
| 8-2-63 | All-Stars 20, Green Bay 17 (65,000) |
| 8-7-64 | Chicago 28, All-Stars 17 (65,000) |
| 8-6-65 | Cleveland 24, All-Stars 16 (68,000) |
| 8-5-66 | Green Bay 38, All-Stars 0 (72,000) |
| 8-4-67 | Green Bay 27, All-Stars 0 (70,934) |
| 8-2-68 | Green Bay 34, All-Stars 17 (69,917) |
| 8-1-69 | NY Jets 26, All-Stars 24 (74,208) |
| 7-31-70 | Kansas City 24, All-Stars 3 (69,940) |
| 7-30-71 | Baltimore 24, All-Stars 17 (52,289) |
| 7-28-72 | Dallas 20, All-Stars 7 (54,162) |
| 7-27-73 | Miami 14, All-Stars 3 (54,103) |
| 1974 | No game |
| 8-1-75 | Pittsburgh 21, All-Stars 14 (54,562) |
| 7-23-76 | Pittsburgh 24, All-Stars 0 (52,895) |

*Discontinued.

# Alltime Winningest NFL Head Coaches

## Most Career Wins

| Coach | Yrs | Teams | Regular Season | | | | Career | | | |
|---|---|---|---|---|---|---|---|---|---|---|
| | | | W | L | T | Pct | W | L | T | Pct |
| Don Shula | 33 | Colts, Dolphins | 328 | 156 | 6 | .676 | 347 | 173 | 6 | .665 |
| George Halas | 40 | Bears | 318 | 148 | 31 | .671 | 324 | 151 | 31 | .671 |
| Tom Landry | 29 | Cowboys | 250 | 162 | 6 | .605 | 270 | 178 | 6 | .601 |
| Curly Lambeau | 33 | Packers, Cardinals, Redskins | 226 | 132 | 22 | .624 | 229 | 134 | 22 | .623 |
| *Paul Brown | 25 | Browns, Bengals | 213 | 104 | 9 | .672 | 222 | 116 | 9 | .668 |
| Chuck Noll | 23 | Steelers | 193 | 148 | 1 | .566 | 209 | 156 | 1 | .572 |
| M. Schottenheimer | 20 | Browns, Chiefs, Redskins, Chargers | 200 | 126 | 1 | .613 | 205 | 139 | 1 | .596 |
| Dan Reeves | 23 | Broncos, Giants, Falcons | 190 | 165 | 2 | .535 | 201 | 174 | 2 | .536 |
| Chuck Knox | 22 | Rams, Bills, Seahawks | 186 | 147 | 1 | .558 | 193 | 158 | 1 | .550 |
| Bill Parcells | 18 | Giants, Patriots, Jets, Cowboys | 172 | 130 | 1 | .569 | 183 | 138 | 1 | .570 |
| †Mike Holmgren | 17 | Packers, Seahawks | 161 | 111 | 0 | .592 | 174 | 122 | 0 | .588 |
| Joe Gibbs | 15 | Redskins | 154 | 94 | 0 | .621 | 171 | 101 | 0 | .629 |
| Bud Grant | 18 | Vikings | 158 | 96 | 5 | .620 | 168 | 108 | 5 | .607 |
| Bill Cowher | 14 | Steelers | 149 | 90 | 1 | .623 | 161 | 99 | 1 | .619 |
| †Mike Shanahan | 16 | Raiders, Broncos | 146 | 98 | 0 | .598 | 154 | 103 | 0 | .599 |
| Marv Levy | 17 | Chiefs, Bills | 143 | 112 | 0 | .561 | 154 | 120 | 0 | .562 |
| †Bill Belichick | 14 | Browns, Patriots | 138 | 86 | 0 | .616 | 153 | 90 | 0 | .630 |
| Steve Owen | 23 | Giants | 151 | 100 | 17 | .595 | 153 | 108 | 17 | .581 |
| †Tony Dungy | 13 | Buccaneers, Colts | 139 | 69 | 0 | .668 | 148 | 79 | 0 | .652 |
| Hank Stram | 17 | Chiefs, Saints | 131 | 97 | 10 | .571 | 136 | 100 | 10 | .573 |
| Weeb Ewbank | 20 | Colts, Jets | 130 | 129 | 7 | .502 | 134 | 130 | 7 | .507 |
| †Jeff Fisher | 15 | Oilers, Titans | 128 | 102 | 0 | .557 | 133 | 108 | 0 | .552 |

## Top Winning Percentages

| | W | L | T | Pct | | W | L | T | Pct |
|---|---|---|---|---|---|---|---|---|---|
| Vince Lombardi | 105 | 35 | 6 | .740 | Don Shula | 347 | 173 | 6 | .665 |
| John Madden | 112 | 39 | 7 | .731 | †Tony Dungy | 148 | 79 | 0 | .652 |
| George Allen | 118 | 54 | 5 | .681 | George Seifert | 124 | 67 | 0 | .650 |
| George Halas | 324 | 151 | 31 | .671 | †Bill Belichick | 153 | 90 | 0 | .630 |
| *Paul Brown | 222 | 116 | 9 | .668 | Joe Gibbs | 162 | 93 | 0 | .629 |

Note: Minimum 100 victories.

†Active in 2008. *Includes a 52–4–3 (5–0 playoff) record with Browns in AAFC and a 7–20–1 record with Bengals in AFL.

# Pro Football Most Valuable Players

| Year | Player/ Team | Position |
|---|---|---|
| 1938 | Mel Hein, NYG (NFL) | C |
| 1939 | Parker Hall, Clev (NFL) | HB |
| 1940 | Ace Parker, Brooklyn (NFL) | QB |
| 1941 | Don Hutson, GB (NFL) | E |
| 1942 | Don Hutson, GB (NFL) | E |
| 1943 | Sid Luckman, Chi Bears (NFL) | QB |
| 1944 | Frank Sinkwich, Det (NFL) | HB |
| 1945 | Bob Waterfield, Clev (NFL) | QB |
| 1946 | Bill Dudley, Pit (NFL) | HB |
| | Glenn Dobbs, Brooklyn (AAFC) | HB |
| 1947 | No Selection (NFL) | |
| | Otto Graham, Clev (AAFC) | QB |
| 1948 | No Selection (NFL) | |
| | Otto Graham, Clev (AAFC-tie) | QB |
| | Frankie Albert, SF (AAFC-tie) | QB |
| 1949 | No Selection (NFL) | |
| 1950 | No Selection (NFL) | |
| 1951 | Otto Graham, Clev (UP) | QB |
| 1952 | No Selection (NFL) | |
| 1953 | Otto Graham, Clev (UP) | QB |
| 1954 | Joe Perry, SF (UP) | FB |
| | Lou Groza, Clev (TSN) | OT/K |

| Year | Player/ Team | Position |
|---|---|---|
| 1955 | Otto Graham, Clev (UP, TSN) | QB |
| | Harlon Hill, Chi Bears (NEA) | E |
| 1956 | Frank Gifford, NYG (UP, NEA, TSN) | HB |
| 1957 | Y.A. Tittle, SF (UP) | QB |
| | Jim Brown, Clev (AP, TSN) | FB |
| | John Unitas, Balt (NEA) | QB |
| 1958 | Jim Brown, Clev (UP, AP, NEA, TSN) | FB |
| 1959 | John Unitas, Balt (UP, MCP, TSN) | QB |
| | Charley Conerly, NYG (AP, NEA) | QB |
| 1960 | Norm Van Brocklin, Phil, NFL (UP, AP, NEA, TSN, MCP) | QB |
| | Joe Schmidt, Det, NFL (UP- tie) | LB |
| | Abner Haynes, Dal Texans, AFL (UP, TSN) | HB |
| 1961 | Paul Hornung, GB, NFL (UP, AP, TSN, MCP) | HB |
| | Y.A. Tittle, NYG (NEA) | QB |
| | George Blanda, Hous (UP, TSN) | QB |
| 1962 | Y.A. Tittle, NYG, NFL (UP, TSN) | QB |
| | Jim Taylor, GB, NFL (AP, NEA) | FB |
| | Andy Robustelli, NYG, NFL (MCP) | DE |
| | Cookie Gilchrist, Buf, AFL (UP) | FB |
| | Len Dawson, Dal Texans, AFL (TSN) | QB |
| 1963 | Jim Brown, Clev, NFL (UP, NEA (tie), MCP) | FB |
| | Y.A. Tittle, NYG, NFL (AP, NEA (tie), TSN) | QB |
| | Lance Alworth, SD, AFL (UP) | WR |
| | Clem Daniels, Oak, AFL (TSN) | HB |

| Year | Player/ Team | Position |
|------|--------------|----------|
| 1964 | Johnny Unitas, Balt, NFL (UP, AP, TSN, MCP) | QB |
| | Lenny Moore, Balt, NFL (NEA) | HB |
| | Gino Cappelletti, Boston, AFL (UP, TSN) | WR |
| 1965 | Jim Brown, Clev, NFL (UP, AP, TSN, NEA) | FB |
| | Pete Retzlaff, Phil, NFL (MCP) | TE |
| | Jack Kemp, Buf, AFL (UP) | QB |
| | Paul Lowe, SD, AFL (TSN) | RB |
| 1966 | Bart Starr, GB, NFL (UP, AP, NEA, TSN) | QB |
| | Don Meredith, Dal, NFL (MCP) | QB |
| | Jim Nance, Boston, AFL (UP, AP, TSN) | FB |
| 1967 | Johnny Unitas, Balt, NFL (UP, AP, NEA, TSN, MCP) | QB |
| | Daryl Lamonica, Oak, AFL (UP, AP, TSN) | QB |
| 1968 | Earl Morrall, Balt, NFL (UP, AP, NEA, TSN, PFW) | QB |
| | Leroy Kelly, Clev, NFL (MCP) | HB |
| | Joe Namath, NY Jets, AFL (UP, TSN, PFW) | QB |
| 1969 | Roman Gabriel, LA Rams, NFL (UP, AP, NEA, MCP, TSN, PFW) | QB |
| | Daryle Lamonica, Oak, AFL (UP, TSN, PFW) | QB |
| | Joe Namath, NY Jets, AFL (AP) | QB |
| 1970 | John Brodie, SF (AP, NEA) | QB |
| | George Blanda, Oak (MCP) | QB/K |
| 1971 | Alan Page, Min (AP) | DT |
| | Bob Griese, Miami (NEA) | QB |
| | Roger Staubach, Dal (MCP) | QB |
| 1972 | Larry Brown, Washington (AP, NEA, MCP) | RB |
| 1973 | O.J. Simpson, Buf (AP, NEA, MCP) | RB |
| 1974 | Ken Stabler, Oak (AP, NEA) | QB |
| | Merlin Olsen, LA Rams (MCP) | DT |
| 1975 | Fran Tarkenton, Min (PFWA, AP, NEA, MCP) | QB |
| 1976 | Bert Jones, Balt (PFWA, AP, NEA) | QB |
| | Ken Stabler, Oak (MCP) | QB |
| 1977 | Walter Payton, Chi (PFWA, AP, NEA) | RB |
| | Bob Griese, Miami (MCP) | QB |
| 1978 | Earl Campbell, Hous (PFWA, NEA) | RB |
| | Terry Bradshaw, Pit (AP, MCP) | QB |
| 1979 | Earl Campbell, Hous (PFWA, AP, NEA, MCP) | RB |
| 1980 | Brian Sipe, Clev (PFWA, AP, TSN) | QB |
| | Earl Campbell, Hous (NEA) | RB |
| | Ron Jaworski, Phil (MCP) | QB |
| 1981 | Ken Anderson, Cin (PFWA, AP, NEA, TSN, MCP) | QB |
| 1982 | Dan Fouts, SD (PFWA, NEA) | QB |
| | Mark Moseley, Washington (AP, TSN) | K |
| | Joe Theismann, Washington (MCP) | QB |
| 1983 | Joe Theismann, Washington (PFWAA, AP, NEA) | QB |

| Year | Player/ Team | Position |
|------|--------------|----------|
| | Eric Dickerson, LA Rams (TSN) | RB |
| | John Riggins, Washington (MCP) | RB |
| 1984 | Dan Marino, Miami (PFWAA, AP, NEA, MCP, TSN) | QB |
| 1985 | Marcus Allen, LA Raiders (PFWAA, AP, TSN) | RB |
| | Walter Payton, Chi Bears (NEA, MCP) | RB |
| 1986 | Lawrence Taylor, NYG (PFWAA, AP, MCP, TSN) | LB |
| | Phil Simms, NYG (NEA) | QB |
| 1987 | Jerry Rice, SF (PFWAA, NEA, MCP, TSN) | WR |
| | John Elway, Den (AP) | QB |
| 1988 | Boomer Esiason, Cin (PFWAA, AP, TSN) | QB |
| | Roger Craig, SF (NEA) | RB |
| | Randall Cunningham, Phil (MCP) | QB |
| 1989 | Joe Montana, SF (PFWAA, AP, NEA, MCP, TSN) | QB |
| 1990 | Randall Cunningham, Phil (PFWAA) | QB |
| | Joe Montana, SF (AP) | QB |
| | Jerry Rice, SF (TSN) | WR |
| 1991 | Thurman Thomas, Buf (PFWAA, AP, TSN) | RB |
| | Barry Sanders, Det (MCP) | RB |
| 1992 | Steve Young, SF (PFWAA, AP, MCP, TSN) | QB |
| 1993 | Emmitt Smith, Dal (PFWAA, AP, MCP, TSN) | RB |
| 1994 | Steve Young, SF (PFWAA, AP, MCP, TSN) | QB |
| 1995 | Brett Favre, GB (PFWAA, AP, MCP, TSN) | QB |
| 1996 | Brett Favre, GB (PFWAA, AP, MCP, TSN) | QB |
| 1997 | Brett Favre, GB (AP – tie) | QB |
| | Barry Sanders, Det (PFWAA, AP (tie), MCP, TSN) | RB |
| 1998 | Terrell Davis, Den (PFWAA, AP, TSN) | RB |
| | Randall Cunningham, Min (MCP) | QB |
| 1999 | Kurt Warner, StL (AP, PFWAA, MCP) | QB |
| 2000 | Marshall Faulk, StL (AP, PFWAA) | RB |
| | Rich Gannon, Oak (MCP) | QB |
| 2001 | Kurt Warner, StL (AP) | QB |
| | Marshall Faulk, StL (PFWAA, MCP, TSN) | RB |
| 2002 | Rich Gannon, Oak (AP) | QB |
| 2003 | Peyton Manning, Ind (AP - tie) | QB |
| | Steve McNair, Ten (AP - tie) | QB |
| 2004 | Peyton Manning, Ind (AP) | QB |
| 2005 | Shaun Alexander, Sea (AP) | RB |
| 2006 | LaDainian Tomlinson, SD (AP) | RB |
| 2007 | Tom Brady, NE (AP) | QB |
| 2008 | Peyton Manning, Ind (AP) | QB |

NOTE: AP-Associated Press, UP-United Press, PFW-*Pro Football Weekly*, TSN-*The Sporting News*, PFWAA-Pro Football Writers Association of America, PFWA-Pro Football Writers of America, MCP-Maxwell Club of Philadelphia, NEA-Newspaper Enterprise Association.

The NFL began awarding its MVP award, the Joe F. Carr Trophy (Carr was league president from 1921-39), in 1938, and continued to do so until 1946. Since that time, the NFL's Most Valuable Players and Players of the Year have been named by a variety of sources, among them, the United Press, the Associated Press, the Maxwell Club of Philadelphia, and the Pro Football Writers Association of America as well as magazines such as *Pro Football Weekly* and *The Sporting News*.

| Year | Player/ Team | Position |
|---|---|---|
| 1955 | Alan Ameche, Balt (UP, TSN) | FB |
| 1956 | Lenny Moore, Balt (UP) | HB |
| | J.C. Caroline, Chi Bears (TSN) | DB |
| 1957 | Jim Brown, Clev (UP, AP, TSN) | FB |
| 1958 | Jimmy Orr, Pit (UP, AP) | OE |
| | Bobby Mitchell, Cleveland (TSN) | HB |
| 1959 | Nick Pietrosante, Det (AP, TSN) | FB |
| | Boyd Dowler, GB (UP) | OE |
| 1960 | Gail Cogdill, Det, NFL (AP, UP, TSN) | OE |
| | Abner Haynes, Dal Texans, AFL (UP, TSN) | HB |
| 1961 | Mike Ditka, Chi Bears, NFL (AP, UP, TSN) | OE |
| | Earl Faison, SD, AFL (UP, TSN) | DE |
| 1962 | Ronnie Bull, Chi Bears, NFL (AP, UP, TSN) | HB |
| | Curtis McClinton, Dal, AFL (UP, TSN) | FB |
| 1963 | Paul Flatley, Min, NFL (AP, UP, TSN) | OE |
| | Billy Joe, Den, AFL (UP, TSN) | FB |
| 1964 | Charley Taylor, Wash, NFL (AP, UP, TSN, NEA) | HB |
| | Matt Snell, NYJ, AFL (UP, TSN) | FB |
| 1965 | Gale Sayers, Chi, NFL (AP, UP, TSN, NEA) | HB |
| | Joe Namath, NYJ, AFL (AP, UP, TSN) | QB |
| 1966 | Johnny Roland, StL, NFL (UP) | HB |
| | Tommy Nobis, Atl, NFL (AP, TSN, NEA) | LB |
| | Bobby Burnett, Buf, AFL (UP, TSN) | HB |
| 1967 | Mel Farr, Det, NFL (AP-Off, UP, TSN, NEA) | HB |
| | Lem Barney, Det NFL (AP-Def) | CB |
| | George Webster, Hous, AFL (UP) | LB |
| | Dickie Post, SD, AFL (TSN) | HB |
| 1968 | Earl McCullouch, Det, NFL (AP-Off, UP, TSN, NEA) | OE |
| | Claude Humphrey NFL (AP-Def) | DE |
| | Paul Robinson, Cin, AFL (UP, TSN) | HB |
| 1969 | Calvin Hill, Dal, NFL (AP-Off, UP, TSN, NEA) | HB |
| | Joe Greene NFL (AP-Def) | RB |
| | Greg Cook, Cin, AFL (UP) | DT |
| | Carl Garrett, Boston, AFL (TSN) | QB |
| | | HB |
| 1970 | Raymond Chester, Oak (NEA) | TE |
| | Dennis Shaw Buf (AP-Off, UP-AFC) | QB |
| | Bruce Taylor, DB SF (AP-Def, UP-NFC) | DB |
| 1971 | Jim Plunkett NE (UP-AFC) | QB |
| | John Brockington GB (AP-Off, UP-NFC) | RB |
| | Isiah Robertson, SF (AP-Def) | LB |
| 1972 | Franco Harris, Pit (AP-Off, PFW, UP-AFC) | RB |
| | Chester Marcol, GB (UP-NFC) | PK |
| | Willie Buchanan, GB (AP-Def) | CB |
| 1973 | Chuck Foreman, Min (AP-Off, PFW) | RB |
| | Wally Chambers, Chi (AP-Def) | DT |
| | Bobbie Clark, Cin (UP-AFC) | RB |
| | Charle Young Phil (UP-NFC) | TE |
| 1974 | Don Woods, SD (AP-Off, PFW, UP-AFC) | RB |
| | John Hicks, NYG (UP-NFC) | G |
| | Jack Lambert, Pit (AP-Def) | LB |
| 1975 | Steve Bartkowski, Atl (PFW) | QB |
| | Robert Brazile, Hous (AP-Def, UP-AFC) | LB |
| | Mike Thomas, Wash (AP-Off, UP-NFC) | RB |
| 1976 | Mike Haynes, DB NE (AP-Def, UP-AFC) | DB |
| | Sammy White, Min (AP-Off, UP-NFC) | WR |
| 1977 | Tony Dorsett, Dal (NEA, AP-Off, UP-NFC) | RB |
| | A.J. Duhe, Mia (AP-Def, UP-AFC) | DE |
| 1978 | Earl Campbell, Hous Oilers (NEA, PFWA, AP-Off, UP-AFC) | RB |
| | Al "Bubba" Baker, Det (AP-Def, UP-NFC) | DE |

| Year | Player/ Team | Position |
|---|---|---|
| 1979 | Ottis Anderson, StL Card (NEA, PFWA, AP-Off, UP-NFC) | RB |
| | Jerry Butler, Buf (UP-AFC) | WR |
| | Jim Haslett, Buf (AP-Def) | LB |
| 1980 | Billy Sims, Det (NEA, TSN, PFWA, AP-Off, UP-NFC) | RB |
| | Joe Cribbs Buf (UP-AFC) | RB |
| | Buddy Curry, Atl (AP-Def tie) | LB |
| | Al Richardson, Atl (AP-Def tie) | LB |
| 1981 | Lawrence Taylor, NYG (NEA, AP-Def) | LB |
| | George Rogers, NO (TSN, PFWA, AP-Off, UP-NFC) | RB |
| | Joe Delaney, KC (UP-AFC) | RB |
| 1982 | Marcus Allen, LA Raiders (NEA, TSN, PFWA, AP-Off, UP-NFC) | RB |
| | Jim McMahon, Chi (UP-NFC) | QB |
| | Chip Banks, Cle (AP-Def) | LB |
| 1983 | Eric Dickerson, LA Rams (NEA, PFWA, AP-Off, UP-NFC) | RB |
| | Dan Marino, Mia (TSN) | QB |
| | Curt Warner, Sea (UP-AFC) | RB |
| | Vernon Maxwell, Balt (AP-Def) | LB |
| 1984 | Louis Lipps, Pit (NEA, TSN, PFWA, AP-Off, UP-NFC) | WR |
| | Paul McFadden, Phil (UP-NFC) | PK |
| | Bill Maas, KC (AP-Def) | DT |
| 1985 | Eddie Brown, Cin (NEA, TSN, AP-Off, PFWA) | WR |
| | Kevin Mack, Clev (UP-AFC) | RB |
| | Jerry Rice, SF (UP-NFC) | WR |
| | Duane Bickett, Ind (AP-Def) | LB |
| 1986 | Reuben Mayes, NO (NEA, TSN, PFWA, AP-Off, UP-NFC) | RB |
| | Leslie O'Neal, SD (AP-Def, UP-AFC) | DE |
| 1987 | Shane Conlan, Buf (PFWA, AP-Def, UP-AFC) | LB |
| | Bo Jackson, LA Raiders (NEA) | RB |
| | Robert Awalt, StL Card (TSN, UP-NFC) | TE |
| | Troy Stradford, Mia (AP-Off) | RB |
| 1988 | John Stephens, NE (NEA, AP-Off, PFWA) | RB |
| | Keith Jackson, Phil (TSN, UP-NFC) | TE |
| | Eric McMillan, NYJ (AP-Def) | S |
| 1989 | Barry Sanders, Det (NEA, TSN, PFWA, AP-Off, UP-NFC) | RB |
| | Derrick Thomas KC (AP-Def, UP-AFC) | LB |
| 1990 | Mark Carrier, Chi (PFWA, UP-NFC, AP-Def) | S |
| | Emmitt Smith, Dal (AP-Off) | RB |
| | Richmond Webb, Mia (TSN, UP-AFC) | OT |
| 1991 | Mike Croel, Den (PFWA, TSN, AP-Def, UP-AFC) | LB |
| | Lawrence Dawsey TB (UP-NFC) | WR |
| | Leonard Russell, NE (AP-Off) | RB |
| 1992 | Dale Carter, KC (PFWA, AP-Def, UP-AFC) | CB |
| | Carl Pickens, Cin (AP-Off) | WR |
| | Santana Dotson, TB (TSN) | DE |
| | Robert Jones, Dal (UP-NFC) | LB |
| 1993 | Jerome Bettis, LA Rams (PFWA, TSN, AP-Off, UP-NFC) | RB |
| | Rick Mirer, Sea (UP-AFC) | QB |
| | Dana Stubblefield, SF (AP-Def) | DT |
| 1994 | Marshall Faulk, Ind (PFWA, TSN, AP-Off, UP-AFC) | RB |
| | Bryant Young, SF (UP-NFC) | DT |
| | Tim Bowens, Mia (AP-Def) | DT |
| 1995 | Curtis Martin, NE (PFWA, TSN, AP-Off, UP-AFC) | RB |
| | Rashaan Salaam Chi (UP-NFC) | RB |
| | Hugh Douglas, NYJ (AP-Def) | DE |

| Year | Player/ Team | Position |
|------|--------------|----------|
| 1996 | Eddie George, Ten (AP, PFWA, AP-Off, TSN) | RB |
| | Terry Glenn, NE (UP-AFC) | WR |
| | Simeon Rice, Ariz (AP-Def, UP-NFC) | DE |
| 1997 | Warrick Dunn, TB (PFWA, AP-Off, TSN) | RB |
| | Peter Boulware, Balt (AP-Def) | LB |
| 1998 | Randy Moss, Min (PFWA, AP-Off, TSN) | WR |
| | Charles Woodson LA Raiders (AP-Def) | CB |
| 1999 | Edgerrin James, Ind (AP-Off, TSN) | RB |
| | Jevon Kearse, Ten (AP-Def) | DE |
| 2000 | Mike Anderson, Den (AP-Off, TSN) | RB |
| | Brian Urlacher, Chi (AP-Def) | LB |
| 2001 | Anthony Thomas, Chi (AP-Off) | RB |
| | Kendrell Bell, Pit (AP-Def) | LB |
| 2002 | Clinton Ports, Den (AP-Off) | RB |
| | Julius Peppers, Car (AP-Def) | DE |

| Year | Player/ Team | Position |
|------|--------------|----------|
| 2003 | Anquan Boldin, Ariz (AP-Off) | WR |
| | Terrell Suggs, Bal (AP-Def) | LB |
| 2004 | Ben Roethlisberger, Pit (AP-Off) | QB |
| | Jonathan Vilma, NYJ (AP-Def) | LB |
| 2005 | Carnell Williams, TB (AP-Off) | RB |
| | Shawne Merriman, SD (AP-Def) | LB |
| 2006 | Vince Young, Ten (AP-Off) | QB |
| | DeMeco Ryans, Hou (AP-Def) | LB |
| 2007 | Adrian Peterson, Min (AP-Off) | RB |
| | Patrick Willis, SF (AP-Def) | LB |
| 2008 | Matt Ryan, Atl (AP-Off) | QB |
| | Jerod Mayo, NE (AP-Def) | LB |

NOTE: AP-Associated Press, UP-United Press, PFW-*Pro Football Weekly*, TSN-*The Sporting News*, PFWAA-Pro Football Writers Association of America, PFWA-Pro Football Writers of America, MCP-Maxwell Club of Philadelphia, NEA-Newspaper Enterprise Association

Starting in1960, the United Press annually awarded two Rookie of the Year awards, one to an AFL player and one to a NFL player. After the AFL-NFL merger, the UP kept the two-award format for the AFC and NFC. The UP stopped awarding RoY awards after the 1996 season.

Starting in 1967, the Associated Press began announcing two annual Rookie of the Year awards, as well. One went to the best offensive rookie in the NFL, the other to the best defensive rookie.

## Alltime Number-One Draft Choices

| Year | Team | Selection | Position |
|------|------|-----------|----------|
| 1936 | Philadelphia | Jay Berwanger, Chicago | HB |
| 1937 | Philadelphia | Sam Francis, Nebraska | FB |
| 1938 | Cleveland | Corbett Davis, Indiana | FB |
| 1939 | Chicago Cardinals | Ki Aldrich, Texas Christian | C |
| 1940 | Chicago Cardinals | George Cafego, Tennessee | HB |
| 1941 | Chicago Bears | Tom Harmon, Michigan | HB |
| 1942 | Pittsburgh | Bill Dudley, Virginia | HB |
| 1943 | Detroit | Frank Sinkwich, Georgia | HB |
| 1944 | Boston | Angelo Bertelli, Notre Dame | QB |
| 1945 | Chicago Cardinals | Charley Trippi, Georgia | HB |
| 1946 | Boston | Frank Dancewicz, Notre Dame | QB |
| 1947 | Chicago Bears | Bob Fenimore, Oklahoma A&M | HB |
| 1948 | Washington | Harry Gilmer, Alabama | QB |
| 1949 | Philadelphia | Chuck Bednarik, Pennsylvania | C |
| 1950 | Detroit | Leon Hart, Notre Dame | E |
| 1951 | New York Giants | Kyle Rote, SMU | HB |
| 1952 | Los Angeles | Bill Wade, Vanderbilt | QB |
| 1953 | San Francisco | Harry Babcock, Georgia | E |
| 1954 | Cleveland | Bobby Garrett, Stanford | QB |
| 1955 | Baltimore | George Shaw, Oregon | QB |
| 1956 | Pittsburgh | Gary Glick, Colorado A&M | DB |
| 1957 | Green Bay | Paul Hornung, Notre Dame | HB |
| 1958 | Chicago Cardinals | King Hill, Rice | QB |
| 1959 | Green Bay | Randy Duncan, Iowa | QB |
| 1960 | Los Angeles | Billy Cannon, LSU | RB |
| 1961 | Minnesota | Tommy Mason, Tulane | RB |
| | Buffalo (AFL) | Ken Rice, Auburn | G |
| 1962 | Washington | Ernie Davis, Syracuse | RB |
| | Oakland (AFL) | Roman Gabriel, North Carolina St | QB |
| 1963 | LA Rams | Terry Baker, Oregon St | QB |
| | Kansas City (AFL) | Buck Buchanan, Grambling | DT |
| 1964 | San Francisco | Dave Parks, Texas Tech | E |
| | Boston (AFL) | Jack Concannon, Boston College | QB |
| 1965 | NY Giants | Tucker Frederickson, Auburn | RB |
| | Houston (AFL) | Lawrence Elkins, Baylor | E |
| 1966 | Atlanta | Tommy Nobis, Texas | LB |
| | Miami (AFL) | Jim Grabowski, Illinois | RB |

| Year | Team | Selection | Position |
|------|------|-----------|----------|
| 1967 | Baltimore | Bubba Smith, Michigan St | DT |
| 1968 | Minnesota | Ron Yary, USC | T |
| 1969 | Buffalo (AFL) | O.J. Simpson, USC | RB |
| 1970 | Pittsburgh | Terry Bradshaw, Louisiana Tech | QB |
| 1971 | New England | Jim Plunkett, Stanford | QB |
| 1972 | Buffalo | Walt Patulski, Notre Dame | DE |
| 1973 | Houston | John Matuszak, Tampa | DE |
| 1974 | Dallas | Ed Jones, Tennessee St | DE |
| 1975 | Atlanta | Steve Bartkowski, California | QB |
| 1976 | Tampa Bay | Lee Roy Selmon, Oklahoma | DE |
| 1977 | Tampa Bay | Ricky Bell, USC | RB |
| 1978 | Houston | Earl Campbell, Texas | RB |
| 1979 | Buffalo | Tom Cousineau, Ohio St | LB |
| 1980 | Detroit | Billy Sims, Oklahoma | RB |
| 1981 | New Orleans | George Rogers, South Carolina | RB |
| 1982 | New England | Kenneth Sims, Texas | DT |
| 1983 | Baltimore | John Elway, Stanford | QB |
| 1984 | New England | Irving Fryar, Nebraska | WR |
| 1985 | Buffalo | Bruce Smith, Virginia Tech | DE |
| 1986 | Tampa Bay | Bo Jackson, Auburn | RB |
| 1987 | Tampa Bay | Vinny Testaverde, Miami (Fla.) | QB |
| 1988 | Atlanta | Aundray Bruce, Auburn | LB |
| 1989 | Dallas | Troy Aikman, UCLA | QB |
| 1990 | Indianapolis | Jeff George, Illinois | QB |
| 1991 | Dallas | Russell Maryland, Miami (Fla.) | DT |
| 1992 | Indianapolis | Steve Emtman, Washington | DT |
| 1993 | New England | Drew Bledsoe, Washington St | QB |
| 1994 | Cincinnati | Dan Wilkinson, Ohio St | DT |
| 1995 | Cincinnati | Ki-Jana Carter, Penn St | RB |
| 1996 | New York Jets | Keyshawn Johnson, USC | WR |
| 1997 | St Louis | Orlando Pace, Ohio St | OT |
| 1998 | Indianapolis | Peyton Manning, Tennessee | QB |
| 1999 | Cleveland | Tim Couch, Kentucky | QB |
| 2000 | Cleveland | Courtney Brown, Penn St | DE |
| 2001 | Atlanta | Michael Vick, Virginia Tech | QB |
| 2002 | Houston | David Carr, Fresno St | QB |
| 2003 | Cincinnati | Carson Palmer, USC | QB |
| 2004 | San Diego | Eli Manning, Mississippi | QB |
| 2005 | San Francisco | Alex Smith, Utah | QB |
| 2006 | Houston | Mario Williams, North Carolina St | DE |
| 2007 | Oakland | JaMarcus Russell, LSU | QB |
| 2008 | Miami | Jake Long, Michigan | OT |
| 2009 | Detroit | Matthew Stafford, Georgia | QB |

From 1947 through 1958, the first selection in the draft was a bonus pick, awarded to the winner of a random draw. That club, in turn, forfeited its last-round draft choice. The winner of the bonus choice was eliminated from future draws. The system was abolished after 1958, by which time all clubs had received a bonus choice.

Herb Adderley
Troy Aikman
George Allen
Marcus Allen
Lance Alworth
Doug Atkins
Morris (Red) Badgro
Lem Barney
Cliff Battles
Sammy Baugh
Chuck Bednarik
Bert Bell
Bobby Bell
Raymond Berry
Elvin Bethea
Charles W. Bidwill Sr.
Fred Biletnikoff
George Blanda
Mel Blount
Terry Bradshaw
Bob (the Boomer) Brown
Jim Brown
Paul Brown
Roosevelt Brown
Willie Brown
Junios (Buck) Buchanan
Nick Buoniconti
Dick Butkus
Earl Campbell
Tony Canadeo
Joe Carr
Harry Carson
Dave Casper
Guy Chamberlin
Jack Christiansen
Earl (Dutch) Clark
George Connor
Jimmy Conzelman
Lou Creekmur
Larry Csonka
Al Davis
Willie Davis
Len Dawson
Fred Dean
Joe DeLamielleure
Eric Dickerson
Dan Dierdorf
Mike Ditka
Art Donovan
Tony Dorsett
John (Paddy) Driscoll
Bill Dudley
Albert Glen (Turk) Edwards
Carl Eller
John Elway
Weeb Ewbank
Tom Fears
Jim Finks
Ray Flaherty
Len Ford
Dan Fortmann
Dan Fouts
Benny Friedman
Frank Gatski
Bill George

Joe Gibbs
Frank Gifford
Sid Gillman
Otto Graham
Harold (Red) Grange
Bud Grant
Darrell Green
Joe Greene
Forrest Gregg
Bob Griese
Lou Groza
Joe Guyon
George Halas
Jack Ham
Dan Hampton
John Hannah
Franco Harris
Bob Hayes
Mike Haynes
Ed Healey
Mel Hein
Ted Hendricks
Wilbur (Pete) Henry
Arnie Herber
Bill Hewitt
Gene Hickerson
Clarke Hinkle
Elroy (Crazylegs) Hirsch
Paul Hornung
Ken Houston
Robert (Cal) Hubbard
Sam Huff
Lamar Hunt
Don Hutson
Michael Irvin
Jimmy Johnson
John Henry Johnson
Charlie Joiner
David (Deacon) Jones
Stan Jones
Henry Jordan
Sonny Jurgensen
Jim Kelly
Leroy Kelly
Walt Kiesling
Frank (Bruiser) Kinard
Paul Krause
Earl (Curly) Lambeau
Jack Lambert
Tom Landry
Dick (Night Train) Lane
Jim Langer
Willie Lanier
Steve Largent
Yale Lary
Dante Lavelli
Bobby Layne
Alphonse (Tuffy) Leemans
Marv Levy
Bob Lilly
Larry Little
James Lofton
Vince Lombardi
Howie Long
Ronnie Lott

Sid Luckman
William Roy (Link) Lyman
Tom Mack
John Mackey
John Madden
Tim Mara
Wellington Mara
Gino Marchetti
Dan Marino
George Preston Marshall
Ollie Matson
Bruce Matthews
Don Maynard
George McAfee
Mike McCormack
Randall McDaniel
Tommy McDonald
Hugh McElhenny
John (Blood) McNally
Mike Michalske
Wayne Millner
Bobby Mitchell
Ron Mix
Art Monk
Joe Montana
Warren Moon
Lenny Moore
Marion Motley
Mike Munchak
Anthony Munoz
George Musso
Bronko Nagurski
Joe Namath
Earle (Greasy) Neale
Ernie Nevers
Ozzie Newsome
Ray Nitschke
Chuck Noll
Leo Nomellini
Merlin Olsen
Jim Otto
Steve Owen
Alan Page
Clarence (Ace) Parker
Jim Parker
Walter Payton
Joe Perry
Pete Pihos
Fritz Pollard
Hugh (Shorty) Ray
Dan Reeves
Mel Renfro
John Riggins
Jim Ringo
Andy Robustelli
Art Rooney
Dan Rooney
Pete Rozelle
Bob St. Clair
Barry Sanders
Charlie Sanders
Gale Sayers
Joe Schmidt
Tex Schramm
Lee Roy Selmon

Billy Shaw
Art Shell
Don Shula
O.J. Simpson
Mike Singletary
Jackie Slater
Bruce Smith
Jackie Smith
John Stallworth
Bart Starr
Roger Staubach
Ernie Stautner
Jan Stenerud
Dwight Stephenson
Hank Stram
Ken Strong
Joe Stydahar
Lynn Swann
Fran Tarkenton
Charley Taylor
Jim Taylor
Lawrence Taylor
Derrick Thomas
Emmitt Thomas
Thurman Thomas
Jim Thorpe
Andre Tippett
Y.A. Tittle
George Trafton
Charley Trippi
Emlen Tunnell
Clyde (Bulldog) Turner
Johnny Unitas
Gene Upshaw
Norm Van Brocklin
Steve Van Buren
Doak Walker
Bill Walsh
Paul Warfield
Bob Waterfield
Mike Webster
Roger Wehrli
Arnie Weinmeister
Randy White
Reggie White
Dave Wilcox
Bill Willis
Larry Wilson
Ralph Wilson
Kellen Winslow
Alex Wojciechowicz
Willie Wood
Rod Woodson
Rayfield Wright
Ron Yary
Steve Young
Jack Youngblood
Gary Zimmerman

### Canadian Football League Grey Cup

| Year | Results | Site | Attendance |
|------|---------|------|------------|
| 1909 | U of Toronto 26, Parkdale 6 | Toronto | 3,807 |
| 1910 | U of Toronto 16, Hamilton Tigers 7 | Hamilton | 12,000 |
| 1911 | U of Toronto 14, Toronto 7 | Toronto | 13,687 |
| 1912 | Hamilton Alerts 11, Toronto 4 | Hamilton | 5,337 |
| 1913 | Hamilton Tigers 44, Parkdale 2 | Hamilton | 2,100 |
| 1914 | Toronto 14, U of Toronto 2 | Toronto | 10,500 |
| 1915 | Hamilton Tigers 13, Toronto RAA 7 | Toronto | 2,808 |
| 1916–19 | No game | — | — |
| 1920 | U of Toronto 16, Toronto 3 | Toronto | 10,088 |
| 1921 | Toronto 23, Edmonton 0 | Toronto | 9,558 |
| 1922 | Queen's U 13, Edmonton 1 | Kingston | 4,700 |
| 1923 | Queen's U 54, Regina 0 | Toronto | 8,629 |
| 1924 | Queen's U 11, Balmy Beach 3 | Toronto | 5,978 |
| 1925 | Ottawa Senators 24, Winnipeg 1 | Ottawa | 6,900 |
| 1926 | Ottawa Senators 10, Toronto U 7 | Toronto | 8,276 |
| 1927 | Balmy Beach 9, Hamilton Tigers 6 | Toronto | 13,676 |
| 1928 | Hamilton Tigers 30, Regina 0 | Hamilton | 4,767 |
| 1929 | Hamilton Tigers 14, Regina 3 | Hamilton | 1,906 |
| 1930 | Balmy Beach 11, Regina 6 | Toronto | 3,914 |
| 1931 | Montreal AAA 22, Regina 0 | Montreal | 5,112 |
| 1932 | Hamilton Tigers 25, Regina 6 | Hamilton | 4,806 |
| 1933 | Toronto 4, Sarnia 3 | Sarnia | 2,751 |
| 1934 | Sarnia 20, Regina 12 | Toronto | 8,900 |
| 1935 | Winnipeg 18, Hamilton Tigers 12 | Hamilton | 6,405 |
| 1936 | Sarnia 26, Ottawa RR 20 | Toronto | 5,883 |
| 1937 | Toronto 4, Winnipeg 3 | Toronto | 11,522 |
| 1938 | Toronto 30, Winnipeg 7 | Toronto | 18,778 |
| 1939 | Winnipeg 8, Ottawa 7 | Ottawa | 11,738 |
| 1940 | Ottawa 8, Balmy Beach 2 | Toronto | 4,998 |
| 1940 | Ottawa 12, Balmy Beach 5 | Ottawa | 1,700 |
| 1941 | Winnipeg 18, Ottawa 16 | Toronto | 19,065 |
| 1942 | Toronto RCAF 8, Winnipeg RCAF 5 | Toronto | 12,455 |
| 1943 | Hamilton F Wild 23, Winnipeg RCAF 14 | Toronto | 16,423 |
| 1944 | Montreal St H-D Navy 7, Hamilton F Wild 6 | Hamilton | 3,871 |
| 1945 | Toronto 35, Winnipeg 0 | Toronto | 18,660 |
| 1946 | Toronto 28, Winnipeg 6 | Toronto | 18,960 |
| 1947 | Toronto 10, Winnipeg 9 | Toronto | 18,885 |
| 1948 | Calgary 12, Ottawa 7 | Toronto | 20,013 |
| 1949 | Montreal Als 28, Calgary 15 | Toronto | 20,087 |
| 1950 | Toronto 13, Winnipeg 0 | Toronto | 27,101 |
| 1951 | Ottawa 21, Saskatchewan 14 | Toronto | 27,341 |
| 1952 | Toronto 21, Edmonton 11 | Toronto | 27,391 |
| 1953 | Hamilton Ticats 12, Winnipeg 6 | Toronto | 27,313 |
| 1954 | Edmonton 26, Montreal 25 | Toronto | 27,321 |
| 1955 | Edmonton 34, Montreal 19 | Vancouver | 39,417 |
| 1956 | Edmonton 50, Montreal 27 | Toronto | 27,425 |
| 1957 | Hamilton 32, Winnipeg 7 | Toronto | 27,051 |
| 1958 | Winnipeg 35, Hamilton 28 | Vancouver | 36,567 |
| 1959 | Winnipeg 21, Hamilton 7 | Toronto | 33,133 |
| 1960 | Ottawa 16, Edmonton 6 | Vancouver | 38,102 |
| 1961 | Winnipeg 21, Hamilton 14 | Toronto | 32,651 |
| 1962 | Winnipeg 28, Hamilton 27 | Toronto | 32,655 |
| 1963 | Hamilton 21, British Columbia 10 | Vancouver | 36,545 |
| 1964 | British Columbia 34, Hamilton 24 | Toronto | 32,655 |
| 1965 | Hamilton 22, Winnipeg 16 | Toronto | 32,655 |
| 1966 | Saskatchewan 29, Ottawa 14 | Vancouver | 36,553 |
| 1967 | Hamilton 24, Saskatchewan 1 | Ottawa | 31,358 |
| 1968 | Ottawa 24, Calgary 21 | Toronto | 32,655 |
| 1969 | Ottawa 29, Saskatchewan 11 | Montreal | 33,172 |
| 1970 | Montreal 23, Calgary 10 | Toronto | 32,669 |
| 1971 | Calgary 14, Toronto 11 | Vancouver | 34,484 |
| 1972 | Hamilton 13, Saskatchewan 10 | Hamilton | 33,993 |
| 1973 | Ottawa 22, Edmonton 18 | Toronto | 36,653 |
| 1974 | Montreal 20, Edmonton 7 | Vancouver | 34,450 |
| 1975 | Edmonton 9, Montreal 8 | Calgary | 32,454 |
| 1976 | Ottawa 23, Saskatchewan 20 | Toronto | 53,467 |
| 1977 | Montreal 41, Edmonton 6 | Montreal | 68,318 |

## Canadian Football League Grey Cup

| Year | Results | Site | Attendance |
|------|---------|------|-----------|
| 1978 | Edmonton 20, Montreal 13 | Toronto | 54,695 |
| 1979 | Edmonton 17, Montreal 9 | Montreal | 65,113 |
| 1980 | Edmonton 48, Hamilton 10 | Toronto | 54,661 |
| 1981 | Edmonton 26, Ottawa 23 | Montreal | 52,478 |
| 1982 | Edmonton 32, Toronto 16 | Toronto | 54,741 |
| 1983 | Toronto 18, British Columbia 17 | Vancouver | 59,345 |
| 1984 | Winnipeg 47, Hamilton 17 | Edmonton | 60,081 |
| 1985 | British Columbia 37, Hamilton 24 | Montreal | 56,723 |
| 1986 | Hamilton 39, Edmonton 15 | Vancouver | 59,621 |
| 1987 | Edmonton 38, Toronto 36 | Vancouver | 59,478 |
| 1988 | Winnipeg 22, British Columbia 21 | Ottawa | 50,604 |
| 1989 | Saskatchewan 43, Hamilton 40 | Toronto | 54,088 |
| 1990 | Winnipeg 50, Edmonton 11 | Vancouver | 46,968 |
| 1991 | Toronto 36, Calgary 21 | Winnipeg | 51,985 |
| 1992 | Calgary 24, Winnipeg 10 | Toronto | 45,863 |
| 1993 | Edmonton 33, Winnipeg 23 | Calgary | 50,035 |
| 1994 | British Columbia 26, Baltimore 23 | Vancouver | 55,097 |
| 1995 | Baltimore 37, Calgary 20 | Regina, Saskatchewan | 52,564 |
| 1996 | Toronto 43, Edmonton 37 | Hamilton, Ontario | 38,595 |
| 1997 | Toronto 47, Saskatchewan 23 | Edmonton | 60,431 |
| 1998 | Calgary 26, Hamilton 24 | Winnipeg | 34,157 |
| 1999 | Hamilton 32, Calgary 21 | Vancouver | 45,118 |
| 2000 | British Columbia 28, Montreal 26 | Calgary | 43,822 |
| 2001 | Calgary 27, Winnipeg 19 | Montreal | 65,255 |
| 2002 | Montreal 25, Edmonton 16 | Edmonton | 62,531 |
| 2003 | Edmonton 34, Montreal 22 | Regina, Saskatchewan | 50,909 |
| 2004 | Toronto 27, British Columbia 19 | Ottawa | 51,242 |
| 2005 | Edmonton 38, Montreal 35 (OT) | Vancouver | 59,157 |
| 2006 | British Columbia 25, Montreal 14 | Winnipeg | 44,786 |
| 2007 | Saskatchewan 23, Winnipeg 19 | Toronto | 52,230 |
| 2008 | Calgary 22, Montreal 14 | Montreal | 66,308 |

In 1909, Earl Grey, the Governor-General of Canada, donated a trophy for the Rugby Football Championship of Canada. The trophy, which subsequently became known as the Grey Cup, was originally open only to teams registered with the Canada Rugby Union. Since 1954, it has been awarded to the winner of the Canadian Football League's championship game.

### AMERICAN FOOTBALL LEAGUE I

| Year | Champion | Record |
|------|----------|--------|
| 1926 | Philadelphia Quakers | 7-2 |

### AMERICAN FOOTBALL LEAGUE II

| Year | Champion | Record |
|------|----------|--------|
| 1936 | Boston Shamrocks | 8-3 |
| 1937 | LA Bulldogs | 8-0 |

### AMERICAN FOOTBALL LEAGUE III

| Year | Champion | Record |
|------|----------|--------|
| 1940 | Columbus Bullies | 8-1-1 |
| 1941 | Columbus Bullies | 5-1-2 |

### ALL-AMERICAN FOOTBALL CONFERENCE

| Year | Championship Game |
|------|-------------------|
| 1946 | Cleveland 14, NY Yankees 9 |
| 1947 | Cleveland 14, NY Yankees 3 |
| 1948 | Cleveland 49, Buffalo 7 |
| 1949 | Cleveland 21, San Francisco 7 |

### WORLD FOOTBALL LEAGUE

| Year | World Bowl Championship |
|------|-------------------------|
| 1974 | Birmingham 22, Florida 21 |
| 1975 | Disbanded midseason |

### UNITED STATES FOOTBALL LEAGUE

| Year | Championship Game |
|------|-------------------|
| 1983 | Michigan 24, Philadelphia 22 |
| 1984 | Philadelphia 23, Arizona 3 |
| 1985 | Baltimore 28, Oakland 24 |

### X FOOTBALL LEAGUE

| Year | Championship Game |
|------|-------------------|
| 2001 | Los Angeles 38, San Francisco 6 |

### NFL EUROPE*

| Year Record | Champion | |
|-------------|----------|---|
| 1991 | London | 9-1-0 |
| 1992 | Sacramento | 8-2-0 |
| 1995 | Frankfurt | 6-4-0 |
| 1996 | Scotland | 7-3-0 |
| 1997 | Barcelona | 5-5-0 |
| 1998 | Rhein | 7-3-0 |
| 1999 | Frankfurt | 6-4-0 |
| 2000 | Rhein | 7-3-0 |
| 2001 | Berlin | 6-4-0 |
| 2002 | Berlin | 6-4-0 |
| 2003 | Frankfurt | 6-4-0 |
| 2004 | Berlin | 9-1-0 |
| 2005 | Amsterdam | 6-4-0 |
| 2006 | Frankfurt | 7-3-0 |
| 2007 | Hamburg | 7-3-0 |

*Known as World League of American Football until 1998. League folded after the 2007 season.

Florida QB Tim Tebow
rallied the Gators to their
second national title
in three years

# College
# Football

# Man on a Mission

While a stacked Big 12 and an undefeated Utah team reignited calls for a playoff, there was no debating the greatness of Tim Tebow's Florida Gators in 2008

**B.J. SCHECTER**

THE LEGEND OF TIM TEBOW grows with every snap, every bulldozing first down, every fist-pumping, gator-chomping display of emotion. From the time Tebow stepped on the campus at the University of Florida, he became a superhero. But unlike most young stars built up by their fans, Tebow never came crashing down. Instead, he kept adding to his awe-inspiring persona (on and off the field), taking a team on his back and carrying it to a second national title in three years.

To say Tebow won the title by himself would hardly be the truth given Florida's abundance of talented athletes (super-speedy wide receiver/running back Percy Harvin is in a league by himself) and a swarming defense that held high-powered Oklahoma to 14 points in the title game. But in an era of me-first athletes, where the "student" in student-athlete is often little more than put-on, and where the police blotter has become as common as a box score, Tebow is a breath a fresh air.

Built like a linebacker (6'3", 245 pounds), Tebow plays quarterback without giving any regard to his body, smashing into anything that stands in his way. After becoming the first sophomore to win the Heisman Trophy in 2007, it would have been easy for Tebow to become complacent. He could have sat back on his laurels, finished his junior season and collected millions by leaving school

early. Instead, he went on a mission to the Philippines the following summer, spoke to church groups, worked harder than ever and came back with one goal in mind: win a national championship.

When Florida lost to unranked Ole Miss 31–30 at home in late September that goal appeared to be dashed. At a press conference after the game, Tebow put everything on his broad shoulders and vowed to salvage the season, not for himself but for his teammates and the fans. The promise has become a piece of Florida lore. "To the fans and everybody in Gator nation, I'm sorry. I'm extremely sorry," Tebow said, verging on tears. "We were hoping for an undefeated season. That was my goal, something Florida has never done here. I promise you one thing, a lot of good will come out of this. You will never see any player in the entire country play as hard as I will play the rest of the season. You will never see someone push the rest of the team as hard as I will push everybody the rest of the season. You will never see another team play as hard as we will the rest of the season. God bless."

From that moment, Florida was a different team, averaging 46.9 points per game and giving up just 13.1. Though his numbers were down, Tebow made another strong case for the Heisman (he would lose to Oklahoma quarterback Sam Bradford), but that award didn't mean that much to him. Tebow was after the crystal football. To get

to the title game, however, Tebow & Co. would have to knock off No. 1 Alabama in the SEC championship game—without Harvin, who sprained his ankle in the regular-season finale against Florida State.

In the most intense and hard-hitting game of the season, Florida and Alabama exchanged punches as the lead changed hands or the score was tied eight times. After the Crimson Tide seized momentum in the third quarter by scoring 10 straight points to take a 20–17 lead, it was Tebow time. "We put it in our quarterback's hands," said Florida coach Urban Meyer. "We told Tim, 'You're going to have to win the game with the receivers' and they did."

Tebow and the Gators outgained Alabama in yardage 130–1 in the final period, and Touchdown Tim was everywhere, willing his way to first downs, throwing shovel passes just when it looked like he was going to get sacked, and threading the needle against a very good Alabama defense. After the go-ahead score, Tebow rushed to the sideline, got in the faces of the Gators' defensive players and implored them to get one final stop. They did. The result was a 31–20 victory that had Alabama

**Oklahoma QB Sam Bradford bested Tebow for the Heisman, but he and his Sooners fell short of the Gators in the BCS title game.**

coach Nick Saban shaking his head.

"That fourth quarter was vintage Tim Tebow," said Meyer. "There's something special inside of him, and I'm not talking about running. I'm talking about the ability to make the level of play of everyone else around him better."

In the first half of the national championship game against Oklahoma, Tebow was uncharacteristically out of sync. After throwing just two interceptions in the first 13 games of the season, Tebow tossed two in the first half. The Sooners were disguising their looks, bringing pressure and rattling the normally unflappable junior quarterback. "I was a little irritated with myself," Tebow said. "The coverages they showed me—I should have read them better. But the key is to not let it faze you."

Tebow regained his composure and put together an impressive 13-play, 75-yard drive midway through the third quarter. Tebow kept the ball on six of those snaps, rushing for 48 yards, to give Florida a 14–7 lead. A

JOHN BIEVER

Tech rose to No. 2 in the nation after beating Texas in Lubbock on a spectacular last-second touchdown by wideout Michael Crabtree.

It was a fitting end to the game of the year. Texas' McCoy had just engineered what appeared to be the game-winning drive. But 1:29 remained and Harrell methodically led the Red Raiders down the field before finding Crabtree, who eluded a defender and took it into the end zone with one second remaining to give the Red Raiders a 39–33 victory. The hyped-up Tech fans, many of whom camped out for days for the biggest game in school history, stormed the field. "We'd get out a rocking chair and reflect and all that, but we have to play next week," said Texas Tech coach Mike Leach. "So it's going to be fun for a couple hours—and then you tell your grandkids."

Three weeks later, Texas Tech was blown out by Oklahoma in Norman 65–21, causing a three-way tie atop the Big 12 South. Oklahoma wound up winning the tiebreaker (and beat Missouri in the Big 12 title game), while Texas Tech ended up in the Cotton Bowl. The series of events, along with the emergence of USC—which got hot after an early loss to Oregon State—and an undefeated Utah team caused many to call for a Bowl Subdivision playoff yet again, especially after the Utes trounced Alabama 31–17 in the Sugar Bowl to finish 13–0. But, alas, the cries for a playoff never went anywhere and all the talk about tweaking the BCS was met with a collective groan.

But Florida won everything that mattered in 2008, and though Harvin left early to go pro, the Gators are stocked to defend their title in 2009. Three days after Florida beat Oklahoma, Tebow stood before a raucous crowd of 40,000 and showed off the championship trophy. He began to walk off the stage before turning around, grabbing the microphone and saying: "Oh, yeah, and by the way, one more thing: I'm coming back next year. Let's do it again."

team as talented as Oklahoma would not go away, but thanks to the speedy Harvin (171 all-purpose yards) and a stout Gators defense (a goal-line stand and an interception in the end zone) Florida held the lead late in the fourth quarter. However, the Gators would still need Tebow to bring the title home.

Clinging to a 17–14 lead late in the game, Florida had the ball on the Oklahoma 4-yard line when the call came in: Trey Left, 341 Stop Bend X Fake, otherwise known as the jump pass, a Tebow signature. Tebow executed the play perfectly, faking the run, stepping back and jumping, before unleashing a perfect pass to junior wideout David Nelson. Touchdown. Ballgame.

Afterward, Meyer was already playing the role of salesman, trying to convince a whole new breed of talented recruits to come to Gainesville. "When you win national championships," Meyer said, "You have to be out of your freaking mind if you don't want to play for the Gators."

College football fans may have felt they were out of their minds while watching the Big 12 in 2008. Three quarterbacks, Oklahoma's Bradford, Texas' Colt McCoy and Texas Tech's Graham Harrell, put up video game-like numbers and made every week must-see TV in the conference. During one stretch, Oklahoma had five straight 60-point outings. Even more shocking, Texas

# FOR THE RECORD • 2008—2009

## Final Polls

### Associated Press

| | Record | Pts | Head Coach | SI Preseason Rank |
|---|---|---|---|---|
| 1. Florida (48) | 13–1 | 1606 | Urban Meyer | 5 |
| 2. Utah (16) | 13–0 | 1519 | Kyle Whittingham | 25 |
| 3. USC (1) | 12–1 | 1481 | Pete Carroll | 3 |
| 4. Texas | 12–1 | 1478 | Mack Brown | 13 |
| 5. Oklahoma | 12–2 | 1391 | Bob Stoops | 6 |
| 6. Alabama | 12–2 | 1264 | Nick Saban | 29 |
| 7. TCU | 11–2 | 1193 | Gary Patterson | 47 |
| 8. Penn St | 11–2 | 1153 | Joe Paterno | 22 |
| 9. Ohio St | 10–3 | 1013 | Jim Tressel | 2 |
| 10. Oregon | 10–3 | 997 | Mike Bellotti | 20 |
| 11. Boise St | 12–1 | 938 | Chris Petersen | 37 |
| 12. Texas Tech | 11–2 | 916 | Mike Leach | 8 |
| 13. Georgia | 10–3 | 903 | Mark Richt | 1 |
| 14. Mississippi | 9–4 | 857 | Houston Nutt | 60 |
| 15. Virginia Tech | 10–4 | 713 | Frank Beamer | 24 |
| 16. Oklahoma St | 9–4 | 534 | Mike Gundy | 43 |
| 17. Cincinnati | 11–3 | 506 | Brian Kelly | 27 |
| 18. Oregon St | 9–4 | 467 | Mike Riley | 18 |
| 19. Missouri | 10–4 | 435 | Gary Pinkel | 4 |
| 20. Iowa | 9–4 | 317 | Kirk Ferentz | 31 |
| 21. Florida St | 9–4 | 246 | Bobby Bowden | 41 |
| 22. Georgia Tech | 9–4 | 223 | Paul Johnson | 80 |
| 23. West Virginia | 9–4 | 144 | Bill Stewart | 14 |
| 24. Michigan St | 9–4 | 138 | Mark Dantonio | 38 |
| 25. BYU | 10–3 | 137 | Bronco Mendenhall | 17 |

Note: As voted by a panel of 65 sportswriters and broadcasters following bowl games (First place votes in parentheses).

### USA Today/ESPN/Coaches

| | Pts | SI Preseason Rank | | Pts | SI Preseason Rank |
|---|---|---|---|---|---|
| 1. Florida (60) | 1524 | 5 | 13. Boise St | 809 | 37 |
| 2. USC | 1393 | 3 | 14. Virginia Tech | 740 | 24 |
| 3. Texas | 1389 | 13 | 14. Mississippi | 620 | 60 |
| 4. Utah (1) | 1375 | 25 | 16. Missouri | 549 | 4 |
| 5. Oklahoma | 1333 | 6 | 17. Cincinnati | 493 | 27 |
| 6. Alabama | 1157 | 29 | 18. Oklahoma St | 480 | 43 |
| 7. TCU | 1114 | 47 | 19. Oregon St | 407 | 18 |
| 8. Penn St | 1091 | 22 | 20. Iowa | 250 | 31 |
| 9. Oregon | 1011 | 20 | 21. BYU | 248 | 17 |
| 10. Georgia | 904 | 1 | 22. Georgia Tech | 219 | 80 |
| 11. Ohio St | 874 | 2 | 23. Florida St | 217 | 41 |
| 12. Texas Tech | 867 | 8 | 24. Michigan St | 179 | 38 |
| | | | 25. California | 116 | 39 |

Note: Voted by a panel of 61 Div. I-A head coaches; 25 points for 1st, 24 for 2nd, etc. (First place votes in parentheses).

## Bowls and Playoffs

### NCAA Division I-A Bowl Results

| Date | Bowl | Result | Payout/Team ($) | Attendance |
|---|---|---|---|---|
| 12-20-08 | EagleBank | Wake Forest 29, Navy 19 | 750,000 | 28,777 |
| 12-20-08 | New Mexico | Colorado St 40, Fresno St 35 | 750,000 | 24,735 |
| 12-20-08 | St. Petersburg | South Florida 41, Memphis 14 | 1 million | 25,205 |
| 12-20-08 | Las Vegas | Arizona 31, BYU 21 | 1 million | 40,047 |
| 12-21-08 | New Orleans | Southern Miss 30, Troy 27 (OT) | 325,000 | 30,197 |
| 12-23-08 | Poinsettia | TCU 17, Boise St 16 | 750,000 | 34,628 |
| 12-24-08 | Hawaii | Notre Dame 49, Hawaii 21 | 750,000 | 43,487 |
| 12-26-08 | Motor City | Florida Atlantic 24, Central Michigan 21 | 750,000 | 41,399 |
| 12-27-08 | Meineke | West Virginia 31, North Carolina 30 | 1 million | 73,712 |
| 12-27-08 | Champs Sports | Florida St 42, Wisconsin 13 | 2.125 million | 52,692 |

### NCAA Division I-A Bowl Results *(Cont.)*

| Date | Bowl | Result | Payout/Team($) | Attendance |
|---|---|---|---|---|
| 12-27-08 | Emerald | California 24, Miami (Fla.) 17 | 750,000 (ACC) 850,000 (Pac-10) | 42,268 |
| 12-28-08 | Independence | Louisiana Tech 17; Northern Illinois 10 | 1.1 million | 41,567 |
| 12-29-08 | Papajohns.com | Rutgers 29, North Carolina St 23 | 300,000 | 38,582 |
| 12-29-08 | Alamo | Missouri 30, Northwestern 23 (OT) | 2.25 million | 55,986 |
| 12-30-08 | Humanitarian | Maryland 42, Nevada 35 | 750,000 | 26,781 |
| 12-30-08 | Texas | Rice 38, Western Michigan 14 | 750,000 | 58,880 |
| 12-30-08 | Holiday | Oregon 42, Oklahoma St 31 | 2.3 million | 59,106 |
| 12-31-08 | Armed Forces | Houston 34, Air Force 28 | 750,000 | 41,127 |
| 12-31-08 | Sun | Oregon St 3, Pittsburgh 0 | 1.9 million | 49,037 |
| 12-31-08 | Music City | Vanderbilt 16, Boston College 14 | 1.7 million | 54,250 |
| 12-31-08 | Insight | Kansas 42, Minnesota 21 | 1.2 million | 49,103 |
| 12-31-08 | Chick-fil-A | LSU 38, Georgia Tech 3 | 3 million | 71,423 |
| 01-01-09 | Outback | Iowa 31, South Carolina 10 | 3.2 million | 55,117 |
| 01-01-09 | Capital One | Georgia 24, Michigan St 12 | 4.25 million | 59,681 |
| 01-01-09 | Gator | Nebraska 26, Clemson 21 | 2.5 million | 67,282 |
| 01-01-09 | Rose | USC 38, Penn St 24 | 17 million | 93,293 |
| 01-01-09 | Orange | Virginia Tech 20, Cincinnati 7 | 17 million | 73,602 |
| 01-02-09 | Cotton | Mississippi 47, Texas Tech 34 | 3 million | 88,175 |
| 01-02-09 | Liberty | Kentucky 25, East Carolina 19 | 1.8 million | 56,125 |
| 01-02-09 | Sugar | Utah 31, Alabama 17 | 17 million | 71,872 |
| 01-03-09 | International | Connecticut 38, Buffalo 20 | 750,000 | 40,184 |
| 01-05-09 | Fiesta | Texas 24, Ohio St 21 | 17 million | 72,047 |
| 01-06-09 | GMAC | Tulsa 45, Ball St 13 | 750,000 | 32,816 |
| 01-08-09 | BCS Championship | Florida 24, Oklahoma 14 | 17 million | 78,468 |

### NCAA FCS (I-AA) Championship Box Score

| | | | | |
|---|---|---|---|---|
| Montana | 0 | 0 | 7—7 | |
| Richmond | 7 | 14 | 0 | 3—24 |

#### FIRST QUARTER
Richmond: TD Ward 23 pass from Crone (Howard kick), 9:02.

#### SECOND QUARTER
Richmond: TD Vaughan 5 run (Howard kick), 11:29.
Richmond: TD Wilkins 13 pass from Ward (Howard kick), 2:13.

#### FOURTH QUARTER
Montana: TD Reynolds 4 run (McKnight kick), 11:56.
Richmond: FG Radford 39, 6:54.

| | MONTANA | RICHMOND |
|---|---|---|
| First downs | 15 | 16 |
| Rushes-net yards | 25-39 | 39-208 |
| Net passing yards | 267 | 119 |
| Comp/Att/Int | 19-38-1 | 13-19-0 |
| Punts/-total yards | 5-175 | 5-190 |
| Fumbles-lost | 1-1 | 0-0 |
| Penalties-yards | 5-57 | 3-40 |
| Time of possession | 28:59 | 31:01 |

12-19-08, Chattanooga, Tennessee; Att: 17,823.

### Small College Championship Summaries

#### NCAA DIVISION II

**First round**: Tusculum 34, Albany St 22; Valdosta St 24, Carson-Newman 20; West Texas A&M 49, Central Washington 42; Pittsburg St 33, Neb.-Omaha 21; West Chester 52, Southern Connecticut St 32; Seton Hill 14, American International 7; Ashland 27, Minn. St-Mankato 16; Chadron St 23, Wayne St (Neb.) 17.
**Second Round**: Delta St 27, Tusculum 19; North Alabama 37, Valdosta St 10; Abilene Christian 93, West Texas A&M 68; NW Missouri St 38, Pittsburg St 35; Bloomsburg 28, West Chester 21; California (Pa.) 48, Seton Hill 7; Grand Valley St 40, Ashland 7; Minn.-Duluth 20, Chadron St 10.
**Quarterfinals**: North Alabama 55, Delta St 34; NW Missouri St 45, Abilene Christian 36; California (Pa.) 28, Bloomsburg 24; Minn.-Duluth 19, Grand Valley St 13.
**Semifinals**: NW Missouri St 41, North Alabama 7; Minn.-Duluth 45, California (Pa.) 7.

#### NCAA DIVISION II

**Championship**: 12-13-08, Florence, Alabama

| | | | | |
|---|---|---|---|---|
| NW Missouri St | 0 | 0 | 0 | 14—14 |
| Minnesota-Duluth | 0 | 7 | 7 | 7—21 |

#### NCAA DIVISION III

**First round**: Mount Union 56, Randolph-Macon 0; Hobart 33, Lycoming 15; Cortland St 31, Plymouth St 14; Curry 26, Ithaca 21; North Central (Ill.) 44, Thomas More 23; Franklin 62, Otterbein 45; Wabash 20, Case Western Reserve 17; Wheaton (Ill.) 14, Trine 0; Willamette 48, Occidental 33; UW-Whitewater 37, St. John's (Minn.) 7; Wartburg 26, UW-Stevens Point 21; Monmouth (Ill.) 42, Aurora 13; Millsaps 51, LaGrange 26; Wash. & Jeff. 35, Chris. Newport 29; Wesley 20, Muhlenberg 0; Mary Hardin-Baylor 38, Hardin-Simmons 35.

### NCAA DIVISION III *(CONT.)*

**Second Round**: Mount Union 42, Hobart 7; Cortland St 42, Curry 0; Franklin 38, North Central (Ill.) 28; Wheaton (Ill.) 59, Wabash 28; UW-Whitewater 30, Willamette 27; Wartburg 30, Monmouth (Ill.) 28; Wash. & Jeff. 35, Millsaps 20; Mary Hardin-Baylor 46, Wesley 14.

**Quarterfinals**: Mount Union 45, Cortland St 14; Wheaton (Ill.) 45, Franklin 28; UW-Whitewater 34, Wartburg 17; Mary Hardin-Baylor 63, Wash. & Jeff. 7.

**Semifinals**: Mount Union 45, Wheaton (Ill.) 24; UW-Whitewater 39, Mary Hardin-Baylor 13.

### NCAA DIVISION III

**Championship**: 12-20-08, Salem, Virginia, Att: 5,344

| | | | | |
|---|---|---|---|---|
| Mount Union | 21 | 3 | 0 | 7—31 |
| UW-Whitewater | 7 | 3 | 3 | 13—26 |

### NAIA CHAMPIONSHIP

12-20-08, Rome, Georgia, Att: 6,500

| | | | | |
|---|---|---|---|---|
| Sioux Falls (S.D.) | 3 | 7 | 0 | 13—23 |
| Carroll (Mont.) | 0 | 0 | 0 | 7—7 |

## Awards

### Heisman Memorial Trophy

| Player, School | Class | Pos | 1st | 2nd | 3rd | Total |
|---|---|---|---|---|---|---|
| Sam Bradford, Oklahoma | So. | QB | 300 | 315 | 196 | 1726 |
| Colt McCoy, Texas | Jr. | QB | 266 | 288 | 230 | 1640 |
| Tim Tebow, Florida | Jr. | QB | 309 | 207 | 234 | 1575 |
| Graham Harrell, Texas Tech | Sr. | QB | 13 | 44 | 86 | 213 |
| Michael Crabtree, Texas Tech | So. | WR | 3 | 27 | 116 | 116 |

Note: Former Heisman winners and the media vote, with ballots allowing for three names (3 points for 1st, 2 for 2nd, 1 for 3rd).

### Other Awards

Maxwell Award (Player) ......................................... Tim Tebow, Florida, QB
*Sporting News* Player of the Year ......................... Sam Bradford, Oklahoma, QB
Walter Camp Player of the Year ............................. Colt McCoy, Texas, QB
Chuck Bednarik Award (Defense) ......................... Rey Maualuga, USC, LB
Vince Lombardi/Rotary Award (Lineman/LB) ......... Brian Orakpo, Texas, DE
Outland Trophy (Interior Lineman) ......................... Andre Smith, Alabama, OT
Davey O'Brien Award (QB) ...................................... Sam Bradford, Oklahoma, QB
Unitas Golden Arm Award (Senior QB) .............. Graham Harrell, Texas Tech, QB
Doak Walker Award (RB) ........................................ Shonn Greene, Iowa, RB
Biletnikoff Award (WR) ............................................ Michael Crabtree, Texas Tech, WR
Butkus Award (Linebacker) .................................... Aaron Curry, Wake Forest, LB
Jim Thorpe Award (Defensive Back) ..................... Malcolm Jenkins, Ohio St, CB
*Associated Press* Player of the Year .................... Sam Bradford, Oklahoma, QB
Walter Payton Award (FCS Player) ........... Armanti Edwards, Appalachian St, QB
Harlon Hill Trophy (Div. II Player) ......... Bernard Scott, Abilene Christian, RB
Gagliardi Trophy (Div. III Player) ........................ Greg Micheli, Mount Union, QB

### Coaches' Awards

Walter Camp Award ...................................... Nick Saban, Alabama
Eddie Robinson Award (FCS) ..... Mickey Matthews, James Madison
Bobby Dodd Award .......................................... Mack Brown, Texas
Bear Bryant Award ...................................... Kyle Whittingham, Utah

### AFCA COACHES OF THE YEAR

FBS (Division I-A) ......................................... Kyle Whittingham, Utah
FCS (Division I-AA) .............................. Mike London, Richmond
Division II ................................................... Mel Tjeerdsma, NW Missouri St
Division III .................................................... Larry Kehres, Mount Union

## Football Writers Association of America All-America Team

### OFFENSE

QB ........ Colt McCoy, Texas, Jr.
RB ........ Shonn Greene, Iowa, Jr.
RB ........ Kendall Hunter, Oklahoma St, So.
WR ...... Michael Crabtree, Texas Tech, So.
WR ...... Jarett Dillard, Rice, Sr.
TE ........ Chase Coffman, Missouri, Sr.
OL ........ Michael Oher, Mississippi, Sr.
OL ........ Duke Robinson, Oklahoma, Sr.
OL ........ Andre Smith, Alabama, Jr..
OL ........ Jason Smith, Baylor, Sr.
C .......... A.Q. Shipley, Penn St, Sr.
K .......... Louie Sakoda, Utah, Sr.
RS ........ Brandon James, Florida, Jr.

### DEFENSE

DL ........ Terrence Cody, Alabama, Jr.
DL ........ Jerry Hughes, TCU, Jr.
DL ........ Aaron Maybin, Penn St, So.
DL ........ Brian Orakpo, Texas, Sr.
LB ........ Rey Maualuga, USC, Sr.
LB ........ Scott McKillop, Pittsburgh, Sr.
LB ........ Brandon Spikes, Florida, Jr.
DB ........ Eric Berry, Tennessee, So.
DB ........ Malcolm Jenkins, Ohio St, Sr.
DB ........ Taylor Mays, USC, Jr.
DB ........ Alphonso Smith, Wake Forest, Sr.
P .......... Kevin Huber, Cincinnati, Sr.

## Football Bowl Subdivision (I-A)

### ATLANTIC COAST CONFERENCE

| ATLANTIC | Conference | | Full Season | | |
|---|---|---|---|---|---|
| | W | L | W | L | Pct |
| Florida St | 5 | 3 | 9 | 4 | .692 |
| Boston College | 5 | 3 | 9 | 5 | .643 |
| Maryland | 4 | 4 | 8 | 5 | .615 |
| Wake Forest | 4 | 4 | 8 | 5 | .615 |
| Clemson | 4 | 4 | 7 | 6 | .538 |
| North Carolina St | 4 | 4 | 6 | 7 | .462 |
| **COASTAL** | | | | | |
| Virginia Tech | 5 | 3 | 10 | 4 | .714 |
| Georgia Tech | 5 | 3 | 9 | 4 | .692 |
| North Carolina | 4 | 4 | 8 | 5 | .615 |
| Miami (Fla.) | 4 | 4 | 7 | 6 | .538 |
| Virginia | 3 | 5 | 5 | 7 | .417 |
| Duke | 1 | 7 | 4 | 8 | .333 |

### BIG EAST CONFERENCE

| | Conference | | Full Season | | |
|---|---|---|---|---|---|
| | W | L | W | L | Pct |
| Cincinnati | 6 | 1 | 11 | 3 | .786 |
| Pittsburgh | 5 | 2 | 9 | 4 | .692 |
| West Virginia | 5 | 2 | 9 | 4 | .692 |
| Rutgers | 5 | 2 | 8 | 5 | .615 |
| Connecticut | 3 | 4 | 8 | 5 | .615 |
| South Florida | 2 | 5 | 8 | 5 | .615 |
| Louisville | 1 | 6 | 5 | 7 | .417 |
| Syracuse | 1 | 6 | 3 | 9 | .250 |

### BIG TEN CONFERENCE

| | Conference | | Full Season | | |
|---|---|---|---|---|---|
| | W | L | W | L | Pct |
| Penn St | 7 | 1 | 11 | 2 | .846 |
| Ohio St | 7 | 1 | 10 | 3 | .769 |
| Michigan St | 6 | 2 | 9 | 4 | .692 |
| Iowa | 5 | 3 | 9 | 4 | .692 |
| Northwestern | 5 | 3 | 9 | 4 | .692 |
| Minnesota | 3 | 5 | 7 | 6 | .538 |
| Wisconsin | 3 | 5 | 7 | 6 | .538 |
| Illinois | 3 | 5 | 5 | 7 | .417 |
| Purdue | 2 | 6 | 4 | 8 | .333 |
| Michigan | 2 | 6 | 3 | 9 | .250 |
| Indiana | 1 | 7 | 3 | 9 | .250 |

### BIG 12 CONFERENCE

| NORTH | Conference | | Full Season | | |
|---|---|---|---|---|---|
| | W | L | W | L | Pct |
| Missouri | 5 | 3 | 10 | 4 | .714 |
| Nebraska | 5 | 3 | 9 | 4 | .692 |
| Kansas | 4 | 4 | 8 | 5 | .615 |
| Kansas St | 2 | 6 | 5 | 7 | .417 |
| Colorado | 2 | 6 | 5 | 7 | .417 |
| Iowa St | 0 | 8 | 2 | 10 | .167 |
| **SOUTH** | | | | | |
| Texas | 7 | 1 | 12 | 1 | .923 |
| Oklahoma | 7 | 1 | 12 | 2 | .857 |
| Texas Tech | 7 | 1 | 11 | 2 | .846 |
| Oklahoma St | 5 | 3 | 9 | 4 | .692 |
| Baylor | 2 | 6 | 4 | 8 | .333 |
| Texas A&M | 2 | 6 | 4 | 8 | .333 |

## Football Bowl Subdivision (I-A) *(Cont.)*

### CONFERENCE USA

| EAST | Conference | | Full Season | | |
|---|---|---|---|---|---|
| | W | L | W | L | Pct |
| East Carolina | 6 | 2 | 9 | 5 | .642 |
| Southern Miss | 4 | 4 | 7 | 6 | .538 |
| Memphis | 4 | 4 | 6 | 7 | .461 |
| Marshall | 3 | 5 | 4 | 8 | .333 |
| Central Florida | 3 | 5 | 4 | 8 | .333 |
| UAB | 3 | 5 | 4 | 8 | .333 |
| **WEST** | | | | | |
| Tulsa | 7 | 1 | 11 | 3 | .786 |
| Rice | 7 | 1 | 10 | 3 | .769 |
| Houston | 6 | 2 | 8 | 5 | .615 |
| UTEP | 4 | 4 | 5 | 7 | .417 |
| Tulane | 1 | 7 | 2 | 10 | .167 |
| SMU | 0 | 8 | 1 | 11 | .083 |

### MID-AMERICAN ATHLETIC CONFERENCE

| EAST | Conference | | Full Season | | |
|---|---|---|---|---|---|
| | W | L | W | L | Pct |
| Buffalo | 5 | 3 | 8 | 6 | .571 |
| Bowling Green | 4 | 4 | 6 | 6 | .500 |
| Temple | 4 | 4 | 5 | 7 | .417 |
| Akron | 3 | 5 | 5 | 7 | .417 |
| Ohio | 3 | 5 | 4 | 8 | .333 |
| Kent St | 3 | 5 | 4 | 8 | .333 |
| Miami (Ohio) | 1 | 7 | 2 | 10 | .167 |
| **WEST** | | | | | |
| Ball St | 8 | 0 | 12 | 2 | .857 |
| Western Michigan | 6 | 2 | 9 | 4 | .692 |
| Central Michigan | 6 | 2 | 8 | 5 | .615 |
| Northern Illinois | 5 | 3 | 6 | 7 | .462 |
| Toledo | 2 | 6 | 3 | 9 | .250 |
| Eastern Michigan | 2 | 6 | 3 | 9 | .250 |

### MOUNTAIN WEST CONFERENCE

| | Conference | | Full Season | | |
|---|---|---|---|---|---|
| | W | L | W | L | Pct |
| Utah | 8 | 0 | 13 | 0 | 1.000 |
| TCU | 7 | 1 | 11 | 2 | .846 |
| BYU | 6 | 2 | 10 | 3 | .769 |
| Air Force | 5 | 3 | 8 | 5 | .615 |
| Colorado St | 4 | 4 | 7 | 6 | .538 |
| UNLV | 2 | 6 | 5 | 7 | .417 |
| New Mexico | 2 | 6 | 4 | 8 | .333 |
| Wyoming | 1 | 7 | 4 | 8 | .333 |
| San Diego St | 1 | 7 | 2 | 10 | .167 |

### PACIFIC 10 CONFERENCE

| | Conference | | Full Season | | |
|---|---|---|---|---|---|
| | W | L | W | L | Pct |
| USC | 8 | 1 | 12 | 1 | .923 |
| Oregon | 7 | 2 | 10 | 3 | .769 |
| Oregon St | 7 | 2 | 9 | 4 | .692 |
| California | 6 | 3 | 9 | 4 | .692 |
| Arizona | 5 | 4 | 8 | 5 | .615 |
| Stanford | 4 | 5 | 5 | 7 | .417 |
| Arizona St | 4 | 5 | 5 | 7 | .417 |
| UCLA | 3 | 6 | 4 | 8 | .333 |
| Washington St | 1 | 8 | 2 | 11 | .154 |
| Washington | 0 | 9 | 0 | 12 | .000 |

## Football Bowl Subdivision (I-A) *(Cont.)*

### SOUTHEASTERN CONFERENCE

| EAST | Conference | | Full Season | | |
|---|---|---|---|---|---|
| | W | L | W | L | Pct |
| Florida | 7 | 1 | 13 | 1 | .929 |
| Georgia | 6 | 2 | 10 | 3 | .769 |
| Vanderbilt | 4 | 4 | 7 | 6 | .538 |
| South Carolina | 4 | 4 | 7 | 6 | .538 |
| Tennessee | 3 | 5 | 5 | 7 | .417 |
| Kentucky | 2 | 6 | 7 | 6 | .538 |
| **WEST** | | | | | |
| Alabama | 8 | 0 | 12 | 2 | .857 |
| Mississippi | 5 | 3 | 9 | 4 | .692 |
| LSU | 3 | 5 | 8 | 5 | .615 |
| Auburn | 2 | 6 | 5 | 7 | .417 |
| Arkansas | 2 | 6 | 5 | 7 | .417 |
| Mississippi St | 2 | 6 | 4 | 12 | .333 |

### SUN BELT CONFERENCE

| | Conference | | Full Season | | |
|---|---|---|---|---|---|
| | W | L | W | L | Pct |
| Troy | 6 | 1 | 8 | 5 | .615 |
| La.-Lafayette | 5 | 2 | 6 | 6 | .500 |
| Florida Atlantic | 4 | 2 | 7 | 6 | .538 |
| Arkansas St | 3 | 3 | 6 | 6 | .500 |
| Florida International | 3 | 4 | 5 | 7 | .417 |
| Middle Tennessee St | 3 | 4 | 5 | 7 | .417 |
| La.-Monroe | 3 | 4 | 4 | 8 | .333 |
| North Texas | 0 | 7 | 1 | 11 | .083 |

### WESTERN ATHLETIC CONFERENCE

| | Conference | | Full Season | | |
|---|---|---|---|---|---|
| | W | L | W | L | Pct |
| Boise St | 8 | 0 | 12 | 1 | .923 |
| Louisiana Tech | 5 | 3 | 8 | 5 | .615 |
| Nevada | 5 | 3 | 7 | 6 | .538 |
| Hawaii | 5 | 3 | 7 | 7 | .500 |
| Fresno St | 4 | 4 | 7 | 6 | .538 |
| San Jose St | 4 | 4 | 6 | 6 | .500 |
| Utah St | 3 | 5 | 3 | 9 | .250 |
| New Mexico St | 1 | 7 | 3 | 9 | .250 |
| Idaho | 1 | 7 | 2 | 10 | .167 |

### INDEPENDENTS

| | Full Season | | |
|---|---|---|---|
| | W | L | Pct |
| Navy | 8 | 5 | .615 |
| Notre Dame | 7 | 6 | .538 |
| Army | 3 | 9 | .250 |
| Western Kentucky | 2 | 10 | .167 |

## Football Championship Subdivision (I-AA)

### BIG SKY CONFERENCE

| | Conference | | Full Season | | |
|---|---|---|---|---|---|
| | W | L | W | L | Pct |
| Montana | 7 | 1 | 14 | 2 | .875 |
| Weber St | 7 | 1 | 10 | 4 | .714 |
| Montana St | 5 | 3 | 7 | 5 | .583 |
| Eastern Washington | 5 | 3 | 6 | 5 | .545 |
| Northern Arizona | 4 | 4 | 6 | 5 | .545 |
| Sacramento St | 3 | 5 | 6 | 6 | .500 |
| Portland St | 3 | 5 | 4 | 7 | .364 |
| Northern Colorado | 1 | 7 | 1 | 10 | .091 |
| Idaho St | 1 | 7 | 1 | 11 | .083 |

### BIG SOUTH CONFERENCE

| | Conference | | Full Season | | |
|---|---|---|---|---|---|
| | W | L | W | L | Pct |
| Liberty | 5 | 0 | 10 | 2 | .833 |
| Charleston Southern | 3 | 2 | 7 | 5 | .583 |
| Stony Brook | 3 | 2 | 5 | 6 | .455 |
| Gardner-Webb | 2 | 3 | 5 | 6 | .455 |
| Coastal Carolina | 1 | 4 | 6 | 6 | .500 |
| Virginia Military Inst. | 1 | 4 | 4 | 7 | .364 |

### COLONIAL CONFERENCE

| NORTH | Conference | | Full Season | | |
|---|---|---|---|---|---|
| | W | L | W | L | Pct |
| New Hampshire | 7 | 2 | 11 | 3 | .786 |
| Maine | 6 | 3 | 9 | 5 | .642 |
| Massachusetts | 4 | 4 | 7 | 5 | .583 |
| Hofstra | 2 | 6 | 4 | 8 | .333 |
| Rhode Island | 1 | 7 | 3 | 9 | .250 |
| Northeastern | 1 | 7 | 2 | 10 | .167 |
| **SOUTH** | | | | | |
| James Madison | 8 | 0 | 12 | 2 | .857 |
| Villanova | 7 | 1 | 10 | 3 | .769 |
| Richmond | 6 | 2 | 13 | 3 | .813 |
| William & Mary | 5 | 3 | 7 | 4 | .636 |
| Delaware | 2 | 6 | 4 | 8 | .333 |
| Towson | 1 | 7 | 3 | 9 | .250 |

### MISSOURI VALLEY CONFERENCE

| | Conference | | Full Season | | |
|---|---|---|---|---|---|
| | W | L | W | L | Pct |
| Northern Iowa | 7 | 1 | 12 | 3 | .800 |
| Southern Illinois | 7 | 1 | 9 | 3 | .750 |
| South Dakota St | 6 | 2 | 7 | 5 | .583 |
| Western Illinois | 4 | 4 | 6 | 5 | .546 |
| North Dakota St | 4 | 4 | 6 | 5 | .546 |
| Missouri St | 3 | 5 | 4 | 7 | .364 |
| Youngstown St | 3 | 5 | 4 | 8 | .333 |
| Illinois St | 2 | 6 | 3 | 8 | .273 |
| Indiana St | 0 | 8 | 0 | 10 | .000 |

### IVY LEAGUE

| | Conference | | Full Season | | |
|---|---|---|---|---|---|
| | W | L | W | L | Pct |
| Harvard | 6 | 1 | 9 | 1 | .900 |
| Brown | 6 | 1 | 7 | 3 | .700 |
| Pennsylvania | 5 | 2 | 6 | 4 | .600 |
| Yale | 4 | 3 | 6 | 4 | .600 |
| Princeton | 3 | 4 | 4 | 6 | .400 |
| Cornell | 2 | 5 | 4 | 6 | .400 |
| Columbia | 2 | 5 | 2 | 8 | .200 |
| Dartmouth | 0 | 7 | 0 | 10 | .000 |

## Football Champ. Subdivision (I-AA) *(Cont.)*

### MID-EASTERN ATHLETIC CONFERENCE

| | Conference | | Full Season | | |
|---|---|---|---|---|---|
| | W | L | W | L | Pct |
| South Carolina St | 8 | 0 | 10 | 3 | .769 |
| Florida A&M | 5 | 3 | 9 | 3 | .750 |
| Bethune-Cookman | 5 | 3 | 8 | 3 | .727 |
| Hampton | 5 | 3 | 6 | 5 | .545 |
| Delaware St | 5 | 3 | 5 | 6 | .455 |
| Morgan St | 4 | 4 | 6 | 6 | .500 |
| Norfolk St | 3 | 5 | 5 | 7 | .417 |
| North Carolina A&T | 1 | 7 | 3 | 9 | .250 |
| Howard. | 0 | 8 | 1 | 10 | .091 |

### NORTHEAST CONFERENCE

| | Conference | | Full Season | | |
|---|---|---|---|---|---|
| | W | L | W | L | Pct |
| Albany | 7 | 0 | 9 | 3 | .750 |
| Monmouth (N.J.) | 6 | 1 | 7 | 5 | .583 |
| Sacred Heart | 4 | 3 | 8 | 3 | .727 |
| Central Connecticut St | 4 | 3 | 7 | 4 | .636 |
| Robert Morris | 4 | 3 | 5 | 6 | .456 |
| Duquesne | 2 | 5 | 3 | 7 | .300 |
| Wagner | 1 | 6 | 3 | 8 | .273 |
| St. Francis (Pa.) | 0 | 7 | 0 | 11 | .000 |

### OHIO VALLEY CONFERENCE

| | Conference | | Full Season | | |
|---|---|---|---|---|---|
| | W | L | W | L | Pct |
| Eastern Kentucky | 7 | 1 | 8 | 4 | .667 |
| Jacksonville St | 6 | 2 | 8 | 3 | .727 |
| Tenn.-Martin | 6 | 2 | 8 | 4 | .667 |
| Tennessee St | 5 | 3 | 8 | 4 | .667 |
| Murray St | 4 | 4 | 5 | 7 | .417 |
| Eastern Illinois | 3 | 5 | 5 | 7 | .417 |
| SE Missouri St | 2 | 6 | 4 | 8 | .333 |
| Austin Peay | 2 | 6 | 2 | 9 | .182 |
| Tennessee Tech | 1 | 7 | 3 | 9 | .250 |

### PATRIOT LEAGUE

| | Conference | | Full Season | | |
|---|---|---|---|---|---|
| | W | L | W | L | Pct |
| Colgate | 5 | 0 | 9 | 3 | .750 |
| Holy Cross | 5 | 1 | 7 | 4 | .636 |
| Lehigh | 4 | 2 | 5 | 6 | .455 |
| Lafayette | 3 | 3 | 7 | 4 | .636 |
| Bucknell | 2 | 4 | 5 | 6 | .455 |
| Fordham | 1 | 5 | 5 | 6 | .455 |
| Georgetown | 0 | 5 | 2 | 8 | .200 |

## Football Champ. Subdivision (I-AA) *(Cont.)*

### PIONEER LEAGUE

| | Conference | | Full Season | | |
|---|---|---|---|---|---|
| | W | L | W | L | Pct |
| Jacksonville | 7 | 1 | 9 | 4 | .692 |
| San Diego | 6 | 2 | 9 | 2 | .818 |
| Dayton | 6 | 2 | 9 | 3 | .750 |
| Butler | 4 | 4 | 6 | 5 | .545 |
| Drake | 4 | 4 | 6 | 5 | .545 |
| Morehead St | 4 | 4 | 6 | 6 | .500 |
| Davidson | 3 | 5 | 4 | 7 | .364 |
| Valparaiso | 2 | 6 | 3 | 8 | .273 |
| Campbell | 0 | 8 | 1 | 10 | .091 |

### SOUTHERN CONFERENCE

| | Conference | | Full Season | | |
|---|---|---|---|---|---|
| | W | L | W | L | Pct |
| Appalachian St | 8 | 0 | 11 | 3 | .786 |
| Wofford | 7 | 1 | 9 | 3 | .750 |
| Elon | 6 | 2 | 8 | 4 | .667 |
| Furman | 4 | 4 | 7 | 5 | .583 |
| Georgia Southern | 4 | 4 | 6 | 5 | .545 |
| Samford | 4 | 4 | 6 | 5 | .545 |
| Citadel | 2 | 6 | 4 | 8 | .333 |
| Western Carolina | 1 | 7 | 3 | 9 | .250 |
| Chattanooga | 0 | 8 | 1 | 11 | .083 |

### SOUTHLAND CONFERENCE

| | Conference | | Full Season | | |
|---|---|---|---|---|---|
| | W | L | W | L | Pct |
| Central Arkansas | 6 | 1 | 10 | 2 | .833 |
| Texas St | 5 | 2 | 8 | 5 | .615 |
| McNeese St | 4 | 3 | 7 | 4 | .636 |
| Northwestern St | 4 | 3 | 7 | 5 | .583 |
| Nicholls St | 3 | 4 | 3 | 6 | .333 |
| SE Louisiana | 2 | 5 | 5 | 7 | .417 |
| Sam Houston St | 2 | 5 | 4 | 6 | .400 |
| Stephen F. Austin | 2 | 5 | 4 | 8 | .333 |

### SOUTHWESTERN ATHLETIC CONFERENCE

| | Conference | | Full Season | | |
|---|---|---|---|---|---|
| EAST | W | L | W | L | Pct |
| Jackson St | 6 | 3 | 7 | 5 | .583 |
| Alabama A&M | 4 | 3 | 5 | 7 | .417 |
| Alabama St | 2 | 5 | 3 | 8 | .273 |
| Alcorn St | 2 | 7 | 2 | 10 | .167 |
| Mississippi Valley St | 1 | 8 | 3 | 8 | .273 |
| **WEST** | | | | | |
| Grambling St | 10 | 0 | 11 | 2 | .846 |
| Prairie View A&M | 7 | 1 | 9 | 1 | .900 |
| Southern Univ. | 6 | 2 | 6 | 5 | .545 |
| Ark.-Pine Bluff | 2 | 6 | 3 | 9 | .250 |
| Texas Southern | 1 | 6 | 4 | 8 | .333 |

### INDEPENDENTS

| | Full Season | | |
|---|---|---|---|
| | W | L | Pct |
| Bryant | 7 | 4 | .636 |
| Savannah St | 5 | 7 | .417 |
| Marist | 4 | 7 | .364 |
| North Carolina Central | 4 | 7 | .364 |
| Presbyterian | 4 | 8 | .333 |
| Winston-Salem | 3 | 8 | .273 |
| Iona | 3 | 8 | .273 |

## Football Bowl Subdivision (Division I-A)

### SCORING

| | Class | GP | TD | XP | FG | Pts | Pts/Game |
|---|---|---|---|---|---|---|---|
| Javon Ringer, Michigan St | Sr. | 13 | 22 | 0 | 0 | 132 | 10.15 |
| LeSean McCoy, Pittsburgh | So. | 13 | 21 | 0 | 0 | 126 | 9.69 |
| Dez Bryant, Oklahoma St | So. | 13 | 21 | 0 | 0 | 126 | 9.69 |
| Graham Gano, Florida St | Sr. | 11 | 0 | 33 | 24 | 105 | 9.55 |
| Tyrell Fenroy, La.-Lafayette | Sr. | 12 | 19 | 0 | 0 | 114 | 9.50 |
| Jeff Wolfert, Missouri | Sr. | 14 | 0 | 73 | 20 | 133 | 9.50 |
| MiQuale Lewis, Ball St | Jr. | 14 | 22 | 0 | 0 | 132 | 9.43 |
| Louie Sakoda, Utah | Sr. | 13 | 0 | 56 | 22 | 122 | 9.38 |
| Jarett Dillard, Rice | Sr. | 13 | 20 | 0 | 0 | 120 | 9.23 |
| Kevin Kelly, Penn St | Sr. | 13 | 0 | 60 | 20 | 120 | 9.23 |
| Shonn Greene, Iowa | Jr. | 13 | 20 | 0 | 0 | 120 | 9.23 |
| Dennis Kennedy, Akron | Sr. | 12 | 18 | 0 | 0 | 110 | 9.17 |
| Chris Brown, Oklahoma | Jr. | 14 | 21 | 0 | 0 | 114 | 9.00 |
| James Casey, Rice | So. | 13 | 19 | 0 | 0 | 114 | 8.77 |
| Michael Crabtree, Texas Tech | So. | 13 | 19 | 0 | 0 | 114 | 8.77 |

### FIELD GOALS

| | Class | GP | FGA | FG | Pct | FG/Game |
|---|---|---|---|---|---|---|
| Graham Gano, Florida St | Sr. | 11 | 26 | 24 | .923 | 2.18 |
| Ben Hartman, East Carolina | Jr. | 11 | 31 | 21 | .677 | 1.91 |
| Ryan Harrison, Air Force | Sr. | 13 | 29 | 24 | .828 | 1.85 |
| Louie Sakoda, Utah | Sr. | 13 | 24 | 22 | .917 | 1.69 |
| Brett Swenson, Michigan St | Jr. | 13 | 28 | 22 | .786 | 1.69 |

### TOTAL OFFENSE

| | | | Rushing | | Passing | | | Total Offense | |
|---|---|---|---|---|---|---|---|---|---|
| | Class | GP | Car | Net | Att | Yds | Yds | Yds/Play | Yds/Game |
| Case Keenum, Houston | So. | 13 | 76 | 221 | 589 | 5020 | 5241 | 7.88 | 403.2 |
| Graham Harrell, Texas Tech | Sr. | 13 | 41 | -15 | 626 | 5111 | 5096 | 7.64 | 392.0 |
| Chase Clement, Rice | Sr. | 13 | 154 | 693 | 490 | 4119 | 4812 | 7.47 | 370.2 |
| Sam Bradford, Oklahoma | So. | 14 | 42 | 47 | 483 | 4720 | 4767 | 9.08 | 340.5 |
| Colt McCoy, Texas | Jr. | 13 | 136 | 561 | 433 | 3859 | 4420 | 7.77 | 340.0 |
| Chase Daniel. Missouri | Sr. | 14 | 69 | 281 | 528 | 4335 | 4616 | 7.73 | 329.7 |
| Juice Williams, Illinois | Jr. | 12 | 175 | 719 | 381 | 3173 | 3892 | 7.00 | 324.3 |
| Todd Reesing, Kansas | Jr. | 13 | 126 | 224 | 495 | 3888 | 4112 | 6.62 | 316.3 |
| Max Hall, BYU | Jr. | 13 | 65 | 115 | 477 | 3957 | 4072 | 7.51 | 313.2 |
| Dan LeFevour, Central Michigan | Jr. | 11 | 168 | 592 | 376 | 2784 | 3376 | 6.21 | 306.9 |

### RUSHING

| | Class | GP | Car | Yds | TD | Avg | Yds/Game |
|---|---|---|---|---|---|---|---|
| Donald Brown, Connecticut | Jr. | 13 | 367 | 2083 | 18 | 5.68 | 160.23 |
| Shonn Greene, Iowa | Jr. | 13 | 307 | 1850 | 20 | 6.03 | 142.31 |
| Jahvid Best, California | So. | 12 | 194 | 1580 | 15 | 8.14 | 131.67 |
| Javon Ringer, Michigan St | Sr. | 13 | 390 | 1637 | 22 | 4.20 | 125.92 |
| MiQuale Lewis, Ball St | Jr. | 14 | 322 | 1736 | 22 | 5.39 | 124.00 |
| Chris Wells, Ohio St | Jr. | 10 | 207 | 1197 | 8 | 5.78 | 119.70 |
| Kendall Hunter, Oklahoma St | So. | 13 | 241 | 1555 | 16 | 6.45 | 119.62 |
| Vai Taua, Nevada | So. | 13 | 236 | 1521 | 15 | 6.44 | 117.00 |
| Tyrell Fenroy, La.-Lafayette | Sr. | 12 | 226 | 1375 | 19 | 6.08 | 114.58 |
| LeSean McCoy, Pittsburgh | So. | 13 | 308 | 1488 | 21 | 4.83 | 114.46 |

### PASSING EFFICIENCY

| | Class | GP | Att | Comp | Pct Comp | Yds | Yds/Att | TD | Int | Rating Pts |
|---|---|---|---|---|---|---|---|---|---|---|
| Sam Bradford, Oklahoma | So. | 14 | 483 | 328 | 67.9 | 4720 | 9.8 | 50 | 8 | 180.8 |
| David Johnson, Tulsa | Sr. | 14 | 400 | 258 | 64.5 | 4059 | 10.2 | 46 | 18 | 178.7 |
| Colt McCoy, Texas | Jr. | 13 | 433 | 332 | 76.7 | 3859 | 8.9 | 34 | 8 | 173.8 |
| Tim Tebow, Florida | Jr. | 14 | 298 | 192 | 64.4 | 2746 | 9.2 | 30 | 4 | 172.4 |
| Zac Robinson, Oklahoma St | Jr. | 13 | 314 | 204 | 65.0 | 3064 | 9.8 | 25 | 10 | 166.8 |
| Mark Sanchez, USC | Jr. | 13 | 366 | 241 | 65.9 | 3207 | 8.8 | 34 | 10 | 164.6 |
| Chase Clement, Rice | Sr. | 13 | 490 | 326 | 66.5 | 4119 | 8.4 | 44 | 7 | 163.9 |
| Graham Harrell, Texas Tech | Sr. | 13 | 626 | 442 | 70.6 | 5111 | 8.2 | 45 | 9 | 160.0 |
| Case Keenum, Houston | So. | 13 | 589 | 397 | 67.4 | 5020 | 8.5 | 44 | 11 | 159.9 |
| Chase Daniel, Missouri | Sr. | 14 | 528 | 385 | 72.9 | 4335 | 8.2 | 39 | 18 | 159.4 |

Note: Minimum 15 attempts per game.

## Football Bowl Subdivision (Division I-A) *(Cont.)*

### RECEPTIONS PER GAME

|  | Class | GP | No. | Yds | TD | R/Game |
|---|---|---|---|---|---|---|
| Casey Fitzgerald, North Texas | Sr. | 12 | 113 | 1119 | 6 | 9.4 |
| James Casey, Rice | So. | 13 | 111 | 1329 | 13 | 8.5 |
| Austin Collie, BYU | Jr. | 13 | 106 | 1538 | 15 | 8.2 |
| Jamarko Simmons, Western Michigan | Sr. | 13 | 104 | 1276 | 7 | 8.0 |
| Chase Coffman, Missouri | Sr. | 12 | 90 | 987 | 10 | 7.5 |

### RECEIVING YARDS PER GAME

|  | Class | GP | No. | Yds | TD | Yds/Game |
|---|---|---|---|---|---|---|
| Austin Collie, BYU | Jr. | 13 | 106 | 1538 | 15 | 118.3 |
| Kenny Britt, Rutgers | Jr. | 12 | 87 | 1371 | 7 | 114.3 |
| Dez Bryant, Oklahoma St. | So. | 13 | 87 | 1480 | 19 | 113.9 |
| Dezmon Briscoe, Kansas | So. | 13 | 92 | 1407 | 15 | 108.2 |
| Chris Williams, New Mexico St | Sr. | 12 | 86 | 1271 | 9 | 105.9 |

### ALL-PURPOSE RUNNING

|  | Class | GP | Rush | Rec | PR | KOR | Yds | Yds/Game |
|---|---|---|---|---|---|---|---|---|
| Jeremy Maclin, Missouri | So. | 14 | 293 | 1260 | 270 | 1010 | 2833 | 202.4 |
| Jahvid Best, California | So. | 12 | 1580 | 246 | 0 | 421 | 2247 | 187.3 |
| T.Y. Hilton, Florida Int'l | Fr. | 12 | 43 | 1013 | 266 | 841 | 2163 | 180.3 |
| Antonio Brown, Central Michigan | So. | 13 | 116 | 998 | 410 | 791 | 2315 | 178.1 |
| Damaris Johnson, Tulsa | Fr. | 14 | 327 | 743 | 23 | 1382 | 2475 | 176.8 |

### INTERCEPTIONS

|  | Class | GP | No. | Int/Game |
|---|---|---|---|---|
| Eric Berry, Tennessee | So. | 12 | 7 | .58 |
| Kevin Sanders UAB | Sr. | 12 | 7 | .58 |
| Trimane Goddard, UNC | Sr. | 13 | 7 | .54 |
| Darcel McBath, Texas Tech | Sr. | 13 | 7 | .54 |
| Morgan Burnett, Ga. Tech | So. | 13 | 7 | .54 |
| Alphonso Smith, Wake Forest | Sr. | 13 | 7 | .54 |
| Ahmad Black, Florida | So. | 14 | 7 | .50 |

### PUNTING

|  | Class | No. | Avg |
|---|---|---|---|
| T.J. Conley, Idaho | Sr. | 58 | 47.4 |
| Ross Thevenot, Tulane | Jr. | 45 | 45.8 |
| Justin Brantly, Texas A&M. | Sr. | 51 | 45.7 |
| Jacob Richardson, Miami (Ohio) | Sr. | 52 | 45.4 |
| Tim Masthay, Kentucky | Sr. | 53 | 45.2 |

Note: Minimum of 3.6 per game.

### PUNT RETURNS

|  | Class | No. | Yds | TD | Avg |
|---|---|---|---|---|---|
| Antonio Brown, Central Mich. | So. | 20 | 410 | 1 | 20.5 |
| Ian Clark, New Mexico | Jr. | 12 | 236 | 0 | 19.7 |
| Dez Bryant, Oklahoma St | So. | 17 | 305 | 2 | 17.9 |
| Kyle Williams, Arizona St | Jr. | 14 | 238 | 0 | 17.0 |
| Robert Dunn, Auburn | Sr. | 15 | 240 | 1 | 16.0 |

Note: Minimum 1.2 per game.

### KICKOFF RETURNS

|  | Class | No. | Yds | TD | Avg |
|---|---|---|---|---|---|
| Travis Shelton, Temple | Sr. | 23 | 720 | 1 | 31.3 |
| Michael Ray Garvin, Florida St | Sr. | 22 | 662 | 1 | 30.1 |
| Perrish Cox, Oklahoma St | Jr. | 30 | 895 | 2 | 29.8 |
| A.J. Jefferson, Fresno St | Jr. | 31 | 908 | 1 | 29.3 |
| Aaron Brown, TCU | Sr. | 18 | 526 | 1 | 29.2 |

Note: Minimum of 1.2 per game.

## Football Bowl Subdivision (I-A) Single-Game Highs

### RUSHING AND PASSING

Rushing and passing yards: 554—Andy Schmitt, Eastern Mich., QB, Nov 28, 2008 (vs Central Mich.)
Rushing and passing plays: 89—Andy Schmitt, Eastern Mich., QB, Nov 28, 2008 (vs Central Mich.)
Rushing plays: 44—Javon Ringer, Michigan St, RB, Sept 27, 2008 (vs Indiana)
Net rushing yards: 348—Shun White, Navy, RB, Aug 30, 2008 (vs Towson)
Passes attempted: 80—Andy Schmitt, Eastern Michigan, QB, Nov 28, 2008 (vs Central Michigan)
Passes completed: 58—Andy Schmitt, Eastern Michigan, QB, Nov 28, 2008 (vs Central Michigan)
Net passing yards: 536—Graham Harrell, Texas Tech, QB, Aug 30, 2008 (vs Eastern Washington)

### RECEIVING AND RETURNS

Passes caught: 23—Tyler Jones, Eastern Michigan, WR, Nov 28, 2008 (vs Central Michigan)
Receiving yards: 269—Dezmon Briscoe, Kansas, WR, Oct 18, 2008 (vs Oklahoma)
Punt return Yards: 163—Trindon Holliday, LSU, Sept 13, 2008 (vs North Texas)
Kickoff return yards: 319—Leonard Johnson, Iowa St, Nov 1, 2008 (vs Oklahoma St)

### Football Championship Subdivision (Division I-AA)

#### SCORING

| | Class | GP | TD | XP | FG | Pts | Pts/Game |
|---|---|---|---|---|---|---|---|
| Trevyn Smith, Weber St | Jr. | 14 | 28 | 0 | 0 | 168 | 12.00 |
| Herb Donaldson, Western Illinois | Sr. | 11 | 22 | 0 | 0 | 132 | 12.00 |
| David Sinisi, Monmouth | Jr. | 11 | 22 | 0 | 0 | 132 | 12.00 |
| Dane Romero, Wofford | Sr. | 12 | 23 | 0 | 0 | 138 | 11.50 |
| John Matthews, San Diego | Sr. | 11 | 21 | 0 | 0 | 126 | 11.45 |

#### FIELD GOALS

| | Class | GP | FGA | FG | Pct | FG/Game |
|---|---|---|---|---|---|---|
| Andrew Wilcox, Elon | Sr. | 12 | 27 | 22 | .815 | 1.83 |
| Taylor Long, Eastern Kentucky | Sr. | 12 | 27 | 20 | .741 | 1.67 |
| Andrew Samson, Pennsylvania | So. | 10 | 19 | 16 | .842 | 1.60 |
| Robbie Dehaze, Northern Arizona | Sr. | 11 | 20 | 16 | .800 | 1.45 |
| Ryan Gates, Gardner-Webb | Fr. | 11 | 22 | 16 | .727 | 1.45 |

#### TOTAL OFFENSE

| | | | Rushing | | Passing | | | Total Offense | |
|---|---|---|---|---|---|---|---|---|---|
| | Class | GP | Car | Net | Att | Yds | Yds | Yds/Play | Yds/Game |
| Dominic Randolph, Holy Cross | Jr. | 11 | 65 | 79 | 520 | 3838 | 3917 | 6.7 | 356.1 |
| Rhett Bomar, Sam Houston St | Sr. | 10 | 81 | 187 | 436 | 3355 | 3542 | 6.9 | 354.2 |
| Jeremy Moses, Stephen F. Austin | So. | 12 | 56 | -74 | 598 | 4026 | 3952 | 6.0 | 329.3 |
| Cameron Higgins, Weber St. | So. | 14 | 55 | -77 | 464 | 4460 | 4383 | 8.5 | 313.1 |
| Matt Nichols, Eastern Washington | Jr. | 11 | 56 | 83 | 451 | 3293 | 3376 | 6.7 | 306.9 |

#### RUSHING

| | Class | GP | Car | Yds | Avg | TD | Yds/Game |
|---|---|---|---|---|---|---|---|
| Herb Donaldson, Western Illinois | Sr. | 11 | 324 | 1784 | 5.5 | 21 | 162.2 |
| David McCarty, SUNY-Albany | Jr. | 12 | 357 | 1852 | 5.2 | 13 | 154.3 |
| David Sinisi, Monmouth | Jr. | 11 | 286 | 1674 | 5.9 | 22 | 152.2 |
| James Mallory, Central Connecticut St. | Jr. | 11 | 288 | 1520 | 5.3 | 15 | 138.2 |
| Rashad Jennings, Liberty | Sr. | 11 | 263 | 1500 | 5.7 | 17 | 136.4 |

#### PASSING EFFICIENCY

| | Class | GP | Att | Comp | Pct Comp | Yds | Yds/Att | TD | Int | Rating Pts |
|---|---|---|---|---|---|---|---|---|---|---|
| Jonathan Dally, Cal Poly | Sr. | 11 | 202 | 116 | 57.4 | 1960 | 9.7 | 23 | 5 | 171.6 |
| Armanti Edwards, Appalachian St. | Jr. | 13 | 306 | 196 | 64.1 | 2902 | 9.5 | 30 | 9 | 170.2 |
| Cameron Higgins, Weber St | So. | 14 | 464 | 304 | 65.5 | 4460 | 9.6 | 36 | 13 | 166.3 |
| Brock Smith, Liberty | Sr. | 12 | 278 | 179 | 64.4 | 2620 | 9.4 | 19 | 6 | 161.8 |
| Sebastian Trujillo, San Diego | Jr. | 11 | 358 | 239 | 66.8 | 2822 | 7.9 | 35 | 9 | 160.2 |

Note: Minimum 15 attempts per game.

#### RECEPTIONS PER GAME

| | Class | GP | No. | Yds | TD | R/G |
|---|---|---|---|---|---|---|
| John Matthews, San Diego | Sr. | 11 | 102 | 1478 | 21 | 9.3 |
| Andre Roberts, Citadel | Jr. | 12 | 95 | 1334 | 14 | 7.9 |
| Tysson Poots, Southern Utah | So. | 11 | 83 | 1236 | 14 | 7.6 |
| Terrell Hudgens, Elon | Jr. | 12 | 86 | 1116 | 10 | 7.2 |
| Steve Tedesco, Sacred Heart | Jr. | 11 | 77 | 891 | 10 | 7.0 |

#### RECEIVING YARDS PER GAME

| | Class | GP | No. | Yds | TD | Yds/G |
|---|---|---|---|---|---|---|
| John Matthews, San Diego | Sr. | 11 | 102 | 1478 | 21 | 134.4 |
| Ramses Barden, Cal Poly | Sr. | 11 | 67 | 1257 | 18 | 114.3 |
| Tysson Poots, Southern Utah | So. | 11 | 83 | 1236 | 14 | 112.4 |
| Andre Roberts, Citadel | Jr. | 12 | 95 | 1334 | 14 | 111.2 |
| Tim Toone, Weber St | Jr. | 14 | 84 | 1525 | 7 | 108.9 |

#### INTERCEPTIONS

| | Class | GP | No. | Yds | TD | Int/G |
|---|---|---|---|---|---|---|
| M. LeGree, Appalachian St. | So. | 13 | 10 | 32 | 0 | .77 |
| D. Washington, Campbell | Fr. | 9 | 6 | 73 | 0 | .67 |
| Anthony Curry, Valparaiso | Jr. | 11 | 7 | 105 | 1 | .64 |
| Rory Foley, Marist | So. | 11 | 7 | 95 | 0 | .64 |
| Dave Casale, SUNY-Albany | Jr. | 12 | 7 | 52 | 1 | .58 |

#### PUNTING

| | Class | No. | Avg |
|---|---|---|---|
| Brett Arnold, Massachusetts | Sr. | 46 | 45.2 |
| Robbie Dehaze, Northern Arizona | Sr. | 49 | 45.1 |
| Doug Spada, SE Missouri St. | Jr. | 47 | 44.7 |
| Robert Ranney, Brown | Sr. | 43 | 43.7 |
| Scott Ravanesi, Southern Illinois | Jr. | 52 | 43.3 |

## Football Championship Subdivision (Division I-AA) (Cont.)

### ALL-PURPOSE RUNNING

| | Class | GP | Rush | Rec | PR | KOR | Yds | Yds/Game |
|---|---|---|---|---|---|---|---|---|
| Nick Miller, Southern Utah | Sr. | 11 | 9 | 763 | 384 | 993 | 2149 | 195.4 |
| William Osborne, Texas Southern | Jr. | 12 | 36 | 1092 | 349 | 831 | 2308 | 192.3 |
| Larry Warner, Southern Illinois | Sr. | 12 | 1265 | 203 | 189 | 592 | 2249 | 187.4 |
| David McCarty, SUNY-Albany | Jr. | 12 | 1852 | 356 | 0 | 0 | 2208 | 184.0 |
| A.J. Kizekai, Bucknell | Jr. | 10 | 484 | 383 | 0 | 973 | 1840 | 184.0 |

## Division II

### SCORING

| | Class | GP | TD | XP | FG | Pts | Pts/Game |
|---|---|---|---|---|---|---|---|
| Bernard Scott, Abilene Christian | Sr. | 12 | 34 | 0 | 0 | 204 | 17.0 |
| LaRon Council, NW Missouri St. | Jr. | 15 | 36 | 0 | 0 | 216 | 14.4 |
| Phil Milbrath, Michigan Tech | So. | 10 | 21 | 0 | 0 | 128 | 12.8 |
| Isaac Odim, Minn.-Duluth | So. | 15 | 30 | 0 | 0 | 180 | 12.0 |
| Andrew Verbancouer, Winona St | Sr. | 11 | 21 | 0 | 0 | 126 | 11.5 |

### FIELD GOALS

| | Class | GP | FGA | FG | Pct | FG/Game |
|---|---|---|---|---|---|---|
| Ryan Ferrell, Harding | Sr. | 11 | 28 | 18 | .643 | 1.6 |
| Zach Wright, Ouachita Baptist | Sr. | 10 | 21 | 16 | .762 | 1.6 |
| Craig Burgess, Indiana (Pa.). | So. | 10 | 22 | 16 | .727 | 1.6 |
| Jared Keating, Mesa St | Sr. | 10 | 18 | 15 | .833 | 1.5 |
| Jeremy Ditzler, Gannon | So. | 11 | 19 | 15 | .789 | 1.4 |
| Mark Petro, Hillsdale | Jr. | 11 | 19 | 15 | .789 | 1.4 |
| Tom Schneider, North Alabama | Sr. | 14 | 26 | 19 | .731 | 1.4 |

### TOTAL OFFENSE

| | Class | GP | Yds | Yds/Game |
|---|---|---|---|---|
| David Knighton, Harding | Sr. | 10 | 3938 | 393.8 |
| Keith Null, West Texas A&M | Sr. | 13 | 4976 | 382.8 |
| Corey Russell, Tusculum | Sr. | 13 | 4907 | 377.5 |
| Scott Buisson, Ark.-Monticello. | So. | 11 | 4019 | 365.4 |
| Steven Gachette, Southwest Baptist | So. | 11 | 4009 | 364.5 |

### RUSHING

| | Class | GP | Car | Yds | TD | Yds/Game |
|---|---|---|---|---|---|---|
| Jerry Seymour, Glenville St. | Sr. | 11 | 295 | 2282 | 19 | 207.5 |
| Bernard Scott, Abilene Christian | Sr. | 12 | 266 | 2156 | 28 | 179.7 |
| Bobby Coy, Mesa St. | Jr. | 11 | 295 | 1600 | 12 | 145.5 |
| Phil Milbrath, Michigan Tech | So. | 10 | 263 | 1343 | 21 | 134.3 |
| Brian McNeil, Neb.-Omaha | Sr. | 11 | 243 | 1445 | 11 | 131.4 |

### PASSING EFFICIENCY

| | Class | GP | Att | Comp | Pct Comp | Yds | TD | Int | Rating Pts |
|---|---|---|---|---|---|---|---|---|---|
| Billy Malone, Abilene Christian | Sr. | 10 | 293 | 183 | .625 | 3213 | 36 | 8 | 189.7 |
| Ted Schlafke, Minn.-Duluth | Sr. | 15 | 328 | 213 | .649 | 3018 | 35 | 10 | 171.3 |
| Billy Cundiff, Ashland | Jr. | 13 | 414 | 279 | .674 | 3776 | 37 | 8 | 169.6 |
| Keith Null, West Texas A&M | Sr. | 13 | 562 | 385 | .685 | 5097 | 48 | 15 | 167.5 |
| Mike Reilly, Central Washington | Sr. | 12 | 414 | 270 | .652 | 3706 | 37 | 6 | 167.0 |

Note: Minimum 15 attempts per game.

### RECEPTIONS PER GAME

| | Class | GP | No. | Yds | TD | R/G |
|---|---|---|---|---|---|---|
| Johnnie King, Southwest Baptist | Jr. | 10 | 89 | 1120 | 9 | 8.9 |
| Dyshaun Edwards, Tiffin | Sr. | 11 | 91 | 1074 | 10 | 8.3 |
| Julius Pruitt, Ouachita Baptist | Sr. | 10 | 77 | 1116 | 11 | 7.7 |
| Garett Manning, Henderson St. | Sr. | 10 | 76 | 1209 | 10 | 7.6 |
| Johnny Spevak, Central Washington | Jr. | 12 | 91 | 1442 | 20 | 7.6 |

### RECEIVING YARDS PER GAME

| | Class | GP | No. | Yds | TD | Yds/G |
|---|---|---|---|---|---|---|
| Charly Martin, West Texas A&M | Sr. | 13 | 95 | 1867 | 22 | 143.6 |
| Garett Manning, Henderson St. | Sr. | 10 | 76 | 1209 | 10 | 120.9 |
| Johnny Spevak, Central Washington | Jr. | 12 | 91 | 1442 | 20 | 120.2 |
| Johnnie King, Southwest Baptist | Jr. | 10 | 89 | 1120 | 9 | 112.0 |
| Julius Pruitt, Ouachita Baptist | Sr. | 10 | 77 | 1116 | 11 | 111.6 |

## Division II *(Cont.)*

### INTERCEPTIONS

| | Class | GP | No. | Yds | Int/Game |
|---|---|---|---|---|---|
| Jeff Franklin, Central St (Ohio) | Sr. | 9 | 8 | 57 | .89 |
| A. Owusu-Ansah, Indiana (Pa.) | Jr. | 10 | 8 | 222 | .80 |
| Darren Banks, West Liberty | Sr. | 10 | 7 | 92 | .70 |
| Caylon Hann, N.C.-Pembroke | Jr. | 10 | 7 | 78 | .70 |
| Eri Schaumburg, Minn. St-Mrhd. | Sr. | 11 | 7 | 192 | .64 |
| Augustus Ashley, Ark.-Monticello | Sr. | 11 | 7 | 65 | .64 |

### PUNTING

| | Class | No. | Avg |
|---|---|---|---|
| Nick Krut, East Stroudsburg | Sr. | 48 | 46.0 |
| Jamie Hanson, Missouri Western St. | Sr. | 38 | 43.6 |
| John Gregory, Tusculum | Jr. | 51 | 43.5 |
| Zach Boyd, Concord | Sr. | 71 | 43.1 |
| Cody Smith, Texas A&M-Kingsville | Jr. | 44 | 43.0 |

Note: Minimum 3.6 per game.

## Division III

### SCORING

| | Class | GP | TD | XP | FG | Pts | Pts/Game |
|---|---|---|---|---|---|---|---|
| Nate Kmic, Mount Union | Sr. | 15 | 44 | 0 | 0 | 264 | 17.6 |
| Adam Anderson, Whitworth | Jr. | 9 | 25 | 0 | 0 | 152 | 16.9 |
| Jack Phelan, Hartwick | Sr. | 10 | 26 | 0 | 0 | 156 | 15.6 |
| Jim Bower, Maine Maritime | Jr. | 11 | 25 | 0 | 0 | 162 | 14.7 |
| Garet Lynch, Brockport | Sr. | 11 | 26 | 0 | 0 | 158 | 14.4 |

### FIELD GOALS

| | Class | GP | FGA | FG | Pct | FG/Game |
|---|---|---|---|---|---|---|
| Jackson Damron, Cal. Lutheran | Fr. | 9 | 23 | 17 | .739 | 1.89 |
| Jay Graham, Christopher Newport | Sr. | 10 | 25 | 16 | .640 | 1.60 |
| Jeff Schebler, UW-Whitewater | Jr. | 15 | 29 | 22 | .759 | 1.47 |
| Ryan Graboski, UW-Stevens Point | Sr. | 11 | 24 | 15 | .625 | 1.36 |
| Bryan Arbes, Waynesburg | Fr. | 10 | 19 | 13 | .684 | 1.30 |

### TOTAL OFFENSE

| | Class | GP | Yds | Yds/Game |
|---|---|---|---|---|
| Jason Boltus, Hartwick | Sr. | 10 | 3934 | 415.5 |
| Chad Rupp, Franklin | Sr. | 13 | 4181 | 355.8 |
| Corey Sedlar, Hampden-Sydney | Sr. | 10 | 3601 | 353.5 |
| Mackenzie McGrady, Alma | Jr. | 10 | 2956 | 343.3 |
| Donald McKillop, Middlebury | So. | 6 | 1940 | 339.3 |

### RUSHING

| | Class | GP | Car | Yds | TD | Yds/Game |
|---|---|---|---|---|---|---|
| Nate Kmic, Mount Union | Sr. | 15 | 377 | 2790 | 43 | 186.0 |
| DeRon Brown, MIT | Jr. | 10 | 275 | 1816 | 22 | 181.6 |
| Tunde Ogun, Christopher Newport | Jr. | 10 | 267 | 1794 | 16 | 179.4 |
| Alex McGrew, Loras | Sr. | 10 | 316 | 1592 | 20 | 159.2 |
| J.T. Harold, Mass.-Dartmouth | Sr. | 10 | 215 | 1567 | 16 | 156.7 |

### PASSING EFFICIENCY

| | Class | GP | Att | Comp | Pct Comp | Yds | TD | Int | Rating Pts |
|---|---|---|---|---|---|---|---|---|---|
| Greg Micheli, Mount Union | Sr. | 15 | 320 | 240 | .750 | 3743 | 36 | 2 | 209.1 |
| Shane McSweeny, Wesley | So. | 11 | 193 | 130 | .674 | 2003 | 18 | 4 | 181.2 |
| Jason Boltus, Hartwick | Sr. | 10 | 405 | 242 | .598 | 3934 | 46 | 10 | 173.9 |
| Justin Feaster, Hardin-Simmons | Jr. | 11 | 331 | 229 | .692 | 3023 | 31 | 8 | 172.0 |
| Grant Leslie, Willamette | Sr. | 12 | 194 | 114 | .588 | 1914 | 19 | 3 | 170.9 |

Note: Minimum 15 attempts per game.

### RECEPTIONS PER GAME

| | Class | GP | No. | Yds | TD | Rec/Game |
|---|---|---|---|---|---|---|
| Tyler Thiems, Hanover | Sr. | 9 | 117 | 1025 | 10 | 13.0 |
| Michael Jennings, Illinois College | Jr. | 10 | 110 | 1416 | 16 | 11.0 |
| Matt Frank, Carleton | Sr. | 9 | 90 | 990 | 12 | 10.0 |
| Royce Winford, Augsburg | Sr. | 10 | 93 | 1139 | 16 | 9.3 |
| Torrey Lowe, Greensboro | Sr. | 10 | 91 | 858 | 8 | 9.1 |

### RECEIVING YARDS PER GAME

| | Class | GP | No. | Yds | TD | Yds/Game |
|---|---|---|---|---|---|---|
| Jack Phelan, Hartwick | Sr. | 10 | 70 | 1533 | 26 | 153.3 |
| Michael Jennings, Illinois College | Jr. | 10 | 110 | 1416 | 16 | 141.6 |
| Kevin Kelley, Pomona-Pitzer | Sr. | 9 | 79 | 1192 | 8 | 132.4 |
| Patrick O'Connor, Dickinson | Jr. | 10 | 81 | 1324 | 8 | 132.4 |
| Kevin Vaughn, Guilford | Sr. | 10 | 76 | 1197 | 11 | 119.7 |

### Division III (Cont.)

**INTERCEPTIONS**

| | Class | GP | No. | Yds | Int/G |
|---|---|---|---|---|---|
| Matt Meyer, Aurora | Sr. | 11 | 10 | 273 | .91 |
| Brandon Rost, Blackburn | Sr. | 10 | 9 | 117 | .90 |
| John Lawrence, Hamilton | Jr. | 8 | 7 | 112 | .88 |
| Edgar Townsend, Greenville | Jr. | 10 | 8 | 111 | .80 |
| Jason Chier, Ithaca | Sr. | 11 | 8 | 61 | .73 |
| Lance Boyington, Hobart | Sr. | 11 | 8 | 35 | .73 |

**PUNTING**

| | Class | No. | Avg |
|---|---|---|---|
| T.J. Grzesikowski, Ferrum | So. | 47 | 43.8 |
| Ryan Patten, Olivet | So. | 45 | 43.5 |
| Bobby Eppleman, Susquehanna | So. | 35 | 42.7 |
| Andrew Smith, Rowan | Jr. | 33 | 41.7 |
| Adam Pucylowski, North Central (Ill.) | Sr. | 44 | 41.3 |

Note: Minimum 3.6 per game.

## 2008 NCAA FBS (Div. I-A) Team Leaders

### Offense

**SCORING**

| | GP | Pts | Avg |
|---|---|---|---|
| Oklahoma | 14 | 716 | 51.14 |
| Tulsa | 14 | 661 | 47.21 |
| Texas Tech | 13 | 569 | 43.77 |
| Florida | 14 | 611 | 43.64 |
| Texas | 13 | 551 | 42.38 |
| Missouri | 14 | 591 | 42.21 |
| Oregon | 13 | 545 | 41.92 |
| Rice | 13 | 537 | 41.31 |
| Oklahoma St | 13 | 530 | 40.77 |
| Houston | 13 | 528 | 40.62 |

**RUSHING**

| | GP | Car | Yds | Avg | TD | Yds/Game |
|---|---|---|---|---|---|---|
| Navy | 13 | 715 | 3801 | 5.32 | 32 | 292.38 |
| Oregon | 13 | 585 | 3641 | 6.22 | 47 | 280.08 |
| Nevada | 13 | 593 | 3611 | 6.09 | 39 | 277.77 |
| Georgia Tech | 13 | 640 | 3552 | 5.55 | 32 | 273.23 |
| Tulsa | 14 | 674 | 3752 | 5.57 | 40 | 268.00 |
| Air Force | 13 | 777 | 3470 | 4.47 | 27 | 266.92 |
| La.-Lafayette | 12 | 533 | 3164 | 5.94 | 32 | 263.67 |
| Oklahoma St | 13 | 582 | 3191 | 5.48 | 38 | 245.46 |
| Army | 12 | 635 | 2897 | 4.56 | 17 | 241.42 |
| Florida | 14 | 545 | 3236 | 5.94 | 42 | 231.14 |

**TOTAL OFFENSE**

| | GP | Plays | Yds | Avg | TD | Yds/Game |
|---|---|---|---|---|---|---|
| Tulsa | 14 | 1097 | 7978 | 7.27 | 90 | 569.86 |
| Houston | 13 | 1016 | 7316 | 7.20 | 71 | 562.77 |
| Oklahoma | 14 | 1106 | 7670 | 6.93 | 99 | 547.86 |
| Texas Tech | 13 | 979 | 6903 | 7.05 | 79 | 531.00 |
| Nevada | 13 | 1011 | 6611 | 6.54 | 64 | 508.54 |
| Oklahoma St | 13 | 908 | 6340 | 6.98 | 69 | 487.69 |
| Oregon | 13 | 959 | 6303 | 6.57 | 71 | 484.85 |
| Missouri | 14 | 982 | 6778 | 6.90 | 76 | 484.14 |
| Texas | 13 | 955 | 6185 | 6.48 | 74 | 475.77 |
| Rice | 13 | 965 | 6122 | 6.34 | 74 | 470.92 |

**PASSING**

| | GP | Att | Comp | Int | Pct Comp | Yds | Yds/Gm | TD |
|---|---|---|---|---|---|---|---|---|
| Texas Tech | 13 | 662 | 465 | 10 | 70.24 | 5371 | 413.2 | 47 |
| Houston | 13 | 610 | 411 | 11 | 67.38 | 5221 | 401.6 | 45 |
| Oklahoma | 14 | 517 | 350 | 9 | 67.70 | 4891 | 349.4 | 51 |
| Missouri | 14 | 565 | 404 | 18 | 71.50 | 4625 | 330.4 | 41 |
| Rice | 13 | 516 | 339 | 7 | 65.70 | 4254 | 327.2 | 48 |
| BYU | 13 | 493 | 338 | 14 | 68.56 | 4035 | 310.4 | 35 |
| Texas | 13 | 447 | 343 | 8 | 76.73 | 4008 | 308.3 | 36 |
| Kansas | 13 | 500 | 333 | 13 | 66.60 | 3973 | 305.6 | 33 |
| Tulsa | 14 | 423 | 270 | 21 | 63.83 | 4226 | 301.9 | 47 |
| New Mexico St | 12 | 492 | 330 | 16 | 67.07 | 3616 | 301.3 | 25 |

### Single-Game Highs

Points Scored: 83—Arkansas St, Sep 6, 2008 (vs Texas Southern)
Net Rushing Yards: 558—Navy, Aug 30, 2008 (vs Towson)
Passing Yards: 536—Texas Tech, Aug 30, 2008 (vs Eastern Washington)
Rushing and Passing Yards: 791—Tulsa, Oct 18, 2008 (vs UTEP)
Fewest Rushing and Passing Yards Allowed: 24—Mississippi, Nov 28, 2008 (vs Mississippi St)

## Defense

### OPPONENTS' SCORING

| | GP | Pts | Avg |
|---|---|---|---|
| USC | 13 | 117 | 9.0 |
| TCU | 13 | 147 | 11.3 |
| Boise St | 13 | 164 | 12.6 |
| Florida | 14 | 181 | 12.9 |
| Iowa | 13 | 169 | 13.0 |
| Ohio St | 13 | 181 | 13.9 |
| Alabama | 14 | 200 | 14.3 |
| Penn St | 13 | 187 | 14.4 |
| Virginia Tech | 14 | 234 | 16.7 |
| Tennessee | 12 | 201 | 16.8 |

### TOTAL DEFENSE

| | GP | Plays | Yds | Avg Y/Play | Avg Y/G |
|---|---|---|---|---|---|
| TCU | 13 | 739 | 2831 | 3.83 | 217.77 |
| USC | 13 | 798 | 2883 | 3.61 | 221.77 |
| Alabama | 14 | 858 | 3689 | 4.30 | 263.50 |
| Tennessee | 12 | 776 | 3162 | 4.07 | 263.50 |
| Boston College | 14 | 889 | 3754 | 4.22 | 268.14 |
| Connecticut | 13 | 791 | 3614 | 4.57 | 278.00 |
| Virginia Tech | 14 | 794 | 3912 | 4.93 | 279.43 |
| Penn St | 13 | 829 | 3641 | 4.39 | 280.08 |
| Florida | 14 | 896 | 3994 | 4.46 | 285.29 |
| South Florida | 13 | 814 | 3739 | 4.59 | 287.62 |

### OPPONENTS' RUSHING

| | GP | Car | Yds | Avg | TD | Yds/Game |
|---|---|---|---|---|---|---|
| TCU | 13 | 355 | 612 | 1.72 | 9 | 47.1 |
| Alabama | 14 | 391 | 1038 | 2.65 | 5 | 74.1 |
| Texas | 13 | 356 | 1086 | 3.05 | 8 | 83.5 |
| Mississippi | 13 | 411 | 1112 | 2.71 | 9 | 85.5 |
| USC | 13 | 416 | 1136 | 2.73 | 8 | 87.4 |
| Nevada | 13 | 377 | 1152 | 3.06 | 17 | 88.6 |
| Boston College | 14 | 454 | 1277 | 2.81 | 14 | 91.2 |
| Penn St | 13 | 430 | 1212 | 2.82 | 12 | 93.2 |
| Iowa | 13 | 397 | 1222 | 3.08 | 7 | 94.0 |
| South Florida | 13 | 436 | 1238 | 2.84 | 12 | 95.2 |

### TURNOVER MARGIN

| | | Turnovers Gained | | | Turnovers Lost | | | |
|---|---|---|---|---|---|---|---|---|
| | GP | Fum | Int | Total | Fum | Int | Total | Mar/Gm |
| Oklahoma | 14 | 15 | 19 | 34 | 2 | 9 | 11 | 1.64 |
| Florida | 14 | 9 | 26 | 35 | 8 | 5 | 13 | 1.57 |
| Buffalo | 14 | 25 | 8 | 33 | 8 | 6 | 14 | 1.36 |
| Baylor | 12 | 11 | 16 | 27 | 6 | 5 | 11 | 1.33 |
| Wake Forest | 13 | 19 | 18 | 37 | 13 | 7 | 20 | 1.31 |
| Ohio St | 13 | 14 | 15 | 29 | 7 | 6 | 13 | 1.23 |
| Navy | 13 | 14 | 16 | 30 | 10 | 5 | 15 | 1.15 |
| California | 13 | 10 | 24 | 34 | 9 | 10 | 19 | 1.15 |
| Rice | 13 | 15 | 16 | 31 | 9 | 7 | 16 | 1.15 |

6 teams tied at 1.00.

### OPPONENTS' PASSING EFFICIENCY

| | GP | Att | Comp | Pct Comp | Int | Pct Int | Yds | Yds/Att | TD | Pct TD | Rating Pts |
|---|---|---|---|---|---|---|---|---|---|---|---|
| USC | 13 | 382 | 199 | 52.09 | 19 | 4.97 | 1747 | 4.57 | 6 | 1.57 | 85.75 |
| Boise St | 13 | 449 | 234 | 52.12 | 22 | 4.90 | 2472 | 5.51 | 8 | 1.78 | 94.43 |
| Florida | 14 | 456 | 242 | 53.07 | 26 | 5.70 | 2518 | 5.52 | 12 | 2.63 | 96.76 |
| TCU | 13 | 384 | 193 | 50.26 | 15 | 3.91 | 2219 | 5.78 | 8 | 2.08 | 97.90 |
| Iowa | 13 | 463 | 256 | 55.29 | 23 | 4.97 | 2565 | 5.54 | 9 | 1.94 | 98.32 |
| California | 13 | 432 | 223 | 51.62 | 24 | 5.56 | 2509 | 5.81 | 12 | 2.78 | 98.44 |
| Boston College | 14 | 435 | 244 | 56.09 | 26 | 5.98 | 2477 | 5.69 | 9 | 2.07 | 98.81 |
| San Jose St | 12 | 356 | 187 | 52.53 | 16 | 4.49 | 2043 | 5.74 | 9 | 2.53 | 100.06 |
| Connecticut | 13 | 368 | 196 | 53.26 | 18 | 4.89 | 2187 | 5.94 | 9 | 2.45 | 101.51 |
| Clemson | 13 | 428 | 239 | 55.84 | 19 | 4.44 | 2243 | 5.24 | 14 | 3.27 | 101.74 |

## NCAA Football Bowl Subdivision* National Champions

| Year | Champion | Record | Bowl Game | Head Coach |
|---|---|---|---|---|
| 1883 | Yale | 8-0-0 | No bowl | Ray Tompkins (Captain) |
| 1884 | Yale | 9-0-0 | No bowl | Eugene L. Richards (Captain) |
| 1885 | Princeton | 9-0-0 | No bowl | Charles DeCamp (Captain) |
| 1886 | Yale | 9-0-1 | No bowl | Robert N. Corwin (Captain) |
| 1887 | Yale | 9-0-0 | No bowl | Harry W. Beecher (Captain) |
| 1888 | Yale | 13-0-0 | No bowl | Walter Camp |
| 1889 | Princeton | 10-0-0 | No bowl | Edgar Poe (Captain) |
| 1890 | Harvard | 11-0-0 | No bowl | George A. Stewart/George C. Adams |
| 1891 | Yale | 13-0-0 | No bowl | Walter Camp |
| 1892 | Yale | 13-0-0 | No bowl | Walter Camp |
| 1893 | Princeton | 11-0-0 | No bowl | Tom Trenchard (Captain) |
| 1894 | Yale | 16-0-0 | No bowl | William C. Rhodes |
| 1895 | Pennsylvania | 14-0-0 | No bowl | George Woodruff |
| 1896 | Princeton | 10-0-1 | No bowl | Garrett Cochran |
| 1897 | Pennsylvania | 15-0-0 | No bowl | George Woodruff |
| 1898 | Harvard | 11-0-0 | No bowl | W. Cameron Forbes |
| 1899 | Harvard | 10-0-1 | No bowl | Benjamin H. Dibblee |
| 1900 | Yale | 12-0-0 | No bowl | Malcolm McBride |
| 1901 | Michigan | 11-0-0 | Won Rose | Fielding Yost |
| 1902 | Michigan | 11-0-0 | No bowl | Fielding Yost |
| 1903 | Princeton | 11-0-0 | No bowl | Art Hillebrand |
| 1904 | Pennsylvania | 12-0-0 | No bowl | Carl Williams |
| 1905 | Chicago | 11-0-0 | No bowl | Amos Alonzo Stagg |
| 1906 | Princeton | 9-0-1 | No bowl | Bill Roper |
| 1907 | Yale | 9-0-1 | No bowl | Bill Knox |
| 1908 | Pennsylvania | 11-0-1 | No bowl | Sol Metzger |
| 1909 | Yale | 10-0-0 | No bowl | Howard Jones |
| 1910 | Harvard | 8-0-1 | No bowl | Percy Houghton |
| 1911 | Princeton | 8-0-2 | No bowl | Bill Roper |
| 1912 | Harvard | 9-0-0 | No bowl | Percy Houghton |
| 1913 | Harvard | 9-0-0 | No bowl | Percy Houghton |
| 1914 | Army | 9-0-0 | No bowl | Charley Daly |
| 1915 | Cornell | 9-0-0 | No bowl | Al Sharpe |
| 1916 | Pittsburgh | 8-0-0 | No bowl | Pop Warner |
| 1917 | Georgia Tech | 9-0-0 | No bowl | John Heisman |
| 1918 | Pittsburgh | 4-1-0 | No bowl | Pop Warner |
| 1919 | Harvard | 9-0-1 | Won Rose | Bob Fisher |
| 1920 | California | 9-0-0 | Won Rose | Andy Smith |
| 1921 | Cornell | 8-0-0 | No bowl | Gil Dobie |
| 1922 | Cornell | 8-0-0 | No bowl | Gil Dobie |
| 1923 | Illinois | 8-0-0 | No bowl | Bob Zuppke |
| 1924 | Notre Dame | 10-0-0 | Won Rose | Knute Rockne |
| 1925 | Alabama (H) | 10-0-0 | Won Rose | Wallace Wade |
|  | Dartmouth (D) | 8-0-0 | No bowl | Jesse Hawley |
| 1926 | Alabama (H) | 9-0-1 | Tied Rose | Wallace Wade |
|  | Stanford (D)(H) | 10-0-1 | Tied Rose | Pop Warner |
| 1927 | Illinois | 7-0-1 | No bowl | Bob Zuppke |
| 1928 | Georgia Tech (H) | 10-0-0 | Won Rose | Bill Alexander |
|  | USC (D) | 9-0-1 | No bowl | Howard Jones |
| 1929 | Notre Dame | 9-0-0 | No bowl | Knute Rockne |
| 1930 | Notre Dame | 10-0-0 | No bowl | Knute Rockne |
| 1931 | USC | 10-1-0 | Won Rose | Howard Jones |
| 1932 | USC (H) | 10-0-0 | Won Rose | Howard Jones |
|  | Michigan (D) | 8-0-0 | No bowl | Harry Kipke |
| 1933 | Michigan | 7-0-1 | No bowl | Harry Kipke |
| 1934 | Minnesota | 8-0-0 | No bowl | Bernie Bierman |
| 1935 | Minnesota (H) | 8-0-0 | No bowl | Bernie Bierman |
|  | SMU (D) | 12-1-0 | Lost Rose | Matty Bell |
| 1936 | Minnesota | 7-1-0 | No bowl | Bernie Bierman |
| 1937 | Pittsburgh | 9-0-1 | No bowl | Jock Sutherland |
| 1938 | TCU (AP) | 11-0-0 | Won Sugar | Dutch Meyer |
|  | Notre Dame (D) | 8-1-0 | No bowl | Elmer Layden |

*In 2007, the NCAA renamed division I-A as the "Football Bowl Subdivision" and division I-AA as the "Football Championship Subdivision."

| Year | Champion | Record | Bowl Game | Head Coach |
|---|---|---|---|---|
| 1939 | USC (D) | 8-0-2 | Won Rose | Howard Jones |
| | Texas A&M (AP) | 11-0-0 | Won Sugar | Homer Norton |
| 1940 | Minnesota | 8-0-0 | No bowl | Bernie Bierman |
| 1941 | Minnesota | 8-0-0 | No bowl | Bernie Bierman |
| 1942 | Ohio St | 9-1-0 | No bowl | Paul Brown |
| 1943 | Notre Dame | 9-1-0 | No bowl | Frank Leahy |
| 1944 | Army | 9-0-0 | No bowl | Red Blaik |
| 1945 | Army | 9-0-0 | No bowl | Red Blaik |
| 1946 | Notre Dame | 8-0-1 | No bowl | Frank Leahy |
| 1947 | Notre Dame | 9-0-0 | No bowl | Frank Leahy |
| | Michigan* | 10-0-0 | Won Rose | Fritz Crisler |
| 1948 | Michigan | 9-0-0 | No bowl | Bennie Oosterbaan |
| 1949 | Notre Dame | 10-0-0 | No bowl | Frank Leahy |
| 1950 | Oklahoma | 10-1-0 | Lost Sugar | Bud Wilkinson |
| 1951 | Tennessee | 10-1-0 | Lost Sugar | Bob Neyland |
| 1952 | Michigan St | 9-0-0 | No bowl | Biggie Munn |
| 1953 | Maryland | 10-1-0 | Lost Orange | Jim Tatum |
| 1954 | Ohio St | 10-0-0 | Won Rose | Woody Hayes |
| | UCLA (UPI) | 9-0-0 | No bowl | Red Sanders |
| 1955 | Oklahoma | 11-0-0 | Won Orange | Bud Wilkinson |
| 1956 | Oklahoma | 10-0-0 | No bowl | Bud Wilkinson |
| 1957 | Auburn | 10-0-0 | No bowl | Shug Jordan |
| | Ohio St (UPI) | 9-1-0 | Won Rose | Woody Hayes |
| 1958 | LSU | 11-0-0 | Won Sugar | Paul Dietzel |
| 1959 | Syracuse | 11-0-0 | Won Cotton | Ben Schwartzwalder |
| 1960 | Minnesota | 8-2-0 | Lost Rose | Murray Warmath |
| 1961 | Alabama | 11-0-0 | Won Sugar | Bear Bryant |
| 1962 | USC | 11-0-0 | Won Rose | John McKay |
| 1963 | Texas | 11-0-0 | Won Cotton | Darrell Royal |
| 1964 | Alabama | 10-1-0 | Lost Orange | Bear Bryant |
| 1965 | Alabama | 9-1-1 | Won Orange | Bear Bryant |
| | Michigan St (UPI) | 10-1-0 | Lost Rose | Duffy Daugherty |
| 1966 | Notre Dame | 9-0-1 | No bowl | Ara Parseghian |
| 1967 | USC | 10-1-0 | Won Rose | John McKay |
| 1968 | Ohio St | 10-0-0 | Won Rose | Woody Hayes |
| 1969 | Texas | 11-0-0 | Won Cotton | Darrell Royal |
| 1970 | Nebraska | 11-0-1 | Won Orange | Bob Devaney |
| | Texas (UPI) | 10-1-0 | Lost Cotton | Darrell Royal |
| 1971 | Nebraska | 13-0-0 | Won Orange | Bob Devaney |
| 1972 | USC | 12-0-0 | Won Rose | John McKay |
| 1973 | Notre Dame | 11-0-0 | Won Sugar | Ara Parseghian |
| | Alabama (UPI) | 11-1-0 | Lost Sugar | Bear Bryant |
| 1974 | Oklahoma | 11-0-0 | No bowl | Barry Switzer |
| | USC (UPI) | 10-1-1 | Won Rose | John McKay |
| 1975 | Oklahoma | 11-1-0 | Won Orange | Barry Switzer |
| 1976 | Pittsburgh | 12-0-0 | Won Sugar | Johnny Majors |
| 1977 | Notre Dame | 11-1-0 | Won Cotton | Dan Devine |
| 1978 | Alabama | 11-1-0 | Won Sugar | Bear Bryant |
| | USC (UPI) | 12-1-0 | Won Rose | John Robinson |
| 1979 | Alabama | 12-0-0 | Won Sugar | Bear Bryant |
| 1980 | Georgia | 12-0-0 | Won Sugar | Vince Dooley |
| 1981 | Clemson | 12-0-0 | Won Orange | Danny Ford |
| 1982 | Penn St | 11-1-0 | Won Sugar | Joe Paterno |
| 1983 | Miami (Fla.) | 11-1-0 | Won Orange | Howard Schnellenberger |
| 1984 | BYU | 13-0-0 | Won Holiday | LaVell Edwards |
| 1985 | Oklahoma | 11-1-0 | Won Orange | Barry Switzer |
| 1986 | Penn St | 12-0-0 | Won Fiesta | Joe Paterno |
| 1987 | Miami (Fla.) | 12-0-0 | Won Orange | Jimmy Johnson |
| 1988 | Notre Dame | 12-0-0 | Won Fiesta | Lou Holtz |
| 1989 | Miami (Fla.) | 11-1-0 | Won Sugar | Dennis Erickson |
| 1990 | Colorado | 11-1-1 | Won Orange | Bill McCartney |
| | Georgia Tech (UPI) | 11-0-1 | Won Citrus | Bobby Ross |
| 1991 | Miami (Fla.) | 12-0-0 | Won Orange | Dennis Erickson |
| | Washington (CNN) | 12-0-0 | Won Rose | Don James |
| 1992 | Alabama | 13-0-0 | Won Sugar | Gene Stallings |
| 1993 | Florida St | 12-1-0 | Won Orange | Bobby Bowden |
| 1994 | Nebraska | 13-0-0 | Won Orange | Tom Osborne |
| 1995 | Nebraska | 12-0-0 | Won Fiesta | Tom Osborne |
| †1996 | Florida | 12–1 | Won Sugar | Steve Spurrier |

| Year | Champion | Record | Bowl Game | Head Coach |
|---|---|---|---|---|
| 1997 | Michigan | 12–0 | Won Rose | Lloyd Carr |
| | Nebraska (ESPN) | 13–0 | Won Orange | Tom Osborne |
| 1998 | Tennessee | 13–0 | Won Fiesta | Phillip Fulmer |
| 1999 | Florida St | 12–0 | Won Sugar | Bobby Bowden |
| 2000 | Oklahoma | 13–0 | Won Orange | Bob Stoops |
| 2001 | Miami (Fla.) | 12–0 | Won Rose | Larry Coker |
| 2002 | Ohio St | 14–0 | Won Fiesta | Jim Tressel |
| 2003 | LSU | 13–1 | Won Sugar | Nick Saban |
| | USC | 12–1 | Won Rose | Pete Carroll |
| 2004 | USC | 13–0 | Won Orange | Pete Carroll |
| 2005 | Texas | 13–0 | Won Rose | Mack Brown |
| ‡2006 | Florida | 13–1 | Won BCS Nat'l Championship | Urban Meyer |
| 2007 | LSU | 12–2 | Won BCS Nat'l Championship | Les Miles |
| 2008 | Florida | 13–1 | Won BCS Nat'l Championship | Urban Meyer |

*The AP, which had voted Notre Dame No. 1, took a second vote, giving the national title to Michigan after its 49–0 win over USC in the Rose Bowl. Note: Selectors: Helms Athletic Foundation (H) 1883–1935, The Dickinson System (D) 1924–40, The Associated Press (AP) 1936–present, United Press International (UPI) 1958–90, *USA Today*/CNN (CNN) 1991–96, and *USA Today*/ESPN (ESPN) 1997–present. †In 1996 the NCAA introduced overtime to break ties. ‡In 2006, the BCS established a separate national championship game in addition to its existing four-bowl structure.

## Results of Major Bowl Games

### Rose Bowl

| | |
|---|---|
| 1-1-02 ............Michigan 49, Stanford 0 | 1-2-50 ............Ohio St 17, California 14 |
| 1-1-16 ............Washington St 14, Brown 0 | 1-1-51 ............Michigan 14, California 6 |
| 1-1-17 ............Oregon 14, Pennsylvania 0 | 1-1-52 ............Illinois 40, Stanford 7 |
| 1-1-18 ............Mare Island 19, Camp Lewis 7 | 1-1-53 ............USC 7, Wisconsin 0 |
| 1-1-19 ............Great Lakes 17, Mare Island 0 | 1-1-54 ............Michigan St 28, UCLA 20 |
| 1-1-20 ............Harvard 7, Oregon 6 | 1-1-55 ............Ohio St 20, USC 7 |
| 1-1-21 ............California 28, Ohio St 0 | 1-2-56 ............Michigan St 17, UCLA 14 |
| 1-2-22 ............Washington & Jefferson 0, California 0 | 1-1-57 ............Iowa 35, Oregon St 19 |
| 1-1-23 ............USC 14, Penn St 3 | 1-1-58 ............Ohio St 10, Oregon 7 |
| 1-1-24 ............Navy 14, Washington 14 | 1-1-59 ............Iowa 38, California 12 |
| 1-1-25 ............Notre Dame 27, Stanford 10 | 1-1-60 ............Washington 44, Wisconsin 8 |
| 1-1-26 ............Alabama 20, Washington 19 | 1-2-61 ............Washington 17, Minnesota 7 |
| 1-1-27 ............Alabama 7, Stanford 7 | 1-1-62 ............Minnesota 21, UCLA 3 |
| 1-2-28 ............Stanford 7, Pittsburgh 6 | 1-1-63 ............USC 42, Wisconsin 37 |
| 1-1-29 ............Georgia Tech 8, California 7 | 1-1-64 ............Illinois 17, Washington 7 |
| 1-1-30 ............USC47, Pittsburgh 14 | 1-1-65 ............Michigan 34, Oregon St 7 |
| 1-1-31 ............Alabama 24, Washington St 0 | 1-1-66 ............UCLA 14, Michigan St 12 |
| 1-1-32 ............USC 21, Tulane 12 | 1-2-67 ............Purdue 14, USC 13 |
| 1-2-33 ............USC 35, Pittsburgh 0 | 1-1-68 ............USC 14, Indiana 3 |
| 1-1-34 ............Columbia 7, Stanford 0 | 1-1-69 ............Ohio St 27, USC16 |
| 1-1-35 ............Alabama 29, Stanford 13 | 1-1-70 ............USC 10, Michigan 3 |
| 1-1-36 ............Stanford 7, Southern Methodist 0 | 1-1-71 ............Stanford 27, Ohio St 17 |
| 1-1-37 ............Pittsburgh 21, Washington 0 | 1-1-72 ............Stanford 13, Michigan 12 |
| 1-1-38 ............California 13, Alabama 0 | 1-1-73 ............USC 42, Ohio St 17 |
| 1-2-39 ............USC 7, Duke 3 | 1-1-74 ............Ohio St 42, USC 21 |
| 1-1-40 ............USC 14, Tennessee 0 | 1-1-75 ............USC 18, Ohio St 17 |
| 1-1-41 ............Stanford 21, Nebraska 13 | 1-1-76 ............UCLA 23, Ohio St 10 |
| 1-1-42 ............Oregon St 20, Duke 16 | 1-1-77 ............USC 14, Michigan 6 |
| 1-1-43 ............Georgia 9, UCLA 0 | 1-2-78 ............Washington 27, Michigan 20 |
| 1-1-44 ............USC 29, Washington 0 | 1-1-79 ............USC 17, Michigan 10 |
| 1-1-45 ............USC 25, Tennessee 0 | 1-1-80 ............USC 17, Ohio St 16 |
| 1-1-46 ............Alabama 34, USC 14 | 1-1-81 ............Michigan 23, Washington 6 |
| 1-1-47 ............Illinois 45, UCLA 14 | 1-1-82 ............Washington 28, Iowa 0 |
| 1-1-48 ............Michigan 49, USC 0 | 1-1-83 ............UCLA 24, Michigan 14 |
| 1-1-49 ............Northwestern 20, California 14 | 1-2-84 ............UCLA 45, Illinois 9 |

Note: The Fiesta, Orange, Rose and Sugar Bowls constitute the Bowl Alliance, formed in 1995 and running through the 2009 regular season and 2010 bowl season. Starting in January 2007, it will include a separate BCS National Championship game as well. The four other BCS Bowls will host the following conference champions with consideration for the following conference tie-ins: the ACC or Big East champion in the FedEx Orange Bowl, the SEC champion in the Allstate Sugar Bowl, the Big Ten and the Pac-10 champions in the Rose Bowl and the Big 12 champion in the Tostitos Fiesta Bowl. rankings. There are also four at-large positions in the BCS that are open to any Division I-A team. This allows any Division I-A school in the nation the opportunity to play in a BCS bowl game.

### Rose Bowl *(Cont.)*

1-1-85 .............USC 20, Ohio St 17
1-1-86 .............UCLA 45, Iowa 28
1-1-87 .............Arizona St 22, Michigan 15
1-1-88 .............Michigan St 20, USC 17
1-2-89 .............Michigan 22, USC 14
1-1-90 .............USC 17, Michigan 10
1-1-91 .............Washington 46, Iowa 34
1-1-92 .............Washington 34, Michigan 14
1-1-93 .............Michigan 38, Washington 31
1-1-94 .............Wisconsin 21, UCLA 16
1-2-95 .............Penn St 38, Oregon 20
1-1-96 .............USC 41, Northwestern 32
1-1-97 .............Ohio St 20, Arizona St 17
1-1-98 .............Michigan 21, Washington St 16
1-1-99 .............Wisconsin 38, UCLA 31
1-1-00 .............Wisconsin 17, Stanford 9
1-1-01 .............Washington 34, Purdue 24
1-3-02 .............Miami 37, Nebraska 14
1-1-03 .............Oklahoma 34, Washington St 14
1-1-04 .............USC 28, Michigan 14
1-1-05 .............Texas 38, Michigan 37
1-4-06 .............Texas 41, USC 38
1-1-07 .............USC 32, Michigan 18
1-1-08 .............USC 49, Illinois 17
1-1-09 .............USC 38, Penn St 24

City: Pasadena. Stadium: Rose Bowl, capacity 96,576. Playing Sites: Tournament Park (1902, 1916–22), Rose Bowl (1923–41, since 1943), Duke Stadium, Durham, NC (1942).

### Orange Bowl

1-1-35 .............Bucknell 26, Miami (Fla.) 0
1-1-36 .............Catholic 20, Mississippi 19
1-1-37 .............Duquesne 13, Mississippi St 12
1-1-38 .............Auburn 6, Michigan St 0
1-2-39 .............Tennessee 17, Oklahoma 0
1-1-40 .............Georgia Tech 21, Missouri 7
1-1-41 .............Mississippi St 14, Georgetown 7
1-1-42 .............Georgia 40, TCU 26
1-1-43 .............Alabama 37, Boston College 21
1-1-44 .............LSU 19, Texas A&M 14
1-1-45 .............Tulsa 26, Georgia Tech 12
1-1-46 .............Miami (Fla.) 13, Holy Cross 6
1-1-47 .............Rice 8, Tennessee 0
1-1-48 .............Georgia Tech 20, Kansas 14
1-1-49 .............Texas 41, Georgia 28
1-2-50 .............Santa Clara 21, Kentucky 13
1-1-51 .............Clemson 15, Miami (Fla.) 14
1-1-52 .............Georgia Tech 17, Baylor 14
1-1-53 .............Alabama 61, Syracuse 6
1-1-54 .............Oklahoma 7, Maryland 0
1-1-55 .............Duke 34, Nebraska 7
1-2-56 .............Oklahoma 20, Maryland 6
1-1-57 .............Colorado 27, Clemson 21
1-1-58 .............Oklahoma 48, Duke 21
1-1-59 .............Oklahoma 21, Syracuse 6
1-1-60 .............Georgia 14, Missouri 0
1-2-61 .............Missouri 21, Navy 14
1-1-62 .............LSU 25, Colorado 7
1-1-63 .............Alabama 17, Oklahoma 0
1-1-64 .............Nebraska 13, Auburn 7
1-1-65 .............Texas 21, Alabama 17
1-1-66 .............Alabama 39, Nebraska 28
1-2-67 .............Florida 27, Georgia Tech 12
1-1-68 .............Oklahoma 26, Tennessee 24
1-1-69 .............Penn St 15, Kansas 14
1-1-70 .............Penn St 10, Missouri 3

### Orange Bowl *(Cont.)*

1-1-71 .............Nebraska 17, LSU 12
1-1-72 .............Nebraska 38, Alabama 6
1-1-73 .............Nebraska 40, Notre Dame 6
1-1-74 .............Penn St 16, LSU 9
1-1-75 .............Notre Dame 13, Alabama 11
1-1-76 .............Oklahoma 14, Michigan 6
1-1-77 .............Ohio St 27, Colorado 10
1-2-78 .............Arkansas 31, Oklahoma 6
1-1-79 .............Oklahoma 31, Nebraska 24
1-1-80 .............Oklahoma 24, Florida St 7
1-1-81 .............Oklahoma 18, Florida St 17
1-1-82 .............Clemson 22, Nebraska 15
1-1-83 .............Nebraska 21, LSU 20
1-2-84 .............Miami (Fla.) 31, Nebraska 30
1-1-85 .............Washington 28, Oklahoma 17
1-1-86 .............Oklahoma 25, Penn St 10
1-1-87 .............Oklahoma 42, Arkansas 8
1-1-88 .............Miami (Fla.) 20, Oklahoma 14
1-2-89 .............Miami (Fla.) 23, Nebraska 3
1-1-90 .............Notre Dame 21, Colorado 6
1-1-91 .............Colorado 10, Notre Dame 9
1-1-92 .............Miami (Fla.) 22, Nebraska 0
1-1-93 .............Florida St 27, Nebraska 14
1-1-94 .............Florida St 18, Nebraska 16
1-1-95 .............Nebraska 24, Miami (Fla.) 17
1-1-96 .............Florida St 31, Notre Dame 26
12-31-96 .........Nebraska 41, Virginia Tech 21
1-2-98 .............Nebraska 42, Tennessee 17
1-2-99 .............Florida 31, Syracuse 10
1-1-00 .............Michigan 35, Alabama 34 (ot)
1-3-01 .............Oklahoma 13, Florida St 2
1-2-02 .............Florida 56, Maryland 23
1-2-03 .............USC 38, Iowa 17
1-1-04 .............Miami (Fla.) 16, Florida St 15
1-4-05 .............USC 55, Oklahoma 19
1-3-06 .............Penn State 26, Florida State 23 (3OT)
1-2-07 .............Louisville 24, Wake Forest 13
1-3-08 .............Kansas 24, Virginia Tech 21
1-1-09 .............Virginia Tech 20, Cincinnati 7

City: Miami. Stadium: Pro Player Stadium, capacity 75,192. Playing Sites: Orange Bowl (1935–96), Pro Player Stadium (since 1996).

### Sugar Bowl

1-1-35 .............Tulane 20, Temple 14
1-1-36 .............TCU 3, LSU 2
1-1-37 .............Santa Clara 21, LSU 14
1-1-38 .............Santa Clara 6, LSU 0
1-2-39 .............TCU 15, Carnegie Tech 7
1-1-40 .............Texas A&M 14, Tulane 13
1-1-41 .............Boston Col 19, Tennessee 13
1-1-42 .............Fordham 2, Missouri 0
1-1-43 .............Tennessee 14, Tulsa 7
1-1-44 .............Georgia Tech 20, Tulsa 18
1-1-45 .............Duke 29, Alabama 26
1-1-46 .............Oklahoma St 33, St. Mary's (Ca.) 13
1-1-47 .............Georgia 20, North Carolina 10
1-1-48 .............Texas 27, Alabama 7
1-1-49 .............Oklahoma 14, North Carolina 6
1-2-50 .............Oklahoma 35, LSU 0
1-1-51 .............Kentucky 13, Oklahoma 7
1-1-52 .............Maryland 28, Tennessee 13
1-1-53 .............Georgia Tech 24, Mississippi 7
1-1-54 .............Georgia Tech 42, W Virginia 19
1-1-55 .............Navy 21, Mississippi 0
1-2-56 .............Georgia Tech 7, Pittsburgh 0

### Sugar Bowl *(Cont.)*

1-1-57..............Baylor 13, Tennessee 7
1-1-58..............Mississippi 39, Texas 7
1-1-59..............LSU 7, Clemson 0
1-1-60..............Mississippi 21, LSU 0
1-2-61..............Mississippi 14, Rice 6
1-1-62..............Alabama 10, Arkansas 3
1-1-63..............Mississippi 17, Arkansas 13
1-1-64..............Alabama 12, Mississippi 7
1-1-65..............LSU 13, Syracuse 10
1-1-66..............Missouri 20, Florida 18
1-2-67..............Alabama 34, Nebraska 7
1-1-68..............LSU 20, Wyoming 13
1-1-69..............Arkansas 16, Georgia 2
1-1-70..............Mississippi 27, Arkansas 22
1-1-71..............Tennessee 34, Air Force 13
1-1-72..............Oklahoma 40, Auburn 22
12-31-72.........Oklahoma 14, Penn St 0
12-31-73.........Notre Dame 24, Alabama 23
12-31-74.........Nebraska 13, Florida 10
12-31-75.........Alabama 13, Penn St 6
1-1-77..............Pittsburgh 27, Georgia 3
1-2-78..............Alabama 35, Ohio St 6
1-1-79..............Alabama 14, Penn St 7
1-1-80..............Alabama 24, Arkansas 9
1-1-81..............Georgia 17, Notre Dame 10
1-1-82..............Pittsburgh 24, Georgia 20
1-1-83..............Penn St 27, Georgia 23
1-2-84..............Auburn 9, Michigan 7
1-1-85..............Nebraska 28, LSU 10
1-1-86..............Tennessee 35, Miami (Fla.) 7
1-1-87..............Nebraska 30, LSU 15
1-1-88..............Syracuse 16, Auburn 16
1-2-89..............Florida St 13, Auburn 7
1-1-90..............Miami (Fla.) 33, Alabama 25
1-1-91..............Tennessee 23, Virginia 22
1-1-92..............Notre Dame 39, Florida 28
1-1-93..............Alabama 34, Miami (Fla.) 13
1-1-94..............Florida 41, West Virginia 7
1-2-95..............Florida St 23, Florida 17
12-31-95.........Virginia Tech 28, Texas 10
1-2-97..............Florida St 52, Florida St 20
1-1-98..............Florida St 31, Ohio St 14
1-1-99..............Ohio St 24, Texas A&M 14
1-4-00..............Florida St 46, Virginia Tech 29
1-2-01..............Miami (Fla.) 37, Florida 20
1-1-02..............LSU 47, Illinois 34
1-1-03.............Georgia 26, Florida St 13
1-4-04..............LSU 21, Oklahoma 14
1-3-05.............Auburn 16, Virginia Tech 13
1-2-06.............West Virginia 38, Georgia 35
1-3-07..............LSU 41, Notre Dame 14
1-1-08.............Georgia 41, Hawaii 10
1-2-09..............Utah 31, Alabama 17

City: New Orleans. Stadium: Louisiana Superdome, capacity 76,791. Playing Sites: Tulane Stadium (1935–74), Louisiana Superdome (since 1975). Due to Hurricane Katrina, 2006 Sugar Bowl played in Atlanta's Georgia Dome.

### Cotton Bowl

1-1-37..............TCU 16, Marquette 6
1-1-38..............Rice 28, Colorado 14
1-2-39..............St. Mary's (Ca.) 20, Texas Tech 13
1-1-40..............Clemson 6, Boston Col 3
1-1-41..............Texas A&M 13, Fordham 12
1-1-42..............Alabama 29, Texas A&M 21

### Cotton Bowl *(Cont.)*

1-1-43..............Texas 14, Georgia Tech 7
1-1-44..............Texas 7, Randolph Field 7
1-1-45..............Oklahoma St 34, TCU 0
1-1-46..............Texas 40, Missouri 27
1-1-47..............Arkansas 0, LSU 0
1-1-48..............Southern Methodist 13, Penn St 13
1-1-49..............Southern Methodist 21, Oregon 13
1-2-50..............Rice 27, North Carolina 13
1-1-51..............Tennessee 20, Texas 14
1-1-52..............Kentucky 20, TCU 7
1-1-53..............Texas 16, Tennessee 0
1-1-54..............Rice 28, Alabama 6
1-1-55..............Georgia Tech 14, Arkansas 6
1-2-56..............Mississippi 14, TCU 13
1-1-57..............TCU 28, Syracuse 27
1-1-58..............Navy 20, Rice 7
1-1-59..............TCU 0, Air Force 0
1-1-60..............Syracuse 23, Texas 14
1-2-61..............Duke 7, Arkansas 6
1-1-62..............Texas 12, Mississippi 7
1-1-63..............LSU 13, Texas 0
1-1-64..............Texas 28, Navy 6
1-1-65..............Arkansas 10, Nebraska 7
1-1-66..............LSU 14, Arkansas 7
12-31-66.........Georgia 24, Southern Methodist 9
1-1-68..............Texas A&M 20, Alabama 16
1-1-69..............Texas 36, Tennessee 13
1-1-70..............Texas 21, Notre Dame 17
1-1-71..............Notre Dame 24, Texas 11
1-1-72..............Penn St 30, Texas 6
1-1-73..............Texas 17, Alabama 13
1-1-74..............Nebraska 19, Texas 3
1-1-75..............Penn St 41, Baylor 20
1-1-76..............Arkansas 31, Georgia 10
1-1-77..............Houston 30, Maryland 21
1-2-78..............Notre Dame 38, Texas 10
1-1-79..............Notre Dame 35, Houston 34
1-1-80..............Houston 17, Nebraska 14
1-1-81..............Alabama 30, Baylor 2
1-1-82..............Texas 14, Alabama 12
1-1-83..............SMU 7, Pittsburgh 3
1-2-84..............Georgia 10, Texas 9
1-1-85..............Boston Col 45, Houston 28
1-1-86..............Texas A&M 36, Auburn 16
1-1-87..............Ohio St 28, Texas A&M 12
1-1-88..............Texas A&M 35, Notre Dame 10
1-2-89..............UCLA 17, Arkansas 3
1-1-90..............Tennessee 31, Arkansas 27
1-1-91..............Miami (Fla.) 46, Texas 3
1-1-92..............Florida St 10, Texas A&M 2
1-1-93..............Notre Dame 28, Texas A&M 3
1-1-94..............Notre Dame 24, Texas A&M 21
1-2-95..............USC 55, Texas Tech 14
1-1-96..............Colorado 38, Oregon 6
1-1-97..............BYU 19, Kansas St 15
1-1-98..............UCLA 29, Texas A&M 23
1-1-99..............Texas 38, Mississippi St 11
1-1-00..............Arkansas 27, Texas 6
1-1-01..............Kansas St 35, Tennessee 21
1-1-02..............Oklahoma 10, Arkansas 3
1-1-03..............Texas 35, LSU 20
1-2-04..............Mississippi 31, Oklahoma St 28
1-1-05..............Tennessee 38, Texas A&M 7
1-2-06..............Alabama 13, Texas Tech 10
1-1-07..............Auburn 17, Nebraska 14
1-1-08..............Missouri 38, Arkansas 7
1-2-09..............Mississippi 47, Texas Tech 34

City: Dallas. Stadium: Cotton Bowl, capacity 68,252.

## Results of Major Bowl Games *(Cont.)*

### Sun Bowl
1-1-36 ...............Hardin-Simmons 14, New Mexico St 14
1-1-37 ...............Hardin-Simmons 34, UTEP 6
1-1-38 ...............W Virginia 7, Texas Tech 6
1-2-39 ...............Utah 26, New Mexico 0
1-1-40 ...............Catholic 0, Arizona St 0
1-1-41 ...............Case Reserve 26, Arizona St 13
1-1-42 ...............Tulsa 6, Texas Tech 0
1-1-43 ...............2nd Air Force 13, Hardin-Simmons 7
1-1-44 ...............Southwestern (Tex.) 7, New Mexico 0
1-1-45 ...............Southwestern (Tex.) 35, New Mexico 0
1-1-46 ...............New Mexico 34, Denver 24
1-1-47 ...............Cincinnati 18, Virginia Tech 6
1-1-48 ...............Miami (OH) 13, Texas Tech 12
1-1-49 ...............W Virginia 21, UTEP 12
1-2-50 ...............UTEP 33, Georgetown 20
1-1-51 ...............W Texas St 14, Cincinnati 13
1-1-52 ...............Texas Tech 25, Pacific 14
1-1-53 ...............Pacific 26, Southern Miss 7
1-1-54 ...............UTEP 37, Southern Miss 14
1-1-55 ...............UTEP 47, Florida St 20
1-2-56 ...............Wyoming 21, Texas Tech 14
1-1-57 ...............George Washington 13, UTEP 0
1-1-58 ...............Louisville 34, Drake 20
12-31-58 ..........Wyoming 14, Hardin-Simmons 6
12-31-59 ..........New Mexico St 28, N Texas 8
12-31-60 ..........New Mexico St 20, Utah St 13
12-30-61 ..........Villanova 17, Wichita St 9
12-31-62 ..........W Texas St 15, Ohio 14
12-31-63 ..........Oregon 21, Southern Methodist 14
12-26-64 ..........Georgia 7, Texas Tech 0
12-31-65 ..........UTEP 13, TCU 12
12-24-66 ..........Wyoming 28, Florida St 20
12-30-67 ..........UTEP 14, Mississippi 7
12-28-68 ..........Auburn 34, Arizona 10
12-20-69 ..........Nebraska 45, Georgia 6
12-19-70 ..........Georgia Tech 17, Texas Tech 9
12-18-71 ..........LSU 33, Iowa St 15
12-30-72 ..........North Carolina 32, Texas Tech 28
12-29-73 ..........Missouri 34, Auburn 17
12-28-74 ..........Mississippi St 26, North Carolina 24
12-26-75 ..........Pittsburgh 33, Kansas 19
1-2-77 .............Texas A&M 37, Florida 14
12-31-77 ..........Stanford 24, LSU 14
12-23-78 ..........Texas 42, Maryland 0
12-22-79 ..........Washington 14, Texas 7
12-27-80 ..........Nebraska 31, Mississippi St 17
12-26-81 ..........Oklahoma 40, Houston 14
12-25-82 ..........North Carolina 26, Texas 10
12-24-83 ..........Alabama 28, Southern Methodist 7
12-22-84 ..........Maryland 28, Tennessee 27
12-28-85 ..........Georgia 13, Arizona 13
12-25-86 ..........Alabama 28, Washington 6
12-25-87 ..........Oklahoma St 35, W Virginia 33
12-24-88 ..........Alabama 29, Army 28
12-30-89 ..........Pittsburgh 31, Texas A&M 28
12-31-90 ..........Michigan St 17, USC 16
12-31-91 ..........UCLA 6, Illinois 3
12-31-92 ..........Baylor 20, Arizona 15
12-24-93 ..........Oklahoma 41, Texas Tech 10
12-30-94 ..........Texas 35, North Carolina 31
12-29-95 ..........Iowa 38, Washington 18
12-31-96 ..........Stanford 38, Michigan St 0
12-31-97 ..........Arizona St 17, Iowa 7
12-31-98 ..........TCU 28, USC 19
12-31-99 ..........Oregon 24, Minnesota 20
12-29-00 ..........Wisconsin 21, UCLA 20
12-31-01 ..........Washington St 33, Purdue 27
12-31-02 ..........Purdue 34, Washington 24

### Sun Bowl
12-31-03 ..........Minnesota 31, Oregon 30
12-31-04 ..........Arizona State 27, Purdue 23
12-30-05 ..........UCLA 50, Northwestern 39
12-29-06 ..........Oregon State 39, Missouri 38
12-31-07 ..........Oregon 56, South Florida 21
12-31-08 ..........Oregon St 3, Pittsburgh 0

City: El Paso. Stadium: Sun Bowl, capacity 51,270.
Name Changes: Sun Bowl (1936–86; 94–), John Hancock Sun Bowl (1987–88), John Hancock Bowl (1989–93). Playing Sites: Kidd Field (1936–62), Sun Bowl (since 1963).

### Gator Bowl
1-1-46 ...............Wake Forest 26, South Carolina 14
1-1-47 ...............Oklahoma 34, North Carolina St 13
1-1-48 ...............Maryland 20, Georgia 20
1-1-49 ...............Clemson 24, Missouri 23
1-2-50 ...............Maryland 20, Missouri 7
1-1-51 ...............Wyoming 20, Washington & Lee 7
1-1-52 ...............Miami (Fla.) 14, Clemson 0
1-1-53 ...............Florida 14, Tulsa 13
1-1-54 ...............Texas Tech 35, Auburn 13
12-31-54 ..........Auburn 33, Baylor 13
12-31-55 ..........Vanderbilt 25, Auburn 13
12-29-56 ..........Georgia Tech 21, Pittsburgh 14
12-28-57 ..........Tennessee 3, Texas A&M 0
12-27-58 ..........Mississippi 7, Florida 3
1-2-60 .............Arkansas 14, Georgia Tech 7
12-31-60 ..........Florida 13, Baylor 12
12-30-61 ..........Penn St 30, Georgia Tech 15
12-29-62 ..........Florida 17, Penn St 7
12-28-63 ..........North Carolina 35, Air Force 0
1-2-65 .............Florida St 36, Oklahoma 19
12-31-65 ..........Georgia St 31, Texas Tech 21
12-31-66 ..........Tennessee 18, Syracuse 12
12-30-67 ..........Penn St 17, Florida St 17
12-28-68 ..........Missouri 35, Alabama 10
12-27-69 ..........Florida 14, Tennessee 13
1-2-71 .............Auburn 35, Mississippi 28
12-31-71 ..........Georgia 7, North Carolina 3
12-30-72 ..........Auburn 24, Colorado 3
12-29-73 ..........Texas Tech 28, Tennessee 19
12-30-74 ..........Auburn 27, Texas 3
12-29-75 ..........Maryland 13, Florida 0
12-27-76 ..........Notre Dame 20, Penn St 9
12-30-77 ..........Pittsburgh 34, Clemson 3
12-29-78 ..........Clemson 17, Ohio St 15
12-28-79 ..........North Carolina 17, Michigan 15
12-29-80 ..........Pittsburgh 37, South Carolina 9
12-28-81 ..........North Carolina 31, Arkansas 27
12-30-82 ..........Florida St 31, W Virginia 12
12-30-83 ..........Florida 14, Iowa 6
12-28-84 ..........Oklahoma St 21, South Carolina 14
12-30-85 ..........Florida St 34, Oklahoma St 23
12-27-86 ..........Clemson 27, Stanford 21
12-31-87 ..........LSU 30, South Carolina 13
1-1-89 .............Georgia 34, Michigan St 27
12-30-89 ..........Clemson 27, W Virginia 7
1-1-91 .............Michigan 35, Mississippi 3
12-29-91 ..........Oklahoma 48, Virginia 14
12-31-92 ..........Florida 27, North Carolina St 10
12-31-93 ..........Alabama 24, North Carolina 10
12-30-94 ..........Tennessee 45, Virginia Tech 23
1-1-96 .............Syracuse 41, Clemson 0
1-1-97 .............North Carolina 20, W Virginia 13

COLLEGE FOOTBALL **203**

### Gator Bowl *(Cont.)*

1-1-98 ..............North Carolina 42, Viginia Tech 13
1-1-99 ..............Georgia Tech 35, Notre Dame 28
1-1-00 ..............Miami 27, Georgia Tech 13
1-1-01 ..............Virginia Tech 41, Clemson 20
1-1-02 ..............Florida St 30, Virginia Tech 17
1-1-03 ..............North Carolina St 28, Notre Dame 6
1-1-04 ..............Maryland 41, W Virginia 7
1-1-05 ..............Florida State 30, West Virginia 18
1-2-06 ..............Virginia Tech 35, Louisville 24
1-1-07 ..............West Virginia 38, Georgia Tech 35
1-1-08 ..............Texas Tech 31, Virginia 28
1-1-09 ..............Nebraska 26, Clemson 21

City: Jacksonville, FL. Stadium: Alltel Stadium, capacity 76,976.

### Florida Citrus Bowl

1-1-47 ..............Catawba 31, Maryville (Tenn.) 6
1-1-48 ..............Catawba 7, Marshall 0
1-1-49 ..............Murray St 21, Sul Ross St 21
1-2-50 ..............St. Vincent 7, Emory & Henry 6
1-1-51 ..............Morris Harvey 35, Emory & Henry 14
1-1-52 ..............Stetson 35, Arkansas St 20
1-1-53 ..............E Texas St 33, Tennessee Tech 0
1-1-54 ..............E Texas St 7, Arkansas St 7
1-1-55 ..............NE-Omaha 7, Eastern Kentucky 6
1-2-56 ..............Juniata 6, Missouri Valley 6
1-1-57 ..............W Texas St 20, Southern Miss 13
1-1-58 ..............E Texas St 10, Southern Miss 9
12-27-58 ..........E Texas St 26, Missouri Valley 7
1-1-60 ..............Middle Tennessee St 21, Presbyterian 12
12-30-60 ..........Citadel 27, Tennessee Tech 0
12-29-61 ..........Lamar 21, Middle Tennessee St 14
12-22-62 ..........Houston 49, Miami (Ohio) 21
12-28-63 ..........Western Kentucky 27, Coast Guard 0
12-12-64 ..........E Carolina 14, Massachusetts 13
12-11-65 ..........E Carolina 31, Maine 0
12-10-66 ..........Morgan St 14, W Chester 6
12-16-67 ..........TN-Martin 25, W Chester 8
12-27-68 ..........Richmond 49, Ohio 42
12-26-69 ..........Toledo 56, Davidson 33
12-28-70 ..........Toledo 40, William & Mary 12
12-28-71 ..........Toledo 28, Richmond 3
12-29-72 ..........Tampa 21, Kent St 18
12-22-73 ..........Miami (Ohio) 16, Florida 7
12-21-74 ..........Miami (Ohio) 21, Georgia 10
12-20-75 ..........Miami (Ohio) 20, South Carolina 7
12-18-76 ..........Oklahoma St 49, BYU 21
12-23-77 ..........Florida St 40, Texas Tech 17
12-23-78 ..........North Carolina St 30, Pittsburgh 17
12-22-79 ..........LSU 34, Wake Forest 10
12-20-80 ..........Florida 35, Maryland 20
12-19-81 ..........Missouri 19, Southern Miss 17
12-18-82 ..........Auburn 33, Boston Col 26
12-17-83 ..........Tennessee 30, Maryland 23
12-22-84 ..........Georgia 17, Florida St 17
12-28-85 ..........Ohio St 10, BYU 7
1-1-87 ..............Auburn 16, USC 7
1-1-88 ..............Clemson 35, Penn St 10
1-2-89 ..............Clemson 13, Oklahoma 6
1-1-90 ..............Illinois 31, Virginia 21
1-1-91 ..............Georgia Tech 45, Nebraska 21
1-1-92 ..............California 37, Clemson 13
1-1-93 ..............Georgia 21, Ohio State 14
1-1-94 ..............Penn State 31, Tennessee 13
1-2-95 ..............Alabama 24, Ohio St 17

### Florida Citrus Bowl *(Cont.)*

1-1-96 ..............Tennessee 20, Ohio St 14
1-1-97 ..............Tennessee 48, Northwestern 28
1-1-98 ..............Florida 21, Penn St 6
1-1-99 ..............Michigan 45, Arkansas 31
1-1-00 ..............Michigan St 37, Florida 34
1-1-01 ..............Michigan 31, Auburn 28
1-1-02 ..............Tennessee 45, Michigan 17
1-1-03 ..............Auburn 13, Penn St 9
1-1-04 ..............Georgia 34, Purdue 27 (OT)
1-1-05 ..............Iowa 30, LSU 25
1-2-06 ..............Wisconsin 24, Auburn 10
1-1-07 ..............Wisconsin 17, Arkansas 14
1-1-08 ..............Michigan 41, Florida 35
1-1-09 ..............Georgia 24, Michigan St 12

City: Orlando, FL. Stadium: Florida Citrus Bowl, capacity 70,000. Name Change: Tangerine Bowl (1947–82). Capital One Bowl (since 2008). Playing Sites: Tangerine Bowl (1947–72, 1974–82); Florida Field, Gainesville (1973); Orlando Stadium/Florida Citrus Bowl-Orlando (1983–2007).

### Liberty Bowl

12-19-59 ..........Penn St 7, Alabama 0
12-17-60 ..........Penn St 41, Oregon 12
12-16-61 ..........Syracuse 15, Miami (Fla.) 14
12-15-62 ..........Oregon St 6, Villanova 0
12-21-63 ..........Mississippi St 16, North Carolina St 12
12-19-64 ..........Utah 32, W Virginia 6
12-18-65 ..........Mississippi 13, Auburn 7
12-10-66 ..........Miami (Fla.) 14, Virginia Tech 7
12-16-67 ..........North Carolina St 14, Georgia 7
12-14-68 ..........Mississippi 34, Virginia Tech 17
12-13-69 ..........Colorado 47, Alabama 33
12-12-70 ..........Tulane 17, Colorado 3
12-20-71 ..........Tennessee 14, Arkansas 13
12-18-72 ..........Georgia Tech 31, Iowa St 30
12-17-73 ..........North Carolina St 31, Kansas 18
12-16-74 ..........Tennessee 7, Maryland 3
12-22-75 ..........USC 20, Texas A&M 0
12-20-76 ..........Alabama 36, UCLA 6
12-19-77 ..........Nebraska 21, North Carolina 17
12-23-78 ..........Missouri 20, LSU 15
12-22-79 ..........Penn St 9, Tulane 6
12-27-80 ..........Purdue 28, Missouri 25
12-30-81 ..........Ohio St 31, Navy 28
12-29-82 ..........Alabama 21, Illinois 15
12-29-83 ..........Notre Dame 19, Boston Col 18
12-27-84 ..........Auburn 21, Arkansas 15
12-27-85 ..........Baylor 21, LSU 7
12-29-86 ..........Tennessee 21, Minnesota 14
12-29-87 ..........Georgia 20, Arkansas 17
12-28-88 ..........Indiana 34, South Carolina 10
12-28-89 ..........Mississippi 42, Air Force 29
12-27-90 ..........Air Force 23, Ohio St 11
12-29-91 ..........Air Force 38, Mississippi St 15
12-31-92 ..........Mississippi 13, Air Force 0
12-28-93 ..........Louisville 18, Michigan St 7
12-31-94 ..........Illinois 30, E Carolina 0
12-30-95 ..........East Carolina 19, Stanford 13
12-27-96 ..........Syracuse 30, Houston 17
12-31-97 ..........Southern Miss 41, Pittsburgh 7
12-31-98 ..........Tulane 41, BYU 27
12-31-99 ..........Southern Miss 23, Colorado St 17
12-29-01 ..........Colorado St 22, Louisville 17
12-31-01 ..........Louisville 28, BYU 10
12-31-02 ..........TCU 17, Colorado St 3
12-31-03 ..........Utah 17, Southern Mississippi 0

## Liberty Bowl *(Cont.)*

12-31-04 ..........Louisville 44, Boise State 40
12-31-05 ..........Tulsa 31, Fresno State 24
12-29-06 ..........South Carolina 44, Houston 36
12-29-07 ..........Mississippi St 10, Central Florida 3
1-2-09 ..............Kentucky 25, East Carolina 19
City: Memphis (since 1965). Stadium: Liberty Bowl
Memorial Stadium, capacity 62,921.
Playing Sites: Philadelphia (Municipal Stadium, 1959–63),
Atlantic City (Convention Center, 1964).

## Bluebonnet Bowl

12-19-59 ..........Clemson 23, TCU 7
12-17-60 ..........Texas 3, Alabama 3
12-16-61 ..........Kansas 33, Rice 7
12-22-62 ..........Missouri 14, Georgia Tech 10
12-21-63 ..........Baylor 14, LSU 7
12-19-64 ..........Tulsa 14, Mississippi 7
12-18-65 ..........Tennessee 27, Tulsa 6
12-17-66 ..........Texas 19, Mississippi 0
12-23-67 ..........Colorado 31, Miami (Fla.) 21
12-31-68 ..........Southern Methodist 28, Oklahoma 27
12-31-69 ..........Houston 36, Auburn 7
12-31-70 ..........Alabama 24, Oklahoma 24
12-31-71 ..........Colorado 29, Houston 17
12-30-72 ..........Tennessee 24, LSU 17
12-29-73 ..........Houston 47, Tulane 7
12-23-74 ..........North Carolina St 31, Houston 31
12-27-75 ..........Texas 38, Colorado 21
12-31-76 ..........Nebraska 27, Texas Tech 24
12-31-77 ..........USC 47, Texas A&M 28
12-31-78 ..........Stanford 25, Georgia 22
12-31-79 ..........Purdue 27, Tennessee 22
12-31-80 ..........North Carolina 16, Texas 7
12-31-81 ..........Michigan 33, UCLA 14
12-31-82 ..........Arkansas 28, Florida 24
12-31-83 ..........Oklahoma St 24, Baylor 14
12-31-84 ..........W Virginia 31, TCU 14
12-31-85 ..........Air Force 24, Texas 16
12-31-86 ..........Baylor 21, Colorado 9
12-31-87 ..........Texas 32, Pittsburgh 27

City: Houston. Playing sites: Rice Stadium (1959–67;
1985–86), Astrodome (1968–84, 1987).
Name change: Astro-Bluebonnet Bowl (1968–76). Bowl
was discontinued after 1987.

## Peach Bowl

12-30-68 ..........LSU 31, Florida St 27
12-30-69 ..........W Virginia 14, South Carolina 3
12-30-70 ..........Arizona St 48, North Carolina 26
12-30-71 ..........Mississippi 41, Georgia Tech 18
12-29-72 ..........North Carolina St 49, W Virginia 13
12-28-73 ..........Georgia 17, Maryland 16
12-28-74 ..........Vanderbilt 6, Texas Tech 6
12-31-75 ..........W Virginia 13, North Carolina St 10
12-31-76 ..........Kentucky 21, North Carolina 0
12-31-77 ..........North Carolina St 24, Iowa St 14
12-25-78 ..........Purdue 41, Georgia Tech 21
12-31-79 ..........Baylor 24, Clemson 18
1-2-81 ..............Miami (Fla.) 20, Virginia Tech 10
12-31-81 ..........W Virginia 26, Florida 6
12-31-82 ..........Iowa 28, Tennessee 22
12-30-83 ..........Florida St 28, North Carolina 3
12-31-84 ..........Virginia 27, Purdue 24
12-31-85 ..........Army 31, Illinois 29
12-31-86 ..........Virginia Tech 25, North Carolina St 24

## Peach Bowl *(Cont.)*

1-2-88 ..............Tennessee 27, Indiana 22
12-31-88 ..........North Carolina St 28, Iowa 23
12-30-89 ..........Syracuse 19, Georgia 18
12-29-90 ..........Auburn 27, Indiana 23
1-1-92 ..............E Carolina 37, North Carolina St 34
1-2-93 ..............North Carolina 21, Mississippi St 17
12-31-93 ..........Clemson 14, Kentucky 13
1-1-95 ..............North Carolina St 28, Mississippi St 24
12-30-95 ..........Virginia 34, Georgia 27
12-28-96 ..........LSU 10, Clemson 7
1-2-98 ..............Auburn 21, Clemson 17
12-31-98 ..........Georgia 35, Virginia 33
12-30-99 ..........Mississippi St 17, Clemson 7
12-29-00 ..........LSU 28, Georgia Tech 14
12-31-01 ..........North Carolina 16, Auburn 10
12-31-02 ..........Maryland 30, Tennessee 3
1-2-04 ..............Clemson 27, Tennessee 14
12-31-04 ..........Miami (Fla.) 27, Florida 10
12-30-05 ..........LSU 40, Miami (Fla.) 3
12-30-06 ..........Georgia 31, Virginia Tech 24
12-31-07 ..........Auburn 23, Clemson 20 (OT)
12-31-08 ..........LSU 38, Georgia Tech 3
City: Atlanta. Stadium: Georgia Dome, capacity 71,500.
Name change: Chick-fil-A Bowl (2006–).Playing Sites:
Grant Field (1968–70), Atlanta–Fulton County Stadium
(1971–92), Georgia Dome (since 1993).

## Fiesta Bowl

12-27-71 ..........Arizona St 45, Florida St 38
12-23-72 ..........Arizona St 49, Missouri 35
12-21-73 ..........Arizona St 28, Pittsburgh 7
12-28-74 ..........Oklahoma St 16, BYU 6
12-26-75 ..........Arizona St 17, Nebraska 14
12-25-76 ..........Oklahoma 41, Wyoming 7
12-25-77 ..........Penn St 42, Arizona St 30
12-25-78 ..........Arkansas 10, UCLA 10
12-25-79 ..........Pittsburgh 16, Arizona 10
12-26-80 ..........Penn St 31, Ohio St 19
1-1-82 ..............Penn St 26, USC 10
1-1-83 ..............Arizona St 32, Oklahoma 21
1-2-84 ..............Ohio St 28, Pittsburgh 23
1-1-85 ..............UCLA 39, Miami (Fla.) 37
1-1-86 ..............Michigan 27, Nebraska 23
1-2-87 ..............Penn St 14, Miami (Fla.) 10
1-1-88 ..............Florida St 31, Nebraska 28
1-2-89 ..............Notre Dame 34, W Virginia 21
1-1-90 ..............Florida St 41, Nebraska 17
1-1-91 ..............Louisville 34, Alabama 7
1-1-92 ..............Penn St 42, Tennessee 17
1-1-93 ..............Syracuse 26, Colorado 22
1-1-94 ..............Arizona 29, Miami (Fla.) 0
1-2-95 ..............Colorado 41, Notre Dame 24
1-2-96 ..............Nebraska 62, Florida 24
1-1-97 ..............Penn St 38, Texas 15
12-31-97 ..........Kansas St 35, Syracuse 18
1-4-99 ..............Tennessee 23, Florida St 16
1-2-00 ..............Nebraska 31, Tennessee 21
1-1-01 ..............Oregon St 41, Notre Dame 9
1-1-02 ..............Oregon 38, Colorado 16
1-3-03 ..............Ohio St 31, Miami (Fla.) 24 [2 OT]
1-2-04 ..............Ohio St 35, Kansas St 28
1-1-05 ..............Utah 35, Pittsburgh 7
1-2-06 ..............Ohio State 34, Notre Dame 20
1-1-07 ..............Boise State 43, Oklahoma 42
1-2-08 ..............West Virginia 48, Oklahoma 28
1-5-09 ..............Texas 24, Ohio St 21
City: Tempe, AZ. Stadium: Sun Devil Stadium,
capacity 73,471.

## Independence Bowl

12-13-76.........McNeese St 20, Tulsa 16
12-17-77.........Louisiana Tech 24, Louisville 14
12-16-78.........E Carolina 35, Louisiana Tech 13
12-15-79.........Syracuse 31, McNeese St 7
12-13-80.........Southern Miss 16, McNeese St 14
12-12-81.........Texas A&M 33, Oklahoma St 16
12-11-82.........Wisconsin 14, Kansas St 3
12-10-83.........Air Force 9, Mississippi 3
12-15-84.........Air Force 23, Virginia Tech 7
12-21-85.........Minnesota 20, Clemson 13
12-20-86.........Mississippi 20, Texas Tech 17
12-19-87.........Washington 24, Tulane 12
12-23-88.........Southern Miss 38, UTEP 18
12-16-89.........Oregon 27, Tulsa 24
12-15-90.........Louisiana Tech 34, Maryland 34
12-29-91.........Georgia 24, Arkansas 15
12-31-92.........Wake Forest 39, Oregon 35
12-31-93.........Virginia Tech 45, Indiana 20
12-28-94.........Virginia 20, TCU 10
12-29-95.........LSU 45, Michigan St 26
12-31-96.........Auburn 32, Army 29
12-28-97.........LSU 27, Notre Dame 9
12-31-98.........Mississippi 35, Texas Tech 18
12-31-99.........Mississippi 27, Oklahoma 25
12-31-00.........Mississippi St 43, Texas A&M 41
12-27-01.........Alabama 14, Iowa St 13
12-27-02.........Mississippi 27, Nebraska 23
12-31-03.........Arkansas 27, Missouri 14
12-28-04.........Iowa State 17, Miami (Ohio) 13
12-30-05.........Missouri 38, South Carolina 31
12-28-06.........Oklahoma State 34, Alabama 31
12-30-07.........Alabama 30, Colorado 24
12-28-08.........Louisiana Tech 17, Northern Ill. 10
City: Shreveport, LA. Stadium: Independence Stadium, capacity 50,459.

## All-American Bowl

12-22-77.........Maryland 17, Minnesota 7
12-20-78.........Texas A&M 28, Iowa St 12
12-29-79.........Missouri 24, South Carolina 14
12-27-80.........Arkansas 34, Tulane 15
12-31-81.........Mississippi St 10, Kansas 0
12-31-82.........Air Force 36, Vanderbilt 28
12-22-83.........W Virginia 20, Kentucky 16
12-29-84.........Kentucky 20, Wisconsin 19
12-31-85.........Georgia Tech 17, Michigan St 14
12-31-86.........Florida St 27, Indiana 13
12-22-87.........Virginia 22, BYU 16
12-29-88.........Florida 14, Illinois 10
12-28-89.........Texas Tech 49, Duke 21
12-28-90.........North Carolina St 31, Southern Miss 27

City: Birmingham, AL. Stadium: Legion Field.
Name Change: Hall of Fame Classic (1977–84). Bowl was discontinued after 1990.

## Holiday Bowl

12-22-78.........Navy 23, BYU 16
12-21-79.........Indiana 38, BYU 37
12-19-80.........BYU 46, SMU45
12-18-81.........BYU 38, Washington St 36
12-17-82.........Ohio St 47, BYU 17
12-23-83.........BYU 21, Missouri 17
12-21-84.........BYU 24, Michigan 17
12-22-85.........Arkansas 18, Arizona St 17
12-30-86.........Iowa 39, San Diego St 38

## Holiday Bowl *(Cont.)*

12-30-87.........Iowa 20, Wyoming 19
12-30-88.........Oklahoma St 62, Wyoming 14
12-29-89.........Penn St 50, BYU 39
12-29-90.........Texas A&M 65, BYU 14
12-30-91.........Iowa 13, BYU 13
12-30-92.........Hawaii 27, Illinois 17
12-30-93.........Ohio St 28, BYU 21
12-30-94.........Michigan 24, Colorado St 14
12-29-95.........Kansas St 54, Colorado St 21
12-30-96.........Colorado 33, Washington 21
12-30-97.........Colorado St 35, Missouri 24
12-30-98.........Arizona 23, Nebraska 20
12-29-99.........Kansas St 24, Washington 20
12-29-00.........Oregon 35, Texas 30
12-28-01.........Texas 47, Washington 43
12-27-02.........Kansas St 34, Arizona St 27
12-30-03.........Washington St 28, Texas 20
12-30-04.........Texas Tech 45, California 31
12-29-05.........Oklahoma 17, Oregon 14
12-28-06.........California 45, Texas A&M 10
12-27-07.........Texas 52, Arizona St 34
12-30-08.........Oregon 42, Oklahoma St 31
City: San Diego. Stadium: Qualcomm Stadium, capacity 70,000.

## Las Vegas Bowl

12-19-81.........Toledo 27, San Jose St 25
12-18-82.........Fresno St 29, Bowling Green 28
12-17-83.........Northern Illinois 20, Cal St-Fullerton 13
12-15-84.........UNLV 30, Toledo 13*
12-14-85.........Fresno St 51, Bowling Green 7
12-13-86.........San Jose St 37, Miami (Ohio) 7
12-12-87.........Eastern Michigan 30, San Jose St 27
12-10-88.........Fresno St 35, Western Michigan 30
12-9-89...........Fresno St 27, Ball St 6
12-8-90...........San Jose St 48, Central Michigan 24
12-14-91.........Bowling Green 28, Fresno St 21
12-18-92.........Bowling Green 35, Nevada 34
12-17-93.........Utah St 42, Ball St 33
12-15-94.........UNLV 52, Central Michigan 24
12-14-95.........Toledo 40, Nevada 37
12-19-96.........Nevada 18, Ball St 15
12-19-97.........Oregon 41, Air Force 13
12-19-98.........North Carolina 20, San Diego St 13
12-18-99.........Utah 17, Fresno St 16
12-21-00.........UNLV 31, Arkansas 14
12-25-01.........Utah 10, USC 6
12-25-02.........UCLA 27, New Mexico 13
12-24-03.........Oregon St 55, New Mexico 14
12-23-04.........Wyoming 24, UCLA, 21
12-22-05.........California 35, BYU 28
12-21-06.........BYU 38, Oregon 8
12-22-07.........BYU 17, UCLA 16
12-20-08.........Arizona 31, BYU 21

* Toledo won later by forfeit. City: Las Vegas (since 1992). Stadium: Sam Boyd Silver Bowl Stadium, capacity 40,000. Name change: California Bowl (1981–91).
Playing sites: Fresno, CA (Bulldog Stadium, 1981–91), Las Vegas.

## Aloha Bowl

12-25-82.........Washington 21, Maryland 20
12-26-83.........Penn St 13, Washington 10
12-29-84.........Southern Methodist 27, Notre Dame 20

### Aloha Bowl *(Cont.)*

12-28-85..........Alabama 24, USC  3
12-27-86..........Arizona 30, North Carolina 21
12-25-87..........UCLA 20, Florida 16
12-25-88..........Washington St 24, Houston 22
12-25-89..........Michigan St 33, Hawaii 13
12-25-90..........Syracuse 28, Arizona 0
12-25-91..........Georgia Tech 18, Stanford 17
12-25-92..........Kansas 23, BYU 20
12-25-93..........Colorado 41, Fresno St 30
12-25-94..........Boston College 12, Kansas St 7
12-25-95..........Kansas 51, UCLA 30
12-25-96..........Navy 42, California 38
12-25-97..........Washington 51, Michigan St 23
12-25-98..........Colorado 51, Oregon 43
12-25-99..........Wake Forest 23, Arizona St 3
12-25-00..........Boston College 31, Arizona St 17

City: Honolulu. Stadium: Aloha Stadium. Bowl was discontinued after 2000.

### Freedom Bowl

12-16-84..........Iowa 55, Texas 17
12-30-85..........Washington 20, Colorado 17
12-30-86..........UCLA 31, BYU 10
12-30-87..........Arizona St 33, Air Force 28
12-29-88..........BYU 20, Colorado 17
12-30-89..........Washington 34, Florida 7
12-29-90..........Colorado St 32, Oregon 31
12-30-91..........Tulsa 28, San Diego St 17
12-29-92..........Fresno St 24, USC  7
12-30-93..........USC 28, Utah 21
12-29-94..........Utah 16, Arizona 13

City: Anaheim. Stadium: Anaheim Stadium. Bowl was discontinued after 1994.

### Outback Bowl

12-23-86..........Boston College 27, Georgia 24
1-2-88..............Michigan 28, Alabama 24
1-2-89..............Syracuse 23, LSU 10
1-1-90..............Auburn 31, Ohio St 14
1-1-91..............Clemson 30, Illinois 0
1-1-92..............Syracuse 24, Ohio St 17
1-1-93..............Tennessee 38, Boston College 23
1-1-94..............Michigan 42, North Carolina St 7
1-2-95..............Wisconsin 34, Duke 20
1-1-96..............Penn St 43, Auburn 14
1-1-97..............Alabama 17, Michigan 14
1-1-98..............Georgia 33, Wisconsin 6
1-1-99..............Penn St 26, Kentucky 14
1-1-00..............Georgia 28, Purdue 25
1-1-01..............South Carolina 24, Ohio St 7
1-1-02..............South Carolina 31, Ohio St 28
1-1-03..............Michigan 38, Florida 30
1-1-04..............Iowa 37, Florida 17
1-1-05..............Georgia 24, Wisconsin 21
1-2-06..............Florida 31, Iowa 24
1-1-07..............Penn State 20, Tennessee 10
1-1-08..............Tennessee 21, Wisconsin 17
1-1-09..............Iowa 31, South Carolina 10

City: Tampa. Stadium: Raymond James Stadium, capacity 75,000. Name change: Hall of Fame Bowl (1986–95).

### Insight Bowl

12-31-89..........Arizona 17, North Carolina St 10

### Insight Bowl *(Cont.)*

12-31-90..........California 17, Wyoming 15
12-31-91..........Indiana 24, Baylor 0
12-29-92..........Washington St 31, Utah 28
12-29-93..........Kansas St 52, Wyoming 17
12-29-94..........BYU 31, Oklahoma 6
12-27-95..........Texas Tech 55, Air Force 41
12-27-96..........Wisconsin 38, Utah 10
12-27-97..........Arizona 20, New Mexico 14
12-26-98..........Missouri 34, W Virginia 31
12-31-99..........Colorado 62, Boston College 28
12-28-00..........Iowa St 37, Pittsburgh 29
12-29-01..........Syracuse 26, Kansas St 3
12-26-02..........Pittsburgh 38, Oregon St 13
12-26-03..........California 52, Virginia Tech 49
12-28-04..........Oregon State 38, Notre Dame 21
12-27-05..........Arizona State 45, Rutgers 40
12-29-06..........Texas Tech 44, Minnesota 41
12-31-07..........Oklahoma St 49, Indiana 33
12-31-08..........Kansas 42, Minnesota 21

City: Tucson.  Stadium: Arizona Stadium, capacity 55,883. Name change: Copper Bowl (1990–97), Insight.com Bowl (1998–2000).

### Tangerine Bowl

12-28-90..........Florida St 24, Penn St 17
12-28-91..........Alabama 30, Colorado 25
1-1-93..............Stanford 24, Penn St 3
1-1-94..............Boston College 31, Virginia 13
1-2-95..............South Carolina 24, W Virginia 21
12-30-95..........North Carolina 20, Arkansas 10
12-27-96..........Miami (Fla.) 31, Virginia 21
12-29-97..........Georgia Tech 35, W Virginia 30
12-29-98..........Miami (Fla.) 46, North Carolina St 23
12-30-99..........Illinois 62, Virginia 21
12-28-00..........North Carolina St 38, Minnesota 30
12-20-01..........Pittsburgh 34, North Carolina St 19
12-23-02..........Texas Tech 55, Clemson 15
12-22-03..........North Carolina St 56, Kansas 26

City: Miami.  Stadium: Pro Player Stadium, capacity 75,192. Name change: Blockbuster Bowl (1990–93), Carquest Bowl (1994–97), Micron PC Bowl (1998–01). Discontinued after 2003.

### Alamo Bowl

12-31-93..........California 37, Iowa 3
12-31-94..........Washington St 10, Baylor 3
12-28-95..........Texas A&M 22, Michigan 20
12-29-96..........Iowa 27, Texas Tech 0
12-30-97..........Purdue 33, Oklahoma St 20
12-29-98..........Purdue 37, Kansas St 34
12-28-99..........Penn St 24, Texas A&M 0
12-30-00..........Nebraska 66, Northwestern 17
12-29-01..........Iowa 16, Texas Tech 13
12-28-02..........Wisconsin 31, Colorado 28 (OT)
12-29-03..........Nebraska 17, Michigan St 3
12-29-04..........Ohio State 33, Oklahoma State 7
12-28-05..........Nebraska 32, Michigan 28
12-30-06..........Texas 26, Iowa 24
12-29-07..........Penn St 24, Texas A&M 17
12-29-08..........Missouri 30, Northwestern 23

City: San Antonio, TX. Stadium: Alamodome, capaciity 67,000.

## 1936

| | | Record | Coach |
|---|---|---|---|
| 1. | Minnesota | 7-1-0 | Bernie Bierman |
| 2. | LSU | 9-0-1 | Bernie Moore |
| 3. | Pittsburgh | 7-1-1 | Jock Sutherland |
| 4. | Alabama | 8-0-1 | Frank Thomas |
| 5. | Washington | 7-1-1 | Jimmy Phelan |
| 6. | Santa Clara | 7-1-0 | Buck Shaw |
| 7. | Northwestern | 7-1-0 | Pappy Waldorf |
| 8. | Notre Dame | 6-2-1 | Elmer Layden |
| 9. | Nebraska | 7-2-0 | Dana X. Bible |
| 10. | Pennsylvania | 7-1-0 | Harvey Harman |
| 11. | Duke | 9-1-0 | Wallace Wade |
| 12. | Yale | 7-1-0 | Ducky Pond |
| 13. | Dartmouth | 7-1-1 | Red Blaik |
| 14. | Duquesne | 7-2-0 | John Smith |
| 15. | Fordham | 5-1-2 | Jim Crowley |
| 16. | TCU | 8-2-2 | Dutch Meyer |
| 17. | Tennessee | 6-2-2 | Bob Neyland |
| 18. | Arkansas | 7-3-0 | Fred Thomsen |
| 19. | Navy | 6-3-0 | Tom Hamilton |
| 20. | Marquette | 7-1-0 | Frank Murray |

## 1937

| | | Record | Coach |
|---|---|---|---|
| 1. | Pittsburgh | 9-0-1 | Jock Sutherland |
| 2. | California | 9-0-1 | Stub Allison |
| 3. | Fordham | 7-0-1 | Jim Crowley |
| 4. | Alabama | 9-0-0 | Frank Thomas |
| 5. | Minnesota | 6-2-0 | Bernie Bierman |
| 6. | Villanova | 8-0-1 | Clipper Smith |
| 7. | Dartmouth | 7-0-2 | Red Blaik |
| 8. | LSU | 9-1-0 | Bernie Moore |
| 9. | Notre Dame | 6-2-1 | Elmer Layden |
| | Santa Clara | 8-0-0 | Buck Shaw |
| 11. | Nebraska | 6-1-2 | Biff Jones |
| 12. | Yale | 6-1-1 | Ducky Pond |
| 13. | Ohio St | 6-2-0 | Francis Schmidt |
| 14. | Holy Cross | 8-0-2 | Eddie Anderson |
| | Arkansas | 6-2-2 | Fred Thomsen |
| 16. | TCU | 4-2-2 | Dutch Meyer |
| 17. | Colorado | 8-0-0 | Bunnie Oakes |
| 18. | Rice | 5-3-2 | Jimmy Kitts |
| 19. | North Carolina | 7-1-1 | Ray Wolf |
| 20. | Duke | 7-2-1 | Wallace Wade |

## 1938

| | | Record | Coach |
|---|---|---|---|
| 1. | TCU | 10-0-0 | Dutch Meyer |
| 2. | Tennessee | 10-0-0 | Bob Neyland |
| 3. | Duke | 9-0-0 | Wallace Wade |
| 4. | Oklahoma | 10-0-0 | Tom Stidham |
| 5. | #Notre Dame | 8-1-0 | Elmer Layden |
| 6. | Carnegie Tech | 7-1-0 | Bill Kern |
| 7. | USC | 8-2-0 | Howard Jones |
| 8. | Pittsburgh | 8-2-0 | Jock Sutherland |
| 9. | Holy Cross | 8-1-0 | Eddie Anderson |
| 10. | Minnesota | 6-2-0 | Bernie Bierman |
| 11. | Texas Tech | 10-0-0 | Pete Cawthon |
| 12. | Cornell | 5-1-1 | Carl Snavely |
| 13. | Alabama | 7-1-1 | Frank Thomas |
| 14. | California | 10-1-0 | Stub Allison |
| 15. | Fordham | 6-1-2 | Jim Crowley |
| 16. | Michigan | 6-1-1 | Fritz Crisler |
| 17. | Northwestern | 4-2-2 | Pappy Waldorf |

## 1938 (Cont.)

| | | Record | Coach |
|---|---|---|---|
| 18. | Villanova | 8-0-1 | Clipper Smith |
| 19. | Tulane | 7-2-1 | Red Dawson |
| 20. | Dartmouth | 7-2-0 | Red Blaik |

#Selected No. 1 by the Dickinson System.

## 1939

| | | Record | Coach |
|---|---|---|---|
| 1. | Texas A&M | 10-0-0 | Homer Norton |
| 2. | Tennessee | 10-0-0 | Bob Neyland |
| 3. | #USC | 7-0-2 | Howard Jones |
| 4. | Cornell | 8-0-0 | Carl Snavely |
| 5. | Tulane | 8-0-1 | Red Dawson |
| 6. | Missouri | 8-1-0 | Don Faurot |
| 7. | UCLA | 6-0-4 | Babe Horrell |
| 8. | Duke | 8-1-0 | Wallace Wade |
| 9. | Iowa | 6-1-1 | Eddie Anderson |
| 10. | Duquesne | 8-0-1 | Buff Donelli |
| 11. | Boston College | 9-1-0 | Frank Leahy |
| 12. | Clemson | 8-1-0 | Jess Neely |
| 13. | Notre Dame | 7-2-0 | Elmer Layden |
| 14. | Santa Clara | 5-1-3 | Buck Shaw |
| 15. | Ohio St | 6-2-0 | Francis Schmidt |
| 16. | Georgia Tech | 7-2-0 | Bill Alexander |
| 17. | Fordham | 6-2-0 | Jim Crowley |
| 18. | Nebraska | 7-1-1 | Biff Jones |
| 19. | Oklahoma | 6-2-1 | Tom Stidham |
| 20. | Michigan | 6-2-0 | Fritz Crisler |

#Selected No. 1 by the Dickinson System.

## 1940

| | | Record | Coach |
|---|---|---|---|
| 1. | Minnesota | 8-0-0 | Bernie Bierman |
| 2. | Stanford | 9-0-0 | C. Shaughnessy |
| 3. | Michigan | 7-1-0 | Fritz Crisler |
| 4. | Tennessee | 10-0-0 | Bob Neyland |
| 5. | Boston College | 10-0-0 | Frank Leahy |
| 6. | Texas A&M | 8-1-0 | Homer Norton |
| 7. | Nebraska | 8-1-0 | Biff Jones |
| 8. | Northwestern | 6-2-0 | Pappy Waldorf |
| 9. | Mississippi St | 9-0-1 | Allyn McKeen |
| 10. | Washington | 7-2-0 | Jimmy Phelan |
| 11. | Santa Clara | 6-1-1 | Buck Shaw |
| 12. | Fordham | 7-1-0 | Jim Crowley |
| 13. | Georgetown | 8-1-0 | Jack Hagerty |
| 14. | Pennsylvania | 6-1-1 | George Munger |
| 15. | Cornell | 6-2-0 | Carl Snavely |
| 16. | SMU | 8-1-1 | Matty Bell |
| 17. | Hard.-Simmons | 9-0-0 | Abe Woodson |
| 18. | Duke | 7-2-0 | Wallace Wade |
| 19. | Lafayette | 9-0-0 | Hooks Mylin |
| 20. | — | | |

Only 19 teams selected.

## 1941

| | | Record | Coach |
|---|---|---|---|
| 1. | Minnesota | 8-0-0 | Bernie Bierman |
| 2. | Duke | 9-0-0 | Wallace Wade |
| 3. | Notre Dame | 8-0-1 | Frank Leahy |
| 4. | Texas | 8-1-1 | Dana X. Bible |
| 5. | Michigan | 6-1-1 | Fritz Crisler |

Note: Except where indicated with an asterisk, the polls from 1936 through 1964 were taken before the bowl games and those from 1965 through the present were taken after the bowl games.

## 1941 *(Cont.)*

| | | Record | Coach |
|---|---|---|---|
| 6. | Fordham | 7-1-0 | Jim Crowley |
| 7. | Missouri | 8-1-0 | Don Faurot |
| 8. | Duquesne | 8-0-0 | Buff Donelli |
| 9. | Texas A&M | 9-1-0 | Homer Norton |
| 10. | Navy | 7-1-1 | Swede Larson |
| 11. | Northwestern | 5-3-0 | Pappy Waldorf |
| 12. | Oregon St | 7-2-0 | Lon Stiner |
| 13. | Ohio St | 6-1-1 | Paul Brown |
| 14. | Georgia | 8-1-1 | Wally Butts |
| 15. | Pennsylvania | 7-1-1 | George Munger |
| 16. | Mississippi St | 8-1-1 | Allyn McKeen |
| 17. | Mississippi | 6-2-1 | Harry Mehre |
| 18. | Tennessee | 8-2-0 | John Barnhill |
| 19. | Washington St | 6-4-0 | Babe Hollingbery |
| 20. | Alabama | 8-2-0 | Frank Thomas |

## 1942

| | | Record | Coach |
|---|---|---|---|
| 1. | Ohio St | 9-1-0 | Paul Brown |
| 2. | Georgia | 10-1-0 | Wally Butts |
| 3. | Wisconsin | 8-1-1 | H. Stuhldreher |
| 4. | Tulsa | 10-0-0 | Henry Frnka |
| 5. | Georgia Tech | 9-1-0 | Bill Alexander |
| 6. | Notre Dame | 7-2-2 | Frank Leahy |
| 7. | Tennessee | 8-1-1 | John Barnhill |
| 8. | Boston College | 8-1-0 | Denny Myers |
| 9. | Michigan | 7-3-0 | Fritz Crisler |
| 10. | Alabama | 7-3-0 | Frank Thomas |
| 11. | Texas | 8-2-0 | Dana X. Bible |
| 12. | Stanford | 6-4-0 | Marchie Schwartz |
| 13. | UCLA | 7-3-0 | Babe Horrell |
| 14. | William & Mary | 9-1-1 | Carl Voyles |
| 15. | Santa Clara | 7-2-0 | Buck Shaw |
| 16. | Auburn | 6-4-1 | Jack Meagher |
| 17. | Washington St | 6-2-2 | Babe Hollingbery |
| 18. | Mississippi St | 8-2-0 | Allyn McKeen |
| 19. | Minnesota | 5-4-0 | George Hauser |
| | Holy Cross | 5-4-1 | Ank Scanlon |
| | Penn St | 6-1-1 | Bob Higgins |

## 1943

| | | Record | Coach |
|---|---|---|---|
| 1. | Notre Dame | 9-1-0 | Frank Leahy |
| 2. | Iowa Pre-Flight | 9-1-0 | Don Faurot |
| 3. | Michigan | 8-1-0 | Fritz Crisler |
| 4. | Navy | 8-1-0 | Billick Whelchel |
| 5. | Purdue | 9-0-0 | Elmer Burnham |
| 6. | Great Lakes | 10-2-0 | Tony Hinkle |
| 7. | Duke | 8-1-0 | Eddie Cameron |
| 8. | Del Monte P-F | 7-1-0 | Bill Kern |
| 9. | Northwestern | 6-2-0 | Pappy Waldorf |
| 10. | March Field | 9-1-0 | Paul Schissler |
| 11. | Army | 7-2-1 | Red Blaik |
| 12. | Washington | 4-0-0 | Ralph Welch |
| 13. | Georgia Tech | 7-3-0 | Bill Alexander |
| 14. | Texas | 7-1-0 | Dana X. Bible |
| 15. | Tulsa | 6-0-1 | Henry Frnka |
| 16. | Dartmouth | 6-1-0 | Earl Brown |
| 17. | Bainbridge NTS | 7-0-0 | Joe Maniaci |
| 18. | Colorado College | 7-0-0 | Hal White |
| 19. | Pacific | 7-2-0 | Amos A. Stagg |
| 20. | Pennsylvania | 6-2-1 | George Munger |

## 1944

| | | Record | Coach |
|---|---|---|---|
| 1. | Army | 9-0-0 | Red Blaik |
| 2. | Ohio St | 9-0-0 | Carroll Widdoes |
| 3. | Randolph Field | 11-0-0 | Frank Tritico |
| 4. | Navy | 6-3-0 | Oscar Hagberg |
| 5. | Bainbridge NTS | 9-0-0 | Joe Maniaci |
| 6. | Iowa Pre-Flight | 10-1-0 | Jack Meagher |
| 7. | USC | 7-0-2 | Jeff Cravath |
| 8. | Michigan | 8-2-0 | Fritz Crisler |
| 9. | Notre Dame | 8-2-0 | Ed McKeever |
| 10. | March Field | 7-1-2 | Paul Schissler |
| 11. | Duke | 5-4-0 | Eddie Cameron |
| 12. | Tennessee | 8-0-1 | John Barnhill |
| 13. | Georgia Tech | 8-2-0 | Bill Alexander |
| | Norman P-F | 6-0-0 | John Gregg |
| 15. | Illinois | 5-4-1 | Ray Eliot |
| 16. | El Toro Marines | 8-1-0 | Dick Hanley |
| 17. | Great Lakes | 9-2-1 | Paul Brown |
| 18. | Fort Pierce | 9-0-0 | Hamp Pool |
| 19. | St. Mary's P-F | 4-4-0 | Jules Sikes |
| 20. | 2nd Air Force | 7-2-1 | Bill Reese |

## 1945

| | | Record | Coach |
|---|---|---|---|
| 1. | Army | 9-0-0 | Red Blaik |
| 2. | Alabama | 9-0-0 | Frank Thomas |
| 3. | Navy | 7-1-1 | Oscar Hagberg |
| 4. | Indiana | 9-0-1 | Bo McMillan |
| 5. | Oklahoma A&M | 8-0-0 | Jim Lookabaugh |
| 6. | Michigan | 7-3-0 | Fritz Crisler |
| 7. | St. Mary's (CA) | 7-1-0 | Jimmy Phelan |
| 8. | Pennsylvania | 6-2-0 | George Munger |
| 9. | Notre Dame | 7-2-1 | Hugh Devore |
| 10. | Texas | 9-1-0 | Dana X. Bible |
| 11. | USC | 7-3-0 | Jeff Cravath |
| 12. | Ohio St | 7-2-0 | Carroll Widdoes |
| 13. | Duke | 6-2-0 | Eddie Cameron |
| 14. | Tennessee | 8-1-0 | John Barnhill |
| 15. | LSU | 7-2-0 | Bernie Moore |
| 16. | Holy Cross | 8-1-0 | John DeGrosa |
| 17. | Tulsa | 8-2-0 | Henry Frnka |
| 18. | Georgia | 8-2-0 | Wally Butts |
| 19. | Wake Forest | 4-3-1 | Peahead Walker |
| 20. | Columbia | 8-1-0 | Lou Little |

## 1946

| | | Record | Coach |
|---|---|---|---|
| 1. | Notre Dame | 8-0-1 | Frank Leahy |
| 2. | Army | 9-0-1 | Red Blaik |
| 3. | Georgia | 10-0-0 | Wally Butts |
| 4. | UCLA | 10-0-0 | B. LaBrucherie |
| 5. | Illinois | 7-2-0 | Ray Eliot |
| 6. | Michigan | 6-2-1 | Fritz Crisler |
| 7. | Tennessee | 9-1-0 | Bob Neyland |
| 8. | LSU | 9-1-0 | Bernie Moore |
| 9. | North Carolina | 8-1-1 | Carl Snavely |
| 10. | Rice | 8-2-0 | Jess Neely |
| 11. | Georgia Tech | 8-2-0 | Bobby Dodd |
| 12. | Yale | 7-1-1 | Howard Odell |
| 13. | Pennsylvania | 6-2-0 | George Munger |
| 14. | Oklahoma | 7-3-0 | Jim Tatum |
| 15. | Texas | 8-2-0 | Dana X. Bible |
| 16. | Arkansas | 6-3-1 | John Barnhill |
| 17. | Tulsa | 9-1-0 | J.O. Brothers |
| 18. | North Carolina St | 8-2-0 | Beattie Feathers |
| 19. | Delaware | 9-0-0 | Bill Murray |
| 20. | Indiana | 6-3-0 | Bo McMillan |

### 1947

| | | Record | Coach |
|---|---|---|---|
| 1. | Notre Dame | 9-0-0 | Frank Leahy |
| 2. | #Michigan | 9-0-0 | Fritz Crisler |
| 3. | SMU | 9-0-1 | Matty Bell |
| 4. | Penn St | 9-0-0 | Bob Higgins |
| 5. | Texas | 9-1-0 | Blair Cherry |
| 6. | Alabama | 8-2-0 | Red Drew |
| 7. | Pennsylvania | 7-0-1 | George Munger |
| 8. | USC | 7-1-1 | Jeff Cravath |
| 9. | North Carolina | 8-2-0 | Carl Snavely |
| 10. | Georgia Tech | 9-1-0 | Bobby Dodd |
| 11. | Army | 5-2-2 | Red Blaik |
| 12. | Kansas | 8-0-2 | George Sauer |
| 13. | Mississippi | 8-2-0 | Johnny Vaught |
| 14. | William & Mary | 9-1-0 | Rube McCray |
| 15. | California | 9-1-0 | Pappy Waldorf |
| 16. | Oklahoma | 7-2-1 | Bud Wilkinson |
| 17. | North Carolina St | 5-3-1 | Beattie Feathers |
| 18. | Rice | 6-3-1 | Jess Neely |
| 19. | Duke | 4-3-2 | Wallace Wade |
| 20. | Columbia | 7-2-0 | Lou Little |

#The AP, which had voted Notre Dame No. 1 before the bowl games, took a second vote, giving the title to Michigan after its 49–0 win over USC in the Rose Bowl.

### 1948

| | | Record | Coach |
|---|---|---|---|
| 1. | Michigan | 9-0-0 | Bennie Oosterbaan |
| 2. | Notre Dame | 9-0-1 | Frank Leahy |
| 3. | North Carolina | 9-0-1 | Carl Snavely |
| 4. | California | 10-0-0 | Pappy Waldorf |
| 5. | Oklahoma | 9-1-0 | Bud Wilkinson |
| 6. | Army | 8-0-1 | Red Blaik |
| 7. | Northwestern | 7-2-0 | Bob Voigts |
| 8. | Georgia | 9-1-0 | Wally Butts |
| 9. | Oregon | 9-1-0 | Jim Aiken |
| 10. | SMU | 8-1-1 | Matty Bell |
| 11. | Clemson | 10-0-0 | Frank Howard |
| 12. | Vanderbilt | 8-2-1 | Red Sanders |
| 13. | Tulane | 9-1-0 | Henry Frnka |
| 14. | Michigan St | 6-2-2 | Biggie Munn |
| 15. | Mississippi | 8-1-0 | Johnny Vaught |
| 16. | Minnesota | 7-2-0 | Bernie Bierman |
| 17. | William & Mary | 6-2-2 | Rube McCray |
| 18. | Penn St | 7-1-1 | Bob Higgins |
| 19. | Cornell | 8-1-0 | Lefty James |
| 20. | Wake Forest | 6-3-0 | Peahead Walker |

### 1949

| | | Record | Coach |
|---|---|---|---|
| 1. | Notre Dame | 10-0-0 | Frank Leahy |
| 2. | Oklahoma | 10-0-0 | Bud Wilkinson |
| 3. | California | 10-0-0 | Pappy Waldorf |
| 4. | Army | 9-0-0 | Red Blaik |
| 5. | Rice | 9-1-0 | Jess Neely |
| 6. | Ohio St | 6-1-2 | Wes Fesler |
| 7. | Michigan | 6-2-1 | Bennie Oosterbaan |
| 8. | Minnesota | 7-2-0 | Bernie Bierman |
| 9. | LSU | 8-2-0 | Gaynell Tinsley |
| 10. | Pacific | 11-0-0 | Larry Siemering |
| 11. | Kentucky | 9-2-0 | Bear Bryant |
| 12. | Cornell | 8-1-0 | Lefty James |
| 13. | Villanova | 8-1-0 | Jim Leonard |
| 14. | Maryland | 8-1-0 | Jim Tatum |

### 1949 *(Cont.)*

| | | Record | Coach |
|---|---|---|---|
| 15. | Santa Clara | 7-2-1 | Len Casanova |
| 16. | North Carolina | 7-3-0 | Carl Snavely |
| 17. | Tennessee | 7-2-1 | Bob Neyland |
| 18. | Princeton | 6-3-0 | Charlie Caldwell |
| 19. | Michigan St | 6-3-0 | Biggie Munn |
| 20. | Missouri | 7-3-0 | Don Faurot |
| | Baylor | 8-2-0 | Bob Woodruff |

### 1950

| | | Record | Coach |
|---|---|---|---|
| 1. | Oklahoma | 10-0-0 | Bud Wilkinson |
| 2. | Army | 8-1-0 | Red Blaik |
| 3. | Texas | 9-1-0 | Blair Cherry |
| 4. | Tennessee | 10-1-0 | Bob Neyland |
| 5. | California | 9-0-1 | Pappy Waldorf |
| 6. | Princeton | 9-0-0 | Charlie Caldwell |
| 7. | Kentucky | 10-1-0 | Bear Bryant |
| 8. | Michigan St | 8-1-0 | Biggie Munn |
| 9. | Michigan | 5-3-1 | Bennie Oosterhaan |
| 10. | Clemson | 8-0-1 | Frank Howard |
| 11. | Washington | 8-2-0 | Howard Odell |
| 12. | Wyoming | 9-0-0 | Bowden Wyatt |
| 13. | Illinois | 7-2-0 | Ray Eliot |
| 14. | Ohio St | 6-3-0 | Wes Fesler |
| 15. | Miami (FL) | 9-0-1 | Andy Gustafson |
| 16. | Alabama | 9-2-0 | Red Drew |
| 17. | Nebraska | 6-2-1 | Bill Glassford |
| 18. | Washington & Lee | 8-2-0 | George Barclay |
| 19. | Tulsa | 9-1-1 | J.O. Brothers |
| 20. | Tulane | 6-2-1 | Henry Frnka |

### 1951

| | | Record | Coach |
|---|---|---|---|
| 1. | Tennessee | 10-0-0 | Bob Neyland |
| 2. | Michigan St | 9-0-0 | Biggie Munn |
| 3. | Maryland | 9-0-0 | Jim Tatum |
| 4. | Illinois | 8-0-1 | Ray Eliot |
| 5. | Georgia Tech | 10-0-1 | Bobby Dodd |
| 6. | Princeton | 9-0-0 | Charlie Caldwell |
| 7. | Stanford | 9-1-0 | Chuck Taylor |
| 8. | Wisconsin | 7-1-1 | Ivy Williamson |
| 9. | Baylor | 8-1-1 | George Sauer |
| 10. | Oklahoma | 8-2-0 | Bud Wilkinson |
| 11. | TCU | 6-4-0 | Dutch Meyer |
| 12. | California | 8-2-0 | Pappy Waldorf |
| 13. | Virginia | 8-1-0 | Art Guepe |
| 14. | San Francisco | 9-0-0 | Joe Kuharich |
| 15. | Kentucky | 7-4-0 | Bear Bryant |
| 16. | Boston University | 6-4-0 | Buff Donelli |
| 17. | UCLA | 5-3-1 | Red Sanders |
| 18. | Washington St | 7-3-0 | Forest Evashevski |
| 19. | Holy Cross | 8-2-0 | Eddie Anderson |
| 20. | Clemson | 7-2-0 | Frank Howard |

### 1952

| | | Record | Coach |
|---|---|---|---|
| 1. | Michigan St | 9-0-0 | Biggie Munn |
| 2. | Georgia Tech | 11-0-0 | Bobby Dodd |
| 3. | Notre Dame | 7-2-1 | Frank Leahy |
| 4. | Oklahoma | 8-1-1 | Bud Wilkinson |
| 5. | USC | 9-1-0 | Jess Hill |
| 6. | UCLA | 8-1-0 | Red Sanders |
| 7. | Mississippi | 8-0-2 | Johnny Vaught |

## 1952 *(Cont.)*

| | | Record | Coach |
|---|---|---|---|
| 8. | Tennessee | 8-1-1 | Bob Neyland |
| 9. | Alabama | 9-2-0 | Red Drew |
| 10. | Texas | 8-2-0 | Ed Price |
| 11. | Wisconsin | 6-2-1 | Ivy Williamson |
| 12. | Tulsa | 8-1-1 | J.O. Brothers |
| 13. | Maryland | 7-2-0 | Jim Tatum |
| 14. | Syracuse | 7-2-0 | Ben Schwartzwalder |
| 15. | Florida | 7-3-0 | Bob Woodruff |
| 16. | Duke | 8-2-0 | Bill Murray |
| 17. | Ohio St | 6-3-0 | Woody Hayes |
| 18. | Purdue | 4-3-2 | Stu Holcomb |
| 19. | Princeton | 8-1-0 | Charlie Caldwell |
| 20. | Kentucky | 5-4-2 | Bear Bryant |

## 1953

| | | Record | Coach |
|---|---|---|---|
| 1. | Maryland | 10-0-0 | Jim Tatum |
| 2. | Notre Dame | 9-0-1 | Frank Leahy |
| 3. | Michigan St | 8-1-0 | Biggie Munn |
| 4. | Oklahoma | 8-1-1 | Bud Wilkinson |
| 5. | UCLA | 8-1-0 | Red Sanders |
| 6. | Rice | 8-2-0 | Jess Neely |
| 7. | Illinois | 7-1-1 | Ray Eliot |
| 8. | Georgia Tech | 8-2-1 | Bobby Dodd |
| 9. | Iowa | 5-3-1 | Forest Evashevski |
| 10. | W Virginia | 8-1-0 | Art Lewis |
| 11. | Texas | 7-3-0 | Ed Price |
| 12. | Texas Tech | 10-1-0 | DeWitt Weaver |
| 13. | Alabama | 6-2-3 | Red Drew |
| 14. | Army | 7-1-1 | Red Blaik |
| 15. | Wisconsin | 6-2-1 | Ivy Williamson |
| 16. | Kentucky | 7-2-1 | Bear Bryant |
| 17. | Auburn | 7-2-1 | Shug Jordan |
| 18. | Duke | 7-2-1 | Bill Murray |
| 19. | Stanford | 6-3-1 | Chuck Taylor |
| 20. | Michigan | 6-3-0 | Bennie Oosterbaan |

## 1954

| | | Record | Coach |
|---|---|---|---|
| 1. | Ohio St | 9-0-0 | Woody Hayes |
| 2. | #UCLA | 9-0-0 | Red Sanders |
| 3. | Oklahoma | 10-0-0 | Bud Wilkinson |
| 4. | Notre Dame | 9-1-0 | Terry Brennan |
| 5. | Navy | 7-2-0 | Eddie Erdelatz |
| 6. | Mississippi | 9-1-0 | Johnny Vaught |
| 7. | Army | 7-2-0 | Red Blaik |
| 8. | Maryland | 7-2-1 | Jim Tatum |
| 9. | Wisconsin | 7-2-0 | Ivy Williamson |
| 10. | Arkansas | 8-2-0 | Bowden Wyatt |
| 11. | Miami (FL) | 8-1-0 | Andy Gustafson |
| 12. | W Virginia | 8-1-0 | Art Lewis |
| 13. | Auburn | 7-3-0 | Shug Jordan |
| 14. | Duke | 7-2-1 | Bill Murray |
| 15. | Michigan | 6-3-0 | Bennie Oosterbaan |
| 16. | Virginia Tech | 8-0-1 | Frank Moseley |
| 17. | USC | 8-3-0 | Jess Hill |
| 18. | Baylor | 7-3-0 | George Sauer |
| 19. | Rice | 7-3-0 | Jess Neely |
| 20. | Penn St | 7-2-0 | Rip Engle |

#Selected No. 1 by UP.

## 1955

| | | Record | Coach |
|---|---|---|---|
| 1. | Oklahoma | 10-0-0 | Bud Wilkinson |
| 2. | Michigan St | 8-1-0 | Duffy Daugherty |
| 3. | Maryland | 10-0-0 | Jim Tatum |
| 4. | UCLA | 9-1-0 | Red Sanders |
| 5. | Ohio St | 7-2-0 | Woody Hayes |
| 6. | TCU | 9-1-0 | Abe Martin |
| 7. | Georgia Tech | 8-1-1 | Bobby Dodd |
| 8. | Auburn | 8-1-1 | Shug Jordan |
| 9. | Notre Dame | 8-2-0 | Terry Brennan |
| 10. | Mississippi | 9-1-0 | Johnny Vaught |
| 11. | Pittsburgh | 7-3-0 | John Michelosen |
| 12. | Michigan | 7-2-0 | Bennie Oosterbaan |
| 13. | USC | 6-4-0 | Jess Hill |
| 14. | Miami (FL) | 6-3-0 | Andy Gustafson |
| 15. | Miami (OH) | 9-0-0 | Ara Parseghian |
| 16. | Stanford | 6-3-1 | Chuck Taylor |
| 17. | Texas A&M | 7-2-1 | Bear Bryant |
| 18. | Navy | 6-2-1 | Eddie Erdelatz |
| 19. | W Virginia | 8-2-0 | Art Lewis |
| 20. | Army | 6-3-0 | Red Blaik |

## 1956

| | | Record | Coach |
|---|---|---|---|
| 1. | Oklahoma | 10-0-0 | Bud Wilkinson |
| 2. | Tennessee | 10-0-0 | Bowden Wyatt |
| 3. | Iowa | 8-1-0 | Forest Evashevski |
| 4. | Georgia Tech. | 9-1-0 | Bobby Dodd |
| 5. | Texas A&M | 9-0-1 | Bear Bryant |
| 6. | Miami (FL) | 8-1-1 | Andy Gustafson |
| 7. | Michigan | 7-2-0 | Bennie Oosterbaan |
| 8. | Syracuse | 7-1-0 | Ben Schwartzwalder |
| 9. | Michigan St | 7-2-0 | Duffy Daugherty |
| 10. | Oregon St | 7-2-1 | Tommy Prothro |
| 11. | Baylor | 8-2-0 | Sam Boyd |
| 12. | Minnesota | 6-1-2 | Murray Warmath |
| 13. | Pittsburgh | 7-2-1 | John Michelosen |
| 14. | TCU | 7-3-0 | Abe Martin |
| 15. | Ohio St | 6-3-0 | Woody Hayes |
| 16. | Navy | 6-1-2 | Eddie Erdelatz |
| 17. | Geo Washington | 7-1-1 | Gene Sherman |
| 18. | USC | 8-2-0 | Jess Hill |
| 19. | Clemson | 7-1-2 | Frank Howard |
| 20. | Colorado | 7-2-1 | Dallas Ward |
| | Penn St | 6-2-1 | Rip Engle |

## 1957

| | | Record | Coach |
|---|---|---|---|
| 1. | Auburn | 10-0-0 | Shug Jordan |
| 2. | #Ohio St | 8-1-0 | Woody Hayes |
| 3. | Michigan St | 8-1-0 | Duffy Daugherty |
| 4. | Oklahoma | 9-1-0 | Bud Wilkinson |
| 5. | Navy | 8-1-1 | Eddie Erdelatz |
| 6. | Iowa | 7-1-1 | Forest Evashevski |
| 7. | Mississippi | 8-1-1 | Johnny Vaught |
| 8. | Rice | 7-3-0 | Jess Neely |
| 9. | Texas A&M | 8-2-0 | Bear Bryant |
| 10. | Notre Dame | 7-3-0 | Terry Brennan |
| 11. | Texas | 6-3-1 | Darrell Royal |
| 12. | Arizona St | 10-0-0 | Dan Devine |
| 13. | Tennessee | 7-3-0 | Bowden Wyatt |
| 14. | Mississippi St | 6-2-1 | Wade Walker |
| 15. | North Carolina St | 7-1-2 | Earle Edwards |
| 16. | Duke | 6-2-2 | Bill Murray |

## 1957 (Cont.)

| | | Record | Coach |
|---|---|---|---|
| 17. | Florida | 6-2-1 | Bob Woodruff |
| 18. | Army | 7-2-0 | Red Blaik |
| 19. | Wisconsin | 6-3-0 | Milt Brunt |
| 20. | VMI | 9-0-1 | John McKenna |

#Selected No. 1 by UP.

## 1958

| | | Record | Coach |
|---|---|---|---|
| 1. | LSU | 10-0-0 | Paul Dietzel |
| 2. | Iowa | 7-1-1 | Forest Evashevski |
| 3. | Army | 8-0-1 | Red Blaik |
| 4. | Auburn | 9-0-1 | Shug Jordan |
| 5. | Oklahoma | 9-1-0 | Bud Wilkinson |
| 6. | Air Force | 9-0-1 | Ben Martin |
| 7. | Wisconsin | 7-1-1 | Milt Bruhn |
| 8. | Ohio St | 6-1-2 | Woody Hayes |
| 9. | Syracuse | 8-1-0 | Ben Schwartzwalder |
| 10. | TCU | 8-2-0 | Abe Martin |
| 11. | Mississippi | 8-2-0 | Johnny Vaught |
| 12. | Clemson | 8-2-0 | Frank Howard |
| 13. | Purdue | 6-1-2 | Jack Mollenkopf |
| 14. | Florida | 6-3-1 | Bob Woodruff |
| 15. | South Carolina | 7-3-0 | Warren Giese |
| 16. | California | 7-3-0 | Pete Elliott |
| 17. | Notre Dame | 6-4-0 | Terry Brennan |
| 18. | SMU | 6-4-0 | Bill Meek |
| 19. | Oklahoma St | 7-3-0 | Cliff Speegle |
| 20. | Rutgers | 8-1-0 | John Stiegman |

## 1959

| | | Record | Coach |
|---|---|---|---|
| 1. | Syracuse | 10-0-0 | Ben Schwartzwalder |
| 2. | Mississippi | 9-1-0 | Johnny Vaught |
| 3. | LSU | 9-1-0 | Paul Dietzel |
| 4. | Texas | 9-1-0 | Darrell Royal |
| 5. | Georgia | 9-1-0 | Wally Butts |
| 6. | Wisconsin | 7-2-0 | Milt Bruhn |
| 7. | TCU | 8-2-0 | Abe Martin |
| 8. | Washington | 9-1-0 | Jim Owens |
| 9. | Arkansas | 8-2-0 | Frank Broyles |
| 10. | Alabama | 7-1-2 | Bear Bryant |
| 11. | Clemson | 8-2-0 | Frank Howard |
| 12. | Penn St | 8-2-0 | Rip Engle |
| 13. | Illinois | 5-3-1 | Ray Eliot |
| 14. | USC | 8-2-0 | Don Clark |
| 15. | Oklahoma | 7-3-0 | Bud Wilkinson |
| 16. | Wyoming | 9-1-0 | Bob Devaney |
| 17. | Notre Dame | 5-5-0 | Joe Kuharich |
| 18. | Missouri | 6-4-0 | Dan Devine |
| 19. | Florida | 5-4-1 | Bob Woodruff |
| 20. | Pittsburgh | 6-4-0 | John Michelosen |

## 1960

| | | Record | Coach |
|---|---|---|---|
| 1. | Minnesota | 8-1-0 | Murray Warmath |
| 2. | Mississippi | 9-0-1 | Johnny Vaught |
| 3. | Iowa | 8-1-0 | Forest Evashevski |
| 4. | Navy | 9-1-0 | Wayne Hardin |
| 5. | Missouri | 9-1-0 | Dan Devine |
| 6. | Washington | 9-1-0 | Jim Owens |
| 7. | Arkansas | 8-2-0 | Frank Broyles |
| 8. | Ohio St | 7-2-0 | Woody Hayes |
| 9. | Alabama | 8-1-1 | Bear Bryant |

## 1960 (Cont.)

| | | Record | Coach |
|---|---|---|---|
| 10. | Duke | 7-3-0 | Bill Murray |
| 11. | Kansas | 7-2-1 | Jack Mitchell |
| 12. | Baylor | 8-2-0 | John Bridgers |
| 13. | Auburn | 8-2-0 | Shug Jordan |
| 14. | Yale | 9-0-0 | Jordan Oliver |
| 15. | Michigan St | 6-2-1 | Duffy Daugherty |
| 16. | Penn St | 6-3-0 | Rip Engle |
| 17. | New Mexico St | 10-0-0 | Warren Woodson |
| 18. | Florida | 8-2-0 | Ray Graves |
| 19. | Syracuse | 7-2-0 | Ben Schwartzwalder |
| | Purdue | 4-4-1 | Jack Mollenkopf |

## 1961

| | | Record | Coach |
|---|---|---|---|
| 1. | Alabama | 10-0-0 | Bear Bryant |
| 2. | Ohio St | 8-0-1 | Woody Hayes |
| 3. | Texas | 9-1-0 | Darrell Royal |
| 4. | LSU | 9-1-0 | Paul Dietzel |
| 5. | Mississippi | 9-1-0 | Johnny Vaught |
| 6. | Minnesota | 7-2-0 | Murray Warmath |
| 7. | Colorado | 9-1-0 | Sonny Grandelius |
| 8. | Michigan St | 7-2-0 | Duffy Daugherty |
| 9. | Arkansas | 8-2-0 | Frank Broyles |
| 10. | Utah St | 9-0-1 | John Ralston |
| 11. | Missouri | 7-2-1 | Dan Devine |
| 12. | Purdue | 6-3-0 | Jack Mollenkopf |
| 13. | Georgia Tech | 7-3-0 | Bobby Dodd |
| 14. | Syracuse | 7-3-0 | Ben Schwartzwalder |
| 15. | Rutgers | 9-0-0 | John Bateman |
| 16. | UCLA | 7-3-0 | Bill Barnes |
| 17. | Rice | 7-3-0 | Jess Neely |
| | Penn St | 7-3-0 | Rip Engle |
| | Arizona | 8-1-1 | Jim LaRue |
| 20. | Duke | 7-3-0 | Bill Murray |

## 1962

| | | Record | Coach |
|---|---|---|---|
| 1. | USC | 10-0-0 | John McKay |
| 2. | Wisconsin | 8-1-0 | Milt Bruhn |
| 3. | Mississippi | 9-0-0 | Johnny Vaught |
| 4. | Texas | 9-0-1 | Darrell Royal |
| 5. | Alabama | 9-1-0 | Bear Bryant |
| 6. | Arkansas | 9-1-0 | Frank Broyles |
| 7. | LSU | 8-1-1 | Charlie McClendon |
| 8. | Oklahoma | 8-2-0 | Bud Wilkinson |
| 9. | Penn St | 9-1-0 | Rip Engle |
| 10. | Minnesota | 6-2-1 | Murray Warmath |

11-20: UPI

| | | Record | Coach |
|---|---|---|---|
| 11. | Georgia Tech | 7-2-1 | Bobby Dodd |
| 12. | Missouri | 7-1-2 | Dan Devine |
| 13. | Ohio St | 6-3-0 | Woody Hayes |
| 14. | Duke | 8-2-0 | Bill Murray |
| | Washington | 7-1-2 | Jim Owens |
| 16. | Northwestern | 7-2-0 | Ara Parseghian |
| | Oregon St | 8-2-0 | Tommy Prothro |
| 18. | Arizona St | 7-2-1 | Frank Kush |
| | Miami (FL) | 7-3-0 | Andy Gustafson |
| | Illinois | 2-7-0 | Pete Elliott |

## 1963

| | | Record | Coach |
|---|---|---|---|
| 1. | Texas | 10-0-0 | Darrell Royal |
| 2. | Navy | 9-1-0 | Wayne Hardin |
| 3. | Illinois | 7-1-1 | Pete Elliott |

## 1963 *(Cont.)*

| | | Record | Coach |
|---|---|---|---|
| 4. | Pittsburgh | 9-1-0 | John Michelosen |
| 5. | Auburn | 9-1-0 | Shug Jordan |
| 6. | Nebraska | 9-1-0 | Bob Devaney |
| 7. | Mississippi | 7-0-2 | Johnny Vaught |
| 8. | Alabama | 8-2-0 | Bear Bryant |
| 9. | Oklahoma | 8-2-0 | Bud Wilkinson |
| 10. | Michigan St | 6-2-1 | Duffy Daugherty |

**11–20: UPI**

| | | | |
|---|---|---|---|
| 11. | Mississippi St | 6-2-2 | Paul Davis |
| 12. | Syracuse | 8-2-0 | Ben Schwartzwalder |
| 13. | Arizona St | 8-1-0 | Frank Kush |
| 14. | Memphis St | 9-0-1 | Billy J. Murphy |
| 15. | Washington | 6-4-0 | Jim Owens |
| 16. | Penn St | 7-3-0 | Rip Engle |
| | USC | 7-3-0 | John McKay |
| | Missouri | 7-3-0 | Dan Devine |
| 19. | North Carolina | 8-2-0 | Jim Hickey |
| 20. | Baylor | 7-3-0 | John Bridgers |

## 1964

| | | Record | Coach |
|---|---|---|---|
| 1. | Alabama | 10-0-0 | Bear Bryant |
| 2. | Arkansas | 11-0-0 | Frank Broyles |
| 3. | Notre Dame | 9-1-0 | Ara Parseghian |
| 4. | Michigan | 8-1-0 | Bump Elliott |
| 5. | Texas | 9-1-0 | Darrell Royal |
| 6. | Nebraska | 9-1-0 | Bob Devaney |
| 7. | LSU | 7-2-1 | Charlie McClendon |
| 8. | Oregon St | 8-2-0 | Tommy Prothro |
| 9. | Ohio St | 7-2-0 | Woody Hayes |
| 10. | USC | 7-3-0 | John McKay |

**11–20: UPI**

| | | | |
|---|---|---|---|
| 11. | Florida St | 8-1-1 | Bill Peterson |
| 12. | Syracuse | 7-3-0 | Ben Schwartzwalder |
| 13. | Princeton | 9-0-0 | Dick Colman |
| 14. | Penn St | 6-4-0 | Rip Engle |
| | Utah | 8-2-0 | Ray Nagel |
| 16. | Illinois | 6-3-0 | Pete Elliott |
| | New Mexico | 9-2-0 | Bill Weeks |
| 18. | Tulsa | 8-2-0 | Glenn Dobbs |
| 19. | Missouri | 6-3-1 | Dan Devine |
| 20. | Mississippi | 5-4-1 | Johnny Vaught |
| | Michigan St | 4-5-1 | Duffy Daugherty |

## 1965

| | | Record | Coach |
|---|---|---|---|
| 1. | Alabama | 9-1-1 | Bear Bryant |
| 2. | #Michigan St | 10-1-0 | Duffy Daugherty |
| 3. | Arkansas | 10-1-0 | Frank Broyles |
| 4. | UCLA | 8-2-1 | Tommy Prothro |
| 5. | Nebraska | 10-1-0 | Bob Devaney |
| 6. | Missouri | 8-2-1 | Dan Devine |
| 7. | Tennessee | 8-1-2 | Doug Dickey |
| 8. | LSU | 8-3-0 | Charlie McClendon |
| 9. | Notre Dame | 7-2-1 | Ara Parseghian |
| 10. | USC | 7-2-1 | John McKay |

**11–20: UPI**

| | | | |
|---|---|---|---|
| 11. | Texas Tech | 8-2-0 | J.T. King |
| 12. | Ohio St | 7-2-0 | Woody Hayes |
| 13. | Florida | 7-3-0 | Ray Graves |
| 14. | Purdue | 7-2-1 | Jack Mollenkopf |
| 15. | Georgia | 6-4-0 | Vince Dooley |
| 16. | Tulsa | 8-2-0 | Glenn Dobbs |
| 17. | Mississippi | 6-4-0 | Johnny Vaught |

## 1965 *(Cont.)*

| | | Record | Coach |
|---|---|---|---|
| 18. | Kentucky | 6-4-0 | Charlie Bradshaw |
| 19 | Syracuse | 7-3-0 | Ben Schwartzwalder |
| 20. | Colorado | 6-2-2 | Eddie Crowder |

#Selected No. 1 by UPI.

## 1966*

| | | Record | Coach |
|---|---|---|---|
| 1. | Notre Dame | 9-0-1 | Ara Parseghian |
| 2. | Michigan St | 9-0-1 | Duffy Daugherty |
| 3. | Alabama | 10-0-0 | Bear Bryant |
| 4. | Georgia | 9-1-0 | Vince Dooley |
| 5. | UCLA | 9-1-0 | Tommy Prothro |
| 6. | Nebraska | 9-1-0 | Bob Devaney |
| 7. | Purdue | 8-2-0 | Jack Mollenkopf |
| 8. | Georgia Tech | 9-1-0 | Bobby Dodd |
| 9. | Miami (FL) | 7-2-1 | Charlie Tate |
| 10. | SMU | 8-2-0 | Hayden Fry |

**11–20: UPI**

| | | | |
|---|---|---|---|
| 11. | Florida | 8-2-0 | Ray Graves |
| 12. | Mississippi | 8-2-0 | Johnny Vaught |
| 13. | Arkansas | 8-2-0 | Frank Broyles |
| 14. | Tennessee | 7-3-0 | Doug Dickey |
| 15. | Wyoming | 9-1-0 | Lloyd Eaton |
| 16. | Syracuse | 8-2-0 | Ben Schwartzwalder |
| 17. | Houston | 8-2-0 | Bill Yeoman |
| 18. | USC | 7-3-0 | John McKay |
| 19. | Oregon St | 7-3-0 | Dee Andros |
| 20. | Virginia Tech | 8-1-1 | Jerry Claiborne |

## 1967*

| | | Record | Coach |
|---|---|---|---|
| 1. | USC | 9-1-0 | John McKay |
| 2. | Tennessee | 9-1-0 | Doug Dickey |
| 3. | Oklahoma | 9-1-0 | Chuck Fairbanks |
| 4. | Indiana | 9-1-0 | John Pont |
| 5. | Notre Dame | 8-2-0 | Ara Parseghian |
| 6. | Wyoming | 10-0-0 | Lloyd Eaton |
| 7. | Oregon St | 7-2-1 | Dee Andros |
| 8. | Alabama | 8-1-1 | Bear Bryant |
| 9. | Purdue | 8-2-0 | Jack Mollenkopf |
| 10. | Penn St | 8-2-0 | Joe Paterno |

**11–20: UPI†**

| | | | |
|---|---|---|---|
| 11. | UCLA | 7-2-1 | Tommy Prothro |
| 12. | Syracuse | 8-2-0 | Ben Schwartzwalder |
| 13. | Colorado | 8-2-0 | Eddie Crowder |
| 14. | Minnesota | 8-2-0 | Murray Warmath |
| 15. | Florida St | 7-2-1 | Bill Peterson |
| 16. | Miami (FL) | 7-3-0 | Charlie Tate |
| 17. | North Carolina St | 8-2-0 | Earle Edwards |
| 18. | Georgia | 7-3-0 | Vince Dooley |
| 19. | Houston | 9-2-0 | Bill Yeoman |
| 20. | Arizona St | 8-2-0 | Frank Kush |

†UPI ranked Penn St 11th and did not rank Alabama, which was on probation.

## 1968

| | | Record | Coach |
|---|---|---|---|
| 1. | Ohio St | 10-0-0 | Woody Hayes |
| 2. | Penn St | 11-0-0 | Joe Paterno |
| 3. | Texas | 9-1-1 | Darrell Royal |
| 4. | USC | 9-1-1 | John McKay |
| 5. | Notre Dame | 7-2-1 | Ara Parseghian |

## 1968 *(Cont.)*

| | | Record | Coach |
|---|---|---|---|
| 6. | Arkansas | 10-1-0 | Frank Broyles |
| 7. | Kansas | 9-2-0 | Pepper Rodgers |
| 8. | Georgia | 8-1-2 | Vince Dooley |
| 9. | Missouri | 8-3-0 | Dan Devine |
| 10. | Purdue | 8-2-0 | Jack Mollenkopf |
| 11. | Oklahoma | 7-4-0 | Chuck Fairbanks |
| 12. | Michigan | 8-2-0 | Bump Elliott |
| 13. | Tennessee | 8-2-1 | Doug Dickey |
| 14. | SMU | 8-3-0 | Hayden Fry |
| 15. | Oregon St | 7-3-0 | Dee Andros |
| 16. | Auburn | 7-4-0 | Shug Jordan |
| 17. | Alabama | 8-3-0 | Bear Bryant |
| 18. | Houston | 6-2-2 | Bill Yeoman |
| 19. | LSU | 8-3-0 | Charlie McClendon |
| 20. | Ohio | 10-1-0 | Bill Hess |

## 1969

| | | Record | Coach |
|---|---|---|---|
| 1. | Texas | 11-0-0 | Darrell Royal |
| 2. | Penn St | 11-0-0 | Joe Paterno |
| 3. | USC | 10-0-1 | John McKay |
| 4. | Ohio St | 8-1-0 | Woody Hayes |
| 5. | Notre Dame | 8-2-1 | Ara Parseghian |
| 6. | Missouri | 9-2-0 | Dan Devine |
| 7. | Arkansas | 9-2-0 | Frank Broyles |
| 8. | Mississippi | 8-3-0 | Johnny Vaught |
| 9. | Michigan | 8-3-0 | Bo Schembechler |
| 10. | LSU | 9-1-0 | Charlie McClendon |
| 11. | Nebraska | 9-2-0 | Bob Devaney |
| 12. | Houston | 9-2-0 | Bill Yeoman |
| 13. | UCLA | 8-1-1 | Tommy Prothro |
| 14. | Florida | 9-1-1 | Ray Graves |
| 15. | Tennessee | 9-2-0 | Doug Dickey |
| 16. | Colorado | 8-3-0 | Eddie Crowder |
| 17. | W Virginia | 10-0-1 | Jim Carlen |
| 18. | Purdue | 8-2-0 | Jack Mollenkopf |
| 19. | Stanford | 7-2-1 | John Ralston |
| 20. | Auburn | 8-3-0 | Shug Jordan |

## 1970

| | | Record | Coach |
|---|---|---|---|
| 1. | Nebraska | 11-0-1 | Bob Devaney |
| 2. | Notre Dame | 10-1-0 | Ara Parseghian |
| 3. | #Texas | 10-1-0 | Darrell Royal |
| 4. | Tennessee | 11-0-1 | Bill Battle |
| 5. | Ohio St | 9-1-0 | Woody Hayes |
| 6. | Arizona St | 11-0-0 | Frank Kush |
| 7. | LSU | 9-3-0 | Charlie McClendon |
| 8. | Stanford | 9-3-0 | John Ralston |
| 9. | Michigan | 9-1-0 | Bo Schembechler |
| 10. | Auburn | 9-2-0 | Shug Jordan |
| 11. | Arkansas | 9-2-0 | Frank Broyles |
| 12. | Toledo | 12-0-0 | Frank Lauterbur |
| 13. | Georgia Tech | 9-3-0 | Bud Carson |
| 14. | Dartmouth | 9-0-0 | Bob Blackman |
| 15. | USC | 6-4-1 | John McKay |
| 16. | Air Force | 9-3-0 | Ben Martin |
| 17. | Tulane | 8-4-0 | Jim Pittman |
| 18. | Penn St | 7-3-0 | Joe Paterno |
| 19. | Houston | 8-3-0 | Bill Yeoman |
| 20. | Oklahoma | 7-4-1 | Chuck Fairbanks |
| | Mississippi | 7-4-0 | Johnny Vaught |

#Selected No. 1 by UPI.

## 1971

| | | Record | Coach |
|---|---|---|---|
| 1. | Nebraska | 13-0-0 | Bob Devaney |
| 2. | Oklahoma | 11-1-0 | Chuck Fairbanks |
| 3. | Colorado | 10-2-0 | Eddie Crowder |
| 4. | Alabama | 11-1-0 | Bear Bryant |
| 5. | Penn St | 11-1-0 | Joe Paterno |
| 6. | Michigan | 11-1-0 | Bo Schembechler |
| 7. | Georgia | 11-1-0 | Vince Dooley |
| 8. | Arizona St | 11-1-0 | Frank Kush |
| 9. | Tennessee | 10-2-0 | Bill Battle |
| 10. | Stanford | 9-3-0 | John Ralston |
| 11. | LSU | 9-3-0 | Charlie McClendon |
| 12. | Auburn | 9-2-0 | Shug Jordan |
| 13. | Notre Dame | 8-2-0 | Ara Parseghian |
| 14. | Toledo | 12-0-0 | John Murphy |
| 15. | Mississippi | 10-2-0 | Billy Kinard |
| 16. | Arkansas | 8-3-1 | Frank Broyles |
| 17. | Houston | 9-3-0 | Bill Yeoman |
| 18. | Texas | 8-3-0 | Darrell Royal |
| 19. | Washington | 8-3-0 | Jim Owens |
| 20. | USC | 6-4-1 | John McKay |

## 1972

| | | Record | Coach |
|---|---|---|---|
| 1. | USC | 12-0-0 | John McKay |
| 2. | Oklahoma | 11-1-0 | Chuck Fairbanks |
| 3. | Texas | 10-1-0 | Darrell Royal |
| 4. | Nebraska | 9-2-1 | Bob Devaney |
| 5. | Auburn | 10-1-0 | Shug Jordan |
| 6. | Michigan | 10-1-0 | Bo Schembechler |
| 7. | Alabama | 10-2-0 | Bear Bryant |
| 8. | Tennessee | 10-2-0 | Bill Battle |
| 9. | Ohio St | 9-2-0 | Woody Hayes |
| 10. | Penn St | 10-2-0 | Joe Paterno |
| 11. | LSU | 9-2-1 | Charlie McClendon |
| 12. | North Carolina | 11-1-0 | Bill Dooley |
| 13. | Arizona St | 10-2-0 | Frank Kush |
| 14. | Notre Dame | 8-3-0 | Ara Parseghian |
| 15. | UCLA | 8-3-0 | Pepper Rodgers |
| 16. | Colorado | 8-4-0 | Eddie Crowder |
| 17. | North Carolina St | 8-3-1 | Lou Holtz |
| 18. | Louisville | 9-1-0 | Lee Corso |
| 19. | Washington St | 7-4-0 | Jim Sweeney |
| 20. | Georgia Tech | 7-4-1 | Bill Fulch |

## 1973

| | | Record | Coach |
|---|---|---|---|
| 1. | Notre Dame | 11-0-0 | Ara Parseghian |
| 2. | Ohio St | 10-0-1 | Woody Hayes |
| 3. | Oklahoma | 10-0-1 | Barry Switzer |
| 4. | #Alabama | 11-1-0 | Bear Bryant |
| 5. | Penn St | 12-0-0 | Joe Paterno |
| 6. | Michigan | 10-0-1 | Bo Schembechler |
| 7. | Nebraska | 9-2-1 | Tom Osborne |
| 8. | USC | 9-2-1 | John McKay |
| 9. | Arizona St | 11-1-0 | Frank Kush |
| | Houston | 11-1-0 | Bill Yeoman |
| 11. | Texas Tech | 11-1-0 | Jim Carlen |
| 12. | UCLA | 9-2-0 | Pepper Rodgers |
| 13. | LSU | 9-3-0 | Charlie McClendon |
| 14. | Texas | 8-3-0 | Darrell Royal |
| 15. | Miami (OH) | 11-0-0 | Bill Mallory |
| 16. | North Carolina St | 9-3-0 | Lou Holtz |
| 17. | Missouri | 8-4-0 | Al Onofrio |
| 18. | Kansas | 7-4-1 | Don Fambrough |

# Annual Associated Press Top 20 (Cont.)

## 1973 (Cont.)

| | | Record | Coach |
|---|---|---|---|
| 19. | Tennessee | 8-4-0 | Bill Battle |
| 20. | Maryland | 8-4-0 | Jerry Claiborne |
| | Tulane | 9-3-0 | Bennie Ellender |

#Selected No. 1 by UPI.

## 1974

| | | Record | Coach |
|---|---|---|---|
| 1. | Oklahoma | 11-0-0 | Barry Switzer |
| 2. | #USC | 10-1-1 | John McKay |
| 3. | Michigan | 10-1-0 | Bo Schembechler |
| 4. | Ohio St | 10-2-0 | Woody Hayes |
| 5. | Alabama | 11-1-0 | Bear Bryant |
| 6. | Notre Dame | 10-2-0 | Ara Parseghian |
| 7. | Penn St | 10-2-0 | Joe Paterno |
| 8. | Auburn | 10-2-0 | Shug Jordan |
| 9. | Nebraska | 9-3-0 | Tom Osborne |
| 10. | Miami (Ohio) | 10-0-1 | Dick Crum |
| 11. | North Carolina St | 9-2-1 | Lou Holtz |
| 12. | Michigan St | 7-3-1 | Denny Stolz |
| 13. | Maryland | 8-4-0 | Jerry Claiborne |
| 14. | Baylor | 8-4-0 | Grant Teaff |
| 15. | Florida | 8-4-0 | Doug Dickey |
| 16. | Texas A&M | 8-3-0 | Emory Ballard |
| 17. | Mississippi St | 9-3-0 | Bob Tyler |
| | Texas | 8-4-0 | Darrell Royal |
| 19. | Houston | 8-3-1 | Bill Yeoman |
| 20. | Tennessee | 7-3-2 | Bill Battle |

#Selected No. 1 by UPI

## 1975

| | | Record | Coach |
|---|---|---|---|
| 1. | Oklahoma | 11-1-0 | Barry Switzer |
| 2. | Arizona St | 12-0-0 | Frank Kush |
| 3. | Alabama | 11-1-0 | Bear Bryant |
| 4. | Ohio St | 11-1-0 | Woody Hayes |
| 5. | UCLA | 9-2-1 | Dick Vermeil |
| 6. | Texas | 10-2-0 | Darrell Royal |
| 7. | Arkansas | 10-2-0 | Frank Broyles |
| 8. | Michigan | 8-2-2 | Bo Schembechler |
| 9. | Nebraska | 10-2-0 | Tom Osborne |
| 10. | Penn St | 9-3-0 | Joe Paterno |
| 11. | Texas A&M | 10-2-0 | Emory Bellard |
| 12. | Miami (OH) | 11-1-0 | Dick Crum |
| 13. | Maryland | 9-2-1 | Jerry Claiborne |
| 14. | California | 8-3-0 | Mike White |
| 15. | Pittsburgh | 8-4-0 | Johnny Majors |
| 16. | Colorado | 9-3-0 | Bill Mallory |
| 17. | USC | 8-4-0 | John McKay |
| 18. | Arizona | 9-2-0 | Jim Young |
| 19. | Georgia | 9-3-0 | Vince Dooley |
| 20. | W Virginia | 9-3-0 | Bobby Bowden |

## 1976

| | | Record | Coach |
|---|---|---|---|
| 1. | Pittsburgh | 12-0-0 | Johnny Majors |
| 2. | USC | 11-1-0 | John Robinson |
| 3. | Michigan | 10-2-0 | Bo Schembechler |
| 4. | Houston | 10-2-0 | Bill Yeoman |
| 5. | Oklahoma | 9-2-1 | Barry Switzer |
| 6. | Ohio St | 9-2-1 | Woody Hayes |
| 7. | Texas A&M | 10-2-0 | Emory Bellard |
| 8. | Maryland | 11-1-0 | Jerry Claiborne |

## 1976 (Cont.)

| | | Record | Coach |
|---|---|---|---|
| 9. | Nebraska | 9-3-1 | Tom Osborne |
| 10. | Georgia | 10-2-0 | Vince Dooley |
| 11. | Alabama | 9-3-0 | Bear Bryant |
| 12. | Notre Dame | 9-3-0 | Dan Devine |
| 13. | Texas Tech | 10-2-0 | Steve Sloan |
| 14. | Oklahoma St | 9-3-0 | Jim Stanley |
| 15. | UCLA | 9-2-1 | Terry Donahue |
| 16. | Colorado | 8-4-0 | Bill Mallory |
| 17. | Rutgers | 11-0-0 | Frank Burns |
| 18. | Kentucky | 9-3-0 | Fran Curci |
| 19. | Iowa St | 8-3-0 | Earle Bruce |
| 20. | Mississippi St | 9-2-0 | Bob Tyler |

## 1977

| | | Record | Coach |
|---|---|---|---|
| 1. | Notre Dame | 11-1-0 | Dan Devine |
| 2. | Alabama | 11-1-0 | Bear Bryant |
| 3. | Arkansas | 11-1-0 | Lou Holtz |
| 4. | Texas | 11-1-0 | Fred Akers |
| 5. | Penn St | 11-1-0 | Joe Paterno |
| 6. | Kentucky | 10-1-0 | Fran Curci |
| 7. | Oklahoma | 10-2-0 | Barry Switzer |
| 8. | Pittsburgh | 9-2-1 | Jackie Sherrill |
| 9. | Michigan | 10-2-0 | Bo Schembechler |
| 10. | Washington | 10-2-0 | Don James |
| 11. | Ohio St | 9-3-0 | Woody Hayes |
| 12. | Nebraska | 9-3-0 | Tom Osborne |
| 13. | USC | 8-4-0 | John Robinson |
| 14. | Florida St | 10-2-0 | Bobby Bowden |
| 15. | Stanford | 9-3-0 | Bill Walsh |
| 16. | San Diego St | 10-1-0 | Claude Gilbert |
| 17. | North Carolina | 8-3-1 | Bill Dooley |
| 18. | Arizona St | 9-3-0 | Frank Kush |
| 19. | Clemson | 8-3-1 | Charley Pell |
| 20. | BYU | 9-2-0 | LaVell Edwards |

## 1978

| | | Record | Coach |
|---|---|---|---|
| 1. | Alabama | 11-1-0 | Bear Bryant |
| 2. | #USC | 12-1-0 | John Robinson |
| 3. | Oklahoma | 11-1-0 | Barry Switzer |
| 4. | Penn St | 11-1-0 | Joe Paterno |
| 5. | Michigan | 10-2-0 | Bo Schembechler |
| 6. | Clemson | 11-1-0 | Charley Pell |
| 7. | Notre Dame | 9-3-0 | Dan Devine |
| 8. | Nebraska | 9-3-0 | Tom Osborne |
| 9. | Texas | 9-3-0 | Fred Akers |
| 10. | Houston | 9-3-0 | Bill Yeoman |
| 11. | Arkansas | 9-2-1 | Lou Holtz |
| 12. | Michigan St | 8-3-0 | Darryl Rogers |
| 13. | Purdue | 9-2-1 | Jim Young |
| 14. | UCLA | 8-3-1 | Terry Donahue |
| 15. | Missouri | 8-4-0 | Warren Powers |
| 16. | Georgia | 9-2-1 | Vince Dooley |
| 17. | Stanford | 8-4-0 | Bill Walsh |
| 18. | North Carolina St | 9-3-0 | Bo Rein |
| 19. | Texas A&M | 8-4-0 | Emory Bellard (4–2) |
| | | | Tom Wilson (4–2) |
| 20. | Maryland | 9-3-0 | Jerry Claiborne |

#Selected No. 1 by UPI.

## 1979

| | | Record | Coach |
|---|---|---|---|
| 1. | Alabama | 12-0-0 | Bear Bryant |
| 2. | USC | 11-0-1 | John Robinson |
| 3. | Oklahoma | 11-1-0 | Barry Switzer |
| 4. | Ohio St | 11-1-0 | Earle Bruce |
| 5. | Houston | 11-1-0 | Bill Yeoman |
| 6. | Florida St | 11-1-0 | Bobby Bowden |
| 7. | Pittsburgh | 11-1-0 | Jackie Sherrill |
| 8. | Arkansas | 10-2-0 | Lou Holtz |
| 9. | Nebraska | 10-2-0 | Tom Osborne |
| 10. | Purdue | 10-2-0 | Jim Young |
| 11. | Washington | 10-1-0 | Don James |
| 12. | Texas | 9-3-0 | Fred Akers |
| 13. | BYU | 11-1-0 | LaVell Edwards |
| 14. | Baylor | 8-4-0 | Grant Teaff |
| 15. | North Carolina | 8-3-1 | Dick Crum |
| 16. | Auburn | 8-3-0 | Doug Barfield |
| 17. | Temple | 10-2-0 | Wayne Hardin |
| 18. | Michigan | 8-4-0 | Bo Schembechler |
| 19. | Indiana | 8-4-0 | Lee Corso |
| 20. | Penn St | 8-4-0 | Joe Paterno |

## 1980

| | | Record | Coach |
|---|---|---|---|
| 1. | Georgia | 12-0-0 | Vince Dooley |
| 2. | Pittsburgh | 11-1-0 | Jackie Sherrill |
| 3. | Oklahoma | 10-2-0 | Barry Switzer |
| 4. | Michigan | 10-2-0 | Bo Schembechler |
| 5. | Florida St | 10-2-0 | Bobby Bowden |
| 6. | Alabama | 10-2-0 | Bear Bryant |
| 7. | Nebraska | 10-2-0 | Tom Osborne |
| 8. | Penn St | 10-2-0 | Joe Paterno |
| 9. | Notre Dame | 9-2-1 | Dan Devine |
| 10. | North Carolina | 11-1-0 | Dick Crum |
| 11. | USC | 8-2-1 | John Robinson |
| 12. | BYU | 12-1-0 | LaVell Edwards |
| 13. | UCLA | 9-2-0 | Terry Donahue |
| 14. | Baylor | 10-2-0 | Grant Teaff |
| 15. | Ohio St | 9-3-0 | Earle Bruce |
| 16. | Washington | 9-3-0 | Don James |
| 17. | Purdue | 9-3-0 | Jim Young |
| 18. | Miami (FL) | 9-3-0 | H. Schnellenberger |
| 19. | Mississippi St | 9-3-0 | Emory Bellard |
| 20. | SMU | 8-4-0 | Ron Meyer |

## 1981

| | | Record | Coach |
|---|---|---|---|
| 1. | Clemson | 12-0-0 | Danny Ford |
| 2. | Texas | 10-1-1 | Fred Akers |
| 3. | Penn St | 10-2-0 | Joe Paterno |
| 4. | Pittsburgh | 11-1-0 | Jackie Sherrill |
| 5. | SMU | 10-1-0 | Ron Meyer |
| 6. | Georgia | 10-2-0 | Vince Dooley |
| 7. | Alabama | 9-2-1 | Bear Bryant |
| 8. | Miami (FL) | 9-2-0 | H. Schnellenberger |
| 9. | North Carolina | 10-2-0 | Dick Crum |
| 10. | Washington | 10-2-0 | Don James |
| 11. | Nebraska | 9-3-0 | Tom Osborne |
| 12. | Michigan | 9-3-0 | Bo Schembechler |
| 13. | BYU | 11-2-0 | LaVell Edwards |
| 14. | USC | 9-3-0 | John Robinson |
| 15. | Ohio St | 9-3-0 | Earle Bruce |
| 16. | Arizona St | 9-2-0 | Darryl Rogers |
| 17. | W Virginia | 9-3-0 | Don Nehlen |

## 1981 *(Cont.)*

| | | Record | Coach |
|---|---|---|---|
| 18. | Iowa | 8-4-0 | Hayden Fry |
| 19. | Missouri | 8-4-0 | Warren Powers |
| 20. | Oklahoma | 7-4-1 | Barry Switzer |

## 1982

| | | Record | Coach |
|---|---|---|---|
| 1. | Penn St | 11-1-0 | Joe Paterno |
| 2. | SMU | 11-0-1 | Bobby Collins |
| 3. | Nebraska | 12-1-0 | Tom Osborne |
| 4. | Georgia | 11-1-0 | Vince Dooley |
| 5. | UCLA | 10-1-1 | Terry Donahue |
| 6. | Arizona St | 10-2-0 | Darryl Rogers |
| 7. | Washington | 10-2-0 | Don James |
| 8. | Clemson | 9-1-1 | Danny Ford |
| 9. | Arkansas | 9-2-1 | Lou Holtz |
| 10. | Pittsburgh | 9-3-0 | Foge Fazio |
| 11. | LSU | 8-3-1 | Jerry Stovall |
| 12. | Ohio St | 9-3-0 | Earle Bruce |
| 13. | Florida St | 9-3-0 | Bobby Bowden |
| 14. | Auburn | 9-3-0 | Pat Dye |
| 15. | USC | 8-3-0 | John Robinson |
| 16. | Oklahoma | 8-4-0 | Barry Switzer |
| 17. | Texas | 9-3-0 | Fred Akers |
| 18. | North Carolina | 8-4-0 | Dick Crum |
| 19. | W Virginia | 9-3-0 | Don Nehlen |
| 20. | Maryland | 8-4-0 | Bobby Ross |

## 1983

| | | Record | Coach |
|---|---|---|---|
| 1. | Miami (Fla.) | 11-1-0 | H. Schnellenberger |
| 2. | Nebraska | 12-1-0 | Tom Osborne |
| 3. | Auburn | 11-1-0 | Pat Dye |
| 4. | Georgia | 10-1-1 | Vince Dooley |
| 5. | Texas | 11-1-0 | Fred Akers |
| 6. | Florida | 9-2-1 | Charlie Pell |
| 7. | BYU | 11-1-0 | LaVell Edwards |
| 8. | Michigan | 9-3-0 | Bo Schembechler |
| 9. | Ohio St | 9-3-0 | Earle Bruce |
| 10. | Illinois | 10-2-0 | Mike White |
| 11. | Clemson | 9-1-1 | Danny Ford |
| 12. | SMU | 10-2-0 | Bobby Collins |
| 13. | Air Force | 10-2-0 | Ken Hatfield |
| 14. | Iowa | 9-3-0 | Hayden Fry |
| 15. | Alabama | 8-4-0 | Ray Perkins |
| 16. | W Virginia | 9-3-0 | Don Nehlen |
| 17. | UCLA | 7-4-1 | Terry Donahue |
| 18. | Pittsburgh | 8-3-1 | Foge Fazio |
| 19. | Boston College | 9-3-0 | Jack Bicknell |
| 20. | E Carolina | 8-3-0 | Ed Emory |

## 1984

| | | Record | Coach |
|---|---|---|---|
| 1. | BYU | 13-0-0 | LaVell Edwards |
| 2. | Washington | 11-1-0 | Don James |
| 3. | Florida | 9-1-1 | Chas Pell (0-1-1) Galen Hall (9-0) |
| 4. | Nebraska | 10-2-0 | Tom Osborne |
| 5. | Boston College | 10-2-0 | Jack Bicknell |
| 6. | Oklahoma | 9-2-1 | Barry Switzer |
| 7. | Oklahoma St | 10-2-0 | Pat Jones |
| 8. | SMU | 10-2-0 | Bobby Collins |
| 9. | UCLA | 9-3-0 | Terry Donahue |

## 1984 *(Cont.)*

| | | Record | Coach |
|---|---|---|---|
| 10. | USC | 10-3-0 | Ted Tollner |
| 11. | South Carolina | 10-2-0 | Joe Morrison |
| 12. | Maryland | 9-3-0 | Bobby Ross |
| 13. | Ohio St | 9-3-0 | Earle Bruce |
| 14. | Auburn | 9-4-0 | Pat Dye |
| 15. | LSU | 8-3-1 | Bill Arnsparger |
| 16. | Iowa | 8-4-1 | Hayden Fry |
| 17. | Florida St | 7-3-2 | Bobby Bowden |
| 18. | Miami (Fla.) | 8-5-0 | Jimmy Johnson |
| 19. | Kentucky | 9-3-0 | Jerry Claiborne |
| 20. | Virginia | 8-2-2 | George Welsh |

## 1985

| | | Record | Coach |
|---|---|---|---|
| 1. | Oklahoma | 11-1-0 | Barry Switzer |
| 2. | Michigan | 10-1-1 | Bo Schembechler |
| 3. | Penn St | 11-1-0 | Joe Paterno |
| 4. | Tennessee | 9-1-2 | Johnny Majors |
| 5. | Florida | 9-1-1 | Galen Hall |
| 6. | Texas A&M | 10-2-0 | Jackie Sherrill |
| 7. | UCLA | 9-2-1 | Terry Donahue |
| 8. | Air Force | 12-1-0 | Fisher DeBerry |
| 9. | Miami (Fla.) | 10-2-0 | Jimmy Johnson |
| 10. | Iowa | 10-2-0 | Hayden Fry |
| 11. | Nebraska | 9-3-0 | Tom Osborne |
| 12. | Arkansas | 10-2-0 | Ken Hatfield |
| 13. | Alabama | 9-2-1 | Ray Perkins |
| 14. | Ohio St | 9-3-0 | Earle Bruce |
| 15. | Florida St | 9-3-0 | Bobby Bowden |
| 16. | BYU | 11-3-0 | LaVell Edwards |
| 17. | Baylor | 9-3-0 | Grant Teaff |
| 18. | Maryland | 9-3-0 | Bobby Ross |
| 19. | Georgia Tech. | 9-2-1 | Bill Curry |
| 20. | LSU | 9-2-1 | Bill Arnsparger |

## 1986

| | | Record | Coach |
|---|---|---|---|
| 1. | Penn St | 12-0-0 | Joe Paterno |
| 2. | Miami (Fla.) | 11-1-0 | Jimmy Johnson |
| 3. | Oklahoma | 11-1-0 | Barry Switzer |
| 4. | Arizona St | 10-1-1 | John Cooper |
| 5. | Nebraska | 10-2-0 | Tom Osborne |
| 6. | Auburn | 10-2-0 | Pat Dye |
| 7. | Ohio St | 10-3-0 | Earle Bruce |
| 8. | Michigan | 11-2-0 | Bo Schembechler |
| 9. | Alabama | 10-3-0 | Ray Perkins |
| 10. | LSU | 9-3-0 | Bill Arnsparger |
| 11. | Arizona | 9-3-0 | Larry Smith |
| 12. | Baylor | 9-3-0 | Grant Teaff |
| 13. | Texas A&M | 9-3-0 | Jackie Sherrill |
| 14. | UCLA | 8-3-1 | Terry Donahue |
| 15. | Arkansas | 9-3-0 | Ken Hatfield |
| 16. | Iowa | 9-3-0 | Hayden Fry |
| 17. | Clemson | 8-2-2 | Danny Ford |
| 18. | Washington | 8-3-1 | Don James |
| 19. | Boston College | 9-3-0 | Jack Bicknell |
| 20. | Virginia Tech. | 9-2-1 | Bill Dooley |

† In 1989 the AP expanded its final poll to 25 teams.

## 1987

| | | Record | Coach |
|---|---|---|---|
| 1. | Miami (Fla.) | 12-0-0 | Jimmy Johnson |
| 2. | Florida St | 11-1-0 | Bobby Bowden |
| 3. | Oklahoma | 11-1-0 | Barry Switzer |
| 4. | Syracuse | 11-0-1 | Dick MacPherson |
| 5. | LSU | 10-1-1 | Mike Archer |
| 6. | Nebraska | 10-2-0 | Tom Osborne |
| 7. | Auburn | 9-1-2 | Pat Dye |
| 8. | Michigan St | 9-2-1 | George Perles |
| 9. | UCLA | 10-2-0 | Terry Donahue |
| 10. | Texas A&M | 10-2-0 | Jackie Sherrill |
| 11. | Oklahoma St | 10-2-0 | Pat Jones |
| 12. | Clemson | 10-2-0 | Danny Ford |
| 13. | Georgia | 9-3-0 | Vince Dooley |
| 14. | Tennessee | 10-2-1 | Johnny Majors |
| 15. | South Carolina | 8-4-0 | Joe Morrison |
| 16. | Iowa | 10-3-0 | Hayden Fry |
| 17. | Notre Dame | 8-4-0 | Lou Holtz |
| 18. | USC | 8-4-0 | Larry Smith |
| 19. | Michigan | 8-4-0 | Bo Schembechler |
| 20. | Arizona St | 7-4-1 | John Cooper |

## 1988

| | | Record | Coach |
|---|---|---|---|
| 1. | Notre Dame | 12-0-0 | Lou Holtz |
| 2. | Miami (Fla.) | 11-1-0 | Jimmy Johnson |
| 3. | Florida St | 11-1-0 | Bobby Bowden |
| 4. | Michigan | 9-2-1 | Bo Schembechler |
| 5. | West Virginia | 11-1-0 | Don Nehlen |
| 6. | UCLA | 10-2-0 | Terry Donahue |
| 7. | USC | 10-2-0 | Larry Smith |
| 8. | Auburn | 10-2-0 | Pat Dye |
| 9. | Clemson | 10-2-0 | Danny Ford |
| 10. | Nebraska | 11-2-0 | Tom Osborne |
| 11. | Oklahoma St | 10-2-0 | Pat Jones |
| 12. | Arkansas | 10-2-0 | Ken Hatfield |
| 13. | Syracuse | 10-2-0 | Dick MacPherson |
| 14. | Oklahoma | 9-3-0 | Barry Switzer |
| 15. | Georgia | 9-3-0 | Vince Dooley |
| 16. | Washington St | 9-3-0 | Dennis Erickson |
| 17. | Alabama | 9-3-0 | Bill Curry |
| 18. | Houston | 9-3-0 | Jack Pardee |
| 19. | LSU | 8-4-0 | Mike Archer |
| 20. | Indiana | 8-3-1 | Bill Mallor |

## †1989

| | | Record | Coach |
|---|---|---|---|
| 1. | Miami (Fla.) | 11-1-0 | Dennis Erickson |
| 2. | Notre Dame | 12-1-0 | Lou Holtz |
| 3. | Florida St | 10-2-0 | Bobby Bowden |
| 4. | Colorado | 11-1-0 | Bill McCartney |
| 5. | Tennessee | 11-1-0 | Johnny Majors |
| 6. | Auburn | 10-2-0 | Pat Dye |
| 7. | Michigan | 10-2-0 | Bo Schembechler |
| 8. | USC | 9-2-1 | Larry Smith |
| 9. | Alabama | 10-2-0 | Bill Curry |
| 10. | Illinois | 10-2-0 | John Mackovic |
| 11. | Nebraska | 10-2-0 | Tom Osborne |
| 12. | Clemson | 10-2-0 | Danny Ford |
| 13. | Arkansas | 10-2-0 | Ken Hatfield |
| 14. | Houston | 9-2-0 | Jack Pardee |
| 15. | Penn St | 8-3-1 | Joe Paterno |
| 16. | Michigan St | 8-4-0 | George Perles |
| 17. | Pittsburgh | 8-3-1 | Mike Gottfried |
| 18. | Virginia | 10-3-0 | George Welsh |

### †1989 *(Cont.)*

| | | Record | Coach |
|---|---|---|---|
| 19. | Texas Tech | 9-3-0 | Spike Dykes |
| 20. | Texas A&M | 8-4-0 | R.C. Slocum |
| 21. | W Virginia | 8-3-1 | Don Nehlen |
| 22. | BYU | 10-3-0 | LaVell Edwards |
| 23. | Washington | 8-4-0 | Don James |
| 24. | Ohio St | 8-4-0 | John Cooper |
| 25. | Arizona | 8-4-0 | Dick Tomey |

### 1990

| | | Record | Coach |
|---|---|---|---|
| 1. | Colorado | 11-1-1 | Bill McCartney |
| 2. | #Ga. Tech (UPI) | 11-0-1 | Bobby Ross |
| 3. | Miami (Fla.) | 10-2-0 | Dennis Erickson |
| 4. | Florida St | 10-2-0 | Bobby Bowden |
| 5. | Washington | 10-2-0 | Don James |
| 6. | Notre Dame | 9-3-0 | Lou Holtz |
| 7. | Michigan | 9-3-0 | Gary Moeller |
| 8. | Tennessee | 9-2-2 | Johnny Majors |
| 9. | Clemson | 10-2-0 | Ken Hatfield |
| 10. | Houston | 10-1-0 | John Jenkins |
| 11. | Penn St | 9-3-0 | Joe Paterno |
| 12. | Texas | 10-2-0 | David McWilliams |
| 13. | Florida | 9-2-0 | Steve Spurrier |
| 14. | Louisville | 10-1-1 | H. Schnellenberger |
| 15. | Texas A&M | 9-3-1 | R.C. Slocum |
| 16. | Michigan St | 8-3-1 | George Perles |
| 17. | Oklahoma | 8-3-0 | Gary Gibbs |
| 18. | Iowa | 8-4-0 | Hayden Fry |
| 19. | Auburn | 8-3-1 | Pat Dye |
| 20. | USC I | 8-4-1 | Larry Smith |
| 21. | Mississippi | 9-3-0 | Billy Brewer |
| 22. | BYU | 10-3-0 | LaVell Edwards |
| 23. | Virginia | 8-4-0 | George Wells |
| 24. | Nebraska | 9-3-0 | Tom Osborne |
| 25. | Illinois | 8-4-0 | John Mackovic |

### 1991

| | | Record | Coach |
|---|---|---|---|
| 1. | Miami (Fla.) | 12-0-0 | Dennis Erickson |
| 2. | #Washington | 12-0-0 | Don James |
| 3. | Penn St | 11-2-0 | Joe Paterno |
| 4. | Florida St | 11-2-0 | Bobby Bowden |
| 5. | Alabama | 11-1-0 | Gene Stallings |
| 6. | Michigan | 10-2-0 | Gary Moeller |
| 7. | Florida | 10-2-0 | Steve Spurrier |
| 8. | California | 10-2-0 | Bruce Snyder |
| 9. | E Carolina | 11-1-0 | Bill Lewis |
| 10. | Iowa | 10-1-1 | Hayden Fry |
| 11. | Syracuse | 10-2-0 | Paul Pasqualoni |
| 12. | Texas A&M | 10-2-0 | R.C. Slocum |
| 13. | Notre Dame | 10-3-0 | Lou Holtz |
| 14. | Tennessee | 9-3-0 | Johnny Majors |
| 15. | Nebraska | 9-2-1 | Tom Osborne |
| 16. | Oklahoma | 9-3-0 | Gary Gibbs |
| 17. | Georgia | 9-3-0 | Ray Goff |
| 18. | Clemson | 9-2-1 | Ken Hatfield |
| 19. | UCLA | 9-3-0 | Terry Donahue |
| 20. | Colorado | 8-3-1 | Bill McCartney |
| 21. | Tulsa | 10-2-0 | David Rader |
| 22. | Stanford | 8-4-0 | Dennis Green |
| 23. | BYU | 8-3-2 | LaVell Edwards |
| 24. | North Carolina St | 9-3-0 | Dick Sheridan |
| 25. | Air Force | 10-3-0 | Fisher DeBerry |

#Selected No. 1 by *USA Today*/CNN.

### 1992

| | | Record | Coach |
|---|---|---|---|
| 1. | Alabama | 13-0-0 | Gene Stallings |
| 2. | Florida St | 11-1-0 | Bobby Bowden |
| 3. | Miami | 11-1-0 | Dennis Erickson |
| 4. | Notre Dame | 10-1-1 | Lou Holtz |
| 5. | Michigan | 9-0-3 | Gary Moeller |
| 6. | Syracuse | 10-2-0 | Paul Pasqualoni |
| 7. | Texas A&M | 12-1-0 | R.C. Slocum |
| 8. | Georgia | 10-2-0 | Ray Goff |
| 9. | Stanford | 10-3-0 | Bill Walsh |
| 10. | Florida | 9-4-0 | Steve Spurrier |
| 11. | Washington | 9-3-0 | Don James |
| 12. | Tennessee | 9-3-0 | Johnny Majors |
| 13. | Colorado | 9-2-1 | Bill McCartney |
| 14. | Nebraska | 9-3-0 | Tom Osborne |
| 15. | Washington St | 9-3-0 | Mike Price |
| 16. | Mississippi | 9-3-0 | Billy Brewer |
| 17. | North Carolina St | 9-3-1 | Dick Sheridan |
| 18. | Ohio St | 8-3-1 | John Cooper |
| 19. | North Carolina | 9-3-0 | Mack Brown |
| 20. | Hawaii | 11-2-0 | Bob Wagner |
| 21. | Boston College | 8-3-1 | Tom Coughlin |
| 22. | Kansas | 8-4-0 | Glen Mason |
| 23. | Mississippi St | 7-5-0 | Jackie Sherrill |
| 24. | Fresno St | 9-4-0 | Jim Sweeney |
| 25. | Wake Forest | 8-4-0 | Bill Dooley |

### 1993

| | | Record | Coach |
|---|---|---|---|
| 1. | Florida St | 12-1-0 | Bobby Bowden |
| 2. | Notre Dame | 11-1-0 | Lou Holtz |
| 3. | Nebraska | 11-1-0 | Tom Osborne |
| 4. | Auburn | 11-0-0 | Terry Bowden |
| 5. | Florida | 11-2-0 | Steve Spurrier |
| 6. | Wisconsin | 10-1-1 | Barry Alvarez |
| 7. | W Virginia | 11-1-0 | Don Nehlen |
| 8. | Penn St | 10-2-0 | Joe Paterno |
| 9. | Texas A&M | 10-2-0 | R.C. Slocum |
| 10. | Arizona | 10-2-0 | Dick Tomey |
| 11. | Ohio St | 10-1-1 | John Cooper |
| 12. | Tennessee | 9-2-1 | Phil Fulmer |
| 13. | Boston College | 9-3-0 | Tom Coughlin |
| 14. | Alabama | 9-3-1 | Gene Stallings |
| 15. | Miami | 9-3-0 | Dennis Erickson |
| 16. | Colorado | 8-3-1 | Bill McCartney |
| 17. | Oklahoma | 9-3-0 | Gary Gibbs |
| 18. | UCLA | 8-4-0 | Terry Donahue |
| 19. | North Carolina | 10-3-0 | Mack Brown |
| 20. | Kansas St | 9-2-1 | Bill Snyder |
| 21. | Michigan | 8-4-0 | Gary Moeller |
| 22. | Virginia Tech | 9-3-0 | Frank Beamer |
| 23. | Clemson | 9-3-0 | Ken Hatfield |
| 24. | Louisville | 9-3-0 | H. Schnellenberger |
| 25. | California | 9-4-0 | Keith Gilbertson |

### 1994

| | | Record | Coach |
|---|---|---|---|
| 1. | Nebraska | 13-0-0 | Tom Osborne |
| 2. | Penn St | 12-0-0 | Joe Paterno |
| 3. | Colorado | 11-1-0 | Bill McCartney |
| 4. | Florida St | 10-1-1 | Bobby Bowden |
| 5. | Alabama | 12-1-0 | Gene Stallings |
| 6. | Miami (Fla.) | 10-2-0 | Dennis Erickson |
| 7. | Florida | 10-2-1 | Steve Spurrier |
| 8. | Texas A&M | 10-0-1 | R.C. Slocum |

†In 1989 the AP expanded its final poll to 25 teams.

### 1994 *(Cont.)*

| | | Record | Coach |
|---|---|---|---|
| 9. | Auburn | 9-1-1 | Terry Bowden |
| 10. | Utah | 10-2-0 | Ron McBride |
| 11. | Oregon | 9-4-0 | Rich Brooks |
| 12. | Michigan | 8-4-0 | Gary Moeller |
| 13. | USC | 8-3-1 | John Robinson |
| 14. | Ohio St | 9-4-0 | John Cooper |
| 15. | Virginia | 9-3-0 | George Welsh |
| 16. | Colorado St | 10-2-0 | Sonny Lubick |
| 17. | North Carolina St | 9-3-0 | Mike O'Cain |
| 18. | BYU | 10-3-0 | LaVell Edwards |
| 19. | Kansas St | 9-3-0 | Bill Snyder |
| 20. | Arizona | 8-4-0 | Dick Tomey |
| 21. | Washington St | 8-4-0 | Mike Price |
| 22. | Tennessee | 8-4-0 | Phillip Fulmer |
| 23. | Boston College | 7-4-1 | Dan Henning |
| 24. | Mississippi St | 8-4-0 | Jackie Sherrill |
| 25. | Texas | 8-4-0 | John Mackovic |

### 1995

| | | Record | Coach |
|---|---|---|---|
| 1. | Nebraska | 12-0-0 | Tom Osborne |
| 2. | Florida | 12-1-0 | Steve Spurrier |
| 3. | Tennessee | 11-1-0 | Phillip Fulmer |
| 4. | Florida St | 10-2-0 | Bobby Bowden |
| 5. | Colorado | 10-2-0 | Rick Neuheisel |
| 6. | Ohio St | 11-2-0 | John Cooper |
| 7. | Kansas St | 10-2-0 | Bill Snyder |
| 8. | Northwestern | 10-2-0 | Gary Barnett |
| 9. | Kansas | 10-2-0 | Glen Mason |
| 10. | Virginia Tech | 10-2-0 | Frank Beamer |
| 11. | Notre Dame | 9-3-0 | Lou Holtz |
| 12. | USC | 9-2-1 | John Robinson |
| 13. | Penn St | 9-3-0 | Joe Paterno |
| 14. | Texas | 10-2-1 | John Mackovic |
| 15. | Texas A&M | 9-3-0 | S.C. Slocum |
| 16. | Virginia | 9-4-0 | George Welsh |
| 17. | Michigan | 9-4-0 | Lloyd Carr |
| 18. | Oregon | 9-3-0 | Mike Bellotti |
| 19. | Syracuse | 9-3-0 | Paul Pasqualoni |
| 20. | Miami (Fla.) | 8-3-0 | Butch Davis |
| 21. | Alabama | 8-3-0 | Gene Stallings |
| 22. | Auburn | 8-4-0 | Terry Bowden |
| 23. | Texas Tech | 9-3-0 | Spike Dykes |
| 24. | Toledo | 11-0-1 | Gary Pinkel |
| 25. | Iowa | 8-4-0 | Hayden Fry |

### 1996

| | | Record* | Coach |
|---|---|---|---|
| 1. | Florida | 12-1 | Steve Spurrier |
| 2. | Ohio St | 11-1 | John Cooper |
| 3. | Florida St | 11-1 | Bobby Bowden |
| 4. | Arizona St | 11-1 | Bruce Snyder |
| 5. | BYU | 14-1 | LaVell Edwards |
| 6. | Nebraska | 11-2 | Tom Osborne |
| 7. | Penn St | 11-2 | Joe Paterno |
| 8. | Colorado | 10-2 | Rick Neuheisel |
| 9. | Tennessee | 10-2 | Phillip Fulmer |
| 10. | North Carolina | 10-2 | Mack Brown |
| 11. | Alabama | 10-3 | Gene Stallings |
| 12. | LSU | 10-2 | Gerry DiNardo |
| 13. | Virginia Tech | 10-2 | Frank Beamer |
| 14. | Miami (Fla.) | 9-3 | Butch Davis |
| 15. | Northwestern | 9-3 | Gary Barnett |

### 1996 *(Cont.)*

| | | Record | Coach |
|---|---|---|---|
| 16. | Washington | 9-3 | Jim Lambright |
| 17. | Kansas St | 9-3 | Bill Snyder |
| 18. | Iowa | 9-3 | Hayden Fry |
| 19. | Notre Dame | 8-3 | Lou Holtz |
| 20. | Michigan | 8-4 | Lloyd Carr |
| 21. | Syracuse | 9-3 | Paul Pasqualoni |
| 22. | Wyoming | 10-2 | Joe Tiller |
| 23. | Texas | 8-5 | John Mackovic |
| 24. | Auburn | 8-4 | Terry Bowden |
| 25. | Army | 10-2 | Bob Sutton |

### 1997

| | | Record | Coach |
|---|---|---|---|
| 1. | Michigan | 12-0 | Lloyd Carr |
| 2. | Nebraska | 13-0 | Tom Osborne |
| 3. | Florida St | 11-1 | Bobby Bowden |
| 4. | Florida | 10-2 | Steve Spurrier |
| 5. | UCLA | 10-2 | Bob Toledo |
| 6. | North Carolina | 11-1 | Mack Brown |
| 7. | Tennessee | 11-2 | Phillip Fulmer |
| 8. | Kansas St | 11-1 | Bill Snyder |
| 9. | Washington St | 10-2 | Mike Price |
| 10. | Georgia | 10-2 | Jim Donnan |
| 11. | Auburn | 10-3 | Terry Bowden |
| 12. | Ohio St | 10-3 | John Cooper |
| 13. | LSU | 9-3 | Gerry DiNardo |
| 14. | Arizona St | 8-3 | Bruce Snyder |
| 15. | Purdue | 9-3 | Joe Tiller |
| 16. | Penn St | 9-3 | Joe Paterno |
| 17. | Colorado St | 11-2 | Sonny Lubick |
| 18. | Washington | 8-4 | Jim Lambright |
| 19. | Southern Mississippi | 9-4 | Jeff Bower |
| 20. | Texas A&M | 9-4 | R. C. Slocum |
| 21. | Syracuse | 9-4 | Paul Pasqualoni |
| 22. | Mississippi | 8-4 | Tommy Tuberville |
| 23. | Missouri | 7-5 | Larry Smith |
| 24. | Oklahoma St | 8-4 | Bob Simmons |
| 25. | Georgia Tech | 7-5 | George O'Leary |

### 1998

| | | Record | Coach |
|---|---|---|---|
| 1. | Tennessee | 13-0 | Phillip Fulmer |
| 2. | Ohio St | 11-1 | John Cooper |
| 3. | Florida St | 11-2 | Bobby Bowden |
| 4. | Arizona | 12-1 | Dick Tomey |
| 5. | Florida | 10-2 | Steve Spurrier |
| 6. | Wisconsin | 11-1 | Barry Alvarez |
| 7. | Tulane | 12-0 | Tommy Bowden |
| 8. | UCLA | 10-2 | Bob Toledo |
| 9. | Georgia Tech | 10-2 | George O'Leary |
| 10. | Kansas St | 11-2 | Bill Snyder |
| 11. | Texas A&M | 11-3 | R.C. Slocum |
| 12. | Michigan | 10-3 | Lloyd Carr |
| 13. | Air Force | 12-1 | Fisher DeBerry |
| 14. | Georgia | 9-3 | Jim Donnan |
| 15. | Texas | 9-3 | Mack Brown |
| 16. | Arkansas | 9-3 | Houston Nutt |
| 17. | Penn St | 9-3 | Joe Paterno |
| 18. | Virginia | 9-3 | George Welsh |
| 19. | Nebraska | 9-4 | Frank Solich |
| 20. | Miami (Fla.) | 9-3 | Butch Davis |
| 21. | Missouri | 8-4 | Larry Smith |
| 22. | Notre Dame | 9-3 | Bob Davie |
| 23. | Virginia Tech | 9-3 | Frank Beamer |

*In 1996 the NCAA introduced overtime to break ties.

### 1998 *(Cont.)*

| | | Record | Coach |
|---|---|---|---|
| 24. | Purdue | 9–4 | Joe Tiller |
| 25. | Syracuse | 8–4 | Paul Pasqualoni |

### 1999

| | | Record | Coach |
|---|---|---|---|
| 1. | Florida St | 12–0 | Bobby Bowden |
| 2. | Virginia Tech | 11–1 | Frank Beamer |
| 3. | Nebraska | 12–1 | Frank Solich |
| 4. | Wisconsin | 10–2 | Barry Alvarez |
| 5. | Michigan | 10–2 | Lloyd Carr |
| 6. | Kansas St | 11–1 | Bill Snyder |
| 7. | Michigan St | 10–2 | Nick Saban |
| 8. | Alabama | 10–3 | Mike DuBose |
| 9. | Tennessee | 9–3 | Phillip Fulmer |
| 10. | Marshall | 13–0 | Bob Pruett |
| 11. | Penn St | 10–3 | Joe Paterno |
| 12. | Florida | 9–4 | Steve Spurrier |
| 13. | Mississippi St | 10–2 | Jackie Sherrill |
| 14. | Southern Miss | 9–3 | Jeff Bower |
| 15. | Miami (Fla.) | 9–4 | Butch Davis |
| 16. | Georgia | 8–4 | Jim Donnan |
| 17. | Arkansas | 8–4 | Houston Nutt |
| 18. | Minnesota | 8–4 | Glen Mason |
| 19. | Oregon | 9–3 | Mike Bellotti |
| 20. | Georgia Tech | 8–4 | Goerge O'Leary |
| 21. | Texas | 9–5 | Mack Brown |
| 22. | Mississippi | 8–4 | David Cutcliffe |
| 23. | Texas A&M | 8–4 | R.C. Slocum |
| 24. | Illinois | 8–4 | Ron Turner |
| 25. | Purdue | 7–5 | Joe Tiller |

### 2000

| | | Record | Coach |
|---|---|---|---|
| 1. | Oklahoma | 13–0 | Bob Stoops |
| 2. | Miami (Fla.) | 11–1 | Butch Davis |
| 3. | Washington | 11–1 | Rick Neuheisel |
| 4. | Oregon St | 11–1 | Dennis Erickson |
| 5. | Florida St | 11–2 | Bobby Bowden |
| 6. | Virginia Tech | 11–1 | Frank Beamer |
| 7. | Oregon | 10–2 | Mike Belotti |
| 8. | Nebraska | 10–2 | Frank Solich |
| 9. | Kansas St | 11–3 | Bill Snyder |
| 10. | Florida | 10–3 | Steve Spurrier |
| 11. | Michigan | 9–3 | Lloyd Carr |
| 12. | Texas | 9–3 | Mack Brown |
| 13. | Purdue | 8–4 | Joe Tiller |
| 14. | Colorado St | 10–2 | Sonny Lubeck |
| 15. | Notre Dame | 9–3 | Bob Davie |
| 16. | Clemson | 9–3 | Tommy Bowden |
| 17. | Georgia Tech | 9–3 | George O'Leary |
| 18. | Auburn | 9–4 | Tommy Tuberville |
| 19. | South Carolina | 8–4 | Lou Holtz |
| 20. | Georgia | 8–4 | Jim Donnan |
| 21. | TCU | 10–2 | Dennis Franchione |
| 22. | LSU | 8–4 | Nick Saban |
| 23. | Wisconsin | 9–4 | Barry Alvarez |
| 24. | Mississippi St | 8–4 | Jackie Sherrill |
| 25. | Iowa St | 9–3 | Dan McCarney |

### 2001

| | | Record | Coach |
|---|---|---|---|
| 1. | Miami (Fla.) | 12–0 | Larry Coker |
| 2. | Oregon | 11–1 | Mike Belotti |
| 3. | Florida | 10–2 | Steve Spurrier |
| 4. | Tennessee | 11–2 | Phillip Fulmer |

### 2001

| | | Record | Coach |
|---|---|---|---|
| 5. | Texas | 11–2 | Mack Brown |
| 6. | Oklahoma | 11–2 | Bob Stoops |
| 7. | LSU | 10–3 | Nick Saban |
| 8. | Nebraska | 11–2 | Frank Solich |
| 9. | Colorado | 10–3 | Gary Barnett |
| 10. | Washington St | 10–2 | Mike Price |
| 11. | Maryland | 10–2 | Ralph Friedgen |
| 12. | Illinois | 10–2 | Ron Turner |
| 13. | South Carolina | 9–3 | Lou Holtz |
| 14. | Syracuse | 10–3 | Paul Pasqualoni |
| 15. | Florida St | 8–4 | Bobby Bowden |
| 16. | Stanford | 9–3 | Tyrone Willingham |
| 17. | Louisville | 11–2 | John Smith |
| 18. | Virginia Tech | 8–4 | Frank Beamer |
| 19. | Washington | 8–4 | Rick Neuheisel |
| 20. | Michigan | 8–4 | Lloyd Carr |
| 21. | Boston College | 8–4 | Tom O'Brien |
| 22. | Georgia | 8–4 | Mark Richt |
| 23. | Toledo | 10–2 | Tom Amstutz |
| 24. | Georgia Tech | 8–5 | George O'Leary |
| 25. | BYU | 12–2 | Gary Crowton |

### 2002

| | | Record | Coach |
|---|---|---|---|
| 1. | Ohio St | 14–0 | Jim Tressel |
| 2. | Miami (Fla.) | 12–1 | Larry Coker |
| 3. | Georgia | 13–1 | Mark Richt |
| 4. | USC | 11–2 | Pete Carroll |
| 5. | Oklahoma | 12–2 | Bob Stoops |
| 6. | Texas | 11–2 | Mack Brown |
| 7. | Kansas St | 11–2 | Bill Snyder |
| 8. | Iowa | 11–2 | Kirk Ferentz |
| 9. | Michigan | 10–3 | Lloyd Carr |
| 10. | Washington St | 10–3 | Mike Price |
| 11. | Alabama | 10–3 | Dennis Franchione |
| 12. | North Carolina St | 11–3 | Chuck Amato |
| 13. | Maryland | 11–3 | Ralph Friedgen |
| 14. | Auburn | 9–4 | Tommy Tuberville |
| 15. | Boise St | 12–1 | Dan Hawkins |
| 16. | Penn St | 9–4 | Joe Paterno |
| 17. | Notre Dame | 10–3 | Tyrone Willingham |
| 18. | Virginia Tech | 10–4 | Frank Beamer |
| 19. | Pittsburgh | 9–4 | Walt Harris |
| 20. | Colorado | 9–5 | Gary Barnett |
| 21. | Florida St | 9–5 | Bobby Bowden |
| 22. | Viriginia | 9–5 | Al Groh |
| 23. | TCU | 10–2 | Gary Patterson |
| 24. | Marshall | 11–2 | Bob Pruett |
| 25. | W Virginia | 9–4 | Rich Rodriguez |

### 2003

| | | Record | Coach |
|---|---|---|---|
| 1. | USC | 12–1 | Pete Carroll |
| 2. | LSU* | 13–1 | Nick Saban |
| 3. | Oklahoma | 12–2 | Bob Stoops |
| 4. | Ohio St | 11–2 | Jim Tressel |
| 5. | Miami (Fla.) | 11–2 | Larry Coker |
| 6. | Michigan | 10–3 | Lloyd Carr |
| 7. | Georgia | 11–3 | Mark Richt |
| 8. | Iowa | 10–3 | Kirk Ferentz |
| 9. | Washington St | 10–3 | Bill Doba |
| 10. | Miami (Ohio) | 13–1 | Terry Hoeppner |
| 11. | Florida St | 10–3 | Bobby Bowden |
| 12. | Texas | 10–3 | Mack Brown |
| 13. | Kansas St | 11–4 | Bill Snyder |
| | Mississippi | 10–3 | David Cutcliffe |

## 2003 *(Cont.)*

| | | Record | Coach |
|---|---|---|---|
| 15. | Tennessee | 10–3 | Phillip Fulmer |
| 16. | Boise St | 13–1 | Dan Hawkins |
| 17. | Maryland | 10–3 | Ralph Friedgen |
| 18. | Nebraska | 10–3 | Frank Solich/Bo Pelini |
| | Purdue | 9–4 | Joe Tiller |
| 20. | Minnesota | 10–3 | Glen Mason |
| 21. | Utah | 10–2 | Urban Meyer |
| 22. | Clemson | 9–4 | Tommy Bowden |
| 23. | Bowling Green | 11–3 | Gregg Brandon |
| 24. | Florida | 8–5 | Ron Zook |
| 25. | TCU | 11–2 | Gary Patterson |

*Ranked No. 1 in *USAToday*/ESPN Poll.

## 2004

| | | Record | Coach |
|---|---|---|---|
| 1. | USC | 13-0 | Pete Carroll |
| 2. | Auburn | 13-0 | Tommy Tuberville |
| 3. | Oklahoma | 12-1 | Bob Stoops |
| 4. | Utah | 12-0 | Kyle Whittingham |
| 5. | Texas | 11-1 | Mack Brown |
| 6. | Louisville | 11-1 | Bobby Petrino |
| 7. | Georgia | 10-2 | Mark Richt |
| 8. | Iowa | 10-2 | Kirk Ferentz |
| 9. | California | 10-2 | Jeff Tedford |
| 10. | Virginia Tech | 10-3 | Frank Beamer |
| 11. | Miami | 9-3 | Larry Coker |
| 12. | Tennessee | 10-3 | Phillip Fulmer |
| 13. | Michigan | 9-3 | Lloyd Carr |
| 14. | Florida | 8-5 | Ron Zook |
| 15. | Michigan | 9-3 | Lloyd Carr |
| 16. | LSU | 9-3 | Les Miles |
| 17. | Wisconsin | 9-3 | Barry Alvarez |
| 18. | Texas Tech | 8-4 | Mike Leach |
| 19. | Arizona St | 9-3 | Dirk Koetter |
| 20. | Ohio St | 8-4 | Jim Tressel |
| 21. | Boston College | 9-3 | Tom O'Brien |
| 22. | Fresno St | 9-3 | Pat Hill |
| 23. | Virginia | 8-4 | Al Groh |
| 24. | Navy | 10-2 | Paul Johnson |
| 25. | Pittsburgh | 8-4 | Walt Harris |

## 2005

| | | Record | Coach |
|---|---|---|---|
| 1. | Texas | 13-0 | Mack Brown |
| 2. | USC | 12-1 | Pete Carroll |
| 3. | Penn St | 11-1 | Joe Paterno |
| 4. | Ohio St | 10-2 | Jim Tressel |
| 5. | Texas | 11-1 | Mack Brown |
| 6. | LSU | 11-2 | Les Miles |
| 7. | Virginia Tech | 10-3 | Frank Beamer |
| 8. | Alabama | 10-2 | Mike Shula |
| 9. | Notre Dame | 9-3 | Charlie Weis |
| 10. | Georgia | 10-3 | Mark Richt |
| 11. | TCU | 11-1 | Gary Patterson |
| 12. | Florida | 9-3 | Urban Meyer |
| 12. | Oregon | 10-2 | Mike Bellotti |
| 14. | Auburn | 9-3 | Tommy Tuberville |
| 15. | Wisconsin | 9-3 | Barry Alvarez |
| 15. | Michigan | 9-3 | Lloyd Carr |
| 16. | UCLA | 10-2 | Karl Dorrell |
| 17. | Miami (Fla.) | 9-3 | Larry Coker |
| 18. | Boston College | 9-3 | Tom O'Brien |
| 19. | Louisville | 9-3 | Bobby Petrino |
| 20. | Texas Tech | 9-3 | Mike Leach |
| 21. | Clemson | 8-4 | Tommy Bowden |
| 22. | Oklahoma | 8-4 | Bob Stoops |

## 2005 *(Cont.)*

| | | Record | Coach |
|---|---|---|---|
| 23. | Florida St | 8-5 | Bobby Bowden |
| 24. | Nebraska | 8-4 | Bill Callahan |
| 25. | California | 8-4 | Jeff Tedford |

## 2006

| | | Record | Coach |
|---|---|---|---|
| 1. | Florida | 13-1 | Urban Meyer |
| 2. | Ohio St | 12-1 | Jim Tressel |
| 3. | LSU | 11-2 | Les Miles |
| 4. | USC | 11-2 | Pete Carroll |
| 5. | Boise St | 13-0 | Chris Petersen |
| 6. | Louisville | 12-1 | Steve Kragthorpe |
| 7. | Wisconsin | 12-1 | Bret Bielema |
| 8. | Michigan | 11-2 | Lloyd Carr |
| 9. | Auburn | 11-2 | Tommy Tuberville |
| 10. | West Virginia | 11-2 | Rich Rodriguez |
| 11. | Oklahoma | 11-3 | Bob Stoops |
| 12. | Rutgers | 11-2 | Greg Schiano |
| 13. | Texas | 10-3 | Mack Brown |
| 14. | California | 10-3 | Jeff Tedford |
| 15. | Arkansas | 10-4 | Houston Nutt |
| 16. | BYU | 11-2 | Bronco Mendenhall |
| 17. | Notre Dame | 10-3 | Charlie Weis |
| 18. | Wake Forest | 11-3 | Jim Grobe |
| 19. | Virginia Tech | 10-3 | Frank Beamer |
| 20. | Boston College | 10-3 | Jeff Jagodzinski |
| 21. | Oregon St | 10-4 | Mike Riley |
| 22. | TCU | 11-2 | Gary Patterson |
| 23. | Georgia | 9-4 | Mark Richt |
| 24. | Penn St | 9-4 | Joe Paterno |
| 25. | Tennessee | 9-4 | Phillip Fulmer |

## 2007

| | | Record | Coach |
|---|---|---|---|
| 1. | LSU | 12-2 | Les Miles |
| 2. | Georgia | 11-2 | Mark Richt |
| 3. | USC | 11-2 | Pete Carroll |
| 4. | Missouri | 12-2 | Gary Pinkel |
| 5. | Ohio St | 11-2 | Jim Tressel |
| 6. | West Virginia | 11-2 | Rich Rodriguez |
| 7. | Kansas | 12-1 | Mark Mangino |
| 8. | Oklahoma | 11-3 | Bob Stoops |
| 9. | Virginia Tech | 11-3 | Frank Beamer |
| 10. | Texas | 10-3 | Mack Brown |
| 10. | Boston College | 11-3 | Jeff Jagodzinski |
| 12. | Tennessee | 10-4 | Philip Fulmer |
| 13. | Florida | 9-4 | Urban Meyer |
| 14. | BYU | 11-2 | Bronco Mendenhall |
| 15. | Auburn | 9-4 | Tommy Tuberville |
| 16. | Arizona St | 10-3 | Dennis Erickson |
| 17. | Cincinnati | 10-3 | Brian Kelly |
| 18. | Michigan | 9-4 | Lloyd Carr |
| 19. | Hawaii | 12-1 | June Jones |
| 20. | Illinois | 9-4 | Ron Zook |
| 21. | Clemson | 9-4 | Tommy Bowden |
| 22. | Texas Tech | 9-4 | Mike Leach |
| 23. | Oregon | 9-4 | Mike Bellotti |
| 24. | Wisconsin | 9-4 | Bret Bielema |
| 25. | Oregon St | 9-4 | Mike Riley |

## Football Championship Subdivision (Div. I-AA)

| Year | Winner | Runner-Up | Score |
|------|--------|-----------|-------|
| 1978 | Florida A&M | Massachusetts | 35–28 |
| 1979 | Eastern Kentucky | Lehigh | 30–7 |
| 1980 | Boise St | Eastern Kentucky | 31–29 |
| 1981 | Idaho St | Eastern Kentucky | 34–23 |
| 1982 | Eastern Kentucky | Delaware | 17–14 |
| 1983 | Southern Illinois | Western Carolina | 43–7 |
| 1984 | Montana St | Louisiana Tech | 19–6 |
| 1985 | Georgia Southern | Furman | 44–42 |
| 1986 | Georgia Southern | Arkansas St | 48–21 |
| 1987 | NE Louisiana | Marshall | 43–42 |
| 1988 | Furman | Georgia Southern | 17–12 |
| 1989 | Georgia Southern | Stephen F. Austin St | 37–34 |
| 1990 | Georgia Southern | Nevada-Reno | 36–13 |
| 1991 | Youngstown St | Marshall | 25–17 |
| 1992 | Marshall | Youngstown St | 31–28 |
| 1993 | Youngstown St | Marshall | 17–5 |
| 1994 | Youngstown St | Boise St | 28–14 |
| 1995 | Montana | Marshall | 22–20 |
| 1996 | Marshall | Montana | 49–29 |
| 1997 | Youngstown St | McNesse St | 10–9 |
| 1998 | Massachusetts | Georgia Southern | 55–43 |
| 1999 | Georgia Southern | Youngstown St | 59–24 |
| 2000 | Georgia Southern | Montana | 27–25 |
| 2001 | Montana | Furman | 13–6 |
| 2002 | Western Kentucky | McNeese St | 34–14 |
| 2003 | Delaware | Colgate | 40–0 |
| 2004 | James Madison | Montana | 31–21 |
| 2005 | Appalachian St | Northern Iowa | 21–16 |
| 2006 | Appalachian St | Massachusetts | 28–17 |
| 2007 | Appalachian St | Delaware | 49–21 |
| 2008 | Richmond | Montana | 24–7 |

## Division II

| Year | Winner | Runner-Up | Score |
|------|--------|-----------|-------|
| 1973 | Louisiana Tech | Western Kentucky | 34–0 |
| 1974 | Central Michigan | Delaware | 54–14 |
| 1975 | Northern Michigan | Western Kentucky | 16–14 |
| 1976 | Montana St | Akron | 24–13 |
| 1977 | Lehigh | Jacksonville St | 33–0 |
| 1978 | Eastern Illinois | Delaware | 10–9 |
| 1979 | Delaware | Youngstown St | 38–21 |
| 1980 | Cal Poly SLO | Eastern Illinois | 21–13 |
| 1981 | SW Texas St | North Dakota St | 42–13 |
| 1982 | SW Texas St | UC–Davis | 34–9 |
| 1983 | North Dakota St | Central St (Ohio) | 41–21 |
| 1984 | Troy St | North Dakota St | 18–17 |
| 1985 | North Dakota St | North Alabama | 35–7 |
| 1986 | North Dakota St | South Dakota | 27–7 |
| 1987 | Troy St | Portland St | 31–17 |
| 1988 | North Dakota St | Portland St | 35–21 |
| 1989 | Mississippi College | Jacksonville St | 3–0 |
| 1990 | N Dakota St | Indiana (Pa.) | 51–11 |
| 1991 | Pittsburg St | Jacksonville St | 23–6 |
| 1992 | Jacksonville St | Pittsburg St | 17–13 |
| 1993 | North Alabama | Indiana (Pa.) | 41–34 |
| 1994 | North Alabama | Texas A&M–Kingsville | 16–10 |
| 1995 | North Alabama | Pittsburg St | 27–7 |
| 1996 | Northern Colorado | Carson-Newman | 23–14 |
| 1997 | Northern Colorado | New Haven | 51–0 |
| 1998 | NW Missouri St | Carson-Newman | 24–6 |
| 1999 | NW Missouri St | Carson-Newman | 58–52 (OT) |
| 2000 | Delta St | Bloomsburg | 63–34 |
| 2001 | Grand Valley St | North Dakota | 17–14 |
| 2002 | Grand Valley St | Valdosta St | 31–24 |
| 2003 | Grand Valley St | North Dakota | 10–3 |
| 2004 | Valdosta State | Pittsburg State | 36–31 |
| 2005 | Grand Valley St | NW Missouri St | 21–17 |

### Division II *(Cont.)*

| Year | Winner | Runner-Up | Score |
|------|--------|-----------|-------|
| 2006 | Grand Valley St | NW Missouri St | 17–14 |
| 2007 | Valdosta St | NW Missouri St | 25-20 |
| 2008 | Minnesota-Duluth | NW Missouri St | 21–14 |

### Division III

| Year | Winner | Runner-Up | Score |
|------|--------|-----------|-------|
| 1973 | Wittenberg | Juniata | 41–0 |
| 1974 | Central (Iowa) | Ithaca | 10–8 |
| 1975 | Wittenberg | Ithaca | 28–0 |
| 1976 | St. John's (Minn.) | Towson St | 31–28 |
| 1977 | Widener | Wabash | 39–36 |
| 1978 | Baldwin-Wallace | Wittenberg | 24–10 |
| 1979 | Ithaca | Wittenberg | 14–10 |
| 1980 | Dayton | Ithaca | 63–0 |
| 1981 | Widener | Dayton | 17–10 |
| 1982 | West Georgia | Augustana (Ill.) | 14–0 |
| 1983 | Augustana (Ill.) | Union (N.Y.) | 21–17 |
| 1984 | Augustana (Ill.) | Central (Iowa) | 21–12 |
| 1985 | Augustana (Ill.) | Ithaca | 20–7 |
| 1986 | Augustana (Ill.) | Salisbury St | 31–3 |
| 1987 | Wagner | Dayton | 19–3 |
| 1988 | Ithaca | Central (Iowa) | 39–24 |
| 1989 | Dayton | Union (N.Y.) | 17–7 |
| 1990 | Allegheny | Lycoming | 21–14 (OT) |
| 1991 | Ithaca | Dayton | 34–20 |
| 1992 | UW-LaCrosse | Washington & Jefferson | 16–12 |
| 1993 | Mount Union | Rowan | 34–24 |
| 1994 | Albion | Washington & Jefferson | 38–15 |
| 1995 | UW-LaCrosse | Rowan | 36–7 |
| 1996 | Mount Union | Rowan | 56–24 |
| 1997 | Mount Union | Lycoming | 61–12 |
| 1998 | Mount Union | Rowan | 44–24 |
| 1999 | Pacific Lutheran | Rowan | 42–13 |
| 2000 | Mount Union | St. John's (Minn.) | 10–7 |
| 2001 | Mount Union | Bridgewater | 30–27 |
| 2002 | Mount Union | Trinity (Tex.) | 48–7 |
| 2003 | St. John's (Minn.) | Mount Union | 24–6 |
| 2004 | Linfield | Mary Hardin-Baylor | 28–21 |
| 2005 | Mount Union | UW-Whitewater | 35–28 |
| 2006 | Mount Union | UW-Whitewater | 35–16 |
| 2007 | UW-Whitewater | Mount Union | 31–21 |
| 2008 | Mount Union | UW-Whitewater | 31–26 |

## NAIA Divisional Championships

### Division I

| Year | Winner | Runner-Up | Score |
|------|--------|-----------|-------|
| 1956 | St. Joseph's (Ind.)/Montana St | | 0–0 |
| 1957 | Pittsburg St (Kan.) | Hillsdale | 27–26 |
| 1958 | NE Oklahoma | Northern Arizona | 19–13 |
| 1959 | Texas A&I | Lenoir-Rhyne | 20–7 |
| 1960 | Lenoir-Rhyne | Humboldt St | 15–14 |
| 1961 | Pittsburg St (Kan.) | Linfield | 12–7 |
| 1962 | Central St (Okla.) | Lenoir-Rhyne | 28–13 |
| 1963 | St. John's (Minn.) | Prairie View | 33–27 |
| 1964 | Concordia-Moorhead/ Sam Houston St | | 7–7 |
| 1965 | St. John's (Minn.) | Linfield | 33–0 |
| 1966 | Waynesburg | UW-Whitewater | 42–21 |
| 1967 | Fairmont St | Eastern Washington | 28–21 |
| 1968 | Troy St (Mich.) | Texas A&I | 43–35 |
| 1969 | Texas A&I | Concordia-Moorhead (Minn.) | 32–7 |
| 1970 | Texas A&I | Wofford | 48–7 |
| 1971 | Livingston (Ala.) | Arkansas Tech | 14–12 |
| 1972 | E Texas St | Carson-Newman | 21–18 |
| 1973 | Abilene Christian | Elon | 42–14 |

## Division I *(Cont.)*

| Year | Winner | Runner-Up | Score |
|------|--------|-----------|-------|
| 1974 | Texas A&I | Henderson St | 34–23 |
| 1975 | Texas A&I | Salem (W.V.) | 37–0 |
| 1976 | Texas A&I | Central Arkansas | 26–0 |
| 1977 | Abilene Christian | SW Oklahoma | 24–7 |
| 1978 | Angelo St | Elon | 34–14 |
| 1979 | Texas A&I | Central St (Okla.) | 20–14 |
| 1980 | Elon | NE Oklahoma | 17–10 |
| 1981 | Elon | Pittsburg St | 3–0 |
| 1982 | Central St (Okla.) | Mesa | 14–11 |
| 1983 | Carson-Newman | Mesa | 36–28 |
| 1984 | Carson-Newman/Central Arkansas | | 19–19 |
| 1985 | Central Arkansas/Hillsdale | | 10–10 |
| 1986 | Carson-Newman | Cameron | 17–0 |
| 1987 | Cameron | Carson-Newman | 30–2 |
| 1988 | Carson-Newman | Adams St (Col.) | 56–21 |
| 1989 | Carson-Newman | Emporia St | 34–20 |
| 1990 | Central St (Ohio) | Mesa St | 38–16 |
| 1991 | Central Arkansas | Central St (Ohio) | 19–16 |
| 1992 | Central St (Ohio) | Gardner-Webb | 19–16 |
| 1993 | East Central (Okla.) | Glenville St | 49–35 |
| 1994 | Northeastern St (Okla.) | Arkansas–Pine Bluff | 13–12 |
| 1995 | Central St (Ohio) | Northeastern St (Okla.) | 37–7 |
| 1996 | SW Oklahoma St | Montana Tech | 33–31 |
| 1997 | Findlay | Willamette | 14–7 |
| 1998 | Azusa Pacific | Olivet Nazarene | 17–14 |
| 1999 | Northwestern Oklahoma St | Georgetown (Ky.) | 34–26 |
| 2000 | Georgetown (Ky.) | Northwestern Oklahoma St | 20–0 |
| 2001 | Georgetown (Ky.) | Sioux Falls | 49–27 |
| 2002 | Carroll (Mont.) | Georgetown (Ky.) | 28–7 |
| 2003 | Carroll (Mont.) | Northwestern Oklahoma St | 41–28 |
| 2004 | Carroll (Mont.) | St. Francis (Ind.) | 15–13 |
| 2005 | Carroll (Mont.) | St. Francis (Ind.) | 27–10 |
| 2006 | Sioux Falls (S.D.) | St. Francis (Ind.) | 23–19 |
| 2007 | Carroll (Mont.) | Sioux Falls (S.D.) | 17–9 |
| 2008 | Sioux Falls (S.D.) | Carroll (Mont.) | 23–7 |

## Division II†

| Year | Winner | Runner-Up | Score |
|------|--------|-----------|-------|
| 1970 | Westminster (Pa.) | Anderson | 21–16 |
| 1971 | California Lutheran | Westminster (Pa.) | 30–14 |
| 1972 | Missouri Southern | Northwestern (Iowa) | 21–14 |
| 1973 | Northwestern (Iowa) | Glenville St | 10–3 |
| 1974 | Texas Lutheran | Missouri Valley | 42–0 |
| 1975 | Texas Lutheran | California Lutheran | 34–8 |
| 1976 | Westminster (Pa.) | Redlands | 20–13 |
| 1977 | Westminster (Pa.) | California Lutheran | 17–9 |
| 1978 | Concordia-Moorhead (Minn.) | Findlay | 7–0 |
| 1979 | Findlay | Northwestern (Iowa) | 51–6 |
| 1980 | Pacific Lutheran | Wilmington (Ohio) | 38–10 |
| 1981 | Austin Coll./Conc.-Moorhead (Minn.) | | 24–24 |
| 1982 | Linfield | William Jewell | 33–15 |
| 1983 | Northwestern (Iowa) | Pacific Lutheran | 25–21 |
| 1984 | Linfield | Northwestern (Iowa) | 33–22 |
| 1985 | UW-La Crosse | Pacific Lutheran | 24–7 |
| 1986 | Linfield | Baker | 17–0 |
| 1987 | Pacific Lutheran | UW-Stevens Point* | 16–16 |
| 1988 | Westminster (Pa.) | UW-La Crosse | 21–14 |
| 1989 | Westminster (Pa.) | UW-La Crosse | 51–30 |
| 1990 | Peru St | Westminster (Pa.) | 17–7 |
| 1991 | Georgetown (Ky.) | Pacific Lutheran | 28–20 |
| 1992 | Findlay | Linfield | 26–13 |
| 1993 | Pacific Lutheran | Westminster (Pa.) | 50–20 |
| 1994 | Westminster (Pa.) | Pacific Lutheran | 27–7 |
| 1995 | Findlay | Central Washington | 21–21 |
| 1996 | Sioux Falls (S.D.) | Western Washington | 47–25 |

*Forfeited 1987 season due to use of an ineligible player.    †In 1997 the NAIA consolidated its two divisions into one.

## Heisman Memorial Trophy

Awarded to the best college player by the Downtown Athletic Club of New York City. The trophy is named after John W. Heisman, who coached Georgia Tech to the national championship in 1917 and later served as DAC athletic director.

| Year | Winner, College, Position | Winner's Season Statistics | Runner-Up, College |
|---|---|---|---|
| 1935 | Jay Berwanger, Chicago, HB | Rush: 119 Yds: 577 TD: 6 | Monk Meyer, Army |
| 1936 | Larry Kelley, Yale, E | Rec: 17 Yds: 372 TD: 6 | Sam Francis, Nebraska |
| 1937 | Clint Frank, Yale, HB | Rush: 157 Yds: 667 TD: 11 | Byron White, Colorado |
| 1938 | †Davey O'Brien, TCU, QB | Att/Comp: 194/110 Yds: 1733 TD: 19 | Marshall Goldberg, Pittsburgh |
| 1939 | Nile Kinnick, Iowa, HB | Rush: 106 Yds: 374 TD: 5 | Tom Harmon, Michigan |
| 1940 | Tom Harmon, Michigan, HB | Rush: 191 Yds: 852 TD: 16 | John Kimbrough, Texas A&M |
| 1941 | †Bruce Smith, Minnesota, HB | Rush: 98 Yds: 480 TD: 6 | Angelo Bertelli, Notre Dame |
| 1942 | Frank Sinkwich, Georgia, HB | Att/Comp: 166/84 Yds: 1392 TD: 10 | Paul Governali, Columbia |
| 1943 | Angelo Bertelli, Notre Dame, QB | Att/Comp: 36/25 Yds: 511 TD: 10 | Bob Odell, Pennsylvania |
| 1944 | Les Horvath, Ohio State, QB | Rush: 163 Yds: 924 TD: 12 | Glenn Davis, Army |
| 1945 | *†Doc Blanchard, Army, FB | Rush: 101 Yds: 718 TD: 13 | Glenn Davis, Army |
| 1946 | Glenn Davis, Army, HB | Rush: 123 Yds: 712 TD: 7 | Charley Trippi, Georgia |
| 1947 | †John Lujack, Notre Dame, QB | Att/Comp: 109/61 Yds: 777 TD: 9 | Bob Chappuis, Michigan |
| 1948 | *Doak Walker, SMU, HB | Rush: 108 Yds: 532 TD: 8 | Charlie Justice, North Carolina |
| 1949 | †Leon Hart, Notre Dame, E | Rec: 19 Yds: 257 TD: 5 | Charlie Justice, North Carolina |
| 1950 | *Vic Janowicz, Ohio St, HB | Att/Comp: 77/32 Yds: 561 TD: 12 | Kyle Rote, SMU |
| 1951 | Dick Kazmaier, Princeton, HB | Rush: 149 Yds: 861 TD: 9 | Hank Lauricella, Tennessee |
| 1952 | Billy Vessels, Oklahoma, HB | Rush: 167 Yds: 1072 TD: 17 | Jack Scarbath, Maryland |
| 1953 | John Lattner, Notre Dame, HB | Rush: 134 Yds: 651 TD: 6 | Paul Giel, Minnesota |
| 1954 | Alan Ameche, Wisconsin, FB | Rush: 146 Yds: 641 TD: 9 | Kurt Burris, Oklahoma |
| 1955 | Howard Cassady, Ohio St, HB | Rush: 161 Yds: 958 TD: 15 | Jim Swink, TCU |
| 1956 | Paul Hornung, Notre Dame, QB | Att/Comp: 111/59 Yds: 917 TD: 3 | Johnny Majors, Tennessee |
| 1957 | John David Crow, Texas A&M, HB | Rush: 129 Yds: 562 TD: 10 | Alex Karras, Iowa |
| 1958 | Pete Dawkins, Army, HB | Rush: 78 Yds: 428 TD: 6 | Randy Duncan, Iowa |
| 1959 | Billy Cannon, LSU, HB | Rush: 139 Yds: 598 TD: 6 | Rich Lucas, Penn St |
| 1960 | Joe Bellino, Navy, HB | Rush: 168 Yds: 834 TD: 18 | Tom Brown, Minnesota |
| 1961 | Ernie Davis, Syracuse, HB | Rush: 150 Yds: 823 TD: 15 | Bob Ferguson, Ohio St |
| 1962 | Terry Baker, Oregon St, QB | Att/Comp: 203/112 Yds: 1738 TD: 15 | Jerry Stovall, LSU |
| 1963 | *Roger Staubach, Navy, QB | Att/Comp: 161/107 Yds: 1474 TD: 7 | Billy Lothridge, Georgia Tech |
| 1964 | John Huarte, Notre Dame, QB | Att/Comp: 205/114 Yds: 2062 TD: 16 | Jerry Rhome, Tulsa |
| 1965 | Mike Garrett, USC, HB | Rush: 267 Yds: 1440 TD: 16 | Howard Twilley, Tulsa |
| 1966 | Steve Spurrier, Florida, QB | Att/Comp: 291/179 Yds: 2012 TD: 16 | Bob Griese, Purdue |
| 1967 | Gary Beban, UCLA, QB | Att/Comp: 156/87 Yds: 1359 TD: 8 | O.J. Simpson, USC |
| 1968 | O.J. Simpson, USC, HB | Rush: 383 Yds: 1880 TD: 23 | Leroy Keyes, Purdue |
| 1969 | Steve Owens, Oklahoma, FB | Rush: 358 Yds: 1523 TD: 23 | Mike Phipps, Purdue |
| 1970 | Jim Plunkett, Stanford, QB | Att/Comp: 358/191 Yds: 2715 TD: 18 | Joe Theismann, Notre Dame |
| 1971 | Pat Sullivan, Auburn, QB | Att/Comp: 281/162 Yds: 2012; 20 TD | Ed Marinaro, Cornell |
| 1972 | Johnny Rodgers, Nebraska, FL | Rec: 55 Yds: 942 TD: 17 | Greg Pruitt, Oklahoma |
| 1973 | John Cappelletti, Penn St, HB | Rush: 286 Yds: 1522 TD: 17 | John Hicks, Ohio St |
| 1974 | *Archie Griffin, Ohio St, HB | Rush: 256 Yds: 1695 TD: 12 | Anthony Davis, USC |
| 1975 | Archie Griffin, Ohio St, HB | Rush: 262 Yds: 1450 TD: 4 | Chuck Muncie, California |
| 1976 | †Tony Dorsett, Pittsburgh, HB | Rush: 370 Yds: 2150 TD: 23 | Ricky Bell, USC |
| 1977 | Earl Campbell, Texas, FB | Rush: 267 Yds: 1744 TD: 19 | Terry Miller, Oklahoma St |
| 1978 | *Billy Sims, Oklahoma, HB | Rush: 231 Yds: 1762 TD: 20 | Chuck Fusina, Penn St |
| 1979 | Charles White, USC, HB | Rush: 332 Yds: 1803 TD: 19 | Billy Sims, Oklahoma |
| 1980 | George Rogers, South Carolina, HB | Rush: 324 Yds: 1894 TD: 14 | Hugh Green, Pittsburgh |
| 1981 | Marcus Allen, USC, HB | Rush: 433 Yds: 2427 TD: 23 | Herschel Walker, Georgia |
| 1982 | *Herschel Walker, Georgia, HB | Rush: 335 Yds: 1752 TD: 17 | John Elway, Stanford |
| 1983 | Mike Rozier, Nebraska, HB | Rush: 275 Yds: 2148 TD: 29 | Steve Young, BYU |
| 1984 | Doug Flutie, Boston College, QB | Att/Comp: 396/233 Yds: 3454 TD: 27 | Keith Byars, Ohio St |
| 1985 | Bo Jackson, Auburn, HB | Rush: 278 Yds: 1786 TD: 17 | Chuck Long, Iowa |
| 1986 | Vinny Testaverde, Miami (Fla.), QB | Att/Comp: 276/175 Yds: 2557 TD: 26 | Paul Palmer, Temple |

### Heisman Memorial Trophy *(Cont.)*

| Year | Winner, College, Position | Winner's Season Statistics | Runner-Up, College |
|------|---------------------------|----------------------------|--------------------|
| 1987 | Tim Brown, Notre Dame, WR | Rec: 39 Yds: 846 TD: 7 | Don McPherson, Syracuse |
| 1988 | *Barry Sanders, Oklahoma St, RB | Rush: 344 Yds: 2628 TD: 39 | Rodney Peete, USC |
| 1989 | *Andre Ware, Houston, QB | Att/Comp: 578/365 Yds: 4699 TD: 46 | Anthony Thompson, Indiana |
| 1990 | *Ty Detmer, BYU, QB | Att/Comp: 562/361 Yds: 5188 TD: 41 | Raghib Ismail, Notre Dame |
| 1991 | *Desmond Howard, Michigan, WR | Rec: 61 Yds: 950 TD: 23 | Casey Weldon, Florida St |
| 1992 | Gino Torretta, Miami (FL), QB | Att/Comp: 402/228 Yds: 3060 TD: 19 | Marshall Faulk, San Diego St |
| 1993 | †Charlie Ward, Florida St, QB | Att/Comp: 380/264 Yds: 3032 TD: 27 | Heath Shuler, Tennessee |
| 1994 | Rashaan Salaam, Colorado, RB | Rush: 298 Yds: 2055 TD: 24 | Ki-Jana Carter, Penn St |
| 1995 | Eddie George, Ohio State, RB | Rush: 303 Yds: 1826 TD: 23 | Tommie Frazier, Nebraska |
| 1996 | †Danny Wuerffel, Florida, QB | Att/Comp: 360/207 Yds: 3625 TD: 39 | Troy Davis, Iowa St |
| 1997 | †Charles Woodson, Michigan, CB/WR | 7 interceptions; Rec: 11 Yds: 231 TD: 4 | Peyton Manning, Tennessee |
| 1998 | Ricky Williams, Texas, RB | Rush: 361 Yds: 2124 TD: 28 | Michael Bishop, Kansas St |
| 1999 | Ron Dayne, Wisconsin, RB | Rush: 303 Yds: 1834 TD: 19 | Joe Hamilton, Georgia Tech |
| 2000 | Chris Weinke, Florida St, QB | Att/Comp: 431/266 Yds: 4167 TD: 33 | Josh Heupel, Oklahoma |
| 2001 | Eric Crouch, Nebraska, QB | Att/Comp: 189/105 Yds: 1510 TD: 7; Rush: 1115 Yds, 18 TD | Rex Grossman, Florida |
| 2002 | Carson Palmer, USC, QB | Att/Comp: 450/228 Yds: 3639 TD: 32 | Brad Banks, Iowa |
| 2003 | Jason White, Oklahoma, QB | Pct. Comp: 64; 3744 Yds; TD: 40 | Larry Fitzgerald, Pittsburgh |
| 2004 | *†Matt Leinart, USC, QB | Att/Comp: 269/412 Yds: 2990 TD: 28 | Adrian Peterson, Oklahoma |
| 2005 | *Reggie Bush, USC, RB | Rush: 200 Rec:478 Ret:179 Yds:1,740 TD: 16 | Vince Young, Texas |
| 2006 | Troy Smith, Ohio State, QB | Att/Comp: 311/203 Yds: 2542 TD: 30 | Darren McFadden, Arkansas |
| 2007 | ^Tim Tebow, Florida, QB | Att/Comp: 350/234 Yds: 3286 TD: 32 | Darren McFadden, Arkansas |
| 2008 | ^Sam Bradford, Oklahoma, QB | Att/Comp: 483/328 Yds: 4720 TD: 50 | Colt McCoy, Texas |

*Juniors; ^Sophomore; (all others seniors). †Winners who played for national championship teams the same year. Note: Former Heisman winners and national media cast votes, with ballots allowing for three names (3 points for first, 2 for second and 1 for third).

### Maxwell Award

Given to the nation's outstanding college football player by the Maxwell Football Club of Philadelphia.

| Year | Player, College, Position | Year | Player, College, Position |
|------|---------------------------|------|---------------------------|
| 1937 | Clint Frank, Yale, HB | 1961 | Bob Ferguson, Ohio St, FB |
| 1938 | Davey O'Brien, TCU, QB | 1962 | Terry Baker, Oregon St, QB |
| 1939 | Nile Kinnick, Iowa, HB | 1963 | Roger Staubach, Navy, QB |
| 1940 | Tom Harmon, Michigan, HB | 1964 | Glenn Ressler, Penn St, C |
| 1941 | Bill Dudley, Virginia, HB | 1965 | Tommy Nobis, Texas, LB |
| 1942 | Paul Governali, Columbia, QB | 1966 | Jim Lynch, Notre Dame, LB |
| 1943 | Bob Odell, Pennsylvania, HB | 1967 | Gary Beban, UCLA, QB |
| 1944 | Glenn Davis, Army, HB | 1968 | O.J. Simpson, USC, RB |
| 1945 | Doc Blanchard, Army, FB | 1969 | Mike Reid, Penn St, DT |
| 1946 | Charley Trippi, Georgia, HB | 1970 | Jim Plunkett, Stanford, QB |
| 1947 | Doak Walker, SMU, HB | 1971 | Ed Marinaro, Cornell, RB |
| 1948 | Chuck Bednarik, Pennsylvania, C | 1972 | Brad Van Pelt, Michigan St, DB |
| 1949 | Leon Hart, Notre Dame, E | 1973 | John Cappelletti, Penn St, RB |
| 1950 | Reds Bagnell, Pennsylvania, HB | 1974 | Steve Joachim, Temple, QB |
| 1951 | Dick Kazmaier, Princeton, HB | 1975 | Archie Griffin, Ohio St, RB |
| 1952 | John Lattner, Notre Dame, HB | 1976 | Tony Dorsett, Pittsburgh, RB |
| 1953 | John Lattner, Notre Dame, HB | 1977 | Ross Browner, Notre Dame, DE |
| 1954 | Ron Beagle, Navy, E | 1978 | Chuck Fusina, Penn St, QB |
| 1955 | Howard Cassady, Ohio St, HB | 1979 | Charles White, USC, RB |
| 1956 | Tommy McDonald, Oklahoma, HB | 1980 | Hugh Green, Pittsburgh, DE |
| 1957 | Bob Reifsnyder, Navy, T | 1981 | Marcus Allen, USC, RB |
| 1958 | Pete Dawkins, Army, HB | 1982 | Herschel Walker, Georgia, RB |
| 1959 | Rich Lucas, Penn St, QB | 1983 | Mike Rozier, Nebraska, RB |
| 1960 | Joe Bellino, Navy, HB | 1984 | Doug Flutie, Boston College, QB |

## Maxwell Award (Cont.)

| Year | Player, College, Position | Year | Player, College, Position |
|---|---|---|---|
| 1985 | Chuck Long, Iowa, QB | 1997 | Peyton Manning, Tennessee, QB |
| 1986 | Vinny Testaverde, Miami (Fla.), QB | 1998 | Ricky Williams, Texas, RB |
| 1987 | Don McPherson, Syracuse, QB | 1999 | Ron Dayne, Wisconsin, RB |
| 1988 | Barry Sanders, Oklahoma St, RB | 2000 | Drew Brees, Purdue, QB |
| 1989 | Anthony Thompson, Indiana, RB | 2001 | Ken Dorsey, Miami (Fla.), QB |
| 1990 | Ty Detmer, BYU, QB | 2002 | Larry Johnson, Penn St, RB |
| 1991 | Desmond Howard, Michigan, WR | 2003 | Eli Manning, Mississippi, QB |
| 1992 | Gino Torretta, Miami (Fla.), QB | 2004 | Jason White, Oklahoma, QB |
| 1993 | Charlie Ward, Florida St, QB | 2005 | Vince Young, Texas, QB |
| 1994 | Kerry Collins, Penn St, QB | 2006 | Brady Quinn, Notre Dame, QB |
| 1995 | Eddie George, Ohio St, RB | 2007 | Tim Tebow, Florida, QB |
| 1996 | Danny Wuerffel, Florida, QB | 2008 | Tim Tebow, Florida, QB |

## Davey O'Brien National Quarterback Award

Given to the top quarterback in the nation by the Davey O'Brien Educational and Charitable Trust of Fort Worth. Named for TCU Hall of Fame quarterback Davey O'Brien (1936–38).

| Year | Player, College | Year | Player, College |
|---|---|---|---|
| 1981 | Jim McMahon, BYU | 1995 | Danny Wuerffel, Florida |
| 1982 | Todd Blackledge, Penn St | 1996 | Danny Wuerffel, Florida |
| 1983 | Steve Young, BYU | 1997 | Peyton Manning, Tennessee |
| 1984 | Doug Flutie, Boston College | 1998 | Michael Bishop, Kansas St |
| 1985 | Chuck Long, Iowa | 1999 | Joe Hamilton, Georgia Tech |
| 1986 | Vinny Testaverde, Miami (Fla.) | 2000 | Chris Weinke, Florida St |
| 1987 | Don McPherson, Syracuse | 2001 | Eric Crouch, Nebraska |
| 1988 | Troy Aikman, UCLA | 2002 | Brad Banks, Iowa |
| 1989 | Andre Ware, Houston | 2003 | Jason White, Oklahoma |
| 1990 | Ty Detmer, BYU | 2004 | Jason White, Oklahoma |
| 1991 | Ty Detmer, BYU | 2005 | Vince Young, Texas |
| 1992 | Gino Torretta, Miami (Fla.) | 2006 | Troy Smith, Ohio St |
| 1993 | Charlie Ward, Florida St | 2007 | Tim Tebow, Florida |
| 1994 | Kerry Collins, Penn St | 2008 | Sam Bradford, Oklahoma |

Note: Originally honored the outstanding football player in the Southwest as follows: 1977—Earl Campbell, Texas, RB; 1978—Billy Sims, Oklahoma, RB; 1979—Mike Singletary, Baylor, LB; 1980—Mike Singletary, Baylor, LB.

## Vince Lombardi/Rotary Award

Given to the outstanding college lineman of the year, the award is sponsored by the Rotary Club of Houston.

| Year | Player, College, Position | Year | Player, College, Position |
|---|---|---|---|
| 1970 | Jim Stillwagon, Ohio St, MG | 1990 | Chris Zorich, Notre Dame, NG |
| 1971 | Walt Patulski, Notre Dame, DE | 1991 | Steve Emtman, Washington, DT |
| 1972 | Rich Glover, Nebraska, MG | 1992 | Marvin Jones, Florida St, LB |
| 1973 | John Hicks, Ohio St, OT | 1993 | Aaron Taylor, Notre Dame, OT |
| 1974 | Randy White, Maryland, DT | 1994 | Warren Sapp, Miami (Fla.), DT |
| 1975 | Lee Roy Selmon, Oklahoma, DT | 1995 | Orlando Pace, Ohio St, OT |
| 1976 | Wilson Whitley, Houston, DT | 1996 | Orlando Pace, Ohio St, OT |
| 1977 | Ross Browner, Notre Dame, DE | 1997 | Grant Wistrom, Nebraska, DE |
| 1978 | Bruce Clark, Penn St, DT | 1998 | Dat Nguyen, Texas A&M, LB |
| 1979 | Brad Budde, USC, G | 1999 | Corey Moore, Virginia Tech, DE |
| 1980 | Hugh Green, Pittsburgh, DE | 2000 | Jamal Reynolds, Florida St, DE |
| 1981 | Kenneth Sims, Texas, DT | 2001 | Julius Peppers, North Carolina, DE |
| 1982 | Dave Rimington, Nebraska, C | 2002 | Terrell Suggs, Arizona St, DL |
| 1983 | Dean Steinkuhler, Nebraska, G | 2003 | Tommie Harris, Oklahoma, DT |
| 1984 | Tony Degrate, Texas, DT | 2004 | David Pollack, Georgia, DE |
| 1985 | Tony Casillas, Oklahoma, NG | 2005 | A.J. Hawk, Ohio St, LB |
| 1986 | Cornelius Bennett, Alabama, LB | 2006 | LaMarr Woodley, Michigan, DE |
| 1987 | Chris Spielman, Ohio St, LB | 2007 | Glenn Dorsey, LSU, DT |
| 1988 | Tracy Rocker, Auburn, DT | 2008 | Brian Orakpo, Texas, DE |
| 1989 | Percy Snow, Michigan St, LB | | |

## Outland Trophy

Given to the outstanding interior lineman, selected by the Football Writers Association of America.

| Year | Player, College, Position | Year | Player, College, Position |
|---|---|---|---|
| 1946 | George Connor, Notre Dame, T | 1949 | Ed Bagdon, Michigan St, G |
| 1947 | Joe Steffy, Army, G | 1950 | Bob Gain, Kentucky, T |
| 1948 | Bill Fischer, Notre Dame, G | 1951 | Jim Weatherall, Oklahoma, T |

## Outland Trophy *(Cont.)*

| Year | Player, College, Position | Year | Player, College, Position |
|------|---------------------------|------|---------------------------|
| 1952 | Dick Modzelewski, Maryland, T | 1981 | Dave Rimington, Nebraska, C |
| 1953 | J.D. Roberts, Oklahoma, G | 1982 | Dave Rimington, Nebraska, C |
| 1954 | Bill Brooks, Arkansas, G | 1983 | Dean Steinkuhler, Nebraska, G |
| 1955 | Calvin Jones, Iowa, G | 1984 | Bruce Smith, Virginia Tech, DT |
| 1956 | Jim Parker, Ohio St, G | 1985 | Mike Ruth, Boston College, NG |
| 1957 | Alex Karras, Iowa, T | 1986 | Jason Buck, BYU, DT |
| 1958 | Zeke Smith, Auburn, G | 1987 | Chad Hennings, Air Force, DT |
| 1959 | Mike McGee, Duke, T | 1988 | Tracy Rocker, Auburn, DT |
| 1960 | Tom Brown, Minnesota, G | 1989 | Mohammed Elewonibi, BYU, G |
| 1961 | Merlin Olsen, Utah St, T | 1990 | Russell Maryland, Miami (Fla.), DT |
| 1962 | Bobby Bell, Minnesota, T | 1991 | Steve Emtman, Washington, DT |
| 1963 | Scott Appleton, Texas, T | 1992 | Will Shields, Nebraska, G |
| 1964 | Steve DeLong, Tennessee, T | 1993 | Rob Waldrop, Arizona, NG |
| 1965 | Tommy Nobis, Texas, G | 1994 | Zach Wiegert, Nebraska, G |
| 1966 | Loyd Phillips, Arkansas, T | 1995 | Jonathan Ogden, UCLA, OT |
| 1967 | Ron Yary, USC, T | 1996 | Orlando Pace, Ohio St, OT |
| 1968 | Bill Stanfill, Georgia, T | 1997 | Aaron Taylor, Nebraska, G |
| 1969 | Mike Reid, Penn St, DT | 1998 | Kris Farris, UCLA, OL |
| 1970 | Jim Stillwagon, Ohio St, MG | 1999 | Chris Samuels, Alabama, OL |
| 1971 | Larry Jacobson, Nebraska, DT | 2000 | John Henderson, Tennessee, DT |
| 1972 | Rich Glover, Nebraska, MG | 2001 | Bryant McKinnie, Miami (Fla.), OT |
| 1973 | John Hicks, Ohio St, OT | 2002 | Rien Long, Washington St, DL |
| 1974 | Randy White, Maryland, DE | 2003 | Robert Gallery, Iowa, OT |
| 1975 | Lee Roy Selmon, Oklahoma, DT | 2004 | Jammal Brown, Oklahoma, OT |
| 1976 | Ross Browner, Notre Dame, DE | 2005 | Greg Eslinger, Minnesota, LB |
| 1977 | Brad Shearer, Texas, DT | 2006 | Joe Thomas, Wisconsin, OT |
| 1978 | Greg Roberts, Oklahoma, G | 2007 | Glenn Dorsey, LSU, DT |
| 1979 | Jim Ritcher, North Carolina St, C | 2008 | Andre Smith, Alabama, OT |
| 1980 | Mark May, Pittsburgh, OT | | |

## Butkus Award

Given to the top collegiate linebacker, the award was established by the Downtown Athletic Club of Orlando and named for college Hall of Famer Dick Butkus of Illinois.

| Year | Player, College | Year | Player, College |
|------|-----------------|------|-----------------|
| 1985 | Brian Bosworth, Oklahoma | 1997 | Andy Katzenmoyer, Ohio St |
| 1986 | Brian Bosworth, Oklahoma | 1998 | Chris Claiborne, USC |
| 1987 | Paul McGowan, Florida St | 1999 | LaVar Arrington, Penn St |
| 1988 | Derrick Thomas, Alabama | 2000 | Dan Morgan, Miami (Fla.) |
| 1989 | Percy Snow, Michigan St | 2001 | Rocky Calmus, Oklahoma |
| 1990 | Alfred Williams, Colorado | 2002 | E.J. Henderson, Maryland |
| 1991 | Erick Anderson, Michigan | 2003 | Teddy Lehman, Oklahoma |
| 1992 | Marvin Jones, Florida St | 2004 | Derrick Johnson, Texas |
| 1993 | Trev Alberts, Nebraska | 2005 | Paul Posluszny, Penn State |
| 1994 | Dana Howard, Illinois | 2006 | Patrick Willis, Mississippi |
| 1995 | Kevin Hardy, Illinois | 2007 | James Laurinaitis, Ohio St |
| 1996 | Matt Russell, Colorado | 2008 | Aaron Curry, Wake Forest, LB |

## Jim Thorpe Award

Given to the best defensive back of the year, the award is presented by the Jim Thorpe Athletic Club of Oklahoma City.

| Year | Player, College | Year | Player, College |
|------|-----------------|------|-----------------|
| 1986 | Thomas Everett, Baylor | 1997 | Charles Woodson, Michigan |
| 1987 | Bennie Blades, Miami (Fla.) | 1998 | Antoine Winfield, Ohio St |
| | Rickey Dixon, Oklahoma | 1999 | Tyrone Carter, Minnesota |
| 1988 | Deion Sanders, Florida St | 2000 | Jamar Fletcher, Wisconsin |
| 1989 | Mark Carrier, USC | 2001 | Roy Williams, Oklahoma |
| 1990 | Darryl Lewis, Arizona | 2002 | Terence Newman, Kansas St |
| 1991 | Terrell Buckley, Florida St | 2003 | Derrick Strait, Oklahoma |
| 1992 | Deon Figures, Colorado | 2004 | Carlos Rogers, Auburn |
| 1993 | Antonio Langham, Alabama | 2005 | Michael Huff, Texas |
| 1994 | Chris Hudson, Colorado | 2006 | Aaron Ross, Texas |
| 1995 | Greg Myers, Colorado St | 2007 | Antoine Cason, Arizona |
| 1996 | Lawrence Wright, Florida | 2008 | Malcolm Jenkins, Ohio St |

# Awards (Cont.)

## Walter Payton Player of the Year Award

Given to the top FCS (I-AA) player, voted by Div. I-AA sports information directors. Sponsored by Sports Network.

| Year | Player, College, Position |
|------|---------------------------|
| 1987 | Kenny Gamble, Colgate, RB |
| 1988 | Dave Meggett, Towson St, RB |
| 1989 | John Friesz, Idaho, QB |
| 1990 | Walter Dean, Grambling, RB |
| 1991 | Jamie Martin, Weber St, QB |
| 1992 | Michael Payton, Marshall, QB |
| 1993 | Doug Nussmeier, Idaho, QB |
| 1994 | Steve McNair, Alcorn St, QB |
| 1995 | Dave Dickenson, Montana, QB |
| 1996 | Archie Amerson, Northern Arizona, RB |
| 1997 | Brian Finneran, Villanova, WR |

| Year | Player, College, Position |
|------|---------------------------|
| 1998 | Jerry Azumah, New Hampshire, RB |
| 1999 | Adrian Peterson, Georgia Southern, RB |
| 2000 | Louis Ivory, Furman, RB |
| 2001 | Brian Westbrook, Villanova, RB |
| 2002 | Tony Romo, Eastern Ilinois, QB |
| 2003 | Jamaal Branch, Colgate, RB |
| 2004 | Lang Campbell, William & Mary, QB |
| 2005 | Erik Meyer, Eastern Washington, QB |
| 2006 | Ricky Santos, New Hampshire, QB |
| 2007 | Jayson Foster, Georgia Southern, QB |
| 2008 | Armanti Edwards, Appalachian St, QB |

# NCAA Football Bowl Subdivision (I-A) Individual Records

## Career

### SCORING

**Most Points Scored:** 468—Travis Prentice, Miami (Ohio), 1996–99
**Most Points Scored per Game:** 12.1—Marshall Faulk, San Diego St, 1991–93
**Most Touchdowns Scored:** 78—Travis Prentice, Miami (Ohio), 1996–99 (73 rushing, 5 receiving)
**Most Touchdowns Scored per Game:** 2.0—Marshall Faulk, San Diego St, 1991–93
**Most Touchdowns Scored, Rushing:** 73—Travis Prentice, Miami (Ohio), 1996–99
**Most Touchdowns Scored, Passing:** 134—Graham Harrell, Texas Tech, 2005–08
**Most Touchdowns Scored, Receiving:** 60—Jarrett Dillard, Rice, 2005–08
**Most Touchdowns Scored, Interception Returns:** 5—Ken Thomas, San Jose St, 1979–82; Jackie Walker, Tennessee, 1969–71; Deltha O'Neal, California, 1996–99; Darrent Williams, Okla St, 2001–04
**Most Touchdowns Scored, Punt Returns:** 8—Wes Welker, Texas Tech, 2000–03; Antonio Perkins, Oklahoma, 2001–04
**Most Touchdowns Scored, Kickoff Returns:** 6—Anthony Davis, USC, 1972–74; Ashlan Davis, Tulsa, 2004–05

### TOTAL OFFENSE

**Most Plays:** 2,587—Timmy Chang, Hawaii, 2000–04
**Most Plays per Game:** 50.1—Kliff Kingsbury, Texas Tech, 1999–2002
**Most Yards Gained:** 16,910—Timmy Chang, Hawaii, 2000–04 (17,072 passing, -162 rushing)
**Most Yards Gained per Game:** 387.9—Colt Brennan, Hawaii, 2005–07
**Most 300+ Yard Games:** 33 —Ty Detmer, BYU, 1988–91

### RUSHING

**Most Rushes:** 1,215—Steve Bartalo, Colorado St, 1983–86 (4813 yds)
**Most Rushes per Game:** 34.0—Ed Marinaro, Cornell, 1969–71
**Most Yards Gained:** 6,397—Ron Dayne, Wisconsin, 1996–99
**Most Yards Gained per Game:** 174.6—Ed Marinaro, Cornell, 1969–71
**Most 100+ Yard Games:** 34—DeAngelo Williams, Memphis, 2002–05

### RUSHING (CONT.)

**Most 200+ Yard Games:** 11—Marcus Allen, USC, 1978–81; Ricky Williams, Texas, 1995–98; Ron Dayne, Wisconsin, 1996–99

### PASSING

**Highest Passing Efficiency Rating:** 168.9—Ryan Dinwiddie, Boise St, 2000–03
**Most Passes Attempted:** 2,436—Timmy Chang, Hawaii, 2000–04
**Most Passes Attempted per Game:** 47.0—Tim Rattay, Louisiana Tech, 1997–99
**Most Passes Completed:** 1,403—Graham Harrell, Texas Tech, 2005–08
**Most Passes Completed per Game:** 31.2—Graham Harrell, Texas Tech, 2005–08
**\*Highest Completion Percentage:** 70.4—Colt Brennan, Hawaii, 2005–07
**Most Yards Gained:** 17,072—Timmy Chang, Hawaii, 2000–04
**Most Yards Gained per Game:** 386.2—Tim Rattay, Louisiana Tech, 1997–99 (3 years); 351.0—Graham Harrell, Texas Tech, 2005–08 (4 years)

### RECEIVING

**Most Passes Caught:** 316—Taylor Stubblefield, Purdue, 2001–04
**Most Passes Caught per Game:** 10.5—Emmanuel Hazard, Houston, 1989–90
**Most Yards Gained:** 5,005—Trevor Insley, Nevada, 1996–99
**Most Yards Gained per Game:** 140.9—Alex Van Dyke, Nevada, 1994–95
**†Highest Average Gain per Reception:** 22.0—Herman Moore, Virginia, 1988–90

### ALL-PURPOSE RUNNING

**Most Plays:** 1,347—Steve Bartalo, Colorado St, 1983-86 (1,215 rushes, 132 receptions)
**Most Yards Gained:** 7,573—DeAngelo Williams, Memphis, 2002–05 (6,026 rushing, 723 receiving, 824 KO retrurns)
**Most Yards Gained per Game:** 237.8—Ryan Benjamin, Pacific, 1990–92
**Highest Average Gain per Play:** 17.4—Anthony Carter, Michigan, 1979–82

\*Minimum 1,000 attempts.
†Minimum 105 receptions.

## Career *(Cont.)*

### INTERCEPTIONS

**Most Passes Intercepted:** 29—Al Brosky, Illinois, 1950–52

**Most Passes Intercepted per Game:** 1.1—Al Brosky, Illinois, 1950–52

**Most Yards on Interception Returns:** 501—Terrell Buckley, Florida St, 1989–91

**Highest Average Gain per Interception:** 26.5—Tom Pridemore, West Virginia, 1975–77

### SPECIAL TEAMS

**Highest Punt Return Average:** 23.6—Jack Mitchell, Oklahoma, 1946–48

**Highest Kickoff Return Average:** 36.2—Forrest Hall, San Francisco, 1946–47

**Highest Average Yards per Punt:** 46.3—Todd Sauerbrun, West Virginia, 1991–93 (150–199 punts). 45.3—Ryan Plackemeier, Wake Forest, 2002–05 (200-250 punts). 45.2—Daniel Sepulveda, Baylor, 2003–06 (250+ punts).

## Single Season

### SCORING

**Most Points Scored:** 234—Barry Sanders, Oklahoma St, 1988

**Most Points Scored per Game:** 21.3—Barry Sanders, Oklahoma St, 1988

**Most Touchdowns Scored:** 39—Barry Sanders, Oklahoma St, 1988

**Most Touchdowns Scored, Rushing:** 37—Barry Sanders, Oklahoma St, 1988

**Most Touchdowns Scored, Passing:** 58—Colt Brennan, Hawaii, 2006

**Most Touchdowns Scored, Receiving:** 27—Troy Edwards, Louisiana Tech, 1998

**Most Touchdowns Scored, Interception Returns:** 4—Deltha O'Neal, California, 1999

**Most Touchdowns Scored, Punt Returns:** 5—Chad Owens, Hawaii, 2004

**Most Touchdowns Scored, Kickoff Returns:** 5—Ashlan Davis, Tulsa, 2004

### TOTAL OFFENSE

**Most Plays:** 814—Kliff Kingsbury, Texas Tech, 2002

**Most Yards Gained:** 5,976—B.J. Symons, Texas Tech, 2003

**Most Yards Gained per Game:** 474.6—David Klingler, Houston, 1990

**Most 300+ Yard Games:** 14—Colt Brennan, Hawaii, 2006; Paul Smith, Tulsa, 2007

### RUSHING

**Most Rushes:** 450—Kevin Smith, Central Florida, 2007

**Most Rushes per Game:** 39.6—Ed Marinaro, Cornell, 1971

**Most Yards Gained:** 2,628—Barry Sanders, Oklahoma St, 1988

**Most Yards Gained per Game:** 238.9—Barry Sanders, Oklahoma St, 1988

**Most 100+ Yard Games:** 13—Shonn Green, Iowa, 2008

### PASSING

**Highest Passing Efficiency Rating:** 186.0—Colt Brennan, Hawaii, 2006

**Most Passes Attempted:** 719—B.J. Symons, Texas Tech, 2003

**Most Passes Attempted per Game:** 58.5—David Klingler, Houston, 1990

**Most Passes Completed:** 512—Graham Harrell, Texas Tech, 2007

### PASSING *(Cont.)*

**Most Passes Completed per Game:** 39.4—Graham Harrell, Texas Tech, 2007

**Highest Completion Percentage:** 76.7—Colt McCoy, Texas, 2008

**Most Yards Gained:** 5,140—David Klingler, Houston, 1990 (11 games); 5,336—B.J. Symons, Texas Tech, 2003 (12 games); 5,833—B.J. Symons, Texas Tech, 2003 (13 games

**Most Yards Gained per Game:** 467.3—David Klingler, Houston, 1990

### RECEIVING

**Most Passes Caught:** 142—Emmanuel Hazard, Houston, 1989

**Most Passes Caught per Game:** 13.4—Howard Twilley, Tulsa, 1965

**Most Yards Gained:** 2,060—Trevor Insley, Nevada, 1999

**Most Yards Gained per Game:** 187.3—Trevor Insley, Nevada, 1999

**Highest Average Gain per Reception:** 31.9—Brennan Marion, Tulsa, 2007 (min. 30 receptions)

### ALL-PURPOSE RUNNING

**Most Plays:** 432—Marcus Allen, USC, 1981

**Most Yards Gained:** 3,250—Barry Sanders, Oklahoma St, 1988

**Most Yards Gained per Game:** 295.5—Barry Sanders, Oklahoma St, 1988

**Highest Average Gain per Play:** 19.8—T.Y. Hilton, Florida International, 2008

### INTERCEPTIONS

**Most Passes Intercepted:** 14—Al Worley, Washington, 1968

**Most Yards on Interception Returns:** 302 — Charles Phillips, USC, 1974

**Highest Average Gain per Interception:** 51.8 — Norm Thompson, Utah, 1969

### SPECIAL TEAMS

**Highest Punt Return Average:** 28.5—Maurice Drew, UCLA, 2005

**Highest Kickoff Return Average:** 40.1 — Paul Allen, BYU, 1961

**Highest Average Yards per Punt:** 50.3 — Chad Kessler, LSU, 1997

*Minimum 1,000 attempts.

## Single Game

### SCORING

**Most Points Scored:** 48—Howard Griffith, Illinois, 1990 (vs Southern Illinois)
**Most Field Goals:** 7—Dale Klein, Nebraska, 1985 (vs Missouri); Mike Prindle, Western Michigan, 1984 (vs Marshall)
**Most Extra Points (Kick):** 13—Derek Mahoney, Fresno St, 1991 (vs New Mexico); Terry Leiweke, Houston, 1968 (vs Tulsa)
**Most Extra Points (2-Pts):** 6—Jim Pilot, New Mexico St, 1961 (vs Hardin-Simmons), all 6 rush

### TOTAL OFFENSE

**Most Yards Gained:** 732—David Klingler, Houston, 1990 (vs Arizona St); (716 pass, 16 rush)

### RUSHING

**Most Yards Gained:** 406—LaDainian Tomlinson, TCU, 1999 (vs UTEP)
**Most Touchdowns Rushed:** 8—Howard Griffith, Illinois, 1990 (vs Southern Illinois)

### PASSING

**Most Passes Completed:** 58—Andy Schmitt, Eastern Michigan, 2008 (vs Central Michigan)
**Most Yards Gained:** 716—David Klingler, Houston, 1990 (vs Arizona St)
**Most Touchdown Passes:** 11—David Klingler, Houston, 1990 [vs Eastern Washington (I-AA)]

### RECEIVING

**Most Passes Caught:** 23—Randy Gatewood, UNLV, 1994 (vs Idaho); Tyler Jones, Eastern Michigan, 2008 (vs Central Michigan)
**Most Yards Gained:** 405—Troy Edwards, Louisiana Tech, 1998 (vs Nebraska)
**Most Touchdown Catches:** 7—Rashaun Woods, Oklahoma St, 2003 (vs SMU)

# NCAA Football Championship Subdivision (I-AA) Ind. Records

## Career

### SCORING

**Most Points Scored:** 544—Brian Westbrook, Villanova, 1997–98, 2000-01
**Most Touchdowns Scored:** 89—Brian Westbrook, Villanova, 1997–98, 2000-01
**Most Touchdowns Scored, Rushing:** 84—Adrian Peterson, Georgia Southern, 1998–2001
**Most Touchdowns Scored, Passing:** 140—Bruce Eugene, Grambling St, 2001–05
**Most Touchdowns Scored, Receiving:** 58—David Ball, New Hampshire, 2003–06

### RUSHING

**Most Rushes:** 1,240—Jordan Scott, Colgate, 2005–08
**Most Rushes per Game:** 38.2—Arnold Mickens, Butler, 1994–95
**Most Yards Gained:** 6,559—Adrian Peterson, Georgia Southern, 1998–2001
**Most Yards Gained per Game:** 190.7—Arnold Mickens, Butler, 1994–95 (2 years); 164.5—Adrian Peterson, Georgia Southern, 1998–2000 (3 years); 156.2—Adrian Peterson, Georgia Southern, 1998–2001 (4 years)

### PASSING

**Highest Passing Efficiency Rating:** 170.8—Shawn Knight, William & Mary, 1991–94 (3 years); 176.7—Josh Johnson, San Diego, 2004–07 (4 years)
**Most Passes Attempted:** 1,680—Marcus Brady, Cal St-Northridge, 1998–2001; Steve McNair, Alcorn St, 1991–94
**Most Passes Completed:** 1,122—Ricky Santos, New Hampsire, 2004–07
**Most Passes Completed per Game:** 26.5—Chris Sanders, Chattanooga, 1999–2000
**Highest Completion Percentage:** 69.6—Eric Sanders, Northern Iowa, 2004–07
**Most Yards Gained:** 14,496—Steve McNair, Alcorn St, 1991–94
**Most Yards Gained per Game:** 350.0—Neil Lomax, Portland St, 1978–80

### RECEIVING

**Most Passes Caught:** 317—Jacquay Nunnally, Florida A&M, 1997–2000
**Most Yards Gained:** 4,693—Jerry Rice, Mississippi Valley St, 1981–84
**Most Yards Gained per Game:** 114.5—Jerry Rice, Mississippi Valley St, 1981–84 (min. 3,000 yds)
**Highest Average Gain per Reception:** 22.0—Dedric Ward, Northern Iowa, 1993–96 (min. 125 rec.)

## Single Season

### SCORING

**Most Points Scored:** 234—Omar Cuff, Delaware, 2007
**Most Touchdowns Scored:** 39—Omar Cuff, Delaware, 2007 (15 games)
**Most Touchdowns Scored, Rushing:** 35—Omar Cuff, Delaware, 2007
**Most Touchdowns Scored, Passing:** 56—Willie Totten, Mississippi Valley St, 1984; Bruce Eugene, Grambling St, 2005
**Most Touchdowns Scored, Receiving:** 27—Jerry Rice, Mississippi Valley St, 1984

### RUSHING

**Most Rushes:** 450—Jamaal Branch, Colgate, 2003
**Most Rushes per Game:** 40.9—Arnold Mickens, Butler, 1994
**Most Yards Gained:** 2,326—Jamaal Branch, Colgate, 2003
**Most Yards Gained per Game:** 225.5—Arnold Mickens, Butler, 1994

## Single Season *(Cont.)*

### PASSING

**Highest Passing Efficiency Rating:** 204.6—Shawn Knight, William & Mary, 1993
**Most Passes Attempted:** 598—Jeremy Moses, Stephen F. Austin, 2008
**Most Passes Completed:** 385—Brett Gordon, Villanova, 2002
**Most Passes Completed per Game:** 32.4—Willie Totten, Mississippi Valley St, 1984
**Highest Completion Percentage:** 75.2—Eric Sanders, Northern Iowa, 2007
**Most Yards Gained:** 4,863—Steve McNair, Alcorn St, 1994
**Most Yards Gained per Game:** 455.7—Willie Totten, Mississippi Valley St, 1984

### RECEIVING

**Most Passes Caught:** 120—Stephen Campbell, Brown, 2000
**Most Yards Gained:** 1,712—Eddie Conti, Delaware, 1998
**Most Yards Gained per Game:** 168.2—Jerry Rice, Mississippi Valley St, 1984
**Highest Average Gain per Reception:** 28.9—Mikhael Ricks, Stephen F. Austin, 1997; (min. 35 receptions); 20.7—Golden Tate, Tennessee St, 1983 (min 60 receptions)

## Single Game

### SCORING

**Most Points Scored:** 42—Omar Cuff, Delaware, 2007 (vs William & Mary); Jesse Burton, McNeese St, 1998 (vs Southern Utah); Archie Amerson, Northern Arizona, 1996 (vs Weber St)
**Most Field Goals:** 8—Goran Lingmerth, Northern Arizona, 1986 (vs Idaho)

### RUSHING

**Most Yards Gained:** 437—Maurice Hicks, North Carolina A&T, 2001 (vs Morgan St)
**Most Touchdowns Rushed:** 7—Archie Amerson, Northern Arizona, 1996 (vs Weber St)

### PASSING

**Most Passes Completed:** 57—Jeremy Moses, Stephen F. Austin, 2008, (vs. Sam Houston St)
**Most Yards Gained:** 624—Jamie Martin, Weber St, 1991 (vs Idaho St)
**Most Touchdown Passes:** 9—Willie Totten, Mississippi Valley St, 1984 (vs Kentucky St); Drew Hubel, Portland St, 2007 (vs Weber St)

### RECEIVING

**Most Passes Caught:** 24—Chas Gessner, Brown, 2002, (vs Rhode Island); Jerry Rice, Mississippi Valley St, 1983 (vs Southern–Birmingham)
**Most Yards Gained:** 376—Kassim Osgood, Cal Poly, 2000 (vs Northern Iowa)
**Most Touchdown Catches:** 6—Cos DeMatteo, Chattanooga, 2000 (vs Mississippi Valley St)

# NCAA Division II Individual Records

## Career

### SCORING

**Most Points Scored:** 656—Germaine Rice, Pittsburg St, 2003–06
**Most Touchdowns Scored:** 109—Germaine Rice, Pittsburg St, 2003–06
**Most Touchdowns Scored, Rushing:** 107—Germaine Rice, Pittsburg St, 2003–06
**Most Touchdowns Scored, Passing:** 148—Jimmy Terwilliger, East Stroudsburg, 2003–06
**Most Touchdowns Scored, Receiving:** 78—Dallas Mall, Bentley, 2001–04

### RUSHING

**Most Rushes:** 1,271—Xavier Omon, NW Missouri St, 2004–07
**Most Rushes per Game:** 29.8—Bernie Peeters, Luther, 1968–71
**Most Yards Gained:** 7,962—Danny Woodhead, Chadron St, 2004–07
**Most Yards Gained per Game:** 183.4—Anthony Gray, Western New Mexico, 1997–98

### PASSING

**Highest Passing Efficiency Rating:** 170.7—Jimmy Terwilliger, East Stroudsburg, 2003–06 (Min. 750 comp.)
**Most Passes Attempted:** 1,898—Andrew Webb, Fort Lewis, 2000–03

### PASSING *(Cont.)*

**Most Passes Completed:** 1,055—Ted Schlafke, Wayne St (Neb.), 2005–08
**Most Passes Completed per Game:** 25.9—Evan Gray, Missouri S&T*, 2003–05
**Highest Completion Percentage:** 69.0—Chris Hatcher, Valdosta St, 1991–94 (min. 1,000 att.)
**Most Yards Gained:** 14,350—Jimmy Terwilliger, East Stroudsburg, 2003–06
**Most Yards Gained per Game:** 323.7—Dusty Bonner, Valdosta St, 2000–01

### RECEIVING

**Most Passes Caught:** 323—Clarence Coleman, Ferris St, 1998–2001
**Most Yards Gained:** 4,983—Clarence Coleman, Ferris St, 1998–2001
**Most Yards Gained per Game:** 160.8—Chris George, Glenville St, 1993–94
**Highest Average Gain per Reception:** 23.2—Romar Crenshaw, SE Oklahoma, 2000–03 (min. 135 receptions)

*Missouri S&T was known then as Missouri-Rolla.

## Single Season

### SCORING

**Most Points Scored:** 234—Bernard Scott, Abilene Christian, 2007
**Most Touchdowns Scored:** 39—Bernard Scott, Abilene Christian, 2007
**Most Touchdowns Scored, Rushing:** 37—Xavier Omon, NW Missouri St, 2007
**Most Touchdowns Scored, Passing:** 54—Dusty Bonner, Valdosta St, 2000
**Most Touchdowns Scored, Receiving:** 35—David Kircus, Grand Valley St, 2002

### RUSHING

**Most Rushes:** 385—Joe Gough, Wayne St (Mich.), 1994
**Most Rushes per Game:** 38.6—Mark Perkins, Hobart, 1968
**Most Yards Gained:** 2,756—Danny Woodhead, Chadron St, 2006
**Most Yards Gained per Game:** 222.0—Anthony Gray, Western New Mexico, 1997

### PASSING

**Highest Passing Efficiency Rating:** 221.63—Curt Anes, Grand Valley St, 2001 (min. 100 comp.); 196.5—Dusty Bonner, Valdosta St, 2001 (min. 200 comp.)

### PASSING *(Cont.)*

**Most Passes Attempted:** 583—Dalton Bell, West Texas A&M, 2006
**Most Passes Completed:** 386—Dalton Bell, West Texas A&M, 2006
**Most Passes Completed per Game:** 32.4—Lance Funderburk, Valdosta St, 1995
**Highest Completion Percentage:** 74.7—Chris Hatcher, Valdosta St, 1994 (min. 250 att.)
**Most Yards Gained:** 5,097—Keith Null, West Texas A&M, .2008
**Most Yards Gained per Game:** 393.4—Grady Benton, West Texas A&M, 1994

### RECEIVING

**Most Passes Caught:** 143—Nick Smart, Southwest Baptist, 2007
**Most Yards Gained:** 1,876—Chris George, Glenville St, 1993
**Most Yards Gained per Game:** 187.6—Chris George, Glenville St, 1993
**Highest Average Gain per Reception:** 32.5—Tyrone Johnson, Western St, 1991 (min. 30 receptions)

## Single Game

### SCORING

**Most Points Scored:** 48—Paul Zaeske, North Park, 1968 (vs North Central [Ill.]); Junior Wolf, Okla. Panhandle St, 1958 (vs St. Mary [Ks.])
**Most Field Goals:** 6—Steve Huff, Central Missouri St, 1985 (vs SE Missouri St); Austin Wellock, Ashland, 2002 (vs. Wayne St)

### RUSHING

**Most Yards Gained:** 418—Jarom Freeman, Southern Connecticut St, 2007 (vs Bryant)
**Most Touchdowns Rushed:** 8—Junior Wolf, Okla. Panhandle St, 1958 (vs St. Mary [Ks.])

### PASSING

**Most Passes Completed:** 76—Jarrod DeGeorgia, Wayne St (Neb.), 1996 (vs Drake)
**Most Yards Gained:** 645—Matt Kohn, Indianapolis, 2003 (vs Michigan Tech)
**Most Touchdowns Passed:** 10—Bruce Swanson, North Park, 1968 (vs North Central [Ill.])

### RECEIVING

**Most Passes Caught:** 23—Chris George, Glenville St, 1994 (vs W.V. Wesleyan); Barry Wagner, Alabama A&M, 1989 (vs Clark Atlanta)
**Most Yards Gained:** 401—Kevin Ingram, West Chester, 1998 (vs Clarion)
**Most Touchdown Catches:** 8—Paul Zaeske, North Park, 1968 (vs North Central [Ill.])

# NCAA Division III Individual Records

## Career

### SCORING

**Most Points Scored:** 780—Nate Kmic, Mount Union, 2005–08
**Most Touchdowns Scored:** 130—Nate Kmic, Mount Union, 2005–08
**Most Touchdowns Scored, Rushing:** 125—Nate Kmic, Mount Union, 2005–08
**Most Touchdowns Scored, Passing:** 148—Justin Peery, Westminster (Mo.), 1996–99
**Most Touchdowns Scored, Receiving:** 75—Scott Pingel, Westminster (Mo.), 1996–99

### RUSHING

**Most Rushes:** 1,190—Steve Tardif, Maine Maritime, 1996–99
**Most Rushes per Game:** 32.7—Chris Sizemore, Bridgewater (Va.), 1972–74

### RUSHING *(Cont.)*

**Most Yards Gained:** 8,074—Nate Kmic, Mount Union, 2005–08
**Most Yards Gained per Game:** 187.1—Tony Sutton, Wooster, 2002–04

### PASSING

**Highest Passing Efficiency Rating:** 194.2—Bill Borchert, Mount Union, 1994–97
**Most Passes Attempted:** 1,982—Josh Vogelbach, Guilford, 2005–08
**Most Passes Completed:** 1,189—Josh Vogelbach, Guilford, 2005–08
**Most Passes Completed per Game:** 49.6—Josh Vogelbach, Guilford, 2005–08
**Highest Completion Percentage:** 74.1—Greg Micheli, Mount Union, 2005–08 (min. 750 att.)

## Career (Cont.)

### PASSING (Cont.)

**Most Yards Gained:** 13,605—Josh Vogelbach, Guilford, 2005–08

**Most Yards Gained per Game:** 358.9—Brett Elliott, Linfield, 2004–05

### RECEIVING

**Most Passes Caught:** 436—Scott Pingel, Westminster (Mo.), 1996–99

**Most Yards Gained:** 6,108—Scott Pingel, Westminster (Mo.), 1996–99

**Most Yards Gained per Game:** 156.6—Scott Pingel, Westminster (Mo.), 1996–99

**Highest Average Gain per Reception:** 23.4—Michael Coleman, Widener, 1998–2001

## Single Season

### SCORING

**Most Points Scored:** 264—Nate Kmic, Mount Union, 2008

**Most Points Scored per Game:** 20.8—James Regan, Pomona-Pitzer, 1997

**Most Touchdowns Scored:** 44—Nate Kmic, Mount Union, 2008

**Most Touchdowns Scored, Rushing:** 43—Nate Kmic, Mount Union, 2008

**Most Touchdowns Scored, Passing:** 61—Brett Elliott, Linfield, 2004

**Most Touchdowns Scored, Receiving:** 26—Scott Pingel, Westminster (Mo.), 1998; Jack Phelan, Hartwick, 2008

### RUSHING

**Most Rushes:** 463—Dante Washington, Carthage, 2004

**Most Rushes per Game:** 38.0—Mike Birosak, Dickinson, 1989

**Most Yards Gained:** 2,790—Nate Kmic, Mount Union, 2008

### PASSING

**Highest Passing Efficiency Rating:** 225.0—Mike Simpson, Eureka, 1994

**Most Passes Attempted:** 575—Brett Dietz, Hanover, 2003

**Most Passes Completed:** 360—Brett Dietz, Hanover, 2003

**Most Passes Completed per Game:** 32.9—Justin Peery, Westminster (Mo.), 1999

**Highest Completion Percentage:** 75.0—Greg Micheli, Mount Union, 2008

**Most Yards Gained:** 4,595—Brett Elliott, Linfield, 2004

**Most Yards Gained per Game:** 450.1—Justin Peery, Westminster (Mo.), 1998

### RECEIVING

**Most Passes Caught:** 136—Scott Pingel, Westminster (Mo.), 1999

**Most Yards Gained:** 2,157—Scott Pingel, Westminster, (Mo.), 1998

**Most Yards Gained per Game:** 215.7—Scott Pingel, Westminster, (Mo.), 1998

**Highest Average Gain per Reception:** 26.9—Marty Redlawsk, Concordia (Ill.), 1985 (min. 35 receptions)

## Single Game

### SCORING

**Most Field Goals:** 6—Jim Hever, Rhodes, 1984 (vs Millsaps)

### PASSING

**Most Passes Completed:** 51—Scott Kello, Sul Ross St, 2002 (vs Howard Payne)

**Most Yards Gained:** 731—Zamir Amin, Menlo, 2000 (vs California Lutheran)

**Most Touchdown Passes:** 9—Joe Zarlinga, Ohio Northern, 1998 (vs Capital)

### RUSHING

**Most Yards Gained:** 441—Dante Brown, Marietta, 1996 (vs Baldwin-Wallace)

**Most Touchdowns Rushed:** 8—Carey Bender, Coe, 1994 (vs Beloit)

### RECEIVING

**Most Passes Caught:** 23—Sean Munroe, Mass-Boston, 1992 (vs Mass-Maritime)

**Most Yards Gained:** 418—Lewis Howes, Principia, 2002 (vs Martin Luther)

**Most Touchdown Catches:** 7—Matt Perceval, Wesleyan (Conn.), 1998 (vs Middlebury)

# NCAA FBS (Div. I-A) Alltime Individual Leaders

## Career

### Scoring

**POINTS (KICKERS)**

| | Years | Pts |
|---|---|---|
| Art Carmody, Louisville | 2004–07 | 433 |
| ‡Kevin Kelly, Penn St | 2005–08 | 425 |
| Roman Anderson, Houston | 1988–91 | 423 |
| Billy Bennett, Georgia | 2000–03 | 409 |
| Jeremy Ito, Rutgers | 2004–07 | 400 |

‡includes one TD and one 2-pt. conversion (rush)

**POINTS (NON-KICKERS)**

| | Years | Pts |
|---|---|---|
| Travis Prentice, Miami (Ohio) | 1996–99 | 468 |
| Ricky Williams, Texas | 1995–98 | 452 |
| Taurean Henderson, Texas Tech | 2002–05 | 414 |
| Brock Forsey, Boise St | 1999–02 | 408 |
| Cedric Benson, Texas | 2001–04 | 404 |

**POINTS PER GAME (NON-KICKERS)**

| | Years | Pts/Game |
|---|---|---|
| Marshall Faulk, San Diego St | 1991–93 | 12.1 |
| Ed Marinaro, Cornell | 1969–71 | 11.8 |
| Bill Burnett, Arkansas | 1968–70 | 11.3 |
| Steve Owens, Oklahoma | 1967–69 | 11.2 |
| Eddie Talboom, Wyoming | 1948–50 | 10.8 |

### Total Offense

**YARDS GAINED**

| | Years | Yds |
|---|---|---|
| Timmy Chang, Hawaii | 2000–04 | 16,910 |
| Graham Harrell, Texas Tech | 2005–08 | 15,599 |
| Colt Brennan, Hawaii | 2005–07 | 14,740 |
| Ty Detmer, BYU | 1988–91 | 14,665 |
| Kevin Kolb, Houston | 2003–06 | 13,715 |

**YARDS PER GAME**

| | Years | Yds/Game |
|---|---|---|
| Colt Brennan, Hawaii | 2005–07 | 387.9 |
| Tim Rattay, Louisiana Tech | 1997–99 | 382.4 |
| Graham Harrell, Texas Tech | 2005–08 | 346.6 |
| Chase Holbrook, New Mexico St | 2005–08 | 321.4 |
| Chris Vargas, Nevada | 1992–93 | 320.9 |

### Rushing

**YARDS GAINED**

| | Years | Yds |
|---|---|---|
| Ron Dayne, Wisconsin | 1996–99 | 6,397 |
| Ricky Williams, Texas | 1995–98 | 6,279 |
| Tony Dorsett, Pittsburgh | 1973–76 | 6,082 |
| DeAngelo Williams, Memphis | 2002–05 | 6,026 |
| Charles White, USC | 1976–79 | 5,598 |
| Travis Prentice, Miami (Ohio) | 1996–99 | 5,596 |

**YARDS PER GAME**

| | Years | Yds/Game |
|---|---|---|
| Ed Marinaro, Cornell | 1969–71 | 174.6 |
| O.J. Simpson, USC | 1967–68 | 164.4 |
| Herschel Walker, Georgia | 1980–82 | 159.4 |
| Garrett Wolfe, Northern Illinois | 2004-06 | 156.5 |
| LeShon Johnson, Northern Illinois | 1992–93 | 150.6 |

**TOUCHDOWNS RUSHING**

| | Years | TD |
|---|---|---|
| Travis Prentice, Miami (Ohio) | 1996–99 | 73 |
| Ricky Williams, Texas | 1995–98 | 72 |
| Anthony Thompson, Indiana | 1986–89 | 64 |
| Cedric Benson, Texas | 2001–04 | 64 |
| Ron Dayne, Wisconsin | 1996–99 | 63 |

### Passing

**PASSING EFFICIENCY**

| | Years | Rating |
|---|---|---|
| Ryan Dinwiddie, Boise St | 2000–03 | 168.9 |
| Colt Brennan, Hawaii | 2005–07 | 167.7 |
| Danny Wuerffel, Florida | 1993–96 | 163.6 |
| Omar Jacobs, Bowling Green | 2003–05 | 163.5 |
| Ty Detmer, BYU | 1988–91 | 162.7 |

Note: Minimum 500 completions.

**YARDS GAINED**

| | Years | Yds |
|---|---|---|
| Timmy Chang, Hawaii | 2000–04 | 17,072 |
| Graham Harrell, Texas Tech | 2005–08 | 15,793 |
| Ty Detmer, BYU | 1988–91 | 15,031 |
| Colt Brennan, Hawaii | 2005–07 | 14,193 |
| Philip Rivers, North Carolina St | 2000–03 | 13,484 |

**COMPLETIONS**

| | Years | Comp |
|---|---|---|
| Graham Harrell, Texas Tech | 2005–08 | 1,403 |
| Timmy Chang, Hawaii | 2000–04 | 1,388 |
| Kliff Kingsbury, Texas Tech | 1999–02 | 1,231 |
| Philip Rivers, North Carolina St | 2000–03 | 1,147 |
| Colt Brennan, Hawaii | 2005–07 | 1,115 |

**TOUCHDOWNS PASSING**

| | Years | TD |
|---|---|---|
| Graham Harrell, Texas Tech | 2005–08 | 134 |
| Colt Brennan, Hawaii | 2005–07 | 131 |
| Ty Detmer, BYU | 1988–91 | 121 |
| Timmy Chang, Hawaii | 2000–04 | 117 |
| Tim Rattay, Louisiana Tech | 1997–99 | 115 |

### Receiving

**CATCHES**

| | Years | No. |
|---|---|---|
| Taylor Stubblefield, Purdue | 2001–04 | 316 |
| Josh Davis, Marshall | 2001–04 | 306 |
| Taurean Henderson, Texas Tech | 2002–05 | 303 |
| Arnold Jackson, Louisville | 1997–00 | 300 |
| Trevor Insley, Nevada | 1996–99 | 298 |

**CATCHES PER GAME**

| | Years | No./Game |
|---|---|---|
| Emmanuel Hazard, Houston | 1989–90 | 10.5 |
| Alex Van Dyke, Nevada | 1994–95 | 10.3 |
| Howard Twilley, Tulsa | 1963–65 | 10.0 |
| Jason Phillips, Houston | 1987–88 | 9.4 |
| Michael Crabtree, Texas Tech | 2007–08 | 8.9 |

**YARDS GAINED**

| | Years | Yds |
|---|---|---|
| Trevor Insley, Nevada | 1996–99 | 5,005 |
| Marcus Harris, Wyoming | 1993–96 | 4,518 |
| Rashaun Woods, Oklahoma St | 2000–03 | 4,412 |
| Ryan Yarborough, Wyoming | 1990–93 | 4,357 |
| Troy Edwards, Louisiana Tech | 1996–98 | 4,352 |

**TOUCHDOWN CATCHES**

| | Years | TD |
|---|---|---|
| Jarrett Dillard, Rice | 2005–08 | 60 |
| Troy Edwards, Louisiana Tech | 1996–98 | 50 |
| Darius Watts, Marshall | 2000–03 | 47 |
| Aaron Turner, Pacific | 1989–92 | 43 |
| Ryan Yarborough, Wyoming | 1990–93 | 42 |
| Rashaun Woods, Oklahoma St | 2000–03 | 42 |

## Career *(Cont.)*

### All-Purpose Running

**YARDS GAINED**

| | Years | Yds |
|---|---|---|
| DeAngelo Williams, Memphis | 2002–05 | 7,573 |
| Ricky Williams, Texas | 1996–98 | 7,206 |
| Napoleon McCallum, Navy | 1981–85 | 7,172 |
| Chris Johnson, East Carolina | 2004–07 | 6,993 |
| Darrin Nelson, Stanford | 1977–78, 80–81 | 6,885 |

| **YARDS PER GAME** | Years | Yds/Game |
|---|---|---|
| Ryan Benjamin, Pacific | 1990–92 | 237.8 |
| Sheldon Canley, San Jose St | 1988–90 | 205.8 |
| Jeremy Maclin, Missouri | 2007–08 | 200.3 |
| Howard Stevens, Louisville | 1971–72 | 193.7 |
| O.J. Simpson, USC | 1967–68 | 192.9 |

### Interceptions

| PLAYER/SCHOOL | Years | Int |
|---|---|---|
| Al Brosky, Illinois | 1950–52 | 29 |
| John Provost, Holy Cross | 1972–74 | 27 |
| Martin Bayless, Bowling Green | 1980–83 | 27 |
| Tom Curtis, Michigan | 1967–69 | 25 |
| Tony Thurman, Boston College | 1981–84 | 25 |
| Tracy Saul, Texas Tech | 1989–92 | 25 |

### Punting Average

| PLAYER/SCHOOL | Years | Avg |
|---|---|---|
| Daniel Sepulveda, Baylor | 2003–06 | 45.2 |
| Shane Lechler, Texas A&M | 1996–99 | 44.7 |
| Bill Smith, Mississippi | 1983–86 | 44.3 |
| Jim Arnold, Vanderbilt | 1979–82 | 43.9 |
| Ralf Mojsiejenko, Michigan St | 1981–84 | 43.6 |

Note: 250+ punts.

### Punt Return Average

| PLAYER/SCHOOL | Years | Avg |
|---|---|---|
| Jack Mitchell, Oklahoma | 1946–48 | 23.6 |
| Gene Gibson, Cincinnati | 1949–50 | 20.5 |
| Eddie Macon, Pacific | 1949–51 | 18.9 |
| Jackie Robinson, UCLA | 1939–40 | 18.8 |
| Dan Shelton, Illinois | 2001–04 | 17.9 |

Note: Minimum 30 returns.

### Kickoff Return Average

| PLAYER/SCHOOL | Years | Avg |
|---|---|---|
| Anthony Davis, USC | 1972–74 | 35.1 |
| Eric Booth, Southern Miss | 1994–97 | 32.4 |
| Overton Curtis, Utah St | 1957–58 | 31.0 |
| Fred Montgomery, New Mexico St | 1991–92 | 30.5 |
| Bryan Williams, Akron | 2005–08 | 30.5 |

Note: Minimum 30 returns.

## Single Season

### Scoring

| POINTS | Year | Pts |
|---|---|---|
| Barry Sanders, Oklahoma St | 1988 | 234 |
| Brock Forsey, Boise St | 2002 | 192 |
| Troy Edwards, Louisiana Tech | 1998 | 186 |
| Kevin Smith, Central Florida | 2007 | 180 |
| Mike Rozier, Nebraska | 1983 | 174 |
| Lydell Mitchell, Penn St | 1971 | 174 |

| FIELD GOALS | Year | FG |
|---|---|---|
| Billy Bennett, Georgia | 2003 | 31 |
| John Lee, UCLA | 1984 | 29 |
| John Sullivan, New Mexico | 2007 | 29 |
| Paul Woodside, West Virginia | 1982 | 28 |
| Luis Zendejas, Arizona St | 1983 | 28 |
| Nick Browne, TCU | 2003 | 28 |
| Justin Medlock, UCLA | 2006 | 28 |

Four tied with 27.

### All-Purpose Running

| YARDS GAINED | Year | Yds |
|---|---|---|
| Barry Sanders, Oklahoma St | 1988 | 3,250 |
| Ryan Benjamin, Pacific | 1991 | 2,995 |
| Chris Johnson, East Carolina | 2007 | 2,960 |
| Reggie Bush, USC | 2005 | 2,890 |
| Jeremy Maclin, Missouri | 2008 | 2,833 |

| YARDS PER GAME | Year | Yds/Game |
|---|---|---|
| Barry Sanders, Oklahoma St | 1988 | 295.5 |
| Ryan Benjamin, Pacific | 1991 | 249.6 |
| Byron (Whizzer) White, Colorado | 1937 | 246.3 |
| Mike Pringle, Fullerton St | 1989 | 244.6 |
| Paul Palmer, Temple | 1986 | 239.4 |

### Total Offense

| YARDS GAINED | Year | Yds |
|---|---|---|
| B.J. Symons, Texas Tech | 2003 | 5,976 |
| Colt Brennan, Hawaii | 2006 | 5,915 |
| Graham Harrell, Texas Tech | 2007 | 5,614 |
| Case Keenum, Houston | 2008 | 5,241 |
| David Klingler, Houston | 1990 | 5,221 |

| YARDS PER GAME | Year | Yds/Game |
|---|---|---|
| David Klingler, Houston | 1990 | 474.6 |
| B.J. Symons, Texas Tech | 2003 | 459.7 |
| Graham Harrell, Texas Tech | 2007 | 431.8 |
| Andre Ware, Houston | 1989 | 423.7 |
| Colt Brennan, Hawaii | 2006 | 422.5 |

### Rushing

| YARDS GAINED | Year | Yds |
|---|---|---|
| Barry Sanders, Oklahoma St | 1988 | 2,628 |
| Kevin Smith, Central Florida | 2007 | 2,567 |
| Marcus Allen, USC | 1981 | 2,342 |
| Troy Davis, Iowa St | 1996 | 2,185 |
| LaDainian Tomlinson, TCU | 2000 | 2,158 |

| YARDS PER GAME | Year | Yds/Game |
|---|---|---|
| Barry Sanders, Oklahoma St | 1988 | 238.9 |
| Marcus Allen, USC | 1981 | 212.9 |
| Ed Marinaro, Cornell | 1971 | 209.0 |
| Troy Davis, Iowa St | 1996 | 198.6 |
| LaDainian Tomlinson, TCU | 2000 | 196.2 |

## Single Season *(Cont.)*

### Rushing *(Cont.)*

| TOUCHDOWNS RUSHING | Year | TD |
|---|---|---|
| Barry Sanders, Oklahoma St | 1988 | 37 |
| Kevin Smith, Central Florida | 2007 | 29 |
| Mike Rozier, Nebraska | 1983 | 29 |
| Willis McGahee, Miami (Fla.) | 2002 | 28 |
| Ricky Williams, Texas | 1998 | 27 |
| Lee Suggs, Virginia Tech | 2000 | 27 |

### Passing

| PASSING EFFICIENCY | Year | Rating |
|---|---|---|
| Colt Brennan, Hawaii | 2006 | 186.0 |
| Shaun King, Tulane | 1998 | 183.3 |
| Stefan LeFors, Louisville | 2004 | 181.7 |
| Sam Bradford, Oklahoma | 2008 | 180.8 |
| Michael Vick, Virginia Tech | 1999 | 180.4 |

| YARDS GAINED | Year | Yds |
|---|---|---|
| B.J. Symons, Texas Tech | 2003 | 5,833 |
| Graham Harrell, Texas Tech | 2007 | 5,705 |
| Colt Brennan, Hawaii | 2006 | 5,549 |
| Ty Detmer, BYU | 1990 | 5,188 |
| David Klingler, Houston | 1990 | 5,140 |

| COMPLETIONS | Year | Att | Comp |
|---|---|---|---|
| Graham Harrell, Texas Tech | 2007 | 713 | 512 |
| Kliff Kingsbury, Texas Tech | 2002 | 712 | 479 |
| B.J. Symons, Texas Tech | 2003 | 719 | 470 |
| Graham Harrell, Texas Tech | 2008 | 626 | 442 |
| Sonny Cumbie, Texas Tech | 2004 | 642 | 421 |

| TOUCHDOWNS PASSING | Year | TD |
|---|---|---|
| Colt Brennan, Hawaii | 2006 | 58 |
| David Klingler, Houston | 1990 | 54 |
| B.J. Symons, Texas Tech | 2003 | 52 |
| Sam Bradford, Oklahoma | 2008 | 50 |
| Graham Harrell, Texas Tech | 2007 | 48 |

### Receiving

| CATCHES | Year | GP | No. |
|---|---|---|---|
| Emmanuel Hazard, Houston | 1989 | 11 | 142 |
| Troy Edwards, Louisiana Tech | 1998 | 12 | 140 |
| Nate Burleson, Nevada | 2002 | 12 | 138 |
| Howard Twilley, Tulsa | 1965 | 10 | 134 |
| Trevor Insley, Nevada | 1999 | 11 | 134 |
| Michael Crabtree, Texas Tech | 2008 | 13 | 134 |

| CATCHES PER GAME | Year | No. | No./Game |
|---|---|---|---|
| Howard Twilley, Tulsa | 1965 | 134 | 13.4 |
| Emmanuel Hazard, Houston | 1989 | 142 | 12.9 |
| Trevor Insley, Nevada | 1999 | 134 | 12.2 |
| Alex Van Dyke, Nevada | 1995 | 129 | 11.7 |
| Troy Edwards, Louisiana Tech | 1998 | 140 | 11.7 |

| YARDS GAINED | Year | Yds |
|---|---|---|
| Trevor Insley, Nevada | 1999 | 2,060 |
| Troy Edwards, Louisiana Tech | 1998 | 1,996 |
| Michael Crabtree, Texas Tech | 2007 | 1,962 |
| Alex Van Dyke, Nevada | 1995 | 1,854 |
| J.R. Tolver, San Diego St | 2002 | 1,785 |

| TOUCHDOWN CATCHES | Year | TD |
|---|---|---|
| Troy Edwards, Louisiana Tech | 1998 | 27 |
| Randy Moss, Marshall | 1997 | 25 |
| Emmanuel Hazard, Houston | 1989 | 22 |
| Larry Fitzgerald, Pittsburgh | 2003 | 22 |
| Michael Crabtree, Texas Tech | 2007 | 22 |

## Single Game

### Scoring

| POINTS | Opponent | Year | Pts |
|---|---|---|---|
| Howard Griffith, Illinois | Southern Illinois | 1990 | 48 |
| Marshall Faulk, San Diego St | Pacific | 1991 | 44 |
| Jim Brown, Syracuse | Colgate | 1956 | 43 |
| Fred Wendt, UTEP* | New Mexico St | 1948 | 42 |
| Arnold Boykin, Mississippi | Mississippi St | 1951 | 42 |
| Rashaun Woods, Okla. St | SMU | 2003 | 42 |

*UTEP was Texas Mines in 1948.

| FIELD GOALS | Opponent | Year | FG |
|---|---|---|---|
| Dale Klein, Nebraska | Missouri | 1985 | 7 |
| Mike Prindle, Western Michigan | Marshall | 1984 | 7 |

Note: 15 tied with 6.

Klein's distances were 32-22-43-44-29-43-43.
Prindle's distances were 32-44-42-23-48-41-27.

### Total Offense

| YARDS GAINED | Opponent | Year | Yds |
|---|---|---|---|
| David Klingler, Houston | Arizona St | 1990 | 732 |
| Matt Vogler, TCU | Houston | 1990 | 696 |
| B.J. Symons, Texas Tech | Mississippi | 2003 | 681 |
| Brian Lindgren, Idaho | Middle Tenn St | 2001 | 657 |
| Graham Harrell, Texas Tech | Oklahoma St | 2007 | 643 |
| David Klingler, Houston | TCU | 1990 | 625 |
| Scott Mitchell, Utah | Air Force | 1988 | 625 |

### Passing

| YARDS GAINED | Opponent | Year | Yds |
|---|---|---|---|
| David Klingler, Houston | Arizona St | 1990 | 716 |
| Matt Vogler, TCU | Houston | 1990 | 690 |
| B.J. Symons, Texas Tech | Mississippi | 2003 | 661 |
| Graham Harrell, Texas Tech | Oklahoma St | 2007 | 646 |
| Cody Hodges, Texas Tech | Kansas St | 2005 | 643 |

| COMPLETIONS | Opponent | Year | Comp |
|---|---|---|---|
| Andy Schmitt, E. Michigan | Central Mich. | 2008 | 58 |
| Drew Brees, Purdue | Wisconsin | 1998 | 55 |
| Rusty LaRue, Wake Forest | Duke | 1995 | 55 |
| Andy Schmitt, E. Michigan | Temple | 2008 | 50 |
| Rusty LaRue, Wake Forest | No.Carolina St | 1995 | 50 |

Note: 5 tied with 49.

| TOUCHDOWNS PASSING | Opponent | Year | TD |
|---|---|---|---|
| David Klingler, Houston | E Wash | 1990 | 11 |

Note: Klingler's TD passes were 5-48-29-7-3-7-40-10-7-8-51.

## Single Game *(Cont.)*

### Rushing

| YARDS GAINED | Opponent | Year | Yds |
|---|---|---|---|
| LaDainian Tomlinson, TCU...UTEP | | 1999 | 406 |
| Tony Sands, Kansas.........Missouri | | 1991 | 396 |
| Marshall Faulk, San Diego St..Pacific | | 1991 | 386 |
| Troy Davis, Iowa St...........Missouri | | 1996 | 378 |
| Anthony Thompson, Indiana..Wisconsin | | 1989 | 377 |
| Robbie Mixon, Cent. Mich...Eastern Mich | | 2002 | 377 |

| TOUCHDOWNS RUSHING | Opponent | Year | TD |
|---|---|---|---|
| Howard Griffith, Illinois .....Southern Illinois | | 1990 | 8 |

Note: Griffith's TD runs were 5-51-7-41-5-18-5-3.

### Receiving

| CATCHES | Opponent | Year | No. |
|---|---|---|---|
| Tyler Jones, E. Michigan.....Central Mich. | | 2008 | 23 |
| Randy Gatewood, UNLV.....Idaho | | 1994 | 23 |
| Jay Miller, BYU ...................New Mexico | | 1973 | 22 |
| Troy Edwards, La. Tech ......Nebraska | | 1998 | 21 |
| Chris Daniels, Purdue.........Michigan St | | 1999 | 21 |

Note: 3 tied with 20.

### Receiving *(Cont.)*

| YARDS GAINED | Opponent | Year | Yds |
|---|---|---|---|
| Troy Edwards, Louisiana Tech...Nebraska | | 1998 | 405 |
| Randy Gatewood, UNLV .........Idaho | | 1994 | 363 |
| Chuck Hughes, UTEP*............North Texas | | 1965 | 349 |
| Donnie Avery, Houston ...........Rice | | 2007 | 346 |
| Casey Fitzgerald, North Texas..SMU | | 2007 | 327 |

*UTEP was Texas Western in 1965.

| TOUCHDOWN CATCHES | Opponent | Year | TD |
|---|---|---|---|
| Rashaun Woods, Okla. St .....SMU | | 2003 | 7 |
| Tim Delaney, San Diego St....New Mex. St | | 1969 | 6 |

## Longest Plays (since 1941)

| PASSING | Opponent | Year | Yds |
|---|---|---|---|
| Fred Owens to Jack Ford, Portland..............................St. Mary's (Ca.) | | 1947 | 99 |
| Bo Burris to Warren McVea, Houston..............................Washington St | | 1966 | 99 |
| Colin Clapton to Eddie Jenkins, Holy Cross ............................Boston Univ. | | 1970 | 99 |
| Terry Peel to Robert Ford, Houston..............................Syracuse | | 1970 | 99 |
| Terry Peel to Robert Ford, Houston..............................San Diego St | | 1972 | 99 |
| Cris Collinsworth to Derrick Gaffney, Florida.....................................Rice | | 1977 | 99 |
| Scott Ankrom to James Maness, TCU.........................................Rice | | 1984 | 99 |
| Gino Torretta to Horace Copeland, Miami (Fla.) ...........................Arkansas | | 1991 | 99 |
| John Paci to Thomas Lewis, Indiana....................................Penn St | | 1993 | 99 |
| Troy DeGar to Wes Caswell Tulsa.......................................Oklahoma | | 1996 | 99 |
| Drew Brees to Vinny Sutherland, Purdue ................................Northwestern | | 1999 | 99 |
| Dan Urban to Justin McCariens, Northern Illinois.....................Ball St | | 2000 | 99 |
| Jason Johnson to Brandon Marshall, Arizona.................................Idaho | | 2001 | 99 |
| Dondrial Pinkins to Troy Williamson, South Carolina .....................Virginia | | 2003 | 99 |
| Jim Sorgi to Lee Evans, Wisconsin...............................Akron | | 2003 | 99 |
| Giovanni Vizza to Casey Fitzgerald, North Texas ...........................La.-Monroe | | 2007 | 99 |

| RUSHING | Opponent | Year | Yd |
|---|---|---|---|
| Gale Sayers, Kansas ............Nebraska | | 1963 | 99 |
| Max Anderson, Arizona St....Wyoming | | 1967 | 99 |
| Ralph Thompson, West Texas St ........................Wichita St | | 1970 | 99 |
| Kelsey Finch, Tennessee ......Florida | | 1977 | 99 |
| Eric Vann, Kansas.................Oklahoma | | 1997 | 99 |
| Terry Caulley, Connecticut....Army | | 2006 | 99 |

| FIELD GOALS | Opponent | Year | Yds |
|---|---|---|---|
| Steve Little, Arkansas ;...........Texas | | 1977 | 67 |
| Russell Erxleben, Texas .........Rice | | 1977 | 67 |
| Joe Williams, Wichita St ........Southern Ill. | | 1978 | 67 |
| Martin Gramatica, Kansas St...Northern Ill. | | 1998 | 65 |
| Tony Franklin, Texas A&M ......Baylor | | 1976 | 65 |

| PUNTS | Opponent | Year | Yds |
|---|---|---|---|
| Pat Brady, Nevada*................Loyola (Ca.) | | 1950 | 99 |
| George O'Brien, Wisconsin ...Iowa | | 1952 | 96 |
| John Hadl, Kansas.................Oklahoma | | 1959 | 94 |
| Carl Knox, TCU .....................Oklahoma St | | 1947 | 94 |
| Preston Johnson, SMU...........Pittsburgh | | 1940 | 94 |

*Nevada was Nevada-Reno in 1950.

## FOOTBALL BOWL SUBDIVISION (DIV. I-A) WINNINGEST TEAMS

### Alltime Winning Percentage

| | Yrs | W | L | T | Pct | GP | Bowl Record |
|---|---|---|---|---|---|---|---|
| Michigan | 129 | 872 | 295 | 36 | .740 | 1,203 | 19-20-0 |
| Notre Dame | 120 | 831 | 284 | 42 | .736 | 1,157 | 13-15-0 |
| Texas | 116 | 832 | 317 | 33 | .718 | 1,182 | 24-21-2 |
| Oklahoma | 114 | 791 | 297 | 53 | .716 | 1,141 | 24-16-1 |
| Ohio St | 119 | 807 | 306 | 53 | .715 | 1,166 | 18-21-0 |
| Alabama | 114 | 799 | 316 | 43 | .709 | 1,158 | 31-21-3 |
| USC | 116 | 766 | 303 | 54 | .706 | 1,123 | 30-16-0 |
| Boise St | 41 | 339 | 144 | 2 | .701 | 485 | 5-3-0 |
| Nebraska | 119 | 817 | 337 | 40 | .701 | 1,194 | 22-22-0 |
| Tennessee | 112 | 775 | 327 | 53 | .694 | 1,155 | 25-22-0 |
| Penn St | 122 | 800 | 349 | 41 | .689 | 1,190 | 26-12-2 |
| Florida St | 62 | 459 | 221 | 17 | .671 | 697 | 20-14-2 |
| Georgia | 115 | 723 | 384 | 54 | .646 | 1,161 | 24-16-3 |
| LSU | 115 | 700 | 383 | 47 | .640 | 1,130 | 20-18-1 |
| Miami (Fla.) | 82 | 544 | 310 | 19 | .634 | 873 | 18-13-0 |
| Auburn | 116 | 681 | 395 | 47 | .627 | 1,123 | 19-13-2 |
| Florida | 102 | 641 | 373 | 40 | .627 | 1,054 | 16-19-0 |
| Miami (Ohio) | 120 | 649 | 379 | 44 | .626 | 1,072 | 6-3-0 |
| South Florida | 12 | 87 | 52 | 0 | .626 | 139 | 1-2-0 |
| Arizona St | 96 | 545 | 334 | 24 | .617 | 903 | 12-11-1 |
| Washington | 119 | 650 | 400 | 50 | .614 | 1,100 | 14-14-1 |
| Central Michigan | 108 | 558 | 353 | 36 | .608 | 947 | 1-3-0 |
| Colorado | 119 | 663 | 426 | 36 | .605 | 1,125 | 12-16-0 |
| Virginia Tech | 115 | 657 | 425 | 46 | .603 | 1,128 | 13-17-0 |
| *Western Kentucky | 89 | 511 | 336 | 30 | .600 | 847 | 0-0-0 |
| Texas A&M | 114 | 659 | 433 | 48 | .599 | 1,140 | 13-17-0 |

Note: Includes bowl games. *Reclassified as FBS (Div. I-A) on November 2, 2006.

### Alltime Victories

| | | | | | |
|---|---|---|---|---|---|
| Michigan | 872 | Georgia | 723 | Arkansas | 651 |
| Texas | 832 | LSU | 700 | Washington | 650 |
| Notre Dame | 831 | Auburn | 681 | Miami (Ohio) | 649 |
| Nebraska | 817 | Syracuse | 674 | Florida | 641 |
| Ohio St | 807 | West Virginia | 673 | North Carolina | 639 |
| Penn St | 800 | Colorado | 663 | Army | 637 |
| Alabama | 799 | Georgia Tech | 662 | Minnesota | 637 |
| Oklahoma | 791 | Texas A&M | 659 | Clemson | 632 |
| Tennessee | 775 | Virginia Tech | 657 | Navy | 632 |
| USC | 766 | Pittsburgh | 653 | California | 614 |

### NUMBER ONE VS NUMBER TWO

The No. 1 and No. 2 teams, according to the Associated Press Poll, have met 33 times, including 13 bowl games, since the poll's inception in 1936. The No. 1 teams have a 20-11-2 record in these matchups. Notre Dame (4-3-2) has played in nine of the games.

| Date | Results | Stadium |
|---|---|---|
| 10-9-43 | No. 1 Notre Dame 35, No. 2 Michigan 12 | Michigan (Ann Arbor) |
| 11-20-43 | No. 1 Notre Dame 14, No. 2 Iowa Pre-Flight 13 | Notre Dame (South Bend) |
| 12-2-44 | No. 1 Army 23, No. 2 Navy 7 | Municipal (Baltimore) |
| 11-10-45 | No. 1 Army 48, No. 2 Notre Dame 0 | Yankee (New York) |
| 12-1-45 | No. 1 Army 32, No. 2 Navy 13 | Municipal (Philadelphia) |
| 11-9-46 | No. 1 Army 0, No. 2 Notre Dame 0 | Yankee (New York) |
| 1-1-63 | No. 1 USC 42, No. 2 Wisconsin 37 (Rose Bowl) | Rose Bowl (Pasadena) |
| 10-12-63 | No. 2 Texas 28, No. 1 Oklahoma 7 | Cotton Bowl (Dallas) |
| 1-1-64 | No. 1 Texas 28, No. 2 Navy 6 (Cotton Bowl) | Cotton Bowl (Dallas) |
| 11-19-66 | No. 1 Notre Dame 10, No. 2 Michigan St 10 | Spartan (East Lansing) |
| 9-28-68 | No. 1 Purdue 37, No. 2 Notre Dame 22 | Notre Dame (South Bend) |
| 1-1-69 | No. 1 Ohio St 27, No. 2 USC 16 (Rose Bowl) | Rose Bowl (Pasadena) |
| 12-6-69 | No. 1 Texas 15, No. 2 Arkansas 14 | Razorback (Fayetteville) |
| 11-25-71 | No. 1 Nebraska 35, No. 2 Oklahoma 31 | Owen Field (Norman) |
| 1-1-72 | No. 1 Nebraska 38, No. 2 Alabama 6 (Orange Bowl) | Orange Bowl (Miami) |
| 1-1-79 | No. 2 Alabama 14, No. 1 Penn St 7 (Sugar Bowl) | Sugar Bowl (New Orleans) |
| 9-26-81 | No. 1 USC 28, No. 2 Oklahoma 24 | Coliseum (Los Angeles) |
| 1-1-83 | No. 2 Penn St 27, No. 1 Georgia 23 (Sugar Bowl) | Sugar Bowl (New Orleans) |
| 10-19-85 | No. 1 Iowa 12, No. 2 Michigan 10 | Kinnick (Iowa City) |

### NUMBER ONE VS NUMBER TWO *(Cont.)*

| Date | Results | Stadium |
|---|---|---|
| 9-27-86 | No. 2 Miami (Fla.) 28, No. 1 Oklahoma 16 | Orange Bowl (Miami) |
| 1-2-87 | No. 2 Penn St 14, No. 1 Miami (FL) 10 (Fiesta Bowl) | Sun Devil (Tempe) |
| 11-21-87 | No. 2 Oklahoma 17, No. 1 Nebraska 7 | Memorial (Lincoln) |
| 1-1-88 | No. 2 Miami (Fla.) 20, No. 1 Oklahoma 14 (Orange Bowl) | Orange Bowl (Miami) |
| 11-26-88 | No. 1 Notre Dame 27, No. 2 USC 10 | Coliseum (Los Angeles) |
| 9-16-89 | No. 1 Notre Dame 24, No. 2 Michigan 19 | Michigan (Ann Arbor) |
| 11-16-91 | No. 2 Miami (Fla.) 17, No. 1 Florida St 16 | Campbell (Tallahassee) |
| 1-1-93 | No. 2 Alabama 34, No. 1 Miami (Fla.) 13 (Sugar Bowl) | Superdome (New Orleans) |
| 11-13-93 | No. 2 Notre Dame 31, No. 1 Florida St 24 | Notre Dame (South Bend) |
| 1-1-94 | No. 1 Florida St 18, No. 2 Nebraska 16 (Orange Bowl) | Orange Bowl (Miami) |
| 1-2-96 | No. 1 Nebraska 62, No. 2 Florida 24 (Fiesta Bowl) | Sun Devil (Tempe) |
| 11-30-96 | No. 2 Florida St 24, No. 1 Florida 21 | Campbell (Tallahassee) |
| 1-4-99 | No. 1 Tennessee 23, No. 2 Florida St 16 (Fiesta Bowl) | Sun Devil (Tempe) |
| 1-4-00 | No. 1 Florida St 46, No. 2 Virginia Tech 29 (Sugar Bowl) | Superdome (New Orleans) |
| 1-3-03 | No. 2 Ohio St 31, No. 1 Miami (Fla.) 24 [2OT] (Fiesta Bowl) | Sun Devil (Tempe) |
| 1-4-05 | No. 1 USC 55, No. 2 Oklahoma 19 (Orange Bowl) | Pro Player Stadium (Miami) |
| 1-5-06 | No. 2 Texas 41, No. 1 USC 38 (Rose Bowl) | Rose Bowl (Pasadena) |
| 9-9-06 | No. 1 Ohio St 24, No. 2 Texas 7 | Texas Memorial (Austin) |
| 11-18-06 | No. 1 Ohio St 42, No. 2 Michigan 39 | Ohio (Columbus) |
| 1-8-07 | No. 2 Florida 41, No. 1 Ohio St 14 (BCS Championship) | Univ. of Phoenix (Glendale) |
| 1-7-08 | No. 2 LSU 38, No. 1 Ohio St. 24 (BCS Championship) | Superdome (New Orleans) |
| 12-6-08 | No. 2 Florida 31, No. 1 Alabama 20 (SEC Championship) | Georgia Dome (Atlanta) |
| 1-8-09 | No. 1 Florida 24, No. 2 Oklahoma 14 (BCS Championship) | Dolphins Stadium (Miami) |

### LONGEST FBS (DIV. I-A) WINNING STREAKS

| Wins | Team | Yrs | Ended by | Score |
|---|---|---|---|---|
| 47 | Oklahoma | 1953–57 | Notre Dame | 7–0 |
| 39 | Washington | 1908–14 | Oregon St | 0–0 |
| 37 | Yale | 1890–93 | Princeton | 6–0 |
| 37 | Yale | 1887–89 | Princeton | 10–0 |
| 35 | Toledo | 1969–71 | Tampa | 21–0 |
| 34 | USC | 2003–05 | Texas | 41–38 |
| 34 | Miami | 2000–03 | Ohio St | 31–24 (2ot) |
| 34 | Pennsylvania | 1894–96 | Lafayette | 6–4 |
| 31 | Oklahoma | 1948–50 | Kentucky | 13–7 |
| 31 | Pittsburgh | 1914–18 | Cleveland Naval Reserve | 10–9 |
| 31 | Pennsylvania | 1896–98 | Harvard | 10–0 |
| 30 | Texas | 1968–70 | Notre Dame | 24–11 |

### LONGEST FBS (DIV. I-A) UNBEATEN STREAKS

| No. | W | T | Team | Yrs | Ended by | Score |
|---|---|---|---|---|---|---|
| 63 | 59 | 4 | Washington | 1907–17 | California | 27–0 |
| 56 | 55 | 1 | Michigan | 1901–05 | Chicago | 2–0 |
| 50 | 46 | 4 | California | 1920–25 | Olympic Club | 15–0 |
| 48 | 47 | 1 | Oklahoma | 1953–57 | Notre Dame | 7–0 |
| 48 | 47 | 1 | Yale | 1885–89 | Princeton | 10–0 |
| 47 | 42 | 5 | Yale | 1879–85 | Princeton | 6–5 |
| 44 | 42 | 2 | Yale | 1894–96 | Princeton | 24–6 |
| 42 | 39 | 3 | Yale | 1904–08 | Harvard | 4–0 |
| 39 | 37 | 2 | Notre Dame | 1946–50 | Purdue | 28–14 |
| 37 | 36 | 1 | Oklahoma | 1972–75 | Kansas | 23–3 |
| 37 | 37 | 0 | Yale | 1890–93 | Princeton | 6–0 |
| 35 | 35 | 0 | Toledo | 1969–71 | Tampa | 21–0 |
| 35 | 34 | 1 | Minnesota | 1903–05 | Wisconsin | 16–12 |
| 34 | 34 | 0 | USC | 2003–05 | Texas | 41–38 |
| 34 | 34 | 0 | Miami | 2000–03 | Ohio St | 31–24 (2ot) |
| 34 | 33 | 1 | Nebraska | 1912–16 | Kansas | 7–3 |
| 34 | 34 | 0 | Pennsylvania | 1894–96 | Lafayette | 6–4 |
| 34 | 32 | 2 | Princeton | 1884–87 | Harvard | 12–0 |
| 34 | 29 | 5 | Princeton | 1877–82 | Harvard | 1–0 |
| 33 | 30 | 3 | Tennessee | 1926–30 | Alabama | 18–6 |
| 33 | 31 | 2 | Georgia Tech | 1914–18 | Pittsburgh | 32–0 |
| 33 | 30 | 3 | Harvard | 1911–15 | Cornell | 10–0 |
| 32 | 31 | 1 | Nebraska | 1969–71 | UCLA | 20–17 |
| 32 | 30 | 2 | Army | 1944–47 | Columbia | 21–20 |
| 32 | 31 | 1 | Harvard | 1898–1900 | Yale | 28–0 |

Note: Includes bowl games.

### LONGEST DIVISION I-A LOSING STREAKS

| Losses | | Seasons | Ended Against | Score |
|---|---|---|---|---|
| 34 | Northwestern | 1979–82 | Northern Illinois | 31–6 |
| 28 | Virginia | 1958–61 | William & Mary | 21–6 |
| 28 | Kansas St | 1945–48 | Arkansas St | 37–6 |
| 27 | New Mexico St | 1988–90 | Cal St–Fullerton | 43–9 |
| 27 | Eastern Michigan | 1980–82 | Kent St | 9–7 |

### MOST-PLAYED DIVISION I-A RIVALRIES

| GP | Opponents (Series Leader Listed First) | Record | First Game | GP | Opponents (Series Leader Listed First) | Record | First Game |
|---|---|---|---|---|---|---|---|
| 118 | Minnesota–Wisconsin | 59-51-8 | 1890 | 106 | Kansas–Kansas St | 65-36-5 | 1902 |
| 117 | Kansas–Missouri | 55-53-9 | 1891 | 105 | Baylor–TCU | 49-49-7 | 1899 |
| 115 | Nebraska–Kansas | 89-23-3 | 1892 | 105 | Michigan–Ohio St | 57-42-6 | 1897 |
| 115 | Texas–Texas A&M | 74-36-5 | 1894 | 105 | Mississippi–Mississippi St | 60-39-6 | 1901 |
| 113 | Miami (Ohio)–Cincinnati | 59-47-7 | 1888 | 104 | Tennessee–Kentucky | 72-23-9 | 1893 |
| 113 | North Carolina–Virginia | †57-52-4 | 1892 | 103 | North Carolina–Wake Forest | 67-34-2 | 1897 |
| 112 | Auburn–Georgia | 53-51-8 | 1892 | 103 | Georgia–Georgia Tech | 59-39-5 | 1893 |
| 112 | Oregon–Oregon St | 56-46-10 | 1894 | 103 | Nebraska–Iowa St | 85-16-2 | 1896 |
| 111 | Purdue–Indiana | 69-36-6 | 1891 | 103 | Texas–Oklahoma | 58-40-5 | 1900 |
| 111 | Stanford–California | 55-45-11 | 1892 | 103 | Oklahoma–Oklahoma St | 80-16-7 | 1904 |
| 109 | Navy–Army | 53-49-7 | 1890 | | | | |
| 108 | Utah–Utah St | 76-28-4 | 1892 | | | | |
| 106 | Clemson–South Carolina | 65-37-4 | 1896 | | | | |

†Disputed series record: Virginia claims North Carolina leads series 55-51-4 based on a forfeited game in 1956.

## 2008 NCAA Coaches' Records

### ALLTIME WINNINGEST FBS (DIV. I-A) COACHES

#### By Percentage

| Coach (Alma Mater) | Colleges Coached | Yrs | W | L | T | Pct |
|---|---|---|---|---|---|---|
| Knute Rockne (Notre Dame '14)† | Notre Dame 1918–30 | 13 | 105 | 12 | 5 | .881 |
| Frank W. Leahy (Notre Dame '31)† | Boston College 1939–40; Notre Dame 1941–43, 1946–53 | 13 | 107 | 13 | 9 | .864 |
| George W. Woodruff (Yale 1889)† | Pennsylvania 1892–01; Illinois 1903; Carlisle 1905 | 12 | 142 | 25 | 2 | .846 |
| Barry Switzer (Arkansas '60) | Oklahoma 1973–88 | 16 | 157 | 29 | 4 | .837 |
| Tom Osborne (Hastings '59)† | Nebraska 1973–97 | 25 | 255 | 49 | 3 | .836 |
| Percy D. Haughton (Harvard 1899)† | Cornell 1899–1900; Harvard 1908–16; Columbia 1923–24 | 13 | 96 | 17 | 6 | .832 |
| Bob Neyland (Army '16)† | Tennessee 1926–34, 1936–40, 1946–52 | 21 | 173 | 31 | 12 | .829 |
| Fielding Yost (West Virginia 1895)† | Ohio Wesleyan 1897; Nebraska 1898; Kansas 1899; Stanford 1900; Michigan 1901–23, 1925–26 | 29 | 196 | 36 | 12 | .828 |
| Bud Wilkinson (Minnesota '37)† | Oklahoma 1947–63 | 17 | 145 | 29 | 4 | .826 |
| *Bob Stoops (Iowa '83) | Oklahoma 1999–2008 | 10 | 109 | 24 | 0 | .820 |
| Jock Sutherland (Pittsburgh '18)† | Lafayette 1919–23; Pittsburgh 1924–38 | 20 | 144 | 28 | 14 | .812 |
| Bob Devaney (Alma [Mich] '39)† | Wyoming 1957–61; Nebraska 1962–72 | 16 | 136 | 30 | 7 | .806 |
| Frank W. Thomas (Notre Dame '23)† | Tenn.-Chattanooga 1925–28; Alabama 1931–42, 1944–46 | 19 | 141 | 33 | 9 | .795 |
| Henry L. Williams (Yale 1891)† | Army 1891; Minnesota 1900–21 | 23 | 141 | 34 | 12 | .786 |
| Gil Dobie (Minnesota '02)† | North Dakota St 1906–07; Washington 1908-16; Navy 1917–19; Cornell 1920–35; Boston College 1936–38 | 33 | 180 | 45 | 15 | .781 |
| Bear Bryant (Alabama '36)† | Maryland 1945, Kentucky 1946–53, | 38 | 323 | 85 | 17 | .780 |
| Fred Folsom (Dartmouth 1895) | Colorado 1895–99, 1901–02; Dartmouth 1903–06; Colorado 1908–15 | 19 | 106 | 28 | 6 | .779 |
| Bo Schembechler (Miami [Ohio] '51) | Miami (Ohio) 1963–68; Michigan 1969–89 | 27 | 234 | 65 | 8 | .775 |
| Fritz Crisler (Chicago '22) | Minnesota 1930–31, Princeton 1931–37– Michigan 1938–47 | 18 | 116 | 32 | 9 | .768 |
| Wallace Wade (Brown, '17) | Alabama 1923–30; Duke 1931–41, 46–50 | 24 | 171 | 49 | 10 | .765 |

*Active in 2008. †Hall of Fame member.

Note: Minimum 10 years as head coach at Division I institutions; record at four-year colleges only; bowl games included; ranked by percentage, ties computed as half won, half lost.

## ALLTIME WINNINGEST FBS (DIV. I-A) COACHES (Cont.)

### By Victories

| | Yrs | W | L | T | Pct | | Yrs | W | L | T | Pct |
|---|---|---|---|---|---|---|---|---|---|---|---|
| *Joe Paterno | 43 | 383 | 127 | 3 | .750 | Hayden Fry | 37 | 232 | 178 | 10 | .564 |
| *Bobby Bowden | 43 | 382 | 123 | 4 | .754 | *Frank Beamer | 28 | 219 | 112 | 4 | .660 |
| Paul (Bear) Bryant | 38 | 323 | 85 | 17 | .780 | *Jim Tressel | 23 | 218 | 76 | 2 | .740 |
| Glenn (Pop) Warner | 44 | 319 | 106 | 32 | .733 | Jess Neely | 40 | 207 | 176 | 19 | .539 |
| Amos Alonzo Stagg | 57 | 314 | 199 | 35 | .605 | Warren Woodson | 31 | 203 | 95 | 14 | .673 |
| LaVell Edwards | 29 | 257 | 100 | 3 | .718 | Don Nehlen | 30 | 202 | 128 | 8 | .609 |
| Tom Osborne | 25 | 255 | 49 | 3 | .836 | Vince Dooley | 25 | 201 | 77 | 10 | .715 |
| Lou Holtz | 33 | 249 | 132 | 7 | .651 | *Mack Brown | 25 | 201 | 100 | 1 | .667 |
| Woody Hayes | 33 | 238 | 72 | 10 | .759 | Eddie Anderson | 39 | 201 | 128 | 15 | .606 |
| Bo Schembechler | 27 | 234 | 65 | 8 | .775 | | | | | | |

*Active in 2008. Record at four-year colleges only.

### Most Bowl Victories

| | W | L | T | | W | L | T |
|---|---|---|---|---|---|---|---|
| *Joe Paterno | 23 | 11 | 1 | Jackie Sherrill | 8 | 6 | 0 |
| *†Bobby Bowden | 21 | 10 | 1 | Darrell Royal | 8 | 7 | 1 |
| Paul (Bear) Bryant | 15 | 12 | 2 | *Philip Fulmer | 8 | 7 | 0 |
| Lou Holtz | 12 | 8 | 2 | Vince Dooley | 8 | 10 | 2 |
| Tom Osborne | 12 | 13 | 0 | Pat Dye | 7 | 2 | 1 |
| *Mack Brown | 11 | 6 | 0 | Tommy Tuberville | 7 | 3 | 0 |
| Don James | 10 | 5 | 0 | Bob Devaney | 7 | 3 | 0 |
| John Vaught | 10 | 8 | 0 | Dan Devine | 7 | 3 | 0 |
| Bobby Dodd | 9 | 4 | 0 | Earle Bruce | 7 | 5 | 0 |
| Johnny Majors | 9 | 7 | 0 | Charlie McClendon | 7 | 6 | 0 |
| John Robinson | 8 | 1 | 0 | *Steve Spurrier | 7 | 7 | 0 |
| Barry Alvarez | 8 | 3 | 0 | Hayden Fry | 7 | 9 | 1 |
| Terry Donahue | 8 | 4 | 1 | Frank Beamer | 7 | 9 | 0 |
| Barry Switzer | 8 | 5 | 0 | LaVell Edwards | 7 | 14 | 1 |

## WINNINGEST ACTIVE FBS (DIV. I-A) COACHES

### By Percentage

| Coach, College | Yrs | W | L | T | Pct. | Bowls W | L | T |
|---|---|---|---|---|---|---|---|---|
| Pete Carroll, USC | 8 | 88 | 15 | 0 | .854 | 6 | 2 | 0 |
| Urban Meyer, Florida | 8 | 83 | 17 | 0 | .830 | 5 | 1 | 0 |
| **Bob Stoops, Oklahoma | 10 | 109 | 24 | 0 | .820 | 4 | 6 | 0 |
| Mark Richt, Georgia | 8 | 82 | 22 | 0 | .788 | 6 | 2 | 0 |
| †Bobby Bowden, Florida St | 43 | 382 | 123 | 4 | .754 | 21 | 10 | 1 |
| Joe Paterno, Penn St | 43 | 383 | 127 | 3 | .750 | 23 | 11 | 1 |
| Bobby Petrino, Arkansas | 5 | 46 | 16 | 0 | .742 | 2 | 2 | 0 |
| Jim Tressel, Ohio St | 23 | 218 | 76 | 2 | .740 | 4 | 4 | 0 |
| Brian Kelly, Cincinnati | 18 | 159 | 57 | 2 | .734 | 2 | 1 | 0 |
| Steve Spurrier, South Carolina | 19 | 170 | 62 | 2 | .731 | 7 | 7 | 0 |
| Paul Johnson, Georgia Tech | 12 | 116 | 43 | 0 | .730 | 2 | 3 | 0 |
| Gary Patterson, TCU | 9 | 73 | 27 | 0 | .730 | 5 | 3 | 0 |
| Dan Hawkins, Colorado | 13 | 105 | 47 | 1 | .690 | 2 | 3 | 0 |
| Nick Saban, Alabama | 13 | 110 | 50 | 1 | .686 | 4 | 6 | 0 |
| Les Miles, LSU | 8 | 70 | 32 | 0 | .686 | 5 | 2 | 0 |
| Chris Ault, Nevada | 24 | 198 | 91 | 1 | .684 | 1 | 5 | 0 |
| Dennis Erickson, Arizona St | 20 | 163 | 75 | 0 | .684 | 5 | 6 | 0 |
| Mack Brown, Texas | 25 | 201 | 100 | 1 | .667 | 11 | 6 | 0 |
| Bill Snyder, Kansas St | 17 | 136 | 68 | 1 | .666 | 6 | 5 | 0 |
| Jeff Tedford, California | 7 | 59 | 30 | 0 | .663 | 5 | 1 | 0 |

#Bowl games included. Ties computed as half win, half loss. Note: Min. five years as Div. I-A head coach at four-year collges only. **One bowl and seven regular-season wins from Stoops' 2005 season at Oklahoma were vacated in 2007 and then restored in 2008. †Fourteen regular season wins from Bowden's 2006 and 2007 seasons at Florida St were vacated in early 2009 but were under appeal as of press time and are still included in Bowden's career totals.

### By Victories

| | | | |
|---|---|---|---|
| Joe Paterno, Penn St | 383 | Dennis Erickson, Arizona St | 163 |
| Bobby Bowden, Florida St | 382 | Brian Kelly, Cincinnati | 159 |
| Frank Beamer, Virginia Tech | 219 | Mike Price, UTEP | 159 |
| Jim Tressel, Ohio St | 218 | Phillip Fulmer, Tennessee | 152 |
| Mack Brown, Texas | 201 | Howard Schellenberger, Fla. Atlantic | 148 |
| Chris Ault, Nevada | 198 | Larry Blakeney, Troy | 143 |
| Dick Tomey, San Jose St | 181 | Mike Bellotti, Oregon | 137 |
| Steve Spurrier, South Carolina | 170 | Bill Snyder, Kansas St | 136 |

*Active in 2008.

## WINNINGEST ACTIVE FCS (DIV. I-AA) COACHES
### By Percentage

| Coach, College | Yrs | W | L | T | Pct* |
|---|---|---|---|---|---|
| Bob Hauck, Montana | 6 | 66 | 16 | 0 | .805 |
| Al Bagnoli, Pennsylvania | 27 | 200 | 73 | 0 | .733 |
| David Bennett, Coastal Carolina | 13 | 108 | 40 | 0 | .730 |
| Mark Farley, Northern Iowa | 8 | 75 | 28 | 0 | .728 |
| K.C. Keeler, Delaware | 16 | 144 | 55 | 1 | .723 |
| Joe Taylor, Florida A&M | 26 | 206 | 79 | 4 | .720 |
| Buddy Pough, South Carolina St | 7 | 57 | 24 | 0 | .704 |
| Pete Richardson, Southern Univ. | 27 | 169 | 71 | 1 | .703 |
| Pete Lembo, Elon | 8 | 64 | 28 | 0 | .696 |
| Dick Biddle, Colgate | 13 | 104 | 49 | 0 | .680 |

*Playoff games included.
Note: Minimum five years as a Division I-A and/or Division I-AA head coach; record at four-year colleges only.

### By Victories

| | | | |
|---|---|---|---|
| Bob Ford, Albany St | 234 | Rob Ash, Montana St | 189 |
| Joe Taylor, Florida A&M | 206 | Walt Hameline, Wagner | 189 |
| Jerry Moore, Appalachian St | 205 | Jimmye Laycock, William & Mary | 189 |
| Al Bagnoli, Pennsylvania | 200 | Pete Richardson, Southern U. | 169 |
| Andy Talley, Villanova | 192 | Mike Ayers, Wofford | 152 |

## WINNINGEST ACTIVE DIVISION II COACHES
### By Percentage

| Coach, College | Yrs | W | L | T | Pct* |
|---|---|---|---|---|---|
| Chuck Martin, Grand Valley St | 5 | 61 | 5 | 0 | .924 |
| Chuck Broyles, Pittsburg St (Kan.) | 19 | 193 | 41 | 2 | .822 |
| Ken Sparks, Carson-Newman | 29 | 276 | 67 | 2 | .803 |
| John Luckhardt, California (Pa.) | 24 | 194 | 61 | 2 | .759 |
| Bill Zwaan, West Chester | 12 | 108 | 35 | 0 | .755 |
| Danny Hale, Bloomsburg | 21 | 176 | 59 | 1 | .748 |
| Mel Tjeerdsma, NW Missouri St | 25 | 216 | 79 | 4 | .729 |
| Tom Sawyer, Winona St | 13 | 109 | 42 | 0 | .722 |
| Bryan Collins, LIU-C.W. Post | 11 | 87 | 34 | 0 | .719 |
| Peter Yetten, Bentley | 21 | 151 | 60 | 1 | .715 |

*Ties computed as half win, half loss. Playoff games included.
Note: Minimum five years as a college head coach; record at four-year colleges only.

### By Victories

| | | | |
|---|---|---|---|
| Ken Sparks, Carson-Newman | 276 | John Luckhardt, California (Pa.) | 194 |
| Billy Joe, Miles | 239 | Chuck Broyles, Pittsburg St | 193 |
| Willard Bailey, St. Paul's | 224 | Monte Cater, Shepherd | 184 |
| Dennis Douds, East Stroudsburg | 218 | Danny Hale, Bloomsburg | 176 |
| Mel Tjeerdsma, NW Missouri St | 216 | Peter Yetten, Bentley | 151 |

## WINNINGEST ACTIVE DIVSION III COACHES
### By Percentage

| Coach, College | Yrs | W | L | T | Pct* |
|---|---|---|---|---|---|
| Larry Kehres, Mount Union | 23 | 275 | 21 | 3 | .925 |
| Mike Sirianni, Washington and Jefferson | 6 | 61 | 10 | 0 | .859 |
| Jim Purthill, St. Norbert | 10 | 91 | 16 | 0 | .850 |
| Rick Willis, Wartburg | 10 | 89 | 20 | 0 | .817 |
| Mike Whalen, Williams | 5 | 32 | 8 | 0 | .800 |
| Joe Fincham, Wittenberg | 13 | 114 | 29 | 0 | .797 |
| Jeff McMartin, Central (Iowa) | 5 | 43 | 12 | 0 | .782 |
| John Gagliardi, St. John's (Minn.) | 60 | 461 | 125 | 11 | .781 |
| Pete Fredenberg, Mary Hardin-Baylor | 11 | 99 | 29 | 0 | .773 |
| Jimmie Keeling, Hardin-Simmons | 19 | 158 | 47 | 0 | .771 |

*Ties computed as half won, half lost. Playoff games included. †Dean Paul's 8–2 season with Ohio Northern in 2004 was later vacated.

Note: Minimum five years as a college head coach; record at four-year colleges only.

### By Victories

| | |
|---|---|
| John Gagliardi, St John's (Minn.) | 461 |
| Larry Kehres, Mount Union | 275 |
| Eric Hamilton, The College of New Jersey | 192 |
| Rick Giancola, Montclair St. | 181 |
| Dale Widolff, Occidental | 162 |
| Rich Lackner, Carnegie Mellon | 160 |
| Jimmie Keeling, Hardin-Simmons | 158 |
| Larry Kindbom, Wash U.-St. Louis | 154 |
| Michael DeLong, Springfield | 154 |
| Steve Mohr, Trinity (Texas) | 153 |
| Barry Streeter, Gettysburg | 152 |
| Mike Hollway, Ohio Wesleyan | 141 |

## WINNINGEST ACTIVE NAIA COACHES
### By Percentage

| Coach, College | Yrs | W | L | T | Pct* |
|---|---|---|---|---|---|
| Mike Van Diest, Carroll (Mont.) | 10 | 117 | 19 | 0 | .860 |
| Bill Cronin, Georgetown (Ky.) | 12 | 118 | 28 | 0 | .808 |
| Mike Gardner, Malone (Ohio) | 5 | 41 | 15 | 0 | .732 |
| Hank Biesiot, Dickinson St (N.D.) | 33 | 235 | 89 | 1 | .725 |
| Patrick Ross, Lindenwood (Mo.) | 7 | 58 | 23 | 0 | .716 |
| Steve Ryan, Morningside (Ia.) | 7 | 56 | 24 | 0 | .700 |
| Mike Cochran, Southern Nazarene (Okla.) | 8 | 62 | 27 | 0 | .697 |
| Carl Poelker, McKendree (Ill.) | 27 | 182 | 80 | 1 | .694 |
| Monty Lewis, Friends (Ks.) | 16 | 104 | 48 | 0 | .684 |
| Kevin Donley, St. Francis (Ind.) | 30 | 229 | 109 | 1 | .677 |
| Paul Troth, Missouri Valley | 13 | 88 | 43 | 0 | .672 |
| Mike Feminis, St. Xavier (Ill.) | 10 | 76 | 38 | 0 | .667 |
| Keith Barefield, Northwestern Oklahoma St. | 11 | 81 | 41 | 2 | .661 |
| Larry Wilcox, Benedictine (Ks.) | 30 | 207 | 114 | 0 | .645 |
| Mac Bryan, Pikeville (Ky.) | 8 | 54 | 30 | 1 | .641 |

*Playoff games included.

Note: Minimum five years as a collegiate head coach and includes record against four-year institutions only.

### By Victories

| | |
|---|---|
| Hank Biesiot, Dickinson St (N.D.) | 235 |
| Kevin Donley, St. Francis (Ind.) | 229 |
| Larry Wilcox, Benedictine (Kan.) | 207 |
| Carl Poelker, McKendree (Ill.) | 182 |
| Jim Dennison, Walsh (Ohio) | 176 |
| Fran Schwenk, William Jewell (Mo.) | 135 |
| Bob Green, Montana Tech | 128 |
| Bill Cronin, Georgetown (Ky.) | 118 |
| Mike Van Dienst, Carroll (Mont.) | 117 |
| Dave Dallas, Kansas Wesleyan | 109 |

Pro Basketball

Finals MVP
Kobe Bryant led the
Los Angeles Lakers
back to a
title in 2009

BOB ROSATO/SPORTS ILLUSTRATED

# Kobe's Beef

After a frustrating loss in the 2008 NBA Finals,
Kobe Bryant willed his Lakers back to the top in 2009,
defeating an Orlando team powered by Howard

## BY CHRIS MANNIX

THE 2008–09 SEASON WAS A TALE of two cities and, in many ways, one of two stars. In Los Angeles, the Lakers began it with the sting of watching the Boston Celtics celebrate their 17th NBA championship still resonating vividly in their memories. And no one replayed it more than Kobe Bryant. It had taken Bryant six years to climb back to the mountaintop that he (along with Shaquille O'Neal) once ruled and from the first day of training camp the frustration of being unable to finish the job was painted on his face. But the Lakers had one big—7'0", 275-pound big, to be exact—reason for optimism: Andrew Bynum, who was in street clothes for the '08 Finals after dislocating his left kneecap in midseason. The knee healed and his confidence restored, Bynum burst out of the gate, averaging 12.8 points and 9.5 rebounds in November and 17.3 points and 7.7 boards in January. With Bynum healthy (at least for the first half of the season), the Lakers shifted Pau Gasol to power forward and moved Lamar Odom (albeit reluctantly) to the bench, giving LA the longest—and arguably most dangerous—three-man frontcourt rotation in the NBA.

The Lakers other (non) addition in 2008 came in the slender 6'6" frame of Trevor Ariza. Ariza was window dressing during L.A.'s '08 Finals run, averaging 2.1 points in the postseason and making little more than cameo appearances in five of the six Finals games. But Ariza seized a spot in the rotation with an 11-point, two-block effort on opening night and by the middle of March the defensive-minded swingman emerged as the Lakers starting small forward. "I'm just really about this team," said Ariza. "I want to win. I feel we have everything, all the tools we need to win a championship."

As it turns out the Lakers would need Bynum, Ariza and every other weapon they could get their hands on. The Western Conference has long been the A-Team to the East's B-Squad and '08-'09 would be no different. There were the usual suspects like San Antonio, Houston and New Orleans, each harboring championship aspirations. There was Denver, which went from the brink of rebuilding to a conference contender when they swapped mercurial guard Allen Iverson for local hero Chauncey Billups one week into the season. And there was Portland, a talented and hungry young team that believed this would be the season they grew up. So despite a 65-win regular season and a lock on the top seed by the All-Star break, a return trip to the Finals for the Lakers would hardly be a cakewalk.

Some 3,000 miles away the Orlando Magic were battling demons of their own. Long considered the most talented young team in the conference with 20-something stars Dwight Howard, Jameer Nelson and Rashard Lewis, Orlando had yet to prove itself in the postseason and was in danger of becoming a footnote in Cleveland and

Thanks to dominant center Dwight Howard, who led the NBA in rebounds and blocks in 2009, Orlando upset Cleveland to win the Eastern Conference.

Boston's annual battle for supremacy. Their struggles were reflected by their star, Howard, who had emerged as the NBA's top center but still couldn't fight his way past LeBron James and Kevin Garnett as the top star in the conference. Indeed, all signs pointed towards a similar result for the Magic entering the 2009 postseason. Despite sitting atop the conference standings for several weeks during the first half, the Magic's playoff hopes took a crippling blow when Nelson was lost for the season with a shoulder injury. Though the Magic were able to right the ship after a midseason trade for Rafer Alston, few gave Orlando more than a puncher's chance of getting by the Cavaliers and Celtics, for very familiar reasons. Too small. Too weak. Too inexperienced. "We know no one thinks we can win," said Rashard Lewis. "But I think we're going to surprise some people."

The Magic stunned Philadelphia in the first round, winning a decisive Game 6 on the road without the services of Howard, who was suspended after swinging an elbow at Sixers center Samuel Dalembert in Game 5. The ride figured to end in the second round against Boston. Despite an undermanned lineup—after missing most of the second half of the regular season, Kevin Garnett was ruled out of the playoffs with a knee injury—the Celtics still played the type of physical style that had given Orlando fits (see Pistons, Detroit) in the past. It started to play out that way, too, with the rough-and-tumble Celtics grabbing a 3–2 advantage thanks to Glen Davis's heroic 18-foot buzzer beater in Game 4.

Refusing to fold, the Magic instead dug in, winning a gritty Game 6 at home before hammering the Celtics on their home floor in Game 7. "Amazing effort," said Magic coach Stan Van Gundy. "These guys are winners."

Orlando was once again a heavy underdog against Cleveland in the conference finals. Though just 1–3 against the Magic in the regular season, the Cavaliers combination of size (Zydrunas Ilgauskas, Anderson Varejao, Joe Smith), skill (that LeBron guy) and home court advantage (where the Cavs lost just once in the regular season) was believed to be enough to overwhelm the

JESSE D. GARRABRANT/NBAE VIA GETTY IMAGE

**Despite being the regular-season MVP, LeBron couldn't carry the Cavs back to the Finals in 2009.**

does best: score. He averaged 27.4 points in helping L.A. dispatch Utah in the first round and the exact same figure in a surprisingly difficult seven-game series against the Rockets. But his biggest challenge would come in the conference finals against the upstart Nuggets, who behind the playoff-savvy Billups had stormed into the West's final round. With Dahntay Jones and Carmelo Anthony draped all over him, Bryant responded. He scored 40, 41 and 22 points in the Lakers first three wins but his finest performance came in Game 6. With the Nuggets loading up on him, Bryant scored from all angles, totaling 35 points and sending the Lakers back to the NBA Finals. Said Nuggets coach George Karl, "He made shots that I think Jesus would have had trouble covering."

The Finals themselves weren't so much a series as they were a coronation. Though buoyed by Nelson's surprising return to the lineup, the Magic were decked in a 25-point Game 1 blowout and were outlasted by the Lakers in a five-point Game 2 defeat. Orlando rallied to take Game 3 at home but suffered a demoralizing loss in Game 4, a game they led by 12 points at halftime only to be upended by two Derek Fisher three-pointers (one in regulation, one in overtime) to fall into a 3–1 hole. With little fight left in them, the Magic crumbled in Game 5 and the Lakers claimed their 15th NBA championship. As Bryant celebrated, the anguish of the '08 defeat replaced by the ecstasy of this victory, Dwight Howard sat silently on the sidelines and soaked it all in. He suffered in silence, perhaps hoping that, like Bryant, this pain could power him next season.

young Magic. It wasn't. Using the pick-and-roll like a surgical scalpel, Orlando carved up the Cavalier defense. Behind 30 points from Howard, the Magic stole Game 1 and would have taken two in Cleveland if not for James's heroic three-point dagger in Game 2. Again undaunted, the Magic took two straight from the Cavs at home before earning the franchise's second trip to the NBA Finals with a Game 6 rout. Said Van Gundy, "I don't think people thought we could be at this level."

Out west, the Kobe Bryant show was in full swing. With Bynum controlling the backboards and Ariza wreaking havoc defensively, Bryant was free to do what he

## NBA Final Standings

### Western Conference

#### NORTHWEST DIVISION

| Team | W | L | Pct | GB |
|---|---|---|---|---|
| †Denver | 54 | 28 | .659 | — |
| *Portland | 54 | 28 | .659 | — |
| *Utah | 48 | 34 | .585 | 6 |
| Minnesota | 24 | 58 | .293 | 30 |
| Oklahoma City | 23 | 59 | .280 | 31 |

#### PACIFIC DIVISION

| Team | W | L | Pct | GB |
|---|---|---|---|---|
| ‡LA Lakers | 65 | 17 | .793 | — |
| Phoenix | 46 | 36 | .561 | 19 |
| Golden State | 29 | 53 | .354 | 36 |
| LA Clippers | 19 | 63 | .232 | 46 |
| Sacramento | 17 | 65 | .207 | 48 |

#### SOUTHWEST DIVISION

| Team | W | L | Pct | GB |
|---|---|---|---|---|
| †San Antonio | 54 | 28 | .659 | — |
| *Houston | 53 | 29 | .646 | 1 |
| *Dallas | 50 | 32 | .610 | 4 |
| *New Orleans | 49 | 33 | .598 | 5 |
| Memphis | 24 | 58 | .293 | 30 |

### Eastern Conference

#### ATLANTIC DIVISION

| Team | W | L | Pct | GB |
|---|---|---|---|---|
| †Boston | 62 | 20 | .756 | — |
| *Philadelphia | 41 | 41 | .500 | 21 |
| New Jersey | 34 | 48 | .415 | 28 |
| Toronto | 33 | 49 | .402 | 29 |
| New York | 32 | 50 | .390 | 30 |

#### CENTRAL DIVISION

| Team | W | L | Pct | GB |
|---|---|---|---|---|
| ‡Cleveland | 66 | 16 | .805 | — |
| *Chicago | 41 | 41 | .500 | 25 |
| *Detroit | 39 | 43 | .476 | 27 |
| Indiana | 36 | 46 | .439 | 30 |
| Milwaukee | 34 | 48 | .415 | 32 |

#### SOUTHEAST DIVISION

| Team | W | L | Pct | GB |
|---|---|---|---|---|
| †Orlando | 59 | 23 | .720 | — |
| *Atlanta | 47 | 35 | .573 | 12 |
| *Miami | 43 | 39 | .524 | 16 |
| Charlotte | 35 | 47 | .427 | 24 |
| Washington | 19 | 63 | .232 | 40 |

†Clinched division title.　*Clinched playoff berth.　‡Clinched conference title.

## 2009 NBA Playoffs

### EASTERN CONFERENCE　　　WESTERN CONFERENCE

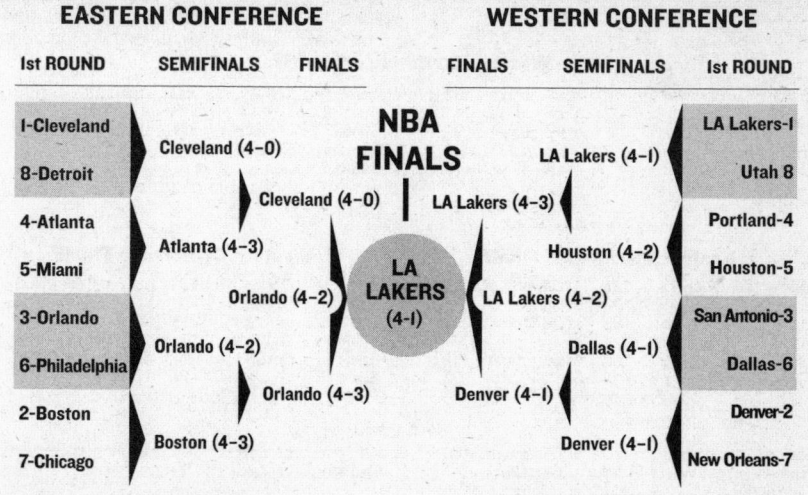

| 1st ROUND | SEMIFINALS | FINALS | FINALS | SEMIFINALS | 1st ROUND |
|---|---|---|---|---|---|

1-Cleveland
8-Detroit
Cleveland (4–0)
Cleveland (4–0)

4-Atlanta
5-Miami
Atlanta (4–3)

3-Orlando
6-Philadelphia
Orlando (4–2)
Orlando (4–2)

2-Boston
7-Chicago
Boston (4–3)
Orlando (4–3)

**NBA FINALS**

LA Lakers (4–3)

**LA LAKERS (4–1)**

LA Lakers (4–1)
LA Lakers (4–3)
Houston (4–2)
LA Lakers (4–2)
Dallas (4–1)
Denver (4–1)
Denver (4–1)

LA Lakers-1
Utah 8
Portland-4
Houston-5
San Antonio-3
Dallas-6
Denver-2
New Orleans-7

## Eastern Conference First Round

| | | | | |
|---|---|---|---|---|
| Game 1......Detroit | 84 | at Cleveland | 102 |
| Game 2......Detroit | 82 | at Cleveland | 94 |
| Game 3......Cleveland | 79 | at Detroit | 68 |
| Game 4......Cleveland | 99 | at Detroit | 78 |

Cleveland won series 4–0.

| | | | | |
|---|---|---|---|---|
| Game 1......Philadelphia | 100 | at Orlando | 98 |
| Game 2......Philadelphia | 87 | at Orlando | 96 |
| Game 3......Orlando | 94 | at Philadelphia | 96 |
| Game 4......Orlando | 84 | at Philadelphia | 81 |
| Game 5......Philadelphia | 78 | at Orlando | 91 |
| Game 6......Orlando | 114 | at Philadelphia | 89 |

Orlando won series 4–2.

| | | | | |
|---|---|---|---|---|
| Game 1......Chicago | 105 | at Boston | 103* |
| Game 2......Chicago | 115 | at Boston | 118 |
| Game 3......Boston | 107 | at Chicago | 86 |
| Game 4......Boston | 118 | at Chicago | 121† |
| Game 5......Chicago | 104 | at Boston | 106* |
| Game 6......Boston | 127 | at Chicago | 128^ |
| Game 7......Chicago | 99 | at Boston | 109 |

Boston won series 4–3.

| | | | | |
|---|---|---|---|---|
| Game 1......Miami | 64 | at Atlanta | 90 |
| Game 2......Miami | 108 | at Atlanta | 93 |
| Game 3......Atlanta | 78 | at Miami | 107 |
| Game 4......Atlanta | 81 | at Miami | 71 |
| Game 5......Miami | 91 | at Atlanta | 106 |
| Game 6......Atlanta | 72 | at Miami | 98 |
| Game 7......Miami | 78 | at Atlanta | 91 |

Atlanta won series 4–3.

## Western Conference First Round

| | | | | |
|---|---|---|---|---|
| Game 1......Utah | 100 | at LA Lakers | 113 |
| Game 2......Utah | 109 | at LA Lakers | 119 |
| Game 3......LA Lakers | 86 | at Utah | 88 |
| Game 4......LA Lakers | 108 | at Utah | 94 |
| Game 5......Utah | 96 | at LA Lakers | 107 |

LA Lakers won series 4–1.

| | | | | |
|---|---|---|---|---|
| Game 1......Dallas | 105 | at San Antonio | 97 |
| Game 2......Dallas | 84 | at San Antonio | 105 |
| Game 3......San Antonio | 67 | at Dallas | 88 |
| Game 4......San Antonio | 90 | at Dallas | 99 |
| Game 5......Dallas | 106 | at San Antonio | 93 |

Dallas won series 4–1.

| | | | | |
|---|---|---|---|---|
| Game 1......New Orleans | 84 | at Denver | 113 |
| Game 2......New Orleans | 93 | at Denver | 108 |
| Game 3......Denver | 93 | at New Orleans | 95 |
| Game 4......Denver | 121 | at New Orleans | 63 |
| Game 5......New Orleans | 86 | at Denver | 107 |

Denver won series 4–1.

| | | | | |
|---|---|---|---|---|
| Game 1......Houston | 108 | at Portland | 81 |
| Game 2......Houston | 103 | at Portland | 107 |
| Game 3......Portland | 83 | at Houston | 86 |
| Game 4......Portland | 88 | at Houston | 89 |
| Game 5......Houston | 77 | at Portland | 88 |
| Game 6......Portland | 76 | at Houston | 92 |

Houston won series 4–2.

## Eastern Conference Semifinals

| | | | | |
|---|---|---|---|---|
| Game 1......Atlanta | 72 | at Cleveland | 99 |
| Game 2......Atlanta | 85 | at Cleveland | 105 |
| Game 3......Cleveland | 97 | at Atlanta | 82 |
| Game 4......Cleveland | 84 | at Atlanta | 74 |

Cleveland won series 4–0.

| | | | | |
|---|---|---|---|---|
| Game 1......Orlando | 95 | at Boston | 90 |
| Game 2......Orlando | 94 | at Boston | 112 |
| Game 3......Boston | 96 | at Orlando | 117 |
| Game 4......Boston | 95 | at Orlando | 94 |
| Game 5......Orlando | 88 | at Boston | 92 |
| Game 6......Boston | 75 | at Orlando | 83 |
| Game 7......Orlando | 101 | at Boston | 82 |

Orlando won series 4–3.

## Western Conference Semifinals

| | | | | |
|---|---|---|---|---|
| Game 1......Houston | 100 | at LA Lakers | 92 |
| Game 2......Houston | 98 | at LA Lakers | 111 |
| Game 3......LA Lakers | 108 | at Houston | 94 |
| Game 4......LA Lakers | 87 | at Houston | 99 |
| Game 5......Houston | 78 | at LA Lakers | 118 |
| Game 6......LA Lakers | 80 | at Houston | 95 |
| Game 7......Houston | 70 | at LA Lakers | 89 |

LA Lakers won series 4–3.

| | | | | |
|---|---|---|---|---|
| Game 1......Dallas | 95 | at Denver | 109 |
| Game 2......Dallas | 105 | at Denver | 117 |
| Game 3......Denver | 106 | at Dallas | 105 |
| Game 4......Denver | 117 | at Dallas | 119 |
| Game 5......Dallas | 110 | at Denver | 124 |

Denver won series 4–1.

## Eastern Conference Finals

| | | | | |
|---|---|---|---|---|
| Game 1......Orlando | 107 | at Cleveland | 106 |
| Game 2......Orlando | 95 | at Cleveland | 96 |
| Game 3......Cleveland | 89 | at Orlando | 99 |
| Game 4......Cleveland | 114 | at Orlando | 116* |
| Game 5......Orlando | 102 | at Cleveland | 112 |
| Game 6......Cleveland | 90 | at Orlando | 103 |

Orlando won series 4–2.

## Western Conference Finals

| | | | | |
|---|---|---|---|---|
| Game 1......Denver | 103 | at LA Lakers | 105 |
| Game 2......Denver | 106 | at LA Lakers | 103 |
| Game 3......LA Lakers | 103 | at Denver | 97 |
| Game 4......LA Lakers | 101 | at Denver | 120 |
| Game 5......Denver | 94 | at LA Lakers | 103 |
| Game 6......LA Lakers | 119 | at Denver | 92 |

LA Lakers won series 4–2.

## NBA Finals

| | | | | |
|---|---|---|---|---|
| Game 1......Orlando | 75 | at LA Lakers | 100 |
| Game 2......Orlando | 96 | at LA Lakers | 101* |
| Game 3......LA Lakers | 104 | at Orlando | 108 |
| Game 4......LA Lakers | 99 | at Orlando | 91* |
| Game 5......LA Lakers | 99 | at Orlando | 86 |

LA Lakers won series 4–1.

* Overtime. †Double overtime. ^Triple overtime.

# NBA Finals Composite Box Score

## ORLANDO MAGIC

| Player | GP | Mpg | FG% | 3FG% | FT% | Reb./per game Off. | Total | Apg | Spg | Bpg | TOpg | Ppg |
|---|---|---|---|---|---|---|---|---|---|---|---|---|
| Hedo Turkoglu | 5 | 41.2 | .492 | .438 | .742 | 0.2 | 4.6 | 3.8 | 0.8 | 0.4 | 2.6 | 18.0 |
| Rashard Lewis | 5 | 42.4 | .405 | .400 | .846 | 1.8 | 7.6 | 4.0 | 0.8 | 0.0 | 2.0 | 17.4 |
| Dwight Howard | 5 | 42.6 | .488 | .000 | .603 | 3.6 | 15.2 | 2.2 | 1.6 | 4.0 | 4.0 | 15.4 |
| Rafer Alston | 5 | 29.4 | .368 | .158 | .800 | 0.2 | 2.2 | 3.0 | 0.8 | 0.0 | 1.6 | 10.6 |
| Mickael Pietrus | 5 | 28.0 | .475 | .333 | .786 | 0.4 | 2.0 | 0.4 | 0.6 | 0.2 | 0.6 | 10.6 |
| Courtney Lee | 5 | 17.6 | .375 | .182 | .750 | 0.4 | 1.4 | 0.2 | 0.6 | 0.0 | 0.6 | 5.8 |
| J.J. Redick | 4 | 16.3 | .400 | .455 | 1.000 | 0.3 | 0.5 | 2.0 | 0.3 | 0.0 | 0.5 | 5.5 |
| Jameer Nelson | 5 | 18.0 | .348 | .167 | .500 | 0.2 | 1.4 | 2.8 | 0.2 | 0.0 | 1.4 | 3.8 |
| Marcin Gortat | 5 | 10.6 | .467 | .000 | .500 | 0.4 | 2.6 | 0.0 | 0.4 | 1.0 | 0.6 | 3.2 |
| Tony Battie | 5 | 7.0 | .455 | .000 | .000 | 0.2 | 0.8 | 0.4 | 0.0 | 0.4 | 0.2 | 2.0 |
| **Avg/Total** | 5 | **250.0** | **.428** | **.330** | **.691** | **7.7** | **38.2** | **18.4** | **6.0** | **6.0** | **14.1** | **91.2** |

## LOS ANGELES LAKERS

| Player | GP | Mpg | FG% | 3FG% | FT% | Reb./per game Off. | Total | Apg | Spg | Bpg | TOpg | Ppg |
|---|---|---|---|---|---|---|---|---|---|---|---|---|
| Kobe Bryant | 5 | 43.8 | .430 | .360 | .841 | 0.6 | 5.6 | 7.4 | 1.4 | 1.4 | 3.2 | 32.4 |
| Pau Gasol | 5 | 42.4 | .600 | .000 | .778 | 2.0 | 9.2 | 2.2 | 0.8 | 1.8 | 1.0 | 18.6 |
| Lamar Odom | 5 | 33.8 | .542 | .500 | .688 | 2.0 | 7.8 | 0.8 | 1.0 | 1.0 | 1.8 | 13.4 |
| Trevor Ariza | 5 | 37.6 | .357 | .417 | .500 | 1.8 | 6.0 | 1.6 | 1.8 | 0.2 | 1.0 | 11.0 |
| Derek Fisher | 5 | 35.8 | .500 | .438 | 1.000 | 0.6 | 3.0 | 1.8 | 1.2 | 0.0 | 0.6 | 11.0 |
| Andrew Bynum | 5 | 19.0 | .364 | .000 | .667 | 2.0 | 4.2 | 0.6 | 0.4 | 0.6 | 0.6 | 6.0 |
| Luke Walton | 5 | 15.2 | .800 | .000 | .500 | 0.6 | 2.0 | 1.0 | 0.2 | 0.0 | 0.4 | 3.8 |
| Jordan Farmar | 5 | 11.4 | .368 | .125 | 1.000 | 0.4 | 1.2 | 0.4 | 0.4 | 0.0 | 0.6 | 3.4 |
| Josh Powell | 2 | 5.5 | .500 | 1.000 | .000 | 1.0 | 2.0 | 0.5 | 0.0 | 0.0 | 1.0 | 2.5 |
| Shannon Brown | 3 | 5.3 | .000 | .000 | .000 | 0.3 | 0.3 | 0.0 | 0.0 | 0.0 | 0.0 | 0.0 |
| D.J. Mbenga | 2 | 2.0 | .000 | .000 | .000 | 0.0 | 0.3 | 0.0 | 0.0 | 0.3 | 0.5 | 0.0 |
| Sasha Vujacic | 5 | 4.4 | .000 | .000 | .000 | 0.0 | 0.4 | 0.4 | 0.0 | 0.0 | 0.2 | 0.0 |
| **Avg/Total** | 5 | **250.0** | **.457** | **.372** | **.758** | **11.3** | **40.6** | **16.4** | **7.2** | **5.2** | **10.9** | **100.6** |

## Game 1

### ORLANDO 75

| Player | Min | FG M-A | FT M-A | Reb O-T | A | PF | S | TO | TP |
|---|---|---|---|---|---|---|---|---|---|
| H. Turkoglu | 33 | 3-11 | 6-6 | 0-4 | 2 | 2 | 1 | 4 | 13 |
| R. Lewis | 36 | 2-10 | 2-2 | 2-5 | 0 | 4 | 0 | 0 | 8 |
| D. Howard | 35 | 1-6 | 10-16 | 5-15 | 2 | 3 | 2 | 2 | 12 |
| C. Lee | 23 | 3-10 | 0-0 | 1-1 | 0 | 3 | 1 | 1 | 7 |
| R. Alston | 25 | 2-9 | 2-2 | 0-2 | 1 | 1 | 1 | 0 | 6 |
| M. Pietrus | 32 | 5-13 | 1-3 | 1-3 | 0 | 4 | 0 | 0 | 14 |
| T. Battie | 5 | 1-3 | 0-0 | 0-1 | 0 | 0 | 0 | 0 | 2 |
| M. Gortat | 20 | 2-4 | 0-0 | 1-8 | 0 | 3 | 2 | 0 | 4 |
| J. Nelson | 23 | 3-9 | 0-0 | 0-2 | 4 | 1 | 0 | 1 | 6 |
| J.J. Redick | 8 | 1-2 | 0-0 | 0-0 | 1 | 0 | 1 | 0 | 3 |
| Totals | 240 | 23-77 | 21-29 | 10-41 | 10 | 21 | 8 | 8 | 75 |

Percentages: FG—.299, FT—.724. 3-pt goals: 8–23, .348 (Turkoglu 1–3, Lewis 2–4, Lee 1–4, Alston 0–4, Nelson 0–2, Pietrus 3–5, Redick 1–1). Team rebounds: 8. Blocked shots: 8 (Gortat 4, Howard 2, Turkoglu, Battie).

### LOS ANGELES 100

| Player | Min | FG M-A | FT M-A | Reb O-T | A | PF | S | TO | TP |
|---|---|---|---|---|---|---|---|---|---|
| T. Ariza | 24 | 1-4 | 0-0 | 1-2 | 2 | 3 | 0 | 0 | 3 |
| P. Gasol | 37 | 7-12 | 2-2 | 3-8 | 3 | 3 | 0 | 2 | 16 |
| A. Bynum | 22 | 3-8 | 3-4 | 3-9 | 0 | 4 | 0 | 0 | 9 |
| K. Bryant | 38 | 16-34 | 8-8 | 1-8 | 8 | 1 | 2 | 1 | 40 |
| D. Fisher | 32 | 4-6 | 0-0 | 1-3 | 1 | 3 | 0 | 0 | 9 |
| L. Odom | 32 | 5-11 | 1-2 | 2-14 | 0 | 3 | 1 | 2 | 11 |
| L. Walton | 24 | 4-5 | 1-2 | 1-2 | 2 | 3 | 0 | 0 | 9 |
| J. Farmar | 13 | 0-3 | 0-0 | 0-2 | 1 | 1 | 0 | 1 | 0 |
| S. Vujacic | 5 | 0-1 | 0-0 | 0-1 | 1 | 2 | 0 | 1 | 0 |
| J. Powell | 3 | 1-2 | 0-0 | 2-4 | 0 | 0 | 0 | 0 | 3 |
| S. Brown | 8 | 0-2 | 0-0 | 1-1 | 0 | 0 | 0 | 0 | 0 |
| D.J. Mbenga | 2 | 0-1 | 0-0 | 0-1 | 0 | 0 | 0 | 1 | 0 |
| Totals | 240 | 41-89 | 15-18 | 15-55 | 18 | 23 | 4 | 8 | 100 |

Percentages: FG—.461, FT—.833. 3-pt goals: 3–9 .333 (Ariza 1–2, Bryant 0–1, Fisher 1–1, Odom 0–3, Farmar 0–1, Powell 1–1). Team rebounds: 9. Blocked shots: 7 (Gasol 2, Bryant 2, Ariza, Bynum, Odom).

A: 18,997. Officials: Crawford, DeRosa, Mauer.

## Game 2

### ORLANDO 96

| Player | Min | FG M-A | FT M-A | Reb O-T | A | PF | S | TO | TP |
|---|---|---|---|---|---|---|---|---|---|
| H. Turkoglu | 47 | 8-17 | 3-4 | 0-6 | 4 | 5 | 0 | 5 | 22 |
| R. Lewis | 45 | 12-21 | 4-4 | 5-11 | 7 | 2 | 1 | 2 | 34 |
| D. Howard | 47 | 5-10 | 7-9 | 3-16 | 4 | 4 | 4 | 7 | 17 |
| C. Lee | 12 | 1-3 | 0-0 | 0-2 | 0 | 2 | 0 | 0 | 2 |
| R. Alston | 26 | 1-8 | 2-2 | 0-1 | 5 | 1 | 0 | 1 | 4 |
| M. Pietrus | 23 | 1-3 | 0-0 | 0-2 | 0 | 6 | 0 | 1 | 2 |
| M. Gortat | 15 | 1-4 | 2-4 | 1-3 | 0 | 1 | 0 | 2 | 4 |
| J.J. Redick | 27 | 2-9 | 0-0 | 1-2 | 1 | 3 | 0 | 1 | 5 |
| J. Nelson | 17 | 1-3 | 2-4 | 0-0 | 1 | 0 | 0 | 1 | 4 |
| T. Battie | 5 | 1-1 | 0-0 | 0-1 | 0 | 0 | 0 | 0 | 2 |
| Totals | 265 | 33-79 | 20-27 | 10-44 | 22 | 24 | 5 | 20 | 96 |

Percentages: FG—.418, FT—.741. 3-pt goals: 10–30, .333 (Turkoglu 3–6, Lewis, 6–12, Alston 0–4, Pietrus 0–1, Redick 1–6, Nelson 0–1). Team rebounds: 11. Blocked shots: 6 (Howard 4, Turkoglu, Pietrus).

### LOS ANGELES 101

| Player | Min | FG M-A | FT M-A | Reb O-T | A | PF | S | TO | TP |
|---|---|---|---|---|---|---|---|---|---|
| T. Ariza | 38 | 3-13 | 0-0 | 1-7 | 2 | 3 | 3 | 0 | 8 |
| P. Gasol | 44 | 7-14 | 10-11 | 0-10 | 3 | 3 | 2 | 0 | 24 |
| A. Bynum | 16 | 2-5 | 1-1 | 0-1 | 2 | 5 | 0 | 1 | 5 |
| K. Bryant | 49 | 10-22 | 8-10 | 0-4 | 8 | 2 | 2 | 7 | 29 |
| D. Fisher | 41 | 4-9 | 2-2 | 0-1 | 3 | 2 | 3 | 2 | 12 |
| L. Odom | 46 | 8-9 | 3-4 | 2-8 | 2 | 5 | 1 | 2 | 19 |
| L. Walton | 5 | 0-0 | 0-0 | 0-2 | 0 | 3 | 0 | 0 | 0 |
| J. Farmar | 6 | 2-5 | 0-0 | 1-1 | 0 | 1 | 1 | 0 | 4 |
| S. Vujacic | 5 | 0-1 | 0-0 | 0-1 | 0 | 0 | 0 | 0 | 0 |
| S. Brown | 6 | 0-0 | 0-0 | 0-0 | 0 | 1 | 0 | 0 | 0 |
| Totals | 265 | 36-78 | 24-28 | 4-35 | 20 | 25 | 12 | 12 | 101 |

Percentages: FG—.462, FT—.857. 3-pt goals: 5–15, .333 (Ariza 2–6, Bryant 1–4, Fisher 2–3, Farmar 0–1, Vujacic 0–1). Team rebounds: 9. Blocked shots: 6 (Bynum 2, Odom 3, Gasol).

A: 18,997. Officials: Javie, Washington, McCutchen.

## Game 3

### LOS ANGELES 104

| Player | Min | FG M-A | FT M-A | Reb O-T | A | PF | S | TO | TP |
|---|---|---|---|---|---|---|---|---|---|
| T. Ariza | 42 | 5-13 | 1-2 | 3-7 | 1 | 4 | 2 | 1 | 13 |
| P. Gasol | 40 | 9-11 | 5-6 | 1-3 | 1 | 3 | 1 | 1 | 23 |
| A. Bynum | 23 | 2-6 | 0-1 | 2-4 | 1 | 2 | 1 | 1 | 4 |
| K. Bryant | 40 | 11-25 | 5-10 | 1-3 | 8 | 5 | 0 | 4 | 31 |
| D. Fisher | 32 | 4-9 | 0-0 | 1-3 | 2 | 2 | 1 | 0 | 9 |
| L. Odom | 32 | 4-6 | 3-5 | 1-2 | 1 | 4 | 1 | 2 | 11 |
| J. Farmar | 16 | 4-6 | 2-2 | 1-3 | 0 | 1 | 0 | 2 | 11 |
| S. Vujacic | 3 | 0-1 | 0-0 | 0-0 | 0 | 1 | 0 | 0 | 0 |
| L. Walton | 11 | 1-1 | 0-0 | 1-2 | 2 | 3 | 0 | 2 | 2 |
| Totals | 240 | 40-78 | 16-26 | 11-27 | 16 | 25 | 6 | 13 | 104 |

Percentages: FG—.513, FT—.615. 3-pt goals: 8–23, .348 (Ariza 2–7, Bryant 4–9, Fisher 1–4, Farmar 1–3). Team rebounds: 15. Blocked shots: 3 (Gasol 2, Odom).

### ORLANDO 108

| Player | Min | FG M-A | FT M-A | Reb O-T | A | PF | S | TO | TP |
|---|---|---|---|---|---|---|---|---|---|
| H. Turkoglu | 42 | 7-12 | 3-4 | 1-6 | 7 | 3 | 1 | 1 | 18 |
| R. Lewis | 41 | 8-14 | 2-2 | 1-5 | 5 | 4 | 0 | 3 | 21 |
| D. Howard | 43 | 5-6 | 11-16 | 2-14 | 2 | 4 | 1 | 1 | 21 |
| C. Lee | 20 | 2-4 | 0-0 | 0-0 | 0 | 3 | 1 | 1 | 4 |
| R. Alston | 37 | 8-12 | 3-4 | 0-2 | 4 | 1 | 0 | 3 | 20 |
| M. Pietrus | 31 | 7-11 | 4-4 | 1-2 | 2 | 3 | 3 | 1 | 18 |
| T. Battie | 9 | 2-3 | 0-0 | 0-0 | 1 | 2 | 0 | 0 | 4 |
| J. Nelson | 11 | 1-1 | 0-0 | 0-0 | 2 | 0 | 1 | 3 | 2 |
| M. Gortat | 5 | 0-0 | 0-0 | 0-0 | 0 | 0 | 0 | 0 | 0 |
| Totals | 240 | 40-64 | 23-30 | 6-29 | 23 | 21 | 7 | 13 | 108 |

Percentages: FG—.625, FT—.767. 3-pt goals: 5–14, .357 (Turkoglu 1–3, Lewis 3–6, Lee 0–1, Alston 1–1, Pietrus 0–3). Team rebounds: 8. Blocked shots: 3 (Howard 2, Battie).

A: 17,461. Officials: Crawford, Stafford, Wunderlich.

## Game 4

### LOS ANGELES 99

| Player | Min | FG M-A | FT M-A | Reb O-T | A | PF | S | TO | TP |
|---|---|---|---|---|---|---|---|---|---|
| T. Ariza | 44 | 6-14 | 1-2 | 3-9 | 2 | 3 | 2 | 1 | 16 |
| P. Gasol | 49 | 7-14 | 2-4 | 2-10 | 1 | 4 | 1 | 1 | 16 |
| A. Bynum | 16 | 2-3 | 2-2 | 1-2 | 0 | 5 | 0 | 0 | 6 |
| K. Bryant | 49 | 11-31 | 8-8 | 1-7 | 8 | 3 | 1 | 3 | 32 |
| D. Fisher | 42 | 5-11 | 0-0 | 1-4 | 1 | 5 | 2 | 0 | 12 |
| L. Odom | 28 | 4-10 | 0-0 | 2-5 | 1 | 5 | 1 | 0 | 9 |
| D.J. Mbenga | 4 | 0-0 | 0-0 | 0-0 | 0 | 0 | 0 | 0 | 0 |
| L. Walton | 11 | 2-2 | 2-4 | 0-2 | 0 | 0 | 0 | 0 | 6 |
| J. Farmar | 9 | 0-2 | 0-0 | 0-0 | 1 | 1 | 0 | 0 | 0 |
| J. Powell | 8 | 1-2 | 0-0 | 0-0 | 1 | 2 | 0 | 2 | 2 |
| S. Vujacic | 4 | 0-2 | 0-0 | 0-0 | 1 | 0 | 0 | 0 | 0 |
| S. Brown | 2 | 0-0 | 0-0 | 0-0 | 0 | 0 | 0 | 0 | 0 |
| Totals | 265 | 38-91 | 15-20 | 10-39 | 15 | 28 | 8 | 7 | 99 |

Percentages: FG—.418, FT—.750. 3-pt goals: 8-23, .348 (Ariza 3-4, Bryant 2-6, Fisher 2-7, Odom 1-2, Farmar 0-2, Vujacic 0-2). Technical Fouls: 3 (Ariza, Gasol, Coach Jackson). Team rebounds: 12. Blocked shots: 2 (Bryant, Mbenga).

### ORLANDO 91

| Player | Min | FG M-A | FT M-A | Reb O-T | A | PF | S | TO | TP |
|---|---|---|---|---|---|---|---|---|---|
| H. Turkoglu | 41 | 8-13 | 8-13 | 0-5 | 3 | 4 | 1 | 1 | 25 |
| R. Lewis | 46 | 2-10 | 0-0 | 0-7 | 4 | 2 | 2 | 3 | 6 |
| D. Howard | 49 | 5-12 | 6-14 | 6-21 | 2 | 4 | 0 | 7 | 16 |
| C. Lee | 7 | 1-4 | 1-2 | 0-0 | 0 | 2 | 0 | 1 | 4 |
| R. Alston | 27 | 5-13 | 0-0 | 0-1 | 2 | 2 | 1 | 1 | 11 |
| M. Pietrus | 37 | 4-8 | 6-7 | 0-2 | 0 | 3 | 0 | 1 | 15 |
| T. Battie | 12 | 1-3 | 0-0 | 0-0 | 0 | 2 | 0 | 1 | 2 |
| J.J. Redick | 17 | 2-6 | 1-1 | 0-0 | 3 | 0 | 0 | 0 | 6 |
| J. Nelson | 26 | 1-3 | 0-0 | 1-3 | 3 | 2 | 0 | 1 | 2 |
| M. Gortat | 4 | 2-2 | 0-0 | 0-2 | 0 | 0 | 0 | 1 | 4 |
| Totals | 265 | 31-74 | 22-37 | 7-41 | 17 | 21 | 4 | 17 | 91 |

Percentages: FG—.419, FT—.595. 3-pt goals: 7-21, .333 (Turkoglu 1-3, Lewis 2-6, Lee 1-4, Alston 1-4, Pietrus 1-2, Redick 1-2). Technical Fouls: 2 (Pietrus, Team–Def. 3 Sec.) Team rebounds: 24. Blocked shots: 10 (Howard 9, Gortat).

A: 17,461. Officials: Callahan, Foster, Salvatore.

## Game 5

### LOS ANGELES 99

| Player | Min | FG M-A | FT M-A | Reb O-T | A | PF | S | TO | TP |
|---|---|---|---|---|---|---|---|---|---|
| T. Ariza | 41 | 5-12 | 3-6 | 1-5 | 1 | 3 | 2 | 3 | 15 |
| P. Gasol | 42 | 6-9 | 2-4 | 4-15 | 3 | 2 | 0 | 1 | 14 |
| A. Bynum | 17 | 3-11 | 0-1 | 4-5 | 0 | 5 | 1 | 1 | 6 |
| K. Bryant | 43 | 10-23 | 8-8 | 0-6 | 5 | 2 | 2 | 1 | 30 |
| D. Fisher | 32 | 4-7 | 4-4 | 0-4 | 2 | 4 | 0 | 1 | 13 |
| L. Odom | 32 | 5-12 | 4-5 | 3-10 | 0 | 4 | 1 | 3 | 17 |
| L. Walton | 14 | 1-2 | 0-0 | 1-2 | 1 | 0 | 0 | 0 | 2 |
| J. Farmar | 14 | 1-3 | 0-0 | 0-0 | 1 | 0 | 0 | 0 | 2 |
| S. Vujacic | 5 | 0-1 | 0-0 | 0-0 | 0 | 0 | 0 | 0 | 0 |
| Totals | 240 | 35-80 | 21-28 | 13-47 | 13 | 20 | 6 | 10 | 99 |

Percentages: FG—.438, FT—.750. 3-pt goals: 8-16, .500 (Ariza 2-5, Bryant 2-5, Fisher 1-1, Odom 3-3, Walton 0-1, Farmar 0-1). Technical Fouls: 1 (Ariza). Team rebounds: 9. Blocked shots: 8 (Gasol 4, Bryant 4).

### ORLANDO 86

| Player | Min | FG M-A | FT M-A | Reb O-T | A | PF | S | TO | TP |
|---|---|---|---|---|---|---|---|---|---|
| H. Turkoglu | 42 | 4-8 | 3-4 | 0-2 | 3 | 5 | 1 | 2 | 12 |
| R. Lewis | 45 | 6-19 | 3-5 | 1-10 | 4 | 3 | 1 | 2 | 18 |
| D. Howard | 39 | 5-9 | 1-3 | 2-10 | 1 | 5 | 1 | 3 | 11 |
| C. Lee | 26 | 5-11 | 2-2 | 1-4 | 1 | 3 | 1 | 0 | 12 |
| R. Alston | 33 | 5-15 | 1-2 | 1-5 | 3 | 5 | 2 | 3 | 12 |
| M. Pietrus | 17 | 2-5 | 0-0 | 0-1 | 0 | 0 | 0 | 0 | 4 |
| J. Nelson | 13 | 2-7 | 0-0 | 0-2 | 4 | 0 | 0 | 1 | 5 |
| T. Battie | 3 | 0-1 | 0-0 | 1-2 | 1 | 1 | 0 | 0 | 0 |
| M. Gortat | 9 | 2-4 | 0-0 | 0-0 | 0 | 0 | 0 | 0 | 4 |
| J.J. Redick | 13 | 3-3 | 0-0 | 0-0 | 3 | 1 | 0 | 1 | 8 |
| Totals | 240 | 34-82 | 10-16 | 6-36 | 20 | 23 | 6 | 12 | 86 |

Percentages: FG—.415, FT—.625. 3-pt goals: 8-27, .296 (Turkoglu 1-1, Lewis 3-12, Lee 0-2, Alston 1-6, Pietrus 0-1, Nelson 1-3, Redick 2-2). Technical Fouls: 1 (Turkoglu). Team rebounds: 14. Blocked shots: 3 (Howard 3).

A: 17,461. Officials: Mauer, Crawford, DeRosa.

# 2008–09 All-NBA Teams

| FIRST TEAM | SECOND TEAM | THIRD TEAM |
|---|---|---|
| F LeBron James, Cle | F Tim Duncan, SA | F Carmelo Anthony, Den |
| F Dirk Nowitzki, Dal | F Paul Pierce, Bos | F Pau Gasol, LAL |
| C Dwight Howard, Orl | C Yao Ming, Hou | C Shaquille O'Neal, Phx |
| G Kobe Bryant, LAL | G Brandon Roy, Por | G Chauncey Billups, Den |
| G Dwyane Wade, Mia | G Chris Paul, NO | G Tony Parker, SA |

## All-Rookie Teams

| FIRST TEAM | SECOND TEAM |
|---|---|
| Derrick Rose, Chi | Eric Gordon, LAC |
| O.J. Mayo, Mem | Kevin Love, Min |
| Russell Westbrook, OKC | Mario Chalmers, Mia |
| Brook Lopez, NJ | Marc Gasol, Mem |
| Michael Beasley, Mia | D.J. Augustin, Cha (tie) |
|  | Rudy Fernandez, Por (tie) |

## All-Defensive Team

| FIRST TEAM | SECOND TEAM |
|---|---|
| F LeBron James, Cle | F Ron Artest, Hou |
| F Kevin Garnett, Bos | F Shane Battier, Hou |
| C Dwight Howard, Orl | C Tim Duncan, SA |
| G Kobe Bryant, LAL | G Dwyane Wade, Mia |
| G Chris Paul, NO | G Rajon Rondo, Bos |

# 2008–09 NBA Regular Season Individual Leaders

## Scoring

| | GP | Pts | Avg |
|---|---|---|---|
| Dwyane Wade, Mia | 79 | 2,386 | 30.2 |
| LeBron James, Cle | 81 | 2,304 | 28.4 |
| Kobe Bryant, LAL | 82 | 2,201 | 26.8 |
| Dirk Nowitzki, Dal | 81 | 2,094 | 25.9 |
| Danny Granger, Ind | 67 | 1,728 | 25.8 |
| Kevin Durant, OKC | 74 | 1,871 | 25.3 |
| Chris Paul, NO | 78 | 1,781 | 22.8 |
| Carmelo Anthony, Den | 66 | 1,504 | 22.8 |
| Chris Bosh, Tor | 77 | 1,746 | 22.7 |
| Brandon Roy, Por | 78 | 1,765 | 22.6 |

## Rebounds

| | GP | Reb | Avg |
|---|---|---|---|
| Dwight Howard, Orl | 79 | 1,093 | 13.8 |
| Troy Murphy, Ind | 73 | 861 | 11.8 |
| David Lee, NY | 81 | 951 | 11.7 |
| Tim Duncan, SA | 75 | 800 | 10.7 |
| Emeka Okafor, Cha | 82 | 827 | 10.1 |
| Chris Bosh, Tor | 77 | 771 | 10.0 |
| Yao Ming, Hou | 77 | 761 | 9.9 |
| Pau Gasol, LAL | 81 | 780 | 9.6 |
| Kevin Love, Min | 81 | 734 | 9.1 |
| Antawn Jamison, Wash | 81 | 721 | 8.9 |

## Assists

| | GP | Ast | Avg |
|---|---|---|---|
| Chris Paul, NO | 78 | 861 | 11.0 |
| Deron Williams, Utah | 68 | 725 | 10.7 |
| Steve Nash, Phx | 74 | 717 | 9.7 |
| Jose Calderon, Tor | 68 | 607 | 8.9 |
| Jason Kidd, Dal | 81 | 702 | 8.7 |
| Rajon Rondo, Bos | 80 | 659 | 8.2 |
| Baron Davis, LAC | 65 | 501 | 7.7 |
| Dwyane Wade, Mia | 79 | 589 | 7.5 |
| LeBron James, Cle | 81 | 587 | 7.2 |
| Chris Duhon, NY | 79 | 566 | 7.2 |

## Field-Goal Percentage

| | FGA | FGM | Pct |
|---|---|---|---|
| Shaquille O'Neal, Phx | 841 | 512 | .609 |
| Nene Hilario, Den | 709 | 428 | .604 |
| Andris Biedrins, GS | 533 | 308 | .578 |
| Dwight Howard, Orl | 979 | 560 | .572 |
| Pau Gasol, LAL | 1,045 | 592 | .567 |
| Emeka Okafor, Cha | 772 | 433 | .561 |
| David Lee, NY | 951 | 522 | .549 |
| Yao Ming, Hou | 1,032 | 566 | .548 |
| Amare Stoudemire, Phx | 749 | 404 | .539 |
| Paul Millsap, Utah | 749 | 400 | .534 |

## Free-Throw Percentage

| | FTA | FTM | Pct |
|---|---|---|---|
| Jose Calderon, Tor | 154 | 151 | .981 |
| Ray Allen, Bos | 249 | 237 | .952 |
| Steve Nash, Phx | 210 | 196 | .933 |
| Chauncey Billups, Det/Den | 458 | 418 | .913 |
| Mo Williams, Cle | 228 | 208 | .912 |
| D.J. Augustin, Cha | 233 | 208 | .893 |
| Dirk Nowitzki, Dal | 545 | 485 | .890 |
| David West, NO | 415 | 367 | .884 |
| Manu Ginobli, SA | 190 | 168 | .884 |
| Leandro Barbosa, Phx | 194 | 171 | .881 |

## Three-Point Field-Goal Percentage

| | 3FGA | 3FGM | Pct |
|---|---|---|---|
| Anthony Morrow, GS | 184 | 86 | .467 |
| Jameer Nelson, Orl | 181 | 82 | .453 |
| Troy Murphy, Ind | 358 | 161 | .450 |
| Kelenna Azubuike, GS | 210 | 94 | .448 |
| Bobby Simmons, NJ | 262 | 117 | .447 |
| Mehmet Okur, Utah | 202 | 90 | .446 |
| Eddie House, Bos | 340 | 151 | .444 |
| Matt Bonner, SA | 268 | 118 | .440 |
| Steve Nash, Phx | 246 | 108 | .439 |
| D.J. Augustin, Cha | 246 | 108 | .439 |

## Steals

| | GP | Steals | Avg |
|---|---|---|---|
| Chris Paul, NO | 78 | 216 | 2.77 |
| Dwyane Wade, Mia | 79 | 173 | 2.19 |
| Jason Kidd, Dal | 81 | 160 | 1.98 |
| Mario Chalmers, Mia | 82 | 160 | 1.95 |
| Rajon Rondo, Bos | 80 | 149 | 1.86 |
| Gerald Wallace, Cha | 71 | 121 | 1.70 |
| Ronnie Brewer, Utah | 81 | 138 | 1.70 |
| LeBron James, Cle | 81 | 137 | 1.69 |
| Trevor Ariza, LAL | 82 | 137 | 1.67 |
| Andre Iguodala, Phil | 82 | 131 | 1.60 |

## Blocked Shots

| | GP | BS | Avg |
|---|---|---|---|
| Dwight Howard, Orl | 79 | 231 | 2.92 |
| Chris Andersen, Den | 71 | 175 | 2.46 |
| Marcus Camby, LAC | 62 | 132 | 2.13 |
| Ronny Turiaf, GS | 79 | 168 | 2.13 |
| Jermaine O'Neal, Mia/Tor | 68 | 136 | 2.00 |
| Kendrick Perkins, Bos | 76 | 150 | 1.97 |
| Yao Ming, Hou | 77 | 150 | 1.95 |
| Tyrus Thomas, Chi | 79 | 151 | 1.91 |
| Brook Lopez, NJ | 82 | 151 | 1.84 |
| Samuel Dalembert, Phil | 82 | 146 | 1.78 |

## Offense

| Team | FG Pct | 3FG Pct | FT Pct | Rebound Avg | | A | TO | Stl | Scoring Avg |
|---|---|---|---|---|---|---|---|---|---|
| | | | | Off | Total | | | | |
| Phoenix | 50.4 | 38.3 | 74.4 | 11.0 | 41.7 | 23.2 | 15.4 | 7.2 | 109.4 |
| Golden State | 45.8 | 37.3 | 79.1 | 11.6 | 42.0 | 20.9 | 14.2 | 7.8 | 108.6 |
| LA Lakers | 47.4 | 36.1 | 77.0 | 12.4 | 43.9 | 23.3 | 13.1 | 8.8 | 106.9 |
| New York | 44.5 | 36.0 | 78.4 | 11.1 | 42.1 | 21.2 | 13.9 | 7.4 | 105.2 |
| Indiana | 45.5 | 37.8 | 80.7 | 11.3 | 43.7 | 21.6 | 14.0 | 7.0 | 105.1 |
| Denver | 47.0 | 37.1 | 76.0 | 11.0 | 41.6 | 22.2 | 14.9 | 8.7 | 104.3 |
| Utah | 47.5 | 34.9 | 77.1 | 11.5 | 41.0 | 24.7 | 14.3 | 8.8 | 103.6 |
| Chicago | 45.7 | 38.1 | 79.6 | 11.8 | 42.1 | 21.1 | 13.9 | 7.5 | 102.2 |
| Dallas | 46.2 | 35.0 | 81.9 | 11.1 | 42.7 | 21.7 | 12.2 | 7.2 | 101.7 |
| Orlando | 45.7 | 38.1 | 71.5 | 10.0 | 43.3 | 19.4 | 13.5 | 7.0 | 101.0 |
| Boston | 48.6 | 39.7 | 76.5 | 10.6 | 42.1 | 22.7 | 15.0 | 7.6 | 100.9 |
| Sacramento | 44.7 | 36.8 | 79.8 | 10.2 | 39.1 | 19.7 | 14.8 | 6.9 | 100.6 |
| Cleveland | 46.8 | 39.3 | 75.7 | 10.8 | 42.2 | 20.3 | 12.0 | 7.2 | 100.3 |
| Portland | 46.5 | 38.3 | 76.5 | 12.9 | 41.7 | 20.3 | 12.1 | 6.7 | 99.4 |
| Milwaukee | 44.5 | 36.3 | 78.0 | 11.9 | 40.7 | 22.0 | 13.6 | 7.4 | 99.3 |
| Toronto | 45.8 | 37.2 | 82.4 | 9.8 | 40.4 | 22.4 | 12.9 | 6.4 | 99.0 |
| Houston | 45.3 | 37.5 | 80.5 | 10.5 | 43.0 | 20.3 | 13.3 | 6.7 | 98.4 |
| Miami | 45.7 | 35.7 | 75.4 | 10.1 | 39.5 | 20.4 | 11.9 | 7.9 | 98.3 |
| Atlanta | 45.8 | 36.6 | 73.7 | 10.6 | 40.0 | 20.2 | 12.2 | 7.4 | 98.1 |
| New Jersey | 44.8 | 37.6 | 77.9 | 10.4 | 39.8 | 20.0 | 12.4 | 6.8 | 98.1 |
| Minnesota | 44.1 | 35.3 | 76.9 | 11.9 | 41.7 | 20.4 | 13.5 | 6.2 | 97.8 |
| Philadelphia | 45.9 | 31.8 | 74.5 | 12.7 | 41.2 | 20.1 | 13.5 | 8.0 | 97.4 |
| San Antonio | 46.6 | 38.6 | 76.1 | 8.9 | 41.0 | 21.2 | 11.1 | 5.8 | 97.0 |
| Oklahoma City | 44.7 | 34.6 | 78.6 | 12.2 | 42.6 | 20.3 | 15.5 | 7.4 | 97.0 |
| Washington | 45.0 | 33.0 | 76.7 | 11.7 | 40.1 | 20.0 | 13.5 | 7.5 | 96.1 |
| New Orleans | 45.7 | 36.4 | 80.7 | 9.8 | 39.7 | 19.6 | 11.7 | 7.2 | 95.8 |
| LA Clippers | 44.1 | 35.4 | 73.6 | 10.9 | 39.8 | 21.0 | 14.2 | 7.0 | 95.1 |
| Detroit | 45.4 | 34.9 | 75.1 | 11.6 | 41.4 | 20.6 | 11.2 | 6.0 | 94.2 |
| Memphis | 45.4 | 36.0 | 75.6 | 10.3 | 38.8 | 17.4 | 14.2 | 7.5 | 93.9 |
| Charlotte | 45.5 | 36.6 | 74.0 | 10.8 | 39.7 | 21.2 | 14.9 | 7.1 | 93.6 |

## Defense (Opponents' Statistics)

| Team | FG Pct | 3FG Pct | FT Pct | Rebound Avg. | | A | TO | Stl | Scoring Avg |
|---|---|---|---|---|---|---|---|---|---|
| | | | | Off | Total | | | | |
| Cleveland | 43.0 | 33.0 | 77.2 | 10.5 | 38.6 | 19.0 | 13.3 | 6.2 | 90.7 |
| San Antonio | 45.3 | 37.9 | 77.4 | 9.1 | 40.5 | 18.0 | 11.2 | 6.5 | 93.5 |
| Houston | 44.4 | 35.9 | 75.0 | 10.6 | 39.7 | 19.4 | 11.8 | 7.1 | 93.9 |
| Portland | 46.1 | 37.4 | 80.0 | 9.5 | 36.5 | 19.3 | 12.6 | 6.2 | 94.0 |
| Orlando | 43.4 | 34.4 | 75.2 | 10.3 | 41.7 | 18.1 | 12.5 | 6.8 | 94.0 |
| Boston | 43.1 | 35.2 | 77.4 | 10.2 | 38.2 | 19.0 | 14.0 | 7.1 | 94.6 |
| Detroit | 45.1 | 35.2 | 77.5 | 10.4 | 40.3 | 20.2 | 11.2 | 5.7 | 94.7 |
| Charlotte | 45.4 | 36.6 | 75.6 | 10.7 | 38.9 | 19.6 | 14.1 | 7.6 | 94.9 |
| New Orleans | 45.3 | 36.2 | 77.2 | 10.0 | 40.1 | 20.4 | 12.5 | 6.0 | 95.1 |
| Atlanta | 45.4 | 36.0 | 76.5 | 11.4 | 41.6 | 20.4 | 12.8 | 6.5 | 96.1 |
| Philadelphia | 46.2 | 36.5 | 77.8 | 11.3 | 39.3 | 21.7 | 14.7 | 7.0 | 97.2 |
| Miami | 45.4 | 39.3 | 76.3 | 11.0 | 41.6 | 19.8 | 14.4 | 6.4 | 97.3 |
| LA Lakers | 44.6 | 34.5 | 75.2 | 11.8 | 41.5 | 22.8 | 14.8 | 7.9 | 99.2 |
| Dallas | 45.5 | 37.2 | 79.4 | 10.7 | 41.2 | 19.4 | 12.3 | 7.1 | 99.2 |
| Memphis | 47.3 | 35.5 | 77.0 | 10.3 | 39.9 | 21.2 | 13.9 | 7.7 | 99.3 |
| Denver | 43.8 | 36.4 | 78.3 | 11.9 | 41.0 | 21.1 | 14.8 | 7.8 | 100.0 |
| Milwaukee | 45.8 | 37.8 | 79.1 | 10.1 | 40.9 | 21.1 | 15.7 | 7.5 | 100.4 |
| New Jersey | 46.3 | 39.1 | 76.2 | 10.6 | 41.4 | 21.9 | 12.8 | 6.9 | 100.5 |
| Utah | 46.6 | 36.6 | 76.1 | 11.1 | 40.3 | 20.1 | 15.6 | 8.1 | 101.2 |
| Toronto | 46.5 | 36.7 | 78.4 | 10.9 | 41.9 | 23.0 | 12.8 | 6.3 | 101.9 |
| Minnesota | 47.4 | 37.7 | 77.8 | 9.9 | 40.9 | 21.5 | 12.1 | 7.4 | 102.7 |
| Oklahoma City | 47.5 | 36.4 | 76.1 | 10.8 | 41.2 | 21.6 | 13.5 | 8.5 | 103.1 |
| Chicago | 45.7 | 35.4 | 78.5 | 12.4 | 42.9 | 21.2 | 13.6 | 7.7 | 103.2 |
| Washington | 48.2 | 38.7 | 75.9 | 11.4 | 41.8 | 24.6 | 13.4 | 7.2 | 103.5 |
| LA Clippers | 47.3 | 37.5 | 76.0 | 11.7 | 44.1 | 23.8 | 12.8 | 8.0 | 103.9 |
| Indiana | 45.8 | 37.5 | 76.4 | 11.1 | 44.1 | 21.1 | 13.4 | 7.7 | 106.2 |
| Phoenix | 46.7 | 38.3 | 77.5 | 12.1 | 40.8 | 21.2 | 13.5 | 8.6 | 107.5 |
| New York | 48.0 | 35.1 | 75.8 | 11.6 | 46.1 | 21.6 | 13.9 | 8.0 | 107.8 |
| Sacramento | 48.3 | 40.6 | 75.6 | 12.4 | 44.0 | 21.9 | 13.7 | 8.6 | 109.3 |
| Golden State | 46.8 | 38.0 | 77.9 | 14.2 | 47.1 | 24.1 | 14.5 | 7.9 | 112.3 |

## Atlanta Hawks

| Player | GP | MPG | FG% | 3Pt% | FT% | OFF | DEF | Total | APG | SPG | BPG | TO | PF | PPG |
|---|---|---|---|---|---|---|---|---|---|---|---|---|---|---|
| Joe Johnson | 79 | 39.5 | 43.7 | 36.0 | 82.6 | 0.8 | 3.6 | 4.4 | 5.8 | 1.1 | 0.2 | 2.5 | 2.2 | 21.4 |
| Josh Smith | 69 | 35.1 | 49.2 | 29.9 | 58.8 | 1.9 | 5.3 | 7.2 | 2.4 | 1.4 | 1.6 | 2.3 | 2.7 | 15.6 |
| Mike Bibby | 79 | 34.7 | 43.5 | 39.0 | 78.9 | -0.5 | 3.0 | 3.5 | 5.0 | 1.2 | 0.1 | 1.6 | 1.8 | 14.9 |
| Marvin Williams | 61 | 34.3 | 45.8 | 35.5 | 80.6 | 1.8 | 4.5 | 6.3 | 1.3 | 0.9 | 0.6 | 1.2 | 2.1 | 13.9 |
| Ronald Murray | 80 | 24.7 | 44.7 | 36.0 | 76.0 | 0.3 | 1.8 | 2.1 | 2.0 | 1.1 | 0.2 | 1.6 | 2.2 | 12.2 |
| Al Horford | 67 | 33.5 | 52.5 | 0.0 | 72.7 | 2.2 | 7.1 | 9.3 | 2.4 | 0.8 | 1.4 | 1.5 | 2.8 | 11.5 |
| Maurice Evans | 80 | 23.0 | 43.2 | 39.5 | 82.2 | 1.1 | 1.9 | 3.0 | 0.7 | 0.6 | 0.1 | 0.5 | 2.0 | 7.2 |
| Zaza Pachulia | 77 | 19.1 | 49.7 | 0.0 | 70.9 | 2.2 | 3.4 | 5.7 | 0.7 | 0.5 | 0.3 | 1.2 | 2.7 | 6.2 |
| Solomon Jones | 63 | 10.7 | 60.4 | 50.0 | 71.6 | 0.8 | 1.4 | 2.3 | 0.2 | 0.1 | 0.5 | 0.4 | 2.0 | 3.0 |
| Acie Law | 55 | 10.2 | 37.4 | 31.0 | 81.7 | 0.1 | 0.9 | 1.1 | 1.6 | 0.2 | 0.1 | 1.5 | 0.8 | 2.9 |
| Speedy Claxton | 2 | 7.5 | 28.6 | 0.0 | 50.0 | 0.0 | 0.0 | 0.0 | 1.5 | 0.0 | 0.0 | 0.0 | 0.5 | 2.5 |
| Thomas Gardner | 16 | 6.1 | 25.0 | 17.4 | -50.0 | 0.0 | 0.4 | 0.4 | 0.1 | 0.3 | 0.1 | 0.2 | 0.3 | 1.5 |
| Othello Hunter | 16 | 5.8 | 55.0 | 0.0 | 0.0 | 0.6 | 0.9 | 1.5 | 0.1 | 0.1 | 0.3 | 0.1 | 0.7 | 1.4 |
| Hawks | 82 | 240.3 | 45.8 | 36.6 | 73.7 | 10.6 | 29.4 | 40.0 | 20.2 | 7.4 | 4.6 | 12.8 | 19.6 | 98.1 |
| Opponents | 82 | 240.3 | 45.4 | 35.3 | 76.9 | 11.6 | 30.3 | 41.9 | 20.8 | 6.5 | 4.3 | 13.7 | 20.5 | 96.5 |

## Boston Celtics

| Player | GP | MPG | FG% | 3Pt% | FT% | OFF | DEF | Total | APG | SPG | BPG | TO | PF | PPG |
|---|---|---|---|---|---|---|---|---|---|---|---|---|---|---|
| Paul Pierce | 81 | 37.5 | 45.7 | 39.1 | 83.0 | 0.7 | 5.0 | 5.6 | 3.6 | 1.0 | 0.3 | 2.8 | 2.7 | 20.5 |
| Ray Allen | 79 | 36.4 | 48.0 | 40.9 | 95.2 | 0.8 | 2.7 | 3.5 | 2.8 | 0.9 | 0.2 | 1.7 | 2.0 | 18.2 |
| Kevin Garnett | 57 | 31.1 | 53.1 | 25.0 | 84.1 | 1.4 | 7.1 | 8.5 | 2.5 | 1.1 | 1.2 | 1.6 | 2.2 | 15.8 |
| Rajon Rondo | 80 | 33.0 | 50.5 | 31.3 | 64.2 | 1.3 | 4.0 | 5.2 | 8.2 | 1.9 | 0.1 | 2.6 | 2.4 | 11.9 |
| Eddie House | 81 | 18.3 | 44.5 | 44.4 | 79.2 | 0.1 | 1.8 | 1.9 | 1.1 | 0.8 | 0.1 | 0.7 | 1.4 | 8.5 |
| Kendrick Perkins | 76 | 29.6 | 57.7 | 0.0 | 60.0 | 2.7 | 5.5 | 8.1 | 1.3 | 0.3 | 2.0 | 2.2 | 3.3 | 8.5 |
| Tony Allen | 46 | 19.3 | 48.2 | 22.2 | 72.5 | 0.5 | 1.8 | 2.3 | 1.4 | 1.2 | 0.5 | 1.7 | 2.1 | 7.6 |
| Leon Powe | 70 | 17.5 | 52.4 | 0.0 | 68.9 | 2.1 | 2.9 | 4.9 | 0.7 | 0.3 | 0.5 | 1.1 | 2.7 | 7.7 |
| Glen Davis | 76 | 21.5 | 44.2 | 40.0 | 73.0 | 1.6 | 2.4 | 4.0 | 0.9 | 0.7 | 0.3 | 0.9 | 3.0 | 7.0 |
| *Mikki Moore | 24 | 19.0 | 60.0 | 0.0 | 73.7 | 1.3 | 3.1 | 4.4 | 1.0 | 0.2 | 0.2 | 0.9 | 4.0 | 4.8 |
| *Stephon Marbury | 23 | 18.0 | 34.2 | 24.0 | 46.2 | 0.1 | 1.1 | 1.2 | 3.3 | 0.4 | 0.1 | 1.6 | 1.5 | 3.8 |
| Brian Scalabrine | 39 | 12.9 | 42.1 | 39.3 | 88.9 | 0.2 | 1.1 | 1.3 | 0.5 | 0.2 | 0.3 | 0.3 | 1.9 | 3.5 |
| Bill Walker | 29 | 7.4 | 62.1 | 0.0 | 69.6 | 0.3 | 0.7 | 1.0 | 0.4 | 0.2 | 0.1 | 0.6 | 1.8 | 3.0 |
| Gabe Pruitt | 27 | 7.8 | 30.7 | 29.2 | 81.0 | 0.2 | 0.7 | 0.9 | 0.8 | 0.3 | 0.1 | 0.4 | 0.7 | 2.0 |
| Celtics | 82 | 242.4 | 48.6 | 39.7 | 76.5 | 10.6 | 31.5 | 42.1 | 22.7 | 7.6 | 4.7 | 15.6 | 23.1 | 100.9 |
| Opponents | 82 | 242.4 | 43.1 | 34.9 | 77.1 | 10.2 | 27.4 | 37.6 | 18.9 | 7.1 | 4.7 | 14.6 | 22.2 | 93.4 |

## Charlotte Bobcats

| Player | GP | MPG | FG% | 3Pt% | FT% | OFF | DEF | Total | APG | SPG | BPG | TO | PF | PPG |
|---|---|---|---|---|---|---|---|---|---|---|---|---|---|---|
| Gerald Wallace | 71 | 37.6 | 48.0 | 29.8 | 80.4 | 1.6 | 6.2 | 7.8 | 2.7 | 1.7 | 0.9 | 2.1 | 3.0 | 16.6 |
| *Boris Diaw | 59 | 37.6 | 49.5 | 41.9 | 68.6 | 1.6 | 4.3 | 5.9 | 4.9 | 0.9 | 0.8 | 3.0 | 2.8 | 15.1 |
| Raymond Felton | 82 | 37.6 | 40.8 | 28.5 | 80.5 | 0.7 | 3.1 | 3.8 | 6.7 | 1.5 | 0.4 | 2.8 | 2.3 | 14.2 |
| Emeka Okafor | 82 | 32.8 | 56.1 | 0.0 | 59.3 | 3.4 | 6.7 | 10.1 | 0.6 | 0.6 | 1.7 | 1.8 | 3.0 | 13.2 |
| *Raja Bell | 45 | 35.6 | 44.0 | 39.5 | 87.7 | 0.7 | 3.2 | 4.0 | 2.5 | 0.8 | 0.1 | 1.5 | 2.4 | 13.0 |
| D.J. Augustin | 72 | 26.5 | 43.0 | 43.9 | 89.3 | 0.2 | 1.6 | 1.8 | 3.5 | 0.6 | 0.0 | 1.7 | 1.9 | 11.8 |
| *V. Radmanovic | 32 | 21.1 | 40.1 | 35.7 | 64.5 | 0.8 | 2.4 | 3.3 | 1.3 | 0.6 | 0.3 | 1.6 | 1.9 | 8.3 |
| Dontell Jefferson | 6 | 14.0 | 50.0 | 50.0 | 66.7 | 0.2 | 1.8 | 2.0 | 1.5 | 0.7 | 0.2 | 1.0 | 1.5 | 4.8 |
| *Juwan Howard | 39 | 11.5 | 51.0 | 0.0 | 67.6 | 0.7 | 1.1 | 1.8 | 0.6 | 0.2 | 0.1 | 0.7 | 1.7 | 4.4 |
| Sean May | 24 | 12.5 | 39.8 | 100.0 | 70.0 | 0.8 | 2.0 | 2.9 | 0.4 | 0.2 | 0.2 | 1.1 | 1.3 | 3.9 |
| *DeSagana Diop | 41 | 14.2 | 46.0 | 0.0 | 27.0 | 1.7 | 2.1 | 3.8 | 0.5 | 0.4 | 0.8 | 0.7 | 1.8 | 2.8 |
| Nazr Mohammed | 39 | 8.7 | 40.6 | 0.0 | 55.0 | 0.9 | 1.1 | 2.0 | 0.2 | 0.1 | 0.4 | 0.6 | 1.6 | 2.7 |
| Cartier Martin | 33 | 8.1 | 36.4 | 30.3 | 80.0 | 0.2 | 0.8 | 1.0 | 0.4 | 0.2 | 0.1 | 0.3 | 1.0 | 2.6 |
| Alexis Ajinca | 31 | 5.9 | 36.2 | 0.0 | 71.4 | 0.7 | 1.0 | 1.0 | 0.1 | 0.2 | 0.2 | 0.4 | 1.1 | 2.3 |
| *Sean Singletary | 24 | 7.5 | 39.6 | 4.0 | 80.0 | 0.2 | 0.6 | 0.8 | 0.7 | 0.2 | 0.0 | 0.8 | 1.3 | 2.3 |
| Bobcats | 82 | 243.0 | 45.5 | 36.6 | 74.0 | 10.8 | 28.9 | 39.7 | 21.2 | 7.1 | 4.8 | 15.6 | 21.4 | 93.6 |
| Opponents | 82 | 243.0 | 45.4 | 36.6 | 75.6 | 10.7 | 28.2 | 38.9 | 19.6 | 7.6 | 6.0 | 14.7 | 20.9 | 94.9 |

* mid-season trade

## Chicago Bulls

| Player | GP | MPG | FG% | 3Pt% | FT% | OFF | DEF | Total | APG | SPG | BPG | TO | PF | PPG |
|---|---|---|---|---|---|---|---|---|---|---|---|---|---|---|
| | | | Field Goals | | | Rebounds | | | | | | | | |
| Ben Gordon ..........82 | 82 | 36.6 | 45.5 | 41.0 | 86.4 | 0.6 | 2.8 | 3.5 | 3.4 | 0.9 | 0.3 | 2.4 | 2.2 | 20.7 |
| *John Salmons ......26 | 26 | 37.7 | 47.3 | 41.5 | 84.3 | 0.6 | 3.7 | 4.3 | 2.0 | 1.0 | 0.6 | 1.7 | 2.3 | 18.3 |
| Derrick Rose ........81 | 81 | 37.0 | 47.5 | 22.2 | 78.8 | 1.2 | 2.7 | 3.9 | 6.3 | 0.8 | 0.2 | 2.5 | 1.5 | 16.8 |
| Luol Deng .............49 | 49 | 34.0 | 44.8 | 40.0 | 79.6 | 1.6 | 4.4 | 6.0 | 1.9 | 1.2 | 0.5 | 1.5 | 1.7 | 14.1 |
| *Brad Miller ..........27 | 27 | 27.6 | 47.8 | 23.1 | 85.3 | 2.5 | 5.0 | 7.4 | 3.2 | 0.8 | 0.4 | 1.7 | 3.3 | 11.8 |
| Tyrus Thomas ......79 | 79 | 27.5 | 45.1 | 33.3 | 78.3 | 1.9 | 4.6 | 6.4 | 1.0 | 1.2 | 1.9 | 1.6 | 2.8 | 10.8 |
| Kirk Hinrich ..........51 | 51 | 26.3 | 43.7 | 40.8 | 79.1 | 0.3 | 2.1 | 2.4 | 3.9 | 1.3 | 0.4 | 1.7 | 2.5 | 9.9 |
| Joakim Noah ........80 | 80 | 24.2 | 55.6 | 0.0 | 67.6 | 3.1 | 4.5 | 7.6 | 1.3 | 0.6 | 1.4 | 1.0 | 3.0 | 6.7 |
| *Tim Thomas .........18 | 18 | 14.1 | 40.0 | 44.2 | 70.0 | 0.4 | 1.9 | 2.3 | 0.7 | 0.3 | 0.0 | 0.6 | 1.5 | 5.8 |
| Aaron Gray ...........56 | 56 | 12.8 | 48.5 | 0.0 | 57.6 | 1.5 | 2.4 | 3.9 | 0.8 | 0.3 | 0.3 | 0.7 | 2.4 | 3.5 |
| Lindsey Hunter .....28 | 28 | 9.5 | 32.9 | 33.3 | 60.0 | 0.1 | 0.4 | 0.4 | 1.3 | 0.7 | 0.0 | 0.7 | 1.0 | 2.6 |
| *Anthony Robertson ..6 | 6 | 3.8 | 29.4 | 20.0 | 0.0 | 0.3 | 0.8 | 1.2 | 0.2 | 0.0 | 0.0 | 0.1 | 0.0 | 2.0 |
| *Linton Johnson ......8 | 8 | 5.3 | 36.4 | 50.0 | 0.0 | 0.4 | 0.6 | 1.0 | 0.3 | 0.1 | 0.0 | 0.3 | 0.8 | 1.1 |
| **Bulls ......................82** | 82 | 243.0 | 45.7 | 38.1 | 79.6 | 11.8 | 30.3 | 42.1 | 21.1 | 7.5 | 5.5 | 14.5 | 20.8 | 102.2 |
| **Opponents ...............82** | 82 | 243.0 | 45.8 | 34.7 | 78.6 | 12.4 | 30.4 | 42.8 | 21.0 | 7.6 | 5.5 | 14.4 | 20.8 | 102.5 |

## Cleveland Cavaliers

| Player | GP | MPG | FG% | 3Pt% | FT% | OFF | DEF | Total | APG | SPG | BPG | TO | PF | PPG |
|---|---|---|---|---|---|---|---|---|---|---|---|---|---|---|
| | | | Field Goals | | | Rebounds | | | | | | | | |
| LeBron James ......81 | 81 | 37.7 | 48.9 | 34.4 | 78.0 | 1.3 | 6.3 | 7.6 | 7.2 | 1.7 | 1.2 | 3.0 | 1.7 | 28.4 |
| Mo Williams ..........81 | 81 | 35.0 | 46.7 | 43.6 | 91.2 | 0.6 | 2.9 | 3.4 | 4.1 | 0.9 | 0.1 | 2.2 | 2.7 | 17.8 |
| Zydrunas Ilgauskas ..65 | 65 | 27.2 | 47.2 | 38.5 | 79.9 | 2.4 | 5.1 | 7.5 | 1.0 | 0.4 | 1.3 | 1.4 | 2.8 | 12.9 |
| Delonte West ........64 | 64 | 33.6 | 45.7 | 39.9 | 83.3 | 0.5 | 2.7 | 3.2 | 3.5 | 1.5 | 0.2 | 1.4 | 2.0 | 11.7 |
| Anderson Varejao ..81 | 81 | 28.5 | 53.6 | 0.0 | 61.6 | 2.0 | 5.1 | 7.2 | 1.0 | 0.9 | 0.8 | 1.0 | 3.0 | 8.6 |
| Daniel Gibson .....75 | 75 | 23.9 | 39.1 | 38.2 | 76.7 | 0.4 | 1.7 | 2.1 | 1.8 | 0.6 | 0.2 | 0.8 | 2.2 | 7.8 |
| Wally Szczerbiak ..74 | 74 | 20.6 | 45.0 | 41.1 | 84.9 | 0.6 | 2.6 | 3.1 | 1.1 | 0.4 | 0.1 | 0.7 | 1.8 | 7.0 |
| *Joe Smith ............21 | 21 | 19.6 | 49.6 | 33.3 | 75.0 | 1.7 | 3.0 | 4.8 | 0.8 | 0.3 | 0.7 | 0.5 | 2.4 | 6.5 |
| Sasha Pavlovic ......66 | 66 | 16.0 | 42.2 | 41.0 | 46.3 | 0.5 | 1.5 | 1.9 | 1.1 | 0.3 | 0.2 | 0.7 | 1.8 | 4.6 |
| J.J. Hickson .........62 | 62 | 11.4 | 51.5 | 0.0 | 67.2 | 0.8 | 1.8 | 2.7 | 0.1 | 0.2 | 0.5 | 0.7 | 1.3 | 4.0 |
| Ben Wallace .........56 | 56 | 23.5 | 44.5 | 0.0 | 42.2 | 2.4 | 4.0 | 6.5 | 0.8 | 0.9 | 1.3 | 0.6 | 1.5 | 2.9 |
| Tarence Kinsey ......50 | 50 | 5.5 | 44.9 | 38.9 | 86.8 | 0.2 | 0.6 | 0.8 | 0.2 | 0.2 | 0.0 | 0.4 | 0.7 | 2.0 |
| Darnell Jackson ....51 | 51 | 8.4 | 43.0 | 0.0 | 68.6 | 0.6 | 1.1 | 1.7 | 0.2 | 0.2 | 0.1 | 0.3 | 1.5 | 1.9 |
| Lorenzen Wright ...17 | 17 | 7.4 | 37.0 | 0.0 | 37.5 | 0.4 | 1.1 | 1.5 | 0.2 | 0.2 | 0.3 | 0.5 | 1.0 | 1.4 |
| Jawad Williams ...10 | 10 | 2.0 | 41.7 | 33.3 | 0.0 | 0.1 | 0.1 | 0.2 | 0.0 | 0.1 | 0.0 | 0.1 | 0.2 | 1.2 |
| Trey Johnson .........4 | 4 | 3.5 | 0.0 | 0.0 | 100.0 | 0.0 | 0.3 | 0.3 | 0.0 | 0.0 | 0.0 | 0.3 | 1.0 | 1.0 |
| **Cavaliers ..................82** | 82 | 241.2 | 46.8 | 39.3 | 75.7 | 10.8 | 31.4 | 42.2 | 20.3 | 7.2 | 5.3 | 12.7 | 20.3 | 100.3 |
| **Opponents ...............82** | 82 | 241.2 | 43.1 | 33.3 | 77.0 | 10.7 | 28.2 | 38.9 | 19.1 | 6.3 | 4.1 | 13.9 | 20.3 | 91.4 |

## Dallas Mavericks

| Player | GP | MPG | FG% | 3Pt% | FT% | OFF | DEF | Total | APG | SPG | BPG | TO | PF | PPG |
|---|---|---|---|---|---|---|---|---|---|---|---|---|---|---|
| | | | Field Goals | | | Rebounds | | | | | | | | |
| Dirk Nowitzki ........81 | 81 | 37.7 | 47.9 | 35.9 | 89.0 | 1.1 | 7.3 | 8.4 | 2.4 | 0.8 | 0.8 | 1.9 | 2.2 | 25.9 |
| Jason Terry ...........74 | 74 | 33.7 | 46.3 | 36.6 | 88.0 | 0.5 | 1.9 | 2.4 | 3.4 | 1.3 | 0.3 | 1.6 | 1.9 | 19.6 |
| Josh Howard ........52 | 52 | 32.0 | 45.1 | 34.5 | 78.2 | 1.1 | 3.9 | 5.1 | 1.6 | 1.2 | 0.6 | 1.7 | 2.6 | 18.0 |
| Jason Kidd ..........81 | 81 | 35.6 | 41.6 | 40.6 | 81.9 | 1.0 | 5.1 | 6.2 | 8.7 | 2.0 | 0.5 | 2.3 | 2.1 | 9.0 |
| Brandon Bass .......81 | 81 | 19.4 | 49.6 | 0.0 | 86.7 | 1.6 | 2.9 | 4.5 | 0.5 | 0.3 | 0.7 | 1.1 | 1.7 | 8.5 |
| Jose Barea ...........79 | 79 | 20.3 | 44.2 | 35.7 | 75.3 | 0.5 | 1.8 | 2.2 | 3.4 | 0.5 | 0.1 | 1.3 | 1.5 | 7.8 |
| Antoine Wright ......65 | 65 | 23.9 | 41.5 | 30.2 | 74.7 | 0.5 | 1.6 | 2.1 | 1.2 | 0.7 | 0.4 | 0.8 | 2.6 | 7.3 |
| Erick Dampier .......80 | 80 | 23.0 | 65.0 | 0.0 | 63.8 | 2.7 | 4.4 | 7.1 | 1.0 | 0.3 | 1.2 | 0.9 | 2.4 | 5.7 |
| Gerald Green .......38 | 38 | 9.9 | 43.9 | 30.4 | 84.4 | 0.4 | 1.1 | 1.4 | 0.4 | 0.3 | 0.1 | 0.9 | 1.3 | 5.2 |
| James Singleton ..62 | 62 | 14.3 | 52.9 | 32.5 | 85.9 | 1.4 | 2.6 | 4.0 | 0.4 | 0.4 | 0.5 | 0.6 | 1.8 | 5.1 |
| Jerry Stackhouse .10 | 10 | 16.2 | 26.7 | 13.8 | 100.0 | 0.5 | 1.2 | 1.7 | 1.2 | 0.4 | 0.1 | 0.9 | 0.6 | 4.2 |
| Devean George ...43 | 43 | 16.5 | 38.0 | 28.9 | 77.3 | 0.6 | 1.2 | 1.8 | 0.3 | 0.5 | 0.3 | 0.4 | 1.3 | 3.4 |
| *Ryan Hollins ........27 | 27 | 9.6 | 52.5 | 0.0 | 51.5 | 1.0 | 1.3 | 2.3 | 0.1 | 0.2 | 0.6 | 0.5 | 1.6 | 2.9 |
| Shawne Williams ...15 | 15 | 11.3 | 28.6 | 5.9 | 81.8 | 1.3 | 1.8 | 3.1 | 0.1 | 0.1 | 0.6 | 0.3 | 1.3 | 2.8 |
| *Matt Carroll .........21 | 21 | 6.7 | 27.3 | 12.5 | 100.0 | 0.1 | 0.6 | 0.7 | 0.1 | 0.1 | 0.1 | 0.3 | 0.7 | 1.2 |
| **Mavericks .................82** | 82 | 241.5 | 46.2 | 35.0 | 81.9 | 11.1 | 31.6 | 42.7 | 21.7 | 7.2 | 5.2 | 12.7 | 19.5 | 101.7 |
| **Opponents ...............82** | 82 | 241.5 | 45.5 | 37.5 | 79.8 | 10.8 | 30.6 | 41.4 | 19.6 | 7.2 | 4.1 | 13.0 | 20.1 | 99.8 |

\* mid-season trade

## Denver Nuggets

| Player | GP | MPG | FG% | 3Pt% | FT% | OFF | DEF | Total | APG | SPG | BPG | TO | PF | PPG |
|---|---|---|---|---|---|---|---|---|---|---|---|---|---|---|
| Carmelo Anthony | 66 | 34.5 | 44.3 | 37.1 | 79.3 | 1.6 | 5.2 | 6.8 | 3.4 | 1.1 | 0.4 | 3.0 | 3.0 | 22.8 |
| *Chauncey Billups | 77 | 35.3 | 42.0 | 41.0 | 91.3 | 0.4 | 2.6 | 3.0 | 6.4 | 1.2 | 0.2 | 2.3 | 2.1 | 17.9 |
| J.R. Smith | 81 | 27.7 | 44.6 | 39.7 | 75.4 | 0.5 | 3.1 | 3.7 | 2.8 | 1.0 | 0.2 | 1.9 | 2.3 | 15.2 |
| Nené | 77 | 32.6 | 60.4 | 20.0 | 72.3 | 2.4 | 5.4 | 7.8 | 1.4 | 1.2 | 1.3 | 1.9 | 3.6 | 14.6 |
| Kenyon Martin | 66 | 32.0 | 49.1 | 36.8 | 60.4 | 1.2 | 4.8 | 6.0 | 2.0 | 1.5 | 1.1 | 1.6 | 3.0 | 11.7 |
| Linas Kleiza | 82 | 22.2 | 44.7 | 32.6 | 72.5 | 1.1 | 2.9 | 4.0 | 0.8 | 0.4 | 0.2 | 1.0 | 1.9 | 9.9 |
| Chris Andersen | 71 | 20.6 | 54.8 | 20.0 | 71.8 | 2.3 | 3.9 | 6.2 | 0.4 | 0.6 | 2.5 | 1.0 | 2.5 | 6.4 |
| Dahntay Jones | 79 | 18.1 | 45.8 | 64.7 | 72.8 | 0.7 | 1.4 | 2.1 | 1.0 | 0.6 | 0.2 | 0.9 | 2.5 | 5.4 |
| Anthony Carter | 78 | 22.9 | 43.3 | 23.9 | 73.1 | 0.5 | 2.1 | 2.6 | 4.7 | 1.2 | 0.2 | 2.0 | 1.8 | 5.3 |
| Renaldo Balkman | 53 | 14.7 | 55.8 | 28.6 | 64.6 | 1.6 | 2.2 | 3.8 | 0.6 | 0.9 | 0.4 | 0.7 | 1.8 | 5.0 |
| *Johan Petro | 27 | 8.0 | 42.9 | 0.0 | 42.9 | 0.6 | 1.8 | 2.3 | 0.4 | 0.1 | 0.4 | 0.5 | 2.1 | 2.2 |
| Sonny Weems | 12 | 4.6 | 32.0 | 0.0 | 37.5 | 0.0 | 0.3 | 0.3 | 0.3 | 0.1 | 0.1 | 0.5 | 0.7 | 1.6 |
| *Jason Hart | 11 | 3.3 | 50.0 | 0.0 | 75.0 | 0.1 | 0.3 | 0.4 | 0.5 | 0.0 | 0.0 | 0.3 | 0.4 | 1.2 |
| **Nuggets** | 82 | 240.6 | 47.0 | 37.1 | 76.0 | 11.0 | 30.6 | 41.6 | 22.2 | 8.7 | 6.0 | 15.3 | 22.9 | 104.3 |
| **Opponets** | 82 | 240.6 | 44.0 | 36.6 | 78.2 | 12.1 | 29.2 | 41.2 | 21.4 | 7.9 | 5.4 | 15.4 | 23.7 | 100.9 |

## Detroit Pistons

| Player | GP | MPG | FG% | 3Pt% | FT% | OFF | DEF | Total | APG | SPG | BPG | TO | PF | PPG |
|---|---|---|---|---|---|---|---|---|---|---|---|---|---|---|
| Richard Hamilton | 67 | 34.0 | 44.7 | 36.8 | 84.8 | 0.7 | 2.4 | 3.1 | 4.4 | 0.6 | 0.1 | 2.0 | 2.6 | 18.3 |
| *Allen Iverson | 54 | 36.5 | 41.6 | 28.6 | 78.6 | 0.5 | 2.6 | 3.1 | 4.9 | 1.6 | 0.1 | 2.5 | 1.5 | 17.4 |
| Tayshaun Prince | 82 | 35.7 | 45.1 | 39.7 | 77.8 | 1.6 | 4.2 | 5.8 | 3.1 | 0.5 | 0.6 | 1.2 | 1.3 | 14.2 |
| Rodney Stuckey | 79 | 31.9 | 43.9 | 29.5 | 80.3 | 0.9 | 2.6 | 3.5 | 4.9 | 1.0 | 0.1 | 2.2 | 2.7 | 13.4 |
| Rasheed Wallace | 66 | 32.2 | 41.9 | 35.4 | 77.2 | 0.8 | 6.6 | 7.4 | 1.4 | 0.9 | 1.3 | 0.9 | 3.0 | 12.0 |
| *Antonio McDyess | 62 | 30.1 | 51.0 | 0.0 | 69.8 | 3.0 | 6.8 | 9.8 | 1.3 | 0.7 | 0.8 | 0.8 | 3.1 | 9.6 |
| Will Bynum | 57 | 14.1 | 45.6 | 15.8 | 79.8 | 0.3 | 1.0 | 1.3 | 2.8 | 0.6 | 0.0 | 1.3 | 1.5 | 7.2 |
| Jason Maxiell | 78 | 18.1 | 57.5 | 0.0 | 53.2 | 2.2 | 2.0 | 4.2 | 0.3 | 0.3 | 0.8 | 0.6 | 2.0 | 5.8 |
| Arron Afflalo | 74 | 16.7 | 43.7 | 40.2 | 81.7 | 0.4 | 1.4 | 1.8 | 0.6 | 0.4 | 0.2 | 0.6 | 1.9 | 4.9 |
| Kwame Brown | 58 | 17.2 | 53.3 | 0.0 | 51.6 | 1.6 | 3.4 | 5.0 | 0.6 | 0.4 | 0.4 | 0.9 | 2.4 | 4.2 |
| Walter Herrmann | 59 | 10.7 | 39.6 | 34.2 | 76.0 | 0.5 | 1.3 | 1.8 | 0.4 | 0.1 | 0.1 | 0.3 | 0.7 | 3.8 |
| Amir Johnson | 62 | 14.7 | 59.5 | 0.0 | 65.7 | 1.6 | 2.1 | 3.7 | 0.3 | 0.3 | 1.0 | 0.5 | 2.8 | 3.5 |
| Walter Sharpe | 8 | 2.5 | 36.4 | 0.0 | 0.0 | 0.0 | 0.4 | 0.4 | 0.0 | 0.0 | 0.3 | 0.0 | 0.4 | 1.0 |
| **Pistons** | 82 | 242.7 | 45.4 | 34.9 | 75.1 | 11.6 | 29.9 | 41.4 | 20.6 | 6.0 | 4.6 | 11.9 | 20.9 | 94.2 |
| **Opponents** | 82 | 242.7 | 45.1 | 35.4 | 77.5 | 10.5 | 29.9 | 40.4 | 20.1 | 5.8 | 4.2 | 11.8 | 19.7 | 94.7 |

## Golden State Warriors

| Player | GP | MPG | FG% | 3Pt% | FT% | OFF | DEF | Total | APG | SPG | BPG | TO | PF | PPG |
|---|---|---|---|---|---|---|---|---|---|---|---|---|---|---|
| Stephen Jackson | 59 | 39.6 | 41.4 | 33.8 | 82.6 | 1.2 | 3.9 | 5.1 | 6.5 | 1.5 | 0.5 | 3.9 | 2.6 | 20.7 |
| *Jamal Crawford | 54 | 38.6 | 40.6 | 33.8 | 88.9 | 0.4 | 2.9 | 3.3 | 4.4 | 0.9 | 0.2 | 2.3 | 1.5 | 19.7 |
| Monta Ellis | 25 | 35.7 | 45.1 | 30.8 | 83.0 | 0.6 | 3.8 | 4.3 | 3.7 | 1.6 | 0.3 | 2.7 | 2.7 | 19.0 |
| Corey Maggette | 51 | 31.1 | 46.1 | 25.3 | 82.4 | 1.0 | 4.6 | 5.5 | 1.8 | 0.9 | 0.2 | 2.4 | 3.8 | 18.6 |
| Kelenna Azubuike | 74 | 32.1 | 46.4 | 44.8 | 80.8 | 1.5 | 3.5 | 5.0 | 1.6 | 0.8 | 0.7 | 1.3 | 2.5 | 14.4 |
| Andris Biedrins | 62 | 30.0 | 57.8 | 0.0 | 55.1 | 3.6 | 7.6 | 11.2 | 2.0 | 1.0 | 1.6 | 1.8 | 3.8 | 11.9 |
| Anthony Morrow | 67 | 22.6 | 47.8 | 46.7 | 87.0 | 1.2 | 1.8 | 3.0 | 1.2 | 0.5 | 0.2 | 0.8 | 1.9 | 10.1 |
| C.J. Watson | 77 | 24.5 | 45.7 | 40.0 | 87.0 | 0.5 | 2.0 | 2.5 | 2.7 | 1.3 | 0.1 | 1.2 | 1.8 | 9.5 |
| Marco Belinelli | 42 | 21.0 | 44.2 | 39.7 | 76.9 | 0.2 | 1.5 | 1.7 | 2.1 | 0.9 | 0.0 | 1.4 | 1.7 | 8.9 |
| Brandan Wright | 39 | 17.6 | 52.8 | 0.0 | 74.1 | 1.6 | 2.4 | 4.0 | 0.5 | 0.6 | 1.0 | 0.6 | 1.9 | 8.3 |
| Ronny Turiaf | 79 | 21.5 | 50.8 | 0.0 | 79.0 | 1.1 | 3.4 | 4.6 | 2.1 | 0.4 | 2.1 | 0.9 | 3.1 | 5.9 |
| Rob Kurz | 40 | 11.1 | 38.9 | 39.5 | 80.0 | 0.8 | 1.2 | 2.0 | 0.5 | 0.4 | 0.5 | 0.4 | 2.0 | 3.9 |
| Jermareo Davidson | 14 | 7.9 | 48.6 | 0.0 | 47.1 | 0.7 | 1.7 | 2.4 | 0.1 | 0.1 | 0.2 | 0.4 | 0.9 | 3.0 |
| Marcus Williams | 9 | 6.0 | 23.5 | 33.3 | 33.3 | 0.0 | 0.4 | 0.4 | 1.4 | 0.1 | 0.1 | 0.4 | 0.7 | 1.3 |
| **Warriors** | 82 | 242.4 | 45.8 | 37.3 | 79.1 | 11.6 | 30.4 | 42.0 | 20.9 | 7.8 | 6.4 | 14.6 | 22.5 | 108.6 |
| **Opponents** | 82 | 242.4 | 46.8 | 38.0 | 77.9 | 14.2 | 32.9 | 47.1 | 24.1 | 7.9 | 5.0 | 15.0 | 23.5 | 112.3 |

* mid-season trade

## Houston Rockets

| Player | GP | MPG | FG% | 3Pt% | FT% | OFF | DEF | Total | APG | SPG | BPG | TO | PF | PPG |
|---|---|---|---|---|---|---|---|---|---|---|---|---|---|---|
| Yao Ming | 77 | 33.6 | 54.8 | 100.0 | 86.6 | 2.6 | 7.2 | 9.9 | 1.8 | 0.4 | 2.0 | 3.0 | 3.3 | 19.7 |
| Ron Artest | 69 | 35.5 | 40.1 | 39.9 | 74.8 | 0.9 | 4.3 | 5.2 | 3.3 | 1.5 | 0.4 | 2.0 | 2.2 | 17.1 |
| Tracy McGrady | 35 | 33.7 | 38.8 | 37.6 | 80.1 | 0.6 | 3.8 | 4.4 | 5.0 | 1.2 | 0.4 | 2.0 | 1.1 | 15.6 |
| Luis Scola | 82 | 30.3 | 53.1 | 0.0 | 76.0 | 2.4 | 6.3 | 8.8 | 1.5 | 0.8 | 0.1 | 1.5 | 3.2 | 12.7 |
| Aaron Brooks | 80 | 25.0 | 40.4 | 36.6 | 86.6 | 0.4 | 1.6 | 2.0 | 3.0 | 0.6 | 0.1 | 1.6 | 1.9 | 11.2 |
| Von Wafer | 63 | 19.4 | 44.7 | 39.0 | 75.2 | 0.3 | 1.5 | 1.8 | 1.1 | 0.6 | 0.1 | 0.9 | 1.1 | 9.7 |
| Carl Landry | 69 | 21.3 | 57.4 | 33.3 | 81.3 | 1.8 | 3.2 | 5.0 | 0.6 | 0.4 | 0.5 | 1.0 | 2.4 | 9.2 |
| *Kyle Lowry | 28 | 21.7 | 47.5 | 27.6 | 80.0 | 0.5 | 2.3 | 2.8 | 3.5 | 0.8 | 0.3 | 1.4 | 2.0 | 7.6 |
| Shane Battier | 60 | 33.9 | 41.0 | 38.4 | 82.1 | 0.9 | 3.9 | 4.8 | 2.3 | 0.8 | 0.9 | 0.8 | 1.9 | 7.3 |
| Brent Barry | 56 | 15.3 | 40.7 | 37.4 | 95.0 | 0.3 | 1.4 | 1.7 | 1.4 | 0.4 | 0.1 | 0.9 | 0.8 | 3.7 |
| James White | 4 | 2.8 | 60.0 | 50.0 | 0.0 | 0.0 | 0.0 | 0.0 | 0.0 | 0.3 | 0.3 | 0.8 | 0.5 | 1.8 |
| Dikembe Mutombo | 9 | 10.7 | 38.5 | 0.0 | 66.7 | 1.3 | 2.3 | 3.7 | 0.0 | 0.0 | 1.2 | 0.7 | 1.2 | 1.8 |
| *Brian Cook | 9 | 2.8 | 31.3 | 40.0 | 0.0 | 0.1 | 0.4 | 0.6 | 0.1 | 0.0 | 0.3 | 0.2 | 0.3 | 1.3 |
| Chuck Hayes | 71 | 12.1 | 37.2 | 0.0 | 36.8 | 1.0 | 2.5 | 3.5 | 0.6 | 0.5 | 0.3 | 0.4 | 1.9 | 1.3 |
| **Rockets** | 82 | 241.5 | 45.3 | 37.5 | 80.5 | 10.5 | 32.5 | 43.0 | 20.3 | 6.7 | 4.3 | 14.1 | 18.9 | 98.4 |
| **Opponents** | 82 | 241.5 | 44.4 | 35.7 | 74.9 | 10.6 | 29.3 | 39.9 | 19.8 | 7.2 | 5.3 | 12.3 | 20.6 | 94.4 |

## Indiana Pacers

| Player | GP | MPG | FG% | 3Pt% | FT% | OFF | DEF | Total | APG | SPG | BPG | TO | PF | PPG |
|---|---|---|---|---|---|---|---|---|---|---|---|---|---|---|
| Danny Granger | 67 | 36.2 | 44.7 | 40.4 | 87.8 | 0.7 | 4.4 | 5.1 | 2.7 | 1.0 | 1.5 | 2.5 | 3.1 | 25.8 |
| Mike Dunleavy | 18 | 27.5 | 40.1 | 35.6 | 81.5 | 0.8 | 3.0 | 3.8 | 2.4 | 0.7 | 0.5 | 2.1 | 2.0 | 15.1 |
| T.J. Ford | 74 | 30.5 | 45.2 | 33.7 | 87.2 | 0.8 | 2.7 | 3.5 | 5.3 | 1.2 | 0.2 | 2.4 | 2.4 | 14.9 |
| Troy Murphy | 73 | 34.0 | 47.5 | 45.0 | 82.6 | 2.0 | 9.8 | 11.8 | 2.4 | 0.8 | 0.5 | 1.6 | 3.1 | 14.3 |
| Marquis Daniels | 54 | 31.5 | 45.1 | 20.0 | 72.1 | 1.5 | 3.1 | 4.6 | 2.1 | 1.2 | 0.5 | 1.7 | 2.2 | 13.6 |
| Jarrett Jack | 82 | 33.1 | 45.3 | 35.3 | 85.2 | 0.5 | 2.8 | 3.4 | 4.1 | 1.1 | 0.2 | 2.2 | 2.2 | 13.1 |
| Brandon Rush | 75 | 24.0 | 42.3 | 37.3 | 69.7 | 0.5 | 2.7 | 3.1 | 0.9 | 0.5 | 0.5 | 1.0 | 1.7 | 8.1 |
| Roy Hibbert | 70 | 14.4 | 47.1 | 0.0 | 66.7 | 1.6 | 1.8 | 3.5 | 0.3 | 0.3 | 1.1 | 0.8 | 3.1 | 7.1 |
| Rasho Nesterovic | 70 | 17.3 | 51.3 | 0.0 | 78.1 | 1.3 | 2.1 | 3.4 | 1.6 | 0.4 | 0.5 | 0.9 | 2.4 | 6.8 |
| Jeff Foster | 74 | 24.7 | 50.1 | 28.6 | 65.8 | 2.9 | 4.0 | 6.9 | 1.8 | 0.7 | 0.7 | 1.2 | 3.1 | 6.1 |
| Stephen Graham | 52 | 13.2 | 41.4 | 30.3 | 80.6 | 0.4 | 1.4 | 1.8 | 0.6 | 0.2 | 0.1 | 0.9 | 1.6 | 5.4 |
| Travis Diener | 55 | 13.1 | 41.3 | 39.0 | 80.0 | 0.1 | 1.5 | 1.6 | 2.2 | 0.5 | 0.1 | 0.4 | 0.8 | 3.7 |
| Maceo Baston | 27 | 8.0 | 54.3 | 0.0 | 63.0 | 0.8 | 1.1 | 1.9 | 0.3 | 0.2 | 0.4 | 0.4 | 1.4 | 2.5 |
| Josh McRoberts | 33 | 8.5 | 42.2 | 0.0 | 76.9 | 0.8 | 1.5 | 2.2 | 0.5 | 0.4 | 0.5 | 0.4 | 1.2 | 2.4 |
| **Pacers** | 82 | 241.8 | 45.5 | 37.8 | 80.7 | 11.3 | 32.5 | 43.7 | 21.6 | 7.0 | 5.3 | 14.5 | 23.1 | 105.1 |
| **Opponents** | 82 | 241.8 | 45.8 | 37.5 | 76.4 | 11.1 | 33.0 | 44.1 | 21.1 | 7.7 | 5.4 | 14.0 | 20.6 | 106.2 |

## Los Angeles Clippers

| Player | GP | MPG | FG% | 3Pt% | FT% | OFF | DEF | Total | APG | SPG | BPG | TO | PF | PPG |
|---|---|---|---|---|---|---|---|---|---|---|---|---|---|---|
| *Zach Randolph | 39 | 35.1 | 48.7 | 34.2 | 70.1 | 3.0 | 6.4 | 9.4 | 2.3 | 0.8 | 0.3 | 2.3 | 2.7 | 20.9 |
| Al Thornton | 71 | 37.4 | 44.6 | 25.3 | 75.4 | 1.7 | 3.5 | 5.2 | 1.5 | 0.8 | 0.9 | 1.8 | 3.2 | 16.8 |
| Eric Gordon | 78 | 34.3 | 45.6 | 38.9 | 85.4 | 0.6 | 2.0 | 2.6 | 2.8 | 1.0 | 0.5 | 2.1 | 2.2 | 16.1 |
| Baron Davis | 65 | 34.6 | 37.0 | 30.2 | 75.7 | 0.7 | 3.0 | 3.7 | 7.7 | 1.7 | 0.5 | 3.0 | 3.0 | 14.9 |
| Chris Kaman | 31 | 29.7 | 52.8 | 0.0 | 68.0 | 2.4 | 5.5 | 8.0 | 1.5 | 0.6 | 1.5 | 2.7 | 3.0 | 12.0 |
| Marcus Camby | 62 | 31.0 | 51.2 | 25.0 | 72.5 | 2.6 | 8.5 | 11.1 | 2.0 | 0.8 | 2.1 | 1.5 | 2.1 | 10.3 |
| Fred Jones | 52 | 28.8 | 40.7 | 36.7 | 81.5 | 0.4 | 2.0 | 2.4 | 3.6 | 1.0 | 0.2 | 1.3 | 2.2 | 7.3 |
| Steve Novak | 71 | 16.4 | 44.4 | 41.6 | 91.3 | 0.3 | 1.5 | 1.8 | 0.6 | 0.3 | 0.1 | 0.3 | 1.0 | 6.9 |
| Ricky Davis | 36 | 21.8 | 33.9 | 31.5 | 86.1 | 0.3 | 1.4 | 1.7 | 2.3 | 0.5 | 0.1 | 1.1 | 1.8 | 6.4 |
| *Mardy Collins | 39 | 20.9 | 43.3 | 46.4 | 64.9 | 0.7 | 1.8 | 2.5 | 2.6 | 0.7 | 0.3 | 1.4 | 1.9 | 5.9 |
| Mike Taylor | 51 | 15.1 | 41.2 | 32.5 | 69.1 | 0.4 | 1.3 | 1.7 | 2.1 | 0.7 | 0.0 | 1.4 | 1.6 | 5.7 |
| DeAndre Jordan | 53 | 14.5 | 63.3 | 0.0 | 38.5 | 1.4 | 3.1 | 4.5 | 0.2 | 0.2 | 1.1 | 0.8 | 1.8 | 4.3 |
| Brian Skinner | 51 | 16.5 | 44.9 | 0.0 | 63.8 | 1.4 | 2.6 | 4.0 | 0.5 | 0.3 | 1.0 | 0.8 | 1.8 | 4.2 |
| Paul Davis | 27 | 11.9 | 40.8 | 0.0 | 79.4 | 1.0 | 1.4 | 2.5 | 0.4 | 0.4 | 0.1 | 0.5 | 1.6 | 4.0 |
| *Alex Acker | 18 | 9.9 | 40.0 | 43.8 | 50.0 | 0.4 | 0.8 | 1.2 | 0.6 | 0.2 | 0.2 | 0.4 | 0.5 | 3.5 |
| **Clippers** | 82 | 242.4 | 44.1 | 35.4 | 73.6 | 10.9 | 29.0 | 39.8 | 21.0 | 7.0 | 5.9 | 14.9 | 20.1 | 95.1 |
| **Opponents** | 82 | 242.4 | 47.3 | 37.5 | 76.0 | 11.7 | 32.4 | 44.1 | 23.8 | 8.0 | 5.0 | 13.3 | 19.6 | 103.9 |

* mid-season trade

### Los Angeles Lakers

| Player | GP | MPG | FG% | 3Pt% | FT% | OFF | DEF | Total | APG | SPG | BPG | TO | PF | PPG |
|---|---|---|---|---|---|---|---|---|---|---|---|---|---|---|
| Kobe Bryant | 82 | 36.1 | 46.7 | 35.1 | 85.6 | 1.1 | 4.1 | 5.2 | 4.9 | 1.5 | 0.5 | 2.6 | 2.3 | 26.8 |
| Pau Gasol | 81 | 37.0 | 56.7 | 50.0 | 78.1 | 3.2 | 6.4 | 9.6 | 3.5 | 0.6 | 1.0 | 1.9 | 2.1 | 18.9 |
| Andrew Bynum | 50 | 28.9 | 56.0 | 0.0 | 70.7 | 2.7 | 5.2 | 8.0 | 1.4 | 0.4 | 1.8 | 1.7 | 3.1 | 14.3 |
| Lamar Odom | 78 | 29.7 | 49.2 | 32.0 | 62.3 | 2.3 | 5.9 | 8.2 | 2.6 | 1.0 | 1.3 | 1.8 | 3.0 | 11.3 |
| Derek Fisher | 82 | 29.8 | 42.4 | 39.7 | 84.6 | 0.3 | 2.0 | 2.3 | 3.2 | 1.2 | 0.1 | 0.9 | 2.3 | 9.9 |
| Trevor Ariza | 82 | 24.4 | 46.0 | 31.9 | 71.0 | 1.4 | 2.9 | 4.3 | 1.8 | 1.7 | 0.3 | 1.1 | 2.0 | 8.9 |
| Jordan Farmar | 65 | 18.3 | 39.1 | 33.6 | 58.4 | 0.3 | 1.5 | 1.8 | 2.4 | 0.9 | 0.2 | 1.3 | 1.6 | 6.4 |
| Sasha Vujacic | 80 | 16.2 | 38.7 | 36.3 | 92.1 | 0.2 | 1.5 | 1.7 | 1.4 | 1.0 | 0.1 | 0.4 | 1.9 | 5.8 |
| Luke Walton | 65 | 17.9 | 43.6 | 29.8 | 71.9 | 0.8 | 1.9 | 2.8 | 2.7 | 0.5 | 0.2 | 1.1 | 1.6 | 5.0 |
| Josh Powell | 60 | 11.7 | 44.4 | 0.0 | 76.0 | 1.2 | 1.8 | 2.9 | 0.5 | 0.2 | 0.3 | 0.9 | 1.6 | 4.2 |
| *Shannon Brown | 18 | 7.6 | 52.4 | 66.7 | 88.9 | 0.2 | 0.9 | 1.1 | 0.6 | 0.2 | 0.1 | 0.5 | 0.5 | 3.2 |
| D.J. Mbenga | 23 | 7.9 | 47.4 | 0.0 | 87.5 | 0.4 | 1.0 | 1.3 | 0.4 | 0.4 | 1.0 | 0.6 | 1.4 | 2.7 |
| *Adam Morrison | 8 | 5.5 | 33.3 | 25.0 | 50.0 | 0.3 | 0.8 | 1.0 | 0.4 | 0.0 | 0.0 | 0.4 | 0.5 | 1.3 |
| Lakers | 82 | 241.2 | 47.4 | 36.1 | 77.0 | 12.4 | 31.5 | 43.9 | 23.3 | 8.8 | 5.1 | 13.4 | 20.7 | 106.9 |
| Opponents | 82 | 241.2 | 44.7 | 34.5 | 75.3 | 11.7 | 29.8 | 41.5 | 22.6 | 7.7 | 4.8 | 15.6 | 22.1 | 99.3 |

### Memphis Grizzlies

| Player | GP | MPG | FG% | 3Pt% | FT% | OFF | DEF | Total | APG | SPG | BPG | TO | PF | PPG |
|---|---|---|---|---|---|---|---|---|---|---|---|---|---|---|
| Rudy Gay | 79 | 37.3 | 45.3 | 35.1 | 76.7 | 1.4 | 4.2 | 5.5 | 1.7 | 1.2 | 0.8 | 2.6 | 2.8 | 18.9 |
| O.J. Mayo | 82 | 38.0 | 43.8 | 38.4 | 87.9 | 0.7 | 3.1 | 3.8 | 3.2 | 1.1 | 0.2 | 2.8 | 2.5 | 18.5 |
| Marc Gasol | 82 | 30.7 | 53.0 | 0.0 | 73.3 | 2.5 | 4.9 | 7.4 | 1.7 | 0.8 | 1.1 | 2.0 | 3.2 | 11.9 |
| Hakim Warrick | 82 | 24.7 | 49.1 | 21.7 | 71.1 | 1.6 | 3.4 | 5.0 | 0.8 | 0.6 | 0.5 | 1.2 | 2.1 | 11.6 |
| Mike Conley | 82 | 30.6 | 44.2 | 40.6 | 81.7 | 0.3 | 3.1 | 3.4 | 4.3 | 1.1 | 0.1 | 1.7 | 1.8 | 10.9 |
| Darrell Arthur | 76 | 19.3 | 43.8 | 0.0 | 66.7 | 1.4 | 3.1 | 4.6 | 0.6 | 0.7 | 0.7 | 0.6 | 2.7 | 5.6 |
| Darko Milicic | 61 | 17.0 | 51.5 | 0.0 | 56.2 | 1.4 | 3.0 | 4.3 | 0.6 | 0.4 | 0.8 | 0.8 | 2.2 | 5.5 |
| Quinton Ross | 68 | 17.1 | 38.2 | 37.5 | 81.0 | 0.4 | 1.4 | 1.9 | 0.7 | 0.5 | 0.2 | 0.5 | 1.7 | 3.9 |
| Darius Miles | 34 | 8.8 | 48.5 | 16.7 | 74.2 | 0.6 | 1.1 | 1.7 | 0.5 | 0.3 | 0.6 | 0.6 | 0.9 | 3.5 |
| Marko Jaric | 53 | 11.4 | 33.1 | 39.3 | 70.7 | 0.4 | 0.8 | 1.2 | 1.4 | 0.6 | 0.2 | 0.9 | 1.2 | 2.6 |
| Greg Buckner | 63 | 13.9 | 38.4 | 25.5 | 80.0 | 0.5 | 1.6 | 2.1 | 0.9 | 0.5 | 0.1 | 0.6 | 1.7 | 2.5 |
| Hamed Haddaji | 19 | 6.3 | 48.4 | 0.0 | 60.0 | 0.8 | 1.6 | 2.5 | 0.4 | 0.1 | 0.6 | 0.5 | 1.1 | 2.5 |
| Grizzlies | 82 | 241.5 | 45.4 | 36.0 | 75.6 | 10.3 | 28.5 | 38.8 | 17.4 | 7.5 | 4.7 | 15.3 | 21.7 | 93.9 |
| Opponents | 82 | 241.5 | 48.0 | 35.5 | 77.0 | 10.3 | 29.6 | 39.9 | 21.2 | 7.7 | 5.4 | 14.6 | 21.8 | 99.3 |

### Miami Heat

| Player | GP | MPG | FG% | 3Pt% | FT% | OFF | DEF | Total | APG | SPG | BPG | TO | PF | PPG |
|---|---|---|---|---|---|---|---|---|---|---|---|---|---|---|
| Dwyane Wade | 79 | 38.6 | 49.1 | 31.7 | 76.5 | 1.1 | 3.9 | 5.0 | 7.5 | 2.2 | 1.3 | 3.4 | 2.3 | 30.2 |
| Michael Beasley | 81 | 24.8 | 47.2 | 40.7 | 77.2 | 1.4 | 4.1 | 5.4 | 1.0 | 0.5 | 0.5 | 1.5 | 2.3 | 13.9 |
| *Jermaine O'Neal | 27 | 30.0 | 47.5 | 0.0 | 75.0 | 2.0 | 3.3 | 5.4 | 2.0 | 0.4 | 2.0 | 1.9 | 3.0 | 13.0 |
| Udonis Haslem | 75 | 34.1 | 51.8 | 0.0 | 75.3 | 2.3 | 6.0 | 8.2 | 1.1 | 0.6 | 0.3 | 1.1 | 2.7 | 10.6 |
| Mario Chalmers | 82 | 32.0 | 42.0 | 36.7 | 76.7 | 0.5 | 2.3 | 2.8 | 4.9 | 2.0 | 0.1 | 2.0 | 2.9 | 10.0 |
| Daequan Cook | 75 | 24.4 | 37.5 | 38.7 | 87.5 | 0.3 | 2.3 | 2.5 | 0.9 | 0.5 | 0.1 | 0.6 | 1.7 | 9.1 |
| *Jamario Moon | 26 | 26.5 | 45.9 | 37.0 | 86.7 | 0.4 | 4.1 | 4.5 | 1.0 | 0.8 | 0.6 | 0.5 | 1.8 | 7.1 |
| Chris Quinn | 66 | 14.6 | 40.8 | 40.9 | 81.0 | 0.1 | 1.0 | 1.1 | 2.0 | 0.4 | 0.0 | 0.5 | 1.2 | 5.1 |
| *Luther Head | 10 | 17.6 | 37.2 | 37.5 | 62.5 | 0.3 | 2.2 | 2.5 | 2.3 | 1.1 | 0.1 | 0.9 | 2.2 | 4.3 |
| James Jones | 40 | 15.8 | 36.9 | 34.4 | 83.9 | 0.3 | 1.3 | 1.6 | 0.5 | 0.3 | 0.4 | 0.3 | 1.5 | 4.2 |
| Mark Blount | 20 | 10.4 | 38.5 | 40.7 | 61.5 | 0.5 | 1.6 | 2.1 | 0.2 | 0.1 | 0.4 | 0.7 | 0.9 | 4.0 |
| Yakhouba Diawara | 63 | 13.5 | 35.0 | 31.3 | 52.6 | 0.4 | 0.9 | 1.3 | 0.4 | 0.2 | 0.1 | 0.3 | 1.2 | 3.4 |
| Dorell Wright | 6 | 12.2 | 40.0 | 0.0 | 33.3 | 0.3 | 3.0 | 3.3 | 0.3 | 0.3 | 0.0 | 1.0 | 1.3 | 3.0 |
| Jamaal Magloire | 55 | 12.9 | 49.6 | 0.0 | 48.3 | 1.5 | 2.5 | 4.0 | 0.4 | 0.2 | 0.5 | 0.6 | 2.2 | 2.9 |
| Joel Anthony | 65 | 16.1 | 48.3 | 0.0 | 65.2 | 1.4 | 1.7 | 3.0 | 0.4 | 0.4 | 1.4 | 0.6 | 2.1 | 2.2 |
| Heat | 82 | 243.4 | 45.7 | 35.7 | 75.4 | 10.1 | 29.4 | 39.5 | 20.4 | 7.9 | 5.5 | 12.5 | 20.7 | 98.3 |
| Opponents | 82 | 243.4 | 45.5 | 38.9 | 77.1 | 10.9 | 30.9 | 41.9 | 20.1 | 6.4 | 4.1 | 15.2 | 19.9 | 98.0 |

* mid-season trade

## Milwaukee Bucks

| Player | GP | MPG | FG% | 3Pt% | FT% | OFF | DEF | Total | APG | SPG | BPG | TO | PF | PPG |
|---|---|---|---|---|---|---|---|---|---|---|---|---|---|---|
| | | | **Field Goals** | | | **Rebounds** | | | | | | | | |
| Michael Redd ......33 | 33 | 36.5 | 45.5 | 36.6 | 81.4 | 0.7 | 2.5 | 3.2 | 2.7 | 1.1 | 0.1 | 1.6 | 1.4 | 21.2 |
| Richard Jefferson..82 | 82 | 35.8 | 43.9 | 39.7 | 80.5 | 0.7 | 3.9 | 4.6 | 2.4 | 0.8 | 0.2 | 2.0 | 3.1 | 19.6 |
| Charlie Villanueva..78 | 78 | 26.9 | 44.7 | 34.5 | 83.8 | 2.0 | 4.7 | 6.7 | 1.8 | 0.6 | 0.7 | 1.8 | 3.3 | 16.2 |
| Ramon Sessions ...79 | 79 | 27.5 | 44.5 | 17.6 | 79.4 | 0.8 | 2.6 | 3.4 | 5.7 | 1.1 | 0.1 | 1.9 | 2.0 | 12.4 |
| Andrew Bogut ......36 | 36 | 31.2 | 57.7 | 0.0 | 57.1 | 3.3 | 7.0 | 10.3 | 2.0 | 0.6 | 1.0 | 2.4 | 3.6 | 11.7 |
| Luke Ridnour........72 | 72 | 28.2 | 40.3 | 35.0 | 86.9 | 0.5 | 2.6 | 3.0 | 5.1 | 1.3 | 0.2 | 1.8 | 2.8 | 9.6 |
| Charlie Bell..........70 | 70 | 25.5 | 41.4 | 36.3 | 82.5 | 0.5 | 1.5 | 1.9 | 2.2 | 0.7 | 0.1 | 1.1 | 2.0 | 8.4 |
| Luc Mbah a Moute..82 | 82 | 25.8 | 46.2 | 0.0 | 72.9 | 2.3 | 3.6 | 5.9 | 1.1 | 1.1 | 0.6 | 1.2 | 2.5 | 7.2 |
| *Keith Bogans.......29 | 29 | 16.7 | 37.6 | 34.8 | 93.9 | 0.6 | 2.6 | 3.1 | 1.1 | 0.7 | 0.1 | 0.8 | 1.5 | 6.0 |
| Joe Alexander......59 | 59 | 12.1 | 41.6 | 34.8 | 69.9 | 0.7 | 1.2 | 1.9 | 0.7 | 0.3 | 0.5 | 0.9 | 1.8 | 4.7 |
| Dan Gadzuric........67 | 67 | 14.0 | 48.0 | 0.0 | 54.4 | 1.4 | 2.4 | 3.8 | 0.6 | 0.5 | 0.6 | 0.6 | 2.4 | 4.0 |
| Francisco Elson ...59 | 59 | 16.6 | 49.1 | 25.0 | 84.6 | 1.7 | 2.2 | 3.9 | 0.5 | 0.6 | 0.6 | 0.8 | 2.4 | 3.4 |
| Malik Allen...........49 | 49 | 11.8 | 42.9 | 0.0 | 47.6 | 0.7 | 1.4 | 2.1 | 0.7 | 0.1 | 0.2 | 0.4 | 1.8 | 3.2 |
| Eddie Gill .............6 | 6 | 7.2 | 66.7 | 66.7 | 0.0 | 0.0 | 0.7 | 0.7 | 1.8 | 0.5 | 0.2 | 0.8 | 1.7 | 2.3 |
| Damon Jones.......18 | 18 | 6.0 | 32.4 | 39.3 | 0.0 | 0.0 | 0.3 | 0.3 | 0.4 | 0.2 | 0.0 | 0.3 | 0.2 | 1.8 |
| **Bucks**...............82 | 82 | 241.2 | 44.5 | 36.3 | 78.0 | 11.9 | 28.9 | 40.7 | 22.0 | 7.4 | 3.8 | 14.1 | 24.2 | 99.3 |
| **Opponents**..............82 | 82 | 241.2 | 45.8 | 37.8 | 79.1 | 10.1 | 30.8 | 41.0 | 21.1 | 7.5 | 4.6 | 16.5 | 22.5 | 100.4 |

## Minnesota Timberwolves

| Player | GP | MPG | FG% | 3Pt% | FT% | OFF | DEF | Total | APG | SPG | BPG | TO | PF | PPG |
|---|---|---|---|---|---|---|---|---|---|---|---|---|---|---|
| | | | **Field Goals** | | | **Rebounds** | | | | | | | | |
| Al Jefferson .........50 | 50 | 36.7 | 49.7 | 0.0 | 73.8 | 3.4 | 7.5 | 11.0 | 1.6 | 0.8 | 1.7 | 1.8 | 2.8 | 23.1 |
| Randy Foye .........70 | 70 | 35.6 | 40.7 | 36.0 | 84.6 | 0.5 | 2.6 | 3.1 | 4.3 | 1.0 | 0.4 | 2.1 | 2.9 | 16.3 |
| Ryan Gomes.........82 | 82 | 31.9 | 43.1 | 37.2 | 80.7 | 1.3 | 3.5 | 4.8 | 1.6 | 0.8 | 0.3 | 1.6 | 2.2 | 13.3 |
| Kevin Love...........81 | 81 | 25.3 | 45.9 | 10.5 | 78.9 | 3.4 | 5.7 | 9.1 | 1.0 | 0.4 | 0.6 | 1.5 | 2.5 | 11.1 |
| Craig Smith..........74 | 74 | 19.7 | 56.2 | 0.0 | 67.7 | 1.3 | 2.5 | 3.8 | 1.1 | 0.4 | 0.3 | 1.4 | 2.5 | 10.1 |
| Mike Miller ...........73 | 73 | 32.3 | 48.2 | 37.8 | 73.2 | 1.0 | 5.6 | 6.6 | 4.5 | 0.4 | 0.4 | 2.0 | 1.9 | 9.9 |
| Sebastian Telfair ...75 | 75 | 27.9 | 38.3 | 34.6 | 81.9 | 0.4 | 1.3 | 1.7 | 4.6 | 1.0 | 0.2 | 2.0 | 2.5 | 9.8 |
| Rodney Carney .....67 | 67 | 17.9 | 41.6 | 35.0 | 75.8 | 0.5 | 1.3 | 1.9 | 0.4 | 0.7 | 0.4 | 0.6 | 1.4 | 7.2 |
| Corey Brewer........15 | 15 | 20.5 | 41.1 | 41.7 | 73.7 | 1.2 | 2.1 | 3.3 | 1.7 | 1.0 | 0.2 | 0.9 | 2.5 | 6.2 |
| *Bobby Brown ......21 | 21 | 12.2 | 41.6 | 38.9 | 88.9 | 0.3 | 0.5 | 0.8 | 1.4 | 0.3 | 0.1 | 0.8 | 1.0 | 5.5 |
| *Shelden Williams.15 | 15 | 13.8 | 44.1 | 0.0 | 66.7 | 1.6 | 3.4 | 5.0 | 0.3 | 0.7 | 0.5 | 0.5 | 1.9 | 4.9 |
| Kevin Ollie ...........50 | 50 | 17.0 | 40.7 | 0.0 | 83.3 | 0.3 | 1.2 | 1.5 | 2.3 | 0.4 | 0.1 | 0.7 | 1.6 | 4.0 |
| Brian Cardinal.......64 | 64 | 14.2 | 38.5 | 32.6 | 85.7 | 0.6 | 1.6 | 2.2 | 1.2 | 0.6 | 0.2 | 0.8 | 2.1 | 3.0 |
| Jason Collins........31 | 31 | 13.6 | 31.4 | 0.0 | 46.4 | 0.9 | 1.4 | 2.3 | 0.4 | 0.3 | 0.4 | 0.4 | 2.4 | 1.8 |
| Mark Madsen........19 | 19 | 6.1 | 21.4 | 0.0 | 0.0 | 0.5 | 0.4 | 0.9 | 0.2 | 0.1 | 0.1 | 0.2 | 0.9 | 0.3 |
| **Timberwolves**............82 | 82 | 241.5 | 44.1 | 35.3 | 76.9 | 11.9 | 29.8 | 41.7 | 20.4 | 6.2 | 3.9 | 14.2 | 21.8 | 97.8 |
| **Opponents** .................82 | 82 | 241.5 | 47.4 | 37.7 | 77.8 | 9.9 | 31.0 | 40.9 | 21.5 | 7.4 | 5.9 | 12.5 | 20.0 | 102.7 |

## New Jersey Nets

| Player | GP | MPG | FG% | 3Pt% | FT% | OFF | DEF | Total | APG | SPG | BPG | TO | PF | PPG |
|---|---|---|---|---|---|---|---|---|---|---|---|---|---|---|
| | | | **Field Goals** | | | **Rebounds** | | | | | | | | |
| Devin Harris.........69 | 69 | 36.1 | 43.8 | 29.1 | 82.0 | 0.4 | 2.9 | 3.3 | 6.9 | 1.7 | 0.2 | 3.1 | 2.4 | 21.3 |
| Vince Carter .........80 | 80 | 36.8 | 43.7 | 38.5 | 81.7 | 0.9 | 4.2 | 5.1 | 4.7 | 1.0 | 0.5 | 2.1 | 2.9 | 20.8 |
| Brook Lopez.........82 | 82 | 30.5 | 53.1 | 0.0 | 79.3 | 2.7 | 5.4 | 8.1 | 1.0 | 0.5 | 1.8 | 1.8 | 3.1 | 13.0 |
| Keyon Dooling .....77 | 77 | 26.9 | 43.6 | 42.1 | 82.5 | 0.3 | 1.7 | 2.0 | 3.5 | 0.9 | 0.1 | 1.4 | 1.8 | 9.7 |
| Jarvis Hayes ........74 | 74 | 24.8 | 44.5 | 38.5 | 69.2 | 0.4 | 3.2 | 3.6 | 0.7 | 0.7 | 0.1 | 0.7 | 2.2 | 8.7 |
| Yi Jianlian.............61 | 61 | 23.3 | 38.2 | 34.3 | 77.2 | 1.1 | 4.2 | 5.3 | 1.0 | 0.5 | 0.6 | 1.2 | 2.6 | 8.6 |
| Bobby Simmons...71 | 71 | 24.4 | 44.9 | 44.7 | 74.1 | 1.0 | 2.9 | 3.9 | 1.3 | 0.7 | 0.1 | 0.9 | 2.6 | 7.8 |
| Ryan Anderson ....66 | 66 | 19.9 | 39.3 | 36.5 | 84.5 | 1.6 | 3.1 | 4.7 | 0.8 | 0.7 | 0.3 | 1.0 | 2.4 | 7.4 |
| C. Douglas-Roberts..44 | 44 | 13.3 | 46.0 | 25.0 | 82.3 | 0.3 | 0.8 | 1.1 | 1.2 | 0.3 | 0.2 | 0.7 | 0.8 | 4.9 |
| Josh Boone ..........62 | 62 | 16.0 | 52.8 | 0.0 | 37.6 | 1.7 | 2.5 | 4.2 | 0.5 | 0.4 | 0.8 | 0.5 | 1.7 | 4.2 |
| Trenton Hassell ...53 | 53 | 20.6 | 45.0 | 25.0 | 80.0 | 0.9 | 1.8 | 2.8 | 1.0 | 0.4 | 0.3 | 0.6 | 1.7 | 3.7 |
| Eduardo Najera....27 | 27 | 11.8 | 44.6 | 20.0 | 36.4 | 0.6 | 1.9 | 2.5 | 0.7 | 0.4 | 0.2 | 0.7 | 1.9 | 2.9 |
| Sean Williams.......33 | 33 | 11.1 | 41.7 | 0.0 | 62.5 | 1.0 | 1.4 | 2.4 | 0.4 | 0.2 | 0.9 | 0.6 | 2.2 | 2.4 |
| Maurice Ager .......20 | 20 | 4.9 | 34.9 | 0.0 | 50.0 | 0.2 | 0.4 | 0.5 | 0.2 | 0.1 | 0.1 | 0.2 | 0.9 | 1.7 |
| **Nets**...........................82 | 82 | 241.8 | 44.8 | 37.6 | 77.9 | 10.4 | 29.5 | 39.8 | 20.0 | 6.8 | 4.8 | 13.1 | 22.4 | 98.1 |
| **Opponents**..................82 | 82 | 241.8 | 46.2 | 39.1 | 76.2 | 10.6 | 30.8 | 41.4 | 21.9 | 6.9 | 4.8 | 13.4 | 20.5 | 100.5 |

\* mid-season trade

### New Orleans Hornets

| Player | GP | MPG | FG% | 3Pt% | FT% | OFF | DEF | Total | APG | SPG | BPG | TO | PF | PPG |
|---|---|---|---|---|---|---|---|---|---|---|---|---|---|---|
| Chris Paul | 78 | 38.5 | 50.3 | 36.4 | 86.8 | 0.9 | 4.7 | 5.5 | 11.0 | 2.8 | 0.1 | 3.0 | 2.7 | 22.8 |
| David West | 76 | 39.2 | 47.2 | 24.0 | 88.4 | 2.1 | 6.4 | 8.5 | 2.3 | 0.6 | 0.9 | 2.1 | 2.7 | 21.0 |
| Peja Stojakovic | 61 | 34.2 | 39.9 | 37.8 | 89.4 | 0.7 | 3.6 | 4.3 | 1.2 | 0.9 | 0.1 | 0.8 | 1.7 | 13.3 |
| Rasual Butler | 82 | 31.9 | 43.3 | 39.0 | 78.2 | 0.6 | 2.7 | 3.3 | 0.9 | 0.6 | 0.7 | 0.7 | 1.9 | 11.2 |
| James Posey | 75 | 28.5 | 41.2 | 36.9 | 82.2 | 0.5 | 4.3 | 4.8 | 1.1 | 0.8 | 0.3 | 1.1 | 2.9 | 8.9 |
| *Tyson Chandler | 45 | 32.1 | 56.5 | 0.0 | 57.9 | 3.6 | 5.1 | 8.7 | 0.5 | 0.3 | 1.2 | 1.6 | 3.2 | 8.8 |
| Devin Brown | 63 | 13.8 | 35.5 | 28.9 | 78.0 | 0.5 | 1.4 | 1.9 | 0.9 | 0.5 | 0.1 | 0.9 | 1.3 | 5.2 |
| Hilton Armstrong | 70 | 15.6 | 56.1 | 0.0 | 63.3 | 1.2 | 1.6 | 2.8 | 0.4 | 0.4 | 0.6 | 1.1 | 2.6 | 4.8 |
| Julian Wright | 54 | 14.3 | 46.6 | 9.5 | 56.7 | 0.9 | 2.0 | 2.8 | 0.8 | 0.7 | 0.4 | 0.8 | 0.9 | 4.4 |
| Morris Peterson | 43 | 12.0 | 39.9 | 38.8 | 63.2 | 0.3 | 1.7 | 2.0 | 0.4 | 0.4 | 0.1 | 0.4 | 1.2 | 4.4 |
| *Antonio Daniels | 61 | 12.0 | 42.4 | 34.7 | 82.1 | 0.1 | 0.8 | 0.9 | 2.1 | 0.3 | 0.0 | 0.8 | 0.7 | 3.8 |
| Sean Marks | 60 | 14.0 | 48.5 | 20.0 | 68.2 | 1.0 | 2.1 | 3.1 | 0.2 | 0.1 | 0.6 | 0.6 | 2.0 | 3.2 |
| Melvin Ely | 31 | 12.0 | 38.9 | 0.0 | 63.9 | 1.0 | 1.1 | 2.1 | 0.6 | 0.1 | 0.3 | 0.7 | 1.9 | 3.1 |
| Ryan Bowen | 21 | 10.4 | 57.9 | 0.0 | 60.0 | 0.5 | 0.7 | 1.1 | 0.4 | 0.7 | 0.2 | 0.2 | 1.8 | 2.2 |
| **Hornets** | 82 | 240.9 | 45.7 | 36.4 | 80.7 | 9.8 | 29.9 | 39.7 | 19.6 | 7.2 | 4.1 | 12.6 | 20.3 | 95.8 |
| **Opponents** | 82 | 240.9 | 45.0 | 35.4 | 77.3 | 10.0 | 30.0 | 40.0 | 20.1 | 5.8 | 3.5 | 13.3 | 20.4 | 94.3 |

### New York Knicks

| Player | GP | MPG | FG% | 3Pt% | FT% | OFF | DEF | Total | APG | SPG | BPG | TO | PF | PPG |
|---|---|---|---|---|---|---|---|---|---|---|---|---|---|---|
| *Al Harrington | 68 | 35.0 | 44.6 | 36.2 | 80.4 | 1.3 | 5.0 | 6.3 | 1.4 | 1.2 | 0.3 | 2.3 | 3.1 | 20.7 |
| Nate Robinson | 74 | 29.9 | 43.7 | 32.5 | 84.1 | 1.3 | 2.6 | 3.9 | 4.1 | 1.3 | 0.1 | 1.9 | 2.8 | 17.2 |
| David Lee | 81 | 34.9 | 54.9 | 0.0 | 75.5 | 3.2 | 8.6 | 11.7 | 2.1 | 1.0 | 0.3 | 1.9 | 3.2 | 16.0 |
| Wilson Chandler | 82 | 33.4 | 43.2 | 32.8 | 79.5 | 1.1 | 4.3 | 5.4 | 2.1 | 0.9 | 0.9 | 1.7 | 3.0 | 14.4 |
| *Larry Hughes | 25 | 27.5 | 39.0 | 38.5 | 79.4 | 0.4 | 2.2 | 2.6 | 2.4 | 1.4 | 0.2 | 1.4 | 1.8 | 11.2 |
| Chris Duhon | 79 | 36.8 | 42.1 | 39.1 | 85.6 | 0.6 | 2.5 | 3.1 | 7.2 | 0.9 | 0.1 | 2.8 | 1.6 | 11.1 |
| Quentin Richardson | 72 | 26.3 | 39.3 | 36.5 | 76.1 | 1.0 | 3.4 | 4.4 | 1.6 | 0.7 | 0.1 | 1.0 | 1.8 | 10.2 |
| Danilo Gallinari | 28 | 14.7 | 44.8 | 44.4 | 96.3 | 0.5 | 1.5 | 2.0 | 0.5 | 0.5 | 0.1 | 0.5 | 1.7 | 6.1 |
| *Courtney Sims | 1 | 11.0 | 50.0 | 0.0 | 0.0 | 2.0 | 2.0 | 4.0 | 0.0 | 0.0 | 1.0 | 1.0 | 1.0 | 6.0 |
| *Chris Wilcox | 25 | 13.2 | 52.9 | 0.0 | 50.9 | 1.2 | 2.0 | 3.3 | 0.6 | 0.3 | 0.2 | 0.8 | 1.9 | 5.4 |
| Jared Jeffries | 56 | 23.4 | 44.0 | 8.3 | 61.1 | 2.3 | 1.8 | 4.1 | 1.4 | 0.8 | 0.6 | 1.2 | 2.7 | 5.3 |
| Joe Crawford | 2 | 11.5 | 30.0 | 25.0 | 100.0 | 0.5 | 1.5 | 2.0 | 0.5 | 0.5 | 0.0 | 0.0 | 1.0 | 4.5 |
| *Mouhamed Sene | 1 | 6.0 | 50.0 | 0.0 | 100.0 | 2.0 | 3.0 | 5.0 | 0.0 | 0.0 | 1.0 | 1.0 | 0.0 | 3.0 |
| *Demetris Nichols | 2 | 4.5 | 40.0 | 0.0 | 50.0 | 0.0 | 1.0 | 1.0 | 0.0 | 0.0 | 0.5 | 0.0 | 0.0 | 2.5 |
| Eddy Curry | 3 | 4.0 | 100.0 | 0.0 | 33.3 | 0.0 | 1.3 | 1.3 | 0.0 | 0.0 | 0.0 | 0.7 | 1.7 | 1.7 |
| **Knicks** | 82 | 241.5 | 44.5 | 36.0 | 78.4 | 11.1 | 31.0 | 42.1 | 21.2 | 7.4 | 2.5 | 14.3 | 20.4 | 105.2 |
| **Opponents** | 82 | 241.5 | 48.0 | 35.1 | 75.8 | 11.6 | 34.5 | 46.1 | 21.6 | 8.0 | 5.3 | 14.5 | 19.4 | 107.8 |

### Oklahoma City Thunder

| Player | GP | MPG | FG% | 3Pt% | FT% | OFF | DEF | Total | APG | SPG | BPG | TO | PF | PPG |
|---|---|---|---|---|---|---|---|---|---|---|---|---|---|---|
| Kevin Durant | 74 | 39.0 | 47.6 | 42.2 | 86.3 | 1.0 | 5.5 | 6.5 | 2.8 | 1.3 | 0.7 | 3.0 | 1.8 | 25.3 |
| Jeff Green | 78 | 36.8 | 44.6 | 38.9 | 78.8 | 1.5 | 5.1 | 6.7 | 2.0 | 1.0 | 0.4 | 2.2 | 2.6 | 16.5 |
| Russell Westbrook | 82 | 32.5 | 39.8 | 27.1 | 81.5 | 2.2 | 2.7 | 4.9 | 5.3 | 1.3 | 0.2 | 3.3 | 2.3 | 15.3 |
| Nenad Krstic | 46 | 24.8 | 46.9 | 0.0 | 79.7 | 1.8 | 3.7 | 5.5 | 0.6 | 0.5 | 1.1 | 1.0 | 2.5 | 9.7 |
| D.J. White | 7 | 18.6 | 52.0 | 0.0 | 76.9 | 1.4 | 3.1 | 4.6 | 0.9 | 0.4 | 0.7 | 0.4 | 1.4 | 8.9 |
| *Thabo Sefolosha | 23 | 31.1 | 41.7 | 24.3 | 83.3 | 1.2 | 4.0 | 5.2 | 2.0 | 1.7 | 1.1 | 1.2 | 2.3 | 8.5 |
| Nick Collison | 71 | 25.8 | 56.8 | 0.0 | 72.1 | 2.5 | 4.3 | 6.9 | 0.9 | 0.7 | 0.7 | 1.0 | 3.4 | 8.2 |
| *Shaun Livingston | 8 | 23.8 | 53.8 | 0.0 | 100.0 | 0.4 | 2.9 | 3.3 | 2.0 | 0.6 | 0.3 | 0.8 | 1.0 | 7.8 |
| Desmond Mason | 39 | 27.3 | 43.5 | 0.0 | 54.1 | 1.1 | 3.0 | 4.0 | 1.2 | 0.4 | 0.8 | 1.4 | 2.5 | 7.5 |
| Earl Watson | 68 | 26.1 | 38.4 | 23.5 | 75.5 | 0.5 | 2.2 | 2.7 | 5.8 | 0.7 | 0.2 | 2.3 | 2.0 | 6.6 |
| Kyle Weaver | 56 | 20.8 | 45.9 | 34.4 | 70.7 | 0.6 | 1.8 | 2.3 | 1.8 | 0.8 | 0.5 | 1.2 | 1.4 | 5.3 |
| Damian Wilkins | 41 | 15.5 | 36.2 | 37.5 | 80.4 | 1.0 | 1.2 | 1.7 | 0.9 | 0.5 | 0.2 | 0.9 | 1.3 | 5.3 |
| *Malik Rose | 20 | 15.7 | 37.8 | 0.0 | 80.0 | 0.7 | 2.6 | 3.3 | 1.0 | 0.5 | 0.1 | 1.0 | 2.4 | 5.0 |
| *Chucky Atkins | 18 | 16.6 | 29.1 | 25.0 | 91.7 | 0.3 | 0.7 | 1.0 | 1.7 | 0.4 | 0.1 | 0.7 | 1.2 | 3.9 |
| Robert Swift | 26 | 13.2 | 52.1 | 0.0 | 75.0 | 0.8 | 2.6 | 3.4 | 0.3 | 0.2 | 0.7 | 0.3 | 1.9 | 3.3 |
| Steven Hill | 1 | 2.0 | 100.0 | 0.0 | 0.0 | 2.0 | 1.0 | 3.0 | 0.0 | 0.0 | 0.0 | 0.0 | 2.0 | 2.0 |
| **Thunder** | 82 | 241.5 | 44.7 | 34.6 | 78.6 | 12.2 | 30.5 | 42.6 | 20.3 | 7.4 | 4.5 | 16.2 | 20.2 | 97.0 |
| **Opponents** | 82 | 241.5 | 47.5 | 36.4 | 76.1 | 10.8 | 30.4 | 41.2 | 21.6 | 8.5 | 5.0 | 13.9 | 20.2 | 103.1 |

\* mid-season trade

## Orlando Magic

| Player | GP | MPG | FG% | 3Pt% | FT% | OFF | DEF | Total | APG | SPG | BPG | TO | PF | PPG |
|---|---|---|---|---|---|---|---|---|---|---|---|---|---|---|
| Dwight Howard ....79 | | 35.7 | 57.2 | 0.0 | 59.4 | 4.3 | 9.6 | 13.8 | 1.4 | 1.0 | 2.9 | 3.0 | 3.4 | 20.6 |
| Rashard Lewis .....79 | | 36.2 | 43.9 | 39.7 | 83.6 | 1.2 | 4.6 | 5.7 | 2.6 | 1.0 | 0.7 | 2.0 | 2.5 | 17.7 |
| Hedo Turkoglu........77 | | 36.6 | 41.3 | 35.6 | 80.7 | 0.6 | 4.7 | 5.3 | 4.9 | 0.8 | 0.3 | 2.7 | 2.8 | 16.8 |
| Jameer Nelson .....42 | | 31.2 | 50.3 | 45.3 | 88.7 | 0.5 | 3.0 | 3.5 | 5.4 | 1.2 | 0.1 | 2.0 | 2.9 | 16.7 |
| *Rafer Alston........29 | | 29.5 | 41.3 | 31.7 | 70.7 | 0.3 | 2.6 | 2.9 | 5.1 | 1.8 | 0.1 | 1.8 | 2.2 | 12.0 |
| Mickael Pietrus.....54 | | 24.6 | 41.3 | 35.9 | 70.9 | 0.8 | 2.4 | 3.3 | 1.2 | 0.6 | 0.4 | 1.0 | 2.3 | 9.4 |
| Courtney Lee .......77 | | 25.2 | 45.0 | 40.4 | 83.0 | 0.2 | 2.1 | 2.3 | 1.2 | 1.0 | 0.2 | 0.9 | 2.0 | 8.4 |
| J.J. Redick .........64 | | 17.4 | 39.1 | 37.4 | 87.1 | 0.1 | 1.6 | 1.7 | 1.1 | 0.3 | 0.0 | 0.8 | 1.1 | 6.0 |
| Anthony Johnson...80 | | 18.5 | 40.4 | 39.1 | 75.3 | 0.4 | 1.5 | 1.8 | 2.5 | 0.6 | 0.1 | 1.0 | 1.4 | 5.3 |
| Tony Battie ..........77 | | 15.6 | 48.9 | 22.2 | 65.9 | 1.2 | 2.4 | 3.6 | 0.4 | 0.3 | 0.3 | 0.6 | 1.5 | 4.8 |
| Marcin Gortat .......63 | | 12.6 | 56.7 | 100.0 | 57.8 | 1.5 | 3.0 | 4.5 | 0.2 | 0.3 | 0.8 | 0.4 | 1.8 | 3.8 |
| Jeremy Richardson..12 | | 7.8 | 28.6 | 35.3 | 50.0 | 0.1 | 1.1 | 1.2 | 0.3 | 0.0 | 0.0 | 0.3 | 0.5 | 3.1 |
| *Tyronn Lue ..........14 | | 9.2 | 39.5 | 35.3 | 66.7 | 0.0 | 0.8 | 0.8 | 1.0 | 0.1 | 0.0 | 0.1 | 0.9 | 3.0 |
| *Adonal Foyle.........9 | | 6.6 | 63.6 | 0.0 | 50.0 | 1.0 | 1.9 | 2.9 | 0.1 | 0.0 | 0.9 | 0.3 | 0.4 | 1.9 |
| **Magic**................82 | | 240.6 | 45.7 | 38.1 | 71.5 | 10.0 | 33.3 | 43.3 | 19.4 | 7.0 | 5.4 | 13.9 | 20.3 | 101.0 |
| **Opponents**.................82 | | 240.6 | 43.3 | 34.2 | 75.5 | 10.5 | 31.6 | 42.1 | 18.1 | 6.9 | 3.8 | 13.1 | 22.4 | 94.4 |

## Philadelphia 76ers

| Player | GP | MPG | FG% | 3Pt% | FT% | OFF | DEF | Total | APG | SPG | BPG | TO | PF | PPG |
|---|---|---|---|---|---|---|---|---|---|---|---|---|---|---|
| Andre Iguodala ....82 | | 39.9 | 47.3 | 30.7 | 72.4 | 1.1 | 4.6 | 5.7 | 5.3 | 1.6 | 0.4 | 2.7 | 1.9 | 18.8 |
| Andre Miller.........82 | | 36.3 | 47.3 | 28.3 | 82.6 | 1.5 | 3.0 | 4.5 | 6.5 | 1.3 | 0.2 | 2.4 | 2.4 | 16.3 |
| Thaddeus Young ..75 | | 34.4 | 49.5 | 34.1 | 73.5 | 1.9 | 3.2 | 5.0 | 1.1 | 1.3 | 0.3 | 1.6 | 2.2 | 15.3 |
| Elton Brand ..........29 | | 31.7 | 44.7 | 0.0 | 67.6 | 2.7 | 6.1 | 8.8 | 1.3 | 0.6 | 1.6 | 2.3 | 2.7 | 13.8 |
| Louis Williams.........81 | | 23.7 | 39.8 | 28.6 | 79.0 | 0.4 | 1.6 | 2.0 | 3.0 | 1.1 | 0.2 | 1.9 | 1.6 | 12.8 |
| Willie Green..........81 | | 22.6 | 43.5 | 31.7 | 72.9 | 0.4 | 1.2 | 1.6 | 2.0 | 0.7 | 0.2 | 0.8 | 1.9 | 8.5 |
| Marreese Speights..79 | | 16.0 | 50.2 | 25.0 | 77.3 | 1.6 | 2.2 | 3.7 | 0.4 | 0.3 | 0.7 | 0.6 | 2.3 | 7.7 |
| Samuel Dalembert..82 | | 24.8 | 49.8 | 0.0 | 73.4 | 2.6 | 5.9 | 8.5 | 0.2 | 0.4 | 1.8 | 1.4 | 3.0 | 6.4 |
| Donyell Marshall ..25 | | 7.6 | 45.2 | 45.5 | 50.0 | 0.2 | 1.4 | 1.6 | 0.6 | 0.2 | 0.2 | 0.2 | 1.0 | 3.8 |
| Reggie Evans.......79 | | 14.4 | 44.4 | 0.0 | 59.4 | 1.7 | 2.9 | 4.6 | 0.3 | 0.5 | 0.1 | 0.9 | 2.0 | 3.3 |
| Royal Ivie .............71 | | 12.1 | 33.2 | 34.2 | 79.1 | 0.3 | 0.8 | 1.1 | 0.6 | 0.5 | 0.1 | 0.3 | 1.1 | 3.0 |
| Kareem Rush ........25 | | 8.0 | 34.5 | 30.3 | 100.0 | 0.0 | 0.6 | 0.6 | 0.6 | 0.2 | 0.0 | 0.4 | 0.4 | 2.2 |
| Theo Ratliff ..........46 | | 12.6 | 53.1 | 0.0 | 60.0 | 1.0 | 1.8 | 2.8 | 0.2 | 0.4 | 1.0 | 0.3 | 1.7 | 1.9 |
| **76ers** ...................82 | | 240.9 | 45.9 | 31.8 | 74.5 | 12.7 | 28.5 | 41.2 | 20.1 | 8.0 | 5.1 | 14.1 | 20.1 | 97.4 |
| **Opponents**.................82 | | 240.9 | 46.2 | 36.7 | 78.2 | 11.4 | 27.9 | 39.3 | 21.9 | 7.0 | 4.9 | 15.6 | 21.8 | 97.3 |

## Phoenix Suns

| Player | GP | MPG | FG% | 3Pt% | FT% | OFF | DEF | Total | APG | SPG | BPG | TO | PF | PPG |
|---|---|---|---|---|---|---|---|---|---|---|---|---|---|---|
| Amare Stoudemire..53 | | 36.8 | 53.9 | 42.9 | 83.5 | 2.2 | 5.9 | 8.1 | 2.0 | 0.9 | 1.1 | 2.8 | 3.1 | 21.4 |
| Shaquille O'Neal ..75 | | 30.0 | 60.9 | 0.0 | 59.5 | 2.5 | 5.9 | 8.4 | 1.7 | 0.7 | 1.4 | 2.2 | 3.4 | 17.8 |
| *Jason Richardson ..58 | | 33.1 | 48.8 | 38.3 | 77.8 | 1.1 | 3.4 | 4.5 | 1.9 | 1.1 | 0.4 | 1.2 | 1.8 | 16.4 |
| Steve Nash .........74 | | 33.6 | 50.3 | 43.9 | 93.3 | 0.3 | 2.8 | 3.0 | 9.7 | 0.7 | 0.1 | 3.4 | 1.5 | 15.7 |
| Leandro Barbosa ..70 | | 24.4 | 48.2 | 37.5 | 88.1 | 0.5 | 2.1 | 2.6 | 2.3 | 1.2 | 0.1 | 1.3 | 1.6 | 14.2 |
| Grant Hill .............82 | | 29.8 | 52.3 | 31.6 | 80.8 | 0.8 | 4.2 | 4.9 | 2.3 | 1.1 | 0.7 | 1.5 | 2.2 | 12.0 |
| Matt Barnes.........77 | | 27.0 | 42.3 | 34.3 | 74.3 | 1.0 | 4.4 | 5.5 | 2.8 | 0.7 | 0.3 | 1.7 | 2.7 | 10.2 |
| *Jared Dudley ......48 | | 15.2 | 48.1 | 39.4 | 69.1 | 1.2 | 1.9 | 3.0 | 0.8 | 0.8 | 0.1 | 0.7 | 1.4 | 5.5 |
| Alando Tucker......30 | | 9.4 | 43.0 | 34.8 | 78.8 | 0.6 | 0.4 | 1.0 | 0.4 | 0.2 | 0.0 | 0.5 | 0.5 | 4.6 |
| Goran Dragic .......55 | | 13.2 | 39.3 | 37.0 | 76.9 | 0.6 | 1.3 | 1.9 | 2.0 | 0.5 | 0.1 | 1.3 | 1.6 | 4.5 |
| Louis Amundson ..76 | | 13.7 | 53.6 | 0.0 | 44.2 | 1.7 | 1.9 | 3.6 | 0.4 | 0.4 | 0.9 | 0.7 | 2.0 | 4.2 |
| Robin Lopez.........60 | | 10.2 | 51.8 | 0.0 | 69.1 | 0.9 | 1.1 | 2.0 | 0.1 | 0.2 | 0.7 | 0.5 | 1.6 | 3.2 |
| *Stromile Swift ......13 | | 9.3 | 36.6 | 100.0 | 53.3 | 0.8 | 1.7 | 2.5 | 0.2 | 0.3 | 0.5 | 0.7 | 1.9 | 3.0 |
| *Dee Brown ............2 | | 14.0 | 20.0 | 25.0 | 100.0 | 0.0 | 0.5 | 0.5 | 1.5 | 0.0 | 0.0 | 1.5 | 3.0 | 2.5 |
| **Suns**...........................82 | | 240.9 | 50.4 | 38.3 | 74.4 | 11.0 | 30.7 | 41.7 | 23.2 | 7.2 | 5.1 | 15.7 | 20.6 | 109.4 |
| **Opponents**.................82 | | 240.9 | 46.7 | 38.3 | 77.5 | 12.1 | 28.7 | 40.8 | 21.2 | 8.6 | 4.5 | 14.2 | 22.9 | 107.5 |

* mid-season trade

## Portland Trail Blazers

| Player | GP | MPG | FG% | 3Pt% | FT% | OFF | DEF | Total | APG | SPG | BPG | TO | PF | PPG |
|---|---|---|---|---|---|---|---|---|---|---|---|---|---|---|
| | | | **Field Goals** | | | **Rebounds** | | | | | | | | |
| Brandon Roy | 78 | 37.2 | 48.0 | 37.7 | 82.4 | 1.3 | 3.4 | 4.7 | 5.1 | 1.1 | 0.3 | 2.0 | 1.6 | 22.6 |
| LaMarcus Aldridge | 81 | 37.1 | 48.4 | 25.0 | 78.1 | 2.9 | 4.6 | 7.5 | 1.9 | 1.0 | 1.0 | 1.5 | 2.6 | 18.1 |
| Travis Outlaw | 81 | 27.7 | 45.3 | 37.7 | 72.3 | 0.9 | 3.2 | 4.1 | 1.0 | 0.6 | 0.7 | 1.2 | 2.1 | 12.8 |
| Steve Blake | 69 | 31.7 | 42.8 | 42.7 | 84.0 | 0.4 | 2.1 | 2.5 | 5.0 | 1.0 | 0.1 | 1.6 | 1.8 | 11.0 |
| Rudy Fernandez | 78 | 25.6 | 42.5 | 39.9 | 83.9 | 0.6 | 2.1 | 2.7 | 2.0 | 0.9 | 0.2 | 1.1 | 1.4 | 10.4 |
| Greg Oden | 61 | 21.5 | 56.4 | 0.0 | 63.7 | 2.8 | 4.2 | 7.0 | 0.5 | 0.4 | 1.1 | 1.4 | 3.9 | 8.9 |
| Joel Przybilla | 82 | 23.8 | 62.5 | 0.0 | 66.3 | 2.5 | 6.3 | 8.7 | 0.3 | 0.4 | 1.2 | 1.0 | 2.6 | 5.5 |
| Nicolas Batum | 79 | 18.4 | 44.6 | 36.9 | 80.8 | 1.1 | 1.7 | 2.8 | 0.9 | 0.6 | 0.5 | 0.6 | 1.8 | 5.4 |
| Sergio Rodriguez | 80 | 15.3 | 39.2 | 32.5 | 79.2 | 0.5 | 1.1 | 1.6 | 3.6 | 0.7 | 0.0 | 1.5 | 1.7 | 4.5 |
| Jerryd Bayless | 53 | 12.4 | 36.5 | 25.9 | 80.6 | 0.2 | 0.9 | 1.1 | 1.5 | 0.3 | 0.0 | 1.1 | 1.5 | 4.3 |
| Channing Frye | 63 | 11.8 | 42.3 | 33.3 | 72.2 | 0.7 | 1.6 | 2.2 | 0.4 | 0.3 | 0.3 | 0.5 | 1.7 | 4.2 |
| Shavlik Randolph | 10 | 3.7 | 61.5 | 100.0 | 25.0 | 1.0 | 0.8 | 1.8 | 0.0 | 0.0 | 0.1 | 0.6 | 0.4 | 1.8 |
| **Trail Blazers** | **82** | **241.8** | **46.5** | **38.3** | **76.5** | **12.9** | **28.8** | **41.7** | **20.3** | **6.7** | **4.9** | **12.9** | **20.4** | **99.4** |
| **Opponents** | **82** | **241.8** | **46.0** | **37.4** | **80.3** | **9.6** | **26.7** | **36.3** | **19.4** | **6.3** | **3.9** | **13.2** | **21.1** | **94.1** |

## Sacramento Kings

| Player | GP | MPG | FG% | 3Pt% | FT% | OFF | DEF | Total | APG | SPG | BPG | TO | PF | PPG |
|---|---|---|---|---|---|---|---|---|---|---|---|---|---|---|
| | | | **Field Goals** | | | **Rebounds** | | | | | | | | |
| Kevin Martin | 51 | 38.2 | 42.0 | 41.5 | 86.7 | 0.6 | 3.0 | 3.6 | 2.7 | 1.2 | 0.2 | 2.9 | 2.3 | 24.6 |
| *Andres Nocioni | 23 | 31.0 | 44.8 | 44.1 | 76.3 | 0.9 | 5.2 | 6.0 | 1.8 | 0.6 | 0.7 | 1.7 | 3.7 | 13.7 |
| Francisco Garcia | 65 | 30.4 | 44.4 | 39.8 | 82.0 | 0.9 | 2.5 | 3.4 | 2.3 | 1.2 | 1.0 | 1.7 | 3.0 | 12.7 |
| Spencer Hawes | 77 | 29.3 | 46.6 | 34.8 | 66.2 | 1.9 | 5.2 | 7.1 | 1.9 | 0.6 | 1.2 | 2.1 | 3.2 | 11.4 |
| Jason Thompson | 82 | 28.1 | 49.7 | 0.0 | 69.2 | 2.9 | 4.5 | 7.4 | 1.1 | 0.6 | 0.7 | 1.8 | 3.8 | 11.1 |
| Beno Udrih | 73 | 31.1 | 46.1 | 31.0 | 82.0 | 0.6 | 2.4 | 3.0 | 4.7 | 1.1 | 0.2 | 2.2 | 2.6 | 11.0 |
| *Rashad McCants | 24 | 19.4 | 44.4 | 35.7 | 78.3 | 0.4 | 1.5 | 2.0 | 1.5 | 0.8 | 0.3 | 0.8 | 1.7 | 10.3 |
| *Ike Diogu | 10 | 14.2 | 60.0 | 50.0 | 75.8 | 1.4 | 2.5 | 3.9 | 0.3 | 0.2 | 0.1 | 0.6 | 1.4 | 9.2 |
| Bobby Jackson | 71 | 20.9 | 39.8 | 30.5 | 85.1 | 0.6 | 2.2 | 2.8 | 2.0 | 0.9 | 0.1 | 0.9 | 1.4 | 7.5 |
| *Will Solomon | 14 | 12.0 | 40.6 | 44.8 | 50.0 | 0.2 | 1.3 | 1.5 | 0.7 | 0.5 | 0.0 | 0.4 | 0.8 | 5.0 |
| Donte Greene | 55 | 13.2 | 32.6 | 26.0 | 85.3 | 0.3 | 1.2 | 1.6 | 0.5 | 0.3 | 0.3 | 0.7 | 1.2 | 3.8 |
| *Calvin Booth | 7 | 7.9 | 50.0 | 0.0 | 75.0 | 0.6 | 0.9 | 1.4 | 0.0 | 0.1 | 0.3 | 0.1 | 1.4 | 2.3 |
| Kenny Thomas | 8 | 7.8 | 37.5 | 0.0 | 0.0 | 0.5 | 1.4 | 1.9 | 0.1 | 0.8 | 0.1 | 0.1 | 1.1 | 0.8 |
| **Kings** | **82** | **242.7** | **44.7** | **36.8** | **79.8** | **10.2** | **28.9** | **39.1** | **19.7** | **6.9** | **4.3** | **15.4** | **23.3** | **100.6** |
| **Opponents** | **82** | **242.7** | **48.3** | **40.6** | **75.6** | **12.4** | **31.6** | **44.0** | **21.9** | **8.6** | **5.2** | **14.4** | **21.2** | **109.3** |

## San Antonio Spurs

| Player | GP | MPG | FG% | 3Pt% | FT% | OFF | DEF | Total | APG | SPG | BPG | TO | PF | PPG |
|---|---|---|---|---|---|---|---|---|---|---|---|---|---|---|
| | | | **Field Goals** | | | **Rebounds** | | | | | | | | |
| Tony Parker | 72 | 34.0 | 50.6 | 29.2 | 78.2 | 0.4 | 2.7 | 3.1 | 6.9 | 0.9 | 0.1 | 2.6 | 1.5 | 22.0 |
| Tim Duncan | 75 | 33.6 | 50.4 | 0.0 | 69.2 | 2.7 | 8.0 | 10.7 | 3.5 | 0.5 | 1.7 | 2.2 | 2.3 | 19.3 |
| Manu Ginobli | 44 | 26.8 | 45.4 | 33.0 | 88.4 | 0.5 | 4.0 | 4.5 | 3.6 | 1.5 | 0.4 | 2.0 | 2.0 | 15.5 |
| Roger Mason | 82 | 30.4 | 42.5 | 42.1 | 89.0 | 0.2 | 2.9 | 3.1 | 2.1 | 0.5 | 0.2 | 1.2 | 2.0 | 11.8 |
| *Drew Gooden | 19 | 16.8 | 49.0 | 0.0 | 78.9 | 1.5 | 2.9 | 4.4 | 0.2 | 0.2 | 0.2 | 0.8 | 2.1 | 9.8 |
| Michael Finley | 81 | 28.8 | 43.7 | 41.1 | 82.3 | 0.3 | 3.0 | 3.3 | 1.4 | 0.5 | 0.2 | 0.8 | 1.0 | 9.7 |
| Matt Bonner | 81 | 23.8 | 49.6 | 44.0 | 73.9 | 1.2 | 3.6 | 4.8 | 1.0 | 0.6 | 0.3 | 0.5 | 2.3 | 8.2 |
| George Hill | 77 | 16.5 | 40.3 | 32.9 | 78.1 | 0.4 | 1.7 | 2.1 | 1.8 | 0.6 | 0.3 | 1.0 | 1.9 | 5.7 |
| Ime Udoka | 67 | 15.4 | 38.3 | 32.8 | 60.9 | 0.4 | 2.4 | 2.8 | 0.8 | 0.5 | 0.2 | 0.6 | 1.3 | 4.3 |
| Kurt Thomas | 79 | 17.8 | 50.3 | 0.0 | 82.2 | 1.7 | 3.4 | 5.1 | 0.8 | 0.4 | 0.7 | 0.5 | 2.2 | 4.3 |
| Desmond Farmer | 3 | 18.0 | 28.6 | 25.0 | 100.0 | 0.0 | 2.0 | 2.0 | 0.7 | 0.0 | 0.0 | 1.3 | 2.0 | 4.3 |
| Malik Hairston | 15 | 10.3 | 49.0 | 0.0 | 28.6 | 0.7 | 1.1 | 1.9 | 0.9 | 0.4 | 0.5 | 0.8 | 1.3 | 3.3 |
| Bruce Bowen | 80 | 18.9 | 42.2 | 42.9 | 53.8 | 0.2 | 1.6 | 1.8 | 0.5 | 0.5 | 0.2 | 0.3 | 1.5 | 2.7 |
| Blake Ahearn | 3 | 6.3 | 33.3 | 50.0 | 100.0 | 0.0 | 0.3 | 0.3 | 0.7 | 0.3 | 0.0 | 0.3 | 1.0 | 2.7 |
| Fabricio Oberto | 54 | 12.5 | 58.7 | 0.0 | 57.1 | 1.2 | 1.4 | 2.6 | 1.1 | 0.1 | 0.2 | 0.7 | 1.8 | 2.6 |
| Jacque Vaughn | 30 | 9.7 | 32.0 | 100.0 | 88.9 | 0.1 | 0.6 | 0.7 | 1.8 | 0.2 | 0.0 | 0.5 | 0.9 | 2.2 |
| Marcus Williams | 2 | 1.5 | 100.0 | 0.0 | 0.0 | 0.0 | 0.0 | 0.0 | 0.0 | 0.0 | 0.0 | 0.0 | 0.5 | 2.0 |
| *Austin Croshere | 3 | 7.7 | 22.2 | 0.0 | 0.0 | 1.3 | 2.0 | 3.3 | 1.0 | 0.0 | 0.0 | 0.7 | 0.3 | 1.3 |
| **Spurs** | **82** | **242.7** | **46.6** | **38.6** | **76.1** | **8.9** | **32.2** | **41.0** | **21.2** | **5.8** | **4.0** | **11.7** | **18.9** | **97.0** |
| **Opponents** | **82** | **242.7** | **45.3** | **37.9** | **76.9** | **9.1** | **31.3** | **40.4** | **18.1** | **6.5** | **4.3** | **11.7** | **18.4** | **93.3** |

* mid-season trade

## Toronto Raptors

| Player | GP | MPG | FG% | 3Pt% | FT% | OFF | DEF | Total | APG | SPG | BPG | TO | PF | PPG |
|---|---|---|---|---|---|---|---|---|---|---|---|---|---|---|
| Chris Bosh | 77 | 38.0 | 48.7 | 24.5 | 81.7 | 2.8 | 7.2 | 10.0 | 2.5 | 0.9 | 1.0 | 2.3 | 2.5 | 22.7 |
| Andrea Bargnani | 78 | 31.4 | 45.0 | 40.9 | 83.1 | 0.9 | 4.4 | 5.3 | 1.2 | 0.4 | 1.2 | 1.7 | 3.1 | 15.4 |
| *Shawn Marion | 27 | 35.3 | 48.8 | 15.4 | 80.6 | 2.7 | 5.6 | 8.3 | 2.3 | 1.2 | 0.8 | 1.8 | 1.5 | 14.3 |
| Jose Calderon | 68 | 34.3 | 49.7 | 40.6 | 98.1 | 0.2 | 2.6 | 2.9 | 8.9 | 1.1 | 0.1 | 2.1 | 1.7 | 12.8 |
| Anthony Parker | 80 | 33.0 | 42.6 | 39.0 | 83.4 | 0.6 | 3.4 | 4.0 | 3.4 | 1.3 | 0.2 | 1.4 | 1.8 | 10.7 |
| Jason Kapono | 80 | 22.9 | 43.2 | 42.8 | 81.0 | 0.3 | 1.7 | 2.0 | 1.3 | 0.3 | 0.0 | 0.9 | 1.8 | 8.2 |
| Joey Graham | 78 | 19.8 | 48.1 | 18.8 | 82.5 | 1.2 | 2.5 | 3.7 | 0.6 | 0.5 | 0.2 | 1.0 | 2.4 | 7.7 |
| *P. Mensah-Bonsu | 19 | 13.8 | 35.4 | 0.0 | 68.3 | 2.6 | 2.8 | 5.4 | 0.3 | 0.5 | 0.2 | 0.9 | 1.9 | 5.1 |
| *Patrick O'Bryant | 13 | 11.3 | 54.7 | 0.0 | 37.5 | 0.5 | 2.0 | 2.5 | 0.2 | 0.2 | 0.9 | 0.4 | 2.5 | 4.7 |
| *Quincy Douby | 7 | 10.4 | 54.5 | 44.4 | 75.0 | 0.4 | 0.6 | 1.0 | 1.7 | 0.4 | 0.0 | 1.0 | 0.6 | 4.4 |
| Roko Ukic | 72 | 12.4 | 38.0 | 17.7 | 73.3 | 0.4 | 0.7 | 1.0 | 2.1 | 0.4 | 0.0 | 0.8 | 1.1 | 4.2 |
| Kris Humphries | 29 | 9.1 | 42.2 | 0.0 | 79.2 | 0.8 | 1.6 | 2.4 | 0.3 | 0.3 | 0.2 | 0.3 | 1.1 | 3.9 |
| *Marcus Banks | 6 | 6.7 | 33.3 | 20.0 | 33.3 | 0.2 | 0.3 | 0.5 | 1.0 | 0.2 | 0.0 | 0.5 | 0.8 | 2.3 |
| Hassan Adams | 12 | 4.3 | 30.8 | 0.0 | 50.0 | 0.1 | 0.5 | 0.6 | 0.1 | 0.1 | 0.1 | 0.3 | 0.3 | 0.9 |
| Jake Voskuhl | 38 | 6.3 | 26.7 | 0.0 | 78.6 | 0.6 | 1.0 | 1.6 | 0.2 | 0.1 | 0.1 | 0.5 | 1.6 | 0.9 |
| **Raptors** | 82 | 241.5 | 45.8 | 37.2 | 82.4 | 9.8 | 30.6 | 40.4 | 22.4 | 6.4 | 4.8 | 13.4 | 19.4 | 99.0 |
| **Opponets** | 82 | 241.5 | 46.5 | 36.7 | 78.4 | 10.9 | 31.0 | 41.9 | 23.0 | 6.4 | 4.7 | 13.3 | 20.1 | 101.9 |

## Utah Jazz

| Player | GP | MPG | FG% | 3Pt% | FT% | OFF | DEF | Total | APG | SPG | BPG | TO | PF | PPG |
|---|---|---|---|---|---|---|---|---|---|---|---|---|---|---|
| Deron Williams | 68 | 36.8 | 47.1 | 31.0 | 84.9 | 0.4 | 2.5 | 2.9 | 10.7 | 1.1 | 0.3 | 3.4 | 2.0 | 19.4 |
| Mehmet Okur | 72 | 33.5 | 48.5 | 44.6 | 81.7 | 1.7 | 6.0 | 7.7 | 1.7 | 0.8 | 0.7 | 1.8 | 3.0 | 17.0 |
| Carlos Boozer | 37 | 32.4 | 49.0 | 0.0 | 69.8 | 3.0 | 7.4 | 10.4 | 2.1 | 1.1 | 0.2 | 2.1 | 3.6 | 16.2 |
| Ronnie Brewer | 81 | 32.2 | 50.8 | 25.9 | 70.2 | 1.2 | 2.5 | 3.7 | 2.2 | 1.7 | 0.4 | 1.4 | 1.6 | 13.7 |
| Paul Millsap | 76 | 30.1 | 53.4 | 0.0 | 69.9 | 3.3 | 5.3 | 8.6 | 1.8 | 1.0 | 1.0 | 1.7 | 3.8 | 13.5 |
| Andrei Kirilenko | 67 | 27.3 | 44.9 | 27.4 | 78.5 | 1.3 | 3.5 | 4.8 | 2.6 | 1.2 | 1.2 | 1.8 | 1.9 | 11.6 |
| C.J. Miles | 72 | 24.0 | 45.9 | 35.2 | 87.6 | 0.6 | 1.7 | 2.3 | 1.5 | 0.6 | 0.2 | 0.9 | 2.6 | 9.1 |
| Kyle Korver | 78 | 24.0 | 43.8 | 38.6 | 88.2 | 0.4 | 2.9 | 3.3 | 1.8 | 0.6 | 0.4 | 1.2 | 2.2 | 9.0 |
| Kosta Koufos | 48 | 11.8 | 50.8 | 0.0 | 70.6 | 1.0 | 1.8 | 2.9 | 0.4 | 0.3 | 0.7 | 0.5 | 1.5 | 4.7 |
| Matt Harpring | 63 | 11.0 | 46.1 | 0.0 | 76.4 | 0.7 | 1.2 | 2.0 | 0.4 | 0.5 | 0.1 | 0.5 | 1.6 | 4.4 |
| Ronnie Price | 52 | 14.2 | 37.9 | 31.1 | 75.6 | 0.2 | 1.1 | 1.3 | 2.1 | 0.8 | 0.1 | 1.2 | 1.4 | 4.0 |
| Morris Almond | 25 | 10.2 | 40.7 | 29.4 | 80.8 | 0.4 | 1.1 | 1.4 | 0.3 | 0.2 | 0.2 | 0.6 | 1.2 | 3.7 |
| Brevin Knight | 74 | 12.7 | 34.9 | 0.0 | 75.0 | 0.2 | 1.0 | 1.2 | 2.6 | 0.9 | 0.1 | 0.9 | 1.3 | 2.4 |
| Kyrylo Fesenko | 21 | 7.4 | 58.3 | 0.0 | 33.3 | 0.7 | 1.1 | 1.8 | 0.2 | 0.3 | 0.7 | 0.4 | 1.7 | 2.3 |
| Jarron Collins | 26 | 7.7 | 45.7 | 0.0 | 72.7 | 0.8 | 0.7 | 1.4 | 0.3 | 0.1 | 0.0 | 0.4 | 1.3 | 1.5 |
| **Jazz** | 82 | 242.4 | 47.5 | 34.9 | 77.1 | 11.5 | 29.5 | 41.0 | 24.7 | 8.8 | 4.6 | 14.8 | 22.3 | 103.6 |
| **Opponents** | 82 | 242.4 | 46.4 | 36.1 | 76.3 | 11.1 | 29.2 | 40.3 | 20.0 | 8.0 | 5.2 | 16.1 | 24.0 | 100.9 |

## Washington Wizards

| Player | GP | MPG | FG% | 3Pt% | FT% | OFF | DEF | Total | APG | SPG | BPG | TO | PF | PPG |
|---|---|---|---|---|---|---|---|---|---|---|---|---|---|---|
| Antawn Jamison | 81 | 38.2 | 46.8 | 35.1 | 75.4 | 2.4 | 6.5 | 8.9 | 1.9 | 1.2 | 0.3 | 1.5 | 2.7 | 22.2 |
| Caron Butler | 67 | 38.6 | 45.3 | 31.0 | 85.8 | 1.8 | 4.4 | 6.2 | 4.3 | 1.6 | 0.3 | 3.1 | 2.5 | 20.8 |
| Gilbert Arenas | 2 | 31.5 | 26.1 | 28.6 | 75.0 | 0.5 | 4.0 | 4.5 | 10.0 | 0.0 | 0.5 | 0.5 | 2.0 | 13.0 |
| Nick Young | 82 | 22.4 | 44.4 | 34.1 | 85.0 | 0.4 | 1.5 | 1.8 | 1.2 | 0.5 | 0.2 | 1.1 | 1.7 | 10.9 |
| Andray Blatche | 71 | 24.0 | 47.1 | 23.8 | 70.4 | 1.8 | 3.5 | 5.3 | 1.7 | 0.8 | 1.0 | 1.7 | 3.0 | 10.0 |
| Brendan Haywood | 6 | 29.2 | 48.0 | 0.0 | 47.6 | 2.2 | 5.2 | 7.3 | 1.3 | 0.7 | 2.5 | 1.5 | 2.3 | 9.7 |
| *Mike James | 53 | 29.7 | 38.7 | 36.7 | 83.8 | 0.5 | 1.9 | 2.4 | 3.6 | 0.8 | 0.1 | 1.7 | 1.9 | 9.6 |
| Darius Songaila | 77 | 19.8 | 53.2 | 0.0 | 88.9 | 1.0 | 2.0 | 2.9 | 1.2 | 0.8 | 0.3 | 1.0 | 2.6 | 7.4 |
| DeShawn Stevenson | 32 | 27.7 | 31.2 | 27.1 | 53.3 | 0.3 | 2.0 | 2.4 | 3.1 | 0.7 | 0.1 | 1.0 | 1.3 | 6.6 |
| JaVale McGee | 75 | 15.2 | 49.4 | 0.0 | 66.0 | 1.6 | 2.3 | 3.9 | 0.3 | 0.4 | 1.0 | 0.8 | 2.1 | 6.5 |
| *Javaris Crittenton | 56 | 20.2 | 45.9 | 14.3 | 59.3 | 0.9 | 1.9 | 2.9 | 2.6 | 0.7 | 0.1 | 1.4 | 1.7 | 5.3 |
| Juan Dixon | 50 | 16.3 | 39.5 | 33.3 | 87.2 | 0.2 | 1.2 | 1.3 | 2.4 | 0.7 | 0.1 | 1.4 | 1.5 | 5.2 |
| Dominic McGuire | 79 | 26.2 | 43.2 | 50.0 | 72.5 | 1.4 | 4.0 | 5.4 | 2.5 | 0.8 | 0.9 | 1.2 | 1.9 | 4.5 |
| Oleksiy Pecherov | 32 | 8.7 | 38.6 | 32.6 | 82.8 | 1.1 | 1.3 | 2.4 | 0.1 | 0.2 | 0.1 | 0.3 | 1.1 | 3.6 |
| Etan Thomas | 26 | 11.8 | 48.5 | 0.0 | 69.6 | 1.0 | 1.6 | 2.5 | 0.2 | 0.1 | 0.7 | 0.7 | 1.3 | 3.1 |
| **Wizards** | 82 | 240.3 | 45.0 | 33.0 | 76.7 | 11.7 | 28.4 | 40.1 | 20.0 | 7.6 | 4.4 | 14.0 | 20.5 | 96.1 |
| **Opponents** | 82 | 240.3 | 48.2 | 38.7 | 75.9 | 11.4 | 30.4 | 41.8 | 24.6 | 7.2 | 5.3 | 13.9 | 20.0 | 103.5 |

* mid-season trade

The 2009 NBA Draft was held on June 25, 2009 in New York City.

### First Round

1. LAC—Blake Griffin, Oklahoma
2. MEM—Hasheem Thabeet, Conn.
3. OKC—James Harden, Ariz. St
4. SAC—Tyreke Evans, Memphis
5. MIN—Ricky Rubio, Spain
   (from WAS)
6. MIN—Jonny Flynn, Syracuse
7. GSW—Stephen Curry, Davidson
8. NYK—Jordan Hill, Arizona
9. TOR—DeMar DeRozan, USC
10. MIL—Brandon Jennings, Italy
11. NJN—Terrence Williams, Lo'sville
12. CHA—Gerald Henderson, Duke
13. IND—Tyler Hansbrough, N.C.
14. PHX—Earl Clark, Louisville
15. DET—Austin Daye, Gonzaga
16. CHI—James Johnson, Wake Forest
17. PHI—Jrue Holiday, UCLA
18. MIN—Ty Lawson, Duke
    (from MIA, traded to DEN)
19. ATL—Jeff Teague, Wake Forest
20. UTAH—Eric Maynor, VCU
21. NOH—Darren Collison, UCLA
22. POR—Victor Claver, Spain
    (from DAL)
23. SAC—Omri Casspi, Israel
    (from HOU)
24. DAL—B.J. Mullens, Ohio St
    (from POR, traded to OKC)
25. OKC—Rodrigue Beaubois, France
    (from SAS, traded to DAL)
26. CHI—Taj Gibson, USC
    (from DEN, through OKC)
27. MEM—DeMarre Carroll, Missouri
    (from ORL)
28. MIN—Wayne Ellington, N.C.
    (from BOS)
29. LAL—Toney Douglas, Fla. St
    (traded to NYK)
30. CLE—Christian Eyenga, Congo

### Second Round

31. SAC—Jeff Pendergraph, Ariz. St
    (traded to POR)
32. WAS—Jermaine Taylor, Cent. Fla.
    (traded to HOU)
33. POR—Dante Cunningham, 'Nova
    (from LAC)
34. DEN—Sergio Llull, Spain
    (from OKC, traded to HOU)
35. DET—DaJuan Summers, G'town
    (from MIN)
36. MEM—Sam Young, Pittsburgh
37. SAS—DeJuan Blair, Pittsburgh
    (from GSW, thru PHX)
38. POR—Jon Brockman, Wash.
    (from NYK thru CHI, traded to SAC)
39. DET—Jonas Jerebko, Sweden
    (from TOR)
40. CHA—Derrick Brown, Xavier
    (from NJN thru OKC)
41. MIL—Jodie Meeks, Kentucky
42. LAL—Patrick Beverley, Ukraine
    (from CHA, traded to MIA)
43. MIA—Marcus Thornton, LSU
    (from IND, traded to NO)
44. DET—Chase Budinger, Arizona
    (traded to HOU)
45. MIN—Nick Calathes, Florida
    (from PHI thru MIA,
    traded to HOU)
46. CLE—Danny Green, N.C.
    (from CHI)
47. MIN—Henk Norel, Netherlands
    (from MIA)
48. PHX—Taylor Griffin,
    Oklahoma
49. ATL—Sergiy Gladyr, Ukraine
50. UTAH—Goran Suton, Mich. St
51. SAS—Jack McClinton, Miami
    (from NOH thru TOR)
52. IND—A.J. Price, Connecticut
    (from DAL)
53. SAS—Nando De Colo, France
    (from HOU)
54. CHA—Robert Vaden, UAB
    (from SAS, traded to OKC)
55. POR—Patrick Mills, St. Mary's
    (from DEN)
56. DAL—Ahmad Nivins, St. Jo's.
    (from POR)
57. PHX—Emir Preldzic, Slovenia
    (from ORL thru OKC,
    traded to CLE)
58. BOS—Lester Hudson, Tenn.-Martin
59. LAL—Chinemelu Elonu, Tex. A&M

## Women's National Basketball Association

### 2009 Final Regular Season Standings

#### EASTERN CONFERENCE

| Team | W | L | Pct | GB |
|---|---|---|---|---|
| †Indiana | 22 | 12 | .647 | — |
| *Atlanta | 18 | 16 | .529 | 4.0 |
| *Detroit | 18 | 16 | .529 | 4.0 |
| *Washington | 16 | 18 | .471 | 6.0 |
| Chicago | 16 | 18 | .471 | 6.0 |
| Connecticut | 16 | 18 | .471 | 6.0 |
| New York | 13 | 21 | .382 | 9.0 |

#### WESTERN CONFERENCE

| Team | W | L | Pct | GB |
|---|---|---|---|---|
| †Phoenix | 23 | 11 | .676 | — |
| *Seattle | 20 | 14 | .588 | 3.0 |
| *Los Angeles | 18 | 16 | .529 | 5.0 |
| *San Antonio | 15 | 19 | .441 | 8.0 |
| Minnesota | 14 | 20 | .412 | 9.0 |
| Sacramento | 12 | 22 | .353 | 11.0 |

†Clinched conference title.  *Clinched playoff berth.

### 2009 Playoffs

#### FIRST ROUND

##### WESTERN CONFERENCE

| Game 1 | Phoenix 91 | at San Antonio 92 |
| Game 2 | San Antonio 78 | at Phoenix 106 |
| Game 3 | San Antonio 92 | at Phoenix 100 |

Phoenix won series 2-1.

| Game 1 | Seattle 63 | at Los Angeles 70 |
| Game 2 | Los Angeles 74 | at Seattle 75 |
| Game 2 | Los Angeles 75 | at Seattle 64 |

Los Angeles won series 2-1.

##### WESTERN CONFERENCE FINALS

| Game 1 | Phoenix 103 | at Los Angeles 94 |
| Game 2 | Los Angeles 87 | at Phoenix 76 |
| Game 3 | Los Angeles 74 | at Phoenix 85 |

Phoenix won series 2-1.

##### EASTERN CONFERENCE

| Game 1 | Indiana 88 | at Washington 79 |
| Game 2 | Washington 74 | at Indiana 81 |

Indiana won series 2-0.

| Game 1 | Atlanta 89 | at Detroit 94 |
| Game 2 | Detroit 94 | at Atlanta 79 |

Detroit won series 2-0.

##### EASTERN CONFERENCE FINALS

| Game 1 | Indiana 56 | at Detroit 72 |
| Game 2 | Detroit 75 | at Indiana 79 |
| Game 3 | Detroit 67 | at Indiana 72 |

Indiana won series 2-1.

#### WNBA FINALS

| Game 1 | Indiana 116 | at Phoenix 120 (OT) |
| Game 2 | Indiana 93 | at Phoenix 84 |
| Game 3 | Phoenix 85 | at Indiana 86 |
| Game 4 | Phoenix 90 | at Indiana 77 |
| Game 5 | Indiana 86 | at Phoenix 94 |

Phoenix won series 3-2.

## NBA Champions

| Season | Winner | Series | Runner-Up | Winning Coach | Finals MVP |
|---|---|---|---|---|---|
| 1946–47 | Philadelphia | 4–1 | Chicago | Eddie Gottlieb | — |
| 1947–48 | Baltimore | 4–2 | Philadelphia | Buddy Jeannette | — |
| 1948–49 | Minneapolis | 4–2 | Washington | John Kundla | — |
| 1949–50 | Minneapolis | 4–2 | Syracuse | John Kundla | — |
| 1950–51 | Rochester | 4–3 | New York | Les Harrison | — |
| 1951–52 | Minneapolis | 4–3 | New York | John Kundla | — |
| 1952–53 | Minneapolis | 4–1 | New York | John Kundla | — |
| 1953–54 | Minneapolis | 4–3 | Syracuse | John Kundla | — |
| 1954–55 | Syracuse | 4–3 | Ft Wayne | Al Cervi | — |
| 1955–56 | Philadelphia | 4–1 | Ft Wayne | George Senesky | — |
| 1956–57 | Boston | 4–3 | St Louis | Red Auerbach | — |
| 1957–58 | St Louis | 4–2 | Boston | Alex Hannum | — |
| 1958–59 | Boston | 4–0 | Minneapolis | Red Auerbach | — |
| 1959–60 | Boston | 4–3 | St Louis | Red Auerbach | — |
| 1960–61 | Boston | 4–1 | St Louis | Red Auerbach | — |
| 1961–62 | Boston | 4–3 | LA Lakers | Red Auerbach | — |
| 1962–63 | Boston | 4–2 | LA Lakers | Red Auerbach | — |
| 1963–64 | Boston | 4–1 | San Francisco | Red Auerbach | — |
| 1964–65 | Boston | 4–1 | LA Lakers | Red Auerbach | — |
| 1965–66 | Boston | 4–3 | LA Lakers | Red Auerbach | — |
| 1966–67 | Philadelphia | 4–2 | San Francisco | Alex Hannum | — |
| 1967–68 | Boston | 4–2 | LA Lakers | Bill Russell | — |
| 1968–69 | Boston | 4–3 | LA Lakers | Bill Russell | Jerry West, LA |
| 1969–70 | New York | 4–3 | LA Lakers | Red Holzman | Willis Reed, NY |
| 1970–71 | Milwaukee | 4–0 | Baltimore | Larry Costello | Kareem Abdul-Jabbar, Mil |
| 1971–72 | LA Lakers | 4–1 | New York | Bill Sharman | Wilt Chamberlain, LA |
| 1972–73 | New York | 4–1 | LA Lakers | Red Holzman | Willis Reed, NY |
| 1973–74 | Boston | 4–3 | Milwaukee | Tommy Heinsohn | John Havlicek, Bos |
| 1974–75 | Golden State | 4–0 | Washington | Al Attles | Rick Barry, GS |
| 1975–76 | Boston | 4–2 | Phoenix | Tommy Heinsohn | JoJo White, Bos |
| 1976–77 | Portland | 4–2 | Philadelphia | Jack Ramsay | Bill Walton, Port |
| 1977–78 | Washington | 4–3 | Seattle | Dick Motta | Wes Unseld, Wash |
| 1978–79 | Seattle | 4–1 | Washington | Lenny Wilkens | Dennis Johnson, Sea |
| 1979–80 | LA Lakers | 4–2 | Philadelphia | Paul Westhead | Magic Johnson, LA |
| 1980–81 | Boston | 4–2 | Houston | Bill Fitch | Cedric Maxwell, Bos |
| 1981–82 | LA Lakers | 4–2 | Philadelphia | Pat Riley | Magic Johnson, LA |
| 1982–83 | Philadelphia | 4–0 | LA Lakers | Billy Cunningham | Moses Malone, Phil |
| 1983–84 | Boston | 4–3 | LA Lakers | K.C. Jones | Larry Bird, Bos |
| 1984–85 | LA Lakers | 4–2 | Boston | Pat Riley | Kareem Abdul-Jabbar, LA |
| 1985–86 | Boston | 4–2 | Houston | K.C. Jones | Larry Bird, Bos |
| 1986–87 | LA Lakers | 4–2 | Boston | Pat Riley | Magic Johnson, LA |
| 1987–88 | LA Lakers | 4–3 | Detroit | Pat Riley | James Worthy, LA |
| 1988–89 | Detroit | 4–0 | LA Lakers | Chuck Daly | Joe Dumars, Det |
| 1989–90 | Detroit | 4–1 | Portland | Chuck Daly | Isiah Thomas, Det |
| 1990–91 | Chicago | 4–1 | LA Lakers | Phil Jackson | Michael Jordan, Chi |
| 1991–92 | Chicago | 4–2 | Portland | Phil Jackson | Michael Jordan, Chi |
| 1992–93 | Chicago | 4–2 | Phoenix | Phil Jackson | Michael Jordan, Chi |
| 1993–94 | Houston | 4–3 | New York | Rudy Tomjanovich | Hakeem Olajuwon, Hou |
| 1994–95 | Houston | 4–0 | Orlando | Rudy Tomjanovich | Hakeem Olajuwon, Hou |
| 1995–96 | Chicago | 4–2 | Seattle | Phil Jackson | Michael Jordan, Chi |
| 1996–97 | Chicago | 4–2 | Utah | Phil Jackson | Michael Jordan, Chi |
| 1997–98 | Chicago | 4–2 | Utah | Phil Jackson | Michael Jordan, Chi |
| 1998–99 | San Antonio | 4–1 | New York | Gregg Popovich | Tim Duncan, SA |
| 1999–00 | LA Lakers | 4–2 | Indiana | Phil Jackson | Shaquille O'Neal, LA |
| 2000–01 | LA Lakers | 4–1 | Philadelphia | Phil Jackson | Shaquille O'Neal, LA |
| 2001–02 | LA Lakers | 4–0 | New Jersey | Phil Jackson | Shaquille O'Neal, LA |
| 2002–03 | San Antonio | 4–2 | New Jersey | Gregg Popovich | Tim Duncan, SA |
| 2003–04 | Detroit | 4–1 | LA Lakers | Larry Brown | Chauncey Billups, Det |
| 2004–05 | San Antonio | 4–3 | Detroit | Gregg Popovich | Tim Duncan, SA |
| 2005–06 | Miami | 4–2 | Dallas | Pat Riley | Dwyane Wade, Mia |
| 2006–07 | San Antonio | 4–0 | Cleveland | Gregg Popovich | Tony Parker, SA |
| 2007–08 | Boston | 4–2 | LA Lakers | Doc Rivers | Paul Pierce, Bos |
| 2008–09 | LA Lakers | 4–2 | Orlando | Phil Jackson | Kobe Bryant, LA |

### Regular Season Most Valuable Player: Maurice Podoloff Trophy

| Season | Player, Team | GP | Field Goals FGM | Pct | 3-Pt FG FGM | Pct | Free Throws FTM | Pct | Rebounds Off | Total | A | Stl | BS | Avg |
|---|---|---|---|---|---|---|---|---|---|---|---|---|---|---|
| 1955–56 | Bob Pettit, StL | 72 | 646 | 42.9 | – | – | 557 | 73.6 | – | 1,164 | 189 | – | – | 25.7 |
| 1956–57 | Bob Cousy, Bos | 64 | 478 | 37.8 | – | – | 363 | 82.1 | – | 309 | 478 | – | – | 20.6 |
| 1957–58 | Bill Russell, Bos | 69 | 456 | 44.2 | – | – | 230 | 51.9 | – | 1,564 | 202 | – | – | 16.6 |
| 1958–59 | Bob Pettit, StL | 72 | 719 | 43.8 | – | – | 667 | 75.9 | – | 1,182 | 221 | – | – | 29.2 |
| 1959–60 | Wilt Chamberlain, Phil | 72 | 1,065 | 46.1 | – | – | 577 | 58.2 | – | 1,941 | 168 | – | – | 37.6 |
| 1960–61 | Bill Russell, Bos | 78 | 532 | 42.6 | – | – | 258 | 55.0 | – | 1,868 | 264 | – | – | 16.9 |
| 1961–62 | Bill Russell, Bos | 76 | 575 | 45.7 | – | – | 286 | 59.5 | – | 1,891 | 341 | – | – | 18.9 |
| 1962–63 | Bill Russell, Bos | 78 | 511 | 43.2 | – | – | 287 | 55.5 | – | 1,843 | 348 | – | – | 16.8 |
| 1963–64 | Oscar Robertson, Cin | 79 | 840 | 48.3 | – | – | 800 | 85.3 | – | 783 | 868 | – | – | 31.4 |
| 1964–65 | Bill Russell, Bos | 78 | 429 | 43.8 | – | – | 244 | 57.3 | – | 1,878 | 410 | – | – | 14.1 |
| 1965–66 | Wilt Chamberlain, Phil | 79 | 1,074 | 54.0 | – | – | 501 | 51.3 | – | 1,943 | 414 | – | – | 33.5 |
| 1966–67 | Wilt Chamberlain, Phil | 81 | 785 | 68.3 | – | – | 386 | 44.1 | – | 1,957 | 630 | – | – | 24.1 |
| 1967–68 | Wilt Chamberlain, Phil | 82 | 819 | 59.5 | – | – | 354 | 38.0 | – | 1,952 | 702 | – | – | 24.3 |
| 1968–69 | Wes Unseld, Balt | 82 | 427 | 47.6 | – | – | 277 | 60.5 | – | 1,491 | 213 | – | – | 13.8 |
| 1969–70 | Willis Reed, NY | 81 | 702 | 50.7 | – | – | 351 | 75.6 | – | 1,126 | 161 | – | – | 21.7 |
| 1970–71 | Lew Alcindor*, Mil | 82 | 1,063 | 57.7 | – | – | 470 | 69.0 | – | 1,311 | 272 | – | – | 31.7 |
| 1971–72 | Kareem Abdul-Jabbar, Mil | 81 | 1,159 | 57.4 | – | – | 504 | 68.9 | – | 1,346 | 370 | – | – | 34.8 |
| 1972–73 | Dave Cowens, Bos | 82 | 740 | 45.2 | – | – | 204 | 77.9 | – | 1,329 | 333 | – | – | 20.5 |
| 1973–74 | Kareem Abdul-Jabbar, Mil | 81 | 948 | 53.9 | – | – | 295 | 70.2 | 287 | 1,178 | 386 | 112 | 283 | 27.0 |
| 1974–75 | Bob McAdoo, Buff | 82 | 1,095 | 51.2 | – | – | 641 | 80.5 | 307 | 1,155 | 179 | 92 | 174 | 34.5 |
| 1975–76 | Kareem Abdul-Jabbar, LAL | 82 | 914 | 52.9 | – | – | 447 | 70.3 | 272 | 1,383 | 413 | 119 | 338 | 27.7 |
| 1976–77 | Kareem Abdul-Jabbar, LAL | 82 | 888 | 57.9 | – | – | 376 | 70.1 | 266 | 1,090 | 319 | 101 | 261 | 26.2 |
| 1977–78 | Bill Walton, Port | 58 | 460 | 52.2 | – | – | 177 | 72.0 | 118 | 766 | 291 | 60 | 146 | 18.9 |
| 1978–79 | Moses Malone, Hou | 82 | 716 | 54.0 | – | – | 599 | 73.9 | 587 | 1,444 | 147 | 79 | 119 | 24.8 |
| 1979–80 | Kareem Abdul-Jabbar, LAL | 82 | 835 | 60.4 | 0 | 00.0 | 364 | 76.5 | 190 | 886 | 371 | 81 | 280 | 24.8 |
| 1980–81 | Julius Erving, Phil | 82 | 794 | 52.1 | 4 | 22.2 | 422 | 78.7 | 244 | 657 | 364 | 173 | 147 | 24.6 |
| 1981–82 | Moses Malone, Hou | 81 | 945 | 51.9 | 0 | 00.0 | 630 | 76.2 | 558 | 1,188 | 142 | 76 | 125 | 31.1 |
| 1982–83 | Moses Malone, Phil | 78 | 654 | 50.1 | 0 | 00.0 | 600 | 76.1 | 445 | 1,194 | 101 | 89 | 157 | 24.5 |
| 1983–84 | Larry Bird, Bos | 79 | 758 | 49.2 | 18 | 24.7 | 374 | 88.8 | 181 | 796 | 520 | 144 | 69 | 24.2 |
| 1984–85 | Larry Bird, Bos | 80 | 918 | 52.2 | 56 | 42.7 | 403 | 88.2 | 164 | 842 | 531 | 129 | 98 | 28.7 |
| 1985–86 | Larry Bird, Bos | 82 | 796 | 49.6 | 82 | 42.3 | 441 | 89.6 | 190 | 805 | 557 | 166 | 51 | 25.8 |
| 1986–87 | Magic Johnson, LAL | 80 | 683 | 52.2 | 8 | 20.5 | 535 | 84.8 | 122 | 504 | 977 | 138 | 36 | 23.9 |
| 1987–88 | Michael Jordan, Chi | 82 | 1,069 | 53.5 | 7 | 13.2 | 723 | 84.1 | 139 | 449 | 485 | 259 | 131 | 35.0 |
| 1988–89 | Magic Johnson, LAL | 77 | 579 | 50.9 | 59 | 31.4 | 513 | 91.1 | 111 | 607 | 988 | 138 | 22 | 22.5 |
| 1989–90 | Magic Johnson, LAL | 79 | 546 | 48.0 | 106 | 38.4 | 567 | 89.0 | 128 | 522 | 907 | 132 | 34 | 22.3 |
| 1990–91 | Michael Jordan, Chi | 82 | 990 | 53.9 | 29 | 31.2 | 571 | 85.1 | 118 | 492 | 453 | 223 | 83 | 31.5 |
| 1991–92 | Michael Jordan, Chi | 80 | 943 | 51.9 | 27 | 27.0 | 491 | 83.2 | 91 | 511 | 489 | 182 | 75 | 30.1 |
| 1992–93 | Charles Barkley, Phx | 76 | 716 | 52.0 | 67 | 30.5 | 445 | 76.5 | 237 | 928 | 385 | 119 | 74 | 25.6 |
| 1993–94 | Hakeem Olajuwon, Hou | 80 | 894 | 52.8 | 8 | 42.1 | 388 | 71.6 | 229 | 955 | 287 | 128 | 297 | 27.3 |
| 1994–95 | David Robinson, SA | 81 | 788 | 53.0 | 6 | 30.0 | 656 | 77.4 | 234 | 877 | 236 | 134 | 262 | 27.6 |
| 1995–96 | Michael Jordan, Chi | 82 | 916 | 49.5 | 111 | 42.7 | 548 | 83.4 | 148 | 543 | 352 | 180 | 42 | 30.4 |
| 1996–97 | Karl Malone, Utah | 82 | 864 | 55.0 | 0 | 00.0 | 521 | 75.5 | 193 | 809 | 368 | 113 | 48 | 27.4 |
| 1997–98 | Michael Jordan, Chi | 82 | 881 | 46.5 | 30 | 23.8 | 565 | 78.4 | 130 | 475 | 283 | 141 | 45 | 28.7 |
| 1998–99 | Karl Malone, Utah | 49 | 393 | 49.3 | 0 | 00.0 | 378 | 78.8 | 107 | 463 | 201 | 62 | 28 | 23.8 |
| 1999–00 | Shaquille O'Neal, LAL | 79 | 956 | 57.4 | 0 | 00.0 | 432 | 52.4 | 336 | 1078 | 299 | 36 | 239 | 29.7 |
| 2000–01 | Allen Iverson, Phil | 71 | 762 | 42.0 | 98 | 32.0 | 585 | 81.4 | 50 | 273 | 325 | 78 | 20 | 31.1 |
| 2001–02 | Tim Duncan, SA | 82 | 764 | 50.8 | 1 | 10.0 | 560 | 79.9 | 268 | 1042 | 307 | 61 | 203 | 25.5 |
| 2002–03 | Tim Duncan, SA | 81 | 714 | 51.3 | 0 | 00.0 | 450 | 71.0 | 260 | 1045 | 316 | 55 | 237 | 23.3 |
| 2003–04 | Kevin Garnett, Minn | 82 | 804 | 49.9 | 11 | 25.6 | 368 | 79.1 | 245 | 1139 | 409 | 120 | 178 | 24.2 |
| 2004–05 | Steve Nash, Phx | 75 | 430 | 50.2 | 94 | 43.1 | 211 | 88.7 | 80 | 330 | 861 | 74 | 6 | 26.0 |
| 2005–06 | Steve Nash, Phx | 79 | 541 | 51.2 | 150 | 43.9 | 257 | 92.1 | 47 | 333 | 826 | 61 | 12 | 18.8 |
| 2006–07 | Dirk Nowitzki, Dal | 78 | 673 | 50.2 | 72 | 41.6 | 498 | 90.4 | 122 | 693 | 263 | 52 | 62 | 24.6 |
| 2007–08 | Kobe Bryant, LAL | 82 | 775 | 45.9 | 150 | 36.1 | 623 | 84.0 | 94 | 517 | 441 | 151 | 40 | 28.3 |
| 2008–09 | LeBron James, Cle | 81 | 789 | 48.9 | 132 | 34.4 | 594 | 78.0 | 106 | 613 | 587 | 137 | 93 | 28.4 |

*Alcindor changed his name to Kareem Abdul-Jabbar after the 1970–71 season.

### Coach of the Year: Arnold (Red) Auerbach Trophy

1962–63...Harry Gallatin, StL
1963–64...Alex Hannum, SF
1964–65...Red Auerbach, Bos
1965–66...Dolph Schayes, Phil
1966–67...Johnny Kerr, Chi
1967–68...Richie Guerin, StL
1968–69...Gene Shue, Balt
1969–70...Red Holzman, NY
1970–71...Dick Motta, Chi
1971–72...Bill Sharman, LA
1972–73...Tom Heinsohn, Bos
1973–74...Ray Scott, Det
1974–75...Phil Johnson, KC-Oma
1975–76...Bill Fitch, Clev
1976–77...Tom Nissalke, Hou
1977–78...Hubie Brown, Atl

1978–79...Cotton Fitzsimmons, KC
1979–80...Bill Fitch, Bos
1980–81...Jack McKinney, Ind
1981–82...Gene Shue, Wash
1982–83...Don Nelson, Mil
1983–84...Frank Layden, Utah
1984–85...Don Nelson, Mil
1985–86...Mike Fratello, Atl
1986–87...Mike Schuler, Port
1987–88...Doug Moe, Den
1988–89...Cotton Fitzsimmons, Phx
1989–90...Pat Riley, LAL
1990–91...Don Chaney, Hou
1991–92...Don Nelson, GS
1992–93...Pat Riley, NY
1993–94...Lenny Wilkens, Atl

1994–95...Del Harris, LAL
1995–96...Phil Jackson, Chi
1996–97...Pat Riley, Mia
1997–98...Larry Bird, Ind
1998–99...Mike Dunleavy, Port
1999–00...Glenn (Doc) Rivers, Orl
2000–01...Larry Brown, Phil
2001–02...Rick Carlisle, Det
2002–03...Gregg Popovich, SA
2003–04...Hubie Brown, Mem
2004–05...Mike D'Antoni, Phx
2005–06...Avery Johnson, Dal
2006–07...Sam Mitchell, Tor
2007–08...Byron Scott, NO
2008–09...Mike Brown, Cle

Note: Award named after Auerbach in 1986.

### Rookie of the Year: Eddie Gottlieb Trophy

1952–53...Don Meineke, FW
1953–54...Ray Felix, Balt
1954–55...Bob Pettit, Mil
1955–56...Maurice Stokes, Roch
1956–57...Tom Heinsohn, Bos
1957–58...Woody Sauldsberry, Phil
1958–59...Elgin Baylor, Minn
1959–60...Wilt Chamberlain, Phil
1960–61...Oscar Robertson, Cin
1961–62...Walt Bellamy, Chi
1962–63...Terry Dischinger, Chi
1963–64...Jerry Lucas, Cin
1964–65...Willis Reed, NY
1965–66...Rick Barry, SF
1966–67...Dave Bing, Det
1967–68...Earl Monroe, Balt
1968–69...Wes Unseld, Balt
1969–70...K. Abdul-Jabbar, Mil
1970–71...Dave Cowens, Bos
       Geoff Petrie, Port

1971–72...Sidney Wicks, Port
1972–73...Bob McAdoo, Buff
1973–74...Ernie DiGregorio, Buf
1974–75...Keith Wilkes, GS
1975–76...Alvan Adams, Phx
1976–77...Adrian Dantley, Buf
1977–78...Walter Davis, Phx
1978–79...Phil Ford, KC
1979–80...Larry Bird, Bos
1980–81...Darrell Griffith, Utah
1981–82...Buck Williams, NJ
1982–83...Terry Cummings, SD
1983–84...Ralph Sampson, Hou
1984–85...Michael Jordan, Chi
1985–86...Patrick Ewing, NY
1986–87...Chuck Person, Ind
1987–88...Mark Jackson, NY
1988–89...Mitch Richmond, GS
1989–90...David Robinson, SA
1990–91...Derrick Coleman, NJ

1991–92...Larry Johnson, Cha
1992–93...Shaquille O'Neal, Orl
1993–94...Chris Webber, GS
1994–95...J. Kidd, Dal/G. Hill, Det
1995–96...Damon Stoudamire, Tor
1996–97...Allen Iverson, Phil
1997–98...Tim Duncan, SA
1998–99...Vince Carter, Tor
1999–00...Steve Francis, Hou
       Elton Brand, Chi
2000–01...Mike Miller, Orl
2001–02...Pau Gasol, Mem
2002–03...Amare Stoudemire, Phx
2003–04...LeBron James, Clev
2004–05...Emeka Okafor, Cha
2005–06...Chris Paul, NO
2006–07...Brandon Roy, Port
2007–08...Kevin Durant, Sea
2008–09...Derrick Rose, Chi

### Defensive Player of the Year

1982–83...Sidney Moncrief, Mil
1983–84...Sidney Moncrief, Mil
1984–85...Mark Eaton, Utah
1985–86...Alvin Robertson, SA
1986–87...Michael Cooper, LAL
1987–88...Michael Jordan, Chi
1988–89...Mark Eaton, Utah
1989–90...Dennis Rodman, Det
1990–91...Dennis Rodman, Det

1991–92...David Robinson, SA
1992–93...Hakeem Olajuwon, Hou
1993–94...Hakeem Olajuwon, Hou
1994–95...Dikembe Mutombo, Den
1995–96...Gary Payton, Sea
1996–97...Dikembe Mutombo, Atl
1997–98...Dikembe Mutombo, Atl
1998–99...Alonzo Mourning, Mia
1999–00...Alonzo Mourning, Mia

2000–01...Dikembe Mutombo, Phil/Atl
2001–02...Ben Wallace, Det
2002–03...Ben Wallace, Det
2003–04...Ron Artest, Ind
2004–05...Ben Wallace, Det
2005–06...Ben Wallace, Det
2006–07...Marcus Camby, Den
2007–08...Kevin Garnett, Bos
2008–09...Dwight Howard, Orl

### Sixth Man Award

1982–83...Bobby Jones, Phil
1983–84...Kevin McHale, Bos
1984–85...Kevin McHale, Bos
1985–86...Bill Walton, Bos
1986–87...Ricky Pierce, Mil
1987–88...Roy Tarpley, Dal
1988–89...Eddie Johnson, Phx
1989–90...Ricky Pierce, Mil
1990–91...Detlef Schrempf, Ind

1991–92...Detlef Schrempf, Ind
1992–93...Cliff Robinson, Port
1993–94...Dell Curry, Cha
1994–95...Anthony Mason, NY
1995–96...Tony Kukoc, Chi
1996–97...John Starks, NY
1997–98...Danny Manning, Phx
1998–99...Darrell Armstrong, Orl
1999–00...Rodney Rogers, Phx

2000–01...Aaron McKie, Phil
2001–02...Corliss Williamson, Det
2002–03...Bobby Jackson, Sac
2003–04...Antawn Jamison, Dal
2004–05...Ben Gordon, Chi
2005–06...Mike Miller, Mem
2006–07...Leandro Barbosa, Phx
2007–08...Manu Ginobli, SA
2008–09...Jason Terry, Dal

## J. Walter Kennedy Citizenship Award

1974–75...Wes Unseld, Wash
1975–76...Slick Watts, Sea
1976–77...Dave Bing, Wash
1977–78...Bob Lanier, Det
1978–79...Calvin Murphy, Hou
1979–80...Austin Carr, Cle
1980–81...Mike Glenn, NY
1981–82...Kent Benson, Det
1982–83...Julius Erving, Phil
1983–84...Frank Layden, Utah
1984–85...Dan Issel, Den
1985–86...Michael Cooper, LAL
         Rory Sparrow, NY

1986–87...Isiah Thomas, Det
1987–88...Alex English, Den
1988–89...Thurl Bailey, Utah
1989–90...Glenn (Doc) Rivers, Atl
1990–91...Kevin Johnson, Phx
1991–92...Magic Johnson, LAL
1992–93...Terry Porter, Port
1993–94...Joe Dumars, Det
1994–95...Joe O'Toole, Atl
1995–96...Chris Dudley, Port
1996–97...P.J. Brown, Mia
1997–98...Steve Smith, Atl

1998–99...Brian Grant, Port
1999–00...Vlade Divac, Sac
2000–01...Dikembe Mutombo, Phil
2001–02...Alonzo Mourning, Mia
2002–03...David Robinson, SA
2003–04...Reggie Miller, Ind
2004–05...Eric Snow, Clev
2005–06...Kevin Garnett, Min
2006–07...Luol Deng, Chi
2007–08...Grant Hill, Phx
2008–09...Dikembe Mutombo, Hou

## Most Improved Player

1985–86...Alvin Robertson, SA
1986–87...Dale Ellis, Sea
1987–88...Kevin Duckworth, Port
1988–89...Kevin Johnson, Phx
1989–90...Rony Seikaly, Mia
1990–91...Scott Skiles, Orl
1991–92...Pervis Ellison, Wash
1992–93...Mahmoud Abdul-Rauf, Den

1993–94...Don MacLean, Wash
1994–95...Dana Barros, Phil
1995–96.....Gheorghe Muresan, Wash
1996–97...Isaac Austin, Mia
1997–98...Alan Henderson, Atl
1998–99...Darrell Armstrong, Orl
1999–00...Jalen Rose, Ind
2000–01...Tracy McGrady, Orl

2001–02...Jermaine O'Neal, Ind
2002–03...Gilbert Arenas, GS
2003–04...Zach Randolph, Port
2004–05...Bobby Simmons, LAC
2005–06...Boris Diaw, Phx
2006–07...Monta Ellis, GS
2007–08...Hedo Turkoglu, Orl
2008–09...Danny Granger, Ind

## Executive of the Year

1972–73...Joe Axelson, KC-Oma
1973–74...Eddie Donovan, Buf
1974–75...Dick Vertlieb, GS
1975–76...Jerry Colangelo, Phx
1976–77...Ray Patterson, Hou
1977–78...Angelo Drossos, SA
1978–79...Bob Ferry, Wash
1979–80...Red Auerbach, Bos
1980–81...Jerry Colangelo, Phx
1981–82...Bob Ferry, Wash
1982–83...Zollie Volchok, Sea
1983–84...Frank Layden, Utah
1984–85...Vince Boryla, Den

1985–86...Stan Kasten, Atl
1986–87...Stan Kasten, Atl
1987–88...Jerry Krause, Chi
1988–89...Jerry Colangelo, Phx
1989–90...Bob Bass, SA
1990–91...Bucky Buckwalter, Port
1991–92...Wayne Embry, Clev
1992–93...Jerry Colangelo, Phx
1993–94...Bob Whitsitt, Sea
1994–95...Jerry West, LAL
1995–96...Jerry Krause, Chi
1996–97...Bob Bass, Cha
1997–98...Wayne Embry, Clev

1998–99...Geoff Petrie, Sac
1999–00...John Gabriel, Orl
2000–01...Geoff Petrie, Sac
2001–02...Rod Thorn, NJ
2002–03...Joe Dumars, Det
2003–04...Jerry West, Mem
2004–05...Bryan Colangelo, Phx
2005–06...Elgin Baylor, LAC
2006–07...Bryan Colangelo, Tor
2007–08...Danny Ainge, Bos
2008–09...Mark Warkentien, Den

# NBA Alltime Individual Leaders

## Scoring

### MOST POINTS, CAREER

| | Pts | Avg |
|---|---|---|
| Kareem Abdul-Jabbar | 38,387 | 24.6 |
| Karl Malone | 36,928 | 25.0 |
| Michael Jordan | 32,292 | 30.1 |
| Wilt Chamberlain | 31,419 | 30.1 |
| *Shaquille O'Neal | 27,619 | 24.7 |
| Moses Malone | 27,409 | 20.6 |
| Elvin Hayes | 27,313 | 21.0 |
| Hakeem Olajuwon | 26,946 | 21.8 |
| Oscar Robertson | 26,710 | 25.7 |
| Dominique Wilkins | 26,668 | 24.8 |

*Active in 2008–09.

### HIGHEST SCORING AVERAGE, CAREER

| | | |
|---|---|---|
| Michael Jordan | 30.1 | 1,072 games |
| Wilt Chamberlain | 30.1 | 1,045 games |
| *LeBron James | 27.5 | 472 games |
| Elgin Baylor | 27.4 | 846 games |
| *Allen Iverson | 27.1 | 886 games |
| Jerry West | 27.0 | 932 games |
| Bob Pettit | 26.4 | 792 games |
| George Gervin | 26.2 | 791 games |
| Oscar Robertson | 25.7 | 1,040 games |
| *Kobe Bryant | 25.1 | 948 games |

*Acitve in 2008–09. Note: Minimum 400 games.

### MOST POINTS, SEASON

| | | |
|---|---|---|
| Wilt Chamberlain, Phil | 4,029 | 1961–62 |
| Wilt Chamberlain, SF | 3,586 | 1962–63 |
| Michael Jordan, Chi | 3,041 | 1986–87 |
| Wilt Chamberlain, Phil | 3,033 | 1960–61 |
| Wilt Chamberlain, SF | 2,948 | 1963–64 |
| Michael Jordan, Chi | 2,868 | 1987–88 |
| Kobe Bryant, LA | 2,832 | 2005–06 |
| Bob McAdoo, Buff | 2,831 | 1974–75 |
| Rick Barry, SF | 2,775 | 1966–67 |
| Michael Jordan, Chi | 2,753 | 1989–90 |

### HIGHEST SCORING AVERAGE, SEASON

| | | |
|---|---|---|
| Wilt Chamberlain, Phil | 50.4 | 1961–62 |
| Wilt Chamberlain, SF | 44.8 | 1962–63 |
| Wilt Chamberlain, Phil | 38.4 | 1960–61 |
| Wilt Chamberlain, Phil | 37.6 | 1959–60 |
| Michael Jordan, Chi | 37.1 | 1986–87 |
| Wilt Chamberlain, SF | 36.9 | 1963–64 |
| Rick Barry, SF | 35.6 | 1966–67 |
| Kobe Bryant, LA | 35.4 | 2005–06 |
| Michael Jordan, Chi | 35.0 | 1987–88 |
| Elgin Baylor, LA | 34.8 | 1960–61 |

Note: Minimum 70 games.

## Scoring *(Cont.)*

### MOST POINTS, SINGLE GAME

| | Player, Team | Opp | Date |
|---|---|---|---|
| 100 | Wilt Chamberlain, Phil | NY | 3/2/62 |
| 81 | Kobe Bryant, LAL | Tor | 1/22/06 |
| 78 | Wilt Chamberlain, Phil | LAL | 12/8/61 |
| 73 | Wilt Chamberlain, Phil | Chi | 1/13/62 |
| 73 | Wilt Chamberlain, SF | NY | 11/16/62 |
| 73 | David Thompson, Den | Det | 4/9/78 |
| 72 | Wilt Chamberlain, SF | LAL | 11/3/62 |
| 71 | David Robinson, SA | LAC | 4/24/94 |
| 71 | Elgin Baylor, LAL | NY | 11/15/60 |
| 70 | Wilt Chamberlain, SF | Syr | 3/10/63 |

### Field-Goal Percentage

Highest FG Percentage, Career: .599—Artis Gilmore
Highest FG Percentage, Season: .727—Wilt Chamberlain, LA Lakers, 1972–73 (426/586)

### Free Throws

#### HIGHEST FREE-THROW PERCENTAGE, CAREER

| | |
|---|---|
| Mark Price | .904 |
| *Steve Nash | .900 |
| Rick Barry | .900 |
| *Peja Stojakovic | .894 |
| *Ray Allen | .893 |

Note: Minimum 1200 free throws made. *Active 2008–09.

#### HIGHEST FREE-THROW PERCENTAGE, SEASON

| | | |
|---|---|---|
| Jose Calderon, Tor | .981 | 2008–09 |
| Calvin Murphy, Hou | .958 | 1980–81 |
| Mahmoud Abdul-Rauf, Den | .956 | 1993–94 |
| Ray Allen, Bos | .952 | 2008–09 |
| Jeff Hornacek, Utah | .950 | 1999–00 |
| Mark Price, Clev | .948 | 1992–93 |

#### MOST FREE THROWS MADE, CAREER

| | No. | Yrs | Pct |
|---|---|---|---|
| Karl Malone | 9,787 | 19 | .742 |
| Moses Malone | 8,531 | 19 | .769 |
| Oscar Robertson | 7,694 | 14 | .838 |
| Michael Jordan | 7,327 | 15 | .835 |
| Jerry West | 7,160 | 14 | .814 |

### Three-Point Field Goals

Most Three-Point Field-Goals, Career: 2,560—Reggie Miller
Highest Three-Point Field-Goal Percentage, Career: .454—Jason Kapono*
Most Three-Point Field Goals, Season: 269—Ray Allen, Sea, 2005–06
Highest Three-Point Field-Goal Percentage, Season: .524—Steve Kerr, Chi, 1994–95
Most Three-Point Field Goals, Game: 12—Kobe Bryant, LA Lakers vs Seattle, 1/7/03; Donyell Marshall, Toronto vs. Philadelphia, 3/13/05

Note: First season of three-point field goal: 1979–80. *Active 2008–09.

### Steals

Most Steals, Career: 3,265—John Stockton
Most Steals, Season: 301—Alvin Robertson, San Antonio, 1985–86
Most Steals, Game: 11—Kendall Gill, New Jersey vs Miami, 4/3/99; Larry Kenon, San Antonio vs Kansas City, 12/26/76

## Rebounds

### MOST REBOUNDS, CAREER

| | No. | Yrs | Avg |
|---|---|---|---|
| Wilt Chamberlain | 23,924 | 14 | 22.9 |
| Bill Russell | 21,620 | 13 | 22.5 |
| Kareem Abdul-Jabbar | 17,440 | 20 | 11.2 |
| Elvin Hayes | 16,279 | 16 | 12.5 |
| Moses Malone | 16,212 | 19 | 12.2 |
| Karl Malone | 14,968 | 19 | 10.1 |
| Robert Parish | 14,715 | 21 | 9.1 |
| Nate Thurmond | 14,464 | 14 | 15.0 |
| Walt Bellamy | 14,241 | 14 | 13.7 |
| Wes Unseld | 13,769 | 13 | 14.0 |

### MOST REBOUNDS, SEASON

| | | |
|---|---|---|
| Wilt Chamberlain, Phil | 2,149 | 1960–61 |
| Wilt Chamberlain, Phil | 2,052 | 1961–62 |
| Wilt Chamberlain, Phil | 1,957 | 1966–67 |
| Wilt Chamberlain, Phil | 1,952 | 1967–68 |
| Wilt Chamberlain, SF | 1,946 | 1962–63 |
| Wilt Chamberlain, Phil | 1,943 | 1965–66 |
| Wilt Chamberlain, Phil | 1,941 | 1959–60 |
| Bill Russell, Bos | 1,930 | 1963–64 |
| Bill Russell, Bos | 1,878 | 1964–65 |
| Bill Russell, Bos | 1,868 | 1960–61 |

### MOST REBOUNDS, GAME

| | Player, Team | Opp | Date |
|---|---|---|---|
| 55 | Wilt Chamberlain, Phil | Bos | 11/24/60 |
| 51 | Bill Russell, Bos | Syr | 02/05/60 |
| 49 | Bill Russell, Bos | Phil | 11/16/57 |
| 49 | Bill Russell, Bos | Det | 03/11/65 |
| 45 | Wilt Chamberlain, Phil | Syr | 02/06/60 |
| 45 | Wilt Chamberlain, Phil | LA | 01/21/61 |

## Assists

### MOST ASSISTS, CAREER

| | |
|---|---|
| John Stockton | 15,806 |
| Mark Jackson | 10,334 |
| *Jason Kidd | 10,199 |
| Magic Johnson | 10,141 |
| Oscar Robertson | 9,887 |

*Active in 2008–09.

### MOST ASSISTS, SEASON

| | | |
|---|---|---|
| John Stockton, Utah | 1,164 | 1990–91 |
| John Stockton, Utah | 1,134 | 1989–90 |
| John Stockton, Utah | 1,128 | 1987–88 |
| John Stockton, Utah | 1,126 | 1991–92 |
| Isiah Thomas, Det | 1,123 | 1984–85 |

**MOST ASSISTS, GAME:** 30—Scott Skiles, Orlando vs Denver, 12/30/90

## Blocked Shots

### MOST BLOCKED SHOTS, CAREER

| | |
|---|---|
| Hakeem Olajuwon | 3,830 |
| *Dikembe Mutombo | 3,289 |
| Kareem Abdul-Jabbar | 3,189 |
| Mark Eaton | 3,064 |
| David Robinson | 2,954 |

*Active in 2008–09.

### MOST BLOCKED SHOTS, SEASON

| | | |
|---|---|---|
| Mark Eaton, Utah | 456 | 1984–85 |
| Manute Bol, Wash | 397 | 1985–86 |
| Elmore Smith, LA | 393 | 1973–74 |

**MOST BLOCKED SHOTS, GAME:** 17—Elmore Smith, LA Lakers vs Portland, 10/28/73

## Scoring

### MOST POINTS, CAREER

| | Pts | App. | Avg |
|---|---|---|---|
| Michael Jordan | 5,987 | 13 | 33.4 |
| Kareem Abdul-Jabbar | 5,762 | 18 | 24.3 |
| *Shaquille O'Neal | 5,121 | 15 | 25.2 |
| Karl Malone | 4,761 | 19 | 24.7 |
| Jerry West | 4,457 | 13 | 29.1 |
| *Kobe Bryant | 4,381 | 12 | 25.0 |
| Larry Bird | 3,897 | 12 | 23.8 |
| John Havlicek | 3,776 | 13 | 22.0 |
| Hakeem Olajuwon | 3,755 | 15 | 25.9 |
| *Tim Duncan | 3,724 | 11 | 23.3 |
| Magic Johnson | 3,701 | 13 | 19.5 |

*Active 2008–09.

### †HIGHEST SCORING AVERAGE, CAREER

| | Avg | Games |
|---|---|---|
| Michael Jordan | 33.4 | 179 |
| *Allen Iverson | 29.7 | 71 |
| *LeBron James | 29.4 | 60 |
| Jerry West | 29.1 | 153 |
| *Tracy McGrady | 28.5 | 38 |
| Elgin Baylor | 27.0 | 134 |
| George Gervin | 27.0 | 59 |
| Hakeem Olajuwon | 25.9 | 145 |
| *Vince Carter | 25.9 | 42 |
| *Dwyane Wade | 25.7 | 61 |
| Bob Pettit | 25.5 | 88 |
| *Dirk Nowitzki | 25.5 | 97 |
| Dominique Wilkins | 25.4 | 55 |
| *Shaquille O'Neal | 25.2 | 203 |
| *Amare Stoudemire | 25.1 | 36 |

†Minimum of 25 games. *Active 2008–09.

### MOST POINTS, GAME

| | Player, Team | Opp | Date |
|---|---|---|---|
| †63 | Michael Jordan, Chi | Bos | 4/20/86 |
| 61 | Elgin Baylor, LA | Bos | 4/14/62 |
| 56 | Wilt Chamberlain, Phil | Syr | 3/22/62 |
| 56 | Michael Jordan, Chi | Mia | 4/29/92 |
| 56 | Charles Barkley, Phx | GS | 5/4/94 |
| 55 | Rick Barry, SF | Phil | 4/18/67 |
| 55 | Michael Jordan, Chi | Cle | 5/1/88 |
| 55 | Michael Jordan, Chi | Phx | 4/16/95 |
| 55 | Michael Jordan, Chi | Wash | 4/27/97 |

†Double overtime game.

## Rebounds

### MOST REBOUNDS, CAREER

| | No. | App. | Avg |
|---|---|---|---|
| Bill Russell | 4,104 | 13 | 24.9 |
| Wilt Chamberlain | 3,913 | 13 | 24.5 |
| Kareem Abdul-Jabbar | 2,481 | 18 | 10.5 |
| Shaquille O'Neal | 2,447 | 15 | 12.1 |
| Karl Malone | 2,062 | 19 | 10.7 |
| *Tim Duncan | 2,015 | 11 | 12.6 |

*Active 2008–09.

### MOST REBOUNDS, GAME

| | Player, Team | Opp | Date |
|---|---|---|---|
| 41 | Wilt Chamberlain, Phil | Bos | 4/5/67 |
| 40 | Bill Russell, Bos | Phil | 3/23/58 |
| 40 | Bill Russell, Bos | StL | 3/29/60 |
| †40 | Bill Russell, Bos | LA | 4/18/62 |

†Overtime game. Three tied at 39.

## Assists

### MOST ASSISTS, CAREER

| | No. | Games |
|---|---|---|
| Magic Johnson | 2,346 | 190 |
| John Stockton | 1,839 | 182 |
| Larry Bird | 1,062 | 164 |
| Scottie Pippen | 1,048 | 208 |
| Michael Jordan | 1,022 | 179 |

### MOST ASSISTS, GAME

| | Player, Team | Opp | Date |
|---|---|---|---|
| 24 | Magic Johnson, LAL | Phx | 5/15/84 |
| 24 | John Stockton, Utah | LAL | 5/17/88 |
| 23 | Magic Johnson, LAL | Port | 5/3/85 |
| 23 | John Stockton, Utah | Port | 4/25/96 |
| 23 | Steve Nash, Phx | LAL | 4/24/07 |

## Games played

| | |
|---|---|
| Robert Horry | 244 |
| Kareem Abdul-Jabbar | 237 |
| Scottie Pippen | 208 |
| *Shaquille O'Neal | 203 |
| Danny Ainge | 193 |
| Karl Malone | 193 |
| Magic Johnson | 190 |
| Robert Parish | 184 |
| Byron Scott | 183 |
| John Stockton | 182 |

## Appearances

| | |
|---|---|
| John Stockton | 19 |
| Karl Malone | 19 |
| Kareem Abdul-Jabbar | 18 |
| Robert Horry | 16 |
| Robert Parish | 16 |
| Scottie Pippen | 16 |
| Terry Porter | 16 |
| Dolph Schayes | 15 |
| Clyde Drexler | 15 |
| Jerome Kersey | 15 |
| Hakeem Olajuwon | 15 |
| *Shaquille O'Neal | 15 |
| Tree Rollins | 15 |

*Active 2008–09.

## Scoring

| | | | | | |
|---|---|---|---|---|---|
| 1946–47 | Joe Fulks, Phil | 1389 | 1978–79 | George Gervin, SA | 29.6 |
| 1947–48 | Max Zaslofsky, Chi | 1007 | 1979–80 | George Gervin, SA | 33.1 |
| 1948–49 | George Mikan, Min | 1698 | 1980–81 | Adrian Dantley, Utah | 30.7 |
| 1949–50 | George Mikan, Min | 1865 | 1981–82 | George Gervin, SA | 32.3 |
| 1950–51 | George Mikan, Min | 1932 | 1982–83 | Alex English, Den | 28.4 |
| 1951–52 | Paul Arizin, Phil | 1674 | 1983–84 | Adrian Dantley, Utah | 30.6 |
| 1952–53 | Neil Johnston, Phil | 1564 | 1984–85 | Bernard King, NY | 32.9 |
| 1953–54 | Neil Johnston, Phil | 1759 | 1985–86 | Dominique Wilkins, Atl | 30.3 |
| 1954–55 | Neil Johnston, Phil | 1631 | 1986–87 | Michael Jordan, Chi | 37.1 |
| 1955–56 | Bob Pettit, StL | 1849 | 1987–88 | Michael Jordan, Chi | 35.0 |
| 1956–57 | Paul Arizin, Phil | 1817 | 1988–89 | Michael Jordan, Chi | 32.5 |
| 1957–58 | George Yardley, Det | 2001 | 1989–90 | Michael Jordan, Chi | 33.6 |
| 1958–59 | Bob Pettit, StL | 2105 | 1990–91 | Michael Jordan, Chi | 31.5 |
| 1959–60 | Wilt Chamberlain, Phil | 2707 | 1991–92 | Michael Jordan, Chi | 30.1 |
| 1960–61 | Wilt Chamberlain, Phil | 3033 | 1992–93 | Michael Jordan, Chi | 32.6 |
| 1961–62 | Wilt Chamberlain, Phil | 4029 | 1993–94 | David Robinson, SA | 29.8 |
| 1962–63 | Wilt Chamberlain, SF | 3586 | 1994–95 | Shaquille O'Neal, Orl | 29.3 |
| 1963–64 | Wilt Chamberlain, SF | 2948 | 1995–96 | Michael Jordan, Chi | 30.4 |
| 1964–65 | Wilt Chamberlain, SF-Phil | 2534 | 1996–97 | Michael Jordan, Chi | 29.6 |
| 1965–66 | Wilt Chamberlain, Phil | 2649 | 1997–98 | Michael Jordan, Chi | 28.7 |
| 1966–67 | Rick Barry, SF | 2775 | 1998–99 | Allen Iverson, Phil | 26.8 |
| 1967–68 | Dave Bing, Det | 2142 | 1999–00 | Shaquille O'Neal, LA Lakers | 29.7 |
| 1968–69 | Elvin Hayes, SD | 2327 | 2000–01 | Allen Iverson, Phil | 31.1 |
| 1969–70 | Jerry West, LA | *31.2 | 2001–02 | Allen Iverson, Phil | 31.4 |
| 1970–71 | Kareem Abdul-Jabbar, Mil | 31.7 | 2002–03 | Tracy McGrady, Orl | 32.1 |
| 1971–72 | Kareem Abdul-Jabbar, Mil | 34.8 | 2003–04 | Tracy McGrady, Orl | 28.0 |
| 1972–73 | Nate Archibald, KC-Oma | 34.0 | 2004–05 | Allen Iverson, Phil | 30.7 |
| 1973–74 | Bob McAdoo, Buff | 30.6 | 2005–06 | Kobe Bryant, LA Lakers | 35.4 |
| 1974–75 | Bob McAdoo, Buff | 34.5 | 2006–07 | Kobe Bryant, LA Lakers | 31.6 |
| 1975–76 | Bob McAdoo, Buff | 31.1 | 2007–08 | LeBron James, Cle | 30.0 |
| 1976–77 | Pete Maravich, NO | 31.1 | 2008–09 | Dwyane Wade, Mia | 30.2 |
| 1977–78 | George Gervin, SA | 27.2 | | | |

*Based on per game average since 1969–70.

## Rebounding

| | | | | | |
|---|---|---|---|---|---|
| 1950–51 | Dolph Schayes, Syr | 1080 | 1981–82 | Moses Malone, Hou | 14.7 |
| 1951–52 | Larry Foust, FW | 880 | 1982–83 | Moses Malone, Phil | 15.3 |
| | Mel Hutchins, Mil | 880 | 1983–84 | Moses Malone, Phil | 13.4 |
| 1952–53 | George Mikan, Min | 1007 | 1984–85 | Moses Malone, Phil | 13.1 |
| 1953–54 | Harry Gallatin, NY | 1098 | 1985–86 | Bill Laimbeer, Det | 13.1 |
| 1954–55 | Neil Johnston, Phil | 1085 | 1986–87 | Charles Barkley, Phil | 14.6 |
| 1955–56 | Bob Pettit, StL | 1164 | 1987–88 | Michael Cage, LAC | 13.0 |
| 1956–57 | Maurice Stokes, Roch | 1256 | 1988–89 | Hakeem Olajuwon, Hou | 13.5 |
| 1957–58 | Bill Russell, Bos | 1564 | 1989–90 | Hakeem Olajuwon, Hou | 14.0 |
| 1958–59 | Bill Russell, Bos | 1612 | 1990–91 | David Robinson, SA | 13.0 |
| 1959–60 | Wilt Chamberlain, Phil | 1941 | 1991–92 | Dennis Rodman, Det | 18.7 |
| 1960–61 | Wilt Chamberlain, Phil | 2149 | 1992–93 | Dennis Rodman, Det | 18.3 |
| 1961–62 | Wilt Chamberlain, Phil | 2052 | 1993–94 | Dennis Rodman, SA | 17.3 |
| 1962–63 | Wilt Chamberlain, SF | 1946 | 1994–95 | Dennis Rodman, SA | 16.8 |
| 1963–64 | Bill Russell, Bos | 1930 | 1995–96 | Dennis Rodman, Chi | 14.9 |
| 1964–65 | Bill Russell, Bos | 1878 | 1996–97 | Dennis Rodman, Chi | 16.1 |
| 1965–66 | Wilt Chamberlain, Phil | 1943 | 1997–98 | Dennis Rodman, Chi | 15.0 |
| 1966–67 | Wilt Chamberlain, Phil | 1957 | 1998–99 | Chris Webber, Sac | 13.0 |
| 1967–68 | Wilt Chamberlain, Phil | 1952 | 1999–00 | Dikembe Mutombo, Atl | 14.1 |
| 1968–69 | Wilt Chamberlain, LA | 1712 | 2000–01 | Dikembe Mutombo, Atl | 13.5 |
| 1969–70 | Elvin Hayes, SD | *16.9 | 2001–02 | Ben Wallace, Det | 13.0 |
| 1970–71 | Wilt Chamberlain, LA | 18.2 | 2002–03 | Ben Wallace, Det | 15.4 |
| 1971–72 | Wilt Chamberlain, LA | 19.2 | 2003–04 | Kevin Garnett, Min | 13.9 |
| 1972–73 | Wilt Chamberlain, LA | 18.6 | 2004–05 | Kevin Garnett, Min | 13.5 |
| 1973–74 | Elvin Hayes, Capital (Wash) | 18.1 | 2005–06 | Kevin Garnett, Min | 12.7 |
| 1974–75 | Wes Unseld, Wash | 14.8 | 2006–07 | Kevin Garnett, Min | 12.8 |
| 1975–76 | Kareem Abdul-Jabbar, LA | 16.9 | 2007–08 | Dwight Howard, Orl | 14.2 |
| 1976–77 | Bill Walton, Port | 14.4 | 2008–09 | Dwight Howard, Orl | 13.8 |
| 1977–78 | Len Robinson, NO | 15.7 | | | |
| 1978–79 | Moses Malone, Hou | 17.6 | | | |
| 1979–80 | Swen Nater, SD | 15.0 | | | |
| 1980–81 | Moses Malone, Hou | 14.8 | | | |

*Based on per game average since 1969–70.

### Assists

| | | | | | |
|---|---|---|---|---|---|
| 1946–47 | Ernie Calverly, Prov | 202 | 1978–79 | Kevin Porter, Det | 13.4 |
| 1947–48 | Howie Dallmar, Phil | 120 | 1979–80 | Micheal Ray Richardson, NY | 10.1 |
| 1948–49 | Bob Davies, Roch | 321 | 1980–81 | Kevin Porter, Wash | 9.1 |
| 1949–50 | Dick McGuire, NY | 386 | 1981–82 | Johnny Moore, SA | 9.6 |
| 1950–51 | Andy Phillip, Phil | 414 | 1982–83 | Magic Johnson, LA | 10.5 |
| 1951–52 | Andy Phillip, Phil | 539 | 1983–84 | Magic Johnson, LA | 13.1 |
| 1952–53 | Bob Cousy, Bos | 547 | 1984–85 | Isiah Thomas, Det | 13.9 |
| 1953–54 | Bob Cousy, Bos | 518 | 1985–86 | Magic Johnson, LA Lakers | 12.6 |
| 1954–55 | Bob Cousy, Bos | 557 | 1986–87 | Magic Johnson, LA Lakers | 12.2 |
| 1955–56 | Bob Cousy, Bos | 642 | 1987–88 | John Stockton, Utah | 13.8 |
| 1956–57 | Bob Cousy, Bos | 478 | 1988–89 | John Stockton, Utah | 13.6 |
| 1957–58 | Bob Cousy, Bos | 463 | 1989–90 | John Stockton, Utah | 14.5 |
| 1958–59 | Bob Cousy, Bos | 557 | 1990–91 | John Stockton, Utah | 14.2 |
| 1959–60 | Bob Cousy, Bos | 715 | 1991–92 | John Stockton, Utah | 13.7 |
| 1960–61 | Oscar Robertson, Cin | 690 | 1992–93 | John Stockton, Utah | 12.0 |
| 1961–62 | Oscar Robertson, Cin | 899 | 1993–94 | John Stockton, Utah | 12.6 |
| 1962–63 | Guy Rodgers, SF | 825 | 1994–95 | John Stockton, Utah | 12.3 |
| 1963–64 | Oscar Robertson, Cin | 868 | 1995–96 | John Stockton, Utah | 11.2 |
| 1964–65 | Oscar Robertson, Cin | 861 | 1996–97 | Mark Jackson, Ind | 11.4 |
| 1965–66 | Oscar Robertson, Cin | 847 | 1997–98 | Rod Strickland, Wash | 10.5 |
| 1966–67 | Guy Rodgers, Chi | 908 | 1998–99 | Jason Kidd, Phx | 10.8 |
| 1967–68 | Wilt Chamberlain, Phil | 702 | 1999–00 | Jason Kidd, Phx | 10.1 |
| 1968–69 | Oscar Robertson, Cin | 772 | 2000–01 | Jason Kidd, Phx | 9.8 |
| 1969–70 | Lenny Wilkens, Sea | *9.1 | 2001–02 | Andre Miller, Cle | 10.9 |
| 1970–71 | Norm Van Lier, Cin | 10.1 | 2002–03 | Jason Kidd, NJ | 8.9 |
| 1971–72 | Jerry West, LA | 9.7 | 2003–04 | Jason Kidd, NJ | 9.2 |
| 1972–73 | Nate Archibald, KC-Oma | 11.4 | 2004–05 | Steve Nash, Phx | 11.5 |
| 1973–74 | Ernie DiGregorio, Buf | 8.2 | 2005–06 | Steve Nash, Phx | 10.5 |
| 1974–75 | Kevin Porter, Wash | 8.0 | 2006–07 | Steve Nash, Phx | 11.6 |
| 1975–76 | Don Watts, Sea | 8.1 | 2007–08 | Chris Paul, NO | 11.6 |
| 1976–77 | Don Buse, Ind | 8.5 | 2008–09 | Chris Paul, NO | 11.0 |
| 1977–78 | Kevin Porter, NJ-Det | 10.2 | | | |

*Based on per game average since 1969–70.

### Field-Goal Percentage

| | | | | | |
|---|---|---|---|---|---|
| 1946–47 | Bob Feerick, Wash | 40.1 | 1978–79 | Cedric Maxwell, Bos | 58.4 |
| 1947–48 | Bob Feerick, Wash | 34.0 | 1979–80 | Cedric Maxwell, Bos | 60.9 |
| 1948–49 | Arnie Risen, Roch | 42.3 | 1980–81 | Artis Gilmore, Chi | 67.0 |
| 1949–50 | Alex Groza, Ind | 47.8 | 1981–82 | Artis Gilmore, Chi | 65.2 |
| 1950–51 | Alex Groza, Ind | 47.0 | 1982–83 | Artis Gilmore, SA | 62.6 |
| 1951–52 | Paul Arizin, Phil | 44.8 | 1983–84 | Artis Gilmore, SA | 63.1 |
| 1952–53 | Neil Johnston, Phil | 45.2 | 1984–85 | James Donaldson, LAC | 63.7 |
| 1953–54 | Ed Macauley, Bos | 48.6 | 1985–86 | Steve Johnson, SA | 63.2 |
| 1954–55 | Larry Foust, FW | 48.7 | 1986–87 | Kevin McHale, Bos | 60.4 |
| 1955–56 | Neil Johnston, Phil | 45.7 | 1987–88 | Kevin McHale, Bos | 60.4 |
| 1956–57 | Neil Johnston, Phil | 44.7 | 1988–89 | Dennis Rodman, Det | 59.5 |
| 1957–58 | Jack Twyman, Cin | 45.2 | 1989–90 | Mark West, Phx | 62.5 |
| 1958–59 | Ken Sears, NY | 49.0 | 1990–91 | Buck Williams, Port | 60.2 |
| 1959–60 | Ken Sears, NY | 47.7 | 1991–92 | Buck Williams, Port | 60.4 |
| 1960–61 | Wilt Chamberlain, Phil | 50.9 | 1992–93 | Cedric Ceballos, Phx | 57.6 |
| 1961–62 | Walt Bellamy, Chi | 51.9 | 1993–94 | Shaquille O'Neal, Orl | 59.9 |
| 1962–63 | Wilt Chamberlain, SF | 52.8 | 1994–95 | Chris Gatling, GS | 63.3 |
| 1963–64 | Jerry Lucas, Cin | 52.7 | 1995–96 | Gheorghe Muresan, Wash | 58.4 |
| 1964–65 | Wilt Chamberlain, SF-Phil | 51.0 | 1996–97 | Gheorghe Muresan, Wash | 60.4 |
| 1965–66 | Wilt Chamberlain, Phil | 54.0 | 1997–98 | Shaquille O'Neal, LAL | 58.4 |
| 1966–67 | Wilt Chamberlain, Phil | 68.3 | 1998–99 | Shaquille O'Neal, LAL | 57.6 |
| 1967–68 | Wilt Chamberlain, Phil | 59.5 | 1999–00 | Shaquille O'Neal, LAL | 57.4 |
| 1968–69 | Wilt Chamberlain, LAL | 58.3 | 2000–01 | Shaquille O'Neal, LAL | 57.2 |
| 1969–70 | Johnny Green, Cin | 55.9 | 2001–02 | Shaquille O'Neal, LAL | 57.9 |
| 1970–71 | Johnny Green, Cin | 58.7 | 2002–03 | Eddy Curry, Chi | 58.5 |
| 1971–72 | Wilt Chamberlain, LAL | 64.9 | 2003–04 | Shaquille O'Neal, LAL | 58.4 |
| 1972–73 | Wilt Chamberlain, LAL | 72.7 | 2004–05 | Shaquille O'Neal, Mia | 60.1 |
| 1973–74 | Bob McAdoo, Buf | 54.7 | 2005–06 | Shaquille O'Neal, Mia | 60.0 |
| 1974–75 | Don Nelson, Bos | 53.9 | 2006–07 | Mikki Moore, NJ | 60.9 |
| 1975–76 | Wes Unseld, Wash | 56.1 | 2007–08 | Andris Biedrins, GS | 62.6 |
| 1976–77 | Kareem Abdul-Jabbar, LAL | 57.9 | 2008–09 | Erick Dampier, Dal | 65.0 |
| 1977–78 | Bobby Jones, Den | 57.8 | | | |

## Free-Throw Percentage

| Season | Player | Pct | Season | Player | Pct |
|---|---|---|---|---|---|
| 1946–47 | Fred Scolari, Wash | 81.1 | 1978–79 | Rick Barry, Hou | 94.7 |
| 1947–48 | Bob Feerick, Wash | 78.8 | 1979–80 | Rick Barry, Hou | 93.5 |
| 1948–49 | Bob Feerick, Wash | 85.9 | 1980–81 | Calvin Murphy, Hou | 95.8 |
| 1949–50 | Max Zaslofsky, Chi | 84.3 | 1981–82 | Kyle Macy, Phx | 89.9 |
| 1950–51 | Joe Fulks, Phil | 85.5 | 1982–83 | Calvin Murphy, Hou | 92.0 |
| 1951–52 | Bob Wanzer, Roch | 90.4 | 1983–84 | Larry Bird, Bos | 88.8 |
| 1952–53 | Bill Sharman, Bos | 85.0 | 1984–85 | Kyle Macy, Phx | 90.7 |
| 1953–54 | Bill Sharman, Bos | 84.4 | 1985–86 | Larry Bird, Bos | 89.6 |
| 1954–55 | Bill Sharman, Bos | 89.7 | 1986–87 | Larry Bird, Bos | 91.0 |
| 1955–56 | Bill Sharman, Bos | 86.7 | 1987–88 | Jack Sikma, Mil | 92.2 |
| 1956–57 | Bill Sharman, Bos | 90.5 | 1988–89 | Magic Johnson, LAL | 91.1 |
| 1957–58 | Dolph Schayes, Syr | 90.4 | 1989–90 | Larry Bird, Bos | 93.0 |
| 1958–59 | Bill Sharman, Bos | 93.2 | 1990–91 | Reggie Miller, Ind | 91.8 |
| 1959–60 | Dolph Schayes, Syr | 89.3 | 1991–92 | Mark Price, Clev | 94.7 |
| 1960–61 | Bill Sharman, Bos | 92.1 | 1992–93 | Mark Price, Clev | 94.8 |
| 1961–62 | Dolph Schayes, Syr | 89.7 | 1993–94 | Mahmoud Abdul-Rauf, Den | 95.6 |
| 1962–63 | Larry Costello, Syr | 88.1 | 1994–95 | Spud Webb, Sac | 93.4 |
| 1963–64 | Oscar Robertson, Cin | 85.3 | 1995–96 | Mahmoud Abdul-Rauf, Den | 93.0 |
| 1964–65 | Larry Costello, Phil | 87.7 | 1996–97 | Mark Price, GS | 90.6 |
| 1965–66 | Larry Siegfried, Bos | 88.1 | 1997–98 | Chris Mullin, Ind | 93.9 |
| 1966–67 | Adrian Smith, Cin | 90.3 | 1998–99 | Reggie Miller, Ind | 91.5 |
| 1967–68 | Oscar Robertson, Cin | 87.3 | 1999–00 | Jeff Hornacek, Utah | 95.0 |
| 1968–69 | Larry Siegfried, Bos | 86.4 | 2000–01 | Reggie Miller, Ind | 92.8 |
| 1969–70 | Flynn Robinson, Mil | 89.8 | 2001–02 | Reggie Miller, Ind | 91.1 |
| 1970–71 | Chet Walker, Chi | 85.9 | 2002–03 | Allan Houston, NY | 91.9 |
| 1971–72 | Jack Marin, Balt | 89.4 | 2003–04 | Peja Stojakovic, Sac | 92.7 |
| 1972–73 | Rick Barry, GS | 90.2 | 2004–05 | Reggie Miller, Ind | 93.3 |
| 1973–74 | Ernie DiGregorio, Buf | 90.2 | 2005–06 | Steve Nash, Phx | 92.1 |
| 1974–75 | Rick Barry, GS | 90.4 | 2006–07 | Kyle Korver, Phil | 91.4 |
| 1975–76 | Rick Barry, GS | 92.3 | 2007–08 | Peja Stojakovic, NO | 92.9 |
| 1976–77 | Ernie DiGregorio, Buf | 94.5 | 2008–09 | Jose Calderon, Tor | 98.1 |
| 1977–78 | Rick Barry, GS | 92.4 | | | |

## Three-Point Field-Goal Percentage

| Season | Player | Pct | Season | Player | Pct |
|---|---|---|---|---|---|
| 1979–80 | Fred Brown, Sea | 44.3 | 1994–95 | Steve Kerr, Chi | 52.4 |
| 1980–81 | Brian Taylor, SD | 38.3 | 1995–96 | Tim Legler, Wash | 52.2 |
| 1981–82 | Campy Russell, NY | 43.9 | 1996–97 | Glen Rice, Cha | 47.0 |
| 1982–83 | Mike Dunleavy, SA | 34.5 | 1997–98 | Dale Ellis, Sea | 46.0 |
| 1983–84 | Darrell Griffith, Utah | 36.1 | 1998–99 | Dell Curry, Mil | 47.6 |
| 1984–85 | Byron Scott, LAL | 43.3 | 1999–00 | Hubert Davis, Dal | 49.1 |
| 1985–86 | Craig Hodges, Mil | 45.1 | 2000–01 | Brent Barry, Sea | 47.6 |
| 1986–87 | Kiki Vandeweghe, Por | 48.1 | 2001–02 | Steve Smith, SA | 47.2 |
| 1987–88 | Craig Hodges, Mil-Phx | 49.1 | 2002–03 | Bruce Bowen, SA | 44.1 |
| 1988–89 | Jon Sundvold, Mia | 52.2 | 2003–04 | Anthony Peeler, Sac | 48.2 |
| 1989–90 | Steve Kerr, Clev | 50.7 | 2004–05 | Fred Hoiberg, Min | 48.3 |
| 1990–91 | Jim Les, Sac | 46.1 | 2005–06 | Richard Hamilton, Det | 45.8 |
| 1991–92 | Dana Barros, Sea | 44.6 | 2006–07 | Jason Kapono, Mia | 51.4 |
| 1992–93 | Chris Mullin, GS | 45.1 | 2007–08 | Jason Kapono, Tor | 48.3 |
| 1993–94 | Tracy Murray, Por | 45.9 | 2008–09 | Anthony Morrow, GS | 46.7 |

## Steals

| Season | Player | Avg | Season | Player | Avg |
|---|---|---|---|---|---|
| 1973–74 | Larry Steele, Por | 2.68 | 1991–92 | John Stockton, Utah | 2.98 |
| 1974–75 | Rick Barry, GS | 2.85 | 1992–93 | Michael Jordan, Chi | 2.83 |
| 1975–76 | Don Watts, Sea | 3.18 | 1993–94 | Nate McMillan, Sea | 2.96 |
| 1976–77 | Don Buse, Ind | 3.47 | 1994–95 | Scottie Pippen, Chi | 2.94 |
| 1977–78 | Ron Lee, Phx | 2.74 | 1995–96 | Gary Payton, Sea | 2.85 |
| 1978–79 | M.L. Carr, Det | 2.46 | 1996–97 | Mookie Blaylock, Atl | 2.72 |
| 1979–80 | Micheal Ray Richardson, NY | 3.23 | 1997–98 | Mookie Blaylock, Atl | 2.61 |
| 1980–81 | Magic Johnson, LAL | 3.43 | 1998–99 | Kendall Gill, NJ | 2.68 |
| 1981–82 | Magic Johnson, LAL | 2.67 | 1999–00 | Eddie Jones, Cha | 2.67 |
| 1982–83 | Micheal Ray Richardson, GS-NJ | 2.84 | 2000–01 | Allen Iverson, Phil | 2.51 |
| 1983–84 | Rickey Green, Utah | 2.65 | 2001–02 | Allen Iverson, Phil | 2.80 |
| 1984–85 | Micheal Ray Richardson, NJ | 2.96 | 2002–03 | Allen Iverson, Phil | 2.74 |
| 1985–86 | Alvin Robertson, SA | 3.67 | 2003–04 | Baron Davis, NO | 2.36 |
| 1986–87 | Alvin Robertson, SA | 3.21 | 2004–05 | Larry Hughes, Wash | 2.89 |
| 1987–88 | Michael Jordan, Chi | 3.16 | 2005–06 | Gerald Wallace, Cha | 2.51 |
| 1988–89 | John Stockton, Utah | 3.21 | 2006–07 | Baron Davis, GS | 2.14 |
| 1989–90 | Michael Jordan, Chi | 2.77 | 2007–08 | Chris Paul, NO | 2.71 |
| 1990–91 | Alvin Robertson, Mil | 3.04 | 2008–09 | Chris Paul, NO | 2.77 |

## Blocked Shots

| | | |
|---|---|---|
| 1973–74 | Elmore Smith, LAL | 4.85 |
| 1974–75 | Kareem Abdul-Jabbar, Mil | 3.26 |
| 1975–76 | Kareem Abdul-Jabbar, LAL | 4.12 |
| 1976–77 | Bill Walton, Port | 3.25 |
| 1977–78 | George Johnson, NJ | 3.38 |
| 1978–79 | Kareem Abdul-Jabbar, LAL | 3.95 |
| 1979–80 | Kareem Abdul-Jabbar, LAL | 3.41 |
| 1980–81 | George Johnson, SA | 3.39 |
| 1981–82 | George Johnson, SA | 3.12 |
| 1982–83 | Wayne Rollins, Atl | 4.29 |
| 1983–84 | Mark Eaton, Utah | 4.28 |
| 1984–85 | Mark Eaton, Utah | 5.56 |
| 1985–86 | Manute Bol, Wash | 4.96 |
| 1986–87 | Mark Eaton, Utah | 4.06 |
| 1987–88 | Mark Eaton, Utah | 3.71 |
| 1988–89 | Manute Bol, GS | 4.31 |
| 1989–90 | Hakeem Olajuwon, Hou | 4.59 |
| 1990–91 | Hakeem Olajuwon, Hou | 3.95 |
| 1991–92 | David Robinson, SA | 4.49 |
| 1992–93 | Hakeem Olajuwon, Hou | 4.17 |
| 1993–94 | Dikembe Mutombo, Den | 4.10 |
| 1994–95 | Dikembe Mutombo, Den | 3.91 |
| 1995–96 | Dikembe Mutombo, Den | 4.49 |
| 1996–97 | Shawn Bradley, NJ | 3.40 |
| 1997–98 | Marcus Camby, Tor | 3.65 |
| 1998–99 | Alonzo Mourning, Mia | 3.91 |
| 1999–00 | Alonzo Mourning, Mia | 3.72 |
| 2000–01 | Theo Ratliff, Phil/Atl | 3.74 |
| 2001–02 | Ben Wallace, Det | 3.48 |
| 2002–03 | Theo Ratliff, Atl | 3.23 |
| 2003–04 | Theo Ratliff, Port | 3.61 |
| 2004–05 | Andrei Kirilenko, Utah | 3.32 |
| 2005–06 | Marcus Camby, Den | 3.29 |
| 2006–07 | Marcus Camby, Den | 3.30 |
| 2007–08 | Marcus Camby, Den | 3.61 |
| 2008–09 | Dwight Howard, Orl | 2.92 |

# NBA All-Star Game Results

| Year | Result | Site | Winning Coach | Most Valuable Player |
|---|---|---|---|---|
| 1951 | East 111, West 94 | Boston | Joe Lapchick | Ed Macauley, Bos |
| 1952 | East 108, West 91 | Boston | Al Cervi | Paul Arizin, Phil |
| 1953 | West 79, East 75 | Ft Wayne | John Kundla | George Mikan, Min |
| 1954 | East 98, West 93 (OT) | New York | Joe Lapchick | Bob Cousy, Bos |
| 1955 | East 100, West 91 | New York | Al Cervi | Bill Sharman, Bos |
| 1956 | West 108, East 94 | Rochester | Charley Eckman | Bob Pettit, StL |
| 1957 | East 109, West 97 | Boston | Red Auerbach | Bob Cousy, Bos |
| 1958 | East 130, West 118 | St Louis | Red Auerbach | Bob Pettit, StL |
| 1959 | West 124, East 108 | Detroit | Ed Macauley | B. Pettit, StL/ E. Baylor, Min |
| 1960 | East 125, West 115 | Philadelphia | Red Auerbach | Wilt Chamberlain, Phil |
| 1961 | West 153, East 131 | Syracuse | Paul Seymour | Oscar Robertson, Cin |
| 1962 | West 150, East 130 | St Louis | Fred Schaus | Bob Pettit, StL |
| 1963 | East 115, West 108 | Los Angeles | Red Auerbach | Bill Russell, Bos |
| 1964 | East 111, West 107 | Boston | Red Auerbach | Oscar Robertson, Cin |
| 1965 | East 124, West 123 | St Louis | Red Auerbach | Jerry Lucas, Cin |
| 1966 | East 137, West 94 | Cincinnati | Red Auerbach | Adrian Smith, Cin |
| 1967 | West 135, East 120 | San Francisco | Fred Schaus | Rick Barry, SF |
| 1968 | East 144, West 124 | New York | Alex Hannum | Hal Greer, Phil |
| 1969 | East 123, West 112 | Baltimore | Gene Shue | Oscar Robertson, Cin |
| 1970 | East 142, West 135 | Philadelphia | Red Holzman | Willis Reed, NY |
| 1971 | West 108, East 107 | San Diego | Larry Costello | Lenny Wilkens, Sea |
| 1972 | West 112, East 110 | Los Angeles | Bill Sharman | Jerry West, LA |
| 1973 | East 104, West 84 | Chicago | Tom Heinsohn | Dave Cowens, Bos |
| 1974 | West 134, East 123 | Seattle | Larry Costello | Bob Lanier, Det |
| 1975 | East 108, West 102 | Phxnix | K.C. Jones | Walt Frazier, NY |
| 1976 | East 123, West 109 | Philadelphia | Tom Heinsohn | Dave Bing, Wash |
| 1977 | West 125, East 124 | Milwaukee | Larry Brown | Julius Erving, Phil |
| 1978 | East 133, West 125 | Atlanta | Billy Cunningham | Randy Smith, Buff |
| 1979 | West 134, East 129 | Detroit | Lenny Wilkens | David Thompson, Den |
| 1980 | East 144, West 135 (OT) | Washington | Billy Cunningham | George Gervin, SA |
| 1981 | East 123, West 120 | Cleveland | Billy Cunningham | Nate Archibald, Bos |
| 1982 | East 120, West 118 | New Jersey | Bill Fitch | Larry Bird, Bos |
| 1983 | East 132, West 123 | Los Angeles | Billy Cunningham | Julius Erving, Phil |
| 1984 | East 154, West 145 (OT) | Denver | K.C. Jones | Isiah Thomas, Det |
| 1985 | West 140, East 129 | Indiana | Pat Riley | Ralph Sampson, Hou |
| 1986 | East 139, West 132 | Dallas | K.C. Jones | Isiah Thomas, Det |
| 1987 | West 154, East 149 (OT) | Seattle | Pat Riley | Tom Chambers, Sea |
| 1988 | East 138, West 133 | Chicago | Mike Fratello | Michael Jordan, Chi |
| 1989 | West 143, East 134 | Houston | Pat Riley | Karl Malone, Utah |
| 1990 | East 130, West 113 | Miami | Chuck Daly | Magic Johnson, LAL |
| 1991 | East 116, West 114 | Charlotte | Chris Ford | Charles Barkley, Phil |
| 1992 | West 153, East 113 | Orlando | Don Nelson | Magic Johnson, LAL |
| 1993 | West 135, East 132 | Salt Lake City | Paul Westphal | K. Malone/J. Stockton, Utah |
| 1994 | East 127, West 118 | Minneapolis | Lenny Wilkens | Scottie Pippen, Chi |

| Year | Result | Site | Winning Coach | Most Valuable Player |
|------|--------|------|---------------|----------------------|
| 1995 | West 139, East 112 | Phoenix | Paul Westphal | Mitch Richmond, Sac |
| 1996 | East 129, West 118 | San Antonio | Phil Jackson | Michael Jordan, Chi |
| 1997 | East 132, West 120 | Cleveland | Doug Collins | Glen Rice, Cha |
| 1998 | East 135, West 114 | New York | Larry Bird | Michael Jordan, Chi |
| 1999 | Cancelled due to lockout. | | | |
| 2000 | West 137, East 126 | Oakland | Phil Jackson | S. O'Neal, LAL/T. Duncan, SA |
| 2001 | East 111, West 110 | Washington | Larry Brown | Allen Iverson, Phill |
| 2002 | West 135, East 120 | Philadelphia | Don Nelson | Kobe Bryant, LAL |
| 2003 | West 155, East 145 (2OT) | Atlanta | Rick Adelman | Kevin Garnett, Min |
| 2004 | West 136, East 132 | Los Angeles | Flip Saunders | Shaquille O'Neal, LAL |
| 2005 | East 125, West 115 | Denver | Stan Van Gundy | Allen Iverson, Phil |
| 2006 | East 122, West 120 | Houston | Flip Saunders | LeBron James, Cle |
| 2007 | West 153, East 132 | Las Vegas | Mike D'Antoni | Kobe Bryant, Cle |
| 2008 | East 134, West 128 | New Orleans | Doc Rivers | LeBron James, Cle |
| 2009 | West 146, East 119 | Phoenix | Phil Jackson | K. Bryant, LAL/S. O'Neal, Phx |

# Members of the Basketball Hall of Fame

## Contributors

Senda Abbott (1984)
Clair F. Bee (1967)
Danny Biasone (2000)
Hubie Brown (2005)
Walter A. Brown (1965)
John W. Bunn (1964)
Jerry Colangelo (2004)
William Davidson (2008)
Bob Douglas (1971)
Al Duer (1981)
Wayne Embry (1999)
Clifford Fagan (1983)
Harry A. Fisher (1973)
Larry Fleisher (1991)
Dave Gavitt (2006)
Edward Gottlieb (1971)
Luther H. Gulick (1959)
Lester Harrison (1979)

Chick Hearn (2003)
Ferenc Hepp (1980)
Edward J. Hickox (1959)
Paul D. (Tony) Hinkle (1965)
Ned Irish (1964)
R. William Jones (1964)
J. Walter Kennedy (1980)
Meadowlark Lemon (2003)
Emil S. Liston (1974)
Earl Lloyd (2003)
Bill Mokray (1965)
Ralph Morgan (1959)
Frank Morgenweck (1962)
James Naismith (1959)
C.M. Newton (2000)
John J. O'Brien (1961)
Larry O'Brien (1991)
Harold G. Olsen (1959)

Maurice Podoloff (1973)
H. V. Porter (1960)
William A. Reid (1963)
Elmer Ripley (1972)
Lynn W. St. John (1962)
Abe Saperstein (1970)
Arthur A. Schabinger (1961)
Amos Alonzo Stagg (1959)
Boris Stankovic (1991)
Edward Steitz (1983)
Chuck Taylor (1968)
Bertha F. Teague (1984)
Oswald Tower (1959)
Arthur L. Trester (1961)
Dick Vitale (2008)
Clifford Wells (1971)
Lou Wilke (1982)
Fred Zollner (1999)

## Players

Kareem Abdul-Jabbar (1995)
Nate (Tiny) Archibald (1991)
Paul J. Arizin (1977)
Charles Barkley (2006)
Thomas B. Barlow (1980)
Rick Barry (1987)
Elgin Baylor (1976)
John Beckman (1972)
Walt Bellamy (1993)
Sergei Belov (1992)
Dave Bing (1990)
Larry Bird (1998)
Carol Blazejowski (1994)
Bennie Borgmann (1961)
Bill Bradley (1982)
Joseph Brennan (1974)
Al Cervi (1984)
Wilt Chamberlain (1978)
Charles (Tarzan) Cooper (1976)
Kresimir Cosic (1996)
Bob Cousy (1970)
Dave Cowens (1991)
Joan Crawford (1997)
Billy Cunningham (1986)

Denise Curry (1997)
Drazen Dalipagic (2004)
Adrian Dantley (2008)
Bob Davies (1969)
Forrest S. DeBernardi (1961)
Dave DeBusschere (1982)
H.G. (Dutch) Dehnert (1968)
Anne Donovan (1995)
Clyde Drexler (2004)
Joe Dumars (2006)
Paul Endacott (1971)
Alex English (1997)
Julius Erving (1993)
Patrick Ewing (2008)
Harold (Bud) Foster (1964)
Walter (Clyde) Frazier (1987)
Max (Marty) Friedman (1971)
Joe Fulks (1977)
Lauren (Laddie) Gale (1976)
Harry (the Horse) Gallatin (1991)
William Gates (1989)
George Gervin (1996)
Tom Gola (1975)
Gail Goodrich (1996)

Hal Greer (1981)
Robert (Ace) Gruenig (1963)
Clifford O. Hagan (1977)
Victor Hanson (1960)
Lusia Harris-Stewart (1992)
John Havlicek (1983)
Connie Hawkins (1992)
Elvin Hayes (1990)
Marques Haynes (1998)
Tom Heinsohn (1986)
Nat Holman (1964)
Robert J. Houbregs (1987)
Bailey Howell (1997)
Chuck Hyatt (1959)
Dan Issel (1993)
Harry (Buddy) Jeannette (1994)
Earvin (Magic) Johnson (2002)
William C. Johnson (1976)
D. Neil Johnston (1990)
K.C. Jones (1989)
Sam Jones (1983)
Michael Jordan (2009)
Edward (Moose) Krause (1975)
Bob Kurland (1961)

## Players *(Cont.)*

Bob Lanier (1992)
Joe Lapchick (1966)
Nancy Lieberman-Cline (1996)
Clyde Lovellette (1988)
Jerry Lucas (1979)
Angelo (Hank) Luisetti (1959)
C. Edward Macauley (1960)
Moses Malone (2001)
Peter P. Maravich (1987)
Hortencia Marcari (2005)
Slater Martin (1981)
Bob McAdoo (2000)
Branch McCracken (1960)
Jack McCracken (1962)
Bobby McDermott (1988)
Dick McGuire (1993)
Kevin McHale (1999)
Dino Meneghin (2003)
Ann Meyers (1993)
George L. Mikan (1959)
Vern Mikkelsen (1995)
Cheryl Miller (1995)
Earl Monroe (1990)

Calvin Murphy (1993)
Charles (Stretch) Murphy (1960)
Hakeem Olajuwon (2008)
H. O. (Pat) Page (1962)
Robert Parish (2003)
Drazen Petrovic (2002)
Bob Pettit (1970)
Andy Phillip (1961)
Jim Pollard (1977)
Frank Ramsey (1981)
Willis Reed (1981)
Arnie Risen (1998)
Oscar Robertson (1979)
David Robinson (2009)
John S. Roosma (1961)
Bill Russell (1974)
John (Honey) Russell (1964)
Adolph Schayes (1972)
Ernest J. Schmidt (1973)
John J. Schommer (1959)
Barney Sedran (1962)
Uljana Semjonova (1993)
Bill Sharman (1975)

Christian Steinmetz (1961)
Lusia Harris Stewart (1992)
John Stockton (2009)
Maurice Stokes (2004)
Isiah Thomas (2000)
David Thompson (1996)
John A. (Cat) Thompson (1962)
Nate Thurmond (1984)
Jack Twyman (1982)
Wes Unseld (1988)
Robert (Fuzzy) Vandivier (1974)
Edward A. Wachter (1961)
Bill Walton (1993)
Robert F. Wanzer (1987)
Jerry West (1979)
Nera White (1992)
Lenny Wilkens (1989)
Dominique Wilkins (2006)
Lynette Woodard (2004)
John R. Wooden (1960)
James Worthy (2003)
George (Bird) Yardley (1996)

## Coaches

Forest C. (Phog) Allen (1959)
Harold Anderson (1984)
Red Auerbach (1968)
Geno Auriemma (2006)
Leon Barmore (2003)
Sam Barry (1978)
Ernest A. Blood (1960)
Jim Boeheim (2005)
Larry Brown (2002)
Jim Calhoun (2005)
Howard G. Cann (1967)
H. Clifford Carlson (1959)
Lou Carnesecca (1992)
Ben Carnevale (1969)
Pete Carril (1997)
Everett Case (1981)
Van Chancellor (2007)
John Chaney (2001)
Jody Conradt (1998)
Denny Crum (1994)
Chuck Daly (1994)
Everett S. Dean (1966)
Antonio Diaz-Miguel (1997)
Edgar A. Diddle (1971)
Bruce Drake (1972)
Pedro Ferrandiz (2007)
Sandro Gamba (2006)
Clarence Gaines (1981)

Jack Gardner (1983)
Amory T. (Slats) Gill (1967)
Aleksandr Gomelsky (1995)
Sue Gunter (2005)
Alex Hannum (1998)
Marv Harshman (1984)
Don Haskins (1997)
Edgar S. Hickey (1978)
Howard A. Hobson (1965)
Red Holzman (1986)
Hank Iba (1968)
Phil Jackson (2007)
Alvin F. (Doggie) Julian (1967)
Frank W. Keaney (1960)
George E. Keogan (1961)
Bob Knight (1991)
Mike Krzyzewski (2001)
John Kundla (1995)
Ward L. Lambert (1960)
Harry Litwack (1975)
Kenneth D. Loeffler (1964)
A.C. (Dutch) Lonborg (1972)
John B. McLendon (1978)
Arad A. McCutchan (1980)
Al McGuire (1992)
Frank McGuire (1976)
Walter E. Meanwell (1959)
Raymond J. Meyer (1978)

Ralph Miller (1988)
Billie Moore (1999)
Peter F. Newell (1978)
Aleksandar Nikolic (1998)
Mirko Novosel (2007)
Lute Olson (2002)
Jack Ramsay (1992)
Pat Riley (2008)
Cesare Rubini (1994)
Adolph F. Rupp (1968)
Cathy Rush (2008)
Leonard D. Sachs (1961)
Bill Sharman (2004)
Everett F. Shelton (1979)
Jerry Sloan (2009)
Dean Smith (1982)
C. Vivian Stringer (2009)
Pat Summitt (2000)
Fred R. Taylor (1985)
John Thompson (1999)
Margaret Wade (1984)
Stanley H. Watts (1985)
Lenny Wilkens (1998)
Roy Williams (2007)
John R. Wooden (1972)
Morgan Wooten (2000)
Phil Woolpert (1992)
Kay Yow (2002)

## Referees

James E. Enright (1978)
George T. Hepbron (1960)
George Hoyt (1961)
Matthew P. Kennedy (1959)
Lloyd Leith (1982)
Zigmund J. Mihalik (1985)
John P. Nucatola (1977)

Ernest C. Quigley (1961)
Marvin Rudolph (2007)
J. Dallas Shirley (1979)
Earl Strom (1995)
David Tobey (1961)
David H. Walsh (1961)

## Teams

Buffalo Germans (1961)
First Team (1959)
Harlem Globetrotters (2002)
Original Celtics (1959)
Renaissance (1963)
1966 Texas Western (2007)

Note: Year of election in parentheses.

# American Basketball Association

## Champions

| Year | Champion | Series | Runner-up | Winning Coach |
|------|----------|--------|-----------|---------------|
| 1968 | Pittsburgh Pipers | 4–3 | New Orleans Bucs | Vince Cazetta |
| 1969 | Oakland Oaks | 4–1 | Indiana Pacers | Alex Hannum |
| 1970 | Indiana Pacers | 4–2 | Los Angeles Stars | Bob Leonard |
| 1971 | Utah Stars | 4–3 | Kentucky Colonels | Bill Sharman |
| 1972 | Indiana Pacers | 4–2 | New York Nets | Bob Leonard |
| 1973 | Indiana Pacers | 4–3 | Kentucky Colonels | Bob Leonard |
| 1974 | New York Nets | 4–1 | Utah Stars | Kevin Loughery |
| 1975 | Kentucky Colonels | 4–1 | Indiana Pacers | Hubie Brown |
| 1976 | New York Nets | 4–2 | Denver Nuggets | Kevin Loughery |

## ABA Postseason Awards

### Most Valuable Player

| | |
|---|---|
| 1967–68 | Connie Hawkins, Pitt |
| 1968–69 | Mel Daniels, Ind |
| 1969–70 | Spencer Haywood, Den |
| 1970–71 | Mel Daniels, Ind |
| 1971–72 | Artis Gilmore, Ken |
| 1972–73 | Billy Cunningham, Car |
| 1973–74 | Julius Erving, NY |
| 1974–75 | Julius Erving, NY |
| | George McGinnis, Ind |
| 1975–76 | Julius Erving, NY |

### Rookie of the Year

| | |
|---|---|
| 1967–68 | Mel Daniels, Minn |
| 1968–69 | Warren Armstrong, Oak |
| 1969–70 | Spencer Haywood, Den |
| 1970–71 | Charlie Scott, Vir |
| | Dan Issel, Ken |
| 1971–72 | Artis Gilmore, Ken |
| 1972–73 | Brian Taylor, NY |
| 1973–74 | Swen Nater, SA |
| 1974–75 | Marvin Barnes, StL |
| 1975–76 | David Thompson, Den |

### Coach of the Year

| | |
|---|---|
| 1967–68 | Vince Cazetta, Pitt |
| 1968–69 | Alex Hannum, Oak |
| 1969–70 | Bill Sharman, LA |
| | Joe Belmont, Den |
| 1970–71 | Al Bianchi, Vir |
| 1971–72 | Tom Nissalke, Dal |
| 1972–73 | Larry Brown, Car |
| 1973–74 | Babe McCarthy, Ken |
| | Joe Mullaney, Utah |
| 1974–75 | Larry Brown, Den |
| 1975–76 | Larry Brown, Den |

## ABA Season Leaders

### Scoring

| | | GP | Pts | Avg |
|---|---|----|-----|-----|
| 1967–68 | Connie Hawkins, Pitt | 70 | 1875 | 26.8 |
| 1968–69 | Rick Barry, Oak | 35 | 1190 | 34.0 |
| 1969–70 | Spencer Haywood, Den | 84 | 2519 | 30.0 |
| 1970–71 | Dan Issel, Ken | 83 | 2480 | 29.9 |
| 1971–72 | Charlie Scott, Vir | 79 | 2637 | 33.4 |
| 1972–73 | Julius Erving, Vir | 71 | 2268 | 31.9 |
| 1973–74 | Julius Erving, NY | 84 | 2299 | 27.4 |
| 1974–75 | George McGinnis, Ind | 79 | 2353 | 29.8 |
| 1975–76 | Julius Erving, NY | 84 | 2462 | 29.3 |

### Rebounds

| | | |
|---|---|---|
| 1967–68 | Mel Daniels, Minn | 15.6 |
| 1968–69 | Mel Daniels, Ind | 16.5 |
| 1969–70 | Spencer Haywood, Den | 19.5 |
| 1970–71 | Mel Daniels, Ind | 18.0 |
| 1971–72 | Artis Gilmore, Ken | 17.8 |
| 1972–73 | Artis Gilmore, Ken | 17.6 |
| 1973–74 | Artis Gilmore, Ken | 18.3 |
| 1974–75 | Swen Nater, SA | 16.4 |
| 1975–76 | Artis Gilmore, Ken | 15.5 |

### Assists

| | | |
|---|---|---|
| 1967–68 | Larry Brown, NO | 6.5 |
| 1968–69 | Larry Brown, Oak | 7.1 |
| 1969–70 | Larry Brown, Wash | 7.1 |
| 1970–71 | Bill Melchionni, NY | 8.3 |
| 1971–72 | Bill Melchionni, NY | 8.4 |
| 1972–73 | Bill Melchionni, NY | 7.4 |
| 1973–74 | Al Smith, Den | 8.2 |
| 1974–75 | Mack Calvin, Den | 7.7 |
| 1975–76 | Don Buse, Ind | 8.2 |

### Steals

| | | |
|---|---|---|
| 1973–74 | Ted McClain, Car | 2.98 |
| 1974–75 | Brian Taylor, NY | 2.80 |
| 1975–76 | Don Buse, Ind | 4.12 |

### Blocked Shots

| | | |
|---|---|---|
| 1973–74 | Caldwell Jones, SD | 4.00 |
| 1974–75 | Caldwell Jones, SD | 3.24 |
| 1975–76 | Billy Paultz, SA | 3.05 |

# World Championship of Basketball

| Year | Winner | Runner-Up | Score | Site |
|------|--------|-----------|-------|------|
| 1950 | Argentina | United States | † | Buenos Aires |
| 1954 | United States | Brazil | † | Rio de Janeiro |
| 1959 | Brazil | United States | † | Santiago, Chile |
| 1963 | Brazil | Yugoslavia | † | Rio de Janeiro |
| 1967 | Soviet Union | Yugoslavia | † | Montevideo, Uruguay |
| 1970 | Yugoslavia | Brazil | † | Ljubljana, Yugoslavia |
| 1974 | Soviet Union | Yugoslavia | † | San Juan |
| 1978 | Yugoslavia | Soviet Union | 82–81 (OT) | Manila |
| 1982 | Soviet Union | United States | 95–94 | Cali, Colombia |
| 1986 | United States | Soviet Union | 87–85 | Madrid |
| 1990 | Yugoslavia | Soviet Union | 92–75 | Buenos Aires |
| *1994 | United States | Russia | 137–91 | Toronto |
| †1998 | Yugoslavia | Russia | 64–62 | Athens |
| 2002 | Yugoslavia | Argentina | 84–77 (OT) | Indianapolis |
| 2006 | Spain | Greece | 70–47 | Saitama, Japan |

*U.S. professionals began competing in 1994.†In 1998, a labor dispute resulted in a boycott of the World Championship by NBA stars; the U.S. roster was filled by members of the CBA and European professional leagues and college players.
†Result determined by overall record in final round of competition.

Tyler Hansbrough
(with ball) led
North Carolina to its
second NCAA title in
five years

College Basketball

# Great Expectations

A season removed from an embarassing Final Four loss,
Tyler Hansbrough and several other Tar Heels starters
eschewed the lure of the NBA for a redemptive title run

## BY B.J. SCHECTER

THE MOST TALENTED TEAMS don't always win and that's why we love sports. But when you combine talent with determination and an unfailing will, it's a tough combination to overcome. Tyler Hansbrough returned to Chapel Hill, N.C., after North Carolina's humiliating 84–66 loss to Kansas in the 2008 Final Four and felt sick. He insisted to coach Roy Williams that he was coming back for his senior year, but Williams refused to believe him. Finally, one day in the weight room that spring, Hansbrough had enough of the doubting and was ready to make it official.

"I've been miserable for two weeks," Hansbrough told Williams. "I'm staying here, and I'm really happy for the first time since the end of the season. So why don't you go on upstairs and write something you think I'd say, and I'll stay here and finish my workout?"

Hansbrough, the 2007–08 Naismith Player of the Year, was the cornerstone of the Tar Heels, but it wasn't until Ty Lawson and Wayne Ellington pulled their names out of the NBA Draft an hour before the deadline that North Carolina became the prohibitive favorite. From that point on the Tar Heels were expected to win the national title

and some wondered whether they'd even lose a game.

The pressure was immense, but Hansbrough & Co. were extremely driven (they spent the offseason flipping 500-pound tractor tires around the Dean Dome) and not a even stress reaction condition in Hansbrough's right shin (which caused him to miss four games) or a Marcus Ginyard stress fracture (which would strip UNC of its best defensive player for the season) could slow the Heels down.

North Carolina drilled Michigan State at Ford Field in December in a dress rehearsal for the Final Four and then learned to play without Lawson, who suffered from turf toe late in the season and reaggravated the injury in the regular-season finale, a win over rival Duke. Lawson missed the ACC Tournament and the first two games of the NCAAs. Though North Carolina played well in his absence, the Tar Heels wouldn't be able to win the title without their floor leader.

Lawson returned for the Sweet 16 and it was like he never left. North Carolina played like the best team in the country and rolled into Detroit like a freight train. After routing Villanova in the national semifinal, the Tar Heels once again met Michigan State (after the Spartans upset UConn in the other

semifinal), which carried the hopes of a state in crisis and was playing a virtual home game. Williams knew that, on the 30th anniversary of Michigan State's last national title, and with the auto industry and economy in shambles, many were calling the Spartans a team of destiny.

"They have a lot of want-to," Williams told his team before the game. "They're playing for their state, their city, for the economy. Well, we're playing for ourselves and everything we've worked for. We're going to exceed their want-to. Invest everything. Don't come back in here with anything left."

The Tar Heels jumped on Michigan State from the start and, led by Ellington, who scored 17 of his 19 points in the first half, soon North Carolina ran the Spartans off the floor. The Tar Heels were simply too deep and too talented. The game was never in doubt and North Carolina cruised to an easy 89–72 victory to win its fifth national title. As the final buzzer sounded, Williams and Hansbrough embraced and the coach was thrilled that the senior who decided to come back ended his career on top.

"Once Tyler decided to come back, I wanted this kid to have the greatest senior year he could possibly have," said Williams.

**Paced by sophomore Maya Moore (r.), the 2009 NCAA Women's Player of the Year, the Huskies went undefeated, dominating the competition on their way to a sixth title.**

"Heck, I'm going to have more chances to win, but this is his last chance. And he's so special."

The UConn women were special once again as well. The Huskies have made national titles and undefeated seasons seem like old hat, but there was something more impressive about this Connecticut team. UConn won its sixth national title and completed its third undefeated season, winning by a mind-boggling average of 35.4 points per game. "I'm not going to say this team was better than the '95 team or the '02 team," said assistant Jamelle Elliott, who was a member of the '95 team and an assistant on the '02 team. "But the way we beat teams this year was really impressive. I don't remember going through the season and beating the Top 25 teams as badly as we beat them this year."

Led by player of the year Maya Moore (only a sophomore) and All-America players Renee Montgomery and Tina Charles, UConn had the star power and depth to overwhelm their opponents. The Huskies

"Our bottom teams would be middle to top tier anywhere else in the country, including the ACC," said Pitt point guard Levance Fields. "Quality teams like Georgetown and Notre Dame [struggled] because of how tough the league is."

Added Syracuse coach Jim Boeheim: "This is the best our conference has ever been." The Big East earned three No. 1 seeds in the NCAAs (Louisville, UConn and Pitt) and two teams from the conference, UConn and Villanova, made the Final Four.

As good as the Big East was, the SEC was as far down as it has been in years. The conference sent just three teams to the NCAA tournament and Kentucky missed the Big Dance for the first time since 1991. It was a sad moment for the blue blood of college basketball when coach Billy Gillespie was fired after just two seasons. Losing to the Gardner-Webbs of the world was simply unacceptable. Kentucky needed to make a big-name hire and found the perfect person in Memphis coach John Calipari, signing him to an astonishing eight-year, $35 million contract. Immediately, Calipari vowed to restore the culture of the program and bring championships to Lexington.

"I'm a regular guy, folks. I do not walk on water," Calipari said at his introductory press conference. "I do not have a magic wand. I'm day to day. I told Dr. Todd and Mitch, if you want something to happen in a year, do not hire me. That's not how I do things. But when we get it right, you notice we're No. 1 in the country, we're playing in Final Fours—when you get it right."

Williams and Auriemma got it right at North Carolina and UConn, respectively. Both teams fulfilled season-long expectations and the Huskies surpassed them. After all, despite what Auriemma might lead you to believe, you can't argue with perfection.

could run, score, wear teams down, and stifle them with defense. Still, coach Geno Auriemma pushed his troops hard, going so far as to make the Huskies do defensive slides for an entire 2½-hour practice after what he deemed was a lackluster effort in a win over LSU.

"The NBA is all about winning, but at this level winning doesn't make you happy," said Auriemma. "You can win, play lousy, and in my program, feel lousy. To me it's about: How good can we be?"

During the men's regular season, the most common question seemed to be 'Just how good is the Big East?' The super conference featured some of the best teams in the country (three of which reached No. 1) and every night was a battle. Even bottom feeders like St. John's, Rutgers and Seton Hall showed they could give the top teams a run. Some speculated that the conference would send a record nine teams to the NCAA tournament, but in the end the Big East sent just seven after Notre Dame and Providence weren't selected.

# FOR THE RECORD • 2008—2009

## NCAA Men's Championship Game Box Score

### North Carolina 89

| | Min | FG M-A | FT M-A | Reb O-T | A | PF | TP |
|---|---|---|---|---|---|---|---|
| D. Thompson | 23 | 3-8 | 3-4 | 0-3 | 0 | 4 | 9 |
| T. Hansbrough | 34 | 6-14 | 6-10 | 1-7 | 2 | 3 | 18 |
| T. Lawson | 37 | 3-10 | 15-18 | 0-4 | 6 | 0 | 21 |
| D. Green | 24 | 2-4 | 0-0 | 2-3 | 4 | 5 | 6 |
| W. Ellington | 35 | 7-12 | 2-2 | 2-4 | 0 | 2 | 19 |
| M. Campbell | 1 | 0-1 | 0-0 | 0-1 | 0 | 0 | 0 |
| B. Frasor | 23 | 1-2 | 0-0 | 1-1 | 1 | 3 | 2 |
| L. Drew II | 4 | 0-1 | 0-0 | 0-0 | 0 | 0 | 0 |
| J. Tanner | 1 | 0-0 | 0-0 | 0-0 | 0 | 0 | 0 |
| J. Watts | 1 | 1-2 | 0-0 | 1-1 | 0 | 0 | 2 |
| E. Davis | 14 | 5-7 | 1-4 | 2-8 | 0 | 4 | 11 |
| P. Moody | 1 | 0-0 | 0-0 | 0-0 | 0 | 0 | 0 |
| M. Copeland | 1 | 0-0 | 0-0 | 0-0 | 0 | 0 | 0 |
| T. Zeller | 1 | 0-0 | 1-2 | 0-1 | 0 | 1 | 1 |
| Totals | | 28-61 | 28-40 | 9-33 | 13 | 22 | 89 |

Percentages: FG-.459, FT-.700. 3-Point Goals: 5–12, .417 (T. Hansbrough 0–2, T. Lawson 0–3, D. Green 2–3, W. Ellington 3–3, B. Frasor 0–1). Team Rebounds: 0. Blocked Shots: 0. Turnovers: 7 (D. Thompson 2, T. Hansbrough 2, T. Lawson 1, D. Green 1). Steals: 9 (T. Lawson 8, D. Green 1). Technical Fouls: None.

Halftime: North Carolina 55, Michigan St 34.
Officials: Tom O'Neill, Curtis Shaw, Tony Greene.
A: 72,922.

### Michigan St 72

| | Min | FG M-A | FT M-A | Reb O-T | A | PF | TP |
|---|---|---|---|---|---|---|---|
| R. Morgan | 19 | 1-2 | 2-2 | 1-1 | 0 | 5 | 4 |
| D. Roe | 17 | 1-1 | 0-1 | 2-8 | 0 | 3 | 2 |
| G. Suton | 31 | 7-10 | 0-0 | 3-11 | 0 | 3 | 17 |
| K. Lucas | 35 | 4-12 | 6-8 | 0-0 | 7 | 2 | 14 |
| T. Walton | 24 | 0-2 | 2-2 | 0-1 | 3 | 3 | 2 |
| I. Ibok | 1 | 0-0 | 0-0 | 0-1 | 0 | 0 | 0 |
| C. Allen | 17 | 0-8 | 3-5 | 1-1 | 1 | 2 | 3 |
| A. Thornton | 3 | 0-1 | 2-2 | 0-3 | 0 | 1 | 2 |
| D. Summers | 21 | 4-10 | 3-4 | 2-5 | 2 | 1 | 13 |
| I. Dahlman | 1 | 1-1 | 0-0 | 1-1 | 0 | 0 | 2 |
| Dr. Green | 12 | 2-2 | 3-5 | 2-7 | 0 | 3 | 7 |
| J. Crandell | 1 | 0-0 | 0-0 | 0-0 | 0 | 0 | 0 |
| K. Lucious | 14 | 2-5 | 0-0 | 0-0 | 0 | 3 | 6 |
| T. Herzog | 1 | 0-0 | 0-0 | 0-0 | 0 | 0 | 0 |
| M. Gray | 3 | 0-1 | 0-0 | 1-1 | 0 | 2 | 0 |
| Totals | | 22-55 | 21-29 | 13-40 | 13 | 28 | 72 |

Percentages: FG-.400, FT-.724. 3-Point Goals: 7–23, .304 (G. Suton 3–4, K. Lucas 0–7, C. Allen 0–7, D. Summers 2–6, K. Lucious 2–5). Team Rebounds: 0. Blocked Shots: 5 (D. Roe 1, G. Suton 2, D. Summers 1, T. Herzog 1). Turnovers: 21 (R. Morgan 1, D. Roe 1, G. Suton 3, K. Lucas 6, T. Walton 4, D. Summers 2, Dr. Green 2, K. Lucious 2). Steals: 1 (Dr. Green 1). Technical Fouls: None.

## Final ESPN/USA Today Top 25 Poll

| | |
|---|---|
| 1. North Carolina (31) ..... 34–4 | 14. Purdue ..... 27–10 |
| 2. Michigan St ..... 31–7 | 15. Xavier ..... 27–8 |
| 3. Connecticut ..... 31–5 | 16. Washington ..... 26–9 |
| 4. Villanova ..... 30–8 | 17. LSU ..... 27–8 |
| 5. Louisville ..... 31–6 | 18. UCLA ..... 26–9 |
| 6. Pittsburgh ..... 31–5 | 19. Arizona St ..... 25–10 |
| 7. Oklahoma ..... 30–6 | 20. Wake Forest ..... 24–7 |
| 8. Missouri ..... 31–7 | 21. Marquette ..... 25–10 |
| 9. Memphis ..... 33–4 | 22. Florida St ..... 25–10 |
| 10. Kansas ..... 27–8 | 23. Texas ..... 23–12 |
| 11. Duke ..... 30–7 | 24. Arizona ..... 21–14 |
| 12. Syracuse ..... 28–10 | 25. Butler ..... 26–6 |
| 13. Gonzaga ..... 28–6 | |

## National Invitation Tournament Scores

**First round:** Penn St 77, George Mason 73 (OT); Rhode Island 68, Niagara 62; Florida 84, Jacksonville 62; Miami (Fla.) 78, Providence 66; Notre Dame 70, UAB 64; New Mexico 83, Nebraska 71; Kentucky 70, UNLV 60; Creighton 73, Bowling Green 71; St. Mary's 68, Washington St 57; Davidson 70, South Carolina 63; San Diego St 65, Weber St 49; Kansas St 83, Illinois St 79 (OT); Auburn 87, Tenn.-Martin 82; Tulsa 68, Northwestern 59; Virginia Tech 116, Duquesne 108 (2OT); Baylor 74, Georgetown 72.
**Second round:** Penn St 83, Rhode Island 72; Florida 74, Miami (Fla.) 60; Notre Dame 70, New Mexico 68; Kentucky 65, Creighton 63; St. Mary's 80, Davidson 68; San Diego St 70, Kansas St 52; Auburn 74, Tulsa 55; Baylor 84, Virginia Tech 66.
**Quarterfinals:** Penn St 71, Florida 62; Notre Dame 77, Kentucky 67; San Diego St 70, St. Mary's 66; Baylor 74, Auburn 72.
**Semifinals:** Penn St 67, Notre Dame 59; Baylor 76, San Diego St 62.
**Championship Game:** Penn St 69, Baylor 63.

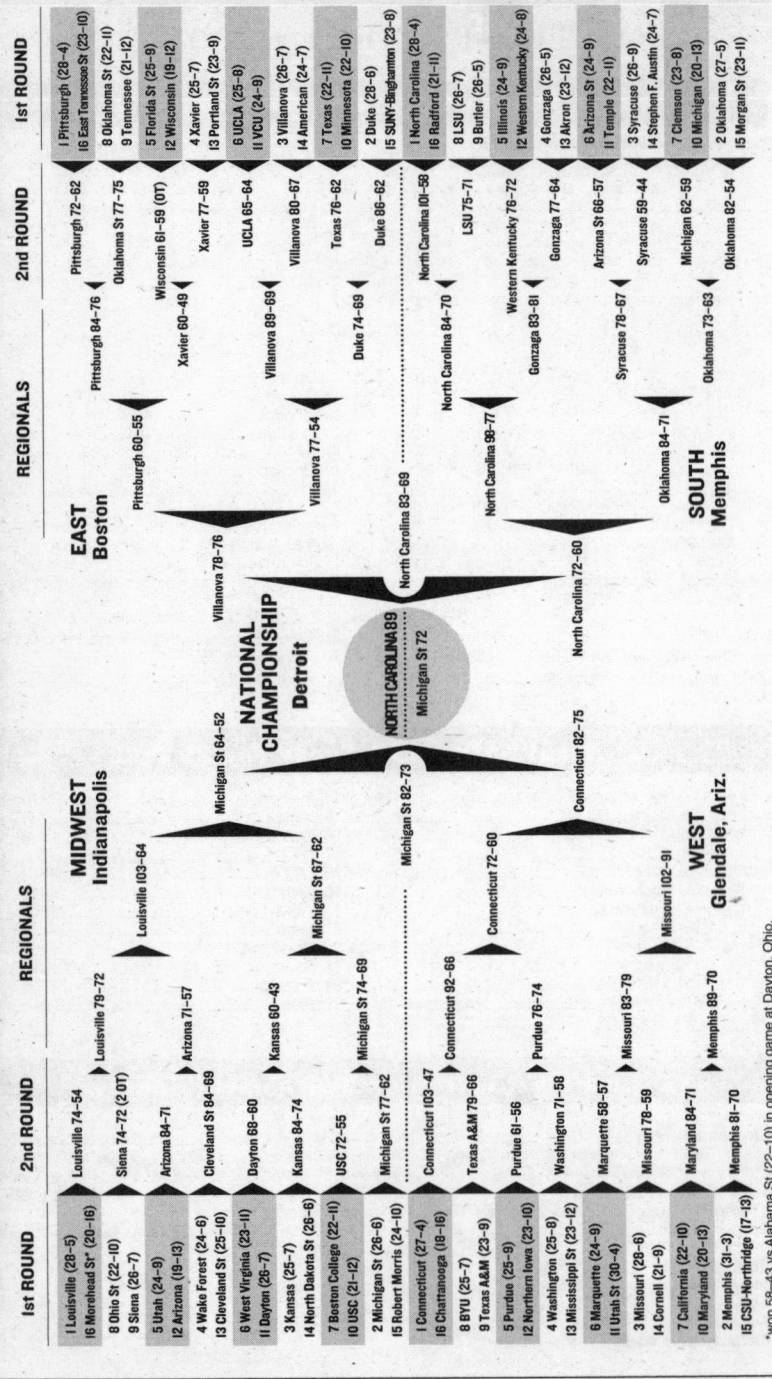

*won 58-43 vs Alabama St (22-10) in opening game at Dayton, Ohio.

## America East

| | Conference | | | All Games | | |
|---|---|---|---|---|---|---|
| | W | L | Pct | W | L | Pct |
| *SUNY-Binghamton | 13 | 3 | .813 | 23 | 8 | .742 |
| Vermont | 13 | 3 | .813 | 23 | 8 | .742 |
| Boston Univ. | 11 | 5 | .688 | 17 | 13 | .567 |
| SUNY-Stony Brook | 8 | 8 | .500 | 16 | 14 | .533 |
| New Hampshire | 8 | 8 | .500 | 14 | 16 | .467 |
| Md.-Baltimore Cty. | 7 | 9 | .438 | 15 | 17 | .469 |
| SUNY-Albany | 6 | 10 | .375 | 15 | 16 | .484 |
| Maine | 4 | 12 | .250 | 9 | 21 | .300 |
| Hartford | 2 | 14 | .125 | 7 | 21 | .212 |

## Atlantic Coast

| | Conference | | | All Games | | |
|---|---|---|---|---|---|---|
| | W | L | Pct | W | L | Pct |
| North Carolina | 13 | 3 | .813 | 28 | 4 | .875 |
| *Duke | 11 | 5 | .688 | 28 | 6 | .824 |
| Wake Forest | 11 | 5 | .688 | 24 | 6 | .800 |
| Florida St | 10 | 6 | .625 | 25 | 9 | .735 |
| Clemson | 9 | 7 | .563 | 23 | 8 | .742 |
| Boston College | 9 | 17 | .563 | 22 | 11 | .667 |
| Maryland | 7 | 9 | .438 | 20 | 13 | .606 |
| Miami (Fla.) | 7 | 9 | .438 | 18 | 12 | .600 |
| Virginia Tech | 7 | 9 | .438 | 18 | 14 | .563 |
| North Carolina St | 6 | 10 | .375 | 16 | 14 | .533 |
| Virginia | 4 | 12 | .250 | 10 | 18 | .357 |
| Georgia Tech | 2 | 14 | .125 | 12 | 19 | .387 |

## Atlantic Sun

| | Conference | | | All Games | | |
|---|---|---|---|---|---|---|
| | W | L | Pct | W | L | Pct |
| Jacksonville | 15 | 5 | .750 | 18 | 13 | .581 |
| *East Tennessee St | 14 | 6 | .700 | 23 | 10 | .697 |
| Belmont | 14 | 6 | .700 | 19 | 12 | .613 |
| Lipscomb | 12 | 8 | .600 | 17 | 14 | .548 |
| Mercer | 11 | 9 | .550 | 17 | 15 | .531 |
| Campbell | 11 | 9 | .550 | 14 | 16 | .467 |
| Stetson | 9 | 11 | .450 | 13 | 17 | .433 |
| S.C.-Upstate | 8 | 12 | .400 | 9 | 21 | .300 |
| Florida Gulf Coast | 7 | 13 | .350 | 11 | 20 | .355 |
| North Florida | 6 | 14 | .300 | 8 | 22 | .267 |
| Kennesaw St. | 3 | 17 | .150 | 7 | 22 | .241 |

## Atlantic 10

| | Conference | | | All Games | | |
|---|---|---|---|---|---|---|
| | W | L | Pct | W | L | Pct |
| Xavier | 12 | 4 | .750 | 25 | 7 | .781 |
| Dayton | 11 | 5 | .688 | 26 | 7 | .788 |
| Rhode Island | 11 | 5 | .688 | 22 | 10 | .688 |
| *Temple | 11 | 5 | .688 | 22 | 11 | .667 |
| Duquesne | 9 | 7 | .563 | 21 | 12 | .636 |
| La Salle | 9 | 7 | .563 | 18 | 13 | .581 |
| Richmond | 9 | 7 | .563 | 18 | 15 | .545 |
| St. Joseph's | 9 | 7 | .563 | 17 | 15 | .531 |
| St. Louis | 8 | 8 | .500 | 18 | 14 | .563 |
| Massachusetts | 7 | 9 | .438 | 12 | 18 | .400 |
| St. Bonaventure | 6 | 12 | .375 | 15 | 15 | .500 |
| Charlotte | 5 | 11 | .313 | 11 | 20 | .355 |
| George Washington | 4 | 12 | .250 | 10 | 18 | .357 |
| Fordham | 1 | 15 | .063 | 3 | 25 | .107 |

## Big East

| | Conference | | | All Games | | |
|---|---|---|---|---|---|---|
| | W | L | Pct | W | L | Pct |
| *Louisville | 16 | 2 | .889 | 28 | 5 | .848 |
| Pittsburgh | 15 | 3 | .833 | 28 | 4 | .875 |
| Connecticut | 15 | 3 | .833 | 27 | 4 | .871 |
| Villanova | 13 | 5 | .722 | 26 | 7 | .788 |
| Marquette | 12 | 6 | .667 | 24 | 9 | .727 |
| Syracuse | 11 | 7 | .611 | 26 | 9 | .743 |
| West Virginia | 10 | 8 | .556 | 23 | 11 | .676 |
| Providence | 10 | 8 | .556 | 19 | 13 | .594 |
| Notre Dame | 8 | 10 | .444 | 18 | 14 | .563 |
| Cincinnati | 8 | 10 | .444 | 18 | 14 | .563 |
| Georgetown | 7 | 11 | .389 | 16 | 14 | .533 |
| Seton Hall | 7 | 11 | .389 | 17 | 15 | .531 |
| St. John's | 6 | 12 | .333 | 16 | 17 | .485 |
| South Florida | 4 | 14 | .222 | 9 | 22 | .290 |
| Rutgers | 2 | 16 | .111 | 11 | 21 | .344 |
| DePaul | 0 | 18 | .000 | 9 | 24 | .273 |

## Big Sky

| | Conference | | | All Games | | |
|---|---|---|---|---|---|---|
| | W | L | Pct | W | L | Pct |
| Weber St | 15 | 1 | .938 | 21 | 9 | .700 |
| *Portland St | 14 | 5 | .688 | 23 | 9 | .719 |
| Montana | 11 | 5 | .688 | 17 | 12 | .586 |
| Idaho St | 9 | 7 | .563 | 13 | 19 | .406 |
| Northern Colorado | 8 | 8 | .500 | 14 | 18 | .438 |
| Montana St | 6 | 10 | .375 | 14 | 17 | .452 |
| Eastern Washington | 6 | 10 | .375 | 12 | 18 | .400 |
| Northern Arizona | 5 | 11 | .313 | 8 | 19 | .296 |
| Sacramento St | 1 | 15 | .063 | 2 | 27 | .069 |

## Big South

| | Conference | | | All Games | | |
|---|---|---|---|---|---|---|
| | W | L | Pct | W | L | Pct |
| *Radford | 15 | 3 | .833 | 21 | 11 | .656 |
| Virginia Military Inst. | 13 | 5 | .722 | 24 | 8 | .750 |
| Liberty | 12 | 6 | .667 | 22 | 11 | .667 |
| UNC-Asheville | 10 | 8 | .556 | 15 | 16 | .484 |
| Gardner-Webb | 9 | 7 | .500 | 13 | 17 | .433 |
| Presbyterian | 9 | 7 | .500 | 12 | 17 | .414 |
| Winthrop | 9 | 7 | .500 | 11 | 19 | .367 |
| Coastal Carolina | 5 | 13 | .278 | 11 | 20 | .355 |
| Charleston Southern | 4 | 14 | .222 | 9 | 20 | .310 |
| High Point | 4 | 14 | .222 | 9 | 21 | .300 |

## Big 10

| | Conference | | | All Games | | |
|---|---|---|---|---|---|---|
| | W | L | Pct | W | L | Pct |
| Michigan St | 15 | 3 | .833 | 26 | 6 | .813 |
| *Purdue | 11 | 7 | .611 | 25 | 9 | .735 |
| Illinois | 11 | 7 | .611 | 24 | 9 | .727 |
| Ohio St | 10 | 8 | .556 | 22 | 10 | .688 |
| Penn St | 10 | 8 | .556 | 22 | 11 | .667 |
| Wisconsin | 10 | 8 | .556 | 19 | 12 | .613 |
| Minnesota | 9 | 9 | .500 | 22 | 10 | .688 |
| Michigan | 9 | 9 | .500 | 20 | 13 | .606 |
| Northwestern | 8 | 10 | .444 | 17 | 13 | .567 |
| Iowa | 5 | 13 | .278 | 15 | 17 | .469 |
| Indiana | 1 | 17 | .056 | 6 | 25 | .194 |

Note: Standings based on regular-season conference play only; overall records include all tournament play.
*Conference tournament winner.

## Big 12

| | Conference | | | All Games | | |
|---|---|---|---|---|---|---|
| | W | L | Pct | W | L | Pct |
| Kansas | 14 | 2 | .875 | 25 | 7 | .781 |
| Oklahoma | 13 | 3 | .813 | 27 | 5 | .844 |
| *Missouri | 12 | 4 | .750 | 28 | 6 | .824 |
| Texas A&M | 9 | 7 | .563 | 23 | 9 | .719 |
| Oklahoma St | 9 | 7 | .563 | 22 | 11 | .667 |
| Texas | 9 | 7 | .563 | 22 | 11 | .667 |
| Kansas St | 9 | 7 | .563 | 21 | 11 | .656 |
| Nebraska | 8 | 8 | .500 | 18 | 12 | .600 |
| Baylor | 5 | 11 | .313 | 20 | 14 | .588 |
| Iowa St | 4 | 12 | .260 | 15 | 17 | .469 |
| Texas Tech | 3 | 13 | .188 | 14 | 19 | .424 |
| Colorado | 1 | 15 | .063 | 9 | 22 | .290 |

## Big West

| | Conference | | | All Games | | |
|---|---|---|---|---|---|---|
| | W | L | Pct | W | L | Pct |
| *CSU-Northridge | 11 | 5 | .688 | 17 | 13 | .567 |
| Pacific | 10 | 6 | .625 | 19 | 12 | .613 |
| Long Beach St | 10 | 6 | .625 | 15 | 15 | .500 |
| UC-Riverside | 8 | 8 | .500 | 17 | 13 | .567 |
| UC-Santa Barbara | 8 | 8 | .500 | 16 | 15 | .516 |
| UC-Irvine | 8 | 8 | .500 | 12 | 19 | .387 |
| *CSU-Fullerton | 7 | 9 | .438 | 15 | 17 | .469 |
| UC-Davis | 7 | 9 | .438 | 13 | 19 | .406 |
| Cal Poly | 3 | 13 | .188 | 7 | 21 | .250 |

## Colonial

| | Conference | | | All Games | | |
|---|---|---|---|---|---|---|
| | W | L | Pct | W | L | Pct |
| *VCU | 14 | 4 | .778 | 24 | 9 | .727 |
| George Mason | 13 | 5 | .722 | 22 | 10 | .688 |
| Old Dominion | 12 | 6 | .667 | 21 | 10 | .677 |
| Northeastern | 12 | 6 | .667 | 18 | 12 | .600 |
| Hofstra | 11 | 7 | .611 | 21 | 11 | .656 |
| Drexel | 10 | 8 | .556 | 15 | 14 | .517 |
| James Madison | 9 | 9 | .500 | 19 | 14 | .576 |
| Georgia St | 8 | 10 | .444 | 12 | 20 | .375 |
| Delaware | 6 | 12 | .333 | 13 | 19 | .406 |
| Towson | 5 | 13 | .278 | 12 | 22 | .353 |
| William & Mary | 5 | 13 | .278 | 10 | 20 | .333 |
| UNC-Wilmington | 3 | 15 | .167 | 7 | 25 | .219 |

## Conference USA

| | Conference | | | All Games | | |
|---|---|---|---|---|---|---|
| | W | L | Pct | W | L | Pct |
| *Memphis | 16 | 0 | 1.000 | 31 | 3 | .912 |
| Tulsa | 12 | 4 | .750 | 24 | 10 | .706 |
| UAB | 11 | 5 | .688 | 22 | 11 | .667 |
| Houston | 10 | 6 | .625 | 21 | 11 | .656 |
| UTEP | 10 | 6 | .625 | 19 | 12 | .613 |
| Central Florida | 7 | 9 | .438 | 17 | 14 | .548 |
| Marshall | 7 | 9 | .438 | 15 | 17 | .469 |
| Tulane | 7 | 9 | .438 | 14 | 17 | .452 |
| East Carolina | 5 | 11 | .313 | 13 | 17 | .433 |
| Southern Miss | 4 | 12 | .250 | 15 | 17 | .469 |
| Rice | 4 | 12 | .250 | 10 | 17 | .313 |
| SMU | 3 | 13 | .188 | 9 | 21 | .300 |

## Horizon League

| | Conference | | | All Games | | |
|---|---|---|---|---|---|---|
| | W | L | Pct | W | L | Pct |
| Butler | 15 | 3 | .833 | 26 | 5 | .839 |
| UW-Green Bay | 13 | 5 | .722 | 22 | 10 | .688 |
| *Cleveland St | 12 | 6 | .667 | 25 | 10 | .714 |
| Wright St | 12 | 6 | .667 | 20 | 13 | .606 |
| UW-Milwaukee | 11 | 7 | .611 | 17 | 14 | .548 |
| Ill.-Chicago | 7 | 11 | .389 | 16 | 15 | .516 |
| Youngstown St | 7 | 11 | .389 | 11 | 19 | .367 |
| Loyola (Ill.) | 6 | 12 | .333 | 14 | 18 | .438 |
| Valparaiso | 5 | 13 | .278 | 9 | 22 | .290 |
| Detroit | 2 | 16 | .111 | 7 | 23 | .233 |

## Ivy League†

| | Conference | | | All Games | | |
|---|---|---|---|---|---|---|
| | W | L | Pct | W | L | Pct |
| Cornell | 11 | 3 | .786 | 21 | 9 | .700 |
| Brown | 8 | 6 | .571 | 13 | 14 | .481 |
| Pennsylvania | 8 | 6 | .571 | 13 | 15 | .464 |
| Columbia | 7 | 7 | .500 | 12 | 16 | .429 |
| Yale | 7 | 7 | .500 | 9 | 19 | .321 |
| Dartmouth | 6 | 8 | .429 | 14 | 14 | .500 |
| Harvard | 6 | 8 | .429 | 10 | 18 | .357 |
| Princeton | 3 | 11 | .214 | 9 | 19 | .321 |

## Metro Atlantic

| | Conference | | | All Games | | |
|---|---|---|---|---|---|---|
| | W | L | Pct | W | L | Pct |
| *Siena | 16 | 2 | .889 | 26 | 7 | .788 |
| Niagara | 14 | 4 | .778 | 26 | 8 | .765 |
| Rider | 12 | 6 | .667 | 19 | 12 | .613 |
| Manhattan | 9 | 9 | .500 | 16 | 14 | .533 |
| Fairfield | 9 | 9 | .500 | 17 | 15 | .531 |
| St. Peter's | 8 | 10 | .444 | 11 | 19 | .367 |
| Iona | 7 | 11 | .389 | 12 | 19 | .387 |
| Loyola (Md.) | 7 | 11 | .389 | 12 | 20 | .375 |
| Canisius | 4 | 14 | .222 | 11 | 20 | .355 |
| Marist | 4 | 14 | .222 | 10 | 23 | .303 |

## Mid-American

| | Conference | | | All Games | | |
|---|---|---|---|---|---|---|
| EAST | W | L | Pct | W | L | Pct |
| Buffalo | 11 | 5 | .688 | 21 | 11 | .656 |
| Bowling Green | 11 | 5 | .688 | 19 | 13 | .594 |
| *Akron | 10 | 6 | .625 | 23 | 12 | .657 |
| Kent St | 10 | 6 | .625 | 19 | 14 | .576 |
| Miami (Ohio) | 10 | 6 | .625 | 17 | 13 | .567 |
| Ohio | 7 | 9 | .438 | 15 | 17 | .469 |
| **WEST** | | | | | | |
| Ball St | 7 | 9 | .438 | 14 | 17 | .452 |
| Central Michigan | 7 | 9 | .438 | 12 | 19 | .387 |
| Western Michigan | 7 | 9 | .438 | 10 | 21 | .323 |
| Eastern Michigan | 6 | 10 | .375 | 8 | 24 | .250 |
| Northern Illinois | 5 | 11 | .313 | 10 | 20 | .333 |
| Toledo | 5 | 11 | .313 | 7 | 25 | .219 |

*Conference tournament winner.
†Does not hold end-of-season conference tournament.

## Summit

| | Conference | | | All Games | | |
|---|---|---|---|---|---|---|
| | W | L | Pct | W | L | Pct |
| *North Dakota St | 16 | 2 | .889 | 26 | 6 | .813 |
| Oral Roberts | 14 | 4 | .778 | 16 | 15 | .516 |
| Oakland | 13 | 5 | .722 | 22 | 12 | .647 |
| IUPUI | 9 | 9 | .500 | 16 | 14 | .533 |
| IPFW | 8 | 10 | .444 | 13 | 17 | .433 |
| Southern Utah | 8 | 10 | .444 | 11 | 20 | .355 |
| South Dakota St | 7 | 11 | .389 | 13 | 20 | .394 |
| Western Illinois | 6 | 12 | .333 | 9 | 20 | .310 |
| Centenary | 6 | 12 | .333 | 8 | 23 | .258 |
| Mo.-Kansas City | 3 | 15 | .167 | 7 | 24 | .226 |

## Mid-Eastern Athletic

| | Conference | | | All Games | | |
|---|---|---|---|---|---|---|
| | W | L | Pct | W | L | Pct |
| *Morgan St | 13 | 3 | .813 | 23 | 11 | .676 |
| South Carolina St | 10 | 6 | .625 | 17 | 14 | .548 |
| Bethune-Cookman | 9 | 7 | .563 | 17 | 16 | .515 |
| North Carolina A&T | 9 | 7 | .563 | 16 | 16 | .500 |
| Norfolk St | 9 | 7 | .563 | 13 | 18 | .419 |
| *Coppin St | 9 | 7 | .563 | 13 | 19 | .406 |
| Hampton | 8 | 8 | .500 | 16 | 16 | .500 |
| Florida A&M | 6 | 10 | .375 | 10 | 21 | .323 |
| Howard | 6 | 10 | .375 | 8 | 23 | .258 |
| Delaware St | 6 | 10 | .375 | 8 | 24 | .250 |
| Md.-Eastern Shore | 3 | 13 | .188 | 7 | 23 | .233 |

## Missouri Valley

| | Conference | | | All Games | | |
|---|---|---|---|---|---|---|
| | W | L | Pct | W | L | Pct |
| Creighton | 14 | 4 | .778 | 26 | 7 | .788 |
| *Northern Iowa | 14 | 4 | .778 | 23 | 10 | .697 |
| Illinois St | 11 | 7 | .611 | 24 | 9 | .727 |
| Bradley | 10 | 8 | .556 | 18 | 14 | .563 |
| Evansville | 8 | 10 | .444 | 17 | 13 | .567 |
| Wichita St | 8 | 10 | .444 | 16 | 16 | .500 |
| Southern Illinois | 8 | 10 | .444 | 13 | 18 | .419 |
| Drake | 7 | 11 | .389 | 17 | 15 | .531 |
| Indiana St | 7 | 11 | .389 | 11 | 21 | .344 |
| Missouri St | 3 | 15 | .167 | 11 | 20 | .355 |

## Mountain West

| | Conference | | | All Games | | |
|---|---|---|---|---|---|---|
| | W | L | Pct | W | L | Pct |
| BYU | 12 | 4 | .750 | 25 | 7 | .781 |
| *Utah | 12 | 4 | .750 | 24 | 9 | .727 |
| New Mexico | 12 | 4 | .750 | 21 | 11 | .656 |
| San Diego St | 11 | 5 | .688 | 23 | 9 | .719 |
| UNLV | 9 | 7 | .563 | 21 | 10 | .677 |
| Wyoming | 7 | 9 | .438 | 19 | 13 | .594 |
| TCU | 5 | 11 | .313 | 14 | 17 | .452 |
| Colorado St | 4 | 12 | .250 | 9 | 22 | .290 |
| Air Force | 0 | 16 | .000 | 10 | 21 | .323 |

## Northeast

| | Conference | | | All Games | | |
|---|---|---|---|---|---|---|
| | W | L | Pct | W | L | Pct |
| *Robert Morris | 15 | 3 | .833 | 24 | 10 | .706 |
| Mount St. Mary's | 12 | 6 | .667 | 19 | 13 | .594 |
| Sacred Heart | 12 | 6 | .667 | 17 | 14 | .548 |
| Long Island | 12 | 6 | .667 | 16 | 14 | .533 |
| Quinnipiac | 10 | 8 | .556 | 15 | 16 | .484 |
| Wagner | 8 | 10 | .444 | 16 | 14 | .533 |
| Central Conn. St | 8 | 10 | .444 | 13 | 17 | .433 |
| St. Francis (N.Y.) | 7 | 11 | .389 | 10 | 20 | .333 |
| Monmouth | 6 | 12 | .333 | 8 | 23 | .258 |
| Fairleigh Dickinson | 6 | 12 | .333 | 7 | 23 | .233 |
| St. Francis (Pa.) | 3 | 15 | .167 | 6 | 23 | .207 |

## Ohio Valley

| | Conference | | | All Games | | |
|---|---|---|---|---|---|---|
| | W | L | Pct | W | L | Pct |
| Tenn.-Martin | 14 | 4 | .778 | 22 | 9 | .710 |
| Murray St | 13 | 5 | .722 | 19 | 12 | .613 |
| Austin Peay | 13 | 5 | .722 | 19 | 13 | .594 |
| *Morehead St | 12 | 6 | .667 | 19 | 15 | .559 |
| Eastern Kentucky | 10 | 8 | .556 | 18 | 13 | .581 |
| Tennessee St | 9 | 9 | .500 | 12 | 18 | .400 |
| Eastern Illinois | 8 | 10 | .444 | 12 | 18 | .400 |
| Tennessee Tech | 6 | 12 | .333 | 12 | 18 | .400 |
| Jacksonville St | 5 | 13 | .278 | 11 | 17 | .393 |
| SE Missouri St | 0 | 18 | .000 | 3 | 27 | .100 |

## Pac 10

| | Conference | | | All Games | | |
|---|---|---|---|---|---|---|
| | W | L | Pct | W | L | Pct |
| Washington | 14 | 4 | .778 | 25 | 8 | .758 |
| UCLA | 13 | 5 | .722 | 25 | 8 | .758 |
| Arizona St | 11 | 7 | .611 | 24 | 9 | .727 |
| California | 11 | 7 | .611 | 22 | 10 | .688 |
| *USC | 9 | 9 | .500 | 21 | 12 | .636 |
| Arizona | 9 | 9 | .500 | 19 | 13 | .594 |
| Washington St | 8 | 10 | .444 | 17 | 15 | .531 |
| Oregon St | 7 | 11 | .389 | 13 | 17 | .433 |
| Stanford | 6 | 12 | .333 | 18 | 13 | .581 |
| Oregon | 2 | 16 | .111 | 8 | 23 | .258 |

## Patriot League

| | Conference | | | All Games | | |
|---|---|---|---|---|---|---|
| | W | L | Pct | W | L | Pct |
| *American | 13 | 1 | .929 | 24 | 7 | .774 |
| Holy Cross | 11 | 3 | .786 | 18 | 14 | .563 |
| Navy | 8 | 6 | .571 | 19 | 11 | .633 |
| Army | 6 | 8 | .429 | 11 | 19 | .367 |
| Lehigh | 5 | 9 | .357 | 15 | 14 | .517 |
| Colgate | 5 | 9 | .357 | 10 | 20 | .333 |
| Lafayette | 4 | 10 | .286 | 8 | 22 | .267 |
| Bucknell | 4 | 10 | .286 | 7 | 23 | .233 |

*Conference tournament winner.

## Southeastern

| EAST | Conference | | | All Games | | |
|---|---|---|---|---|---|---|
| | W | L | Pct | W | L | Pct |
| South Carolina | 10 | 6 | .625 | 21 | 9 | .700 |
| Tennessee | 10 | 6 | .625 | 21 | 12 | .636 |
| Florida | 9 | 7 | .563 | 23 | 10 | .697 |
| Vanderbilt | 8 | 8 | .500 | 19 | 12 | .613 |
| Kentucky | 8 | 8 | .500 | 20 | 13 | .606 |
| Georgia | 3 | 13 | .188 | 12 | 20 | .375 |
| **WEST** | | | | | | |
| LSU | 13 | 3 | .813 | 26 | 7 | .788 |
| Auburn | 10 | 6 | .625 | 22 | 11 | .667 |
| *Mississippi St | 9 | 7 | .563 | 23 | 12 | .657 |
| Alabama | 7 | 9 | .438 | 18 | 14 | .563 |
| Mississippi | 7 | 9 | .438 | 16 | 15 | .516 |
| Arkansas | 2 | 14 | .125 | 14 | 16 | .467 |

## Southern

| NORTH | Conference | | | All Games | | |
|---|---|---|---|---|---|---|
| | W | L | Pct | W | L | Pct |
| *Chattanooga | 11 | 9 | .550 | 18 | 16 | .529 |
| Western Carolina | 11 | 9 | .550 | 16 | 15 | .516 |
| Samford | 9 | 11 | .450 | 16 | 16 | .500 |
| Appalachian St | 9 | 11 | .450 | 13 | 18 | .419 |
| Elon | 7 | 13 | .350 | 11 | 20 | .355 |
| UNC-Greensboro | 4 | 16 | .200 | 5 | 25 | .167 |
| **SOUTH** | | | | | | |
| Davidson | 18 | 2 | .900 | 26 | 7 | .788 |
| Coll. of Charleston | 15 | 5 | .750 | 26 | 8 | .765 |
| Citadel | 15 | 5 | .750 | 20 | 12 | .625 |
| Wofford | 12 | 8 | .600 | 16 | 14 | .533 |
| Georgia Southern | 5 | 15 | .250 | 8 | 22 | .267 |
| Furman | 4 | 16 | .200 | 6 | 24 | .200 |

## Southland

| EAST | Conference | | | All Games | | |
|---|---|---|---|---|---|---|
| | W | L | Pct | W | L | Pct |
| *Stephen F. Austin | 13 | 3 | .813 | 24 | 7 | .774 |
| Nicholls St | 12 | 4 | .750 | 20 | 11 | .645 |
| SE Louisiana | 7 | 9 | .438 | 13 | 17 | .433 |
| McNeese St | 5 | 11 | .313 | 11 | 18 | .379 |
| Northwestern St | 3 | 13 | .188 | 11 | 20 | .355 |
| Central Arkansas | 3 | 13 | .188 | 10 | 19 | .345 |
| **WEST** | | | | | | |
| Sam Houston St | 12 | 4 | .750 | 18 | 12 | .600 |
| Tex. A&M-Corp. Chrs. | 11 | 5 | .688 | 18 | 15 | .545 |
| Tex.-Arlington | 9 | 7 | .563 | 16 | 14 | .533 |
| Tex.-San Antonio | 8 | 8 | .500 | 19 | 13 | .594 |
| Texas St | 7 | 9 | .438 | 14 | 16 | .467 |
| Lamar | 6 | 10 | .375 | 15 | 15 | .500 |

## Southwestern Athletic

| | Conference | | | All Games | | |
|---|---|---|---|---|---|---|
| | W | L | Pct | W | L | Pct |
| *Alabama St | 16 | 2 | .899 | 22 | 9 | .710 |
| Jackson St | 15 | 3 | .833 | 18 | 15 | .545 |
| Prairie View A&M | 12 | 6 | .667 | 17 | 16 | .515 |
| Ark.-Pine Bluff | 11 | 7 | .611 | 13 | 18 | .419 |
| Southern Univ. | 8 | 10 | .444 | 8 | 23 | .258 |
| Mississippi Valley St | 7 | 11 | .389 | 7 | 25 | .219 |
| Texas Southern | 7 | 11 | .389 | 7 | 25 | .219 |
| Alabama A&M | 6 | 12 | .333 | 8 | 19 | .296 |
| Grambling St | 4 | 14 | .222 | 6 | 23 | .207 |
| Alcorn St | 4 | 14 | .222 | 6 | 25 | .194 |

## Sun Belt

| EAST | Conference | | | All Games | | |
|---|---|---|---|---|---|---|
| | W | L | Pct | W | L | Pct |
| *Western Kentucky | 15 | 3 | .833 | 24 | 8 | .750 |
| Troy | 14 | 4 | .778 | 19 | 12 | .613 |
| South Alabama | 10 | 8 | .556 | 20 | 13 | .606 |
| Mid. Tennessee St | 10 | 8 | .556 | 18 | 14 | .563 |
| Florida Int'l | 7 | 11 | .389 | 13 | 20 | .394 |
| Florida Atlantic | 2 | 16 | .111 | 6 | 26 | .188 |
| **WES** | | | | | | |
| Ark.-Little Rock | 15 | 3 | .833 | 23 | 8 | .742 |
| North Texas | 11 | 7 | .611 | 20 | 12 | .625 |
| Denver | 9 | 9 | .500 | 15 | 16 | .484 |
| La.-Lafayette | 7 | 11 | .389 | 10 | 20 | .333 |
| New Orleans | 6 | 12 | .333 | 11 | 19 | .367 |
| La.-Monroe | 6 | 12 | .333 | 10 | 20 | .333 |
| Arkansas St | 5 | 13 | .278 | 13 | 17 | .433 |

## West Coast

| | Conference | | | All Games | | |
|---|---|---|---|---|---|---|
| | W | L | Pct | W | L | Pct |
| *Gonzaga | 14 | 0 | 1.000 | 26 | 5 | .839 |
| St. Mary's (Ca.) | 10 | 4 | .714 | 26 | 6 | .813 |
| Portland | 9 | 5 | .643 | 19 | 12 | .613 |
| Santa Clara | 7 | 7 | .500 | 16 | 17 | .485 |
| San Diego | 6 | 8 | .429 | 16 | 16 | .500 |
| Pepperdine | 5 | 9 | .357 | 9 | 23 | .281 |
| San Francisco | 3 | 11 | .214 | 11 | 19 | .367 |
| Loyola Marymount | 2 | 12 | .143 | 3 | 28 | .097 |

## Western Athletic

| | Conference | | | All Games | | |
|---|---|---|---|---|---|---|
| | W | L | Pct | W | L | Pct |
| *Utah St | 14 | 2 | .875 | 30 | 4 | .882 |
| Nevada | 11 | 5 | .688 | 21 | 12 | .636 |
| Boise St | 9 | 7 | .563 | 19 | 12 | .613 |
| New Mexico St | 9 | 7 | .563 | 17 | 15 | .531 |
| Idaho | 9 | 7 | .563 | 16 | 15 | .516 |
| Louisiana Tech | 6 | 10 | .375 | 15 | 18 | .455 |
| San Jose St | 6 | 10 | .375 | 13 | 17 | .433 |
| Hawaii | 5 | 11 | .313 | 13 | 17 | .433 |
| Fresno St | 3 | 13 | .188 | 13 | 21 | .382 |

## Independents

| | All Games | | |
|---|---|---|---|
| | W | L | Pct |
| Seattle | 21 | 8 | .724 |
| South Dakota | 20 | 9 | .690 |
| Utah Valley St | 17 | 11 | .607 |
| Chicago St | 19 | 13 | .594 |
| North Dakota | 16 | 12 | .571 |
| Longwood | 17 | 14 | .548 |
| Savannah St | 15 | 14 | .517 |
| Tex.-Pan American | 10 | 17 | .370 |
| SIU-Edwardsville | 10 | 20 | .333 |
| CSU-Bakersfield | 8 | 21 | .276 |
| Bryant | 8 | 21 | .276 |
| Winston-Salem | 8 | 2 | .267 |
| Houston Baptist | 5 | 25 | .167 |
| North Carolina Central | 4 | 27 | .129 |
| New Jersey Inst. of Tech. | 1 | 30 | .032 |

*Conference tournament winner.

## Scoring

| | Class | GP | FG | 3FG | FT | Pts | Avg |
|---|---|---|---|---|---|---|---|
| Stephen Curry, Davidson. | Jr. | 34 | 312 | 130 | 220 | 974 | 28.6 |
| Lester Hudson, Tenn.-Martin | Sr. | 32 | 313 | 106 | 148 | 880 | 27.5 |
| Jermaine Taylor, Central Florida | Sr. | 31 | 291 | 92 | 138 | 812 | 26.2 |
| David Holston, Chicago St | Sr. | 32 | 269 | 147 | 145 | 830 | 25.9 |
| Stefon Jackson, UTEP | Sr. | 37 | 282 | 32 | 312 | 908 | 24.5 |
| Josh Akognon, Cal St-Fullerton | Sr. | 32 | 248 | 136 | 132 | 764 | 23.9 |
| Jodie Meeks, Kentucky | Jr. | 36 | 263 | 117 | 211 | 854 | 23.7 |
| Luke Harangody, Notre Dame | Jr. | 34 | 300 | 14 | 178 | 792 | 23.3 |
| Ben Woodside, North Dakota St | Sr. | 33 | 234 | 67 | 231 | 766 | 23.2 |
| Jeremy Hazell, Seton Hall | So. | 32 | 235 | 105 | 151 | 726 | 22.7 |
| Blake Griffin, Oklahoma | So. | 35 | 300 | 3 | 191 | 794 | 22.7 |
| Eric Maynor, VCU | Sr. | 34 | 248 | 66 | 198 | 760 | 22.4 |
| Chavis Holmes, Virginia Military Institute | Sr. | 31 | 212 | 83 | 174 | 681 | 22.0 |
| Drake Reed, Austin Peay | Sr. | 33 | 275 | 17 | 156 | 723 | 21.9 |
| Michael Deloach, Norfolk St | Sr. | 31 | 244 | 35 | 143 | 666 | 21.5 |
| Toney Douglas, Florida St | Sr. | 35 | 239 | 85 | 188 | 751 | 21.5 |
| Kevin Tiggs, East Tennessee St | Sr. | 34 | 248 | 37 | 196 | 729 | 21.4 |
| Marcus Thornton, LSU | Sr. | 35 | 256 | 78 | 149 | 739 | 21.1 |
| James Florence, Mercer | Jr. | 32 | 229 | 63 | 145 | 666 | 20.8 |
| Tyler Hansbrough, North Carolina | Sr. | 34 | 223 | 9 | 249 | 704 | 20.7 |
| Seth Curry, Liberty | Fr. | 35 | 243 | 102 | 119 | 707 | 20.2 |
| Craig Brackins, Iowa St | So. | 32 | 243 | 21 | 138 | 645 | 20.2 |
| Dior Lowhorn, San Francisco | Jr. | 30 | 231 | 38 | 104 | 604 | 20.1 |
| James Harden, Arizona St | So. | 35 | 221 | 58 | 204 | 704 | 20.1 |
| Troy Jackson, Alcorn St | Jr. | 30 | 193 | 36 | 178 | 600 | 20.0 |
| Darryl Proctor, Md.-Baltimore County | Sr. | 32 | 254 | 2 | 129 | 639 | 20.0 |
| D.J. Rivera, Binghamton | Jr. | 32 | 230 | 47 | 132 | 639 | 20.0 |
| Mike Rose, Eastern Kentucky | Sr. | 31 | 208 | 99 | 104 | 619 | 20.0 |

### FIELD-GOAL PERCENTAGE

| | Class | GP | FG | FGA | Pct |
|---|---|---|---|---|---|
| Jeff Pendergraph, Arizona St | Sr. | 35 | 198 | 300 | 66.0 |
| Blake Griffin, Oklahoma | So. | 35 | 300 | 459 | 65.4 |
| Joey Henley, Sacred Heart | Sr. | 31 | 196 | 313 | 62.6 |
| Keith Benson, Oakland | So. | 36 | 191 | 307 | 62.2 |
| Ahmad Nivins, St. Joseph's | Sr. | 32 | 205 | 335 | 61.2 |
| Marqus Blakely, Vermont | Jr. | 33 | 199 | 326 | 61.0 |
| Robert Glenn, IUPUI | Jr. | 30 | 155 | 254 | 61.0 |
| Luke Nevill, Utah | Sr. | 34 | 201 | 331 | 60.7 |
| Matt Mullery, Brown | Jr. | 28 | 174 | 287 | 60.6 |
| Justin Rutty, Quinnipiac | So. | 30 | 194 | 321 | 60.4 |

Note: Minimum 5 made per game.

### FREE-THROW PERCENTAGE

| | Class | GP | FT | FTA | Pct |
|---|---|---|---|---|---|
| Brett Harvey, Loyola (Md.) | Jr. | 32 | 142 | 156 | 91.0 |
| Josh White, North Texas | So. | 32 | 96 | 106 | 90.6 |
| Jodie Meeks, Kentucky | Jr. | 36 | 211 | 234 | 90.2 |
| Darren Collison, UCLA | Sr. | 35 | 113 | 126 | 89.7 |
| Alan Voskuil, Texas Tech | Sr. | 33 | 86 | 96 | 89.6 |
| David Kool, Western Michigan | Jr. | 31 | 161 | 180 | 89.4 |
| Josn Akognon, CSU-Fullerton | Sr. | 32 | 132 | 148 | 89.2 |
| Taylor Rochestie, Washington St | Sr. | 33 | 90 | 101 | 89.1 |
| Mike Schachtner, Green Bay | Sr. | 33 | 120 | 135 | 88.9 |
| Jack McClinton, Miami (Fla.) | Sr. | 32 | 116 | 131 | 88.5 |

Note: Minimum 2.5 made per game.

### REBOUNDS

| | Class | GP | Reb | Avg |
|---|---|---|---|---|
| Blake Griffin, Oklahoma | So. | 35 | 504 | 14.4 |
| John Bryant, Santa Clara | Sr. | 33 | 467 | 14.2 |
| Kenneth Faried, Morehead St | So. | 36 | 468 | 13.0 |
| DeJuan Blair, Pittsburgh | So. | 35 | 432 | 12.3 |
| Ahmad Nivins, St. Joseph's | Sr. | 32 | 378 | 11.8 |
| Luke Harangody, Notre Dame | Jr. | 34 | 401 | 11.8 |
| Jon Brockman, Washington | Sr. | 34 | 391 | 11.5 |
| Joseph Harris, Coastal Carolina | Sr. | 31 | 352 | 11.4 |
| Artsiom Parakhouski, Radford | Jr. | 33 | 369 | 11.2 |
| Cole Aldrich, Kansas | Sr. | 35 | 387 | 11.1 |

### ASSISTS

| | Class | GP | A | Avg |
|---|---|---|---|---|
| Jonathan Jones, Oakland | Jr. | 36 | 290 | 8.1 |
| Brock Young, East Carolina | So. | 30 | 227 | 7.6 |
| Levance Fields, Pittsburgh | Sr. | 36 | 270 | 7.5 |
| DiJuan Harris, Charlotte | Jr. | 31 | 223 | 7.2 |
| Ashton Mitchell, Sam Houston St | Jr. | 30 | 205 | 6.8 |
| Jonny Flynn, Syracuse | So. | 38 | 254 | 6.7 |
| Brandon Brooks, Alabama St | Sr. | 32 | 212 | 6.6 |
| Ty Lawson, North Carolina | Jr. | 35 | 230 | 6.6 |
| Chris Lowe, Massachusetts | Sr. | 30 | 193 | 6.4 |
| John Roberston, Texas Tech | Sr. | 33 | 212 | 6.4 |
| Nick Calathes, Florida | So. | 36 | 231 | 6.4 |
| Ronald Moore, Siena | Jr. | 35 | 224 | 6.4 |
| Julyan Stone, UTEP | So. | 37 | 236 | 6.4 |
| David Holston, Chicago St | Sr. | 32 | 204 | 6.4 |

*Includes games played in tournaments.

## THREE-POINT FIELD-GOAL PERCENTAGE

| | Class | GP | 3FG | 3FGA | Avg |
|---|---|---|---|---|---|
| Mike Rose, Eastern Kentucky ...Sr. | | 31 | 99 | 206 | 49.8 |
| Booker Woodfox, Creighton ......Sr. | | 34 | 91 | 191 | 48.0 |
| Jared Stohl, Portland...............So. | | 32 | 89 | 195 | 47.9 |
| Ryan Tillema, Green Bay...........Sr. | | 26 | 74 | 163 | 47.9 |
| Jimmy Baron, Rhode Island......Sr. | | 34 | 118 | 260 | 47.7 |
| Jack McClinton, Miami (Fla.)....Sr. | | 32 | 101 | 223 | 47.5 |
| Brandon Hazzard, Troy ..............Jr. | | 32 | 83 | 185 | 47.0 |
| Rihards Kuksiks, Arizona St........So. | | 34 | 93 | 210 | 46.9 |
| Chavis Holmes, Virg. Mil. Inst. ......Sr. | | 31 | 83 | 188 | 45.9 |
| Andrew Goudelock, Col. of Charl..So. | | 36 | 95 | 216 | 45.7 |

Note: Minimum 2.5 made per game.

## BLOCKED SHOTS

| | Class | GP | BS | Avg |
|---|---|---|---|---|
| Jarvis Varnado, Mississippi St.........Jr. | | 36 | 170 | 4.7 |
| Hasheem Thabeet, Connecticut......Jr. | | 36 | 152 | 4.2 |
| Tony Gaffney, Massachusetts..........Sr. | | 30 | 115 | 3.8 |
| Kleon Penn, McNeese St ................Sr. | | 29 | 102 | 3.5 |
| Taj Gibson, USC ..........................Jr. | | 35 | 100 | 2.9 |
| Cruz Daniels, High Point..................Jr. | | 30 | 83 | 2.8 |
| Chief Kickingstallionsims, Alabama St..Sr. | | 32 | 88 | 2.8 |
| Chris Johnson, LSU.........................Sr. | | 35 | 95 | 2.7 |
| Luke Nevill, Utah ...........................Sr. | | 34 | 92 | 2.7 |
| Larry Sanders, VCU ......................So. | | 34 | 92 | 2.7 |
| Andrew Nicholson, St. Bonaventure...Fr. | | 30 | 81 | 2.7 |
| Cole Aldrich, Kansas .....................So. | | 35 | 94 | 2.7 |
| Marqus Blakely, Vermont ................Jr. | | 33 | 88 | 2.7 |
| Thomas Coleman, N.C. A&T..........So. | | 31 | 85 | 2.7 |

## THREE-POINT FIELD GOALS MADE PER GAME

| | Class | GP | 3FG | Avg |
|---|---|---|---|---|
| David Holston, Chicago St ..............Sr. | | 32 | 147 | 4.6 |
| Josh Akognon, CSU-Fullerton .........Sr. | | 32 | 136 | 4.3 |
| Erik Kangas, Oakland .......................Sr. | | 35 | 135 | 3.9 |
| Stephen McDowell, Chattanooga ....Sr. | | 35 | 135 | 3.9 |
| Stephen Curry, Davidson .................Jr. | | 34 | 130 | 3.8 |
| Austin Kenon, Virginia Military Inst. So. | | 32 | 119 | 3.7 |
| Garrison Carr, American ..................Sr. | | 32 | 114 | 3.6 |
| Craig Moore, Northwestern ............Sr. | | 31 | 110 | 3.5 |
| Jimmy Baron, Rhode Island.............Sr. | | 34 | 118 | 3.5 |
| Kyle McAlarney, Notre Dame..........Sr. | | 36 | 124 | 3.4 |
| Jamarco Warren, Charleston South. ..So. | | 29 | 99 | 3.4 |

## STEALS

| | Class | GP | Stl | Avg |
|---|---|---|---|---|
| Chavis Holmes, Virginia Military Inst. ..Sr. | | 31 | 105 | 3.4 |
| Travis Holmes, Viginia Military Inst.....Sr. | | 27 | 87 | 3.2 |
| Devin Gibson, Tex.-San Antonio ...So. | | 27 | 82 | 3.0 |
| David Holston, Chicago St..............Sr. | | 32 | 97 | 3.0 |
| Cedric Jackson, Cleveland St.........Sr. | | 37 | 112 | 3.0 |
| Devan Downey, South Carolina .......Jr. | | 31 | 89 | 2.9 |
| Tywain McKee, Coppin St ..............Sr. | | 32 | 91 | 2.8 |
| Chase Adams, Centenary ...............Jr. | | 31 | 83 | 2.7 |
| Paul Gause, Seton Hall ...................Sr. | | 32 | 85 | 2.7 |
| Brigham Waginger, West. Carolina.....Jr. | | 31 | 71 | 2.6 |
| Kevin Palmer, Tex A&M-Corp. Chr....Jr. | | 33 | 86 | 2.6 |
| Tyrone Lewis, Niagara ....................Jr. | | 35 | 91 | 2.6 |

### Single-Game Highs

#### POINTS

60.........Ben Woodside, North Dakota St, Dec. 12, 2008  (vs Stephen F. Austin)
54.........Jodie Meeks, Kentucky, January 13, 2009 (vs Tennessee)
46.........Aaron Jackson, Duquesne, March 18, 2009 (vs Virginia Tech)
46.........Jodie Meeks, Kentucky, December 20, 2008 (vs Appalachian St)
45.........Jermaine Taylor, Central Florida, February 25, 2009 (vs Rice)
45.........Jodie Meeks, Kentucky, February 14, 2009 (vs Arkansas)

#### REBOUNDS

27.........John Bryant, Santa Clara, March 7, 2009 (vs San Diego)
25.........Chris Badley, Canisius, December 30, 2008, (vs Maine)
24.........Kenneth Faried, Morehead St, November 23, 2008 (vs Florida A&M)
23.........DeJuan Blair, Pittsburgh, February 16, 2009 (vs Connecticut)
23.........Blake Griffin, Oklahoma, February 14, 2009 (vs Texas Tech)

#### ASSISTS

17.........Michael Vogler, Troy, November 29, 2008 (vs Northwestern St)
16.........Levance Fields, Pittsburgh, February 7, 2009 (vs DePaul)
Five tied with15.

#### THREE POINT FIELD GOALS

11 ........Joey Mundweiler, Wagner, February 28, 2009 (vs Monmouth)
10.........Roburt Sallie, Memphis, March 19, 2009, (vs Cal St.-Northridge)
10 ........Courtney Pilgrim, East Tennessee St, February 28, 2009 (vs Mercer)
10.........Jodie Meeks, Kentucky, January 13, 2009 (vs Tennessee)
10 ........Kyle McAlarney, Notre Dame, November 26, 2008 (vs North Carolina)

#### STEALS

9..........Stephen Curry, Davidson, November 14, 2008 (vs Guilford)
Eleven tied with 8.

#### BLOCKED SHOTS

11 ........Chief Kickingstallionsims, Alabama St, February 7, 2009 (vs Ark.-Pine Bluff)
10.........Cole Aldrich, Kansas, March 22, 2009 (vs Dayton)
10 ........Hasheem Thabeet, Connecticut, January 31, 2009 (vs Providence)
Nine tied with 9.

## SCORING OFFENSE

| | GP | W | L | Pts | Avg |
|---|---|---|---|---|---|
| Virginia Military Institute | 32 | 24 | 8 | 3002 | 93.8 |
| North Carolina | 38 | 24 | 4 | 3413 | 89.8 |
| Chicago St | 32 | 19 | 13 | 2693 | 84.2 |
| Texas St | 30 | 14 | 16 | 2445 | 81.5 |
| Missouri | 38 | 31 | 7 | 3096 | 81.5 |
| Wake Forest | 31 | 24 | 7 | 2510 | 81.0 |
| Oklahoma St | 35 | 23 | 12 | 2830 | 80.9 |
| North Dakota St | 33 | 26 | 7 | 2659 | 80.6 |
| Syracuse | 38 | 28 | 10 | 3046 | 80.2 |
| Rhode Island | 34 | 23 | 11 | 2696 | 79.3 |

## SCORING DEFENSE

| | GP | W | L | Pts | Avg |
|---|---|---|---|---|---|
| Washington St | 33 | 17 | 16 | 1829 | 55.4 |
| Stephen F. Austin | 32 | 24 | 8 | 1795 | 56.1 |
| Illinois | 34 | 24 | 10 | 1944 | 57.2 |
| Princeton | 27 | 13 | 14 | 1545 | 57.2 |
| Wright St | 33 | 20 | 13 | 1897 | 57.5 |
| Butler | 32 | 26 | 6 | 1854 | 57.9 |
| Memphis | 37 | 33 | 4 | 2176 | 58.8 |
| Bethune-Cookman | 33 | 17 | 16 | 1941 | 58.8 |
| Miami (Ohio) | 30 | 17 | 13 | 1766 | 58.9 |
| Wisconsin | 33 | 20 | 13 | 1948 | 59.0 |

## SCORING MARGIN

| | Off | Def | Mar |
|---|---|---|---|
| North Carolina | 89.8 | 72.0 | 17.8 |
| Memphis | 75.1 | 58.8 | 16.3 |
| Gonzaga | 78.9 | 63.0 | 15.9 |
| Connecticut | 78.3 | 64.3 | 14.1 |
| Missouri | 81.5 | 67.7 | 13.8 |
| Pittsburgh | 77.4 | 64.4 | 13.0 |
| Louisville | 74.3 | 61.8 | 12.5 |
| Davidson | 77.8 | 65.9 | 11.9 |
| BYU | 77.1 | 65.2 | 11.9 |
| Duke | 77.5 | 65.9 | 11.6 |

## FIELD-GOAL PERCENTAGE

| | FGM | FGA | Pct |
|---|---|---|---|
| Utah St | 899 | 1813 | 49.6 |
| Oklahoma | 982 | 1997 | 49.2 |
| UCLA | 967 | 1973 | 49.0 |
| Wake Forest | 906 | 1849 | 49.0 |
| Gonzaga | 967 | 1982 | 48.8 |
| Syracuse | 1110 | 2277 | 48.7 |
| North Dakota St | 943 | 1936 | 48.7 |
| BYU | 909 | 1879 | 48.4 |
| Sacred Heart | 857 | 1772 | 48.4 |
| California | 892 | 1848 | 48.3 |

## FIELD-GOAL PERCENTAGE DEFENSE

| | Opp FG | Opp FGA | Opp Pct |
|---|---|---|---|
| Memphis | 755 | 2033 | 37.1 |
| Stephen F. Austin | 615 | 1634 | 37.6 |
| Connecticut | 888 | 2353 | 37.7 |
| Gonzaga | 748 | 1981 | 37.8 |
| Kansas | 773 | 2019 | 38.3 |
| Wright St | 633 | 1652 | 38.3 |
| Butler | 639 | 1659 | 38.5 |
| Xavier | 767 | 1985 | 38.6 |
| Florida St | 771 | 1994 | 38.7 |
| Washington St | 626 | 1616 | 38.7 |

## FREE-THROW PERCENTAGE

| | FT | FTA | Pct |
|---|---|---|---|
| Southern Utah | 484 | 608 | 79.6 |
| UW-Green Bay | 539 | 685 | 78.7 |
| Utah | 541 | 693 | 78.1 |
| UC-Davis | 508 | 652 | 77.9 |
| Loyola (Md.) | 522 | 673 | 77.6 |
| Kentucky | 601 | 777 | 77.3 |
| Washington St | 343 | 446 | 76.9 |
| Ill.-Chicago | 440 | 574 | 76.7 |
| Maryland | 463 | 611 | 75.8 |
| UC-Irvine | 397 | 524 | 75.8 |

## THREE-POINT FIELD GOALS MADE PER GAME

| | GP | 3FG | Avg |
|---|---|---|---|
| Virginia Military Institute | 32 | 438 | 13.7 |
| Eastern Kentucky | 31 | 320 | 10.3 |
| Belmont | 33 | 336 | 10.2 |
| Portland St | 33 | 317 | 9.6 |
| Oklahoma St | 35 | 327 | 9.3 |
| Liberty | 35 | 321 | 9.2 |
| Boston Univ. | 30 | 267 | 8.9 |
| Notre Dame | 36 | 319 | 8.9 |
| St. Francis (N.Y.) | 30 | 263 | 8.8 |
| Illinois St | 34 | 297 | 8.7 |
| Massachusetts | 30 | 262 | 8.7 |
| Michigan | 35 | 305 | 8.7 |
| Davidson | 35 | 305 | 8.7 |
| Duquesne | 34 | 296 | 8.7 |
| East Carolina | 30 | 261 | 8.7 |

## REBOUNDING MARGIN

| | GP | Reb | Opp Reb | Margin Avg |
|---|---|---|---|---|
| Michigan St | 38 | 1482 | 1128 | 9.3 |
| Pittsburgh | 36 | 1433 | 1099 | 9.3 |
| Connecticut | 36 | 1559 | 1237 | 8.9 |
| SUNY-Albany | 31 | 1206 | 937 | 8.7 |
| Xavier | 35 | 1378 | 1089 | 8.3 |
| Washington | 35 | 1437 | 1150 | 8.2 |
| Morehead St | 36 | 1400 | 1106 | 8.2 |
| Appalachian St | 31 | 1220 | 988 | 7.5 |
| South Carolina St | 31 | 1232 | 1002 | 7.4 |
| Kansas | 35 | 1371 | 1119 | 7.2 |

# 2009 NCAA Basketball Women's Division I Tournament

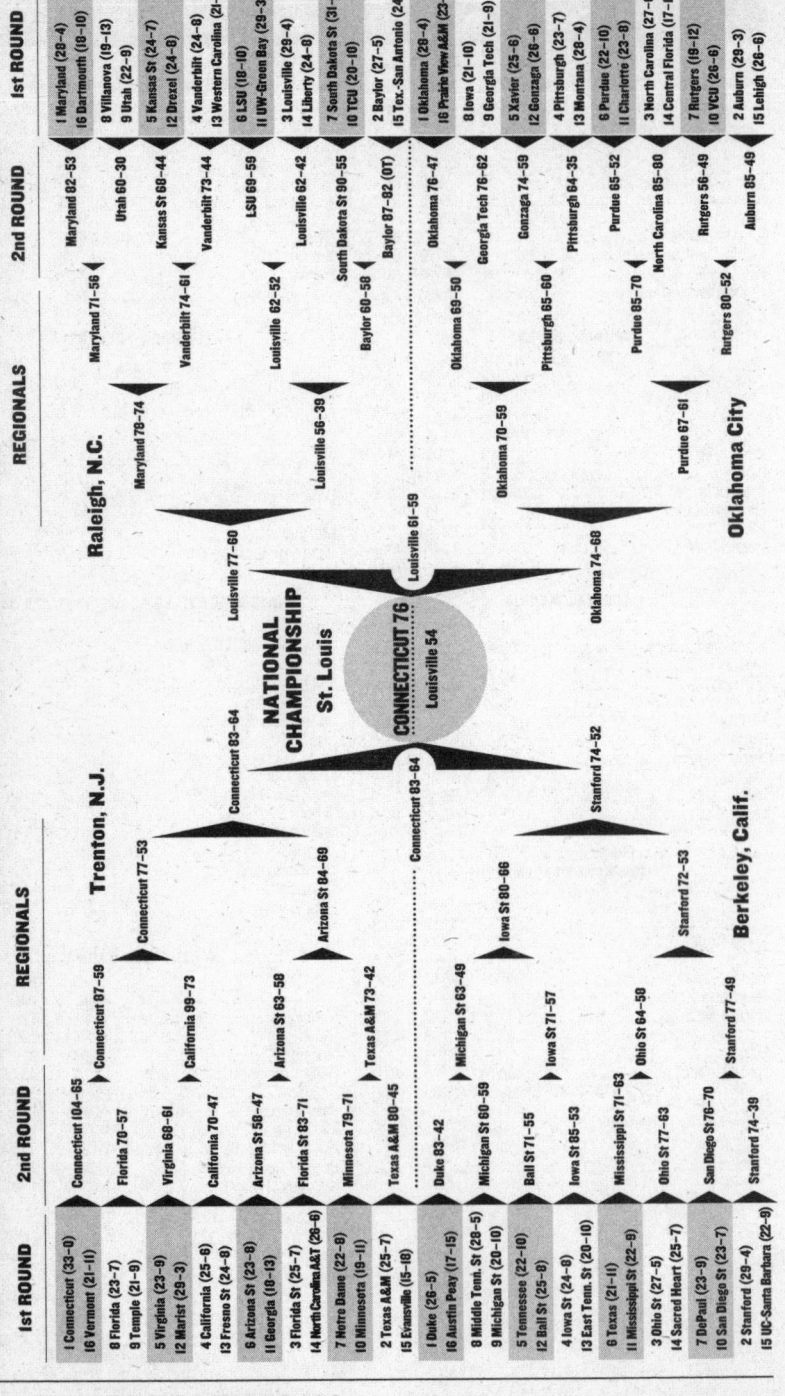

## 1st ROUND

1 Connecticut (33–0)
16 Vermont (21–11)
8 Florida (23–7)
9 Temple (21–9)
5 Virginia (23–9)
12 Marist (29–3)
4 California (25–6)
13 Fresno St (24–8)
6 Arizona St (23–8)
11 Georgia (18–13)
3 North Carolina A&T (26–6)
14 Notre Dame (22–8)
7 Minnesota (19–11)
10 Texas A&M (25–7)
2 Texas A&M (25–7)
15 Evansville (15–18)

1 Duke (26–5)
16 Austin Peay (17–15)
8 Middle Tenn. St (28–5)
9 Michigan St (20–10)
5 Tennessee (22–10)
12 Ball St (25–8)
4 Iowa St (24–8)
13 East Tenn. St (20–10)
6 Texas (21–11)
11 Mississippi St (22–9)
3 Ohio St (27–5)
14 Sacred Heart (25–7)
7 DePaul (23–9)
10 San Diego St (23–7)
2 Stanford (29–4)
15 UC-Santa Barbara (22–9)

## 2nd ROUND

Connecticut 104–65

Florida 70–57

Virginia 60–61

California 70–47

Arizona St 58–47

Florida St 83–71

Minnesota 79–71

Texas A&M 80–45

Duke 83–42

Michigan St 60–59

Ball St 71–55

Iowa St 85–53

Mississippi St 71–63

Ohio St 77–63

San Diego St 76–70

Stanford 74–39

## REGIONALS

### Trenton, N.J.

Connecticut 87–59

California 99–73

Arizona St 63–58

Texas A&M 73–42

Michigan St 63–49

Iowa St 71–57

Ohio St 64–58

Stanford 77–49

Connecticut 77–53

Arizona St 84–69

Iowa St 80–66

Stanford 72–53

Connecticut 83–64

Stanford 74–52

### Berkeley, Calif.

Connecticut 83–64

## NATIONAL CHAMPIONSHIP
### St. Louis

CONNECTICUT 76
Louisville 54

Louisville 77–60

Oklahoma 74–68

Louisville 61–59

## REGIONALS

### Raleigh, N.C.

Maryland 78–74

Louisville 56–39

Oklahoma 70–59

Purdue 67–61

### Oklahoma City

Maryland 71–56

Vanderbilt 74–61

Louisville 62–52

Baylor 60–58

Oklahoma 69–50

Pittsburgh 65–60

Purdue 85–70

Rutgers 56–49

## 2nd ROUND

Maryland 82–53

Utah 60–30

Kansas St 68–44

Vanderbilt 73–44

LSU 69–59

Louisville 62–42

South Dakota St 90–55

Baylor 87–82 (OT)

Oklahoma 76–47

Georgia Tech 76–62

Pittsburgh 64–35

Purdue 65–52

North Carolina 85–80

Rutgers 80–52

Auburn 85–49

## 1st ROUND

1 Maryland (28–4)
16 Dartmouth (10–18)
8 Villanova (19–13)
9 Utah (22–9)
5 Kansas St (24–7)
12 Drexel (24–8)
4 Vanderbilt (24–8)
13 Western Carolina (21–10)
6 LSU (18–10)
11 UW-Green Bay (29–3)
3 Louisville (29–4)
14 Liberty (24–8)
7 South Dakota St (31–2)
10 TCU (20–10)
2 Baylor (27–5)
15 Tex.-San Antonio (24–8)

1 Oklahoma (28–4)
16 Prairie View A&M (23–10)
8 Iowa (21–10)
9 Georgia Tech (21–9)
5 Xavier (25–6)
12 Gonzaga (26–6)
4 Pittsburgh (23–7)
13 Montana (28–4)
6 Purdue (22–10)
11 Charlotte (23–8)
3 North Carolina (27–6)
14 Central Florida (17–16)
7 Rutgers (19–12)
10 VCU (26–6)
2 Auburn (29–3)
15 Lehigh (26–6)

# NCAA Women's Championship Game Box Score

## Connecticut 76

| | Min | FG M-A | FT M-A | Reb O-T | A | PF | TP |
|---|---|---|---|---|---|---|---|
| M. Moore | 39 | 7–18 | 1–4 | 1–9 | 5 | 2 | 18 |
| T. Charles | 35 | 11–13 | 3–3 | 4–19 | 0 | 3 | 25 |
| T. Hayes | 31 | 2–4 | 0–0 | 0–1 | 4 | 2 | 15 |
| R. Montgomery | 39 | 5–14 | 6–10 | 0–3 | 4 | 1 | 18 |
| K. Greene | 37 | 4–7 | 1–1 | 4–5 | 2 | 3 | 9 |
| T. Williams | 1 | 0–0 | 0–0 | 1–1 | 0 | 0 | 0 |
| J. Fernandes | 1 | 0–0 | 0–0 | 0–0 | 0 | 0 | 0 |
| M. Gardler | 1 | 0–0 | 0–0 | 0–0 | 0 | 0 | 0 |
| L. Dixon | 1 | 0–1 | 0–0 | 0–0 | 0 | 0 | 0 |
| K. McLaren | 14 | 0–1 | 1–2 | 0–1 | 2 | 2 | 1 |
| C. Kerns | 1 | 0–0 | 0–0 | 0–0 | 0 | 0 | 0 |
| Totals | | 29–58 | 14–20 | 13–39 | 17 | 14 | 76 |

Percentages: FG-.500, FT-.700, 3-pt goals: 4–14, .286 (M. Moore 1–4, T. Hayes 1–2, R. Montgomery 2–7, L. Dixon 0–1). Blocked shots: 7 (M. Moore 1, T. Charles 1. K. McLaren 5). Turnovers: 12 (M. Moore 2, T. Charles 2, T. Hayes 1, R. Montgomery 5, K. Greene 1, K. McLaren 1). Steals: 6 (M. Moore 3, T. Hayes 2, R. Montgomery 3). Technical Fouls: None.

Halftime: Connecticut 39, Louisville 25.
Final Four Most Outstanding Player: Tina Charles.

## Louisville 54

| | Min | FG M-A | FT M-A | Reb O-T | A | PF | TP |
|---|---|---|---|---|---|---|---|
| C. Bingham | 33 | 4–14 | 2–2 | 7–11 | 0 | 2 | 10 |
| A. McCoughtry | 39 | 9–24 | 3–4 | 2–6 | 1 | 2 | 23 |
| G. Rucker | 6 | 1–1 | 0–0 | 1–1 | 0 | 0 | 2 |
| T. Stephen | 4 | 0–0 | 0–0 | 0–1 | 0 | 1 | 0 |
| D. Byrd | 34 | 1–10 | 0–0 | 1–5 | 4 | 5 | 2 |
| B. Burke | 36 | 2–4 | 0–0 | 2–3 | 1 | 2 | 5 |
| J. Howard | 5 | 1–2 | 0–0 | 0–0 | 0 | 1 | 3 |
| M. Jackson | 1 | 0–1 | 0–0 | 0–0 | 0 | 0 | 0 |
| L. Terry | 1 | 0–0 | 0–0 | 0–0 | 0 | 0 | 0 |
| M. Reid | 24 | 2–9 | 3–4 | 2–3 | 0 | 1 | 7 |
| K. Hines | 17 | 1–3 | 0–0 | 1–3 | 0 | 1 | 2 |
| Totals | | 21–68 | 8–10 | 16–33 | 6 | 15 | 54 |

Percentages: FG-.309, FT-.800, 3-pt goals: 4–11, .364 (C. Bingham 0–2, A. McCoughtry 2–4, B. Burke 1–3, J. Howard 1–2). Blocked shots: 0. Turnovers: 9 (C. Bingham 1, A. McCoughtry 3, T. Stephen 2, D. Byrd 3). Steals: 6 (A. McCoughtry 3, D. Byrd 1, B. Burke 1, K. Hines 1). Technical Fouls: 1 (Team).

Officials: Lisa Mattingly, Dee Kantner, Clarke Stevens.
A: 18,478.

# NCAA Women's Division I Individual Leaders

## SCORING

| Player and Team | Class | GP | TFG | 3FG | FT | Pts | Avg |
|---|---|---|---|---|---|---|---|
| Alysha Clark, Middle Tennessee St | Jr. | 34 | 343 | 12 | 237 | 935 | 27.5 |
| Dawn Evans, James Madison | So. | 31 | 246 | 92 | 154 | 738 | 23.8 |
| Gabriela Marginean, Drexel | Jr. | 33 | 252 | 22 | 243 | 769 | 23.3 |
| Angel McCoughtry, Louisville | Sr. | 39 | 329 | 43 | 200 | 901 | 23.1 |
| Andrea Riley, Oklahoma St | Jr. | 32 | 228 | 60 | 219 | 735 | 23.0 |
| Shavonte Zellous, Pittsburgh | Sr. | 33 | 245 | 59 | 198 | 747 | 22.6 |
| Ashley Nichole Hayes, Murray St | Sr. | 32 | 273 | 64 | 113 | 723 | 22.6 |
| Danielle McCray, Kansas | Jr. | 36 | 274 | 81 | 148 | 777 | 21.6 |
| DeWanna Bonner, Auburn | Sr. | 34 | 239 | 20 | 218 | 716 | 21.1 |
| Amber Guffey, Murray St | Sr. | 32 | 197 | 57 | 221 | 672 | 21.0 |
| Jantel Lavender, Ohio St | So. | 35 | 290 | 0 | 148 | 728 | 20.8 |
| Sade Logan, Robert Morris | Sr. | 24 | 177 | 79 | 66 | 499 | 20.8 |
| Monica Wright, Virginia | Jr. | 34 | 271 | 37 | 117 | 696 | 20.5 |
| Rachele Fitz, Marist | Jr. | 33 | 251 | 4 | 169 | 675 | 20.5 |
| Carlee Cassidy, Md.-Baltimore County | Jr. | 30 | 179 | 90 | 175 | 613 | 20.4 |
| Megan Frazee, Liberty | Sr. | 25 | 185 | 27 | 99 | 496 | 19.8 |
| Ashley Walker, California | Sr. | 34 | 264 | 13 | 131 | 672 | 19.8 |
| Tyra Grant, Penn St | Jr. | 29 | 201 | 55 | 110 | 567 | 19.6 |
| Epiphanny Price, Rutgers | Jr. | 33 | 216 | 46 | 166 | 644 | 19.5 |
| Heather Bowman, Gonzaga | Jr. | 33 | 237 | 1 | 166 | 641 | 19.4 |
| Britney Jones, UAB | Sr. | 30 | 208 | 46 | 120 | 582 | 19.4 |
| Maya Moore, Connecticut | So. | 39 | 284 | 90 | 96 | 754 | 19.3 |
| Kara Murphy, Akron | So. | 30 | 186 | 42 | 166 | 580 | 19.3 |
| Kara Ayers, St. Francis (N.Y.) | Sr. | 26 | 158 | 47 | 137 | 500 | 19.2 |
| Theresa Lisch, St. Louis | Jr. | 30 | 173 | 59 | 169 | 574 | 19.1 |

## FIELD-GOAL PERCENTAGE

| Player and Team | Class | GP | FG | FGA | Pct |
|---|---|---|---|---|---|
| Carolyn Swords, Boston College | So. | 35 | 230 | 339 | 67.8 |
| Natasha Williams, DePaul | Sr. | 31 | 191 | 308 | 62.0 |
| Tina Charles, Connecticut | Jr. | 39 | 259 | 418 | 62.0 |
| Ta'Shia Phillips, Xavier | So. | 32 | 184 | 300 | 61.3 |
| Alysha Clark, Middle Tenn. St | Jr. | 34 | 343 | 565 | 60.7 |
| Marshae Dotson, Florida | So. | 32 | 181 | 300 | 60.3 |
| Jayne Appel, Stanford | Jr. | 38 | 251 | 417 | 60.2 |
| Rachele Fitz, Marist | Jr. | 33 | 251 | 420 | 59.8 |
| Kourtney Brown, Buffalo | So. | 32 | 220 | 376 | 58.5 |
| Jessica Adair, Geo. Washington | Sr. | 31 | 167 | 286 | 58.4 |
| Jess Fuller, Hofstra | Jr. | 30 | 150 | 257 | 58.4 |

Note: Minimum 5 FG per game.

## REBOUNDS

| Player and Team | Class | GP | Reb | Avg |
|---|---|---|---|---|
| Judie Lomax, Connecitcut | So. | 28 | 401 | 14.3 |
| Courtney Paris, Oklahoma | Sr. | 37 | 503 | 13.6 |
| Phyllisha Mitchell, Tenn.-Martin | Sr. | 29 | 372 | 12.8 |
| Ta'Shia Phillips, Xavier | So. | 32 | 286 | 12.1 |
| Arnika Brown, Western Kentucky | So. | 29 | 337 | 11.6 |
| Ify Ibekwe, Arizona | So. | 29 | 336 | 11.6 |
| Emma Cannon, Central Florida | So. | 34 | 393 | 11.6 |
| Tiffany Benson, William & Mary | Jr. | 31 | 357 | 11.5 |
| Yinka Olorunnife, Idaho | So | 28 | 311 | 11.1 |
| Jernisha Cann, IUPUI | Sr. | 29 | 315 | 10.9 |

## FREE-THROW PERCENTAGE

| Player and Team | Class | GP | FT | FTA | Pct |
|---|---|---|---|---|---|
| Lauren Prochaska, Bowl. Green | So. | 34 | 167 | 179 | 93.3 |
| Morgan Warburton, Utah | Sr. | 33 | 161 | 178 | 90.4 |
| Emily London, Samford | So. | 29 | 83 | 92 | 90.2 |
| Danielle Robinson, Oklahoma | So. | 37 | 119 | 132 | 90.2 |
| Mercedes Fox-Griffin, Oregon St | Sr. | 32 | 81 | 90 | 90.0 |
| Jessica Pike, Oakland | Sr. | 31 | 88 | 98 | 89.8 |
| Gabriela Marginean, Drexel | Jr. | 33 | 243 | 271 | 89.7 |
| Amber Guffey, Murray St | Jr. | 32 | 122 | 137 | 89.1 |
| Theresa Lisch, St. Louis | Jr. | 30 | 169 | 190 | 88.9 |
| Dymond Simon, Arizona St | Jr. | 29 | 90 | 102 | 88.2 |

Note: Minimum 2.5 made per game.

## ASSISTS

| Player and Team | Class | GP | Ast | Avg |
|---|---|---|---|---|
| Whitney Boddie, Auburn | Sr. | 33 | 262 | 7.9 |
| Shalee Lehning, Kansas St | Sr. | 30 | 229 | 7.6 |
| Courtney Vandersloot, Gonzaga | So. | 32 | 239 | 7.5 |
| Monica Gibbs, Tex.-San Antonio | Sr. | 33 | 221 | 6.7 |
| Tonya Schnibbe, Weber St | Jr. | 29 | 194 | 6.7 |
| Claire Faucher, Portland St | Jr. | 33 | 220 | 6.7 |
| Marisah Henderson, Wichita St | Jr. | 31 | 205 | 6.6 |
| Tonicia Tademy, CSU-Northridge | Sr. | 31 | 204 | 6.6 |
| Skye Johnson, Bradley | Jr. | 31 | 196 | 6.3 |
| Andrea Riley, Oklahoma St | Jr. | 32 | 193 | 6.0 |
| Andrea Barber, Southern Miss. | Sr. | 28 | 167 | 6.0 |

## THREE-POINT FIELD-GOAL PERCENTAGE

| Player and Team | Class | GP | 3FG | 3FGA | Pct |
|---|---|---|---|---|---|
| Melissa Liebschwager, Furman | Sr. | 30 | 70 | 149 | 47.0 |
| Emily London, Samford | So. | 29 | 64 | 138 | 46.4 |
| Jill Young, South Dakota St | Sr. | 34 | 82 | 178 | 46.1 |
| Jena Stutzman, Kent St | Fr. | 29 | 68 | 154 | 44.2 |
| Maggie McCloskey, Loyola (Ill.) | Jr. | 28 | 78 | 178 | 43.8 |
| Jessica Williams, Toledo | So. | 31 | 62 | 143 | 43.4 |
| Amber Bland, N.C. A&T | Sr. | 32 | 66 | 153 | 43.1 |
| Tracy Pontius, Bowling Green | So. | 34 | 77 | 179 | 43.0 |
| Alexandra Thompson, Davidson | Jr. | 30 | 65 | 152 | 42.8 |
| Dietra Caldwell, UTEP | Fr. | 29 | 64 | 150 | 42.7 |

Note: Minimum 2.0 made per game.

## BLOCKED SHOTS

| Player and Team | Class | GP | BS | Avg |
|---|---|---|---|---|
| Brittany Pittman, Morehead St | Jr. | 29 | 164 | 5.7 |
| Louella Tomlinson, St. Mary's (Ca.) | So. | 30 | 161 | 5.4 |
| Allyssa DeHaan, Michigan St | Jr. | 33 | 107 | 3.2 |
| Jess Fuller, Hofstra | Jr. | 30 | 97 | 3.2 |
| Amy Jaeschke, Northwestern | So. | 30 | 96 | 3.2 |
| Stephanie Geehan, Fairfield | Jr. | 31 | 96 | 3.1 |
| Jessica Breland, North Carolina | Jr. | 35 | 108 | 3.1 |
| Danielle Wilson, Baylor | Jr. | 27 | 83 | 3.1 |
| Chanel Mokango, Mississippi St | Jr. | 33 | 97 | 2.9 |
| Kaitlin Sowinski, Sacred Heart | Sr. | 33 | 97 | 2.9 |

# NCAA Men's Division II Individual Leaders

## SCORING

| Player and Team | Class | GP | TFG | 3FG | FT | Pts | Avg |
|---|---|---|---|---|---|---|---|
| LaVontay Fenderson, UW-Parkside | Sr. | 27 | 249 | 44 | 167 | 709 | 26.3 |
| Thad McFadden, Fairmont St | Sr. | 29 | 233 | 106 | 164 | 736 | 25.4 |
| Ted Scott, West Virginia St | Sr. | 30 | 251 | 65 | 135 | 702 | 23.4 |
| Ben Howlett, West Liberty St | Sr. | 30 | 256 | 50 | 129 | 691 | 23.0 |
| Stan Hall, Alderson-Broaddus | Sr. | 33 | 299 | 20 | 141 | 759 | 23.0 |
| Jake Linton, St. Martin's | Sr. | 30 | 183 | 86 | 237 | 689 | 23.0 |
| Anthony Hilliard, Elizabeth City St | Sr. | 28 | 217 | 9 | 197 | 640 | 22.9 |
| Brandon Hopf, Oakland City | Jr. | 29 | 278 | 1 | 93 | 650 | 22.4 |
| Tim Turner, Davis & Elkins | So. | 28 | 212 | 106 | 95 | 625 | 22.3 |
| Chris Hall, Lynn | So. | 28 | 201 | 74 | 147 | 623 | 22.3 |
| Drake Beranek, Neb.-Kearney | Jr. | 26 | 211 | 52 | 96 | 570 | 21.9 |
| Stephen Dennis, Kutztown | Jr. | 33 | 254 | 32 | 170 | 710 | 21.5 |
| Brandon Brown, CSU-San Bernardino | Jr. | 23 | 198 | 7 | 91 | 494 | 21.5 |
| Joseph Jones, Edinboro | Sr. | 28 | 221 | 52 | 104 | 598 | 21.4 |
| Kendrick Easley, Mount Olive | Jr. | 28 | 184 | 96 | 129 | 593 | 21.2 |
| Nick Kohs, Christian Brothers | Sr. | 32 | 255 | 0 | 167 | 677 | 21.2 |

## REBOUNDS

| Player and Team | Class | GP | Reb | Avg |
|---|---|---|---|---|
| Nathan Schumacher, Oakland City | ...Jr. | 29 | 369 | 12.7 |
| Laurence Ekperigin, Le Moyne | ...........Jr. | 31 | 354 | 11.4 |
| Anthony Hilliard, Elizabeth City St | ...Sr. | 28 | 309 | 11.0 |
| Tyler Cain, South Dakota | ...................Jr. | 29 | 320 | 11.0 |
| Anthony Wynn, St. Paul's | ..................Sr. | 28 | 306 | 10.9 |
| Blake Poole, St. Martin's | ..................So. | 30 | 317 | 10.6 |
| William Slones, SE Oklahoma | ...........Jr. | 27 | 283 | 10.5 |
| Mariniz Woody, Benedict | ....................Sr. | 30 | 312 | 10.4 |
| Larry Gordon, Cal Poly-Pomona | .......Jr. | 33 | 343 | 10.4 |
| Michel Vidal, Lynn | ..........................So. | 28 | 289 | 10.3 |

## ASSISTS

| Player and Team | Class | GP | Ast | Avg |
|---|---|---|---|---|
| Kyle Camper, Slippery Rock | .........Sr. | 29 | 305 | 10.5 |
| Darren Duncan, Merrimack | ...........Jr. | 30 | 230 | 7.7 |
| D.J. Ferguson, Flagler | .................So. | 26 | 185 | 7.1 |
| Anthony Anderson, Charleston (W.V.) | ...Sr. | 27 | 186 | 6.9 |
| Chad Akins, Delta St | .....................Jr. | 30 | 205 | 6.8 |
| Evan Hutchinson, Oakland City | ....So. | 27 | 180 | 6.7 |
| Mario Burns, Mont. St-Billings | .......Jr. | 26 | 166 | 6.4 |
| Devin Stewart, Western New Mexico | .Sr. | 27 | 171 | 6.3 |
| Darren Jones, West Virginia St | .......Jr. | 30 | 187 | 6.2 |
| Ryan Troutman, Tusculum | .............Sr. | 31 | 192 | 6.2 |

## FIELD-GOAL PERCENTAGE

| Player and Team | Class | GP | FG | FGA | Pct |
|---|---|---|---|---|---|
| Garret Siler, Augusta St | .............Sr. | 35 | 225 | 285 | 78.9 |
| Joey Cameron, Carson-Newman | ...Jr. | 21 | 115 | 168 | 68.5 |
| James Dillard, Johnson C. Smith | ..Jr. | 26 | 180 | 263 | 68.4 |
| Laurence Ekperigin, Le Moyne | ..Jr. | 31 | 221 | 323 | 68.4 |
| Brian Metz, Wayne St (Neb.) | .....Jr. | 27 | 142 | 210 | 67.6 |
| Tyler Cain, South Dakota | .............Jr. | 29 | 185 | 278 | 66.5 |
| Ricky Jackson, West Virginia St | ..Jr. | 29 | 173 | 264 | 65.5 |
| Taylor Mullenax, St. Edward's | ....Sr. | 25 | 165 | 252 | 65.5 |
| Justin Neuhaus, Colo. Christian | ..Jr. | 34 | 194 | 300 | 64.7 |
| Jordan Armstrong, Mercyhurst | .....Jr. | 27 | 136 | 212 | 64.2 |

Note: Minimum 5 made per game.

## FREE-THROW PERCENTAGE

| Player and Team | Class | GP | FT | FTA | Pct |
|---|---|---|---|---|---|
| Dustin Maguire, Northern Kent. | ..So. | 31 | 88 | 94 | 93.6 |
| Cedric Harris, Wheeling Jesuit | ....Fr. | 29 | 88 | 95 | 92.6 |
| Jake Linton, St. Martin's | .............Sr. | 30 | 237 | 259 | 91.5 |
| Robby Springborn, Michigan Tech | .Sr. | 29 | 80 | 88 | 90.9 |
| Nolan Richardson, Midwestern St | ..Sr. | 32 | 184 | 203 | 90.6 |
| Josh Rudder, Lenoir-Rhyne | ..........Sr. | 29 | 134 | 148 | 90.5 |
| Cody Schilling, Augustana (S.D.) | ..Fr. | 31 | 85 | 94 | 90.4 |
| Jamal Holden, Glenville St | ............Jr. | 29 | 103 | 114 | 90.4 |
| Pierce Caldwell, Incarnate Word | ..Jr. | 30 | 98 | 109 | 89.9 |
| Zac Tiedeman, Humboldt St | ........Jr. | 32 | 137 | 153 | 89.5 |

Note: Minimum 2.5 made per game.

# NCAA Women's Division II Individual Leaders

## SCORING

| Player and Team | Class | GP | TFG | 3FG | FT | Pts | Avg |
|---|---|---|---|---|---|---|---|
| Britney Jordan, Texas A&M-Commerce | ...................Sr. | 29 | 302 | 78 | 227 | 909 | 31.3 |
| Katie Cezat, Hillsdale | .............................................Sr. | 31 | 333 | 5 | 237 | 908 | 29.3 |
| Latoya Wily, BYU-Hawaii | ............................Sr. | 27 | 253 | 0 | 186 | 692 | 25.6 |
| Shantrell Moss, Clark Atlanta | ........................Sr. | 31 | 228 | 31 | 264 | 751 | 24.2 |
| Johannah Leedham, Franklin Pierce | ...................Jr. | 34 | 269 | 79 | 182 | 799 | 23.5 |
| Renee Renz, Texas Woman's | .............................Sr. | 21 | 147 | 11 | 170 | 475 | 22.6 |
| Alira Carpenter, Mont. St-Billings | ....................Sr. | 27 | 196 | 81 | 128 | 601 | 22.3 |
| Brittany Mingo, West Virginia St | .......................Sr. | 28 | 237 | 24 | 121 | 619 | 22.1 |
| Brooque Williams, California (Pa.) | ....................Jr. | 34 | 303 | 2 | 136 | 744 | 21.9 |
| Tatiana Ellis, St. Paul's | .....................................Jr. | 28 | 185 | 63 | 178 | 611 | 21.8 |
| Lauren Beckley, Shippensburg | ..........................Jr. | 27 | 192 | 64 | 133 | 581 | 21.5 |
| Stephanie Sarosi, Nova Southeastern | .................Jr. | 29 | 262 | 6 | 91 | 621 | 21.4 |
| Esty Flores, Barton | .........................................Jr. | 25 | 178 | 49 | 116 | 521 | 20.8 |
| Sarah Van Horn, West Virginia Wesleyan | ..............Sr. | 30 | 228 | 0 | 161 | 617 | 20.6 |
| Kierah Kimbrough, North Dakota | ..........................Sr. | 29 | 248 | 0 | 95 | 591 | 20.4 |

## REBOUNDS

| Player and Team | Class | GP | Reb | Avg |
|---|---|---|---|---|
| Katie Cezat, Hillsdale | .......................Sr. | 31 | 521 | 16.8 |
| Latoya Wily, BYU-Hawaii | ....................Sr. | 27 | 375 | 13.9 |
| Jennifer Dichiara, Queens (N.Y.) | .........Sr. | 29 | 360 | 12.4 |
| Kymira Woodberry, Molloy | ...................Jr. | 28 | 338 | 12.1 |
| Britni Rathke, Notre Dame de Namur | ...Sr. | 26 | 306 | 11.8 |
| Delmara Reece, Mercy | .....................So. | 27 | 315 | 11.7 |
| Renee Renz, Texas Woman's | .........Sr. | 21 | 243 | 11.6 |
| Destiny Brown, SE Oklahoma | .........Jr. | 30 | 346 | 11.5 |
| Lauren Beckley, Shippensburg | ........Jr. | 27 | 308 | 11.4 |
| Phebe Smith, Columbus St | ..............Jr. | 32 | 353 | 11.0 |
| Erica Biel, Fort Hays St | ...................Jr. | 28 | 308 | 11.0 |
| Jessica Romano, Philadelphia U. | ....Jr. | 31 | 340 | 11.0 |

## ASSISTS

| Player and Team | Class | GP | Ast | Avg |
|---|---|---|---|---|
| Bug Cooper, Delta St | ...................So. | 36 | 282 | 7.8 |
| Ashley Orphey, Miles | ....................So. | 29 | 194 | 6.7 |
| Kath. Kundermueller, Abilene Christian | ..Jr. | 29 | 193 | 6.7 |
| Anna Atkinson, Wingate | ................Sr. | 28 | 186 | 6.6 |
| Brooke Knight, Hillsdale | .................Jr. | 31 | 196 | 6.3 |
| Shantell Marquis, Mont. St-Billings | ....Jr. | 26 | 160 | 6.2 |
| Christina Baxter, Mercy | ..................Sr. | 27 | 164 | 6.1 |
| Molly Anderson, Winona St | ..............Sr. | 30 | 181 | 6.0 |
| Tammy Acosta, Tex.-Permian Basin | ..Fr. | 25 | 147 | 5.9 |
| Jasmine Gunn, Tusculum | ................So. | 31 | 181 | 5.8 |

## FIELD-GOAL PERCENTAGE

| Player and Team | Class | GP | FG | FGA | Pct |
|---|---|---|---|---|---|
| Shari Buford, Carson-Newman ...Jr. | | 30 | 173 | 283 | 61.1 |
| Latoya Wily, BYU-Hawaii ..............Sr. | | 27 | 253 | 425 | 59.5 |
| Amy Achesinski, Mercyhurst...........So. | | 27 | 142 | 239 | 59.4 |
| Amanda Milner, North Greenville ...Sr. | | 27 | 135 | 231 | 58.4 |
| Amber Rutherford, N. Alabama....Sr. | | 28 | 165 | 283 | 58.3 |
| Kierah Kimbrough, North Dakota .Sr. | | 29 | 248 | 427 | 58.1 |
| Allison Rosel, Fort Lewis ...............Jr. | | 32 | 189 | 330 | 57.3 |
| Ida Edwards, Emporia St.........Sr. | | 32 | 194 | 241 | 56.9 |
| Jahzinga Tracey, Indiana (Pa.)......Sr. | | 32 | 258 | 456 | 56.6 |
| Anita Bulcher, Newberry .............Fr. | | 28 | 147 | 261 | 56.3 |
| Erin Chesnavich, Phila. Sci........Jr. | | 28 | 189 | 336 | 56.3 |
| Stephanie Delgado, Mesa St ....Sr. | | 27 | 135 | 240 | 56.3 |

Note: Minimum 5 FG per game.

## FREE-THROW PERCENTAGE

| Player and Team | Class | GP | FT | FTA | Pct |
|---|---|---|---|---|---|
| Jamey Gelhar, St. Martin's ..............Jr. | | 28 | 94 | 97 | 96.9 |
| Jessie Slack, Northern Kentucky....Sr. | | 32 | 96 | 103 | 93.2 |
| Britney Cruse, St. Joseph's (Ind.) ..Fr. | | 24 | 66 | 71 | 93.0 |
| Bethany Tighe, Stonehill.................Sr. | | 31 | 91 | 99 | 91.9 |
| Amber Rutherford, North Alabama..Sr. | | 28 | 133 | 145 | 91.7 |
| Samantha Saito, Chaminade .........Jr. | | 27 | 94 | 103 | 91.3 |
| Kelsey Deacon, Northern Michigan...Sr. | | 28 | 73 | 80 | 91.3 |
| Kim Wyngaard, Grand Valley St......Sr. | | 30 | 79 | 87 | 90.8 |
| Allison Weiss, Phila. Sciences .....Sr. | | 28 | 92 | 102 | 90.2 |
| Lindsay Cale, Pitt.-Johnstown ....Sr. | | 29 | 110 | 122 | 90.2 |

Note: Minimum 2.5 made per game.

## SCORING

| Player and Team | Class | GP | TFG | 3FG | FT | Pts | Avg |
|---|---|---|---|---|---|---|---|
| John Grotberg, Grinnell..........................................Sr. | | 25 | 245 | 154 | 131 | 775 | 31.0 |
| Steve Djurickovic, Carthage.................................So. | | 25 | 207 | 38 | 239 | 691 | 27.6 |
| Jimmy Bartolotta, MIT............................................Sr. | | 29 | 260 | 95 | 185 | 800 | 27.6 |
| Bobby Long, Grinnell ..............................................Sr. | | 25 | 193 | 123 | 171 | 680 | 27.2 |
| Jose Guitian, Lasell.................................................Sr. | | 29 | 256 | 46 | 144 | 702 | 24.2 |
| John Hoch, Carroll (Wis.)......................................Jr. | | 23 | 178 | 18 | 180 | 554 | 24.1 |
| Rashawn Johnson, Wesley.....................................Sr. | | 27 | 224 | 83 | 116 | 647 | 24.0 |
| Kent Raymond, Wheaton (Ill.)................................Sr. | | 27 | 211 | 58 | 166 | 646 | 23.9 |
| Arjun Ohri, Polytechnic (N.Y.)...............................So. | | 24 | 190 | 74 | 99 | 553 | 23.0 |
| Marvin Billups, SUNY-Purchase ...........................So. | | 26 | 217 | 8 | 156 | 598 | 23.0 |
| Maurice Horton, Worcester St...............................Jr. | | 26 | 208 | 21 | 160 | 597 | 23.0 |
| Tyler Gordon, Finlandia..........................................Jr. | | 19 | 161 | 59 | 53 | 434 | 22.8 |
| Zach Johnson, Carleton .........................................Sr. | | 26 | 202 | 49 | 139 | 592 | 22.8 |
| Justin White, Bard..................................................Jr. | | 24 | 166 | 56 | 148 | 536 | 22.3 |
| J.J. Walsh, St. Joseph's (N.Y.) .............................Sr. | | 22 | 177 | 11 | 124 | 489 | 22.2 |

## REBOUNDS

| Player and Team | Class | GP | Reb | Avg |
|---|---|---|---|---|
| Mark Carson, Rochester Inst. Tech. ..Sr. | | 28 | 395 | 14.1 |
| Jose Guitian, Lasell.......................Sr. | | 29 | 398 | 13.7 |
| Tyler Sanborn, Guilford..................Jr. | | 31 | 399 | 12.9 |
| Jesus Trejo, Lesley .......................So. | | 25 | 319 | 12.8 |
| Derek Mitchell, Ferrum...................So. | | 26 | 323 | 12.4 |
| Marcel Esonwune, York (N.Y.).......So. | | 23 | 275 | 12.0 |
| Daniel Waajid, Pitt.-Greensburg ....Jr. | | 20 | 238 | 11.9 |
| Cameron Mitchell, Willamette.........Jr. | | 23 | 272 | 11.8 |
| Rod Sykes, Blackburn....................Jr. | | 24 | 274 | 11.4 |
| Jon Greenberg, Mass. Liberal Arts..So. | | 25 | 285 | 11.4 |
| John Fraase, Concordia-Moorhead ..So. | | 25 | 284 | 11.4 |

## FIELD-GOAL PERCENTAGE

| Player and Team | Class | GP | FG | FGA | Pct |
|---|---|---|---|---|---|
| Matt Wayne, Adrian .....................Jr. | | 25 | 128 | 178 | 71.9 |
| Jeremy Off, Milwaukee Engr. ......Jr. | | 24 | 136 | 202 | 67.3 |
| Josh Tanguay, Me.-Farmington....Jr. | | 25 | 138 | 208 | 66.3 |
| Alex Imer, St. Mary's (Md.)..........Sr. | | 22 | 121 | 185 | 65.4 |
| Bryan Johnson, Mississippi Coll..Sr. | | 21 | 165 | 253 | 65.2 |
| David Smith, Gwynedd-Mercy ....Sr. | | 29 | 191 | 296 | 64.5 |
| Tom Callen, DePauw.....................Sr. | | 26 | 131 | 205 | 63.9 |
| Nick Sales, Defiance. ...............Jr. | | 27 | 166 | 260 | 63.8 |
| Kori Vernon, UW-Whitewater ......Sr. | | 29 | 153 | 240 | 63.8 |
| Jeff Skemp, UW-Platteville ...........Sr. | | 29 | 203 | 321 | 63.2 |

Note: Minimum 5 made per game.

## ASSISTS

| Player and Team | Class | GP | Ast | Avg |
|---|---|---|---|---|
| David Arseneault, Grinnell...............Sr. | | 23 | 234 | 10.2 |
| Ajani Edwards, SUNY-IT ..................Sr. | | 30 | 243 | 8.1 |
| Sean Wallis, Wash.-St. Louis ...........Sr. | | 31 | 251 | 8.1 |
| Sean Burton, Ithaca.........................Sr. | | 27 | 212 | 7.9 |
| Corey McAdam, Nazareth ...............Jr. | | 27 | 206 | 7.6 |
| Robert Moreno, McMurry..................Sr. | | 25 | 182 | 7.3 |
| Aswad Thomas, Elms .......................Sr. | | 28 | 201 | 7.2 |
| Shane Denully, SUNY-Old Westbury ..Jr. | | 26 | 183 | 7.0 |
| Bradley Gampel, MIT ........................Sr. | | 30 | 207 | 6.9 |
| Mike Floyd, Defiance .......................Jr. | | 26 | 178 | 6.8 |
| Kevin Richard, Lasell ......................Fr. | | 29 | 197 | 6.8 |

## FREE-THROW PERCENTAGE

| Player and Team | Class | GP | FT | FTA | Pct |
|---|---|---|---|---|---|
| Matt Miller, UW-Oshkosh.........Sr. | | 27 | 89 | 96 | 92.7 |
| Todd Doyle, Wentworth Inst. ....Sr. | | 26 | 100 | 108 | 92.6 |
| Ben Huntington, Plymouth St..Sr. | | 26 | 85 | 82 | 92.4 |
| Tony Mane, UW-La Crosse ....So. | | 25 | 71 | 77 | 92.2 |
| John Hoch, Carroll (Wis.) .........Jr. | | 23 | 180 | 196 | 91.8 |
| Arjun Ohri, Polytechnic (N.Y.)...So. | | 24 | 99 | 108 | 91.7 |
| Sean Burton, Ithaca..................Sr. | | 27 | 128 | 140 | 91.4 |
| Roshawn Russell, North Park...Fr. | | 25 | 105 | 116 | 90.5 |
| Joe McCoy, Grove City. ...........Sr. | | 25 | 74 | 82 | 90.2 |
| Aaron Gallant, Tufts ...............Sr. | | 24 | 66 | 74 | 89.2 |

Note: Minimum 2.5 made per game.

## SCORING

| Player and Team | Class | GP | TFG | 3FG | FT | Pts | Avg |
|---|---|---|---|---|---|---|---|
| Kimberly Blakney, Farmingdale St | Jr. | 27 | 234 | 47 | 138 | 653 | 24.2 |
| Megan Scheele, Edgewood | Sr. | 26 | 222 | 1 | 131 | 576 | 22.2 |
| Chelsie Schweers, Christopher Newport | So. | 29 | 230 | 80 | 96 | 636 | 21.9 |
| Kristen Camuso, Centenary (N.J.) | Jr. | 26 | 187 | 95 | 99 | 568 | 21.8 |
| Brianna Peterson, Catholic | So. | 25 | 215 | 29 | 86 | 545 | 21.8 |
| Pamela Robinson, SUNY-Old Westbury | Sr. | 24 | 176 | 25 | 146 | 523 | 21.8 |
| Kortney Kin, Wilmington (Ohio) | Jr. | 27 | 195 | 16 | 166 | 572 | 21.2 |
| Marche Smith, Concordia-Chicago | So. | 24 | 165 | 29 | 143 | 502 | 20.9 |
| Mackenzie Hunter, UW-La Crosse | Sr. | 26 | 195 | 28 | 117 | 535 | 20.6 |
| LeighAnn Burke, DeSales | Sr. | 28 | 210 | 81 | 69 | 570 | 20.4 |
| Kim Vennera, Delaware Valley | Jr. | 25 | 176 | 49 | 106 | 507 | 20.3 |
| Hillary Klimowicz, The College of New Jersey | Sr. | 29 | 232 | 0 | 123 | 587 | 20.2 |
| Melanie Auguste, Colorado College | Sr. | 25 | 169 | 25 | 136 | 499 | 20.0 |
| Christine Tucker, Eastern Nazarene | Jr. | 24 | 163 | 25 | 127 | 478 | 19.9 |
| Melissa Martinelli, Coast Guard | Jr. | 25 | 179 | 0 | 138 | 496 | 19.8 |

## REBOUNDS

| Player and Team | Class | GP | Reb | Avg |
|---|---|---|---|---|
| Courtney Bailey, Penn St-Berks | Jr. | 26 | 383 | 14.7 |
| Lindsey Newcombe, Hardin-Simmons | So. | 28 | 385 | 13.8 |
| Kathryn Stockbower, Swarthmore | So. | 25 | 340 | 13.6 |
| Becky Taylor, Texas-Tyler | Jr. | 26 | 346 | 13.3 |
| Jessica Hunt, Bay Path | Jr. | 25 | 324 | 13.0 |
| Krista Prato Matthews, Trinity (Tex.) | Sr. | 24 | 309 | 12.9 |
| Sharon Dennis, Roch. Inst. Tech. | Fr. | 22 | 282 | 12.8 |
| Adrian Demchenko, Rosemont | Jr. | 25 | 320 | 12.8 |
| Margaux Pickell, Polytechinc (N.Y.) | Fr. | 25 | 317 | 12.7 |
| Brittany Whetts, Neumann | Jr. | 27 | 342 | 12.7 |

## ASSISTS

| Player and Team | Class | GP | Ast | Avg |
|---|---|---|---|---|
| Monique Salmon, Baruch | So. | 30 | 261 | 8.7 |
| Keli Ward, York (Pa.) | Sr. | 30 | 214 | 7.1 |
| Melanie Auguste, Colorado College | Sr. | 25 | 176 | 7.0 |
| Cory Boyd, Wesley | So. | 30 | 207 | 6.9 |
| Dani Dudek, Stevens Inst. of Tech. | Sr. | 29 | 190 | 6.6 |
| Brittany Holden, Green Mountain | Sr. | 25 | 157 | 6.3 |
| Mandy Seward, Anderson (Ind.) | Sr. | 26 | 162 | 6.2 |
| Jessica Jamrogowicz, Washington (Md.) | Jr. | 25 | 155 | 6.2 |
| Christine Tucker, Eastern Nazarene | Jr. | 24 | 148 | 6.2 |
| Selin Whitham, Union (N.Y.) | Sr. | 26 | 159 | 6.1 |
| Lisa Morrissey, Loras | Jr. | 27 | 165 | 6.1 |

## FIELD-GOAL PERCENTAGE

| Player and Team | Class | GP | FG | FGA | Pct |
|---|---|---|---|---|---|
| Hilary Klimowicz, TCNJ | Sr. | 29 | 232 | 346 | 67.1 |
| Kristen Shielee, George Fox | Sr. | 32 | 166 | 265 | 62.6 |
| Nicole Dickman, Thomas More | So. | 31 | 180 | 288 | 62.5 |
| Michelle Rogers, Union (N.Y.) | Sr. | 24 | 161 | 259 | 62.2 |
| Christina Solari, Illinois Wesleyan | Jr. | 31 | 160 | 263 | 60.8 |
| Lisa Nassin, Lake Forest | Jr. | 23 | 126 | 209 | 60.3 |
| Lora Turner, Emory | Sr. | 25 | 174 | 292 | 59.6 |
| Angie Owens, Wesley | So. | 30 | 196 | 330 | 59.4 |
| Megan Scheele, Edgewood | Sr. | 26 | 222 | 376 | 59.0 |
| Christina Speer, Principia | Sr. | 25 | 172 | 293 | 58.7 |

Note: Minimum 5 made per game.

## FREE-THROW PERCENTAGE

| Player and Team | Class | GP | FT | FTA | Pct |
|---|---|---|---|---|---|
| Kathryn Kirby, Fontbonne | Sr. | 27 | 82 | 87 | 94.3 |
| Amanda Hiltunen, Randolph-Macon | Sr. | 29 | 96 | 106 | 90.6 |
| Emily Nelson, Gustavus Adolphus | Sr. | 26 | 67 | 74 | 90.5 |
| Kim Rarick, DeSales | Sr. | 25 | 92 | 102 | 90.2 |
| Margo Muhlbauer, Buena Vista | Jr. | 27 | 146 | 162 | 90.1 |
| Pam Quigley, Ohio Wesleyan | So. | 29 | 82 | 91 | 90.1 |
| Alyssa Bisci, Moravian | Jr. | 27 | 130 | 145 | 89.7 |
| Katie Jarger, Carthage | Sr. | 27 | 68 | 76 | 89.8 |
| Anna Findley, Oglethorpe | Sr. | 31 | 90 | 101 | 89.1 |
| Jen Hnatuck, Juniata | So. | 29 | 73 | 82 | 89.0 |

Note: Minimum 2.5 made per game.

## NCAA Men's Division I Championship Results

### NCAA Final Four Results

| Year | Winner | Score | Runner-up | Third Place | Fourth Place | Winning Coach |
|---|---|---|---|---|---|---|
| 1939 | Oregon | 46–33 | Ohio St | *Oklahoma | *Villanova | Howard Hobson |
| 1940 | Indiana | 60–42 | Kansas | *Duquesne | *USC | Branch McCracken |
| 1941 | Wisconsin | 39–34 | Washington St | *Pittsburgh | *Arkansas | Harold Foster |
| 1942 | Stanford | 53–38 | Dartmouth | *Colorado | *Kentucky | Everett Dean |
| 1943 | Wyoming | 46–34 | Georgetown | *Texas | *DePaul | Everett Shelton |
| 1944 | Utah | 42–40 (OT) | Dartmouth | *Iowa St | *Ohio St | Vadal Peterson |
| 1945 | Oklahoma St | 49–45 | NYU | *Arkansas | *Ohio St | Hank Iba |
| 1946 | Oklahoma St | 43–40 | North Carolina | Ohio St | California | Hank Iba |
| 1947 | Holy Cross | 58–47 | Oklahoma | Texas | CCNY | Alvin Julian |
| 1948 | Kentucky | 58–42 | Baylor | Holy Cross | Kansas St | Adolph Rupp |
| 1949 | Kentucky | 46–36 | Oklahoma St | Illinois | Oregon St | Adolph Rupp |
| 1950 | CCNY | 71–68 | Bradley | North Carolina St | Baylor | Nat Holman |
| 1951 | Kentucky | 68–58 | Kansas St | Illinois | Oklahoma St | Adolph Rupp |
| 1952 | Kansas | 80–63 | St. John's (N.Y.) | Illinois | Santa Clara | Forrest Allen |
| 1953 | Indiana | 69–68 | Kansas | Washington | LSU | Branch McCracken |
| 1954 | La Salle | 92–76 | Bradley | Penn St | USC | Kenneth Loeffler |
| 1955 | San Francisco | 77–63 | La Salle | Colorado | Iowa | Phil Woolpert |
| 1956 | San Francisco | 83–71 | Iowa | Temple | SMU | Phil Woolpert |
| 1957 | North Carolina | 54–53 (3OT) | Kansas | San Francisco | Michigan St | Frank McGuire |
| 1958 | Kentucky | 84–72 | Seattle | Temple | Kansas St | Adolph Rupp |
| 1959 | California | 71–70 | West Virginia | Cincinnati | Louisville | Pete Newell |
| 1960 | Ohio St | 75–55 | California | Cincinnati | NYU | Fred Taylor |
| 1961 | Cincinnati | 70–65 (OT) | Ohio St | Vacated‡ | Utah | Edwin Jucker |
| 1962 | Cincinnati | 71–59 | Ohio St | Wake Forest | UCLA | Edwin Jucker |
| 1963 | Loyola (Ill.) | 60–58 (OT) | Cincinnati | Duke | Oregon St | George Ireland |
| 1964 | UCLA | 98–83 | Duke | Michigan | Kansas St | John Wooden |
| 1965 | UCLA | 91–80 | Michigan | Princeton | Wichita St | John Wooden |
| 1966 | UTEP | 72–65 | Kentucky | Duke | Utah | Don Haskins |
| 1967 | UCLA | 79–64 | Dayton | Houston | North Carolina | John Wooden |
| 1968 | UCLA | 78–55 | North Carolina | Ohio St | Houston | John Wooden |
| 1969 | UCLA | 92–72 | Purdue | Drake | North Carolina | John Wooden |
| 1970 | UCLA | 80–69 | Jacksonville | New Mexico St | St. Bonaventure | John Wooden |
| 1971 | UCLA | 68–62 | Vacated‡ | Vacated‡ | Kansas | John Wooden |
| 1972 | UCLA | 81–76 | Florida St | North Carolina | Louisville | John Wooden |
| 1973 | UCLA | 87–66 | Memphis St | Indiana | Providence | John Wooden |
| 1974 | North Carolina St | 76–64 | Marquette | UCLA | Kansas | Norm Sloan |
| 1975 | UCLA | 92–85 | Kentucky | Louisville | Syracuse | John Wooden |
| 1976 | Indiana | 86–68 | Michigan | UCLA | Rutgers | Bob Knight |
| 1977 | Marquette | 67–59 | North Carolina | UNLV | UNC-Charlotte | Al McGuire |
| 1978 | Kentucky | 94–88 | Duke | Arkansas | Notre Dame | Joe Hall |
| 1979 | Michigan St | 75–64 | Indiana St | DePaul | Penn | Jud Heathcote |
| 1980 | Louisville | 59–54 | Vacated‡ | Purdue | Iowa | Denny Crum |
| 1981 | Indiana | 63–50 | North Carolina | Virginia | LSU | Bob Knight |
| 1982 | North Carolina | 63–62 | Georgetown | *Houston | *Louisville | Dean Smith |
| 1983 | North Carolina St | 54–52 | Houston | *Georgia | *Louisville | Jim Valvano |
| 1984 | Georgetown | 84–75 | Houston | *Kentucky | *Virginia | John Thompson |
| 1985 | Villanova | 66–64 | Georgetown | St. John's (N.Y.) | Vacated‡ | Rollie Massimino |
| 1986 | Louisville | 72–69 | Duke | *Kansas | *LSU | Denny Crum |
| 1987 | Indiana | 74–73 | Syracuse | *UNLV | *Providence | Bob Knight |
| 1988 | Kansas | 83–79 | Oklahoma | *Arizona | *Duke | Larry Brown |
| 1989 | Michigan | 80–79 (OT) | Seton Hall | *Duke | *Illinois | Steve Fisher |
| 1990 | UNLV | 103–73 | Duke | *Arkansas | *Georgia Tech | Jerry Tarkanian |
| 1991 | Duke | 72–65 | Kansas | *UNLV | *North Carolina | Mike Krzyzewski |
| 1992 | Duke | 71–51 | Michigan | *Cincinnati | *Indiana | Mike Krzyzewski |
| 1993 | North Carolina | 77–71 | Michigan | *Kansas | *Kentucky | Dean Smith |
| 1994 | Arkansas | 76–72 | Duke | *Arizona | *Florida | Nolan Richardson |
| 1995 | UCLA | 89–78 | Arkansas | *North Carolina | *Oklahoma St | Jim Harrick |
| 1996 | Kentucky | 76–67 | Syracuse | Vacated‡ | Mississippi St | Rick Pitino |
| 1997 | Arizona | 84–79 (OT) | Kentucky | *Minnesota | *North Carolina | Lute Olson |
| 1998 | Kentucky | 78–69 | Utah | *Stanford | *North Carolina | Tubby Smith |
| 1999 | Connecticut | 77–74 | Duke | *Michigan St | *Ohio St | Jim Calhoun |
| 2000 | Michigan St | 89–76 | Florida | *Wisconsin | *North Carolina | Tom Izzo |
| 2001 | Duke | 82–72 | Arizona | *Maryland | *Michigan St | Mike Krzyzewski |

## NCAA Final Four Results (Cont.)

| Year | Winner | Score | Runner-up | Third Place | Fourth Place | Winning Coach |
|---|---|---|---|---|---|---|
| 2002 | Maryland | 64–52 | Indiana | *Kansas | *Oklahoma | Gary Williams |
| 2003 | Syracuse | 81–78 | Kansas | *Marquette | *Texas | Jim Boeheim |
| 2004 | Connecticut | 82–73 | Georgia Tech | *Oklahoma St | *Duke | Jim Calhoun |
| 2005 | North Carolina | 75-70 | Illinois | *Louisville | *Michigan St | Roy Williams |
| 2006 | Florida | 73–57 | UCLA | *George Mason | *LSU | Billy Donovan |
| 2007 | Florida | 84–75 | Ohio St | *UCLA | *Georgetown | Billy Donovan |
| 2008 | Kansas | 75–68 (OT) | Vacated‡ | *UCLA | *North Carolina | Bill Self |
| 2009 | North Carolina | 89–72 | Michigan St | *Villanova | *Connecticut | Roy Williams |

*Tied for third place. ‡Student-athletes representing St. Joseph's (Pa.) in 1961, Villanova in 1971, Western Kentucky in 1971, UCLA in 1980, Memphis State in 1985, Massachusetts in 1996, and Memphis in 2008 were declared ineligible subsequent to the tournament. Under NCAA rules, the teams' and ineligible student-athletes' records were deleted, and the teams' places in the standings were vacated.

## NCAA Final Four Most Outstanding Players

| Year | Winner, School | GP | Field Goals FGM | Field Goals Pct | 3-Pt FG FGA | 3-Pt FG FGM | Free Throws FTM | Free Throws Pct | Reb | Asst | Stl | BS | Avg |
|---|---|---|---|---|---|---|---|---|---|---|---|---|---|
| 1939 | None selected | | | | | | | | | | | | |
| 1940 | Marv Huffman, Indiana | 2 | 7 | — | — | — | 4 | — | — | — | — | — | 9.0 |
| 1941 | John Kotz, Wisconsin | 2 | 8 | — | — | — | 6 | — | — | — | — | — | 11.0 |
| 1942 | Howard Dallmar, Stanford | 2 | 8 | — | — | — | 4 | 66.7 | — | — | — | — | 10.0 |
| 1943 | Ken Sailors, Wyoming | 2 | 10 | — | — | — | 8 | 72.7 | — | — | — | — | 14.0 |
| 1944 | Arnie Ferrin, Utah | 2 | 11 | — | — | — | 6 | — | — | — | — | — | 14.0 |
| 1945 | Bob Kurland, Oklahoma St | 2 | 16 | — | — | — | 5 | — | — | — | — | — | 18.5 |
| 1946 | Bob Kurland, Oklahoma St | 2 | 21 | — | — | — | 10 | 66.7 | — | — | — | — | 26.0 |
| 1947 | George Kaftan, Holy Cross | 2 | 18 | — | — | — | 12 | 70.6 | — | — | — | — | 24.0 |
| 1948 | Alex Groza, Kentucky | 2 | 16 | — | — | — | 5 | — | — | — | — | — | 18.5 |
| 1949 | Alex Groza, Kentucky | 2 | 19 | — | — | — | 14 | — | — | — | — | — | 26.0 |
| 1950 | Irwin Dambrot, CCNY | 2 | 12 | 42.9 | — | — | 4 | 50.0 | — | — | — | — | 14.0 |
| 1951 | None selected | | | | | | | | | | | | |
| 1952 | Clyde Lovellette, Kansas | 2 | 24 | — | — | — | 18 | — | — | — | — | — | 33.0 |
| 1953 | *B.H. Horn, Kansas | 2 | 17 | — | — | — | 17 | — | — | — | — | — | 25.5 |
| 1954 | Tom Gola, La Salle | 2 | 12 | — | — | — | 14 | — | — | — | — | — | 19.0 |
| 1955 | Bill Russell, San Francisco | 2 | 19 | — | — | — | 9 | — | — | — | — | — | 23.5 |
| 1956 | *Hal Lear, Temple | 2 | 32 | — | — | — | 16 | — | — | — | — | — | 40.0 |
| 1957 | *Wilt Chamberlain, Kansas | 2 | 18 | 51.4 | — | — | 19 | 70.4 | 25 | — | — | — | 32.5 |
| 1958 | *Elgin Baylor, Seattle | 2 | 18 | 34.0 | — | — | 12 | 75.0 | 41 | — | — | — | 24.0 |
| 1959 | *Jerry West, West Virginia | 2 | 22 | 66.7 | — | — | 22 | 68.8 | 25 | — | — | — | 33.0 |
| 1960 | Jerry Lucas, Ohio St | 2 | 16 | 66.7 | — | — | 3 | 100.0 | 23 | — | — | — | 17.5 |
| 1961 | *Jerry Lucas, Ohio St | 2 | 20 | 71.4 | — | — | 16 | 94.1 | 25 | — | — | — | 28.0 |
| 1962 | Paul Hogue, Cincinnati | 2 | 23 | 63.9 | — | — | 12 | 63.2 | 38 | — | — | — | 29.0 |
| 1963 | Art Heyman, Duke | 2 | 18 | 41.0 | — | — | 15 | 68.2 | 19 | — | — | — | 25.5 |
| 1964 | Walt Hazzard, UCLA | 2 | 11 | 55.0 | — | — | 8 | 66.7 | 10 | — | — | — | 15.0 |
| 1965 | *Bill Bradley, Princeton | 2 | 34 | 63.0 | — | — | 19 | 95.0 | 24 | — | — | — | 43.5 |
| 1966 | *Jerry Chambers, Utah | 2 | 25 | 53.2 | — | — | 20 | 83.3 | 35 | — | — | — | 35.0 |
| 1967 | Lew Alcindor, UCLA | 2 | 14 | 60.9 | — | — | 11 | 45.8 | 38 | — | — | — | 19.5 |
| 1968 | Lew Alcindor, UCLA | 2 | 22 | 62.9 | — | — | 9 | 90.0 | 34 | — | — | — | 26.5 |
| 1969 | Lew Alcindor, UCLA | 2 | 23 | 67.7 | — | — | 16 | 64.0 | 41 | — | — | — | 31.0 |
| 1970 | Sidney Wicks, UCLA | 2 | 15 | 71.4 | — | — | 9 | 60.0 | 34 | — | — | — | 19.5 |
| 1971 | *†Howard Porter, Villanova | 2 | 20 | 48.8 | — | — | 7 | 77.8 | 24 | — | — | — | 23.5 |
| 1972 | Bill Walton, UCLA | 2 | 20 | 69.0 | — | — | 17 | 73.9 | 41 | — | — | — | 28.5 |
| 1973 | Bill Walton, UCLA | 2 | 28 | 82.4 | — | — | 2 | 40.0 | 30 | — | — | — | 29.0 |
| 1974 | David Thompson, N.C. St | 2 | 19 | 51.4 | — | — | 11 | 78.6 | 17 | — | — | — | 24.5 |
| 1975 | Richard Washington, UCLA | 2 | 23 | 54.8 | — | — | 8 | 72.7 | 20 | — | — | — | 27.0 |
| 1976 | Kent Benson, Indiana | 2 | 17 | 50.0 | — | — | 7 | 63.6 | 18 | — | — | — | 20.5 |
| 1977 | Butch Lee, Marquette | 2 | 11 | 34.4 | — | — | 8 | 100.0 | 6 | 2 | 1 | 1 | 15.0 |
| 1978 | Jack Givens, Kentucky | 2 | 28 | 65.1 | — | — | 8 | 66.7 | 17 | 4 | 1 | 3 | 32.0 |
| 1979 | Earvin Johnson, Michigan St | 2 | 17 | 68.0 | — | — | 19 | 86.4 | 17 | 3 | 0 | 2 | 26.5 |
| 1980 | Darrell Griffith, Louisville | 2 | 23 | 62.2 | — | — | 11 | 68.8 | 7 | 15 | 0 | 2 | 28.5 |
| 1981 | Isiah Thomas, Indiana | 2 | 14 | 56.0 | — | — | 9 | 81.8 | 4 | 9 | 3 | 0 | 18.5 |
| 1982 | James Worthy, North Carolina | 2 | 20 | 74.1 | — | — | 2 | 28.6 | 8 | 9 | 0 | 4 | 21.0 |
| 1983 | *Akeem Olajuwon, Houston | 2 | 16 | 55.2 | — | — | 9 | 64.3 | 40 | 3 | 2 | 5 | 20.5 |
| 1984 | Patrick Ewing, Georgetown | 2 | 8 | 57.1 | — | — | 2 | 100.0 | 18 | 1 | 1 | 15 | 9.0 |
| 1985 | Ed Pinckney, Villanova | 2 | 8 | 57.1 | — | — | 12 | 75.0 | 15 | 6 | 3 | 0 | 14.0 |
| 1986 | Pervis Ellison, Louisville | 2 | 15 | 60.0 | — | — | 6 | 75.0 | 24 | 2 | 3 | 1 | 18.0 |
| 1987 | Keith Smart, Indiana | 2 | 14 | 63.6 | 1 | 0 | 7 | 77.8 | 7 | 7 | 0 | 2 | 17.5 |
| 1988 | Danny Manning, Kansas | 2 | 25 | 55.6 | 1 | 0 | 6 | 66.7 | 17 | 4 | 8 | 9 | 28.0 |

*Not a member of the championship-winning team. †Record later vacated.

## NCAA Final Four MOPs (Cont.)

| Year | Winner, School | GP | Field Goals | | 3-Pt FG | | Free Throws | | Reb | Asst | Stl | BS | Avg |
|------|----------------|----|------|-----|-----|-----|-----|------|-----|------|-----|----|-----|
| | | | FGM | Pct | FGA | FGM | FTM | Pct | | | | | |
| 1989 | ....Glen Rice, Michigan | 2 | 24 | 49.0 | 16 | 7 | 4 | 100.0 | 16 | 1 | 0 | 3 | 29.5 |
| 1990 | ....Anderson Hunt, UNLV | 2 | 19 | 61.3 | 16 | 9 | 2 | 50.0 | 4 | 9 | 1 | 1 | 24.5 |
| 1991 | ....Christian Laettner, Duke | 2 | 12 | 54.5 | 1 | 1 | 21 | 91.3 | 17 | 2 | 1 | 2 | 23.0 |
| 1992 | ....Bobby Hurley, Duke | 2 | 10 | 41.7 | 12 | 7 | 8 | 80.0 | 3 | 11 | 0 | 3 | 17.5 |
| 1993 | ....Donald Williams, North Carolina | 2 | 15 | 65.2 | 14 | 10 | 10 | 100.0 | 4 | 2 | 2 | 0 | 25.0 |
| 1994 | ....Corliss Williamson, Arkansas | 2 | 21 | 50.0 | 0 | 0 | 10 | 71.4 | 21 | 8 | 4 | 3 | 26.0 |
| 1995 | ....Ed O'Bannon, UCLA | 2 | 16 | 45.7 | 8 | 3 | 10 | 76.9 | 25 | 3 | 7 | 1 | 22.5 |
| 1996 | ....Tony Delk, Kentucky | 2 | 15 | 41.7 | 16 | 8 | 6 | 54.6 | 9 | 2 | 3 | 2 | 22.0 |
| 1997 | ....Miles Simon, Arizona | 2 | 17 | 45.9 | 10 | 3 | 17 | 77.3 | 8 | 6 | 0 | 1 | 27.0 |
| 1998 | ....Jeff Sheppard, Kentucky | 2 | 16 | 55.2 | 10 | 4 | 7 | 77.8 | 10 | 7 | 4 | 0 | 21.5 |
| 1999 | ....Richard Hamilton, Connecticut | 2 | 20 | 51.3 | 7 | 3 | 8 | 72.7 | 12 | 4 | 2 | 1 | 25.5 |
| 2000 | ....Mateen Cleaves, Michigan St | 2 | 8 | 44.4 | 4 | 3 | 10 | 83.3 | 6 | 5 | 2 | 0 | 14.5 |
| 2001 | ....Shane Battier, Duke | 2 | 13 | 50.0 | 12 | 5 | 12 | 70.6 | 19 | 8 | 2 | 6 | 21.5 |
| 2002 | ....Juan Dixon, Maryland | 2 | 16 | 59.3 | 15 | 7 | 12 | 80.0 | 8 | 5 | 7 | 0 | 25.5 |
| 2003 | ....Carmelo Anthony, Syracuse | 2 | 19 | 54.3 | 6 | 9 | 9 | 81.1 | 24 | 8 | 4 | 0 | 26.5 |
| 2004 | ....Emeka Okafor, Connecticut | 2 | 17 | 65.4 | 0 | 0 | 8 | 53.3 | 22 | 2 | 1 | 4 | 21.0 |
| 2005 | ....Sean May, North Carolina | 2 | 19 | 65.5 | 0 | 0 | 10 | 71.4 | 17 | 5 | 1 | 2 | 24.0 |
| 2006 | ....Joakim Noah, Florida | 2 | 12 | 60.0 | 1 | 0 | 4 | 100.0 | 17 | 5 | 2 | 10 | 14.0 |
| 2007 | ....Corey Brewer, Florida | 2 | 9 | 47.3 | 13 | 7 | 7 | 87.5 | 10 | 2 | 3 | 5 | 16.0 |
| 2008 | ....Mario Chalmers, Kansas | 2 | 10 | 43.5 | 9 | 3 | 6 | 75.0 | 7 | 6 | 7 | 0 | 14.5 |
| 2009 | ....Wayne Ellington, North Carolina | 2 | 14 | 53.8 | 11 | 8 | 3 | 75.0 | 13 | 4 | 0 | 0 | 19.5 |

## Best NCAA Tournament Single-Game Scoring Performances

| Player and Team | Year | Round | FG | 3FG | FT | TP |
|-----------------|------|-------|----|----|----|----|
| Austin Carr, Notre Dame vs Ohio | 1970 | 1st | 25 | — | 11 | 61 |
| Bill Bradley, Princeton vs Wichita St | 1965 | C* | 22 | — | 14 | 58 |
| Oscar Robertson, Cincinnati vs Arkansas | 1958 | C | 21 | — | 14 | 56 |
| Austin Carr, Notre Dame vs Kentucky | 1970 | 2nd | 22 | — | 8 | 52 |
| Austin Carr, Notre Dame vs TCU | 1971 | 1st | 20 | — | 12 | 52 |
| David Robinson, Navy vs Michigan | 1987 | 1st | 22 | 0 | 6 | 50 |
| Elvin Hayes, Houston vs Loyola (Ill.) | 1968 | 1st | 20 | — | 9 | 49 |
| Hal Lear, Temple vs SMU | 1956 | C* | 17 | — | 14 | 48 |
| Austin Carr, Notre Dame vs Houston | 1971 | C | 17 | — | 13 | 47 |
| Dave Corzine, DePaul vs Louisville | 1978 | 2nd | 18 | — | 10 | 46 |

C=regional third place; C*=third-place game.

## NIT Championship Results

| Year | Winner | Score | Runner-up | Year | Winner | Score | Runner-up |
|------|--------|-------|-----------|------|--------|-------|-----------|
| 1938 | .......Temple | 60–36 | Colorado | 1965 | .....St. John's (N.Y.) | 55–51 | Villanova |
| 1939 | .......Long Island U. | 44–32 | Loyola (Ill.) | 1966 | .......BYU | 97–84 | NYU |
| 1940 | .......Colorado | 51–40 | Duquesne | 1967 | .......Southern Illinois | 71–56 | Marquette |
| 1941 | .......Long Island U. | 56–42 | Ohio U | 1968 | .......Dayton | 61–48 | Kansas |
| 1942 | .......West Virginia | 47–45 | W. Kentucky | 1969 | .......Temple | 89–76 | Boston College |
| 1943 | .......St. John's (N.Y.) | 48–27 | Toledo | 1970 | .......Marquette | 65–53 | St. John's (N.Y.) |
| 1944 | .......St. John's (N.Y.) | 47–39 | DePaul | 1971 | .......North Carolina | 84–66 | Georgia Tech |
| 1945 | .......DePaul | 71–54 | Bowling Green | 1972 | .......Maryland | 100–69 | Niagara |
| 1946 | .......Kentucky | 46–45 | Rhode Island | 1973 | .......Virginia Tech | 92–91 (OT) | Notre Dame |
| 1947 | .......Utah | 49–45 | Kentucky | 1974 | .......Purdue | 97–81 | Utah |
| 1948 | .......St. Louis | 65–52 | NYU | 1975 | .......Princeton | 80–69 | Providence |
| 1949 | .......San Francisco | 48–47 | Loyola (Ill.) | 1976 | .......Kentucky | 71–67 | UNC-Charlotte |
| 1950 | .......CCNY | 69–61 | Bradley | 1977 | .......St. Bonaventure | 94–91 | Houston |
| 1951 | .......BYU | 62–43 | Dayton | 1978 | .......Texas | 101–93 | North Carolina St |
| 1952 | .......La Salle | 75–64 | Dayton | 1979 | .......Indiana | 53–52 | Purdue |
| 1953 | .......Seton Hall | 58–46 | St. John's (N.Y.) | 1980 | .......Virginia | 58–55 | Minnesota |
| 1954 | .......Holy Cross | 71–62 | Duquesne | 1981 | .......Tulsa | 86–84 (OT) | Syracuse |
| 1955 | .......Duquesne | 70–58 | Dayton | 1982 | .......Bradley | 67–58 | Purdue |
| 1956 | .......Louisville | 93–80 | Dayton | 1983 | .......Fresno St | 69–60 | DePaul |
| 1957 | .......Bradley | 84–83 | Memphis St | 1984 | .......Michigan | 83–63 | Notre Dame |
| 1958 | .......Xavier (Ohio) | 78–74 (OT) | Dayton | 1985 | .......UCLA | 65–62 | Indiana |
| 1959 | .......St. John's (N.Y.) | 76–71 (OT) | Bradley | 1986 | .......Ohio St | 73–63 | Wyoming |
| 1960 | .......Bradley | 88–72 | Providence | 1987 | .......Southern Miss | 84–80 | La Salle |
| 1961 | .......Providence | 62–59 | St. Louis | 1988 | .......Connecticut | 72–67 | Ohio St |
| 1962 | .......Dayton | 73–67 | St. John's (N.Y.) | 1989 | .......St. John's (N.Y.) | 73–65 | St. Louis |
| 1963 | .......Providence | 81–66 | Canisius | 1990 | .......Vanderbilt | 74–72 | St. Louis |
| 1964 | .......Bradley | 86–54 | New Mexico | 1991 | .......Stanford | 78–72 | Oklahoma |

## NIT Championship Results (Cont.)

| Year | Winner | Score | Runner-up | Year | Winner | Score | Runner-up |
|------|--------|-------|-----------|------|--------|-------|-----------|
| 1992 | Virginia | 81–76 | Notre Dame | 2001 | Tulsa | 79–60 | Alabama |
| 1993 | Minnesota | 62–61 | Georgetown | 2002 | Memphis | 72–62 | South Carolina |
| 1994 | Villanova | 80–73 | Vanderbilt | 2003 | St. John's | 70–67 | Georgetown |
| 1995 | Virginia Tech | 65–64 (OT) | Marquette | 2004 | Michigan | 62–55 | Rutgers |
| 1996 | Nebraska | 60–56 | St. Joseph's | 2005 | South Carolina | 60–57 | Saint Joseph's |
| 1997 | Michigan | 82–73 | Florida St | 2006 | South Carolina | 76–64 | Michigan |
| 1998 | Minnesota | 79–72 | Penn St | 2007 | West Virginia | 78–73 | Clemson |
| 1999 | California | 61–60 | Clemson | 2008 | Ohio St | 92–85 | Massachusetts |
| 2000 | Wake Forest | 71–61 | Notre Dame | 2009 | Penn St | 69–63 | Baylor |

# NCAA Men's Division I Season Leaders

## Scoring Average

| Year | Player and Team | Ht | Class | GP | FG | 3FG | FT | Pts | Avg |
|------|-----------------|-----|-------|-----|-----|-----|-----|-----|-----|
| 1948 | Murray Wier, Iowa | 5-9 | Sr. | 19 | 152 | — | 95 | 399 | 21.0 |
| 1949 | Tony Lavelli, Yale | 6-3 | Sr. | 30 | 228 | — | 215 | 671 | 22.4 |
| 1950 | Paul Arizin, Villanova | 6-3 | Sr. | 29 | 260 | — | 215 | 735 | 25.3 |
| 1951 | Bill Mlkvy, Temple | 6-4 | Sr. | 25 | 303 | — | 125 | 731 | 29.2 |
| 1952 | Clyde Lovellette, Kansas | 6-9 | Sr. | 28 | 315 | — | 165 | 795 | 28.4 |
| 1953 | Frank Selvy, Furman | 6-3 | Jr. | 25 | 272 | — | 194 | 738 | 29.5 |
| 1954 | Frank Selvy, Furman | 6-3 | Sr. | 29 | 427 | — | 355 | 1209 | 41.7 |
| 1955 | Darrell Floyd, Furman | 6-1 | Jr. | 25 | 344 | — | 209 | 897 | 35.9 |
| 1956 | Darrell Floyd, Furman | 6-1 | Sr. | 28 | 339 | — | 268 | 946 | 33.8 |
| 1957 | Grady Wallace, South Carolina | 6-4 | Sr. | 29 | 336 | — | 234 | 906 | 31.2 |
| 1958 | Oscar Robertson, Cincinnati | 6-5 | So. | 28 | 352 | — | 280 | 984 | 35.1 |
| 1959 | Oscar Robertson, Cincinnati | 6-5 | Jr. | 30 | 331 | — | 316 | 978 | 32.6 |
| 1960 | Oscar Robertson, Cincinnati | 6-5 | Sr. | 30 | 369 | — | 273 | 1011 | 33.7 |
| 1961 | Frank Burgess, Gonzaga | 6-1 | Sr. | 26 | 304 | — | 234 | 842 | 32.4 |
| 1962 | Billy McGill, Utah | 6-9 | Sr. | 26 | 394 | — | 221 | 1009 | 38.8 |
| 1963 | Nick Werkman, Seton Hall | 6-3 | Jr. | 22 | 221 | — | 208 | 650 | 29.5 |
| 1964 | Howard Komives, Bowling Green | 6-1 | Sr. | 23 | 292 | — | 260 | 844 | 36.7 |
| 1965 | Rick Barry, Miami (Fla.) | 6-7 | Sr. | 26 | 340 | — | 293 | 973 | 37.4 |
| 1966 | Dave Schellhase, Purdue | 6-4 | Sr. | 24 | 284 | — | 213 | 781 | 32.5 |
| 1967 | Jim Walker, Providence | 6-3 | Sr. | 28 | 323 | — | 205 | 851 | 30.4 |
| 1968 | Pete Maravich, LSU | 6-5 | So. | 26 | 432 | — | 274 | 1138 | 43.8 |
| 1969 | Pete Maravich, LSU | 6-5 | Jr. | 26 | 433 | — | 282 | 1148 | 44.2 |
| 1970 | Pete Maravich, LSU | 6-5 | Sr. | 31 | 522 | — | 337 | 1381 | 44.5 |
| 1971 | Johnny Neumann, Mississippi | 6-6 | So. | 23 | 366 | — | 191 | 923 | 40.1 |
| 1972 | Dwight Lamar, SW Louisiana | 6-1 | Jr. | 29 | 429 | — | 196 | 1054 | 36.3 |
| 1973 | William Averitt, Pepperdine | 6-1 | Sr. | 25 | 352 | — | 144 | 848 | 33.9 |
| 1974 | Larry Fogle, Canisius | 6-5 | So. | 25 | 326 | — | 183 | 835 | 33.4 |
| 1975 | Bob McCurdy, Richmond | 6-7 | Sr. | 26 | 321 | — | 213 | 855 | 32.9 |
| 1976 | Marshall Rodgers, Tex.-Pan American | 6-2 | Sr. | 25 | 361 | — | 197 | 919 | 36.8 |
| 1977 | Freeman Williams, Portland St | 6-4 | Jr. | 26 | 417 | — | 176 | 1010 | 38.8 |
| 1978 | Freeman Williams, Portland St | 6-4 | Sr. | 27 | 410 | — | 149 | 969 | 35.9 |
| 1979 | Lawrence Butler, Idaho St | 6-3 | Sr. | 27 | 310 | — | 192 | 812 | 30.1 |
| 1980 | Tony Murphy, Southern-Birmingham | 6-3 | Sr. | 29 | 377 | — | 178 | 932 | 32.1 |
| 1981 | Zam Fredrick, South Carolina | 6-2 | Sr. | 27 | 300 | — | 181 | 781 | 28.9 |
| 1982 | Harry Kelly, Texas Southern | 6-7 | Jr. | 29 | 336 | — | 190 | 862 | 29.7 |
| 1983 | Harry Kelly, Texas Southern | 6-7 | Sr. | 29 | 333 | — | 169 | 835 | 28.8 |
| 1984 | Joe Jakubick, Akron | 6-5 | Sr. | 27 | 304 | — | 206 | 814 | 30.1 |
| 1985 | Xavier McDaniel, Wichita St | 6-8 | Sr. | 31 | 351 | — | 142 | 844 | 27.2 |
| 1986 | Terrance Bailey, Wagner | 6-2 | Jr. | 29 | 321 | — | 212 | 854 | 29.4 |
| 1987 | Kevin Houston, Army | 5-11 | Sr. | 29 | 311 | 63 | 268 | 953 | 32.9 |
| 1988 | Hersey Hawkins, Bradley | 6-3 | Sr. | 31 | 377 | 87 | 284 | 1125 | 36.3 |
| 1989 | Hank Gathers, Loyola Marymount | 6-7 | Jr. | 31 | 419 | 0 | 177 | 1015 | 32.7 |
| 1990 | Bo Kimble, Loyola Marymount | 6-5 | Sr. | 32 | 404 | 92 | 231 | 1131 | 35.3 |
| 1991 | Kevin Bradshaw, U.S. Int'l | 6-6 | Sr. | 28 | 358 | 60 | 278 | 1054 | 37.6 |
| 1992 | Brett Roberts, Morehead St | 6-8 | Sr. | 29 | 278 | 66 | 193 | 815 | 28.1 |
| 1993 | Greg Guy, Tex.-Pan American | 6-1 | Jr. | 19 | 189 | 67 | 111 | 556 | 29.3 |
| 1994 | Glenn Robinson, Purdue | 6-8 | Jr. | 34 | 368 | 79 | 215 | 1030 | 30.3 |
| 1995 | Kurt Thomas, TCU | 6-9 | Sr. | 27 | 288 | 3 | 202 | 781 | 28.9 |
| 1996 | Kevin Granger, Texas Southern | 6-3 | Sr. | 24 | 194 | 30 | 230 | 648 | 27.0 |
| 1997 | Charles Jones, LIU-Brooklyn | 6-3 | Jr. | 30 | 338 | 109 | 118 | 903 | 30.1 |
| 1998 | Charles Jones, LIU-Brooklyn | 6-3 | Sr. | 30 | 326 | 116 | 101 | 869 | 29.0 |
| 1999 | Alvin Young, Niagara | 6-3 | Sr. | 29 | 253 | 65 | 157 | 728 | 25.1 |

## Scoring Average (Cont.)

| Year | Player and Team | Ht | Class | GP | FG | 3FG | FT | Pts | Avg |
|------|-----------------|-----|-------|-----|-----|-----|-----|-----|-----|
| 2000 | Courtney Alexander, Fresno St | 6-6 | Sr. | .27 | 252 | 58 | 107 | 669 | 24.8 |
| 2001 | Ronnie McCollum, Centenary | 6-4 | Sr. | 27 | 244 | 85 | 214 | 787 | 29.1 |
| 2002 | Jason Conley, Virginia Military | 6-5 | Fr. | 28 | 285 | 79 | 171 | 820 | 29.3 |
| 2003 | Ruben Douglas, New Mexico | 6-5 | Sr. | 28 | 218 | 94 | 253 | 783 | 28.0 |
| 2004 | Keydren Clark, St. Peter's | 5-8 | So. | 29 | 233 | 112 | 197 | 775 | 26.7 |
| 2005 | Keydren Clark, St. Peter's | 5-9 | Jr. | 28 | 230 | 109 | 152 | 721 | 25.8 |
| 2006 | Adam Morrison, Gonzaga | 6-8 | Jr. | 33 | 306 | 74 | 240 | 926 | 28.1 |
| 2007 | Reggie Williams, Virginia Military Institute | 6-5 | Jr. | 33 | 338 | 76 | 176 | 928 | 28.1 |
| 2008 | Stephen Curry, Davidson | 6-3 | Jr. | 34 | 312 | 130 | 220 | 974 | 28.6 |

## Rebounds

| Year | Player and Team | Ht | Class | GP | Reb | Avg |
|------|-----------------|-----|-------|-----|-----|-----|
| 1951 | Ernie Beck, Pennsylvania | 6-4 | So. | 27 | 556 | 20.6 |
| 1952 | Bill Hannon, Army | 6-3 | So. | 17 | 355 | 20.9 |
| 1953 | Ed Conlin, Fordham | 6-5 | So. | 26 | 612 | 23.5 |
| 1954 | Art Quimby, Connecticut | 6-5 | Jr. | 26 | 588 | 22.6 |
| 1955 | Charlie Slack, Marshall | 6-5 | Jr. | 21 | 538 | 25.6 |
| 1956 | Joe Holup, George Washington | 6-6 | Sr. | 26 | 604 | †.256 |
| 1957 | Elgin Baylor, Seattle | 6-6 | Jr. | 25 | 508 | †.235 |
| 1958 | Alex Ellis, Niagara | 6-5 | Sr. | 25 | 536 | †.262 |
| 1959 | Leroy Wright, Pacific | 6-8 | Jr. | 26 | 652 | †.238 |
| 1960 | Leroy Wright, Pacific | 6-8 | Sr. | 17 | 380 | †.234 |
| 1961 | Jerry Lucas, Ohio St | 6-8 | Jr. | 27 | 470 | †.198 |
| 1962 | Jerry Lucas, Ohio St | 6-8 | Sr. | 28 | 499 | †.211 |
| 1963 | Paul Silas, Creighton | 6-7 | Sr. | 27 | 557 | 20.6 |
| 1964 | Bob Pelkington, Xavier (Ohio) | 6-7 | Sr. | 26 | 567 | 21.8 |
| 1965 | Toby Kimball, Connecticut | 6-8 | Sr. | 23 | 483 | 21.0 |
| 1966 | Jim Ware, Oklahoma City | 6-8 | Sr. | 29 | 607 | 20.9 |
| 1967 | Dick Cunningham, Murray St | 6-10 | Jr. | 22 | 479 | 21.8 |
| 1968 | Neal Walk, Florida | 6-10 | Jr. | 25 | 494 | 19.8 |
| 1969 | Spencer Haywood, Detroit | 6-8 | So. | 22 | 472 | 21.5 |
| 1970 | Artis Gilmore, Jacksonville | 7-2 | Jr. | 28 | 621 | 22.2 |
| 1971 | Artis Gilmore, Jacksonville | 7-2 | Sr. | 26 | 603 | 23.2 |
| 1972 | Kermit Washington, American | 6-8 | Jr. | 23 | 455 | 19.8 |
| 1973 | Kermit Washington, American | 6-8 | Sr. | 22 | 439 | 20.0 |
| 1974 | Marvin Barnes, Providence | 6-9 | Sr. | 32 | 597 | 18.7 |
| 1975 | John Irving, Hofstra | 6-9 | So. | 21 | 323 | 15.4 |
| 1976 | Sam Pellom, Buffalo | 6-8 | So. | 26 | 420 | 16.2 |
| 1977 | Glenn Mosley, Seton Hall | 6-8 | Sr. | 29 | 473 | 16.3 |
| 1978 | Ken Williams, North Texas St | 6-7 | Sr. | 28 | 411 | 14.7 |
| 1979 | Monti Davis, Tennessee St | 6-7 | Jr. | 26 | 421 | 16.2 |
| 1980 | Larry Smith, Alcorn St | 6-8 | Sr. | 26 | 392 | 15.1 |
| 1981 | Darryl Watson, Miss. Valley St | 6-7 | Sr. | 27 | 379 | 14.0 |
| 1982 | LaSalle Thompson, Texas | 6-10 | Jr. | 27 | 365 | 13.5 |
| 1983 | Xavier McDaniel, Wichita St | 6-7 | So. | 28 | 403 | 14.4 |
| 1984 | Akeem Olajuwon, Houston | 7-0 | Jr. | 37 | 500 | 13.5 |
| 1985 | Xavier McDaniel, Wichita St | 6-8 | Sr | 31 | 460 | 14.8 |
| 1986 | David Robinson, Navy | 6-11 | Jr. | 35 | 455 | 13.0 |
| 1987 | Jerome Lane, Pittsburgh | 6-6 | So. | 33 | 444 | 13.5 |
| 1988 | Kenny Miller, Loyola (Ill.) | 6-9 | Fr. | 29 | 395 | 13.6 |
| 1989 | Hank Gathers, Loyola (Calif.) | 6-7 | Jr. | 31 | 426 | 13.7 |
| 1990 | Anthony Bonner, St. Louis | 6-8 | Sr. | 33 | 456 | 13.8 |
| 1991 | Shaquille O'Neal, LSU | 7-1 | So. | 28 | 411 | 14.7 |
| 1992 | Popeye Jones, Murray St | 6-8 | Sr. | 30 | 431 | 14.4 |
| 1993 | Warren Kidd, Middle Tenn. St | 6-9 | Sr. | 26 | 386 | 14.8 |
| 1994 | Jerome Lambert, Baylor | 6-8 | Jr. | 24 | 355 | 14.8 |
| 1995 | Kurt Thomas, TCU | 6-9 | Sr. | 27 | 393 | 14.6 |
| 1996 | Marcus Mann, Miss. Valley St | 6-8 | Sr. | 29 | 394 | 13.6 |
| 1997 | Tim Duncan, Wake Forest | 6-11 | Sr. | 31 | 457 | 14.7 |
| 1998 | Ryan Perryman, Dayton | 6-7 | Sr. | 33 | 412 | 12.5 |
| 1999 | Ian McGinnis, Dartmouth | 6-8 | So. | 26 | 317 | 12.2 |
| 2000 | Darren Phillips, Fairfield | 6-7 | Sr. | 29 | 405 | 14.0 |
| 2001 | Chris Marcus, Western Kentucky | 7-1 | Jr. | 31 | 374 | 12.1 |
| 2002 | Jeremy Bishop, Quinnipiac | 6-6 | J.. | 29 | 347 | 12.0 |
| 2003 | Brandon Hunter, Ohio | 6-7 | Sr. | 30 | 378 | 12.6 |
| 2004 | Paul Millsap, Louisiana Tech | 6-7 | Fr. | 30 | 374 | 12.5 |

†From 1956–1962, title was based on highest individual recoveries out of total by both teams in all games.

## Rebounds (Cont.)

| Year | Player and Team | Ht | Class | GP | Reb | Avg |
|---|---|---|---|---|---|---|
| 2005 | Paul Millsap, Louisiana Tech | 6-8 | So. | 29 | 360 | 12.4 |
| 2006 | Paul Millsap, Louisiana Tech | 6-8 | Jr. | 33 | 438 | 13.3 |
| 2007 | Rashad Jones-Jennings, Ark.-Little Rock | 6-8 | Sr. | 30 | 392 | 13.3 |
| 2008 | Blake Griffin, Oklahoma | 6-10 | So. | 35 | 504 | 14.4 |

## Assists

| Year | Player and Team | Class | GP | Ast | Avg |
|---|---|---|---|---|---|
| 1984 | Craig Lathen, Ill.-Chicago | Jr. | 29 | 274 | 9.45 |
| 1985 | Rob Weingard, Hofstra | Sr. | 24 | 228 | 9.50 |
| 1986 | Mark Jackson, St. John's (N.Y.) | Jr. | 36 | 328 | 9.11 |
| 1987 | Avery Johnson, Southern-Birm. | Jr. | 31 | 333 | 10.74 |
| 1988 | Avery Johnson, Southern-Birm. | Sr. | 30 | 399 | 13.30 |
| 1989 | Glenn Williams, Holy Cross | Sr. | 28 | 278 | 9.93 |
| 1990 | Todd Lehmann, Drexel | Sr. | 28 | 260 | 9.29 |
| 1991 | Chris Corchiani, North Carolina St | Sr. | 31 | 299 | 9.65 |
| 1992 | Van Usher, Tennessee Tech | Sr. | 29 | 254 | 8.76 |
| 1993 | Sam Crawford, New Mex. St | Sr. | 34 | 310 | 9.12 |
| 1994 | Jason Kidd, California | So. | 30 | 272 | 9.06 |
| 1995 | Nelson Haggerty, Baylor | Sr. | 28 | 284 | 10.10 |
| 1996 | Raimonds Miglinieks, UC-Irvine | Sr. | 27 | 230 | 8.52 |
| 1997 | Kenny Mitchell, Dartmouth | Sr. | 26 | 203 | 7.81 |
| 1998 | Ahlon Lewis, Arizona St | Sr. | 32 | 294 | 9.19 |
| 1999 | Doug Gottlieb, Oklahoma St | Jr. | 34 | 299 | 8.79 |
| 2000 | Mark Dickel, UNLV | Sr. | 31 | 280 | 9.03 |
| 2001 | Markus Carr, CSU–Northridge | Jr. | 32 | 286 | 8.94 |
| 2002 | T.J. Ford, Texas | Fr. | 33 | 273 | 8.27 |
| 2003 | Martell Bailey, Ill.-Chicago | Jr. | 30 | 244 | 8.13 |
| 2004 | Greg Davis, Troy St | Sr. | 31 | 256 | 8.26 |
| 2005 | Damitrius Coleman, Mercer | Jr. | 28 | 224 | 8.00 |
| | Will Funn, Portland St | Sr. | 28 | 224 | 8.00 |
| 2006 | Jared Jordan, Marist | Jr. | 29 | 247 | 8.52 |
| 2007 | Jared Jordan, Marist | Sr. | 31 | 274 | 8.83 |
| 2008 | Johnathon Jones, Oakland | Jr. | 36 | 290 | 8.06 |

## Blocked Shots

| Year | Player and Team | Class | GP | BS | Avg |
|---|---|---|---|---|---|
| 1986 | David Robinson, Navy | Jr. | 35 | 207 | 5.91 |
| 1987 | David Robinson, Navy | Sr. | 32 | 144 | 4.50 |
| 1988 | Rodney Blake, St. Joseph's (Pa.) | Sr. | 29 | 116 | 4.00 |
| 1989 | Alonzo Mourning, Georgetown | Fr. | 34 | 169 | 4.97 |
| 1990 | Kenny Green, Rhode Island | Sr. | 26 | 124 | 4.77 |
| 1991 | Shawn Bradley, BYU | Fr. | 34 | 177 | 5.21 |
| 1992 | Shaquille O'Neal, LSU | Jr. | 30 | 157 | 5.23 |
| 1993 | Theo Ratliff, Wyoming | Jr. | 28 | 124 | 4.43 |
| 1994 | Grady Livingston, Howard | Jr. | 26 | 115 | 4.42 |
| 1995 | Keith Closs, Central Conn. St | Fr. | 26 | 139 | 5.35 |
| 1996 | Keith Closs, Central Conn. St | So. | 28 | 178 | 6.36 |
| 1997 | Adonal Foyle, Colgate | Jr. | 28 | 180 | 6.43 |
| 1998 | Jerome James, Florida A&M | Sr. | 27 | 125 | 4.63 |
| 1999 | Tarvis Williams, Hampton | Jr. | 27 | 135 | 5.00 |
| 2000 | Ken Johnson, Ohio St | Sr. | 30 | 161 | 5.37 |
| 2001 | Tarvis Williams, Hampton | Sr | 32 | 147 | 4.59 |
| 2002 | Wojciech Myrda, La.-Monroe | Sr. | 32 | 172 | 5.38 |
| 2003 | Emeka Okafor, Connecticut | So. | 33 | 156 | 4.73 |
| 2004 | Anwar Ferguson, Houston | Sr. | 27 | 111 | 4.11 |
| 2005 | Deng Gai, Fairfield | Sr. | 30 | 165 | 5.50 |
| 2006 | Shawn James, Northeastern | So. | 30 | 196 | 6.53 |
| 2007 | Mickell Gladness, Ala.-A&M | Jr. | 30 | 188 | 6.26 |
| 2008 | Jarvis Varnado, Mississippi St | Jr. | 36 | 170 | 4.72 |

## Steals

| Year | Player and Team | Class | GP | Stl | Avg |
|---|---|---|---|---|---|
| 1986 | Darron Brittman, Chicago St | Sr. | 28 | 139 | 4.96 |
| 1987 | Tony Fairley, Charleston South. | Sr. | 28 | 114 | 4.07 |
| 1988 | Aldwin Ware, Florida A&M | Sr. | 29 | 142 | 4.90 |
| 1989 | Kenny Robertson, Cleveland St | Jr. | 28 | 111 | 3.96 |
| 1990 | Ronn McMahon, E. Washington | Sr. | 29 | 130 | 4.48 |
| 1991 | Van Usher, Tennessee Tech | Jr. | 28 | 104 | 3.71 |
| 1992 | Victor Snipes, NE Illinois | So. | 25 | 86 | 3.44 |

## Steals (Cont.)

| Year | Player and Team | Class | GP | Stl | Avg |
|------|-----------------|-------|-----|-----|-----|
| 1993 | Jason Kidd, California | Fr. | 29 | 110 | 3.80 |
| 1994 | Shawn Griggs, SW Louisiana | Sr. | 30 | 120 | 4.00 |
| 1995 | Roderick Anderson, Texas | Sr. | 30 | 101 | 3.37 |
| 1996 | Pointer Williams, McNeese St | Sr. | 27 | 118 | 4.37 |
| 1997 | Joel Hoover, Md.-Eastern Shore | Fr. | 28 | 90 | 3.21 |
| 1998 | Bonzi Wells, Ball St | Sr. | 29 | 103 | 3.55 |
| 1999 | Shawnta Rogers, George Wash. | Sr. | 29 | 103 | 3.55 |
| 2000 | Carl Williams, Liberty | Sr. | 28 | 107 | 3.82 |
| 2001 | Greedy Daniels, TCU | Jr. | 25 | 108 | 4.32 |
| 2002 | Desmond Cambridge, Ala. A&M | Sr. | 29 | 160 | 5.52 |
| 2003 | Alexis McMillan, Stetson | Sr. | 22 | 87 | 3.95 |
| 2004 | Marques Green, St. Bonaventure | Sr. | 27 | 107 | 3.96 |
| 2005 | Obie Trotter, Alabama A&M | Jr. | 32 | 125 | 3.91 |
| 2006 | Tim Smith, East Tennessee St | Sr. | 28 | 95 | 3.39 |
| 2007 | Travis Holmes, Virginia Military Inst. | So.. | 33 | 111 | 3.36 |
| 2008 | Chavis Holmes, Virg. Mil. Inst. | Sr. | 31 | 105 | 3.39 |

# NCAA Men's Division I Alltime Individual Leaders

## Single Game Records

### SCORING HIGHS VS DIVISION I OPPONENT

| Pts | Player and Team vs Opponent | Date |
|-----|------------------------------|------|
| 72 | Kevin Bradshaw, U.S. Int'l vs Loyola Marymount | 1-5-91 |
| 69 | Pete Maravich, LSU vs Alabama | 2-7-70 |
| 68 | Calvin Murphy, Niagara vs Syracuse | 12-7-68 |
| 66 | Jay Handlan, Washington & Lee vs Furman | 2-17-51 |
| 66 | Pete Maravich, LSU vs Tulane | 2-10-69 |
| 66 | Anthony Roberts, Oral Roberts vs North Carolina A&T | 2-19-77 |
| 65 | Anthony Roberts, Oral Roberts vs Oregon | 3-9-77 |
| 65 | Scott Haffner, Evansville vs Dayton | 2-18-89 |
| 64 | Pete Maravich, LSU vs Kentucky | 2-21-70 |
| 63 | Johnny Neumann, Mississippi vs LSU | 1-30-71 |
| 63 | Hersey Hawkins, Bradley vs Detroit | 2-22-88 |

### SCORING HIGHS VS NON-DIVISION I OPPONENT

| Pts | Player and Team vs Opponent | Date |
|-----|------------------------------|------|
| 100 | Frank Selvy, Furman vs Newberry | 2-13-54 |
| 85 | Paul Arizin, Villanova vs Philadelphia NAMC | 2-12-49 |
| 81 | Freeman Williams, Portland St vs Rocky Mountain | 2-3-78 |
| 73 | Bill Mlkvy, Temple vs Wilkes | 3-3-51 |
| 71 | Freeman Williams, Portland St vs S. Oregon | 2-9-77 |

### REBOUNDING HIGHS ALL-TIME

| Reb | Player and Team vs Opponent | Date |
|-----|------------------------------|------|
| 51 | Bill Chambers, William & Mary vs Virginia | 2-14-53 |
| 43 | Charlie Slack, Marshall vs Morris Harvey | 1-12-54 |
| 42 | Tom Heinsohn, Holy Cross vs Boston College | 3-1-55 |
| 40 | Art Quimby, Connecticut vs Boston University | 1-11-55 |
| 39 | Maurice Stokes, St. Francis (Pa.) vs John Carroll | 1-28-55 |
| 39 | Dave DeBusschere, Detroit vs C. Michigan | 1-30-60 |
| 39 | Keith Swagerty, Pacific vs UC-Santa Barbara | 3-5-65 |

### REBOUNDING HIGHS SINCE 1973*

| Reb | Player and Team vs Opponent | Date |
|-----|------------------------------|------|
| 35 | Larry Abney, Fresno St vs SMU | 2-17-00 |
| 34 | David Vaughn, Oral Roberts vs Brandeis | 1-8-73 |
| 32 | Jervaughn Scales, Southern-Birm. vs Grambling | 2-7-94 |
| 32 | Durand Macklin, LSU vs Tulane | 11-26-76 |
| 31 | Jim Bradley, Northern Illinois vs UW-Milwaukee | 2-19-73 |
| 31 | Calvin Natt, NE Louisiana vs Georgia Southern | 12-29-76 |

### ASSISTS

| Asst | Player and Team vs Opponent | Date |
|------|------------------------------|------|
| 22 | Tony Fairley, Baptist vs Armstrong St | 2-9-87 |
| 22 | Avery Johnson, Southern-Birm. vs Texas Southern | 1-25-88 |
| 22 | Sherman Douglas, Syracuse vs Providence | 1-28-89 |
| 21 | Kelvin Scarborough, New Mexico vs Hawaii | 2-13-87 |

*Freshmen became eligible for varsity play in 1973

## Single Game Records (Cont.)

### ASSISTS

| Asst | Player and Team vs Opponent | Date |
|---|---|---|
| 21 | Anthony Manuel, Bradley vs UC-Irvine | 12-19-87 |
| 21 | Avery Johnson, Southern-Birm. vs Alabama St | 1-16-88 |

### STEALS

| Stl | Player and Team vs Opponent | Date |
|---|---|---|
| 13 | Mookie Blaylock, Oklahoma vs Centenary | 12-12-87 |
| 13 | Mookie Blaylock, Oklahoma vs Loyola Marymount | 12-17-88 |
| 12 | Kenny Robertson, Cleveland St vs Wagner | 12-3-88 |
| 12 | Terry Evans, Oklahoma vs Florida A&M | 1-27-93 |
| 12 | Richard Duncan, Middle Tenn. St vs Eastern Kentucky | 2-20-99 |
| 12 | Greedy Daniels, Texas Christian vs Ark.–Pine Bluff | 12-30-00 |
| 12 | Jehiel Lewis, Navy vs Bucknell | 1-12-02 |
| 12 | Carldell Johnson, Ala.-Birmingham vs. South Carolina St | 11-27-05 |

### BLOCKED SHOTS

| BS | Player and Team vs Opponent | Date |
|---|---|---|
| 16 | Mickell Gladness, Alabama A&M vs Texas Southern | 2-24-07 |
| 14 | David Robinson, Navy vs UNC–Wilmington | 1-4-86 |
| 14 | Shawn Bradley, BYU vs Eastern Kentucky | 12-7-90 |
| 14 | Roy Rogers, Alabama vs Georgia | 2-10-96 |
| 14 | Loren Woods, Arizona vs Oregon | 2-3-00 |
| Ten tied with 13 | | |

## Single Season Records

### POINTS

| Player and Team | Year | GP | FG | 3FG | FT | Pts |
|---|---|---|---|---|---|---|
| Pete Maravich, LSU | 1970 | 31 | 522 | — | 337 | 1381 |
| Elvin Hayes, Houston | 1968 | 33 | 519 | — | 176 | 1214 |
| Frank Selvy, Furman | 1954 | 29 | 427 | — | 355 | 1209 |
| Pete Maravich, LSU | 1969 | 26 | 433 | — | 282 | 1148 |
| Pete Maravich, LSU | 1968 | 26 | 432 | — | 274 | 1138 |
| Bo Kimble, Loyola Marymount | 1990 | 32 | 404 | 92 | 231 | 1131 |
| Hersey Hawkins, Bradley | 1988 | 31 | 377 | 87 | 284 | 1125 |
| Austin Carr, Notre Dame | 1970 | 29 | 444 | — | 218 | 1106 |
| Austin Carr, Notre Dame | 1971 | 29 | 430 | — | 241 | 1101 |
| Otis Birdsong, Houston | 1977 | 36 | 452 | — | 186 | 1090 |

### SCORING AVERAGE

| Player and Team | Year | GP | FG | 3FG | FT | Pts |
|---|---|---|---|---|---|---|
| Pete Maravich, LSU | 1970 | 31 | 522 | 337 | 1381 | 44.5 |
| Pete Maravich, LSU | 1969 | 26 | 433 | 282 | 1148 | 44.2 |
| Pete Maravich, LSU | 1968 | 26 | 432 | 274 | 1138 | 43.8 |
| Frank Selvy, Furman | 1954 | 29 | 427 | 355 | 1209 | 41.7 |
| Johnny Neumann, Mississippi | 1971 | 23 | 366 | 191 | 923 | 40.1 |
| Freeman Williams, Portland St | 1977 | 26 | 417 | 176 | 1010 | 38.8 |
| Billy McGill, Utah | 1962 | 26 | 394 | 221 | 1009 | 38.8 |
| Calvin Murphy, Niagara | 1968 | 24 | 337 | 242 | 916 | 38.2 |
| Austin Carr, Notre Dame | 1970 | 29 | 444 | 218 | 1106 | 38.1 |
| Austin Carr, Notre Dame | 1971 | 29 | 430 | 241 | 1101 | 38.0 |

### REBOUNDS

| Player and Team | Year | GP | Reb | Player and Team | Year | GP | Reb |
|---|---|---|---|---|---|---|---|
| Walt Dukes, Seton Hall | 1953 | 33 | 734 | Artis Gilmore, Jacksonville | 1970 | 28 | 621 |
| Leroy Wright, Pacific | 1959 | 26 | 652 | Tom Gola, La Salle | 1955 | 31 | 618 |
| Tom Gola, La Salle | 1954 | 30 | 652 | Ed Conlin, Fordham | 1953 | 26 | 612 |
| Charlie Tyra, Louisville | 1956 | 29 | 645 | Art Quimby, Connecticut | 1955 | 25 | 611 |
| Paul Silas, Creighton | 1964 | 29 | 631 | Bill Russell, San Francisco | 1956 | 29 | 609 |
| Elvin Hayes, Houston | 1968 | 33 | 624 | Jim Ware, Oklahoma City | 1966 | 29 | 607 |

### REBOUND AVERAGE ALL-TIME

| Player and Team | Year | GP | Reb | Avg |
|---|---|---|---|---|
| Charlie Slack, Marshall | 1955 | 21 | 538 | 25.6 |
| Leroy Wright, Pacific | 1959 | 26 | 652 | 25.1 |
| Art Quimby, Connecticut | 1955 | 25 | 611 | 24.4 |
| Charlie Slack, Marshall | 1956 | 22 | 520 | 23.6 |
| Ed Conlin, Fordham | 1953 | 26 | 612 | 23.5 |

### REBOUND AVERAGE SINCE 1973*

| Player and Team | Year | GP | Reb | Avg |
|---|---|---|---|---|
| Kermit Washington, American | 1973 | 22 | 439 | 20.0 |
| Marvin Barnes, Providence | 1973 | 30 | 571 | 19.0 |
| Marvin Barnes, Providence | 1974 | 32 | 597 | 18.7 |
| Pete Padgett, Nev.-Reno | 1973 | 26 | 462 | 17.8 |
| Jim Bradley, Northern Illinois | 1973 | 24 | 426 | 17.8 |

## Single Season Records (Cont.)

### ASSISTS

| Player and Team | Year | GP | Asst | Player and Team | Year | GP | Asst |
|---|---|---|---|---|---|---|---|
| Mark Wade, UNLV | 1987 | 38 | 406 | Sherman Douglas, Syracuse | 1989 | 38 | 326 |
| Avery Johnson, Southern-Birm. | 1988 | 30 | 399 | Sam Crawford, New Mex. St | 1993 | 34 | 310 |
| Anthony Manuel, Bradley | 1988 | 31 | 373 | Greg Anthony, UNLV | 1991 | 35 | 310 |
| Avery Johnson, Southern-Birm. | 1987 | 31 | 333 | Reid Gettys, Houston | 1984 | 37 | 309 |
| Mark Jackson, St. John's (N.Y.) | 1986 | 32 | 328 | Carl Golston, Loyola (Ill.) | 1985 | 33 | 305 |

### ASSIST AVERAGE

| Player and Team | Year | GP | Asst | Avg | Player and Team | Year | GP | Asst | Avg |
|---|---|---|---|---|---|---|---|---|---|
| Avery Johnson, Southern-Birm. | 1988 | 30 | 399 | 13.3 | Chris Corchiani, North Carolina St | 1991 | 31 | 299 | 9.6 |
| Anthony Manuel, Bradley | 1988 | 31 | 373 | 12.0 | Tony Fairley, Charleston South.* | 1987 | 28 | 270 | 9.6 |
| Avery Johnson, Southern-Birm. | 1987 | 31 | 333 | 10.7 | Tyrone Bogues, Wake Forest | 1987 | 29 | 276 | 9.5 |
| Mark Wade, UNLV | 1987 | 38 | 406 | 10.7 | Ron Weingard, Hofstra | 1985 | 24 | 228 | 9.5 |
| Nelson Haggerty, Baylor | 1995 | 28 | 284 | 10.1 | Craig Neal, Georgia Tech | 1988 | 32 | 303 | 9.5 |
| Glenn Williams, Holy Cross | 1989 | 28 | 278 | 9.9 | | | | | |

### FIELD-GOAL PERCENTAGE

| Player and Team | Year | GP | FG | FGA | Pct |
|---|---|---|---|---|---|
| Steve Johnson, Oregon St | 1981 | 28 | 235 | 315 | 74.6 |
| Dwayne Davis, Florida | 1989 | 33 | 179 | 248 | 72.2 |
| Keith Walker, Utica | 1985 | 27 | 154 | 216 | 71.3 |
| Steve Johnson, Oregon St | 1980 | 30 | 211 | 297 | 71.0 |
| Adam Mark, Belmont | 2002 | 26 | 150 | 212 | 70.8 |
| Oliver Miller, Arkansas | 1991 | 38 | 254 | 361 | 70.4 |
| Alan Williams, Princeton | 1987 | 25 | 163 | 232 | 70.3 |
| Mark McNamara, California | 1982 | 27 | 231 | 329 | 70.2 |
| Warren Kidd, Middle Tennessee St | 1991 | 30 | 173 | 247 | 70.0 |
| Pete Freeman, Akron | 1991 | 28 | 175 | 250 | 70.0 |

Based on qualifiers for annual championship.

### FREE-THROW PERCENTAGE

| Player and Team | Year | GP | FT | FTA | Pct |
|---|---|---|---|---|---|
| Blake Ahearn SW Missouri St† | 2004 | 33 | 117 | 120 | 97.5 |
| Ryan Toolson, Utah Valley St | 2006 | 29 | 96 | 99 | 97.0 |
| Derek Raivio, Gonzaga | 2006 | 33 | 146 | 152 | 96.1 |
| Craig Cellins, Penn St | 1985 | 27 | 94 | 98 | 95.9 |
| A.J. Graves, Butler | 2006 | 32 | 137 | 143 | 95.8 |
| J.J. Redick, Duke | 2004 | 37 | 143 | 150 | 95.3 |
| Steve Drabyn, Belmont | 2003 | 29 | 78 | 82 | 95.1 |
| Rod Foster, UCLA | 1982 | 27 | 95 | 100 | 95.0 |
| Clay McKnight, Pacific | 2000 | 24 | 74 | 78 | 94.9 |
| Matt Logie, Lehigh | 2003 | 28 | 91 | 96 | 94.8 |
| Blake Ahearn, Missouri State | 2005 | 32 | 90 | 95 | 94.7 |

### THREE-POINT FIELD-GOAL PERCENTAGE

| Player and Team | Year | GP | 3FG | 3FGA | Pct |
|---|---|---|---|---|---|
| Glenn Tropf, Holy Cross | 1988 | 29 | 52 | 82 | 63.4 |
| Sean Wightman, Western Michigan | 1992 | 30 | 48 | 76 | 63.2 |
| Keith Jennings, East Tennessee St | 1991 | 33 | 84 | 142 | 59.2 |
| Dave Calloway, Monmouth (N.J.) | 1989 | 28 | 48 | 82 | 58.5 |
| Steve Kerr, Arizona | 1988 | 38 | 114 | 199 | 57.3 |
| Reginald Jones, Prairie View | 1987 | 28 | 64 | 112 | 57.1 |
| Jim Cantamessa, Siena | 1998 | 29 | 66 | 117 | 56.4 |
| Joel Tribelhorn, Colorado St | 1989 | 33 | 76 | 135 | 56.3 |
| Mike Joseph, Bucknell | 1988 | 28 | 65 | 116 | 56.0 |
| Brian Jackson, Evansville | 1995 | 27 | 53 | 95 | 55.8 |

Based on qualifiers for annual championship.

*Formerly Baptist
†Southwest Missouri State changed name to Missouri State after 2004–05 season
Based on qualifiers for annual championship.

## Single Season Records (Cont.)

### STEALS

| Player and Team | Year | GP | Stl |
|---|---|---|---|
| Desmond Cambridge, Alabama A&M ..2002 | | 29 | 160 |
| Mookie Blaylock, Oklahoma | 1988 | 39 | 150 |
| Aldwin Ware, Florida A&M | 1988 | 29 | 142 |
| Darron Brittman, Chicago St. | 1986 | 28 | 139 |
| John Linehan, Providence | 2002 | 31 | 139 |

### BLOCKED SHOTS

| Player and Team | Year | GP | BS |
|---|---|---|---|
| David Robinson, Navy | 1986 | 35 | 207 |
| Shawn James, Northeastern | 2005 | 30 | 196 |
| Mickell Gladness, Alabama A&M | 2006 | 30 | 188 |
| Adonal Foyle, Colgate | 1997 | 28 | 180 |
| Keith Closs, Central Conn. St | 1996 | 28 | 178 |

### STEAL AVERAGE

| Player and Team | Year | GP | Stl | Avg |
|---|---|---|---|---|
| D. Cambridge, Alabama A&M ....2002 | | 29 | 160 | 5.52 |
| Darron Brittman, Chicago St | 1986 | 28 | 139 | 4.96 |
| Aldwin Ware, Florida A&M | 1988 | 29 | 142 | 4.90 |
| John Linehan, Providence | 2002 | 31 | 139 | 4.48 |
| Ronn McMahon, E. Washington..1990 | | 29 | 130 | 4.48 |

### BLOCKED-SHOT AVERAGE

| Player and Team | Year | GP | BS | Avg |
|---|---|---|---|---|
| Shawn James, Northeastern | 2005 | 30 | 196 | 6.53 |
| Adonal Foyle, Colgate | 1997 | 28 | 180 | 6.43 |
| Keith Closs, Central Conn. St | 1996 | 28 | 178 | 6.36 |
| Mickell Gladness, Alabama A&M | 2006 | 28 | 188 | 6.26 |
| David Robinson, Navy | 1986 | 35 | 207 | 5.91 |

## Career Records

### POINTS

| Player and Team | Ht | Final Year | GP | FG | 3FG* | FT | Pts |
|---|---|---|---|---|---|---|---|
| Pete Maravich, LSU | 6-5 | 1970 | 83 | 1387 | — | 893 | 3667 |
| Freeman Williams, Portland St. | 6-4 | 1978 | 106 | 1369 | — | 511 | 3249 |
| Lionel Simmons, La Salle | 6-7 | 1990 | 131 | 1244 | 56 | 673 | 3217 |
| Alphonso Ford, Mississippi Valley St. | 6-2 | 1993 | 109 | 1121 | 333 | 590 | 3165 |
| Harry Kelly, Texas Southern | 6-7 | 1983 | 110 | 1234 | — | 598 | 3066 |
| Keydren Clark, St. Peter's | 5-9 | 2006 | 118 | 967 | 435 | 689 | 3058 |
| Hersey Hawkins, Bradley | 6-3 | 1988 | 125 | 1100 | 118 | 690 | 3008 |
| Oscar Robertson, Cincinnati | 6-5 | 1960 | 88 | 1052 | — | 869 | 2973 |
| Danny Manning, Kansas | 6-10 | 1988 | 147 | 1216 | 10 | 509 | 2951 |
| Alfredrick Hughes, Loyola (Ill.) | 6-5 | 1985 | 120 | 1226 | — | 462 | 2914 |
| Elvin Hayes, Houston | 6-8 | 1968 | 93 | 1215 | — | 454 | 2884 |
| Tyler Hansbrough, North Carolina | 6-9 | 2009 | 142 | 939 | 12 | 982 | 2872 |
| Larry Bird, Indiana St. | 6-9 | 1979 | 94 | 1154 | — | 542 | 2850 |
| Otis Birdsong, Houston | 6-4 | 1977 | 116 | 1176 | — | 480 | 2832 |
| Kevin Bradshaw, Bethune-Cookman, U.S. Int'l | 6-6 | 1991 | 111 | 1027 | 132 | 618 | 2804 |
| Allan Houston, Tennessee | 6-6 | 1993 | 128 | 902 | 346 | 651 | 2801 |
| J.J. Redick, Duke | 6-4 | 2006 | 139 | 825 | 457 | 662 | 2769 |
| Hank Gathers, USC, Loyola Marymount | 6-7 | 1990 | 117 | 1127 | 0 | 469 | 2723 |
| Reggie Lewis, Northeastern | 6-7 | 1987 | 122 | 1043 | 30 (1) | 592 | 2708 |
| Daren Queenan, Lehigh | 6-5 | 1988 | 118 | 1024 | 29 | 626 | 2703 |
| Byron Larkin, Xavier (Ohio) | 6-3 | 1988 | 121 | 1022 | 51 | 601 | 2696 |
| Bo McCalebb, New Orleans | 6-0 | 2008 | 128 | 977 | 115 | 610 | 2679 |

*Listed is the number of three-pointers scored since it became the national rule in 1987; the number in the parentheses is number scored prior to 1987—these counted as three points in the game but counted as two-pointers in the national rankings. The three-pointers in the parentheses are not included in total points.

### SCORING AVERAGE

| Player and Team | Final Year | GP | FG | FT | Pts | Avg |
|---|---|---|---|---|---|---|
| Pete Maravich, LSU | 1968 | 83 | 1387 | 893 | 3667 | 44.2 |
| Austin Carr, Notre Dame | 1971 | 74 | 1017 | 526 | 2560 | 34.6 |
| Oscar Robertson, Cincinnati | 1960 | 88 | 1052 | 869 | 2973 | 33.8 |
| Calvin Murphy, Niagara | 1970 | 77 | 947 | 654 | 2548 | 33.1 |
| Dwight Lamar, SW Louisiana | 1973 | 57 | 768 | 326 | 1862 | 32.7 |
| Frank Selvy, Furman | 1954 | 78 | 922 | 694 | 2538 | 32.5 |
| Rick Mount, Purdue | 1970 | 72 | 910 | 503 | 2323 | 32.3 |
| Darrell Floyd, Furman | 1956 | 71 | 868 | 545 | 2281 | 32.1 |
| Nick Werkman, Seton Hall | 1964 | 71 | 812 | 649 | 2273 | 32.0 |
| Willie Humes, Idaho St. | 1971 | 48 | 565 | 380 | 1510 | 31.5 |
| William Averitt, Pepperdine | 1973 | 49 | 615 | 311 | 1541 | 31.4 |
| Elgin Baylor, Coll. of Idaho, Seattle | 1958 | 80 | 956 | 588 | 2500 | 31.3 |
| Elvin Hayes, Houston | 1968 | 93 | 1215 | 454 | 2884 | 31.0 |
| Freeman Williams, Portland St. | 1978 | 106 | 1369 | 511 | 3249 | 30.7 |
| Larry Bird, Indiana St. | 1979 | 94 | 1154 | 542 | 2850 | 30.3 |

## Career Records (Cont.)
### REBOUNDS ALL-TIME

| Player and Team | Final Year | GP | Reb |
|---|---|---|---|
| Tom Gola, La Salle | 1955 | 118 | 2201 |
| Joe Holup, George Washington | 1956 | 104 | 2030 |
| Charlie Slack, Marshall | 1956 | 88 | 1916 |
| Ed Conlin, Fordham | 1955 | 102 | 1884 |
| Dickie Hemric, Wake Forest | 1955 | 104 | 1802 |

### REBOUNDS SINCE 1973*

| Player and Team | Final Year | GP | Reb |
|---|---|---|---|
| Tim Duncan, Wake Forest | 1997 | 128 | 1570 |
| Derrick Coleman, Syracuse | 1990 | 143 | 1537 |
| Malik Rose, Drexel | 1996 | 120 | 1514 |
| Ralph Sampson, Virginia | 1983 | 132 | 1511 |
| Pete Padgett, Nev.-Reno | 1976 | 104 | 1464 |

### ASSISTS

| Player and Team | Final Year | GP | Asst |
|---|---|---|---|
| Bobby Hurley, Duke | 1993 | 140 | 1076 |
| Chris Corchiani, North Carolina St. | 1991 | 124 | 1038 |
| Ed Cota, North Carolina | 2000 | 138 | 1030 |
| Keith Jennings, East Tennessee St. | 1991 | 127 | 983 |
| Steve Blake, Maryland | 2003 | 138 | 972 |

### FIELD-GOAL PERCENTAGE

| Player and Team | Final Year | FG | FGA | Pct |
|---|---|---|---|---|
| Steve Johnson, Oregon St | 1981 | 828 | 1222 | 67.8 |
| Michael Bradley, Kentucky/Villanova | 2001 | 441 | 651 | 67.7 |
| Murray Brown, Florida St | 1980 | 566 | 847 | 66.8 |
| Lee Campbell, SW Missouri St | 1990 | 411 | 618 | 66.5 |
| Warren Kidd, Middle Tennessee St | 1993 | 496 | 747 | 66.4 |

Note: Minimum 400 field goals and 4 FG made per game.

### FREE-THROW PERCENTAGE

| Player and Team | Final Year | FT | FTA | Pct |
|---|---|---|---|---|
| Blake Ahearn, Missouri St | 2007 | 435 | 460 | 94.6 |
| Derek Raivio, Gonzaga | 2007 | 343 | 370 | 92.7 |
| Gary Buchanan, Villanova | 2003 | 324 | 355 | 91.3 |
| J.J. Redick, Duke | 2006 | 662 | 726 | 91.2 |
| Greg Starrick, Kentucky/Southern Illinois | 1972 | 341 | 375 | 90.9 |

Note: Minimum 300 free throws made.
*Freshmen became eligible for varsity play in 1973.

### THREE-POINT FIELD GOALS MADE

| Player and Team | Final Year | GP | 3FG |
|---|---|---|---|
| J.J. Redick, Duke | 2006 | 139 | 457 |
| David Holston, Chicago St | 2009 | 119 | 450 |
| Keydren Clark, St. Peter's | 2006 | 118 | 435 |
| Chris Lofton, Tennessee | 2008 | 128 | 431 |
| Stephen Curry, Davidson | 2009 | 104 | 414 |

### THREE-POINT FIELD-GOAL PERCENTAGE

| Player and Team | Final Year | 3FG | 3FGA | Pct |
|---|---|---|---|---|
| Tony Bennett, UW–Green Bay | 1992 | 290 | 584 | 49.7 |
| Stephen Sir, San Diego St/Northern Ariz. | 2007 | 323 | 689 | 46.9 |
| David Olson, Eastern Illinois | 1992 | 262 | 562 | 46.6 |
| Jaycee Carroll, Utah St | 2008 | 369 | 793 | 46.5 |
| Ross Land, Northern Arizona | 2000 | 308 | 664 | 46.4 |

Note: Minimum 200 3-point field goals and 2.0 3FG/G.

## Career Records (Cont.)

### STEALS

| Player and Team | Final Year | GP | Stl |
|---|---|---|---|
| John Linehan, Providence | 2002 | 122 | 385 |
| Desmond Cambridge, Alabama A&M | 2002 | 111 | 377 |
| Eric Murdock, Providence | 1991 | 117 | 376 |
| Pepe Sanchez, Temple | 2000 | 116 | 365 |
| Cookie Belcher, Nebraska | 2001 | 131 | 353 |

### BLOCKED SHOTS

| Player and Team | Final Year | GP | BS |
|---|---|---|---|
| Wojciech Myrda, La.-Monroe | 2002 | 115 | 535 |
| Adonal Foyle, Colgate | 1997 | 87 | 492 |
| Tim Duncan, Wake Forest | 1997 | 128 | 481 |
| Alonzo Mourning, Georgetown | 1992 | 120 | 453 |
| Tarvis Williams, Hampton | 2001 | 114 | 452 |

# NCAA Men's Division I Team Leaders

## Division I Team Alltime Wins

| Team | First Year | Yrs | W | L | T |
|---|---|---|---|---|---|
| Kentucky | 1903 | 106 | 1988 | 635 | 1 |
| North Carolina | 1911 | 99 | 1984 | 703 | 0 |
| Kansas | 1899 | 111 | 1970 | 793 | 0 |
| Duke | 1906 | 104 | 1877 | 817 | 0 |
| Syracuse | 1901 | 108 | 1753 | 806 | 0 |
| Temple | 1895 | 113 | 1711 | 960 | 0 |
| St. John's (N.Y.) | 1908 | 102 | 1686 | 868 | 0 |
| UCLA | 1920 | 90 | 1658 | 726 | 0 |
| Pennsylvania | 1897 | 109 | 1651 | 949 | 2 |
| Notre Dame | 1898 | 104 | 1641 | 908 | 1 |
| Indiana | 1901 | 109 | 1637 | 909 | 0 |
| Utah | 1909 | 101 | 1637 | 858 | 0 |
| Illinois | 1906 | 104 | 1609 | 853 | 0 |
| Western Kentucky | 1915 | 90 | 1602 | 780 | 0 |
| Oregon St | 1902 | 108 | 1594 | 1180 | 0 |

Note: Minimum of 25 years in Division I.

## Division I Alltime Winning Percentage

| Team | First Year | Yrs | W | L | T | Pct |
|---|---|---|---|---|---|---|
| Kentucky | 1903 | 106 | 1988 | 635 | 1 | .758 |
| North Carolina | 1911 | 99 | 1984 | 703 | 0 | .738 |
| Kansas | 1899 | 111 | 1970 | 793 | 0 | .713 |
| UNLV | 1959 | 51 | 1058 | 429 | 0 | .711 |
| UCLA | 1920 | 90 | 1672 | 726 | 0 | .697 |
| Duke | 1906 | 104 | 1877 | 817 | 0 | .697 |
| Syracuse | 1901 | 108 | 1753 | 806 | 0 | .685 |
| Western Kentucky | 1915 | 90 | 1602 | 780 | 0 | .673 |
| St. John's (N.Y.) | 1908 | 102 | 1686 | 868 | 0 | .660 |
| Louisville | 1912 | 95 | 1587 | 831 | 0 | .656 |
| Utah | 1909 | 101 | 1637 | 858 | 0 | .656 |
| Illinois | 1906 | 104 | 1609 | 853 | 0 | .654 |
| Arizona | 1905 | 104 | 1568 | 858 | 1 | .646 |
| Notre Dame | 1898 | 104 | 1651 | 908 | 1 | .645 |
| Arkansas | 1924 | 86 | 1487 | 822 | 0 | .644 |
| Indiana | 1901 | 109 | 1641 | 909 | 0 | .644 |

# NCAA Men's Division I Winning Streaks

## Longest—Full Season

| Team | Games | Years | Ended by |
|---|---|---|---|
| UCLA | 88 | 1971–74 | Notre Dame (71–70) |
| San Francisco | 60 | 1955–57 | Illinois (62–33) |
| UCLA | 47 | 1966–68 | Houston (71–69) |
| UNLV | 45 | 1990–91 | Duke (79–77) |
| Texas | 44 | 1913–17 | Rice (24–18) |
| Seton Hall | 43 | 1939–41 | LIU-Brooklyn (49–26) |
| LIU-Brooklyn | 43 | 1935–37 | Stanford (45–31) |
| UCLA | 41 | 1968–69 | USC (46–44) |
| Marquette | 39 | 1970–71 | Ohio St (60–59) |
| Cincinnati | 37 | 1962–63 | Wichita St (65–64) |
| North Carolina | 37 | 1957–58 | W Virginia (75–64) |

## Longest—Regular Season

| Team | Games | Years | Ended by |
|---|---|---|---|
| UCLA | 76 | 1971–74 | Notre Dame (71–70) |
| Indiana | 57 | 1975–77 | Toledo (59–57) |
| Marquette | 56 | 1970–72 | Detroit (70–49) |
| Kentucky | 54 | 1952–55 | Georgia Tech (59–58) |
| San Francisco | 51 | 1955–57 | Illinois (62–33) |
| Pennsylvania | 48 | 1970–72 | Temple (57–52) |
| Ohio State | 47 | 1960–62 | Wisconsin (86–67) |
| Texas | 44 | 1913–17 | Rice (24–18) |
| UCLA | 43 | 1966–68 | Houston (71–69) |
| LIU-Brooklyn | 43 | 1935–37 | Stanford (45–31) |
| Seton Hall | 42 | 1939–41 | LIU-Brooklyn (49–26) |

## Longest—Home Court

| Team | Games | Years | Team | Games | Years |
|------|-------|-------|------|-------|-------|
| Kentucky | 129 | 1943–55 | Lamar | 80 | 1978–84 |
| St. Bonaventure | 99 | 1948–61 | Long Beach St | 75 | 1968–74 |
| UCLA | 98 | 1970–76 | UNLV | 72 | 1974–78 |
| Cincinnati | 86 | 1957–64 | Arizona | 71 | 1987–92 |
| Marquette | 81 | 1967–73 | Cincinnati | 68 | 1972–78 |
| Arizona | 81 | 1945–51 | Western Kentucky | 67 | 1949–55 |

# NCAA Men's Division I Winningest Coaches

## Active Coaches*

### WINS

| Coach and Team | W |
|----------------|---|
| Mike Krzyzewski, Duke | 833 |
| Jim Calhoun, Connecticut | 805 |
| Jim Boeheim, Syracuse | 799 |
| Bob Huggins, West Virginia | 639 |
| Tom Penders, Houston | 629 |
| Gary Williams, Maryland | 625 |
| Homer Drew, Valparaiso | 602 |
| Roy Williams, North Carolina | 594 |
| Bo Ryan, Wisconsin | 576 |
| Mike Montgomery, California | 569 |

### WINNING PERCENTAGE

| Coach and Team | Yrs | W | L | Pct |
|----------------|-----|---|---|-----|
| Roy Williams, North Carolina | 21 | 594 | 138 | .811 |
| Mark Few, Gonzaga | 10 | 264 | 66 | .800 |
| Jamie Dixon, Pittsburgh | 6 | 163 | 45 | .784 |
| Bruce Pearl, Tennessee | 17 | 415 | 121 | .774 |
| Bo Ryan, Wisconsin | 25 | 576 | 176 | .766 |
| John Calipari, Memphis | 17 | 441 | 139 | .760 |
| Mike Krzyzewski, Duke | 34 | 833 | 274 | .752 |
| Thad Matta, Ohio St | 9 | 229 | 77 | .748 |
| Mark Fox, Georgia | 5 | 123 | 43 | .741 |
| Rick Pitino, Louisville | 23 | 552 | 197 | .737 |

Note: Minimum 5 years as a Division I head coach; includes record at 4-year colleges only.

Note: Minimum 5 years as a Division I head coach; includes record at 4-year colleges only.

## Alltime Winningest Men's Division I Coaches

| | W |
|---|---|
| Bob Knight (Army, Indiana, Texas Tech) | 902 |
| Dean Smith (North Carolina) | 879 |
| Adolph Rupp (Kentucky) | 876 |
| *Mike Krzyzewski (Army, Duke) | 833 |
| Jim Phelan (Mt. St. Mary's) | 830 |
| *Jim Calhoun (Northeastern, Connecticut) | 805 |
| Eddie Sutton (Creighton, Arkansas, Kentucky, Oklahoma St) | 804 |
| *Jim Boeheim (Syracuse) | 799 |
| Lefty Driesell (Davidson, Maryland, James Madison, Georgia St) | 786 |
| Lute Olson (Long Beach St, Iowa, Arizona) | 780 |
| Lou Henson (Hardin-Simmons, New Mexico St, Illinois, New Mexico St) | 779 |
| Henry Iba (NW Missouri St, Colorado, Oklahoma St) | 764 |
| Ed Diddle (Western Kentucky) | 759 |
| Phog Allen (Baker, Kansas, Haskell, Central Missouri St, Kansas) | 746 |
| John Chaney (Cheyney St, Temple) | 741 |
| Jerry Tarkanian (Long Beach St, UNLV, Fresno St) | 729 |
| Norm Stewart (Northern Iowa, Missouri) | 728 |
| Ray Meyer (DePaul) | 724 |
| Don Haskins (Oklahoma St, UTEP) | 719 |
| Denny Crum (UCLA, Louisville) | 675 |
| John Wooden (Purdue, Indiana St, UCLA) | 664 |
| Ralph Miller (Wichita St, Iowa, Oregon St) | 657 |
| Gene Bartow (C. Missouri St, Valparaiso, Memphis, Illinois, UCLA, UAB) | 647 |
| Billy Tubbs (Lamar, Southwestern [Tex.], Oklahoma, TCU) | 641 |
| *Bob Huggins (Akron, Cincinnati, Kansas St, West Virginia) | 639 |
| Marv Harshman (Pacific Lutheran, Washington St, Washington) | 637 |

Note: Minimum 10 head coaching seasons in Division I.
*Active in 2008–09.

## Alltime Winningest Men's Division I Coaches (Cont.)
### WINNING PERCENTAGE

| Coach (Team, Years) | Yrs | W | L | Pct |
|---|---|---|---|---|
| Clair Bee (Rider 1929–31, LIU-Brooklyn 1932–45, 1946–51) | .21 | 412 | 87 | .826 |
| Adolph Rupp (Kentucky 1931–72) | .41 | 876 | 190 | .822 |
| *Roy Williams (Kansas 1989–2003, North Carolina 2003–) | .21 | 594 | 138 | .811 |
| John Wooden (Indiana St 1947–48, UCLA 1949–75) | .29 | 664 | 162 | .804 |
| *Mark Few (Gonzaga 1999–) | .10 | 264 | 66 | .800 |
| John Kresse (College of Charleston 1980–2002) | .23 | 560 | 143 | .797 |
| Jerry Tarkanian (Long Beach St 1969–73, UNLV 1974–92, Fresno St 1995–2002) | .31 | 729 | 201 | .784 |
| Francis Schmidt (Tulsa 1916–17, Arkansas 1924–29, TCU 1930–34) | .17 | 258 | 72 | .782 |
| Dean Smith (North Carolina 1962–97) | .36 | 879 | 254 | .776 |
| *Bo Ryan (UW-Milwaukee 1999–2001, Wisconsin 2001–) | .25 | 576 | 176 | .766 |
| Jack Ramsay (St. Joseph's [Pa.] 1956–66) | .11 | 231 | 71 | .765 |
| Frank Keaney (Rhode Island 1921–48) | .28 | 401 | 124 | .764 |
| George Keogan (St. Louis 1916, Allegheny 1919, Valparaiso 1920–21, Notre Dame 1924–43) | .27 | 414 | 127 | .764 |
| Vic Bubas (Duke 1960–69) | .10 | 213 | 67 | .761 |
| *John Calipari (Massachusetts 1989–96, Memphis 2001–09) | .17 | 441 | 139 | .760 |
| Harry Fisher (Columbia 1907–16, Army 1922–23, 1925) | .16 | 189 | 60 | .759 |
| Fred Bennion (Brigham Young 1909–10, Utah 1911-14, Montana St 1915-19) | .11 | 95 | 31 | .756 |
| *Mike Krzyzewski (Army 1976–80, Duke 1981–) | .34 | 833 | 274 | .752 |
| Charles (Chick) Davies (Duquesne 1925–43, 1947–48) | .21 | 314 | 106 | .748 |
| Ray Mears (Wittenberg 1957–62, Tennessee 1963–77) | .21 | 399 | 135 | .747 |
| Edward McNichol (Penn 1921-30) | .10 | 186 | 63 | .747 |
| Al McGuire (Belmont Abbey 1958–64, Marquette 1965–77) | .20 | 406 | 142 | .741 |
| Phog Allen (Baker 1906–08, Haskell 1909, C. Mo. St 1913–19, Kansas 1908–09, 1920–56) | .50 | 746 | 264 | .739 |
| Everett Case (North Carolina St 1947–65) | .19 | 377 | 134 | .738 |
| *Rick Pitino (Boston Univ. 1979–83, Prov. 1986–87, Kent'y 1990–97, Lo'ville 2002–) | .23 | 552 | 197 | .737 |
| Lute Olson (Long Beach St 1973–74, Iowa 1974–83, Arizona 1983–) | .34 | 780 | 280 | .736 |
| Arthur Schabinger (Ottawa 1917–20, Emporia St 1921–22, Creighton 1924–25) | .19 | 245 | 88 | .736 |
| G. Ott Romney (Montana St 1923–28, BYU 1929–35) | .13 | 283 | 102 | .735 |
| *Jim Boeheim (Syracuse 1977–) | .33 | 799 | 288 | .735 |

*Active in 2008–09. Note: Minimum 10 head coaching seasons in Division I.

## Alltime Winningest Women's Division I Coaches
### WINNING PERCENTAGE

| Coach (Team, Years) | Yrs | W | L | Pct |
|---|---|---|---|---|
| Leon Barmore (Louisiana Tech 1983–02) | .20 | 576 | 87 | .869 |
| *Geno Auriemma (Connecticut 1986–) | .24 | 696 | 122 | .851 |
| *Pat Summitt (Tennessee 1975–) | .35 | 1005 | 193 | .839 |
| *Tara VanDerveer (Idaho 1979-80, Ohio St 1981–85, Stanford 1986–95, 97–) | .30 | 757 | 193 | .797 |
| Bill Sheahan (Mt. St. Mary's 1982–98) | .17 | 372 | 104 | .782 |
| *Robin Selvig (Montana 1979–) | .31 | 725 | 204 | .780 |
| *Gail Goestenkors (Duke 1993–07, Texas 2007–) | .17 | 439 | 124 | .780 |
| *Wes Moore (Maryville 1988–93, Francis Marion 1996–98, Chattanooga 1999–) | .20 | 466 | 132 | .779 |
| *Carey Green (Liberty 2000–) | .10 | 237 | 77 | .755 |
| *Andy Landers (Georgia 1980–) | .30 | 725 | 239 | .752 |

Note: Minimum 10 head coaching seasons in Division I.

*Active in 2008–09.

## Alltime Winningest Women's Division I Coaches

| | W |
|---|---|
| *Pat Summitt (Tennessee) | 1,005 |
| Jody Conradt (Sam Houston St, Tex.-Arlington, Texas) | 900 |
| *C. Vivian Stringer (Cheyney St, Iowa, Rutgers) | 825 |
| *Sylvia Rhyne Hatchell (Francis Marison, North Carolina) | 812 |
| *Tara VanDerveer (Idaho, Ohio St, Stanford) | 757 |
| Kay Yow (Elon, North Carolina St) | 737 |
| *Robin Selvig (Montana) | 725 |
| *Andy Landers (Georgia) | 725 |
| Sue Gunter (Stephen F. Austin, LSU) | 708 |
| *Debbie Ryan (Virginia) | 699 |
| *Geno Auriemma (Connecticut) | 696 |

Note: Minimum 10 head coaching seasons in Division I.

*Active in 2008–09.

| Year | Winner | Score | Runner-up | Winning Coach |
|------|--------|-------|-----------|---------------|
| 1982 | Louisiana Tech | 76–62 | Cheyney | Sonja Hogg/Leon Barmore |
| 1983 | USC | 69–67 | Louisiana Tech | Linda Sharp |
| 1984 | USC | 72–61 | Tennessee | Linda Sharp |
| 1985 | Old Dominion | 70–65 | Georgia | Marianne Stanley |
| 1986 | Texas | 97–81 | USC | Jody Conradt |
| 1987 | Tennessee | 67–44 | Louisiana Tech | Pat Summitt |
| 1988 | Louisiana Tech | 56–54 | Auburn | Leon Barmore |
| 1989 | Tennessee | 76–60 | Auburn | Pat Summitt |
| 1990 | Stanford | 88–81 | Auburn | Tara VanDerveer |
| 1991 | Tennessee | 70–67 (OT) | Virginia | Pat Summitt |
| 1992 | Stanford | 78–62 | Western Kentucky | Tara VanDerveer |
| 1993 | Texas Tech | 84–82 | Ohio State | Marsha Sharp |
| 1994 | North Carolina | 60–59 | Louisiana Tech | Sylvia Hatchell |
| 1995 | Connecticut | 70–64 | Tennessee | Geno Auriemma |
| 1996 | Tennessee | 83–65 | Georgia | Pat Summitt |
| 1997 | Tennessee | 68–59 | Old Dominion | Pat Summitt |
| 1998 | Tennessee | 93–75 | Louisiana Tech | Pat Summitt |
| 1999 | Purdue | 62–45 | Duke | Carolyn Peck |
| 2000 | Connecticut | 71–52 | Tennessee | Geno Auriemma |
| 2001 | Notre Dame | 68–66 | Purdue | Muffet McGraw |
| 2002 | Connecticut | 82–70 | Oklahoma | Geno Auriemma |
| 2003 | Connecticut | 73–68 | Tennessee | Geno Auriemma |
| 2004 | Connecticut | 70–61 | Tennessee | Geno Auriemma |
| 2005 | Baylor | 84–62 | Michigan St | Kim Mulkey-Robinson |
| 2006 | Maryland | 78–75 | Duke | Brenda Frese |
| 2007 | Tennessee | 59–46 | Rutgers | Pat Summitt |
| 2008 | Tennessee | 64–48 | Stanford | Pat Summitt |
| 2009 | Connecticut | 76–54 | Louisville | Geno Auriemma |

## NCAA Women's Division I Alltime Individual Leaders

### Single-Game Records

#### SCORING HIGHS

| Pts | Player and Team vs Opponent | Year |
|-----|------------------------------|------|
| 60 | Cindy Brown, Long Beach St vs San Jose St | 1987 |
| 58 | Kim Perrot, SW Louisiana vs SE Louisiana | 1990 |
| 58 | Lorri Bauman, Drake vs SW Missouri St* | 1984 |
| 56 | Jackie Stiles, SW Missouri St vs Evansville | 2000 |
| 55 | Patricia Hoskins, Mississippi Valley St vs Southern-Birm. | 1989 |
| 55 | Patricia Hoskins, Mississippi Valley St vs Alabama St | 1989 |
| 54 | Anjinea Hopson, Grambling vs Jackson St | 1994 |
| 54 | Mary Lowry, Baylor vs Texas | 1994 |
| 54 | Wanda Ford, Drake vs SW Missouri St* | 1986 |

Three tied with 53.

#### REBOUNDS

| Reb | Player and Team vs Opponent | Year |
|-----|------------------------------|------|
| 40 | Deborah Temple, Delta St vs UAB | 1983 |
| 37 | Rosina Pearson, Bethune-Cookman vs Florida Memorial | 1985 |
| 33 | Maureen Formico, Pepperdine vs Loyola (Calif.) | 1985 |
| 32 | Lachelle Lyles, Southeast Mo. St. vs Tennessee St. | 2006 |
| 31 | Darlene Beale, Howard vs South Carolina St | 1987 |
| 30 | Cindy Bonforte, Wagner vs Queens (N.Y.) | 1983 |
| 30 | Kayone Hankins, New Orleans vs. Nicholls St | 1994 |
| 30 | Wanda Ford, Drake vs Eastern Illinois | 1985 |
| 30 | Jennifer Butler, Massachusetts vs Florida | 2003 |

Three tied with 29.

#### ASSISTS

| Asst | Player and Team vs Opponent | Year |
|------|------------------------------|------|
| 23 | Michelle Burden, Kent St vs Ball St | 1991 |
| 22 | Shawn Monday, Tennessee Tech vs Morehead St | 1988 |
| 22 | Veronica Pettry, Loyola (Ill.) vs Detroit | 1989 |
| 22 | Tine Freil, Pacific vs Wichita St | 1991 |
| 21 | Tine Freil, Pacific vs Fresno St | 1992 |
| 21 | Amy Bauer, Wisconsin vs Detroit | 1989 |
| 21 | Neacole Hall, Alabama St vs Southern-Birm. | 1989 |

Six tied with 20.

*school changed name to Missouri State after 2004–05 season

## Single Season Records

### POINTS

| Player and Team | Year | GP | FG | 3FG | FT | Pts |
|---|---|---|---|---|---|---|
| Jackie Stiles, SW Missouri St* | 2001 | 35 | 365 | 65 | 267 | 1062 |
| Cindy Brown, Long Beach St | 1987 | 35 | 362 | — | 250 | 974 |
| Genia Miller, CSU-Fullerton | 1991 | 33 | 376 | 0 | 217 | 969 |
| Sheryl Swoopes, Texas Tech | 1993 | 34 | 356 | 32 | 211 | 955 |
| Alysha Clark, Middle Tennessee St | 2008 | 34 | 343 | 12 | 237 | 935 |
| Andrea Congreaves, Mercer | 1992 | 28 | 353 | 77 | 142 | 925 |
| Wanda Ford, Drake | 1986 | 30 | 390 | — | 139 | 919 |
| Chamique Holdsclaw, Tennessee | 1998 | 39 | 370 | 9 | 166 | 915 |
| Barbara Kennedy, Clemson | 1982 | 31 | 392 | — | 124 | 908 |
| Patricia Hoskins, Mississippi Valley St | 1989 | 27 | 345 | 13 | 205 | 908 |
| LaTaunya Pollard, Long Beach St | 1983 | 31 | 376 | — | 155 | 907 |

### SEASON SCORING AVERAGE

| Player and Team | Year | GP | FG | 3FG | FT | Pts | Avg |
|---|---|---|---|---|---|---|---|
| Patricia Hoskins, Mississippi Valley St | 1989 | 27 | 345 | 13 | 205 | 908 | 33.6 |
| Andrea Congreaves, Mercer | 1992 | 28 | 353 | 77 | 142 | 925 | 33.0 |
| Deborah Temple, Delta St | 1984 | 28 | 373 | — | 127 | 873 | 31.2 |
| Andrea Congreaves, Mercer | 1993 | 26 | 302 | 51 | 150 | 805 | 31.0 |
| Wanda Ford, Drake | 1986 | 30 | 390 | — | 139 | 919 | 30.6 |
| Anucha Browne, Northwestern | 1985 | 28 | 341 | — | 173 | 855 | 30.5 |
| LeChandra LeDay, Grambling | 1988 | 28 | 334 | 36 | 146 | 850 | 30.4 |
| Jackie Stiles, SW MIssouri St* | 2001 | 35 | 365 | 65 | 267 | 1062 | 30.3 |
| Kim Perrot, SW Louisiana | 1990 | 28 | 308 | 95 | 128 | 839 | 30.0 |
| Tina Hutchinson, San Diego St | 1984 | 30 | 383 | — | 132 | 898 | 29.9 |
| Jan Jensen, Drake | 1991 | 30 | 358 | 6 | 166 | 888 | 29.6 |
| Genia Miller, CSU-Fullerton | 1991 | 33 | 376 | 0 | 217 | 969 | 29.4 |
| Barbara Kennedy, Clemson | 1982 | 31 | 392 | — | 124 | 908 | 29.3 |
| LaTaunya Pollard, Long Beach St | 1983 | 31 | 376 | — | 155 | 907 | 29.3 |
| Lisa McMullen, Alabama St | 1991 | 28 | 285 | 126 | 119 | 815 | 29.1 |

### REBOUNDS

| Player and Team | Year | GP | Reb | Player and Team | Year | GP | Reb |
|---|---|---|---|---|---|---|---|
| Courtney Paris, Oklahoma | 2006 | 36 | 539 | Darlene Jones, Miss Valley St | 1983 | .31 | 487 |
| Wanda Ford, Drake | 1985 | 30 | 534 | Melanie Simpson, Okla. City | 1982 | 37 | 481 |
| Lachelle Lyles, SE Missouri St | 2006 | 30 | 517 | R. Pearson, Beth.-Cookman | 1985 | 26 | 480 |
| Wanda Ford, Drake | 1986 | 30 | 506 | Patricia Hoskins, Miss. Valley St | 1987 | 28 | 476 |
| Anne Donovan, Old Dominion | 1983 | 35 | 504 | Cheryl Miller, USC | 1985 | 30 | 474 |

### REBOUND AVERAGE

| Player and Team | Year | GP | Reb | Avg |
|---|---|---|---|---|
| Rosina Pearson, Bethune-Cookman | 1985 | 26 | 480 | 18.5 |
| Wanda Ford, Drake | 1985 | 30 | 534 | 17.8 |
| Katie Beck, East Tennessee St | 1988 | 25 | 441 | 17.6 |
| DeShawne Blocker, East Tennessee St | 1994 | 26 | 450 | 17.3 |
| Lachelle Lyles, SE Missouri St. | 2006 | 30 | 517 | 17.2 |
| Patricia Hoskins, Mississippi Valley St | 1987 | 28 | 476 | 17.0 |
| Wanda Ford, Drake | 1986 | 30 | 506 | 16.9 |
| Patricia Hoskins, Mississippi Valley St | 1989 | 27 | 440 | 16.3 |
| Joy Kellogg, Oklahoma City | 1984 | 23 | 373 | 16.2 |
| Courtney Paris, Oklahoma | 2006 | 30 | 485 | 16.2 |
| Deborah Mitchell, Mississippi Coll. | 1983 | 28 | 447 | 16.0 |
| Cheryl Miller, USC | 1985 | 30 | 474 | 15.8 |

*school changed name to Missouri State after 2004–05 season

## Single Season Records (Cont.)

### FIELD-GOAL PERCENTAGE

| Player and Team | Year | GP | FG | FGA | Pct |
|---|---|---|---|---|---|
| Myndee Larsen, Southern Utah | 1998 | 28 | 249 | 344 | 72.4 |
| Chantelle Anderson, Vanderbilt | 2001 | 34 | 292 | 404 | 72.3 |
| Deneka Knowles, SE Louisiana | 1996 | 26 | 199 | 276 | 72.1 |
| Crystal Langhorne, Maryland | 2006 | 32 | 202 | 280 | 72.1 |
| Barbara Farris, Tulane | 1998 | 27 | 151 | 210 | 71.9 |
| Renay Adams, Tennessee Tech | 1991 | 30 | 185 | 258 | 71.7 |
| Regina Days, Georgia Southern | 1986 | 27 | 234 | 332 | 70.5 |
| Kim Wood, UW-Green Bay | 1994 | 27 | 188 | 271 | 69.4 |
| Kelly Lyons, Old Dominion | 1990 | 31 | 308 | 444 | 69.4 |
| Alisha Hill, Howard | 1995 | 28 | 194 | 281 | 69.0 |

Based on qualifiers for annual championship.

### FREE-THROW PERCENTAGE

| Player and Team | Year | GP | FT | FTA | Pct |
|---|---|---|---|---|---|
| Adrienne Squire, Penn St | 2006 | 29 | 80 | 83 | 96.4 |
| Shanna Zolman, Tennessee | 2004 | 35 | 88 | 92 | 95.7 |
| Ginny Doyle, Richmond | 1992 | 29 | 96 | 101 | 95.0 |
| Jill Marano, La Salle | 2003 | 29 | 88 | 93 | 94.6 |
| Sue Bird, Connecticut | 2002 | 39 | 98 | 104 | 94.2 |
| Paula Corder-King, SE Missouri St | 1999 | 28 | 111 | 118 | 94.1 |
| Kandi Brown, Morehead St | 2003 | 28 | 104 | 111 | 93.7 |
| Linda Cyborski, Delaware | 1991 | 29 | 74 | 79 | 93.7 |
| Kandi Brown, Morehead St | 2002 | 29 | 74 | 79 | 93.7 |
| Kristin Iwanaga, California | 2005 | 29 | 85 | 91 | 93.4 |

Based on qualifiers for annual championship.

## Career Records

### POINTS

| Player and Team | Yrs | GP | Pts |
|---|---|---|---|
| Jackie Stiles, SW Missouri St* | 1997–01 | 129 | 3393 |
| Patricia Hoskins, Mississippi Valley St | 1985–89 | 110 | 3122 |
| Lorri Bauman, Drake | 1981–84 | 120 | 3115 |
| Chamique Holdsclaw, Tennessee | 1995–99 | 148 | 3025 |
| Cheryl Miller, USC | 1983–86 | 128 | 3018 |
| Cindy Blodgett, Maine | 1994–98 | 118 | 3005 |
| LaToya Thomas, Mississippi St | 1999–2003 | 125 | 2981 |
| Valorie Whiteside, Appalachian St | 1984–88 | 116 | 2944 |
| Kelly Mazzante, Penn St | 2000–04 | 133 | 2919 |
| Joyce Walker, LSU | 1981–84 | 117 | 2906 |

### SCORING AVERAGE

| Player and Team | Yrs | GP | FG | 3FG | FT | Pts | Avg |
|---|---|---|---|---|---|---|---|
| Patricia Hoskins, Mississippi Valley St | 1985–89 | 110 | 1196 | 24 | 706 | 3122 | 28.4 |
| Sandra Hodge, New Orleans | 1981–84 | 107 | 1194 | — | 472 | 2860 | 26.7 |
| Jackie Stiles, SW Missouri St* | 1997–01 | 129 | 1160 | 221 | 852 | 3393 | 26.3 |
| Lorri Bauman, Drake | 1981–84 | 120 | 1104 | — | 907 | 3115 | 26.0 |
| Andrea Congreaves, Mercer | 1989–93 | 108 | 1107 | 153 | 429 | 2796 | 25.9 |
| Cindy Blodgett, Maine | 1994–98 | 118 | 1055 | 219 | 676 | 3005 | 25.5 |
| Valorie Whiteside, Appalachian St | 1984–88 | 116 | 1153 | 0 | 638 | 2944 | 25.4 |
| Joyce Walker, LSU | 1981–84 | 117 | 1259 | — | 388 | 2906 | 24.8 |
| Tarcha Hollis, Grambling | 1989–91 | 84 | 891 | 3 | 246 | 2031 | 24.2 |
| Korie Hlede, Duquesne | 1994–98 | 109 | 1045 | 162 | 379 | 2631 | 24.1 |
| Karen Pelphrey, Marshall | 1983–86 | 114 | 1175 | — | 396 | 2746 | 24.1 |
| Erma Jones, Bethune-Cookman | 1982–84 | 87 | 961 | — | 173 | 2095 | 24.1 |

| Year | Winner | Score | Runner-up | Third Place | Fourth Place |
|---|---|---|---|---|---|
| 1957 | Wheaton (Ill.) | 89–65 | Kentucky Wesleyan | Mt. St. Mary's (Md.) | CSU-Los Angeles |
| 1958 | South Dakota | 75–53 | St. Michael's | Evansville | Wheaton (Ill.) |
| 1959 | Evansville | 83–67 | SW Missouri St | North Carolina A&T | CSU-Los Angeles |
| 1960 | Evansville | 90–69 | Chapman | Kentucky Wesleyan | Cornell College |
| 1961 | Wittenberg | 42–38 | SE Missouri St | South Dakota St | Mt. St. Mary's (Md.) |
| 1962 | Mt. St. Mary's (Md.) | 58–57 (OT) | CSU-Sacramento | Southern Illinois | Nebraska Wesleyan |
| 1963 | South Dakota St | 44–42 | Wittenberg | Oglethorpe | Southern Illinois |
| 1964 | Evansville | 72–59 | Akron | North Carolina A&T | Northern Iowa |
| 1965 | Evansville | 85–82 (OT) | Southern Illinois | North Dakota | St. Michael's |
| 1966 | Kentucky Wesleyan | 54–51 | Southern Illinois | Akron | North Dakota |
| 1967 | Winston-Salem | 77–74 | SW Missouri St | Kentucky Wesleyan | Illinois St |
| 1968 | Kentucky Wesleyan | 63–52 | Indiana St | Trinity (Tex.) | Ashland |
| 1969 | Kentucky Wesleyan | 75–71 | SW Missouri St | †Vacated | Ashland |
| 1970 | Philadelphia Textile | 76–65 | Tennessee St | UC-Riverside | Buffalo St |
| 1971 | Evansville | 97–82 | Old Dominion | †Vacated | Kentucky Wesleyan |
| 1972 | Roanoke | 84–72 | Akron | Tennessee St | Eastern Mich |
| 1973 | Kentucky Wesleyan | 78–76 (OT) | Tennessee St | Assumption | Brockport St |
| 1974 | Morgan St | 67–52 | SW Missouri St | Assumption | New Orleans |
| 1975 | Old Dominion | 76–74 | New Orleans | Assumption | Tenn.-Chattanooga |
| 1976 | Puget Sound | 83–74 | Tenn.-Chattanooga | Eastern Illinois | Old Dominion |
| 1977 | Tenn.-Chattanooga | 71–62 | Randolph-Macon | North Alabama | Sacred Heart |
| 1978 | Cheyney | 47–40 | UW-Green Bay | Eastern Illinois | Central Florida |
| 1979 | North Alabama | 64–50 | UW-Green Bay | Cheyney | Bridgeport |
| 1980 | Virginia Union | 80–74 | New York Tech | Florida Southern | North Alabama |
| 1981 | Florida Southern | 73–68 | Mt. St. Mary's (Md.) | Cal Poly-SLO | UW-Green Bay |
| 1982 | District of Columbia | 73–63 | Florida Southern | Kentucky Wesleyan | CSU-Bakersfield |
| 1983 | Wright St | 92–73 | District of Columbia | *CSU-Bakersfield | *Morningside |
| 1984 | Central Missouri St | 81–77 | St. Augustine's | *Kentucky Wesleyan | *N Alabama |
| 1985 | Jacksonville St | 74–73 | South Dakota St | *Kentucky Wesleyan | *Mt. St. Mary's (Md.) |
| 1986 | Sacred Heart | 93–87 | SE Missouri St | *Cheyney | *Florida Southern |
| 1987 | Kentucky Wesleyan | 92–74 | Gannon | *Delta St | *Eastern Montana |
| 1988 | Lowell | 75–72 | Ak.-Anchorage | Florida Southern | Troy St |
| 1989 | North Carolina Central | 73–46 | SE Missouri St | UC-Riverside | Jacksonville St |
| 1990 | Kentucky Wesleyan | 93–79 | CSU-Bakersfield | North Dakota | Morehouse |
| 1991 | North Alabama | 79–72 | Bridgeport (Conn.) | *CSU-Bakersfield | *Virginia Union |
| 1992 | Virginia Union | 100–75 | Bridgeport (Conn.) | *CSU-Bakersfield | *California (Pa.) |
| 1993 | CSU-Bakersfield | 85–72 | Troy St (Ala.) | *New Hampshire Coll | *Wayne St (Mich.) |
| 1994 | CSU-Bakersfield | 92–86 | Southern Indiana | *New Hampshire Coll | *Washburn |
| 1995 | Southern Indiana | 71–63 | UC–Riverside | Norfolk St | *Indiana (Pa.) |
| 1996 | Fort Hays St | 70–63 | Northern Kentucky | *California (Pa.) | *Virginia Union |
| 1997 | CSU-Bakersfield | 57–56 | Northern Kentucky | *Lynn | *Salem-Teikyo |
| 1998 | UC-Davis | 83–77 | Kentucky Wesleyan | *St. Rose | *Virginia Union |
| 1999 | Kentucky Wesleyan | 75–60 | Metropolitan St | *Truman St | *Florida Southern |
| 2000 | Metropolitan St | 97–79 | Kentucky Wesleyan | *Missouri Southern | *Seattle Pacific |
| 2001 | Kentucky Wesleyan | 72–63 | Washburn | *Western Washington | *Tampa |
| 2002 | Metropolitan St | 80–72 | Kentucky Wesleyan | *Shaw | *Indiana (Pa.) |
| 2003 | Northeastern St (Okla.) | 75–64 | †Vacated | *Bowie St | *Queens (N.Y.) |
| 2004 | Kennesaw St | 84–59 | Southern Indiana | *Humboldt St | *Metropolitan St |
| 2005 | Virginia Union | 63–58 | Bryant | *Lynn | *Tarleton St |
| 2006 | Winona St (Minn.) | 73–61 | Virginia Union | *Seattle Pacific | *Stonehill |
| 2007 | Barton | 77–75 | Winona St (Minn.) | *CSU-San Bernardino | *Central Missouri |
| 2008 | Winona St (Minn.) | 87–76 | Augusta St | *Bentley | *Ak.-Anchorage |
| 2009 | Findlay | 56–53 (OT) | Cal Poly.-Pomona | *Augusta St | *Central Missouri |

*tied for third place

*Indicates tied for third. †Student-athletes representing American International in 1969, Southwestern Louisiana in 1971, and Kentucky Wesleyan in 2003 were declared ineligible subsequent to the tournament. Under NCAA rules, the teams' and ineligible student-athletes' records were deleted, and the teams' places in the final standings were vacated.

## SINGLE-GAME SCORING HIGHS

| Pts | Player and Team vs Opponent | Date |
|---|---|---|
| 113 | Bevo Francis, Rio Grande vs Hillsdale | 1954 |
| 84 | Bevo Francis, Rio Grande vs Alliance | 1954 |
| 82 | Bevo Francis, Rio Grande vs Bluffton | 1954 |
| 80 | Paul Crissman, USC vs Pacific Christian | 1966 |
| 77 | William English, Winston-Salem vs Fayetteville St | 1968 |

## Single Season Records

### SCORING AVERAGE

| Player and Team | Year | GP | FG | FT | Pts | Avg |
|---|---|---|---|---|---|---|
| Bevo Francis, Rio Grande | 1954 | 27 | 444 | 367 | 1255 | 46.5 |
| Earl Glass, Mississippi Industrial | 1963 | 19 | 322 | 171 | 815 | 42.9 |
| Earl Monroe, Winston-Salem | 1967 | 32 | 509 | 311 | 1329 | 41.5 |
| John Rinka, Kenyon | 1970 | 23 | 354 | 234 | 942 | 41.0 |
| Willie Shaw, Lane | 1964 | 18 | 303 | 121 | 727 | 40.4 |

### REBOUND AVERAGE

| Player and Team | Year | GP | Reb | Avg |
|---|---|---|---|---|
| Tom Hart, Middlebury | 1956 | 21 | 620 | 29.5 |
| Tom Hart, Middlebury | 1955 | 22 | 649 | 29.5 |
| Frank Stronczek, American Int'l | 1966 | 26 | 717 | 27.6 |
| R.C. Owens, College of Idaho | 1954 | 25 | 677 | 27.1 |
| Maurice Stokes, St. Francis (Pa.) | 1954 | 26 | 689 | 26.5 |

### ASSISTS

| Player and Team | Year | GP | Asst |
|---|---|---|---|
| Steve Ray, Bridgeport | 1989 | 32 | 400 |
| Steve Ray, Bridgeport | 1990 | 33 | 385 |
| Tony Smith, Pfeiffer | 1992 | 35 | 349 |
| Jim Ferrer, Bentley | 1989 | 31 | 309 |
| Rob Paternostro, New Hamp. Coll. | 1995 | 33 | 309 |

### ASSIST AVERAGE

| Player and Team | Year | GP | Asst | Avg |
|---|---|---|---|---|
| Steve Ray, Bridgeport | 1989 | 32 | 400 | 12.5 |
| Steve Ray, Bridgeport | 1990 | 33 | 385 | 11.7 |
| Demetri Beekman, Assumption | 1993 | 23 | 264 | 11.5 |
| Ernest Jenkins, N.M.-Highlands | 1995 | 27 | 291 | 10.8 |
| Brian Gregory, Oakland | 1989 | 28 | 300 | 10.7 |

### FIELD-GOAL PERCENTAGE

| Player and Team | Year | Pct |
|---|---|---|
| Garret Siler, Augusta St | 2008 | 78.9 |
| Todd Linder, Tampa | 1987 | 75.2 |
| Maurice Stafford, North Alabama | 1984 | 75.0 |
| Matthew Cornegay, Tuskegee | 1982 | 74.8 |
| Callistus Eziukwu, Grand Valley St | 2005 | 73.7 |

### FREE-THROW PERCENTAGE

| Player and Team | Year | Pct |
|---|---|---|
| Paul Cluxton, Northern Kentucky | 1997 | 100.0 |
| Tomas Rimkus, Pace | 1997 | 95.6 |
| C.J. Cowgill, Chaminade | 2001 | 95.0 |
| Billy Newton, Morgan St | 1976 | 94.4 |
| Kent Andrews, McNeese St | 1968 | 94.4 |

## Career Records

### POINTS

| Player and Team | Yrs | Pts |
|---|---|---|
| Travis Grant, Kentucky St | 1969–72 | 4045 |
| Bob Hopkins, Grambling | 1953–56 | 3759 |
| Tony Smith, Pfeiffer | 1989–92 | 3350 |
| Earnest Lee, Clark Atlanta | 1984–87 | 3298 |
| Joe Miller, Alderson-Broaddus | 1954–57 | 3294 |

### CAREER SCORING AVERAGE

| Player and Team | Yrs | GP | Pts | Avg |
|---|---|---|---|---|
| Travis Grant, Kentucky St | 1969–72 | 121 | 4045 | 33.4 |
| John Rinka, Kenyon | 1967–70 | 99 | 3251 | 32.8 |
| Florindo Vieira, Quinnipiac | 1954–57 | 69 | 2263 | 32.8 |
| Willie Shaw, Lane | 1961–64 | 76 | 2379 | 31.3 |
| Mike Davis, Virginia Union | 1966–69 | 89 | 2758 | 31.0 |

### REBOUND AVERAGE

| Player and Team | Yrs | GP | Reb | Avg |
|---|---|---|---|---|
| Tom Hart, Middlebury | 1953, 55–56 | 63 | 1738 | 27.6 |
| Maurice Stokes, St. Francis (Pa.) | 1953–55 | 72 | 1812 | 25.2 |
| Frank Stronczek, American Int'l | 1965–67 | 62 | 1549 | 25.0 |
| Bill Thieben, Hofstra | 1954–56 | 76 | 1837 | 24.2 |
| Hank Brown, Lowell Tech | 1965–67 | 49 | 1129 | 23.0 |

### Career Records (Cont.)

#### ASSISTS

| Player and Team | Yrs | Asst |
|---|---|---|
| Demetri Beekman, Assumption | 1990–93 | 1044 |
| Adam Kaufman, Edinboro | 1998–01 | 936 |
| Rob Paternostro, New Hamp. Coll. | 1992–95 | 919 |
| Luke Cooper, Alaska-Anchorage | 2005–08 | 880 |
| Tony Smith, Pfeiffer | 1989–92 | 828 |

#### ASSIST AVERAGE

| Player and Team | Yrs | GP | Asst | Avg |
|---|---|---|---|---|
| Steve Ray, Bridgeport | 1989–90 | 65 | 785 | 12.1 |
| Demetri Beekman, Assumption | 1990–93 | 119 | 1044 | 8.8 |
| Ernest Jenkins, N.M.-Highlands | 1992–95 | 84 | 699 | 8.3 |
| Zack Whiting, Chaminade | 2004–07 | 86 | 703 | 8.2 |
| Adam Kaufman, Edinboro | 1998–01 | 116 | 936 | 8.1 |

Note: Minimum 550 Assists.

#### FIELD-GOAL PERCENTAGE

| Player and Team | Yrs | Pct |
|---|---|---|
| Garrett Siler, Augusta St | 2006–09 | 74.5 |
| Todd Linder, Tampa | 1984–87 | 70.8 |
| Tom Schurfranz, Bellarmine | 1989–92 | 70.2 |
| Chad Scott, California (Pa.) | 1991–94 | 70.0 |
| Ed Phillips, Alabama A&M | 1968–71 | 68.9 |

Note: Minimum 400 FGM.

#### FREE-THROW PERCENTAGE

| Player and Team | Yrs | Pct |
|---|---|---|
| Paul Cluxton, Northern Kentucky | 1994-97 | 93.5 |
| Jake Linton, St. Martin's | 2006–09 | 92.4 |
| Kent Andrews, McNeese St | 1967-69 | 91.6 |
| Chris Brunson, Souther Ind. | 2002–05 | 90.1 |
| Jon Hagen, Minnesota St–Mankato | 1963-65 | 90.0 |

Note: Minimum 250 FTM.

## NCAA Men's Division III Championship Results

| Year | Winner | Score | Runner-up | Third Place | Fourth Place |
|---|---|---|---|---|---|
| 1975 | LeMoyne-Owen | 57–54 | Glassboro St | Augustana (Ill.) | Brockport St |
| 1976 | Scranton | 60–57 | Wittenberg | Augustana (Ill.) | Plattsburgh St |
| 1977 | Wittenberg | 79–66 | Oneonta St | Scranton | Hamline |
| 1978 | North Park | 69–57 | Widener | Albion | Stony Brook |
| 1979 | North Park | 66–62 | Potsdam St | Franklin & Marshall | Centre |
| 1980 | North Park | 83–76 | Upsala | Wittenberg | Longwood |
| 1981 | Potsdam St | 67–65 (OT) | Augustana (Ill.) | Ursinus | Otterbein |
| 1982 | Wabash | 83–62 | Potsdam St | Brooklyn | CSU-Stanislaus |
| 1983 | Scranton | 64–63 | Wittenberg | Roanoke | UW–Whitewater |
| 1984 | UW–Whitewater | 103–86 | Clark (Mass.) | DePauw | Upsala |
| 1985 | North Park | 72–71 | Potsdam St | Nebraska Wesleyan | Widener |
| 1986 | Potsdam St | 76–73 | LeMoyne-Owen | Nebraska Wesleyan | Jersey City St |
| 1987 | North Park | 106–100 | Clark (Mass.) | Wittenberg | Stockton St |
| 1988 | Ohio Wesleyan | 92–70 | Scranton | Nebraska Wesleyan | Hartwick |
| 1989 | UW–Whitewater | 94–86 | Trenton St | Southern Maine | Centre |
| 1990 | Rochester | 43–42 | DePauw | Washington (Md.) | Calvin |
| 1991 | UW–Platteville | 81–74 | Franklin & Marshall | Otterbein | Ramapo (N.J.) |
| 1992 | Calvin | 62–49 | Rochester | UW–Platteville | Jersey City St |
| 1993 | Ohio Northern | 71–68 | Augustana | Mass.–Dartmouth | Rowan |
| 1994 | Lebanon Valley Coll | 66–59 (OT) | NYU | Wittenberg | St Thomas (Minn.) |
| 1995 | UW–Platteville | 69–55 | Manchester | Rowan | Trinity (Conn.) |
| 1996 | Rowan | 100–93 | Hope (Mich.) | Illinois Wesleyan | Franklin & Marshall |
| 1997 | Illinois Wesleyan | 89–86 | Nebraska Wesleyan | Williams | Alvernia |
| 1998 | UW–Platteville | 69–56 | Hope (Mich.) | Williams | Wilkes |
| 1999 | UW–Platteville | 76–75 (2 OT) | Hampden-Sydney | William Paterson | Connecticut Coll. |
| 2000 | Calvin | 79–74 | UW–Eau Claire | Salem St | Franklin & Marshall |
| 2001 | Catholic | 76–62 | William Paterson | Illinois Wesleyan | Ohio Northern |
| 2002 | Otterbein | 102–83 | Elizabethtown | Carthage | Rochester |
| 2003 | Williams | 67–65 | Gustavus Adolphus | Wooster | Hampden Sydney |
| 2004 | UW–Stevens Point | 84–82 | Williams | John Carroll | Amherst |
| 2005 | UW–Stevens Point | 73–49 | Rochester | Calvin | York |
| 2006 | Virginia Wesleyan | 59–56 | Wittenberg | Illinois Wesleyan | Amherst |
| 2007 | Amherst | 80–67 | Virginia Wesleyan | Washington (Mo.) | Wooster |
| 2008 | Washington-St. Louis | 90–86 | Amherst | Hope | Ursinus |
| 2009 | Washington-St. Louis | 61–52 | Richard Stockton | Guilford | Franklin & Marshall |

## SINGLE-GAME SCORING HIGHS

| Pts | Player and Team vs Opponent | Year |
|---|---|---|
| 77 | Jeff Clement, Grinnell vs Illinois College | 1998 |
| 69 | Steve Diekmann, Grinnell vs Simpson | 1995 |
| 64 | Tim Russell, Albertus Magnus | 2005 |
| 63 | Ryan Hodges, Cal-Lutheran | 2005 |
| 63 | Joe DeRoche, Thomas vs St. Joseph's (Me.) | 1988 |
| 62 | Kyle Myrick, Lincoln (Pa.) vs. Penn St.-Abington | 2006 |
| 62 | Nick Pelotte, Plymouth St | 2005 |
| 62 | Shannon Lilly, Bishop vs Southwest Assembly of God | 1983 |
| 61 | Steve Honderd, Calvin vs Kalamazoo | 1993 |
| 61 | Dana Wilson, Husson vs Ricker | 1974 |

## Single Season Records

### SCORING AVERAGE

| Player and Team | Year | GP | FG | FT | Pts | Avg |
|---|---|---|---|---|---|---|
| Steve Diekmann, Grinnell | 1995 | 20 | 223 | 162 | 745 | 37.3 |
| Rickey Sutton, Lyndon St | 1976 | 14 | 207 | 93 | 507 | 36.2 |
| Shannon Lilly, Bishop | 1983 | 26 | 345 | 218 | 908 | 34.9 |
| Dana Wilson, Husson | 1974 | 20 | 288 | 122 | 698 | 34.9 |
| Rickey Sutton, Lyndon St | 1977 | 16 | 223 | 112 | 558 | 34.9 |

### REBOUND AVERAGE

| Player and Team | Year | GP | Reb | Avg |
|---|---|---|---|---|
| Joe Manley, Bowie St | 1976 | 29 | 579 | 20.0 |
| Fred Petty, New Hampshire Coll. | 1974 | 22 | 436 | 19.8 |
| Larry Williams, Pratt | 1977 | 24 | 457 | 19.0 |
| Charles Greer, Thomas | 1977 | 17 | 318 | 18.7 |
| Larry Parker, Plattsburgh St | 1975 | 23 | 430 | 18.7 |

### ASSISTS

| Player and Team | Year | GP | Asst |
|---|---|---|---|
| Robert James, Kean | 1989 | 29 | 391 |
| Tennyson Whitted, Ramapo | 2002 | 29 | 319 |
| Ricky Spicer, UW-Whitewater | 1989 | 31 | 295 |
| Joe Marcotte, New Jersey Tech | 1995 | 30 | 292 |
| Andre Bolton, Chris. Newport | 1996 | 30 | 289 |

### ASSIST AVERAGE

| Player and Team | Year | GP | Asst | Avg |
|---|---|---|---|---|
| Robert James, Kean | 1989 | 29 | 391 | 13.5 |
| Albert Kirchner, Mt. St. Vincent | 1990 | 24 | 267 | 11.1 |
| Tennyson Whitted, Ramapo | 2002 | 29 | 319 | 11.0 |
| Ron Torgalski, Hamilton | 1989 | 26 | 275 | 10.6 |
| Louis Adams, Rust | 1989 | 22 | 227 | 10.3 |

### FIELD-GOAL PERCENTAGE

| Player and Team | Year | Pct |
|---|---|---|
| Travis Weiss, St. John's (Minn.) | 1994 | 76.6 |
| Brian Schmitting, Ripon | 2006 | 76.3 |
| Pete Metzelaars, Wabash | 1982 | 75.3 |
| Tony Rychlec, Mass. Maritime | 1981 | 74.9 |
| Tony Rychlec, Mass. Maritime | 1982 | 73.1 |

### FREE-THROW PERCENTAGE

| Player and Team | Year | Pct |
|---|---|---|
| Korey Coon, Illinois Wesleyan | 2000 | 96.3 |
| Chanse Young, Manchester | 1998 | 95.6 |
| Andy Enfield, Johns Hopkins | 1991 | 95.3 |
| Nick Wilkins, Coe | 2003 | 95.7 |
| Chris Carideo, Widener | 1992 | 95.2 |

## Career Records

### POINTS

| Player and Team | Yrs | Pts |
|---|---|---|
| Andre Foreman, Salisbury St | 1989–92 | 2940 |
| Willie Chandler, Misericordia | 2000–03 | 2898 |
| John Grotberg, Grinnell | 2006–09 | 2848 |
| Lamont Strothers, Chris. Newport | 1988–91 | 2709 |
| Matt Hancock, Colby | 1987–90 | 2678 |

### SCORING AVERAGE

| Player and Team | Yrs | GP | Avg |
|---|---|---|---|
| Dwain Govan, Bishop | 1974–75 | 55 | 32.8 |
| Dave Russell, Shepherd | 1974–75 | 60 | 30.6 |
| Kyle Myrick, Lincoln (Pa.) | 2005–06 | 57 | 30.2 |
| Rickey Sutton, Lyndon St | 1976–79 | 80 | 29.7 |
| John Grotberg, Grinnell | 2006–09 | 96 | 29.7 |

### REBOUND AVERAGE

| Player and Team | Yrs | GP | Reb | Avg |
|---|---|---|---|---|
| Larry Parker, Plattsburgh St | 1975–78 | 85 | 1482 | 17.4 |
| Charles Greer, Thomas | 1975–77 | 58 | 926 | 16.0 |
| Willie Parr, LeMoyne-Owen | 1974–76 | 76 | 1182 | 15.6 |
| Michael Smith, Hamilton | 1989–92 | 107 | 1632 | 15.2 |
| Dave Kufeld, Yeshiva | 1977–80 | 81 | 1222 | 15.1 |

### ASSIST AVERAGE

| Player and Team | Yrs | Avg |
|---|---|---|
| David Arsenault, Grinnell | 2006–09 | 9.4 |
| Phil Dixon, Shenandoah | 1993–96 | 8.6 |
| Tennyson Whitted, Ramapo | 2000–03 | 8.5 |
| Steve Artis, Chris. Newport | 1990–93 | 8.1 |
| David Genovese, Mt. St. Vincent | 1992–95 | 7.5 |

# Hockey

verizon wi

**Sidney Crosby,
of the 2009 Stanley Cup
champion
Pittsburgh Penguins**

# Kid Makes Good

## Detroit's smothering defense and a late knee injury were not enough to derail Sid "The Kid" Crosby's climb to the top of Lord Stanley's summit

### BY B.J. SCHECTER

IT WAS THE BIGGEST MOMENT of his life and all he could do was sit back and watch. Game 7 of the Stanley Cup finals. Tight game on the road. Hostile crowd. Time winding down. This was the situation Sidney Crosby dreamed about while growing up in Canada, but in order for the Pittsburgh Penguins to hoist the Cup, Crosby had to become a cheerleader. Crosby injured his left knee 5½ minutes into the second period and after being carried to the locker room he was only able to play 32 seconds in the third (he could neither stop nor turn). As the seconds counted down, it seemed like an eternity, but Crosby's teammates held on for a 2–1 victory to dethrone the defending champion Detroit Red Wings.

"I don't recommend anyone trying to watch a Stanley Cup Finals Game 7 from the bench," said Crosby.

Added Crosby's mother, Tina: "This is probably not the way you dream about it, but we're taking it."

A year after losing to the Red Wings in the finals, the Penguins climbed back to hockey's summit and this time they left with the ultimate prize. It was a defining moment for hockey's brightest star. Four years after coming into the league as Sid the Kid, Crosby had become the youngest captain of a Stanley Cup team. Wayne Gretzky, the person Crosby has most often been compared to, took five seasons to win a Cup. Penguins owner Mario Lemieux took seven. "When you have Sid anything is possible," said Lemieux, who cried after the game.

It didn't look good for Pittsburgh after Detroit took the first two games of the series at home by identical 3–1 scores. But the Penguins didn't lose their composure, evening the series by winning the next two games at home and providing an answer for everything Detroit threw at them. The Red Wings executed a brilliant game plan, having defensive pest Henrik Zetterberg shadow Crosby wherever he went. In one way it worked, as Crosby had a statistically insignificant series with one goal, two assists and a -3 rating.

But the extra attention paid to Crosby opened things up for Conn Smythe-winner Evgeni Malkin (36 points in 24 playoff games) and Maxime Talbot, who scored the game-winner in Game 6 and both goals in Game 7. Crosby, who still finished with a playoff-leading 15 goals and 16 assists, refused to crack under the pressure and never got frustrated. He was happy for his teammates to get the glory.

"Everything he does is about hockey," said Talbot of Crosby. "Yes, he's not flashy like other players in the NHL, and

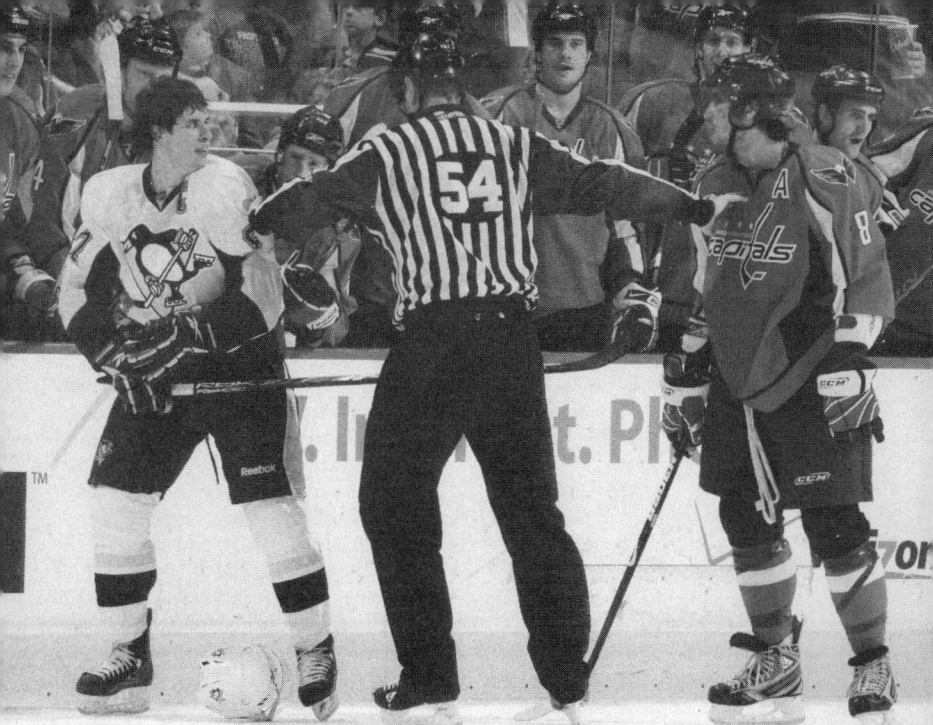

maybe the media think he's boring...but he loves the game."

After celebrating with his teammates on the ice, Crosby felt no pain and got caught up in the moment. He was late joining the handshake line, drawing the ire of several Red Wings after Crosby didn't shake the hand of Detroit captain Nicklas Lindstrom. "Nick's there, one of the greatest defensemen ever, and he's waiting and waiting and Crosby doesn't come over to shake his hand," said Detroit's Kris Draper. Crosby later said that the slight wasn't intentional and apologized for any offense he caused.

There was plenty of tension between Crosby and the Washington Capitals' Alex Ovechkin. Two of the league's brightest young stars, the players are polar opposites and don't like one another. At the All-Star game, Ovechkin mocked Crosby during a skills competition event. Then, during a 5–2 Capitals win in February, Ovechkin and Crosby got tangled up and exchanged shoves. Ovechkin ripped off Crosby's helmet

**After this on-ice scuffle in February and a contentious seven-game Eastern Conf. semifinals in May, it became clear that there's no love lost between Crosby (l.) and '09 Hart Trophy winner Alex Ovechkin.**

and the pair had to be separated by linesmen. Crosby accused Ovechkin of pointing at the Penguins' bench and causing a fight. Ovechkin shot back by saying that Crosby "talks too much."

"We're emotional guys, and we play hard, and when we have something on our mind, we say it," Ovechkin told the *Washington Post.*

"A lot of things happen on the ice, and that's where they need to stay," Crosby told the *Post.* "But there's a certain point, too, a certain respect level. There's just things you don't do."

It was fitting that the two teams met in the Eastern Conference semifinal. In a thrilling series that lived up to the hype, Ovechkin and Crosby put on a dazzling display, pushing one another to the limit. The series went seven games and in the finale

**Devils goalie Martin Brodeur further cemented his venerable legacy in 2009, reaching an NHL milestone for career victories.**

Early in the season, Avery made more waves when he told a television reporter that some players in the league were enjoying his "sloppy seconds." He was referring to a pair of ex-girlfriends, actress Elisha Cuthbert (who was dating the Flames' Dion Phaneuf) and model Rachel Hunter (who was engaged to the Kings' Jarrett Stoll) and the comments immediately drew the ire of the league. Instead of brushing it off as Sean being Sean, the league labeled Avery a pariah. Commissioner Gary Bettman suspended him for six games and the Stars banished him, though they still honored his contract. Avery was eventually picked up by the Rangers and played for their farm team, but he never made his way back to the NHL.

ESPN analyst Barry Melrose made his way back to the league after a 13-year absence when he was hired as the Tampa Bay Lightning's coach. It was an odd move and Melrose quickly alienated his players, blaming everyone but himself for Tampa's woes. He was fired after just 16 games. The league was hoping for a banner year for the Montreal Canadiens, which was celebrating its 100-year anniversary, but the Canadiens had a frustrating season and were swept from the playoffs by the (gasp!) Bruins.

But for a league with struggling television ratings and a niche fan base, Crosby winning his first Stanley Cup was a blessing. When Crosby is in the mix, the NHL is guaranteed name recognition, and any sports league is only as good as its stars. Though he was injured as he skated over to accept the Cup, Crosby could feel no pain. When commissioner Gary Bettman handed Crosby the 35-pound chalice, he congratulated him and asked, "How do you feel?" Crosby didn't hesitate, saying: "I feel great."

Crosby and the Penguins—literally—stole the show. Crosby scored two goals in Game 7, and got the last laugh when he picked Ovechkin's pocket in the third period and raced in for a breakaway goal.

Not many goals have made it by Devils netminder Martin Brodeur over the years. After missing four months of the season with a torn bicep tendon in his left elbow, Brodeur returned in March and made history. Brodeur passed Patrick Roy's record of 551 regular-season victories and came within two shutouts of Terry Sawchuk's career mark of 103. Brodeur's contract runs through the 2011–12 season and when he's done he'll go down in history as the greatest goaltender of all time.

Sean Avery will never be mentioned among the greats of anything, except maybe as having one of the great mouths. Avery has always had a way of getting under people's skin, on and off the ice. Avery caused a ruckus in 2008 when he camped in front of Brodeur and repeatedly waved his stick to distract the goalie. Though it was considered unethical, there was nothing anyone could do about it. After the season, the league passed a rule making the move illegal and it became known as the Avery rule.

# FOR THE RECORD•2008–2009

### Western Conference

#### CENTRAL DIVISION

|  | GP | W | L | OTL | Pts | GF | GA |
|---|---|---|---|---|---|---|---|
| †Detroit | 82 | 51 | 21 | 10 | 112 | 295 | 244 |
| *Chicago | 82 | 46 | 24 | 12 | 104 | 264 | 216 |
| *St. Louis | 82 | 41 | 31 | 10 | 92 | 233 | 233 |
| *Columbus | 82 | 41 | 31 | 10 | 92 | 226 | 230 |
| Nashville | 82 | 40 | 34 | 8 | 88 | 213 | 233 |

#### NORTHWEST DIVISION

|  | GP | W | L | OTL | Pts | GF | GA |
|---|---|---|---|---|---|---|---|
| †Vancouver | 82 | 45 | 27 | 10 | 100 | 246 | 220 |
| *Calgary | 82 | 46 | 30 | 6 | 98 | 254 | 248 |
| Minnesota | 82 | 40 | 33 | 9 | 89 | 219 | 200 |
| Edmonton | 82 | 38 | 35 | 9 | 85 | 234 | 248 |
| Colorado | 82 | 32 | 45 | 5 | 69 | 199 | 257 |

#### PACIFIC DIVISION

|  | GP | W | L | OTL | Pts | GF | GA |
|---|---|---|---|---|---|---|---|
| †San Jose | 82 | 53 | 18 | 11 | 117 | 257 | 204 |
| *Anaheim | 82 | 42 | 33 | 7 | 91 | 245 | 238 |
| Dallas | 82 | 36 | 35 | 11 | 83 | 230 | 257 |
| Phoenix | 82 | 36 | 39 | 7 | 79 | 208 | 252 |
| Los Angeles | 82 | 34 | 37 | 11 | 79 | 207 | 234 |

OTL=overtime loss; worth 1 pt.

### Eastern Conference

#### NORTHEAST DIVISION

|  | GP | W | L | OTL | Pts | GF | GA |
|---|---|---|---|---|---|---|---|
| †Boston | 82 | 53 | 19 | 10 | 116 | 274 | 196 |
| *Montreal | 82 | 41 | 30 | 11 | 93 | 249 | 247 |
| Buffalo | 82 | 41 | 32 | 9 | 91 | 250 | 234 |
| Ottawa | 82 | 36 | 35 | 11 | 83 | 217 | 237 |
| Toronto | 82 | 34 | 35 | 13 | 81 | 250 | 293 |

#### ATLANTIC DIVISION

|  | GP | W | L | OTL | Pts | GF | GA |
|---|---|---|---|---|---|---|---|
| †New Jersey | 82 | 51 | 27 | 4 | 106 | 244 | 209 |
| *Pittsburgh | 82 | 45 | 28 | 9 | 99 | 264 | 239 |
| *Philadelphia | 82 | 44 | 27 | 11 | 99 | 264 | 238 |
| *NY Rangers | 82 | 43 | 30 | 9 | 95 | 210 | 218 |
| NY Islanders | 82 | 26 | 47 | 9 | 61 | 201 | 279 |

#### SOUTHEAST DIVISION

|  | GP | W | L | OTL | Pts | GF | GA |
|---|---|---|---|---|---|---|---|
| †Washington | 82 | 50 | 24 | 8 | 108 | 272 | 245 |
| *Carolina | 82 | 45 | 30 | 7 | 97 | 239 | 226 |
| Florida | 82 | 41 | 30 | 11 | 93 | 234 | 231 |
| Atlanta | 82 | 35 | 41 | 6 | 76 | 257 | 280 |
| Tampa Bay | 82 | 24 | 40 | 18 | 66 | 210 | 279 |

†Division winner. *Playoff team.

## 2009 Stanley Cup Playoffs

Note: Playoff teams are re-seeded after quarterfinals

## Stanley Cup Playoff Results

### Conference Quarterfinals

#### EASTERN CONFERENCE

| | | | | | | | |
|---|---|---|---|---|---|---|---|
| April 15 | NY Rangers | 4 | at Washington | 3 | | | |
| April 18 | NY Rangers | 1 | at Washington | 0 | | | |
| April 20 | Washington | 4 | at NY Rangers | 0 | | | |
| April 22 | Washington | 1 | at NY Rangers | 2 | | | |
| April 24 | NY Rangers | 0 | at Washington | 4 | | | |
| April 26 | Washington | 5 | at NY Rangers | 3 | | | |
| April 28 | NY Rangers | 1 | at Washington | 2 | | | |

Washington won series 4–3.

## Conference Quarterfinals *(Cont.)*

### EASTERN CONFERENCE *(CONT.)*

| | | | |
|---|---|---|---|
| April 16 | Montreal | 2 | at Boston | 4 |
| April 18 | Montreal | 1 | at Boston | 5 |
| April 20 | Boston | 4 | at Montreal | 2 |
| April 22 | Boston | 4 | at Montreal | 1 |

Boston won series 4–0.

| April 15 | Philadelphia | 1 | at Pittsburgh | 4 |
|---|---|---|---|---|
| April 17 | Philadelphia | 2 | at Pittsburgh | 3* |
| April 19 | Pittsburgh | 3 | at Philadelphia | 6 |
| April 21 | Pittsburgh | 3 | at Philadelphia | 1 |
| April 23 | Philadelphia | 3 | at Pittsburgh | 0 |

| April 25 | Pittsburgh | 5 | at Philadelphia | 3 |
|---|---|---|---|---|

Pittsburgh won series 4–2.

| April 15 | Carolina | 1 | at New Jersey | 4 |
|---|---|---|---|---|
| April 17 | Carolina | 2 | at New Jersey | 1* |
| April 19 | New Jersey | 3 | at Carolina | 2* |
| April 21 | New Jersey | 3 | at Carolina | 4 |
| April 23 | Carolina | 0 | at New Jersey | 1 |
| April 26 | New Jersey | 0 | at Carolina | 4 |
| April 28 | Carolina | 4 | at New Jersey | 3 |

Carolina won series 4–3.

### WESTERN CONFERENCE

| April 16 | Anaheim | 2 | at San Jose | 0 |
|---|---|---|---|---|
| April 18 | Anaheim | 3 | at San Jose | 2 |
| April 21 | San Jose | 4 | at Anaheim | 3 |
| April 23 | San Jose | 0 | at Anaheim | 4 |
| April 25 | Anaheim | 2 | at San Jose | 3* |
| April 27 | San Jose | 1 | at Anaheim | 4 |

Anaheim won series 4–2.

| April 16 | Columbus | 1 | at Detroit | 4 |
|---|---|---|---|---|
| April 18 | Columbus | 0 | at Detroit | 4 |
| April 21 | Detroit | 4 | at Columbus | 1 |
| April 23 | Detroit | 6 | at Columbus | 5 |

Detroit won series 4–0.

| April 15 | St. Louis | 1 | at Vancouver | 2 |
|---|---|---|---|---|
| April 17 | St. Louis | 0 | at Vancouver | 3 |
| April 19 | Vancouver | 3 | at St. Louis | 2 |
| April 21 | Vancouver | 3 | at St. Louis | 2* |

Vancouver won series 4–0.

| April 16 | Calgary | 2 | at Chicago | 3* |
|---|---|---|---|---|
| April 18 | Calgary | 2 | at Chicago | 3 |
| April 20 | Chicago | 2 | at Calgary | 4 |
| April 22 | Chicago | 4 | at Calgary | 6 |
| April 25 | Calgary | 1 | at Chicago | 5 |
| April 27 | Chicago | 4 | at Calgary | 1 |

Chicago won series 4–2.

## Conference Semifinals

### EASTERN CONFERENCE

| May 1 | Carolina | 1 | at Boston | 4 |
|---|---|---|---|---|
| May 3 | Carolina | 3 | at Boston | 0 |
| May 6 | Boston | 2 | at Carolina | 3* |
| May 8 | Boston | 1 | at Carolina | 4 |
| May 10 | Carolina | 0 | at Boston | 4 |
| May 12 | Boston | 4 | at Carolina | 2 |
| May 14 | Carolina | 3 | at Boston | 2* |

Carolina won series 4–3.

| May 2 | Pittsburgh | 2 | at Washington | 3 |
|---|---|---|---|---|
| May 4 | Pittsburgh | 3 | at Washington | 4 |
| May 6 | Washington | 2 | at Pittsburgh | 3* |
| May 8 | Washington | 3 | at Pittsburgh | 5 |
| May 9 | Pittsburgh | 4 | at Washington | 3* |
| May 11 | Washington | 5 | at Pittsburgh | 4* |
| May 13 | Washington | 2 | at Pittsburgh | 6 |

Pittsburgh won series 4–3.

### WESTERN CONFERENCE

| May 1 | Anaheim | 2 | at Detroit | 3 |
|---|---|---|---|---|
| May 3 | Anaheim | 4 | at Detroit | 3** |
| May 5 | Detroit | 1 | at Anaheim | 2 |
| May 7 | Detroit | 6 | at Anaheim | 3 |
| May 10 | Anaheim | 1 | at Detroit | 4 |
| May 12 | Detroit | 1 | at Anaheim | 2 |
| May 14 | Anaheim | 3 | at Detroit | 4 |

Detroit won series 4–3.

| April 30 | Chicago | 3 | at Vancouver | 5 |
|---|---|---|---|---|
| May 2 | Chicago | 6 | at Vancouver | 3 |
| May 5 | Vancouver | 1 | at Chicago | 2 |
| May 7 | Vancouver | 1 | at Chicago | 2* |
| May 9 | Chicago | 4 | at Vancouver | 2 |
| May 11 | Vancouver | 5 | at Chicago | 7 |

Chicago won series 4–2.

## Eastern Conference Finals

| May 18 | Carolina | 2 | at Pittsburgh | 3 |
|---|---|---|---|---|
| May 21 | Carolina | 4 | at Pittsburgh | 7 |
| May 23 | Pittsburgh | 6 | at Carolina | 2 |
| May 26 | Pittsburgh | 4 | at Carolina | 1 |

Pittsburgh won series 4–0.

## Western Conference Finals

| May 17 | Chicago | 2 | at Detroit | 5 |
|---|---|---|---|---|
| May 19 | Chicago | 2 | at Detroit | 3* |
| May 22 | Detroit | 3 | at Chicago | 4* |
| May 24 | Detroit | 6 | at Chicago | 1 |
| May 27 | Chicago | 1 | at Detroit | 2* |

Detroit won series 4–1.

## Stanley Cup Finals

| May 30 | Pittsburgh | 1 | at Detroit | 3 |
|---|---|---|---|---|
| May 31 | Pittsburgh | 1 | at Detroit | 3 |
| June 2 | Detroit | 2 | at Pittsburgh | 4 |
| June 4 | Detroit | 2 | at Pittsburgh | 4 |

| June 6 | Pittsburgh | 0 | at Detroit | 5 |
|---|---|---|---|---|
| June 9 | Detroit | 1 | at Pittsburgh | 2 |
| June 12 | Pittsburgh | 2 | at Detroit | 1 |

Pittsburgh won series 4–3.

*Overtime game. †Double overtime game. **Triple overtime game. ‡Quadruple overtime game.

## Game 1

| Pittsburgh | 1 | 0 | 0—1 |
| Detroit | 1 | 1 | 1—3 |

**FIRST PERIOD**
Scoring: 1, Detroit, B Stuart, 13:38; 1, Pittsburgh, R Fedotenko (Malkin), 18:37. Penalties: None.

**SECOND PERIOD**
Scoring: 1, Detroit, J Franzen (Rafalski, Zetterberg), 19:02. Penalties: B Ledba, Det (slashing), 4:38; M Samuelsson, Det (holding), 7:05; C Adams, Pit (hooking), 13:44.

**THIRD PERIOD**
Scoring: 1, Detroit, J Abdelkader (Leino), 2:46. Penalties: None.

Shots on goal: DET 11–11–8—30; PIT 7–13–12—32.

Power-play opportunities: DET 0–1, PIT 0–2.

Goalies: Det, C Osgood (32 shots, 31 saves).
Pit, M. Fleury (30 shots, 27 saves).

Referees: Devorski, LaRue. Linesmen: Amell, Racicot.

A: 20,066.

## Game 2

| Pittsburgh | 1 | 0 | 0—1 |
| Detroit | 0 | 2 | 1—3 |

**FIRST PERIOD**
Scoring: 1, Pittsburgh, E Malkin (PP–Letang, Guerin), 16:50. Penalties: Kronwall, Det (cross-checking), 16:08.

**SECOND PERIOD**
Scoring: 2, Detroit, J Ericsson (Hudler, Helm), 4:21; V Filppula (Holmstrom, Hossa), 10:29. Penalties: Malkin, Pit (interference), 8:15.

**THIRD PERIOD**
Scoring: 1, Detroit, J Abdelkader, Det (Holmstrom, Hossa), 2:47. Penalties: Malkin, Pit (instigator, fighting), 19:41; Talbot, Pit (slashing), 19:41; Zetterberg, Det (fighting), 19:41.

Shots on goal: DET 7–16–3—26; PIT 11–9–12—32.

Power-play opportunities: DET 0–2, PIT 1–1.

Goalies: Det, C Osgood (32 shots, 31 saves).
Pit, M Fleury (26 shots, 23 saves).

Referees: McCreary, Joannette. Linesmen: Morin, Miller.

A: 20,066.

## Game 3

| Detroit | 2 | 0 | 0—2 |
| Pittsburgh | 2 | 0 | 2—4 |

**FIRST PERIOD**
Scoring: 2, Pittsburgh, M Talbot (Malkin, Letang), 4:48; K Letang (PP–Malkin, Gonchar), 15:57; 2, Detroit, H Zetterberg (Leino, Franzen), 6:19; J Franzen (PP-Zetterberg, Kronwall), 11:33. Penalties: B Orpik, Pit (interference), 9:42; D Cleary, Det (holding), 14:46; J Franzen, Det, (tripping), 18:02.

**SECOND PERIOD**
Scoring: None. Penalties: M Satan, Pit (holding), 15:35.

**THIRD PERIOD**
Scoring: 2, Pittsburgh, S Gonchar (PP–Malkin, Crosby), 10:29; M Talbot (EN-Fedotenko), 19:03. Penalties: J Ericsson, Det (interference), 9:06.

Shots on goal: DET 12–14–3—29; PIT 7–4–10—21.

Power-play opportunities: DET 1–2, PIT 2–3.

Goalies: Det, C Osgood (20 shots, 17 saves).
Pit, M Fleury (29 shots, 27 saves).

Referees: Devorski, LaRue. Linesmen: Amell, Racicot.

A: 17,132.

## Game 4

| Detroit | 1 | 1 | 0—2 |
| Pittsburgh | 1 | 3 | 0—4 |

**FIRST PERIOD**
Scoring: 1, Pittsburgh, E Malkin (PP–Letang, Staal), 2:39; 1, Detroit, Helm, 18:19. Penalties: N Kronwall, Det (tripping), 1:12; M Eaton, Pit (cross-checking), 11:09; J Ericsson, Det (high-sticking), 16:27; B Guerin, Pit (high-sticking), 16:37.

**SECOND PERIOD**
Scoring: 1, Detroit, B Stuart (Zetterberg, Rafalski), 00:46; 3, Pittsburgh, J Staal (Talbot, Eaton), 8:35; Crosby (Malkin), 10:34; T Kennedy (Crosby, Kunitz), 14:12. Penalties: E Malkin, Pit (hooking), 5:44; B Orpik, Pit (tripping ), 7:43.

**THIRD PERIOD**
Scoring: None. Penalties: N Kronwall, Det (hooking), 18:27; D Cleary, Det (tripping), 20:00; B Orpik, Pit (roughing), 20:00.

Shots on goal: DET 19–9–11—39; PIT 11–11–9—31.

Power-play opportunities: DET 0–4, PIT 1–3.

Goalies: Det, C Osgood (31 shots, 27 saves).
Pit, M Fleury (39 shots, 37 saves).

Referees: McCreary, Joannette. Linesmen: Morin, Miller.

A: 17,132.

## Game 5

```
Pittsburgh.................0        0        0——0
Detroit.......................1        4        0——5
```

### FIRST PERIOD

Scoring: 1, Detroit, D Cleary (Patsyuk, Rafalski), 13:32. Penalties: N Kronwall, Det (tripping), 7:16; C Kunitz, Pit, (interference), 19:39.

### SECOND PERIOD

Scoring: 4, Detroit, V Filppula (Hossa, Osgood), 1:44; N Kronwall (PP–Franzen, Zetterberg), 6:11; B Rafalski (PP–Datsyuk, Lidstrom), 8:26; H Zetterberg (PP–Hudler, Samuelsson), 15:40. Penalties: S Gonchar, Pit (slashing), 5:53; E Malkin, Pit (elbowing), 6:48; C Kunitz, Pit (roughing), 13:50; S Crosby, Pit (slashing), 17:37; M Talbot, Pit (slashing), 17:57.

### THIRD PERIOD

Scoring: None. Penalties: M Hossa, Det (roughing), 1:53; E Malkin, Pit (hooking), 7:14; P Dupuis, Pit (high-sticking), 15:50; C Adams, Pit (misconduct), 15:50; E Malkin (cross-checking), 18:08; B Lebda, Det (misconduct), 18:08; M Cooke, Pit (misconduct), 18:08; M Talbot, Pit (misconduct), 18:08.

Shots on goal: DET 8–15–6—29; PIT 10–6–6–22.

Power-play Opportunities: DET 3–9, PIT 0–2.

Goalies : Det, C Osgood (22 shots, 22 saves). Pit, M Fleury (21 shots, 16 saves); M Garon (8 shots, 8 saves).

Referees: Devorksi, LaRue. Linesmen: Amell, Racicot.

A: 20,066.

## Game 6

```
Detroit .........................0        0        1——1
Pittsburgh..................0        1        1——2
```

### FIRST PERIOD

Scoring: None. Penalties: H Zetterberg, Det (interference), 3:35; V Filppula, Det (tripping), 13:29.

### SECOND PERIOD

Scoring: 1, Pittsburgh, J Staal (Kennedy, Scuderi), 0:51. Penalties: None.

### THIRD PERIOD

Scoring: 1, Pittsburgh, T Kennedy (Talbot, Fedotenko), 5:35; 1, Detroit, K Draper (Ericsson, Lidstrom), 8:01. Penalties: E Malkin, Pit (cross-checking), 9:18; B Guerin, Pit (high-sticking), 12:40.

Shots on goal: DET 3–9–14—26; PIT 12–12–7—31.

Power-play Opportunities: DET 0–2, PIT 0–2.

Goalies : Det, C Osgood (31 shots, 29 saves). Pit, M Fleury (26 shots, 25 saves).

Referees: McCreary, Joannette. Linesmen: Morin, Miller.

A: 17,132.

## Game 7

```
Pittsburgh..................0        2        0——2
Detroit .........................0        0        1——1
```

### FIRST PERIOD

Scoring: None. Penalties: B Stuart, Pit (slashing), 11:24.

### SECOND PERIOD

Scoring: 2, Pittsburgh, M Talbot (Malkin), 1:13; M Talbot (Kunitz, Scuder), 10:07. Penalties: J Staal, Pit (hooking), 1:59; T Holmstrom, Det (holding), 1:59; H Gill, Pit (holding), 6:16.

### THIRD PERIOD

Scoring: 1, Detroit, J Ericsson (Lidstrom, Hudler), 13:53. Penalties: M Eaton, Det (tripping), 2:36.

Shots on goal: DET 6–11–7—24; PIT 10–7–1—18.

Power-play Opportunities: DET 0–2, PIT 0–1.

Goalies : Det, C Osgood (18 shots, 16 saves). Pit, M Fleury (24 shots, 23 saves).

Referees: Devorksi, McCreary. Linesmen: Morin, Racicot.

A: 20,066.

# Individual 2009 Playoff Leaders

## Scoring

### POINTS

| Player and Team | GP | G | Ast | Pts | +/– | PM | Player and Team | GP | G | Ast | Pts | +/– | PM |
|---|---|---|---|---|---|---|---|---|---|---|---|---|---|
| Evgeni Malkin, Pit | 24 | 14 | 22 | 36 | 3 | 51 | Marian Hossa, Det | 23 | 6 | 9 | 15 | 5 | 10 |
| Sidney Crosby, Pit | 24 | 15 | 16 | 31 | 9 | 14 | Martin Havlat, Chi | 16 | 5 | 10 | 15 | 0 | 8 |
| Henrik Zetterberg, Det | 23 | 11 | 13 | 24 | 13 | 13 | Nicklas Backstrom, Wsh | 14 | 3 | 12 | 15 | 3 | 8 |
| Johan Franzen, Det | 23 | 12 | 11 | 23 | 8 | 12 | Patrick Kane, Chi | 16 | 9 | 5 | 14 | -9 | 12 |
| Alexander Ovechkin, Wsh | 14 | 11 | 10 | 21 | 10 | 8 | Corey Perry, Ana | 13 | 6 | 8 | 14 | 2 | 36 |
| Ryan Getzlaf, Ana | 13 | 4 | 14 | 18 | 3 | 25 | Ruslan Fedotenko, Pit | 24 | 7 | 7 | 14 | 9 | 4 |
| Nicklas Lidstrom, Det | 21 | 4 | 12 | 16 | 11 | 6 | Alexander Semin, Wsh | 14 | 5 | 9 | 14 | -1 | 16 |
| Valtteri Filppula, Det | 23 | 3 | 13 | 16 | 8 | 8 | Sergei Gonchar, Pit | 22 | 3 | 11 | 14 | 3 | 12 |
| Eric Staal, Car | 18 | 10 | 5 | 15 | -3 | 4 | Chris Kunitz, Pit | 24 | 1 | 13 | 14 | 3 | 19 |
| Dan Cleary, Det | 23 | 9 | 6 | 15 | 17 | 12 | | | | | | | |
| Bill Guerin, Pit | 24 | 7 | 8 | 15 | 8 | 15 | Five tied at 13 points. | | | | | | |

### GOALS

| Player and Team | GP | G |
|---|---|---|
| Sidney Crosby, Pit | 24 | 15 |
| Evgeni Malkin, Pit | 24 | 14 |
| Johan Franzen, Det | 23 | 12 |
| Henrik Zetterberg, Det | 23 | 11 |
| Alexander Ovechkin, Wsh | 14 | 11 |
| Eric Staal, Car | 18 | 10 |
| Dan Cleary, Det | 24 | 9 |
| Patrick Kane, Chi | 16 | 9 |

### SHORT-HANDED GOALS

| Player and Team | GP | SH |
|---|---|---|
| Seven players tied at 1 SH goal. | | |

### POWER PLAY GOALS

| Player and Team | GP | PP |
|---|---|---|
| Evgeni Malkin, Pit | 24 | 7 |
| Jonathan Toews, Chi | 17 | 5 |
| Sidney Crosby, Pit | 24 | 5 |
| Johan Franzen, Det | 23 | 4 |
| Henrik Zetterberg, Det | 23 | 4 |

### ASSISTS

| Player and Team | GP | A |
|---|---|---|
| Evgeni Malkin, Pit | 24 | 22 |
| Sidney Crosby, Pit | 24 | 16 |
| Ryan Getzlaf, Ana | 13 | 14 |
| Henrik Zetterberg, Det | 23 | 13 |
| Valtteri Filppula, Det | 23 | 13 |
| Chris Kunitz, Pit | 24 | 13 |

### PLUS/MINUS

| Player and Team | GP | +/– |
|---|---|---|
| Dan Cleary, Det | 23 | 17 |
| Henrik Zetterberg, Det | 23 | 13 |
| Milan Lucic, Bos | 9 | 12 |
| Nicklas Lidstrom, Det | 23 | 11 |
| Brian Rafalski, Det | 18 | 11 |
| Alexander Ovechkin, Wsh | 16 | 10 |
| Jonathan Ericsson, Det | 22 | 9 |
| Sidney Crosby, Pit | 24 | 9 |
| Ruslan Fedotenko, Pit | 24 | 9 |

Seven tied at 8.

## Goaltending*

### GOALS AGAINST AVERAGE

| Player and Team | GP | W-L | Avg |
|---|---|---|---|
| Tim Thomas, Bos | 11 | 7–4 | 1.85 |
| Chris Osgood, Det | 23 | 15–8 | 2.01 |
| Jonas Hiller, Ana | 13 | 7–6 | 2.23 |
| Martin Brodeur, NJ | 7 | 3–4 | 2.39 |
| Roberto Luongo, Van | 10 | 6–4 | 2.52 |
| Simeon Varlamov, Wsh | 13 | 7–6 | 2.53 |

*minimum of 420 minutes

### SAVE PERCENTAGE

| Player and Team | GP | W-L | GAA | GA | SV | SV% | SA |
|---|---|---|---|---|---|---|---|
| Jonas Hiller, Ana | 13 | 7–6 | 2.23 | 30 | 494 | .943 | 524 |
| Tim Thomas, Bos | 11 | 7–4 | 1.85 | 21 | 302 | .935 | 323 |
| Martin Brodeur, NJ | 7 | 3–4 | 2.39 | 17 | 222 | .929 | 239 |
| Chris Osgood, Det | 23 | 15–8 | 2.01 | 47 | 590 | .926 | 637 |
| Sim. Varlamov, Wsh | 13 | 7–6 | 2.53 | 32 | 357 | .918 | 389 |
| Cam Ward, Car | 18 | 8–10 | 2.67 | 49 | 527 | .914 | 576 |
| Roberto Luongo, Van | 10 | 6–4 | 2.52 | 26 | 278 | .908 | 304 |

# NHL Awards

| Award | Player and Team | Award | Player and Team |
|---|---|---|---|
| Hart Trophy (MVP) | Alexander Ovechkin, Wsh | Adams Award (top coach) | Claude Julien, Bos |
| Pearson Award (NHLPA MOP) | Alexander Ovechkin, Wsh | Selke Trophy (top defensive forward) | Pavel Datsyuk, Det |
| Calder Trophy (top rookie) | Steve Mason, CBJ | Jennings Trophy (goaltender on club allowing fewest goals) | Tim Thomas, Bos |
| Vezina Trophy (top goaltender) | Tim Thomas, Bos | | |
| Norris Trophy (top defenseman) | Zdeno Chara, Bos | Conn Smythe Trophy (playoff MVP) | Evgeni Malkin, Pit |
| Lady Byng Trophy (for gentlemanly play) | Pavel Datsyuk, Det | | |

# Individual 2008-09 Regular Season Leaders

## Scoring

### POINTS

| Player and Team | GP | G | Ast | Pts | +/– | PIM | Player and Team | GP | G | Ast | Pts | +/– | PIM |
|---|---|---|---|---|---|---|---|---|---|---|---|---|---|
| Evgeni Malkin, Pit | 82 | 35 | 78 | 113 | 17 | 80 | Jeff Carter, Phi | 82 | 46 | 38 | 84 | 23 | 68 |
| Alex Ovechkin, Wsh | 79 | 56 | 54 | 110 | 8 | 72 | Mike Cammalleri, Cgy | 81 | 39 | 43 | 82 | -2 | 44 |
| Sidney Crosby, Pit | 77 | 33 | 70 | 103 | 3 | 76 | Daniel Sedin, Van | 82 | 31 | 51 | 82 | 24 | 36 |
| Pavel Datsyuk, Det | 81 | 32 | 65 | 97 | 34 | 22 | Henrik Sedin, Van | 82 | 22 | 60 | 82 | 22 | 48 |
| Zach Parise, NJ | 82 | 45 | 49 | 94 | 30 | 24 | Martin St. Louis, TB | 82 | 30 | 50 | 80 | 4 | 14 |
| Ilya Kovalchuk, Atl | 79 | 43 | 48 | 91 | -12 | 50 | Mike Richards, Phi | 79 | 30 | 50 | 80 | 22 | 63 |
| Ryan Getzlaf, Ana | 81 | 25 | 66 | 91 | 5 | 121 | Rick Nash, CBJ | 78 | 40 | 39 | 79 | 11 | 52 |
| Jarome Iginla, Cgy | 82 | 35 | 54 | 89 | -2 | 37 | Alexander Semin, Wsh | 62 | 34 | 45 | 79 | 25 | 77 |
| Marc Savard, Bos | 82 | 25 | 63 | 88 | 25 | 70 | Patrik Elias, NJ | 77 | 31 | 47 | 78 | 18 | 32 |
| Nicklas Backstrom, Wsh | 82 | 22 | 66 | 88 | 16 | 46 | Mike Ribeiro, Dal | 82 | 22 | 56 | 78 | -4 | 52 |
| Joe Thornton, SJ | 82 | 25 | 61 | 86 | 16 | 56 | | | | | | | |

## Scoring *(Cont.)*

### GOALS

| Player and Team | GP | G |
|---|---|---|
| Alex Ovechkin, Wsh | 79 | 56 |
| Jeff Carter, Phi | 82 | 46 |
| Zach Parise, NJ | 82 | 45 |
| Ilya Kovalchuk, Atl | 79 | 43 |
| Rick Nash, CBJ | 78 | 40 |
| Eric Staal, Car | 82 | 40 |
| Marian Hossa, Det | 74 | 40 |
| Thomas Vanek, Buf | 73 | 40 |
| Mike Cammalleri, Cgy | 81 | 39 |
| Dany Heatley, Ott | 82 | 39 |

### POWER PLAY GOALS

| Player and Team | GP | PP |
|---|---|---|
| Thomas Vanek, Buf | 73 | 20 |
| Alex Ovechkin, Wsh | 79 | 19 |
| Mike Cammalleri, Cgy | 81 | 19 |
| Mike Green, Wsh | 68 | 18 |
| Teemu Selanne, Ana | 65 | 16 |
| Brad Boyes, StL | 82 | 16 |

### ASSISTS

| Player and Team | GP | Ast |
|---|---|---|
| Evgeni Malkin, Pit | 82 | 78 |
| Sidney Crosby, Pit | 77 | 70 |
| Ryan Getzlaf, Ana | 81 | 66 |
| Nicklas Backstrom, Wsh | 82 | 66 |
| Pavel Datsyuk, Det | 81 | 65 |
| Marc Savard, Bos | 82 | 63 |
| Joe Thornton, SJ | 82 | 61 |
| Henrik Sedin, Van | 82 | 60 |
| Mike Ribeiro, Dal | 82 | 56 |
| Alex Ovechkin, Wsh | 79 | 54 |
| Jarome Iginla, Cgy | 82 | 54 |

### SHORT-HANDED GOALS

| Player and Team | GP | SHG |
|---|---|---|
| Mike Richards, Phi | 79 | 7 |
| Patrick Marleau, SJ | 76 | 5 |
| Rick Nash, CBJ | 78 | 5 |

Seven tied with 4.

### GAME-WINNING GOALS

| Player and Team | GP | GW |
|---|---|---|
| Jeff Carter, Phi | 82 | 12 |
| Brad Boyes, StL | 82 | 11 |
| Patrick Marleau, SJ | 76 | 10 |
| Alex Ovechkin, Wsh | 79 | 10 |
| Petr Sykora, Pit | 76 | 10 |
| Derek Roy, Buf | 82 | 9 |

Seven tied with 8.

### PLUS/MINUS

| Player and Team | GP | +/- |
|---|---|---|
| David Krejci, Bos | 82 | 37 |
| Blake Wheeler, Bos | 81 | 36 |
| Pavel Datsyuk, Det | 81 | 34 |
| Travis Zajac, NJ | 82 | 33 |
| Duncan Keith, Chi | 77 | 33 |
| Dennis Wideman, Bos | 79 | 32 |
| Nicklas Lidstrom, Det | 78 | 31 |
| Zach Parise, NJ | 82 | 30 |
| Willie Mitchell, Van | 82 | 29 |
| Martin Havlat, Chi | 81 | 29 |

## Goaltending
### (Minimum 25 games)

### GOALS AGAINST AVERAGE

| Player and Team | GP | W-L | GAA | GA |
|---|---|---|---|---|
| Tim Thomas, Bos | 54 | 36-11 | 2.10 | 114 |
| Steve Mason, CBJ | 61 | 33-20 | 2.29 | 140 |
| Niklas Backstrom, Min | 71 | 37-24 | 2.33 | 159 |
| Nikolai Khabibulin, Chi | 42 | 25-8 | 2.33 | 96 |
| Roberto Luongo, Van | 54 | 33-13 | 2.34 | 124 |
| Pekka Rinne, Nsh | 52 | 29-15 | 2.38 | 119 |
| Jonas Hiller, Ana | 46 | 23-15 | 2.39 | 99 |
| Scott Clemmensen, NJ | 40 | 25-13 | 2.39 | 94 |

### WINS

| Player and Team | GP | GAA | W | L |
|---|---|---|---|---|
| Miikka Kiprusoff, Cgy | 76 | 2.84 | 45 | 24 |
| Evgeni Nabokov, SJ | 62 | 2.44 | 41 | 12 |
| Cam Ward, Car | 68 | 2.44 | 39 | 23 |
| Henrik Lundqvist, NYR | 70 | 2.43 | 38 | 25 |
| Niklas Backstrom, Min | 71 | 2.33 | 37 | 24 |
| Tim Thomas, Bos | 54 | 2.10 | 36 | 11 |
| Marc-Andre Fleury, Pit | 62 | 2.67 | 35 | 18 |

### SAVE PERCENTAGE

| Player and Team | GP | W-L | GA | SV | SV% |
|---|---|---|---|---|---|
| Tim Thomas, Bos | 54 | 36-11 | 114 | 1580 | .933 |
| Tomas Vokoun, Fla | 59 | 26-23 | 138 | 1718 | .926 |
| Craig Anderson, Fla | 31 | 15-7 | 74 | 903 | .924 |
| Niklas Backstrom, Min | 71 | 37-24 | 159 | 1900 | .923 |
| Roberto Luongo, Van | 54 | 33-13 | 124 | 1418 | .920 |
| Nik. Khabibulin, Chi | 42 | 25-8 | 96 | 1096 | .919 |
| Jonas Hiller, Ana | 46 | 23-15 | 99 | 1118 | .919 |
| Ryan Miller, Buf | 59 | 34-18 | 145 | 1628 | .918 |

### SHUTOUTS

| Player and Team | GP | W | L | SO |
|---|---|---|---|---|
| Steve Mason, CBJ | 61 | 33 | 20 | 10 |
| Roberto Luongo, Van | 54 | 33 | 13 | 9 |
| Niklas Backstrom, Min | 71 | 37 | 24 | 8 |
| Evgeni Nabokov, SJ | 62 | 41 | 12 | 7 |
| Pekka Rinne, Nsh | 52 | 29 | 15 | 7 |

Four tied with 6.

# NHL Team-by-Team Statistical Leaders

## Anaheim Ducks

### SCORING

| Player | GP | G | Ast | Pts | +/- | PM |
|---|---|---|---|---|---|---|
| Ryan Getzlaf, C | 81 | 25 | 66 | 91 | 5 | 121 |
| Corey Perry, RW | 78 | 32 | 40 | 72 | 10 | 109 |
| Scott Niedermayer, D | 82 | 14 | 45 | 59 | -8 | 70 |
| Bobby Ryan, RW | 64 | 31 | 26 | 57 | 13 | 33 |
| Teemu Selanne, RW | 65 | 27 | 27 | 54 | -3 | 36 |
| Chris Pronger, D | 82 | 11 | 37 | 48 | E | 88 |
| Chris Kunitz, LW | 62 | 16 | 19 | 35 | 9 | 55 |
| Andrew Ebbett, C | 48 | 8 | 24 | 32 | 8 | 24 |
| Brendan Morrison, C | 62 | 10 | 12 | 22 | E | 16 |
| Rob Niedermayer, C | 79 | 14 | 7 | 21 | -17 | 42 |
| Steve Montador, D | 65 | 4 | 16 | 20 | 14 | 125 |
| Todd Marchant, C | 72 | 5 | 13 | 18 | -2 | 34 |
| Samuel Pahlsson, C | 52 | 5 | 10 | 15 | -16 | 32 |
| Travis Moen, LW | 63 | 4 | 7 | 11 | -17 | 77 |
| James Wisniewski, LW | 17 | 1 | 10 | 11 | 3 | 16 |
| George Parros, RW | 74 | 5 | 5 | 10 | 8 | 135 |
| Ryan Whitney, D | 20 | 0 | 10 | 10 | 1 | 12 |

### SCORING *(CONT.)*

| Player | GP | G | Ast | Pts | +/- | PM |
|---|---|---|---|---|---|---|
| Drew Miller, LW | 27 | 4 | 6 | 10 | E | 17 |
| Erik Christensen, C | 17 | 2 | 7 | 9 | -2 | 6 |
| Ryan Carter, C | 48 | 3 | 6 | 9 | 3 | 52 |
| Bret Hedican, D | 51 | 1 | 5 | 6 | -7 | 36 |
| Brian Sutherby, C | 17 | 3 | 3 | 6 | 6 | 19 |
| Kent Huskins, D | 33 | 2 | 4 | 6 | 6 | 27 |
| Petteri Nokelainen, C | 17 | 4 | 2 | 6 | 3 | 6 |
| Brad May, LW | 20 | 0 | 5 | 5 | 5 | 28 |
| Francois Beauchemin, D | 20 | 4 | 1 | 5 | -3 | 12 |
| Brett Festerling, D | 40 | 0 | 5 | 5 | 5 | 18 |
| Sheldon Brookbank, D | 29 | 1 | 3 | 4 | 3 | 51 |
| Mike Brown, RW | 28 | 2 | 1 | 3 | -2 | 60 |

### GOALTENDING

| Player | GP | Mins | W | L | TGA | GAA | SO |
|---|---|---|---|---|---|---|---|
| J-S. Giguere | 46 | 2458 | 19 | 18 | 127 | 3.10 | 2 |
| Jonas Hiller | 46 | 2489 | 23 | 15 | 99 | 2.39 | 4 |

## Atlanta Thrashers

### SCORING

| Player | GP | G | Ast | Pts | +/- | PM |
|---|---|---|---|---|---|---|
| Ilya Kovalchuk, LW | 79 | 43 | 48 | 91 | -12 | 50 |
| Slava Kozlov, LW | 82 | 26 | 50 | 76 | -14 | 44 |
| Todd White, C | 82 | 22 | 51 | 73 | -9 | 24 |
| Bryan Little, C | 79 | 31 | 20 | 51 | -5 | 24 |
| Colby Armstrong, RW | 82 | 22 | 18 | 40 | -5 | 75 |
| Ron Hainsey, D | 81 | 6 | 33 | 39 | -16 | 32 |
| Rich Peverley, C | 39 | 13 | 22 | 35 | 16 | 18 |
| Tobias Enstrom, D | 82 | 5 | 27 | 32 | 14 | 52 |
| Marty Reasoner, C | 79 | 14 | 16 | 30 | 11 | 36 |
| Eric Perrin, C | 78 | 7 | 16 | 23 | -2 | 36 |
| Erik Christensen, C | 47 | 5 | 14 | 19 | -7 | 14 |
| Zach Bogosian, D | 47 | 9 | 10 | 19 | 11 | 47 |
| Jason Williams, RW | 41 | 7 | 11 | 18 | -9 | 8 |
| Jim Slater, C | 60 | 8 | 10 | 18 | E | 52 |
| Niclas Havelid, D | 63 | 2 | 13 | 15 | 4 | 42 |
| Matheiu Schneider, D | 44 | 4 | 11 | 15 | -10 | 50 |
| Chris Thorburn, RW | 82 | 7 | 8 | 15 | -10 | 104 |
| Eric Boulton, LW | 76 | 3 | 10 | 13 | -3 | 176 |
| Nathan Oystrick, D | 53 | 4 | 8 | 12 | -2 | 50 |
| Joey Crabb, RW | 29 | 4 | 5 | 9 | -2 | 28 |
| Colin Stuart, LW | 33 | 5 | 3 | 8 | 3 | 18 |
| Garnet Exelby, D | 59 | 0 | 7 | 7 | -2 | 120 |
| Boris Valabik, D | 50 | 0 | 5 | 5 | -14 | 132 |
| Anssi Salmela, D | 9 | 1 | 2 | 3 | E | 2 |
| Joe Motzko, LW | 6 | 1 | 0 | 1 | 1 | 0 |
| Brett Sterling, LW | 6 | 1 | 0 | 1 | -3 | 2 |

### GOALTENDING

| Player | GP | Mins | W | L | TGA | GAA | SO |
|---|---|---|---|---|---|---|---|
| Kari Lehtonen | 46 | 2624 | 19 | 22 | 134 | 3.06 | 3 |
| Johan Hedberg | 33 | 1717 | 13 | 12 | 100 | 3.49 | 0 |
| Ondrej Pavelec | 13 | 599 | 3 | 7 | 36 | 3.60 | 0 |

## Boston Bruins

### SCORING

| Player | GP | G | Ast | Pts | +/- | PM |
|---|---|---|---|---|---|---|
| Marc Savard, C | 82 | 25 | 63 | 88 | 25 | 70 |
| David Krejci, C | 82 | 22 | 51 | 73 | 37 | 26 |
| Phil Kessel, RW | 70 | 36 | 24 | 60 | 23 | 16 |
| Michael Ryder, RW | 74 | 27 | 26 | 53 | 28 | 26 |
| Zdeno Chara, D | 80 | 19 | 31 | 50 | 23 | 95 |
| Dennis Wideman, D | 79 | 13 | 37 | 50 | 32 | 34 |
| Blake Wheeler, LW | 81 | 21 | 24 | 45 | 36 | 46 |
| Chuck Kobasew, RW | 68 | 21 | 21 | 42 | 5 | 56 |
| Milan Lucic, LW | 72 | 17 | 25 | 42 | 17 | 136 |
| Patrice Bergeron, C | 64 | 8 | 31 | 39 | 2 | 16 |
| P.J. Axelsson, LW | 75 | 6 | 24 | 30 | -1 | 16 |
| Matt Hunwick, D | 53 | 6 | 21 | 27 | 15 | 31 |
| Stephane Yelle, C | 77 | 7 | 11 | 18 | 6 | 32 |
| Mark Stuart, D | 82 | 5 | 12 | 17 | 20 | 76 |
| Andrew Ference, D | 47 | 1 | 15 | 16 | 7 | 40 |
| Mark Recchi, RW | 18 | 10 | 6 | 16 | -3 | 2 |
| Marco Sturm, LW | 19 | 7 | 6 | 13 | 9 | 8 |
| Shane Hnidy, D | 65 | 3 | 9 | 12 | 6 | 45 |
| Shawn Thornton, LW | 79 | 6 | 5 | 11 | -2 | 123 |
| Aaron Ward, D | 65 | 3 | 7 | 10 | 16 | 44 |
| Byron Bitz, RW | 35 | 4 | 3 | 7 | E | 18 |
| Vladimir Sobotka, C | 25 | 1 | 4 | 5 | -10 | 10 |
| Martin St. Pierre, C | 14 | 2 | 2 | 4 | -1 | 4 |
| Petteri Nokelainen, C | 33 | 0 | 3 | 3 | -1 | 10 |
| Steve Montador, D | 13 | 0 | 1 | 1 | 3 | 18 |
| Matt Lashoff, D | 16 | 0 | 1 | 1 | 1 | 10 |
| Martin Karsums, RW | 6 | 0 | 1 | 1 | -3 | 0 |

### GOALTENDING

| Player | GP | Mins | W | L | TGA | GAA | SO |
|---|---|---|---|---|---|---|---|
| Tim Thomas | 54 | 3259 | 36 | 11 | 114 | 2.10 | 5 |
| Manny Fernandez | 28 | 1644 | 16 | 8 | 71 | 2.59 | 1 |
| Tuukka Rask | 1 | 60 | 1 | 0 | 0 | 0.00 | 1 |

## Buffalo Sabres

### SCORING

| Player | GP | G | Ast | Pts | +/- | PM |
|---|---|---|---|---|---|---|
| Derek Roy, C | 82 | 28 | 42 | 70 | -5 | 38 |
| Jason Pominville, RW | 82 | 20 | 46 | 66 | -4 | 18 |
| Thomas Vanek, LW | 73 | 40 | 24 | 64 | -1 | 44 |
| Tim Connolly, C | 48 | 18 | 29 | 47 | 12 | 22 |
| Jaroslav Spacek, D | 80 | 8 | 37 | 45 | 2 | 38 |
| Drew Stafford, RW | 79 | 20 | 25 | 45 | 3 | 29 |
| Ales Kotalik, RW | 56 | 13 | 19 | 32 | -7 | 28 |
| Clarke MacArthur, LW | 71 | 17 | 14 | 31 | -4 | 56 |
| Paul Gaustad, C | 62 | 12 | 17 | 29 | 4 | 108 |
| Jochen Hecht, C | 70 | 12 | 15 | 27 | -9 | 33 |
| Daniel Paille, LW | 73 | 12 | 15 | 27 | E | 20 |
| Craig Rivet, D | 64 | 2 | 22 | 24 | 4 | 125 |
| Toni Lydman, D | 80 | 3 | 20 | 23 | E | 70 |
| M. Afinogenov, RW | 48 | 6 | 14 | 20 | -7 | 20 |
| Adam Mair, C | 75 | 8 | 11 | 19 | 4 | 95 |
| Andrej Sekera, D | 69 | 3 | 16 | 19 | -11 | 22 |

### SCORING (CONT.)

| Player | GP | G | Ast | Pts | +/- | PM |
|---|---|---|---|---|---|---|
| Teppo Numminen, D | 57 | 2 | 15 | 17 | -4 | 22 |
| Henrik Tallinder, D | 66 | 1 | 11 | 12 | -2 | 36 |
| Matt Ellis, LW | 45 | 7 | 5 | 12 | 4 | 12 |
| Patricka Kaleta, RW | 51 | 4 | 5 | 9 | 1 | 89 |
| Nathan Paetsch, D | 23 | 2 | 4 | 6 | 3 | 25 |
| Chris Butler, D | 47 | 2 | 4 | 6 | 11 | 18 |
| Dominic Moore, C | 18 | 1 | 3 | 4 | -1 | 23 |
| Mark Mancari, RW | 7 | 1 | 1 | 2 | -4 | 4 |
| Andrew Peters, LW | 28 | 0 | 1 | 1 | -2 | 81 |
| Nathan Gerbe, C | 10 | 0 | 1 | 1 | 3 | 4 |

### GOALTENDING

| Player | GP | Mins | W | L | TGA | GAA | SO |
|---|---|---|---|---|---|---|---|
| Ryan Miller | 59 | 3443 | 34 | 18 | 145 | 2.53 | 5 |
| Patrick Lalime | 24 | 1297 | 5 | 13 | 67 | 3.10 | 0 |
| Mikael Tellqvist | 6 | 230 | 2 | 1 | 9 | 2.35 | 0 |

## Calgary Flames

### SCORING

| Player | GP | G | Ast | Pts | +/– | PM |
|---|---|---|---|---|---|---|
| Jarome Iginla, RW | 82 | 35 | 54 | 89 | -2 | 37 |
| Michael Cammalleri, LW | 81 | 39 | 43 | 82 | -2 | 44 |
| Daymond Langkow, C | 73 | 21 | 28 | 49 | 1 | 20 |
| Craig Conroy, C | 82 | 12 | 36 | 48 | 20 | 28 |
| Dion Phaneuf, D | 80 | 11 | 36 | 47 | -11 | 100 |
| Todd Bertuzzi, RW | 66 | 15 | 29 | 44 | -13 | 74 |
| Curtis Glencross, LW | 74 | 13 | 27 | 40 | 14 | 42 |
| Rene Bourque, LW | 58 | 21 | 19 | 40 | 18 | 70 |
| David Moss, RW | 81 | 20 | 19 | 39 | -5 | 22 |
| Adrian Aucoin, D | 81 | 10 | 24 | 34 | -8 | 46 |
| Matthew Lombardi, C | 50 | 9 | 21 | 30 | 11 | 30 |
| Dustin Boyd, C | 71 | 11 | 11 | 22 | -11 | 10 |
| Cory Sarich, D | 76 | 2 | 18 | 20 | 12 | 112 |
| Mark Giordano, D | 58 | 2 | 17 | 19 | 2 | 59 |
| Jamie Lundmark, C | 27 | 8 | 8 | 16 | 2 | 17 |
| Olli Jokinen, C | 19 | 8 | 7 | 15 | -7 | 18 |
| Eric Nystrom, LW | 76 | 5 | 5 | 10 | -7 | 89 |
| Adam Pardy, D | 60 | 1 | 9 | 10 | 3 | 69 |
| Robyn Regehr, D | 75 | 0 | 8 | 8 | 10 | 73 |
| Jim Vandermeer, D | 45 | 1 | 6 | 7 | 1 | 108 |
| Wayne Primeau, C | 24 | 0 | 4 | 4 | -3 | 14 |
| Jordan Leopold, D | 19 | 1 | 3 | 4 | -5 | 6 |
| Andre Roy, LW | 44 | 3 | 0 | 3 | -1 | 83 |
| Matt Pelech, D | 5 | 0 | 3 | 3 | 1 | 9 |
| Brandon Prust, RW | 25 | 1 | 1 | 2 | -4 | 79 |
| D. Van der Gulik, RW | 6 | 0 | 2 | 2 | -1 | 0 |
| Warren Peters, C | 16 | 1 | 0 | 1 | -2 | 12 |
| Brett Sutter, LW | 4 | 1 | 0 | 1 | -2 | 2 |
| John Negrin, D | 3 | 0 | 1 | 1 | -2 | 2 |

### GOALTENDING

| Player | GP | Mins | W | L | TGA | GAA | SO |
|---|---|---|---|---|---|---|---|
| Miikka Kiprusoff | 76 | 4418 | 45 | 24 | 209 | 2.84 | 4 |
| Curtis McElhinney | 14 | 518 | 1 | 6 | 31 | 3.59 | 0 |

## Carolina Hurricanes

### SCORING

| Player | GP | G | Ast | Pts | +/– | PM |
|---|---|---|---|---|---|---|
| Ray Whitney, LW | 82 | 24 | 53 | 77 | 2 | 32 |
| Eric Staal, C | 82 | 40 | 35 | 75 | 15 | 50 |
| Tuomo Ruutu, LW | 79 | 26 | 28 | 54 | E | 79 |
| Rod Brind'Amour, C | 80 | 16 | 35 | 51 | -23 | 36 |
| Sergei Samsonov, LW | 81 | 16 | 32 | 48 | -8 | 28 |
| Matt Cullen, C | 69 | 22 | 21 | 43 | 11 | 20 |
| Joe Corvo, D | 81 | 14 | 24 | 38 | -1 | 18 |
| Anton Babchuk, D | 72 | 16 | 19 | 35 | 13 | 16 |
| Joni Pitkanen, D | 71 | 7 | 26 | 33 | 11 | 58 |
| Chad LaRose, LW | 81 | 19 | 12 | 31 | 6 | 35 |
| Dennis Seidenberg, D | 70 | 5 | 25 | 30 | -9 | 37 |
| Scott Walker, RW | 41 | 5 | 10 | 15 | -4 | 39 |
| Erik Cole, RW | 17 | 2 | 13 | 15 | 3 | 10 |
| Patrick Eaves, RW | 74 | 6 | 8 | 14 | 7 | 31 |
| Tim Gleason, D | 70 | 0 | 12 | 12 | 3 | 68 |
| Ryan Bayda, LW | 70 | 5 | 7 | 12 | 2 | 26 |
| Jussi Jokinen, LW | 25 | 1 | 10 | 11 | -2 | 12 |
| Niclas Wallin, D | 64 | 2 | 8 | 10 | -1 | 42 |
| Justin Williams, RW | 32 | 3 | 7 | 10 | -9 | 9 |
| Frantisek Kaberle, D | 30 | 1 | 7 | 8 | -4 | 8 |
| Brandon Sutter, C | 50 | 1 | 5 | 6 | -1 | 16 |
| Josef Melichar, D | 15 | 0 | 4 | 4 | -1 | 8 |
| Dan LaCouture, LW | 11 | 2 | 0 | 2 | -1 | 10 |
| Michael Ryan, C | 18 | 0 | 2 | 2 | -3 | 2 |
| Dwight Helminen, C | 23 | 1 | 1 | 2 | -2 | 0 |
| Bryan Rodney, D | 8 | 0 | 2 | 2 | -3 | 2 |
| Wade Brookbank, LW | 27 | 1 | 0 | 1 | E | 40 |
| Tim Conboy, D | 28 | 0 | 1 | 1 | -1 | 37 |
| Patrick Dwyer, RW | 13 | 1 | 0 | 1 | -2 | 0 |
| Jakub Petruzalek, RW | 2 | 0 | 1 | 1 | 1 | 0 |

### GOALTENDING

| Player | GP | Mins | W | L | TGA | GAA | SO |
|---|---|---|---|---|---|---|---|
| Cam Ward | 68 | 3928 | 39 | 23 | 160 | 2.44 | 6 |
| Michael Leighton | 19 | 1029 | 6 | 7 | 50 | 2.92 | 0 |

## Chicago Blackhawks

### SCORING

| Player | GP | G | Ast | Pts | +/– | PM |
|---|---|---|---|---|---|---|
| Martin Havlat, RW | 81 | 29 | 48 | 77 | 29 | 30 |
| Patrick Kane, RW | 80 | 25 | 45 | 70 | -2 | 42 |
| Jonathan Toews, C | 82 | 34 | 35 | 69 | 12 | 51 |
| Kris Versteeg, RW | 78 | 22 | 31 | 53 | 15 | 55 |
| Brian Campbell, D | 82 | 7 | 45 | 52 | 5 | 22 |
| Andrew Ladd, LW | 82 | 15 | 34 | 49 | 26 | 28 |
| Dave Bolland, C | 81 | 19 | 28 | 47 | 19 | 52 |
| Patrick Sharp, LW | 61 | 26 | 18 | 44 | 6 | 41 |
| Duncan Keith, D | 77 | 8 | 36 | 44 | 33 | 60 |
| Cam Barker, D | 68 | 6 | 34 | 40 | -6 | 65 |
| Dustin Byfuglien, D | 77 | 15 | 16 | 31 | 7 | 81 |
| Brent Seabrook, D | 82 | 8 | 18 | 26 | 23 | 62 |
| Troy Bouwer, LW | 69 | 10 | 16 | 26 | 7 | 50 |
| Colin Fraser, C | 81 | 6 | 11 | 17 | 3 | 55 |
| Ben Eager, LW | 75 | 11 | 4 | 15 | 1 | 161 |
| Matt Walker, D | 65 | 1 | 13 | 14 | 7 | 79 |

### SCORING *(CONT.)*

| Player | GP | G | Ast | Pts | +/– | PM |
|---|---|---|---|---|---|---|
| James Wisniewski, D | 31 | 2 | 11 | 13 | 6 | 14 |
| Adam Burish, RW | 66 | 6 | 3 | 9 | 3 | 93 |
| Aaron Johnson, D | 38 | 3 | 5 | 8 | 19 | 33 |
| Craig Adams, RW | 36 | 2 | 4 | 6 | -3 | 22 |
| Samuel Pahlsson, C | 13 | 2 | 1 | 3 | -1 | 2 |
| Niklas Hjalmarsson, D | 21 | 1 | 2 | 3 | 4 | 0 |
| Brent Sopel, D | 23 | 1 | 1 | 2 | -4 | 8 |
| Jack Skille, RW | 8 | 1 | 0 | 1 | -3 | 5 |

### GOALTENDING

| Player | GP | Mins | W | L | TGA | GAA | SO |
|---|---|---|---|---|---|---|---|
| Nikolai Khabibulin | 42 | 2467 | 25 | 8 | 96 | 2.33 | 3 |
| Cristobal Huet | 41 | 2351 | 20 | 15 | 99 | 2.53 | 3 |
| Antti Niemi | 3 | 141 | 1 | 1 | 8 | 3.40 | 0 |

## Colorado Avalanche

### SCORING

| Player | GP | G | Ast | Pts | +/- | PM |
|---|---|---|---|---|---|---|
| Milan Hejduk, RW........82 | 27 | 32 | 59 | -19 | 16 |
| Ryan Smyth, LW.........77 | 26 | 33 | 59 | -15 | 62 |
| Wojtek Wolski, LW ........78 | 14 | 28 | 42 | -13 | 28 |
| John-Michael Liles, D ..75 | 12 | 27 | 39 | -19 | 31 |
| Paul Stastny, C...........45 | 11 | 25 | 36 | -9 | 22 |
| Marek Svatos, RW........69 | 14 | 20 | 34 | -6 | 34 |
| Tyler Arnason, C...........71 | 5 | 17 | 22 | -16 | 14 |
| Ruslan Salei, D...........70 | 4 | 17 | 21 | -4 | 72 |
| T.J. Hensick, C .............61 | 4 | 17 | 21 | -7 | 14 |
| Jordan Leopold, D ....64 | 6 | 14 | 20 | -10 | 18 |
| Cody McLeod, LW ......79 | 15 | 5 | 20 | -11 | 162 |
| Ian Laperriere, RW ...74 | 7 | 12 | 19 | E | 163 |
| Chris Stewart, RW.....53 | 11 | 8 | 19 | -18 | 54 |
| Darcy Tucker, RW.......63 | 8 | 8 | 16 | -13 | 67 |
| David Jones, LW........40 | 8 | 5 | 13 | -8 | 8 |
| Brett Clark, D...........76 | 2 | 10 | 12 | -16 | 32 |
| Joe Sakic, C..............15 | 2 | 10 | 12 | -6 | 6 |
| Cody McCormick, C ...55 | 1 | 11 | 12 | -5 | 92 |
| Ben Guite, RW..........50 | 5 | 7 | 12 | 2 | 30 |
| Scott Hannan, D..........81 | 1 | 9 | 10 | -21 | 26 |
| Adam Foote, D..........42 | 1 | 6 | 7 | -12 | 30 |
| Brian Willsie, RW ........42 | 1 | 3 | 4 | -6 | 14 |
| Daniel Tjarnqvist, D......37 | 2 | 2 | 4 | 1 | 8 |
| T.J. Galiardi, C...........11 | 3 | 1 | 4 | -4 | 6 |
| Ray Macias, D...............6 | 0 | 1 | 1 | E | 0 |

### GOALTENDING

| Player | GP | Mins | W | L | TGA | GAA | SO |
|---|---|---|---|---|---|---|---|
| Peter Budaj............56 | 3232 | 20 | 29 | 154 | 2.86 | 2 |
| Andrew Raycroft....31 | 1722 | 12 | 16 | 90 | 3.14 | 0 |

## Dallas Stars

### SCORING

| Player | GP | G | Ast | Pts | +/- | PM |
|---|---|---|---|---|---|---|
| Mike Ribeiro, C ...........82 | 22 | 56 | 78 | -4 | 52 |
| Loui Eriksson, LW .......82 | 36 | 27 | 63 | 14 | 14 |
| Brad Richards, C .........56 | 16 | 32 | 48 | -4 | 6 |
| Mike Modano, C ........80 | 15 | 31 | 46 | -13 | 46 |
| Steve Ott, C ...............64 | 19 | 27 | 46 | 3 | 135 |
| James Neal, LW...........77 | 24 | 13 | 37 | -11 | 51 |
| Matt Niskanen, D ........80 | 6 | 29 | 35 | -11 | 52 |
| Fabian Brunnstrom, LW..55 | 17 | 12 | 29 | -8 | 8 |
| Stephane Robidas, D ..72 | 3 | 23 | 26 | 10 | 76 |
| Trevor Daley, D..........75 | 7 | 18 | 25 | 2 | 73 |
| Jere Lehtinen, RW........48 | 8 | 16 | 24 | 1 | 8 |
| Brenden Morrow, LW ..18 | 5 | 10 | 15 | -4 | 49 |
| Mark Parrish, RW ........44 | 8 | 5 | 13 | -3 | 18 |
| Darryl Sydor, D............65 | 2 | 11 | 13 | -2 | 16 |
| Chris Conner, RW.........38 | 3 | 10 | 13 | -5 | 10 |
| Nicklas Grossman, D...81 | 2 | 10 | 12 | -8 | 51 |
| Toby Petersen, C .........57 | 4 | 7 | 11 | 1 | 14 |
| Sean Avery, LW...........23 | 3 | 7 | 10 | 2 | 77 |
| Brendan Morrrison, C ..19 | 6 | 3 | 9 | 3 | 16 |
| Brian Sutherby, C........42 | 5 | 4 | 9 | -5 | 52 |
| Krys Barch, RW ..........72 | 4 | 5 | 9 | 1 | 133 |
| Landon Wilson, RW .....27 | 2 | 6 | 8 | 5 | 21 |
| Joel Lundqvist, C.........43 | 1 | 5 | 6 | -9 | 20 |
| Andrew Hutchinson, D..38 | 2 | 3 | 5 | -4 | 12 |
| B.J. Crombeen, RW .....15 | 1 | 4 | 5 | -1 | 26 |
| Sergei Zubov, D...........10 | 0 | 4 | 4 | -4 | 0 |
| Mark Fistric, D............36 | 0 | 4 | 4 | -1 | 42 |
| Tom Wandell, C.............14 | 1 | 2 | 3 | -1 | 4 |

### GOALTENDING

| Player | GP | Mins | W | L | TGA | GAA | SO |
|---|---|---|---|---|---|---|---|
| Marty Turco ............74 | 4327 | 33 | 31 | 203 | 2.81 | 3 |
| Tobias Stephen ......10 | 438 | 1 | 3 | 17 | 3.70 | 0 |
| Matt Climie.................3 | 185 | 2 | 1 | 9 | 2.92 | 0 |

## Columbus Blue Jackets

### SCORING

| Player | GP | G | Ast | Pts | +/- | PM |
|---|---|---|---|---|---|---|
| Rick Nash, LW..............78 | 40 | 39 | 79 | 11 | 52 |
| Kristian Huselius, LW ..74 | 21 | 35 | 56 | 1 | 44 |
| R. J. Umberger, C ........82 | 26 | 20 | 46 | -10 | 53 |
| Jakub Voracek, RW.....80 | 9 | 29 | 38 | 11 | 44 |
| Manny Malhotra, C.......77 | 11 | 24 | 35 | 9 | 28 |
| Fedor Tyutin, D............82 | 9 | 25 | 34 | 1 | 81 |
| Jason Williams, RW......39 | 12 | 17 | 29 | 5 | 16 |
| Fredrik Modin, LW........50 | 9 | 16 | 25 | 2 | 28 |
| Derick Brassard, C......31 | 10 | 15 | 25 | 12 | 17 |
| Mike Commodore, D.....81 | 5 | 19 | 24 | 11 | 100 |
| Michael Peca, C ..........71 | 4 | 18 | 22 | -6 | 58 |
| Jason Chimera, LW.....49 | 8 | 14 | 22 | 8 | 41 |
| Kris Russell, D.............66 | 2 | 19 | 21 | -10 | 28 |
| Jan Hejda, D................82 | 3 | 18 | 21 | 23 | 38 |
| Rafi Torres, LW............51 | 12 | 8 | 20 | -4 | 23 |
| Marc Methot, D ............66 | 4 | 13 | 17 | 7 | 55 |
| Jared Boll, RW .............75 | 4 | 10 | 14 | -6 | 180 |
| Antoine Vermette, LW...17 | 7 | 6 | 13 | 5 | 8 |
| Andrew Murray, C ........67 | 8 | 3 | 11 | -6 | 10 |
| Rostislav Klesla, D........34 | 1 | 8 | 9 | 2 | 38 |
| Christian Backman, D..56 | 2 | 5 | 7 | 5 | 32 |
| Jiri Novotny, C ............42 | 4 | 3 | 7 | 4 | 14 |
| Derek Dorsett, RW ......52 | 4 | 1 | 5 | -1 | 150 |
| Nikita Filatov, LW..........8 | 4 | 0 | 4 | 3 | 0 |
| Craig MacDonald, C ......8 | 1 | 1 | 2 | 1 | 0 |
| Christ Gratton, C............6 | 0 | 1 | 1 | 2 | 2 |
| Aaron Rome, D..............8 | 0 | 1 | 1 | 1 | 0 |

### GOALTENDING

| Player | GP | Mins | W | L | TGA | GAA | SO |
|---|---|---|---|---|---|---|---|
| Steve Mason........61 | 3664 | 33 | 20 | 140 | 2.29 | 10 |
| Pascal Leclaire ....12 | 674 | 4 | 6 | 43 | 3.83 | 0 |
| Fredrik Norrena......8 | 323 | 1 | 3 | 17 | 3.16 | 0 |

## Detroit Red Wings

### SCORING

| Player | GP | G | Ast | Pts | +/- | PM |
|---|---|---|---|---|---|---|
| Pavel Datsyuk, C ..........81 | 32 | 65 | 97 | 34 | 22 |
| Henrik Zetterberg, LW ..77 | 31 | 42 | 73 | 13 | 36 |
| Marian Hossa, RW.......74 | 40 | 31 | 71 | 27 | 63 |
| Nicklas Lidstrom, D ......78 | 16 | 43 | 59 | 31 | 30 |
| Brian Rafalski, D..........78 | 10 | 49 | 59 | 17 | 20 |
| Johan Franzen, LW......71 | 34 | 25 | 59 | 21 | 44 |
| Jiri Hudler, RW ..............82 | 23 | 34 | 57 | 7 | 16 |
| Niklas Kronwall, D........80 | 6 | 45 | 51 | 2 | 50 |
| Daniel Cleary, RW.......74 | 14 | 26 | 40 | E | 46 |
| Mikael Samuelsson, RW..81 | 19 | 21 | 40 | E | 50 |
| Valtteri Filppula, C ......80 | 12 | 28 | 40 | 9 | 42 |
| T. Holmstrom, RW.....53 | 14 | 23 | 37 | 18 | 38 |
| Tomas Kopecky, RW.....79 | 6 | 13 | 19 | -7 | 46 |
| Kris Draper, C..............79 | 7 | 10 | 17 | -13 | 40 |
| Brett Lebda, D..............65 | 6 | 10 | 16 | 9 | 48 |
| Brad Stuart, D...............67 | 2 | 13 | 15 | -3 | 26 |
| Andreas Lilja, D............60 | 2 | 11 | 13 | 13 | 66 |
| Kirk Maltby, LW............78 | 5 | 6 | 11 | -9 | 28 |
| Ville Leino, LW .............13 | 5 | 4 | 9 | 5 | 6 |
| Derek Meech, D ...........41 | 2 | 5 | 7 | -12 | 12 |
| Jonathan Ericsson, D ...19 | 1 | 3 | 4 | -1 | 15 |
| Aaron Downey, RW.........4 | 1 | 1 | 2 | E | 7 |
| Darren McCarty, RW.....13 | 1 | 0 | 1 | -2 | 25 |
| Darren Helm, C..............16 | 0 | 1 | 1 | -7 | 4 |

### GOALTENDING

| Player | GP | Mins | W | L | TGA | GAA | SO |
|---|---|---|---|---|---|---|---|
| Chris Osgood.........46 | 2663 | 26 | 9 | 137 | 2.98 | 2 |
| Ty Conklin ............40 | 2246 | 25 | 11 | 94 | 2.35 | 6 |

## Edmonton Oilers

### SCORING

| Player | GP | G | Ast | Pts | +/– | PM |
|---|---|---|---|---|---|---|
| Ales Hemsky, RW | 72 | 23 | 43 | 66 | 1 | 32 |
| Sheldon Souray, D | 81 | 23 | 30 | 53 | 1 | 98 |
| Shawn Horcoff, C | 80 | 17 | 36 | 53 | 7 | 39 |
| Tom Gilbert, D | 82 | 5 | 40 | 45 | 6 | 26 |
| Sam Gagner, C | 76 | 16 | 25 | 41 | -1 | 51 |
| Denis Grebeshkov, D | 72 | 7 | 32 | 39 | 12 | 38 |
| Andrew Cogliano, C | 82 | 18 | 20 | 38 | -6 | 22 |
| Dustin Penner, LW | 78 | 17 | 20 | 37 | 7 | 61 |
| Lubomir Visnovsky, D | 50 | 8 | 23 | 31 | 6 | 30 |
| Robert Nilsson, LW | 64 | 9 | 20 | 29 | 1 | 26 |
| Erik Cole, RW | 63 | 16 | 11 | 27 | -3 | 63 |
| Kyle Brodziak, C | 79 | 11 | 16 | 27 | 4 | 21 |
| Ethan Moreau, LW | 77 | 14 | 12 | 26 | E | 133 |
| Marc-Antoine Pouliot, C | 63 | 8 | 12 | 20 | 1 | 23 |
| Fernando Pisani, RW | 38 | 7 | 8 | 15 | -1 | 14 |
| Steve Staios, D | 80 | 2 | 12 | 14 | -5 | 92 |
| Liam Reddox, LW | 46 | 5 | 7 | 12 | -6 | 10 |
| Ales Kotalik, RW | 19 | 7 | 4 | 11 | 2 | 6 |
| Zack Stortini, RW | 52 | 6 | 5 | 11 | -3 | 181 |
| Ladislav Smid, D | 60 | 0 | 11 | 11 | -6 | 57 |
| Jason Strudwick, D | 71 | 2 | 7 | 9 | -4 | 60 |
| Patrick O'Sullivan, LW | 19 | 2 | 4 | 6 | -7 | 12 |
| Rob Schremp, C | 4 | 0 | 3 | 3 | 2 | 2 |
| Gilbert Brule, C | 11 | 2 | 1 | 3 | -3 | 12 |
| Ryan Potulny, C | 8 | 0 | 3 | 3 | 2 | 0 |
| Steve McIntyre, LW | 22 | 2 | 0 | 2 | -2 | 40 |
| Jean-Francois Jacques | 7 | 1 | 0 | 1 | E | 9 |

### GOALTENDING

| Player | GP | Mins | W | L | TGA | GAA | SO |
|---|---|---|---|---|---|---|---|
| Dwayne Roloson | 63 | 3597 | 28 | 24 | 166 | 2.77 | 1 |
| Mathieu Garon | 15 | 815 | 6 | 8 | 43 | 3.17 | 0 |
| J. Drouin-Deslariers | 10 | 540 | 4 | 3 | 30 | 3.34 | 0 |

## Florida Panthers

### SCORING

| Player | GP | G | Ast | Pts | +/– | PM |
|---|---|---|---|---|---|---|
| Stephen Weiss, C | 78 | 14 | 47 | 61 | 18 | 22 |
| David Booth, LW | 72 | 31 | 29 | 60 | 10 | 38 |
| Cory Stillman, LW | 63 | 17 | 32 | 49 | 1 | 37 |
| Nathan Horton, RW | 67 | 22 | 23 | 45 | -5 | 48 |
| Michael Frolik, C | 79 | 21 | 24 | 45 | 9 | 22 |
| Jay Bouwmeester, D | 82 | 15 | 27 | 42 | -2 | 68 |
| Bryan McCabe, D | 69 | 15 | 24 | 39 | -1 | 41 |
| Radek Dvorak, RW | 81 | 15 | 21 | 36 | E | 42 |
| Keith Ballard, D | 82 | 6 | 28 | 34 | 14 | 72 |
| Richard Zednik, RW | 70 | 17 | 16 | 33 | 2 | 46 |
| Gregory Campbell, C | 77 | 13 | 19 | 32 | E | 76 |
| Ville Peltonen, LW | 79 | 12 | 19 | 31 | 6 | 31 |
| Nick Boynton, D | 68 | 5 | 16 | 21 | 7 | 91 |
| Brett McLean, C | 80 | 7 | 12 | 19 | -11 | 29 |
| Kamil Kreps, C | 66 | 4 | 15 | 19 | 3 | 18 |
| Karlis Skrastins, D | 80 | 4 | 14 | 18 | 9 | 30 |
| Jassen Cullimore, D | 68 | 2 | 8 | 10 | -10 | 37 |
| Rostislav Olesz, LW | 37 | 4 | 5 | 9 | -5 | 8 |
| Anthony Stewart, C | 59 | 2 | 5 | 7 | -6 | 34 |
| Nick Taransky, C | 34 | 1 | 5 | 6 | -2 | 33 |
| Noah Welch, D | 23 | 1 | 1 | 2 | -5 | 11 |
| Shawn Matthias, C | 16 | 0 | 2 | 2 | -3 | 2 |
| Michal Repik, RW | 5 | 2 | 0 | 2 | 1 | 2 |
| Bryan Allen, D | 2 | 0 | 1 | 1 | 2 | 0 |
| Steve Emminger, D | 9 | 1 | 0 | 1 | 1 | 6 |
| Cory Murphy, D | 7 | 0 | 1 | 1 | -1 | 22 |

### GOALTENDING

| Player | GP | Mins | W | L | TGA | GAA | SO |
|---|---|---|---|---|---|---|---|
| Tomas Vokoun | 59 | 3324 | 26 | 23 | 138 | 2.49 | 6 |
| Craig Anderson | 31 | 1636 | 15 | 7 | 74 | 2.71 | 3 |

## Los Angeles Kings

### SCORING

| Player | GP | G | Ast | Pts | +/– | PM |
|---|---|---|---|---|---|---|
| Anze Kopitar, C | 82 | 27 | 39 | 66 | -17 | 32 |
| Alexander Frolov, LW | 77 | 32 | 27 | 59 | -6 | 30 |
| Dustin Brown, RW | 80 | 24 | 29 | 53 | -15 | 64 |
| Michal Handzus, C | 82 | 18 | 24 | 42 | -7 | 32 |
| Jarret Stoll, C | 74 | 18 | 23 | 41 | -7 | 68 |
| Kyle Quincey, D | 72 | 4 | 34 | 38 | -5 | 63 |
| Patrick O'Sullivan, C | 62 | 14 | 23 | 37 | 1 | 16 |
| Kyle Calder, LW | 74 | 8 | 19 | 27 | -1 | 41 |
| Drew Doughty, D | 81 | 6 | 21 | 27 | -17 | 56 |
| Wayne Simmonds, RW | 82 | 9 | 14 | 23 | -8 | 73 |
| Teddy Purcell, RW | 40 | 4 | 12 | 16 | 4 | 4 |
| Oscar Moller, RW | 40 | 7 | 8 | 15 | -3 | 16 |
| Matt Greene, D | 82 | 2 | 12 | 14 | 1 | 111 |
| Sean O'Donnell, D | 82 | 0 | 12 | 12 | 2 | 71 |
| Peter Harrold, D | 69 | 4 | 8 | 12 | -13 | 28 |
| Jack Johnson, D | 41 | 6 | 5 | 11 | -18 | 46 |

### SCORING *(CONT.)*

| Player | GP | G | Ast | Pts | +/– | PM |
|---|---|---|---|---|---|---|
| Derek Armstrong, C | 56 | 5 | 4 | 9 | -11 | 63 |
| Tom Preissing, D | 22 | 3 | 4 | 7 | -7 | 6 |
| Brad Richardson, C | 31 | 0 | 5 | 5 | -6 | 11 |
| Brian Boyle, C | 28 | 4 | 1 | 5 | -9 | 42 |
| Denis Gauthier, D | 65 | 2 | 2 | 4 | -11 | 90 |
| Justin Williams, RW | 12 | 1 | 3 | 4 | 1 | 8 |
| Trevor Lewis, C | 6 | 1 | 2 | 3 | E | 0 |
| Davis Drewiskie, D | 17 | 0 | 3 | 3 | 1 | 18 |
| Raitis Ivanans, LW | 76 | 2 | 0 | 2 | -8 | 145 |
| Matt Moulson, LW | 7 | 1 | 0 | 1 | -4 | 2 |
| John Zeiler, RW | 27 | 0 | 1 | 1 | -2 | 42 |

### GOALTENDING

| Player | GP | Mins | W | L | TGA | GAA | SO |
|---|---|---|---|---|---|---|---|
| Jonathan Quick | 44 | 2495 | 21 | 18 | 103 | 2.48 | 4 |
| Jason LaBarbera | 28 | 1477 | 8 | 11 | 65 | 2.64 | 0 |
| Erik Ersberg | 19 | 995 | 5 | 8 | 47 | 2.83 | 2 |

## Minnesota Wild

### SCORING

| Player | GP | G | Ast | Pts | +/- | PM |
|---|---|---|---|---|---|---|
| Mikko Koivu, C .............79 | 20 | 47 | 67 | 2 | 66 |
| Andrew Burnette, LW...80 | 22 | 28 | 50 | -5 | 18 |
| P. Bouchard, RW ..........79 | 17 | 16 | 30 | 46 | -5 | 20 |
| Owen Nolan, RW ..........59 | 25 | 20 | 45 | 5 | 26 |
| Antti Miettinen, RW ......82 | 15 | 29 | 44 | -1 | 32 |
| Marek Zidlikcy, D..........76 | 12 | 30 | 42 | -12 | 76 |
| Eric Belanger, C ...........79 | 13 | 23 | 36 | -5 | 26 |
| Marc-Andre Bergeron, D..72 | 14 | 18 | 32 | 5 | 30 |
| Brent Burns, D..............59 | 8 | 19 | 27 | -7 | 45 |
| Kim Johnsson, D .........81 | 2 | 22 | 24 | -3 | 44 |
| James Sheppard, C .....82 | 5 | 19 | 24 | -14 | 41 |
| Marian Gaborik, RW .....17 | 13 | 10 | 23 | 3 | 2 |
| Stephane Veilleux, LW..81 | 13 | 10 | 23 | -17 | 40 |
| Cal Clutterbuck, RW.....78 | 11 | 7 | 18 | -5 | 76 |
| Martin Skoula, D...........81 | 4 | 12 | 16 | -12 | 10 |
| Nick Schultz, D.............79 | 2 | 9 | 11 | -4 | 31 |
| Benoit Pouliot, LW ........37 | 5 | 6 | 11 | 1 | 18 |
| Dan Fritsche, RW .........34 | 4 | 5 | 9 | -3 | 10 |
| Peter Olvecky, LW ........31 | 2 | 5 | 7 | 1 | 12 |
| Colton Gillies, C...........45 | 2 | 5 | 7 | -2 | 18 |
| Krys Kolanos, C ...........21 | 3 | 3 | 6 | 3 | 16 |
| Kurtis Foster, D............10 | 1 | 5 | 6 | 7 | 6 |
| Craig Weller, D .............36 | 1 | 2 | 3 | -3 | 47 |
| Derej Boogaard, LW.......51 | 0 | 3 | 3 | 3 | 87 |
| Erik Reitz, D.................31 | 1 | 1 | 2 | -2 | 41 |

### GOALTENDING

| Player | GP | Mins | W | L | TGA | GAA | SO |
|---|---|---|---|---|---|---|---|
| Niklas Backstrom..71 | 4088 | 37 | 24 | 159 | 2.33 | 8 |
| Josh Harding ........19 | 870 | 3 | 9 | 32 | 2.21 | 0 |

## Nashville Predators

### SCORING

| Player | GP | G | Ast | Pts | +/- | PM |
|---|---|---|---|---|---|---|
| J.P. Dumont, RW ..........82 | 16 | 49 | 65 | 1 | 20 |
| Jason Arnott, C.............65 | 33 | 24 | 57 | 2 | 49 |
| Shea Weber, D .............81 | 23 | 30 | 53 | 1 | 80 |
| Martin Erat, RW ...........71 | 17 | 33 | 50 | -7 | 48 |
| Ryan Suter, D................82 | 7 | 38 | 45 | 16 | 73 |
| David Legwand, C ........73 | 20 | 22 | 42 | -3 | 32 |
| Joel Ward, RW ..............79 | 17 | 18 | 35 | 1 | 29 |
| Steve Sullivan, RW........41 | 11 | 21 | 32 | 2 | 30 |
| Dan Hamhuis, D............82 | 3 | 23 | 26 | -4 | 67 |
| Radek Bonk, C .............66 | 9 | 16 | 25 | -12 | 34 |
| Vernon Fiddler, LW .......78 | 11 | 6 | 17 | -13 | 24 |
| Ryan Jones, RW ...........46 | 7 | 10 | 17 | 1 | 22 |
| Jordin Tootoo, RW .........72 | 4 | 12 | 16 | -15 | 124 |
| Jerred Smithson, C.......82 | 4 | 9 | 13 | -6 | 49 |
| Kevin Klein, D...............63 | 4 | 8 | 12 | -2 | 19 |
| Greg Zanon, D..............82 | 4 | 7 | 11 | 8 | 38 |
| Ville Koistinen, D...........38 | 3 | 18 | 11 | E | 14 |
| Scott Nichol, C .............43 | 4 | 6 | 10 | E | 41 |
| Rich Peverley, C ...........27 | 2 | 7 | 9 | -3 | 15 |
| Patric Hornqvist, RW .....28 | 2 | 5 | 7 | -3 | 16 |
| Antti Pihlstrom, LW........53 | 2 | 5 | 7 | -1 | 10 |
| Greg de Vries, D...........71 | 1 | 4 | 5 | -15 | 65 |
| Cal O'Reilly, C...............11 | 3 | 2 | 5 | 2 | 2 |
| Wade Belak, RW............38 | 0 | 2 | 2 | -1 | 54 |
| Nick Taransky, C...........11 | 0 | 1 | 1 | -1 | 17 |

### GOALTENDING

| Player | GP | Mins | W | L | TGA | GAA | SO |
|---|---|---|---|---|---|---|---|
| Pekka Rinne........52 | 2999 | 29 | 15 | 119 | 2.38 | 7 |
| Dan Ellis..............35 | 1965 | 11 | 19 | 96 | 2.93 | 3 |

## Montreal Canadiens

### SCORING

| Player | GP | G | Ast | Pts | +/- | PM |
|---|---|---|---|---|---|---|
| Alexei Kovalev, RW ......78 | 26 | 39 | 65 | -4 | 74 |
| Andrei Markov, D .........78 | 12 | 52 | 64 | -2 | 36 |
| Saku Koivu, C ..............65 | 16 | 34 | 50 | 4 | 44 |
| Alex Tanguay, LW..........50 | 16 | 25 | 41 | 13 | 34 |
| Andrei Kostitsyn, LW......74 | 23 | 18 | 41 | -7 | 50 |
| Robert Lang, C .............50 | 18 | 21 | 39 | 6 | 36 |
| Tomas Plekanec, C .......80 | 20 | 19 | 39 | -9 | 54 |
| Roman Hamrlik, D........81 | 6 | 27 | 33 | 5 | 62 |
| Maxim Lapierre, C.........79 | 15 | 13 | 28 | 9 | 76 |
| G. Latendresse, RW ......56 | 14 | 12 | 26 | 4 | 45 |
| Chris. Higgins, LW........57 | 12 | 11 | 23 | -1 | 22 |
| Josh Gorges, D.............81 | 4 | 19 | 23 | 12 | 37 |
| Sergei Kostitsyn, LW .....56 | 8 | 15 | 23 | -3 | 64 |
| Tom Kostopoulos, RW..78 | 8 | 14 | 22 | -1 | 106 |
| Matt D'Agostini, RW.......53 | 12 | 9 | 21 | -17 | 16 |
| Patrice Brisebois, D.......62 | 5 | 13 | 18 | -3 | 19 |
| Mathieu Schneider, D...23 | 5 | 12 | 17 | -2 | 14 |
| M. Dandenault, RW.......41 | 4 | 8 | 12 | 6 | 17 |
| Mike Komisarek, D........66 | 2 | 9 | 11 | E | 121 |
| Max Pacioretty, LW.......34 | 3 | 8 | 11 | -3 | 27 |
| Steve Begin, LW............42 | 6 | 4 | 10 | -5 | 27 |
| Francis Bouillon, D........54 | 5 | 4 | 9 | -7 | 53 |
| Ryan O'Byrne, D ..........37 | 0 | 5 | 5 | -7 | 58 |
| Glen Metropolit, C........21 | 2 | 1 | 3 | -5 | 13 |
| Kyle Chipchura, C.........13 | 0 | 3 | 3 | -5 | 5 |

### GOALTENDING

| Player | GP | Mins | W | L | TGA | GAA | SO |
|---|---|---|---|---|---|---|---|
| Carey Price ...........52 | 3036 | 23 | 16 | 143 | 2.83 | 1 |
| Jaroslav Halak.......34 | 1931 | 18 | 14 | 92 | 2.86 | 1 |

## New Jersey Devils

### SCORING

| Player | GP | G | Ast | Pts | +/- | PM |
|---|---|---|---|---|---|---|
| Zach Parise, LW...........82 | 45 | 49 | 94 | 30 | 24 |
| J. Langenbrunner, RW..77 | 31 | 47 | 78 | 18 | 32 |
| Patrik Elias, LW ...........81 | 29 | 40 | 69 | 25 | 56 |
| Travis Zajac, C .............82 | 20 | 42 | 62 | 33 | 29 |
| Brian Gionta, RW ..........81 | 20 | 40 | 60 | 12 | 32 |
| Dainius Zubrus, C ........82 | 15 | 25 | 40 | 6 | 69 |
| Paul Martin, D .............73 | 5 | 28 | 33 | 21 | 36 |
| Brian Rolston, C ...........64 | 15 | 17 | 32 | 2 | 30 |
| David Clarkson, RW.....82 | 17 | 15 | 32 | -1 | 164 |
| Johnny Oduya, D..........82 | 7 | 22 | 29 | 21 | 30 |
| John Madden, C ...........76 | 7 | 16 | 23 | -7 | 26 |
| Colin White, D .............71 | 1 | 17 | 18 | 18 | 46 |
| Bryce Salvador, D.........76 | 3 | 13 | 16 | -1 | 78 |
| Mike Mottau, D.............80 | 1 | 14 | 15 | 24 | 35 |
| Brendan Shanahan, LW..34 | 6 | 8 | 14 | -2 | 29 |
| Jay Pandolfo, LW ..........61 | 5 | 5 | 10 | -12 | 10 |
| Bobby Holik, C .............62 | 4 | 5 | 9 | -2 | 66 |
| Mike Rupp, C ...............72 | 3 | 6 | 9 | -2 | 136 |
| Andy Greene, D............49 | 2 | 7 | 9 | 3 | 22 |
| Niclas Havelid, D..........15 | 0 | 4 | 4 | -2 | 6 |
| Anssi Salmela, D..........17 | 0 | 3 | 3 | 1 | 6 |
| Jay Leach, D.................24 | 0 | 1 | 1 | E | 21 |
| Petr Vrana, LW .............16 | 1 | 0 | 1 | -4 | 2 |
| Nicklas Bergfors, RW.....8 | 1 | 0 | 1 | -1 | 0 |
| P. Letourneau-Leblond, D..8 | 0 | 1 | 1 | 3 | 22 |

### GOALTENDING

| Player | GP | Mins | W | L | TGA | GAA | SO |
|---|---|---|---|---|---|---|---|
| Scott Clemmensen..40 | 2356 | 25 | 13 | 94 | 2.39 | 2 |
| Martin Brodeur ....31 | 1814 | 19 | 9 | 73 | 2.42 | 5 |
| Kevin Weekes .....16 | 795 | 7 | 5 | 32 | 2.42 | 0 |

## New York Islanders
### SCORING

| Player | GP | G | Ast | Pts | +/- | PM |
|---|---|---|---|---|---|---|
| Mark Streit, D | 74 | 16 | 40 | 56 | 6 | 62 |
| Kyle Okposo, RW | 65 | 18 | 21 | 39 | -6 | 36 |
| Doug Weight, C | 53 | 10 | 28 | 38 | -15 | 55 |
| Bill Guerin, RW | 61 | 16 | 20 | 36 | -15 | 63 |
| Frans Nielsen, C | 59 | 9 | 24 | 33 | -4 | 18 |
| Richard Park, RW | 71 | 14 | 17 | 31 | -13 | 34 |
| Trent Hunter, RW | 55 | 14 | 17 | 31 | -8 | 41 |
| Andy Hilbert, C | 67 | 11 | 16 | 27 | -3 | 22 |
| Blake Comeau, LW | 53 | 7 | 18 | 25 | -17 | 32 |
| Josh Bailey, C | 68 | 7 | 18 | 25 | -14 | 16 |
| Sean Bergenheim, LW | 59 | 15 | 9 | 24 | -2 | 64 |
| Mike Comrie, C | 41 | 7 | 13 | 20 | -8 | 26 |
| Bruno Gervais, D | 69 | 3 | 16 | 19 | -15 | 33 |
| Chris Campoli, D | 51 | 6 | 11 | 17 | -20 | 43 |
| Jon Sim, LW | 49 | 9 | 6 | 15 | -12 | 42 |
| Jeff Tambellini, LW | 65 | 7 | 8 | 15 | -20 | 32 |
| Tim Jackman, RW | 69 | 5 | 7 | 12 | -17 | 155 |
| Andy Sutton, D | 23 | 2 | 8 | 10 | 3 | 40 |
| Radek Martinek, D | 51 | 6 | 4 | 10 | -16 | 28 |
| Dean McAmmond, C | 18 | 2 | 7 | 9 | 5 | 8 |
| Brendan Witt, D | 65 | 0 | 9 | 9 | -34 | 94 |
| Freddy Meyer, D | 27 | 4 | 5 | 9 | -19 | 14 |
| Jack Hillen, D | 40 | 1 | 5 | 6 | -9 | 16 |
| Mike Iggulden, C | 11 | 1 | 4 | 5 | -3 | 4 |
| Nate Thompson, C | 43 | 2 | 2 | 4 | -11 | 49 |

### GOALTENDING

| Player | GP | Mins | W | L | TGA | GAA | SO |
|---|---|---|---|---|---|---|---|
| Joey McDonald | 49 | 2792 | 14 | 26 | 157 | 3.37 | 1 |
| Yann Davis | 31 | 1760 | 10 | 17 | 84 | 2.86 | 2 |
| Rick DiPietro | 5 | 256 | 1 | 3 | 15 | 3.52 | 0 |
| Peter Mannino | 3 | 133 | 1 | 1 | 10 | 4.52 | 0 |

## Ottawa Senators
### SCORING

| Player | GP | G | Ast | Pts | +/- | PM |
|---|---|---|---|---|---|---|
| Daniel Alfredsson, RW | 79 | 24 | 50 | 74 | 7 | 24 |
| Jason Spezza, C | 82 | 32 | 41 | 73 | -14 | 79 |
| Dany Heatley, LW | 82 | 39 | 33 | 72 | -11 | 88 |
| Filip Kuba, D | 71 | 3 | 37 | 40 | 4 | 28 |
| Mike Fisher, C | 78 | 13 | 19 | 32 | E | 66 |
| Nick Foligno, C | 81 | 17 | 15 | 32 | -10 | 59 |
| Antoine Vermette, LW | 62 | 9 | 19 | 28 | -12 | 42 |
| Chris Kelly, C | 82 | 12 | 11 | 23 | -10 | 38 |
| Chris Phillips, D | 82 | 6 | 16 | 22 | -14 | 66 |
| Jarkko Ruutu, LW | 78 | 7 | 14 | 21 | E | 144 |
| Brendan Bell, D | 53 | 6 | 15 | 21 | -5 | 24 |
| Ryan Shannon, C | 35 | 8 | 12 | 20 | -1 | 2 |
| Jesse Winchester, RW | 76 | 3 | 15 | 18 | E | 33 |
| Alexandre Picard, D | 47 | 6 | 8 | 14 | -2 | 8 |
| Chris Campoli, D | 25 | 5 | 8 | 13 | 4 | 12 |
| Brian Lee, D | 53 | 2 | 11 | 13 | -2 | 33 |
| Shean Donovan, RW | 65 | 5 | 5 | 10 | -2 | 34 |
| Chris Neil, RW | 60 | 3 | 7 | 10 | -13 | 146 |
| Anton Volchenkov, D | 68 | 2 | 8 | 10 | -10 | 36 |
| Dean McAmmond, C | 44 | 3 | 4 | 7 | -2 | 16 |
| Mike Comrie, C | 22 | 3 | 4 | 7 | -6 | 6 |
| Christopher Schubert, D | 50 | 3 | 3 | 6 | -8 | 26 |
| Ilya Zubov, C | 10 | 0 | 2 | 2 | -1 | 0 |
| Peter Regin, C | 11 | 1 | 1 | 2 | E | 2 |

### GOALTENDING

| Player | GP | Mins | W | L | TGA | GAA | SO |
|---|---|---|---|---|---|---|---|
| Alex Auld | 43 | 2449 | 16 | 18 | 101 | 2.47 | 1 |
| Brian Elliott | 31 | 1667 | 16 | 8 | 77 | 2.77 | 1 |
| Martin Gerber | 14 | 839 | 4 | 9 | 40 | 2.86 | 1 |

## New York Rangers
### SCORING

| Player | GP | G | Ast | Pts | +/- | PM |
|---|---|---|---|---|---|---|
| Scott Gomez, C | 77 | 16 | 42 | 58 | -2 | 60 |
| Nikolai Zherdev, RW | 82 | 23 | 35 | 58 | 6 | 39 |
| Chris Drury, C | 81 | 22 | 34 | 56 | -8 | 32 |
| Markus Naslund, LW | 82 | 24 | 22 | 46 | -10 | 57 |
| Brandon Dubinsky, C | 82 | 13 | 28 | 41 | -6 | 112 |
| Ryan Callahan, RW | 81 | 22 | 18 | 40 | 7 | 45 |
| Michal Rozsival, D | 76 | 8 | 22 | 30 | -7 | 52 |
| Wade Redden, D | 81 | 3 | 23 | 26 | -5 | 51 |
| Daniel Girardi, D | 82 | 4 | 18 | 22 | -14 | 53 |
| Paul Mara, D | 76 | 5 | 16 | 21 | 2 | 94 |
| Nigel Dawes, LW | 52 | 10 | 9 | 19 | -2 | 15 |
| Aaron Voros, LW | 54 | 8 | 8 | 16 | -9 | 122 |
| Marc Staal, D | 82 | 3 | 12 | 15 | -7 | 64 |
| Lauri Korpikoski, C | 68 | 6 | 8 | 14 | -10 | 14 |
| Nik Antropov, RW | 18 | 7 | 6 | 13 | -1 | 6 |
| Dmitri Kalinin, D | 58 | 1 | 12 | 13 | -7 | 26 |
| Fredrik Sjostrom, RW | 79 | 7 | 6 | 13 | -11 | 30 |
| Sean Avery, LW | 18 | 5 | 7 | 12 | 4 | 34 |
| Blair Betts, C | 81 | 6 | 4 | 10 | -5 | 16 |
| Petr Prucha, LW | 28 | 4 | 5 | 9 | -2 | 16 |
| Derek Morris, D | 18 | 0 | 8 | 8 | 3 | 16 |
| Colton Orr, RW | 82 | 1 | 4 | 5 | -15 | 193 |
| Dan Fritsche, RW | 16 | 1 | 3 | 4 | -2 | 2 |
| Corey Potter, RW | 5 | 1 | 1 | 2 | -1 | 0 |

### GOALTENDING

| Player | GP | Mins | W | L | TGA | GAA | SO |
|---|---|---|---|---|---|---|---|
| Henrik Lundqvist | 70 | 4153 | 38 | 25 | 168 | 2.43 | 3 |
| Steve Valiquette | 15 | 823 | 5 | 5 | 39 | 2.84 | 1 |

## Philadelphia Flyers
### SCORING

| Player | GP | G | Ast | Pts | +/- | PM |
|---|---|---|---|---|---|---|
| Jeff Carter, C | 82 | 46 | 38 | 84 | 23 | 68 |
| Mike Richards, C | 79 | 30 | 50 | 80 | 22 | 63 |
| Simon Gagne, LW | 79 | 34 | 40 | 74 | 21 | 42 |
| Scott Hartnell, LW | 82 | 30 | 30 | 60 | 14 | 143 |
| Joffrey Lupul, RW | 79 | 25 | 15 | 50 | 1 | 58 |
| Mike Knuble, RW | 82 | 27 | 20 | 47 | 5 | 62 |
| Kimmo Timonen, D | 77 | 3 | 40 | 43 | 19 | 54 |
| Braydon Coburn, D | 80 | 7 | 21 | 28 | 7 | 97 |
| Claude Giroux, RW | 42 | 9 | 18 | 27 | 10 | 14 |
| Daniel Briere, C | 29 | 11 | 14 | 25 | -1 | 26 |
| Matt Carle, D | 64 | 4 | 20 | 24 | 2 | 16 |
| Scottie Upshall, RW | 55 | 7 | 14 | 21 | 5 | 63 |
| Arron Asham, RW | 78 | 8 | 12 | 20 | E | 155 |
| Glen Metropoli, C | 55 | 4 | 10 | 14 | -1 | 15 |
| Andrew Alberts, D | 79 | 1 | 12 | 13 | 6 | 61 |
| Darroll Powe, LW | 60 | 6 | 5 | 11 | -8 | 35 |
| Ossi Vaananen, D | 46 | 1 | 9 | 10 | 7 | 22 |
| Randy Jones, D | 47 | 4 | 4 | 8 | 8 | 22 |
| Luca Sbisa, D | 39 | 0 | 7 | 7 | -6 | 36 |
| Daniel Carcillo, LW | 20 | 0 | 4 | 4 | -2 | 80 |
| Ryan Parent, D | 31 | 0 | 4 | 4 | 3 | 10 |
| Andreas Nodl, LW | 38 | 1 | 3 | 4 | -15 | 2 |
| Riley Cote, LW | 63 | 0 | 3 | 3 | -7 | 174 |
| Josh Gratton, LW | 19 | 1 | 2 | 3 | -2 | 57 |
| Jonathan Kalinski, LW | 12 | 1 | 2 | 3 | -2 | 0 |
| Steve Eminger, D | 12 | 0 | 2 | 2 | E | 8 |
| Lasse Kukkonen, D | 22 | 0 | 2 | 2 | -2 | 10 |

### GOALTENDING

| Player | GP | Mins | W | L | TGA | GAA | SO |
|---|---|---|---|---|---|---|---|
| Martin Biron | 55 | 3177 | 29 | 19 | 146 | 2.76 | 2 |
| Antero Niittymaki | 32 | 1805 | 15 | 8 | 83 | 2.76 | 1 |

## Phoenix Coyotes

### SCORING

| Player | GP | G | Ast | Pts | +/− | PM |
|---|---|---|---|---|---|---|
| Shane Doan, RW | 82 | 31 | 42 | 73 | 5 | 72 |
| Olli Jokinen, C | 57 | 21 | 21 | 42 | -5 | 49 |
| Steve Reinprecht, C | 73 | 14 | 27 | 41 | E | 20 |
| Ed Jovanovski, D | 82 | 9 | 27 | 36 | -15 | 106 |
| Peter Mueller, C | 72 | 13 | 23 | 36 | -7 | 24 |
| Martin Hanzal, C | 74 | 11 | 20 | 31 | -4 | 40 |
| Keith Yandle, D | 69 | 4 | 26 | 30 | -4 | 37 |
| Mikkel Boedker, RW | 78 | 11 | 17 | 28 | -6 | 18 |
| Zbynek Michalek, D | 82 | 6 | 21 | 27 | -13 | 28 |
| Enver Lisin, RW | 48 | 13 | 8 | 21 | -13 | 24 |
| Joakim Lindstrom, LW | 44 | 9 | 11 | 20 | -6 | 28 |
| Kyle Turris, C | 63 | 8 | 12 | 20 | -15 | 21 |
| Matthew Lombardi, C | 19 | 5 | 11 | 16 | 2 | 14 |
| Viktor Tikhonov, LW | 61 | 8 | 8 | 16 | -3 | 20 |
| Todd Fedoruk, LW | 72 | 6 | 7 | 13 | -9 | 72 |
| Scottie Upshall, LW | 19 | 8 | 5 | 13 | 2 | 26 |
| Derek Morris, D | 57 | 5 | 7 | 12 | -13 | 24 |
| Ken Klee, D | 68 | 1 | 10 | 11 | 9 | 24 |
| Petr Prucha, LW | 19 | 2 | 8 | 10 | 1 | 6 |
| Daniel Carcillo, LW | 54 | 3 | 7 | 10 | -13 | 174 |
| Kevin Porter, C | 34 | 5 | 5 | 10 | -2 | 4 |
| David Hale, D | 48 | 3 | 6 | 9 | -11 | 36 |
| Kurt Sauer, D | 68 | 1 | 6 | 7 | -1 | 36 |
| Daniel Winnik, C | 49 | 3 | 4 | 7 | 1 | 63 |
| Dmitri Kalinin, D | 15 | 1 | 3 | 4 | -2 | 6 |
| Steven Goetzen, RW | 16 | 2 | 2 | 4 | -2 | 24 |

### GOALTENDING

| Player | GP | Mins | W | L | TGA | GAA | SO |
|---|---|---|---|---|---|---|---|
| Ilya Bryzgalov | 65 | 3760 | 26 | 31 | 187 | 2.98 | 3 |
| Mikael Tellqvist | 15 | 798 | 7 | 5 | 38 | 2.86 | 0 |
| Al Montoya | 5 | 259 | 3 | 1 | 9 | 2.08 | 1 |
| Josh Tordjman | 2 | 118 | 0 | 2 | 8 | 4.08 | 0 |

## Pittsburgh Penguins

### SCORING

| Player | GP | G | Ast | Pts | +/− | PM |
|---|---|---|---|---|---|---|
| Evgeni Malkin, C | 82 | 35 | 78 | 113 | 17 | 80 |
| Sidney Crosby, C | 77 | 33 | 70 | 103 | 3 | 76 |
| Jordan Staal, C | 82 | 22 | 27 | 49 | 5 | 37 |
| Petr Sykora, RW | 76 | 25 | 21 | 46 | 3 | 36 |
| Ruslan Fedotenko, LW | 65 | 16 | 23 | 39 | 18 | 44 |
| Miroslav Satan, RW | 65 | 17 | 19 | 36 | 3 | 36 |
| Tyler Kennedy, C | 67 | 15 | 20 | 35 | 15 | 30 |
| Kris Letang, D | 74 | 10 | 23 | 33 | -7 | 24 |
| Matt Cooke, LW | 76 | 13 | 18 | 31 | E | 101 |
| Pascal Dupuis, LW | 71 | 12 | 16 | 28 | 1 | 30 |
| Maxime Talbot, C | 75 | 12 | 10 | 22 | -9 | 63 |
| Alex Goligoski, D | 45 | 6 | 14 | 20 | 5 | 16 |
| Sergei Gonchar, D | 25 | 6 | 13 | 19 | 6 | 26 |
| Brooks Orpik, D | 79 | 2 | 17 | 19 | 10 | 73 |
| Chris Kunitz, LW | 20 | 7 | 11 | 18 | 3 | 16 |
| Robert Scuderi, D | 81 | 1 | 15 | 16 | 23 | 18 |
| Ryan Whitney, D | 28 | 2 | 11 | 13 | -15 | 16 |
| Bill Guerin, RW | 17 | 5 | 7 | 12 | 3 | 18 |
| Hal Gill, D | 62 | 2 | 8 | 10 | 11 | 53 |
| Mark Eaton, D | 68 | 4 | 5 | 9 | 3 | 36 |
| Philippe Boucher, D | 25 | 3 | 3 | 6 | 10 | 24 |
| Mike Zigomannis, C | 22 | 2 | 4 | 6 | -2 | 27 |
| Eric Godard, RW | 71 | 2 | 2 | 4 | -3 | 171 |
| Bill Thomas, RW | 16 | 2 | 1 | 3 | -4 | 2 |
| Chris Minard, C | 20 | 1 | 2 | 3 | E | 4 |
| Dustin Jeffrey, C | 14 | 1 | 2 | 3 | 4 | 0 |

### GOALTENDING

| Player | GP | Mins | W | L | TGA | GAA | SO |
|---|---|---|---|---|---|---|---|
| Marc-Andre Fleury | 62 | 3641 | 35 | 18 | 162 | 2.67 | 4 |
| Dany Sabourin | 19 | 989 | 6 | 8 | 47 | 2.85 | 0 |
| Mathieu Garon | 4 | 205 | 2 | 1 | 10 | 2.91 | 0 |
| John Curry | 3 | 150 | 2 | 1 | 6 | 2.40 | 0 |

## San Jose Sharks

### SCORING

| Player | GP | G | Ast | Pts | +/− | PM |
|---|---|---|---|---|---|---|
| Joe Thornton, C | 82 | 25 | 61 | 86 | 16 | 56 |
| Patrick Marleau, C | 76 | 38 | 33 | 71 | 16 | 18 |
| Devin Setoguchi, RW | 81 | 31 | 34 | 65 | 16 | 25 |
| Joe Pavelski, C | 80 | 25 | 34 | 59 | 5 | 46 |
| Dan Boyle, D | 77 | 16 | 41 | 57 | 6 | 52 |
| Milan Michalek, LW | 77 | 23 | 34 | 57 | 11 | 52 |
| Ryane Clowe, LW | 71 | 22 | 30 | 52 | 8 | 51 |
| Rob Blake, D | 73 | 10 | 35 | 45 | 15 | 110 |
| Christian Ehrhoff, D | 77 | 8 | 34 | 42 | -12 | 63 |
| Marc-Eduoard Vlasic, D | 82 | 6 | 30 | 36 | 15 | 42 |
| Jonathan Cheechoo, RW | 66 | 12 | 17 | 29 | -3 | 59 |
| Mike Grier, RW | 62 | 10 | 13 | 23 | 8 | 25 |
| Jeremy Roenick, C | 42 | 4 | 9 | 13 | -1 | 24 |
| Tomas Plihal, C | 64 | 5 | 8 | 13 | -4 | 22 |
| Marcel Goc, C | 55 | 2 | 9 | 11 | -6 | 18 |

### SCORING (CONT.)

| Player | GP | G | Ast | Pts | +/− | PM |
|---|---|---|---|---|---|---|
| Brad Lukovich, D | 58 | 0 | 8 | 8 | 5 | 12 |
| Alexei Semenov, D | 47 | 1 | 7 | 8 | 3 | 57 |
| Douglas Murray, D | 75 | 0 | 7 | 6 | 6 | 38 |
| Jamie McGinn, LW | 35 | 4 | 2 | 6 | -6 | 2 |
| Travis Moen, LW | 19 | 3 | 2 | 5 | -1 | 14 |
| Jody Shelley, LW | 70 | 2 | 2 | 4 | -6 | 116 |
| Lukas Kaspar, RW | 13 | 2 | 2 | 4 | E | 8 |
| Brad Staubitz, D | 35 | 1 | 2 | 3 | E | 76 |
| Tom Cavanagh, RW | 17 | 1 | 1 | 2 | -2 | 4 |
| Claude Lemieux | 18 | 0 | 1 | 1 | -5 | 21 |

### GOALTENDING

| Player | GP | Mins | W | L | TGA | GAA | SO |
|---|---|---|---|---|---|---|---|
| Evgeni Nabokov | 62 | 3687 | 41 | 12 | 150 | 2.44 | 7 |
| Brian Boucher | 22 | 1291 | 12 | 6 | 47 | 2.18 | 2 |

## St. Louis Blues

### SCORING

| Player | GP | G | Ast | Pts | +/- | PM |
|---|---|---|---|---|---|---|
| Brad Boyes, RW | 82 | 33 | 39 | 72 | -20 | 26 |
| David Backes, RW | 82 | 31 | 23 | 54 | -3 | 165 |
| David Perron, LW | 81 | 15 | 35 | 50 | 13 | 50 |
| Keith Tkachuk, C | 79 | 25 | 24 | 49 | -11 | 61 |
| Patrik Berglund, C | 76 | 21 | 26 | 47 | 19 | 16 |
| Andy McDonald, C | 46 | 15 | 29 | 44 | -13 | 24 |
| T.J. Oshie, C | 57 | 14 | 25 | 39 | 16 | 30 |
| Carlo Coaiacovo, D | 63 | 3 | 26 | 29 | 2 | 29 |
| Jay McClement, C | 82 | 12 | 14 | 26 | -10 | 29 |
| Alexander Steen, LW | 61 | 6 | 18 | 24 | -6 | 24 |
| Barret Jackman, D | 82 | 4 | 17 | 21 | -17 | 86 |
| Brad Winchester, LW | 64 | 13 | 8 | 21 | -1 | 89 |
| Jeff Woywitka, D | 65 | 3 | 15 | 18 | 8 | 57 |
| B.J. Crombeen, RW | 66 | 11 | 6 | 17 | -8 | 122 |
| Paul Kariya, LW | 11 | 2 | 13 | 15 | 1 | 2 |
| Roman Polak, D | 69 | 1 | 14 | 15 | -15 | 45 |
| Lee Stempniak, RW | 14 | 3 | 10 | 13 | -3 | 2 |
| Jay McKee, D | 69 | 1 | 7 | 8 | 11 | 44 |
| Mike Weaver, D | 58 | 0 | 7 | 7 | -3 | 12 |
| Yan Stastny, C | 34 | 3 | 4 | 7 | -14 | 20 |
| Eric Brewer, D | 28 | 1 | 5 | 6 | -14 | 24 |
| Dan Hinote, RW | 51 | 1 | 4 | 5 | -7 | 64 |
| Cam Janssen, RW | 56 | 1 | 3 | 4 | -5 | 131 |
| Steve Regier, LW | 8 | 3 | 1 | 4 | -1 | 4 |
| Steve Wagner, D | 22 | 2 | 2 | 4 | -5 | 18 |
| Cam Paddock, C | 16 | 2 | 1 | 3 | -4 | 0 |
| Tyson Strachan, D | 30 | 0 | 3 | 3 | 8 | 39 |
| Chris Porter, C | 6 | 1 | 1 | 2 | -1 | 0 |

### GOALTENDING

| Player | GP | Mins | W | L | TGA | GAA | SO |
|---|---|---|---|---|---|---|---|
| Chris Mason | 57 | 3215 | 27 | 21 | 129 | 2.41 | 6 |
| Manny Legace | 29 | 1452 | 13 | 9 | 77 | 3.18 | 0 |
| Ben Bishop | 6 | 245 | 1 | 1 | 12 | 2.94 | 0 |

## Tampa Bay Lightning

### SCORING

| Player | GP | G | Ast | Pts | +/- | PM |
|---|---|---|---|---|---|---|
| Martin St. Louis, RW | 82 | 30 | 50 | 80 | 4 | 14 |
| Vincent Lecavalier, C | 77 | 29 | 38 | 67 | -9 | 54 |
| Steve Stamkos, C | 79 | 23 | 23 | 46 | -18 | 39 |
| Vaclav Prospal, LW | 82 | 19 | 26 | 45 | -20 | 52 |
| Mark Recchi, RW | 62 | 13 | 32 | 45 | -15 | 20 |
| Ryan Malone, LW | 70 | 26 | 19 | 45 | 4 | 98 |
| Steve Eminger, D | 50 | 4 | 19 | 23 | -4 | 36 |
| Lukas Krajicek, D | 71 | 2 | 17 | 19 | -8 | 48 |
| Jeff Halpern, C | 52 | 7 | 9 | 16 | -13 | 32 |
| Evgeny Artyukhin, RW | 73 | 6 | 10 | 16 | 1 | 151 |
| Andrej Meszaros, D | 52 | 2 | 14 | 16 | -4 | 36 |
| Jussi Jokinen, LW | 46 | 6 | 10 | 16 | -8 | 16 |
| Matt Pettinger, LW | 59 | 8 | 7 | 15 | -14 | 24 |
| Cory Murphy, D | 25 | 5 | 10 | 15 | -3 | 12 |
| Paul Ranger, D | 42 | 12 | 11 | 13 | -5 | 56 |
| Adam Hall, RW | 74 | 5 | 5 | 10 | -9 | 29 |
| Paul Szczechura, C | 31 | 4 | 5 | 9 | -1 | 12 |
| Gary Roberts, LW | 30 | 4 | 3 | 7 | -11 | 27 |
| Matt Lashoff, D | 12 | 0 | 7 | 7 | -7 | 10 |
| Radim Vrbata, RW | 18 | 3 | 3 | 6 | -1 | 8 |
| Ryan Craig, C | 54 | 2 | 4 | 6 | -7 | 60 |
| Steve Downie, RW | 23 | 3 | 3 | 6 | 2 | 54 |
| Marek Malik, D | 42 | 0 | 5 | 5 | -3 | 36 |
| Josef Melichar, D | 24 | 0 | 5 | 5 | 1 | 29 |
| Martins Karsums, RW | 18 | 1 | 4 | 5 | -5 | 6 |
| Matt Smaby, D | 43 | 0 | 4 | 4 | -11 | 50 |

### GOALTENDING

| Player | GP | Mins | W | L | TGA | GAA | SO |
|---|---|---|---|---|---|---|---|
| Mike Smith | 41 | 2471 | 14 | 18 | 108 | 2.62 | 2 |
| Karri Ramo | 24 | 1312 | 4 | 10 | 80 | 3.66 | 0 |
| Mike McKenna | 15 | 776 | 4 | 8 | 46 | 3.56 | 1 |
| Olaf Kolzig | 8 | 410 | 2 | 4 | 25 | 3.66 | 0 |

## Toronto Maple Leafs

### SCORING

| Player | GP | G | Ast | Pts | +/- | PM |
|---|---|---|---|---|---|---|
| Jason Blake, LW | 78 | 25 | 38 | 63 | -2 | 40 |
| A. Ponikarovsky, LW | 82 | 23 | 38 | 61 | 6 | 38 |
| Matt Stajan, C | 76 | 15 | 40 | 55 | -4 | 54 |
| Mikhail Grabovski, C | 78 | 20 | 28 | 48 | -8 | 92 |
| Nik Antropov, C | 63 | 21 | 25 | 46 | -13 | 24 |
| Niklas Hagman, RW | 65 | 22 | 20 | 42 | -5 | 4 |
| Dominic Moore, C | 63 | 12 | 29 | 41 | -1 | 69 |
| Pavel Kubina, D | 82 | 14 | 26 | 40 | -15 | 94 |
| Tomas Kaberle, D | 57 | 4 | 27 | 31 | -8 | 8 |
| Lee Stempniak, RW | 61 | 11 | 20 | 31 | -9 | 31 |
| Nikolai Kulemin, LW | 73 | 15 | 16 | 31 | -8 | 18 |
| John Mitchell, C | 76 | 12 | 17 | 29 | -16 | 33 |
| Ian White, D | 71 | 10 | 16 | 26 | 6 | 57 |
| Jeff Finger, D | 66 | 6 | 17 | 23 | -7 | 43 |
| Jamal Mayers, RW | 71 | 7 | 9 | 16 | -7 | 82 |
| Luke Schenn, D | 70 | 2 | 12 | 14 | -12 | 71 |

### SCORING *(CONT.)*

| Player | GP | G | Ast | Pts | +/- | PM |
|---|---|---|---|---|---|---|
| Anton Stralman, D | 38 | 1 | 12 | 13 | -2 | 20 |
| Boyd Devereaux, C | 23 | 6 | 5 | 11 | 3 | 2 |
| Mike Van Ryn, D | 27 | 3 | 8 | 11 | 2 | 14 |
| Jonas Frogren, D | 41 | 1 | 6 | 7 | E | 28 |
| Jeremy Williams, RW | 11 | 5 | 2 | 7 | 2 | 2 |
| Jeff Hamilton, C | 15 | 3 | 3 | 6 | 2 | 4 |
| Alexander Steen, LW | 20 | 2 | 2 | 4 | -4 | 6 |
| Jiri Tlusty, C | 14 | 0 | 4 | 4 | E | 0 |

### GOALTENDING

| Player | GP | Mins | W | L | TGA | GAA | SO |
|---|---|---|---|---|---|---|---|
| Vesa Toskala | 53 | 3056 | 22 | 17 | 166 | 3.26 | 1 |
| Curtis Joseph | 21 | 841 | 5 | 9 | 50 | 3.57 | 0 |
| Martin Gerber | 12 | 706 | 6 | 5 | 38 | 3.23 | 0 |
| Justin Pogge | 7 | 372 | 1 | 4 | 27 | 4.36 | 0 |

## Vancouver Canucks

### SCORING

| Player | GP | G | Ast | Pts | +/- | PM |
|---|---|---|---|---|---|---|
| Daniel Sedin, LW | 82 | 31 | 51 | 82 | 24 | 36 |
| Henrik Sedin, C | 82 | 22 | 60 | 82 | 22 | 48 |
| Ryan Kesler, C | 82 | 26 | 33 | 59 | 8 | 61 |
| Pavol Demitra, RW | 69 | 20 | 33 | 53 | 6 | 20 |
| Alex Burrows, LW | 82 | 28 | 23 | 51 | 23 | 150 |
| Kevin Bieksa, D | 72 | 11 | 32 | 43 | -4 | 97 |
| Alexander Edler, D | 80 | 10 | 27 | 37 | 11 | 54 |
| Steve Bernier, RW | 81 | 15 | 17 | 32 | 4 | 27 |
| Mats Sundin, C | 41 | 9 | 19 | 28 | -5 | 28 |
| Kyle Wellwood, C | 74 | 18 | 9 | 27 | 2 | 4 |
| Mattias Ohlund, D | 82 | 6 | 19 | 25 | 14 | 105 |
| Sami Salo, D | 60 | 5 | 20 | 25 | 5 | 26 |
| Willie Mitchell, D | 82 | 3 | 20 | 23 | 29 | 59 |
| Mason Raymond, LW | 72 | 11 | 12 | 23 | 2 | 24 |
| Jannik Hansen, RW | 55 | 6 | 15 | 21 | 5 | 37 |

### SCORING

| Player | GP | G | Ast | Pts | +/- | PM |
|---|---|---|---|---|---|---|
| Taylor Pyatt, LW | 69 | 10 | 9 | 19 | E | 43 |
| Shane O'Brien, D | 76 | 0 | 10 | 10 | 6 | 196 |
| Ryan Johnson, C | 62 | 2 | 7 | 9 | 1 | 12 |
| Darcy Hordichuk, LW | 73 | 4 | 1 | 5 | 1 | 109 |
| Jason Jaffray, LW | 14 | 2 | 2 | 4 | -2 | 14 |
| Rick Rypien, C | 12 | 3 | 0 | 3 | -3 | 19 |
| Rob Davison, D | 23 | 0 | 2 | 2 | -4 | 51 |

### GOALTENDING

| Player | GP | Mins | W | L | TGA | GAA | SO |
|---|---|---|---|---|---|---|---|
| Roberto Luongo | 54 | 3181 | 33 | 13 | 124 | 2.34 | 9 |
| Curtis Sanford | 19 | 973 | 7 | 8 | 42 | 2.59 | 1 |
| Jason LaBarbera | 9 | 451 | 3 | 2 | 20 | 2.66 | 0 |
| Cory Schneider | 8 | 355 | 2 | 4 | 20 | 3.38 | 0 |

## Washington Capitals

### SCORING

| Player | GP | G | Ast | Pts | +/- | PM |
|---|---|---|---|---|---|---|
| Alexander Ovechkin, LW | 79 | 56 | 54 | 110 | 8 | 72 |
| Nicklas Backstrom, C | 82 | 22 | 66 | 88 | 16 | 46 |
| Alexander Semin, LW | 62 | 34 | 45 | 79 | 25 | 77 |
| Mike Green, D | 68 | 31 | 42 | 73 | 24 | 68 |
| Brooks Laich, C | 82 | 23 | 30 | 53 | -1 | 31 |
| Viktor Kozlov, C | 67 | 13 | 28 | 41 | -9 | 16 |
| T. Fleischmann, RW | 73 | 19 | 18 | 37 | -3 | 20 |
| Sergei Fedorov, C | 52 | 11 | 22 | 33 | 4 | 50 |
| Michael Nylander, C | 72 | 9 | 24 | 33 | E | 32 |
| Eric Fehr, RW | 61 | 12 | 13 | 25 | 8 | 22 |
| Dave Steckel, C | 76 | 8 | 11 | 19 | 2 | 34 |
| Boyd Gordon, C | 63 | 5 | 9 | 14 | -4 | 16 |
| Milan Jurcina, D | 79 | 3 | 11 | 14 | 1 | 68 |
| Tom Poti, D | 52 | 3 | 10 | 13 | 3 | 28 |
| Shaone Morrisonn, D | 72 | 3 | 10 | 13 | 4 | 77 |
| Jeff Schultz, D | 64 | 1 | 11 | 12 | 13 | 21 |
| Matt Bradley, RW | 81 | 5 | 6 | 11 | -1 | 59 |

### SCORING

| Player | GP | G | Ast | Pts | +/- | PM |
|---|---|---|---|---|---|---|
| Chris Clark, RW | 32 | 1 | 5 | 6 | -3 | 32 |
| Keith Aucoin, C | 12 | 2 | 4 | 6 | 5 | 4 |
| Tyler Sloan, D | 26 | 1 | 4 | 5 | 4 | 14 |
| Karl Alzner, D | 30 | 1 | 4 | 5 | -1 | 2 |
| Donald Brashear, LW | 63 | 1 | 3 | 4 | -6 | 121 |
| John Erksine, D | 52 | 0 | 4 | 4 | 1 | 63 |
| Sami Lepisto, D | 7 | 0 | 4 | 4 | -3 | 6 |
| Bryan Helmer, D | 12 | 0 | 3 | 3 | -1 | 2 |
| Brian Pothier, D | 9 | 1 | 2 | 3 | E | 4 |
| Alexandre Giroux, C | 12 | 1 | 1 | 2 | 4 | 10 |

### GOALTENDING

| Player | GP | Mins | W | L | TGA | GAA | SO |
|---|---|---|---|---|---|---|---|
| Jose Theodore | 57 | 3287 | 32 | 17 | 157 | 2.87 | 2 |
| Brent Johnson | 21 | 1131 | 12 | 6 | 53 | 2.81 | 0 |
| Simeon Varlamov | 6 | 329 | 4 | 0 | 13 | 2.37 | 0 |
| Michal Neuvirth | 5 | 220 | 2 | 1 | 11 | 3.00 | 0 |

# 2009 NHL Draft

## First Round

The opening round of the 2009 NHL entry draft was held on June 26 in Montreal, Quebec, Canada.

| Team | Selection | Position | Team | Selection | Position |
|---|---|---|---|---|---|
| 1. NY Islanders | John Tavares | C | 16. Minnesota | Nick Leddy | D |
| 2. Tampa Bay | Victor Hedman | D | 17. St. Louis | David Rundblad | D |
| 3. Colorado | Matt Duchene | C | 18. Montreal | Louis Leblanc | C |
| 4. Atlanta | Evander Kane | C | 19. NY Rangers | Chris Kreider | C |
| 5. Los Angeles | Brayden Schenn | C | 20. New Jersey | Jacob Josefson | C |
| 6. Phoenix | Ekman Larsson | D | 21. Columbus | John Moore | D |
| 7. Toronto | Nazem Kadri | C | 22. Vancouver | Jordan Schroeder | RW |
| 8. Dallas | Scott Glennie | C | 23. Calgary | Tim Erixon | D |
| 9. Ottawa | Jared Cowen | D | 24. Washington | Marcus Johansson | LW |
| 10. Edmonton | Paajarvi Svensson | LW | 25. Boston | Jordan Caron | C |
| 11. Nashville | Ryan Ellis | D | 26. Anaheim | Kyle Palmieri | C |
| 12. NY Islanders | Calvin deHaan | D | 27. Carolina | Philippe Paradis | C |
| 13. Buffalo | Zack Kassian | RW | 28. Chicago | Dylan Olsen | D |
| 14. Florida | Dmitry Kulikov | D | 29. Tampa Bay | Carter Ashton | LW |
| 15. Anaheim | Peter Holland | C | 30. Pittsburgh | Simon Despres | D |

## The Stanley Cup

Awarded annually to the team that wins the NHL's best-of-seven final-round playoffs. The Stanley Cup is the oldest trophy competed for by professional athletes in North America. It was donated in 1893 by Frederick Arthur, Lord Stanley of Preston.

### Results

| | |
|---|---|
| 1892–93 | Montreal A.A.A. |
| 1893–94 | Montreal A.A.A. |
| 1894–95 | Montreal Victorias |
| 1895–96 | Winnipeg Victorias (Feb) |
| 1895–96 | Montreal Victorias (Dec) |
| 1896–97 | Montreal Victorias |
| 1897–98 | Montreal Victorias |
| 1898–99 | Montreal Victorias (Feb) |
| 1898–99 | Montreal Shamrocks (Mar) |
| 1899–1900 | Montreal Shamrocks |
| 1900–01 | Winnipeg Victorias |
| 1901–02 | Winnipeg Victorias (Jan) |
| 1901–02 | Montreal A.A.A. (Mar) |
| 1902–03 | Montreal A.A.A. (Feb) |
| 1902–03 | Ottawa Silver Seven (Mar) |
| 1903–04 | Ottawa Silver Seven |
| 1904–05 | Ottawa Silver Seven |
| 1905–06 | Ottawa Silver Seven (Feb) |
| 1905–06 | Montreal Wanderers (Mar) |
| 1906–07 | Kenora Thistles (Jan) |
| 1906–07 | Montreal Wanderers (Mar) |
| 1907–08 | Montreal Wanderers |
| 1908–09 | Ottawa Senators |
| 1909–10 | Montreal Wanderers |
| 1910–11 | Ottawa Senators |
| 1911–12 | Quebec Bulldogs |
| 1912–13 | Quebec Bulldogs |
| 1913–14 | Toronto Blueshirts |
| 1914–15 | Vancouver Millionaires |
| 1915–16 | Montreal Canadiens |
| 1916–17 | Seattle Metropolitans |

### NHL WINNERS AND FINALISTS

| Season | Champion | Finalist | GP in Final |
|---|---|---|---|
| 1917–18 | Toronto Arenas | Vancouver Millionaires | 5 |
| 1918–19 | No decision* | No decision* | 5 |
| 1919–20 | Ottawa Senators | Seattle Metropolitans | 5 |
| 1920–21 | Ottawa Senators | Vancouver Millionaires | 5 |
| 1921–22 | Toronto St. Pats | Vancouver Millionaires | 5 |
| 1922–23 | Ottawa Senators | Vancouver Maroons, Edmonton Eskimos | 2, 4 |
| 1923–24 | Montreal Canadiens | Vancouver Maroons, Calgary Tigers | 2, 2 |
| 1924–25 | Victoria Cougars | Montreal Canadiens | 4 |
| 1925–26 | Montreal Maroons | Victoria Cougars | 4 |
| 1926–27 | Ottawa Senators | Boston Bruins | 4 |
| 1927–28 | New York Rangers | Montreal Maroons | 5 |
| 1928–29 | Boston Bruins | New York Rangers | 2 |
| 1929–30 | Montreal Canadiens | Boston Bruins | 2 |
| 1930–31 | Montreal Canadiens | Chicago Black Hawks | 5 |
| 1931–32 | Toronto Maple Leafs | New York Rangers | 3 |
| 1932–33 | New York Rangers | Toronto Maple Leafs | 4 |
| 1933–34 | Chicago Black Hawks | Detroit Red Wings | 4 |
| 1934–35 | Montreal Maroons | Toronto Maple Leafs | 3 |
| 1935–36 | Detroit Red Wings | Toronto Maple Leafs | 4 |
| 1936–37 | Detroit Red Wings | New York Rangers | 5 |
| 1937–38 | Chicago Black Hawks | Toronto Maple Leafs | 4 |
| 1938–39 | Boston Bruins | Toronto Maple Leafs | 5 |
| 1939–40 | New York Rangers | Toronto Maple Leafs | 6 |
| 1940–41 | Boston Bruins | Detroit Red Wings | 4 |
| 1941–42 | Toronto Maple Leafs | Detroit Red Wings | 7 |
| 1942–43 | Detroit Red Wings | Boston Bruins | 4 |
| 1943–44 | Montreal Canadiens | Chicago Black Hawks | 4 |
| 1944–45 | Toronto Maple Leafs | Detroit Red Wings | 7 |
| 1945–46 | Montreal Canadiens | Boston Bruins | 5 |
| 1946–47 | Toronto Maple Leafs | Montreal Canadiens | 6 |
| 1947–48 | Toronto Maple Leafs | Detroit Red Wings | 4 |
| 1948–49 | Toronto Maple Leafs | Detroit Red Wings | 4 |
| 1949–50 | Detroit Red Wings | New York Rangers | 7 |
| 1950–51 | Toronto Maple Leafs | Montreal Canadiens | 5 |
| 1951–52 | Detroit Red Wings | Montreal Canadiens | 4 |
| 1952–53 | Montreal Canadiens | Boston Bruins | 5 |
| 1953–54 | Detroit Red Wings | Montreal Canadiens | 7 |
| 1954–55 | Detroit Red Wings | Montreal Canadiens | 7 |

## NHL WINNERS AND FINALISTS

| Season | Champion | Finalist | GP in Final |
|---|---|---|---|
| 1955–56 | Montreal Canadiens | Detroit Red Wings | 5 |
| 1956–57 | Montreal Canadiens | Boston Bruins | 5 |
| 1957–58 | Montreal Canadiens | Boston Bruins | 6 |
| 1958–59 | Montreal Canadiens | Toronto Maple Leafs | 5 |
| 1959–60 | Montreal Canadiens | Toronto Maple Leafs | 4 |
| 1960–61 | Chicago Blackhawks | Detroit Red Wings | 6 |
| 1961–62 | Toronto Maple Leafs | Chicago Blackhawks | 6 |
| 1962–63 | Toronto Maple Leafs | Detroit Red Wings | 5 |
| 1963–64 | Toronto Maple Leafs | Detroit Red Wings | 7 |
| 1964–65 | Montreal Canadiens | Chicago Blackhawks | 7 |
| 1965–66 | Montreal Canadiens | Detroit Red Wings | 6 |
| 1966–67 | Toronto Maple Leafs | Montreal Canadiens | 6 |
| 1967–68 | Montreal Canadiens | St. Louis Blues | 4 |
| 1968–69 | Montreal Canadiens | St. Louis Blues | 4 |
| 1969–70 | Boston Bruins | St. Louis Blues | 4 |
| 1970–71 | Montreal Canadiens | Chicago Blackhawks | 7 |
| 1971–72 | Boston Bruins | New York Rangers | 6 |
| 1972–73 | Montreal Canadiens | Chicago Blackhawks | 6 |
| 1973–74 | Philadelphia Flyers | Boston Bruins | 6 |
| 1974–75 | Philadelphia Flyers | Buffalo Sabres | 6 |
| 1975–76 | Montreal Canadiens | Philadelphia Flyers | 4 |
| 1976–77 | Montreal Canadiens | Boston Bruins | 4 |
| 1977–78 | Montreal Canadiens | Boston Bruins | 6 |
| 1978–79 | Montreal Canadiens | New York Rangers | 5 |
| 1979–80 | New York Islanders | Philadelphia Flyers | 6 |
| 1980–81 | New York Islanders | Minnesota North Stars | 5 |
| 1981–82 | New York Islanders | Vancouver Canucks | 4 |
| 1982–83 | New York Islanders | Edmonton Oilers | 4 |
| 1983–84 | Edmonton Oilers | New York Islanders | 5 |
| 1984–85 | Edmonton Oilers | Philadelphia Flyers | 5 |
| 1985–86 | Montreal Canadiens | Calgary Flames | 5 |
| 1986–87 | Edmonton Oilers | Philadelphia Flyers | 7 |
| 1987–88 | Edmonton Oilers | Boston Bruins | 4 |
| 1988–89 | Calgary Flames | Montreal Canadiens | 6 |
| 1989–90 | Edmonton Oilers | Boston Bruins | 5 |
| 1990–91 | Pittsburgh Penguins | Minnesota North Stars | 6 |
| 1991–92 | Pittsburgh Penguins | Chicago Blackhawks | 4 |
| 1992–93 | Montreal Canadiens | Los Angeles Kings | 5 |
| 1993–94 | New York Rangers | Vancouver Canucks | 7 |
| 1994–95 | New Jersey Devils | Detroit Red Wings | 4 |
| 1995–96 | Colorado Avalanche | Florida Panthers | 4 |
| 1996–97 | Detroit Red Wings | Philadelphia Flyers | 4 |
| 1997–98 | Detroit Red Wings | Washington Capitals | 4 |
| 1998–99 | Dallas Stars | Buffalo Sabres | 6 |
| 1999–2000 | New Jersey Devils | Dallas Stars | 6 |
| 2000–01 | Colorado Avalanche | New Jersey Devils | 7 |
| 2001–02 | Detroit Red Wings | Carolina Hurricanes | 5 |
| 2002–03 | New Jersey Devils | Anaheim Mighty Ducks | 7 |
| 2003–04 | Tampa Bay Lightning | Calgary Flames | 7 |
| 2004–05 | No Stanley Cup due to season lockout | | |
| 2005–06 | Carolina Hurricanes | Edmonton Oilers | 7 |
| 2006–07 | Anaheim Ducks | Ottawa Senators | 5 |
| 2007–08 | Detroit Red Wings | Pittsburgh Penguins | 6 |
| 2008–09 | Pittsburgh Penguins | Detroit Red Wings | 7 |

*In 1919 the Montreal Canadiens traveled to meet Seattle, the PCHL champions. After five games had been played—the teams were tied at two wins and one tie—the series was called off by the local Department of Health because of the influenza epidemic and the death of Canadiens defenseman Joe Hall from influenza.

## Conn Smythe Trophy

Awarded to the Most Valuable Player of the Stanley Cup playoffs, as selected by the Professional Hockey Writers Association. The trophy is named after the former coach, general manager, president and owner of the Toronto Maple Leafs.

| | | | |
|---|---|---|---|
| 1965 | Jean Beliveau, Mtl | 1988 | Wayne Gretzky, Edm |
| 1966 | Roger Crozier, Det | 1989 | Al MacInnis, Cgy |
| 1967 | Dave Keon, Tor | 1990 | Bill Ranford, Edm |
| 1968 | Glenn Hall, StL | 1991 | Mario Lemieux, Pit |
| 1969 | Serge Savard, Mtl | 1992 | Mario Lemieux, Pit |
| 1970 | Bobby Orr, Bos | 1993 | Patrick Roy, Mtl |
| 1971 | Ken Dryden, Mtl | 1994 | Brian Leetch, NYR |
| 1972 | Bobby Orr, Bos | 1995 | Claude Lemieux, NJ |
| 1973 | Yvan Cournoyer, Mtl | 1996 | Joe Sakic, Col |
| 1974 | Bernie Parent, Phi | 1997 | Mike Vernon, Det |
| 1975 | Bernie Parent, Phi | 1998 | Steve Yzerman, Det |
| 1976 | Reggie Leach, Phi | 1999 | Joe Nieuwendyk, Dal |
| 1977 | Guy Lafleur, Mtl | 2000 | Scott Stevens, NJ |
| 1978 | Larry Robinson, Mtl | 2001 | Patrick Roy, Col |
| 1979 | Bob Gainey, Mtl | 2002 | Nicklas Lidstrom, Det |
| 1980 | Bryan Trottier, NYI | 2003 | J.-S. Giguere, Ana |
| 1981 | Butch Goring, NYI | 2004 | Brad Richards, TB |
| 1982 | Mike Bossy, NYI | 2005 | No Award–No Season |
| 1983 | Bill Smith, NYI | 2006 | Cam Ward, Car |
| 1984 | Mark Messier, Edm | 2007 | Scott Niedermayer, Ana |
| 1985 | Wayne Gretzky, Edm | 2008 | Henrik Zetterberg, Det |
| 1986 | Patrick Roy, Mtl | 2009 | Evgeni Malkin, Pit |
| 1987 | Ron Hextall, Phi | | |

## Alltime Stanley Cup Playoff Leaders

### Points

| Playoff Seasons | GP | G | Ast | Pts | Playoff Seasons | GP | G | Ast | Pts |
|---|---|---|---|---|---|---|---|---|---|
| Wayne Gretzky, four teams ...16 | 208 | 122 | 260 | 382 | *Sergei Fedorov, Det, Wsh ...15 | 183 | 52 | 124 | 176 |
| Mark Messier, Edm, Van, NYR...18 | 236 | 109 | 186 | 295 | Denis Savard, Chi, Mtl ...16 | 169 | 66 | 109 | 175 |
| Jari Kurri, four teams ...15 | 200 | 106 | 127 | 233 | Mario Lemieux, Pit ...8 | 107 | 76 | 96 | 172 |
| Glenn Anderson, four teams....15 | 225 | 93 | 121 | 214 | *Nicklas Lidstrom, Det ...17 | 235 | 46 | 119 | 165 |
| Paul Coffey, six teams ...16 | 194 | 59 | 137 | 196 | Peter Forsberg, Que, Col, Phi ...13 | 151 | 64 | 107 | 171 |
| Brett Hull, four teams ...19 | 202 | 103 | 87 | 190 | Denis Potvin, NYI ...14 | 185 | 56 | 108 | 164 |
| Doug Gilmour, seven teams....18 | 182 | 60 | 128 | 188 | Mike Bossy, NYI ...10 | 129 | 85 | 75 | 160 |
| *Joe Sakic, Que, Col ...13 | 172 | 84 | 104 | 188 | Gordie Howe, Det, Hart ...20 | 157 | 68 | 92 | 160 |
| Steve Yzerman, Det ...20 | 196 | 70 | 115 | 185 | Bobby Smith, Min, Mtl ...13 | 184 | 64 | 96 | 160 |
| Bryan Trottier, NYI, Pit ...17 | 221 | 71 | 113 | 184 | Al MacInnis, Cgy, StL ...19 | 177 | 39 | 121 | 160 |
| Jaromir Jagr, Pit, Wsh, NYR .....15 | 169 | 77 | 104 | 181 | *Claude Lemieux, six teams ...18 | 234 | 80 | 77 | 157 |
| Ray Bourque, Bos, Col ...21 | 214 | 41 | 139 | 180 | Adam Oates, six teams ...15 | 163 | 42 | 114 | 156 |
| Jean Beliveau, Mtl ...17 | 162 | 79 | 97 | 176 | | | | | |

### Goals

| Playoff Seasons | GP | G |
|---|---|---|
| Wayne Gretzky, four teams ...16 | 208 | 122 |
| Mark Messier, Edm, NYR ...18 | 236 | 109 |
| Jari Kurri, five teams ...15 | 200 | 106 |
| Brett Hull, Cgy, StL, Dal, Det...19 | 202 | 103 |
| Glenn Anderson, four teams...15 | 225 | 93 |
| Mike Bossy, NYI ...10 | 129 | 85 |
| *Joe Sakic, Que, Col ...13 | 172 | 84 |
| Maurice Richard, Mtl ...15 | 133 | 82 |
| *Claude Lemieux, six teams ...18 | 234 | 80 |
| Jean Beliveau, Mtl ...17 | 162 | 79 |
| Jaromir Jagr, Pitt, Wsh, NYR...15 | 169 | 77 |
| Mario Lemieux, Pitt ...8 | 107 | 76 |
| Dino Ciccarelli, Min, Wsh, Det ...14 | 141 | 73 |
| Esa Tikkanen, five teams ...13 | 186 | 72 |
| Bryan Trottier, NYI, Pit ...17 | 221 | 71 |

### Assists

| Playoff Seasons | GP | Ast |
|---|---|---|
| Wayne Gretzky, four teams ...16 | 208 | 260 |
| Mark Messier, Edm, NYR ...18 | 236 | 186 |
| Ray Bourque, Bos, Col ...21 | 214 | 139 |
| Paul Coffey, six teams ...16 | 194 | 137 |
| Doug Gilmour, seven teams ...18 | 182 | 128 |
| Jari Kurri, five teams ...15 | 200 | 127 |
| *Sergei Fedorov, Det, Wsh ...15 | 183 | 124 |
| Glenn Anderson, four teams...15 | 225 | 121 |
| Al MacInnis, Cgy, StL ...19 | 177 | 121 |
| Larry Robinson, Mtl, LA ...20 | 227 | 116 |
| Steve Yzerman, Det ...20 | 196 | 115 |
| Lawrence Murphy, six teams ...20 | 215 | 115 |
| Adam Oates, six teams ...15 | 163 | 114 |
| Bryan Trottier, NYI, Pit ...17 | 221 | 113 |
| *Chris Chelios, Mtl, Chi, Det ...24 | 266 | 113 |

*Active in 2008–09.

## Alltime Stanley Cup Playoff Goaltending Leaders

| WINS | W | L | Pct |  | SHUTOUTS | GP | W | SO |
|---|---|---|---|---|---|---|---|---|
| Patrick Roy, Mtl, Col | 151 | 94 | .616 |  | Patrick Roy, Mtl, Col | 247 | 151 | 23 |
| *Martin Brodeur, NJ | 98 | 78 | .557 |  | *Martin Brodeur, NJ | 176 | 98 | 23 |
| Grant Fuhr, five teams | 92 | 50 | .648 |  | *Curtis Joseph, four teams | 133 | 63 | 16 |
| Billy Smith, LA, NYI | 88 | 36 | .710 |  | Four tied with 14 shutouts. | | | |
| Ed Belfour, four teams | 88 | 68 | .564 |  | | | | |
| Ken Dryden, Mtl | 80 | 32 | .714 |  | **GOALS AGAINST AVG** | | | Avg |
| Mike Vernon, four teams | 77 | 56 | .579 |  | George Hainsworth, Mtl, Tor | | | 1.93 |
| *Chris Osgood, NYI, StL, Det | 74 | 49 | .602 |  | *Martin Brodeur, NJ | | | 1.98 |
| Jacques Plante, five teams | 71 | 36 | .663 |  | Turk Broda, Tor | | | 1.98 |
| Andy Moog, four teams | 68 | 57 | .544 |  | Dominik Hasek, Chi, Buf, Det | | | 2.02 |
| Dominik Hasek, Chi, Buf, Det | 65 | 49 | .570 |  | *Jean-Sebastien Giguere, Ana | | | 2.08 |
| *Curtis Joseph, four teams | 63 | 66 | .488 |  | *Chris Osgood, NYI, StL, Det | | | 2.09 |
| Tom Barrasso, Buf, Pit, Ott | 61 | 54 | .530 |  | | | | |
| Turk Broda, Tor | 60 | 39 | .606 |  | Note: At least 50 games played. | | | |

*Active in 2008–09.

Note: At least 50 games played.
*Active in 2008–09.

## Alltime Stanley Cup Team Playoff Record, by Wins

| TEAM | W | L | Pct |  | TEAM | W | L | Pct |
|---|---|---|---|---|---|---|---|---|
| Montreal | 398 | 277 | .590 |  | Calgary* | 94 | 114 | .452 |
| Detroit | 300 | 262 | .534 |  | Washington | 79 | 96 | .451 |
| Boston | 252 | 275 | .478 |  | Vancouver | 77 | 100 | .435 |
| Toronto | 251 | 269 | .483 |  | Los Angeles | 65 | 105 | .382 |
| Pittsburgh | 211 | 185 | .533 |  | San Jose | 59 | 66 | .472 |
| NY Rangers | 197 | 212 | .482 |  | Carolina§ | 59 | 68 | .465 |
| Chicago | 197 | 226 | .465 |  | Anaheim | 53 | 39 | .576 |
| Philadelphia | 191 | 177 | .519 |  | Ottawa | 49 | 54 | .476 |
| Edmonton | 152 | 99 | .606 |  | Phoenix†† | 29 | 63 | .315 |
| Dallas# | 148 | 149 | .498 |  | Tampa Bay | 26 | 25 | .551 |
| St. Louis | 138 | 169 | .450 |  | Florida | 13 | 18 | .419 |
| NY Islanders | 131 | 102 | .562 |  | Minnesota | 10 | 14 | .417 |
| Colorado** | 130 | 113 | .535 |  | Nashville | 5 | 12 | .294 |
| Buffalo | 119 | 124 | .490 |  | Columbus | 0 | 4 | .000 |
| New Jersey† | 121 | 104 | .538 |  | | | | |

*Atlanta Flames 1972–80. †Colorado Rockies 1976–82, Kansas City Scouts 1974–76. #Minnesota North Stars 1967–93.
**Quebec Nordiques 1979–95. ††Winnipeg Jets 1979–96. §Hartford Whalers 1979–97.

## Stanley Cup Playoff Coaching Records

| Coach | Team | Yrs | Series | Series W | Series L | Games | Games W | Games L | T | Cups | Pct |
|---|---|---|---|---|---|---|---|---|---|---|---|
| Glen Sather | Edm | 10 | 27 | 21 | 6 | †126 | 89 | 37 | 0 | 4 | .706 |
| Toe Blake | Mtl | 13 | 23 | 18 | 5 | 119 | 82 | 37 | 0 | 8 | .689 |
| Scott Bowman | Five teams | 28 | 68 | 49 | 19 | 353 | 223 | 130 | 0 | 9 | .632 |
| Hap Day | Tor | 9 | 14 | 10 | 4 | 80 | 49 | 31 | 0 | 5 | .613 |
| Al Arbour | StL, NYI | 16 | 42 | 30 | 12 | 209 | 123 | 86 | 0 | 4 | .589 |
| Bob Hartley | Col, Atl | 5 | 14 | 10 | 4 | 84 | 49 | 35 | 0 | 1 | .583 |
| Fred Shero | Phi, NYR | 8 | 21 | 15 | 6 | 110 | 63 | 47 | 0 | 2 | .573 |
| *Mike Keenan | five teams | 13 | 30 | 18 | 12 | 173 | 96 | 77 | 0 | 1 | .555 |
| *Ken Hitchcock | Dal, Phi, CBJ | 9 | 21 | 13 | 8 | 121 | 66 | 55 | 0 | 1 | .545 |
| *Jacques Lemaire | Mtl, NJ, Min | 9 | 20 | 12 | 8 | 112 | 60 | 54 | 0 | 1 | .526 |

†Does not include suspended game, May 24, 1988. *Active in 2008–09.
Note: Coaches ranked by winning percentage. Minimum: 65 games.

## The 10 Longest Overtime Games

| Date | Result | OT | Scorer | Series | Series Winner |
|---|---|---|---|---|---|
| 3-24-36 | Det 1 vs Mtl M 0 | 116:30 | Mud Bruneteau | SF | Det |
| 4-3-33 | Tor 1 vs Bos 0 | 104:46 | Ken Doraty | SF | Tor |
| 5-4-00 | Phi 2 vs Pit 1 | 92:01 | Keith Primeau | CSF | Phil |
| 4-24-03 | Ana 4 vs Dal 3 | 80:48 | Petr Sykora | CSF | Ana |
| 4-24-96 | Pit 3 vs Wsh 2 | 79:15 | Petr Nedved | CQF | Pitt |
| 3-23-43 | Tor 3 vs Det 2 | 70:18 | Jack McLean | SF | Det |
| 3-28-30 | Mtl 2 vs NYR 1 | 68:52 | Gus Rivers | SF | Mtl |
| 4-18-87 | NYI 3 vs Wsh 2 | 68:47 | Pat LaFontaine | DSF | NYI |
| 4-27-94 | Buf 1 vs NJ 0 | 65:43 | Dave Hannan | CQF | NJ |
| 3-27-51 | Mtl 3 vs Det 2 | 61:09 | Maurice Richard | SF | Mtl |

## Hart Memorial Trophy

Awarded annually "to the player adjudged to be the most valuable to his team." The original trophy was donated by Dr. David A. Hart, father of Cecil Hart, former manager-coach of the Montreal Canadiens. In the 1980s Wayne Gretzky won the award nine times.

| Year | Winner | Key Statistics | Runner-Up |
|---|---|---|---|
| 1924 | Frank Nighbor, Ott | 10 goals, 3 assists in 20 games | Sprague Cleghorn, Mtl |
| 1925 | Billy Burch, Ham | 20 goals, 4 assists in 27 games | Howie Morenz, Mtl |
| 1926 | Nels Stewart, Mtl M | 42 points in 36 games | Sprague Cleghorn, Mtl |
| 1927 | Herb Gardiner, Mtl | 12 points in 44 games as defenseman | Bill Cook, NYR |
| 1928 | Howie Morenz, Mtl | 33 goals, 18 assists | Roy Worters, Pitt |
| 1929 | Roy Worters, NYA | 1.21 goals against, 13 shutouts | Ace Bailey, Tor |
| 1930 | Nels Stewart, Mtl M | 39 goals, 16 assists | Lionel Hitchman, Bos |
| 1931 | Howie Morenz, Mtl | 28 goals, 23 assists | Eddie Shore, Bos |
| 1932 | Howie Morenz, Mtl | 24 goals, 25 assists | Ching Johnson, NYR |
| 1933 | Eddie Shore, Bos | 27 assists in 48 games as defenseman | Bill Cook, NYR |
| 1934 | Aurel Joliat, Mtl | 27 points | Lionel Conacher, Chi |
| 1935 | Eddie Shore, Bos | 26 assists in 48 games as defenseman | Charlie Conacher, Tor |
| 1936 | Eddie Shore, Bos | 16 assists in 46 games as defenseman | Hooley Smith, Mtl M |
| 1937 | Babe Siebert, Mtl | 28 points | Lionel Conacher, Mtl M |
| 1938 | Eddie Shore, Bos | 17 points in 47 games as defenseman | Paul Thompson, Chi |
| 1939 | Toe Blake, Mtl | led NHL in points (47) | Syl Apps, Tor |
| 1940 | Ebbie Goodfellow, Det | 28 points | Syl Apps, Tor |
| 1941 | Bill Cowley, Bos | led NHL in assists (45) and points (62) | Dit Clapper, Bos |
| 1942 | Tom Anderson, Bos | 41 points | Syl Apps, Tor |
| 1943 | Bill Cowley, Bos | led NHL in assists (45) | Doug Bentley, Chi |
| 1944 | Babe Pratt, Tor | 57 points in 50 games | Bill Cowley, Bos |
| 1945 | Elmer Lach, Mtl | led NHL in assists (54) and points (80) | Maurice Richard, Mtl |
| 1946 | Max Bentley, Chi | 61 points in 47 games | Gaye Stewart, Tor |
| 1947 | Maurice Richard, Mtl | led NHL in goals (45); 26 assists | Milt Schmidt, Bos |
| 1948 | Buddy O'Connor, NYR | 60 points in 60 games | Frank Brimsek, Bos |
| 1949 | Sid Abel, Det | 28 goals, 26 assists | Bill Durnan, Mtl |
| 1950 | Charlie Rayner, NYR | 6 shutouts | Ted Kennedy, Tor |
| 1951 | Milt Schmidt, Bos | 61 points in 62 games | Maurice Richard, Mtl |
| 1952 | Gordie Howe, Det | led NHL in goals (47) and points (86) | Elmer Lach, Mtl |
| 1953 | Gordie Howe, Det | led NHL in goals (49) and points (95) | Al Rollins, Chi |
| 1954 | Al Rollins, Chi | 5 shutouts | Red Kelly, Det |
| 1955 | Ted Kennedy, Tor | 52 points | Harry Lumley, Tor |
| 1956 | Jean Beliveau, Mtl | led NHL in goals (47) and points (88) | Tod Sloan, Tor |
| 1957 | Gordie Howe, Det | led NHL in goals (44) and points (89) | Jean Beliveau, Mtl |
| 1959 | Andy Bathgate, NYR | 74 points in 70 games | Gordie Howe, Det |
| 1960 | Gordie Howe, Det | 45 assists, 73 points | Bobby Hull, Chi |
| 1961 | Bernie Geoffrion, Mtl | 50 goals, 95 points | Johnny Bower, Tor |
| 1962 | Jacques Plante, Mtl | 42 wins, 2.37 goals against avg. | Doug Harvey, NYR |
| 1963 | Gordie Howe, Det | 47 assists, 73 points | Stan Mikita, Chi |
| 1964 | Jean Beliveau, Mtl | 50 assists, 78 points | Bobby Hull, Chi |
| 1965 | Bobby Hull, Chi | 39 goals, 32 assists | Norm Ullman, Det |
| 1966 | Bobby Hull, Chi | led NHL in assists (54) and points (97) | Jean Beliveau, Mtl |
| 1967 | Stan Mikita, Chi | led NHL in assists (62) and points (97) | Ed Giacomin, NYR |
| 1968 | Stan Mikita, Chi | 40 goals, 47 assists | Jean Beliveau, Mtl |
| 1969 | Phil Esposito, Bos | led NHL in assists (77) and points (126) | Jean Beliveau, Mtl |
| 1970 | Bobby Orr, Bos | led NHL in assists (87) and points (120) | Tony Esposito, Chi |
| 1971 | Bobby Orr, Bos | 102 assists, 139 points | Phil Esposito, Bos |
| 1972 | Bobby Orr, Bos | 80 assists, 117 points | Ken Dryden, Mtl |
| 1973 | Bobby Clarke, Phi | 67 assists, 104 points | Phil Esposito, Bos |
| 1974 | Phil Esposito, Bos | led NHL in goals (68) and points (145) | Bernie Parent, Phi |
| 1975 | Bobby Clarke, Phi | 89 assists, 116 points | Rogatien Vachon, LA |
| 1976 | Bobby Clarke, Phi | 89 assists, 119 points | Denis Potvin, NYI |
| 1977 | Guy Lafleur, Mtl | led NHL in assists (80) and points (136) | Bobby Clarke, Phi |
| 1978 | Guy Lafleur, Mtl | led NHL in goals (60) and points (132) | Bryan Trottier, NYI |
| 1979 | Bryan Trottier, NYI | led NHL in assists (87) and points (134) | Guy Lafleur, Mtl |
| 1980 | Wayne Gretzky, Edm | 51 goals, 86 points | Marcel Dionne, LA |
| 1981 | Wayne Gretzky, Edm | led NHL in assists (109) and points (164) | Mike Liut, StL |
| 1982 | Wayne Gretzky, Edm | NHL-record 92 goals and 212 points | Bryan Trottier, NYI |
| 1983 | Wayne Gretzky, Edm | led NHL in goals (71) and points (196) | Pete Peeters, Bos |
| 1984 | Wayne Gretzky, Edm | led NHL in goals (87) and points (205) | Rod Langway, Wsh |
| 1985 | Wayne Gretzky, Edm | led NHL in goals (73) and points (208) | Dale Hawerchuk, Win |
| 1986 | Wayne Gretzky, Edm | NHL-record 163 assists and 215 points | Mario Lemieux, Pit |
| 1987 | Wayne Gretzky, Edm | led NHL in assists (121) and points (183) | Ray Bourque, Bos |
| 1988 | Mario Lemieux, Pit | led NHL in goals (70) and points (168) | Grant Fuhr, Edm |

## Hart Memorial Trophy *(Cont.)*

| Year | Winner | Key Statistics | Runner-Up |
|------|--------|----------------|-----------|
| 1989 | Wayne Gretzky, LA | 114 assists, 168 points | Mario Lemieux, Pit |
| 1990 | Mark Messier, Edm | 84 assists, 129 points | Ray Bourque, Bos |
| 1991 | Brett Hull, StL | led NHL in goals (86); 131 points | Wayne Gretzky, LA |
| 1992 | Mark Messier, NYR | 72 assists, 107 points | Patrick Roy, Mtl |
| 1993 | Mario Lemieux, Pitt | 69 goals, 91 assists in 60 games | Doug Gilmour, Tor |
| 1994 | Sergei Fedorov, Det | 56 goals, 64 assists | Dominik Hasek, Buf |
| 1995 | Eric Lindros, Phi | 29 goals, 41 assists in 46 games | Jaromir Jagr, Pit |
| 1996 | Mario Lemieux, Pit | led NHL in goals (69) and points (161) | Mark Messier, NYR |
| 1997 | Dominik Hasek, Buf | 5 shutouts, 2.27 goals against avg. | Paul Kariya, Ana |
| 1998 | Dominik Hasek, Buf | 13 shutouts, 2.09 goals against avg. | Jaromir Jagr, Pit |
| 1999 | Jaromir Jagr, Pit | 44 goals, 127 points | Alexei Yashin, Ott |
| 2000 | Chris Pronger, StL | 62 points, +52 plus/minus rating | Jaromir Jagr, Pit |
| 2001 | Joe Sakic, Col | 118 points, +45 plus/minus rating | Mario Lemieux, Pit |
| 2002 | Jose Theodore, Mtl | 2.11 goals against avg./7 shutouts | Jarome Iginla, Cal |
| 2003 | Peter Forsberg, Col | 77 assists, +52 plus/minus rating | Markus Naslund, Van |
| 2004 | Martin St. Louis, TB | 94 points, +35 plus/minus rating | Jarome Iginla, Cal |
| 2005 | No Award–No Season. | | |
| 2006 | Joe Thornton, Bos/SJ | 29 goals, 96 assists; 125 points | Jaromir Jagr, NYR |
| 2007 | Sidney Crosby, Pit | 36 goals, 84 assists; 120 points | Roberto Luongo, Van |
| 2008 | Alexander Ovechkin, Wsh | 65 goals, 47 assists; 112 points | Evgeni Malkin, Pit |
| 2009 | Alexander Ovechkin, Wsh | 56 goals, 54 assists; 110 points | Evgeni Malkin, Pit |

## Art Ross Trophy

Awarded annually "to the player who leads the league in scoring points at the end of the regular season." The trophy was presented to the NHL in 1947 by Arthur Howie Ross, former manager-coach of the Boston Bruins. The tie-breakers, in order, are: (1) most goals, (2) fewer games played, (3) first goal of the season. Bobby Orr is the only defenseman in NHL history to win this trophy, and he won it twice (1970 and 1975).

| Year | Winner | Pts | Year | Winner | Pts |
|------|--------|-----|------|--------|-----|
| 1919 | Newsy Lalonde, Mtl | 44 | 1959 | Dickie Moore, Mtl | 96 |
| 1920 | Joe Malone, Que | 30 | 1960 | Bobby Hull, Chi | 81 |
| 1921 | Newsy Lalonde, Mtl | 48 | 1961 | Bernie Geoffrion, Mtl | 95 |
| 1922 | Punch Broadbent, Ott | 41 | 1962 | Bobby Hull, Chi | 84 |
| 1923 | Babe Dye, Tor | 46 | 1963 | Gordie Howe, Det | 86 |
| 1924 | Cy Denneny, Ott | 37 | 1964 | Stan Mikita, Chi | 89 |
| 1925 | Babe Dye, Tor | 23 | 1965 | Stan Mikita, Chi | 87 |
| 1926 | Nels Stewart, Mtl M | 44 | 1966 | Bobby Hull, Chi | 97 |
| 1927 | Bill Cook, NYR | 42 | 1967 | Stan Mikita, Chi | 97 |
| 1928 | Howie Morenz, Mtl | 37 | 1968 | Stan Mikita, Chi | 87 |
| 1929 | Ace Bailey, Tor | 51 | 1969 | Phil Esposito, Bos | 126 |
| 1930 | Cooney Weiland, Bos | 32 | 1970 | Bobby Orr, Bos | 120 |
| 1931 | Howie Morenz, Mtl | 73 | 1971 | Phil Esposito, Bos | 152 |
| 1932 | Harvey Jackson, Tor | 51 | 1972 | Phil Esposito, Bos | 133 |
| 1933 | Bill Cook, NYR | 53 | 1973 | Phil Esposito, Bos | 130 |
| 1934 | Charlie Conacher, Tor | 50 | 1974 | Phil Esposito, Bos | 145 |
| 1935 | Charlie Conacher, Tor | 57 | 1975 | Bobby Orr, Bos | 135 |
| 1936 | Sweeney Schriner, NYA | 45 | 1976 | Guy Lafleur, Mtl | 125 |
| 1937 | Sweeney Schriner, NYA | 46 | 1977 | Guy Lafleur, Mtl | 136 |
| 1938 | Gordie Drillon, Tor | 52 | 1978 | Guy Lafleur, Mtl | 132 |
| 1939 | Toe Blake, Mtl | 47 | 1979 | Bryan Trottier, NYI | 134 |
| 1940 | Milt Schmidt, Bos | 52 | 1980 | Marcel Dionne, LA | 137 |
| 1941 | Bill Cowley, Bos | 62 | 1981 | Wayne Gretzky, Edm | 164 |
| 1942 | Bryan Hextall, NYR | 56 | 1982 | Wayne Gretzky, Edm | 212 |
| 1943 | Doug Bentley, Chi | 73 | 1983 | Wayne Gretzky, Edm | 196 |
| 1944 | Herb Cain, Bos | 82 | 1984 | Wayne Gretzky, Edm | 205 |
| 1945 | Elmer Lach, Mtl | 80 | 1985 | Wayne Gretzky, Edm | 208 |
| 1946 | Max Bentley, Chi | 61 | 1986 | Wayne Gretzky, Edm | 215 |
| 1947 | *Max Bentley, Chi | 72 | 1987 | Wayne Gretzky, Edm | 183 |
| 1948 | Elmer Lach, Mtl | 61 | 1988 | Mario Lemieux, Pit | 168 |
| 1949 | Roy Conacher, Chi | 68 | 1989 | Mario Lemieux, Pit | 199 |
| 1950 | Ted Lindsay, Det | 78 | 1990 | Wayne Gretzky, LA | 142 |
| 1951 | Gordie Howe, Det | 86 | 1991 | Wayne Gretzky, LA | 163 |
| 1952 | Gordie Howe, Det | 86 | 1992 | Mario Lemieux, Pit | 131 |
| 1953 | Gordie Howe, Det | 95 | 1993 | Mario Lemieux, Pit | 160 |
| 1954 | Gordie Howe, Det | 81 | 1994 | Wayne Gretzky, LA | 130 |
| 1955 | Bernie Geoffrion, Mtl | 75 | 1995 | Jaromir Jagr, Pit | 70 |
| 1956 | Jean Beliveau, Mtl | 88 | 1996 | Mario Lemieux, Pit | 161 |
| 1957 | Gordie Howe, Det | 89 | 1997 | Mario Lemieux, Pit | 122 |
| 1958 | Dickie Moore, Mtl | 84 | 1998 | Jaromir Jagr, Pit | 102 |

## Art Ross Trophy *(Cont.)*

| Year | Winner | Pts | Year | Winner | Pts |
|------|--------|-----|------|--------|-----|
| 1999 | Jaromir Jagr, Pit | 127 | 2005 | No award/no season | |
| 2000 | Jaromir Jagr, Pit | 96 | 2006 | Joe Thornton, Bos/SJ | 125 |
| 2001 | Jaromir Jagr, Pit | 121 | 2007 | Sidney Crosby, Pit | 120 |
| 2002 | Jarome Iginla, Cgy | 96 | 2008 | Alexander Ovechkin, Wsh | 112 |
| 2003 | Peter Forsberg, Col | 106 | 2009 | Evgeni Malkin, Pit | 113 |
| 2004 | Martin St. Louis, TB | 94 | | | |

Note: Listing includes scoring leaders prior to inception of Art Ross Trophy in 1947–48.

## Lady Byng Memorial Trophy

Awarded annually "to the player adjudged to have exhibited the best type of sportsmanship and gentlemanly conduct combined with a high standard of playing ability." Lady Byng, who first presented the trophy in 1925, was the wife of Canada's Governor-General. She donated a second trophy in 1936 after the first was given permanently to Frank Boucher of the New York Rangers, who won it seven times in eight seasons. Stan Mikita, one of the league's most penalized players during his early years in the NHL, won the trophy twice late in his career (1967 and 1968).

| | | |
|---|---|---|
| 1925 Frank Nighbor, Ott | 1954 Red Kelly, Det | 1982 Rick Middleton, Bos |
| 1926 Frank Nighbor, Ott | 1955 Sid Smith, Tor | 1983 Mike Bossy, NYI |
| 1927 Billy Burch, NYA | 1956 Earl Reibel, Det | 1984 Mike Bossy, NYI |
| 1928 Frank Boucher, NYR | 1957 Andy Hebenton, NYR | 1985 Jari Kurri, Edm |
| 1929 Frank Boucher, NYR | 1958 Camille Henry, NYR | 1986 Mike Bossy, NYI |
| 1930 Frank Boucher, NYR | 1959 Alex Delvecchio, Det | 1987 Joe Mullen, Cgy |
| 1931 Frank Boucher, NYR | 1960 Don McKenney, Bos | 1988 Mats Naslund, Mtl |
| 1932 Joe Primeau, Tor | 1961 Red Kelly, Tor | 1989 Joe Mullen, Cgy |
| 1933 Frank Boucher, NYR | 1962 Dave Keon, Tor | 1990 Brett Hull, StL |
| 1934 Frank Boucher, NYR | 1963 Dave Keon, Tor | 1991 Wayne Gretzky, LA |
| 1935 Frank Boucher, NYR | 1964 Ken Wharram, Chi | 1992 Wayne Gretzky, LA |
| 1936 Doc Romnes, Chi | 1965 Bobby Hull, Chi | 1993 Pierre Turgeon, NYI |
| 1937 Marty Barry, Det | 1966 Alex Delvecchio, Det | 1994 Wayne Gretzky, LA |
| 1938 Gordie Drillon, Tor | 1967 Stan Mikita, Chi | 1995 Ron Francis, Pit |
| 1939 Clint Smith, NYR | 1968 Stan Mikita, Chi | 1996 Paul Kariya, Ana |
| 1940 Bobby Bauer, Bos | 1969 Alex Delvecchio, Det | 1997 Paul Kariya, Ana |
| 1941 Bobby Bauer, Bos | 1970 Phil Goyette, StL | 1998 Ron Francis, Pit |
| 1942 Syl Apps, Tor | 1971 John Bucyk, Bos | 1999 Wayne Gretzky, NYR |
| 1943 Max Bentley, Chi | 1972 Jean Ratelle, NYR | 2000 Pavol Demitra, StL |
| 1944 Clint Smith, Chi | 1973 Gilbert Perreault, Buf | 2001 Joe Sakic, Col |
| 1945 Billy Mosienko, Chi | 1974 John Bucyk, Bos | 2002 Ron Francis, Car |
| 1946 Toe Blake, Mtl | 1975 Marcel Dionne, Det | 2003 Alexander Mogilny, Det |
| 1947 Bobby Bauer, Bos | 1976 Jean Ratelle, NYR-Bos | 2004 Brad Richards, TB |
| 1948 Buddy O'Connor, NYR | 1977 Marcel Dionne, LA | 2005 No Award |
| 1949 Bill Quackenbush, Det | 1978 Butch Goring, LA | 2006 Pavel Datsyuk, Det |
| 1950 Edgar Laprade, NYR | 1979 Bob MacMillan, Atl | 2007 Pavel Datsyuk, Det |
| 1951 Red Kelly, Det | 1980 Wayne Gretzky, Edm | 2008 Pavel Datsyuk, Det |
| 1952 Sid Smith, Tor | 1981 Rick Kehoe, Pitt | 2009 Pavel Datsyuk, Det |
| 1953 Red Kelly, Det | | |

## James Norris Memorial Trophy

Awarded annually "to the defense player who demonstrates throughout the season the greatest all-around ability in the position." James Norris was the former owner-president of the Detroit Red Wings. Bobby Orr holds the record for most consecutive times winning the award (eight, 1968–1975).

| | | |
|---|---|---|
| 1954 Red Kelly, Det | 1973 Bobby Orr, Bos | 1992 Brian Leetch, NYR |
| 1955 Doug Harvey, Mtl | 1974 Bobby Orr, Bos | 1993 Chris Chelios, Chi |
| 1956 Doug Harvey, Mtl | 1975 Bobby Orr, Bos | 1994 Ray Bourque, Bos |
| 1957 Doug Harvey, Mtl | 1976 Denis Potvin, NYI | 1995 Paul Coffey, Det |
| 1958 Doug Harvey, Mtl | 1977 Larry Robinson, Mtl | 1996 Chris Chelios, Chi |
| 1959 Tom Johnson, Mtl | 1978 Denis Potvin, NYI | 1997 Brian Leetch, NYR |
| 1960 Doug Harvey, Mtl | 1979 Denis Potvin, NYI | 1998 Rob Blake, LA |
| 1961 Doug Harvey, Mtl | 1980 Larry Robinson, Mtl | 1999 Al MacInnis, StL |
| 1962 Doug Harvey, NYR | 1981 Randy Carlyle, Pit | 2000 Chris Pronger, StL |
| 1963 Pierre Pilote, Chi | 1982 Doug Wilson, Chi | 2001 Nicklas Lidstrom, Det |
| 1964 Pierre Pilote, Chi | 1983 Rod Langway, Wsh | 2002 Nicklas Lidstrom, Det |
| 1965 Pierre Pilote, Chi | 1984 Rod Langway, Wsh | 2003 Nicklas Lidstrom, Det |
| 1966 Jacques Laperriere, Mtl | 1985 Paul Coffey, Edm | 2004 Scott Niedermayer, NJ |
| 1967 Harry Howell, NYR | 1986 Paul Coffey, Edm | 2005 No Award |
| 1968 Bobby Orr, Bos | 1987 Ray Bourque, Bos | 2006 Nicklas Lidstrom, Det |
| 1969 Bobby Orr, Bos | 1988 Ray Bourque, Bos | 2007 Nicklas Lidstrom, Det |
| 1970 Bobby Orr, Bos | 1989 Chris Chelios, Mtl | 2008 Nicklas Lidstrom, Det |
| 1971 Bobby Orr, Bos | 1990 Ray Bourque, Bos | 2009 Zdeno Chara, Bos |
| 1972 Bobby Orr, Bos | 1991 Ray Bourque, Bos | |

## Calder Memorial Trophy

Awarded annually "to the player selected as the most proficient in his first year of competition in the National Hockey League." Frank Calder was a former NHL president. Sergei Makarov, who won the award in 1989–90, was the oldest recipient of the trophy, at 31. Players are no longer eligible for the award if they are 26 or older as of September 15th of the season in question.

| | | |
|---|---|---|
| 1933 .......Carl Voss, Det | 1959 .......Ralph Backstrom, Mtl | 1985 .......Mario Lemieux, Pit |
| 1934 ......Russ Blinko, Mtl M | 1960 .....Bill Hay, Chi | 1986 .......Gary Suter, Cgy |
| 1935 .......Dave Schriner, NYA | 1961 .......Dave Keon, Tor | 1987 .......Luc Robitaille, LA |
| 1936 .......Mike Karakas, Chi | 1962 .......Bobby Rousseau, Mtl | 1988 .......Joe Nieuwendyk, Cgy |
| 1937 .......Syl Apps, Tor | 1963 .......Kent Douglas, Tor | 1989 .......Brian Leetch, NYR |
| 1938 .......Cully Dahlstrom, Chi | 1964 .......Jacques Laperriere, Mtl | 1990 .......Sergei Makarov, Cgy |
| 1939 .......Frank Brimsek, Bos | 1965 .......Roger Crozier, Det | 1991 .......Ed Belfour, Chi |
| 1940 .......Kilby MacDonald, NYR | 1966 .......Brit Selby, Tor | 1992 .......Pavel Bure, Van |
| 1941 .......Johnny Quilty, Mtl | 1967 .......Bobby Orr, Bos | 1993 .......Teemu Selanne, Win |
| 1942 .......Grant Warwick, NYR | 1968 .......Derek Sanderson, Bos | 1994 .......Martin Brodeur, NJ |
| 1943 .......Gaye Stewart, Tor | 1969 .......Danny Grant, Min | 1995 .......Peter Forsberg, Que |
| 1944 .......Gus Bodnar, Tor | 1970 .......Tony Esposito, Chi | 1996 .......Daniel Alfredsson, Ott |
| 1945 .......Frank McCool, Tor | 1971 .......Gilbert Perreault, Buf | 1997 .......Bryan Berard, NYI |
| 1946 .......Edgar Laprade, NYR | 1972 .......Ken Dryden, Mtl | 1998 .......Sergei Samsonov, Bos |
| 1947 .......Howie Meeker, Tor | 1973 .......Steve Vickers, NYR | 1999 .......Chris Drury, Col |
| 1948 .......Jim McFadden, Det | 1974 .......Denis Potvin, NYI | 2000 .......Scott Gomez, NJ |
| 1949 .......Pentti Lund, NYR | 1975 .......Eric Vail, Atl | 2001 .......Evgeni Nabokov, SJ |
| 1950 .......Jack Gelineau, Bos | 1976 .......Bryan Trottier, NYI | 2002 .......Dany Heatley, Atl |
| 1951 .......Terry Sawchuk, Det | 1977 .......Willi Plett, Atl | 2003 .......Barret Jackman, StL |
| 1952 .......Bernie Geoffrion, Mtl | 1978 .......Mike Bossy, NYI | 2004 .......Andrew Raycroft, Bos |
| 1953 .......Gump Worsley, NYR | 1979 .......Bobby Smith, Min | 2005 .......No Award |
| 1954 .......Camille Henry, NYR | 1980 .......Ray Bourque, Bos | 2006.........Alexander Ovechkin, Wsh |
| 1955 .......Ed Litzenberger, Chi | 1981 .......Peter Stastny, Que | 2007.........Evgeni Malkin, Pit |
| 1956 .......Glenn Hall, Det | 1982 .......Dale Hawerchuk, Win | 2008.........Patrick Kane, Chi |
| 1957 .......Larry Regan, Bos | 1983 .......Steve Larmer, Chi | 2009.........Steve Mason, CBJ |
| 1958 .......Frank Mahovlich, Tor | 1984 .......Tom Barrasso, Buf | |

## Vezina Trophy

Awarded annually "to the goalkeeper adjudged to be the best at his position." The trophy is named after Georges Vezina, an outstanding goalie for the Montreal Canadiens who collapsed during a game on November 28, 1925, and died four months later of tuberculosis. The general managers of the NHL teams vote on the award.

| | | |
|---|---|---|
| 1927 ........George Hainsworth, Mtl | 1960 .......Jacques Plante, Mtl | 1981 ........Richard Sevigny, Mtl |
| 1928 ........George Hainsworth, Mtl | 1961 .......Johnny Bower, Tor | Michel Larocque, Mtl |
| 1929 ........George Hainsworth, Mtl | 1962 .......Jacques Plante, Mtl | 1982 ........Billy Smith, NYI |
| 1930 .......Tiny Thompson, Bos | 1963 ........Glenn Hall, Chi | Denis Herron, Mtl |
| 1931 .......Roy Worters, NYA | 1964 .......Charlie Hodge, Mtl | 1983 ........Pete Peeters, Bos |
| 1932 .......Charlie Gardiner, Chi | 1965 ........Terry Sawchuk, Tor | 1984 ........Tom Barrasso, Buf |
| 1933 .......Tiny Thompson, Bos | Johnny Bower, Tor | 1985 ........Pelle Lindbergh, Phi |
| 1934 .......Charlie Gardiner, Chi | 1966 .......Gump Worsley, Mtl | 1986 ........John Vanbiesbrouck, NYR |
| 1935 .......Lorne Chabot, Chi | Charlie Hodge, Mtl | 1987 ........Ron Hextall, Phi |
| 1936 .......Tiny Thompson, Bos | 1967 ........Glenn Hall, Chi | 1988 ........Grant Fuhr, Edm |
| 1937 .......Normie Smith, Det | Denis DeJordy, Chi | 1989 ........Patrick Roy, Mtl |
| 1938 .......Tiny Thompson, Bos | 1968 .......Lorne Worsley, Mtl | 1990 ........Patrick Roy, Mtl |
| 1939 .......Frank Brimsek, Bos | 1969 ........Jacques Plante, StL | 1991 ........Ed Belfour, Chi |
| 1940 .......Dave Kerr, NYR | Glenn Hall, StL | 1992 ........Patrick Roy, Mtl |
| 1941 .......Turk Broda, Tor | 1970 .......Tony Esposito, Chi | 1993 ........Ed Belfour, Chi |
| 1942 .......Frank Brimsek, Bos | 1971 ........Ed Giacomin, NYR | 1994 .......Dominik Hasek, Buf |
| 1943 .......Johnny Mowers, Det | Gilles Villemure, NYR | 1995 .......Dominik Hasek, Buf |
| 1944 .......Bill Durnan, Mtl | 1972 .......Tony Esposito, Chi | 1996 ........Jim Carey, Wsh |
| 1945 .......Bill Durnan, Mtl | Gary Smith, Chi | 1997 ........Dominik Hasek, Buf |
| 1946 .......Bill Durnan, Mtl | 1973 ........Ken Dryden, Mtl | 1998 .......Dominik Hasek, Buf |
| 1947 .......Bill Durnan, Mtl | 1974 .......Bernie Parent, Phi | 1999 .......Dominik Hasek, Buf |
| 1948 .......Turk Broda, Tor | Tony Esposito, Chi | 2000 ........Olaf Kolzig, Wash |
| 1949 .......Bill Durnan, Mtl | 1975 .......Bernie Parent, Phi | 2001 .......Dominik Hasek, Buf |
| 1950 .......Bill Durnan, Mtl | 1976 .......Ken Dryden, Mtl | 2002 ........Jose Theodore, Mtl |
| 1951 .......Al Rollins, Tor | 1977 ........Ken Dryden, Mtl | 2003 ........Martin Brodeur, NJ |
| 1952 .......Terry Sawchuk, Det | Michel Larocque, Mtl | 2004 ........Martin Brodeur, NJ |
| 1953 .......Terry Sawchuk, Det | 1978 ........Ken Dryden, Mtl | 2005 .......No Award |
| 1954 .......Harry Lumley, Tor | Michel Larocque, Mtl | 2006 ........Miikka Kiprusoff, Cgy |
| 1955 .......Terry Sawchuk, Det | 1979 ........Ken Dryden, Mtl | 2007 ........Martin Brodeur, NJ |
| 1956 .......Jacques Plante, Mtl | Michel Larocque, Mtl | 2008 ........Martin Brodeur, NJ |
| 1957 .......Jacques Plante, Mtl | 1980 ........Bob Sauve, Buf | 2009 ........Tim Thomas, Bos |
| 1958 .......Jacques Plante, Mtl | Don Edwards, Buf | |
| 1959 .......Jacques Plante, Mtl | | |

## Selke Trophy

Awarded annually "to the forward who best excels in the defensive aspects of the game." The trophy is named after Frank J. Selke, the architect of the Montreal Canadians dynasty that won five consecutive Stanley Cups in the late '50s. The winner is selected by a vote of the Professional Hockey Writers Association.

| | | |
|---|---|---|
| 1978.......Bob Gainey, Mtl | 1989........Guy Carbonneau, Mtl | 2000........Steve Yzerman, Det |
| 1979........Bob Gainey, Mtl | 1990........Rick Meagher, StL | 2001........John Madden, NJ |
| 1980.......Bob Gainey, Mtl | 1991........Dirk Graham, Chi | 2002........Michael Peca, NYI |
| 1981.......Bob Gainey, Mtl | 1992........Guy Carbonneau, Mtl | 2003........Jere Lehtinen, Dal |
| 1982........Steve Kasper, Bos | 1993........Doug Gilmour, Tor | 2004........Kris Draper, Det |
| 1983........Bobby Clarke, Phi | 1994........Sergei Fedorov, Det | 2005........No Award |
| 1984.......Doug Jarvis, Wsh | 1995........Ron Francis, Pit | 2006........Rod Brind'Amour, Car |
| 1985........Craig Ramsay, Buf | 1996........Sergei Fedorov, Det | 2007........Rod Brind'Amour, Car |
| 1986........Troy Murray, Chi | 1997........Michael Peca, Buf | 2008........Pavel Datsyuk, Det |
| 1987........Dave Poulin, Phi | 1998........Jere Lehtinen, Dal | 2009........Pavel Datsyuk, Det |
| 1988........Guy Carbonneau, Mtl | 1999........Jere Lehtinen, Dal | |

## Adams Award

Awarded annually "to the NHL coach adjudged to have contributed the most to his team's success." The trophy is named in honor of Jack Adams, longtime coach and general manager of the Detroit Red Wings. The winner is selected by a vote of the National Hockey League Broadcasters' Association.

| | | |
|---|---|---|
| 1974 .....Fred Shero, Phi | 1986 .....Glen Sather, Edm | 1998 .....Pat Burns, Bos |
| 1975 .....Bob Pulford, LA | 1987 .....Jacques Demers, Det | 1999 .....Jacques Martin, Ott |
| 1976 .....Don Cherry, Bos | 1988 .....Jacques Demers, Det | 2000 .....Joel Quenneville, StL |
| 1977 .....Scott Bowman, Mtl | 1989 .....Pat Burns, Mtl | 2001 .....Bill Barber, Phi |
| 1978 .....Bobby Kromm, Det | 1990 .....Bob Murdoch, Win | 2002 .....Bob Francis, Phx |
| 1979 .....Al Arbour, NYI | 1991 .....Brian Sutter, StL | 2003 .....Jacques Lemaire, Min |
| 1980 .....Pat Quinn, Phi | 1992 .....Pat Quinn, Van | 2004 .....John Tortorella, TB |
| 1981 .....Red Berenson, StL | 1993 .....Pat Burns, Tor | 2005 .....No Award |
| 1982 .....Tom Watt, Win | 1994 .....Jacques Lemaire, NJ | 2006 .....Lindy Ruff, Buf |
| 1983 .....Orval Tessier, Chi | 1995 .....Marc Crawford, Que | 2007 .....Alain Vigneault, Van |
| 1984 .....Bryan Murray, Wsh | 1996 .....Scotty Bowman, Det | 2008 .....Bruce Boudreau, Wsh |
| 1985 .....Mike Keenan, Phi | 1997 .....Ted Nolan, Buf | 2009 .....Claude Julien, Bos |

# Career Records

## Alltime Point Leaders

| Player | Yrs | GP | G | A | Pts | Pts/game |
|---|---|---|---|---|---|---|
| Wayne Gretzky, Edm, LA, StL, NYR...............20 | | 1487 | 894 | 1963 | 2857 | 1.921 |
| Mark Messier, Edm, NYR, Van ......................25 | | 1756 | 694 | 1193 | 1887 | 1.074 |
| Gordie Howe, Det, Hfd ..................................26 | | 1767 | 801 | 1049 | 1850 | 1.047 |
| Ron Francis, four teams ................................23 | | 1731 | 549 | 1249 | 1798 | 1.039 |
| Marcel Dionne, Det, LA, NYR .......................18 | | 1348 | 731 | 1040 | 1771 | 1.314 |
| Steve Yzerman, Det ......................................22 | | 1514 | 692 | 1063 | 1755 | 1.159 |
| Mario Lemieux, Pit .......................................17 | | 915 | 690 | 1033 | 1723 | 1.883 |
| *Joe Sakic, Que, Col.....................................20 | | 1378 | 625 | 1016 | 1641 | 1.191 |
| Jaromir Jagr, Pit, Wsh, NYR..........................17 | | 1273 | 646 | 953 | 1599 | 1.256 |
| Phil Esposito, Chi, Bos, NYR ........................18 | | 1282 | 717 | 873 | 1590 | 1.240 |
| Ray Bourque, Bos, Col ..................................22 | | 1612 | 410 | 1169 | 1579 | .980 |
| Paul Coffey, eight teams ...............................21 | | 1409 | 396 | 1135 | 1531 | 1.087 |
| Stan Mikita, Chi ...........................................22 | | 1394 | 541 | 926 | 1467 | 1.052 |
| *Mark Recchi, seven teams ..........................20 | | 1490 | 545 | 897 | 1442 | .968 |
| Bryan Trottier, NYI, Pit ..................................18 | | 1279 | 524 | 901 | 1425 | 1.114 |

## Alltime Goal-Scoring Leaders

| Player | Yrs | GP | G | G/game |
|---|---|---|---|---|
| Wayne Gretzky, Edm, LA, StL, NYR....................................20 | | 1487 | 894 | .601 |
| Gordie Howe, Det, Hfd........................................................26 | | 1767 | 801 | .453 |
| Brett Hull, Cgy, StL, Dal, Det..............................................19 | | 1269 | 741 | .584 |
| Marcel Dionne, Det, LA, NYR .............................................18 | | 1348 | 731 | .542 |
| Phil Esposito, Chi, Bos, NYR..............................................18 | | 1282 | 717 | .559 |
| Mike Gartner, Wsh, Min, NYR, Tor, Phx...............................19 | | 1432 | 708 | .494 |
| Mark Messier, Edm, NYR, Van ...........................................25 | | 1756 | 694 | .395 |
| Steve Yzerman, Det. ...........................................................22 | | 1514 | 692 | .457 |
| Mario Lemieux, Pit...............................................................17 | | 915 | 690 | .754 |
| Luc Robitaille, LA, Pit, NYR, Det.........................................19 | | 1431 | 668 | .467 |
| *Brendan Shanahan, NJ, StL, Hfd, Det, NYR ....................21 | | 1524 | 656 | .430 |
| Jaromir Jagr, Pitt, Wsh, NYR...............................................17 | | 1273 | 646 | .507 |

*Active in 2008–09.

## Alltime Assist Leaders

| Player | Yrs | GP | A | A/game |
|---|---|---|---|---|
| Wayne Gretzky, Edm, LA, StL, NYR | 20 | 1487 | 1963 | 1.320 |
| Ron Francis, Hfd, Pit, Car | 23 | 1731 | 1249 | .722 |
| Mark Messier, Edm, NYR, Van | 25 | 1756 | 1193 | .679 |
| Ray Bourque, Bos, Col | 22 | 1612 | 1169 | .725 |
| Paul Coffey, eight teams | 21 | 1409 | 1135 | .806 |
| Adam Oates, seven teams | 22 | 1337 | 1079 | .807 |
| Steve Yzerman, Det | 22 | 1514 | 1063 | .702 |
| Gordie Howe, Det, Hfd | 26 | 1767 | 1049 | .594 |
| Marcel Dionne, Det, LA, NYR | 18 | 1348 | 1040 | .772 |
| Mario Lemieux, Pit | 17 | 915 | 1033 | 1.129 |
| *Joe Sakic, Que, Col | 20 | 1378 | 1016 | .737 |
| Doug Gilmour, seven teams | 20 | 1474 | 964 | .654 |

## Alltime Penalty Minutes Leaders

| Player | Yrs | GP | PIM | Min/game |
|---|---|---|---|---|
| Dave Williams, Tor, Van, Det, LA, Hfd | 14 | 962 | 3966 | 4.12 |
| Dale Hunter, Que, Wsh, Col | 19 | 1407 | 3565 | 2.53 |
| Tie Domi, Tor, NYR, Win | 16 | 1020 | 3515 | 3.45 |
| Marty McSorley, Pit, Edm, LA, NYR, SJ, Bos | 17 | 961 | 3381 | 3.52 |
| Bob Probert, Det, Chi | 16 | 935 | 3300 | 3.53 |
| Rob Ray, Buf, Ott | 15 | 900 | 3207 | 3.56 |
| Craig Berube, Phi, Tor, Cgy, Wsh, NYI | 17 | 1054 | 3149 | 2.99 |
| Tim Hunter, Cgy, Que, Van, SJ | 16 | 815 | 3146 | 3.86 |
| Chris Nilan, Mtl, NYR, Bos | 13 | 688 | 3043 | 4.42 |
| Rick Tocchet, Phi, Pit, LA, Bos, Wsh, Phx | 18 | 1144 | 2972 | 2.60 |
| Patrick Verbeek, NJ, Hfd, NYR, Dal, Det | 19 | 1424 | 2905 | 2.04 |
| *Chris Chelios, Mtl, Chi, Det | 25 | 1644 | 2891 | 1.76 |

## Goaltending Records

### ALLTIME GOALTENDING LEADERS, BY WINS

| Goaltender | W | L | T/OTL | Pct |
|---|---|---|---|---|
| *Martin Brodeur, NJ | 557 | 299 | 150 | .628 |
| Patrick Roy, Mtl, Col | 551 | 315 | 131 | .618 |
| Ed Belfour, five teams | 484 | 320 | 121 | .590 |
| *Curtis Joseph, five teams | 454 | 352 | 96 | .557 |
| Terry Sawchuk, five teams | 447 | 330 | 172 | .562 |
| Jacques Plante, five teams | 437 | 246 | 145 | .615 |
| Tony Esposito, Mtl, Chi | 423 | 306 | 151 | .566 |
| Glenn Hall, Det, Chi, StL | 407 | 326 | 163 | .545 |
| Grant Fuhr, six teams | 403 | 295 | 114 | .567 |
| *Chris Osgood, Det, NYI, StL, Det | 389 | 204 | 89 | .636 |
| Dominik Hasek, Chi, Buf, Ott, Det | 389 | 223 | 91 | .618 |

### ACTIVE GOALTENDING LEADERS, BY PERCENTAGE

| Goaltender | W | L | T/OTL | Pct |
|---|---|---|---|---|
| Manny Legace, LA, Det, StL | 177 | 92 | 36 | .639 |
| Chris Osgood, Det, NYI, StL, Det | 389 | 204 | 89 | .636 |
| Martin Brodeur, NJ | 557 | 299 | 150 | .628 |
| Marty Turco, Dal | 240 | 134 | 52 | .624 |
| Ryan Miller, Buf | 146 | 86 | 26 | .616 |
| Henrik Lundqvist, NY | 142 | 83 | 34 | .614 |
| Miikka Kiprusoff, SJ, Cgy | 204 | 125 | 42 | .606 |
| Evgeni Nabokov, SJ | 249 | 162 | 56 | .593 |
| Curtis Joseph, five teams | 454 | 352 | 96 | .557 |
| Jean-Seb. Giguere, Hfd, Cgy, Ana | 210 | 169 | 56 | .547 |

Note: Ranked by winning percentage; minimum 250 games played. All players active in 2008–09.

### ALLTIME SHUTOUT LEADERS

| Goaltender | Team | Yrs | GP | SO |
|---|---|---|---|---|
| Terry Sawchuk | Det, Bos, Tor, LA, NYR | 21 | 971 | 103 |
| *Martin Brodeur | NJ | 16 | 999 | 101 |
| George Hainsworth | Mtl, Tor | 11 | 465 | 94 |
| Glenn Hall | Det, Chi, StL | 18 | 906 | 84 |
| Jacques Plante | Mtl, NYR, StL, Tor, Bos | 18 | 837 | 82 |
| Tiny Thompson | Bos, Det | 12 | 553 | 81 |
| Alex Connell | Ott, Det, NYA, Mtl M | 12 | 417 | 81 |
| Dominik Hasek | Chi, Buf, Ott, Det | 16 | 735 | 81 |
| Tony Esposito | Mtl, Chi | 16 | 886 | 76 |
| Ed Belfour | Chi, SJ, Dal, Tor | 17 | 963 | 76 |

### ALLTIME GOALS AGAINST AVERAGE LEADERS (PRE-1950)

| Goaltender | Team | Yrs | GP | GA | GAA |
|---|---|---|---|---|---|
| Alec Connell | Ott, Det, NYA, Mtl M | 12 | 417 | 830 | 1.91 |
| George Hainsworth | Mtl, Tor | 11 | 465 | 937 | 1.93 |
| Chuck Gardiner | Chi | 7 | 316 | 664 | 2.02 |
| Lorne Chabot | NYR, Tor, Mtl, Chi, Mtl M, NYA | 11 | 411 | 860 | 2.04 |
| Tiny Thompson | Bos, Det | 12 | 553 | 1183 | 2.08 |

*Active in 2008–09.

## ALLTIME GOALS AGAINST AVERAGE LEADERS (POST-1950)

| Goaltender | Team | Yrs | GP | GA | GAA |
|---|---|---|---|---|---|
| *Marty Turco | Dal | 8 | 382 | 775 | 2.15 |
| *Martin Brodeur | NJ | 16 | 968 | 2099 | 2.20 |
| Dominik Hasek | Chi, Buf, Det, Ott | 16 | 735 | 1572 | 2.20 |
| Ken Dryden | Mtl | 8 | 397 | 870 | 2.24 |
| Roman Turek | Dal, StL, Cgy | 8 | 328 | 734 | 2.31 |
| *Manny Legace | LA, Det, StL | 10 | 308 | 663 | 2.31 |

*Active in 2008–09. Note: Minimum 250 games played. GAA equals goals against per 60 minutes played.

## Alltime Coaching Leaders

| Coach | Team | Seasons | W | L | T | OTL | Pct |
|---|---|---|---|---|---|---|---|
| Scotty Bowman | five teams | 1967–87, 91–2002 | 1244 | 584 | 313 | 0 | .654 |
| Toe Blake | Mtl | 1955–68 | 500 | 255 | 159 | 0 | .634 |
| Fred Shero | Phi, NYR | 1971–81 | 390 | 225 | 119 | 0 | .612 |
| Glen Sather | Edm, NYR | 1979-89, 93-94, 2003–04 | 497 | 314 | 121 | 0 | .598 |
| *Joel Quenneville | StL, Col, Chi | 1996– | 483 | 323 | 77 | 34 | .587 |
| *Ken Hitchcock | Dal, Phi, CBJ | 1995– | 511 | 345 | 88 | 39 | .584 |
| Emile Francis | NYR, StL | 1965–77, 81–83 | 388 | 273 | 117 | 0 | .574 |
| Billy Reay | Tor, Chi | 1957–59, 63–77 | 542 | 385 | 175 | 0 | .571 |
| Pat Burns | Mtl, Tor, Bos, NJ | 1988–2001, 2002–05 | 501 | 367 | 151 | 0 | .566 |
| Al Arbour | StL, NYI | 1970–94 | 781 | 577 | 248 | 0 | .564 |
| Pat Quinn | Phi, LA, Van, Tor | 1978–2006 | 657 | 499 | 154 | 8 | .560 |

*Active in 2008–09. Note: Minimum 600 regular-season games. Ranked by win percentage. Overtime losses up through 2004 are counted as losses. After 2004, ties were eliminated and overtime losses were awarded one point and so are listed in separate OTL column (and counted like ties).

# Single-Season Records

## Goals

| Player | Season | GP | G | Player | Season | GP | G |
|---|---|---|---|---|---|---|---|
| Wayne Gretzky, Edm | 1981–82 | 80 | 92 | Wayne Gretzky, Edm | 1982–83 | 80 | 71 |
| Wayne Gretzky, Edm | 1983–84 | 74 | 87 | Brett Hull, StL | 1991–92 | 73 | 70 |
| Brett Hull, StL | 1990–91 | 78 | 86 | Mario Lemieux, Pit | 1987–88 | 77 | 70 |
| Mario Lemieux, Pit | 1988–89 | 76 | 85 | Bernie Nicholls, LA | 1988–89 | 79 | 70 |
| Alexander Mogilny, Buf | 1992–93 | 77 | 76 | Mario Lemieux, Pit | 1992–93 | 60 | 69 |
| Phil Esposito, Bos | 1970–71 | 78 | 76 | Mario Lemieux, Pit | 1995–96 | 70 | 69 |
| Teemu Selanne, Win | 1992–93 | 84 | 76 | Mike Bossy, NYI | 1978–79 | 80 | 69 |
| Wayne Gretzky, Edm | 1984–85 | 80 | 73 | Phil Esposito, Bos | 1973–74 | 78 | 68 |
| Brett Hull, StL | 1989–90 | 80 | 72 | Jari Kurri, Edm | 1985–86 | 78 | 68 |
| Jari Kurri, Edm | 1984–85 | 73 | 71 | Mike Bossy, NYI | 1980–81 | 79 | 68 |

## Assists

| Player | Season | GP | Asst | Player | Season | GP | Asst |
|---|---|---|---|---|---|---|---|
| Wayne Gretzky, Edm | 1985–86 | 80 | 163 | Bobby Orr, Bos | 1970–71 | 78 | 102 |
| Wayne Gretzky, Edm | 1984–85 | 80 | 135 | Mario Lemieux, Pit | 1987–88 | 77 | 98 |
| Wayne Gretzky, Edm | 1982–83 | 80 | 125 | Adam Oates, Bos | 1992–93 | 84 | 97 |
| Wayne Gretzky, LA | 1990–91 | 78 | 122 | Joe Thornton, SJ | 2005-06 | 81 | 96 |
| Wayne Gretzky, Edm | 1986–87 | 79 | 121 | Doug Gilmour, Tor | 1992–93 | 83 | 95 |
| Wayne Gretzky, Edm | 1981–82 | 80 | 120 | Pat LaFontaine, Buf | 1992–93 | 84 | 95 |
| Wayne Gretzky, Edm | 1983–84 | 74 | 118 | Mario Lemieux, Pit | 1985–86 | 79 | 93 |
| Mario Lemieux, Pit | 1988–89 | 76 | 114 | Peter Stastny, Que | 1981–82 | 80 | 93 |
| Wayne Gretzky, LA | 1988–89 | 78 | 114 | Wayne Gretzky, LA | 1993–94 | 81 | 92 |
| Wayne Gretzky, Edm | 1987–88 | 64 | 109 | Mario Lemieux, Pit | 1995–96 | 70 | 92 |
| Wayne Gretzky, Edm | 1980–81 | 80 | 109 | Ron Francis, Pit | 1995–96 | 77 | 92 |
| Wayne Gretzky, LA | 1989–90 | 73 | 102 | Joe Thornton, SJ | 2006-07 | 82 | 92 |

## Points

| Player | Season | G | Asst | Pts | Player | Season | G | Asst | Pts |
|---|---|---|---|---|---|---|---|---|---|
| Wayne Gretzky, Edm | 1985–86 | 52 | 163 | 215 | Wayne Gretzky, LA | 1990–91 | 41 | 122 | 163 |
| Wayne Gretzky, Edm | 1981–82 | 92 | 120 | 212 | Mario Lemieux, Pit | 1995–96 | 69 | 92 | 161 |
| Wayne Gretzky, Edm | 1984–85 | 73 | 135 | 208 | Mario Lemieux, Pit | 1992–93 | 69 | 91 | 160 |
| Wayne Gretzky, Edm | 1983–84 | 87 | 118 | 205 | Steve Yzerman, Det | 1988–89 | 65 | 90 | 155 |
| Mario Lemieux, Pit | 1988–89 | 85 | 114 | 199 | Phil Esposito, Bos | 1970–71 | 76 | 76 | 152 |
| Wayne Gretzky, Edm | 1982–83 | 71 | 125 | 196 | Bernie Nicholls, NYI | 1988–89 | 70 | 80 | 150 |
| Wayne Gretzky, Edm | 1986–87 | 62 | 121 | 183 | Wayne Gretzky, Edm | 1987–88 | 40 | 109 | 149 |
| Mario Lemieux, Pit | 1987–88 | 70 | 98 | 168 | Pat LaFontaine, Buf | 1992–93 | 53 | 95 | 148 |
| Wayne Gretzky, LA | 1988–89 | 54 | 114 | 168 | Mike Bossy, NYI | 1981–82 | 64 | 83 | 147 |
| Wayne Gretzky, Edm | 1980–81 | 55 | 109 | 164 | Phil Esposito, Bos | 1973–74 | 68 | 77 | 145 |

## Single-Season Records *(Cont.)*

### Points per Game

| Player | Season | GP | Pts | Avg |
|---|---|---|---|---|
| Wayne Gretzky, Edm | 1983–84 | 74 | 205 | 2.77 |
| Wayne Gretzky, Edm | 1985–86 | 80 | 215 | 2.69 |
| Mario Lemieux, Pit | 1992–93 | 60 | 160 | 2.67 |
| Wayne Gretzky, Edm | 1981–82 | 80 | 212 | 2.65 |
| Mario Lemieux, Pit | 1988–89 | 76 | 199 | 2.62 |
| Wayne Gretzky, Edm | 1984–85 | 80 | 208 | 2.60 |
| Wayne Gretzky, Edm | 1982–83 | 80 | 196 | 2.45 |
| Wayne Gretzky, Edm | 1987–88 | 64 | 149 | 2.33 |
| Wayne Gretzky, Edm | 1986–87 | 79 | 183 | 2.32 |
| Mario Lemieux, Pitt | 1995–96 | 70 | 161 | 2.30 |
| Mario Lemieux, Pit | 1987–88 | 77 | 168 | 2.18 |
| Wayne Gretzky, LA | 1988–89 | 78 | 168 | 2.15 |
| Wayne Gretzky, LA | 1990–91 | 78 | 163 | 2.09 |
| Mario Lemieux, Pit | 1989–90 | 59 | 123 | 2.08 |
| Wayne Gretzky, Edm | 1980–81 | 80 | 164 | 2.05 |
| Mario Lemieux, Pit | 1991–92 | 64 | 131 | 2.05 |
| Bill Cowley, Bos | 1943–44 | 36 | 71 | 1.97 |
| Phil Esposito, Bos | 1970–71 | 78 | 152 | 1.95 |
| Wayne Gretzky, LA | 1989–90 | 73 | 142 | 1.95 |
| Steve Yzerman, Det | 1988–89 | 80 | 155 | 1.94 |

Note: Minimum 50 points in one season.

### Goals per Game

| Player | Season | GP | G | Avg |
|---|---|---|---|---|
| Joe Malone, Mtl | 1917–18 | 20 | 44 | 2.20 |
| Cy Denneny, Ott | 1917–18 | 20 | 36 | 1.80 |
| Newsy Lalonde, Mtl | 1917–18 | 14 | 23 | 1.64 |
| Joe Malone, Que | 1919–20 | 24 | 39 | 1.63 |
| Newsy Lalonde, Mtl | 1919–20 | 23 | 36 | 1.57 |
| Reg Noble, Tor | 1917–18 | 20 | 30 | 1.50 |
| Babe Dye, Ham-Tor | 1920–21 | 24 | 35 | 1.46 |
| Cy Denneny, Ott | 1920–21 | 24 | 34 | 1.42 |
| Joe Malone, Ham | 1920–21 | 20 | 28 | 1.40 |
| Newsy Lalonde, Mtl | 1920–21 | 24 | 33 | 1.38 |

Note: Minimum 20 goals in one season.

### Assists per Game

| Player | Season | GP | Asst | Avg |
|---|---|---|---|---|
| Wayne Gretzky, Edm | 1985–86 | 80 | 163 | 2.04 |
| Wayne Gretzky, Edm | 1987–88 | 64 | 109 | 1.70 |
| Wayne Gretzky, Edm | 1984–85 | 80 | 135 | 1.69 |
| Wayne Gretzky, Edm | 1983–84 | 74 | 118 | 1.59 |
| Wayne Gretzky, Edm | 1982–83 | 80 | 125 | 1.56 |
| Wayne Gretzky, LA | 1990–91 | 78 | 122 | 1.56 |
| Wayne Gretzky, Edm | 1986–87 | 79 | 121 | 1.53 |
| Mario Lemieux, Pit | 1992–93 | 60 | 91 | 1.52 |
| Wayne Gretzky, Edm | 1981–82 | 80 | 120 | 1.50 |
| Mario Lemieux, Pit | 1988–89 | 76 | 114 | 1.50 |

Note: Minimum 35 assists in one season.

### Shutout Leaders

| | Season | SO | Length of Schedule |
|---|---|---|---|
| George Hainsworth, Mtl | 1928–29 | 22 | 44 |
| Alec Connell, Ott | 1925–26 | 15 | 36 |
| Alec Connell, Ott | 1927–28 | 15 | 44 |
| Hal Winkler, Bos | 1927–28 | 15 | 44 |
| Tony Esposito, Chi | 1969–70 | 15 | 76 |
| George Hainsworth, Mtl | 1926–27 | 14 | 44 |
| Clint Benedict, Mtl M | 1926–27 | 13 | 44 |
| Alec Connell, Ott | 1926–27 | 13 | 44 |
| George Hainsworth, Mtl | 1927–28 | 13 | 44 |
| John Roach, NYR | 1928–29 | 13 | 44 |
| Roy Worters, NYA | 1928–29 | 13 | 44 |
| Harry Lumley, Tor | 1953–54 | 13 | 70 |
| Dominik Hasek, Buf | 1997–98 | 13 | 82 |
| Tiny Thompson, Bos | 1928–29 | 12 | 44 |
| Chuck Gardiner, Chi | 1930–31 | 12 | 44 |
| Terry Sawchuk, Det | 1951–52 | 12 | 70 |
| Terry Sawchuk, Det | 1953–54 | 12 | 70 |
| Terry Sawchuk, Det | 1954–55 | 12 | 70 |
| Glenn Hall, Det | 1955–56 | 12 | 70 |
| Bernie Parent, Phi | 1973–74 | 12 | 78 |
| Bernie Parent, Phi | 1974–75 | 12 | 80 |
| Martin Brodeur, NJ | 2006–07 | 12 | 82 |
| Lorne Chabot, NYR | 1927–28 | 11 | 44 |
| Harry Holmes, Det | 1927–28 | 11 | 44 |
| Roy Worters, Pit Pirates | 1927–28 | 11 | 44 |
| Lorne Chabot, Tor | 1928–29 | 11 | 44 |
| Clint Benedict, Mtl M | 1928–29 | 11 | 44 |
| Joe Miller, Pit Pirates | 1928–29 | 11 | 44 |
| Tiny Thompson, Bos | 1932–33 | 11 | 48 |
| Terry Sawchuck, Det | 1950–51 | 11 | 70 |
| Dominik Hasek, Buf | 2000–01 | 11 | 82 |
| Martin Brodeur, NJ | 2003–04 | 11 | 82 |
| Lorne Chabot, NYR | 1926–27 | 10 | 44 |
| Clarence Dolson, Det | 1928–29 | 10 | 44 |
| John Roach, Det | 1932–33 | 10 | 48 |
| Chuck Gardiner, Chi | 1933–34 | 10 | 48 |
| Tiny Thompson, Bos | 1935–36 | 10 | 48 |
| Frank Brimsek, Bos | 1938–39 | 10 | 48 |
| Bill Durnan, Mtl | 1948–49 | 10 | 60 |
| Gerry McNeil, Mtl | 1952–53 | 10 | 70 |
| Harry Lumley, Tor | 1952–53 | 10 | 70 |
| Tony Esposito, Chi | 1973–74 | 10 | 78 |
| Ken Dryden, Mtl | 1976–77 | 10 | 80 |
| Martin Brodeur, NJ | 1996–97 | 10 | 82 |
| Martin Brodeur, NJ | 1997–98 | 10 | 82 |
| Roman Cechmanek, Phi | 2000–01 | 10 | 82 |
| Byron Dafoe, Bos | 1998–99 | 10 | 82 |
| Ed Belfour, Tor | 2003–04 | 10 | 82 |
| Miikka Kiprusoff, Cgy | 2005–06 | 10 | 82 |
| Henrik Lundqvist, NYR | 2007–08 | 10 | 82 |
| Steve Mason, CBJ | 2008–09 | 10 | 82 |

### Wins

| | Season | Record* |
|---|---|---|
| Martin Brodeur, NJ | 2006–07 | 48–23 |
| Roberto Luongo, Van | 2006–07 | 47–22 |
| Bernie Parent, Phi | 1973–74 | 47–13–12 |
| Evgeni Nabokov, SJ | 2007–08 | 46–21 |
| Miikka Kiprusoff, Cgy | 2008–09 | 45–24 |
| Bernie Parent, Phi | 1974–75 | 44–14–9 |
| Terry Sawchuk, Det | 1950–51 | 44–13–13 |
| Terry Sawchuk, Det | 1951–52 | 44–14–12 |
| Martin Brodeur, NJ | 2007–08 | 44–27 |
| Tom Barrasso, Pit | 1992–93 | 43–14–5 |
| Ed Belfour, Chi | 1990–91 | 43–19–7 |
| Martin Brodeur, NJ | 1997–98 | 43–17–8 |
| Martin Brodeur, NJ | 1999–00 | 43–20–8 |
| Martin Brodeur, NJ | 2005-06 | 43–23 |
| Jacques Plante, Mtl | 1955–56 | 42–12–10 |
| Jacques Plante, Mtl | 1961–62 | 42–14–14 |
| Ken Dryden, Mtl | 1975–76 | 42–10–8 |
| Mike Richter, NYR | 1993–94 | 42–12–6 |
| Roman Turek, StL | 1999–00 | 42–15–9 |
| Martin Brodeur, NJ | 2000–01 | 42–17–11 |
| Miikka Kiprusoff, Cgy | 2005–06 | 42–20 |

*Starting with the 2005–06 season, ties were eliminated.

## Goals Against Average

| (PRE-1950) | Season | GP | GAA |
|---|---|---|---|
| George Hainsworth, Mtl | 1928–29 | 44 | 0.92 |
| George Hainsworth, Mtl | 1927–28 | 44 | 1.05 |
| Alec Connell, Ott | 1925–26 | 36 | 1.12 |
| Tiny Thompson, Bos | 1928–29 | 44 | 1.15 |
| Roy Worters, NYA | 1928–29 | 38 | 1.15 |

| (POST-1950) | Season | GP | GAA |
|---|---|---|---|
| Miika Kiprusoff, Cal | 2003–04 | 38 | 1.69 |
| Marty Turco, Dal | 2002–03 | 55 | 1.73 |
| Tony Esposito, Chi | 1971–72 | 48 | 1.770 |
| Al Rollins, Tor | 1950–51 | 40 | 1.774 |
| Ron Tugnutt, Ott | 1998–99 | 43 | 1.79 |

# Single-Game Records

## Goals

| | Date | G |
|---|---|---|
| Joe Malone, Que vs Tor | 1-31-20 | 7 |
| Newsy Lalonde, Mtl vs Tor | 1-10-20 | 6 |
| Joe Malone, Que vs Ott | 3-10-20 | 6 |
| Corb Denneny, Tor vs Ham | 1-26-21 | 6 |
| Cy Denneny, Ott vs Ham | 3-7-21 | 6 |
| Syd Howe, Det vs NYR | 2-3-44 | 6 |
| Red Berenson, StL vs Phi | 11-7-68 | 6 |
| Darryl Sittler, Tor vs Bos | 2-7-76 | 6 |

## Assists

| | Date | A |
|---|---|---|
| Billy Taylor, Det vs Chi | 3-16-47 | 7 |
| Wayne Gretzky, Edm vs Wsh | 2-15-80 | 7 |
| Wayne Gretzky, Edm vs Chi | 12-11-85 | 7 |
| Wayne Gretzky, Edm vs Que | 2-14-86 | 7 |

Note: 24 tied with 6.

## Points

| | Date | G | A | Pts |
|---|---|---|---|---|
| Darryl Sittler, Tor vs Bos | 2-7-76 | 6 | 4 | 10 |
| Maurice Richard, Mtl vs Det | 12-28-44 | 5 | 3 | 8 |
| Bert Olmstead, Mtl vs Chi | 1-9-54 | 4 | 4 | 8 |
| Tom Bladon, Phi vs Clev | 12-11-77 | 4 | 4 | 8 |
| Bryan Trottier, NYI vs NYR | 12-23-78 | 5 | 3 | 8 |
| Peter Stastny, Que vs Wsh | 2-22-81 | 4 | 4 | 8 |
| Anton Stastny, Que vs Wsh | 2-22-81 | 3 | 5 | 8 |
| Wayne Gretzky, Edm vs NJ | 11-19-83 | 3 | 5 | 8 |
| Wayne Gretzky, Edm vs Min | 1-4-84 | 4 | 4 | 8 |
| Paul Coffey, Edm vs Det | 3-14-86 | 2 | 6 | 8 |
| Mario Lemieux, Pit vs StL | 10-15-88 | 2 | 6 | 8 |
| Bernie Nicholls, LA vs Tor | 12-1-88 | 2 | 6 | 8 |
| Mario Lemieux, Pit vs NJ | 12-31-88 | 5 | 3 | 8 |

# NHL Season Leaders

## Points

| Season | Player and Club | Pts |
|---|---|---|
| 1917–18 | Joe Malone, Mtl | 44 |
| 1918–19 | Newsy Lalonde, Mtl | 30 |
| 1919–20 | Joe Malone, Que | 48 |
| 1920–21 | Newsy Lalonde, Mtl | 41 |
| 1921–22 | Punch Broadbent, Ott | 46 |
| 1922–23 | Babe Dye, Tor | 37 |
| 1923–24 | Cy Denneny, Ott | 23 |
| 1924–25 | Babe Dye, Tor | 44 |
| 1925–26 | Nels Stewart, Mtl M | 42 |
| 1926–27 | Bill Cook, NY | 37 |
| 1927–28 | Howie Morenz, Mtl | 51 |
| 1928–29 | Ace Bailey, Tor | 32 |
| 1929–30 | Cooney Weiland, Bos | 73 |
| 1930–31 | Howie Morenz, Mtl | 51 |
| 1931–32 | Harvey Jackson, Tor | 53 |
| 1932–33 | Bill Cook, NY | 50 |
| 1933–34 | Charlie Conacher, Tor | 52 |
| 1934–35 | Charlie Conacher, Tor | 57 |
| 1935–36 | Sweeney Schriner, NYA | 45 |
| 1936–37 | Sweeney Schriner, NYA | 46 |
| 1937–38 | Gord Drillon, Tor | 52 |
| 1938–39 | Hector Blake, Mtl | 47 |
| 1939–40 | Milt Schmidt, Bos | 52 |
| 1940–41 | Bill Cowley, Bos | 62 |
| 1941–42 | Bryan Hextall, NY | 54 |
| 1942–43 | Doug Bentley, Chi | 73 |
| 1943–44 | Herb Cain, Bos | 82 |
| 1944–45 | Elmer Lach, Mtl | 80 |
| 1945–46 | Max Bentley, Chi | 61 |
| 1946–47 | Max Bentley, Chi | 72 |
| 1947–48 | Elmer Lach, Mtl | 61 |
| 1948–49 | Roy Conacher, Chi | 68 |
| 1949–50 | Ted Lindsay, Det | 78 |

| Season | Player and Club | Pts |
|---|---|---|
| 1950–51 | Gordie Howe, Det | 86 |
| 1951–52 | Gordie Howe, Det | 86 |
| 1952–53 | Gordie Howe, Det | 95 |
| 1953–54 | Gordie Howe, Det | 81 |
| 1954–55 | Bernie Geoffrion, Mtl | 75 |
| 1955–56 | Jean Beliveau, Mtl | 88 |
| 1956–57 | Gordie Howe, Det | 89 |
| 1957–58 | Dickie Moore, Mtl | 84 |
| 1958–59 | Dickie Moore, Mtl | 96 |
| 1959–60 | Bobby Hull, Chi | 81 |
| 1960–61 | Bernie Geoffrion, Mtl | 95 |
| 1961–62 | Andy Bathgate, NY | 84 |
|  | Bobby Hull, Chi | 84 |
| 1962–63 | Gordie Howe, Det | 86 |
| 1963–64 | Stan Mikita, Chi | 89 |
| 1964–65 | Stan Mikita, Chi | 87 |
| 1965–66 | Bobby Hull, Chi | 97 |
| 1966–67 | Stan Mikita, Chi | 97 |
| 1967–68 | Stan Mikita, Chi | 87 |
| 1968–69 | Phil Esposito, Bos | 126 |
| 1969–70 | Bobby Orr, Bos | 120 |
| 1970–71 | Phil Esposito, Bos | 152 |
| 1971–72 | Phil Esposito, Bos | 133 |
| 1972–73 | Phil Esposito, Bos | 130 |
| 1973–74 | Phil Esposito, Bos | 145 |
| 1974–75 | Bobby Orr, Bos | 135 |
| 1975–76 | Guy Lafleur, Mtl | 125 |
| 1976–77 | Guy Lafleur, Mtl | 136 |
| 1977–78 | Guy Lafleur, Mtl | 132 |
| 1978–79 | Bryan Trottier, NYI | 134 |
| 1979–80 | Marcel Dionne, LA | 137 |
|  | Wayne Gretzky, Edm | 137 |
| 1980–81 | Wayne Gretzky, Edm | 164 |

## Points *(Cont.)*

| Season | Player and Club | Pts | Season | Player and Club | Pts |
|---|---|---|---|---|---|
| 1981–82 | Wayne Gretzky, Edm | 212 | 1995–96 | Mario Lemieux, Pit | 161 |
| 1982–83 | Wayne Gretzky, Edm | 196 | 1996–97 | Mario Lemieux, Pit | 122 |
| 1983–84 | Wayne Gretzky, Edm | 205 | 1997–98 | Jaromir Jagr, Pit | 102 |
| 1984–85 | Wayne Gretzky, Edm | 208 | 1998–99 | Jaromir Jagr, Pit | 127 |
| 1985–86 | Wayne Gretzky, Edm | 215 | 1999–00 | Jaromir Jagr, Pit | 96 |
| 1986–87 | Wayne Gretzky, Edm | 183 | 2000–01 | Jaromir Jagr, Pit | 121 |
| 1987–88 | Mario Lemieux, Pit | 168 | 2001–02 | Jarome Iginla, Cgy | 96 |
| 1988–89 | Mario Lemieux, Pit | 199 | 2002–03 | Peter Forsberg, Col | 106 |
| 1989–90 | Wayne Gretzky, LA | 142 | 2003–04 | Martin St. Louis, TB | 94 |
| 1990–91 | Wayne Gretzky, LA | 163 | 2004–05 | No season | |
| 1991–92 | Mario Lemieux, Pit | 131 | 2005–06 | Joe Thornton, Bos/SJ | 125 |
| 1992–93 | Mario Lemieux, Pit | 160 | 2006–07 | Sidney Crosby, Pit | 120 |
| 1993–94 | Wayne Gretzky, LA | 130 | 2007–08 | Alexander Ovechkin, Wsh | 112 |
| 1994–95 | Jaromir Jagr, Pit | 70 | 2008–09 | Evgeni Malkin, Pit | 113 |

## Goals

| Season | Player and Club | G | Season | Player and Club | G |
|---|---|---|---|---|---|
| 1917–18 | Joe Malone, Mtl | 44 | 1963–64 | Bobby Hull, Chi | 43 |
| 1918–19 | Odie Cleghorn, Mtl | 23 | 1964–65 | Norm Ullman, Det | 42 |
| 1919–20 | Joe Malone, Que | 39 | 1965–66 | Bobby Hull, Chi | 54 |
| 1920–21 | Babe Dye, Ham-Tor | 35 | 1966–67 | Bobby Hull, Chi | 52 |
| 1921–22 | Punch Broadbent, Ott | 32 | 1967–68 | Bobby Hull, Chi | 44 |
| 1922–23 | Babe Dye, Tor | 26 | 1968–69 | Bobby Hull, Chi | 58 |
| 1923–24 | Cy Denneny, Ott | 22 | 1969–70 | Phil Esposito, Bos | 43 |
| 1924–25 | Babe Dye, Tor | 38 | 1970–71 | Phil Esposito, Bos | 76 |
| 1925–26 | Nels Stewart, Mtl | 34 | 1971–72 | Phil Esposito, Bos | 66 |
| 1926–27 | Bill Cook, NY | 33 | 1972–73 | Phil Esposito, Bos | 55 |
| 1927–28 | Howie Morenz, Mtl | 33 | 1973–74 | Phil Esposito, Bos | 68 |
| 1928–29 | Ace Bailey, Tor | 22 | 1974–75 | Phil Esposito, Bos | 61 |
| 1929–30 | Cooney Weiland, Bos | 43 | 1975–76 | Guy Lafleur, Mtl | 56 |
| 1930–31 | Charlie Lonacher, Tor | 31 | 1976–77 | Steve Shutt, Mtl | 60 |
| 1931–32 | Charlie Conacher, Tor | 34 | 1977–78 | Guy Lafleur, Mtl | 60 |
| | Bill Cook, NY | 34 | 1978–79 | Mike Bossy, NYI | 69 |
| 1932–33 | Bill Cook, NY | 28 | 1979–80 | Charlie Simmer, LA | 56 |
| 1933–34 | Charlie Conacher, Tor | 32 | | Blaine Stoughton, Hart | 56 |
| 1934–35 | Charlie Conacher, Tor | 36 | 1980–81 | Mike Bossy, NYI | 68 |
| 1935–36 | Charlie Conacher, Tor | 23 | 1981–82 | Wayne Gretzky, Edm | 92 |
| | Bill Thoms, Tor | 23 | 1982–83 | Wayne Gretzky, Edm | 71 |
| 1936–37 | Larry Aurie, Det | 23 | 1983–84 | Wayne Gretzky, Edm | 87 |
| | Nels Stewart, Bos-NYA | 23 | 1984–85 | Wayne Gretzky, Edm | 73 |
| 1937–38 | Gord Drillon, Tor | 26 | 1985–86 | Jari Kurri, Edm | 68 |
| 1938–39 | Roy Conacher, Bos | 26 | 1986–87 | Wayne Gretzky, Edm | 62 |
| 1939–40 | Bryan Hextall, NY | 24 | 1987–88 | Mario Lemieux, Pit | 70 |
| 1940–41 | Bryan Hextall, NY | 26 | 1988–89 | Mario Lemieux, Pit | 85 |
| 1941–42 | Lynn Patrick, NY | 32 | 1989–90 | Brett Hull, StL | 72 |
| 1942–43 | Doug Bentley, Chi | 33 | 1990–91 | Brett Hull, StL | 86 |
| 1943–44 | Doug Bentley, Chi | 38 | 1991–92 | Brett Hull, StL | 70 |
| 1944–45 | Maurice Richard, Mtl | 50 | 1992–93 | Alexander Mogilny, Buf | 76 |
| 1945–46 | Gaye Stewart, Tor | 37 | | Teemu Selanne, Win | 76 |
| 1946–47 | Maurice Richard, Mtl | 45 | 1993–94 | Pavel Bure, Van | 60 |
| 1947–48 | Ted Lindsay, Det | 33 | 1994–95 | Peter Bondra, Wsh | 34 |
| 1948–49 | Sid Abel, Det | 28 | 1995–96 | Mario Lemieux, Pit | 69 |
| 1949–50 | Maurice Richard, Mtl | 43 | 1996–97 | Keith Tkachuk, Phx | 52 |
| 1950–51 | Gordie Howe, Det | 43 | 1997–98 | Teemu Selanne, Ana | 52 |
| 1951–52 | Gordie Howe, Det | 47 | | Peter Bondra, Wsh | 52 |
| 1952–53 | Gordie Howe, Det | 49 | 1998–99 | Teemu Selanne, Ana | 47 |
| 1953–54 | Maurice Richard, Mtl | 37 | 1999–00 | Pavel Bure, Fla | 58 |
| 1954–55 | Bernie Geoffrion, Mtl | 38 | 2000–01 | Pavel Bure, Fla | 59 |
| | Maurice Richard, Mtl | 38 | 2001–02 | Jarome Iginla, Cgy | 52 |
| 1955–56 | Jean Beliveau, Mtl | 47 | 2002–03 | Milan Hejduk, Col | 50 |
| 1956–57 | Gordie Howe, Det | 44 | 2003–04 | Jarome Iginla, Cgy | 41 |
| 1957–58 | Dickie Moore, Mtl | 36 | | Rick Nash, CBJ | 41 |
| 1958–59 | Jean Beliveau, Mtl | 45 | | Ilya Kovalchuk, Atl | 41 |
| 1959–60 | Bobby Hull, Chi | 39 | 2004–05 | No season | |
| | Bronco Horvath, Bos | 39 | 2005–06 | Jonathan Cheechoo, SJ | 56 |
| 1960–61 | Bernie Geoffrion, Mtl | 50 | 2006–07 | Vincent Lecavalier, TB | 52 |
| 1961–62 | Bobby Hull, Chi | 50 | 2007–08 | Alexander Ovechkin, Wsh | 65 |
| 1962–63 | Gordie Howe, Det | 38 | 2008–09 | Alexander Ovechkin, Wsh | 56 |

## Assists

| Season | Player and Club | Asst | Season | Player and Club | Asst |
|---|---|---|---|---|---|
| 1917–18 | statistic not kept | | 1966–67 | Stan Mikita, Chi | 62 |
| 1918–19 | Newsy Lalonde, Mtl | 9 | 1967–68 | Phil Esposito, Bos | 49 |
| 1919–20 | Corbett Denneny, Tor | 12 | 1968–69 | Phil Esposito, Bos | 77 |
| 1920–21 | Louis Berlinquette, Mtl | 9 | 1969–70 | Bobby Orr, Bos | 87 |
| 1921–22 | Punch Broadbench, Ott | 14 | 1970–71 | Bobby Orr, Bos | 102 |
| 1922–23 | Babe Dye, Tor | 11 | 1971–72 | Bobby Orr, Bos | 80 |
| 1923–24 | Billy Boucher, Mtl | 6 | 1972–73 | Phil Esposito, Bos | 75 |
| 1924–25 | Cy Denneny, Ott | 15 | 1973–74 | Bobby Orr, Bos | 90 |
| 1925–26 | Frank Nighbor, Ott | 13 | 1974–75 | Bobby Clarke, Phi | 89 |
| 1926–27 | Dick Irvin, Chi | 18 | | Bobby Orr, Bos | 89 |
| 1927–28 | Howie Morenz, Mtl | 18 | 1975–76 | Bobby Clarke, Phi | 89 |
| 1928–29 | Frank Boucher, NY | 16 | 1976–77 | Guy Lafleur, Mtl | 80 |
| 1929–30 | Frank Boucher, NY | 36 | 1977–78 | Bryan Trottier, NYI | 77 |
| 1930–31 | Joe Primeau, Tor | 32 | 1978–79 | Bryan Trottier, NYI | 87 |
| 1931–32 | Joe Primeau, Tor | 37 | 1979–80 | Wayne Gretzky, Edm | 86 |
| 1932–33 | Frank Boucher, NY | 28 | 1980–81 | Wayne Gretzky, Edm | 109 |
| 1933–34 | Joe Primeau, Tor | 32 | 1981–82 | Wayne Gretzky, Edm | 120 |
| 1934–35 | Art Chapman, NYA | 34 | 1982–83 | Wayne Gretzky, Edm | 125 |
| 1935–36 | Art Chapman, NYA | 28 | 1983–84 | Wayne Gretzky, Edm | 118 |
| 1936–37 | Syl Apps, Tor | 29 | 1984–85 | Wayne Gretzky, Edm | 135 |
| 1937–38 | Syl Apps, Tor | 29 | 1985–86 | Wayne Gretzky, Edm | 163 |
| 1938–39 | Bill Cowley, Bos | 34 | 1986–87 | Wayne Gretzky, Edm | 121 |
| 1939–40 | Milt Schmidt, Bos | 30 | 1987–88 | Wayne Gretzky, Edm | 109 |
| 1940–41 | Bill Cowley, Bos | 45 | 1988–89 | Wayne Gretzky, LA | 114 |
| 1941–42 | Phil Watson, NY | 37 | | Mario Lemieux, Pit | 114 |
| 1942–43 | Bill Cowley, Bos | 45 | 1989–90 | Wayne Gretzky, LA | 102 |
| 1943–44 | Clint Smith, Chi | 49 | 1990–91 | Wayne Gretzky, LA | 122 |
| 1944–45 | Elmer Lach, Mtl | 54 | 1991–92 | Wayne Gretzky, LA | 90 |
| 1945–46 | Elmer Lach, Mtl | 34 | 1992–93 | Adam Oates, Bos | 97 |
| 1946–47 | Billy Taylor, Det | 46 | 1993–94 | Wayne Gretzky, LA | 92 |
| 1947–48 | Doug Bentley, Chi | 37 | 1994–95 | Ron Francis, Pit | 48 |
| 1948–49 | Doug Bentley, Chi | 43 | 1995–96 | Mario Lemieux, Pit | 92 |
| 1949–50 | Ted Lindsay, Det | 55 | | Ron Francis, Pit | 92 |
| 1950–51 | Gordie Howe, Det | 43 | 1996–97 | Mario Lemieux, Pit | 72 |
| | Ted Kennedy, Tor | 43 | 1997–98 | Jaromir Jagr, Pit | 67 |
| 1951–52 | Elmer Lach, Mtl | 50 | | Wayne Gretzky, NYR | 67 |
| 1952–53 | Gordie Howe, Det | 46 | 1998–99 | Jaromir Jagr, Pit | 83 |
| 1953–54 | Gordie Howe, Det | 48 | 1999–00 | Mark Recchi, Phi | 63 |
| 1954–55 | Bert Olmstead, Mtl | 48 | 2000–01 | Jaromir Jagr, Pit | 69 |
| 1955–56 | Bert Olmstead, Mtl | 56 | | Adam Oates, Wsh | 69 |
| 1956–57 | Ted Lindsay, Det | 55 | 2001–02 | Adam Oates, Wsh | 64 |
| 1957–58 | Henri Richard, Mtl | 52 | 2002–03 | Peter Forsberg, Col | 77 |
| 1958–59 | Dickie Moore, Mtl | 55 | 2003–04 | Scott Gomez, NJ | 56 |
| 1959–60 | Bobby Hull, Chi | 42 | | Martin St. Louis, TB | 56 |
| 1960–61 | Jean Beliveau, Mtl | 58 | 2004–05 | No season | |
| 1961–62 | Andy Bathgate, NY | 56 | 2005–06 | Joe Thornton, Bos/SJ | 96 |
| 1962–63 | Henri Richard, Mtl | 50 | 2006–07 | Joe Thornton, SJ | 92 |
| 1963–64 | Andy Bathgate, NY-Tor | 58 | 2007–08 | Joe Thornton, SJ | 67 |
| 1964–65 | Stan Mikita, Chi | 59 | 2008–09 | Evgeni Malkin, Pit | 78 |
| 1965–66 | Stan Mikita, Chi | 48 | | | |
| | Bobby Rousseau, Mtl | 48 | | | |
| | Jean Beliveau, Mtl | 48 | | | |

## Goals Against Average

| Season | Goaltender and Club | GP | Min | GA | SO | Avg |
|---|---|---|---|---|---|---|
| 1917–18 | Georges Vezina, Mtl | 21 | 1282 | 84 | 1 | 3.93 |
| 1918–19 | Clint Benedict, Ott | 18 | 1113 | 53 | 2 | 2.86 |
| 1919–20 | Clint Benedict, Ott | 24 | 1444 | 64 | 5 | 2.66 |
| 1920–21 | Clint Benedict, Ott | 24 | 1457 | 75 | 2 | 3.09 |
| 1921–22 | Clint Benedict, Ott | 24 | 1508 | 84 | 2 | 3.34 |
| 1922–23 | Clint Benedict, Ott | 24 | 1478 | 54 | 4 | 2.18 |
| 1923–24 | Georges Vezina, Mtl | 24 | 1459 | 48 | 3 | 1.97 |
| 1924–25 | Georges Vezina, Mtl | 30 | 1860 | 56 | 5 | 1.81 |
| 1925–26 | Alec Connell, Ott | 36 | 2251 | 42 | 15 | 1.12 |
| 1926–27 | Clint Benedict, Mtl M | 43 | 2748 | 65 | 13 | 1.42 |
| 1927–28 | George Hainsworth, Mtl | 44 | 2730 | 48 | 13 | 1.05 |
| 1928–29 | George Hainsworth, Mtl | 44 | 2800 | 43 | 22 | 0.92 |
| 1929–30 | Tiny Thompson, Bos | 44 | 2680 | 98 | 3 | 2.19 |

## Goals Against Average *(Cont.)*

| Season | Goaltender and Club | GP | Min | GA | SO | Avg |
|---|---|---|---|---|---|---|
| 1930–31 | Roy Worters, NYA | 44 | 2760 | 74 | 8 | 1.61 |
| 1931–32 | Chuck Gardiner, Chi | 48 | 2989 | 92 | 4 | 1.85 |
| 1932–33 | Tiny Thompson, Bos | 48 | 3000 | 88 | 11 | 1.76 |
| 1933–34 | Wilf Cude, Det-Mtl | 30 | 1920 | 47 | 5 | 1.47 |
| 1934–35 | Lorne Chabot, Chi | 48 | 2940 | 88 | 8 | 1.80 |
| 1935–36 | Tiny Thompson, Bos | 48 | 2930 | 82 | 10 | 1.68 |
| 1936–37 | Normie Smith, Det | 48 | 2980 | 102 | 6 | 2.05 |
| 1937–38 | Tiny Thompson, Bos | 48 | 2970 | 89 | 7 | 1.80 |
| 1938–39 | Frank Brimsek, Bos | 43 | 2610 | 68 | 10 | 1.56 |
| 1939–40 | Dave Kerr, NYR | 48 | 3000 | 77 | 8 | 1.54 |
| 1940–41 | Turk Broda, Tor | 48 | 2970 | 99 | 5 | 2.00 |
| 1941–42 | Frank Brimsek, Bos | 47 | 2930 | 115 | 3 | 2.35 |
| 1942–43 | Johnny Mowers, Det | 50 | 3010 | 124 | 6 | 2.47 |
| 1943–44 | Bill Durnan, Mtl | 50 | 3000 | 109 | 2 | 2.18 |
| 1944–45 | Bill Durnan, Mtl | 50 | 3000 | 121 | 1 | 2.42 |
| 1945–46 | Bill Durnan, Mtl | 40 | 2400 | 104 | 4 | 2.60 |
| 1946–47 | Bill Durnan, Mtl | 60 | 3600 | 138 | 4 | 2.30 |
| 1947–48 | Turk Broda, Tor | 60 | 3600 | 143 | 5 | 2.38 |
| 1948–49 | Bill Durnan, Mtl | 60 | 3600 | 126 | 10 | 2.10 |
| 1949–50 | Bill Durnan, Mtl | 64 | 3840 | 141 | 8 | 2.20 |
| 1950–51 | Al Rollins, Tor | 40 | 2367 | 70 | 5 | 1.77 |
| 1951–52 | Terry Sawchuk, Det | 70 | 4200 | 133 | 12 | 1.90 |
| 1952–53 | Terry Sawchuk, Det | 63 | 3780 | 120 | 9 | 1.90 |
| 1953–54 | Harry Lumley, Tor | 69 | 4140 | 128 | 13 | 1.86 |
| 1954–55 | Harry Lumley, Tor | 69 | 4140 | 134 | 8 | 1.94 |
| 1955–56 | Jacques Plante, Mtl | 64 | 3840 | 119 | 7 | 1.86 |
| 1956–57 | Jacques Plante, Mtl | 61 | 3660 | 122 | 9 | 2.00 |
| 1957–58 | Jacques Plante, Mtl | 57 | 3386 | 119 | 9 | 2.11 |
| 1958–59 | Jacques Plante, Mtl | 67 | 4000 | 144 | 9 | 2.16 |
| 1959–60 | Jacques Plante, Mtl | 69 | 4140 | 175 | 3 | 2.54 |
| 1960–61 | Charlie Hodge, Mtl | 30 | 1800 | 74 | 4 | 2.47 |
| 1961–62 | Jacques Plante, Mtl | 70 | 4200 | 166 | 4 | 2.37 |
| 1962–63 | Don Simmons, Tor | 28 | 1680 | 69 | 1 | 2.46 |
| 1963–64 | Johnny Bower, Tor | 51 | 3009 | 106 | 5 | 2.11 |
| 1964–65 | Johnny Bower, Tor | 34 | 2040 | 81 | 3 | 2.38 |
| 1965–66 | Johnny Bower, Tor | 35 | 1998 | 75 | 3 | 2.25 |
| 1966–67 | Glenn Hall, Chi | 32 | 1664 | 66 | 2 | 2.38 |
| 1967–68 | Gump Worsley, Mtl | 40 | 2213 | 73 | 6 | 1.98 |
| 1968–69 | Jacques Plante, StL | 37 | 2139 | 70 | 5 | 1.96 |
| 1969–70 | Ernie Wakely, StL | 30 | 1651 | 58 | 4 | 2.11 |
| 1970–71 | Jacques Plante, Tor | 40 | 2329 | 73 | 4 | 1.88 |
| 1971–72 | Tony Esposito, Chi | 48 | 2780 | 82 | 9 | 1.77 |
| 1972–73 | Ken Dryden, Mtl | 54 | 3165 | 119 | 6 | 2.26 |
| 1973–74 | Bernie Parent, Phi | 73 | 4314 | 136 | 12 | 1.89 |
| 1974–75 | Bernie Parent, Phi | 68 | 4041 | 137 | 12 | 2.03 |
| 1975–76 | Ken Dryden, Mtl | 62 | 3580 | 121 | 8 | 2.03 |
| 1976–77 | Michel Larocque, Mtl | 26 | 1525 | 53 | 4 | 2.09 |
| 1977–78 | Ken Dryden, Mtl | 52 | 3071 | 105 | 5 | 2.05 |
| 1978–79 | Ken Dryden, Mtl | 47 | 2814 | 108 | 5 | 2.30 |
| 1979–80 | Bob Sauve, Buff | 32 | 1880 | 74 | 4 | 2.36 |
| 1980–81 | Richard Sevigny, Mtl | 33 | 1777 | 71 | 2 | 2.40 |
| 1981–82 | Denis Herron, Mtl | 27 | 1547 | 68 | 3 | 2.64 |
| 1982–83 | Pete Peeters, Bos | 62 | 3611 | 142 | 8 | 2.36 |
| 1983–84 | Pat Riggin, Wsh | 41 | 2299 | 102 | 4 | 2.66 |
| 1984–85 | Tom Barrasso, Buf | 54 | 3248 | 144 | 5 | 2.66 |
| 1985–86 | Bob Froese, Phi | 51 | 2728 | 116 | 5 | 2.55 |
| 1986–87 | Brian Hayward, Mtl | 37 | 2178 | 102 | 1 | 2.81 |
| 1987–88 | Pete Peeters, Wsh | 35 | 1896 | 88 | 2 | 2.78 |
| 1988–89 | Patrick Roy, Mtl | 48 | 2744 | 113 | 4 | 2.47 |
| 1989–90 | Patrick Roy, Mtl | 54 | 3173 | 134 | 3 | 2.53 |
| | Mike Liut, Hfd-Wsh | 37 | 2161 | 91 | 4 | 2.53 |
| 1990–91 | Ed Belfour, Chi | 74 | 4127 | 170 | 4 | 2.47 |
| 1991–92 | Patrick Roy, Mtl | 67 | 3935 | 155 | 5 | 2.36 |
| 1992–93 | Felix Potvin, Tor | 48 | 2781 | 116 | 2 | 2.50 |
| 1993–94 | Dominik Hasek, Buf | 58 | 3358 | 109 | 7 | 1.95 |
| 1994–95 | Dominik Hasek, Buf | 41 | 2416 | 85 | 5 | 2.11 |

## Goals Against Average (Cont.)

| Season | Goaltender and Club | GP | Min | GA | SO | Avg |
|---|---|---|---|---|---|---|
| 1995–96 | Ron Hextall, Phi | 53 | 3102 | 112 | 4 | 2.17 |
| | Chris Osgood, Det | 50 | 2932 | 106 | 5 | 2.17 |
| 1996–97 | Martin Brodeur, NJ | 67 | 3838 | 120 | 10 | 1.88 |
| 1997–98 | Ed Belfour, Dal | 61 | 3581 | 112 | 9 | 1.88 |
| 1998–99 | Ron Tugnutt, Ott | 43 | 2508 | 75 | 3 | 1.79 |
| 1999–00 | Brian Boucher, Phi | 35 | 2038 | 65 | 4 | 1.91 |
| 2000–01 | Marty Turco, Dal | 26 | 1266 | 40 | 3 | 1.90 |
| 2001–02 | Patrick Roy, Col | 63 | 3773 | 122 | 9 | 1.94 |
| 2002–03 | Marty Turco, Dal | 55 | 3202 | 92 | 7 | 1.72 |
| 2003–04 | Miikka Kiprusoff, Cgy | 38 | 2301 | 65 | 4 | 1.69 |
| 2004–05 | No season | | | | | |
| 2005–06 | Miikka Kiprusoff, Cgy | 74 | 4379 | 151 | 10 | 2.07 |
| 2006–07 | Niklas Backstrom, Min | 41 | 2226 | 73 | 5 | 1.97 |
| 2007–08 | Chris Osgood, Det | 43 | 2409 | 84 | 4 | 2.09 |
| 2008–09 | Tim Thomas, Bos | 54 | 3259 | 114 | 5 | 2.10 |

## Penalty Minutes

| Season | Player and Club | GP | PIM | Season | Player and Club | GP | PIM |
|---|---|---|---|---|---|---|---|
| 1918–19 | Joe Hall, Mtl | 17 | 135 | 1964–65 | Carl Brewer, Tor | 70 | 177 |
| 1919–20 | Cully Wilson, Tor | 23 | 79 | 1965–66 | Reggie Fleming, Bos-NYR | 69 | 166 |
| 1920–21 | Bert Corbeau, Mtl | 24 | 86 | 1966–67 | John Ferguson, Mtl | 67 | 177 |
| 1921–22 | Sprague Cleghorn, Mtl | 24 | 63 | 1967–68 | Barclay Plager, StL | 49 | 153 |
| 1922–23 | Billy Boucher, Mtl | 24 | 55 | 1968–69 | Forbes Kennedy, Phi-Tor | 77 | 219 |
| 1923–24 | Bert Corbeau, Tor | 24 | 55 | 1969–70 | Keith Magnuson, Chi | 76 | 213 |
| 1924–25 | Billy Boucher, Mtl | 30 | 92 | 1970–71 | Keith Magnuson, Chi | 76 | 291 |
| 1925–26 | Bert Corbeau, Tor | 36 | 121 | 1971–72 | Brian Watson, Pit | 75 | 212 |
| 1926–27 | Nels Stewart, Mtl M | 44 | 133 | 1972–73 | Dave Schultz, Phi | 76 | 259 |
| 1927–28 | Eddie Shore, Bos | 44 | 165 | 1973–74 | Dave Schultz, Phi | 73 | 348 |
| 1928–29 | Red Dutton, Mtl M | 44 | 139 | 1974–75 | Dave Schultz, Phi | 76 | 472 |
| 1929–30 | Joe Lamb, Ott | 44 | 119 | 1975–76 | Steve Durbano, Pit-KC | 69 | 370 |
| 1930–31 | Harvey Rockburn, Det | 42 | 118 | 1976–77 | Dave Williams, Tor | 77 | 338 |
| 1931–32 | Red Dutton, NYA | 47 | 107 | 1977–78 | Dave Schultz, LA-Pit | 74 | 405 |
| 1932–33 | Red Horner, Tor | 48 | 144 | 1978–79 | Dave Williams, Tor | 77 | 298 |
| 1933–34 | Red Horner, Tor | 42 | 126 | 1979–80 | Jimmy Mann, Win | 72 | 287 |
| 1934–35 | Red Horner, Tor | 46 | 125 | 1980–81 | Dave Williams, Van | 77 | 343 |
| 1935–36 | Red Horner, Tor | 43 | 167 | 1981–82 | Paul Baxter, Pit | 76 | 409 |
| 1936–37 | Red Horner, Tor | 48 | 124 | 1982–83 | Randy Holt, Wsh | 70 | 275 |
| 1937–38 | Red Horner, Tor | 47 | 82 | 1983–84 | Chris Nilan, Mtl | 76 | 338 |
| 1938–39 | Red Horner, Tor | 48 | 85 | 1984–85 | Chris Nilan, Mtl | 77 | 358 |
| 1939–40 | Red Horner, Tor | 30 | 87 | 1985–86 | Joey Kocur, Det | 59 | 377 |
| 1940–41 | Jimmy Orlando, Det | 48 | 99 | 1986–87 | Tim Hunter, Cgy | 73 | 361 |
| 1941–42 | Pat Egan, Bklyn | 48 | 124 | 1987–88 | Bob Probert, Det | 74 | 398 |
| 1942–43 | Jimmy Orlando, Det | 40 | 89 | 1988–89 | Tim Hunter, Cgy | 75 | 375 |
| 1943–44 | Mike McMahon, Mtl | 42 | 98 | 1989–90 | Basil McRae, Min | 66 | 351 |
| 1944–45 | Pat Egan, Bos | 48 | 86 | 1990–91 | Rob Ray, Buf | 66 | 350 |
| 1945–46 | Jack Stewart, Det | 47 | 73 | 1991–92 | Mike Peluso, Chi | 63 | 408 |
| 1946–47 | Gus Mortson, Tor | 60 | 133 | 1992–93 | Marty McSorley, LA | 81 | 399 |
| 1947–48 | Bill Barilko, Tor | 57 | 147 | 1993–94 | Tie Domi, Win | 81 | 347 |
| 1948–49 | Bill Ezinicki, Tor | 52 | 145 | 1994–95 | Enrico Ciccone, TB | 41 | 225 |
| 1949–50 | Bill Ezinicki, Tor | 67 | 144 | 1995–96 | Matthew Barnaby, Buf | 73 | 335 |
| 1950–51 | Gus Mortson, Tor | 60 | 142 | 1996–97 | Gino Odjick, Van | 70 | 371 |
| 1951–52 | Gus Kyle, Bos | 69 | 127 | 1997–98 | Donald Brashear, Van | 77 | 372 |
| 1952–53 | Maurice Richard, Mtl | 70 | 112 | 1998–99 | Rob Ray, Buf | 76 | 261 |
| 1953–54 | Gus Mortson, Chi | 68 | 132 | 1999–00 | Denny Lambert, Atl | 73 | 219 |
| 1954–55 | Fern Flaman, Bos | 70 | 150 | 2000–01 | Matthew Barnaby, TB | 76 | 265 |
| 1955–56 | Lou Fontinato, NYR | 70 | 202 | 2001–02 | Peter Worrell, Fla | 79 | 354 |
| 1956–57 | Gus Mortson, Chi | 70 | 147 | 2002–03 | Jody Shelley, CBJ | 68 | 249 |
| 1957–58 | Lou Fontinato, NYR | 70 | 152 | 2003–04 | Sean Avery, LA | 76 | 261 |
| 1958–59 | Ted Lindsay, Chi | 70 | 184 | 2004–05 | No season | | |
| 1959–60 | Carl Brewer, Tor | 67 | 150 | 2005–06 | Sean Avery, LA | 75 | 257 |
| 1960–61 | Pierre Pilote, Chi | 70 | 165 | 2006–07 | Ben Eager, Phi | 63 | 233 |
| 1961–62 | Lou Fontinato, Mtl | 54 | 167 | 2007–08 | Daniel Carcillo, Phx | 57 | 324 |
| 1962–63 | Howie Young, Det | 64 | 273 | 2008–09 | Daniel Carcillo, Phi | 74 | 254 |
| 1963–64 | Vic Hadfield, NYR | 69 | 151 | | | | |

First played in 1947, this game started before the regular season and was used to match the defending Stanley Cup champions against the league All-Stars from other teams. In 1966 the game was moved to midseason, although there was no game that year. The format changed to a inter-conference showdown in 1969.

## Results

| Year | Site | Score | MVP | Attendance |
|---|---|---|---|---|
| 1947 | Toronto | All-Stars 4, Toronto 3 | None named | 14,169 |
| 1948 | Chicago | All-Stars 3, Toronto 1 | None named | 12,794 |
| 1949 | Toronto | All-Stars 3, Toronto 1 | None named | 13,541 |
| 1950 | Detroit | Detroit 7, All-Stars 1 | None named | 9,166 |
| 1951 | Toronto | 1st team 2, 2nd team 2 | None named | 11,469 |
| 1952 | Detroit | 1st team 1, 2nd team 1 | None named | 10,680 |
| 1953 | Montreal | All-Stars 3, Montreal 1 | None named | 14,153 |
| 1954 | Detroit | All-Stars 2, Detroit 2 | None named | 10,689 |
| 1955 | Detroit | Detroit 3, All-Stars 1 | None named | 10,111 |
| 1956 | Montreal | All-Stars 1, Montreal 1 | None named | 13,095 |
| 1957 | Montreal | All-Stars 5, Montreal 3 | None named | 13,003 |
| 1958 | Montreal | Montreal 6, All-Stars 3 | None named | 13,989 |
| 1959 | Montreal | Montreal 6, All-Stars 1 | None named | 13,818 |
| 1960 | Montreal | All-Stars 2, Montreal 1 | None named | 13,949 |
| 1961 | Chicago | All-Stars 3, Chicago 1 | None named | 14,534 |
| 1962 | Toronto | Toronto 4, All-Stars 1 | Eddie Shack, Tor | 14,236 |
| 1963 | Toronto | All-Stars 3, Toronto 3 | Frank Mahovlich, Tor | 14,034 |
| 1964 | Toronto | All-Stars 3, Toronto 2 | Jean Beliveau, Mtl | 14,232 |
| 1965 | Montreal | All-Stars 5, Montreal 2 | Gordie Howe, Det | 13,529 |
| 1967 | Montreal | Montreal 3, All-Stars 0 | Henri Richard, Mtl | 14,284 |
| 1968 | Toronto | Toronto 4, All-Stars 3 | Bruce Gamble, Tor | 15,753 |
| 1969 | Montreal | East 3, West 3 | Frank Mahovlich, Det | 16,260 |
| 1970 | St. Louis | East 4, West 1 | Bobby Hull, Chi | 16,587 |
| 1971 | Boston | West 2, East 1 | Bobby Hull, Chi | 14,790 |
| 1972 | Minnesota | East 3, West 2 | Bobby Orr, Bos | 15,423 |
| 1973 | NY Rangers | East 5, West 4 | Greg Polis, Pit | 16,986 |
| 1974 | Chicago | West 6, East 4 | Garry Unger, StL | 16,426 |
| 1975 | Montreal | Wales 7, Campbell 1 | Syl Apps Jr, Pit | 16,080 |
| 1976 | Philadelphia | Wales 7, Campbell 5 | Pete Mahovlich, Mtl | 16,436 |
| 1977 | Vancouver | Wales 4, Campbell 3 | Rick Martin, Buf | 15,607 |
| 1978 | Buffalo | Wales 3, Campbell 2 (OT) | Billy Smith, NYI | 16,433 |
| 1980 | Detroit | Wales 6, Campbell 3 | Reg Leach, Phi | 21,002 |
| 1981 | Los Angeles | Campbell 4, Wales 1 | Mike Liut, StL | 15,761 |
| 1982 | Washington | Wales 4, Campbell 2 | Mike Bossy, NYI | 18,130 |
| 1983 | NY Islanders | Campbell 9, Wales 3 | Wayne Gretzky, Edm | 15,230 |
| 1984 | New Jersey | Wales 7, Campbell 6 | Don Maloney, NYR | 18,939 |
| 1985 | Calgary | Wales 6, Campbell 4 | Mario Lemieux, Pit | 16,825 |
| 1986 | Hartford | Wales 4, Campbell 3 (OT) | Grant Fuhr, Edm | 15,100 |
| 1988 | St. Louis | Wales 6, Campbell 5 (OT) | Mario Lemieux, Pit | 17,878 |
| 1989 | Edmonton | Campbell 9, Wales 5 | Wayne Gretzky, LA | 17,503 |
| 1990 | Pittsburgh | Wales 12, Campbell 7 | Mario Lemieux, Pit | 16,236 |
| 1991 | Chicago | Campbell 11, Wales 5 | Vince Damphousse, Tor | 18,472 |
| 1992 | Philadelphia | Campbell 10, Wales 6 | Brett Hull, StL | 17,380 |
| 1993 | Montreal | Wales 16, Campbell 6 | Mike Gartner, NYR | 17,137 |
| 1994 | NY Rangers | East 9, West 8 | Mike Richter, NYR | 18,200 |
| 1996 | Boston | East 5, West 4 | Ray Bourque, Bos | 17,565 |
| 1997 | San Jose | East 11, West 7 | Mark Recchi, Mtl | 17,422 |
| 1998 | Vancouver | North America 8, World 7 | Teemu Selanne, Ana (World) | 18,422 |
| 1999 | Tampa Bay | North America 8, World 6 | Wayne Gretzky, NYR (N. America) | 19,758 |
| 2000 | Toronto | World 9, North America 4 | Pavel Bure, Fla (World) | 19,300 |
| 2001 | Denver | North America 14, World 12 | Bill Guerin, Bos (North America) | 18,646 |
| 2002 | Los Angeles | World 8, North America 5 | Eric Daze, Chi (North America) | 18,118 |
| 2003 | Sunrise, Fla. | West 6, East 5 (shootout) | Dany Heatley, Atl (East) | 19,250 |
| 2004 | St. Paul, Minn. | East 6, West 4 | Joe Sakic, Col (West) | 19,434 |
| 2005 | No game played† | | | |
| 2006 | No game played‡ | | | |
| 2007 | Dallas | West 12, East 9 | Daniel Briere, Buf (East) | 18,532 |
| 2008 | Atlanta | East 8, West 7 | Eric Staal, Car (East) | 18,644 |
| 2009 | Montreal | East 12, West 11 | Alexei Kovalev, Mtl (East) | 21,273 |

Note: The Challenge Cup, a series between the NHL All-Stars and the Soviet Union, was played instead of the All-Star Game in 1979. Eight years later, Rendez-Vous '87, a two-game series matching the Soviet Union and the NHL All-Stars, replaced the All-Star Game. The 1995 NHL All-Star game was cancelled due to a labor dispute. The 1998 NHL All-Star game, billed as a preview to the 1998 Winter Olympics in Nagano, Japan, matched North Amercian–born All-Stars and All-Stars born elsewhere. †In 2005, no game was played due to season-long lockout. ‡In 2006, no game was played due to the simultaneous occurence of the Winter Olympics.

Located in Toronto, the Hockey Hall of Fame was officially opened on August 26, 1961. The current chairman is William C. Hay. There are, at present, 306 members of the Hockey Hall of Fame—209 players, 84 "builders," and 14 on-ice officials. (One member, Alan Eagleson, resigned from the Hall March 25, 1998.) To be eligible, player and referee/linesman candidates should have been out of the game for three years, but the Hall's Board of Directors can make exceptions.

## Players

Sid Abel (1969)
Jack Adams (1959)
Glenn Anderson (2008)
Charles (Syl) Apps (1961)
George Armstrong (1975)
Irvine (Ace) Bailey (1975)
Donald H. (Dan) Bain (1945)
Hobey Baker (1945)
Bill Barber (1990)
Marty Barry (1965)
Andy Bathgate (1978)
Bobby Bauer (1996)
Jean Beliveau (1972)
Clint Benedict (1965)
Douglas Bentley (1964)
Max Bentley (1966)
Hector (Toe) Blake (1966)
Leo Boivin (1986)
Dickie Boon (1952)
Mike Bossy (1991)
Emile (Butch) Bouchard (1966)
Frank Boucher (1958)
George (Buck) Boucher (1960)
Ray Bourque (2004)
Johnny Bower (1976)
Russell Bowie (1945)
Frank Brimsek (1966)
Harry L. (Punch) Broadbent (1962)
Walter (Turk) Broda (1967)
John Bucyk (1981)
Billy Burch (1974)
Harry Cameron (1962)
Gerry Cheevers (1985)
Francis (King) Clancy (1958)
Aubrey (Dit) Clapper (1947)
Bobby Clarke (1987)
Sprague Cleghorn (1958)
Paul Coffey (2004)
Neil Colville (1967)
Charlie Conacher (1961)
Lionel Conacher (1994)
Roy Conacher (1998)
Alex Connell (1958)
Bill Cook (1952)
Fred (Bun) Cook (1995)
Arthur Coulter (1974)
Yvan Cournoyer (1982)
Bill Cowley (1968)
Samuel (Rusty) Crawford (1962)
Jack Darragh (1962)
Allan M. (Scotty) Davidson (1950)
Clarence (Hap) Day (1961)
Alex Delvecchio (1977)
Cy Denneny (1959)
Marcel Dionne (1992)
Gordie Drillon (1975)
Charles Drinkwater (1950)
Ken Dryden (1983)
Terrance (Dick) Duff (2006)
Woody Dumart (1992)
Thomas Dunderdale (1974)

Bill Durnan (1964)
Mervyn A. (Red) Dutton (1958)
Cecil (Babe) Dye (1970)
Phil Esposito (1984)
Tony Esposito (1988)
Arthur F. Farrell (1965)
Bernie Federko (2002)
Viacheslav Fetisov (2001)
Ferdinand (Fern) Flaman (1990)
Frank Foyston (1958)
Ron Francis (2007)
Frank Frederickson (1958)
Grant Fuhr (2003)
Bill Gadsby (1970)
Bob Gainey (1992)
Chuck Gardiner (1945)
Herb Gardiner (1958)
Jimmy Gardner (1962)
Mike Gartner (2001)
Bernie (Boom Boom) Geoffrion (1972)
Eddie Gerard (1945)
Ed Giacomin (1987)
Rod Gilbert (1982)
Clark Gillies (2002)
Hamilton (Billy) Gilmour (1962)
Frank (Moose) Goheen (1952)
Ebenezer R. (Ebbie) Goodfellow (1963)
Michel Goulet (1998)
Mike Grant (1950)
Wilfred (Shorty) Green (1962)
Jim Gregory (2007)
Wayne Gretzky (1999)
Si Griffis (1950)
George Hainsworth (1961)
Glenn Hall (1975)
Joe Hall (1961)
Doug Harvey (1973)
Dale Hawerchuk (2001)
George Hay (1958)
William (Riley) Hern (1962)
Bryan Hextall (1969)
Harry (Hap) Holmes (1972)
Tom Hooper (1962)
George (Red) Horner (1965)
Miles (Tim) Horton (1977)
Gordie Howe (1972)
Syd Howe (1965)
Harry Howell (1979)
Bobby Hull (1983)
Brett Hull (2009)
John (Bouse) Hutton (1962)
Harry M. Hyland (1962)
James (Dick) Irvin (1958)
Harvey (Busher) Jackson (1971)
Ernest (Moose) Johnson (1952)
Ivan (Ching) Johnson (1958)
Tom Johnson (1970)
Aurel Joliat (1947)
Gordon (Duke) Keats (1958)

## Players *(Cont.)*

Leonard (Red) Kelly (1969)
Ted (Teeder) Kennedy (1966)
Dave Keon (1986)
Valeri Kharlamov (2005)
Jari Kurri (2001)
Elmer Lach (1966)
Guy Lafleur (1988)
Pat LaFontaine (2003)
Edouard (Newsy) Lalonde (1950)
Rod Langway (2002)
Jacques Laperriere (1987)
Guy Lapointe (1993)
Edgar Laprade (1993)
Igor Larionov (2008)
Jean (Jack) Laviolette (1962)
Brian Leetch (2009)
Hugh Lehman (1958)
Jacques Lemaire (1984)
Mario Lemieux (1997)
Percy LeSueur (1961)
Herbert A. Lewis (1989)
Ted Lindsay (1966)
Harry Lumley (1980)
Lanny McDonald (1992)
Frank McGee (1945)
Billy McGimsie (1962)
George McNamara (1958)
Al MacInnis (2007)
Duncan (Mickey) MacKay (1952)
Frank Mahovlich (1981)
Joe Malone (1950)
Sylvio Mantha (1960)
Jack Marshall (1965)
Fred G. (Steamer) Maxwell (1962)
Mark Messier (2007)
Stan Mikita (1983)
Dicky Moore (1974)
Patrick (Paddy) Moran (1958)
Howie Morenz (1945)
Billy Mosienko (1965)
Joe Mullen (2000)
Larry Murphy (2004)
Cam Neely (2005)
Frank Nighbor (1947)
Reg Noble (1962)
Herbert (Buddy) O'Connor (1988)
Harry Oliver (1967)
Bert Olmstead (1985)
Bobby Orr (1979)
Bernie Parent (1984)
Brad Park (1988)
Lester Patrick (1947)
Lynn Patrick (1980)
Gilbert Perreault (1990)
Tommy Phillips (1945)
Pierre Pilote (1975)
Didier (Pit) Pitre (1962)
Jacques Plante (1978)
Denis Potvin (1991)
Walter (Babe) Pratt (1966)
Joe Primeau (1963)
Marcel Pronovost (1978)
Bob Pulford (1991)
Harvey Pulford (1945)

Hubert (Bill) Quackenbush (1976)
Frank Rankin (1961)
Jean Ratelle (1985)
Claude (Chuck) Rayner (1973)
Kenneth Reardon (1966)
Henri Richard (1979)
Maurice (Rocket) Richard (1961)
George Richardson (1950)
Gordon Roberts (1971)
Larry Robinson (1995)
Luc Robitaille (2009)
Art Ross (1945)
Patrick Roy (2006)
Blair Russel (1965)
Ernest Russell (1965)
Jack Ruttan (1962)
Borje Salming (1996)
Denis Savard (2000)
Serge Savard (1986)
Terry Sawchuk (1971)
Fred Scanlan (1965)
Milt Schmidt (1961)
Dave (Sweeney) Schriner (1962)
Earl Seibert (1963)
Oliver Seibert (1961)
Eddie Shore (1947)
Steve Shutt (1993)
Albert C. (Babe) Siebert (1964)
Harold (Bullet Joe) Simpson (1962)
Daryl Sittler (1989)
Alfred E. Smith (1962)
Billy Smith (1993)
Clint Smith (1991)
Reginald (Hooley) Smith (1972)
Thomas Smith (1973)
Allan Stanley (1981)
Russell (Barney) Stanley (1962)
Peter Stastny (1998)
Scott Stevens (2007)
John (Black Jack) Stewart (1964)
Nels Stewart (1962)
Bruce Stuart (1961)
Hod Stuart (1945)
Frederic (Cyclone) (O.B.E.)
    Taylor (1947)
Cecil R. (Tiny) Thompson (1959)
Vladislav Tretiak (1989)
Harry J. Trihey (1950)
Bryan Trottier (1997)
Norm Ullman (1982)
Georges Vezina (1945)
Jack Walker (1960)
Marty Walsh (1962)
Harry Watson (1994)
Harry E. Watson (1962)
Ralph (Cooney) Weiland (1971)
Harry Westwick (1962)
Fred Whitcroft (1962)
Gordon (Phat) Wilson (1962)
Lorne (Gump) Worsley (1980)
Roy Worters (1969)
Steve Yzerman (2009)

Note: Year of election to the Hall of Fame is in parentheses after the member's name.

## Builders

Charles Adams (1960)
Weston W. Adams (1972)
Thomas (Frank) Ahearn (1962)
John (Bunny) Ahearne (1977)
Montagu Allan (C.V.O.) (1945)
Keith Allen (1992)
Al Arbour (1996)
Harold Ballard (1977)
David Bauer (1989)
John Bickell (1978)
Scott Bowman (1991)
Herb Brooks (2006)
George V. Brown (1961)
Walter A. Brown (1962)
Frank Buckland (1975)
Walter L. Bush (2000)
Jack Butterfield (1980)
Frank Calder (1947)
Angus D. Campbell (1964)
Clarence Campbell (1966)
Joe Cattarinich (1977)
Ed Chynoweth (2008)
Bob Cole (1996, Media)
Murray Costello (2005)
Joseph (Leo) Dandurand (1963)
Francis Dilio (1964)
George S. Dudley (1958)
James A. Dunn (1968)
*Robert Alan Eagleson (1989–98)
Cliff Fletcher (2004)
Emile Francis (1982)
Jack Gibson (1976)
Tommy Gorman (1963)
Frank Griffiths (1993)
William Hanley (1986)
Charles Hay (1974)
James C. Hendy (1968)
Foster Hewitt (1965)
William Hewitt (1947)
Harley Hotchkiss (2006)
Fred J. Hume (1962)
Mike Ilitch (2003)
George (Punch) Imlach (1984)
Tommy Ivan (1974)
William M. Jennings (1975)
Bob Johnson (1992)
Gordon W. Juckes (1979)
John Kilpatrick (1960)
Brian Kilrea (2003)
Seymour Knox III (1993)

Lou Lamoriello (2009)
George Leader (1969)
Robert LeBel (1970)
Thomas F. Lockhart (1965)
Paul Loicq (1961)
Frederic McLaughlin (1963)
John Mariucci (1985)
Frank Mathers (1992)
John (Jake) Milford (1984)
Hartland Molson (1973)
Scotty Morrison (1999)
Mngr. Athol (Pere) Murray (1998)
Roger Neilson (2002)
Francis Nelson (1947)
Bruce A. Norris (1969)
James Norris, Sr. (1958)
James D. Norris (1962)
William M. Northey (1947)
John O'Brien (1962)
Brian O'Neill (1994)
Fred Page (1993)
Craig Patrick (1996)
Frank Patrick (1958)
Allan W. Pickard (1958)
Rudy Pilous (1985)
Norman (Bud) Poile (1990)
Samuel Pollock (1978)
Donat Raymond (1958)
John Robertson (1947)
Claude C. Robinson (1947)
Philip D. Ross (1976)
Gunther Sabetzki (1995)
Glen Sather (1997)
Frank J. Selke (1960)
Harry Sinden (1983)
Frank D. Smith (1962)
Conn Smythe (1958)
Edward M. Snider (1988)
Lord Stanley of Preston (1945)
James T. Sutherland (1947)
Anatoli V. Tarasov (1974)
Bill Torrey (1995)
Lloyd Turner (1958)
William Tutt (1978)
Carl Potter Voss (1974)
Fred C. Waghorn (1961)
Arthur Wirtz (1971)
Bill Wirtz (1976)
John A. Ziegler, Jr. (1987)

## Referees/Linesmen

Neil Armstrong (1991)
John Ashley (1981)
William L. Chadwick (1964)
John D'Amico (1993)
Chaucer Elliott (1961)
George Hayes (1988)
Robert W. Hewitson (1963)
Fred J. (Mickey) Ion (1961)

Matt Pavelich (1987)
Mike Rodden (1962)
Ray Scapinello (2008)
J. Cooper Smeaton (1961)
Roy (Red) Storey (1967)
Frank Udvari (1973)
Andy Van Hellemond (1999)

*Eagleson resigned from Hall March 25, 1998.

# Tennis

Roger Federer regained his World No. 1 ranking in 2009, winning the French and Wimbledon singles titles

# Return to Form

In 2009, Roger Federer and Serena Williams reasserted their dominance with two Grand Slam victories apiece, but both suffered public meltdowns at the U.S. Open

## BY B.J. SCHECTER

DRAMA. HISTORY. MELTDOWNS. Rivalries. When tennis historians look back on 2009, they'll recall a year in which the sport regained the headlines and—for one year at least—broke from the mold of boring and predictable. Even the ultra-conservative All England Club unveiled a retractable roof on Centre Court. Despite the way the year began and ended (with losses in Grand Slam finals) 2009 still belonged to Roger Federer. That's because Federer finally overcame the clay and won his first French Open (albeit with Rafael Nadal injured) and surpassed Pete Sampras' career record with his 15th Grand Slam title after an epic five-set victory over Andy Roddick at Wimbledon.

Like Sampras, Federer has been criticized for his lack of emotion and people have often called him a robot, given the precision with which he puts away opponents and his ability to effortlessly dominate in every facet of the game. But during his record-breaking Wimbledon run, Federer showed another side: brash, cocky and self-assured. Federer arrived in England by private jet, entered the court wearing a Rolex and donned gold-accented sneakers with his initials on the side. When he finally beat Roddick in the final he slipped on a warmup jacket with the gold number 15 etched onto the back.

Given the way he plays, Federer can be forgiven for the occasional bravado. For when he steps between the lines, his game is a thing of beauty. He has proven that he can win with his serve, from the baseline and at the net. He can win easily and grind it out in five-setters. But most importantly, Federer proved that he is human. Following his defeat to Nadal in the 2008 Wimledon final, Federer lost to Nadal again in the 2009 Australian Open final and for the first time in his career showed self-doubt. Nadal had finally gotten into his head on the court and Federer—who was tentative, almost diffident during the match—broke down. "God, it's killing me," Federer said after the match, unable to finish his thought.

But like all champions, Federer quickly composed himself and regained his winning moxie. In the Wimbledon final, Roddick played as well as you could possibly play, yet still lost in five sets, including 16–14 in the fifth when it became a match of wills. "[Federer] gets credit for a lot of things," said Roddick. "But not a lot of the time is [for] how many matches he kind of digs deep and toughs it out."

Serena and Venus Williams toughed it out throughout the year and continue to carve their names in women's tennis history. Serena won the Australian in blistering heat and then boldly said, "You never should be surprised by anything I do."

Here's what we have come to expect from Serena (and to some extent, Venus): In Grand Slams she is the most fierce competitor in the game; during other tournaments she doesn't seem to care. At Wimbledon, Venus and Serena wiped away the field with

neither Williams coming close to losing a set. The sisters met in the final, where Serena beat her older sister, 7–6, 6–2, to win her 11th Grand Slam title. It was the eighth time this decade a Williams sister has won Wimbledon.

After the match, Serena wore a T-shirt with the message "Are you looking at my titles?" on the front, a jab at the WTA rankings in which Dinara Safina (who Serena embarrassed at Wimbledon, 6–1, 6–0) was No. 1 though Safina has yet to win a Grand Slam. Serena has never been afraid to rock the establishment, but rarely has she crossed the line.

But after cruising to the U.S. Open semifinal Serena lost her cool in a despicable public display. Down one set and trailing 5–6 in the third against Kim Clijsters, Williams was called for a foot fault on a second serve giving Clijsters a match point. It was a questionable call, especially at that point in the match, and Williams went berserk. "You'd better be f------ right," Williams screamed at the line judge, waving her racket in the air. "You don't f------ know me. I swear to God I'm going to take this ball and shove it down your f------ throat."

The linesperson went to the chair umpire and after a brief discussion Williams was assessed a point penalty for unsportsmanlike conduct (she had been warned after throwing her racket earlier), thus ending

**A resurgent Serena Williams beat World No. 1 Dinara Safina to take the Australian Open and then defeated sister Venus to win Wimbledon.**

the match. The incident unfortunately overshadowed a brilliant tournament for Clijsters, who came back from a 27-month absence after giving birth to her daughter, Jada. Williams' outburst aside, the Open shone on the women, particularly 17-year-old American Melanie Oudin who was unseeded and captivated audiences by making it to the quarterfinals. "I've gone from a normal tennis player to almost anyone in the U.S. knowing who I am now," she said.

Everybody in the world knows Federer, but 20-year-old Argentine Juan Martin del Potro burst into the spotlight in New York by beating Nadal in the U.S. Open semifinal, followed by a five-set victory over Federer in the final. Del Potro showed remarkable poise and maturity, while Federer, much like Williams, lost his cool at one point in the match and cursed at the chair umpire.

But Federer's loss in the U.S. Open final couldn't take away from the historic year he had. Even if he doesn't win another Slam (which is highly unlikely considering he's made an astonishing 22 consecutive Grand Slam finals) Federer will go down in history as the greatest to ever play the game.

## 2009 Grand Slam Champions

# Australian Open

### Men's Singles

| | Winner | Runner-up | Score |
|---|---|---|---|
| Quarterfinals | Rafael Nadal ..........................Gilles Simon | | 6–2, 7–5, 7–5 |
| | Fernando Verdasco ................Jo-Wilfried Tsonga | | 7–6 (7–2), 3–6, 6–3, 6–2 |
| | Roger Federer........................Juan Martin del Potro | | 6–3, 6–0, 6–0 |
| | Andy Roddick .......................Novak Djokovic† | | 6–7 (3–7), 6–4, 6–2, 2–1 |
| Semifinals | Rafael Nadal ..........................Fernando Verdasco | | 6–7 (4–7), 6–4, 7–6 (6–2) 6–7 (1–7), 6–4 |
| | Roger Federer........................Andy Roddick | | 6–2, 7–5, 7–5 |
| Final | Rafael Nadal ..........................Roger Federer | | 7–5, 3–6, 7–6 (7–3), 3–6, 6–2 |

† retired match in fourth set due to heat stress

### Women's Singles

| | Winner | Runner-up | Score |
|---|---|---|---|
| Quarterfinals | Serena Williams......................Svetlana Kuznetsova | | 7–5, 5–7, 6–1 |
| | Vera Zvonareva ......................Marion Bartoli | | 6–3, 6–0 |
| | Dinara Safina .........................Jelena Dokic | | 6–4, 4–6, 6–4 |
| | Elena Dementieva ..................Carla Suarez Navarro | | 6–2, 6–2 |
| Semifinals | Serena Williams......................Elena Dementieva | | 6–3, 6–4 |
| | Dinara Safina .........................Vera Zvonareva | | 6–3, 7–6 (7–4) |
| Final | Serena Williams......................Dinara Safina | | 6–0, 6–3 |

### Doubles

| | Winner | Runner-up | Score |
|---|---|---|---|
| Men's Final | Bob Bryan/............................Mahesh Bhupathi/ Mike Bryan Mark Knowles | | 2–6, 7–5, 6–0 |
| Women's Final | Serena Williams/.....................Daniela Hantuchova/ Venus Williams Ai Sugiyama | | 6–3, 6–3 |
| Mixed Final | Sania Mirza/ ..........................Nathalie Dechy/ Mahesh Bhupathi Andy Ram | | 6–3, 6–1 |

# French Open

### Men's Singles

| | Winner | Runner-up | Score |
|---|---|---|---|
| Quarterfinals | Roger Federer........................Gael Monfils | | 7–6 (8–6), 6–2, 6–4 |
| | Fernando Gonzalez ................Andy Murray | | 6–3, 3–6, 6–0, 6–4 |
| | Juan Martin del Potro..............Tommy Robredo | | 6–3, 6–4, 6–2 |
| | Robin Soderling .....................Nikolay Davydenko | | 6–1, 6–3, 6–1 |
| Semifinals | Roger Federer........................Juan Martin del Potro | | 3–6, 7–6 (7–2), 2–6, 6–1, 6–4 |
| | Robin Soderling .....................Fernando Gonzalez | | 6–3, 7–5, 5–7, 4–6, 6–4 |
| Final | Roger Federer........................Robin Soderling | | 6–1, 7–6 (7–1), 6–4 |

### Women's Singles

| | Winner | Runner-up | Score |
|---|---|---|---|
| Quarterfinals | Svetlana Kuznetsova .............Serena Williams | | 7–6 (7–3), 5–7, 7–5 |
| | Dinara Safina .........................Victoria Azarenka | | 1–6, 6–4, 6–2 |
| | Dominika Cibulkova ................Maria Sharapova | | 6–0, 6–2 |
| | Samantha Stosur....................Sorana Cirstea | | 6–1, 6–3 |
| Semifinals | Dinara Safina .........................Dominika Cibulkova | | 6–3, 6–3 |
| | Svetlana Kuznetsova .............Samantha Stosur | | 6–4, 6–7 (5–7), 6–3 |
| Final | Svetlana Kuznetsova .............Dinara Safina | | 6–4, 6–2 |

### Doubles

| | Winner | Runner-Up | Score |
|---|---|---|---|
| Men's Final | Lukas Dlouhy/ .......................Wesley Moodie/ Leander Paes Dick Norman | | 3–6, 6–3, 6–2 |
| Women's Final | Anabel Medina Garrigues/......Victoria Azarenka/ Virginia Ruano Pascual Elena Vesnina | | 6–1, 6–1 |
| Mixed Final | Liezel Huber/..........................Vania King/ Bob Bryan Marcelo Melo | | 5–7, 7–6 (7–5), 10–7 |

## Wimbledon

### Men's Singles

| | Winner | Runner-Up | Score |
|---|---|---|---|
| Quarterfinals | Roger Federer | Ivo Karlovic | 6–3, 7–5, 7–6 (7–3) |
| | Andy Murray | Juan Carlos Ferrero | 7–5, 6–3, 6–2 |
| | Andy Roddick | Lleyton Hewitt | 6–3, 6–7 (10–12), 7–6 (7–1), 4–6, 6–4 |
| | Tommy Haas | Novak Djokovic | 7–5, 7–6 (8–6), 4–6, 6–3 |
| Semifinals | Roger Federer | Tommy Haas | 7–6 (7–3), 7–5, 6–3 |
| | Andy Roddick | Andy Murray | 6–4, 4–6, 7–6 (9–7), 7–6 (7–5) |
| Final | Roger Federer | Andy Roddick | 5–7, 7–6 (8–6), 7–6 (7–5), 3–6, 16–14 |

### Women's Singles

| | Winner | Runner-Up | Score |
|---|---|---|---|
| Quarterfinals | Dinara Safina | Sabine Lisicki | 6–7 (5–7), 6–4, 6–1 |
| | Serena Williams | Victoria Azarenka | 6–2, 6–3 |
| | Elena Dementieva | Francesca Schiavone | 6–2, 6–2 |
| | Venus Williams | Agnieszka Radwanska | 6–1, 6–2 |
| Semifinals | Serena Williams | Elena Dementieva | 6–7 (4–7), 7–5, 8–6 |
| | Venus Williams | Dinara Safina | 6–1, 6–0 |
| Final | Serena Williams | Venus Williams | 7–6 (7–3), 6–2 |

### Doubles

| | Winner | Runner-Up | Score |
|---|---|---|---|
| Men's Final | Daniel Nestor/ Nenad Zimonjic | Bob Bryan/ Mike Bryan | 7–6 (9–7), 6–7 (3–7), 7–6 (7–3), 6–3 |
| Women's Final | Serena Williams/ Venus Williams | Rennae Stubbs/ Samantha Stosur | 7–6 (7–4), 6–4 |
| Mixed Final | Mark Knowles/ Anna-Lena Groenefeld | Leander Paes/ Cara Black | 7–5, 6–3 |

## U.S. Open

### Men's Singles

| | Winner | Runner-Up | Score |
|---|---|---|---|
| Quarterfinals | Juan Martin del Potro | Marin Cilic | 4–6, 6–3, 6–2, 6–1 |
| | Rafael Nadal | Fernando Gonzalez | 7–6 (7–4), 7–6 (7–2), 6–0 |
| | Roger Federer | Robin Soderling | 6–0, 6–3, 6–7 (6–8), 7–6 (8–6) |
| | Novak Djokovic | Fernando Verdasco | 7–6 (7–2), 1–6, 7–5, 6–2 |
| Semifinals | Juan Martin del Potro | Rafael Nadal | 6–2, 6–2, 6–2 |
| | Roger Federer | Novak Djokovic | 7–6 (7–3), 7–5, 7–5 |
| Final | Juan Martin del Potro | Roger Federer | 3–6, 7–6 (7–5), 4–6, 7–6 (7–4), 6–2 |

### Women's Singles

| | Winner | Runner-Up | Score |
|---|---|---|---|
| Quarterfinals | Kim Clijsters | Na Lie | 6–2, 6–4 |
| | Serena Williams | Flavia Pennetta | 6–4, 6–3 |
| | Caroline Wozniacki | Melanie Oudin | 6–2, 6–2 |
| | Yanina Wickmayer | Kateryna Bondarenko | 7–5, 6–4 |
| Semifinals | Kim Clijsters | Serena Williams† | 6–4, 7–5 |
| | Caroline Wozniacki | Yanina Wickmayer | 6–3, 6–3 |
| Final | Kim Clijsters | Caroline Wozniacki | 7–5, 6–3 |

† lost match point due to penalty for misconduct

### Doubles

| | Winner | Runner-Up | Score |
|---|---|---|---|
| Men's Final | Lukas Dlouhy/ Leander Paes | Mark Knowles/ Mahesh Bhupathi | 3–6, 6–3, 6–2 |
| Women's Final | Serena Williams/ Venus Williams | Cara Black/ Liezel Huber | 6–2, 6–2 |
| Mixed Final | Carly Gullickson/ Travis Parrott | Cara Black/ Leander Paes | 6–2, 6–4 |

## Men's Tour (Late 2008 through September 14, 2009)

| Date | Tournament | Site | Singles Winner | Surface | Total Purse |
|---|---|---|---|---|---|
| Oct 5 | Japan Open | Tokyo, Japan | Tomas Berdych | Outdoor Hard | $869,000 |
| Oct 5 | Moselle Open | Metz, France | Dmitry Tursunov | Indoor Hard | €370,000 |
| Oct 12 | Kremlin Cup | Moscow, Russia | Igor Kunitsyn | Indoor Hard | $1,049,000 |
| Oct 12 | BA-CA Trophy | Vienna, Austria | Philipp Petzschner | Indoor Hard | €674,000 |
| Oct 12 | Stockholm Open | Stockholm, Sweden | David Nalbandian | Indoor Hard | €713,000 |
| Oct 19 | Madrid Masters | Madrid, Spain | Andy Murray | Indoor Hard | €2,270,000 |
| Oct 26 | Swiss Indoor | Basel, Switzerland | Roger Federer | Indoor Hard | €891,000 |
| Oct 26 | Lyon Grand Prix | Lyon, France | Robin Soderling | Indoor Carpet | €713,000 |
| Oct 26 | St. Petersburg Open | St. Petersburg, Russia | Andy Murray | Indoor Carpet | $1,049,000 |
| Nov 2 | Paris Masters | Paris, France | Jo Wilfried Tsonga | Indoor Hard | €2,270,000 |
| Nov 16 | China Masters | Shanghai, China | Novak Djokovic | Indoor Hard | $3,800,000 |
| Jan 11 | Qatar Open | Doha, Qatar | Andy Murray | Outdoor Hard | $1,110,250 |
| Jan 11 | Brisbane International | Brisbane, Australia | Radek Stepanek | Outdoor Hard | $484,750 |
| Jan 11 | Chennai Open | Chennai, India | Marin Cilic | Outdoor Hard | $450,000 |
| Jan 18 | Heineken Open | Auckland, New Zealand | Juan Martin del Potro | Outdoor Hard | $480,750 |
| Jan 18 | Medibank International | Sydney, Australia | David Nalbandian | Outdoor Hard | $484,750 |
| Feb 1 | Australian Open | Melbourne, Australia | Rafael Nadal | Outdoor Hard | A$10,712,240 |
| Feb 8 | SA Open | Johannesburg, S. Africa | Jo Wilfried Tsonga | Outdoor Hard | $500,000 |
| Feb 14 | Brasil Open | Costa de Sauipe, Brazil | Tommy Robredo | Outdoor Clay | $562,500 |
| Feb 15 | SAP Open | San Jose, California | Radek Stepanek | Indoor Hard | $600,000 |
| Feb 15 | ABM/Amro | Rotterdam, Neth. | Andy Murray | Indoor Hard | €1,445,000 |
| Feb 22 | Regions Championships | Memphis, Tennessee | Andy Roddick | Indoor Hard | $1,226,500 |
| Feb 22 | Telmex Copa | Buenos Aires, Argentina | Tommy Robredo | Outdoor Clay | $600,000 |
| Feb 22 | Open 13 | Marseille, France | Jo Wilfried Tsonga | Indoor Hard | €576,000 |
| Feb 28 | Dubai Open | Dubai, U.A.E. | Novak Djokovic | Outdoor Hard | $2,233,000 |
| Feb 28 | Mexican Open | Acapulco, Mexico | Nicolas Almagro | Outdoor Clay | $1,226,500 |
| Mar 1 | Delray Beach Int'l | Delray Beach, Fla. | Mardy Fish | Outdoor Hard | $500,000 |
| Mar 22 | BNP Paribas Open | Indian Wells, Calif. | Rafael Nadal | Outdoor Hard | $4,500,000 |
| Apr 5 | Sony Ericsson Open | Miami, Fla. | Andy Murray | Outdoor Hard | $4,500,000 |
| Apr 12 | Grand Prix Hassan II | Casablanca, Morocco | Juan Carlos Ferrero | Outdoor Clay | €450,000 |
| Apr 12 | US Clay Champ'ship | Houston, Texas | Lleyton Hewitt | Outdoor Clay | $500,000 |
| Apr 19 | Monte Carlo Masters | Monte Carlo, Monaco | Rafael Nadal | Outdoor Clay | €2,750,000 |
| Apr 26 | Barcelona Open | Barcelona, Spain | Rafael Nadal | Outdoor Clay | €1,995,000 |
| May 3 | Italia International | Rome, Italy | Rafael Nadal | Outdoor Clay | €2,750,000 |
| May 10 | Estoril Open | Estoril, Portugal | Albert Montanes | Outdoor Clay | €450,000 |
| May 10 | BMW Open | Munich, Germany | Tomas Berdych | Outdoor Clay | €450,000 |
| May 10 | Serbia Open | Belgrade, Serbia | Novak Djokovic | Outdoor Clay | €450,000 |
| May 17 | Madrid Masters | Madrid, Spain | Roger Federer | Outdoor Clay | €3,700,000 |
| May 23 | Austrian Open | Kitzbuhel, Austria | Guillermo Lopez | Outdoor Clay | €450,000 |
| June 7 | French Open | Paris, France | Roger Federer | Outdoor Clay | €16,150,460 |
| June 14 | Gerry Weber Open | Halle, Germany | Tommy Haas | Outdoor Grass | €750,000 |
| June 14 | AEGON Championships | London, England | Andy Murray | Outdoor Grass | €750,000 |
| June 20 | Ordina Open | 's-Hertogenbosch, Netherlands | Benjamin Becker | Outdoor Grass | €450,000 |
| June 20 | AEGON International | Eastbourne, England | Dmitry Tursunov | Outdoor Grass | £450,000 |
| July 5 | Wimbledon | Wimbledon, England | Roger Federer | Outdoor Grass | £12,550,000 |
| July 12 | Hall of Fame Champ's | Newport, R.I. | Rajeev Ram | Outdoor Grass | $500,000 |
| July 19 | Swedish Open | Bastad, Sweden | Robin Soderling | Outdoor Clay | €450,000 |
| July 19 | Mercedes Cup | Stuttgart, Germany | Jeremy Chardy | Outdoor Clay | €450,000 |
| July 26 | RCA Championship | Indianapolis, Indiana | Robby Ginepri | Outdoor Hard | $519,000 |
| July 26 | German Open | Hamburg, Germany | Nikolay Davydenko | Outdoor Clay | €1,115,000 |
| Aug 2 | Allianz Suisse Open | Gstaad, Switzerland | Thomaz Bellucci | Outdoor Clay | €450,000 |
| Aug 2 | Los Angeles Open | Los Angeles | Sam Querrey | Outdoor Hard | $630,500 |
| Aug 2 | Croatia Open | Umag, Croatia | Nikolay Davydenko | Outdoor Clay | €450,000 |
| Aug 9 | Legg Mason Classic | Washington, D.C. | Juan Martin del Potro | Outdoor Hard | $1,402,000 |
| Aug 16 | Rogers Cup | Toronto, Canada | Andy Murray | Outdoor Hard | $3,000,000 |
| Aug 23 | Western & Southern | Cincinnati, Ohio | Roger Federer | Outdoor Hard | $3,000,000 |
| Aug 29 | Pilot Pen Championship | New Haven, Conn. | Fernando Verdasco | Outdoor Hard | $750,000 |
| Sept 14 | U.S. Open | New York City | Juan Martin del Potro | Outdoor Hard | $14,912,000 |

### Women's Tour (Late 2008 through September 14, 2009)

| Date | Tournament | Site | Winner | Runner-Up | Total Purse |
|---|---|---|---|---|---|
| Sep 28 | China Open | Beijing, China | Jelena Jankovic | Svetlana Kuznetsova | $600,000 |
| Oct 5 | Porsche Grand Prix | Stuttgart, Germany | Jelena Jankovic | Nadia Petrova | $650,000 |
| Oct 5 | Japan Open | Tokyo, Japan | Caroline Wozniacki | Kaia Kanepi | $175,000 |
| Oct 12 | Ladies Kremlin Cup | Moscow, Russia | Jelena Jankovic | Vera Zvonareva | $1,340,000 |
| Oct 13 | Zurich Open | Zurich, Switzerland | Justine Henin | Tatiana Golovin | $600,000 |
| Oct 26 | Generali Ladies Open | Linz, Austia | Ana Ivanonic | Vera Zvonareva | $600,000 |
| Nov 2 | Bell Challenge | Quebec City, Can. | Nadia Petrova | Bethanie Mattek | $175,000 |
| Nov 9 | Tour Championships | Doha, Qatar | Venus Williams | Vera Zvonareva | $4,550,000 |
| Jan 10 | ASB Classic | Auckland, N.Z. | Elena Dementieva | Elena Vesnina | $220,000 |
| Jan 11 | Brisbane Int'l | Brisbane, Australia | Victoria Azarenka | Marion Bartoli | $220,000 |
| Jan 16 | Medibank Int'l | Sydney, Australia | Elena Dementieva | Dinara Safina | $600,000 |
| Jan 16 | Hobart Int'l | Hobart, Australia | Petra Kvitova | Iveta Benesova | $220,000 |
| Feb 1 | Australian Open | Melbourne, Australia | Serena Williams | Dinara Safina | $7,262,963 |
| Feb 15 | GDF Suez Open | Paris, France | Amelie Mauresmo | Elena Dementieva | $700,000 |
| Feb 15 | Pattaya Open | Patttaya, Thailand | Vera Zvonareva | Sania Mirza | $220,000 |
| Feb 21 | Dubai Championships | Dubai, U.A.E. | Venus Williams | Virginie Razzano | $2,000,000 |
| Feb 21 | Regions Championships | Memphis, Tenn. | Victoria Azarenka | Caroline Wozniacki | $220,000 |
| Feb 22 | Copa Colsanitas | Bogota, Colombia | Maria M. Sanchez | Gisela Dulko | $220,000 |
| Feb 28 | Mexican Open | Acapulco, Mexico | Venus Williams | Flavia Pennetta | $220,000 |
| Mar 8 | Monterrey Open | Monterrey, Mexico | Marion Bartoli | Na Li | $220,000 |
| Mar 22 | BNP Paribas Open | Indian Wells, Calif. | Vera Zvonareva | Ana Ivanovic | $4,500,000 |
| Apr 5 | Sony Ericsson Open | Miami, Florida | Victoria Azarenka | Serena Williams | $4,500,000 |
| Apr 12 | Andalucia Int'l | Marbella, Spain | Jelena Jankovic | Carla Suarez Navarro | $500,000 |
| Apr 12 | MPS Championships | Ponta Vedra Beach, Fla. | Caroline Wozniacki | Aleksandra Wozniack | $220,000 |
| Apr 19 | Family Circle Cup | Charleston, S.C. | Sabine Lisicki | Caroline Wozniacki | $1,000,000 |
| Apr 19 | Barcelona Open | Barcelona, Spain | Roberta Vinci | Maria Kirilenko | $220,000 |
| May 2 | Morocco Grand Prix | Fez, Morocco | Medina Garrigues | Alisa Kleybanova | $220,000 |
| May 3 | Porsche Grand Prix | Stuttgart, Germany | Svetlana Kuznetsova | Dinara Safina | $700,000 |
| May 9 | Italian International | Rome, Italy | Dinara Safina | Svetlana Kuznetsova | $2,000,000 |
| May 9 | Estoril Open | Estoril, Portugal | Yanina Wickmayer | Ekaterina Makarova | $220,000 |
| May 17 | Madrid Open | Madrid, Spain | Dinara Safina | Caroline Wozniacki | $3,500,000 |
| May 23 | Warsaw Open | Warsaw, Poland | Alexandra Dulgheru | Alona Bondarenko | $600,000 |
| May 23 | Strasbourg Int'l | Strasbourg, France | Aravane Rezai | Lucie Hradecka | $220,000 |
| June 6 | French Open | Paris, France | Svetlana Kuznetsova | Dinara Safina | $10,009,638 |
| June 14 | AEGON Classic | Birmingham, England | Magd. Rybarikova | Na Li | $220,000 |
| June 20 | AEGON Int'l | Eastbourne, England | Caroline Wozniacki | Virginie Razzano | $600,000 |
| June 20 | Ordina Open | 's-Hertogenbosch, Neth. | Tam. Tanasugarn | Yanina Wickmayer | $220,000 |
| July 4 | Wimbledon | Wimbledon, England | Serena Williams | Venus Williams | $9,487,267 |
| July 11 | Swedish Open | Bastad, Sweden | Maria M. Sanchez | Caroline Wozniacki | $220,000 |
| July 12 | GDF Suez Grand Prix | Budapest, Hungary | Agnes Szavay | Patty Schnyder | $220,000 |
| July 19 | Palermo International | Palermo, Italy | Flavia Pennetta | Sara Errani | $220,000 |
| July 19 | Prague Open | Prague, Czech Rep. | Sybille Bammer | Francesca Schiavone | $220,000 |
| July 26 | Slovenia Open | Portoroz, Slovenia | Dinara Safina | Sara Errani | $220,000 |
| July 26 | Gastein International | Bad Gastein, Austria | Andrea Petkovic | Ioana Olaru | $220,000 |
| Aug 2 | Bank of the West Classic | Stanford, California | Marion Bartoli | Venus Wiliams | $700,000 |
| Aug 2 | Istanbul Cup | Istanbul, Turkey | Vera Dushevina | Lucie Hradecka | $220,000 |
| Aug 9 | L.A. Championships | Los Angeles, Calif.. | Flavia Pennetta | Samantha Stosur | $700,000 |
| Aug 16 | Western & Southern Open | Cincinnati, Ohio | Jelena Jankovic | Dinara Safina | $2,000,000 |
| Aug 16 | Rogers Cup | Toronto, Canada | Elena Dementieva | Maria Sharapova | $2,000,000 |
| Aug 29 | Pilot Pen Int'l | New Haven, Conn. | Caroline Wozniacki | Elena Vesnina | $600,000 |
| Sept 13 | U.S. Open | New York City | Kim Clijsters | Caroline Wozniacki | $9,756,000 |

## 2008 Final Season Singles Points Leaders

### Men

| Rank | Player | Country | Points | Events |
|---|---|---|---|---|
| 1. | Rafael Nadal | ESP | 6675 | 19 |
| 2. | Roger Federer | SUI | 5305 | 19 |
| 3. | Novak Djokovic | SRB | 5295 | 19 |
| 4. | Andy Murray | GBR | 3720 | 23 |
| 5. | Nikolay Davydenko | RUS | 2715 | 23 |
| 6. | Jo-Wilfried Tsonga | FRA | 2050 | 21 |
| 7. | Gilles Simon | FRA | 1980 | 29 |
| 8. | Andy Roddick | USA | 1970 | 23 |
| 9. | Juan Martin del Potro | ARG | 1945 | 22 |
| 10. | James Blake | USA | 1975 | 23 |

Note: Compiled by the ATP Tour, through the 2008 season.

### Women

| Rank | Player | Country | Points |
|---|---|---|---|
| 1. | Jelena Jankovic | SRB | 4786 |
| 2. | Dinara Safina | RUS | 3823 |
| 3. | Serena Williams | USA | 3681 |
| 4. | Elena Dementieva | RUS | 3400 |
| 5. | Ana Ivanovic | SRB | 3353 |
| 6. | Vera Zvonareva | RUS | 2626 |
| 7. | Svetlana Kuznetsova | RUS | 2623 |
| 8. | Venus Williams | USA | 2522 |
| 9. | Maria Sharapova | RUS | 2515 |
| 10. | Agnieszka Radwanska | POL | 2256 |

Note: Compiled by the WTA, through the 2008 season.

## Grand Slam Tournaments

### MEN

### Australian Championships

| Year | Winner | Finalist | Score |
|---|---|---|---|
| 1905 | Rodney Heath | A. H. Curtis | 4–6, 6–3, 6–4, 6–4 |
| 1906 | Tony Wilding | H. A. Parker | 6–0, 6–4, 6–4 |
| 1907 | Horace M. Rice | H. A. Parker | 6–3, 6–4, 6–4 |
| 1908 | Fred Alexander | A. W. Dunlop | 3–6, 3–6, 6–0, 6–2, 6–3 |
| 1909 | Tony Wilding | E. F. Parker | 6–1, 7–5, 6–2 |
| 1910 | Rodney Heath | Horace M. Rice | 6–4, 6–3, 6–2 |
| 1911 | Norman Brookes | Horace M. Rice | 6–1, 6–2, 6–3 |
| 1912 | J. Cecil Parke | A. E. Beamish | 3–6, 6–3, 1–6, 6–1, 7–5 |
| 1913 | E. F. Parker | H. A. Parker | 2–6, 6–1, 6–2, 6–3 |
| 1914 | Pat O'Hara Wood | G. L. Patterson | 6–4, 6–3, 5–7, 6–1 |
| 1915 | Francis G. Lowe | Horace M. Rice | 4–6, 6–1, 6–1, 6–4 |
| 1916–18 | No tournament | | |
| 1919 | A. R. F. Kingscote | E. O. Pockley | 6–4, 6–0, 6–3 |
| 1920 | Pat O'Hara Wood | Ron Thomas | 6–3, 4–6, 6–8, 6–1, 6–3 |
| 1921 | Rhys H. Gemmell | A. Hedeman | 7–5, 6–1, 6–4 |
| 1922 | Pat O'Hara Wood | Gerald Patterson | 6–0, 3–6, 3–6, 6–3, 6–2 |
| 1923 | Pat O'Hara Wood | C. B. St John | 6–1, 6–1, 6–3 |
| 1924 | James Anderson | R. E. Schlesinger | 6–3, 6–4, 3–6, 5–7, 6–3 |
| 1925 | James Anderson | Gerald Patterson | 11–9, 2–6, 6–2, 6–3 |
| 1926 | John Hawkes | J. Willard | 6–1, 6–3, 6–1 |
| 1927 | Gerald Patterson | John Hawkes | 3–6, 6–4, 3–6, 18–16, 6–3 |
| 1928 | Jean Borotra | R. O. Cummings | 6–4, 6–1, 4–6, 5–7, 6–3 |
| 1929 | John C. Gregory | R. E. Schlesinger | 6–2, 6–2, 5–7, 7–5 |
| 1930 | Gar Moon | Harry C. Hopman | 6–3, 6–1, 6–3 |
| 1931 | Jack Crawford | Harry C. Hopman | 6–4, 6–2, 2–6, 6–1 |
| 1932 | Jack Crawford | Harry C. Hopman | 4–6, 6–3, 3–6, 6–3, 6–1 |
| 1933 | Jack Crawford | Keith Gledhill | 2–6, 7–5, 6–3, 6–2 |
| 1934 | Fred Perry | Jack Crawford | 6–3, 7–5, 6–1 |
| 1935 | Jack Crawford | Fred Perry | 2–6, 6–4, 6–4, 6–4 |
| 1936 | Adrian Quist | Jack Crawford | 6–2, 6–3, 4–6, 3–6, 9–7 |
| 1937 | Vivian B. McGrath | John Bromwich | 6–3, 1–6, 6–0, 2–6, 6–1 |
| 1938 | Don Budge | John Bromwich | 6–4, 6–2, 6–1 |
| 1939 | John Bromwich | Adrian Quist | 6–4, 6–1, 6–3 |
| 1940 | Adrian Quist | Jack Crawford | 6–3, 6–1, 6–2 |
| 1941–45 | No tournament | | |
| 1946 | John Bromwich | Dinny Pails | 5–7, 6–3, 7–5, 3–6, 6–2 |
| 1947 | Dinny Pails | John Bromwich | 4–6, 6–4, 3–6, 7–5, 8–6 |
| 1948 | Adrian Quist | John Bromwich | 6–4, 3–6, 6–3, 2–6, 6–3 |
| 1949 | Frank Sedgman | Ken McGregor | 6–3, 6–3, 6–2 |
| 1950 | Frank Sedgman | Ken McGregor | 6–3, 6–4, 4–6, 6–1 |
| 1951 | Richard Savitt | Ken McGregor | 6–3, 2–6, 6–3, 6–1 |
| 1952 | Ken McGregor | Frank Sedgman | 7–5, 12–10, 2–6, 6–2 |
| 1953 | Ken Rosewall | Mervyn Rose | 6–0, 6–3, 6–4 |
| 1954 | Mervyn Rose | Rex Hartwig | 6–2, 0–6, 6–4, 6–2 |
| 1955 | Ken Rosewall | Lew Hoad | 9–7, 6–4, 6–4 |
| 1956 | Lew Hoad | Ken Rosewall | 6–4, 3–6, 6–4, 7–5 |
| 1957 | Ashley Cooper | Neale Fraser | 6–3, 9–11, 6–4, 6–2 |
| 1958 | Ashley Cooper | Mal Anderson | 7–5, 6–3, 6–4 |
| 1959 | Alex Olmedo | Neale Fraser | 6–1, 6–2, 3–6, 6–3 |
| 1960 | Rod Laver | Neale Fraser | 5–7, 3–6, 6–3, 8–6, 8–6 |
| 1961 | Roy Emerson | Rod Laver | 1–6, 6–3, 7–5, 6–4 |
| 1962 | Rod Laver | Roy Emerson | 8–6, 0–6, 6–4, 6–4 |
| 1963 | Roy Emerson | Ken Fletcher | 6–3, 6–3, 6–1 |
| 1964 | Roy Emerson | Fred Stolle | 6–3, 6–4, 6–2 |
| 1965 | Roy Emerson | Fred Stolle | 7–9, 2–6, 6–4, 7–5, 6–1 |
| 1966 | Roy Emerson | Arthur Ashe | 6–4, 6–8, 6–2, 6–3 |
| 1967 | Roy Emerson | Arthur Ashe | 6–4, 6–1, 6–1 |
| 1968 | Bill Bowrey | Juan Gisbert | 7–5, 2–6, 9–7, 6–4 |
| 1969* | Rod Laver | Andres Gimeno | 6–3, 6–4, 7–5 |

*Became Open (amateur and professional) in 1969.

## MEN *(Cont.)*

### Australian Championships *(Cont.)*

| Year | Winner | Finalist | Score |
|------|--------|----------|-------|
| 1970 | Arthur Ashe | Dick Crealy | 6–4, 9–7, 6–2 |
| 1971 | Ken Rosewall | Arthur Ashe | 6–1, 7–5, 6–3 |
| 1972 | Ken Rosewall | Mal Anderson | 7–6, 6–3, 7–5 |
| 1973 | John Newcombe | Onny Parun | 6–3, 6–7, 7–5, 6–1 |
| 1974 | Jimmy Connors | Phil Dent | 7–6, 6–4, 4–6, 6–3 |
| 1975 | John Newcombe | Jimmy Connors | 7–5, 3–6, 6–4, 7–5 |
| 1976 | Mark Edmondson | John Newcombe | 6–7, 6–3, 7–6, 6–1 |
| 1977 (Jan) | Roscoe Tanner | Guillermo Vilas | 6–3, 6–3, 6–3 |
| 1977 (Dec) | Vitas Gerulaitis | John Lloyd | 6–3, 7–6, 5–7, 3–6, 6–2 |
| 1978 | Guillermo Vilas | John Marks | 6–4, 6–4, 3–6, 6–3 |
| 1979 | Guillermo Vilas | John Sadri | 7–6, 6–3, 6–2 |
| 1980 | Brian Teacher | Kim Warwick | 7–5, 7–6, 6–3 |
| 1981 | Johan Kriek | Steve Denton | 6–2, 7–6, 6–7, 6–4 |
| 1982 | Johan Kriek | Steve Denton | 6–3, 6–3, 6–2 |
| 1983 | Mats Wilander | Ivan Lendl | 6–1, 6–4, 6–4 |
| 1984 | Mats Wilander | Kevin Curren | 6–7, 6–4, 7–6, 6–2 |
| 1985 (Dec) | Stefan Edberg | Mats Wilander | 6–4, 6–3, 6–3 |
| 1987 (Jan) | Stefan Edberg | Pat Cash | 6–3, 6–4, 3–6, 5–7, 6–3 |
| 1988 | Mats Wilander | Pat Cash | 6–3, 6–7, 3–6, 6–1, 8–6 |
| 1989 | Ivan Lendl | Miloslav Mecir | 6–2, 6–2, 6–2 |
| 1990 | Ivan Lendl | Stefan Edberg | 4–6, 7–6, 5–2, ret. |
| 1991 | Boris Becker | Ivan Lendl | 1–6, 6–4, 6–4, 6–4 |
| 1992 | Jim Courier | Stefan Edberg | 6–3, 3–6, 6–4, 6–2 |
| 1993 | Jim Courier | Stefan Edberg | 6–2, 6–1, 2–6, 7–5 |
| 1994 | Pete Sampras | Todd Martin | 7–6, 6–4, 6–4 |
| 1995 | Andre Agassi | Pete Sampras | 4–6, 6–1, 7–6, 6–4 |
| 1996 | Boris Becker | Michael Chang | 6–2, 6–4, 2–6, 6–2 |
| 1997 | Pete Sampras | Carlos Moya | 6–2, 6–3, 6–3 |
| 1998 | Petr Korda | Marcelo Ríos | 6–2, 6–2, 6–2 |
| 1999 | Yevgeny Kafelnikov | Thomas Enqvist | 4–6, 6–0, 6–3, 7–6 |
| 2000 | Andre Agassi | Yevgeny Kafelnikov | 3–6, 6–3, 6–2, 6–4 |
| 2001 | Andre Agassi | Arnaud Clement | 6–4, 6–2, 6–2 |
| 2002 | Thomas Johansson | Marat Safin | 3–6, 6–4, 6–4, 7–6 (7-4) |
| 2003 | Andre Agassi | Rainer Schuettler | 6–2, 6–2, 6–1 |
| 2004 | Roger Federer | Marat Safin | 7–6 (7-3), 6–4, 6–2 |
| 2005 | Marat Safin | Lleyton Hewitt | 1–6, 6–3, 6–4, 6–4 |
| 2006 | Roger Federer | Marcos Baghdatis | 5–7, 7–5, 6–0, 6–2 |
| 2007 | Roger Federer | Fernando Gonzalez | 7–6 (7-2), 6–4, 6–4 |
| 2008 | Novak Djokovic | Jo-Wilfried Tsonga | 4–6, 6–4, 6–3, 7–6 (7-2) |
| 2009 | Rafael Nadal | Roger Federer | 7–5, 3–6, 7–6 (7-3), 3–6, 6–2 |

### French Championships

| Year | Winner | Finalist | Score |
|------|--------|----------|-------|
| 1925† | Rene Lacoste | Jean Borotra | 7–5, 6–1, 6–4 |
| 1926 | Henri Cochet | Rene Lacoste | 6–2, 6–4, 6–3 |
| 1927 | Rene Lacoste | Bill Tilden | 6–4, 4–6, 5–7, 6–3, 11–9 |
| 1928 | Henri Cochet | Rene Lacoste | 5–7, 6–3, 6–1, 6–3 |
| 1929 | Rene Lacoste | Jean Borotra | 6–3, 2–6, 6–0, 2–6, 8–6 |
| 1930 | Henri Cochet | Bill Tilden | 3–6, 8–6, 6–3, 6–1 |
| 1931 | Jean Borotra | Claude Boussus | 2–6, 6–4, 7–5, 6–4 |
| 1932 | Henri Cochet | Giorgio de Stefani | 6–0, 6–4, 4–6, 6–3 |
| 1933 | Jack Crawford | Henri Cochet | 8–6, 6–1, 6–3 |
| 1934 | Gottfried von Cramm | Jack Crawford | 6–4, 7–9, 3–6, 7–5, 6–3 |
| 1935 | Fred Perry | Gottfried von Cramm | 6–3, 3–6, 6–1, 6–3 |
| 1936 | Gottfried von Cramm | Fred Perry | 6–0, 2–6, 6–2, 2–6, 6–0 |
| 1937 | Henner Henkel | Henry Austin | 6–1, 6–4, 6–3 |
| 1938 | Don Budge | Roderick Menzel | 6–3, 6–2, 6–4 |
| 1939 | Don McNeill | Bobby Riggs | 7–5, 6–0, 6–3 |
| 1940 | No tournament | | |
| 1941‡ | Bernard Destremau | n/a | n/a |
| 1942‡ | Bernard Destremau | n/a | n/a |
| 1943‡ | Yvon Petra | n/a | n/a |
| 1944‡ | Yvon Petra | n/a | n/a |
| 1945‡ | Yvon Petra | Bernard Destremau | 7–5, 6–4, 6–2 |

†1925 was the first year that entries were accepted from all countries.
‡From 1941 to 1945 the event was called Tournoi de France and was closed to all foreigners.

## MEN *(Cont.)*

### French Championships *(Cont.)*

| Year | Winner | Finalist | Score |
|---|---|---|---|
| 1946 | Marcel Bernard | Jaroslav Drobny | 3–6, 2–6, 6–1, 6–4, 6–3 |
| 1947 | Joseph Asboth | Eric Sturgess | 8–6, 7–5, 6–4 |
| 1948 | Frank Parker | Jaroslav Drobny | 6–4, 7–5, 5–7, 8–6 |
| 1949 | Frank Parker | Budge Patty | 6–3, 1–6, 6–1, 6–4 |
| 1950 | Budge Patty | Jaroslav Drobny | 6–1, 6–2, 3–6, 5–7, 7–5 |
| 1951 | Jaroslav Drobny | Eric Sturgess | 6–3, 6–3, 6–3 |
| 1952 | Jaroslav Drobny | Frank Sedgman | 6–2, 6–0, 3–6, 6–4 |
| 1953 | Ken Rosewall | Vic Seixas | 6–3, 6–4, 1–6, 6–2 |
| 1954 | Tony Trabert | Arthur Larsen | 6–4, 7–5, 6–1 |
| 1955 | Tony Trabert | Sven Davidson | 2–6, 6–1, 6–4, 6–2 |
| 1956 | Lew Hoad | Sven Davidson | 6–4, 8–6, 6–3 |
| 1957 | Sven Davidson | Herbie Flam | 6–3, 6–4, 6–4 |
| 1958 | Mervyn Rose | Luis Ayala | 6–3, 6–4, 6–4 |
| 1959 | Nicola Pietrangeli | Ian Vermaak | 3–6, 6–3, 6–4, 6–1 |
| 1960 | Nicola Pietrangeli | Luis Ayala | 3–6, 6–3, 6–4, 4–6, 6–3 |
| 1961 | Manuel Santana | Nicola Pietrangeli | 4–6, 6–1, 3–6, 6–0, 6–2 |
| 1962 | Rod Laver | Roy Emerson | 3–6, 2–6, 6–3, 9–7, 6–2 |
| 1963 | Roy Emerson | Pierre Darmon | 3–6, 6–1, 6–4, 6–4 |
| 1964 | Manuel Santana | Nicola Pietrangeli | 6–3, 6–1, 4–6, 7–5 |
| 1965 | Fred Stolle | Tony Roche | 3–6, 6–0, 6–2, 6–3 |
| 1966 | Tony Roche | Istvan Gulyas | 6–1, 6–4, 7–5 |
| 1967 | Roy Emerson | Tony Roche | 6–1, 6–4, 2–6, 6–2 |
| 1968* | Ken Rosewall | Rod Laver | 6–3, 6–1, 2–6, 6–2 |
| 1969 | Rod Laver | Ken Rosewall | 6–4, 6–3, 6–4 |
| 1970 | Jan Kodes | Zeljko Franulovic | 6–2, 6–4, 6–0 |
| 1971 | Jan Kodes | Ilie Nastase | 8–6, 6–2, 2–6, 7–5 |
| 1972 | Andres Gimeno | Patrick Proisy | 4–6, 6–3, 6–1, 6–1 |
| 1973 | Ilie Nastase | Nikki Pilic | 6–3, 6–3, 6–0 |
| 1974 | Bjorn Borg | Manuel Orantes | 6–7, 6–0, 6–1, 6–1 |
| 1975 | Bjorn Borg | Guillermo Vilas | 6–2, 6–3, 6–4 |
| 1976 | Adriano Panatta | Harold Solomon | 6–1, 6–4, 4–6, 7–6 |
| 1977 | Guillermo Vilas | Brian Gottfried | 6–0, 6–3, 6–0 |
| 1978 | Bjorn Borg | Guillermo Vilas | 6–1, 6–1, 6–3 |
| 1979 | Bjorn Borg | Victor Pecci | 6–3, 6–1, 6–7, 6–4 |
| 1980 | Bjorn Borg | Vitas Gerulaitis | 6–4, 6–1, 6–2 |
| 1981 | Bjorn Borg | Ivan Lendl | 6–1, 4–6, 6–2, 3–6, 6–1 |
| 1982 | Mats Wilander | Guillermo Vilas | 1–6, 7–6, 6–0, 6–4 |
| 1983 | Yannick Noah | Mats Wilander | 6–2, 7–5, 7–6 |
| 1984 | Ivan Lendl | John McEnroe | 3–6, 2–6, 6–4, 7–5, 7–5 |
| 1985 | Mats Wilander | Ivan Lendl | 3–6, 6–4, 6–2, 6–2 |
| 1986 | Ivan Lendl | Mikael Pernfors | 6–3, 6–2, 6–4 |
| 1987 | Ivan Lendl | Mats Wilander | 7–5, 6–2, 3–6, 7–6 |
| 1988 | Mats Wilander | Henri Leconte | 7–5, 6–2, 6–1 |
| 1989 | Michael Chang | Stefan Edberg | 6–1, 3–6, 4–6, 6–4, 6–2 |
| 1990 | Andres Gomez | Andre Agassi | 6–3, 2–6, 6–4, 6–4 |
| 1991 | Jim Courier | Andre Agassi | 3–6, 6–4, 2–6, 6–1, 6–4 |
| 1992 | Jim Courier | Petr Korda | 7–5, 6–2, 6–1 |
| 1993 | Sergi Bruguera | Jim Courier | 6–4, 2–6, 6–2, 3–6, 6–3 |
| 1994 | Sergi Bruguera | Alberto Berasategui | 6–3, 7–5, 2–6, 6–1 |
| 1995 | Thomas Muster | Michael Chang | 7–5, 6–2, 6–4 |
| 1996 | Yevgeny Kafelnikov | Michael Stich | 7–6, 7–5, 7–6 |
| 1997 | Gustavo Kuerten | Sergi Bruguera | 6–3, 6–4, 6–2 |
| 1998 | Carlos Moya | Alex Corretja | 6–3, 7–5, 6–3 |
| 1999 | Andre Agassi | Andrei Medvedev | 1–6, 2–6, 6–4, 6–3, 6–4 |
| 2000 | Gustavo Kuerten | Magnus Norman | 6–2, 6–3, 2–6, 7–6 |
| 2001 | Gustavo Kuerten | Alex Corretja | 6–7, 7–5, 6–2, 6–0 |
| 2002 | Albert Costa | Juan Carlos Ferrero | 6–1, 6–0, 4–6, 6–3 |
| 2003 | Juan Carlos Ferrero | Martin Verkerk | 6–1, 6–3, 6–2 |
| 2004 | Gaston Gaudio | Guillermo Coria | 0–6, 3–6, 6–4, 6–1, 8–6 |
| 2005 | Rafael Nadal | Mariano Puerta | 6–7, 6–3, 6–1, 7–5 |
| 2006 | Rafael Nadal | Roger Federer | 1–6, 6–1, 6–4, 7–6 |
| 2007 | Rafael Nadal | Roger Federer | 6–3, 4–6, 6–3, 6–4 |
| 2008 | Rafael Nadal | Roger Federer | 6–1, 6–3, 6–0 |
| 2009 | Roger Federer | Robin Soderling | 6–1, 7–6 (7–1), 6–4 |

*Became Open (amateur and professional) in 1968, but restricted to only contract professionals in 1972.

## MEN (Cont.)

### Wimbledon Championships

| Year | Winner | Finalist | Score |
|------|--------|----------|-------|
| 1877 | Spencer W. Gore | William C. Marshall | 6–1, 6–2, 6–4 |
| 1878 | P. Frank Hadow | Spencer W. Gore | 7–5, 6–1, 9–7 |
| 1879 | John T. Hartley | V. St Leger Gould | 6–2, 6–4, 6–2 |
| 1880 | John T. Hartley | Herbert F. Lawford | 6–0, 6–2, 2–6, 6–3 |
| 1881 | William Renshaw | John T. Hartley | 6–0, 6–2, 6–1 |
| 1882 | William Renshaw | Ernest Renshaw | 6–1, 2–6, 4–6, 6–2, 6–2 |
| 1883 | William Renshaw | Ernest Renshaw | 2–6, 6–3, 6–3, 4–6, 6–3 |
| 1884 | William Renshaw | Herbert F. Lawford | 6–0, 6–4, 9–7 |
| 1885 | William Renshaw | Herbert F. Lawford | 7–5, 6–2, 4–6, 7–5 |
| 1886 | William Renshaw | Herbert F. Lawford | 6–0, 5–7, 6–3, 6–4 |
| 1887 | Herbert F. Lawford | Ernest Renshaw | 1–6, 6–3, 3–6, 6–4, 6–4 |
| 1888 | Ernest Renshaw | Herbert F. Lawford | 6–3, 7–5, 6–0 |
| 1889 | William Renshaw | Ernest Renshaw | 6–4, 6–1, 3–6, 6–0 |
| 1890 | William J. Hamilton | William Renshaw | 6–8, 6–2, 3–6, 6–1, 6–1 |
| 1891 | Wilfred Baddeley | Joshua Pim | 6–4, 1–6, 7–5, 6–0 |
| 1892 | Wilfred Baddeley | Joshua Pim | 4–6, 6–3, 6–3, 6–2 |
| 1893 | Joshua Pim | Wilfred Baddeley | 3–6, 6–1, 6–3, 6–2 |
| 1894 | Joshua Pim | Wilfred Baddeley | 10–8, 6–2, 8–6 |
| 1895 | Wilfred Baddeley | Wilberforce V. Eaves | 4–6, 2–6, 8–6, 6–2, 6–3 |
| 1896 | Harold S. Mahoney | Wilfred Baddeley | 6–2, 6–8, 5–7, 8–6, 6–3 |
| 1897 | Reggie F. Doherty | Harold S. Mahoney | 6–4, 6–4, 6–3 |
| 1898 | Reggie F. Doherty | H. Laurie Doherty | 6–3, 6–3, 2–6, 5–7, 6–1 |
| 1899 | Reggie F. Doherty | Arthur W. Gore | 1–6, 4–6, 6–2, 6–3, 6–3 |
| 1900 | Reggie F. Doherty | Sidney H. Smith | 6–8, 6–3, 6–1, 6–2 |
| 1901 | Arthur W. Gore | Reggie F. Doherty | 4–6, 7–5, 6–4, 6–4 |
| 1902 | H. Laurie Doherty | Arthur W. Gore | 6–4, 6–3, 3–6, 6–0 |
| 1903 | H. Laurie Doherty | Frank L. Riseley | 7–5, 6–3, 6–0 |
| 1904 | H. Laurie Doherty | Frank L. Riseley | 6–1, 7–5, 8–6 |
| 1905 | H. Laurie Doherty | Norman E. Brookes | 8–6, 6–2, 6–4 |
| 1906 | H. Laurie Doherty | Frank L. Riseley | 6–4, 4–6, 6–2, 6–3 |
| 1907 | Norman E. Brookes | Arthur W. Gore | 6–4, 6–2, 6–2 |
| 1908 | Arthur W. Gore | H. Roper Barrett | 6–3, 6–2, 4–6, 3–6, 6–4 |
| 1909 | Arthur W. Gore | M. J. G. Ritchie | 6–8, 1–6, 6–2, 6–2, 6–2 |
| 1910 | Anthony F. Wilding | Arthur W. Gore | 6–4, 7–5, 4–6, 6–2 |
| 1911 | Anthony F. Wilding | H. Roper Barrett | 6–4, 4–6, 2–6, 6–2, ret. |
| 1912 | Anthony F. Wilding | Arthur W. Gore | 6–4, 6–4, 4–6, 6–4 |
| 1913 | Anthony F. Wilding | Maurice E. McLoughlin | 8–6, 6–3, 10–8 |
| 1914 | Norman E. Brookes | Anthony F. Wilding | 6–4, 6–4, 7–5 |
| 1915–18 | No tournament | | |
| 1919 | Gerald L. Patterson | Norman E. Brookes | 6–3, 7–5, 6–2 |
| 1920 | Bill Tilden | Gerald L. Patterson | 2–6, 6–3, 6–2, 6–4 |
| 1921 | Bill Tilden | Brian I. C. Norton | 4–6, 2–6, 6–1, 6–0, 7–5 |
| 1922 | Gerald L. Patterson | Randolph Lycett | 6–3, 6–4, 6–2 |
| 1923 | Bill Johnston | Francis T. Hunter | 6–0, 6–3, 6–1 |
| 1924 | Jean Borotra | Rene Lacoste | 6–1, 3–6, 6–1, 3–6, 6–4 |
| 1925 | Rene Lacoste | Jean Borotra | 6–3, 6–3, 4–6, 8–6 |
| 1926 | Jean Borotra | Howard Kinsey | 8–6, 6–1, 6–3 |
| 1927 | Henri Cochet | Jean Borotra | 4–6, 4–6, 6–3, 6–4, 7–5 |
| 1928 | Rene Lacoste | Henri Cochet | 6–1, 4–6, 6–4, 6–2 |
| 1929 | Henri Cochet | Jean Borotra | 6–4, 6–3, 6–4 |
| 1930 | Bill Tilden | Wilmer Allison | 6–3, 9–7, 6–4 |
| 1931 | Sidney B. Wood Jr | Francis X. Shields | walkover |
| 1932 | Ellsworth Vines | Henry Austin | 6–4, 6–2, 6–0 |
| 1933 | Jack Crawford | Ellsworth Vines | 4–6, 11–9, 6–2, 2–6, 6–4 |
| 1934 | Fred Perry | Jack Crawford | 6–3, 6–0, 7–5 |
| 1935 | Fred Perry | Gottfried von Cramm | 6–2, 6–4, 6–4 |
| 1936 | Fred Perry | Gottfried von Cramm | 6–1, 6–1, 6–0 |
| 1937 | Don Budge | Gottfried von Cramm | 6–3, 6–4, 6–2 |
| 1938 | Don Budge | Henry Austin | 6–1, 6–0, 6–3 |
| 1939 | Bobby Riggs | Elwood Cooke | 2–6, 8–6, 3–6, 6–3, 6–2 |
| 1940–45 | No tournament | | |
| 1946 | Yvon Petra | Geoff E. Brown | 6–2, 6–4, 6–7 (7–9), 5–7, 6–4 |
| 1947 | Jack Kramer | Tom P. Brown | 6–1, 6–3, 6–2 |
| 1948 | Bob Falkenburg | John Bromwich | 7–5, 0–6, 6–2, 3–6, 7–5 |
| 1949 | Ted Schroeder | Jaroslav Drobny | 3–6, 6–0, 6–3, 4–6, 6–4 |

Note: Prior to 1922 the tournament was run on a challenge-round system. The previous year's winner "stood out" of an All Comers event, which produced a challenger to play him for the title.

## MEN *(Cont.)*

### Wimbledon Championships *(Cont.)*

| Year | Winner | Finalist | Score |
|------|--------|----------|-------|
| 1950 | Budge Patty | Frank Sedgman | 6–1, 6–7 (8–10), 6–2, 6–3 |
| 1951 | Dick Savitt | Ken McGregor | 6–4, 6–4, 6–4 |
| 1952 | Frank Sedgman | Jaroslav Drobny | 4–6, 6–3, 6–2, 6–3 |
| 1953 | Vic Seixas | Kurt Nielsen | 9–7, 6–3, 6–4 |
| 1954 | Jaroslav Drobny | Ken Rosewall | 13–11, 4–6, 6–2, 9–7 |
| 1955 | Tony Trabert | Kurt Nielsen | 6–3, 7–5, 6–1 |
| 1956 | Lew Hoad | Ken Rosewall | 6–2, 4–6, 7–5, 6–4 |
| 1957 | Lew Hoad | Ashley Cooper | 6–2, 6–1, 6–2 |
| 1958 | Ashley Cooper | Neale Fraser | 3–6, 6–3, 6–4, 13–11 |
| 1959 | Alex Olmedo | Rod Laver | 6–4, 6–3, 6–4 |
| 1960 | Neale Fraser | Rod Laver | 6–4, 3–6, 9–7, 7–5 |
| 1961 | Rod Laver | Chuck McKinley | 6–3, 6–1, 6–4 |
| 1962 | Rod Laver | Martin Mulligan | 6–2, 6–2, 6–1 |
| 1963 | Chuck McKinley | Fred Stolle | 9–7, 6–1, 6–4 |
| 1964 | Roy Emerson | Fred Stolle | 6–4, 12–10, 4–6, 6–3 |
| 1965 | Roy Emerson | Fred Stolle | 6–2, 6–4, 6–4 |
| 1966 | Manuel Santana | Dennis Ralston | 6–4, 11–9, 6–4 |
| 1967 | John Newcombe | Wilhelm Bungert | 6–3, 6–1, 6–1 |
| 1968* | Rod Laver | Tony Roche | 6–3, 6–4, 6–2 |
| 1969 | Rod Laver | John Newcombe | 6–4, 5–7, 6–4, 6–4 |
| 1970 | John Newcombe | Ken Rosewall | 5–7, 6–3, 6–2, 3–6, 6–1 |
| 1971 | John Newcombe | Stan Smith | 6–3, 5–7, 2–6, 6–4, 6–4 |
| 1972 | Stan Smith | Ilie Nastase | 4–6, 6–3, 6–3, 4–6, 7–5 |
| 1973 | Jan Kodes | Alex Metreveli | 6–1, 9–8, 6–3 |
| 1974 | Jimmy Connors | Ken Rosewall | 6–1, 6–1, 6–4 |
| 1975 | Arthur Ashe | Jimmy Connors | 6–1, 6–1, 5–7, 6–4 |
| 1976 | Bjorn Borg | Ilie Nastase | 6–4, 6–2, 9–7 |
| 1977 | Bjorn Borg | Jimmy Connors | 3–6, 6–2, 6–1, 5–7, 6–4 |
| 1978 | Bjorn Borg | Jimmy Connors | 6–2, 6–2, 6–3 |
| 1979 | Bjorn Borg | Roscoe Tanner | 6–7, 6–1, 3–6, 6–3, 6–4 |
| 1980 | Bjorn Borg | John McEnroe | 1–6, 7–5, 6–3, 6–7, 8–6 |
| 1981 | John McEnroe | Bjorn Borg | 4–6, 7–6, 7–6, 6–4 |
| 1982 | Jimmy Connors | John McEnroe | 3–6, 6–3, 6–7, 7–6, 6–4 |
| 1983 | John McEnroe | Chris Lewis | 6–2, 6–2, 6–2 |
| 1984 | John McEnroe | Jimmy Connors | 6–1, 6–1, 6–2 |
| 1985 | Boris Becker | Kevin Curren | 6–3, 6–7, 7–6, 6–4 |
| 1986 | Boris Becker | Ivan Lendl | 6–4, 6–3, 7–5 |
| 1987 | Pat Cash | Ivan Lendl | 7–6, 6–2, 7–5 |
| 1988 | Stefan Edberg | Boris Becker | 4–6, 7–6, 6–4, 6–2 |
| 1989 | Boris Becker | Stefan Edberg | 6–0, 7–6, 6–4 |
| 1990 | Stefan Edberg | Boris Becker | 6–2, 6–2, 3–6, 3–6, 6–4 |
| 1991 | Michael Stich | Boris Becker | 6–4, 7–6, 6–4 |
| 1992 | Andre Agassi | Goran Ivanisevic | 6–7, 6–4, 6–4, 1–6, 6–4 |
| 1993 | Pete Sampras | Jim Courier | 7–6, 7–6, 3–6, 6–3 |
| 1994 | Pete Sampras | Goran Ivanisevic | 7–6, 7–6, 6–0 |
| 1995 | Pete Sampras | Boris Becker | 6–7, 6–2, 6–4, 6–2 |
| 1996 | Richard Krajicek | MaliVai Washington | 6–3, 6–4, 6–3 |
| 1997 | Pete Sampras | Cedric Pioline | 6–4, 6–2, 6–4 |
| 1998 | Pete Sampras | Goran Ivanisevic | 6–7, 7–6, 6–4, 3–6, 6–2 |
| 1999 | Pete Sampras | Andre Agassi | 6–3, 6–4, 7–5 |
| 2000 | Pete Sampras | Patrick Rafter | 6–7, 7–6, 6–4, 6–2 |
| 2001 | Goran Ivanisevic | Patrick Rafter | 6–3, 3–6, 6–3, 2–6, 9–7 |
| 2002 | Lleyton Hewitt | David Nalbandian | 6–1, 6–3, 6–2 |
| 2003 | Roger Federer | Mark Philippoussis | 7–6 (7-5), 6–2, 7–6 (7-3) |
| 2004 | Roger Federer | Andy Roddick | 4–6, 7–5, 7–6 (7-3), 6–4 |
| 2005 | Roger Federer | Andy Roddick | 6–2, 7–6 (7-2), 6–4 |
| 2006 | Roger Federer | Rafael Nadal | 6–0, 7–6, (7–5), 6–7 (2–7), 6–3 |
| 2007 | Roger Federer | Rafael Nadal | 7–6 (9–7), 4–6, 7–6 (7–3), 2–6, 6–2 |
| 2008 | Rafael Nadal | Roger Federer | 6–4, 6–4, 6–7 (5–7), 6–7 (8–10) 9–7 |
| 2009 | Roger Federer | Andy Roddick | 5–7, 7–6 (8–6), 7–6 (7–5), 3–6, 16–14 |

*Became Open (amateur and professional) in 1968, but restricted to only contract professionals in 1972.

## MEN *(Cont.)*
### United States Championships

| Year | Winner | Finalist | Score |
|---|---|---|---|
| 1881 | Richard D. Sears | W.E. Glyn | 6–0, 6–3, 6–2 |
| 1882 | Richard D. Sears | C.M. Clark | 6–1, 6–4, 6–0 |
| 1883 | Richard D. Sears | James Dwight | 6–2, 6–0, 9–7 |
| 1884 | Richard D. Sears | H.A. Taylor | 6–0, 1–6, 6–0, 6–2 |
| 1885 | Richard D. Sears | G.M. Brinley | 6–3, 4–6, 6–0, 6–3 |
| 1886 | Richard D. Sears | R.L. Beeckman | 4–6, 6–1, 6–3, 6–4 |
| 1887 | Richard D. Sears | H.W. Slocum Jr | 6–1, 6–3, 6–2 |
| 1888† | H. W. Slocum Jr | H.A. Taylor | 6–4, 6–1, 6–0 |
| 1889 | H. W. Slocum Jr | Q.A. Shaw | 6–3, 6–1, 4–6, 6–2 |
| 1890 | Oliver S. Campbell | H.W. Slocum Jr | 6–2, 4–6, 6–3, 6–1 |
| 1891 | Oliver S. Campbell | Clarence Hobart | 2–6, 7–5, 7–9, 6–1, 6–2 |
| 1892 | Oliver S. Campbell | Frederick H. Hovey | 7–5, 3–6, 6–3, 7–5 |
| 1893† | Robert D. Wrenn | Frederick H. Hovey | 6–4, 3–6, 6–4, 6–4 |
| 1894 | Robert D. Wrenn | M.F. Goodbody | 6–8, 6–1, 6–4, 6–4 |
| 1895 | Frederick H. Hovey | Robert D. Wrenn | 6–3, 6–2, 6–4 |
| 1896 | Robert D. Wrenn | Frederick H. Hovey | 7–5, 3–6, 6–0, 1–6, 6–1 |
| 1897 | Robert D. Wrenn | Wilberforce V. Eaves | 4–6, 8–6, 6–3, 2–6, 6–2 |
| 1898† | Malcolm D. Whitman | Dwight F. Davis | 3–6, 6–2, 6–2, 6–1 |
| 1899 | Malcolm D. Whitman | J. Parmly Paret | 6–1, 6–2, 3–6, 7–5 |
| 1900 | Malcolm D. Whitman | William A. Larned | 6–4, 1–6, 6–2, 6–2 |
| 1901† | William A. Larned | Beals C. Wright | 6–2, 6–8, 6–4, 6–4 |
| 1902 | William A. Larned | Reggie F. Doherty | 4–6, 6–2, 6–4, 8–6 |
| 1903 | H. Laurie Doherty | William A. Larned | 6–0, 6–3, 10–8 |
| 1904† | Holcombe Ward | William J. Clothier | 10–8, 6–4, 9–7 |
| 1905 | Beals C. Wright | Holcombe Ward | 6–2, 6–1, 11–9 |
| 1906 | William J. Clothier | Beals C. Wright | 6–3, 6–0, 6–4 |
| 1907† | William A. Larned | Robert LeRoy | 6–2, 6–2, 6–4 |
| 1908 | William A. Larned | Beals C. Wright | 6–1, 6–2, 8–6 |
| 1909 | William A. Larned | William J. Clothier | 6–1, 6–2, 5–7, 1–6, 6–1 |
| 1910 | William A. Larned | Thomas C. Bundy | 6–1, 5–7, 6–0, 6–8, 6–1 |
| 1911 | William A. Larned | Maurice E. McLoughlin | 6–4, 6–4, 6–2 |
| 1912‡ | Maurice E. McLoughlin | Bill Johnson | 3–6, 2–6, 6–2, 6–4, 6–2 |
| 1913 | Maurice E. McLoughlin | Richard N. Williams | 6–4, 5–7, 6–3, 6–1 |
| 1914 | Richard N. Williams | Maurice E. McLoughlin | 6–3, 8–6, 10–8 |
| 1915 | Bill Johnston | Maurice E. McLoughlin | 1–6, 6–0, 7–5, 10–8 |
| 1916 | Richard N. Williams | Bill Johnston | 4–6, 6–4, 0–6, 6–2, 6–4 |
| 1917# | R.L. Murray | N. W. Niles | 5–7, 8–6, 6–3, 6–3 |
| 1918 | R.L. Murray | Bill Tilden | 6–3, 6–1, 7–5 |
| 1919 | Bill Johnston | Bill Tilden | 6–4, 6–4, 6–3 |
| 1920 | Bill Tilden | Bill Johnston | 6–1, 1–6, 7–5, 5–7, 6–3 |
| 1921 | Bill Tilden | Wallace F. Johnson | 6–1, 6–3, 6–1 |
| 1922 | Bill Tilden | Bill Johnston | 4–6, 3–6, 6–2, 6–3, 6–4 |
| 1923 | Bill Tilden | Bill Johnston | 6–4, 6–1, 6–4 |
| 1924 | Bill Tilden | Bill Johnston | 6–1, 9–7, 6–2 |
| 1925 | Bill Tilden | Bill Johnston | 4–6, 11–9, 6–3, 4–6, 6–3 |
| 1926 | Rene Lacoste | Jean Borotra | 6–4, 6–0, 6–4 |
| 1927 | Rene Lacoste | Bill Tilden | 11–9, 6–3, 11–9 |
| 1928 | Henri Cochet | Francis T. Hunter | 4–6, 6–4, 3–6, 7–5, 6–3 |
| 1929 | Bill Tilden | Francis T. Hunter | 3–6, 6–3, 4–6, 6–2, 6–4 |
| 1930 | John H. Doeg | Francis X. Shields | 10–8, 1–6, 6–4, 16–14 |
| 1931 | Ellsworth Vines | George M. Lott Jr | 7–9, 6–3, 9–7, 7–5 |
| 1932 | Ellsworth Vines | Henri Cochet | 6–4, 6–4, 6–4 |
| 1933 | Fred Perry | Jack Crawford | 6–3, 11–13, 4–6, 6–0, 6–1 |
| 1934 | Fred Perry | Wilmer L. Allison | 6–4, 6–3, 1–6, 8–6 |
| 1935 | Wilmer L. Allison | Sidney B. Wood Jr | 6–2, 6–2, 6–3 |
| 1936 | Fred Perry | Don Budge | 2–6, 6–2, 8–6, 1–6, 10–8 |
| 1937 | Don Budge | Gottfried von Cramm | 6–1, 7–9, 6–1, 3–6, 6–1 |
| 1938 | Don Budge | Gene Mako | 6–3, 6–8, 6–2, 6–1 |
| 1939 | Bobby Riggs | Welby Van Horn | 6–4, 6–2, 6–4 |
| 1940 | Don McNeill | Bobby Riggs | 4–6, 6–8, 6–3, 6–3, 7–5 |
| 1941 | Bobby Riggs | Francis Kovacs II | 5–7, 6–1, 6–3, 6–3 |
| 1942 | Ted Schroeder | Frank Parker | 8–6, 7–5, 3–6, 4–6, 6–2 |
| 1943 | Joseph R. Hunt | Jack Kramer | 6–3, 6–8, 10–8, 6–0 |
| 1944 | Frank Parker | William F. Talbert | 6–4, 3–6, 6–3, 6–3 |
| 1945 | Frank Parker | William F. Talbert | 14–12, 6–1, 6–2 |

†No challenge round played. ‡Challenge round abolished. #National Patriotic Tournament.

## MEN *(Cont.)*
### United States Championships *(Cont.)*

| Year | Winner | Finalist | Score |
|---|---|---|---|
| 1946 | Jack Kramer | Tom P. Brown | 9–7, 6–3, 6–0 |
| 1947 | Jack Kramer | Frank Parker | 4–6, 2–6, 6–1, 6–0, 6–3 |
| 1948 | Pancho Gonzales | Eric W. Sturgess | 6–2, 6–3, 14–12 |
| 1949 | Pancho Gonzales | Ted Schroeder | 16–18, 2–6, 6–1, 6–2, 6–4 |
| 1950 | Arthur Larsen | Herbie Flam | 6–3, 4–6, 5–7, 6–4, 6–3 |
| 1951 | Frank Sedgman | Vic Seixas | 6–4, 6–1, 6–1 |
| 1952 | Frank Sedgman | Gardnar Mulloy | 6–1, 6–2, 6–3 |
| 1953 | Tony Trabert | Vic Seixas | 6–3, 6–2, 6–3 |
| 1954 | Vic Seixas | Rex Hartwig | 3–6, 6–2, 6–4, 6–4 |
| 1955 | Tony Trabert | Ken Rosewall | 9–7, 6–3, 6–3 |
| 1956 | Ken Rosewall | Lew Hoad | 4–6, 6–2, 6–3, 6–3 |
| 1957 | Mal Anderson | Ashley J. Cooper | 10–8, 7–5, 6–4 |
| 1958 | Ashley J. Cooper | Mal Anderson | 6–2, 3–6, 4–6, 10–8, 8–6 |
| 1959 | Neale Fraser | Alex Olmedo | 6–3, 5–7, 6–2, 6–4 |
| 1960 | Neale Fraser | Rod Laver | 6–4, 6–4, 9–7 |
| 1961 | Roy Emerson | Rod Laver | 7–5, 6–3, 6–2 |
| 1962 | Rod Laver | Roy Emerson | 6–2, 6–4, 5–7, 6–4 |
| 1963 | Rafael Osuna | Frank Froehling III | 7–5, 6–4, 6–2 |
| 1964 | Roy Emerson | Fred Stolle | 6–4, 6–2, 6–4 |
| 1965 | Manuel Santana | Cliff Drysdale | 6–2, 7–9, 7–5, 6–1 |
| 1966 | Fred Stolle | John Newcombe | 4–6, 12–10, 6–3, 6–4 |
| 1967 | John Newcombe | Clark Graebner | 6–4, 6–4, 8–6 |
| 1968* | Arthur Ashe | Tom Okker | 14–12, 5–7, 6–3, 3–6, 6–3 |
| 1968** | Arthur Ashe | Bob Lutz | 4–6, 6–3, 8–10, 6–0, 6–4 |
| 1969 | Rod Laver | Tony Roche | 7–9, 6–1, 6–3, 6–2 |
| 1969** | Stan Smith | Bob Lutz | 9–7, 6–3, 6–1 |
| 1970 | Ken Rosewall | Tony Roche | 2–6, 6–4, 7–6, 6–3 |
| 1971 | Stan Smith | Jan Kodes | 3–6, 6–3, 6–2, 7–6 |
| 1972 | Ilie Nastase | Arthur Ashe | 3–6, 6–3, 6–7, 6–4, 6–3 |
| 1973 | John Newcombe | Jan Kodes | 6–4, 1–6, 4–6, 6–2, 6–3 |
| 1974 | Jimmy Connors | Ken Rosewall | 6–1, 6–0, 6–1 |
| 1975 | Manuel Orantes | Jimmy Connors | 6–4, 6–3, 6–3 |
| 1976 | Jimmy Connors | Bjorn Borg | 6–4, 3–6, 7–6, 6–4 |
| 1977 | Guillermo Vilas | Jimmy Connors | 2–6, 6–3, 7–6, 6–0 |
| 1978 | Jimmy Connors | Bjorn Borg | 6–4, 6–2, 6–2 |
| 1979 | John McEnroe | Vitas Gerulaitis | 7–5, 6–3, 6–3 |
| 1980 | John McEnroe | Bjorn Borg | 7–6, 6–1, 6–7, 5–7, 6–4 |
| 1981 | John McEnroe | Bjorn Borg | 4–6, 6–2, 6–4, 6–3 |
| 1982 | Jimmy Connors | Ivan Lendl | 6–3, 6–2, 4–6, 6–4 |
| 1983 | Jimmy Connors | Ivan Lendl | 6–3, 6–7, 7–5, 6–0 |
| 1984 | John McEnroe | Ivan Lendl | 6–3, 6–4, 6–1 |
| 1985 | Ivan Lendl | John McEnroe | 7–6, 6–3, 6–4 |
| 1986 | Ivan Lendl | Miloslav Mecir | 6–4, 6–2, 6–0 |
| 1987 | Ivan Lendl | Mats Wilander | 6–7, 6–0, 7–6, 6–4 |
| 1988 | Mats Wilander | Ivan Lendl | 6–4, 4–6, 6–3, 5–7, 6–4 |
| 1989 | Boris Becker | Ivan Lendl | 7–6, 1–6, 6–3, 7–6 |
| 1990 | Pete Sampras | Andre Agassi | 6–4, 6–3, 6–2 |
| 1991 | Stefan Edberg | Jim Courier | 6–2, 6–4, 6–0 |
| 1992 | Stefan Edberg | Pete Sampras | 3–6, 6–4, 7–6, 6–2 |
| 1993 | Pete Sampras | Cedric Pioline | 6–4, 6–4, 6–3 |
| 1994 | Andre Agassi | Michael Stich | 6–1, 7–6, 7–5 |
| 1995 | Pete Sampras | Andre Agassi | 6–4, 6–3, 4–6, 7–5 |
| 1996 | Pete Sampras | Michael Chang | 6–1, 6–4, 7–6 |
| 1997 | Patrick Rafter | Greg Rusedski | 6–3, 6–2, 4–6, 7–5 |
| 1998 | Patrick Rafter | Mark Philippoussis | 6–3, 3–6, 6–2, 6–0 |
| 1999 | Andre Agassi | Todd Martin | 6–4, 6–7, 6–7, 6–3, 6–2 |
| 2000 | Marat Safin | Pete Sampras | 6–4, 6–3, 6–3 |
| 2001 | Lleyton Hewitt | Pete Sampras | 7–6, 6–1, 6–1 |
| 2002 | Pete Sampras | Andre Agassi | 6–3, 6–4, 5–7, 6–4 |
| 2003 | Andy Roddick | Juan Carlos Ferrero | 6–3, 7–6 (7–2), 6–3 |
| 2004 | Roger Federer | Lleyton Hewitt | 6–0, 7–6 (7–3), 6–0 |
| 2005 | Roger Federer | Andre Agassi | 6–3, 2–6, 7–6 (7–1), 6–1 |
| 2006 | Roger Federer | Andy Roddick | 6–2, 4–6, 7–5, 6–1 |
| 2007 | Roger Federer | Novak Djokovic | 7–6 (7–4), 7–6 (7–2), 6–4 |
| 2008 | Roger Federer | Andy Murray | 6–2, 7–5, 6–2 |
| 2009 | Juan Martin del Potro | Roger Federer | 3–6, 7–6 (7–5), 4–6, 7–6 (7–4), 6–2 |

*Became Open (amateur and professional) in 1968. **Amateur event held.

## WOMEN
### Australian Championships

| Year | Winner | Finalist | Score |
|------|--------|----------|-------|
| 1922 | Margaret Molesworth | Esna Boyd | 6–3, 10–8 |
| 1923 | Margaret Molesworth | Esna Boyd | 6–1, 7–5 |
| 1924 | Sylvia Lance | Esna Boyd | 6–3, 3–6, 6–4 |
| 1925 | Daphne Akhurst | Esna Boyd | 1–6, 8–6, 6–4 |
| 1926 | Daphne Akhurst | Esna Boyd | 6–1, 6–3 |
| 1927 | Esna Boyd | Sylvia Harper | 5–7, 6–1, 6–2 |
| 1928 | Daphne Akhurst | Esna Boyd | 7–5, 6–2 |
| 1929 | Daphne Akhurst | Louise Bickerton | 6–1, 5–7, 6–2 |
| 1930 | Daphne Akhurst | Sylvia Harper | 10–8, 2–6, 7–5 |
| 1931 | Coral Buttsworth | Margorie Crawford | 1–6, 6–3, 6–4 |
| 1932 | Coral Buttsworth | Kathrine Le Messurier | 9–7, 6–4 |
| 1933 | Joan Hartigan | Coral Buttsworth | 6–4, 6–3 |
| 1934 | Joan Hartigan | Margaret Molesworth | 6–1, 6–4 |
| 1935 | Dorothy Round | Nancye Wynne Bolton | 1–6, 6–1, 6–3 |
| 1936 | Joan Hartigan | Nancye Wynne Bolton | 6–4, 6–4 |
| 1937 | Nancye Wynne Bolton | Emily Westacott | 6–3, 5–7, 6–4 |
| 1938 | Dorothy Bundy | D. Stevenson | 6–3, 6–2 |
| 1939 | Emily Westacott | Nell Hopman | 6–1, 6–2 |
| 1940 | Nancye Wynne Bolton | Thelma Coyne | 5–7, 6–4, 6–0 |
| 1941–45 | No tournament | | |
| 1946 | Nancye Wynne Bolton | Joyce Fitch | 6–4, 6–4 |
| 1947 | Nancye Wynne Bolton | Nell Hopman | 6–3, 6–2 |
| 1948 | Nancye Wynne Bolton | Marie Toomey | 6–3, 6–1 |
| 1949 | Doris Hart | Nancye Wynne Bolton | 6–3, 6–4 |
| 1950 | Louise Brough | Doris Hart | 6–4, 3–6, 6–4 |
| 1951 | Nancye Wynne Bolton | Thelma Long | 6–1, 7–5 |
| 1952 | Thelma Long | H. Angwin | 6–2, 6–3 |
| 1953 | Maureen Connolly | Julia Sampson | 6–3, 6–2 |
| 1954 | Thelma Long | J. Staley | 6–3, 6–4 |
| 1955 | Beryl Penrose | Thelma Long | 6–4, 6–3 |
| 1956 | Mary Carter | Thelma Long | 3–6, 6–2, 9–7 |
| 1957 | Shirley Fry | Althea Gibson | 6–3, 6–4 |
| 1958 | Angela Mortimer | Lorraine Coghlan | 6–3, 6–4 |
| 1959 | Mary Carter-Reitano | Renee Schuurman | 6–2, 6–3 |
| 1960 | Margaret Smith | Jan Lehane | 7–5, 6–2 |
| 1961 | Margaret Smith | Jan Lehane | 6–1, 6–4 |
| 1962 | Margaret Smith | Jan Lehane | 6–0, 6–2 |
| 1963 | Margaret Smith | Jan Lehane | 6–2, 6–2 |
| 1964 | Margaret Smith | Lesley Turner | 6–3, 6–2 |
| 1965 | Margaret Smith | Maria Bueno | 5–7, 6–4, 5–2, ret. |
| 1966 | Margaret Smith | Nancy Richey | Default |
| 1967 | Nancy Richey | Lesley Turner | 6–1, 6–4 |
| 1968 | Billie Jean King | Margaret Smith | 6–1, 6–2 |
| 1969* | Margaret Smith Court | Billie Jean King | 6–4, 6–1 |
| 1970 | Margaret Smith Court | Kerry Melville Reid | 6–3, 6–1 |
| 1971 | Margaret Smith Court | Evonne Goolagong | 2–6, 7–6, 7–5 |
| 1972 | Virginia Wade | Evonne Goolagong | 6–4, 6–4 |
| 1973 | Margaret Smith Court | Evonne Goolagong | 6–4, 7–5 |
| 1974 | Evonne Goolagong | Chris Evert | 7–6, 4–6, 6–0 |
| 1975 | Evonne Goolagong | Martina Navratilova | 6–3, 6–2 |
| 1976 | Evonne Goolagong Cawley | Renata Tomanova | 6–2, 6–2 |
| 1977 (Jan) | Kerry Melville Reid | Dianne Balestrat | 7–5, 6–2 |
| 1977 (Dec) | Evonne Goolagong Cawley | Helen Gourlay | 6–3, 6–0 |
| 1978 | Chris O'Neil | Betsy Nagelsen | 6–3, 7–6 |
| 1979 | Barbara Jordan | Sharon Walsh | 6–3, 6–3 |
| 1980 | Hana Mandlikova | Wendy Turnbull | 6–0, 7–5 |
| 1981 | Martina Navratilova | Chris Evert Lloyd | 6–7, 6–4, 7–5 |
| 1982 | Chris Evert Lloyd | Martina Navratilova | 6–3, 2–6, 6–3 |
| 1983 | Martina Navratilova | Kathy Jordan | 6–2, 7–6 |
| 1984 | Chris Evert Lloyd | Helena Sukova | 6–7, 6–1, 6–3 |
| 1985 (Dec) | Martina Navratilova | Chris Evert Lloyd | 6–2, 4–6, 6–2 |
| 1987 (Jan) | Hana Mandlikova | Martina Navratilova | 7–5, 7–6 |
| 1988 | Steffi Graf | Chris Evert | 6–1, 7–6 |
| 1989 | Steffi Graf | Helena Sukova | 6–4, 6–4 |
| 1990 | Steffi Graf | Mary Joe Fernandez | 6–3, 6–4 |
| 1991 | Monica Seles | Jana Novotna | 5–7, 6–3, 6–1 |

*Became Open (amateur and professional) in 1969.

## WOMEN *(Cont.)*
### Australian Championships *(Cont.)*

| Year | Winner | Finalist | Score |
|---|---|---|---|
| 1992 | Monica Seles | Mary Joe Fernandez | 6–2, 6–3 |
| 1993 | Monica Seles | Steffi Graf | 4–6, 6–3, 6–2 |
| 1994 | Steffi Graf | Arantxa Sánchez Vicario | 6–0, 6–2 |
| 1995 | Mary Pierce | Arantxa Sánchez Vicario | 6–3, 6–2 |
| 1996 | Monica Seles | Anke Huber | 6–4, 6–1 |
| 1997 | Martina Hingis | Mary Pierce | 6–2, 6–2 |
| 1998 | Martina Hingis | Conchita Martinez | 6–3, 6–3 |
| 1999 | Martina Hingis | Amelie Mauresmo | 6–2, 6–3 |
| 2000 | Lindsay Davenport | Martina Hingis | 6–1, 7–5 |
| 2001 | Jennifer Capriati | Martina Hingis | 6–4, 6–3 |
| 2002 | Jennifer Capriati | Martina Hingis | 4–6, 7–6 (9–7), 6–2 |
| 2003 | Serena Williams | Venus Williams | 7–6 (7–4), 3–6, 6–4 |
| 2004 | Justine Henin-Hardenne | Kim Clijsters | 6–3, 4–6, 6–3 |
| 2005 | Serena Williams | Lindsay Davenport | 2–6, 6–3, 6–0 |
| 2006 | Amelie Mauresmo | Justine Henin-Hardenne | 6–1, 2–0, ret. |
| 2007 | Serena Williams | Maria Sharapova | 6–1, 6–2 |
| 2008 | Maria Sharapova | Ana Ivanovic | 7–5, 6–3 |
| 2009 | Serena Williams | Dinara Safina | 6–0, 6–3 |

### French Championships

| Year | Winner | Finalist | Score |
|---|---|---|---|
| 1925† | Suzanne Lenglen | Kathleen McKane | 6–1, 6–2 |
| 1926 | Suzanne Lenglen | Mary K. Browne | 6–1, 6–0 |
| 1927 | Kea Bouman | Irene Peacock | 6–2, 6–4 |
| 1928 | Helen Wills | Eileen Bennett | 6–1, 6–2 |
| 1929 | Helen Wills | Simone Mathieu | 6–3, 6–4 |
| 1930 | Helen Wills Moody | Helen Jacobs | 6–2, 6–1 |
| 1931 | Cilly Aussem | Betty Nuthall | 8–6, 6–1 |
| 1932 | Helen Wills Moody | Simone Mathieu | 7–5, 6–1 |
| 1933 | Margaret Scriven | Simone Mathieu | 6–2, 4–6, 6–4 |
| 1934 | Margaret Scriven | Helen Jacobs | 7–5, 4–6, 6–1 |
| 1935 | Hilde Sperling | Simone Mathieu | 6–2, 6–1 |
| 1936 | Hilde Sperling | Simone Mathieu | 6–3, 6–4 |
| 1937 | Hilde Sperling | Simone Mathieu | 6–2, 6–4 |
| 1938 | Simone Mathieu | Nelly Landry | 6–0, 6–3 |
| 1939 | Simone Mathieu | Jadwiga Jedrzejowska | 6–3, 8–6 |
| 1940–45 | No tournament | | |
| 1946 | Margaret Osborne | Pauline Betz | 1–6, 8–6, 7–5 |
| 1947 | Patricia Todd | Doris Hart | 6–3, 3–6, 6–4 |
| 1948 | Nelly Landry | Shirley Fry | 6–2, 0–6, 6–0 |
| 1949 | Margaret Osborne duPont | Nelly Adamson | 7–5, 6–2 |
| 1950 | Doris Hart | Patricia Todd | 6–4, 4–6, 6–2 |
| 1951 | Shirley Fry | Doris Hart | 6–3, 3–6, 6–3 |
| 1952 | Doris Hart | Shirley Fry | 6–4, 6–4 |
| 1953 | Maureen Connolly | Doris Hart | 6–2, 6–4 |
| 1954 | Maureen Connolly | Ginette Bucaille | 6–4, 6–1 |
| 1955 | Angela Mortimer | Dorothy Knode | 2–6, 7–5, 10–8 |
| 1956 | Althea Gibson | Angela Mortimer | 6–0, 12–10 |
| 1957 | Shirley Bloomer | Dorothy Knode | 6–1, 6–3 |
| 1958 | Zsuzsi Kormoczi | Shirley Bloomer | 6–4, 1–6, 6–2 |
| 1959 | Christine Truman | Zsuzsi Kormoczi | 6–4, 7–5 |
| 1960 | Darlene Hard | Yola Ramirez | 6–3, 6–4 |
| 1961 | Ann Haydon | Yola Ramirez | 6–2, 6–1 |
| 1962 | Margaret Smith | Lesley Turner | 6–3, 3–6, 7–5 |
| 1963 | Lesley Turner | Ann Haydon Jones | 2–6, 6–3, 7–5 |
| 1964 | Margaret Smith | Maria Bueno | 5–7, 6–1, 6–2 |
| 1965 | Lesley Turner | Margaret Smith | 6–3, 6–4 |
| 1966 | Ann Jones | Nancy Richey | 6–3, 6–1 |
| 1967 | Francoise Durr | Lesley Turner | 4–6, 6–3, 6–4 |
| 1968* | Nancy Richey | Ann Jones | 5–7, 6–4, 6–1 |
| 1969 | Margaret Smith Court | Ann Jones | 6–1, 4–6, 6–3 |
| 1970 | Margaret Smith Court | Helga Niesseri | 6–2, 6–4 |
| 1971 | Evonne Goolagong | Helen Gourlay | 6–3, 7–5 |

†1925 was the first year that entries were accepted from all countries. *Became Open (amateur and professional) in 1968, but restricted to only contract professionals in 1972.

### WOMEN *(Cont.)*

### French Championships *(Cont.)*

| Year | Winner | Finalist | Score |
|---|---|---|---|
| 1972 | Billie Jean King | Evonne Goolagong | 6–3, 6–3 |
| 1973 | Margaret Smith Court | Chris Evert | 6–7, 7–6, 6–4 |
| 1974 | Chris Evert | Olga Morozova | 6–1, 6–2 |
| 1975 | Chris Evert | Martina Navratilova | 2–6, 6–2, 6–1 |
| 1976 | Sue Barker | Renata Tomanova | 6–2, 0–6, 6–2 |
| 1977 | Mima Jausovec | Florenza Mihai | 6–2, 6–7, 6–1 |
| 1978 | Virginia Ruzici | Mima Jausovec | 6–2, 6–2 |
| 1979 | Chris Evert Lloyd | Wendy Turnbull | 6–2, 6–0 |
| 1980 | Chris Evert Lloyd | Virginia Ruzici | 6–0, 6–3 |
| 1981 | Hana Mandlikova | Sylvia Hanika | 6–2, 6–4 |
| 1982 | Martina Navratilova | Andrea Jaeger | 7–6, 6–1 |
| 1983 | Chris Evert Lloyd | Mima Jausovec | 6–1, 6–2 |
| 1984 | Martina Navratilova | Chris Evert Lloyd | 6–3, 6–1 |
| 1985 | Chris Evert Lloyd | Martina Navratilova | 6–3, 6–7, 7–5 |
| 1986 | Chris Evert Lloyd | Martina Navratilova | 2–6, 6–3, 6–3 |
| 1987 | Steffi Graf | Martina Navratilova | 6–4, 4–6, 8–6 |
| 1988 | Steffi Graf | Natalia Zvereva | 6–0, 6–0 |
| 1989 | Arantxa Sánchez Vicario | Steffi Graf | 7–6, 3–6, 7–5 |
| 1990 | Monica Seles | Steffi Graf | 7–6, 6–4 |
| 1991 | Monica Seles | Arantxa Sánchez Vicario | 6–3, 6–4 |
| 1992 | Monica Seles | Steffi Graf | 6–2, 3–6, 10–8 |
| 1993 | Steffi Graf | Mary Joe Fernandez | 4–6, 6–2, 6–4 |
| 1994 | Arantxa Sánchez Vicario | Mary Pierce | 6–4, 6–4 |
| 1995 | Steffi Graf | Arantxa Sánchez Vicario | 7–5, 4–6, 6–0 |
| 1996 | Steffi Graf | Arantxa Sánchez Vicario | 6–3, 6–7 (4–7), 10–8 |
| 1997 | Iva Majoli | Martina Hingis | 6–4, 6–2 |
| 1998 | Arantxa Sánchez Vicario | Monica Seles | 7–6 (7–5), 0–6, 6–2 |
| 1999 | Steffi Graf | Martina Hingis | 4–6, 7–5, 6–2 |
| 2000 | Mary Pierce | Conchita Martinez | 6–2, 7–5 |
| 2001 | Jennifer Capriati | Kim Clijsters | 1–6, 6–4, 12–10 |
| 2002 | Serena Williams | Venus Williams | 7–5, 6–3 |
| 2003 | Justine Henin-Hardenne | Kim Clijsters | 6–0, 6–4 |
| 2004 | Anastasia Myskina | Elena Dementieva | 6–1, 6–2 |
| 2005 | Justine Henin-Hardenne | Mary Pierce | 6–1, 6–1 |
| 2006 | Justine Henin-Hardenne | Svetlana Kuznetsova | 6–4, 6–4 |
| 2007 | Justine Henin | Ana Ivanovic | 6–1, 6–2 |
| 2008 | Ana Ivanovic | Dinara Safina | 6–4, 6–3 |
| 2009 | Svetlana Kuznetsova | Dinara Safina | 6–4, 6–2 |

### Wimbledon Championships

| Year | Winner | Finalist | Score |
|---|---|---|---|
| 1884 | Maud Watson | Lilian Watson | 6–8, 6–3, 6–3 |
| 1885 | Maud Watson | Blanche Bingley | 6–1, 7–5 |
| 1886 | Blanche Bingley | Maud Watson | 6–3, 6–3 |
| 1887 | Charlotte Dod | Blanche Bingley | 6–2, 6–0 |
| 1888 | Charlotte Dod | Blanche Bingley Hillyard | 6–3, 6–3 |
| 1889 | Blanche Bingley Hillyard | n/a | n/a |
| 1890 | Lena Rice | n/a | n/a |
| 1891 | Charlotte Dod | n/a | n/a |
| 1892 | Charlotte Dod | Blanche Bingley Hillyard | 6–1, 6–1 |
| 1893 | Charlotte Dod | Blanche Bingley Hillyard | 6–8, 6–1, 6–4 |
| 1894 | Blanche Bingley Hillyard | n/a | n/a |
| 1895 | Charlotte Cooper | n/a | |
| 1896 | Charlotte Cooper | Mrs. W. H. Pickering | 6–2, 6–3 |
| 1897 | Blanche Bingley Hillyard | Charlotte Cooper | 5–7, 7–5, 6–2 |
| 1898 | Charlotte Cooper | n/a | n/a |
| 1899 | Blanche Bingley Hillyard | Charlotte Cooper | 6–2, 6–3 |
| 1900 | Blanche Bingley Hillyard | Charlotte Cooper | 4–6, 6–4, 6–4 |
| 1901 | Charlotte Cooper Sterry | Blanche Bingley Hillyard | 6–2, 6–2 |
| 1902 | Muriel Robb | Charlotte Cooper Sterry | 7–5, 6–1 |
| 1903 | Dorothea Douglass | n/a | n/a |
| 1904 | Dorothea Douglass | Charlotte Cooper Sterry | 6–0, 6–3 |
| 1905 | May Sutton | Dorothea Douglass | 6–3, 6–4 |
| 1906 | Dorothea Douglass | May Sutton | 6–3, 9–7 |
| 1907 | May Sutton | Dorothea Douglass | 6–1, 6–4 |

## WOMEN (Cont.)

### Wimbledon Championships (Cont.)

| Year | Winner | Finalist | Score |
|---|---|---|---|
| | | Lambert Chambers | |
| 1908 | Charlotte Cooper Sterry | n/a | n/a |
| 1909 | Dora Boothby | n/a | n/a |
| 1910 | Dorothea Douglass Lambert Chambers | Dora Boothby | 6–2, 6–2 |
| 1911 | Dorothea Douglass Lambert Chambers | Dora Boothby | 6–0, 6–0 |
| 1912 | Ethel Larcombe | n/a | n/a |
| 1913 | Dorothea Douglass Lambert Chambers | | |
| 1914 | Dorothea Douglass Lambert Chambers | Ethel Larcombe | 7–5, 6–4 |
| 1915–18 | No tournament | | |
| 1919 | Suzanne Lenglen | Dorothea Douglass Lambert Chambers | 10–8, 4–6, 9–7 |
| 1920 | Suzanne Lenglen | Dorothea Douglass Lambert Chambers | 6–3, 6–0 |
| 1921 | Suzanne Lenglen | Elizabeth Ryan | 6–2, 6–0 |
| 1922 | Suzanne Lenglen | Molla Mallory | 6–2, 6–0 |
| 1923 | Suzanne Lenglen | Kathleen McKane | 6–2, 6–2 |
| 1924 | Kathleen McKane | Helen Wills | 4–6, 6–4, 6–2 |
| 1925 | Suzanne Lenglen | Joan Fry | 6–2, 6–0 |
| 1926 | Kathleen McKane Godfree | Lili de Alvarez | 6–2, 4–6, 6–3 |
| 1927 | Helen Wills | Lili de Alvarez | 6–2, 6–4 |
| 1928 | Helen Wills | Lili de Alvarez | 6–2, 6–3 |
| 1929 | Helen Wills | Helen Jacobs | 6–1, 6–2 |
| 1930 | Helen Wills Moody | Elizabeth Ryan | 6–2, 6–2 |
| 1931 | Cilly Aussem | Hilde Kranwinkel | 7–5, 7–5 |
| 1932 | Helen Wills Moody | Helen Jacobs | 6–3, 6–1 |
| 1933 | Helen Wills Moody | Dorothy Round | 6–4, 6–8, 6–3 |
| 1934 | Dorothy Round | Helen Jacobs | 6–2, 5–7, 6–3 |
| 1935 | Helen Wills Moody | Helen Jacobs | 6–3, 3–6, 7–5 |
| 1936 | Helen Jacobs | Hilde Kranwinkel Sperling | 6–2, 4–6, 7–5 |
| 1937 | Dorothy Round | Jadwiga Jedrzejowska | 6–2, 2–6, 7–5 |
| 1938 | Helen Wills Moody | Helen Jacobs | 6–4, 6–0 |
| 1939 | Alice Marble | Kay Stammers | 6–2, 6–0 |
| 1940–45 | No tournament | | |
| 1946 | Pauline Betz | Louise Brough | 6–2, 6–4 |
| 1947 | Margaret Osborne | Doris Hart | 6–2, 6–4 |
| 1948 | Louise Brough | Doris Hart | 6–3, 8–6 |
| 1949 | Louise Brough | Margaret Osborne duPont | 10–8, 1–6, 10–8 |
| 1950 | Louise Brough | Margaret Osborne duPont | 6–1, 3–6, 6–1 |
| 1951 | Doris Hart | Shirley Fry | 6–1, 6–0 |
| 1952 | Maureen Connolly | Louise Brough | 6–4, 6–3 |
| 1953 | Maureen Connolly | Doris Hart | 8–6, 7–5 |
| 1954 | Maureen Connolly | Louise Brough | 6–2, 7–5 |
| 1955 | Louise Brough | Beverly Fleitz | 7–5, 8–6 |
| 1956 | Shirley Fry | Angela Buxton | 6–3, 6–1 |
| 1957 | Althea Gibson | Darlene Hard | 6–3, 6–2 |
| 1958 | Althea Gibson | Angela Mortimer | 8–6, 6–2 |
| 1959 | Maria Bueno | Darlene Hard | 6–4, 6–3 |
| 1960 | Maria Bueno | Sandra Reynolds | 8–6, 6–0 |
| 1961 | Angela Mortimer | Christine Truman | 4–6, 6–4, 7–5 |
| 1962 | Karen Hantze Susman | Vera Sukova | 6–4, 6–4 |
| 1963 | Margaret Smith | Billie Jean Moffitt | 6–3, 6–4 |
| 1964 | Maria Bueno | Margaret Smith | 6–4, 7–9, 6–3 |
| 1965 | Margaret Smith | Maria Bueno | 6–4, 7–5 |
| 1966 | Billie Jean King | Maria Bueno | 6–3, 3–6, 6–1 |
| 1967 | Billie Jean King | Ann Haydon Jones | 6–3, 6–4 |
| 1968* | Billie Jean King | Judy Tegart | 9–7, 7–5 |
| 1969 | Ann Haydon Jones | Billie Jean King | 3–6, 6–3, 6–2 |
| 1970 | Margaret Smith Court | Billie Jean King | 14–12, 11–9 |

Note: Prior to 1922 the tournament was run on a challenge-round system. The previous year's winner "stood out" of an All-Comers event, which produced a challenger to play her for the title.

*Became Open (amateur and professional) in 1968, but restricted to only contract professionals in 1972.

### WOMEN *(Cont.)*
### Wimbledon Championships *(Cont.)*

| Year | Winner | Finalist | Score |
|---|---|---|---|
| 1971 | Evonne Goolagong | Margaret Smith Court | 6–4, 6–1 |
| 1972 | Billie Jean King | Evonne Goolagong | 6–3, 6–3 |
| 1973 | Billie Jean King | Chris Evert | 6–0, 7–5 |
| 1974 | Chris Evert | Olga Morozova | 6–0, 6–4 |
| 1975 | Billie Jean King | Evonne Goolagong Cawley | 6–0, 6–1 |
| 1976 | Chris Evert | Evonne Goolagong Cawley | 6–3, 4–6, 8–6 |
| 1977 | Virginia Wade | Betty Stove | 4–6, 6–3, 6–1 |
| 1978 | Martina Navratilova | Chris Evert | 2–6, 6–4, 7–5 |
| 1979 | Martina Navratilova | Chris Evert Lloyd | 6–4, 6–4 |
| 1980 | Evonne Goolagong Cawley | Chris Evert Lloyd | 6–1, 7–6 |
| 1981 | Chris Evert Lloyd | Hana Mandlikova | 6–2, 6–2 |
| 1982 | Martina Navratilova | Chris Evert Lloyd | 6–1, 3–6, 6–2 |
| 1983 | Martina Navratilova | Andrea Jaeger | 6–0, 6–3 |
| 1984 | Martina Navratilova | Chris Evert Lloyd | 7–6, 6–2 |
| 1985 | Martina Navratilova | Chris Evert Lloyd | 4–6, 6–3, 6–2 |
| 1986 | Martina Navratilova | Hana Mandlikova | 7–6, 6–3 |
| 1987 | Martina Navratilova | Steffi Graf | 7–5, 6–3 |
| 1988 | Steffi Graf | Martina Navratilova | 5–7, 6–2, 6–1 |
| 1989 | Steffi Graf | Martina Navratilova | 6–2, 6–7, 6–1 |
| 1990 | Martina Navratilova | Zina Garrison | 6–4, 6–1 |
| 1991 | Steffi Graf | Gabriela Sabatini | 6–4, 3–6, 8–6 |
| 1992 | Steffi Graf | Monica Seles | 6–2, 6–1 |
| 1993 | Steffi Graf | Jana Novotna | 7–6, 1–6, 6–4 |
| 1994 | Conchita Martinez | Martina Navratilova | 6–4, 3–6, 6–3 |
| 1995 | Steffi Graf | Arantxa Sánchez Vicario | 4–6, 6–1, 7–5 |
| 1996 | Steffi Graf | Arantxa Sánchez Vicario | 6–3, 7–5 |
| 1997 | Martina Hingis | Jana Novotna | 2–6, 6–3, 6–3 |
| 1998 | Jana Novotna | Nathalie Tauziat | 6–4, 7–6 |
| 1999 | Lindsay Davenport | Steffi Graf | 6–4, 7–5 |
| 2000 | Venus Williams | Lindsay Davenport | 6–3, 7–6 |
| 2001 | Venus Williams | Justine Henin | 6–1, 3–6, 6–0 |
| 2002 | Serena Williams | Venus Williams | 7–6 (7–4), 6–3 |
| 2003 | Serena Williams | Venus Williams | 4–6, 6–4, 6–2 |
| 2004 | Maria Sharapova | Serena Williams | 6–1, 6–4 |
| 2005 | Venus Williams | Lindsay Davenport | 4–6, 7–6 (7–4), 9–7 |
| 2006 | Amelie Mauresmo | Justine Henin-Hardenne | 2–6, 6–3, 6–4 |
| 2007 | Venus Williams | Marion Bartoli | 6–4, 6–1 |
| 2008 | Venus Williams | Serena Williams | 7–5, 6–4 |
| 2009 | Serena Williams | Venus Williams | 7–6 (7–3), 6–2 |

### United States Championships

| Year | Winner | Finalist | Score |
|---|---|---|---|
| 1887 | Ellen Hansell | Laura Knight | 6–1, 6–0 |
| 1888 | Bertha L. Townsend | Ellen Hansell | 6–3, 6–5 |
| 1889 | Bertha L. Townsend | Louise Voorhes | 7–5, 6–2 |
| 1890 | Ellen C. Roosevelt | Bertha L. Townsend | 6–2, 6–2 |
| 1891 | Mabel Cahill | Ellen C. Roosevelt | 6–4, 6–1, 4–6, 6–3 |
| 1892 | Mabel Cahill | Elisabeth Moore | 5–7, 6–3, 6–4, 4–6, 6–2 |
| 1893 | Aline Terry | Alice Schultze | 6–1, 6–3 |
| 1894 | Helen Hellwig | Aline Terry | 7–5, 3–6, 6–0, 3–6, 6–3 |
| 1895 | Juliette Atkinson | Helen Hellwig | 6–4, 6–2, 6–1 |
| 1896 | Elisabeth Moore | Juliette Atkinson | 6–4, 4–6, 6–2, 6–2 |
| 1897 | Juliette Atkinson | Elisabeth Moore | 6–3, 6–3, 4–6, 3–6, 6–3 |
| 1898 | Juliette Atkinson | Marion Jones | 6–3, 5–7, 6–4, 2–6, 7–5 |
| 1899 | Marion Jones | Maud Banks | 6–1, 6–1, 7–5 |
| 1900 | Myrtle McAteer | Edith Parker | 6–2, 6–2, 6–0 |
| 1901 | Elisabeth Moore | Myrtle McAteer | 6–4, 3–6, 7–5, 2–6, 6–2 |
| 1902* | Marion Jones | Elisabeth Moore | 6–1, 1–0, ret. |
| 1903 | Elisabeth Moore | Marion Jones | 7–5, 8–6 |
| 1904 | May Sutton | Elisabeth Moore | 6–1, 6–2 |
| 1905 | Elisabeth Moore | Helen Homans | 6–4, 5–7, 6–1 |
| 1906 | Helen Homans | Maud Barger-Wallach | 6–4, 6–3 |
| 1907 | Evelyn Sears | Carrie Neely | 6–3, 6–2 |
| 1908 | Maud Barger–Wallach | Evelyn Sears | 6–3, 1–6, 6–3 |
| 1909 | Hazel Hotchkiss | Maud Barger–Wallach | 6–0, 6–1 |

*Five-set final abolished;

## WOMEN *(Cont.)*

### United States Championships *(Cont.)*

| Year | Winner | Finalist | Score |
|---|---|---|---|
| 1910 | Hazel Hotchkiss | Louise Hammond | 6–4, 6–2 |
| 1911 | Hazel Hotchkiss | Florence Sutton | 8–10, 6–1, 9–7 |
| 1912† | Mary K. Browne | Eleanora Sears | 6–4, 6–2 |
| 1913 | Mary K. Browne | Dorothy Green | 6–2, 7–5 |
| 1914 | Mary K. Browne | Marie Wagner | 6–2, 1–6, 6–1 |
| 1915 | Molla Bjurstedt | Hazel Hotchkiss Wightman | 4–6, 6–2, 6–0 |
| 1916 | Molla Bjurstedt | Louise Hammond Raymond | 6–0, 6–1 |
| 1917‡ | Molla Bjurstedt | Marion Vanderhoef | 4–6, 6–0, 6–2 |
| 1918 | Molla Bjurstedt | Eleanor Goss | 6–4, 6–3 |
| 1919 | Hazel Hotchkiss Wightman | Marion Zinderstein | 6–1, 6–2 |
| 1920 | Molla Bjurstedt Mallory | Marion Zinderstein | 6–3, 6–1 |
| 1921 | Molla Bjurstedt Mallory | Mary K. Browne | 4–6, 6–4, 6–2 |
| 1922 | Molla Bjurstedt Mallory | Helen Wills | 6–3, 6–1 |
| 1923 | Helen Wills | Molla Bjurstedt Mallory | 6–2, 6–1 |
| 1924 | Helen Wills | Molla Bjurstedt Mallory | 6–1, 6–3 |
| 1925 | Helen Wills | Kathleen McKane | 3–6, 6–0, 6–2 |
| 1926 | Molla Bjurstedt Mallory | Elizabeth Ryan | 4–6, 6–4, 9–7 |
| 1927 | Helen Wills | Betty Nuthall | 6–1, 6–4 |
| 1928 | Helen Wills | Helen Jacobs | 6–2, 6–1 |
| 1929 | Helen Wills | Phoebe Holcroft Watson | 6–4, 6–2 |
| 1930 | Betty Nuthall | Anna McCune Harper | 6–1, 6–4 |
| 1931 | Helen Wills Moody | Eileen Whitingstall | 6–4, 6–1 |
| 1932 | Helen Jacobs | Carolin Babcock | 6–2, 6–2 |
| 1933 | Helen Jacobs | Helen Wills Moody | 8–6, 3–6, 3–0, ret. |
| 1934 | Helen Jacobs | Sarah Palfrey | 6–1, 6–4 |
| 1935 | Helen Jacobs | Sarah Palfrey Fabyan | 6–2, 6–4 |
| 1936 | Alice Marble | Helen Jacobs | 4–6, 6–3, 6–2 |
| 1937 | Anita Lizane | Jadwiga Jedrzejowska | 6–4, 6–2 |
| 1938 | Alice Marble | Nancye Wynne | 6–0, 6–3 |
| 1939 | Alice Marble | Helen Jacobs | 6–0, 8–10, 6–4 |
| 1940 | Alice Marble | Helen Jacobs | 6–2, 6–3 |
| 1941 | Sarah Palfrey Cooke | Pauline Betz | 7–5, 6–2 |
| 1942 | Pauline Betz | Louise Brough | 4–6, 6–1, 6–4 |
| 1943 | Pauline Betz | Louise Brough | 6–3, 5–7, 6–3 |
| 1944 | Pauline Betz | Margaret Osborne | 6–3, 8–6 |
| 1945 | Sarah Palfrey Cooke | Pauline Betz | 3–6, 8–6, 6–4 |
| 1946 | Pauline Betz | Patricia Canning | 11–9, 6–3 |
| 1947 | Louise Brough | Margaret Osborne | 8–6, 4–6, 6–1 |
| 1948 | Margaret Osborne duPont | Louise Brough | 4–6, 6–4, 15–13 |
| 1949 | Margaret Osborne duPont | Doris Hart | 6–4, 6–1 |
| 1950 | Margaret Osborne duPont | Doris Hart | 6–4, 6–3 |
| 1951 | Maureen Connolly | Shirley Fry | 6–3, 1–6, 6–4 |
| 1952 | Maureen Connolly | Doris Hart | 6–3, 7–5 |
| 1953 | Maureen Connolly | Doris Hart | 6–2, 6–4 |
| 1954 | Doris Hart | Louise Brough | 6–8, 6–1, 8–6 |
| 1955 | Doris Hart | Patricia Ward | 6–4, 6–2 |
| 1956 | Shirley Fry | Althea Gibson | 6–3, 6–4 |
| 1957 | Althea Gibson | Louise Brough | 6–3, 6–2 |
| 1958 | Althea Gibson | Darlene Hard | 3–6, 6–1, 6–2 |
| 1959 | Maria Bueno | Christine Truman | 6–1, 6–4 |
| 1960 | Darlene Hard | Maria Bueno | 6–4, 10–12, 6–4 |
| 1961 | Darlene Hard | Ann Haydon | 6–3, 6–4 |
| 1962 | Margaret Smith | Darlene Hard | 9–7, 6–4 |
| 1963 | Maria Bueno | Margaret Smith | 7–5, 6–4 |
| 1964 | Maria Bueno | Carole Graebner | 6–1, 6–0 |
| 1965 | Margaret Smith | Billie Jean Moffitt | 8–6, 7–5 |
| 1966 | Maria Bueno | Nancy Richey | 6–3, 6–1 |
| 1967 | Billie Jean King | Ann Haydon Jones | 11–9, 6–4 |
| 1968** | Virginia Wade | Billie Jean King | 6–4, 6–4 |
| 1968# | Margaret Smith Court | Maria Bueno | 6–2, 6–2 |
| 1969 | Margaret Smith Court | Nancy Richey | 6–2, 6–2 |
| 1969# | Margaret Smith Court | Virginia Wade | 4–6, 6–3, 6–0 |
| 1970 | Margaret Smith Court | Rosie Casals | 6–2, 2–6, 6–1 |

†Challenge round abolished. ‡National Patriotic Tournament.
**Became Open (amateur and professional) in 1968. #Amateur event held.

## WOMEN *(Cont.)*

### United States Championships *(Cont.)*

| Year | Winner | Finalist | Score |
|---|---|---|---|
| 1971 | Billie Jean King | Rosie Casals | 6–4, 7–6 |
| 1972 | Billie Jean King | Kerry Melville | 6–3, 7–5 |
| 1973 | Margaret Smith Court | Evonne Goolagong | 7–6, 5–7, 6–2 |
| 1974 | Billie Jean King | Evonne Goolagong | 3–6, 6–3, 7–5 |
| 1975 | Chris Evert | Evonne Goolagong Cawley | 5–7, 6–4, 6–2 |
| 1976 | Chris Evert | Evonne Goolagong Cawley | 6–3, 6–0 |
| 1977 | Chris Evert | Wendy Turnbull | 7–6, 6–2 |
| 1978 | Chris Evert | Pam Shriver | 7–6, 6–4 |
| 1979 | Tracy Austin | Chris Evert Lloyd | 6–4, 6–3 |
| 1980 | Chris Evert Lloyd | Hana Mandlikova | 5–7, 6–1, 6–1 |
| 1981 | Tracy Austin | Martina Navratilova | 1–6, 7–6, 7–6 |
| 1982 | Chris Evert Lloyd | Hana Mandlikova | 6–3, 6–1 |
| 1983 | Martina Navratilova | Chris Evert Lloyd | 6–1, 6–3 |
| 1984 | Martina Navratilova | Chris Evert Lloyd | 4–6, 6–4, 6–4 |
| 1985 | Hana Mandlikova | Martina Navratilova | 7–6, 1–6, 7–6 |
| 1986 | Martina Navratilova | Helena Sukova | 6–3, 6–2 |
| 1987 | Martina Navratilova | Steffi Graf | 7–6, 6–1 |
| 1988 | Steffi Graf | Gabriela Sabatini | 6–3, 3–6, 6–1 |
| 1989 | Steffi Graf | Martina Navratilova | 3–6, 6–4, 6–2 |
| 1990 | Gabriela Sabatini | Steffi Graf | 6–2, 7–6 |
| 1991 | Monica Seles | Martina Navratilova | 7–6, 6–1 |
| 1992 | Monica Seles | Arantxa Sánchez Vicario | 6–3, 6–2 |
| 1993 | Steffi Graf | Helena Sukova | 6–3, 6–3 |
| 1994 | Arantxa Sánchez Vicario | Steffi Graf | 1–6, 7–6, 6–4 |
| 1995 | Steffi Graf | Monica Seles | 7–6, 0–6, 6–3 |
| 1996 | Steffi Graf | Monica Seles | 7–5, 7–4 |
| 1997 | Martina Hingis | Venus Williams | 6–0, 6–4 |
| 1998 | Lindsay Davenport | Martina Hingis | 6–3, 7–5 |
| 1999 | Serena Williams | Martina Hingis | 6–3, 7–6 |
| 2000 | Venus Williams | Lindsay Davenport | 6–4, 7–5 |
| 2001 | Venus Williams | Serena Williams | 6–2, 6–4 |
| 2002 | Serena Williams | Venus Williams | 6–4, 6–3 |
| 2003 | Justine Henin-Hardenne | Kim Clijsters | 7–5, 6–1 |
| 2004 | Svetlana Kuznetsova | Elena Dementieva | 6–3, 7–5 |
| 2005 | Kim Clijsters | Mary Pierce | 6–3, 6–1 |
| 2006 | Maria Sharapova | Justine Henin-Hardenne | 6–4, 6–4 |
| 2007 | Justine Henin | Svetlana Kuznetsova | 6–1, 6–3 |
| 2008 | Serena Williams | Jelena Jankovic | 6–4, 7–5 |
| 2009 | Kim Clijsters | Caroline Wozniacki | 7–5, 6–3 |

## Single-Year Grand Slam Winners

### Singles

Don Budge, 1938
Maureen Connolly, 1953
Rod Laver, 1962, 1969
Margaret Smith Court, 1970
Steffi Graf, 1988

### Doubles

Frank Sedgman and Ken McGregor, 1951
Martina Navratilova and Pam Shriver, 1984
Maria Bueno and two partners, 1960
Christine Truman (Australian),
Darlene Hard (French, Wimbledon
and U.S.)
Martina Hingis and two partners, 1998
Mirjana Lucic (Australian),
Jana Novotna (French, Wimbledon
and U.S.)

### Mixed Doubles

Margaret Smith and Ken Fletcher, 1963
Owen Davidson and two partners, 1967
Lesley Turner (Australian),
Billie Jean King (French, Wimbledon
and U.S.)

## Alltime Grand Slam Champions (Singles, Doubles, and Mixed Doubles)

### MEN

| Player | Aus.<br>S-D-M | French<br>S-D-M | Wim.<br>S-D-M | U.S.<br>S-D-M | Total |
|---|---|---|---|---|---|
| Roy Emerson | 6-3-0 | 2-6-0 | 2-3-0 | 2-4-0 | 28 |
| John Newcombe | 2-5-0 | 0-3-0 | 3-6-0 | 2-3-1 | 25 |
| Frank Sedgman | 2-2-2 | 0-3-2 | 1-2-2 | 2-2-2 | 22 |
| Todd Woodbridge | 0-3-1 | 0-1-1 | 0-9-1 | 0-3-3 | 22 |
| Bill Tilden | † | 0-0-1 | 3-1-0 | 7-5-4 | 21 |
| Rod Laver | 3-4-0 | 2-1-1 | 4-1-2 | 2-0-0 | 20 |
| John Bromwich | 2-8-1 | 0-0-0 | 0-2-2 | 0-3-1 | 19 |
| Jean Borotra | 1-1-1 | 1-5-2 | 2-3-1 | 0-0-1 | 18 |
| Fred Stolle | 0-3-1 | 1-2-0 | 0-2-3 | 1-3-2 | 18 |
| Ken Rosewall | 4-3-0 | 2-2-0 | 0-2-0 | 2-2-1 | 18 |
| Neale Fraser | 0-3-1 | 0-3-0 | 1-2-0 | 2-3-3 | 18 |
| Adrian Quist | 3-10-0 | 0-1-0 | 0-2-0 | 0-1-0 | 17 |
| John McEnroe | 0-0-0 | 0-0-1 | 3-4-0 | 4-5-0 | 17 |
| Jack Crawford | 4-4-3 | 1-1-1 | 1-1-1 | 0-0-0 | 17 |
| Mark Woodforde | 0-2-2 | 0-1-1 | 0-6-1 | 0-3-1 | 17 |

†Did not compete.

### WOMEN

| Player | Aus.<br>S-D-M | French<br>S-D-M | Wim.<br>S-D-M | U.S.<br>S-D-M | Total |
|---|---|---|---|---|---|
| Margaret Smith Court | 11-8-2 | 5-4-4 | 3-2-5 | 5-5-8 | 62 |
| Martina Navratilova | 3-8-1 | 2-7-2 | 9-7-4 | 4-9-3 | 59 |
| Billie Jean King | 1-0-1 | 1-1-2 | 6-10-4 | 4-5-4 | 39 |
| Doris Hart | 1-1-2 | 2-5-3 | 1-4-5 | 2-4-5 | 35 |
| Helen Wills Moody | † | 4-2-0 | 8-3-1 | 7-4-2 | 31 |
| Louise Brough | 1-1-0 | 0-3-0 | 4-5-4 | 1-8-3 | 30** |
| Margaret Osborne duPont | † | 2-3-0 | 1-5-1 | 3-8-6 | 29** |
| Elizabeth Ryan | † | 0-4-0 | 0-12-7 | 0-1-2 | 26 |
| *Serena Williams | 4-3-0 | 1-1-0 | 3-4-1 | 3-2-1 | 23 |
| Steffi Graf | 4-0-0 | 6-0-0 | 7-1-0 | 5-0-0 | 23 |
| Pam Shriver | 0-7-0 | 0-4-1 | 0-5-0 | 0-5-0 | 22 |
| Chris Evert | 2-0-0 | 7-2-0 | 3-1-0 | 6-0-0 | 21 |
| Darlene Hard | † | 1-3-2 | 0-4-3 | 2-6-0 | 21 |
| Suzanne Lenglen | † | 2-2-2# | 6-6-3 | 0-0-0 | 21 |
| Nancye Wynne Bolton | 6-10-4 | 0-0-0 | 0-0-0 | 0-0-0 | 20 |
| *Venus Williams | 0-3-1 | 0-1-1 | 5-4-0 | 2-2-0 | 19 |
| Maria Bueno | 0-1-0 | 0-1-1 | 3-5-0 | 4-4-0 | 19 |
| Thelma Coyne Long | 2-12-4 | 0-0-1 | 0-0-0 | 0-0-0 | 19 |

*Active player in 2009. †Did not compete. #Suzanne Lenglen won four singles titles at the French Championships before competition was opened to entries from all nations in 1925. **From 1940–45, with competition in the U.S. Championships thinned due to war, Louise Brough Clapp won four doubles titles (1942–45) and one mixed doubles title (1942); and Margaret Osborne duPont won five doubles titles (1941–45) and three mixed doubles titles (1943–45).

## Alltime Grand Slam Singles Champions

### MEN

| Player | Aus. | French | Wim. | U.S. | Total |
|---|---|---|---|---|---|
| *Roger Federer | 3 | 1 | 6 | 5 | 15 |
| Pete Sampras | 2 | 0 | 7 | 5 | 14 |
| Roy Emerson | 6 | 2 | 2 | 2 | 12 |
| Bjorn Borg | 0 | 6 | 5 | 0 | 11 |
| Rod Laver | 3 | 2 | 4 | 2 | 11 |
| Bill Tilden | † | 0 | 3 | 7 | 10 |
| Jimmy Connors | 1 | 0 | 2 | 5 | 8 |
| Ivan Lendl | 2 | 3 | 0 | 3 | 8 |
| Fred Perry | 1 | 1 | 3 | 3 | 8 |
| Ken Rosewall | 4 | 2 | 0 | 2 | 8 |
| Andre Agassi | 4 | 1 | 1 | 2 | 8 |
| Henri Cochet | † | 4 | 2 | 1 | 7 |
| Rene Lacoste | † | 3 | 2 | 2 | 7 |
| Bill Larned | † | † | 0 | 7 | 7 |
| John McEnroe | 0 | 0 | 3 | 4 | 7 |
| John Newcombe | 2 | 0 | 3 | 2 | 7 |
| Willie Renshaw | † | † | 7 | † | 7 |
| Dick Sears | † | † | 0 | 7 | 7 |

### WOMEN

| Player | Aus. | French | Wim. | U.S. | Total |
|---|---|---|---|---|---|
| Margaret Smith Court | 11 | 5 | 3 | 5 | 24 |
| Steffi Graf | 4 | 6 | 7 | 5 | 22 |
| Helen Wills Moody | † | 4 | 8 | 7 | 19 |
| Chris Evert | 2 | 7 | 3 | 6 | 18 |
| Martina Navratilova | 3 | 2 | 9 | 4 | 18 |
| Billie Jean King | 1 | 1 | 6 | 4 | 12 |
| *Serena Williams | 4 | 1 | 3 | 3 | 11 |
| Maureen Connolly | 1 | 2 | 3 | 3 | 9 |
| Monica Seles | 4 | 3 | 0 | 2 | 9 |
| Suzanne Lenglen | † | 2# | 6 | 0 | 8 |
| Molla Bjurstedt Mallory | † | † | 0 | 8 | 8 |
| Maria Bueno | 0 | 0 | 3 | 4 | 7 |
| Evonne Goolagong | 4 | 1 | 2 | 0 | 7 |
| Dorothea D.L. Chambers | † | † | 7 | 0 | 7 |
| Justine Henin | 1 | 4 | 0 | 2 | 7 |
| *Venus Williams | 0 | 0 | 5 | 2 | 7 |

*Active player in 2009. †Did not compete.

ROBERT BECK

# Golf

**Phil Mickelson (l.) and Tiger Woods both closed out a disappointing 2009 on an upbeat note at the PGA TOUR Championship**

# Tiger's Sweet, but in Minor Key

Golf's dominating figure roared back from injury in '09 and won the FedEx Cup playoffs, but Woods' brilliant play on Tour still didn't net him a victory at a major

## BY MERRELL NODEN

THE GOLF SEASON ENDED WITH A sponsor's dream: Tiger Woods and Phil Mickelson posing side by side at East Lake Golf Club in Atlanta, each with a trophy, a big smile, and mixed feelings about the past year. Mickelson had played exceptionally well in the season-ending Tour Championship, going 12-under par over the final three rounds to come from behind and beat Woods by three strokes. That was a fantastic end to a trying summer during which both his wife, Amy, and his mother, Mary, had been diagnosed with breast cancer. With the two undergoing treatment, Mickelson had played sporadically, finishing tied for second in an emotional U.S. Open at Bethpage Black, but then skipping the British Open and finishing 73rd at the PGA. After finding his putting stroke at East Lake, he reclaimed second place in the world rankings.

For Woods, winning the season-ending FedEx Cup was a somewhat muted victory at the end of a somewhat muted season. Sure, it was nice to be going home with the $10-million first prize, but Woods has never played for money. He did not play especially well on the weekend of this final event, losing the 36-hole lead to 49-year-old Kenny Perry and then getting passed by Mickelson in the final round. Granted, there had been serious questions about how Woods would fare after the season-ending knee surgery and eight-month layoff that followed his dramatic win at the 2008 U.S. Open. At East Lake the brilliant shots never materialized for Woods and for the first time since 2004 he finished the year without winning a single major. Despite his six Tour victories—more than twice any other golfer's total—by Woods's own exacting standards 2009 had to have been a disappointing year.

Despite the tendency of this pair to suck up all the attention, there were other stories—a deluged U.S. Open that only Noah could love; an astonishing resurgence by 59-year-old Tom Watson, not to mention the season-long brilliance of Perry; and the indifferent play of Lorena Ochoa. Like Woods, Ochoa finished the year the way she started it—ranked No. 1 in the world—but just didn't seem to be the same golfer she was in 2008. She too won no majors, which were instead scattered among four women.

No one is surprised any more when Woods does something amazing. In his first tournament back in 2009, Woods lost to Tim Clark in the second round of the World Match Play but he looked good. So, when he won the Arnold Palmer Invitational two weeks before the Masters, expectations were as high as ever.

FRED VUICH

At age 59, Tom Watson dazzled at Turnberry, but he fell just short of his sixth British Open, losing in a four-hole playoff to Stewart Cink.

But at Augusta, despite benign weather, Woods failed to break 70 until the final round and was never really a threat to win. He and Mickelson did thrill the galleries by playing their final round together, with Mickelson getting the better of him by one stroke to finish fifth with Woods tied for sixth. As it turned out, crowd favorite Perry would have won the Masters with a par on either the 71st or 72nd hole. Instead, he bogeyed both to fall into a playoff with Chad Campbell and Argentina's Angel Cabrera. Campbell was dropped on the first playoff hole, while Cabrera got a stroke of luck to hang in. After slicing his tee shot into the woods and getting a lucky bounce off a tree and back into the fairway on his second, Cabrera got up and down for par and then beat Perry on the second playoff hole.

Cabrera's nickname is "El Pato," or "The Duck," for his wide-stance walk, and it would have helped to be a duck or some other waterfowl at this year's foul U.S. Open. The rain fell in sheets, forcing the first round to be suspended after only a few holes and the tournament to finish on a Monday. In these atrocious conditions, a variety of players made a run at the lead. There was young, muscular Ricky Barnes, who self-destructed on the final round's front nine. There was Mickelson, who took a share of the lead in the final round before fading with bogeys at Nos. 15 and 17. And wonder and wonders, there was David Duval, who had slipped from No. 1 in 1999 to No. 882, tied for the lead on the 71st hole. He lost it when Lucas Glover birdied the 16th and ended up tied for second with Barnes and Mickelson. Glover would win by two strokes, another surprise since he had voluntarily taken a three-month break from the game in 2008.

Even after those surprises, no one was prepared for what transpired at Turnberry in mid-July. Watson, who won the first of his five Claret Jugs in 1975 and the last in 1983, actually led the British Open through 71 holes. Indeed, even after Stewart Cink had sunk a 15-foot birdie putt on the 72nd hole, Watson had an eight-foot par putt to win his sixth Open. He missed. That set up a four-hole playoff where, by his own admission, Watson "hit one bad shot after another," losing by six strokes. It was Cink's first major win.

That brought the world's top golfers to Hazeltine, in Chaska, Minnesota, where the course measured a whopping 7,674 yards, the longest ever for a major. The final round started with Woods holding a two-stroke lead over Y.E. Yang of South Korea, who was ranked just 110th. After Woods bogeyed No. 8, the two were tied and would remain that way until the 14th hole, when Yang sank a 60-foot chip for eagle to take a two-stroke lead. Then on 18, Yang hit a hybrid from 197 yards out to 10 feet and sunk his birdie putt to become the first Asian player to win a major.

Did Woods flinch in the biggest tournaments? It's hard to tell. But there seemed to be no problem with his knee. Woods's scoring average for his 16 tournaments was 68.05 and he topped the money list with $10,508.163. But using the yardstick Woods himself values most—majors won—it was a disappointing year. He remains at 14 career majors, four behind Jack Nicklaus's record. He'll resume his quest next year, pursued by Mickelson and a growing group of players emboldened by what they saw this year.

## Men's Majors

### The Masters
**Augusta National GC (par 72; 7,435 yds);**
**Augusta, Ga., April 9–12, 2009**

| Player | Score | Earnings ($) |
| --- | --- | --- |
| *Angel Cabrera | 68-68-69-71--276 | 1,350,000 |
| Chad Campbell | 65-70-72-69--276 | 660,000 |
| Kenny Perry | 68-67-70-71--276 | 660,000 |
| Shingo Katayama | 67-73-70-68--278 | 360,000 |
| Phil Mickelson | 73-68-71-67--279 | 300,000 |
| Steve Flesch | 71-74-68-67--280 | 242,813 |
| John Merrick | 68-74-72-66--280 | 242,813 |
| Steve Stricker | 72-69-68-71--280 | 242,813 |
| Tiger Woods | 70-72-70-68--280 | 242,813 |
| Jim Furyk | 66-74-68-73--281 | 187,500 |
| Hunter Mahan | 66-75-71-69--281 | 187,500 |
| Sean O'Hair | 68-76-68-69--281 | 187,500 |
| Tim Clark | 68-71-72-71--282 | 150,000 |
| Camilo Villegas | 73-69-71-69--282 | 150,000 |
| Todd Hamilton | 68-70-72-73--283 | 131,250 |
| Geoff Ogilvy | 71-70-73-69--283 | 131,250 |
| Aaron Baddeley | 68-74-73-69--284 | 116,250 |
| Graeme McDowell | 69-73-73-69--284 | 116,250 |
| Nick Watney | 70-71-71-73--285 | 105,000 |
| Stephen Ames | 73-68-71-74--286 | 71,400 |
| Paul Casey | 72-72-73-69--286 | 71,400 |
| Ryuji Imada | 73-72-72-69--286 | 71,400 |
| Trevor Immelman | 71-74-72-69--286 | 71,400 |
| Anthony Kim | 75-65-72-74--286 | 71,400 |
| Sandy Lyle | 72-70-73-71--286 | 71,400 |
| Rory McIlroy | 72-73-71-70--286 | 71,400 |
| Ian Poulter | 71-73-68-74--286 | 71,400 |
| Justin Rose | 74-70-71-71--286 | 71,400 |
| Rory Sabbatini | 73-67-70-76--286 | 71,400 |

*Winner on second hole of sudden-death playoff.

### U.S. Open
**Bethpage S.P.–Black Course (par 70; 7,445 yds);**
**Farmingdale, N.Y., June 18–22*, 2009**

| Player | Score | Earnings ($) |
| --- | --- | --- |
| Lucas Glover | 69-64-70-73--276 | 1,350,000 |
| Phil Mickelson | 69-70-69-70--278 | 559,830 |
| David Duval | 67-70-70-71--278 | 559,830 |
| Ricky Barnes | 67-65-70-76--278 | 559,830 |
| Ross Fisher | 70-68-69-72--279 | 289,146 |
| Tiger Woods | 74-69-68-69--280 | 233,350 |
| Soren Hansen | 70-71-70-69--280 | 233,350 |
| Hunter Mahan | 72-68-68-72--280 | 233,350 |
| Henrik Stenson | 73-70-70-68--281 | 197,794 |
| Rory McIlroy | 72-70-72-68--282 | 154,600 |
| Matt Bettencourt | 75-67-71-69--282 | 154,600 |
| Sergio Garcia | 70-70-72-70--282 | 154,600 |
| Ryan Moore | 70-69-72-71--282 | 154,600 |
| Stephen Ames | 74-66-70-72--282 | 154,600 |
| Mike Weir | 64-70-74-74--282 | 154,600 |
| Anthony Kim | 71-71-71-70--283 | 122,128 |
| Retief Goosen | 73-68-68-74--283 | 122,128 |
| Ian Poulter | 70-74-73-67--284 | 100,308 |
| Michael Sim | 71-70-71-72--284 | 100,308 |
| Peter Hanson | 66-71-73-74--284 | 100,308 |
| Graeme McDowell | 69-72-69-74--284 | 100,308 |
| Bubba Watson | 72-70-67-75--284 | 100,308 |
| Lee Westwood | 72-66-74-73--285 | 76,422 |
| Steve Stricker | 73-66-72-74--285 | 76,422 |
| Oliver Wilson | 70-70-71-74--285 | 76,422 |
| Sean O'Hair | 69-69-71-76--285 | 76,422 |

*Because of rain delays, final round finished on Monday, June 22.

### British Open
**Turnberry GC-Ailsa Course (par 70; 7,204 yds);**
**Ayrshire, Scotland, July 16–19, 2009**

| Player | Score | Earnings ($) |
| --- | --- | --- |
| ‡Stewart Cink | 66-72-71-69--278 | 1,221,005 |
| Tom Watson | 65-70-71-72--278 | 732,603 |
| Chris Wood | 70-70-72-67--279 | 415,142 |
| Lee Westwood | 68-70-70-71--279 | 415,142 |
| Luke Donald | 71-72-70-67--280 | 255,597 |
| Retief Goosen | 67-70-71-72--280 | 255,597 |
| Mathew Goggin | 66-72-69-73--280 | 255,597 |
| Soren Hansen | 68-72-74-67--281 | 147,172 |
| Justin Leonard | 69-72-72-68--281 | 147,172 |
| Ernie Els | 70-70-73-68--281 | 147,172 |
| Thomas Aiken | 71-72-69-69--281 | 147,172 |
| Richard S. Johnson | 70-72-69-70--281 | 147,172 |
| Jeff Overton | 70-69-76-67--282 | 82,866 |
| Andres Romero | 68-74-73-67--282 | 82,866 |
| Miguel Angel Jimenez | 64-73-76-69--282 | 82,866 |
| †Matteo Manassero | 71-70-72-69--282 | – |
| Camilo Villegas | 66-73-73-70--282 | 82,866 |
| Justin Rose | 69-72-71-70--282 | 82,866 |
| Francesco Molinari | 71-70-71-70--282 | 82,866 |
| Henrik Stenson | 71-70-71-70--282 | 82,866 |
| Boo Weekley | 67-72-72-71--282 | 82,866 |
| Thongchai Jaidee | 69-72-69-72--282 | 82,866 |
| Ross Fisher | 69-68-70-75--282 | 82,866 |

† Amateur. ‡ Winner after four-hole playoff.

### PGA Championship
**Hazeltine National GC (par 72; 7,674 yds);**
**Chaska, Minn., August 13–16, 2009**

| Player | Score | Earnings ($) |
| --- | --- | --- |
| Y.E. Yang | 73-70-67-70--280 | 1,350,000 |
| Tiger Woods | 67-70-71-75--283 | 810,000 |
| Lee Westwood | 70-72-73-70--285 | 435,000 |
| Rory McIlroy | 71-73-71-70--285 | 435,000 |
| Lucas Glover | 71-70-71-74--286 | 300,000 |
| Martin Kaymer | 73-70-71-73--287 | 233,125 |
| Ernie Els | 75-68-70-74--287 | 233,125 |
| Soren Kjeldsen | 70-73-70-74--287 | 233,125 |
| Henrik Stenson | 73-71-68-75--287 | 233,125 |
| John Merrick | 72-72-74-70--288 | 150,633 |
| Dustin Johnson | 72-73-73-70--288 | 150,633 |
| Zach Johnson | 74-73-70-71--288 | 150,633 |
| Francesco Molinari | 74-73-69-72--288 | 150,633 |
| Graeme McDowell | 70-75-71-72--288 | 150,633 |
| Padraig Harrington | 68-73-69-78--288 | 150,633 |
| Hunter Mahan | 69-75-74-71--289 | 106,567 |
| Vijay Singh | 69-72-75-73--289 | 106,567 |
| Tim Clark | 76-68-71-74--289 | 106,567 |
| Ian Poulter | 72-70-76-72--290 | 81,760 |
| Oliver Wilson | 74-72-72-72--290 | 81,760 |
| Michael Allen | 74-71-72-73--290 | 81,760 |
| Corey Pavin | 73-71-71-75--290 | 81,760 |
| Ross Fisher | 73-68-73-76--290 | 81,760 |

## Late 2008 PGA Tour Events

| Tournament | Final Round | Winner | Score/ Under Par | Earnings ($) |
|---|---|---|---|---|
| Turning Stone Championship | Oct 5 | Dustin Johnson | 279/-9 | 1,080,000 |
| Valero Texas Open | Oct 12 | Zach Johnson | 261/-19 | 810,000 |
| Shriners Hosptials for Children Open | Oct 19 | Marc Turnesa | 263/-25 | 756,000 |
| *Frys.com Open | Oct 26 | Cameron Beckman | 262/-18 | 900,000 |
| Ginn sur Mer Classic | Nov 2 | Ryan Palmer | 281/-7 | 828,000 |
| Children's Miracle Network Classic | Nov 9 | Davis Love III | 263/-25 | 828,000 |

## 2009 PGA Tour Events

| Tournament | Final Round | Winner | Score/ Under Par | Earnings ($) |
|---|---|---|---|---|
| Mercedes-Benz Championship | Jan 11 | Geoff Ogilvy | 268/-24 | 1,120,000 |
| Sony Open in Hawaii | Jan 18 | Zach Johnson | 265/-15 | 972,000 |
| †Bob Hope Chrysler Classic | Jan 25 | Pat Perez | 327/-33 | 918,000 |
| *FBR Open | Feb 1 | Kenny Perry | 270/-14 | 1,080,000 |
| Buick Invitational | Feb 8 | Nick Watney | 277/-11 | 954,000 |
| **AT&T Pebble Beach National Pro-Am | Feb 15 | Dustin Johnson | 201/-15 | 1,098,000 |
| Northern Trust Open | Feb 22 | Phil Mickelson | 269/-15 | 1,134,000 |
| Mayakoba Classic at Riviera Maya | Mar 1 | Mark Wilson | 267/-13 | 648,000 |
| WGC Match Play Championship | Mar 1 | Geoff Ogilvy | 4 & 3 | 1,400,000 |
| Honda Classic | Mar 8 | Y.E. Yang | 271/-9 | 1,008,000 |
| Puerto Rico Open | Mar 15 | Michael Bradley | 274/-14 | 630,000 |
| WGC-CA Championship | Mar 15 | Phil Mickelson | 269/-19 | 1,400,000 |
| Transitions Championship | Mar 22 | Retief Goosen | 276/-8 | 972,000 |
| Arnold Palmer Invitational | Mar 29 | Tiger Woods | 275/-5 | 1,080,000 |
| *Shell Houston Open | Apr 5 | Paul Casey | 277/-11 | 1,026,000 |
| *The Masters | Apr 12 | Angel Cabrera | 276/-12 | 1,350,000 |
| Verizon Heritage | Apr 19 | Brian Gay | 264/-20 | 1,026,000 |
| Zurich Classic | Apr 26 | Jerry Kelly | 274/-14 | 1,134,000 |
| Quail Hollow Championship | May 3 | Sean O'Hair | 277/-11 | 1,170,000 |
| The Players Championship | May 10 | Henrik Stenson | 276/-12 | 1,710,000 |
| Valero Texas Open | May 17 | Zach Johnson | 265/-15 | 1,098,000 |
| Byron Nelson Championship | May 24 | Rory Sabbatini | 261/-19 | 1,170,000 |
| *Crowne Plaza Invitational at Colonial | May 31 | Steve Stricker | 263/-17 | 1,116,000 |
| Memorial Tournament | June 7 | Tiger Woods | 276/-12 | 1,080,000 |
| St. Jude Classic | June 14 | Brian Gay | 262/-18 | 1,080,000 |
| U.S. Open Championship | June 21 | Lucas Glover | 276/-4 | 1,350,000 |
| Travelers Championship | June 28 | Kenny Perry | 258/-22 | 1,080,000 |
| AT&T National | July 5 | Tiger Woods | 267/-13 | 1,080,000 |
| John Deere Classic | July 12 | Steve Stricker | 264/-20 | 774,000 |
| *U.S. Bank Championship | July 19 | Bo Van Pelt | 267/-13 | 720,000 |
| *The Open Championship (British Open) | July 19 | Stewart Cink | 278/-2 | 1,221,005 |
| *Canadian Open | July 26 | Nathan Green | 270/-18 | 918,000 |
| Buick Open | Aug 2 | Tiger Woods | 268/-20 | 918,000 |
| Reno-Tahoe Open | Aug 9 | John Rollins | 271/-17 | 540,000 |
| WGC Bridgestone Invitational | Aug 9 | Tiger Woods | 268/-12 | 1,400,000 |
| PGA Championship | Aug 16 | Y.E. Yang | 280/-8 | 1,350,000 |
| *Wyndham Championship | Aug 23 | Ryan Moore | 264/-16 | 936,000 |
| ‡The Barclays | Aug 30 | Heath Slocum | 275/-9 | 1,350,000 |
| ‡Deutsche Bank Championship | Sept 7 | Steve Stricker | 267/-17 | 1,350,000 |
| ‡BMW Championship | Sept 13 | Tiger Woods | 265/-19 | 1,350,000 |
| ‡TOUR Championship | Sept 27 | Phil Mickelson | 271/-9 | 1,350,000 |

† Five-round tournament. * Won in playoff. **Rain-shortend tournament to three rounds. ‡Events part of four-tournament FedEx Cup, the PGA Tour's 30-player playoff.

# 2009 FedEx Cup Playoff Results

| Player | Points | Earnings ($) |
|---|---|---|
| 1. Tiger Woods | 4,000 | 10,000,000 |
| 2. Phil Mickelson | 2,920 | 3,000,000 |
| 3. Steve Stricker | 2,750 | 2,000,000 |
| 4. Jim Furyk | 2,438 | 1,500,000 |
| 5. Sean O'Hair | 2,200 | 1,000,000 |
| 6. Zach Johnson | 2,073 | 800,000 |
| 7. Padraig Harrington | 2,050 | 700,000 |
| 8. Heath Slocum | 1,855 | 600,000 |
| 9. Kenny Perry | 1,450 | 550,000 |
| 10. Scott Verplank | 1,245 | 500,000 |

## Kraft Nabisco Championship

### Mission Hills CC (par 72; 6,673 yds); Rancho Mirage, Ca., April 2–5, 2009

| Player | Score | Earnings ($) |
|---|---|---|
| Brittany Lincicome | 66-74-70-69--279 | 300,000 |
| Kristy McPherson | 68-70-70-72--280 | 161,853 |
| Cristie Kerr | 71-68-70-71--280 | 161,853 |
| Lindsey Wright | 70-71-71-70--282 | 105,281 |
| Suzann Pettersen | 71-72-74-66--283 | 77,036 |
| Meaghen Francella | 72-73-69-69--283 | 77,036 |
| Christina Kim | 69-69-75-72--285 | 58,034 |
| Pat Hurst | 71-71-73-71--286 | 44,167 |
| Karrie Webb | 73-72-72-69--286 | 44,167 |
| Katherine Hull | 69-74-71-72--286 | 44,167 |
| Jimin Kang | 71-70-71-74--286 | 44,167 |
| Sun Young Yoo | 70-78-73-66--287 | 31,841 |
| Lorena Ochoa | 73-73-72-69--287 | 31,841 |
| Michele Redman | 72-73-72-70--287 | 31,841 |
| Angela Stanford | 67-75-74-71--287 | 31,841 |
| Helen Alfredsson | 72-70-72-73--287 | 31,841 |
| Paula Creamer | 70-72-77-69--288 | 25,542 |
| Yani Tseng | 69-75-75-69--288 | 25,542 |
| Brittany Lang | 67-80-71-70--288 | 25,542 |
| Jee Young Lee | 69-80-72-68--289 | 23,624 |
| †Alexis Thompson | 72-72-77-69--290 | – |
| †Tiffany Joh | 71-75-73-71--290 | – |
| Jiyai Shin | 72-76-71-71--290 | 22,392 |
| Song-Hee Kim | 69-78-72-71--290 | 22,392 |
| Sakura Yokomine | 72-73-74-72--291 | 20,372 |
| Nicole Castrale | 71-75-73-72--291 | 20,372 |
| Allison Fouch | 76-73-69-73--291 | 20,372 |
| Hee-Won Han | 75-73-72-72--292 | 18,540 |
| In-Kyung Kim | 70-73-75-74--292 | 18,540 |

† Amateur.

## LPGA Championship

### Bulle Rock GC (par 72; 6,641 yds); Havre de Grace, Md., June 11–14, 2009

| Player | Score | Earnings ($) |
|---|---|---|
| Anna Nordqvist | 66-70-69-68--273 | 300,000 |
| Lindsey Wright | 70-68-69-70--277 | 182,950 |
| Jiyai Shin | 73-68-69-68--278 | 132,717 |
| Kyeong Bee | 70-69-72-68--279 | 102,668 |
| Nicole Castrale | 65-72-74-69--280 | 68,947 |
| Angela Stanford | 70-71-70-69--280 | 68,947 |
| Kristy McPherson | 70-70-70-70--280 | 68,947 |
| Na Yeon Choi | 68-71-70-72--281 | 49,582 |
| Song-Hee Kim | 73-72-68-69--282 | 39,440 |
| Amy Yang | 68-74-70-70--282 | 39,440 |
| Stacy Lewis | 68-72-71-71--282 | 39,440 |
| Jin Young Pak | 69-71-69-73--282 | 39,440 |
| Brandie Burton | 73-71-72-67--283 | 32,853 |
| Inbee Park | 70-72-73-69--284 | 29,949 |
| Irene Cho | 72-75-65-72--284 | 29,949 |
| Shi Hyun Ahn | 73-70-72-70--285 | 25,041 |
| Paula Creamer | 74-70-71-70--285 | 25,041 |
| Katherine Hull | 69-69-76-71--285 | 25,041 |
| Sophie Gustafson | 69-74-70-72--285 | 25,041 |
| In-Kyung Kim | 72-74-68-71--286 | 21,836 |
| Natalie Gulbis | 72-75-69-70--286 | 21,836 |
| Hee-Won Han | 70-69-73-74--287 | 18,105 |
| Maria Hjorth | 71-75-72-69--287 | 18,105 |
| Michelle Wie | 70-74-73-70--287 | 18,105 |
| Eun-Hee Ji | 74-69-73-71--287 | 18,105 |
| Mindy Kim | 74-69-72-72--287 | 18,105 |
| Allison Hanna-Williams | 72-74-69-72--287 | 18,105 |
| Paige McKenzie | 68-77-69-73--287 | 18,105 |
| Lorena Ochoa | 72-69-73-73--287 | 18,105 |
| Yani Tseng | 73-71-69-74--287 | 18,105 |

## U.S. Women's Open

### Saucon Valley CC–Old Course (par 71; 7,126 yds); Bethlehem, Pa., July 9–12, 2009

| Player | Score | Earnings ($) |
|---|---|---|
| Eun-Hee Ji | 71-72-70-71--284 | 585,000 |
| Candie Kung | 71-77-68-69--285 | 350,000 |
| In-Kyung Kim | 72-72-72-70--286 | 183,568 |
| Cristie Kerr | 69-70-72-75--286 | 183,568 |
| Brittany Lincicome | 72-72-73-70--287 | 122,415 |
| Paula Creamer | 72-68-79-69--288 | 99,126 |
| Ai Miyazato | 74-74-71-69--288 | 99,126 |
| Suzann Pettersen | 74-71-72-71--288 | 99,126 |
| Na Yeon Choi | 68-74-76-71--289 | 76,711 |
| Kyeong Bae | 75-73-69-72--289 | 76,711 |
| Hee Young Park | 70-74-72-73--289 | 76,711 |
| Song-Hee Kim | 74-69-75-72--290 | 66,769 |
| Jiyai Shin | 72-75-76-68--291 | 59,428 |
| †Jennifer Song | 72-74-73-72--291 | – |
| Sun Ju Ahn | 75-71-72-73--291 | 59,428 |
| Morgan Pressel | 74-75-69-73--291 | 59,428 |
| Lindsey Wright | 74-70-77-71--292 | 42,724 |
| Jimin Kang | 76-71-74-71--292 | 42,724 |
| Laura Davies | 72-75-73-72--292 | 42,724 |
| Akiko Fukushima | 76-72-72-72--292 | 42,724 |
| Meaghan Francella | 73-72-74-73--292 | 42,724 |
| Nicole Castrale | 74-71-74-73--292 | 42,724 |
| Anna Grzebien | 73-77-69-73--292 | 42,724 |
| Jean Reynolds | 69-72-74-77--292 | 42,724 |
| Teresa Lu | 76-69-70-77--292 | 42,724 |

† Amateur.

## Women's British Open

### Royal Lytham & St. Anne's GC (par 72; 6,492 yds); Berkshire, England, July 30–August 2, 2009

| Player | Score | Earnings ($) |
|---|---|---|
| Catriona Matthew | 74-67-71-73--285 | 335,000 |
| Karrie Webb | 77-71-72-68--288 | 210,000 |
| Hee-Won Han | 77-73-69-70--289 | 109,500 |
| Paula Creamer | 74-74-70-71--289 | 109,500 |
| Ai Miyazato | 75-71-70-73--289 | 109,500 |
| Christina Kim | 73-71-71-74--289 | 109,500 |
| Kristy McPherson | 74-74-72-70--290 | 74,000 |
| Cristie Kerr | 76-71-75-69--291 | 61,000 |
| Na-Yeon Choi | 80-71-70-70--291 | 61,000 |
| Jiyai Shin | 77-71-68-75--291 | 61,000 |
| Michelle Wie | 73-76-74-69--292 | 40,750 |
| Maria Hjorth | 72-76-73-71--292 | 40,750 |
| Giulia Sergas | 74-67-78-73--292 | 40,750 |
| Hee Young Park | 71-75-73-73--292 | 40,750 |
| Song-Hee Kim | 70-73-74-75--292 | 40,750 |
| Mika Miyazato | 76-72-69-75--292 | 40,750 |
| Michele Redman | 75-75-73-70-293 | 30,000 |
| Kyeong Bae | 73-71-74-75--293 | 30,000 |
| Jane Park | 74-72-72-75--293 | 30,000 |
| Yani Tseng | 74-70-78-72--294 | 25,500 |
| In-Kyung Kim | 81-70-70-73--294 | 25,500 |
| Angela Stanford | 70-76-74-74--294 | 25,500 |
| Se Ri Pak | 76-71-73-74--294 | 25,500 |
| Inbee Park | 76-72-76-71--295 | 23,000 |
| Jeong Jang | 79-73-72-72--296 | 21,625 |
| Shinobu Moromizato | 74-73-71-78--296 | 21,625 |

## Late 2008 LPGA Tour Events

| Tournament | Final Round | Winner | Score/ Under Par | Earnings ($) |
|---|---|---|---|---|
| Samsung World Championship | Oct 5 | Paula Creamer | 279/-9 | 250,000 |
| Longs Drug Challenge | Oct 12 | In-Kyung Kim | 278/-10 | 180,000 |
| Kapalua Classic | Oct 19 | Morgan Pressel | 280/-8 | 225,000 |
| Grand China Air LPGA | Oct 26 | Helen Alfredsson | 204/-12 | 270,000 |
| Hana Bank Championship | Nov 2 | Candie Kung | 210/-6 | 240,000 |
| Mizuno Classic | Nov 9 | Jiyai Shin | 201/-15 | 210,000 |
| Lorena Ochoa Invitational | Nov 16 | Angela Stanfod | 275/-13 | 200,000 |
| ADT Championship | Nov 23 | Jiyai Shin | 286/-2 | 1,000,000 |

## 2009 LPGA Tour Events

| Tournament | Final Round | Winner | Score/ Under Par | Earnings ($) |
|---|---|---|---|---|
| SBS Open | Feb 14 | Angela Stanford | 206/-10 | 180,000 |
| Honda LPGA Thailand | Mar 1 | Lorena Ochoa | 274/-14 | 217,500 |
| HSBC Championship | Mar 8 | Jiyai Shin | 277/-11 | 300,000 |
| MasterCard Classic | Mar 22 | Pat Hurst | 206/-10 | 195,000 |
| Phoenix International | Mar 29 | Karrie Webb | 274/-14 | 225,000 |
| Kraft Nabisco Championship | Apr 5 | Brittany Lincicome | 279/-9 | 300,000 |
| Corona Morelia Championship | Apr 26 | Lorena Ochoa | 267/-25 | 195,000 |
| Michelob Ultra Open | May 10 | Cristie Kerr | 268/-16 | 330,000 |
| Sybase Classic | May 17 | Ji Young Oh | 274/-14 | 300,000 |
| LPGA Corning Classic | May 24 | Yani Tseng | 267/-21 | 225,000 |
| State Farm Classic | June 7 | In-Kyung Kim | 271/-17 | 255,000 |
| McDonald's LPGA Championship | June 14 | Anna Nordqvist | 273/-4 | 300,000 |
| Wegman's Rochester LPGA | June 28 | Jiyai Shin | 271/-17 | 300,000 |
| *Jamie Farr Owens Corning Classic | July 5 | Eunjung Yi | 266/-18 | 210,000 |
| U.S. Women's Open | July 12 | Eun-Hee Ji | 284/E | 585,000 |
| *Evian Masters | July 26 | Ai Miyazato | 274/-14 | 487,500 |
| Women's British Open | Aug 2 | Catriona Matthew | 285/-3 | 335,000 |
| Safeway Classic | Aug 30 | M.J. Hur | 203/-7 | 255,000 |
| Canadian Women's Open | Sept 6 | Suzann Pettersen | 269/-15 | 412,500 |
| *NW Arkansas Championship | Sept 13 | Jiyai Shin | 204/-9 | 270,000 |
| Samsung World Championship | Sept 20 | Na Yeon Choi | 272/-16 | 250,000 |
| CVS LPGA Challenge | Sept 27 | Sophie Gustafson | 268/-20 | 165,000 |
| Navistar LPGA Challenge | Oct 4 | Lorena Ochoa | 270/-218 | 195,000 |

* Won in playoff.

# Champions Tour Results

## Late 2008 Champions Tour Events

| Tournament | Final Round | Winner | Score/ Under Par | Earnings ($) |
|---|---|---|---|---|
| Administaff Small Business Classic | Oct 19 | Bernhard Langer | 204/-12 | 255,000 |
| AT&T Championship | Oct 26 | John Cook | 197/-16 | 247,500 |
| Charles Schwab Cup Championship | Nov 2 | Andy Bean | 268/-20 | 442,000 |

## 2009 Champions Tour Events

| Tournament | Final Round | Winner | Score/ Under Par | Earnings ($) |
|---|---|---|---|---|
| Mitsubishi Electric Championship | Jan 23 | Bernhard Langer | 198/-18 | 315,000 |
| Allianz Championship | Feb 15 | Mike Goodes | 201/-15 | 255,000 |
| ACE Group Classic | Feb 22 | Loren Roberts | 209/-7 | 240,000 |
| Toshiba Senior Classic | Mar 8 | Eduardo Romero | 202/-11 | 255,000 |
| *AT&T Champions Classic | Mar 15 | Dan Forsman | 205/-11 | 240,000 |
| Cap Cana Championship | Mar 29 | Keith Fergus | 203/-13 | 315,000 |
| Outback Steakhouse Pro-Am | Apr 19 | Nick Price | 204/-9 | 255,000 |
| Legends of Golf | Apr 26 | Bernhard Langer/Tom Lehman | 189/-27 | 225,000 each |
| **Regions Charity Classic | May 17 | Keith Fergus | 132/-12 | 255,000 |
| Senior PGA Championship | May 24 | Michael Allen | 274/-6 | 360,000 |
| *Principal Charity Classic | May 31 | Mark McNulty | 203/-10 | 258,750 |
| Triton Financial Classic | June 7 | Bernhard Langer | 201/-15 | 240,000 |
| Dick's Sporting Goods Open | June 28 | Lonnie Nielsen | 195/-21 | 247,500 |
| 3M Championship | July 12 | Bernhard Langer | 200/-16 | 262,500 |
| *Senior Open Championship (British) | July 26 | Loren Roberts | 268/-12 | 315,600 |
| U.S. Senior Open Championship | Aug 2 | Fred Funk | 268/-20 | 470,000 |
| *JELD-WEN Tradition | Aug 23 | Mike Reid | 272/-16 | 392,000 |
| Boeing Classic | Aug 30 | Loren Roberts | 198/-18 | 240,000 |
| Wal-Mart First Tee Open | Sept 6 | Jeff Sluman | 206/-10 | 315,000 |
| Greater Hickory Classic | Sept 20 | Jay Haas | 198/-18 | 262,500 |
| SAS Championship | Sept 27 | Tom Pernice Jr. | 203/-13 | 315,000 |
| Senior Players Championship | Oct 4 | Jay Haas | 267/-13 | 405,000 |

* Won in playoff. **Rain-shortend tournament to two rounds.

## 2009 U.S. Amateur Championships Results*

| Tournament | Final Round | Winner | Score | Runner-Up |
|---|---|---|---|---|
| Women's Amateur Public Links | June 27 | Jennifer Song | 7 & 6 | Kimberly Kim |
| Men's Amateur Public Links | July 18 | Brad Benjamin | 7 & 6 | Nick Taylor |
| Girls' Junior Amateur | July 25 | Amy Anderson | 6 & 5 | Kimberly Kim |
| Boys' Junior Amateur | July 25 | Jordan Spieth | 4 & 3 | Jay Hwang |
| Women's Amateur | Aug 9 | Jennifer Song | 3 & 1 | Jennifer Johnson |
| Men's Amateur | Aug 30 | Byeong-Hun An | 7 & 5 | Ben Martin |
| Women's Mid-Amateur | Oct 8 | Martha Stacy Leach | 3 & 2 | Laura Coblee |
| Men's Mid-Amateur | Oct 9 | Nathan Smith | 7 & 6 | Tim Spitz |

*Results through 10/09/09.

## 2009 International Results

| Tournament | Final Round | Winner | Score | Runner-Up |
|---|---|---|---|---|
| Solheim Cup | Aug 23 | United States | 16–12 | Europe |
| Walker Cup | Sept 13 | United States | 16½–9½ | Great Britain & Ireland |
| President's Cup | Oct 11 | United States | 19½–14½ | International |

## PGA Tour Final 2008 Money Leaders

| Name | Events | Best Finish | Scoring Average* | Money ($) |
|---|---|---|---|---|
| Vijay Singh | 23 | 1 (3) | 69.58 | 6,601,094 |
| Tiger Woods | 6 | 1 (4) | 68.90 | 5,775,000 |
| Phil Mickelson | 21 | 1 (2) | 69.17 | 5,188,875 |
| Sergio Garcia | 19 | 1 (1) | 69.12 | 4,858,224 |
| Kenny Perry | 26 | 1 (3) | 69.83 | 4,663,794 |
| Anthony Kim | 22 | 1 (2) | 69.28 | 4,656,265 |
| Camilo Villegas | 22 | 1 (2) | 69.49 | 4,422,641 |
| Padraig Harrington | 15 | 1 (2) | 69.28 | 4,313,551 |
| Stewart Cink | 23 | 1 (1) | 70.02 | 3,979,301 |
| Justin Leonard | 25 | 1 (1) | 69.77 | 3,943,542 |

*Adjusted for average score of field in each tournament entered.

## LPGA Tour Final 2008 Money Leaders

| Name | Events | Best Finish | Scoring Average | Money ($) |
|---|---|---|---|---|
| Lorena Ochoa | 22 | 1 (7) | 69.70 | 2,763,193 |
| Paula Creamer | 26 | 1 (4) | 70.56 | 1,823,992 |
| Yani Tseng | 27 | 1 (1) | 70.77 | 1,752,086 |
| Annika Sorenstam | 22 | 1 (3) | 70.47 | 1,735,912 |
| Helen Alfredsson | 26 | 1 (2) | 72.16 | 1,431,408 |
| Seon Hwa Lee | 30 | 1 (2) | 71.51 | 1,187,294 |
| Suzann Pettersen | 24 | 2 (3) | 70.96 | 1,177,809 |
| Inbee Park | 26 | 1 (1) | 71.78 | 1,138,370 |
| Angela Stanford | 27 | 1 (2) | 71.22 | 1,134,753 |
| Cristie Kerr | 26 | 1 (1) | 70.88 | 1,108,839 |

## Champions Tour Final 2008 Money Leaders

| Name | Events | Best Finish | Scoring Average | Money ($) |
|---|---|---|---|---|
| Bernhard Langer | 20 | 1 (3) | 69.65 | 2,035,073 |
| Jay Haas | 21 | 1 (2) | 69.66 | 1,991,726 |
| Fred Funk | 18 | 1 (2) | 69.73 | 1,825,931 |
| Jeff Sluman | 26 | 1 (2) | 70.01 | 1,728,443 |
| John Cook | 26 | 1 (1) | 69.76 | 1,721,038 |
| Loren Roberts | 25 | 1 (1) | 69.69 | 1,674,939 |
| Eduardo Romero | 18 | 1 (3) | 69.79 | 1,615,099 |
| Andy Bean | 25 | 1 (2) | 70.42 | 1,506,789 |
| Scott Hoch | 25 | 1 (2) | 70.17 | 1,497,530 |
| Tom Kite | 28 | 1 (1) | 70.78 | 1,284,592 |

# FOR THE RECORD • Year by Year

## THE MAJOR TOURNAMENTS
### The Masters

| Year | Winner | Score | Runner-Up |
|---|---|---|---|
| 1934 | Horton Smith | 284 | Craig Wood |
| 1935 | Gene Sarazen* (144) (only 36-hole playoff) | 282 | Craig Wood (149) |
| 1936 | Horton Smith | 285 | Harry Cooper |
| 1937 | Byron Nelson | 283 | Ralph Guldahl |
| 1938 | Henry Picard | 285 | Ralph Guldahl / Harry Cooper |
| 1939 | Ralph Guldahl | 279 | Sam Snead |
| 1940 | Jimmy Demaret | 280 | Lloyd Mangrum |
| 1941 | Craig Wood | 280 | Byron Nelson |
| 1942 | Byron Nelson* (69) | 280 | Ben Hogan (70) |
| 1943–45 | No tournament | | |
| 1946 | Herman Keiser | 282 | Ben Hogan |
| 1947 | Jimmy Demaret | 281 | Byron Nelson / Frank Stranahan |
| 1948 | Claude Harmon | 279 | Cary Middlecoff |
| 1949 | Sam Snead | 282 | Johnny Bulla / Lloyd Mangrum |
| 1950 | Jimmy Demaret | 283 | Jim Ferrier |
| 1951 | Ben Hogan | 280 | Skee Riegel |
| 1952 | Sam Snead | 286 | Jack Burke Jr. |
| 1953 | Ben Hogan | 274 | Ed Oliver Jr. |
| 1954 | Sam Snead* (70) | 289 | Ben Hogan (71) |
| 1955 | Cary Middlecoff | 279 | Ben Hogan |
| 1956 | Jack Burke Jr. | 289 | Ken Venturi |
| 1957 | Doug Ford | 282 | Sam Snead |
| 1958 | Arnold Palmer | 284 | Doug Ford / Fred Hawkins |
| 1959 | Art Wall Jr. | 284 | Cary Middlecoff |
| 1960 | Arnold Palmer | 282 | Ken Venturi |
| 1961 | Gary Player | 280 | Charles R. Coe / Arnold Palmer |
| 1962 | Arnold Palmer* (68) | 280 | Gary Player (71) / D. Finsterwald (77) |
| 1963 | Jack Nicklaus | 286 | Tony Lema |
| 1964 | Arnold Palmer | 276 | Dave Marr / Jack Nicklaus |
| 1965 | Jack Nicklaus | 271 | Arnold Palmer / Gary Player |
| 1966 | Jack Nicklaus* (70) | 288 | Tommy Jacobs (72) / Gay Brewer Jr. (78) |
| 1967 | Gay Brewer Jr. | 280 | Bobby Nichols |
| 1968 | Bob Goalby | 277 | Roberto DeVicenzo |
| 1969 | George Archer | 281 | Billy Casper / George Knudson / Tom Weiskopf |
| 1970 | Billy Casper* (69) | 279 | Gene Littler (74) |
| 1971 | Charles Coody | 279 | Johnny Miller / Jack Nicklaus |
| 1972 | Jack Nicklaus | 286 | Bruce Crampton / Bobby Mitchell / Tom Weiskopf |
| 1973 | Tommy Aaron | 283 | J.C. Snead |
| 1974 | Gary Player | 278 | Tom Weiskopf / Dave Stockton |
| 1975 | Jack Nicklaus | 276 | Johnny Miller / Tom Weiskopf |
| 1976 | Ray Floyd | 271 | Ben Crenshaw |
| 1977 | Tom Watson | 276 | Jack Nicklaus |
| 1978 | Gary Player | 277 | Hubert Green / Rod Funseth / Tom Watson |
| 1979 | Fuzzy Zoeller* (4–3)† | 280 | Ed Sneed (4–4) / Tom Watson (4–4) |
| 1980 | Seve Ballesteros | 275 | Gibby Gilbert / Jack Newton |
| 1981 | Tom Watson | 280 | Johnny Miller / Jack Nicklaus |
| 1982 | Craig Stadler* (4) | 284 | Dan Pohl (5) |
| 1983 | Seve Ballesteros | 280 | Ben Crenshaw / Tom Kite |
| 1984 | Ben Crenshaw | 277 | Tom Watson |
| 1985 | Bernhard Langer | 282 | Curtis Strange / Seve Ballesteros / Ray Floyd |
| 1986 | Jack Nicklaus | 279 | Greg Norman / Tom Kite |
| 1987 | Larry Mize* (4–3) | 285 | Seve Ballesteros (5) / Greg Norman (4–4) |
| 1988 | Sandy Lyle | 281 | Mark Calcavecchia |
| 1989 | Nick Faldo* (5–3) | 283 | Scott Hoch (5–4) |
| 1990 | Nick Faldo* (4–4) | 278 | Ray Floyd (4–x) |
| 1991 | Ian Woosnam | 277 | José María Olazábal |
| 1992 | Fred Couples | 275 | Ray Floyd |
| 1993 | Bernhard Langer | 277 | Chip Beck |
| 1994 | José María Olazábal | 279 | Tom Lehman |
| 1995 | Ben Crenshaw | 274 | Davis Love III |
| 1996 | Nick Faldo | 276 | Greg Norman |
| 1997 | Tiger Woods | 270 | Tom Kite |
| 1998 | Mark O'Meara | 279 | David Duval / Fred Couples |
| 1999 | José María Olazábal | 280 | Davis Love III |
| 2000 | Vijay Singh | 278 | Ernie Els |
| 2001 | Tiger Woods | 272 | David Duval |
| 2002 | Tiger Woods | 276 | Retief Goosen |
| 2003 | Mike Weir | 281 | Len Mattiace |
| 2004 | Phil Mickelson | 279 | Ernie Els |
| 2005 | Tiger Woods | 276 | Chris DiMarco |
| 2006 | Phil Mickelson | 281 | Tim Clark |
| 2007 | Zach Johnson | 289 | Tiger Woods / Retief Goosen / Rory Sabbatini |
| 2008 | Trevor Immelman | 280 | Tiger Woods |
| 2009 | Angel Cabrera | 276 | Chad Campbell / Kenny Perry |

*Winner in playoff. Playoff scores are in parentheses. †Playoff cut from 18 holes to sudden death.
Note: Played at Augusta National Golf Club, Augusta, GA.

## United States Open Championship

| Year | Winner | Score | Runner-Up | Site |
|------|--------|-------|-----------|------|
| 1895 | Horace Rawlins | †173 | Willie Dunn | Newport GC, Newport, RI |
| 1896 | James Foulis | †152 | Horace Rawlins | Shinnecock Hills GC, Southampton, NY |
| 1897 | Joe Lloyd | †162 | Willie Anderson | Chicago GC, Wheaton, IL |
| 1898 | Fred Herd | 328 | Alex Smith | Myopia Hunt Club, Hamilton, MA |
| 1899 | Willie Smith | 315 | George Low | Baltimore CC, Baltimore, MD |
|      |             |      | Val Fitzjohn | |
|      |             |      | W.H. Way | |
| 1900 | Harry Vardon | 313 | John H. Taylor | Chicago GC, Wheaton, IL |
| 1901 | Willie Anderson* (85) | 331 | Alex Smith (86) | Myopia Hunt Club, Hamilton, MA |
| 1902 | Laurie Auchterlonie | 307 | Stewart Gardner | Garden City GC, Garden City, NY |
| 1903 | Willie Anderson* (82) | 307 | David Brown (84) | Baltusrol GC, Springfield, NJ |
| 1904 | Willie Anderson | 303 | Gil Nicholls | Glen View Club, Golf, IL |
| 1905 | Willie Anderson | 314 | Alex Smith | Myopia Hunt Club, Hamilton, MA |
| 1906 | Alex Smith | 295 | Willie Smith | Onwentsia Club, Lake Forest, IL |
| 1907 | Alex Ross | 302 | Gil Nicholls | Philadelphia Cricket Club, Chestnut Hill, PA |
| 1908 | Fred McLeod* (77) | 322 | Willie Smith (83) | Myopia Hunt Club, Hamilton, MA |
| 1909 | George Sargent | 290 | Tom McNamara | Englewood GC, Englewood, NJ |
| 1910 | Alex Smith* (71) | 298 | John McDermott (75) | Philadelphia Cricket Club, Chestnut Hill, PA |
|      |             |      | Macdonald Smith (77) | |
| 1911 | John McDermott* (80) | 307 | Mike Brady (82) | Chicago GC, Wheaton, IL |
|      |             |      | George Simpson (85) | |
| 1912 | John McDermott | 294 | Tom McNamara | CC of Buffalo, Buffalo, NY |
| 1913 | Francis Ouimet* (72) | 304 | Harry Vardon (77) | The Country Club, Brookline, MA |
|      |             |      | Edward Ray (78) | |
| 1914 | Walter Hagen | 290 | Chick Evans | Midlothian CC, Blue Island, IL |
| 1915 | Jerry Travers | 297 | Tom McNamara | Baltusrol GC, Springfield, NJ |
| 1916 | Chick Evans | 286 | Jock Hutchison | Minikahda Club, Minneapolis. MN |
| 1917–18 | No tournament | | | |
| 1919 | Walter Hagen* (77) | 301 | Mike Brady (78) | Brae Burn CC, West Newton, MA |
| 1920 | Edward Ray | 295 | Harry Vardon | Inverness CC, Toledo, OH |
|      |             |      | Jack Burke | |
|      |             |      | Leo Diegel | |
|      |             |      | Jock Hutchison | |
| 1921 | Jim Barnes | 289 | Walter Hagen | Columbia CC, Chevy Chase, MD |
|      |             |      | Fred McLeod | |
| 1922 | Gene Sarazen | 288 | John L. Black | Skokie CC, Glencoe, IL |
|      |             |      | Bobby Jones | |
| 1923 | Bobby Jones* (76) | 296 | Bobby Cruickshank (78) | Inwood CC, Inwood, NY |
| 1924 | Cyril Walker | 297 | Bobby Jones | Oakland Hills CC, Birmingham, MI |
| 1925 | W. MacFarlane* (75–72) | 291 | Bobby Jones (75–73) | Worcester CC, Worcester, MA |
| 1926 | Bobby Jones | 293 | Joe Turnesa | Scioto CC, Columbus, OH |
| 1927 | Tommy Armour* (76) | 301 | Harry Cooper (79) | Oakmont CC, Oakmont, PA |
| 1928 | Johnny Farrell* (143) | 294 | Bobby Jones (144) | Olympia Fields CC, Matteson, IL |
| 1929 | Bobby Jones* (141) | 294 | Al Espinosa (164) | Winged Foot GC, Mamaroneck, NY |
| 1930 | Bobby Jones | 287 | Macdonald Smith | Interlachen CC, Hopkins, MN |
| 1931 | Billy Burke* (149–148) | 292 | George Von Elm | Inverness Club, Toledo, OH |
|      |             |      | (149–149) | |
| 1932 | Gene Sarazen | 286 | Phil Perkins | Fresh Meadows CC, Flushing, NY |
|      |             |      | Bobby Cruickshank | |
| 1933 | Johnny Goodman | 287 | Ralph Guldahl | North Shore CC, Glenview, IL |
| 1934 | Olin Dutra | 293 | Gene Sarazen | Merion Cricket Club, Ardmore, PA |
| 1935 | Sam Parks Jr. | 299 | Jimmy Thompson | Oakmont CC, Oakmont, PA |
| 1936 | Tony Manero | 282 | Harry Cooper | Baltusrol GC (Upper Course), Springfield, NJ |
| 1937 | Ralph Guldahl | 281 | Sam Snead | Oakland Hills CC, Birmingham, MI |
| 1938 | Ralph Guldahl | 284 | Dick Metz | Cherry Hills CC, Denver, CO |
| 1939 | Byron Nelson* (68–70) | 284 | Craig Wood (68–73) | Philadelphia CC, Philadelphia, PA |
|      |             |      | Denny Shute (76) | |
| 1940 | Lawson Little* (70) | 287 | Gene Sarazen (73) | Canterbury GC, Cleveland, OH |
| 1941 | Craig Wood | 284 | Denny Shute | Colonial Club, Fort Worth, TX |
| 1942–45 | No tournament | | | |
| 1946 | Lloyd Mangrum* (72–72) | 284 | Vic Ghezzi (72–73) | Canterbury GC, Cleveland, OH |
|      |             |      | Byron Nelson (72–73) | |
| 1947 | Lew Worsham* (69) | 282 | Sam Snead (70) | St. Louis CC, Clayton, MO |
| 1948 | Ben Hogan | 276 | Jimmy Demaret | Riviera CC, Los Angeles, CA |
| 1949 | Cary Middlecoff | 286 | Sam Snead | Medinah CC, Medinah, IL |
|      |             |      | Clayton Heafner | |
| 1950 | Ben Hogan* (69) | 287 | Lloyd Mangrum (73) | Merion GC, Ardmore, PA |
|      |             |      | George Fazio (75) | |

## United States Open Championship *(Cont.)*

| Year | Winner | Score | Runner-Up | Site |
|------|--------|-------|-----------|------|
| 1951 | Ben Hogan | 287 | Clayton Heafner | Oakland Hills CC, Birmingham, MI |
| 1952 | Julius Boros | 281 | Ed Oliver | Northwood CC, Dallas, TX |
| 1953 | Ben Hogan | 283 | Sam Snead | Oakmont CC, Oakmont, PA |
| 1954 | Ed Furgol | 284 | Gene Littler | Baltusrol GC (Lower Course), Springfield, NJ |
| 1955 | Jack Fleck* (69) | 287 | Ben Hogan (72) | Olympic Club (Lake Course), San Fran., CA |
| 1956 | Cary Middlecoff | 281 | Ben Hogan Julius Boros | Oak Hill CC, Rochester, NY |
| 1957 | Dick Mayer* (72) | 282 | Cary Middlecoff (79) | Inverness Club, Toledo, OH |
| 1958 | Tommy Bolt | 283 | Gary Player | Southern Hills CC, Tulsa, OK |
| 1959 | Billy Casper | 282 | Bob Rosburg | Winged Foot GC, Mamaroneck, NY |
| 1960 | Arnold Palmer | 280 | Jack Nicklaus | Cherry Hills CC, Denver, CO |
| 1961 | Gene Littler | 281 | Bob Goalby Doug Sanders | Oakland Hills CC, Birmingham, MI |
| 1962 | Jack Nicklaus* (71) | 283 | Arnold Palmer (74) | Oakmont CC, Oakmont, PA |
| 1963 | Julius Boros* (70) | 293 | Jacky Cupit (73) Arnold Palmer (76) | The Country Club, Brookline, MA |
| 1964 | Ken Venturi | 278 | Tommy Jacobs | Congressional CC, Bethesda, MD |
| 1965 | Gary Player* (71) | 282 | Kel Nagle (74) | Bellerive CC, St. Louis, MO |
| 1966 | Billy Casper* (69) | 278 | Arnold Palmer (73) | Olympic Club (Lake Course), San Fran., CA |
| 1967 | Jack Nicklaus | 275 | Arnold Palmer | Baltusrol GC (Lower Course), Springfield, NJ |
| 1968 | Lee Trevino | 275 | Jack Nicklaus | Oak Hill CC, Rochester, NY |
| 1969 | Orville Moody | 281 | Deane Beman Al Geiberger Bob Rosburg | Champions GC (Cypress Creek Course), Houston, TX |
| 1970 | Tony Jacklin | 281 | Dave Hill | Hazeltine GC, Chaska, MN |
| 1971 | Lee Trevino* (68) | 280 | Jack Nicklaus (71) | Merion GC (East Course), Ardmore, PA |
| 1972 | Jack Nicklaus | 290 | Bruce Crampton | Pebble Beach GL, Pebble Beach, CA |
| 1973 | Johnny Miller | 279 | John Schlee | Oakmont CC, Oakmont, PA |
| 1974 | Hale Irwin | 287 | Forrest Fezler | Winged Foot GC, Mamaroneck, NY |
| 1975 | Lou Graham* (71) | 287 | John Mahaffey (73) | Medinah CC, Medinah, IL |
| 1976 | Jerry Pate | 277 | Tom Weiskopf Al Geiberger | Atlanta Athletic Club, Duluth, GA |
| 1977 | Hubert Green | 278 | Lou Graham | Southern Hills CC, Tulsa, OK |
| 1978 | Andy North | 285 | Dave Stockton J.C. Snead | Cherry Hills CC, Denver, CO |
| 1979 | Hale Irwin | 284 | Gary Player Jerry Pate | Inverness Club, Toledo, OH |
| 1980 | Jack Nicklaus | 272 | Isao Aoki | Baltusrol GC (Lower Course), Springfield, NJ |
| 1981 | David Graham | 273 | George Burns Bill Rogers | Merion GC, Ardmore, PA |
| 1982 | Tom Watson | 282 | Jack Nicklaus | Pebble Beach GL, Pebble Beach, CA |
| 1983 | Larry Nelson | 280 | Tom Watson | Oakmont CC, Oakmont, PA |
| 1984 | Fuzzy Zoeller* (67) | 276 | Greg Norman (75) | Winged Foot GC, Mamaroneck, NY |
| 1985 | Andy North | 279 | Dave Barr T.C. Chen Denis Watson | Oakland Hills CC, Birmingham, MI |
| 1986 | Ray Floyd | 279 | Lanny Wadkins Chip Beck | Shinnecock Hills GC, Southampton, NY |
| 1987 | Scott Simpson | 277 | Tom Watson | Olympic Club (Lake Course), San Fran., CA |
| 1988 | Curtis Strange* (71) | 278 | Nick Faldo (75) | The Country Club, Brookline, MA |
| 1989 | Curtis Strange | 278 | Chip Beck Mark McCumber Ian Woosnam | Oak Hill CC, Rochester, NY |
| 1990 | Hale Irwin* (74) (3) | 280 | Mike Donald (74) (4) | Medinah CC, Medinah, IL |
| 1991 | Payne Stewart* (75) | 282 | Scott Simpson (77) | Hazeltine GC, Chaska, MN |
| 1992 | Tom Kite | 285 | Jeff Sluman | Pebble Beach GL, Pebble Beach, CA |
| 1993 | Lee Janzen | 272 | Payne Stewart | Baltusrol GC, Springfield, NJ |
| 1994 | Ernie Els* | 279 | Loren Roberts Colin Montgomerie | Oakmont CC, Oakmont, PA |
| 1995 | Corey Pavin | 280 | Greg Norman | Shinnecock Hills GC, Southampton, NY |
| 1996 | Steve Jones | 278 | Davis Love III Tom Lehman | Oakland Hills CC, Birmingham, MI |
| 1997 | Ernie Els | 276 | Colin Montgomerie | Congressional CC, Bethesda, MD |
| 1998 | Lee Janzen | 280 | Payne Stewart | Olympic Club (Lake Course), San Fran., CA |
| 1999 | Payne Stewart | 279 | Phil Mickelson | Pinehurst Resort and CC, Pinehurst, NC |
| 2000 | Tiger Woods | 272 | Miguel Angel Jiménez Ernie Els | Pebble Beach GL, Pebble Beach, CA |
| 2001 | Retief Goosen* (70) | 276 | Mark Brooks (72) | Southern Hills CC, Tulsa, OK |

## United States Open Championship *(Cont.)*

| Year | Winner | Score | Runner-Up | Site |
|------|--------|-------|-----------|------|
| 2002 | Tiger Woods | 277 | Phil Mickelson | Bethpage State Park (Black), Farmingdale, NY |
| 2003 | Jim Furyk | 272 | Stephen Leaney | Olympia Fields CC, Olympia Fields, IL |
| 2004 | Retief Goosen | 276 | Phil Mickelson | Shinnecock Hills GC, Southampton, NY |
| 2005 | Michael Campbell | 280 | Tiger Woods | Pinehurst Resort and CC, Pinehurst, NC |
| 2006 | Geoff Ogilvy | 285 | Jim Furyk | Winged Foot GC, Mamaroneck, NY |
|  |  |  | Colin Montgomerie |  |
|  |  |  | Phil Mickelson |  |
| 2007 | Angel Cabrera | 285 | Jim Furyk | Oakmont CC, Oakmont, PA |
|  |  |  | Tiger Woods |  |
| 2008 | Tiger Woods* (71) (4) | 283 | Rocco Mediate | Torrey Pines GC (South), San Diego, CA |
| 2009 | Lucas Glover | 276 | Phil Mickelson | Bethpage State Park (Black), Farmingdale, NY |
|  |  |  | David Duval |  |
|  |  |  | Ricky Barnes |  |

*Winner in playoff. Playoff scores are in parentheses. The 1990 and 2008 playoffs went to one hole of sudden death after an 18-hole playoff. In the 1994 playoff, Montgomerie was eliminated after 18 playoff holes, and Els beat Roberts on the 20th.
†Before 1898, 36 holes. From 1898 on, 72 holes.

## The Open Championship (British Open)

| Year | Winner | Score | Runner-Up | Site |
|------|--------|-------|-----------|------|
| 1860† | Willie Park | 174 | Tom Morris Sr. | Prestwick, Scotland |
| 1861‡ | Tom Morris Sr. | 163 | Willie Park | Prestwick, Scotland |
| 1862 | Tom Morris Sr. | 163 | Willie Park | Prestwick, Scotland |
| 1863 | Willie Park | 168 | Tom Morris Sr. | Prestwick, Scotland |
| 1864 | Tom Morris, Sr. | 160 | Andrew Strath | Prestwick, Scotland |
| 1865 | Andrew Strath | 162 | Willie Park | Prestwick, Scotland |
| 1866 | Willie Park | 169 | David Park | Prestwick, Scotland |
| 1867 | Tom Morris Sr. | 170 | Willie Park | Prestwick, Scotland |
| 1868 | Tom Morris Jr. | 154 | Tom Morris Sr. | Prestwick, Scotland |
| 1869 | Tom Morris Jr. | 157 | Tom Morris Sr. | Prestwick, Scotland |
| 1870 | Tom Morris Jr. | 149 | David Strath | Prestwick, Scotland |
|  |  |  | Bob Kirk |  |
| 1871 | No tournament |  |  |  |
| 1872 | Tom Morris Jr. | 166 | David Strath | Prestwick, Scotland |
| 1873 | Tom Kidd | 179 | Jamie Anderson | St. Andrews, Scotland |
| 1874 | Mungo Park | 159 | No record | Musselburgh, Scotland |
| 1875 | Willie Park | 166 | Bob Martin | Prestwick, Scotland |
| 1876 | Bob Martin# | 176 | David Strath | St. Andrews, Scotland |
| 1877 | Jamie Anderson | 160 | Bob Pringle | Musselburgh, Scotland |
| 1878 | Jamie Anderson | 157 | Robert Kirk | Prestwick, Scotland |
| 1879 | Jamie Anderson | 169 | Andrew Kirkaldy | St. Andrews, Scotland |
|  |  |  | James Allan |  |
| 1880 | Robert Ferguson | 162 | No record | Musselburgh, Scotland |
| 1881 | Robert Ferguson | 170 | Jamie Anderson | Prestwick, Scotland |
| 1882 | Robert Ferguson | 171 | Willie Fernie | St. Andrews, Scotland |
| 1883 | Willie Fernie* | 159 | Robert Ferguson | Musselburgh, Scotland |
| 1884 | Jack Simpson | 160 | Douglas Rolland | Prestwick, Scotland |
|  |  |  | Willie Fernie |  |
| 1885 | Bob Martin | 171 | Archie Simpson | St. Andrews, Scotland |
| 1886 | David Brown | 157 | Willie Campbell | Musselburgh, Scotland |
| 1887 | Willie Park Jr. | 161 | Bob Martin | Prestwick, Scotland |
| 1888 | Jack Burns | 171 | Bernard Sayers | St. Andrews, Scotland |
|  |  |  | David Anderson |  |
| 1889 | Willie Park Jr.* (158) | 155 | Andrew Kirkaldy (163) | Musselburgh, Scotland |
| 1890 | John Ball | 164 | Willie Fernie | Prestwick, Scotland |
| 1891 | Hugh Kirkaldy | 166 | Andrew Kirkaldy | St. Andrews, Scotland |
|  |  |  | Willie Fernie |  |
| 1892 | Harold Hilton | **305 | John Ball | Muirfield, Scotland |
|  |  |  | Hugh Kirkaldy |  |
| 1893 | William Auchterlonie | 322 | John E. Laidlay | Prestwick, Scotland |
| 1894 | John H. Taylor | 326 | Douglas Rolland | Royal St. George's, England |
| 1895 | John H. Taylor | 322 | Alexander Herd | St. Andrews, Scotland |
| 1896 | Harry Vardon* (157) | 316 | John H. Taylor (161) | Muirfield, Scotland |
| 1897 | Harold Hilton | 314 | James Braid | Royal Liverpool (Hoylake), England |
| 1898 | Harry Vardon | 307 | Willie Park Jr. | Prestwick, Scotland |
| 1899 | Harry Vardon | 310 | Jack White | Royal St. George's, England |
| 1900 | John H. Taylor | 309 | Harry Vardon | St. Andrews, Scotland |
| 1901 | James Braid | 309 | Harry Vardon | Muirfield, Scotland |

## The Open Championship (British Open) *(Cont.)*

| Year | Winner | Score | Runner-Up | Site |
|---|---|---|---|---|
| 1902 ...........Alexander Herd | | 307 | Harry Vardon | Royal Liverpool (Hoylake), England |
| 1903 ...........Harry Vardon | | 300 | Tom Vardon | Prestwick, Scotland |
| 1904 ...........Jack White | | 296 | John H. Taylor | Royal St. George's, England |
| 1905 ...........James Braid | | 318 | John H. Taylor | St. Andrews, Scotland |
| | | | Rolland Jones | |
| 1906 ...........James Braid | | 300 | John H. Taylor | Muirfield, Scotland |
| 1907 ...........Arnaud Massy | | 312 | John H. Taylor | Royal Liverpool (Hoylake), England |
| 1908 ...........James Braid | | 291 | Tom Ball | Prestwick, Scotland |
| 1909 ...........John H. Taylor | | 295 | James Braid | Deal, England |
| | | | Tom Ball | |
| 1910 ...........James Braid | | 299 | Alexander Herd | St. Andrews, Scotland |
| 1911 ...........Harry Vardon | | 303 | Arnaud Massy | Royal St. George's, England |
| 1912 ...........Ted Ray | | 295 | Harry Vardon | Muirfield, Scotland |
| 1913 ...........John H. Taylor | | 304 | Ted Ray | Royal Liverpool (Hoylake), England |
| 1914 ...........Harry Vardon | | 306 | John H. Taylor | Prestwick, Scotland |
| 1915–19......No tournament | | | | |
| 1920 ...........George Duncan | | 303 | Alexander Herd | Deal, England |
| 1921 ...........Jock Hutchison* (150) | | 296 | Roger Wethered (159) | St. Andrews, Scotland |
| 1922 ...........Walter Hagen | | 300 | George Duncan | Royal St. George's, England |
| | | | Jim Barnes | |
| 1923 ...........Arthur G. Havers | | 295 | Walter Hagen | Troon, Scotland |
| 1924 ...........Walter Hagen | | 301 | Ernest Whitcombe | Royal Liverpool (Hoylake), England |
| 1925 ...........Jim Barnes | | 300 | Archie Compston | Prestwick, Scotland |
| | | | Ted Ray | |
| 1926............Bobby Jones | | 291 | Al Watrous | Royal Lytham & St. Annes, England |
| 1927............Bobby Jones | | 285 | Aubrey Boomer | St. Andrews, Scotland |
| 1928 ...........Walter Hagen | | 292 | Gene Sarazen | Royal St. George's, England |
| 1929 ...........Walter Hagen | | 292 | Johnny Farrell | Muirfield, Scotland |
| 1930 ...........Bobby Jones | | 291 | Macdonald Smith | Royal Liverpool (Hoylake), England |
| | | | Leo Diegel | |
| 1931 ...........Tommy Armour | | 296 | Jose Jurado | Carnoustie, Scotland |
| 1932 ...........Gene Sarazen | | 283 | Macdonald Smith | Prince's, England |
| 1933 ...........Denny Shute* (149) | | 292 | Craig Wood (154) | St. Andrews, Scotland |
| 1934 ...........Henry Cotton | | 283 | Sidney F. Brews | Royal St. George's, England |
| 1935 ...........Alfred Perry | | 283 | Alfred Padgham | Muirfield, Scotland |
| 1936 ...........Alfred Padgham | | 287 | James Adams | Royal Liverpool (Hoylake), England |
| 1937 ...........Henry Cotton | | 290 | Reginald A. Whitcombe | Carnoustie, Scotland |
| 1938 ...........Reginald A. Whitcombe | | 295 | James Adams | Royal St. George's, England |
| 1939 ...........Richard Burton | | 290 | Johnny Bulla | St. Andrews, Scotland |
| 1940–45......No tournament | | | | |
| 1946 ...........Sam Snead | | 290 | Bobby Locke | St. Andrews, Scotland |
| | | | Johnny Bulla | |
| 1947 ...........Fred Daly | | 293 | Reginald W. Horne | Royal Liverpool (Hoylake), England |
| | | | Frank Stranahan | |
| 1948 ...........Henry Cotton | | 294 | Fred Daly | Muirfield, Scotland |
| 1949 ...........Bobby Locke* (135) | | 283 | Harry Bradshaw (147) | Royal St. George's, England |
| 1950 ...........Bobby Locke | | 279 | Roberto DeVicenzo | Troon, Scotland |
| 1951 ...........Max Faulkner | | 285 | Tony Cerda | Portrush, Ireland |
| 1952............Bobby Locke | | 287 | Peter Thomson | Royal Lytham & St. Annes, England |
| 1953 ...........Ben Hogan | | 282 | Frank Stranahan | Carnoustie, Scotland |
| | | | Dai Rees | |
| | | | Peter Thomson | |
| | | | Tony Cerda | |
| 1954 ...........Peter Thomson | | 283 | Sidney S. Scott | Royal Birkdale, Southport, England |
| | | | Dai Rees | |
| | | | Bobby Locke | |
| 1955 ...........Peter Thomson | | 281 | John Fallon | St. Andrews, Scotland |
| 1956 ...........Peter Thomson | | 286 | Flory Van Donck | Royal Liverpool (Hoylake), England |
| 1957 ...........Bobby Locke | | 279 | Peter Thomson | St. Andrews, Scotland |
| 1958 ...........Peter Thomson* (139) | | 278 | Dave Thomas (143) | Royal Lytham & St. Annes, England |
| 1959 ...........Gary Player | | 284 | Fred Bullock | Muirfield, Scotland |
| | | | Flory Van Donck | |
| 1960 ...........Kel Nagle | | 278 | Arnold Palmer | St. Andrews, Scotland |
| 1961 ...........Arnold Palmer | | 284 | Dai Rees | Royal Birkdale, Southport, England |
| 1962 ...........Arnold Palmer | | 276 | Kel Nagle | Troon, Scotland |
| 1963 ...........Bob Charles* (140) | | 277 | Phil Rodgers (148) | Royal Lytham & St. Annes, England |
| 1964 ...........Tony Lema | | 279 | Jack Nicklaus | St. Andrews, Scotland |

## The Open Championship (British Open) *(Cont.)*

| Year | Winner | Score | Runner-Up | Site |
|------|--------|-------|-----------|------|
| 1965 | Peter Thomson | 285 | Brian Huggett<br>Christy O'Connor | Royal Birkdale, Southport, England |
| 1966 | Jack Nicklaus | 282 | Doug Sanders<br>Dave Thomas | Muirfield, Scotland |
| 1967 | Robert DeVicenzo | 278 | Jack Nicklaus | Royal Liverpool (Hoylake), England |
| 1968 | Gary Player | 289 | Jack Nicklaus<br>Bob Charles | Carnoustie, Scotland |
| 1969 | Tony Jacklin | 280 | Bob Charles | Royal Lytham & St. Annes, England |
| 1970 | Jack Nicklaus* (72) | 283 | Doug Sanders (73) | St. Andrews, Scotland |
| 1971 | Lee Trevino | 278 | Lu Liang Huan | Royal Birkdale, Southport, England |
| 1972 | Lee Trevino | 278 | Jack Nicklaus | Muirfield, Scotland |
| 1973 | Tom Weiskopf | 276 | Johnny Miller | Troon, Scotland |
| 1974 | Gary Player | 282 | Peter Oosterhuis | Royal Lytham & St. Annes, England |
| 1975 | Tom Watson* (71) | 279 | Jack Newton (72) | Carnoustie, Scotland |
| 1976 | Johnny Miller | 279 | Jack Nicklaus<br>Seve Ballesteros | Royal Birkdale, Southport, England |
| 1977 | Tom Watson | 268 | Jack Nicklaus | Turnberry, Scotland |
| 1978 | Jack Nicklaus | 281 | Ben Crenshaw<br>Tom Kite<br>Ray Floyd<br>Simon Owen | St. Andrews, Scotland |
| 1979 | Seve Ballesteros | 283 | Ben Crenshaw<br>Jack Nicklaus | Royal Lytham & St. Annes, England |
| 1980 | Tom Watson | 271 | Lee Trevino | Muirfield, Scotland |
| 1981 | Bill Rogers | 276 | Bernhard Langer | Royal St. George's, England |
| 1982 | Tom Watson | 284 | Nick Price<br>Peter Oosterhuis | Troon, Scotland |
| 1983 | Tom Watson | 275 | Andy Bean | Royal Birkdale, Southport, England |
| 1984 | Seve Ballesteros | 276 | Tom Watson<br>Bernhard Langer | St. Andrews, Scotland |
| 1985 | Sandy Lyle | 282 | Payne Stewart | Royal St. George's, England |
| 1986 | Greg Norman | 280 | Gordon Brand | Turnberry, Scotland |
| 1987 | Nick Faldo | 279 | Paul Azinger<br>Rodger Davis | Muirfield, Scotland |
| 1988 | Seve Ballesteros | 273 | Nick Price | Royal Lytham & St. Annes, England |
| 1989†† | Mark Calcavecchia* (4-3-3-3) | 275 | Wayne Grady (4-4-4-4)<br>Greg Norman (3-3-4-x) | Troon, Scotland |
| 1990 | Nick Faldo | 270 | Payne Stewart<br>Mark McNulty | St. Andrews, Scotland |
| 1991 | Ian Baker-Finch | 272 | Mike Harwood | Royal Birkdale, Southport, England |
| 1992 | Nick Faldo | 272 | John Cook | Muirfield, Scotland |
| 1993 | Greg Norman | 267 | Nick Faldo | Royal St. George's, England |
| 1994 | Nick Price | 268 | Jesper Parnevik | Turnberry, Scotland |
| 1995 | John Daly* (4-3-4-4) | 282 | C. Rocca (5-4-7-3) | St. Andrews, Scotland |
| 1996 | Tom Lehman | 271 | Mark McCumber<br>Ernie Els | Royal Lytham & St. Annes, England |
| 1997 | Justin Leonard | 272 | Jesper Parnevik<br>Darren Clarke | Troon, Scotland |
| 1998 | Mark O'Meara* (4-4-5-4) | 280 | Brian Watts (5-4-5-5) | Royal Birkdale, Southport, England |
| 1999 | Paul Lawrie* (5-4-3-3) | 290 | Jean Van de Velde (6-4-3-5)<br>Justin Leonard (5-4-4-5) | Carnoustie, Scotland |
| 2000 | Tiger Woods | 269 | Thomas Bjorn<br>Ernie Els | St. Andrews, Scotland |
| 2001 | David Duval | 274 | Niclas Fasth | Royal Lytham & St. Annes, England |
| 2002 | Ernie Els* | 278 | Stuart Appleby | Muirfield, Scotland |
| 2003 | Ben Curtis | 283 | Vijay Singh | Royal St. George's, England |
| 2004 | Todd Hamilton* | 274 | Ernie Els | Troon, Scotland |
| 2005 | Tiger Woods | 274 | Colin Montgomerie | St. Andrews, Scotland |
| 2006 | Tiger Woods | 270 | Chris DiMarco | Royal Liverpool (Hoylake), England |
| 2007 | Padraig Harrington* | 277 | Sergio Garcia | Carnoustie, Scotland |
| 2008 | Padraig Harrington | 283 | Ian Poulter | Royal Birkdale, Southport, England |
| 2009 | Stewart Cink* | 278 | Tom Watson | Turnberry, Scotland |

*Winner in playoff. †The first event was open only to professional golfers.
‡The second annual open was open to amateurs and pros. #Tied, but refused playoff.
**Championship extended from 36 to 72 holes. ††Playoff cut from 18 holes to 4 holes.

## PGA Championship

| Year | Winner | Score | Runner-Up | Site |
|------|--------|-------|-----------|------|
| 1916 | Jim Barnes | 1 up | Jock Hutchison | Siwanoy CC, Bronxville, NY |
| 1917–18 | No tournament | | | |
| 1919 | Jim Barnes | 6 & 5 | Fred McLeod | Engineers CC, Roslyn, NY |
| 1920 | Jock Hutchison | 1 up | J. Douglas Edgar | Flossmoor CC, Flossmoor, IL |
| 1921 | Walter Hagen | 3 & 2 | Jim Barnes | Inwood CC, Far Rockaway, NY |
| 1922 | Gene Sarazen | 4 & 3 | Emmet French | Oakmont CC, Oakmont, PA |
| 1923 | Gene Sarazen | 1 up 38 holes | Walter Hagen | Pelham CC, Pelham, NY |
| 1924 | Walter Hagen | 2 up | Jim Barnes | French Lick CC, French Lick, IN |
| 1925 | Walter Hagen | 6 & 5 | William Mehlhorn | Olympia Fields CC, Olympia Fields, IL |
| 1926 | Walter Hagen | 5 & 3 | Leo Diegel | Salisbury GC, Westbury, NY |
| 1927 | Walter Hagen | 1 up | Joe Turnesa | Cedar Crest CC, Dallas, TX |
| 1928 | Leo Diegel | 6 & 5 | Al Espinosa | Five Farms CC, Baltimore, MD |
| 1929 | Leo Diegel | 6 & 4 | Johnny Farrell | Hillcrest CC, Los Angeles, CA |
| 1930 | Tommy Armour | 1 up | Gene Sarazen | Fresh Meadow CC, Flushing, NY |
| 1931 | Tom Creavy | 2 & 1 | Denny Shute | Wannamoisett CC, Rumford, RI |
| 1932 | Olin Dutra | 4 & 3 | Frank Walsh | Keller GC, St. Paul, MN |
| 1933 | Gene Sarazen | 5 & 4 | Willie Goggin | Blue Mound CC, Milwaukee, WI |
| 1934 | Paul Runyan | 1 up | Craig Wood | Park CC, Williamsville, NY |
| 1935 | Johnny Revolta | 5 & 4 38 holes | Tommy Armour | Twin Hills CC, Oklahoma City, OK |
| 1936 | Denny Shute | 3 & 2 | Jimmy Thomson | Pinehurst CC, Pinehurst, NC |
| 1937 | Denny Shute | 1 up 37 holes | Harold McSpaden | Pittsburgh FC, Aspinwall, PA |
| 1938 | Paul Runyan | 8 & 7 | Sam Snead | Shawnee CC, Shawnee-on-Delaware, PA |
| 1939 | Henry Picard | 1 up 37 holes | Byron Nelson | Pomonok CC, Flushing, NY |
| 1940 | Byron Nelson | 1 up | Sam Snead | Hershey CC, Hershey, PA |
| 1941 | Vic Ghezzi | 1 up 38 holes | Byron Nelson | Cherry Hills CC, Denver, CO |
| 1942 | Sam Snead | 2 & 1 | Jim Turnesa | Seaview CC, Atlantic City, NJ |
| 1943 | No tournament | | | |
| 1944 | Bob Hamilton | 1 up | Byron Nelson | Manito G & CC, Spokane, WA |
| 1945 | Byron Nelson | 4 & 3 | Sam Byrd | Morraine CC, Dayton, OH |
| 1946 | Ben Hogan | 6 & 4 | Ed Oliver | Portland GC, Portland, OR |
| 1947 | Jim Ferrier | 2 & 1 | Chick Harbert | Plum Hollow CC, Detroit, MI |
| 1948 | Ben Hogan | 7 & 6 | Mike Turnesa | Norwood Hills CC, St. Louis, MO |
| 1949 | Sam Snead | 3 & 2 | Johnny Palmer | Hermitage CC, Richmond, VA |
| 1950 | Chandler Harper | 4 & 3 | Henry Williams Jr. | Scioto CC, Columbus, OH |
| 1951 | Sam Snead | 7 & 6 | Walter Burkemo | Oakmont CC, Oakmont, PA |
| 1952 | Jim Turnesa | 1 up | Chick Harbert | Big Spring CC, Louisville, KY |
| 1953 | Walter Burkemo | 2 & 1 | Felice Torza | Birmingham CC, Birmingham, MI |
| 1954 | Chick Harbert | 4 & 3 | Walter Burkemo | Keller GC, St. Paul, MN |
| 1955 | Doug Ford | 4 & 3 | Cary Middlecoff | Meadowbrook CC, Detroit, MI |
| 1956 | Jack Burke | 3 & 2 | Ted Kroll | Blue Hill CC, Boston, MA |
| 1957 | Lionel Hebert | 2 & 1 | Dow Finsterwald | Miami Valley CC, Dayton, OH |
| 1958 | Dow Finsterwald | 276 | Billy Casper | Llanerch CC, Havertown, PA |
| 1959 | Bob Rosburg | 277 | Jerry Barber Doug Sanders | Minneapolis GC, St. Louis Park, MN |
| 1960 | Jay Hebert | 281 | Jim Ferrier | Firestone CC, Akron, OH |
| 1961 | Jerry Barber* (67) | 277 | Don January (68) | Olympia Fields CC, Olympia Fields, IL |
| 1962 | Gary Player | 278 | Bob Goalby | Aronimink GC, Newton Square, PA |
| 1963 | Jack Nicklaus | 279 | Dave Ragan Jr. | Dallas Athletic Club, Dallas, TX |
| 1964 | Bobby Nichols | 271 | Jack Nicklaus Arnold Palmer | Columbus CC, Columbus, OH |
| 1965 | Dave Marr | 280 | Billy Casper Jack Nicklaus | Laurel Valley CC, Ligonier, PA |
| 1966 | Al Geiberger | 280 | Dudley Wysong | Firestone CC, Akron, OH |
| 1967 | Don January* (69) | 281 | Don Massengale (71) | Columbine CC, Littleton, CO |
| 1968 | Julius Boros | 281 | Bob Charles Arnold Palmer | Pecan Valley CC, San Antonio, TX |
| 1969 | Ray Floyd | 276 | Gary Player | NCR CC, Dayton, OH |
| 1970 | Dave Stockton | 279 | Arnold Palmer Bob Murphy | Southern Hills CC, Tulsa, OK |
| 1971 | Jack Nicklaus | 281 | Billy Casper | PGA Nat'l GC, Palm Beach Gardens, FL |

## PGA Championship *(Cont.)*

| Year | Winner | Score | Runner-Up | Site |
|------|--------|-------|-----------|------|
| 1972 | Gary Player | 281 | Tommy Aaron<br>Jim Jamieson | Oakland Hills CC, Birmingham, MI |
| 1973 | Jack Nicklaus | 277 | Bruce Crampton | Canterbury GC, Cleveland, OH |
| 1974 | Lee Trevino | 276 | Jack Nicklaus | Tanglewood GC, Winston-Salem, NC |
| 1975 | Jack Nicklaus | 276 | Bruce Crampton | Firestone CC, Akron, OH |
| 1976 | Dave Stockton | 281 | Ray Floyd<br>Don January | Congressional CC, Bethesda, MD |
| 1977† | Lanny Wadkins* (4-4-4) | 282 | Gene Littler (4-4-5) | Pebble Beach GL, Pebble Beach, CA |
| 1978 | John Mahaffey* (4–3) | 276 | Jerry Pate (4–4)<br>Tom Watson (4–5) | Oakmont CC, Oakmont, PA |
| 1979 | David Graham* (4-4-2) | 272 | Ben Crenshaw (4-4-4) | Oakland Hills CC, Birmingham, MI |
| 1980 | Jack Nicklaus | 274 | Andy Bean | Oak Hill CC, Rochester, NY |
| 1981 | Larry Nelson | 273 | Fuzzy Zoeller | Atlanta Athletic Club, Duluth, GA |
| 1982 | Raymond Floyd | 272 | Lanny Wadkins | Southern Hills CC, Tulsa, OK |
| 1983 | Hal Sutton | 274 | Jack Nicklaus | Riviera CC, Pacific Palisades, CA |
| 1984 | Lee Trevino | 273 | Gary Player<br>Lanny Wadkins | Shoal Creek, Birmingham, AL |
| 1985 | Hubert Green | 278 | Lee Trevino | Cherry Hills CC, Denver, CO |
| 1986 | Bob Tway | 276 | Greg Norman | Inverness CC, Toledo, OH |
| 1987 | Larry Nelson* (4) | 287 | Lanny Wadkins (5) | PGA Natl GC, Palm Beach Gardens, FL |
| 1988 | Jeff Sluman | 272 | Paul Azinger | Oak Tree GC, Edmond, OK |
| 1989 | Payne Stewart | 276 | Mike Reid | Kemper Lakes GC, Hawthorn Woods, IL |
| 1990 | Wayne Grady | 282 | Fred Couples | Shoal Creek, Birmingham, AL |
| 1991 | John Daly | 276 | Bruce Lietzke | Crooked Stick GC, Carmel, IN |
| 1992 | Nick Price | 278 | Jim Gallagher Jr. | Bellerive CC, St. Louis, MO |
| 1993 | Paul Azinger* (4–4) | 272 | Greg Norman (4–5) | Inverness CC, Toledo, OH |
| 1994 | Nick Price | 269 | Corey Pavin | Southern Hills CC, Tulsa, OK |
| 1995 | Steve Elkington* (3) | 267 | Colin Montgomerie (4) | Riviera CC, Pacific Palisades, CA |
| 1996 | Mark Brooks* (3) | 277 | Kenny Perry (x) | Valhalla GC, Louisville, KY |
| 1997 | Davis Love III | 269 | Justin Leonard | Winged Foot GC, Mamaroneck, NY |
| 1998 | Vijay Singh | 271 | Steve Stricker | Sahalee CC, Redmond, WA |
| 1999 | Tiger Woods | 277 | Sergio Garcia | Medinah CC, Medinah, IL |
| 2000 | Tiger Woods* (3-4-5) | 270 | Bob May (4-4-x) | Valhalla GC, Louisville, KY |
| 2001 | David Toms | 265 | Phil Mickelson | Atlanta AC, Duluth, GA |
| 2002 | Rich Beem | 278 | Tiger Woods | Hazeltine National GC, Shaska, MN |
| 2003 | Shaun Micheel | 276 | Chad Campbell | Oak Hill CC, Rochester, NY |
| 2004 | Vijay Singh* | 280 | Chris DiMarco | Whistling Straits GC, Kohler, WI |
| 2005 | Phil Mickelson | 276 | Steve Elkington | Baltusrol GC, Springfield, NJ |
| 2006 | Tiger Woods | 270 | Shaun Micheel | Medinah CC, Medinah, IL |
| 2007 | Tiger Woods | 272 | Woody Austin | Southern Hills CC, Tulsa, OK |
| 2008 | Padraig Harrington | 277 | Sergio Garcia | Oakland Hills CC, Birmingham, MI |
| 2009 | Y.E. Yang | 280 | Tiger Woods | Hazeltine National GC, Shaska, MN |

*Winner in playoff. †Playoff changed from 18 holes to sudden death.

## Alltime Major Championship Winners

| | Masters | U.S. Open | British Open | PGA Champ. | U.S. Amateur | British Amateur | Total |
|---|---|---|---|---|---|---|---|
| Jack Nicklaus | 6 | 4 | 3 | 5 | 2 | 0 | 20 |
| *Tiger Woods | 4 | 3 | 3 | 4 | 3 | 0 | 17 |
| Bobby Jones | 0 | 4 | 3 | 0 | 5 | 1 | 13 |
| Walter Hagen | 0 | 2 | 4 | 5 | 0 | 0 | 11 |
| Ben Hogan | 2 | 4 | 1 | 2 | 0 | 0 | 9 |
| Gary Player | 3 | 1 | 3 | 2 | 0 | 0 | 9 |
| John Ball | 0 | 0 | 1 | 0 | 0 | 8 | 9 |
| Arnold Palmer | 4 | 1 | 2 | 0 | 1 | 0 | 8 |
| Tom Watson | 2 | 1 | 5 | 0 | 0 | 0 | 8 |
| Harold Hilton | 0 | 0 | 2 | 0 | 1 | 4 | 7 |
| Gene Sarazen | 1 | 2 | 1 | 3 | 0 | 0 | 7 |
| Sam Snead | 3 | 0 | 1 | 3 | 0 | 0 | 7 |
| Harry Vardon | 0 | 1 | 6 | 0 | 0 | 0 | 7 |

*Active PGA Tour player.

## Alltime Multiple Professional Major Winners

| MASTERS | | U.S. OPEN *(Cont.)* | | BRITISH OPEN *(Cont.)* | | PGA CHAMPIONSHIP | |
|---|---|---|---|---|---|---|---|
| Jack Nicklaus | 6 | Hale Irwin | 3 | Peter Thomson | 5 | Walter Hagen | 5 |
| Arnold Palmer | 4 | *Tiger Woods | 3 | Tom Watson | 5 | Jack Nicklaus | 5 |
| *Tiger Woods | 4 | Julius Boros | 2 | Walter Hagen | 4 | *Tiger Woods | 4 |
| Jimmy Demaret | 3 | Billy Casper | 2 | Bobby Locke | 4 | Gene Sarazen | 3 |
| Nick Faldo | 3 | *Ernie Els | 2 | Tom Morris Sr. | 4 | Sam Snead | 3 |
| Gary Player | 3 | *Retief Goosen | 2 | Tom Morris Jr. | 4 | Jim Barnes | 2 |
| Sam Snead | 3 | Ralph Guldahl | 2 | Willie Park | 4 | Leo Diegel | 2 |
| Seve Ballesteros | 2 | Walter Hagen | 2 | Jamie Anderson | 3 | Raymond Floyd | 2 |
| Ben Crenshaw | 2 | *Lee Janzen | 2 | Seve Ballesteros | 3 | Ben Hogan | 2 |
| Ben Hogan | 2 | John McDermott | 2 | Henry Cotton | 3 | Byron Nelson | 2 |
| *Bernhard Langer | 2 | Cary Middlecoff | 2 | Nick Faldo | 3 | Larry Nelson | 2 |
| *Phil Mickelson | 2 | Andy North | 2 | Robert Ferguson | 3 | Gary Player | 2 |
| Byron Nelson | 2 | Gene Sarazen | 2 | Bobby Jones | 3 | Paul Runyan | 2 |
| *José María Olazábal | 2 | Alex Smith | 2 | Jack Nicklaus | 3 | Denny Shute | 2 |
| Horton Smith | 2 | Payne Stewart | 2 | Gary Player | 3 | Dave Stockton | 2 |
| Tom Watson | 2 | Curtis Strange | 2 | *Tiger Woods | 3 | Lee Trevino | 2 |
| | | Lee Trevino | 2 | *Padraig Harrington | 2 | *Vijay Singh | 2 |
| **U.S. OPEN** | | | | Harold Hilton | 2 | | |
| Willie Anderson | 4 | **BRITISH OPEN** | | Bob Martin | 2 | | |
| Ben Hogan | 4 | Harry Vardon | 6 | *Greg Norman | 2 | | |
| Bobby Jones | 4 | James Braid | 5 | Arnold Palmer | 2 | | |
| Jack Nicklaus | 4 | J.H. Taylor | 5 | Willie Park Jr. | 2 | | |
| | | | | Lee Trevino | 2 | | |

* Active player.

# THE PGA TOUR
## Most Career Wins†

| | Wins | | Wins | | Wins |
|---|---|---|---|---|---|
| Sam Snead | 82 | Billy Casper | 51 | *Phil Mickelson | 37 |
| Jack Nicklaus | 73 | Walter Hagen | 44 | *Vijay Singh | 34 |
| *Tiger Woods | 71 | Cary Middlecoff | 40 | Horton Smith | 32 |
| Ben Hogan | 64 | Gene Sarazen | 39 | Harry Cooper | 31 |
| Arnold Palmer | 62 | Tom Watson | 39 | Jimmy Demaret | 31 |
| Byron Nelson | 52 | Lloyd Mangrum | 36 | Leo Diegel | 30 |

† Through 10/05/09. * Active player.

## Season Money Leaders

| | Earnings ($) | | Earnings ($) | | Earnings ($) |
|---|---|---|---|---|---|
| 1934 ...Paul Runyan | 6,767.00 | 1959 ...Art Wall | 53,167.60 | 1984 ...Tom Watson | 476,260.00 |
| 1935 ...Johnny Revolta | 9,543.00 | 1960 ...Arnold Palmer | 75,262.85 | 1985 ...Curtis Strange | 542,321.00 |
| 1936 ...Horton Smith | 7,682.00 | 1961 ...Gary Player | 64,540.45 | 1986 ...Greg Norman | 653,296.00 |
| 1937 ...Harry Cooper | 14,138.69 | 1962 ...Arnold Palmer | 81,448.33 | 1987 ...Curtis Strange | 925,941.00 |
| 1938 ...Sam Snead | 19,534.49 | 1963 ...Arnold Palmer | 128,230.00 | 1988 ...Curtis Strange | 1,147,644.00 |
| 1939 ...Henry Picard | 10,303.00 | 1964 ...Jack Nicklaus | 113,284.50 | 1989 ...Tom Kite | 1,395,278.00 |
| 1940 ...Ben Hogan | 10,655.00 | 1965 ...Jack Nicklaus | 140,752.14 | 1990 ...Greg Norman | 1,165,477.00 |
| 1941 ...Ben Hogan | 18,358.00 | 1966 ...Billy Casper | 121,944.92 | 1991 ...Corey Pavin | 979,430.00 |
| 1942 ...Ben Hogan | 13,143.00 | 1967 ...Jack Nicklaus | 188,998.08 | 1992 ...Fred Couples | 1,344,188.00 |
| 1943 ...No statistics compiled | | 1968 ...Billy Casper | 205,168.67 | 1993 ...Nick Price | 1,478,557.00 |
| 1944 ...Byron Nelson* | 37,967.69 | 1969 ...Frank Beard | 164,707.11 | 1994 ...Nick Price | 1,499,927.00 |
| 1945 ...Byron Nelson* | 63,335.66 | 1970 ...Lee Trevino | 157,037.63 | 1995 ...Greg Norman | 1,654,959.00 |
| 1946 ...Ben Hogan | 42,556.16 | 1971 ...Jack Nicklaus | 244,490.50 | 1996 ...Tom Lehman | 1,780,159.00 |
| 1947 ...Jimmy Demaret | 27,936.83 | 1972 ...Jack Nicklaus | 320,542.26 | 1997 ...Tiger Woods | 2,066,833.00 |
| 1948 ...Ben Hogan | 32,112.00 | 1973 ...Jack Nicklaus | 308,362.10 | 1998 ...David Duval | 2,591,031.00 |
| 1949 ...Sam Snead | 31,593.83 | 1974 ...Johnny Miller | 353,021.59 | 1999 ...Tiger Woods | 6,616,585.00 |
| 1950 ...Sam Snead | 35,758.83 | 1975 ...Jack Nicklaus | 298,149.17 | 2000 ...Tiger Woods | 9,188,321.00 |
| 1951 ...Lloyd Mangrum | 26,088.83 | 1976 ...Jack Nicklaus | 266,438.57 | 2001 ...Tiger Woods | 5,687,777.00 |
| 1952 ...Julius Boros | 37,032.97 | 1977 ...Tom Watson | 310,653.16 | 2002 ...Tiger Woods | 6,912,625.00 |
| 1953 ...Lew Worsham | 34,002.00 | 1978 ...Tom Watson | 362,428.93 | 2003 ...Vijay Singh | 7,573,907.00 |
| 1954 ...Bob Toski | 65,819.81 | 1979 ...Tom Watson | 462,636.00 | 2004 ...Vijay Singh | 10,905,166.00 |
| 1955 ...Julius Boros | 63,121.55 | 1980 ...Tom Watson | 530,808.33 | 2005 ...Tiger Woods | 10,628,024.00 |
| 1956 ...Ted Kroll | 72,835.83 | 1981 ...Tom Kite | 375,698.84 | 2006 ...Tiger Woods | 9,941,563.00 |
| 1957 ...Dick Mayer | 65,835.00 | 1982 ...Craig Stadler | 446,462.00 | 2007 ...Tiger Woods | 10,867,052.00 |
| 1958 ...Arnold Palmer | 42,607.50 | 1983 ...Hal Sutton | 426,668.00 | 2008 ...Vijay Singh | 6,601,094.00 |

* War bonds. Note: Total money listed from 1968 through 1974. Official money listed from 1975 on.

## Year by Year Statistical Leaders

### SCORING AVERAGE

| | | |
|---|---|---|
| 1980 | Lee Trevino | 69.73 |
| 1981 | Tom Kite | 69.80 |
| 1982 | Tom Kite | 70.21 |
| 1983 | Raymond Floyd | 70.61 |
| 1984 | Calvin Peete | 70.56 |
| 1985 | Don Pooley | 70.36 |
| 1986 | Scott Hoch | 70.08 |
| 1987 | David Frost | 70.09 |
| 1988 | Greg Norman | 69.38 |
| 1989 | Payne Stewart | 69.485† |
| 1990 | Greg Norman | 69.10 |
| 1991 | Fred Couples | 69.59 |
| 1992 | Fred Couples | 69.38 |
| 1993 | Greg Norman | 68.90 |
| 1994 | Greg Norman | 68.81 |
| 1995 | Greg Norman | 69.06 |
| 1996 | Tom Lehman | 69.32 |
| 1997 | Nick Price | 68.98 |
| 1998 | David Duval | 69.13 |
| 1999 | Tiger Woods | 68.43 |
| 2000 | Tiger Woods | 67.79 |
| 2001 | Tiger Woods | 68.81 |
| 2002 | Tiger Woods | 68.13 |
| 2003 | Tiger Woods | 68.41 |
| 2004 | Vijay Singh | 69.19 |
| 2005 | Tiger Woods | 68.66 |
| 2006 | Tiger Woods | 68.11 |
| 2007 | Tiger Woods | 67.79 |
| 2008 | Sergio Garcia | 69.12 |

Note: Scoring average per round, with adjustments made at each round for the field's course scoring average.

### DRIVING DISTANCE

| | | Yds |
|---|---|---|
| 1980 | Dan Pohl | 274.3 |
| 1981 | Dan Pohl | 280.1 |
| 1982 | Bill Calfee | 275.3 |
| 1983 | John McComish | 277.4 |
| 1984 | Bill Glasson | 276.5 |
| 1985 | Andy Bean | 278.2 |
| 1986 | Davis Love III | 285.7 |
| 1987 | John McComish | 283.9 |
| 1988 | Steve Thomas | 284.6 |
| 1989 | Ed Humenik | 280.9 |
| 1990 | Tom Purtzer | 279.6 |
| 1991 | John Daly | 288.9 |
| 1992 | John Daly | 283.4 |
| 1993 | John Daly | 288.9 |
| 1994 | Davis Love III | 283.8 |
| 1995 | John Daly | 289.0 |
| 1996 | John Daly | 288.8 |
| 1997 | John Daly | 302.0 |
| 1998 | John Daly | 299.4 |
| 1999 | John Daly | 305.6 |
| 2000 | John Daly | 301.4 |
| 2001 | John Daly | 306.7 |
| 2002 | John Daly | 306.8 |
| 2003 | Hank Kuehne | 321.4 |
| 2004 | Hank Kuehne | 314.4 |
| 2005 | Scott Hend | 318.9 |
| 2006 | Bubba Watson | 319.6 |
| 2007 | Bubba Watson | 315.2 |
| 2008 | Bubba Watson | 315.1 |

† Number had to be carried to extra decimal place to determine winner.

Note: Average computed by charting distance of two tee shots on a predetermined par-four or par-five hole (one on front nine, one on back nine).

### DRIVING ACCURACY

| | | |
|---|---|---|
| 1980 | Mike Reid | 79.5 |
| 1981 | Calvin Peete | 81.9 |
| 1982 | Calvin Peete | 84.6 |
| 1983 | Calvin Peete | 81.3 |
| 1984 | Calvin Peete | 77.5 |
| 1985 | Calvin Peete | 80.6 |
| 1986 | Calvin Peete | 81.7 |
| 1987 | Calvin Peete | 83.0 |
| 1988 | Calvin Peete | 82.5 |
| 1989 | Calvin Peete | 82.6 |
| 1990 | Calvin Peete | 83.7 |
| 1991 | Hale Irwin | 78.3 |
| 1992 | Doug Tewell | 82.3 |
| 1993 | Doug Tewell | 82.5 |
| 1994 | David Edwards | 81.6 |
| 1995 | Fred Funk | 81.3 |
| 1996 | Fred Funk | 78.7 |
| 1997 | Allen Doyle | 80.8 |
| 1998 | Bruce Fleisher | 81.4 |
| 1999 | Fred Funk | 80.2 |
| 2000 | Fred Funk | 79.7 |
| 2001 | Joe Durant | 81.1 |
| 2002 | Fred Funk | 81.2 |
| 2003 | Fred Funk | 77.9 |
| 2004 | Fred Funk | 77.2 |
| 2005 | Jeff Hart | 76.0 |
| 2006 | Joe Durant | 78.4 |
| 2007 | Jose Coceres | 75.5 |
| 2008 | Olin Browne | 80.4 |

Note: Percentage of fairways hit on number of par-four and par-five holes played; par-three holes excluded.

### GREENS IN REGULATION

| | | |
|---|---|---|
| 1980 | Jack Nicklaus | 72.1 |
| 1981 | Calvin Peete | 73.1 |
| 1982 | Calvin Peete | 72.4 |
| 1983 | Calvin Peete | 71.4 |
| 1984 | Andy Bean | 72.1 |
| 1985 | John Mahaffey | 71.9 |
| 1986 | John Mahaffey | 72.0 |
| 1987 | Gil Morgan | 73.3 |
| 1988 | John Adams | 73.9 |
| 1989 | Bruce Lietzke | 72.6 |
| 1990 | Doug Tewell | 70.9 |
| 1991 | Bruce Lietzke | 73.3 |
| 1992 | Tim Simpson | 74.0 |
| 1993 | Fuzzy Zoeller | 73.6 |
| 1994 | Bill Glasson | 73.0 |
| 1995 | Lenny Clements | 72.3 |
| 1996 | Fred Couples | 71.8 |
| | Mark O'Meara | 71.8 |
| 1997 | Tom Lehman | 72.7 |
| 1998 | Hal Sutton | 71.3 |
| 1999 | Tiger Woods | 71.4 |
| 2000 | Tiger Woods | 75.2 |
| 2001 | Tom Lehman | 74.5 |
| 2002 | Tiger Woods | 74.0 |

### GREENS IN REGULATION (Cont.)

| | | |
|---|---|---|
| 2003 | Joe Durant | 72.9 |
| 2004 | Joe Durant | 73.3 |
| 2005 | Sergio Garcia | 71.8 |
| 2006 | Tiger Woods | 74.2 |
| 2007 | Tiger Woods | 71.0 |
| 2008 | Joe Durant | 71.1 |

Note: Average of greens reached in regulation out of total holes played; hole is considered hit in regulation if any part of the ball rests on the putting surface in two shots less than the hole's par—a par-5 hit in two shots is one green in regulation.

### PUTTING

| | | |
|---|---|---|
| 1980 | Jerry Pate | 28.81 |
| 1981 | Alan Tapie | 28.70 |
| 1982 | Ben Crenshaw | 28.65 |
| 1983 | Morris Hatalsky | 27.96 |
| 1984 | Gary McCord | 28.57 |
| 1985 | Craig Stadler | 28.627† |
| 1986 | Greg Norman | 1.736 |
| 1987 | Ben Crenshaw | 1.743 |
| 1988 | Don Pooley | 1.729 |
| 1989 | Steve Jones | 1.734 |
| 1990 | Larry Rinker | 1.7467† |
| 1991 | Jay Don Blake | 1.7326† |
| 1992 | Mark O'Meara | 1.731 |
| 1993 | David Frost | 1.739 |
| 1994 | Loren Roberts | 1.737 |
| 1995 | Jim Furyk | 1.708 |
| 1996 | Brad Faxon | 1.709 |
| 1997 | Don Pooley | 1.718 |
| 1998 | Rick Fehr | 1.722 |
| 1999 | Brad Faxon | 1.723 |
| 2000 | Brad Faxon | 1.704 |
| 2001 | David Frost | 1.708 |
| 2002 | Bob Heintz | 1.682 |
| 2003 | John Huston | 1.713 |
| 2004 | Stewart Cink | 1.723 |
| 2005 | Arjun Atwal | 1.710 |
| 2006 | Daniel Chopra | 1.712 |
| 2007 | Tim Clark | 1.727 |
| 2008 | Bob Tway | 1.718 |

Note: Average number of putts taken on greens reached in regulation; prior to 1986, based on average number of putts per 18 holes.

### SAND SAVES

| | | |
|---|---|---|
| 1980 | Bob Eastwood | 65.4 |
| 1981 | Tom Watson | 60.1 |
| 1982 | Isao Aoki | 60.2 |
| 1983 | Isao Aoki | 62.3 |
| 1984 | Peter Oosterhuis | 64.7 |
| 1985 | Tom Purtzer | 60.8 |
| 1986 | Paul Azinger | 63.8 |
| 1987 | Paul Azinger | 63.2 |
| 1988 | Greg Powers | 63.5 |
| 1989 | Mike Sullivan | 66.0 |
| 1990 | Paul Azinger | 67.2 |
| 1991 | Ben Crenshaw | 64.9 |
| 1992 | Mitch Adcock | 66.9 |
| 1993 | Ken Green | 64.4 |

## Year by Year Statistical Leaders *(Cont.)*

### SAND SAVES *(Cont.)*

| | | |
|---|---|---|
| 1994 | Corey Pavin | 65.4 |
| 1995 | Billy Mayfair | 68.6 |
| 1996 | Gary Rusnak | 64.0 |
| 1997 | Bob Estes | 70.3 |
| 1998 | Keith Fergus | 71.0 |
| 1999 | Jeff Sluman | 67.3 |
| 2000 | Fred Couples | 67.0 |
| 2001 | Franklin Langham | 68.9 |
| 2002 | J. Olazabal | 64.9 |
| 2003 | Stuart Appleby | 62.1 |
| 2004 | Dan Forsman | 62.3 |
| 2005 | Pat Perez | 63.0 |
| 2006 | Luke Donald | 63.6 |
| 2007 | Tim Clark | 68.1 |
| 2008 | Dudley Hart | 63.7 |

Note: Percentage of up-and-down efforts from greenside sand traps only—fairway bunkers excluded.

### EAGLES

| | | |
|---|---|---|
| 1980 | Dave Eichelberger | 16 |
| 1981 | Bruce Lietzke | 12 |
| 1982 | Tom Weiskopf | 10 |
| | J.C. Snead | 10 |
| | Andy Bean | 10 |
| 1983 | Chip Beck | 15 |
| 1984 | Gary Hallberg | 15 |
| 1985 | Larry Rinker | 14 |
| 1986 | Joey Sindelar | 16 |
| 1987 | Phil Blackmar | 20 |
| 1988 | Ken Green | 21 |
| 1989 | Lon Hinkle | 14 |
| | Duffy Waldorf | 14 |
| 1990 | Paul Azinger | 14 |
| 1991 | Andy Bean | 15 |
| 1992 | Dan Forsman | 18 |
| 1993 | Davis Love III | 15 |
| 1994 | Davis Love III | 18 |
| 1995 | Kelly Gibson | 16 |
| 1996 | Tom Watson | 97.2 |
| 1997 | Tiger Woods | 104.1 |

### EAGLES *(Cont.)*

| | | |
|---|---|---|
| 1998 | Davis Love III | 83.3 |
| 1999 | Vijay Singh | 104.8 |
| 2000 | Tiger Woods | 72.0 |
| 2001 | Phil Mickelson | 73.8 |
| 2002 | John Daly | 78.4 |
| 2003 | Tiger Woods | 76.5 |
| 2004 | Nick Price | 90.0 |
| 2005 | Brenden Pappas | 70.6 |
| 2006 | J.B. Holmes | 72.9 |
| 2007 | Chris Tidland | 88.5 |
| 2008 | Chad Campbell | 105.8 |

Note: Total of eagles scored 1980–1995. Since 1996 winner determined by number of holes played per eagle.

### BIRDIES

| | | |
|---|---|---|
| 1980 | Andy Bean | 388 |
| 1981 | Vance Heafner | 388 |
| 1982 | Andy Bean | 392 |
| 1983 | Hal Sutton | 399 |
| 1984 | Mark O'Meara | 419 |
| 1985 | Joey Sindelar | 411 |
| 1986 | Joey Sindelar | 415 |
| 1987 | Dan Forsman | 409 |
| 1988 | Dan Forsman | 465 |
| 1989 | Ted Schulz | 415 |
| 1990 | Mike Donald | 401 |
| 1991 | Scott Hoch | 446 |
| 1992 | Jeff Sluman | 417 |
| 1993 | John Huston | 426 |
| 1994 | Brad Bryant | 397 |
| 1995 | Steve Lowery | 410 |
| 1996 | Fred Couples | 4.20 |
| 1997 | Tiger Woods | 4.25 |
| 1998 | David Duval | 4.29 |
| 1999 | Tiger Woods | 4.46 |
| 2000 | Tiger Woods | 4.92 |
| 2001 | Phil Mickelson | 4.49 |
| 2002 | Tiger Woods | 4.47 |
| 2003 | Vijay Singh | 4.41 |

### BIRDIES *(Cont.)*

| | | |
|---|---|---|
| 2004 | Vijay Singh | 4.40 |
| 2005 | Tiger Woods | 4.57 |
| 2006 | Tiger Woods | 4.65 |
| 2007 | Tiger Woods | 4.03 |
| 2008 | Ryan Palmer | 4.16 |

Note: Total of birdies scored 1980–95. Since 1996, winner determined by average number of birdies per round.

### ALL-AROUND

| | | |
|---|---|---|
| 1987 | Dan Pohl | 170 |
| 1988 | Payne Stewart | 170 |
| 1989 | Paul Azinger | 250 |
| 1990 | Paul Azinger | 162 |
| 1991 | Scott Hoch | 283 |
| 1992 | Fred Couples | 256 |
| 1993 | Gil Morgan | 252 |
| 1994 | Bob Estes | 227 |
| 1995 | Justin Leonard | 323 |
| 1996 | Fred Couples | 214 |
| 1997 | Bill Glasson | 282 |
| 1998 | John Huston | 151 |
| 1999 | Tiger Woods | 120 |
| 2000 | Tiger Woods | 113 |
| 2001 | Phil Mickelson | 174 |
| 2002 | Phil Mickelson | 259 |
| 2003 | Tiger Woods | 206 |
| 2004 | Jeff Ogilvy | 268 |
| 2005 | Tiger Woods | 265 |
| 2006 | Tiger Woods | 216 |
| 2007 | Tiger Woods | 240 |
| 2008 | Pat Perez | 323 |

Note: Sum of the places of standing from the other statistical egories; the player with the number closest to zero leads.

## PGA Player of the Year Award

| | |
|---|---|
| 1948 | Ben Hogan |
| 1949 | Sam Snead |
| 1950 | Ben Hogan |
| 1951 | Ben Hogan |
| 1952 | Julius Boros |
| 1953 | Ben Hogan |
| 1954 | Ed Furgol |
| 1955 | Doug Ford |
| 1956 | Jack Burke |
| 1957 | Dick Mayer |
| 1958 | Dow Finsterwald |
| 1959 | Art Wall |
| 1960 | Arnold Palmer |
| 1961 | Jerry Barber |
| 1962 | Arnold Palmer |
| 1963 | Julius Boros |
| 1964 | Ken Venturi |
| 1965 | Dave Marr |
| 1966 | Billy Casper |
| 1967 | Jack Nicklaus |
| 1968 | Not awarded |

| | |
|---|---|
| 1969 | Orville Moody |
| 1970 | Billy Casper |
| 1971 | Lee Trevino |
| 1972 | Jack Nicklaus |
| 1973 | Jack Nicklaus |
| 1974 | Johnny Miller |
| 1975 | Jack Nicklaus |
| 1976 | Jack Nicklaus |
| 1977 | Tom Watson |
| 1978 | Tom Watson |
| 1979 | Tom Watson |
| 1980 | Tom Watson |
| 1981 | Bill Rogers |
| 1982 | Tom Watson |
| 1983 | Hal Sutton |
| 1984 | Tom Watson |
| 1985 | Lanny Wadkins |
| 1986 | Bob Tway |
| 1987 | Paul Azinger |
| 1988 | Curtis Strange |
| 1989 | Tom Kite |

| | |
|---|---|
| 1990 | Wayne Levi |
| 1991 | Fred Couples |
| 1992 | Fred Couples |
| 1993 | Nick Price |
| 1994 | Nick Price |
| 1995 | Greg Norman |
| 1996 | Tom Lehman |
| 1997 | Tiger Woods |
| 1998 | David Duval |
| 1999 | Tiger Woods |
| 2000 | Tiger Woods |
| 2001 | Tiger Woods |
| 2002 | Tiger Woods |
| 2003 | Tiger Woods |
| 2004 | Vijay Singh |
| 2005 | Tiger Woods |
| 2006 | Tiger Woods |
| 2007 | Tiger Woods |
| 2008 | Padraig Harrington |

## Vardon Trophy: Scoring Average

| Year | Winner | Avg | Year | Winner | Avg | Year | Winner | Avg |
|------|--------|-----|------|--------|-----|------|--------|-----|
| 1937 | Harry Cooper | *500 | 1964 | Arnold Palmer | 70.01 | 1987 | Don Pohl | 70.25 |
| 1938 | Sam Snead | 520 | 1965 | Billy Casper | 70.85 | 1988 | Chip Beck | 69.46 |
| 1939 | Byron Nelson | 473 | 1966 | Billy Casper | 70.27 | 1989 | Greg Norman | 69.49 |
| 1940 | Ben Hogan | 423 | 1967 | Arnold Palmer | 70.18 | 1990 | Greg Norman | 69.10 |
| 1941 | Ben Hogan | 494 | 1968 | Billy Casper | 69.82 | 1991 | Fred Couples | 69.59 |
| 1942–46 | No award | | 1969 | Dave Hill | 70.34 | 1992 | Fred Couples | 69.38 |
| 1947 | Jimmy Demaret | 69.90 | 1970 | Lee Trevino | 70.64 | 1993 | Nick Price | 69.11 |
| 1948 | Ben Hogan | 69.30 | 1971 | Lee Trevino | 70.27 | 1994 | Greg Norman | 68.81 |
| 1949 | Sam Snead | 69.37 | 1972 | Lee Trevino | 70.89 | 1995 | Steve Elkington | 69.62 |
| 1950 | Sam Snead | 69.23 | 1973 | Bruce Crampton | 70.57 | 1996 | Tom Lehman | 69.32 |
| 1951 | Lloyd Mangrum | 70.05 | 1974 | Lee Trevino | 70.53 | 1997 | Nick Price | 68.98 |
| 1952 | Jack Burke | 70.54 | 1975 | Bruce Crampton | 70.51 | 1998 | David Duval | 69.13 |
| 1953 | Lloyd Mangrum | 70.22 | 1976 | Don January | 70.56 | 1999 | Tiger Woods | 68.43 |
| 1954 | E.J. Harrison | 70.41 | 1977 | Tom Watson | 70.32 | 2000 | Tiger Woods | 67.79 |
| 1955 | Sam Snead | 69.86 | 1978 | Tom Watson | 70.16 | 2001 | Tiger Woods | 68.81 |
| 1956 | Cary Middlecoff | 70.35 | 1979 | Tom Watson | 70.27 | 2002 | Tiger Woods | 68.13 |
| 1957 | Dow Finsterwald | 70.30 | 1980 | Lee Trevino | 69.73 | 2003 | Tiger Woods | 68.41 |
| 1958 | Bob Rosburg | 70.11 | 1981 | Tom Kite | 69.80 | 2004 | Vijay Singh | 68.84 |
| 1959 | Art Wall | 70.35 | 1982 | Tom Kite | 70.21 | 2005 | Tiger Woods | 68.66 |
| 1960 | Billy Casper | 69.95 | 1983 | Raymond Floyd | 70.61 | 2006 | Jim Furyk | 68.86 |
| 1961 | Arnold Palmer | 69.85 | 1984 | Calvin Peete | 70.56 | 2007 | Tiger Woods | 67.79 |
| 1962 | Arnold Palmer | 70.27 | 1985 | Don Pooley | 70.36 | 2008 | Sergio Garcia | 69.12 |
| 1963 | Billy Casper | 70.58 | 1986 | Scott Hoch | 70.08 | | | |

*Point system used, 1937–41. NOTE: As of 1988, based on minimum of 60 rounds per year. Adjusted for average score of field in tournaments entered.

# Women's Golf

# THE MAJOR TOURNAMENTS

## LPGA Championship

| Year | Winner | Score | Runner-Up | Site |
|------|--------|-------|-----------|------|
| 1955 | Beverly Hanson† (4 & 3) | 220 | Louise Suggs | Orchard Ridge CC, Ft Wayne, IN |
| 1956 | Marlene Hagge* | 291 | Patty Berg | Forest Lake CC, Detroit, MI |
| 1957 | Louise Suggs | 285 | Wiffi Smith | Churchill Valley CC, Pittsburgh, PA |
| 1958 | Mickey Wright | 288 | Fay Crocker | Churchill Valley CC, Pittsburgh, PA |
| 1959 | Betsy Rawls | 288 | Patty Berg | Sheraton Hotel CC, French Lick, IN |
| 1960 | Mickey Wright | 292 | Louise Suggs | Sheraton Hotel CC, French Lick, IN |
| 1961 | Mickey Wright | 287 | Louise Suggs | Stardust CC, Las Vegas, NV |
| 1962 | Judy Kimball | 282 | Shirley Spork | Stardust CC, Las Vegas, NV |
| 1963 | Mickey Wright | 294 | Mary Lena Faulk Mary Mills Louise Suggs | Stardust CC, Las Vegas, NV |
| 1964 | Mary Mills | 278 | Mickey Wright | Stardust CC, Las Vegas, NV |
| 1965 | Sandra Haynie | 279 | Clifford A. Creed | Stardust CC, Las Vegas, NV |
| 1966 | Gloria Ehret | 282 | Mickey Wright | Stardust CC, Las Vegas, NV |
| 1967 | Kathy Whitworth | 284 | Shirley Englehorn | Pleasant Valley CC, Sutton, MA |
| 1968 | Sandra Post* | 294 | Kathy Whitworth (75) | Pleasant Valley CC, Sutton, MA |
| 1969 | Betsy Rawls | 293 | Susie Berning Carol Mann | Concord GC, Kiameshia Lake, NY |
| 1970 | Shirley Englehorn* | 285 | Kathy Whitworth (78) | Pleasant Valley CC, Sutton, MA |
| 1971 | Kathy Whitworth | 288 | Kathy Ahern | Pleasant Valley CC, Sutton, MA |
| 1972 | Kathy Ahern | 293 | Jane Blalock | Pleasant Valley CC, Sutton, MA |
| 1973 | Mary Mills | 288 | Betty Burfeindt | Pleasant Valley CC, Sutton, MA |
| 1974 | Sandra Haynie | 288 | JoAnne Carner | Pleasant Valley CC, Sutton, MA |
| 1975 | Kathy Whitworth | 288 | Sandra Haynie | Pine Ridge GC, Baltimore, MD |
| 1976 | Betty Burfeindt | 287 | Judy Rankin | Pine Ridge GC, Baltimore, MD |
| 1977 | Chako Higuchi | 279 | Pat Bradley Sandra Post Judy Rankin | Bay Tree Golf Plantation, N Myrtle Beach, SC |
| 1978 | Nancy Lopez | 275 | Amy Alcott | Jack Nicklaus GC, Kings Island, OH |
| 1979 | Donna Caponi | 279 | Jerilyn Britz | Jack Nicklaus GC, Kings Island, OH |

### LPGA Championship (Cont.)

| Year | Winner | Score | Runner-Up | Site |
|---|---|---|---|---|
| 1980 | Sally Little | 285 | Jane Blalock | Jack Nicklaus GC, Kings Island, OH |
| 1981 | Donna Caponi | 280 | Jerilyn Britz | Jack Nicklaus GC, Kings Island, OH |
| | | | Pat Meyers | |
| 1982 | Jan Stephenson | 279 | JoAnne Carner | Jack Nicklaus GC, Kings Island, OH |
| 1983 | Patty Sheehan | 279 | Sandra Haynie | Jack Nicklaus GC, Kings Island, OH |
| 1984 | Patty Sheehan | 272 | Beth Daniel | Jack Nicklaus GC, Kings Island, OH |
| | | | Pat Bradley | |
| 1985 | Nancy Lopez | 273 | Alice Miller | Jack Nicklaus GC, Kings Island, OH |
| 1986 | Pat Bradley | 277 | Patty Sheehan | Jack Nicklaus GC, Kings Island, OH |
| 1987 | Jane Geddes | 275 | Betsy King | Jack Nicklaus GC, Kings Island, OH |
| 1988 | Sherri Turner | 281 | Amy Alcott | Jack Nicklaus GC, Kings Island, OH |
| 1989 | Nancy Lopez | 274 | Ayako Okamoto | Jack Nicklaus GC, Kings Island, OH |
| 1990 | Beth Daniel | 280 | Rosie Jones | Bethesda CC, Bethesda, MD |
| 1991 | Meg Mallon | 274 | Pat Bradley | Bethesda CC, Bethesda, MD |
| | | | Ayako Okamoto | |
| 1992 | Betsy King | 267 | Karen Noble | Bethesda CC, Bethesda, MD |
| 1993 | Patty Sheehan | 275 | Lauri Merten | Bethesda CC, Bethesda, MD |
| 1994 | Laura Davies | 279 | Alice Ritzman | DuPont CC, Wilmington, DE |
| 1995 | Kelly Robbins | 274 | Laura Davies | DuPont CC, Wilmington, DE |
| 1996 | Laura Davies | 213† | Julie Piers | DuPont CC, Wilmington, DE |
| 1997 | Chris Johnson* | 281 | Leta Lindley | DuPont CC, Wilmington, DE |
| 1998 | Se Ri Pak | 273 | Donna Andrews | DuPont CC, Wilmington, DE |
| 1999 | Juli Inkster | 268 | Liselotte Neumann | DuPont CC, Wilmington, DE |
| 2000 | Juli Inkster* | 281 | Stefania Croce | DuPont CC, Wilmington, DE |
| 2001 | Karrie Webb | 270 | Laura Diaz | DuPont CC, Wilmington, DE |
| 2002 | Se Ri Pak | 279 | Beth Daniel | DuPont CC, Wilmington, DE |
| 2003 | Annika Sorenstam* | 278 | Grace Park | DuPont CC, Wilmington, DE |
| 2004 | Annika Sorenstam | 271 | Shi Hyun Ahn | DuPont CC, Wilmington, DE |
| 2005 | Annika Sorenstam | 277 | Michelle Wie | Bulle Rock GC, Havre de Grace, MD |
| 2006 | Se Ri Pak* | 280 | Karrie Webb | Bulle Rock GC, Havre de Grace, MD |
| 2007 | Suzann Pettersen | 274 | Karrie Webb | Bulle Rock GC, Havre de Grace, MD |
| 2008 | Yani Tseng* | 276 | Maria Hjorth | Bulle Rock GC, Havre de Grace, MD |
| 2009 | Anna Nordqvist | 273 | Lindsey Wright | Bulle Rock GC, Havre de Grace, MD |

*Won playoff. †Won match-play final. #Shortened due to rain.

### U.S. Women's Open

| Year | Winner | Score | Runner-Up | Site |
|---|---|---|---|---|
| 1946 | Patty Berg | 5 & 4 | Betty Jameson | Spokane CC, Spokane, WA |
| 1947 | Betty Jameson | 295 | Sally Sessions | Starmount Forest CC, Greensboro, NC |
| | | | Polly Riley | |
| 1948 | Babe Zaharias | 300 | Betty Hicks | Atlantic City CC, Northfield, NJ |
| 1949 | Louise Suggs | 291 | Babe Zaharias | Prince George's G & CC, Landover, MD |
| 1950 | Babe Zaharias | 291 | Betsy Rawls | Rolling Hills GC, Wichita, KS |
| 1951 | Betsy Rawls | 293 | Louise Suggs | Druid Hills GC, Atlanta, GA |
| 1952 | Louise Suggs | 284 | Marlene Bauer | Bala GC, Philadelphia, PA |
| | | | Betty Jameson | |
| 1953 | Betsy Rawls* (71) | 302 | Jackie Pung (77) | CC of Rochester, Rochester, NY |
| 1954 | Babe Zaharias | 291 | Betty Hicks | Salem CC, Peabody, MA |
| 1955 | Fay Crocker | 299 | Mary Lena Faulk | Wichita CC, Wichita, KS |
| | | | Louise Suggs | |
| 1956 | Kathy Cornelius* (75) | 302 | Barbara McIntire (82) | Northland CC, Duluth, MN |
| 1957 | Betsy Rawls | 299 | Patty Berg | Winged Foot GC, Mamaroneck, NY |
| 1958 | Mickey Wright | 290 | Louise Suggs | Forest Lake CC, Detroit, MI |
| 1959 | Mickey Wright | 287 | Louise Suggs | Churchill Valley CC, Pittsburgh |
| 1960 | Betsy Rawls | 292 | Joyce Ziske | Worcester CC, Worcester, MA |
| 1961 | Mickey Wright | 293 | Betsy Rawls | Baltusrol GC (Lower Course), Springfield, NJ |
| 1962 | Murle Breer | 301 | Jo Ann Prentice | Dunes GC, Myrtle Beach, SC |
| | | | Ruth Jessen | |
| 1963 | Mary Mills | 289 | Sandra Haynie | Kenwood CC, Cincinnati, OH |
| | | | Louise Suggs | |
| 1964 | Mickey Wright* (70) | 290 | Ruth Jessen (72) | San Diego CC, Chula Vista, CA |
| 1965 | Carol Mann | 290 | Kathy Cornelius | Atlantic City CC, Northfield, NJ |
| 1966 | Sandra Spuzich | 297 | Carol Mann | Hazeltine Natl GC, Chaska, MN |
| 1967 | Catherine LaCoste | 294 | Susie Berning | Hot Springs GC (Cascades Course), Hot Springs, VA |
| | | | Beth Stone | |
| 1968 | Susie Berning | 289 | Mickey Wright | Moslem Springs GC, Fleetwood, PA |
| 1969 | Donna Caponi | 294 | Peggy Wilson | Scenic Hills CC, Pensacola, FL |

## U.S. Women's Open *(Cont.)*

| Year | Winner | Score | Runner-Up | Site |
|---|---|---|---|---|
| 1970 | Donna Caponi | 287 | Sandra Haynie<br>Sandra Spuzich | Muskogee CC, Muskogee, OK |
| 1971 | JoAnne Carner | 288 | Kathy Whitworth | Kahkwa CC, Erie, PA |
| 1972 | Susie Berning | 299 | Kathy Ahern<br>Pam Barnett<br>Judy Rankin | Winged Foot GC, Mamaroneck, NY |
| 1973 | Susie Berning | 290 | Gloria Ehret<br>Shelley Hamlin | CC of Rochester, Rochester, NY |
| 1974 | Sandra Haynie | 295 | Carol Mann<br>Beth Stone | La Grange CC, La Grange, IL |
| 1975 | Sandra Palmer | 295 | JoAnne Carner<br>Sandra Post<br>Nancy Lopez | Atlantic City CC, Northfield, NJ |
| 1976 | JoAnne Carner* (76) | 292 | Sandra Palmer (78) | Rolling Green CC, Springfield, PA |
| 1977 | Hollis Stacy | 292 | Nancy Lopez | Hazeltine Natl GC, Chaska, MN |
| 1978 | Hollis Stacy | 289 | JoAnne Carner<br>Sally Little | CC of Indianapolis, Indianapolis, IN |
| 1979 | Jerilyn Britz | 284 | Debbie Massey<br>Sandra Palmer | Brooklawn CC, Fairfield, CT |
| 1980 | Amy Alcott | 280 | Hollis Stacy | Richland CC, Nashville, TN |
| 1981 | Pat Bradley | 279 | Beth Daniel | La Grange CC, La Grange, IL |
| 1982 | Janet Anderson | 283 | Beth Daniel<br>Sandra Haynie<br>Donna White<br>JoAnne Carner | Del Paso CC, Sacramento,CA |
| 1983 | Jan Stephenson | 290 | JoAnne Carner<br>Patty Sheehan | Cedar Ridge CC, Tulsa, OK |
| 1984 | Hollis Stacy | 290 | Rosie Jones | Salem CC, Peabody, MA |
| 1985 | Kathy Baker | 280 | Judy Dickinson | Baltusrol GC (Upper Course), Springfield, NJ |
| 1986 | Jane Geddes* (71) | 287 | Sally Little (73) | NCR GC, Dayton, OH |
| 1987 | Laura Davies* (71) | 285 | Ayako Okamoto (73)<br>JoAnne Carner (74) | Plainfield CC, Plainfield, NJ |
| 1988 | Liselotte Neumann | 277 | Patty Sheehan | Baltimore CC, Baltimore, MD |
| 1989 | Betsy King | 278 | Nancy Lopez | Indianwood G & CC, Lake Orion, MI |
| 1990 | Betsy King | 284 | Patty Sheehan | Atlanta Athletic Club, Duluth, GA |
| 1991 | Meg Mallon | 283 | Pat Bradley | Colonial Club, Fort Worth, TX |
| 1992 | Patty Sheehan* (72) | 280 | Juli Inkster | Oakmont CC, Oakmont, PA |
| 1993 | Lauri Merten | 280 | Donna Andrew<br>Helen Alfredsson | Crooked Stick, Carmel, IN |
| 1994 | Patty Sheehan | 277 | Tammie Green | Indianwood G & CC, Lake Orion, MI |
| 1995 | Annika Sorenstam | 278 | Meg Mallon | The Broadmoor GC, Colorado Springs,CO |
| 1996 | Annika Sorenstam | 272 | Kris Tschetter | Pine Needles GC, Southern Pines, NC |
| 1997 | Alison Nicholas | 274 | Nancy Lopez | Pumpkin Ridge CC, North Plains, OR |
| 1998 | Se Ri Pak† | 290 | Jenny Chuasiriporn | Blackwolf Run Golf Resort, Kohler, WI |
| 1999 | Juli Inkster | 272 | Sherri Turner | Old Waverly GC, West Point, MS |
| 2000 | Karrie Webb | 282 | Cristie Kerr/ Meg Mallon | Merit GC, Libertyville, IL |
| 2001 | Karrie Webb | 273 | Se Ri Pak | Pine Needles GC, Southern Pines, NC |
| 2002 | Juli Inkster | 276 | Annika Sorenstam | Prairie Dunes CC, Hutchinson, KS |
| 2003 | Hilary Lunke* | 283 | Kelly Robbins | Pumpkin Ridge GC, North Plains, OR |
| 2004 | Meg Mallon | 274 | Annika Sorenstam | The Orchards GC, South Hadley, MA |
| 2005 | Birdie Kim | 287 | Brittany Lang<br>Morgan Pressel | Cherry Hills CC, Cherry Hills Village, CO |
| 2006 | Annika Sorenstam* | 284 | Pat Hurst | Newport CC, Newport, RI |
| 2007 | Cristie Kerr | 279 | Angela Park<br>Lorena Ochoa | Pine Needles GC, Southern Pines, NC |
| 2008 | Inbee Park | 283 | Helen Alfredsson | Interlachen CC, Edina, MN |
| 2009 | Eun-Hee Ji | 284 | Candie Kung | Saucon Valley CC-Old Course, Bethlehem, PA |

* Winner in playoff. † Winner on second hole of sudden death after 18-hole playoff ended in a tie.

## Kraft Nabisco Championship

| Year | Winner | Score | Runner-Up | Year | Winner | Score | Runner-Up |
|------|--------|-------|-----------|------|--------|-------|-----------|
| 1972 | Jane Blalock | 213 | Carol Mann | 1991 | Amy Alcott | 273 | Dottie Mochrie |
|      |          |     | Judy Rankin | 1992 | Dottie Mochrie* | 279 | Juli Inkster |
| 1973 | Mickey Wright | 284 | Joyce Kazmierski | 1993 | Helen Alfredsson | 284 | Amy Benz |
| 1974 | Jo Ann Prentice* | 289 | Jane Blalock |      |          |     | Tina Barrett |
|      |          |     | Sandra Haynie |      |          |     | Betsy King |
| 1975 | Sandra Palmer | 283 | Kathy McMullen | 1994 | Donna Andrews | 276 | Laura Davies |
| 1976 | Judy Rankin | 285 | Betty Burfeindt | 1995 | Nanci Bowen | 285 | Susie Redman |
| 1977 | Kathy Whitworth | 289 | JoAnne Carner | 1996 | Patti Sheehan | 281 | Kelly Robbins |
|      |          |     | Sally Little |      |          |     | Meg Mallon |
|      |          |     | Penny Pulz |      |          |     | Annika Sorenstam |
| 1978 | Sandra Post* | 283 |          | 1997 | Betsy King | 276 | Kris Tschetter |
| 1979 | Sandra Post | 276 | Nancy Lopez | 1998 | Pat Hurst | 281 | Helen Dobson |
| 1980 | Donna Caponi | 275 | Amy Alcott | 1999 | Dottie Pepper | 269 | Meg Mallon |
| 1981 | Nancy Lopez | 277 | Carolyn Hill | 2000 | Karrie Webb | 274 | Dottie Pepper |
| 1982 | Sally Little | 278 | Hollis Stacy | 2001 | Annika Sorenstam | 281 | five players |
|      |          |     | Sandra Haynie | 2002 | Annika Sorenstam | 280 | Liselotte Neumann |
| 1983 | Amy Alcott | 282 | Beth Daniel | 2003 | P. Meunier-Lebouc | 281 | Annika Sorenstam |
|      |          |     | Kathy Whitworth | 2004 | Grace Park | 277 | Aree Song |
| 1984 | Juli Inkster* | 280 | Pat Bradley | 2005 | Annika Sorenstam | 273 | Rosie Jones |
| 1985 | Alice Miller | 275 | Jan Stephenson | 2006 | Karrie Webb* | 279 | Lorena Ochoa |
| 1986 | Pat Bradley | 280 | Val Skinner | 2007 | Morgan Pressel | 285 | Catriona Matthew |
| 1987 | Betsy King* | 283 | Patty Sheehan |      |          |     | Brittany Lincicome |
| 1988 | Amy Alcott | 274 | Colleen Walker |      |          |     | Suzann Pettersen |
| 1989 | Juli Inkster | 279 | Tammie Green |      |          |     |          |
|      |          |     | JoAnne Carner | 2008 | Lorena Ochoa | 277 | Annika Sorenstam |
| 1990 | Betsy King | 283 | Kathy Postlewait | 2009 | Brittany Lincicome | 279 | Kristy McPherson |
|      |          |     | Shirley Furlong |      |          |     | Cristie Kerr |

*Winner in sudden-death playoff. Note: Designated fourth major in 1983; played at Mission Hills CC, Rancho Mirage, CA.

## du Maurier Classic

| Year | Winner | Score | Runner-Up | Site |
|------|--------|-------|-----------|------|
| 1973 | Jocelyne Bourassa* | 214 | Sandra Haynie | Montreal GC, Montreal |
|      |          |     | Judy Rankin |          |
| 1974 | Carole Jo Callison | 208 | JoAnne Carner | Candiac GC, Montreal |
| 1975 | JoAnne Carner* | 214 | Carol Mann | St. George's CC, Toronto |
| 1976 | Donna Caponi* | 212 | Judy Rankin | Cedar Brae G & CC, Toronto |
| 1977 | Judy Rankin | 214 | Pat Meyers | Lachute G & CC, Montreal |
|      |          |     | Sandra Palmer |          |
| 1978 | JoAnne Carner | 278 | Hollis Stacy | St. George's CC, Toronto |
| 1979 | Amy Alcott | 285 | Nancy Lopez | Richelieu Valley CC, Montreal |
| 1980 | Pat Bradley | 277 | JoAnne Carner | St. George's CC, Toronto |
| 1981 | Jan Stephenson | 278 | Nancy Lopez | Summerlea CC, Dorion, Quebec |
|      |          |     | Pat Bradley |          |
| 1982 | Sandra Haynie | 280 | Beth Daniel | St. George's CC, Toronto |
| 1983 | Hollis Stacy | 277 | JoAnne Carner | Beaconsfield GC, Montreal |
|      |          |     | Alice Miller |          |
| 1984 | Juli Inkster | 279 | Ayako Okamoto | St. George's G & CC, Toronto |
| 1985 | Pat Bradley | 278 | Jane Geddes | Beaconsfield CC, Montreal |
| 1986 | Pat Bradley* | 276 | Ayako Okamoto | Board of Trade CC, Toronto |
| 1987 | Jody Rosenthal | 272 | Ayako Okamoto | Islesmere GC, Laval, Quebec |
| 1988 | Sally Little | 279 | Laura Davies | Vancouver GC, Coquitlam, British Columbia |
| 1989 | Tammie Green | 279 | Pat Bradley | Beaconsfield GC, Montreal |
|      |          |     | Betsy King |          |
| 1990 | Cathy Johnston | 276 | Patty Sheehan | Westmount G & CC, Kitchener, Ontario |
| 1991 | Nancy Scranton | 279 | Debbie Massey | Vancouver GC, Coquitlam, British Columbia |
| 1992 | Sherri Steinhauer | 277 | Judy Dickinson | St. Charles CC, Winnipeg, Manitoba |
| 1993 | Brandie Burton | 277 | Betsy King | London Hunt and CC, London, Ontario |
| 1994 | Martha Nause | 279 | Michelle McGann | Ottawa Hunt and GC, Ottawa, Ont. |
| 1995 | Jenny Lidback | 280 | Liselotte Neumann | Beaconsfield GC, Pointe-Claire, Quebec |
| 1996 | Laura Davies | 277 | Nancy Lopez | Edmonton CC, Edmonton, Alberta |
|      |          |     | Karrie Webb |          |
| 1997 | Colleen Walker | 278 | Liselotte Neumann | Glen Abbey GC, Oakville, Ontario |
| 1998 | Brandie Burton | 270 | Annika Sorenstam | Essex G & CC, Windsor, Ontario |
| 1999 | Karrie Webb | 277 | Laura Davies | Priddis Greens G & CC, Calgary, Alberta |
| 2000 | Meg Mallon | 282 | Rosie Jones | Royal Ottawa GC, Aylmer, Quebec |

*Winner in sudden-death playoff. Note: Designated third major in 1979. Tournament discontinued in 2001.

### Women's British Open

| Year | Winner | Score | Runner-Up | Site |
|------|--------|-------|-----------|------|
| 2001 | Se Ri Pak | 277 | Mi Hyun Kim | Sunningdale GC, Berkshire, England |
| 2002 | Karrie Webb | 273 | Michelle Ellis | Turnberry GC, Ailsa, Scotland |
|      |        |     | Paula Marti |  |
| 2003 | Annika Sorenstam | 278 | Se Ri Pak | Royal Lytham & St. Annes, England |
| 2004 | Karen Stupples | 269 | Rachel Teske | Sunningdale GC, Berklshire, England |
| 2005 | Jeong Jang | 272 | Sophie Gustafson | Royal Birkdale CC, Merseyside, England |
| 2006 | Sherri Steinhauer | 281 | Cristie Kerr | Royal Lytham & St. Anne's, England |
| 2007 | Lorena Ochoa | 287 | Jee Young Lee | Old Course, St. Andrew's, Scotland |
|      |        |     | Maria Hjorth |  |
| 2008 | Ji-Yai Shin | 270 | Yanj Tseng | Sunningdale GC, Berkshire, England |
| 2009 | Catriona Matthew | 285 | Karrie Webb | Royal Lytham & St. Annes, England |

Note: Designated fourth major in 2001.

### Alltime Major Championship Winners

| | LPGA | U.S. Open | Nabisco | Brit. Open | ‡du Maurier | #Titleholders | †Western | U.S. Am | Brit. Am | Total |
|---|---|---|---|---|---|---|---|---|---|---|
| Patty Berg | 0 | 1 | 0 | 0 | 0 | 7 | 7 | 1 | 0 | 16 |
| Mickey Wright | 4 | 4 | 0 | 0 | 0 | 2 | 3 | 0 | 0 | 13 |
| Louise Suggs | 1 | 2 | 0 | 0 | 0 | 4 | 4 | 1 | 1 | 13 |
| Babe Zaharias | 0 | 3 | 0 | 0 | 0 | 3 | 4 | 1 | 1 | 12 |
| *Juli Inkster | 2 | 2 | 2 | 0 | 1 | 0 | 0 | 3 | 0 | 10 |
| Annika Sorenstam | 3 | 3 | 3 | 1 | 0 | 0 | 0 | 0 | 0 | 10 |
| Betsy Rawls | 2 | 4 | 0 | 0 | 0 | 0 | 2 | 0 | 0 | 8 |
| JoAnne Carner | 0 | 2 | 0 | 0 | 0 | 0 | 0 | 5 | 0 | 7 |
| *Karrie Webb | 1 | 2 | 2 | 1 | 1 | 0 | 0 | 0 | 0 | 7 |
| Kathy Whitworth | 3 | 0 | 0 | 0 | 0 | 2 | 1 | 0 | 0 | 6 |
| Pat Bradley | 1 | 1 | 1 | 0 | 3 | 0 | 0 | 0 | 0 | 6 |
| Patty Sheehan | 3 | 2 | 1 | 0 | 0 | 0 | 0 | 0 | 0 | 6 |
| Glenna Vare | 0 | 0 | 0 | 0 | 0 | 0 | 0 | 6 | 0 | 6 |
| Betsy King | 1 | 2 | 3 | 0 | 0 | 0 | 0 | 0 | 0 | 6 |

*Active LPGA player.
#Major from 1937–1972. †Major from 1937–1967. ‡Major from 1979–2000.

### Alltime Multiple Professional Major Winners

| LPGA | | U.S. OPEN | | NABISCO/DINAH SHORE | | WESTERN OPEN | |
|------|--|-----------|--|---------------------|--|--------------|--|
| Mickey Wright | 4 | Betsy Rawls | 4 | Amy Alcott | 3 | Patty Berg | 7 |
| Nancy Lopez | 3 | Mickey Wright | 4 | Betsy King | 3 | Louise Suggs | 4 |
| Se Ri Pak | 3 | Susie Maxwell Berning | 3 | Annika Sorenstam | 3 | Babe Zaharias | 4 |
| Patty Sheehan | 3 | Hollis Stacy | 3 | *Juli Inkster | 2 | Mickey Wright | 3 |
| Annika Sorenstam | 3 | Babe Zaharias | 3 | *Karrie Webb | 2 | June Beebe | 2 |
| Kathy Whitworth | 3 | Annika Sorenstam | 3 | | | Opal Hill | 2 |
| Donna Caponi | 2 | JoAnne Carner | 2 | TITLEHOLDERS | | Betty Jameson | 2 |
| Sandra Haynie | 2 | Donna Caponi | 2 | Patty Berg | 7 | Betsy Rawls | 2 |
| Mary Mills | 2 | Betsy King | 2 | Louise Suggs | 4 | | |
| Betsy Rawls | 2 | Meg Mallon | 2 | Babe Zaharias | 3 | DU MAURIER | |
| Laura Davies | 2 | Patty Sheehan | 2 | Dorothy Kirby | 2 | Pat Bradley | 3 |
| *Juli Inkster | 2 | Louise Suggs | 2 | Marilynn Smith | 2 | Brandie Burton | 2 |
| | | Karrie Webb | 2 | Kathy Whitworth | 2 | JoAnne Carner | 2 |
| | | *Juli Inkster | 2 | Mickey Wright | 2 | | |

*Active player.

# THE LPGA TOUR

### Most Career Wins†

| | Wins | | Wins | | Wins |
|---|------|---|------|---|------|
| Kathy Whitworth | 88 | Sandra Haynie | 42 | *Juli Inkster | 31 |
| Mickey Wright | 82 | Babe Zaharias | 41 | Amy Alcott | 29 |
| Annika Sorenstam | 72 | Carol Mann | 38 | Jane Blalock | 29 |
| Patty Berg | 60 | *Karrie Webb | 36 | *Lorena Ochoa | 27 |
| Louise Suggs | 58 | Patty Sheehan | 35 | Marlene Hagge | 26 |
| Betsy Rawls | 55 | Betsy King | 34 | Judy Rankin | 26 |
| Nancy Lopez | 48 | Beth Daniel | 33 | Donna Caponi | 24 |
| JoAnne Carner | 43 | Pat Bradley | 31 | *Se Ri Pak | 24 |

†Through 10/05/09. *Active player.

## Season Money Leaders

| | Earnings ($) | | Earnings ($) | | Earnings ($) |
|---|---|---|---|---|---|
| 1950...Babe Zaharias | 14,800 | 1970...Kathy Whitworth | 30,235 | 1990...Beth Daniel | 863,578 |
| 1951...Babe Zaharias | 15,087 | 1971...Kathy Whitworth | 41,181 | 1991...Pat Bradley | 763,118 |
| 1952...Betsy Rawls | 14,505 | 1972...Kathy Whitworth | 65,063 | 1992...Dottie Mochrie | 693,335 |
| 1953...Louise Suggs | 19,816 | 1973...Kathy Whitworth | 82,864 | 1993...Betsy King | 595,992 |
| 1954...Patty Berg | 16,011 | 1974...JoAnne Carner | 87,094 | 1994...Laura Davies | 687,201 |
| 1955...Patty Berg | 16,492 | 1975...Sandra Palmer | 76,374 | 1995...Annika Sorenstam | 666,533 |
| 1956...Marlene Hagge | 20,235 | 1976...Judy Rankin | 150,734 | 1996...Karrie Webb | 1,002,000 |
| 1957...Patty Berg | 16,272 | 1977...Judy Rankin | 122,890 | 1997...Annika Sorenstam | 1,236,789 |
| 1958...Beverly Hanson | 12,639 | 1978...Nancy Lopez | 189,814 | 1998...Annika Sorenstam | 1,092,748 |
| 1959...Betsy Rawls | 26,774 | 1979...Nancy Lopez | 197,489 | 1999...Karrie Webb | 1,591,959 |
| 1960...Louise Suggs | 16,892 | 1980...Beth Daniel | 231,000 | 2000...Karrie Webb | 1,876,853 |
| 1961...Mickey Wright | 22,236 | 1981...Beth Daniel | 206,998 | 2001...Annika Sorenstam | 2,105,868 |
| 1962...Mickey Wright | 21,641 | 1982...JoAnne Carner | 310,400 | 2002...Annika Sorenstam | 2,863.904 |
| 1963...Mickey Wright | 31,269 | 1983...JoAnne Carner | 291,404 | 2003...Annika Sorenstam | 2,029,506 |
| 1964...Mickey Wright | 29,800 | 1984...Betsy King | 266,771 | 2004...Annika Sorenstam | 2,544,707 |
| 1965...Kathy Whitworth | 28,658 | 1985...Nancy Lopez | 416,472 | 2005...Annika Sorenstam | 2,588,240 |
| 1966...Kathy Whitworth | 33,517 | 1986...Pat Bradley | 492,021 | 2006...Lorena Ochoa | 2,592,872 |
| 1967...Kathy Whitworth | 32,937 | 1987...Ayako Okamoto | 466,034 | 2007...Lorena Ochoa | 4,364,994 |
| 1968...Kathy Whitworth | 48,379 | 1988...Sherri Turner | 350,851 | 2008...Lorena Ochoa | 2,763,193 |
| 1969...Carol Mann | 49,152 | 1989...Betsy King | 654,132 | | |

## LPGA Player of the Year

| | | | | | |
|---|---|---|---|---|---|
| 1966 | Kathy Whitworth | 1981 | JoAnne Carner | 1996 | Laura Davies |
| 1967 | Kathy Whitworth | 1982 | JoAnne Carner | 1997 | Annika Sorenstam |
| 1968 | Kathy Whitworth | 1983 | Patty Sheehan | 1998 | Annika Sorenstam |
| 1969 | Kathy Whitworth | 1984 | Betsy King | 1999 | Karrie Webb |
| 1970 | Sandra Haynie | 1985 | Nancy Lopez | 2000 | Karrie Webb |
| 1971 | Kathy Whitworth | 1986 | Pat Bradley | 2001 | Annika Sorenstam |
| 1972 | Kathy Whitworth | 1987 | Ayako Okamoto | 2002 | Annika Sorenstam |
| 1973 | Kathy Whitworth | 1988 | Nancy Lopez | 2003 | Annika Sorenstam |
| 1974 | JoAnne Carner | 1989 | Betsy King | 2004 | Annika Sorenstam |
| 1975 | Sandra Palmer | 1990 | Beth Daniel | 2005 | Annika Sorenstam |
| 1976 | Judy Rankin | 1991 | Pat Bradley | 2006 | Lorena Ochoa |
| 1977 | Judy Rankin | 1992 | Dottie Mochrie | 2007 | Lorena Ochoa |
| 1978 | Nancy Lopez | 1993 | Betsy King | 2008 | Lorena Ochoa |
| 1979 | Nancy Lopez | 1994 | Beth Daniel | | |
| 1980 | Beth Daniel | 1995 | Annika Sorenstam | | |

## Vare Trophy: Best Scoring Average*

| | Avg | | Avg | | Avg |
|---|---|---|---|---|---|
| 1953...Patty Berg | 75.00 | 1972...Kathy Whitworth | 72.38 | 1991...Pat Bradley | 70.76 |
| 1954...Babe Zaharias | 75.48 | 1973...Judy Rankin | 73.08 | 1992...Dottie Mochrie | 70.80 |
| 1955...Patty Berg | 74.47 | 1974...JoAnne Carner | 72.87 | 1993...Nancy Lopez | 70.83 |
| 1956...Patty Berg | 74.57 | 1975...JoAnne Carner | 72.40 | 1994...Beth Daniel | 70.90 |
| 1957...Louise Suggs | 74.64 | 1976...Judy Rankin | 72.25 | 1995...Annika Sorenstam | 71.00 |
| 1958...Beverly Hanson | 74.92 | 1977...Judy Rankin | 72.16 | 1996...Annika Sorenstam | 70.47 |
| 1959...Betsy Rawls | 74.03 | 1978...Nancy Lopez | 71.76 | 1997...Karrie Webb | 70.00 |
| 1960...Mickey Wright | 73.25 | 1979...Nancy Lopez | 71.20 | 1998...Annika Sorenstam | 69.99 |
| 1961...Mickey Wright | 73.55 | 1980...Amy Alcott | 71.51 | 1999...Karrie Webb | 69.43 |
| 1962...Mickey Wright | 73.67 | 1981...JoAnne Carner | 71.75 | 2000...Karrie Webb | 70.05 |
| 1963...Mickey Wright | 72.81 | 1982...JoAnne Carner | 71.49 | 2001...Annika Sorenstam | 69.42 |
| 1964...Mickey Wright | 72.46 | 1983...JoAnne Carner | 71.41 | 2002...Annika Sorenstam | 68.70 |
| 1965...Kathy Whitworth | 72.61 | 1984...Patty Sheehan | 71.40 | 2003...Se Ri Pak | 70.03 |
| 1966...Kathy Whitworth | 72.60 | 1985...Nancy Lopez | 70.73 | 2004...Grace Park | 69.99 |
| 1967...Kathy Whitworth | 72.74 | 1986...Pat Bradley | 71.10 | 2005...Annika Sorenstam | 69.33 |
| 1968...Carol Mann | 72.04 | 1987...Betsy King | 71.14 | 2006...Lorena Ochoa | 69.23 |
| 1969...Kathy Whitworth | 72.38 | 1988...Colleen Walker | 71.26 | 2007...Lorena Ochoa | 69.69 |
| 1970...Kathy Whitworth | 72.26 | 1989...Beth Daniel | 70.38 | 2008...Lorena Ochoa | 69.70 |
| 1971...Kathy Whitworth | 72.88 | 1990...Beth Daniel | 70.54 | | |

*Must play 70 rounds or more to qualify; Annika Sorenstam compiled an average of 69.02 in 60 rounds in 2003.

### U.S. Senior Open

| Year | Winner | Score | Runner-Up | Site |
|------|--------|-------|-----------|------|
| 1980 | Roberto DeVicenzo | 285 | William C. Campbell | Winged Foot GC, Mamaroneck, NY |
| 1981 | Arnold Palmer* (70) | 289 | Bob Stone (74) | Oakland Hills CC, Birmingham, MI |
| | | | Billy Casper (77) | |
| 1982 | Miller Barber | 282 | Gene Littler, Dan Sikes, Jr. | Portland GC, Portland, OR |
| 1983 | Billy Casper* (75) (3) | 288 | Rod Funseth (75) (4) | Hazeltine GC, Chaska, MN |
| 1984 | Miller Barber | 286 | Arnold Palmer | Oak Hill CC, Rochester, NY |
| 1985 | Miller Barber | 285 | Roberto DeVicenzo | Edgewood Tahoe GC, Stateline, NV |
| 1986 | Dale Douglass | 279 | Gary Player | Scioto CC, Columbus, OH |
| 1987 | Gary Player | 270 | Doug Sanders | Brooklawn CC, Fairfield, CT |
| 1988 | Gary Player* (68) | 288 | Bob Charles (70) | Medinah CC, Medinah, IL |
| 1989 | Orville Moody | 279 | Frank Beard | Laurel Valley GC, Ligonier, PA |
| 1990 | Lee Trevino | 275 | Jack Nicklaus | Ridgewood CC, Paramus, NJ |
| 1991 | Jack Nicklaus* (65) | 282 | Chi Chi Rodriguez (69) | Oakland Hills CC, Birmingham, MI |
| 1992 | Larry Laoretti | 275 | Jim Colbert | Saucon Valley CC, Bethlehem, PA |
| 1993 | Jack Nicklaus | 278 | Tom Weiskopf | Cherry Hills CC, Englewood, CO |
| 1994 | Simon Hobday | 274 | Jim Albus | Pinehurst Resort & CC, Pinehurst, NC |
| 1995 | Tom Weiskopf | 275 | Jack Nicklaus | Congressional CC, Bethesda, MD |
| 1996 | Dave Stockton | 277 | Hale Irwin | Canterbury GC, Beachwood, OH |
| 1997 | Graham Marsh | 280 | Hale Irwin | Olympia Fields CC, Olympia Fields, IL |
| 1998 | Hale Irwin | 285 | Vicente Fernandez | Riviera CC, Pacific Palisades, CA |
| 1999 | Dave Eichelberger | 281 | Ed Dougherty | Des Moines G & CC, Des Moines, IA |
| 2000 | Hale Irwin | 267 | Bruce Fleisher | Saucon Valley CC, Bethlehem, PA |
| 2001 | Bruce Fleisher | 280 | Isao Aoki, Gil Morgan | Salem CC, Peabody, MA |
| 2002 | Don Pooley* (19) (5) | 274 | Tom Watson (18) | Caves Valley GC, Owings Mill, MD |
| 2003 | Bruce Lietzke | 277 | Tom Watson | Inverness GC, Toledo, OH |
| 2004 | Peter Jacobsen | 272 | Hale Irwin | Bellerive CC, St. Louis, MO |
| 2005 | Allen Doyle | 274 | D.A. Weibring | NCR GC, Kettering, OH |
| | | | Loren Roberts | |
| 2006 | Allen Doyle | 272 | Tom Watson | Prairie Dunes CC, Hutchinson, KS |
| 2007 | Brad Bryant | 282 | Ben Crenshaw | Whistling Straits GC, Kohler, WI |
| 2008 | Eduardo Romero | 274 | Fred Funk | Broadmoor GC, Colorado Springs, CO |
| 2009 | Fred Funk | 268 | Joey Sindelar | Crooked Stick GC, Carmel, IN |

*Winner in playoff. Playoff scores are in parentheses. The 1983 playoff went to one hole of sudden death after an 18-hole playoff.

## CHAMPIONS TOUR

### Season Money Leaders

| | Earnings ($) | | Earnings ($) | | Earnings ($) |
|---|---|---|---|---|---|
| 1980...Don January | 44,100 | 1990...Lee Trevino | 1,190,518 | 2000...Larry Nelson | 2,708,005 |
| 1981...Miller Barber | 83,136 | 1991...Mike Hill | 1,065,657 | 2001...Allen Doyle | 2,553,582 |
| 1982...Miller Barber | 106,890 | 1992...Lee Trevino | 1,027,002 | 2002...Hale Irwin | 3,028,304 |
| 1983...Don January | 237,571 | 1993...Dave Stockton | 1,175,944 | 2003...Tom Watson | 1,853,108 |
| 1984...Don January | 328,597 | 1994...Dave Stockton | 1,402,519 | 2004...Craig Stadler | 2,306,066 |
| 1985...Peter Thomson | 386,724 | 1995...Jim Colbert | 1,444,386 | 2005...Dana Quigley | 2,170,258 |
| 1986...Bruce Crampton | 454,299 | 1996...Jim Colbert | 1,627,890 | 2006...Jay Haas | 2,420,227 |
| 1987...Chi Chi Rodriguez | 509,145 | 1997...Hale Irwin | 2,449,420 | 2007...Jay Haas | 2,581,001 |
| 1988...Bob Charles | 533,929 | 1998...Hale Irwin | 2,861,945 | 2008...Bernhard Langer | 2,035,073 |
| 1989...Bob Charles | 725,887 | 1999...Bruce Fleisher | 2,515,705 | | |

### Most Career Wins†

| | Wins | | Wins |
|---|---|---|---|
| Hale Irwin | 45 | Jim Colbert | 20 |
| Lee Trevino | 29 | Bruce Crampton | 20 |
| Gil Morgan | 25 | George Archer | 19 |
| Miller Barber | 24 | Gary Player | 19 |
| Bob Charles | 23 | Larry Nelson | 19 |
| Don January | 22 | Bruce Fleisher | 18 |
| Chi Chi Rodriguez | 22 | Mike Hill | 18 |

*Active player.
†Through 10/05/09.

## Ryder Cup Matches

| Year | Results | Site |
|------|---------|------|
| 1927 | United States 9½, Great Britain 2½ | Worcester CC, Worcester, MA |
| 1929 | Great Britain 7, United States 5 | Moortown GC, Leeds, England |
| 1931 | United States 9, Great Britain 3 | Scioto CC, Columbus, OH |
| 1933 | Great Britain 6½, United States 5½ | Southport and Ainsdale Courses, Southport, England |
| 1935 | United States 9, Great Britain 3 | Ridgewood CC, Ridgewood, NJ |
| 1937 | United States 8, Great Britain 4 | Southport and Ainsdale Courses, Southport, England |
| 1939–1945 | No tournament | |
| 1947 | United States 11, Great Britain 1 | Portland GC, Portland, OR |
| 1949 | United States 7, Great Britain 5 | Ganton GC, Scarborough, England |
| 1951 | United States 9½, Great Britain 2½ | Pinehurst CC, Pinehurst, NC |
| 1953 | United States 6½, Great Britain 5½ | Wentworth Club, Surrey, England |
| 1955 | United States 8, Great Britain 4 | Thunderbird Ranch & CC, Palm Springs, CA |
| 1957 | Great Britain 7½, United States 4½ | Lindrick GC, Yorkshire, England |
| 1959 | United States 8½, Great Britain 3½ | Eldorado CC, Palm Desert, CA |
| 1961 | United States 14½, Great Britain 9½ | Royal Lytham & St. Annes GC, St Anne's-on-the-Sea, England |
| 1963 | United States 23, Great Britain 9 | East Lake CC, Atlanta |
| 1965 | United States 19½, Great Britain 12½ | Royal Birkdale GC, Southport, England |
| 1967 | United States 23½, Great Britain 8½ | Champions GC, Houston |
| 1969 | United States 16, Great Britain 16 | Royal Birkdale GC, Southport, England |
| 1971 | United States 18½, Great Britain 13½ | Old Warson CC, St. Louis |
| 1973 | United States 19, Great Britain 13 | Hon Co of Edinburgh Golfers, Muirfield, Scotland |
| 1975 | United States 21, Great Britain 11 | Laurel Valley GC, Ligonier, PA |
| 1977 | United States 12½, Great Britain 7½ | Royal Lytham & St. Annes GC, St. Annes-on-the-Sea, Eng. |
| 1979 | United States 17, Europe 11 | Greenbrier, White Sulphur Springs, WV |
| 1981 | United States 18½, Europe 9½ | Walton Heath GC, Surrey, England |
| 1983 | United States 14½, Europe 13½ | PGA National GC, Palm Beach Gardens, FL |
| 1985 | Europe 16½, United States 11½ | Belfry GC, Sutton Coldfield, England |
| 1987 | Europe 15, United States 13 | Muirfield GC, Dublin, OH |
| 1989 | Europe 14, United States 14 | Belfry GC, Sutton Coldfield, England |
| 1991 | United States 14½, Europe 13½ | Ocean Course, Kiawah Island, SC |
| 1993 | United States 15, Europe 13 | Belfry GC, Sutton Coldfield, England |
| 1995 | Europe 14½, United States 13½ | Oak Hill CC, Rochester, NY |
| 1997 | Europe 14½, United States 13½ | Valderrama GC, Sotogrande, Spain |
| 1999 | United States 14½, Europe 13½ | The Country Club, Brookline, MA |
| 2002 | Europe 15½, Unites States 12½ | Belfry GC, Sutton Coldfield, England |
| 2004 | Europe 18½, United States 9½ | Oakland Hills CC, Bloomfield Hills, MI |
| 2006 | Europe 18½, United States 9½ | The K Club, County Kildare, Ireland |
| 2008 | United States 16½, Europe 11½ | Valhalla GC, Louisville, KY |

Team matches held every odd year between U.S. professionals and those of Great Britain/Europe. Team members selected on basis of finishes in PGA and European tour events. Match in 2001 canceled due to 9/11 terrorist attacks.

## Presidents Cup Matches

| Year | Results | Site |
|------|---------|------|
| 1994 | United States 20, International 12 | Robert Trent Jones GC, Lake Manassas, VA |
| 1996 | United States 16½, International 15½ | Robert Trent Jones GC, Lake Manassas, VA |
| 1998 | International 20½ United States 11½ | Royal Melbourne GC, Melbourne, Australia |
| 2000 | United States 21½, International 10½ | Robert Trent Jones GC, Lake Manassas, VA |
| 2003 | International 17, United States 17 | Fan Court Hotel CC, George, South Africa |
| 2005 | United States 18½, International 15½ | Robert Trent Jones GC, Lake Manassas, VA |
| 2007 | United States 19½, International 14½ | Royal Montreal GC, Bizard, Quebec |
| 2009 | United States 19½, International 14½ | Harding Park GC, San Francisco, CA |

A biennial event played in non-Ryder Cup years designed to provide non-European players with international team and match play.

## Walker Cup Matches

| Year | Results | Site |
|---|---|---|
| 1922 | United States 8, Great Britain 4 | Nat'l Golf Links of America, Southampton, NY |
| 1923 | United States 6, Great Britain 5 | St. Andrews, Scotland |
| 1924 | United States 9, Great Britain 3 | Garden City GC, Garden City, NY |
| 1926 | United States 6, Great Britain 5 | St. Andrews, Scotland |
| 1928 | United States 11, Great Britain 1 | Chicago GC, Wheaton, IL |
| 1930 | United States 10, Great Britain 2 | Royal St. George GC, Sandwich, England |
| 1932 | United States 8, Great Britain 1 | The Country Club, Brookline, MA |
| 1934 | United States 9, Great Britain 2 | St. Andrews, Scotland |
| 1936 | United States 9, Great Britain 0 | Pine Valley GC, Clementon, NJ |
| 1938 | Great Britain 7, United States 4 | St. Andrews, Scotland |
| 1940–46 | No tournament | |
| 1947 | United States 8, Great Britain 4 | St. Andrews, Scotland |
| 1949 | United States 10, Great Britain 2 | Winged Foot GC, Mamaroneck, NY |
| 1951 | United States 6, Great Britain 3 | Birkdale GC, Southport, England |
| 1953 | United States 9, Great Britain 3 | The Kittansett Club, Marion, MA |
| 1955 | United States 10, Great Britain 2 | St. Andrews, Scotland |
| 1957 | United States 8, Great Britain 3 | Minikahda Club, Minneapolis |
| 1959 | United States 9, Great Britain 3 | Muirfield, Scotland |
| 1961 | United States 11, Great Britain 1 | Seattle GC, Seattle |
| 1963 | United States 12, Great Britain 8 | Ailsa Course, Turnberry, Scotland |
| 1965 | Great Britain 11, United States 11 | Baltimore CC, Five Farms, Baltimore, MD |
| 1967 | United States 13, Great Britain 7 | Royal St. George's GC, Sandwich, England |
| 1969 | United States 10, Great Britain 8 | Milwaukee CC, Milwaukee, WI |
| 1971 | Great Britain 13, United States 11 | St. Andrews, Scotland |
| 1973 | United States 14, Great Britain 10 | The Country Club, Brookline, MA |
| 1975 | United States 15½, Great Britain 8½ | St. Andrews, Scotland |
| 1977 | United States 16, Great Britain 8 | Shinnecock Hills GC, Southampton, NY |
| 1979 | United States 15½, Great Britain 8½ | Muirfield, Scotland |
| 1981 | United States 15, Great Britain 9 | Cypress Point Club, Pebble Beach, CA |
| 1983 | United States 13½, Great Britain 10½ | Royal Liverpool GC, Hoylake, England |
| 1985 | United States 13, Great Britain 11 | Pine Valley GC, Pine Valley, NJ |
| 1987 | United States 16½, Great Britain 7½ | Sunningdale GC, Berkshire, England |
| 1989 | Great Britain 12½, United States 11½ | Peachtree Golf Club, Atlanta |
| 1991 | United States 14, Great Britain 10 | Portmarnock GC, Dublin, Ireland |
| 1993 | United States 19, Great Britain 5 | Interlachen CC, Edina, MN |
| 1995 | Great Britain & Ireland 14, United States 10 | Royal Porthcawl, Porthcawl, Wales |
| 1997 | United States 18, Great Britain & Ireland 6 | Quaker Ridge GC, Scarsdale, NY |
| 1999 | Great Britai & Ireland 15, United States 9 | Nairn GC, Nairn, Scotland |
| 2001 | Great Britain & Ireland 15, United States 9 | Ocean Forest GC, Sea Island, GA |
| 2003 | Great Britain & Ireland 12½, United States 11½ | Ganton GC, Ganton, England |
| 2005 | United States 12½, Great Britain & Ireland 11½ | Chicago GC, Wheaton IL |
| 2007 | United States 12½, Great Britain & Ireland 11½ | Royal County Down, Newcastle, N. Ireland |
| 2009 | United States 16½, Great Britain & Ireland 9½ | Merion Golf Club, Ardmore, PA |

Men's amateur team competition every other year between United States and Great Britain/Ireland. U.S. team members selected by USGA.

## Solheim Cup Matches

| Year | Results | Site |
|---|---|---|
| 1990 | United States 11½, Europe 4½ | Lake Nona GC, Orlando, FL |
| 1992 | Europe 11½, United States 6½ | Dalmahoy Hotel GC, Edinburgh |
| 1994 | United States 13, Europe 7 | The Greenbriar, White Sulpher Springs, WV |
| 1996 | United States 17, Europe 11 | Marriot St Pierre Hotel & CC, Chepstow, Wales |
| 1998 | United States 16, Europe 12 | Muirfield Village GC, Dublin, OH |
| 2000 | Europe 14½, United States, 11 ½ | Loch Lomond GC, Luss, Scotand |
| 2002 | United States 15½, Europe 12 ½ | Interlachen CC, Minneapolis, MN |
| 2003 | Europe 17½, United States 10 ½ | Barseback G&CC, Malmo, Sweden |
| 2005 | United States 15½, Europe 12 ½ | Crooked Stick GC, Carmel IN |
| 2007 | United States 16, Europe 12 | Halmstad GC, Halmstad, Sweden |
| 2009 | United States 16, Europe 12 | Rich Harvest Farms GC, Sugar Grove, IL |

Women's team matches held every other year between U.S. professionals and those of Europe. Team members selected on the basis of finishes in LPGA and European tour events.

## Curtis Cup Matches

| Year | Results | Site |
|------|---------|------|
| 1932 | United States 5½, British Isles 3½ | Wentworth GC, Wentworth, England |
| 1934 | United States 6½, British Isles 2½ | Chevy Chase Club, Chevy Chase, MD |
| 1936 | United States 4½ British Isles 4½ | King's Course, Gleneagles, Scotland |
| 1938 | United States 5½, British Isles 3½ | Essex CC, Manchester, MA |
| 1940–46 | No tournament | |
| 1948 | United States 6½, British Isles 2½ | Birkdale GC, Southport, England |
| 1950 | United States 7½, British Isles 1½ | CC of Buffalo, Williamsville, NY |
| 1952 | British Isles 5, United States 4 | Muirfield, Scotland |
| 1954 | United States 6, British Isles 3 | Merion GC, Ardmore, PA |
| 1956 | British Isles 5, United States 4 | Prince's GC, Sandwich Bay, England |
| 1958 | British Isles 4½, United States 4½ | Brae Burn CC, West Newton, Mass. |
| 1960 | United States 6½, British Isles 2½ | Lindrick GC, Worksop, England |
| 1962 | United States 8, British Isles 1 | Broadmoor CG, Colorado Springs,CO |
| 1964 | United States 10½, British Isles 7½ | Royal Porthcawl GC, Porthcawl, South Wales |
| 1966 | United States 13, British Isles 5 | Va. Hot Springs G & TC, Hot Springs, VA |
| 1968 | United States 10½, British Isles 7½ | Royal County Down GC, Newcastle, N. Ire. |
| 1970 | United States 11½, British Isles 6½ | Brae Burn CC, West Newton, MA |
| 1972 | United States 10, British Isles 8 | Western Gailes, Ayrshire, Scotland |
| 1974 | United States 13, British Isles 5 | San Francisco GC, San Francisco |
| 1976 | United States 11½, British Isles 6½ | Royal Lytham & St. Annes GC, England |
| 1978 | United States 12, British Isles 6 | Apawamis Club, Rye, NY |
| 1980 | United States 13, British Isles 5 | St. Pierre G & CC, Chepstow, Wales |
| 1982 | United States 14½, British Isles 3½ | Denver CC, Denver |
| 1984 | United States 9½ British Isles 8½ | Muirfield, Scotland |
| 1986 | British Isles 13, United States 5 | Prairie Dunes CC, Hutchinson, KS |
| 1988 | British Isles 11, United States 7 | Royal St. George's GC, Sandwich, England |
| 1990 | United States 14, British Isles 4 | Somerset Hills CC, Bernardsville, NJ |
| 1992 | Great Britain/Ireland 10, United States 8 | Royal Liverpool GC, Hoylake, England |
| 1994 | Great Britain/Ireland 9, United States 9 | The Honors Course, Ooltewah, TN |
| 1996 | Great Britain/Ireland 11½, United States 6½ | Killarney Golf & Fishing Club, Killarney, Ireland |
| 1998 | United States 10, Great Britain/Ireland 8 | The Minikahda Club, Minneapolis |
| 2000 | United States 10, Great Britain/Ireland 8 | Ganton GC, North Yorkshire, England |
| 2002 | United States 11, Great Britain/Ireland 7 | Fox Chapel GC, Pittsburgh, PA |
| 2004 | United States 10, Great Britain/Ireland 8 | Formby GC, Merseyside, England |
| 2006 | United States 11½, Great Britain/Ireland 6½ | Bandon Dunes GC, Bandon, OR |
| 2008 | United States 13, Great Britain/Ireland 7 | Old Course, St. Andrews, Scotland |

Women's amateur team competition every other year between the United States and Great Britain/Ireland. U.S. team members selected by USGA.

# Boxing/ MMA

Manny Pacquiao (l.) laid claim to the unofficial title of world's best pound-for-pound boxer in 2009

# Fighting For Eyeballs

MMA bouts again bubbled over with drama in 2009, but with Pacquiao's arrival and Mayweather's return, the sport of boxing showed it's not to be counted out yet

**BY CHRIS MANNIX**

THE RELATIONSHIP BETWEEN boxing and mixed martial arts has long been one filled with conflict, an almost daily battle fueled by vitriolic rhetoric. Whether it's Top Rank boxing promoter Bob Arum describing an MMA show as "a bunch of skinhead white guys watching people in the ring who also look like skinhead white guys" or UFC head honcho Dana White opining that boxing is "dying a horrible death right now," neither side seemed to be able to resist the temptation of bashing the other. But as competitive as boxing and MMA have become, the world's premier combat sports had never gone head-to-head with major pay-per-view events. Never, that is, until September 19th, when Floyd Mayweather, boxing's former pound-for-pound king, and current lightweight champ Juan Manuel Marquez faced off in Las Vegas on the same night that UFC 103 was broadcast from Dallas. With the stakes high for both sides, it didn't take long for the verbal sparring to heat up. "I don't think it will be any competition," said Golden Boy Promotions CEO Richard Schaefer, predicting boxing would get the bigger draw. Countered UFC's White, "They're giving you the fight that you don't want. Nobody asked for this fight with Mayweather and—what's his name? What's his name? Nobody even knows."

Competition aside, 2009 was a banner year for both boxing and MMA. With the spectacle of the viral but very overrated Kimbo Slice behind them, MMA organizations began luring fans with high quality action. In April, World Extreme Cagefighting bantamweight champion Miguel Torres put his title on the line in a bloody brawl with Takeya Mizugaki at WEC 40. Mizugaki opened a gruesome cut over Torres's left eye in the third round that threatened to stop the fight. After a tepid approval by the ringside doctors, Torres launched a brutal counterattack, battering Mizugaki's face with precision punches that earned him a narrow decision win. The following month fans were treated to another action-filled slugfest when featherweight champion Mike Brown took on Urijah Faber at WEC 41. In one of the most action-packed fights of the year, Brown battered and bruised the weary challenger to earn a unanimous decision.

All of this was a prelude to the biggest MMA show of them all: UFC 100. The biggest prize of all was on the line when former WWE star Brock Lesnar faced Frank Mir in a rematch of their UFC 81 clash for the heavyweight title. Lesnar was aggressive from the opening bell, smothering Mir and pounding him with thudding haymakers. In the second round Lesnar violently pinned Mir against the cage and unleashed a bar-

**The headline bout at UFC 100—a rematch of a fight from UFC 81—saw Lesnar (top) score a quick, second-round win over Mir.**

rage of punches until the referee stepped in to stop the fight. The show was a smashing success, with UFC reporting 1.6 million pay-per-view buys and a $5.1 million live gate.

While MMA continued to grow, boxing found itself facing a crisis. Before his welterweight showdown with Shane Mosley in January, Antonio Margarito was caught trying to slip a plaster-like substance into his gloves. Though Mosley won the fight with a ninth-round knockout, Margarito was vilified in the press and had his license suspended for a year.

Margarito was still a hot topic in May when Manny Pacquiao, fresh off a stunning upset of Oscar De La Hoya, faced junior welterweight king Ricky Hatton. The heavy-handed Hatton, who had never lost at 140 pounds, was supposed to be Pacquiao's greatest challenge to date. But like 48 others before him, Hatton failed to meet the challenge. Applying his trademark pressure from the opening bell, Pacquiao knocked the British champ down twice in the first round. With the clock winding down in the second, Pacquiao pulverized Hatton with a vicious left hand that left Hatton lying prone on the canvas. "That was as impressive a knockout as I have ever seen," said Pacquiao's trainer, Freddie Roach.

While Pacquiao reignited boxing's spark, Mayweather's return poured gasoline on it. Few expected Mayweather to remain retired when he announced he was walking away from the sport in June 2008. And they were

right. Facing Marquez, universally recognized as the No. 2 pound-for-pound fighter in the world, Mayweather showed none of the rust that was expected following a 21-month layoff. He dropped Marquez in the second round with a short left hook and flustered Marquez with brilliant counter-punching and impenetrable defense. By the end of the fight, Mayweather had connected on 59% of his shots while Marquez landed only 12%, giving Mayweather a unanimous decision victory. "The king is back," admitted De La Hoya after the fight. "And he is back with a vengeance."

While Mayweather has long proclaimed himself as the top draw in boxing, he finally had the numbers to back it up. In the days after the fight HBO reported more than one-million PPV buys, numbers that added up to more than $52 million in domestic revenue. Those numbers reportedly trounced the UFC card by a more than two-to-one margin. Even White confessed to being impressed. "What they did was phenomenal and I'm happy for them," said White. "Bottom line, we did a good number and we still got our asses kicked."

With Mayweather-Marquez, boxing won the first head-to-head battle. But with these two combat sports, the war is far from over.

# FOR THE RECORD • 2008—2009

## Current World Champions

| Division | Weight Limit | WBA Champion | WBC Champion | IBF Champion |
|---|---|---|---|---|
| Heavyweight | None | Nikolay Valuev | Vitali Klitschko | Wladimir Klitschko |
| Cruiserweight | 200 | Guillermo Jones | Giacobbe Fragomeni | Tomasz Adamek |
| Light Heavyweight | 175 | Gabriel Campillo | Jean Pascal | Tavoris Cloud |
| Super Middleweight | 168 | Mikkel Kessler | Carl Froch | Lucian Bute |
| Middleweight | 160 | Felix Sturm | Kelly Pavlik | Sebastian Sylvester |
| Super Welterweight | 154 | Daniel Santos | Sergio Martinez | Cory Spinks |
| Welterweight | 147 | Shane Mosley* | Andre Berto | Isaac Hlatshwayo |
| Super Lightweight | 140 | Amir Khan | Devon Alexander | Juan Urango |
| Lightweight | 135 | Juan Manuel Marquez* | Edwin Valero | Vacant |
| Super Featherweight | 130 | Juan Carlos Salgado | Humbeto Soto | Robert Gurerero |
| Featherweight | 126 | Chris John | Elio Rojas* | Cristobal Cruz |
| Super Bantamweight | 122 | Celestino Caballero* | Toshiaki Nishioka | Cellestino Caballero |
| Bantamweight | 118 | Anselmo Moreno | Hozumi Hasegawa | Joseph Agbeko |
| Super Flyweight | 115 | Vic Darchinyan* | Vic Darchinyan* | Simphiwe Nongqayi |
| Flyweight | 112 | Denkaosan Kaovichit* | Daisuke Naito | Vacant |
| Light Flyweight | 108 | Giovanni Segura | Edgar Sosa | Brian Viloria |
| Strawweight | 105 | Roman Gonzalez | Oley. Sithsamerchai | Raul Garcia |

Note: WBC=World Boxing Council; WBA=World Boxing Association; IBF=International Boxing Federation. Champions as of October 20, 2009. *Denotes unified, mulit-title or super champion.

## Title and Major Boxing Matches of Late 2008 and 2009

Abbreviations: WBC=World Boxing Council; WBA= World Boxing Association; IBF=International Boxing Federation; KO=knockout; TKO=technical knockout; UD=unanimous decision; SD=split decision; DQ=disqualification; MD=majority decision; TD=technical decision. Bouts from Oct. 1, 2008 to Oct. 1, 2009.

| | Date | Winner | Loser | Result | Title/Org. | Site |
|---|---|---|---|---|---|---|
| **HEAVYWEIGHT** | Dec 13 | Wladimir Klitschko | Hasim Rahman | TKO 7 | IBF | Mannheim, Germany |
| | Dec 20 | Nikolai Valuev | Evander Holyfield | MD | WBA | Zurich, Switzerland |
| | Feb 7 | Ruslan Chagaev | Carl Drummond | TKO 6 | WBA | Rostock, Germany |
| | Mar 21 | Vitali Klitschko | Juan Carlos Gomez | TKO 9 | WBC | Stuttgart, Germany |
| | June 20 | Wladimir Klitschko | Ruslan Chagaev | TKO 10 | IBF | Gelsenkirchen, Germany |
| | Sept 26 | Vitali Klitschko | Chris Arreola | TKO 10 | WBC | Los Angeles |
| **CRUISERWEIGHT** | Dec 11 | Tomasz Adamek | Steve Cunningham | SD | IBF | Newark, New Jersey |
| | Feb 27 | Tomasz Adamek | Johnathon Banks | TKO 8 | IBF | Newark, New Jersey |
| | May 16 | Giacobbe Fragomeni | Krzysztof Wlodarczyk | SD | WBC | Rome |
| | July 11 | Tomasz Adamek | Bobby Gunn | TKO 4 | IBF | Newark, New Jersey |
| **LIGHT HEAVYWEIGHT** | Oct 11 | Chad Dawson | Antonio Tarver | UD | IBF | Las Vegas |
| | Nov 22 | Hugo Garay | Jurgen Braehmer | UD | WBA | Rostock, Germany |
| | May 9 | Chad Dawson | Antonio Tarver | UD | IBF | Las Vegas |
| | June 19 | Jean Pascal | Adrian Diaconu | UD | WBC | Montreal |
| | June 20 | Gabriel Campillo | Hugo Garay | MD | WBA | Sunchales, Argentina |
| | Aug 15 | Gabriel Campillo | Biebut Shumerov | MD | WBA | Astana, Kazakhstan |
| | Sept 25 | Jean Pascal | Silvio Branco | TKO 10 | WBC | Montreal |
| **SUPER MIDDLEWEIGHT** | Oct 23 | Lucian Bute | Librado Andrade | UD | IBF | Montreal |
| | Oct 25 | Mikkel Kessler | Danilo Haussler | KO 3 | WBA | Oldenburg, Germany |
| | Feb 25 | Carl Froch | Jermain Taylor | TKO 12 | WBC | Mashantucket, Conn. |
| | Mar 13 | Lucian Bute | Fulgencio Zuniga | TKO 4 | IBF | Montreal |
| | Sept 12 | Mikkel Kessler | Gusmyl Perdomo | TKO 4 | WBA | Herning, Denmark |
| **MIDDLEWEIGHT** | Nov 1 | Felix Sturm | Sebastian Sylvester | UD | WBA | Oberhausen, Germany |
| | Nov 8 | Arthur Abraham | Raul Marquez | TKO 6 | IBF | Bamberg, Germany |
| | Feb 21 | Kelly Pavlik | Marco Antiono Rubio | TKO 9 | WBC | Youngstown, Ohio |
| | Mar 14 | Arthur Abraham | Lajuan Simon | UD | IBF | Kiel, Germany |
| | Apr 25 | Felix Sturm | Koji Sato | TKO 7 | WBA | Krefeld, Germany |
| | June 27 | Arthur Abraham | Mahir Oral | TKO 10 | IBF | Berlin |
| | July 11 | Felix Sturm | Khoren Gevor | UD | WBA | Nuerburg, Germany |
| **JR. MIDDLEWT. (SUPER WELTERT.)** | Feb 14 | Sergio Martinez | Kermit Cintron | Draw | Interim WBC | Sunris, Florida |
| | Aug 30 | Nobuhiro Ishida | Marco Avendano | UD | Interim WBA | Osaka, Japan |
| **WELTERWEIGHT** | Jan 17 | Andre Berto | Luis Collazo | UD | WBC | Biloxi, Mississippi |
| | Jan 24 | Shane Mosley | Antonio Margarito | TKO 9 | WBA | Los Angeles |
| | Apr 10 | Vyacheslav Senchenko | Yuriy Nuzhnenko | UD | WBA | Donetsk, Ukraine |
| | May 30 | Andre Berto | Juan Urango | UD | WBC | Hollywood, Florida |
| | Sept 19 | Floyd Mayweather Jr. | Juan Manuel Marquez | UD | WBA | Las Vegas |

| | Date | Winner | Loser | Result | Title/Org. | Site |
|---|---|---|---|---|---|---|
| **SUPER LIGHTWEIGHT (JUNIOR WELTERWEIGHT)** | Feb 7 | Andriy Kotelnik | Marcos Maidena | SD | WBA | Rostock, Germany |
| | Apr 4 | Timothy Bradley | Kendall Holt | UD | WBC | Montreal |
| | July 18 | Amir Khan | Andriy Kotelnik | UD | WBA | Manchester, England |
| | Aug 28 | Juan Urango | Randall Bailey | TKO 11 | IBF | Hollywood, Florida |
| **LIGHTWEIGHT** | Jan 3 | Paulus Moses | Yusuke Kobori | UD | WBA | Yokohama, Japan |
| | Feb 14 | Nate Campbell | Ali Funeka | MD | WBA/IBF | Sunrise, Florida |
| | July 25 | Paulus Moses | Takehiro Shimada | UD | WBA | Windhoek, Namibia |
| **SUPER FEATHERWEIGHT (JUNIOR LIGHTWEIGHT)** | Mar 28 | Humberto Soto | Antonio Davis | TKO 4 | WBC | Tijuana, Mexico |
| | Apr 18 | Malcom Klassen | Cassius Baloyi | TKO 7 | IBF | Mafikeng, South Africa |
| | May 2 | Humberto Soto | Benoit Gaudet | TKO 9 | WBC | Las Vegas |
| | June 27 | Jorge Linares | Josaphat Perez | TKO 8 | WBA | Nuevo Laredo, Mexico |
| | Aug 22 | Robert Guerrero | Malcolm Klassen | UD | IBF | Houston |
| **FEATHERWEIGHT** | Oct 16 | Oscar Larios | Takahiro Aoh | SD | WBC | Tokyo |
| | Oct 24 | Chris John | Hiroyuki Enoki | UD | WBA | Tokyo |
| | Feb 14 | Cristobal Cruz | Cyril Thomas | UD | IBF | Saint-Quentin, France |
| | Feb 28 | Chris John | Rocky Juarez | Draw | WBA | Houston |
| | Mar 12 | Takahiro Aoh | Oscar Larios | UD | WBC | Tokyo |
| | July 11 | Cristobal Cruz | Jorge Solis | UD | IBF | Tuxtla Gutierrez, Mexico |
| | July 14 | Elio Rojas | Takahiro Aoh | UD | WBC | Tokyo |
| **SUPER BANTAMWEIGHT (JUNIOR FEATHERWEIGHT)** | Nov 21 | Celestino Caballero | Steve Molitor | TKO 4 | WBA/IBF | Orillia, Canada |
| | Jan 3 | Toshiaki Nishioka | Genaro Garcia | TKO 12 | WBC | Yokohama, Japan |
| | Mar 21 | Bernard Dunne | Ricardo Cordoba | TKO 11 | WBA | Dublin, Ireland |
| | Apr 30 | Celestino Caballero | Jeffrey Mathebula | SD | WBA/IBF | Panama City, Panama |
| | May 23 | Toshiaki Nishioka | Jhonny Gonzalez | TKO 3 | WBC | Monterrey, Mexico |
| | Aug 29 | Celestino Caballero | Francisco Leal | TKO 7 | WBA/IBF | Mexicali, Mexico |
| | Sept 15 | Humberto Soto | Aristedes Perez | TKO 2 | WBC | Cancun, Mexcio |
| | Sept 26 | P. Kratingdaenggym | Bernard Dunne | KO 3 | WBA | Dublin, Ireland |
| **BANTAMWEIGHT** | Oct 16 | Hozumi Hasegawa | Alejandro Valdez | TKO 2 | WBC | Tokyo, Japan |
| | Oct 30 | Anselmo Moreno | Rolly Lunas | UD | WBA | Panama City, Panama |
| | Dec 11 | Joseph Agbeko | William Gonzalez | MD | IBF | Newark, New Jersey |
| | Mar 12 | Hozumi Hasegawa | Vusi Malinga | TKO 1 | WBC | Kobe, Japan |
| | Mar 14 | Nehomar Cermeno | Cristian Mijares | SD | Interim WBA | Torreon, Mexico |
| | May 2 | Anselmo Moreno | Wladimir Sidorenko | SD | WBA | Bremen, Germany |
| | July 4 | Anselmo Moreno | Mahyar Monshippur | SD | WBA | Poitiers, France |
| | July 11 | Joseph Agbeko | Vic Darchinyan | UD | IBF | Sunrise, Florida |
| | July 14 | Hozumi Hasegawa | Nestor Rocha | TKO 1 | WBC | Kobe, Japan |
| | Sept 12 | Nehomar Cermeno | Cristian Mijares | UD | Interim WBA | Monterrey, Mexico |
| **SUPER FLYWEIGHT (JUNIOR BANTAMWEIGHT)** | Nov 1 | Vic Daychinyan | Cristian Mijares | KO 9 | Unified | Carson, California |
| | Feb 7 | Vic Darchinyan | Jorge Arce | TKO 11 | Unified | Anaheim, California |
| | Apr 11 | Nobuo Nashiro | Konosuke Tomiyama | TKO 8 | WBA | Osaka, Japan |
| | Sept 15 | Simphiwe Nongqayi | Jorge Arce | UD | IBF | Cancun, Mexico |
| | Sept 30 | Nobuo Nashiro | Hugo Cazares | Draw | WBA | Osaka, Japan |
| **FLYWEIGHT** | Nov 1 | Nonito Donaire | Moruti Mthalane | TKO 6 | IBF | Las Vegas |
| | Dec 23 | Daisuke Naito | Shingo Yamaguchi | TKO 11 | WBC | Tokyo |
| | Dec 31 | Denkaosan Kaovichit | Takefumi Sakata | KO 2 | WBA | Hiroshima, Japan |
| | Apr 19 | Nonito Donaire | Raul Martinez | TKO 4 | IBF | Manila, Philippines |
| | May 26 | Daisuke Naito | Xiong Zhao Zhong | UD | WBC | Tokyo |
| | May 26 | Denkaosan Kaovichit | Hiroyuki Hisataka | SD | WBA | Uttaradit, Thailand |
| **LIGHT FLYWEIGHT (JUNIOR FLYWEIGHT)** | Nov 2 | Ulises Solis | Nerys Espinoza | UD | IBF | Aguascalientes, Mexico |
| | Nov 29 | Edgar Sosa | Juanito Rubillar | TKO 7 | WBC | Mexico City |
| | Apr 4 | Edgar Sosa | P. Porpramook | TKO 4 | WBC | Ciudad Victoria, Mexico |
| | Apr 19 | Brian Viloria | Ulises Solis | KO 11 | IBF | Manila, Philippines |
| | June 20 | Edgar Sosa | Carlos Melo | TKO 5 | WBC | Mexico City |
| | July 25 | Giovanni Segura | Juanito Rubillar | TKO 6 | WBA | Nuevo Vallarta, Mexico |
| | Aug 29 | Brian Viloria | Jesus Iribe | UD | IBF | Honolulu, Hawaii |
| | Sept 15 | Edgar Sosa | Omar Soto | KO 6 | WBC | Puebla, Mexico |
| **STRAWWEIGHT (MINI FLYWT.) (MINIMUM WT.)** | Nov 27 | O. Sithsamerchai | P. Porpramook | UD | WBC | Phitsanulok, Thailand |
| | Dec 13 | Raul Garcia | Jose Luis Varela | UD | IBF | Loreto, Mexico |
| | Feb 28 | Roman Gonzalez | Franscisco Rojas | MD | WBA | Oaxaca, Mexico |
| | Apr 11 | Raul Garcia | Ronald Barrera | TKO 6 | IBF | La Paz, Mexico |
| | May 29 | O. Sithsamerchai | M. Rachman | TD 11 | WBC | Phuket, Thailand |
| | July 14 | Roman Gonzalez | Katsunari Takayama | UD | WBA | Kobe, Japan |

## World Champions

Sanctioning bodies: the National Boxing Association (NBA), the New York State Athletic Commission (NY), the World Boxing Association (WBA), the World Boxing Council (WBC), and the International Boxing Federation (IBF).

### Heavyweights (Weight: Unlimited)

| Champion | Reign | Champion | Reign | Champion | Reign | Champion | Reign |
|---|---|---|---|---|---|---|---|
| John L. Sullivan* | 1885–92 | Muhammad Ali* | 1964–70† | Trevor Berbick WBC | 1986 | Hasim Rahman* WBC, | |
| James J. Corbett* | 1892–97 | Ernie Terrell WBA | 1965–67 | Mike Tyson WBC | 1986–87 | IBF | 2001–05 |
| Bob Fitzsimmons* | 1897–99 | Joe Frazier* NY | 1968–70 | James Smith WBA | 1986–87 | Chris Byrd IBF | 2002–06 |
| James J. Jeffries* | 1899–05 | Jimmy Ellis WBA | 1968–70 | Tony Tucker IBF | 1987 | Roy Jones Jr. WBA | 2003–05 |
| Marvin Hart* | 1905–06 | Joe Frazier* | 1970–73 | Mike Tyson* | 1987–90 | Lennox Lewis* WBC | 2001–04 |
| Tommy Burns* | 1906–08 | George Foreman* | 1973–74 | Buster Douglas* | 1990 | John Ruiz, WBA | 2003–05 |
| Jack Johnson* | 1908–15 | Muhammad Ali* | 1974–78 | Evander Holyfield* | 1990–92 | Vitali Klitschko WBC | 2004–05 |
| Jess Willard* | 1915–19 | Leon Spinks* | 1978 | Lennox Lewis WBC | 1993–95 | Hasim Rahman WBC | 2005–06 |
| Jack Dempsey* | 1919–26 | Ken Norton WBC | 1978 | Riddick Bowe* | 1992–93 | Nikolay Valuev WBA | 2005–07 |
| Gene Tunney* | 1926–28† | Larry Holmes WBC | 1978–80 | Evander Holyfield* | 1993–94 | Oleg Maskaev WBC | 2006–08 |
| Max Schmeling* | 1930–32 | Muhammad Ali* | 1978–79† | Michael Moorer* | 1994 | Wladimir Klitschko. | |
| Jack Sharkey* | 1932–33 | John Tate WBA | 1979–80 | George Foreman* | 1994–95 | IBF | 2006– |
| Primo Carnera* | 1933–34 | Mike Weaver WBA | 1980–82 | Oliver McCall WBC | 1995 | Ruslan Chagaev WBA | 2007–08 |
| Max Baer* | 1934–35 | Larry Holmes* | 1980–85 | Frank Bruno WBC | 1995–96 | Samuel Peter WBC | 2008 |
| James J. Braddock* | 1935–37 | Michael Dokes WBA | 1982–83 | Bruce Seldon WBA | 1995–96 | Nikolai Valuev WBA | 2008– |
| Joe Louis* | 1937–49† | Gerrie Coetzee WBA | 1983–84 | Mike Tyson WBA | 1996 | Vitali Klitschko WBC | 2008– |
| Ezzard Charles* | 1949–51 | Tim Witherspoon | | Michael Moorer IBF | 1996–97 | | |
| Jersey Joe Walcott* | 1951–52 | WBC | 1984 | Shannon Briggs* | 1997–98 | | |
| Rocky Marciano* | 1952–56† | Pinklon Thomas WBC | 1984–86 | Lennox Lewis* WBC | 1997–01 | | |
| Floyd Patterson* | 1956–59 | Greg Page WBA | 1984–85 | E. Holyfield WBA, IBF | 1996–99 | | |
| Ingemar Johansson* | 1959–60 | Michael Spinks* | 1985–87 | Lennox Lewis | 1999–01 | | |
| Floyd Patterson* | 1960–62 | Tim Witherspoon | | E. Holyfield WBA | 2000–01 | | |
| Sonny Liston* | 1962–64 | WBA | 1986 | John Ruiz WBA | 2001–03 | | |

### Cruiserweights (Weight Limit: 200 pounds)

| Champion | Reign | Champion | Reign | Champion | Reign | Champion | Reign |
|---|---|---|---|---|---|---|---|
| Marvin Camel* WBC | 1980 | Evander Holyfield* | | M. Dominguez* | | O'Neil Bell IBF | 2005–06 |
| Carlos De Leon* WBC | 1980–82 | WBA, IBF | 1987–88 | WBC | 1996–98 | O'Neil Bell WBC/WBA | 2006–07 |
| Ossie Ocasio WBA | 1982–84 | Evander Holyfield* | 1988† | A. Washington IBF | 1996–97 | Steve Cunningham | |
| S.T. Gordon* WBC | 1982–83 | Toufik Belbouli WBA | 1989 | Uriah Grant IBF | 1997 | IBF | 2006–08 |
| Carlos De Leon* WBC | 1983–85 | Robert Daniels WBA | 1989–91 | Imamu Mayfield IBF | 1997–98 | J.M. Mormeck | |
| Marvin Camel IBF | 1983–84 | Carlos De Leon* WBC | 1989–90 | Fabrice Tiozzo WBA | 1997–00 | WBC/WBA | 2007 |
| Lee Roy Murphy IBF | 1984–86 | Glenn McCrory IBF | 1989–90 | J.C. Gomez* WBC | 1998–02† | David Haye WBC | 2007–08 |
| Piet Crous WBA | 1984–85 | Jeff Lampkin IBF | 1990 | Arthur Williams IBF | 1998–99 | David Haye WBA | 2007– |
| Alfonso Ratliff* | | M. Duran* WBC | 1990–91 | Vassiliy Girov* IBF | 1999–03 | Guillermo Jones | |
| WBC | 1985 | Bobby Czyz WBA | 1991–92† | James Toney* IBF | 2003 | WBA | 2009 |
| Dwight Braxton WBA | 1985–86 | Anaclet Wamba* WBC | 1991–95† | Virgil Hill WBA | 2000–02 | Giacobbe Fragomeni | |
| Bernard Benton* WBC | 1985–86 | James Pritchard IBF | 1991 | Wayne Braithwaite | | WBC | 2009– |
| Carlos DeLeon* WBC | 1986–88 | James Warring IBF | 1991–92 | WBC | 2002–05 | Tomasz Adamek IBF | 2008– |
| Evander Holyfield* | | Alfred Cole IBF | 1992–96 | J.M. Mormeck WBA | 2002–06 | | |
| WBA | 1986–88 | Orlin Norris WBA | 1993–95 | J.M. Mormeck IBF | 2005–06 | | |
| Ricky Parkey IBF | 1986–87 | Nate Miller WBA | 1995–97 | Melvin Davis IBF | 2004–05 | | |

### Light Heavyweights (Weight Limit: 175 pounds)

| Champion | Reign | Champion | Reign | Champion | Reign | Champion | Reign |
|---|---|---|---|---|---|---|---|
| Jack Root* | 1903 | Tommy Loughran* | 1927–29† | Archie Moore* | 1952–62† | Mike Rossman* | |
| George Gardner* | 1903 | Maxie Rosenbloom* | 1930–34 | Harold Johnson NBA | 1961 | WBA | 1978–79 |
| Bob Fitzsimmons* | 1903–05 | George Nichols NBA | 1932 | Harold Johnson* | 1962–63 | Victor Galindez* | |
| Jack O'Brien* | 1905–12† | Bob Godwin NBA | 1933 | Willie Pastrano* | 1963–65 | WBA | 1979 |
| Jack Dillon* | 1914–16 | Bob Olin* | 1934–35 | Jose Torres* | 1965–66 | Marvin Johnson* | |
| Battling Levinsky* | 1916–20 | John Henry Lewis* | 1935–38† | Dick Tiger* | 1966–68 | WBC | 1978–79 |
| Georges Carpentier* | 1920–22 | Melio Bettina | 1939 | Bob Foster* | 1968–74† | M.S. Muhammad* | |
| Battling Siki* | 1922–23 | Billy Conn* | 1939–40† | Vicente Rondon WBA | 1971–72 | WBC | 1979–81 |
| Mike McTigue* | 1923–25 | Anton Christoforidis | 1941 | John Conteh WBC | 1974–77 | Marvin Johnson | |
| Paul Berlenbach* | 1925–26 | Gus Lesnevich* | 1941–48 | Victor Galindez* WBA | 1974–78 | WBA | 1979–80 |
| Jack Delaney* | 1926–27† | Freddie Mills* | 1948–50 | Miguel A. Cuello WBC | 1977–78 | E.M. Muhammad* | |
| Jimmy Slattery NBA | 1927 | Joey Maxim* | 1950–52 | Mate Parlov WBC | 1978 | WBA | 1980–81 |

*Lineal champion.   †Champion relinquished title to retire or switch weight classes, or had title stripped by boxing organization.

### Light Heavyweights *(Cont.)*

| Champion | Reign | Champion | Reign | Champion | Reign | Champion | Reign |
|---|---|---|---|---|---|---|---|
| Michael Spinks* WBA | 1981–83 | Dennis Andries WBC.. | 1989 | Bruno Girard WBA | 2001–03 | Danny Green WBA | 2007–08 |
| Dwight Qawi WBC | 1981–83 | Jeff Harding WBC | 1989–90 | Mehdi Sahnoune | | Hugo Garay WBA | 2008–09 |
| Michael Spinks* | 1983–85† | Dennis Andries WBC.. | 1990–91 | WBA | 2003 | Antonio Tarver IBF | 2008 |
| J. B. Williamson WBC. | 1985–86 | Thomas Hearns WBC | 1991–92 | Silvio Branco WBA | 2003–04 | Adrian Diaconu WBC | 2008–09 |
| Slobodan Kacar IBF | 1985–86 | Jeff Harding WBC | 1991–94 | Antonio Tarver | | Gabriel Campillo WBA. | 2009– |
| Marvin Johnson* | | Iran Barkley* WBA | 1992 | WBC, IBF | 2003 | Jean Pascal WBC | 2009– |
| WBA | 1986–87 | Virgil Hill* WBA | 1992–97 | Roy Jones Jr. WBC | 2003 | Tavoris Cloud IBF | 2009– |
| Dennis Andries WBC.. | 1986–87 | Henry Maske IBF | 1993–96 | Glencoffe Johnson | | | |
| Bobby Czyz IBF | 1986–87 | Mike McCallum WBC. | 1994–95 | IBF | 2004–05 | | |
| Leslie Stewart WBA | 1987 | Fabrice Tiozzo WBC | 1995–96 | Fabrice Tiozzo WBA | 2004–5 | | |
| Virgil Hill* WBA | 1987–91 | D. Michalczewski* | | Antonio Tarver* WBC. | 2004–05 | | |
| Pr Charles Williams | | IBF | 1997† | Silvio Branco WBA | 2005–07 | | |
| IBF | 1987–93 | Roy Jones Jr. | | Clinton Woods IBF | 2005–08 | | |
| Thomas Hearns WBC.. | 1987† | WBC, WBA | 1997–03 | Tomasz Adamek WBC | 2005–07 | | |
| Donny Lalonde WBC | 1987–88 | William Guthrie IBF | 1997–98 | Stipe Drews WBA | 2007 | | |
| Sugar Ray Leonard | | Reggie Johnson IBF | 1998–99 | Chad Dawson WBC | 2007–08 | | |
| WBC | 1988 | Roy Jones Jr.* | 1999–03 | | 2008–09† | | |

### Super Middleweights  (Weight Limit: 168 pounds)

| Champion | Reign | Champion | Reign | Champion | Reign | Champion | Reign |
|---|---|---|---|---|---|---|---|
| Murray Sutherland* IBF | | Nigel Benn WBC | 1992–96 | Markus Beyer WBC | 1999–00 | Mikkel Kessler WBC | 2006–07 |
| 1984 | | James Toney IBF | 1992–94 | Bruno Girard* WBA | 2000–01† | Robert Stieglitz IBF | 2007 |
| Chong-Pal Park* IBF | 1984–87 | Michael Nunn* WBA | 1992–94 | Glenn Catley WBC | 2000–01 | Alejandro Berrio IBF | 2007 |
| Chong-Pal Park* WBA | 1987–88 | Steve Little* WBA | 1994 | Eric Lucas WBC | 2000–03 | Joe Calzaghe, WBC | 2007–08 |
| G. Rocchigiani IBF | 1988–89 | Frank Liles* WBA | 1994–99 | Byron Mitchell WBA | 2000–03 | Lucian Bute, IBF | 2007– |
| F. Obelmejias* WBA | 1988–89 | Roy Jones Jr. IBF | 1994–96 | Sven Ottke WBA | 2003† | Joe Calzaghe, WBA | 2007–08 |
| Sugar Ray Leonard | | Thulane Malinga WBC. | 1996 | Anthony Mundine WBA | 2003 | Carl Froch WBC | 2008– |
| WBC | 1988–90† | V. Nardiello WBC | 1996 | Markus Beyer WBC | 2003–04 | Mikkel Kessler WBA | 2008– |
| In-Chul Baek* WBA | 1989–90 | Robin Reid WBC | 1996–97 | Sven Ottke, IBF | 2003–05 | | |
| Lindell Holmes IBF | 1990–91 | Charles Brewer IBF | 1997–98 | Cristian Sanavia WBC | 2004 | | |
| Chris Tiozzo* WBA | 1990–91 | Thulane Malinga | | Manny Siaca WBA | 2004 | | |
| Mauro Galvano WBC | 1990–92 | WBC | 1997–98 | Mikel Kessler WBA | 2004–07 | | |
| Victor Cordova* WBA | 1991 | Richie Woodhall WBC. | 1998–99 | Markus Beyer WBC | 2004–06 | | |
| Darrin Van Horn IBF | 1991–92 | Sven Ottke IBF | 1998–03 | Jeff Lacy IBF | 2005 | | |
| Iran Barkley IBF | 1992 | Byron Mitchell* WBA. | 1999–00 | Joe Calzaghe IBF | 2006–07 | | |

### Middleweights  (Weight Limit: 160 pounds)

| Champion | Reign | Champion | Reign | Champion | Reign | Champion | Reign |
|---|---|---|---|---|---|---|---|
| Jack Dempsey* | 1884–91 | Rocky Graziano* | 1947–48 | Rodrigo Valdez WBC | 1974–76 | Bernard Hopkins* | |
| Bob Fitzsimmons* | 1891–97† | Tony Zale* | 1948 | Rodrigo Valdez* | 1977–78 | IBF | 1994– |
| Kid McCoy | 1897–98 | Marcel Cerdan* | 1948–49 | Hugo Corro* | 1978–79 | Keith Holmes WBC | 1996–98 |
| Tommy Ryan* | 1898–07† | Jake La Motta* | 1949–51 | Vito Antuofermo* | 1979–80 | William Joppy WBA | 1996–97 |
| Stanley Ketchel* | 1908 | Sugar Ray Robinson* | 1951 | Alan Minter* | 1980 | J.C. Green WBA | 1997 |
| Billy Papke* | 1908 | Randy Turpin* | 1951 | Marvin Hagler* | 1980–87 | William Joppy WBA | 1998–01 |
| Stanley Ketchel* | 1908–10† | Sugar Ray Robinson* | 1951–52† | Sugar Ray Leonard* | 1987† | Hassine Cherifi WBC | 1998–99 |
| Frank Klaus* | 1913 | Bobo Olson* | 1953–55 | Frank Tate IBF | 1987–88 | Keith Holmes WBC | 1999–00 |
| George Chip* | 1913–14 | Sugar Ray Robinson* | 1955–57 | Sumbu Kalambay | | Felix Trinidad WBA | 2001 |
| Al McCoy* | 1914–17 | Gene Fullmer* | 1957 | WBA | 1987–89 | William Joppy WBA | 2001–03 |
| Mike O'Dowd* | 1917–20 | Sugar Ray Robinson* | 1957 | Thomas Hearns* | | Bernard Hopkins* | |
| Johnny Wilson* | 1920–23 | Carmen Basilio* | 1957–58 | WBC | 1987–88 | WBC/IBF | 2001–05 |
| Harry Greb* | 1923–26 | Sugar Ray Robinson* | 1958–60 | Iran Barkley* WBC | 1988–89 | Bernard Hopkins WBA | 2003–05 |
| Tiger Flowers* | 1926 | Gene Fullmer NBA | 1959–62 | Michael Nunn IBF | 1988–91 | Jermain Taylor IBF | 2005 |
| Mickey Walker* | 1926–31† | Paul Pender* | 1960–61 | Roberto Duran* WBC | 1989–90† | Jermain Taylor WBA | 2005–06 |
| Gorilla Jones* | 1931–32 | Terry Downes* | 1961–62 | Michael Nunn* IBF | 1991 | Jermain Taylor WBC | 2005–07 |
| Marcel Thil* | 1932–37 | Paul Pender* | 1962–63† | Mike McCallum WBA | 1989–91 | Arthur Abraham IBF | 2005–09† |
| Fred Apostoli* | 1937–39 | Dick Tiger WBA | 1962–63 | Julian Jackson WBC | 1990–93 | Felix Sturm WBA | 2006 |
| Al Hostak NBA | 1938 | Dick Tiger* | 1963 | James Toney* IBF | 1991–93† | Javier Castillejo WBA | 2006–07 |
| Solly Krieger NBA | 1938–39 | Joey Giardello* | 1963–65 | Reggie Johnson WBA | 1992–94 | Felix Sturm WBA | 2007– |
| Al Hostak NBA | 1939–40 | Dick Tiger* | 1965–66 | Roy Jones Jr.* IBF | 1993–95† | Kelly Pavlik WBC | 2007– |
| Ceferino Garcia* | 1939–40 | Emile Griffith* | 1966–67 | G. McClellan WBC | 1993–95† | Sebastian Sylvester | |
| Ken Overlin* | 1940–41 | Nino Benvenuti* | 1967 | Jorge Castro WBA | 1994–95 | IBF | 2009– |
| Tony Zale NBA | 1940–41 | Emile Griffith* | 1967–68 | Shinji Takehara WBC | 1995–96 | | |
| Billy Soose* | 1941 | Nino Benvenuti* | 1968–70 | Julian Jackson WBC | 1995 | | |
| Tony Zale* | 1941–47 | Carlos Monzon* | 1970–77† | Quincy Taylor WBC | 1995–96 | | |

*Lineal champion. †Champion retired or relinquished title.

## Junior Middleweights (Weight Limit: 154 pounds)

| Champion | Reign |
|---|---|
| Emile Griffith (EBU) | 1962–63 |
| Dennis Moyer* | 1962–63 |
| Ralph Dupas* | 1963 |
| Sandro Mazzinghi* | 1963–65 |
| Nino Benvenuti | 1965–66 |
| Ki-Soo Kim* | 1966–68 |
| Sandro Mazzinghi* | 1968 |
| Freddie Little* | 1969–70 |
| Carmelo Bossi* | 1970–71 |
| Koichi Wajima* | 1971–74 |
| Oscar Albarado* | 1974–75 |
| Koichi Wajima* | 1975 |
| Miguel de Oliveira WBC | 1975–76 |
| Jae-Do Yuh* | 1975–76 |
| Elisha Obed WBC | 1975–76 |
| Koichi Wajima* | 1976 |
| Jose Duran* | 1976 |
| Eckhard Dagge WBC | 1976–77 |
| Miguel Angel Castellini* | 1976–77 |
| Eddie Gazo* | 1977–78 |
| Rocky Mattioli WBC | 1977–79 |
| Masashi Kudo* | 1978–79 |
| Maurice Hope WBC | 1979–81 |
| Ayub Kalule* | 1979–81 |
| Wilfred Benitez WBC | 1981–82 |
| Sugar Ray Leonard* | 1981–82† |
| Tadashi Mihara WBA | 1981–82 |
| Davey Moore WBA | 1982–83 |
| Thomas Hearns* WBC | 1982–84 |
| Roberto Duran WBA | 1983–84 |
| Mark Medal IBF | 1984 |
| Thomas Hearns* | 1984–86† |
| Mike McCallum* WBA | 1984–87† |
| Carlos Santos IBF | 1984–86 |
| Buster Drayton IBF | 1986–87 |
| Duane Thomas WBC | 1986–87 |
| Matthew Hilton IBF | 1987–88 |
| Lupe Aquino WBC | 1987 |
| Gianfranco Rosi WBC | 1987–88 |
| Julian Jackson WBA | 1987–90 |
| Donald Curry WBC | 1988–89 |
| Robert Hines IBF | 1988–89 |
| Darrin Van Horn IBF | 1989 |
| Rene Jacquot WBC | 1989 |
| John Mugabi* WBC | 1989–90 |
| Gianfranco Rosi IBF | 1989–94 |
| Terry Norris* WBC | 1990–93 |
| Gilbert Dele WBA | 1991 |
| Vinny Pazienza WBA | 1991–92 |
| Julio C. Vasquez WBA | 1992–95 |
| Simon Brown* WBC | 1993–94 |
| Terry Norris* WBC | 1994 |
| Luis Santana* WBC | 1995–95 |
| Vincent Pettway IBF | 1994–95 |
| Paul Vaden IBF | 1995 |
| Carl Daniels WBA | 1995 |
| Terry Norris* WBC | 1995–97 |
| Terry Norris* IBF | 1995–96† |
| L. Boudouani WBA | 1996–99 |
| Raul Marquez IBF | 1997 |
| Keith Mullings* WBC | 1997–99 |
| Yori Boy Campas IBF | 1997–98 |
| Fernando Vargas IBF | 1998–00 |
| F. Javier Castillejo* WBC | 1999–01 |
| David Reid WBA | 1999–00 |
| Felix Trinidad WBA | 2000–01 |
| Felix Trinidad WBA, IBF | 2001† |
| Oscar De La Hoya* WBC | 2001–03 |
| Fernando Vargas WBA | 2001–02 |
| Ronald Wright IBF† | 2001–04 |
| Oscar De La Hoya* WBC/WBA | 2002–03 |
| Shane Mosley* WBC | 2003–04 |
| Alejandro Garcia WBA | 2003–05 |
| Ronald Wright WBA/WBC | 2004–05 |
| Verno Phillips IBF | 2004–05 |
| Ricardo Mayora WBC | 2005–06 |
| Alex T. Garcia WBA | 2005–06 |
| Roman Karmazin IBF | 2005–06 |
| Jose A. Rivera WBA | 2006–07 |
| Oscar De La Hoya WBC | 2006–07 |
| Cory Spinks IBF | 2006–08 |
|  | 2009– |
| Travis Simms WBA | 2007 |
| Floyd Mayweather Jr. WBC | 2007 |
| Joachim Alcine WBA | 2007–08 |
| Vernon Forrest WBC | 2007–08 |
| Sergio Mora WBC | 2008 |
| Verno Phillips IBF | 2008† |
| Daniel Santos WBA | 2008– |
| Vernon Forrest WBC | 2008–09 |
| Sergio Gabriel Martinez WBC | 2009– |

## Welterweights (Weight Limit: 147 pounds)

| Champion | Reign |
|---|---|
| Paddy Duffy* | 1888–90† |
| Mysterious Billy Smith* | 1892–94 |
| Tommy Ryan* | 1894–98† |
| Mysterious Billy Smith* | 1898–1900 |
| Rube Ferns* | 1900 |
| Matty Matthews* | 1900–01 |
| Rube Ferns* | 1901 |
| Joe Walcott* | 1901–04 |
| The Dixie Kid* | 1904–05† |
| Honey Mellody* | 1906–07 |
| Mike Sullivan* | 1907–08† |
| Jimmy Gardner* | 1908† |
| Jimmy Clabby* | 1910–1† |
| Waldemar Holberg* | 1914 |
| Tom McCormick* | 1914 |
| Matt Wells* | 1914–15 |
| Mike Glover* | 1915 |
| Jack Britton* | 1915 |
| Ted "Kid" Lewis* | 1915–16 |
| Jack Britton* | 1916–17 |
| Ted "Kid" Lewis* | 1917–19 |
| Jack Britton* | 1919–22 |
| Mickey Walker* | 1922–26 |
| Pete Latzo* | 1926–27 |
| Joe Dundee* | 1927–29 |
| Jackie Fields* | 1929–30 |
| Young Jack Thompson* | 1930 |
| Tommy Freeman* | 1930–31 |
| Young Jack Thompson* | 1931 |
| Lou Brouillard* | 1931–32 |
| Jackie Fields* | 1932–33 |
| Young Corbett III* | 1933 |
| Jimmy McLarnin* | 1933–34 |
| Barney Ross* | 1934 |
| Jimmy McLarnin* | 1934–35 |
| Barney Ross* | 1935–38 |
| Henry Armstrong* | 1938–40 |
| Fritzie Zivic* | 1940–41 |
| Red Cochrane* | 1941–46 |
| Marty Servo* | 1946 |
| Sugar Ray Robinson* | 1946–51† |
| Johnny Bratton* | 1951 |
| Kid Gavilan* | 1951–54 |
| Johnny Saxton* | 1954–55 |
| Tony DeMarco* | 1955 |
| Carmen Basilio* | 1955–56 |
| Johnny Saxton* | 1956 |
| Carmen Basilio* | 1956–57† |
| Virgil Akins* | 1958 |
| Don Jordan* | 1958–60 |
| Kid Paret* | 1960–61 |
| Emile Griffith* | 1961 |
| Kid Paret* | 1961–62 |
| Emile Griffith* | 1962–63 |
| Luis Rodriguez* | 1963 |
| Emile Griffith* | 1963–66† |
| Curtis Cokes* | 1966–69 |
| Jose Napoles* | 1969–70 |
| Billy Backus* | 1970–71 |
| Jose Napoles* | 1971–75 |
| Hedgemon Lewis NY | 1972–73 |
| Angel Espada WBA | 1975–76 |
| John H. Stracey* | 1975–76 |
| Carlos Palomino* | 1976–79 |
| Pipino Cuevas WBA | 1976–80 |
| Wilfredo Benitez* | 1979 |
| Sugar Ray Leonard* | 1979–80 |
| Roberto Duran* | 1980 |
| Thomas Hearns WBA | 1980–81 |
| Sugar Ray Leonard* | 1980–82† |
| Donald Curry* WBA | 1983–85 |
| Milton McCrory WBC | 1983–85 |
| Donald Curry* | 1985–86 |
| Lloyd Honeyghan* | 1986–87 |
| Jorge Vaca* WBC | 1987–88 |
| Lloyd Honeyghan* WBC | 1988–89 |
| Mark Breland WBA | 1987 |
| Marlon Starling WBA | 1987–88 |
| Tomas Molinares WBA | 1988–89 |
| Simon Brown IBF | 1988–91 |
| Mark Breland WBA | 1989–90 |
| Marlon Starling* WBC | 1989–90 |
| Aaron Davis WBA | 1990–91 |
| Maurice Blocker* WBC | 1990–91 |
| Meldrick Taylor WBA | 1991–92 |
| Simon Brown* WBC | 1991 |
| Buddy McGirt* WBC | 1991–93 |
| Felix Trinidad IBF | 1993–00 |
| Pernell Whitaker* WBC | 1993–97 |
| Crisanto Espana WBA | 1992–94 |
| Ike Quartey WBA | 1994–97† |
| Oscar De La Hoya* WBC | 1997–99 |
| James Page WBA | 1998–01 |
| Felix Trinidad* IBF, WBC | 1999–00† |
| Shane Mosley* WBC | 2000–02 |
| Andrew Lewis WBA | 2001–02 |
| Vernon Forrest IBF | 2001 |
| Vernon Forrest* WBC | 2001–03 |
| Ricardo Mayorga WBA | 2002 |
| Ricardo Mayorga* WBC | 2003–05 |
| Michele Piccirillo IBF | 2002–03 |
| Jose Rivera WBA | 2003 |
| Cory Spinks IBF, WBC, WBA | 2003–05 |
| Zab Judah WBA/WBC/IBF | 2005–06 |
| Luis Collazo WBA | 2006 |
| Ricky Hatton WBA | 2006 |
| Carlos Baldomir WBC | 2006 |
| F. Mayweather, Jr. IBF | 2006 |
| Miguel Cotto WBA | 2006–08 |
| F. Mayweather Jr. WBC | 2006–08 |

*Lineal champion. †Champion relinquished title to retire or switch weight classes, or had title stripped by boxing organization.

## Welterweights *(Cont.)*

| Champion | Reign | Champion | Reign | Champion | Reign | Champion | Reign |
|---|---|---|---|---|---|---|---|
| Kermit Cintron IBF | 2006–08 | Joshua Clottey IBF | 2008–09† | Andre Berto WBC | 2008– | Isaac Hlatshwayo IBF | 2009– |
| A. Margarito IBF | 2008 | Ant. Margarito WBA | 2008–09 | Shane Mosley WBA | 2009– | | |

## Super Lightweights (Weight Limit: 140 pounds)

| Champion | Reign | Champion | Reign | Champion | Reign | Champion | Reign |
|---|---|---|---|---|---|---|---|
| Pinkey Mitchell* | 1922–25 | S. Muangsurin WBC | 1976–78 | Julio César Chávez* | | Kostya Tszyu* IBF | 2003–05 |
| Red Herring | 1925 | A. Cervantes WBA | 1977–80 | IBF | 1990–91 | Vivian Harris WBA | 2003–05 |
| Mushy Callahan* | 1926–30 | Sang-Hyun Kim WBC | 1978–80 | Loreto Garza WBA | 1990–91 | Arturo Gatti WBC | 2004–05 |
| Jack (Kid) Berg* | 1930–31 | Saoul Mamby WBC | 1980–82 | Juan Coggi WBA | 1991 | F. Mayweather Jr. | |
| Tony Canzoneri* | 1931–32 | Aaron Pryor* WBA | 1980–83 | Edwin Rosario WBA | 1991–92 | WBC | 2005–06 |
| Johnny Jadick* | 1932–33 | Leroy Haley WBC | 1982–83 | Rafael Pineda IBF | 1991–92 | Carlos Maussa | |
| Sammy Fuller | 1932–33 | Aaron Pryor* IBF | 1983–85† | Akinobu Hiranaka | | WBA | 2005–06 |
| Battling Shaw* | 1933 | Bruce Curry WBC | 1983–84 | WBA | 1992 | Ricky Hatton IBF | 2005–06 |
| Tony Canzoneri* | 1933 | Johnny Bumphus | | Pernell Whitaker IBF | 1992–93† | Souleymane M'baye | |
| Barney Ross* | 1933–35† | WBA | 1984 | Charles Murray IBF | 1993–94 | WBA | 2006–07 |
| Tippy Larkin* | 1946 | Bill Costello WBC | 1984–85 | Jake Rodriguez IBF | 1994–95 | Juan Urango IBF | 2006–07 |
| Carlos Ortiz* | 1959–60 | Gene Hatcher WBA | 1984–85 | Frankie Randall* WBC | 1994 | Junior Witter WBC | 2006–08 |
| Duilio Loi* | 1960–62 | Ubaldo Sacco WBA | 1985–86 | Frankie Randall WBA | 1994–96 | Gavin Rees WBA | 2007–08 |
| Eddie Perkins* | 1962 | Lonnie Smith* WBC | 1985–86 | Juan Coggi WBA | 1996 | Ricky Hatton IBF | 2007 |
| Duilio Loi* | 1962–63† | Patrizio Oliva WBA | 1986–87 | Julio César Chávez* | | Lovemore N'Dou | |
| Roberto Cruz WBA | 1963 | Gary Hinton IBF | 1986 | WBC | 1994–96 | IBF | 2007 |
| Eddie Perkins* | 1963–65 | Rene Arredondo* | | Kostya Tszyu IBF | 1995–97 | Paul Malignaggi | |
| Carlos Hernandez* | 1965–66 | WBC | 1986 | Frankie Randall WBA | 1996–97 | IBF | 2007–09† |
| Sandro Lopopolo* | 1966–67 | Tsuyoshi Hamada | | Oscar De La Hoya* | | Timothy Bradley | |
| Paul Fujii* | 1967–68 | WBC | 1986–87 | WBC | 1996–97† | WBC | 2008–09 |
| Nicolino Loche* | 1968–72 | Joe Louis Manley | | Khalid Rahilou WBA | 1997–98 | Andreas Kotelnik | |
| Pedro Adigue WBC | 1968–70 | IBF | 1986–87 | Vincent Phillips* IBF | 1997–99 | WBA | 2008–09 |
| Bruno Arcari WBC | 1970–74 | Terry Marsh IBF | 1987 | Sharmba Mitchell | | Devon Alexander | |
| Alfonso Frazer* | 1972 | Juan Coggi WBA | 1987–90 | WBA | 1998–01 | WBC | 2009– |
| Antonio Cervantes* | 1972–76 | Rene Arredondo WBC | 1987 | Kostya Tszyu WBC | 1998– | Amir Khan WBA | 2009– |
| Perico Fernandez | | R. Mayweather* WBC | 1987–89 | Terronn Millett* IBF | 1999–00 | Juan Urango IBF | 2009– |
| WBC | 1974–75 | James McGirt IBF | 1988 | Zab Judah* IBF | 2000–01 | | |
| S. Muangsurin WBC | 1975–76 | Meldrick Taylor IBF | 1988–90 | Kostya Tszyu*† | | | |
| Wilfred Benitez* | 1976–79† | Julio César Chávez* | | WBA/C | 2001–03 | | |
| M. Velasquez WBC | 1976 | WBC | 1989–94 | | | | |

## Lightweights (Weight Limit: 135 pounds)

| Champion | Reign | Champion | Reign | Champion | Reign | Champion | Reign |
|---|---|---|---|---|---|---|---|
| Jack McAuliffe* | 1886–94† | Henry Armstrong* | 1938–39 | Joe Brown* | 1956–62 | Hilmer Kenty WBA | 1980–81 |
| Kid Lavigne* | 1896–99 | Lou Ambers* | 1939–40 | Carlos Ortiz* | 1962–65 | Sean O'Grady WBA | 1981 |
| Frank Erne* | 1899–1902 | Sammy Angott NBA | 1940–41 | Ismael Laguna* | 1965 | Claude Noel WBA | 1981 |
| Joe Gans* | 1902–04 | Lew Jenkins* | 1940–41 | Carlos Ortiz* | 1965–68 | Alexis Arguello* | |
| Jimmy Britt* | 1904–05 | Sammy Angott** | 1941–42† | Carlos Teo Cruz* | 1968–69 | WBC | 1981–82† |
| Battling Nelson* | 1905–06 | Beau Jack* NY | 1942–43 | Mando Ramos* | 1969–70 | Arturo Frias WBA | 1981–82 |
| Joe Gans* | 1906–08 | Bob Montgomery* | | Ismael Laguna* | 1970 | Ray Mancini* WBA | 1982–84 |
| Battling Nelson* | 1908–10 | NY | 1943 | Ken Buchanan* | 1970–72 | Alexis Arguello* | 1982–83 |
| Ad Wolgast* | 1910–12 | Sammy Angott NBA | 1943–44 | Roberto Duran* | 1972–79† | Edwin Rosario WBC | 1983–84 |
| Willie Ritchie* | 1912–14 | Beau Jack* NY | 1943–44 | Chango Carmona | | Choo Choo Brown | |
| Freddie Welsh* | 1915–17 | Bob Montgomery* | | WBC | 1972 | IBF | 1984 |
| Benny Leonard* | 1917–25† | NY | 1944–47 | Rodolfo Gonzalez | | L. Bramble* WBA | 1984–86 |
| Jimmy Goodrich* | 1925 | Juan Zurita NBA | 1944–45 | WBC | 1972–74 | Jose Luis Ramirez | |
| Rocky Kansas* | 1925–26 | Ike Williams* | 1947–51 | Ishimatsu Suzuki | | WBC | 1984–85 |
| Sammy Mandell* | 1926–30 | James Carter* | 1951–52 | WBC | 1974–76 | Harry Arroyo IBF | 1984–85 |
| Al Singer* | 1930 | Lauro Salas* | 1952 | Estaban DeJesus | | Jimmy Paul IBF | 1985–86 |
| Tony Canzoneri* | 1930–33 | James Carter* | 1952–54 | WBC | 1976–78 | Hector Camacho | |
| Barney Ross* | 1933–35† | Paddy DeMarco* | 1954 | Jim Watt WBC* | 1979–81 | WBC | 1985–86 |
| Tony Canzoneri* | 1935–36 | James Carter* | 1954–55 | Ernesto Espana | | Greg Haugen IBF | 1986–87 |
| Lou Ambers* | 1936–38 | Wallace Smith* | 1955–56 | WBA | 1979–80 | Edwin Rosario* WBA | 1986–87 |

*Lineal champion. †Champion relinquished title to retire or switch weight classes, or had title stripped by boxing organization.

## Lightweights *(Cont.)*

| Champion | Reign |
|---|---|
| Julio César Chávez* | |
| WBA | 1987–88 |
| Jose Luis Ramirez | |
| WBC | 1987–88 |
| Julio César Chávez* | 1988–89† |
| Vinny Pazienza IBF | 1987–88 |
| Greg Haugen IBF | 1988–89 |
| P. Whitaker* | |
| WBC, IBF | 1989–90 |
| Edwin Rosario WBA | 1989–90 |
| Juan Nazario WBA | 1990 |
| P. Whitaker* | |
| WBA, WBC | 1990–92† |
| Pernell Whitaker* | |
| IBF | 1991–92† |
| Julio César Chávez | |
| IBF | 1990–91 |
| Edwin Rosario WBA | 1991–92 |
| Julio César Chávez | |
| WBC | 1990–92 |

| Champion | Reign |
|---|---|
| Miguel Gonzalez | |
| WBC | 1992–95 |
| Joey Gamache | |
| WBA | 1992–93 |
| Dingaan Thobela | |
| WBA | 1993 |
| Fred Pendleton* IBF | 1993–94 |
| Orzubek Nazarov | |
| WBA | 1993–98 |
| Rafael Ruelas* IBF | 1994–95 |
| Oscar De La Hoya* | |
| IBF | 1995† |
| Phillip Holiday IBF | 1995–97 |
| Jean B. Mendy* | |
| WBC | 1996–97 |
| Steve Johnston* | |
| WBC | 1997–98 |
| Shane Mosley IBF | 1997–99† |
| Jean B. Mendy WBA | 1998–99 |
| Cesar Bazan* WBC | 1998–99 |

| Champion | Reign |
|---|---|
| Steve Johnston* | |
| WBC | 1999–00 |
| Julien Lorcy WBA | 1999 |
| Stefano Zoff WBA | 1999 |
| Paul Spadafora IBF | 1999–03 |
| Gilbert Serrano WBA | 1999–00 |
| T. Hatakeyama WBA | 2000–01 |
| Jose Luis Castillo* | |
| WBC | 2000–02 |
| Julien Lorcy WBA | 2001 |
| Raul Balbi WBA | 2001 |
| F. Mayweather* WBC | 2002–03 |
| Leonard Dorin WBA | 2002–03 |
| Javier Jauregui IBF | 2003–04 |
| Julio Diaz IBF | 2004–05 |
| Lakva Sim WBA | 2004 |
| Juan Diaz WBA | 2004–08 |
| Jose Luis Castillo | |
| WBC | 2004–05 |
| Diego Corrales WBC | 2005–06 |

| Champion | Reign |
|---|---|
| Jesus Chavez IBF | 2005–07 |
| Joel Casamayor | |
| WBC | 2006–08 |
| Julio Diaz IBF | 2007 |
| Juan Diaz | 2007–08 |
| David Diaz WBC | 2008 |
| Yusuke Kobori WBA | 2008– |
| Nate Campbell IBF | 2008–09† |
| Manny Pacquiao | |
| WBC | 2008–09† |
| Juan Manuel Marquez | |
| WBA | 2009– |
| Edwin Valero WBC | 2009– |

## Super Featherweights (Weight Limit: 130 pounds)

| Champion | Reign |
|---|---|
| Johnny Dundee* | 1921–23 |
| Jack Bernstein* | 1923 |
| Johnny Dundee* | 1923–24 |
| Steve (Kid) Sullivan* | 1924–25 |
| Mike Ballerino* | 1925 |
| Tod Morgan* | 1925–29 |
| Benny Bass* | 1929–31 |
| Kid Chocolate* | 1931–33 |
| Frankie Klick* | 1933–34† |
| Sandy Saddler* | 1949–50† |
| Harold Gomes* | 1959–60 |
| Gabriel (Flash) Elorde* | 1960–67 |
| Yoshiaki Numata* | 1967 |
| Hiroshi Kobayashi* | 1967–71 |
| Rene Barrientos WBC | 1969–70 |
| Yoshiaki Numata WBC | 1970–71 |
| Alfredo Marcano* | 1971–72 |
| R. Arredondo WBC | 1971–74 |
| Ben Villaflor* | 1972–73 |
| Kuniaki Shibata* | 1973 |
| Ben Villaflor* | 1973–76 |
| Kuniaki Shibata WBC | 1974–75 |
| Alfredo Escalera IBF | 1975–78 |
| Samuel Serrano* | 1976–80 |
| Alexis Arguello WBC | 1978–80 |
| Yasutsune Uehara* | 1980–81 |
| Rafael Limon WBC | 1980–81 |
| C. Boza-Edwards WBC | 1981 |
| Samuel Serrano* | 1981–83 |
| R. Navarrete WBC | 1981–82 |
| Rafael Limon WBC | 1982 |

| Champion | Reign |
|---|---|
| Bobby Chacon WBC | 1982–83 |
| Roger Mayweather* | 1983–84 |
| Hector Camacho WBC | 1983–84 |
| Rocky Lockridge* | 1984–85 |
| Hwan-Kil Yuh IBF | 1984–85 |
| Julio César Chávez WBC | 1984–87 |
| Lester Ellis IBF | 1985 |
| Wilfredo Gomez* | 1985–86 |
| Barry Michael IBF | 1985–87 |
| Alfredo Layne* WBA | 1986 |
| Brian Mitchell* WBA | 1986–91† |
| Rocky Lockridge IBF | 1987–88 |
| Azumah Nelson* WBC | 1988–94 |
| Tony Lopez IBF | 1988–89 |
| Juan Molina IBF | 1989–90 |
| Tony Lopez IBF | 1990–91 |
| Joey Gamache WBA | 1991 |
| Brian Mitchell IBF | 1991 |
| Genaro Hernandez WBA | 1991–95 |
| James Leija* WBC | 1994 |
| Juan Molina IBF | 1991–95 |
| Gabriel Ruelas* WBC | 1994–95 |
| Eddie Hopson IBF | 1995 |
| Tracy Patterson IBF | 1995 |
| Azumah Nelson* WBC | 1995–97 |
| Choi Yong-Soo WBA | 1995–98 |
| Arturo Gatti IBF | 1995–98† |
| Genaro Hernandez* WBC | 1997–98 |
| Roberto Garcia IBF | 1998–99 |
| Floyd Mayweather Jr.* WBC | 1998–01† |
| T. Hatakeyama WBA | 1998–99 |

| Champion | Reign |
|---|---|
| Lakva Sim WBA | 1999 |
| Diego Corrales IBF | 1999–01 |
| Jong Kwon Baek WBA | 1999–00 |
| Joel Casamayor WBA | 2000–02 |
| Steve Forbes IBF | 2000–02† |
| Acelino Freitas* WBA | 2002–04 |
| Y. Nantchachai WBA | 2002–05 |
| S. Singmanassak WBC | 2002–03 |
| Jesus Chavez WBC | 2003–04 |
| Carlos Hernandez IBF | 2003–04 |
| Erik Morales WBC/IBF | 2004–05 |
| Erik Morales IBF | 2004–05 |
| Marco A. Barrera WBC | 2005–07 |
| Vicente Mosquera WBA | 2005–06 |
| Robbie Peden IBF | 2005 |
| Marco A. Barrera, IBF | 2005–06 |
| Cassius Baloyi IBF | 2006 |
| Edwin Valero WBA | 2006–08 |
| Gairy St. Clair IBF | 2006 |
| Malcolm Klassen IBF | 2006–07 |
| Mzonke Fana IBF | 2007–08 |
| Juan Manuel Marquez WBC | 2007–08 |
| Manny Pacquiao WBC | 2008 |
| Jorge Linares WBA | 2008–09 |
| Cassius Baloyi IBF | 2008–09 |
| Malcom Klassen IBF | 2009 |
| Humberto Soto WBC | 2008– |
| Juan Carlos Salgado IBF | 2009– |
| Robert Guerrero IBF | 2009– |

## Featherweights (Weight Limit: 126 pounds)

| Champion | Reign |
|---|---|
| Torpedo Billy Murphy* | 1890 |
| Young Griffo* | 1890–92† |
| George Dixon* | 1892–97 |
| Solly Smith* | 1897–98 |
| Dave Sullivan* | 1898 |
| George Dixon* | 1898–1900 |
| Terry McGovern* | 1900–01 |

| Champion | Reign |
|---|---|
| Young Corbett II* | 1901–03† |
| Abe Attell* | 1903–04 |
| Tommy Sullivan* | 1904–05† |
| Abe Attell* | 1906–12 |
| Johnny Kilbane* | 1912–23 |
| Eugene Criqui* | 1923 |
| Johnny Dundee* | 1923–24† |

| Champion | Reign |
|---|---|
| "Kid" Kaplan* | 1925–26† |
| Tony Canzoneri* | 1927–28 |
| Andre Routis* | 1928–29 |
| Battling Battalino* | 1929–32† |
| Tommy Paul NBA | 1932–33 |
| Kid Chocolate NY | 1932–33† |
| Freddie Miller NBA | 1933–36 |

*Lineal champion. †Champion relinquished title to retire or switch weight classes, or had title stripped by boxing organization.

### Featherweights *(Cont.)*

| Champion | Reign |
|---|---|
| Mike Beloise NY | 1936–37 |
| Petey Sarron NBA | 1936–37 |
| Maurice Holtzer | 1937–38 |
| Henry Armstrong* | 1937–38† |
| Joey Archibald* NY | 1938–39 |
| Leo Rodak NBA | 1938–39 |
| Joey Archibald | 1939–40 |
| Petey Scalzo NBA | 1940–41 |
| Harry Jeffra* | 1940–41 |
| Joey Archibald* | 1941 |
| Richie Lamos NBA | 1941 |
| Chalky Wright* | 1941–42 |
| Jackie Wilson NBA | 1941–43 |
| Willie Pep* | 1942–48 |
| Jackie Callura NBA | 1943 |
| Phil Terranova NBA | 1943–44 |
| Sal Bartolo NBA | 1944–46 |
| Sandy Saddler* | 1948–49 |
| Willie Pep* | 1949–50 |
| Sandy Saddler* | 1950–57† |
| Kid Bassey* | 1957–59 |
| Davey Moore* | 1959–63 |
| Sugar Ramos* | 1963–64 |
| Vicente Saldivar* | 1964–67† |
| Paul Rojas WBA | 1968 |
| Jose Legra WBC | 1968–69 |
| Shozo Saijyo WBA | 1968–71 |
| J. Famechon* WBC | 1969–70 |
| Vicente Saldivar* WBC | 1970 |
| Kuniaki Shibata* WBC | 1970–72 |
| Antonio Gomez WBA | 1971–72 |
| C. Sanchez* WBC | 1972 |
| Ernesto Marcel WBA | 1972–74 |
| Jose Legra* WBC | 1972–73 |
| Eder Jofre* WBC | 1973–74† |
| Ruben Olivares WBA | 1974 |

| Champion | Reign |
|---|---|
| Bobby Chacon WBC | 1974–75 |
| Alexis Arguello* WBA | 1974–76† |
| Ruben Olivares WBC | 1975 |
| Poison Kotey WBC | 1975–76 |
| Danny Lopez* WBC | 1976–80 |
| Rafael Ortega WBA | 1977 |
| Cecilio Lastra WBA | 1977–78 |
| Eusebio Pedroza* WBA | 1978–85 |
| S. Sanchez* WBC | 1980–82† |
| Juan LaPorte WBC | 1982–84 |
| Wilfredo Gomez WBC | 1984 |
| Min-Keun Oh IBF | 1984–85 |
| Azumah Nelson WBC | 1984–88 |
| Barry McGuigan* WBA | 1985–86 |
| Ki Young Chung IBF | 1985–86 |
| Steve Cruz* WBA | 1986–87 |
| Antonio Rivera WBA | 1986–88 |
| A. Esparragoza* WBA | 1987–91 |
| Calvin Grove IBF | 1988 |
| Jorge Paez IBF | 1988–91 |
| Jeff Fenech WBC | 1988–90† |
| Marcos Villasana WBC | 1990–91 |
| Paul Hodkinson WBC | 1991–93 |
| Troy Dorsey IBF | 1991 |
| Manuel Medina IBF | 1991–93 |
| Yung Kyun Park* WBA | 1991–93 |
| Gregorio Vargas WBC | 1993 |
| Tom Johnson IBF | 1993–97† |
| Eloy Rojas* WBA | 1993–96 |
| Kevin Kelley WBC | 1993–95 |
| A. Gonzalez WBC | 1995 |
| Manuel Medina WBC | 1995–95 |
| Luisito Espinosa WBC | 1995–99 |
| Wilfredo Vazquez* WBA | 1996–98 |
| Hector Lizarraga IBF | 1997–98 |
| Naseem Hamed* WBA | 1998† |

| Champion | Reign |
|---|---|
| Naseem Hamed* | 1998–01 |
| Freddy Norwood WBA | 1998 |
| Manuel Medina IBF | 1998–99 |
| Antonio Cermeno WBA | 1998–99 |
| Cesar Soto WBC | 1999 |
| Freddy Norwood WBA | 1999–00 |
| Naseem Hamed* WBC | 1999† |
| Paul Ingle IBF | 1999–00 |
| Guty Espadas WBC | 2000–01 |
| Erik Morales WBC | 2000–02 |
| Derrick Gainer WBA | 2000–03 |
| Mbulelo Botile IBF | 2001 |
| Frankie Toledo IBF | 2001 |
| Manuel Medina IBF | 2001–02 |
| Marco A. Barrera WBA/WBC | 2001–03 |
| Johnny Tapia IBF | 2002 |
| Marco A. Barrera* WBC | 2002† |
| Erik Morales WBC | 2002–03 |
| Juan Marquez IBF | 2003–06 |
| Chris John WBA | 2003– |
| In Jin Chi WBC | 2004–06 |
| Valdemir Pereira, IBF | 2006 |
| Eric Aiken IBF | 2006 |
| T. Koshimoto, WBC | 2006 |
| Rudolfo Lopez WBC | 2006 |
| Robert Guerrero IBF | 2006 |
| Orlando Salido IBF | 2006 |
| In Jin Chi WBC | 2006–07 |
| Robert Guerrero IBF | 2007–08† |
| Jorge Linares WBC | 2007–08 |
| Oscar Larios WBC | 2008–09 |
| Cristobal Cruz IBF | 2008– |
| Takahiro Aoh WBC | 2009 |
| Elio Rojas WBC | 2009– |

### Super Bantamweights (Weight Limit: 122 pounds)

| Champion | Reign |
|---|---|
| Jack (Kid) Wolfe* | 1922–23 |
| Carl Duane* | 1923–24 |
| Rigoberto Riasco* WBC | 1976 |
| R. Kobayashi* WBC | 1976 |
| Dong-Kyun Yum* WBC | 1976–77 |
| Wilfredo Gomez* WBC | 1977–83† |
| Soo-Hwan Hong WBA | 1977–78 |
| Ricardo Cardona WBA | 1978–80 |
| Leo Randolph WBA | 1980 |
| Sergio Palma WBA | 1980–82 |
| Leonardo Cruz WBA | 1982–84 |
| Jaime Garza* WBC | 1983 |
| Bobby Berna IBF | 1983–84 |
| Loris Stecca WBA | 1984 |
| Seung-Il Suh IBF | 1984–85 |
| Victor Callejas WBA | 1984–86 |
| Juan Meza* WBC | 1984–85 |
| Ji-Won Kim IBF | 1985–86 |
| Lupe Pintor* WBC | 1985–86 |
| S. Payakaroon* WBC | 1986–87 |
| Seung-Hoon Lee IBF | 1987–88 |
| Louie Espinoza WBA | 1987 |
| Jeff Fenech* WBC | 1987† |
| Julio Gervacio WBA | 1987–88 |
| Daniel Zaragoza* WBC | 1988–90 |

| Champion | Reign |
|---|---|
| Jose Sanabria IBF | 1988–89 |
| B. Pinango WBA | 1988 |
| J.J. Estrada WBA | 1988–89 |
| Fabrice Benichou IBF | 1989–90 |
| Jesus Salud WBA | 1989–90 |
| Welcome Ncita IBF | 1990–92 |
| Paul Banke* WBC | 1990 |
| Luis Mendoza WBA | 1990–91 |
| Raul Perez WBA | 1992 |
| Pedro Decima* WBC | 1990–91 |
| K. Hatanaka* WBC | 1991 |
| Daniel Zaragoza* WBC | 1991–92 |
| Thiery Jacob* WBC | 1992 |
| Tracy Patterson* WBC | 1992–94 |
| Kennedy McKinney IBF | 1993–94 |
| Wilfredo Vasquez WBA | 1992–95 |
| Vuyani Bungu IBF | 1994–99† |
| H. Acero* Sanchez WBC | 1994–95 |
| Antonio Cermeno WBA | 1995–98† |
| Daniel Zaragoza* WBC | 1995–97 |
| Erik Morales* WBC | 1997–00† |
| Enrique Sanchez WBA | 1998 |
| Nestor Garza WBA | 1998–00 |
| Benedict Ledwaba IBF | 1999–01 |
| Clarence Adams WBA | 2000–01† |

| Champion | Reign |
|---|---|
| Willie Jorrin WBC | 2000–02 |
| Manny Pacquiao IBF | 2001–04 |
| Yober Ortega WBA | 2001–02 |
| Y. Sithyodthong WBA | 2002 |
| Osamu Sato WBA | 2002 |
| Salim Medjkoune WBA | 2002–03 |
| Mahyar Monshipour WBA | 2003–06 |
| Oscar Larios WBC | 2002–05 |
| Israel Vazquez IBF | 2004–05 |
| S. Sithchatchawal WBA | 2006 |
| Israel Vazquez WBC | 2005–07 |
| C. Caballero WBA, | 2006– |
| IBF | 2008– |
| Michael Hunter IBF | 2006 |
| Steve Molitor IBF | 2006–08 |
| Rafael Marquez WBC | 2007 |
| Israel Vazquez WBC | 2007–08 |
| Toshiaki Nishioka WBC | 2008– |

*Lineal champion. †Champion relinquished title to retire or switch weight classes, or had title stripped by boxing organization.

# World Champions (Cont.)

## Bantamweights (Weight Limit: 118 pounds)

| Champion | Reign |
|---|---|
| Spider Kelly | 1887 |
| Hughey Boyle | 1887–88 |
| Spider Kelly | 1889 |
| Chappie Moran | 1889–90 |
| George Dixon | 1890–91 |
| Pedlar Palmer | 1895–99 |
| Terry McGovern* | 1899–00† |
| Harry Harris | 1901 |
| Harry Forbes* | 1901–03 |
| Frankie Neil* | 1903–04 |
| Joe Bowker* | 1904–05† |
| Jimmy Walsh* | 1905–06† |
| Owen Moran | 1907–08 |
| Monte Attell | 1909–10 |
| Frankie Conley | 1910–11 |
| Johnny Coulon* | 1910–14 |
| Kid Williams* | 1914–17 |
| Kewpie Ertle | 1915 |
| Pete Herman* | 1917–20 |
| Joe Lynch* | 1920–21 |
| Pete Herman* | 1921 |
| Johnny Buff* | 1921–22 |
| Joe Lynch* | 1922–24 |
| Abe Goldstein* | 1924 |
| Cannonball Martin* | 1924–25 |
| Phil Rosenberg* | 1925–27† |
| Bud Taylor NBA | 1927–28 |
| Bushy Graham NY | 1928–29 |
| Panama Al Brown* | 1929–35 |
| Sixto Escobar NBA | 1934–35 |
| Baltazar Sangchilli* | 1935–36 |
| Lou Salica NBA | 1935 |
| Sixto Escobar NBA | 1935–36 |
| Tony Marino* | 1936 |
| Sixto Escobar* | 1936–37 |
| Harry Jeffra* | 1937–38 |
| Sixto Escobar* | 1938–39† |
| Georgie Pace NBA | 1939–40 |
| Lou Salica* | 1940–42 |
| Manuel Ortiz* | 1942–47 |
| Harold Dade* | 1947 |
| Manuel Ortiz* | 1947–50 |
| Vic Toweel* | 1950–52 |
| Jimmy Carruthers* | 1952–54† |
| Robert Cohen* | 1954–56 |
| Paul Macias NBA | 1955–57 |
| Mario D'Agata* | 1956–57 |
| Alphonse Halimi* | 1957–59 |
| Joe Becerra* | 1959–60† |
| Eder Jofre* | 1961–65 |
| Fighting Harada* | 1965–68 |
| Lionel Rose* | 1968–69 |
| Ruben Olivares* | 1969–70 |
| Chucho Castillo* | 1970–71 |
| Ruben Olivares* | 1971–72 |
| Rafael Herrera* | 1972 |
| Enrique Pinder* | 1972–73 |
| Romeo Anaya* | 1973 |
| Arnold Taylor* | 1973–74 |
| Rafael Herrera WBC | 1973–74 |
| Soo-Hwan Hong* | 1974–75 |
| Rodolfo Martinez WBC | 1974–76 |
| Alfonso Zamora* | 1975–77 |
| Carlos Zarate* WBC | 1976–79 |
| Jorge Lujan | 1977–80 |
| Lupe Pintor* WBC | 1979–83† |
| Julian Solis | 1980 |
| Jeff Chandler* | 1980–84 |
| Albert Davila WBC | 1983–85 |
| Richard Sandoval* | 1984–86 |
| Satoshi Shingaki IBF | 1984–85 |
| Jeff Fenech IBF | 1985 |
| Daniel Zaragoza WBC | 1985 |
| Miguel Lora WBC | 1985–88 |
| Gaby Canizales* | 1986 |
| Bernardo Pinango* | 1986–87† |
| W. Vasquez WBA | 1987–88 |
| Kevin Seabrooks* IBF | 1987–88 |
| Kaokor Galaxy WBA | 1988 |
| Moon Sung-Kil WBA | 1988–89 |
| Kaokor Galaxy WBA | 1989 |
| Raul Perez WBC | 1988–91 |
| O. Canizales* IBF | 1988–95† |
| Luisito Espinosa WBA | 1989–91 |
| Israel Contreras WBA | 1991–92 |
| Eddie Cook WBA | 1992–93 |
| Greg Richardson WBC | 1991 |
| J. Tatsuyoshi, WBC | 1991–92 |
| Victor Rabanales WBC | 1992–93 |
| Jung-Il Byun WBC | 1993 |
| Jorge Julio WBA | 1993 |
| Yasuei Yakushiji WBC | 1993–95 |
| Junior Jones WBA | 1994 |
| John M. Johnson WBA | 1994 |
| D. Chuvatana WBA | 1994–95 |
| V. Sahaprom* WBA | 1995–96 |
| W. McCullough WBC | 1995–96 |
| Harold Mestre IBF | 1995 |
| Mbulelo Botile IBF | 1995–97 |
| Nana Konadu* WBA | 1996–98 |
| S. Singmanassak WBC | 1996–97 |
| Tim Austin IBF | 1997–03 |
| J.Tatsuyoshi WBC | 1997–98 |
| Johnny Tapia* WBA | 1998–99 |
| V. Sahaprom* WBC | 1999–01† |
| Paulie Ayala* WBA | 1999–01† |
| Eidy Moya WBA | 2001–02 |
| Johnny Bredahl WBA | 2002–05 |
| Rafael Marquez IBF | 2003–07 |
| W. Sidorenko WBA | 2005–08 |
| H. Hasegawa WBC | 2005– |
| Luis Perez IBF | 2007 |
| Joseph Agbeko IBF | 2007– |
| Anselmo Moreno WBA | 2008– |

## Super Flyweights (Weight Limit: 115 pounds)

| Champion | Reign |
|---|---|
| Rafael Orono* WBC | 1980–81 |
| Chul-Ho Kim* WBC | 1981–82 |
| Gustavo Ballas WBA | 1981 |
| Rafael Pedroza WBA | 1981–82 |
| Jiro Watanabe WBA | 1982–84 |
| Rafael Orono* WBC | 1982–83 |
| Payao Poontarat* WBC | 1983–84 |
| Joo-Do Chun IBF | 1983–85 |
| Jiro Watanabe* | 1984–86 |
| Kaosai Galaxy WBA | 1984 |
| Ellyas Pica IBF | 1985–86 |
| Cesar Polanco IBF | 1986 |
| Gilberto Roman* WBC | 1986–87 |
| Ellyas Pical IBF | 1986 |
| Santos Laciar* WBC | 1987 |
| Tae-Il Chang IBF | 1987 |
| Sugar Rojas* WBC | 1987–88 |
| Ellyas Pical IBF | 1987–89 |
| Giberto Roman* WBC | 1988–89 |
| Juan Polo Perez IBF | 1989–90 |
| Nana Konadu* WBC | 1989–90 |
| Sung-Kil Moon* WBC | 1990–93 |
| Robert Quiroga IBF | 1990–93 |
| Julio Borboa IBF | 1993–94 |
| Katsuya Onizuka WBA | 1993–94 |
| Lee Hyung-Chul WBA | 1994–95 |
| Jose Luis Bueno* WBC | 1993–94 |
| H. Kawashima* WBC | 1994–97 |
| Harold Grey IBF | 1994–95 |
| Alimi Goitia WBA | 1995–96 |
| Yokthai Sith-Oar WBA | 1996–97 |
| Carlos Salazar IBF | 1995–96 |
| Harold Grey IBF | 1996 |
| Danny Romero IBF | 1996–97 |
| Gerry Penalosa* WBC | 1997–98 |
| Johnny Tapia IBF | 1997–99† |
| Satoshi Iida WBA | 1997–98 |
| In-Joo Cho* WBC | 1998–00 |
| Jesus Rojas WBA | 1998–99 |
| Mark Johnson IBF | 1999–00 |
| Hideki Todaka WBA | 1999–00 |
| Felix Machado IBF | 2000–03 |
| M. Tokuyama* WBC | 2000–04 |
| Leo Gamez WBA | 2000–01 |
| Celes Kobayashi WBA | 2001–02 |
| Alexander Munoz WBA | 2002–05 |
| Luis Alberto Perez IBF | 2003–06 |
| Katsushige Kawashima WBC | 2004–05 |
| M. Tokuyama WBC | 2005–06 |
| Jose M. Castillo WBA | 2005–06 |
| Nobuo Nashiro WBA | 2006–08 |
| Cristian Mijares WBC | 2006–08 |
| Dmitri Kirilov IBF | 2007–08 |
| Vic Darchinyan WBC, WBA | 2008– |
| IBF | 2006–09† |
| Simphiwe Nongqayi IBF | 2009– |

## Flyweights (Weight Limit: 112 pounds)

| Champion | Reign |
|---|---|
| Sid Smith* | 1913 |
| Bill Ladbury* | 1913–14 |
| Percy Jones* | 1914† |
| Joe Symonds* | 1914–16 |
| Jimmy Wilde* | 1916–23 |
| Pancho Villa* | 1923–25† |
| Fidel La Barba* | 1925–27† |
| Frenchy Belanger* NBA | 1927–28 |
| Izzy Schwartz NY | 1927–29 |
| Frankie Genaro* NBA | 1928–29 |
| Spider Pladner* NBA | 1929 |
| Frankie Genaro* NBA | 1929–31 |
| Midget Wolgast NY | 1930–35 |
| Young Perez* NBA | 1931–32 |
| Jackie Brown* NBA | 1932–35 |
| Benny Lynch* | 1935–38† |
| Small Montana NY | 1935–37 |
| Peter Kane* | 1938–43 |
| Little Dado NY | 1938–40 |
| Jackie Paterson* | 1943–48 |
| Rinty Monaghan* | 1948–50† |

*Lineal champion. †Champion relinquished title to retire or switch weight classes, or had title stripped by boxing organization.

**424** BOXING

## Flyweights *(Cont.)*

| Champion | Reign | Champion | Reign | Champion | Reign | Champion | Reign |
|---|---|---|---|---|---|---|---|
| Terry Allen* | 1950 | Erbito Salavarria | | Chong-Kwan Chung | | Chatchai Sasakul* | |
| Dado Marino* | 1950–52 | WBA | 1975–76 | IBF | 1985–86 | WBC | 1997–98 |
| Yoshio Shirai* | 1952–54 | Alfonso Lopez WBA | 1976 | Bi-Won Chung IBF | 1986 | Hugo Soto WBA | 1998–99 |
| Pascual Perez* | 1954–60 | G. Espadas WBA | 1976–78 | Hi-Sup Shin IBF | 1986–87 | Manny Pacquiao* WBC | 1998–99 |
| Pone Kingpetch* | 1960–62 | B. Gonzalez WBA | 1978–79 | Dodie Penalosa IBF | 1987 | Leo Gamez WBA | 1999 |
| Masahiko Harada* | 1962–63 | Chan-Hee Park* | | Fidel Bassa WBA | 1987–89 | Irene Pacheco IBF | 1999–05 |
| Pone Kingpetch* | 1963 | WBC | 1979–80 | Choi-Chang Ho IBF | 1987–88 | S. Pisnurachan WBA | 1999–00 |
| Hiroyuki Ebihara* | 1963–64 | Luis Ibarra WBA | 1979–80 | Rolando Bohol IBF | 1988 | M. Sinsurat* WBC | 1999–00 |
| Pone Kingpetch* | 1964–65 | Tae-Shik Kim WBA | 1980 | Yong-Kang Kim* | | Malcolm Tunacao* WBC | 2000–01 |
| Salvatore Burrini* | 1965–66 | Shoji Oguma* WBC | 1980–81 | WBC | 1988–89 | Eric Morel WBA | 2000–03 |
| H. Accavallo WBA | 1966–68 | Peter Mathebula WBA | 1980–81 | Duke McKenzie IBF | 1988–89 | P. Wonjongkam* | |
| Walter McGowan* | 1966 | Santos Laciar WBA | 1981 | Sot Chitalada* WBC | 1989–91 | WBC | 2001–03 |
| Chartchai Chionoi* | 1966–69 | Antonio Avelar* WBC | 1981–82 | Dave McAuley IBF | 1989–92 | Lorenzo Parra WBA | 2003–07 |
| Efren Torres* | 1969–70 | Luis Ibarra WBA | 1981 | Jesus Rojas WBA | 1989–90 | Vic Darchinyan IBF | 2005–07 |
| Hiroyuki Ebihara WBA | 1969 | Juan Herrera WBA | 1981–82 | Yul-Woo Lee WBA | 1990 | Takefumi Sakata | |
| B. Villacampo WBA | 1969–70 | P. Cardona* WBC | 1982 | L. Tamakuma WBA | 1990–91 | WBA | 2007–08 |
| Chartchai Chionoi* | 1970 | Santos Laciar WBA | 1982–85 | M. Kittikasem* WBC | 1991–92 | Daisuke Naito WBC | 2007– |
| B. Chartvanchai | | Freddie Castillo* WBC | 1982 | Yuri Arbachakov* | | Nonito Donaire IBF | 2007–09† |
| WBA | 1970 | E. Mercedes* WBC | 1982–83 | WBC | 1992–97 | Denkaosan Kaovichit | |
| Masao Ohba WBA | 1970–73 | Charlie Magri* WBC | 1983 | Yong Kang Kim | | WBA | 2008– |
| Erbito Salavarria* | 1970–73† | Frank Cedeno* WBC | 1983–84 | WBA | 1991–92 | | |
| B. Gonzalez WBA | 1972 | Soon-Chun Kwon | | Rodolfo Blanco IBF | 1992–93 | | |
| V. Borkorsor WBC | 1972–73† | IBF | 1983–85 | P. Sithbangprachan IBF | 1993–95 | | |
| Venice Borkorsor* | 1973† | Koji Kobayashi* | | David Griman WBA | 1992–94 | | |
| Chartchai Chionoi WBA | 1973–74 | WBC | 1984 | S.S. Ploenchit WBA | 1994–96 | | |
| B. Gonzalez* WBA | 1973–74 | Gabriel Bernal* | | Francisco Tejedor IBF | 1995 | | |
| Shoji Oguma* WBC | 1974–75 | WBC | 1984 | Danny Romero IBF | 1995–96 | | |
| S. Hanagata WBA | 1974–75 | Sot Chitalada* WBC | 1984–88 | Mark Johnson IBF | 1996–99† | | |
| Miguel Canto* WBC | 1975–79 | Hilario Zapate WBA | 1985–87 | Jose Bonilla WBA | 1996–98 | | |

## Light Flyweights (Weight Limit: 108 pounds)

| Champion | Reign | Champion | Reign | Champion | Reign |
|---|---|---|---|---|---|
| Franco Udella WBC | 1975 | Tacy Macalos IBF | 1988–89 | Ricardo Lopez IBF | 1999–02 |
| Jaime Rios WBA | 1975–76 | German Torres WBC | 1988–89 | Yo-Sam Choi* WBC | 1999–02 |
| Luis Estaba* WBC | 1975–78 | Yul-Woo Lee WBC | 1989 | Beibis Mendoza WBA | 2000–01 |
| Juan Guzman WBA | 1976 | M. Kittikasem IBF | 1989–90 | Rosendo Alvarez WBA | 2001–05 |
| Yoko Gushiken WBA | 1976–81 | H. Gonzalez WBC | 1989–90 | Jorge Arce* WBC | 2002–05 |
| Freddy Castillo* WBC | 1978 | Michael Carbajal IBF | 1990–94 | Jose Burgos IBF | 2003–05 |
| Sor Vorasingh* WBC | 1978 | R. Pascua WBC | 1990 | Brian Viloria WBC | 2005–06 |
| Sung-Jun Kim* WBC | 1978–80 | M. C. Castro WBC | 1991 | R. Vasquez WBA | 2005–06 |
| Shigeo Nakajima* WBC | 1980 | H. Gonzalez WBC | 1991–93 | Will Grigsby IBF | 2005–06 |
| Hilario Zapata* WBC | 1980–82 | Hirokia Ioka* WBA | 1991–92 | Koki Kameda WBA | 2006–07 |
| Pedro Flores WBA | 1981 | Myung-Woo Yuh* WBA | 1993† | Omar Nino Rivero WBC | 2006–07 |
| Hwan-Jin Kim WBA | 1981 | Michael Carbajal* WBC | 1993–94 | Ulises Solis IBF | 2006–09 |
| Katsuo Tokashiki WBA | 1981–83 | Leo Gamez WBA | 1993–95 | Juan Carlos Reveco WBA | 2007 |
| Amado Urzua* WBC | 1982 | H. Gonzalez* WBC, IBF | 1994–95 | Edgar Sosa WBC | 2007– |
| Tadashi Tomori* WBC | 1982 | Choi Hi-Yong WBA | 1995–96 | Brahim Asloum WBA | 2007–09† |
| Hilario Zapata* WBC | 1982–83 | S. Sor Jaturong WBC, IBF | 1995–96 | Giovanni Segura WBA | 2009– |
| Jung-Koo Chang* WBC | 1983–88† | Carlos Murillo WBA | 1996 | Brian Viloria IBF | 2009– |
| Lupe Madera WBA | 1983–84 | Keiji Yamaguchi WBA | 1996 | | |
| Dodie Penalosa IBF | 1983–86 | Michael Carbajal IBF | 1996–97 | | |
| Francisco Quiroz WBA | 1984–85 | Saman Jaturong* WBC | 1995–99 | | |
| Joey Olivo WBA | 1985 | Phichitchor Siriwat WBA | 1996–00 | | |
| Myung-Woo Yuh* WBA | 1985–91 | Mauricio Pastrana IBF | 1997–98† | | |
| Jum-Hwan Choi IBF | 1986–88 | Will Grigsby IBF | 1998–99 | | |

*Lineal champion.    †Champion relinquished title to retire or switch weight classes, or had title stripped by boxing organization.

### Strawweights (Weight Limit: 105 pounds)

| Champion | Reign |
|---|---|
| Kyung-Yun Lee* IBF | 1987 |
| Hiroki Ioka* WBC | 1987–88 |
| Leo Gamez WBA | 1988–89 |
| S. Sithnaruepol IBF | 1988–89 |
| N. Kiatwanchai* WBC | 1988–89 |
| Bong-Jun Kim WBA | 1989–91 |
| Nico Thomas IBF | 1989 |
| Eric Chavez IBF | 1989–90 |
| Jum-Hwan Choi* WBC | 1989–90 |
| Hideyuki Ohashi* WBC | 1990 |
| F. Lookmingkwan IBF | 1990–92 |
| Ricardo Lopez* WBC | 1990–98† |
| Hi-Yong Choi WBA | 1991–92 |
| Manny Melchor IBF | 1992 |
| Hideyuki Ohashi WBA | 1992–93 |
| R.S. Voraphin IBF | 1992–96 |
| Chana Porpaoin WBA | 1993–95 |

| Champion | Reign |
|---|---|
| Rosendo Alvarez WBA | 1995–98 |
| R. Sor Vorapin IBF | 1996–97 |
| Zolani Petelo* IBF | 1997–00† |
| W. Chor Charoen WBC | 1998–00 |
| R. Lopez* WBA, WBC | 1998–99† |
| Songkram Popaoin WBA | 1999 |
| Noel Arambulet WBA | 1999–00 |
| Jose Aguirre* WBC | 2000–04 |
| Joma Gamboa WBA | 2000 |
| Keitaro Hoshino WBA | 2000–01 |
| Chana Porpaoin WBA | 2001 |
| Roberto Leyva IBF | 2001–02 |
| Yutaka Niida WBA | 2001† |
| Miguel Barrera IBF | 2002–03 |
| Edgar Cardenas IBF | 2003 |
| Noel Arambulet WBA | 2002–04 |
| Daniel Reyes IBF | 2003–05 |

| Champion | Reign |
|---|---|
| Eagle Junlaphan WBC | 2004 |
| Isaac Bustos WBC | 2004–05 |
| Yukata Niida WBA | 2004–08 |
| K. Takayama WBC | 2005 |
| Eagle Junlaphan WBC | 2005–07 |
| M. Rachman IBF | 2005–07 |
| Florante Condes IBF | 2007–08 |
| O. Sithsamerchai WBC | 2007– |
| Roman Gonzalez WBA | 2008– |
| Raul Garcia IBF | 2008– |

*Lineal champion. †Champion relinquished title to retire or switch weight classes, or had title stripped by boxing organization.

## Lineal Heavyweight Champions

| Champion | Reign | Age* | Career | W-L-D (KO) | SD |
|---|---|---|---|---|---|
| John L. Sullivan | 1885–92 | 26 | 1878–92 | 38-1-3 (33) | 0 |
| James J. Corbett | 1892–97 | 26 | 1884–03 | 11-4-2 (7) | 1 |
| Bob Fitzsimmons | 1897–99 | 33 | 1880–16 | 74-8-3 (67) | 0 |
| James J. Jeffries† | 1899–05 | 24 | 1896–10 | 18-1-2 (15) | 7 |
| Marvin Hart | 1905–06 | 28 | 1899–10 | 28-7-4 (19) | 0 |
| Tommy Burns | 1906–08 | 24 | 1900–20 | 46-5-8 (37) | 11 |
| Jack Johnson | 1908–15 | 30 | 1894–28 | 77-13-14 (48) | 9 |
| Jess Willard | 1915–19 | 33 | 1911–23 | 23-6-1 (20) | 1 |
| Jack Dempsey | 1919–26 | 24 | 1914–27 | 60-6-8 (50) | 5 |
| Gene Tunney† | 1926–28 | 29 | 1915–28 | 61-1-1 (45) | 2 |
| Max Schmeling | 1930–32 | 24 | 1924–48 | 56-10-4 (39) | 1 |
| Jack Sharkey | 1932–33 | 29 | 1924–36 | 38-13-3 (14) | 0 |
| Primo Carnera | 1933–34 | 26 | 1928–37 | 88-14-0 (69) | 2 |
| Max Baer | 1934–35 | 25 | 1929–41 | 72-12-0 (53) | 0 |
| James J. Braddock | 1935–37 | 29 | 1926–38 | 51-26-7 (26) | 0 |
| Joe Louis† | 1937–49 | 23 | 1934–51 | 68-3-0 (54) | 25 |
| Ezzard Charles | 1949–51 | 27 | 1940–59 | 96-25-1 (59) | 8 |
| Jersey Joe Walcott | 1951–52 | 37 | 1930–53 | 53-18-1 (33) | 1 |
| Rocky Marciano† | 1952–56 | 29 | 1947–56 | 49-0-0 (43) | 6 |
| Floyd Patterson | 1956–59 | 21 | 1952–72 | 55-8-1 (40) | 4 |
| Ingemar Johansson | 1959–60 | 26 | 1952–63 | 26-2-0 (17) | 0 |
| Floyd Patterson | 1960–62 | 25 | 1952–72 | 55-8-1 (40) | 2 |
| Sonny Liston | 1962–64 | 30 | 1953–70 | 50-4-0 (39) | 1 |
| Muhammad Ali | 1964–71 | 22 | 1960–81 | 56-5-0 (37) | 9 |
| Joe Frazier | 1971–73 | 27 | 1965–81 | 32-4-1 (27) | 2 |
| George Foreman | 1973–74 | 24 | 1969–97 | 76-5-0 (68) | 2 |
| Muhammad Ali | 1974–78 | 32 | 1960–81 | 56-5-0 (37) | 10 |
| Leon Spinks | 1978 | 24 | 1977–95 | 26-17-3 (14) | 0 |
| Muhammad Ali† | 1978–79 | 36 | 1960–81 | 56-5-0 (37) | 0 |
| Larry Holmes | 1980–85 | 29 | 1973–2002 | 69-6-0 (44) | 20 |
| Michael Spinks | 1985–88 | 29 | 1977–88 | 32-1-0 (21) | 3 |
| Mike Tyson | 1988–90 | 21 | 1985–2005 | 49-4-0 (43) | 2 |
| Buster Douglas | 1990 | 29 | 1981–99 | 38-6-1 (25) | 0 |
| Evander Holyfield | 1990–92 | 28 | 1984– | 38-5-2 (26) | 3 |
| Riddick Bowe | 1992–93 | 25 | 1989–96 | 40-1-0 (32) | 2 |
| Evander Holyfield | 1993–94 | 31 | 1984– | 38-5-2 (26) | 0 |
| Michael Moorer | 1994 | 26 | 1988–97 | 39-2-0 (31) | 0 |
| George Foreman | 1994–97 | 45 | 1969–97 | 76-5-0 (68) | 3 |
| Shannon Briggs | 1997–98 | 25 | 1992–00 | 32-3-1 (25) | 0 |
| Lennox Lewis | 1998–01 | 32 | 1989–2004 | 40-2-1 (31) | 5 |
| Hasim Rahman | 2001 | 28 | 1994– | 35-4-0 (29) | 0 |
| Lennox Lewis† | 2001–04 | 36 | 1989–2004 | 41-2-1 (32) | 2 |
| Chris Byrd | 2002–06 | 35 | 1993– | 38-2-1 (20) | 3 |
| John Ruiz | 2001–03 | 31 | 1992– | 38-5-1 (28) | 2 |
| Roy Jones, Jr. | 2003 | 34 | 1989– | 49-3-0 (38) | 0 |
| John Ruiz | 2003–05 | 33 | 1992– | 41-6-1 (28) | 2 |
| Vitali Klitschko† | 2004–05 | 34 | 1996–2005; 2007– | 34-2-0 (33) | 1 |
| Hasim Rahman | 2005-06 | 33 | 1994– | 41-5-2 (33) | 1 |
| Oleg Maskaev | 2006-08 | 37 | 1993– | 32-5-0 (26) | 0 |
| Wladimir Klitschko | 2006– | 33 | 1996– | 53-3-0 (47) | 0 |
| Nikolay Valuev | 2005–07 | 32 | 1993– | 44-0-0 (32) | 1 |
| Ruslan Chagaev | 2007–08 | 28 | 2001 | 24-0-1 (17) | 1 |
| Samuel Peter | 2008 | 28 | 2004– | 30-2-0 (23) | 0 |
| Vitali Klitschko^ | 2008– | 38 | 1996–2005; 2007– | 38-2-0 (37) | 0 |
| Nikolay Valuev | 2008– | 36 | 1993– | 50-1-0 (34) | 0 |

*Age when boxer won world championship.
† Boxer retired or relinquished world title.
^ Boxer returned from retirement.

# Horse Racing

Jockey Calvin Borel won the
2009 Kentucky Oaks and
Preakness Stakes (above) on
filly Rachel Alexandra

# What a Long, Strange Trip

Jockey Calvin Borel rejuvenated the sport by winning the Derby and the Preakness on different mounts, but his unique Triple Crown quest fell short at Belmont

## BY CHRIS MANNIX

HYPE IS AN INTEGRAL PART OF any sport but few rely on the media buildup to generate interest more than horse racing. There was Smarty Jones's survival tale in 2004, Street Senses's '07 surge under venerable trainer Carl Nafzger and the powerful Big Brown's quest in '08 to etch his name in the history books as the greatest thoroughbred of all time. But in the weeks leading up to the 2009 Kentucky Derby, the only storylines that were emerging were negative ones. There was owner-breeder Ernie Paragallo's arrest in April on charges of cruelty to animals and reports that trainer Jeff Mullins was pumping one of his horses with performance enhancers during an April 4th race at Aqueduct, the track where another of his colts, early Derby favorite I Want Revenge, claimed a victory on that same day. Indeed, while the crowds were still predicted to gather in record numbers, many casual observers—who make up a sizeable chunk of the television audience—were left to wonder if any of the Triple Crown races were going to be worth watching.

However, as it has so many times before, the Derby quickly and emphatically injected life back into the sport. At 50–1, Mine That Bird was the longest of long shots in a rela-

tively anonymous 19-horse field. Trained in obscurity and driven to Churchill Downs in a cramped three-horse trailer that arrived 11 days before the start of the race, Mine That Bird was predicted by most experts to finish at the back of the pack. That's where he started, too, before making one of the most memorable surges in Derby history. With jockey Calvin Borel squeezing him through splinter-sized cracks along the rail, Mine That Bird passed 18 horses in 21 seconds and exploded down the stretch to win by 6¾ lengths, stunning the 153,563 in attendance with the largest margin of victory since 1946. Said 2008 Derby-winning jockey Kent Desormeaux, "It was one of the most patient, skilled rides ever."

In the wake of Mine That Bird's victory the attention shifted to his jockey. The Derby was Borel's second race of the weekend and it could be argued his least important. One day earlier Borel had saddled filly Rachel Alexandra to a staggering 20¼-lengths victory in the Kentucky Oaks. Now he was faced with a choice: Does he continue to ride Mine That Bird in the Preakness and pursue the elusive Triple Crown or does he try to make history and sit Rachel Alexandra? In the end, Borel chose the filly. "I got no choice," Borel said eight days before the Preakness. "She's the best horse I've ever ridden."

Borel's words proved prophetic. In front of a sparse crowd of 77,850 (down from last year's 112,222, after Pimilico instituted a no-BYOB rule), Rachel Alexandra opened a four-length lead going into the stretch and held off a late charge from (yes) Mine That Bird to become the first filly in 85 years to win the Preakness Stakes. "She's got so much determination," Borel said. "When you look in the filly's eyes, it's unbelievable. You win."

With the possibility of a traditional Triple Crown once again removed (31 years and counting), the racing world once again fixated on Borel. The diminutive jockey had already made history by winning the first two legs of the Triple Crown on different horses and by winning the Belmont Stakes he could secure his own version of the crown.

With Rachel Alexandra's owners bowing her out of the race, Borel was back on Mine That Bird, who had gone from a 50–1 long

**Riding 50–1 longshot Mine That Bird, jockey Calvin Borel came back from next to last to gallop home and win the '09 Kentucky Derby.**

shot at the Derby to a 6–5 favorite at Belmont. The buzz in New York grew louder when Mine That Bird jumped out to an early lead and was in front at the top of the homestretch. But the trademark burst that was Mine That Bird's staple in the Derby and Preakness was missing in the agonizing 1½-mile Belmont. Summer Bird caught up to Mine That Bird at the 16th pole and the colt that had captivated the nation for two months faded to a third-place finish. "He was a little bit too aggressive," explained Borel afterwards. "He wouldn't drop the bit."

Still, Mine That Bird's sudden rise to stardom had taught even the most casual of horse racing fans a valuable lesson, one that will likely be repeated for many years to come: A great race doesn't always need the hype.

## THOROUGHBRED RACING

### The Triple Crown

#### 135th Kentucky Derby

May 2, 2009. Grade I, 3-year-olds; 11th race, Churchill Downs, Louisville. All 126 lbs. Distance: 1¼ miles. Purse: $2,000,000 guaranteed. Track: Sloppy (sealed). Off: 6:28 p.m. Winner: Mine That Bird (By Birdstone out of Mining My Own by Smart Strike); Times: 0:22.98, 0:47.23, 1:12.09, 1:37.49, 2:02.66. Won: Driving. Breeder: Lamantia, Blackburn & Needham/Betz Thoroughbreds. Scratched: I Want Revenge.

| Horse | Finish-PP | Margin | Jockey/Trainer |
|---|---|---|---|
| Mine That Bird | 1–8 | 6¾ | Calvin Borel/Bennie "Chip" Woolley Jr. |
| Pioneerof the Nile | 2–15 | nose | Garrett Gomez/Bob Baffert |
| Musket Man | 3–2 | head | Eibar Coa/Derek Ryan |
| Papa Clem | 4–7 | 6 | Rafael Bejarano/Gary Stute |
| Chocolate Candy | 5–11 | head | Mike Smith/Jerry Hollendorfer |
| Summer Bird | 6–16 | 1¼ | Chris Rosier/Tim Ice |
| Join in the Dance | 7–9 | ½ | Chris DeCarlo/Todd Pletcher |
| Regal Ransom | 8–10 | ¾ | Alan Garcia/Saeed bin Suroor |
| West Side Bernie | 9–1 | 2 | Stewart Elliott/Kelly Breen |
| General Quarters | 10–12 | 1½ | Julien Leparoux/Thomas McCarthy |
| Dunkirk | 11–14 | 1½ | Edgar Prado/Todd Pletcher |
| Hold Me Back | 12–5 | ½ | Kent Desormeaux/Bill Mott |
| Advice | 13–4 | ¾ | Rene Douglas/Todd Pletcher |
| Desert Party | 14–18 | 1¼ | Ramon Dominguez/Saeed bin Suroor |
| Mr. Hot Stuff | 15–3 | 8½ | John Velazquez/Eoin Harty |
| Atomic Rain | 16–13 | 3½ | Joe Bravo/Kelly Breen |
| Nowhere to Hide | 17–17 | 7½ | Shaun Bridgmohan/Nick Zito |
| Friesan Fire | 18–6 | 1¼ | Gabriel Saez/Larry Jones |
| Flying Private | 19–19 | — | Robbie Albarado/D. Wayne Lukas |

#### 134th Preakness Stakes

May 16, 2009. Grade I, 3-year-olds; 12th race, Pimlico Race Course, Baltimore. All 126 lbs. Distance: 1³⁄₁₆ miles; Stakes value: $1,100,000. Track: Fast. Off: 6:15 p.m. Winner: Rachel Alexandra (By Medaglia d'Oro out of Lotta Kim by Roar); Times: 0:23.10, 0:46.71, 1:11.01, 1:35.82, 1:55.08. Won: Driving. Breeder: Dolphus Morrison

| Horse | Finish-PP | Margin | Jockey/Trainer |
|---|---|---|---|
| Rachel Alexandra | 1-13 | 1 | Calvin Borel/Steve Asmussen |
| Mine That Bird | 2–2 | ½ | Mike Smith/Bennie "Chip" Woolley Jr. |
| Musket Man | 3–3 | 2½ | Eibar Coa/Derek Ryan |
| Flying Private | 4–10 | 1½ | Alan Garcia/D. Wayne Lukas |
| Big Drama | 5–1 | 2¼ | John Velazquez/David Fawkes |
| Papa Clem | 6–7 | neck | Rafael Bejarano/Gary Stute |
| Terrain | 7–6 | ¾ | Jeremy Rose/Albert Stall Jr. |
| Luv Gov | 8–4 | 2¼ | Jamie Theriot/D. Wayne Lukas |
| General Quarters | 9–8 | 7¾ | Julien Leparoux/Thomas McCarthy |
| Friesan Fire | 10–5 | 7¼ | Gabriel Saez/Larry Jones |
| Pioneerof the Nile | 11–9 | 6¼ | Garrett Gomez/Bob Baffert |
| Tone It Down | 12–12 | ½ | Kent Desormeaux/William Kolmo |
| Take the Points | 13–11 | — | Edgar Prado/Todd Pletcher |

#### 141st Belmont Stakes

June 6, 2009. Grade I, 3-year-olds; 11th race, Belmont Park, Elmont, NY. All 126 lbs. Distance: 1½ miles. Stakes value: $1,000,000. Track: Fast. Off: 6:29 p.m. Winner: Summer Bird (By Birdstone out of Hong Kong Squall by Summer Squall); Times: 0:23.41, 47.13, 1:12.43, 1:37.86, 2:01.66, 2:27.54. Won: Driving. Breeder: K.K. and V.D. Jayamaran.

| Horse | Finish-PP | Margin | Jockey/Trainer |
|---|---|---|---|
| Summer Bird | 1–4 | 2¾ | Kent Desormeaux/Tim Ice |
| Dunkirk | 2–2 | neck | John Velazquez/Todd Pletcher |
| Mine That Bird | 3–7 | 3¾ | Calvin Borel/Bennie "Chip" Woolley Jr. |
| Charitable Man | 3–6 | 3¾ | Alan Garcia/Kiaran McLaughlin |
| Luv Gov | 5–5 | 4½ | Miguel Mena/D. Wayne Lukas |
| Flying Private | 6–8 | 2 | Julien Leparoux/D. Wayne Lukas |
| Brave Victory | 7–10 | 1¼ | Rajiv Maragh/Nick Zito |
| Mr. Hot Stuff | 9–3 | 7 | Edgar Prado/Eoin Harty |
| Chocolate Candy | 10–1 | 29¾ | Garrett Gomez/Jerry Hollendorfer |
| Miner's Escape | 10–9 | — | Jose Lezcano/Nick Zito |

## Late 2008

| Date | Race | Track | Distance | Winner | Trainer/Jockey | Purse ($) |
|---|---|---|---|---|---|---|
| Oct 4 | Champagne Stakes | Belmont | 1 mile | Vineyard Haven | R. Frankel/ E. Prado | 400,000 |
| Oct 4 | Shadwell Turf Mile | Keeneland | 1 mile | Thorn Song | D. Romans/ R. Albarado | 600,000 |
| Oct 4 | Indiana Derby | Hoosier | 1¹⁄₁₆ miles | Tin Cup Chalice | M. Lecesse/ P. Rodriguez | 514,100 |
| Oct 4 | Lane's End B. Futurity | Keeneland | 1¹⁄₁₆ miles | Square Eddie | J. Best/ R. Bejarano | 500,000 |
| Oct 4 | Frizette Stakes | Belmont | 1 mile | Sky Diva | S. Klesaris/ R. Dominguez | 400,000 |
| Oct 4 | First Lady Stakes | Keeneland | 1 mile | Vacare | C. Clement/ C. Nakatani | 432,000 |
| Oct 4 | E.P. Taylor Stakes | Woodbine | 1¼ miles | Folk Opera | S. B. Suroor/ L. Dettori | 936,352 |
| Oct 4 | Nearctic Stakes | Woodbine | 6 furlongs | True to Tradition | S. Lake/ K. Carmouche | 464,941 |
| Oct 4 | Pattison Canadian International | Woodbine | 1½ miles | Marsh Side | N. Drysdale/ J. Castellano | 1,851,250 |
| Oct 5 | Juddmonte Spinster Stakes | Keeneland | 1¼ miles | Carriage Trail | C. McGaughey/ K. Desormeaux | 500,000 |
| Oct 5 | Prix de L'Arc De Triomphe | Longchamp | 1½ miles | Zarkava | A. de Royer-Dupre/ C. Soumillon | 4,000,000 |
| Oct 11 | Queen Elizabeth II Challenge Cup | Keeneland | 1¹⁄₁₆ miles | Alwajeeha | J. Velazquez/ K. McLaughlin | 500,000 |
| Oct 24 | Breeders Cup Juvenile Fillies | Santa Anita | 1¹⁄₁₆ miles | Stardom Bound | C. Paasch/ M. Smith | 2,000,000 |
| Oct 24 | Breeders Cup Juvenile Fillies Turf | Santa Anita | 1 mile | Maram | C. Brown/ J. Lexcano | 1,000,000 |
| Oct 24 | Breeders Cup F & M Turf | Santa Anita | 1¼ miles | Forever Together | J. Sheppard/ J. Leparoux | 2,000,000 |
| Oct 24 | Breeders Cup Ladies' Classic | Santa Anita | 1¹⁄₈ miles | Zenyatta | J. Shirreffs/ M. Smith | 2,000,000 |
| Oct 25 | Breeders Cup F & M Sprint | Santa Anita | 7 furlongs | Ventura | R. Frankel/ R. Frankel | 1,000,000 |
| Oct 25 | Breeders Cup Classic | Santa Anita | 1¼ miles | Raven's Pass | J. Gosden/ F. Dettori | 4,580,000 |
| Oct 25 | Breeders Cup Turf | Santa Anita | 1½ miles | Conduit | M. Stoute/ R. Moore | 2,926,620 |
| Oct 25 | Breeders Cup Turf Sprint | Santa Anita | 6½ furlongs | Desert Code | D. Hofmans/ R. Migliore | 1,094,620 |
| Oct 25 | Breeders Cup Distaff | Santa Anita | 1¹⁄₈ miles | Ginger Punch | R. Frankel/ R. Bejarano | 2,070,160 |
| Oct 25 | Breeders Cup Mile | Santa Anita | 1 mile | Goldikova | F. Head/ O. Peslier | 1,951,080 |
| Oct 25 | Breeders Cup Dirt Mile | Santa Anita | 1 mile | Albertus Maximus | V. Cerin/ G. Gomez | 916,000 |
| Oct 25 | Breeders Cup Juvenile | Santa Anita | 1¹⁄₁₆ miles | Midshipman | B. Baffert/ G. Gomez | 1,951,080 |
| Oct 25 | Breeders Cup Juvenile Turf | Santa Anita | 1 miles | Donativum | J. Gosden/ F. Dettori | 1,035,080 |
| Oct 25 | Breeders Cup Sprint | Santa Anita | 6 furlongs | Mignight Lute | B. Baffert/ G. Gomez | 1,832,000 |
| Oct 25 | Breeders Cup Marathon | Santa Anita | 1½ miles | Muhannak | R. Beckett/ P. Smullen | 517,540 |
| Nov 23 | Clark Handicap | Churchill Downs | 1¹⁄₈ miles | Einstein | H. Pitts/ J. Leparoux | 440,400 |

### 2009

| Date | Race | Track | Distance | Winner | Trainer/Jockey | Purse ($) |
|---|---|---|---|---|---|---|
| Jan 24 | Sunshine Millions Classic | Gulfstream | 1¹⁄₈ miles | It's a Bird | M. Wolfson/ J. Leparoux | 1,000,000 |
| Jan 24 | Sunshine Millions Filly & Mare Sprint | Gulfstream | 6 furlongs | High Resolve | G. Gilchrist/ R. Albarado | 300,000 |
| Jan 24 | Sunshine Millions Filly & Mare Turf | Gulfstream | 1¹⁄₈ miles | Wild Promises | G. Gilchrist/ A. Gryder | 500,000 |
| Jan 24 | Sunshine Millions Dash | Gulfstream | 6 furlongs | This Ones For Phil | R. Dutrow Jr./ E. Prado | 250,000 |
| Jan 24 | Sunshine Millions Turf | Santa Anita | 1¹⁄₈ miles | Soldier's Dancer | D. Vivian/ R. Bejarano | 500,000 |

# Major Stakes Races (*Cont.*)

## 2009 (*Cont.*)

| Date | Race | Track | Distance | Winner | Trainer/Jockey | Purse ($) |
|---|---|---|---|---|---|---|
| Jan 24 | Sunshine Millions Distaff | Santa Anita | 1 1/16 miles | Leah's Secret | T. Pletcher/ E. Coa | 500,000 |
| Jan 24 | Sunshine Milions Sprint | Santa Anita | 6 furlongs | Georgie Boy | K. Walsh/ G. Gomez | 300,000 |
| Jan 24 | Sunshine Millions Oaks | Santa Anita | 6 furlongs | Beltene | J. Carava/ J. Rosario | 250,000 |
| Mar 3 | Santa Anita Handicap | Santa Anita | 1 1/4 miles | Einstein | H. Pitts Blasi J. Leparoux | 1,000,000 |
| Mar 3 | Santa Anita Oaks | Santa Anita | 1 1/16 miles | Stardom Bound | R. Frankel/ M. Smith | 300,000 |
| Mar 14 | Louisiana Derby | La. Fair Grounds | 1 1/16 miles | Friesan Fire | L. Jones/ G. Saez | 600,000 |
| Mar 14 | Fair Grounds Oaks | La. Fair Grounds | 1 1/16 miles | Rachel Alexandra | H. Wiggins/ C. Borel | 400,000 |
| Mar 14 | New Orleans Handicap | La. Fair Grounds | 1 1/8 miles | Macho Again | D. Stewart/ R. Albarado | 500,000 |
| Mar 14 | Mervyn Muniz Jr. Memorial Turf | La. Fair Grounds | 1 1/8 miles | Proudinsky | R. Frankel/ V. Espinoza | 500,000 |
| Mar 21 | Lane's End Stakes | Turfway | 1 1/8 miles | Hold Me Back | W. Mott/ K. Desormeaux | 500,000 |
| Mar 28 | Dubai World Cup | Nad al Sheba | 1 1/4 miles | Well Armed | E. Harty/ A. Gryder | 6,000,000 |
| Mar 28 | Dubai Duty Free Turf | Nad al Sheba | 1 1/8 miles | Gladiatorus | M. Shafya/ A. Ajtebi | 5,000,000 |
| Mar 28 | Dubai Sheema Classic | Nad al Sheba | 1 1/2 miles | Eastern Anthem | M. Shafa/ A. Ajtebi | 5,000,000 |
| Mar 28 | Dubai Golden Shaheen | Nad al Sheba | 6 furlongs | Big City Man | J. Barton/ J. Verenzuela | 2,000,000 |
| Mar 28 | UAE Derby | Nad al Sheba | 1 1/8 miles | Regal Ransom | S. bin Suroor/ A. Garcia | 2,000,000 |
| Mar 28 | Godolphin Mile | Nad al Sheba | 1 mile | Two Step Salsa | S. bin Suroor/ L. Dettori | 1,000,000 |
| Mar 28 | Florida Derby | Gulfstream | 1 1/8 miles | Quality Road | J. Jerkens/ J. Velazquez | 750,000 |
| Apr 4 | Wood Memorial Stakes | Aqueduct | 1 1/8 miles | I Want Revenge | J. Mullins/ J. Talamo | 750,000 |
| Apr 4 | Santa Anita Derby | Santa Anita | 1 1/8 miles | Pioneerof The Nile | B. Baffert/ G. Gomez | 750,000 |
| Apr 4 | Ashland Stakes | Keeneland | 1 1/16 miles | Hooh Why | D. Dupuy/ C. Lanerie | 400,000 |
| Apr 4 | Apple Blossom Handicap | Oaklawn | 1 1/16 miles | Seventh Street | K. McLaughlin/ R. Maragh | 490,000 |
| Apr 4 | Illinois Derby | Hawthorne | 1 1/8 miles | Musket Man | D. Ryan/ E. Coa | 500,000 |
| Apr 4 | Oaklawn Handicap | Oaklawn | 1 1/8 miles | It's a Bird | M. Wolfson/ J. Leparoux | 500,000 |
| Apr 11 | Blue Grass Stakes | Keeneland | 1 1/8 miles | General Quarters | T. McCarthy/ E. Coa | 750,000 |
| Apr 11 | Arkansas Derby | Oaklawn | 1 1/8 miles | Papa Clem | G. Stute/ R. Bejarano | 1,000,000 |
| Apr 18 | Charles Town Classic | Charles Town | 1 1/8 miles | Researcher | J. Runco/ K. Carmouche | 615,000 |
| May 1 | Kentucky Oaks | Churchill Downs | 1 1/8 miles | Rachel Alexandra | H. Wiggins/ C. Borel | 554,500 |
| May 2 | Kentucky Derby | Churchill Downs | 1 1/4 miles | Mine That Bird | B. Woolley/ C. Borel | 2,177,200 |
| May 2 | Woodford Reserve Turf Classic | Churchill Downs | 1 1/8 miles | Einstein | H. Pitts/ J. Leparoux | 557,600 |
| May 9 | Lone Star Derby | Lone Star | 1 1/16 miles | Mythical Power | B. Baffert/ V. Espinoza | 400,000 |
| May 16 | Preakness Stakes | Pimlico | 1 3/16 miles | Rachel Alexandra | S. Asmussen/ C. Borel | 1,100,000 |
| May 25 | Metropolitan Handicap | Belmont | 1 mile | Bribon | R. Ribaudo/ A. Garcia | 600,000 |
| May 25 | Lone Star Handicap | Lone Star | 1 1/16 miles | It's a Bird | M. Wolfson/ J. Leparoux | 400,000 |
| June 6 | Belmont Stakes | Belmont | 1 1/2 miles | Summer Bird | T. Ice/ K. Desormeaux | 1,000,000 |

## 2009 (through September 30 ) *(Cont.)*

| Date | Race | Track | Distance | Winner | Trainer/Jockey | Purse ($) |
|------|------|-------|----------|--------|----------------|-----------|
| June 6 | Just a Game Stakes | Belmont | 1 mile | Diamondrella | A. Penna Jr./ R. Maragh | 400,000 |
| June 6 | Manhattan Handicap Turf | Belmont | 1¼ miles | Gio Ponti | C. Clement/ G. Gomez | 400,000 |
| June 7 | Woodbine Oaks | Woodbine | 1⅛ miles | Milwaukee Appeal | S. Fairlie/ S. Elliott | 449,657 |
| June 13 | Stephen Foster Handicap | Churchill Downs | 1⅛ miles | Macho Again | D. Stewart/ R. Albarado | 660,000 |
| June 20 | Colonial Turf Cup | Colonial | 1³⁄₁₆ miles | Battle of Hastings | J. Mulins/ T. Baze | 500,000 |
| June 21 | Queen's Plate Stakes | Woodbine | 1¼ miles | Eye of the Leopard | M. Frostad/ E. DaSilva | 986,737 |
| July 4 | United Nations Stakes | Monmouth | 1⅜ miles | Presious Passion | M. Hartmann/ E. Trujillo | 750,000 |
| July 4 | Suburban Handicap | Belmont | 1¼ miles | Dry Martini | B. Tagg/ E. Prado | 400,000 |
| July 5 | American Oaks Inv'l Turf | Hollywood | 1¼ miles | Gozzip Girl | T. Albertrani/ K. Desormeaux | 700,000 |
| July 11 | Gold Cup Handicap | Hollywood | 1¼ miles | Rail trip | R. Ellis/ J. Valdiva Jr. | 700,000 |
| July 11 | Man O'War Stakes Turf | Belmont | 1⅜ miles | Gio Ponti | C. Clement/ R. Dominguez | 500,000 |
| July 12 | Prince of Wales Stakes | Fort Erie | 1³⁄₁₆ miles | Gallant | M. Casse/ C. Fraser | 429,351 |
| July 18 | Virginia Derby | Colonial Downs | 1¼ miles | Battle of Hastings | J. Mulins/ T. Baze | 750,000 |
| July 19 | Delaware Handicap | Delaware | 1¼ miles | Swift Temper | D. Romans/ A. Garcia | 1,000,350 |
| Aug 1 | Diana Stakes Turf | Saratoga | 1⅛ miles | Forever Together | J. Sheppard/ J. Leparoux | 500,000 |
| Aug 1 | Jim Dandy Stakes | Saratoga | 1⅛ miles | Kensei | S. Asmussen/ E. Prado | 500,000 |
| Aug 1 | West Virginia Derby | Mountaineer | 1⅛ miles | Soul Warrior | S. Asmussen/ D, Beckner | 750,000 |
| Aug 2 | Haskell Invitational | Monmouth | 1⅛ miles | Rachel Alexandra | S. Asmussen/ C. Borel | 1,000,000 |
| Aug 2 | Breeder's Stakes Turf | Woodbine | 1½ miles | Perfect Shower | R. Attfield/ J. Jones | 467,019 |
| Aug 8 | Arlington Million Stakes Turf | Arlington | 1¼ miles | Gio Ponti | C. Clement/ R. Dominguez | 1,000,000 |
| Aug 8 | Whitney Handicap | Saratoga | 1⅛ miles | Bullsbay | H. G. Motion/ J. Rose | 750,000 |
| Aug 8 | Beverly D. Stakes | Arlington | 1³⁄₁₆ miles | Dyanforce | W. Mott/ K. Desormeaux | 750,000 |
| Aug 8 | Secretariat Stakes | Arlington | 1¼ miles | Take The Points | T. Pletcher/ K. Desormeaux | 400,000 |
| Aug 15 | Sword Dancer Invitational | Saratoga | 1½ miles | Telling | S. Hobby/ J. Castellano | 500,000 |
| Aug 22 | Alabama Stakes | Saratoga | 1¼ miles | Careless Jewel | J. Carroll/ R. Landry | 600,000 |
| Aug 29 | Travers Stakes | Saratoga | 1¼ miles | Summer Bird | T. Ice/ K. Desormeaux | 1,000,000 |
| Aug 29 | Personal Ensign Stakes | Saratoga | 1¼ miles | Icon Project | M. Wolfson/ J. Leparoux | 400,000 |
| Sept 5 | Woodward Stakes | Saratoga | 1⅛ miles | Rachel Alexandra | S. Asmussen/ C. Borel | 750,000 |
| Sept 6 | Pacific Classic | Del Mar | 1¼ miles | Richard's Kid | B. Baffert/ M. Smith | 1,000,000 |
| Aug 31 | Del Mar Derby | Del Mar | 1⅛ miles | Madeo | J. Shireffs/ M. Smith | 350,000 |
| Sept 19 | Super Derby XXX | Louisiana Downs | 1⅛ miles | Regal Ransom | S. bin Suroor/ R. Migliore | 750,000 |
| Sept 20 | Woodbine Mile | Woodbine | 1 mile | Ventura | R. Frankel/ G. Gomez | 954,742 |
| Sept 20 | Northern Dancer Stakes Turf | Woodbine | 1½ miles | Just As Well | J. Sheppard/ J. Leparoux | 688,544 |
| Oct 3 | Jockey Club Gold Cup | Belmont | 1¼ miles | Summer Bird | T. Ice/ K. Desormeaux | 750,000 |

# FOR THE RECORD • Year by Year

## THOROUGHBRED RACING

### Kentucky Derby

Run at Churchill Downs, Louisville, KY, on the first Saturday in May.

| Year | Winner (Margin) | Jockey | Second | Third | Time |
|---|---|---|---|---|---|
| 1875 | Aristides (1) | Oliver Lewis | Volcano | Verdigris | 2:37¾ |
| 1876 | Vagrant (2) | Bobby Swim | Creedmoor | Harry Hill | 2:38¼ |
| 1877 | Baden-Baden (2) | William Walker | Leonard | King William | 2:38 |
| 1878 | Day Star (2) | Jimmie Carter | Himyar | Leveler | 2:37¼ |
| 1879 | Lord Murphy (1) | Charlie Shauer | Falsetto | Strathmore | 2:37 |
| 1880 | Fonso (1) | George Lewis | Kimball | Bancroft | 2:37½ |
| 1881 | Hindoo (4) | Jimmy McLaughin | Lelex | Alfambra | 2:40 |
| 1882 | Apollo (½) | Babe Hurd | Runnymede | Bengal | 2:40¼ |
| 1883 | Leonatus (3) | Billy Donohue | Drake Carter | Lord Raglan | 2:43 |
| 1884 | Buchanan (2) | Isaac Murphy | Loftin | Audrain | 2:40¼ |
| 1885 | Joe Cotton (Neck) | Erskine Henderson | Bersan | Ten Booker | 2:37¼ |
| 1886 | Ben Ali (½) | Paul Duffy | Blue Wing | Free Knight | 2:36½ |
| 1887 | Montrose (2) | Isaac Lewis | Jim Gore | Jacobin | 2:39¼ |
| 1888 | MacBeth II (1) | George Covington | Gallifet | White | 2:38¼ |
| 1889 | Spokane (Nose) | Thomas Kiley | Proctor Knott | Once Again | 2:34½ |
| 1890 | Riley (2) | Isaac Murphy | Bill Letcher | Robespierre | 2:45 |
| 1891 | Kingman (1) | Isaac Murphy | Balgowan | High Tariff | 2:52¼ |
| 1892 | Azra (Nose) | Alonzo Clayton | Huron | Phil Dwyer | 2:41½ |
| 1893 | Lookout (5) | Eddie Kunze | Plutus | Boundless | 2:39¼ |
| 1894 | Chant (2) | Frank Goodale | Pearl Song | Sigurd | 2:41 |
| 1895 | Halma (3) | Soup Perkins | Basso | Laureate | 2:37½ |
| 1896 | Ben Brush (Nose) | Willie Simms | Ben Eder | Semper Ego | 2:07¼ |
| 1897 | Typhoon II (Head) | Buttons Garner | Ornament | Dr. Catlett | 2:12½ |
| 1898 | Plaudit (Neck) | Willie Simms | Lieber Karl | Isabey | 2:09 |
| 1899 | Manuel (2) | Fred Taral | Corsini | Mazo | 2:12 |
| 1900 | Lieut. Gibson (4) | Jimmy Boland | Florizar | Thrive | 2:06¼ |
| 1901 | His Eminence (2) | Jimmy Winkfield | Sannazarro | Driscoll | 2:07¾ |
| 1902 | Alan-a-Dale (Nose) | Jimmy Winkfield | Inventor | The Rival | 2:08¾ |
| 1903 | Judge Himes (¾) | Hal Booker | Early | Bourbon | 2:09 |
| 1904 | Elwood (½) | Frankie Prior | Ed Tierney | Brancas | 2:08½ |
| 1905 | Agile (3) | Jack Martin | Ram's Horn | Layson | 2:10¾ |
| 1906 | Sir Huon (2) | Roscoe Troxler | Lady Navarre | James Reddick | 2:08⅕ |
| 1907 | Pink Star (2) | Andy Minder | Zal | Ovelando | 2:12⅗ |
| 1908 | Stone Street (1) | Arthur Pickens | Sir Cleges | Dunvegan | 2:15⅕ |
| 1909 | Wintergreen (4) | Vincent Powers | Miami | Dr. Barkley | 2:08⅕ |
| 1910 | Donau (½) | Fred Herbert | Joe Morris | Fighting Bob | 2:06⅖ |
| 1911 | Meridian (¾) | George Archibald | Governor Gray | Colston | 2:05 |
| 1912 | Worth (Neck) | Carroll H. Schilling | Duval | Flamma | 2:09⅖ |
| 1913 | Donerail (½) | Roscoe Goose | Ten Point | Gowell | 2:04⅘ |
| 1914 | Old Rosebud (8) | John McCabe | Hodge | Bronzewing | 2:03⅖ |
| 1915 | Regret (2) | Joe Notter | Pebbles | Sharpshooter | 2:05⅖ |
| 1916 | George Smith (Neck) | Johnny Loftus | Star Hawk | Franklin | 2:04 |
| 1917 | Omar Khayyam (2) | Charles Borel | Ticket | Midway | 2:04⅗ |
| 1918 | Exterminator (1) | William Knapp | Escoba | Viva America | 2:10⅘ |
| 1919 | Sir Barton (5) | Johnny Loftus | Billy Kelly | Under Fire | 2:09⅘ |
| 1920 | Paul Jones (Head) | Ted Rice | Upset | On Watch | 2:09 |
| 1921 | Behave Yourself (Head) | Charles Thompson | Black Servant | Prudery | 2:04⅕ |
| 1922 | Morvich (½) | Albert Johnson | Bet Mosie | John Finn | 2:04⅗ |
| 1923 | Zev (1½) | Earl Sande | Martingale | Vigil | 2:05⅖ |
| 1924 | Black Gold (½) | John Mooney | Chilhowee | Beau Butler | 2:05⅕ |
| 1925 | Flying Ebony (1½) | Earl Sande | Captain Hal | Son of John | 2:07⅗ |
| 1926 | Bubbling Over (5) | Albert Johnson | Bagenbaggage | Rock Man | 2:03⅗ |
| 1927 | Whiskery (Head) | Linus McAtee | Osmond | Jock | 2:06 |
| 1928 | Reigh Count (3) | Chick Lang | Misstep | Toro | 2:10⅖ |
| 1929 | Clyde Van Dusen (2) | Linus McAtee | Naishapur | Panchio | 2:10⅘ |
| 1930 | Gallant Fox (2) | Earl Sande | Gallant Knight | Ned O. | 2:07⅗ |
| 1931 | Twenty Grand (4) | Charles Kurtsinger | Sweep All | Mate | 2:01⅘ |

## Kentucky Derby *(Cont.)*

| Year | Winner (Margin) | Jockey | Second | Third | Time |
|---|---|---|---|---|---|
| 1932 | Burgoo King (5) | Eugene James | Economic | Stepenfetchit | 2:05⅕ |
| 1933 | Brokers Tip (Nose) | Don Meade | Head Play | Charley O. | 2:06⅘ |
| 1934 | Cavalcade (2½) | Mack Garner | Discovery | Agrarian | 2:04 |
| 1935 | Omaha (1½) | Willie Saunders | Roman Soldier | Whiskolo | 2:05 |
| 1936 | Bold Venture (Head) | Ira Hanford | Brevity | Indian Broom | 2:03⅗ |
| 1937 | War Admiral (1¾) | Charles Kurtsinger | Pompoon | Reaping Reward | 2:03⅕ |
| 1938 | Lawrin (1) | Eddie Arcaro | Dauber | Can't Wait | 2:04⅘ |
| 1939 | Johnstown (8) | James Stout | Challedon | Heather Broom | 2:03⅗ |
| 1940 | Gallahadion (1½) | Carroll Bierman | Bimelech | Dit | 2:05 |
| 1941 | Whirlaway (8) | Eddie Arcaro | Staretor | Market Wise | 2:01⅖ |
| 1942 | Shut Out (2½) | Wayne Wright | Alsab | Valdina Orphan | 2:04⅖ |
| 1943 | Count Fleet (3) | John Longden | Blue Swords | Slide Rule | 2:04 |
| 1944 | Pensive (4½) | Conn McCreary | Broadcloth | Stir Up | 2:04⅕ |
| 1945 | Hoop Jr. (6) | Eddie Arcaro | Pot o' Luck | Darby Dieppe | 2:07 |
| 1946 | Assault (8) | Warren Mehrtens | Spy Song | Hampden | 2:06⅗ |
| 1947 | Jet Pilot (Head) | Eric Guerin | Phalanx | Faultless | 2:06⅘ |
| 1948 | Citation (3½) | Eddie Arcaro | Coaltown | My Request | 2:05⅖ |
| 1949 | Ponder (3) | Steve Brooks | Capot | Palestinian | 2:04⅕ |
| 1950 | Middleground (1¼) | William Boland | Hill Prince | Mr. Trouble | 2:01⅗ |
| 1951 | Count Turf (4) | Conn McCreary | Royal Mustang | Ruhe | 2:02⅗ |
| 1952 | Hill Gail (2) | Eddie Arcaro | Sub Fleet | Blue Man | 2:01⅗ |
| 1953 | Dark Star (Head) | Hank Moreno | Native Dancer | Invigorator | 2:02 |
| 1954 | Determine (1½) | Ray York | Hasty Road | Hasseyampa | 2:03 |
| 1955 | Swaps (1½) | Bill Shoemaker | Nashua | Summer Tan | 2:01⅘ |
| 1956 | Needles (¾) | Dave Erb | Fabius | Come On Red | 2:03⅖ |
| 1957 | Iron Liege (Nose) | Bill Hartack | Gallant Man | Round Table | 2:02⅕ |
| 1958 | Tim Tam (½) | Ismael Valenzuela | Lincoln Road | Noureddin | 2:05 |
| 1959 | Tomy Lee (Nose) | Bill Shoemaker | Sword Dancer | First Landing | 2:02⅕ |
| 1960 | Venetian Way (3½) | Bill Hartack | Bally Ache | Victoria Park | 2:02⅖ |
| 1961 | Carry Back (¾) | John Sellers | Crozier | Bass Clef | 2:04 |
| 1962 | Decidedly (2¼) | Bill Hartack | Roman Line | Ridan | 2:00⅖ |
| 1963 | Chateaugay (1¼) | Braulio Baeza | Never Bend | Candy Spots | 2:01⅘ |
| 1964 | Northern Dancer (Neck) | Bill Hartack | Hill Rise | The Scoundrel | 2:00 |
| 1965 | Lucky Debonair (Neck) | Bill Shoemaker | Dapper Dan | Tom Rolfe | 2:01⅕ |
| 1966 | Kauai King (½) | Don Brumfield | Advocator | Blue Skyer | 2:02 |
| 1967 | Proud Clarion (1) | Bobby Ussery | Barbs Delight | Damascus | 2:00⅗ |
| 1968 | Forward Pass (Disq.) | Ismael Valenzuela | Francie's Hat | T.V. Commercial | 2:02⅕ |
| 1969 | Majestic Prince (Neck) | Bill Hartack | Arts and Letters | Dike | 2:01⅘ |
| 1970 | Dust Commander (5) | Mike Manganello | My Dad George | High Echelon | 2:03⅖ |
| 1971 | Canonero II (3¾) | Gustavo Avila | Jim French | Bold Reason | 2:03⅕ |
| 1972 | Riva Ridge (3¼) | Ron Turcotte | No Le Hace | Hold Your Peace | 2:01⅘ |
| 1973 | Secretariat (2½) | Ron Turcotte | Sham | Our Native | 1:59⅖ |
| 1974 | Cannonade (2¼) | Angel Cordero Jr. | Hudson County | Agitate | 2:04 |
| 1975 | Foolish Pleasure (1¾) | Jacinto Vasquez | Avatar | Diabolo | 2:02 |
| 1976 | Bold Forbes (1) | Angel Cordero Jr. | Honest Pleasure | Elocutionist | 2:01⅗ |
| 1977 | Seattle Slew (1¾) | Jean Cruguet | Run Dusty Run | Sanhedrin | 2:02⅕ |
| 1978 | Affirmed (1½) | Steve Cauthen | Alydar | Believe It | 2:01⅕ |
| 1979 | Spectacular Bid (2¾) | Ronald J. Franklin | General Assembly | Golden Act | 2:02⅖ |
| 1980 | Genuine Risk (1) | Jacinto Vasquez | Rumbo | Jaklin Klugman | 2:02 |
| 1981 | Pleasant Colony (¾) | Jorge Velasquez | Woodchopper | Partez | 2:02 |
| 1982 | Gato Del Sol (2½) | Eddie Delahoussaye | Laser Light | Reinvested | 2:02⅕ |
| 1983 | Sunny's Halo (2) | Eddie Delahoussaye | Desert Wine | Caveat | 2:02⅕ |
| 1984 | Swale (3¼) | Laffit Pincay Jr. | Coax Me Chad | At the Threshold | 2:02⅖ |
| 1985 | Spend A Buck (5) | Angel Cordero Jr. | Stephan's Odyssey | Chief's Crown | 2:00⅕ |
| 1986 | Ferdinand (2¼) | Bill Shoemaker | Bold Arrangement | Broad Brush | 2:02⅘ |
| 1987 | Alysheba (¾) | Chris McCarron | Bet Twice | Avies Copy | 2:03⅖ |
| 1988 | Winning Colors (Neck) | Gary Stevens | Forty Niner | Risen Star | 2:02⅕ |
| 1989 | Sunday Silence (2½) | Pat Valenzuela | Easy Goer | Awe Inspiring | 2:05 |
| 1990 | Unbridled (3½) | Craig Perret | Summer Squall | Pleasant Tap | 2:02 |
| 1991 | Strike the Gold (1¾) | Chris Antley | Best Pal | Mane Minister | 2:03 |
| 1992 | Lil E. Tee (1) | Pat Day | Casual Lies | Dance Floor | 2:03 |
| 1993 | Sea Hero (2½) | Jerry Bailey | Prairie Bayou | Wild Gale | 2:02⅖ |
| 1994 | Go for Gin (2½) | Chris McCarron | Strodes Creek | Blumin Affair | 2:03⅗ |
| 1995 | Thunder Gulch (2¼) | Gary Stevens | Tejano Run | Timber Country | 2:01⅕ |
| 1996 | Grindstone (Nose) | Jerry Bailey | Cavonnier | Prince of Thieves | 2:01 |
| 1997 | Silver Charm (Head) | Gary Stevens | Captain Bodgit | Free House | 2:02⅖ |

## Kentucky Derby *(Cont.)*

| Year | Winner (Margin) | Jockey | Second | Third | Time |
|---|---|---|---|---|---|
| 1998 | Real Quiet (½) | Kent Desormeaux | Victory Gallop | Indian Charlie | 2:02⅒ |
| 1999 | Charismatic (Neck) | Chris Antley | Menifee | Cat Thief | 2:03⅕ |
| 2000 | Fusaichi Pegasus (1½) | Kent Desormeaux | Aptitude | Impeachment | 2:01.12 |
| 2001 | Monarchos (4¾) | Jorge Chavez | Invisible Ink | Congaree | 1:59.97 |
| 2002 | War Emblem (4) | Victor Espinoza | Proud Citizen | Perfect Drift | 2:01.13 |
| 2003 | Funny Cide (1¾) | Jose Santos | Empire Maker | Peace Rules | 2:01.19 |
| 2004 | Smarty Jones (2¾) | Stewart Elliott | Lion Heart | Imperialism | 2:04.06 |
| 2005 | Giacomo (½) | Mike Smith | Closing Argument | Afleet Alex | 2:02.75 |
| 2006 | Barbaro (1½) | Edgar Prado | Bluegrass Cat | Steppenwolfer | 2:01.36 |
| 2007 | Street Sense (2¼) | Calvin Borel | Hard Spun | Curlin | 2:02.17 |
| 2008 | Big Brown (4¾) | Kent Desormeaux | Eight Belles | Denis of Cork | 2:01.82 |
| 2009 | Mine That Bird (6¾) | Calvin Borel | Pioneerof the Nile | Musket Man | 2:02.66 |

Note: Distance: 1½ miles (1875–95), 1¼ miles (1896–present).

## Preakness

Run at Pimlico Race Course, Baltimore, Md., two weeks after the Kentucky Derby.

| Year | Winner (Margin) | Jockey | Second | Third | Time |
|---|---|---|---|---|---|
| 1873 | Survivor (10) | G. Barbee | John Boulger | Artist | 2:43 |
| 1874 | Culpepper (¾) | W. Donohue | King Amadeus | Scratch | 2:56½ |
| 1875 | Tom Ochiltree (2) | L. Hughes | Viator | Bay Final | 2:43½ |
| 1876 | Shirley (4) | G. Barbee | Rappahannock | Algerine | 2:44¾ |
| 1877 | Cloverbrook (4) | C. Holloway | Bombast | Lucifer | 2:45½ |
| 1878 | Duke of Magenta (6) | C. Holloway | Bayard | Albert | 2:41¾ |
| 1879 | Harold (3) | L. Hughes | Jericho | Rochester | 2:40½ |
| 1880 | Grenada (¾) | L. Hughes | Oden | Emily F. | 2:40½ |
| 1881 | Saunterer (½) | T. Costello | Compensation | Baltic | 2:40½ |
| 1882 | Vanguard (Neck) | T. Costello | Heck | Col Watson | 2:44½ |
| 1883* | Jacobus (4) | G. Barbee | Parnell | | 2:42½ |
| 1884* | Knight of Ellerslie (2) | S. Fisher | Welcher | | 2:39½ |
| 1885 | Tecumseh (2) | Jim McLaughlin | Wickham | John C. | 2:49 |
| 1886 | The Bard (3) | S. Fisher | Eurus | Elkwood | 2:45 |
| 1887 | Dunboyne (1) | W. Donohue | Mahoney | Raymond | 2:39½ |
| 1888 | Refund (3) | F. Littlefield | Judge Murray | Glendale | 2:49 |
| 1889* | Buddhist (8) | W. Anderson | Japhet | * | 2:17½ |
| 1890* | Montague (3) | W. Martin | Philosophy | Barrister | 2:36¾ |
| 1894 | Assignee (3) | Fred Taral | Potentate | Ed Kearney | 1:49¼ |
| 1895 | Belmar (1) | Fred Taral | April Fool | Sue Kittie | 1:50½ |
| 1896 | Margrave (1) | H. Griffin | Hamilton II | Intermission | 1:51 |
| 1897 | Paul Kauvar (1½) | C. Thorpe | Elkins | On Deck | 1:51¼ |
| 1898 | Sly Fox (2) | C. W. Simms | The Huguenot | Nuto | 1:49⅗ |
| 1899 | Half Time (1) | R. Clawson | Filigrane | Lackland | 1:47 |
| 1900 | Hindus (Head) | H. Spencer | Sarmation | Ten Candles | 1:48⅖ |
| 1901 | The Parader (2) | F. Landry | Sadie S. | Dr. Barlow | 1:47⅕ |
| 1902 | Old England (Nose) | L. Jackson | Major Daingerfield | Namtor | 1:45⅘ |
| 1903 | Flocarline (½) | W. Gannon | Mackey Dwyer | Rightful | 1:44⅘ |
| 1904 | Bryn Mawr (1) | E. Hildebrand | Wotan | Dolly Spanker | 1:44⅕ |
| 1905 | Cairngorm (Head) | W. Davis | Kiamesha | Coy Maid | 1:45⅘ |
| 1906 | Whimsical (4) | Walter Miller | Content | Larabie | 1:45 |
| 1907 | Don Enrique (1) | G. Mountain | Ethon | Zambesi | 1:45⅖ |
| 1908 | Royal Tourist (4) | E. Dugan | Live Wire | Robert Cooper | 1:46⅖ |
| 1909 | Effendi (1) | Willie Doyle | Fashion Plate | Hilltop | 1:39⅘ |
| 1910 | Layminster (½) | R. Estep | Dalhousie | Sager | 1:40⅗ |
| 1911 | Watervale (1) | E. Dugan | Zeus | The Nigger | 1:51 |
| 1912 | Colonel Holloway (5) | C. Turner | Bwana Tumbo | Tipsand | 1:56⅗ |
| 1913 | Buskin (Neck) | J. Butwell | Kleburne | Barnegat | 1:53⅖ |
| 1914 | Holiday (¾) | A. Schuttinger | Brave Cunarder | Defendum | 1:53⅘ |
| 1915 | Rhine Maiden (1½) | Douglas Hoffman | Half Rock | Runes | 1:58 |
| 1916 | Damrosch (1½) | Linus McAtee | Greenwood | Achievement | 1:54⅘ |
| 1917 | Kalitan (2) | E. Haynes | Al M. Dick | Kentucky Boy | 1:54⅖ |
| 1918* | War Cloud (¾) | Johnny Loftus | Sunny Slope | Lanius | 1:53⅗ |
| 1918* | Jack Hare, Jr (2) | C. Peak | The Porter | Kate Bright | 1:53⅖ |
| 1919 | Sir Barton (4) | Johnny Loftus | Eternal | Sweep On | 1:53 |
| 1920 | Man o' War (1½) | Clarence Kummer | Upset | Wildair | 1:51⅗ |

## Preakness (*Cont.*)

| Year | Winner (Margin) | Jockey | Second | Third | Time |
|---|---|---|---|---|---|
| 1921 | Broomspun (¾) | F. Coltiletti | Polly Ann | Jeg | 1:54⅕ |
| 1922 | Pillory (Head) | L. Morris | Hea | June Grass | 1:51⅗ |
| 1923 | Vigil (1¼) | B. Marinelli | General Thatcher | Rialto | 1:53⅗ |
| 1924 | Nellie Morse (1½) | J. Merimee | Transmute | Mad Play | 1:57⅕ |
| 1925 | Coventry (4) | Clarence Kummer | Backbone | Almadel | 1:59 |
| 1926 | Display (Head) | J. Maiben | Blondin | Mars | 1:59⅘ |
| 1927 | Bostonian (½) | A. Abel | Sir Harry | Whiskery | 2:01⅗ |
| 1928 | Victorian (Nose) | Sonny Workman | Toro | Solace | 2:00⅕ |
| 1929 | Dr. Freeland (1) | Louis Schaefer | Minotaur | African | 2:01⅗ |
| 1930 | Gallant Fox (¾) | Earl Sande | Crack Brigade | Snowflake | 2:00⅗ |
| 1931 | Mate (1½) | G. Ellis | Twenty Grand | Ladder | 1:59 |
| 1932 | Burgoo King (Head) | E. James | Tick On | Boatswain | 1:59⅘ |
| 1933 | Head Play (4) | Charles Kurtsinger | Ladysman | Utopian | 2:02 |
| 1934 | High Quest (Nose) | R. Jones | Cavalcade | Discovery | 1:58⅕ |
| 1935 | Omaha (6) | Willie Saunders | Firethorn | Psychic Bid | 1:58⅖ |
| 1936 | Bold Venture (Nose) | George Woolf | Granville | Jean Bart | 1:59 |
| 1937 | War Admiral (Head) | Charles Kurtsinger | Pompoon | Flying Scot | 1:58⅖ |
| 1938 | Dauber (7) | M. Peters | Cravat | Menow | 1:59⅘ |
| 1939 | Challedon (1¼) | George Seabo | Gilded Knight | Volitant | 1:59⅘ |
| 1940 | Bimelech (3) | F. A. Smith | Mioland | Gallahadion | 1:58⅗ |
| 1941 | Whirlaway (5½) | Eddie Arcaro | King Cole | Our Boots | 1:58⅘ |
| 1942 | Alsab (1) | B. James | Requested | (dead heat | 1:57 |
| | | | Sun Again | for second) | |
| 1943 | Count Fleet (8) | Johnny Longden | Blue Swords | Vincentive | 1:57⅖ |
| 1944 | Pensive (¾) | Conn McCreary | Platter | Stir Up | 1:59⅕ |
| 1945 | Polynesian (2½) | W. D. Wright | Hoop Jr. | Darby Dieppe | 1:58⅘ |
| 1946 | Assault (Neck) | Warren Mehrtens | Lord Boswell | Hampden | 2:01⅖ |
| 1947 | Faultless (1¼) | Doug Dodson | On Trust | Phalanx | 1:59 |
| 1948 | Citation (5½) | Eddie Arcaro | Vulcan's Forge | Boyard | 2:02⅖ |
| 1949 | Capot (Head) | Ted Atkinson | Palestinian | Noble Impulse | 1:56 |
| 1950 | Hill Prince (5) | Eddie Arcaro | Middleground | Dooley | 1:59⅕ |
| 1951 | Bold (7) | Eddie Arcaro | Counterpoint | Alerted | 1:56⅖ |
| 1952 | Blue Man (3½) | Conn McCreary | Jampol | One Count | 1:57⅖ |
| 1953 | Native Dancer (Neck) | Eric Guerin | Jamie K. | Royal Bay Gem | 1:57⅘ |
| 1954 | Hasty Road (Neck) | Johnny Adams | Correlation | Hasseyampa | 1:57⅖ |
| 1955 | Nashua (1) | Eddie Arcaro | Saratoga | Traffic Judge | 1:54⅗ |
| 1956 | Fabius (¾) | Bill Hartack | Needles | No Regrets | 1:58⅖ |
| 1957 | Bold Ruler (2) | Eddie Arcaro | Iron Liege | Inside Tract | 1:56⅕ |
| 1958 | Tim Tam (1½) | I. Valenzuela | Lincoln Road | Gone Fishin' | 1:57⅕ |
| 1959 | Royal Orbit (4) | William Harmatz | Sword Dancer | Dunce | 1:57 |
| 1960 | Bally Ache (4) | Bobby Ussery | Victoria Park | Celtic Ash | 1:57⅗ |
| 1961 | Carry Back (¾) | Johnny Sellers | Globemaster | Crozier | 1:57⅗ |
| 1962 | Greek Money (Nose) | John Rotz | Ridan | Roman Line | 1:56⅕ |
| 1963 | Candy Spots (3½) | Bill Shoemaker | Chateaugay | Never Bend | 1:56⅕ |
| 1964 | Northern Dancer (2¼) | Bill Hartack | The Scoundrel | Hill Rise | 1:56⅘ |
| 1965 | Tom Rolfe (Neck) | Ron Turcotte | Dapper Dan | Hail to All | 1:56⅕ |
| 1966 | Kauai King (1¾) | Don Brumfield | Stupendous | Amberoid | 1:55⅖ |
| 1967 | Damascus (2¼) | Bill Shoemaker | In Reality | Proud Clarion | 1:55⅕ |
| 1968 | Forward Pass (6) | I. Valenzuela | Out of the Way | Nodouble | 1:56⅘ |
| 1969 | Majestic Prince (Head) | Bill Hartack | Arts and Letters | Jay Ray | 1:55⅗ |
| 1970 | Personality (Neck) | Eddie Belmonte | My Dad George | Silent Screen | 1:56⅕ |
| 1971 | Canonero II (1½) | Gustavo Avila | Eastern Fleet | Jim French | 1:54 |
| 1972 | Bee Bee Bee (1¼) | Eldon Nelson | No Le Hace | Key to the Mint | 1:55⅗ |
| 1973 | Secretariat (2½) | Ron Turcotte | Sham | Our Native | 1:54⅖ |
| 1974 | Little Current (7) | Miguel Rivera | Neapolitan Way | Cannonade | 1:54⅗ |
| 1975 | Master Derby (1) | Darrel McHargue | Foolish Pleasure | Diabolo | 1:56⅖ |
| 1976 | Elocutionist (3) | John Lively | Play the Red | Bold Forbes | 1:55 |
| 1977 | Seattle Slew (1½) | Jean Cruguet | Iron Constitution | Run Dusty Run | 1:54⅖ |
| 1978 | Affirmed (Neck) | Steve Cauthen | Alydar | Believe It | 1:54⅖ |
| 1979 | Spectacular Bid (5½) | Ron Franklin | Golden Act | Screen King | 1:54⅕ |
| 1980 | Codex (4¾) | Angel Cordero Jr. | Genuine Risk | Colonel Moran | 1:54⅕ |
| 1981 | Pleasant Colony (1) | Jorge Velasquez | Bold Ego | Paristo | 1:54⅗ |
| 1982 | Aloma's Ruler (½) | Jack Kaenel | Linkage | Cut Away | 1:55⅖ |
| 1983 | Deputed Testamony (2¾) | Donald Miller Jr. | Desert Wine | High Honors | 1:55⅖ |
| 1984 | Gate Dancer (1½) | Angel Cordero Jr. | Play On | Fight Over | 1:53⅗ |
| 1985 | Tank's Prospect (Head) | Pat Day | Chief's Crown | Eternal Prince | 1:53⅖ |
| 1986 | Snow Chief (4) | Alex Solis | Ferdinand | Broad Brush | 1:54⅘ |
| 1987 | Alysheba (½) | Chris McCarron | Bet Twice | Cryptoclearance | 1:55⅘ |

## Preakness (*Cont.*)

| Year | Winner (Margin) | Jockey | Second | Third | Time |
|---|---|---|---|---|---|
| 1988 | Risen Star (1¼) | E. Delahoussaye | Brian's Time | Winning Colors | 1:56⅕ |
| 1989 | Sunday Silence (Nose) | Pat Valenzuela | Easy Goer | Rock Point | 1:53⅘ |
| 1990 | Summer Squall (2¼) | Pat Day | Unbridled | Mister Frisky | 1:53⅗ |
| 1991 | Hansel (Head) | Jerry Bailey | Corporate Report | Mane Minister | 1:54 |
| 1992 | Pine Bluff (¾) | Chris McCarron | Alydeed | Casual Lies | 1:55⅗ |
| 1993 | Prairie Bayou (½) | Mike Smith | Cherokee Run | El Bakan | 1:56⅗ |
| 1994 | Tabasco Cat (¾) | Pat Day | Go For Gin | Concern | 1:56⅖ |
| 1995 | Timber Country (½) | Pat Day | Oliver's Twist | Thunder Gulch | 1:54⅖ |
| 1996 | Louis Quatorze (3¼) | Pat Day | Skip Away | Editor's Note | 1:53⅖ |
| 1997 | Silver Charm (Head) | Gary Stevens | Free House | Captain Bodgit | 1:54⅖ |
| 1998 | Real Quiet (2¼) | Kent Desormeaux | Victory Gallop | Classic Cat | 1:54⅗ |
| 1999 | Charismatic (1½) | Chris Antley | Menifee | Badge | 1:55⅕ |
| 2000 | Red Bullet (3¾) | Jerry Bailey | Fusaichi Pegasus | Impeachment | 1:56.04 |
| 2001 | Point Given (2¼) | Gary Stevens | A P Valentine | Congaree | 1:55.51 |
| 2002 | War Emblem (¾) | Victor Espinoza | Magic Weisner | Proud Citizen | 1:56.36 |
| 2003 | Funny Cide (9¾) | Jose Santos | Midway Road | Scrimshaw | 1:55.61 |
| 2004 | Smarty Jones (11½) | Stewart Elliott | Rock Hard Ten | Eddington | 1:55.59 |
| 2005 | Afleet Alex (7) | Jeremy Rose | Scrappy T | Giacomo | 1:55.04 |
| 2006 | Bernardini (5¼) | Javier Castellano | Sweetnorthernsaint | Hemingway's Key | 1:54.65 |
| 2007 | Curlin (Head) | Robby Albarado | Street Sense | Hard Spun | 1:53.46 |
| 2008 | Big Brown (5¼) | Kent Desormeaux | Macho Again | Icabad Crane | 1:54.80 |
| 2009 | Rachel Alexandra (1) | Calvin Borel | Mine That Bird | Musket Man | 1:55.08 |

*Preakness was a two-horse race in 1883, '84 and '89. It was not run 1891–1893; and in 1918, it was run in two divisions.

Note: Distance: 1½ miles (1873–88), 1¼ miles (1889), 1½ miles (1890), 1 1/16 miles (1894–1900), 1 mile and 70 yards (1901–1907), 1 1/16 miles (1908), 1 mile (1909–10), 1⅛ miles (1911–24), 1 3/16 miles (1925–present).

## Belmont

Run at Belmont Park, Elmont, NY, three weeks after the Preakness Stakes. Held previously at two locations in the Bronx (NY): Jerome Park (1867–1889) and Morris Park (1890–1904).

| Year | Winner (Margin) | Jockey | Second | Third | Time |
|---|---|---|---|---|---|
| 1867 | Ruthless (Head) | J. Gilpatrick | De Courcy | Rivoli | 3:05 |
| 1868 | General Duke (2) | R. Swim | Northumberland | Fannie Ludlow | 3:02 |
| 1869 | Fenian (Unknown) | C. Miller | Glenelg | Invercauld | 3:04¼ |
| 1870 | Kingfisher (½) | E. Brown | Foster | Midday | 2:59½ |
| 1871 | Harry Bassett (3) | W. Miller | Stockwood | By-the-Sea | 2:56 |
| 1872 | Joe Daniels (¾) | James Rowe | Meteor | Shylock | 2:58¼ |
| 1873 | Springbok (4) | James Rowe | Count d'Orsay | Strachino | 3:01¾ |
| 1874 | Saxon (Neck) | G. Barbee | Grinstead | Aaron Pennington | 2:39½ |
| 1875 | Calvin (2) | R. Swim | Aristides | Milner | 2:40¼ |
| 1876 | Algerine (Head) | W. Donahue | Fiddlestick | Barricade | 2:40½ |
| 1877 | Cloverbrook (1) | C. Holloway | Loiterer | Baden-Baden | 2:46 |
| 1878 | Duke of Magenta (2) | L. Hughes | Bramble | Sparta | 2:43½ |
| 1879 | Spendthrift (5) | S. Evans | Monitor | Jericho | 2:42¾ |
| 1880 | Grenada (½) | L. Hughes | Ferncliffe | Turenne | 2:47 |
| 1881 | Saunterer (Neck) | T. Costello | Eole | Baltic | 2:47 |
| 1882 | Forester (5) | James McLaughlin | Babcock | Wyoming | 2:43 |
| 1883 | George Kinney (2) | James McLaughlin | Trombone | Renegade | 2:42½ |
| 1884 | Panique (½) | James McLaughlin | Knight of Ellerslie | Himalaya | 2:42 |
| 1885 | Tyrant (3½) | Paul Duffy | St. Augustine | Tecumseh | 2:43 |
| 1886 | Inspector B (1) | James McLaughlin | The Bard | Linden | 2:41 |
| 1887* | Hanover (28-32) | James McLaughlin | Oneko | | 2:43½ |
| 1888* | Sir Dixon (12) | James McLaughlin | Prince Royal | | 2:40¼ |
| 1889 | Eric (Head) | W. Hayward | Diable | Zephyrus | 2:47 |
| 1890 | Burlington (1) | S. Barnes | Devotee | Padishah | 2:07¾ |
| 1891 | Foxford (Neck) | E. Garrison | Montana | Laurestan | 2:08¾ |
| 1892* | Patron (Unknown) | W. Hayward | Shellbark | | 2:17 |
| 1893 | Comanche (Head) | Willie Simms | Dr. Rice | Rainbow | 1:53¼ |
| 1894 | Henry of Navarre (2-4) | Willie Simms | Prig | Assignee | 1:56½ |
| 1895 | Belmar (Head) | Fred Taral | Counter Tenor | Nanki Pooh | 2:11½ |
| 1896 | Hastings (Neck) | H. Griffin | Handspring | Hamilton II | 2:24½ |
| 1897 | Scottish Chieftain (1) | J. Scherrer | On Deck | Octagon | 2:23¼ |
| 1898 | Bowling Brook (8) | P. Littlefield | Previous | Hamburg | 2:32 |
| 1899 | Jean Bereaud (Head) | R. R. Clawson | Half Time | Glengar | 2:23 |

## Belmont (*Cont.*)

| Year | Winner (Margin) | Jockey | Second | Third | Time |
|---|---|---|---|---|---|
| 1900 | Ildrim (Head) | N. Turner | Petrucio | Missionary | 2:21½ |
| 1901 | Commando (½) | H. Spencer | The Parader | All Green | 2:21 |
| 1902 | Masterman (2) | John Bullmann | Ranald | King Hanover | 2:22½ |
| 1903 | Africander (2) | John Bullmann | Whorler | Red Knight | 2:23⅕ |
| 1904 | Delhi (3½) | George Odom | Graziallo | Rapid Water | 2:06⅗ |
| 1905 | Tanya (1/2) | E. Hildebrand | Blandy | Hot Shot | 2:08 |
| 1906 | Burgomaster (4) | L. Lyne | The Quail | Accountant | 2:20 |
| 1907 | Peter Pan (1) | G. Mountain | Superman | Frank Gill | Unknown |
| 1908 | Colin (Head) | Joe Notter | Fair Play | King James | Unknown |
| 1909 | Joe Madden (8) | E. Dugan | Wise Mason | Donald MacDonald | 2:21⅗ |
| 1910* | Sweep (6) | J. Butwell | Duke of Ormonde | | 2:22 |
| 1913 | Prince Eugene (½) | Roscoe Troxler | Rock View | Flying Fairy | 2:18 |
| 1914 | Luke McLuke (8) | M. Buxton | Gainer | Charlestonian | 2:20 |
| 1915 | The Finn (4) | G. Byrne | Half Rock | Pebbles | 2:18⅖ |
| 1916 | Friar Rock (3) | E. Haynes | Spur | Churchill | 2:22 |
| 1917 | Hourless (10) | J. Butwell | Skeptic | Wonderful | 2:17⅘ |
| 1918 | Johren (2) | Frank Robinson | War Cloud | Cum Sah | 2:20⅖ |
| 1919 | Sir Barton (5) | Johnny Loftus | Sweep On | Natural Bridge | 2:17⅖ |
| 1920* | Man o' War (20) | Clarence Kummer | Donnacona | | 2:14⅕ |
| 1921 | Grey Lag (3) | Earl Sande | Sporting Blood | Leonardo II | 2:16⅘ |
| 1922 | Pillory (2) | C. H. Miller | Snob II | Hea | 2:18⅘ |
| 1923 | Zev (1½) | Earl Sande | Chickvale | Rialto | 2:19 |
| 1924 | Mad Play (2) | Earl Sande | Mr. Mutt | Modest | 2:18⅘ |
| 1925 | American Flag (8) | Albert Johnson | Dangerous | Swope | 2:16⅘ |
| 1926 | Crusader (1) | Albert Johnson | Espino | Haste | 2:32⅕ |
| 1927 | Chance Shot (1½) | Earl Sande | Bois de Rose | Flambino | 2:32⅖ |
| 1928 | Vito (3) | Clarence Kummer | Genie | Diavolo | 2:33⅕ |
| 1929 | Blue Larkspur (¾) | Mack Garner | African | Jack High | 2:32⅘ |
| 1930 | Gallant Fox (3) | Earl Sande | Whichone | Questionnaire | 2:31⅗ |
| 1931 | Twenty Grand (10) | Charles Kurtsinger | Sun Meadow | Jamestown | 2:29⅗ |
| 1932 | Faireno (1½) | T. Malley | Osculator | Flag Pole | 2:32⅘ |
| 1933 | Hurryoff (1½) | Mack Garner | Nimbus | Union | 2:32⅗ |
| 1934 | Peace Chance (6) | W. D. Wright | High Quest | Good Goods | 2:29⅕ |
| 1935 | Omaha (1½) | Willie Saunders | Firethorn | Rosemont | 2:30⅗ |
| 1936 | Granville (Nose) | James Stout | Mr. Bones | Hollyrood | 2:30 |
| 1937 | War Admiral (3) | Charles Kurtsinger | Sceneshifter | Vamoose | 2:28⅗ |
| 1938 | Pasteurized (Neck) | James Stout | Dauber | Cravat | 2:29⅖ |
| 1939 | Johnstown (5) | James Stout | Belay | Gilded Knight | 2:29⅗ |
| 1940 | Bimelech (¾) | F. A. Smith | Your Chance | Andy K | 2:29⅗ |
| 1941 | Whirlaway (2½) | Eddie Arcaro | Robert Morris | Yankee Chance | 2:31 |
| 1942 | Shut Out (2) | Eddie Arcaro | Alsab | Lochinvar | 2:29⅕ |
| 1943 | Count Fleet (25) | Johnny Longden | Fairy Manhurst | Deseronto | 2:28⅕ |
| 1944 | Bounding Home (½) | G. L. Smith | Pensive | Bull Dandy | 2:32⅕ |
| 1945 | Pavot (5) | Eddie Arcaro | Wildlife | Jeep | 2:30⅕ |
| 1946 | Assault (3) | Warren Mehrtens | Natchez | Cable | 2:30⅘ |
| 1947 | Phalanx (5) | R. Donoso | Tide Rips | Tailspin | 2:29⅖ |
| 1948 | Citation (8) | Eddie Arcaro | Better Self | Escadru | 2:28⅕ |
| 1949 | Capot (½) | Ted Atkinson | Ponder | Palestinian | 2:30⅕ |
| 1950 | Middleground (1) | William Boland | Lights Up | Mr. Trouble | 2:28⅗ |
| 1951 | Counterpoint (4) | D. Gorman | Battlefield | Battle Morn | 2:29 |
| 1952 | One Count (2½) | Eddie Arcaro | Blue Man | Armageddon | 2:30⅕ |
| 1953 | Native Dancer (Neck) | Eric Guerin | Jamie K. | Royal Bay Gem | 2:38⅗ |
| 1954 | High Gun (Neck) | Eric Guerin | Fisherman | Limelight | 2:30⅘ |
| 1955 | Nashua (9) | Eddie Arcaro | Blazing Count | Portersville | 2:29 |
| 1956 | Needles (Neck) | David Erb | Career Boy | Fabius | 2:29⅘ |
| 1957 | Gallant Man (8) | Bill Shoemaker | Inside Tract | Bold Ruler | 2:26⅗ |
| 1958 | Cavan (6) | Pete Anderson | Tim Tam | Flamingo | 2:30⅕ |
| 1959 | Sword Dancer (¾) | Bill Shoemaker | Bagdad | Royal Orbit | 2:28⅖ |
| 1960 | Celtic Ash (5½) | Bill Hartack | Venetian Way | Disperse | 2:29⅗ |
| 1961 | Sherluck (2¼) | Braulio Baeza | Globemaster | Guadalcanal | 2:29⅕ |
| 1962 | Jaipur (Nose) | Bill Shoemaker | Admiral's Voyage | Crimson Satan | 2:28⅘ |
| 1963 | Chateaugay (2½) | Braulio Baeza | Candy Spots | Choker | 2:30⅕ |
| 1964 | Quadrangle (2) | Manuel Ycaza | Roman Brother | Northern Dancer | 2:28⅖ |
| 1965 | Hail to All (Neck) | John Sellers | Tom Rolfe | First Family | 2:28⅖ |
| 1966 | Amberold (2½) | William Boland | Buffle | Advocator | 2:29⅗ |
| 1967 | Damascus (2½) | Bill Shoemaker | Cool Reception | Gentleman | 2:28⅘ |

## Belmont *(Cont.)*

| Year | Winner (Margin) | Jockey | Second | Third | Time |
|---|---|---|---|---|---|
| 1968 | Stage Door Johnny (1¼) | Hellodoro Gustines | Forward Pass | James Call Me Prince | 2:27⅕ |
| 1969 | Arts and Letters (5½) | Braulio Baeza | Majestic Prince | Dike | 2:28⅘ |
| 1970 | High Echelon (¾) | John L. Rotz | Needles N Pins | Naskra | 2:34 |
| 1971 | Pass Catcher (¾) | Walter Blum | Jim French | Bold Reason | 2:30⅖ |
| 1972 | Riva Ridge (7) | Ron Turcotte | Ruritania | Cloudy Dawn | 2:28 |
| 1973 | Secretariat (31) | Ron Turcotte | Twice a Prince | My Gallant | 2:24 |
| 1974 | Little Current (7) | Miguel A. Rivera | Jolly Johu | Cannonade | 2:29⅕ |
| 1975 | Avatar (Neck) | Bill Shoemaker | Foolish Pleasure | Master Derby | 2:28⅕ |
| 1976 | Bold Forbes (Neck) | Angel Cordero Jr. | McKenzie Bridge | Great Contractor | 2:29 |
| 1977 | Seattle Slew (4) | Jean Cruguet | Run Dusty Run | Sanhedrin | 2:29⅗ |
| 1978 | Affirmed (Head) | Steve Cauthen | Alydar | Darby Creek Road | 2:26⅘ |
| 1979 | Coastal (3¼) | Ruben Hernandez | Golden Act | Spectacular Bid | 2:28⅗ |
| 1980 | Temperence Hill (2) | Eddie Maple | Genuine Risk | Rockhill Native | 2:29⅘ |
| 1981 | Summing (Neck) | George Martens | Highland Blade | Pleasant Colony | 2:29 |
| 1982 | Conquistador Cielo (14½) | Laffit Pincay, Jr. | Gato Del Sol | Illuminate | 2:28⅕ |
| 1983 | Caveat (3½) | Laffit Pincay Jr. | Slew o'Gold | Barberstown | 2:27⅘ |
| 1984 | Swale (4) | Laffit Pincay Jr. | Pine Circle | Morning Bob | 2:27⅕ |
| 1985 | Creme Fraiche (½) | Eddie Maple | Stephan's Odyssey | Chief's Crown | 2:27 |
| 1986 | Danzig Connection (1¼) | Chris McCarron | Johns Treasure | Ferdinand | 2:29⅘ |
| 1987 | Bet Twice (14) | Craig Perret | Cryptoclearance | Gulch | 2:28⅕ |
| 1988 | Risen Star (14¾) | Eddie Delahoussaye | Kingpost | Brian's Time | 2:26⅖ |
| 1989 | Easy Goer (8) | Pat Day | Sunday Silence | Le Voyageur | 2:26 |
| 1990 | Go and Go (8¼) | Michael Kinane | Thirty Six Red | Baron de Vaux | 2:27⅕ |
| 1991 | Hansel (Head) | Jerry Bailey | Strike the Gold | Mane Minister | 2:28 |
| 1992 | A.P. Indy (¾) | Eddie Delahoussaye | My Memoirs | Pine Bluff | 2:26 |
| 1993 | Colonial Affair (2¼) | Julie Krone | Kissin Kris | Wild Gale | 2:29⅘ |
| 1994 | Tabasco Cat (2) | Pat Day | Go For Gin | Strodes Creek | 2:26⅘ |
| 1995 | Thunder Gulch (2) | Gary Stevens | Star Standard | Citadeed | 2:32 |
| 1996 | Editor's Note (1) | Rene Douglas | Skip Away | My Flag | 2:28⅘ |
| 1997 | Touch Gold (¾) | Chris McCarron | Silver Charm | Free House | 2:28⅘ |
| 1998 | Victory Gallop (Nose) | Gary Stevens | Real Quiet | Thomas Jo | 2:28⅘ |
| 1999 | Lemon Drop Kid (Head) | Jose Santos | Vision and Verse | Charismatic | 2:27⅘ |
| 2000 | Commendable (1½) | Pat Day | Aptitude | Unshaded | 2:31.19 |
| 2001 | Point Given (12¼ ) | Gary Stevens | A P Valentine | Monarchos | 2:26.56 |
| 2002 | Sarava (½) | Edgar Prado | Medaglia d'Oro | Sunday Break | 2:29.71 |
| 2003 | Empire Maker (¾) | Jerry Bailey | Ten Most Wanted | Funny Cide | 2:28.26 |
| 2004 | Birdstone (1) | Edgar Prado | Smarty Jones | Royal Assault | 2:27.59 |
| 2005 | Afleet Alex(4¾) | Jeremy Rose | Andromeda's Hero | Nolan's Cat | 2:28.75 |
| 2006 | Jazil (1¼) | Fernando Jara | Bluegrass Cat | Sunriver | 2:27.86 |
| 2007 | Rags to Riches (Head) | John Velazquez | Curlin | Tiago | 2:28.74 |
| 2008 | Da' Tara (5¼) | Alan Garcia | Denis of Cork | Ready's Echo | 2:29.65 |
| 2009 | Summer Bird (2¾) | Kent Desormeaux | Dunkirk | Mine That Bird | 2:27.54 |

*Belmont was a two-horse race in 1887, '88, '92, 1910 and '20; and was not held in 1911–1912.

Note: Distance: 1 mile 5 furlongs (1867–89), 1¼ miles (1890–1905), 1⅜ miles (1906–25), 1½ miles (1926–present).

## Triple Crown Winners

| Year | Horse | Jockey | Owner | Trainer |
|---|---|---|---|---|
| 1919 | Sir Barton | John Loftus | J. K. L. Ross | H. G. Bedwell |
| 1930 | Gallant Fox | Earle Sande | Belair Stud | James Fitzsimmons |
| 1935 | Omaha | William Saunders | Belair Stud | James Fitzsimmons |
| 1937 | War Admiral | Charles Kurtsinger | Samuel D. Riddle | George Conway |
| 1941 | Whirlaway | Eddie Arcaro | Calumet Farm | Ben Jones |
| 1943 | Count Fleet | John Longden | Mrs J. D. Hertz | Don Cameron |
| 1946 | Assault | Warren Mehrtens | King Ranch | Max Hirsch |
| 1948 | Citation | Eddie Arcaro | Calumet Farm | Jimmy Jones |
| 1973 | Secretariat | Ron Turcotte | Meadow Stable | Lucien Laurin |
| 1977 | Seattle Slew | Jean Cruguet | Karen L. Taylor | William H. Turner Jr. |
| 1978 | Affirmed | Steve Cauthen | Harbor View Farm | Laz Barrera |

Motor Sports

After a rocky start to 2009,
Helio Castroneves found
redemption at the Indy 500

3

FRED VUICH

# Big Comebacks, On and Off Track

In 2009, redemption was the theme for the victorious drivers at Indy and Daytona, but thanks to the economy, NASCAR and Formula One suffered through down seasons.

## BY MARK BEECH

NOT EVEN THE SPECTRE OF the slumping global economy could hold back the tears of joy that flowed this year at Indianapolis and Daytona. The two biggest days in American racing ended in drastically different ways—steady rain washed out Daytona after 380 miles—but both redeemed their respective champions. Not bad for nearly 1,000 miles of all out driving.

The season's most compelling moment occurred at the 93rd running of the Indy 500 on May 24, where two-time race winner Helio Castroneves roared to a victory that reclaimed both his personal reputation, as well as his status as one of the best drivers in the sport's history. A month earlier, the Brazilian native had been found not guilty by a Miami jury on six counts of tax evasion, a result that brought an end to six months of agonizing limbo. Facing up to 35 years in prison, his life and career were in jeopardy. The 5'7", 145-pound Castroneves lost 12 pounds during his ordeal, and missed the first two races of the IndyCar season. "I've been through a hurricane and survived," he told *Sports Illustrated* last May. "I feel like the luckiest man alive."

Lucky and fast. Along with his Penske Racing teammate Ryan Briscoe, Castroneves, 35, dominated the Indy speed charts for the better part of a month, winning the pole with an average speed of 224.864 miles per hour. And he won going away, leading 66 laps en route to his third 500 win. Castroneves's victory was also the 15th for 72-year-old team owner Roger Penske, a record in the sport. "This one might be the most special of all because it closes the book on everything that Helio has gone through," he told *SI* afterwards.

In NASCAR, the hype going into the season-opening Daytona 500 concerned Jimmie Johnson's quest to win a record fourth-straight Sprint Cup title. But the only thing anybody was talking about afterwards was Matt Kenseth's first victory in the Great American Race. The 2003 Cup champion, coming off his worst career finish in the Chase for the Cup (11th), was mired in a 36-race winless streak. His career seemed on the decline. "I'm tired of not winning," he told his wife Katie before the race. "Maybe I'm starting to lose it."

Kenseth took the lead with 54 laps remaining on the 2.5-mile speedway and hit the pits with the lead under the yellow caution flag when the rain began to fall. He then waited 20 minutes for NASCAR to call the race and and declare him the winner, at which point the normally reserved 36-year-old Wisconsin native began to weep.

The spotlight for most of the Cup season

FRED VUICH

focused on Tony Stewart, whose new Stewart-Haas Racing team was an instant sensation. In a year during which the economy forced more contraction in NASCAR than at any time in recent memory, Stewart-Haas was an expansion sensation. Stewart, a two-time Cup champ, won three of the year's first 26 races and led the points standings for more than three months.

Another driver who enjoyed a superlative campaign was 50-year-old Mark Martin. Racing for powerful Hendrick Motorsports, Martin gave hope to senior citizens everywhere, winning a series-best four races heading into the Chase in pursuit of his first Cup title. "He is a phenomenon," team owner Rick Hendrick told *SI* in June.

The big story in Formula One last season should have been the emergence of U.K driver Jenson Button, a virtual unknown who won six of the year's first seven races. Instead, F/1 was plagued by dissent and scandal. Upset over a proposal by FIA president Max Mosely to cap spending in 2010, eight teams, including Ferrari and McLaren, threatened to form their own circuit. The split was avoided when Mosely abandoned the plan and announced his intention to step down following the season.

But more trouble was in store. In September, FIA slammed Renault with a two-year

**In 2009, Matt Kenseth (17) won his first Daytona 500, but thanks to the rain, he claimed his victory sitting on pit road.**

suspended ban from the F/1 World Championships after the manufacturer admitted to charges of race fixing, including an incident where the team ordered Nelson Piquet Jr. to wreck during the 2008 Singapore Grand Prix in order to allow Fernando Alonso to win.

Back home in IndyCar, Danica Patrick—she of the one career victory and the sky-high Q-rating—flirted for most of the season with a move to NASCAR. She even went so far as to pay a visit to the Stewart-Haas racing shop. Though she signed a three-year deal with her Andretti-Green team in September, the door seemed to remain open for her to compete in upcoming seasons on a limited basis in NASCAR's Nationwide Series.

After Patrick's visit to his race shop, Stewart said he could "pretty much guarantee at some point she's going to be in [NASCAR]." He went on to add, "I know that she's serious about it. "She looked me straight in the eye and said, 'This is what I want to do. It looks like a lot of work, but it looks like fun.' I don't think she has some misguided idea that it's going to be easy. She wants to do it the right way."

## Indy Racing League

### Indianapolis 500

Results of the 93rd running of the Indianapolis 500 and fourth race of the 2009 Indy Racing League season. Held Sunday, May 24, 2009, at the 2.5-mile Indianapolis Motor Speedway in Indianapolis, Indiana. Distance, 500 miles; starters, 33; winning time of race, 3 hours, 19 mins., 34.6427 seconds; average speed, 150.318 mph; margin of victory, 1.9819 seconds; caution flags, 8 for 61 laps; lead changes, six among four drivers.

#### TOP 10 FINISHERS

| Pos. | Driver (start pos.) | C/E/T | Qual. Speed | Laps | Status |
|------|---------------------|-------|-------------|------|--------|
| 1 | Helio Castroneves (1) | D/H/F | 224.864 | 200 | running |
| 2 | Dan Wheldon (18) | D/H/F | 222.777 | 200 | running |
| 3 | Danica Patrick (10) | D/H/F | 222.822 | 200 | running |
| 4 | Townsend Bell (24) | D/H/F | 221.195 | 200 | running |
| 5 | Will Power (9) | D/H/F | 223.028 | 200 | running |
| 6 | Scott Dixon (5) | D/H/F | 223.867 | 200 | running |
| 7 | Dario Franchitti (3) | D/H/F | 224.010 | 200 | running |
| 8 | Ed Carpenter (17) | D/H/F | 222.780 | 200 | running |
| 9 | Paul Tracy (13) | D/H/F | 223.111 | 200 | running |
| 10 | Hideki Mutoh (16) | D/H/F | 222.805 | 200 | running |

### 2009 Indy Racing League Results

| Date | Race | Winner (start pos.) | C/E/T | Qual. Speed |
|------|------|---------------------|-------|-------------|
| Apr 5 | Grand Prix of St. Petersburg | Ryan Briscoe (4) | D/H/F | 103.564 |
| Apr 19 | Grand Prix of Long Beach | Dario Franchitti (2) | D/H/F | 101.403 |
| Apr 27 | Kansas 300 | Scott Dixon (4) | D/H/F | 210.368 |
| May 24 | Indianapolis 500 | Helio Castroneves (1) | D/H/F | 224.864 |
| May 31 | Milwaukee 225 | Scott Dixon (4) | D/H/F | 167.089 |
| June 6 | Texas 550 | Helio Castroneves (4) | D/H/F | 214.228 |
| June 21 | Iowa 250 | Dario Franchitti (4) | D/H/F | 0.000† |
| June 27 | Richmond 300* | Scott Dixon (2) | D/H/F | 166.638 |
| July 5 | Grand Prix of Watkins Glen | Justin Wilson (2) | D/H/F | 135.841 |
| July 12 | Toronto 200 | Dario Franchitti (1) | D/H/F | 103.532 |
| July 26 | Edmonton 95* | Will Power (1) | D/H/F | 116.414 |
| Aug 1 | Kentucky 300 | Ryan Brisoce (3) | D/H/F | 0.000† |
| Aug 9 | Mid-Ohio 200 | Scott Dixon (3) | D/H/F | 121.282 |
| Aug 23 | Sonoma Grand Prix | Dario Franchitti (1) | D/H/F | 107.955 |
| Aug 29 | Chicago 300 | Ryan Briscoe (1) | D/H/F | 215.364 |
| Sept 19 | Japan 300 | Scott Dixon (1) | D/H/F | 202.031 |
| Oct 10 | Miami 300 | Dario Franchitti (1) | D/H/F | 212.696 |

Note: Distances are in miles unless followed by * (laps). †Qualification round rained out.

### 2009 Final IRL Standings

| Driver | Pts |
|--------|-----|
| Dario Franchitti | 616 |
| Scott Dixon | 605 |
| Ryan Briscoe | 604 |
| Helio Castroneves | 433 |
| Danica Patrick | 393 |
| Tony Kanaan | 386 |
| Graham Rahal | 385 |
| Marco Andretti | 380 |
| Justin Wilson | 354 |
| Dan Wheldon | 354 |
| Hideki Mutoh | 353 |
| Ed Carpenter | 321 |

## Daytona 500†

Results of the 51st Daytona 500, the opening round of the 2009 Sprint Cup series. Held Sunday, February 15, 2009, at the 2.5-mile high-banked Daytona International Speedway. Distance, 500 miles; starters, 43; winning time of race, 2:15.40; average speed, 132.816 mph; margin of victory, caution; caution flags, 8 for 35 laps; lead changes, 9. -

†Note: race called after 152 laps because of inclement weather.

### TOP 10 FINISHERS

| Pos. | Driver (start pos.) | Car | Laps | Winnings ($) |
|---|---|---|---|---|
| 1 | Matt Kenseth (39) | Ford | 152 | 1,530,390 |
| 2 | Kevin Harvick (32) | Chevrolet | 152 | 1,115,720 |
| 3 | A.J. Allmendinger (20) | Dodge | 152 | 786,563 |
| 4 | Clint Bowyer (22) | Chevrolet | 152 | 632,013 |
| 5 | Elliott Sadler (30) | Dodge | 152 | 515,113 |
| 6 | David Regan (33) | Ford | 152 | 412,163 |
| 7 | Michael Waltrip (27) | Toyota | 152 | 371,238 |
| 8 | Tony Stewart (5) | Chevrolet | 152 | 371,371 |
| 9 | Reed Sorenson (34) | Dodge | 152 | 362,324 |
| 10 | Kurt Busch (13) | Dodge | 152 | 325,713 |

## 2008 Sprint Chase for the Cup* Final Season Standings

| Driver | Pts | Starts | Wins | Top 5 | Top 10 |
|---|---|---|---|---|---|
| Jimmie Johnson | 6684 | 36 | 7 | 15 | 22 |
| Carl Edwards | 6615 | 36 | 9 | 19 | 27 |
| Greg Biffle | 6467 | 36 | 2 | 12 | 17 |
| Kevin Harvick | 6408 | 36 | 0 | 7 | 19 |
| Clint Bowyer | 6381 | 36 | 1 | 7 | 17 |
| Jeff Burton | 6335 | 36 | 2 | 7 | 18 |
| Jeff Gordon | 6316 | 36 | 0 | 13 | 19 |
| Denny Hamlin | 6214 | 36 | 1 | 12 | 18 |
| Tony Stewart | 6202 | 36 | 1 | 10 | 16 |
| Kyle Busch | 6186 | 36 | 8 | 17 | 21 |
| Matt Kenseth | 6184 | 36 | 0 | 9 | 20 |
| Dale Earnhardt Jr. | 6127 | 36 | 1 | 10 | 16 |

## 2008 Sprint Cup* Final Season Driver Winnings

| Driver | Winnings ($) |
|---|---|
| Carl Edwards | 8,095,200 |
| Jimmie Johnson | 7,354,860 |
| Kyle Busch | 6,617,590 |
| Kasey Kahne | 6,272,460 |
| Tony Stewart | 6,268,430 |
| Ryan Newman | 6,179,560 |
| Jeff Gordon | 5,944,140 |
| Kevin Harvick | 5,603,650 |
| Jeff Burton | 5,542,180 |
| Denny Hamlin | 5,494,360 |
| Greg Biffle | 4,906,160 |
| Bobby Labonte | 4,668,830 |

## 2009 Sprint Chase for the Cup Late-Season Standings†

| Driver | Pts | Starts | Wins | Top 5 | Top 10 |
|---|---|---|---|---|---|
| Jimmie Johnson | 5728 | 30 | 5 | 12 | 19 |
| Mark Martin | 5716 | 30 | 5 | 12 | 18 |
| Juan Pablo Montoya | 5670 | 30 | 0 | 6 | 16 |
| Tony Stewart | 5644 | 30 | 4 | 15 | 21 |
| Jeff Gordon | 5623 | 30 | 1 | 14 | 21 |
| Kurt Busch | 5607 | 30 | 1 | 8 | 17 |
| Greg Biffle | 5540 | 30 | 0 | 9 | 14 |
| Carl Edwards | 5536 | 30 | 0 | 7 | 13 |
| Denny Hamlin | 5509 | 30 | 2 | 11 | 16 |
| Ryan Newman | 5505 | 30 | 0 | 5 | 14 |
| Kasey Kahne | 5422 | 30 | 2 | 5 | 12 |
| Brian Vickers | 5377 | 30 | 1 | 4 | 13 |

*Series name changed from Winston Cup to Nextel Cup after 2003 season, then to Sprint Cup beginning in 2008.
†2009 Sprint Chase for the Cup standings through October 11, 2009 (30 of 36 races).

# 2008-09 NASCAR Sprint Cup Results

## Late 2008 Sprint Cup Series Results

| Date | Track/Distance | Winner (start pos.) | Car | Laps | Winnings ($) |
|------|----------------|---------------------|-----|------|--------------|
| *Oct 11..........Charlotte 500 | | Jeff Burton (4) | Chevrolet | 334 | 280,208 |
| *Oct 19..........Martinsville 500 | | Jimmie Johnson (1) | Chevrolet504 | 121,975 | |
| *Oct 26..........Atlanta 500 | | Carl Edwards (4) | Ford325 | 357,800 | |
| *Nov 2 ...........Texas 500 | | Carl Edwards (16) | Ford | 334 | 496,300 |
| *Nov 9 ...........Phoenix 500 | | Jimmie Johnson (1) | Chevrolet | 313 | 261,711 |
| *Nov 16 ..........Homestead/Miami 400 | | Carl Edwards (4) | Ford | 267 | 365,225 |

## 2009 Sprint Cup Series Results†

| Date | Track/Distance | Winner (start pos.) | Car | Laps | Winnings ($) |
|------|----------------|---------------------|-----|------|--------------|
| Feb 15............Daytona 500 | | Matt Kenseth (39) | Ford | 152 | 1,530,390 |
| Feb 22............Fontana 500 | | Matt Kenseth (24) | Ford | 250 | 346,615 |
| Mar 1............Las Vegas 427 | | Kyle Busch (1) | Toyota | 285 | 461,273 |
| Mar 8.............Atlanta 500 | | Kurt Busch (2) | Dodge | 330 | 164,175 |
| Mar 22............Bristol 500 | | Kyle Busch (19) | Toyota | 503 | 232,998 |
| Mar 29............Martinsville 500 | | Jimmie Johnson (9) | Chevrolet | 500 | 213,626 |
| Apr 5 .............Texas 500 | | Jeff Gordon (2) | Chevrolet | 334 | 541,874 |
| Apr 18 ............Phoenix 500 | | Mark Martin (1) | Chevrolet | 312 | 232,150 |
| Apr 26 ............Talladega 499 | | Brad Keselowski (9) | Chevrolet | 188 | 312,075 |
| May 2.............Richmond 400 | | Kyle Busch (14) | Toyota | 400 | 257,248 |
| May 9 ............Darlington 500 | | Mark Martin (12) | Chevrolet | 367 | 295,150 |
| May 16............All-Star Race | | Tony Stewart (15) | Chevrolet | 100 | N/A |
| May 25 ...........Charlotte 600 | | David Reutimann (21) | Toyota | 227 | 403,748 |
| May 31 ...........Dover 400 | | Jimmie Johnson (8) | Chevrolet | 400 | 351,151 |
| June 7............Pocono 500 | | Tony Stewart (1) | Chevrolet | 200 | 238,798 |
| June 14 ..........Michigan 400 | | Mark Martin (32) | Chevrolet | 200 | 189,125 |
| June 21 ..........Sonoma 350 | | Kasey Kahne (5) | Dodge | 113 | 345,071 |
| June 28 ..........New Hampshire 301 | | Joey Logano (24) | Toyota | 273 | 276,201 |
| July 4.............Daytona 400 | | Tony Stewart (1) | Chevrolet | 160 | 349,873 |
| July 11............Chicagoland 400 | | Mark Martin (14) | Chevrolet | 267 | 317,825 |
| July 26............Brickyard 400 | | Jimmie Johnson (16) | Chevrolet | 160 | 448,001 |
| Aug 3 ............Pocono 500 | | Denny Hamlin (6) | Toyota | 200 | 235,725 |
| Aug 10 ...........Watkins Glen 220 | | Tony Stewart (13) | Chevrolet | 90 | 234,648 |
| Aug 16 ...........Michigan 400 | | Brian Vickers (1) | Toyota | 200 | 180,873 |
| Aug 22 ...........Bristol 500 | | Kyle Busch (15) | Toyota | 500 | 341,073 |
| Aug 31 ...........California 500 | | Jimmie Johnson (1) | Chevrolet | 250 | 314,611 |
| *Sept 6 ...........Atlanta 500 | | Kasey Kahne (2) | Dodge | 325 | 363,073 |
| *Sept 12 .........Richmond 400 | | Denny Hamlin (3) | Toyota | 400 | 238,075 |
| *Sept 20 .........New Hampshire 300 | | Mark Martin (14) | Chevrolet | 300 | 232,750 |
| *Sept 27 .........Dover 400 | | Jimmie Johnson (1) | Chevrolet | 400 | 341,151 |
| *Oct 4.............Kansas 400 | | Tony Stewart (5) | Chevrolet | 267 | 332,498 |
| *Oct 11...........Fontana 500 | | Jimmie Johnson (3) | Chevrolet | 250 | 302,801 |

† Through October 11, 2009.
* Part of 10-race Chase for the Cup.

# Formula One Grand Prix Racing

## 2009 Formula One Results†

| Grand Prix | Date | Winner | Car | Laps | Time |
|---|---|---|---|---|---|
| Australia | Mar 29 | Jenson Button | Brawn-Mercecdes | 58 | 1:34:15.784 |
| Malaysia | Apr 5 | Jenson Button | Brawn-Mercecdes | 31 | 55:30.622 |
| China | Apr 19 | Sebastian Vettel | RBR-Renault | 56 | 1:57:43.485 |
| Bahrain | Apr 26 | Jenson Button | Brawn-Mercecdes | 57 | 1:31:48.182 |
| Spain | May 10 | Jenson Button | Brawn-Mercecdes | 66 | 1:37:19.202 |
| Monaco | May 24 | Jenson Button | Brawn-Mercecdes | 78 | 1:40:44.282 |
| Turkey | June 7 | Jenson Button | Brawn-Mercecdes | 58 | 1:26:24.848 |
| Great Britain | June 21 | Sebastian Vettel | RBR-Renault | 60 | 1:22:49.328 |
| Germany | July 12 | Mark Webber | RBR-Renault | 60 | 1:36:43.310 |
| Hungary | July 26 | Lewis Hamilton | McLaren-Mercedes | 70 | 1:38:23.876 |
| Europe | Aug 23 | Rubens Barrichello | Brawn-Mercecdes | 57 | 1:35:51.289 |
| Belguim | Aug 30 | Kimi Raikkonen | Ferrari | 44 | 1:23:50.995 |
| Italy | Sept 13 | Rubens Barrichello | Brawn-Mercecdes | 53 | 1:16:21.706 |
| Singapore | Sept 27 | Lewis Hamilton | McLaren-Mercedes | 61 | 1:56:06.337 |
| Japan | Oct 4 | Sebastian Vettel | RBR-Renault | 53 | 1:28:20.443 |

† Through October 5, 2009.

## 2008 World Championship Final Standings

Drivers compete in Grand Prix races for the title of World Driving Champion. Below are the top 10 drivers from the 2008 season. Points are awarded for places 1–6 as follows: 10-6-4-3-2-1.

| Driver | Country | Team | Pts |
|---|---|---|---|
| Lewis Hamilton | Great Britain | McLaren-Mercedes | 98 |
| Felipe Massa | Brazil | Ferrari | 97 |
| Kimi Raikkonen | Finland | Ferrari | 75 |
| Robert Kubica | Poland | BMW Sauber | 75 |
| Fernando Alonso | Spain | Renault | 61 |
| Nick Heidfeld | Germany | BMW Sauber | 60 |
| Heikki Kovalainen | Finland | McLaren-Mercedes | 53 |
| Sebastian Vettel | Germany | STR-Ferrari | 35 |
| Jarno Trulli | Italy | Toyota | 31 |
| Timo Glock | Germany | Toyota | 25 |

# Professional Sports Car Racing

## The 24 Hours of Daytona

Held at the Daytona International Speedway on Jan 24–25, 2009, the 24 Hours of Daytona serves as the opening round of the Grand American Road Racing Association's season.

| Place | Drivers | Car (Class) | Distance |
|---|---|---|---|
| 1 | D. Law, D. Donohue, B. Ride, A. Garcia | Porsche Riley | 735 laps (108.994 mph) |
| 2 | S. Pruett, M. Rojas, J. Montoya | Lexus Riley | 735 |
| 3 | J.C. France, J. Barbosa, T. Borcheller, H. Haywood | Porsche Riley | 735 |
| 4 | W. Taylor, M. Angelelli, B. Frisselle, P. Lamy | Ford Dallara | 735 |
| 5 | S. Dixon, D. Franchitti, A. Lloyd | Lexus Riley | 731 |

## 2009 American Le Mans Series—Prototype Class

| Date | Race | Winners | Car |
|---|---|---|---|
| Mar 21 | 12 Hours of Sebring | R. Capello, T. Kristensen, A. McNish | Audi R15 TDI |
| April 4 | St. Petersburg Challenge | S. Sharp, D. Brabham | Acura ARX-02a |
| April 19 | Grand Prix of Long Beach | G. de Ferran, S. Pagenaud | Acura ARX-02a |
| May 17 | Utah Grand Prix | G. de Ferran, S. Pagenaud | Acura ARX-02a |
| July 18 | Northeast Grand Prix | G. de Ferran, S. Pagenaud | Acura ARX-02a |
| Aug 9 | Mid Ohio | G. de Ferran, S. Pagenaud | Acura ARX-02a |
| Aug 16 | Road America 500 | S. Sharp, D. Brabham | Acura ARX-02a |
| Aug 30 | Grand Prix of Mosport | S. Sharp, D. Brabham | Acura ARX-02a |
| Sept 26 | Petit Le Mans | S. Sarrazin, F. Montagny | Peugeot 908 HDI |
| Oct 11 | Monterey Championships | G. de Ferran, S. Pagenaud | Acura ARX-02a |

## 2009 American Le Mans Series—GTS Class

| Date | Race | Winners | Car |
|---|---|---|---|
| Mar 21 | 12 Hours of Sebring | J. O'Connell, J. Magnussen, A. Garcia | Corvette C6R |
| April 19 | Grand Prix of Long Beach | O. Beretta, O. Gavin | Corvette C6R |

# Professional Sports Car Racing *(Cont.)*

## 2009 American Le Mans Series—GT Class

| Date | Race | Winners | Car |
|---|---|---|---|
| Mar 21 | 12 Hours of Sebring | M. Salo, P. Kaffer, J. Melo | Ferrari F430GT |
| April 4 | St. Petersburg Challenge | P. Long, J. Bergmeister | Porsche 911 GT3 |
| April 19 | Grand Prix of Long Beach | P. Long, J. Bergmeister | Porsche 911 GT3 |
| May 17 | Utah Grand Prix | P. Long, J. Bergmeister | Porsche 911 GT3 |
| July 18 | Northeast Grand Prix | P. Long, J. Bergmeister | Porsche 911 GT3 |
| Aug 9 | Mid Ohio | P. Long, J. Bergmeister | Porsche 911 GT3 |
| Aug 16 | Road America 500 | B. Auberlen, J. Hand | BMW E92 M3 |
| Aug 30 | Grand Prix of Mosport | J. Magnussen, J. O'Connell | Corvette C6R |
| Sept 26 | Petit Le Mans | M. Salo, P. Kaffer, J. Melo | Ferrari F430GT |
| Oct 11 | Monterey Championships | P. Long, J. Bergmeister | Porsche 911 GT3 |

## 2009 American Le Mans Series Championship Final Standings

| PROTOTYPE CLASS | Pts | GTS CLASS | Pts | GT CLASS | Pts |
|---|---|---|---|---|---|
| David Brabham | 158 | Oliver Gavin | 46 | Jorg Bergmeister | 156 |
| Scott Sharp | 158 | Olivier Beretta | 46 | Patrick Long | 156 |
| Gil de Ferran | 137 | Johnny O'Connell | 30 | Jaime Melo | 137 |
| Simon Pagenaud | 137 | Jan Magnussen | 30 | Pierre Kaffer | 137 |
| Jon Field | 103 | Antonio Garcia | 30 | Dick Muller | 89 |
| Clint Field | 103 | Marcel Fassler | 26 | Tom Milner Jr. | 89 |

# 24 Hours of Le Mans

Held at Le Mans, France, on June 13–14, 2009, the 24 Hours of Le Mans is the most prestigious international event in endurance racing.

| Place | Drivers | Car | Laps |
|---|---|---|---|
| 1 | M. Gene, A. Wurz, D. Brabham | Peugeot 908 | 382 (134.63 mph) |
| 2 | S. Sarrazin, F. Montagny, S. Bourdais | Peugeot 908 | 381 |
| 3 | R. Capello, T. Kristensen, A. McNish | Audi R15 | 376 |
| 4 | J. Charouz, T. Enge, S. Mucke | Lola Aston Martin | 373 |
| 5 | O. Panis, N. Lapierre, S. Ayari | Oreca AIM | 370 |

## Indianapolis 500

First held in 1911, the Indianapolis 500—200 laps of the 2.5-mile Indianapolis Motor Speedway Track (called the Brickyard in honor of its original pavement)—grew to become the most famous auto race in the world. Though the Memorial Day weekend event lost participants and prestige in the mid-1990s due to feuding in the world of U.S. open-wheel racing, it annually attracts crowds of over 100,000.

| Year | Winner (start pos.) | Chassis-Engine | Avg Speed | Pole Winner | Speed |
|------|---------------------|----------------|-----------|-------------|-------|
| 1911 | Ray Harroun (28) | Marmon-Marmon | 74.590 | Lewis Strang | First entered |
| 1912 | Joe Dawson (7) | National-National | 78.720 | Gil Anderson | First entered |
| 1913 | Jules Goux (7) | Peugeot-Peugeot | 75.930 | Caleb Bragg | Drew pole |
| 1914 | Rene Thomas (15) | Delage-Delage | 82.470 | Jean Chassagne | Drew pole |
| 1915 | Ralph DePalma (2) | Mercedes-Mercedes | 89.840 | Howard Wilcox | 98.90 |
| 1916 | Dario Resta (4) | Peugeot-Peugeot | 84.000 | John Aitken | 96.69 |
| 1917–18 | No race | | | | |
| 1919 | Howard Wilcox (2) | Peugeot-Peugeot | 88.050 | Rene Thomas | 104.78 |
| 1920 | Gaston Chevrolet (6) | Frontenac-Frontenac | 88.620 | Ralph DePalma | 99.15 |
| 1921 | Tommy Milton (20) | Frontenac-Frontenac | 89.620 | Ralph DePalma | 100.75 |
| 1922 | Jimmy Murphy (1) | Duesenberg-Miller | 94.480 | Jimmy Murphy | 100.50 |
| 1923 | Tommy Milton (1) | Miller-Miller | 90.950 | Tommy Milton | 108.17 |
| 1924 | L.L. Corum / Joe Boyer (21) | Duesenberg-Duesenberg | 98.230 | Jimmy Murphy | 108.037 |
| 1925 | Peter DePaolo (2) | Duesenberg-Duesenberg | 101.130 | Leon Duray | 113.196 |
| 1926 | Frank Lockhart (20) | Miller-Miller | 95.904 | Earl Cooper | 111.735 |
| 1927 | George Souders (22) | Duesenberg-Duesenberg | 97.545 | Frank Lockhart | 120.100 |
| 1928 | Louis Meyer (13) | Miller-Miller | 99.482 | Leon Duray | 122.391 |
| 1929 | Ray Keech (6) | Miller-Miller | 97.585 | Cliff Woodbury | 120.599 |
| 1930 | Billy Arnold (1) | Summers-Miller | 100.448 | Billy Arnold | 113.268 |
| 1931 | Louis Schneider (13) | Stevens-Miller | 96.629 | Russ Snowberger | 112.796 |
| 1932 | Fred Frame (27) | Wetteroth-Miller | 104.144 | Lou Moore | 117.363 |
| 1933 | Louis Meyer (6) | Miller-Miller | 104.162 | Bill Cummings | 118.524 |
| 1934 | Bill Cummings (10) | Miller-Miller | 104.863 | Kelly Petillo | 119.329 |
| 1935 | Kelly Petillo (22) | Wetteroth-Offy | 106.240 | Rex Mays | 120.736 |
| 1936 | Louis Meyer (28) | Stevens-Miller | 109.069 | Rex Mays | 119.664 |
| 1937 | Wilbur Shaw (2) | Shaw-Offy | 113.580 | Bill Cummings | 123.343 |
| 1938 | Floyd Roberts (1) | Wetteroth-Miller | 117.200 | Floyd Roberts | 125.681 |
| 1939 | Wilbur Shaw (3) | Maserati-Maserati | 115.035 | Jimmy Snyder | 130.138 |
| 1940 | Wilbur Shaw (2) | Maserati-Maserati | 114.277 | Rex Mays | 127.850 |
| 1941 | Floyd Davis / Mauri Rose (17) | Wetteroth-Offy | 115.117 | Mauri Rose | 128.691 |
| 1942–45 | No race | | | | |
| 1946 | George Robson (15) | Adams-Sparks | 114.820 | Cliff Bergere | 126.471 |
| 1947 | Mauri Rose (3) | Deidt-Offy | 116.338 | Ted Horn | 126.564 |
| 1948 | Mauri Rose (3) | Deidt-Offy | 119.814 | Rex Mays | 130.577 |
| 1949 | Bill Holland (4) | Deidt-Offy | 121.327 | Duke Nalon | 132.939 |
| 1950 | Johnnie Parsons (5) | Kurtis-Offy | 124.002 | Walt Faulkner | 134.343 |
| 1951 | Lee Wallard (2) | Kurtis-Offy | 126.244 | Duke Nalon | 136.498 |
| 1952 | Troy Ruttman (7) | Kuzma-Offy | 128.922 | Fred Agabashian | 138.010 |
| 1953 | Bill Vukovich (1) | KK500A-Offy | 128.740 | Bill Vukovich | 138.392 |
| 1954 | Bill Vukovich (19) | KK500A-Offy | 130.840 | Jack McGrath | 141.033 |
| 1955 | Bob Sweikert (14) | KK500C-Offy | 128.209 | Jerry Hoyt | 140.045 |
| 1956 | Pat Flaherty (1) | Watson-Offy | 128.490 | Pat Flaherty | 145.596 |
| 1957 | Sam Hanks (13) | Salih-Offy | 135.601 | Pat O'Connor | 143.948 |
| 1958 | Jim Bryan (7) | Salih-Offy | 133.791 | Dick Rathmann | 145.974 |
| 1959 | Rodger Ward (6) | Watson-Offy | 135.857 | Johnny Thomson | 145.908 |
| 1960 | Jim Rathmann (2) | Watson-Offy | 138.767 | Eddie Sachs | 146.592 |
| 1961 | A.J. Foyt (7) | Trevis-Offy | 139.130 | Eddie Sachs | 147.481 |
| 1962 | Rodger Ward (2) | Watson-Offy | 140.293 | Parnelli Jones | 150.370 |
| 1963 | Parnelli Jones (1) | Watson-Offy | 143.137 | Parnelli Jones | 151.153 |
| 1964 | A.J. Foyt (5) | Watson-Offy | 147.350 | Jim Clark | 158.828 |
| 1965 | Jim Clark (2) | Lotus-Ford | 150.686 | A.J. Foyt | 161.233 |
| 1966 | Graham Hill (15) | Lola-Ford | 144.317 | Mario Andretti | 165.899 |
| 1967 | A.J. Foyt (4) | Coyote-Ford | 151.207 | Mario Andretti | 168.982 |
| 1968 | Bobby Unser (3) | Eagle-Offy | 152.882 | Joe Leonard | 171.559 |
| 1969 | Mario Andretti (2) | Hawk-Ford | 156.867 | A.J. Foyt | 170.568 |
| 1970 | Al Unser (1) | PJ Colt-Ford | 155.749 | Al Unser | 170.221 |
| 1971 | Al Unser (5) | PJ Colt-Ford | 157.735 | Peter Revson | 178.696 |
| 1972 | Mark Donohue (3) | McLaren-Offy | 162.962 | Bobby Unser | 195.940 |

| Year | Winner (start pos.) | Chassis-Engine | Avg speed | Pole Winner | Speed |
|---|---|---|---|---|---|
| 1973 | Gordon Johncock (11) | Eagle-Offy | 159.036 | Johnny Rutherford | 198.413 |
| 1974 | Johnny Rutherford (25) | McLaren-Offy | 158.589 | A.J. Foyt | 191.632 |
| 1975 | Bobby Unser (3) | Racers Eagle-Offy | 149.213 | A.J. Foyt | 193.976 |
| 1976 | Johnny Rutherford (1) | McLaren-Offy | 148.725 | Johnny Rutherford | 188.957 |
| 1977 | A.J. Foyt (4) | Coyote-Ford | 161.331 | Tom Sneva | 198.884 |
| 1978 | Al Unser (5) | Lola-Cosworth | 161.361 | Tom Sneva | 202.156 |
| 1979 | Rick Mears (1) | Penske-Cosworth | 158.899 | Rick Mears | 193.736 |
| 1980 | Johnny Rutherford (1) | Chaparral-Cosworth | 142.862 | Johnny Rutherford | 192.256 |
| 1981 | Bobby Unser (1) | Penske-Cosworth | 139.084 | Bobby Unser | 200.546 |
| 1982 | Gordon Johncock (5) | Wildcat-Cosworth | 162.026 | Rick Mears | 207.004 |
| 1983 | Tom Sneva (4) | March-Cosworth | 162.117 | Teo Fabi | 207.395 |
| 1984 | Rick Mears (3) | March-Cosworth | 163.612 | Tom Sneva | 210.029 |
| 1985 | Danny Sullivan (8) | March-Cosworth | 152.982 | Pancho Carter | 212.583 |
| 1986 | Bobby Rahal (4) | March-Cosworth | 170.722 | Rick Mears | 216.828 |
| 1987 | Al Unser (20) | March-Cosworth | 162.175 | Mario Andretti | 215.390 |
| 1988 | Rick Mears (1) | Penske-Chevrolet | 144.809 | Rick Mears | 219.198 |
| 1989 | Emerson Fittipaldi (3) | Penske-Chevrolet | 167.581 | Rick Mears | 223.885 |
| 1990 | Arie Luyendyk (3) | Lola-Chevrolet | 185.981* | Emerson Fittipaldi | 225.301 |
| 1991 | Rick Mears (1) | Penske-Chevrolet | 176.457 | Rick Mears | 224.113 |
| 1992 | Al Unser Jr. (12) | Galmer-Chevrolet | 134.477 | Roberto Guerrero | 232.482 |
| 1993 | Emerson Fittipaldi (9) | Penske-Chevrolet | 157.207 | Arie Luyendyk | 223.967 |
| 1994 | Al Unser Jr. (1) | Penske-Mercedes | 160.872 | Al Unser Jr. | 228.011 |
| 1995 | Jacques Villeneuve (5) | Reynard-Ford | 153.616 | Scott Brayton | 231.616 |
| 1996 | Buddy Lazier (5) | Reynard-Ford | 147.956 | Tony Stewart | 233.100† |
| 1997 | Arie Luyendyk (1) | G Force-Oldsmobile | 145.827 | Arie Luyendyk | 231.468 |
| 1998 | Eddie Cheever (17) | Dallara-Oldsmobile | 145.155 | Billy Boat | 223.503 |
| 1999 | Kenny Brack (8) | Dallara-Oldsmobile | 153.176 | Arie Luyendyk | 225.179 |
| 2000 | Juan Montoya (2) | G Force-Oldsmobile | 167.607 | Greg Ray | 223.471 |
| 2001 | Helio Castroneves (11) | Dallara-Oldsmobile | 153.601 | Scott Sharp | 226.037 |
| 2002 | Helio Castroneves (13) | Dallara-Chevrolet | 166.499 | Bruno Junqueira | 231.342 |
| 2003 | Gil de Ferran | Panoz-Toyota | 156.291 | Helio Castroneves | 231.725 |
| 2004 | Buddy Rice (1) | G Force-Honda | 138.518 | Buddy Rice | 222.024 |
| 2005 | Dan Wheldon | Dallara-Honda | 157.603 | Tony Kanaan | 227.566 |
| 2006 | Sam Hornish Jr.(1) | Dallara-Honda | 157.085 | Sam Hornish Jr. | 228.985 |
| 2007 | Dario Franchitti (3) | Dallara-Honda | 151.744 | Helio Castroneves | 225.817 |
| 2008 | Scott Dixon (1) | Dallara-Honda | 143.567 | Scott Dixon | 226.366 |
| 2009 | Helio Castroneves (1) | Dallara-Honda | 150.138 | Helio Castroneves | 224.864 |

*Track record, winning speed. †Track record, qualifying speed.

## Indianapolis 500 Rookie of the Year Award

| | | |
|---|---|---|
| 1952 ............Art Cross | 1973 ............Graham McRae | 1992 ............Lyn St. James |
| 1953 ............Jimmy Daywalt | 1974 ............Pancho Carter | 1993 ............Nigel Mansell |
| 1954 ............Larry Crockett | 1975 ............Bill Puterbaugh | 1994 ............Jacques Villeneuve* |
| 1955 ............Al Herman | 1976 ............Vern Schuppan | 1995 ............Gil de Ferran* |
| 1956 ............Bob Veith | 1977 ............Jerry Sneva | 1996 ............Tony Stewart |
| 1957 ............Don Edmunds | 1978 ............Rick Mears* | 1997 ............Jeff Ward |
| 1958 ............George Amick | ............Larry Rice | 1998 ............Steve Knapp |
| 1959 ............Bobby Grim | 1979 ............Howdy Holmes | 1999 ............Robby McGehee |
| 1960 ............Jim Hurtubise | 1980 ............Tim Richmond | 2000 ............Juan Montoya* |
| 1961 ............Parnelli Jones* | 1981 ............Josele Garza | 2001 ............Helio Castroneves* |
| ............Bobby Marshman | 1982 ............Jim Hickman | 2002 ............Alex Barron |
| 1962 ............Jimmy McElreath | 1983 ............Teo Fabi | ............Tomas Scheckter |
| 1963 ............Jim Clark* | 1984 ............Michael Andretti | 2003 ............Tora Tagaki |
| 1964 ............Johnny White | ............Roberto Guerrero | 2004 ............Kosuke Matsuura |
| 1965 ............Mario Andretti* | 1985 ............Arie Luyendyk* | 2005 ............Danica Patrick |
| 1966 ............Jackie Stewart | 1986 ............Randy Lanier | 2006 ............Marco Andretti |
| 1967 ............Denis Hulme | 1987 ............Fabrizio Barbazza | 2007 ............Phil Giebler |
| 1968 ............Billy Vukovich | 1988 ............Billy Vukovich III | 2008 ............Ryan Hunter-Reay |
| 1969 ............Mark Donohue* | 1989 ............Bernard Jourdain | 2009 ............Alex Tagliani |
| 1970 ............Donnie Allison | ............Scott Pruett | |
| 1971 ............Denny Zimmerman | 1990 ............Eddie Cheever* | |
| 1972 ............Mike Hiss | 1991 ............Jeff Andretti | |

*Future winner of Indy 500.

## Champ Car World Series Champions

From 1909 to 1955, this championship was awarded by the American Automobile Association (AAA), and from 1956 to 1979 by the United States Auto Club (USAC). Since 1979, Championship Auto Racing Teams (CART) has conducted the championship. Known as PPG CART World Series until 1998. Series name changed to Champ Car World Series for 2005 racing season. On Februray 22, 2008, the Champ Car World Series merged with the Indy Racing League.

| | | |
|---|---|---|
| 1909 ............George Robertson | 1941 ............Rex Mays | 1977 ............Tom Sneva |
| 1910 ............Ray Harroun | 1942–45 ....No racing | 1978 ............Tom Sneva |
| 1911 ............Ralph Mulford | 1946 ............Ted Horn | 1979 ............A.J. Foyt |
| 1912 ............Ralph DePalma | 1947 ............Ted Horn | 1979 ............Rick Mears |
| 1913 ............Earl Cooper | 1948 ............Ted Horn | 1980 ............Johnny Rutherford |
| 1914 ............Ralph DePalma | 1949 ............Johnnie Parsons | 1981 ............Rick Mears |
| 1915 ............Earl Cooper | 1950 ............Henry Banks | 1982 ............Rick Mears |
| 1916 ............Dario Resta | 1951 ............Tony Bettenhausen | 1983 ............Al Unser |
| 1917 ............Earl Cooper | 1952 ............Chuck Stevenson | 1984 ............Mario Andretti |
| 1918 ............Ralph Mulford | 1953 ............Sam Hanks | 1985 ............Al Unser |
| 1919 ............Howard Wilcox | 1954 ............Jimmy Bryan | 1986 ............Bobby Rahal |
| 1920 ............Tommy Milton | 1955 ............Bob Sweikert | 1987 ............Bobby Rahal |
| 1921 ............Tommy Milton | 1956 ............Jimmy Bryan | 1988 ............Danny Sullivan |
| 1922 ............Jimmy Murphy | 1957 ............Jimmy Bryan | 1989 ............Emerson Fittipaldi |
| 1923 ............Eddie Hearne | 1958 ............Tony Bettenhausen | 1990 ............Al Unser Jr. |
| 1924 ............Jimmy Murphy | 1959 ............Rodger Ward | 1991 ............Michael Andretti |
| 1925 ............Peter DePaolo | 1960 ............A.J. Foyt | 1992 ............Bobby Rahal |
| 1926 ............Harry Hartz | 1961 ............A.J. Foyt | 1993 ............Nigel Mansell |
| 1927 ............Peter DePaolo | 1962 ............Rodger Ward | 1994 ............Al Unser Jr. |
| 1928 ............Louis Meyer | 1963 ............A.J. Foyt | 1995 ............Jacques Villeneuve |
| 1929 ............Louis Meyer | 1964 ............A.J. Foyt | 1996 ............Jimmy Vasser |
| 1930 ............Billy Arnold | 1965 ............Mario Andretti | 1997 ............Alex Zanardi |
| 1931 ............Louis Schneider | 1966 ............Mario Andretti | 1998 ............Alex Zanardi |
| 1932 ............Bob Carey | 1967 ............A.J. Foyt | 1999 ............Juan Montoya |
| 1933 ............Louis Meyer | 1968 ............Bobby Unser | 2000 ............Gil de Ferran |
| 1934 ............Bill Cummings | 1969 ............Mario Andretti | 2001 ............Gil de Ferran |
| 1935 ............Kelly Petillo | 1970 ............Al Unser | 2002 ............Cristiano da Matta |
| 1936 ............Mauri Rose | 1971 ............Joe Leonard | 2003 ............Paul Tracy |
| 1937 ............Wilbur Shaw | 1972 ............Joe Leonard | 2004 ............Sebastian Bourdais |
| 1938 ............Floyd Roberts | 1973 ............Roger McCluskey | 2005 ............Sebastian Bourdais |
| 1939 ............Wilbur Shaw | 1974 ............Bobby Unser | 2006 ............Sebastian Bourdais |
| 1940 ............Rex Mays | 1975 ............A.J. Foyt | 2007 ............Sebastian Bourdais |
| | 1976 ............Gordon Johncock | |

## Alltime Champ Car* Leaders

### WINS

| | |
|---|---|
| A.J. Foyt............67 |
| Mario Andretti ............52 |
| Michael Andretti............42 |
| Al Unser............39 |
| Bobby Unser............35 |
| Al Unser Jr ............31 |
| †Paul Tracy ............31 |
| Rick Mears............29 |
| †Sebastian Bourdais............29 |
| Johnny Rutherford ............27 |
| Rodger Ward ............26 |
| Gordon Johncock ............25 |
| Bobby Rahal ............24 |
| Ralph DePalma............24 |
| Tommy Milton ............23 |
| Tony Bettenhausen ............22 |
| Emerson Fittipaldi............22 |
| Earl Cooper ............20 |
| Jimmy Bryan ............19 |
| Jimmy Murphy ............19 |
| Danny Sullivan ............17 |
| Ralph Mulford ............17 |

### POLE POSITIONS

| | |
|---|---|
| Mario Andretti ............67 |
| A.J. Foyt............53 |
| Bobby Unser............49 |
| Rick Mears ............40 |
| Michael Andretti............32 |
| †Sebastian Bourdais............28 |
| Al Unser ............27 |
| †Paul Tracy ............25 |
| Johnny Rutherford ............23 |
| Gordon Johncock ............20 |
| Rex Mays ............19 |
| Danny Sullivan ............19 |
| Bobby Rahal ............18 |
| Emerson Fittipaldi ............17 |
| Gil de Ferran............16 |
| Tony Bettenhausen ............14 |
| Juan Montoya ............14 |
| Don Branson............14 |
| Tom Sneva ............14 |
| Parnelli Jones ............12 |

*Series known as CART prior to 2003 season

## Stock Car Racing's Major Events

In 1985, Winston began offering a $1 million bonus to any driver to win three of the top four NASCAR events in the same season. A fifth event, the Brickyard 400 (in Indianapolis) was added in 1994. As of 1998 the Winston million was awarded to any driver who won three of the five events. The other four races are the richest (Daytona 500), the fastest (Talladega 500), the longest (Charlotte 600) and the oldest (Southern 500 at Darlington). Only five drivers, Lee Roy Yarbrough (1969), David Pearson (1976), Bill Elliott (1985), Dale Jarrett (1996) and Jeff Gordon (1997, '98) have scored the three-track hat trick.

### Daytona 500

| Year | Winner (start pos.) | Chassis-Engine | Avg speed | Pole Winner | Qual. speed |
|---|---|---|---|---|---|
| 1959 | Lee Petty | Oldsmobile | 135.520 | Cotton Owens | 143.198 |
| 1960 | Junior Johnson | Chevrolet | 124.740 | Fireball Roberts | 151.556 |
| 1961 | Marvin Panch | Pontiac | 149.601 | Fireball Roberts | 155.709 |
| 1962 | Fireball Roberts | Pontiac | 152.529 | Fireball Roberts | 156.995 |
| 1963 | Tiny Lund | Ford | 151.566 | Johnny Rutherford | 165.183 |
| 1964 | Richard Petty | Plymouth | 154.345 | Paul Goldsmith | 174.910 |
| 1965 | Fred Lorenzen | Ford | 141.539 | Darel Dieringer | 171.151 |
| 1966 | Richard Petty | Plymouth | 160.627 | Richard Petty | 175.165 |
| 1967 | Mario Andretti | Ford | 149.926 | Curtis Turner | 180.831 |
| 1968 | Cale Yarborough | Mercury | 143.251 | Cale Yarborough | 189.222 |
| 1969 | Lee Roy Yarbrough | Ford | 157.950 | David Pearson | 190.029 |
| 1970 | Pete Hamilton | Plymouth | 149.601 | Cale Yarborough | 194.015 |
| 1971 | Richard Petty | Plymouth | 144.462 | A.J. Foyt | 182.744 |
| 1972 | A.J. Foyt | Mercury | 161.550 | Bobby Isaac | 186.632 |
| 1973 | Richard Petty | Dodge | 157.205 | Buddy Baker | 185.662 |
| 1974 | Richard Petty | Dodge | 140.894 | David Pearson | 185.017 |
| 1975 | Benny Parsons | Chevrolet | 153.649 | Donnie Allison | 185.827 |
| 1976 | David Pearson | Mercury | 152.181 | A.J. Foyt | 185.943 |
| 1977 | Cale Yarborough | Chevrolet | 153.218 | Donnie Allison | 188.048 |
| 1978 | Bobby Allison | Ford | 159.730 | Cale Yarborough | 187.536 |
| 1979 | Richard Petty | Oldsmobile | 143.977 | Buddy Baker | 196.049 |
| 1980 | Buddy Baker | Oldsmobile | 177.602* | A.J. Foyt | 195.020 |
| 1981 | Richard Petty | Buick | 169.651 | Bobby Allison | 194.624 |
| 1982 | Bobby Allison | Buick | 153.991 | Benny Parsons | 196.317 |
| 1983 | Cale Yarborough | Pontiac | 155.979 | Ricky Rudd | 198.864 |
| 1984 | Cale Yarborough | Chevrolet | 150.994 | Cale Yarborough | 201.848 |
| 1985 | Bill Elliott | Ford | 172.265 | Bill Elliott | 205.114 |
| 1986 | Geoff Bodine | Chevrolet | 148.124 | Bill Elliott | 205.039 |
| 1987 | Bill Elliott | Ford | 176.263 | Bill Elliott | 210.364† |
| 1988 | Bobby Allison | Buick | 137.531 | Ken Schrader | 193.823 |
| 1989 | Darrell Waltrip | Chevrolet | 148.466 | Ken Schrader | 196.996 |
| 1990 | Derrike Cope | Chevrolet | 165.761 | Ken Schrader | 196.515 |
| 1991 | Ernie Irvan | Chevrolet | 148.148 | Davey Allison | 195.955 |
| 1992 | Davey Allison | Ford | 160.256 | Sterling Marlin | 192.213 |
| 1993 | Dale Jarrett | Chevrolet | 154.972 | Kyle Petty | 189.426 |
| 1994 | Sterling Marlin | Chevrolet | 156.931 | Loy Allen Jr | 190.158 |
| 1995 | Sterling Marlin | Chevrolet | 141.710 | Dale Jarrett | 193.498 |
| 1996 | Dale Jarrett | Ford | 154.308 | Dale Earnhardt | 189.510 |
| 1997 | Jeff Gordon | Chevrolet | 148.295 | Mike Skinner | 189.813 |
| 1998 | Dale Earnhardt | Chevrolet | 172.712 | Bobby Labonte | 192.415 |
| 1999 | Jeff Gordon | Chevrolet | 161.551 | Jeff Gordon | 195.067 |
| 2000 | Dale Jarrett | Ford | 155.669 | Dale Jarrett | 191.091 |
| 2001 | Michael Waltrip | Chevrolet | 161.783 | Bill Elliott | 183.570 |
| 2002 | Ward Burton | Dodge | 142.971 | Jimmie Johnson | 185.831 |
| 2003 | Michael Waltrip | Chevrolet | 133.870 | Jeff Green | 186.606 |
| 2004 | Dale Earnhardt Jr. | Chevrolet | 156.345 | Greg Biffle | 188.387 |
| 2005 | Jeff Gordon | Chevrolet | 135.173 | Dale Jarrett | 188.312 |
| 2006 | Jimmie Johnson | Chevrolet | 142.667 | Jeff Burton | 188.887 |
| 2007 | Kevin Harvick | Chevrolet | 149.335 | David Gilliland | 186.320 |
| 2008 | Ryan Newman | Dodge | 152.672 | Jimmie Johnson | 187.075 |
| 2009 | Matt Kenseth | Ford | 132.816 | Martin Truex Jr. | 188.001 |

Note: The Daytona 500, held annually in February, now opens the NASCAR season with 200 laps around the 2.5-mile high-banked Daytona International Speedway. Starting in 1988, cars racing at Daytona have used restrictor plates that lower power and acceleration.

*Track record, winning speed. †Track record, qualifying speed.

## Brickyard 400

| Year | Winner | Car | Avg Speed | Pole Winner | Speed |
|---|---|---|---|---|---|
| 1994 | Jeff Gordon | Chevrolet | 131.977 | Rick Mast | 172.414 |
| 1995 | Dale Earnhardt | Chevrolet | 155.206 | Jeff Gordon | 172.536 |
| 1996 | Dale Jarrett | Ford | 139.508 | Jeff Gordon | 176.419 |
| 1997 | Ricky Rudd | Ford | 130.814 | Ernie Irvan | 177.736 |
| 1998 | Jeff Gordon | Chevrolet | 126.772 | Ernie Irvan | 179.394 |
| 1999 | Dale Jarrett | Ford | 148.194 | Jeff Gordon | 179.612 |
| 2000 | Bobby Labonte | Pontiac | 155.912* | Ricky Rudd | 181.068 |
| 2001 | Jeff Gordon | Chevrolet | 130.790 | Jimmy Spencer | 179.666 |
| 2002 | Bill Elliott | Dodge | 125.033 | Tony Stewart | 182.960 |
| 2003 | Kevin Harvick | Chevrolet | 134.554 | Kevin Harvick | 184.343 |
| 2004 | Jeff Gordon | Chevrolet | 115.037 | Casey Mears | 186.293† |
| 2005 | Tony Stewart | Chevrolet | 148.782 | Elliott Sadler | 184.117 |
| 2006 | Jimmie Johnson | Chevrolet | 137.182 | Jeff Burton | 182.778 |
| 2007 | Tony Stewart | Chevrolet | 117.379 | Reed Sorenson | 184.207 |
| 2008 | Jimmie Johnson | Chevrolet | 115.117 | Jimmie Johnson | 181.763 |
| 2009 | Jimmie Johnson | Chevrolet | 145.882 | Mark Martin | 182.054 |

Note: Held at the 2.5-mile Indianapolis Motor Speedway.
*Track record, winning speed. †Track record, qualifying speed

## Talladega 500

| Year | Winner | Car | Avg Speed | Pole Winner | Speed |
|---|---|---|---|---|---|
| 1970 | Pete Hamilton | Plymouth | 152.321 | Bobby Isaac | 199.658 |
| 1971 | Donnie Allison | Mercury | 147.419 | Donnie Allison | 185.869 |
| 1972 | David Pearson | Mercury | 134.400 | Bobby Isaac | 192.428 |
| 1973 | David Pearson | Mercury | 131.956 | Buddy Baker | 193.435 |
| 1974 | David Pearson | Mercury | 130.220 | David Pearson | 186.086 |
| 1975 | Buddy Baker | Ford | 144.94 | Buddy Baker | 189.947 |
| 1976 | Buddy Baker | Ford | 169.887 | Dave Marcis | 189.197 |
| 1977 | Darrell Waltrip | Chevrolet | 164.887 | A.J. Foyt | 192.424 |
| 1978 | Cale Yarborough | Oldsmobile | 155.699 | Cale Yarborough | 191.904 |
| 1979 | Bobby Allison | Ford | 154.770 | Darrell Waltrip | 195.644 |
| 1980 | Buddy Baker | Oldsmobile | 170.481 | David Pearson | 197.704 |
| 1981 | Bobby Allison | Buick | 149.376 | Bobby Allison | 195.864 |
| 1982 | Darrell Waltrip | Buick | 156.697 | Benny Parsons | 200.176 |
| 1983 | Richard Petty | Pontiac | 135.936 | Cale Yarborough | 202.650 |
| 1984 | Cale Yarborough | Chevrolet | 172.988 | Cale Yarborough | 202.692 |
| 1985 | Bill Elliott | Ford | 186.288 | Bill Elliott | 209.398 |
| 1986 | Bobby Allison | Buick | 157.698 | Bill Elliott | 212.229 |
| 1987 | Davey Allison | Ford | 154.228 | Bill Elliott | 221.809† |
| 1988 | Phil Parsons | Oldsmobile | 156.547 | Davey Allison | 198.969 |
| 1989 | Davey Allison | Ford | 155.869 | Mark Martin | 193.061 |
| 1990 | Dale Earnhardt | Chevrolet | 159.571 | Bill Elliott | 199.388 |
| 1991 | Harry Gant | Oldsmobile | 165.620 | Ernie Irvan | 195.186 |
| 1992 | Davey Allison | Ford | 167.609 | Ernie Irvan | 192.831 |
| 1993 | Ernie Irvan | Chevrolet | 155.412 | Dale Earnhardt | 192.355 |
| 1994 | Dale Earnhardt | Chevrolet | 157.478 | Ernie Irvan | 193.298 |
| 1995 | Mark Martin | Ford | 178.902 | Terry Labonte | 196.532 |
| 1996 | Sterling Marlin | Chevrolet | 149.999 | Ernie Irvan | 192.855 |
| 1997 | Mark Martin | Ford | 188.354* | John Andretti | 193.627 |
| 1998 | Dale Jarrett | Ford | 159.318 | Ken Schrader | 196.153 |
| 1999 | Dale Earnhardt | Chevrolet | 166.632 | Joe Nemechek | 198.331 |
| 2000 | Dale Earnhardt | Chevrolet | 165.681 | Joe Nemechek | 190.279 |
| 2001 | Dale Earnhardt Jr. | Chevrolet | 164.185 | Stacy Compton | 185.240 |
| 2002 | Dale Earnhardt Jr. | Chevrolet | 183.665 | qualifying cancelled | — |
| 2003 | Michael Waltrip | Chevrolet | 156.045 | Elliott Sadler | 189.943 |
| 2004 | Jeff Gordon | Chevrolet | 129.396 | Ricky Rudd | 191.180 |
| 2005 | Dale Jarrett | Ford | 143.818 | Elliott Sadler | 189.260 |
| 2006 | Brian Vickers | Chevrolet | 157.602 | David Gilliland | 191.712 |
| 2007 | Jeff Gordon | Chevrolet | 143.438 | Michael Waltrip | 189.070 |
| 2008 | Kyle Busch | Toyota | 157.409 | Joe Nemechek | 187.396 |
| 2009 | Brad Keselowski | Chevrolet | 147.565 | Juan Pablo Montoya | 188.171 |

*Track record, winning speed. †Track record, qualifying speed.

## Charlotte 600

| Year | Winner | Car | Avg Speed | Pole Winner |
|------|--------|-----|-----------|-------------|
| 1960 | Joe Lee Johnson | Chevrolet | 107.752 | Joe Lee Johnson |
| 1961 | David Pearson | Pontiac | 111.634 | Richard Petty |
| 1962 | Nelson Stacy | Ford | 125.552 | Fireball Roberts |
| 1963 | Fred Lorenzen | Ford | 132.418 | Junior Johnson |
| 1964 | Jim Paschal | Plymouth | 125.772 | Junior Johnson |
| 1965 | Fred Lorenzen | Ford | 121.772 | Fred Lorenzon |
| 1966 | Marvin Panch | Plymouth | 135.042 | Paul Goldsmith |
| 1967 | Jim Paschal | Plymouth | 135.832 | Cale Yarborough |
| 1968 | Buddy Baker | Dodge | 104.207 | Donnie Allison |
| 1969 | Lee Roy Yarbrough | Mercury | 134.631 | Donnie Allison |
| 1970 | Donnie Allison | Ford | 129.680 | Bobby Isaac |
| 1971 | Bobby Allison | Mercury | 140.442 | Charlie Glotzbach |
| 1972 | Buddy Baker | Dodge | 142.255 | Bobby Allison |
| 1973 | Buddy Baker | Dodge | 134.890 | Buddy Baker |
| 1974 | David Pearson | Mercury | 135.720 | David Pearson |
| 1975 | Richard Petty | Dodge | 145.327 | David Pearson |
| 1976 | David Pearson | Mercury | 137.352 | David Pearson |
| 1977 | Richard Petty | Dodge | 137.636 | David Pearson |
| 1978 | Darrell Waltrip | Chevrolet | 138.355 | David Pearson |
| 1979 | Darrell Waltrip | Chevrolet | 136.674 | Neil Bonnet |
| 1980 | Benny Parsons | Chevrolet | 119.265 | Cale Yarborough |
| 1981 | Bobby Allison | Buick | 129.326 | Neil Bonnett |
| 1982 | Neil Bonnett | Ford | 130.508 | David Pearson |
| 1983 | Neil Bonnett | Chevrolet | 140.406 | Buddy Baker |
| 1984 | Bobby Allison | Buick | 129.233 | Harry Gant |
| 1985 | Darrell Waltrip | Chevrolet | 141.807 | Bill Elliott |
| 1986 | Dale Earnhardt | Chevrolet | 140.406 | Geoff Bodine |
| 1987 | Kyle Petty | Ford | 131.483 | Bill Elliott |
| 1988 | Darrell Waltrip | Chevrolet | 124.460 | Davey Allison |
| 1989 | Darrell Waltrip | Chevrolet | 144.077 | Alan Kulwicki |
| 1990 | Rusty Wallace | Pontiac | 137.650 | Ken Schrader |
| 1991 | Davey Allison | Ford | 138.951 | Mark Martin |
| 1992 | Dale Earnhardt | Chevrolet | 132.980 | Bill Elliott |
| 1993 | Dale Earnhardt | Chevrolet | 145.504 | Ken Schrader |
| 1994 | Jeff Gordon | Chevrolet | 139.445 | Jeff Gordon |
| 1995 | Bobby Labonte | Chevrolet | 151.952* | Jeff Gordon |
| 1996 | Dale Jarrett | Ford | 147.581 | Jeff Gordon |
| 1997 | Jeff Gordon | Chevrolet | 136.745 | Jeff Gordon |
| 1998 | Jeff Gordon | Chevrolet | 136.424 | Jeff Gordon |
| 1999 | Jeff Burton | Ford | 151.367 | Bobby Labonte |
| 2000 | Matt Kenseth | Ford | 142.640 | Dale Earnhardt Jr |
| 2001 | Jeff Burton | Ford | 138.107 | Ryan Newman |
| 2002 | Mark Martin | Ford | 137.729 | Jimmie Johnson |
| 2003 | Jimmie Johnson | Chevrolet | 126.198 | Ryan Newman |
| 2004 | Jimmie Johnson | Chevrolet | 142.763 | Jimmie Johnson |
| 2005 | Jimmie Johnson | Chevrolet | 114.698 | Ryan Newman |
| 2006 | Kasey Kahne | Dodge | 128.840 | Scott Riggs |
| 2007 | Casey Mears | Chevrolet | 130.222 | Ryan Newman |
| 2008 | Kasey Kahne | Dodge | 135.772 | Kyle Busch |
| 2009 | David Reutimann | Toyota | 120.899 | Ryan Newman |

Note: Held at the 1.5 mile high-banked Lowe's Motor Speedway in Charlotte on Memorial Day weekend.
*Track record, winning speed.

## Darlington 500

Note: Formerly the Winston 500, held at the 2.66-mile Talladega Superspeedway. Starting in 1988, cars racing at Talladega have used restrictor plates that lower power and acceleration.

| Year | Winner | Car | Avg Speed | Pole Winner |
|------|--------|-----|-----------|-------------|
| 1950 | Johnny Mantz | Plymouth | 76.260 | Wally Campbell |
| 1951 | Herb Thomas | Hudson | 76.900 | Marshall Teague |
| 1952 | Fonty Flock | Oldsmobile | 74.510 | Dick Rathman |
| 1953 | Buck Baker | Oldsmobile | 92.780 | Fonty Flock |
| 1954 | Herb Thomas | Hudson | 94.930 | Buck Baker |
| 1955 | Herb Thomas | Chevrolet | 92.281 | Tim Flock |
| 1956 | Curtis Turner | Ford | 95.067 | Buck Baker |
| 1957 | Speedy Thompson | Chevrolet | 100.100 | Paul Goldsmith |
| 1958 | Fireball Roberts | Chevrolet | 102.590 | Fireball Roberts |
| 1959 | Jim Reed | Chevrolet | 111.836 | Fireball Roberts |
| 1960 | Buck Baker | Pontiac | 105.901 | Cotton Owens |
| 1961 | Nelson Stacy | Ford | 117.880 | Fireball Roberts |
| 1962 | Larry Frank | Ford | 117.965 | Fireball Roberts |
| 1963 | Fireball Roberts | Ford | 129.784 | Fireball Roberts |
| 1964 | Buck Baker | Dodge | 117.757 | Richard Petty |
| 1965 | Ned Jarrett | Ford | 115.924 | Junior Johnson |
| 1966 | Darel Dieringer | Mercury | 114.830 | Lee Yarborough |
| 1967 | Richard Petty | Plymouth | 131.933 | David Pearson |
| 1968 | Cale Yarborough | Mercury | 126.132 | Charlie Glotzbach |
| 1969 | Lee Roy Yarbrough | Ford | 105.612 | Cale Yarborough |
| 1970 | Buddy Baker | Dodge | 128.817 | David Pearson |
| 1971 | Bobby Allison | Mercury | 131.398 | Bobby Allison |
| 1972 | Bobby Allison | Chevrolet | 128.124 | David Pearson |
| 1973 | Cale Yarborough | Chevrolet | 134.033 | David Pearson |
| 1974 | Cale Yarborough | Chevrolet | 111.075 | Richard Petty |
| 1975 | Bobby Allison | Matador | 116.825 | David Pearson |
| 1976 | David Pearson | Mercury | 120.534 | David Pearson |
| 1977 | David Pearson | Mercury | 106.797 | Darrell Waltrip |
| 1978 | Cale Yarborough | Oldsmobile | 116.828 | David Pearson |
| 1979 | David Pearson | Chevrolet | 126.259 | Bobby Allison |
| 1980 | Terry Labonte | Chevrolet | 115.210 | Darrell Waltrip |
| 1981 | Neil Bonnett | Ford | 126.410 | Harry Gant |
| 1982 | Cale Yarborough | Buick | 126.703 | David Pearson |
| 1983 | Bobby Allison | Buick | 123.343 | Neil Bonnett |
| 1984 | Harry Gant | Chevrolet | 128.270 | Harry Gant |
| 1985 | Bill Elliott | Ford | 121.254 | Bill Elliott |
| 1986 | Tim Richmond | Chevrolet | 121.068 | Tim Richmond |
| 1987 | Dale Earnhardt | Chevrolet | 115.520 | Davey Allison |
| 1988 | Bill Elliott | Ford | 128.297 | Bill Elliott |
| 1989 | Dale Earnhardt | Chevrolet | 135.462 | Alan Kulwicki |
| 1990 | Dale Earnhardt | Chevrolet | 123.141 | Dale Earnhardt |
| 1991 | Harry Gant | Oldsmobile | 133.508 | Davey Allison |
| 1992 | Darrell Waltrip | Chevrolet | 129.114 | Sterling Marlin |
| 1993 | Mark Martin | Ford | 137.932 | Ken Schrader |
| 1994 | Bill Elliott | Ford | 127.915 | Geoff Bodine |
| 1995 | Jeff Gordon | Chevrolet | 121.231 | John Andretti |
| 1996 | Jeff Gordon | Chevrolet | 135.757 | Dale Jarrett |
| 1997 | Jeff Gordon | Chevrolet | 121.149 | Bobby Labonte |
| 1998 | Jeff Gordon | Chevrolet | 139.031* | Dale Jarrett |
| 1999 | Jeff Burton | Ford | 100.816 | Kenny Irwin |
| 2000 | Bobby Labonte | Pontiac | 108.275 | Jeremy Mayfield |
| 2001 | Ward Burton | Dodge | 122.773 | Kurt Busch |
| 2002 | Jeff Gordon | Chevrolet | 118.617 | Sterling Marlin |
| 2003 | Terry Labonte | Chevrolet | 120.744 | Ryan Newman |
| 2004 | Jimmie Johnson | Chevrolet | 125.044 | Kurt Busch |
| 2005 | Greg Biffle | Ford | 135.127 | Kasey Kahne |
| 2006 | Greg Biffle | Ford | 123.031 | Kasey Kahne |
| 2007 | Jeff Gordon | Chevrolet | 124.372 | Clint Bowyer |
| 2008 | Kyle Busch | Toyota | 140.350 | Greg Biffle |
| 2009 | Mark Martin | Chevrolet | 119.687 | Matt Kenseth |

Through 2004, results listed were for the Southern 500, traditionally the second race of the year at the 1.366-mile Darlington (S.C.) Raceway. Starting in 2005, Darlington only hosted one race a year, in May.

*Track record, winning speed.

## Sprint Cup* NASCAR Champions

| Year | Driver | Car | Wins | Poles | Winnings ($) |
|---|---|---|---|---|---|
| 1949 | Red Byron | Oldsmobile | 2 | 1 | 5,800 |
| 1950 | Bill Rexford | Oldsmobile | 1 | 0 | 6,175 |
| 1951 | Herb Thomas | Hudson | 7 | 4 | 18,200 |
| 1952 | Tim Flock | Hudson | 8 | 4 | 20,210 |
| 1953 | Herb Thomas | Hudson | 11 | 10 | 27,300 |
| 1954 | Lee Petty | Dodge | 7 | 3 | 26,706 |
| 1955 | Tim Flock | Chrysler | 18 | 19 | 33,750 |
| 1956 | Buck Baker | Chrysler | 14 | 12 | 29,790 |
| 1957 | Buck Baker | Chevrolet | 10 | 5 | 24,712 |
| 1958 | Lee Petty | Oldsmobile | 7 | 4 | 20,600 |
| 1959 | Lee Petty | Plymouth | 10 | 2 | 45,570 |
| 1960 | Rex White | Chevrolet | 6 | 3 | 45,260 |
| 1961 | Ned Jarrett | Chevrolet | 1 | 4 | 27,285 |
| 1962 | Joe Weatherly | Pontiac | 9 | 6 | 56,110 |
| 1963 | Joe Weatherly | Mercury | 3 | 6 | 58,110 |
| 1964 | Richard Petty | Plymouth | 9 | 8 | 98,810 |
| 1965 | Ned Jarrett | Ford | 13 | 9 | 77,966 |
| 1966 | David Pearson | Dodge | 14 | 7 | 59,205 |
| 1967 | Richard Petty | Plymouth | 27 | 18 | 130,275 |
| 1968 | David Pearson | Ford | 16 | 12 | 118,824 |
| 1969 | David Pearson | Ford | 11 | 14 | 183,700 |
| 1970 | Bobby Isaac | Dodge | 11 | 13 | 121,470 |
| 1971 | Richard Petty | Plymouth | 21 | 9 | 309,225 |
| 1972 | Richard Petty | Plymouth | 8 | 3 | 227,015 |
| 1973 | Benny Parsons | Chevrolet | 1 | 0 | 114,345 |
| 1974 | Richard Petty | Dodge | 10 | 7 | 299,175 |
| 1975 | Richard Petty | Dodge | 13 | 3 | 378,865 |
| 1976 | Cale Yarborough | Chevrolet | 9 | 2 | 387,173 |
| 1977 | Cale Yarborough | Chevrolet | 9 | 3 | 477,499 |
| 1978 | Cale Yarborough | Oldsmobile | 10 | 8 | 530,751 |
| 1979 | Richard Petty | Chevrolet | 5 | 1 | 531,292 |
| 1980 | Dale Earnhardt | Chevrolet | 5 | 0 | 588,926 |
| 1981 | Darrell Waltrip | Buick | 12 | 11 | 693,342 |
| 1982 | Darrell Waltrip | Buick | 12 | 7 | 873,118 |
| 1983 | Bobby Allison | Buick | 6 | 0 | 828,355 |
| 1984 | Terry Labonte | Chevrolet | 2 | 2 | 713,010 |
| 1985 | Darrell Waltrip | Chevrolet | 3 | 4 | 1,318,735 |
| 1986 | Dale Earnhardt | Chevrolet | 5 | 1 | 1,783,880 |
| 1987 | Dale Earnhardt | Chevrolet | 11 | 1 | 2,099,243 |
| 1988 | Bill Elliott | Ford | 6 | 6 | 1,574,639 |
| 1989 | Rusty Wallace | Pontiac | 6 | 4 | 2,247,950 |
| 1990 | Dale Earnhardt | Chevrolet | 9 | 4 | 3,083,056 |
| 1991 | Dale Earnhardt | Chevrolet | 4 | 0 | 2,396,685 |
| 1992 | Alan Kulwicki | Ford | 2 | 6 | 2,322,561 |
| 1993 | Dale Earnhardt | Chevrolet | 6 | 2 | 3,353,789 |
| 1994 | Dale Earnhardt | Chevrolet | 4 | 2 | 3,400,733 |
| 1995 | Jeff Gordon | Chevrolet | 7 | 9 | 4,347,343 |
| 1996 | Terry Labonte | Chevrolet | 2 | 4 | 4,030,648 |
| 1997 | Jeff Gordon | Chevrolet | 10 | 1 | 4,201,227 |
| 1998 | Jeff Gordon | Chevrolet | 13 | 7 | 6,175,867 |
| 1999 | Dale Jarrett | Ford | 4 | 0 | 3,608,829 |
| 2000 | Bobby Labonte | Pontiac | 4 | 2 | 4,041,750 |
| 2001 | Jeff Gordon | Chevrolet | 6 | 8 | 6,649,076 |
| 2002 | Tony Stewart | Pontiac | 3 | 4 | 4,695,150 |
| 2003 | Matt Kenseth | Ford | 1 | 2 | 4,038,120 |
| 2004 | Kurt Busch | Ford | 3 | 1 | 4,200,330 |
| 2005 | Tony Stewart | Chevrolet | 5 | 3 | 6,987,530 |
| 2006 | Jimmie Johnson | Chevrolet | 5 | 1 | 8,909,140 |
| 2007 | Jimmie Johnson | Chevrolet | 10 | 4 | 7,646,420 |
| 2008 | Jimmie Johnson | Chevrolet | 7 | 6 | 7,354,860 |

*Series name changed from Winston Cup after 2003 season, then to Sprint Cup beginning in 2008.

### Alltime NASCAR Leaders

| WINS | | WINS | | POLE POSITIONS | | POLE POSITIONS | |
|---|---|---|---|---|---|---|---|
| Richard Petty | 200 | Lee Petty | 54 | Richard Petty | 126 | Junior Johnson | 47 |
| David Pearson | 105 | Ned Jarrett | 50 | David Pearson | 113 | *Mark Martin | 47 |
| Bobby Allison | 84 | Junior Johnson | 50 | Cale Yarborough | 70 | Buck Baker | 44 |
| Darrell Waltrip | 84 | Herb Thomas | 48 | *Jeff Gordon | 67 | *Ryan Newman | 44 |
| Cale Yarborough | 83 | Buck Baker | 46 | Darrell Waltrip | 59 | Buddy Baker | 40 |
| *Jeff Gordon | 82 | *Jimmie Johnson | 45 | Bobby Allison | 57 | Tim Flock | 39 |
| Dale Earnhardt | 76 | Bill Elliott | 44 | Bill Elliott | 54 | Herb Thomas | 39 |
| Rusty Wallace | 55 | *Mark Martin | 40 | Bobby Isaac | 51 | Geoff Bodine | 37 |

*Active drivers. Note: NASCAR wins leaders and pole position leaders through Oct 11, 2009.

## Formula One Grand Prix Racing

### World Driving Champions

| Year | Winner | Car | Year | Winner | Car |
|---|---|---|---|---|---|
| 1950 | Guiseppe Farina, Italy | Alfa Romeo | 1977 | Niki Lauda, Austria | Ferrari |
| 1951 | Juan-Manuel Fangio, Argentina | Alfa Romeo | 1978 | Mario Andretti, U.S. | Lotus-Ford |
| | | | 1979 | Jody Scheckter, S Africa | Ferrari |
| 1952 | Alberto Ascari, Italy | Ferrari | 1980 | Alan Jones, Australia | Williams-Ford |
| 1953 | Alberto Ascari, Italy | Ferrari | 1981 | Nelson Piquet, Brazil | Brabham-Ford |
| 1954 | Juan-Manuel Fangio, Argentina | Maserati-Mercedes | 1982 | Keke Rosberg, Finland | Williams-Ford |
| | | | 1983 | Nelson Piquet, Brazil | Brabham-BMW |
| 1955 | Juan-Manuel Fangio, Argentina | Mercedes | 1984 | Niki Lauda, Austria | McLaren-Porsche |
| | | | 1985 | Alain Prost, France | McLaren-Porsche |
| 1956 | Juan-Manuel Fangio, Argentina | Ferrari | 1986 | Alain Prost, France | McLaren-Porsche |
| | | | 1987 | Nelson Piquet, Brazil | Williams-Honda |
| 1957 | Juan-Manuel Fangio, Argentina | Maserati | 1988 | Ayrton Senna, Brazil | McLaren-Honda |
| | | | 1989 | Alain Prost, France | McLaren-Honda |
| 1958 | Mike Hawthorn, Grt Britain | Ferrari | 1990 | Ayrton Senna, Brazil | McLaren-Honda |
| 1959 | Jack Brabham, Australia | Cooper-Climax | 1991 | Ayrton Senna, Brazil | McLaren-Honda |
| 1960 | Jack Brabham, Australia | Cooper-Climax | 1992 | Nigel Mansell, Grt. Britain | Williams-Renault |
| 1961 | Phil Hill, U.S. | Ferrari | 1993 | Alain Prost, France | Williams-Renault |
| 1962 | Graham Hill, Grt Britain | BRM | 1994 | Michael Schumacher, Ger | Benetton-Ford |
| 1963 | Jim Clark, Scotland | Lotus-Climax | 1995 | Michael Schumacher, Ger | Benetton-Renault |
| 1964 | John Surtees, Grt Britain | Ferrari | 1996 | Damon Hill, Grt Britain | Williams-Renault |
| 1965 | Jim Clark, Scotland | Lotus-Climax | 1997 | Jacques Villeneuve, Can | Williams-Renault |
| 1966 | Jack Brabham, Australia | Brabham-Repco | 1998 | Mika Hakkinen, Finland | McLaren-Mercedes |
| 1967 | Denny Hulme, New Zealand | Brabham-Repco | 1999 | Mika Hakkinen, Finland | McLaren-Mercedes |
| | | | 2000 | Michael Schumacher, Ger | Ferrari |
| 1968 | Graham Hill, Grt Britain | Lotus-Ford | 2001 | Michael Schumacher, Ger | Ferrari |
| 1969 | Jackie Stewart, Scotland | Matra-Ford | 2002 | Michael Schumacher, Ger | Ferrari |
| 1970 | Jochen Rindt, Austria* | Lotus-Ford | 2003 | Michael Schumacher, Ger | Ferrari |
| 1971 | Jackie Stewart, Scotland | Tyrell-Ford | 2004 | Michael Schumacher, Ger | Ferrari |
| 1972 | Emerson Fittipaldi, Brazil | Lotus-Ford | 2005 | Fernando Alonso, Spain | Renault |
| 1973 | Jackie Stewart, Scotland | Tyrell-Ford | 2006 | Fernando Alonso, Spain | Renault |
| 1974 | Emerson Fittipaldi, Brazil | McLaren-Ford | 2007 | Kimi Raikkonen, Finland | Ferrari |
| 1975 | Niki Lauda, Austria | Ferrari | 2008 | Lewis Hamilton, Great Britain | McLaren-Mercedes |
| 1976 | James Hunt, Grt Britain | McLaren-Ford | | | |

*The championship was awarded posthumously, after Rindt was killed during practice for the Italian Grand Prix.

### Alltime F/I Grand Prix Winners

| Driver | Wins | Driver | Wins |
|---|---|---|---|
| Michael Schumacher, Germany | 91 | Jim Clark, Great Britain | 25 |
| Alain Prost, France | 51 | Niki Lauda, Austria | 25 |
| Ayrton Senna, Brazil | 41 | Juan Manuel Fangio, Argentina | 24 |
| Nigel Mansell, Great Britain | 31 | Nelson Piquet, Brazil | 23 |
| Jackie Stewart, Great Britain | 27 | Damon Hill, Great Britain | 22 |

### Alltime F/I Grand Prix Pole Winners

| Driver | Poles | Driver | Poles |
|---|---|---|---|
| Michael Schumacher, Germany | 68 | Juan Manuel Fangio, Argentina | 29 |
| Ayrton Senna, Brazil | 65 | Mika Hakkinen, Finland | 26 |
| Alain Prost, France | 33 | Niki Lauda, Austria | 24 |
| Jim Clark, Great Britain | 33 | Nelson Piquet, Brazil | 24 |
| Nigel Mansell, Great Britain | 31 | Damon Hill, Great Britain | 20 |

*Active driver in 2009. Note: Grand Prix winners through Oct 4, 2009.

## The 24 Hours of Daytona

| Year | Winner | Car | Avg Speed | Distance |
|---|---|---|---|---|
| 1962 | Dan Gurney | Lotus 19-Class SP11 | 104.101 mph | 3 hrs (312.42 mi) |
| 1963 | Pedro Rodriguez | Ferrari-Class 12 | 102.074 mph | 3 hrs (308.61 mi) |
| 1964 | Pedro Rodriguez/Phil Hill | Ferrari 250 LM | 98.230 mph | 2,000 km |
| 1965 | Ken Miles/Lloyd Ruby | Ford | 99.944 mph | 2,000 km |
| 1966 | Ken Miles/Lloyd Ruby | Ford Mark II | 108.020 mph | 24 hrs (2,570.63 mi) |
| 1967 | Lorenzo Bandini/Chris Amon | Ferrari 330 P4 | 105.688 mph | 24 hrs (2,537.46 mi) |
| 1968 | Vic Elford/Jochen Neerpasch | Porsche 907 | 106.697 mph | 24 hrs (2,565.69 mi) |
| 1969 | Mark Donohue/Chuck Parsons | Chevy Lola | 99.268 mph | 24 hrs (2,383.75 mi) |
| 1970 | Pedro Rodriguez/Leo Kinnunen | Porsche 917 | 114.866 mph | 24 hrs (2,758.44 mi) |
| 1971 | Pedro Rodriguez/Jackie Oliver | Porsche 917K | 109.203 mph | 24 hrs (2,621.28 mi) |
| 1972* | Mario Andretti/Jacky Ickx | Ferrari 312/P | 122.573 mph | 6 hrs (738.24 mi) |
| 1973 | Peter Gregg/Hurley Haywood | Porsche Carrera | 106.225 mph | 24 hrs (2,552.7 mi) |
| 1974 | (No race) | | | |
| 1975 | Peter Gregg/Hurley Haywood | Porsche Carrera | 108.531 mph | 24 hrs (2,606.04 mi) |
| 1976† | Peter Gregg/Brian Redman/ John Fitzpatrick | BMW CSL | 104.040 mph | 24 hrs (2,092.8 mi) |
| 1977 | John Graves/Hurley Haywood/ Dave Helmick | Porsche Carrera | 108.801 mph | 24 hrs (2,615 mi) |
| 1978 | Rolf Stommelen/ Antoine Hezemans/Peter Gregg | Porsche Turbo | 108.743 mph | 24 hrs (2,611.2 mi) |
| 1979 | Ted Field/Danny Ongais/ Hurley Haywood | Porsche Turbo | 109.249 mph | 24 hrs (2,626.56 mi) |
| 1980 | Volkert Meri/Rolf Stommelen/ Reinhold Joest | Porsche Turbo | 114.303 mph | 24 hrs |
| 1981 | Bob Garretson/Bobby Rahal/ Brian Redman | Porsche Turbo | 113.153 mph | 24 hrs |
| 1982 | John Paul Jr/John Paul Sr/ Rolf Stommelen | Porsche Turbo | 114.794 mph | 24 hrs |
| 1983 | Preston Henn/Bob Wollek/ Claude Ballot-Lena/A.J. Foyt | Porsche Turbo | 98.781 mph | 24 hrs |
| 1984 | Sarel van der Merwe/ Graham Duxbury/Tony Martin | Porsche March | 103.119 mph | 24 hrs (2,476.8 mi) |
| 1985 | A.J. Foyt/Bob Wollek/ Al Unser/Thierry Boutsen | Porsche 962 | 104.162 mph | 24 hrs (2,502.68 mi) |
| 1986 | Al Holbert/Derek Bell/Al Unser Jr. | Porsche 962 | 105.484 mph | 24 hrs (2,534.72 mi) |
| 1987 | Chip Robinson/Derek Bell/ Al Holbert/Al Unser Jr. | Porsche 962 | 111.599 mph | 24 hrs (2,680.68 mi) |
| 1988 | Martin Brundle/John Nielsen/ Raul Boesel | Jaguar XJR-9 | 107.943 mph | 24 hrs (2,591.68 mi) |
| 1989 | John Andretti/Derek Bell/ Bob Wollek | Porsche 962 | 92.009 mph | 24 hrs (2,210.76 mi) |
| 1990 | Davy Jones/ Jan Lammers/ Andy Wallace | Jaguar XJR-12 | 112.857 mph | 24 hrs (2,709.16 mi) |
| 1991 | Hurley Haywood/ John Winter/ Frank Jelinski/ Henri Pescarolo/ Bob Wollek | Porsche 962C | 106.633 mph | 24 hrs (2,559.64 mi) |
| 1992 | Massahiro Hasemi/ Kazuoyshi Hoshino/ Toshio Suzuki/ Anders Olofsson | Nissan R91CP | 112.987 mph | 24 hrs (2,712.72 mi) |
| 1993 | P.J. Jones/Mark Dismore/ Rocky Moran | Toyota Eagle MK III | 103.537 mph | 24 hrs (2,484.88 mi) |
| 1994 | Paul Gentilozzi/ Scott Pruett/ Butch Leitzinger/ Steve Millen | Nissan 300 ZX | 104.80 mph | 24 hrs (2,693.67 mi) |
| 1995 | Jurgen Lassig/ Christophe Buochut/ Giovanni Lavaggi/ Marco Werner | Porsche Spyder K8 | 102.28 mph | 690 laps (2,456.4 mi) |
| 1996 | Wayne Taylor/ Scott Sharp/ Jim Pace | Oldsmobile Mark III | 103.32 mph | 697 laps (2,481.32 mi) |
| 1997 | Elliot Forbes-Robinson/ John Schneider/Rob Dyson/ John Paul Jr/Butch Leitzinger/James Weaver/Andy Wallace | Ford R & S MK III | 102.292 mph | 690 laps (2,456.4 mi) |
| 1998 | Arie Luyendyk/Didier Theys/ Mauro Baldi | Ferrari 333 SP | 105.565 mph | 711 laps (2,531.16 mi) |
| 1999 | Elliott Forbes-Robinson/ Butch Leitzinger/ Andy Wallace | Ford R & S MK III | 104.9 mph | 708 laps (2,520.48 mi) |
| 2000 | Olivier Beretta/Karl Wendlinger/ Dominique Dupuy | Dodge Viper | 107.207 mph | 723 laps (2,573.88 m) |

## The 24 Hours of Daytona *(Cont.)*

| Year | Winner | Car | Speed | Laps |
|------|--------|-----|-------|------|
| 2001 | Ron Fellows/Chris Kneifel/ Franck Freon/Johnny O'Connell | Corvette | 97.293 mph | 656 laps (2,335.360 mi) |
| 2002 | Didier Theys/Fredy Lienhard/ Max Papis/Mauro Baldi· | Dallara-Judd (SRP) | 106.143 mph | 716 laps (2,548.96 mi) |
| 2003 | Kevin Buckler/Michael Schrom Timo Bernhard/Jorg Bergmeister | Porsche GT3 RS | 114.068 mph‡ | 694 laps (2,470.64 mi) |
| 2004 | Forest Barber/Terry Borcheller Andy Pilgrim/Christian Fittipaldi | Pontiac Doran | 117.651 mph | 526 laps (1,872.56 mi) |
| 2005 | Wayne Taylor, Max Angelelli, Emmanuel Collard | Pontiac Riley | 119.397 mph | 710 laps (2,527.60 mi) |
| 2006 | Scott Dixon/Dan Wheldon Casey Mears | Lexus Riley | 108.826 mph | 734 laps (2,613.04 mi) |
| 2007 | Scott Pruett/Salvador Duran Juan Pablo Montoya | Lexus Riley | 99.020 mph | 668 laps (2,378.08 mi) |
| 2008 | Scott Pruett/Memo Rojas Juan Pablo Montoya Dario Franchitti | Lexus Riley | 103.057 mph | 695 laps (2,474.20 mi) |
| 2009 | Darren Law/David Donohue Buddy Rice/Antonio Garcia | Porsche Riley | 108.994 mph | 735 laps (2,616.60 mi.) |

*Race shortened due to fuel crisis. †Course lengthened from 3.81 miles to 3.84 miles. ‡Top speed.

## World SportsCar Champions*

| Year | Winner | Car | Year | Winner | Car |
|------|--------|-----|------|--------|-----|
| 1978 | Peter Gregg | Porsche 935 | 1989 | Geoff Brabham | Nissan GTP |
| 1979 | Peter Gregg | Porsche 935 | 1990 | Geoff Brabham | Nissan GTP |
| 1980 | John Fitzpatrick | Porsche 935 | 1991 | Geoff Brabham | Nissan NPT |
| 1981 | Brian Redman | Chevy Lola | 1992 | Juan Fangio II | Toyota EGL MKII |
| 1982 | John Paul Jr | Chevy Lola | 1993 | Juan Fangio II | Toyota EGL MKIII |
| 1983 | Al Holbert | Chevy March | 1994 | Wayne Taylor | Mazda Kudzu |
| 1984 | Randy Lanier | Chevy March | 1995 | Fermin Velez | Ferrari 333 SP |
| 1985 | Al Holbert | Porsche 962 | 1996 | Wayne Taylor | Mazda Kudzu |
| 1986 | Al Holbert | Porsche 962 | 1997 | Butch Leitzinger | Ford R&S MKIII |
| 1987 | Chip Robinson | Porsche 962 | 1998 | Butch Leitzinger | Ford R&S MKIII |
| 1988 | Geoff Brabham | Nissan GTP | | | |

| Year | Prototype | GTS | GT |
|------|-----------|-----|-----|
| 1999 | Elliott Forbes-Robinson | Olivier Beretta | Cort Wagner |
| 2000 | Allan McNish | Olivier Beretta | Sascha Maassen |
| 2001 | Emanuele Pirro | Terry Borcheller | Jörg Müller |
| 2002 | Tom Kristensen | Ron Fellows | Lucas Luhr |
| 2003 | Frank Biela/Marco Werner | Ron Fellows/John O'Connell | Sascha Maassen/L. Luhr |
| 2004 | Frank Biela/Emanuele Pirro | Olivier Gavin/Olivier Beretta | Patrick Long/Jorg Bergmeister |
| 2005 | Frank Biela/Emanuele Pirro | Olivier Gavin/Olivier Beretta | Patrick Long/Jorg Bergmeister |
| 2006 | R. Capello/A. McNish | Olivier Gavin/Olivier Beretta | Johannes van Overbeek |
| 2007 | R. Capello/A. McNish | Olivier Gavin/Olivier Beretta | Mika Salo/Jaime Melo |
| 2008 | Lucas Luhr/Marco Werner | Jan Magnussen/J. O'Connell | Jorg Bergmeister/Wolf Henzler |
| 2009 | David Brabham/Scott Sharp | Olivier Gavin/Olivier Beretta | Jorg Bergmeister/Patrick Long |

*1978–93 champions raced in the GT series, which in 1994 was replaced by the World SportsCar series. Beginning in 1999, racing was reclassified according to the American Le Mans Series. The Series is comprised of two different types of race cars divided into two categories and five separate classes. The Prototype category features open-cockpit prototype as well as Grand Touring Prototype (GTP) class cars. The Grand Touring category features the Grand Touring S (GTS) class cars, formerly known as GT2, and Grand Touring (GT) cars, formerly known as GT3. Both classes feature purpose-built race cars with an emphasis on spectator car identification.

## Alltime SportsCar Leaders

### PROTOTYPE WINS

| | |
|---|---|
| *Rinaldo Capello | 34 |
| *Allan McNish | 27 |
| *Marco Werner | 25 |
| *Frank Biela | 22 |
| J.J. Lehto | 19 |
| *Emanuele Pirro | 19 |
| James Weaver | 16 |

### GTS AND GT WINS

| | |
|---|---|
| Al Holbert | 49 |
| Peter Gregg | 41 |
| *Olivier Beretta | 41 |
| *Johnny O'Connell | 37 |
| *Oliver Gavin | 32 |
| Hurley Haywood | 31 |
| *Jorg Bergmeister | 29 |

* Active driver in 2009.

| Year | Winning Drivers | Car |
|------|-----------------|-----|
| 1923 | André Lagache/René Léonard | Chenard & Walker |
| 1924 | John Duff/Francis Clement | Bentley |
| 1925 | Gérard de Courcelles/André Rossignol | La Lorraine |
| 1926 | Robert Bloch/André Rossignol | La Lorraine |
| 1927 | J. Dudley Benjafield/Sammy Davis | Bentley |
| 1928 | Woolf Barnato/Bernard Rubin | Bentley |
| 1929 | Woolf Barnato/Sir Henry Birkin | Bentley Speed 6 |
| 1930 | Woolf Barnato/Glen Kidston | Bentley Speed 6 |
| 1931 | Earl Howe/Sir Henry Birkin | Alfa Romeo 8C-2300 sc |
| 1932 | Raymond Sommer/Luigi Chinetti | Alfa Romeo 8C-2300 sc |
| 1933 | Raymond Sommer/Tazio Nuvolari | Alfa Romeo 8C-2300 sc |
| 1934 | Luigi Chinetti/Philippe Etancelin | Alfa Romeo 8C-2300 sc |
| 1935 | John Hindmarsh/Louis Fontés | Lagonda M45R |
| 1936 | RACE CANCELLED | |
| 1937 | Jean-Pierre Wimille/Robert Benoist | Bugatti 57G sc |
| 1938 | Eugene Chaboud/Jean Tremoulet | Delahaye 135M |
| 1939 | Jean-Pierre Wimille/Pierre Veyron | Bugatti 57G sc |
| 1940–48 | RACES CANCELLED | |
| 1949 | Luigi Chinetti/Lord Selsdon | Ferrari 166MM |
| 1950 | Louis Rosier/Jean-Louis Rosier | Talbot-Lago |
| 1951 | Peter Walker/Peter Whitehead | Jaguar C |
| 1952 | Hermann Lang/Fritz Reiss | Mercedes-Benz 300 SL |
| 1953 | Tony Rolt/Duncan Hamilton | Jaguar C |
| 1954 | Froilan Gonzales/Maurice Trintignant | Ferrari 375 |
| 1955 | Mike Hawthorn/Ivor Bueb | Jaguar D |
| 1956 | Ron Flockhart/Ninian Sanderson | Jaguar D |
| 1957 | Ron Flockhart/Ivor Bueb | Jaguar D |
| 1958 | Olivier Gendebien/Phil Hill | Ferrari 250 TR58 |
| 1959 | Carroll Shelby/Roy Salvadori | Aston Martin DBR1 |
| 1960 | Olivier Gendebien/Paul Frère | Ferrari 250 TR59/60 |
| 1961 | Olivier Gendebien/Phil Hill | Ferrari 250 TR61 |
| 1962 | Olivier Gendebien/Phil Hill | Ferrari 250P |
| 1963 | Lodovico Scarfiotti/Lorenzo Bandini | Ferrari 250P |
| 1964 | Jean Guichel/Nino Vaccarella | Ferrari 275P |
| 1965 | Jochen Rindt/Masten Gregory | Ferrari 250LM |
| 1966 | Chris Amon/Bruce McLaren | Ford Mk2 |
| 1967 | Dan Gurney/A.J. Foyt | Ford Mk4 |
| 1968 | Pedro Rodriguez/Lucien Bianchi | Ford GT40 |
| 1969 | Jacky Ickx/Jackie Oliver | Ford GT40 |
| 1970 | Hans Herrmann/Richard Attwood | Porsche 917 |
| 1971 | Helmut Marko/Gijs van Lennep | Porsche 917 |
| 1972 | Henri Pescarolo/Graham Hill | Matra-Simca MS670 |
| 1973 | Henri Pescarolo/Gérard Larrousse | Matra-Simca MS670B |
| 1974 | Henri Pescarolo/Gérard Larrousse | Matra-Simca MS670B |
| 1975 | Jacky Ickx/Derek Bell | Mirage-Ford MB |
| 1976 | Jacky Ickx/Gijs van Lennep | Porsche 936 |
| 1977 | Jacky Ickx/Jurgen Barth/Hurley Haywood | Porsche 936 |
| 1978 | Jean-Pierre Jaussaud/Didier Pironi | Renault-Alpine A442 |
| 1979 | Klaus Ludwig/Bill Whittington/Don Whittington | Porsche 935 |
| 1980 | Jean-Pierre Jaussaud/Jean Rondeau | Rondeau-Ford M379B |
| 1981 | Jacky Ickx/Derek Bell | Porsche 936-81 |
| 1982 | Jacky Ickx/Derek Bell | Porsche 956 |
| 1983 | Vern Schuppan/Hurley Haywood/Al Holbert | Porsche 956-83 |
| 1984 | Klaus Ludwig/Henri Pescarolo | Porsche 956B |
| 1985 | Klaus Ludwig/Paolo Barilla/John Winter | Porsche 956B |
| 1986 | Derek Bell/Hans-Joachim Stuck/Al Holbert | Porsche 962C |
| 1987 | Derek Bell/Hans-Joachim Stuck/Al Holbert | Porsche 962C |
| 1988 | Jan Lammers/Johnny Dumfries/Andy Wallace | Jaguar XJR9LM |
| 1989 | Jochen Mass/Manuel Reuter/Stanley Dickens | Sauber-Mercedes C9-88 |
| 1990 | John Nielsen/Price Cobb/Martin Brundle | TWR Jaguar XJR-12 |
| 1991 | Volker Weidler/Johnny Herbert/Bertrand Gachot | Mazda 787B |
| 1992 | Derek Warwick/Yannick Dalmas/Mark Blundell | Peugeot 905B |
| 1993 | Geoff Brabham/Christophe Bouchut/Eric Helary | Peugeot 905 |
| 1994 | Yannick Dalmas/Hurley Haywood/Mauro Baldi | Porsche 962 |
| 1995 | Yannick Dalmas/J.J. Lehto/Masanori Sekiya | McLaren BMW |
| 1996 | Manuel Reuter/Davy Jones/Alexander Wurz | TWR Porsche |
| 1997 | Michele Alboreto/Stefan Johansson/Tom Kristensen | TWR Porsche |
| 1998 | Allan McNish/Laurent Aiello/Stephane Ortelli | Porsche GT One |
| 1999 | Yannick Dalmas/Joachim Winkelhock/Pierluigi Martini | BMW V12 LMR |
| 2000 | Frank Biela/Tom Kristensen/Emanuele Pirro | Audi R8 |
| 2001 | Frank Biela/Tom Kristensen/Emanuele Pirro | Audi R8 |
| 2002 | Frank Biela/Tom Kristensen/Emanuele Pirro | Audi R8 |
| 2003 | Rinaldo Capello/Tom Kristensen/Guy Smith | Bentley EXP Speed 8 |
| 2004 | Rinaldo Capello/Seiji Ara/Tom Kristensen | Audi R8 |
| 2005 | J.J. Lehto/Marco Werner/Tom Kristensen | Audi R8 |
| 2006 | Frank Biela/Emanuele Pirro/Marco Werner | Audi R10 |
| 2007 | Frank Biela/Emanuele Pirro/Marco Werner | Audi R10 |
| 2008 | Rinaldo Capello/Tom Kristensen/Allan McNish | Audi R10 |
| 2009 | Marc Gene/Alexander Wurz/David Brabham | Peugeot 908 |

# Soccer

Jozy Altidore (l.) scored early and led the U.S. national team to a stunning upset over top-ranked Spain at the '09 Confederations Cup

# Miracle on Grass

In undoubtedly the biggest win in U.S. soccer history, the Americans stunned Spain at the Confederations Cup and served notice that they could be a real force in 2010

BY HANK HERSCH

THROUGH THE SUMMER, THE reign of Spain stayed mainly over the futbol-loving world. In May, powerhouse Barcelona—led by 21-year-old Argentine wiz Lionel Messi—beat Manchester United 2–0 in the final of the Champions League, the most prestigious club tournament on the planet. Meanwhile, the Spanish national team, long known for its depth of talent and meagerness of achievement, continued to build on its first major international success in 44 years, the 2008 UEFA European Championship. Stretching its winning streak to a record 15 games, La Furia Roja (or the Red Fury) became the first team not to have won the World Cup to be ranked No. 1 in the FIFA rankings.

So it was no surprise in June that Spain roared into the semifinals of the Confederations Cup in South Africa, a quadrennial tournament that serves as a dry run for the coming World Cup and whose elite field is comprised of the World Cup's host, its reigning champion and the title holders from FIFA's six confederations. What was surprising was Spain's opponent: the U.S.,

which lost twice in three matches during first-round play. The Americans squeaked through on goal differential thanks to their improbable 3–0 victory over Egypt and Italy's even more improbable 3–0 loss to Brazil: The Azzurri had suffered a three-goal defeat only once since 1970 in a major tournament. As U.S. defender Jonathan Bornstein said afterward, "It's like that quote from *Dumb and Dumber* [after Lauren Holly tells Jim Carrey he has a million-to-one shot of landing her]: 'So you're telling me there's a chance!' That's what we kept saying."

So how to decipher what happened next in the semis? That the team with the one-game winning streak dominated the one that hadn't lost in 35 matches? That 19-year-old striker Jozy Altidore, who could not get off the bench for his team in Spain's second division, would score the first goal allowed by Spain in 451 minutes? That American centerbacks Jay DeMerit and Oguchi Onyewu, fronting for goalkeeper Tim Howard, would shut down the most dynamic midfield in the world as well as premier goal-scorer Fernando Torres? That despite being outshot 11–4 the

U.S. midfielder Landon Donovan celebrates the American victory over Spain by leaping into teammate Benny Feilhaber's arms.

SHAUN BOTTERILL · FIFA/FIFA VIA GETTY IMAGES

U.S. would prevail 2–0, so frustrating the Spaniards that they refused to engage in the customary exchange of jerseys afterward?

"It just shows we can compete with the best," said team captain and left full-back Carlos Bocanegra. "To do it on a consistent basis is our biggest thing moving forward. We have showed we can play with the big boys. We can beat them."

The victory ranked as one of the greatest in U.S. history; just four days later the U.S. was poised to surpass it. At halftime of the final in Johannesburg, the Yanks held a 2–0 lead over five-time World Cup champion Brazil, which had thoroughly outclassed the U.S. 3–0 in the opening round. Yet what could have turned into an epic achievement—the nation's first major international championship—instead ended in heart break. Missing defensive midfielder Michael Bradley, who had been red-carded late in the win over Spain, the U.S. surrendered its lead on a pair of goals to Luis Fabiano. Lucio's header past Howard in the 84th minute then proved decisive in Brazil's 3–2 victory.

At the least, the moments of brilliance and the lessons learned at the Confederations Cup helped prepare the Americans for a return trip to South Africa in 2010; they roared through qualifying by beating up on lesser North American opponents (although they still couldn't solve Mexico at Azteca Stadium) to clinch a berth in World Cup. Will they be able to sustain the sort of effort in South Africa next year that served them so well against Spain?

"We're at the point where we don't want respect," said U.S. midfielder Landon Donovan after the frustrating loss to Brazil in the Confederations Cup final. "We want to win."

## 2008 Major League Soccer

### 2008 Final Standings

#### EASTERN CONFERENCE

| Team | GP | W | L | T | Pts | GF | GA |
|---|---|---|---|---|---|---|---|
| †Columbus | 30 | 17 | 7 | 6 | 57 | 50 | 36 |
| *Chicago | 30 | 13 | 10 | 7 | 46 | 44 | 33 |
| *New England | 30 | 12 | 11 | 7 | 43 | 40 | 43 |
| *Kansas City | 30 | 11 | 10 | 9 | 42 | 37 | 39 |
| *New York | 30 | 10 | 11 | 9 | 39 | 42 | 48 |
| D.C. United | 30 | 14 | 15 | 4 | 37 | 43 | 51 |
| Toronto FC | 30 | 9 | 13 | 8 | 35 | 34 | 43 |

#### WESTERN CONFERENCE

| Team | GP | W | L | T | Pts | GF | GA |
|---|---|---|---|---|---|---|---|
| †Houston | 30 | 13 | 5 | 12 | 51 | 45 | 32 |
| *Chivas USA | 30 | 12 | 11 | 7 | 43 | 40 | 41 |
| *Real Salt Lake | 30 | 10 | 10 | 10 | 40 | 40 | 39 |
| Colorado | 30 | 11 | 14 | 5 | 38 | 44 | 45 |
| FC Dallas | 30 | 8 | 10 | 12 | 36 | 45 | 41 |
| Los Angeles | 30 | 8 | 13 | 9 | 33 | 55 | 62 |
| San Jose | 30 | 8 | 13 | 9 | 33 | 32 | 38 |

Note: Three points for a win. One point for a tie. †Conference champion. *Qualified for playoffs

#### SCORING LEADERS

| Player, Team | GP | G | A | Pts |
|---|---|---|---|---|
| Landon Donovan, LA | 25 | 20 | 9 | 29 |
| Guillermo Schelotto, CLB | 26 | 7 | 19 | 26 |
| Kenny Cooper, DAL | 30 | 18 | 3 | 21 |
| Javier Morales, RSL | 29 | 6 | 15 | 21 |
| Jaime Moreno, DC | 25 | 10 | 10 | 20 |
| Edson Buddle, LA | 27 | 15 | 3 | 18 |
| Brian Ching, HOU | 25 | 13 | 5 | 18 |
| Cuauhtemoc Blanco, CHI | 27 | 7 | 11 | 18 |
| Juan Pablo Angel, NY | 23 | 14 | 3 | 17 |
| Luciano Emillio, DC | 27 | 11 | 5 | 16 |

#### ASSISTS LEADERS

| Player, Team | GP | A |
|---|---|---|
| Guillermo Schelotto, CLB | 27 | 19 |
| Javier Morales, RSL | 29 | 15 |
| Terry Cooke, COL | 24 | 12 |
| Cuauhtemoc Blanco, CHI | 27 | 11 |
| David Beckahm, LA | 25 | 10 |
| Jaime Moreno, DC | 25 | 10 |
| Landon Donovan, LA | 25 | 9 |
| Brad Davis, HOU | 26 | 8 |
| Andre Rocha, DAL | 27 | 8 |
| Justin Mapp, CHI | 30 | 8 |

#### GOALS LEADERS

| Player, Team | GP | G |
|---|---|---|
| Landon Donovan, LA | 25 | 20 |
| Kenny Cooper, DAL | 30 | 18 |
| Edson Buddle, LA | 27 | 15 |
| Juan Pablo Angel, NY | 23 | 14 |
| Brian Ching, HOU | 25 | 13 |
| Conor Casey, COL | 21 | 11 |
| Luciano Emilio, DC | 27 | 11 |
| Jaime Moreno, DC | 25 | 10 |
| Chad Barrett, TOR | 29 | 9 |

#### GOALS-AGAINST-AVERAGE LEADERS

| Player, Team | GAA |
|---|---|
| Pat Onstad, HOU | 1.03 |
| Jon Busch, CHI | 1.10 |
| William Hesmer, CLB | 1.14 |
| Bouna Coundoul, COL | 1.24 |
| Joe Cannon, SJ | 1.27 |
| Kevin Hartman, KC | 1.30 |
| Nick Rimando, RSL | 1.30 |
| Dario Sala, DAL | 1.32 |
| Brad Guzan, CHV | 1.33 |

### Western Conference Playoffs

#### 1ST ROUND (TWO LEGS)

| Columbus | 1 | 2—3 |
| Kansas City | 1 | 0—1 |

| Chicago | 0 | 3—3 |
| New England | 0 | 0—0 |

#### CONF. FINALS

| Columbus | 2 |
| Chicago | 1 |

### Eastern Conference Playoffs

#### 1ST ROUND (TWO LEGS)

| Chivas USA | 0 | 2—2 |
| Real Salt Lake | 1 | 2—3 |

| New York | 1 | 3—4 |
| Houston | 1 | 0—1 |

#### CONF. FINALS

| New York | 2 |
| Real Salt Lake | 0 |

### 2008 MLS CUP

#### (November 23, 2008; Home Depot Center, Los Angeles, Calif.)

| Columbus | 1 | 2 — — 3 |
| New York | 0 | 1 — — 1 |

**FIRST HALF:** Scoring: 1, Columbus, Moreno (31).

**SECOND HALF:** Scoring: 1, New York, Wolyniec (51); 2, Columbus, Marshall (53), Hejduk (82).

**Columbus:** Hesmer, Hejduk, Padula, Marshall, O'Rourke, Carroll, Gaven (Lenhart 90), Evans, Rogers, Moreno, Schelotto (Iro 90).

**New England:** Cepero, Leitch, Mendes, Goldthwaite, Jimenez, Van den Berch, Richards, Ubiparipovic, Sassano (Rojas 78), Angel, Wolyniec (Kandji 83).

Attendance: 27,000. Referee: Baldomero Toledo.

**MLS Cup MVP:** Guillermo Schelotto, Columbus.

## Europe

### GROUP 1

| Country | GP | W | L | T | Pts |
|---|---|---|---|---|---|
| *Denmark | 9 | 6 | 0 | 3 | 21 |
| Portugal | 9 | 4 | 1 | 4 | 16 |
| Sweden | 9 | 4 | 2 | 3 | 15 |
| Hungary | 9 | 4 | 4 | 1 | 13 |
| Albania | 9 | 1 | 4 | 4 | 7 |
| Malta | 9 | 0 | 8 | 1 | 1 |

### GROUP 2

| Country | GP | W | L | T | Pts |
|---|---|---|---|---|---|
| Switzerland | 9 | 6 | 1 | 2 | 20 |
| Greece | 9 | 5 | 2 | 2 | 17 |
| Israel | 9 | 4 | 2 | 3 | 15 |
| Latvia | 9 | 4 | 3 | 2 | 14 |
| Luxembourg | 9 | 1 | 6 | 2 | 5 |
| Moldova | 9 | 0 | 6 | 3 | 3 |

### GROUP 3

| Country | GP | W | L | T | Pts |
|---|---|---|---|---|---|
| Slovakia | 9 | 6 | 2 | 1 | 19 |
| Slovenia | 9 | 5 | 2 | 2 | 17 |
| Czech Republic | 9 | 4 | 2 | 3 | 15 |
| Northern Ireland | 9 | 4 | 3 | 2 | 14 |
| Poland | 9 | 3 | 4 | 2 | 11 |
| San Marino | 9 | 0 | 9 | 0 | 0 |

### GROUP 4

| Country | GP | W | L | T | Pts |
|---|---|---|---|---|---|
| *Germany | 9 | 8 | 0 | 1 | 25 |
| Russia | 9 | 7 | 2 | 0 | 21 |
| Finland | 9 | 5 | 2 | 2 | 17 |
| Wales | 9 | 3 | 6 | 0 | 9 |
| Azerbaijan | 9 | 1 | 7 | 1 | 4 |
| Liechtenstein | 9 | 0 | 7 | 2 | 2 |

### GROUP 5

| Country | GP | W | L | T | Pts |
|---|---|---|---|---|---|
| *Spain | 9 | 9 | 0 | 0 | 27 |
| Bosnia & Herz. | 9 | 6 | 2 | 1 | 19 |
| Turkey | 9 | 3 | 3 | 3 | 12 |
| Belgium | 9 | 3 | 5 | 1 | 10 |
| Estonia | 9 | 1 | 6 | 2 | 5 |
| Armenia | 9 | 1 | 7 | 1 | 4 |

### GROUP 6

| Country | GP | W | L | T | Pts |
|---|---|---|---|---|---|
| *England | 9 | 8 | 1 | 0 | 24 |
| Ukraine | 9 | 5 | 1 | 3 | 18 |
| Croatia | 9 | 5 | 2 | 2 | 17 |
| Belarus | 9 | 4 | 4 | 1 | 13 |
| Kazakhstan | 9 | 2 | 7 | 0 | 6 |
| Andorra | 9 | 0 | 9 | 0 | 0 |

### GROUP 7

| Country | GP | W | L | T | Pts |
|---|---|---|---|---|---|
| *Serbia | 9 | 7 | 1 | 1 | 22 |
| France | 9 | 5 | 1 | 3 | 18 |
| Austria | 9 | 4 | 3 | 2 | 14 |
| Lithuania | 9 | 3 | 6 | 0 | 9 |
| Romania | 9 | 2 | 4 | 3 | 9 |
| Faroe Islands | 9 | 1 | 7 | 1 | 4 |

### GROUP 8

| Country | GP | W | L | T | Pts |
|---|---|---|---|---|---|
| *Italy | 9 | 6 | 0 | 3 | 21 |
| Ireland | 9 | 4 | 0 | 5 | 17 |
| Bulgaria | 9 | 2 | 2 | 5 | 11 |
| Cyprus | 9 | 2 | 4 | 3 | 9 |
| Montenegro | 9 | 1 | 3 | 5 | 8 |
| Georgia | 9 | 0 | 6 | 3 | 3 |

### GROUP 9

| Country | GP | W | L | T | Pts |
|---|---|---|---|---|---|
| *Netherlands | 8 | 8 | 0 | 0 | 24 |
| Norway | 8 | 2 | 2 | 4 | 10 |
| Scotland | 8 | 3 | 4 | 1 | 10 |
| Macedonia | 8 | 2 | 5 | 1 | 7 |
| Iceland | 8 | 1 | 5 | 2 | 5 |

## Africa

### GROUP A

| Country | GP | W | L | T | Pts |
|---|---|---|---|---|---|
| Cameroon | 5 | 3 | 1 | 1 | 10 |
| Gabon | 5 | 3 | 2 | 0 | 9 |
| Togo | 5 | 1 | 2 | 2 | 5 |
| Morocco | 5 | 0 | 2 | 3 | 3 |

### GROUP B

| Country | GP | W | L | T | Pts |
|---|---|---|---|---|---|
| Tunisia | 5 | 3 | 0 | 2 | 11 |
| Nigeria | 5 | 2 | 0 | 3 | 9 |
| Mozambique | 5 | 1 | 3 | 1 | 4 |
| Kenya | 5 | 1 | 4 | 0 | 3 |

### GROUP C

| Country | GP | W | L | T | Pts |
|---|---|---|---|---|---|
| Algeria | 5 | 4 | 0 | 1 | 13 |
| Egypt | 5 | 3 | 1 | 1 | 10 |
| Zambia | 5 | 1 | 3 | 1 | 4 |
| Rwanda | 5 | 0 | 4 | 1 | 1 |

### GROUP D

| Country | GP | W | L | T | Pts |
|---|---|---|---|---|---|
| *Ghana | 5 | 4 | 1 | 0 | 12 |
| Mali | 5 | 2 | 1 | 2 | 8 |
| Benin | 5 | 2 | 2 | 1 | 7 |
| Sudan | 5 | 0 | 4 | 1 | 1 |

### GROUP E

| Country | GP | W | L | T | Pts |
|---|---|---|---|---|---|
| *Cote D'Ivoire | 5 | 4 | 0 | 1 | 13 |
| Burkina Faso | 5 | 3 | 2 | 0 | 9 |
| Malawi | 5 | 1 | 3 | 1 | 4 |
| Guinea | 5 | 1 | 4 | 0 | 3 |

## Asia & Australia

### GROUP 1

| Country | GP | W | L | T | Pts |
|---|---|---|---|---|---|
| *Australia | 8 | 6 | 0 | 2 | 20 |
| *Japan | 8 | 4 | 1 | 3 | 15 |
| †Bahrain | 8 | 3 | 4 | 1 | 10 |
| Qatar | 8 | 1 | 4 | 3 | 6 |
| Uzbekistan | 8 | 1 | 6 | 1 | 4 |

### GROUP 2

| Country | GP | W | L | T | Pts |
|---|---|---|---|---|---|
| *South Korea | 8 | 4 | 0 | 4 | 16 |
| *North Korea | 8 | 3 | 2 | 3 | 12 |
| †Saudi Arabia | 8 | 3 | 2 | 3 | 12 |
| Iran | 8 | 2 | 1 | 5 | 11 |
| United Arab Emirates | 8 | 0 | 7 | 1 | 1 |

## North & Central America, Caribbean

| Country | GP | W | L | T | Pts |
|---|---|---|---|---|---|
| *United States | 9 | 6 | 2 | 1 | 19 |
| *Mexico | 9 | 6 | 3 | 0 | 18 |
| Costa Rica | 9 | 5 | 4 | 0 | 15 |
| Honduras | 9 | 4 | 4 | 1 | 13 |
| El Salvador | 9 | 2 | 5 | 2 | 8 |
| Trinidad & Tobago | 9 | 1 | 6 | 3 | 5 |

## South America

| Country | GP | W | L | T | Pts |
|---|---|---|---|---|---|
| *Brazil | 17 | 9 | 2 | 6 | 33 |
| *Paraguay | 17 | 10 | 4 | 3 | 33 |
| *Chile | 17 | 9 | 5 | 3 | 30 |
| Argentina | 17 | 7 | 6 | 4 | 25 |
| Uruguay | 17 | 6 | 5 | 6 | 24 |
| Ecuador | 17 | 6 | 6 | 5 | 23 |
| Venezuela | 17 | 6 | 8 | 3 | 21 |
| Colombia | 17 | 5 | 7 | 5 | 20 |
| Bolivia | 17 | 4 | 10 | 3 | 15 |
| Peru | 17 | 2 | 11 | 4 | 10 |

*Qualified for 2010 FIFA World Cup as of Oct. 11, 2009. †Bahrain and Saudi Arabia will compete in a two-leg playoff with the winner qualifying for the 2010 World Cup. Note: in group play, three points are awarded for a win, one for a tie.

## The World Cup

### Results—Men

| Year | Champion | Score | Runner-Up | Winning Coach |
|------|----------|-------|-----------|---------------|
| 1930 | Uruguay | 4–2 | Argentina | Alberto Supicci |
| 1934 | Italy | 2–1 | Czechoslovakia | Vittorio Pozzo |
| 1938 | Italy | 4–2 | Hungary | Vittorio Pozzo |
| 1950 | Uruguay | 2–1 | Brazil | Juan Lopez |
| 1954 | W Germany | 3–2 | Hungary | Sepp Herberger |
| 1958 | Brazil | 5–2 | Sweden | Vicente Feola |
| 1962 | Brazil | 3–1 | Czechoslovakia | Aymore Moreira |
| 1966 | England | 4–2 | W Germany | Alf Ramsey |
| 1970 | Brazil | 4–1 | Italy | Mario Zagalo |
| 1974 | W Germany | 2–1 | Netherlands | Helmut Schoen |
| 1978 | Argentina | 3–1 | Netherlands | César Menotti |
| 1982 | Italy | 3–1 | W Germany | Enzo Bearzot |
| 1986 | Argentina | 3–2 | W Germany | Carlos Bilardo |
| 1990 | W Germany | 1–0 | Argentina | Franz Beckenbauer |
| 1994 | Brazil | 0–0 (3–2) | Italy | Carlos Alberto Parreira |
| 1998 | France | 3–0 | Brazil | Aime Jacquet |
| 2002 | Brazil | 2–0 | Germany | Luis Felipe Scolari |
| 2006 | Italy | 1–1 (5–3) | France | Marcello Lippi |

### Alltime World Cup Participation

| Nation | Matches | W | T | L | Goals For | Goals Against | Nation | Matches | W | T | L | Goals For | Goals Against |
|--------|---------|---|---|---|-----------|---------------|--------|---------|---|---|---|-----------|---------------|
| Brazil | 92 | 64 | 14 | 14 | 201 | 84 | Senegal | 5 | 2 | 2 | 1 | 7 | 6 |
| *Germany | 92 | 55 | 19 | 18 | 190 | 112 | Ukraine | 5 | 2 | 1 | 1 | 5 | 7 |
| Italy | 77 | 44 | 19 | 14 | 122 | 69 | E Germany | 6 | 2 | 2 | 2 | 5 | 5 |
| Argentina | 65 | 33 | 13 | 19 | 113 | 73 | Ghana | 4 | 2 | 0 | 2 | 4 | 6 |
| England | 55 | 25 | 17 | 13 | 74 | 47 | Norway | 8 | 2 | 3 | 3 | 7 | 8 |
| France | 51 | 25 | 10 | 16 | 95 | 64 | Algeria | 6 | 2 | 1 | 3 | 6 | 10 |
| Spain | 49 | 22 | 12 | 15 | 80 | 60 | Morocco | 10 | 2 | 4 | 4 | 10 | 13 |
| †Russia | 37 | 17 | 6 | 14 | 64 | 44 | Japan | 10 | 2 | 2 | 6 | 8 | 14 |
| Yugoslavia | 37 | 17 | 6 | 14 | 60 | 46 | Saudi Arabia | 13 | 2 | 2 | 9 | 9 | 32 |
| Netherlands | 35 | 16 | 10 | 9 | 58 | 36 | Cuba | 3 | 1 | 1 | 1 | 5 | 12 |
| Poland | 31 | 15 | 5 | 11 | 44 | 40 | S Africa | 6 | 1 | 3 | 2 | 8 | 11 |
| Hungary | 32 | 15 | 3 | 14 | 87 | 57 | N Korea | 4 | 1 | 1 | 2 | 5 | 9 |
| Uruguay | 40 | 15 | 10 | 15 | 65 | 57 | Ivory Coast | 3 | 1 | 0 | 2 | 5 | 6 |
| Sweden | 45 | 15 | 11 | 19 | 70 | 69 | Jamaica | 3 | 1 | 0 | 2 | 3 | 9 |
| Austria | 29 | 12 | 4 | 13 | 42 | 48 | Israel | 3 | 1 | 0 | 2 | 1 | 3 |
| Czech Republic | 33 | 12 | 5 | 16 | 47 | 49 | Republic of Ireland | 13 | 2 | 7 | 4 | 10 | 10 |
| Portugal | 19 | 11 | 1 | 7 | 32 | 21 | Australia | 7 | 1 | 2 | 4 | 5 | 11 |
| Mexico | 45 | 11 | 12 | 22 | 48 | 84 | Iran | 9 | 1 | 2 | 6 | 6 | 18 |
| Belgium | 36 | 10 | 9 | 17 | 46 | 63 | Tunisia | 12 | 1 | 4 | 7 | 8 | 17 |
| Romania | 21 | 8 | 5 | 8 | 30 | 32 | Honduras | 3 | 0 | 2 | 1 | 2 | 3 |
| Switzerland | 26 | 8 | 5 | 13 | 37 | 51 | Angola | 3 | 0 | 2 | 1 | 1 | 2 |
| Denmark | 13 | 7 | 2 | 4 | 24 | 18 | Dutch East Indies | 1 | 0 | 0 | 1 | 0 | 6 |
| Chile | 25 | 7 | 6 | 12 | 31 | 40 | Egypt | 4 | 0 | 2 | 2 | 3 | 6 |
| Paraguay | 22 | 6 | 7 | 9 | 27 | 36 | Kuwait | 3 | 0 | 1 | 2 | 2 | 6 |
| United States | 25 | 6 | 3 | 16 | 27 | 51 | Trinidad and Tobago | 3 | 0 | 1 | 2 | 0 | 4 |
| Turkey | 10 | 5 | 1 | 4 | 20 | 17 | Slovenia | 3 | 0 | 0 | 3 | 2 | 7 |
| Croatia | 12 | 5 | 2 | 5 | 13 | 10 | Serbia & Montenegro | 3 | 0 | 0 | 3 | 2 | 10 |
| Nigeria | 11 | 4 | 1 | 6 | 14 | 16 | United Arab Emirates | 3 | 0 | 0 | 3 | 2 | 11 |
| Cameroon | 17 | 4 | 7 | 6 | 16 | 28 | New Zealand | 3 | 0 | 0 | 3 | 2 | 12 |
| Peru | 15 | 4 | 3 | 8 | 19 | 31 | Haiti | 3 | 0 | 0 | 3 | 2 | 14 |
| Scotland | 23 | 4 | 7 | 12 | 25 | 41 | Iraq | 3 | 0 | 0 | 3 | 1 | 4 |
| S. Korea | 24 | 4 | 7 | 13 | 21 | 53 | Togo | 3 | 0 | 0 | 3 | 1 | 6 |
| Ecuador | 7 | 3 | 0 | 4 | 7 | 8 | Canada | 3 | 0 | 0 | 3 | 0 | 5 |
| Northern Ireland | 13 | 3 | 5 | 5 | 13 | 23 | Greece | 3 | 0 | 0 | 3 | 0 | 8 |
| Costa Rica | 10 | 3 | 1 | 6 | 12 | 21 | China | 3 | 0 | 0 | 3 | 0 | 9 |
| Colombia | 13 | 3 | 2 | 8 | 14 | 23 | Zaire | 3 | 0 | 0 | 3 | 0 | 14 |
| Bulgaria | 25 | 3 | 8 | 14 | 22 | 49 | Bolivia | 6 | 0 | 1 | 5 | 1 | 20 |
| Wales | 5 | 2 | 6 | 1 | 10 | 7 | El Salvador | 6 | 0 | 0 | 6 | 1 | 22 |

*Includes West Germany 1950–90. †Includes USSR 1930–1990.
Note: Matches decided by penalty kicks are shown as drawn games.

## World Cup Final Box Scores *(Cont.)*

### URUGUAY 1930

| | | | |
|---|---|---|---|
| Uruguay.................1 | 3 | ——4 |
| Argentina.............2 | 0 | ——2 |

**FIRST HALF:** Scoring: 1, Uruguay, Dorado (12); 2, Argentina, Peucelle (20); 3, Argentina, Stabile (37).

**SECOND HALF:** Scoring: 4, Uruguay, Cea (57); 5, Uruguay, Iriarte (68); 6, Uruguay, Castro (89).

**Argentina:** Botosso, Della Toree, Paternoster, J. Evaristo, Monti, Suarez, Peucelle, Varallo, Stabile, Ferreira, M. Evaristo.

**Uruguay:** Ballesteros, Nasazzi, Mascheroni, Andrade, Fernandez, Gestido, Dorado, Scarone, Castro, Cea, Iriarte.

Referee: Langenus (Belgium).

### ITALY 1934

| | | | |
|---|---|---|---|
| Italy ........................0 | 1 | 1——2 |
| Czechoslovakia...........0 | 1 | 0——1 |

**SECOND HALF:** Scoring: 1, Czech., Puc (70); 2, Italy, Orsi (80).

**OVERTIME:** Scoring: 3, Italy, Schiavio (95).

**Italy:** Combi, Monzeglio, Allemandi, Ferraris Monti, Monti, Bertolini, Guaita, Meazza, Schiavio, Ferrari, Orsi.

**Czechoslovakia:** Planicka, Zenisek, Ctyroky, Kostalek, Cambal, Cambal, Krcil, Junek, Svoboda, Sobotka, Nejedly, Puc.

Referee: Eklind (Sweden).

### FRANCE 1938

| | | | |
|---|---|---|---|
| Italy ........................3 | 1 | ——4 |
| Hungary..................1 | 1 | ——2 |

**FIRST HALF:** Scoring: 1, Italy, Colaussi (5); 2, Hungary, Titkos (7); 3, Italy, Piola (16); 4, Italy, Piola (35).

**SECOND HALF:** Scoring: 5, Hungary, Sarosi (70); 6, Italy, Colaussi (82).

**Italy:** Olivieri, Foni, Rava, Serantoni, Andreolo, Locatelli, Biavati, Meazza, Piola, Ferrari, Colaussi.

**Hungary:** Szabo, Polger, Biro, Szalay, Szucs, Lazar, Sas, Vincze, Sarosi, Zsengeller, Titkos.

Referee: Capdeville (France).

### BRAZIL 1950

| | | | |
|---|---|---|---|
| Uruguay.................0 | 2 | ——2 |
| Brazil ......................0 | 1 | ——1 |

**SECOND HALF:** Scoring: 1, Brazil, Friaca (47); 2, Uruguay, Schiaffino (66); 3, Uruguay, Ghiggia (79).

**Uruguay:** Maspoli, Gonzales, Tejera, Gambretta, Varela, Andrade, Ghiggia, Perez, Miguez, Schiffiano, Moran.

**Brazil:** Barbosa, Augusto, Juvenal, Bauer, Banilo, Bigode, Friaca, Zizinho, Ademir, Jair, Chico.

Referee: Reader (England).

### SWITZERLAND 1954

| | | | |
|---|---|---|---|
| W Germany ...........2 | 1 | ——3 |
| Hungary..................2 | 0 | ——2 |

**FIRST HALF:** Scoring: 1, Hungary, Puskas (6); 2, Hungary, Czibor (8); 3, W Germ., Morlock (10); 4, W Germ., Rahn (18).

**SECOND HALF:** Scoring: 5, W Germany, Rahn (84).

**W Germany:** Turek, Posipal, Kohlmeyer, Eckel, Liebrich, Mai, Rahn, Morlock, O.Walter, F. Walter, Schaefer.

**Hungary:** Grosics, Buzansky, Lantos, Bozsik, Lorant, Zakarias, Czibor, Kocsis, Hidegkuti, Puskas, Toth.

Referee: Ling (England).

### SWEDEN 1958

| | | | |
|---|---|---|---|
| Brazil......................2 | 3 | ——5 |
| Sweden..................1 | 1 | ——2 |

**FIRST HALF:** Scoring:1, Sweden, Liedholm (3); 2, Brazil, Vava (9); 3, Brazil, Vava (32).

**SECOND HALF:** Scoring: 4, Brazil, Pelé (55); 5, Brazil, Zagalo (68); 6, Sweden Simonsson (80); 7, Brazil, Pelé (90).

**Brazil:** Glymar, D. Santos, N. Santos, Zito, Bellini, Orlando, Garrincha, Didi, Vava, Pelé, Zagalo.

**Sweden:** Svensson, Bergmark, Axbom, Boerjesson, Gustavsson, Parling, Hamrin, Gren, Simonsson, Liedholm, Skoglund.

Referee: Guigue (France).

### CHILE 1962

| | | | |
|---|---|---|---|
| Brazil............1 | 2 | ——3 |
| Czechoslovakia ...1 | 0 | ——1 |

**FIRST HALF:** Scoring: 1, Czech., Masopust (15); 2, Brazil, Amarildo (17).

**SECOND HALF:** Scoring: 3, Brazil, Zito (68); 4, Brazil, Vava (77).

**Brazil:** Glymar, D. Santos, N. Santos, Zito, Mauro, Zozimo, Garrincha, Didi, Vava, Amarildo, Zagalo.

**Czechoslovakia:** Schroiff, Tichy, Novak, Pluskal, Popluhar, Masopust, Pospichal, Scherer, Kvasnak, Kadraba, Jelinek.

Referee: Latychev (USSR).

### ENGLAND 1966

| | | | |
|---|---|---|---|
| England.............1 | 1 | 2——4 |
| W Germany......1 | 1 | 0——2 |

**FIRST HALF:** Scoring: 1, W Germany, Haller (12); 2, England, Hurst (18).

**SECOND HALF:** Scoring: 3, England, Peters (78); 4, W. Germany, Weber (90).

**OVERTIME:** Scoring: 5, England, Hurst (101); 6, England, Hurst (120).

**England:** Banks, Cohen, Wilson, Stiles, J. Charlton, Moore, Ball, Hurst, Hunt, R. Charlton, Peters.

**W Germany:** Tilkowski, Hottges, Schmellinger, Beckenbauer, Schulz, Weber, Held, Haller, Seeler, Overath, Emmerich.

Referee: Dienst (Switzerland).

### MEXICO 1970

| | | | |
|---|---|---|---|
| Brazil......................1 | 3 | ——4 |
| Italy ........................1 | 0 | ——1 |

**FIRST HALF:** Scoring: 1, Brazil, Pelé (18); 2, Italy, Boninsegna (32).

**SECOND HALF:** Scoring: 3, Brazil, Gerson (65); 4, Brazil, Jairzinho (70); 5, Brazil, Alberto (86).

**Brazil:** Feliz, Alberto, Brito, Wilson, Piazza, Everaldo, Clodoaldo, Gerson, Jairzinho, Tostao, Pelé, Rivelino.

**Italy:** Albertosi, Burgnich, Cera, Rosato, Facchetti, Bertini (Juliano), Mazzola, De Sisti, Domenghini, Boninsegna (Rivera), Riva.

Referee: Glockner (E Germany).

### W GERMANY 1974

| | | | |
|---|---|---|---|
| W Germany ...........2 | 0 | ——2 |
| Netherlands...........1 | 0 | ——1 |

**FIRST HALF:** Scoring: 1, Netherlands, Neeskens, PK (1); 2, W Germany, Breitner, PK (26); 3, W Germany, Müller (44).

## World Cup Final Box Scores (Cont.)

### W GERMANY 1974 (CONT.)

**W Germany:** Maier, Vogts, Beckenbauer, Schwarzenbeck, Breitner, Hoeness, Bonhof, Overath, Grabowski, Müller, Holzenbein.

**Netherlands:** Jongbloed, Suurbier, Rijsbergen (de Jong), Haan, Krol, Jansen, Neeskens, van Hanagem, Cruyff, Rensenbrink (van der Kerkhof).

Referee: Taylor (England).

### ARGENTINA 1978

| | | | |
|---|---|---|---|
| Argentina ...............1 | 0 | 2 | ——3 |
| Netherlands ...........0 | 1 | 0 | ——1 |

**FIRST HALF:** Scoring: 1, Argentina, Kempes (38).

**SECOND HALF:** Scoring: 2, Netherlands, Nanninga (81).

**OVERTIME:** Scoring: 3, Arg., Kempes (104); 4, Arg., Bertoni (114).

### ARGENTINA 1978 (Cont.)

**Argentina:** Fillol, Olguin, Galvan, Passarella, Tarantini, Ardiles (Larrosa), Gallego, Kempes, Bertoni, Luque, Ortiz (Houseman).

**Netherlands:** Jongbloed, Jansen (Suurbier), Krol, Brandts, Poortvliet, Neeskens, Haan, W. van der Kerkhoff, R. van der Kerkhoff, Rep (Nanninga), Rensenbrink.

Referee: Gonella (Italy).

### ITALY 1982

| | | | |
|---|---|---|---|
| Italy ........................0 | 3 | ——3 |
| W Germany ............0 | 1 | ——1 |

**SECOND HALF:** Scoring: 1, Italy, Rossi (57); 2, Italy, Tardelli (68); 3, Italy, Altobelli (81); 4, W Germany, Breitner (83).

**Italy:** Zoff, Bergomi, Scirea, Collovati, Cabrini, Oriali, Gentile, Tardelli, Conti, Rossi, Graziani (Altobelli, Causio).

**W Germany:** Schumacher, Kaltz, Stielike, K. Foerster, B. Foerster, Dremmler (Hrubesch), Breitner, Briegel, Rummenigge (Müller), Fischer (Littbarski).

Referee: Coelho (Brazil).

### MEXICO 1986

| | | | |
|---|---|---|---|
| Argentina ...............1 | 2 | ——3 |
| W Germany ...........0 | 2 | ——2 |

**FIRST HALF:** Scoring: 1, Argentina, Brown (22).

**SECOND HALF:** Scoring: 2, Arg., Valdano (55); 3, W Germ., Rummenigge (73); 4, W Germ., Voller (81); 5, Arg., Burruchaga (83).

**Argentina:** Pumpido, Brown, Cuciuffo, Ruggeri, Olarticoecha, Bastista, Giusti, Burruchaga (Trobbiani 90), Enrique, Maradona, Valdona.

**W Germany:** Schumacher, Jakobs, Forster, Eder, Brehme, Matthaus, Berthold, Magath (Hoeness 62), Briegel, Rummenigge, Allofs (Voller 46).

Referee: Filho (Brazil).

### ITALY 1990

| | | | |
|---|---|---|---|
| W Germany ..............0 | 1 | —— 1 |
| Argentina ...............0 | 0 | ——0 |

**SECOND HALF:** Scoring: 1, W Germany, Brehme, PK (84).

**W Germany:** Illgner, Brehme, Kohler, Augenthaler, Buchwald, Berthold (Reuter), Littbarski, Haessler, Mattaeus, Voeller, Klinsmann.

**Argentina:** Goychoechea, Lorenzo, Serrizuela, Sensini, Ruggeri (Monzon), Simon, Basualdo, Burruchag (Calderon), Maradona, Troglio, Dezottir.

Referee: Coelho (Brazil).

### UNITED STATES 1994

| | | | |
|---|---|---|---|
| Italy ........................0 | 0 | 0——0 |
| Brazil.......................0 | 0 | 0——0 |

Scoring: None. Shootout goals: Italy—2: Albertini, Evani; Brazil—3: Romario, Branco, Dunga.

**Italy:** Pagliuca, Benarrivo, Maldini, Baresi, Mussi

### UNITED STATES 1994 (Cont.)

(Apolloni 35), Albertini, D. Baggio (Evani 95), Berti, Donadoni, Baggio, Massaro.

**Brazil:** Taffarel, Jorginho (Cafu 21), Branco, Aldair, Santos, Silva, Dunga, Zinho (Viola 106), Mazinho, Bebeto, Romario.

Referee: Puhl (Hungary).

### FRANCE 1998

| | | |
|---|---|---|
| Brazil .........................0 | 0——0 |
| France.........................2 | 1——3 |

**FIRST HALF:** Scoring: 1, France, Zidane (27); 2, France, Zidane (45).

**SECOND HALF:** Scoring: 3, France, Petit (90).

**Brazil:** Taffarel, Cafu, Aldair, Baiano, Carlos, Sampaio (Edmundo 74), Dunga, Rivaldo, Leonardo, (Denilson 46), Bebeto, Ronaldo.

**France:** Barthez, Lizarazu, Desailly, Thuram, Leboeuf, Djorkaeff (Vieira 75) Deschamps, Zidane, Petit, Karembeu (Boghossian 57), Guivarc'h (Dugarry 66).

Referee: Belqola (Morocco).

### KOREA/JAPAN 2002

| | | |
|---|---|---|
| Brazil ....................0 | 2——2 |
| Germany ..............0 | 0——0 |

**SECOND HALF:** Scoring: 1, Brazil, Ronaldo (67); 2, Brazil, Ronaldo (79).

**Brazil:** Marcos, Cafu, Lucio, Roque Junior, Edmilson, Carlos, Silva, Ronaldo (Denilson, 90), Rivaldo, Ronaldinho (Juninho, 85), Kleberson.

**Germany:** Kahn, Linke, Ramelow, Neuville, Hamann, Klose (Bierhoff, 74), Jeremies (Asamoah, 77), Bode (Ziege, 84), Schneider, Metzelder, Frings.

Referee: Collina (Italy).

### GERMANY 2006

| | | | |
|---|---|---|---|
| Italy.............1 | 0 | 0 ——1 |
| France ........1 | 0 | 0 ——1 |

**Italy won on penalty kicks, 5–3.**

**FIRST HALF:** Scoring: 1, France, Zidane (7); 1, Italy, Materazzi (19).

SHOOTOUT GOALS: Italy—Pirlo, Materazzi, De Rossi, Del Piero, Grosso; France—Wiltord, Abidal, Sagnol.

**Italy:** Buffon, Zambrotta, Cannavaro, Materazzi, Grosso, Camoranesi (Del Piero 86), Pirlo, Gattuso, Perrotta (Iaquinta 61), Totti (De Rossi 61), Toni.

**France:** Barthez, Sagnol, Thuram, Gallas, Abidal, Ribery (Trezeguet 100), Vieira (Diarra 56), Makelele, Zidane, Malouda, Henry (Wiltord 107).

Referee: Elizondo (Argentina).

## Alltime Leaders
### GOALS

| Player, Nation | Tournaments | Goals | Player, Nation | Tournaments | Goals |
|---|---|---|---|---|---|
| Ronaldo, Brazil | 1998, 2002, '04, '06 | 15 | Miroslav Klose, Germany | 2002, '04 | 10 |
| Gerd Müller, W Germany | 1970, '74 | 14 | Ademir, Brazil | 1950 | 9 |
| Just Fontaine, France | 1958 | 13 | Eusebio, Portugal | 1966 | 9 |
| Pelé, Brazil | 1958, '62, '66, '70 | 12 | Jairzinho, Brazil | 1970, '74 | 9 |
| Sandor Kocsis, Hungary | 1954 | 11 | Paolo Rossi, Italy | 1982, '86 | 9 |
| Teofilo Cubillas, Peru | 1970, '78 | 10 | K.H. Rummenigge, W Germany | 1978, '82, '86 | 9 |
| Gregorz Lato, Poland | 1974, '78, '82 | 10 | Uwe Seeler, W Germany | 1958, '62, '66, '70 | 9 |
| Helmut Rahn, W Germany | 1954, '58 | 10 | Vava, Brazil | 1958, '62 | 9 |
| Gary Lineker, England | 1986, '90 | 10 | | | |

### LEADING SCORER, CUP BY CUP

| Year | Player, Nation | Goals | Year | Player, Nation | Goals |
|---|---|---|---|---|---|
| 1930 | Guillermo Stabile, Argentina | 8 | 1970 | Gerd Müller, W Germany | 10 |
| 1934 | Oldrich Nejedly, Czechoslovakia | 5 | 1974 | Gregorz Lato, Poland | 7 |
| 1938 | Leonidas da Silva, Brazil | 8 | 1978 | Mario Kempes, Argentina | 6 |
| 1950 | Ademir de Menezes, Brazil | 9 | 1982 | Paolo Rossi, Italy | 6 |
| 1954 | Sandor Kocsis, Hungary | 11 | 1986 | Gary Lineker, England | 6 |
| 1958 | Just Fontaine, France | 13 | 1990 | Salvatore Schillaci, Italy | 6 |
| 1962 | Florian Albert, Hungary | 4 | 1994 | Hristo Stoichkov, Bulgaria | 6 |
| | Valentin Ivanov, USSR, Garrincha, Brazil, | | | Oleg Salenko, Russia | |
| | Vava, Brazil, Drazan Jerkovic, Yugoslavia, | | 1998 | Davor Suker, Croatia | 6 |
| | Leonel Sanchez, Chile | | 2002 | Ronaldo, Brazil | 8 |
| 1966 | Eusebio Ferreira, Portugal | 9 | 2006 | Miroslav Klose, Germany | 5 |

## Most Goals, Individual, One Game

| Goals | Player, Nation | Score | Date |
|---|---|---|---|
| 5 | Oleg Salenko, Russia | Russia–Cameroon, 6–1 | 6-28-94 |
| 4 | Leonidas, Brazil | Brazil–Poland, 6–5 | 6-5-38 |
| 4 | Ernest Willimowski, Poland | Brazil–Poland, 6–5 | 6-5-38 |
| 4 | Gustav Wetterström, Sweden | Sweden–Cuba, 8–0 | 6-12-38 |
| 4 | Juan Alberto Schiaffino, Uruguay | Uruguay–Bolivia, 8–0 | 7-2-50 |
| 4 | Ademir, Brazil | Brazil–Sweden, 7–1 | 7-9-50 |

## Most Goals, Individual, One Game (*Cont.*)

| Goals | Player, Nation | Score | Date |
|---|---|---|---|
| 4 | Sandor Kocsis, Hungary | Hungary–W Germany, 8–3 | 6-20-54 |
| 4 | Just Fontaine, France | France–W Germany, 6–3 | 6-28-58 |
| 4 | Eusebio, Portugal | Portugal–N Korea, 5–3 | 7-23-66 |
| 4 | Emilio Butragueño, Spain | Spain–Denmark, 5–1 | 6-18-86 |

Note: 31 players have scored 32 World Cup hat tricks. Gerd Müller of West Germany is the only man to have two World Cup hat tricks, both in 1970. The last hat tricks were 6-1-02, Miroslav Klose (Ger) vs. Saudi Arabia; 6-21-98, Gabriel Batistuta (Arg) vs. Jamaica; 6-23-90, Tomas Skuhravy (Czech) vs. Costa Rica; and 6-17-90, Michel (Spain) vs. S Korea.

## Attendance and Goal Scoring, Year by Year

| Year | Site | No. of Games | Goals | Goals/Game | Attendance | Avg Att |
|---|---|---|---|---|---|---|
| 1930 | Uruguay | 18 | 70 | 3.89 | 434,500 | 24,139 |
| 1934 | Italy | 17 | 70 | 4.12 | 395,000 | 23,235 |
| 1938 | France | 18 | 84 | 4.67 | 483,000 | 26,833 |
| 1950 | Brazil | 22 | 88 | 4.00 | 1,337,000 | 60,773 |
| 1954 | Switzerland | 26 | 140 | 5.38 | 943,000 | 36,269 |
| 1958 | Sweden | 35 | 126 | 3.60 | 868,000 | 24,800 |
| 1962 | Chile | 32 | 89 | 2.78 | 776,000 | 24,250 |
| 1966 | England | 32 | 89 | 2.78 | 1,614,677 | 50,459 |
| 1970 | Mexico | 32 | 95 | 2.97 | 1,673,975 | 52,312 |
| 1974 | W Germany | 38 | 97 | 2.55 | 1,774,022 | 46,685 |
| 1978 | Argentina | 38 | 102 | 2.68 | 1,610,215 | 42,374 |
| 1982 | Spain | 52 | 146 | 2.80 | 1,856,277 | 35,698 |
| 1986 | Mexico | 52 | 132 | 2.54 | 2,441,731 | 46,956 |
| 1990 | Italy | 52 | 115 | 2.21 | 2,514,443 | 48,354 |
| 1994 | United States | 52 | 140 | 2.69 | 3,567,415 | 68,604 |
| 1998 | France | 64 | 171 | 2.67 | 2,775,400 | 43,366 |
| 2002 | Korea/Japan | 64 | 161 | 2.52 | 2,705,216 | 42,269 |
| 2006 | Germany | 64 | 147 | 2.23 | 3,353,655 | 52,40 |
| Totals | | 644 | 1,901 | 2.95 | 28,418,310 | 44,128 |

## Results—Women's World Cup

| Year | Champion | Score | Runner-Up | Third Place | Fourth Place |
|------|----------|-------|-----------|-------------|--------------|
| 1991 | United States | 2–1 | Norway | Sweden | Germany |
| 1995 | Norway | 2–0 | Germany | United States | China |
| 1999 | United States | 0–0 (5–4 pk) | China | Brazil | Norway |
| 2003 | Germany | 2–1 | Sweden | United States | Canada |
| 2007 | Germany | 2–0 | Brazil | United States | Norway |

# Major League Soccer Finals

## MLS Cup Results

| Year | Champion | Score | Runner-up | Regular Season MVP |
|------|----------|-------|-----------|--------------------|
| 1996 | D.C. United | 3–2 (ot) | Los Angeles | Carlos Valderrama, TB |
| 1997 | D.C. United | 2–1 | Colorado | Preki, Kansas City |
| 1998 | Chicago | 2–0 | D.C. United | Marco Etcheverry, D.C. |
| 1999 | D.C. United | 2–0 | Los Angeles | Jason Kreis, Dallas |
| 2000 | Kansas City | 1–0 | Chicago | Tony Meola, Kansas City |
| 2001 | San Jose | 2–1 (ot) | Los Angeles | Alex Pineda Chacon, Miami |
| 2002 | Los Angeles | 1–0 (ot) | New England | Carlos Ruiz, Los Angeles |
| 2003 | San Jose | 4–2 | Chicago | Preki, Kansas City |
| 2004 | D.C. United | 3–2 | Kansas City | Amado Guevara, MetroStars |
| 2005 | Los Angeles | 1–0 (ot) | New England | Taylor Twellman, NE |
| 2006 | Houston | 1–1 (ot, 4-3 PKs) | New England | Christian Gomez, D.C. |
| 2007 | Houston | 2–1 | New England | Luciano Emilio, D.C. |
| 2008 | Columbus | 3–1 | New York | Guillermo Schelotto, Clb |

# United Soccer League Finals

| Year | Champion | Score | Runner-Up | Regular Season MVP |
|------|----------|-------|-----------|--------------------|
| 1991 | San Francisco | 1–3, 2–0 (1–0 on PKs) | Albany | Jean Harbor, Maryland |
| 1992 | Colorado | 1–0 | Tampa Bay | Taifour Diane, Colorado |
| 1993 | Colorado | 3–1 (OT) | Los Angeles | Taifour Diane, Colorado |
| 1994 | Montreal | 1–0 | Colorado | Paulinho, Los Angeles |
| 1995 | Seattle | 1–2 (SO), 3–0, 2–1 (SO) | Atlanta | Peter Hattrup, Seattle |
| 1996 | Seattle | 2–0 | Rochester | Wolde Harris, Colorado |
| 1997 | Milwaukee | 2–1 (SO) | Carolina | Doug Miller, Rochester |
| 1998 | Rochester | 3–1 | Minnesota | Mark Baena, Seattle |
| 1999 | Minnesota | 2–1 | Rochester | John Swallen, Minnesota |
| 2000 | Rochester | 3–1 | Minnesota | Vitalis Takawira, Mil |
| 2001 | Rochester | 2–0 | Vancouver | Paul Conway, Charleston |
| 2002 | Milwaukee | 2–1 (2 OT) | Richmond | Leighton O'Brien, Seattle |
| 2003 | Charleston | 3–0 | Minnesota | Thiago Martins, Pittsburgh |
| 2004 | Montreal | 2–0 | Seattle | Greg Sutton, Montreal |
| 2005 | Seattle | 1–1 (4–3 on PKs) | Richmond | Jason Jordan, Vancouver |
| 2006 | Vancouver | 3–0 | Rochester | Joey Gjertsen, Vancouver |
| 2007 | Seattle | 4–0 | Atlanta | Sebastien Le Toux, Seattle |
| 2008 | Vancouver | 2–1 | Puerto Rico | Jonathan Steele, Puerto Rico |
| 2009 | Montreal | 6–3 (two legs) | Vancouver | Cristian Arietta, Puerto Rico |

# NCAA Sports

Last minute heroics
helped the Boston Univ.
Terriers take the 2009
NCAA hockey title

# Start Fast, Finish Hard

## From early swings to last-minute goals, these three NCAA championship teams took decidedly different routes to the title

### BY HANK HERSCH

WHO KNOWS WHEN THE decisive moment will come in an NCAA title game? Or if there will only be one defining moment? During 2008–09, three champions made their marks at every possible juncture—the beginning, the middle, and at the very end.

### MEN'S HOCKEY

Down 3–1 in the Frozen Four final against Miami of Ohio with a minute to play, Boston University was finished; even the Terriers' mascot had removed his costume. But with 59.5 seconds left, forward Zach Cohen found the top shelf with a backhander off a rebound. Then, with just over 17 ticks remaining, BU forward Nick Bonino blasted a one-timer off a pass from Hobey Baker Award-winner Matt Gilroy. No wonder the Terriers celebrated wildly after Bonino's goal: In every game in which he had registered a point during the season, they had prevailed. "They were all excited like they'd just won," coach Jack Parker said. "I told them to relax and get ready. They hadn't won it yet."

The winning tally came 11:47 into overtime. BU defenseman Colby Cohen (no relation to Zach) got the puck on the left point. He considered faking and going around a charging Red Hawk, but he worried about losing possession on the chewed-up ice. So the sophomore opted to unleash his 100-mph slap shot instead. Cohen's blast deflected off Miami defenseman Kevin Roeder's leg pads and fluttered into the right corner of the net. The celebration of BU's first title in 14 years was on in earnest. "I've been getting close," Cohen said. "I hit a couple of [goal posts] this week. I saw it go in. It's an unbelievable feeling."

"Wow, what a hockey game," said Parker, who won his record 30th tournament game. "What a finish."

### MEN'S SOCCER

Ah, the virtues of studying video. After winning the ACC tournament, Maryland coach Sasho Cirovski watched some tape and noticed that his attacking midfielder, Graham Zusi, had a tendency to drift wide, so he had him pinch in more; Zusi went on a scoring spree that included the only goal in a double-overtime defeat of St. John's in the NCAA semifinal. Then, before the final against rival North Carolina in Frisco, Texas, Cirovski noticed something else: a high frequency of deflected balls within the Tar Heels' 18-yard box. Armed with all that information, Zusi would say later, "I was in the right place at the right time."

The only goal of the championship match came in the 67th minute. Maryland's Doug Rodkey crossed to Jeremy Hall, who launched a rocket toward the Tar Heels' goal. Defender Eddie Ababio blocked the shot, and the rebound fell to Zusi at the top of the box. With a calm left foot he drove the ball into the lower left corner of the net.

"I tried to get over there," said UNC goalkeeper Brooks Haggerty, "but he placed it really well." Freshman keeper Zac MacMath finished with his 15th shutout of the season, and Maryland (23–3–0) had it second title in four years.

Zusi had six goals on the year; five were game-winners. "This season was a marathon," said Cirovski, "and our 26th game was the 26th mile."

## BASEBALL

LSU was constantly feeling pressure against Texas during the first two games of their College World Series final, rallying to win the first encounter in 11 innings and struggling futilely to climb out of a deep hole in the sec-

**In the deciding third game of the 2009 College World Series, LSU rightfielder Jared Mitchell mashed a three-run homer, helping the Tigers to the title.**

ond. In the decisive game, the top-seeded Tigers desperately needed a lead to work with.

The key blow came in the first inning. With two on and two out, junior right fielder Jared Mitchell pulled an inside fastball from righty Cole Green down the right field line, providing a 3–0 cushion. "This game was played on a lot of emotion," said Mitchell. "Starting fast, that helped us." Though the Longhorns would rally to tie the game at 4–4 in the fifth, LSU was able to burn through the Texas bullpen and rebuild its advantage. The Tigers' relievers, meanwhile, hurled 3⅔ shutout innings in support of starter Anthony Ranaudo for an 11–4 victory.

It was Mitchell's second NCAA championship ring; he'd won a BCS title as a receiver for the Tigers in 2007. Said the Most Outstanding Player of the CWS, "I may have to start putting them on my toes."

## NCAA Team Champions

### Fall 2008

| | | | Champion | Runner-Up |
|---|---|---|---|---|
| **Cross-Country** | MEN | Division I: | Oregon | Iona |
| | | Division II: | Adams St | Western St |
| | | Division III: | SUNY Cortland | North Central Illinois |
| | WOMEN | Division I: | Washington | Oregon |
| | | Division II: | Adams St | Grand Valley St |
| | | Division III: | Middlebury | Calvin |
| **Field Hockey** | WOMEN | Division I: | Maryland | Wake Forest |
| | | Division II | Bloomsburg | UMass-Lowell |
| | | Division III: | Bowdoin | Tufts |
| **Football** | MEN | FCS (I-AA): | Richmond | Montana |
| | | Division II: | Minn.-Duluth | NW Missouri St |
| | | Division III: | Mount Union | UW-Whitewater |
| **Soccer** | MEN | Division I: | Maryland | North Carolina |
| | | Division II: | Cal.St-Dominguez Hills | Dowling |
| | | Division III: | Messiah | Stevens Institute |
| | WOMEN | Division I: | North Carolina | Notre Dame |
| | | Division II: | Seattle Pacific | West Florida |
| | | Division III: | Messiah | Wheaton (Ill.) |
| **Volleyball** | WOMEN | Division I: | Penn St | Stanford |
| | | Division II: | Concordia-St. Paul | Cal. St-San Bernardino |
| | | Division III: | Emory | La Verne |
| **Water Polo** | MEN | | USC | Stanford |

### Winter 2008-2009

| | | | Champion | Runner-Up |
|---|---|---|---|---|
| **Bowling** | WOMEN | | Nebraska | Central Missouri |
| **Basketball** | MEN | Division I: | North Carolina | Michigan St |
| | | Division II: | Findlay | Cal. Poly-Pomona |
| | | Division III: | Washington-St. Louis | Richard Stockton |
| | WOMEN | Division I: | Connecticut | Louisville |
| | | Division II: | Minn. St-Mankato | Franklin Pierce |
| | | Division III: | George Fox | Washington-St. Louis |
| **Fencing** | | | Penn St | Notre Dame |
| **Gymnastics** | MEN | | Stanford | Michigan |
| | WOMEN | | Georgia | Alabama |
| **Ice Hockey** | MEN | Division I: | Boston University | Miami (Ohio) |
| | | Division III: | Neumann | Gustavus Adolphus |
| | WOMEN | Division I: | Wisconsin | Mercyhurst |
| | | Division III: | Amherst | Elmira |
| **Rifle** | | | West Virginia | Kentucky |
| **Skiing** | | | Denver | Colorado |
| **Swimming and Diving** | MEN | Division I: | Auburn | Texas |
| | | Division II: | Drury | Wayne St |
| | | Division III: | Kenyon | Emory |
| | WOMEN | Division I: | California | Georgia |
| | | Division II: | Drury | Wayne St |
| | | Division III: | Kenyon | Emory |

## Winter 2008-2009 *(Cont.)*

| | | | Champion | Runner-Up |
|---|---|---|---|---|
| **Wrestling** | MEN | Division I: | Iowa | Ohio St |
| | | Division II: | Neb.-Omaha | Newberry |
| | | Division III: | Wartburg | Augsburg (Minn.) |
| **Indoor Track and Field** | MEN | Division I: | Oregon | Florida |
| | | Division II: | Saint Augustine's (N.C.) | Adams St |
| | | Division III: | UW-La Crosse/ UW-Oshkosh | Whitworth |
| | WOMEN | Division I: | Tennessee | Texas A&M |
| | | Division II: | Lincoln (Mo.) | Grand Valley St |
| | | Division III: | Wartburg | UW-La Crosse |

## Spring 2009

| | | | Champion | Runner-Up |
|---|---|---|---|---|
| **Baseball** | | Division I: | LSU | Texas |
| | | Division II: | Lynn | Emporia St |
| | | Division III: | St. Thomas (Minn.) | Wooster |
| **Golf** | MEN | Division I: | Texas A&M | Arkansas |
| | | Division II: | Sonoma St | Cal. St-San Bernardino |
| | | Division III: | Oglethorpe | La Verne |
| | WOMEN | Division I: | Arizona St | UCLA |
| | | Division II: | Nova Southeastern | Grand Valley St |
| | | Division III | Methodist | UW-Stevens Pt. |
| **Lacrosse** | MEN | Division I: | Syracuse | Cornell |
| | | Division II: | LIU-C.W. Post | Le Moyne |
| | | Division III: | Cortland St | Gettysburg |
| | WOMEN | Division I: | Northwestern | North Carolina |
| | | Division II | Adelphi | Lock Haven |
| | | Division III: | Franklin & Marshall | Salisbury |
| **Rowing** | WOMEN | Division I: | Stanford | California |
| | | Division II | Western Washington | Mercyhurst |
| | | Division III: | Williams | Bates |
| **Softball** | | Division I: | Washington | Florida |
| | | Division II: | Lock Haven | Ala.-Huntsville |
| | | Division III: | Messiah | Coe |
| **Tennis** | MEN | Division I: | USC | Ohio St |
| | | Division II: | Armstrong Atlantic St | Barry |
| | | Division III: | UC-Santa Cruz | Amherst |
| | WOMEN | Division I: | Duke | California |
| | | Division II: | Armstrong Atlantic St | Lynn |
| | | Division III: | Williams | Amherst |
| **Outdoor Track and Field** | MEN | Division I: | Texas A&M | Oregon/Florida/ Florida St |
| | | Division II: | Saint Augustine's (N.C.) | Abilene Christian |
| | | Division III: | UW-Oshkosh | McMurry |
| | WOMEN | Division I: | Texas A&M | Oregon |
| | | Division II: | Lincoln (Mo.) | Angelo St |
| | | Division III: | Wartburg | UW-Oshkosh |
| **Volleyball** | MEN | | UC-Irvine | USC |
| **Water Polo** | WOMEN | | UCLA | USC |

### Cross Country

| | Champion | Runner-Up |
|---|---|---|
| MEN | Galen Rupp, Oregon | Samuel Chelanga, Liberty |
| WOMEN | Sally Kipyego, Texas Tech | Susan Kuijken, Florida St |

## Winter 2008-2009

### Gymnastics

| MEN | | Champion | Runner-Up |
|---|---|---|---|
| | All-around | Steve Legendre, Oklahoma | Glen Ishino, California |
| | Vault | Steven Legendre, Oklahoma | Geoff Reins, Iowa |
| | Parallel bars | Paul Ruggeri, Illinois | Kyle Brady, California |
| | Horizontal bar | Paul Ruggeri, Illinois | Thomas Kelly, Michigan |
| | Floor exercise | Steve Legendre, Oklahoma | Paul Ruggeri, Illinois |
| | Pommel horse | Daniel Ribeiro, Illinois | Steven Spencer, Ohio St |
| | Rings | Evan Roth, California | Philip Goldberg, Michigan |
| WOMEN | All-around | Courtney Kupets, Georgia | Kristina Baskett, Utah |
| | Balance beam | Courtney Kupets, Georgia | Courtney McCool, Georgia |
| | Uneven bars | Courtney Kupets, Georgia | Carly Janiga, Stanford |
| | Floor exercise | Courtney Kupets, Georgia | Ashleigh Clare-Kearney, LSU |
| | Vault | Ashleigh Clare-Kearney, LSU | Susan Jackson, LSU |

### Skiing

| MEN | | Champion | Runner-Up |
|---|---|---|---|
| | Slalom | Gabriel Rivas, Colorado | Petter Brenna, New Mexico |
| | Giant slalom | David Donaldson, Vermont | Leif Haugen, Denver |
| | 10-kilometer classic | Juergen Uhl, Vermont | Raphael Wunderle, Ak.-Anchorage |
| | 20-kilometer free | Vegard Kjoelhamar, Colorado | Lex Treinen, Ak.-Anchorage |
| WOMEN | Slalom | Malin Hemmingsson, New Mexico | Estelle Pecherand, New Mexico |
| | Giant slalom | Lindsay Cone, St. Lawrence | Estelle Pecherand, New Mexico |
| | 5-kilometer classic | Antje Maempel, Denver | Polina Ermoshina, New Mexico |
| | 15-kilometer free | Antje Maempel, Denver | Alexa Turzian, Colorado |

### Wrestling

| | Champion | Runner-Up |
|---|---|---|
| 125 lb | Troy Nickerson, Cornell | Paul Donahoe, Edinboro |
| 133 lb | Franklin Gomez, Michigan St | Reece Humphrey, Ohio St |
| 141 lb | J Jaggers, Ohio St | Ryan Williams, Old Dominion |
| 149 lb | Darrion Caldwell, North Carolina St | Brent Metcalf, Iowa |
| 157 lb | Jordan Burroughs, Nebraska | Michael Poeta, Illinois |
| 165 lb | Jarrod King, Edinboro | Andrew Howe, Wisconsin |
| 174 lb | Steve Luke, Michigan | Mike Miller, Central Michigan |
| 184 lb | Jake Herbert, Northwestern | Mike Pucillo, Ohio St |
| 197 lb | Jake Varner, Iowa St | Craig Brester, Nebraska |
| 285 lb | Mark Ellis, Missouri | Konrad Dudziak, Duke |

### Swimming and Diving — Men

| | Champion | Time | Runner-Up | Time |
|---|---|---|---|---|
| 50-yd freestyle | Nathan Adrian, California | 18.71 | James Feigen, Texas | 18.84 |
| 100-yd freestyle | Nathan Adrian, California | 41.08a | James Feigen, Texas | 41.49 |
| 200-yd freestyle | Shaune Fraser, Florida | 1:31.70 | Dave Walters, Texas | 1:32.59 |
| 500-yd freestyle | Jean Basson, Arizona | 4:08.92 | Michael Klueh, Texas | 4:09.32 |
| 1650-yd freestyle | Troy Prinsloo, Georgia | 14:30.91 | Chad La Tourette, Stanford | 14:33.55 |
| 100-yd backstroke | Kohlton Norys, Auburn | 45.26 | David Russell, California | 45.30 |
| 200-yd backstroke | Tyler Clary, Michigan | 1:37.58* | Jake Tapp, Arizona | 1:38.67 |
| 100-yd breaststroke | Damir Dugonjic, California | 50.86* | Adam Klein, Auburn | 51.80 |
| 200-yd breaststroke | Neil Versfeld, Georgia | 1:51.40* | Sean Mahoney, California | 1:52.34 |
| 100-yd butterfly | Austin Staab, Stanford | 44.18* | Tyler McGill, Auburn | 44.63a |
| 200-yd butterfly | Shaune Fraser, Florida | 1:40.75* | Mark Dylla, Georgia | 1:40.85 |
| 200-yd IM | Bradley Ally, Florida | 1:40.49* | Tyler Clary, Michigan | 1:41.67 |
| 400-yd IM | Tyler Clary, Michigan | 3:35.98a | Gal Nevo, Georgia Tech | 3:38.00 |
| 200-yd free relay | Auburn | 1:14.08* | Stanford | 1:14.22 |
| 400-yd free relay | Auburn | 2:46.67 | Texas | 2:47.02a |
| 800-yd free relay | Texas | 6:10.16* | Arizona | 6:11.82 |
| 200-yd medley relay | Auburn | 1:22.36* | California | 1:22.50 |
| 400-yd medley relay | Auburn | 3:01.39* | California | 3:01.69 |
| 1-meter diving | Drew Livingston, Texas | 442.70 | David Boudia, Purdue | 420.80 |
| 3-meter diving | David Boudia, Purdue | 493.10 | Kelly Marx, Auburn | 454.85 |
| Platform | David Boudia, Purdue | 530.45 | Drew Livingston, Texas | 493.20 |

a-American recod. *-NCAA record.

## Swimming and Diving — Women

| | Champion | Time/Pts | Runner-Up | Time/Pts |
|---|---|---|---|---|
| 50-yd freestyle | Lara Jackson, Arizona | 21.40 | Anne-marie Botek, Georgia | 21.80 |
| 100-yd freestyle | Dana Vollmer, California | 47.17 | Karlee Bispo, Texas | 47.48 |
| 200-yd freestyle | Dana Vollmer, California | 1:42.01 | Morgan Scroggy, Georgia | 1:42.90 |
| 500-yd freestyle | Allison Schmitt, Georgia | 4:35.17 | Wendy Trott, Georgia | 4:36.20 |
| 1650-yd freestyle | Wendy Trott, Georgia | 15:45.59 | Whitney Sprague, N. Carolina | 15:46.57 |
| 100-yd backstroke | Gemma Spofforth, Florida | 50.55 | Rachel Goh, Auburn | 51.61 |
| 200-yd backstroke | Gemma Spofforth, Florida | 1:49.11 | Teresa Crippen, Florida | 1:51.59 |
| 100-yd breaststroke | Rebecca Soni, USC | 58.36 | Jillian Tyler, Minnesota | 58.53 |
| 200-yd breaststroke | Rebecca Soni, USC | 2:05.52 | Alia Atkinson, Texas A&M | 2:06.99 |
| 100-yd butterfly | Amanda Sims, California | 51.28 | Elaine Breeden, Stanford | 51.34 |
| 200-yd butterfly | Elaine Breeden, Stanford | 1:50.98 | Kathleen Hersey, Texas | 1:51.18 |
| 200-yd IM | Julia Smit, Stanford | 1:52.79* | Kathleen Hersey, Texas | 1:53.33 |
| 400-yd IM | Julia Smit, Stanford | 4:00.56* | Katinka Hosszu, USC | 4:01.49 |
| 200-yd free relay | Arizona | 1:26.20* | California | 1:26.48 |
| 400-yd free relay | California | 3:09.88* | Stanford | 3:11.14 |
| 800-yd free relay | California | 6:52.69* | Georgia | 6:55.05 |
| 200-yd medley relay | Georgia | 1:36.45 | Wisconsin | 1:36.53 |
| 400-yd medley relay | Arizona | 3:28.31* | California | 3:30.27 |
| 1-meter diving | A. Pozdniakova, Hawaii | 351.15 | Christina Loukas, Indiana | 339.80 |
| 3-meter diving | Christina Loukas, Indiana | 437.75 | A. Pozdniakova, Hawaii | 386.10 |
| Platform | Kristen Davies, N. Carolina St | 339.65 | Jessica Livingston, Texas | 321.50 |

## Indoor Track and Field — Men

| | Champion | Time/Mark | Runner-Up | Time/Mark |
|---|---|---|---|---|
| 60-meter dash | Jacoby Ford, Clemson | 6.52 | Trindon Holliday, LSU | 6.55 |
| 60-meter hurdles | Ronnie Ash, Bethune-Cookman | 7.63 | Omo Osaghee, Texas Tech | 7.64 |
| 200-meter dash | Trey Harts, Baylor | 20.63 | Charles Clark, Florida St | 20.67 |
| 400-meter dash | Michael Bingham, Wake Forest | 45.69 | Gil Roberts, Texas Tech | 45.71 |
| 800-meter run | Jacob Hernandez, Texas | 1:48.04 | Andrew Wheating, Oregon | 1:48.54 |
| 4x400-meter relay | Baylor | 3:05.81 | Florida St | 3:05.97 |
| Mile run | Lee Emanuel, New Mexico | 4:00.36 | Craig Miller, Wisconsin | 4:01.34 |
| 3,000-meter run | Galen Rupp, Oregon | 7:48.94 | Michael Coe, California | 7:54.42 |
| 5,000-meter run | Galen Rupp, Oregon | 13:41.45 | Sam Chelanga, Liberty | 13:44.57 |
| Distance medley | Oregon | 9:29.59 | Arkansas | 9:30.31 |
| High jump | Scott Sellers, Kansas St | 2.25m | Derek Drouin, Indiana | 2.14m |
| Pole Vault | Jason Colwick, Rice | 5.60m | Yavgeniy Olhovsky, Virginia Tech | 5.45m |
| Long jump | Nicholas Gordon, Nebraska | 8.03m | Jeremy Hicks, LSU | 8.01m |
| Triple jump | Christian Taylor, Florida | 16.98m | Will Claye, Oklahoma | 16.80m |
| Shot put | Ryan Whiting, Arizona St | 20.16m | Aaron Studt, Minnesota | 19.36m |
| 35-pound wt throw | Jason Lewis, Arizona St | 22.88m | Steffen Nerdal, Memphis | 22.54m |
| Heptathlon | Ashton Eaton, Oregon | 5,988 pts | Gonzalo Barroilhet, Florida St | 5,879 pts |

## Indoor Track and Field — Women

| | Champion | Time/Mark | Runner-Up | Time/Mark |
|---|---|---|---|---|
| 60-meter dash | LaKya Brookins, South Carolina | 7.13 | Alexandria Anderson, Texas | 7.24 |
| 60-meter hurdles | Tiffany Ofili, Michigan | 8.00 | Celriece Law, Tennessee | 8.04 |
| 200-meter dash | Murielle Ahoure, Miami (Fla.) | 22.80 | Porscha Lucas, Texas A&M | 22.83 |
| 400-meter dash | Francena McCrory, Hampton | 51.55 | Jessica Beard, Texas A&M | 51.77 |
| 800-meter run | Lacey Cramer, BYU | 2:04.27 | Phoebe Wright, Tennessee | 2:04:38 |
| 4x400-meter relay | Texas A&M | 3:32.52 | Arizona St | 3:34.30 |
| Mile run | Sarah Bowman, Tennessee | 4:29.72 | Sally Kipyego, Texas Tech | 4:29.75 |
| 3,000-meter run | Jenny Barringer, Colorado | 8:42.03* | Susan Kuijken, Florida St | 8:56.27 |
| 5,000-meter run | Sally Kipyego, Texas Tech | 15:51.14 | Frances Koons, Villanova | 15:58.92 |
| Distance medley | Tennessee | 10:50.98* | North Carolina | 10:56.19a |
| High jump | Destinee Hooker, Texas | 1.98m | Elizabeth Patterson, Arizona | 1.95m |
| Pole vault | Kylie Hutson, Indiana St | 4.35m | Alicia Rue, Minnesota | 4.30m |
| Long jump | Eleni Kafourou, Boise St | 6.53m | Jeomi Maduka, Cornell | 6.50m |
| Triple jump | Kimberly Williams, Florida St | 13.81m | Sarah Nambawa, Mid. Tenn. St | 13.51m |
| Shot Put | Miriam Kevkhishvili, Florida | 17.84m | Sarah Stevens, Arizona St | 17.74m |
| 20-pound wt throw | D'Ana McCarty, Louisville | 22.09m | Stevi Large, Akron | 21.79m |
| Pentathlon | Amy Menlove, BYU | 4,365 pts | Gayle Hunter, Penn St | 4,342 pts |

## Rifle

| | Champion | Pts | Runner-Up | Pts |
|---|---|---|---|---|
| Smallbore | Brian Carstensen, Jacksonville St | 682.2 | Ashley Jackson, Kentucky | 682.1 |
| Air rifle | Jenna Compton, Akron | 691.6 | Bryant Wallizer, West Virginia | 691 |

a-American record. *-NCAA record.

## Spring 2009

### Golf

| | Champion | Score | Runners-Up | Score |
|---|---|---|---|---|
| MEN | Matt Hill, North Carolina St | 207 | Kyle Stanley, Clemson | 209 |
| WOMEN | Maria Hernandez, Purdue | 289 | Jennifer Song, USC | 290 |

### Outdoor Track and Field

#### MEN

| | Champion | Mark | Runner-Up | Mark |
|---|---|---|---|---|
| 100-meter dash | Trindon Holliday, LSU | 10.00 | Ahmad Rashad, USC | 10.10 |
| 200-meter dash | Charles Clark, Florida St | 20.55 | Rondel Sorrillo, Kentucky | 20.70 |
| 400-meter dash | Jonathan Borlee, Florida St | 44.78 | Michael Bingham, Wake Forest | 45.09 |
| 4x100-meter relay | Florida | 38.58 | LSU | 38.67 |
| 800-meter run | Andrew Wheating, Oregon | 1:46.21 | Tevan Everett, Texas | 1:46.27 |
| 1,500-meter run | German Fernandez, Oklahoma St | 3:39.00 | Garrett Heath, Stanford | 3:39.51 |
| 4x400-meter relay | Florida St | 2:59.99 | Texas A&M | 3:00.91 |
| 5,000-meter run | Galen Rupp, Oregon | 14:04.12 | David McNeil, Northern Arizona | 14:05.79 |
| 10,000-meter run | Galen Rupp, Oregon | 28:21.45 | Shawn Forrest, Arkansas | 28:24.53 |
| 110-meter hurdles | Ronnie Ash, Bethune-Cookman | 13.27 | Jason Richardson, South Carolina | 13.49 |
| 400-meter hurdles | Jeshua Anderson, Washington St | 48.47 | Johnny Dutch, South Carolina | 48.62 |
| 3,000-meter steeple | Kyle Perry, BYU | 8:29.24 | Hillary Bor, Iowa St | 8:35.12 |
| High jump | Scott Sellers, Kansas St | 2.26m | Ryan Fleck, Auburn | 2.23m |
| Pole vault | Jason Colwick, Rice | 5.70m | Scott Roth, Washington | 5.55m |
| Long jump | Ngonidzashe Makusha, Florida St | 8.11m | Stanley Gbagbeke, Mid. Tenn. St | 8.00m |
| Triple jump | Will Claye, Oklahoma | 17.24m | Julian Reid, Texas A&M | 17.10m |
| Shot put | Ryan Whiting, Arizona St | 20.11m | Zack Lloyd, Arizona | 19.86m |
| Discus throw | Martin Maric, California | 59.82m | Ryan Whiting, Arizona St | 59.80m |
| Hammer throw | Marcel Lomnicky, Virginia Tech | 71.78m | Walter Henning, LSU | 70.72m |
| Javelin throw | Chris Hill, Georgia | 81.80m | Corey White, USC | 75.72m |
| Decathlon | Ashton Eaton, Oregon | 8,241 pts | Matteo Sossah, North Carolina | 8,044 pts |

#### WOMEN

| | Champion | Mark | Runner-Up | Mark |
|---|---|---|---|---|
| 100-meter dash | Alexandria Anderson, Texas | 11.20 | Jessica Young, TCU | 11.22 |
| 200-meter dash | Porscha Lucas, Texas A&M | 22.81 | Charonda Williams, Arizona St | 22.84 |
| 400-meter dash | Joanna Atkins, Auburn | 50.39 | Jessica Beard, Texas A&M | 50.56 |
| 4x100-meter relay | Texas A&M | 42.36* | Florida St | 43.33 |
| 800-meter run | Geena Gall, Michigan | 2:00.80 | Laura Hermanson, N. Dakota St | 2:01.37 |
| 1,500-meter run | Susan Kuijken, Florida St | 4:13.05 | Brenda Martinez, UC-Riverside | 4:13.97 |
| 4x400-meter relay | Texas | 3:28.51 | LSU | 3:28.82 |
| 5,000-meter run | Angela Bizzarri, Illinois | 16:17.94 | Nicole Blood, Oregon | 16:26.58 |
| 10,000-meter run | Danette Doetzel, Providence | 33:25.71 | Cecily Lemmon, BYU | 33:39.97 |
| 100-meter hurdles | Tiffany Ofili, Michigan | 12.96 | Kristi Castlin, Virginia Tech | 13.15 |
| 400-meter hurdles | Nicole Leach, UCLA | 55.39 | Ti'erra Brown, Miami (Fla.) | 55.68 |
| 3,000-meter steeple | Jenny Barringer, Colorado | 9:25.54* | Nicole Bush, Michigan St | 9:40.49 |
| High jump | Destinee Hooker, Texas | 1.95m | Elizabeth Patterson, Arizona | 1.89m |
| Pole vault | Kylie Hutson, Indiana St | 4.40m | Vera Neuenswander, Indiana | 4.30m |
| Long jump | Kimberly Williams, Florida St | 6.54m† | Karoline Koehler, San Diego St | 6.54m† |
| Triple jump | Kimberly Williams, Florida St | 14.38m | Yasmine Regis, Texas A&M | 13.82m |
| Shot put | Mariam Kevkhishvili, Florida | 17.79m | Sarah Stevens, Arizona St | 17.58m |
| Discus throw | D'Andra Carter, Texas Tech | 55.62m | Sarah Stevens, Arizona St | 53.98m |
| Hammer throw | Stevi Large, Akron | 68.08m | Eva Orban, USC | 67.45m |
| Javelin throw | Rachel Yurkovich, Oregon | 59.62m | Kara Patterson, Purdue | 57.96m |
| Heptathlon | Brianne Theisen, Oregon | 6,086 pts | Liz Roehrig, Minnesota | 5,892 pts |

### Tennis

| | | Champion | Score | Runner-Up |
|---|---|---|---|---|
| MEN | Singles | Devin Britton, Mississippi | 3–6, 6–2, 6–3 | Steven Moneke, Ohio St |
| | Doubles | D. Inglot/M. Shabaz, Virginia | 3–6, 7–6 (4), 6–4 | D. Sandgren/J.P. Smith, Tennessee |
| WOMEN | Singles | Mallory Cecil, Duke | 7–5, 6–4 | Laura Vallverdu, Miami (Fla.) |
| | Doubles | M. Andersson/J. Jurikova, California | 6–3, 6–4 | H. Barte/L. Burdette, Stanford |

*NCAA meet record. †-Place determined by best 12 and ties from qualifying through finals.

# CHAMPIONSHIP RESULTS

## Baseball

### DIVISION I

| Year | Champion | Coach | Score | Runner-Up | Most Outstanding Player |
|------|----------|-------|-------|-----------|-------------------------|
| 1947 | California* | Clint Evans | 8–7 | Yale | No award |
| 1948 | USC | Sam Barry | 9–2 | Yale | No award |
| 1949 | Texas* | Bibb Falk | 10–3 | Wake Forest | Charles Teague, Wake Forest, 2B |
| 1950 | Texas | Bibb Falk | 3–0 | Washington St | Ray VanCleef, Rutgers, CF |
| 1951 | Oklahoma* | Jack Baer | 3–2 | Tennnessee | Sidney Hatfield, Tennessee, P-1B |
| 1952 | Holy Cross | Jack Barry | 8–4 | Missouri | James O'Neill, Holy Cross, P |
| 1953 | Michigan | Ray Fisher | 7–5 | Texas | J.L. Smith, Texas, P |
| 1954 | Missouri | John (Hi) Simmons | 4–1 | Rollins | Tom Yewcic, Michigan St, C |
| 1955 | Wake Forest | Taylor Sanford | 7–6 | Western Michigan | Tom Borland, Oklahoma St, P |
| 1956 | Minnesota | Dick Siebert | 12–1 | Arizona | Jerry Thomas, Minnesota, P |
| 1957 | California* | George Wolfman | 1–0 | Penn St | Cal Emery, Penn St, P-1B |
| 1958 | USC | Rod Dedeaux | 8–7† | Missouri | Bill Thom, USC, P |
| 1959 | Oklahoma St | Toby Greene | 5–3 | Arizona | Jim Dobson, Oklahoma St, 3B |
| 1960 | Minnesota | Dick Siebert | 2–1‡ | USC | John Erickson, Minnesota, 2B |
| 1961 | USC* | Rod Dedeaux | 1–0 | Oklahoma St | Littleton Fowler, Oklahoma St, P |
| 1962 | Michigan | Don Lund | 5–4 | Santa Clara | Bob Garibaldi, Santa Clara, P |
| 1963 | USC | Rod Dedeaux | 5–2 | Arizona | Bud Hollowell, USC, C |
| 1964 | Minnesota | Dick Siebert | 5–1 | Missouri | Joe Ferris, Maine, P |
| 1965 | Arizona St | Bobby Winkles | 2–1# | Ohio St | Sal Bando, Arizona St, 3B |
| 1966 | Ohio St | Marty Karow | 8–2 | Oklahoma St | Steve Arlin, Ohio St, P |
| 1967 | Arizona St | Bobby Winkles | 11–2 | Houston | Ron Davini, Arizona St, C |
| 1968 | USC* | Rod Dedeaux | 4–3 | Southern Illinois | Bill Seinsoth, USC, 1B |
| 1969 | Arizona St | Bobby Winkles | 10–1 | Tulsa | John Dolinsek, Arizona St, LF |
| 1970 | USC | Rod Dedeaux | 2–1 | Florida St | Gene Ammann, Florida St, P |
| 1971 | USC | Rod Dedeaux | 7–2 | Southern Illinois | Jerry Tabb, Tulsa, 1B |
| 1972 | USC | Rod Dedeaux | 1–0 | Arizona St | Russ McQueen, USC, P |
| 1973 | USC* | Rod Dedeaux | 4–3 | Arizona St | Dave Winfield, Minnesota, P-OF |
| 1974 | USC | Rod Dedeaux | 7–3 | Miami (Fla.) | George Milke, USC, P |
| 1975 | Texas | Cliff Gustafson | 5–1 | S Carolina | Mickey Reichenbach, Texas, 1B |
| 1976 | Arizona | Jerry Kindall | 7–1 | Eastern Michigan | Steve Powers, Arizona, P-DH |
| 1977 | Arizona St | Jim Brock | 2–1 | S Carolina | Bob Horner, Arizona St, 3B |
| 1978 | USC* | Rod Dedeaux | 10–3 | Arizona St | Rod Boxberger, USC, P |
| 1979 | CSU–Fullerton | Augie Garrido | 2–1 | Arkansas | Tony Hudson, CSU–Fullerton, P |
| 1980 | Arizona | Jerry Kindall | 5–3 | Hawaii | Terry Francona, Arizona, LF |
| 1981 | Arizona St | Jim Brock | 7–4 | Oklahoma St | Stan Holmes, Arizona St, LF |
| 1982 | Miami (Fla.)* | Ron Fraser | 9–3 | Wichita St | Dan Smith, Miami (Fla.), P |
| 1983 | Texas* | Cliff Gustafson | 4–3 | Alabama | Calvin Schiraldi, Texas, P |
| 1984 | CSU–Fullerton | Augie Garrido | 3–1 | Texas | John Fishel, CSU–Fullerton, LF |
| 1985 | Miami (Fla.) | Ron Fraser | 10–6 | Texas | Greg Ellena, Miami (Fla.), DH |
| 1986 | Arizona | Jerry Kindall | 10–2 | Florida St | Mike Senne, Arizona, LF |
| 1987 | Stanford | Mark Marquess | 9–5 | Oklahoma St | Paul Carey, Stanford, RF |
| 1988 | Stanford | Mark Marquess | 9–4 | Arizona St | Lee Plemel, Stanford, P |
| 1989 | Wichita St | Gene Stephenson | 5–3 | Texas | Greg Brummett, Wichita St, P |
| 1990 | Georgia | Steve Webber | 2–1 | Oklahoma St | Mike Rebhan, Georgia, P |
| 1991 | LSU | Skip Bertman | 6–3 | Wichita St | Gary Hymel, LSU, C |
| 1992 | Pepperdine | Andy Lopez | 3–2 | CSU–Fullerton | Phil Nevin, CSU–Fullerton, 3B |
| 1993 | LSU | Skip Bertman | 8–0 | Wichita St | Todd Walker, LSU, 2B |
| 1994 | Oklahoma | Larry Cochell | 13–5 | Georgia Tech | Chip Glass, Oklahoma, CF |
| 1995 | CSU–Fullerton* | Augie Garrido | 11–5 | USC | Mark Kotsay, CSU–Fullerton, CF-P |
| 1996 | LSU* | Skip Bertman | 9–8 | Miami (Fla.) | Pat Burrell, Miami (Fla.), 3B |
| 1997 | LSU* | Skip Bertman | 13–6 | Alabama | Brandon Larson, LSU, SS |
| 1998 | USC | Mike Gillespie | 21–14 | Arizona St | Wes Rachels, USC, 2B |
| 1999 | Miami (Fla.) | Jim Morris | 6–5 | Florida St | Marshall McDougall, FSU 3B/2B |
| 2000 | LSU* | Skip Bertman | 6–5 | Stanford | Trey Hodges, LSU, P |
| 2001 | Miami (Fla.)* | Jim Morris | 12–1 | Stanford | Charlton Jimerson, Miami (Fla.), OF |
| 2002 | Texas | Augie Garrido | 12–6 | South Carolina | Huston Street, Texas, P |
| 2003 | Rice | Wayne Graham | 14–2^ | Stanford | John Hudgins, Stanford, P |
| 2004 | CSU–Fullerton | George Horton | 3–2^ | Texas | Jason Windsor, CSU–Fullerton |

*Undefeated teams in College World Series play.
†12 innings.   ‡10 innings.   #15 innings.   ^Score of decisive game of best-of-three series.

## DIVISION I *(CONT.)*

| Year | Champion | Coach | Score | Runner-Up | Most Outstanding Player |
|------|----------|-------|-------|-----------|-------------------------|
| 2005 ....Texas | Augie Garrido | 6–2^ | Florida | David Maroul, Texas |
| 2006 ....Oregon St | Pat Casey | 3–2^ | North Carolina | Jonah Nickerson, Oregon St, P |
| 2007 ....Oregon St | Pat Casey | 9–3^ | North Carolina | Jorge Reyes, Oregon St, P |
| 2008 ....Fresno St | Mike Batesole | 6–1 | Georgia | Tommy Mendonca. Fresno St, 3B |
| 2009 ....LSU | Paul Mainieri | 11–4^ | Texas | Jared Mitchell, LSU, OF |

*Undefeated teams in College World Series play.

†12 innings.    ‡10 innings.    #15 innings.    ^Score of decisive game of best-of-three series.

## DIVISION II

| Year | Champion | Year | Champion | Year | Champion |
|------|----------|------|----------|------|----------|
| 1968 ...Chapman* | | 1982 ...UC–Riverside* | | 1996 ...Kennesaw St* | |
| 1969 ...Illinois St* | | 1983 ...Cal Poly–Pomona* | | 1997 ...CSU–Chico* | |
| 1970 ...CSU-Northridge | | 1984 ...CSU-Northridge | | 1998 ...Tampa* | |
| 1971 ...Florida Southern | | 1985 ...Florida Southern* | | 1999 ...CSU–Chico | |
| 1972 ...Florida Southern | | 1986 ...Troy St | | 2000 ...SE Oklahoma St | |
| 1973 ...UC–Irvine* | | 1987 ...Troy St* | | 2001 ...St. Mary's (Tex.) | |
| 1974 ...UC–Irvine | | 1988 ...Florida Southern* | | 2002 ...Columbus St | |
| 1975 ...Florida Southern | | 1989 ...Cal Poly–SLO | | 2003 ...Central Missouri St | |
| 1976 ...Cal Poly–Pomona | | 1990 ...Jacksonville St | | 2004 ...Kennesaw St | |
| 1977 ...UC–Riverside | | 1991 ...Jacksonville St | | 2005 ...Florida Southern | |
| 1978 ...Florida Southern | | 1992 ...Tampa* | | 2006 ...Tampa | |
| 1979 ...Valdosta St | | 1993 ...Tampa | | 2007 ...Tampa | |
| 1980 ...Cal Poly–Pomona* | | 1994 ...Central Missouri St | | 2008 ...Mount Olive | |
| 1981 ...Florida Southern* | | 1995 ...Florida Southern* | | 2009 ...Lynn | |

## DIVISION III

| Year | Champion | Year | Champion | Year | Champion |
|------|----------|------|----------|------|----------|
| 1976 .........CSU-Stanislaus | | 1987 .........Montclair St | | 1998 .........Eastern Connecticut St | |
| 1977 .........CSU-Stanislaus | | 1988 .........Ithaca | | 1999 .........N.Carolina Wesleyan | |
| 1978 .........Glassboro St | | 1989 .........N. Carolina Wesleyan | | 2000 .........Montclair St | |
| 1979 .........Glassboro St | | 1990 .........Eastern Connecticut St | | 2001 .........St. Thomas (Minn.) | |
| 1980 .........Ithaca | | 1991 .........Southern Maine | | 2002 .........Eastern Connecticut St | |
| 1981 .........Marietta | | 1992 .........William Paterson | | 2003 .........Chapman | |
| 1982 .........Eastern Connecticut St | | 1993 .........Montclair St | | 2004 .........UW-Stevens Pt | |
| 1983 .........Marietta | | 1994 .........UW-Oshkosh | | 2005 .........Wisconsin | |
| 1984 .........Ramapo | | 1995 .........La Verne | | 2006 .........Marietta | |
| 1985 .........UW-Oshkosh | | 1996 .........William Paterson | | 2007 .........Kean | |
| 1986 .........Marietta | | 1997 .........Southern Maine | | 2008 .........Trinity (Conn.) | |
| | | | | 2009 .........St. Thomas (Minn.) | |

*Undefeated teams in final series.

# Ice Hockey

## Men

### DIVISION I

| Year | Champion | Coach | Score | Runner-Up | Most Outstanding Player |
|------|----------|-------|-------|-----------|-------------------------|
| 1948 .....Michigan | Vic Heyliger | 8–4 | Dartmouth | Joe Riley, Dartmouth, F |
| 1949 .....Boston College | John Kelley | 4–3 | Dartmouth | Dick Desmond, Dartmouth, G |
| 1950 .....Colorado College | Cheddy Thompson | 13–4 | Boston University | Ralph Bevins, Boston University, G |
| 1951 .....Michigan | Vic Heyliger | 7–1 | Brown | Ed Whiston, Brown, G |
| 1952 .....Michigan | Vic Heyliger | 4–1 | Colorado College | Kenneth Kinsley, Colorado Coll, G |
| 1953 .....Michigan | Vic Heyliger | 7–3 | Minnesota | John Matchefts, Michigan, F |
| 1954 .....Rensselaer | Ned Harkness | 5–4 (OT) | Minnesota | Abbie Moore, Rensselaer, F |
| 1955 .....Michigan | Vic Heyliger | 5–3 | Colorado College | Philip Hilton, Colorado College, D |
| 1956 .....Michigan | Vic Heyliger | 7–5 | Michigan Tech | Lorne Howes, Michigan, G |
| 1957 .....Colorado College | Thomas Bedecki | 13–6 | Michigan | Bob McCusker, Colorado Coll, F |
| 1958 .....Denver | Murray Armstrong | 6–2 | North Dakota | Murray Massier, Denver, F |
| 1959 .....North Dakota | Bob May | 4–3 (OT) | Michigan St | Reg Morelli, North Dakota, F |
| 1960 .....Denver | Murray Armstrong | 5–3 | Michigan Tech | Bob Marquis, Boston University, F |
| 1961 .....Denver | Murray Armstrong | 12–2 | St. Lawrence | Barry Urbanski, Boston Univ, G |
| 1962 .....Michigan Tech | John MacInnes | 7–1 | Clarkson | Louis Angotti, Michigan Tech, F |
| 1963 .....North Dakota | Barney Thorndycraft | 6–5 | Denver | Al McLean, North Dakota, F |
| 1964 .....Michigan | Allen Renfrew | 6–3 | Denver | Bob Gray, Michigan, G |
| 1965 .....Michigan Tech | John MacInnes | 8–2 | Boston College | Gary Milroy, Michigan Tech, F |
| 1966 .....Michigan St | Amo Bessone | 6–1 | Clarkson | Gaye Cooley, Michigan St, G |
| 1967 .....Cornell | Ned Harkness | 4–1 | Boston University | Walt Stanowski, Cornell, D |

## Men (Cont.)

### DIVISION I (CONT.)

| Year | Champion | Coach | Score | Runner-Up | Most Outstanding Player |
|------|----------|-------|-------|-----------|-------------------------|
| 1968 | Denver | Murray Armstrong | 4–0 | North Dakota | Gerry Powers, Denver, G |
| 1969 | Denver | Murray Armstrong | 4–3 | Cornell | Keith Magnuson, Denver, D |
| 1970 | Cornell | Ned Harkness | 6–4 | Clarkson | Daniel Lodboa, Cornell, D |
| 1971 | Boston University | Jack Kelley | 4–2 | Minnesota | Dan Brady, Boston University, G |
| 1972 | Boston University | Jack Kelley | 4–0 | Cornell | Tim Regan, Boston University, G |
| 1973 | Wisconsin | Bob Johnson | 4–2 | Vacated | Dean Talafous, Wisconsin, F |
| 1974 | Minnesota | Herb Brooks | 4–2 | Michigan Tech | Brad Shelstad, Minnesota, G |
| 1975 | Michigan Tech | John MacInnes | 6–1 | Minnesota | Jim Warden, Michigan Tech, G |
| 1976 | Minnesota | Herb Brooks | 6–4 | Michigan Tech | Tom Vanelli, Minnesota, F |
| 1977 | Wisconsin | Bob Johnson | 6–5 (OT) | Michigan | Julian Baretta, Wisconsin, G |
| 1978 | Boston University | Jack Parker | 5–3 | Boston College | Jack O'Callahan, Boston Univ, D |
| 1979 | Minnesota | Herb Brooks | 4–3 | North Dakota | Steve Janaszak, Minnesota, G |
| 1980 | North Dakota | John Gasparini | 5–2 | Northern Michigan | Doug Smail, North Dakota, F |
| 1981 | Wisconsin | Bob Johnson | 6–3 | Minnesota | Marc Behrend, Wisconsin, G |
| 1982 | North Dakota | John Gasparini | 5–2 | Wisconsin | Phil Sykes, North Dakota, F |
| 1983 | Wisconsin | Jeff Sauer | 6–2 | Harvard | Marc Behrend, Wisconsin, G |
| 1984 | Bowling Green | Jerry York | 5–4 (OT) | Minn.–Duluth | Gary Kruzich, Bowling Green, G |
| 1985 | Rensselaer | Mike Addesa | 2–1 | Providence | Chris Terreri, Providence, G |
| 1986 | Michigan St | Ron Mason | 6–5 | Harvard | Mike Donnelly, Michigan St, F |
| 1987 | North Dakota | John Gasparini | 5–3 | Michigan St | Tony Hrkac, North Dakota, F |
| 1988 | Lake Superior St | Frank Anzalone | 4–3 (OT) | St. Lawrence | Bruce Hoffort, Lake Superior St, G |
| 1989 | Harvard | Bill Cleary | 4–3 (OT) | Minnesota | Ted Donato, Harvard, F |
| 1990 | Wisconsin | Jeff Sauer | 7–3 | Colgate | Chris Tancill, Wisconsin, F |
| 1991 | Northern Michigan | Rick Comley | 8–7 (3OT) | Boston University | Scott Beattie, Northern Michigan, F |
| 1992 | Lake Superior St | Jeff Jackson | 4–2 | Wisconsin | Paul Constantin, Lake Superior St, F |
| 1993 | Maine | Shawn Walsh | 5–4 | Lake Superior St | Jim Montgomery, Maine, F |
| 1994 | Lake Superior St | Jeff Jackson | 9–1 | Boston University | Sean Tallaire, Lake Superior St, F |
| 1995 | Boston University | Jack Parker | 6–2 | Maine | Chris O'Sullivan, Boston Univ, F |
| 1996 | Michigan | Red Berenson | 3–2 (OT) | Colorado College | Brendan Morrison, Michigan, F |
| 1997 | North Dakota | Dean Blais | 6–4 | Boston University | Matt Henderson, North Dakota, F |
| 1998 | Michigan | Red Berenson | 3–2 (OT) | Boston College | Marty Turco, Michigan, G |
| 1999 | Maine | Shawn Walsh | 3–2 (OT) | New Hampshire | Alfie Michaud, Maine, G |
| 2000 | North Dakota | Dean Blais | 4–2 | Boston College | Lee Goren, North Dakota, F |
| 2001 | Boston College | Jerry York | 3–2 (OT) | North Dakota | Chuck Kobasew, Boston Coll, F |
| 2002 | Minnesota | Don Lucia | 4–3 (OT) | Maine | Grant Potulny, Minnesota, F |
| 2003 | Minnesota | Don Lucia | 5–1 | New Hampshire | Thomas Vanek, Minnesota, F |
| 2004 | Denver | George Gwozdecky | 1–0 | Maine | Adam Berkhoel, Denver, G |
| 2005 | Denver | George Gwozdecky | 4–1 | North Dakota | Peter Mannino, Denver |
| 2006 | Wisconsin | Mike Eaves | 2–1 | Boston College | Robbie Earl, Wisconsin, F |
| 2007 | Michigan St | Rick Comley | 3–1 | Boston College | Justin Abdelkader, Michigan St, F |
| 2008 | Boston College | Jerry York | 4–1 | Notre Dame | Nathan Gerbe, Boston Coll, F |
| 2009 | Boston University | Jack Parker | 4–3 (OT) | Miami (Ohio) | Colby Cohen, Boston University, D |

### DIVISION II (Discontinued)

| Year | Champion | Coach | Score | Runner-Up |
|------|----------|-------|-------|-----------|
| 1978 | Merrimack | Thom Lawler | 12–2 | Lake Forest |
| 1979 | Lowell | Bill Riley Jr | 6–4 | Mankato St |
| 1980 | Mankato St | Don Brose | 5–2 | Elmira |
| 1981 | Lowell | Bill Riley Jr | 5–4 | Plattsburgh St |
| 1982 | Lowell | Bill Riley Jr | 6–1 | Plattsburgh St |
| 1983 | RIT | Brian Mason | 4–2 | Bemidji St |
| 1984 | Bemidji St | R.H. (Bob) Peters | 14–4* | Merrimack |
| 1993 | Bemidji St | R.H. (Bob) Peters | 15–6* | Mercyhurst |
| 1994 | Bemidji St | R.H. (Bob) Peters | 7–6* | Ala.–Huntsville |
| 1995 | Bemidji St | R.H. (Bob) Peters | 11–6* | Mercyhurst |
| 1996 | Ala.–Huntsville | Doug Ross | 10–1* | Bemidji St |
| 1997 | Bemidji St | R.H. (Bob) Peters | 7–4* | Ala.–Huntsville |
| 1998 | Ala.–Huntsville | Doug Ross | 11–4* | Bemidji St |
| 1999 | St. Michael's (Vt.) | Lou DiMasi | 12–9* | New Hamp. Coll |

*Two-game, total-goal series.

## Men *(Cont.)*

### DIVISION III

| Year | Champion | Coach | Score | Runner-Up |
|------|----------|-------|-------|-----------|
| 1984 | Babson | Bob Riley | 8–0 | Union (N.Y.) |
| 1985 | RIT | Bruce Delventhal | 5–1 | Bemidji St |
| 1986 | Bemidji St | R.H. (Bob) Peters | 8–5 | Vacated |
| 1987 | Vacated | | | Oswego St |
| 1988 | UW-River Falls | Rick Kozuback | 7–1, 3–5, 3–0 | Elmira |
| 1989 | UW-Stevens Point | Mark Mazzoleni | 3–3, 3–2 | RIT |
| 1990 | UW-Stevens Point | Mark Mazzoleni | 10–1, 3–6, 1–0 | Plattsburgh St |
| 1991 | UW-River Falls | Mark Mazzoleni | 6–2 | Mankato St |
| 1992 | Plattsburgh St | Bob Emery | 7–3 | UW-Stevens Point |
| 1993 | UW-Stevens Point | Joe Baldarotta | 4–3 | UW-River Falls |
| 1994 | UW-River Falls | Dean Talafous | 6–4 | UW-Superior |
| 1995 | Middlebury | Bill Beaney | 1–0 | Fredonia St |
| 1996 | Middlebury | Bill Beaney | 3–2 | RIT |
| 1997 | Middlebury | Bill Beaney | 3–2 | UW-Superior |
| 1998 | Middlebury | Bill Beaney | 2–1 | UW-Stevens Point |
| 1999 | Middlebury | Bill Beaney | 5–0 | UW-Superior |
| 2000 | Norwich | Michael McShane | 2–1 | St. Thomas (Minn.) |
| 2001 | Plattsburgh | Bob Emery | 6–2 | RIT |
| 2002 | UW-Superior | Dan Stauber | 3–2 | Norwich |
| 2003 | Norwich | Michael McShane | 2–1 | Oswego St |
| 2004 | Middlebury | Bill Beaney | 1–0 | St. Norbert |
| 2005 | Middlebury | Bill Beaney | 5–0 | St. Thomas (Minn.) |
| 2006 | Middlebury | Bill Beaney | 3–0 | St. Norbert |
| 2007 | Oswego | Ed Gosek | 4–3 | Middlebury |
| 2008 | St. Norbert | Tim Coghlin | 2–0 | Plattsburgh St |
| 2009 | Neumann | Dominick Dawes | 4–1 | Gustavus Adolphus |

## Women - DIVISION I

| Year | Champion | Coach | Score | Runner-Up |
|------|----------|-------|-------|-----------|
| 2001 | Minn.-Duluth | Shannon Miller | 4–2 | St. Lawrence |
| 2002 | Minn.-Duluth | Shannon Miller | 3–2 | Brown |
| 2003 | Minn.-Duluth | Shannon Miller | 4–3 (2 OT) | Harvard |
| 2004 | Minnesota | Laura Holldorson | 6–2 | Harvard |
| 2005 | Minnesota | Laura Holldorson | 4–3 | Harvard |
| 2006 | Wisconsin | Mark Johnson | 3–0 | Minnesota |
| 2007 | Wisconsin | Mark Johnson | 4–1 | Minnesota |
| 2008 | Minn.-Duluth | Shannon Miller | 4–0 | Wisconsin |
| 2009 | Wisconsin | Mark Johnson | 5–0 | Mercyhurst |

# Soccer

## Men - DIVISION I

| Year | Champion | Coach | Score | Runner-Up |
|------|----------|-------|-------|-----------|
| 1959 | St. Louis | Bob Guelker | 5–2 | Bridgeport |
| 1960 | St. Louis | Bob Guelker | 3–2 | Maryland |
| 1961 | West Chester | Mel Lorback | 2–0 | St. Louis |
| 1962 | St. Louis | Bob Guelker | 4–3 | Maryland |
| 1963 | St. Louis | Bob Guelker | 3–0 | Navy |
| 1964 | Navy | F.H. Warner | 1–0 | Michigan St |
| 1965 | St. Louis | Bob Guelker | 1–0 | Michigan St |
| 1966 | San Francisco | Steve Negoesco | 5–2 | LIU–Brooklyn |
| 1967 | Michigan St | Gene Kenney | 0–0 | Game called due to |
|      | St. Louis | Harry Keough | | inclement weather |
| 1968 | Maryland | Doyle Royal | 2–2 (2 OT) | |
|      | Michigan St | Gene Kenney | | |
| 1969 | St. Louis | Harry Keough | 4–0 | San Francisco |
| 1970 | St. Louis | Harry Keough | 1–0 | UCLA |
| 1971 | Vacated | | 3–2 | St. Louis |
| 1972 | St. Louis | Harry Keough | 4–2 | UCLA |
| 1973 | St. Louis | Harry Keough | 2–1 (OT) | UCLA |
| 1974 | Howard | Lincoln Phillips | 2–1 (4 OT) | St. Louis |
| 1975 | San Francisco | Steve Negoesco | 4–0 | SIU–Edwardsville |
| 1976 | San Francisco | Steve Negoesco | 1–0 | Indiana |
| 1977 | Hartwick | Jim Lennox | 2–1 | San Francisco |
| 1978 | Vacated | | 2–0 | Indiana |

## Men - DIVISION I *(CONT.)*

| Year | Champion | Coach | Score | Runner-Up |
|---|---|---|---|---|
| 1979 | SIU–Edwardsville | Bob Guelker | 3–2 | Clemson |
| 1980 | San Francisco | Steve Negoesco | 4–3 (OT) | Indiana |
| 1981 | Connecticut | Joe Morrone | 2–1 (OT) | Alabama A&M |
| 1982 | Indiana | Jerry Yeagley | 2–1 (8 OT) | Duke |
| 1983 | Indiana | Jerry Yeagley | 1–0 (2 OT) | Columbia |
| 1984 | Clemson | I.M. Ibrahim | 2–1 | Indiana |
| 1985 | UCLA | Sigi Schmid | 1–0 (8 OT) | American |
| 1986 | Duke | John Rennie | 1–0 | Akron |
| 1987 | Clemson | I.M. Ibrahim | 2–0 | San Diego St |
| 1988 | Indiana | Jerry Yeagley | 1–0 | Howard |
| 1989 | Santa Clara | Steve Sampson | 1–1 (2 OT) | |
|  | Virginia | Bruce Arena | | |
| 1990 | UCLA | Sigi Schmid | 1–0 (OT) | Rutgers |
| 1991 | Virginia | Bruce Arena | 0–0* | Santa Clara |
| 1992 | Virginia | Bruce Arena | 2–0 | San Diego |
| 1993 | Virginia | Bruce Arena | 2–0 | South Carolina |
| 1994 | Virginia | Bruce Arena | 1–0 | Indiana |
| 1995 | Wisconsin | Jim Launder | 2–0 | Duke |
| 1996 | St. John's (N.Y.) | Dave Masur | 4–1 | Florida International |
| 1997 | UCLA | Sigi Schmid | 2–1 | Virginia |
| 1998 | Indiana | Jerry Yeagley | 3–1 | Stanford |
| 1999 | Indiana | Jerry Yeagley | 1–0 | Santa Clara |
| 2000 | Connecticut | Ray Reid | 2–0 | Creighton |
| 2001 | N.Carolina | Elmar Bolowich | 2–0 | Indiana |
| 2002 | UCLA | Tom Fitzgerald | 1–0 | Stanford |
| 2003 | Indiana | Jerry Yeagley | 2–1 | St. John's (N.Y.) |
| 2004 | Indiana | Jerry Yeagley | 1–1 (2 OT 3-2) | UC-Santa Barbara |
| 2005 | Maryland | Sasho Cirovski | 1–0 | New Mexico |
| 2006 | UC-Santa Barbara | Tim Vom Steeg | 2–1 | UCLA |
| 2007 | Wake Forest | Tony da Luz | 2–0 | Ohio St |
| 2008 | Maryland | Sasha Cirovski | 1–0 | North Carolina |

*Under a rule passed in 1991, the NCAA determined that when a score is tied after regulation and overtime, and the championship is determined by penalty kicks, the official score will be 0–0.

## Men - DIVISION II

| Year | Champion | Year | Champion | Year | Champion |
|---|---|---|---|---|---|
| 1972 | SIU–Edwardsville | 1984 | Florida International | 1996 | Grand Canyon |
| 1973 | Missouri–St. Louis | 1985 | Seattle Pacific | 1997 | CSU-Bakersfield |
| 1974 | Adelphi | 1986 | Seattle Pacific | 1998 | Southern Conn St |
| 1975 | Baltimore | 1987 | Southern Conn St | 1999 | Southern Conn St |
| 1976 | Loyola (Md.) | 1988 | Florida Tech | 2000 | CSU–Dominguez Hills |
| 1977 | Alabama A&M | 1989 | New Hampshire College | 2001 | Tampa |
| 1978 | Seattle Pacific | 1990 | Southern Conn St | 2002 | Sonoma St |
| 1979 | Alabama A&M | 1991 | Florida Tech | 2003 | Lynn |
| 1980 | Lock Haven | 1992 | Southern Conn St | 2004 | Seattle |
| 1981 | Tampa | 1993 | Seattle Pacific | 2005 | Fort Lewis |
| 1982 | Florida International | 1994 | Tampa | 2006 | Dowling (N.Y.) |
| 1983 | Seattle Pacific | 1995 | Southern Conn St | 2007 | Franklin Pierce |
| | | | | 2008 | Cal St.-Dominguez Hills |

## Men - DIVISION III

| Year | Champion | Year | Champion | Year | Champion |
|---|---|---|---|---|---|
| 1974 | Brockport St | 1987 | NC–Greensboro | 2000 | Messiah |
| 1975 | Babson | 1988 | UC–San Diego | 2001 | Richard Stockton |
| 1976 | Brandeis | 1989 | Elizabethtown | 2002 | Messiah |
| 1977 | Lock Haven | 1990 | Glassboro St | 2003 | Trinity (Tex.) |
| 1978 | Lock Haven | 1991 | UC–San Diego | 2004 | Messiah |
| 1979 | Babson | 1992 | Kean | 2005 | Messiah |
| 1980 | Babson | 1993 | UC–San Diego | 2006 | Messiah |
| 1981 | Glassboro St | 1994 | Bethany (W.V.) | 2007 | Middlebury |
| 1982 | NC–Greensboro | 1995 | Williams | 2008 | Messiah |
| 1983 | NC–Greensboro | 1996 | College of New Jersey* | | |
| 1984 | Wheaton (Ill.) | 1997 | Wheaton (Ill.) | | |
| 1985 | NC–Greensboro | 1998 | Ohio Wesleyan | | |
| 1986 | NC–Greensboro | 1999 | St. Lawrence | | |

*Formerly Trenton St

## Women

### DIVISION I

| Year | Champion | Coach | Score | Runner-Up |
|------|----------|-------|-------|-----------|
| 1982 | North Carolina | Anson Dorrance | 2–0 | Central Florida |
| 1983 | North Carolina | Anson Dorrance | 4–0 | George Mason |
| 1984 | North Carolina | Anson Dorrance | 2–0 | Connecticut |
| 1985 | George Mason | Hank Leung | 2–0 | North Carolina |
| 1986 | North Carolina | Anson Dorrance | 2–0 | Colorado College |
| 1987 | North Carolina | Anson Dorrance | 1–0 | Massachusetts |
| 1988 | North Carolina | Anson Dorrance | 4–1 | North Carolina St |
| 1989 | North Carolina | Anson Dorrance | 2–0 | Colorado College |
| 1990 | North Carolina | Anson Dorrance | 6–0 | Connecticut |
| 1991 | North Carolina | Anson Dorrance | 3–1 | Wisconsin |
| 1992 | North Carolina | Anson Dorrance | 9–1 | Duke |
| 1993 | North Carolina | Anson Dorrance | 6–0 | George Mason |
| 1994 | North Carolina | Anson Dorrance | 5–0 | Notre Dame |
| 1995 | Notre Dame | Chris Petrucelli | 1–0 | Portland |
| 1996 | North Carolina | Anson Dorrance | 1–0 | Notre Dame |
| 1997 | North Carolina | Anson Dorrance | 2–0 | Connecticut |
| 1998 | Florida | Becky Burleigh | 1–0 | North Carolina |
| 1999 | North Carolina | Anson Dorrance | 2–0 | Notre Dame |
| 2000 | North Carolina | Anson Dorrance | 2–1 | UCLA |
| 2001 | Santa Clara | Jerry Smith | 1–0 | North Carolina |
| 2002 | Portland | Clive Charles | 2–1 | Santa Clara |
| 2003 | North Carolina | Anson Dorrance | 6–0 | Connecticut |
| 2004 | Norte Dame | Randy Waldrum | 1–1 (OT 4–3) | UCLA |
| 2005 | Portland | Garrett Smith | 4–0 | UCLA |
| 2006 | North Carolina | Anson Dorrance | 2–1 | Notre Dame |
| 2007 | USC | Ali Khosroshahin | 2–0 | Florida St |
| 2008 | North Carolina | Anson Dorrance | 2–1 | Notre Dame |

### DIVISION II

| Year | Champion | Year | Champion | Year | Champion |
|------|----------|------|----------|------|----------|
| 1988 | CSU–Hayward | 1995 | Franklin Pierce | 2002 | Christian Brothers |
| 1989 | Barry | 1996 | Franklin Pierce | 2003 | Kennesaw St |
| 1990 | Sonoma St | 1997 | Franklin Pierce | 2004 | Metro St |
| 1991 | CSU–Dominguez Hills | 1998 | Lynn | 2005 | Nebraska-Omaha |
| 1992 | Barry | 1999 | Franklin Pierce | 2006 | Metro St |
| 1993 | Barry | 2000 | UC-San Diego | 2007 | Tampa |
| 1994 | Franklin Pierce | 2001 | UC-San Diego | 2008 | Seattle Pacific |

### DIVISION III

| Year | Champion | Year | Champion | Year | Champion |
|------|----------|------|----------|------|----------|
| 1986 | Rochester | 1994 | Trenton St | 2002 | Ohio Wesleyan |
| 1987 | Rochester | 1995 | UC-San Diego | 2003 | Oneonta St |
| 1988 | William Smith | 1996 | UC-San Diego | 2004 | Wheaton College |
| 1989 | UC-San Diego | 1997 | UC-San Diego | 2005 | Messiah |
| 1990 | Ithaca | 1998 | Macalester | 2006 | Wheaton (Ill.) |
| 1991 | Ithaca | 1999 | UC-San Diego | 2007 | Wheaton (Ill.) |
| 1992 | Cortland St | 2000 | College of New Jersey* | 2008 | Messiah |
| 1993 | Trenton St | 2001 | Ohio Wesleyan | | |

# Olympics

Brazil's Rio de Janeiro won the right to host the 2016 Summer Olympics

# Lakeshore–No, Beachfront–*Sim!*

Chicago bid for the 2016 Summer Olympics fell short and Rio's first-Games in-South-America pitch won out, but which city will benefit the most in the long run?

**BY MERRELL NODEN**

THE SHOCKING NEWS CAME fast: Not only would Chicago not be getting the 2016 Summer Olympics, it was the first city to be eliminated. No one had expected this, not the excited crowds awaiting the Windy City's coronation in Daley Plaza nor the London bookies, who picked Chicago as the odds-on favorite even before President Obama decided at the last minute to fly to Copenhagen and join a delegation that already included the First Lady and Oprah. Some insiders were convinced that a few hours of presidential glad-handing would put Chicago over the top.

Wrong. Chicago was gone before things even got interesting, the victim, many surmised, of either USOC bumbling or bloc voting by Asian delegates supporting Tokyo. If the latter, they too were soon disappointed: Tokyo was next to go. In the final vote, Rio de Janeiro beat Madrid, 66–32. For the first time ever, the Olympic Games would be going to South America. It was hard to tell who was more delighted by this result, the bikini-clad, samba-dancing celebrants packing Rio's famed Copacabana beach or Obama critics like Rush Limbaugh, who declared himself "gleeful" at this supposed blow to Obama's prestige.

In fact, the choice of Rio probably had little to do with Obama or, indeed, with his hometown of Chicago, which now follows New York as great American cities that did not even come close. Rio's best argument for hosting the Games was not what it has—fabulous natural beauty and those glorious beaches—but what all of South America has never had, an Olympics. Those five Olympic rings are supposed to stand for the five continents, and lately the IOC has been trying to make those rings more than mere symbolism. The IOC sees its great sports festival as fairy dust sprinkled on the annointed city, bringing not only fabulous venues but also upgrades to infrastructure and mass transit and, most importantly, respect.

Rio needs it. It is a beautiful city, but probably the poorest ever to get the Games. Its airport is crumbling, it has barely half the estimated 50,000 hotel rooms it will need, and it will have to drastically upgrade its public transportation system. Not to mention, there are only two barely passable golf courses within 50 miles of the city, making the re-introduc-

REUTERS/ANDY CLARK (CANADA SPORT OLYMPICS)

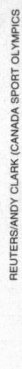

tion of golf to the Games in 2016 another yet-to-be resolved matter. (Rugby will be be added to the Olympic slate in 2016 as well.) In addition, the crime rate in Rio's hillside *favelas*, or slums, is notorious: In 2008 there were 2,069 murders in this city of seven million people. But despite those drawbacks, Rio was determined to get the Games. By the time Obama had begun calling around to IOC leaders like Jacques Rogge, it was clear that the Brazilian president Luiz Inacio Lula da Silva had already done so. The charismatic Lula is the rare leader with a life story as interesting as Obama's. Though he never finished high school and once supported himself by selling peanuts on the street, now, near the end of his second term, he's worked wonders with the largest economy on the continent. He has already been rewarded by

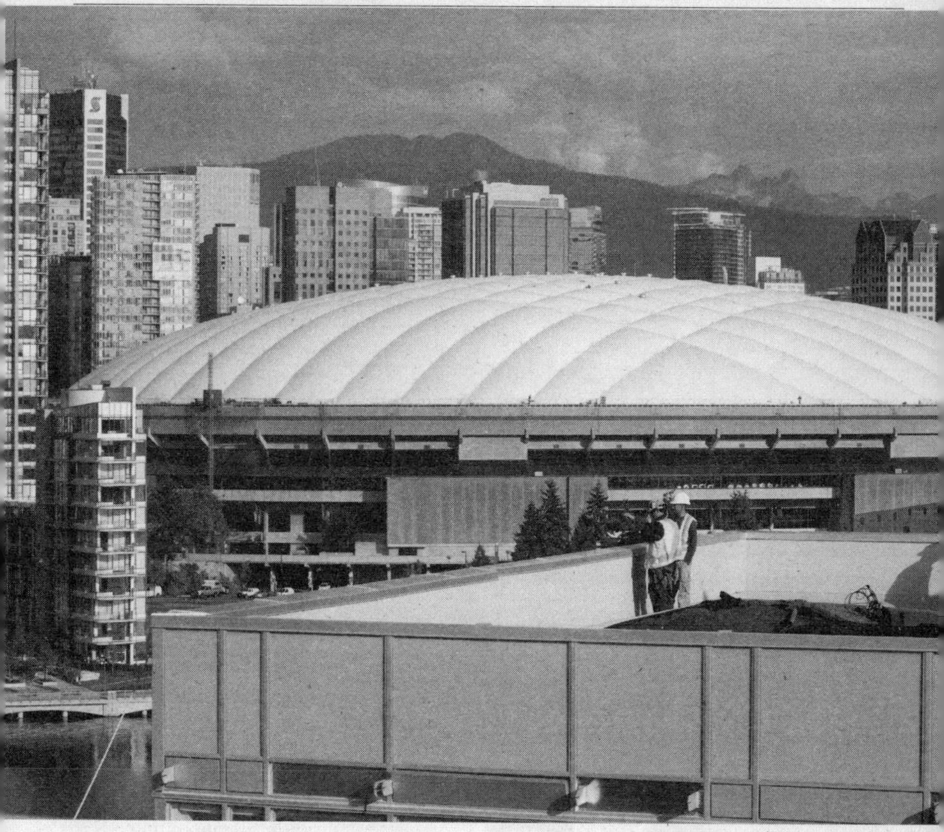

**Vancouver is putting the final touches on preparations to host the Winter Games in 2010, but the world economic slowdown might make the city's host duties costly.**

Rio's hosting the 2007 Pan Am Games and by Brazil's getting picked to host the FIFA World Cup in 2014.

Chicago, by contrast, wasn't sure how it felt about the Games. Though the Chicago City Council voted 49–0 to guarantee funding in the event of cost overruns, Chicagoans seemed to have mixed feelings. A poll in the *Chicago Tribune* found that 84% did not want the "Games in the Parks," as the bid team, Chicago 2016, chose to style them. The Chicago plan called for building the Olympic village and many venues near the city's beautiful waterfront. But Chicago's chances weren't

AP PHOTO/CHARLES DHARAPAK, POOL

Rogge at the IAAF World Track and Field Championships in Berlin and announced that the network had been put on hold. But the damage to Chicago's chances had been done.

Perhaps those wary Chicagoans were reading the newspapers from Vancouver, where the next Winter Games are scheduled to open on February 12. The news about preparations had been mostly good, marked by startling news of budget surpluses. But with the local lumber industry struggling due to U.S. construction woes, unemployment over 8%, and a decline in tax revenues, British Columbia's provincial finance minister announced on September 1 a projected loss of $2.5 billion for this fiscal year. Some 300 jobs were cut and a wage freeze threatened. What's more, only one third of the 1,100 apartments in the waterfront Olympic village had

helped by the actions of the new team at the USOC. The biggest strike against an American city was perhaps the USOC's announcement, on July 6, that it was starting an Olympic television network. The news miffed both NBC and the IOC. A mere six weeks later USOC chairman Larry Probst met with IOC President Jacques

been sold.

It's news like that that makes cities wary of the Olympics. Many insiders were predicting that future Games would of necessity be much humbler affairs than those past. Just don't bet on those proud Brazilians settling for anything less than a carnival of Olympic proportions.

## 2008 Summer Games

### TRACK AND FIELD
### Men

#### 100 METERS
1. ...Usain Bolt Jamaica — 9.69 WR
2. ...Richard Thompson, Trinidad — 9.89
3. ...Walter Dix, United States — 9.91

#### 200 METERS
1. ...Usain Bolt, Jamaica — ·19.30 WR
2. ...Shawn Crawford, United States — 19.96
3. ...Walter Dix, United States — 19.98

#### 400 METERS
1. ...Lashawn Merritt, United States — 43.75
2. ...Jeremy Wariner, United States — 44.74
3. ...David Neville, United States — 44.80

#### 800 METERS
1. ...Wilfred Kipkemboi Bungei, Kenya — 1:44.65
2. ...Ismail Ahmed Ismail, Sudan — 1:44.70
3. ...Alfred Kirwa Yego, Kenya — 1:44.82

#### 1,500 METERS
1. ...Rasheed Ramzi, Bahrain — 3:32.94
2. ...Asbel Kipruto Kiprop, Kenya — 3:33.11
3. ...Nick Willis, New Zealand — 3:34.16

#### 5,000 METERS
1. ...Kenenisa Bekele, Ethiopia — 12:57.82 OR
2. ...Eliud Kipchoge, Kenya — 13:02.80
3. ...Edwin Cheruiyot Soi , Kenya — 13:06.22

#### 10,000 METERS
1. ...Kenenisa Bekele, Ethiopia — 27:01.17 OR
2. ...Sileshi Sihine, Ethiopia — 27:02.77
3. ...Micah Kikemboi Kogo, Kenya — 27:04.11

#### MARATHON
1. ...Samuel Kamau, Kenya — 2:06:32 OR
2. ...Jaouad Gharib, Morocco — 2:07:16
3. ...Tsegay Kebede, Ethiopia — 2:l0:00

#### 110-METER HURDLES
1. ...Dayron Robles, Cuba — 12.93
2. ...David Payne, United States — 13.17
3. ...David Oliver, United States — 13.18

#### 400-METER HURDLES
1. ...Angelo Taylor, United States — 47.25
2. ...Kerron Clement, United States — 47.98
3. ...Bershawn Jackson, United States — 48.06

#### 3,000-METER STEEPLECHASE
1. ...Brimin Kipruto, Kenya — 8:10.34
2. ...Mahiedine Mekissi-Banabbad, France — 8:10.49
3. ...Richard Kipkemboi Mateelong, Kenya — 8:11.01

#### 4 X 100-METER RELAY
1. ...Jamaica (A. Powell, M. Frater — 37.10 WR
Usain Bolt, N. Carter)
2. ...Trinidad & Tobago — 38.06
3. ...Japan — 38.15

#### 4 X 400-METER RELAY
1. ...United States: (A. Taylor — 2.55.39 OR
J. Wariner, L. Merritt, D. Neville)
2. ...Bahamas — 2.58.03
3. ...Russia — 2.58.06

#### 20-KILOMETER WALK
1. ...Valeriy Borchin, Russia — 1:19.01
2. ...Jefferson Perez, Ecuador — 1:19.15
3. ...Jared Tallent, Australia — 1:19.42

#### 50-KILOMETER WALK
1. ...Alex Schwazer, Italy — 3:37.09 OR
2. ...Jared Tallent, Australia — 3:39.27
3. ...Denis Nizhegorodov, Russia — 3:40.14

#### HIGH JUMP
1. ...Andrey Silnov, Russia — 7 ft 9 in
2. ...Germaine Mason, Great Britian — 7 ft 8 in
3. ...Yaroslav Rybakov, Russia — 7 ft 8 in

#### POLE VAULT
1. ...Steve Hooker, Australia — 19 ft 6½ in OR
2. ...Eugeny Lukyanenko, Russia — 19 ft 2¼ in
3. ...Denys Yurchenko, Ukraine — 18 ft 8½ in

#### LONG JUMP
1. ...Irving Jahir Saladino, Panama — 27 ft 4¼ in
2. ...Godfrey Khotso Mokoena, S. Africa — 27 ft ½ in
3. ...Ibrahim Camejo, Cuba — 26 ft 10¾ in

#### TRIPLE JUMP
1. ...Nelson Evora, Portugal — 57 ft 11½ in
2. ...Phillips Idowa, Great Britian — 57 ft 9¾ in
3. ...Leevan Sands, Bahamas — 57 ft 8½ in

#### SHOT PUT
1. ...Tomasz Majewski, Poland — 70 ft 6¾ in
2. ...Christian Cantwell, United States — 69 ft 2¼ in
3. ...Andrei Mikhnevich, Belarus — 69 ft ¾ in

#### DISCUS THROW
1. ...Gerd Kanter, Estonia — 225 ft 9½ in
2. ...Piotr Malachowski, Poland — 222 ft 6 in
3. ...Virgilijus Alekna, Lithuania — 222 ft 4¾ in

#### HAMMER THROW
1. ...Primoz Kozmus, Slovenia — 269 ft 1 in
2. ...Vadim Devyaovskiy, Belarus — 267 ft 9 in
3. ...Ivan Tsikhan, Belarus — 267 ft 5 in

#### JAVELIN
1. ...Andreas Thorkildsen, Norway — 297 ft 1¾ in OR
2. ...Ainars Kovals, Latvia — 284 ft 3 in
3. ...Tero Pitkamaki, Finland — 282 ft 8 in

#### DECATHLON
| | Pts |
| --- | --- |
| 1. ...Bryan Clay, United States | 8791 |
| 2. ...Andrei Krauchanka,Belarus | 8551 |
| 3. ...Leonel Suarez, Cuba | 8527 |

### TRACK AND FIELD
### Women

#### 100 METERS
1. ...Shelly-Ann Fraser, Jamaica — 10.78
2. ...Sherone Simpson, Jamaica — 10.98
2. ...Kerron Stewart, Jamaica — 10.98

#### 200 METERS
1. ...Veronica Campbell-Brown, Jamaica — 21.74
2. ...Allyson Felix, United States — 21.93
3. ...Kerron Stewart, Jamaica — 22.00

Note: OR=Olympic Record.  WR=World Record.  EOR=Equals Olympic Record.  EWR=Equals World Record.

## TRACK AND FIELD (CONT.)
### Women *(Cont.)*

**400 METERS**

1. ...Christine Ohuruogo, Great Britain — 49.62
2. ...Shericka Williams, Jamaica — 49.69
3. ...Sanya Richards, United States — 49.93

**800 METERS**

1. ...Pamela Jelimo, Kenya — 1:54.87
2. ...J. Jepkosgei Busienei, Kenya — 1:56.07
3. ...Hasna Benhassi, Morocco — 1:56.73

**1,500 METERS**

1. ...Nancy Jebet Lagat, Kenya — 4:00.23
2. ...Iryna Lishchynska, Ukraine — 4:01.63
3. ...Nataliya Tobias, Ukraine — 4:01.78

**5,000 METERS**

1. ...Tirunesh Dibaba Kenene, Ethiopia — 15:41.40
2. ...Elvan Abeylegesse, Turkey — 15:42.74
3. ...Meseret Defar Tola, Ethiopia — 15:44.96

**10,000 METERS**

1. ...Tirunesh Dibaba Kenene, Ethiopia — 29:54.66 OR
2. ...Elvan Abeylegesse, Turkey — 29:56.34
3. ...Shalane Flanagan, United States — 30:22.22

**MARATHON**

1. ...Constantina Tomescu Dita, Romania — 2:26:44
2. ...Nyambura Wincatherine, Kenya — 2:27:06
3. ...Zhou Chunxiu, China — 2:27:07

**100-METER HURDLES**

1. ...Dawn Harper, United States — 12.54
2. ...Sally McLellan, Australia — 12.64
3. ...Priscilla Lopes-Schliep, Canada — 12.64

**400-METER HURDLES**

1. ...Melaine Walker, Jamaica — 52.64 OR
2. ...Sheena Tosta, United States — 53.70
3. ...Tasha Danvers, Great Britain — 53.84

**3,000-METER STEEPLECHASE**

1. ...Gulnara Samitova-Galkina, Russia — 8:58.81 WR
2. ...Eunice Jepkorir, Kenya — 9:07.41
3. ...Yekaterina Volkova, Russia — 9:07.64

**4 X 100-METER RELAY**

1. ...Russia (Y. Chermoshanskaya, — 42.31
   Y. Gushchina, E. Polyakova, A. Fedoriva)
2. ...Belgium — 42.54
3. ...Nigeria — 43.04

**4 X 400-METER RELAY**

1. ...United States (A. Felix, S. Richards, — 3:18.54
   M. Henderson, M. Wineberg)
2. ...Russia — 3:18.82
3. ...Jamaica — 3:20.40

**20-KILOMETER WALK**

1. ...Olga Kaniskina, Russia — 1:26:31 OR
2. ...Kjersti Tysse Platzer, Norway — 1:27:07
3. ...Elisa Rigaudo, Italy — 1:27:12

**HIGH JUMP**

1. ...Tia Hellebaut, Belgium — 6 ft 8¾ in
2. ...Blanka Vlasic, Croatia — 6 ft 8¾ in
3. ...Anna Chicherova, Russia — 6 ft 8 in

**POLE VAULT**

1. ...Yelena Isinbayeva, Russia — 16 ft 6¾ in WR
2. ...Jennifer Stuczynski, United States — 15 ft 9 in
3. ...Svetlana Feofanova, Russia — 15 ft 7 in

**LONG JUMP**

1. ...Maurren Higa Maggi, Brazil — 23 ft 1 in
2. ...Tatiana Lebedeva, Russia — 23 ft
3. ...Blessing Okhagbare, Nigeria — 22 ft 8 in

**TRIPLE JUMP**

1. ...Francoise Mbango Etone, Cameroon — 50 ft 5 in
2. ...Tatiana Lebedva, Russia — 50 ft 3 in
3. ...Hrysopiyi Devetzi, Greece — 49 ft 11½ in

**SHOT PUT**

1. ...Valerie Vili, New Zealand — 67 ft 5½ in
2. ...Natallia Mikhnevich, Belarus — 66 ft 6½ in
3. ...Nadzeya Ostapchuk, Belarus — 65 ft 2 in

**DISCUS THROW**

1. ...Stephanie Brown-Trafton, United States — 212 ft 4¾ in
2. ...Yarelys Barrios, Cuba — 208 ft 9½ in
3. ...Olena Antonova, Ukraine — 205 ft 4 in

**JAVELIN**

1. ...Barbora Spotakova, Czech Republic — 234 ft 3¾ in
2. ...Maria Abakumova, Russia — 232 ft 2½ in
3. ...Christina Obergfoll, Germany — 216 ft 11½ in

**HEPTATHLON** — Pts

1. ...Natalia Dobrynska, Ukraine — 6733
2. ...Hyleas Fountain, United States — 6619
3. ...Tatiana Chernova, Russia — 6591

**HAMMER THROW**

1. ...Aksana Miankova, Belarus — 250 ft 5½ in OR
2. ...Yipsi Moreno, Cuba — 246 ft 8½ in
3. ...Zhang Wenxiu, China — 243 ft 10 in

## INDIVIDUAL ARCHERY

### Men

1. ...Viktor Ruban, Ukraine
2. ...Kyung-Mo Park, South Korea
3. ...Bair Badenov, Russia

### Women

1. ...Zhang Juan Juan, China
2. ...Sung-Hyun Park, South Korea
3. ...Ok-Hee Yun, South Korea

## TEAM ARCHERY

### Men

1. ....South Korea
2. ....Italy
3. ....China

### Women

1. ....South Korea
2. ....China
3. ....France

Note: OR=Olympic Record. WR=World Record. EOR=Equals Olympic Record. EWR=Equals World Record.

## BADMINTON

### Men
**SINGLES**
1. ....Lin Dan, China
2. ....Chong Wei Lee, Malaysia
3. ....Chen Jin, China

**DOUBLES**
1. ....M.Kido/H. Setiawan, Indonesia
2. ....H. Fu/Y. Yun, China
3. ....L.Jaejin/H. Jiman, South Korea

### Women
**SINGLES**
1. .... Zhang Ning, China
2. ....Xingfang Xie, China
3. ....Maria Kristin Yulianti, Indonesia

**DOUBLES**
1. ......D. Jing/Yu Yang, China
2. ....H. Lee/K. Lee, South Korea
3. .... Y. Wei/Y. Zhang, China

**MIXED DOUBLES**
1.   Y. Lee/H. Lee, South Korea
2.   N. Widianto/
     L. Natsir, Indonesia
3.   He Hanbin/
     Yu Yang, China

## BMX

### Men
1. ....Maris Strombergs, Latvia
2. ....Mike Day, United States
3. ....Donny Robinson, United States

### Women
1. ....Anne-Caroline Chausson, France
2. ....Laetitia le Corquille, France
3. ....Jill Kintner, United States

## BASEBALL
1. .....South Korea
2. .....Cuba
3. .....United States

## BASKETBALL

### Men
Final: United States 118, Spain 107
Argentina (3rd)
United States: Carmelo Anthony, Carlos Boozer,
Chris Bosh, Kobe Bryant, Dwight Howard, LeBron
James, Jason Kidd, Chris Paul, Tayshaun Prince,
Michael Redd, Dwyane Wade, Deron Williams

### Women
Final: United States 92, Australia 65
Russia (3rd)
United States: Seimone Augustus, Sue Bird, Sylvia
Fowles, Lisa Leslie, DeLisha Milton-Jones, Candace
Parker, Cappie Pondexter, Tamika Catchings, Tina
Thompson, Diana Taurasi, Katie Smith

## BOXING

**LIGHT FLYWEIGHT (106 LB)**
1. ......Zou Shiming, China
2. ......Serdamba Pureydori, Mongolia
3. ......Paddy Barnes, Ireland
3. ......Yampier Hernandez, Cuba

**FLYWEIGHT (112 LB)**
1. ......Somit Jongjohor, Thailand
2. ......Andris Laffita Hernandez, Cuba
3. ......Vincenzo Picardi, Italy
3. ......Georgy Balakshin, Russia

**BANTAMWEIGHT (119 LB)**
1. ......Badar-Uugan Enkhbat, Mongolia
2. ......Yankiel Leon Alarcon, Cuba
3. ......Veaceslav Gojan, Moldova
3. ......Bruno Julie, Mauritius

**FEATHERWEIGHT (125 LB)**
1. ......Vasyl Lomachenko, Ukraine
2. ......Khedafi Djelkhir, France
3. ......Shahin Imranov, Azerbaijan
3. ......Yakup Kilic, Turkey

**LIGHTWEIGHT (132 LB)**
1. ......Alexey Tishchenko, Russia
2. ......Daouda Sow, France
3. ......Hrachik Javakhyan, Armenia
3. ......Yordenis Ugas, Cuba

**LIGHT WELTERWEIGHT (139 LB)**
1. ......Felix Diaz, Dominican Republic
2. ......Manus Boonjumnong, Thailand
3. ......Alexis Vastine, France
3. ......Roniel Iglesias Sotolongo, Cuba

**WELTERWEIGHT (147 LB)**
1. ......Bakhyt Sarsekbayev, Kazakhstan
2. ......Carlos Banteaux Suarez, Cuba
3. ......Hanati Silamu, China
3. ......Kim Jungjoo, South Korea

**MIDDLEWEIGHT (165 LB)**
1. ......James Degale, Great Britain
2. ......Emilio Correa Bayeaux, Cuba
3. ......Vjender, India
3. :......Darren John Sutherland, Ireland

**LIGHT HEAVYWEIGHT (178 LB)**
1. ......Zhang Xiaoping, China
2. ......Kenny Egan, Ireland
3. ......Tony Jeffries, Great Britain
3. ......Yerkebulan Shynaliyev, Kazakhstan

**HEAVYWEIGHT (201 LB)**
1. ......Rakhim Chakhkiev, Russia
2. ........Clemente Russo, Italy
3. ......Deontay Wilder, United States
3. ......Osmai Acosta Duarte, Cuba

**SUPERHEAVYWEIGHT (201+ LB)**
1. ......Roberto Cammarelle, Italy
2. ......Zhang Zhilei, China
3. ......David Price, Great Britain
3. ......Vyacheslav Glazkov, Ukraine

## CANOE/KAYAK
### Men

**C-1 FLATWATER 500 METERS**
| | | |
|---|---|---|
| 1. ...Maxim Opalev, Russia | | 1:47.140 |
| 2. ...David Cal, Spain | | 1:48.397 |
| 3. ...Iurli Cheban, Ukraine | | 1:48.766 |

**C-1 FLATWATER 1,000 METERS**
| | | |
|---|---|---|
| 1. ....Attila Sandor Vajda, Hungary | | 3:50.467 |
| 2. ....David Cal, Spain | | 3:52.751 |
| 3. ....Thomas Hall, Canada | | 3:53.653 |

**C-2 FLATWATER 500 METERS**
| | | |
|---|---|---|
| 1. ....M. Guanliang/Y. Wenjun, China | | 1:41.025 |
| 2. ....A. Kostogold/S. Ulegin, Russia | | 1:41.282 |
| 3. ....C. Gille/T. Wylenzek, Germany | | 1:41.964 |

**C-2 FLATWATER 1,000 METERS**
| | | |
|---|---|---|
| 1. ...Aliaksandr/Andrei Bahdanovich, Belarus | | 3:36.365 |
| 2. ....C. Gille/T. Wylenzek, Germany | | 3:36.588 |
| 3. ....G. Kozmann/T. Kiss, Hungary | | 3:40.258 |

**C-1 WHITEWATER SLALOM** — Pts
| | | |
|---|---|---|
| 1. ....Michal Martikan, Slovakia | | 176.65 |
| 2. ....David Florence, Great Britain | | 178.61 |
| 3. ....Robin Bell, Australia | | 180.59 |

**C-2 WHITEWATER SLALOM** — Pts
| | | |
|---|---|---|
| 1. ....Pavel/Peter Hochschorner, Slovakia | | 190.82 |
| 2. ....J. Volf/O. Stepanek, Czech Republic | | 192.89 |
| 3. ....M. Kuznetsov/D. Larionov, Russia | | 197.37 |

## CANOE/KAYAK
### Men (Cont.)

**K-1 FLATWATER 500 METERS**
1. ...Ken Wallace, Australia — 1:37.252
2. ...Adam van Koeverden, Canada — 1:37.630
3. ...Tim Brabants, Great Britain — 1:37.671

**K-1 FLATWATER 1,000 METERS**
1. ...Tim Brabants, Great Britain — 3:26.323
2. ...Erik Veraas Larsen, Norway — 3:27.342
3. ...Ken Wallace, Australia — 3:27.485

**K-2 FLATWATER 1,000 METERS**
1. ...A. Ihle/M. Hollstein, Germany — 3:11.809
2. ...K. Knudsen/R. Poulsen, Denmark — 3:13.580
3. ...A. Facchin/A. Scaduto, Italy — 3:14.750

**K-2 FLATWATER 5000 METERS**
1. ...S. Cravlotto/C. Perez, Spain — 1:28.736
2. ...R. Rauhe/T. Wieskotler, Germany — 1:28.827
3. ...P. Piatrushenka/V. Makehneu, Belarus — 1:30.005

**K-4 FLATWATER 1,000 METERS**
1. ...Belarus — 2:55.714
2. ...Slovakia — 2:56.593
3. ...Germany — 2:56.676

### Women

**K-1 FLATWATER 500 METERS**
1. ...Inna Osypenko-Radomska, Ukraine — 1:50.673
2. ...Josefa Idem, Italy — 1:50.677
3. ...Katrin Wagner-Augustin, Germany — 1:51.022

**K-2 FLATWATER 500 METERS**
1. ...K. Kovacs/N. Janic, Hungary — 1:41.308
2. ...A. Konieczna/B. Mikolajczyk, Poland — 1:42.092
3. ...M. Delattre/A. Viard, France — 1:42.128

**K-4 FLATWATER 500 METERS**
1. ...Germany — 1:32.231
2. ...Hungary — 1:32.971
3. ...Australia — 1:34.704

**K-1 WHITEWATER SLALOM** — Pts
1. ...Elena Kaliska, Slovakia — 192.64
2. ...Jacqueline Lawrence, Australia — 206.94
3. ...Violetta Oblinger Peters, Austria — 214.77

## CYCLING–Men

**ROAD RACE**
1. ...Samuel Sanchez, Spain — 6:23:49
2. ...David Rebellin, Italy — 6:23:49
3. ...Fabian Cancellara, Switzerland — 6:23:49

**INDIVIDUAL TIME TRIAL**
1. ...Fabian Cancellara, Switzerland — 1:02:11.43
2. ...Gustav Larsson, Sweden — 1:02:44.79
3. ...Levi Leipheimer, United States — 1:03:21.11

**4,000-METER INDIVIDUAL PURSUIT**
1. ...Bradley Wiggins, Great Britain — 4:16.977
2. ...Hayden Roulston, New Zealand — 4:19.611
3. ...Steven Burke, Great Britain — 4:20.947

**4,000-METER TEAM PURSUIT**
1. ...Great Britain (Ed Clancy, Paul Manning, Geraint Thomas, Bradley Wiggins) — 3:53.314 WR
2. ...Denmark — 4:00.040
3. ...New Zealand — 3:57.776

**SPRINT**
1. ...Chris Hoy, Great Britain — 9.815 OR
2. ...Jason Kenny, Great Britain — 9.857
3. ...Stefan Nimke, Germany — 10.064

**POINTS RACE**
1. ...Juan Llaneras, Spain — 60,2
2. ...Roger Kluge, Germany — 58,2
3. ...Chris Newton, Great Britain — 56,2

**KIERIN**
1. ...Chris Hoy, Great Britain
2. ...Ross Edgar, Great Britain
3. ...Kiyofumi Nagai, Japan

**MADISON**
1. ...J. Curuchet/W. Perez, Argentina — 8,0
2. ...J. Llaneras/A. Tauler, Spain — 7,0
3. ...M. Ignatyev/A. Markov, Russia — 6,0

**OLYMPIC SPRINT**
1. ...Great Britain — 43.128
2. ...France — 43.651
3. ...Germany — 44.014

**CROSS COUNTRY**
1. ...Julien Absalon, France — 1:55.59
2. ...Jean-Christophe Peraud, France — 1:57.06
3. ...Nino Schwurter, Switzerland — 1:57.52

### Women

**POINTS RACE**
1. ...Marianne Vos, Netherlands — 30,1
2. ...Yoanka Gonzalez, Cuba — 18,0
3. ...Leire Olaverria, Spain — 13,0

**INDIVIDUAL TIME TRIAL**
1. ...Kristin Armstrong, United States — 34:51.72
2. ...Emma Pooley, Great Britain — 35:16.01
3. ...Karin Thurig, Switzerland — 35:50.99

**3,000-METER INDIVIDUAL PURSUIT**
1. ...Rebecca Romero, Great Britain — 3:28.321
2. ...Wendy Houvenaghel, Great Britain — 3:30.395
3. ...Lesya Kalitovska, Ukraine — 3:31.413

**SPRINT**
1. ...Victoria Pendleton, Great Britain — 11.118
2. ...Anna Meares, Australia — —
3. ...Shuang Guo, China — 11.617

**ROAD RACE**
1. ...Nicole Cooke, Great Britain — 3:32:24
2. ...Emma Johansson, Sweden — 3:32:24
3. ...Tatiana Guderzo, Italy — 3:32:24

**CROSS COUNTRY**
1. ...Sabine Spitz, Germany — 1:45.11
2. ...Maja Wloszczowska, Poland — 1:45.52
3. ...Irina Kalentyeva, Russia — 1:46.28

## DIVING
### Men

| SPRINGBOARD | Pts | PLATFORM | Pts |
|---|---|---|---|
| 1.....Chong He, China | 572.90 | 1.....Matthew Mitcham, Australia | 537.95 |
| 2.....Alexandre Despatie, Canada | 536.65 | 2.....Luxin Zhou, China | 533.15 |
| 3.....Kai Oin, China | 530.10 | 3.....Gleb Galperin, Russia | 525.80 |

### Women

| SPRINGBOARD | Pts | PLATFORM | Pts |
|---|---|---|---|
| 1.....Jingjing Guo, China | 415.35 | 1.....Ruoulin Chen, China | 447.70 |
| 2.....Julia Pakhalina, Russia | 398.60 | 2.....Emilie Heymans, Canada | 437.05 |
| 3.....Minxia Wu, China | 389.85 | 3. ....Xin Wang, China | 429.90 |

## EQUESTRIAN

| TEAM EVENTING | | INDIVIDUAL DRESSAGE | Pts |
|---|---|---|---|
| 1. ......Germany | | 1. ......Anky van Grunsven, Netherlands | 82.400 |
| 2. ......Australia | | 2. ......Isabell Werth, Germany | 78.100 |
| 3. ......Great Britain | | 3. ......Heike Kemmer, Germany | 75.950 |

| INDIVIDUAL EVENTING | Pts | TEAM JUMPING | |
|---|---|---|---|
| 1. ......Hinrich Romeike, Germany | 54.20 | 1.....United States | |
| 2. ......Gina Miles, United States | 56.10 | 2. ......Canada | |
| 3. ......Kristina Cook, Great Britain | 57.40 | 3. ......Norway | |

| TEAM DRESSAGE | | INDIVIDUAL JUMPING | Pen. Pts |
|---|---|---|---|
| 1. ......Germany | | 1. ......Eric Lamaze, Canada | 0.00 |
| 2. ......Netherlands | | 2. ......Rolf-Goran Bengtsson, Sweden | 0.00 |
| 3. ......Denmark | | 3. ......Beezie Madden, United States | 4.00 |

## FENCING
### Men

| FOIL | ÉPÉE | TEAM ÉPÉE |
|---|---|---|
| 1. ......Benjamin Kleibrink, Germany | 1. ......Matteo Tagliariol, Italy | 1. ......France |
| 2. ......Yuki Ota, Japan | 2. ......Fabrice Jeannet, France | 2. ......Poland |
| 3. ......Salvatore Sanzo, Italy | 3. ......Jose Luis Abajo, Spain | 3. ......Italy |
| SABRE | TEAM SABRE | |
| 1. ......Man Zhong, China | 1. ......France | |
| 2. ......Nicolas Lopez, France | 2. .....United States | |
| 3. ......Mihai Covaliu, Romania | 3. ......Italy | |

### Women

| FOIL | ÉPÉE | TEAM FOIL |
|---|---|---|
| 1.....Maria Valentina Vezzali, Italy | 1. ......Britta Heidemann, Germany | 1. ....................Russia |
| 2.....Hyunhee Nam, South Korea | 2. ......Ana Maria Branza, Romania | 2. ....................United States |
| 3.....Margherita Granbassi, Italy | 3. ......I. Mincza-Nebald, Hungary | 3. ....................Italy |
| SABRE | TEAM SABRE | |
| 1.....Mariel Zagunis, United States | 1. ....................Ukraine | |
| 2.....Sada Jacobson, United States | 2. ....................China | |
| 3.....Becca Ward, United States | 3. ....................United States | |

## FIELD HOCKEY

| Men | | Women | |
|---|---|---|---|
| 1. | Germany | 1. | Netherlands |
| 2. | Spain | 2. | China |
| 3. | Australia | 3. | Argentina |

## GYMNASTICS
### Men

| ALL-AROUND | Pts | PARALLEL BARS | Pts |
|---|---|---|---|
| 1. ..........Yang Wei, China | 94.575 | 1. ..........Li Xiaopeng, China | 16.450 |
| 2. ..........Kohei Uchimura, Japan | 91.975 | 2. ..........Yoo Wonchul, South Korea | 16.250 |
| 3. ..........Benoit Caranobe, France | 91.925 | 3. ..........Anton Fokin, Uzbekistan | 16.200 |

| HORIZONTAL BAR | Pts | VAULT | Pts |
|---|---|---|---|
| 1. ..........Zou Kai, China | 16.200 | 1. ..........Leszek Blanik, Poland | 16.537 |
| 2. ..........Jonathan Horton, United States | 16.175 | 2. ..........Thomas Bouhail, France | 16.537 |
| 3. ..........Fabian Hambuchen, Germany | 15.875 | 3. ..........Anton Golotsutskov, Russia | 16.475 |

### GYMNASTICS (Cont.)

## Men

| POMMEL HORSE | Pts | | FLOOR EXERCISE | Pts |
|---|---|---|---|---|
| 1. ..........Xiao Oin, China | 15.875 | | 1. ..........Zou Kai, China | 16.050 |
| 2. ..........Filip Ude, Croatia | 15.725 | | 2. ..........Gervasio Deferr, Spain | 15.775 |
| 3. ..........Louis Smith, Great Britain | 15.725 | | 3. ..........Anton Golotsutskov, Russia | 15.725 |

| RINGS | Pts | | TEAM COMBINED EXERCISES | |
|---|---|---|---|---|
| 1. ..........Chen Yibing, China | 16.600 | | 1. ..........China | |
| 2. ..........Wei Yang, China | 16.425 | | 2. ..........Japan | |
| 3. ..........Oleksandr Vorobiov, Ukraine | 16.325 | | 3. ..........United States | |

## Women

| ALL-AROUND | Pts | | BALANCE BEAM | Pts |
|---|---|---|---|---|
| 1. ..........Nastia Liukin, United States | 63.325 | | 1. ..........Shawn Johnson, United States | 16.225 |
| 2. ..........Shawn Johnson, United States | 62.725 | | 2. ..........Nastia Liukin, United States | 16.025 |
| 3. ..........Yang Yilin, China | 62.650 | | 3. ..........Cheng Fei, China | 15.950 |

| VAULT | Pts | | FLOOR EXERCISE | Pts |
|---|---|---|---|---|
| 1. ..........Un Jong Hong, North Korea | 15.650 | | 1. ..........Sandra Izbasa, Romania | 15.650 |
| 2. ..........Oksana Chusovitina, Germany | 15.575 | | 2. ..........Shawn Johnson, United States | 15.500 |
| 3. ..........Cheng Fei, China | 15.562 | | 3. ..........Nastia Liukin, United States | 15.425 |

| UNEVEN BARS | Pts | | TEAM COMBINED EXERCISES | |
|---|---|---|---|---|
| 1. ..........He Kexin, China | 16.725 | | 1. ..........China | |
| 2. ..........Nastia Liukin, United States | 16.725 | | 2. ..........United States | |
| 3. ..........Yang Yilin, China | 16.650 | | 3. ..........Romania | |

## JUDO

| Men | Women |
|---|---|
| **EXTRA-LIGHTWEIGHT** | **EXTRA-LIGHTWEIGHT** |
| 1. ..........Minho Choi, South Korea | 1. ..........Alina Alexandra Dumitru, Romania |
| 2. ..........Ludwig Paischer, Austria | 2. ..........Yanet Bermoy, Cuba |
| 3. ..........Rishod Sobirov, Uzbekistan | 3. ..........Paula Belen Pareto, Argentina |
| 3. ..........Ruben Houkes, Netherlands | 3. ..........Ryoko Tani, Japan |
| **HALF-LIGHTWEIGHT** | **HALF-LIGHTWEIGHT** |
| 1. ..........Masato Uchishiba, Japan | 1. ..........Dongmei Xien, China |
| 2. ..........Benjamin Darbelet, France | 2. ..........Ae Kum An, North Korea |
| 3. ..........Yordanis Arencibia, Cuba | 3. ..........Soraya Haddad, Algeria |
| 3. ..........Choi Min Pak, North Korea | 3. ..........Misato Nakamura, Japan |
| **LIGHTWEIGHT** | **LIGHTWEIGHT** |
| 1. ..........Elnur Mammadli, Azerbaijan | 1. ..........Giulia Quintavalle, Italy |
| 2. ..........Kichyn Wang, South Korea | 2. ..........Deborah Gravenstijn, Netherlands |
| 3. ..........Rasul Booiev, Tajikistan | 3. ..........Ketleyn Quadros, Brazil |
| 3. ..........Leandro Guilhero, Brazil | 3. ..........Yan Xu, China |
| **HALF-MIDDLEWEIGHT** | **HALF-MIDDLEWEIGHT** |
| 1. ..........Ole Bischof, Germany | 1. ..........Ayumi Tanimoto, Japan |
| 2. ..........Jaebum Kim, South Korea | 2. ..........Lucie Decosse, France |
| 3. ..........Tiago Camilo, Brazil | 3. ..........Elisabeth Willeboordse, Netherlands |
| 3. ..........Roman Gontiuk, Ukraine | 3. ..........Ok Im Won, North Korea |
| **MIDDLEWEIGHT** | **MIDDLEWEIGHT** |
| 1. ..........Irakli Tsirekidze, Georgia | 1. ..........Masae Ueno, Japan |
| 2. ..........Amar Benikhlef, Algeria | 2. ..........Anaysi Hernandez, Cuba |
| 3. ..........Hesham Mesbah, Egypt | 3. ..........Ronda Rousey, United States |
| 3. ..........Sergei Aschwanden, Switzerland | 3. ..........Edith Bosch, Netherlands |
| **HALF-HEAVYWEIGHT** | **HALF-HEAVYWEIGHT** |
| 1. ..........Tuyshinbayar Naidan, Mongolia | 1. ..........Yang Xiuli, China |
| 2. ..........Askhat Zhitkeyev, Kazakhstan | 2. ..........Yalennis Castillo, Cuba |
| 3. ..........Movlud Miraliyev, Azerbaijan | 3. ..........Gyeongmi Jeong, South Korea |
| 3. ..........Henk Grol, Netherlands | 3. ..........Stephanie Possamai, France |
| **HEAVYWEIGHT** | **HEAVYWEIGHT** |
| 1. ..........Satoshi Ishii, Japan | 1. ..........Tong Wen, China |
| 2. ..........Abdullo Tangriev, Uzbekistan | 2. ..........Maki Tsukada, Japan |
| 3. ..........Oscar Brayson, Cuba | 3. ..........Lucija Polavder, Slovenia |
| 3. ..........Teddy Riner, France | 3. ..........Idalys Ortiz, Cuba |

## MODERN PENTATHLON

### Men

1. ......Andrev Moiseev, Russia
2. ......Edvinas Krungolcas, Lituania
3. ......Andreius Zadneprovskis, Lithuania

### Women

1. ......Lena Schoneborn, Germany
2. ......Heather Fell, Great Britain
3. ......Victoria Tereshuk, Ukraine

## MOUNTAIN BIKING

### Men

1. ......Julien Absalon, France          1:55.59
2. ......Jean-Christophe Peraud, France  1:57.06
3. ......Nino Schurter, Switzerland      1:57.52

### Women

1. ......Sabine Spitz, Germany           1:45.11
2. ......Maia Wloszczowska, Poland       1:45.52
3. ......Irina Kalentyeva, Russia        1:46.28

## ROWING

### Men

#### SINGLE SCULLS

1. ...Olaf Tufte, Norway          6:59.83
2. ...Ondrej Synek, Estonia       7:00.63
3. ...Mahe Drysdale, New Zealand  7:01.56

#### COXLESS PAIR

1. ...D. Ginn/D. Free, Australia                        6:37.44
2. ...D. Calder/S. Frandsen, Canada                     6:39.55
3. ...N. Twaddle/G. Bridgewater, New Zealand 6:44.19

#### DOUBLE SCULLS

1. ...D. Crawshay/S. Brennan, Australia       6:27.77
2. ...T. Endrekson/J. Jaanson, Estonia        6:29.05
3. ...M. Wells/S. Rowbotham, Great Britain    6:29.10

#### COXLESS FOUR

1. ...Great Britain  6:06.57
2. ...Australia       6:07.85
3. ...France          6:09.31

#### LIGHTWEIGHT DOUBLE SCULLS

1. ...Z. Purchase/M. Hunter, Great Britain    6:10.99
2. ...D. Mougios/V. Polymeros, Greece         6:11.72
3. ...M. Rasmussen/R. Hansen, Denmark         6:12.45

#### LIGHTWEIGHT COXLESS FOUR

1. ...Denmark  5:47.76
2. ...Poland   5:49.39
3. ...Canada   5:50.09

#### QUADRUPLE SCULLS

1. ...Poland  5:41.33
2. ...Italy   5:43.57
3. ...France  5:44.34

#### EIGHT-OARS

1. ...Canada         5:23.89
2. ...Great Britain  5:25.11
3. ...United States  5:25.34

### Women

#### SINGLE SCULLS

1. ...Rumyana Neykova, Bulgaria         7:22.34
2. ...Michelle Guerette, United States  7:22.78
3. ...Ekaterina Karsten, Belarus        7:23.98

#### QUADRUPLE SCULLS

1. ...China          6:16.06
2. ...Great Britain  6:17.37
3. ...Germany        6:19.56

#### DOUBLE SCULLS

1. ...Caroline/Georgina Evers-Swindell, N.Z.  7:07.32
2. ...A. Thiele/C. Huth, Germany               7:07.33
3. ...E. Laverick/A. Bebington, Great Britain  7:07.55

#### COXLESS PAIR

1. ...G. Andrunache/V. Susanu, Romania  7:20.60
2. ...W. You/G. Youlan, China            7:22.28
3. ...Y. Bichyk/N. Helakh, Belarus       7:22.91

#### LIGHTWEIGHT DOUBLE SCULLS

1. ...K. van der Kolk/M. van Eupen, Neth  6:54.74
2. ...S. Stern/M. Nieminen, Finland        6:56.03
3. ...M. Kok/T. Cameron, Canada            6:56.68

#### EIGHT-OARS

1. ...United States  6:05.34
2. ...Netherlands    6:07.22
3. ...Romania        6:07.25

## SHOOTING- Men

| RAPID-FIRE PISTOL | Pts |
|---|---|
| 1. ........Oleksandr Petriy, Ukraine | 780.2 |
| 2. ........Ralf Schumann, Germany | 779.5 |
| 3. ........Christian Rietz, Germany | 779.3 |

| SMALL-BORE RIFLE, THREE-POSITION | Pts |
|---|---|
| 1. ........Oiu Jian, China | 1272.5 |
| 2. ........Yuriy Sukhorukov, Ukraine | 1272.4 |
| 3. ........Raimond Debevec, Slovenia | 1271.7 |

| FREE PISTOL | Pts |
|---|---|
| 1. ........Jin Jongoh, South Korea | 660.4 |
| 2. ........Zongliang Tan, China | 659.5 |
| 3. ........Vladimir Isakov, Russia | 658.9 |

| SMALL-BORE RIFLE, PRONE | Pts |
|---|---|
| 1. ........Artur Ayvazyan, Ukraine | 702.7 |
| 2. ........Matt Emmons, United States | 701.7 |
| 3. ........Warren Potent, Australia | 700.5 |

| AIR PISTOL | Pts |
|---|---|
| 1. ........Pang Wei, China | 688.2 |
| 2. ........Jin Jongoh, South Korea | 684.5 |
| 3. ........Jason Turner, United States | 682.0 |

| AIR RIFLE | Pts |
|---|---|
| 1. ........Abhinav Bindra, India | 700.5 |
| 2. ........Zhu Oinan, China | 699.7 |
| 3. ........Henri Hakkinen, Finland | 699.4 |

| TRAP | Pts |
|---|---|
| 1. ........David Kostelecky, Czech Republic | 146.0 |
| 2. ........Giovanni Pellielo, Italy | 143.0 |
| 3. ........Aleksey Alipov, Russia | 142.0 |

| DOUBLE TRAP | Pts |
|---|---|
| 1. ........Walton Eller, United States | 190.0 |
| 2. ........Francesco D'aniello, Italy | 187.0 |
| 3. ........Hu Binyuan, China | 184.0 |

| SKEET | Pts |
|---|---|
| 1. ........Vincent Hancock, United States | 145.0 |
| 2. ........Tore Brovold, Norway | 145.0 |
| 3. ........Anthony Terras, France | 144.0 |

## SHOOTING - Women

| SPORT PISTOL | Pts |
|---|---|
| 1. ......Ying Chen, China | 793.4 |
| 2. ......Gundegmaa Otryad, Mongolia | 792.2 |
| 3. ......Munkhbayar Dorisuren, Germany | 789.2 |

| AIR PISTOL | Pts |
|---|---|
| 1. ......Wenjun Guo, China | 492.3 OR |
| 2. ......Natalia Paderina, Russia | 489.1 |
| 3. ......Nino Salukvadze, Georgia | 487.4 |

| SMALL-BORE RIFLE, THREE-POSITION | Pts |
|---|---|
| 1. ......Du Li, China | 690.3 |
| 2. ......Katerina Emmons, Czech Republic | 687.7 |
| 3. ......Eglys Cruz, Cuba | 687.6 |

| AIR RIFLE | Pts |
|---|---|
| 1. ......Katerina Emmons, Czech Republic | 503.5 |
| 2. ......Lyoubov Galkina, Russia | 502.1 |
| 3. ......Snjezana Pejic, Croatia | 500.9 |

| TRAP | Pts |
|---|---|
| 1. ......Satu Makela-Nummela, Finland | 91.0 |
| 2. ......Zuzana Stefecekova, Slovakia | 89.0 |
| 3. ......Corey Cogdell, United States | 86.0 |

| SKEET | Pts |
|---|---|
| 1. ......Chiara Cainero, Italy | 93.0 |
| 2. ......Kimberly Rhode, United States | 93.0 |
| 3. ......Christine Brinker, Germany | 93.0 |

## SOCCER

| Men | Women |
|---|---|
| 1. ....................Argentina | 1. ...................United States |
| 2. ...................Nigeria | 2. ..................Brazil |
| 3. ...................Brazil | 3. ...................Germany |

## SOFTBALL

1. .....Japan
2. .....United States
3. .....Australia

## SWIMMING - Men

| 50-METER FREESTYLE | |
|---|---|
| 1. ...Cesar Cielo Filho, Brazil | 21.30 OR |
| 2. ...Amaury Leveaux, France | 21.45 |
| 3. ...Alain Bernard, France | 21.49 |

| 100-METER FREESTYLE | |
|---|---|
| 1. ...Alain Bernard, France | 47.21 |
| 2. ...Eamon Sullivan, Australia | 47.32 |
| 3. ...Cesar Cielo Filho, Brazil | 47.67 |
| 3. ....Jason Lezak, United States | 47.67 |

| 200-METER FREESTYLE | |
|---|---|
| 1. ...Michael Phelps, United States | 1:42.96 WR |
| 2. ...Park Taehwan, South Korea | 1:44.85 |
| 3. ...Peter Vanderkaay, United States | 1:45.14 |

| 400-METER FREESTYLE | |
|---|---|
| 1. ...Park Taehwan, South Korea | 3:41.86 |
| 2. ...Zhang Lin, China | 3:42.44 |
| 3. ...Larsen Jensen, United States | 3:42.78 |

| 1,500-METER FREESTYLE | |
|---|---|
| 1. ...Oussama Mellouli, Tunisia | 14:40.84 |
| 2. ...Grant Hackett, Australia | 14:41.53 |
| 3. ...Ryan Cochrane, Canada | 14:42.69 |

| 100-METER BACKSTROKE | |
|---|---|
| 1. ...Aaron Peirsol, United States | 52.54 WR |
| 2. ...Matt Greyers, United States | 53.11 |
| 3. ...Hayden Stoeckel, Australia | 53.18 |
| 3. ...Arkady Vyatchanin, Russia | 53.18 |

| 200-METER BACKSTROKE | |
|---|---|
| 1. ...Ryan Lochte, United States | 1:53.94 WR |
| 2. ...Aaron Peirsol, United States | 1:54.33 |
| 3. ...Arkady Vyatchanin, Russia | 1:54.93 |

| 100-METER BREASTSTROKE | |
|---|---|
| 1. ...Kosuke Kitajima, Japan | 58.91 WR |
| 2. ...Alexander Dale Oen, Norway | 59.20 |
| 3. ...Hugues Duboscq, France | 59.37 |

| 200-METER BREASTSTROKE | |
|---|---|
| 1. ...Kosuke Kitajima, Japan | 2:07.64 OR |
| 2. ...Brenton Rickard, Australia | 2:08.88 |
| 3. ...Hugues Duboscq, France | 2:08.94 |

| 100-METER BUTTERFLY | |
|---|---|
| 1. ...Michael Phelps, United States | 50.58 OR |
| 2. ...Milorad Cavic, Serbia | 50.59 |
| 3. ...Andrew Lauterstein, Australia | 51.12 |

| 200-METER BUTTERFLY | |
|---|---|
| 1. ...Michael Phelps, United States | 1:52.03 WR |
| 2. ...Laszlo Cseh, Hungary | 1:52.70 |
| 3. ...Takeshi Matsuda, Japan | 1:52.97 |

| 200-METER INDIVIDUAL MEDLEY | |
|---|---|
| 1. ...Michael Phelps, United States | 1:54.23 WR |
| 2. ...Laszlo Cseh, Hungary | 1:56.52 |
| 3. ...Ryan Lochte, United States | 1:56.53 |

| 400-METER INDIVIDUAL MEDLEY | |
|---|---|
| 1. ...Michael Phelps, United States | 4:03.84 WR |
| 2. ...Laszlo Cseh, Hungary | 4:06.16 |
| 3. ...Ryan Lochte, United States | 4:08.09 |

| 4 X 100-METER MEDLEY RELAY | |
|---|---|
| 1. ...United States (Peirsol, Hansen, Lezak, Phelps) | 3:29.34 WR |
| 2. ...Australia | 3:30.04 |
| 3. ...Japan | 3:31.18 |

| 4 X 100-METER FREESTYLE RELAY | |
|---|---|
| 1. ...United States (Lezak, Phelps, Weber-Gale, Jones) | 3:08.24 WR |
| 2. ...France | 3:08.32 |
| 3. ...Australia | 3:09.91 |

## SWIMMING - Men *(Cont.)*

### 4 X 200-METER FREESTYLE RELAY
1. ...United States (Lochte, Phelps, Vanderkaay, Berens)   6:58.56 WR
2. ...Russia   7:03.70
3. ...Australia   7:04.98

### 10 KM MARATHON
1. ...Maarten van der Weijden, Netherlands   1:51:51.60
2. ...David Davies, Great Britain   1:51:53.10
3. ...Thomas Lurz, Germany   1:51:53.60

## SWIMMING - Women

### 50-METER FREESTYLE
1. ...Britta Steffen, Germany   24.06 OR
2. ...Dara Torres, United States   24.07
3. ...Cate Campbell, Australia   24.17

### 100-METER FREESTYLE
1. ...Britta Steffen, Germany   53.12 OR
2. ...Lisbeth Trickett, Australia   53.16
3. ...Natalie Coughlin, United States   53.39

### 200-METER FREESTYLE
1. ...Frederica Pellegrini, Italy   1:54.82 WR
2. ...Sara Isakovic, Slovenia   1:54.97
3. ...Jiaying Pang, China   1:55.05

### 400-METER FREESTYLE
1. ...Rebecca Adlington, Great Britain   4:03.22
2. ...Katie Hoff, United States   4:03.29
3. ...Joanne Jackson, Great Britain   4:03.52

### 800-METER FREESTYLE
1. ...Rebecca Adlington, Great Britain   8:14.10 WR
2. ...Alessia Filippi, Italy   8:20.23
3. ...Lotte Friis, Denmark   8:23.03

### 100-METER BACKSTROKE
1. ...Natalie Coughlin, United States   58.96
2. ...Kirsty Coventry, Zimbabwe   59.19
3. ...Margaret Hoelzer, United States   59.34

### 200-METER BACKSTROKE
1. ...Kirsty Coventry, Zimbabwe   2:05.24 WR
2. ...Margaret Hoelzer, United States   2:06.23
3. ...Reiko Nakamura, Japan   2:07.13

### 100-METER BREASTSTROKE
1. ...Leisel Jones, Australia   1:05.17 WR
2. ...Rebecca Soni, United States   1:06.73
3. ...Mirna Jukic, Austria   1:07.34

### 200-METER BREASTSTROKE
1. ...Rebecca Soni, United States   2:20.22 WR
2. ...Leisel Jones, Australia   2:22.05
3. ...Sara Nordenstam, Norway   2:23.02

### 100-METER BUTTERFLY
1. ...Lisbeth Trickett, Australia   56.73
2. ...Christine Magnuson, United States   57.10
3. ...Jessicah Schipper, Australia   57.25

### 200-METER BUTTERFLY
1. ...Liu Zige, China   2:04.18 WR
2. ...Jiao Liuyang, China   2:04.72
3. ...Jessicah Schipper, Australia   2:06.26

### 200-METER INDIVIDUAL MEDLEY
1. ...Stephanie Rice, Australia   2:08.45 WR
2. ...Kirsty Coventry, Zimbabwe   2:08.59
3. ...Natalie Coughlin, United States   2:10.34

### 400-METER INDIVIDUAL MEDLEY
1. ...Stephanie Rice, Australia   4:29.45 WR
2. ...Kirsty Coventry, Zimbabwe   4:29.89
3. ...Katie Hoff, United States   4:31.71

### 4 X 100-METER MEDLEY RELAY
1. ...Australia (Jones, Schipper, Seebohm, Trickett)   3:52.69 WR
2. ...United States   3:53.30
3. ...China   3:56.11

### 4 X 100-METER FREESTYLE RELAY
1. ...Netherlands (Dekker, Veldhuis, Heemserk, Kromowidjojo)   3:33.76 OR
2. ...United States   3:34.33
3. ...Australia   3:35.05

### 4 X 200-METER FREESTYLE RELAY
1. ...Australia (Mackenzie, Rice, Barratt, Palmer)   7:44.31 WR
2. ...China   7:45.93
3. ...United States   7:46.33

### 10-KM MARATHON
1. ...Larisa Ilchenko, Russia   1:59.27.70
2. ...Keri-Anne Payne, Great Britain   1:59.29.20
3. ...Cassandra Patten, Great Britain   1:59.31.00

## SYNCHRONIZED DIVING

### Men

#### 3M SPRINGBOARD

| | Pts |
|---|---|
| 1. .........W. Feng/K. Qin, China | 469.08 |
| 2. .........D. Sautin/Y. Kunakov, Russia | 421.98 |
| 3. .........I. Kvasha/O. Prygorov, Ukraine | 415.05 |

#### 10M PLATFORM

| | Pts |
|---|---|
| 1. .........Y. Lin/L. Huo, China | 468.18 |
| 2. .........P. Hausding/S. Klein, Germany | 450.42 |
| 3. .........G. Galperin/D. Dobroskok, Russia | 445.26 |

### Women

#### 3M SPRINGBOARD

| | Pts |
|---|---|
| 1. .........J. Guo/M. Wu, China | 343.50 |
| 2. .........J.Pakhalina/A. Pozdnyakova, Russia | 323.61 |
| 3. .........D. Kotzian/H. Fischer, Germany | 318.90 |

#### 10M PLATFORM

| | Pts |
|---|---|
| 1. .........X. Wang/R. Chen, China | 363.54 |
| 2. .........B. Cole/M. Wu, Australia | 335.16 |
| 3. .........P. Espinosa/T. Ortiz, Mexico | 330.06 |

Note: OR=Olympic record. WR=world record. EOR=equals Olympic record. EWR=equals world record.

## SYNCHRONIZED SWIMMING

| DUET | | TEAM | |
|---|---|---|---|
| 1. | Russia | 1. | Russia |
| 2. | Spain | 2. | Spain |
| 3. | Japan | 3. | China |

## TABLE TENNIS

### Men

**SINGLES**

1. Ma Lin, China
2. Hao Wang, China
3. Ligin Wang, China

**DOUBLES**

1. H. Wang/L. Wang, China
2. C. Suss/T. Boll, Germany
3. J. Yoon/S. Oh, South Korea

### Women

**SINGLES**

1. Zhang Yining, China
2. Nan Wang, China
3. Guo Yue, China

**DOUBLES**

1. G. Yue/Z. Yining, China
2. Y. Wang/J. Li, Singapore
3. M. Park/K. Kim, South Korea

## TAEKWONDO

### Men

**FLYWEIGHT**

1. Guillermo Perez, Mexico
2. Yulis Gabriel Mercedes, Dom. Republic
3. Chu Mu-Yen, Taiwan
3. Rohulla Nikpai, Afghanistan

**FEATHERWEIGHT**

1. Son Taejin, South Korea
2. Mark Lopez, United States
3. Sung Yu-Chi, Taiwan
3. Servet Tazegul, Turkey

**WELTERWEIGHT**

1. Hadi Saei, Iran
2. Mauro Sarmiento, Italy
3. Zhu Guo, China
3. Steven Lopez, United States

**HEAVYWEIGHT**

1. Cha Dongmin, South Korea
2. Alexandros Nikolaidis, Greece
3. Arman Chilmanov, Kazakhstan
3. Chika Yagazie Chukwumerije, Nigeria

### Women

**FLYWEIGHT**

1. Wu Jingyu, China
2. Buttree Puedpong, Thailand
3. Dalia Contreras Rivero, Venezuela
3. Daynellis Montejo, Cuba

**FEATHERWEIGHT**

1. Lim Sujeong, South Korea
2. Azize Tanrikulu, Turkey
3. Martina Zubcic, Croatia
3. Diana Lopez, United States

**WELTERWEIGHT**

1. Hwang Kyungseon, South Korea
2. Karine Sergerie, Canada
3. Sandra Saric, Croatia
3. Gwladys Patience Epangue, France

**HEAVYWEIGHT**

1. Maria del Rosario Espinoza, Mexico
2. Nina Solheim, Norway
3. Natalia Falavigna, Brazil
3. Sarah Stevenson, Great Britain

## TEAM HANDBALL

### Men

1. France
2. Iceland
3. Spain

### Women

1. Norway
2. Russia
3. South Korea

## TENNIS

### Men

**SINGLES**

1. Rafael Nadal, Spain
2. Fernando Gonzalez, Chile
3. Novak Djokovic, Serbia

**DOUBLES**

1. Roger Federer/Stanislas Wawrinka, Switzerland
2. Thomas Johansson/Simon Aspelin, Sweden
3. Bob Bryan/Mike Bryan, United States

### Women

**SINGLES**

1. Elena Dementieva, Russia
2. Dinara Safina, Russia
3. Vera Zvonareva, Russia

**DOUBLES**

1. Serena Williams/Venus Williams, United States
2. Virginia Ruano/Anabel Medina, Spain
3. Yan Zi/Zheng Jie, China

## TRAMPOLINE

### Men

| | | |
|---|---|---|
| 1. | Lu Chunlong, China | 41.00 |
| 2. | Jason Burnett, Canada | 40.70 |
| 3. | Dong Dong, China | 40.60 |

### Women

| | | |
|---|---|---|
| 1. | Ha Wenna, China | 37.80 |
| 2. | Karen Cockburn, Canada | 37.00 |
| 3. | Ekaterina Khilko, Uzbekistan | 36.90 |

## TRIATHLON

### Men
1..........Jan Frodeno, Germany — 1:48:53
2..........Simon Whitfield, Canada — 1:48:58
3..........Bevan Docherty, New Zealand — 1:49:05

### Women
1..........Emma Snowsill, Australia — 1:58:27
2..........Vanessa Fernandes, Portugal — 1:59:34
3..........Emma Moffatt, Australia — 1:59:55

## VOLLEYBALL

### Men
1..........United States
2..........Brazil
3..........Russia

### Women
1..........Brazil
2..........United States
3..........China

## BEACH VOLLEYBALL

### Men
1..........Phil Dalhausser/Todd Rogers, United States
2..........Marcio Araujo/Fabio Magalhaes, Brazil
3..........Emanuel Rego/Ricardo Santos, Brazil

### Women
1..........Misty May-Treanor/Kerri Walsh, United States
2..........Tian Jia/Wang Jie, China
3..........Zhang Xi/Xue Chen, China

## WATER POLO

### Men
1..........Hungary
2..........United States
3..........Serbia

### Women
1..........Netherlands
2..........United States
3..........Australia

## WEIGHTLIFTING - Men

### 123 POUNDS
1..........Long Oingguan, China — 644 lb
2..........Anh Tuan Hoang, Vietnam — 639 lb
3..........Eko Yuli Irawan, Indonesia — 635 lb

### 137 POUNDS
1..........Zhang Xiangxiang, China — 703 lb
2..........Diego Salazar, Colombia — 672 lb
3..........Triyatno, Indonesia — 657 lb

### 152 POUNDS
1..........Liao Hui, China — 767 lb
2..........Vancelas Dabaya-Tientcheu, France — 745 lb
3..........Tigran G. Martirosyan, Armenia — 745 lb

### 170 POUNDS
1..........Sa Jaehyouk, South Korea — 807 lb
2..........Li Hongli, China — 807 lb
3..........Geyorg Davtyan, Armenia — 793.5 lb

### 187 POUNDS
1..........Lu Yong, China — 868.5 lb WR
2..........Andrei Rybakou, Belarus — 868.5 lb
3..........Tigran V. Martirosyan, Armenia — 838 lb

### 207 POUNDS
1..........Ilya Ilin, Kazakhstan — 895 lb
2..........Szymon Kolecki, Poland — 888.5 lb
3..........Khadzhimurat Akkaev, Russia — 886 lb

### 231 POUNDS
1..........Andrei Aramnau, Belarus — 961 lb WR
2..........Dmitriy Klokov, Russia — 932.5 lb
3..........Dmitry Lapikov, Russia — 926 lb

### 231+ POUNDS
1..........Matthias Steiner, Germany — 1016 lb
2..........Evgeny Chigishev, Russia — 1014 lb
3..........Viktors Scerbatihs, Latvia — 987 lb

## WEIGHTLIFTING - Women

### 106 POUNDS
1..........Chen Xiexia, China — 467 lb OR
2..........Sibel Ozkan, Turkey — 439 lb
3..........Chen Wei-Ling, Taiwan — 432 lb

### 117 POUNDS
1..........P. Jaroenrattanatarakoon, Thailand — 487 lb
2..........Yoon Jinhee, South Korea — 469.5 lb
3..........Natassia Novikava, Belarus — 469.5 lb

### 128 POUNDS
1..........Chen Yanging, China — 538 lb OR
2..........Marina Shainova, Russia — 500.5 lb
3..........O Jong Ae, North Korea — 498 lb

### 139 POUNDS
1..........Pak Hyon Suk, North Korea — 531.5 lb
2..........Irina Nekrassova, Kazakhstan — 529 lb
3..........Lu Ying-Chi, Taiwan — 509 lb

### 152 POUNDS
1..........Liu Chunhong, China — 630.5 lb WR
2..........Oxana Silvenko, Russia — 562 lb
3..........Natalya Davydova, Ukraine — 551 lb

### 165 POUNDS
1..........Cao Lei, China — 622 lb OR
2..........Alla Vazhenina, Kazakhstan — 586.5 lb
3..........Nadezda Evstyukhina, Russia — 582 lb

### 165+ POUNDS
1..........Jang Miran, South Korea — 719 lb WR
2..........Olha Korobka, Ukraine — 611 lb
3..........Mariya Grabovetskaya, Kazakhstan — 595 lb

Note: OR=Olympic Record.  WR=World Record.  EOR=Equals Olympic Record.  EWR=Equals World Record.

## FREESTYLE WRESTLING

### 121 POUNDS
1. ....................Henry Cejudo, United States
2. ....................Tomohiro Matsunaga, Japan
3. ....................Radoslav Velikov, Bulgaria
3. ....................Besik Kudukhov, Russia

### 132 POUNDS
1. ....................Mavlet Batirov, Russia
2. ....................Vasyl Fedoryshyn, Ukraine
3. ....................Seyedmorad Mohammadi, Iran
3. ....................Kenichi Yumoto, Japan

### 145.5 POUNDS
1. ....................Ramazan Sahin, Turkey
2. ....................Andriy Stadnik, Ukraine
3. ....................Otar Tushishvili, Georgia
3. ....................Sushil Kumar, India

### 163 POUNDS
1. ....................Buvaysa Saytive, Russia
2. ....................Soslan Tigiev, Uzbekistan
3. ....................Murad Gaidarov, Belarus
3. ....................Kiril Terziev, Bulgaria

### 185 POUNDS
1. ....................Revazi Mindorashvili, Georgia
2. ....................Yusup Abdusalomov, Tajikistan
3. ....................Georgy Ketoev, Russia
3. ....................Taras Danko, Ukraine

### 211.5 POUNDS
1. ....................Shirvani Muradov, Russia
2. ....................Taimuraz Tigiyev, Kazakhstan
3. ....................Khetag Gazyumov, Azerbaijan
3. ....................George Gogshelidze, Georgia

### 264.5 POUNDS
1. ....................Artur Taymazov, Uzbekistan
2. ....................Bakhtivar Akhmedov, Russia
3. ....................Marid Mutalimov, Kazakhstan
3. ....................David Musulbes, Slovakia

## GRECO-ROMAN WRESTLING

### 121 POUNDS
1. ....................Islam-Beka Albiev, Russia
2. ....................Vitaliy Rahimov, Azerbaijan
3. ....................Nurbakyt Tengizbayev, Kazakhstan
3. ....................Ruslan Tiumenbaev, Kyrgyzstan

### 132 POUNDS
1. ....................Nazyr Mankiev, Russia
2. ....................Royshan Bayramov, Azerbaijan
3. ....................Roman Amoyan, Armenia
3. ....................Park Eunchol, South Korea

### 145.5 POUNDS
1. ....................Steeve Guenot, France
2. ....................Kanatbek Begaliev, Kyrgyzstan
3. ....................Mikhail Siamionau, Belarus
3. ....................Armen Varandyan, Ukraine

### 163 POUNDS
1. ....................Manuchar Kyirkelia, Georgia
2. ....................Chang Yongxiang, China
3. ....................Yavor Yanakiev, Bulgaria
3. ....................Christophe Guenot, France

### 185 POUNDS
1. ....................Andrea Minguzzi, Italy
2. ....................Zoltan Fodor, Hungary
3. ....................Nazmi Avluca, Turkey

### 211.5 POUNDS
1. ....................Aslanbek Khushtov, Russia
2. ....................Mirko Englich, Germany
3. ....................Asset Mambetov, Kazakhstan
3. ....................Adam Wheeler, United States

### 264.5 POUNDS
1. ....................Mijain Lopez, Cuba
2. ....................Khasan Baroev, Russia
3. ....................Yuri Patrikeev, Armenia
3. ....................Mindaugas Mizgaitis, Lithuania

## YACHTING
### Men

#### DINGHY 470
1. ....................Australia
2. ....................Great Britain
3. ....................France

#### FINN
1. ....................Great Britain
2. ....................Denmark
3. ....................Spain

#### DINGHY
1. ....................Paul Goodison, G.B.
2. ....................Vasilji Zbogar, Slvn.
3. ....................Diego Romero, Ita.

#### TORNADO
1. ....................Spain
2. ....................Australia
3. ....................Argentina

#### LASER
1. ....................New Zealand
2. ....................Slovenia
3. ....................Argentina

#### 49ER
1. ....................Denmark
2. ....................Spain
3. ....................Germany

#### STAR
1. ....................Great Britain
2. ....................Brazil
3. ....................Sweden

#### MISTRAL
1. ....................Tom Ashley, N.Z.
2. ....................J. Bontemps, Fra.
3. ....................Shaher Zubari, Isr.

#### HW DINGHY
1. ....................Ben Ainslie, G.B.
2. ....................Zach Railey, U.S.
3. ....................G. Florent, France

### Women

#### MISTRAL
1. ....................Yin Jian, China
2. ....................Alessandra Sensini, Italy
3. ....................Bryonny Shaw, Great Britain

#### 470
1. ....................Australia
2. ....................Netherlands
3. ....................Brazil

#### EUROPE
1. ....................Anna Tunnicliffe, United States
2. ....................Gintare Volungeviciute, Lithuania
3. ....................Xin Lijia, China

#### KEEL
1. ....................Great Britain
2. ....................Netherlands
3. ....................Greece

Note: OR=Olympic Record.  WR=World Record.  EOR=Equals Olympic Record.  EWR=Equals World Record.

## Summer Olympic Games Locations and Dates

| | Year | Site | Dates | COMPETITORS Men | Women | Nations | Most Medals | US Medals |
|---|---|---|---|---|---|---|---|---|
| I | 1896 | Athens, Greece | Apr 6–15 | 311 | 0 | 13 | Greece (10-19-18—47) | 11-6-2—19 (2nd) |
| II | 1900 | Paris, France | May 20–Oct 28 | 1319 | 11 | 22 | France (29-41-32—102) | 20-14-19—53 (2nd) |
| III | 1904 | St Louis, United States | July 1–Nov 23 | 681 | 6 | 12 | United States (80-86-72—238) | |
| — | 1906 | Athens, Greece | Apr 22–May 28 | 77 | 7 | 20 | France (15-9-16—40) | 12-6-5—23 (4th) |
| IV | 1908 | London, Great Britain | Apr 27–Oct 31 | 1999 | 36 | 23 | Britain (56-50-39—145) | 23-12-12—47 (2nd) |
| V | 1912 | Stockholm, Sweden | May 5–July 22 | 2490 | 57 | 28 | Sweden (24-24-17—65) | 23-19-19—61 (2nd) |
| VI | 1916 | Berlin, Germany | Canceled because of war | | | | | |
| VII | 1920 | Antwerp, Belgium | Apr 20–Sep 12 | 2543 | 64 | 29 | United States (41-27-28—96) | |
| VIII | 1924 | Paris, France | May 4–July 27 | 2956 | 136 | 44 | United States (45-27-27—99) | |
| IX | 1928 | Amsterdam, Netherlands | May 17–Aug 12 | 2724 | 290 | 46 | United States (22-18-16—56) | |
| X | 1932 | Los Angeles, United States | July 30–Aug 14 | 1281 | 127 | 37 | United States (41-32-31—104) | |
| XI | 1936 | Berlin, Germany | Aug 1–16 | 3738 | 328 | 49 | Germany (33-26-30—89) | 24-20-12—56 (2nd) |
| XII | 1940 | Tokyo, Japan | CANCELED BECAUSE OF WAR | | | | | |
| XIII | 1944 | London, Great Britain | CANCELED BECAUSE OF WAR | | | | | |
| XIV | 1948 | London, Great Britain | July 29–Aug 14 | 3714 | 385 | 59 | United States (38-27-19—84) | |
| XV | 1952 | Helsinki, Finland | July 19–Aug 3 | 4407 | 518 | 69 | United States (40-19-17—76) | |
| XVI | 1956 | Melbourne, Australia* | Nov 22–Dec 8 | 2958 | 384 | 67 | USSR (37-29-32—98) | 32-25-17—74 (2nd) |
| XVII | 1960 | Rome, Italy | Aug 25–Sep 11 | 4738 | 610 | 83 | USSR (43-29-31—103) | 34-21-16—71 (2nd) |
| XVIII | 1964 | Tokyo, Japan | Oct 10–24 | 4457 | 683 | 93 | United States (36-26-28—90) | |
| XIX | 1968 | Mexico City, Mexico | Oct 12–27 | 4750 | 781 | 112 | United States (45-28-34—107) | |
| XX | 1972 | Munich, W Germany | Aug 26–Sep 10 | 5848 | 1299 | 122 | USSR (50-27-22—99) | 33-31-30—94 (2nd) |
| XXI | 1976 | Montreal, Canada | July 17–Aug 1 | 4834 | 1251 | 92† | USSR (49-41-35—125) | 34-35-25—94 (3rd) |
| XXII | 1980 | Moscow, USSR | July 19–Aug 3 | 4265 | 1088 | 81‡ | USSR (80-69-46—195) | Did not compete |
| XXIII | 1984 | Los Angeles, United States | July 28–Aug 12 | 5458 | 1620 | 141# | United States (83-61-30—174) | |
| XXIV | 1988 | Seoul, S Korea | Sep 17–Oct 2 | 7105 | 2476 | 160 | USSR (55-31-46—132) | 36-31-27—94 (3rd) |
| XXV | 1992 | Barcelona, Spain | July 25–Aug. 9 | 7555 | 3008 | 172 | Unified Team (45-38-29—112) | 37-34-37—108 (2nd) |
| XXVI | 1996 | Atlanta, United States | July 19–Aug 4 | 6984 | 3766 | 197 | United States (44-32-25—101) | |
| XXVII | 2000 | Sydney, Australia | Sept 15–Oct 1 | 6862 | 4254 | 199 | United States (39-25-33—97) | |
| XXVIII | 2004 | Athens, Greece | Aug 11–Aug 29 | 11099 total | | 202 | United States (35-39-29—103) | |

| | Year | Site | Dates | Men | Women | Nations | Most Medals | US Medal |
|---|---|---|---|---|---|---|---|---|
| | | | | **COMPETITORS** | | | | |
| XXIX | 2008 | Beijing, China | Aug 8–<br>Aug 24 | 11028 total | | 204 | United States<br>(36-38-36—1]0) | |

*The equestrian events were held in Stockholm, Sweden, June 10–17, 1956.

†This figure includes Cameroon, Egypt, Morocco, and Tunisia, countries that boycotted the 1976 Olympics after some of their athletes had already competed.

‡The U.S. was among 65 countries that did not participate in the 1980 Summer Games in Moscow.

#The USSR, East Germany, and 14 other countries did not participate in the 1984 Summer Games in Los Angeles.

# Alltime Olympic Medal Winners

## Summer

### NATIONS

| Nation | Gold | Silver | Bronze | Total | Nation | Gold | Silver | Bronze | Total |
|---|---|---|---|---|---|---|---|---|---|
| United States | 934 | 730 | 643 | 2307 | Japan | 123 | 112 | 125 | 360 |
| USSR (1952–88) | 395 | 319 | 296 | 1010 | Russia | 109 | 101 | 112 | 322 |
| Great Britain | 209 | 259 | 258 | 725 | Finland | 103 | 80 | 113 | 296 |
| Germany | 196 | 222 | 241 | 659 | Romania | 86 | 89 | 117 | 292 |
| (1896–1936, 1992– ) | | | | | Poland | 62 | 80 | 119 | 261 |
| France | 191 | 208 | 241 | 640 | Canada | 57 | 95 | 106 | 258 |
| Italy | 190 | 158 | 173 | 523 | The Netherlands | 72 | 80 | 96 | 248 |
| Sweden | 142 | 160 | 173 | 475 | South Korea | 68 | 74 | 73 | 215 |
| Hungary | 159 | 141 | 160 | 460 | Bulgaria | 51 | 84 | 77 | 212 |
| Australia | 134 | 141 | 169 | 444 | West Germany (1952–88) | 56 | 67 | 81 | 204 |
| East Germany (1956–88) | 153 | 129 | 127 | 409 | Cuba | 67 | 62 | 60 | 189 |
| China | 163 | 117 | 106 | 386 | Switzerland | 45 | 69 | 65 | 179 |

### INDIVIDUALS — OVERALL

#### Men

| Athlete, Nation | Sport | G | S | B | Tot | Athlete, Nation | Sport | G | S | B | Tot |
|---|---|---|---|---|---|---|---|---|---|---|---|
| Michael Phelps, United States | Swim | 14 | 0 | 2 | 16 | Matt Biondi, United States | Swim | 8 | 2 | 1 | 11 |
| Nikolai Andrianov, USSR | Gym | 7 | 5 | 3 | 15 | Viktor Chukarin, USSR | Gym | 7 | 3 | 1 | 11 |
| Boris Shakhlin, USSR | Gym | 7 | 4 | 2 | 13 | Carl Osburn, United States | Shoot | 5 | 4 | 2 | 11 |
| Edoardo Mangiarotti, Italy | Fen | 6 | 5 | 2 | 13 | Ray Ewry, United States | Track | 10 | 0 | 0 | 10 |
| Takashi Ono, Japan | Gym | 5 | 4 | 4 | 13 | Carl Lewis, United States | Track | 9 | 1 | 0 | 10 |
| Paavo Nurmi, Finland | Track | 9 | 3 | 0 | 12 | Aladár Gerevich, Hungary | Fen | 7 | 1 | 2 | 10 |
| Sawao Kato, Japan | Gym | 8 | 3 | 1 | 12 | Akinori Nakayama, Japan | Gym | 6 | 2 | 2 | 10 |
| Alexei Nemov, Russia | Gym | 4 | 2 | 6 | 12 | Vitaly Scherbo, UT/Belarus | Gym | 6 | 0 | 4 | 10 |
| Mark Spitz, United States | Swim | 9 | 1 | 1 | 11 | Aleksandr Dityatin, USSR | Gym | 3 | 6 | 1 | 10 |

#### Women

| Athlete, Nation | Sport | G | S | B | Tot | Athlete, Nation | Sport | G | S | B | Tot |
|---|---|---|---|---|---|---|---|---|---|---|---|
| Larissa Latynina, USSR | Gym | 9 | 5 | 4 | 18 | Lyudmila Tourischeva, USSR | Gym | 4 | 3 | 2 | 9 |
| Jenny Thompson, United States | Swim | 8 | 3 | 1 | 12 | Kornelia Ender, E Germany | Swim | 4 | 4 | 0 | 8 |
| Vera Cáslavská, Czech | Gym | 7 | 4 | 0 | 11 | Dawn Fraser, Australia | Swim | 4 | 4 | 0 | 8 |
| Agnes Keleti, Hungary | Gym | 5 | 3 | 2 | 10 | Shirley Babashoff, United States | Swim | 2 | 6 | 0 | 8 |
| Polina Astaknova, USSR | Gym | 5 | 2 | 3 | 10 | Sofia Muratova, USSR | Gym | 2 | 2 | 4 | 8 |
| Dara Torres, United States | Swim | 4 | 1 | 4 | 9 | Inge de Bruijn, Netherlands | Swim | 4 | 2 | 2 | 8 |
| Nadia Comaneci, Romania | Gym | 5 | 3 | 1 | 9 | Eight tied with seven. | | | | | |

### INDIVIDUALS — GOLD

#### Men

| | | | | | |
|---|---|---|---|---|---|
| Micheal Phelps, United States | 14 | Mark Spitz, United States | 9 | Boris Shakhlin, USSR | 7 |
| Ray Ewry, United States | 10 | Sawao Kato, Japan | 8 | Viktor Chukarin, USSR | 7 |
| Paavo Nurmi, Finland | 9 | Matt Biondi, United States | 8 | Aladár Gerevich, Hungary | 7 |
| Carl Lewis, United States | 9 | Nikolai Andrianov, USSR | 7 | | |

#### Women

| | | | | | |
|---|---|---|---|---|---|
| Larissa Latynina, USSR | 9 | Krisztina Egerszegi, Hungary | 5 | Betty Cuthbert, Australia | 4 |
| Jenny Thompson, U.S. | 8 | Kornelia Ender, E Germany | 4 | Pat McCormick, United States | 4 |
| Vera Cáslavská, Czech | 7 | Dawn Fraser, Australia | 4 | Bärbel Eckert Wöckel, E Ger | 4 |
| Kristin Otto, E Germany | 6 | Lyudmila Tourischeva, USSR | 4 | Amy Van Dyken, United States | 4 |
| Agnes Keleti, Hungary | 5 | Evelyn Ashford, United States | 4 | Inge de Bruijn, Netherlands | 4 |
| Nadia Comaneci, Romania | 5 | Janet Evans, United States | 4 | Yana Klochkova, Ukraine | 4 |
| Polina Astaknova, USSR | 5 | Fanny Blankers-Koen, Neth | 4 | Dara Torres, United States | 4 |

## TRACK AND FIELD — Men

### 100 METERS

| | |
|---|---|
| 1896....Thomas Burke, United States | 12.0 |
| 1900....Frank Jarvis, United States | 11.0 |
| 1904....Archie Hahn, United States | 11.0 |
| 1906....Archie Hahn, United States | 11.2 |
| 1908....Reginald Walker, S Africa | 10.8 OR |
| 1912....Ralph Craig, United States | 10.8 |
| 1920....Charles Paddock, United States | 10.8 |
| 1924....Harold Abrahams, Great Britain | 10.6 OR |
| 1928....Percy Williams, Canada | 10.8 |
| 1932....Eddie Tolan, United States | 10.3 OR |
| 1936....Jesse Owens, United States | 10.3 |
| 1948....Harrison Dillard, United States | 10.3 |
| 1952....Lindy Remigino, United States | 10.4 |
| 1956....Bobby Morrow, United States | 10.5 |
| 1960....Armin Hary, W Germany | 10.2 OR |
| 1964....Bob Hayes, United States | 10.0 EWR |
| 1968....Jim Hines, United States | 9.95 WR |
| 1972....Valery Borzov, USSR | 10.14 |
| 1976....Hasely Crawford, Trinidad | 10.06 |
| 1980....Allan Wells, Great Britain | 10.25 |
| 1984....Carl Lewis, United States | 9.99 |
| 1988....Carl Lewis, United States* | 9.92 WR |
| 1992....Linford Christie, Great Britain | 9.96 |
| 1996....Donovan Bailey, Canada | 9.84 WR |
| 2000....Maurice Greene, United States | 9.87 |
| 2004....Justin Gatlin, United States | 9.85 |
| 2008....Usain Bolt, Jamaica | 9.69 WR |

*Ben Johnson, Canada, disqualified.

### 200 METERS

| | |
|---|---|
| 1900....John Walter Tewksbury, United States | 22.2 |
| 1904....Archie Hahn, United States | 21.6 OR |
| 1906....Not held | |
| 1908....Robert Kerr, Canada | 22.6 |
| 1912....Ralph Craig, United States | 21.7 |
| 1920....Allen Woodring, United States | 22.0 |
| 1924....Jackson Scholz, United States | 21.6 |
| 1928....Percy Williams, Canada | 21.8 |
| 1932....Eddie Tolan, United States | 21.2 OR |
| 1936....Jesse Owens, United States | 20.7 OR |
| 1948....Mel Patton, United States | 21.1 |
| 1952....Andrew Stanfield, United States | 20.7 |
| 1956....Bobby Morrow, United States | 20.6 OR |
| 1960....Livio Berruti, Italy | 20.5 EWR |
| 1964....Henry Carr, United States | 20.3 OR |
| 1968....Tommie Smith, United States | 19.83 WR |
| 1972....Valery Borzov, USSR | 20.00 |
| 1976....Donald Quarrie, Jamaica | 20.23 |
| 1980....Pietro Mennea, Italy | 20.19 |
| 1984....Carl Lewis, United States | 19.80 OR |
| 1988....Joe DeLoach, United States | 19.75 OR |
| 1992....Mike Marsh, United States | 20.01 |
| 1996....Michael Johnson, United States | 19.32 WR |
| 2000....Konstadinos Kederis, Greece | 20.09 |
| 2004....Shawn Crawford, United States | 19.79 |
| 2008....Usain Bolt, Jamaica | 19.30 WR |

### 400 METERS

| | |
|---|---|
| 1896....Thomas Burke, United States | 54.2 |
| 1900....Maxey Long, United States | 49.4 OR |
| 1904....Harry Hillman, United States | 49.2 OR |
| 1906....Paul Pilgrim, United States | 53.2 |
| 1908....Wyndham Halswelle, Great Britain | 50.0 |
| 1912....Charles Reidpath, United States | 48.2 OR |
| 1920....Bevil Rudd, South Africa | 49.6 |
| 1924....Eric Liddell, Great Britain | 47.6 OR |
| 1928....Ray Barbuti, United States | 47.8 |
| 1932....William Carr, United States | 46.2 WR |
| 1936....Archie Williams, United States | 46.5 |
| 1948....Arthur Wint, Jamaica | 46.2 |

### 400 METERS (Cont.)

| | |
|---|---|
| 1952....George Rhoden, Jamaica | 45.9 |
| 1956....Charles Jenkins, United States | 46.7 |
| 1960    Otis Davis, United States | 44.9 WR |
| 1964....Michael Larrabee, United States | 45.1 |
| 1968....Lee Evans, United States | 43.86 WR |
| 1972....Vincent Matthews, United States | 44.66 |
| 1976....Alberto Juantorena, Cuba | 44.26 |
| 1980....Viktor Markin, USSR | 44.60 |
| 1984....Alonzo Babers, United States | 44.27 |
| 1988....Steve Lewis, United States | 43.87 |
| 1992....Quincy Watts, United States | 43.50 OR |
| 1996....Michael Johnson, United States | 43.49 OR |
| 2000....Michael Johnson, United States | 43.84 |
| 2004....Jeremy Wariner, United States | 44.00 |
| 2008....Lashawn Merritt, United States | 43.75 |

### 800 METERS

| | |
|---|---|
| 1896....Edwin Flack, Australia | 2:11 |
| 1900....Alfred Tysoe, Great Britain | 2:01.2 |
| 1904....James Lightbody, United States | 1:56 OR |
| 1906....Paul Pilgrim, United States | 2:01.5 |
| 1908....Mel Sheppard, United States | 1:52.8 WR |
| 1912....James Meredith, United States | 1:51.9 WR |
| 1920....Albert Hill, Great Britain | 1:53.4 |
| 1924....Douglas Lowe, Great Britain | 1:52.4 |
| 1928....Douglas Lowe, Great Britain | 1:51.8 OR |
| 1932....Thomas Hampson, Great Britain | 1:49.8 WR |
| 1936....John Woodruff, United States | 1:52.9 |
| 1948....Mal Whitfield, United States | 1:49.2 OR |
| 1952....Mal Whitfield, United States | 1:49.2 EOR |
| 1956....Thomas Courtney, United States | 1:47.7 OR |
| 1960....Peter Snell, New Zealand | 1:46.3 OR |
| 1964....Peter Snell, New Zealand | 1:45.1 OR |
| 1968....Ralph Doubell, Australia | 1:44.3 EWR |
| 1972....Dave Wottle, United States | 1:45.9 |
| 1976....Alberto Juantorena, Cuba | 1:43.50 WR |
| 1980....Steve Ovett, Great Britain | 1:45.40 |
| 1984....Joaquim Cruz, Brazil | 1:43.00 OR |
| 1988....Paul Ereng, Kenya | 1:43.45 |
| 1992....William Tanui, Kenya | 1:43.66 |
| 1996....Vebjoern Rodal, Norway | 1:42.58 OR |
| 2000....Nils Schumann, Germany | 1:45.08 |
| 2004....Yuriy Borzakovskiy, Russia | 1:44.45 |
| 2008....Wilfred Kipkemboi Bungei, Kenya | 1:44.65 |

### 1,500 METERS

| | |
|---|---|
| 1896....Edwin Flack, Australia | 4:33.2 |
| 1900....Charles Bennett, Great Britain | 4:06.2 WR |
| 1904....James Lightbody, United States | 4:05.4 WR |
| 1906....James Lightbody, United States | 4:12.0 |
| 1908....Mel Sheppard, United States | 4:03.4 OR |
| 1912....Arnold Jackson, Great Britain | 3:56.8 OR |
| 1920....Albert Hill, Great Britain | 4:01.8 |
| 1924....Paavo Nurmi, Finland | 3:53.6 OR |
| 1928....Harry Larva, Finland | 3:53.2 OR |
| 1932....Luigi Beccali, Italy | 3:51.2 OR |
| 1936....Jack Lovelock, New Zealand | 3:47.8 WR |
| 1948....Henri Eriksson, Sweden | 3:49.8 |
| 1952....Josef Barthel, Luxemburg | 3:45.1 OR |
| 1956....Ron Delany, Ireland | 3:41.2 OR |
| 1960....Herb Elliott, Australia | 3:35.6 WR |
| 1964....Peter Snell, New Zealand | 3:38.1 |
| 1968....Kipchoge Keino, Kenya | 3:34.9 OR |
| 1972....Pekkha Vasala, Finland | 3:36.3 |
| 1976....John Walker, New Zealand | 3:39.17 |
| 1980....Sebastian Coe, Great Britain | 3:38.4 |
| 1984....Sebastian Coe, Great Britain | 3:32.53 OR |
| 1988....Peter Rono, Kenya | 3:35.96 |
| 1992....Fermin Cacho, Spain | 3:40.12 |
| 1996....Noureddine Morceli, Algeria | 3:35.78 |
| 2000....Noah Ngeni, Kenya | 3:32.07 OR |

Note: OR=Olympic Record. WR=World Record. EOR=Equals Olympic Record. EWR=Equals World Record. WB=World Best.

## TRACK AND FIELD — Men (Cont.)

### 1,500 METERS (Cont.)

| | | |
|---|---|---|
| 2004 | Hicham El Guerrouj, Morocco | 3:34.18 |
| 2008 | Rasheed Ramzi, Bahrain | 3:32.94 |

### 5,000 METERS

| | | |
|---|---|---|
| 1912 | Hannes Kolehmainen, Finland | 14:36.6 WR |
| 1920 | Joseph Guillemot, France | 14:55.6 |
| 1924 | Paavo Nurmi, Finland | 14:31.2 OR |
| 1928 | Villie Ritola, Finland | 14:38 |
| 1932 | Lauri Lehtinen, Finland | 14:30 OR |
| 1936 | Gunnar Hickert, Finland | 14:22.2 OR |
| 1948 | Gaston Reiff, Belgium | 14:17.6 OR |
| 1952 | Emil Zatopek, Czechoslovakia | 14:06.6 OR |
| 1956 | Vladimir Kuts, USSR | 13:39.6 OR |
| 1960 | Murray Halberg, New Zealand | 13:43.4 |
| 1964 | Bob Schul, United States | 13:48.8 |
| 1968 | Mohamed Gammoudi, Tunisia | 14:05.0 |
| 1972 | Lasse Viren, Finland | 13:26.4 OR |
| 1976 | Lasse Viren, Finland | 13:24.76 |
| 1980 | Miruts Yifter, Ethiopia | 13:21.0 |
| 1984 | Said Aouita, Morocco | 13:05.59 OR |
| 1988 | John Ngugi, Kenya | 13:11.70 |
| 1992 | Dieter Baumann, Germany | 13:12.52 |
| 1996 | Venuste Niyongabo, Burundi | 13:07.96 |
| 2000 | Millon Wolde, Ethiopia | 13:35.49 |
| 2004 | Hicham El Guerrouj, Morocco | 13:14.39 |
| 2008 | Kenenisa Bekele, Ethiopia | 12:57.82OR |

### 10,000 METERS

| | | |
|---|---|---|
| 1912 | Hannes Kolehmainen, Finland | 31:20.8 |
| 1920 | Paavo Nurmi, Finland | 31:45.8 |
| 1924 | Vilho (Ville) Ritola, Finland | 30:23.2 WR |
| 1928 | Paavo Nurmi, Finland | 30:18.8 OR |
| 1932 | Janusz Kusocinski, Poland | 30:11.4 OR |
| 1936 | Ilmari Salminen, Finland | 30:15.4 |
| 1948 | Emil Zatopek, Czechoslovakia | 29:59.6 OR |
| 1952 | Emil Zatopek, Czechoslovakia | 29:17.0 OR |
| 1956 | Vladimir Kuts, USSR | 28:45.6 OR |
| 1960 | Pyotr Bolotnikov, USSR | 28:32.2 OR |
| 1964 | Billy Mills, United States | 28:24.4 OR |
| 1968 | Naftali Temu, Kenya | 29:27.4 |
| 1972 | Lasse Viren, Finland | 27:38.4 WR |
| 1976 | Lasse Viren, Finland | 27:40.38 |
| 1980 | Miruts Yifter, Ethiopia | 27:42.7 |
| 1984 | Alberto Cova, Italy | 27:47.54 |
| 1988 | Brahim Boutaib, Morocco | 27:21.46 OR |
| 1992 | Khalid Skah, Morocco | 27:46.70 |
| 1996 | Haile Gebrselassie, Ethiopia | 27:07.34 OR |
| 2000 | Haile Gebrselassie, Ethiopia | 27:18.20 |
| 2004 | Kenenisa Bekele, Ethiopia | 27:05.10 OR |
| 2008 | Kenenisa Bekele, Ethiopia | 27:01.17 OR |

### MARATHON

| | | |
|---|---|---|
| 1896 | Spiridon Louis, Greece | 2:58:50 |
| 1900 | Michel Theato, France | 2:59:45 |
| 1904 | Thomas Hicks, United States | 3:28:53 |
| 1906 | William Sherring, Canada | 2:51:23.6 |
| 1908 | John Hayes, United States | 2:55:18.4 OR |
| 1912 | Kenneth McArthur, S Africa | 2:36:54.8 |
| 1920 | Hannes Kolehmainen, Finland | 2:32:35.8 WB |
| 1924 | Albin Stenroos, Finland | 2:41:22.6 |
| 1928 | Boughera El Ouafi, France | 2:32:57 |
| 1932 | Juan Zabala, Argentina | 2:31:36 OR |
| 1936 | Kijung Son, Japan (Korea) | 2:29:19.2 OR |
| 1948 | Delfo Cabrera, Argentina | 2:34:51.6 |
| 1952 | Emil Zatopek, Czechoslovakia | 2:23:03.2 OR |
| 1956 | Alain Mimoun O'Kacha, France | 2:25:00.0 |
| 1960 | Abebe Bikila, Ethiopia | 2:15:16.2 WB |
| 1964 | Abebe Bikila, Ethiopia | 2:12:11.2 WB |
| 1968 | Mamo Wolde, Ethiopia | 2:20:26.4 |
| 1972 | Frank Shorter, United States | 2:12:19.8 |
| 1976 | Waldemar Cierpinski, E Germ. | 2:09:55 OR |
| 1980 | Waldemar Cierpinski, E Germ. | 2:11:03.0 |
| 1984 | Carlos Lopes, Portugal | 2:09:21.0 OR |
| 1988 | Gelindo Bordin, Italy | 2:10:32 |

### MARATHON (Cont.)

| | | |
|---|---|---|
| 1992 | Hwang Young-Cho, S Korea | 2:13:23 |
| 1996 | Josia Thugwane, S Africa | 2:12:36 |
| 2000 | Gezahgne Abera, Ethiopia | 2:10:11 |
| 2004 | Stefano Baldini, Italy | 2:10:55 |
| 2008 | Samuel Kamau, Kenya | 2:06:32 OR |

### 110-METER HURDLES

| | | |
|---|---|---|
| 1896 | Thomas Curtis, United States | 17.6 |
| 1900 | Alvin Kraenzlein, United States | 15.4 OR |
| 1904 | Frederick Schule, United States | 16.0 |
| 1906 | Robert Leavitt, United States | 16.2 |
| 1908 | Forrest Smithson, United States | 15.0 WR |
| 1912 | Frederick Kelly, United States | 15.1 |
| 1920 | Earl Thomson, Canada | 14.8 WR |
| 1924 | Daniel Kinsey, United States | 15.0 |
| 1928 | Sydney Atkinson, S Africa | 14.8 |
| 1932 | George Saling, United States | 14.6 |
| 1936 | Forrest Towns, United States | 14.2 |
| 1948 | William Porter, United States | 13.9 OR |
| 1952 | Harrison Dillard, United States | 13.7 OR |
| 1956 | Lee Calhoun, United States | 13.5 OR |
| 1960 | Lee Calhoun, United States | 13.8 |
| 1964 | Hayes Jones, United States | 13.6 |
| 1968 | Willie Davenport, United States | 13.3 OR |
| 1972 | Rod Milburn, United States | 13.24 EWR |
| 1976 | Guy Drut, France | 13.30 |
| 1980 | Thomas Munkelt, E Germany | 13.39 |
| 1984 | Roger Kingdom, United States | 13.20 OR |
| 1988 | Roger Kingdom, United States | 12.98 OR |
| 1992 | Mark McKoy, Canada | 13.12 |
| 1996 | Allen Johnson, United States | 12.95 OR |
| 2000 | Anier Garcia, Cuba | 13.00 |
| 2004 | Xiang Liu, China | 12.91 EWR |
| 2008 | Dayron Robles, Cuba | 12.93 |

### 400-METER HURDLES

| | | |
|---|---|---|
| 1900 | John Walter Tewksbury, U.S. | 57.6 |
| 1904 | Harry Hillman, United States | 53.0 |
| 1906 | Not held | |
| 1908 | Charles Bacon, United States | 55.0 WR |
| 1912 | Not held | |
| 1920 | Frank Loomis, United States | 54.0 WR |
| 1924 | F. Morgan Taylor, United States | 52.6 |
| 1928 | David Burghley, Great Britain | 53.4 OR |
| 1932 | Robert Tisdall, Ireland | 51.7 |
| 1936 | Glenn Hardin, United States | 52.4 |
| 1948 | Roy Cochran, United States | 51.1 OR |
| 1952 | Charles Moore, United States | 50.8 OR |
| 1956 | Glenn Davis, United States | 50.1 EOR |
| 1960 | Glenn Davis, United States | 49.3 EOR |
| 1964 | Rex Cawley, United States | 49.6 |
| 1968 | Dave Hemery, Great Britain | 48.12 WR |
| 1972 | John Akii-Bua, Uganda | 47.82 WR |
| 1976 | Edwin Moses, United States | 47.64 WR |
| 1980 | Volker Beck, E Germany | 48.70 |
| 1984 | Edwin Moses, United States | 47.75 |
| 1988 | Andre Phillips, United States | 47.19 OR |
| 1992 | Kevin Young, United States | 46.78 WR |
| 1996 | Derrick Adkins, United States | 47.54 |
| 2000 | Angelo Taylor, United States | 47.50 |
| 2004 | Felix Sanchez, Dominican Rep | 47.63 |
| 2008 | Angelo Taylor, United States | 47.25 |

### 3,000-METER STEEPLECHASE

| | | |
|---|---|---|
| 1920 | Percy Hodge, Great Britain | 10:00.4 OR |
| 1924 | Vilho (Ville) Ritola, Finland | 9:33.6 OR |
| 1928 | Toivo Loukola, Finland | 9:21.8 WR |
| 1932 | Volmari Iso-Hollo, Finland | 10:33.4* |
| 1936 | Volmari Iso-Hollo, Finland | 9:03.8 WR |
| 1948 | Thore Sjöstrand, Sweden | 9:04.6 |
| 1952 | Horace Ashenfelter, U.S. | 8:45.4 WR |
| 1956 | Chris Brasher, Great Britain | 8:41.2 OR |
| 1960 | Zdzislaw Krzyszkowiak, Poland | 8:34.2 OR |
| 1964 | Gaston Roelants, Belgium | 8:30.8 OR |

## TRACK AND FIELD — Men *(Cont.)*

### 3,000-METER STEEPLECHASE *(Cont.)*

| | | |
|---|---|---|
| 1968 | ....Amos Biwott, Kenya | 8:51 |
| 1972 | ....Kipchoge Keino, Kenya | 8:23.6 OR |
| 1976 | ....Anders Gärderud, Sweden | 8:08.2 WR |
| 1980 | ....Bronislaw Malinowski, Poland | 8:09.7 |
| 1984 | ....Julius Korir, Kenya | 8:11.8 |
| 1988 | ....Julius Kariuki, Kenya | 8:05.51 OR |
| 1992 | ....Matthew Birir, Kenya | 8:08.84 |
| 1996 | ....Joseph Keter, Kenya | 8:07.12 |
| 2000 | ....Reuben Kosgei, Kenya | 8:21.43 |
| 2004 | ....Ezekiel Kemboi, Kenya | 8:05.81 |
| 2008 | ....Brimin Kipruto, Kenya | 8:10.34 |

*About 3,450 meters; extra lap by error.

### 4 X 100-METER RELAY

| | | |
|---|---|---|
| 1912 | .................Great Britain | 42.4 OR |
| 1920 | .................United States | 42.2 WR |
| 1924 | .................United States | 41.0 EWR |
| 1928 | .................United States | 41.0 EWR |
| 1932 | .................United States | 40.0 EWR |
| 1936 | .................United States | 39.8 WR |
| 1948 | .................United States | 40.6 |
| 1952 | .................United States | 40.1 |
| 1956 | .................United States | 39.5 WR |
| 1960 | .................W Germany | 39.5 EWR |
| 1964 | .................United States | 39.0 WR |
| 1968 | .................United States | 38.2 WR |
| 1972 | .................United States | 38.19 EWR |
| 1976 | .................United States | 38.33 |
| 1980 | .................USSR | 38.26 |
| 1984 | .................United States | 37.83 WR |
| 1988 | .................USSR | 38.19 |
| 1992 | .................United States | 37.40 WR |
| 1996 | .................Canada | 37.69 |
| 2000 | .................United States | 37.61 |
| 2004 | .................Great Britain | 38.07 |
| 2008 | .................Jamaica | 37.10 WR |

### 4 X 400-METER RELAY

| | | |
|---|---|---|
| 1908 | .................United States | 3:29.4 |
| 1912 | .................United States | 3:16.6 WR |
| 1920 | .................Great Britain | 3:22.2 |
| 1924 | .................United States | 3:16.0 WR |
| 1928 | .................United States | 3:14.2 WR |
| 1932 | .................United States | 3:08.2 WR |
| 1936 | .................Great Britain | 3:09.0 |
| 1948 | .................United States | 3:10.4 WR |
| 1952 | .................Jamaica | 3:03.9 WR |
| 1956 | .................United States | 3:04.8 |
| 1960 | .................United States | 3:02.2 WR |
| 1964 | .................United States | 3:00.7 WR |
| 1968 | .................United States | 2:56.16 WR |
| 1972 | .................Kenya | 2:59.8 |
| 1976 | .................United States | 2:58.65 |
| 1980 | .................USSR | 3:01.1 |
| 1984 | .................United States | 2:57.91 |
| 1988 | .................United States | 2:56.16 EWR |
| 1992 | .................United States | 2:55.74 WR |
| 1996 | .................United States | 2:55.99 |
| 2000 | .................United States | 2:56.35 |
| 2004 | .................United States | 2:55.91 |
| 2008 | .................United States | 2:55.39 OR |

### 20-KILOMETER WALK

| | | |
|---|---|---|
| 1956 | ....Leonid Spirin, USSR | 1:31:27.4 |
| 1960 | ....Vladimir Golubnichiy, USSR | 1:33:07.2 |
| 1964 | ....Kenneth Mathews, Great Britain | 1:29:34.0 OR |
| 1968 | ....Vladimir Golubnichiy, USSR | 1:33:58.4 |
| 1972 | ....Peter Frenkel, E Germany | 1:26:42.4 OR |
| 1976 | ....Daniel Bautista, Mexico | 1:24;40.6 OR |
| 1980 | ....Maurizio Damilano, Italy | 1:23:35.5 OR |
| 1984 | ....Ernesto Canto, Mexico | 1:23:13.0 OR |

### 20-KILOMETER WALK *(Cont.)*

| | | |
|---|---|---|
| 1988 | ....Jozef Pribilinec, Czechoslovakia | 1:19:57.0 OR |
| 1992 | ....Daniel Plaza, Spain | 1:21:45.0 |
| 1996 | ....Jefferson Pérez, Ecuador | 1:20:07 |
| 2000 | ....Robert Korzeniowski, Poland | 1:18:59 OR |
| 2004 | ....Ivano Brugnetti, Italy | 1:19:40 |
| 2008 | ....Valeriy Borchin, Russia | 1:19:01 |

### 50-KILOMETER WALK

| | | |
|---|---|---|
| 1932 | ....Thomas Green, Great Britain | 4:50:10 |
| 1936 | ....Harold Whitlock, Great Britain | 4:30:41.4 OR |
| 1948 | ....John Ljunggren, Sweden | 4:41:52 |
| 1952 | ....Giuseppe Dordoni, Italy | 4:28:07.8 OR |
| 1956 | ....Norman Read, New Zealand | 4:30:42.8 |
| 1960 | ....Donald Thompson, Great Britain | 4:25:30 OR |
| 1964 | ....Abdon Parnich, Italy | 4:11:12.4 OR |
| 1968 | ....Christoph Höhne, E Germany | 4:20:13.6 |
| 1972 | ....Bernd Kannenberg, W Germany | 3:56:11.6 OR |
| 1980 | ....Hartwig Gauder, E Germany | 3:49:24.0 OR |
| 1984 | ....Raul Gonzalez, Mexico | 3:47:26.0 OR |
| 1988 | ....Viacheslav Ivanenko, USSR | 3:38:29.0 OR |
| 1992 | ....Andrey Perlov, Unified Team | 3:50:13 |
| 1996 | ....Robert Korzeniowski, Poland | 3:43:30 |
| 2000 | ....Robert Korzeniowski, Poland | 3:42:22 OR |
| 2004 | ....Robert Korzeniowski, Poland | 3:38:46 |
| 2008 | ....Alex Schwazer, Italy | 3:37:09 OR |

### HIGH JUMP

| | | |
|---|---|---|
| 1896 | ....Ellery Clark, United States | 5 ft 11¼ in |
| 1900 | ....Irving Baxter, United States | 6 ft 2¾ in OR |
| 1904 | ....Samuel Jones, United States | 5 ft 11 in |
| 1906 | ...Cornelius Leahy, Great Britain/Ireland | 5 ft 10 in |
| 1908 | ....Harry Porter, United States | 6 ft 3 in OR |
| 1912 | ....Alma Richards, United States | 6 ft 4 in OR |
| 1920 | ...Richmond Landon, United States | 6 ft 4 in OR |
| 1924 | ....Harold Osborn, United States | 6 ft 6 in OR |
| 1928 | ....Robert W. King, United States | 6 ft 4½ in |
| 1932 | ....Duncan McNaughton, Canada | 6 ft 5½ in |
| 1936 | ....Cornelius Johnson, United States | 6 ft 8 in OR |
| 1948 | ....John L. Winter, Australia | 6 ft 6 in |
| 1952 | ....Walter Davis, United States | 6 ft 8½ in OR |
| 1956 | ....Charles Dumas, United States | 6 ft 11½ in OR |
| 1960 | ....Robert Shavlakadze, USSR | 7 ft 1 in OR |
| 1964 | ....Valery Brumel, USSR | 7 ft 1¾ in OR |
| 1968 | ....Dick Fosbury, United States | 7 ft 4¼ in OR |
| 1972 | ....Yuri Tarmak, USSR | 7 ft 3¾ in |
| 1976 | ....Jacek Wszola, Poland | 7 ft 4½ in OR |
| 1980 | ....Gerd Wessig, E Germany | 7 ft 8¾ in WR |
| 1984 | ....Dietmar Mögenburg, W Ger | 7 ft 8½ in |
| 1988 | ....Gennadiy Avdeyenko, USSR | 7 ft 9¾ in OR |
| 1992 | ....Javier Sotomayor, Cuba | 7 ft 8 in. |
| 1996 | ....Charles Austin, United States | 7 ft 10 in OR |
| 2000 | ....Sergey Kliugin, Russia | 7 ft 8¼ in |
| 2004 | ....Stefan Holm, Sweden | 7 ft 8¾ in |
| 2008 | ....Andrey Silnov, Russia | 7 ft 9 in |

### POLE VAULT

| | | |
|---|---|---|
| 1896 | ....William Hoyt, United States | 10 ft 10 in |
| 1900 | ....Irving Baxter, United States | 10 ft 10 in |
| 1904 | ....Charles Dvorak, United States | 11 ft 5¾ in |
| 1906 | ....Fernand Gonder, France | 11 ft 5¾ in |
| 1908 | ....Alfred Gilbert, United States | 12 ft 2 in OR |
| | Edward Cooke Jr., United States | |
| 1912 | ....Harry Babcock, United States | 12 ft 11½ in |
| 1920 | ....Frank Foss, United States | 13 ft 5 in WR |
| 1924 | ....Lee Barnes, United States | 12 ft 11½ in |
| 1928 | ....Sabin Carr, United States | 13 ft 9¼ in OR |
| 1932 | ....William Miller, United States | 14 ft 1¾ in OR |

Note: OR=Olympic Record. WR=World Record. EOR=Equals Olympic Record. EWR=Equals World Record. WB=World Best.

## TRACK AND FIELD — Men (Cont.)

### POLE VAULT (Cont.)

| | |
|---|---|
| 1936...Earle Meadows, United States | 14 ft 3¼ in OR |
| 1948...Guinn Smith, United States | 14 ft 1¼ in |
| 1952...Robert Richards, United States | 14 ft 11 in OR |
| 1956...Robert Richards, United States | 14 ft 11½ in OR |
| 1960...Don Bragg, United States | 15 ft 5 in OR |
| 1964...Fred Hansen, United States | 16 ft 8¾ in OR |
| 1968...Bob Seagren, United States | 17 ft 8½ in OR |
| 1972...Wolfgang Nordwig, E Germany | 18 ft ½ in OR |
| 1976...Tadeusz Slusarski, Poland | 18 ft ½ in EOR |
| 1980...Wladyslaw Kozakiewicz, Pol | 18 ft 11½ in WR |
| 1984...Pierre Quinon, France | 18 ft 10¼ in |
| 1988...Sergei Bubka, USSR | 19 ft 4¼ in OR |
| 1992...Maksim Tarasov, Unified Team | 19 ft ¼ in |
| 1996...Jean Galfione, France | 19 ft 5 ¼ in OR |
| 2000...Nick Hysong, United States | 19 ft 4¼ in |
| 2004...Timothy Mack, United States | 19 ft 6¼ in |
| 2008...Steve Hooker, Australia | 19 ft 6½ in OR |

### LONG JUMP

| | |
|---|---|
| 1896...Ellery Clark, United States | 20 ft 10 in |
| 1900...Alvin Kraenzlein, United States | 23 ft 6¾ in OR |
| 1904...Meyer Prinstein, United States | 24 ft 1 in OR |
| 1906...Meyer Prinstein, United States | 23 ft 7½ in |
| 1908...Frank Irons, United States | 24 ft 6½ in OR |
| 1912...Albert Gutterson, United States | 24 ft 11¼ in OR |
| 1920...William Peterssen, Sweden | 23 ft 5½ in |
| 1924...DeHart Hubbard, United States | 24 ft 5 in |
| 1928...Edward B. Hamm, United States | 25 ft 4½ in OR |
| 1932...Edward Gordon, United States | 25 ft ¾ in |
| 1936...Jesse Owens, United States | 26 ft 5½ in OR |
| 1948...William Steele, United States | 25 ft 8 in |
| 1952...Jerome Biffle, United States | 24 ft 10 in |
| 1956...Gregory Bell, United States | 25 ft 8¼ in |
| 1960...Ralph Boston, United States | 26 ft 7¾ in OR |
| 1964...Lynn Davies, Great Britain | 26 ft 5¾ in |
| 1968...Bob Beamon, United States | 29 ft 2½ in WR |
| 1972...Randy Williams, United States | 27 ft ½ in |
| 1976...Arnie Robinson, United States | 27 ft 4¾ in |
| 1980...Lutz Dombrowski, E Germany | 28 ft ¼ in |
| 1984...Carl Lewis, United States | 28 ft ¼ in |
| 1988...Carl Lewis, United States | 28 ft 7½ in |
| 1992...Carl Lewis, United States | 28 ft 5½ in |
| 1996...Carl Lewis, United States | 27 ft 10¾ in |
| 2000...Ivan Pedrosa, Cuba | 28 ft ¾ in |
| 2004...Dwight Phillips, United States | 28 ft 2¼ in |
| 2008...Irving Jahir Saladino, Panama | 27 ft 4¼ in |

### TRIPLE JUMP

| | |
|---|---|
| 1896...James Connolly, United States | 44 ft 11¾ in |
| 1900...Meyer Prinstein, United States | 47 ft 5¾ in OR |
| 1904...Meyer Prinstein, United States | 47 ft 1 in |
| 1906...Peter O'Connor, GB/ Ire | 46 ft 2¼ in |
| 1908...Timothy Ahearne, GB/ Ire | 48 ft 11¼ in OR |
| 1912...Gustaf Lindblom, Sweden | 48 ft 5¼ in |
| 1920...Vilho Tuulos, Finland | 47 ft 7 in |
| 1924...Anthony Winter, Australia | 50 ft 11¼ in WR |
| 1928...Mikio Oda, Japan | 49 ft 11 in |
| 1932...Chuhei Nambu, Japan | 51 ft 7 in WR |
| 1936...Naoto Tajima, Japan | 52 ft 6 in WR |
| 1948...Arne Ahman, Sweden | 50 ft 6¼ in |
| 1952...Adhemar da Silva, Brazil | 53 ft 2¾ in WR |
| 1956...Adhemar da Silva, Brazil | 53 ft 7¾ in OR |
| 1960...Jozef Schmidt, Poland | 55 ft 2 in |
| 1964...Jozef Schmidt, Poland | 55 ft 3½ in OR |
| 1968...Viktor Saneyev, USSR | 57 ft ¾ in WR |
| 1972...Viktor Saneyev, USSR | 56 ft 11¾ in |
| 1976...Viktor Saneyev, USSR | 56 ft 8¾ in |
| 1980...Jaak Uudmae, USSR | 56 ft 11¼ in |
| 1984...Al Joyner, United States | 56 ft 7½ in |

### TRIPLE JUMP (Cont.)

| | |
|---|---|
| 1988...Khristo Markov, Bulgaria | 57 ft 9½ in OR |
| 1992...Mike Conley, United States | 59 ft 7½ in (w) |
| 1996...Kenny Harrison, United States | 59 ft 4¼ in OR |
| 2000...Jonathon Edwards, G. Britain | 58 ft 1¼ in |
| 2004...Christian Olsson, Sweden | 58 ft 4½ in |
| 2008...Nelson Evora, Portugal | 57 ft 11½ in |

### SHOT PUT

| | |
|---|---|
| 1896...Robert Garrett, United States | 36 ft 9¾ in |
| 1900...Richard Sheldon, United States | 46 ft 3¼ in OR |
| 1904...Ralph Rose, United States | 48 ft 7 in WR |
| 1906...Martin Sheridan, United States | 40 ft 5¼ in |
| 1908...Ralph Rose, United States | 46 ft 7½ in |
| 1912...Pat McDonald, United States | 50 ft 4 in OR |
| 1920...Ville Porhola, Finland | 48 ft 7¼ in |
| 1924...Clarence Houser, United States | 49 ft 2¼ in |
| 1928...John Kuck, United States | 52 ft ¾ in WR |
| 1932...Leo Sexton, United States | 52 ft 6 in OR |
| 1936...Hans Woellke, Germany | 53 ft 1¾ in OR |
| 1948 ...Wilbur Thompson, United States | 56 ft 2 in OR |
| 1952...Parry O'Brien, United States | 57 ft ½ in OR |
| 1956...Parry O'Brien, United States | 60 ft 11¼ in OR |
| 1960...William Nieder, United States | 64 ft 6¾ in OR |
| 1964...Dallas Long, United States | 66 ft 8½ in OR |
| 1968...Randy Matson, United States | 67 ft 4¾ in |
| 1972...Wladyslaw Komar, Poland | 69 ft 6 in OR |
| 1976...Udo Beyer, E Germany | 69 ft ¾ in |
| 1980...Vladimir Kiselyov, USSR | 70 ft ½ in OR |
| 1984...Alessandro Andrei, Italy | 69 ft 9 in |
| 1988...Ulf Timmermann, E Germany | 73 ft 8¾ in OR |
| 1992...Mike Stulce, United States | 71 ft 2½ in |
| 1996...Randy Barnes, United States | 70 ft 11 in |
| 2000...Arsi Harju, Finland | 69 ft 10¼ in |
| 2004...Yuriy Bilonog, Ukraine | 69 ft 5¼ in |
| 2008...Tomasz Majewski, Poland | 70 ft 6¾ in |

### DISCUS THROW

| | |
|---|---|
| 1896...Robert Garrett, United States | 95 ft 7½ in |
| 1900...Rudolf Bauer, Hungary | 118 ft 3 in OR |
| 1904 ....Martin Sheridan, United States | 128 ft 10½ in OR |
| 1906...Martin Sheridan, United States | 136 ft |
| 1908...Martin Sheridan, United States | 134 ft 2 in OR |
| 1912...Armas Taipele, Finland | 148 ft 3 in OR |
| 1920...Elmer Niklander, Finland | 146 ft 7 in |
| 1924...Clarence Houser, United States | 151 ft 4 in OR |
| 1928...Clarence Houser, United States | 155 ft 3 in OR |
| 1932...John Anderson, United States | 162 ft 4 in OR |
| 1936...Ken Carpenter, United States | 165 ft 7 in OR |
| 1948...Adolfo Consolini, Italy | 173 ft 2 in OR |
| 1952...Sim Iness, United States | 180 ft 6 in OR |
| 1956...Al Oerter, United States | 184 ft 11 in OR |
| 1960...Al Oerter, United States | 194 ft 2 in OR |
| 1964...Al Oerter, United States | 200 ft 1 in OR |
| 1968...Al Oerter, United States | 212 ft 6 in OR |
| 1972...Ludvik Danek, Czechoslovakia | 211 ft 3 in |
| 1976...Mac Wilkins, United States | 221 ft 5 in OR |
| 1980...Viktor Rashchupkin, USSR | 218 ft 8 in |
| 1984...Rolf Dannenberg, W Ger | 218 ft 6 in |
| 1988...Jürgen Schult, E Germany | 225 ft 9 in OR |
| 1992...Romas Ubartas, Lithuania | 213 ft 8 in |
| 1996...Lars Riedel, Germany | 227 ft 8 in OR |
| 2000...Virgilijus Alekna, Lithuania | 227 ft 4 in |
| 2004...Virgilijus Alekna, Lithuania | 229 ft 3 in |
| 2008...Gerd Kanter, Estonia | 225 ft 9½ in |

### HAMMER THROW

| | |
|---|---|
| 1900...John Flanagan, United States | 163 ft 1 in |
| 1904...John Flanagan, United States | 168 ft 1 in OR |
| 1906...Not held | |
| 1908...John Flanagan, United States | 170 ft 4 in OR |
| 1912...Matt McGrath, United States | 179 ft 7 in OR |

(w)-wind aided

## TRACK AND FIELD — Men *(Cont.)*

### HAMMER THROW *(Cont.)*

| | |
|---|---|
| 1920...Pat Ryan, United States | 173 ft 5 in |
| 1924...Fred Tootell, United States | 174 ft 10 in |
| 1928...Patrick O'Callaghan, Ireland | 168 ft 7 in |
| 1932...Patrick O'Callaghan, Ireland | 176 ft 11 in |
| 1936...Karl Hein, Germany | 185 ft 4 in OR |
| 1948...Imre Nemeth, Hungary | 183 ft 11 in |
| 1952...Jozsef Csermak, Hungary | 197 ft 11 in WR |
| 1956...Harold Connolly, United States | 207 ft 3 in OR |
| 1960...Vasily Rudenkov, USSR | 220 ft 2 in OR |
| 1964...Romuald Klim, USSR | 228 ft 10 in OR |
| 1968...Gyula Zsivotsky, Hungary | 240 ft 8 in OR |
| 1972...Anatoli Bondarchuk, USSR | 247 ft 8 in OR |
| 1976...Yuri Sedykh, USSR | 254 ft 4 in OR |
| 1980...Yuri Sedykh, USSR | 268 ft 4 in WR |
| 1984...Juha Tiainen, Finland | 256 ft 2 in |
| 1988...Sergei Litvinov, USSR | 278 ft 2 in OR |
| 1992...Andrey Abduvaliyev, Unified T | 270 ft 9 in |
| 1996...Balazs Kiss, Hungary | 266 ft 6 in |
| 2000...Szymon Ziolkowski, Poland | 262 ft 6 in |
| 2004...Adrian Zsolt, Hungary | 272 fr 11 in |
| 2008...Primoz Kozmus, Slovenia | 269 ft 1 in |

### JAVELIN

| | |
|---|---|
| 1908...Erik Lemming, Sweden | 179 ft 10 in |
| 1912...Erik Lemming, Sweden | 198 ft 11 in OR |
| 1920...Jonni Myyrä, Finland | 215 ft 10 in OR |
| 1924...Jonni Myyrä, Finland | 206 ft 6 in |
| 1928...Eric Lundkvist, Sweden | 218 ft 6 in OR |
| 1932...Matti Jarvinen, Finland | 238 ft 6 in OR |
| 1936...Gerhard Stöck, Germany | 235 ft 8 in |
| 1948...Kai Rautavaara, Finland | 228 ft 10½ in |
| 1952...Cy Young, United States | 242 ft 1 in OR |
| 1956...Egil Danielson, Norway | 281 ft 2¼ in WR |
| 1960...Viktor Tsibulenko, USSR | 277 ft 8 in |
| 1964...Pauli Nevala, Finland | 271 ft 2 in |
| 1968...Janis Lusis, USSR | 295 ft 7 in OR |
| 1972...Klaus Wolfermann, W Germany | 296 ft 10 in OR |

### JAVELIN *(Cont.)*

| | |
|---|---|
| 1976...Miklos Nemeth, Hungary | 310 ft 4 in WR |
| 1980...Dainis Kuta, USSR | 299 ft 2⅜ in |
| 1984...Arto Härkönen, Finland | 284 ft 8 in |
| 1988...Tapio Korjus, Finland | 276 ft 6 in |
| 1992...Jan Zelezny, Czechoslovakia | 294 ft 2 in OR |
| 1996...Jan Zelezny, Czech Republic | 289 ft 3 in |
| 2000...Jan Zelezny, Czech Republic | 295 ft 9½ in OR |
| 2004...Andreas Thorkildsen, Norway | 283 ft 9 in |
| 2008...Andreas Thorkildsen, Norway | 297 ft 1¾ in OR |

### DECATHLON

| | | Pts |
|---|---|---|
| 1904 ...Thomas Kiely, Ireland | | 6036 |
| 1912 ...Jim Thorpe, United States* | | 8412 WR |
| 1920 ...Helge Lövland, Norway | | 6803 |
| 1924 ...Harold Osborn, United States | | 7711 WR |
| 1928 ...Paavo Yrjölä, Finland | | 8053.29 WR |
| 1932 ...James Bausch, United States | | 8462 WR |
| 1936 ...Glenn Morris, United States | | 7900 WR |
| 1948 ...Robert Mathias, United States | | 7139 |
| 1952 ...Robert Mathias, United States | | 7887 WR |
| 1956 ...Milton Campbell, United States | | 7937 OR |
| 1960 ...Rafer Johnson, United States | | 8392 OR |
| 1964 ...Willi Holdorf, W Germany | | 7887 |
| 1968 ...Bill Toomey, United States | | 8193 OR |
| 1972 ...Nikolai Avilov, USSR | | 8454 WR |
| 1976 ...Bruce Jenner, United States | | 8617 WR |
| 1980 ...Daley Thompson, Great Britain | | 8495 |
| 1984 ...Daley Thompson, Great Britain | | 8798 EWR |
| 1988 ...Christian Schenk, E Germany | | 8488 |
| 1992 ...Robert Zmelik, Czechoslovakia | | 8611 |
| 1996 ...Dan O'Brien, United States | | 8824 OR |
| 2000 ...Erki Nool, Estonia | | 8641 |
| 2004 ...Roman Seberle, Czech Rep | | 8893 OR |
| 2008 ...Bryan Clay, United States | | 8791 |

*In 1913, Thorpe was disqualified for having played professional baseball in 1910. His record was restored in 1982.

## TRACK AND FIELD — Women

### 100 METERS

| | |
|---|---|
| 1928 ....Elizabeth Robinson, US | 12.2 EWR |
| 1932 ....Stella Walsh, Poland | 11.9 EWR |
| 1936 ....Helen Stephens, United States | 11.5 |
| 1948 ....Francina Blankers-Koen, Neth | 11.9 |
| 1952 ....Marjorie Jackson, Australia | 11.5 EWR |
| 1956 ....Betty Cuthbert, Australia | 11.5 EWR |
| 1960 ....Wilma Rudolph, United States | 11.0 |
| 1964 ....Wyomia Tyus, United States | 11.4 |
| 1968 ....Wyomia Tyus, United States | 11.0 WR |
| 1972 ....Renate Stecher, E Germany | 11.07 |
| 1976 ....Annegret Richter, W Germany | 11.08 |
| 1980 ....Lyudmila Kondratyeva, USSR | 11.06 |
| 1984 ....Evelyn Ashford, United States | 10.97 OR |
| 1988 ....Florence Griffith Joyner, United States | 10.54 WR |
| 1992 ....Gail Devers, United States | 10.82 |
| 1996 ....Gail Devers, United States | 10.94 |
| 2000 ....Vacant* | |
| 2004 ....Yuliya Nesterenko, Belarus | 10.93 |
| 2008 ....Shelly-Ann Fraser, Jamaica | 10.78 |

### 200 METERS

| | |
|---|---|
| 1948 ....Francina Blankers-Koen, Neth | 24.4 |
| 1952 ....Marjorie Jackson, Australia | 23.7 |
| 1956 ....Betty Cuthbert, Australia | 23.4 EOR |
| 1960 ....Wilma Rudolph, United States | 24.0 |

### 200 METERS *(Cont.)*

| | |
|---|---|
| 1964 ....Edith McGuire, United States | 23.0 OR |
| 1968 ....Irena Szewinska, Poland | 22.5 WR |
| 1972 ....Renate Stecher, E Germany | 22.40 EWR |
| 1976 ....Bärbel Eckert, E Germany | 22.37 OR |
| 1980 ....Bärbel Wöckel (Eckert), E Germ. | 22.03 OR |
| 1984 ....Valerie Brisco-Hooks, U.S. | 21.81 OR |
| 1988 ....Florence Griffith Joyner, U.S. | 21.34 WR |
| 1992 ....Gwen Torrence, United States | 21.81 |
| 1996 ....Marie-José Pérec, France | 22.12 |
| 2000 ....Vacant* | |
| 2004 ....Veronica Campbell, Jamaica | 22.05 |
| 2008 ....Veronica Campbell-Brown, Jamaica | 21.74 |

### 400 METERS

| | |
|---|---|
| 1964 ....Betty Cuthbert, Australia | 52.0 OR |
| 1968 ....Colette Besson, France | 52.0 EOR |
| 1972 ....Monika Zehrt, E Germany | 51.08 OR |
| 1976 ....Irena Szewinska, Poland | 49.29 WR |
| 1980 ....Marita Koch, E Germany | 48.88 OR |
| 1984 ....Valerie Brisco-Hooks, U.S. | 48.83 OR |
| 1988 ....Olga Bryzgina, USSR | 48.65 OR |
| 1992 ....Marie-José Pérec, France | 48.83 |
| 1996 ....Marie-José Pérec, France | 48.25 OR |
| 2000 ....Cathy Freeman, Australia | 49.11 |
| 2004 ....T. Williams-Darling, Bahamas | 49.41 |
| 2004 ....T. Williams-Darling, Bahamas | 49.41 |

Note: OR=Olympic Record. WR=World Record. EOR=Equals Olympic Record. EWR=Equals World Record. WB=World Best.
*Marion Jones was stripped of her medals from the 2000 Olympics, no decision on replacing her victories has been made.

## TRACK AND FIELD — Women *(Cont.)*

### 800 METERS

| | | |
|---|---|---|
| 1928 | Lina Radke, Germany | 2:16.8 WR |
| 1932-56 | Not held | |
| 1960 | Lyudmila Shevtsova, USSR | 2:04.3 EWR |
| 1964 | Ann Packer, Great Britain | 2:01.1 OR |
| 1968 | Madeline Manning, United States | 2:00.9 OR |
| 1972 | Hildegard Falck, W Germany | 1:58.55 OR |
| 1976 | Tatyana Kazankina, USSR | 1:54.94 WR |
| 1980 | Nadezhda Olizarenko, USSR | 1:53.42 WR |
| 1984 | Doina Melinte, Romania | 1:57.6 |
| 1988 | Sigrun Wodars, E Germany | 1:56.10 |
| 1992 | Ellen Van Langen, Netherlands | 1:55.54 |
| 1996 | Svetlana Masterkova, Russia | 1:57.73 |
| 2000 | Maria Mutola, Mozambique | 1:56.15 |
| 2004 | Kelly Holmes, Great Britain | 1:56.38 |
| 2008 | Pamela Jelimo, Kenya | 1:54.87 |

### 1,500 METERS

| | | |
|---|---|---|
| 1972 | Lyudmila Bragina, USSR | 4:01.4 WR |
| 1976 | Tatyana Kazankina, USSR | 4:05.48 |
| 1980 | Tatyana Kazankina, USSR | 3:56.6 OR |
| 1984 | Gabriella Dorio, Italy | 4:03.25 |
| 1988 | Paula Ivan, Romania | 3:53.96 OR |
| 1992 | Hassiba Boulmerka, Algeria | 3:55.30 |
| 1996 | Svetlana Masterkova, Russia | 4:00.83 |
| 2000 | Nouria Merah-Benida, Algeria | 4:05.10 |
| 2004 | Kelly Holmes, Great Britain | 3:57.90 |
| 2008 | Nancy Jebet Lagat, Kenya | 4:00.23 |

### 3,000 METERS

| | | |
|---|---|---|
| 1984 | Maricica Puica, Romania | 8:35.96 OR |
| 1988 | Tatyana Samolenko, USSR | 8:26.53 OR |
| 1992 | Elena Romanova, Unified Team | 8:46.04 |

### 5,000 METERS

| | | |
|---|---|---|
| 1996 | Wang Junxia, China | 14:57.88 |
| 2000 | Gabriela Szabo, Romania | 14:40.79 OR |
| 2004 | Meseret Defar, Ethiopia | 14:45.65 |
| 2008 | Tirunesh Dibaba Kenene, Ethiopia | 15:41.40 |

### 10,000 METERS

| | | |
|---|---|---|
| 1988 | Olga Bondarenko, USSR | 31:05.21 OR |
| 1992 | Derartu Tulu, Ethiopia | 31:06.02 |
| 1996 | Fernanda Ribeiro, Portugal | 31:01.63 OR |
| 2000 | Derartu Tulu, Ethiopia | 30:17.49 OR |
| 2004 | Huina Xing, China | 30:24.36 |
| 2008 | Tirunesh Dibaba Kenene, Ethiopia | 29:54.66 OR |

### MARATHON

| | | |
|---|---|---|
| 1984 | Joan Benoit, United States | 2:24:52 OR |
| 1988 | Rosa Mota, Portugal | 2:25:40 |
| 1992 | Valentin Yegorova, Unified Team | 2:32:41 |
| 1996 | Fatuma Roba, Ethiopia | 2:26:05 |
| 2000 | Naoko Takahashi, Japan | 2:23:14 OR |
| 2004 | Noguchi Mizuki, Japan | 2:26:20 |
| 2008 | Constantina Tomescu Dita, Romania | 2:26:44 |

### 80-METER HURDLES

| | | |
|---|---|---|
| 1932 | Babe Didrikson, United States | 11.7 WR |
| 1936 | Trebisonda Valla, Italy | 11.7 |
| 1948 | Francina Blankers-Koen, Neth | 11.2 OR |
| 1952 | Shirley Strickland, Australia | 10.9 WR |
| 1956 | Shirley Strickland, Australia | 10.7 OR |
| 1960 | Irina Press, USSR | 10.8 |
| 1964 | Karin Balzer, E Germany | 10.5 |
| 1968 | Maureen Caird, Australia | 10.3 OR |

### 100-METER HURDLES

| | | |
|---|---|---|
| 1972 | Annelie Ehrhardt, E Germany | 12.59 WR |
| 1976 | Johanna Schaller, E Germany | 12.77 |

### 100-METER HURDLES *(Cont.)*

| | | |
|---|---|---|
| 1980 | Vera Komisova, USSR | 12.56 OR |
| 1984 | Benita Fitzgerald-Brown, U.S. | 12.84 |
| 1988 | Yordanka Donkova, Bulgaria | 12.38 OR |
| 1992 | Paraskevi Patoulidou, Greece | 12.64 |
| 1996 | Lyudmila Engqvist, Sweden | 12.58 |
| 2000 | Olga Shishigina, Kazakhstan | 12.65 |
| 2004 | Joanna Hayes, United States | 12.37 OR |
| 2008 | Dawn Harper, United States | 12.54 |

### 400-METER HURDLES

| | | |
|---|---|---|
| 1984 | Nawal el Moutawakel, Morocco | 54.61 OR |
| 1988 | Debra Flintoff-King, Australia | 53.17 OR |
| 1992 | Sally Gunnell, Great Britain | 53.23 |
| 1996 | Deon Hemmings, Jamaica | 52.82 OR |
| 2000 | Irina Privalova, Russia | 53.02 |
| 2004 | Faní Halkiá, Greece | 52.82 |
| 2008 | Melaine Walker, Jamaica | 52.64 |

### 4 X 100-METER RELAY

| | | |
|---|---|---|
| 1928 | Canada | 48.4 WR |
| 1932 | United States | 46.9 WR |
| 1936 | United States | 46.9 |
| 1948 | Netherlands | 47.5 |
| 1952 | United States | 45.9 WR |
| 1956 | Australia | 44.5 WR |
| 1960 | United States | 44.5 |
| 1964 | Poland | 43.6 |
| 1968 | United States | 42.8 WR |
| 1972 | W Germany | 42.81 EWR |
| 1976 | E Germany | 42.55 OR |
| 1980 | E Germany | 41.60 WR |
| 1984 | United States | 41.65 |
| 1988 | United States | 41.98 |
| 1992 | United States | 42.11 |
| 1996 | United States | 41.95 |
| 2000 | Bahamas | 41.95 |
| 2004 | Jamaica | 41.73 |
| 2008 | Russia | 42.31 |

### 4 X 400-METER RELAY

| | | |
|---|---|---|
| 1972 | E Germany | 3:23 WR |
| 1976 | E Germany | 3:19.23 WR |
| 1980 | USSR | 3:20.02 |
| 1984 | United States | 3:18.29 OR |
| 1988 | USSR | 3:15.18 WR |
| 1992 | Unified Team | 3:20.20 |
| 1996 | United States | 3:20.91 |
| 2000 | Vacant† | |
| 2004 | United States | 3:19.01 |
| 2008 | United States | 3:18.54 |

### 10-KILOMETER WALK

| | | |
|---|---|---|
| 1992 | Chen Yueling, China | 44:32 |
| 1996 | Elena Nikolayeva, Russia | 41:49 OR |

### 20-KILOMETER WALK

| | | |
|---|---|---|
| 2000 | Liping Wang, China | 1:29:05 |
| 2004 | Athanasía Tsouméléka, Greece | 1:29:12 |
| 2008 | Olga Kaniskina, Russia | 1:26:31 OR |

### HIGH JUMP

| | | |
|---|---|---|
| 1928 | Ethel Catherwood, Canada | 5 ft 2½ in |
| 1932 | Jean Shiley, United States | 5 ft 5¼ in WR |
| 1936 | Ibolya Csak, Hungary | 5 ft 3 in |
| 1948 | Alice Coachman, United States | 5 ft 6 in |
| 1952 | Esther Brand, South Africa | 5 ft 5¾ in |
| 1956 | Mildred L. McDaniel, U.S. | 5 ft 9¼ in WR |
| 1960 | Iolanda Balas, Romania | 6 ft ¾ in OR |
| 1964 | Iolanda Balas, Romania | 6 ft 2¾ in OR |

Note: OR=Olympic Record; WR=World Record; EOR=Equals Olympic Record; EWR=Equals World Record; WB=World Best.

†Marion Jones was stripped of her medals from the 2000 Olympics, no decision on replacing her victories has been made.

## TRACK AND FIELD — Women *(Cont.)*

### HIGH JUMP *(Cont.)*

| | | |
|---|---|---|
| 1968 | Miloslava Reskova, Czech. | 5 ft 11½ in |
| 1972 | Ulrike Meyfarth, W. Germany | 6 ft 3½ in EWR |
| 1976 | Rosemarie Ackermann, E Germ | 6 ft 4 in OR |
| 1980 | Sara Simeoni, Italy | 6 ft 5½ in OR |
| 1984 | Ulrike Meyfarth, W Germany | 6 ft 7½ in OR |
| 1988 | Louise Ritter, United States | 6 ft 8 in OR |
| 1992 | Heike Henkel, Germany | 6 ft 7½ in |
| 1996 | Stefka Kostadinova, Bulgaria | 6 ft 8¾ in OR |
| 2000 | Yelena Yelesina, Russia | 6 ft 7 in |
| 2004 | Yelena Slesarenko, Russia | 6 ft 9 in |
| 2008 | Tia Hellebaut, Belgium | 6 ft 8¾ in |

### POLE VAULT

| | | |
|---|---|---|
| 2000 | Stacy Dragila, United States | 15 ft 1 in OR |
| 2004 | Yelena Isinbayeva, Russia | 16 ft 1¼ in WR |
| 2008 | Yelena Isinbayeva, Russia | 16 ft 6¾ in WR |

### LONG JUMP

| | | |
|---|---|---|
| 1948 | Olga Gyarmati, Hungary | 18 ft 8¼ in |
| 1952 | Yvette Williams, New Zealand | 20 ft 5¾ in OR |
| 1956 | Elzbieta Krzeskinska, Poland | 20 ft 10 in EWR |
| 1960 | Vyera Krepkina, USSR | 20 ft 10¾ in OR |
| 1964 | Mary Rand, Great Britain | 22 ft 2¼ in WR |
| 1968 | Viorica Viscopoleanu, Rom | 22 ft 4½ in WR |
| 1972 | Heidemarie Rosendahl, W Ger | 22 ft 3 in |
| 1976 | Angela Voigt, E Germany | 22 ft ¾ in |
| 1980 | Tatyana Kolpakova, USSR | 23 ft 2 in OR |
| 1984 | Anisoara Stanciu, Romania | 22 ft 10 in |
| 1988 | Jackie Joyner-Kersee, U.S. | 24 ft 3½ in OR |
| 1992 | Heike Drechsler, Germany | 23 ft 5¼ in |
| 1996 | Chioma Ajunwa, Nigeria | 23 ft 4½ in |
| 2000 | Heike Drechsler, Germany | 22 ft 11¼ in |
| 2004 | Tatyana Lebedeva, Russia | 23 ft 2½ in |
| 2008 | Maurren Higa Maggi, Brazil | 23 ft 1 in |

### TRIPLE JUMP

| | | |
|---|---|---|
| 1996 | Inessa Kravets, Ukraine | 50 ft 3½ in |
| 2000 | Tereza Marinova, Bulgaria | 49 ft 10½ in |
| 2004 | Francoise M. Etone, Cameroon | 50 ft 2½ in |
| 2008 | Francoise M. Etone, Cameroon | 50 ft 5 in |

### SHOT PUT

| | | |
|---|---|---|
| 1948 | Micheline Ostermeyer, France | 45 ft 1½ in |
| 1952 | Galina Zybina, USSR | 50 ft 1¾ in WR |
| 1956 | Tamara Tyshkevich, USSR | 54 ft 5 in OR |
| 1960 | Tamara Press, USSR | 56 ft 10 in OR |
| 1964 | Tamara Press, USSR | 59 ft 6¼ in OR |
| 1968 | Margitta Gummel, E Germany | 64 ft 4 in WR |
| 1972 | Nadezhda Chizhova, USSR | 69 ft WR |
| 1976 | Ivanka Hristova, Bulgaria | 69 ft 5¼ in OR |
| 1980 | Ilona Slupianek, E Germany | 73 ft 6¼ in |
| 1984 | Claudia Losch, W Germany | 67 ft 2¼ in |
| 1988 | Natalya Lisovskaya, USSR | 72 ft 11¾ in |
| 1992 | Svetlana Kriveleva, Unified Team | 69 ft 1¼ in |
| 1996 | Astrid Kumbernuss, Germany | 67 ft 5½ in |
| 2000 | Yanina Korolchik, Belarus | 67 ft 5½ in |
| 2004 | Yumileidi Cumba Jay, Cuba | 64 ft 3¼ in |
| 2008 | Valerie Vili, New Zealand | 67 ft 5½ in |

### DISCUS THROW

| | | |
|---|---|---|
| 1928 | Helena Konopacka, Poland | 129 ft 11¾ in WR |
| 1932 | Lillian Copeland, United States | 133 ft 2 in OR |
| 1936 | Gisela Mauermayer, Germany | 156 ft 3 in OR |
| 1948 | Micheline Ostermeyer, France | 137 ft 6 in |
| 1952 | Nina Romaschkova, USSR | 168 ft 8 in OR |
| 1956 | Olga Fikotova, Czechoslovakia | 176 ft 1 in OR |
| 1960 | Nina Ponomaryeva, USSR | 180 ft 9 in OR |
| 1964 | Tamara Press, USSR | 187 ft 10 in OR |
| 1968 | Lia Manoliu, Romania | 191 ft 2 in OR |
| 1972 | Faina Melnik, USSR | 218 ft 7 in OR |
| 1976 | Evelin Schlaak, E Germany | 226 ft 4 in OR |
| 1980 | Evelin Jahl (Schlaak), E. Germ. | 229 ft 6 in OR |
| 1984 | Ria Stalman, Netherlands | 214 ft 5 in |
| 1988 | Martina Hellmann, E Germany | 237 ft 2 in OR |
| 1992 | Maritza Martén, Cuba | 229 ft 10 in |
| 1996 | Ilke Wyludda, Germany | 228 ft 6 in |
| 2000 | Ellina Zvereva, Belarus | 224 ft 5 in |
| 2004 | Natalya Sadova, Russia | 219 ft 10 in |
| 2008 | S. Brown-Trafton, United States | 212 ft 4¾ in |

### HAMMER THROW

| | | |
|---|---|---|
| 2000 | Kamila Skolimowska, Russia | 233 ft 5 in OR |
| 2004 | Olga Kuzenkova, Russia | 246 ft 1½ in OR |
| 2008 | Aksana Miankova, Belarus | 250 ft 5½ in OR |

### JAVELIN THROW

| | | |
|---|---|---|
| 1932 | Babe Didrikson, United States | 143 ft 4 in OR |
| 1936 | Tilly Fleischer, Germany | 148 ft 3 in OR |
| 1948 | Herma Bauma, Austria | 149 ft 6 in |
| 1952 | Dana Zatopkova, Czechoslovakia | 165 ft 7 in |
| 1956 | Inese Jaunzeme, USSR | 176 ft 8 in |
| 1960 | Elvira Ozolina, USSR | 183 ft 8 in OR |
| 1964 | Mihaela Penes, Romania | 198 ft 7 in |
| 1968 | Angela Nemeth, Hungary | 198 ft |
| 1972 | Ruth Fuchs, E Germany | 209 ft 7 in OR |
| 1976 | Ruth Fuchs, E Germany | 216 ft 4 in OR |
| 1980 | Maria Colon, Cuba | 224 ft 5 in OR |
| 1984 | Tessa Sanderson, Great Britain | 228 ft 2 in OR |
| 1988 | Petra Felke, E Germany | 245 ft OR |
| 1992 | Silke Renk, Germany | 224 ft 2 in |
| 1996 | Heli Rantanen, Finland | 222 ft 11 in |
| 2000 | Trine Hattestad, Norway | 226 ft ½ in OR |
| 2004 | Osleidys Menendez, Cuba | 234 ft 8 in OR |
| 2008 | B. Spotakova, Czech Republic | 234 ft 3¾ in |

### PENTATHLON

| | | | Pts |
|---|---|---|---|
| 1964 | Irina Press, USSR | | 5246 WR |
| 1968 | Ingrid Becker, W Germany | | 5098 |
| 1972 | Mary Peters, Great Britain | | 4801 WR |
| 1976 | Siegrun Siegl, E Germany | | 4745 |
| 1980 | Nadezhda Tkachenko, USSR | | 5083 WR |

### HEPTATHLON

| | | | Pts |
|---|---|---|---|
| 1984 | Glynis Nunn, Australia | | 6390 OR |
| 1988 | Jackie Joyner-Kersee, U.S. | | 7291 WR |
| 1992 | Jackie Joyner-Kersee, U.S. | | 7044 |
| 1996 | Ghada Shouaa, Syria | | 6780 |
| 2000 | Denise Lewis, Great Britain | | 6584 |
| 2004 | Carolina Kluft, Sweden | | 6952 |
| 2008 | Natalia Dobrynska, Ukraine | | 6733 |

## BASKETBALL — Men *(Cont.)*

### 1936
Final: United States 19, Canada 8
United States: Ralph Bishop, Joe Fortenberry, Carl Knowles, Jack Ragland, Carl Shy, William Wheatley, Francis Johnson, Samuel Balter, John Gibbons, Frank Lubin, Arthur Mollner, Donald Piper, Duane Swanson, Willard Schmidt

### 1948
Final: United States 65, France 21
United States: Cliff Barker, Don Barksdale, Ralph Beard, Lewis Beck, Vince Boryla, Gordon Carpenter, Alex Groza, Wallace Jones, Bob Kurland, Ray Lumpp, Robert Pitts, Jesse Renick, Bob Robinson, Ken Rollins

### 1952
Final: United States 36, USSR 25
United States: Charles Hoag, Bill Hougland, Melvin Dean Kelley, Bob Kenney, Clyde Lovellette, Marcus Freiberger, Victor Wayne Glasgow, Frank McCabe, Daniel Pippen, Howard Williams, Ronald Bontemps, Bob Kurland, William Lienhard, John Keller

### 1956
Final: United States 89, USSR 55
United States: Carl Cain, Bill Hougland, K.C. Jones, Bill Russell, James Walsh, William Evans, Burdette Haldorson, Ron Tomsic, Dick Boushka, Gilbert Ford, Bob Jeangerard, Charles Darling

### 1960
Final: United States 90, Brazil 63
United States: Jay Arnette, Walt Bellamy, Bob Boozer, Terry Dischinger, Jerry Lucas, Oscar Robertson, Adrian Smith, Burdette Haldorson, Darrall Imhoff, Allen Kelley, Lester Lane, Jerry West

### 1964
Final: United States 73, USSR 59
United States: Jim Barnes, Bill Bradley, Larry Brown, Joe Caldwell, Mel Counts, Richard Davies, Walt Hazzard, Lucius Jackson, John McCaffrey, Jeff Mullins, Jerry Shipp, George Wilson

### 1968
Final: United States 65, Yugoslavia 50
United States: John Clawson, Ken Spain, Jo-Jo White, Michael Barrett, Spencer Haywood, Charles Scott, William Hosket, Calvin Fowler, Michael Silliman, Glynn Saulters, James King, Donald Dee

### 1972
Final: USSR 51, United States 50
United States: Kenneth Davis, Doug Collins, Thomas Henderson, Mike Bantom, Bobby Jones, Dwight Jones, James Forbes, James Brewer, Tom Burleson, Tom McMillen, Kevin Joyce, Ed Ratleff

### 1976
Final: United States 95, Yugoslavia 74
United States: Phil Ford, Steve Sheppard, Adrian Dantley, Walter Davis, Quinn Buckner, Ernie Grunfield, Kenny Carr, Scott May, Michel Armstrong, Tom La Garde, Phil Hubbard, Mitch Kupchak

### 1980
Final: Yugoslavia 86, Italy 77
U.S. participated in boycott.

### 1984
Final: United States 96, Spain 65
United States: Steve Alford, Leon Wood, Patrick Ewing, Vern Fleming, Alvin Robertson, Michael Jordan, Joe Kleine, Jon Koncak, Wayman Tisdale, Chris Mullin, Sam Perkins, Jeff Turner

### 1988
Final: USSR 76, Yugoslavia 63
U.S. (3rd): Mitch Richmond, Charles E. Smith IV, Vernell Coles, Hersey Hawkins, Jeff Grayer, Charles D. Smith, Willie Anderson, Stacey Augmon, Dan Majerle, Danny Manning, J.R. Reid, David Robinson

### 1992
Final: United States 117, Croatia 85
United States: David Robinson, Christian Laettner, Patrick Ewing, Larry Bird, Scottie Pippen, Michael Jordan, Clyde Drexler, Karl Malone, John Stockton, Chris Mullin, Charles Barkley, Earvin Johnson

### 1996
Final: United States 95, Yugoslavia 69
United States: Charles Barkley, Anfernee Hardaway, Grant Hill, Karl Malone, Reggie Miller, Hakeem Olajuwon, Shaquille O'Neal, Scottie Pippen, Mitch Richmond, John Stockton, David Robinson, Gary Payton

### 2000
Final: United States 85, France 75
United States: Shareef Abdur-Rahim, Ray Allen, Vin Baker, Vince Carter, Kevin Garnett, Tim Hardaway, Allan Houston, Jason Kidd, Antonio McDyess, Alonzo Mourning, Gary Payton, Steve Smith

### 2004
Final: Argentina 84, Italy 69
U.S. (3rd): Allen Iverson, LeBron James, Tim Duncan, Carmelo Anthony, Dwyane Wade, Richard Jefferson, Lamar Odom, Stephon Marbury, Carlos Boozer, Emeka Okafor, Amare Stoudemire, Shawn Marion

### 2008
Final: United States 118, Spain 107
U.S.: Carmelo Anthony, Carlos Boozer, Chris Bosh, Kobe Bryant, Dwight Howard, LeBron James, Jason Kidd, Chirs Paul, Tayshaun Prince, Michael Redd, Dwyane Wade, Deron Williams

## BASKETBALL — Women

### 1976
Gold, USSR; Silver, United States*
United States: Cindy Brogdon, Susan Rojcewicz, Ann Meyers, Lusia Harris, Nancy Dunkle, Charlotte Lewis, Nancy Lieberman, Gail Marquis, Patricia Roberts, Mary Anne O'Connor, Patricia Head, Julienne Simpson

*In 1976 the women played a round-robin tournament, with the gold medal going to the team with the best record. The USSR won with a 5–0 record, and the USA, with a 3–2 record, was given the silver by virtue of a 95–79 victory over Bulgaria, which was also 3–2.

### 1980
Final: USSR 104, Bulgaria 73
U.S. participated in boycott.

### 1984
Final: United States 85, Korea 55
United States: Teresa Edwards, Lea Henry, Lynette Woodard, Anne Donovan, Cathy Boswell, Cheryl Miller, Janice Lawrence, Cindy Noble, Kim Mulkey, Denise Curry, Pamela McGee, Carol Menken-Schaudt

### 1988
Final: United States 77, Yugoslavia 70
United States: Teresa Edwards, Mary Ethridge, Cynthia Brown, Anne Donovan, Teresa Weatherspoon, Bridgette Gordon, Victoria Bullett, Andrea Lloyd, Katrina McClain, Jennifer Gillom, Cynthia Cooper, Suzanne McConnell

### 1992
Final: Unified Team 76, China 66
United States (3rd): Teresa Edwards, Teresa Weatherspoon, Victoria Bullett, Katrina McClain, Cynthia Cooper, Suzanne McConnell, Daedra Charles, Clarissa Davis, Tammy Jackson, Vickie Orr, Carolyn Jones, Medina Dixon

### 1996
Final: United States 111, Brazil 87
United States: Jennifer Azzi, Ruthie Bolton, Teresa Edwards, Lisa Leslie, Rebecca Lobo, Katrina McClain, Nikki McCray, Carla McGhee, Dawn Staley, Katy Steding, Sheryl Swoopes, Venus Lacey

### 2000
Final: United States 76, Australia 54
United States: Ruthie Bolton-Holifield, Teresa Edwards, Yolanda Griffith, Chamique Holdsclaw, Lisa Leslie, Nikki McCray, Delisha Milton, Katie Smith, Dawn Staley, Sheryl Swoopes, Natalie Williams, Kara Wolters

### 2004
Final: United States 74, Australia 63
United States: Dawn Staley, Diana Taurasi, Lisa Leslie, Sheryl Swoopes, Tamika Catchings, Sue Bird, Ruth Riley, Shannon Johnson, Katie Smith, Yolanda Griffith, Swintayla Cash, Tina Thompson

### 2008
Final: United States 92, Australia 65
United States: Seimone Augustus, Sue Bird, Sylvia Fowles, Lisa Leslie, DeLisha Milton-Jones, Candace Parker, Cappie Pondexter, Tamika Catchings, Tina Thompson, Diana Taurasi, Katie Smith

## BOXING

### LIGHT FLYWEIGHT (106 LB)
| | |
|---|---|
| 1968 | Francisco Rodriguez, Venezuela |
| 1972 | Gyorgy Gedo, Hungary |
| 1976 | Jorge Hernandez, Cuba |
| 1980 | Shamil Sabyrov, USSR |
| 1984 | Paul Gonzalez, United States |
| 1988 | Ivailo Hristov, Bulgaria |
| 1992 | Rogelio Marcelo, Cuba |
| 1996 | Daniel Petrov, Bulgaria |
| 2000 | Brahim Asloum, France |
| 2004 | Yan Bhartelemy Varela, Cuba |
| 2008 | Zou Shiming, China |

### FLYWEIGHT (112 LB)
| | |
|---|---|
| 1904 | George Finnegan, United States |
| 1920 | Frank Di Gennara, United States |
| 1924 | Fidel LaBarba, United States |
| 1928 | Antal Kocsis, Hungary |
| 1932 | Istvan Enekes, Hungary |
| 1936 | Willi Kaiser, Germany |
| 1948 | Pascual Perez, Argentina |
| 1952 | Nathan Brooks, United States |
| 1956 | Terence Spinks, Great Britain |
| 1960 | Gyula Torok, Hungary |
| 1964 | Fernando Atzori, Italy |
| 1968 | Ricardo Delgado, Mexico |
| 1972 | Georgi Kostadinov, Bulgaria |
| 1976 | Leo Randolph, United States |
| 1980 | Peter Lessov, Bulgaria |
| 1984 | Steve McCrory, United States |
| 1988 | Kim Kwang Sun, S Korea |
| 1992 | Su Choi Chol, N Korea |
| 1996 | Maikro Romero, Cuba |

### FLYWEIGHT (112 LB) (Cont.)
| | |
|---|---|
| 2000 | Wijan Ponlid, Thailand |
| 2004 | Yuriokis Toledano, Cuba |
| 2008 | Somit Jongjohor, Thailand |

### BANTAMWEIGHT (119 LB)
| | |
|---|---|
| 1904 | Oliver Kirk, United States |
| 1908 | A. Henry Thomas, Great Britain |
| 1920 | Clarence Walker, S Africa |
| 1924 | William Smith, S Africa |
| 1928 | Vittorio Tamagnini, Italy |
| 1932 | Horace Gwynne, Canada |
| 1936 | Ulderico Sergo, Italy |
| 1948 | Tibor Csik, Hungary |
| 1952 | Pentti Hamalainen, Finland |
| 1956 | Wolfgang Behrendt, E Germany |
| 1960 | Oleg Grigoryev, USSR |
| 1964 | Takao Sakurai, Japan |
| 1968 | Valery Sokolov, USSR |
| 1972 | Orlando Martinez, Cuba |
| 1976 | Yong Jo Gu, N Korea |
| 1980 | Juan Hernandez, Cuba |
| 1984 | Maurizio Stecca, Italy |
| 1988 | Kennedy McKinney, United States |
| 1992 | Joel Casamayor, Cuba |
| 1996 | István Kovács, Hungary |
| 2000 | Guillermo Ortiz, Cuba |
| 2004 | Guillermo Ortiz, Cuba |
| 2008 | Badar-Uugan Enkhbat, Mongolia |

### FEATHERWEIGHT (125 LB)
| | |
|---|---|
| 1904 | Oliver Kirk, United States |
| 1908 | Richard Gunn, Great Britain |
| 1920 | Paul Fritsch, France |

## BOXING *(Cont.)*

### FEATHERWEIGHT (125 LB) *(Cont.)*

| | |
|---|---|
| 1924 | John Fields, United States |
| 1928 | Lambertus van Klaveren, Netherlands |
| 1932 | Carmelo Robledo, Argentina |
| 1936 | Oscar Casanovas, Argentina |
| 1948 | Ernesto Formenti, Italy |
| 1952 | Jan Zachara, Czechoslovakia |
| 1956 | Vladimir Safronov, USSR |
| 1960 | Francesco Musso, Italy |
| 1964 | Stanislav Stephashkin, USSR |
| 1968 | Antonio Roldan, Mexico |
| 1972 | Boris Kousnetsov, USSR |
| 1976 | Angel Herrera, Cuba |
| 1980 | Rudi Fink, E Germany |
| 1984 | Meldrick Taylor, United States |
| 1988 | Giovanni Parisi, Italy |
| 1992 | Andreas Tews, Germany |
| 1996 | Somluck Kamsing, Thailand |
| 2000 | Bekzat Sattarkhanox, Kazakhsta |
| 2004 | Alexei Tichtchenko, Russia |
| 2008 | Vasyl Lomachenko, Ukraine |

### LIGHTWEIGHT (132 LB)

| | |
|---|---|
| 1904 | Harry Spanger, United States |
| 1908 | Frederick Grace, Great Britain |
| 1920 | Samuel Mosberg, United States |
| 1924 | Hans Nielsen, Denmark |
| 1928 | Carlo Orlandi, Italy |
| 1932 | Lawrence Stevens, S Africa |
| 1936 | Imre Harangi, Hungary |
| 1948 | Gerald Dreyer, S Africa |
| 1952 | Aureliano Bolognesi, Italy |
| 1956 | Richard McTaggart, Great Britain |
| 1960 | Kazimierz Pazdzior, Poland |
| 1964 | Jozef Grudzien, Poland |
| 1968 | Ronald Harris, United States |
| 1972 | Jan Szczepanski, Poland |
| 1976 | Howard Davis, United States |
| 1980 | Angel Herrera, Cuba |
| 1984 | Pernell Whitaker, United States |
| 1988 | Andreas Zuelow, E Germany |
| 1992 | Oscar De La Hoya, United States |
| 1996 | Hocine Soltani, Algeria |
| 2000 | Mario Mesa, Cuba |
| 2004 | Mario Mesa, Cuba |
| 2008 | Alexey Tishchenko, Russia |

### LIGHT WELTERWEIGHT (139 LB)

| | |
|---|---|
| 1952 | Charles Adkins, United States |
| 1956 | Vladimir Yengibaryan, USSR |
| 1960 | Bohumil Nemecek, Czechoslovakia |
| 1964 | Jerzy Kulej, Poland |
| 1968 | Jerzy Kulej, Poland |
| 1972 | Ray Seales, United States |
| 1976 | Ray Leonard, United States |
| 1980 | Patrizio Oliva, Italy |
| 1984 | Jerry Page, United States |
| 1988 | Viatcheslav Janovski, USSR |
| 1992 | Hector Vinent, Cuba |
| 1996 | Hector Vinent, Cuba |
| 2000 | Mahamadkadyz Abdullaev, Uzbekistan |
| 2004 | Manus Boonjumnong, Thailand |
| 2008 | Felix Diaz, Dominican Rebublic |

### WELTERWEIGHT (147 LB)

| | |
|---|---|
| 1904 | Albert Young, United States |
| 1920 | Albert Schneider, Canada |
| 1924 | Jean Delarge, Belgium |
| 1928 | Edward Morgan, New Zealand |
| 1932 | Edward Flynn, United States |
| 1936 | Sten Suvio, Finland |
| 1948 | Julius Torma, Czechoslovakia |

### WELTERWEIGHT (147 LB)

| | |
|---|---|
| 1952 | Zygmunt Chychla, Poland |
| 1956 | Nicolae Linca, Romania |
| 1960 | Giovanni Benvenuti, Italy |
| 1964 | Marian Kasprzyk, Poland |
| 1968 | Manfred Wolke, E Germany |
| 1972 | Emilio Correa, Cuba |
| 1976 | Jochen Bachfeld, E Germany |
| 1980 | Andres Aldama, Cuba |
| 1984 | Mark Breland, United States |
| 1988 | Robert Wangila, Kenya |
| 1992 | Michael Carruth, Ireland |
| 1996 | Oleg Saitov, Russia |
| 2000 | Oleg Saitov, Russia |
| 2004 | Bakhtiyar Artayev, Kazakhstan |
| 2008 | Bakhyt Sarsekbayev, Kazakhstan |

### LIGHT MIDDLEWEIGHT (156 LB)

| | |
|---|---|
| 1952 | Laszlo Papp, Hungary |
| 1956 | Laszlo Papp, Hungary |
| 1960 | Wilbert McClure, United States |
| 1964 | Boris Lagutin, USSR |
| 1968 | Boris Lagutin, USSR |
| 1972 | Dieter Kottysch, W Germany |
| 1976 | Jerzy Rybicki, Poland |
| 1980 | Armando Martinez, Cuba |
| 1984 | Frank Tate, United States |
| 1988 | Park Si-Hun, S Korea |
| 1992 | Juan Lemus, Cuba |
| 1996 | David Reid, United States |
| 2000 | Yermakhan Ibraimov, Kazakhstan |

### MIDDLEWEIGHT (165 LB)

| | |
|---|---|
| 1904 | Charles Mayer, United States |
| 1908 | John Douglas, Great Britain |
| 1920 | Harry Mallin, Great Britain |
| 1924 | Harry Mallin, Great Britain |
| 1928 | Piero Toscani, Italy |
| 1932 | Carmen Barth, United States |
| 1936 | Jean Despeaux, France |
| 1948 | Laszlo Papp, Hungary |
| 1952 | Floyd Patterson, United States |
| 1956 | Gennady Schatkov, USSR |
| 1960 | Edward Crook, United States |
| 1964 | Valery Popenchenko, USSR |
| 1968 | Christopher Finnegan, Great Britain |
| 1972 | Vyacheslav Lemechev, USSR |
| 1976 | Michael Spinks, United States |
| 1980 | Jose Gomez, Cuba |
| 1984 | Shin Joon Sup, S Korea |
| 1988 | Henry Maske, E Germany |
| 1992 | Ariel Hernandez, Cuba |
| 1996 | Ariel Hernandez, Cuba |
| 2000 | Jorge Gutierrez, Cuba |
| 2004 | Gaydarbek Gaydarbekov, Russia |
| 2008 | James Degale, Great Britain |

### LIGHT HEAVYWEIGHT (178 LB)

| | |
|---|---|
| 1920 | Edward Eagan, United States |
| 1924 | Harry Mitchell, Great Britain |
| 1928 | Victor Avendano, Argentina |
| 1932 | David Carstens, S Africa |
| 1936 | Roger Michelot, France |
| 1948 | George Hunter, S Africa |
| 1952 | Norvel Lee, United States |
| 1956 | James Boyd, United States |
| 1960 | Cassius Clay, United States |
| 1964 | Cosimo Pinto, Italy |
| 1968 | Dan Poznyak, USSR |
| 1972 | Mate Parlov, Yugoslavia |
| 1976 | Leon Spinks, United States |
| 1980 | Slobodan Kacer, Yugoslavia |

## BOXING *(Cont.)*

### LIGHT HEAVYWEIGHT (178 LB) *(Cont.)*

| | |
|---|---|
| 1984 | Anton Josipovic, Yugoslavia |
| 1988 | Andrew Maynard, United States |
| 1992 | Torsten May, Germany |
| 1996 | Vassili Jirov, Kazakhstan |
| 2000 | Alexander Lebziak, Russia |
| 2004 | Andre Ward, United States |
| 2008 | Zhang Xiaoping, China |

### HEAVYWEIGHT (OVER 201 LB)

| | |
|---|---|
| 1904 | Samuel Berger, United States |
| 1908 | Albert Oldham, Great Britain |
| 1920 | Ronald Rawson, Great Britain |
| 1924 | Otto von Porat, Norway |
| 1928 | Arturo Rodriguez Jurado, Argentina |
| 1932 | Santiago Lovell, Argentina |
| 1936 | Herbert Runge, Germany |
| 1948 | Rafael Inglesias, Argentina |
| 1952 | H. Edward Sanders, United States |
| 1956 | T. Peter Rademacher, United States |
| 1960 | Franco De Piccoli, Italy |
| 1964 | Joe Frazier, United States |
| 1968 | George Foreman, United States |
| 1972 | Teofilo Stevenson, Cuba |
| 1976 | Teofilo Stevenson, Cuba |

| | |
|---|---|
| 1980 | Teofilo Stevenson, Cuba |
| 1984 | Henry Tillman, United States |
| 1988 | Ray Mercer, United States |
| 1992 | Félix Sávon, Cuba |
| 1996 | Félix Sávon, Cuba |
| 2000 | Félix Sávon, Cuba |
| 2004 | Odlanier Fonte, Cuba |
| 2008 | Rakhim Chakhiev, Russia |

### SUPERHEAVYWEIGHT (UNLIMITED)

| | |
|---|---|
| 1984 | Tyrell Biggs, United States |
| 1988 | Lennox Lewis, Canada |
| 1992 | Roberto Balado, Cuba |
| 1996 | Vladimir Klitschko, Ukraine |
| 2000 | Audley Harrison, Great Britain |
| 2004 | Alexander Povetkin, Russia |
| 2008 | Roberto Cammarelle, Italy |

*Until 1984 the heavyweight division was unlimited. With the addition of the super heavyweight division, a limit of 201 pounds was imposed.

## SWIMMING— Men

### 50-METER FREESTYLE

| | |
|---|---|
| 1904 | Zoltan Halmay, Hungary (50 yds) 28.0 |
| 1988 | Matt Biondi, United States 22.14 WR |
| 1992 | Aleksandr Popov, Unified Team 22.30 |
| 1996 | Aleksandr Popov, Russia 22.13 |
| 2000 | Anthony Ervin, United States 21.98 |
| | Gary Hall Jr, United States 21.98 |
| 2004 | Gary Hall Jr, United States 21.93 |
| 2008 | Cesar Cielo Filho, Brazil 21.30 OR |

### 100-METER FREESTLYE

| | |
|---|---|
| 1896 | Alfred Hajos, Hungary 1:22.2 OR |
| 1904 | Zoltan Halmay, Hungary (100 yds) 1:02.8 |
| 1906 | Charles Daniels, United States 1:13.4 |
| 1908 | Charles Daniels, United States 1:05.6 WR |
| 1912 | Duke Kahanamoku, United States 1:03.4 |
| 1920 | Duke Kahanamoku, United States 1:00.4 WR |
| 1924 | John Weissmuller, United States 59.0 OR |
| 1928 | John Weissmuller, United States 58.6 OR |
| 1932 | Yasuji Miyazaki, Japan 58.2 |
| 1936 | Ferenc Csik, Hungary 57.6 |
| 1948 | Wally Ris, United States 57.3 OR |
| 1952 | Clarke Scholes, United States 57.4 |
| 1956 | Jon Henricks, Australia 55.4 OR |
| 1960 | John Devitt, Australia 55.2 OR |
| 1964 | Don Schollander, United States 53.4 OR |
| 1968 | Mike Wenden, Australia 52.2 WR |
| 1972 | Mark Spitz, United States 51.22 WR |
| 1976 | Jim Montgomery, United States 49.99 WR |
| 1980 | Jörg Woithe, E Germany 50.40 |
| 1984 | Rowdy Gaines, United States 49.80 OR |
| 1988 | Matt Biondi, United States 48.63 OR |
| 1992 | Aleksandr Popov, Unified Team 49.02 |
| 1996 | Aleksandr Popov, Russia 48.74 |
| 2000 | P. van den Hoogenband, Neth 48.30 |
| 2004 | P. van den Hoogenband, Neth 48.17 |
| 2008 | Alain Bernard, France 47.21 |

### 200-METER FREESTYLE

| | |
|---|---|
| 1900 | Frederick Lane, Australia 2:25.2 OR |
| 1904 | Charles Daniels, United States 2:44.2 |
| 1968 | Michael Wenden, Australia 1:55.2 OR |
| 1972 | Mark Spitz, United States 1:52.78 WR |

### 200-METER FREESTLYE *(CONT.)*

| | |
|---|---|
| 1976 | Bruce Furniss, United States 1:50.29 WR |
| 1980 | Sergei Kopliakov, USSR 1:49.81 OR |
| 1984 | Michael Gross, W Germany 1:47.44 WR |
| 1988 | Duncan Armstrong, Australia 1:47.25 WR |
| 1992 | Evgueni Sadovyi, Unified Team 1:46.70 OR |
| 1996 | Danyon Loader, New Zealand 1:47.63 |
| 2000 | Pieter van den Hoogenband, Neth 1:45.35 EWR |
| 2004 | Ian Thorpe, Australia 1:44.71 OR |
| 2008 | Michael Phelps, United States 1:42.96 WR |

### 400-METER FREESTYLE

| | |
|---|---|
| 1896 | Paul Neumann, Austria (500 yds) 8:12.6 |
| 1904 | Charles Daniels, U.S. (440 yds) 6:16.2 |
| 1906 | Otto Scheff, Austria (440 yds) 6:23.8 |
| 1908 | Henry Taylor, Great Britain 5:36.8 |
| 1912 | George Hodgson, Canada 5:24.4 |
| 1920 | Norman Ross, United States 5:26.8 |
| 1924 | John Weissmuller, United States 5:04.2 OR |
| 1928 | Albert Zorilla, Argentina 5:01.6 OR |
| 1932 | Buster Crabbe, United States 4:48.4 OR |
| 1936 | Jack Medica, United States 4:44.5 OR |
| 1948 | William Smith, United States 4:41.0 OR |
| 1952 | Jean Boiteux, France 4:30.7 OR |
| 1956 | Murray Rose, Australia 4:27.3 OR |
| 1960 | Murray Rose, Australia 4:18.3 OR |
| 1964 | Don Schollander, United States 4:12.2 WR |
| 1968 | Mike Burton, United States 4:09.0 OR |
| 1972 | Brad Cooper, Australia 4:00.27 OR |
| 1976 | Brian Goodell, United States 3:51.93 WR |
| 1980 | Vladimir Salnikov, USSR 3:51.31 OR |
| 1984 | George DiCarlo, United States 3:51.23 OR |
| 1988 | Uwe Dassler, E Germany 3:46.95 WR |
| 1992 | Evgueni Sadovyi, Unified Team 3:45.00 WR |
| 1996 | Danyon Loader, New Zealand 3:47.97 |
| 2000 | Ian Thorpe, Australia 3:40.59 WR |
| 2004 | Ian Thorpe, Australia 3:43.10 |
| 2008 | Park Taehwan, South Korea 3:41.86 |

### 1,500-METER FREESTYLE

| | |
|---|---|
| 1908 | Henry Taylor, Great Britain 22:48.4 WR |
| 1912 | George Hodgson, Canada 22:00.0 WR |
| 1920 | Norman Ross, United States 22:23.2 |

## SWIMMING— Men *(Cont.)*

### 1,500-METER FREESTLYE *(CONT.)*

| | | |
|---|---|---|
| 1924 | Andrew Charlton, Australia | 20:06.6 WR |
| 1928 | Arne Borg, Sweden | 19:51.8 WR |
| 1932 | Kusuo Kitamura, Japan | 19:12.4 OR |
| 1936 | Noboru Terada, Japan | 19:13.7 |
| 1948 | James McLane, United States | 19:18.5 |
| 1952 | Ford Konno, United States | 18:30.3 OR |
| 1956 | Murray Rose, Australia | 17:58.9 |
| 1960 | John Konrads, Australia | 17:19.6 OR |
| 1964 | Robert Windle, Australia | 17:01.7 OR |
| 1968 | Mike Burton, United States | 16:38.9 OR |
| 1972 | Mike Burton, United States | 15:52.58 OR |
| 1976 | Brian Goodell, United States | 15:02.40 WR |
| 1980 | Vladimir Salnikov, USSR | 14:58.27 WR |
| 1984 | Michael O'Brien, United States | 15:05.20 |
| 1988 | Vladimir Salnikov, USSR | 15:00.40 |
| 1992 | Kieren Perkins, Australia | 14:43.48 WR |
| 1996 | Kieren Perkins, Australia | 14:56.40 |
| 2000 | Grant Hackett, Australia | 14:48.33 |
| 2004 | Grant Hackett, Australia | 14:43.40 OR |
| 2008 | Ousama Mellouli, Tunisia | 14:40.84 |

### 100-METER BACKSTROKE

| | | |
|---|---|---|
| 1904 | Walter Brack, Germany (100 yds) | 1:16.8 |
| 1908 | Arno Bieberstein, Germany | 1:24.6 WR |
| 1912 | Harry Hebner, United States | 1:21.2 |
| 1920 | Warren Kealoha, United States | 1:15.2 |
| 1924 | Warren Kealoha, United States | 1:13.2 OR |
| 1928 | George Kojac, United States | 1:08.2 WR |
| 1932 | Masaji Kiyokawa, Japan | 1:08.6 |
| 1936 | Adolph Kiefer, United States | 1:05.9 OR |
| 1948 | Allen Stack, United States | 1:06.4 |
| 1952 | Yoshi Oyakawa, United States | 1:05.4 OR |
| 1956 | David Thiele, Australia | 1:02.2 OR |
| 1960 | David Thiele, Australia | 1:01.9 OR |
| 1968 | Roland Matthes, E Germany | 58.7 OR |
| 1972 | Roland Matthes, E Germany | 56.58 OR |
| 1976 | John Naber, United States | 55.49 WR |
| 1980 | Bengt Baron, Sweden | 56.33 |
| 1984 | Rick Carey, United States | 55.79 |
| 1988 | Daichi Suzuki, Japan | 55.05 |
| 1992 | Mark Tewksbury, Canada | 53.98 WR |
| 1996 | Jeff Rouse, United States | 54.10 |
| 2000 | Lenny Krayzelburg, United States | 53.72 OR |
| 2004 | Aaron Peirsol, United States | 54.06 |
| 2008 | Aaron Peirsol, United States | 52.54 WR |

### 200-METER BACKSTROKE

| | | |
|---|---|---|
| 1900 | Ernst Hoppenberg, Germany | 2:47.0 |
| 1964 | Jed Graef, United States | 2:10.3 WR |
| 1968 | Roland Matthes, E Germany | 2:09.6 OR |
| 1972 | Roland Matthes, E Germany | 2:02.82 EWR |
| 1976 | John Naber, United States | 1:59.19 WR |
| 1980 | Sandor Wladar, Hungary | 2:01.93 |
| 1984 | Rick Carey, United States | 2:00.23 |
| 1988 | Igor Polianski, USSR | 1:59.37 |
| 1992 | Martin Lopez-Zubero, Spain | 1:58.47 OR |
| 1996 | Brad Bridgewater, United States | 1:58.54 |
| 2000 | Lenny Krayzelburg, United States | 1:56.76 OR |
| 2004 | Aaron Peirsol, United States | 1:54.95 OR |
| 2008 | Ryan Lochte, United States | 1:53.94 WR |

### 100-METER BREASTSTROKE

| | | |
|---|---|---|
| 1968 | Don McKenzie, United States | 1:07.7 OR |
| 1972 | Nobutaka Taguchi, Japan | 1:04.94 WR |
| 1976 | John Hencken, United States | 1:03.11 WR |
| 1980 | Duncan Goodhew, Great Britain | 1:03.44 |
| 1984 | Steve Lundquist, United States | 1:01.65 WR |
| 1988 | Adrian Moorhouse, Great Britain | 1:02.04 |

### 100-METER BREASTSTROKE *(CONT.)*

| | | |
|---|---|---|
| 1992 | Nelson Diebel, United States | 1:01.50 OR |
| 1996 | Fred DeBurghgraeve, Belgium | 1:00.65 |
| 2000 | Domenico Fioravanti, Italy | 1:00.46 OR |
| 2004 | Kosuke Kitajima, Japan | 1:00.08 |
| 2008 | Kosuke Kitajima, Japan | 58.91 WR |

### 200-METER BREASTSTROKE

| | | |
|---|---|---|
| 1908 | Frederick Holman, Great Britain | 3:09.2 WR |
| 1912 | Walter Bathe, Germany | 3:01.8 WR |
| 1920 | Haken Malmroth, Sweden | 3:04.4 |
| 1924 | Robert Skelton, United States | 2:56.6 |
| 1928 | Yoshiyuki Tsuruta, Japan | 2:48.8 OR |
| 1932 | Yoshiyuki Tsuruta, Japan | 2:45.4 |
| 1936 | Tetsuo Hamuro, Japan | 2:41.5 OR |
| 1948 | Joseph Verdeur, United States | 2:39.3 OR |
| 1952 | John Davies, Australia | 2:34.4 OR |
| 1956 | Masaru Furukawa, Japan | 2:34.7 OR |
| 1960 | William Mulliken, United States | 2:37.4 |
| 1964 | Ian O'Brien, Australia | 2:27.8 WR |
| 1968 | Felipe Munoz, Mexico | 2:28.7 |
| 1972 | John Hencken, United States | 2:21.55 WR |
| 1976 | David Wilkie, Great Britain | 2:15.11 WR |
| 1980 | Robertas Zhulpa, USSR | 2:15.85 |
| 1984 | Victor Davis, Canada | 2:13.34 WR |
| 1988 | Jozsef Szabo, Hungary | 2:13.52 |
| 1992 | Mike Barrowman, United States | 2:10.16 WR |
| 1996 | Norbert Rózsa, Hungary | 2:12.57 |
| 2000 | Domenico Fioravanti, Italy | 2:10.87 |
| 2004 | Kosuke Kitajima, Japan | 2:09.44 OR |
| 2008 | Kosuke Kitajima, Japan | 2:07.64 OR |

### 100-METER BUTTERFLY

| | | |
|---|---|---|
| 1968 | Doug Russell, United States | 55.9 OR |
| 1972 | Mark Spitz, United States | 54.27 WR |
| 1976 | Matt Vogel, United States | 54.35 |
| 1980 | Pär Arvidsson, Sweden | 54.92 |
| 1984 | Michael Gross, W Germany | 53.08 WR |
| 1988 | Anthony Nesty, Suriname | 53.00 OR |
| 1992 | Pablo Morales, United States | 53.32 |
| 1996 | Denis Pankratov, Russia | 52.27 WR |
| 2000 | Lars Froelander, Sweden | 52.00 |
| 2004 | Michael Phelps, United States | 51.25 OR |
| 2008 | Michael Phelps, United States | 50.58 OR |

### 200-METER BUTTERFLY

| | | |
|---|---|---|
| 1956 | William Yorzyk, United States | 2:19.3 OR |
| 1960 | Michael Troy, United States | 2:12.8 WR |
| 1964 | Kevin Berry, Australia | 2:06.6 WR |
| 1968 | Carl Robie, United States | 2:08.7 |
| 1972 | Mark Spitz, United States | 2:00.70 WR |
| 1976 | Mike Bruner, United States | 1:59.23 WR |
| 1980 | Sergei Fesenko, USSR | 1:59.76 |
| 1984 | Jon Sieben, Australia | 1:57.04 WR |
| 1988 | Michael Gross, W Germany | 1:56.94 OR |
| 1992 | Melvin Stewart, United States | 1:56.26 OR |
| 1996 | Denis Pankratov, Russia | 1:56.51 |
| 2000 | Tom Malchow, United States | 1:55.35 OR |
| 2004 | Michael Phelps, United States | 1:54.04 OR |
| 2008 | Michael Phelps, United States | 1:52.03 WR |

### 200-METER INDIVIDUAL MEDLEY

| | | |
|---|---|---|
| 1968 | Charles Hickcox, United States | 2:12.0 OR |
| 1972 | Gunnar Larsson, Sweden | 2:07.17 WR |
| 1984 | Alex Baumann, Canada | 2:01.42 WR |
| 1988 | Tamas Darnyi, Hungary | 2:00.17 WR |
| 1992 | Tamas Darnyi, Hungary | 2:00.76 |
| 1996 | Attila Czene, Hungary | 1:59.91 OR |
| 2000 | Massimiliano Rosolino, Italy | 1:58.98 OR |
| 2004 | Michael Phelps, United States | 1:57.14 OR |

Note: OR=Olympic Record. WR=World Record. EOR=Equals Olympic Record. EWR=Equals World Record. WB=World Best.

## SWIMMING — Men *(Cont.)*

### 200-METER INDIVIDUAL MEDLEY *(Cont.)*

| | | |
|---|---|---|
| 2008 | Michael Phelps, United States | 1:54.23 WR |

### 400-METER INDIVIDUAL MEDLEY

| | | |
|---|---|---|
| 1964 | Richard Roth, United States | 4:45.4 WR |
| 1968 | Charles Hickcox, United States | 4:48.4 |
| 1972 | Gunnar Larsson, Sweden | 4:31.98 OR |
| 1976 | Rod Strachan, United States | 4:23.68 WR |
| 1980 | Aleksandr Sidorenko, USSR | 4:22.89 OR |
| 1984 | Alex Baumann, Canada | 4:17.41 WR |
| 1988 | Tamas Darnyi, Hungary | 4:14.75 WR |
| 1992 | Tamas Darnyi, Hungary | 4:14.23 OR |
| 1996 | Tom Dolan United States | 4:14.90 |
| 2000 | Tom Dolan, United States | 4:11.76 WR |
| 2004 | Michael Phelps, United States | 4:08.26 WR |
| 2008 | Michael Phelps, United States | 4:03.84 WR |

### 4 X 100-METER MEDLEY RELAY

| | | |
|---|---|---|
| 1960 | United States | 4:05.4 WR |
| 1964 | United States | 3:58.4 WR |
| 1968 | United States | 3:54.9 WR |
| 1972 | United States | 3:48.16 WR |
| 1976 | United States | 3:42.22 WR |
| 1980 | Australia | 3:45.70 |
| 1984 | United States | 3:39.30 WR |
| 1988 | United States | 3:36.93 WR |
| 1992 | United States | 3:36.93 EWR |
| 1996 | United States | 3:34.84 WR |
| 2000 | United States | 3:33.73 WR |
| 2004 | United States | 3:30.68 WR |
| 2008 | United States | 3:29.34 WR |

### 4 X 100-METER FREESTYLE RELAY

| | | |
|---|---|---|
| 1964 | United States | 3:32.2 WR |
| 1968 | United States | 3:31.7 WR |
| 1972 | United States | 3:26.42 WR |
| 1984 | United States | 3:19.03 WR |

### 4 X 100-METER FREESTYLE RELAY *(Cont.)*

| | | |
|---|---|---|
| 1988 | United States | 3:16.53 WR |
| 1992 | United States | 3:16.74 |
| 1996 | United States | 3:15.41 OR |
| 2000 | Australia | 3:13.67 WR |
| 2004 | S Africa | 3:13.17 WR |
| 2008 | United States | 3:08.24 WR |

### 4 X 200-METER FREESTYLE RELAY

| | | |
|---|---|---|
| 1906 | Hungary (1,000 m) | 16:52.4 |
| 1908 | Great Britain | 10:55.6 |
| 1912 | Australia/New Zealand | 10:11.6 WR |
| 1920 | United States | 10:04.4 WR |
| 1924 | United States | 9:53.4 WR |
| 1928 | United States | 9:36.2 WR |
| 1932 | Japan | 8:58.4 WR |
| 1936 | Japan | 8:51.5 WR |
| 1948 | United States | 8:46.0 WR |
| 1952 | United States | 8:31.1 OR |
| 1956 | Australia | 8:23.6 WR |
| 1960 | United States | 8:10.2 WR |
| 1964 | United States | 7:52.1 WR |
| 1968 | United States | 7:52.33 |
| 1972 | United States | 7:35.78 WR |
| 1976 | United States | 7:23.22 WR |
| 1980 | USSR | 7:23.50 |
| 1984 | United States | 7:15.69 WR |
| 1988 | United States | 7:12.51 WR |
| 1992 | Unified Team | 7:11.95 WR |
| 1996 | United States | 7:14.84 |
| 2000 | Australia | 7:07.05 WR |
| 2004 | United States | 7:07.33 |
| 2008 | United States | 6:58.56 WR |

## SWIMMING — Women

### 50-METER FREESTYLE

| | | |
|---|---|---|
| 1988 | Kristin Otto, E Germany | 25.49 OR |
| 1992 | Yang Wenyi, China | 24.79 WR |
| 1996 | Amy Van Dyken, United States | 24.87 |
| 2000 | Inge de Bruijn, Netherlands | 24.32 WR |
| 2004 | Inge de Bruijn, Netherlands | 24.58 |
| 2008 | Britta Steffen, Germany | 24.06 OR |

### 100-METER FREESTYLE

| | | |
|---|---|---|
| 1912 | Fanny Durack, Australia | 1:22.2 |
| 1920 | Ethelda Bleibtrey, United States | 1:13.6 WR |
| 1924 | Ethel Lackie, United States | 1:12.4 |
| 1928 | Albina Osipowich, United States | 1:11.0 OR |
| 1932 | Helene Madison, United States | 1:06.8 OR |
| 1936 | Hendrika Mastenbroek, Neth | 1:05.9 OR |
| 1948 | Greta Andersen, Denmark | 1:06.3 |
| 1952 | Katalin Szöke, Hungary | 1:06.8 |
| 1956 | Dawn Fraser, Australia | 1:02.0 WR |
| 1960 | Dawn Fraser, Australia | 1:01.2 OR |
| 1964 | Dawn Fraser, Australia | 59.5 OR |
| 1968 | Jan Henne, United States | 1:00.0 |
| 1972 | Sandra Neilson, United States | 58.59 OR |
| 1976 | Kornelia Ender, E Germany | 55.65 WR |
| 1980 | Barbara Krause, E Germany | 54.79 WR |
| 1984 | Carrie Steinseifer, United States | 55.92 |
| | Nancy Hogshead, United States | 55.92 |
| 1988 | Kristin Otto, E Germany | 54.93 |
| 1992 | Zhuang Yong, China | 54.64 OR |

### 100-METER FREESTYLE *(CONT.)*

| | | |
|---|---|---|
| 1996 | Le Jingyi, China | 54.50 OR |
| 2000 | Inge de Bruijn, Netherlands | 53.83 OR |
| 2004 | Jodie Henry, Australia | 53.84 |
| 2008 | Britta Steffen, Germany | 53.12 OR |

### 200-METER FREESTYLE

| | | |
|---|---|---|
| 1968 | Debbie Meyer, United States | 2:10.5 OR |
| 1972 | Shane Gould, Australia | 2:03.56 WR |
| 1976 | Kornelia Ender, E Germany | 1:59.26 WR |
| 1980 | Barbara Krause, E Germany | 1:58.33 OR |
| 1984 | Mary Wayte, United States | 1:59.23 |
| 1988 | Heike Friedrich, E Germany | 1:57.65 OR |
| 1992 | Nicole Haislett, United States | 1:57.90 |
| 1996 | Claudia Poll, Costa Rica | 1:58.16 |
| 2000 | Susie O'Neill, Australia | 1:58.24 |
| 2004 | Camelia Potec, Romania | 1:58.03 |
| 2008 | Frederica Pellegrini, Italy | 1:54.82 WR |

### 400-METER FREESTYLE

| | | |
|---|---|---|
| 1924 | Martha Norelius, United States | 6:02.2 OR |
| 1928 | Martha Norelius, United States | 5:42.8 WR |
| 1932 | Helene Madison, United States | 5:28.5 WR |
| 1936 | Hendrika Mastenbroek, Neth | 5:26.4 OR |
| 1948 | Ann Curtis, United States | 5:17.8 OR |
| 1952 | Valeria Gyenge, Hungary | 5:12.1 OR |
| 1956 | Lorraine Crapp, Australia | 4:54.6 OR |
| 1960 | Chris von Saltza, United States | 4:50.6 OR |
| 1964 | Virginia Duenkel, United States | 4:43.3 OR |

Note: OR=Olympic Record. WR=World Record. EOR=Equals Olympic Record. EWR=Equals World Record. WB=World Best.

## SWIMMING — Women *(Cont.)*

### 400-METER FREESTYLE *(CONT.)*

| | | |
|---|---|---|
| 1968 | Debbie Meyer, United States | 4:31.8 OR |
| 1972 | Shane Gould, Australia | 4:19.44 WR |
| 1976 | Petra Thümer, E Germany | 4:09.89 WR |
| 1980 | Ines Diers, E Germany | 4:08.76 WR |
| 1984 | Tiffany Cohen, United States | 4:07.10 OR |
| 1988 | Janet Evans, United States | 4:03.85 WR |
| 1992 | Dagmar Hase, Germany | 4:07.18 |
| 1996 | Michelle Smith, Ireland | 4:07.25 |
| 2000 | Brooke Bennett, United States | 4:05.80 |
| 2004 | Laure Manaudou, France | 4:05.34 |
| 2008 | Rebecca Adlington, Great Britain | 4:03.22 |

### 800-METER FREESTYLE

| | | |
|---|---|---|
| 1968 | Debbie Meyer, United States | 9:24.0 OR |
| 1972 | Keena Rothhammer, United States | 8:53.68 WR |
| 1976 | Petra Thümer, E Germany | 8:37.14 WR |
| 1980 | Michelle Ford, Australia | 8:28.90 OR |
| 1984 | Tiffany Cohen, United States | 8:24.95 OR |
| 1988 | Janet Evans, United States | 8:20.20 OR |
| 1992 | Janet Evans, United States | 8:25.52 |
| 1996 | Brooke Bennett, United States | 8:27.89 |
| 2000 | Brooke Bennett, United States | 8:19.67 OR |
| 2004 | Ai Shibata, Japan | 8:24.54 |
| 2008 | Rebecca Adlington, Great Britain | 8:14.10 WR |

### 100-METER BACKSTROKE

| | | |
|---|---|---|
| 1924 | Sybil Bauer, United States | 1:23.2 OR |
| 1928 | Marie Braun, Netherlands | 1:22.0 |
| 1932 | Eleanor Holm, United States | 1:19.4 |
| 1936 | Dina Senff, Netherlands | 1:18.9 |
| 1948 | Karen Harup, Denmark | 1:14.4 OR |
| 1952 | Joan Harrison, South Africa | 1:14.3 |
| 1956 | Judy Grinham, Great Britain | 1:12.9 OR |
| 1960 | Lynn Burke, United States | 1:09.3 OR |
| 1964 | Cathy Ferguson, United States | 1:07.7 WR |
| 1968 | Kaye Hall, United States | 1:06.2 WR |
| 1972 | Melissa Belote, United States | 1:05.78 OR |
| 1976 | Ulrike Richter, E Germany | 1:01.83 OR |
| 1980 | Rica Reinisch, E Germany | 1:00.86 WR |
| 1984 | Theresa Andrews, United States | 1:02.55 |
| 1988 | Kristin Otto, E Germany | 1:00.89 |
| 1992 | Krisztina Egerszegi, Hungary | 1:00.68 OR |
| 1996 | Beth Botsford, United States | 1:01.19 |
| 2000 | Diana Iuliana Mocanu, Romania | 1:00.21 OR |
| 2004 | Natalie Coughlin, United States | 1:00.37 |
| 2008 | Natalie Coughlin, United States | 58.96 |

### 200-METER BACKSTROKE

| | | |
|---|---|---|
| 1968 | Pokey Watson, United States | 2:24.8 OR |
| 1972 | Melissa Belote, United States | 2:19.19 WR |
| 1976 | Ulrike Richter, E Germany | 2:13.43 OR |
| 1980 | Rica Reinisch, E Germany | 2:11.77 WR |
| 1984 | Jolanda De Rover, Netherlands | 2:12.38 |
| 1988 | Krisztina Egerszegi, Hungary | 2:09.29 OR |
| 1992 | Krisztina Egerszegi, Hungary | 2:07.06 OR |
| 1996 | Krisztina Egerszegi, Hungary | 2:07.83 |
| 2000 | Diana Iuliana Mocanu, Romania | 2:08.16 |
| 2004 | Kirsty Coventry, Zimbabwe | 2:09.19 |
| 2008 | Kirsty Coventry, Zimbabwe | 2:05.24 WR |

### 100-METER BREASTSTROKE

| | | |
|---|---|---|
| 1968 | Djurdjica Bjedov, Yugoslavia | 1:15.8 OR |
| 1972 | Catherine Carr, United States | 1:13.58 WR |
| 1976 | Hannelore Anke, E Germany | 1:11.16 |
| 1980 | Ute Geweniger, E Germany | 1:10.22 |
| 1984 | Petra Van Staveren, Netherlands | 1:09.88 OR |
| 1988 | Tania Dangalakova, Bulgaria | 1:07.95 OR |
| 1992 | Elena Roudkovskaia, Unified Team | 1:08.00 |
| 1996 | Penelope Heyns, S Africa | 1:07.73 |
| 2000 | Megan Quann, United States | 1:07.05 |

### 100-METER BREASTSTROKE *(CONT.)*

| | | |
|---|---|---|
| 2004 | Xue Juan Luo, China | 1:06.64 |
| 2008 | Liesel Jones, Australia | 1:05.17 WR |

### 200-METER BREASTSTROKE

| | | |
|---|---|---|
| 1924 | Lucy Morton, Great Britain | 3:33.2 OR |
| 1928 | Hilde Schrader, Germany | 3:12.6 |
| 1932 | Clare Dennis, Australia | 3:06.3 OR |
| 1936 | Hideko Maehata, Japan | 3:03.6 |
| 1948 | Petronella Van Vliet, Netherlands | 2:57.2 |
| 1952 | Eva Szekely, Hungary | 2:51.7 OR |
| 1956 | Ursula Happe, W Germany | 2:53.1 OR |
| 1960 | Anita Lonsbrough, Great Britain | 2:49.5 WR |
| 1964 | Galina Prozumenshikova, USSR | 2:46.4 OR |
| 1968 | Sharon Wichman, United States | 2:44.4 OR |
| 1972 | Beverly Whitfield, Australia | 2:41.71 OR |
| 1976 | Marina Koshevaia, USSR | 2:33.35 WR |
| 1980 | Lina Kaciusyte, USSR | 2:29.54 OR |
| 1984 | Anne Ottenbrite, Canada | 2:30.38 |
| 1988 | Silke Hoerner, E Germany | 2:26.71 WR |
| 1992 | Kyoko Iwasaki, Japan | 2:26.65 OR |
| 1996 | Penelope Heyns, S Africa | 2:25.41 OR |
| 2000 | Agnes Kovacs, Hungary | 2:24.35 OR |
| 2004 | Amanda Beard, United States | 2:23.37 OR |
| 2008 | Rebecca Soni, United States | 2:20.22 WR |

### 100-METER BUTTERFLY

| | | |
|---|---|---|
| 1956 | Shelley Mann, United States | 1:11.0 OR |
| 1960 | Carolyn Schuler, United States | 1:09.5 OR |
| 1964 | Sharon Stouder, United States | 1:04.7 WR |
| 1968 | Lynn McClements, Australia | 1:05.5 |
| 1972 | Mayumi Aoki, Japan | 1:03.34 WR |
| 1976 | Kornelia Ender, E Germany | 1:00.13 EWR |
| 1980 | Caren Metschuck, E Germany | 1:00.42 |
| 1984 | Mary T. Meagher, United States | 59.26 |
| 1988 | Kristin Otto, E Germany | 59.00 OR |
| 1992 | Qian Hong, China | 58.62 OR |
| 1996 | Amy Van Dyken, United States | 59.13 |
| 2000 | Inge de Bruijn, Netherlands | 56.61 WR |
| 2004 | Petria Thomas, Australia | 57.72 |
| 2008 | Lisbeth Trickett, Australia | 56.73 |

### 200-METER BUTTERFLY

| | | |
|---|---|---|
| 1968 | Ada Kok, Netherlands | 2:24.7 OR |
| 1972 | Karen Moe, United States | 2:15.57 WR |
| 1976 | Andrea Pollack, E Germany | 2:11.41 OR |
| 1980 | Ines Geissler, E Germany | 2:10.44 OR |
| 1984 | Mary T. Meagher, United States | 2:06.90 OR |
| 1988 | Kathleen Nord, E Germany | 2:09.51 |
| 1992 | Summer Sanders, United States | 2:08.67 |
| 1996 | Susan O'Neill, Australia | 2:07.76 |
| 2000 | Misty Hyman, United States | 2:05.88 OR |
| 2004 | Otylia Jedrzegczak, Poland | 2:06.05 |
| 2008 | Liu Zige, China | 2:04.18 WR |

### 200-METER INDIVIDUAL MEDLEY

| | | |
|---|---|---|
| 1968 | Claudia Kolb, United States | 2:24.7 OR |
| 1972 | Shane Gould, Australia | 2:23.07 WR |
| 1984 | Tracy Caulkins, United States | 2:12.64 OR |
| 1988 | Daniela Hunger, E Germany | 2:12.59 OR |
| 1992 | Lin Li, China | 2:11.65 WR |
| 1996 | Michelle Smith, Ireland | 2:13.93 |
| 2000 | Yana Klochkova, Ukraine | 2:10.68 OR |
| 2004 | Yana Klochkova, Ukraine | 2:11.14 |
| 2008 | Stephanie Rice, Australia | 2:08.45 WR |

### 400-METER INDIVIDUAL MEDLEY

| | | |
|---|---|---|
| 1964 | Donna de Varona, United States | 5:18.7 OR |
| 1968 | Claudia Kolb, United States | 5:08.5 OR |
| 1972 | Gail Neall, Australia | 5:02.97 WR |
| 1976 | Ulrike Tauber, E Germany | 4:42.77 WR |

Note: OR=Olympic Record. WR=World Record. EOR=Equals Olympic Record. EWR=Equals World Record. WB=World Best.

## SWIMMING — Women *(Cont.)*

### 400-METER INDIVIDUAL MEDLEY *(CONT.)*

| | | |
|---|---|---|
| 1980 | Petra Schneider, E Germany | 4:36.29 WR |
| 1984 | Tracy Caulkins, United States | 4:39.24 |
| 1988 | Janet Evans, United States | 4:37.76 |
| 1992 | Krisztina Egerszegi, Hungary | 4:36.54 |
| 1996 | Michelle Smith, Ireland | 4:39.18 |
| 2000 | Yana Klochkova, Ukraine | 4:33.59 WR |
| 2004 | Yana Klochkova, Ukraine | 4:34.83 |
| 2008 | Stephanie Rice, Australia | 4:29.45 WR |

### 4 X 100-METER MEDLEY RELAY

| | | |
|---|---|---|
| 1960 | United States | 4:41.1 WR |
| 1964 | United States | 4:33.9 WR |
| 1968 | United States | 4:28.3 OR |
| 1972 | United States | 4:20.75 WR |
| 1976 | E Germany | 4:07.95 WR |
| 1980 | E Germany | 4:06.67 WR |
| 1984 | United States | 4:08.34 |
| 1988 | E Germany | 4:03.74 OR |
| 1992 | United States | 4:02.54 WR |
| 1996 | United States | 4:02.88 |
| 2000 | United States | 3:58:30 WR |
| 2004 | Australia | 3:57.32 WR |
| 2008 | Australia | 3:52.69 WR |

### 4 X 100-METER FREESTYLE RELAY

| | | |
|---|---|---|
| 1912 | Great Britain | 5:52.8 WR |
| 1920 | United States | 5:11.6 WR |

### 4 X 100-METER FREESTYLE RELAY *(CONT.)*

| | | |
|---|---|---|
| 1924 | United States | 4:58.8 WR |
| 1928 | United States | 4:47.6 WR |
| 1932 | United States | 4:38.0 WR |
| 1936 | Netherlands | 4:36.0 OR |
| 1948 | United States | 4:29.2 OR |
| 1952 | Hungary | 4:24.4 WR |
| 1956 | Australia | 4:17.1 WR |
| 1960 | United States | 4:08.9 WR |
| 1964 | United States | 4:03.8 WR |
| 1968 | United States | 4:02.5 OR |
| 1972 | United States | 3:55.19 WR |
| 1976 | United States | 3:44.82 WR |
| 1980 | E Germany | 3:42.71 WR |
| 1984 | United States | 3:43.43 |
| 1988 | E Germany | 3:40.63 OR |
| 1992 | United States | 3:39.46 WR |
| 1996 | United States | 3:39.29 OR |
| 2000 | United States | 3:36.61 WR |
| 2004 | Australia | 3:35.94 WR |
| 2008 | Netherlands | 3:33.76 OR |

### 4 X 200-METER FREESTYLE RELAY

| | | |
|---|---|---|
| 1996 | United States | 7:59.87 |
| 2000 | United States | 7:57.80 OR |
| 2004 | United States | 7:53.42 WR |
| 2008 | Australia | 7:44.31 WR |

## DIVING — Men

| SPRINGBOARD | | Pts |
|---|---|---|
| 1908 | Albert Zürner, Germany | 85.5 |
| 1912 | Paul Günther, Germany | 79.23 |
| 1920 | Louis Kuehn, United States | 675.40 |
| 1924 | Albert White, United States | 97.46 |
| 1928 | Pete DesJardins, United States | 185.04 |
| 1932 | Michael Galitzen, United States | 161.38 |
| 1936 | Richard Degener, United States | 163.57 |
| 1948 | Bruce Harlan, United States | 163.64 |
| 1952 | David Browning, United States | 205.29 |
| 1956 | Robert Clotworthy, United States | 159.56 |
| 1960 | Gary Tobian, United States | 170.00 |
| 1964 | Kenneth Sitzberger, United States | 159.90 |
| 1968 | Bernie Wrightson, United States | 170.15 |
| 1972 | Vladimir Vasin, USSR | 594.09 |
| 1976 | Phil Boggs, United States | 619.05 |
| 1980 | Aleksandr Portnov, USSR | 905.02 |
| 1984 | Greg Louganis, United States | 754.41 |
| 1988 | Greg Louganis, United States | 730.80 |
| 1992 | Mark Lenzi, United States | 676.53 |
| 1996 | Xiong Ni, China | 701.46 |
| 2000 | Xiong Ni, China | 708.72 |
| 2004 | Bo Peng, China | 787.38 |
| 2008 | He Chong, China | 572.90 |

| PLATFORM | | Pts |
|---|---|---|
| 1904 | George Sheldon, United States | 12.66 |
| 1906 | Gottlob Walz, Germany | 156.0 |
| 1908 | Hjalmar Johansson, Sweden | 83.75 |
| 1912 | Erik Adlerz, Sweden | 73.94 |
| 1920 | Clarence Pinkston, United States | 100.67 |
| 1924 | Albert White, United States | 97.46 |
| 1928 | Pete DesJardins, United States | 98.74 |
| 1932 | Harold Smith, United States | 124.80 |
| 1936 | Marshall Wayne, United States | 113.58 |
| 1948 | Sammy Lee, United States | 130.05 |
| 1952 | Sammy Lee, United States | 156.28 |
| 1956 | Joaquin Capilla, Mexico | 152.44 |
| 1960 | Robert Webster, United States | 165.56 |
| 1964 | Robert Webster, United States | 148.58 |
| 1968 | Klaus Dibiasi, Italy | 164.18 |
| 1972 | Klaus Dibiasi, Italy | 504.12 |
| 1976 | Klaus Dibiasi, Italy | 600.51 |
| 1980 | Falk Hoffmann, E Germany | 835.65 |
| 1984 | Greg Louganis, United States | 710.91 |
| 1988 | Greg Louganis, United States | 638.61 |
| 1992 | Sun Shuwei, China | 677.31 |
| 1996 | Dmitri Sautin, Russia | 692.34 |
| 2000 | Tian Liang, China | 724.53 |
| 2004 | Jia Hu, China | 748.08 |
| 2008 | Matthew Mitcham, Australia | 537.95 |

## DIVING — Women

| | SPRINGBOARD | Pts |
|---|---|---|
| 1920 | Aileen Riggin, United States | 539.90 |
| 1924 | Elizabeth Becker, United States | 474.50 |
| 1928 | Helen Meany, United States | 78.62 |
| 1932 | Georgia Coleman, United States | 87.52 |
| 1936 | Marjorie Gestring, United States | 89.27 |
| 1948 | Victoria Draves, United States | 108.74 |
| 1952 | Patricia McCormick, United States | 147.30 |
| 1956 | Patricia McCormick, United States | 142.36 |
| 1960 | Ingrid Krämer, E Germany | 155.81 |
| 1964 | Ingrid Engel Krämer, E Germany | 145.00 |
| 1968 | Sue Gossick, United States | 150.77 |
| 1972 | Micki King, United States | 450.03 |
| 1976 | Jennifer Chandler, United States | 506.19 |
| 1980 | Irina Kalinina, USSR | 725.91 |
| 1984 | Sylvie Bernier, Canada | 530.70 |
| 1988 | Gao Min, China | 580.23 |
| 1992 | Gao Min, China | 572.40 |
| 1996 | Fu Mingxia, China | 547.68 |
| 2000 | Fu Mingxia, China | 609.42 |
| 2004 | Guo Jingjing, China | 633.15 |
| 2008 | Guo Jingjing, China | 415.35 |

| | PLATFORM | Pts |
|---|---|---|
| 1912 | Greta Johansson, Sweden | 39.90 |
| 1920 | Stefani Fryland-Clausen, Denmark | 34.60 |
| 1924 | Caroline Smith, United States | 33.20 |
| 1928 | Elizabeth B. Pinkston, United States | 31.60 |
| 1932 | Dorothy Poynton, United States | 40.26 |
| 1936 | Dorothy Poynton Hill, United States | 33.93 |
| 1948 | Victoria Draves, United States | 68.87 |
| 1952 | Patricia McCormick, United States | 79.37 |
| 1956 | Patricia McCormick, United States | 84.85 |
| 1960 | Ingrid Krämer, E Germany | 91.28 |
| 1964 | Lesley Bush, United States | 99.80 |
| 1968 | Milena Duchkova, Czechoslovakia | 109.59 |
| 1972 | Ulrika Knape, Sweden | 390.00 |
| 1976 | Elena Vaytsekhovskaya, USSR | 406.59 |
| 1980 | Martina Jäschke, E Germany | 596.25 |
| 1984 | Zhou Jihong, China | 435.51 |
| 1988 | Xu Yanmei, China | 445.20 |
| 1992 | Mingxia Fu, China | 461.43 |
| 1996 | Mingxia Fu, China | 521.58 |
| 2000 | Laura Wilkinson, United States | 543.75 |
| 2004 | Chantelle Newbery, Australia | 590.31 |
| 2008 | Chen Ruoulin, China | 447.70 |

## GYMNASTICS — Men

| | ALL-AROUND | Pts |
|---|---|---|
| 1900 | Gustave Sandras, France | 302 |
| 1904 | Julius Lenhart, Austria | 69.80 |
| 1906 | Pierre Paysse, France | 97 |
| 1908 | Alberto Braglia, Italy | 317.0 |
| 1912 | Alberto Braglia, Italy | 135.0 |
| 1920 | Giorgio Zampori, Italy | 88.35 |
| 1924 | Leon Stukelj, Yugoslavia | 110.340 |
| 1928 | Georges Miez, Switzerland | 247.500 |
| 1932 | Romeo Neri, Italy | 140.625 |
| 1936 | Alfred Schwarzmann, Germany | 113.100 |
| 1948 | Veikko Huhtanen, Finland | 229.70 |
| 1952 | Viktor Chukarin, USSR | 115.70 |
| 1956 | Viktor Chukarin, USSR | 114.25 |
| 1960 | Boris Shakhlin, USSR | 115.95 |
| 1964 | Yukio Endo, Japan | 115.95 |
| 1968 | Sawao Kato, Japan | 115.90 |
| 1972 | Sawao Kato, Japan | 114.65 |
| 1976 | Nikolai Andrianov, USSR | 116.65 |
| 1980 | Aleksandr Dityatin, USSR | 118.65 |
| 1984 | Koji Gushiken, Japan | 118.70 |
| 1988 | Vladimir Artemov, USSR | 119.125 |
| 1992 | Vitaly Scherbo, Unified Team | 59.025 |
| 1996 | Li Xiaoshuang, China | 58.423 |
| 2000 | Alexei Nemov, Russia | 58.474 |
| 2004 | Paul Hamm, United States | 57.823 |
| 2008 | Yang Wei, China | 94.575 |

| | HORIZONTAL BAR | Pts |
|---|---|---|
| 1896 | Hermann Weingärtner, Germany | — |
| 1904 | Anton Heida, United States | 40 |
| 1924 | Leon Stukelj, Yugoslavia | 19.73 |
| 1928 | Georges Miez, Switzerland | 19.17 |
| 1932 | Dallas Bixler, United States | 18.33 |
| 1936 | Aleksanteri Saarvala, Finland | 19.367 |
| 1948 | Josef Stalfer, Switzerland | 19.85 |
| 1952 | Jack Günthard, Switzerland | 19.55 |
| 1956 | Takashi Ono, Japan | 19.60 |

| | HORIZONTAL BAR *(CONT)* | Pts |
|---|---|---|
| 1960 | Takashi Ono, Japan | 19.60 |
| 1964 | Boris Shakhlin, USSR | 19.625 |
| 1968 | Akinori Nakayama, Japan | 19.55 |
| 1972 | Mitsuo Tsukahara, Japan | 19.725 |
| 1976 | Mitsuo Tsukahara, Japan | 19.675 |
| 1980 | Stoyan Deltchev, Bulgaria | 19.825 |
| 1984 | Shinji Morisue, Japan | 20.00 |
| 1988 | Vladimir Artemov, USSR | 19.90 |
| 1992 | Trent Dimas, United States | 9.875 |
| 1996 | Andreas Wecker, Germany | 9.850 |
| 2000 | Alexei Nemov, Russia | 9.787 |
| 2004 | Igor Cassina, Italy | 9.812 |
| 2008 | Zou Kai, China | 16.200 |

| | PARALLEL BARS | Pts |
|---|---|---|
| 1896 | Alfred Flatow, Germany | — |
| 1904 | George Eyser, United States | 44 |
| 1924 | August Güttinger, Switzerland | 21.63 |
| 1928 | Ladislav Vacha, Czechoslovakia | 18.83 |
| 1932 | Romeo Neri, Italy | 18.97 |
| 1936 | Konrad Frey, Germany | 19.067 |
| 1948 | Michael Reusch, Switzerland | 19.75 |
| 1952 | Hans Eugster, Switzerland | 19.65 |
| 1956 | Viktor Chukarin, USSR | 19.20 |
| 1960 | Boris Shakhlin, USSR | 19.40 |
| 1964 | Yukio Endo, Japan | 19.675 |
| 1968 | Akinori Nakayama, Japan | 19.475 |
| 1972 | Sawao Kato, Japan | 19.475 |
| 1976 | Sawao Kato, Japan | 19.675 |
| 1980 | Aleksandr Tkachyov, USSR | 19.775 |
| 1984 | Bart Conner, United States | 19.95 |
| 1988 | Vladimir Artemov, USSR | 19.925 |
| 1992 | Vitaly Scherbo, Unified Team | 9.900 |
| 1996 | Rustan Sharipov, Ukraine | 9.837 |
| 2000 | Li Xiaopeng, China | 9.825 |
| 2004 | Valeri Goncharov, Ukraine | 9.787 |
| 2008 | Li Xiaopeng, China | 16.450 |

## GYMNASTICS — Men *(Cont.)*

| VAULT | | Pts |
|---|---|---|
| 1896 | Karl Schumann, Germany | — |
| 1904 | George Eyser, United States | 36 |
| 1924 | Frank Kriz, United States | 9.98 |
| 1928 | Eugen Mack, Switzerland | 9.58 |
| 1932 | Savino Guglielmetti, Italy | 18.03 |
| 1936 | Alfred Schwarzmann, Germany | 19.20 |
| 1948 | Paavo Aaltonen, Finland | 19.55 |
| 1952 | Viktor Chukarin, USSR | 19.20 |
| 1956 | Helmut Bantz, Germany | 18.85 |
| 1960 | Takashi Ono, Japan | 19.35 |
| 1964 | Haruhiro Yamashita, Japan | 19.60 |
| 1968 | Mikhail Voronin, USSR | 19.00 |
| 1972 | Klaus Köste, E Germany | 18.85 |
| 1976 | Nikolai Andrianov, USSR | 19.45 |
| 1980 | Nikolai Andrianov, USSR | 19.825 |
| 1984 | Lou Yun, China | 19.95 |
| 1988 | Lou Yun, China | 19.875 |
| 1992 | Vitaly Scherbo, Unified Team | 9.856 |
| 1996 | Alexei Nemov, Russia | 9.787 |
| 2000 | Gervasio Deferr, Spain | 9.712 |
| 2004 | Gervasio Deferr, Spain | 9.737 |
| 2008 | Leszek Blanik, Poland | 16.537 |

| POMMEL HORSE | | Pts |
|---|---|---|
| 1896 | Louis Zutter, Switzerland | — |
| 1904 | Anton Heida, United States | 42 |
| 1924 | Josef Wilhelm, Switzerland | 21.23 |
| 1928 | Hermann Hänggi, Switzerland | 19.75 |
| 1932 | Istvan Pelle, Hungary | 19.07 |
| 1936 | Konrad Frey, Germany | 19.333 |
| 1948 | Paavo Aaltonen, Finland | 19.35 |
| 1952 | Viktor Chukarin, USSR | 19.50 |
| 1956 | Boris Shakhlin, USSR | 19.25 |
| 1960 | Eugen Ekman, Finland | 19.375 |
| 1964 | Miroslav Cerar, Yugoslavia | 19.525 |
| 1968 | Miroslav Cerar, Yugoslavia | 19.325 |
| 1972 | Viktor Klimenko, USSR | 19.125 |
| 1976 | Zoltan Magyar, Hungary | 19.70 |
| 1980 | Zoltan Magyar, Hungary | 19.925 |
| 1984 | Li Ning, China | 19.95 |
| 1988 | Dmitri Bilozerchev, USSR | 19.95 |
| 1992 | Vitaly Scherbo, Unified Team | 9.925 |
| 1996 | Donghua Li, Switzerland | 9.875 |
| 2000 | Marius Urzica, Romania | 9.862 |
| 2004 | Haibin Teng, China | 9.837 |
| 2008 | Xiao Oin, China | 15.875 |

| RINGS | | Pts |
|---|---|---|
| 1896 | Ioannis Mitropoulos, Greece | — |
| 1904 | Hermann Glass, United States | 45 |
| 1924 | Francesco Martino, Italy | 21.553 |
| 1928 | Leon Stukelj, Yugoslavia | 19.25 |
| 1932 | George Gulack, United States | 18.97 |
| 1936 | Alois Hudec, Czechoslovakia | 19.433 |
| 1948 | Karl Frei, Switzerland | 19.80 |
| 1952 | Grant Shaginyan, USSR | 19.75 |
| 1956 | Albert Azaryan, USSR | 19.35 |
| 1960 | Albert Azaryan, USSR | 19.725 |
| 1964 | Takuji Haytta, Japan | 19.475 |

| RINGS *(CONT.)* | | Pts |
|---|---|---|
| 1968 | Akinori Nakayama, Japan | 19.45 |
| 1972 | Akinori Nakayama, Japan | 19.35 |
| 1976 | Nikolai Andrianov, USSR | 19.65 |
| 1980 | Aleksandr Dityatin, USSR | 19.875 |
| 1984 | Koji Gushiken, Japan | 19.85 |
| 1988 | Holger Behrendt, E Germany | 19.925 |
| 1992 | Vitaly Scherbo; Unified Team | 9.937 |
| 1996 | Yuri Chechi, Italy | 9.887 |
| 2000 | Szilveszter Csollany, Hungary | 9.862 |
| 2004 | Dimosthenis Tampakos, Greece | 9.862 |
| 2008 | Chen Yibing, China | 16.600 |

| FLOOR EXERCISE | | Pts |
|---|---|---|
| 1932 | Istvan Pelle, Hungary | 9.60 |
| 1936 | Georges Miez, Switzerland | 18.666 |
| 1948 | Ferenc Pataki, Hungary | 19.35 |
| 1952 | K. William Thoresson, Sweden | 19.25 |
| 1956 | Valentin Muratov, USSR | 19.20 |
| 1960 | Nobuyuki Aihara, Japan | 19.45 |
| 1964 | Franco Menichelli, Italy | 19.45 |
| 1968 | Sawao Kato, Japan | 19.475 |
| 1972 | Nikolai Andrianov, USSR | 19.175 |
| 1976 | Nikolai Andrianov, USSR | 19.45 |
| 1980 | Roland Brückner, E Germany | 19.75 |
| 1984 | Li Ning, China | 19.925 |
| 1988 | Sergei Kharkov, USSR | 19.925 |
| 1992 | Li Xiaoshuang, China | 9.925 |
| 1996 | Ioannis Melissanidis, Greece | 9.850 |
| 2000 | Igors Vihrovs, Latvia | 9.812 |
| 2004 | Kyle Shewfelt, Canada | 9.787 |
| 2008 | Zou Kai, China | 16.050 |

| TEAM COMBINED EXERCISES | | Pts |
|---|---|---|
| 1904 | Turngemeinde Philadelphia | 374.43 |
| 1906 | Norway | 19.00 |
| 1908 | Sweden | 438 |
| 1912 | Italy | 265.75 |
| 1920 | Italy | 359.855 |
| 1924 | Italy | 839.058 |
| 1928 | Switzerland | 1718.625 |
| 1932 | Italy | 541.850 |
| 1936 | Germany | 657.430 |
| 1948 | Finland | 1358.30 |
| 1952 | USSR | 574.40 |
| 1956 | USSR | 568.25 |
| 1960 | Japan | 575.20 |
| 1964 | Japan | 577.95 |
| 1968 | Japan | 575.90 |
| 1972 | Japan | 571.25 |
| 1976 | Japan | 576.85 |
| 1980 | USSR | 598.60 |
| 1984 | United States | 591.40 |
| 1988 | USSR | 593.35 |
| 1992 | Unified Team | 585.45 |
| 1996 | Russia | 576.778 |
| 2000 | China | 231.919 |
| 2004 | Japan | 173.821 |
| 2008 | China | 286.125 |

## GYMNASTICS — Women

| ALL-AROUND | | Pts |
|---|---|---|
| 1952 | Maria Gorokhovskaya, USSR | 76.78 |
| 1956 | Larissa Latynina, USSR | 74.933 |
| 1960 | Larissa Latynina, USSR | 77.031 |
| 1964 | Vera Caslavska, Czechoslovakia | 77.564 |
| 1968 | Vera Caslavska, Czechoslovakia | 78.25 |
| 1972 | Lyudmila Tousischeva, USSR | 77.025 |
| 1976 | Nadia Comaneci, Romania | 79.275 |
| 1980 | Yelena Davydova, USSR | 79.15 |
| 1984 | Mary Lou Retton, United States | 79.175 |
| 1988 | Yelena Shushunova, USSR | 79.662 |
| 1992 | Tatiana Gutsu, Unified Team | 39.737 |
| 1996 | Lilia Podkopayeva, Ukraine | 39.255 |
| 2000 | Simona Amanar, Romania | 38.642 |
| 2004 | Carly Patterson, United States | 38.387 |
| 2008 | Nastia Liukin, United States | 63.325 |

### GYMNASTICS - Women *(Cont.)*

| VAULT | | Pts |
|---|---|---|
| 1952 | Yekaterina Kalinchuk, USSR | 19.20 |
| 1956 | Larissa Latynina, USSR | 18.833 |
| 1960 | Margarita Nikolayeva, USSR | 19.316 |
| 1964 | Vera Caslavska, Czechoslovakia | 19.483 |
| 1968 | Vera Caslavska, Czechoslovakia | 19.775 |
| 1972 | Karin Janz, E Germany | 19.525 |
| 1976 | Nelli Kim, USSR | 19.80 |
| 1980 | Natalya Shaposhnikova, USSR | 19.725 |
| 1984 | Ecaterina Szabo, Romania | 19.875 |
| 1988 | Svetlana Boginskaya, USSR | 19.905 |
| 1992 | Henrietta Onodi, Hungary | 9.925 |
| | Lavinia Milosovici, Romania | 9.925 |
| 1996 | Simona Amanar, Romania | 9.825 |
| 2000 | Yelena Zamolodtchikova, Russia | 9.731 |
| 2004 | Monica Rosu, Romania | 9.656 |
| 2008 | Un Jong Hong, North Korea | 15.650 |

| UNEVEN BARS | | Pts |
|---|---|---|
| 1952 | Margit Korondi, Hungary | 19.40 |
| 1956 | Agnes Keleti, Hungary | 18.966 |
| 1960 | Polina Astakhova, USSR | 19.616 |
| 1964 | Polina Astakhova, USSR | 19.332 |
| 1968 | Vera Caslavska, Czechoslovakia | 19.65 |
| 1972 | Karin Janz, E Germany | 19.675 |
| 1976 | Nadia Comaneci, Romania | 20.00 |
| 1980 | Maxi Gnauck, E Germany | 19.875 |
| 1984 | Ma Yanhong, China | 19.95 |
| 1988 | Daniela Silivas, Romania | 20.00 |
| 1992 | Lu Li, China | 10.00 |
| 1996 | Svetlana Khorkina, Russia | 9.850 |
| 2000 | Svetlana Khorkina, Russia | 9.862 |
| 2004 | Emilie Lepennec, France | 9.687 |
| 2008 | He Kexin, China | 16.725 |

| BALANCE BEAM | | Pts |
|---|---|---|
| 1952 | Nina Bocharova, USSR | 19.22 |
| 1956 | Agnes Keleti, Hungary | 18.80 |
| 1960 | Eva Bosakova, Czechoslovakia | 19.283 |
| 1964 | Vera Caslavska, Czechoslovakia | 19.449 |
| 1968 | Natalya Kuchinskaya, USSR | 19.65 |
| 1972 | Olga Korbut, USSR | 19.40 |
| 1976 | Nadia Comaneci, Romania | 19.95 |
| 1980 | Nadia Comaneci, Romania | 19.80 |
| 1984 | Simona Pauca, Romania | 19.80 |
| 1988 | Daniela Silivas, Romania | 19.924 |
| 1992 | Tatiana Lisenko, Unified Team | 9.975 |
| 1996 | Shannon Miller, United States | 9.862 |
| 2000 | Xuan Li, China | 9.825 |
| 2004 | Catalina Ponor, Romania | 9.787 |
| 2008 | Shawn Johnson, United States | 16.225 |

| FLOOR EXERCISE | | Pts |
|---|---|---|
| 1952 | Agnes Keleti, Hungary | 19.36 |
| 1956 | Agnes Keleti, Hungary | 18.733 |
| 1960 | Larissa Latynina, USSR | 19.583 |
| 1964 | Larissa Latynina, USSR | 19.599 |
| 1968 | Vera Caslavska, Czechoslovakia | 19.675 |
| 1972 | Olga Korbut, USSR | 19.575 |
| 1976 | Nelli Kim, USSR | 19.85 |
| 1980 | Nadia Comaneci, Romania | 19.875 |
| 1984 | Ecaterina Szabo, Romania | 19.975 |
| 1988 | Daniela Silivas, Romania | 19.937 |
| 1992 | Lavinia Milosovici, Romania | 10.00 |
| 1996 | Lilia Podkopayeva, Ukraine | 9.887 |
| 2000 | Yelena Zamolodtchikova, Russia | 9.850 |
| 2004 | Catalina Ponor, Romania | 9.750 |
| 2008 | Sandra Izbasa, Romania | 15.650 |

| TEAM COMBINED EXERCISES | | Pts |
|---|---|---|
| 1928 | The Netherlands | 316.75 |
| 1932 | Not held | |
| 1936 | Germany | 506.50 |
| 1948 | Czechoslovakia | 445.45 |
| 1952 | USSR | 527.03 |
| 1956 | USSR | 444.800 |
| 1960 | USSR | 382.320 |
| 1964 | USSR | 280.890 |
| 1968 | USSR | 382.85 |
| 1972 | USSR | 380.50 |
| 1976 | USSR | 466.00 |
| 1980 | USSR | 394.90 |
| 1984 | Romania | 392.02 |
| 1988 | USSR | 395.475 |
| 1992 | Unified Team | 395.666 |
| 1996 | United States | 389.225 |
| 2000 | Romania | 154.608 |
| 2004 | Romania | 114.283 |
| 2004 | China | 188.900 |

| RHYTHMIC ALL-AROUND | | Pts |
|---|---|---|
| 1984 | Lori Fung, Canada | 57.95 |
| 1988 | Marina Lobach, USSR | 60.00 |
| 1992 | A. Timoshenko, Unified Team | 59.037 |
| 1996 | E. Serebrianskaya, Ukraine | 39.683 |
| 2000 | Yulia Barsukova, Russia | 39.632 |
| 2004 | Alina Kabaeva, Russia | 108.400 |
| 2008 | Evgeniya Kanaeva, Russia | 75.500 |

| RHYTHMIC TEAM COMBINED EXERCISES | | Pts |
|---|---|---|
| 1996 | Spain | 38.933 |
| 2000 | Russia | 39.500 |
| 2004 | China | 249.750 |
| 2008 | Russia | 35.550 |

## SOCCER

### Men

| | | | |
|---|---|---|---|
| 1900 | Great Britain | 1928 | Uruguay |
| 1904 | Canada | 1936 | Italy |
| 1908 | Great Britain | 1948 | Sweden |
| 1912 | Great Britain | 1952 | Hungary |
| 1920 | Belgium | 1956 | USSR |
| 1924 | Uruguay | 1960 | Yugoslavia |

| | | | |
|---|---|---|---|
| 1964 | Hungary | 1988 | USSR |
| 1968 | Hungary | 1992 | Spain |
| 1972 | Poland | 1996 | Nigeria |
| 1976 | E Germany | 2000 | Cameroon |
| 1980 | Czechoslovakia | 2004 | Argentina |
| 1984 | France | 2008 | Argentina |

### Women

| | |
|---|---|
| 1996 | United States |
| 2000 | Norway |
| 2004 | United States |
| 2008 | United States |

# Track &
# Field

Jamaican phenom Usain Bolt
smashed two (of his own) world
sprinting records in 2009

# Striking Twice

In 2009, lightning-fast Jamaican Usain Bolt once again sprinted to world records, proving Beijing was no fluke

BY MERRELL NODEN

LIGHTNING, WE KNOW *CAN* STRIKE twice. Just as he did last year at the Olympics, Usain Bolt tore up the track at the World Championships, setting world records in both the 100 (9.58) and 200 (19.19) and running a key leg on Jamaica's winning 4 x 100-meter relay team. In doing so, the tall, jocular Jamaican looked, quite simply, like an entirely new species of runner. In the 100, defending champion Tyson Gay ran a U.S. record of 9.71 and still managed to be out of the race by the 50-meter mark. Bolt's .11-second lowering of his own world record in the 100 was the largest in that event since the sport began keeping official records to the hundredth of a second.

That Bolt performed these heroics in Berlin's Olympic Stadium conjured up inevitable memories of Jesse Owens and the four gold medals he won 73 years ago, when Germany was in the throes of Nazi propaganda. Bolt had no ugly racial theories to disprove, but this young man, who turned 23 the day after the 200 final, seems to have every chance of joining Owens in the all-time pantheon of mythic athletes, if he hasn't already. One poll ranked him third among the world's most recognized athletes, behind Tiger Woods and David Beckham. That's heady stuff for track and field, which hasn't had a star of Bolt's potential reach in years.

Though he left no doubt that we still haven't seen his absolute best, Bolt's performances in Berlin dominated the meet, which featured the usual mix of surprises and disappointments, blunders by U.S. relay teams, and an excruciating, drawn-out controversy over one young athlete's gender.

Had it not been for Bolt, the world's attention would surely have focused on Kenenisa Bekele, who was the only other athlete to win two individual gold medals in Berlin. The 27-year-old Ethiopian ran a fantastically controlled final lap in the 10,000 meters to float away from Zerseney Tadese of Eritrea. His winning time of 26:46.31 was mind-boggling given how effortless it looked. The 5,000, contested six days later, was, by contrast, a real race, with Bekele leading Bernard Lagat of the U.S. into the homestretch before losing the lead and then ultimately retaking it to win by a meter. Bekele's time, 13:17.09, was almost 12 seconds slower than the second half of his 10,000, but no matter. With the win, he became the first man to pull off this double at the World Championships.

The greatest shock of the year was the failure of Yelena Isinbayeva to clear a height in the pole vault in Berlin. The 27-year-old Russian had won two Olympic gold medals and the last two outdoor world titles, not to mention setting a slew of world records along the way. When, a month before the Worlds, she was beaten by Anna Rogowska of Poland, it seemed like a fluke. But it was Rogowska who won the gold in Berlin. Still, Isinbayeva got revenge the following week in Zurich, where she jumped a world record 16' 7¼" to beat Rogowska.

The most wrenching situation of the year

**After running a mind-boggling 9.58 in the 100 meters, Bolt may be tempted to try his abilites over longer distance races.**

MICHAEL KAPPELER/AFP/GETTY IMAGES

followed the women's 800, where a muscular South African teenager named Caster Semenya destroyed the field in 1:55.45. There had already been nasty questions about Semenya's build, and the ease with which she won only increased them. "These kind of people should not run with us," said Elisa Cusma of Italy, who finished sixth. "For me, she's not a woman. She's a man." The muscular 18-year-old had come from nowhere this season, dropping her personal best by seven seconds in winning the African Junior Championships less than a month before the Worlds.

After her Berlin performance, the International Amateur Athletic Federationa hastily assembled a team of experts to judge whether Semenya was woman enough to compete. Subsequent news reports claimed that the tests revealed Semenya had both male and female reproductive organs. But whatever the IAAF finally decides regarding her status, it's hard to feel anything other than queasy at such treatment of an athlete whom no one accused of deliberately cheating.

The U.S. team had a good meet, winning ten gold medals. Six of those came in sweeps of the men's and women's long jump, the 400s, and the 4 x 400-meter relays. With Olympic champion Brian Clay absent due to injury, Trey Hardee won the decathlon. Not so surprising was Allison Felix's win in the 200 or Kerron Clement's victory in the men's 400 hurdles. Shannon Rowbury claimed bronze in the 1500 (after the apparent winner was disqualified for decking a competitor on the final turn!), and Dathan Ritzenheim came in sixth in the 10,000. He later broke the U.S. record in the 5,000 in Zurich to underscore improvements by U.S. distance runners. Still, it was hard to stomach

yet another botched exchange in both the shorter relays. After passing out of the exchange zone, both U.S. teams were disqualified, just as they had been in Beijing.

But there's no doubt who is now the sport's great star. Not that the transition from star-in–the-making to world celebrity has been easy: Bolt now travels with two bodyguards and in late April rolled his Mercedes into a ditch near Kingston. He managed to escape with minor injuries to his left foot but had to withdraw from a meet. In other words, his preparation wasn't perfect and we still don't know his real limits. Many fans would love to see him give the 400 a serious try, though it is the long jump that Bolt himself says he plans to try.

Late in the summer Bekele offered to race Bolt over a neutral distance—say, 600 or 800 meters—predicting he'd beat him there. It would be a freak show, for sure, but an intriguing one between two fantastic runners who also happen to be the biggest stars in the sport. So, purism be damned: Didn't Jesse Owens race against horses? Both Bolt and Bekele may soon know how that feels.

# FOR THE RECORD • 2009

## 2009 IAAF World Championships

### Berlin, Germany, August 15–23, 2009

### Men

**100 METERS**
1. ....Usain Bolt, Jamaica ........... 9.59WR
2. ....Tyson Gay, United States .......... 9.71
3. ....Asafa Powell, Jamaica .......... 9.84

**200 METERS**
1. ....Usain Bolt, Jamaica .......... 19.19WR
2. ....Alonso Edward, Panama .......... 19.81
3. ....Wallace Spearmon, United States .. 19.85

**400 METERS**
1. ....LaShawn Merritt, United States .. 44.06
2. ....Jeremy Wariner, United States .. 44.60
3. ....Renny Quow, Trinidad & Tobago .. 45.02

**800 METERS**
1. ....Mbulaeni Mulaudzi, South Africa 1:45.29
2. ....Alfred Kirwa Yego, Kenya ..... 1:45.35
3. ....Yusuf Saak Kamel, Bahrain .... 1:45.35

**1,500 METERS**
1. ....Yusuf Saad Kamel, Bahrain .... 3:35.93
2. ....Deresse Mekonnen, Ethiopia ... 3:36.01
3. ....Bernard Lagat, United States . 3:36.20

**3,000-METER STEEPLECHASE**
1. ....Ezekiel Kemboi, Kenya ........ 8:00.43
2. ....Richard Mateelong, Kenya ..... 8:00.89
3. ....Bouabdellah Tahri, France .... 8:01.18

**5,000 METERS**
1. ....Kenenisa Bekele, Ethiopia ... 13:17.09
2. ....Bernard Lagat, United States 13:17.33
3. ....James Kwalia C'Kurui, Bahrain 13:17.78

**10,000 METERS**
1. ....Kenenisa Bekele, Ethiopia ... 26:46.31
2. ....Zersenay Tadese, Eritrea .... 26:50.12
3. ....Moses Ndiema Masai, Kenya ... 26:57.39

**110-METER HURDLES**
1. ....Ryan Brathwaite, Barbados ....... 13.14
2. ....Terrence Trammell, United States 13.15
3. ....David Payne, United States ...... 13.15

**400-METER HURDLES**
1. ....Kerron Clement, United States .. 47.91
2. ....Javier Culson, Puerto Rico ..... 48.09
3. ....Bershawn Jackson, United States 48.23

**4 x 100-METER RELAY**
1. ....Jamaica .......................... 37.31
   (Mullings, Frater, Bolt, Powell)
2. ....Trinidad & Tobago ................ 37.62
   (Brown, Burns, Callander, Thompson)
3. ....United Kingdom ................... 38.02
   (Williamson, Edgar, Devonish,
   Alkines-Aryeetey)

**4 x 400-METER RELAY**
1. ....United States .................. 2:57.86
   (Taylor, Wariner, Clement, Merritt)
2. ....United Kingdom ................. 3:00.53
   (Williams, Bingham, Tobin, Rooney)
3. ....Australia ...................... 3:00.90
   (Steffensen, Offereins, Thomas, Wroe)

**20-KILOMETER RACE WALK**
1. ....Valeriy Borchin, Russia ....... 1:18:41
2. ....Hao Wang, China ............... 1:19:06
3. ....Eder Sanchez, Mexico .......... 1:19:22

**50-KILOMETER RACE WALK**
1. ....Sergey Kirdyapkin, Russia ..... 3:38:35
2. ....Trond Nymark, Norway .......... 3:41:16
3. ....Jesus Angel Garcia, Spain ..... 3:41:37

**MARATHON**
1. ....Able Kirui, Kenya ............. 2:06:54
2. ....Emmanuel Mutai, Kenya ......... 2:07:48
3. ....Tsegay Kebede, Ethiopia ....... 2:08:35

**POLE VAULT**
1. ....Steven Hooker, Australia ....... 5.90m
2. ....Romain Mesnil, France .......... 5.85m
3. ....Renaud Lavillenie, France ...... 5.80m

**LONG JUMP**
1. ....Dwight Phillips, United States .. 8.54m
2. ....Godfrey Mokoena, South Africa 8.47m
3. ....Mitchell Watt, Australia ....... 8.37m

**TRIPLE JUMP**
1. ....Phillips Idowu, United Kingdom 17.73m
2. ....Nelson Evora, Portugal ........ 17.55m
3. ....Alexis Copello, Cuba .......... 17.36m

**HIGH JUMP**
1. ....Yaroslav Rybakov, Russia ..... §2.32m
2. ....Kyriakos Ioannau, Cyprus ..... §2.32m
*3. ...Raul Spank, Germany .......... §2.32m
*3. ...Sylwester Bednarek, Poland ... §2.32m

**SHOT PUT**
1. ....Christian Cantwell, United States 22.03m
2. ....Tomasz Majewski, Poland ...... 21.91m
3. ....Ralf Bartels, Germany ........ 21.37m

**DISCUS THROW**
1. ....Robert Harting, Germany ...... 69.43m
2. ....Piotr Malachowski, Poland .... 69.15m
3. ....Gerd Kanter, Estonia ......... 66.88m

**HAMMER THROW**
1. ....Primoz Kozmus, Slovenia ...... 80.84m
2. ....Szymon Ziolkowski, Poland .... 79.30m
3. ....Aleksey Zagornyi, Russia ..... 78.09m

**JAVELIN THROW**
1. ....Andreas Thorkildsen, Norway .. 89.59m
2. ....Guillermo Martinez, Cuba ..... 86.41m
3. ....Yukifumi Murakami, Japan ..... 82.97m

**DECATHLON**
1. ....Trey Hardee, United States ... 8790pts
2. ....Leonel Suarez, Cuba .......... 8640pts
3. ....Aleksandr Pogorelov, Russia .. 8528pts

### Women

**100 METERS**
1. ....Shelly-Ann Fraser, Jamaica ..... 10.73
2. ....Kerron Stewart, Jamaica ........ 10.75
3. ....Carmeltia Jeter, United States . 10.90

**200 METERS**
1. ....Allyson Felix, United States ... 22.02
2. ....Veronica Campbell-Brown, Jamaica 22.35
3. ....Debbie Ferguson-McKenzie, Bahamas 22.41

**400 METERS**
1. ....Sanya Richards, United States .. 49.00
2. ....Shericka Williams, Jamaica ..... 49.32
3. ....Antonina Krivoshapka, Russia ... 49.71

**800 METERS**
1. ....Caster Semenya, South Africa 1:55.45
2. ....Janeth Busienei, Kenya ....... 1:57.90
3. ....Jennifer Meadows, U.K. ....... 1:57.93

**1,500 METERS**
1. ....Maryam Yusuf Jamal, Bahrain 4:03.74
2. ....Lisa Dobriskey, United Kingdom 4:03.75
3. ....Shannon Rowbury, United States 4:04.18

**3,000-METER STEEPLECHASE**
1. ....Marta Dominguez, Spain ....... 9:07.32
2. ....Yuliya Zarudneva, Russia ..... 9:08.39
3. ....Milcah Chemos Cheyma, Kenya 9:08.57

**5,000 METERS**
1. ....Vivian Cheruiyot, Kenya ..... 14:57.97
2. ....Sylvia Jebiwott Kibet, Kenya 14:58.33
3. ....Meseret Defar, Ethiopia ..... 14:58.41

**10,000 METERS**
1. ....Linet Masai, Kenya .......... 30:51.24
2. ....Meselech Melkamu, Ethiopia .. 30:51.34
3. ....Wude Ayalew, Ethiopia ....... 30:51.95

**100-METER HURDLES**
1. ....Brigitte Foster-Hylton, Jamaica 12.51
2. ....Priscilla Lopes-Schilep, Canada 12.54
3. ....Delloreen Ennis-London, Jamaica 12.55

**400-METER HURDLES**
1. ....Melaine Walker, Jamaica ....... 52.42
2. ....Lashinda Demus, United States 52.96
3. ....Josanne Lucas, Trin. & Tob. ... 53.20

**4 x 100-METER RELAY**
1. ....Jamaica .......................... 42.06
   (Facey, Fraser, Bailey, Stewart)
2. ....Bahamas .......................... 42.29
   (Ferguson, Sturrup, Amertil,
   Ferguson-Mckenzie)
3. ....Germany .......................... 42.87
   (Wagner, Mollinger, Tschirch, Sailer)

WR–World record. *Athletes tied after clearing same height same number of times. §Place decided by which athlete cleared height first.

### Berlin, Germany, August 15–23, 2009
### Women (*Cont.*)

**4 x 400-METER RELAY**
1. ....United States                    3:17.83
   (Dunn, Felix, Demus, Richards)
2. ....Jamaica                          3:21.15
   (Whyte, Williams-Mills, Lloyd, Williams)
3. ....Russia                           3:21.64
   (Kapachinskaya, Firova, Litvinova,
   Krivoshapka)

**20-KILOMETER RACE WALK**
1. ....Olga Kaniskina, Russia           1:28:09
2. ....Olive Loughnane, Ireland         1:28:58
3. ....Hong Liu, China                  1:29:10

**MARATHON**
1. ....Xue Bai, China                   2:25:15
2. ....Yoshimi Ozaki, Japan             2:25:25
3. ....Aselefech Mergia, Ethiopia       2:25:32

**HIGH JUMP**
1. ....Blanka Vlasic, Croatia           2.04m
2. ....Anna Chicherova, Russia          §2.02m
3. ....Ariane Friedrich, Germany        §2.02m

**POLE VAULT**
1. ....Anna Rogowska, Poland            4.75m
*2. ....Monika Pyrek, Poland            4.65m
*2. ....Chelsea Johnson, United States  4.65m

**LONG JUMP**
1. ....Brittney Reese, United States    7.10m
2. ....Tatyana Lebedeva, Russia         6.97m
3. ....Karin May Melis, Turkey          6.80m

**TRIPLE JUMP**
1. ....Yargeris Savigne, Cuba           14.95m
2. ....Mabel Gay, Cuba                  14.61m
3. ....Anna Pyatykh, Russia             14.58m

**SHOT PUT**
1. ....Valerie Vili, New Zealand        20.44m
2. ....Nadine Kleinert, Germany         20.20m
3. ....Lijiao Gong, China               19.89m

**DISCUS THROW**
1. ....Dani Samuels, Australia          65.44m
2. ....Yarelis Barrios, Cuba            65.31m
3. ....Nicoleta Grasu, Romania          65.20m

**HAMMER THROW**
1. ....Anita Wlodarczyk, Poland         77.96mWR
2. ....Betty Heidler, Germany           77.12m
3. ....Martina Hrasnova, Slovakia       74.79m

**JAVELIN THROW**
1. ....Steffi Nerius, Germany           67.30m
2. ....Barbora Spotakova, Czech Rep.    66.42m
3. ....Maria Abakumova, Russia          66.06m

**HEPTATHLON**
1. ....Jessica Ennis, United Kingdom    6731pts
2. ....Jennifer Oeser, Germany          6493pts
3. ....Kamila Chudzik, Poland           6471pts

WR–World record. *Athletes tied after clearing same height same number of times. § Final place decided by which athlete cleared height first.

## World and American Outdoor Records

As of October 1, 2009. World outdoor records are recognized by the International Amateur Athletics Federation (IAAF). American records recognized by U.S.A. Track & Field.

### Men

| Event | Mark | Record Holder | Date | Site |
|---|---|---|---|---|
| 100 meters | 9.58 | Usain Bolt, Jamaica (W) | 8-16-09 | Berlin |
| | 9.71 | Tyson Gay (A) | 8-16-09 | Berlin |
| 200 meters | 19.19 | Usain Bolt, Jamaica (W) | 8-20-09 | Berlin |
| | 19.32 | Michael Johnson (A) | 8-01-96 | Atlanta |
| 400 meters | 43.18 | Michael Johnson, U.S. (W,A) | 8-26-99 | Seville, Spain |
| 800 meters | 1:41.11 | Wilson Kipketer, Denmark (W) | 8-24-97 | Cologne |
| | 1:42.60 | Johnny Gray (A) | 8-28-85 | Koblenz, Germany |
| 1,000 meters | 2:11.96 | Noah Ngeny, Kenya (W) | 9-05-99 | Rieti, Italy |
| | 2:13.90 | Rick Wohlhuter (A) | 7-20-74 | Oslo |
| 1,500 meters | 3:26.00 | Hicham El Guerrouj, Morocco (W) | 7-14-98 | Rome |
| | 3:69.30 | Bernard Lagat (A) | 8-28-05 | Rieti, Italy |
| Mile | 3:43.13 | Hicham El Guerrouj, Morocco (W) | 7-07-99 | Rome |
| | 3:46.91 | Alan Webb (A) | 7-21-07 | Brasschaat, Belguim |
| 2,000 meters | 4:44.79 | Hicham El Guerrouj, Morocco (W) | 9-07-99 | Berlin |
| | 4:52.44 | Jim Spivey (A) | 9-15-87 | Lausanne, Switzerland |
| 3,000 meters | 7:20.67 | Daniel Komen, Kenya (W) | 9-01-96 | Rieti, Italy |
| | 7:30.84 | Bob Kennedy (A) | 8-08-98 | Fontvielle, Monaco |
| 3,000-m Steeplechase | 7:53.63 | Saif Saaeed Shaheen, Qatar (W) | 9-03-04 | Brussels |
| | 8:08.82 | Daniel Lincoln (A) | 7-14-06 | Rome |
| 5,000 meters | 12:37.35 | Kenenisa Bekele, Ethiopia (W) | 5-31-04 | Hengelo, Netherlands |
| | 12:58.21 | Bob Kennedy (A) | 8-14-96 | Zurich |
| 10,000 meters | 26:17.53 | Kenenisa Bekele, Ehtiopia (W) | 8-26-05 | Brussels |
| | 27:13.98 | Meb Keflezighi (A) | 5-04-01 | Stanford, California |
| Marathon | 2:03:59 | Haile Gebrselassie, Ethiopia (W) | 9-28-08 | Berlin |
| | 2:05.38 | Khalid Khannouchi (A) | 4-14-02 | London |
| 110-meter hurdles | 12.87 | Dayron Robles, Cuba (W) | 6-12-08 | Ostrava, Czech Republic |
| | 12.90 | Dominique Arnold (A) | 7-11-06 | Lausanne, Switzerland |
| 400-meter hurdles | 46.78 | Kevin Young, United States (W,A) | 8-6-92 | Barcelona |
| 20-kilometer walk | 1:17.16 | Vladimir Kanaykin, Russia (W) | 9-29-07 | Saransk, Russia |
| | 1:23:40 | Tim Seaman (A) | 3-07-99 | Chula Vista, California |
| 50-kilometer walk | 3:34:14 | Denis Nizhegorodov, Russia (W) | 5-11-08 | Cheboksary, Russia |
| 4 x 100-meter relay | 37.10 | Jamaica (Nesta Carter, (W) Michael Prater, Usain Bolt, Asafa Powell) | 8-22-08 | Beijing |

## Men (*Cont.*)

| Event | Mark | Record Holder | Date | Site |
|---|---|---|---|---|
| 4 x 100-meter relay | 37.40 | Mike Marsh, Leroy Burrell, (A) Dennis Mitchell, Carl Lewis | 8-08-92 | Barcelona |
| | 37.40 | Jon Drummond, Andrew Canson, (A) Dennis Mitchell, Leroy Burrell | 8-21-93 | Stuttgart, Germany |
| 4 x 200-meter relay | 1:18.68 | U.S. (Mike Marsh, Leroy Burrell, (W,A) Floyd Heard, Carl Lewis) | 4-17-94 | Walnut, California |
| 4 x 400-meter relay | 2:54.29 | United States (Andrew Valmon, (W,A) Quincy Watts, Harry Reynolds, Michael Johnson) | 7-22-93 | Stuttgart, Germany |
| 4 x 800-meter relay | 7:02.43 | Kenya (Wilfred Bungei, (W) William Yiampoy, Joseph Mutua, Ismael Kombich) | 8-25-06 | Brussels |
| | 7:02.82 | Jebreh Harris, Khadevis Robinson, (A) Sam Burley, David Krummenacker | 8-25-06 | Brussels |
| 4 x 1,500-meter relay | 14:38.8 | West Germany (W) (Thomas Wessinghage, Harald Hudak, Michael Lederer, Karl Fleschen) | 8-17-77 | Cologne, Germany |
| High jump | 2.45m | Javier Sotomayor, Cuba (W) | 7-27-93 | Salamanca, Spain |
| | 2.40m | Charles Austin (A) | 8-07-91 | Zurich |
| Pole vault | 6.14m | Sergei Bubka, Ukraine (W) | 7-31-94 | Sestriere, Italy |
| | 6.04m | Brad Walker (A) | 6-08-08 | Eugene, Oregon |
| Long jump | 8.95m | Mike Powell, United States (W,A) | 8-30-91 | Tokyo |
| Triple jump | 18.29m | Jonathan Edwards, U.K. (W) | 8-07-95 | Göteborg, Sweden |
| | 18.09m | Kenny Harrison (A) | 7-27-96 | Atlanta |
| Shot put | 23.12m | Randy Barnes, United States (W,A) | 5-20-90 | Westwood, California |
| Discus throw | 74.08m | Jürgen Schult, East Germany (W) | 6-06-86 | Neubrandenburg, Germ. |
| | 72.34m | Ben Plucknett (A) | 7-07-81 | Stockholm |
| Hammer throw | 86.74m | Yuri Syedykh, USSR (W) | 8-30-86 | Stuttgart, Germany |
| | 82.52m | Lance Deal (A) | 9-17-96 | Milan |
| Javelin throw | 98.48m | Jan Zelezny, Czech Republic (W) | 5-25-96 | Jena, Germany |
| | 91.29m | Breaux Greer (A) | 6-21-07 | Indianapolis |
| Decathlon | 9026 pts | Roman Sebrle, Czech Rep. (W) | 5-27-01 | Goetzis, Austria |
| | 8891pts | Dan O'Brien (A) | 9-04-92 | Talence, France |

Note: The decathlon consists of 10 events: the 100 meters, long jump, shot put, high jump and 400 meters on the first day; the 110-meter hurdles, discus, pole vault, javelin and 1,500 meters on the second.

## Women

| Event | Mark | Record Holder | Date | Site |
|---|---|---|---|---|
| 100 meters | 10.49 | Florence Griffith Joyner, U.S. (W,A) | 7-16-88 | Indianapolis |
| 200 meters | 21.34 | Florence Griffith Joyner, U.S. (W,A) | 9-29-88 | Seoul |
| 400 meters | 47.60 | Marita Koch, E Germany (W) | 10-6-85 | Canberra, Australia |
| | 48.70 | Sanya Richards (A) | 9-17-06 | Athens |
| 800 meters | 1:53.28 | Jarmila Kratochvílová, Czech. (W) | 7-26-83 | Munich |
| | 1:56.40 | Jearl Miles-Clark (A) | 8-11-99 | Zurich |
| 1,000 meters | 2:28.98 | Svetlana Masterkova, Russia (W) | 8-23-96 | Brussels |
| | 2:31.80 | Regina Jacobs (A) | 7-02-99 | Brunswick, Maine |
| 1,500 meters | 3:50.46 | Yunxia Qu, China (W) | 9-11-93 | Beijing |
| | 3:57.12 | Mary Slaney (A) | 7-26-83 | Stockholm |
| Mile | 4:12.56 | Svetlana Masterkova, Russia (W) | 8-14-96 | Zurich |
| | 4:16.71 | Mary Slaney (A) | 8-21-85 | Zurich |
| 2,000 meters | 5:25.36 | Sonia O'Sullivan, Ireland (W) | 7-08-94 | Edinburgh |
| | 5:32.70 | Mary Slaney (A) | 8-03-84 | Eugene, Oregon |
| 3,000 meters | 8:06.11 | Junxia Wang, China (W) | 9-13-93 | Beijing |
| | 8:25.83 | Mary Slaney (A) | 9-07-85 | Rome |
| 3,000-m Steeplechase | 8:58.81 | Gulnara Samitova-Galkina, Russia (W) | 8-17-08 | Beijing |
| | 9:12.50 | Jenny Barringer (A) | 8-17-09 | Berlin |
| 5,000 meters | 14:11.15 | Tirunesh Dibaba, Ethiopia (W) | 6-06-08 | Oslo |
| | 14:44.80 | Shalane Flanagan (A) | 5-14-07 | Walnut Creek, California |
| 10,000 meters | 29:31.78 | Junxia Wang, China (W) | 9-08-93 | Beijing |
| | 30:22.22 | Shalane Flanagan (A) | 8-15-08 | Beijing |
| Marathon | 2:15:25 | Paula Radcliffe, Great Britain (W) | 4-13-03 | London |
| | 2:19:36 | Deena Kastor (A) | 4-23-06 | London |
| 100-meter hurdles | 12.21 | Yordanka Donkova, Bulgaria (W) | 8-20-88 | Stara Zagora, Bulgaria |
| | 12.33 | Gail Devers (A) | 7-23-00 | Sacramento, California |
| 400-meter hurdles | 52.34 | Yuliya Nosova, Russia (W) | 8-08-03 | Tula, Russia |
| | 52.61 | Kim Batten (A) | 8-11-95 | Gothenburg, Sweden |
| 20-kilometer walk | 1:25:41 | Olimpiada Ivanova, Russia (W) | 8-07-05 | Helsinki |
| | 1:33:28.15 | Teresa Vaill (A) | 6-25-05 | Carson, California |

## Women *(Cont.)*

| | | | | |
|---|---|---|---|---|
| 4 x 100-meter relay | 41.37 | East Germany (Silke Gladisch, (W) | 10-6-85 | Canberra, Australia |
| | | Sabine Reiger, Ingrid Auerswald, Marlies Göhr) | | |
| | 41.47 | Chrsyte Gaines, Marion Jo nes, (A) | 8-08-97 | Athens |
| | | Inger Miller, Gail Devers | | |
| 4 x 200-meter relay | 1:27.46 | United States (LaTasha Jenkins, (W,A) | 4-29-00 | Philadelphia |
| | | LaTasha Colander-Richardson, | | |
| | | Nanceen Perry, Marion Jones) | | |
| 4 x 400-meter relay | 3:15.17 | USSR (Tatyana Ledovskaya, (W) | 10-01-88 | Seoul |
| | | Olga Nazarova, Maria Pinigina, | | |
| | | Olga Bryzgina) | | |
| | 3:15.51 | Denean Howard, Diane Dixon (A) | 10-01-88 | Seoul |
| | | Valerie Brisco, Florence Griffith-Joyner | | |
| 4 x 800-meter relay | 7:50.17 | USSR (Nadezhda Olizarenko, | 8-05-84 | Moscow |
| | | Lyubov Gurina, Lyudmila Borisova, | | |
| | | Irina Podyalovskaya) | | |
| | 8:19.90 | Robin Campbell, Joetta Clark (A) | 6-24-79 | Bourges, France |
| | | Chris Gregorek, Essie Kelley | | |
| High jump | 2.09m | Stefka Kostadinova, Bulgaria (W) | 8-30-87 | Rome |
| | 2.03m | Louise Ritter (A) | 9-30-88 | Seoul |
| Pole vault | 5.06m | Yelena Isinbayeva, Russia (W) | 8-28-09 | Zurich |
| | 4.92m | Jenn Stuczynski (A) | 7-06-08 | Eugene, Oregon |
| Long jump | 7.52m | Galina Chistyakova, USSR (W) | 6-11-88 | Leningrad |
| | 7.49m | Jackie Joyner-Kersee (A) | 7-31-94 | Sestriere, Italy |
| Triple jump | 15.50m | Inessa Kravets, Ukraine (W) | 8-10-95 | Gothenburg, Sweden |
| | 14.45m | Tiombe Hurd (A) | 7-11-04 | Sacramento, California |
| Shot put | 22.63m | Natalya Lisovskaya, USSR (W) | 6-07-87 | Moscow |
| | 20.18m | Ramona Pagel (A) | 6-25-88 | San Diego, California |
| Discus throw | 76.80m | Gabriele Reinsch, East Germany (W) | 7-09-88 | Neubrandenburg, Germ. |
| | 67.67m | Suzy Powell-Roos (A) | 4-14-07 | Wailuku, Hawaii |
| Hammer throw | 77.96m | Anita Wlodarczyk, Poland (W) | 8-22-09 | Berlin |
| | 73.87m | Erin Gilreath (A) | 6-25-05 | Carson, California |
| Javelin throw | 72.28m | Barbora Spotakova, Czech Rep. (W) | 9-13-08 | Stuttgart |
| | 64.19m | Kim Kreiner (A) | 5-16-07 | Fortaleza, Brazil |
| Heptathlon | 7291 pts | Jackie Joyner-Kersee, U.S. (W,A) | 9-24-88 | Seoul |

Note: The heptathlon consists of 7 events: the 100-meter hurdles, high jump, shot put and 200 meters on the first day; the long jump, javelin and 800 meters on the second.

As of October 1, 2009. American indoor records are recognized by USA Track and Field. World Indoor records are recognized by the International Amateur Athletics Federation (IAAF). (A) represents an American record, (W) represents a World record.

## Men

| Event | Mark | Record Holder | Date | Site |
|---|---|---|---|---|
| 50 meters | 5.56 | Donovan Bailey, Canada (W) | 2-09-96 | Reno, Nev. |
| | 5.56 | Maurice Greene (A) | 2-12-99 | Los Angeles |
| 55 meters* | 6.00 | Lee McRae (A) | 3-14-86 | Oklahoma City |
| 60 meters | 6.39 | Maurice Greene (W, A) | 2-03-98 | Madrid |
| | 6.39 | Maurice Greene (W, A) | 3-03-01 | Atlanta |
| 200 meters | 19.92 | Frankie Fredericks, Namibia (W) | 2-18-96 | Liévin, France |
| | 20.10 | Wallace Spearmon(A) | 3-11-05 | Fayetteville, Ark. |
| 400 meters | 44.57 | Kerron Clement (W, A) | 3-12-05 | Fayetteville, Ark. |
| 800 meters | 1:42.67 | Wilson Kipketer, Denmark (W) | 3-09-97 | Paris |
| | 1:45.00 | Johnny Gray (A) | 3-08-92 | Sindelfingen, Germany |
| 1,000 meters | 2:14.96 | Wilson Kipketer, Denmark (W) | 2-20-00 | Birmingham, England |
| | 2:17.86 | David Krummenacker (A) | 1-27-02 | Boston |
| 1,500 meters | 3:31.18 | Hicham El Guerrouj, Morocco (W) | 2-02-97 | Stuttgart, Germany |
| | 3:33.34 | Bernard Lagat (A) | 2-11-05 | Fayetteville, Ark. |
| Mile | 3:48.45 | Hicham El Guerrouj, Morocco (W) | 2-12-97 | Ghent, Belgium |
| | 3:49.89 | Bernard Lagat (A) | 2-11-05 | Fayetteville, Ark. |
| 3,000 meters | 7:24.90 | Daniel Komen, Kenya (W) | 2-06-98 | Budapest, Hungary |
| | 7:32.43 | Bernard Lagat (A) | 2-17-07 | Birmingham, England |
| 5,000 meters | 12:49.60 | Kenenisa Bekele, Ethiopia (W) | 2-20-04 | Birmingham, England |
| | 13:20.55 | Doug Padilla (A) | 2-12-82 | New York City |
| 50-meter hurdles | 6.25 | Mark McKoy, Canada (W) | 3-05-86 | Kobe, Japan |
| | 6.35 | Greg Foster (A) | 1-31-87 | Ottawa |
| | 6.35 | Greg Foster (A) | 1-27-85 | Rosemont, Illinois |
| 55-meter hurdles* | 6.89 | Renaldo Nehemiah (A) | 1-20-79 | New York City |
| 60-meter hurdles | 7.30 | Colin Jackson, Great Britain (W) | 3-6-94 | Sindelfingen, Germany |
| | 7.36 | Greg Foster (A) | 1-16-87 | Los Angeles |
| | 7.36 | Allen Johnson (A) | 3-06-04 | Budapest, Hungary |
| 5,000-meter walk | 18:07.08 | Mikhail Shchennikov, Russia (W) | 2-14-95 | Moscow |
| | 19:15.88 | Tim Seaman (A) | 3-07-87 | Indianapolis |
| 4 x 200-meter relay | 1:22.11 | United Kingdom (Linford Christie, (W) Darren Braithwaite, Ade Mafe, John Regis) | 3-03-91 | Glasgow |
| | 1:22.71 | National Team (A) (Thomas Jefferson, Raymond Pierre, Antonio McKay Kevin Little) | 3-03-91 | Glasgow |
| 4 x 400-meter relay | 3:01.96 | United States (W, A) (Andre Morris, Dameon Johnson, Deon Minor, Milton Campbell | 3-07-99 | Maebashi, Japan |
| 4 x 800-meter relay | 7:13.94 | United States (W, A) (Joey Woody, Karl Paranya, Rich Kenah, David Krummenacker) | 2-06-00 | Boston |
| High jump | 2.43m | Javier Sotomayor, Cuba (W) | 3-4-89 | Budapest, Hungary |
| | 2.40m | Hollis Conway (A) | 3-10-91 | Seville |
| Pole vault | 6.15m | Sergei Bubka, Ukraine (W) | 2-21-93 | Donetsk, Ukraine |
| | 6.02m | Jeff Hartwig (A) | 3-10-02 | Sindelfingen, Germany |
| Long jump | 8.79m | Carl Lewis (W, A) | 1-27-84 | New York City |
| Triple jump | 17.83m | Alicier Urrutia, Cuba (W) | 3-01-97 | Sindelfingen, Germany |
| | 17.83m | Christian Olsson, Sweden (W) | 3-07-04 | Budapest, Hungary |
| | 17.76m | Mike Conley (A) | 2-27-87 | New York City |
| Shot put | 22.66m | Randy Barnes (W, A) | 1-20-89 | Los Angeles |
| Weight throw* | 25.86m | Lance Deal (A) | 3-04-95 | Atlanta |
| Pentathlon* | 4478 pts | Steve Fritz, (A) | 1-14-95 | Lawrence, Kan. |
| Heptathlon | 6476 pts | Dan O'Brien (W, A) | 3-13-93 | Toronto |

*No recognized world record.

## Women

| Event | Mark | Record Holder | Date | Site |
|---|---|---|---|---|
| 50 meters | 5.96 | Irina Privolova, Russia (W) | 2-09-95 | Madrid |
| | 6.02 | Gail Devers (A) | 2-22-99 | Liévin, France |
| 55 meters* | 6.56 | Gwen Torrence (A) | 3-14-87 | Oklahoma City, Okla. |
| 60 meters | 6.92 | Irina Privalova, Russia (W) | 2-11-93 | Madrid |
| | 6.92 | Irina Privalova, Russia (W) | 2-09-95 | Madrid |
| | 6.95 | Gail Devers (A) | 3-12-93 | Toronto |
| | 6.95 | Marion Jones (A) | 3-07-98 | Maebashi, Japan |
| 200 meters | 21.87 | Merlene Ottey, Jamaica (W) | 2-13-93 | Liévin, France |
| | 22.18 | Michelle Collins (A) | 3-15-03 | Birmingham, England |
| 400 meters | 49.59 | Jarmila Kratochvílová, Czecho. (W) | 3-07-82 | Milan |
| | 50.64 | Diane Dixon (A) | 3-10-91 | Seville |
| 800 meters | 1:55.82 | Jolanda Ceplak, Slovenia (W) | 3-02-02 | Vienna |
| | 1:58.71 | Nicole Teter (A) | 3-02-02 | New York City |
| 1,000 meters | 2:30.94 | Maria Mutola, Mozambique (W) | 2-25-99 | Stockholm |
| | 2:34.19 | Jennifer Toomey (A) | 2-20-04 | Birmingham, England |
| 1,500 meters | 3:57.71 | Yelena Soboleva, Russia (W) | 3-09-08 | Valencia, Spain |
| | 3:59.98 | Regina Jacobs, United States ( A) | 2-01-03 | Boston |
| Mile | 4:17.14 | Doina Melinte, Romania (W) | 2-09-90 | East Rutherford, N.J. |
| | 4:20.50 | Mary Slaney (A) | 2-19-82 | San Diego |
| 3,000 meters | 8:23.72 | Meseret Defar, Ethiopia (W) | 2-03-07 | Stuttgart |
| | 8:33.25 | Shalane Flanagan (A) | 1-27-07 | Boston |
| 5,000 meters | 14:24.37 | Meseret Defar, Ethiopia (W) | 2-18-09 | Stockholm |
| | 14:47.62 | Shalane Flanagan (A) | 2-07-09 | Boston |
| 50-meter hurdles | 6.58 | Cornelia Oschkenat, E Germany (W) | 2-20-88 | Berlin |
| | 6.67 | Jackie Joyner-Kersee (A) | 2-10-95 | Reno, Nev. |
| 55-meter hurdles* | 7.37 | Jackie Joyner-Kersee (A) | 2-03-89 | New York City |
| 60-meter hurdles | 7.68 | Susanna Kallur, Sweden (W) | 2-20-08 | Berlin |
| | 7.74 | Gail Devers (A) | 3-01-03 | Boston |
| 3,000-meter walk | 11:40.33 | Claudia Stef, Romania | 1-30-99 | Bucharest, Romania |
| | 12:20.79 | Debbi Lawrence (A) | 3-12-93 | Toronto |
| 4 x 200-meter relay | 1:32.41 | Russia (Y, Kondratyeva, (W) I. Khabarova, Y.Pechonkina, Y. Gushchina) | 1-29-05 | Glasgow |
| | 1:33.24 | Flirtisha Harris, Chryste Gaines, (A) Terri Dendy, Michele Collins | 2-12-94 | Glasgow |
| 4 x 400-meter relay | 3:23.37 | Russia (Y. Gushchina, (W) O. Kotlyarova, O. Zaytseva, O. Krasnomovets) | 1-28-06 | Glasgow |
| | 3:27.59 | Michelle Collins, Monique Hennagan (A) Zundra Feagin-Alexander, Shanelle Porter | 3-07-99 | Maebashi, Japan |
| 4 x 800-meter relay | 8:14.53 | Russia, (Y. Zinorova, (W) O. Kotlyarova, M. Savinova, N. Ignatova) | 2-10-08 | Moscow, Russia |
| | 8:28.41 | Univ. of Wisconsin (Sarah Renk, (A) Kim Sherman, Sue Gentes, Amy Wickus) | 3-14-92 | Indianapolis |
| High jump | 2.08m | Kajsa Bergqvist, Sweden (W) | 2-4-06 | Arnstadt, Germany |
| | 2.01m | Tisha Waller (A) | 2-28-98 | Atlanta |
| Pole vault | 5.00m | Yelena Isinbaeva, Russia (W) | 2-15-09 | Donetsk, Ukraine |
| | 4.83m | Jenn Stuczynski (A) | 3-01-09 | Boston |
| Long jump | 7.37m | Heike Drechsler, East Germany (W) | 2-13-88 | Vienna |
| | 7.13m | Jackie Joyner-Kersee (A) | 3-5-94 | Atlanta |
| Triple jump | 15.36m | Tatyana Lebedeva, Russia (W) | 3-6-04 | Budapest, Hungary |
| | 14.23m | Sheila Hudson-Strudwick (A) | 3-4-95 | Atlanta |
| Shot put | 22.50m | Helena Fibingerová, Czecho. (W) | 2-19-77 | Jablonec, Czecho. |
| | 19.83m | Ramona Pagel (A) | 2-20-87 | Inglewood, Calif. |
| Weight throw* | 24.56m | Brittany Riley (A) | 3-10-07 | Fayetteville, Ark. |
| Pentathlon | 4991 pts | Irina Belova, Russia (W) | 2-15-92 | Berlin |
| | 4753 pts | DeDee Nathan (A) | 3-4/5-99 | Maebashi, Japan |

*No recognized world record.

# World Track and Field Championships

## Men

### 100 METERS

| | | |
|---|---|---|
| 1983 | Carl Lewis, United States | 10.07 |
| 1987* | Carl Lewis, United States | 9.93 WR |
| 1991 | Carl Lewis, United States | 9.86 WR |
| 1993 | Linford Christie, Great Britain | 9.87 |
| 1995 | Donovan Bailey, Canada | 9.97 |
| 1997 | Maurice Greene, United States | 9.86 |
| 1999 | Maurice Greene, United States | 9.80 |
| 2001 | Maurice Greene, United States | 9.82 |
| 2003 | Kim Collins, St. Kitts & Nevis | 10.07 |
| 2005 | Justin Gatlin, United States | 9.88 |
| 2007 | Tyson Gay, United States | 9.85 |
| 2009 | Usain Bolt, Jamaica | 9.58WR |

### 200 METERS

| | | |
|---|---|---|
| 1983 | Calvin Smith, United States | 20.14 |
| 1987 | Calvin Smith, United States | 20.16 |
| 1991 | Michael Johnson, United States | 20.01 |
| 1993 | Frank Fredericks, Namibia | 19.85 |
| 1995 | Michael Johnson, United States | 19.79 |
| 1997 | Ato Boldon, Trinidad and Tobago | 20.04 |
| 1999 | Maurice Greene, United States | 19.90 |
| 2001 | Konstadínos Kedéris, Greece | 20.04 |
| 2003 | John Capel, United States | 20.30 |
| 2005 | Justin Gatlin, United States | 20.04 |
| 2007 | Tyson Gay, United States | 19.76 |
| 2009 | Usain Bolt, Jamaica | 19.19WR |

### 400 METERS

| | | |
|---|---|---|
| 1983 | Bert Cameron, Jamaica | 45.05 |
| 1987 | Thomas Schoenlebe, E Germany | 44.33 |
| 1991 | Antonio Pettigrew, United States | 44.57 |
| 1993 | Michael Johnson, United States | 43.65 |
| 1995 | Michael Johnson, United States | 43.39 |
| 1997 | Michael Johnson, United States | 44.12 |
| 1999 | Michael Johnson, United States | 43.18 WR |
| 2001 | Avard Moncur, Bahamas | 44.64 |
| 2003 | Jerome Young, United States | 44.50 |
| 2005 | Jeremy Wariner, United States | 43.93 |
| 2007 | Jeremy Wariner, United States | 43.45 |
| 2009 | LaShawn Merritt, United States | 44.06 |

### 800 METERS

| | | |
|---|---|---|
| 1983 | Willi Wulbeck, W Germany | 1:43.65 |
| 1987 | Billy Konchellah, Kenya | 1:43.06 |
| 1991 | Billy Konchellah, Kenya | 1:43.99 |
| 1993 | Paul Ruto, Kenya | 1:44.71 |
| 1995 | Wilson Kipketer, Denmark | 1:45.08 |
| 1997 | Wilson Kipketer, Denmark | 1:43.38 |
| 1999 | Wilson Kipketer, Denmark | 1:43.30 |
| 2001 | André Bucher, Switzerland | 1:43.70 |
| 2003 | Djabir Saïd-Guerni, Algeria | 1:44.81 |
| 2005 | Rashid Ramzi, Brunei | 1:44.24 |
| 2007 | Alfred Kirwa Yego | 1:47.09 |
| 2009 | Mbulaeni Mulaudzi, South Africa | 1:45.29 |

### 1,500 METERS

| | | |
|---|---|---|
| 1983 | Steve Cram, Great Britain | 3:41.59 |
| 1987 | Abdi Bile, Somalia | 3:36.80 |
| 1991 | Noureddine Morceli, Algeria | 3:32.84 |
| 1993 | Noureddine Morceli, Algeria | 3:34.24 |
| 1995 | Noureddine Morceli, Algeria | 3:33.73 |
| 1997 | Hicham El Guerrouj, Morocco | 3:35.83 |
| 1999 | Hicham El Guerrouj, Morocco | 3:27.65 |
| 2001 | Hicham El Guerrouj, Morocco | 3:30.68 |
| 2003 | Hicham El Guerrouj, Morocco | 3:31.77 |
| 2005 | Rashid Ramzi, Brunei | 3:37.88 |
| 2007 | Bernard Lagat, United States | 3:34.77 |
| 2009 | Yusuf Kamel, Bahrain | 3:35.93 |

### 3,000-METER STEEPLECHASE

| | | |
|---|---|---|
| 1983 | Patriz Ilg, W Germany | 8:15.06 |
| 1987 | Francesco Panetta, Italy | 8:08.57 |
| 1991 | Moses Kiptanui, Kenya | 8:12.59 |
| 1993 | Moses Kiptanui, Kenya | 8:06.36 |
| 1995 | Moses Kiptanui, Kenya | 8:04.16 |
| 1997 | Wilson Boit Kipketer, Kenya | 8:05.84 |
| 1999 | Christopher Koskei, Kenya | 8:11.76 |
| 2001 | Reuben Kosgei, Kenya | 8:15.16 |
| 2003 | Saif Saaeed Shaheen, Qatar | 8:04.39 |
| 2005 | Saif Saaeed Shaheen, Qatar | 8:13.31 |
| 2007 | Brimin Kipruto, Kenya | 8:13.82 |
| 2009 | Ezekiel Kemboi, Kenya | 8:00.43 |

### 5,000 METERS

| | | |
|---|---|---|
| 1983 | Eamonn Coghlan, Ireland | 13:28.53 |
| 1987 | Said Aouita, Morocco | 13:26.44 |
| 1991 | Yobes Ondieki, Kenya | 13:14.45 |
| 1993 | Ismael Kirui, Kenya | 13:02.75 |
| 1995 | Ismael Kirui, Kenya | 13:16.77 |
| 1997 | Daniel Komen, Kenya | 13:07.38 |
| 1999 | Salah Hissou, Morocco | 12:58.13 |
| 2001 | Richard Limo, Kenya | 13:00.77 |
| 2003 | Eliud Kipchoge, Kenya | 12:52.79 |
| 2005 | Benjamin Limo, Kenya | 13:32.55 |
| 2007 | Bernard Lagat, United States | 13:45.87 |
| 2009 | Kenenisa Bekele, Ethiopia | 13:17.09 |

### 10,000 METERS

| | | |
|---|---|---|
| 1983 | Alberto Cova, Italy | 28:01.04 |
| 1987 | Paul Kipkoech, Kenya | 27:38.63 |
| 1991 | Moses Tanui, Kenya | 27:38.74 |
| 1993 | Haile Gebrselassie, Ethiopia | 27:46.02 |
| 1995 | Haile Gebrselassie, Ethiopia | 27:12.95 |
| 1997 | Haile Gebrselassie, Ethiopia | 27:24.58 |
| 1999 | Haile Gebrselassie, Ethiopia | 27:57.27 |
| 2001 | Charles Kamathi, Kenya | 27:53.25 |
| 2003 | Kenenisa Bekele, Ethiopia | 26:49.57 |
| 2005 | Kenenisa Bekele, Ethiopia | 27:08.33 |
| 2007 | Kenenisa Bekele, Ethiopia | 27:05.90 |
| 2009 | Kenenisa Bekele, Ethiopia | 26:46.31 |

### MARATHON

| | | |
|---|---|---|
| 1983 | Rob de Castella, Australia | 2:10:03 |
| 1987 | Douglas Wakiihuri, Kenya | 2:11:48 |
| 1991 | Hiromi Taniguchi, Japan | 2:14:57 |
| 1993 | Mark Plaatjes, United States | 2:13:57 |
| 1995 | Martín Fiz, Spain | 2:11:41 |
| 1997 | Abel Anton, Spain | 2:13:16 |
| 1999 | Abel Anton, Spain | 2:13:36 |
| 2001 | Gezahegne Abera, Ethiopia | 2:12:42 |
| 2003 | Jaouad Gharib, Morocco | 2:08:31 |
| 2005 | Jaouad Gharib, Morocco | 2:10:10 |
| 2007 | Luke Kibet, Kenya | 2:15:59 |
| 2009 | Abel Kirui, Kenya | 2:06:54 |

### 110-METER HURDLES

| | | |
|---|---|---|
| 1983 | Greg Foster, United States | 13.42 |
| 1987 | Greg Foster, United States | 13.21 |
| 1991 | Greg Foster, United States | 13.06 |
| 1993 | Colin Jackson, Great Britain | 12.91 WR |
| 1995 | Allen Johnson, United States | 13.00 |
| 1997 | Allen Johnson, United States | 12.93 |
| 1999 | Colin Jackson, Great Britain | 13.04 |
| 2001 | Allen Johnson, United States | 13.04 |
| 2003 | Allen Johnson, United States | 13.12 |
| 2005 | Ladji Doucoure, France | 13.07 |
| 2007 | Liu Xiang, China | 12.95 |
| 2009 | Ryan Brathwaite, Barbados | 13.14 |

WR=World record.   *Ben Johnson, Canada, disqualified.

### Men *(Cont.)*

#### 400-METER HURDLES

| | | |
|---|---|---|
| 1983 | Edwin Moses, United States | 47.50 |
| 1987 | Edwin Moses, United States | 47.46 |
| 1991 | Samuel Matete, Zambia | 47.64 |
| 1993 | Kevin Young, United States | 47.18 |
| 1995 | Derrick Adkins, United States | 47.98 |
| 1997 | Stéphane Diagana, France | 47.70 |
| 1999 | Fabrizio Mori, Italy | 47.72 |
| 2001 | Felix Sánchez, Dominican Rep. | 47.49 |
| 2003 | Felix Sánchez, Dominican Rep. | 47.25 |
| 2005 | Bershawn Jackson, United States | 47.30 |
| 2007 | Kerron Clement, United States | 47.61 |
| 2009 | Kerron Clement, United States | 47.91 |

#### 20-KILOMETER WALK

| | | |
|---|---|---|
| 1983 | Ernesto Canto, Mexico | 1:20:49 |
| 1987 | Maurizio Damilano, Italy | 1:20:45 |
| 1991 | Maurizio Damilano, Italy | 1:19:37 |
| 1993 | Valentin Massana, Spain | 1:22:31 |
| 1995 | Michele Didoni, Italy | 1:19:59 |
| 1997 | Daniel Garcia, Mexico | 1:21:43 |
| 1999 | Ilya Markov, Russia | 1:23:34 |
| 2001 | Roman Rasskazov, Russia | 1:20:31 |
| 2003 | Jefferson Pérez, Ecuador | 1:17.21 WR |
| 2005 | Jefferson Pérez, Ecuador | 1:18:35 |
| 2007 | Jefferson Pérez, Ecuador | 1:22:20 |
| 2009 | Valeriy Borchin, Russia | 1:18.41 |

#### 50-KILOMETER WALK

| | | |
|---|---|---|
| 1983 | Ronald Weigel, East Germany | 3:43:08 |
| 1987 | Hartwig Gauder, East Germany | 3:40:53 |
| 1991 | Aleksandr Potashov, USSR | 3:53:09 |
| 1993 | Jesus Angel Garcia, Spain | 3:41:41 |
| 1995 | Valentin Kononen, Finland | 3:43:42 |
| 1997 | Robert Korzeniowski, Poland | 3:44:46 |
| 1999 | German Skurygin, Russia | 3:44:23 |
| 2001 | Robert Korzeniowski, Poland | 3:42:08 |
| 2003 | R. Korzeniowski, Poland | 3:36:03 WR |
| 2005 | S. Kirdyapkin, Russia | 3:38:08 |
| 2007 | Nathan Deakes, Australia | 3:43:53 |
| 2009 | Sergey Kirdyapkin, Russia | 3:38.35 |

#### 4 X 100-METER RELAY

| | | |
|---|---|---|
| 1983 | United States (Emmit King, Willie Gault, Calvin Smith, Carl Lewis) | 37.86 |
| 1987 | United States (Lee McRae, Lee McNeil, Harvey Glance, Carl Lewis) | 37.90 |
| 1991 | United States (A. Cason L. Burrell, D. Mitchell, C. Lewis) | 37.50 WR |
| 1993 | United States (J. Drummond, A. Cason, D. Mitchell, L. Burrell) | 37.48 |
| 1995 | Canada (Robert Esmie, Glenroy Gilbert, Bruny Surin, Donovan Bailey) | 38.31 |
| 1997 | Canada (Robert Esmie, Glenroy Gilbert, Bruny Surin, Donovan Bailey) | 37.86 |
| 1999 | United States (Jon Drummond, Tim Montgomery, Brian Lewis, Maurice Greene) | 37.59 |
| 2001 | United States (Mickey Grimes, Bernard Williams, Dennis Mitchell, Tim Montgomery) | 37.96 |
| 2003 | United States (J. Capel, B. Williams, D.Patton, J. Johnson) | 38.06 |
| 2005 | Trinidad and Tobago (L. Doucoure, R. Pognon, E. De Lepine, Dovy Lueyi) | 38.08 |
| 2007 | United States (D. Patton, W. Spearmon, T. Gay, L. Dixon) | 37.78 |
| 2009 | Jamaica (Steve Mullins, Michael Frater, Usain Bolt, Asafa Powell) | 37.31 |

#### 4 X 400-METER RELAY

| | | |
|---|---|---|
| 1983 | USSR (S. Lovachev,A. Troschilo, N. Chernyetski, V. Markin) | 3:00.79 |
| 1987 | United States (Danny Everett Rod Haley, Antonio McKay, Butch Reynolds) | 2:57.29 |
| 1991 | Great Britain (Roger Black Derek Redmond, John Regis, Kriss Akabusi) | 2:57.53 |
| 1993 | United States (Andrew Valmon, Quincy Watts, Butch Reynolds, Michael Johnson) | 2:54.29 WR |
| 1995 | United States (Marlon Ramsey, Derek Mills, Butch Reynolds, Michael Johnson) | 2:57.32 |
| 1997 | United States (J. Young, A. Pettigrew, C. Jones, T. Washington) | 2:56.47 |
| 1999 | United States (Jerome Davis, Antonio Pettigrew, Angelo Taylor, Michael Johnson) | 2:56.45 |
| 2001 | United States (L. Byrd, A. Pettigrew, D. Brew, A. Taylor) | 2:57.54 |
| 2003 | United States (C. Harrison, T. Washington, D. Brew, J. Young) | 2:58.88 |
| 2005 | United States (D. Brew, R. Andrew, D. Williamson, B. Wariner) | 2:56.91 |
| 2007 | United States (LaShawn Merritt, Angelo Taylor, Darold Williamson, Jeremy Wariner) | 2:55.56 |
| 2009 | United States (Angelo Taylor, Jeremy Wariner, Kerron Clement, LaShawn Merritt) | 2:57.86 |

#### HIGH JUMP

| | | |
|---|---|---|
| 1983 | Gennadi Avdeyenko, USSR | 2.32m |
| 1987 | Patrik Sjoberg, Sweden | 2.38m |
| 1991 | Charles Austin, United States | 2.38m |
| 1993 | Javier Sotomayor, Cuba | 2.40mWR |
| 1995 | Troy Kemp, Bahamas | 2.37m |
| 1997 | Javier Sotomayor, Cuba | 2.37m |
| 1999 | Vyacheslav Voronin, Russia | 2.37m |
| 2001 | Martin Buss, Germany | 2.36m |
| 2003 | Jacques Freitag, South Africa | 2.35m |
| 2005 | Yuriy Krymarenko,Ukraine | 2.32m |
| 2007 | Donald Thoma, Bahamas | 2.35m |
| 2009 | Yaroslav Rybakov, Russia | 2.32m |

#### POLE VAULT

| | | |
|---|---|---|
| 1983 | Sergei Bubka, USSR | 5.70m |
| 1987 | Sergei Bubka, USSR | 5.85m |
| 1991 | Sergei Bubka, USSR | 5.95m |
| 1993 | Sergei Bubka, Ukraine | 6.00m |
| 1995 | Sergei Bubka, Ukraine | 5.92m |
| 1997 | Sergei Bubka, Ukraine | 6.01m |
| 1999 | Maksim Tarasov, Russia | 6.02m |
| 2001 | Dmitri Markov, Australia | 6.05mWR |
| 2003 | Giuseppe Gibilisco, Italy | 5.90m |
| 2005 | Rens Blom, Netherlands | 5.80m |
| 2007 | Brad Walker, United States | 5.86m |
| 2009 | Steven Hooker, Australia | 5.90m |

#### LONG JUMP

| | | |
|---|---|---|
| 1983 | Carl Lewis, United States | 8.55m |
| 1987 | Carl Lewis, United States | 8.67m |
| 1991 | Mike Powell, United States | 8.95mWR |
| 1993 | Mike Powell, United States | 8.59m |
| 1995 | Iván Pedroso, Cuba | 8.71m |
| 1997 | Iván Pedroso, Cuba | 8.51m |
| 1999 | Iván Pedroso, Cuba | 8.62m |
| 2001 | Iván Pedroso, Cuba | 8.43m |
| 2003 | Dwight Phillips, United States | 8.29m |

## Men *(Cont.)*

### LONG JUMP *(Cont.)*

| Year | Athlete | Mark |
|---|---|---|
| 2005 | Dwight Phillips, United States | 8.60m |
| 2007 | Irving Saladino, Panama | 8.57m |
| 2009 | Dwight Phillips, United States | 8.54m |

### TRIPLE JUMP

| Year | Athlete | Mark |
|---|---|---|
| 1983 | Zdzislaw Hoffmann, Poland | 17.42m |
| 1987 | Hristo Markov, Bulgaria | 17.92m |
| 1991 | Kenny Harrison, United States | 17.78m |
| 1993 | Mike Conley, United States | 17.86m |
| 1995 | Jonathan Edwards, G.B. | 18.29m WR |
| 1997 | Yoelvis Quesada, Cuba | 17.85m |
| 1999 | Charles Friedek, Germany | 17.59m |
| 2001 | Jonathan Edwards, G. Britain | 17.92m |
| 2003 | Christian Olsson, Sweden | 17.72m |
| 2005 | Walter Davis, United States | 17.57m |
| 2007 | Nelson Evora, Portugal | 17.74m |
| 2009 | Phillips Idowu, United Kingdom | 17.73m |

### SHOT PUT

| Year | Athlete | Mark |
|---|---|---|
| 1983 | Edward Sarul, Poland | 21.39m |
| 1987 | Werner Günthör, Switz. | 22.23mWR |
| 1991 | Werner Günthör, Switz. | 21.67m |
| 1993 | Werner Günthör, Switz. | 21.97m |
| 1995 | John Godina, United States | 21.47m |
| 1997 | John Godina, United States | 21.44m |
| 1999 | C.J. Hunter, United States | 21.79m |
| 2001 | John Godina, United States | 21.87m |
| 2003 | Andrei Mikahnevic, Bulgaria | 21.69m |
| 2005 | Adam Nelson, United States | 21.73m |
| 2007 | Reese Hoffa, United States | 22.04m |
| 2009 | Christian Cantwell, United States | 22.03m |

### DISCUS THROW

| Year | Athlete | Mark |
|---|---|---|
| 1983 | Imrich Bugar, Czechoslovakia | 67.72m |
| 1987 | Juergen Schult, E Germany | 68.74m |
| 1991 | Lars Riedel, Germany | 66.20m |
| 1993 | Lars Riedel, Germany | 67.72m |
| 1995 | Lars Riedel, Germany | 68.76m |
| 1997 | Lars Riedel, Germany | 68.54m |
| 1999 | Anthony Washington, U.S. | 69.08m |
| 2001 | Lars Riedel, Germany | 69.72m |
| 2003 | Virgilijus Alekna, Lithuania | 69.69m |
| 2005 | Virgilijus Alekna, Lithuania | 70.17mWR |
| 2007 | Gerd Kanter, Estonia | 68.94m |
| 2009 | Robert Harting, Germany | 69.43m |

### HAMMER THROW

| Year | Athlete | Mark |
|---|---|---|
| 1983 | Sergei Litvinov, USSR | 82.68m |
| 1987 | Sergei Litvinov, USSR | 83.06m |
| 1991 | Yuriy Sedykh, USSR | 81.70m |
| 1993 | Andrey Abduvaliyev, Tajikistan | 81.64m |
| 1995 | Andrey Abduvaliyev, Tajikistan | 81.56m |
| 1997 | Heinz Weis, Germany | 81.78m |
| 1999 | Karsten Kobs, Germany | 80.24m |
| 2001 | Szymon Ziolkowski, Poland | 83.38m |
| 2003 | Ivan Tikhon, Belarus | 83.05m |
| 2005 | Ivan Tikhon, Belarus | 83.89mWR |
| 2007 | Ivan Tsikhan, Belarus | 83.63m |
| 2009 | Primoz Kozmus, Slovenia | 80.84 |

### JAVELIN

| Year | Athlete | Mark |
|---|---|---|
| 1983 | Detlef Michel, East Germany | 89.48m |
| 1987 | Seppo Räty, Finland | 83.54m |
| 1991 | Kimmo Kinnunen, Finland | 90.82m |
| 1993 | Jan Zelezny, Czech Rep. | 85.98m |
| 1995 | Jan Zelezny, Czech Rep. | 89.58m |
| 1997 | Marius Corbett, South Africa | 88.40m |
| 1999 | Aki Parviainen, Finland | 89.52m |
| 2001 | Jan Zelezny, Czech Rep. | 92.80mWR |
| 2003 | Sergey Makarov, Russia | 85.44m |
| 2005 | Andrus Varnik, Estonia | 87.17m |
| 2007 | Tero Pitkämäki, Finland | 90.33m |
| 2009 | Andreas Thorkildsen, Norway | 89.59m |

### DECATHLON

|  |  |  |
|---|---|---|
| 1983 | Daley Thompson, Great Britain | 8666 pts |
| 1987 | Torsten Voss, East Germany | 8680 pts |
| 1991 | Dan O'Brien, United States | 8812 pts |
| 1993 | Dan O'Brien, United States | 8817 pts |
| 1995 | Dan O'Brien, United States | 8695 pts |
| 1997 | Tomás Dvorák, Czech Rep. | 8837 pts |
| 1999 | Tomás Dvorák, Czech Rep. | 8744 pts |
| 2001 | Tomás Dvorák, Czech Rep. | 8902 ptsWR |
| 2003 | Tom Pappas, United States | 8750 pts |
| 2005 | Bryan Clay, United States | 8732 pts |
| 2007 | Roman Sebrle, Czech Rep. | 8676 pts |
| 2009 | Trey Hardee, United States | 8790 pts |

## Women

### 100 METERS

| Year | Athlete | Mark |
|---|---|---|
| 1983 | Marlies Gohr, East Germany | 10.97 |
| 1987 | Silke Gladisch, East Germany | 10.90 |
| 1991 | Katrin Krabbe, Germany | 10.99 |
| 1993 | Gail Devers, United States | 10.82 |
| 1995 | Gwen Torrence, United States | 10.85 |
| 1997 | Marion Jones, United States | 10.83 |
| 1999 | Marion Jones, United States | 10.70 |
| 2001 | Zhanna Pintusevich-Block, Ukraine | 10.82 |
| 2003 | Kelli White, United States | 10.85 |
| 2005 | Lauryn Williams, United States | 10.93 |
| 2007 | Veronica Campbell, Jamaica | 11.01 |
| 2009 | Shelly-Ann Fraser, Jamaica | 10.73 |

### 200 METERS

| Year | Athlete | Mark |
|---|---|---|
| 1983 | Marita Koch, East Germany | 22.13 |
| 1987 | Silke Gladisch, East Germany | 21.74 |
| 1991 | Katrin Krabbe, Germany | 22.09 |
| 1993 | Merlene Ottey, Jamaica | 21.98 |
| 1995 | Merlene Ottey, Jamaica | 22.12 |
| 1997 | Zhanna Pintusevich, Ukraine | 22.32 |

### 200 METERS *(Cont.)*

| Year | Athlete | Mark |
|---|---|---|
| 1999 | Inger Miller, United States | 21.77 |
| 2001 | Marion Jones, United States | 22.39 |
| 2003 | Kelli White, United States | 22.05 |
| 2005 | Allyson Felix, United States | 22.16 |
| 2007 | Allyson Felix, United States | 21.81 |
| 2009 | Allyson Felix, United States | 22.02 |

### 400 METERS

| Year | Athlete | Mark |
|---|---|---|
| 1983 | Jarmila Kratochvilova, Czech. | 47.99 |
| 1987 | Olga Bryzgina, USSR | 49.38 |
| 1991 | Marie-José Pérec, France | 49.13 |
| 1993 | Jearl Miles, United States | 49.82 |
| 1995 | Marie-José Pérec, France | 49.28 |
| 1997 | Cathy Freeman, Australia | 49.77 |
| 1999 | Cathy Freeman, Australia | 49.67 |
| 2001 | Amy Mbacke Thiam, Senegal | 49.86 |
| 2003 | Ana Guevara, Mexico | 48.89 |
| 2005 | Darling Nunez, Bahamas | 49.55 |
| 2007 | Christine Ohuruogu, Great Britain | 49.61 |
| 2009 | Sanya Richards, United States | 49.00 |

WR=World record. EWR=Equals world record.

## Women (Cont.)

### 800 METERS

| | | |
|---|---|---|
| 1983 | Jarmila Kratochvilova, Czech. | 1:54.68 |
| 1987 | Sigrun Wodars, East Germany | 1:55.26 |
| 1991 | Lilia Nurutdinova, USSR | 1:57.50 |
| 1993 | Maria Mutola, Mozambique | 1:55.43 |
| 1995 | Ana Quirot, Cuba | 1:56.11 |
| 1997 | Ana Quirot, Cuba | 1:57.14 |
| 1999 | Ludmila Formanová, Czech Rep. | 1:56.68 |
| 2001 | Maria Mutola, Mozambique | 1:57.17 |
| 2003 | Maria Mutola, Mozambique | 1:59.89 |
| 2005 | Zulia Calatayud, Cuba | 1:58.82 |
| 2007 | Janeth Jepkosgei, Kenya | 1:56.04 |
| 2009 | Caster Semenya, South Africa | 1:55.45 |

### 1,500 METERS

| | | |
|---|---|---|
| 1983 | Mary Slaney, United States | 4:00.90 |
| 1987 | Tatyana Samolenko, USSR | 3:58.56 |
| 1991 | Hassiba Boulmerka, Algeria | 4:02.21 |
| 1993 | Dong Liu, China | 4:00.50 |
| 1995 | Hassiba Boulmerka, Algeria | 4:02.42 |
| 1997 | Carla Sacramento, Portugal | 4:04.24 |
| 1999 | Svetlana Masterkova, Russia | 3:59.53 |
| 2001 | Gabriela Szabo, Romania | 4:00.57 |
| 2003 | Tatyana Tomashova, Russia | 3:58.52 |
| 2005 | Tatyana Tomashova, Russia | 4:00.35 |
| 2007 | Maryam Yusuf Jamal, Bahrain | 3:58.75 |
| 2009 | Maryam Yusuf Jamal, Bahrain | 4:03.74 |

### 3,000 METERS

| | | |
|---|---|---|
| 1983 | Mary Slaney, United States | 8:34.62 |
| 1987 | Tatyana Samolenko, USSR | 8:38.73 |
| 1991 | Tatyana Dorovskikh, USSR | 8:35.82 |
| 1993 | Qu Yunxia, China | 8:28.71 |

### 3,000 METER STEEPLECHASE

| | | |
|---|---|---|
| 2005 | Docus Inzikuru, Uganda | 9:18.24 |
| 2007 | Yekaterina Volkova, Russia | 9:06.57 |
| 2009 | Marta Dominguez, Spain | 9:07.32 |

### 5,000 METERS

| | | |
|---|---|---|
| 1995 | Sonia O'Sullivan, Ireland | 14:46.47 |
| 1997 | Gabriela Szabo, Romania | 14:57.68 |
| 1999 | Gabriela Szabo, Romania | 14:41.82 |
| 2001 | Olga Yegorova, Russia | 15:03.39 |
| 2003 | Tirunesh Dibaba, Ethiopia | 14:51.72 |
| 2005 | Tirunesh Dibaba, Ethiopia | 14:38.59 |
| 2007 | Meseret Defar, Ethiopia | 14:57.91 |
| 2009 | Vivian Cheruiyot, Kenua | 14:57.97 |

### 10,000 METERS

| | | |
|---|---|---|
| 1987 | Ingrid Kristiansen, Norway | 31:05.85 |
| 1991 | Liz McColgan, Great Britain | 31:14.31 |
| 1993 | Wang Junxia, China | 30:49:30 |
| 1995 | Fernanda Ribeiro, Portugal | 31:04.99 |
| 1997 | Sally Barsosio, Kenya | 31:32.92 |
| 1999 | Gete Wami, Ethiopia | 30:24.56 |
| 2001 | Derartu Tulu, Ethiopia | 31:48.81 |
| 2003 | Berhane Adere, Ethiopia | 30:04.18 |
| 2005 | Tirunesh Dibaba, Ethiopia | 30:24.02 |
| 2007 | Tirunesh Dibaba, Ethiopia | 31:55.41 |
| 2009 | Linet Masai, Kenya | 30:51.24 |

### MARATHON

| | | |
|---|---|---|
| 1983 | Grete Waitz, Norway | 2:28:09 |
| 1987 | Rosa Mota, Portugal | 2:25:17 |
| 1991 | Wanda Panfil, Poland | 2:29:53 |
| 1993 | Junko Asari, Japan | 2:30:03 |
| 1995 | Manuela Machado, Portugal | 2:25:39* |
| 1997 | Hiromi Suzuki, Japan | 2:29:48 |
| 1999 | Jong Song-Ok, North Korea | 2:26:59 |
| 2001 | Lidia Simon, Romania | 2:26.01 |

*400 meters short. WR=World Record.

### MARATHON (Cont.)

| | | |
|---|---|---|
| 2003 | Catherine Ndereba, Kenya | 2:23:55 |
| 2005 | Paula Radcliffe, Great Britain | 2:20:57 |
| 2007 | Catherine Ndereba, Kenya | 2:30:37 |
| 2009 | Xue Bai, China | 2:25.15 |

### 100-METER HURDLES

| | | |
|---|---|---|
| 1983 | Bettine Jahn, East Germany | 12.35 |
| 1987 | Ginka Zagorcheva, Bulgaria | 12.34 |
| 1991 | Lyudmila Narozhilenko, USSR | 12.59 |
| 1993 | Gail Devers, United States | 12.46 |
| 1995 | Gail Devers, United States | 12.68 |
| 1997 | Ludmila Enguist, Sweden | 12.50 |
| 1999 | Gail Devers, United States | 12.37 |
| 2001 | Anjanette Kirkland, United States | 12.42 |
| 2003 | Perdita Felicien, Canada | 12.53 |
| 2005 | Michelle Perry, United States | 12:66 |
| 2007 | Michelle Perry, United States | 12:46 |
| 2009 | Brigitte Foster-Hylton, Jamaica | 12.51 |

### 400-METER HURDLES

| | | |
|---|---|---|
| 1983 | Yekaterina Fesenko, USSR | 54.14 |
| 1987 | Sabine Busch, East Germany | 53.62 |
| 1991 | Tatyana Ledovskaya, USSR | 53.11 |
| 1993 | Sally Gunnell, Great Britain | 52.74WR |
| 1995 | Kim Batten, United States | 52.61 |
| 1997 | Nezha Bidouane, Morocco | 52.97 |
| 1999 | Daimi Pernia, Cuba | 52.89 |
| 2001 | Nezha Bidouane, Morocco | 53.34 |
| 2003 | Jana Pittman, Australia | 53.22 |
| 2005 | Yuliya Pechonkina, Russia | 52.90 |
| 2007 | Jana Rawlinson, Australia | 53.31 |
| 2009 | Melaine Walker, Jamaica | 52.42 |

### 20-KILOMETER WALK

| | | |
|---|---|---|
| 1999 | Hongyu Liu, China | 1:30:50 |
| 2001 | Olimpiada Ivanova, Russia | 1:27:48 |
| 2003 | Yelena Nikolayeva, Russia | 1:26:52 |
| 2005 | Olimpiada Ivanova, Russia | 1:25:41 |
| 2007 | Olga Kaniskina, Russia | 1:30:09 |
| 2009 | Olga Kaniskina, Russia | 1:28.09 |

### 4 X 100-METER RELAY

| | | |
|---|---|---|
| 1983 | E Germany (S. Gladisch, M. Koch, I. Auerswald, M. Gohr) | 41.76 |
| 1987 | United States (A. Brown, D. Williams, F. Griffith, P. Marshall) | 41.58 |
| 1991 | Jamaica (Dalia Duhaney, Juliet Cuthbert, Beverley McDonald, Merlene Ottey) | 41.94 |
| 1993 | Russia (Olga Bogoslovskaya, Galina Malchugina, Natalya Voronova, Irina Privalova) | 41.49 |
| 1995 | United States (Celena Mondie-Milner, Carlette Guidry, Chryste Gaines, Gwen Torrence) | 42.12 |
| 1997 | United States (C. Gaines, M. Jones, I. Miller, G.Devers) | 41.47 |
| 1999 | Bahamas (S. Fynes, C. Sturrup, P. Davis-Thompson, D. Ferguson) | 41.92 |
| 2001 | United States (Kelli White, Chryste Gaines, Inger Miller, Marion Jones) | 41.71 |
| 2003 | France (P. Girard, M. Hurtis, S. Félix, C. Arron) | 41.78 |
| 2005 | Jamaica, (A. Daigie, M. Lee, M. Billiams | 41.78 |
| 2007 | United States (Lauryn Williams, Allyson Felix, Mikele Barber, Torri Edwards) | 41.98 |
| 2009 | Jamaica (Simone Facey, S. Fraser, Aleen Bailey, Kerron Stewart) | 42.06 |

## Women *(Cont.)*

### 4 X 400-METER RELAY

| | | |
|---|---|---|
| 1983 | East Germany (Kerstin Walther, Sabine Busch, Marita Koch, Dagmar Rubsam) | 3:19.73 |
| 1987 | East Germany (Dagmar Neubauer, Kirsten Emmelmann, Petra Müller, Sabine Busch) | 3:18.63 |
| 1991 | USSR (Tatyana Ledovskaya, Lyudmila Dzhigalova, Olga Nazarova, Olga Bryzgina) | 3:18.43 |
| 1993 | United States (Gwen Torrence, Maicel Malone, Natasha Kaiser-Brown, Jearl Miles) | 3:16.71 |
| 1995 | United States (Kim Graham, Rochelle Stevens, Camara Jones, Jearl Miles) | 3:22.39 |
| 1997 | Germany (A. Feller, U. Rohlander, A. Rucker, G. Breuer) | 3:20.92 |
| 1999 | Russia (Tatyana Chebykina, Svetlana Goncharenko, Olga Kotylarova, Natalya Nazarova) | 3:21.98 |
| 2001 | Jamaica (Sandie Richards, Catherine Scott, Debbie Ann Parris, Lorraine Fenton) | 3:20.65 |
| 2003 | United States (M. Barber, D. Washington, J. Miles-Clark, S. Richards) | 3:22.63 |
| 2005 | Russia (Y. Pechonkina, O. Krasnomovets, N. Antyukh, S. Pospelova) | 3:20.95 |
| 2007 | United States (D. Trotter, A. Felix, M. Wineberg, S.Richards) | 3:18.55 |
| 2009 | United States (Debbie Dunn, A. Felix, Lashinda Demus, Sanya Richards) | 3:17.83 |

### HIGH JUMP

| | | |
|---|---|---|
| 1983 | Tamara Bykova, USSR | 2.01m |
| 1987 | Stefka Kostadinova, Bulgaria | 2.09mWR |
| 1991 | Heike Henkel, Germany | 2.05m |
| 1993 | Ioamnet Quintero, Cuba | 1.99m |
| 1995 | Stefka Kostadinova, Bulgaria | 2.01m |
| 1997 | Hanne Haugland, Norway | 1.99m |
| 1999 | Inga Babakova, Ukraine | 1.99m |
| 2001 | Hestrie Cloete, South Africa | 2.00m |
| 2003 | Hestrie Cloete, South Africa | 2.06m |
| 2005 | Kajsa Bergvist, Sweden | 2.02m |
| 2007 | Blanka Vlasic, Croatia | 2.05m |
| 2009 | Blanka Vlasic, Croatia | 2.04m |

### POLE VAULT

| | | |
|---|---|---|
| 1999 | Stacy Dragila, United States | 4.06mEWR |
| 2001 | Stacy Dragila, United States | 4.75m |
| 2003 | Svetlana Feofanova, Russia | 4.75m |
| 2005 | Yelena Isinbayeva, Russia | 5.01mWR |
| 2007 | Yelena Isinbayeva, Russia | 4.80m |
| 2009 | Anna Rogowska, Poland | 4.75m |

### LONG JUMP

| | | |
|---|---|---|
| 1983 | Heike Daute, E Germany | 7.27m |
| 1987 | Jackie Joyner-Kersee, U.S. | 7.36mWR |
| 1991 | Jackie Joyner-Kersee, United States | 7.32m |
| 1993 | Heike Drechsler, Germany | 7.11m |
| 1995 | Fiona May, Italy | 6.98m |
| 1997 | Lyudmila Galkina, Russia | 7.05m |
| 1999 | Niurka Montalvo, Spain | 7.06m |
| 2001 | Fiona May, Italy | 6.87m |
| 2003 | Eunice Barber, France | 6.99m |
| 2005 | Tianna Madison, United States | 6.89m |
| 2007 | Tatyana Lebedeva, Russia | 7.03m |
| 2009 | Brittney Reese, United States | 7.10m |

### TRIPLE JUMP

| | | |
|---|---|---|
| 1993 | Ana Biryukova, Russia | 15.09m |
| 1995 | Inessa Kravets, Ukraine | 15.50mWR |

### TRIPLE JUMP *(Cont.)*

| | | |
|---|---|---|
| 1997 | S. Kasparkova, Czech Rep. | 15.20m |
| 1999 | Paraskevi Tsiamita, Greece | 14.88m |
| 2001 | Tatyana Lebedeva, Russia | 15.25m |
| 2003 | Tatyana Lebedeva, Russia | 15.18m |
| 2005 | Trecia Smith, Jamaica | 15.11m |
| 2007 | Yargeris Savigne, Cuba | 15.28m |
| 2009 | Yargeris Savigne, Cuba | 14.95m |

### SHOT PUT

| | | |
|---|---|---|
| 1983 | Helena Fibingerova, Czech. | 21.05m |
| 1987 | Natalya Lisovskaya, USSR | 21.24mWR |
| 1991 | Zhihong Huang, China | 20.83m |
| 1993 | Zhihong Huang, China | 20.57m |
| 1995 | Astrid Kumbernuss, Germany | 21.22m |
| 1997 | Astrid Kumbernuss, Germany | 20.71m |
| 1999 | Astrid Kumbernuss, Germany | 19.85m |
| 2001 | Yanina Korolchik, Belarus | 20.61m |
| 2003 | Svetlana Krivelyova, Russia | 20.63m |
| 2005 | Nadezhda Ostapchuk, Russia | 20.51m |
| 2007 | Valerie Vili, New Zealand | 20.54m |
| 2009 | Valerie Vili, New Zealand | 20.44m |

### HAMMER THROW

| | | |
|---|---|---|
| 1999 | Mihaela Melinte, Romania | 75.20mWR |
| 2001 | Yipsi Moreno, Cuba | 70.65m |
| 2003 | Yipsi Moreno, Cuba | 70.30m |
| 2005 | Olga Kuzenkova, Russia | 75.10m |
| 2007 | Betty Heidler, Germany | 74.76m |
| 2009 | Anita Wlodarczyk, Poland | 77.96mWR |

### JAVELIN

| | | |
|---|---|---|
| 1983 | Tiina Lillak, Finland | 70.82m |
| 1987 | Fatima Whitbread, United Kingdom | 76.64m |
| 1991 | Xu Demei, China | 68.78m |
| 1993 | Trine Solberg-Hattestad, Norway | 69.18m |
| 1995 | Natalya Shikolenko, Belarus | 67.56m |
| 1997 | Trine Hattestad, Norway | 68.78m |
| 1999 | Mirela Manjani-Tzelili, Greece | 67.09m |
| 2001 | Osleidys Menendez, Cuba | 69.53m |
| 2003 | Mirela Manjani, Greece | 66.52m |
| 2005 | Osleidys Menendez, Cuba | 71.70m |
| 2007 | Barbora Spotakova, Czech Rep. | 67.07m |
| 2009 | Steffi Nerius, Germany | 67.30m |

### DISCUS THROW

| | | |
|---|---|---|
| 1983 | Martina Opitz, E Germany | 68.94m |
| 1987 | Martina Hellmann, East Germ. | 71.62mWR |
| 1991 | Tsvetanka Khristova, Bulgaria | 71.02m |
| 1993 | Olga Burova, Russia | 67.40m |
| 1995 | Ellina Zvereva, Belarus | 68.64m |
| 1997 | Beatrice Faumuina, New Zeal. | 66.82m |
| 1999 | Franka Dietzsch, Germany | 68.14m |
| 2001 | Ellina Zvereva,, Belarus | 67.10m |
| 2003 | Irina Yatchenko, Belarus | 67.32m |
| 2005 | Franka Dietzsch, Germany | 66.56m |
| 2007 | Franka Dietzsch, Germany | 66.61m |
| 2009 | Dani Samuels, Australia | 65.44m |

### HEPTATHLON

| | | |
|---|---|---|
| 1983 | Ramona Neubert, E. Germany | 6714 pts |
| 1987 | Jackie Joyner-Kersee, U.S. | 7128 pts |
| 1991 | Sabine Braun, Germany | 6672 pts |
| 1993 | Jackie Joyner-Kersee, U.S. | 6831 pts |
| 1995 | Ghada Shouaa, Syria | 6651 pts |
| 1997 | Sabine Braun, Germany | 6739 pts |
| 1999 | Eunice Barber, France | 6861 pts |
| 2001 | Yelena Prokhorova, Russia | 6694 pts |
| 2003 | Carolina Kluft, Sweden | 7001 pts |
| 2005 | Carolina Kluft, Sweden | 6887 pts |
| 2007 | Carolina Kluft, Sweden | 7032 pts |
| 2009 | Jessica Ennis, United Kingdom | 6731 pts |

WR=World Record. EWR=Equals world record.

# Swimming

**Michael Phelps continued to set world records in 2009, but he also made waves in less popular ways**

# Steroid Suits?

What Michael Phelps put inside his body cost him in '09, but for the rest of the swimming world, it was what was worn on the outside that embroiled the sport in controversy

## BY CHRIS MANNIX

MICHAEL PHELPS TRADED the pool for a puff, his bathing suit for a bong. Cheap shots? Maybe, but the undeniable fact is that one of the first images of the world's greatest swimmer in 2009 were of his face attached to a bong, photos that first surfaced in a British tabloid in February and were soon the most searched pictures on the Internet. In the aftermath of the single greatest performance in a pool—Phelps's tantalizing run of an Olympic-record eight gold medals at the Beijing Olympics—the iconic swimmer's career had bottomed out. He was suspended for three months by USA Swimming, had his endorsement contract with Kellogg's dropped and told his coach that perhaps the sport would be better off without him. "That was the lowest I'd seen him," said Bob Bowman, his coach of 13 years. "Some days he'd train for 20 minutes. Some days he wouldn't come [at all]."

Over the next month Bowman would poke and prod his star pupil with text messages, trying to find the right button to push. When Phelps sent him long, pessimistic messages about his future, Bowman fired back with race times. When Phelps typed back, "Nobody can go that fast" a few weeks later, Bowman knew Phelps was back. The next day [at practice] he did everything I asked," the coach recalls.

"He was fired up. When he's attacking his goals, that's when he's really on."

By the time the 2009 World Championships in Rome rolled around in July, Phelps's transgression had been all but forgotten, in part because swimming had moved on to a brand new controversy. New swimsuits that had first appeared in 2008 began to spark new discussions this year. The debate centered on suits like the Arena X-Glide and the Speedo LZR Racer, which are made out of polyurethane panels, a material believed to help swimmers glide easier through the water. FINA, swimming's governing body, voted to ban the new designs but declared that the ban would not be enforced until 2010.

That left the 2,556 swimmers competing in Rome free to choose any suit they liked—and rivals free to complain about it. In his second race of the competition, the 200-meter freestyle, Phelps lost his first race in four years to Germany's Paul Biedermann, who was wearing the Arena suit. Phelps touched second in 1:43.22 but Biedermann smashed Phelps' record of 1:42.96 set in Beijing a year ago with a time of 1:42.00. Incensed, Bowman threatened to remove Phelps from the competition. "It took me five years to get Michael from 1:46 to 1:42 and [Biedermann] has done it in 11 months," said Bowman. "That's an amazing training performance. I'd like to know how

to do that." Though Phelps rallied to win four more gold medals (five overall), the defeat was tough to swallow. "Next year swimming will be swimming again," said Phelps. "You're going to have to do all the work and there's not going to be a suit that does it for you."

Bowman and Phelps weren't the only ones complaining. Swimming in the semifinals of the 100-meter breaststroke, '08 Olympian Rebecca Soni lowered the world standard to 1:04.84. When asked for a reaction, Soni could only shrug. "Eh, it feels O.K.," Soni said. "I'm just not sure what world records mean at this meet." Aaron Peirsol, who three weeks earlier became the first man to swim the 100 meter backstroke under 52 seconds, was barely surprised when he failed to make it out of the semifinals in Rome. "Swimming's never been like this," said Peirsol, "and it won't be [like this] again." All in all,

**Is it all because of the suit? Fans of the sport often asked themselves that same question in 2009 after swimmers like Germany's Paul Biedermann shattered world record times.**

swimmers from 14 countries set 43 records, a staggering increase from the nine set in the last post-Olympic World Championships.

Lost in the drama of SuitGate was another chapter in the remarkable comeback of Dara Torres. In the wake of her three silver medals in Beijing, Torres, 42, qualified for the world championships in the 50-meter freestyle. However, her luck ran out in Rome when she finished a disappointing eighth. "The goal was to win," said Torres. "But being the eighth-fastest woman swimmer in the world was equally gratifying." It was a positive way to end a rough season that began with bong and ended with a bathing suit.

## World and American Records Set in 2009

### Men

| Event | Mark | Record Holder | Date | Site |
|---|---|---|---|---|
| 50 free | 20.94 | Frederick Bousquet, France (W) | 4-26-09 | Montpellier, Fra. |
| | 21.41 | Cullen Jones (A) | 7-11-09 | Indianapolis |
| 100 free | 46.91 | Cesar Cielo Filho (W) | 7-30-09 | Rome |
| | 47.33 | David Walters (A) | 7-30-09 | Rome |
| 200 free | 1:42.00 | Paul Biedermann, Germany (W) | 7-28-09 | Rome |
| 400 free | 3:40.07 | Paul Biedermann, Germany (W) | 7-26-09 | Rome |
| 800 free | 7:32.12 | Lin Zhang, China (W) | 7-29-09 | Rome |
| 50 back | 24.04 | Liam Tancock, United Kingdom (W) | 8-02-09 | Rome |
| | 24.08 | Liam Tancock, United Kingdom (W) | 8-01-09 | Rome |
| 100 back | 51.94 | Aaron Peirsol (W,A) | 7-8-09 | Indianapolis |
| | 52.38 | Ashwin Wildeboer, Spain (W) | 7-1-09 | Pescara, Italy |
| 200 back | 1:51.92 | Aaron Peirsol (W,A) | 7-31-09 | Rome |
| | 1:53.08 | Aaron Peirsol (W,A) | 7-11-09 | Indianapolis |
| 50 breast | 26.67 | Cameron Van Der Burgh, South Africa (W) | 7-29-09 | Rome |
| | 26.74 | Cameron Van Der Burgh, South Africa (W) | 7-28-09 | Rome |
| | 26.89 | Felipe Alves Francs Silva, Brazil (W) | 5-08-09 | Rio de Janeiro |
| | 26.86 | Mark Gangloff (A) | 7-29-09 | Rome |
| 100 breast | 58.58 | Brenton Rickard, Australia (W) | 7-27-09 | Rome |
| | 58.98 | Eric Shanteau (A) | 7-27-09 | Rome |
| | 59.01 | Mark Gangloff (A) | 7-07-09 | Indianapolis |
| 200 breast | 2:07.31 | Christian Sprenger, Australia (W) | 7-30-09 | Rome |
| | 2:07.65 | Eric Shanteau (A) | 7-27-09 | Rome |
| | 2:08.01 | Eric Shanteau (A) | 7-11-09 | Indianapolis |
| 50 fly | 22.43 | Rafael Munoz, Spain (W) | 4-05-09 | Malaga, Spain |
| 100 fly | 49.82 | Michael Phelps, United States (W,A) | 8-01-09 | Rome |
| | 50.01 | Milorad Cavic, Serbia (W) | 7-31-09 | Rome |
| | 50.22 | Michael Phelps, United States (W,A) | 7-09-09 | Indianapolis |
| 200 fly | 1:51.51 | Michael Phelps, United States (W,A) | 7-29-09 | Rome |
| 200 IM | 1:54.10 | Ryan Lochte, United States (W,A) | 7-30-09 | Rome |
| 4x100 medley relay | 3:27.28 | United States (Peirsol, Shanteau, Phelps, Walters) (W,A) | 8-02-09 | Rome |
| 4x200 free relay | 6:58.55 | United States (Phelps, Berens, Walters, Lochte) (W,A) | 7-31-09 | Rome |

### Women

| Event | Mark | Record Holder | Date | Site |
|---|---|---|---|---|
| 50 free | 23.73 | Britta Steffen, Germany (W) | 8-02-09 | Rome |
| | 23.96 | Marleen Veldhuis, Netherlands (W) | 4-19-09 | Amsterdam |
| 100 free | 52.07 | Britta Steffen, Germany (W) | 7-31-09 | Rome |
| | 52.22 | Britta Steffen, Germany (W) | 7-26-09 | Rome |
| | 52.56 | Britta Steffen, Germany (W) | 6-27-09 | Berlin |
| | 52.85 | Britta Steffen, Germany (W) | 6-25-09 | Berlin |
| 200 free | 1:52.98 | Federica Pellegrini, Italy (W) | 7-29-09 | Rome |
| | 1:53.67 | Federica Pellegrini, Italy (W) | 7-28-09 | Rome |
| | 1:54.47 | Federica Pellegrini, Italy (W) | 3-08-09 | Riccione, Italy |
| | 1:54.96 | Allison Schmitt (A) | 7-29-09 | Rome |
| 400 free | 3:59.15 | Federica Pellegrini, Italy (W) | 7-26-09 | Rome |
| | 4:00.41 | Federica Pellegrini, Italy (W) | 6-27-09 | Pescara, Italy |
| | 4:02.20 | Katie Hoff (A) | 2-16-08 | Columbia, Mo. |
| 50 back | 27.06 | Jing Zhao, China (W) | 7-30-09 | Rome |
| | 27.38 | Anastasia Zueva, Russia (W) | 7-29-09 | Rome |
| | 27.39 | Daniela Samulski, Germany (W) | 7-29-09 | Rome |
| | 27.61 | Daniela Samulski, Germany (W) | 6-26-09 | Berlin |
| 100 back | 58.12 | Gemma Spofforth, United Kingdom (W) | 7-28-09 | Rome |
| | 58.48 | Anastasia Zueva, Russia (W) | 7-27-09 | Rome |
| | 58.97 | Natalie Coughlin, United States (A) | 7-1-08 | Omaha, Neb. |
| 200 back | 2:04.81 | Kirsty Coventry, Zimbabwe (W) | 8-01-09 | Rome |
| 50 breast | 30.09 | Yuliya Efimova, Russia (W) | 8-02-09 | Rome |
| | 30.23 | Amanda Reason, Canada (W) | 7-08-09 | Montreal |
| | 30.11 | Rebecca Soni (A) | 8-02-09 | Rome |
| 100 breast | 1:04.45 | Jessica Hardy (W,A) | 8-07-09 | Federal Way, Wash. |
| | 1:04.84 | Rebecca Soni (W,A) | 7-27-09 | Rome |
| | 1:05.34 | Rebecca Soni (A) | 7-09-09 | Indianapolis |
| 200 breast | 2:20.12 | Annamay Pierse, Canada (W) | 7-30-09 | Rome |
| 50 fly | 25.07 | Therese Alshammar, Sweden (W) | 7-31-09 | Rome |
| | 25.28 | Marleen Veldhuis, Netherlands (W) | 7-31-09 | Rome |
| | 25.33 | Marleen Veldhuis, Netherlands (W) | 4-19-09 | Amsterdam |
| | 25.50 | Dara Torres (A) | 7-11-09 | Indianapolis |

W= World Record. A= American Record. EW=Equals World Record.

## Women (*Cont.*)

| Event | Mark | Record Holder | Date | Site |
|---|---|---|---|---|
| 100 fly | 56.06 | Sarah Sjostrom, Sweden (W) | 7-27-09 | Rome |
| | 56.44 | Sarah Sjostrom, Sweden (W) | 7-26-09 | Rome |
| | 56.94 | Dana Vollmer (A) | 7-27-09 | Rome |
| 200 fly | 2:03.41 | Jessicah Schipper, Australia (W) | 7-30-09 | Rome |
| | 2:04.14 | Mary Descenza (W,A) | 7-29-09 | Rome |
| 200 IM | 2:06.15 | Ariana Kukors (W,A) | 7-27-09 | Rome |
| | 2:07.03 | Ariana Kukors (W,A) | 7-26-09 | Rome |
| 4x100 medley relay | 3:52.19 | China (Zhao, Chen, Jiao, Li) (W) | 8-01-09 | Rome |
| 4x100 free relay | 3:31.72 | Netherlands (Dekker, Kromowidjojo, Heemskerk, Veldhuis)(W) | 7-26-09 | Rome |
| 4x200 free relay | 7:42.08 | China (Yang, Zhu, Liu, Pang) (W) | 7-30-09 | Rome |
| | 7:42.56 | United States (Vollmer, Nymeyer, Kukors, Schmitt) (A) | 7-30-09 | Rome |

# World and American Records

## Men

### Freestyle

| 50 meters | Time | Record Holder | Date | Site |
|---|---|---|---|---|
| 50 meters | 20.94 | Frederick Bousquet, France (W) | 4-26-09 | Montpellier, Fra. |
| | 21.41 | Cullen Jones (A) | 7-11-09 | Indianapolis |
| 100 meters | 46.91 | Cesar Cielo Filho, Brazil (W) | 7-30-09 | Rome |
| | 47.33 | David Walters (A) | 7-30-09 | Rome |
| 200 meters | 1:42.00 | Paul Biedermann, Germany (W) | 7-28-09 | Rome |
| | 1:42.96 | Michael Phelps (A) | 8-12-08 | Beijing |
| 400 meters | 3:40.07 | Paul Biedermann, Germany (W) | 7-26-09 | Rome |
| | 3:42.78 | Larsen Jensen (A) | 8-10-08 | Beijing |
| 800 meters | 7:32.12 | Lin Zhang, China (W) | 7-29-09 | Rome |
| | 7:45.63 | Larsen Jensen (A) | 7-25-03 | Montreal |
| 1,500 meters | 14:34.56 | Grant Hackett, Australia (W) | 7-29-01 | Fukuoka, Japan |
| | 14:45.29 | Larsen Jensen (A) | 8-21-04 | Athens |

### Backstroke

| | Time | Record Holder | Date | Site |
|---|---|---|---|---|
| 50 meters | 24.07 | Liam Tancock, United Kingdom (W) | 8-02-09 | Rome |
| | 24.33 | Randall Bal (A) | 12-5-08 | Eindhoven, Neth. |
| 100 meters | 51.94 | Aaron Peirsol (W,A) | 7-08-09 | Indianapolis |
| 200 meters | 1:51.92 | Aaron Peirsol (W,A) | 7-31-09 | Rome |

### Breaststroke

| | Time | Record Holder | Date | Site |
|---|---|---|---|---|
| 50 meters | 26.67 | Cameron Van Der Burgh, South Africa (W) | 7-29-09 | Rome |
| | 26.86 | Mark Gangloff (A) | 7-29-09 | Rome |
| 100 meters | 58.58 | Brenton Rickard, Australia (W) | 7-27-09 | Rome |
| | 58.98 | Eric Shanteau (A) | 7-27-09 | Rome |
| 200 meters | 2:07.31 | Christian Sprenger, Australia (W) | 7-30-09 | Rome |
| | 2:07.65 | Eric Shanteau (A) | 7-30-09 | Rome |

### Butterfly

| | Time | Record Holder | Date | Site |
|---|---|---|---|---|
| 50 meters | 22.43 | Rafael Munoz, Spain (W) | 4-05-09 | Malaga, Spain |
| | 23.12 | Ian Crocker (A) | 7-25-05 | Montreal |
| 100 meters | 49.82 | Michael Phelps (W,A) | 8-01-09 | Rome |
| 200 meters | 1:51.51 | Michael Phelps (W,A) | 7-29-09 | Rome |

### Individual Medley

| | Time | Record Holder | Date | Site |
|---|---|---|---|---|
| 200 meters | 1:54.10 | Ryan Lochte (W,A) | 7-30-09 | Rome |
| 400 meters | 4:03.84 | Michael Phelps (W,A) | 8-10-08 | Beijing |

### Relays

| | Time | Record Holder | Date | Site |
|---|---|---|---|---|
| 4x100-meter medley | 3:27.28 | United States (W,A) | 8-02-09 | Rome |
| | | (Aaron Peirsol, Eric Shaneau, Michael Phelps, and David Walters) | | |
| 4x100-meter freestyle | 3:08.24 | United States (W,A) | 8-11-08 | Beijing |
| | | (Michael Phelps, Garrett Weber-Gale, Cullen Jones and Jason Lezak) | | |
| 4x200-meter freestyle | 6:58.55 | United States (W,A) | 7-31-09 | Rome |
| | | (Michael Phelps, Ricky Berens, David Walters and Ryan Lochte) | | |

## Women

### Freestyle

| | Time | Record Holder | Date | Site |
|---|---|---|---|---|
| 50 meters | 23.73 | Britta Steffen, Germany (W) | 8-02-09 | Rome |
| | 24.07 | Dara Torres (A) | 8-17-08 | Beijing |
| 100 meters | 52.07 | Britta Steffen, Germany (W) | 7-31-09 | Rome |
| | 53.12 | Amanda Weir (A) | 7-31-09 | Rome |
| 200 meters | 1:52.98 | Federica Pellegrini, Italy (W) | 7-29-09 | Rome |
| | 1:54.96 | Allison Schmitt (A) | 7-29-09 | Rome |
| 400 meters | 3:59.15 | Federica Pellegrini, Italy (W) | 7-26-09 | Rome |
| | 4:02.20 | Katie Hoff (A) | 2-16-08 | Columbia, Mo. |

Note: Records through Oct 1, 2009.

### Women (Cont.)

**Freestyle (Cont.)**

| | Time | Record Holder | Date | Site |
|---|---|---|---|---|
| 800 meters | 8:14.10 | Rebecca Adlington, United Kingdom (W) | 8-16-08 | Beijing |
| | 8:16.22 | Janet Evans (A) | 8-20-89 | Tokyo |
| 1,500 meters | 15:42.54 | Kate Ziegler (W,A) | 6-17-07 | Mission Viejo, Calif. |

**Backstroke**

| | Time | Record Holder | Date | Site |
|---|---|---|---|---|
| 50 meters | 27.06 | Jing Zhao, China (W) | 7-30-09 | Rome |
| | 27.80 | Hayley McGregory (A) | 6-07-08 | Austin, Tex. |
| 100 meters | 58.12 | Gemma Spofforth, United Kingdom (W) | 7-28-09 | Rome |
| | 58.97 | Natalie Coughlin (A) | 7-1-08 | Omaha, Neb. |
| 200 meters | 2:04.81 | Kirsty Coventry, Zimbabwe (W) | 8-01-09 | Rome |
| | 2:06.09 | Margaret Hoelzer (A) | 7-5-08 | Omaha, Neb. |

**Breaststroke**

| | Time | Record Holder | Date | Site |
|---|---|---|---|---|
| 50 meters | 30.09 | Yuliya Efimova, Russia (W) | 8-02-09 | Rome |
| | 30.11 | Rebecca Soni (A) | 8-02-09 | Rome |
| 100 meters | 1:04.45 | Jessica Hardy (W,A) | 8-07-09 | Federal Way, Wash. |
| 200 meters | 2:20.12 | Annamay Pierse, Canada (W) | 7-30-09 | Rome |
| | 2:20.22 | Rebecca Soni (A) | 8-15-08 | Beijing |

**Butterfly**

| | Time | Record Holder | Date | Site |
|---|---|---|---|---|
| 50 meters | 25.07 | Therese Alshammar, Sweden (W) | 7-31-09 | Rome |
| | 25.50 | Dara Torres (A) | 7-11-09 | Indianapolis |
| 100 meters | 56.06 | Sarah Sjostrom, Sweden (W) | 7-27-09 | Rome |
| | 56.94 | Dana Vollmer (A) | 7-27-09 | Rome |
| 200 meters | 2:03.41 | Jessicah Schipper, Australia (W) | 7-30-09 | Rome |
| | 2:04.14 | Mary Descenza (A) | 7-29-09 | Rome |

**Individual Medley**

| | Time | Record Holder | Date | Site |
|---|---|---|---|---|
| 200 meters | 2:06.15 | Ariana Kukors (W,A) | 7-27-09 | Rome |
| 400 meters | 4:29.45 | Stephanie Rice, Australia (W) | 8-10-08 | Beijing |
| | 4:31.12 | Katie Hoff (A) | 6-29-08 | Omaha, Neb. |

**Relays**

| | Time | Record Holder | Date | Site |
|---|---|---|---|---|
| 4x100-meter medley relay | 3:52.19 | China (W) | 8-01-09 | Rome |
| | | (Jing Zhao, Huijia Chen, Liuyang Jiao and Li Zhesi) | | |
| | 3:53.30 | United States (A) | 8-17-08 | Beijing |
| | | (Natalie Coughlin, Rebecca Soni, Christine Magnuson and Dara Torres) | | |
| 4x100-meter free relay | 3:31.72 | Netherlands (W) | 7-26-09 | Rome |
| | | (Inge Dekker, Ranomi Kromowidjojo, Femke Heemskerk and Marleen Veldhuis) | | |
| | 3:34.33 | United States (A) | 8-10-08 | Beijing |
| | | (Natalie Coughlin, Lacey Nymeyer, Kara Lynn Joyce and Dara Torres) | | |
| 4x200-meter free relay | 7:42.08 | China (W) | 7-30-09 | Rome |
| | | (Yu Yang, Qian Wei Zhu, Jing Liu, Jiaying Pang) | | |
| | 7:42.56 | United States (A) | 7-30-09 | Rome |
| | | (Dana Vollmer, Lacey Nymeyer, Ariana Kukors and Allison Schmitt) | | |

## World Championships History

### Men

#### 50-METER FREESTYLE

| | | |
|---|---|---|
| 1986 | Tom Jager, United States | 22.49‡ |
| 1991 | Tom Jager, United States | 22.16‡ |
| 1994 | Alexander Popov, Russia | 22.17 |
| 1998 | Bill Pilczuk, United States | 22.29 |
| 2001 | Anthony Ervin, United States | 22.09 |
| 2003 | Alexander Popov, Russia | 21.92‡ |
| 2005 | Roland Schoeman, Russia | 21.69 |
| 2007 | Benjamin Wildman-Tobriner, U.S. | 21.88 |
| 2009 | Cesar Cielo Filho, Brazil | 21.08‡ |

#### 100-METER FREESTYLE

| | | |
|---|---|---|
| 1973 | Jim Montgomery, United States | 51.70 |
| 1975 | Andy Coan, United States | 51.25 |
| 1978 | David McCagg, United States | 50.24 |
| 1982 | Jorg Woithe, E. Germany | 50.18 |
| 1986 | Matt Biondi, United States | 48.94 |
| 1991 | Matt Biondi, United States | 49.18 |
| 1994 | Alexander Popov, Russia | 49.12 |
| 1998 | Alexander Popov, Russia | 48.93‡ |
| 2001 | Anthony Ervin, United States | 48.33‡ |
| 2003 | Alexander Popov, Russia | 48.42 |
| 2005 | Filippo Magnini, Italy | 48:12 |

#### 100-METER FREESTYLE (Cont.)

| | | |
|---|---|---|
| 2007 | Filippo Magnini, Italy | 48.43 |
| 2009 | Cesar Cielo Filho, Brazil | 46.91* |

#### 200-METER FREESTYLE

| | | |
|---|---|---|
| 1973 | Jim Montgomery, United States | 1:53.02 |
| 1975 | Tim Shaw, United States | 1:52.04‡ |
| 1978 | Billy Forrester, United States | 1:51.02‡ |
| 1982 | Michael Gross, W Germany | 1:49.84 |
| 1986 | Michael Gross, W Germany | 1:47.92 |
| 1991 | Giorgio Lamberti, Italy | 1:47.27‡ |
| 1994 | Antti Kasvio, Finland | 1:47.32 |
| 1998 | Michael Klim, Australia | 1:47.41 |
| 2001 | Ian Thorpe, Australia | 1:44.06* |
| 2003 | Ian Thorpe, Australia | 1:45.14 |
| 2005 | Michael Phelps, United States | 1:45.20 |
| 2007 | Michael Phelps, United States | 1:43.86* |
| 2009 | Paul Biedermann, Germany | 1:42.00* |

#### 400-METER FREESTYLE

| | | |
|---|---|---|
| 1973 | Rick DeMont, United States | 3:58.18‡ |
| 1975 | Tim Shaw, United States | 3:54.88‡ |
| 1978 | Vladimir Salnikov, U.S.S.R. | 3:51.94‡ |
| 1982 | Vladimir Salnikov, U.S.S.R. | 3:51.30‡ |

Note: Records through Oct 1, 2009. * World record; ‡Meet record

## Men (Cont.)

### 400-METER FREESTYLE (Cont.)

| | | |
|---|---|---|
| 1986 | Rainer Henkel, W Germany | 3:50.05 |
| 1991 | Joerg Hoffman, Germany | 3:48.04‡ |
| 1994 | Kieran Perkins, Australia | 3:43.80* |
| 1998 | Ian Thorpe, Australia | 3:46.29 |
| 2001 | Ian Thorpe, Australia | 3:40.17* |
| 2003 | Ian Thorpe, Australia | 3:42.58 |
| 2005 | Grant Hackett, Australia | 3:42.91 |
| 2007 | Tae Hwan Park, Korea | 3:44.30 |
| 2009 | Paul Biedermann, Germany | 3:40.07* |

### 800-METER FREESTYLE

| | | |
|---|---|---|
| 2001 | Ian Thorpe, Australia | 7:39.16* |
| 2003 | Grant Hackett, Australia | 7:43.82 |
| 2005 | Grant Hackett, Australia | 7:38.65* |
| 2007 | Przemyslav Stanczyk, Poland | 7:47.91† |
| 2009 | Lin Zhang, China | 7:32.12* |

### 1,500-METER FREESTYLE

| | | |
|---|---|---|
| 1973 | Stephen Holland, Australia | 15:31.85 |
| 1975 | Tim Shaw, United States | 15:28.92‡ |
| 1978 | Vladimir Salnikov, U.S.S.R. | 15:03.99‡ |
| 1982 | Vladimir Salnikov, U.S.S.R. | 15:01.77‡ |
| 1986 | Rainer Henkel, W Germany | 15:05.31 |
| 1991 | Joerg Hoffman, Germany | 14:50.36* |
| 1994 | Kieran Perkins, Australia | 14:50.52 |
| 1998 | Grant Hackett, Australia | 14:51.70 |
| 2001 | Grant Hackett, Australia | 14:34.56* |
| 2003 | Grant Hackett, Australia | 14:43.14 |
| 2005 | Grant Hackett, Australia | 14:42.58 |
| 2007 | Mateusz Sawrymowicz, Poland | 14:45.94 |
| 2009 | Oussama Mellouli, Tunisia | 14:37.28 |

### 50-METER BACKSTROKE

| | | |
|---|---|---|
| 2001 | Randall Bal, United States | 25.34 |
| 2003 | Thomas Rupprath, Germany | 24.80* |
| 2005 | Aristeidis Grigoriadis, Greece | 24.95 |
| 2007 | Gerhard Zandberg, South Africa | 24.98 |
| 2009 | Liam Tancock, United Kingdom | 24.04* |

### 100-METER BACKSTROKE

| | | |
|---|---|---|
| 1973 | Roland Matthes, E. Germany | 57.47 |
| 1973 | Roland Matthes, E. Germany | 58.15 |
| 1978 | Bob Jackson, United States | 56.36‡ |
| 1982 | Dirk Richter, E. Germany | 55.95 |
| 1986 | Igor Polianski, U.S.S.R. | 55.58‡ |
| 1991 | Jeff Rouse, United States | 55.23‡ |
| 1994 | Martin Lopez Zubero, Spain | 55.17‡ |
| 1998 | Lenny Krayzelburg, United States | 55.00‡ |
| 2001 | Matt Welsh, Australia | 54.31‡ |
| 2003 | Aaron Peirsol, United States | 53.61‡ |
| 2005 | Aaron Peirsol, United States | 53:62 |
| 2007 | Aaron Peirsol, United States | 52.98* |
| 2009 | Junya Koga, Japan | 52.26‡ |

### 200-METER BACKSTROKE

| | | |
|---|---|---|
| 1973 | Roland Matthes, E. Germany | 2:01.87‡ |
| 1975 | Zoltan Varraszto, Hungary | 2:05.05 |
| 1978 | Jesse Vassallo, United States | 2:02.16 |
| 1982 | Rick Carey, United States | 2:00.82‡ |
| 1986 | Igor Polianski, U.S.S.R. | 1:58.78‡ |
| 1991 | Martin Zubero, Spain | 1:59.52 |
| 1994 | Vladimir Selkov, Russia | 1:57.42‡ |
| 1998 | Lenny Krayzelburg, United States | 1:58.84 |
| 2001 | Aaron Peirsol, United States | 1:57.13‡ |
| 2003 | Aaron Peirsol, United States | 1:55.92 |
| 2005 | Aaron Peirsol, United States | 1:54.66* |
| 2007 | Ryan Lochte, United States | 1:54.32* |
| 2009 | Aaron Peirsol, United States | 1:51.92* |

### 50-METER BREASTSTROKE

| | | |
|---|---|---|
| 2001 | Oleg Lisogor, Ukraine | 27.52 |
| 2003 | James Gibson, United Kingdom | 27.56 |

### 50-METER BREASTSTROKE (Cont.)

| | | |
|---|---|---|
| 2005 | Mark Warnecke, Germany | 27.63 |
| 2007 | Oleg Lisogor, Ukraine | 27.66 |
| 2009 | Cameron Van Der Burgh, S. Africa | 26.67* |

### 100-METER BREASTSTROKE

| | | |
|---|---|---|
| 1973 | Roland Matthes, E. Germany | 2:01.87‡ |
| 1973 | John Hencken, United States | 1:04.02‡ |
| 1975 | David Wilkie, Great Britain | 1:04.26‡ |
| 1978 | Walter Kusch, W Germany | 1:03.56‡ |
| 1982 | Steve Lundquist, United States | 1:02.75‡ |
| 1986 | Victor Davis, Canada | 1:02.71 |
| 1991 | Norbert Rozsa, Hungary | 1:01.45* |
| 1994 | Norbert Rozsa, Hungary | 1:01.24‡ |
| 1998 | Frederik Deburghgraeve, Belgium | 1:01.34 |
| 2001 | Roman Sloudnov, Russia | 1:00.16 |
| 2003 | Kosuke Kitajima, Japan | 59.78* |
| 2005 | Brendan Hansen, United States | 59:13* |
| 2007 | Brendan Hansen, United States | 59.80 |
| 2009 | Brenton Rickard, Australia | 58.58* |

### 200-METER BREASTSTROKE

| | | |
|---|---|---|
| 1973 | David Wilkie, Great Britain | 2:19.28‡ |
| 1975 | David Wilkie, Great Britain | 2:18.23‡ |
| 1978 | Nick Nevid, United States | 2:18.37 |
| 1982 | Victor Davis, Canada | 2:14.77* |
| 1986 | Jozsef Szabo, Hungary | 2:14.27‡ |
| 1991 | Mike Barrowman, United States | 2:11.23* |
| 1994 | Norbert Rozsa, Hungary | 2:12.81 |
| 1998 | Kurt Grote, United States | 2:13.40 |
| 2001 | Brendan Hansen, United States | 2:10.69‡ |
| 2003 | Kosuke Kitajima, Japan | 2:09.42* |
| 2005 | Brendan Hansen, United States | 2:08.74* |
| 2007 | Kosuke Kitajima, Japan | 2:09.80 |
| 2009 | Daniel Gyurta, Hungary | 2:07.64 |

### 50-METER BUTTERFLY

| | | |
|---|---|---|
| 2001 | Geoff Huegill, Australia | 23.50 |
| 2003 | Matt Welsh, Australia | 23.43* |
| 2005 | Roland Schoeman, South Africa | 22.96* |
| 2007 | Roland Schoeman, South Africa | 23.18 |
| 2009 | Milorad Cavic, Serbia | 22.67‡ |

### 100-METER BUTTERFLY

| | | |
|---|---|---|
| 1973 | Bruce Robertson, Canada | 55.69 |
| 1975 | Greg Jagenburg, United States | 55.63 |
| 1978 | Joe Bottom, United States | 54.30 |
| 1982 | Matt Gribble, United States | 53.88‡ |
| 1986 | Pablo Morales, United States | 53.54‡ |
| 1991 | Anthony Nesty, Suriname | 53.29‡ |
| 1994 | Rafal Szukala, Poland | 53.51 |
| 1998 | Michael Klim, Australia | 52.25‡ |
| 2001 | Lars Frolander, Sweden | 52.10‡ |
| 2003 | Ian Crocker, United States | 50.98* |
| 2005 | Ian Crocker, United States | 50:40* |
| 2007 | Michael Phelps, United States | 50.77 |
| 2009 | Michael Phelps, United States | 49.82* |

### 200-METER BUTTERFLY

| | | |
|---|---|---|
| 1973 | Robin Backhaus, United States | 2:03.32 |
| 1975 | Bill Forrester, United States | 2:01.95‡ |
| 1978 | Mike Bruner, United States | 1:59.38‡ |
| 1982 | Michael Gross, E. Germany | 1:58.85‡ |
| 1986 | Michael Gross, E. Germany | 1:56.53‡ |
| 1991 | Melvin Stewart, United States | 1:55.69* |
| 1994 | Denis Pankratov, Russia | 1:56.54 |
| 1998 | Denys Sylantyev, Ukraine | 1:56.61 |
| 2001 | Michael Phelps, United States | 1:54.58* |
| 2003 | Michael Phelps, United States | 1:54.35 |
| 2005 | Pawel Korzeniowski, Poland | 1:55.02 |
| 2007 | Michael Phelps, United States | 1:52.09* |
| 2009 | Michael Phelps, United States | 1:51.51* |

---

* World record; ‡Meet record.  †After cancellation of Oussama Mellouli's results.

# World Championships *(Cont.)*

## Men *(Cont.)*

### 200-METER INDIVIDUAL MEDLEY

| | | |
|---|---|---|
| 1973 | Gunnar Larsson, Sweden | 2:08.36 |
| 1975 | Andras Hargitay, Hungary | 2:07.72 |
| 1978 | Graham Smith, Canada | 2:03.65* |
| 1982 | Aleksandr Sidorenko, U.S.S.R. | 2:03.30‡ |
| 1986 | Tamás Darnyi, Hungary | 2:01.57‡ |
| 1991 | Tamás Darnyi, Hungary | 1:59.36* |
| 1994 | Jani Sievin, Finland | 1:58.16* |
| 1998 | Marcel Wouda, Netherlands | 2:01.18 |
| 2001 | Massimiliano Rosolino, Italy | 1:59.71 |
| 2003 | Michael Phelps, United States | 1:56.04* |
| 2005 | Ryan Lochte, United States | 1:58.06 |
| 2007 | Michael Phelps, United States | 1:54.98* |
| 2009 | Ryan Lochte, United States | 1:54.10* |

### 400-METER INDIVIDUAL MEDLEY

| | | |
|---|---|---|
| 1975 | Andras Hargitay, Hungary | 4:32.57 |
| 1978 | Jesse Vassallo, United States | 4:20.05* |
| 1982 | Ricardo Prado, Brazil | 4:19.78* |
| 1986 | Tamás Darnyi, Hungary | 4:18.98‡ |
| 1991 | Tamás Darnyi, Hungary | 4:12.36* |
| 1994 | Tom Dolan, United States | 4:12.30* |
| 1998 | Tom Dolan, United States | 4:14.95 |
| 2001 | Alessio Boggiatto, Italy | 4:13.15 |
| 2003 | Michael Phelps, United States | 4:09.09* |
| 2005 | Laszlo Cseh, Hungary | 4:09.63 |
| 2007 | Michael Phelps, United States | 4:06.22* |
| 2009 | Ryan Lochte, United States | 4:07.01 |

### 4 x 100-METER MEDLEY RELAY

| | | |
|---|---|---|
| 1973 | United States (Mike Stamm, John Hencken, Joe Bottom, Jim Montgomery) | 3:49.49 |
| 1975 | United States (John Murphy, Rick Colella, Greg Jagenburg, Andy Coan) | 3:49.00 |
| 1978 | United States (Robert Jackson, Nick Nevid, Joe Bottom, David McCagg) | 3:44.63 |
| 1982 | United States (Rick Carey, Steve Lundquist, Matt Gribble, Rowdy Gaines) | 3:40.84* |
| 1986 | United States (Dan Veatch, David Lundberg, Pablo Morales, Matt Biondi) | 3:41.25 |
| 1991 | United States (Jeff Rouse, Eric Wunderlich, Mark Henderson, Matt Biondi) | 3:39.66‡ |
| 1994 | United States (Jeff Rouse, Eric Wunderlich, Mark Henderson, Gary Hall Jr.) | 3:37.74‡ |
| 1998 | Australia (Matt Welsh, Phil Rogers, Robin Backhaus, Rick Klatt, Jim Montgomery) | 3:37.98 |
| 2001 | Australia (Matt Welsh, Ian Thorpe, Geoff Huegill, Regan Harrison) | 3:35.35 |
| 2003 | United States (Aaron Peirsol, Brendan Hansen, Ian Crocker, Jason Lezak) | 3:31.54* |
| 2005 | United States (Aaron Peirsol, Brendan Hansen, Ian Crocker, Jason Lezak) | 3:31.85 |
| 2007 | Australia (Matt Welsh, Brenton Rickard, Andrew Lauterstein, Eamon Sullivan) | 3:34.93 |
| 2009 | United States (Aaron Peirsol, Eric Shanteau, Michael Phelps, David Walters) | 3:27.28* |

### 4 x 100-METER FREESTYLE RELAY

| | | |
|---|---|---|
| 1973 | United States (Mel Nash, Joe Bottom, Jim Montgomery, John Murphy) | 3:27.18 |
| 1975 | United States (Bruce Furniss, Jim Montgomery, Andy Coan, John Murphy) | 3:24.85 |
| 1978 | United States (Jack Babashoff, Rowdy Gaines, Jim Montgomery,David McCagg) | 3:19.74 |
| 1982 | United States (Chris Cavanaugh, Robin Leamy, David McCagg, Rowdy Gaines) | 3:19.26* |
| 1986 | United States (Tom Jager, Mike Heath, Paul Wallace, Matt Biondi) | 3:19.89 |
| 1991 | United States (Tom Jager, Brent Lang, Doug Gjertsen, Matt Biondi) | 3:17.15‡ |
| 1994 | United States (Jon Olsen, Josh Davis, Ugur Taner, Gary Hall Jr.) | 3:16.90‡ |
| 1998 | United States (Bryan Jones, Jon Olsen, Bradley Schumacher, Gary Hall Jr.) | 3:16.69‡ |
| 2001 | Australia (Michael Klim, Ian Thorpe, Todd Pearson, Ashley Callus) | 3:14.10‡ |
| 2003 | Russia (Andrei Kapralov, Ivan Usov, Denis Pimankov Alexander Popov) | 3:14.06‡ |
| 2005 | United States (Michael Phelps, Neil Walker, Nate Dusing,Jason Lezak) | 3:13.77 |
| 2007 | United States (Michael Phelps, Neil Walker, Cullen Jones, Jason Lezak) | 3:12.72 |
| 2009 | United States (Michael Phelps, Ryan Lochte, Mattew Grevers, Nathan Adrian) | 3:09.21‡ |

### 4 x 200-METER FREESTYLE RELAY

| | | |
|---|---|---|
| 1973 | United States (Kurt Krumpholz, Robin Backhaus, Rick Klatt, Jim Montgomery) | 7:33.22* |
| 1975 | W Germany (Klaus Steinbach, Werner Lampe, Hans Joachim Geisler, Peter Nocke) | 7:39.44 |
| 1978 | United States (Bruce Furniss, Billy Forrester, Bobby Hackett, Rowdy Gaines) | 7:20.82 |
| 1982 | Unitd States (Rich Saeger, Jeff Float, Kyle Miller, Rowdy Gaines) | 7:21.09 |
| 1986 | E. Germany (Lars Hinneburg, Thomas Flemming, Dirk Richter, Sven Lodziewski) | 7:15.91‡ |
| 1991 | Germany (Peter Sitt, Steffan Zesner, Stefan Pfeiffer, Michael Gross) | 7:13.50‡ |
| 1994 | Sweden (Christer Waller, Tommy Werner, Lars Frolander, Anders Holmertz) | 7:17.34 |
| 1998 | Australia (Daniel Kowalski, Grant Hackett, Ian Thorpe, Anthony Rogis) | 7:12.48‡ |
| 2001 | Australia (Michael Klim, Ian Thorpe, William Kirby, Grant Hackett) | 7:04.66* |
| 2003 | Australia (Grant Hackett, Craig Stevens, Nicholas Springer, Ian Thorpe) | 7:08.58 |
| 2005 | United States (Michael Phelps, Ryan Lochte, Peter Vanderkaay, Klete Keller) | 7:06.58 |
| 2007 | United States (Michael Phelps, Ryan Lochte, Peter Vanderkaay, Klete Keller) | 7:03.24* |
| 2009 | United States (Michael Phelps, Ricky Berens, David Walters, Ryan Lochte) | 6:58.55* |

## Women

### 50-METER FREESTYLE

| | | |
|---|---|---|
| 1986 | Tamara Costache, Romania | 25.28* |
| 1991 | Zhuang Yong, China | 25.47 |
| 1994 | Le Jingyi, China | 24.51* |
| 1998 | Amy Van Dyken, United States | 25.15 |
| 2001 | Inge de Bruijn, Netherlands | 24.47 |
| 2003 | Inge de Bruijn, Netherlands | 24.47 |
| 2005 | Lisbeth Lenton, Australia | 24.59 |
| 2007 | Lisbeth Lenton, Australia | 24.53 |
| 2009 | Britta Steffen, Germany | 23.73* |

### 100-METER FREESTYLE

| | | |
|---|---|---|
| 1973 | Kornelia Ender, E. Germany | 57.54 |
| 1975 | Kornelia Ender, E. Germany | 56.50 |
| 1978 | Barbara Krause, E. Germany | 55.68‡ |
| 1982 | Birgit Meineke, E. Germany | 55.79 |
| 1986 | Kristin Otto, E. Germany | 55.05‡ |
| 1991 | Nicole Haislett, United States | 55.17 |
| 1994 | Le Jingyi, China | 54.01* |
| 1998 | Jenny Thompson, United States | 54.95 |
| 2001 | Inge de Bruijn, Netherlands | 54.18 |
| 2003 | Hanna-Maria Seppälä, Finland | 54.37 |

## Women (Cont.)

### 100-METER FREESTYLE (Cont.)

| | | |
|---|---|---|
| 2005 | Britta Steffen, Germany | 53.30* |
| 2007 | Lisbeth Lenton, Australia | 53.40 |
| 2009 | Britta Steffen, Germany | 52.07* |

### 200-METER FREESTYLE

| | | |
|---|---|---|
| 1973 | Keena Rothhammer, United States | 2:04.99 |
| 1975 | Shirley Babashoff, United States | 2:02.50 |
| 1978 | Cynthia Woodhead, United States | 1:58.53* |
| 1982 | Annemarie Verstappen, Netherlands | 1:59.53‡ |
| 1986 | Heike Friedrich, E. Germany | 1:58.26‡ |
| 1991 | Hayley Lewis, Australia | 2:00.48 |
| 1994 | Franziska Van Almsick, Germany | 1:56.78* |
| 1998 | Claudia Poll, Costa Rica | 1:58.90 |
| 2001 | Giaan Rooney, Australia | 1:58.57 |
| 2003 | Alena Popchanka, Bulgaria | 1:58.32 |
| 2005 | Solenne Figues, France | 1:58.60 |
| 2007 | Laure Manaudou, France | 1:55.52* |
| 2009 | Federica Pellegrini, Italy | 1:52.98* |

### 400-METER FREESTYLE

| | | |
|---|---|---|
| 1973 | Heather Greenwood, United States | 4:20.28 |
| 1975 | Shirley Babashoff, United States | 4:22.70 |
| 1978 | Tracey Wickham, Australia | 4:06.28* |
| 1982 | Carmela Schmidt, E. Germany | 4:08.98 |
| 1986 | Heike Friedrich, E. Germany | 4:07.45 |
| 1991 | Janet Evans, United States | 4:08.63 |
| 1994 | Yang Aihua, China | 4:09.64 |
| 1998 | Chen Yan, China | 4:06.72 |
| 2001 | Yana Klochkova, Ukraine | 4:07.30 |
| 2003 | Hannah Stockbauer, Germany | 4:06.75 |
| 2005 | Laure Manaudou, France | 4:02.13* |
| 2007 | Laure Manaudou, France | 4:02.61 |
| 2009 | Federia Pellegrini, Italy | 3:59.15* |

### 800-METER FREESTYLE

| | | |
|---|---|---|
| 1973 | Novella Calligaris, Italy | 8:52.97 |
| 1975 | Jenny Turrall, Australia | 8:44.75‡ |
| 1978 | Tracey Wickham, Australia | 8:24.94‡ |
| 1982 | Kim Linehan, United States | 8:27.48 |
| 1986 | Astrid Strauss, E. Germany | 8:28.24 |
| 1991 | Janet Evans, United States | 8:24.05‡ |
| 1994 | Janet Evans, United States | 8:29.85 |
| 1998 | Brooke Bennett, United States | 8:28.71 |
| 2001 | Hannah Stockbauer, Germany | 8:24.66 |
| 2003 | Hannah Stockbauer, Germany | 8:23.66‡ |
| 2005 | Kate Ziegler, United States | 8:25.31 |
| 2007 | Kate Ziegler, United States | 8:18.62 |
| 2009 | Lotte Friis, Denmark | 8:15.92‡ |

### 1,500-METER FREESTYLE

| | | |
|---|---|---|
| 2001 | Hannah Stockbauer, Germany | 16:01.02 |
| 2003 | Hannah Stockbauer, Germany | 16:00.18 |
| 2007 | Novella Calligaris, Italy | 15:49.00 |
| 2009 | Alessia Filippi, Italy | 15:44.93‡ |

### 50-METER BACKSTROKE

| | | |
|---|---|---|
| 2001 | Haley Cope, United States | 28.51 |
| 2003 | Nina Zhivanevskaya, Spain | 28.48 |
| 2005 | Giaan Rooney, Australia | 28.63 |
| 2007 | Leila Vaziri, United States | 28.16e |
| 2009 | Jiing Zhao, China | 27.06* |

### 100-METER BACKSTROKE

| | | |
|---|---|---|
| 1973 | Ulrike Richter, E. Germany | 1:05.42 |
| 1975 | Ulrike Richter, E. Germany | 1:03.30‡ |
| 1978 | Linda Jezek, United States | 1:02.55‡ |
| 1982 | Kristin Otto, E. Germany | 1:01.30‡ |
| 1986 | Betsy Mitchell, United States | 1:01.74 |
| 1991 | Krisztina Egerszegi, Hungary | 1:01.78 |
| 1994 | He Cihong, China | 1:00.57 |

### 100-METER BACKSTROKE (Cont.)

| | | |
|---|---|---|
| 1998 | Lea Maurer, United States | 1:01.16 |
| 2001 | Natalie Coughlin, United States | 1:00.37 |
| 2003 | Antje Buschschulte, Germany | 1:00.50 |
| 2005 | Kirsty Coventry, Zimbabwe | 1:00.24 |
| 2007 | Natalie Coughlin, United States | 59.44* |
| 2009 | Gemma Spofforth, United Kingdom | 58.12* |

### 200-METER BACKSTROKE

| | | |
|---|---|---|
| 1973 | Melissa Belote, United States | 2:20.52 |
| 1975 | Birgit Treiber, E. Germany | 2:15.46* |
| 1978 | Linda Jezek, United States | 2:11.93* |
| 1982 | Cornelia Sirch, E. Germany | 2:09.91* |
| 1986 | Cornelia Sirch, E. Germany | 2:11.37 |
| 1991 | Krisztina Egerszegi, Hungary | 2:09.15‡ |
| 1994 | He Cihong, China | 2:07.40 |
| 1998 | Roxanna Maracineanu, France | 2:11.26 |
| 2001 | Diana Mocanu, Romania | 2:09.94 |
| 2003 | Katy Sexton, Great Britain | 2:08.74 |
| 2005 | Kirsty Coventry, Zimbabwe | 2:08.52 |
| 2007 | Margaret Hoelzer, United States | 2:07.16 |
| 2009 | Kirsty Coventry, Zimbabwe | 2:04.81* |

### 50-METER BREASTSTROKE

| | | |
|---|---|---|
| 2001 | Xuejuan Luo, China | 30.84 |
| 2003 | Xuejuan Luo, China | 30.67 |
| 2005 | Jade Edmistone, Australia | 30.45* |
| 2007 | Jessica Hardy, United States | 30.63 |
| 2009 | Yuliya Efimova, Russia | 30.09* |

### 100-METER BREASTSTROKE

| | | |
|---|---|---|
| 1973 | Renate Vogel, E. Germany | 1:13.74 |
| 1975 | Hannalore Anke, E. Germany | 1:12.72 |
| 1978 | Julia Bogdanova, U.S.S.R. | 1:10.31* |
| 1982 | Ute Geweniger, E. Germany | 1:09.14‡ |
| 1986 | Sylvia Gerasch, E. Germany | 1:08.11* |
| 1991 | Linley Frame, Australia | 1:08.81 |
| 1994 | Samantha Riley, Australia | 1:07.96* |
| 1998 | Kristy Kowal, United States | 1:08.42 |
| 2001 | Xuejuan Luo, China | 1:07.18‡ |
| 2003 | Xuejuan Luo, China | 1:06.80 |
| 2005 | Leisel Jones, Australia | 1:05.09* |
| 2007 | Leisel Jones, Australia | 1:05.72 |
| 2009 | Rebecca Soni, United States | 1:04.93 |

### 200-METER BREASTSTROKE

| | | |
|---|---|---|
| 1973 | Renate Vogel, E. Germany | 2:40.01 |
| 1975 | Hannalore Anke, E. Germany | 2:37.25‡ |
| 1978 | Lina Kachushite, U.S.S.R. | 2:31.42* |
| 1982 | Svetlana Varganova, U.S.S.R. | 2:28.82‡ |
| 1986 | Silke Hoerner, E. Germany | 2:27.40* |
| 1991 | Elena Volkova, U.S.S.R. | 2:29.53 |
| 1994 | Samantha Riley, Australia | 2:26.87‡ |
| 1998 | Agnes Kovacs, Hungary | 2:25.45‡ |
| 2001 | Agnes Kovacs, Hungary | 2:24.90 |
| 2003 | Amanda Beard, United States | 2:22.99* |
| 2005 | Leisel Jones, Australia | 2:20.54* |
| 2007 | Leisel Jones, Australia | 2:21.84 |
| 2009 | Nadja Higl, Serbia | 2:21.62 |

### 50-METER BUTTERFLY

| | | |
|---|---|---|
| 2001 | Inge De Bruijn, Netherlands | 25.90 |
| 2003 | Inge De Bruijn, Netherlands | 25.84 |
| 2005 | Danni Miatke, Australia | 26.11 |
| 2007 | Therese Alshammar, Sweden | 25.91 |
| 2009 | Marieke Guehrer, Australia | 25.48 |

### 100-METER BUTTERFLY

| | | |
|---|---|---|
| 1973 | Kornelia Ender, E. Germany | 1:02.53 |
| 1975 | Kornelia Ender, E. Germany | 1:01.24* |
| 1978 | Joan Pennington, United States | 1:00.20‡ |

---

* World record. e Equals World Record. ‡ Meet record.

### 100-METER BUTTERFLY *(Cont.)*

| | | |
|---|---|---|
| 1982 | Mary T. Meagher, United States | 59.41‡ |
| 1986 | Kornelia Gressler, E. Germany | 59.51 |
| 1991 | Qian Hong, China | 59.68 |
| 1994 | Liu Limin, China | 58.98‡ |
| 1998 | Jenny Thompson, United States | 58.46‡ |
| 2001 | Petria Thomas, Australia | 58:27 |
| 2003 | Jenny Thompson, United States | 57.96‡ |
| 2005 | Jessicah Schipper, Australia | 57.23‡ |
| 2007 | Lisbeth Lenton, Australia | 57.15 |
| 2009 | Sarah Sjostrom, Sweden | 56.06* |

### 200-METER BUTTERFLY

| | | |
|---|---|---|
| 1973 | Rosemarie Kother, E. Germany | 2:13.76‡ |
| 1975 | Rosemarie Kother, E. Germany | 2:15.92 |
| 1978 | Tracy Caulkins, United States | 2:09.87* |
| 1982 | Ines Geissler, E. Germany | 2:08.66‡ |
| 1986 | Mary T. Meagher, United States | 2:08.41‡ |
| 1991 | Summer Sanders, United States | 2:09.24 |
| 1994 | Liu Limin, China | 2:07.25‡ |
| 1998 | Susie O'Neill, Australia | 2:07.93‡ |
| 2001 | Petria Thomas, Australia | 2:06.73‡ |
| 2003 | Otylia Jedrzejczak, Poland | 2:07.56 |
| 2005 | Otylia Jedrzejczak, Poland | 2:05.61* |
| 2007 | Jessicah Schipper, Australia | 2:06.39 |
| 2009 | Jessicah Schipper, Australia | 2:03.41* |

### 200-METER INDIVIDUAL MEDLEY

| | | |
|---|---|---|
| 1973 | Andrea Huebner, E. Germany | 2:20.51 |
| 1975 | Kathy Heddy, United States | 2:19.80 |
| 1978 | Tracy Caulkins, United States | 2:14.07* |
| 1982 | Petra Schneider, E. Germany | 2:11.79 |
| 1986 | Kristin Otto, E. Germany | 2:15.56 |
| 1991 | Li Lin, China | 2:13.40 |
| 1994 | Lu Bin, China | 2:12.34‡ |
| 1998 | Wu Yanyan, China | 2:10.88 |
| 2001 | Martha Bowen, United States | 2:11.93 |
| 2003 | Yana Klochkova, Ukraine | 2:10.75‡ |
| 2005 | Katie Hoff, United States | 2:10.41‡ |
| 2007 | Katie Hoff, United States | 2:10.13 |
| 2009 | Ariana Kukors, United States | 2:06.15* |

### 400-METER INDIVIDUAL MEDLEY

| | | |
|---|---|---|
| 1973 | Gudrun Wegner, E. Germany | 4:57.71 |
| 1975 | Ulrike Tauber, E. Germany | 4:52.76‡ |
| 1978 | Tracy Caulkins, United States | 4:40.83* |
| 1982 | Petra Schneider, E. Germany | 4:36.10* |
| 1986 | Kathleen Nord, E. Germany | 4:43.75 |
| 1991 | Lin Li, China | 4:41.45 |
| 1994 | Dai Guohong, China | 4:39.14 |
| 1998 | Chen Yan, China | 4:36.66 |
| 2001 | Yana Klochkova, Ukraine | 4:36.98 |
| 2003 | Yana Klochkova, Ukraine | 4:36.74 |
| 2005 | Katie Hoff, United States | 4:36.07‡ |
| 2007 | Katie Hoff, United States | 4:32.89* |
| 2009 | Katinka Hosszu, Hungary | 4:30.31‡ |

### 4 x 100-METER MEDLEY RELAY

| | | |
|---|---|---|
| 1973 | E. Germany (Ulrike Richter, Renate Vogel, Rosemarie Kother, Kornelia Ender) | 4:16.84 |
| 1975 | E. Germany (Ulrike Richter, Hannelore Anke, Rosemarie Kother, Kornelia Ender) | 4:14.74 |
| 1978 | United States (Linda Jezek, Tracy Caulkins, Joan Pennington, Cynthia Woodhead) | 4:08.21‡ |
| 1982 | E. Germany (K. Otto, U. Gewinger, I. Geissler, B. Meineke) | 4:05.8* |
| 1986 | E. Germany (K. Zimmermann, S. Gerasch, K. Gressler, K. Otto) | 4:04.82 |

### 4 x 100-METER MEDLEY RELAY *(Cont.)*

| | | |
|---|---|---|
| 1991 | United States (Janie Wagstaff, Tracey McFarlane, Crissy Ahmann-Leighton, Nicole Haislett) | 4:06.51 |
| 1994 | China (He Cihong, Dai Guohong, Liu Limin, Lu Bin) | 4:01.67* |
| 1998 | United States (K. Kowal, L.Maurer, J.Thompson, A. Van Dyken) | 4:01.93 |
| 2001 | Australia (Dyana Calub, Sarah Ryan, Petria Thomas, Leisel Jones) | 4:07.30 |
| 2003 | China (Shu Xhan, Xuejuan Luo Yafei Zhou, Yu Yang) | 3:59.89‡ |
| 2005 | Australia (S. Edington, L. Jones, J. Schipper, L. Lenton) | 3:56.30* |
| 2007 | Australia (E. Seebohm, L. Jones, J. Schipper, L. Lenton) | 3:55.74* |
| 2009 | China (Jing Zhao, Huijia Chen, Liuyang Jiao, Zhesi Li) | 3:52.19* |

### 4 x 100-METER FREESTYLE RELAY

| | | |
|---|---|---|
| 1973 | E. Germany (K. Ender, A. Eife, A. Huebner, S. Eichner) | 3:52.45 |
| 1975 | E. Germany (K. Ender, B.Krause, C. Hempel, U. Bruckner) | 3:49.37 |
| 1978 | United States (T. Caulkins, S. Elkins, J. Pennington, C. Woodhead) | 3:43.43* |
| 1982 | E. Germany (B. Meineke, S. Link, K. Otto, C. Metschuk) | 3:43.97 |
| 1986 | E. Germany (K. Otto, M. Stellmach, S. Schulze, H. Friedrich) | 3:40.57* |
| 1991 | United States (N. Haislett, J.Cooper, W. Hedgepeth, J. Thompson) | 3:43.26 |
| 1994 | China (Le Jingyi, Ying Shan, Le Ying, Lu Bin) | 3:37.91* |
| 1998 | United States (C. Fox, L. Farella, M. Valerio, B.J. Bedford) | 3:42.11 |
| 2001 | Germany (P.Dallman, A. Buschschulte, K. Meissner, S. Volkner) | 3:39.58 |
| 2003 | United States (N. Coughlin, L. Benko, R. Jeffrey, J.Thompson) | 3:38.09 |
| 2005 | Germany (P. Dallman, D. Goetz, B. Steffen, A. Liebs) | 3:35.22* |
| 2007 | Netherlands (I. Dekker, R. Kromowidjojo, F. Heemskerk, M. Veldhuis) | 3:35.48 |
| 2009 | Netherlands (I. Dekker, R. Kromowidjojo, F. Heemskerk, M. Veldhuis) | 3:31.72* |

### 4 x 200-METER FREESTYLE RELAY

| | | |
|---|---|---|
| 1986 | E. Germany (Manuela Stellmach, Astrid Strauss, Nadja Bergknecht, Heike Friedrich) | 7:59.33* |
| 1991 | Germany (Kerstin Kielgass, Manuela Stellmach, Dagmar Hase, Stephanie Ortwig) | 8:02.56 |
| 1994 | China (Le Ying, Yang Alhua, Zhou Guabin, Lu Bin) | 7:57.96 |
| 1998 | Germany (Silvia Szalai, Antje Buschschulte, Janina Goetz, Franziska Van Almsick) | 8:02.56 |
| 2001 | Great Britain (Nicola Jackson, Janine Belton, Karen Legg, Karen Pickering) | 7:58.69 |
| 2003 | United States (L. Benko, R. Komisarz R. Jeffrey, D. Munz) | 7:55.70‡ |
| 2005 | Germany (Petra Dallman, Daniela Samulski, Britta Steffen, Annika Liebs) | 7:50.82* |
| 2007 | United States (Natalie Coughlin, Dana Vollmer, Lacey Nymeyer, Katie Hoff) | 7:50.09* |
| 2009 | China (Yu Yang, Qian Wei Zhu, Jing Liu, Jiaying Pang) | 7:42.08* |

* World record; ‡Meet record.

Seven-time champion Lance Armstrong (r.) returned to the Tour de France in 2009, but Astana teammate Alberto Contador (c.) took the title

# Miscellaneous Sports

# "Next Year, Different Story"

Lance Armstrong's 2009 comeback was remarkable, but his third-place finish at the Tour de France only fueled his determination to win it once more in 2010

## BY MERRELL NODEN

THE YEAR IN CYCLING REACHED a breathtaking peak, literally, on July 19, in the Swiss Alps, when Alberto Contador stormed up a steep ascent at the Verbier at such a rate—1850 meters per hour—that even his Astana teammate and bitter rival Lance Armstrong had to admit that this was pretty special stuff. With that astonishing climb—Armstrong had once averaged 1700 meters over the same stretch—the 24-year-old Spaniard claimed the yellow jersey for good in this year's Tour de France and set up a grudge match in next year's race that promises to be one for the ages.

The year took shape, calendar be damned, back in September of 2008. That's when Armstrong announced that after a three-year absence he was returning to the sport he had so utterly dominated, winning the Tour seven straight years, from 1999 to 2005, before retiring. In retirement he had been as industrious as ever, tirelessly raising money for cancer research, dating celebrities like actress Kate Hudson, running the New York City Marathon twice and, in June, becoming a father for the fourth time. But through it all, Armstrong has continued to be dogged by accusations of drug use during his cycling career. So, in announcing his

comeback, he also announced that he'd be subjecting himself to his own one-man drug-testing program. It was to be overseen by one of the top drug testing experts in the world, UCLA professor Don Catlin, and it was to be as thorough and transparent as possible. Armstrong's reasoning seemed to be that if he were to perform well under such stringent conditions—not to mention at age 37—he'd have made a very strong case against all those rumors.

Unfortunately, the much ballyhooed testing program never got going. In February, not long after Armstrong had finished 29th in the Tour Down Under, his first competition since the end of the 2005 season, Catlin announced that the program was going to be too complex and expensive to maintain, and that he and Armstrong had decided to call it off before it ever began.

The comeback, however, was on. Armstrong finished 7th in the Tour de California in February and, after breaking his collarbone in a fall in Spain, came in 12th in the Giro d'Italia. His return seemed to promise an embarrassment of riches for the Astana team he was joining. Not only did it feature Armstrong and Contador, who had won the Tour in 2007 (but sat out the 2008 race when his Astana team was banned due to prior doping that did not involve current

In 2009, American skier Lindsey Vonn repeated as World Cup champion, giving the U.S. ski team high hopes for Vancouver in 2010.

team members), it also featured Andreas Klöden, who would wind up sixth overall, and Armstrong's fellow American, Levi Leipheimer, who, until a nasty fall midway through the race produced a broken wrist and forced him to withdraw, was in fourth place. Many considered this year's Astana team the best ever to compete in the Tour.

If so, that was not due to its bubbly team spirit. Even before the Tour began, on July 4th in Monaco, there were questions about who would lead Astana and who would serve as *domestique*: Would it be the young Spaniard, who until Armstrong's reappearance looked to be this year's favorite? Or would it be the Tour's seven-time champ? Contador was chosen to lead the team, but Armstrong began well, sitting second through six stages. When, on the first mountain stage, Contador ignored his team's plan and launched an attack that carried him past Armstrong, it ruffled feathers.

When asked what had been the most difficult point for him, Contador answered, "It was in the team hotel." He did not elaborate further but from the cold congratulations Armstrong later gave him on the victory stand it was plain the two did not get along. Armstrong did not quite look like his old self, but would finish a very impressive third overall, 5:24 behind Contador and 1:13 behind Andy Schleck of Luxembourg, who will be another strong rival next year.

"My relationship with Lance is zero," said Contador. "He is a great rider and has completed another great race, but it is another thing on a personal level, where I have never had great admiration for him and never will."

The feeling was mutual, which means fans are already drooling over next year's race. Even before the *peloton* rolled into Paris, Armstrong had made it clear he'd be back, though for a newly formed team, Team RadioShack, which was to be based in the U.S. He was also predicting a different result. "Next year, different story," said Armstrong.

Whatever its outcome, that story will be well worth watching.

## Miscellaneous Sport Champions

**Archery**

| 2009 U.S. Outdoor Championships | Winner (Recurve) | Winner (Compound) |
|---|---|---|
| MEN | Vic Wunderle | Dave Cousins |
| WOMEN | Heather Koehl | Jamie VaNatta |

**Bowling**

| 2008–09 PBA Tour | Money Winner ($) | Highest Average (pts.) |
|---|---|---|
| TOUR LEADERS | Norm Duke ($199,130) | Wes Mallott (222.98) |

| 2008–09 PBA Senior Tour | Money Winner ($) | Highest Average (pts.) |
|---|---|---|
| TOUR LEADERS | Wayne Webb ($41,850) | Brian Voss (223.99) |

**Curling**

| 2009 World Championships | Country | Skip |
|---|---|---|
| MEN | Scotland | David Murdoch |
| WOMEN | China | Bingyu Wang |

| 2009 U.S. Club National Championships | Club | Skip |
|---|---|---|
| MEN | Wisconsin | Mike Fraboni |
| WOMEN | Minnesota I | Norma O'Leary |

**Cycling**

| | Winner | Time |
|---|---|---|
| 2009 ROAD RACE WORLD CHAMPIONSHIP | Cadel Evans, Australia | 6:56:26 |
| 2009 TOUR DE FRANCE | Alberto Contador, Spain | 85:48:35 |

**Sled Dog Racing**

| | Winner | Time |
|---|---|---|
| 2009 IDITAROD | Lance Mackey | 9 days, 21:38:46 |

**Figure Skating**

| 2009 ISU World Championships | Winner | Country |
|---|---|---|
| MEN | Evan Lysacek | United States |
| WOMEN | Yu-Na Kim | South Korea |
| PAIRS | Aliona Savchenko/ Robin Szolkowy | Germany |
| ICE DANCING | Oksana Domnina/ Maxim Shabalin | Russia |

| 2009 U.S. Figure Skating Nat'l Championships | Winner | Club |
|---|---|---|
| MEN | Jeremy Abbott | Broadmoor SC |
| WOMEN | Alissa Czisny | Detroit SC |
| PAIRS | Keauna McLaughlin/ Rockne Brubaker | Los Angeles FSC/ Broadmoor SC |
| ICE DANCING | Meryl Davis/ Charlie White | Arctic FSC/ Detroit SC |

**Handball**

| 2009 U.S.One-Wall Nat'l Championships | Winner | Runner-up |
|---|---|---|
| MEN | Satish Jagnandan | Cesar Sala |
| WOMEN | Tracy Davis | Theresa McCourt |
| 2009 U.S.Three-Wall Nat'l Championships | Winner | Runner-up |
| MEN | Emmett Peixoto | David Chapman |
| WOMEN | Megan Mehilos | Tracy Davis |

**Lacrosse**

| League | Winner (Score) | Runner-up |
|---|---|---|
| AMERICAN LACROSSE LEAGUE | New York A.C. (14–4) | Dewalt |
| NATIONAL LACROSSE LEAGUE | Calgary Roughnecks (12–10) | New York Titans |
| MAJOR LEAGUE LACROSSE | Toronto Nationals (10–9) | Denver Outlaws |

**Little League Baseball**

| | Winner | Runner-up | Score |
|---|---|---|---|
| WORLD SERIES CHAMPION | Chula Vista, California | Taoyuan, Taiwan | 6–3 |

**Motor Boat Racing**

| American Boat Racing Association | Winning Boat | Winning Driver |
|---|---|---|
| GOLD CUP CHAMPION | U-16 Ellstrom Elam Plus | Dave Villwock |

**Polo**

| 2009 U.S. Open | Winner | Runner-up |
|---|---|---|
| U.S. POLO ASSOCIATION | Audi (9–8, OT) | Las Monjitas |

## Miscellaneous Sport Champions

**Rodeo**

| 2008 PRCA World Champions | Winner(s) | |
|---|---|---|
| ALL-AROUND | Trevor Brazile | |
| SADDLE BRONC RIDING | Cody Wright | |
| BAREBACK RIDING | Justin McDaniel | |
| BULL RIDING | J.W. Harris | |
| STEER WRESTLING | Luke Branquinho | |
| STEER ROPING | Scott Snedecor | |
| CALF TIE-DOWN ROPING | Stran Smith | |
| TEAM ROPING (Header, Heeler) | Matt Sherwood, Random Adams | |

**Rowing**

| 2009 Intercollegiate Rowing Association | Winner | Runner-Up |
|---|---|---|
| MEN | Washington | California |

**Rugby**

| 2009 Rugby Union | Winner | Runner-Up |
|---|---|---|
| MEN'S CLUB (DIV. I) | Gentlemen of Aspen | Las Vegas Blackjacks |
| MEN'S COLLEGIATE (DIV. I) | BYU | California |

| 2009 American National Rugby League | Winner | Runner-Up |
|---|---|---|
| U.S. CHAMPION | New York Knights | Jacksonville Axemen |

**Skiing**

| FIS World Champion | Men's Winner (Season) | Women's Winner (Season) |
|---|---|---|
| OVERALL | Aksel Svindal (NOR) | Lindsey Vonn (USA) |
| DOWNHILL | Mic. Walchoffer (GER) | Lindsey Vonn (USA) |
| SLALOM | J.-Baptiste Grange (FRA) | Maria Riesch (GER) |
| GIANT SLALOM | Didier Cuche (SUI) | Tania Poutiainen (FIN) |
| SUPER G | Aksel Svindal (NOR) | Lindsey Vonn (USA) |
| COMBINED | Carlo Janka (SUI) | Anja Paerson (SWE) |

**Softball**

| 2009 U.S. ASA Championship | Major Fast Pitch Winner | Major Slow Pitch Winner |
|---|---|---|
| MEN | Farm Tavern | Flashback |
| WOMEN | None (tournament cancelled) | |

**Speed Skating**

| 2009 ISU All-Around World Champion | Winner | |
|---|---|---|
| MEN | Sven Kramer (NET) | |
| WOMEN | Martina Sablikova (CZE) | |

**Squash**

| U.S. Championship | Hard Ball Winner | Soft Ball Winner |
|---|---|---|
| MEN | Eric Pearson | Julian Illingworth |
| WOMEN | N/A | Natalie Grainger |

**Triathlon**

| 2009 Ironman World Championship | Winner | Time |
|---|---|---|
| MEN | Craig Alexander (AUS) | 8:20:21 |
| WOMEN | Crissie Wellington (UK) | 8:54:02 |

| 2009 U.S. Elite Triathlon Championship | Winner | Time |
|---|---|---|
| MEN | Matt Chrabot | 1:48:14 |
| WOMEN | Jasmine Oeinck | 2:02:49 |

**Volleyball**

| 2009 U.S. Adult Championship (Open Div.) | Winner | Runner-Up |
|---|---|---|
| MEN | Paul Mitchell | BC |
| WOMEN | Huskies VBC | USA Red |

**Wrestling**

| 2009 U.S. Championship | Freestyle | Greco-Roman |
|---|---|---|
| 121 LBS. | Nick Simmons | Jermaine Hodge |
| 132 LBS. | Mike Zadick | Joe Betterman |
| 145.5 LBS. | Trent Paulson | Frank Sahin |
| 163 LBS. | Travis Paulson | Harry Lester* |
| 185 LBS. | Jake Herbert* | T.C. Dantzler |
| 211.5 LBS. | Jake Varner | Brad Ahearn |
| 264.5 LBS. | Steve Mocco | Dremiel Byers |
| TEAM | Sunkist Kids (Div. I) | U.S. Army (Div. I) |
| | Gator WC (Div. II) | Sunkist Kids (Div. II) |
| | *Most Outstanding Wrestler | |

## Bowling

### PBA TOUR RESULTS
### 2008–09 Tour

| Date | Event | Winner | Earnings ($) | Runner-Up |
|---|---|---|---|---|
| Oct. 19–26 | PBA World Championship | Norm Duke | 50,000 | Chris Barnes |
| Oct 29–Nov 2 | Viper Championship | Brad Angelo | 25,000 | Chris Loschetter |
| Nov 4–9 | Lake County Indiana Championship | Walter Ray Williams Jr. | 25,000 | Bill O'Neill |
| Nov 9–11 | Ultimate Scoring Championship | Mike Wolfe | 25,000 | Mike Scroggins |
| Nov 12–16 | Chameleon Championship | Michael Machuga | 25,000 | Bill O'Neill |
| Nov 26–30 | Scorpion Championship | Wes Malott | 25,000 | Ken Simard |
| Dec 3–7 | Cheetah Championship | Parker Bohn III | 25,000 | Mike Scroggins |
| Dec 10–14 | Shark Championship | Rhino Page | 25,100 | Wes Malott |
| Jan 4–6 | Mixed Doubles Championship | Norm Duke | 25,000 | Steve Harman |
| Jan 7–11 | National Bowling Stadium Champ. | Patrick Allen | 25,000 | Walter Ray Williams, Jr. |
| Jan 14–18 | Earl Anthony Medford Classic | Wes Malott | 25,000 | Tommy Jones |
| Jan 20–25 | PGA Tournament of Champions | Patrick Allen | 50;100 | Rhino Page |
| Feb 3–8 | Dick Weber Open | Norm Duke | 35,000 | Michael Fagan |
| Feb 9–15 | USBC Masters | John Nolen | 60,000 | Danny Wiseman |
| Feb. 18–22 | GEICO Plastic Ball Championship | Jeff Carter | 25,000 | Pete Weber |
| Feb 23–March 1 | Etonic Marathon Open | Wes Malott | 35,000 | Ronnie Russell |
| March 2–8 | Buckeye State Eliminator | Chris Barnes | 25,000 | Mika Koivuniemi |
| March 18–22 | Match Play Championship | Chris Barnes | 25,000 | Walter Ray Williams, Jr. |
| March 25–29 | Long Island Classic | Jason Belmonte | 25,000 | Michael Fagan |
| March 29–April 5 | 66th U.S. Open | Mike Scroggins | 100,000 | Norm Duke |
| April 9–10 | King of Bowling | Wes Malott | 50,000* | Parker Bohn III |
| April 23–26 | Japan Cup | Patrick Allen | 50,500* | Wes Malott |

*not counted in tour's season earnings

### TOUR LEADERS - PBA: 2008–09

| MONEY LEADERS | Events | Earnings ($) | AVERAGE | Events | Average |
|---|---|---|---|---|---|
| Norm Duke | 18 | 199,130 | Wes Malott | 20 | 222.98 |
| Rhino Page | 20 | 197,760 | Bill O'Neill | 20 | 222.96 |
| Mike Scroggins | 21 | 179,820 | Patrick Allen | 21 | 222.75 |
| Patrick Allen | 21 | 175,900 | Chris Barnes | 21 | 222.20 |
| Wes Malott | 20 | 174,680 | Walter Ray Williams Jr. | 21 | 221.27 |

### PBA Career Statistics

| CAREER EARNINGS | | CAREER TITLES | |
|---|---|---|---|
| Walter Ray Williams Jr. | $3,917,402 | Walter Ray Williams Jr. | 45 |
| Pete Weber | $3,121,303 | Earl Anthony | 43 |
| Parker Bohn III | $2,632,264 | Mark Roth | 34 |
| Norm Duke | $2,740,596 | Pete Weber | 34 |
| Brian Voss | $2,352,192 | Parker Bohn III | 32 |
| Note: Career leaders through Sept. 1, 2009. | | Norm Duke | 32 |

## Cycling

### Tour de France Winners

| Year | Winner | Time | Year | Winner | Time |
|---|---|---|---|---|---|
| 1903 | Maurice Garin, France | 94 hrs, 33 min | 1923 | Henri Pelissier, France | 222 hrs, 15 min, 30 sec |
| 1904 | Henry Cornet, France | 96 hrs, 5 min, 56 sec | 1924 | Ottavio Bottechia, Italy | 226 hrs, 18 min, 21 sec |
| 1905 | Louis Trousselier, France | 110 hrs, 26 min, 58 sec | 1925 | Ottavio Bottechia, Italy | 219 hrs, 10 min, 18 sec |
| 1906 | Rene Pottier, France | Not available | 1926 | Lucien Buysse, Belgium | 238 hrs, 44 min, 25 sec |
| 1907 | Lucien Petit-Breton, France | 158 hrs, 54 min, 5 sec | 1927 | Nicolas Frantz, Luxembourg | 198 hrs, 16 min, 42 sec |
| 1908 | Lucien Petit-Breton, France | Not available | 1928 | Nicolas Frantz, Luxembourg | 192 hrs, 48 min, 58 sec |
| 1909 | Francois Faber, Luxembourg | 157 hrs, 1 min, 22 sec | 1929 | Maurice Dewaele, Belgium | 186 hrs, 39 min, 16 sec |
| 1910 | Octave Lapize, France | 162 hrs, 41 min, 30 sec | 1930 | Andre Leducq, France | 172 hrs, 12 min, 16 sec |
| 1911 | Gustave Garrigou, France | 195 hrs, 37 min | 1931 | Antonin Magne, France | 177 hrs, 10 min, 3 sec |
| 1912 | Odile Defraye, Belgium | 190 hrs, 30 min, 28 sec | 1932 | Andre Leducq, France | 154 hrs, 12 min, 49 sec |
| 1913 | Philippe Thys, Belgium | 197 hrs, 54 min | 1933 | Georges Speicher, France | 147 hrs, 51 min, 37 sec |
| 1914 | Philippe Thys, Belgium | 200 hrs, 28 min, 48 sec | 1934 | Antonin Magne, France | 147 hrs, 13 min, 58 sec |
| 1915–18 NO RACE | | | 1935 | Romain Maes, Belgium | 141 hrs, 32 min |
| 1919 | Firmin Lambot, Belgium | 231 hrs, 7 min, 15 sec | 1936 | Sylvere Maes, Belgium | 142 hrs, 47 min, 32 sec |
| 1920 | Philippe Thys, Belgium | 228 hrs, 36 min, 13 sec | 1937 | Roger Lapebie, France | 138 hrs, 58 min, 31 sec |
| 1921 | Leon Scieur, Belgium | 221 hrs, 50 min, 26 sec | 1938 | Gino Bartali, Italy | 148 hrs, 29 min, 12 sec |
| 1922 | Firmin Lambot, Belgium | 222 hrs, 8 min, 6 sec | 1939 | Sylvere Maes, Belgium | 132 hrs, 3 min, 17 sec |

## Tour de France Winners *(Cont.)*

| Year | Winner | Time | Year | Winner | Time |
|------|--------|------|------|--------|------|
| 1940–46 | NO RACE | | 1978 | Bernard Hinault, France | 108 hrs, 18 min |
| 1947 | Jean Robic, France | 148 hrs, 11 min, 25 sec | 1979 | Bernard Hinault, France | 103 hrs, 6 min, 50 sec |
| 1948 | Gino Bartali, Italy | 147 hrs, 10 min, 36 sec | 1980 | Joop Zoetemelk, Netherlands | 109 hrs, 19 min, 14 sec |
| 1949 | Fausto Coppi, Italy | 149 hrs, 40 min, 49 sec | 1981 | Bernard Hinault, France | 96 hrs, 19 min, 38 sec |
| 1950 | Ferdi Kubler, Switzerland | 145 hrs, 36 min, 56 sec | 1982 | Bernard Hinault, France | 92 hrs, 8 min, 46 sec |
| 1951 | Hugo Koblet, Switzerland | 142 hrs, 20 min, 14 sec | 1983 | Laurent Fignon, France | 105 hrs, 7 min, 52 sec |
| 1952 | Fausto Coppi, Italy | 151 hrs, 57 min, 20 sec | 1984 | Laurent Fignon, France | 112 hrs, 3 min, 40 sec |
| 1953 | Louison Bobet, France | 129 hrs, 23 min, 25 sec | 1985 | Bernard Hinault, France | 113 hrs, 24 min, 23 sec |
| 1954 | Louison Bobet, France | 140 hrs, 6 min, 5 sec | 1986 | Greg LeMond, United States | 110 hrs, 35 min, 19 sec |
| 1955 | Louison Bobet, France | 130 hrs, 29 min, 26 sec | 1987 | Stephen Roche, Ireland | 115 hrs, 27 min, 42 sec |
| 1956 | Roger Walkowiak, France | 124 hrs, 1 min, 16 sec | 1988 | Pedro Delgado, Spain | 84 hrs, 27 min, 53 sec |
| 1957 | Jacques Anquetil, France | 129 hrs, 46 min, 11 sec | 1989 | Greg LeMond, United States | 87 hrs, 38 min, 35 sec |
| 1958 | Charly Gaul, Luxembourg | 116 hrs, 59 min, 5 sec | 1990 | Greg LeMond, United States | 90 hrs, 43 min, 20 sec |
| 1959 | Federico Bahamontes, Spain | 123 hrs, 46 min, 45 sec | 1991 | Miguel Induráin, Spain | 101 hrs, 1 min, 20 sec |
| 1960 | Gastone Nencini, Italy | 112 hrs, 8 min, 42 sec | 1992 | Miguel Induráin, Spain | 100 hrs, 49 min, 30 sec |
| 1961 | Jacques Anquetil, France | 122 hrs, 1 min, 33 sec | 1993 | Miguel Induráin, Spain | 95 hrs, 57 min, 9 sec |
| 1962 | Jacques Anquetil, France | 114 hrs, 31 min, 54 sec | 1994 | Miguel Induráin, Spain | 103 hrs, 38 min, 38 sec |
| 1963 | Jacques Anquetil, France | 113 hrs, 30 min, 5 sec | 1995 | Miguel Induráin, Spain | 92 hrs, 44 min, 59 sec |
| 1964 | Jacques Anquetil, France | 127 hrs, 9 min, 44 sec | 1996 | Bjarne Riis, Denmark | 95 hrs, 57 min, 16 sec |
| 1965 | Felice Gimondi, Italy | 116 hrs, 42 min, 6 sec | 1997 | Jan Ullrich, Germany | 100 hrs, 30 min, 35 sec |
| 1966 | Lucien Aimar, France | 117 hrs, 34 min, 21 sec | 1998 | Marco Pantani, Italy | 92 hrs, 49 min, 46 sec |
| 1967 | Roger Pingeon, France | 136 hrs, 53 min, 50 sec | 1999 | Lance Armstrong, United States | 91 hrs, 32 min, 16 sec |
| 1968 | Jan Janssen, Netherlands | 133 hrs, 49 min, 32 sec | 2000 | Lance Armstrong, United States | 92 hrs, 33 min, 8 sec |
| 1969 | Eddy Merckx, Belgium | 116 hrs, 16 min, 2 sec | 2001 | Lance Armstrong, United States | 86 hrs, 17 min, 28 sec |
| 1970 | Eddy Merckx, Belgium | 119 hrs, 31 min, 49 sec | 2002 | Lance Armstrong, United States | 82 hrs, 5 min, 12 sec |
| 1971 | Eddy Merckx, Belgium | 96 hrs, 45 min, 14 sec | 2003 | Lance Armstrong, United States | 83 hrs, 41 min, 12 sec |
| 1972 | Eddy Merckx, Belgium | 108 hrs, 17 min, 18 sec | 2004 | Lance Armstrong, United States | 83 hrs, 36 min, 2 sec |
| 1973 | Luis Ocana, Spain | 122 hrs, 25 min, 34 sec | 2005 | Lance Armstrong, United States | 82 hrs, 34 min, 5 sec |
| 1974 | Eddy Merckx, Belgium | 116 hrs, 16 min, 58 sec | 2006 | Oscar Pereiro, Spain† | 82 hrs, 48 min, 30 sec |
| 1975 | Bernard Thevenet, France | 114 hrs, 35 min, 31 sec | 2007 | Alberto Contador, Spain | 91 hrs, 26 min |
| 1976 | Lucien Van Impe, Belgium | 116 hrs, 22 min, 23 sec | 2008 | Carlos Sastre, Spain | 87 hrs, 52 min, 52 sec |
| 1977 | Bernard Thevenet, France | 115 hrs, 38 min, 30 sec | 2009 | Alberto Contador, Spain | 85 hrs, 48 min, 35 sec |

†Floyd Landis, the initial winner, was officially stripped of his title on Sept. 20, 2007 by the ICU after a hearing affirmed that he had tested positive for using banned substances during Stage 17 of the 2006 Tour.

# Figure Skating

## WORLD CHAMPIONS
### Women

| Year | Winner | Year | Winner | Year | Winner |
|------|--------|------|--------|------|--------|
| 1906 | Madge Sayers-Cave, Great Britain | 1938 | Megan Taylor, Great Britain | 1970 | Gabriele Seyfert, E. Germany |
| 1907 | Madge Sayers-Cave, Great Britain | 1939 | Megan Taylor, Great Britain | 1971 | Beatrix Schuba, Austria |
| 1908 | Lily Kronberger, Hungary | 1940–46 | NO COMPETITION | 1972 | Beatrix Schuba, Austria |
| 1909 | Lily Kronberger, Hungary | 1947 | Barbara Ann Scott, Canada | 1973 | Karen Magnussen, Canada |
| 1910 | Lily Kronberger, Hungary | 1948 | Barbara Ann Scott, Canada | 1974 | Christine Errath, E. Germany |
| 1911 | Lily Kronberger, Hungary | 1949 | Alena Vrzanova, Czechoslovakia | 1975 | Dianne DeLeeuw, Netherlands |
| 1912 | Opika von Meray Horvath, Hungary | 1950 | Alena Vrzanova, Czechoslovakia | 1976 | Dorothy Hamill, United States |
| 1913 | Opika von Meray Horvath, Hungary | 1951 | Jeannette Altwegg, Great Britain | 1977 | Linda Fratianne, United States |
| 1914 | Opika von Meray Horvath, Hungary | 1952 | Jacqueline duBief, France | 1978 | Annett Poetzsch, E. Germany |
| 1915–21 | NO COMPETITION | 1953 | Tenley Albright, United States | 1979 | Linda Fratianne, United States |
| 1922 | Herma Plank-Szabo, Austria | 1954 | Gundi Busch, W. Germany | 1980 | Annett Poetzsch, E. Germany |
| 1923 | Herma Plank-Szabo, Austria | 1955 | Tenley Albright, United States | 1981 | Denise Biellmann, Switzerland |
| 1924 | Herma Plank-Szabo, Austria | 1956 | Carol Heiss, United States | 1982 | Elaine Zayak, United States |
| 1925 | Herma Jaross-Szabo, Austria | 1957 | Carol Heiss, United States | 1983 | Rosalynn Sumners, United States |
| 1926 | Herma Jaross-Szabo, Austria | 1958 | Carol Heiss, United States | 1984 | Katarina Witt, E. Germany |
| 1927 | Sonja Henie, Norway | 1959 | Carol Heiss, United States | 1985 | Katarina Witt, E. Germany |
| 1928 | Sonja Henie, Norway | 1960 | Carol Heiss, United States | 1986 | Debi Thomas, United States |
| 1929 | Sonja Henie, Norway | 1961 | NO COMPETITION | 1987 | Katarina Witt, E. Germany |
| 1930 | Sonja Henie, Norway | 1962 | Sjoukje Dijkstra, Netherlands | 1988 | Katarina Witt, E. Germany |
| 1931 | Sonja Henie, Norway | 1963 | Sjoukje Dijkstra, Netherlands | 1989 | Midori Ito, Japan |
| 1932 | Sonja Henie, Norway | 1964 | Sjoukje Dijkstra, Netherlands | 1990 | Jill Trenary, United States |
| 1933 | Sonja Henie, Norway | 1965 | Petra Burka, Canada | 1991 | Kristi Yamaguchi, United States |
| 1934 | Sonja Henie, Norway | 1966 | Peggy Fleming, United States | 1992 | Kristi Yamaguchi, United States |
| 1935 | Sonja Henie, Norway | 1967 | Peggy Fleming, United States | 1993 | Oksana Baiul, Ukraine |
| 1936 | Sonja Henie, Norway | 1968 | Peggy Fleming, United States | 1994 | Yuka Sato, Japan |
| 1937 | Cecilia Colledge, Great Britain | 1969 | Gabriele Seyfert, E. Germany | 1995 | Chen Lu, China |

# Figure Skating *(Cont.)*

## WORLD CHAMPIONS *(Cont.)*
### Women *(Cont.)*

1996 .....Michelle Kwan, United States
1997 .....Tara Lipinski, United States
1998 .....Michelle Kwan, United States
1999 .....Maria Butyrskaya, Russia
2000 .....Michelle Kwan, United States

2001 .....Michelle Kwan, United States
2002 .....Irina Slutskaya, Russia
2003 .....Michelle Kwan, United States
2004 .....Shizuka Arakawa, Japan
2005 .....Irina Slutskaya, Russia

2006 .....Kimmie Meissner, United States
2007 .....Miki Ando, Japan
2008 .....Mao Asada, Japan
2009 .....Yu-Na Kim, South Korea

### Men

1896 .....Gilbert Fuchs, Germany
1897 .....Gustav Hugel, Austria
1898 .....Henning Grenander, Sweden
1899 .....Gustav Hugel, Austria
1900 .....Gustav Hugel, Austria
1901 .....Ulrich Salchow, Sweden
1902 .....Ulrich Salchow, Sweden
1903 .....Ulrich Salchow, Sweden
1904 .....Ulrich Salchow, Sweden
1905 .....Ulrich Salchow, Sweden
1906 .....Gilbert Fuchs, Germany
1907 .....Ulrich Salchow, Sweden
1908 .....Ulrich Salchow, Sweden
1909 .....Ulrich Salchow, Sweden
1910 .....Ulrich Salchow, Sweden
1911 .....Ulrich Salchow, Sweden
1912 ....Fritz Kachler, Austria
1913 .....Fritz Kachler, Austria
1914 ....Gosta Sandhal, Sweden
1915—21     NO COMPETITION
1922 .....Gillis Grafstrom, Sweden
1923 .....Fritz Kachler, Austria
1924 .....Gillis Grafstrom, Sweden
1925 .....Willy Bockl, Austria
1926 .....Willy Bockl, Austria
1927 .....Willy Bockl, Austria
1928 .....Willy Bockl, Austria
1929 .....Gillis Grafstrom, Sweden
1930 .....Karl Schafer, Austria
1931 .....Karl Schafer, Austria
1932 .....Karl Schafer, Austria
1933 .....Karl Schafer, Austria
1934 ....Karl Schafer, Austria
1935 ....Karl Schafer, Austria

1936 .....Karl Schafer, Austria
1937 .....Felix Kaspar, Austria
1938 .....Felix Kaspar, Austria
1939 .....Graham Sharp, Great Britain
1940—46     NO COMPETITION
1947 .....Hans Gerschwiler, Switzerland
1948 .....Dick Button, United States
1949 .....Dick Button, United States
1950 .....Dick Button, United States
1951 .....Dick Button, United States
1952 .....Dick Button, United States
1953 .....Hayes Alan Jenkins, United States
1954 .....Hayes Alan Jenkins, United States
1955 .....Hayes Alan Jenkins, United States
1956 .....Hayes Alan Jenkins, United States
1957 .....David W. Jenkins, United States
1958 .....David W. Jenkins, United States
1959 .....David W. Jenkins, United States
1960 .....Alan Giletti, France
1961 .....No competition
1962 ....Donald Jackson, Canada
1963 ....Donald McPherson, Canada
1964 .....Manfred Schneldorfer, W. Germany
1965 .....Alain Calmat, France
1966 .....Emmerich Danzer, Austria
1967 .....Emmerich Danzer, Austria
1968 .....Emmerich Danzer, Austria
1969 .....Tim Wood, United States
1970 .....Tim Wood, United States
1971 .....Andrej Nepela, Czechoslovakia
1972 .....Andrej Nepela, Czechoslovakia
1973 .....Andrej Nepela, Czechoslovakia
1974 .....Jan Hoffmann, E. Germany
1975 .....Sergei Volkov, USSR

1976 .....John Curry, Great Britain
1977 .....Vladimir Kovalev, USSR
1978 ....Charles Tickner, United States
1979 .....Vladimir Kovalev, USSR
1980 .....Jan Hoffmann, E. Germany
1981 .....Scott Hamilton, United States
1982 .....Scott Hamilton, United States
1983 .....Scott Hamilton, United States
1984 .....Scott Hamilton, United States
1985 .....Aleksandr Fadeev, USSR
1986 .....Brian Boitano, United States
1987 .....Brian Orser, Canada
1988 .....Brian Boitano, United States
1989 .....Kurt Browning, Canada
1990 .....Kurt Browning, Canada
1991 .....Kurt Browning, Canada
1992 .....Viktor Petrenko, CIS
1993 .....Kurt Browning, Canada
1994 .....Elvis Stojko, Canada
1995 .....Elvis Stojko, Canada
1996 .....Todd Eldredge, United States
1997 .....Elvis Stojko, Canada
1998 .....Alexei Yagudin, Russia
1999 .....Alexei Yagudin, Russia
2000 .....Alexei Yagudin, Russia
2001 .....Evgeni Plushenko, Russia
2002 .....Alexei Yagudin, Russia
2003 .....Evgeni Plushenko, Russia
2004 .....Evgeni Plushenko, Russia
2005 ....Stephane Lambiel, Switzerland
2006 ....Stephane Lambiel, Switzerland
2007 .....Brian Joubert, France
2008 .....Jeffrey Buttle, Canada
2009 .....Evan Lysacek, United States

### Pairs

1908 .....Anna Hubler, Heinrich Burger, Germany
1909 .....Phyllis Johnson, James H. Johnson, Great Britain
1910 .....Anna Hubler, Heinrich Burger, Germany
1911 .....Ludowika Eilers, Walter Jakobsson, Germany/Finland
1912 .....Phyllis Johnson, James H. Johnson, Great Britain
1913 .....Helene Engelmann, Karl Majstrik, Germany
1914 ....Ludowika Jakobsson-Eilers, Walter Jakobsson-Eilers, Finland
1915—21     NO COMPETITION
1922 .....Helene Engelmann, Alfred Berger, Germany
1923 .....Ludowika Jakobsson-Eilers, Walter Jakobsson-Eilers, Finland
1924 ....Helene Engelmann, Alfred Berger, Germany
1925 .....Herma Jaross-Szabo, Ludwig Wrede, Austria
1926 .....Andree Joly, Pierre Brunet, France
1927 ....Herma Jaross-Szabo, Ludwig Wrede, Austria
1928 .....Andree Joly, Pierre Brunet, France
1929 .....Lilly Scholz, Otto Kaiser, Austria
1930 ....Andree Brunet-Joly, Pierre Brunet-Joly, France
1931 .....Emilie Rotter, Laszlo Szollas, Hungary
1932 .....Andree Brunet-Joly, Pierre Brunet-Joly, France

1933 .....Emilie Rotter, Laszlo Szollas, Hungary
1934 ....Emilie Rotter, Laszlo Szollas, Hungary
1935 .....Emilie Rotter, Laszlo Szollas, Hungary
1936 .....Maxi Herber, Ernst Bajer, Germany
1937 .....Maxi Herber, Ernst Bajer, Germany
1938 .....Maxi Herber, Ernst Bajer, Germany
1939 .....Maxi Herber, Ernst Bajer, Germany
1940—46     NO COMPETITION
1947 .....Micheline Lannoy, Pierre Baugniet, Belgium
1948 .....Micheline Lannoy, Pierre Baugniet, Belgium
1949 .....Andrea Kekessy, Ede Kiraly, Hungary
1950 .....Karol Kennedy, Peter Kennedy, United States
1951 ....Ria Baran, Paul Falk, W. Germany
1952 .....Ria Baran Falk, Paul Falk, W. Germany
1953 .....Jennifer Nicks, John Nicks, Great Britain
1954 .....Frances Dafoe, Norris Bowden, Canada
1955 .....Frances Dafoe, Norris Bowden, Canada
1956 .....Sissy Schwarz, Kurt Oppelt, Austria
1957 .....Barbara Wagner, Robert Paul, Canada
1958 .....Barbara Wagner, Robert Paul, Canada
1959 .....Barbara Wagner, Robert Paul, Canada

## WORLD CHAMPIONS
### Pairs

1960.....Barbara Wagner, Robert Paul, Canada
1961.....NO COMPETITION
1962.....Maria Jelinek, Otto Jelinek, Canada
1963.....Marika Kilius, Hans-Jurgen Baumler, W Germany
1964.....Marika Kilius, Hans-Jurgen Baumler, W Germany
1965.....Ljudmila Protopopov, Oleg Protopopov, USSR
1966.....Ljudmila Protopopov, Oleg Protopopov, USSR
1967.....Ljudmila Protopopov, Oleg Protopopov, USSR
1968.....Ljudmila Protopopov, Oleg Protopopov, USSR
1969.....Irina Rodnina, Aleksey Ulanov, USSR
1970.....Irina Rodnina, Aleksey Ulanov, USSR
1971.....Irina Rodnina, Aleksey Ulanov, USSR
1972.....Irina Rodnina, Aleksey Ulanov, USSR
1973.....Irina Rodnina, Aleksandr Zaytsev, USSR
1974.....Irina Rodnina, Aleksandr Zaytsev, USSR
1975.....Irina Rodnina, Aleksandr Zaytsev, USSR
1976.....Irina Rodnina, Aleksandr Zaytsev, USSR
1977.....Irina Rodnina, Aleksandr Zaytsev, USSR
1978.....Irina Rodnina, Aleksandr Zaytsev, USSR
1979.....Tai Babilonia, Randy Gardner, United States
1980.....Maria Cherkasova, Sergei Shakhrai, USSR
1981.....Irina Vorobieva, Igor Lisovsky, USSR
1982.....Sabine Baess, Tassilio Thierbach, E. Germany
1983.....Elena Valova, Oleg Vasiliev, USSR
1984.....Barbara Underhill, Paul Martini, Canada

1985.....Elena Valova, Oleg Vasiliev, USSR
1986.....Ekaterina Gordeeva, Sergei Grinkov, USSR
1987.....Ekaterina Gordeeva, Sergei Grinkov, USSR
1988.....Elena Valova, Oleg Vasiliev, USSR
1989.....Ekaterina Gordeeva, Sergei Grinkov, USSR
1990.....Ekaterina Gordeeva, Sergei Grinkov, USSR
1991.....Natalia Mishkutienok, Artur Dmitriev, USSR
1992.....Natalia Mishkutienok, Artur Dmitriev, CIS
1993.....Isabelle Brasseur, Lloyd Eisler, Canada
1994.....Evgenia Shishkova, Vadim Naumov, Russia
1995.....Radka Kovarikova, Rene Novotny, Czech Republic
1996.....Marina Eltsova, Andrey Buskhov, Russia
1997.....Mandy Wötzel, Ingo Steuer, Germany
1998.....Jenni Meno, Todd Sand, United States
1999.....Elena Berezhnaya, Anton Sikharulidze, Russia
2000.....Maria Petrova, Aleksei Tikhonov, Russia
2001.....Jamie Salé, David Pelletier, Canada
2002.....Xue Shen, Hongbo Zhao, China
2003.....Xue Shen, Hongbo Zhao, China
2004.....Tatiana Totmianina, Maxim Marinin, Russia
2005.....Tatiana Totmianina, Maxim Marinin, Russia
2006.....Qing Pang, Jian Tong, China
2007.....Shen Xue, Zhao Hongbo, China
2008.....Aliona Savchenko, Robin Szolkowy, Germany
2009.....Aliona Savchenko, Robin Szolkowy, Germany

### Dance

1950....Lois Waring, Michael McGean, United States
1951....Jean Westwood, Lawrence Demmy, Great Britain
1952....Jean Westwood, Lawrence Demmy, Great Britain
1953....Jean Westwood, Lawrence Demmy, Great Britain
1954....Jean Westwood, Lawrence Demmy, Great Britain
1955....Jean Westwood, Lawrence Demmy, Great Britain
1956....Pamela Wieght, Paul Thomas, Great Britain
1957....June Markham, Courtney Jones, Great Britain
1958....June Markham, Courtney Jones, Doreen D. Denny, Courtney Jones, Great Britain
1960....Doreen D. Denny, Courtney Jones, Great Britain
1961....NO COMPETITION
1962....Eva Romanova, Pavel Roman, Czechoslovakia
1963....Eva Romanova, Pavel Roman, Czechoslovakia
1964....Eva Romanova, Pavel Roman, Czechoslovakia
1965....Eva Romanova, Pavel Roman, Czechoslovakia
1966....Diane Towler, Bernard Ford, Great Britain
1967....Diane Towler, Bernard Ford, Great Britain
1968....Diane Towler, Bernard Ford, Great Britain
1969....Diane Towler, Bernard Ford, Great Britain
1970....Ljudmila Pakhomova, Aleksandr Gorshkov, USSR
1971....Ljudmila Pakhomova, Aleksandr Gorshkov USSR
1972....Ljudmila Pakhomova, Aleksandr Gorshkov USSR
1973....Ljudmila Pakhomova, Aleksandr Gorshkov USSR
1974....Ljudmila Pakhomova, Aleksandr Gorshkov USSR
1975....Irina Moiseeva, Andreij Minenkov, USSR
1976....Ljudmila Pakhomova, Aleksandr Gorshkov USSR
1977....Irina Moiseeva, Andreij Minenkov, USSR
1978....Natalia Linichuk, Gennadi Karponosov, USSR
1979....Natalia Linichuk, Gennadi Karponosov, USSR

1980....Krisztina Regoeczy, Andras Sallai, Hungary
1981....Jayne Torvill, Christopher Dean, Great Britain
1982....Jayne Torvill, Christopher Dean, Great Britain
1983....Jayne Torvill, Christopher Dean, Great Britain
1984....Jayne Torvill, Christopher Dean, Great Britain
1985....Natalia Bestemianova, Andrei Bukin, USSR
1986....Natalia Bestemianova, Andrei Bukin, USSR
1987....Natalia Bestemianova, Andrei Bukin, USSR
1988....Natalia Bestemianova, Andrei Bukin, USSR
1989....Marina Klimova, Sergei Ponomarenko, USSR
1990....Marina Klimova, Sergei Ponomarenko, USSR
1991....Isabelle Duchesnay, Paul Duchesnay, France
1992....Marina Klimova, Sergei Ponomarenko, CIS
1993....Renee Roca, Gorsha Sur, United States
1994....Oksana Grishuk, Evgeny Platov, Russia
1995....Oksana Grishuk, Evgeny Platov, Russia
1996....Oksana Grishuk, Evgeny Platov, Russia
1997....Oksana Grishuk, Evgeny Platov, Russia
1998....Anjelika Krylova, Oleg Ovsyannikov, Russia
1999....Anjelika Krylova, Oleg Ovsyannikov, Russia
2000....Marina Anissina, Gwendal Peizerat, France
2001....Barbara Fusar Poli, Maurizio Margaglio, Italy
2002....Irina Lobacheva, Ilia Averbukh, Russia
2003....Shae-Lynn Bourne, Victor Kraatz, Canada
2004....Tatiana Navka, Roman Kostomarov, Russia
2005....Tatiana Navka, Roman Kostomarov, Russia
2006....Albena Denkova, Maxim Staviski, Bulgaria
2007....Albena Denkova ,Maxim Staviski, Bulgaria
2008....Isabelle Delobel, Olivier Schoenfelder, France
2009....Oksana Domnina, Maxim Shabalin, Russia

## CHAMPIONS OF THE UNITED STATES

The championships held in 1914, 1918, 1920 and 1921 under the auspices of the International Skating Union of America were open to Canadians, although the competitions were considered to be United States championships. Beginning in 1922, the championships have been held under the auspices of the United States Figure Skating Association.

### Women

1914....Theresa Weld, SC of Boston
1915–17   NO COMPETITION
1918....Rosemary S. Beresford,
    New York SC
1919   NO COMPETITION
1920....Theresa Weld, SC of Boston
1921....Theresa Weld Blanchard,
    SC of Boston
1922....Theresa Weld Blanchard,
    SC of Boston
1923....Theresa Weld Blanchard,
    SC of Boston
1924....Theresa Weld Blanchard,
    SC of Boston
1925....Beatrix Loughran, New York SC
1926....Beatrix Loughran, New York SC
1927....Beatrix Loughran, New York SC
1928....Maribel Y. Vinson, SC of Boston
1929....Maribel Y. Vinson, SC of Boston
1930....Maribel Y. Vinson, SC of Boston
1931....Maribel Y. Vinson, SC of Boston
1932....Maribel Y. Vinson, SC of Boston
1933....Maribel Y. Vinson, SC of Boston
1934....Suzanne Davis, SC of Boston
1935....Maribel Y. Vinson, SC of Boston
1936....Maribel Y. Vinson, SC of Boston
1937....Maribel Y. Vinson, SC of Boston
1938....Joan Tozzer, SC of Boston
1939....Joan Tozzer, SC of Boston
1940....Joan Tozzer, SC of Boston
1941....Jane Vaughn, Philadelphia
    SC & HS
1942....Jane Vaughn Sullivan,
    Philadelphia SC & HS
1943....Gretchen Van Zandt Merrill,
    SC of Boston
1944....Gretchen Van Zandt Merrill,
    SC of Boston
1945....Gretchen Van Zandt Merrill,
    SC of Boston

1946....Gretchen Van Zandt Merrill,
    SC of Boston
1947....Gretchen Van Zandt Merrill,
    SC of Boston
1948....Gretchen Van Zandt Merrill,
    SC of Boston
1949....Yvonne Claire Sherman,
    SC of New York
1950....Yvonne Claire Sherman,
    SC of New York
1951....Sonya Klopfer,
    Junior SC of New York
1952....Tenley E. Albright, SC of Boston
1953....Tenley E. Albright, SC of Boston
1954....Tenley E. Albright, SC of Boston
1955....Tenley E. Albright, SC of Boston
1956....Tenley E. Albright, SC of Boston
1957....Carol E. Heiss, SC of New York
1958....Carol E. Heiss, SC of New York
1959....Carol E. Heiss, SC of New York
1960....Carol E. Heiss, SC of New York
1961....Laurence R. Owen,
    SC of Boston
1962....Barbara Roles Pursley,
    Arctic Blades FSC
1963....Lorraine G. Hanlon,
    SC of Boston
1964....Peggy Fleming,
    Arctic Blades FSC
1965....Peggy Fleming,
    Arctic Blades FSC
1966....Peggy Fleming,
    City of Colorado Springs
1967....Peggy Fleming, Broadmoor SC
1968....Peggy Fleming, Broadmoor SC
1969....Janet Lynn, Wagon Wheel FSC
1970....Janet Lynn, Wagon Wheel FSC
1971....Janet Lynn, Wagon Wheel FSC
1972....Janet Lynn, Wagon Wheel FSC
1973....Janet Lynn, Wagon Wheel FSC

1974....Dorothy Hamill, SC of New York
1975....Dorothy Hamill, SC of New York
1976....Dorothy Hamill, SC of New York
1977....Linda Fratianne, Los Angeles FSC
1978....Linda Fratianne, Los Angeles FSC
1979....Linda Fratianne, Los Angeles FSC
1980....Linda Fratianne, Los Angeles FSC
1981....Elaine Zayak, SC of New York
1982....Rosalynn Sumners, Seattle SC
1983....Rosalynn Sumners, Seattle SC
1984....Rosalynn Sumners, Seattle SC
1985....Tiffany Chin, San Diego FSC
1986....Debi Thomas, Los Angeles FSC
1987....Jill Trenary, Broadmoor SC
1988....Debi Thomas, Los Angeles FSC
1989....Jill Trenary, Broadmoor SC
1990....Jill Trenary, Broadmoor SC
1991....Tonya Harding, Carousel FSC
1992....Kristi Yamaguchi, St Moritz ISC
1993....Nancy Kerrigan, Colonial FSC
1994....Tonya Harding, Portland FSC
1995....Nicole Bobek, Los Angeles FSC
1996....Michelle Kwan, Los Angeles FSC
1997....Tara Lipinski, Detroit SC
1998....Michelle Kwan, Los Angeles FSC
1999....Michelle Kwan, Los Angeles FSC
2000....Michelle Kwan, Los Angeles FSC
2001....Michelle Kwan, Los Angeles FSC
2002....Michelle Kwan, Los Angeles FSC
2003....Michelle Kwan, Los Angeles FSC
2004....Michelle Kwan, Los Angeles FSC
2005....Michelle Kwan, Los Angeles FSC
2006....Sasha Cohen, Orange County FSC
2007....Kimmie Meissner,
    Univ. of Delaware FSC
2008.....Mirai Nagasu, Pasadena FSC
2009.....Alissa Czisny, Detroit SC

### Men

1914   Norman M. Scott,
    WC of Montreal
1915–17   NO COMPETITION
1918....Nathaniel W. Niles, SC of Boston
1919   NO COMPETITION
1920....Sherwin C. Badger, SC of Boston
1921....Sherwin C. Badger, SC of Boston
1922....Sherwin C. Badger, SC of Boston
1923....Sherwin C. Badger, SC of Boston
1924....Sherwin C. Badger, SC of Boston
1925....Nathaniel W. Niles, SC of Boston
1926   Chris I. Christenson,
    Twin City FSC
1927....Nathaniel W. Niles, SC of Boston
1928....Roger F. Turner, SC of Boston
1929....Roger F. Turner, SC of Boston
1930....Roger F. Turner, SC of Boston

1931....Roger F. Turner, SC of Boston
1932....Roger F. Turner, SC of Boston
1933....Roger F. Turner, SC of Boston
1934....Roger F. Turner, SC of Boston
1935....Robin H. Lee, SC of New York
1936....Robin H. Lee, SC of New York
1937....Robin H. Lee, SC of New York
1938....Robin H. Lee, Chicago FSC
1939....Robin H. Lee, St Paul FSC
1940....Eugene Turner, Los Angeles FSC
1941....Eugene Turner, Los Angeles FSC
1942....Robert Specht, Chicago FSC
1943   Arthur R. Vaughn Jr.,
    Phila. SC & HS
1944–45   NO COMPETITION
1946   Dick Button,
    Philadelphia SC & HS

1947....Dick Button,
    Philadelphia SC & HS
1948....Dick Button,
    Philadelphia SC & HS
1949....Dick Button,
    Philadelphia SC & HS
1950....Dick Button, SC of Boston
1951....Dick Button, SC of Boston
1952....Dick Button, SC of Boston
1953....Hayes Alan Jenkins,
    Cleveland SC
1954....Hayes Alan Jenkins,
    Broadmoor SC
1955....Hayes Alan Jenkins,
    Broadmoor SC
1956....Hayes Alan Jenkins,
    Broadmoor SC

## CHAMPIONS OF THE UNITED STATES *(Cont.)*

### Men *(Cont.)*

| | | |
|---|---|---|
| 1957....David Jenkins, Broadmoor SC | 1974....Gordon McKellen Jr., SC of Lake Placid | 1990....Todd Eldredge, Los Angeles FSC |
| 1958....David Jenkins, Broadmoor SC | 1975....Gordon McKellen Jr., SC of Lake Placid | 1991....Todd Eldredge, Los Angeles FSC |
| 1959....David Jenkins, Broadmoor SC | 1976....Terry Kubicka, Arctic Blades FSC | 1992....Christopher Bowman, Los Angeles FSC |
| 1960....David Jenkins, Broadmoor SC | 1977....Charles Tickner, Denver FSC | 1993....Scott Davis, Broadmoor SC |
| 1961....Bradley R. Lord, SC of Boston | 1978....Charles Tickner, Denver FSC | 1994....Scott Davis, Broadmoor SC |
| 1962....Monty Hoyt, Broadmoor SC | 1979....Charles Tickner, Denver FSC | 1995....Todd Eldredge, Detroit SC |
| 1963....Thomas Litz, Hershey FSC | 1980....Charles Tickner, Denver FSC | 1996....Rudy Galindo, St Moritz ISC |
| 1964....Scott Ethan Allen, SC of New York | 1981....Scott Hamilton, Philadelphia SC & HS | 1997....Todd Eldredge, Detroit SC |
| 1965....Gary C. Visconti, Detroit SC | 1982....Scott Hamilton, Philadelphia SC & HS | 1998....Todd Eldredge, Detroit SC |
| 1966....Scott Ethan Allen, SC of New York | 1983....Scott Hamilton, Philadelphia SC & HS | 1999....Michael Weiss, Washington FSC |
| 1967....Gary C. Visconti, Detroit SC | 1984....Scott Hamilton, Philadelphia SC & HS | 2000....Michael Weiss, Washington FSC |
| 1968....Tim Wood, Detroit SC | 1985....Brian Boitano, Peninsula FSC | 2001....Timothy Goebel, Winterhurst FSC |
| 1969....Tim Wood, Detroit SC | 1986....Brian Boitano, Peninsula FSC | 2002....Todd Eldredge, Los Angeles FSC |
| 1970....Tim Wood, City of Colorado Springs | 1987....Brian Boitano, Peninsula FSC | 2003....Michael Weiss, Washington FSC |
| 1971....John Misha Petkevich, Great Falls FSC | 1988....Brian Boitano, Peninsula FSC | 2004....Johnny Weir, SC of New York |
| 1972....Kenneth Shelley, Arctic Blades FSC | 1989....Christopher Bowman, Los Angeles FSC | 2005....Johnny Weir, SC of New York |
| 1973....Gordon McKellen Jr., SC of Lake Placid | | 2006....Johnny Weir, SC of New York |
| | | 2007....Evan Lysacek, DuPage FSC |
| | | 2008....Evan Lysacek, DuPage FSC |
| | | 2009....Jeremy Abbott, Broadmoor, SC |

### Pairs

| | | |
|---|---|---|
| 1914 Jeanne Chevalier, Norman M. Scott, WC of Montreal | 1938 Joan Tozzer, M. Bernard Fox, SC of Boston | 1957 Nancy Rouillard Ludington, Ronald Ludington, Commonwealth FSC/SC of Boston |
| 1915–17 NO COMPETITION | 1939 Joan Tozzer, M. Bernard Fox, SC of Boston | 1958 Nancy Rouillard Ludington, Ronald Ludington, Commonwealth FSC/SC of Boston |
| 1918 Theresa Weld, Nathaniel W. Niles, SC of Boston | 1940 Joan Tozzer, M. Bernard Fox, SC of Boston | 1959 Nancy Rouillard Ludington, Ronald Ludington, Commonwealth FSC |
| 1919 No competition | 1941 Donna Atwood, Eugene Turner, Mercury FSC/Los Angeles FSC | 1960 Nancy Rouillard Ludington, Ronald Ludington, Commonwealth FSC |
| 1920 Theresa Weld, Nathaniel W. Niles, SC of Boston | 1942 Doris Schubach, Walter Noffke, Springfield Ice Birds | 1961 Maribel Y. Owen, Dudley S. Richards, SC of Boston |
| 1921 Theresa Weld Blanchard, Nathaniel W. Niles, SC of Boston | 1943 Doris Schubach, Walter Noffke, Springfield Ice Birds | 1962 Dorothyann Nelson, Pieter Kollen, Village of Lake Placid |
| 1922 Theresa Weld Blanchard, Nathaniel W. Niles, SC of Boston | 1944 Doris Schubach, Walter Noffke, Springfield Ice Birds | 1963 Judianne Fotheringill, Jerry J. Fotheringill, Broadmoor SC |
| 1923 Theresa Weld Blanchard, Nathaniel W. Niles, SC of Boston | 1945 Donna Jeanne Pospisil, Jean-Pierre Brunet, SC of New York | 1964 Judianne Fotheringill, Jerry J. Fotheringill, Broadmoor SC |
| 1924 Theresa Weld Blanchard, Nathaniel W. Niles, SC of Boston | 1946 Donna Jeanne Pospisil, Jean-Pierre Brunet, SC of New York | 1965 Vivian Joseph, Ronald Joseph, Chicago FSC |
| 1925 Theresa Weld Blanchard, Nathaniel W. Niles, SC of Boston | 1947 Yvonne Claire Sherman, Robert J. Swenning, SC of New York | 1966 Cynthia Kauffman, Ronald Kauffman, Seattle SC |
| 1926 Theresa Weld Blanchard, Nathaniel W. Niles, SC of Boston | 1948 Karol Kennedy, Peter Kennedy, Seattle SC | 1967 Cynthia Kauffman, Ronald Kauffman, Seattle SC |
| 1927 Theresa Weld Blanchard, Nathaniel W. Niles, SC of Boston | 1949 Karol Kennedy, Peter Kennedy, Seattle SC | 1968 Cynthia Kauffman, Ronald Kauffman, Seattle SC |
| 1928 Maribel Y. Vinson, Thornton L. Coolidge, SC of Boston | 1950 Karol Kennedy, Peter Kennedy, Broadmoor SC | 1969 Cynthia Kauffman, Ronald Kauffman, Seattle SC |
| 1929 Maribel Y. Vinson, Thornton L. Coolidge, SC of Boston | 1951 Karol Kennedy, Peter Kennedy, Broadmoor SC | 1970 Jo Jo Starbuck, Kenneth Shelley, Arctic Blades FSC |
| 1930 Beatrix Loughran, Sherwin C. Badger, SC of New York | 1952 Karol Kennedy, Peter Kennedy, Broadmoor SC | 1971 Jo Jo Starbuck, Kenneth Shelley, Arctic Blades FSC |
| 1931 Beatrix Loughran, Sherwin C. Badger, SC of New York | 1953 Carole Ann Ormaca, Robin Greiner, SC of Fresno | 1972 Jo Jo Starbuck, Kenneth Shelley, Arctic Blades FSC |
| 1932 Beatrix Loughran, Sherwin C. Badger, SC of New York | 1954 Carole Ann Ormaca, Robin Greiner, SC of Fresno | 1973 Melissa Militano, Mark Militano, SC of New York |
| 1933 Maribel Y. Vinson, George E. B. Hill, SC of SC of Boston | 1955 Carole Ann Ormaca, Robin Greiner, St Moritz ISC | |
| 1936 Maribel Y. Vinson, George E. B. Hill, SC of Boston | 1956 Carole Ann Ormaca, Robin Greiner, St Moritz ISC | |
| 1937 Maribel Y. Vinson, George E. B. Hill, SC of Boston | | |

## CHAMPIONS OF THE UNITED STATES *(CONT.)*
### Pairs *(Cont.)*

| | | |
|---|---|---|
| 1974 Melissa Militano, Johnny Johns, SC of New York/Detroit SC | 1985 Jill Watson, Peter Oppegard, LA FSC | 1997 Kyoko Ina, Jason Dungjen, SC of New York |
| 1975 Melissa Militano, Johnny Johns, SC of New York/Detroit SC | 1986 Gillian Wachsman, Todd Waggoner, SC of Wilmington | 1998 Kyoko Ina, Jason Dungjen, SC of New York |
| 1976 Tai Babilonia, Randy Gardner, LA FSC | 1987 Jill Watson, Peter Oppegard, LA FSC | 1999 Danielle Hartsell, Steve Hartsell, Detroit SC |
| 1977 Tai Babilonia, Randy Gardner, LA FSC | 1988 Jill Watson, Peter Oppegard, LA FSC | 2000 Kyoko Ina, John Zimmerman, SC of New York/Birmingham FSC |
| 1978 Tai Babilonia, Randy Gardner, Los Angeles FSC/ Santa Monica FSC | 1989 Kristi Yamaguchi, Rudy Galindo, St Mortiz ISC | 2001 Kyoko Ina, John Zimmerman, SC of New York/Birmingham FSC |
| 1979 Tai Babilonia, Randy Gardner, Los Angeles FSC/ Santa Monica FSC | 1990 Kristi Yamaguchi, Rudy Galindo, St Mortiz ISC | 2002 Kyoko Ina, John Zimmerman, SC of New York/Birmingham FSC |
| 1980 Tai Babilonia, Randy Gardner, Los Angeles FSC/ Santa Monica FSC | 1991 Natasha Kuchiki, Todd Sand, LA FSC | 2003 Tiffany Scott, Philip Dulebohn, Colonial FSC/ Univ of Delaware FSC |
| 1981 Caitlin Carruthers, Peter Carruthers, SC of Wilmington | 1992 Calla Urbanski, Rocky Marval, U of Delaware FSC/ SC of New York | 2004 Rena Inoue, John Baldwin, All Year FSC |
| 1982 Caitlin Carruthers, Peter Carruthers, SC of Wilmington | 1993 Calla Urbanski, Rocky Marval, U of Delaware FSC/ SC of New York | 2005 Kathryn Orscher, Garrett Lucash, Charter Oak FSC |
| 1983 Caitlin Carruthers, Peter Carruthers, SC of Wilmington | 1994 Jenni Meno, Todd Sand, Winterhurst FSC/ Los Angeles FSC | 2006 Rena Inoue, John Baldwin, All Year FSC |
| 1984 Caitlin Carruthers, Peter Carruthers, SC of Wilmington | 1995 Jenni Meno, Todd Sand, Winterhurst FSC/ Los Angeles FSC | 2007 Brooke Castile, Benjamin Okolski, Arctic FSC |
| | 1996 Jenni Meno, Todd Sand, Winterhurst FSC/ Los Angeles FSC | 2008 Keauna McLaughlin, Los Angeles FSC/ Rockne Brubaker, Broadmoor SC |
| | | 2009 Keauna McLaughlin, Los Angeles FSC/ Rockne Brubaker, Broadmoor SC |

### Dance

| | | |
|---|---|---|
| 1914 Waltz: Theresa Weld, Nathaniel W. Niles, SC of Boston | 1928 Waltz: Rosaline Dunn, Joseph K. Savage, New York SC | 1939 Sandy Macdonald, Harold Hartshorne,SC of New York |
| 1915–19  NO COMPETITION | Fourteenstep: Ada Bauman Kelly, George T. Braakman, New York SC | 1940 Sandy Macdonald, Harold Hartshorne, SC of New York |
| 1920 Waltz: Theresa Weld, Nathaniel W. Niles, SC of Boston | 1929 Waltz and Original Dance combined: Edith C. Secord, Joseph K. Savage, SC of New York | 1941 Sandy Macdonald, Harold Hartshorne, SCNY |
| Fourteenstep: Gertrude Cheever Porter, Irving Brokaw, New York SC | 1930 Waltz: Edith C. Secord, Joseph K. Savage, SC of New York | 1942 Edith B. Whetstone, Alfred N. Richards, Jr, Philadelphia SC & HS |
| 1921 Waltz and Fourteenstep: Theresa Weld-Blanchard, Nathaniel W. Niles, SC of Boston | Original: Clara Rotch Frothingham, George E. B. Hill, SC of Boston | 1943 Marcella May, James Lochead Jr., Skate & Ski Club |
| 1922 Waltz: Beatrix Loughran, Edward M. Howland, New York SC/ SC of Boston | 1931 Waltz: Edith C. Secord, Ferrier T. Martin, SC of New York | 1944 Marcella May, James Lochead Jr., Skate & Ski Club |
| Fourteenstep: Theresa Weld Blanchard, Nathaniel W. Niles, SC of Boston | Original: Theresa Weld Blanchard, Nathaniel W. Niles, SC of Boston | 1945 Kathe Mehl Williams, Robert J. Swenning,SC of New York |
| 1923 Waltz: Mr. & Mrs. Henry W. Howe, New York SC | 1932 Waltz: Edith C. Secord, Joseph K. Savage, SC of New York | 1946 Anne Davies, Carleton C. Hoffner Jr., Washington FSC |
| Fourteenstep: Sydney Goode, James B. Greene, New York SC | Original: Clara Rotch Frothingham, George E. B. Hill, SC of Boston | 1947 Lois Waring, Walter H. Bainbridge Jr., Baltimore FSC/Washiton FSC |
| 1924 Waltz: Rosaline Dunn, Frederick Gabel, New York SC | 1933 Waltz: Ilse Twaroschk, Frederick F. Fleishmann, Brooklyn FSC | 1948 Lois Waring, Walter H. Bainbridge Jr.,Baltimore FSC/Washington FSC |
| Fourteenstep: Sydney Goode, James B. Greene, New York SC | Original: Suzanne Davis, Frederick Goodridge, SC of Boston | 1949 Lois Waring, Walter H. Bainbridge Jr.,Baltimore FSC/Washington FSC |
| 1925 Waltz and Fourteenstep: Virginia Slattery, Ferrier T. Martin, New York SC | 1934 Waltz: Nettie C. Prantel, Roy Hunt, SC of New York | 1950 Lois Waring, Michael McGean, Baltimore FSC |
| | Original: Suzanne Davis, Frederick Goodridge, SC of Boston | 1951 Carmel Bodel, Edward L. Bodel, St. Mortiz ISC |
| 1926 Waltz: Rosaline Dunn, Joseph K. Savage, New York SC | 1935 Waltz: Nettie C. Prantel, Roy Hunt, SC of New York | 1952 Lois Waring, Michael McGean, Baltimore FSC |
| Fourteenstep: Sydney Goode, James B.Greene, New York SC | 1936 Marjorie Parker, Joseph K. Savage, SC of New York | 1953 Carol Ann Peters, Daniel C. Ryan, Washington FSC |
| 1927 Waltz and Fourteenstep: Rosaline Dunn, Joseph K. Savage, New York SC | 1937 Nettie C. Prantel, Harold Hartshorne, SC of New York | 1954 Carmel Bodel, Edward L. Bodel, St Moritz ISC |
| | 1938 Nettie C. Prantel, Harold Hartshorne, SC of New York | 1955 Carmel Bodel, Edward L. Bodel, St Moritz ISC |

## CHAMPIONS OF THE UNITED STATES *(CONT.)*

### Dance *(Cont.)*

| Year | Champion | Year | Champion | Year | Champion |
|------|----------|------|----------|------|----------|
| 1956 | Joan Zamboni, Roland Junso, Arctic Blades FSC | 1974 | Colleen O'Connor, Jim Millns, Broadmoor SC/ City of Colorado Springs | 1992 | April Sargent, Russ Witherby, Ogdensburg FSC/ U of Delaware FSC |
| 1957 | Sharon McKenzie, Bert Wright, Los Angeles FSC | 1975 | Colleen O'Connor, Jim Millns, Broadmoor SC | 1993 | Renee Roca, Gorsha Sur, Broadmoor SC |
| 1958 | Andree Anderson, Donald Jacoby, Buffalo SC | 1976 | Colleen O'Connor, Jim Millns, Broadmoor SC | 1994 | Elizabeth Punsalan, Jerod Swallow, Broadmoor SC/Detroit SC |
| 1959 | Andree Anderson Jacoby, Donald Jacoby, Buffalo SC | 1977 | Judy Genovesi, Kent Weigle, SC of Hartford/Charter Oak FSC | 1995 | Renee Roca, Gorsha Sur, Broadmoor SC |
| 1960 | Margie Ackles, Charles W. Phillips Jr., Los Angeles FSC/Arctic Blades FSC | 1978 | Stacey Smith, John Summers, SC of Wilmington | 1996 | Elizabeth Punsalan, Jerod Swallow, Detroit SC |
| 1961 | Diane C. Sherbloom, Larry Pierce, Los Angeles FSC/ WC of Indianapolis | 1979 | Stacey Smith, John Summers, SC of Wilmington | 1997 | Elizabeth Punsalan, Jerod Swallow, Detroit SC |
| 1962 | Yvonne N. Littlefield, Peter F. Betts, Arctic Blades FSC/ Paramount, CA | 1980 | Stacey Smith, John Summers, SC of Wilmington | 1998 | Elizabeth Punsalan, Jerod Swallow, Detroit SC |
| 1963 | Sally Schantz, Stanley Urban, SC of Boston/Buffalo SC | 1981 | Judy Blumberg, Michael Seibert, Broadmoor SC/ISC of Indianapolis | 1999 | Naomi Lang, Peter Tchernyshev, Detroit SC |
| 1964 | Darlene Streich, Charles D. Fetter Jr., WC of Indianapolis | 1982 | Judy Blumberg, Michael Seibert, Broadmoor SC/ISC of Indianapolis | 2000 | Naomi Lang, Peter Tchernyshev, Detroit SC |
| 1965 | Kristin Fortune, Dennis Sveum, Los Angeles FSC | 1983 | Judy Blumberg, Michael Seibert, Pittsburgh FSC | 2001 | Naomi Lang, Peter Tchernyshev, Detroit SC |
| 1966 | Kristin Fortune, Dennis Sveum, Los Angeles FSC | 1984 | Judy Blumberg, Michael Seibert, Pittsburgh FSC | 2002 | Naomi Lang, Peter Tchernyshev, American Academy FSC |
| 1967 | Lorna Dyer, John Carrell, Broadmoor SC | 1985 | Judy Blumberg, Michael Seibert, Pittsburgh FSC | 2003 | Naomi Lang, Peter Tchernyshev, American Academy FSC |
| 1968 | Judy Schwomeyer, James Sladky, WC of Indianapolis/Academy FSC | 1986 | Renee Roca, Donald Adair, Genesee FSC/Academy FSC | 2004 | Tanith Belbin, Ben Agosto, Detroit SC |
| 1969 | Judy Schwomeyer, James Sladky, WC of Indianapolis/Genesee FSC | 1987 | Suzanne Semanick, Scott Gregory, U of Delaware SC | 2005 | Tanith Belbin, Ben Agosto, Detroit SC |
| 1970 | Judy Schwomeyer, James Sladky, WC of Indianapolis/Genesee FSC | 1988 | Suzanne Semanick, Scott Gregory, U of Delaware SC | 2006 | Tanith Belbin, Ben Agosto, Arctic FSC |
| 1971 | Judy Schwomeyer, James Sladky, WC of Indianapolis/Genesee FSC | 1989 | Susan Wynne, Joseph Druar, Broadmoor SC/Seattle SC | 2007 | Tanith Belbin, Ben Agosto, Arctic FSC |
| 1972 | Judy Schwomeyer, James Sladky, WC of Indianapolis/Genesee FSC | 1990 | Susan Wynne, Joseph Druar, Broadmoor SC/Seattle SC | 2008 | Tanith Belbin, Ben Agosto, Arctic FSC |
| 1973 | Mary Karen Campbell, Johnny Johns, Lansing SC/Detroit SC | 1991 | Elizabeth Punsalan, Jerod Swallow, Broadmoor SC | 2009 | Meryl Davis, Arctic FSC/ Charlie White, Detroit SC |

# Gymnastics

## World Champions — Men

### All-Around

| Year | Champion, Nation |
|------|------------------|
| 1903 | Joseph Martinez, France |
| 1905 | Marcel Lalue, France |
| 1907 | Joseph Czada, Czechoslovakia |
| 1909 | Marcos Torres, France |
| 1911 | Ferdinand Steiner, Czechoslovakia |
| 1913 | Marcos Torres, France |
| 1922 | Peter Sumi, Yugoslavia F. Pechacek, Czechoslovakia |
| 1926 | Peter Sumi, Yugoslavia |
| 1930 | Josip Primozic, Yugoslavia |
| 1934 | Eugene Mack, Switzerland |
| 1938 | Jan Gajdos, Czechoslovakia |
| 1950 | Walter Lehmann, Switzerland |
| 1954 | Valentin Mouratov, USSR Victor Chukarin, USSR |
| 1958 | Boris Shaklin, USSR |
| 1962 | Yuri Titov, USSR |
| 1966 | Mikhail Voronin, USSR |
| 1970 | Eizo Kenmotsu, Japan |
| 1974 | Shigeru Kasamatsu, Japan |
| 1978 | Nikolai Andrianov, USSR |

### All-Around *(Cont.)*

| Year | Champion, Nation |
|------|------------------|
| 1979 | Alexander Ditiatin, USSR |
| 1981 | Yuri Korolev, USSR |
| 1983 | Dimitri Bilozertchev, USSR |
| 1985 | Yuri Korolev, USSR |
| 1987 | Dimitri Bilozertchev, USSR |
| 1989 | Igor Korobchinsky, USSR |
| 1991 | Grigori Misutin, CIS |
| 1993 | Vitaly Scherbo, Belarus |
| 1994 | Ivan Ivankov, Belarus |
| 1995 | Li Xiaoshuang, China |
| 1997 | Ivan Ivankov, Belarus |
| 1999 | Nicolae Krukov, Russia |
| 2001 | Feng Jing, China |
| 2003 | Paul Hamm, United States |
| 2005 | Hiroyuki Tomita, Japan |
| 2007 | Yang Wei, China |
| 2009 | Kohei Uchimura, Japan |

### Pommel Horse

| Year | Champion, Nation |
|------|------------------|
| 1930 | Josip Primozic, Yugoslavia |

### Pommel Horse *(Cont.)*

| Year | Champion, Nation |
|------|------------------|
| 1934 | Eugene Mack, Switzerland |
| 1938 | Michael Reusch, Switzerland |
| 1950 | Josef Stalder, Switzerland |
| 1954 | Grant Chaguinjan, USSR |
| 1958 | Boris Shaklin, USSR |
| 1962 | Miroslav Cerar, Yugoslavia |
| 1966 | Miroslav Cerar, Yugoslavia |
| 1970 | Miroslav Cerar, Yugoslavia |
| 1974 | Zoltan Magyar, Hungary |
| 1978 | Zoltan Magyar, Hungary |
| 1979 | Zoltan Magyar, Hungary |
| 1981 | Michael Mikolai, East Germany |
| 1983 | Dmitri Bilozertchev, USSR |
| 1985 | Valentin Moguilny, USSR |
| 1987 | Zsolt Borkai, Hungary Dmitri Bilozertchev, USSR |
| 1989 | Valentin Moguilny, USSR |
| 1991 | Valeri Belenki, USSR |
| 1992 | Pae Gil Su, North Korea Vitaly Scherbo, CIS Li Jing, China |

## World Champions — Men

### Pommel Horse (Cont.)

| Year | Champion, Nation |
|------|------------------|
| 1993 | Pae Gil Su, North Korea |
| 1994 | Marius Urzica, Romania |
| 1995 | Li Donghua, Switzerland |
| 1996 | Pae Gil Su, North Korea |
| 1997 | Valeri Belenki, Germany |
| 1999 | Alexei Nemov, Russia |
| 2001 | Marius Urzica, Romania |
| 2003 | Teng Haibin, China |
|      | Takehiro Kashima, Japan |
| 2005 | Qin Xiao, China |
| 2007 | Qin Xiao, China |
| 2009 | Hongtao Zhang, China |

### Floor Exercise

| Year | Champion, Nation |
|------|------------------|
| 1930 | Josip Primozic, Yugoslavia |
| 1934 | Georges Miesz, Switzerland |
| 1938 | Jan Gajdos, Czechoslovakia |
| 1950 | Josef Stalder, Switzerland |
| 1954 | Valentin Mouratov, USSR |
|      | Masao Takemoto, Japan |
| 1958 | Masao Takemoto, Japan |
| 1962 | Nobuyuki Aihara, Japan |
|      | Yukio Endo, Japan |
| 1966 | Akinori Nakayama, Japan |
| 1970 | Akinori Nakayama, Japan |
| 1974 | Shigeru Kasamatsu, Japan |
| 1978 | Kurt Thomas, United States |
| 1979 | Kurt Thomas, United States |
|      | Roland Brucker, East Germ. |
| 1981 | Yuri Korolev, USSR, Li Yuejui, China |
| 1983 | Tong Fei, China |
| 1985 | Tong Fei, China |
| 1987 | Lou Yun, China |
| 1989 | Igor Korobchinsky, USSR |
| 1991 | Igor Korobchinsky, USSR |
| 1993 | Grigori Misutin, Ukraine |
| 1994 | Vitaly Scherbo, Belarus |
| 1995 | Vitaly Scherbo, Belarus |
| 1996 | Vitaly Scherbo, Belarus |
| 1997 | Alexei Nemov, Russia |
| 1999 | Alexei Nemov, Russia |
| 2001 | Marian Dragulescu, Romania |
| 2003 | Paul Hamm, United States |
|      | Jordan Jovtchev, Bulgaria |
| 2005 | Diego Hypolito, Brazil |
| 2007 | Zou Kai, China |
| 2009 | Marian Dragulescu, Romania |

### Rings

| Year | Champion, Nation |
|------|------------------|
| 1930 | Emanuel Loffler, Czechoslovakia |
| 1934 | Alois Hudec, Czechoslovakia |
| 1938 | Alois Hudec, Czechoslovakia |
| 1950 | Walter Lehmann, Switzerland |
| 1954 | Albert Azarian, USSR |
| 1958 | Albert Azarian, USSR |
| 1962 | Yuri Titov, USSR |
| 1966 | Mikhail Voronin, USSR |
| 1970 | Akinori Nakayama, Japan |
| 1974 | N. Andrianov, USSR D. Grecu, Rom. |
| 1978 | Nikolai Andrianov, USSR |
| 1979 | Alexander Ditiatin, USSR |
| 1981 | Alexander Ditiatin, USSR |
| 1983 | Dimitri Bilozertchev, USSR |
| 1985 | Li Ning, China, Yuri Korolev, USSR |

### Rings (Cont.)

| Year | Champion, Nation |
|------|------------------|
| 1987 | Yuri Korolev, USSR |
| 1989 | Andreas Aguilar, West Germ. |
| 1991 | Grigory Misutin, USSR |
| 1992 | Vitaly Scherbo, CIS |
| 1993 | Yuri Chechi, Italy |
| 1994 | Yuri Chechi, Italy |
| 1995 | Yuri Chechi, Italy |
| 1996 | Yuri Chechi, Italy |
| 1997 | Yuri Chechi, Italy |
| 1999 | Zhen Dong, China |
| 2001 | Jordan Jovtchev, Bulgaria |
| 2003 | Jordan Jovtchev, Bulgaria |
|      | Dimosthenis Tampakos, Greece |
| 2005 | Yuri Van Gelder, Netherlands |
| 2007 | Diego Hypolito, Brazil |
| 2009 | Mingyong Yan, China |

### Parallel Bars

| Year | Champion, Nation |
|------|------------------|
| 1930 | Josip Primozic, Yugoslavia |
| 1934 | Eugene Mack, Switzerland |
| 1938 | Michael Reusch, Switzerland |
| 1950 | Hans Eugster, Switzerland |
| 1954 | Victor Chukarin, USSR |
| 1958 | Boris Shaklin, USSR |
| 1962 | Miroslav Cerar, Yugoslavia |
| 1966 | Sergei Diamidov, USSR |
| 1970 | Akinori Nakayama, Japan |
| 1974 | Eizo Kenmotsu, Japan |
| 1978 | Eizo Kenmotsu, Japan |
| 1979 | Bart Conner, United States |
| 1981 | Koji Gushiken, Japan |
|      | Alexandr Ditiatin, USSR |
| 1983 | Vladimir Artemov, USSR |
|      | Lou Yun, China |
| 1985 | Sylvio Kroll, East Germany |
|      | Valentin Moguilny, USSR |
| 1987 | Vladimir Artemov, USSR |
| 1989 | Li Jing, China |
|      | Vladimir Artemov, USSR |
| 1991 | Li Jing, China |
| 1992 | Li Jin, China, Alexei Voropaev, CIS |
| 1993 | Vitaly Scherbo, Belarus |
| 1994 | Huang Liping, China |
| 1995 | Vitaly Scherbo, Belarus |
| 1996 | Rustam Sharipov, Ukraine |
| 1997 | Zhang Jinjing, China |
| 1999 | Joo-Hyung Lee, South Korea |
| 2001 | Sean Townsend, U.S. |
| 2003 | Li Xiao-Peng, China |
| 2005 | Mitja Petkovsek, Slovenia |
| 2007 | Mitja Petkovsek, Slovenia |
| 2009 | Guanyin Yang, China |

### High Bar

| Year | Champion, Nation |
|------|------------------|
| 1930 | Istvan Pelle, Hungary |
| 1934 | Ernst Winter, Germany |
| 1938 | Michael Reusch, Switzerland |
| 1950 | Paavo Aaltonen, Finland |
| 1954 | Valentin Mouratov, USSR |
| 1958 | Boris Shaklin, USSR |
| 1962 | Takashi Ono, Japan |
| 1966 | Akinori Nakayama, Japan |
| 1970 | Eizo Kenmotsu, Japan |
| 1974 | Eberhard Gienger, W Germany |

### High Bar (Cont.)

| Year | Champion, Nation |
|------|------------------|
| 1978 | Shigeru Kasamatsu, Japan |
| 1979 | Kurt Thomas, United States |
| 1981 | Alexander Takchev, USSR |
| 1983 | Dimitri Bilozertchev, USSR |
| 1985 | Tong Fei, China |
| 1987 | Dimitri Bilozertchev, USSR |
| 1989 | Li Chunyang, China |
| 1991 | Li Chunyang, China |
|      | R. Buechner, Germ |
| 1992 | Grigori Misutin, CIS |
| 1993 | Sergei Kharkov, Russia |
| 1994 | Vitaly Scherbo, Belarus |
| 1995 | Andreas Wecker, Germany |
| 1996 | Jesús Carballo, Spain |
| 1997 | Jani Tanskanen, Finland |
| 1999 | Jesus Carballo, Spain |
| 2001 | Vlasios Maras, Greece |
| 2003 | Takehiro Kashima, Japan |
| 2005 | Vlasios Maras, Greece |
| 2007 | Fabian Hambuechen, Germ. |
| 2009 | Kai Zou, China |

### Vault

| Year | Champion, Nation |
|------|------------------|
| 1934 | Eugene Mack, Switzerland |
| 1938 | Eugene Mack, Switzerland |
| 1950 | Ernst Gebendinger, Switzerland |
| 1954 | Leo Sotornik, Czechoslovakia |
| 1958 | Yuri Titov, USSR |
| 1962 | Premysel Krbec, Czechoslovakia |
| 1966 | Haruhiro Yamashita, Japan |
| 1970 | Mitsuo Tsukahara, Japan |
| 1974 | Shigeru Kasamatsu, Japan |
| 1978 | Junichi Shimizu, Japan |
| 1979 | Alexander Ditiatin, USSR |
| 1981 | Ralf-Peter Hemmann, East Germany |
| 1983 | Arthur Akopian, USSR |
| 1985 | Yuri Korolev, USSR |
| 1987 | Lou Yun, China |
|      | Sylvio Kroll, East Germany |
| 1989 | Joreg Behrend, East Germany |
| 1991 | Yoo Ok Youl, South Korea |
| 1992 | Yoo Ok Youl, South Korea |
| 1993 | Vitaly Scherbo, Belarus |
| 1994 | Vitaly Scherbo, Belarus |
| 1995 | G. Misutin, Ukraine |
|      | A. Nemov, Russia |
| 1996 | Alexei Nemov, Russia |
| 1997 | Sergei Fedorchenko, Kazakhstan |
| 1999 | Li Xiao-Peng, China |
| 2001 | Marian Dragulescu, Romania |
| 2003 | Li Xiao-Peng, China |
| 2005 | Eichi Sekiguchi, Japan |
| 2007 | Leszek Blanik, Poland |
| 2009 | Marian Dragulescu, Romania |

## World Champions — Women

### All-Around

| Year | Champion, Nation |
|---|---|
| 1934 | Vlasta Dekanova, Czechoslovakia |
| 1938 | Vlasta Dekanova, Czechoslovakia |
| 1950 | Helena Rakoczy, Poland |
| 1954 | Galina Roudiko, USSR |
| 1958 | Larissa Latynina, USSR |
| 1962 | Larissa Latynina, USSR |
| 1966 | Vera Caslavska, Czechoslovakia |
| 1970 | Ludmilla Tourischeva, USSR |
| 1974 | Ludmilla Tourischeva, USSR |
| 1978 | Elena Mukhina, USSR |
| 1979 | Nelli Kim, USSR |
| 1981 | Olga Bicherova, USSR |
| 1983 | Natalia Yurchenko, USSR |
| 1985 | Elena Shoushounova, USSR |
| | Oksana Omeliantchik, USSR |
| 1987 | Aurelia Dobre, Romania |
| 1989 | Svetlana Bouguinskaia, USSR |
| 1991 | Kim Zmeskal, United States |
| 1993 | Shannon Miller, United States |
| 1994 | Shannon Miller, United States |
| 1995 | Lilia Podkopayeva, Ukraine |
| 1997 | Svetlana Khorkina, Russia |
| 1999 | Maria Olaru, Romania |
| 2001 | Svetlana Khorkina, Russia |
| 2003 | Svetlana Khorkina, Russia |
| 2005 | Chellsie Memmel, United States |
| 2007 | Shawn Johnson, United States |
| 2009 | Bridget Sloan, United States |

### Floor Exercise

| Year | Champion, Nation |
|---|---|
| 1950 | Helena Rakoczy, Poland |
| 1954 | Tamara Manina, USSR |
| 1958 | Eva Bosakava, Czechoslovakia |
| 1962 | Larissa Latynina, USSR |
| 1966 | Natalia Kuchinskaya, USSR |
| 1970 | Ludmilla Tourischeva, USSR |
| 1974 | Ludmilla Tourischeva, USSR |
| 1978 | Nelli Kim, USSR |
| | Elena Mukhina, USSR |
| 1979 | Emilia Eberle, Romania |
| 1981 | Natalia Ilenko, USSR |
| 1983 | Ecaterina Szabo, Romania |
| 1985 | Oksana Omeliantchik, USSR |
| 1987 | Elena Shoushounova, USSR |
| | Daniela Silivas, Romania |
| 1989 | Svetlana Bouguinskaia, USSR |
| | Daniela Silivas, Romania |
| 1991 | Cristina Bontas, Romania |
| | Oksana Tchusovitina, USSR |
| 1992 | Kim Zmeskal, United States |
| 1993 | Shannon Miller, United States |
| 1994 | Dina Kochetkova, Russia |

### Floor Exercise *(Cont.)*

| Year | Champion, Nation |
|---|---|
| 1995 | Gina Gogean, Romania |
| 1996 | Gina Gogean, Romania |
| 1997 | Gina Gogean, Romania |
| 1999 | Andreea Raducan, Romania |
| 2001 | Andreea Raducan, Romania |
| 2003 | Daiane Dos Santos, Brazil |
| 2005 | Nastia Liukin, United States |
| 2007 | Shawn Johnson, United States |
| 2009 | Elizabeth Tweddle, United Kingdom |

### Uneven Bars

| Year | Champion, Nation |
|---|---|
| 1950 | Gertchen Kolar, Austria |
| | Anna Pettersson, Sweden |
| 1954 | Agnes Keleti, Hungary |
| 1958 | Larissa Latynina, USSR |
| 1962 | Irina Pervuschina, USSR |
| 1966 | Natalia Kuchinskaya, USSR |
| 1970 | Karin Janz, East Germany |
| 1974 | Annelore Zinke, East Germany |
| 1978 | Marcia Frederick, United States |
| 1979 | Ma Yanhong, China |
| | Maxi Gnauck, East Germany |
| 1981 | Maxi Gnauck, East Germany |
| 1983 | Maxi Gnauck, East Germany |
| 1985 | Gabriele Fahnrich, East Germany |
| 1987 | Daniela Silivas, Romania |
| | Doerte Thuemmler, East Germany |
| 1989 | Fan Di, China |
| | Daniela Silivas, Romania |
| 1991 | Gwang Suk Kim, North Korea |
| 1992 | Lavinia Milosivici, Romania |
| 1993 | Shannon Miller, United States |
| 1994 | Luo Li, China |
| 1995 | Svetlana Khorkina, Russia |
| 1996 | Svetlana Khorkina, Russia |
| 1997 | Svetlana Khorkina, Russia |
| 1999 | Svetlana Khorkina, Russia |
| 2001 | Svetlana Khorkina, Russia |
| 2003 | Chellsie Memmel, U.S. |
| | Hollie Vise, United States |
| 2005 | Nastia Liukin, United States |
| 2007 | Ksenia Semenov, Russia |
| 2009 | Kexin He, China |

### Balance Beam

| Year | Champion, Nation |
|---|---|
| 1950 | Helena Rakoczy, Poland |
| 1954 | Keiko Tanaka, Japan |
| 1958 | Larissa Latynina, USSR |
| 1962 | Eva Bosakova, Czech. |
| 1966 | Natalia Kuchinskaya, USSR |
| 1970 | Erika Zuchold, East Germany |

### Balance Beam *(Cont.)*

| Year | Champion, Nation |
|---|---|
| 1974 | Ludmilla Tourischeva, USSR |
| 1978 | Nadia Comaneci, Romania |
| 1979 | Vera Cerna, Czechoslovakia |
| 1981 | Maxi Gnauck, East Germany |
| 1983 | Olga Mostepanova, USSR |
| 1985 | Daniela Silivas, Romania |
| 1987 | Aurelia Dobre, Romania |
| 1989 | Daniela Silivas, Romania |
| 1991 | Svetlana Boguinskaia, USSR |
| 1992 | Kim Zmeskal, United States |
| 1993 | Lavinia Milosovici, Romania |
| 1994 | Shannon Miller, United States |
| 1995 | Mo Huilan, China |
| 1996 | Dina Kochetkova, Russia |
| 1997 | Gina Gogean, Romania |
| 1999 | E. Zamolodchikova, Russia |
| 2001 | Andreea Raducan, Romania |
| 2003 | Fan Ye, China |
| 2005 | Nan Zhang, China |
| 2007 | Nastia Liukin, United States |
| 2009 | Linlin Deng, China |

### Vault

| Year | Champion, Nation |
|---|---|
| 1950 | Helena Rakoczy, Poland |
| 1954 | T. Manina, USSR |
| | Anna Pettersson, Sweden |
| 1958 | Larissa Latynina, USSR |
| 1962 | Vera Caslavska, Czech. |
| 1966 | Vera Caslavska, Czech. |
| 1970 | Erika Zuchold, East Germany |
| 1974 | Olga Korbut, USSR |
| 1978 | Nelli Kim, USSR |
| 1979 | Dumitrita Turner, Romania |
| 1981 | Maxi Gnauck, East Germany |
| 1983 | Boriana Stoyanova, Bulgaria |
| 1985 | Elena Shoushounova, USSR |
| 1987 | Elena Shoushounova, USSR |
| 1989 | Olesia Durnik, USSR |
| 1991 | Lavinia Milosovici, Romania |
| 1992 | Henrietta Onodi, Hungary |
| 1993 | Elena Piskun, Belarus |
| 1994 | Gina Gogean, Romania |
| 1995 | L. Podkopayeva, Ukraine |
| | Simona Amanar, Rom. |
| 1996 | Gina Gogean, Romania |
| 1997 | Simona Amanar, Romania |
| 1999 | Jie Ling, China |
| 2001 | Svetlana Khorkina, Russia |
| 2003 | Oksana Chusovitina, Uzbekistan |
| 2005 | Fei Cheng, China |
| 2007 | Fei Cheng, China |
| 2009 | Kayla Williams, United States |

## National Champions — Men

### All-Around

| Year | Champion |
|---|---|
| 1963 | Art Shurlock |
| 1964 | Rusty Mitchell |
| 1965 | Rusty Mitchell |
| 1966 | Rusty Mitchell |
| 1967 | Katsuoki Kanzaki |
| 1968 | Yoshi Hayasaki |
| 1969 | Steve Hug |

### All-Around *(Cont.)*

| Year | Champion |
|---|---|
| 1970 | Makoto Sakamoto, Mas Watanabe |
| 1971 | Yoshi Takei |
| 1972 | Yoshi Takei |
| 1973 | Marshall Avener |
| 1974 | John Crosby |
| 1975 | Tom Beach, Bart Conner |

### All-Around *(Cont.)*

| Year | Champion |
|---|---|
| 1976 | Kurt Thomas |
| 1977 | Kurt Thomas |
| 1978 | Kurt Thomas |
| 1979 | Bart Conner |
| 1980 | Peter Vidmar |
| 1981 | Jim Hartung |
| 1982 | Peter Vidmar |

### All-Around *(Cont.)*

| Year | Champion |
|---|---|
| 1983 | Mitch Gaylord |
| 1984 | Mitch Gaylord |
| 1985 | Brian Babcock |
| 1986 | Tim Daggett |
| 1987 | Scott Johnson |
| 1988 | Dan Hayden |
| 1989 | Tim Ryan |

## National Champions — Men *(Cont.)*

### All-Around *(Cont.)*

| Year | Champion |
|---|---|
| 1990 | John Roethlisberger |
| 1991 | Chris Waller |
| 1992 | John Roethlisberger |
| 1993 | John Roethlisberger |
| 1994 | Scott Keswick |
| 1995 | John Roethlisberger |
| 1996 | Blaine Wilson |
| 1997 | Blaine Wilson |
| 1998 | Blaine Wilson |
| 1999 | Blaine Wilson |
| 2000 | Blaine Wilson |
| 2001 | Sean Townsend |
| 2002 | Paul Hamm |
| 2003 | Paul Hamm |
| 2004 | Paul Hamm |
| 2005 | Todd Thornton |
| 2006 | Alexander Artemev |
| 2007 | David Durante |
| 2008 | David Sender |
| 2009 | Jonathan Horton |

### Floor Exercise

| Year | Champion |
|---|---|
| 1963 | Tom Seward |
| 1964 | Rusty Mitchell |
| 1965 | Rusty Mitchell |
| 1966 | Dan Millman |
| 1967 | Katsuoki Kanzaki Ron Aure |
| 1968 | Katsuoki Kanzaki |
| 1969 | Steve Hug, Dave Thor |
| 1970 | Makoto Sakamoto |
| 1971 | John Crosby |
| 1972 | Yoshi Takei |
| 1973 | John Crosby |
| 1974 | John Crosby |
| 1975 | Peter Korman |
| 1977 | Ron Galimore |
| 1978 | Kurt Thomas |
| 1979 | Ron Galimore |
| 1980 | Ron Galimore |
| 1981 | Jim Hartung |
| 1982 | Jim Hartung |
| 1983 | Mitch Gaylord |
| 1984 | Peter Vidmar |
| 1985 | Mark Oates |
| 1986 | Robert Sundstrom |
| 1987 | John Sweeney |
| 1988 | Mark Oates Charles Lakes |
| 1989 | Mike Racanelli |
| 1990 | Bob Stelter |
| 1991 | Mike Racanelli |
| 1992 | Gregg Curtis |
| 1993 | Kerry Huston |
| 1994 | Jeremy Killen |
| 1995 | Daniel Stover |
| 1996 | Jay Thornton |
| 1997 | Jason Gatson |
| 1998 | Jason Gatson |
| 1999 | Jason Gatson |
| 2000 | Blaine Wilson |
| 2001 | Sean Townsend |
| 2002 | Morgan Hamm |
| 2003 | Morgan Hamm |
| 2004 | Paul Hamm |

### Floor Exercise *(Cont.)*

| Year | Champion |
|---|---|
| 2005 | Guillermo Alvarez |
| 2006 | Jonathan Horton |
| 2007 | Paul Hamm |
| 2008 | Morgan Hamm |
| 2009 | Steven Legendre |

### Pommel Horse

| Year | Champion |
|---|---|
| 1963 | Larry Spiegel |
| 1964 | Sam Bailie |
| 1965 | Jack Ryan |
| 1966 | Jack Ryan |
| 1967 | Paul Mayer/Dave Doty |
| 1968 | Katsuoki Kanzaki |
| 1969 | Dave Thor |
| 1970 | Mas Watanabe |
| 1971 | Leonard Caling |
| 1972 | Sadao Hamada |
| 1973 | Marshall Avener |
| 1974 | Marshall Avener |
| 1975 | Bart Conner |
| 1977 | Gene Whelan |
| 1978 | Jim Hartung |
| 1979 | Bart Conner |
| 1980 | Jim Simons |
| 1981 | Jim Hartung |
| 1982 | Jim Hartung |
| 1983 | Bart Conner |
| 1984 | Tim Daggett |
| 1985 | Phil Cahoy |
| 1986 | Phil Cahoy |
| 1987 | Tim Daggett |
| 1988 | Kevin Davis |
| 1989 | Kevin Davis |
| 1990 | Patrick Kirksey |
| 1991 | Chris Waller |
| 1992 | Chris Waller |
| 1993 | Chris Waller |
| 1994 | Mihai Begiu |
| 1995 | Mark Sohn |
| 1996 | Josh Stein |
| 1997 | John Roethlisberger |
| 1998 | John Roethlisberger |
| 1999 | John Roethlisberger |
| 2000 | John Roethlisberger |
| 2001 | Brett McClure |
| 2002 | Paul Hamm |
| 2003 | Paul Hamm |
| 2004 | Brett McClure |
| 2005 | Yewki Tomita |
| 2006 | Alexander Artemev |
| 2007 | Alexander Artemev |
| 2008 | Yewki Tomita |
| 2009 | Luke Stannard |

### Rings

| Year | Champion |
|---|---|
| 1963 | Art Shurlock |
| 1964 | Glen Gailis |
| 1965 | Glen Gailis |
| 1966 | Glen Gailis |
| 1967 | Fred Dennis, Don Hatch |
| 1968 | Yoshi Hayasaki |
| 1969 | Fred Dennis, Bob Emery |
| 1970 | Makoto Sakamoto |
| 1971 | Yoshi Takei |

### Rings *(Cont.)*

| Year | Champion |
|---|---|
| 1972 | Yoshi Takei |
| 1973 | Jim Ivicek |
| 1974 | Tom Weeder |
| 1975 | Tom Beach |
| 1977 | Kurt Thomas |
| 1978 | Mike Silverstein |
| 1979 | Bart Conner |
| 1980 | Jim Hartung |
| 1981 | Jim Hartung |
| 1982 | Jim Hartung Peter Vidmar |
| 1983 | Mitch Gaylord |
| 1984 | Jim Hartung |
| 1985 | Dan Hayden |
| 1986 | Dan Hayden |
| 1987 | Scott Johnson |
| 1988 | Dan Hayden |
| 1989 | Scott Keswick |
| 1990 | Scott Keswick |
| 1991 | Scott Keswick |
| 1992 | Tim Ryan |
| 1993 | John Roethlisberger |
| 1994 | Scott Keswick |
| 1995 | Paul O'Neill |
| 1996 | Kip Simons |
| 1997 | Blaine Wilson |
| 1998 | Jeff Johnson |
| 1999 | Blaine Wilson |
| 2000 | Blaine Wilson |
| 2001 | Sean Townsend |
| 2002 | Blaine Wilson |
| 2003 | Blaine Wilson |
| 2004 | Raj Bhavsar |
| 2005 | Sean Golden |
| 2006 | Kevin Tan |
| 2007 | Kevin Tan |
| 2008 | Kevin Tan |
| 2009 | Jonathan Horton |

### Vault

| Year | Champion |
|---|---|
| 1963 | Art Shurlock |
| 1964 | Gary Hery |
| 1965 | Brent Williams |
| 1966 | Dan Millman |
| 1967 | Jack Kenan, Sid Jensen |
| 1968 | Rich Scorza |
| 1969 | Dave Butzman |
| 1970 | Makoto Sakamoto |
| 1971 | Gary Morava |
| 1972 | Mike Kelley |
| 1973 | Gary Morava |
| 1974 | John Crosby |
| 1975 | Tom Beach |
| 1977 | Ron Galimore |
| 1978 | Jim Hartung |
| 1979 | Ron Galimore |
| 1980 | Ron Galimore |
| 1981 | Ron Galimore |
| 1982 | Jim Hartung/Jim Mikus |
| 1983 | Chris Reigel |
| 1984 | Chris Reigel |
| 1985 | Scott Johnson Mark Oates |
| 1986 | Scott Wilbanks |
| 1987 | John Sweeney |

### Vault *(Cont.)*

| Year | Champion |
|---|---|
| 1988 | John Sweeney/Bill Paul |
| 1989 | Bill Roth |
| 1990 | Lance Ringnald |
| 1991 | Scott Keswick |
| 1992 | Trent Dimas |
| 1993 | Bill Roth |
| 1994 | Keith Wiley |
| 1995 | David St. Pierre |
| 1996 | Blaine Wilson |
| 1997 | Blaine Wilson |
| 1998 | Brent Klaus |
| 1999 | Guard Young |
| 2000 | Blaine Wilson |
| 2001 | Jason Furr |
| 2002 | Paul Hamm |
| 2003 | Raj Bhavsar |
| 2004 | David Sender |
| 2005 | Sean Golden |
| 2006 | David Sender |
| 2007 | Sean Golden |
| 2008 | David Sender |
| 2009 | Jake Dalton |

### Parallel Bars

| Year | Champion |
|---|---|
| 1963 | Tom Seward |
| 1964 | Rusty Mitchell |
| 1965 | Glen Gailis |
| 1966 | Ray Hadley |
| 1967 | Katsuoki Kanzaki Tom Goldsborough |
| 1968 | Yoshi Hayasaki |
| 1969 | Steve Hug |
| 1970 | Makoto Sakamoto |
| 1971 | Brent Simmons |
| 1972 | Yoshi Takei |
| 1973 | Marshall Avener |
| 1974 | Jim Ivicek |
| 1975 | Bart Conner |
| 1977 | Kurt Thomas |
| 1978 | Bart Conner |
| 1979 | Bart Conner |
| 1980 | Phil Cahoy/Larry Gerard |
| 1981 | Bart Conner |
| 1982 | Peter Vidmar |
| 1983 | Mitch Gaylord |
| 1984 | Peter Vidmar, Mitch Gaylord, Tim Daggett |
| 1985 | Tim Daggett |
| 1986 | Tim Daggett |
| 1987 | Scott Johnson |
| 1988 | D. Hayden/K. Davis |
| 1989 | Conrad Voorsanger |
| 1990 | Trent Dimas |
| 1991 | Scott Keswick |
| 1992 | Jair Lynch |
| 1993 | Chainey Umphrey |
| 1994 | Steve McCain |
| 1995 | John Roethlisberger |
| 1996 | Jair Lynch |
| 1997 | Blaine Wilson |
| 1998 | Blaine Wilson |
| 1999 | Jason Gatson |
| 2000 | Trent Wells |
| 2001 | Sean Townsend |
| 2002 | Sean Townsend |

## National Champions — Men *(Cont.)*

### Parallel Bars *(Cont.)*

| Year | Champion |
|------|----------|
| 2003 | Jason Gatson |
| 2004 | Alexander Artemev |
| 2005 | D.J. Bucher |
| 2006 | Alexander Artemev |
| 2007 | David Durante |
| 2008 | Justin Spring |
| 2009 | Tim McNeill |

### High Bars

| Year | Champion |
|------|----------|
| 1963 | Art Shurlock |
| 1964 | Glen Gailis |
| 1965 | Rusty Mitchell |
| 1966 | Katsuzoki Kanzaki |
| 1967 | Katsuzoki Kanzaki |
|  | Jerry Fontana |

### High Bars *(Cont.)*

| Year | Champion |
|------|----------|
| 1968 | Yoshi Hayasaki |
| 1969 | Rich Grisby |
| 1970 | Makoto Sakamoto |
| 1971 | Yoshi Takei |
| 1972 | Tom Lindner |
| 1973 | John Crosby |
| 1974 | Brent Simmons |
| 1975 | Tom Beach |
| 1977 | Kurt Thomas |
| 1978 | Kurt Thomas |
| 1979 | Yoichi Tomita |
| 1980 | Jim Hartung |
| 1981 | Bart Conner |
| 1982 | Mitch Gaylord |
| 1983 | Mario McCutcheon |
| 1983 | Mario McCutcheon |

### High Bars *(Cont.)*

| Year | Champion |
|------|----------|
| 1984 | Peter Vidmar |
|  | Tim Daggett |
|  | Mitch Gaylord |
| 1985 | Dan Hayden |
| 1986 | D. Hayden/D. Moriel |
| 1987 | David Moriel |
| 1988 | Dan Hayden |
| 1989 | Tim Ryan |
| 1990 | Trent Dimas |
|  | Lance Ringnald |
| 1991 | Lance Ringnald |
| 1992 | Jair Lynch |
| 1993 | Steve McCain |
| 1994 | Scott Keswick |
| 1995 | John Roethlisberger |
| 1996 | Bill Roth |

### High Bars *(Cont.)*

| Year | Champion |
|------|----------|
| 1997 | Douglas Stibel |
| 1998 | Jason Gatson |
| 1999 | Jamie Natalie |
| 2000 | Trent Wells |
|  | Jamie Natalie |
| 2001 | Daniel Diaz-Luong |
| 2002 | Blaine Wilson |
| 2003 | Paul Hamm |
| 2004 | Paul Hamm |
| 2005 | D.J. Bucher |
| 2006 | Chris Brooks |
| 2007 | Justin Spring |
| 2008 | Joseph Hagerty |
| 2009 | Jonathan Horton |

## National Champions — Women

### All-Around

| Year | Champion |
|------|----------|
| 1963 | Donna Schanezer |
| 1965 | Gail Daley |
| 1966 | Donna Schanezer |
| 1968 | Linda Scott |
| 1969 | Joyce Tanac |
|  | Schroeder |
| 1970 | Cathy Rigby |
| 1971 | Joan Moore Gnat |
|  | Linda Metheny Mulvihill |
| 1972 | Joan Moore Gnat |
|  | Cathy Rigby |
| 1973 | Joan Moore Gnat |
| 1974 | Joan Moore Gnat |
| 1975 | Tammy Manville |
| 1976 | Denise Cheshire |
| 1977 | Donna Turnbow |
| 1978 | Kathy Johnson |
| 1979 | Leslie Pyfer |
| 1980 | Julianne McNamara |
| 1981 | Tracee Talavera |
| 1982 | Tracee Talavera |
| 1983 | Dianne Durham |
| 1984 | Mary Lou Retton |
| 1985 | Sabrina Mar |
| 1986 | Jennifer Sey |
| 1987 | Kristie Phillips |
| 1988 | Phoebe Mills |
| 1989 | Brandy Johnson |
| 1990 | Kim Zmeskal |
| 1991 | Kim Zmeskal |
| 1992 | Kim Zmeskal |
| 1993 | Shannon Miller |
| 1994 | Dominique Dawes |
| 1995 | Dominique Moceanu |
| 1996 | Shannon Miller |
| 1997 | V. Adler/ K. Powell |
| 1998 | Kristen Maloney |
| 1999 | Kristen Maloney |
| 2000 | Elise Ray |
| 2001 | Tasha Schwikert |
| 2002 | Tasha Schwikert |
| 2003 | Courtney Kupets |
| 2004 | Courtney Kupets/Carly Patterson |
| 2005 | Nastia Liukin |
| 2006 | Nastia Liukin |

### All-Around *(Cont.)*

| Year | Champion |
|------|----------|
| 2007 | Shawn Johnson |
| 2008 | Shawn Johnson |
| 2009 | Bridget Sloan |

### Vault

| Year | Champion |
|------|----------|
| 1963 | Donna Schanezer |
| 1965 | Gail Daley |
| 1966 | Donna Schanezer |
| 1968 | Terry Spencer |
| 1969 | Joyce Tanac Schroeder |
|  | Cleo Carver |
| 1970 | Cathy Rigby |
| 1971 | Joan Moore Gnat/Adele Gleaves |
| 1972 | Cindy Eastwood |
| 1973 | Roxanne Pierce Mancha |
| 1974 | Dianne Dunbar |
| 1975 | Kolleen Casey |
| 1976 | Debbie Wilcox |
| 1977 | Lisa Cawthron |
| 1978 | Rhonda Schwandt/Sharon Shapiro |
| 1979 | Christa Canary |
| 1980 | J. McNamara/B. Kline |
| 1981 | Kim Neal |
| 1982 | Yumi Mordre |
| 1983 | Dianne Durham |
| 1984 | Mary Lou Retton |
| 1985 | Yolanda Mavity |
| 1986 | Joyce Wilborn |
| 1987 | Rhonda Faehn |
| 1988 | Rhonda Faehn |
| 1989 | Brandy Johnson |
| 1990 | Brandy Johnson |
| 1991 | Kerri Strug |
| 1992 | Kerri Strug |
| 1993 | Dominique Dawes |
| 1994 | Dominique Dawes |
| 1995 | Shannon Miller |
| 1996 | Dominique Dawes |
| 1997 | Vanessa Atler |
| 1998 | Dominique Moceanu |
| 1999 | Vanessa Atler |
| 2000 | Kristen Maloney |
| 2001 | Mohini Bhardwaj |
| 2002 | Elizabeth Tricase |

### Vault *(Cont.)*

| Year | Champion |
|------|----------|
| 2003 | Annia Hatch |
| 2004 | Liz Tricase |
| 2005 | Alicia Sacramone |
| 2006 | Alicia Sacramone |
| 2007 | Alicia Sacramone |
| 2008 | Alicia Sacramone |
| 2009 | Kayla Williams |

### Uneven Bars

| Year | Champion |
|------|----------|
| 1963 | Donna Schanezer |
| 1965 | Irene Haworth |
| 1966 | Donna Schanezer |
| 1968 | Linda Scott |
| 1969 | Joyce Tanac Schroeder |
|  | Lisa Nelson |
| 1970 | Roxanne Pierce Mancha |
| 1971 | Joan Moore Gnat |
| 1972 | Cathy Rigby |
| 1973 | Roxanne Pierce Mancha |
| 1974 | Diane Dunbar |
| 1975 | Leslie Wolfsberger |
| 1976 | Leslie Wolfsberger |
| 1977 | Donna Turnbow |
| 1978 | Marcia Frederick |
| 1979 | Marcia Frederick |
| 1980 | Marcia Frederick |
| 1981 | Julianne McNamara |
| 1982 | Marie Roethlisberger |
| 1983 | Julianne McNamara |
| 1984 | Julianne McNamara |
| 1985 | Sabrina Mar |
| 1986 | Marie Roethlisberger |
| 1987 | Melissa Marlowe |
| 1988 | Chelle Stack |
| 1989 | Chelle Stack |
| 1990 | Sandy Woolsey |
| 1991 | Elisabeth Crandall |
| 1992 | Dominique Dawes |
| 1993 | Shannon Miller |
| 1994 | Dominique Dawes |
| 1995 | Dominique Dawes |
| 1996 | Dominique Dawes |
| 1997 | Kristy Powell |

### National Champions — Women

#### Uneven Bars *(Cont.)*

| Year | Champion |
|---|---|
| 1998 | Elise Ray |
| 1999 | Jamie Dantzscher |
| | Jennie Thompson |
| 2000 | Elise Ray |
| 2001 | Katie Heenan |
| 2002 | Tasha Schwikert |
| 2003 | Katie Heenan |
| 2004 | Courtney Kupets |
| 2005 | Nastia Liukin |
| 2006 | Nastia Liukin |
| 2007 | Nastia Liukin |
| 2008 | Nastia Liukin |
| 2009 | Bridget Sloan |

#### Balance Beam

| Year | Champion |
|---|---|
| 1963 | Leissa Krol |
| 1965 | Gail Daley |
| 1966 | Irene Haworth |
| | Linda Scott |
| 1968 | Linda Scott |
| 1969 | Lonna Woodward |
| 1970 | Joyce Tanac Schroeder |
| 1971 | Linda Metheny Mulvihill |
| 1972 | Kim Chace |
| 1973 | Nancy Thies Marshall |
| 1974 | Joan Moore Gnat |
| 1975 | Kyle Gayner |
| 1976 | Carrie Englert |
| 1977 | Donna Turnbow |
| 1978 | Christa Canary |
| 1979 | Heidi Anderson |
| 1980 | Kelly Garrison-Steves |
| 1981 | Tracee Talavera |
| 1982 | Julianne McNamara |
| 1983 | Dianne Durham |
| 1984 | Pam Bileck |
| | Tracee Talavera |
| 1986 | Angie Denkins |

#### Balance Beam *(Cont.)*

| Year | Champion |
|---|---|
| 1987 | Kristie Phillips |
| 1985 | Kelly Garrison-Steves |
| 1988 | Kelly Garrison-Steves |
| 1989 | Brandy Johnson |
| 1990 | Betty Okino |
| 1991 | Shannon Miller |
| 1992 | Kerri Strug |
| | Kim Zmeskal |
| 1993 | Dominique Dawes |
| 1994 | Dominique Dawes |
| 1995 | Doni Thompson |
| | Monica Flammer |
| 1996 | Dominique Dawes |
| 1997 | Kendall Beck |
| 1998 | Dominique Moceanu |
| 1999 | Vanessa Atler |
| 2000 | Alyssa Beckerman |
| | Amy Chow |
| 2001 | Tasha Schwikert |
| 2002 | Tasha Schwikert |
| 2003 | Hollie Vise |
| 2004 | Courtney Kupets |
| 2005 | Nastia Liukin |
| 2006 | Nastia Liukin |
| 2007 | Shawn Johnson |
| 2008 | Nastia Liukin |
| 2009 | Ivana Hong |

#### Floor Exercise

| Year | Champion |
|---|---|
| 1963 | Donna Schanezer |
| 1965 | Gail Daley |
| 1966 | Donna Schanezer |
| 1968 | Linda Scott |
| 1970 | Cathy Rigby |
| 1971 | Joan Moore Gnat |
| | Linda Metheny Mulvihill |
| 1972 | Joan Moore Gnat |
| 1973 | Joan Moore Gnat |

#### Floor Exercise *(Cont.)*

| Year | Champion |
|---|---|
| 1974 | Joan Moore Gnat |
| 1975 | Kathy Howard |
| 1976 | Carrie Englert |
| 1977 | Kathy Johnson |
| 1978 | Kathy Johnson |
| 1979 | Heidi Anderson |
| 1980 | Beth Kline |
| 1981 | Michelle Goodwin |
| 1982 | Amy Koopman |
| 1983 | Dianne Durham |
| 1984 | Mary Lou Retton |
| 1985 | Sabrina Mar |
| 1986 | Yolanda Mavity |
| 1987 | Kristie Phillips |
| 1988 | Phoebe Mills |
| 1989 | Brandy Johnson |
| 1990 | Brandy Johnson |
| 1991 | Kim Zmeskal |
| | Dominique Dawes |
| 1992 | Kim Zmeskal |
| 1993 | Shannon Miller |
| 1994 | Dominique Dawes |
| 1995 | Dominique Dawes |
| 1996 | Dominique Dawes |
| 1997 | Lindsay Wing |
| 1998 | Vanessa Atler |
| 1999 | Elise Ray |
| 2000 | Kristen Maloney |
| 2001 | Tabitha Yim |
| 2002 | Tasha Schwikert |
| 2003 | Ashley Postell |
| 2004 | Carly Patterson |
| 2005 | Alicia Sacramone |
| 2006 | Alicia Sacramone |
| | Randi Stageberg |
| 2007 | Shawn Johnson |
| 2008 | Shawn Johnson |
| 2009 | Bridget Sloan |

## Skiing

### 2009 World Cup Alpine Final Season Standings

| Men | | Pts | Women | | Pts |
|---|---|---|---|---|---|
| **OVERALL** | Aksel Lund Svindal, Norway | 1009 | **OVERALL** | Lindsey Vonn, United States | 1788 |
| **DOWNHILL** | Michael Walchhofer, Austria | 470 | **DOWNHILL** | Lindsey Vonn, United States | 502 |
| **SLALOM** | Jean-Baptiste Grange, France | 571 | **SLALOM** | Maria Riesch, Germany | 670 |
| **GIANT SLALOM** | Didier Cuche, Switzerland | 474 | **GIANT SLALOM** | Tania Poutiainen, Finland | 508 |
| **SUPER G** | Aksel Lund Svindal, Norway | 292 | **SUPER G** | Lindsey Vonn, United States | 461 |
| **COMBINED** | Carlo Janka, Switzerland | 242 | **COMBINED** | Anja Paerson, Sweden | 251 |

## World Cup Season Title Holders

### Men – OVERALL

| Year | Champion | Year | Champion |
|---|---|---|---|
| 1967 | Jean-Claude Killy, France | 1975 | Gustavo Thoeni, Italy |
| 1968 | Jean-Claude Killy, France | 1976 | Ingemar Stenmark, Sweden |
| 1969 | Karl Schranz, Austria | 1977 | Ingemar Stenmark, Sweden |
| 1970 | Karl Schranz, Austria | 1978 | Ingemar Stenmark, Sweden |
| 1971 | Gustavo Thoeni, Italy | 1979 | Peter Lüscher, Switzerland |
| 1972 | Gustavo Thoeni, Italy | 1980 | Andreas Wenzel, Liechtenstein |
| 1973 | Gustavo Thoeni, Italy | 1981 | Phil Mahre, United States |
| 1974 | Piero Gros, Italy | 1982 | Phil Mahre, United States |

## Men – OVERALL (Cont.)

| | |
|---|---|
| 1983 .....................Phil Mahre, United States | 1997 .....................Luc Alphand, France |
| 1984 .....................Pirmin Zurbriggen, Switzerland | 1998 .....................Hermann Maier, Austria |
| 1985 .....................Marc Girardelli, Luxembourg | 1999 .....................Lasse Kjus, Norway |
| 1986 .....................Marc Girardelli, Luxembourg | 2000 .....................Hermann Maier, Austria |
| 1987 .....................Pirmin Zurbriggen, Switzerland | 2001 .....................Hermann Maier, Austria |
| 1988 .....................Pirmin Zurbriggen, Switzerland | 2002 .....................Stephan Eberharter, Austria |
| 1989 .....................Marc Girardelli, Luxembourg | 2003 .....................Stephan Eberharter, Austria |
| 1990 .....................Pirmin Zurbriggen, Switzerland | 2004 .....................Hermann Maier, Austria |
| 1991 .....................Marc Girardelli, Luxembourg | 2005 .....................Bode Miller, United States |
| 1992 .....................Paul Accola, Switzerland | 2006 .....................Benjamin Raich, Austria |
| 1993 .....................Marc Girardelli, Luxembourg | 2007 .....................Aksel Lund Svindal, Norway |
| 1994 .....................Kjetil André Aamodt, Norway | 2008 .....................Bode Miller, United States |
| 1995 .....................Alberto Tomba, Italy | 2009 .....................Aksel Lund Svindal, Norway |
| 1996 .....................Lasse Kjus, Norway | |

## Women – OVERALL

| | |
|---|---|
| 1967 ...............Nancy Greene, Canada | 1989 ...............Vreni Schneider, Switzerland |
| 1968 ...............Nancy Greene, Canada | 1990 ...............Petra Kronberger, Austria |
| 1969 ...............Gertrud Gabl, Austria | 1991 ...............Petra Kronberger, Austria |
| 1970 ...............Michèle Jacot, France | 1992 ...............Petra Kronberger, Austria |
| 1971 ...............Annemarie Pröll, Austria | 1993 ...............Anita Wachter, Austria |
| 1972 ...............Annemarie Pröll, Austria | 1994 ...............Vreni Schneider, Switzerland |
| 1973 ...............Annemarie Pröll, Austria | 1995 ...............Vreni Schneider, Switzerland |
| 1974 ...............Annemarie Moser-Proell, Austria | 1996 ...............Katja Seizinger, Germany |
| 1975 ...............Annemarie Moser-Proell, Austria | 1997 ...............Pernilla Wiberg, Sweden |
| 1976 ...............Rosi Mitermaier, W Germany | 1998 ...............Katja Seizinger, Germany |
| 1977 ...............Lise-Marie Morerod, Switzerland | 1999 ...............Alexandra Meissnitzer, Austria |
| 1978 ...............Hanni Wenzel, Liechtenstein | 2000 ...............Renate Goetschl, Austria |
| 1979 ...............Annemarie Moser-Proell, Austria | 2001 ...............Janica Kostelic, Croatia |
| 1980 ...............Hanni Wenzel, Liechtenstein | 2002 ...............Michaela Dorfmeister, Austria |
| 1981 ...............Marie-Thérèse Nadig, Switzerland | 2003 ...............Janica Kostelic, Austria |
| 1982 ...............Erika Hess, Switzerland | 2004 ...............Anja Paerson, Sweden |
| 1983 ...............Tamara McKinney, United States | 2005 ...............Anja Paerson, Sweden |
| 1984 ...............Erika Hess, Switzerland | 2006 ...............Janica Kostelic, Croatia |
| 1985 ...............Michela Figini, Switzerland | 2007 ...............Nicole Hosp, Austria |
| 1986 ...............Maria Walliser, Switzerland | 2008 ...............Lindsey Vonn, United States |
| 1987 ...............Maria Walliser, Switzerland | 2009 ...............Lindsey Vonn, United States |
| 1988 ...............Michela Figini, Switzerland | |

# Wrestling

## United States National Champions

| 1983 FREESTYLE | 1984 FREESTYLE | 1985 FREESTYLE |
|---|---|---|
| 105.5 .......Rich Salamone | 105.5 .......Rich Salamone | 105.5 .......Tim Vanni |
| 114.5 .......Joe Gonzales | 114.5 .......Charlie Heard | 114.5 .......Jim Martin |
| 125.5 .......Joe Corso | 125.5 .......Joe Corso | 125.5 .......Charlie Heard |
| 136.5 .......Rich Dellagatta* | 136.5 .......Rich Dellagatta* | 136.5 .......Darryl Burley |
| 149.5 .......Bill Hugent | 149.5 .......Andre Metzger | 149.5 .......Bill Nugent* |
| 163 .........Lee Kemp | 163 .........Dave Schultz* | 163 .........Kenny Monday |
| 180.5 .......Chris Campbell | 180.5 .......Mark Schultz | 180.5 .......Mike Sheets |
| 198 .........Pete Bush | 198 .........Steve Fraser | 198 .........Mark Schultz |
| 220 .........Greg Gibson | 220 .........Harold Smith | 220 .........Greg Gibson |
| Hvy .........Bruce Baumgartner | Hvy .........Bruce Baumgartner | 286 .........Bruce Baumgartner |
| Team.......Sunkist Kids | Team.......Sunkist Kids | Team.......Sunkist Kids |
| **GRECO-ROMAN** | **GRECO-ROMAN** | **GRECO-ROMAN** |
| 105.5 .......T.J. Jones | 105.5 .......T.J. Jones | 105.5 .......T.J. Jones |
| 114.5 .......Mark Fuller | 114.5 .......Mark Fuller | 114.5 .......Mark Fuller |
| 125.5 .......Rob Hermann | 136.5 .......Dan Mello | 125.5 .......Eric Seward* |
| 136.5 .......Dan Mello | 149.5 .......Jim Martinez* | 136.5 .......Buddy Lee |
| 149.5 .......Jim Martinez | 163 .........John Matthews | 149.5 .......Jim Martinez |
| 163 .........James Andre | 180.5 .......Tom Press | 163 .........David Butler |
| 180.5 .......Steve Goss | 198 .........Mike Houck | 180.5 .......Chris Catallo |
| 198 .........Steve Fraser* | 220 .........No champion | 198 .........Mike Houck |
| 220 .........Dennis Koslowski | Hvy .........No champion | 220 .........Greg Gibson |
| Hvy .........No champion | Team.......Adirondack 3-Style, Wash. | 286 .........Dennis Koslowski |
| Team.......Minn. Wrestling Club | | Team.......U.S. Marine Corps |

## United States National Champions

### 1986

**FREESTYLE**

| | |
|---|---|
| 105.5 | Rich Salamone |
| 114.5 | Joe Gonzales |
| 125.5 | Kevin Darkus |
| 136.5 | John Smith |
| 149.5 | Andre Metzger* |
| 163 | Dave Schultz |
| 180.5 | Mark Schultz |
| 198 | Jim Scherr |
| 220 | Dan Severn |
| 286 | Bruce Baumgartner |
| Team | Sunkist Kids (Div. I) |
| | Hawkeye Wrestling |
| | Club (Div. II) |

**GRECO-ROMAN**

| | |
|---|---|
| 105.5 | Eric Wetzel |
| 114.5 | Shawn Sheldon |
| 125.5 | Anthony Amado |
| 136.5 | Frank Famiano |
| 149.5 | Jim Martinez |
| 163 | David Butler* |
| 180.5 | Darryl Gholar |
| 198 | Derrick Waldroup |
| 220 | Dennis Koslowski |
| 286 | Duane Koslowski |
| Team | U.S. Marine Corps (Div. I) |
| | U.S. Navy (Div. II) |

### 1987

**FREESTYLE**

| | |
|---|---|
| 105.5 | Takashi Irie |
| 114.5 | Mitsuru Sato |
| 125.5 | Barry Davis |
| 136.5 | Takumi Adachi |
| 149.5 | Andre Metzger |
| 163 | Dave Schultz* |
| 180.5 | Mark Schultz |
| 198 | Jim Scherr |
| 220 | Bill Scherr |
| 286 | Bruce Baumgartner |
| Team | Sunkist Kids (Div. I) |
| | Team Foxcatcher (Div. II) |

**GRECO-ROMAN**

| | |
|---|---|
| 105.5 | Eric Wetzel |
| 114.5 | Shawn Sheldon |
| 125.5 | Eric Seward |
| 136.5 | Frank Famiano |
| 149.5 | Jim Martinez |
| 163 | David Butler |
| 180.5 | Chris Catallo |
| 198 | Derrick Waldroup* |
| 220 | Dennis Koslowski |
| 286 | Duane Koslowski |
| Team | U.S. Marine Corp (Div. I) |
| | U.S. Army (Div. II) |

### 1988

**FREESTYLE**

| | |
|---|---|
| 105.5 | Tim Vanni |
| 114.5 | Joe Gonzales |
| 125.5 | Kevin Darkus |
| 136.5 | John Smith* |
| 149.5 | Nate Carr |
| 163 | Kenny Monday |
| 180.5 | Dave Schultz |
| 198 | Melvin Douglas III |
| 220 | Bill Scherr |
| 286 | Bruce Baumgartner |

### 1988 *(Cont.)*

**FREESTYLE *(CONT)***

| | |
|---|---|
| Team | Sunkist Kids (Div. I) |
| | Team Foxcatcher (Div. II) |

**GRECO-ROMAN**

| | |
|---|---|
| 105.5 | T.J. Jones |
| 114.5 | Shawn Sheldon |
| 125.5 | Gogi Parseghian* |
| 136.5 | Dalen Wasmund |
| 149.5 | Craig Pollard |
| 163 | Tony Thomas |
| 180.5 | Darryl Gholar |
| 198 | Mike Carolan |
| 220 | Dennis Koslowski |
| 286 | Duane Koslowski |
| Team | U.S. Marine Corps (Div. I) |
| | Sunkist Kids (Div. II) |

### 1989

**FREESTYLE**

| | |
|---|---|
| 105.5 | Tim Vanni |
| 114.5 | Zeke Jones |
| 125.5 | Brad Penrith |
| 136.5 | John Smith |
| 149.5 | Nate Carr |
| 163 | Rob Koll |
| 180.5 | Rico Chiapparelli |
| 198 | Jim Scherr* |
| 220 | Bill Scherr |
| 286 | Bruce Baumgartner |
| Team | Sunkist Kids (Div. I) |
| | Team Foxcatcher (Div. II) |

**GRECO-ROMAN**

| | |
|---|---|
| 105.5 | Lew Dorrance |
| 114.5 | Mark Fuller |
| 125.5 | Gogi Parseghian |
| 136.5 | Isaac Anderson |
| 149.5 | Andy Seras* |
| 163 | David Butler |
| 180.5 | John Morgan |
| 198 | Michial Foy |
| 220 | Steve Lawson |
| 286 | Craig Pittman |
| Team | USMC (I) Jets USA (II) |

### 1990

**FREESTYLE**

| | |
|---|---|
| 105.5 | Rob Eiter |
| 114.5 | Zeke Jones |
| 125.5 | Joe Melchiore |
| 136.5 | John Smith |
| 149.5 | Nate Carr |
| 163 | Rob Koll |
| 180.5 | Royce Alger |
| 198 | Chris Campbell* |
| 220 | Bill Scherr |
| 286 | Bruce Baumgartner |
| Team | Sunkist Kids (Div. I) |
| | Team Foxcatcher (Div. II) |

**GRECO-ROMAN**

| | |
|---|---|
| 105.5 | Lew Dorrance |
| 114.5 | Sam Henson |
| 125.5 | Mark Pustelnik |
| 136.5 | Isaac Anderson |
| 149.5 | Andy Seras |
| 163 | David Butler |
| 180.5 | Derrick Waldroup |
| 198 | Randy Couture* |
| 220 | Chris Tironi |

### 1990 *(Cont.)*

**GRECO-ROMAN *(CONT)***

| | |
|---|---|
| 286 | Matt Ghaffari |
| Team | Jets USA (Div. I) |
| | California Jets (Div. II) |

### 1991

**FREESTYLE**

| | |
|---|---|
| 105.5 | Tim Vanni |
| 114.5 | Zeke Jones |
| 125.5 | Brad Penrith |
| 136.5 | John Smith* |
| 149.5 | Townsend Saunders |
| 163 | Kenny Monday |
| 180.5 | Kevin Jackson |
| 198 | Chris Campbell |
| 220 | Mark Coleman |
| 286 | Bruce Baumgartner |
| Team | Sunkist Kids (Div. I) |
| | Jets USA (Div. II) |

**GRECO-ROMAN**

| | |
|---|---|
| 105.5 | Eric Wetzel |
| 114.5 | Shawn Sheldon |
| 125.5 | Frank Famiano |
| 136.5 | Buddy Lee |
| 149.5 | Andy Seras |
| 163 | Gordy Morgan |
| 180.5 | John Morgan* |
| 198 | Michial Foy |
| 220 | Dennis Koslowski |
| 286 | Craig Pittman |
| Team | Jets USA (Div. I) |
| | Sunkist Kids (Div. II) |

### 1992

**FREESTYLE**

| | |
|---|---|
| 105.5 | Rob Eiter |
| 114.5 | Jack Griffin |
| 125.5 | Kendall Cross* |
| 136.5 | John Fisher |
| 149.5 | Matt Demaray |
| 163 | Greg Elinsky |
| 180.5 | Royce Alger |
| 198 | Dan Chaid |
| 220 | Bill Scherr |
| 286 | Bruce Baumgartner |
| Team | Sunkist Kids (Div. I) |
| | Team Foxcatcher (Div. II) |

**GRECO-ROMAN**

| | |
|---|---|
| 105.5 | Eric Wetzel |
| 114.5 | Mark Fuller |
| 125.5 | Dennis Hall |
| 136.5 | Buddy Lee* |
| 149.5 | Rodney Smith |
| 163 | Travis West |
| 180.5 | John Morgan |
| 198 | Michial Foy |
| 220 | Dennis Koslowski |
| 286 | Matt Ghaffari |
| Team | N.Y. Athletic Club (Div. I) |
| | Sunkist Kids (Div. II) |

### 1993

**FREESTYLE**

| | |
|---|---|
| 105.5 | Rob Eiter |
| 114.5 | Zeke Jones |
| 125.5 | Brad Penrith |
| 136.5 | Tom Brands |
| 149.5 | Matt Demaray |
| 163 | Dave Schultz* |

*Outstanding wrestler.

## United States National Champions

### 1993 *(Cont.)*

**FREESTYLE**

| | |
|---|---|
| 180.5 | Kevin Jackson |
| 198 | Melvin Douglas |
| 220 | Kirk Trost |
| 286 | Bruce Baumgartner |
| Team | Sunkist Kids (Div. I) |
| | Team Foxcatcher (Div. II) |

**GRECO-ROMAN**

| | |
|---|---|
| 105.5 | Eric Wetzel |
| 114.5 | Shawn Sheldon |
| 125.5 | Dennis Hall* |
| 136.5 | Shon Lewis |
| 149.5 | Andy Seras |
| 163 | Gordy Morgan |
| 180.5 | Dan Henderson |
| 198 | Randy Couture |
| 220 | James Johnson |
| 286 | Matt Ghaffari |
| Team | N.Y. Athletic Club (Div. I) |
| | Sunkist Kids (Div. II) |

### 1994

**FREESTYLE**

| | |
|---|---|
| 105.5 | Tim Vanni |
| 114.5 | Zeke Jones |
| 125.5 | Terry Brands |
| 136.5 | Tom Brands |
| 149.5 | Matt Demaray |
| 163 | Dave Schultz |
| 180.5 | Royce Alger |
| 198 | Melvin Douglas |
| 220 | Mark Kerr |
| 286 | Bruce Baumgartner* |
| Team | Sunkist Kids (Div. I) |
| | Team Foxcatcher (Div. II) |

**GRECO-ROMAN**

| | |
|---|---|
| 105.5 | Isaac Ramaswamy |
| 114.5 | Shawn Sheldon |
| 125.5 | Dennis Hall |
| 136.5 | Shon Lewis |
| 149.5 | Andy Seras* |
| 163 | Gordy Morgan |
| 180.5 | Dan Henderson |
| 198 | Derrick Waldroup |
| 220 | James Johnson |
| 286 | Matt Ghaffari |
| Team | Armed Forces (Div. I) |
| | N.Y. Athletic Club (Div. II) |

### 1995

**FREESTYLE**

| | |
|---|---|
| 105.5 | Tim Vanni |
| 114.5 | Zeke Jones |
| 125.5 | Terry Brands |
| 136.5 | Tom Brands |
| 149.5 | Matt Demaray |
| 163 | Dave Schultz |
| 180.5 | Royce Alger |
| 198 | Melvin Douglas |
| 220 | Mark Kerr |
| 286 | Bruce Baumgartner* |
| Team | Sunkist Kids (Div. I) |
| | Team Foxcatcher (Div. II) |

**GRECO-ROMAN**

| | |
|---|---|
| 105.5 | Isaac Ramaswamy |
| 114.5 | Shawn Sheldon |
| 125.5 | Dennis Hall |
| 136.5 | Shon Lewis |

### 1995 *(Cont.)*

**GRECO-ROMAN *(CONT)***

| | |
|---|---|
| 149.5 | Andy Seras* |
| 163 | Gordy Morgan |
| 180.5 | Dan Henderson |
| 198 | Derrick Waldroup |
| 220 | James Johnson |
| 286 | Matt Ghaffari |
| Team | Armed Forces (Div. I) |
| | N.Y. Athletic Club (Div. II) |

### 1996

**FREESTYLE**

| | |
|---|---|
| 105.5 | Rob Eiter |
| 114.5 | Lou Rosselli |
| 125.5 | Kendall Cross* |
| 136.5 | Tom Brands |
| 149.5 | Matt Demaray |
| 163 | Dave Schultz |
| 180.5 | Kevin Jackson |
| 198 | Melvin Douglas |
| 220 | Kurt Angle |
| 286 | Bruce Baumgartner |
| Team | Sunkist Kids (Div. I) |
| | Team Foxcatcher (Div. II) |

**GRECO-ROMAN**

| | |
|---|---|
| 105.5 | Isaac Ramaswamy |
| 114.5 | Shawn Sheldon |
| 125.5 | Dennis Hall* |
| 136.5 | Van Fronhofer |
| 149.5 | Heath Sims |
| 163 | Matt Lindland |
| 180.5 | Marty Morgan |
| 198 | Michial Foy |
| 220 | James Johnson |
| 286 | Rulon Gardner |
| Team | Armed Forces (Div. I) |
| | Sunkist Kids (Div. II) |

### 1997

**FREESTYLE**

| | |
|---|---|
| 110 | Kanamti Soloman |
| 119 | Zeke Jones |
| 127.75 | Terry Brands |
| 138.75 | Carl Kolat |
| 152 | Lincoln McIlravy* |
| 167.5 | Dan St. John |
| 187.25 | Les Gutches |
| 213.75 | Melvin Douglas |
| 275.5 | Tom Erikson |
| Team | Sunkist Kids (Div. I) |
| | N.Y. Athletic Club (Div. II) |

**GRECO-ROMAN**

| | |
|---|---|
| 110 | Mark Yanagihara |
| 119 | Broderick Lee |
| 127.75 | Dennis Hall |
| 138.75 | Kevin Bracken |
| 152 | Chris Saba |
| 167.5 | Miguel Spencer |
| 187.25 | Dan Henderson |
| 213.75 | Randy Couture* |
| 275.5 | Rulon Gardner |
| Team | Armed Forces (Div. I) |
| | N.Y. Athletic Club (Div. II) |

### 1998

**FREESTYLE**

| | |
|---|---|
| 119 | Sam Henson |
| 127.75 | Tony Purler |

### 1998 *(Cont.)*

**FREESTYLE *(CONT)***

| | |
|---|---|
| 138.75 | Shawn Charles |
| 152 | Lincoln McIlravy |
| 167.5 | Steve Marianetti |
| 187.25 | Les Gutches* |
| 213.75 | Melvin Douglas |
| 286 | Tolly Thompson |
| Team | Sunkist Kids (Div. I) |
| | N.Y. Athletic Club (Div. II) |

**GRECO-ROMAN**

| | |
|---|---|
| 119 | Shawn Sheldon |
| 127.75 | Dennis Hall |
| 138.75 | Shon Lewis |
| 152 | Chris Saba |
| 167.5 | Matt Lindland |
| 187.25 | Dan Niebuhr* |
| 213.75 | Jason Klohs |
| 286 | Matt Ghaffari |
| Team | Armed Forces (Div. I) |
| | Sunkist Kids (Div. II) |

### 1999

**FREESTYLE**

| | |
|---|---|
| 119 | Lou Rosselli |
| 127.75 | Terry Brands |
| 138.75 | Cary Kolat |
| 152 | Lincoln McIlravy |
| 167.5 | Joe Williams |
| 187.25 | Les Gutches |
| 213.75 | Dominic Black |
| 286 | Stephen Neal* |
| Team | Sunkist Kids (Div. I) |
| | N.Y. Athletic Club (Div. II) |

### 1999 *(Cont.)*

**GRECO-ROMAN**

| | |
|---|---|
| 119 | Steven Mays |
| 127.75 | Dennis Hall |
| 138.75 | Glen Nieradka |
| 152 | David Zuniga |
| 167.5 | Matt Lindland |
| 187.25 | Quincey Clark |
| 213.75 | Randy Couture |
| 286 | Dremiel Byers* |
| Team | Minnesota Storm (Div. I) |
| | Sunkist Kids (Div. II) |

### 2000

**FREESTYLE**

| | |
|---|---|
| 119 | Sammie Henson |
| 127.75 | Keyy Boumans |
| 138.75 | Cary Kolat |
| 152 | Lincoln McIlravy |
| 167.5 | Brandon Slay* |
| 187.25 | Les Gutches |
| 213.75 | Melvin Douglas |
| 286 | Kerry McCoy |
| Team | Sunkist Kids (Div. I) |
| | N.Y. Athletic Club (Div. II) |

**GRECO-ROMAN**

| | |
|---|---|
| 119 | Brandon Paulson |
| 127.75 | Dennis Hall |
| 138.75 | Kevin Bracken |
| 152 | Heath Sims |
| 167.5 | Matt Lindland |
| 187.25 | Quincey Clark* |
| 213.75 | Jason Gleasman |
| 286 | Rulon Gardner |

## United States National Champions

### 2000 *(Cont.)*
#### GRECO-ROMAN *(CONT.)*
Team........Armed Forces (Div. I)
Sunkist Kids (Div. II)

### 2001
#### FREESTYLE
119 ..........Eric Akin
127.75 .....Eric Guerrero
138.75 .....Bill Zadick
152 ..........Ramico Blackmon
167.5 ........Joe Williams
187.25 .....Cael Sanderson*
213.75 ......Dominic Black
286 ..........Kerry McCoy
Team........Sunkist Kids (Div. I)
New York A.C. (Div. II)

#### GRECO-ROMAN
119 ..........Jeff Cervone
127.75 .....Dennis Hall
138.75 .....Kevin Bracken
152 ..........Marcel Cooper
167.5 .......Keith Sieracki
187.25 .....Matt Lindland*
213.75 ......Garrett Lowney
286 ..........Rulon Gardner
Team........U.S. Army (Div. I)
Sunkist Kids (Div. II)

### 2002
#### FREESTYLE
121 ..........Teague Moore
132 ..........Eric Guerrero
145.5 ........Bill Zadick
163 ..........Joe Williams*
185 ..........Cael Sanderson
211.5 ........Tim Hartung
264.5 ........Kerry McCoy
Team........Sunkist Kids (Div. I)
New York A.C. (Div. II)

#### GRECO-ROMAN
121 ..........Brandon Paulson
132 ..........Glenn Nieradka*
145.5 ........Kevin Bracken
163 ..........Keith Sieracki
185 ..........Ethan Bosch
211.75 ......Garrett Lowney
264.5 ........Dremiel Byers
Team........U.S. Army (Div. I)
New York A.C. (Div. II)

### 2003
#### FREESTYLE
121 ..........Stephen Abas
132 ..........Eric Guerrero*
145.5 ........Chris Bono
163 ..........Joe Williams
185 ..........Cael Sanderson
211.5 ........Daniel Cormier
264.5 ........Kerry McCoy
Team........Sunkist Kids (Div. I)
Gator WC (Div. II)

#### GRECO-ROMAN
121 ..........Brandon Paulson
132 ..........James Gruenwald*
145.5 ........Kevin Bracken
163 ..........Keith Sieracki
185 ..........Brad Vering
211.5 ........Garrett Lowney
264.5 ........Dremiel Byers

### 2003 *(Cont.)*
#### GRECO-ROMAN *(CONT.)*
Team........U.S. Army (Div. I)
Air Force (Div. II)

### 2004
#### FREESTYLE
121 ..........Stephen Abbas
132 ..........Eric Guerrero
145.5 ........Jamill Kelly
163 ..........Joe Williams
185 ..........Lee Fullhart*
211.5 ........Daniel Cormier
264.5 ........Kerry McCoy
Team........Sunkist Kids (Div. I)
Gator WC (Div. II)

#### GRECO-ROMAN
121 ..........Brandon Paulson
132 ..........James Gruenwald
145.5 ........Faruk Sahin
163 ..........Darryl Christian
185 ..........Brad Vering
211.5 ........Justin Ruiz
264.5 ........Dremiel Byers*
Team........New York A.C. (Div. I)
Air Force (Div. II)

### 2005
#### FREESTYLE
121 ..........Sam Henson
132 ..........Michael Lightner*
145.5 ........Chris Bono
163 ..........Joe Williams
185 ..........Mo Lawal
211.5 ........Daniel Cormier
264.5 ........Tolly Thompson
Team........Sunkist Kids (Div. I)
Gator WC (Div. II)

#### GRECO-ROMAN
121 ..........Sam Hazewinkel
132 ..........Joseph Warren
145.5 ........Harry Lester
163 ..........Darryl Christian
185 ..........Brad Vering
211.5 ........Justin Ruiz
264.5 ........Dremiel Byers*
Team........New York A.C. (Div.I)
Air Force (Div. II)

### 2006
#### FREESTYLE
121 ..........Henry Cejudo
132 ..........Zach Roberson
145.5 ........Chris Bono
163 ..........Donny Pritzlaff*
185 ..........Mo Lawal
211.5 ........Daniel Cormier
264.5 ........Tolly Thompson
Team........Sunkist Kids (Div. I)
Gator WC (Div. II)

#### GRECO-ROMAN
121 ..........Lindsey Durlacher
132 ..........Joseph Warren
145.5 ........Marcel Cooper
163 ..........T.C. Dantzler
185 ..........Jacob Clark*
211.5 ........Justin Ruiz
264.5 ........Dremiel Byers

### 2006 *(Cont.)*
#### GRECO-ROMAN *(CONT.)*
Team........U.S. Army (Div. I)
New York A.C. (Div. II)

### 2007
#### FREESTYLE
121 ..........Henry Cejudo
132 ..........Nate Gallick*
145.5 ........Chris Bono
163 ..........Joe Heskett
185 ..........Joe Williams
211.5 ........Daniel Cormier
264.5 ........Tommy Rowlands
Team........Sunkist Kids (Div. I)
Gator WC (Div. II)

#### GRECO-ROMAN
121 ..........Sam Hazewinkel*
132 ..........Joseph Warren
145.5 ........Glenn Garrison
163 ..........T.C. Dantzler
185 ..........Brad Vering
211.5 ........Justin Ruiz
264.5 ........Russ Davie
Team........U.S. Army (Div. I)
New York A.C. (Div. II)

### 2008
#### FREESTYLE
121 ..........Matt Azevedo*
132 ..........Shawn Bunch
145.5 ........Doug Schwab
163 ..........Ben Askren
185 ..........Mo Lawal
211.5 ........Daniel Cormier
264.5 ........Tommy Rowlands
Team........Sunkist Kids (Div. I)
New York A.C. (Div. II)

#### GRECO-ROMAN
121 :........Spencer Mango*
132 ..........Jim Gruenwald
145.5 ........Mark Rial
163 ..........T.C. Dantzler
185 ..........Brad Ahearn
211.5 ........Justin Ruiz
264.5 ........Dremiel Byers
Team........U.S. Army (Div. I)
New York A.C. (Div. II)

### 2009
#### FREESTYLE
121 ..........Nick Simmons
132 ..........Mike Zadick
145.5 ........Trent Paulson
163 ..........Travis Paulson
185 ..........Jake Herbert*
211.5 ........Jake Varner
264.5 ........Steve Mocco
Team........Sunkist Kids (Div. I)
Gator WC (Div. II)

#### GRECO-ROMAN
121 ..........Jermaine Hodge
132 ..........Joe Betterman
145.5 ........Faruk Sahin
163 ..........Harry Lester*
185 ..........T.C. Dantzler
211.5 ........Brad Ahearn
264.5 ........Dremiel Byers
Team........U.S. Army (Div. I)
Sunkist Kids (Div. II)

*Outstanding wrestler.

# Awards

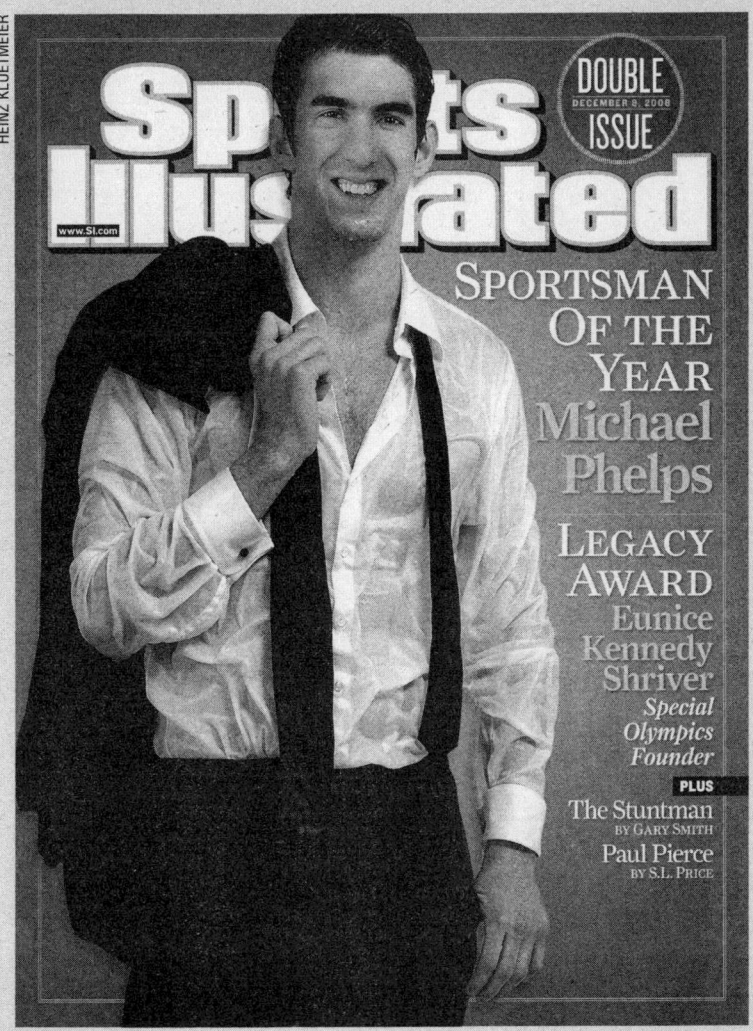

**Sports Illustrated**

www.SI.com

DOUBLE
DECEMBER 8, 2008
ISSUE

SPORTSMAN
OF THE
YEAR
Michael
Phelps

LEGACY
AWARD
Eunice
Kennedy
Shriver
*Special
Olympics
Founder*

**PLUS**

The Stuntman
BY GARY SMITH

Paul Pierce
BY S.L. PRICE

*SPORTS ILLUSTRATED'S*
**2008 Sportsman of the Year
Michael Phelps**

## Athlete Awards

### Sports Illustrated Sportsman of the Year

| Year | Recipient | Year | Recipient | Year | Recipient |
|---|---|---|---|---|---|
| 1954 | Roger Bannister, Track and Field | 1977 | Steve Cauthen, Horse Racing | 1990 | Joe Montana, Pro Football |
| 1955 | Johnny Podres, Baseball | 1978 | Jack Nicklaus, Golf | 1991 | Michael Jordan, Pro Basketball |
| 1956 | Bobby Morrow, Track and Field | 1979 | Terry Bradshaw, Pro Football | 1992 | Arthur Ashe, Tennis |
| 1957 | Stan Musial, Baseball | | Willie Stargell, Baseball | 1993 | Don Shula, Pro Football |
| 1958 | Rafer Johnson, Track and Field | 1980 | U.S. Olympic Hockey Team | 1994 | Bonnie Blair, Speed Skating |
| 1959 | Ingemar Johansson, Boxing | 1981 | Sugar Ray Leonard, Boxing | | Johann Olav Koss, Speed Skating |
| 1960 | Arnold Palmer, Golf | 1982 | Wayne Gretzky, Hockey | 1995 | Cal Ripken Jr, Baseball |
| 1961 | Jerry Lucas, Basketball | 1983 | Mary Decker, Track and Field | 1996 | Tiger Woods, Golf |
| 1962 | Terry Baker, Football | 1984 | Mary Lou Retton, Gymnastics | 1997 | Dean Smith, College Basketball |
| 1963 | Pete Rozelle, Pro Football | | Edwin Moses, Track and Field | 1998 | Mark McGwire, Sammy Sosa, |
| 1964 | Ken Venturi, Golf | 1985 | Kareem Abdul-Jabbar, Pro Basketball | | Baseball |
| 1965 | Sandy Koufax, Baseball | 1986 | Joe Paterno, Football | 1999 | U.S. Women's Soccer Team |
| 1966 | Jim Ryun, Track and Field | 1987 | Athletes Who Care: | 2000 | Tiger Woods, Golf |
| 1967 | Carl Yastrzemski, Baseball | | Bob Bourne, Hockey | 2001 | C. Schilling/ R. Johnson, Baseball |
| 1968 | Bill Russell, Pro Basketball | | Kip Keino, Track and Field | 2002 | Lance Armstrong, Cycling |
| 1969 | Tom Seaver, Baseball | | Judi Brown King, Track and Field | 2003 | Tim Duncan/David Robinson, |
| 1970 | Bobby Orr, Hockey | | Dale Murphy, Baseball | | Basketball |
| 1971 | Lee Trevino, Golf | | Chip Rives, Football | 2004 | Boston Red Sox, Baseball |
| 1972 | B.J. King, Tennis/ J. Wooden, Bask | | Patty Sheehan, Golf | 2005 | Tom Brady, Pro Football |
| 1973 | Jackie Stewart, Auto Racing | | Rory Sparrow, Pro Basketball | 2006 | Dwyane Wade, Pro Basketball |
| 1974 | Muhammad Ali, Boxing | | Reggie Williams, Pro Football | 2007 | Brett Favre, Pro Football |
| 1975 | Pete Rose, Baseball | 1988 | Orel Hershiser, Baseball | 2008 | Michael Phelps, Swimming |
| 1976 | Chris Evert, Tennis | 1989 | Greg LeMond, Cycling | | |

### Associated Press Athletes of the Year

| Year | MEN | WOMEN | Year | MEN | WOMEN |
|---|---|---|---|---|---|
| 1931 | Pepper Martin, Baseball | Helene Madison, Swimming | 1958 | Herb Elliott, Track and Field | Althea Gibson, Tennis |
| 1932 | Gene Sarazen, Golf | Babe Didrikson, Track and Field | 1959 | Ingemar Johansson, Boxing | Maria Bueno, Tennis |
| 1933 | Carl Hubbell, Baseball | Helen Jacobs, Tennis | 1960 | Rafer Johnson, Track and Field | Wilma Rudolph, Track and Field |
| 1934 | Dizzy Dean, Baseball | Virginia Van Wie, Golf | 1961 | Roger Maris, Baseball | Wilma Rudolph, Track and Field |
| 1935 | Joe Louis, Boxing | Helen Wills Moody, Tennis | | | |
| 1936 | Jesse Owens, Track and Field | Helen Stephens, Track and Field | 1962 | Maury Wills, Baseball | Dawn Fraser, Swimming |
| | | | 1963 | Sandy Koufax, Baseball | Mickey Wright, Golf |
| 1937 | Don Budge, Tennis | Katherine Rawls, Swimming | 1964 | Don Schollander, Swimming | Mickey Wright, Golf |
| | | | 1965 | Sandy Koufax, Baseball | Kathy Whitworth, Golf |
| 1938 | Don Budge, Tennis | Patty Berg, Golf | 1966 | Frank Robinson, Baseball | Kathy Whitworth, Golf |
| 1939 | Nile Kinnick, Football | Alice Marble, Tennis | 1967 | Carl Yastrzemski, Baseball | Billie Jean King, Tennis |
| 1940 | Tom Harmon, Football | Alice Marble, Tennis | 1968 | Denny McLain, Baseball | Peggy Fleming, Skating |
| 1941 | Joe DiMaggio, Baseball | Betty Hicks Newell, Golf | 1969 | Tom Seaver, Baseball | Debbie Meyer, Swimming |
| 1942 | Frank Sinkwich, Football | Gloria Callen, Swimming | 1970 | George Blanda, Pro Football | Chi Cheng, Track and Field |
| 1943 | Gunder Haegg, Track and Field | Patty Berg, Golf | 1971 | Lee Trevino, Golf | Evonne Goolagong, Tennis |
| | | | 1972 | Mark Spitz, Swimming | Olga Korbut, Gymnastics |
| 1944 | Byron Nelson, Golf | Ann Curtis, Swimming | 1973 | O.J. Simpson, Pro Football | Billie Jean King, Tennis |
| 1945 | Bryon Nelson, Golf | Babe Didrikson Zaharias, Golf | 1974 | Muhammad Ali, Boxing | Chris Evert, Tennis |
| | | | 1975 | Fred Lynn, Baseball | Chris Evert, Tennis |
| 1946 | Glenn Davis, Football | Babe Didrikson Zaharias, Golf | 1976 | Bruce Jenner, Track and Field | Nadia Comaneci, Gymnastics |
| 1947 | Johnny Lujack, Football | Babe Didrikson Zaharias, Golf | 1977 | Steve Cauthen, Horse Racing | Chris Evert, Tennis |
| 1948 | Lou Boudreau, Baseball | Fanny Blankers-Koen, Track and Field | 1978 | Ron Guidry, Baseball | Nancy Lopez, Golf |
| 1949 | Leon Hart, Football | Marlene Bauer, Golf | 1979 | Willie Stargell, Baseball | Tracy Austin, Tennis |
| 1950 | Jim Konstanty, Baseball | Babe Didrikson Zaharias, Golf | 1980 | U.S. Olympic Hockey Team | Chris Evert Lloyd, Tennis |
| | | | 1981 | John McEnroe, Tennis | Tracy Austin, Tennis |
| 1951 | Dick Kazmaier, Football | Maureen Connolly, Tennis | 1982 | Wayne Gretzky, Hockey | Mary Decker, Track and Field |
| 1952 | Bob Mathias, Track and Field | Maureen Connolly, Tennis | | | |
| 1953 | Ben Hogan, Golf | Maureen Connolly, Tennis | 1983 | Carl Lewis, Track and Field | Martina Navratilova, Tennis |
| 1954 | Willie Mays, Baseball | Babe Didrikson Zaharias, Golf | 1984 | Carl Lewis, Track and Field | Mary Lou Retton, Gymnastics |
| 1955 | Hopalong Cassidy, Football | Patty Berg, Golf | 1985 | Dwight Gooden, Baseball | Nancy Lopez, Golf |
| 1956 | Mickey Mantle, Baseball | Pat McCormick, Diving | 1986 | Larry Bird, Pro Basketball | Martina Navratilova, Tennis |
| 1957 | Ted Williams, Baseball | Althea Gibson, Tennis | 1987 | Ben Johnson, Track and Field | Jackie Joyner-Kersee, Track and Field |

### Associated Press Athletes of the Year *(Cont.)*

| | MEN | WOMEN |
|---|---|---|
| 1988 | Orel Hershiser, Baseball | Florence Griffith Joyner, Track and Field |
| 1989 | Joe Montana, Pro Football | Steffi Graf, Tennis |
| 1990 | Joe Montana, Pro Football | Beth Daniel, Golf |
| 1991 | Michael Jordan, Pro Basketball | Monica Seles, Tennis |
| 1992 | Michael Jordan, Pro Basketball | Monica Seles, Tennis |
| 1993 | Michael Jordan, Pro Basketball | Sheryl Swoopes, Basketball |
| 1994 | George Foreman, Boxing | Bonnie Blair, Speed Skating |
| 1995 | Cal Ripken Jr, Baseball | Rebecca Lobo, Basketball |
| 1996 | Michael Johnson, Track and Field | Amy Van Dyken, Swimming |
| 1997 | Tiger Woods, Golf | Martina Hingis, Tennis |
| 1998 | Mark McGwire, Baseball | Se Ri Pak, Golf |
| 1999 | Tiger Woods, Golf | U.S. Women's Soccer Team |
| 2000 | Tiger Woods, Golf | Marion Jones, Track and Field |
| 2001 | Barry Bonds, Baseball | Jennifer Capriati, Tennis |
| 2002 | Lance Armstrong, Cycling | Serena Williams, Tennis |
| 2003 | Lance Armstrong, Cycling | Annika Sorenstam, Golf |
| 2004 | Lance Armstrong, Cycling | Annika Sorenstam, Golf |
| 2005 | Lance Armstrong, Cycling | Annika Sorenstam, Golf |
| 2006 | Tiger Woods, Golf | Lorena Ochoa, Golf |
| 2007 | Tom Brady, Pro Football | Lorena Ochoa, Golf |
| 2008 | Michael Phelps, Swimming | Candace Parker, Basketball |

### James E. Sullivan Award

Presented annually by the AAU to the athlete who "by his or her performance, example and influence as an amateur, has done the most during the year to advance the cause of sportsmanship."

|  |  |
|---|---|
| 1930 | Bobby Jones, Golf |
| 1931 | Barney Berlinger, Track and Field |
| 1932 | Jim Bausch, Track and Field |
| 1933 | Glenn Cunningham, Track and Field |
| 1934 | Bill Bonthron, Track and Field |
| 1935 | Lawson Little, Golf |
| 1936 | Glenn Morris, Track and Field |
| 1937 | Don Budge, Tennis |
| 1938 | Don Lash, Track and Field |
| 1939 | Joe Burk, Rowing |
| 1940 | Greg Rice, Track and Field |
| 1941 | Leslie MacMitchell, Track and Field |
| 1942 | Cornelius Warmerdam, Track |
| 1943 | Gilbert Dodds, Track and Field |
| 1944 | Ann Curtis, Swimming |
| 1945 | Doc Blanchard, Football |
| 1946 | Arnold Tucker, Football |
| 1947 | John B. Kelly Jr, Rowing |
| 1948 | Bob Mathias, Track and Field |
| 1949 | Dick Button, Skating |
| 1950 | Fred Wilt, Track and Field |
| 1951 | Bob Richards, Track and Field |
| 1952 | Horace Ashenfelter, Track and Field |
| 1953 | Sammy Lee, Diving |
| 1954 | Mal Whitfield, Track and Field |
| 1955 | Harrison Dillard, Track and Field |
| 1956 | Pat McCormick, Diving |
| 1957 | Bobby Morrow, Track and Field |
| 1958 | Glenn Davis, Track and Field |
| 1959 | Parry O'Brien, Track and Field |
| 1960 | Rafer Johnson, Track and Field |
| 1961 | Wilma Rudolph, Track and Field |
| 1962 | Jim Beatty, Track and Field |
| 1963 | John Pennel, Track and Field |
| 1964 | Don Schollander, Swimming |
| 1965 | Bill Bradley, Basketball |
| 1966 | Jim Ryun, Track and Field |
| 1967 | Randy Matson, Track and Field |
| 1968 | Debbie Meyer, Swimming |
| 1969 | Bill Toomey, Track and Field |
| 1970 | John Kinsella, Swimming |
| 1971 | Mark Spitz, Swimming |
| 1972 | Frank Shorter, Track and Field |
| 1973 | Bill Walton, Basketball |
| 1974 | Rich Wohlhuter, Track and Field |
| 1975 | Tim Shaw, Swimming |
| 1976 | Bruce Jenner, Track and Field |
| 1977 | John Naber, Swimming |
| 1978 | Tracy Caulkins, Swimming |
| 1979 | Kurt Thomas, Gymnastics |
| 1980 | Eric Heiden, Speed Skating |
| 1981 | Carl Lewis, Track and Field |
| 1982 | Mary Decker, Track and Field |
| 1983 | Edwin Moses, Track and Field |
| 1984 | Greg Louganis, Diving |
| 1985 | Joan B.-Samuelson, T & F |
| 1986 | Jackie Joyner-Kersee, T & F |
| 1987 | Jim Abbott, Baseball |
| 1988 | Florence Griffith Joyner, Track |
| 1989 | Janet Evans, Swimming |
| 1990 | John Smith, Wrestling |
| 1991 | Mike Powell, Track and Field |
| 1992 | Bonnie Blair, Speed Skating |
| 1993 | Charlie Ward, Football, Basketball |
| 1994 | Dan Jansen, Speed Skating |
| 1995 | Bruce Baumgartner, Wrestling |
| 1996 | Michael Johnson, Track and Field |
| 1997 | Peyton Manning, Football |
| 1998 | Chamique Holdsclaw, Basketball |
| 1999 | Kelly and Coco Miller, Basketball |
| 2000 | Rulon Gardner, Wrestling |
| 2001 | Michelle Kwan, Figure Skating |
| 2002 | Sarah Hughes, Figure Skating |
| 2003 | Michael Phelps, Swimming |
| 2004 | Paul Hamm, Gymnastics |
| 2005 | J. J. Redick, College Basketball |
| 2006 | Jessica Long, Paralympic Swimmer |
| 2007 | Tim Tebow, College Football |
| 2008 | Shawn Johnson, Gymnastics |

### *The Sporting News* Sportsman of the Year

|  |  |
|---|---|
| 1968 | Denny McLain, Baseball |
| 1969 | Tom Seaver, Baseball |
| 1970 | John Wooden, Basketball |
| 1971 | Lee Trevino, Golf |
| 1972 | Charles O. Finley, Baseball |
| 1973 | O.J. Simpson, Pro Football |
| 1974 | Lou Brock, Baseball |
| 1975 | Archie Griffin, Football |
| 1976 | Larry O'Brien, Pro Basketball |
| 1977 | Steve Cauthen, Horse Racing |
| 1978 | Ron Guidry, Baseball |
| 1979 | Willie Stargell, Baseball |
| 1980 | George Brett, Baseball |
| 1981 | Wayne Gretzky, Hockey |
| 1982 | Whitey Herzog, Baseball |
| 1983 | Bowie Kuhn, Baseball |
| 1984 | Peter Ueberroth, LA Olympics |
| 1985 | Pete Rose, Baseball |
| 1986 | Larry Bird, Pro Basketball |
| 1987 | No award |
| 1988 | Jackie Joyner-Kersee, T & F |
| 1989 | Joe Montana, Pro Football |
| 1990 | Nolan Ryan, Baseball |
| 1991 | Michael Jordan, Pro Basketball |
| 1992 | Mike Krzyzewski, Basketball |
| 1993 | Pat Gillick/Cito Gaston, Baseball |
| 1994 | Emmitt Smith, Pro Football |
| 1995 | Cal Ripken Jr, Baseball |
| 1996 | Joe Torre, Baseball |
| 1997 | Michael Jordan, Basketball |
| 1998 | Mark McGwire, Baseball |
| 1999 | New York Yankees, Baseball |
| 2000 | Kurt Warner/Marshall Faulk, Pro Football |
| 2001 | Curt Schilling, Baseball |
| 2002 | Tyrone Willingham, Football |
| 2003 | Jack McKeon, Baseball / Dick Vermeil, Pro Football |
| 2004 | Tom Brady, Pro Football |
| 2005 | Matt Leinart, College Football |
| 2006 | LaDainian Tomlinson, Pro Football |
| 2007 | Tom Brady, Pro Football |
| 2008 | Eli Manning, Pro Football |

### United Press International Male and Female Athlete of the Year

| | MEN | WOMEN |
|---|---|---|
| 1974 | Muhammad Ali, Boxing | Irena Szewinska, Track and Field |
| 1975 | Joao Oliveira, Track and Field | Nadia Comaneci, Gymnastics |
| 1976 | Alberto Juantorena, Track and Field | Nadia Comaneci, Gymnastics |
| 1977 | Alberto Juantorena, Track and Field | Rosie Ackermann, Track and Field |
| 1978 | Henry Rono, Track and Field | Tracy Caulkins, Swimming |
| 1979 | Sebastian Coe, Track and Field | Marita Koch, Track and Field |
| 1980 | Eric Heiden, Speed Skating | Hanni Wenzel, Alpine Skiing |
| 1981 | Sebastian Coe, Track and Field | Chris Evert Lloyd, Tennis |
| 1982 | Daley Thompson, Track and Field | Marita Koch, Track and Field |
| 1983 | Carl Lewis, Track and Field | Jarmila Kratochvilova, Track and Field |
| 1984 | Carl Lewis, Track and Field | Martina Navratilova, Tennis |
| 1985 | Steve Cram, Track and Field | Mary Decker Slaney, Track and Field |
| 1986 | Diego Maradona, Soccer | Heike Drechsler, Track and Field |
| 1987 | Ben Johnson, Track and Field | Steffi Graf, Tennis |
| 1988 | Matt Biondi, Swimming | Florence Griffith Joyner, Track and Field |
| 1989 | Boris Becker, Tennis | Steffi Graf, Tennis |
| 1990 | Stefan Edberg, Tennis | Merlene Ottey, Track and Field |
| 1991 | Michael Jordan, Pro Basketball | Monica Seles, Tennis |
| 1992 | Mario Lemieux, Hockey | Monica Seles, Tennis |
| 1993 | Michael Jordan, Pro Basketball | Steffi Graf, Tennis |
| 1994 | Nick Price, Golf | Bonnie Blair, Speed Skating |
| 1995 | Cal Ripken Jr, Baseball | Steffi Graf, Tennis |

Note: Award not given since 1995.

### Dial Award

Presented by the Dial Corporation to the male and female national high school athlete/scholar of the year.

| | BOYS | GIRLS |
|---|---|---|
| 1979 | Herschel Walker, Football | No award |
| 1980 | Bill Fralic, Football | Carol Lewis, Track and Field |
| 1981 | Kevin Willhite, Football | Cheryl Miller, Basketball |
| 1982 | Mike Smith, Basketball | Elaine Zayak, Skating |
| 1983 | Chris Spielman, Football | Melanie Buddemeyer, Swimming |
| 1984 | Hart Lee Dykes, Football | Nora Lewis, Basketball |
| 1985 | Jeff George, Football | Gea Johnson, Track and Field |
| 1986 | Scott Schaffner, Football | Mya Johnson, Track and Field |
| 1987 | Todd Marinovich, Football | Kristi Overton, Water Skiing |
| 1988 | Carlton Gray, Football | Courtney Cox, Basketball |
| 1989 | Robert Smith, Football | Lisa Leslie, Basketball |
| 1990 | Derrick Brooks, Football | Vicki Goetze, Golf |
| 1991 | Jeff Buckey, Football, Track and Field | Katie Smith, Basketball, Volleyball, Track |
| 1992 | Jacque Vaughn, Basketball | Amanda White, Track and Field, Swimming |
| 1993 | Tiger Woods, Golf | Kristin Folkl, Basketball |
| 1994 | Taymon Domzalski, Basketball | Shannon Miller, Gymnastics |
| 1995 | Brent Abernathy, Baseball | Shea Ralph, Basketball |
| 1996 | Grant Irons, Football | Grace Park, Golf |
| 1997 | Ronald Curry, Football | Michelle Kwan, Figure Skating |

Note: Award not given since 1997.

# Obituaries

Chuck Daly
1930–2009

**Myles Brand, 67, college administrator.** *NCAA President. SI writes:*

"Before he became the NCAA President in 2002, Brand was the president of Indiana Universtiy; in 2000 he fired basketball coach Bob Knight for violating a zero-tolerance behavior policy. Brand played a year of lacrosse and basketball in college but otherwise had little athletic pedigree. His mandate, he told *SI* in 2003, was to show that 'athletics are not at odds with the greatest academic mission of a university; quite the contrary, in fact.' To that end, he created the Academic Progress Rate, stripping programs of scholarships when their APR fell below an acceptable level. 'I believe Myles will be remembered as a person who helped us refocus on the student in student-athlete, and his academic reforms will long outlive him,' said University of Georgia president Michael Adams."

In Indianapolis, Indiana, of pancreatic cancer, on September 16, 2009.

**Eunice Kennedy Shriver, 88, athlete and sports pioneer.** *Founder of the Special Olympics. SI writes:*

"Eunice Kennedy Shriver, the oldest of Joseph Kennedy's five daughters and sister to John, Robert, and Edward, received *SI*'s first Sportsman of the Year Legacy Award in 2008, recognizing her as the founder of the Special Olympics and the single most important person to have advanced the rights and enriched the lives of people with intellectual disabilities. But while Special Olympics was unquestionably her legacy, Eunice is remembered by her family as much for being an athlete herself. She sailed, she swam, she was a graceful runner, she played tennis at Stanford, and she played quarterback in the family's celebrated touch football games on the lawn at Hyannisport.

"'One of the first things Mrs. Shriver ever told me after we met,' says 56-year-old Loretta Claiborne, one of the most celebrated Special Olympic athletes, 'was that she was going to come out and watch me run. She took the sports seriously and looked on us as athletes. That's important.'"

In Hyannis, Massachusetts, of complications from strokes, on August 11, 2009.

**Jim Johnson, 68, football coach.** *Philadelphia Eagles defensive coordinator. SI writes:*

"In 22 years as an NFL assistant Johnson gained a reputation as one of the league's sharpest defensive minds, and Philadelphia's unit was consistently one of the NFL's best during his 10 seasons in charge (1999–2008). During the playoffs in January 2009, Johnson worked from the coaches' box because of back pain; it was discovered after the season that he had a tumor on his spine. Johnson's initials were painted on the field at Eagles preseason camp. 'Jim was tailor-made to coach in Philadelphia,' said Broncos safety Brian Dawkins, an Eagle from 1996 to 2008. 'He was a tough coach...[but] he cared about us deeply.'"

In Philadelphia, Pennsylvania, of skin cancer, on July 28, 2009.

**Steve McNair, 36, football player.** *Former Pro Bowl quarterback. SI writes:*

"Both soft-spoken and supremely confident, with a throwback attitude and a disciplined mobility that set a new standard for black—and white—quarterbacks, the country boy out of Mount Olive, Mississippi, and Alcorn State inspired awed devotion from hard-core fans and universal admiration from teammates and opponents. His let-it-all-hang-out throwing style earned him the nickname 'Air' McNair in college and in the NFL, McNair threw for 31,304 yards and 174 touchdowns over a riveting 13-year career with Tennessee and Baltimore. He made three Pro Bowls, led the Titans to Super Bowl XXXIV and was named co-MVP of the league in 2003.

"'I always felt that Steve McNair was indestructible,' said former Titans tight end and teammate Frank Wycheck. Indeed, McNair endured more than his share of injuries, including back surgery, painful bouts of turf toe, a bruised sternum, and dislocated fingers. But even before the retired McNair's shocking death at the alleged hands of his mistress—shot twice in the head, twice in the chest, while sleeping in an apartment he had rented for her—the married father of four had exhibited questionable judgment, having been charged with DUI and illegal gun possession in 2003 and DUI by consent in 2007. All charges had been subesuently dropped and the dings to his image had never lasted.

"'Everybody makes mistakes,' McNair said after his arrival in Baltimore in 2006. 'Just because [someone] got caught in the wrong place at the wrong time doesn't mean he's a bad guy.'"

In Nashville, Tennessee, of gunshot wounds, on July 4, 2009.

**Ed Thomas, 58, football coach.** *Longtime football coach at Aplington-Parkersburg High School in Iowa. SI writes:*

"The most recognizable figure in a small northern Iowa farm town of 1,900, Coach Thomas was allegedly gunned down by a former Aplington-Parkersburg football player in the high school's weight room. Thomas, who had won 297 games in 37 seasons coaching the Falcons, had also claimed two state titles and produced four current NFL players. After a tornado devastated the community in May of 2008, leveling the high school campus as well as the coach's own home, Thomas was instrumental in leading the town's recovery and rallying his Falcons to a 11–1 record that year.

"'You know how the Bible says to build your house on the rock?' said Chris Luhring, the Parkersburg police chief, who also once played for Thomas. 'He was the rock that this community was built on.'"

In Parkersburg, Iowa, of gunshot wounds, on June 24, 2009.

**Richard Quick, 66, swimming coach.** *Three-time Olympic women's swimming coach. SI writes:*

"Quick won more NCAA Division I championships than any other coach—13, including five straight women's titles at Texas in the 1980s, seven women's titles at Stanford after that, and the men's crown at Auburn in the spring of 2009—and in three terms as U.S. Olympic coach (1988, '96, 2000) his swimmers won 59 medals. Among his top pupils were gold-medal winners Jenny Thompson, Summer Sanders, and Rowdy Gaines. He was known for his innovative and grueling workouts and he was willing to try any new gimmick that might give his swimmers an edge. But Sanders says Quick's greatest gift was his ability to instill confidence in his swimmers. 'Richard was in a league of his own when it came to making people believe they can do the impossible,' she said."

In Austin, Texas, of an inoperable brain tumor, on June 10, 2009.

**Wayman Tisdale, 44, basketball player.** *Former three-time All-America center. SI writes:*

"The son of a Tulsa preacher, Tisdale was so highly regarded in high school that Oklahoma hoops coach Billy Tubbs agreed to move Sooners' Sunday practice to the evening so that Tisdale could attend services at his father's church, where he played bass guitar. At Norman, Tisdale became the first—and still only—player to be named first-team All-America as a freshman, sophomore, and junior. Tisdale turned pro and averaged 15.3 points with three teams over 12 NBA seasons, then retired to pursue his other love: music. His first album was released in 1995 and sold a quarter of a millions copies. His most recent album—*Rebound*—was inspired by his battle with cancer, which was diagnosed in 2007."

In Tulsa, Oklahoma, of complications from cancer on May 15, 2009.

**Chuck Daly, 78, basketball coach.** *Two-time NBA Finals winner and coach of the legendary 1992 Olympic Dream Team.*

Daly was renowned for his ability to create harmony out of diverse personalities at all levels of the game, whether they were Ivy Leaguers at Pennsylvania, Dream Teamers Michael Jordan and Charles Barkley, or members of the "Bad Boy" Detroit Pistons as dissimilar as Dennis Rodman and Joe Dumars.

Daly had a career regular-season record of 638–437 in 13 NBA seasons. In 12 playoff appearances, his teams went 75–51, winning back-to-back titles in 1989 and '90. Two years later he led the legendary Dream Team to Olympic gold at the Summer Games in Barcelona. Daly was voted one of the 10 greatest coaches of the NBA's first half-century in 1996, two years after being inducted into the Basketball Hall of Fame. He was the first coach to win both NBA and Olympic titles. 'Chuck was a great leader,' Michael Jordan said.

'I only wish I could have played for him outside of the Dream Team.'

In Jupiter, Florida, of pancreatic cancer, on May 9, 2009.

**Dom DiMaggio, 92, baseball player.** *Former Boston Red Sox centerfielder. SI writes:*

Dimaggio, the bespectacled Red Sox centerfielder made his own mark on the major leagues despite playing in the shadow of Hall of Fame brother Joe and teammate Ted Williams. Known as the "Little Professor" because of his eyeglasses and 5'9", 168-pound frame, Dimaggio spent his entire 10-year career with the Red Sox and was a seven-time All-Star who put together his own hitting streak when he batted safely in 34 consecutive games in 1949. He was also a founding partner of the AFL's Boston Patriots.

In Marion, Massachusetts, of pneumonia on May 8, 2009.

**Doc Blanchard, 84, football player.** *1945 Heisman Trophy winner. SI writes:*

"After being turned down by the Naval Academy in 1942 for, among other things, being overweight, Felix Anthony Blanchard ended up enrolling at West Point, where he led Army's football team to three wins over Navy in as many years. Blanchard teamed with Glenn Davis to form the most feared and famed backfield of their day. (They appeared on covers of *Time* and *Life*.) A battering ram of a fullback, Blanchard was known as Mr. Inside to the athletic Davis' Mr. Outside. Blanchard became the first junior to win the Heisman in 1945, then Davis won it the next year. In their three years together the pair led the Cadets to 27 wins and one tie in 28 games."

In Bulverde, Texas, of pneumonia, on April 18, 2009.

**Harry Kalas, 73, broadcaster.** *Hall of Fame broadcaster for the Philadelphia Phillies. SI writes:*

"Blessed with a deep baritone that became one of the most recognizable voices in sports, Phillies play-by-play man Kalas reached a national audience doing voiceovers for NFL films and narration for *Inside the NFL*. Harry the K, as he was known in Philadelphia, was inducted into the broadcasters' wing of the Baseball Hall of Fame in 2002. He collapsed in the broadcast booth before a Phillies-Nationals afternoon game and died shortly thereafter at the hospital. 'We lost our voice today,' said Phillies team president David Montgomery."

In. Washington, D.C., of a heart attack, on April 13, 2009.

**Mark Fidrych, 54, baseball player.** *1976 AL Rookie of the Year and All-Star pitcher. SI writes:*

"Fidrych burst onto the scene as a gangly, mop-headed rookie with the Detroit Tigers in 1976, acquiring his nickname "The Bird" because he resembled the *Sesame Street* character Big Bird. He became hugely popular as much for his quirky behavior—he appeared to talk to baseballs and himself, and manicured the mound by hand—as for his pitching success. He went 19–9, won the AL Rookie of the Year award and became a pop culture phenomenon worthy of covers of *SI* and *Rolling Stone*. Fidrych flamed out nearly as suddenly as he arrived, however. Due to several injuries he pitched only 27 more big league games before retiring in 1983. 'I just think I was in exactly the right place at the right time,' Fidrych, referring to his rookie year, told *SI* in 2001. 'I really didn't know how big it was until the season was over.'

In Northborough, Massachusetts, of a farm accident, on April 13, 2009.

**Nick Adenhart, 22, baseball player.** *Los Angeles Angels pitcher. SI writes:*

"On April 8, in his fourth major league start, Adenhart threw six scoreless innings against the A's, by far the best performance of his brief career. Little more than two hours later, at 12:30 a.m., the car he was in was struck by an allegedly drunk driver, who ran a red light. 'I feel like a got punched in the heart,' Angels owner Arte Moreno said.

"Adenhart was among the best prospects in the Angels system—*Baseball America* ranked him the No. 1 high school player in the country before his senior season at Williamsport High in Maryland—but he was largely unknown outside of Baltimore and Los Angeles.

"Adenhart had called his father, Jim, in Maryland the day before his first start of the season and told him, 'You better come here because something special is going to happen.' Jim was there to see his son stand triumphantly on the mound at Angel Stadium."

In Fullerton, California, of injuries sustained in a hit-and-run car accident, on April 9, 2009.

**Andrea Mead Lawrence, 76, skier.** *Olympic gold medalist and environmentalist. SI writes:*

"After competing at the 1948 Winter Games as a pigtailed 15-year-old, Lawrence won the giant slalom and then the slalom four years later in Oslo, earning her the distinction of being the only American skier to win two gold medals in a single Olympics. She spent her later years working to preserve and protect the Eastern Sierra Nevada range."

In Mammoth Lakes, California, of complications from cancer, on March 30, 2009.

**Lou Saban, 87, football coach.** *Peripatetic football coach and administrator. SI writes:*

"After playing quarterback at Indiana and linebacker for the Cleveland Browns, Saban went on to coach the AFL's Boston Patriots and the NFL's Buffalo Bills and Denver Broncos. His college gigs included major programs such as Miami (Fla.), Army and Maryland. He also found time to run the Yankees in 1981 and '82, thanks to a close relationship with George Steinbrenner. Following a 0–10 season at Chowan in 2002, Saban resigned, but said he'd be open to coaching again (though he didn't). 'Hell, I don't know anything else but coaching, know what I'm saying?' he said. 'That's where I belong.'"

In North Myrtle Beach, South Carolina, of complications from a fall, on March 29, 2009.

**Alysheba, 25, thoroughbred.** *1987 Kentucky Derby and Preakness Stakes winner.*

Known as 'America's Horse,' Alysheba, the son of Alydar, was the three-year-old male champion in 1987, thanks to victories at the first two legs of the Triple Crown. In 1988 he won six major stakes races, inlcuding the Breeders' Cup Classic, and was named Horse of the Year. 'He's the most talented horse I ever rode,' said jockey Chris McCarron, who rode Alysheba to victory at Churchill Downs in 1987.

In Lexington, Kentucky, of euthanasia after falling and breaking his right hind leg, on March 27, 2009.

**Colleen Howe, 76, hockey agent.** *SI writes:*

"One of the first women to represent a pro athlete as an agent, Howe negotiated her husband Gordie's deals with the Houston Aeros and the New England Whalers of the WHA. Known as Mrs. Hockey, Howe was also the agent for her sons Mark and Marty, who played alongside their father for seven seasons. She was inducted into the U.S. Hockey Hall of Fame in 2000 for her work in promoting youth hockey."

In Bloomfield Hills, Michigan, of complications from Pick's disease, on March 6, 2009.

**Betty Jameson, 89, golfer.** *Co-founder of the LPGA. SI writes:*

"An oil painter who enjoyed reading T.S. Eliot to friends, the graceful and statuesque Jameson won the first of two consecutive Women's Amateur titles in 1939 and she turned pro in 1945. Five years later she helped formalize the women's professional tour when she joined 12 others to co-found the LPGA. She became the first woman to break 300 in a 72-hole tournament and she won the 1947 U.S. Women's Open with a score of 295. She finished her career with 13 pro victories and was a charter member of the LPGA Tour Hall of Fame."

In Boynton Beach, Florida, of complications from surgery to remove a tumor, on February 7, 2009.

**Dante Lavelli, 85 football player.** *Hall of Fame NFL end. SI writes:*

"A native of Hudson, Ohio, Lavelli played three games for Paul Brown at Ohio State in 1942 before enlisting in the Army. When Lavelli returned from the war, he rejoined his old coach, then with the Cleveland Browns, playing four years in the All-American Football Conference and seven in the NFL. Nicknamed Gluefingers, Lavelli caught 386 passes for 6,488 yards in his career and was enshrined in Canton in 1975.

"'If I had to throw the ball to get a first down and I had to pick any receiver in history, it would be Dante,' Cleveland quarterback Otto Graham once said. 'He had the best hands the game has ever seen.'"

In Cleveland, Ohio, of congestive heart failure, on January 20, 2009.

**Ingemar Johansson, 76, boxer.** *Former heavyweight champion.*

Swedish boxer Johansson stunned the boxing world in 1959 by defeating then heavyweight champion Floyd Patterson. Known as "Ingo" to Swedes, Johansson knocked out Patterson in the third round at Yankee Stadium on June 26, 1959 to take the title. He floored the American seven times before referee Ruby Goldstein stopped the fight, becoming only the fifth heavyweight champion born outside the United States, a feat that earned him *Associated Press'* Male Athlete of Year honors.

In Kungsbacka, Sweden, of complications from Alzheimer's disease, on January 30, 2009.

**Kay Yow, 66, college basketball coach.** *Hall of Fame and Olympic basketball coach. SI writes:*

"In 38 years as a head coach, Yow racked up 737 wins against 344 losses; during her 34 years at North Carolina State she was 680–325, making her one of only three Division I women's coaches with 1,000 games at a single institution. Her Wolfpack teams went to 20 NCAA tournaments, 11 Sweet 16s, and one Final Four. In 1988 Yow coached the U.S. Olympic women's team to a gold medal in Seoul, and in 2002 she became the fifth women's coach inducted into the Basketball Hall of Fame.

"Yow's hallmark was her positivity, a quality she sustained even during her trying 2006–07 season, when chemotherapy treatments robbed her of her hair, appetite, fingernails and much of her famous energy even as she was inspiring her team to reach the Sweet 16. 'She lived by what she always told us, and I will try to do the same,' said former N.C. State center Gillian Goring in 2007."

In Cary, North Carolina, of breast cancer, on January 24, 2009.

**Jose Torres, 72, boxer.** *1956 Olympic light heavyweight silver medalist and pro boxing champion. SI writes:*

"The native Puerto Rican won the Olympic light heavyweight silver medal for the U.S. in 1956. Torres knocked out Willie Pastrano for the light heavyweight title in '65 and was champion for 21 months before losing to Dick Tiger; he retired in 1969 with a 41–3–1 record. He was later chairman of the New York State Athletic Commission and wrote acclaimed biographies of boxers Muhammad Ali (*Sting Like a Bee*) and Mike Tyson (*Fire and Fear*)."

In Ponce, Puerto Rico, of a heart attack, on January 19, 2009.

**Joe Hirsch, 80, horse racing journalist.** *SI writes:*

"Hirsch joined the *Daily Racing Form* in 1955 and quickly became the nation's preeminent turf writer, known for his wit ('Once there was a horse named Kelso,' he wrote about the five-time Horse of the Year. 'But only once.') and for being an ambassador for the sport of kings. In the '60s New York Jets owner Sonny Werblin, a close friend, asked him to live with Joe Namath to help keep the young QB on the straight and narrow. 'Joe learned a lot about women from me over the years,' said Namath, 'but I learned so much more from him.'"

In New York City, New York, of complications from Parkinson's disease, on January 9, 2009.

**Sam McQuagg, 73, race car driver.** *1965 NASCAR rookie of the Year. SI writes:*

"McQuagg dominated his local racetrack in Valdosta, Georgia, and parlayed that success into a full-time NASCAR ride in 1965, earning Rookie of the Year honors. He won only one race in his career—the 1966 Firecracker 400 at Daytona—but was best known for an incident in a race he didn't win. He was leading the 1965 Southern 500 in Darlington when Cale Yarborough bumped him while trying to make a pass. Yarborough's car went over the guard rail and out of the track, and the footage was used for years at the beginning of *Wide World of Sports* to illustrate the 'agony of defeat.'"

In Columbus, Georgia, of complications from cancer, on January 3, 2009.

**Sammy Baugh, 94, football player.** *Hall of Fame Washington Redskins quarterback.*

After starring at TCU, where he picked up the nickname 'Slingin' Sammy,' Baugh played with the Redskins from 1937 to 1952, leading them to the NFL title in his rookie season and again in 1942. When Baugh entered the NFL the forward pass was a rarity, but Baugh turned the pass into a regular feature of the offensive game plan. He still holds Redskins records for career touchdown passes (187) and completion percentage in a season (70.3) and his No. 33 is the only jersey number Washington has ever retired.

Baugh was also the best all-around player in an era when such versatility was essential. In 1943 he led the league in passing, punting and defensive interceptions. His 51.4-yard punting average in 1940 is still the NFL single-season record. Baugh was the last surviving member of the Pro Football Hall of Fame's inaugural class.

In Rotan, Texas, of complications from kidney disease and pneumonia, on December 17, 2008.

**Carole Caldwell Graebner, 65, tennis player.** *Two-time Grand Slam doubles champion. SI writes:*

"Known more for her doubles play—she and partner Nancy Richey were the top-ranked tandem in the world in 1965 and won two Grand Slam titles at the U.S. and Australian Opens—Graebner was an upstart finalist in the singles draw at the 1964 U.S. Open. Playing through a brutal case of sunburn that forced her to wear white cotton gloves, she lost the final in straight sets to Maria Bueno."

In New York City, New York , of complications from cancer, on November 19, 2008.

**Preacher Roe, 92, baseball player.** *Five-time All-Star pitcher. SI writes:*

"A high school math teacher in Arkansas before becoming a major leaguer in 1938, Roe made five All-Star teams in 12 seasons with the Cardinals, Pirates, and Brooklyn Dodgers. The lefthander was a pivotal figure in *The Boys of Summer*, Roger Kahn's 1972 memoir of his years as a Dodgers beat reporter in the 1950s, and after retiring made headlines by admitting that he owed much of his success to the mound to an illegal spitball."

In West Plains, Missouri, of complications from colon cancer, on November 11, 2008.

**Pete Newell, 93, basketball coach.** *Hall of Fame coach that won both an NIT and NCAA title. SI writes:*

"From 1946 to '60 Newell coached at the University of San Francisco, Michigan State and California; he won the 1949 NIT title with San Francisco and the 1959 title with Cal. In 1960 Newell coached Team USA to an Olympic gold medal. He then retired, but in '76 he began hosting an annual summer camp to help big men work on their technique. Bill Walton, Hakeem Olajuwon and Shaquille O'Neal are among the many inside players Newell tutored."

In Rancho Santa Fe, Calif., after a long illness, on November 17, 2008.

**Doreen Wilber, 78, archer.** *1972 Olympic gold medalist.*

Wilber became the first Iowan to win a gold medal when she upset heavily favored archers from Poland and Russia at the Munich Summer Games in 1972, a year that marked the sport's reintroduction after a more than 50-year absence from the Olympics. After her gold-medal triumph, Wilber spent the rest of her life running a junior Olympic development program and teaching archery in her backyard.

In Jefferson, Iowa, of Alzheimer's disease, on October 19, 2008.

**Ben Weider, 85, bodybuilder.** *Co-founded the International Brotherhood of Body Builders . SI writes:*

"In 1946 Weider and his brother Joe started their organization to sanction amateur and professional body building competitions. The Weider brothers went on to become the sport's greatest promoters, building a business empire that included lines of equipment and nutritional supplements and *Muscle and Fitness* magazine. (And in '68 they brought an unknown Austrian bodybuilder named Arnold Schwarzenegger to California and helped him become a champion.)"

In Montreal, Canada, of natural causes, on October 17, 2008.

**George Kissell, 88, baseball scout, coach, and executive.** *SI writes:*

"Longtime St. Louis Cardinals official Kissell never made it to the majors—he played three seasons in the minors before serving in the Navy in World War II—but he was a Cardinals fixture for the past six decades as a minor league instructor and big league coach. (Former manager Whitey Herzog once said, 'George Kissell is the only man I know who can talk for 15 minutes about a ground ball.') Kissell was a player development coordinator until his death."

In Pinellas Park, Fla., of injuries from a car crash, on October 7, 2008.

# 2010 MAJOR EVENTS

## JANUARY

| | |
|---|---|
| Major College BCS Bowl Games | Jan 1–5 |
| BCS Championship Game | Jan 7 |
| NFL Wild-Card Playoffs | Jan 9–10 |
| U.S. Figure Skating Championships | Jan 15–23 |
| NFL Divisional Playoffs | Jan 16–17 |
| NFL Conference Championships | Jan 24 |
| Australian Open | Jan 18–31 |
| Millrose Games | Jan 29 |
| NFL Pro Bowl | Jan 31 |

## FEBRUARY

| | |
|---|---|
| Millrose Games | Feb 6 |
| Super Bowl XLIV | Feb 7 |
| Winter Olympic Games | Feb 12–28 |
| NBA All-Star Game | Feb 14 |
| Daytona 500 | Feb 14 |
| *MLB Spring Training Begins* | *Feb 24** |

## MARCH

| | |
|---|---|
| March Madness Begins | March 18 |
| World Figure Skating Championships | March 20–29 |
| *Major League Soccer Season Begins* | *March 25** |

## APRIL

| | |
|---|---|
| Kraft Nabisco Championship | April 1–4 |
| Major League Baseball Opening Day | April 2 |
| NCAA Men's Basketball Final Four | April 3 & 5 |
| NCAA Women's Basketball Final Four | April 4 & 6 |
| NCAA Men's Hockey Frozen Four | April 8 & 10 |
| *NHL Playoffs Begin* | *April 14** |
| The Masters | April 8–11 |
| *NBA Playoffs Begin* | *April 17** |
| Boston Marathon | April 19 |
| NFL Draft | April 22–24 |

## MAY

| | |
|---|---|
| Kentucky Derby | May 1 |
| The Players Championship (Golf) | May 6–9 |
| Preakness Stakes | May 15 |
| NBA Draft Lottery | May 18 |
| *WNBA Season Begins* | *May 20** |
| NASCAR All-Star Race | May 22 |
| *NHL Stanley Cup Final Begins* | *May 29** |
| Indianapolis 500 | May 30 |

## JUNE

| | |
|---|---|
| French Open | May 23–June 6 |
| *NBA Finals Begin* | *June 3** |
| *LPGA Championship* | *June 3–6** |
| Belmont Stakes | June 5 |
| MLB First-Year Player Draft | June 7–9 |
| U.S. Men's Open (Golf) | June 17–20 |
| NHL Entry Draft | June 18–19 |
| College World Series | June 19–30 |
| US Outdoor Track & Field Championships | June 23–27 |
| NBA Draft | June 24 |

*\* Approximate date.*

## JULY

| | |
|---|---|
| FIFA World Cup | June 11–July 11 |
| Wimbledon | June 21–July 4 |
| Tour de France | July 3–25 |
| U.S. Women's Open (Golf) | July 8–11 |
| MLB All-Star Game | July 13 |
| Men's British Open | July 15–18 |
| FINA World Swimming Championships | July 15–23 |
| Brickyard 400 | July 25 |

## AUGUST

| | |
|---|---|
| Women's British Open | July 29– Aug 1 |
| NFL Hall of Fame Induction | Aug 7 |
| PGA Championship | Aug 12–15 |
| *PGA Tour FedEx Playoffs Begin* | *Aug 19** |
| Little League World Series | Aug 20–29 |

## SEPTEMBER

| | |
|---|---|
| U.S. Open (Tennis) | Aug 23–Sept 5 |
| *College Football Season Begins* | *Sep 2** |
| *NFL Season Begins* | *Sept 9** |
| *NASCAR Chase for the Cup Begins* | *Sept 12** |
| PGA TOUR Championship | Sep 23–26 |
| *WNBA Finals Begin* | *Sep 28** |

## OCTOBER

| | |
|---|---|
| Ryder Cup (Men's Golf) | Oct 1–3 |
| *MLB Divisional Series Begin* | *Oct 6** |
| *NHL Season Begins* | *Oct 7** |
| *MLB League Championship Series Begin* | *Oct 14** |
| World Gymnastics Championships | Oct 18–24 |
| *NBA Regular Season Begins* | *Oct 25** |
| Women's World Tour Championships (Tennis) | Oct 25–31 |
| *World Series Begins* | *Oct 27** |

## NOVEMBER

| | |
|---|---|
| Breeders' Cup | Nov 5–6 |
| New York Marathon | Nov 7 |
| *NASCAR Chase for the Cup Ends* | *Nov 14** |
| *Men's World Tour Championships (Tennis)* | *Nov 21–28** |
| MLS Cup | Nov 21 |

## DECEMBER

| | |
|---|---|
| Davis Cup Final (Tennis) | Dec 3–5 |
| Heisman Trophy Presentation | Dec 11 |
| *Major College Bowl Games Begin* | *Dec 18** |